Encyclopædia

of

Religion and Ethics

Encyclopædia of Religion and Ethics

EDITED BY

JAMES HASTINGS

WITH THE ASSISTANCE OF

JOHN A. SELBIE

AND

LOUIS H. GRAY

VOLUME VIII

LIFE AND DEATH—MULLA

T&T CLARK
EDINBURGH

T&T CLARK LTD
59 GEORGE STREET
EDINBURGH EH2 2LQ
SCOTLAND

Edition Completed and Corrected Editions 1926–1976
Reprinted 1994

ISBN 0 567 06508 1

British Library Cataloguing-in-Publication Data
A catalogue record for this book is available from the British Library

Printed and bound in Great Britain by Antony Rowe Ltd, Wiltshire

AUTHORS OF ARTICLES IN THIS VOLUME

ABELSON (JOSHUA), M.A., D.Lit. (London).
Principal of Aria College, Portsmouth; author of *Immanence of God in Rabbinical Literature, Jewish Mysticism, Maimonides on the Jewish Creed.*
Maimonides.

ABRAHAMS (ISRAEL), M.A. (Lond. and Camb.), D.D. (Heb. Union Coll., Cincin.).
Reader in Talmudic and Rabbinic Literature in the University of Cambridge; formerly Senior Tutor in the Jews' College, London; editor of the *Jewish Quarterly Review*, 1888–1908.
Marriage (Jewish).

ADLER (E. N.), M.A.
Member of the Council of the Jewish Historical Society; Corresponding Member of the Royal Academy of History of Spain and of the Jewish Historical Society of America; author of *Jews in Many Lands, Auto-de-fé and Jew.*
Mendelssohn.

ALEXANDER (HARTLEY BURR), Ph.D.
Professor of Philosophy in the University of Nebraska.
Literature (American).

ALLAN (JOHN), M.A., M.R.A.S.
Assistant in the Department of Coins and Medals in the British Museum; Assistant to the Professor of Sanskrit at University College, London.
Magadha, Maya.

ANESAKI (MASAHARU), M.A., D.Litt.
Professor of the Science of Religion in the Imperial University of Tokyo; Professor of Japanese Literature and Life in the University of Harvard, 1913–15.
Life and Death (Japanese), **Missions** (Buddhist).

ANWYL (Sir EDWARD), M.A. (Oxon.).
Late Professor of Welsh and Comparative Philology, and Dean of the Faculty of Arts, in the University College of Wales, Aberystwyth; author of *Celtic Religion.*
Merlin.

ARMITAGE-SMITH (GEORGE), M.A., D.Lit.
Principal of Birkbeck College, London; formerly Dean of the Faculty of Economics in the University of London; Fellow of Statistical Society; Member of Council of the Royal Economics Society; Lecturer on Economics and Mental Science at Birkbeck College.
Money.

ARNOLD (THOMAS WALKER), C.I.E., Litt.D., M.A.
Professor of Arabic, University of London, University College; author of *The Preaching of Islam*; editor of *The Encyclopædia of Islām.*
Missions (Muhammadan), **Muhammadanism** (in India).

BAIKIE (JAMES).
Fellow of the Royal Astronomical Society; Minister of the United Free Church at Edinburgh; author of *Lands and Peoples of the Bible* (1914).
Literature (Egyptian), **Manetho.**

BALL (JAMES DYER), I.S.O., M.R.A.S., M. Ch. Br. R.A.S.
Of the Hongkong Civil Service (retired); author of *Things Chinese, The Chinese at Home*, and other works; editor of *Friend of China.*
Life and Death (Chinese), **Light and Darkness** (Chinese).

BARBER (WILLIAM THEODORE AQUILA), B.A. (Lond.), M.A. (Camb.), D.D. (Dublin).
Headmaster of the Leys School, Cambridge.
Lullists.

BARKER (HENRY), M.A.
Lecturer in Moral Philosophy in the University of Edinburgh.
Locke.

BARNS (THOMAS), M.A. (Oxon.).
Vicar of Hilderstone, Staffordshire.
Michaelmas.

BARTON (GEORGE AARON), A.M., Ph.D., LL.D.
Professor of Biblical Literature and Semitic Languages in Bryn Mawr College, Pennsylvania; author of *A Sketch of Semitic Origins*, 'Ecclesiastes' in the *International Critical Commentary, Commentary on Job, The Origin and Development of Babylonian Writing.*
Marriage (Semitic), **Milk** (Civilized Religions).

BEAZLEY (CHARLES RAYMOND), D.Litt. (Oxford), F.R.G.S.
Professor of Modern History in the University of Birmingham; formerly Fellow of Merton College, Oxford; Member of Council of the Royal Historical Society; Member of the Royal Asiatic Society; author of *Dawn of Modern Geography*, and other works.
Missions (Christian, Early and Mediæval).

BEVAN (ANTHONY ASHLEY), M.A.
Fellow of Trinity College, Cambridge; Lord Almoner's Reader in Arabic in the University of Cambridge; author of *A Short Commentary on the Book of Daniel* (1892); editor of *The Hymn of the Soul* in the 'Cambridge Texts and Studies' (1897), and of the *Naḳā'iḍ* of Jarir and al-Farazdaḳ (1905–12).
Manichæism.

BEZOLD (CARL), Ph.D., LL.D.
Geheimer Hofrat; Ordinary Professor of Oriental Philology and Director of the Oriental Seminary in the University of Heidelberg; Ordinary Member of the Heidelberg Akademie der Wissenschaften; editor of *Zeitschrift für Assyriologie*.
Literature (Babylonian).

BEZZENBERGER (Dr. ADALBERT).
Professor der Sanskrit und vergl. Sprachwissenschaften an der Universität Königsberg.
Lithuanians and Letts.

BLOOMFIELD (MAURICE), Ph.D., LL.D.
Professor of Sanskrit and Comparative Philology in Johns Hopkins University, Baltimore; President of the American Oriental Society.
Literature (Vedic and Classical Sanskrit).

BOSANQUET (ROBERT C.), M.A., F.S.A.
Professor of Classical Archæology in the University of Liverpool; formerly Director of the British School of Archæology at Athens.
Minotaur.

BRANDT (Dr. WILHELM).
Late Professor of Old and New Testament and the History of Religion in the University of Amsterdam.
Mandæans, Masbothæans.

BROUGH (JOSEPH), B.A., LL.D. (Cantab.), M.Sc. (Wales).
Lecturer on Logic at Bedford College, London; formerly Professor of Logic and Philosophy in the University College of Wales, Aberystwyth; author of *The Study of Mental Science*.
Logic, Method (Logical).

BRYANT (Mrs. SOPHIE), D.Sc. (London), Litt.D. (Dublin).
Headmistress of the North London Collegiate School; author of *Studies in Character*, and other works.
Loyalty.

BURNET (JOHN), M.A. (Oxon.), LL.D. (Edin.), Ph.D. (Prag).
Professor of Greek in the United College of St. Salvator and St. Leonard, St. Andrews; Hon. Fellow of Merton College, Oxford; author of *Early Greek Philosophy* (1892); editor of *Platonis Opera* (1899–1907), and other works.
Megarics.

CABROL (FERNAND).
Abbot of Farnborough, Hants.
Monasticism.

CARNOY (ALBERT JOSEPH), Docteur en Philosophie et Lettres (Louvain).
Professor of Zend and Pahlavi and Greek Palæography in the University of Louvain; Research Professor in the University of Pennsylvania (1915–16).
Magic (Iranian).

CARPENTER (J. ESTLIN), M.A., D.Litt., D.D., D.Theol.
Wilde Lecturer in Natural and Comparative Religion in the University of Oxford; formerly Principal of Manchester College, Oxford; author of *The Bible in the Nineteenth Century*, and other works; joint-editor of *The Hexateuch according to the Revised Version*.
Martineau.

CARTER (JESSE BENEDICT), Ph.D. (Halle).
Director of the American Academy in Rome.
Love (Roman).

COBB (WILLIAM FREDERICK), D.D.
Rector of the Church of St. Ethelburga the Virgin, London; author of *Mysticism and the Creed* (1914).
Life and Death (Christian).

CODRINGTON (ROBERT HENRY), D.D. (Oxon.).
Hon. Fellow of Wadham College, Oxford; Prebendary of Chichester; formerly Missionary in Melanesia; author of *The Melanesian Languages* (1885), *The Melanesians: their Anthropology and Folklore* (1891).
Melanesians.

COE (GEORGE ALBERT), Ph.D., LL.D.
Professor of Religious Education and Psychology in the Union Theological Seminary, New York; author of *The Spiritual Life*, *The Religion of a Mature Mind*, *Education in Religion and Morals*.
Morbidness.

COLEMAN (ALEXIS IRÉNÉE DU PONT), M.A. (Oxon.).
Assistant Professor of English Literature, College of the City of New York.
Miracle-Plays.

COMPTON (ALFRED DONALDSON), B.Sc.
Assistant Professor of English Literature, College of the City of New York.
Miracle-Plays.

CONWAY (R. SEYMOUR), Litt.D.
Professor of Latin and Indo-European Philology in the University of Manchester; sometime Fellow of Gonville and Caius College, Cambridge; Corresponding Member of the German Imperial Institute of Archæology; editor of *The Italic Dialects*.
Ligurian Religion.

COOPER (JAMES), D.D. (Aberd.), Hon. D.Litt. (Dublin), D.C.L. (Durham).
Professor of Ecclesiastical History in the University of Glasgow.
Mary.

CRAWLEY (ALFRED ERNEST), M.A. (Camb.).
Fellow of the Sociological Society; Examiner to the University of London; author of *The Mystic Rose*, *The Tree of Life*, *The Idea of the Soul*, *The Book of the Ball*.
Life and Death (Primitive, American), **Locust, Love** (Primitive, American), **Magical Circle, Mask, May, Metals and Minerals, Mirror.**

CROOKE (WILLIAM), B.A.
Ex-Scholar of Trinity College, Dublin; Fellow of the Royal Anthropological Institute; President of the Anthropological Section of the British Association, 1910; President of the Folklore Society, 1911–12; late of the Bengal Civil Service.
Magh, Mahaban, Mahar, Majhwar, Mal, Mishmis.

CRUICKSHANK (WILLIAM), M.A., B.D.
Minister of the Church of Scotland at Kinneff, Bervie; author of *The Bible in the Light of Antiquity* (1913).
Light and Darkness (Semitic and Egyptian).

DAVIDS (T. W. RHYS), LL.D., Ph.D., D.Sc., F.B.A.
Formerly Professor of Comparative Religion, Manchester; President of the Pāli Text Society; author of *Buddhism* (1878), *Questions of King Milinda* (1890–94), *American Lectures on Buddhism* (1896), *Buddhist India* (1902), *Early Buddhism* (1908).
Lumbini, Milinda, Moggallana.

DAVIDS (MRS. RHYS), M.A.
Formerly Lecturer on Indian Philosophy in the University of Manchester; Fellow of University College, London; author of *Buddhist Psychological Ethics* (1900), *Psalms of the Early Buddhists* (1909, 1913), *Buddhism* (1912), *Buddhist Psychology* (1914).
Logic (Buddhist), **Love** (Buddhist), **Moksa.**

DAVIDSON (WILLIAM LESLIE), M.A., LL.D.
Professor of Logic and Metaphysics in the University of Aberdeen; author of *The Logic of Definition, Theism as Grounded in Human Nature, The Stoic Creed, Political Thought in England: the Utilitarians from Bentham to J. S. Mill.*
Mill, James and John Stuart.

DENNEY (JAMES), D.D.
Principal, and Professor of New Testament Language, Literature, and Theology, United Free Church College, Glasgow; author of *Studies in Theology, The Death of Christ, Jesus and the Gospel.*
Mediation.

DEUTSCH (GOTTHARD), Ph.D. (Vienna).
Professor of History in the Hebrew Union College, Cincinnati; author of *Philosophy of Jewish History* (1897).
Love (Jewish).

DOTTIN (GEORGES), Docteur ès-Lettres.
Professeur de langue et littérature grecques à l'Université de Rennes.
Marriage (Celtic).

DUCKWORTH (W. LAURENCE H.), M.A., M.D., Sc.D.
Fellow of Jesus College, Cambridge; University Lecturer in Physical Anthropology; Senior Demonstrator of Anatomy.
Monsters (Biological).

EDGELL (BEATRICE), M.A. (Wales), Ph.D. (Würzburg).
Lecturer in Philosophy in Bedford College, and University Reader in Psychology in the University of London.
Memory.

ELBOGEN (DR. I.).
Dozent in der Geschichte und Literatur der Juden an der Lehranstalt für die Wissenschaft des Judentums, Berlin.
Literature (Jewish).

EMMET (CYRIL WILLIAM), M.A.
Vicar of West Hendred, Berks; formerly Scholar of Corpus Christi College, Oxford; author of *The Eschatological Question in the Gospels, The Epistle to the Galatians* (Readers' Commentary).
Messiah.

ENTHOVEN (REGINALD E.), I.C.S.
Commissioner, 2nd Grade, Bombay Presidency.
Lingayats.

EUCKEN (RUDOLF CHRISTOPH), Dr. theol. u. philos.
Geheimer Rat; ordentlicher Professor der Philosophie an der Universität zu Jena; author of *Hauptprobleme der Religionsphilosophie der Gegenwart*, and other works.
Monism.

FINDLAY (GEORGE GILLANDERS), B.A. (Lond.), D.D. (St. Andrews).
Tutor in New Testament Literature and Classics in Headingley College, Leeds.
Methodism (Doctrine).

FOAKES-JACKSON (FREDERICK JOHN), D.D.
Fellow of Jesus College, Cambridge, and Hon. Canon of Peterborough Cathedral; author of *The History of the Christian Church to A.D. 461, A Bible History of the Hebrews*, and other works.
Meletianism.

FOLEY (WILLIAM MALCOLM), B.D.
Rector of Tralee, Co. Kerry; Archdeacon of Ardfert; Canon of St. Patrick's Cathedral, Dublin; Canon of St. Mary's Cathedral, Limerick; Examining Chaplain to the Bishop of Limerick; formerly Donnellan Lecturer (1892–93) in the University of Dublin.
Marriage (Christian).

FORKE (ALFRED), LL.D.
Agassiz Professor of Oriental Languages and Literature in the University of California, Berkeley; Hon. Member of the Royal Asiatic Society at Shanghai.
Materialism (Chinese).

FOWLER (WILLIAM WARDE), M.A., Hon. D.Litt. (Manchester), Hon. LL.D. (Edin.).
Fellow and late Subrector of Lincoln College, Oxford; Gifford Lecturer in Edinburgh University (1909–10).
Marriage (Roman).

FRANCKE (AUGUST HERMANN), Ph.D. h. c. (Breslau).
Hon. Foreign Member of the British and Foreign Bible Society; Moravian Missionary.
gLing Chos.

FRANKS (ROBERT SLEIGHTHOLME), M.A., B.Litt.
Principal of the Western College, Bristol; author of *The New Testament Doctrines of Man, Sin, and Salvation* (1908).
Merit (Christian).

FRAZER (ROBERT WATSON), LL.B., C.E., I.C.S. (retired).
Lecturer in Tamil and Telugu, University College, London; formerly Principal Librarian, London Institution; author of *A Literary History of India, Indian Thought Past and Present.*
Literature (Dravidian).

GARBE (RICHARD), Ph.D.
Professor des Sanskrit und der allgemeinen Religionsgeschichte an der Universität zu Tübingen.
Lokayata, Mimamsa.

GARDINER (ALAN HENDERSON), D.Litt. (Oxon.).
Formerly Reader in Egyptology at Manchester University; Laycock Student of Egyptology at Worcester College, Oxford; sub-editor of the Hieroglyphic Dictionary of the German Academies at Berlin.
Life and Death (Egyptian), **Magic** (Egyptian).

GASTER (MOSES), Ph.D.
Chief Rabbi, Spanish and Portuguese Congregations, London; formerly President of the Folklore Society, and of the Jewish Historical Society; Vice-President of the Royal Asiatic Society.
Magic (Jewish).

GEDEN (ALFRED S.), M.A. (Oxon.), D.D. (Aberd.).
Professor of Old Testament Languages and Literature and of Comparative Religion in the Wesleyan College, Richmond, Surrey; author of *Studies in the Religions of the East*; translator of Deussen's *Philosophy of the Upanishads*.
Mercy (Indian), **Monasticism** (Buddhist, Hindu).

GEFFCKEN (Dr. JOHANNES).
Ordentlicher Professor der Klass. Philologie an der Universität Rostock.
Mænads.

GERIG (JOHN LAWRENCE), M.A., Ph.D.
Associate Professor of Romance Languages and Celtic in Columbia University, New York.
Love (Celtic).

GIBSON (WILLIAM RALPH BOYCE), M.A., D.Sc.
Professor of Mental and Moral Philosophy in the University of Melbourne; author of *A Philosophical Introduction to Ethics* (1904), and other works.
Love (Psychological and Ethical).

GIESE (Dr. FRIEDRICH).
Professor für Ural-Altaische Sprachen an der Universität Konstantinopel; ehemals Professor für die Türkische Sprache an der Universität Berlin.
Muhammadanism (in Turkey).

GOMME (Sir LAURENCE), F.S.A.
Fellow of the Anthropological Institute; Vice-President of the Folklore Society; Hon. Member of Glasgow Archæological Society.
Milk (Primitive Religions).

GOULD (FREDERICK JAMES).
Lecturer and Demonstrator for the Moral Education League; author of *Moral Instruction: its Theory and Practice*.
Moral Education League.

GRANDIDIER (GUILLAUME CHARLES AUGUSTE), Docteur ès-Sciences.
Correspondant du Museum d'Histoire naturelle chargé de missions scientifiques par le Gouvernement français à Madagascar.
Madagascar.

GRASS (KARL KONRAD), Dr.Theol.
Professor of New Testament Exegesis in the Imperatorskij Jurjevskij University, Dorpat, Russia.
Men of God.

GRAY (LOUIS HERBERT), Ph.D. (Columbia).
Sometime Member of the Editorial Staff of the *New International Encyclopædia*; assistant editor of the present work; author of *Indo-Iranian Phonology* (1902); translator of *Vāsavadattā, a Sanskrit Romance by Subandhu* (1913).
Life and Death (Iranian), **Light and Darkness** (Iranian), **Literature** (Pahlavi), **Marriage** (Iranian), **Mazandaran, Mean** (Chinese), **Merit** (Introductory and Non-Christian), **Missions** (Zoroastrian).

GRIERSON (Sir GEORGE ABRAHAM), K.C.I.E., Ph.D., (Halle), D.Litt. (Dublin), I.C.S. (retired).
Honorary Member of the American Oriental Society, Honorary Fellow of the Asiatic Society of Bengal; Foreign Associate Member of the Société Asiatique de Paris; Superintendent of the Linguistic Society of India.
Literature (Indian Vernacular), **Madhvas, Maluk Dasis.**

GRIERSON (HERBERT JOHN CLIFFORD), M.A., LL.D.
Professor of Rhetoric and English Literature in the University of Edinburgh; editor of *The Poems of John Donne* (1912).
Milton.

GRIFFITH (FRANCIS LLEWELLYN), M.A., F.S.A., Hon. Ph.D. (Leipzig).
Reader in Egyptology in the University of Oxford; editor of the Archæological Survey of the Egypt Exploration Fund; Corresponding Member of the Royal Academy of Sciences at Berlin; Foreign Associate of the Société Asiatique; Member of the Imperial Academy of Sciences of Vienna.
Marriage (Egyptian).

HÄLSIG (Dr. F.).
Leipzig.
Magic (Teutonic).

HALL (THOMAS CUMING), B.A., D.D.
Professor of Christian Ethics in Union Theological Seminary, New York.
Moral Obligation.

HAMILTON-GRIERSON (Sir PHILIP JAMES, Kt.), B.A. (Oxon.).
Fellow of the Society of Scottish Antiquaries; Fellow of the Royal Anthropological Institute; Solicitor for Scotland to the Board of Inland Revenue.
Market.

HARRISON (JANE ELLEN), LL.D. (Aberd.), D.Litt. (Durham).
Staff Lecturer and sometime Fellow of Newnham College, Cambridge; author of *The Religion of Ancient Greece* (1905), *Prolegomena to the Study of Greek Religion* (1907), *Themis: a Study of the Social Origins of Greek Religion* (1912).
Mountain-Mother.

HARTLAND (EDWIN SIDNEY), F.S.A.
President of the Folklore Society, 1899; President of the Anthropological Section of the British Association, 1906; President of Section I (Religions of the Lower Culture) at the Oxford International Congress for the History of Religions, 1908; author of *The Legend of Perseus, Primitive Paternity, Ritual and Belief.*
Life-Token.

HARTMANN (Dr. MARTIN).
Professor der Syrisch-Arab. Islamkunde an der Universität Berlin.
Muhammadanism (in China).

HASSÉ (EVELYN R.), D.D.
Bishop of the Moravian Church; President of the Directory Board of the Moravian Church in Great Britain and Ireland.
Moravians.

HERFORD (R. TRAVERS), B.A.
Librarian of the Dr. Williams Library, London; author of *Christianity in Talmud and Midrash, Pharisaism: its Aim and its Method.*
Minim.

HICKS (ROBERT DREW), M.A.
Fellow and formerly Classical Lecturer of Trinity College, Cambridge.
Lucretius.

HILLEBRANDT (A. F. ALFRED), Ph.D. (Munich), LL.D.
Ord. Professor of Sanskrit and Comparative Philology in the University of Breslau; Corresponding Member of the Königliche Gesellschaft der Wissenschaften zu Göttingen, and of the Royal Bavarian Academy of Sciences; Geheimer Regierungsrat.
Light and Darkness (Hindu).

HODSON (THOMAS CALLAN), I.C.S. (retired).
Hon. Secretary of the Royal Anthropological Institute; author of *The Meitheis* (1908), *The Nāga Tribes of Manipur* (1911).
Lushais, Manipuris.

HOPE (JOHN MAURICE VAIZEY), M.A. (Cantab. et Oxon.).
Clare College; sometime Scholar of Trinity College, Cambridge; late Fellow of St. Augustine's College, Canterbury.
Lying.

HOPKINS (EDWARD WASHBURN), Ph.D., LL.D.
Professor of Sanskrit and Comparative Philology in Yale University; former President of the American Oriental Society; author of *The Religions of India, The Great Epic of India, India Old and New, Epic Mythology.*
Mahabharata, Manitu.

HORROCKS (ARTHUR JAMES), M.A., D.D.
Minister of the Congregational Church at Camden Town.
Meekness.

HURWITZ (SOLOMON THEODORE HALÉVY), M.A., Ph.D. (Columbia).
Gustav Gottheil Lecturer in Semitic Languages in Columbia University; formerly Librarian of Jewish Literature in the New York Public Library; author of *Root-Determinatives in Semitic Speech.*
Midrash and Midrashic Literature.

HYAMSON (ALBERT MONTEFIORE), F.R.Hist.S.
Corresponding Member of the American Jewish Historical Society; Member of Council of the Jewish Historical Society of England; author of *A History of the Jews in England.*
Messiahs (Pseudo-).

HYSLOP (JAMES HERVEY), Ph.D., LL.D.
Secretary of the American Society for Psychical Research; formerly Professor of Logic and Ethics in Columbia University.
Moral Argument.

INGE (WILLIAM RALPH), D.D.
Dean of St. Paul's; author of *Christian Mysticism* (1899), *Studies of English Mystics* (1906), *Personal Idealism and Mysticism* (1907), *Faith and its Psychology* (1908).
Logos.

JACOBS (HENRY EYSTER), S.T.D., LL.D.
Dean and Professor of Systematic Theology in the Lutheran Theological Seminary at Philadelphia.
Luther, Lutheranism.

JOHNSTON (Sir HARRY HAMILTON), G.C.M.G., K.C.B., D.Sc. (Camb.).
Vice-President of the African Society; author of *The Uganda Protectorate* (1902), *Liberia* (1906).
Masai.

JOHNSTON (REGINALD FLEMING), M.A. (Oxon.), F.R.G.S.
District Officer and Magistrate, Weihaiwei; formerly Private Secretary to the Governor of Hongkong; Member of the Royal Asiatic Society and of the Folklore Society; author of *From Peking to Mandalay* (1908), *Lion and Dragon in Northern China* (1910), *Buddhist China* (1913).
Magic (Chinese).

JONES (H. STUART), M.A.
Fellow of Trinity College, Oxford; Fellow of the British Academy; formerly Director of the British School at Rome.
Mithraism.

JONES (J. P.), M.A., D.D.
Professor of Indian Missions in the Kennedy School of Missions, Hartford, Conn.; editor of *The Year Book of Missions in India.*
Madura.

JOSEPH (MORRIS).
Senior Minister of the West London Synagogue; author of *Judaism as Creed and Life* (1910).
Life and Death (Jewish), **Meir.**

JOYCE (GEORGE HAYWARD), S.J., M.A. (Oxon.).
Professor of Dogmatic Theology at St. Beuno's College, St. Asaph, N. Wales.
Mental Reservation.

JUYNBOLL (TH. W.), Dr. juris et phil.
Adjutor interpretis 'Legati Warneriani,' Leyden.
Malik ibn Anas.

KAY (D. MILLER), B.Sc., D.D.
Regius Professor of Hebrew and Oriental Languages in the University of St. Andrews.
Massebhah.

KEITH (ARTHUR BERRIEDALE), D.C.L., D.Litt.
Barrister-at-law; Regius Professor of Sanskrit and Comparative Philology in the University of Edinburgh.
Marriage (Hindu).

KENNETT (ROBERT HATCH), D.D.
Regius Professor of Hebrew in the University of Cambridge; Canon of Ely; Fellow of Queens' College, Cambridge; Examining Chaplain to the Bishops of Ely and Manchester.
Moab.

KERN (JOHAN HENDRIK CASPAR), LL.D. (Leyden), Hon. Dr.Phil. (Leipzig, Christiania).
Formerly Professor of Sanskrit and Comparative Philology in the University of Leyden.
Malay Archipelago.

KING (LEONARD WILLIAM), M.A., Litt.D., F.S.A.
Assistant Keeper of Egyptian and Assyrian Antiquities, British Museum; Professor of Assyrian and Babylonian Archæology in the University of London; author of *A History of Babylonia and Assyria*.
Magic (Babylonian).

KROLL (WILHELM), Dr. Phil.
Professor der Klass. Philologie an der Universität Münster.
Momentary Gods.

KRÜGER (Dr. GUSTAV).
Professor der Kirchengeschichte an der Universität Giessen.
Monophysitism, Monotheletism.

KÜHLER (WILHELMUS JOHANNES).
Professor of Theology in the University of Amsterdam, and of the Seminary of the Mennonites in Amsterdam.
Mennonites.

LATTE (KURT).
Königsberg.
Love (Greek).

LAWLOR (HUGH JACKSON), D.D., Litt.D.
Beresford Professor of Ecclesiastical History in the University of Dublin; Canon and Precentor of St. Patrick's Cathedral, Dublin; Sub-Dean of the Chapel Royal, Dublin.
Montanism.

LILLEY (ALFRED LESLIE), M.A.
Canon of Hereford and Archdeacon of Ludlow.
Modernism.

LOOFS (FRIEDRICH), Lic. Theol., Dr. Phil. u. Theol.
Ordentlicher Professor der Kirchengeschichte an der Universität zu Halle; Geheimer Konsistorialrat; Mitglied des Konsistoriums der Provinz Sachsen.
Macedonianism.

LYALL (Sir CHARLES JAMES), K.C.S.I., C.I.E., Hon. LL.D. (Edin.), Ph.D. (Strassburg), D.Litt. (Oxford), F.B.A., I.C.S. (retired).
Hon. Member of the Asiatic Society of Bengal; Hon. Member of the Deutsche Morgenländische Gesellschaft; Member of Council of the Royal Asiatic Society; Judicial and Public Secretary to the India Office (1898–1910).
Mikirs.

MACCULLOCH (JOHN ARNOTT), Hon. D.D. (St. Andrews).
Rector of St. Saviour's, Bridge of Allan; Hon. Canon of the Cathedral of the Holy Spirit, Cumbrae; Examiner in Comparative Religion and Philosophy of Religion, Victoria University, Manchester; author of *The Religion of the Ancient Celts*.
Light and Darkness (Primitive), **Locks and Keys, Lycanthropy, Magic** (Celtic), **Metamorphosis, Miracles, Monsters** (Ethnic), **Mountains and Mountain-Gods, Mouth.**

MACDONELL (ARTHUR ANTHONY), M.A. (Oxon.), Ph.D. (Leipzig).
Boden Professor of Sanskrit in the University of Oxford; Fellow of Balliol College; Fellow of the British Academy; Fellow of the Royal Danish Academy; Keeper of the Indian Institute, Oxford.
Literature (Buddhist), **Lotus** (Indian), **Magic** (Vedic).

MÁCHAL (JAN), D.Ph.
Ord. Professor of Slavic Literatures in the Bohemian University, Prague; ord. Member of the Bohemian Academy; Member of the Royal Bohemian Society of Sciences.
Marriage (Slavic).

MCINTYRE (JAMES LEWIS), M.A. (Edin. and Oxon.), D.Sc. (Edin.).
Anderson Lecturer in Comparative Psychology to the University of Aberdeen; Lecturer in Psychology, Logic, and Ethics to the Aberdeen Provincial Committee for the Training of Teachers; formerly Examiner in Philosophy to the University of Edinburgh; author of *Giordano Bruno* (1903).
Melancholy.

MACKENZIE (JOHN STUART), LL.D., Litt.D.
Professor of Logic and Philosophy in University College of South Wales and Monmouthshire; author of *An Introduction to Social Philosophy, A Manual of Ethics, Outlines of Metaphysics, Lectures on Humanism*.
Metaphysics.

MACKINTOSH (HUGH ROSS), M.A., D.Phil. (Edin.), D.D. (Edin.).
Professor of Systematic Theology in New College, Edinburgh; author of *The Doctrine of the Person of Jesus Christ* (1912).
Mercy.

MACKINTOSH (ROBERT), M.A., D.D. (Glas.), B.D. (Edin.).
Professor of Ethics, Christian Sociology, and Apologetics in the Lancashire Independent College, and Lecturer in the University of Manchester.
Monolatry and Henotheism.

MACLAGAN (P. J.), M.A., D.Phil.
Of the English Presbyterian Mission, Swatow.
Literature (Chinese), **Love** (Chinese), **Mencius, Micius.**

MACLEAN (ARTHUR JOHN), D.D. (Camb.), Hon. D.D. (Glas.).
Bishop of Moray, Ross, and Caithness; author of *Dictionary and Grammar of Vernacular Syriac*; editor of *East Syrian Liturgies*.
Light and Darkness (Christian), **Ministry** (Early Christian).

MCLEAN (NORMAN), M.A.
Fellow and Senior Tutor of Christ's College; Lecturer in Aramaic in the University of Cambridge; joint-editor of *The Larger Cambridge Edition of the Septuagint*.
Marcionism.

MACPHAIL (GEORGE R.), M.A.
Minister of the United Free Church at Dundee.
Men, The.

MAGNUS (LEONARD A.), LL.B.
London; editor of *Russian Folk-Tales* (1915).
Magic (Slavic).

MAIR (ALEXANDER WILLIAM), M.A. (Aberd. and Camb.), Litt.D. (Aberd.).
Sometime Fellow of Gonville and Caius College, Cambridge; Professor of Greek in the University of Edinburgh; editor of *Hesiod*.
Life and Death (Greek and Roman).

MARETT (ROBERT RANULPH), M.A., F.R.A.I.
Fellow of Exeter College, and Reader in Social Anthropology in the University of Oxford; author of *The Threshold of Religion*.
Magic (Introductory), **Mana.**

MARGOLIOUTH (DAVID SAMUEL), M.A., D.Litt., F.B.A.
Fellow of New College, and Laudian Professor of Arabic in the University of Oxford; author of *Mohammed and the Rise of Islam*, *Mohammedanism*, *The Early Development of Mohammedanism*.
Magic (Arabian and Muslim), **Mahdi**, **Mecca**, **Medina**, **Muhammad**, **Muhammadanism** (in Central Africa, in North Africa, in Arabia).

MARSHALL (JOHN TURNER), M.A., D.D.
Principal of Manchester Baptist College; Lecturer in History of Christian Doctrine in Manchester University.
Life and Death (Hebrew), **Mammon.**

MAUDE (JOSEPH HOOPER), M.A.
Rector of Pusey, Berks.; Late Fellow and Dean of Hertford College, Oxford.
Litany.

MELLONE (S. H.), M.A. (Lond.), D.Sc. (Edin.).
Principal of the Unitarian Home Missionary College, Manchester; Lecturer in the History of Christian Doctrine in the University of Manchester; author of *Studies in Philosophical Criticism*, *Leaders of Religious Thought in the Nineteenth Century*.
Mean.

MODI (SHAMS-UL-ULMA JIVANJI JAMSHEDJI), B.A., Hon. Ph.D. (Heidelberg).
Fellow of the University of Bombay; Dipl. Litteris et Artibus (Sweden); Officier d'Académie, France; Officier de l'Instruction Publique, France; Secretary of the Anthropological Society of Bombay; Vice-President of the Bombay Branch of the Royal Asiatic Society.
Marriage (Iranian).

MOULTON (JAMES HOPE), M.A. (Cantab.), D.Lit. (Lond.), D.D. (Edin., Berlin, and Groningen), D.C.L. (Durham).
Late Fellow of King's College, Cambridge; Greenwood Professor of Hellenistic Greek and Indo-European Philology in the University of Manchester; Tutor in Didsbury Wesleyan College; author of *Grammar of New Testament Greek* (3rd ed. 1908), *Religion and Religions* (1913), *Early Zoroastrianism* (Hibbert Lectures, 1914).
Magi.

NAKAJIMA (TAMAKICHI).
Professor of Civil Law in the Imperial University, Kyoto.
Marriage (Japanese and Korean).

NICHOLSON (REYNOLD ALLEYNE), M.A., Litt.D., LL.D.
Lecturer in Persian in the University of Cambridge; sometime Fellow of Trinity College; author of *A Literary History of the Arabs* (1907), the *Tarjuman al-Ashwaq* of Ibn al-Arabi, with translation and commentary (1911), *The Mystics of Islam* (1914).
Love (Muhammadan), **Ma'arri**, **Mazdak**, **Muhyi al-din ibn al-Arabi.**

OTTLEY (ROBERT LAURENCE), D.D.
Regius Professor of Pastoral Theology, and Canon of Christ Church, Oxford; author of *The Doctrine of the Incarnation* (1895), *Aspects of the Old Testament* (1897), *The Religion of Israel* (1905), and other works.
Moderation.

PAASONEN (HENRY), Ph.D.
Professor of Finno-Ugric Philology in the University of Helsingfors; Vice-President of the Finno-Ugric Society.
Mordvins.

PARKER (EDWARD HARPER), M.A.
Professor of Chinese in the Victoria University, Manchester; formerly H.M. Consul at Kiungchow.
Mongols.

PATON (JOHN LEWIS), M.A.
High Master, Manchester Grammar School; Late Fellow of St. John's College, Cambridge; Member of Consultative Committee of the Board of Education.
Mission (Inner).

PATON (LEWIS BAYLES), Ph.D., D.D.
Nettleton Professor of Old Testament Exegesis and Criticism, and Instructor in Assyrian, in Hartford Theological Seminary; formerly Director of the American School of Archæology in Jerusalem; author of *The Early History of Syria and Palestine*, *Jerusalem in Bible Times*, *The Early Religion of Israel*.
Love (Semitic and Egyptian).

PEARSON (A. C.), M.A.
Sometime Scholar of Christ's College, Cambridge; editor of *Fragments of Zeno and Cleanthes*, Euripides' *Helena*, *Heraclidæ*, and *Phœnissæ*.
Love (Greek), **Mother of the Gods** (Greek and Roman).

PETRIE (WILLIAM MATTHEW FLINDERS), D.C.L. (Oxon.), LL.D. (Edin. and Aberd.), Litt.D. (Camb.), Ph.D. (Strassburg).
Fellow of the Royal Society and of the British Academy; Edwards Professor of Egyptology in the University of London.
Lotus (Egyptian).

POPE (HUGH), O.P., S.T.M., D.S.S.
Formerly Professor of New Testament Exegesis in the Collegio Angelico, Rome.
Monarchianism.

POPPER (WILLIAM), Ph.D.
Associate Professor of Semitic Languages in the University of California, Berkeley.
Mulla.

POUSSIN (LOUIS DE LA VALLÉE), Docteur en philosophie et lettres (Liége), en langues orientales (Louvain).
Professor de sanscrit à l'université de Gand; Membre de l'Académie royale de Belgique; Co-Directeur du Muséon; Membre de la R.A.S. et de la Société asiatique.
Lotus of the True Law, **Madhyamaka**, **Magic** (Buddhist), **Mahavastu**, **Mahayana**, **Manjusri**, **Mara**, **Materialism** (Indian).

REID (JAMES SMITH), M.A., LL.D., Litt.D.
Fellow and late Tutor of Gonville and Caius College, Cambridge; Professor of Ancient History in the University of Cambridge; editor of the *Academica* and other works of Cicero; author of *Municipalities of the Roman Empire*.
Light and Darkness (Greek and Roman).

RENDALL (GERALD HENRY), B.D., Litt.D., LL.D.
Headmaster of Charterhouse, Cambridge; formerly Principal and Professor of Greek, University of Liverpool; Examining Chaplain to the Lord Bishop of Chelmsford.
Marcus Aurelius Antoninus.

REVON (MICHEL), LL.D., D.Lit.
Professor of History of the Civilization of the Far East in the University of Paris; formerly Professor of Law in the Imperial University of Tokyo and Legal Adviser to the Japanese Government; author of *Le Shinntöisme.*
Magic (Japanese).

RIVERS (W. H. R.), M.A., M.D., F.R.S., F.R.C.P.
Fellow of St. John's College, Cambridge; President of the Anthropological Section of the British Association in 1911; author of *The Todas, History of Melanesian Society, Kinship and Social Organisation.*
Marriage (Introductory and Primitive), **Mother-Right.**

ROSE (H. A.), I.C.S.
Panjab, India.
Life and Death (Indian), **Magic** (Indian).

ROYCE (JOSIAH), Ph.D., LL.D.
Alford Professor of Natural Religion, Moral Philosophy, and Civil Polity in Harvard University; Gifford Lecturer at the University of Aberdeen, 1898–1900.
Mind, Monotheism.

SAYCE (ARCHIBALD HENRY), D.Litt. (Oxon.), LL.D. (Dublin), D.D. (Edin. and Aberd.), D.Phil. (Christiania).
Fellow of Queen's College and Professor of Assyriology in the University of Oxford; President of the Society of Biblical Archæology.
Median Religion.

SCHULHOF (JOHN MAURICE). See HOPE (JOHN MAURICE VAIZEY).

SCOTT (WILLIAM ROBERT), M.A., D.Phil., Litt.D., F.B.A.
Adam Smith Professor of Political Economy in the University of Glasgow; President of the Economics and Statistics Section of the British Association, 1915; author of *Francis Hutcheson* (1900), *The Constitution and Finance of English, Scottish, and Irish Stock Companies to 1720* (1910–12).
Luxury, Malthusianism.

SEATON (MARY ETHEL).
Mediæval and Modern Languages Tripos, Class I., 1909 and 1910; Lecturer at Girton College, Cambridge.
Life and Death (Teutonic).

SELER (EDUARD), Dr.Phil.
Professor für Amerikanische Sprache, Völker- und Altertumskunde an der Universität zu Berlin; Mitglied der Königl. Preussischen Akademie der Wissenschaften; Abt. Direktor des Königl. Museums für Völkerkunde; Professor onor. Mus.-Nac., Mexico.
Mayans, Mexicans (Ancient).

SELL (EDWARD), B.D., D.D., M.R.A.S.
Fellow of the University of Madras; Hon. Canon of St. George's Cathedral, Madras; Secretary of the Church Missionary Society, Madras; author of *The Faith of Islam, The Historical Development of the Qur'ān, The Life of Muḥammad, The Religious Orders of Islam.*
Mercy (Muslim).

SHAW (CHARLES GRAY), Ph.D.
Professor of Philosophy in the University of New York; author of *Christianity and Modern Culture, The Precinct of Religion, The Value and Dignity of Human Life.*
Moral Sense.

SHEDD (WILLIAM A.), M.A.
Of the Presbyterian Mission, Urumia, Persia.
Muhammadanism (in Persia).

SIMON (JOHN SMITH), D.D.
President of the Wesley Historical Society; ex-President of the Wesleyan Methodist Conference.
Methodism (History and Polity).

SKEAT (WALTER W.), M.A.
Official Lecturer at the British Museum; sometime Scholar of Christ's College, Cambridge; formerly of the Civil Service of the Federated Malay States; author of *Malay Magic* (1900); joint-author of *Pagan Races of the Malay Peninsula* (1906).
Malay Peninsula.

SMITH (KIRBY FLOWER), Ph.D. (Johns Hopkins), LL.D. (Vermont).
Professor of Latin in the Johns Hopkins University, Baltimore.
Magic (Greek and Roman).

SMITH (VINCENT ARTHUR), M.A.
Of the Indian Civil Service (retired); author of *Asoka* in 'Rulers of India,' *Early History of India, A History of Fine Art in India and Ceylon.*
Mathura.

SPITZ (MATERNUS), O.S.B.
Professor of Church History at St. Thomas' Abbey, Erdington, Birmingham; Hon. Member of the International Association of Mission-Science.
Missions (Christian, Roman Catholic).

STOKES (GEORGE J.), M.A. (Trinity College, Dublin).
Of Lincoln's Inn, Barrister-at-Law; Professor of Philosophy and Jurisprudence in University College, Cork, National University of Ireland.
Motive.

STRAHAN (JAMES), M.A., D.D.
Professor of Hebrew and Biblical Criticism in Magee College, Londonderry; Cunningham Lecturer; author of *Hebrew Ideals, The Book of Job.*
Love (Christian and New Testament).

SUFFRIN (AARON EMMANUEL), M.A. (Oxon.).
Vicar of Waterlooville, Hants.
Memra.

SYMES (JOHN ELLIOTSON), M.A. (Cantab.).
Formerly Principal of University College, Nottingham; author of *Political Economy, The Prelude to Modern History.*
Maurice.

TASKER (JOHN G.), D.D.
Principal, and Professor of Church History and Apologetics, Wesleyan College, Handsworth, Birmingham.
Longsuffering.

TENNANT (FREDERICK ROBERT), D.D., B.Sc.
Fellow and Lecturer of Trinity College, Cambridge.
Materialism, Matter.

THOMAS (FREDERICK WILLIAM), M.A. (Camb.), Hon. Ph.D. (Munich).
Librarian of the India Office; Reader in Tibetan in the University of London; Lecturer in Comparative Philology in University College, London; formerly Fellow of Trinity College, Cambridge.
Matrcheta.

THOMSON (J. ARTHUR), M.A., LL.D.
Regius Professor of Natural History in the University of Aberdeen; author of *The Study of Animal Life, The Science of Life, Heredity, The Bible of Nature, Darwinism and Human Life, Outlines of Zoology, The Biology of the Seasons, Introduction to Science, The Wonder of Life.*
Life and Death (Biological).

THURSTON (HERBERT), B.A., S.J.
Joint-editor of the Westminster Library for Priests and Students; author of *Life of St. Hugh of Lincoln, The Holy Year of Jubilee, The Stations of the Cross.*
Liguori, Loreto, Lourdes, Loyola.

TOZZER (ALFRED MARSTON), Ph.D., F.R.G.S.
Assistant Professor of Anthropology in the University of Harvard; Curator of Middle American Archæology in Peabody Museum, Harvard.
Mexicans (Modern).

VAMBÉRY (ARMINIUS).
Late Professor of Oriental Languages in the University of Budapesth; author of *Travels in Central Asia.*
Muhammadanism (in Central Asia).

WADDELL (L. AUSTINE), C.B., C.I.E., LL.D., F.L.S., F.R.A.I., M.R.A.S., M.S.B.A., Lt.-Colonel I.M.S. (retired).
Formerly Professor of Tibetan in University College, London; author of *The Buddhism of Tibet, Tribes of the Brahmaputra Valley, Lhasa and its Mysteries.*
Lotus (Indian [in Buddhism]).

WEIR (THOMAS HUNTER), B.D., M.R.A.S.
Lecturer in Arabic in the University of Glasgow; Examiner in Hebrew and Aramaic in the University of London.
Muhammadanism (in Syria, Egypt, and Mesopotamia).

WEITBRECHT (HERBERT UDNY), Ph.D., D.D.
Superintendent and Warden of the Mildmay Institutions, North London; Hon. Fellow of the Panjab University; chief Reviser of the Urdu New Testament.
Missions (Christian, Protestant).

WENTSCHER (Dr. MAX).
Professor der Philosophie an der Universität Bonn.
Lotze.

WHITACRE (ÆLRED), O.P., Sac. Theol. Lector.
Professor of Dogmatic Theology at the Dominican House of Studies, Hawkesyard Priory, Staffordshire.
Molinism.

WHITEHEAD (HENRY), D.D. (Oxon.).
Bishop of Madras; formerly Fellow of Trinity College, Oxford.
Madras and Coorg.

WHITLEY (WILLIAM THOMAS), M.A., LL.D., F.R.Hist.S., F.T.S.
Secretary of the Baptist Historical Society; formerly Principal of the Baptist College of Victoria, and Secretary of the Victorian Baptist Foreign Mission.
Muggletonians.

WILDE (NORMAN), Ph.D.
Professor of Philosophy and Psychology in the University of Minnesota.
Moral Law.

WOODHOUSE (WILLIAM J.), M.A.
Professor of Greek in the University of Sydney, New South Wales.
Marriage (Greek).

CROSS-REFERENCES

In addition to the cross-references throughout the volume, the following list of minor references may be useful:

Topic.	Probable Title of Article.
Life, Wheel of	Wheel of Life.
Light, Friends of	Deutsch-Katholicismus.
Lizard	Animals.
Los von Rom	Sects (Christian).
Love, Family of	,, ,,
Low Church	Church, Doctrine of the (Anglican).
Lust	Desire.
Mabinogion	Celts.
Madness	Insanity.
Magpie	Animals.
Manes	Ancestor-worship (Roman).
Mang'anjas	Bantu and S. Africa.
Man-tigers	Lycanthropy.
Mantis	Animals.
Marcellians	Sects (Christian).
Marcites	,, ,,
Marcosians	,, ,,
Mariavites	Old Catholicism.
Marks	Symbols.
Maronites	Syrian Christians.
Martinists	Sects (Russian).
Maruts	Vedic Religion.
Maṣṣôth	Festivals and Fasts (Hebrew).
Mathurists	Religious Orders (Christian).
Maundy Thursday	Feet-washing.
Maurists	Religious Orders (Christian).
Maximilianists	Sects (Christian).
Mazdæism	Zoroastrianism.
Melanchthon	Synergism.
Meliorism	Probabiliorism.
Mendelism	Heredity.
Mendicants	Religious Orders (Christian).
Menhirs	Stones.
Mermaid	Water, Water-gods.
Michael	Demons.
Micronesia	Australasia.
Midsummer	May.
Minorites	Religious Orders (Christian).
Mixtecs	Mexicans.
Mock King	King (Introductory).
Moiræ	Fate (Greek and Roman).
Molech, Moloch	Ammonites.
Moluccas	Indonesians, Malay Archipelago.
Monergism	Synergism.
Monogamy	Marriage.
Moors	Muhammadanism (in Arabia).
More (Henry)	Cambridge Platonists.
Morelstshiki	Sects (Russian).
Moses	Israel.
Mother of God	Mary.
Mountain of the World	Cosmogony and Cosmology.

LISTS OF ABBREVIATIONS

I. General

A.H. = Anno Hijrae (A.D. 622).
Ak. = Akkadian.
Alex. = Alexandrian.
Amer. = American.
Apoc. = Apocalypse, Apocalyptic.
Apocr. = Apocrypha.
Aq. = Aquila.
Arab. = Arabic.
Aram. = Aramaic.
Arm. = Armenian.
Ary. = Aryan.
As. = Asiatic.
Assyr. = Assyrian.
AT = Altes Testament.
AV = Authorized Version.
AVm = Authorized Version margin.
A.Y. = Anno Yazdagird (A.D. 639).
Bab. = Babylonian.
c. = *circa*, about.
Can. = Canaanite.
cf. = compare.
ct. = contrast.
D = Deuteronomist.
E = Elohist.
edd. = editions or editors.
Egyp. = Egyptian.
Eng. = English.
Eth. = Ethiopic.
EV, EVV = English Version, Versions.
f. = and following verse or page.
ff. = and following verses or pages.
Fr. = French.
Germ. = German.
Gr. = Greek.
H = Law of Holiness.
Heb. = Hebrew.
Hel. = Hellenistic.
Hex. = Hexateuch.
Himy. = Himyaritic.
Ir. = Irish.
Iran. = Iranian.
Isr. = Israelite.
J = Jahwist.
J″ = Jehovah.
Jerus. = Jerusalem.
Jos. = Josephus.
LXX = Septuagint.
Min. = Minæan.
MSS = Manuscripts.
MT = Massoretic Text.
n. = note.
NT = New Testament.
Onḳ. = Onkelos.
OT = Old Testament.
P = Priestly Narrative.
Pal. = Palestine, Palestinian.
Pent. = Pentateuch.
Pers. = Persian.
Phil. = Philistine.
Phœn. = Phœnician.
Pr. Bk. = Prayer Book.
R = Redactor.
Rom. = Roman.
RV = Revised Version.
RVm = Revised Version margin.
Sab. = Sabæan.
Sam. = Samaritan.
Sem. = Semitic.
Sept. = Septuagint.
Sin. = Sinaitic.
Skr. = Sanskrit.
Symm. = Symmachus.
Syr. = Syriac.
t. (following a number) = times.
Talm. = Talmud.
Targ. = Targum.
Theod. = Theodotion.
TR = Textus Receptus, Received Text.
tr. = translated or translation.
VSS = Versions.
Vulg., Vg. = Vulgate.
WH = Westcott and Hort's text.

II. Books of the Bible

Old Testament.

Gn = Genesis.
Ex = Exodus.
Lv = Leviticus.
Nu = Numbers.
Dt = Deuteronomy.
Jos = Joshua.
Jg = Judges.
Ru = Ruth.
1 S, 2 S = 1 and 2 Samuel.
1 K, 2 K = 1 and 2 Kings.
1 Ch, 2 Ch = 1 and 2 Chronicles.
Ezr = Ezra.
Neh = Nehemiah.
Est = Esther.
Job.
Ps = Psalms.
Pr = Proverbs.
Ec = Ecclesiastes.
Ca = Canticles.
Is = Isaiah.
Jer = Jeremiah.
La = Lamentations.
Ezk = Ezekiel.
Dn = Daniel.
Hos = Hosea.
Jl = Joel.
Am = Amos.
Ob = Obadiah.
Jon = Jonah.
Mic = Micah.
Nah = Nahum.
Hab = Habakkuk.
Zeph = Zephaniah.
Hag = Haggai.
Zec = Zechariah.
Mal = Malachi.

Apocrypha.

1 Es, 2 Es = 1 and 2 Esdras.
To = Tobit.
Jth = Judith.
Ad. Est = Additions to Esther.
Wis = Wisdom.
Sir = Sirach or Ecclesiasticus.
Bar = Baruch.
Three = Song of the Three Children.
Sus = Susanna.
Bel = Bel and the Dragon.
Pr. Man = Prayer of Manasses.
1 Mac, 2 Mac = 1 and 2 Maccabees.

New Testament.

Mt = Matthew.
Mk = Mark.
Lk = Luke.
Jn = John.
Ac = Acts.
Ro = Romans.
1 Co, 2 Co = 1 and 2 Corinthians.
Gal = Galatians.
Eph = Ephesians.
Ph = Philippians.
Col = Colossians.
1 Th, 2 Th = 1 and 2 Thessalonians.
1 Ti, 2 Ti = 1 and 2 Timothy.
Tit = Titus.
Philem = Philemon.
He = Hebrews.
Ja = James.
1 P, 2 P = 1 and 2 Peter.
1 Jn, 2 Jn, 3 Jn = 1, 2, and 3 John.
Jude.
Rev = Revelation.

III. For the Literature

1. The following authors' names, when unaccompanied by the title of a book, stand for the works in the list below.

Baethgen = *Beiträge zur sem. Religionsgesch.*, 1888.
Baldwin = *Dict. of Philosophy and Psychology*, 3 vols. 1901–1905.
Barth = *Nominalbildung in den sem. Sprachen*, 2 vols. 1889, 1891 ([2]1894).
Benzinger = *Heb. Archäologie*, 1894.
Brockelmann = *Gesch. d. arab. Litteratur*, 2 vols. 1897–1902.
Bruns-Sachau = *Syr.-Röm. Rechtsbuch aus dem fünften Jahrhundert*, 1880.
Budge = *Gods of the Egyptians*, 2 vols. 1903.
Daremberg-Saglio = *Dict. des ant. grec. et rom.*, 1886–90.
De la Saussaye = *Lehrbuch der Religionsgesch.*[3], 1905.
Denzinger = *Enchiridion Symbolorum*[11], Freiburg im Br., 1911.
Deussen = *Die Philos. d. Upanishads*, 1899 [Eng. tr., 1906].
Doughty = *Arabia Deserta*, 2 vols. 1888.
Grimm = *Deutsche Mythologie*[4], 3 vols. 1875–1878, Eng. tr. *Teutonic Mythology*, 4 vols. 1882–1888.
Hamburger = *Realencyclopädie für Bibel u. Talmud*, i. 1870 ([2]1892), ii. 1883, suppl. 1886, 1891 f., 1897.
Holder = *Altceltischer Sprachschatz*, 1891 ff.
Holtzmann-Zöpffel = *Lexicon f. Theol. u. Kirchenwesen*[2], 1895.
Howitt = *Native Tribes of S. E. Australia*, 1904.
Jubainville = *Cours de Litt. celtique*, i.–xii., 1883 ff.
Lagrange = *Études sur les religions sémitiques*[2], 1904.
Lane = *An Arabic-English Dictionary*, 1863 ff.
Lang = *Myth, Ritual and Religion*[2], 2 vols. 1899.
Lepsius = *Denkmäler aus Ægypten u. Æthiopien*, 1849–1860.
Lichtenberger = *Encyc. des sciences religieuses*, 1876.
Lidzbarski = *Handbuch der nordsem. Epigraphik*, 1898.
McCurdy = *History, Prophecy, and the Monuments*, 2 vols. 1894–1896.
Muir = *Orig. Sanskrit Texts*, 1858–1872.
Muss-Arnolt = *A Concise Dict. of the Assyrian Language*, 1894 ff.
Nowack = *Lehrbuch d. heb. Archäologie*, 2 vols 1894.
Pauly-Wissowa = *Realencyc. der classischen Altertumswissenschaft*, 1894 ff.
Perrot-Chipiez = *Hist. de l'Art dans l'Antiquité*, 1881 ff.
Preller = *Römische Mythologie*, 1858.
Réville = *Religion des peuples non-civilisés*, 1883.
Riehm = *Handwörterbuch d. bibl. Altertums*[2], 1893–1894.
Robinson = *Biblical Researches in Palestine*[2], 1856.
Roscher = *Lex. d. gr. u. röm. Mythologie*, 1884 ff.
Schaff-Herzog = *The New Schaff-Herzog Encyclopedia of Relig. Knowledge*, 1908 ff.
Schenkel = *Bibel-Lexicon*, 5 vols. 1869–1875.
Schürer = *GJV*[3], 3 vols. 1898–1901 [*HJP*, 5 vols. 1890 ff.].
Schwally = *Leben nach dem Tode*, 1892.
Siegfried-Stade = *Heb. Wörterbuch zum AT*, 1893.
Smend = *Lehrbuch der alttest. Religionsgesch.*[2], 1899.
Smith (G. A.) = *Historical Geography of the Holy Land*[4], 1896.
Smith (W. R.) = *Religion of the Semites*[2], 1894.
Spencer (H.) = *Principles of Sociology*[3], 1885–1896.
Spencer-Gillen[a] = *Native Tribes of Central Australia*, 1899.
Spencer-Gillen[b] = *Northern Tribes of Central Australia*, 1904.
Swete = *The OT in Greek*, 3 vols. 1893 ff.
Tylor (E. B.) = *Primitive Culture*[3], 1891 [[4]1903].
Ueberweg = *Hist. of Philosophy*, Eng. tr., 2 vols. 1872–1874.
Weber = *Jüdische Theologie auf Grund des Talmud u. verwandten Schriften*[2], 1897.
Wiedemann = *Die Religion der alten Aegypter*, 1890 [Eng. tr., revised, *Religion of the Anc. Egyptians*, 1897].
Wilkinson = *Manners and Customs of the Ancient Egyptians*, 3 vols. 1878.
Zunz = *Die gottesdienstlichen Vorträge der Juden*[2], 1892.

2. Periodicals, Dictionaries, Encyclopædias, and other standard works frequently cited.

AA = Archiv für Anthropologie.
AAOJ = American Antiquarian and Oriental Journal.
ABAW = Abhandlungen d. Berliner Akad. d. Wissenschaften.
AE = Archiv für Ethnographie.
AEG = Assyr. and Eng. Glossary (Johns Hopkins University).
AGG = Abhandlungen der Göttinger Gesellschaft der Wissenschaften.
AGPh = Archiv für Geschichte der Philosophie.
AHR = American Historical Review.
AHT = Ancient Hebrew Tradition (Hommel).
AJPh = American Journal of Philology.
AJPs = American Journal of Psychology.
AJRPE = American Journal of Religious Psychology and Education.
AJSL = American Journal of Semitic Languages and Literature.
AJTh = American Journal of Theology.
AMG = Annales du Musée Guimet.
APES = American Palestine Exploration Society.
APF = Archiv für Papyrusforschung.
AR = Anthropological Review.
ARW = Archiv für Religionswissenschaft.
AS = Acta Sanctorum (Bollandus).
ASG = Abhandlungen der Sächsischen Gesellschaft der Wissenschaften.
ASoc = L'Année Sociologique.
ASWI = Archæological Survey of W. India.
AZ = Allgemeine Zeitung.
BAG = Beiträge zur alten Geschichte.
BASS = Beiträge zur Assyriologie u. sem. Sprachwissenschaft (edd. Delitzsch and Haupt).
BCH = Bulletin de Correspondance Hellénique.
BE = Bureau of Ethnology.
BG = Bombay Gazetteer.
BJ = Bellum Judaicum (Josephus).
BL = Bampton Lectures.
BLE = Bulletin de Littérature Ecclésiastique.
BOR = Bab. and Oriental Record.
BS = Bibliotheca Sacra.
BSA = Annual of the British School at Athens.
BSAA = Bulletin de la Soc. archéologique à Alexandrie.
BSAL = Bulletin de la Soc. d'Anthropologie de Lyon.
BSAP = Bulletin de la Soc. d'Anthropologie, etc., Paris.
BSG = Bulletin de la Soc. de Géographie.
BTS = Buddhist Text Society.
BW = Biblical World.
BZ = Biblische Zeitschrift.

CAIBL=Comptes rendus de l'Académie des Inscriptions et Belles-Lettres.
CBTS=Calcutta Buddhist Text Society.
CE=Catholic Encyclopædia.
CF=Childhood of Fiction (MacCulloch).
CGS=Cults of the Greek States (Farnell).
CI=Census of India.
CIA=Corpus Inscrip. Atticarum.
CIE=Corpus Inscrip. Etruscarum.
CIG=Corpus Inscrip. Græcarum.
CIL=Corpus Inscrip. Latinarum.
CIS=Corpus Inscrip. Semiticarum.
COT=Cuneiform Inscriptions and the OT [Eng. tr. of *KAT*²; see below].
CR=Contemporary Review.
CeR=Celtic Review.
ClR=Classical Review.
CQR=Church Quarterly Review.
CSEL=Corpus Script. Eccles. Latinorum.
DACL = Dict. d'Archéologie chrétienne et de Liturgie (Cabrol).
DB=Dict. of the Bible.
DCA=Dict. of Christian Antiquities (Smith-Cheetham).
DCB=Dict. of Christian Biography (Smith-Wace).
DCG=Dict. of Christ and the Gospels.
DI=Dict. of Islam (Hughes).
DNB=Dict. of National Biography.
DPhP=Dict. of Philosophy and Psychology.
DWAW=Denkschriften der Wiener Akad. der Wissenschaften.
EBi=Encyclopædia Biblica.
EBr=Encyclopædia Britannica.
EEFM=Egyp. Explor. Fund Memoirs.
EI=Encyclopædia of Islām.
ERE=The present work.
Exp=Expositor.
ExpT=Expository Times.
FHG=Fragmenta Historicorum Græcorum (coll. C. Müller, Paris, 1885).
FL=Folklore.
FLJ=Folklore Journal.
FLR=Folklore Record.
GA=Gazette Archéologique.
GB=Golden Bough (Frazer).
GGA=Göttingische Gelehrte Anzeigen.
GGN=Göttingische Gelehrte Nachrichten (Nachrichten der königl. Gesellschaft der Wissenschaften zu Göttingen).
GIAP=Grundriss d. Indo-Arischen Philologie.
GIrP=Grundriss d. Iranischen Philologie.
GJV=Geschichte des jüdischen Volkes.
GVI=Geschichte des Volkes Israel.
HAI=Handbook of American Indians.
HDB=Hastings' Dict. of the Bible.
HE=Historia Ecclesiastica.
HGHL=Historical Geography of the Holy Land (G. A. Smith).
HI=History of Israel.
HJ=Hibbert Journal.
HJP=History of the Jewish People.
HN=Historia Naturalis (Pliny).
HWB=Handwörterbuch.
IA=Indian Antiquary.
ICC=International Critical Commentary.
ICO=International Congress of Orientalists.
ICR=Indian Census Report.
IG=Inscrip. Græcæ (publ. under auspices of Berlin Academy, 1873 ff.).
IGA=Inscrip. Græcæ Antiquissimæ.
IGI=Imperial Gazetteer of India² (1885); new edition (1908–1909).
IJE=International Journal of Ethics.
ITL=International Theological Library.
JA=Journal Asiatique.
JAFL=Journal of American Folklore.
JAI=Journal of the Anthropological Institute.
JAOS=Journal of the American Oriental Society.
JASB=Journal of the Anthropological Society of Bombay.
JASBe=Journ. of As. Soc. of Bengal.
JBL=Journal of Biblical Literature.
JBTS=Journal of the Buddhist Text Society.
JD=Journal des Débats.
JDTh=Jahrbücher f. deutsche Theologie.
JE=Jewish Encyclopedia.
JGOS=Journal of the German Oriental Society.
JHC=Johns Hopkins University Circulars.
JHS=Journal of Hellenic Studies.
JLZ=Jenäer Litteraturzeitung.
JPh=Journal of Philology.
JPTh=Jahrbücher für protestantische Theologie.
JPTS=Journal of the Pāli Text Society.
JQR=Jewish Quarterly Review.
JRAI=Journal of the Royal Anthropological Institute.
JRAS=Journal of the Royal Asiatic Society.
JRASBo=Journal of the Royal Asiatic Society, Bombay branch.
JRASC=Journal of the Royal Asiatic Society, Ceylon branch.
JRASK=Journal of the Royal Asiatic Society, Korean branch.
JRGS=Journal of the Royal Geographical Society.
JThSt=Journal of Theological Studies.
*KAT*² = Die Keilinschriften und das AT² (Schrader), 1883.
*KAT*³=Zimmern-Winckler's ed. of the preceding (really a totally distinct work), 1903.
KB or *KIB*=Keilinschriftliche Bibliothek (Schrader), 1889 ff.
KGF = Keilinschriften und die Geschichtsforschung, 1878.
LCBl=Literarisches Centralblatt.
LOPh=Literaturblatt für Oriental. Philologie.
LOT=Introduction to Literature of OT (Driver).
LP=Legend of Perseus (Hartland).
LSSt=Leipziger sem. Studien.
M=Mélusine.
MAIBL = Mémoires de l'Acad. des Inscriptions et Belles-Lettres.
MBAW = Monatsbericht d. Berliner Akad. d. Wissenschaften.
MGH=Monumenta Germaniæ Historica (Pertz).
MGJV=Mittheilungen der Gesellschaft für jüdische Volkskunde.
MGWJ=Monatsschrift für Geschichte und Wissenschaft des Judentums.
MI=Origin and Development of the Moral Ideas (Westermarck).
MNDPV = Mittheilungen u. Nachrichten des deutschen Palästina-Vereins.
MR=Methodist Review.
MVG=Mittheilungen der vorderasiatischen Gesellschaft.
MWJ = Magazin für die Wissenschaft des Judentums.
NBAC=Nuovo Bulletino di Archeologia Cristiana.
NC=Nineteenth Century.
NHWB=Neuhebräisches Wörterbuch.
NINQ=North Indian Notes and Queries.
NKZ=Neue kirchliche Zeitschrift.
NQ=Notes and Queries.
NR=Native Races of the Pacific States (Bancroft).
NTZG=Neutestamentliche Zeitgeschichte.
OED=Oxford English Dictionary.
OLZ=Orientalische Litteraturzeitung.
OS=Onomastica Sacra.
OTJC=Old Testament in the Jewish Church (W. R. Smith).
OTP=Oriental Translation Fund Publications.
PAOS=Proceedings of American Oriental Society.
PASB=Proceedings of the Anthropological Soc. of Bombay.

PB=Polychrome Bible (English).
PBE=Publications of the Bureau of Ethnology.
PC=Primitive Culture (Tylor).
PEFM=Palestine Exploration Fund Memoirs.
PEFSt = Palestine Exploration Fund Quarterly Statement.
PG=Patrologia Græca (Migne).
PJB=Preussische Jahrbücher.
PL=Patrologia Latina (Migne).
PNQ=Punjab Notes and Queries.
PR=Popular Religion and Folklore of N. India (Crooke).
*PRE*³=Prot. Realencyclopädie (Herzog-Hauck).
PRR=Presbyterian and Reformed Review.
PRS=Proceedings of the Royal Society.
PRSE=Proceedings Royal Soc. of Edinburgh.
PSBA=Proceedings of the Society of Biblical Archæology.
PTS=Pāli Text Society.
RA=Revue Archéologique.
RAnth=Revue d'Anthropologie.
RAS=Royal Asiatic Society.
RAssyr=Revue d'Assyriologie.
RB=Revue Biblique.
RBEW=Reports of the Bureau of Ethnology (Washington).
RC=Revue Critique.
RCel=Revue Celtique.
RCh=Revue Chrétienne.
RDM=Revue des Deux Mondes.
RE=Realencyclopädie.
REG=Revue des Études Grecques.
REg=Revue Égyptologique.
REJ=Revue des Études Juives.
REth=Revue d'Ethnographie.
RHLR=Revue d'Histoire et de Littérature Religieuses.
RHR=Revue de l'Histoire des Religions.
RN=Revue Numismatique.
RP=Records of the Past.
RPh=Revue Philosophique.
RQ=Römische Quartalschrift.
RS = Revue sémitique d'Épigraphie et d'Hist. ancienne.
RSA=Recueil de la Soc. archéologique.
RSI=Reports of the Smithsonian Institution.
RTAP=Recueil de Travaux rélatifs à l'Archéologie et à la Philologie.
RTP=Revue des traditions populaires.
RThPh=Revue de Théologie et de Philosophie.
RTr=Recueil de Travaux.
RVV=Religionsgeschichtliche Versuche und Vorarbeitungen.
RWB=Realwörterbuch.
SBAW=Sitzungsberichte d. Berliner Akademie d. Wissenschaften.
SBB=Sacred Books of the Buddhists.
SBE=Sacred Books of the East.
SBOT=Sacred Books of the OT (Hebrew).
SDB=Single-vol. Dict. of the Bible (Hastings).
SK=Studien und Kritiken.
SMA=Sitzungsberichte d. Münchener Akademie.
SSGW=Sitzungsberichte d. Kgl. Sächs. Gesellsch. d. Wissenschaften.
SWAW=Sitzungsberichte d. Wiener Akademie d. Wissenschaften.
TAPA = Transactions of American Philological Association.
TASJ = Transactions of the Asiatic Soc. of Japan.
TC=Tribes and Castes.
TES=Transactions of Ethnological Society.
ThLZ=Theologische Litteraturzeitung.
ThT=Theol. Tijdschrift.
TRHS=Transactions of Royal Historical Society.
TRSE=Transactions of Royal Soc. of Edinburgh.
TS=Texts and Studies.
TSBA=Transactions of the Soc. of Biblical Archæology.
TU=Texte und Untersuchungen.
WAI=Western Asiatic Inscriptions.
WZKM=Wiener Zeitschrift f. Kunde des Morgenlandes.
ZA=Zeitschrift für Assyriologie.
ZÄ=Zeitschrift für ägyp. Sprache u. Altertumswissenschaft.
ZATW = Zeitschrift für die alttest. Wissenschaft.
ZCK=Zeitschrift für christliche Kunst.
ZCP=Zeitschrift für celtische Philologie.
ZDA=Zeitschrift für deutsches Altertum.
ZDMG = Zeitschrift der deutschen morgenländischen Gesellschaft.
ZDPV = Zeitschrift des deutschen Palästina-Vereins.
ZE=Zeitschrift für Ethnologie.
ZKF=Zeitschrift für Keilschriftforschung.
ZKG=Zeitschrift für Kirchengeschichte.
ZKT=Zeitschrift für kathol. Theologie.
ZKWL=Zeitschrift für kirchl. Wissenschaft und kirchl. Leben.
ZM=Zeitschrift für die Mythologie.
ZNTW = Zeitschrift für die neutest. Wissenschaft.
ZPhP = Zeitschrift für Philosophie und Pädagogik.
ZTK=Zeitschrift für Theologie und Kirche.
ZVK=Zeitschrift für Volkskunde.
ZVRW = Zeitschrift für vergleichende Rechtswissenschaft.
ZWT = Zeitschrift für wissenschaftliche Theologie.

[A small superior number designates the particular edition of the work referred to, as *KAT*², *LOT*⁶, etc.]

ENCYCLOPÆDIA

OF

RELIGION AND ETHICS

L

LIFE AND DEATH.

LIFE AND DEATH (Biological).—The characteristic quality, common to plants, animals, and man, which distinguishes them from all other things, is what we call 'life.' It cannot be defined in terms of anything else, but what the concept implies may be illustrated; and that is the aim of this article. The word 'life' is often used to denote the living creature's complete sequence of activities and experiences throughout the period during which it is alive; as when we say that an eagle has a very long, busy, and free life. It is also used as a short word for what is almost always going on in connexion with living creatures—their acting upon their environment and reacting to it; and it is, of course, quite clear and useful to say that life consists of action and reaction between organism and environment. We must, indeed, be careful never to lose sight of the fact that life is a relation. But what we wish to discern is the characteristic quality of organisms, one term in the relation. It may also be noted that 'life' is a distinctively biological concept, and that there is always a risk in transferring it to other fields. No harm is done, perhaps, in speaking of mental, moral, social, and spiritual life; but one may beg important questions in speaking of the life of crystals. By death we mean here the cessation of an organism's individual life, a fatal disruption of the unity of the organism. There is no confusion in using the same word for the end of the individual as such, and for the apparently irreversible process which leads to the end.

1. General characteristics of living organisms.—Many biologists have sought to sum up the characteristics of living organisms, but no formulation has won general acceptance. This doubtless means that the insignia of life have not yet been discerned either wholly or in their proper perspective. One of the clearest statements is given by Roux (*VII Internat. Zoological Congress Boston*, Cambridge, U.S.A., 1912, p. 436), who recognizes five 'elementary functions': (1) self-dissimilation; (2) self-preservation, including assimilation, growth, movement, etc.; (3) self-multiplication; (4) self-development; and (5) self-regulation in the exercise of all functions, including self-differentiation, self-adjustment, self-adaptation, and, in many organisms, distinctly recognizable psychical functions. The persistent use of the prefix self, on the part of the founder of *Entwicklungsmechanik*, is very interesting. Przibram (*Experimentelle Zoologie*, iv.) arranges 'the criteria of life' in three groups—morphological, chemical, and physiological. The morphological characteristic is some measure of differentiation or heterogeneity of structure, which distinguishes even the simplest organism from a crystal. The chemical characteristic is the invariable presence of albuminoid substances in a colloid state. The physiological characteristic is to be found in growth and in the movement of parts. Another way of stating the general characteristics of organisms will now be expounded—under three heads.

(1) *Persistence of complex specific metabolism and of specific organization.*—We place in the forefront the fact that the organism is typically in continual flux and yet retains its integrity. Chemical change is the rule of the world, but the

peculiarities in the case of organisms are (*a*) that many of the changes are very complex, having in part to do with proteids; (*b*) that they are specific for each kind of creature; and (*c*) that they are correlated in such a way that they continue and the associated structure persists. Each of these peculiarities requires some exposition. (*a*) Many chemical changes occur in the living organism, and some of them are relatively simple, but the essential changes appear to be concerned with proteid or albuminoid substances, which are always present. These compounds are peculiarly intricate, with a large number of atoms or atom-groups in their molecules; they diffuse very slowly and do not readily pass through membranes; they occur in a colloid state, and, although some are crystallizable, *e.g.* hæmoglobin, they are not known in a crystalloid state in the living organism; they are relatively stable bodies, yet they are continually breaking down and being built up again in the living body, partly under the direct influence of ferments or enzymes. The constructive, synthetic, up-building, winding-up processes are summed up in the term 'anabolism'; the disruptive, analytic, down-breaking, running-down processes are summed up in the term 'katabolism,' both sets of processes being included in the term 'metabolism,' for which we have, unfortunately, no English equivalent like the fine German word *Stoffwechsel*, 'change of stuff.'

(*b*) It is a noteworthy fact that each kind of organism, so far as we know, has its specific metabolism, its own chemical individuality. This is often well illustrated by the difference in the analogous chemical products of related species. There is chemical specificity in the milk of nearly related animals and in the grapes of nearly related vines. It has become possible of recent years to make absolutely sure, within given limits, of the kind of animal to which a blood-stain is due—*e.g.*, whether horse or ass. The familiar fact that there are people who cannot eat certain kinds of food—*e.g.*, eggs, milk, oysters, crabs—without more or less serious symptoms is an illustration of specificity which is actually individual. It looks as if a man is individual not only to his finger-prints, but to his chemical molecules. We come back to what was said of old: 'All flesh is not the same flesh: but there is one kind of flesh of men, another flesh of beasts, another of fishes, and another of birds' (1 Co 15[39]).

(*c*) In the ordinary chemical changes of the inorganic world, as in the weathering of rocks into soil, one substance changes into another. The same sort of thing goes on in the living body, but the characteristic feature is a balancing of accounts so that the specific activity continues. We lay emphasis on this characteristic since it seems fundamental—the capacity of continuing in spite of change, of continuing, indeed, through change. An organism was not worthy of the name until it showed, for a short time at least, not merely activity, but persistent activity. The organism is like a clock, inasmuch as it is always running down and always being wound up; but, unlike a clock, it can wind itself up, if it gets food and rest. The chemical processes are so correlated that up-building makes further down-breaking possible; the pluses balance the minuses; and the creature lives on. We are familiar with the self-preservative activities of higher animals, but not less important is the continual maintenance of the specific chemical activity of each cell and of the correlated invisible structure or organization. It is an extraordinary fact that a particular functional activity in a nervous system may be restored after the destruction of the nerve-cells and fibres on which the activity previously depended—a fact all the more remarkable since in higher animals there is no regeneration of nerve-cells. But not less important is the manner in which a unicellular organism can spend its substance and yet, as it were, have it, because of the fundamental capacity for self-renewal.

To what has just been said several saving clauses must be added to prevent misunderstanding. (*α*) The organism is no exception to the law of the conservation of energy. In doing work and even in mere living it expends energy and suffers wear and tear. It cannot continue active unless it captures more energy and has time for rest and repairs. But its chemical activities are so correlated that it remains for a considerable time a going concern. Fatigue, senescence, and death show that its fundamental capacity for self-maintenance is not perfect. (*β*) A particular chemical reaction that takes place in an organism may sometimes be repeated in artificial isolation, and, when this can be done, it is plain that there is nothing characteristically vital about it. It is the same in the eagle as in the test-tube. But in the living organism it is a link in a concatenated series which makes for self-repair and continuance. The riddle of life is that of the burning bush—'nec tamen consumebatur.' (*γ*) If a living organism were to be minced up quickly, no change of chemical composition would necessarily occur for some little time. But what exhibition would there be of the alleged fundamental characteristic of self repair? It may be answered that the minced-up organism would be dead, whereas we are dealing at present with living organisms. Or it may be more shrewdly pointed out that the living units of the body are adapted to chemical self-repair in particular conditions—*e.g.*, an environment of other cells, which have been abolished by the mincing. But perhaps the most instructive answer is the experimental one, that, if a sponge be minced up and forced through a cloth filter, little drops of the débris, placed in appropriate environment, will at once proceed to build themselves up into new sponges. (*δ*) It has to be admitted that the criterion of life to which we are giving prominence is relative. Some organisms can keep going for a hundred years, and some for only a hundred days, and some for only a hundred hours—the question rises as to the limit. Among the primeval organisms may there not have been some which lived only for a hundred seconds? How then would these hypothetical creatures have differed from the pill of potassium which flares itself out, rushing over the surface of the basin of water on which it has been thrown? The answer must be that an organism did not begin to be until alongside of disruptive processes associated with proteid substances there were also correlated constructive processes, making for repair and self-maintenance.

(2) *Growth, reproduction, and development.*—When an inorganic thing is affected by an external influence inducing chemical change, the result is apt to be destructive. It changes into something else—the bar of iron into rust, and the barrel of gunpowder mostly into gas. The organism's responses to stimuli—in most cases a more accurate phrasing than 'reactions to external forces'—also involve disruptions, but these are not destructive. As we have seen, they are correlated with self-maintaining processes. Now we can conceive of an organism which balanced its accounts from hour to hour, but never had much margin. There are such organisms which live, to use a homely expression, from hand to mouth. They are viable, going concerns, but they are trading on a very restricted basis of capital. It is plain that organisms could not have gone very far on such dangerous lines. They could not have survived any crisis. There is

obvious advantage, therefore, in storing energy in potential form, and this accumulation of reserves is fundamentally characteristic of organisms—especially of plants. As regards income and output of energy, an organism is far and away more efficient than any engine that man has yet invented. The organism can make its income go farther. It allows a smaller proportion of energy to sink into unavailable form. It can turn potential energy into useful form in a way that engines cannot do without enormous waste. More than this, however, there is a power of laying by what can be used later on. J. Joly ('The Abundance of Life,' *Scient. Proc. Roy. Soc. Dublin*, vii. [1891] 55–90) expressed the dynamic contrast long ago when he said that, whereas the transfer of energy into an inanimate material system was attended with effects conducive to dissipation and retardative to further transfer, the transfer of energy into an animate material system is attended with effects retardative of dissipation and conducive to further transfer. This seems to lead on to the criterion of growth. A surplus of income over expenditure is the primal condition of organic growth, and in this respect plants are pre-eminent, since they accumulate such rich reserves (potential energy of chemical substances) and are so very economical in the getting of them. It must not be forgotten that it is the existence of the plant world that has made it possible for animals to dispense, relatively speaking, with intra-organismal stores. In the art. GROWTH it has been pointed out that the growth of living creatures, as contrasted with that of crystals, is at the expense of materials different from those which compose the organism; that it implies active assimilation, not passive accretion; and that it is, in quite a new sense, a regulated process. An organism does not grow like a snowball rolling down a hill. To sum up, the power of sustained metabolism—of balancing accounts with some margin to go on with—makes growth possible.

But growth naturally leads on to multiplication or reproduction. As Haeckel clearly pointed out in his *Generelle Morphologie* (Berlin, 1866), reproduction is discontinuous growth. It seems impossible to draw any hard-and-fast line between a fragmentation which separates off overgrowths and the more specialized modes of reproduction. We seem to be looking back to near the beginning of organic life when we see the breakage of a protoplasmic mass which has grown too large to be a unity. It was long ago pointed out by Herbert Spencer and others that a living unit would tend to divide when the increase of volume outran—as it soon must if it continues—the increase of surface. In a sphere, for instance, the volume must increase as the cube, and the surface only as the square, of the radius. Thus, if it grew beyond a certain size, a spherical organism would get into serious functional difficulties, the volume of material to be kept alive having increased out of proportion to the surface by which it is kept alive. By division into two units, the disproportion is counteracted. It has also been suggested that there is a certain normal proportion between the nucleus and the cell-substance or cytoplasm, which is disturbed if the cytoplasm increases beyond a certain limit. A non-nucleated piece of cytoplasm cut off from a large protozoon can move about for a time, but it can neither feed nor grow. There are facts which indicate that the nucleus is a trophic and respiratory centre of the cell. It may be then that the division of a cell is a means of restoring the balance between volume and surface and between cytoplasm and nucleoplasm. The balance may also be restored by the emission of processes from the surface of the cell, as in rhizopod protozoa (Amœbæ, Foraminifera, Radiolaria, etc.); or by a multiplication of nuclei, as often happens. But what has been suggested is a theory of the advantage of cell-division, not of the immediate physiological reason for its occurrence. As to this, it has been mooted that a period of growth is followed automatically by a process of 'autokatalysis,' but precise data are wanting. It cannot be gainsaid that the division of a cell remains one of the deep problems of biology. W. Bateson writes:

> 'I know nothing which to a man well trained in scientific knowledge and method brings so vivid a realisation of our ignorance of the nature of life as the mystery of cell-division. . . . The greatest advance I can conceive in biology would be the discovery of the nature of the instability which leads to the continual division of the cell. When I look at a dividing cell I feel as an astronomer might do if he beheld the formation of a double star: that an original act of creation is taking place before me' (*Problems of Genetics*, p. 39).

In most cases a cell divides into two precisely similar daughter cells; this is associated with an exceedingly complicated division of the nucleus, which secures that each of the two daughter cells gets a very accurate half of each part of the original nucleus. But the difficulty of the problem is increased by the fact that a cell may also divide into two dissimilar halves, one with and another without one or more of the constituent parts of the original nucleus. In some cases among higher animals and in many unicellular organisms the cell-division may be apparently less complicated than in the usual 'indirect' method. The cell constricts in a dumb-bell-like fashion, and the nucleus likewise. In some unicellular organisms there is fragmentation of the unit. It is probable that the complicated methods of cell-division which are now the rule are the results of a long process of evolution, and that the fundamental characteristic is simply division. In any case there is no doubt that the power of spontaneous division is one of the most distinctive features of living units.

A consideration of effective activity led us to the idea of self-repair and the accumulation of reserves; this led us to the fact of growth; and this to multiplication, which takes place by division. It is characteristic of organisms to multiply, and, since what is separated off is in many cases a fragment, a group of cells, or a single cell, we are brought face to face with development—the power that a part has of growing and differentiating until it has literally reproduced the whole. Development is the expression of the latent possibilities of an imperfect organism in an appropriate environment. It is the making visible of the intrinsic manifoldness of some primordium—a bud, a fragment, a sample, or a germ-cell—and, as it appears to us, it should be thought of as a continuation (under special circumstances and with a special result, namely, a new individual) of the restitution and regrowth which goes on always to make good the body's wear and tear. Every gradation between the two may be illustrated by the phenomena of regeneration, which is exhibited when a lost part is replaced. It is a noteworthy fact that a starfish, which practises autotomy or self-mutilation in the spasms of capture and finds safety in its reflex device (for it often escapes and can regrow at leisure what it has lost), may also (e.g., *Linckia guildingii*) habitually multiply in this rather expensive fashion.

Bateson quotes Sir Michael Foster's definition: 'A living thing is a vortex of chemical and molecular change,' and points out that 'the living "vortex" differs from all others in the fact that it can divide and throw off other "vortices," through which again matter continually swirls. We may perhaps take the parallel a stage further. A simple vortex, like a smoke-ring, if projected in a suitable way will twist and form two rings. If each loop as it is formed could grow and then twist again to form more loops, we should have a model representing several of the essential features of living things' (*op. cit.* p. 40).

It has to be added, as we have seen, that the living

'vortex' is the seat of complex and specific chemical changes which are correlated in such a way that the creature *lasts*. But more has to be added still.

(3) *Effective behaviour, registration of experience, and variability.*—The common idea in this grouping is self-expression. (*a*) Life is a kind of activity, reaching a climax in behaviour, *i.e.* in an organically determined, correlated series of acts which make towards a definite result. Behaviour concerns the organism as a whole, as in locomotion, or a considerable part of an organism, and differs from a reflex action in being a concatenation. It has different modes (tropisms, taxisms, instinctive behaviour, intelligent behaviour), but there is the common feature of correlation, of purposiveness (not necessarily purposefulness), and, usually, of individuality. When an amœba appears to go on the hunt, follows another, catches it, loses it, re-captures it, we must say either 'behaviour' or 'magic.' We need not suppose that the amœba knows what it is about, but it is very difficult not to say that its awareness is accompanied by some analogue of 'will.' In the case of instinctive behaviour there is often an extraordinary adherence to routine, and this may defeat itself, but in ninety-nine cases out of a hundred what is done is effective, and the individuality probably finds expression in ways that escape us. (*b*) The effectiveness which characterizes the behaviour of organisms (*i.e.* of those that show behaviour enough to be studied) seems to depend on profiting by experience in the individual lifetime, or on the results of successful ancestral experiments, or, usually, on both. It appears to us to be one of the insignia of life that the organism registers its experiments or the results of its experiences. We must here include under the term 'organism' the germ-cell, which is an organism implicit or *in potentia*, and may be said to make experiments in internal organization just as much as, in reality far more than, a protozoon which makes experiments in its skeletal architecture or in its behaviour. As W. K. Clifford said,

> 'It is the peculiarity of living things not merely that they change under the influence of surrounding circumstances, but that any change which takes place in them is not lost, but retained, and as it were built into the organism to serve as the foundation for future actions' (*Lectures and Essays*, London, 1879, i. 83).

As Bergson puts it,

> 'Its past, in its entirety, is prolonged into its present, and abides there, actual and acting' (*Creative Evolution*, p. 16).

As Jennings says, from the physiological point of view, in discussing the behaviour of the starfish,

> 'The precise way each part shall act under the influence of the stimulus must be determined by the past history of that part; by the stimuli that have acted upon it, by the reactions which it has given, by the results which these reactions have produced (as well as by the present relations of this part to other parts, and by the immediate effects of its present action). . . . We know as solidly as we know anything in physiology that the history of an organism does modify it and its actions—in ways not yet thoroughly understood, doubtless, yet none the less real' ('Behavior of the Starfish,' *University of California Publications in Zoology*, iv. [1907] 177).

(*c*) The organism's variability or power of producing some distinctively new character must, in the present state of science, be taken as 'given.' The only capacity like it that we know of is our own power of mental experiment—the secret of the artist, the musician, the thinker, or the inventor. It may be noted that 'modifications' wrought on the body by some peculiarity of nurture, environment, or habit are to be distinguished from germinal variations. They are important individually, but they are not known to affect the progeny in any representative fashion. We may also distinguish those negative variations which are due to the loss of an ancestral character, like horns or a tail, for there are various opportunities in the history of the germ-cells for the dropping out of an hereditary item. Similarly, in regard to those variations which are plainly interpretable as new arrangements of previously expressed ancestral characters, there is no theoretical difficulty. What is baffling, however, is the origin of something definitely novel, especially when there is reason to believe that it originates brusquely. We can hardly do more at present than assume that the organism is essentially creative. Just as the intact organism, from amœba to elephant, tries experiments, so the germ-cell, which is no ordinary cell but an implicit organism, a condensed individuality, may perhaps make experiments in self-expression, which we call variations or mutations. This completes our statement of the general characteristics of organisms.

2. Death.—It is convenient to distinguish, from a biological point of view, three different kinds of death. (1) There is *violent* death, when some external influence shatters, or dissolves, or benumbs the organization. A wound, a sudden change of temperature, or being swallowed by another organism may involve the irrecoverable cessation of bodily life. For many animals in open nature the end seems to be always violent. (2) There is *microbic* death, when some intruding micro-organism, establishing itself in the body, multiplies exceedingly and produces fatal effects. The intruders cause lesions, or destroy important elements, or produce fatal toxins, and so on. In wild nature there is little microbic death except when man effects disarrangements in distribution, so that organisms are exposed to the attack of new microbes. (3) There is *natural* death, which results from some breakdown in the correlation of vital processes. Hard-worked organs, such as the heart, may suffer from the imperfect recuperation of their wear and tear. The highly specialized cells of the nervous system tend to lose early in life their power of dividing and therefore of replacement; thus in higher animals there is not after birth any increase in the number of nerve-cells. In various ways there arises within the body an accumulation of physiological arrears which eventually implies physiological insolvency. Especially does the process of reproduction strain the resources of the organism.

In spite of criticisms, Weismann's doctrine of the immortality of the protozoa remains acceptable. Not that these unicellular organisms live any charmed life; they are continually being killed by accidents, vicissitudes, and enemies; some of them are occasionally consumed by microbes; but it seems to be the case that in their normal conditions (when waste-products do not accumulate in the surrounding medium and when there is opportunity for conjugation) many of them at least are not subject to natural death in the same degree as higher animals are. Some of them, indeed, may be exempt from natural death altogether. The reasons for this immunity are to be found in the relative simplicity of structure, for unicellular organisms can continuously and completely make good their wear and tear, and in the relatively simple modes of multiplication, which do not involve the nemesis so frequent in higher organisms. Though it is not improbable that very simple multicellular organisms, such as the freshwater hydra, may enjoy some measure of immunity from natural death, there is doubtless general truth in the epigram that, in the course of evolution, natural death was the price paid for a body. The relative immunity of unicellular organisms strongly suggests that natural death is not to be regarded simply as an intrinsic necessity—the fate of all life.

Life was described by Bichât as 'the sum of the functions which resist death,' but this is a one-sided emphasis. For, while it is characteristic of organisms that they are continually at work in securing the persistence of their specific organization, it is equally characteristic that they spend themselves in securing the continuance of their kind. Instead of seeking to avoid death, to speak metaphorically, they often rather invite it, sacrificing themselves in producing and providing for the next generation. Their reproductive activities put an end to their self-preservation. Natural death is not to be thought of as like the running down of a clock. It is more than an individual physiological problem; it is adjusted in reference to the welfare of the species. As has been noted in art. AGE, there is good reason for regarding the occurrence of death at a particular time as adaptive. Constitutions which lose their correlation at the end of a year have been selected in certain conditions; constitutions which lose their correlation at the end of ten years have been selected in others. It is certain, as Weismann says, that 'worn-out individuals are not only valueless to the species, but they are even harmful' (*Essays upon Heredity*, etc. i. 24). As Goethe put it, 'Death is Nature's expert contrivance to get plenty of life' ('Aphorisms on Nature,' tr. Huxley, in *Nature*, i. [1869] 1).

3. Organism and mechanism.—The task of mechanics, as G. Kirchhoff said, is 'to describe completely and in the simplest manner the motions which take place in nature' (*Vorlesungen über mathematische Physik*, Leipzig, 1876, i. 1). A mechanical description is satisfactory as such when it enables us to formulate a process as a continuous series of necessarily concatenated mechanical operations like those of an automatic machine or of a volcano. We shall use the term 'mechanical' throughout as meaning a matter-and-motion description, and as equivalent to physico-chemical, for chemical and physical descriptions are (ideally at least) reducible to mechanical terms. The question before us is how far mechanical description can be usefully employed in the study of organisms. The question is twofold: (1) how far we can describe characteristically vital events in terms of those concepts and formulæ which certainly serve us well when we study the tides or eclipses, the fashioning of a dewdrop, or the making of a star; and (2) how far a mechanical description answers the distinctly biological questions as to the correlation of an organism's activities, its behaviour, its growth and reproduction, its development and evolution.

There is no doubt that chemical and physical laws apply to living creatures—to what has been called their inorganic aspect. Chemically regarded, living involves a complex of reactions in or associated with the material which we call 'protoplasm,' and some of these can be reproduced apart from the organism altogether. Some vital processes illustrate J. H. van't Hoff's rule of chemical reactions, for they increase in rapidity as the temperature increases. This may serve as an instance of the solidarity of the organism's chemical processes with those that occur in things in general, but it must be carefully noticed that we cannot assert that the movements of molecules in a living protoplasmic system are the same as those in an inorganic system. In his posthumously published *Prinzipien der Mechanik* (Leipzig, 1894) H. Hertz emphasized the need of caution.

'It is certainly a justified caution with which we confine the realm of mechanics expressly to inanimate nature and leave the question open how far its laws can be extended beyond. In truth, the matter stands thus, that we can neither maintain that the internal phenomena of animated beings obey the same laws nor that they follow other laws' (quoted by J. T. Merz, *History of European Thought*, iii. [Edinburgh and London, 1912] 584).

It is plain that many physical processes occur in the body which are comparable to those observable in the inorganic domain—processes of diffusion, capillarity, surface-tension, and so on. And, just as the living body illustrates conservation of matter, so is it with the conservation of energy. One mode may change into another mode, but no energy ceases or is lost in the transformation. Careful experiments with a calorimeter show that it is possible to square accounts of the energy-income and energy-expenditure of an organism, the slight discrepancy that is sometimes observed being reasonably explained as due to the inevitable imperfections of instruments and observations. It should be noticed, however, that, according to some physicists, the second Law of Thermodynamics does not apply to living creatures. While no fact securely established in regard to organisms has been shown to be inconsistent with the generalizations of chemistry and physics, and while many results of importance, both theoretically and practically, have rewarded the application of chemico-physical methods to living creatures, we believe it to be quite inaccurate to say that mechanical concepts and formulæ suffice for more than a partial and abstract description of the life of organisms. We shall proceed to test this.

(*a*) *Everyday functions.*—As things stand at present, there is not forthcoming any physico-chemical description of any total vital operation, even of everyday functions such as the interchange of gases in the lungs, the passage of digested food from the alimentary canal into the blood-vessels, or the filtering processes that go on in the kidneys. The co-ordination involved in the discharge of a function and the correlation of one function with another are characteristic physiological facts which are not made clearer when the chemistry or physics of an artificially isolated corner is worked out.

Even in such a familiar occurrence as a response to a stimulus 'there is in reality no experimental evidence whatsoever that the process can be understood as one of physical and chemical causation. . . . In the case of physiological stimulus and response no real quantitative relation can be traced between the supposed physical or chemical cause, and its effect. When we attempt to trace a connection we are lost in an indefinite maze of complex conditions, out of which the response emerges' (J. S. Haldane, *Mechanism, Life, and Personality*, p. 34).

A very familiar fact is that the same stimulus applied to two apparently similar animals, or to the same animal at different times, evokes different answers. We can indeed give reasons for this, but the reasons are not mechanical reasons.

(*b*) *Behaviour.*—When we think of a collie dog controlling a flock of sheep according to instructions, or of a swallow returning from its winter in the South to the place of its birth, or of the spider spinning a typical web without experience or model, or of the larval freshwater mussels fastening themselves to minnows, or of the larval liver-fluke responding to the contact of the water-snail by which alone it can successfully continue its life, or of the amœba capturing its prey, losing it, following it, re-capturing it, and so on, we are face to face with animal behaviour which transcends mechanical description. The behaviour is made up of a succession of acts which are correlated in a particular sequence. This is true even in instances where we know nothing of the associated mentality. It goes without saying that the behaviour implies chemical and physical events, but the bond of union eludes the chemist and physicist. There are elements of spontaneity, plasticity, adaptiveness, and purposiveness that are foreign to mechanical reasoning. We can make nothing of behaviour without new concepts, notably that of the organism as an historical being that trades with time.

(*c*) *Development.*—The condensation of the inheritance into microscopic germ-cells, the combination of two inheritances in fertilization, the subsequent division of the inheritance involved in the segmentation of the ovum, the process of differentiation wherein from the apparently simple the obviously complex emerges, the embryo's power of righting itself when the building materials of its edifice are artificially disarranged, the way in which different parts are correlated and, as it were, conspire together towards some future result—these and many other facts lead towards a convincing impression that development far transcends mechanism.

In his *Science and Philosophy of the Organism* (1908), Driesch has with unexampled thoroughness and subtlety tested the possibilities of mechanical description with particular reference to the facts of development, and reached a conclusion of the first importance.

'No kind of causality based upon the constellations of single physical and chemical acts can account for organic individual development; this development is not to be explained by any hypothesis about configuration of physical and chemical agents. . . . Life, at least morphogenesis, is not a specialised arrangement of inorganic events; biology, therefore, is not applied physics and chemistry; life is something apart, and biology is an independent science' (i. 142).

But, if the description of development is beyond mechanics, what, it may be asked, is the rôle of the young and vigorous science of 'developmental mechanics' (*Entwicklungsmechanik*) so well represented by the work of Roux? It may be answered that the developing embryo, as a material system, does of course exhibit chemical and physical processes which may be analyzed apart and treated singly; that development shows a continuous action and reaction between an implicit organism and the environing conditions; and that developmental mechanics so-called is in great part concerned with discovering the correlation between steps in development and their appropriate external stimulation and nurture. But a further answer is this, that the term 'mechanical' or 'mechanistic' is often, unfortunately, applied to a systematic or connected description which displays a series of events in causal coherence without any intervention of mentality. Given certain properties of organisms in general and of nerve-cells in particular, we may give a more or less connected and complete account of a reflex action without implying any psychical agency. But this should not be called a mechanical or mechanistic description; it is simply what it pretends to be, a physiological or biological description, and it implies various non-mechanical concepts. Similarly, given the organism's power of registration and of persistently reproducing its specific organization, given the cell's mysterious power of dividing—of dividing now into similar and again into dissimilar halves—given the power of utilizing nurtural stimuli to educe the inherent manifoldness, and so on, we can begin to discover the connectedness of the successive stages in development. But this should not be called mechanical description.

(*d*) *Evolution.*—The adequacy of mechanical description may also be tested in reference to evolution. There is apt to be fallacy in speaking of organic evolution as a continuation of 'evolution' in the inorganic domain. For it is more accurate, probably, to speak of the development than of the evolution of the solar system, since it is the differentiation of one mass into explicit manifoldness. The originative nebula, if such it was, is comparable to a great world-egg which developed into several embryos, as eggs sometimes do, but there was no struggle between the various planets, or between them and their environmental limitations, no sifting process which eliminated some and left others surviving. There were no alternatives, no trial and error methods. There was nothing comparable to that staking of individual lives and losing of them which is so characteristic of that sublime adventure which we call organic evolution. The theory of organic evolution starts with the mystery of variability, which is more like experimenting in self-expression than anything in the inorganic world, though it is not without its analogies even there. In natural selection the organism is often anything but a passive pawn. It does not simply submit to the apparently inevitable. It often evades its fate by a change of habit or of environment; it compromises, it experiments, it is full of device and endeavour. It not only adapts itself to its environment, it adapts its environment. The evolving organism is an historical being, a genuine agent which trades with its talents. Such mechanical description as is possible leaves the essential features undescribed.

4. The uniqueness of life.—The negative conclusion has been arrived at that mechanical or physico-chemical concepts do not suffice for answering biological questions. This is because organisms show a certain apartness or uniqueness, the various theories of which may be roughly designated vitalistic. Before considering these, however, we must refer, practically rather than philosophically, to three preliminary points. (*a*) It is maintained by some that mechanical formulation, legitimate and useful for certain purposes, apparently adequate for things as they are in certain cases, such as the tides, is not the ideal formulation even within the domain of the not-living. But, if it is not adequate there, it will be still less adequate within the realm of organisms. Practically, however, it may be answered that this is not a biologist's business. All will admit that mechanical formulæ work very usefully within the inorganic domain; but the biologist finds that they do not help him to answer his particular questions. He therefore seeks for formulæ of his own. (*b*) It is often pointed out that, although we cannot at present translate vital happenings, such as growth and division, into terms of any known mechanics, we may be able to do so in the course of time. It may be, for instance, that the concepts of chemistry and physics will undergo profound modification in centuries to come, and no one can say that they have not changed in the past. The practical answer to this question is that we can speak only of the chemistry and physics that we know. (*c*) It is held by some that it is consciousness, or mind, that gives organisms their apartness or uniqueness. But, without entering into a discussion of this, we may again give a practical answer, that the problem 'vitalism or mechanism' is the same for plants as for animals, and that we do not know anything about the mind or consciousness of plants.

There are three well-known positions in regard to the apartness of living creatures, which may be roughly described as the three grades of vitalism. (1) The first finds the differentia of organisms in the greater complexity in the configurations of elementary particles; protoplasmic metabolism is extremely intricate. New concepts are not required, but the activities of organisms cannot be predicted from a formulation of what occurs in the inorganic domain. Biology may be allowed a laboratory of its own, but it should be called biochemical. The main objection to this view is simply a matter of fact—that no headway has been made in giving mechanical answers to characteristically biological questions. (2) The second view is that there is a peculiar kind of physical energy operative in living creatures and nowhere else. Organisms have a monopoly of some power in the same series as, say, electricity. This theory is a lineal descendant of one form of the old theory of 'vital force,' but it has been brought up to date. It has been suggested that there may be a specific intra-organismal form of energy evolved by and peculiar to the complex nature of the molecule of protoplasm or of protoplasms, which exhibits an unceasing alternation of unipolar and bipolar states, the latter resulting in cell-division.

'The attraction and repulsion observed between cell and cell are certain of the manifestations of this supposed form of energy—but probably not by any means all; just as attraction and repulsion are manifestations of electrical energy under certain conditions, but are not by any means the only manifestations. In nerve impulses we may, for instance, really be experiencing manifestations in another way of the same form of energy which under other conditions produces the attractions and repulsions and the figures of strain in the dividing cells, and the actual cell-division. . . . By this supposed form of energy, I do not mean a mysterious metaphysical influence, but a form of energy comparable to gravity, electricity, or magnetism—in some respects similar to these but in other respects differing from each, and a form which could be investigated by the ordinary methods of mensuration and computation available to the mathematician' (Assheton, *Archiv für Entwicklungsmechanik*, xxix. 68 f.).

(3) The third view is thoroughgoing vitalism, best represented by the work of Driesch. Its postulate is a non-perceptual vital agency or entelechy, which does not occur in not-living things, but is associated with organisms, where it operates in certain cases, directing the chemico-physical processes so that their results are different from what they would have been apart from its intervention. The postulated entelechy is not the outcome of more complex physical conditions, 'not a new elemental consequence of some constellation'; it intervenes only at certain steps, introducing an occasional indeterminism; it is supposed to be a genuine agent, counting for something, 'at work,' as Driesch says. On this view, there is a deep-lying distinction—a difference in principle—between the flight of a bird and the movement of a comet, and biology is by hypothesis autonomous. We cannot enter into a discussion of Driesch's ingenious and consistently-worked-out theory of entelechy, or of the three proofs which he gives of the autonomy of life. The first is based on a study of morphogenesis, *i.e.* of the way in which an organism realizes in development its specific form and structure; the second is based on a study of inheritance; the third is based on a study of the movements of organisms. That they show the impossibility of 'a machine-theory of life' will be admitted by many who are not disposed to postulate an organismal entity. According to Driesch, entelechy is 'an autonomous agent,' 'of a non-spatial nature,' without a seat or localization. It is immaterial and it is not energy; it is not inconsistent in its agency with the laws of energy; its function is to suspend and to set free, in a regulatory manner, pre-existing faculties of inorganic interaction.

'There is something in the organism's behaviour—in the widest sense of the word—which is opposed to an inorganic resolution of the same, and which shows that the living organism is more than a sum or an aggregate of its parts. . . . This something we call entelechy' (*op. cit.* ii. 338).

In illustration of the criticisms of Driesch's position, reference may be made to three points. (*a*) It is argued that, if entelechy is effective, it implies a breach in the fundamental law of the conservation of energy. But it is like begging the question to press this difficulty, and Poynting has suggested, in discussing the analogous case of the operation of our will, that a merely deflecting force does no work, though it changes configuration. The will may introduce a constraint which guides molecules to glide past one another instead of clashing—a slight change of spin which may be compensated for by a slight opposite spin put on the rest of the body.

'The will may act as a guiding power changing the direction of motion of the atoms and molecules in the brain, and we can imagine such a guiding power without having to modify our ideas of the constancy of matter or the constancy of motion, or even the constancy of energy' (*HJ* i. 745).

The same may apply to the action of entelechy, and attention must be directed to the care that Driesch has taken to state his doctrine so that it does not violate the principle of the conservation of energy. He supposes entelechy to suspend reactions which are possible 'with such compounds as are present, and which would happen without entelechy. And entelechy may regulate this suspending of reactions now in one direction and now in another, suspending and permitting possible becoming whenever required for its purposes' (*op. cit.* ii. 180). Entelechy stops a movement, and the energy of the latter becomes potential. Later on the movement may continue, the potential energy being reconverted into kinetic. Thus no violence is done to the principle.

(*b*) A recurrent argument in Driesch's exposition of his doctrine of vitalism is that no machine-like arrangement can possibly account for the facts of development, inheritance, or behaviour. A machine is defined as 'a given specific combination of specific chemical and physical agents,' and Driesch seeks to reduce to absurdity the theory that any machine could do what is required. His argument is very convincing, and of course we can argue only about machines that we know and imaginative combinations or improvements of these, but it seems open to the critic to reply that no one knows all possible machines, and to urge that proving the untenability of a machine-theory does not prove the necessity of postulating an entelechy. Concerning the ingenious machines invented by man, it may not be needless to remind ourselves that their introduction into the present argument is apt to be fallacious. For they, like the wonderful achievements of the synthetic chemists, are the fruits of intelligence, not fair samples of the inorganic world. An ingenious machine, like a type-writing or a calculating machine, is an elaborated tool, an extended hand, and has inside of it, so to speak, a human thought. It is because of these qualities that it is a little like an organism. Practically, however, most of those who have a near acquaintance with living creatures will agree with Driesch that their behaviour is not very like the working of machines. For certain purposes it is useful to think of the organism as an engine, but we must recognize that it is a self-stoking, self-repairing, self-preserving, self-adjusting, self-increasing, self-reproducing engine.

(*c*) Another objection is stated by J. S. Haldane:

'In order to "guide" effectually the excessively complex physical and chemical phenomena occurring in living material, and at many different parts of a complex organism, the vital principle would apparently require to possess a superhuman knowledge of these processes. Yet the vital principle is assumed to act unconsciously. The very nature of the vitalistic assumption is thus totally unintelligible' (*op. cit.* p. 28).

Similarly Jennings urges the difficulty of understanding how entelechy gets its power of co-ordinating and individualizing:

'To accept the Entelechy unanalysed and unexplained is merely to give up the problem as insoluble'; and, if we try to work out a development of entelechies, 'then surely we are merely transferring our problem from the complex that we actually find in time and space to a sort of manufactured copy of this problem, presenting the same difficulties, with the additional one that it is impalpable and cannot be directly dealt with at all. The entelechy simply adds to our difficulties' ('Behavior of the Starfish,' *loc. cit.* p. 180).

Jennings also points out that, according to Driesch, two living systems absolutely identical in every physico-chemical respect may behave differently under absolutely identical conditions, this depending upon whether, and how, the entelechy takes part in the process. This leads to a very serious admission of experimental indeterminism, which for some minds is enough to condemn the theory. It should be stated that Driesch has replied vigorously to the criticisms brought against his position, and that he never for a moment pretended that we could understand 'even in the slightest degree' how entelechy is able to discharge its function as regulator and guide.

Differing from Driesch's position, according to which entelechy is not identical with the psychical, is the animism so ably expounded by McDougall in his *Body and Mind* (1911). The panpsychism of Paulsen and the very distinctive position of Bergson should also be considered.

According to McDougall, 'not only conscious thinking, but also morphogenesis, heredity, and evolution are psycho-physical processes. All alike are conditioned and governed by psychical dispositions that have been built up in the course of the experience of the race' (p. 379).

5. Provisional conclusion.—Looking backwards, we cannot admit that the study of animal behaviour, for instance, is no more than the study of very subtle problems in chemistry and physics; we do not find evidence to justify the view that organisms exhibit a new kind of physical energy in a line with electricity and the like; and we do not share the opinion of many recognized authorities that the facts cannot be met except by a theory of entelechy. What then is our position? It is that of 'descriptive' or 'methodological' vitalism.

Making no pronouncement whatsoever in regard to the essence of the difference between organisms and things in general, we hold to what we believe to be a fact, that mechanical formulæ do not begin to answer the distinctively biological questions. Bio-chemistry and bio-physics added together do not give us one biological answer. We need new concepts, such as that of the organism as an historic being, a genuine agent, a concrete individuality, which has traded with time and has enregistered within itself past experiences and experiments, and which has its conative bow ever bent towards the future. We need new concepts because there are new facts to describe, which we cannot analyze away into simpler processes. In the present state of knowledge we cannot tell in what the newness or apartness essentially consists, and this appears to us to be a quite legitimate, though provisional, stopping-place, without pressing on to any positive vitalistic theory, which must be, from the nature of the case, metaphysical.

If we go beyond science in the endeavour to form some connected reconstruction, we should say that those constellations of 'matter' and 'energy' called organisms afford opportunity for the expression of aspects of reality which are not patent in the inorganic domain. We must not think of 'matter' and 'energy' as the exclusive stones and mortar of the ever-growing cosmic edifice; they are abstract concepts, defined by certain methods, which serve well in the description of the physical universe. They certainly represent reality, for we safely make prophecies and risk our lives on the strength of this. But it is quite another thing to say that they are exhaustive. An aspect of reality which may safely be neglected in astronomy and navigation, in chemistry and engineering, becomes patent in the realm of organisms, and we call it 'life.' It is neither a product of 'matter' and 'energy' nor an outcome of the increasing complexity of constellations; it is an expression of the reality of which atoms and their movements are also but conceptual aspects. It may be regarded as that aspect of reality which is clearly manifested only in protoplasmic systems—and in normal conditions in all of them. May it not be that the qualities which render the postulation of entelechy or vital impetus necessary to some minds have been in kind present throughout the history of the Nature that we know? We say 'in kind,' since it is plain that we share in a movement which is not the unrolling of something originally given, but a creative evolution in which time counts. Instead of supposing the intervention of a non-material agency which controls chemical and physical processes in organisms, we suppose that a new aspect of reality is revealed in organisms—that capacity for correlation, persistence, and individuality, for growing, multiplying, and developing, for behaviour, experience, and experiment, which we call 'life,' which can nowise be explained in terms of anything simpler than itself.

To the biologist the actualities are organisms and their doings, and life is a generalized concept denoting their peculiar quality. What life in essence or principle is he does not know. Taking life in the abstract, therefore, as 'given,' we have had to be content in this article with stating the general characteristics of living creatures. It is plain, however, that analytical and formal discussion falls far short of giving any adequate idea of life in its concrete fullness. For that requires a synthesis, and that, again, is impossible without sympathy. We must use our everyday experience of livingness in ourselves and in other organisms, not for knowledge alone, but as a source of sympathy wherewith to enliven the larger data of biology; and we need not be afraid of exaggerating the wonder of life. Sympathetically and imaginatively, therefore, as well as with precision, we must seek to envisage the variety of life—hundreds of thousands of distinct individualities or species; the abundance of life—like a river always tending to overflow its banks; the diffusion of life—exploring and exploiting every corner of land and sea; the insurgence of life—self-assertive, persistent, defiant, continually achieving the apparently impossible; the cyclical development of life—ever passing from birth, through love, to death; the intricacy of life—every cell a microcosm; the subtlety of life—every drop of blood an index of idiosyncrasies; the inter-relatedness of life—with myriad threads woven into a patterned web; the drama of life—plot within plot, age after age, with every conceivable illustration of the twin motives of hunger and love; the flux of life—even under our short-lived eyes; the progress of life—slowly creeping upwards through unthinkable time, expressing itself in ever nobler forms; the beauty of life—every finished organism an artistic harmony; the morality of life—spending itself to the death for other than individual ends; the mentality of life—sometimes quietly dreaming, sometimes sleep-walking, sometimes wide awake; and the victory of life—subduing material things to its will and in its highest reaches controlling itself towards an increasing purpose.

See, further, ABIOGENESIS, AGE, BIOLOGY, DEVELOPMENT, GROWTH, HEREDITY.

LITERATURE.—R. Assheton, *Archiv für Entwicklungsmechanik*, xxix. [1910] 46–78; W. Bateson, *Problems of Genetics*, London, 1913; H. Bergson, *Creative Evolution*, Eng. tr., do. 1911; G. Bunge, *Physiological and Pathological Chemistry*, Eng. tr., London, 1890 (esp. Lect. i. 'Vitalism and Mechanism'); O. Bütschli, *Mechanismus und Vitalismus*, Leipzig, 1901; F. Czapek, *Chemical Phenomena in Life*, London and New York, 1911; A. Dastre, *La Vie et la mort*, Paris, 1903; H. Driesch, *The Science and Philosophy of the Organism*, 2 vols., London, 1908, *The Problem of Individuality*, do. 1914; J. S. Haldane, *Mechanism, Life, and Personality*, do. 1913; M. M. Hartog, *Problems of Life and Reproduction*, do. 1913; L. T. Hobhouse, *Development and Purpose*, do. 1913; J. W. Jenkinson, *Experimental Embryology*, Oxford, 1909 (with a discussion of vitalism); H. S. Jennings, 'Doctrines held as Vitalism,' in *American Naturalist*, xlvii. [1913] 385–417; J. Johnstone, *The Philosophy of Biology*, Cambridge, 1914; Oliver Lodge, *Life and Matter*[4], London, 1906; J. Loeb, *The Mechanistic Conception of Life*, Chicago, 1912; W. McDougall, *Body and Mind*, London, 1911; J. T. Merz, *A History of European Thought in the Nineteenth Century*, esp. vol. ii., Edinburgh and London, 1902; C. S. Minot, *The Problem of Age, Growth, and Death*, London, 1908; B. Moore, *The Origin and Nature of Life*, do. 1913; C. Lloyd Morgan, *The Interpretation of Nature*, Bristol, 1905, *Instinct and Experience*,

London, 1912; T. Percy Nunn, 'Animism and the Doctrine of Energy' in *Proc. Aristotelian Society*, 1911-12; Karl Pearson, *Grammar of Science*, revised ed., London, 1911; J. H. Poynting, 'Physical Law and Life' in *HJ* i. [1903] 728-746; Hans Przibram, *Experimentelle Zoologie*, pt. iv. 'Vitalität,' Leipzig and Vienna, 1913; E. Radl, *Geschichte der biologischen Theorien*, Leipzig, 1905; W. Roux, *Gesammelte Abhandlungen über Entwickelungsmechanik der Organismen*, 2 vols., Leipzig, 1895; E. S. Russell, 'Vitalism' in *Scientia*, ix. [1911] 329-345; E. A. Schäfer, *Presidential Address British Association*, Dundee, 1912; Herbert Spencer, *Principles of Biology*, London, 1866, new ed., vol. i., 1898; D'Arcy W. Thompson, 'Magnalia Naturæ; or, The Greater Problems of Biology,' *Pres. Address Section D, Brit. Association*, Portsmouth, 1911; J. Arthur Thomson, *Introduction to Science*, London, 1912, *The Wonder of Life*, do. 1914; M. Verworn, *General Physiology*, Eng. tr., do. 1899; J. Ward, *Naturalism and Agnosticism*³, do. 1906; A. Weismann, *Essays upon Heredity and Kindred Biological Problems*², 2 vols., Oxford, 1891-92, esp. Essay iii. on 'Life and Death.'

J. ARTHUR THOMSON.

LIFE AND DEATH (Primitive).—In primitive thought, so far as we can analyze it, life and death are not the balanced opposites which civilized contemplation has made them. To early man life is the normal condition, death an abnormal catastrophe, unnatural, miraculous, and terrible. An exception is to be made when a man kills his quarry or his foe; here the satisfaction of an end achieved inhibits the feelings aroused by the non-violent death of a tribesman. According to Australian philosophy, men would live on indefinitely, except for the result of actual physical violence or of sorcery, a refined form of it.[1] This is the usual view of the savage, though it is hardly a reasoned opinion. The savage, like the majority of civilized men, lives in the present; this fact involves a certain inertia of thought as to the contrast between life and death, and it is true of both stages of culture that 'the fear of death is as nothing.'[2] The primitive mind, when it exercised itself on the subject of life, was concerned with the acquisition of physical strength and moral influence rather than with the problem of the nature of vitality; but the constant rage and terror which characterized its attitude towards death involved a permanent concern with the supposed causes of an event which, though inevitable, remained a mystery and a violation of natural law.

1. The nature of life.—The distinction between life and soul is in some cases confused, and in others not drawn. Again, the latter concept includes several ideas. We have, however, to deal with a 'life-principle' whenever there is a clear connexion between a concept and facts of life. For the earliest stage of thought the chief datum is the difference observed between the dead body and the living and moving body. It is inferred that something has departed from the body when dead; the something is a concrete object or substance, ideated vaguely at first, later with some precision, as a special entity, or identified with one or other part of the living organism.

Certain Australians speak of 'something,' a *yowee*, not described, which never leaves the body of the living man; it grows as he grows, and decays as he decays.[3] This illustrates well the primary stage. Put in another form, the inference is that the 'soul' does not finally leave the body until decomposition is well advanced.[4] Such cases indicate that the inference of life from observed movement is not in itself primary. Many peoples regard inanimate objects as 'alive,' but the meaning of this is clearly shown by the Tongan and West African notion that these objects 'die' when they are broken or destroyed.[5] The view

¹ W. E. Roth, *Ethnological Studies among the North-West Central Queensland Aborigines*, Brisbane, 1897, p. 161; cf. art. DEATH AND DISPOSAL OF THE DEAD (Introductory), vol. iv. p. 412 f.

² Roth, p. 161.

³ K. L. Parker, *The Euahlayi Tribe*, London, 1905, p. 35.

⁴ L. Fison, *JAI* x. [1880-81] 141.

⁵ W. Mariner, *The Tonga Islands*², London, 1818, ii. 130; M. H. Kingsley, *FL* viii. [1897] 145.

that so vaguely ideated a content is concrete is supported by the fact that any haphazard identification serves as 'life'; examples will be found below. But the primal concept is, as the first Australian instance shows, very near to a result in which a man's 'life' is himself in replica.

This perhaps is to be regarded as the second stage of analysis. The Hervey Islanders considered that fat men had fat souls, thin men thin souls.[1] According to the Karo Battak of Sumatra, a man's *tendi* disappears at death. It is a 'copy' of the owner, his 'other self.'[2] According to the Karens, that which 'personates the varied phenomena of life' is the *kelah* or *là*, which 'is not the soul,' but 'is distinct from the body and its absence from the body is death.' It is also the individuality of the animated being.[3] 'It merely gives life,' and 'cannot be distinguished from the person himself.'[4] The Iroquois conceived of 'an exceedingly subtle and refined image, . . . possessing the form of the body, with a head, teeth, arms, legs,' etc.[5]

The next stage is characteristic of Papuan and Malayan belief.

> 'The Dayak idea of life is this, that in mankind there is a living principle called *sĕmangat* or *semungi*; that sickness is caused by the temporary absence and death by the total departure of this principle from the body.'[6]

But this 'principle' is a replica of the individual, and a miniature replica. This is the *tanoana*, or 'little man,' of the Torajas of Celebes.[7] The *sĕmangat* of the wild Malayan tribes is a 'shape,' exactly like the man himself, but no bigger than a grain of maize.[8] The *sĕmangat* of the Malays is a 'thumbling,' and corresponds exactly in shape, proportion, and complexion to its embodiment or casing (*sarong*), *i.e.* the body. It is the cause of life; it is itself an individual person, as it were, and is separable from the body in sleep, sickness, and death.[9] A similar conception is found in S. Africa,[10] America,[11] and other localities sporadically, but is general enough to be regarded as typical.

The problem of its origin is not clear. J. G. Frazer thus describes the conception:

> 'As the savage commonly explains the processes of inanimate nature by supposing that they are produced by living beings working in or behind the phenomena, so he explains the phenomena of life itself. If an animal lives and moves, it can only be, he thinks, because there is a little animal inside which moves it: if a man lives and moves, it can only be because he has a little man or animal inside who moves him.'[12]

The argument agrees with the fact that the miniature replica is usually supposed to be the cause of life, but it is difficult to understand how the idea of an inner being, whether in inanimate things or in living men, could have arisen in the first instance. Only the contrast between the dead and the living body seems adequate to produce it; later, the idea could be applied to all natural objects. As for the miniature size of the replica, this is probably a refinement of an earlier conception, in which such qualities were distinguished, and it would be naturally deduced from the fact that the man's body is still present, without any reduction; that which has departed, therefore, must be infinitesimally small. The same result is

¹ W. W. Gill, *Myths and Songs from the South Pacific*, London, 1876, p. 171.

² J. H. Neumann, *Mededeelingen van wege het nederlandsch Zendelinggenootschap*, xlvi. [1902] 127 f.

³ E. B. Cross, *JAOS* iv. [1854] 309 ff.

⁴ F. Mason, *JASBe* xxxiv. [1865] 195.

⁵ J. N. B. Hewitt, *JAFL* viii. [1895] 107.

⁶ S. St. John, *Life in the Forests of the Far East*², London, 1863, i. 177 ff.

⁷ A. C. Kruijt, *Het Animisme in den ind. Archipel*, The Hague, 1906, p. 12.

⁸ W. W. Skeat and C. O. Blagden, *Pagan Races of the Malay Peninsula*, London, 1906, ii. 1, 194.

⁹ W. W. Skeat, *Malay Magic*, London, 1900, p. 47 ff.

¹⁰ J. Macdonald, *Religion and Myth*, London, 1893, p. 33.

¹¹ J. G. Swan, *Smithsonian Contributions*, xvi. [1870] 84.

¹² *GB*³, pt. ii., *Taboo and the Perils of the Soul*, London, 1911, p. 26.

necessitated by the idea that the life must take its departure by some one of the orifices of the body, and it is possible also that certain characteristics of the memory-image may have exercised an influence.[1]

In these early stages the life-principle is, though 'refined,' always material; the conception of insubstantiality is quite a late achievement of thought.[2] But certain natural confusions occur. Thus, the *sĕmangat* of the wild Malays differs from the conception held by other races in the same regions, for that which gives life is the *jiwa*. The Pataui Malays also believe in a 'life breath,' *nyawa*; the *sĕmangat*, in their view, is not the vital principle, but is possessed by every object in the universe.[3]

In his study of the animism of the Moluccas and neighbouring districts, A. C. Kruijt finds a permanent distinction between the soul of a living man and the soul of a dead man. The former he considers to be impersonal, though in many cases it is certainly itself a person, and always is a miniature replica of the owner; it gives him life. Its material is fine, ethereal substance; it has various seats in the body where its action is most conspicuous, such as the pulses. It dies when the man dies. The other soul is a continuation of the individual after life and does not appear till death. In the latter conception we seem to have a combined result of the memory-image and the hallucinational ghost.

A later detail, which involves the idea that all things in nature either are animate or possess 'souls,' is also attached to the theory of the *sĕmangat*, though it is chiefly things concerning or interesting man that possess the miniature replica.[4]

The *sĕmangat* of the Eastern Semang is red like blood, or is in the blood.[5] Life is usually regarded as being closely connected with the blood—a natural inference from observation of wounds or of death by loss of blood. Life and blood are identified.[6] A vaguer identification is frequently found with various parts or states of the living organism. To some, as the Iroquois, life is the flesh[7]—a concept which probably originated from experience of nutrition. The heart is a seat of life; in some cases it, like blood, has a 'soul' of its own.[8] The Australians regard the kidney-fat as an important seat of life,[9] and the caul-fat and omentum are so regarded.[10]

The absence of breath in the case of the dead is a fact naturally assisting a belief that the breath is the life, or that the life is in the breath. In the Marquesas it was the custom to hold the nose and lips of dying persons, in order to prevent death.[11] In primitive thought there is no explicit inconsistency in the identification of life with various things; the early books of the OT hold, now the breath,[12] now the blood, to be the 'life.' Primitive biology, in its secondary stages, has a larger list.[13] In this is to be included the shadow of a man, which is (like everything connected with personality) 'a vital part,'[14] and a man's reflexion is also closely akin to, if not identified with, his life.

In Melanesia is a pool 'into which if any one looks he dies; the malignant spirit takes hold upon his life by means of his reflection on the water.'[15]

The lore of shadow, mirror-image, and portrait becomes prominent, however, only in the third stage of culture—that of the higher barbarism. The Chinese place the dying man's picture upon his body, in the hope of saving his life.[16] In Siam, 'when a copy of the face of a person is made and taken away from him, a portion of his life goes with the picture.'[1] The comparison of the life-essence with fire is the best known of many metaphorical analogies, and occupies a prominent place in myth—*e.g.*, the fire of life infused by Prometheus into the clay figures which became men—and in metaphysical theology.

Until modern times, speculation has concerned itself with the source of life rather than with its origin. In early mythology conceptions like that of the Hervey Islanders, who regard a 'point'[2] as the beginning of existence, are rare. Rare also are such pseudo-biological ideas as the Maori concept that the life of a man is contained in the catamenia,[3] but the usual conclusion is that the 'soul' is the source of life or is itself life.

2. The life of nature.—Life in the vegetable kingdom has probably always been recognized, and primitive thought doubtless distinguished it as being different in character from that of animals. The same may have been the case with its attitude to inanimate things, unless it merely 'personalized' them.

The view of Tylor, that in primitive animism there is 'a belief in the animation of all nature,' and that 'man recognizes in every detail of his world the operation of personal life and will,'[4] can be applied only to certain developments of the higher barbaric stage.

'It is not likely that at one stage man regarded everything as alive, and at a later stage gradually discriminated between animate and inanimate. The fact is, that he began by regarding everything as neutral, merely as given. Yet though he never thought about the matter at all, in his acts . . . he distinguished as well as we do between animate and inanimate.'[5] 'Whatever power and importance he [primitive man] may have ascribed to inanimate objects, he drew the strongest of lines between such objects and what was endowed with life.'[6]

An excellent observer remarks of the Kafirs of S. Africa, in regard to the question whether they 'imagine everything in nature to be alive,' that they very rarely think of the matter at all. When questioned on the subject of the animation of stones, they laughed, and said, 'It would never enter a Kafir's head to think stones felt in that sort of way.'[7]

Throughout the fluid and ill-defined psychology of primitive man we may distinguish a tendency to mark off the concept of things as living from the concept of them as ideas, whether in life or after death. The latter aspect is ideational, the former perceptual. An excellent illustration of the distinction is the Indonesian view, expounded by Kruijt, that the life-soul of creatures is never confused or compounded with the after-death soul. In later psychologies, on the other hand, Tylor's hypothesis, that eventually the 'life' of a thing and its 'phantom' are combined, holds good. Language has probably had much to do with the combination. The view of Kruijt, however, that the Indonesian 'life-soul' is but a part of the world-soul, applies only to the higher developments of animism.[8] Here we have a parallel with the pantheistic theories of the world.

3. Regard for life.—Another parallel with these is the regard for life generally, a regard which develops with culture but is more pronounced in Oriental than in Western morality. At first this feeling is a vague altruism, but later it is fused

1 A. E. Crawley, *The Idea of the Soul*, London, 1909, p. 200 ff.
2 *Ib.* pp. 57, 209; the Kinjin Dayak term is in point, *urip-ok* = 'fine ethereal life' (p. 110).
3 Skeat-Blagden, ii. 194; N. Annandale, *Man*, iii. [1903] 27.
4 Crawley, p. 132.
5 Skeat-Blagden, *loc. cit.*
6 Gn 9[4], Lv 17[11-14]; Crawley, p. 112; Frazer, p. 240.
7 Hewitt, *loc. cit.*
8 Crawley, pp. 120, 136.
9 See references in Crawley, *Mystic Rose*, London, 1902, p. 101 ff.
10 W. R. Smith, *Religion of the Semites*[2], London, 1894, p. 379.
11 Frazer, p. 31.
12 Gn 2[7].
13 Crawley, *Idea of the Soul*, p. 238.
14 Frazer, p. 77 ff.
15 R. H. Codrington, in *JAI* x. 313.
16 Crawley, *Idea of the Soul*, p. 225.

1 E. Young, *The Kingdom of the Yellow Robe*, London, 1898, p. 140.
2 Crawley, *Idea of the Soul*, p. 93, quoting Gill.
3 *Ib.* p. 90.
4 *PC*[3] i. 285 ff., 424 ff.
5 Crawley, *Idea of the Soul*, p. 20.
6 E. J. Payne, *History of the New World called America*, Oxford, 1892–99, ii. 265.
7 D. Kidd, *Savage Childhood*, London, 1906, p. 145 f.
8 See Crawley, *Idea of the Soul*, p. 262. In Semitic thought living water is running water, living flesh raw flesh (W. R. Smith, pp. 190, 339). These phrases are probably metaphorical only.

with metaphysical estimates of the intrinsic value of life, as such.

'In Buddhism, Jainism, and Taouism the respect for animal life is extreme.'[1] 'A disciple of Buddha may not knowingly deprive any creature of life, not even a worm or an ant. He may not drink water in which animal life of any kind whatever is contained, and must not even pour it out on grass or clay.'[2] 'The Jain is stricter still in his regard for animal life. He sweeps the ground before him as he goes, lest animate things be destroyed; he walks veiled, lest he inhale a living organism; he considers that the evening and night are not times for eating, since one might then swallow a live thing by mistake; and he rejects not only meat but even honey, together with various fruits that are supposed to contain worms, not because of his distaste for worms, but because of his regard for life.'[3] Throughout Japan, 'the life of animals has always been held more or less sacred.'[4] In China it is regarded as 'meritorious to save animals from death—even insects if the number mounts to a hundred. . . . to set at liberty animals intended to be slaughtered.' 'To kill ten insects . . . without great reason to kill . . . animals for food . . . "to be foremost to encourage the slaughter of animals"' are regarded as errors 'of the same magnitude as the crime of devising a person's death or of drowning or murdering a child.'[5] The Burmese 'laugh at the suggestion made by Europeans, that Buddhists abstain from taking life because they believe in the transmigration of souls, having never heard of it before.'[6] The same position may be assumed with regard to the Brāhman doctrine of *ahiṁsā*, which includes the sanctity of all life. On the other hand, 'no creed in Christendom teaches kindness to animals as a dogma of religion.' 'The Manichæans prohibited all killing of animals, but Manichæism did not originate on Christian ground.'[7]

4. The life deposit.—A remarkable belief is that of the 'life-index' or 'external soul,' which is found with some regularity in all the stages of the lower civilizations. An early example is the sex totems of Australia.

The Wotjobaluk tribe of South-Eastern Australia 'held that "the life of Ngŭnŭngŭnŭt (the Bat) is the life of a man and the life of Yártatgŭrk (the Nightjar) is the life of a woman," and that when either of these creatures is killed the life of some man or of some woman is shortened. In such a case every man or every woman in the camp feared that he or she might be the victim, and from this cause great fights arose in this tribe.'[8]

In later folk-lore the idea is crystallized into the talisman, but previously a host of objects are regarded as eligible for the safe-deposit of the individual life. It is noteworthy that the subject is more frequent in mythology than in practical life. The fact that, according to the common-sense view, the more 'deposits' of life a man has, the more is he liable to death, may explain this natural difference. A remarkable aspect of the belief is connected with the growth of children and the growth of plants. The inception of this idea can hardly be attributed to any other influence than the observation of the facts of growth. It is therefore probably not originated by the notion of life.

But the sympathetic relation soon develops into a life-interest.

'In folk-tales the life of a person is sometimes so bound up with the life of a plant that the withering of the plant will immediately follow or be followed by the death of the person.'[9] 'Among the M'Bengas in Western Africa, about the Gaboon, when two children are born on the same day, the people plant two trees of the same kind and dance round them. The life of each of the children is believed to be bound up with the life of one of the trees: and if the tree dies or is thrown down, they are sure that the child will soon die. In Sierra Leone also it is customary at the birth of a child to plant a shoot of a *malep*-tree, and they think that the tree will grow with the child and be its god. If a tree which has been thus planted withers away, the people consult a sorcerer on the subject. . . . Some of the Papuans unite the life of a new-born child sympathetically with that of a tree by driving a pebble into the bark of the tree. This is supposed to give them complete mastery over the child's life; if the tree is cut down, the child will die. . . . In Bali a coco-palm is planted at the birth of a child. It is believed to grow up equally with the child, and is called its "life-plant."'[10]

---

1 Westermarck, *MI* ii. 497.
2 *Ib.* quoting H. Oldenberg, *Buddha*, Berlin, 1881, pp. 290, 351.
3 *Ib.* p. 498 f., quoting E. W. Hopkins, *Religions of India*, London, 1896, p. 288.
4 E. J. Reed, *Japan*, London, 1880, i. 61.
5 *Indo-Chinese Gleaner*, iii. [1821] 164, 205 f., quoted by Westermarck, *loc. cit.*
6 H. F. Hall, *The Soul of a People*, London, 1902, p. 232 f.
7 *MI* ii. 506.
8 A. W. Howitt, *JAI* xiv. [1883–84] 145, xviii. [1887–88] 58.
9 Frazer, *GB*³, pt. vii., *Balder the Beautiful*, London, 1913, ii. 159, 102, 105, 110, 117 f., 135 f.
10 *Ib.* ii. 160–164.

Similar customs are still frequent in Europe, and 'life-trees,' as Frazer styles them, have always been a prominent feature of European folk-lore. 'The life of Simeon, prince of Bulgaria, was bound up with a certain column in Constantinople, so that if the capital of the column were removed, Simeon would immediately die. The emperor took the hint and removed the capital, and at the same hour . . . Simeon died of heart-disease in Bulgaria.'[1]

The conclusion of these ideas supplies a constant motive in fairy-tales and the mythology which is their basis.

Thus, 'Koshchei the Deathless is killed by a blow from the egg or the stone in which his life or death is secreted; . . . the magician dies when the stone in which his life or death is contained is put under his pillow; and the Tartar hero is warned that he may be killed by the golden arrow or golden sword in which his soul has been stowed away.'[2] A remarkable instance occurs in the myth of the god Balder. His life was bound up in the mistletoe. The apparent inconsistency that he was slain by a blow from the plant is explained by Frazer: 'When a person's life is conceived as embodied in a particular object, with the existence of which his own existence is inseparably bound up, and the destruction of which involves his own, the object in question may be regarded and spoken of indifferently as his life or his death. . . . Hence if a man's death is in an object, it is perfectly natural that he should be killed by a blow from it.'[3]

The idea that the mistletoe itself is the life of the tree on which it grows is of the same order as the Malay and Chinese idea with regard to the knobs and excrescences on tree trunks.[4] Two converse ideas may be noted. A person whose life is magically isolated has one weak spot, *e.g.* the heel of Achilles. Death, no less than life, may be 'deposited,' as in the stories where it is kept in a bottle. See, further, art. LIFE-TOKEN.

5. Life magic.—When the conception of life as a magical essence is established, the formula is applied all round the social and religious spheres. The elementary facts of nutrition thus become the basis of an elaborate vitalistic philosophy. In its more primitive forms this appears as a practical science of life insurance. 'Food . . . during thousands of years occupied the largest space in man's mental area of vision.'[5] This consideration helps to explain the existence of so large a body of superstitions concerning food. And into these enter the magical and, later, the vitalistic theory. Particular creatures are eaten because of their particular vital force.[6] The slayer eats part of his foe in order to assimilate his life and strength (see, further, art. CANNIBALISM, §§ 3–7). In order to procure longevity the Zulus ate the flesh of long-lived animals.[7] Medea injected into the veins of Æson an infusion of the long-lived deer and crow.[8] In the lower culture special virtue is assigned to human flesh.[9] Besides the eating of flesh and the drinking of blood, there are various methods of acquiring the 'life essence.' The Caribs transfer the life of an animal to a boy by rubbing its juices into his body.[10] Anointing with *amṛta* oil and with gold-grease are methods of procuring life found in Indian and Chinese folk-lore respectively.[11] The Tibetan Buddhist acquires 'life' by drinking the 'ambrosia' from the 'Vase of Life'[12] (see, further, artt. FOOD and EATING THE GOD).

Long life is often the subject of charms. The Chinese wear a longevity garment on birthdays.[13] The Hindus ascribed long life to continence.[14] Most religions include prayers for long life. After

---

1 Frazer, *Balder*, ii. 156 f. 2 *Ib.* p. 279. 3 *Ib.*
4 Skeat, *Malay Magic*, p. 194; Crawley, *Idea of the Soul*, p. 164, quoting de Groot.
5 Payne, i. 279.
6 Frazer, *GB*³, pt. v., *Spirits of the Corn and of the Wild*, London, 1912, ii. 138 ff.
7 H. Callaway, *Nursery Tales of the Zulus*, London, 1868, p. 175.
8 Ovid, *Metam.* vii. 271 ff. 9 Parker, p. 38.
10 J. G. Frazer, *Totemism*, London, 1910, i. 42.
11 *The Bower MS*, ed. A. F. R. Hoernle, Calcutta, 1893–97, ii. 107; J. J. M. de Groot, *The Rel. System of China*, Leyden, 1892 ff., iv. 331.
12 L. A. Waddell, *The Buddhism of Tibet*, London, 1895, p. 447.
13 De Groot, i. 60 ff. 14 *Bower MS*, ii. 142.

a death, magic is employed to prolong the life of the survivors.[1]

Magical persons, and later the gods, are regarded as both possessing a richer store of life and being able to impart it to others; the savage medicine-man is able to infuse life into an inanimate fetish. Breathing upon the object gives it the breath of life (as in Ezekiel's apologue of the dead bones); smearing it with blood gives it the life of the blood.[2] According to the Tantras, a king may slay his enemy by infusing life into his foe's effigy and then destroying it.[3] Divine persons naturally tend to become long-lived or immortal.

But, though divine persons throughout bear a more or less 'charmed life,' absolute immortality is a late conception. The gods of the Homeric pantheon maintained their life by eating ambrosia, the 'food of deathlessness,' and by drinking nectar;[4] and similar ideas were connected with the Persian *haoma* and the Hindu *soma*. In Scandinavian myth the apples of Iðunn are eaten by the gods in order to perpetuate their life.[5] The Egyptian gods were mortal.[6] The tendency to immortality, however, is carried out in the higher religions, probably in connexion with the natural attribution to the gods of a general power over life and a control of creation. In the end the gods assume in themselves the ultimate hopes and fears of men, and they become 'lords and givers of life.'

6. Renewal of life.—A crude form of the ideas connected with a renewed earthly life after death, or resurrection, may be seen among the Australian aborigines, who speak of the ghost returning at times to the grave and contemplating its mortal remains.[7] Similarly, on the W. Coast of Africa 'it is the man himself in a shadowy or ghostly form that continues his existence after death.'[8] The belief in the revivification of a dead person does not appear until the thaumaturgic stages of barbarous religion, when it becomes a favourite miracle, performed by a word of power or by the life-giving touch or contact with the body of the divine person. But the belief in a second life, or, rather, a series of lives, is a remarkable and regular feature of primitive thought. It takes the form of reincarnation; the dead are born again in their descendants, the idea being a natural inference from the resemblance of children to their parents and grandparents.[9] The Central Australians have developed it into an elaborate theory of heredity, in which the 'life' is a germ-plasm.[10] Other Australians evolved the notion that white men were blackfellows returned to life; 'tumble down blackfellow, jump up whitefellow' is a familiar phrase. The whiteness of the native corpse after cremation has been suggested as the basis of the notion.[11]

The idea of reincarnation refers also to living parents. Thus an old blackfellow of Australia cries to his son, 'There you stand with my body!' The son is recognized as 'the actual re-incarnation of the father.'[12] This frequent belief has been suggested as an explanation of certain customs of which killing the first-born is a culmination—the child is supposed to have robbed the father of a portion of his life (cf. *ERE* vi. 33[a]).

7. The nature of death.—Primitive thought has no definition of the nature of death, but the usual attitude towards it, as may be inferred from mourning customs, is a mystic terror. The catastrophic nature of the event is perhaps the fundamental reason for this attitude, but various emotions and ideas are superimposed. Grief and sympathy occur among the lowest races, and they develop with culture. Another emotion is fear of the corpse as a mysterious personality; a parallel fear is that of the departed 'something,' ghost or spirit. Like other tabu states and social crises, death has not only its *rites de passage*, such as mourning, but a mysterious power of pollution. This is partly connected with a fear that the survivors may also become victims, a fear which develops into an avoidance of infection.[1] These ideas reach their climax in the Zoroastrian conception of the absolute impurity of death, a type of all uncleanness.[2] In others of the higher religions, particularly Christianity, the material notions of the state of death give way to spiritual. The departed soul has less connexion with the body, although even here a physiological fact has kept up the idea of 'the odour of sanctity.'

Fear of dying has no connexion with the primitive fear of death.[3] Suicide for trivial reasons is very common among the lower races.

> 'Many savages meet death with much indifference, or regard it as no great evil, but merely as a change to a life very similar to this. But it is a fact often noticed among ourselves, that a person on the verge of death may resign himself to his fate with the greatest calmness, although he has been afraid to die throughout his life. Moreover, the fear of death may be disguised by thoughtlessness, checked by excitement, or mitigated by dying in company. There are peoples who are conspicuous for their bravery, and yet have a great dread of death. Nobody is entirely free from this feeling, though it varies greatly in strength among different races and in different individuals. In many savages it is so strongly developed that they cannot bear to hear death mentioned.'[4] The last objection, however, may often be due to mystical notions.

Christianity esteems death as the passage to a better life, and the higher religions, generally, mitigate the inevitable lot.

Speculation on the origin of death is considerable in early thought, and myths innumerable have been invented to explain it (cf. art. DEATH AND DISPOSAL OF THE DEAD [Introductory], vol. iv. p. 411 f.). A common motive of these is a misunderstanding or a trick. At a higher stage death is attributed to the malevolence of demons, often supposed to eat the life of men and so produce death.[5] Otherwise, the separation of the life-giving soul from the body as a fact, not as a theory of origin, is usually explained as the result of sorcery, except in cases of obvious violence or accident.[6] By various means the human sorcerer, like the supernatural demon, destroys or abstracts the life.

In the higher barbarism death appears as a punishment for breaking tabu or other supernatural injunctions. The greater religions connect its origin with sin, Christianity with the primal sin of disobedience.[7] Throughout, humanity is instinctively agreed that death *is* unnatural, and the conception of a second life is a protest against it.

8. Mythological and ethical applications.—Apart from myths in explanation of the origin of death and the less frequent fancies of a mystical or magical life-source, primitive thought makes little use of the concepts of life and death as motives of

1 Rājendralāla Mitra, *Indo-Aryans*, Calcutta, 1881, ii. 145.
2 Cf. A. B. Ellis, *The Tshi-speaking Peoples*, London, 1887, p. 101 f.; J. G. Müller, *Gesch. der amer. Urreligionen*, Basel, 1855, p. 606; W. R. Smith, pp. 339, 344.
3 R. Mitra, ii. 110.
4 *Il.* v. 339 f., *Od.* v. 199.
5 J. Grimm, *Teutonic Mythology*, Eng. tr., London, 1882–88, p. 318 f.
6 A. Wiedemann, *Religion of the Ancient Egyptians*, Eng. tr., London, 1897, p. 173; cf. Frazer, *GB*[3], pt. iii., *The Dying God*, do. 1911, p. 1 ff.
7 Howitt, *JAI* xiii. [1883–84] 188.
8 Crawley, *Idea of the Soul*, p. 175, quoting A. B. Ellis.
9 J. Parkinson, *JAI* xxxvi. [1906] 312 ff. (Africa); Kruijt, p. 175; Crawley, *Idea of the Soul*, pp. 101, 110, 161 (S. America, Melanesia, Indonesia).
10 Crawley, *Idea of the Soul*, p. 88.
11 L. Fison and A. W. Howitt, *Kamilaroi and Kurnai*, Melbourne, 1880, p. 248; Howitt, *Native Tribes of South-East Australia*, London, 1904, p. 442.
12 Howitt, *JAI* xiv. 145; Manu, ix. 8.

1 Crawley, *Mystic Rose*, p. 95 ff.; *MI* ii. 537.
2 *SBE* iv. [1895] p. lxxv f.
3 For the contrary view see *MI* ii. 535 f.
4 *MI* ii. 535.
5 J. G. F. Riedel, *De sluik- en kroesharige rassen tusschen Selebes en Papua*, The Hague, 1886, p. 271.
6 *MI* i. 24, 29, ii. 534, 651.
7 Gn 2 and 3; cf. Manu, v. 4.

story. Their deification is rarer still. In some stories one or more remarkable personages are brought into close connexion with the facts of life and death. Thus, the Maoris tell how men would have been deathless if Maui, the culture-hero, had succeeded in passing through the body of Night. In Scandinavian story Líf and Lífþrasir ('life' and 'desiring life') survive the destruction of the world.[1] The usual result is that some great deity possesses control over life, as in Hebraism, Christianity, and Islām. There is a tendency also to connect vitality with the sun-god; the Rigveda speaks of the sun in the character of Savitar, the Vivifier.[2] In Hindu theology Yama, the first of mortal men, became 'King of the Dead.'[3] In Christian theology a contrast is drawn between the old Adam, by whom death entered the world, and the new, who re-introduced 'life' on a higher plane. A less refined moral is drawn in the Babylonian epic; the conclusion is that Gilgamesh must die and cannot escape the universal lot.

'Let him hope for and, if possible, provide for proper burial. . . . He will then, at least, not suffer the pangs of hunger in the world of spirits.'[4]

The Scandinavian figures, Líf and Lífþrasir, are among the rare cases where life is personified. Death is more frequently deified. Old Slavic myth seems to have had a goddess Smrt,[5] and the Baganda are said to have a god of death, Walumbe.[6] The Etruscan figure of Charun may be similar to the last, the conception being derived from human executioners, and the god being a slayer rather than a god of death. The Thanatos of Greek poetry, the brother of Sleep, is hardly a religious personification. The Sheol of the OT and the Hel of the Eddas are originally places which receive the dead. As a rule, the figure later described as Death is either a messenger of the gods or a god whose office is indirectly connected with the death of men. So Yama has his messengers, and the Tatars believe in an 'angel' of death. The latter is the type of Christian ideas. The Greeks had both Charon and Hermes Psychopompos, but in modern Greek folk-lore Charon has become a figure of terror, Death himself.[7] Death with his scythe seems to be a transference from a personification of Time.

A certain control over life is assumed in primitive ritual drama, as in the pretended death and revivification of youths at initiation, and of candidates for the priesthood.[8] Ideas of a magical vitality grew up out of sacred meals; at the same time there appears the connexion of sin and death, and the consequent aspiration towards a purging of sin accompanied by a renewal of life. Out of these elements arises the ethical view of the renewal, but still undivorced from a mystical idea of a spiritual prolongation of existence. 'Salvation' in the life after death was promised by the Greek mysteries.[9] In its lowest terms the salvation resulting from belief in Christ was eternal life. Faith and morality meet when eternal life is the reward for a good life on earth. Life is identified with goodness.

The fear of retribution in a future existence has been impressed by several of the great religions, notably by Christianity. But there is no justification for connecting the origins of religion with either this fear (long posterior to the inception of religious ideas, and a late and special ethical development) or the worship of death or the dead. The dead are more or less feared in early thought; the infection of death is carefully avoided; the ghosts of the dead are intensely dreaded, and therefore carefully propitiated. Many ghosts, it is true, have been developed into gods, but there are many keys which fit the doors of religion.

1 P. D. Chantepie de la Saussaye, *Religion of the Teutons*, Boston, 1902, p. 352.
2 M. Monier-Williams, *Religious Thought and Life in India*, London, 1883, p. 17; A. A. Macdonell, *Ved. Myth.*, Strassburg, 1897, p. 34.
3 Hopkins, *Religions of India*, p. 128.
4 M. Jastrow, *Religions of Babylonia and Assyria*, Boston, 1898, p. 512.
5 Grimm, iv. 1560.
6 J. Roscoe, *The Baganda*, London, 1911, p. 315.
7 J. C. Lawson, *Modern Greek Folklore and Anc. Greek Religion*, Cambridge, 1910, p. 98 ff.
8 Cf. Spencer-Gillen[a], p. 523 f.; J. Maclean, *Compendium of Kafir Laws and Customs*, Mt. Coke, 1858, p. 79; art. INITIATION (Introductory and Primitive), 4 (1), (2).
9 Pindar, frag. 102; Cicero, *Legg.* ii. 14.

LITERATURE.—This is cited in the article, but the whole of E. B. Tylor's exposition of animism in his *Primitive Culture*[3], London, 1891, applies to the subject.

A. E. CRAWLEY.

LIFE AND DEATH (American).

—The beliefs of the aborigines of America agree in the main with those of other peoples at the same stages of development; but there are a few interesting features of an individual character.

With regard to ideas of the life which informs the organism, the Eskimos identify it or its action with the 'life-warmth.'[1] So the Navahos regarded the warmth of the body as the living soul; the 'shade' or 'double,' a distinct concept, was supposed to wander away when a man was sick or dying.[2] The Sauk identified the soul with 'vitality,' and supposed it to exist after death.[3] The Toltec explained that it was 'something within them which made them live: . . . which caused death when it quitted them.'[4] Identifying breath or air with the vital principle, the Acagchemems are represented as crediting the atmosphere with a mortiferous quality.[5]

'In many American languages the Great Spirit and the Great Wind are one and the same both in word and signification.'[6]

The Aztec word *ehecatl*, e.g., means 'wind, air, life, soul, shadow.' A phrase attributed to an Indian orator is: 'The fire in your huts and the life in your bodies are one and the same thing.' Spirits and human magicians, such as the shamans, devour men's souls; the result is death.[7] Death is 'infectious'; a dead man's belongings decay quickly. Such is the ancient opinion among the Irish also, who hold that a dead man's clothes wear out more quickly than those of a living man.[8] The belief in the reincarnation of the dead in children is widely spread and firmly held. The Haida refine upon it by saying that after five such reincarnations the individual 'soul' is annihilated.[9]

A special feature of American religious theory, on which practically the whole ritual of the central nations was founded, was developed from the usual primitive idea that divine persons are subject to senility, death, and decay. Alone among the Mexican gods Tezcatlipoca 'is credited with perpetual juvenility.'[10] The principle was developed that the gods, in particular the sun, would die if deprived of food. Hence the perpetual round of human sacrifices offered on Maya and Nahua altars. This daily 'feast of flowers,' as it was euphemistically termed, kept the gods alive. A serious result was the equally perpetual carrying on of warfare for the sole purpose of obtaining captives to serve as victims. The heart, as the symbol of life, was the choicest portion.[11]

1 E. W. Nelson, *18 RBEW*, pt. i. [1899], p. 422.
2 A. G. Morice, *Proc. Can. Inst.*, vii. [Toronto, 1888-89] 158 f.
3 W. H. Keating, *Narrative of an Expedition to the Source of St. Peter's River*, etc., Philadelphia, 1824, i. 229, 232, ii. 154.
4 E. J. Payne, *History of the New World called America*, Oxford, 1892-99, i. 468, quoting Oviedo.
5 *NR* iii. 525.
6 *Ib.* iii. 117.
7 J. Jetté, *JRAI* xxxvii. [1907] 161, 176.
8 F. Boas, *JAFL* vi. [1893] 40; *ib.* viii. [1895] 110.
9 G. M. Dawson, 'The Haida Indians,' in *Geol. Survey of Canada*, Toronto, 1880, p. 121 f.
10 Payne, i. 429.
11 *Ib.* i. 523; cf. L. Spence, *The Myths of Mexico and Peru*, London, 1913, pp. 74, 98.

It is natural that an old chronicler should say:

'The Maya have an immoderate fear of death, and they seem to have given it a figure peculiarly repulsive.'[1] 'In the Dresden and other codices god A is represented as a figure with exposed vertebræ and skull-like countenance, with the marks of corruption on his body, and displaying every sign of mortality. On his head he wears a snail-symbol, the Aztec sign of birth, perhaps to typify the connection between birth and death. He also wears a pair of cross-bones. The hieroglyph which accompanies his figure represents a corpse's head with closed eyes, a skull, and a sacrificial knife. His symbol is that for the calendar day Cimi, which means death. He presides over the west, the home of the dead, the region towards which they invariably depart with the setting sun. That he is a death-god there can be no doubt, but of his name we are ignorant. He is probably identical with the Aztec god of death and hell, Mictlan, and is perhaps one of those Lords of Death and Hell who invite the heroes to the celebrated game of ball in the Kiche *Popol Vuh*, and hold them prisoners in their gloomy realm.'[2]

Like Hel and Hades, Mictlan seems to have developed from a place into a person. He is a 'grisly monster with capacious mouth,' like the mediæval European identification of the whale and hell. Mediæval Europe evolved also, but by poetical rather than religious imagination, a figure akin to that of the American god A. For similar reasons the Sinaloa are said to have devoted most of their worship to Cocohuame, who is Death.[3]

Another detail of the human sacrifice is this:

'The idea that the god thus slain in the person of his representative comes to life again immediately, was graphically represented in the Mexican ritual by skinning the slain man-god and clothing in his skin a living man, who thus became the new representative of the godhead.'[4]

This principle, probable enough, is, however, a secondary development; the revivification of the god was the primary meaning of the sacrifice.

In Mexican theology the supreme deity Tloque-Nahuaque (of Molina) is 'he upon whom depends the existence of all things.' As is the case elsewhere, the sun is connected with vitality, 'animating and keeping alive all creatures.' An interesting point is the connexion of Mexican food-goddesses with the idea of life and its bestowal.[5]

The aboriginal creation of a Great Spirit has been discredited. Equally unreliable are such forms as the Master of Life (of Lafitau), and Master of Breath, though such phrases may have been applied sporadically by the Northern Indians to some 'great medicine.'

A feature of the eschatology[6] is the other-world paradise for the brave, comparable only with the belief of Islām, although European chivalry shares the aversion from dying in bed.

The 'happy hunting-grounds,' which have become a proverb, are typified in the Comanche belief—here is 'the orthodox American paradise, in its full glory. In the direction of the setting sun lie the happy prairies, where the buffalo lead the hunter in the glorious chase, and where the horse of the pale-face aids those who have excelled in scalping and horse-stealing, to attain supreme felicity.'[7]

LITERATURE.—In addition to the works cited in the text cf. D. G. Brinton, *Myths of the New World*, New York, 1868; de Nadaillac (J. F. A. du Pouget), *Prehistoric America*, do. 1884.

A. E. CRAWLEY.

LIFE AND DEATH (Chinese).—**1. Popular ideas.**—Life and death are more intimately associated in the Chinese mind than in the Western. The curtain separating life and death is thinner. The future life to the average Chinese, taught as he is by popular Buddhism and Taoism, is largely a replica of this life on a different plane of existence, but death is no theme of beauty. After passing through the Judgment Halls of the Ten Judges of Hades (a hell with many furies), the victims are supposed to require food, clothing, houses, servants, means of travelling both on land and on water, and money. All these are sent to them by their friends and relatives by means of burning paper models and imitations.

2. Ancient beliefs.—The ancient Chinese were unable to distinguish between death, sleep, and a swoon. They therefore tried to resuscitate the dead by calling them by name to return,[1] etc., by providing food for them, by keeping their bodies in the dress that they wore, and, at first, by tightly covering the corpse.[2] Many customs now in vogue in China are due to this belief. Death was a prolonged sleep (or due to suspended animation); and, as the sleeper will wake, so the corpse may do the same, should the soul return to its habitation.[3] Articles which were believed to promote vitality, such as jade, gold, silver, pearls, and cowries, were stuffed into the mouths of the dead.[4] No methods of disposing of the dead were employed which would quickly destroy the body, and coffins were made of such materials as pine and cypress, for they 'were intended to preserve human bodies from putrefaction and to facilitate their resurrection by enveloping them thus air-tight in a material which, being possessed of vital energy, was considered capable of transmitting life once more into the clay.'[5]

The ancient Chinese were most scrupulous in washing and dressing the dead, so that the body might be ready at any time for the soul to return to its fleshly dwelling-place.[6]

The strong Chinese reprobation of the mutilation of the body had its origin in these ancient ideas, for mutilation prevents the body from being in a fit state for the soul to return to it, or to appear in the next world. Hence criminals were beheaded as a severe punishment, and strangling was considered a lesser one.[7] The mode since the revolution seems to be that of shooting.

In the belief of the Chinese life 'remains after the soul has left the body.'[8] There is thus a belief in a life in death itself, or, as de Groot graphically describes it, a cohabitation of the soul and the body after death.[9] In accordance with this idea, there is not a complete separation of soul and body. In the popular ideas of the people, one of the three souls is in the grave. Thus death dominates life, and life lives in death and is not extinguished by it. One of the other souls is believed to inhabit the ancestral tablet, while the third passes to the other world.[10]

3. Classical ideas.—If we turn now to the ancient classics, which throw a light on the early life of the Chinese, we find, besides the views already expressed, higher conceptions as well, or, at all events, less gross ones. Amidst all the ceremonial and ritual, the belief in immortality is clearly seen.[11] Ancestor-worship alone is enough to prove this. Even before the days of Taoism and Buddhism, the souls of the ancestors were believed to be in heaven.[12] Confucianism 'teaches the existence of the soul after death,' but nothing regarding the character of that existence.[13] The knowledge of a future life was hazy and indefinite in the old religion of China.[14]

'Thus they looked up to heaven (whither the spirit was gone), and buried (the body) in the earth,'[15] for, it is added, 'the body and animal soul go downward; the intelligent spirit is on high.'[16]

---

1 Payne, i. 172, 97.
2 *Ib.* p. 172 f.
3 *NR* iii. 180.
4 J. G. Frazer, *GB*[2], London, 1900, iii. 136.
5 *NR* iii. 195, 423; J. Dunn, *Hist. of the Oregon Territory*, London, 1844, p. 284.
6 On the ideas of a future life see *NR* iii. 530 ff.
7 *NR* iii. 528.

---

1 J. Legge, *Chinese Classics*, Hongkong, 1861–72; *SBE* xxvii. [1885] 108, 112, 129, 157, etc.
2 J. J. M. de Groot, *Religious System of China*, Leyden, 1892 ff., i. 243 ff., 29 f., 356 ff., 46 ff.; Legge, *SBE* xxvii. 368 f.
3 De Groot, i. 243 ff.
4 *Ib.* p. 269 ff.
5 *Ib.* p. 293 ff.
6 *Ib.* p. 331 ff.
7 *Ib.* p. 342 ff.
8 *Ib.* p. 348 ff.
9 *Ib.*
10 *Ib.* iv. 74.
11 Cf. J. Legge, *Religions of China*, London, 1880, p. 13 f.
12 J. Dyer Ball, *The Religious Aspect in China*, Hongkong, 1906, p. 49.
13 *Ib.* p. 50.
14 Cf. Legge, *Religions of China*, p. 117.
15 Legge, *SBE* xxvii. 368; see also p. 444.
16 Legge, *Religions of China*, p. 119.

The attitude of Confucius towards death was that of an agnostic.

He virtually avoided a direct answer to the question asked him by one of his disciples about death, his reply being, 'While we do not know life, how can we know about death?'[1] The older commentators say that the master gave 'no answer, because spirits and death are obscure and unprofitable subjects to talk about.' Some of the modern Confucian writers agree with this opinion, but the majority say that the answer was profound, and showed the proper order in which such inquiries should be prosecuted, for 'death is only the natural termination of life.'[2] To the ordinary reader, however, it would appear that this reply was only an exemplification of a passage in the *Doctrine of the Mean* (xii. 2), 'There is that which even the Sage does not know.'[3]

The followers of Confucius have not risen above the agnostic position which he took, and here it was that Buddhism came to satisfy the longings of the ignorant as to the future with its scheme of rewards and punishments, its firm beliefs and precise statements, its apparent knowledge of futurity, and its assurance of lives to come and the influence of this life on them.

The duration of life and its early or late ending were believed by most of the Confucian school to be dependent on man's proper use of life, and this is a very general belief among the Chinese.

'Heaven does not cut short men's lives—they bring them to an end in the midst themselves.'[4] 'A man of great virtue is sure to have long life.'[5] A concrete example of this is the Great Shun (*c.* 2300 B.C.), whose filial piety was so great that he attained the age of 100.[6]

Length of days, therefore, was regarded by the Chinese as the reward of virtue, and longevity is one of the five blessings earnestly desired. Over many a door is pasted a piece of red paper, renewed at the New Year, bearing the wish, 'May the five blessings descend on this door.'

Though what is stated above is the general opinion, all have not subscribed to it.

The materialistic Wang Ch'ung (*c.* A.D. 97) says, 'Worthies are taken ill and die early, and wicked people may be strong and robust and become very old.' 'Human diseases and death are not a retribution for evil doing.' 'When a man expires, his fate is fulfilled. After his death he does not live again.' 'Human life and death depend on the length of the span [of life], not on good or bad actions.'[7]

The Chinese temperament is one which enjoys life to the full. The people are generally contented and happy, and the deep hidden meanings of life are largely wanting.

4. Taoism.—In the 3rd and 4th centuries B.C. Chinese philosophy was in its golden period. It critically examined life and its connotations, and evolved original conceptions of the nature, motives, and mysteries of existence. This 'pursuit of truth and wisdom' claimed not a few noted men among its adherents. Later, Confucianism, with its love of rites and ceremonies and its reverence for former sages, had the effect of turning men's minds from the inquiries which a philosophical spirit delights to make, and Taoism, under whose ægis such inquiries had arisen, to a large extent changed to a system of rites and idolatry.[8]

Primitive Taoism—that shown to us as developed through the sayings and mind of its founder, Lao-tsŭ (b. 604 B.C.), and its earlier writers—knew little more than Confucianism as to the great subjects of life and death.

Licius (Lieh-tzŭ, 4th cent. B.C.) says: 'The living and the dead . . . know nothing of each other's state.'[9] 'We all have an end, but whither the end leads us is unknown.'[10] Chuancius (Chuang-tzŭ, 3rd and 4th cent. B.C.) asks: 'What should the dead know of the living or the living know of the dead? You and I may be in a dream from which we have not yet awaked.'[1] 'To him who can penetrate the mystery of life, all things are revealed.'[2]

The prolongation of life and the cheating of death of its due, or, rather, the raising of mortal life above death by the transforming of life into a higher existence,[3] has been one of the aims of Taoism, to be attained 'by quietism and dispassionativism, by regulating one's breath and using medicines.'[4]

Lao-tzŭ is stated to have said that, to a perfect man, 'life and death . . . are but as night and day, and cannot destroy his peace.'[5] In Licius we find (as the statement of one almost a sage) that life and death were looked upon in the same light. Licius says that 'the source of life is death.'[6] 'There is no such thing as absolute life or death';[7] *i.e.*, 'from the standpoint of the Absolute, since there is no such principle as life in itself, it follows there can be no such thing as death.'[8] On the other hand, we have such statements as 'Great indeed is death! . . . It gives rest to the noble-hearted and causes the base to cower.'[9] The sage looks upon life and death 'merely as waking and sleeping.'[10]

In the idealistic and mystical writings of Chuancius (Chuang-tzŭ), one of the great Taoist philosophers, who lived about two centuries after the founder Lao-tzŭ, there are some striking statements.

He says that for the sage 'life means death to all that men think life, the life of *seeming* or reputation, of *doing* or action, of *being* or individual selfhood.'[11] 'He who clearly apprehends the scheme of existence does not rejoice over life, nor repine at death; if he knows that terms are not final.' In other words, 'life and death are but links in an endless chain.'[12] Life is inevitable, for it 'comes and cannot be declined. It goes and cannot be stopped.'[13] The quick passage of life is thus expressed: 'Man passes through this sublunary life as a white horse passes a crack. Here one moment, gone the next.'[14] 'The life of man is but as a stoppage at an inn.'[15] 'The living are men on a journey.'[16] 'Life is a loan.'[17]

Taoism borrowed largely from Buddhism, and developed its scheme of life and death, amplifying its descriptions of renewed lives, which are to succeed death itself.[18]

In the Epicurean Yang Chu's philosophy (*c.* 300 B.C.) life is to be lived for the possessor's own self and to be an expression of his individuality. There is to be a disregard of life and death; life is of importance only to him who lives it, and that solely during his brief existence.[19] The Chinese have not followed this philosopher.

Wang Ch'ung, who holds a mid position between Confucianism and Taoism, was of the opinion that the dead do not become ghosts, and are unconscious,[20] and that 'sleep, a trance, and death are essentially the same.'[21]

He also says that 'human death is like the extinction of fire. . . . To assert that a person after death is still conscious is like saying that an extinguished light shines again. . . . The soul of a dead man cannot become a body again.'[22]

5. Buddhism.—For the general attitude of Buddhism as regards life and death see artt. DEATH AND DISPOSAL OF THE DEAD (Buddhist) and KARMA. It is, however, more than questionable whether esoteric Buddhism, with its metaphysical aspect towards the world of senses, has much or any hold on the mass of the people.[23] Accordingly, many of

1 Legge, *Chinese Classics*, i. 104 (*Confucian Analects*, xi. 11).
2 *Ib.* i. 104 f., note.
3 *Ib.* i. 256.
4 *Ib.* iii. 264 ff. (*Shu King Book of Shang*, xi. 11).
5 J. H. S. Lockhart, *A Manual of Chinese Quotations*, Hongkong, 1893, p. 150.
6 Legge, *Chinese Classics*, i. 262 f. and note (*Doct. of Mean*, xvii. 1).
7 A. Forke, *Lun Heng*, pt. ii. (Berlin, 1911) p. 162.
8 See A. Forke, *Yang Chu's Garden of Pleasure*, London, 1912, Introd. p. 7 f.
9 L. Giles, *Taoist Teachings*, London, 1912, p. 32.
10 *Ib.* p. 23.

1 H. A. Giles, *Chuang Tzŭ*, London, 1889, p. 86.
2 *Ib.* p. 433.
3 L. Wieger, *Taoisme*, Paris, 1911, i., Introd. p. 12 f.; Legge, *Texts of Tâoism* (*SBE* xxxix. [1891], Introd. p. 23 f.).
4 See refutation of such ideas by Wang Ch'ung in A. Forke, *Lun Hêng*, pt. i. (London, 1911) p. 346 ff.
5 H. A. Giles, *Chuang Tzŭ*, p. 267; cf. Legge, *SBE* xxxix. 22.
6 L. Giles, *Taoist Teachings*, p. 21.
7 *Ib.* p. 22.
8 *Ib.* p. 23.
9 *Ib.* p. 27.
10 *Ib.* p. 29.
11 H. A. Giles, *Chuang Tzŭ*, Introd. p. xx.
12 *Ib.* p. 203; see also p. 223 ff.
13 *Ib.* p. 229.
14 *Ib.* p. 285.
15 *Ib.* p. 293.
16 L. Giles, *Taoist Teachings*, p. 28.
17 H. A. Giles, *Chuang Tzŭ*, p. 224; cf. Legge, *SBE* xxxix., Introd. p. 22, *SBE* xl. [1891] 6.
18 See Legge, *Religions of China*, p. 189 ff.
19 A. Forke, *Yang Chu's Garden of Pleasure*, p. 25; see also pp. 26 f., 35, 39 ff.
20 See A. Forke, *Lun Hêng*, pt. i. p. 191 ff., pt. ii. 369 ff.
21 *Ib.* i. 195.
22 *Ib.* i. 196.
23 For Chinese Buddhism see art. CHINA (Buddhism in) and the lit. there cited, to which may be added E. J. Eitel, *Three Lectures on Buddhism*², London, 1873; J. Edkins, *Religion in China*², London, 1878; J. Dyer Ball, *Religious Aspect in China*.

its votaries in the Northern branch of that religion believe in the glorious Paradise of the West, to which the souls of the believers in Amida (Amitābha) Buddha can ascend and escape the long catena of lives and deaths supposed to be the lot of the aspirant to Nirvāṇa on his weary road thither.

To vie with its sister religion, Taoism evolved in its turn a nine-storeyed heaven with the Dragon King as ruler to await the arrival of pious souls.

6. Conclusion. — Thus, with the multiplicity of lives to which Buddhism has accustomed the Chinese mind, death looms largely in the purview of life, not only to the Buddhist, but also to the Taoist and even the Confucianist; for Buddhism has entered into the religious life of the whole people and tinctured their ideas and thoughts. The Chinese is practical in his outlook on life. He finds himself in the midst of it, he has to accept it, and his thoughts turn more naturally to what its outcome is to be than to its source and origin. More fantastic than his visions of his future are those of his past. With no inkling, for the most part, as to whence he came, he has given full play to his fancy to conjure up the origin of the human race.[1] One of the fairy-like tales of his mythology is that the vermin on the body of a colossal giant, who brought order out of chaos, were the progenitors of mankind;[2] while in another account the mountains produced the lowest of the lower creation, and these, in turn, developed higher forms, culminating in man, who was evolved from the ape.[3]

We find higher ideas in the ancient classics; for, though covering but limited ground, the rudimentary knowledge of the Supreme Being possessed by the ancient Chinese embraced the idea that He gave 'birth to the multitudes of the people,'[4] so that in the State worship by the Emperors He has been addressed as the maker of heaven, earth, man, and all animate beings.[5]

LITERATURE.—Authorities are cited in the footnotes.

J. DYER BALL.

LIFE AND DEATH (Christian).—In passing from the OT view to that of the NT there is no abrupt or startling gap, although a delicate tact is conscious of a difference of atmosphere, and becomes aware that the elements common to both are not in the same proportion, and appear to have been subjected to some organic change in the later form. In the OT words denoting 'life' occur in 166 passages, and in the Apocrypha in 24; words denoting 'death' occur in 354 passages, and in the Apocrypha in 33; on the other hand, in the NT words denoting 'life' occur in 135 passages, and words denoting 'death' in 128. In this quantitative analysis the striking fact is that death occupied the OT mind more predominantly than life. Qualitatively taken, however, a striking difference at once appears. Life in the OT for the most part refers to existence here in the flesh, and comparatively rarely rises above it, being summed up in the LXX phrase in Sir 37^{25}: 'the life of man is in the number of his days.' Instances occur, of course, especially in the later Psalms and Wisdom literature, of life being regarded as independent of bodily conditions, but these are to be treated as indications of a transition in thought to a higher plane, as a *præparatio evangelica*.

The significant feature of the NT allusions to life (and death) is their want of any real interest in mere earthly living, and this feature is plain even where the necessities of experience compel reference to the fact of physical death. Thus, out of the 135 passages where 'life' (ζωή) occurs, not more than seven can be referred to physical life. In one (Lk 1^{75}) the text varies, and the life referred to might be heavenly. In Lk 16^{25} the life of Dives is sharply contrasted with the life of Lazarus. Ac 8^{33} is a quotation from the LXX; Ac 17^{25} is inspired by Stoic thought. In Ro 8^{38}, 1 Co 3^{22}, and Ph 1^{21}, where life and death are conjoined as correlative powers, the reference may be to earthly life and death, but the probability is that in each case the meaning is that spiritual life and spiritual death face us. In the first passage it is invisible powers personified that are declared incapable of sundering the Christian from Christ; in the second passage the words are equally patient of either meaning; and in the third, if Theophylact may be followed,[1] the spiritual meaning prevails. Besides these seven passages, the word 'life' in the NT does not seem to be used anywhere in the lower sense.

The case is different with the term 'death' (θάνατος), for in something less than a score of passages in the Gospels, and in eight passages of Acts, the death of Jesus is referred to; in nine passages of Heb. physical death, especially that of Jesus, is the subject; and in Rev. 'death' is personified in conjunction with Hades, or is described as being followed by a second death, or is regarded as the term of this life. On the other hand, St. Paul and St. John, with hardly an exception, when they refer to death at all, mean spiritual death, not physical. Our task is to examine the passages where the terms ζωή and θάνατος, or their cognates, occur in the NT, in order to ascertain their precise meaning.

1. Life.—(*a*) The first mode of expression for the 'life' which Christ gives is to be found in the use of the definite article. Examples of this are Mt 7^{14}, 'straitened is the way that leadeth unto the life'; $18^{8f.}$, Mk $9^{43.45}$, 'to enter into the life maimed,' 'to enter into the life with one eye'; Mt 19^{17}, 'thou wouldst enter into the life'; Jn 5^{24} (cf. Jn 3^{15}), 'hath passed out of the death into the life'; 6^{48}, 'the bread of the life'; 8^{12}, 'shall have the light of the life'; 11^{25} 14^{6}, 'I am the life'; Ac 3^{15}, 'the prince of the life'; Ro 8^{2}, 'the law of the spirit of the life'; 2 Co 4^{12}, 'the life worketh in you'; 5^{4}, 'the mortal may be swallowed up by the life'; 1 Ti 6^{12}, 'lay hold of the aeonian life'; 1 Jn 1^{1}, 'the word of the life'; 5^{12}, 'he that hath the Son hath the life'; Rev $2^{7.10}$ 3^{5} 13^{8}, 'the tree,' 'the crown,' 'the book of the life'; 21^{6}, 'the water of the life.'

In all these cases the article is used in what grammarians call the anaphoric sense, by which the substantive is pointed to as referring to an object already definitely known. Thus, in the instances given the implication is that the life mentioned is that with which the readers were already familiar as the subject of Evangelic preaching, and an object of their own religious experience. It is also implicitly contrasted with another and a lower kind of life—that of the natural man, of the man of this world (cf. F. W. Blass, *Grammar of NT Greek*[2], London, 1905, p. 146).

(*b*) Life which is unreal and fleeting is set aside in favour of the life which is real and abiding: 1 Ti 4^{8}, 'life that is now and life which is to come'; 6^{19}, 'the life that really is.'

(*c*) It is assigned a heavenly nature by a predicative clause: Ro 5^{10}, 'we shall be saved by his [the Son's] life'; 2 Co $4^{10f.}$, 'the life of Jesus'; Eph 4^{18}, 'the life of God'; 2 Ti 1^{1}, 'life that is in Christ Jesus'; 1 Jn 5^{11}, 'the life in his Son.'

(*d*) The characteristic NT expression qualifying life, however, is 'æonian,' rendered in AV 'everlasting' 24 times, and 'eternal' 42 times, but both terms are misleading, as giving a quantitative in-

[1] For the philosophical theory see art. COSMOGONY AND COSMOLOGY (Chinese).

[2] Cf. J. Dyer Ball, *Scraps from Chinese Mythology*, annotated in *China Review*, Hongkong, 1872–1901, xi. 76 ff.

[3] A. M. Fielde, *A Corner of Cathay*, New York, 1894, p. 158 ff.

[4] Legge, *Religions of China*, p. 28.

[5] *Ib.* p. 47 ff.

[1] 'A kind of new life I live, and Christ is all things to me, breath and life and light' (see M. R. Vincent, 'Philippians and Philemon,' *ICC*, 1897, *in loco*).

stead of a qualitative category. 'Æonian' as an adjective occurs in all 71 times in the NT, and in 43 of these it qualifies 'life.' These passages (in addition to 17 in the Fourth Gospel) are Mt 19$^{16. 29}$ 25^{46}, Mk 10$^{17. 30}$, Lk 10^{25} 18$^{18. 30}$, Ac 13$^{46. 48}$, Ro 2^{7} 5^{21} 6$^{22f.}$, Gal 6^{8}, 1 Ti 1^{16} 6^{12}, Tit 1^{2} 3^{7}, 1 Jn 1^{2} 2^{25} 3^{15} 5$^{11. 13. 20}$, Jude ^{21}. In all these passages it is not the duration of the life that is in question, but its nature and its source. Hence, though the rendering 'eternal' may be permissible, that of 'everlasting' is erroneous, and even 'eternal' can be allowed only where eternity is understood as by Boethius:

'Whatsoever, therefore, comprehendeth and possesseth the whole plenitude of unlimited life at once, to which nought of the future is wanting, and from which nought of the past hath flowed away, this may rightly be deemed eternal' (*Phil. Consol.*, v. prosa 6 [*PL* lxiii. 859]; cf. Dante, *Parad.* xxii. 61-69).

It is in the prominence given to this view of life that we are to find the superiority of the NT teaching on it over that of the OT.

The transition from the sense of 'æonian' in the LXX (where it [or its cognates] is used about 330 times) to its sense in the NT is of the nature of an evolution. The NT sense of 'spiritual,' or 'divine,' is not wanting in the OT,[1] yet the more usual sense of the term is that of duration. Out of this lower sense there gradually unfolds, at first tentatively, but at length surely and fully, the ground on which duration rests, viz. the possession of an essence which is superior to the category of time. What endures is that of which time is but the changing expression, and the great gift of Christ is seen to consist in the power which He confers of escaping from the jurisdiction of 'the prince of the power of the air' into the higher realm where the 'æon' or the 'æonian' king rules.

The use of the term 'æon' in the NT is important for our present purpose; for, in addition to the passages in which the temporal meaning of the term is required, there are a number which are ambiguous, and also a further number where 'æon' is certainly used in a personal sense. Different ages, or different regions of the universe, are placed by God under the control of rulers to whom the name of 'æon' is given. In Ac 15^{18} the rendering should in all probability be 'God maketh these things known from æon.' So in Ac 3^{21} and Lk 1^{70} the prophets are said to receive their inspiration 'from æon.' The sense of Jn 9^{32} is best reached by paraphrasing it: 'From the realm of the æon the news has not been heard of anybody opening the eyes of a man born blind.' In Eph 2^{2} no question can be raised, for the 'æon of this world' there is clearly a personal being, since he is given as a sub-title 'the prince of the power of the air.' In 1 Ti 1^{17} God is distinguished as the 'King of the æons.' In Col 1^{26} the revelation given to the saints is exalted above that given to the æons. The latter knew nothing of the mystery of the indwelling Christ, the hope of glory. The knowledge of this was the prerogative of the saints. In 2 P 3^{18} the 'day of æon' can be nothing but the 'day of the Lord,' and hence the æon here is Jesus (cf. also He 1^{2}, 1 Co 10^{11}, Gal 1^{4}, and the appendix to Mk in the Freer-logion).

When we remember that Christianity grew up in a Gnostic environment, that among the Gnostics the doctrine of personal æons was universal, and that 1 Clem. 35, Origen (*c. Celsum*, vi. 31), Ignatius (*Eph.* 19), Clem. Alex. (*Strom.* iv. 13), Irenæus (*Hær.* i. 17), and Hippolytus (*Ref.* vi. 26) all refer to the doctrine explicitly as worthy of note and demanding correction, we shall not be surprised if echoes of it are found within the Canon. Further, the same fluidity of meaning which attaches to the use of the term outside the Canon attaches to it also within the Canon. Omitting temporal significance as too general to need exemplification, it is enough to say that the word 'æon' may stand for a superhuman being who is good or evil, supreme or subordinate. Hippolytus (*Ref.* iv. 2) mentions speculators who 'speak of a sedition of æons and of a revolt of good powers to evil, and of a concord of good and wicked æons.' Irenæus (*Hær.* i. 1) relates that the Valentinians taught the existence of 'a certain perfect, pre-existent æon whom they call Proarche, Propator, and Bythos.' So Epictetus (ii. 5) says: 'I am not God (*æon*) but man,' and, therefore, mortal; and pseudo-Dionysius (*de Div. Nom.* v. 4) says: 'God is called Arche and Measure of Æons and Essence of Times and Æon of things that are . . . for He is the æon of æons, He that is before all æons.' The Valentinians further taught, according to Irenæus, that the supreme Æon emanated eight æons, the ogdoad, and these ten others, after which twelve more were produced, making thirty in all; they also saw in the visit of Jesus to the Temple when He was twelve years old, and in His baptism when He was thirty, a cryptic reference to the system of æons. R. Reitzenstein (*Poimandres*, Leipzig, 1904, p. 270) quotes a Hermetic hymn addressed to Isis as the moon-goddess in which it is said: 'Thou art the beginning and the end, and thou rulest over all, for of thee are all things and to (thee as) *æon* do they run as to their end.' So in the Hermetic tractate *Mind unto Hermes*, 2, it is said: 'God makes æon, the æon makes the world, the world makes time, time makes generation.' Here 'æon' is the name of the ideal principle which ultimately takes form in the world of becoming. Similarly, Plato (*Tim.* 37) says: 'When the father and creator saw the creature which he had made moving and living, the created image of the eternal gods (τῶν ἀϊδίων θεῶν), he rejoiced, and in his joy determined to make the copy still more like the original; and, as this was eternal (ἀΐδιον), he sought to make the universe eternal, so far as might be.' In this passage, where Plato wants to express the idea of everlastingness, he has the word ἀΐδιος ready to his hand. But, when he goes on to express a different idea, he uses a different term (αἰώνιος): 'Now the nature of the ideal being was æonian (αἰώνιος), but to bestow this attribute in its fullness on a creature was impossible. Wherefore he resolved to make a moving image of the æon (αἰῶνος), and, setting in order at the same time the heaven, he made this æonian image of the æon abiding in unity (μένοντος αἰῶνος) [an image that in itself was æonian] to move in accordance with number; and this image we call time.' In the latter passage, as is obvious, Plato is dealing with the *quality* of the archetypal order, and, therefore, he uses the word αἰώνιος. In the former passage he was dealing with a category of *quantity*, and, accordingly, he employed the word ἀΐδιος, 'everlasting.' J. Adam (*Vitality of Platonism*, Cambridge, 1911, p. 35 f.) translates αἰῶνος in Pindar (fr. 131, ed. Bergk) as the 'living man,' and says that it never means 'eternity' in Pindar. The passage is ζῷον δ' ἔτι λείπεται αἰῶνος εἴδωλον· τὸ γάρ ἐστι μόνον ἐκ θεῶν (cf. *Il.* xix. 27). Plato's antithesis of æon and time reappears in Philo (ed. T. Mangey, London, 1742, i. 496), who makes the three first days of creation, before sun and moon were created, an image of 'æon' and the last three of time, 'for He set the three days before the sun for the æon, and the three after the sun for time, which is a copy of æon.' Similarly, he says (i. 619) that 'the life of the intelligible world is called æon, as that of the sensible is called time.'

The question whether 'æon' and 'æonian' are to be rendered qualitatively or quantitatively is not identical with the question whether a Jewish or Greek conception is the determinant, for the Hellenization of Christianity was active, even if not in its acute form, from the earliest NT days. Greek thought had penetrated Jewish before NT times (W. Bousset, *Die Religion des Judentums im neutest. Zeitalter*, Berlin, 1903, p. 493; cf. 'æonian torment,' in 4 Mac 9^{9}; 'æonian life' in Enoch 10^{10}; 'judgment of the æon of æons,' 10^{12}; 'the King of the æon,' 27^{3}), and is embedded in the NT itself. Moreover, the Rabbinical antithesis of 'this world' and 'that world' lay on the border-line of Greek thought, and might pass easily into it. The witness of Philo must be added to that of the Synoptic Gospels (with their many isolated sayings redolent of Greek thought and their record of the teaching of a mystery-religion), the Fourth Gospel as a whole, Eph. and Col., and the constant tendency of the Greek in St. Paul to burst its Jewish fetters. We conclude, therefore, that 'æonian life' in the NT is life that belongs to a higher order than animal or ordinary human life; it is from above, and the recipient of it is lifted, by possessing it, into a higher state of consciousness. It is not this present life indefinitely or infinitely prolonged, nor is it life beyond the grave distinguished as such from life on this side of the grave.

It is not possible here to do more than allude to the central place which the fact and truth of regeneration (*q.v.*) occupy in the religion of Jesus Christ. All that is required is a reminder of the close connexion of regeneration with the æonian

[1] *e.g.*, in Ec 3^{11} we are told that God has placed the æon in the heart of man, *i.e.*, has given him a seed of a higher order of being.

life which forms the theme of the NT. To be born from above (ἄνωθεν, Jn 3^{3}); to be turned and to become as little children (Mt 18^{3}); to come out into the resurrection of life (Jn 5^{29}); to put on Christ (Gal 3^{27}); to be quickened together with Christ (Eph 2^{5}); to be in Christ (2 Co 5^{17}); to put on the new man (Eph 4^{24}); to be a new creature (Gal 6^{15})—these and many similar passages describe that dynamic process of which the result is æonian life, or salvation, or the Kingdom of God, or blessedness.

2. Death.—Christian theology has been at once oppressed and confused by its failure to note that in the NT it is not physical life cleared of its experienced ills that is called life, and that it is not physical death as such that is connected with sin. (1) Reflexion would assure us that, when life is used in a super-physical sense, it is at least probable that the death referred to is always something more than the death which dissolves the connexion between the self and its physical vehicle. If one be of the transcendental order, so must the other be. (2) It has never been easy to maintain a causal nexus between sin as a wrong act of will and death as an event of the natural order. Modern science has convinced itself that death has reigned not only since Adam's transgression, but from the first appearance of life. Death indeed, apart from sin, is a process of nature and not a super-natural punishment for sin. (3) Christianity is admittedly a religion whose home is in the spiritual order, and its interest, therefore, in the physical, though real, is only indirect. From its superior standpoint it may have something to say as to the origin and meaning of physical death, but, if it speaks of death as intimately bound up with its own life, that death will not be of the physical order. (4) The law of analogy points in the same direction. A principle which is operative on one level repeats itself analogously at other levels. Just as gravity may be described without straining as love embryonic in matter, or, conversely, as love in the spiritual world exercises an attraction which binds spiritual beings as surely as gravity binds together atoms, so death as physical is a reflexion of a similar principle in the world where life is life indeed. (5) All philosophy assures us of the existence of an infinite principle or truth in the finite event or fact, of the existence of a universal in the particular. But a physical death is a fact in the world of space and time; hence it conceals what is more than a fact—a truth or idea, or a fragment of reality presented under the guise of the actual. If, therefore, a religion which proclaims itself as having the real for its object speaks of death, or attributes to death any place in its world, it cannot be supposed to limit its reference to the death which is merely physical.

It will be found on examination that the conclusion thus reached *a priori* is confirmed by a careful scrutiny of the evidence. (*a*) We may conveniently begin with passages in which death is obviously treated as acting in the spiritual sphere. The following passages in the Fourth Gospel may be cited: 'He hath passed out of the death into the life' (5^{24}; cf. 1 Jn 3^{14}); 'If a man keep my word, he shall never see death' ($8^{51f.}$); in ch. 11 the difficulty caused by the apparent indifference of Jesus in the beginning, by the reference to sleep, and by the affirmation that the believer should never die can be fairly met only by the hypothesis that the story in form moves on the physical plane, but that in substance it is the story of the resurrection of the soul from spiritual death; the reference to the manner of death in 12^{33} is contained in what is certainly a gloss. In 1 Jn we have similar references to spiritual death: 'He that loveth not abideth in the death' (3^{14}), where the death is clearly on the same plane of being as love; in 5^{16} the sin unto death (or not unto death) is also clearly a sin which is followed by death of the same order, viz. in the world of free will, for it is said in explanation that God will give life for them that sin not unto death—a sentence which is meaningless if physical life is meant, since that is *ex hypothesi* there already. In Rev. the second death, which is spiritual, is distinguished from the first death, which is physical (2^{11} $20^{6.\ 14}$ 21^{8}).

In the Epp. also many passages occur in which death must be interpreted as spiritual. In Ro 1^{32} St. Paul, speaking not as a jurist but as a preacher (cf. W. Sanday and A. C. Headlam, *Romans*[5], Edinburgh, 1903, *ad loc.*), sets up an ideal standard with ideal consequences for violation of it. Those who outrage the plainly expressed mind of God as to what righteousness is do so with the full knowledge that they deserve death ('und meint damit den ewigen Tod' [H. A. W. Meyer, *Der Brief an die Römer*, ed. B. Weiss[9], Göttingen, 1899, *ad loc.*]). In the striking passage Ro 5^{12-21}, unless St. Paul is guilty of inexcusable logical confusion, the death which in vv.$^{17.\ 21}$ is obviously spiritual must be of the same kind in vv.$^{12.\ 14}$. The current exegesis which assumes such looseness of thought in St. Paul is itself responsible for the confusion. The meaning is simple, plain, and consistent throughout: Adam was guilty of a sin which was spiritual in its character, being a misuse of free will; therefore he brought on himself spiritual death, and this death has afflicted mankind ever since. But now at last the Christ of God, by Himself entering into vital union with a race self-deprived of the higher life, that is, by sharing in some sense their loss, has restored what they had lost; He has, that is, obeyed the law that only through death do we enter into life. The death He has undone is that which consists in the absence of spiritual life; and the death He has borne is that which consists in the process of taming the lower nature, in the process of the mystic crucifixion. The one lost æonian life by self-will; the other gained it by obedience, and gave it through love.

Similarly, the linking of baptism with Christ's death and life in Ro 6 is explicable only if it is æonian life and æonian death that are in question, and the best proof of this view is to be found in the difficulties into which exegesis has long been implicated through its mistaken assumption that the life and death referred to are physical. Hence it has to say that St. Paul's 'thought glides backwards and forwards from the different senses of "life" and "death" almost imperceptibly' (Sanday-Headlam on 6^{8}). But, from the facts that Christ's death was transacted in the spiritual order, that baptism in its genuine meaning was a moment in a dynamic process, that the life which Christ truly lived was an æonian life, it follows that, the life being the same both in the Lord and in His disciples, they both were united in the mystic Vine, since one and the same life was in it and in its branches. Therefore, St. Paul concludes, since it is now æonian life that rules in both Christ and His members, death is automatically excluded. While 'the seed abideth' in the believer, he not only does not sin, but he cannot sin; or, if he sins, the sin is proof that the life is not yet dominant.

The argument in Ro 7 is similar. Using the image of marriage being valid for life, St. Paul says that the natural man has law for a husband and sin for his child, and sin in turn begets death, *i.e.* spiritual death (v.^{9}). This spiritual death is in turn undone by the Spirit of life in Christ Jesus (8^{2}). We are given even an exact definition of death as being identical with the mind of the flesh, and of life as being spiritual-mindedness (8^{6}).

Even the famous passage in 1 Co 15 is given a coherent meaning only when the thought of spiritual life and spiritual death is kept in the foreground. It is true that here the thought is less pure, and that the physical death of Christ and His resurrection from physical death are made the proofs of the reality of the heavenly order. But, even so, it is not the physical resurrection that is the vital point, but the spiritual, of which the physical is but an expression. The argument is as follows. To be still in your sins is death; faith, however, when it comes, annuls this (spiritual) death, for it is essentially life. This living faith (the life of God in the soul) is what filled Christ, and constituted His title to the higher state of being, as is proved by the fact that He overcame (spiritual) death; the proof that He did so overcome spiritual death is to be seen in the fact that He could not be holden by physical death. Hence death in both senses is abolished, or is in the process of being abolished, but the death which is *the* enemy is spiritual, and, if physical death comes into question at all, it is incidental only or by way of illustration. That this is the true interpretation becomes clear when we observe that the remainder of the chapter (vv.$^{35-58}$) is concerned only with affirming that this higher spiritual, or risen, life will require a cognate spiritual body, and that as God gave the life so He will give the suitable body.

(*b*) There are, however, unquestionably many passages in the NT which seem, on the surface at all events, to refer exclusively to a physical death. They are those which in the Gospels (12 times) and the Acts (8 times) deal with the death of Jesus Christ. But even here a sound exegesis will compel us to distinguish between what is said and what is signified. What is said is that Jesus suffered physical death at the hands of the civil and ecclesiastical authorities of His day. What is signified is that His sufferings as witnessed had a hidden counterpart and a universal validity because, He being a heavenly subject, what He experienced in strong crying and tears affects all who are united to Him as a transcendental subject by being made sharers of His life, partakers of His divine nature. What is signified is that His crucifixion is a mystic process before it takes shape in the moment of a physical death, and that this process of crucifixion, therefore, goes on necessarily in all those who are made one with His life (Gal 5^{24} 6^{14}). What is signified is that the physical death and burial of Christ are a reflexion of a spiritual death and burial which He underwent in order that He might be a radiating centre of heavenly life to all men. The real death and burial are to be found in the æonian world; the death and burial that fall under history are shadows of the real.

The Epistle to the Hebrews also refers explicitly to the physical death and sufferings, but here we must allow for the exigencies of the line of argument adopted. This compelled the author to place the physical death of the man Christ Jesus over against the physical death of the animals slain in OT sacrifices. Yet, even so, the force of the argument depends on the superior worth of the former. His sacrifice was all-compelling, partly because it was voluntary (7^{27} $9^{11f.}$ 10^{9}), still more because of its transcendent worth, it being the offering of One whose life was divine, and made in accordance with the power of an indissoluble life (7^{16}) and through an æonian spirit (9^{14}). The life, we may say, that even here is dealt with is essentially spiritual, and is physical only in a secondary and subordinate sense.

(*c*) A third and small class of passages alone remains where death is of an ambiguous appearance. In Rev 1^{18} 6^{8} 9^{6} $20^{13f.}$ Death is personified and joined with Hades, and both may attack man on his physical or on his spiritual side. In Mt 4^{16} and Lk 1^{79} the shadow of death falls across the heathen world, where spiritual death is surely meant. In Mt 16^{28}, Mk 9^{1}, and Lk 9^{27} contemporaries of Jesus, it is said, should not taste of death till they saw the Kingdom of God. It is impossible to say what was the original context of this triplicated passage, but it is improbable that the passage itself is to be regarded as a falsified prophecy of a historical fact. The 'Kingdom of God' and the 'Son of Man' are terms which express inner realities, and it is at least likely, then, that 'death' is also æonian. In this case the meaning of the passage is that there were some (a 'remnant,' the few who were 'chosen') who would not taste the bitterness of spiritual death, because to them would be vouchsafed the mystic vision of the King in His beauty, of the land that to most men remains far off.

It will be clear, from what has been said, that the NT and Christian antithesis is not that of the OT and Judaism, between this world and the next, but between two kinds of life both here and there. It is a qualitative and not a quantitative difference. On one side is the life of sense, of intellect, of static forms, of fixed perceptions and well-defined conceptions—the life, in short, whose boundaries are set by the practical needs of the empirical Ego. On the other side is the life which creates the very power by which sense and intellect discharge their limited functions, which is in itself defiant of forms, is only partially grasped by perceptions, and for the most part remains outside conceptions—the life, in short, which Jesus came to reveal and to give, which is called æonian, or spiritual, or heavenly, or divine, and is that ever-flowing stream from the life of God of which all expressions of life are at all levels fragmentary flashes. We pass from the fragment towards the complete and perfect in exact proportion to our surrender of our lower and separated self to the life of the whole, which is God. It is this enhanced life and expanded consciousness that the religion of Jesus Christ and His Church is primarily concerned with. Its interest in eschatology, in theories about resurrection, in hypotheses such as that of universalism, of conditional immortality, of the nature of the ultimate union of soul and body, or of reincarnation, though real, is subordinate only. It is concerned with a higher life experienced here and now, and to grow hereafter more and more towards the perfect day. It is interested in theories about that life, but its interest in them is not vital.

LITERATURE.—Boethius, *Philosophiæ Consolatio*; Augustine, *Confessions*, esp. bks. x., xi., xiii.; Aquinas, *Sum.* i. qu. x. artt. 4–6; Philo, *Quod Deus sit immut.*, esp. § 6 (Mangey, p. 277); D. Petavius, *de Deo Deique propr.* iii. 3, 4, and esp. notes to pp. 258–260, ed. L. Guérin, Bar-le-Duc, vol. i., 1864; Greg. Naz. *Orat.* 38; John Damascene, *de Fide orthod.*, bk. ii. ch. i.; Alcuin, *Ep.* 162, in *PL*, c. 419; F. D. E. Schleiermacher, *Reden* (1799), Göttingen, 1906; C. v. Orelli, *Die heb. Syn. der Zeit und Ewigkeit*, Leipzig, 1871; W. W. Harvey, *S. Irenæi adv. Hær.*, Cambridge, 1857, esp. his 'Preliminary Observations'; F. von Hügel, *Eternal Life*, Edinburgh, 1912; W. R. Alger, *Crit. Hist. of the Doctrine of a Future Life*[10], New York, 1878, with copious bibliography.

W. F. COBB.

LIFE AND DEATH (Egyptian).—The Egyptian conceptions of life and death seem at first sight to be full of inexplicable contradictions. No wonder is felt when these states are found to be alternately praised and execrated, for in such praise and execration personal preferences are involved, and these may vary. But it is more perplexing to find diametrically opposite views expressed or implied with regard to questions of fact or belief, as when the same being is described almost in one breath both as alive and as dead, or when men who fear the dead are seen to have used magical means to kill their enemies, thinking thus to be rid of them. Such inconsistencies arise from the blending of the simple distinction between physical life and death with the extremely ancient and almost universal belief in immortality—a belief that is rooted partly in the passionate abhorrence which death inspires as an indignity inflicted upon the living,[1] and partly in the fact that death is known to us only through observation of the external world, and not by conscious inner experience.

Life and death are facts, since they are ever being forced upon our notice; death is a falsehood, however, because we have never known it to be true of ourselves, and, furthermore, because we will not admit that it can be true of ourselves. But, if after the physical death we are not dead, then we must be alive. The words 'life' and 'death' thus both acquire a double meaning, and a wide field for speculation opens out; the achievements of the Egyptians within this field have here to be considered.

A. FORMS OF THE HIEROGLYPHIC SIGN FOR 'nḫ (LIFE)

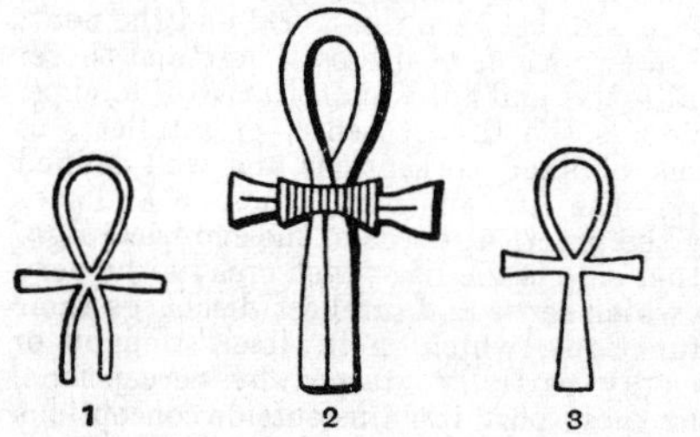

B. THE OBJECT 'nḫ (SANDAL-STRINGS) AND SANDAL FROM THE FOOT-END OF MIDDLE KINGDOM COFFINS

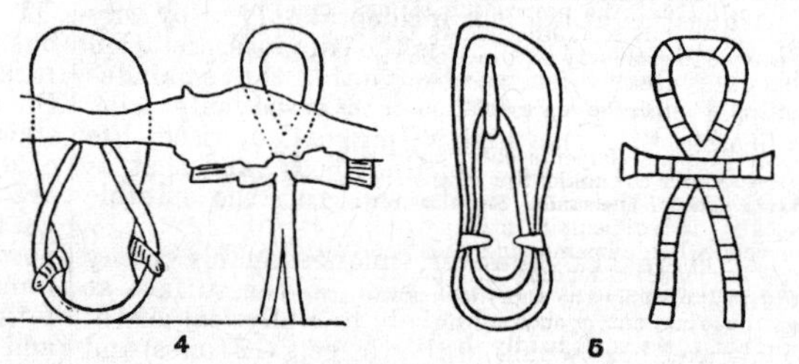

C. SOME SANDALS AS SHOWN ON OLD KINGDOM MONUMENTS

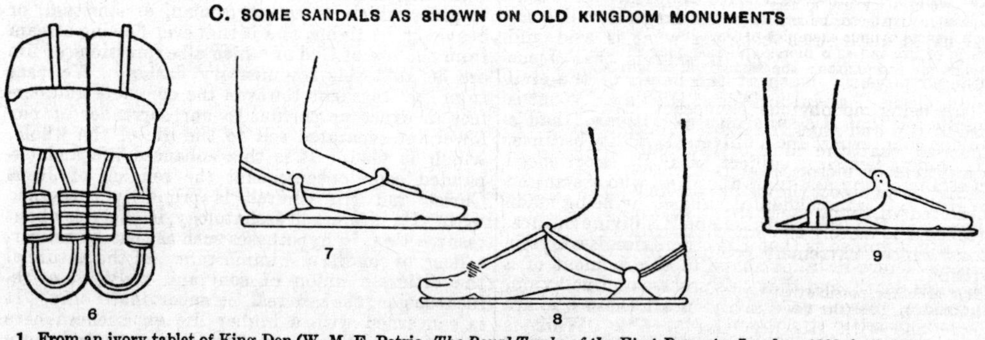

1. From an ivory tablet of King Den (W. M. F. Petrie, *The Royal Tombs of the First Dynasty*, London, 1900, i. pl. 14).
2. Elaborate form of hieroglyph in Old Kingdom inscriptions (Margaret A. Murray, *Saqqara Mastabas*, London, 1905, pl. 11, fig. 86).
3. Simplified form of hieroglyph (Petrie, *Medum*, London, 1892, pl. 14).
4. J. Garstang, *The Burial Customs of Ancient Egypt*, London, 1907, pl. 6, opposite p. 168; over the sandal-strings the original has the superscription, 'the two 'nḫ (sandal-strings) under his feet.'
5. H. Schäfer, *Priestergräber vom Totentempel des Ne-user-rê*, Leipzig, 1908, p. 54.
6. From the slate-palette of Nar-mer, Ist dyn. (J. E. Quibell, *Hierakonpolis*, i., London, 1900, pl. 29).
7. N. de G. Davies, *Deir el Gebrâwi*, London, 1902, i. pl. 11, completed from ii. pl. 6.
8. F. W. von Bissing, *Die Mastaba des Gem-ni-kai*, Berlin, 1905, i. pl. 16.
9. Davies, *The Rock Tombs of Sheikh Saïd*, London, 1901, i. pl. 15.

1. Philological.—Whereas the Egyptian word for 'to die,' *mwt*, Coptic ⲙⲟⲩ (infinitive), ⲙⲟⲟⲩⲧ (qualitative), is shared with all the Semitic languages, the verb for 'to live,' '*nḫ*, Coptic ⲱⲛϩ, ⲱⲛϩ̄, is of doubtful affinities. Several derivatives from the same stem, such as '*nḫ*, 'sandal-string,' '*nḫ*, 'goat,' '*nḫ*, 'ear,' fail to suggest any earlier or more concrete meaning for it, while other words having the same radical letters, such as '*nḫ*, 'oath' (Coptic ⲁⲛⲁϣ), or '*nḫ*, 'mirror,' clearly derive their meaning from '*nḫ*, 'to live.' Closely related in sense are the verbs *wnn*, 'to exist,' and *ḫpr* (Coptic ϣⲱⲡⲉ), 'to become,' 'come into existence.' For 'death' there are various euphemistic expressions, such as *ḫpyt* or *swḏꜣ*, 'passing away,' *mỉnỉ*, 'reaching port'; 'my dying day' is once expressed by *hrw nfr-nỉ ỉm*, 'the day on which it went well with me' (*Sphinx*, iv. [1901] 16); the phrase *sbt r ỉmꜣḫ*, 'to attain to beatitude,' is ambiguous, sometimes referring to honoured old age and sometimes to death. The dead are described as *ntỉw ỉm*, 'those who are yonder,' or as *bꜣgy nnyw*, 'the weary ones.' Theological is the phrase *s n kꜣ-f*, 'to go to one's *ka*, or double'; so, too, are the words *ꜣḫ*, 'glorified being,' *sꜣḥ*, 'noble,' and *ḥsy*, 'blessed,' applied to the illustrious dead. Two epithets that from the early Middle Kingdom onwards are appended to the names of dead persons reflect, the one the identification of the dead with Osiris, and the other the belief in immortality; these are *mꜣ'-ḫrw*, 'the justified,'[1] and *wḥm 'nḫ*, 'who repeats life,' respectively. The deceased Pharaoh was called 'the great God,' like his great prototype Osiris, while the living king is 'the good god.'

2. Writing and figured representation.—(*a*) The symbol of life, which is also the hieroglyph used for writing the words 'life' and 'live,' is the so-called *crux ansata*, ☥, popularly known as the '*ankh* ('*nḫ*), or 'key of life.' Its origin has been much discussed, most scholars agreeing that the sign represents a tie or knot of some kind, though in V. Loret's opinion (*Sphinx*, v. [1902] 138) it depicts a mirror. The true explanation, hinted at but immediately rejected by G. Daressy (*RTAP*

[1] See particularly R. Hertz, 'La Représentation collective de la mort,' in *ASoc* x. [1905–06] 124.

[1] See art. ETHICS AND MORALITY (Egyptian), § 7.

xxvi. [1904] 130), was first enunciated by Battiscombe Gunn, who proves the symbol to depict the strings or straps of the sandal.

No demonstration of Gunn's discovery (acknowledged by A. Erman in his *Ägyptische Grammatik*[3], Berlin, 1911, p. viii) has yet found its way into print: the crucial evidence in the following argumentation has been supplied by Gunn himself. There is an object called *'nḫ*, exactly resembling the symbol and hieroglyph for 'life,' which is often represented pair-wise at the foot-end of Middle Kingdom coffins. These coffins are covered with pictures of articles deemed necessary for the happiness of the dead in the after-life, and care is taken in most cases to place each object in its appropriate position as regards the body of the dead man within the coffin; thus necklaces are shown on the level of his neck, sceptres within reach of his hand, and so forth. *A priori*, therefore, it is to be concluded that the object was connected with the feet—a point clinched by the fact that a pair of these objects is usually shown next one or more pairs of sandals, while the other articles depicted (anklets, bowls for washing, etc.) are more or less clearly connected with the feet (see J. Garstang, *Burial Customs of Anc. Egypt*, London, 1907, pl. 6, opposite p. 168; P. Lacau, *Sarcophages antérieurs au nouvel empire*, Paris, 1904, no. 28034 [p. 90 f.]; H. Schäfer, *Priestergräber*, Leipzig, 1908, fig. 73 [p. 54], 83 [p. 59], and pl. 11). In several instances the accompanying inscriptions describe the pair of objects as 'the two *'nḫ* on the ground under his feet' (cf. Garstang, *loc. cit.*; Lacau, ii. 158; the preposition 'under' must not be pressed too closely, but it at least shows that the *'nḫ* was part of, or belonged in some way to, the sandals). If now we compare the object 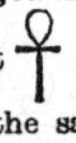 with the representation of the sandals, we shall see that the same elements enter into both—the long loop that passes round the ankle, the straps that serve to bind this loop to the sides of the sandal, and possibly a kind of ribbed bow or buckle. It is difficult to make the representations harmonize in detail, but, remembering that the sign is a very old one, that the modes of binding the sandal to the foot vary greatly, and that possibly the sign depicts the straps not as actually worn but laid out in such a way as to exhibit them to the best advantage, we shall hardly doubt that the objects shown on the Middle Kingdom coffins and called *'nḫ* are a spare pair of sandal-strings for use in the event of those attached to the sandals requiring to be replaced. The cut on the preceding page depicts various examples of the sandal-strings both as an article of use and as a hieroglyph, together with pictures of sandals for comparison; the hieroglyph is normally painted black.

There being no obvious connexion between the idea of life and that of sandal-strings, it must be supposed that the idea of life, not being itself susceptible of pictorial representation, was symbolized by an object the name of which fortuitously coincided in sound with the word for 'life'; this procedure is merely the procedure called 'phonetic transference,' extremely common in hieroglyphic writing.

It is, of course, possible that *'nḫ* (*'ankh?*), 'sandal-strings,' and *'nḫ* (*'ankh?*), 'life' (the vowel in both cases is hypothetic), are ultimately connected etymologically, but, as said above, the original meaning of the stem *'nḫ* is unknown. It would certainly be wrong to advance the hypothesis that the sandal-strings were called *'nḫ* because they resembled the symbol for life, the origin of that symbol itself being regarded as undiscoverable. The evidence of the earliest writing (the absence of the stroke-determinative[1]) shows that the *'ankh*-sign was regarded as a phonetic and not as a pictorial sign.

As a symbol the *'ankh* is everywhere to be found on the Egyptian monuments. Gods and goddesses hold it in their hands, or present it to the nose of their favourites. It appears with arms supporting a standard (*e.g.*, E. Naville, *The Temple of Deir el-Bahari*, v., London, 1906, pl. 149) or as itself representing the legs of a human figure (*Louvre, C 15*); such religious representations have still to be collected and classified. As a mere ornamental device the *'ankh*-sign is frequently found on furniture, jewellery, etc., often in association with other auspicious symbols, *e.g.*, 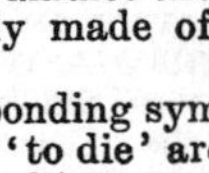, 'life, stability, and prosperity.' As an amulet the *'ankh* is fairly common, and is usually made of green or blue faience.

(*b*) There is no corresponding symbol for 'death.' The words 'death' and 'to die' are in early times followed (or 'determined,' to use the technical expression) by a sign representing a man fallen upon his knees, and bleeding from a wound on the head; later this sign is merged into another of wider application and varying form—the commonest form is —which accompanies various words meaning 'prisoner' or 'enemy.' Very often, however, these hieroglyphs are mutilated or suppressed because of their ill-omened associations (*ZÄ* li. [1914] 19).

3. Literal views of life and death.—How life was envisaged may best be learned from the following wishes on behalf of a dead man:

'May there be given to thee thy eyes to see, thy ears to hear what is spoken; thy mouth to speak, and thy feet to walk. May thy hands and arms move, and thy flesh be firm. May thy members be pleasant, and mayest thou have joy of all thy limbs. Mayest thou scan thy flesh (and find it) whole and sound, without any blemish upon thee; thy true heart being with thee, even the heart that thou didst have heretofore' (K. Sethe, *Urkunden des ägyp. Altertums*, Leipzig, 1904–09, iv. 114 f.).

Death is the negation of life; in slaying their foes, the Egyptians sought to make them 'as though they had never been' (*Urkunden*, iv. 7, and *passim*), and the custom of cutting off their hands and phalli indicates of what activities it was intended to deprive them. Further light is thrown on these materialistic conceptions of life and death in a passage of the 175th chapter of the *Book of the Dead*, where the state of death is described:

'Of a truth it is without water, it is without air—deep, dark, and void, a place where one lives in quietude. Pleasure of love is not there to be had, nay, but beatitude is given to me in lieu of water and air and love, quietude in lieu of bread and beer.'

Inertia is the chief characteristic of the dead, wherefore they were called 'the weary,' 'the inert' (§ 1); elsewhere we find death compared with sleep (e.g., *Pyramid Texts*, ed. Sethe, Leipzig, 1908, 721). Life, on the other hand, is full of activity, and chief among its needs are air to breathe ('breath of life' is a common expression) and food and drink for sustenance. Here, again, the wishes for the dead are the best evidence of the things deemed needful for the living; 'bread and beer, oxen and geese, cloth and linen, incense and myrrh, and things good and pure whereon a god lives'—so runs the common formula, which hardly less often mentions 'the sweet breeze of the North-wind' as a necessity of life. The place of life was pre-eminently the earth; 'O all ye who live upon earth,' begins a favourite invocation.

Various views were held as to the whereabouts of the dead, but their habitation was normally not the earth; 'those who are yonder' is, as we have seen, a common designation of the dead. That the land of death is a land whence there is no returning was early said; already in the Pyramid Texts (2175) we find the warning, 'Go not upon those western ways, for those who have gone yonder come not back again'[1] (the same thought recurs later; cf. *Harris 500*, recto 7, 2). Reflexions as to the duration of life and death are often encountered in the texts. The Egyptian prayed that, like Joseph, he might attain to the age of 110 years (see *RTAP* xxxiv. [1912] 16–18). In comparison with death, the endlessness of which was constantly alluded to (cf. 'the city of eternity' for the necropolis, 'the lords of eternity' for the funerary gods), 'the span of things done upon earth is but as a dream' (*PSBA* xxxv. [1913] 169; cf. *Pap. Petersburg 1116 A*, recto 55 [*Les Papyrus hiératiques . . . de l'Ermitage*, 1913]; it should be said parenthetically that this comparison of life with a dream refers only to the dreamlike fugitiveness of its events, not to any speculations concerning its reality). With regard to the extension of the idea of life, it seems to have included man and the animal

1 Except where 'the symbol life' is meant.

1 For this and other valuable references the writer is indebted to Professor Sethe of Göttingen.

kingdom only (cf. the words quoted from a Memphite text in § 11); it is doubtful whether an Egyptian would have spoken of plants as living; nor is there any expression found to describe the neutral inanimate state of things not belonging to the animal world.

4. The hatred of death.—The opening words of the gravestone-formula, 'O ye who love life and hate death,' strike to the root of the most profound feelings of the Egyptians, whose intense love of life and detestation of death made them devote more time and thought to funerary things than has been done by any other people before or since. The best expression of these feelings is on a stele dating only from the year 46 B.C., but wholly Egyptian in feeling; a woman speaks from the tomb to the husband who has survived her:

'O brother, husband, friend, highpriest—thy heart shall not grow weary of drinking and eating, drunkenness and love. Celebrate a happy day; follow thy heart by day and night; put no care in thy heart. What are thy years upon the earth? The West [*i.e.* the place of burial] is a land of slumber, dark and heavy, the habitation of those who are yonder, who sleep in their mummy-shapes, nor wake to see their brethren, nor regard their fathers and mothers, and their hearts are reft of their wives and children. The living water of which all have a share, for me it is thirst, but it comes to him who is upon earth. Thirst have I, though water is beside me, and I know not the place where I am, since I came to this valley. . . . Turn my face to the North wind on the bank of the water; perchance so my heart shall be relieved of its affliction. Nay but Death, his name is "Come"; every one to whom he hath called comes to him straightway, their hearts affrighted, through fear of him. There is none can see him either of gods or of men; great and small alike rest with him, nor can any stay his finger. He loveth all, and robbeth the son from his mother. The old man moves to meet him, and all men fear and make petition before him. Yet he turns not his face towards them, he comes not to him who implores him, he hearkens not when he is worshipped, he shows himself not, even though any manner of bribe is given to him' (R. Lepsius, *Auswahl der wichtigsten Urkunden des ägyp. Alterthums*, Leipzig, 1842, pl. 16).

This is perhaps the only passage in which death is personified, though the Egyptians were not averse to a sort of fictitious deification of abstract ideas; Life, *e.g.*, is found beside Health in the outward guise of a Nile-god (J. E. Gautier and G. Jéquier, *Mémoire sur les fouilles de Licht*, Paris, 1902, p. 25). The exhortation 'celebrate a happy day' recurs again and again in the songs of the harpers at Egyptian banquets, together with the reminder that life is short, death inevitable and eternal. Herodotus tells us (ii. 78) that at the entertainments of the rich a wooden figure of a dead body in a coffin was borne around and shown to the guests, with the words: 'When thou lookest upon this, drink and be merry, for thou shalt be such as this when thou art dead.' No reference is made to this custom in our texts, but it is thoroughly Egyptian in spirit (see also Plut. *de Is. et Osir.* xvii.). The old songs collected by W. Max Müller, *Die Liebespoesie der alten Ägypter*, Leipzig, 1899 (pp. 29-37), recall the wretched fate of the dead:

'The nobles and glorified ones . . . buried in their pyramids, who built themselves chapels, their place is no more; what is become of them? I have heard the words of Imhotpe and Hardedef, told and told again; where is their place? Their walls are destroyed, their place is no more, as though they had never been. None cometh thence who can relate how they fare. . . .' Then comes the inevitable moral: 'Be of good cheer, forget and enjoy thyself. Follow thy heart, so long as thou livest; place myrrh on thy head, clothe thyself with fine linen, anoint thyself; forget sorrow and remember joy, until arrives that day of putting to shore in the land that loveth silence.'

5. The hope of immortality.—From the same Theban tomb from which the last words are drawn (tomb of the priest Neferhotpe [50], XIXth dyn.) comes a song expressing widely different sentiments:

'I have heard those songs that are in the ancient tombs, and what they tell extolling life on earth, and belittling the region of the dead. Yet wherefore do they thus as concerns the land of Eternity, the just and fair, where terrors are not? Wrangling is its abhorrence, nor does any gird himself against his fellow. That land free of foes, all our kinsmen rest within it from the earliest day of time. The children of millions of millions come thither, every one. For none may tarry in the land of Egypt; none there is that passes not yonder. The span of earthly deeds is but as a dream; but a fair welcome awaits him who has reached the West' (*PSBA* xxxv. 169).

This pretty poem voices the opinions of those who, holding a firm faith in immortality, rejected the cold comfortless views of death already illustrated. No doubt that faith was born of a revulsion of feeling against the pitiless cruelty of death; and, being the offspring of the will rather than of the reason, it did not supersede or drive out the opposite belief. There is an argumentative, controversial note in the asseveration of the old funerary texts, 'Thou hast departed living, thou hast not departed dead' (*Pyramid Texts*, 134; cf. 833); or we may quote the reiterated assurance, 'Thou diest not,' in the same texts (657, 775, 781, 792, 810, 875, 1464, 1477, 1810, 1812, 2201). The multifarious funerary rites, the contracts made with *ka*-priests, and the petitions or threats to passers-by and visitors to the tombs all imply that the benefits of immortality were not to be obtained except by elaborate forethought and deliberate effort. It is true that a discontinuance of the funerary cult might not entail complete annihilation; the Egyptians dreaded, for instance, lest the cessation of the offerings made to them might compel them to devour their own excrements (*ZÄ* xlvii. [1910] 100-111). Nevertheless, there was ever lurking in the background the fear that a man might perish altogether, and that his corpse might decay and fall to pieces (*Book of the Dead*, titles of chs. 45, 163), this fear giving rise to the strange apprehension of a 'second death in the necropolis' (*ib.* chs. 44, 175, 176).

Similar conclusions might perhaps be drawn from the variety of the theories concerning the fate of the departed, who were alternately (or even simultaneously) believed to be stars in the sky, dwellers in the nether world, incarnations of Osiris, or spirits living in the tomb or revisiting their earthly homes (see art. STATE OF THE DEAD [Egyptian]). It is unthinkable that all these divergent views were accepted and believed with a fervent sincerity; rather they were conjectures sanctioned by ancient tradition, half-believed, half-doubted, and expressed with a naive and credulous thoughtlessness, which at the same time failed to silence the haunting suspicion that absolute death, after all, might be a reality.

6. Secondary views of life and death.—Under the influence of the conception of immortality the terms 'life' and 'death' became so impregnated each with the meaning of the other that they no longer contradicted and excluded one another as they had originally done; 'life' was not necessarily the short term of existence upon earth, and 'death' was perhaps but another mode of living. Sometimes, of course, by the abstraction which language permits, the words were used in their old strictly contrasted senses, but often there is left only a shadow of the original meaning; 'living' may be any form of existence vaguely analogous to physical, terrestrial existence, and 'death,' 'die,' 'dead,' are terms that might be applied to various states from which some characteristic feature of living was absent. A few examples, mainly of philological interest, may serve to illustrate this transition of meaning. Not only was prolongation of life the reward of moral conduct (see ETHICS AND MORALITY [Egyptian], § 6), but in a sense the moral life was the only true life; in the *Teaching of Ptahhotpe* we read:

'As for the fool who hearkens not, he achieves not anything, he looks upon him who knows as one who is ignorant, and upon things useful as things harmful, . . . he lives upon that wherewith men die, . . . his character is told (?) in the opinion of the nobles in that he dies living every day' (*Le Papyrus Prisse*, ed. G. Jéquier, Paris, 1911, 17. 4–8).

Such was the fear felt by him who was admitted to the presence of Pharaoh that he knew not whether he was alive or dead (*Sinuhe*, 255; *Koller* [ed. A. H. Gardiner, *Literary Texts of the New Kingdom*, Leipzig, 1911], 5. 1). The verb 'to live' was applied to other things besides human beings and animals; thus, whatever else in a man might die, his name, if properly tended, would continue to live (*Pyramid Texts*, 764, 899, 1024, and in later texts *passim*). 'Living soul' (*b; 'nḫy*) is a collocation of words which frequently occurs; yet, from its association with the dead, the word 'soul' is often determined with the hieroglyph that implies death. Pictures, statues, and images of all kinds were imbued with a sort of life,[1] by virtue of a principle common to all early superstition; the sculptor was called 'he who makes to live' (*s'nḫ*); hieroglyphs representing animals and human beings were sometimes mutilated or suppressed, obviously because they were considered to have the same power to injure as living things (*ZÄ* li. 1–64).

7. Death and the gods.—Could the gods be said to live? In a sense, no doubt, they were considered to live more fully, more truly, than human beings. The solar deity in particular was full of vitality; the Pharaoh is said to be 'granted life like Rē'; Rē 'lives upon truth'; the solar hymns, especially those to the Aten (the solar god of the heretic king Akhenaten) represent all life as emanating from the god; and all gods and goddesses were dispensers of life. On a closer view, however, we find that the kind of life that was predicated of the gods is more analogous to the life of the blessed dead than to the life of human beings; to the virtuous dead it is promised, 'he who is yonder shall be a living god' (Erman, *Gespräch eines Lebensmüden mit seiner Seele*, Berlin, 1896, p. 142; cf. *Pap. Petersburg, 1116A*, recto 56). That the gods dwell afar off together with the dead is shown by the following sentence from a sepulchral stele of the Middle Kingdom: 'I have gone down to the city of eternity, to the place where the gods are' (*Cairo*, 20485). Various dead Pharaohs and celebrities were posthumously deified (see art. HEROES AND HERO-GODS [Egyptian]), and the green or black complexions of their images suggest that they were not regarded as wholly alive. Osiris, as King of Eternity, chief of the Westerners, led but a shadowy existence, and similar conclusions are implied by the fact that certain deities had their 'living' terrestrial representatives. The Pharaoh ruled as Horus 'on the throne-of-Horus of the living'; under another aspect he was the 'living sphinx-image of Atum' (*sšp 'nḫ n 'Itm*). Alternately regarded as 'son of Rē' and as identical with Rē, the King did not die, but 'flew to heaven and joined the sun, the flesh of the god becoming merged in its creator' (*Sinuhe*, R 7 f.). The Apis and Mnevis bulls were respectively living emanations of Ptah and Atum, and other sacred animals whose cult was celebrated in late times doubtless stood in a similar relation to the gods whom they represented. Lastly, the historical aspect from which the gods were sometimes regarded represented them as rulers of a far-distant age, and, in consequence, as beings long since dead.

8. The dead as a class of beings.—In the *Book of the Dead* and elsewhere we find the following classification: men, gods, blessed dead (*ı͗;ḫw*, 'bright' ones), and dead (*mtw*) (see E. A. W. Budge, *Book of the Dead*, London, 1898, pp. 113, 293, 298, 308, 366, 389, 477). In this classification there is a kind of chronological hierarchical arrangement; the dead of the most remote times are holier, and partake more of divinity, than those recently deceased. So, too, the Turin Canon of Kings conceived the earliest rulers of Egypt to have been the gods of the first ennead; then came the lesser gods, and, lastly, the followers of Horus and earliest historical kings. Manetho records a similar sequence of 'gods' and 'semi-divine dead' (νέκυες οἱ ἡμίθεοι). In the *Book of the Dead* and elsewhere 'the dead' are spoken of in a way that clearly assumes them to enjoy a kind of existence; they 'see,' 'hear,' and so forth.

9. Relations of the living and the dead.—Some Egyptologists, influenced more by anthropological theorists than by the unambiguous evidence of the Egyptian texts, have asserted that the funerary rites and practices of the Egyptians were in the main precautionary measures serving to protect the living against the dead (*e.g.*, J. Capart, in *Trans. Third Congr. Hist. Rel.*, Oxford, 1908, i. 203). Nothing could be farther from the truth; it is of fundamental importance to realize that the vast stores of wealth and thought expended by the Egyptians on their tombs—that wealth and that thought which created not only the pyramids, but also the practice of mummification and a very extensive funerary literature—were due to the anxiety of each member of the community with regard to his own individual future welfare, and not to the feelings of respect, or fear, or duty felt towards the other dead. We have only to read the story of the exile Sinuhe to realize the horror felt by an Egyptian at the prospect of dying abroad, and of being thus deprived of the usual funerary honours; it is a feeling akin to this that created the whole system of funereal observances.

It does not vitiate the assertion here made that the dead cannot bury themselves, and are to that extent at the mercy of the living. Death does not absolutely snap all relations; and motives of filial piety, the calculation that one's own funeral rites are dependent on others, liberal inducements in the form of legacies, previous contracts with the deceased, and also a certain modicum of fear and hope—all these things afforded a certain guarantee to the dying man that his own wishes with regard to burial and a *post mortem* cult would be carried out. But there was no real ancestor-worship or objective cult of the dead in ancient Egypt.[1] The feelings of the living towards the other-dead, if they may be so called, constitute, therefore, a question apart from the question of funerary rites (see art. DEATH AND DISPOSAL OF THE DEAD [Egyptian]). The Egyptians wailed and mourned at the death of relatives, not merely out of grief, but as a matter of propriety; under the New Kingdom, mourning-clothes of a bluish colour were worn by women at the funeral (*ZÄ* xlvii. 162); we have at least one possible allusion to fasting on the occasion of a death (*Pap. Petersburg, 1116B*, recto 42); friends as well as relatives attended the funeral. It was thought that after death the deceased might return 'to afford protection to their children upon earth' (*Urkunden*, iv. 491; Nina de Garis Davies and A. H. Gardiner, *Tomb of Amenemhēt*, London, 1914, pl. 27); and we have a number of pathetic letters to departed relatives craving their intervention and help (Cairo, 25,975, hieratic text on linen, Old Kingdom; Cairo, 25,375, and Petrie collection, bowls with hieratic inscription, before Middle Kingdom; Pitt-Rivers collection, cup with hieratic inscription, before XVIIIth dyn. = *PSBA* xiv. [1892] 328). In one of these letters (*Pap. Leyden 371*, XXth dyn.; see Maspero, *Études égyptiennes*, Paris, 1879–91, i. 145–159)

[1] It has often been stated, especially by G. Maspero, that objects found in the tombs have been deliberately broken in order to 'kill' them, and so to send them into the realms of the dead for the use of the deceased. No authentic evidence in favour of this statement seems to be forthcoming.

[1] See, further, art. ETHICS AND MORALITY (Egyptian), § 13 (18).

bitter reproaches are addressed to a dead woman by her widower, who has fallen ill, blaming her for her neglect of him after all his kindness towards her while she was alive.

10. The dead as malignant beings.—In the magical and medical papyri incantations are often directed against 'every enemy male or female, every dead person male or female,' who shall come to injure N, the son of M. The dead are conceived of as the cause of disease, though perhaps only those dead are meant who still wandered homeless over the earth. The evidence seems fairly clear that actual 'possession' by the dead, conceived of as haunting spirits, is meant in such cases; for the demon is charged to 'flow forth,' and honey is said to be a useful medicament 'which is sweet to men, but bitter to the dead' (Erman, *Zaubersprüche für Mutter und Kind*, Berlin, 1901, p. 12 f.). At the same time, the duly-buried dead also had power to take vengeance on those who injured their property or violated their tombs (H. Sottas, *La Préservation de la propriété funéraire*, Paris, 1913). Evidently in Egypt, as in other lands, there was a danger inherent in death and in the dead, as also in blood, the symbol of death; in a Leyden papyrus it is lamented that 'plague is throughout the land, blood is everywhere, death is not lacking' (Gardiner, *The Admonitions of an Egyptian Sage*, Leipzig, 1909, p. 25); and, perhaps because of its association with blood, red colour is in many papyri avoided for writing the names of the gods, except in the case of the evil god Seth.

11. Origin and nature of life and death.—The Pyramid Texts (1466) recall a time 'when heaven was not, when earth was not, when mankind was not, before the gods were born, before death had come into existence.' Many cosmogonic legends were told by the Egyptians (see Erman, *Ägyptische Religion*², Berlin, 1909, pp. 32–36, for best summary); most of these referred the origin of life to some god, but there was a superstition which attributed self-generative powers to various small forms of animal life, such as mice, snakes, or flies. The frog was particularly prominent in this connexion, doubtless owing to the numbers in which tadpoles appear, just as though they had come into existence by themselves out of the wet mud. Hence not only did the frog become a symbol of the resurrection (*wḥm ʿnḫ*, 'living again'), but it was intimately associated with the beginning of things; in the Hermopolitan myth the eight primitive creatures had the heads of frogs or snakes, and in the Abydene tale the frog-headed goddess Heket was associated with Khnum in the creation (see W. Spiegelberg and A. Jacoby, in *Sphinx*, vii. [1903] 215–228). Life, once being started, was continued by the physical methods of reproduction (see esp. *Song of Harper*, l. 1; *Admonitions*, 12, 2–4), but the gods, especially the sun-god, Rē, were none the less the cause and mainspring of life (the birth-scenes in the temples of Luxor and Deir el Bahri are very instructive in this connexion).

A daringly speculative attempt to follow up this train of thought is found in an inscription from Memphis, a late copy of a text of early date (J. H. Breasted, 'The Philosophy of a Memphite Priest,' in *ZÄ* xxxix. [1901] 39),[1] which seeks to explain how Ptah, having primitively divided himself into 'Heart' (the seat of the imaginative, judging faculty), as impersonated by Horus, and 'Tongue' (the organ of command, *i.e.* the executive, willing faculty), as impersonated by Thoth, henceforward pervaded all that lives, 'all gods, all men, all cattle, and all reptiles.' It is then shown how all actions and reactions to sense-impressions presuppose the functions of 'heart' and 'tongue': when the eyes see, or the ears hear, or the nose smells, they convey (this sensation) to the heart, and it is the heart that causes every recognition (judgment) to go forth; it is the tongue that iterates (in the form of a command or act of the will) what the heart devises. In this way Ptah necessarily appears to be the cause of all things done by living creatures; he is, in other words, the vital principle itself. This psychological analysis of human, or rather animal, activity is up to the present unique, and perhaps represents the thought of some unusually gifted individual rather than that of the priests and learned men generally.

The medical papyri show that a serious attempt was early made to understand the workings of the body, but no other effort to reconcile semi-scientific views with the current mythology has yet come to light.

12. Magico-medical views.—A certain pre-natal existence is assumed in many hyperbolical expressions, as 'he ruled (already) in the egg' (*Sinuhe*, R 93). The normal view, of course, was that life began with birth; a writer speaks of the 'children who are broken in the egg, who have seen the face of the crocodile before they ever lived' (*Lebensmüde*, 79). The medical papyri contain prognostications for telling whether a child will live or not; 'if it says *ny* [a sound like the word for 'yes'], it will live; if it says *embi* [a sound like the word for 'no'], it will die' (*Pap. Ebers*, ed. L. Stern, Leipzig, 1875, 97. 13 f.). Spells were used to prevent women from conceiving, and there are various other ways in which birth is touched upon by the magico-medical literature. Amulets and charms of all sorts were employed to protect life; and, conversely, magic was secretly employed to bring about an enemy's death (*e.g.*, by means of waxen images [*Pap. Lee*; see P. E. Newberry, *The Amherst Papyri*, London, 1899]). A Turin papyrus attempts to cover all contingencies by enumerating all the possible kinds of death that may happen to a man (W. Pleyte and F. Rossi, *Pap. de Turin*, Leyden, 1869–76, p. 120 f.). Some kinds of death were considered happier than others; death by drowning, *e.g.*, was a kind of apotheosis, doubtless because Osiris had perished in this way, and those who died thus were called *ḥasye*, 'blessed' (*ZÄ* xlvi. [1909] 132). Curses were considered efficient magical means of affecting life (for a good collection of curses see Sottas, *op. cit.*). Oaths are conditional curses; it was usual to swear 'by the life of Rē,' and so common was this style of oath that the verb *ʿōnḫ*, 'to live,' was used transitively in the sense of 'to swear by,' and the Coptic word for an oath is *anash.* Most contracts and judicial depositions during the New Kingdom begin with the words, 'As Amūn endures, and as the Sovereign endures.' In the law-courts witnesses often swore oaths affecting their own life and property (conditional self-curses; see Spiegelberg, *Studien und Materialien zum Rechtswesen des Pharaohenreiches*, Hanover, 1892, pp. 71–81).

13. Life and the law.—On this subject consult the art. ETHICS AND MORALITY (Egyptian), § 13 (1–3), from which it will be seen that the sanctity of human life was strongly felt, as far at least as Egyptians were concerned. A few details may be added here. Abortion was considered a crime (*Pap. Turin*, 55. 1), unless the charge made in the passage here quoted was one of brutality leading to a miscarriage. Particularly abhorrent was bloodshed between close relatives, as father and son, or a man and his maternal brothers (see Gardiner, *Admonitions*, p. 9). Capital punishment was less favourably considered than punishment by imprisonment and the bastinado (*Pap. Petersburg, 1116A*, recto 48 f.), and persons condemned to death were allowed to make away with themselves.

14. Life as a thing undesirable.—The Egyptians' intense love of life and appreciation of its value are reflected in many of the passages that have been quoted. There is, however, a limited pessimistic literature (see art. ETHICS AND MORALITY [Egyptian], § 6) in which life is regarded as undesirable. This point of view may have been inspired originally by some such anarchical con-

[1] See also Erman, *SBAW*, 1911, p. 916 ff.; a new ed. is promised by Sethe.

ditions as prevailed after the fall of the Memphite dynasties. By the beginning of the Middle Kingdom the pessimistic style of literature was a recognized *genre*. Sometimes the despondent attitude towards life finds expression in the wish for a total cessation of life:

'Would that there might be an end of men, no conception, no birth! O that the earth would cease from noise, and tumult be no more!' (*Leyden Admonitions*, 5. 14–6. 1).

Elsewhere the misery of life is eloquently contrasted with the desirability of death; in a composition containing the dialogue between a misanthrope and his soul, death is described as follows:

'Death is before me to-day like the recovery of a sick man, like going forth abroad after lying prostrate.
Death is before me to-day like the scent of myrrh, like sitting beneath the sail on a windy day.
Death is before me to-day like the scent of lilies, like sitting on the shore of the land of intoxication.
Death is before me to-day like a trodden road, like the return of men from a campaign to their homes.
Death is before me to-day like the clearing of the sky, or as when a man becomes enlightened concerning that which he did not know.
Death is before me to-day as a man longs to see his home, when he has spent many years in captivity' (Erman, *Lebensmüde*, 130 ff.).

In the sequel it appears that the death here so highly praised is not non-existence, but the untroubled existence 'yonder.' And so it mostly was; the Egyptian remains true to his love of life—not perhaps the life on earth with its mingled joys and sorrows, but the life of his dreams in the land of Eternity, 'the just and fair, where terrors are not,' and where 'none girds himself against his fellow.'

LITERATURE.—There is no published monograph on the subject; such references as are needful have been given in the text. For the sign *'ankh* see a detailed discussion by G. Jéquier, in *Bull. de l'institut français d'archéologie orientale*, xi. (Cairo, 1914) 121–136.

ALAN H. GARDINER.

LIFE AND DEATH (Greek and Roman).—The outlook on life of the average Greek of the 5th cent. B.C. may be illustrated by the language which Herodotus, i. 30 ff., puts into the mouth of Solon of Athens in his interview with Crœsus, King of Lydia.

When Solon visited Sardis, after all the grandeur of the royal palace had been exhibited for his admiration, he was asked by Crœsus whom he considered the happiest man (ὀλβιώτατος) he had ever seen. To the surprise of Crœsus, Solon answered, 'Tellus of Athens,' because, 'on the one hand, Tellus lived in a prosperous city, and had sons handsome and good (καλοὶ καὶ ἀγαθοί), and saw children born to them all and all surviving; on the other hand, after a life affluent as we count affluence in Hellas, he died a most glorious death. He fought in a battle between the Athenians and their neighbours at Eleusis, and, routing the enemy, died most nobly; and the Athenians gave him a public burial where he fell, and honoured him greatly.'

Crœsus then asked whom he considered second in happiness. Solon answered, 'Cleobis and Biton.' These were natives of Argos, possessed of sufficient fortune, and, moreover, endowed with such strength of body that both were prize-winners in the games. It is further related of them that on one occasion, when the Argives were celebrating a festival in honour of Hera, it was necessary that their mother, as priestess of Hera, should be conveyed to the temple on an ox-waggon. The oxen not arriving from the field in time, the young men harnessed themselves to the waggon and drew it to the temple, a distance of forty-five stades. After they had performed this feat in view of the assembly, there came upon them a most excellent end of life, wherein God clearly revealed that death is better for a man than life. For the men of Argos standing round praised the strength of the young men, and the women of Argos called their mother blessed in that she had such sons. Then their mother rejoiced exceedingly in her sons' deeds and in the speech of the citizens, and, standing before the image of the goddess, besought her to grant to her children, who had done her such honour, the best thing that man can receive. After this prayer, when her sons had sacrificed and feasted, they fell asleep in the temple and awaked no more, but there ended their days. The Argives, in commemoration of their piety, caused their statues to be made and dedicated at Delphi.

Crœsus was indignant that Solon should not assign to him even the second place among happy men. Then Solon said: 'O Crœsus, you ask me regarding human affairs—me who know that the deity (τὸ θεῖον) is always jealous and delights in confounding mankind. For in the length of days men are constrained to see many things they would not willingly see, and to suffer many things they would not willingly suffer. I put the term of a man's life at seventy years. . . . Now in all these days of seventy years . . . no one day brings us at all anything like another. Thus, O Crœsus, man is altogether the sport of chance (πᾶν ἐστιν ἄνθρωπος συμφορή). You appear to me to be master of immense treasures and king of many nations; but I cannot say that of you which you demand, till I hear you have ended your life happily. For the richest of men is not more happy (ὀλβιώτερος) than he that has sufficient for the day, unless good fortune attend him to the grave and he end his life in happiness. Many men who abound in wealth are unhappy (ἀνόλβιοι); and many who have only a moderate competency are fortunate (εὐτυχέες). He that abounds in riches, and is yet unhappy (ἀνόλβιος), excels the other only in two things; but the other surpasses him in many things. The wealthy man, indeed, is better able to gratify his desires and to bear a great blow of adversity. But the other surpasses him in these respects: although he is not able to meet the blows of misfortune or the claims of his desires, yet his good fortune (εὐτυχίη) wards off these things from him, and he enjoys the full use of his limbs; he is free from diseases, unscathed by evil, blessed with a fine form (εὐειδής), happy in his children (εὔπαις); and, if all these things come at last to be crowned by a decent end, such a one is the man you seek, and may justly be called happy (ὄλβιος). For until that time we ought to suspend our judgment, and not to pronounce him happy (ὄλβιος), but only fortunate (εὐτυχής). Now because no man can possibly attain to this perfection of happiness; as no one region yields all good things, but produces some and wants others, that country being best which affords the greatest plenty; and, further, because no human body is in all respects self-sufficient, but, possessing some advantages, is destitute of others; he therefore who continues to enjoy the greatest number of these and then ends his life graciously, in my judgment, O King, deserves the name of happy. We ought to consider in every matter how the end shall be; for many to whom God has given a glimpse of happiness (ὑποδέξας ὄλβον), He has afterwards utterly overthrown.'

In reviewing these passages we may begin with the last point: 'Consider the end of everything.' This is a favourite sentiment in Greek writers, and there seems to be a note of conscious pride in the words with which Herodotus concludes the episode:

'When he made this reply, he found no favour with Crœsus, who held him of no account and dismissed him, considering him a very foolish man (ἀμαθής) who, overlooking present blessings, bade men look to the end of everything.'

Life is to be viewed as a whole. Already in Homer we find it a mark of the wise man that he 'looks before and after.'[1] It is a favourite notion in Pindar:

'There hang around the minds of men unnumbered errors, and this is the hopeless thing to discover—what is best for a man both now and in the end' (*Ol.* vii. 24 ff.).

Hence the distinction here drawn between the 'happy' man (ὄλβιος· ὁ διὰ τοῦ ὅλου βίου μακαριστός [Hesychius]) and the merely fortunate (εὐτυχής). A man may be prosperous, as Crœsus was. The Asiatic straightway calls him happy, but the 'foolish' Greek refuses that title till he has seen the end of all:

'Behold, this is Oedipus; this is he who solved the famous riddle and was a man most mighty . . . into what a sea of dire calamity is he fallen! Therefore, while a mortal waits to see that final day, call no man happy (μηδέν' ὀλβίζειν) till he have passed the final bourne of life, having suffered no evil' (Sophocles, *Œd. Rex*, 1524 ff.; cf. *Trach.* 1 ff.; Eurip. *Androm* 100 ff., etc.).[2]

Aristotle discusses the saying of Solon in *Eth. Nic.* i. 10:

πότερον οὖν οὐδ' ἄλλον οὐδένα ἀνθρώπων εὐδαιμονιστέον ἕως ἂν ζῇ, κατὰ Σόλωνα δὲ χρεὼν τέλος ὁρᾶν;

He begins by asking what the saying means. Does it mean that a man is happy (εὐδαίμων) only when he is dead, but not before? If so, then it is absurd, especially if we hold that happiness (εὐδαιμονία) is an activity (ἐνέργειά τις). Does it mean that only when a man is dead is one safe to call him happy, as being at last beyond the reach of evil and misfortune? Even if this is the meaning intended, the saying is open to dispute. In estimating a man's life, as happy or unhappy, we cannot confine our view to the individual. Man is a social being (φύσει πολιτικὸς ἄνθρωπος [*Eth. Nic.* i. 7; cf. *Pol.* i. 2]). If happiness, then, as we have

[1] ἅμα πρόσσω καὶ ὀπισσω (*Il.* iii. 109; cf. i. 343, xviii. 250, *Od.* xxiv. 452).

[2] The sentiment is not, of course, specifically Greek; cf. Sir 11^{28}: πρὸ τελευτῆς μὴ μακάριζε μηδένα; Ovid, *Met.* iii. 135: 'Ultima semper | Expectanda dies homini; dicique beatus | Ante obitum nemo supremaque funera debet.'

seen, is characterized by self-sufficiency (*αὐτάρκεια*), it is a self-sufficiency which includes children and other relatives and friends—within certain limits, of course; otherwise it would have to include the relatives of relatives, the friends of friends, and so on indefinitely (*Eth. Nic.* i. 7). When we are estimating the happiness of a man's life, then, we must include in the estimate a consideration of the fortunes or misfortunes of relatives and friends; but, here again, within limits. A man may have lived happily until old age and have died happily. But after his death (1) all sorts of things may happen to his relatives, and (2) these relatives will be of all degrees of nearness and remoteness of relation to the dead man. Now it is equally absurd either (1) to suppose that we must include in our consideration all sorts of degrees of distant relations, which would mean an indefinite postponement of our verdict, or (2) to refuse to take into account any posthumous happenings at all.

The ground of our refusal to bestow the title of 'happy' on a living man is that we consider happiness as something stable and abiding, whereas life is subject to continual change. Consequently, if we judge a man by his condition at any one given time, we shall have to call him sometimes happy, sometimes unhappy. Is not our true solution that we must neglect accidents in our estimate? Most accidents are not determinative of *εὐδαιμονία*. What determines happiness or the reverse is *ἐνέργειαι κατ' ἀρετήν* or the reverse. This view is supported by our present problem. So long as we judge by accidents, we are no better off when the individual is dead than when he was alive. We are driven, then, to judge by the stable things, *i.e.* by the *ἐνέργειαι κατ' ἀρετήν*, and the higher of these are the more abiding, as it is in these chiefly that the happy live out their lives (*καταζῆν*).[1] Hence these are more stable and abiding even than our knowledge of special sciences, which we are not living in and are therefore liable to forget. Thus the stability and permanence which we desire will belong to the *εὐδαίμων*, and he will be *εὐδαίμων* all his life. His happiness may be tarnished by untoward accidents, but it will not be extinguished. He will never become *ἄθλιος*, or truly unhappy, for he will never do things which are *φαῦλα καὶ μισητά*. If overwhelming misfortune, such as overtook Priam—*τύχαι Πριαμικαί*—should come to him, he will cease to be *μακάριος*, but he will not become *ἄθλιος*. Happiness can be affected only by the greatest things, whether for good or evil.

We may, then, define the happy man (*εὐδαίμων*) as a man who energizes *κατ' ἀρετήν* and is adequately equipped in externals, not for a moment, but for a *χρόνος τέλειος*. Or, since the future is uncertain, and *εὐδαιμονία* is a *τέλος* and *τέλειον*, perhaps we may add the proviso 'if it continue.' If so, we shall say that those who have goods and shall continue to have them are *μακάριοι*, but *μακάριοι ἄνθρωποι*—always liable to *τύχαι Πριαμικαί*. We need not defer our judgment, but we may qualify it by saying that they are happy, but with a mortal happiness.

To confine our view to the individual's life, and take no account of what happens after his death to those near and dear to him, is to take too unsocial a view. On the other hand, we must make some limitation. There are two further considerations: (1) posthumous events must be regarded as modifying our judgment of a man's life much less than if the same things had happened while he still lived; he, at any rate, was spared the knowledge of them; (2) we do not know whether the dead *αἰσθάνονται*—whether they are aware of what goes on here. If they are, the news that penetrates to them must be supposed to be slight in itself or at any rate of little moment to them. It follows, then, that posthumous events have no determining effect on our estimate of the individual's life.

[1] The proposal to read *ζῆν* for *καταζῆν* is completely mistaken. *καταζῆν* is the regular word for describing a fixed manner of existence: 'to be a spinster' is *καταζῆν ἄνυμφος*. So *καταβιοῦν* as contrasted with *βιοῦν*.

The doctrine of the jealousy of the gods appears often in Greek literature, and deserves special notice. It is a mistake to suppose that the Greek view is that the deity acts in an arbitrary and, so to say, spiteful fashion. It is true that the conception is sometimes so baldly expressed as to lend colour to such an interpretation.

Thus in Herod. vii. 10 Artabanos, the uncle of Xerxes, tries to dissuade Xerxes from invading Greece: 'Do you see how God strikes with His lightning those animals which rise above others, and suffers them not to vaunt themselves, while the lowly do not at all excite His jealousy? Do you see how He hurls His bolts against the most stately edifices and the most lofty trees? For God is wont to cut down whatsoever is too highly exalted. Thus a great army is often defeated by a small number of men; when God in His jealousy (*φθονήσας*) strikes them with fear or with thunder, they often perish in a manner unworthy of themselves, because God suffers none to be proud save Himself.'

But, while this may have been a popular conception, the underlying idea is a much deeper one. It is, in fact, nothing more than the expression of the Greek idea of justice, or Dike. The definition of justice (*δικαιοσύνη*) which Plato gives in the *Republic*[1] is nothing new, but is implied in the whole Greek attitude to life, as Plato says:

ὅτι γε τὸ τὰ αὑτοῦ πράττειν καὶ μὴ πολυπραγμονεῖν δικαιοσύνη ἐστί, καὶ τοῦτο ἄλλων τε πολλῶν ἀκηκόαμεν καὶ αὐτοὶ πολλάκις εἰρήκαμεν (433 A).

Now, as applied to the relation of God and man, justice lies in the recognition that the divine and the human destinies are utterly unlike. The gods and men are alike the children of earth (mother) and heaven (father): 'from one source spring gods and mortal men' (Hesiod, *Works and Days*, 107); but the lot of the gods is altogether different from that of mankind. Pindar emphasizes this distinction in a beautiful passage:

'One is the race of men, one the race of gods, and from one mother do we both have breath. But separate altogether is the power [faculty, *ingenium*, *indoles*] that sunders us; for one is naught, but the brazen heaven abides, an habitation unshaken for ever. Yet do we resemble somewhat, in mighty mind or in bodily form, the deathless gods, albeit we know not unto what line sovereign Destiny hath appointed us to run either by day or by night' (*Nem.* vi. 1 ff.).

Here we have the two characteristic distinctions which the average Greek drew between the gods and mankind: the gods are deathless and ageless, and untouched of evil; the years of man are few and full of sorrow, and the certain end is death; the gods have knowledge of the future; for man 'the river of prevision is set afar' (Pind. *Nem.* xi. 46). Now it is implied in the very nature of mortality that human life is a chequer-work of good and evil. A life of unbroken success, even if not attained by or attended with wickedness, is already a breach of nature, an injustice, an encroachment on the attributes of divinity, and so excites the jealousy of God, who allows none save Himself to be proud.

A life of unbroken happiness is no portion for men:

'Happy (*ὄλβιος*) is he to whom God hath given a portion of glory (*καλά*, especially success in the national games), and to live all his life with enviable fortune and in opulence; for no mortal is happy in all things' (Bacchylid. v. 50 ff.).

Hence it is a condition of abiding prosperity that a man's happiness should not be uninterrupted; only by being interrupted will it conform to the law of nature, the demands of justice:

'In thy new success I rejoice, but also I am grieved that jealousy [here, human jealousy] requites glorious deeds. But only thus, they say, will a man's happiness (*εὐδαιμονία*) prosper abidingly, if it wins both these things and those' [*i.e.* good and evil] (Pind. *Pyth.* vii. 14 ff.). 'Not one is without lot in sorrow nor shall be; yet the ancient prosperity (*ὄλβος*) of Battos attends them, giving them these and those' (*ib.* v. 54 f.).

[1] *ὅτι ἕνα ἕκαστον ἓν δέοι ἐπιτηδεύειν . . . εἰς ὃ αὐτοῦ ἡ φύσις ἐπιτηδειοτάτη πεφυκυῖα εἴη* (433 A).

This is the point of Clytæmnestra's words in Æsch. *Agam.* 904 f.:

'Let there be no jealousy: for many were the evils that we endured aforetime.' That is, our present good fortune should not excite jealousy. It is but the offset to former adversity.

So Nikias in Thucyd. vii. 77. 3:

'Our calamities are likely to abate: for the enemy have had enough success; and if our expedition provoked the jealousy of any of the gods, we have now been sufficiently punished.'

If a man is attended by an unbroken felicity, he must restore the balance by a voluntary sacrifice of some portion of his happiness.

This is the point of the famous story of Polycrates of Samos (Herod. iii. 40 ff.). His continued prosperity (εὐτυχία) excited the anxiety of his friend Amasis, who wrote to him in these terms: 'It is pleasant to hear of the good fortune of a friend and ally. But the excess of thy prosperity does not please me, because I know how jealous the deity is. As for me, I would choose that my affairs and those of my friends should sometimes be fortunate and sometimes stumble, rather than be fortunate in everything. For I cannot remember that I ever heard of a man who was fortunate in everything, who did not in the end finish in utter ruin. Be advised, therefore, by me, and in view of your good fortune do this: think what it is that you value most and the loss of which would most grieve you, and cast it away, so that it may never be seen again among men; and if after that your good fortune does not alternate with misfortune, repeat the remedy which you have now from me.' It is well known how Polycrates cast a valuable ring into the sea, but, unfortunately, afterwards recovered it in the belly of a fish—which so convinced Amasis that his friend's ruin was inevitable that he sent a herald to Samos to renounce his friendship and dissolve all obligations of hospitality between them, 'lest, if any great and dreadful calamity should befall Polycrates, he might himself be grieved for him, as for a friend.' So in Æsch. *Agam.* 1005 ff.: 'A man's destiny while sailing straight strikes a hidden reef. And, if betimes fear with well-measured (εὐμέτρου) sling makes jettison of a portion of his goods, the whole house sinks not, overladen with woe, nor is the ship engulfed.' The epithet 'well-measured' suggests the restoration of the balance, of the μέτρον which justice demands. The use of σφενδόνη, which is here in its usual sense of 'sling' but elsewhere occurs with the meaning 'bezel of a ring,' may possibly indicate that Æschylus had in mind the story of Polycrates.

The crude popular conception of the jealousy of the gods is refined by Æschylus in a remarkable passage of the *Agamemnon*:

'There is an ancient saying spoken of old among men, that a man's prosperity (ὄλβος), when it grows big, breeds and does not die childless, but from great fortune (τύχη) there springs for his race insatiable woe. But apart from others I hold an opinion of my own. It is the impious deed that breeds others like to its own kind, but the lot of the house which observes straight justice is blest in its children for ever. But old pride (ὕβρις) is wont to breed a young pride that wantons in the woes of men, now or anon, whensoever the appointed day of birth comes; breeds, too, that spirit (δαίμων) unconquerable, undefeatable, even unholy boldness (θράσος), dark curses (ἆται) for the house, like unto their parents' (750 ff.).

The teaching of Æschylus amounts to this. It is not mere prosperity that is sinful and brings evil in its train. Æschylus would, no doubt, admit that great prosperity has its temptations, that hardly shall a rich man enter into the Kingdom of Heaven, as Plato in the *Gorgias* tells us that the incurable souls who are hung up in the prison-house of Hades as deterrent examples to evildoers will mostly be the souls of tyrants and kings and potentates and politicians: 'for these, owing to the licence which they enjoy, commit the greatest and most unholy crimes' (525 D). That, in fact, Æschylus had this idea in mind seems to be proved by the immediately following words of the ode (772 ff.):

'But Justice (Δίκη) shines in smoky homes and honours the righteous (ἐναίσιμος) man; while from gold-bespangled dwellings of unclean hands she turns with averted eyes, and goes to pious homes, regarding not the power of wealth stamped with a false stamp of praise.'

We find the same thought in Pindar, *Pyth.* xi. 50 ff.:

'May I desire glory by the grace of Heaven, seeking things possible at my time of life. For, finding that the middle estate (τὰ μέσα) blooms with the more abiding prosperity (ὄλβος), I dislike the lot of the tyrant and am zealous for the common excellences. But the curses of jealousy are warded off, if one attaining the highest success and using it quietly avoids dread pride. So finds he the verge of death fairer, leaving to his dear children the best of possessions, the grace of a good name.'

If, however, continued prosperity leads a man to pride (ὕβρις), then pride leads to further pride or acts of pride, and by repetition come boldness (θράσος) and more daring deeds of sin: 'then he changed to thoughts of utter daring; for wretched base-devising infatuation, fount of woes, makes men bold (θρασύνει)' (Æsch. *Agam.* 221 ff.). To the Greek mind the Persian invasion of Greece was a typical example of pride and the effects of pride. Æschylus declares of the Persians who fell at Salamis:

'The heaps of corpses shall dumbly declare to the eyes of men even to the third generation that a mortal should not think thoughts too high; for pride flowers, and its fruit is an ear of doom (ἄτη), whence it reaps a harvest of tears' (*Pers.* 818 ff.).

The jealousy of God in the OT is exactly parallel to the Greek doctrine. It is not a capricious spite, but merely the justice which punishes any invasion of the prerogatives of the Deity by man: 'I the Lord thy God am a jealous God, visiting the iniquity of the fathers upon the children, upon the third and upon the fourth generation of them that hate me; and shewing mercy unto thousands, of them that love me and keep my commandments' (Ex 20[5f.]). One form of the breach of justice is that a man should desert the God to whom he belongs and follow after strange gods. Just as the civil law recognized the duty owing from a metic to his προστάτης, or patron, and provided for the punishment of the neglect of these duties by a δίκη ἀποστασίου (Dem. xxv. 65, xxxv. 48, etc.), so neglect of a man's duty to his gods or the following after strange gods was ἀσέβεια, or impiety (cf. Dt 32[15ff.]).

The wise and good man is the man who recognizes the conditions of mortality. The fool refuses this recognition and kicks against the pricks.

'Not for happiness in everything did Atreus beget thee, Agamemnon: thou must have grief as well as joy. For thou art mortal,' says the old man to Agamemnon (Eurip. *Iph. in Aul.* 28 ff.). 'If thou, Hiero, understandest a pithy saying, thou hast heard from them who were of old and knowest that for one good the deathless gods give to mortals two evils. This fools cannot endure with decency, but only the good, turning the fair side out' (Pind. *Pyth.* iii. 80 ff.). 'We with mortal minds should seek from the gods the things that are meet for us, knowing that which lies before our feet, to what destiny we are born. Seek not, my soul, deathless life, but exhaust thy practicable means' (*ib.* 59 f.).

Pindar illustrates the doctrine by the story of Asclepius, whom Zeus slew with the thunderbolt because he tried to bring a man (Hippolytus) back from the dead—an attempt to overstep the limits of mortality, and therefore demanding punishment. The same story is referred to by Æsch. *Agam.* 984 ff., in a passage which excellently illustrates the Greek doctrine:

Excessive prosperity demands voluntary jettison, says Æschylus. Then he proceeds: 'Abundant bounty given of Zeus from the yearly field destroys the plague of famine. But the blood of death that has once fallen on the ground at a man's feet—who shall call that back by any incantation? Did not Zeus for safety's sake [*i.e.* repelling an invasion of his divine prerogative of immortality] stop him who was skilled to bring back from the dead? And were it not that one fate is appointed by the gods to check another fate from going too far, my tongue would have outrun my heart,' etc. All life is based on the principle of justice, compensation, balance, that each should have his own.

Hence, too, it is τὰ ἀπὸ τύχης, the gifts of good-luck, that excite jealousy, not the good things which are won by toil.

The doctrine of the jealousy of the gods is repudiated as a 'poetic falsehood' by Aristotle, *Met.* i. 2, 983[a].

The things which make up human happiness are, according to Solon, adequate endowment of worldly goods, health, beauty of person, prosperous children, and a death in accord with these goods.

This enumeration of the elements of happiness is consonant with general Greek feeling. Similar catalogues occur frequently. Thus the distich inscribed in the temple of Leto at Delos (Aristotle, *Eth. Eudem.* 1214[a] 1 ff., *Eth. Nic.* i. 8, 1099[a] 25):

'Fairest (κάλλιστον) is justice, best (λῷστον) is health, and sweetest (ἥδιστον) of all is to attain what one desires.'

The same order is given in Theognis, 255 f. (cf.

Sophocles, frag. 328 f.). A popular *scolion*, or drinking-song, says:[1]

'Health is best for a mortal man; second, to be fair of body (φυὰν καλός); third, to have wealth without guile; fourth, to be young with one's friends.'

Philemon, frag. 163, gives (1) health, (2) success (εὐπραξία), (3) joy (χαίρειν), and (4) to owe no man. Pindar (*Pyth.* i. 99 f.) says:

'Success (εὖ παθεῖν, practically = prosperity or happiness) is the first of prizes; a fair fame (εὖ ἀκούειν) is the second lot; he who hath chanced on both and taken them to be his hath received the highest crown.' Cf. *Isth.* iv. 12, v. 12, *Nem.* i. 33, ix. 46, *Pyth.* iii. 104; Aristoph. *Av.* 605; Soph. *Œd. Col.* 144; Phocylid. frag. 10; Theocrit. xvii. 116; Bacchylid. i. 27 ff.

According to Aristotle, happiness is an ἐνέργεια κατ' ἀρετήν. But he admits, in *Eth. Nic.* i. 8, that 'nevertheless it does appear that happiness has need also of the external goods as aforesaid. For it is impossible or not easy for a man unprovided with these to do noble things. For many things are performed by friends, wealth, political power, the instruments, as it were, of action. The lack of some things mars happiness—the lack of birth, children, beauty. You could not well apply the term "happy" to a man who was utterly ugly, or low-born, or solitary and childless. Again, less still, if his children or his friends are altogether bad, or if he had good friends or children who are now dead. As we have said, happiness seems to need such outward prosperity. Hence some identify good fortune (εὐτυχία) with happiness, others identify happiness with virtue (ἀρετή).' In the *Rhetoric* (i. 5), where happiness is defined more popularly, such 'external' goods as the above are termed 'parts of happiness,' and the list is εὐγένεια, πολυφιλία, χρηστοφιλία, πλοῦτος, εὐτεκνία, πολυτεκνία, εὐγηρία; the physical excellences, as ὑγίεια, κάλλος, ἰσχύς, μέγεθος, δύναμις ἀγωνιστική; and δόξα, τιμή, εὐτυχία, ἀρετή.

He proceeds to explain what he means by the several terms here employed.

(*a*) εὐγένεια, good birth, may be predicated of a nation or a State, or of an individual. As applied to a nation or a State, it means that it is autochthonous or at any rate ancient, and had as its earliest leaders distinguished men, and has had many distinguished members in the course of its history. As applied to an individual, it refers to descent on either the male or the female side; it implies legitimacy, *i.e.* both father and mother must be citizens (ἀστός, ἀστή) in lawful wedlock (Arist. *Pol.* iii. 1. 4 f.; Dem. *adv. Neær.*; Aristoph. *Av.* 1660 ff.); it implies, further, that the earliest ancestors of the family were famous for virtue or wealth or some such distinction, and that many members of the family, both men and women, have in the course of its history distinguished themselves.

The high importance attached to heredity is evident on every page of Greek literature (see art. PINDAR).

(*b*) πολυφιλία and χρηστοφιλία, the possession of many and good friends, a friend being defined as 'one who, if he consider anything to be good for another, is ready to do it for the other's sake' (Arist. *Rhet.*, *loc. cit.*). Friendship takes a prominent place in the Greek ideal of life.

'Of all kinds are the uses of friends; above all in trouble, but joy also seeks to behold its own assurance' (Pindar, *Nem.* viii. 42 ff.). 'To cast away a good friend I count even as that a man should cast away the life in his own bosom, which he loves most' (Soph. *Œd. Rex*, 611 f.).

We hear of many celebrated friendships—Achilles and Patroclus, Orestes and Pylades, Castor and Pollux. The last is the theme of one of the most beautiful of Pindar's poems, *Nem.* x.

When Castor, the mortal one of the Twins, is slain, Pollux asks to be allowed to die with him: 'Grant me, O Lord, to die with him! A man's honour is departed when he is reft of his friends, and few there be that are faithful in the day of trouble to share the travail' (76 ff.).

The false friend is the object of bitter scorn (Pind. *Isth.* ii. 11; Æsch. *Agam.* 798, etc.). We hear, of course, of a more cynical view, that one should always look upon a friend as a possible enemy (Soph. *Aj.* 677 ff.; Eurip. *Hippol.* 253 ff.).

(*c*) πλοῦτος, wealth.

(*d*) εὐτεκνία and πολυτεκνία: these may be predicated either of the community or of the individual. In the case of the community, they mean the possession of a numerous body of splendid youth, splendid physically—in stature, beauty, strength, and athletic prowess—and splendid morally, the moral qualities desirable in a young man being self-restraint and courage. In the case of the individual, they imply that his children, male and female, are many and good. In a woman, the physical excellences are beauty and stature; the moral excellences are 'self-control and industry without illiberality' (φιλεργία ἄνευ ἀνελευθερίας).

'The high standard of female excellence is very important for the state; for where the condition of the women is vicious, as at Lacedæmon, there is no happiness in half the state.'

The importance of having children lies partly in keeping property within the family, since the bitterest thought of the childless man when dying is that his wealth will go to an outsider:

'Even as a child by his wife is longed for by his father who has reached the other side of youth, and greatly warms his heart, since wealth that falls to an outside alien's keeping is most hateful for a dying man' (Pind. *Ol.* x. [xi.] 94 ff.);

partly in that there will be no one to pay the memorial offerings to the dead (ἐναγίσματα). These motives find their consequence in the frequency of adoption (εἰσποίησις).[1]

(*e*) εὐγηρία, a good old age. This denotes an old age which approaches gradually and without 'pain'; if it comes rapidly, or slowly but accompanied with pain, it is not a good old age. This requires both physical excellences and good fortune. It is incompatible with weakness or disease, and a man must have good fortune to live long and remain ἄλυπος. 'It is indeed true that some attain long life without physical excellences.'

(*f*) The physical excellences: (1) ὑγίεια, health, *i.e.* freedom from disease, full possession of bodily faculties. Such valetudinarianism as that of Herodicus (Plato, *Rep.* iii. 406) is not desirable, as it means the denial of all, or nearly all, human pleasures. (2) κάλλος, beauty. A different kind of beauty is appropriate to different periods of life: the young man must be adapted to exercises of speed and strength, and pleasant and delightful to look upon. Hence pentathletes are most beautiful. The man in the prime of life must be fit for military exercises, combining grace with sternness in his appearance. The old man must be equal to such exertions as are inevitable, and his appearance must not be repulsive, *i.e.* must be free from the disfigurements of age. (3) ἰσχύς, strength. (4) μέγεθος, stature—but not so as to be unwieldy. (5) δύναμις ἀγωνιστική, athletic excellence—size, strength, speed; good running, wrestling, and boxing.

[1] Plato, *Gorg.* 451 E, *Legg.* 631 C, 661 A; cf. schol. *Gorg.*, *loc. cit.*: 'this *scolion* is attributed by some to Simonides, by others to Epicharmus.'

[1] Cf. Isæus, ii. 45 ff.: 'I have shown you that the laws give power to childless men to adopt sons. It is clear, moreover, that I paid attention to him while he lived and buried him when he died. My opponent wishes to turn me out of my father's estate, be it great or small; wishes to make the dead man childless and nameless, so that there shall be none to honour in his behalf the ancestral holies, none to make annual offerings to him (ἐναγίζῃ αὐτῷ καθ' ἕκαστον ἐνιαυτόν), but to rob him of his honours. Providing for this, Menecles, being master of his property, adopted a son, that he might get these things. Do not, then, be persuaded by these men to rob me of the title of heirship, which is all that is left, and make my adoption by him invalid. But, since the matter has come to you and you have power to dispose of it, help us and help him who is now in the house of Hades and do not, in the name of gods and *daimones*, allow him to be insulted by them' (see, further art. ADOPTION [Greek]).

(*g*) δόξα or εὐδοξία, *i.e.* to be regarded as a good man (σπουδαῖος), or as 'the possessor of something which all men or most men or good men or wise men desire.'

(*h*) τιμή, or honour, *i.e.* honours paid for benefactions either great in themselves or great in the circumstances (cf. Dem. *adv. Lept.* § 41). Such honours are sacrifices, memorials in verse and prose, privileges, allotments in land, foremost seats on public occasions, tombs, statues, maintenance at the public charges, barbaric compliments—*e.g.*, prostrations and giving place—local compliments. Τιμαί, as being both honourable and valuable intrinsically, appeal equally to the φιλοχρήματος and the φιλότιμος.

(*i*) εὐτυχία, or good fortune. It is the gifts of fortune that especially excite envy.

(*j*) ἀρετή, virtue. This is discussed in *Rhet.* ch. ix. Virtue is not merely desirable—as gifts of τύχη —but also ἐπαινετόν. It is 'a faculty of providing and preserving good things and a faculty of conferring benefits,' and its elements are justice, bravery, self-control, 'magnificence' (μεγαλοπρέπεια), highmindedness, liberality, gentleness, wisdom practical (φρόνησις) and speculative (σοφία).

The virtues which go to make up virtue, the μέρη ἀρετῆς, are given by Aristotle in the *Rhet.* i. 9 as δικαιοσύνη, ἀνδρία, σωφροσύνη, μεγαλοπρέπεια, μεγαλοψυχία, ἐλευθεριότης, πραότης, φρόνησις, σοφία. Plato, *Rep.* 402 C, gives σωφροσύνη, ἀνδρεία, μεγαλοπρέπεια, ἐλευθεριότης, καὶ ὅσα τούτων ἀδελφά, *Meno*, 73 E – 74 A, δικαιοσύνη, ἀνδρεία, σωφροσύνη, σοφία, μεγαλοπρέπεια καὶ ἄλλαι πάμπολλαι.

The four cardinal virtues, according to Plato, are courage, justice, temperance, and wisdom (*Rep.* 427 E); but the sovereign virtue, which involves all these,[1] is justice, which, as we have seen, Plato defines as τὸ τὰ αὑτοῦ πράττειν καὶ μὴ πολυπραγμονεῖν.[2]

In the famous passage of Pindar (*Nem.* iii. 74 ff.) the first three virtues are that of youth, that of men, and that of the old, while the fourth seems to be nothing else than justice, which is the sovereign and governing principle of all the rest: ἐλᾷ δὲ καὶ τέσσαρας ἀρετὰς ὁ θνατὸς αἰών, φρονεῖν δ' ἐνέπει τὸ παρκείμενον = τὸ τὰ αὑτοῦ πράττειν.

However this may be, justice includes all the other virtues. And the moral conscience of man demands in the name of justice that the just man shall have his reward. So Hesiod, *Works and Days*, 270 ff.:

'Now may neither I nor son of mine be just among men! For it is an ill thing to be just, if the unjust shall have the greater justice. *Howbeit these things I deem not that Zeus will bring to pass.*' Injustice may prevail for a time, but justice is better in the end (*ib.* 217 f.). 'On that which is pleasant but contrary to justice a most bitter end awaits' (Pind. *Isth.* vi. 47 f.). 'Too swift are the minds of men to accept a guileful gain in preference to justice, albeit they travel to a harsh reckoning' (τραχεῖαν ἐπίβδαν [Pind. *Pyth.* iv. 139 ff.]). On the other hand, end and beginning are alike pleasant if God speed.

How, then, and where shall it be better for the just man? The typical answer of the Greek moralist is 'Here and in this life.' Hesiod expresses the prevailing view of the Greek as of the Hebrew wisdom when he says:

'But whoso to stranger and to townsman deal straight judgments, and no whit depart from justice, their city flourisheth, and the people prosper therein. And in their land is peace, the nurse of children, and Zeus doth never decree war for them. Neither doth Famine ever consort with men who deal straight judgments, nor Doom; but with mirth they tend the works that are their care. For them earth beareth much livelihood, and on the hills the oak's top beareth acorns, the oaks midst bees; their fleecy sheep are heavy with wool; their wives bear children like unto their parents; they flourish with good things continually, neither go they on ships, but bounteous earth beareth fruit for them' (*Works and Days*, 225 ff.).

Even so the punishment of the wicked is in this world, whether in their own persons or in the persons of their descendants:

'But whoso ensue evil, insolence, and froward works, for them doth Zeus of the far-seeing eye, the son of Cronus, decree justice. Yea, oftentimes a whole city reapeth the recompense of the evil man, who sinneth and worketh the works of foolishness. On them doth the son of Cronus bring from heaven a grievous visitation, even famine and plague together, and the people perish. Their women bear not children; their houses decay by devising of Olympian Zeus; or anon he destroyeth a great host of them, within a wall it may be, or the son of Cronus taketh vengeance on their ships in the sea' (*ib.* 238 ff.).

In *Republic*, 363 A ff., Plato discusses this view of justice and its rewards. Goods are classified as of three sorts: (1) those desirable for their own sakes, (2) those desirable for their own sakes and for their consequences, and (3) those desirable for their consequences alone. Whereas Socrates would place justice in the second of these classes, the many would place it in the third. Popular morality says that justice is desirable because it leads to reward in this life—a position which is open to the objection that 'seeming to be just' is preferable to 'being just.' Parents exhort their children to be just for the sake of office and other advancement, and because, according to Hesiod (*loc. cit.*) and Homer (*Od.* xix. 109 ff.), the gods prosper the just in this life. Then follows a striking passage:

'Still grander are the gifts of heaven which Musæus and his son (Eumolpus) offer to the just: they take them down into the world below, where they have the saints lying on couches at a feast, everlastingly drunk, crowned with garlands; their idea seems to be that an immortality of drunkenness is the highest reward of virtue. Some extend their rewards yet further; the posterity, as they say, of the faithful and just shall survive to the third and fourth generation. This is the style in which they praise justice. But about the wicked there is another strain; they bury them in a slough in Hades, and make them carry water in a sieve; also while they are yet living they bring them to infamy, and inflict upon them the punishments which Glaucon described as the portion of the just who are reputed to be unjust; nothing else does their invention supply.'

According to Homeric eschatology, there remains for the dead only a shadowy existence in a dim under world, in dank places which even the gods abhor. This life after death, if it can be called life, holds nothing lovely or desirable:

'Speak not comfortably to me of Death, glorious Odysseus. Rather would I be on earth a servant with a landless man of no great livelihood than king over all the dead which are perished' (*Od.* xi. 488 ff.).

There seems to be no distinction of destiny between the good and the wicked, except, indeed, that perjury is said to be punished in the world below (*Il.* iii. 279, xix. 260). We have, it is true, some traces of a brighter fancy.

The poets told of an 'Elysian plain at the ends of earth, where fair-haired Rhadamanthus is; where life is most easy for men; neither snow nor great storm nor rain is there, but ever as the shrill West wind blows, Ocean sends forth breezes to refresh men' (*Od.* iv. 563); but Homer assigns this fate only to Menelaus, 'to whom it was decreed that he should not die nor meet his fate in Argos, the pastureland of horses,' because he 'had Helen to wife and was the son-in-law of Zeus.' They told of certain Islands of the Blest far in the Western Ocean where the heroes of the Theban and Trojan Wars dwelt under the kindly rule of Cronus—'happy (ὄλβιοι) heroes, for whom the bounteous earth bears honeysweet fruit, blooming thrice a year' (Hesiod, *Works and Days*, 166 ff.; cf. also art. BLEST, ABODE OF THE [Greek and Roman]).

But such a lot was apparently reserved for the heroes of old, who, without suffering dissolution of soul and body, were by the favour of the gods transported to a terrestrial paradise.

The introduction to Greece of mystic and orgiastic worship, and the rise of the Orphic and Pythagorean teaching towards the end of the 6th cent., gave a new and heightened meaning to the doctrine of the soul's survival after death. In the mysteries, of which those at Eleusis were the most celebrated, it would seem that a fairer prospect was offered to the initiated—a reward for righteousness in a life of perpetual felicity beyond the grave. Hence we find in Pindar, alongside of the language of orthodox Greek belief, glimpses of a larger and brighter hope, expressed in passages

[1] ὃ πᾶσιν ἐκείνοις τὴν δύναμιν παρέσχεν, ὥστε ἐγγενέσθαι, καὶ ἐγγενομένοις γε σωτηρίαν παρέχειν, ἕωσπερ ἂν ἐνῇ (*Rep.* 433 B).

[2] *Rep.* 433 A; cf. Aristotle, *Rhet.* i. 9. 7, ἔστι δὲ δικαιοσύνη μὲν ἀρετὴ δι' ἣν τὰ αὑτῶν ἕκαστοι ἔχουσι καὶ ὡς ὁ νόμος.

which are among the most striking in the range of Greek literature:

'Wealth adorned with deeds of prowess . . . is a conspicuous star, a most true light for a man, if he that hath it knoweth that which is to come: that the helpless minds of the dead pay straightly here their penance, while the sins done in this kingdom of Zeus one judges under earth, pronouncing doom by abhorred constraint. But equally evermore by night and day the good enjoy the sun, receiving a life free from toil, vexing not the earth with might of hand, neither the waters of the sea in that ghostly life, but with the honoured of the gods they that rejoiced in keeping their oaths live a tearless life, while those others endure woe too dire to behold. But whoso thrice on either side have endured to refrain their souls utterly from unrighteousness, travel by the Way of Zeus unto the tower of Cronus, where round the Islands of the Blest the Ocean breezes blow, and flowers of gold are glowing, some on the land from glorious trees, while others the water feedeth, with wreaths and garlands whereof they entwine their hands by the true counsels of Rhadamanthus, whom the father Cronus hath as his ready assessor, Cronus, husband of Rhea, throned highest of all. Peleus and Cadmus are numbered among these, and thither his mother brought Achilles, when she had with her prayers persuaded the heart of Zeus' (*Ol.* ii. 58 ff.).

Pindar's teaching here appears to be that the soul passes through three successive incarnations, alternating with a disembodied state, and that only after passing through all these blamelessly is it finally redeemed. Such souls, according to another passage of Pindar (frag. 133), receive a final embodiment as kings and wise men and athletes, and after death become, not indeed gods, but heroes:

'From whom Persephone in the ninth year accepts the atonement of ancient woe, the souls of them she sends back into the upper sunlight. From them spring glorious kings and men swift and strong and mightiest in wisdom; and for the future they are called by men holy heroes.'

Again, in frag. 137 Pindar says, in reference to the mysteries:

'Happy is he who beholds these things before he goes beneath the earth; he knows the end of life, he knows its god-given beginning.'

According to this view, the soul lives on after death, it alone being of divine origin:

'By happy dispensation (ὀλβίᾳ αἴσᾳ) all travel to an end which sets free from woe. And the body, indeed, of all goes with mighty Death. But there remaineth alive a phantom of life; for that alone cometh from the gods. It sleepeth when the limbs are active, but to men asleep in many a dream it reveals the coming judgment of pleasant things and hard.'

For the souls of the good there awaits a paradise which is imagined in terms of human bliss:

'For them shines the strength of the sun below while here it is night. And in meadows of red roses their suburb is shady with frankincense and laden with golden fruits. And some in horses, some in games, some in draughts, some in the lyre take their delight, and by them flourisheth all the fair flower of blessedness. And a fragrance spreads above the lovely place, while they evermore mingle all manner of incense in far-shining fire on the altars of the gods' (frag. 129).

'By happy dispensation'! Strange, indeed, would this have sounded to the Homeric hero, and hardly less strange, it would seem, to the orthodox Greek of the 5th century. It is not easy to estimate how far the ideas to which Pindar here gives expression had affected the general body of his countrymen, but it would not appear that they had done so very deeply. The general attitude to death continues much as in Homer. A state of bliss after death is not held out as an incentive to righteousness in this world. Nor is the hope of a blessed immortality offered to comfort the dying or mitigate the grief of the bereaved. When death is spoken of as desirable, it is merely as a κακῶν καταφυγή, a refuge from evil, a dreamless sleep:

'Would that some fate might come, speedy, not over-painful, nor with lingering bed, bringing to us the everlasting, endless sleep!' (Æsch. *Agam.* 1448 ff.).

It does not seem probable that the conception of the state after death exercised any determining influence on the average man's conduct of his life.

When one attempts to discuss Roman views of life and death, there occurs at the outset the comparative paucity of genuinely Roman evidence. The general attitude of the Roman towards life and death presupposes the same general framework as we have outlined in the case of Greece; the same conception of the goods which make up the content of human happiness; the same conception of death as the end and not the beginning; the same belief in the duty of paying solemn offerings (*parentalia*) to the dead. When we advance beyond orthodox opinion to the region of poetic fancy or philosophic speculation, we find that we are merely encountering Greek ideas in a Roman dress.

Greek and Roman alike believed in gods who had a very real regard for the sins and the virtues of mankind, rewarding the good and punishing the evil, *but in this life*, in their own persons or in those of their immediate descendants. Greek and Roman alike believed that the dead in some sense survive and that it was the duty of the living to make offerings to the dead. But for Roman as for Greek, the after-world was but a dim shadow of the present. There was no lively conviction that it would fare worse in the after-world with the bad than with the good; there was no lively conviction that there was any true after-life at all, certainly no such conviction of an immortal felicity as could prompt to martyrdom or self-sacrifice, or alleviate the hour of bereavement with the hope of a blessed reunion hereafter. When Cicero lost by death his beloved daughter Tullia, in the letter of condolence written to him by his friend Servius Sulpicius (*ad Fam.* iv. 5) the topics of consolation are drawn from practical and secular considerations: that she has been taken away from the evil to come, and that she has but shared the common lot, not of individuals only, but of cities:

'Ex Asia rediens, cum ab Ægina Megaram versus navigarem, cœpi regiones circumcirca prospicere: post me erat Ægina, ante me Megara, dextra Piræus, sinistra Corinthus; quæ oppida quodam tempore florentissima fuerunt, nunc prostrata et diruta ante oculos iacent. Cœpi egomet mecum sic cogitare: "hem! nos homunculi indignamur, si quis nostrum interiit aut occisus est, quorum vita brevior esse debet, cum uno loco tot oppidum cadavera proiecta iacent? visne tu te, Servi, cohibere et meminisse hominem te esse natum?"'

Nor in Cicero's most touching reply is there any hint of other consolation.

Nothing, perhaps, in the consideration of the conception of life and death is more significant than the attitude adopted in the question of suicide. The general feeling both in Greece and in Rome seems to have been one of pity for the suicide rather than condemnation. Thus, *e.g.*, Pindar, who three times refers to the suicide of Ajax, in no case hints at any moral wrong in the act, nor does Sophocles in the case of Jocasta. And the fact that Aristotle, in his Πολιτεία Θηβαίων (1553^b 31 f.), and other writers noted that suicide was condemned by the Thebans points clearly to a different attitude on the part of the Greeks in general. Naturally the Orphic-Pythagorean school, insisting on the reality of a true existence conditioned for weal or woe by the account of the present life, condemned suicide. In the *Phædo*, 61 C ff., Plato says that the good man will desire to be dead in order to free his soul from the cumbering influence of the body, which hinders him in the pursuit of truth: 'only, perhaps, he will not do violence to himself, for this, they say, is not lawful' (οὐ θεμιτόν); and he proceeds to refer to a 'secret doctrine' (ἐν ἀπορρήτοις λεγόμενος λόγος) that man is here 'in a sort of prison' (ἔν τινι φρουρᾷ), from which he has no right to free himself or run away' (cf. Cicero, *Cat. Maj.* 20; Plato, *Phædr.* 250 C, *Cratyl.* 400 C, *Gorgias*, 493 A). Macrobius (*Comm. in Somn. Scip.* i. 13) tells us that Plotinus objected to suicide on two grounds: (1) it implies a perturbed state of mind at the moment of dissolution; (2) it is a step which, once taken, is irretrievable. On the other hand, in the *Laws*, 854 C, Plato recognizes that in certain circumstances suicide is a duty. Sacrilege, he tells us, is an inherited malady.

When a man is tempted to commit such an offence, he should 'go and perform expiations, go as a suppliant to the temples of the gods who avert evils, go to the society of those who are called good men amongst you; hear them tell, and yourself try to repeat after them, that every man should honour the noble and the just. Fly from the company of the wicked—fly and turn not back; and if your disease is lightened by these remedies, well and good; but if not, then acknowledge death to be nobler than life, and depart hence.'

Similarly Cicero, *de Offic.* i. 31, holds that in the same circumstances suicide is for one man a duty, for another a crime. A man must decide in consonance with his character. Thus Cato committed suicide, as did Ajax; Ulysses did not.

This question, like the question of the life after death, seems to have been in general considered open. It is always to be remembered that religious formulæ and religious practices lag behind the true and genuine beliefs of those who practise them, and ritual is an unsafe index of the inner meaning of the worshipper. Thus we hear much of oracles in Greek history, and undoubtedly they exercised an enormous influence. Yet even so early as Homer we find it considered an open question whether one should obey an oracle or not:

'If it were some other and a child of earth that bade me this, whether some seer or of the priests that divine from sacrifice, then would we declare it false and rather turn our backs upon it' (*Il.* xxiv. 220 ff.).

In Hector's mouth is put the famous declaration that 'One omen is best—to fight for one's country' (*Il.* xii. 243). So in Rome Cæsar, while holding the office of Pontifex Maximus, delivered himself in the Senate of the doctrine that after death there was no place either for trouble or for joy:

'In luctu atque miseriis mortem ærumnarum requiem, non cruciatum, esse; eam cuncta mortalium mala dissolvere; ultra neque curæ neque gaudio locum esse' (Sall. *Catil.* li.).

So widely divorced, indeed, was outward practice from inward belief that Cato 'wondered how, when one soothsayer met another, he could help laughing' (Cicero, *de Div.* ii. 52). But the better minds, persuaded as they were that death meant either extinction or a true after-life in which the good should fare better than the wicked, prepared themselves for the great change much in the spirit of the Platonic Socrates, by setting their house in order. Thus Cicero:

'Id spero vivis nobis fore. Quamquam tempus est nos de perpetua illa iam, non de hac exigua vita cogitare' (*ad Att.* x. 8).

See, further, art. HAPPINESS (Greek and Roman).

LITERATURE.—C. A. Lobeck, *Aglaophamus*, Königsberg, 1829; E. Rohde, *Psyche*⁴, Tübingen, 1907; E. Buchholz, *Die sittliche Weltanschauung des Pindaros und Aischylos*, Leipzig 1869; J. A. Stewart, *Myths of Plato*, London, 1905; John Masson, *Lucretius, Epicurean and Poet*, do. 1907; G. L. Dickinson, *The Greek View of Life*, do. 1896.

A. W. MAIR.

LIFE AND DEATH (Hebrew).—There are two words which in the English OT are very often translated 'life': *nephesh* and *ḥayyîm*. *Nephesh* denotes the inner occult cause of life's activities. A *nephesh* is a concrete entity, resident in the body, which, if scarcely coming within the range of man's senses, is at any rate thinkable. It is a psychical something, endowed with many attributes, of which life is the chief, though it may also have others, physical and psychical. *Ḥayyîm* represents life abstractly, as a state or condition—vitality, mental and moral activity.

1. **Nephesh.**—OT psychology has always been a crux for Biblical scholars, because they have too often desired (as Franz Delitzsch) to form a 'system' of Biblical psychology. They have too often expected to find everywhere the same grade of civilization and the same type of approach and outlook. They have presupposed far more uniformity of thought than is actually present, and have not (until recently) allowed for primitive, ethnic modes of conception. The word *nephesh* is found in all Semitic languages, in much the same senses as in Hebrew; and therefore we must not be surprised if some extremely primitive beliefs, not taught—perhaps even discouraged—as doctrines by the men who were organs of revelation, have survived in occasional metaphors or modes of speech.

There were three ways in which the phenomena of life were regarded by early man: (1) objectively, by external observation, noting the manifestations of life in other men and in animals; (2) subjectively, by self-consciousness, through which man became aware of many different emotions and appetites, thoughts, and activities which were taking place within him; and (3) by the consciousness that he was being acted on by forces or beings extraneous to himself. We can scarcely point to a time when man did not fancy himself an object of interest, often of assault, to spirits good or evil, by whom he was surrounded. When the external influence came gently, the Hebrew called it *nᵉshāmāh*, 'breath'; when violently, he called it *rūaḥ*, 'wind'; and that part of his nature which was accessible to these gentle or violent invasions, by God or by spirits, he called respectively his *nᵉshāmāh* and his *rūaḥ*.

(1) *The objective method.*—Life is the antithesis of death; and from the beginning the thoughts of man were directed to the phenomena of life by their startling contrast with death. There were two ways in which death must have impressed primeval man: as the cessation of breathing, and as being caused by the shedding of blood.

(*a*) The universal and inevitable accompaniment of death is cessation of breathing; and this, by the force of contrast, would certainly direct the close attention of early man to the phenomena of breathing: the rising and falling of the chest, the varying rapidity of the inhalations, in rest and exercise, and the vapour visible from the mouth and nostrils at every exhalation. How did he account for this? Beyond all doubt, on principles of animism, which ascribed all internal movement, energy, and activity to an indwelling, living entity. *Nephesh* is often defined as 'the inner principle of life.' The vague term 'principle,' however, is much too modern. Early man personalized all our abstractions. The cause of breathing to him—and thus the cause of life—was a living spirit or soul, dwelling in man's chest, the breath-soul, which Semites called the *nephesh*, *i.e.* a semi-physical, semi-spiritual something, a potent reality, not to be identified with the breath, but the occult cause of the breathing; and, when it left the body for a considerable time, death was the result. To die, or 'yield up the ghost,' is to 'breathe out the *nephesh*' (Jer 15[9], Job 11[20]). When Rachel was dying and gave a name to her infant son, 'her *nephesh* was departing' (Gn 35[18]). When Elijah prayed for the recovery of the Shunammite's son, he stretched himself on the child and the child's *nephesh* came into him again (1 K 17[22]). When the Psalmist is sinking in a morass and in danger of drowning, he cries, 'Save me, for the waters are come in even unto my *soul*' (Ps 69[1]).

(*b*) The second startling phenomenon of life was the pulse, and the beat of the heart, which ceased when the blood was shed, in battle or in any other way. The occult cause of the heart-beat was conceived to be another *nephesh*—the blood-soul, resident in the blood; and, when the blood was shed, the *nephesh* was released. The shedding of blood received much scrutiny and thought in connexion with sacrifice, and the Hebrew priests assigned the efficacy of sacrifice to the blood-soul. This is most accurately expressed in Lv 17[11], 'The *nephesh* of the flesh is *in* the blood. . . . The blood maketh atonement by reason of the *nephesh*,' more laxly in Dt 12^{23}, 'The blood *is* the *nephesh*.' This is elucidated in Lv 17^{14}, where we read, 'The *nephesh* of all flesh is its blood, by reason of its *nephesh*' (so Kn., Kal.), *i.e.* we may say that the blood *is* the *nephesh* of the flesh, if we bear in mind that there is a *nephesh* resident in the blood, which is the cause of the vitality of the blood, and therefore also of the flesh. Hence the repellent feature in eating the flesh of animals whose blood had not been shed before death was that, in eating such flesh, from which the *nephesh* had not been allowed to escape, one would eat the *nephesh*, and this is strongly forbidden in the words: 'But flesh with the *nephesh* . . . shall ye not eat' (Gn 9^{4}; cf. Dt 12^{23}).

Human nature was not at first considered as a unity, but attention was directed to the centres of activity, where a mysterious energy was at work; and, long before man used the word *nephesh* as we use the word 'soul,' the several organs were considered separately, as so many independent centres of vitality. The heart, the liver, the kidneys, and the eye were regarded as distinct potencies,[1] endowed with life, not interrelated or unified one with another. The word *nephesh* is not used in the OT of the cause of the vitality resident in each of these organs, but it would be quite analogous to the ideas of other ancient peoples if they did ascribe to each a *nephesh*.

It was a very general belief in old times that a *nephesh* might go out from its abode without causing death for some considerable time. What is to us poetry and metaphor was in the hoary past often accepted as solid fact, as, *e.g.*, when we read of Jacob in Gn 44^{30}, 'His life (*nephesh*) is bound up with the lad's *nephesh*'; and of Jonathan in 1 S 18^{1}, 'his *nephesh* was knit to the *nephesh* of David.' In the statement that the soul of Shechem clave to Dinah (Gn 34^{3}) we have reference to the primitive belief that in love the (or a) *nephesh* leaves the body and enters into union with the soul of its beloved; and a similar belief underlies the phrase which compares peril to 'putting one's soul in one's hand' (Job 13^{14}, Jg 12^{3}, 1 S 19^{5} 28^{21}, Ps 119^{109}).

The consequences of the temporary departure of a soul were believed to be giddiness, mental derangement, sickness, or dotage (Tylor, *PC*^{3} i. 435 f.). There seems to be an allusion to this in the words of Saul in 2 S 1^{9}, if, with Graetz, we may alter the difficult, if not impossible, words כל עוד into בל עוד. Saul has been wounded and is bleeding to death, and his words would then be: 'Giddiness hath taken hold of me, for my *nephesh* is *no longer* in me.' We have a similar underlying belief in the phrase which we use metaphorically: 'I have poured out my soul,' as Hannah said to Eli (1 S 1^{15}); as Job also says: 'My soul is poured out upon me' (30^{16}); and as is said of the righteous servant: 'He poured out his soul unto death' (Is 53^{12}). In the first two cases the result is extreme prostration of mind and body, and in the third case death. It is the voluntary surrender of life.

The blood-soul may be 'smitten' when a wound inflicted causes bloodshed (Gn 37^{21}, Dt 19^{11}); or this *nephesh* may be 'slain' in unintentional homicide (Nu 31^{19} 35^{11}), or in murder (2 S 4^{8}); while in Dt 27^{25} a curse is pronounced on one who should accept a bribe 'to *slay* a *nephesh* of innocent blood.' The Hebrews were forbidden to make 'an incision *to the nephesh*,' *i.e.* to incur the loss of the *nephesh* by the loss of blood (Lv 19^{28}).

(2) *The subjective method.*—It is quite certain that men practised observation long before they practised introspection. When man habituated himself to turn his thoughts within, he became conscious of himself as a unity; the various organs were *his* organs. He was no longer an assemblage of vital organs, as observation led him to suppose; he was a unity, an organism; and the mysterious cause of his internal activities was his *nephesh*, his soul, the cause of his energies and emotions. Thus the *nephesh* in this sense is the seat of appetites, such as hunger (La 1^{11}) and thirst (Is 29^{8}), and also of the outgoings of life in desires, longings, and wishes (1 S 20^{4} 23^{20}, 2 S 3^{21}). It is also the centre of all sensibilities, as disgust (Nu 21^{5}), weariness (Jg 16^{16}), love (Gn 44^{30}), hatred (2 S 5^{8}), anger (2 S 17^{8}), wrath (Jg 18^{25}), and sorrow (Jer 13^{17}); but in all these and similar cases *nephesh* approaches the meaning of our word 'soul' (*q.v.*), and is so rendered.

Most ancient peoples believed that the souls of the departed lingered some days near the corpse; and, while some peoples had no dread of the departing spirit, others, including the Hebrews, had a great terror as to the mischief it might effect; and their boisterous funeral practices were designed to scare the spirit away. We have indications of this belief in the lingering of a soul in the fact that a Nazirite is forbidden during his vow to come near the *nephesh* of a dead man (Nu 6^{6}); a man rendered unclean through a *nephesh* was not allowed to eat the Passover at the statutory time, but might eat it a month later (9^{10}). Indeed, any one, male or female, who was unclean by a *nephesh* must go and remain outside the camp until purified (5^{2}), and a high priest was forbidden at any time to enter a room where the *nephesh* of a dead person was at large (Lv 21^{11}).

Eventually, after or before the funeral, the soul was believed to pass into Sheol, and to be gathered unto its fathers. Hebrew has a distinct word for wraiths or ghosts, *r^{e}phâîm*, but *nephesh* is also used of the soul as a disembodied psychical entity. 'Gather not my *soul* with the wicked,' the Psalmist prays (26^{9}); 'Thou wilt not abandon my *soul* to Sheol,' says another (16^{10}); 'He hath delivered my *soul* from Sheol,' says a third (86^{13}; so Job $33^{18\text{-}28}$, Is 38^{17}). By this time the *nephesh* has become the man's self, his personality.

(3) *The objective-subjective method.*—Man believed himself to be the object of attack or of benign influences from other spirits, or from the one great Spirit, God. When the influence was gentle, he conceived of it as 'breath' (*n^{e}shāmāh*); and when it was violent he spoke of it as a 'wind' (*rūaḥ*), partly, no doubt, because it caused him to pant with excitement. The stronger emotions of man were traced to the *rūaḥ*, or spirit of man, while the gentler emotions and the inspirations from the Divine were due to the action of the Divine *n^{e}shāmāh* or the human *n^{e}shāmāh*. See SPIRIT.

2. Ḥayyîm.—*Ḥayyîm* is a plural form, for which no singular is extant (the root is חיי or חיה, 'to live'). It is an intensive plural, denoting diversity in unity. As the plural form *Elôhîm* seems to express the conception of one God with many manifestations, so *ḥayyîm* expresses life in its many manifestations and modes. G. H. A. Ewald truly says that the word 'life' is 'most expressive and crowded with meaning.'[1] Its various meanings it is now our purpose to deploy.

(1) *Physical life.*—*Ḥayyîm* is used of physical existence (*a*) in relation to time only, representing the continuance of the existence of God or man, in possession of their varied activities; thus we read of 'the days of one's life' (Dt 4^{9}, 1 S 7^{15}), 'the years of one's life' (Gn 23^{1}, Ex 6^{16}), and 'the days of the years of one's life' (Gn 25^{7} 47^{9}); (*b*) in relation to its antithesis, physical death (Jos 2^{13}, Jer 21^{8}, Ps 89^{48}); and (*c*) in relation to the events

[1] H. W. Robinson, *Christian Doctrine of Man*, p. 22.

[1] *OT and NT Theology*, Eng. tr., Edinburgh, 1888, p. 183.

which occur in one's lifetime, or are the outcome of one's energies or activities, as marriage (Lv 18^{18}), deeds of valour (Jg 16^{30}), singing God's praises (Ps 104^{33}), sensuous enjoyments (Ec 3^{12}). 'They were lovely and beautiful in their *lives*' (2 S 1^{23}); 'My soul is weary of my *life*' (Job 10^{1}); 'Preserve my *life* from fear of the enemy' (Ps 64^{1}).

The remarkable thing as to the Hebrew usage of *ḥayyîm* is the clear conviction that 'life' is something more than a continuance of physical existence. There is a clear recognition of the dignity of man—that man was not meant to live the life of an animal or a life of sensuous gratification. Such a life is unworthy of so dignified a creature as man is. As man's sense of dignity developed, the word 'life' became filled with deeper connotation. Roughly speaking, man's view of 'life' passed through the same three stages as we have found in regard to the word *nephesh*: (*a*) man's life consists in what he *has*, 'the abundance of the good things that he possesses'—the objective regard; (*b*) man's life consists in what he *is*, his character—the subjective regard; and (*c*) man's life consists in his relation to God, the influences which come to him from communion with the Divine—the objective-subjective regard. In passing through this development, Israel was subconsciously discussing the problem of the *summum bonum*—What is man's highest good? Wherein does man's true life consist? And his three answers were: (*a*) happiness, (*b*) goodness of character, and (*c*) fellowship with God.

(2) *Joyous life.*—Life, to be worthy of the name, must not be existence merely, but exuberant, joyous life. Life is not the humdrum of physical existence; it is the possession of goods, family, and wealth, which can contribute to man's enjoyment. It is the exhilaration of the red-letter days, when life is sublimely worth living. A life of joy and felicity is alone worthy to be called 'life.' This was always implied in the Oriental salutation: 'Let the king live' (1 K 1^{25}, 2 S 16^{16}). It is associated with largesses of the gold of Sheba (Ps 72^{15}), with riches and honour (Pr 22^{4}), with prosperity and large possessions (Dt 5^{33} [Heb. v.^{30}]). In Ec 9^{9} the Hebrew reads: 'See life with the wife whom thou lovest,' but AV and RV both correctly interpret: 'Live joyfully with the wife'; and, when a man is honoured with an invitation to the court, that is a day of days: 'In the light of the king's countenance is life' (Pr 16^{15}).

(3) *Ethical life.*—True life consists in what a man is and not in what he has. The ideal life is a good life, a life of righteousness. 'In the way of righteousness is life' (Pr 12^{28}); 'Wisdom and discretion are life to the soul' (3^{22}); 'Keep her [wisdom]; for she is thy life' (4^{13}); 'The words of wisdom are life to those that find them' (4^{22}); 'Whoso findeth wisdom findeth life' (8^{35}). There are three things which 'tend to life': righteousness (11^{19}), the labour of the righteous (10^{16}), and the fear of the Lord (19^{23}). In the same pregnant sense of the word 'life' we read of 'the way of life.' 'Torah is light; the reproofs of instruction are the way of life' (6^{23}); 'He that heedeth instruction is in the way of life' (10^{17}). Similarly, the sages speak of a 'fountain of life.' 'The Torah of the wise is a fountain of life' (13^{14}); so is the 'fear of the Lord' (14^{27}) and 'understanding' disciplined by correction (16^{22}). In Lv 18^{5} in the Code of Holiness there is a statement, quoted in Neh 9^{29} and developed at length by Ezk 18^{21}: 'Ye shall keep my statutes, and my judgments: which if a man do, he shall live by them.' The statutes and judgments are considered, not as the rule and guide of life merely, but as providing the pabulum of the moral life. This appears more strikingly in Dt 8^{3}: 'Man doth not live by bread only, but by every word that proceedeth out of the mouth of the Lord doth man live.' Revealed truth is the sustenance of character—of that moral life which is acceptable to God. Similarly, Hezekiah in his Psalm, speaking of the promises of God, says: 'By these things men live, and wholly therein is the life of my spirit' (Is 38^{16}), and in 55^{3} the Lord calls men through His prophet, saying: 'Incline your ear, and come unto me: hear, and your soul shall live.'

(4) *Religious life.*—The passages hitherto considered refer to the moral life nurtured by the instruction of the wise and by obedience to the revealed will of God; but the OT saints rose to a higher conception of life than even this—the life which is nourished by fellowship with God, the life concerning which the Psalmist could say: 'The Lord is the strength of my life' (27^{1}); 'I love thee, O Lord, my strength' (18^{1}); 'The Lord is my strength and my shield' (28^{7}); 'My prayer shall be unto the God of my life' (42^{8}). 'In God's favour is life' (30^{5}); the only life fully worthy of the name is that spent in the consciousness of His favour. Deuteronomy promises repeatedly a long and prosperous life on earth as the token of God's approbation, but the mystics soar above and beyond this present sphere. 'The righteous hath hope in his death,' says one of the sages (Pr 14^{32}). They rejoiced that God was their 'portion' (Ps 119^{57}), 'in the land of the living' (Ps 142^{5}), that God was their 'guest-friend' (Ps 15^{1}), and therefore there is an eternal covenant between Him and them. The high-water mark of a sense of unending frendship with God is found in Ps 73: 'Whom have I in heaven but thee? And there is none upon earth that I desire beside thee'; and from this the inference is drawn: 'I am continually with thee. Thou shalt guide me with thy counsel and afterward receive me to glory' (v.$^{23ff.}$). God's friendship is the only true abiding good. This enables a man to triumph over death. 'Thou wilt show me the path of life: in thy presence is fulness of joy; in thy right hand there are pleasures for evermore' (16^{11}); 'I shall behold thy face in righteousness: I shall be satisfied, when I awake, with thy likeness' (17^{15}).

'In all these Psalms,' says Dillmann,[1] 'there is a full sense of a ζωὴ αἰώνιος already begun in this life, which to their authors gives the assurance that Sheol cannot be the end of such a life, but only blessedness with God. But it is always expressed as a personal conviction, not as a dogma, and we need not wonder that such deep experiences are somewhat rare.'

In conclusion, we turn to the significance of the word 'life' in Ezekiel. The prophet looks forward with great expectancy to the return from exile, but it is under the glamour of vastly improved religious conditions. The Kingdom of God is to be with men. The Lord's servant David shall be the benign prince and ruler ($37^{24f.}$ $34^{23f.}$). Jahweh will take people from among the nations and sprinkle clean water upon them, give them a new heart and put a new spirit within them, and cause them to walk in His statutes and keep His judgments ($36^{24ff.}$). Ezekiel contemplates a new age—a Kingdom of God on earth. But, before that is established, he sees intervening a period of terrible conflict with the powers of evil, in which the wicked who are unfit to form part of the new Kingdom shall perish. Those who do wickedly shall not live, they shall surely die (18^{10-13}). Those who 'do that which is lawful and right,' being endowed with the new heart and the new spirit, 'shall surely live' (18^{5-9}). The Kingdom of God with its great moral and religious privileges is ever before the prophet's thoughts. To 'live' is to pass safely through the impending conflict with evil

[1] *AT Theologie*, p. 400.

and to enter on the new Kingdom, in which God's presence will be much more real and evident (48[35]); to 'die' is to perish in the crisis and to be excluded from the Kingdom.

LITERATURE.—H. Wheeler Robinson, *The Christian Doctrine of Man*, Edinburgh, 1911, ch. i., *Religious Ideas of the OT*, London, 1913, ch. iv.; E. B. Tylor, *PC*[3], do., 1891, chs. xi.–xvii.; T. K. Cheyne, *Origin and Religious Contents of the Psalter*, London, 1891, lect. viii.; R. H. Charles, *Eschatology*[2], do., 1913, ch. i. f.; S. D. F. Salmond, *Christian Doctrine of Immortality*[4], Edinburgh, 1901, ch. ii.; the works on *Old Testament Theology* by H. Schultz (Eng. tr., Edinburgh, 1892), R. Smend (Freiburg, 1899), H. Stade (Tübingen, 1905), C. F. A. Dillmann (Leipzig, 1895); artt. BLOOD, BREATH, DEATH AND DISPOSAL OF THE DEAD (Jewish); *HDB*, art. 'Life and Death,' sect. on 'OT Teaching.'

J. T. MARSHALL.

LIFE AND DEATH (Indian).—The earliest Aryans to enter India worshipped a vast number of petty spirits, but they learned, rather later, to revere a number of the greater phenomena of nature, and also laid much stress on the worship of their ancestors. This ritual formed the foundation on which all the institutions of the Aryan family were built,[1] though it may well be that the religious belief had its own ultimate origin in the natural organization of the family. At all events, the belief in the power of ancestors profoundly modified that organization. The father was the family priest, and controlled the worship of the ancestors of the family in all details. Centuries after their entry into India, when the Aryans were engaged in the imperial work of bringing all the peoples of N. India under their political and intellectual domination, the great doctrine of *karma* and re-birth took shape. With Farquhar[2] we may conjecture that

'among the many animistic tribes the invaders met on the broad plains of the North, there must have been some who held the common primitive belief that the souls of men may become incarnate in animals. There were probably totemistic clans who believed that at death a man became, like his totem, a tiger, an ox, a frog, or a snake.'

Whether the transmigration idea came from this source or not it is impossible to say, and, indeed, it is more probable that it was at first a deduction from the physical resemblances which were observed among kindred.

'But, even if the idea that human souls might undergo animal births came from the aborigines, that is but one element in the complex doctrine. That which gave the belief its power over the intellect, and also its value for the moral life, was the connexion of this fairy-tale idea with the powerful ethical conception of retribution; and we may be certain that that was the work of the Aryan mind.'[3]

The doctrine first appears in the earliest Upaniṣads. Thus, while transmigration has been believed in many lands, the Hindu doctrine of *karma* (*q.v.*) is, as far as we can yet say, unique.[4]

Inextricably, though by no means consistently, intertwined with this moral theory of retribution is the more primitive and far more wide-spread belief that souls are something almost material, although they may not be always palpable or tangible.

1. Vedas and Brāhmaṇas.—In the Rigveda the conceptions of death are not entirely consistent, but the principal belief relating to the *aja bhāga*, or 'unborn part,' was as follows. When the remains of the deceased had been placed on the funeral pile and the process of cremation had begun, Agni, the god of fire, was prayed not to scorch or consume the departed, not to tear asunder his skin or limbs, but, after the flames had done their work, to convey to the fathers or ancestors the mortal who had been presented to him as an offering. His eye was bidden to go to the sun,[5] his breath to the wind, and so on. As for his unborn part, Agni was supplicated to kindle it with his heat and flame, and, assuming his most auspicious form, to convey it to the world of the righteous.[1] Before this unborn part can complete its course from earth to the third heaven, however, it has to traverse a vast gulf of darkness. Leaving behind on earth all that is evil and imperfect, and proceeding by the paths which the fathers trod,[2] the spirit, invested with a lustre like that of the gods, soars to the realms of eternal light in a car or on wings, on the undecaying pinions wherewith Agni slays the Rakṣasas, wafted upwards by the Maruts, recovers then its ancient body in a complete and glorified form, meets with the ancestors who are living in festivity with Yama, obtains from him, when recognized as one of his own, a delectable abode, and enters upon a more perfect life.

In the Vedic era death was held 'to be the going-forth from the living of his breath, or of the thinking part, the mind, which was held to reside in the heart. . . . Heaven, a happy hereafter, was all that was looked forward to by these Vedic Aryans. Throughout the hymns there is no weariness of life, no pessimism.'[3]

From death there is no awakening; the shade, the breath, soul, or spirit has gone forth and returns not.

'In the "*Taittirīya Brāhmana*" the souls of the deceased are said to dwell in the heavens above as stars, and again in the stars are "the lights of those righteous men who go to the celestial world." In the "*Śatapatha Brāhmana*" death is the sun whose rays attach to mortals their life breath, yet, as the "*Katha Upanishad*" declares: "No mortal lives by the breath that goes up and the breath that goes down. We live by another in whom these two repose." There was something which went out of man in sleep and death; something underlying the Ego, the I, the vital breath, more subtle than life. In the "*Rig Veda*," the sun, though it holds the life breath of mortals, is something more. It is the Self, or the Ātman, of all that moves and moves not, of all that fills the heavens and the earth. So of man there is also the Ātman, "the Self, smaller than small, greater than great, hidden in the heart of that creature." A man who is free from desires and free from grief sees the majesty of the Self by the grace of the Creator. It is this Ātman, or Self, more abstract in its conception than soul, Psyche, or "anima," that becomes also the Universal Self, the Self of the World, "bhūmivāh ātman," of which the "Veda" speaks: "When that which had no bones bore him who has bones, when that which was formless took shape and form." The Indian sage . . . had first to sweep away all that which had been produced, even the gods themselves, and to his gaze there remained but the neuter essence, Brahman, from which all things issued forth, and into which all things resolve themselves. There remained also the Self, the Soul, the Ātman of man. There was but one step further to be reached by the Indian mind, and that was taken when all duality vanished, and the Brahman became the Great Self, the "Paramātman," the Universal Self, into which was merged the Ātman, or Self, of man.'[4]

In other words, the Hindu conception of the soul approached that of the modern monists (see, further, art. ĀTMAN).

2. Upaniṣads.—In the pre-Buddhistic Upaniṣads the soul is supposed to exist inside each human body and to be the one sufficient explanation of life and motion. In the living body it dwells ordinarily in a cavity in the heart, and is of the size of a grain of rice or barley. In later speculation it grows to the size of a thumb and is, therefore, called 'the dwarf.' In shape it is like a man. Beliefs varied as to its appearance and as to its composition. One passage says that it consists of consciousness, mind, breath; eye and ears; earth, water, fire, and ether; heat and no heat; desire and no desire; anger and no anger; law and no law—in a word, of all things.[5] Thus the soul was conceived as material, although it also possessed selected mental qualities. It could quit the body in dream sleep, and certain diseases were supposed

[1] J. N. Farquhar, *Crown of Hinduism*, London, 1913, p. 66; cf. *ERE* ii. 28 f.

[2] *Op. cit.* p. 135. [3] *Ib.*

[4] Cf. A. B. Keith's paper on 'Pythagoras and Transmigration,' in *JRAS*, 1909, p. 569.

[5] In Rigveda, x. lviii. 8, the souls of the departed are said to go to the sun and to Uṣas, the dawn.

[1] Rigveda, x. xvi. 1–5. [2] *Ib.* x. xiv. 7.

[3] R. W. Frazer, *Literary History of India*, London, 1898, pp. 36, 38.

[4] Frazer, *op. cit.* p. 105 f.

[5] *Bṛhadāraṇyaka Upan.*, IV. iv. 5; see also III. vii. 14–22. Speculation in the Upaniṣad times was very free and it veered round even to the denial of the soul as a substance (R. G. Bhandarkar, *Vaiṣṇavism, Śaivism and Minor Religious Systems*, Strassburg, 1913, p. 2). Buddhism also practically denied the existence of the human soul as a substance, as Bhandarkar points out (p. 2). But in the end it taught a very different doctrine (see below).

to be due to its having escaped from the body, so that charms had to be employed to bring it back. In some passages the soul is supposed to have existed before birth in some other body, and opinions varied as to how it got into its first body. We also find a curious speculation, with three variants,[1] on the transfer of the soul by generation, through the seed. One of these is the theory that certain human souls, on going to the moon, become the food of the gods as a consequence of their good deeds. When the efficacy of those deeds is exhausted, they pass from the gods to the ether, from the ether into the air, from that into the rain, thence on to the earth, and from it into plants which become food to males, whence they pass into females. At an ordinary man's death the top part of the heart is lighted up, and the soul, guided by that light, departs from the heart into the eye, and through it into some other body, exalted or not according to deeds done in the body which it is leaving. The soul of the man whose cravings have ceased goes to Brahman. The Upaniṣads are almost unanimous that the soul will not obtain release from re-birth either by sacrifice or by penance.

'It must be by a sort of theosophic or animistic insight, by the perception, the absolute knowledge and certainty, that one's own soul is identical with the Great Soul, the only permanent reality, the ultimate basis and cause of all phenomena.'[2]

In the *Kauṣītaki Brāhmaṇa Upan.* the belief in transmigration is combined with a notion that souls go first to the moon. All who depart from this world go to the moon. In the bright fortnight it is gladdened by their spirits, but in the dark one it sends them forth into new births. It is the door of heaven. Him who rejects it it sends on beyond, but whoso rejects it not, him it rains down upon this world; and here he is born as a worm, a grasshopper, fish, bird, lion, boar, serpent, tiger, or a man or some other creature, according to his deeds or his knowledge.[3]

3. Jainism.—The philosophy of Jainism, probably the oldest living Indian creed, defines the universe as not created and not controlled by any individual god. As substance it is without beginning and without end, but it is not homogeneous, since it consists of substance (*dravya*), which is either *jīva*, 'alive,' or *ajīva*, which may be translated 'inorganic.' There are five kinds of substance not alive, viz. matter, space, the two ethers, and (figuratively) time; but living beings are compounded of two kinds of substance, viz. soul and body, and the Jain belief is that nearly everything, even plants, particles of earth, fire, and wind, is possessed of life. In other words, the Jain philosophy is pure animism. *Jīva* is sometimes translated 'living being' and sometimes 'soul,' yet it is not one individual universal world-soul, but a mass of mutually exclusive, individual souls, and every soul having attained its highest state (*mokṣa*) is styled *paramātman*, or 'great soul,' a term only very roughly translatable by the word 'god.' Jainism thus fails to draw any definable distinction between 'life' and the soul. *Dravya* may be defined from several points of view. From the standpoint of its own unchanging nature it is that which ever exists. For example, the soul now embodied as a cat may in its next life be incarnated as a dog, man, insect, or what not, yet remain, in spite of all these changes, the same individual soul all the time; and thus, while the body is merely a vast multitude of cells which come and go, the soul is a homogeneous substance whose qualities (*guṇa*) do not come and go, and which is always itself, never becoming or merging into another, though in their modifications (*paryāya*) the *guṇas* are ceaselessly changing. The soul in its pure state is invisible, but, when compounded in a subtle way with visible, tangible matter, it is rendered visible, and men, angels, etc., are examples of it in this impure state. We do not, however, know when these conceptions were formed by Jainism, and we cannot say that Jain philosophy evolved them unaided. They were apparently borrowed from the common stock of ideas current in India and were modified by the Jains in their own way. The earliest Indo-Aryan conception of life as a series of re-births was far more primitive, and was developed not on metaphysical lines but for ethical purposes.

4. Buddhism.—Buddhism, as an organized creed, has disappeared from India, but the ideas which it adopted or promulgated are still living and form one of the sources from which the Indian beliefs as to the origin of life are drawn. For instance, the Buddhist teaching that all life is due to a common source appears to find expression in the legend that with Buddha himself was born his horse, as well as his wife, his companions, and even the Mahābodhi tree and the four treasure-vases. These are the seven that were born simultaneously, but to make up seven one must count the four vases as one. Another legend declares that with the Bodhisattva were born 500 Śākya princes, 500 maidens, 500 servants, 500 horses, 500 elephants, and as many treasures came to light.[1] A very similar conception has survived in modern India.

Thus in the legend of Gūga, his mother is destined never to bear a son, but Bhagwān rubs some of the dirt out of his head and gives it to her. She divides it among a Brāhman woman, another of the lowest caste, a gray mare, and herself; and all four females, hitherto barren, become fruitful. In another cult-legend a Brāhman gives a Rāja three grains of rice, and each of his three queens swallows one and bears a son. A stock incident in folk-tales is the gift by a *faqīr* of a barleycorn to a barren widow whereby she conceives. For the Buddhist doctrines see art. DEATH AND DISPOSAL OF THE DEAD (Buddhist).

5. Mediæval.—Three or four centuries before the Christian era a religion with Vāsudeva as its central figure and a school of his followers known as Bhāgavata was founded in India. According to the *Mahābhārata*, the sun is the gate, and after entrance those who are free from sin, all their material impurities being burnt, remain as atoms in him (it); then, released from him, they enter the Aniruddha (self-consciousness) form and, becoming mind, they enter the Pradyumna (mind) form. Leaving this, they enter that of Saṁkarṣaṇa, *i.e.* the form of the individual soul (*jīva*), and afterwards, freed from the three *guṇas*, they enter the Supreme Soul, who is everywhere and who is Vāsudeva, 'he who covers the whole world and is the resting-place (*adhivāsa*) of all beings.' Vāsudeva next became identified with Kṛṣṇa and Viṣṇu, and finally with Nārāyaṇa; and the Bhakti system or Ekāntika Dharma (monotheism) was attached to the Vaiṣṇava creeds. Its earliest exposition in the *Bhāgavad-Gīta* teaches that they who know the incarnations and the deeds of Bhagavat are released from the body and not born again. The discipline prescribed, however, for the attainment of the Brahmā condition is religious, not merely moral, and this differentiates the Bhakti doctrine from that of the *Kaṭha* and *Bṛhadāraṇyaka Upaniṣads.* Mention is made of two paths, and those who die while the sun is in his northern course (Uttarāyana) go to Brahmā, while those who die while he is in his southern course go to the orb of the moon, from which the soul returns. Again, the whole

[1] T. W. Rhys Davids, *Buddhist India*, London, 1903, p. 254.
[2] *Ib.* p. 255.
[3] T. W. Rhys Davids, *Lectures on the Origin and Growth of Religion as illustrated by some Points in the History of Buddhism*, London, 1891, p. 81; cf. Appendix VII. for parallel beliefs on souls going to the moon.

[1] J. P. Vogel, 'A Græco-Buddhist Sculpture in the Lahore Museum,' in *Journal of the Punjab Historical Society*, i. [1902] 135.

creation (Saṁsāra) is compared to a *pipal*-tree, which is to be cut by the weapon of indifference or detachment. When a soul departs from a body it takes away the *indriyas* (senses), of which *manas* (mind) is the sixth, and brings them in when it assumes another body. The soul itself is a part of Bhagavat and is eternal. By becoming *soma* (hemp) Bhagavat raises all herbs. By becoming fire he aids digestion. There are two souls in the world, one changeable, the other not, and besides these there is another, the highest or Paramātman, who, as the unchangeable lord, supports all three worlds after entering into them. Hence it appears that it is the animal soul that goes out of the body along with the six senses and enters new ones in that condition.

6. Modern Aryan.—The multiplicity and, it must be confessed, inconsistencies of the older doctrines current in India regarding life and death are reflected in the countless beliefs now existing, but through all the bewildering variations which prevail a few dominant conceptions can generally be traced, and a remote and savage tribe will be found professing a creed which is based on the fundamentals of orthodox Hinduism. Even the regular terminology will reappear in forms more or less mutilated. So numerous are these beliefs that only a few of them can be given.

The basic idea of life in all India is that it is indestructible. This leads to a readiness to take life which to the European appears callous and brutal indifference to it. Thus in 1841 S. C. Macpherson was deputed to Ganjām in Madras to suppress female infanticide and human sacrifices among the Khonds, a tribe which believed that souls return to human form in the same family, but that they do not do so if the naming ceremony on the 7th day after birth has not been performed. As the Khonds ardently desire sons, they saw in this belief a perfect justification for female infanticide as a means of reducing the number of female souls to be re-born in the family.[1] A very similar belief prevails in the Panjāb, where a girl child is or was killed with rites and an incantation bidding her 'send a brother instead.' Exchange is not murder.

How far this and similar beliefs account for the reluctance to cremate young children does not appear. But the souls of those dying after infancy or childhood are very widely believed to pass into another world, at least for a term. Thus in the Panjāb the Kanets of the Kulū valley sometimes after a cremation make a small foot-bridge over running water in the neighbourhood to help the passing of the soul of the deceased.[2] Yet the same people practise a form of divination, which is very widely spread, to ascertain, immediately after death, what animal the soul will enter or has entered.

This belief is perfectly consistent with a belief in metempsychosis and yet compatible with the worship or propitiation of the dead, who may be benevolent or the reverse. Among the kindly dead may be numbered the spirits of ancestors, of pure ones (*siddhs*), and saints, of dutiful widows who have committed *satī*, and so on. But the propitiation of the malevolent dead is much more necessary, and therefore prevalent. For example, in the Kumaon division of the United Provinces the lowest class, the Ḍoms, and even the lower classes of Brāhmans, the Khas Brāhmans and Rajputs—in fact, the bulk of the population—believe in the powers of the malevolent or vindictive dead. Thus, if a man has two wives and drives one to suicide, any disease afflicting the other wife's children is

[1] E. A. Gait, *Census Rep. India*, 1913, p. 216.

[2] H. A. Rose, *Glossary of Punjab Tribes and Castes*, Lahore, 1911, ii. 463.

ascribed to her ghost, which must be propitiated, and gradually comes to be treated as a god. If a man is killed in a quarrel, every misfortune befalling his slayer or his children is ascribed to the ghost.

'There is reason to believe that the emotion caused by the dread of the effects of *karma* is much stronger in the hills than in the plains. In particular dying in debt is dreaded as the debtor will, it is believed, be re-born as the ox or pony of his creditor. If a man's son die it is believed that he was his father's creditor in a former life, and the debt being now extinguished there is no necessity of his further life.' The latter belief is said to provide a great consolation, since the death of an ordinary son is a much more serious matter.

The certainty of the operation of *karma* is not without considerable effect on practical morality.[1] It is automatic, so that specific condemnation by Parmeśwar (God) of any sin is hardly required. Similarly, the idea of forgiveness is absolutely wanting; evil done may be outweighed by meritorious deeds only so far as to ensure a better existence in the future, but it is not effaced, and must be atoned for. As to the objection raised to the theory of transmigration—that it does not follow from it that the soul remembers previous existences—such a consciousness is recognized in the case of great ascetics; and even a person born in a degraded position knows that the reason for this is his wrong-doing in a previous existence. The nature of the next incarnation can also be divined, when a man has died, by placing ashes from a potter's kiln in a shallow vessel and smoothing them. Next morning they will be found marked with human foot-prints, claws, wavy lines, and so on, according as the soul is to be re-born as a man, a bird, a tree, etc. To ensure that they shall be married to each other in a future existence, a man and his wife bathe together in the Ganges with their clothes tied together. The important difference in the teachings of theoretical Hinduism and popular religion in regard to heaven and hell is that the former declares that there are transitory stages of existence in the chain of transmigration, while in the latter there is generally an idea that the soul, when sufficiently purified, goes to dwell for ever in heaven, which is regarded as a place where the soul will enjoy material comforts. In popular Hinduism there is no idea of absorption in the deity or of recurring cycles of existence and non-existence.[2]

The conception of life as something impalpable, yet apparently material and certainly transferable, is extremely common in India, and may, indeed, be described as the most popular. Thus a woman who has lost a child will bathe above its grave, pouring water over herself through a sieve, in order to ensure a fresh conception. For the same reason very young children are sometimes buried under the threshold, so that the life may come back again. This idea leads to the popular belief that life may be stolen, and so on the night of the Dīvāli, or feast of lamps, male children are occasionally stolen and killed so that a barren woman may bathe over the body and conceive a son of her own.[3] As in other ritual murders, it is desirable to kill the child with as much pain as possible. And during the *śrāddhas*, the ancestral fortnight when the sun is in Virgo (Kanyā), occurs the Kanāgatān *laṛan*, or 'fighting in Kanyāgat,' also termed *sāñjhi pāwan* ('sharing with others'), in which women of good Hindu caste, even Khatrīs and Brāhmans, of the Central Panjāb, take part. On the first day of the *śrāddhas*, the goddess Lakṣmī's image in the house or lane is painted with cow-dung, and the women belonging to it go out early in the day to a bathing-place, reviling on the way

[1] *Census Rep. United Provinces*, 1901, i. 77.

[2] *Ib.* p. 76.

[3] No one would think a female soul worth stealing, although a girl's soul is expected to return in a boy.

women who are known to have sons. This leads to tussles in which garments are often rent to pieces, but men must not interfere. The belief is that by cursing the sons of others the female attracts the male souls to herself through the intervention of the goddess, whose image is worshipped daily and thrown into the river at the end of the fortnight which is held sacred to the spouse of Śiva the destroyer as well as to the dead. Married women are also cursed to become widows, in order to prolong one's own wedlock. On the *Amāwas* day regular fights take place between large gangs of women on their way to the river, and the affair is treated as a festival.

LITERATURE.—This has been given in the footnotes.

H. A. ROSE.

LIFE AND DEATH (Iranian).—With their marked tendency towards optimism, the Iranians loved life (*anghu, gaya, jyātu, jīti, uštāna*) and abhorred death (*mahrka, mereθyu*); the one is the creation of Ahura Mazda, the other of Angra Mainyu (*Ys.* xxx. 4), who have been at variance since 'the beginning of life' (*Ys.* xlv. 2). Not only was life first created by Ahura Mazda (*Ys.* xliii. 5, xlvi. 6, xlviii. 6), and not only did he give life to the body (*Ys.* xxxi. 11), so that Zarathushtra asks him how the 'first [*i.e.* the earthly] life' is to be (*Ys.* xxviii. 11; cf. xxxiii. 1), but he is 'the lord of the deeds of life' (*Ys.* xxxi. 8), and from him come the joys of life (*Ys.* xxxiii. 10; cf. xxxiv. 14). The Amesha Spentas (*q.v.*) give aid to the life of man (*Ys.* xxx. 7), so that Zarathushtra fittingly presents the 'life of his own body' as a 'holy offering' (*rātā*) to Ahura Mazda and Asha (*Ys.* xxxiii. 14). On the other hand, the demon Wrath (Aēshma) injures the life of man, and the wicked and unbelievers mar it (*Ys.* xxx. 6, xxxii. 9, 11).

Life in this world is not all; indeed, though Zoroastrianism teaches that all good things are to be enjoyed in full measure, life here below is but a preparation for the richer life beyond. For this reason Zarathushtra asks from Vohu Manah and Asha the 'words of life' (*uxδā anghēuš*), while the 'right ways of weal' (*erezūš savanghō paθō*) are to be learned from the religious teacher in the present life (*Ys.* xliv. 8, xliii. 3).

If life on earth is the 'first life,' the 'second life' is in heaven, and that life the *dregvant* (the 'man of the Lie,' 'the perpetual term for those who take the devil's side in human life' [J. H. Moulton, *Early Zoroastrianism*, London, 1913, pp. 146, 131]) seeks to destroy (*Ys.* xlv. 1, xlvi. 11, liii. 6). Heaven is the place of 'long life' (*Ys.* xliii. 2, 13). Most significant of all is the presence, among the Amesha Spentas, of the godling Immortality, Ameretāt (*Ys.* xliv. 17, xlv. 5, 10, xlvii. 1, li. 7), for in heaven life is to be for eternity (*Ys.* xlv. 7).

When we turn to the Younger Avesta, we find the outlook upon life unchanged. Long life in this world is a blessing and an object of prayer (*Ys.* lxviii. 11; *Āfrīnakān*, i. 18), while both Ahura Mazda and the Gāthās are honoured with life and body (*Ys.* v. 3, lv. 1; cf. lviii. 3). Life is twofold: 'this' or 'the corporeal' (lit. 'osseous') and 'the spiritual' (*ahmāicā ahuyē manahyāicā*, *Ys.* xl. 2, xli. 6; *uvaēibya . . . ahubya . . . aheca anghēuš yō astvatō yasca asti manahyō*, *Ys.* lvii. 25), so that prayer is made to Ahura Mazda to be 'life and corporeality for both lives' (*gayascā astentāoscā . . . ubōyō anghvō*, *Ys.* xli. 3). The 'best life' (*vahišta ahu*, *Ys.* ix. 19, and often) is actually a synonym for 'heaven,' as the 'worst life' (*acišta ahu*, e.g. *Vend.* iii. 35) is for 'hell,' and this concept still survives in the ordinary Persian term for 'heaven,' *bihišt*. The 'best of the best life' is the 'righteousness of Asha' (*Vend.* xviii. 6); and in the time of the final Saoshyant, Astvaṭ-ereta, men will live for ever, for there shall be no more death (*Yt.* xix. 89), even as was the case in the happy days of Yima's reign (*Ys.* ix. 5; *Yt.* xix. 33; *Vend.* ii. 5).

In the Gāthās death is seldom mentioned. The whole stress of Zarathushtra is on life, to be devoted to overcoming the powers of evil and gaining the eternal joys of heaven. Even the wicked do not die; they are damned to the everlasting torments of hell (*Ys.* xlv. 7, xlvi. 11). In the Younger Avesta, on the contrary, death is an important feature. We need not detail the corruption wrought by the 'corpse demon' (Nasu; cf. Gr. νέκυς, 'corpse'), which forms the main theme of *Vend.* v.–xii. (see also art. DEATH AND DISPOSAL OF THE DEAD [Parsi]), and we need only mention that a standing epithet of Haoma (*q.v.*) is *dūraoša* ('from whom destruction [especially death] remains afar,' *Ys.* ix. 2, 19, x. 21, xi. 3, 10, xxxii. 14 [on the latter passage see Moulton, 71 f., 358]). Death is one of the worst of evils (*Yt.* iii. 7–12; cf. ix. 10), and the first to stay it was Thrita (*Vend.* xx. 2), while it is the Druj (the Lie, the negation of the truth of Ahura Mazda [?]) who destroys life (*Ys.* lvii. 15), 'life' here probably being meant in the eschatological sense. As we have seen, in the blessed future there will be no death, but in this present world only the wicked forget death; the man of piety prepares for it (*Aogemadaēcā*, 32 ff.), for it is inevitable (*ib.* 53 ff.).

According to the Pahlavi *Dīnā-ī Maīnōg-ī Xraṭ* (viii. 20), which is not strictly orthodox, being markedly fatalistic in tone (cf. art. FATE [Iranian]), the seven planets 'pervert every creature and creation, and deliver them up to death and every evil.' According to the *Bundahišn* (i. 7; cf. xxx. 20 ff.), the creatures of Ahriman will perish at the Last Day, when the heavens and the earth shall be created anew and when the creation of Ahura Mazda shall reign supreme, after wicked men shall have been purified by the flood of molten metal which at that time will cover the world.

Of mythological concepts of life and death there is scant trace in Zoroastrianism, the sole allusion, evidently borrowed from a Semitic source, being to the tree Gōkarṭ (the Gaokerena of *Yt.* i. 30, *Vend.* xx. 4, etc.), or white Hōm, which is 'the counteractor of decrepitude, the reviver of the dead, and the immortalizer of the living' (*Selections of Zāṭ-Sparam*, viii. 5), and from which, at the ἀποκατάστασις, is obtained one of the components of the food which will give undying life to all (*Bundahišn*, xxx. 25; cf. ix. 6, xviii. 1, and see F. Windischmann, *Zor. Studien*, Berlin, 1863, pp. 169, 253; F. Spiegel, *Erân. Alterthumskunde*, Leipzig, 1871–78, i. 464 ff.).

LITERATURE.—The principal references are given by C. Bartholomae, *Altiran. Wörterbuch*, Strassburg, 1904, *s.vv.* 'Anghav-, 'Gaya-,' 'Jītay-,' 'Jyātav-,' 'Uštana-,' 'Mahrka-, 'Mereθyav-,' 'Pourumahrka-,' etc. No special study of the subject has yet been written.

LOUIS H. GRAY.

LIFE AND DEATH (Japanese).—As might be expected, the early Japanese conceived of life and death as being entirely dependent on breathing. The word for 'to live,' *iku*, is associated with *iki*, 'breath'; and *i-no-chi*, the expression for life and vitality, is believed to mean *iki-no-uchi*, 'during breathing,' or *iki-no-michi*, 'the way of respiration.' Similarly, the word for 'to die,' *shinu*, seems to mean *shi-inu*, 'the wind goes' (a derivation of the word from *sugi-inu*, 'to pass away,' is disputable). These very ancient words are still in common use, though the people think little of their etymology.

The mythology opens with the primal power of production. Three deities are said to have sprung out of the primeval chaos. One of these is the Eternal-Ruling (Ame-no-minaka-nushi), and the other two are the High-Producing (Taka-mimusubi) and the Divine- (or Mysterious-) Producing (Kami-mimusubi). The last two are identified with the Divinity-Male (Kami-ro-gi) and the Divinity-Female (Kami-ro-mi), the terminations *gi* and *mi* representing 'male' and 'female' respectively. It has not unreasonably been suspected that this triad may have been borrowed from the Chinese ideas of the primal entity and the two principles, positive and negative, flowing out of it; but the Divinity-Male and the Divinity-Female are constantly invoked in the ritual or prayers, some of which are of remote origin. It is undeniable that in the pristine faith of the Japanese the generative powers played a great part, but these divinities themselves were thought to have been generated spontaneously, and the first pair are followed by a series of similar deities. They were all generated independently from one another and in turn disappeared or hid themselves.

The last of these pairs are the Male-Who-Invites (Izana-gi) and the Female-Who-Invites (Izana-mi), who are doubtless counterparts of the first pair. They were united in marriage, by order of the celestial deities, and brought forth the islands which make up the Japanese archipelago, and nearly all sorts of elements and objects (see, further, art. COSMOGONY AND COSMOLOGY [Japanese]). The stories of these births show that many objects of nature were believed to be animated, as was, in fact, whatever manifested any power, good or evil, on men. The female deity becomes ill from bearing fire as a child and consequently dies. This death, however, is not to be taken as a natural death in our modern sense of the word. After her death the goddess is found in Yomotsu-kuni, *i.e.* 'the dark country,' which is thought to be in a subterranean region. The male deity visits her there and, against her will, looks on her body by torchlight. Enraged at his importunity, she, accompanied by her attendants of the darkness, pursues him, in order to catch him and to make him a member of the realm where death and darkness rule. Their dialogue on the boundary of the world and the dark region tells of the life and death of human beings. The female deity, now the genius of death, threatens the male that she will take the lives of one thousand men every day, while he expresses his counter-determination that he will give birth to one thousand and five hundred men a day. Thus we see how the pair of generative powers were divided and metamorphosed into the powers of life and death. A similar antithesis is attributed to the Heaven-Shining (Ama-terasu), the goddess of light and culture, and the Swift-Impetuous (Susa-no-wo), the god of darkness and outrage. These two are said to have been born of the Male-Who-Invites, either alone or in union with his consort. These divisions, however, are not thoroughgoing. Usually, in popular belief, life is ascribed to the power of the Producing deity or deities, and death to the power of evil spirits, who are indefinite in their personalities.

The stories told of the deities, of their generation and death, and of life and death in general, show neither definite sequence nor unity of conception. They are coloured by ethnological incidents, and are also possibly mingled with foreign elements. Still it is certain that the pristine beliefs contained the ideas of spontaneous generation and generative reproduction, on the one side, and the belief in unnatural death, caused by evil forces, on the other. This idea of death as the violent cessation of life survived the belief in spontaneous generation, and still remains in the observances of purity, which are intended as a means of avoiding the contagion of pollution or to prevent evil influences of all kinds.

Life is coeval with breathing, but vitality endures longer and acts beyond bodily limitations. Soul, the source of vitality, is considered to be a thing precious and mysterious like a jewel or ball. It is called *tama* or *tama-shii*, 'subtle aerial ball.' But it is not always a unity or a homogeneous whole, for double manifestations of it, or double entities, are spoken of. They are either *nigi-tama* and *ara-tama* or *saki-mitama* and *kushi-mitama*. The *nigi*, 'mild,' 'quiet,' 'refined,' is contrasted with the *ara*, which is 'wild,' 'raging,' 'raw.' Similarly, *saki* means 'happy,' 'flourishing,' while *kushi* means 'wonderful,' 'hidden,' or 'hideous.' The latter set is believed to be the two aspects of the *ara-tama*, the active side of the soul, but in fact the relation between these two sets is not clearly defined. The existence of these double souls in every man is also obscure. We know only that in some cases one of them appears, even to the astonishment of the possessor. Whether or not the double souls were borrowed from the Chinese conception of souls, aerial and terrestrial, or of the two principles, positive and negative, is uncertain.

The soul is sometimes personified as, *e.g.*, Uga-no-mitama, the spirit of vegetable production, or as Iki-kuni-dama, the living-land-soul. In post-Buddhistic ages the souls of trees, rocks, springs, etc. are more in vogue. They appear in human form, but they are distinguished from human souls, being specially named the *sei*, or 'essence.' The double souls were almost forgotten, having been overshadowed by Buddhistic ideas, and they were revived by the Shintoists of the 18th cent., but with little influence upon popular belief. Buddhism teaches that there is only one soul to one living being.

As to future conditions, there is a kind of heavenly world, Takama-no-hara ('Plain of High Heaven'), where celestial deities reign. Yomotsu-kuni, mentioned above, is the opposite pole. Besides these, there are two worlds beyond this, Hi-no-waka-miya ('Solar Young Palace') and Toko-yo ('Eternal World'). The former is mentioned only as the abode of the Male-Who-Invites, and it is sometimes explained as meaning the shrine marking the place of burial. The latter meant any place beyond the sea. Moreover, we are not told whether a deity, when he hides himself, or a human being, when he dies, is destined to be born in one of these worlds beyond. Nothing definite or detailed is told of these conditions. A definite systematization of the eschatology, after the models of Buddhist ideas, was made only by the later Shintoists.

The Japanese remained in rather primitive conditions as to the conceptions of life and death, until Buddhism introduced an elaborate system of ideas in the 6th cent. A.D. Contact with the civilization of the Asiatic continent and the importation of Confucianism with its writings may have influenced Japanese ideas in some respects, as pointed out above. But these influences did not materially change the ideas, because Confucianism was not particular in such matters. On the other hand, the Buddhist influence upon the people of the East consisted chiefly in its elaborate eschatological doctrines. It taught the composite nature of human life, made up of the five components (*skandha*), in order to convince the people of its impermanency. Life, thus made up, is only a knot in a long chain of causation, of deeds and their fruits (*karma*), which stretches out endlessly before and behind. Along this chain our souls have passed through all possible forms of existence, and will continue to transmigrate further on. There are five or six courses (*gati*) of transmigration, ranging from the highest heaven of pleasurable life to the nethermost inferno; and these are again classified according to the three conditions of existence (*bhava*), which are subdivided into twenty-five. Beyond these courses and conditions there are the lands of eternal bliss, prepared by various Buddhas to receive believers. Every one may be born in one of these, according to his faith and merit. The Tuṣitā heaven of Maitreya and the Sukhāvatī of Amitābha were the most popular Buddha-lands (*kṣetra*) in the Buddhism brought to the East. There the soul, no longer subject to causation and transmigration, will enjoy full communion with the saints, and may come back to the earthly worlds in order to save relatives and friends. We can imagine how wonderful and attractive these teachings must have appeared to the people, simple and credulous as they were. Thus, an inscription dated A.D. 622 expresses a belief in *karma* and a devout wish to be taken to the Land of Purity by the grace of Buddha. It is questionable how much impression these ideas left upon the mind of the people at large a hundred years after their introduction; but the change and widening of thought are undeniable.

Steadily progressive Buddhist influence, first among the higher classes and then among the lower, gradually suppressed the old national ideas as well as the Confucianist conceptions of life and death. The romances, stories, and lyrical poems of the 10th cent. and later abound in ideas of *karma*, transmigration, and birth in Buddha-lands. Those ideas and beliefs became and remain to-day the most important factors of popular beliefs, in spite of hostile endeavours made by the Confucianists to depose them, ever since the 17th century. They can be detected in many songs sung by street musicians, and the words alluding to them are used in daily affairs, consciously or unconsciously.

Nevertheless, the native ideas have never died out, but have remained rather as a kind of matrix into which the adopted conceptions have been laid. The national beliefs, so to speak, look upon the sun as the source of all vitality. But here the sun is not exactly the goddess of light (Ama-terasu) of the mythology. It is sexless and without any other attributes than that of the life-giver. It is invoked as the Great Divinity (Oho-mi-kami) or the August Heavenly Way (O-tentō-sama), and is worshipped every morning by some, or on New Year's morning and at sunset on the equinoxes by the majority. They breathe deep breaths facing the sun, meaning to inhale thereby the vital essence (*yōki*) emanating from it. At the same time prayers, either Shintoist or Buddhist, are uttered. The power opposing life is darkness, which, however, means not merely absence of light, but an evil power or pollution (*kegare* or *yinki*), the cause of ills and death.

This belief in the sun as the life-giver is certainly a survival of that in the Producing-Divinity, who follows the Heaven-Shining goddess as her noumenon. The ideas and practices have been influenced by the Buddhist cult of Vairochana (the Great Illuminator) and also by the Confucian dualism of the *yin* and *yang*, but we can see here a tendency to continue primitive beliefs.

These ideas have been systematized in recent times into a cult by some Shintō reformers. One section of Buddhists favours this cult, while the other disregards it, though without opposing it. To the former belong the Shingon sect, the most Hinduistic form of Buddhism, which has tried to amalgamate Shintō, and the Nichiren sect, the most Japanized Buddhism. To the latter category belong the Jōdo and the Shin sects, the Buddhist Pietists and Puritans, and the Zen sect, the school of meditation and introspection.

On an average, the prevailing conceptions of the modern Japanese are based on the Buddhistic Shintō. *Karma* and fate are still believed in by many, but transmigration is not strictly adhered to in the details of its teaching. The majority, in fact, think little of life and of its origin; but evils and diseases are, in many cases and by many people, ascribed to spirits or devils indiscriminately. Among the educated classes and educational circles agnosticism, so common to the Japanese mind and to Confucianists in this connexion, is a recognized principle. Young Buddhists, who are now eagerly engaged in reconstructing their faith in Buddha, are not strict in the doctrines of *karma* and transmigration.

LITERATURE.—B. H. Chamberlain, *Kojiki*, Tokyo, 1882; W. G. Aston, *Nihongi*, London, 1896, *Shinto*, do. 1905, pp. 84 f., 282, 292 f.; L. Hearn, *Gleanings in Buddha-Fields*, Boston, 1897; A. B. Mitford, *Tales of Old Japan*, London, 1874, pp. 193–278.

M. ANESAKI.

LIFE AND DEATH (Jewish).—Optimism is the keynote of post-Biblical Judaism. Everything that God does is for the best (*Berakhoth*, 60*b*), and this life is essentially good, to be contemplated with joy and gratitude. 'For every breath that a man draws,' say the Rabbis, 'let him praise God' (*Midr. Rab.* to Gn 2^7). Yet life is not an end in itself, for it must be lived under a sense of responsibility to the Giver, and all its worth resides in this aspect of it. At death a man loses the opportunity of obeying the Torah and the Commandments (*Shab.* 30*a*). 'Morality,' says M. Lazarus, summing up the teaching of Judaism on this subject, 'is man's vocation' (*Ethics of Judaism*, § 116), and the Rabbinical legend tells of God's saying at Sinai: 'If Israel accept not the Commandments, it is better that the earth revert to chaos' (*Shab.* 88*a*). 'The world,' say the Rabbis elsewhere, 'stands upon three pillars: the Torah, Worship, and Benevolence' (*Aboth*, i. 2); or, according to another maxim, 'upon Justice, Truth, and Peace' (*ib.* i. 18). 'The Torah is the medicine of life' (*Yoma*, 72*b*); in other words, life is made sane and efficient by religion. God, according to the Talmudic doctors, says to Israel: 'My light, the Torah, is in thy hands; thy light, the soul, is in Mine. Tend My light, and I will tend thine' (*Midr. Rab.* to Lv 24^2). The supreme hope of the Jew is to behold the Kingdom of God established on earth, and thus, in a notable passage of the Liturgy for the New Year Festival, he prays:

> 'Put Thy fear, O Lord God, we beseech Thee, upon all Thy works, so that all mankind may bow before Thee, and become one band united to do Thy will with a perfect heart; for we know, O Lord, that dominion is Thine, and that strength is in Thy right hand. And so give glory, O Lord, to Thy people, hope to those that fear Thee, and the opening of the mouth to those that trust in Thee. For then the righteous shall see and be glad, and iniquity shall shut its mouth, and all wickedness shall be wholly consumed like smoke, for the proud rule of sin shall pass away from off the earth. Then every creature shall own Thee as its Creator, and everything that hath breath shall cry, The Lord, the God of Israel, reigneth, and His dominion ruleth over all' (cf. Sir $36^{1ff.}$).

But, though the true life is the life of service, it must be glad service, for 'the view of life taught by Judaism is serious, but cheerful' (Lazarus, § 253). The Shekinah (the Divine Presence), says the Talmud, does not come in response either to grief or to levity, but to glad performance of duty (*Shab.* 30*b*). This is the essence of Jewish doctrine on the subject; neither asceticism nor hedonism, but joy springing from and tempered by the religious idea, is the characteristic Jewish temper. 'There should be no unrestrained laughter in this world' (*Ber.* 31*a*). The history of Israel, with all its tragedy, is sufficient to forbid such mirth; and the pious Jew denies himself many a pleasure in memory of desolate Jerusalem. Moreover, unlimited enjoyment is incompatible with a religious outlook on life; the good man will conceive of himself as living under a Divine law, with which his pleasures must be made conformable. On the other hand, the ascetic idea is alien to the true Jewish spirit. The desire for happiness is no evil thing, and its indulgence, under right conditions, is commendable. Even the impulses that make for physical pleasure are the Divine handiwork, and to gratify them is a duty; without them life would be impossible. 'If it were not for desire, the world could not stand; a man would not take a wife, nor build a house, nor plant a vineyard' (*Midr. Tᵉhillim*, ed. S. Buber, Wilna, 1891, to Ps 37[1]). But indulgence of these lower instincts must have as its motive, not the satisfaction which it yields, but the desire to promote the Divine purpose for which they were created. That indulgence is a duty, but a religious duty.

Thus the Rabbinical law, following the general rule laid down in *Ber.* 35*a*, prescribes a number of prayers to be recited by the Jew on indulging in various pleasures more or less sensuous in character—on partaking, *e.g.*, of various kinds of food, on inhaling the scent of a flower, on looking upon the sea, on beholding a rainbow, on taking possession of a new house, and on wearing new clothes for the first time. By such means physical gratification, while sanctioned, is also sanctified. The tendency to self-indulgence is not rebuked, but restrained; natural desire is tempered, not extirpated or suppressed. 'Material comfort and æsthetical pleasures are regarded as integral parts of an ethically sound life' (Lazarus, § 245). It is a Jewish boast that the Hebrew language is particularly rich in words connoting joy. The Rabbis count ten such synonyms (*Aboth dᵉ Rabbi Nathan* [ed. S. Schechter, Vienna, 1887], 52*a*). The Feast of Tabernacles is called the 'season of our gladness' *par excellence* (see *Authorised Prayer Book*, ed. S. Singer, p. 228); 'it would seem as though the Festival was instituted for the specific purpose of gladness, as though the religiousness of joy was to be indicated by ordaining a special celebration in its honour' (M. Joseph, *Judaism as Creed and Life*[2], p. 185). Joy is itself service; but it must be transmuted into service by being purified. Pleasure must be dignified by piety and self-restraint. At meals, the Rabbis teach, words of Torah must be spoken, otherwise it is as if the assembled company ate of the sacrifices of the dead (*Aboth*, iii. 3). A man should eat only when he is hungry, and drink only when he is thirsty, and always in moderation (*Hullin*, 84*a*, *b*). The Talmud inveighs against gluttony and luxury (*Pesachim*, 114*a*). In fine, Judaism commends the golden mean between unbridled self-gratification and extreme self-denial. Indulgence and renunciation must be allies, not antagonists; something of both must go to the making of the daily life; and each must find its justification in the higher utility. 'Here,' says Moses Luzzatto (18th cent.), 'is the true rule on this subject:—The worldly pleasures which a man needs not it is his duty to eschew; but those which, for one reason or another, he does need he cannot renounce without sin. This is the safe rule. But its application to the various circumstances of life must be left to the intelligence and the conscience' (*Mesilath Yesharim*, ch. 13). A far older teacher, Jehudah Halevi (12th cent.), aptly says: 'Our law, as a whole, is divided between fear, love, and joy, by each of which one can approach God. Thy contrition on a fast day does nothing to bring thee nearer to God than thy joy on the Sabbath and holy days, if it [the latter] is the outcome of a devout heart' (*Kitāb al-Khazari*, tr. H. Hirschfeld, London, 1905, p. 113).

It is due partly to the difficulty of defining the *via media* of moderation, and partly to the sorrowful experiences of the Jewish race, that occasionally temperance has overstepped the safe line, and lost itself in austerity. The Talmud tells of a Rabbi (Ze'ra) who fasted a hundred days (*Baba meṣi'a*, 85*a*), and of another (Mar ben Rabina) who fasted practically all the year round (*Pes.* 68*b*). There have been Jewish sects, like the Essenes and the Ḳaraites (*qq.v.*), which have been marked more or less strongly by austere practices. In Judaism, as in other religions, mysticism has had contempt for the world and its joys as its corollary. The disciples of Hillel and Shammai even formally discussed the question whether life is worth living (*Erubin*, 13*b*). This uncertainty is often visible. The devotee who gives himself to fasting is called, now a saint, and now a sinner (*Ta'anith*, 11*a*, 22*b*); a man must die for the Torah, and yet he must not (*Baba kama*, 61*a*; *Erubin*, 6*b*); to sleep on the earth is commended in one place (*Baraitha* of R. Meir), and discouraged in another (*Ber.* 62*b*). But these contradictions are either passing or incidental phases of Jewish thought; a firmer note is the rule, and the ascetic and the pessimist are only by-products of Judaism. It is a bad sign, say the Rabbis, to despise life (*Tana dᵉbe Eliyahu*, ch. 14); and they account for the sin-offering brought by the Nazirite (Nu 6[14]) by contending that his very abstinence from strong drink was a sin (*Ta'anith*, 11*a*).

'According to our view,' says Jehudah Halevi (*op. cit.* p. 135), 'a servant of God is not one who detaches himself from the world, or hates life, which is one of God's bounties. On the contrary, he loves the world and a long life because it affords him the opportunity of deserving the world to come.'

According to a striking Talmudic utterance, in the next world men will be called to account for the lawful pleasures which they have refused in this life (Jer. *Ḳiddushin*, ch. 4). And the real Jew speaks in these maxims. Judaism fixes the thoughts of its adherents upon the future world, but not to the exclusion of this world. 'It has revealed heaven to men, but earth as well' (M. Güdemann, *Das Judenthum*, Vienna, 1902, p. 56). It has no sympathy with self-mortification for its own sake, no commendation for the temper that voluntarily courts pain and abridges life for the greater glory of God. Suffering has to be patiently endured when it comes; it has even to be welcomed as the seed of moral regeneration. 'With thy very wounds I will heal thee,' God, according to the Rabbis, cries to man (*Midr. Rab.* to Lv 15[2] [the reference is to Jer 30[17]]), and 'those whom God afflicts bear his name' (*Midr. Tᵉhillim* to Ps 94[1]); 'if thou desirest life, hope for affliction' (*ib.* to Ps 16[11]). Such utterances betoken not a worship of sorrow, but a recognition of its disciplinary power, of its value for the character, its significance for the life. Judaism sees no merit in suffering, but only in the right bearing of it; and between its teachings and the ideas of the self-tormenting Hindu there is an impassable gulf. Suicide is a crime, and its perpetrator is not to be mourned (*Midr. Rab.* to Gn 9[5]; Maimonides, *Hil. Roṣeach*, xi. 4); but the slow suicide that comes of self-mortification or of the neglect of health is also reprehensible. 'Ye shall keep my statutes, and my judgments: which if a man do, he shall live by them' (Lv 18[5])—'live by them,' says the Rabbinical gloss, 'not die by them' (*Yoma*, 85*b*).

Scattered among the motley contents of the Talmud are the materials for an entire treatise on medicine and hygiene; and the fact is itself a proof of the importance attached to the physical life by the old Jewish sages. Personal cleanliness is exalted into a religious duty. Hillel (1st cent. B.C.), on his way to the bath-house, tells his disciples that he is about to perform a sacred rite; it is a religious duty, he explains, to tend the body, upon which God has stamped a divine beauty (*Midr. Rab.* to Lv 25[35]). Personal cleanliness, the Talmud teaches, is the avenue to spiritual purity (*Aboda Zara*, 20*b*). The duty of preserving life, it further declares, overrides the religious law (*Yoma*, 85*b*). It is not only allowable, but a duty, to extinguish a dangerous fire on the Sabbath day, and to ask permission of the religious authorities is to incur delay and to be guilty of murder. The heads of the community are to be foremost in the humane task (*ib.* 84*b*). For the dead, even though he be King David himself, the Sabbath must not be broken; but it may be broken for the living, even for a child a day old. 'Put out,' says the Talmud, 'the light of a lamp on the Sabbath day rather than extinguish God's light of life' (*Shab.* 30*b*). In a well-known passage in 1 Mac (2[39-41]) the Jewish patriots are described as resolving to defend themselves on the Sabbath instead of passively sacrificing their lives, as their brethren had done hitherto. Self-preservation is a duty. To slay a fellow-creature at the command of another is a crime (*Pes.* 25*b*); but to slay him in self-defence is justifiable. If we are called upon to choose between saving our own life and that of another, we must save our own (*Baba meṣi'a*, 62*a*). Self-torture is forbidden (*Baba kama*, 91*b*), as is the courting of needless danger to life—by sleeping, *e.g.*, on the ground, or remaining in a dilapidated house (*Ta'anith*, 20*b*; *Ber.* 62*b*). In certain ailments 'unclean' meats, usually forbidden to Jews, may be given to the patient (*Yoma*, 83*a*).

There are limits, however, to this regard for the physical life. A man may break every law to save his life except those which forbid the three cardinal sins, idolatry, incest, and murder (*Sanh.* 74*a*). Those who suffer martyrdom for the faith are justly lauded by the Talmud (*Giṭṭin*, 57*b*). But, with these reservations, the duty of preserving life is paramount. Nothing must be done to abridge the duration of life even in the case of the dying (*Shab.* 151*b*).

The Talmud has the story of a sage who, suffering martyrdom at the stake, is adjured by his disciples to end his agony by giving himself to the flames forthwith. He refuses. 'God,' he says, 'alone can take my life; I may not' (*Aboda Zara*, 18*a*).

Regard for life is exalted into reverence. The gift of God, life must be treated with the utmost consideration. The Talmudic laws prescribing kindness to the lower animals are in part actuated by this motive. God has created the various types of animal life, and desires their perpetuation. It is man's duty to pay homage to the Divine will in this as in every other respect, and to make himself the instrument for its fulfilment (see Aaron of Barcelona, *Sepher Haḥinnukh* [13th cent.], §§ 284, 545).

Life, then, according to the Jewish idea, is not evil, but supremely good; it is not a burden to be shuffled off with a sigh of relief.

'This world is not a vale of tears. It is a beautiful world, and men must keep it beautiful by the inherent graciousness of their own lives and by the joy they weave into the lives of others. On the other hand, the true Israelite does not think of this world as his home. It is but a halting-place on the journey from one point in eternity to the other, "the ante-chamber to the palace" (*Aboth*, iv. 16), "a wayside inn" (*Mo'ed ḳaṭon*, 9*b*), the port where we must equip our bark if we would fare safely on our fateful voyage in the great Beyond' (Joseph, p. 287).

Life is not to be clung to unduly, or to be yielded up grudgingly. When the Master's call comes, it must be obeyed cheerfully; for, since He does everything well, the decree that removes us is as wise and good as is the ordinance that places us here. 'Fear not,' says Ben Sira, 'the sentence of death. . . . Why dost thou refuse, when it is the good pleasure of the Most High?' (Sir 41[3f.]). This acceptance of death as the dispensation of Divine justice is the keynote of the ancient Jewish burial service, which takes the form of a theodicy, and, indeed, is so styled. Its distinctive name is *ṣidduḳ haddin*, 'justification of the Divine sentence,' and its essence is expressed in the following quotation:

'Righteous art Thou, O Lord, both when Thou killest and when Thou makest alive. . . . It is not for us to murmur at Thy method of judging. . . . Blessed, then, be the righteous Judge, all Whose judgments are righteous and true. . . . The Lord gave, and the Lord hath taken away; blessed be the name of the Lord' (*Authorised Prayer Book*, p. 318 f.). On hearing of the death of one dear to him, the devout Jew utters the benediction: 'Blessed be the righteous Judge' (*ib.* p. 292).

The Israelite, then, is taught not to desire death, but also not to fear it. If in life he sees the opportunity for service, in death he discerns the signal for ceasing his labours. He is so to live as to be ready for that signal whenever it is given; his 'garments are always to be white,' for 'who knoweth when the King may come?' (*Shab.* 153*a*). And, so prepared, he can await the unknown hour calmly.

G. H. Dalman is not warranted in charging the Jew, as does Max Müller also in his Gifford Lectures (*Anthropological Religion*, London, 1892, p. 369), with an undue dread of death. 'The celebration of the New Year and the Day of Atonement,' says Dalman, 'according to the notions attached to it by orthodox Judaism, instead of mitigating or banishing the fear of death, strengthens it' (*Christianity and Judaism*, Eng. tr., Oxford, 1901, p. 40). He is doubtless thinking of the passionate prayers for life which fill so large a place in the liturgy for those solemn days. But those days are essentially days of penitence; and, if the Jew supplicates for life, it is in order that by repentance and amendment he may put life to noble uses henceforth. Death itself has no greater terrors for him than it has for any other religionist. Judaism, at any rate, does not encourage such fears, but exhorts the Jew to contemplate death with a tranquil mind as the end and the climax of the well-spent life.

Such a death, coming in its due season, is likened to the gathering of fully-ripened fruit or the quenching of the flame of a burnt-out lamp. The death to be dreaded is the morally premature one, which is compared to the gathering of the half-ripened fruit or the untimely extinction of the lamp (*Midr. Rab.* to Gn 25[8]). Death is a natural ordinance; his work finished, the worker must go and make room for his successor—Abraham for Isaac, Moses for Joshua, David for Solomon (*Midr. Tᵉhillim* to Ps 116[15]). 'And God saw all that He had made, and behold it was very good'—it is death that is meant, says a Rabbi (*Midr. Rab.* to Gn 1[31]). The death of the righteous is like the act of one who gently draws a hair from the surface of milk (*Ber.* 8*a*); this is called 'death by a kiss' (*Baba bathra*, 17*a*). The death of the wicked, on the other hand, is like the painful disentangling of a thorn from wool (*Ber.* 8*a*). Death is the liberator (*Shab.* 30*a*); it is like the entering into port of a well-laden vessel (*Midr. Rab.* to Ec 7[1]); hence it is that the Wise Man declares that 'the day of death is better than the day of one's birth' (*ib.*). It is fulfilment as compared with mere promise. Far from being the primeval curse, death is a blessing. The day that Adam died was made a holiday (*Tana dᵉbe Eliyahu*, ch. 16). 'The death of the righteous,' God says, 'is a grief to Me, and never should they die if they did not themselves ask for death; for did not Abraham say, "I would be dust and ashes," and Jacob, "Let me die now"?' (*Midr. Tᵉhillim* to Ps 116[15]).

The idea, however, that life is desirable as the opportunity for obedience persistently recurs in the Rabbinical literature. The thought of its cessation, therefore, is not welcome.

Even Abraham, who, as already indicated, prays for death, is represented (in the apocryphal *Testament of Abraham*) as being averse to it. He refuses to surrender his soul when the archangel Michael claims it; and to win his compliance the angel, at the Divine bidding, puts off his fierce aspect, and appears to the patriarch clothed in light. In like manner the Angel of Death, finding David absorbed in religious study and, therefore, invincible, has to divert his attention by a stratagem before he can perform his mission (*Shab.* 30*b*).

The Angel of Death is a familiar figure in the Rabbinical literature, and, as in the later Biblical writings (*e.g.*, 1 Ch 21[16]), he is armed with a sword. Its point is tipped with gall, and it is this bitter drop that slays (*Aboda Zara*, 20*b*). Sometimes the weapon is described as a knife (*Ketuboth*, 77*b*); sometimes Death is pictured as strangling his victim with a cord. His presence in a town is betokened by the howling of dogs (*Baba kama*, 60*b*). According to some ideas, Death is a fallen angel (*Pirḳe R. Eliezer*, ch. 13), and identical with the Serpent in Eden (Wis 2[23f.]). His name, which often occurs in Rabbinical literature, is *Sammael*, *i.e.* 'the drug of God,' a reference to the gall on his sword. Liberal opinion, however, denied the existence of an Angel of Death, just as it scouted the idea of a personal Devil. 'Satan, the Angel of Death, and Evil Desire are one and the same' (*Baba bathra*, 16*a*). In other words, it is ignoble impulse alone that tempts and destroys. Death, however, is the friend of men, especially of the righteous. Benevolence disarms him (*Derekh ereṣ zuṭa*, ch. 8); and he instructs the learned in religious lore (*Ber.* 51*a*). He respects the wishes of the just as to when and where he delivers his summons (*Mo'ed ḳaṭon*, 28*a*).

A Talmudic legend tells how a famous sage, Joshua ben Levi, appointed to die, and permitted beforehand to see his place in paradise, seizes the knife of the destroying angel, whereupon a heavenly voice rings out the command, 'Give back the knife; the children of men have need of it' (*Ketuboth*, 77*b*). Longfellow has made good use of the story in his *Legend of Rabbi ben Levi*.

The necessity of death, however, applies only to the existing worldly order. In the Golden Age there will be no death; Messiah Himself will slay it (*Pesiḳta Rabbathi* [ed. M. Friedmann, Vienna, 1880], 161*b* [the Scripture proof cited is Is 25[8]]).

As to the origin of death, various opinions are expressed. The familiar idea that death was brought into the world by Adam's sin has its place in Rabbinical literature (see *Shab.* 55*b*; *Erubin*, 18*b*; *Tana dᵉbe Eliyahu*, ch. 5); but we find it much earlier in Sir 25[24]. Closely connected with this idea is the legend, possibly of Persian origin, that the Serpent, when tempting Eve, infected her and, through her, all mankind with his death-dealing poison (*Shab.* 55*b*, 146*a* ; *Aboda Zara*, 22*b* ; cf., further, Wis 2[24]). According to another view, death was ordained at creation, and the primeval sin merely hastened its coming (*Tanchuma* to Gn 39[1]). Certain sages held that sin is the cause of death, and that there cannot be death without it; but this opinion was controverted by the majority. There were saintly men, it was objected, who had died without sin; like tribulation, death is no proof of transgression (*Shab.* 55*a*, *b* ; *Baba bathra*, 17*a*). But the good man, when he has finished his work, must make way, as already stated, for his successor (*ib.* 30*a*). The saints of old, however, did not die in the same way as did other men. Over Moses, *e.g.*, the Angel of Death had no power ; God Himself took his soul from him ; and the same blessed death was vouchsafed to the patriarchs and to other Scriptural heroes (*Baba bathra*, 17*a*). Some great Biblical figures escaped death altogether, and went living into paradise ; Enoch, Elijah, and Hiram were among them (*Derekh ereṣ zuṭa*, ch. 1). Of Elijah it was believed that he was still to be seen on earth, and there are stories in the Talmud describing his apparitions (see, e.g., *Ta'anith*, 22*a*). Death, moreover, has no power over the phœnix, which renews its youth every thousand years, this being its reward for refusing, alone among the creatures, to eat of the forbidden fruit offered it by Eve (*Midr. Rab.* to Gn 3[6]).

LITERATURE.—Talmud and Midrashim ; A. P. Bender, 'Beliefs, Rites, and Customs of the Jews, connected with Death, Burial, and Mourning,' *JQR* vi. [1893–94] and vii. [1894–95] ; S. Suwalski, *Chaye Hayehudi*, Warsaw, 1898 ; Hamburger's *RE*, art. 'Tod' ; *JE*, art. 'Death' ; M. Joseph, *Judaism as Creed and Life*[2], London, 1910 ; K. Kohler, *Grundriss einer systematischen Theologie des Judenthums*, Leipzig, 1910 ; M. Lazarus, *Ethics of Judaism*, Eng. ed., London, 1901; F. Weber, *System der altsynagog. palästin. Theologie*, Leipzig, 1880, 2nd ed. under title *Jüd. Theol. auf Grund des Talmud*, etc., do., 1897.

MORRIS JOSEPH.

LIFE AND DEATH (Teutonic).—Our knowledge of the conceptions of life and death among primitive Teutonic peoples can be gleaned from three fields : (1) the fragmentary information on Teutonic beliefs and practices given by classical and early Christian writers ; (2) the organized religious belief of the Norse peoples, particularly the cult of the chief gods, which embodies beliefs common to the general Teutonic stock, and reveals traces of earlier ideas ; and (3) the great mass of Teutonic tradition, folklore, superstition, and custom, both in early times and in modern survivals. From a study of this material it would appear that the processes of thought on these subjects among the early Teutons were very similar to those now formulated for all primitive peoples. The early Teuton, in dividing all that affected him into animate and inanimate, probably took for his criterion the power of motion ; from the confusion of this power with the faculty of volition animistic ideas would arise in connexion with active natural phenomena, and, later, even with inanimate objects, while a still further development would appear in personification, with inevitable sex-distinction, and in symbolistic beliefs. The criteria for the attribution of death would be the loss of the power of motion and the phenomena arising from it ; from the observation of sleep, dreams, trances, etc., would spring animistic beliefs. A further stage would appear in the identification of the principle of life with those intangible or tangible manifestations, such as breath, warmth, colour, pulsation, or blood, with whose immanence in the body life is obviously connected ; hence the belief in a material form of the soul, leading to the idea of the 'external soul.' Of the later forms of belief Teutonic folklore and myth give ample evidence, allowing one to presuppose the earlier stages.

1. The principle of life in nature.—The four elements are constantly represented as imbued with life, and as able to transmit or to produce it. The strength of the belief in running water is shown by the wide-spread Teutonic worship of streams and springs (cf. Grimm, *Teut. Mythol.*, p. 101), and the practice of bathing in magic springs testifies to the power of water to give life and health (cf. Frazer, *GB*[3], pt. vii., *Balder the Beautiful*, ii. 29). The personification of the living element in water is generally feminine.

The belief in life inherent in fire is shown by the general Teutonic myth of Wieland, originally doubtless a fire demon, and by the Norse personification of fire as Logi, later confused with, and superseded by, Loki. The life-transmitting powers of fire appear in the customs still practised throughout Teutonic Europe, at the ceremonial bonfires, especially at Easter and Midsummer (*ib.* ch. iv. ; note that Frazer admits the existence and significance of these customs, although he deviates [ch. v.] from Mannhardt's explanation of fire-festivals).[1] Akin to fire-beliefs is the belief in the quickening power of the sun, shown in the connexion between the summer solstice and the Midsummer fires, and in the custom of rolling fiery wheels or other sun-symbols. A curious example of belief in the generative power of lightning occurs in the superstition that mistletoe is produced by a lightning-stroke. The connexion between fire and human life appears in the representation of souls as flames or will-o'-the-wisps.

Air has always had an important connexion with the principle of life under two chief aspects : first, breath, the symbol of life (cf. *Voluspá*, 18); secondly, wind or whirlwind. Wind made known the presence of mysterious beings, and in Oðinn, as god of the wind, the slain, and the 'Wild Host,' is the culmination of the connexion of wind with the continuance of life in the soul.

The primitive conception of the earth as Mother of all appears widely in Teutonic belief (cf. art. EARTH, EARTH-GODS, § 6 f.). Early personifications of her occur (Nerthus, Erce), and her life-giving and restoring power appears in charms in which sods, turfs, or handfuls of earth figure ; many of these, whether in Old English or in modern survivals, are Christianized, but their origin is unmistakable. The earth's living power is transferred even to inanimate objects resting on or discovered within her, such as stones and metals ; we find a life-stone that heals wounds (*Laxdœla Saga*, 58 f.). Stones and metals, like plants, fire, and water, were credited with volition, as in the story of Balder, and the early idea of the conscious power of weapons (cf. 'the sword that fights of itself' [*Skírnismál*, 8 f.]) was long retained in poetry and folk-tales.

The close connexion of trees with the principle of life is proved by the well-attested Teutonic worship of trees, and by the idea of the World-Tree, with its popular parallels in the identification of trees with the guardian-spirits of peoples, tribes, families, or individuals (see HAMADRYADS [Teutonic]). The use of plants and fruits to convey life is frequent even in modern superstition, and an early instance occurs in the *Volsunga Saga* (ch. i.), where the queen becomes pregnant after eating one of Freyja's apples. The ashes of the Yule and Midsummer logs were touched and kept for the same purpose (cf. BRANCHES AND TWIGS, § 5).

Certain animals, particularly the boar, had a special connexion with the power of life and its transmission ; others had an intimate connexion with individual human beings, and from this arises the power of transference or of shape-

[1] W. Mannhardt, *Baumkultus der Germanen*, Berlin, 1875, p. 521 ff.

changing. Another form of this sympathetic connexion appears in the 'external soul'; but totemistic ideas, the logical conclusion of depositing the external soul in animals, seem never to have developed among the Teutons (K. Helm, *Altgerm. Religionsgesch.*, i. 23 ff.). In heroic saga the infant hero is sometimes suckled by an animal, as were Wolfdietrich and Sigurðr Sven. The serpent, in other cults so important a symbol of life, because of the renewal of its skin, has little connexion with life-conceptions in Teutonic mythology. The tenacity of the belief in individual life in the natural world appears in frequent personification, though it is sometimes difficult to distinguish between nature-personifications and those local deities which abound in Teutonic belief, but which may be a later development.

It is a moot point whether the primitive Teuton believed in a universal life-giving spirit; without going so far as to assume a monotheistic origin for Teutonic mythology, we can yet believe that the principle of life was early personified, though whether as earth-spirit or as sky-spirit it is impossible to decide. Animistic thought generally tends to the latter, but the Nerthus evidence, the Nerthus-Freyr combination, and the Swedish worship of Freyr as a fertility deity all point to the former. All the chief gods had some connexion with productivity, and traces of phallic worship are not lacking (*ib.* i. 214–225). The origin of world-life has already been treated (see COSMOGONY AND COSMOLOGY [Teutonic]); the revival of world-life and its different phases were celebrated at the Easter, Midsummer, and Yule festivals.

2. The origin of individual life.—The Teutonic conception was prevented from becoming metaphysical by that material view of the soul which is illustrated by the ceremonies followed at birth (see BIRTH [Teutonic]); and the lack of individualism in the life-conception is shown by the importance attached to blood-kinship, heredity, and re-birth. Blood-kinship was the closest of ties, and the mingling of blood was the symbolic ceremonial for sworn brotherhood (cf. art. BROTHERHOOD [Artificial], i. 7). The power of heredity consisted in the transmission of racial qualities, especially courage and hardihood, as in the case of Sinfjötli (*Volsunga Saga*, 8). The idea of re-birth, which still persists, was deeply rooted in Norse belief, and accounts for the constant pre-Christian custom of naming children after dead ancestors; the name was of great efficacy in the attraction of ancestral qualities, and even implied the transmission of a personality. The impossibility of re-birth was considered a misfortune (cf. P. Herrmann, *Nord. Mythol.*, p. 35 ff.). Similarly, the *hamingja*, or genius in female form, could transfer itself from the dead to a beloved kinsman (*Víga Glúms Saga*, 9). The different stages of human life were little regarded; we know of no initiatory ceremonies at adolescence, although Karl Pearson (*Chances of Death*, London, 1897, vol. ii. ch. ix.) considers that the licentious character of mediæval Walpurgisnacht revels proved their origin as sexual festivities; otherwise we hear only of military ceremonies (Tac. *Germ.* 13) or of heirship feasts (*Ynglinga Saga*, 40).

The material representation of the soul was probably induced by the observation of dreams and similar phenomena, where the soul appears to have an independent existence, or by the location of the soul in various organs of the body, as the liver, heart, or head. An extension of this material representation appears in the doctrine, common to all Teutonic peoples, of the 'external soul'; the chief evidence is the story told by Paulus Diaconus (*de Gest. Langobardorum*, iii. 33) of King Gunthram, whose soul was once observed to issue 'in modum reptilis' from his mouth during sleep. Survivals of this idea in fairy-tales show the control exercised by the individual over his external soul, generally by depositing the soul in a place of apparent safety, in an object or plant, and thereby prolonging indefinitely the body's existence (cf. Frazer, ii. 116 ff.; *CF*, ch. v.). A case of control exercised by an external and malignant power is that of Nornagestr, whose life was identified with a burning candle (*Saga af Nornagesti*, 11). The soul's power to assume animal form and to go on journeys (*hamfarir*), leaving the body sleeping, accounts for *hamramir*, or shape-changers, and confusion of such ideas with the observation of states of supernormal activity appears in accounts of *berserksgangr* and shape-changing (see TRANSMIGRATION [Teutonic] and LYCANTHROPY, § 1).

An extensive power over the principle of life was acquired by magic, chiefly sympathetic, prophylactic, or coercive, and it was possible to induce animal and vegetable fecundity, as by the sympathetic magic of the Midsummer fires. Instances of the sacrifice of human life to ensure vegetable fecundity occur in the immolation of the kings Domaldi and Oláfr (*Ynglinga Saga*, 18, 47); a slightly different case is that of Aunn, who gained an added ten years of life for each son sacrificed (*ib.* 29). Magic use of plants, etc., and of charms could induce prolific human life, and facilitate the soul's coming (*Sigrdrífumál*, 9). Life could be protected or prolonged by various practices, such as passing the individual through a cleft tree or hollow stone (cf. Grimm, p. 1167; Frazer, ii. 168 ff.); the story of Balder exemplifies prophylactic magic to secure invulnerability. By spells poison could be rendered innocuous (*Egils Saga*, 44, 75, 79), and sickness prevented or cured, while the perpetual battle of the Hjaðninga exemplifies the power to renew life indefinitely (*Skáldskaparmál*, 47). Charms also had power to suspend life (cf. the sleepthorn), and to harm or destroy it; metamorphoses were often compulsory, the result of external magic.

3. The conception of death in nature.—The elements have all a death-dealing as well as a life-giving power, especially fire and water; water acquires a maleficent power on Midsummer Day, and demands a human victim; similarly, many vegetable and animal objects had death-dealing powers, inherent or temporarily acquired.

4. The conception of individual death.—This arose from the phenomena attending sleep, which foreshadowed the soul's departure; the soul is still materially represented as issuing from the mouth in the form of a bird or mouse, and its exit is facilitated in every way. In Norse mythology the dead made an actual journey, and needed shoes to travel the Hel road. The idea of cessation of activity after death, if it ever existed, was soon superseded, as is proved by the universal custom of providing the dead with material implements; the earliest tombs contain cups and vessels, not armour and weapons—a sign that at first feasting, not fighting, was to be the chief occupation. Activity after death could be exercised still on earth, but it was then frequently malignant, and could be prevented only by burning the corpse (*Laxdœla Saga*, 17, 24). Spirits could return in animal or in human form (*Erbyggja Saga*, 51, 53), and hauntings show the power of ghosts to affect the living; fear was probably as great an incentive to ancestor-worship as reverence. Activity in another world was materially conceived as a close parallel to mortal life, as is proved by the nature of the implements provided, and such activity was often localized in sepulchral howes (*ib.* 11). The Valhalla belief is the final poetic development of the conception of Oðinn as god of the slain; in a less warlike age a more peaceful prefigurement arises, the *Rosengarten* of the later German poets; Saxo Grammaticus's account (*Gesta Danorum*, i. 31) of Hadding's voyage to the under world represents an intermediate stage (cf. art. BLEST, ABODE OF THE [Teutonic]). The power of death was inexorable and inevitable, even the gods being doomed to perish at the world-death. Death was personified in many forms: as a messenger, or as an enemy. The Norse Hela was certainly at first a Teutonic Proserpine, however shadowy: subsequently, her personality was not distinguished from her abode. Popular and grotesque personifications of death prevailed later, and gave rise to the idea of weakening death's power by insulting or beating a tangible representation (Grimm, p. 767).

In spite of the undoubted fatalism of Teutonic peoples (see art. DOOM, DOOM MYTHS [Teutonic]), the belief, born of instinct and desire, prevailed that magic enabled man to exercise a twofold power over death: first, in retarding or hastening death; secondly, in controlling and summoning spirits (*Erbyggja Saga*, 55). Preventive magic against death might include the wide range of charms to preserve health, prevent barrenness, heal sickness, or stanch blood. Coercive magic to compel death was apparently as frequent as preventive, though naturally more secret. It was possible to foresee the doom of death upon others, and also to have the premonition of it in oneself—to be fey. The summoning of spirits (*helrúna*), performed by means of the *valgaldr*, became in Norse mythology an important branch of magic art (see MAGIC [Teutonic]).

5. The ethical aspect of life and death.—It is difficult to deduce the ethical outlook of the average Teuton on life and death because of the extremely objective character of the literature, but the non-moral aspect of world-life and world-death is proved by the fact that the end of the world comes 'automatically,' involving the gods also. Respect for the principle of life is presupposed by the importance attached to fertility and all that promotes it; but this was instinctive, and originally entirely non-moral. Respect for individual life rarely appears, except in kinship; the slaughter of kin was abhorred as violating the blood-tie (Saxo Grammaticus, *Gesta Danorum*, ii. 1; *Beowulf*, 2436 ff.); but even this was probably due more to tribal than to moral instinct. Custom rather than morality governed the sacrifice or the retention of life, as in the case of the Gothic widows (Procopius, *de Bello Goth.* ii. 14). Chivalrous sparing of life was little known, for Saxo Grammaticus's assertion to the contrary can hardly be substantiated from earlier literature (*Gesta Danorum*, v. 160). The fatalism so deeply ingrained in the Teutons coloured their whole outlook, but it was untinged by remorse for an ill-spent life or by fear of coming punishment; and the lack of a moral division after death is so general that it is tempting to explain apparent inconsistencies by the theory of Christian influence. Suicide was allowable when due to grief for a friend or kinsman, and was more honourable than an ignoble death (cf. Saxo Grammaticus, tr. O. Elton, London, 1894, p. xxxvi). The practice of human sacrifice points to little respect for human life in the abstract (see art. HUMAN SACRIFICE [Teutonic]); the fact that such sacrifices were prophylactic or propitiatory was held sufficient justification, if indeed any were necessary. There certainly seems to have been a strong idea of sacrificing the life and welfare of the one to that of the many. It would add greatly to our knowledge and the interest of the subject if, in the account of prophylactic sacrifices, the least clue were given to the mood and temper of the victim—whether he were merely passive under compulsion or a willing and exalted sufferer.

LITERATURE.—J. G. Frazer, *GB*³, pt. vii., *Balder the Beautiful*, 2 vols., London, 1913; J. Grimm, *Teut. Mythol.*, tr. J. S. Stallybrass, do. 1882–88, chs. xix.–xxix., xxxiv.–xxxviii.; P. Herrmann, *Nord. Mythol.*, Leipzig, 1903, pp. 31–99, 538–567; K. Helm, *Altgerm. Religionsgesch.*, Heidelberg, 1913, i., sections vi.–xi.; W. Golther, *Handb. der germ. Mythol.*, Leipzig, 1895, pp. 72–116; P. D. Chantepie de la Saussaye, *Rel. of the Teutons*, Boston, 1902, chs. iii., xi., xviii., xx., xxi.; E. Mogk, 'Mythologie,' in H. Paul, *Grundr. der germ. Philologie*², iii. Strassburg, 1900, chs. v., xv.; E. H. Meyer, *Germ. Mythol.*, Berlin, 1891, ch. iv.

M. E. SEATON.

LIFE, FUTURE.—See STATE OF THE DEAD.

LIFE-TOKEN.—'Life-token' or 'life-index' is the technical name given to an object the condition of which is in popular belief bound up with that of some person, and indicates his state of health or safety. The object may be an artifact, such as a tool, a weapon, or an ornament; or it may be a tree or plant, an animal, or even a well, or a vessel of water or some other liquid. The most familiar examples are found in the *Arabian Nights*. In the story of 'The Two Sisters who envied their Cadette,' with which Galland concluded his version (cf. R. F. Burton, *Supplemental Nights*, London, 1886–88, iv. 491 ff.), Prince Bahman, on departing in search of the talking bird, the golden water, and the singing tree, leaves with his sister a hunting-knife, the blade of which will remain clean and bright so long as he continues safe and sound, but will be stained with blood if he be slain. His brother, following him, leaves a string of pearls, which will run loose upon the string while he is alive, but after his death will be found fixed and adhering together.

The incident is, in fact, common in folk-tales all over the world where the hero goes on a perilous adventure, and his friends require early information, that they may in case of need sally forth to rescue or avenge him. It is necessary here to draw attention only to one wide-spread cycle—that of the modern variants of the ancient Greek story of Perseus. In these tales Perseus is often represented by three sons, born in consequence of their mother's having partaken of a magical fish. Some portion of the offal of the fish is buried in the garden; a tree grows on the spot and becomes the life-token of the children. Sometimes a portion of the fish's blood is preserved, by its direction, in phials, one for each of the children, to boil or become turbid in case of misfortune. In a story from Pisa the fish-bone is fastened to a beam in the kitchen, and sweats blood when anything untoward happens to any of the boys.

There is thus an original organic connexion between the life-token and the person whose condition it exhibits. This connexion supplies the interpretation. The life-token is derived from the doctrine of sympathetic magic, according to which any portion of a living being, though severed, remains in mystic union with the bulk, and is affected by whatever may affect the bulk. Sympathetic magic, however, is not confined to folk-tales: it has a practical bearing. It is applied in witchcraft and folk-medicine to the injury or to the benefit of human beings and every object that comes into relation with them. Accordingly, we find the life-token not only in folk-tales, but also in everyday custom and superstition.

A striking and pathetic example of a severed portion of a human being employed as his life-token is recorded in the United States. Early in the last century a boy in Grafton County, New Hampshire, was so badly scalded that a piece of his skin, fully an inch in diameter, sloughed off, and was carefully treasured by his mother. When he grew up, he left home and was never heard of after; but his mother used from time to time to examine the fragment of skin, persuaded that, so long as it was sound, her son was alive and well, and that it would not begin to decay until his death. For thirty years, until her death about the year 1843, she kept it; and thenceforth her daughters continued to do so under the influence of the same belief (*JAFL* vi. [1893] 69).

This convenient method of providing a life-token from the substance of one's own body is, however, not always available. Fortunately, the doctrine of sympathetic magic applies equally to objects derived less directly from the person. Just as in the tale the offal of the fish buried in the garden grows up into the tree and becomes the life-token of the children who owe their birth to, or perhaps are a transformation of, the fish, so trees are in actual life planted for the purpose.

The navel-string of a Maori child was buried in a sacred place, and a young sapling planted over it expressly as the babe's 'sign of life' or life-token (R. Taylor, *Te Ika a Maui: New Zealand and its Inhabitants*[2], London, 1870, p. 184). Sometimes it was buried at the foot of a tree or bush. If the tree or bush afterwards 'showed signs of decay or died, the results would be similar to the child' (*Journ. Ethnol. Soc.* i. [1869] 73). In the latter case an already existing tree is appropriated as the life-token by uniting the child with it through the medium of the cord. In the same way, in Germany the afterbirth is thrown or buried at the foot of a young tree, and the child is expected to grow with the tree and thrive as it thrives (K. Bartsch, *Sagen, Märchen und Gebräuche aus Meklenburg*, Vienna, 1880, ii. 43; *Am Urquell*, v. [1894] 253). Though it is not now common thus to unite the child with the tree, the practice of planting a tree at the birth of a child is still frequent in Europe. In Aargau (Switzerland) an apple-tree is planted for a boy, a pear-tree for a girl; and it is definitely believed that the babe will thrive or die like the young tree (W. Mannhardt, *Wald- und Feldkulte*, Berlin, 1875, i. 'Baumkultus,' p. 50, citing Rochholz). Numerous remains of this practice and belief are found in tradition all over Europe.

The caul with which some children are born also becomes an index of their health and prosperity. For this purpose great care is taken of it.

Among the Letts of Russia to lose it betokens misfortune for the child (R. Kobert, *Hist. Studien aus dem pharmakol. Inst. der kais. Universität Dorpat*, iv. [Halle, 1894] 229). In England and Scotland its condition, whether soft and flabby or hard, dry, and stiff, indicates coming misfortune or prosperity (S. O. Addy, *Household Tales*, London, 1895, p. 120; J. G. Dalyell, *Darker Superstitions of Scotland*, Glasgow, 1835, p. 326).

But, as in the stories, the life-token is not always determined at the birth of the person whose fate is indicated by it. When a child has been passed through a young ash-tree split for the purpose, in order to cure infantile hernia, the tree is bound up and plastered, in the hope that it may grow together again; and according to the success of the treatment the child is expected to recover or not. More than this, so intimate has the connexion between the tree and the child become by the operation that, if the tree be afterwards felled, the child will die. Thus the tree is not merely dependent upon the fate of the child; the child is also dependent on the fate of the tree. This mutual dependence is sometimes expressly mentioned in the stories also. It results from the close connexion established between the human being and the object constituted as the life-token. In the stories it is often forgotten; generally in practice it is at least implicit.

On the Eastern peninsula of Maryland, opposite Baltimore, when a member of a family leaves home, a bit of live-for-ever is stuck in the ground to indicate the fortune of the absent one. It will flourish if he prospers; otherwise it will wither and die (*JAFL* iv. [1891] 152). At Rome every Emperor solemnly planted on the Capitol a laurel, which was said to wither when he was about to die. A successful general to whom a triumph was accorded also planted on the occasion, in the shrubbery set by Livia, a laurel, similarly believed to wither when he was about to die. Two myrtle-trees grew before the temple of Quirinus, one called the Patrician tree, the other the Plebeian. So long as the Senate maintained its power as the supreme authority of the State, the Patrician tree flourished. But it began to fail at the time of the Social War, when the Plebs successfully asserted their rights, and the Plebeian tree, hitherto sickly and shrivelled, gained the superiority (Pliny, *HN* xv. 36). The Dayaks of Borneo are accustomed on certain occasions to plant a sort of palm, which is regarded, in the fullest sense of the word, as a life-token. If it grows prosperously, they can reckon on good fortune; but, when it fades or dies, the person concerned has to expect the reverse (Wilken, *Verspreide Geschriften*, iii. 562 n.). In Germany, at Hochheim, Einzingen, and other places near Gotha, two young trees are planted at a wedding by the bridal pair, on the property of the commune. If either of the trees withers, one or the other of the spouses will shortly die (Mannhardt, p. 48).

Turning now to artificial objects—an illustration may be given from a somewhat unexpected quarter.

Father George Eich, reporting in the *Annales de la Propagation de la Foi* (1898) a recent visit to Easter Island, relates that the native converts persistently inquired after another Roman Catholic missionary, Father Albert Montiton, who had previously visited them. They said that he had caused the great stone cross in the cemetery of Hangaroa to be set up, and told them: 'When you see this cross fall, you will say, Father Albert has just died; let us pray for him.' Father Eich went to see the cross, and found that it had in fact fallen, but had been set up again, and bore traces of its fall. On questioning them to ascertain the precise date of its fall, he found that it coincided exactly with that of Father Albert's death in Spain, 25th Feb. 1894 (*FL* xi. [1900] 436, quoting the *Annales* at length).

This kind of life-token easily lends itself to divination concerning the health or prosperity of absent friends, or even the prospects of life of actual members of the household.

In Thuringia, when it is desired to know whether absent children or other kinsmen are still living, all that is necessary is to stick a loaf of bread with ears of corn before putting it into the oven. Each of the ears is designated by the name of one of the absent persons concerning whom inquiry is made; and, if any of them be scorched in the process of baking, the person symbolized is assuredly dead (A. Witzschel, *Sagen, Sitten und Gebräuche aus Thüringen*, Vienna, 1878, ii. 251). Zulu women, when their husbands go to war, hang the conjugal sleeping-mat on the wall of their hut. So long as it casts a shadow on the wall, the husband is safe; when it ceases to do so, he is believed to be dead (T. Arbousset and F. Daumas, *Exploratory Tour*, Cape Town, 1846, p. 145; cf. H. Callaway, *Rel. System of the Amazulu*, Natal, 1870, p. 126). Fire or a candle is often employed. In Brittany a sailor's wife who has been long without tidings of her husband makes a pilgrimage to some shrine and lights a taper before the saint. If her husband is yet alive and well, it burns well; otherwise the flame will be poor and intermittent, and will go out (A. Le Braz, *Légende de la mort en Basse-Bretagne*, Paris, 1893, p. 6). The Kei Islanders in the Moluccas perform a similar ceremony. When men are absent on a voyage, rude lamps, consisting of sea-shells filled with oil and containing wicks, are lighted with a sort of solemn ritual at the sacred fire. Each lamp represents one of the absent men. A straight and steady flame indicates that the man represented is well in body and soul; but, if the flame wavers or burns badly, an evil augury is drawn (*Anthropos*, v. [1910] 354). When the men go from Yule Island, off the coast of New Guinea, to the Papuan Gulf for sago, a fire is lit; if it goes out, 'there will be bad luck for the voyagers, consequently care is taken to keep the fire alight during the whole time the men are away' (A. C. Haddon, *Head-hunters*, London, 1901, p. 259). A Shawnee prophet tried to persuade Tanner, when living among the Indians, that the fire in his lodge was intimately connected with his life. At all seasons and in all weathers it was to remain alight; for, if he suffered it to be extinguished, his life would be at an end (J. Tanner, *Captivity and Adventures*, New York, 1830, p. 155).

The last two cases are interesting examples of the ambiguity already noticed in the relation between the object and the person with whose life it is bound up. They naturally act and react upon one another. Whatever affects the one affects the other also. The object thus connected by a mystic bond with a human life has sometimes been called the 'external soul.' It is perfectly true that in the stories the life of ogre or hero is frequently said to depend on an object hidden safely away, and that this object is occasionally described as the owner's soul. Sometimes, as in the ancient Egyptian story of 'The Two Brothers,' it is called by the equivalent name of his heart. More commonly it is referred to simply as his life. It is also true that in savage belief the soul is separable from the body: it goes forth in dreams; sickness is caused by its absence; a complete severance is death. Care is taken on important occasions, as at marriage or change of dwelling, or at a funeral, to cage and retain the soul, and in sickness to recall it from wandering and restore it to the patient's body. But, as in the stories, so in the practices and superstitions, the object in mystic relation with a man is by no means always called his soul, or said to contain his soul. It seems, therefore, to be going somewhat beyond the facts to apply to it a word expressing a definite conception when it is not applied by the people holding the superstition or exercising the custom. Ideas are often vague, and, where they are so, to affix terms to them which connote to us something definite is to darken counsel.

In Nigeria a great tree frequently stands in a village, and is hung with medicine and votive offerings. It is described by the villagers as 'our Life,' and it is in some sense worshipped as a god (C. Partridge, *Cross River Natives*, London, 1905, pp. 194, 205). The Ibo-speaking Negroes of Awka declared that such a tree had 'the life or breath of the priest in it.' Not long ago the tree died and the priest 'died at the same time because the tree had died' (N. W. Thomas, *Ibo-speaking Peoples*, London, 1913, i. 29). The Montols of Northern Nigeria believe that at the birth of every individual of their race, male or female, a snake of a certain non-poisonous species which haunts the dwellings is also born. From the moment of birth the snake and the man share a life of common duration, and the measure of the one is the measure of the other. Hence every care is taken to protect these animals from injury; and it is said that they are quite harmless to human beings (*Journ. Afr. Soc.* x. [1910] 30). So at Rome every man was deemed to be accompanied throughout life by a *genius*, to which he owed all his gifts and good fortune. The genius was represented by, or incorporated in, a snake, which was never killed, but encouraged in the house, and even in the sleeping-chamber. The result was, according to Pliny, that snakes multiplied to such an extent that, if they had not been kept down by frequent fires, it would have been impossible to make headway against their fecundity (L. Preller, *Röm. Myth.*, Berlin, 1883, ii. 196–198; Pliny, *HN* xxix. 22). Tiberius Gracchus once caught a pair of snakes upon his bed, and was advised by the soothsayers to kill one of them, but warned that his life was bound up with that of the one, and his wife's with that of the other. Rather than put an end to his wife's life, he killed the male and himself died in a short time (Plutarch, *Tiberius Gracchus*). At the monastery of Saint Maurice, on the borders of Burgundy, near the Rhone, was a fishpond stocked with as many fish as there were monks. When any of the monks fell sick, one of the fish floated on the surface of the water, half-dead; and, if the monk was going to die, the fish would die three days before him (J. W. Wolf, *Niederl. Sagen*, Leipzig, 1843, p. 259, citing Leonard Vair, *Trois Livres des charmes*, Paris, 1583, p. 387). On the island of Buru, one of the Moluccas, the same belief seems to be attached to the cayman. No Burunese, we are told, would dare kill a cayman, lest he should unwittingly cause the death of one of his nearest kinsmen (Wilken, iii. 82). In fact, the belief that the lives of human beings are bound up with those of certain of the lower animals as well as of trees and plants is very wide-spread; and the latter are not necessarily viewed as the guardians or incarnations of the souls of the former.

Lakes and streams also serve as life-tokens, independently of the animals that haunt or inhabit them.

On a mountain in Franconia a fountain issues near the ancestral home of an ancient noble family. The clear stream gushes forth incessantly the whole year round; and it was believed to fail only when one of the family was about to die (J. Grimm, *Deutsche Sagen*, Berlin, 1816–18, i. 162). The waters of the crater-lake of Tritriva in Madagascar are of a deep green colour, almost black. It is believed that, when a member of the neighbouring tribe, the Zanatsara, is taken ill, if the water is troubled and becomes of a brown colour, his death is presaged; if it remains clear, he will have a chance of life (*RTP* vii. [1892] 760, quoting J. Sibree).

The present writer has elsewhere (*LP* ii. [1895] 13 ff.) pointed out that the custom of scrying or crystal-gazing (*q.v.*) is intimately related to those of looking into the depths of a well or a pool of water or ink, and into a magical mirror, for the purpose of gaining tidings of absent friends or distant events. It will suffice to say here that the hallucination on which it is founded is equally capable of being produced by gazing intently on any dark and polished surface like that of standing water, a mirror, or a piece of stone, and that the superstition is practically world-wide.

The march between the life-token and the belief in omens drawn from objects not specially connected with any individual is ill-defined. It is by no means necessary to appoint one's own life-token: the health or prosperity of the absent may be divined by the condition of a life-token arbitrarily appointed by anxious relatives or friends at home. There is but a step between this and the drawing of auguries from events and objects not appointed at all. The step is often taken both in tales and in real life.

In an Icelandic tale three drops of blood appearing on the knife while eating are a token to one brother of another's peril or death (*Am Urquell*, iii. [1892] 5, citing Arnason). The sudden falling of three drops of blood from the nose is recorded in recent years in countries as wide apart as Scotland and Transylvania to be regarded as an omen of the death of a near relative (W. Gregor, *Folklore of N.E. of Scotland*, London, 1881, p. 204; H. von Wlislocki, *Volksglaube und Volksbrauch der Siebenbürger Sachsen*, Berlin, 1893, p. 190). At Rauen, about 30 miles from Frankfort-on-the-Oder, a crack in a newly-baked loaf portends the death of one of the family (A. Kuhn and W. Schwartz, *Norddeutsche Sagen*, Leipzig, 1848, p. 436). In Thuringia, if an altar-light goes out, one of the clergy will die (Witzschel, ii. 254). In Brunswick, when a plant in the garden, usually green, puts forth white leaves, it betokens the speedy death of some one in the house (R. Andree, *Braunschw. Volkskunde*, Brunswick, 1896, p. 224). The list of such omens might be continued indefinitely.

Further, if my life be united to any external object, whether physically (so to speak), as in the case of an ailing child passed through a split sapling, or by the arbitrary appointment of myself or another, it is obvious that injuries intentionally inflicted on the object in question will react upon me. The felling of the sapling causes the death of the child. In the classic story of Meleager the hero's life came to an end with the burning and extinction of the fateful brand. This belief is the foundation of that department of magic which is used for injuring others by damaging or destroying things which have been closely attached to them, or to which identity with them is imputed. Fragments of the hair, nails, food, or clothing, portions of the blood or saliva, and earth from the footprints of the victim are all impregnated with his life, are still a portion of himself, though detached; and he may be injured or even done to death by the appropriate treatment of any of these objects. So also to stick pins or daggers into, or to burn, the effigy of a man is to wound or kill the person represented. These are all well-known magical rites. Parallel with them is the treatment of such objects for the purpose of benefiting the person to whom they belong.

The navel-string of an infant, taken by a mother to church at her churching, and laid down behind the altar or in some other suitable place, is deemed in Mecklenburg and Thuringia to be effectual in surrounding the child with such holy influences that he will grow up God-fearing and pious (Witzschel, ii. 249; Bartsch, ii. 45). For some such reason Athenian women who became pregnant for the first time hung up their girdles in the temple of Artemis. Probably for a similar purpose fragments of clothing and other things are hung by votaries on a sacred tree, and pins are deposited in sacred wells. To the same order of thought belongs the sympathetic treatment of wounds by means of the instrument inflicting them. This treatment, formerly accepted by physicians and philosophers, is now left in Europe to the peasantry. It originates in savagery. The Lkungen or Songish of Vancouver Island are very careful to keep concealed the arrow that has wounded a friend, and not to bring it near the fire; for he would become very ill if the weapon, while still covered with his blood, were thrown into the flame (F. Boas, *Rep. Brit. Assoc.*, London, 1890, p. 577). Melanesians keep the arrow, when extracted, in a damp place or in cool leaves, believing that the inflammation will then be slight and will soon subside. But, if the enemy who has shot another can get back his arrow, he puts it into the fire, with intent to irritate the wound and cause fatal results (R. H. Codrington, *The Melanesians*, Oxford, 1891, p. 310). Similar practices are very wide-spread among the European peasantry, and not least in our own island.

By a very natural extension of the idea of the life-token the cognate idea of the faith-token has been evolved. It is not enough for one of a pair of lovers to know that the other is living; there must be constant assurance of the absent one's fidelity. The token of fidelity is, therefore, a common incident both in tales and in actual life.

It is well-known in India. In the *Kathā-sarit-sāgara*, or 'Ocean of the Streams of Story,' a famous collection of Indian tales, the god Śiva appears in a dream to Guhasena and his wife Devasmitā when they are about to part, and gives each of them a red lotus, saying: 'Take each of you one of these lotuses in your hand. And, if either of you shall be unfaithful during your separation, the lotus in the hand of the other shall fade, but not otherwise.' When they awoke, each beheld in the other's hand a red lotus; 'and it seemed if they had got one another's hearts' (C. H. Tawney's tr., Calcutta, 1880, i. 86). In European folk-tales, ballads, and romances the faith-token is by no means an unusual piece of machinery. It has found its way on to the stage. Among other dramas, the plot of P. Massinger's play of *The Picture* (1629) turns upon it. Nor is its vogue in practice less wide. The Mech are a Mongoloid tribe in Bengal. Every Mech has in the court-yard of his house a *sij* plant (*Euphorbia*

Indica), which is carefully tended as the abode of Śiva and the emblem of conjugal fidelity. If its leaves wither, something is wrong with one of the women of the household (H. H. Risley, *TC*, Calcutta, 1892, ii. 89). In Peru the husband knots a branch of Euphorbia before going on a journey. If on his return he finds the knots withered up, his wife has been unfaithful; if they are fresh and living, she has been true (*ZE* xxxvii. [1905] 439). At Siena formerly a maiden who wished to know how her love progressed kept and tended a plant of rue. While it flourished, all went well; but, if it withered, it was a sign that the love she desired had failed her (*Archivio*, x. [1891] 30). Losing a garter in the street means, according to belief in some districts of England and Germany, that the owner's lover is unfaithful (Addy, p. 98; J. Grimm, *Teut. Myth.*, tr. J. S. Stallybrass, London, 1882–88, pp. 1782, 1824). Elsewhere, on the contrary, he is thinking of her (Andree, p. 215; cf. F. D. Bergen, *Current Superstitions*, Boston, 1896, p. 63). Certain sacred wells in France have or had the property of certifying the loved one's fidelity to a jealous lover. All that was necessary was to abstract a pin (which was often nothing but a thorn) from her dress and lay it on the surface of the water. If it floated, all was well; if it sank to the bottom, she was unfaithful (P. Sébillot, *Folklore de France*, ii. [Paris, 1905] 252). In all such cases the faith-token exactly corresponds with the life-token.

LITERATURE.—René Basset, *Nouveaux Contes berbères*, Paris. 1897, gives in a note (pp. 309–316) an extensive list of stories in which the incident occurs. Many of these are abstracted and discussed by F. J. Child, *English and Scottish Popular Ballads*, 5 vols., Boston, 1882–98, in the introductions to the ballads of Hind Horn (i. 187), and Bonny Bee Hom (ii. 317), and by W. A. Clouston, *Popular Tales and Fictions*, 2 vols., Edinburgh, 1887, i. 169, and in his dissertation appended to *John Lane's Continuation of Chaucer's 'Squire's Tale'* (published by the Chaucer Society, London, 1888–90), 299, 334. Discussions will be found on the incident and its relation to custom and superstition by G. A. Wilken in his monographs on 'Het Animisme bij de volken van den Indischen Archipel,' 'De betrekking tusschen menschen-, dieren- en plantenleven naar het volksgeloof,' and 'De Simsonsage,' collected in his *Verspreide Geschriften*, 4 vols., The Hague, 1912, iii.; and E. S. Hartland, *The Legend of Perseus*, 3 vols., London, 1894–96, ii. ch. viii. See also art. LIFE AND DEATH (Primitive), § 4.

E. SIDNEY HARTLAND.

LIGHT AND DARKNESS.

LIGHT AND DARKNESS (Primitive). — Among the lower races the nature and origin of light and darkness gave rise to many questions, and the answers to these are found in a great variety of myths. Frequently light and darkness are assumed to be substances—*e.g.*, 'a hard darkness,' as in an Australian myth [1]—or the sun, often regarded as the cause of light, is thought of as a fire or fiery substance, larger or smaller. Among the primitive peoples the dualism of light and darkness or of beings representing these—so frequently found at higher stages of civilization—can hardly be said to exist.

1. Primordial darkness.—A wide-spread idea seems to be that night precedes or gives rise to day, darkness precedes or gives rise to light. Light, the light of day, appears to come gradually out of the darkness of night, whereas darkness falls over the light of day and extinguishes it, but does not come from it. Man also, asleep and inert during darkness, rises to fresh activity with the light. A pre-existing state of darkness, out of which light and life have proceeded, is thus usually presupposed. Many Australian tribes believe that long ago darkness or semi-darkness prevailed, until the sun was made or released. An emu's egg was thrown up to the sky, and either itself gave a great light or set fire to a wood-pile belonging to a sky-being. The latter sees how beautiful earth now is, and therefore he makes a fire every day. There is little warmth in the morning, because it is not fully kindled, and it is cold at night when the fire dies out. The jackass rouses men to the light. If he did not, or if children imitated him, there would be nothing but darkness. Or the sun is created as the result of certain obscene rites performed by men who complained of having no heat or light; or there is darkness until the magpie props up the sky and so sets free the sun.[2] The last-mentioned myth, that heaven and earth are close together, and that, until they are separated, their offspring are in perpetual and universal night, prevails over Oceania. The children, or gods, or a serpent, or trees force them apart and so let in light and air.[3]

[1] Howitt, p. 426.

[2] K. L. Parker, *More Aust. Legendary Tales*, London, 1898, p. 28; N. W. Thomas, *Natives of Aust.*, do. 1906, p. 249; Howitt, p. 427; E. M. Curr, *Aust. Race*, Melbourne, 1886–87, ii. 48; T. Waitz and G. Gerland, *Anthrop. der Naturvölker*, vi. [Leipzig, 1872] 197; R. Lasch, *ARW* iii. [1900] 99.

[3] B. Thomson, *Savage Island*. London, 1902, p. 84; G. Turner, *Samoa*, do. 1884, p. 296 f.; R. Taylor, *Te Ika a Maui*[2], do. 1870, p. 120; Waitz-Gerland, vi. 245; G. Grey, *Polynes. Myth.*, do., n.d., p. 1 ff.; cf. EARTH, § 3.

Maori mythology relates that the Atua o te po, gods of Hades or darkness, existed before heaven was lifted up, and were more ancient than the Atua o te ra, gods of light, because darkness precedes light. Their chief was Hine nui te po, great mother night, or Hades. Light and life are represented by Tama mir te ra, the great son of day. A creation epic describes the cosmogonic periods, the first of which is that of thought, the second that of night or darkness:

> 'The word became fruitful;
> It dwelt with the feeble glimmering;
> It brought forth night,
> The great night, the long night,
> The lowest night, the loftiest night,
> The thick night, to be felt,
> The night to be touched, the night unseen,
> The night following on,
> The night ending in death.'

Then follows the third period, that of light, and the fourth, in which sun, moon, and stars are created, 'thrown up as the eyes of Heaven, then the heaven became light.'[1] This idea that chaos and darkness—the state of Po, Hades, or night—precede all gods and all things is wide-spread in Polynesia. Even a heaven-god like Taaroa, creator of sun, moon, etc., springs from it;[2] or he sprang out of an egg and so brought light to the world.[3]

The Garos say that earth was at first a huge watery plain, and darkness lay over all. Tatara-Rabuga created earth through a lesser spirit and, at the latter's request, placed sun and moon in the sky to give light.[4]

The myth of Heaven and Earth as a divine pair is common in W. Africa, but its most significant expression is found among the Yorubas, who say that Obutala and Odudua, their chief god and goddess, were shut up in darkness in a calabash in the beginning. She blamed him for this, whereupon he blinded her.[5]

Among the Eskimos, a people dwelling for a great part of the year in darkness, many myths deal with this subject. According to one of these, men came out of the earth, lived in perpetual darkness, and knew no death. There came a flood which destroyed all but two old women, one of whom desired both light and death. Death came,

[1] Taylor, p. 100 ff.

[2] W. Ellis, *Polynes. Researches*[2], London, 1832, i. 322; Waitz-Gerland, vi. 240, 266 f.

[3] L. Frobenius, *Die Weltanschauung der Naturvölker*, p. 10.

[4] A. Playfair, *The Garos*, London, 1909, p. 82 f.

[5] A. B. Ellis, *Yoruba-speaking Peoples*, London, 1894, p. 42; *ARW* xi. [1908] 402 f.; Frobenius, pp. 350, 354, 359

and with it sun, moon, and stars.[1] Another wide-spread myth is that of the brother who, in the time when darkness covered the earth, ravished his sister. In her anger at his brutal conduct, she pursued him to the sky with a brand. He became the moon and she the sun, ever pursuing the moon, except in winter, when she remains in her house and there is darkness. The stars are sparks from the brand.[2]

A well-known Chinese myth relates that in the beginning all was darkness. From a great mundane egg, which divided in two, came Poon-Koo Wong, who made the sky out of the upper and earth out of the lower half. He also made sun and moon.[4] Chinese philosophy speaks of T'ai-Kih, the 'Most Ultimate,' which produced the cosmic souls Yang and Yin, male and female, heaven and earth, warmth and cold, light and darkness.[5] In Japan an old myth in the *Kojiki* speaks of a time when Heaven and Earth were not separated and the In and Yo (= Yin and Yang) not yet divided. All was chaos and presumably darkness.[6]

A Finnish cosmogonic myth in the *Kalevala* relates that from the upper and lower parts of an egg which fell into the primeval waters were formed heaven and earth, from the yolk the sun, from the white the moon, and from the darkness in the egg the clouds.[7]

Scandinavian mythology contains an elaborate myth of beginnings. There was first a void world of mist, *ginnunga-gap*. On its southern extremity was *muspell*, fire, on its northern, *nifl*, fog; from the one proceeded light and warmth, from the other darkness and cold. According to Grimm, *ginnunga-gap* is the equivalent of the Gr. *χάος*, meaning both 'abyss' and 'darkness.'[8] In the Edda, Day personified is the son of Night, each of them having a horse and car, in which they journey round the earth. The primitive method of counting time with Scandinavians, Teutons, and Celts was on the principle that night preceded day, the moon, which 'governs the night,' being the measurer of time. Tacitus says of the Teutons that they count the number of nights, not of days, for the night seems to precede the day. Cæsar writes of the Celts that they define the divisions of seasons not by days but by nights, and observe times in such an order that day follows night.[9] A Celtic myth embodying these ideas has not come down to us.

2. Origin of light.—In some of the myths just cited the origin of light from darkness, or from the creation of sun and moon, is already found. As in the Maori myth, light is sometimes prior to the sun (cf. Gn 1[3. 14]). Some other examples of such myths may be cited. In Bushman belief the sun was a mortal on earth from whose body light radiated for a short distance round his house. Some children were sent to throw him up to the sky as he slept, and now he lightens the earth.[10]

[1] K. Rasmussen, *People of the Polar North*, London, 1908, p. 101.

[2] *Ib.* p. 173; *11 RBEW* [1894], pp. 266, 481; H. Rink, *Tales and Trad. of the Eskimo*, London, 1875, p. 237; cf. the idea of the Ticunus that stars are emanations from the face of the supreme God.

[3] Cf. *HAI*, Washington, 1907–10, i. 971; J. A. Farrer, *Prim. Manners and Customs*, London, 1879, p. 244; E. R. Emerson, *Indian Myths*, do. 1884, p. 102; *1 RBEW* [1881], p. 25; *5 RBEW* [1887], p. 540; Frobenius, p. 30.

[4] J. H. Gray, *China*, London, 1878, i. 1; see also CHINA, vol. iii. p. 551b.

[5] J. J. M. de Groot, *Religion in China*, New York, 1912, p. 9.

[6] W. G. Aston, *Shinto*, London, 1905, p. 85.

[7] *Kalevala*, rune 1.

[8] J. Grimm, *Teut. Myth.*, tr. J. S. Stallybrass, London, 1882–88, p. 558.

[9] *Ib.* p. 735; Tac. *Germ.* 11; Cæsar, *de Bell. Gall.* vi. 18; cf. Pliny, *HN* xvi. 44, and see CALENDAR (Celtic) and CALENDAR (Teutonic).

[10] W. H. I. Bleek, *Bushman Folklore*, London, 1911, pp. 45–55.

The Baronga think that the reflexion of light on the sea after the sun's rising is a kind of source of light whence the sun is renewed daily. It is 'cut out from the provision of fire,' and dies in the West nightly. Light is also called 'that which makes to appear.'[1] An E. African myth tells how two men came to a cave, looked in, and saw the sun. One of them removed a stone, and was burned up. Then the sun ascended on high to light the world.[2] According to the Ja-Luo, Apōdtho, father of mankind, appeared from heaven on earth together with the sun, moon, and wind, which fled to the sky when he was angry, and have remained there ever since. The heaven-land has people as bright as fire, and men will go there when they die.[3]

3. Succession of light and darkness, day and night.—In some instances light, not darkness, is primordial; or after creation, while day exists, night is still unknown. Numerous myths relate how darkness is produced and the regular alternation of day and night follows. The Wümbaio, an Australian tribe, say that at one time the sun never moved. Nurelli, tired of eternal day, bade it go down by the west.[4] In Banks Island, Qat, after making all things, did not know how to make night, and it was always day. He heard that there was night at Vava, and went there to get it from I Qong, Night. Returning with it, he bade his brothers prepare for night. The sun now moved westwards; he let go the night, and it was dark. After a time he cut it with a knife, and daylight again shone out. In Lepers' Island this is told of Tagaro.[5] The Meitheis say that at first there were two suns which rose and set alternately. A slave, tired of getting no rest, shot one of them. There was now always darkness. The other sun refused to come forth, but at last did so as a result of certain ceremonies.[6] The savage Malays of Malacca have a myth of three suns, one of which was always left in the sky, The female sun was induced to swallow her husband and child, and now there was night.[7] A native Brazilian myth tells that at first there was no night. Night, or a cobra who owned night, slept at the bottom of the waters. His daughter would not sleep with her husband till he procured darkness from her father. Servants were sent to bring a *tucuman* fruit from him. In spite of all warnings, they opened it, and all grew dark. The daughter now separated day from night.[8] In Santa Cruz sun and moon are said to have travelled together, but by a trick the sun caused the moon to fall into a marsh and went on before her. Night is the result of a part of the moon becoming black through this trick.[9] A Finnish myth says that in the beginning there was nothing but water and light—an unusual version of the cosmogonic idea.[10] In some instances night is formed as the result of a dualism. The Yezidis say that God made the world beautiful. Then Malik-Taūs appeared before Him and said that there could be no light without darkness, no day without night, and accordingly He caused night to follow day.[11] In a Wallachian *Märchen* God sends a bee to inquire of the devil, the master of night,

[1] A. Junod, *Life of a S. African Tribe*, Neuchatel, 1913, p. 282.

[2] D. Macdonald, *Africana*, London, 1882, i. 280.

[3] C. W. Hobley, *JAI* xxxiii. [1903] 328, 331.

[4] Howitt, p. 428; cf. A. Lang, *Myth, Ritual, and Religion*[2], London, 1899, i. 124 f.

[5] R. H. Codrington, *The Melanesians*, Oxford, 1891, pp. 156, 171.

[6] T. C. Hodson, *The Meitheis*, London, 1908, p. 125 ff.

[7] W. W. Skeat and C. O. Blagden, *Pagan Races of the Malay Peninsula*, London, 1906, ii. 338.

[8] F. J. de Santa-Anna Nery, *Folk-lore brésilien*, Paris, 1888, p. 55; Couto de Magalhães, *Contes indiens du Brésil*, Rio de Janeiro, 1883, p. 1.

[9] W. O'Ferrall, *JAI* xxxiv. [1904] 224.

[10] O. Dähnhardt, *Natursagen*, i. 69.

[11] *Ib.* p. 27.

whether there should be one sun or more. The bee rests on the devil's head and hears his cogitations to the effect that, if there are several suns, men will get so accustomed to heat that there will be no fear of hell; night will be as clear as day; and the works of darkness will be brought to an end.[1] In Breton folk-belief God created the day, and the devil made night as an offset to it.[2] The same dualism is found in a Melanesian story in which all that Tagaro makes is good. Suqe, who makes evil things, wished to have six nights to one day, but Tagaro sent him underground to rule the souls of the dead.[3] An extremely naive Macedonian *Märchen* tells how all creation, grateful to the sun for his light and warmth, proposed to reward him with a wife. But the lion said that several suns would be born and all would be burned up. All agreed that it was better for the sun not to marry. In disgust he hid himself in the sea, and all became dark, to the consternation of the animals. But the hen, persuading him that marriage was a disgrace, caused him to rise from the sea every morning.[4] This myth obviously originates from the apparent disappearance of the sun into the sea at night, and his apparent rising from it in the morning. An Eskimo myth relates that sun and moon were once removed, causing darkness which no shaman could dispel. A boy is sent by his aunt to go south, where he will find the light. He arrives at a hut where light like a ball of fire is lying, but it is hidden by a man shovelling snow, which causes obscurity. He steals the light and is pursued. He breaks off pieces, each of which produces day, which is then followed by night. They are of unequal lengths because sometimes he travels a longer time without throwing out light, sometimes a shorter time.[5] This myth exactly reproduces the phenomena of the Arctic dark winter, and the phenomena of days and nights of varying lengths.

4. Gods of light and darkness; sun and moon.—Day and night or their rulers or representatives, sun and moon, are often personified as male and female, or as husband and wife, as in the Eskimo myths already cited (§ 1). This is found in American Indian mythology; and in Australian belief, *e.g.* among the Arunta, the sun is female, the moon male.[6] It is also found among the Andaman Islanders (the sun is the wife of the moon), the Indians of Guatemala, in Central Celebes, in Cumana, among the Ewe and Yoruba, in Tahiti, among the Piutes, among the Ainus, and among the peasants of Oberpfalz.[7] In another American myth day and night are two wives who produce light and darkness by sitting alternately at the door of their tent.[8]

In New Britain sun and moon, to whom belong respectively day and night, are children of Ilu and Mamao, and, having gone up to the sky, have stayed there ever since.[9]

In a Tongan myth Vatea and Tonga-iti quarrel about the parentage of the first-born of Papa, each claiming it as his own. The child is cut in two. Vatea throws one part up to the sky, where it becomes the sun; Tonga-iti throws the other to the dark sky, whence the moon. This is explained as Day and Night alternately embracing Earth, their joint offspring being sun and moon.[1]

In Norse mythology Night and Day are mother and son, set in the sky by All-Father, who gives each a horse and chariot to drive round the earth. The sun also has a chariot.[2]

In many of the myths just cited sun and moon are not always regarded as causing light and darkness, or rather day and night. These exist apart from them, though the two are associated together. A clear connexion between them, however, is seen in another group of myths—those of the sun-catcher. In some of these the sun is tied down, as in a Toda instance, by a demi-god. There is at once darkness on the earth and in the under world, whither the sun goes at night. The people of both implore the demi-god for the sun's release.[3] More usually the sun is captured because his course is far too rapid and darkness comes too soon—found in many Polynesian myths—or too erratic, as in a Ute myth.[4] Sometimes, however, he is captured in order to lengthen the ordinary day, and this group is then connected with magical rites which have also this for their purpose.[5] Again, he is captured by some persons who wish to amuse themselves, but it becomes so hot that the captors run away.[6] The second group of myths is obviously suggested in answer to such a question as was raised by the Inca prince: Why cannot the sun wander freely about? Clearly because he obeys the will of a superior being. This is an idea found also in the mythologies of the higher culture.

For further examples see *Mélusine*, ii. [1884–85] 556; Lang, *Myth, Rit. and Rel.*[2] i. 124 f.; E. B. Tylor, *Early Hist. of Mankind*[2], London, 1870, p. 346 ff.

Light and darkness, day and night, sun, moon, and stars are often personified or worshipped as gods, or the sun, moon, and stars, as sources of light, are the dwellings of gods. Thus the Ainus believe in a spirit of light who lives in the sun or animates it (*ERE* i. 242[a]). Many African tribes have a high god, often the sky personified, and many of them worship the heavenly bodies as sources of light. Loba, the high god of the Bakwīrī, has a name signifying originally Heaven or Sun, and so in many other instances.[7] Shango of the Yoruba is the sun, dwelling in a flaming house of brass; one of his train is Biri, the darkness.[8] The Kavirondo worship the moon and the sun, the latter regarded as apathetic, occasionally beneficent, but usually malignant.[9] Among the ancient Teutons and Celts sun and moon were also divinities to whom a cult was paid.[10] Among the Polynesians Ka-ne is the sunlight and Tangaloa is the lord of light, his brother being Rongo, god of dark and night.[11] The Andaman Islanders connect Puluga, their high god, with the sky, where he set the sun and moon, who give light by his command and have their meals near his house.[12] Among the Hottentots Tsuni-Goam, the red dawn, is opposed to the dark sky personified as Gaunah.[13] With the

1 A. Schott, *Walach. Märchen*, Stuttgart, 1845, p. 283 f.
2 P. Sébillot, *Folk-lore de France*, Paris, 1904–07, i. 135.
3 Codrington, p. 169.
4 Dähnhardt, p. 130.
5 *18 RBEW* [1899], pt. 1, p. 484.
6 *21 RBEW* [1903], p. 174; Spencer-Gillen[a], p. 561.
7 E. H. Man, *JAI* xii. [1882–83] 160; O. Stoll, *Guatemala*, Leipzig, 1885, p. 275; Lasch, *ARW* iii. 134, 107; Ellis, *Ewe-speaking Peoples*, London, 1890, p. 66, *Yoruba-speaking Peoples*, do. 1894, p. 83; A. Bastian, *Inselgruppen von Oceanien*, Berlin, 1883, p. 46; Lang, *Myth, Rit. and Rel.*[2], i. 131; *ERE* i. 242[a]; Lasch, *ARW* iii. 139.
8 E. Petitot, *Trad. ind. du Canada nord-ouest*, Paris, 1886, p. 16 ff.
9 G. Brown, *Melanesians and Polynesians*, London, 1910, p. 363.

1 W. W. Gill, *Myths and Songs from the S. Pacific*, London, 1876, p. 45.
2 Grimm, pp. 735, 737.
3 W. H. R. Rivers, *The Todas*, London, 1906, p. 592.
4 G. Turner, *Nineteen Years in Polynesia*, London, 1861, p. 248; Taylor, *Te Ika a Maui*[2], p. 100 (in this case Maui beats the sun and makes it lame); Gill, pp. 62, 70; Grey, *Polynes. Myth.*, p. 24 f.; *1 RBEW*, p. 24.
5 Waitz-Gerland, vi. 253; cf. *GB*[3], pt. i., *The Magic Art*, London, 1911, i. 311 ff.
6 E. Nordenskiöld, *Indianerleben*, Leipzig, 1912, p. 294 (Chané Indians).
7 W. Schneider, *Die Rel. der afrik. Naturvölker*, Münster, 1891, pp. 43, 62, 80.
8 Ellis, *Yoruba-speaking Peoples*, p. 46 f.; Frobenius, p. 232 f.
9 G. A. S. Northcote, *JRAI* xxxvii. [1907] 63.
10 Grimm, p. 704.
11 Gill, pp. 10–14; Grey, p. 1 ff.
12 E. H. Man, *JAI* xii. 160 f., 166.
13 T. Hahn, *Tsuni-Goam*, London, 1881, pp. 124, 126.

Fijians Ndauthina is god of light and fire, whose love of light in his infancy was so great that his mother bound lighted reeds to his head.[1]

5. Regions of light and darkness.—As in the higher religions the beneficent or loftier gods are connected with light or dwell in the sky (cf. 1 Ti 6[16], 'dwelling in the light which no man can approach unto'), so it is also in savage belief. The Australian high gods, Būnjil, Mūngun-ngaur, and Baiame, dwell in the sky or in Keladi, 'eternal brightness,' and the Nurali of the Murray River tribes is an embodiment of light.[2] The higher Polynesian gods, Tangaroa, Tangaloa, Tii, etc., dwell in the light heavens, seven or ten in number.[3] The Khonds reverence Būra Pennu, god of light, or Bella Poona, the sun-god, whose dwellings are the sun and the place where it rises. Puluga, the Andaman high god, lives in the sky. This is true also of many African gods; *e.g.*, the Zulus hold that the creator lives in heaven, and Nzambi Mpungu of the Fiort dwells behind the firmament.[4] Similarly one of the names of the supreme being of the Indians of Guiana signifies 'the Ancient One in Skyland.'[5] Many of the Teutonic gods, some of them gods of light, dwelt in the sky, where Valhalla was situated.

'From the sky the gods descend to earth, along the sky they make their journeys, and through the sky they survey unseen the doings of men.'[6]

So also Elysium, the abode of the blest, whether it is in the sky or on or below the earth, is always a region of light and brightness. In contradistinction to this, the abode of unhappy spirits in all mythologies is dark and gloomy, in this resembling the abode of the shades in religions where no distinction had yet been made between good and bad spirits—the Bab. Arallu, the Heb. Sheôl, the Greek Hades (see the series of artt. on BLEST, ABODE OF THE).

The subterranean Pueliko or Tartarus of the Caroline Islanders is cold and dark.[7] In Polynesia, as Po, or darkness, was the primal source of light and of the gods of light, so it is also conceived as the subterranean place of night whither departed spirits go.[8] In Nanumea the wicked go to a place of mud and darkness.[9] The Japanese Yomi, or Hades, means 'darkness,' and it is presided over by Susa-no-wo, a personification of the rain-storm, and a moon-god, ruling also the darkness of night.[10] The Scandinavian Niflhel is a place of darkness surrounded by fogs and gloom (see BLEST, ABODE OF THE [Teutonic]).

6. Evil powers and darkness.—Evil gods, gods of death, etc., are often associated with darkness, or divinities who are not evil have often acquired a sinister aspect in so far as they are associated with the night or even with the moon, the ruler of the night. The Sakai believe that the lord of hell, a cavern in the interior of the earth, is a friend of darkness and cannot bear the light.[11] In Polynesia Rongo, brother of Tangaroa, is god of darkness and night; Hine-nui-te-po, the great mother night, into which all must fall, is a personification of night and death.[12] Some Australian divinities to whom evil powers are ascribed are connected with darkness and night.[13] The Japanese Susa-no-wo, already referred to, is another instance. Much more generally all evil spirits, demons, ghosts, and the like are associated with darkness, which men's fears peopled with them.[14]

In S.E. Guinea evil spirits called *werabana* inhabit dark places and wander about at night; and in New Britain Kaia, a spirit causing disease, earthquake, etc., lives in craters and dark places.[1] The Tasmanians thought that lower spirits concealed themselves in dark ravines by day and came forth at night to do harm.[2] The Australians also peopled the darkness with a variety of horrible beings ready to pounce upon men.[3] Innumerable other examples from savage belief might be cited. Similarly, among the Celts and Teutons a variety of demoniac and supernatural beings were associated with the darkness, and in folk-superstition generally fairies, witches, demons, werwolves, vampires, and ghosts are most powerful in the hours of darkness, especially 'at the lone midnight hour when bad spirits have power.'[4] See artt. DEMONS AND SPIRITS, FAIRY, LYCANTHROPY, VAMPIRE.

Among savages, as also among higher races, there is a wide-spread fear of the darkness. Many savages will not travel or even leave their huts or camp at night; or, if they do so, they must be armed with firebrands and the like to keep evil spirits at a distance, since these fear the light. Thus we find magical rites to overcome the terror of darkness; *e.g.*, in New Caledonia the priest, when cutting the umbilical cord of a boy, had a vessel of water before him, dyed black as ink, in order that when the child grew up he might not fear to go anywhere on a dark night.[5] For similar reasons an eclipse of the sun or the moon is universally feared. Generally a monster is supposed to be destroying these bodies, and, since they are so often regarded as the sources of light, it is feared that their destruction would mean a return to the primordial darkness. Every precaution is therefore taken to scare off the destroying monster or to bring to an end whatever other mythical cause is attributed to an eclipse.[6] In connexion with the belief that evil spirits have power in the dark must be noted the wide-spread idea that their power ceases at dawn, or that, if they are surprised by daylight, they are destroyed. This applies to all evil beings, demons, witches, fairies, etc. See art. FAIRY.

7. Dualism of light and darkness.—The contrary nature of light and darkness, the qualities instinctively associated with each—life with light,[7] death and terror with darkness—might easily suggest to primitive minds a species of natural dualism. The day seems to be swallowed up by night, again to appear and drive it away; at an eclipse sun or moon is wholly or partially concealed by darkness, figured as a beast or demon, but again emerges victorious. Hence in some instances on the lower levels of culture light, or day, and darkness, or night, may be personified and regarded as in conflict. That this was the case is obvious from such a dualistic system as the Parsi, which is fundamentally concerned with an older natural dualism of light and darkness, giving rise to a moral dualism of good and evil. The same dualism is found sporadically in other higher religions, and in faiths in which the influence of Parsiism was felt,[8] also perhaps in such a dualism as exists in the religion of the Buriats (*q.v.*). On the other hand, since light, day, sun, seem to rise out of night, they are perhaps more often regarded as produced by darkness, rather than hostile to it, as in Polynesian mythology and elsewhere (§ 1). It is also probable that modern inquirers into savage myths have too readily assumed that mythical personages represented, on the one hand, light, sun, or dawn, and, on the other, darkness and night, and that myths of a contest between a hero and a demoniac being necessarily meant a contest between light and dark-

1 E. Thomson, *The Fijians*, London, 1908, p. 113.
2 *JAI* xiv. [1885] 313, xiii. [1884] 193; R. Brough Smyth, *Abor. of Victoria*, Melbourne, 1878, i. 423.
3 Gill, pp. 4, 13; Ellis, i. 114, 325; Waitz-Gerland, vi. 240 f., 299.
4 H. Callaway, *Rel. System of the Amazulu*, Natal, 1870, p. 49 f.; A. Lang, *Making of Religion*², London, 1900, p. 228.
5 E. F. im Thurn, *Among the Indians of Guiana*, London, 1883, p. 365.
6 Grimm, p. 698.
7 F. W. Christian, *Caroline Islands*, London, 1899, p. 75.
8 Ellis, i. 396; Waitz-Gerland, vi. 267 f.
9 Turner, *Samoa*, p. 292.
10 Aston, pp. 53, 137 f.
11 Skeat-Blagden, ii. 286.
12 Gill, pp. 4, 10–14; Taylor, p. 100; Ellis, i. 323 f.
13 Waitz-Gerland, vi. 800 f.
14 See *ERE* iv. 623a.

1 Brown, *Melanesians and Polynesians*, pp. 235, 357.
2 A. Ling Roth, *Abor. of Tasmania*, London, 1899, p. 53.
3 Waitz-Gerland, vi. 801; Brough Smyth, i. 457; Spencer-Gillen^b, 496.
4 Sir W. Scott, *Eve of St. John*, verse 24.
5 Turner, *Samoa*, p. 341.
6 Lasch, *ARW* iii. 97–152; also art. PRODIGIES AND PORTENTS.
7 Cf. P. Giran, *Magie et rel. annamite*, Paris, 1912, p. 118.
8 See Dähnhardt, pp. 27 ff., 48.

ness. While it is possible that certain American myths adumbrate such a contest, it is likely that, on arbitrary philological grounds, such an interpretation has been too easily applied to them.[1] One aspect of such a mythic strife may be seen in the beings associated with light and darkness rather than in these themselves personified. Thus the demoniac beings who have power in the darkness are generally powerless and are not feared by day (§ 6), or those connected with gloom and darkness are often regarded as opposite in nature or opposed to divinities or spirits of light—*e.g.*, gods residing in the heavens. In primitive religion decisive examples of a conflict between light and darkness are few in number, but the mythic method is seen in the words of a Basuto who described nature as given up to perpetual strife—the wind chasing the clouds, darkness pursuing night, winter summer, etc.[2] If, as has been supposed, the Polynesian Maui is the sun (though, as has been seen, Maui captures the sun), then the story of how he intended to pass through the body of Hine-nui-te-po, but was unsuccessful and died, and so brought death into the world, might be a myth of the sun or light being swallowed up by darkness.[3] In Khond belief the supreme creator, Būra Pennu, the light- or sun-god, is opposed, not by darkness, but by Tari Pennu, the earth-goddess, the bringer of disease, death, and other evils.[4] Japanese mythology preserves a story of the retirement of the sun-goddess to the rock cave of heaven, leaving the world to darkness, because of the misconduct of her brother Susa-no-wo, the storm-god and later ruler of Yomi (the dark Hades). The gods dance in front of the cave, and she comes out to see them and is prevented from re-entering. Light is thus restored to the world. This suggests a myth of the strife between light and darkness. Later Shinto theologians allegorize the goddess's retirement as emblematic of the darkness of sin, and the renewal of light as signifying repentance.[5] Grimm has suggested that many phrases in Teutonic languages used of light and darkness, day and night, show the one as a hostile, evil power in contrast to the kindly character of the other, and that there is perennial strife between the two.[6]

LITERATURE.—O. Dähnhardt, *Natursagen*, i. 'Sagen zum Alten Test.,' Leipzig and Berlin, 1907; L. Frobenius, *Die Weltanschauung der Naturvölker*, Weimar, 1898; R. Lasch, 'Die Finsternisse in der Myth. und im rel. Brauch der Völker,' *ARW* iii. [1900] 97–152; *Mélusine*, ii. [Paris, 1884–85] 554 ff.; E. B. Tylor, *PC*³, London, 1891, *passim*.

J. A. MACCULLOCH.

LIGHT AND DARKNESS (Chinese).—The Chinese outlook on life and attitude towards religion give more prominence to light than to darkness.

The two principles which pervade all nature and to which everything is assigned—the *yin* and *yang* principles, the dualistic elements of Chinese philosophy—are also the two headings into which light and darkness are differentiated. *Yin*, it may be said, is darkness, and *yang* light. The latter stands for the upper world of light; the former for the nether world of gloom and semi-darkness.

It is difficult to classify as gods of darkness any of the gods of the Chinese, unless Yāma (Yen-ma, Yen-lo), the ruler of Hades, with his entourage of officials and demons, be considered as such. The light of the sun is wanting in the Chinese nether world; it is a land of shades and of the shadow of death, for a twilight gloom prevails. The idea of hells in Taoism was derived from Buddhism; but the conception was developed on different lines. Utter darkness reigns in eight hells out of the millions of various abodes of punishment in the future world of Chinese Buddhism.[1]

In the primitive religion of the ancient Chinese nature-worship was prominently apparent, and remnants of this are still found: in the erstwhile Forbidden City, or Inner City, of Peking there is a splendid altar to Light. The sun, according to the Chinese, is the source of all brightness, and the masculine principle in nature is embodied in it, while the moon is considered to be the essence of the female principle. The philosopher Chu Hsi said:

> 'In the beginning heaven and earth were just the light and dark air. . . . The subtle portion of the air . . . became heaven and the sun, moon, and stars. . . . Light and darkness have no beginning.'[2]

The 'visible darkness' that engulfs the sun and moon at an eclipse is supposed popularly to be the effect of a monster swallowing them. Mandarins under the old regime offered worship as an official duty during an eclipse, soldiers fired muskets, and priests clanged cymbals and chanted prayers to the sun and moon. While all this was going on, the populace fired crackers and clashed pots and pans to frighten the monster away.[3]

There is an altar to the sun to the east of the Tatar City of Peking. That to the moon is outside the west wall.[4]

In that ancient Chinese classic, the *Yi King*, or *Book of Changes*, one of the trigrams is an emblem of light or brightness.[5] Light and brightness are the symbols of, or attributes applied to, goodness and virtue.[6] The rising of the brightest object in the sky is suggestive of advancing, and Hû Ping-wăn of the Yuan dynasty (A.D. 1280–1367) thus applies it:

> 'Of bright things there is none so bright as the sun, and after its pattern he [the superior man] makes himself bright.'[7]

These instances show that the Chinese early seized on the striking symbolism of light and darkness to represent a mental or moral condition as well as a physical one; and this expressive language has continued in use. It appears now and again in the *Tâo Teh Ching*:

> 'We should attemper our brightness, and bring ourselves into agreement with the obscurity of others.'[8] 'Use the light that is within you to revert to your natural clearness of sight.'[9]

There is the goddess of lightning, worshipped by both Buddhists and Taoists, who, according to the popular mythology, was appointed to accompany the god of thunder on his expeditions to prevent his making a mistake, for on one occasion, finding the white rind of a melon flung away, in the darkness of a smoke-begrimed Chinese kitchen, he mistook it for rice and killed with his chisel and hammer the supposed waster of good food. To prevent the recurrence of such an event the goddess carries a mirror in each hand, or one in her two hands, and flashes light on objects before the god strikes. This is the explanation of 'the lightning's fiery wing.'

The god of fire is another of the gods connected with light. His name, Hwa Kwang, may be rendered 'Beautiful Light.' Unlike the majority of the popular gods, he was not originally a human

1 For these myths see D. G. Brinton, *Myths of the New World*, Philadelphia, 1896, p. 198 ff.; Tylor, *PC*³, ii. 290 ff. For some arguments against these views see A. Lang, *Nineteenth Cent.* xix. [1886] 50–65, and *Custom and Myth*², London, 1893, p. 197 ff. (against Hahn's theory of a contest of light and darkness in Hottentot mythology).

2 E. Casalis, *Les Bassoutos*, Paris, 1859, p. 253.

3 Grey, *Polynes. Myth.*, p. 38 f.; Waitz-Gerland, vi. 261, 267.

4 S. C. MacPherson, *Memorials of Service in India*, London, 1865, p. 84.

5 Aston, p. 100 f.

6 Grimm, p. 752.

1 E. J. Eitel, *Handbook of Chinese Buddhism*², London, 1888, p. 105b.

2 T. McClatchie, *Confucian Cosmogony*, p. 53 ff., quoted in S. Wells Williams, *Middle Kingdom*, revised ed., London, 1883, ii. 141.

3 See H. C. Du Bose, *The Dragon, Image, and Demon*, London, 1886, p. 71.

4 See Mrs. A. Little, *Guide to Peking*, Tientsin, 1904, p. 33 ff.; cf. Ezk 8¹⁶.

5 J. Legge, *Yi King*, *SBE* xvi. [1882] 136, note.

6 *Ib.* p. 310.

7 *Ib.* p. 311, note.

8 J. Legge, *Texts of Taoism*, *SBE* xxxix. [1891] 50.

9 H. A. Giles, *Chuang Tzŭ*, London, 1889, p. 19; see *Tâo Teh Ching*, ch. lii.

being, but a lamp, of which the snuffings of the wick were turned into a man by the recital of a charm. He is the form and soul of fire.[1] Both Buddhists and Taoists claim him.

The Buddhists deify light by personification in the *bodhisattva* Marīchī Dēva. The Chinese represent her with eight arms. In two of her hands she holds up emblems of the sun and moon. She is the goddess of light, and protects nations from war. Among her other titles is that of Queen of Heaven. The Taoists also claim her as one of their deities, and fix her residence in a star in the constellation of Sagittarius.[2]

Buddha after Buddha, commencing with Śākyamuni Buddha, has light as one of his attributes, or some manifestation of light appears in the course of his life in connexion with him. Five-coloured lights flashed at his birth, and flame burst from his dead body.[3] Every Buddha has, among his characteristics, a circle of hairs between his eyebrows by which he can illuminate the universes.[4]

'Light' and 'Brightness' often appear in the names given to different Buddhas, as well as occasionally to others, and to different objects. Among these names of Buddhas, present or to come, supposed to be real or fictitious, are such as 'Brightness of the Law,' 'One whose feet display myriads of Luminous Figures,' 'The Buddha of Fixed Light,' 'Light and Bright,' 'The Bright Effulgence of Sun and Moon,' 'The Clear and Bright Efficacy of Sun and Moon.' The 930th Buddha of the present *kalpa* is called 'The Buddha of Wonderful Light.' Some twenty billions of Buddhas have the title of 'Cloud Sovereign Illuminating King.' Five hundred *arhats* will reappear as Buddhas with the name of 'Wide-spreading Brightness.'[5] Some of the demons in which Buddhism believes shed a glare of light.[6] A realm mentioned in Buddhism is 'The Realm of Great Light.'[7] One of the sixteen (or eighteen in Northern Buddhism) celestial worlds is that of 'Light and Sound,'[8] and another is that of 'Unlimited Light.'[9] Buddhism has five 'Luminous Treatises.'[10] A fictitious degree of *samādhi* is also called 'Pure Light and Brightness,' and another 'Pure Light.'[11]

In Northern Buddhism the 'Buddha of Boundless Light,' diffusing great light, Amitā (Amitābha), originated in the ideal of boundless light, and was thought of at first as impersonal. He is the most popular of all the Buddhas among the Chinese people. In his heaven, the wonderful and glorious Paradise of the West, two Buddhas 'radiate light over three thousand great worlds.'[12] Amitā Buddha himself, in the words of the Chinese poem singing his praises, has a

> '. . . halo of light that encircles his head,
> . . . .
> The sun at noonday is less glorious than he.'[13]

As to those who enter that heaven,

> 'The material body of men while on earth
> Is exchanged for another ethereal and bright,
> That is seen from afar to be glowing with light.'[14]

This new mystical school makes use of the symbolism of light in its description of religious states of its devotees.[1] In some cases light plays an important part in the advent to earth of a god on his incarnation, and even one of the mythical emperors of China, the Yellow Emperor (2698 B.C.), owed his origin to this.

With the Taoist gods, a ray of light shoots down arrow-like from heaven to the future mother shortly to be delivered of a child, and thus the divine is blended with the human in the infant, who has sometimes to expiate some sin from which his godlike nature has not saved him, or to cure or to eradicate some infirmity still inherent in his moral nature.

We find a brilliant light in connexion with the preparations for the birth of the Taoist Gemmeous Sovereign, the Supreme Ruler, and in his later incarnations a golden light or a glimmering light[2] descends. Somewhat similar experiences occurred when the Taoist Aged Sire united with light, and became dust and was born on earth.[3] A Taoist writer of the Yuan dynasty says that light broke forth spontaneously in the primordial void, springing from itself in the heart of the void, and his idea would appear to be that to attain illumination one must empty oneself as the primordial void of which he speaks was empty.[4]

The word 'Light' is used as one of the Chinese clan-names or surnames, as it is in English, but it also appears sometimes as an individual name bestowed on an infant, and occasionally in union with some other character in a name selected later in life.

LITERATURE.—This is sufficiently cited in the footnotes.

J. DYER BALL.

LIGHT AND DARKNESS (Christian).

—The symbolical use of the words 'light' and 'darkness' is very common in early Christian literature, and in the main was derived from the OT, as will be seen by the references given below. As time went on, the metaphor of light served as one method of expressing the theological conception of the Persons of the Holy Trinity.

1. The symbolism in the NT.—We may pass by the obvious metaphor by which to speak or act 'in the light' is to do so 'openly,' and to speak or act 'in the darkness' is to do so 'secretly,' as in Mt 10^{27}, Lk 12^{3} (cf. Jn 18^{20}, and Eph 3^{9}, 1 Co 4^{5}). More to our purpose are the numerous passages where 'light' denotes knowledge, truth, and holiness, and 'darkness' denotes ignorance and sin—ignorance in all its phases being included in the latter simile: absence of knowledge, spiritual blindness, error, and wickedness; for blindness, if wilful, becomes sin. The opposition between light and darkness is expressed in Jn $3^{19f.}$; men had the opportunity, for light is come into the world, but they loved the darkness rather than the light, for their works were evil—'every one that doeth ill hateth the light.' 'Darkness' expresses the state of the world before the Incarnation (Jn 1^{5}, Lk 1^{79}); the idea is taken from Is 9^{2}, where it is said that 'the people that walked in darkness have seen a great light.' To be in a state of sin and ignorance is to walk, or sit, or be in darkness (1 Jn $1^{6.\,8}$ 2^{9}, Jn 8^{12}, 1 Th $5^{4f.}$, Ro 2^{19}, Lk 1^{79}). In Jn 8^{12} the 'light of life' is the light 'which both springs from life and issues in life' (B. F. Westcott, *Gospel according to St. John*, London, 1908, *in loc.*). The metaphor is very common in the Johannine writings, but it is frequently found elsewhere. In Mt $6^{22f.}$ the 'body full of light' (φωτεινόν) denotes purity and holiness, and the 'body full of darkness' (σκοτεινόν) denotes evil; so Lk $11^{34f.}$ (cf. Pr 14^{18}).

[1] See Dyer Ball, 'Scraps from Chinese Mythology,' in *China Review*, Hongkong, 1872–1901, xii. 188 ff., 324 ff., 402 ff.

[2] Eitel, *Handbook*, p. 97 f.

[3] *Ib.* pp. 136^{a}, 138^{b}.

[4] *Ib.* p. 188^{b}.

[5] *Ib.* pp. 38^{b} (1st ed.; the 2nd ed., 55^{b}, does not translate the Chinese), 46^{a}, 129^{a}, 50^{b}, 55^{b}, 173^{b} (the 1st ed. [1870] gives 'The Bright Effulgence,' etc., as translation of the Chinese; the 2nd ed. gives only the Chinese), p. 173^{b} (the same difference between the two editions). Also see pp. 129^{a}, 140^{b}, 116^{a} (1st ed., 141^{a} in 2nd ed.), 165^{b} (here again the Chinese is not translated in the 2nd ed.).

[6] *Ib.* p. 172^{b} f. of 1st ed., 206^{b} of 2nd (the 1st ed. is here fuller).

[7] *Ib.* p. 170^{b} of 1st ed., 204^{b} of 2nd (here again the Chinese is not translated in 2nd ed.).

[8] *Ib.* p. 1^{a}.

[9] *Ib.* p. 15^{b}.

[10] *Ib.* p. 44^{b} of 1st ed., where the term is translated; it is not translated in the 2nd ed., p. 63^{b}.

[11] *Ib.* p. 200^{b}.

[12] J. Edkins, *Chinese Buddhism*², London, 1893, p. 234.

[13] *Ib.* p. 173.

[14] *Ib.*

[1] See T. Richards, *The New Test. of Higher Buddhism*, Edinburgh, 1910, pp. 55, 149, 151, etc.

[2] Dyer Ball, 'Scraps from Chinese Mythology,' in *China Review* xi. 72 ff., 207, 213, 282, 287.

[4] *Ib.* p. 85 f.

[3] See L. Wieger, *Le Canon taoïste*, Paris, 1911, i. 65, no. 246.

In Ac 26^{18} the preaching of the gospel is to turn the people from darkness to light and from the power of Satan unto God. St. Paul uses the metaphor freely. The 'works of darkness' are the evil deeds of the present 'night,' and the 'armour of light' is to be put on in view of the approach of the day (Ro 13^{12}; cf. Eph 5^{11}; for 'night' and 'day' in this connexion see 1 Th $5^{4f. 8}$). We are partakers of the inheritance of the saints in light, and have been delivered out of the power of darkness (Col $1^{12f.}$). The fruit of the light is in all goodness, righteousness, and truth (Eph 5^9 RV). Light has no communion with darkness, and therefore Christians are not to be unequally yoked with unbelievers (2 Co 6^{14}, quoted in *Apost. Const.* viii. 34, to forbid Christians to pray with heretics). So St. Paul uses the verb 'to darken' (σκοτίζω or σκοτόω) in Ro 1^{21} 11^{10} and Eph 4^{18} metaphorically of the hardening of the heart or the blinding of the eyes by ignorance, just as he uses 'to enlighten' (φωτίζω) in a metaphorical sense in Eph 1^{18} (cf. Jn 1^9; see below, § 4). St. Peter speaks of our being called out of darkness into God's marvellous light (1 P 2^9). The curious passage 2 P 1^{19}, where prophecy is as 'a lamp shining in a squalid (αὐχμηρῷ) place,' may be compared with Mic 3^6, where 'darkness' is used of want of spiritual perception in a prophet.[1]

The name 'Light' is given to God. Not only is light a gift of God, but God is by nature 'light' (1 Jn 1^5 φῶς anarthrous); therefore He can be known by His creatures, and is all-holy, for in Him is no darkness at all. This goes much further than Is 10^{17}, where God is called 'the light of Israel,' or Ja 1^{17}, where He is called the 'Father of lights' (τῶν φώτων = the heavenly bodies [?]).

This divine attribute is claimed by or ascribed to our Lord in Jn 8^{12} ('I am the light of the world') 9^5 $12^{35. 46}$, Lk 2^{32}, Mt 4^{16} (from Is 9^2). St. John says that in the Word was life, and the life was the light of men, shining in the darkness; He was 'the true light which lighteth every man, coming into the world,' *i.e.* by His Incarnation (but see Westcott's note), in contrast to the Baptist, who was but a witness of the light (Jn 1^{4-9}). Because He is the light, He will shine (ἐπιφαύσει) on the awakened sleeper (Eph 5^{14}). He is to be a light to all men (Ac 13^{47}, quoting Is 49^6 [the reference is to Jesus, not to St. Paul, though the Apostle identifies his mission with that of his Master]; cf. Is 42^6, where the Servant of Jahweh is to be a light of the Gentiles—a phrase repeated of the 'Son of Man' in *Ethiopic Enoch*, xlviii. 4 [1st cent. B.C. ?]). The phrase 'dwelling in light unapproachable' (1 Ti 6^{16}) might be applied to the Son (so Chrysostom, *Hom. xviii. in 1 Tim., in loc.*) or to the Father, but probably it refers to the Father (cf. Ps 104^2, Dn 2^{22}). See also § 3, below.

In an inferior sense the servants of the Incarnate are 'lights.' The Baptist (see above) is 'a lamp that burneth and shineth,' in whose light the disciples were willing to rejoice for a season (Jn 5^{35}). All Christians are the light of the world (Mt 5^{14} φῶς, cf. Ph 2^{15} φωστῆρες), and are sons or children of light (Lk 16^8, Jn 12^{36}, 1 Th 5^5, Eph 5^8 ['once darkness . . . now light in the Lord']). The angels are angels of light (2 Co 11^{14}; we may compare the light which shone when the angel released St. Peter, Ac 12^7). In contrast to this, the devil and his angels are 'world-rulers of this darkness' (Eph 6^{12}), *i.e.*, as the Peshiṭta paraphrases, 'rulers of the world of this darkness' (meaning 'of this dark world'), and their realm is the 'outer darkness' mentioned in Mt 8^{12} (for Jewish parallels see W. C. Allen's note *in loc.*, *ICC* [³1912]) 22^{13} 25^{30}; this is the place of punishment of sinners, and we may compare Jude ^{6}, where the fallen angels are said to be 'kept in everlasting bonds under darkness (ζόφον) unto the judgement of the great day,' and 2 P 2^{17}, where the 'blackness of the darkness' (ὁ ζόφος τοῦ σκότους) is said to have been kept for evil men. The same idea of punishment is found in *Eth. Enoch*, lxiii. 6, where the wicked say: 'Light has vanished from before us, and darkness is our dwelling-place for ever and ever'; on the other hand, God will for the elect 'transform the heaven and make it an eternal blessing and light' (xlv. 4).

2. The same symbolism in the Fathers.—The symbolism of light and darkness is not so common in Patristic writings as in the NT, but a few examples may be given from the first four or five centuries. At the close of the Apostolic period the *Epistle of Barnabas* (§§ 18–20) describes the two ways, of light and darkness, *i.e.* of good and evil (cf. Dt 30^{15}); over the former are stationed the light-giving (φωταγωγοί) angels of God, over the latter the angels of Satan. In the 3rd cent. Origen calls Celsus's arguments darkness, the truth light (*c. Cels.* vi. 67). Lecturing A.D. 348, Cyril of Jerusalem says (*Cat.* vi. 9) that the Father is eternal light, beaming inexhaustibly. The metaphor is found in the Ancient Church Orders —*e.g.*, in the *Egyptian* (Coptic) *Church Order* (§ 62), the *Verona Fragments of the Didascalia*, etc. (ed. E. Hauler, Leipzig, 1900, p. 119), and the *Testament of our Lord*, ii. 24: 'The Father hath sent His Word [and Wisdom] to enlighten the saints.' In the last-mentioned work (Eng. tr., J. Cooper and A. J. Maclean, Edinburgh, 1902) the symbolism is very common, both in the apocalyptic prologue (where it probably comes from an original apocalypse, perhaps of the 2nd cent.; see *JThSt* xiv. [1913] 601–604) and in the Church Order proper. Christians are children of light (i. pref., 1, 3, 12, 37). In the liturgy of this work (i. 23) God is called 'the Father of lights' (Ja 1^{17}), 'King of the treasuries of light,' 'Illuminator of the perfect,' 'Giver of light eternal.' Elsewhere in the book He is called 'Giver or Maker of light' (i. 26, 43), 'God of the lights . . . Whose veil is the light' (ii. 7). Our Lord is 'Begetter of light . . . Guardian of light eternal,' who has 'shed light on the darkness within us' (i. 26). Jesus is the name of light (ii. 27). The illumination of the heart is frequently referred to (i. 15, 21, 23, 31, 32, 38, ii. 5, 7, 9). Somewhat more sparingly the simile is used in the *Apostolic Constitutions.* Christians are 'children of light' (i. 2, ii. 32, 46, 54), as in the parallel passages of the *Older Didascalia* (see these, arranged on opposite pages, in F. X. Funk, *Didasc. et Const. Apostolorum*, Paderborn, 1905). The Father inhabits light inaccessible (*Apost. Const.* vi. 11, viii. 15, from 1 Ti 6^{16}). Jesus is the true light (v. 16), and the bishop must be a student, and enlighten himself with the light of knowledge (ii. 5; cf. viii. 37). These phrases (except v. 16) are not in the *Older Didascalia.* In *Sarapion's Sacramentary* God is called the 'Fount of light,' and is prayed to give us the (or a) Spirit of light (§ 1; *JThSt* i. [1899] 105, in Funk [*op. cit.* ii. 172], numbered § 13). Gregory of Nazianzus (*Orat.* xl. 5 f. [A.D. 381]) calls angels and men 'light' in an inferior sense, though in the highest sense God alone is light.

In the *Clementine Recognitions*, now thought to be of the 4th cent., Simon Magus, denying that God has a Son, says that there is a power of infinite and ineffable light (*i.e.* God), of which power even the Demiurge, Moses, and Jesus are ignorant (ii. 49).

[1] The metaphor from the contrast between the dimness of a reflected light and the clearness of an open vision, a metaphor which was more obvious, no doubt, in the days of unscientific reflectors than it is now, is used by St. Paul in 1 Co 13^{12}, where he describes our partial knowledge in the present world as seeing 'in a mirror' instead of 'face to face'; but the words which we translate 'darkly' (lit. 'in a riddle') do not carry on the simile.

3. Light as describing the relation of the Father and the Son.—We may now investigate the use of the phrase 'Light of Light' (φῶς ἐκ φωτός) applied to our Lord. In the NT the Father is Light, and the Son is Light; but the above phrase is not used, though in He 1[3] our Lord is the effulgence (ἀπαύγασμα) of the Father's glory and the very image of His substance; the reference seems to be to Wis 7[26], where Wisdom is 'an effulgence from everlasting light . . . and an image of [God's] goodness.' (For various Patristic comments on He 1[3] see Westcott's note, *Epistle to the Hebrews*, London, 1889, p. 11.)

An early approximation to the phrase 'Light of Light' is found in Origen (*de Prin.* i. 1), who says that God is light, illuminating man, and interprets 'thy light' in Ps 36[9] of the Son. In the 2nd cent. Justin had used the illustration of fire kindled from fire with reference to the Son and the Father (*Dial.* 11, 128); and Tatian (*c. Græc.* 5) re-echoes his words. So also Tertullian (*Apol.* 21) says that a ray of the sun is still part of the sun; there is no division of substance, but only an extension; thus Christ is Spirit of Spirit, and God of God, as light of light is kindled. But Athanasius sees a danger in the metaphor of fire. He says (*de Decretis*, v. 23) that the Son is not as fire kindled from the heat of the sun, which is commonly put out again, but is 'effulgence' (ἀπαύγασμα), signifying that He is from the essence, proper and indivisible, of the Father, and is one with Him (see A. Robertson's note on the passage in *Nicene and Post-Nicene Fathers*, iv. [1892] 165). Arius in his letter to Alexander had quoted Hieracas as saying that the Son was from the Father as a light from a light (λύχνον ἀπὸ λύχνου), or a lamp divided into two (quoted by Epiphanius, *Hær.* lxix. 7). In the small treatise *In illud 'Omnia,'* 3 (on Lk 10[22]), Athanasius says that Christ, the Light, can never be separated from the Father. In *Orat. c. Arian.* iv. 2 the writer speaks of the Word as 'Light from Fire,' and in iv. 10 compares the Father and the Son to fire and the effulgence from it, 'which are two in being and in appearance, but one in that its effulgence is from it indivisibly'; but it is uncertain if this fourth Oration is by Athanasius.

Later in the 4th cent. (A.D. 381), Ambrose says that 'the Father is Light, and the Son is Light, and the Holy Ghost is Light, and the Holy Ghost is both Light and Fire,' referring to Is 10[17] (*de Spir. Sanct.* i. 14 [160 ff.]). The well-known hymn φῶς ἱλαρόν ('Hail, gladdening Light'), sung at the Lamp-lighting, calls the Son the 'gladdening Light of the holy glory of the immortal, heavenly Father'; it is older than Basil, who apparently quotes it (*de Spir. Sanct.* xxix. [73], A.D. 374).

The phrase 'Light of Light' is found in the creed of Nicæa and in the enlarged creed (called the creed 'of Constantinople') which came into general use. It was derived by the former from the creed of Eusebius of Cæsarea, which, as Eusebius told the Nicene Fathers, had been handed down from preceding bishops of that see, and used in the baptismal catechesis; this creed had 'God of God, Light of Light, Life of Life' (Socrates, *HE* i. 8). On the other hand, the phrase 'Light of Light' is not in the creed of Gregory Thaumaturgus (*c.* A.D. 265), which has only 'Sole of Sole (μόνος ἐκ μόνου), God of God' (it is given in *Ante-Nicene Chr. Lib.* xx. [1882] 5). In Cyril of Jerusalem (*Cat.* iv. 7) the Son is called 'begotten Life of Life, begotten Light of Light'; in xi. 4 Cyril repeats this phrase and adds 'Truth of Truth, and Wisdom of Wisdom, and King of King, and God of God, and Power of Power' (cf. xi. 18). The phrase 'Light of Light' occurs in R. H. Connolly's reconstruction of Aphraates' creed (4th cent.; *JThSt* ix. [1908] 280), but not in the creeds of the various Church Orders, though those of the *Apost. Const.* (vii. 41) and of the *Egyptian* (Coptic) and *Ethiopic Church Orders* are of the Eastern type (those of the *Testament of our Lord*, the *Canons of Hippolytus*, and the *Verona Fragments* are the Western or Roman creed). It is instructive to note the different creeds of the Council of Antioch in Encæniis, A.D. 341. The second creed has 'God of God, Whole of Whole, Sole of Sole, Perfect of Perfect, King of King, Lord of Lord, the living Word, the living Wisdom, [Life], the true Light,' etc. The third creed has merely 'perfect God of perfect God.' The fourth creed, drawn up by a continuation of the Synod, has 'God of God, Light of Light . . . who is the Word and Wisdom and Power and Life, and the true Light' (these creeds are given in Athanasius, *de Synodis*, 23, 24, 25, and the second and fourth in Socrates, *HE* ii. 10, 18; see them also in Hefele, *Councils*, Eng. tr., Edinburgh, 1876, ii. 77–80). With reference to the phrase in question Basil, when dealing with the relation of the Son to the Father, and speaking of the phrase 'like in substance' (ὅμοιον κατ' οὐσίαν), says that he will accept the phrase if the word ἀπαραλλάκτως ('without any difference') be added, as equivalent to the Homoousion:

> 'Being of this mind the Fathers at Nicæa spoke of the Only-begotten as "Light of Light," "Very God of Very God," and so on, and then consistently added the Homoousion. It is impossible for any one to entertain the idea of variableness of light in relation to light, of truth in relation to truth, or of the essence of the Only-begotten in relation to that of the Father' (*Ep.* ix. 3, to Maximus).

Passing to later times, we note the curious fact that the phrase does not occur in the present Nestorian Creed (F. E. Brightman, *Lit. East. and West.*, Oxford, 1896, p. 270), though it is in that of the Nestorian Catholicos Ishuyaw (Īshō'yahbh) I., A.D. 595, which is given by W. A. Wigram, *The Assyrian Church*, London, 1910, p. 291.

Reviewing the evidence, we conclude that the appearance of the phrase in a creed cannot be affirmed before the 3rd cent., though perhaps (in view of Eusebius's word 'bishops' in the plural as above) it was so used early in that century; Cæsarea was perhaps its first home. But before this there is earlier evidence (in the 2nd cent.) of the use of the symbolism of 'Light of Light,' though not of the phrase itself. Even after Nicæa it was not by any means universally adopted into creeds. It will be remembered that the creed of Nicæa was a test of orthodoxy, and was not at first used liturgically; it was not, apparently, for some time used at baptisms, and was not introduced into the Eucharistic service till the end of the 5th century. It is not surprising therefore that, in spite of the great authority of the Council of Nicæa, the phrase in question did not at once spread very rapidly.

4. Baptism and light.—In the early Church the symbolism of light was closely connected with the sacrament of initiation. Baptism was, especially by the Greeks, called 'illumination,' φωτισμός or φώτισμα, as in Justin (*Apol.* i. 61), in Gregory of Nazianzus (*Orat.* xl. 1; cf. ii. 36), once in the *Apost. Const.* (ii. 32, where it expressly includes the laying on of hands; in vi. 1 and viii. 12 the word is used literally, of the pillar of fire, and in ii. 5, v. 1 metaphorically, of knowledge; cf. 2 Co 4[4, 6]), and in the *Older Didascalia* (*Verona Latin Fragments*, ed. Hauler, p. 87: 'post inluminationem quod dicit Græcus fotisma,' with reference to He 6[4] [not in the corresponding passage of *Apost. Const.*]). Similarly the selected candidates for baptism were called φωτιζόμενοι, 'those who are in process of being illuminated' (Lat. *competentes*), and the baptized were called 'the illuminated' (οἱ φωτισθέντες)—as in Justin (*Apol.* i. 61, 65, *Dial.* 122), Clement of Alexandria (*Pæd.* i. 6), who quotes Eph 5[8] of baptism, and wrongly derives φώς, 'man,' from φῶς, 'light,' Cyril of Jerusalem (*Cat.*, Introd. I. xi. 1, xiii. 21), and the *Apost. Const.* (viii. 8 and 35); Eusebius says that Constantine at his baptism 'was filled with heavenly light' (*Vit. Const.* iv. 62). For this reason the baptistery was often called in Greek φωτιστήριον; the *Arabic Didascalia* (§ 35), which derives its account of the church buildings from the *Testament of our Lord*, i. 19, transliterates this name into Arabic (Funk, *Did. et Const. Ap.* ii. 124 f.).

This symbolism is found also in the NT. In He 6[4] 10[32] the aorist participle φωτισθέντες ('illuminated'), denoting a definite act, clearly refers to the Christian act of initiation, and the Syriac versions, both the Peshiṭta and the Ḥarqleian, in translating these passages, explicitly refer them to baptism. The metaphor has been thought to have been derived from the Greek mysteries, though the NT μυστήρια are quite unlike the heathen ones in that in the former the *revelation* of the unknown is what is emphasized (cf. Mk 4[11], 1 Co 4[1] 13[2] 14[2], and Col 1[26], where see Lightfoot's note).

The custom of the candidates for baptism carrying torches probably came from the metaphor, not the metaphor from the custom, which is perhaps alluded to by Cyril of Jerusalem (*Cat.*, Introd. and i. 1) and certainly in pseudo-Ambrose (*de Laps. Virg.* v. [19], A.D. 374 [?]).

There is a 2nd cent. legend, mentioned by Justin (*Dial.* 88), that, when Jesus was baptized, 'a fire was kindled in Jordan.' It is mentioned in the apocryphal *Preaching of Paul*, in the Ebionite Gospel, and in the Old Latin codices 'a' 'g' (in Mt 3[16] they read 'lumen ingens' or 'magnum'; see H. B. Swete, *Holy Spirit in NT*², London, 1910, p. 43 n.), and is a commonplace of Syriac literature. In the Diatessaron it was related that a light flashed on Jordan and the river was girdled with white clouds. This reading is attested by Barṣalībī and Īshō'dādh (see F. C. Burkitt, *Evangelion da-mepharreshe*, Cambridge, 1904, p. 115).

From the baptismal metaphor, Epiphany was called 'The Holy Lights' (cf. Greg. Naz. *Orat.* xxxix. and xl. 1); our Lord's baptism is the event principally commemorated at that festival in the East (see, further, art. EPIPHANY).

5. **Liturgical use of lights.**—There are many traces of the symbolic use of lights in Christian services, from the 4th cent. onwards. Perhaps the earliest is in connexion with funerals. At the Spanish Council of Elvira (*c.* A.D. 305, can. 34) the custom of burning candles in the day-time in a cemetery was forbidden, lest the spirits of the saints should be disturbed—a custom probably borrowed from the heathen (see Hefele, *op. cit.* i. 150). But in some form the custom continued. Lights were carried, as in heathen, so in Christian, funeral processions; see Gregory of Nyssa, *de Vita S. Macrinæ* (near the end, ed. Paris, 1638, ii. 201 A; *c.* A.D. 380), and *Funeral Oration on Meletius* (near the end; A.D. 381). Eusebius says (*Vit. Const.* iv. 66) that Constantine's body lay in state 'surrounded by candles burning in candlesticks of gold, presenting a marvellous spectacle'; and Gregory the Great (*Ep.* ix. 3, to Januarius, A.D. 598) speaks of relatives at a funeral offering lights for churches.

About the 4th cent. we find the symbolic use of lights in other Christian services. In the *Testament of our Lord* (i. 19) it is directed that all parts of the church 'be lighted, both for a type, and also for reading.' The derived *Arabic Didascalia* expands this phrase thus: 'Let them be lighted with many lights as a figure of heavenly things, especially in the reading of the pericopae of the sacred books' (§ 35; Funk, *op. cit.* ii. 125). It has been suggested that lights had necessarily been in use in the catacombs and in the assemblies before dawn in times of persecution, and that, when churches were built above ground in times of peace, the usage was continued and was given a symbolic turn (W. E. Scudamore, in *DCA* ii. 993 f.). This may be partly true, though it does not explain all the circumstances of the case. For we find lights also used as a decoration at festivals, as when Paulinus of Nola (*c.* A.D. 407; † A.D. 431) describes the innumerable festal lights burning night and day as a sign of rejoicing (*Poem.* xiv. [*de S. Felicis Natalit.*, carm. iii.] line 99 ff.). 'Etheria,' or 'Silvia' (whose *Peregrinatio* has usually been dated at the very end of the 4th cent., though many scholars think it is somewhat later), describes the same thing as happening daily at Jerusalem (part of this work is given in App. 5 of L. Duchesne, *Christian Worship*, Eng. tr.³, London, 1912; see pp. 493, 498). This was also a heathen custom (Juvenal, *Sat.* xii. 92). Again, we find lights carried processionally in front of a person, as in the *Ordo Romanus Primus* (*c.* A.D. 770), where seven candles are carried before the pope before mass (ed. E. G. C. F. Atchley, *Ordo Rom. Prim.* §§ 7 f., 21). In the *Ordo* in the MS of St. Amand (Duchesne, p. 457) two candles are lighted when the pope says mass, and are placed behind the altar in candlesticks, right and left. A 5th cent. ivory at Trèves exhibits candles carried in procession (W. C. Bishop, in the *Prayer Book Dictionary*, p. 435). In these cases the Christian custom comes straight from the heathen—in the case of the processional lights from the custom of carrying lights before the emperor—and we cannot trace them to the usage in the catacombs.

Three other symbolical usages in connexion with lights may be noticed. (*a*) *Gospel lights, i.e.* lights used at the reading of the liturgical Gospel at the Eucharist, are mentioned by Jerome (*c. Vigilant.* 7; A.D. 378), and are said by him to have been universal in the East, 'not so as to put darkness to flight, but by way of showing our joy' (he also attests the use of lighted tapers in honour of martyrs). Later on these lights at the Gospel are often mentioned—*e.g.*, in the *Ordo Rom. Prim.* § 11. (*b*) *The Paschal candle* was blessed on Easter Even ('benedictio cerei'), and is alluded to, perhaps by Augustine (*de Civ. Dei*, xv. 22; A.D. 413–426: read 'in laude . . . *cerei*'), certainly by Gregory of Nazianzus (*Orat.* xlv. 2) and Gregory the Great:

> 'the prayers . . . said over the wax taper, and the exposition of the Gospels given by priests about the time of the Paschal solemnity' (*Ep.* xi. 33).

The candle was carried before the *competentes* to the font (cf. § 4, above), and denoted the rising of the Sun of righteousness. The *Liber Pontificalis* says that Pope Zosimus (A.D. 417) extended the custom of blessing the Paschal candle to the parish churches of Rome. (*c*) The office of *Tenebræ* is found from the 7th or 8th cent. onwards—an extremely symbolic service on the night which ushers in Good Friday. After each of the three nocturns one-third of the lights were extinguished, except that seven remained, which were gradually put out during matins, the last when the Gospel was read (*DCA* ii. 994ᵃ).

We may ask what is the meaning of this symbolism of lights when transferred to Christianity, and used in its services. Putting aside the lights carried before a dignitary, we gather that the general idea was that, on the one hand, Christ is the Light of the world, and that, on the other, Christianity is the religion of light and Christians are children of light. Theirs is an open religion, not confined to the few, like the Greek mysteries, not hiding itself, as those cults which became so common in the heathen world, and loved darkness rather than light. Such seems to be the symbolism of the liturgical use of lights.

LITERATURE.—(1) For the subject of light as expressing the relation of the Father and the Son see especially the works of Athanasius, and the edition of A. Robertson, *Select Writings and Letters of Athanasius*, tr. and notes, Oxford, 1892 (the Index, *s.v.* 'Light' and 'Simile,' gives a useful list of passages); see also E. C. S. Gibson, *The Three Creeds*, London, 1908, iii. 1. (2) For the liturgical use of lights see W. E. Scudamore, *Notitia Eucharistica*², London, 1876, and art. 'Lights, Ceremonial Use of,' in *DCA*; E. G. C. F. Atchley, *Ordo Romanus Primus*, London, 1905; W. C. Bishop, art. 'Lights' in the *Prayer Book Dictionary*, do. 1912; C. E. Hammond, art. 'Paschal Taper' in *DCA*. (3) The symbolism of the NT is treated by F. H. Woods in *HDB* and J. Moffatt in *DCG*, artt. 'Light.' On the whole subject see also the works mentioned in the course of the article. A. J. MACLEAN.

LIGHT AND DARKNESS (Greek and Roman).—In the fields of the Hellenic and the Italic civilizations we have in historic times a divinity recognized as supreme, Zeus or Jupiter, who is a personification of the sky and the daylight that fills it. He has counterparts in the religious systems of kindred races. Among Greeks and Romans and peoples subjected to their influence there are two groups of contrasted divinities, those of the upper world (*θεοὶ οὐράνιοι, di superi*) and those of the under world (*θεοὶ χθόνιοι, di inferi*), the former the authors of life and increase and prosperity, the latter of death and waning and misery to mortal creatures.

1. Greek.—Certain varying waves of tendency, changing the behaviour of believers towards these two classes, may be discerned in the history of the Greeks. There was a time when the chief sacred centres had mysterious connexion with the realms of darkness, when the fear of obscurity had more power over the religious consciousness than the delight in heavenly radiance. The spots at which there were reputed entrances to the domain of Hades and darkness were numerous in early Greek days. In many instances, subterranean phenomena, earthquakes, sulphurous or mephitic emanations, disappearing rivers, or medicinal waters had much to do with the superstitions that gathered round such places. Even in historic Greece practices of a primitive character were maintained in such localities, for in religions the new never entirely drives out the old; there is always superposition of strata. At Tænarum, a promontory of Laconia, there was a cleft through which Herakles and Orpheus had both passed when they visited the infernal shades. In the *Frogs* (186), Aristophanes puts an absurd speech in the mouth of Charon, the ferryman of the Styx, ridiculing these popular ideas. Most of the ancient oracles were connected with sites where there was communication with the nether darkness. This is illustrated by the story of the visit of Æneas to the Cumæan Sibyl, as told by Virgil, and by the behaviour at Delphi of the Pythian priestess, the mouthpiece of the oracular Apollo. The secrets of the future have been supposed in all ages to be in the keeping of spirits below, while in Greek literature the sun has knowledge of all the secrets of the present. The name 'necromancer' indicates the persistence of the belief about the dwellers in the regions of darkness.

As time went on, many of the places which had been principally associated with the powers of darkness passed into the possession of divinities who were mostly of the light. This was strikingly the case with Delphi, where, as the later Greeks said, the worship of the chthonian deity Earth (Gē or Gaia) was succeeded by that of Apollo, god of brightness. As civilization and culture strengthened, the reverence paid to the gods beneath was apt to be left to the uninstructed, and to pass into the backwater of superstition. Some of the figures of the dark were partially transformed into figures of the light. Thus it was with Demeter and Persephone as they appeared in the historic age in the mysteries celebrated at Eleusis. Hades, the consort of Persephone, underwent a like change, indicated by his later name Plouton (Pluto), *i.e.* god of wealth or prosperity. The change of view was sometimes aided by euphemism, causing dreaded deities to be propitiated by well-sounding titles. So the avenging spirits of gloom, the Furies, were venerated as 'Eumenides,' 'benevolent ones' (cf. artt. EUMENIDES, ERINYES; EUPHEMISM).

A profound alteration was wrought in the religious conceptions of the Greeks by the rein given to their myth-making fancy and to their artistic genius, working on things divine. As human traits were inwrought into the texture of dimly apprehended superhuman existences, and were enwrapped by the clouds of poetry and the dreams of art, their original connexion with natural objects became veiled, and in some cases was forgotten. The process had already been carried far when the Homeric poetry arose in its glory. Some figures that did not very readily lend themselves to transformation received little notice in later worship. Eos, the dawn-goddess, is prominent in Homer, but, as she is also too obviously the dawn, she is present but little in later ritual. Ovid remarked that her temples were the rarest in the world (*Metam.* xiii. 588). But the divine being who is wreathed in poetry and art does not generally lose that particular contact with nature which gave him his origin. Zeus remained the actual source of events in the sky. Where we say 'it rains' or 'it snows,' the Greek said 'he rains,' or 'he snows,' and sometimes mentioned the name of Zeus. Horace speaks of the hunter camping at night 'under the chilling Jove' (*Od.* I. i. 25). Apollo was always connected with the sunlight, Artemis with the moon, and so with many others. When the overgrowth of legend became abundant, there was an impulse to return to the veneration of actual heavenly bodies. Thus the worship of Helios, the sun, went on side by side with that of Apollo. Naturally, in historic times the development of mythology produced a mixture of attributes, and the interference of many divinities with one and the same function. The appearance and disappearance of the heavenly bodies suggested that the realms of light and darkness had intercommunication. Hermes, in the main a god of brightness, becomes a conductor of souls to regions below. Moreover, light was sometimes really baneful and at other times was thought so. Therefore Apollo, the sun-god, has a mission to destroy life, as well as to preserve it by medicine and to enhance its value by poetry and music. Dionysos, whose connexion with the sun is clear, also has to do with the shades; and so with other divinities. The bad effects of heat led to the idea that Pan, the god of the open country, is most to be dreaded at noon-day, for then he can inflict madness. The mild gleams of the moon and the divinities who guide them were usually beneficent, but sometimes had the contrary activity. The waxing moon is of good intent, the waning moon brings sickness and death. Hekate, a moon-goddess, kindly and supernal in the earlier age of Greece, became later a malignant power of darkness. It may be remarked that the reverence paid, with clear consciousness, to astral bodies as such was never at any time so marked in historic Hellas as among Babylonians and Semites. As a religious motive it belongs rather to the late Hellenic age, and the age of Græco-Roman civilization, and even then, as we shall see, it affected the outer fringes of Greek civilization, where it was wrestling with barbarism, rather than its heart and centre.

Besides the light of heavenly luminaries, great and small, there is the irregular and alarming fire from heaven, the lightning. The deities who rule the regular light also send lightning, especially Zeus, one of whose chief emblems is the thunderbolt, and also Athene and Apollo. It is sometimes a sign of divine anger, as when Semele died by its stroke, sometimes an indication that the god has signified his will and given a presage of the future. To interpret the sign is, of course, a matter for an expert. Lightning was thus connected with divination and prophecy, and spots struck by the sacred bolt were revered.

The fire which is of use to men on earth could not but be regarded as in its origin divine, and as venerable, being a symbol of the eternal. The apparent everlastingness of the fire of which sun, moon, and stars are the manifestations doubtless contributed to the importance of fire in the ritual of worship. A vein of thought which lies deep in the nature of men in the earlier stages of religion, that the gods are envious of human beings and grudge them the things of which they wish to possess themselves, is illustrated by the legends of which Prometheus was the centre. The gift of fire was one which the gods would fain have withheld, and they punished him who outwitted them. A number of Greek divinities have relations with the earthly fire. Hephaistos, the great metal-worker, uses the fierce subterranean flames which find vent in the crests of Ætna and the Lipari Isles. In Homer and the poets generally he is the maker of all the weapons, emblems, and equipments of the Olympians, of the sceptre of Zeus, of the arrows of Apollo and Artemis. Hestia, goddess of the family hearth, has an especial connexion with earthly fire. She is the only one of the greater divine beings whose name has a transparent significance in life, equivalent to the hearth of the house, always regarded as in some sense an altar. As every house had this altar, so the great State family had its central hearth-altar for all the burgesses. When a city sent out some of its sons to found a colony afar, the central fire of the new community was lighted from the central fire of the old home. When a city was under a monarch or despot, its common hearth was in his dwelling; in a republican community it was in the town-hall (πρυτανεῖον) (see, further, art. HEARTH, HEARTH-GODS [Greek]). The conception of Hestia remained one of the clearest and simplest in the range of Greek religion. Where the name of a divinity retains an obvious meaning, he does not lend himself to a covering of myth. Another divinity in whose ritual fire was conspicuous was Dionysos or Bacchus. The pine-tree and the torches that it provides figure in the Bacchic revels, as depicted, for instance, by Euripides in his *Bacchæ*. What we call the St. Elmo's fire was connected with the great twin-gods, the Dioscuri, Castor and Pollux.

The gods of light and darkness must have a potent influence on life, and especially on the beginnings of life. The hearth-fire itself was treated as a symbol of the generation of the human being, and a growth of legend and ritual was developed from this idea. The light-bringing divinities are very naturally those who bring the child out of the pre-natal darkness into the light of life, and many deities were at different times and in different places supposed to exercise this function (cf. art. BIRTH [Greek and Roman]). Zeus himself to the latest age was a god of birth; but the powers that guide the milder radiance of the moon rather than those that wield the fiercer splendour of the sun had chiefly this duty, and the greatest among them was Artemis.

The mysteries of the darkness beyond the grave, in which departed souls were hidden, gave rise to multifarious practices and beliefs. There were many divine beings who either ruled the dead or guarded souls against the perils of the passage from this world to the next. There is no portion of the field of Greek religion in which the development of ideas from Homer's age to the time of the latest Greek philosophic speculation was more complex. The notion of a possible deliverance from the bonds of death prompted a series of beautiful tales, such as that of the restoration of Alcestis to Admetus, the theme of the fine tragedy of Euripides, the recovery of Eurydice by Orpheus, or of Persephone by Demeter. In this connexion the most interesting evolution, from a religious and social point of view, is to be found in the Greek mysteries. They represent the striving of souls on earth to be assured of safety in the perilous passage from the bed of death to a happy abiding-place in the world beyond. Starting from gross forms, in which enchantment had a great part, the mysteries were refined and moralized so as to satisfy the higher yearnings of the spirit, and to instil that better hope in death which, Cicero says, was given by initiation at Eleusis (*de Legibus*, ii. 36).

During the great age of Greece there was among the Hellenes no wide-spread conception of such a mysterious influence of heavenly bodies on human life as was systematized by the Chaldæan astrologers. This lore came from Eastern lands, especially Babylon, and was only in loose contact with religion; it was devotedly followed only in a later time, and then more in the sphere of Roman than in that of Greek civilization. The same is true of the real religious veneration of sun, moon, and stars. But mystic ideas concerning these entered into the earliest Greek thought—that of the Orphic and Pythagorean schools. The express attribution, however, of divinity to the heavenly bodies appears comparatively late in the history of Greek philosophy. Plato, in his *Timæus* (p. 38 f.), describes the fixed stars as divine existences brought into being by the 'Workman' (Demiurgus) of the universe at the bidding of the supreme god. In other passages he assigns divine character to the sun, moon, and planets. He was followed, with variations, by later thinkers—Xenokrates, Herakleides of Pontos, and many others. Aristotle described the celestial bodies as containing a great divine element, and pointed out that this belief, now explicitly declared by philosophers, was implicit, in an obscure form, in the popular mythology. Like doctrine was taught by the Stoics and particularly by Cleanthes, who considered that in the sun lay the guiding principle (ἡγεμονικόν) of the universe. It was common to call the heavenly bodies 'visible gods' as opposed to the unseen divine power. These notions were prevalent among the Neo-Pythagoreans. Apollonius of Tyana (*q.v.*), the seer and wonder-worker of the late 1st cent. A.D., venerated the sun at dawn, like many an Oriental of to-day. That the practice was popular in Greece is shown by the salute which Sokrates offers to the rising luminary, at the end of his great drinking-bout, in the *Symposium* of Plato. The Neo-Platonists, who powerfully affected the thought and religion of the Roman imperial period, embraced and developed beliefs like those that have been cited. Philo, the great Alexandrian Jewish philosopher, was in this respect fully in accord with the Greeks. An idea that was wide-spread in the philosophic schools, and especially favoured by the Stoics, was that the contemplation of the heavenly bodies in their purity and in the regularity of their operations had an ethical value for the regulation of human conduct.

2. Roman.—Among the Romans notions concerning the regions of light and darkness were clothed in some distinctive forms. The dread of evil that might befall if the inhabitants of the nether world, the departed spirits of mortals, did not receive their due from the living was much more marked than in Hellenic communities. In the historic time, till Christianity prevailed, the bodies of the dead were cremated, but some of the attendant ceremonies pointed to a remote age when inhumation was the rule (cf. art. DEATH AND DISPOSAL OF THE DEAD [Greek]). In primitive days the tomb must have been regarded as the only place haunted by the ghosts, and down to the latest age it was so treated in many ceremonial practices. But quite early a conception must have sprung up of a general habitation for those who were colloquially called 'the majority.' The Romans, however, never imagined for themselves a judgment beyond the tomb, which should assign one dwelling-place for the good, another for the bad. The great scheme pictured by Virgil in *Æneid* vi., which has stimulated the imagination not only of poets but of many religionists ever since, was drawn after Greek patterns. The genuine Roman under world was a tract of gloom, and the spirits were minded to do harm to the living unless their wants were supplied, though to avoid offence they were called 'good people' (*manes*). The ritual for the foundation of a new city required that somewhere near its centre an underground chamber called *mundus* should be provided, into which were cast fruits of the earth, probably to satisfy the hunger of the dead, though that may not have been the only purpose of the *mundus*. This chamber was opened at stated times mentioned in the calendar, when fresh offerings were made to the departed, who were thus kept in order and restricted to appearances on the days set apart. These gifts, presented by the nation as a whole to the nation's dead, were parallel to the private presentations at each of the family tombs. Special days for the service of the dead existed in Greece, but they were never so general or so precisely ordered as among the Romans. There was one *mundus* on the Palatine Hill supposed to have been the work of Romulus when he founded Rome ; there was another in the Forum, and others elsewhere. Offerings at these places were made to all the *di inferi*—a phrase in which dead mortals are included, as being in some sort divine. Every Roman tombstone was inscribed 'Dis manibus,' 'to the divine spirits.' The *Larvæ* and *Lemures*, to whom propitiatory offerings were made, are merely the ghosts regarded collectively, in their unsatisfied and therefore terrifying aspect.

As to special divinities of the realms beneath, the earliest worshipped at Rome seems to have been Tellus, Mother Earth, 'the parent of all things and their common tomb,' as Lucretius calls her (v. 259). In the later age she was less and less regarded, in consequence of the attractiveness of Greek invasions in the sphere of religion. Names like Genita Mana, Lara, and others invoked in the *indigitamenta* (*q.v.*), appear to have been epithets of Earth. So, in Greece, Gaia was in some sense a goddess of the dead, and the same attribute was, of course, given to the divinized figure of Earth in other mythologies (cf. art. EARTH, EARTH-GODS, § 8).

A curious place of communication with the infernal regions was a spot called 'Terentus' in the Campus Martius, where probably at one time mephitic vapours escaped. This became in 249 B.C. the centre for a cult newly imported from Greece—that of Dis (whose name is a rendering of Pluto or Plouton) and Proserpina. The cult was probably grafted on to more ancient and purely Roman ceremonial. The blend gave rise to the characteristically Roman 'secular games,' celebrated theoretically, but not always in practice, at intervals of a century, to ensure the safety of the city. The most famous celebration is that ordered by Augustus in 17 B.C., when Horace acted as laureate and supplied the *Carmen Sæculare*.

The idea of a communication with the realms of darkness through an opening in the earth can be traced in other directions. The *devotio*, whereby a citizen could give himself up to the powers of gloom and thereby secure a favour for his country, is an example. Livy (vii. 6) and other ancient writers have told how, in 362 B.C., Curtius, riding in full armour, made his horse jump with him into a chasm in the Forum, which closed up after him. The spot retained the name of 'the pool of Curtius.' Here in the reign of Augustus the populace cast down coins every year on the emperor's birthday, to secure his welfare (Suetonius, *Aug.* 57). The *devotio* of the Decii, who vowed themselves to death by the enemy, thereby binding the powers to favour the safety of the country, was somewhat different. But, should the devoted man fail to find his death, the terms of his vow were satisfied by burying a lay figure in the earth with due ceremony—a curious example of the ease with which the gods might be cheated in Roman ritual. The walling up of the erring Vestal Virgin is an instance of the penal application of the *devotio*.

It is hard to discover in Roman religion the worship of divinities clearly connected with heavenly objects before the time when Greek and Oriental influences became powerful. Even the relation of Jupiter to the light of the sun does not come out with distinctness. The word 'Leucesie' addressed to him in the very primitive hymn that survived in the ritual of the 'Arval Brothers' (*q.v.*) refers to him as god of light, and a corresponding epithet 'Lucetia' was applied to Juno, indicating a connexion between her and the moon. The antiquarian scholars of the late Republic declared that Titus Tatius, the Sabine king of Rome, had introduced the worship of the sun and moon into Rome from his own country, and that a temple of the sun on the Aventine was founded by him. This was the opinion of Varro (*de Ling. Lat.* v. 74), and Tacitus (*Ann.* xv. 41) attributed a temple of the moon (Luna) on the Capitol to Servius Tullius. But the official Roman calendar of festivals, which is known to enshrine very ancient usage, gives no sign of official reverence paid to sun or moon, nor have we any sound evidence of a public priesthood devoted to them either at Rome or elsewhere among Italic peoples, though Varro assigned such an office in old days to the *gens* of the Aurelii. They were supposed to have come from the country of the Sabines, in whose tongue *ausel* denoted the sun. The Aventine, as is well known, was a home of cults introduced from Greece. The existence of a deity called Noctiluca (the 'night-shining one') on the Palatine is hard to explain. The situation implies high antiquity, for no god realized as foreign was allowed to take up an abode within the *pomerium* of the city before the age of the Second Punic War. The name may have been an epithet of Juno, who was connected with the sky. In a ceremony connected with the fixing of the calendar she was addressed as Juno Covella, 'Juno, goddess of the sky.' The name Lucina (closely connected with *lux*) was attached to her as the power which brought the child to light and birth. When the ancient Italic goddess Diana was equated with Artemis, the function of the Greek goddess, as superintending human birth, was transferred to Diana.

The veneration of Volcanus as god of fire belongs to an old stratum in Roman religion ; but, unlike Hephaistos, he was worshipped, it seems exclusively, as protector against danger to men from fire. He was a popular divinity, and his cult was one of those which longest survived the introduction of Christianity. The forms with which another divinity, Vesta, was venerated were remarkably characteristic of the Roman people. Her affinity with fire and her kinship with the Greek Hestia are obvious; but the worship of Vesta among Romans is far more conspicuous than that of Hestia among Greeks, possibly because the structure of the Roman family resisted the assaults of time more stoutly than that of the Greek family. A great feature of Roman religion is the parallelism in many respects of the religious ceremonial of the family and that of the State. And the private and public worships of Vesta resemble each other not a little. Every house had a cult of Vesta, and the name was restricted to the divinity; it had no connotation like the name Hestia, which meant 'hearth' as well as goddess. So thoroughly is Vesta a Latin deity that outside Latium hardly any signs of her existence have been found—a surprising fact when the similarity between Hestia and Vesta is remembered. In the home the cult of the goddess belonged to the matron and the virgin daughters, whose duty it was to see that the fire on the hearth was not extinguished. The centre of worship for the great State family was the ancient shrine of Vesta in the Forum, and no other public temple or altar devoted to her service existed before the end of the Republican period. The temple of Vesta was of the antique round shape derived from that of the earliest Roman house. Close by dwelt her priestesses, the Vestals, of whose abode important remains have come to light in recent days. The temple never contained an image, for Vesta was the one ancient divinity in Rome who never succumbed to the anthropomorphic impulses of her worshippers. The only symbol of the goddess was the eternal fire, whose extinction imported calamity to the land. Lapse of duty or impurity of life on the part of a Vestal was an omen of disaster, only to be averted by the sacrifice of the sinner. The Vestals were the daughters of the community, regarded as one vast family. Augustus, who loved to present himself as the restorer and maintainer of the most ancient Roman rites, connected Vesta with the dwelling-place of the imperial family on the Palatine. The Pontifex Maximus had a public residence close to the house of the Vestals. Augustus made this office an appanage of the emperor, and made over the official house to the Vestals. He then set aside with proper ceremony a portion of his palace on the Palatine to replace it and established there a second State temple of the goddess (see, further, art. HEARTH, HEARTH-GODS [Roman]).

We turn now to the later age of Rome. The conscious worship of the sun marked distinctively the dying days of Roman paganism. The oldest shrine dedicated to the sun was on the Quirinal, and seems to belong to the time of the Second Punic War, and to be a result of the mighty tide of religious influence which then invaded Rome from Hellas. A desire to venerate the sun was manifested, however, earlier, when he appeared with his attributes on the Roman coinage. Augustus placed in Rome two Egyptian obelisks before the temple of Cæsar, and they were supposed to be devoted to the sun. Vespasian transformed into a representation of the sun a great colossal figure erected by Nero in his own honour. Several influences contributed to increase Roman reverence for the luminary, to which inscriptions from the end of the 1st cent. A.D. bear increasing evidence. Some of the most powerful divine invaders who came from the East to conquer the West were solar divinities. Also, as mentioned above, philosophers and mystics had preached the divine nature of the sun and other celestial bodies. Immigrants from the East, and Romans, especially soldiers, who had resided there, brought the religion of the sun with them. The notable drift of sentiment towards monotheism aided the movement, for the one god was often, and not unnaturally, identified with the sun. It was not, however, till after Caracalla, by his universal gift of Roman citizenship to the inhabitants of the cities of the empire, had cut away the ground for fencing off the civic gods of Rome from those of other communities that public and formal recognition was given to these Oriental beliefs. A remarkable event in the history of Roman religion was the accession to the throne of Elagabalus, who bore the name of an eastern solar god, whose priest he had been, like his ancestors before him. This was the divinity of the Syrian city of Emesa. The boy-emperor deposed Jupiter from his supremacy among Roman deities, and, placing his own god in the vacant seat, brought to Rome the round black stone which was the symbol (τύπος) of the god. In his array of titles the emperor made his office as 'priest of the unconquerable sun Elagabalus' (*Sacerdos invicti solis Elagabali*) take precedence of the ancient designation of Pontifex Maximus. This was done in spite of the fact that the divine ruler of Emesa was sometimes correlated with Jupiter, probably because the eagle was an emblem of both. A temple was built contiguous to the Palatine residence of the emperor, and to it were removed the fire of Vesta and other venerable possessions, the Palladium that came from Troy, the shields of the Salii, archaic priests of Mars, and the stone which symbolized the Great Mother (Magna Mater), whose essentially Oriental divinity had been, curiously, recognized four centuries earlier than that of any other immigrant from the East. To give completeness to his innovation, Elagabalus made the foundation-day of the temple the same as the traditional foundation-day of Rome itself, the twenty-first day of April. He also ousted Vesta from the Palatine, where Augustus had planted her, and gave her place to the god Elagabalus. The ritual of the usurping god contained Oriental features revolting to the Roman mind. Among the emperor's pranks was a marriage between his divinity and the goddess of Carthage, sometimes identified with Juno and called 'the heavenly,' sometimes with Venus. It was about this time that 'Juno Cælestis' came to be widely venerated in the West, as connected with the moon. The religious revolution of Elagabalus found some favour in the army, always a nursery of Orientalism. But, when his memory was laid under condemnation, the divinity of Emesa suffered with him and was exiled from Rome.

The sun-god was to be glorified again, but in a saner fashion, in a later part of the same century, by Aurelian. He erected a fine temple in honour of 'the unconquerable god of the sun.' His biographer (*Hist. Aug.* 25) narrates a miracle which occurred when Aurelian defeated Zenobia and her host under the walls of Emesa. At a critical moment he was encouraged by a divine form, which appeared again to him in the temple of Elagabalus within the city and was identified with that divinity. The writer supposed that the god established at Rome by Aurelian was Elagabalus; but the condemnation that this divinity had undergone makes the idea improbable. Some scholars have thought that Aurelian's god was the god of Palmyra, also connected with the sun. But it is most likely that the emperor did not wish to correlate him with any particular Oriental manifestation. The only indication connected with the East is the epithet 'unconquerable' (*invictus*). Aurelian specially associated the god with old Roman practice by denominating the new College of priests as 'Pontifices.' The sun was selected by the emperor as embodying the monotheistic conception; and, in so far as that is concerned, he may be said to have borrowed from the East. An interesting inscription recently discovered in Mœsia records how Licinius the elder and Licinius the younger ordered the consecration of an image of the sun and the establishment of a ceremony in his honour just before the great crowning victory of Constantine, won near Adrianople in 323 B.C. Some years before, Constantine had ceased to place the sun on his coins, a practice common since Aurelian's time.

We come now to the most dominant of all the representatives of the sun in the Roman sphere—Mithra, who is named 'Mithra the unconquerable sun' in many inscriptions. The Mithraic system was complex and many-sided, however, and this is only one aspect of the god. His cult embraced elements derived from many sources, not only from the Persian religion in which his origin is to be found, but from Babylon and elsewhere. Sun, moon, and stars were prominent in the ritual. The extraordinary spread of Mithraism in the Roman empire was mainly the result of tendencies which we have noted in other directions. The vogue of Mithra was especially notable on the frontiers of the empire and in the camps situated there. But many of his shrines have been found in the inner lands, especially on the sites of seaports. At Rome he was venerated on the Janiculum, where M. Gauckler a few years ago discovered a remarkable shrine. Another lies under the church of San Clemente, and memorials have been found also where the Vatican now stands. The popularity of the Mithraic worship was specially due to the provision which it made for satisfying some yearnings which afterwards found a fuller gratification in Christianity. So many were the resemblances between the religion of Christ and that of Mithra that Christians attributed them to the subtle malevolence of evil demons. The religion spread rapidly among the freedmen and soldiers, but also attracted the educated and the officials, and found favour with princes. Its close-knit organization, with its official priests and its ascending grades of illumination, kept believers together in the manner of the Christian rites. It owed much of its hold over the West to the moral element which its mysteries embodied. It instilled into its votaries a higher aim in life and a better hope in death than any other form of pagan creed. The conversion of Constantine, however, gave it its deathblow. Like other heathen cults, it lingered on to the end of the 4th cent., revived a little in the intervening time through the restoration of the forbidden gods by Julian, who himself entertained a religious veneration for the sun. It may be observed that Mithraism never took any great hold on Greek lands where the Greek culture had been long established. It is found in contact with Hellenism chiefly on the outskirts of Greek civilization in the East and on the Danube (see, further, art. MITHRAISM).

In conclusion, we may note that the evil associated with the darkness left its mark on some usages connected with the administration of the Roman State. The taking of augury, which preceded the carrying out of many public affairs, originally took place at dawn. It was just as the sun was rising that Romulus saw the flight of eagles which gave him the kingship. No public business was valid unless conducted between sunrise and sunset—neither meetings of assemblies or of the Senate, nor the administration of justice. Cicero reproached Mark Antony for having carried through decrees of the Senate after the sun had sunk ('Senatus consulta vespertina,' *Phil.* iii. 24). Something of the same usage can be seen in Greece, but the rules there were never so rigid.

LITERATURE.—All information in matters connected with this article can be found in a few publications, in which the results of recent investigation are put together. W. H. Roscher's *Lexicon*, now approaching completion, is invaluable. O. Gruppe, *Griechische Mythologie und Religionsgeschichte*, Munich, 1906, is important on the Greek side, and G. Wissowa, *Religion und Kultus der Römer*², do. 1912, on the Roman. Roman religion has been interestingly treated by W. Warde Fowler, *Roman Festivals*, London, 1908, and *Religious Experience of the Roman People*, do. 1911. Many illustrations of the topics here treated will be found in *GB*³.

J. S. REID.

LIGHT AND DARKNESS (Hindu).—The great contrast between light and darkness with their life-stirring and life-suppressing influence has naturally in all ages taken deep root in the human mind, which welcomed the reappearance of light as the release from the night or the long darkness of winter, and transformed the contrast of light and dark into one of life and death, freedom and bondage, good and evil, virtue and sin. The great representative of light, life, freedom, and goodness was to the mind of ancient India Uṣas, the goddess of dawn, and her rival Rātri, the night, or, in a sense more averse to human life, *tamas*, the darkness. The imperishability of light found its expression in the personification of Aditi, which other scholars explain merely as eternity (cf. Hillebrandt, *Ved. Myth.* iii. 105 ff.).

Uṣas is not only a goddess of the dawn of every day; in many songs that glorify her reappearance the turn of the year is alluded to, and Uṣas means the first dawn of the New Year (cf. A. Ludwig, *Der Rigveda*, Prague, 1876–88, iv. p. xi, vi. 173ᵃ; Hillebrandt, *Ved. Myth.* ii. 25 ff.). Uṣas is partly the Ōstara of the Rigveda poems (F. Kluge, *Zeitschrift für deutsche Wortforschung*, ii. [1901] 42). She brings back the sun, the fire, the sacrifice which has been discontinued during the decaying period of the year; sometimes she is also called *sūryā* or *ekāṣṭakā*, and under the name *saramā* she became the mother of the two heavenly dogs, the *sārameyas*.

The Indians divide the year into two periods, the Uttarāyaṇa, when the sun proceeds towards the north, and the Dakṣiṇāyana, when he goes towards the south, the light half of the year being sacred to the gods, the dark half to the dead. Sometimes (e.g., *Śatapatha Brāhmaṇa*, II. i. 3. 1) it is said that spring, summer, and the rains are the god-seasons, while autumn, winter, and the cold season are the *pitaraḥ*-seasons, sacred to the *manes*. We may begin the New Year with the winter solstice or with Easter time, according as we lay greater stress upon an astronomical or a practical point of view. Indian writers also oscillated between the two possibilities, and faced the problem in the same manner as their brothers did among Teutonic, Slavic, and Italian tribes (cf., *e.g.*, F. M. Müller, *Contributions to the Science of Mythology*, London, 1897, ii. 715). The Vedic authors speak of the dark half of the year as *tamas*, and originally meant thereby the winter, the personification of which was Vṛtra, not the retainer of the heavenly rain, as has generally been believed, but the demon of winter, who was slain by Indra, and who regains the light and sets free the streams bound by the fetters of frost and ice. This idea was inherited from pre-historic times, and formed under the influences of a more northern climate than that of the Indian plains. The farther the Aryan tribes advanced towards the south, and the longer they settled under a milder climate, the less that idea harmonized with the surroundings and the actual climate; the notion of *tamas* was transferred to the really dark season of India—the rains; and the residue of the past and the germ of a new time were thus equally precipitated in the ancient literature. In later times the Holī festival seems to have absorbed most of the customs connected with the New Year festival, though even now the celebration of the Saṁkrānti is by no means forgotten in India; and the splendid spectacle of the bathing festival held about the 12th of January on the banks of the Ganges in Benares will not be forgotten by any one who has happened to witness it.

LITERATURE.—A. Hillebrandt, *Vedische Mythologie*, Breslau, 1891–1902, ii. 25 ff., 77 ff., iii. 188 ff., 204 ff., *Die Sonnwendfeste in Alt-Indien*, Erlangen, 1889 (=*Romanische Forschungen*, v.), p. 299 ff.; H. H. Wilson, 'Religious Festivals of the Hindus' (*Works*, London, 1862–77, ii. 158 ff., on the Uttarāyaṇa; 222 ff., on the Holī rites). On the Holī festival: W. Crooke, *PR*², Westminster, 1896, ii. 313 ff., *Things Indian*, London, 1906, p. 211; J. A. Dubois, *Hindu Manners, Customs, and Ceremonies*², do. 1899, p. 575 ff.; Naṭeśa Sāstri, *Hindu Feasts and Ceremonies*, with an Introduction by H. K. Beauchamp, Madras, 1903, p. 115 ff. ('The Hindu New Year's Day'); F. S. Growse, *Mathurā*³, Allahabad, 1883, *passim*.

A. HILLEBRANDT.

LIGHT AND DARKNESS (Iranian).—The antithesis between light and darkness among the Iranians was closely connected with the antagonism between Ahura Mazda and Ahriman. This feature attracted the attention of Plutarch, who says (*de Is. et Osir.* xlvi.) that Ahura Mazda was born of purest light and Angra Mainyu of darkness, so that τὸν μὲν ἐοικέναι φωτὶ μάλιστα τῶν αἰσθητῶν, τὸν δὲ ἔμπαλιν σκότῳ καὶ ἀγνοίᾳ (cf. Porphyry, *Vit. Pythag.*, p. 41, ed. A. Nauck, Leipzig, 1860; Hippol. *Refut.* i. 2, iv. 43; A. Rapp, *ZDMG* xix. [1865] 48 f.). This view recurs not only in the late *'Ulamā-i-Islām* (tr. E. Blochet, *RHR* xxxvii. [1898] 41) and in al-Shahrastānī's *Kitāb al-milal w'al-niḥal* (tr. T. Haarbrücker, Halle, 1850–51, i. 275), but also in the Armenian writers (*e.g.* Thomas Artsruni, i. 3), while Dio Chrysostom (*Orat.* xxxvi.) goes so far as to make the assertion—not thus far substantiated elsewhere—that, in order to create, Ahura Mazda had to surrender much of his light.

In the Gāthās we find the striking statement that Ahura, 'well-working, created both light(s) and darkness(es)' (*Ys.* xliv. 5). This at once recalls the passage in Is 45⁷, 'I [the Lord] form the light, and create darkness,' but it seems advisable to assume, with J. H. Moulton (*Early Zoroastrianism*, London, 1913, p. 291), that the Iranian and the Hebrew developments are only parallel and not connected (cf., further, E. Stave, *Einfluss des Parsismus auf das Judentum*, Haarlem, 1898, pp. 46 ff., 64 ff., and the 'Semitic and Egyptian' section below, p. 65ᵃ, note 3).

Be the origin of the two what it may—and the true explanation of the Gāthic passage doubtless is, as Moulton maintains, that it is the protest of Zarathushtra against Magian dualism—light is, as is but natural, associated with Ahura Mazda and his supporters, while darkness is connected with Angra Mainyu and his rabble. It was Ahura Mazda who in the beginning filled the blessed realms (*xvāθrā*) with light (*Ys.* xxxi. 7), and in the realms of light (*raocēbīš*) beatitude will be beheld by him whose thought is right (*Ys.* xxx. 1), while the light of the sun is one of the things that glorify Ahura Mazda (*Ys.* i. 11). Apart from the passage already noted, darkness (*temah*) is mentioned only once in the Gāthās, in *Ys.* xxxi. 20, where it refers to the blackness of hell (on the blackness of hell see Moulton, p. 172 f.; F. Spiegel, *Erân. Alterthumskunde*, Leipzig, 1871–78, ii. 121).

In the Younger Avesta the dualism between light and darkness appears in full vigour, so that Spiegel is amply justified (ii. 20 ff.) in dividing his discussion of the Iranian theology and demonology into 'the light side' and 'the dark side' respectively. A phrase which constantly recurs in beginning the laudation of all good deities is 'for his magnificence and his glory' (*ahe raya xvarenanghaca*; for an admirable discussion of the latter word see E. Wilhelm, 'Hvarenō,' in *Jubilee Vol. of the Sir Jamsetjee Jejeebhoy Zarthoshti Madressa*, Bombay, 1914). Light was created by Ahura Mazda (*Ys.* v. 1, xxxvii. 1), and is one of his prerogatives (*Ys.* xii. 1); hence prayer is made to behold 'the creative light of the creative Creator' (*Ys.* lviii. 6), and the light of the sun praises him (*Ys.* lxiv. 6). Together with Asha, Ahura Mazda created 'the shining light and sunny abodes' (*Yt.* iii. 1 f.), so that the abodes of Asha are light (*Ys.* xvi. 7). In these abodes the souls of the righteous dead dwell (*Ys.* xvi. 7; cf. lxviii. 11; *Āfrīnakān*, i. 18; *Vend.* xix. 36), for paradise (*vahišta ahu*; see art. LIFE AND DEATH [Iranian]) is light (*Ys.* lxii. 6, lxviii. 11), and, as such, receives worship (*Visprat*, xxiii. 1; *Sīh rōcak*, ii. 27). Indeed, 'light' (*raocāo*) is a synonym for 'heaven' (*Ys.* xix. 6), another synonym being 'the shining house of praise' (*raoxšna garō-nmāna* [*Yt.* x. 124, xix. 44]) to which worship is paid (*Sīh rōcak*, ii. 30). Still another synonym is 'the light without beginning' (*anaγra raocāo* [*Ys.* lxxi. 9; *Yt.* xxii. 15; *Vend.* xi. 1 f., 13, xix. 35; *Pursišnīhā*, xxxviii.]), which is likewise an object of veneration (*Gāh*, iii. 6, *Sīh rōcak*, ii. 30; cf. Spiegel, ii. 17 f.). Accordingly, in the *Patēt Īrānī* (ed. E. K. Antiā, *Pâzand Texts*, Bombay, 1909, p. 145, tr. J. Darmesteter, *Zend-Avesta*, Paris, 1892–93, iii. 178), the righteous man hopes to attain to 'the place of light' (*rōšn-jāē*), not to 'the place of darkness' (*tārīk-jāē*).

The good creation is given the epithet of 'bright'—Asha (*Ys.* v. 4), the Amesha Spentas and their paths (*Yt.* xiii. 82, 84, xix. 15, 17), Ashi (*Yt.* xvii. 1, 6), Apām Napāṭ (*Yt.* xix. 52; *Sīh rōcak*, ii. 30), the 'glory' (*xvarenah* [*Yt.* xix. 35]), and especially Yima, whose conventional epithet *xšaēta* ('shining') is so completely blended with his name that in modern Persian he is known only as Jamshīd.

The sun, moon, and stars are bidden to give light (*Vend.* xxi. 5, 9, 13), and the light of the moon is lauded (*Nyāyišn*, iii. 7), while so great are the blessings of the light of the sun that, if the sun no longer rose, 'the demons would destroy everything that is in the seven regions [of the world], and the spiritual angels would find no tarrying place and no abiding place in this corporeal existence' (*Yt.* vi. 3; *Nyāyišn*, i. 13; cf. in general *Nyāyišn*, i.–iii.; *Yt.* vi.–viii.). Indeed, the fairest of the forms of Ahura Mazda are the earthly and the heavenly light, *i.e.* the fire and the sun (*Ys.* xxxvi. 6, lviii. 8); and in the palace which Ahura Mazda built for Mithra there is neither night nor darkness (*Yt.* x. 50).

Darkness is a special attribute of hell (*Vend.* iii. 35; *Aogemadaēcā*, xxviii.), for which 'darkness without beginning' is a synonym (*Yt.* xxii. 33; cf. Spiegel, ii. 18 f.). The demons are 'spawn of darkness' (or, perhaps, 'possess the seed of darkness,' *temasciθra* [*Yt.* vi. 4; *Nyāyišn*, i. 14; *Vend.* viii. 80]), and seek refuge in darkness (*Ys.* lvii. 18), or hide in the earth (*zemare-gūz* [*Ys.* ix. 15; *Yt.* xix. 81; *Westergaard Frag.* iv. 3]) or in caverns (*Vend.* iii. 7, 10)—a phrase which may possibly point to survivals of an old chthonic cult (cf. Moulton, pp. 57, 128 f., 132, 399). Properly enough, therefore, divine aid is sought to resist 'darkness, woe, and suffering' (*Ys.* lxxi. 17; cf. *Nyāyišn*, i. 14).

Turning to the Pahlavi texts, we are told that 'the region of light is the place of Aūharmazd, which they call "endless light"' (*Bundahišn*, i. 2), and that the place of the Amesha Spentas is 'in that best existence of light' (*Dāṭistān-ī-Dīnīk*, lxxiv. 2), while Arṭā-ī-Vīrāf, when in the presence of Ahura Mazda, perceived only brilliant light (*Arṭā-ī-Vīrāf Nāmak*, ci.), and the radiance of

Zarathushtra within his mother, during the three days before his birth, was so great as to illumine his father's whole village (*Dīnkarṭ*, V. ii. 2, VII. ii. 56–58).

According to the same texts, hell is full of darkness (*Dāṭistān-ī-Dīnīk*, xxvii. 2, 6, xxxiii. 2, 4, xxxvii. 28, 45), so intense that it 'is fit to grasp with the hand' (*Bundahišn*, xxviii. 47; cf. *Dīnā-ī-Maīnōg-ī-Xrat*, vii. 31). This 'endlessly dark' is the abode of Angra Mainyu (*Bundahišn*, i. 3), and when, in his fruitless endeavour to destroy the light of Ahura Mazda, he emerged from hell, he made the world at mid-day as dark as midnight, returning, after his defeat, to the darkness, where he formed many demons (*ib.* i. 10, iii. 14). In fact, 'the most steadfast quality of the demon himself is darkness, the evil of which is so complete that they shall call the demons also those of a gloomy race' (*Dāṭistān-ī-Dīnīk*, xxxvii. 85). In contrast, although sun, moon, and stars will continue to exist after the renovation of the world, they will no longer be necessary, 'for the world is a dispenser of all light, and all creatures, too, are brilliant' (*ib.* xxxvii. 126). The power of the demons during the darkness has already been noted. Therefore, 'when in the dark it is not allowable to eat food; for the demons and fiends seize upon one-third of the wisdom and glory of him who eats food in the dark' (*Šāyast-lā-Šāyast*, ix. 8; two-thirds are taken if one also eats with unwashed hands); and the eighteenth section of the lost *Sūṭkar Nask* of the Avesta dealt, among other topics, with 'the hussy who spills anything after sunset, or who scatters a morsel of food to the north, at night, without a recital of the Ahunavair' (*Dīnkarṭ*, IX. xix. 2). To the same category of concepts belongs a short Parsi poem contained in the second volume of the collection of Rivāyats of Dārāb Hormazdyār (ed. M. R. Unwallā, 207. 19–208. 4; the edition is not yet published, but the writer has a set of the proofs through the courtesy of the editor and J. J. Modi). According to this 'Rivāyat on the Lighting of a Lamp,' the lamp-light drives away all demons, and it adds:

'From that light of the Fire the world is bright, since it is hostile to the demons of Ahriman; if there were not always the light of the Fire, there would not be a single man in the world.' This little poem is immediately followed, it may be remarked, by another of nine distichs, recounting the miraculous cure of a dying child by the lighting of a lamp on the roof of the house.

The problem of the relation of light and darkness was even more vital than the extant Iranian texts would lead one to suppose; for it gave rise to philosophical speculations which materially helped to form the leading Zoroastrian sects.

Al-Shahrastānī goes so far as to declare (i. 275) that 'all problems of the Magians turn upon two main points: why the light mingled with darkness, and why the light cleansed itself from darkness; they posit the mingling as the beginning, and the cleansing as the aim.'

The Gayōmartian sect maintained, according to al-Shahrastānī, that light had no beginning, but that darkness was created. Whence, was their problem—whether from light, which, however, could not produce anything even partially evil, or from something else, though there was nothing which shared with light the properties of creation and eternity. Their rather lame solution was that Ahura Mazda thought to himself: 'If I had an opponent, how would he be formed?' From this thought, which did not harmonize with the goodness of light, Angra Mainyu was produced. The mingling of light and darkness was due to the fact that the light gave men, before they were embodied, the choice of degradation to the realms of Angra Mainyu or battle with him. They chose corporeal existence and battle, on condition that they were aided by the light to eventual victory and to the final resurrection at his defeat.

The Zarvanite sect held that the light produced a number of creatures of bright, divine nature, the most important of whom was Zarvan (Time), who, after murmuring prayers for a son during 9999 years, entertained the thought: 'Perchance this world is nothing.' From this evil doubt Angra Mainyu was born, and from Zarvan's wisdom sprang Ahura Mazda. There were a number of minor speculations among this sect—*e.g.*, that Angra Mainyu was originally in heaven, but meditated upon treachery until, like Satan, he fell. The Mashītes thought that a portion of light had transformed itself into darkness.

The Zarathushtrians (Zoroastrians) entertained, according to al-Shahrastānī, the views of light and darkness which we would naturally infer from the Avesta and Pahlavi texts. Both light and darkness had existed from the beginning. Good and evil, purity and impurity, etc., had arisen from the mingling of light and darkness; and, had there been no such mingling, the world would not have existed. God was the source of both (cf. *Ys.* xliv. 5, cited above), and in His wisdom had mingled them; but light alone is real, darkness being, in fact, only its necessary antithesis; and, since they are antithetic, they must war against one another until the light shall be victorious over darkness.

Thus in Zoroastrianism the problem of the relation between light and darkness becomes part of the greater question of the origin of good and evil; and from this point of view the antithesis of light and darkness is found again—whether independent or derived—in several Gnostic systems (cf. *ERE*, vol. vi. p. 238 f.), as well as in Mandæanism (A. J. H. W. Brandt, *Mandäische Religion*, Leipzig, 1889, p. 39 ff.) and Manichæism (K. Kessler, *PRE*[3] xii. [1903] 205 ff.). See art. MĀZANDARĀN.

LITERATURE.—In addition to the references given in the art., other citations from the Avesta may be gathered from C. Bartholomae, *Altiran. Wörterbuch*, Strassburg, 1904, *s.vv.* 'Raok-,' 'Raoxšna-,' 'Raocah-,' and 'Taθra-,' 'Temah-,' etc. (coll. 1487–1492, 648–650). No special treatise on the subject has as yet been written.

LOUIS H. GRAY.

LIGHT AND DARKNESS (Semitic and Egyptian).—**I. Peoples and period.**—Babylonian (Assyrian), Egyptian, and Hebrew beliefs on the subject of light and darkness may all be taken together. Although in course of time they became widely divergent, at the outset and for a considerable period they showed many points of similarity—a fact to be ascribed to the contact and the common origin, in part if not in whole, of the peoples inhabiting the countries of the Near East. For the Babylonians and the Hebrews this affinity is generally admitted, both being of the Semitic stock. Further, in the words of Cheyne, 'a primitive contact between the early Egyptian race and the Babylonians has been made extremely probable by Hommel. Winckler, too, remarks with justice that the cultus of the Horus-child belongs to the same religion as the Babylonian, and is in this sense Semitic.'[1] Sayce, while tracing many analogies of the same kind between Babylonian and Egyptian beliefs, takes a further step, and sees in 'the triumph of the gods of light and order over the monsters of chaos not only the birth of the present creation, but also the theological victory of the Semite over the Sumerian.'[2] Without going so far as this, other scholars admit that the mythological compositions of the Babylonians were derived from Sumerian sources.[3] The upper limit of the period to be considered may therefore be placed in Sumerian times, about the middle of the

[1] T. K. Cheyne, *Bible Problems*, London, 1904, p. 200. Linguistic affinities are worked out by C. J. Ball in the *Hilprecht Anniversary Volume*, Leipzig, 1909. For 'darkness' see p. 34, and for 'light,' pp. 37 f., 47 f., and 51.

[2] A. H. Sayce, *The Religions of Ancient Egypt and Babylonia* (Gifford Lectures), Edinburgh, 1902, p. 496.

[3] L. W. King and H. R. Hall, *Egypt and Western Asia in the Light of Recent Discoveries*, London, 1907, p. 220.

fourth millennium B.C., and the lower limit may with propriety be fixed about the time of the Hebrew Exile, before the influence of Persia, followed by Greece, could have been felt.[1] Throughout this period of three millennia the predominant feature of religion in Babylonia and Egypt is the cult of the sun-god. We should therefore expect to find in the records that have survived much that is cognate to at least the first member of our subject. Owing to syncretistic tendencies always present, and the ease with which those ancient peoples tolerated antinomies in belief, no uniform presentation of their views about light and darkness can be given.

2. Various relationships of light and darkness.—While the words 'light' and 'darkness' appear to stand in a co-ordinate relation, in reality they are contrasted terms, to be compared with 'day' and 'night,' 'life' and 'death,' 'good' and 'evil.' In all these cases the co-ordinate relation holds good in the sense that light and darkness, etc., can be regarded as complementary terms, conveying the idea of the whole—*e.g.*, the daily round, the sum-total of existence, and the ethical contents of life. The exceptional view whereby both light and darkness are traced to the same creative source (as in Is 45[7]) may also be brought into this connexion. In general, however, the relation between light and darkness continues to be regarded in Semitic thought as adversative, slightly veiling a dualism which perhaps has been inherited from pre-historic times, and which is not resolved (Jahwism excluded), even theoretically, into a monism until the limit of our period has been passed.[2] We have throughout to reckon with that 'Oriental resignation to the contrasts in life' which marked all the peoples of the Ancient East.[3] The theory that prevailed might at best be termed 'optimistic dualism.'[4] With special reference to light and darkness there was a contest present in the beginning (cosmology), and this is daily and yearly renewed, with every day and night, every spring and autumn (or summer and winter), and it may even extend through the course of the world cycle.[5] While light and darkness have, therefore, each a separate kingdom, the one being for day and for life, the other for night and for death, there is evidence in the development of religious thought in Egypt of an invasion of each upon the other's domain, resulting in a measure of fusion. This is concisely summed up by saying that the solar cult was osirianized and the Osiris myth was celestialized.[6] A subtle theory of a similar kind has been formulated for Babylonia, as an instance of which we may quote the representation of the sun as under-world divinity, 'because in his light the stars disappear and perish.'[7] There is much less warrant for such crossing over of the ideas of light and darkness in Babylonian thought. Regarding the 'Astral Theory' as a whole, it may be remarked that, were it accepted, it would greatly extend the possibilities of our subject. It requires, however, more agreement than at present exists as to the date of the origin of scientific astronomy among the Babylonians before its findings can be used with any measure of confidence.

3. No science of light.—Judging from present data, the likelihood is that the peoples of antiquity were not conscious of the fact that the universe is under the dominion of natural law. Theirs was 'the cosmography of appearances'[1]—a view of the world resting at the empirical stage. They had no scientific theory of light; darkness was not merely the absence of light. Both were 'material entities':[2]

> 'The matter of light issues forth from its place and spreads over the earth; at night it withdraws, and darkness comes forth from its place, each in a hidden, mysterious way.'[3]

The 'substantiality of darkness'[4] may be specially remarked in Ex 10[21] 14[20]. A higher conception of the quality of light was indeed reached. According to Hehn, in the later parts of the OT light is used as a symbol of deity because it is the finest and most immaterial substance known, and there is no danger of corporeal form being attached to it.

> 'The deity as light gives the transition to the deity as spirit.'[5]

Bearing in mind that the peoples of the Ancient East were accustomed to concrete views of what are accepted by us as abstract qualities, we shall understand how they received the phenomena of light and darkness mainly according to their physical effects and their bearing upon life. Light was of service to them; darkness formed a hindrance. This was transferred to the realm of feeling: light they rejoiced in; darkness they dreaded. Love of the light and hatred of the darkness lie at the root of many of the myths of antiquity, and are evident in the metaphorical usage of the two terms. By an inevitable transition light is associated with warmth, and darkness is linked with cold. This applies to the cycle of the year, which is of more importance in ancient belief and practice, as appears in the Tammuz-cult, than the cycle of the day. From warmth again there is an easy passage to life and growth, and from cold to decay and death.

4. Light and darkness as associated with deities.—Like great natural forces, such as thunder and tempest, light and darkness were seen to lie beyond human control, and thus they came to be associated with deity or deities, and with beings more than human. Light is the creation of good gods, although it has also a hurtful side, when found in conjunction with the scorching heat of summer, and when bound up with lightning and fire. Darkness is viewed less as a creation of the gods than as an environment for monsters and evil spirits, who could not exercise their baneful power apart from darkness. Still there are gods specially associated with darkness, both in Babylonia and in Egypt. Many deities bear names and attributes compounded with words signifying 'light,' and their temples are similarly termed (*e.g.* E-Babbara, 'the shining house' [sun-temple at Sippar]). In addition to Shamash, the sun-god (and other deities who in their original function are merely aspects of the sun), Nannar or Sin, the moon-god, and Ishtar, 'the light of the heavens,' the foremost place must here be given to Marduk or Merodach (Amar-Ud, or Amar-Uduk), 'son of the sun,' or 'child of the day,' as being the god of light by pre-eminence. He, too, is generally regarded as a solar deity, although an attempt has been made to prove that he is independent of the sun, being simply the god of light.[6] Although appearing at the summit of the Babylonian pantheon, he

[1] M. Jastrow, *Aspects of Religious Belief and Practice in Babylonia and Assyria*, New York and London, 1911, p. 60 ff.
[2] Cf. *ERE*, art. 'Dualism (Iranian)' and 'Dualism (Jewish),' vol. v. p. 111 ff.
[3] J. H. Breasted, *Development of Religion and Thought in Ancient Egypt*, London, 1912, p. 357.
[4] A. Jeremias, *Die Panbabylonisten; Der alte Orient und die ägyptische Religion*[2], Leipzig, 1907, p. 23.
[5] See *ERE*, art. 'Ages of the World (Babylonian),' vol. i. p. 184[b].
[6] Breasted, p. 149 ff.
[7] A. Jeremias, *The Old Testament in the Light of the Ancient East*, London, 1911, i. 30.

[1] G. Schiaparelli, *Astronomy in the Old Testament*, Oxford, 1905, p. 22.
[2] T. K. Cheyne, *Traditions and Beliefs of Ancient Israel*, London, 1907, p. 10.
[3] S. R. Driver, *The Book of Genesis with Introduction and Notes*[7], London, 1909, p. 6.
[4] *JE*, art. 'Darkness.'
[5] J. Hehn, *Die biblische und die babylonische Gottesidee*, Leipzig, 1913, p. 292.
[6] H. Zimmern and H. Winckler, *Die Keilinschriften und das Alte Testament*[3], Berlin, 1902–03, p. 370 n.

certainly did not hold undisputed sway, either at the beginning or afterwards, and the fight between light and darkness, typified by Marduk (or Bel) and the Dragon, was continued down the ages.[1] How this should be is perhaps best explained on the theory of Radau,[2] who contends that Marduk is the god of light considered not as an illuminative power, but as a life-giving principle, which appears in the warmth of the spring. His fight with Tiāmat is a fight of the light, *i.e.* the warmth, against the darkness, *i.e.* the cold. By this line of argument Marduk comes into relation to the Tammuz-Adonis (and Ishtar) cycle of myths, and is also to be placed in opposition to Nabū, the god of the darker half of the year.[3] Viewed as a solar deity, then, Marduk stands for the sun-god of spring, who brings 'blessing and favours after the sorrows and tribulations of the stormy season.'[4] Before Marduk was exalted to the chief place, Anu, Ninib, Enlil, and Ea fulfilled a similar rôle in the myths of creation,[5] and in later times Ashur arose to dispute the glory. The nearest approach to a god of darkness, energizing in the world of nature, is Ramman, or Addu (Adad, in West Semitic), 'the thunderer.'[6] The darkness which he causes (*e.g.*, in the Flood Story, ii. 46 f.) is relieved by the lightning, in virtue of which he has some title to be regarded as a god of light also. With him may be classed Girru (Gibil) = Nusku, the god of fire,[7] whose symbol, a lighted lamp, is as old as the 14th cent. B.C.[8]

Of the evil spirits that love the darkness, mention may be made of the seven evil demons who, aided by certain of the great gods, were thought to be responsible for the darkening of the moon by eclipse or storm, and even for the disappearance of the orb of night at the end of the month.

'From city to city darkness work they,
A hurricane, which mightily hunts in the heavens, are they,
Thick clouds, that bring darkness in heaven, are they,
Gusts of wind rising, which cast gloom over the bright day, are they. . . .'[9]

In the official cults of Egypt sun-worship was all-important. Less is said about the moon, although it finds a place.[10] Within his own domain, which is the upper world, Rā (Amon-Rā), the sun, figures as a life-giving power, a set-off to the equally great power of death and darkness in the under world, to which so much importance was attached in Egypt. Here, it would seem, light and darkness are concomitants of the fuller notions of life and death. We must include in this even the apparent exception of the 'Aton' cult of the XVIIIth dynasty (in the reign of Ikhnaton). In the 'Solar universalism' of that period, which finds expression in a series of magnificent hymns,[11] while the whole activity and beneficence of the sun are rehearsed, its life-giving power is still in the forefront. In Egypt the part of Marduk is taken by Horus the elder.[12] An equivalent to Ishtar is found in Hathor, who by some scholars is called 'the goddess of light.'[1] Specific gods of darkness appear in Set[2] (or Set-Apōpi), and in one member of the Hermopolitan ennead, Kek (fem. Keket).[3] (For the gods of the under world see below, § 7.) In Egypt the demons of darkness were, like those of Babylonia, an awful power for evil to the living, and conspicuously active in the realm of the dead.[4]

The Hebrew conception of God is frequently conveyed by means of language (much of which is metaphorical and poetical) drawn from the realm of light (see Hehn, *loc. cit.*; cf. Ex 24^{10}, Ps 104^{2}, Is 10^{17} 51^{4} $60^{1-5.\ 19.\ 20}$, Ezk $1^{13.\ 28}$, Hos 6^{5}).[5] But, while light is readily employed as a symbol of Jahweh, from first to last there is no idea of identifying Him with this manifestation of nature (as in the case of Marduk). While God is conceived of as luminous above measure, He is at the same time thought of as hidden, and His ways are reckoned to be mysterious. For this reason darkness, the 'natural antithesis' of light, also enters into the imagery of the OT (Ex 20^{21}, Dt 4^{11} 5^{23}, 1 K 8^{12}, Ps $18^{9.\ 11}$ 97^{2}, Am 5^{18}, Zeph 1^{15}).[6]

It is surprising that, though the Hebrews were surrounded by races more or less allied to them, who shared the Babylonian and Egyptian belief in demons and evil spirits, hardly a trace of such powers of darkness is evident in the religious literature of ancient Israel.[7]

5. Light and darkness in cosmology.—According to the main version of the Babylonian Story of Creation, Marduk, the god of light, prevails over Tiāmat, the personification of chaos, of which darkness presumably forms part.[8] Sayce finds in Mummu (tablet I. 4) 'the flood,' or chaos, the equivalent of 'the "darkness" which in Gn 1^{2} is said to have been "upon the face of the deep."'[9] In both the Hebrew and the Babylonian accounts of what was in the beginning, darkness is reckoned as primeval, *i.e.* before the cosmos. It is an element not to be reckoned as good. While this may be asserted of darkness as diffused through space, it does not hold true of darkness as a division of time, when darkness means no more than night (Gn $1^{4.\ 5}$).[10] According to Hebrew cosmology, one function of the heavenly orbs was to divide the light from the darkness; 'and God saw that it was good' (Gn 1^{18}; cf. Ps 104^{20}). In the Babylonian account there is no mention of the creation of light, perhaps to be explained by the fact that Marduk is himself the god of light and consequently its creator[11]—a view which might well have been entertained in spite of the contradiction, as we see it, that the 'son of the sun' is also made the creator of the sun and all the other orbs of light. In the Hebrew account light is given as the first act in the creation of the world, wrought by the word of God. This, Cheyne thinks, formed no part of the traditional Hebrew cosmogony, but is due to the priestly writer's reflective turn of mind.[12] Be that as it may, this light, which is diffused through space, wherever darkness is not present, is evidently to be distinguished from the 'lights'—sun, moon, and stars—in which light is, as it were, localized (Gn $1^{14ff.}$). In Egypt there is no detailed account of creation.[13] Sayce[14] and

1 T. G. Pinches, *The Old Testament in the Light of the Historical Records and Legends of Assyria and Babylonia*³, London, 1908, p. 530 f.
2 H. Radau, *Bel, the Christ of Ancient Times*, Chicago, 1908, p. 46 f. (with reference to the same writer's *Creation Story*, do., 1902, p. 5 f.).
3 *ERE*, art. 'Babylonians and Assyrians,' vol. ii. p. 312ᵃ; Jastrow regards him rather as a water-deity (*op. cit.* p. 97 f.).
4 Jastrow, p. 39. 5 *Ib.* p. 100 f.
6 L. W. King, *Babylonian Religion and Mythology*², London, 1903, p. 130.
7 *ERE*, art. 'Babylonians and Assyrians,' vol. ii. p. 313ᵃ.
8 A. H. Sayce, in *Hilprecht Anniversary Volume*, p. 79 ff.
9 R. W. Rogers, *Cuneiform Parallels to the Old Testament*, New York, 1912, p. 64 f.; cf. Jastrow, pp. 215, 333 ff.
10 A. H. Sayce, *The Religion of Ancient Egypt*, Edinburgh, 1913, p. 130 ff.; G. Maspero, *The Dawn of Civilization*², London, 1896, p. 92 f.
11 See *ExpT* xxii. [1911] 485. For a revised tr. of the most important of Ikhnaton's hymns see Breasted, *op. cit.* p. 324 ff.
12 Sayce, p. 165.

1 Sayce, p. 146.
2 *ERE*, art. 'Dualism (Egyptian),' vol. v. p. 106ᵇ; Breasted, p. 40.
3 Sayce, p. 132. 4 Breasted, p. 290 ff.
5 *HDB*, art. 'Light,' vol. iii. p. 119.
6 *Ib.*, art. 'Darkness,' vol. i. p. 559.
7 F. Delitzsch, *Mehr Licht*, Leipzig, 1907, p. 51.
8 Cf. Berossus: τὸ πᾶν σκότος καὶ ὕδωρ.
9 *ERE*, art. 'Cosmogony and Cosmology (Babylonian),' vol. iv. p. 129ᵇ.
10 *HDB*, art. 'Cosmogony,' vol. i. p. 502ᵃ.
11 J. Skinner, *Genesis* (*ICC*), Edinburgh, 1910, p. 46.
12 *EBi*, art. 'Light,' col. 2795 f.
13 *HDB*, art. 'Religion of Egypt,' vol. v. p. 179ᵇ.
14 *Religion of Ancient Egypt*, pp. 166, 238 ff.

Jeremias[1] remark on sectional parallels to the Babylonian main version. Different conceptions of the origin of light appear. According to one, primeval chaos is an ocean from which the sun-god (Atum) arises, bringing his own light with him; according to another, light is laid up in the world-egg, waiting to be revealed.

The story of a second creation would seem to be found in the narrative of Berossus, according to whom the animals apparently were not able to bear the light of the first creation, and a second was rendered necessary of such a kind that they could bear the light.[2]

Deutero-Isaiah's exalted conception (45^7), whereby the creation of light and darkness is referred to the same divine source, is the logical outcome of monotheism.[3] It has an anthropomorphic parallel in the words ascribed to Rā: 'When I open my eyes, there is light; when I close them, there is darkness.'[4] This, of course, applies to the daily renewal of light and its withdrawal every night.

A reduction of earth to primeval conditions would involve among other things the extinction of light and by inference the return of the darkness of chaos (Jer 4^{23}). An Egyptian myth, found in the *Book of the Dead*, represents Atum (see above) as defacing what he had made, bringing a return of water, as it was at the beginning. Over this Osiris (lord of darkness) is to rule.[5]

6. Light and darkness in human experience.—The cosmology, although relating to what is first in the order of things, is itself the product of reflexion upon the phenomena of the present. The processes of thought which give origin to the myths connected with the world's beginning, and to mythology in general, may be placed in times antecedent to the Semitic period. The myths, having been invented and reduced to writing, were now exercising a certain counter-influence on current ideas. They were never absent from the background of thought, and in a way they hindered development. We may suppose that light and darkness, especially light, would in time have been accepted as in the course of nature, and have ceased to attract attention. But there came interruptions of the usual order—*e.g.*, in the eclipse of moon or of sun—and on such occasions the mythology was speedily recalled. The cults also were of such a kind that they kept the mythology alive. The great hymns to Shamash, Sin, Ishtar, etc.; the transcription and frequent recitation of funerary literature in Egypt, much of which had been handed down from very early times; the festivals attending new moon, full moon, and the new year, and every occasion of national or local assembly—all must have exercised much influence towards the preservation of traditional beliefs. There was thus but slight opportunity of escaping from the legacy of the past. When the Egyptians looked upon the fiery clouds that attended the rising sun, their minds reverted to the pits of fire that were supposed to mark the eleventh division of the Ṭuat.[6] The multiform representations on cylinder seals of the orbs of night and day, especially of the figure of the sun-god rising between the mountains of the East, depicted with streams of light flowing from both sides, or with rays of light protruding

1 *OT in Light of the Anc. East*, i. 158 ff., and, in more detail, *Die Panbabylonisten*, etc.

2 T. G. Pinches, *The Religion of Babylonia and Assyria*, London, 1906, p. 42.

3 *ERE*, art. 'Cosmogony and Cosmology (Hebrew),' vol. iv. p. 155. Delitzsch, *op. cit.* p. 55, regards this verse as combating Old Persian dualism; similarly Jeremias, *OT in Light of the Anc. East*, ii. 276. A different view is taken by H. Gunkel, *Schöpfung und Chaos*, Göttingen, 1895, p. 136 n.

4 Quoted in *ERE* iv. 228; cf. Sayce, *Religion of Anc. Egypt*, p. 218.

5 E. Naville, *The Old Egyptian Faith*, London, 1909, p. 220 ff.

6 E. A. W. Budge, *The Egyptian Heaven and Hell*, London, 1905, iii. 178 f.

from his shoulders,[1] give a vivid conception of the ideas constantly at work in the minds of the Semites and their neighbours. In addition to anthropomorphic representations of the deities of light, their symbols, especially the sun's disk, winged or unwinged, abounded both in Egypt and in Babylonia. More telling still were the obelisks and pyramids of Egypt, which were symbols of the sun in addition to their other uses. Temples to these deities of light were also present to bear their witness. Very impressive was the thought current so long in Egypt that the sun died every evening, and every morning was resurrected. In the interval he moved with difficulty through the realm of darkness, and, as a passive body, had to be lighted through the under world by other creatures of light.[2] In Babylonia the phases of the moon seem to have attracted attention even more than the daily course of the sun. As king of the night, Sin (Nannar), 'the bright one,' may have had an even older sovereignty than Shamash, who was reckoned to be his son. This sequence has been explained in various ways,[3] but it would seem that the rejoicing which attended the moon's appearance every month, and the lamentation which accompanied its disappearance, point to the belief that in the presence and ascendancy of light, by night no less than by day, the ancient Babylonians found safety and happiness, whereas in darkness there lurked danger and woe. In this connexion it is curious to note that Saturn was regarded as a second sun, to whom (apart from the moon) the illumination of the night was due.[4]

In spite of these efforts to extend the sovereignty of light, there remained a sufficiently terrifying residuum of darkness. To overcome this, resort was had to other agencies, viz. magical rites and a due fulfilment of the duties owing to the dead. Darkness both of earth and of the underground being the *milieu* of demons and the spirits of the deceased, contrariwise they could not have their dwelling in the light. Inasmuch as natural light was not always available, artificial means had to be adopted to overcome the disabilities attaching to darkness. The energy of fire was here of great significance. It is noteworthy that a certain part of the temple where purification was wrought was termed 'the house of light' (Assyr. *bît nûri*). The light is associated with Girru or Nusku, the fire-god, which may be taken to mean that the purification was by fire.[5] The subject of artificial lights is closely related to this branch of our subject. The peoples of antiquity being obsessed by the terror of darkness, it was natural that they should have safeguarded themselves, so far as they could, by having lights in their dwellings and out-of-doors. From the number of lamps found during excavation, notably in Palestine, many of them belonging to the Semitic period, it has been inferred that these were in general use. Out-of-doors torches served the purpose. The torches of the Anunnaki (gods of a lower order) are mentioned in the Babylonian Flood Story (col. ii. 44). A graphic description of the festival 'illumination' of New Year's Eve and days following, given by Breasted,[6] affords an excellent idea of the part played by artificial lights in the ritual of Egypt. One of the duties of the priests and ministrants in the temples was to attend to the fires and lamps (cf. 1 S 3^3, 1 K 7^{49}).

Thoughts of light and darkness were further kept in the minds of these ancient peoples by the terms assigned to the

1 Jastrow, plates 6 and 7 (at p. 16).

2 Budge, iii. 107, 174, 187, 194. According to the Babylonian conception, the sun seems to have entered on a better fate at night-fall, feasting and resting in the abode of the gods (King, *Bab. Religion and Mythology*, p. 33).

3 Jastrow, p. 65.

4 *Ib.* p. 223.

5 *Ib.* p. 313 ff.

6 *Op. cit.* p. 261 ff.

day (Assyr. *urru*, Heb. *ôr*, 'light'); to the morning, or East (Assyr. *ṣît Šamši*, Heb. *mizrāḥ*, 'the rising of the sun'); to the evening, or West (Assyr. *erêb Šamši*, Heb. *mᵉbô hash-shemesh*, 'the setting of the sun'); and by certain Babylonian month names (Âru, Ajjaru, the second or 'bright' month; Addâru, the eleventh, the 'dark' or 'gloomy' month). One series of directions in Hebrew gives north (=*ṣāfôn*) as the 'obscure' or 'dark' place, and south (=*dārôm*) as the 'bright' or 'illuminated' place.[1]

7. Light and darkness in relation to the state after death.—The contrast between light and darkness in the idea of the ancients is most strikingly revealed in their views about the state of the living and of the dead. 'Darkness without light' is one of the curses invoked by Ḫammurabi on any one who should venture to deface his stele. This is synonymous with death. The grave to which the dead are consigned is 'the dark dwelling' (Sumerian *Unugi*), which in its extended meaning is applied to the under world, the abode of the shades (cf. Ps $88^{6.\ 12.\ 18}$).[2] The departed soul itself is a 'creation of darkness' (Sumerian, *gidim*, Semitic, *edimmu*).[3] The darkness attending death was to some extent relieved in the practice of the living by the use of artificial lights in the preliminaries to burial and by occasional illuminations in proximity to the tomb. From Palestinian excavation it has been ascertained that lamps are exceedingly common in graves, where their intention is evidently symbolical. Their purpose has been variously explained, and one and the same interpretation will hardly suit every era. The readiest explanation would place them—at least in the earlier period—on a level with food and drink vessels deposited with the dead. Whatever was of service to the living might also serve the dead.[4]

Among the Babylonians the general idea was that it was a misfortune for the dead again to be brought to the light of day. Unless decent burial were given, their spirits would return to earth, but only to plague the living.[5] In the under world (or preferably the other world) was their home, and there their spirits found rest. The classic description of this abode of the dead is found in the myth of Ishtar's Descent to Hades, to the land of no-return (cf. *Gilgamesh Epic*, ii. $4^{30ff.}$):

> 'To the house of darkness, Irkalla's dwelling-place,
> To the house from which he who enters never returns,
> To the road whose path turns not back,
> To the house where he who enters is deprived of light,
> Where dust is their sustenance, their food clay,
> Light they see not, in darkness do they sit. . . .'[6]

Over this gloomy realm of the Babylonian dead the god Nergal presides, with his consort Ereshkigal, the 'dark' goddess. In Egypt Osiris was lord of the under world, and there held his court. This also was a world lying in darkness, which was relieved one hour in twenty-four, during the passage of the sun-god and his train through each division of the Ṭuat.[7] The entrance to this realm of the dead lay, for both Babylonians and Egyptians, in the west, where the sun goes down. On the other hand, the east, as the point of sunrise, is the abode of life; but this has an interest only for the sun-god and the privileged few who shared his daily recurring glory. Although the point of departure to the under world and the point of return therefrom are clear, there is doubt as to the location, relatively to earth, of the region of the dead. The Egyptians placed it beyond the circle of mountains girding the earth, perhaps on the same plane with earth, perhaps at a lower level. In the Babylonian and Hebrew conception it seems to have lain beneath earth, even lower than the

[1] Schiaparelli, p. 34.
[2] A. Jeremias, *Hölle und Paradies bei den Babyloniern*, Leipzig, 1900, p. 14.
[3] *ERE*, art. 'Death, etc. (Babylonian),' vol. iv. p. 445^{a}.
[4] H. Vincent, *Canaan d'après l'exploration récente*, Paris, 1907, p. 289 ff.; cf. S. A. Cook, *The Religion of Ancient Palestine*, London, 1908, p. 40 ff.
[5] Sayce, *Religions of Anc. Egypt and Babylonia*, pp. 283, 285.
[6] Rogers, p. 121 f.
[7] Budge, iii. 198 f.

waters of the abyss (*apsû*), themselves associated with darkness.[1] This was a region which the sun, living or dead, could not pierce.

A better fate for departed spirits, some if not all, was also conceived of—symbolized, *e.g.*, in the recovery of Tammuz from the under world and in the sun-bark with its occupants who returned to the region of day. Light here plays the principal part, although the obstacle of darkness has to be surmounted before the goal of light can be reached. One of the charms in the *Book of the Dead* is for making the transformation into the god that giveth light (in) the darkness, or light for darkness.[2] The 'island of the blessed,' in the *Gilgamesh Epic*, is cut off from mortals by many barriers, including twelve double-hours of travelling through thick darkness.

The Babylonian heaven was the reserve of the gods, save in exceptional cases. In Egypt, at an early date, the king shared in the delights of heaven, and was exalted to life with the gods in the sky. Later this was qualified by the Osirian doctrine, whereby the realm of the blessed could be attained only by redemption from the under world through faith in Osiris or Amon-Rā. This other world is a realm of light for the most part. The crested ibis, whose name is equivalent to 'light,' is used as a symbol of the soul, including that of the sun-god.[3] The *khu*, or beatified spirits, feed upon the divine grain (*i.e.* the body of Osiris) in the land of the Light-god.[4] Later, 'the followers of the Sun-god, who travelled with him in the Boat of Millions of Years, eventually became beings consisting of nothing but light'[5] (cf. Is 60^{20}).

Hebrew thought about the state of the dead in the under world shows close kinship to the Babylonian, and is less developed than that of Egypt. The utmost allowed, even in the later books of the OT, falling within our period, is that the shades may emerge from Shᵉôl back to the light of the upper world (Is 26^{19}).[6]

LITERATURE.—This is sufficiently given in the footnotes.

WILLIAM CRUICKSHANK.

LIGHTNING. — See PRODIGIES AND PORTENTS.

LIGUORI.—Saint Alfonso Maria di Liguori was born 27 Sept. 1696 at Marianella, near Naples. He was the eldest son of a rather impoverished noble family, and, according to his biographers, was from earliest youth remarkable for his piety, his charm of manner, and his precocious ability. A strain of Spanish blood seems to have lent him a greater seriousness of mind and tenacity of purpose than are common among natives of Southern Italy. He devoted himself to the law, and took the degree of Doctor of Laws at the age of sixteen, being then so small of stature that, to the amusement of the spectators, his doctor's gown hid him almost completely from view. He afterwards practised in the courts of Naples for nearly eight years with extraordinary success; but it would seem that in 1723, in a case in which large pecuniary interests were at stake, Liguori, in the interpretation of an important document, was guilty of an oversight which, when brought home to him, covered him with confusion, and disgusted him with his career and with all worldly ambition. He had always led a most innocent life, and now, giving himself up to solitude and prayer, he had what he believed to be a

[1] For different locations of Shᵉôl, relatively to the Abyss, see charts in *HDB* i. 503^{b} and Schiaparelli, p. 38.
[2] E. A. W. Budge, *The Book of the Dead*, London, 1901, ii. 261 f. Naville (p. 182) considers this an evident reference to the moon.
[3] Sayce, *Religion of Anc. Egypt*, p. 122.
[4] Budge, *Egyp. Heaven and Hell*, iii. 164.
[5] *Ib.* iii. 166.
[6] *SDB*, art. 'Eschatology,' p. 236^{a}.

supernatural intimation to consecrate the rest of his days to God in the ecclesiastical state. He wished to become an Oratorian, but his father, who had already been much distressed on two different occasions by his son's unwillingness to fall in with an advantageous project of marriage that had been suggested, obstinately opposed his design. Yielding eventually to his father's entreaties, and acting on the advice of his confessor, himself an Oratorian, the young lawyer gave up his idea of leaving home, but began to study for an ecclesiastical career, and in December 1726 was ordained priest. In the first six years of his ministry Alfonso worked under the direction of an association of missionary priests, and devoted himself at Naples to the care of the *lazzaroni*, among whom his labours bore extraordinary fruit. He converted many hundreds from a life of sin, and formed a sort of confraternity, the 'Association of the Chapels,' for these poor outcasts, to ensure their perseverance in good. In 1729 Liguori was brought into relation with a certain Father Thomas Falcoia of the 'Pii Operarii,' who conceived a deep respect for the young man, and, when he himself was shortly afterwards made bishop of Castellamare, he was led to the conviction that Alfonso was an instrument divinely sent him to carry out a project which he had long secretly cherished of founding a preaching Order to evangelize the goatherds and peasants of that part of Italy. The scheme eventually took shape in the little town of Scala, near Amalfi, twenty miles from Naples. There the 'Congregation of the Most Holy Redeemer,' from which name the members are most commonly called Redemptorists, was founded in 1732. Bishop Falcoia was at first its nominal superior, but he lived at a distance, while Alfonso resided with the community. Hence, on the bishop's death in 1743, Alfonso was formally elected to preside over his brethren. In 1749 the rule was authoritatively approved by Pope Benedict XIV., and the rule of an Order of nuns, which had been closely associated with the Redemptorist congregation from the beginning, was approved in the following year. But this measure of success was not achieved without numerous disappointments, and several of Liguori's first companions broke away from the Institute. A document drawn up in those very early days by the hand of Alfonso himself in the vain hope of obtaining the approbation of the king of Naples, Don Carlos (afterwards Charles III. of Spain), supplies a concise account of the special characteristics of the new Order.

'The principal aim of the priests so associated is to imitate as closely as possible . . . the life and virtues of Our Lord Jesus Christ. In this they set before themselves their own spiritual advantage and that of the people of this kingdom—especially the most forsaken of these, to whom they render spiritual aid.

In their houses they lead a perfect community life, under obedience to their superior, and perform the functions of the sacred ministry, such as instructions, confessions, the superintendence of schools, confraternities, and other devout gatherings.

They go about the dioceses in which they are established, giving missions, and, as a means of preserving the good results which they have been enabled by the grace of God to effect, they return from time to time to the districts which have been evangelized, to hear confessions and confirm the people in their good resolutions by another series of instructions and sermons as well as by spiritual advice and so forth.

In the monastery as well as abroad they endeavour, with the help of divine grace, to follow closely in the footsteps of the Most Holy Redeemer, Jesus Crucified, in order to instruct the people by example as well as by precept.

As a means of attaining this end, there are twelve points of rule set forth in their constitutions. The headings of these are: Faith, Hope, Love of God, Concord and Charity among themselves, Poverty, Purity of Heart, Obedience, Meekness and Humility of Heart, Mortification, Recollection, Prayer, Abnegation of Self, and Love of the Cross.

Each of the associates passes one day every week [now one day every month] in retreat, thus treating alone with God in the interests of his soul, in order to be able to employ himself afterwards with more ardour in securing the spiritual welfare of his neighbour.

In their houses they consecrate a large part of each day to silence, recollection, the choir, mortification, and to meditation, which is practised three times a day. . . .

Their houses are to contain but a small number of subjects. As for their subsistence, they endeavour not to be a burden on anybody; they live on their family resources, which they have handed over to their superiors, and on such offerings as may be made spontaneously for the love of Jesus Christ, by the piety of the faithful' (Berthe, *Saint Alphonse de Liguori*, Eng. tr., i. 166).

Despite domestic anxieties and contradictions in the government of the new Institute, Liguori, down to about the year 1752, devoted himself indefatigably to the actual work of preaching, while leading at the same time a life of extreme abnegation and austerity. At that period his health began somewhat to fail, and henceforward he devoted more time to literary activities, composing a number of books of piety and instruction, as well as the comprehensive work on moral theology by which he is especially remembered. As early as 1747 the king had wished to make Alfonso archbishop of Palermo, but by earnest representations he had succeeded in evading the proffered honour. The Redemptorists, in point of fact, take a special vow to accept no ecclesiastical dignities, but in 1762 influence was used with the Holy See to dispense the saint from his vow, and, sorely against his will, he was compelled by the pope to accept the bishopric of Sant' Agata dei Goti, a tiny see to the north of Naples, among a peasant population unpleasantly notorious for their barbarism and irreligion. Here he worked wonders for the reform of morals, but after an episcopate of more than thirteen years he persuaded Pope Pius VI. in 1775 to allow him to resign in order that he might end his days among a community of his own Order. Broken with years, with apostolic labours, and with the incredible austerities which he practised, he retired to Nocera dei Pagani, but twelve years were still to pass before he was called to his reward. In the meantime he was destined to endure trials which probably cost him more severe mental suffering than any of the difficulties which he had previously encountered. For forty years and more, mainly owing to the influence of the anti-clerical but all-powerful minister Bernard Tanucci, who was the virtual ruler of Naples, the formal recognition of the Redemptorists as a religious Order had been withheld by the Government. This had always been an obstacle in the way of its expansion, reducing it, as it did, to the position of an illegal association. At the time of Tanucci's downfall in 1776, the Order numbered only nine houses—four in Naples, one in Sicily, and four in the States of the Church. In 1779, under a different administration, everything seemed to point to the adoption of a more generous policy. Promises of favour were made on behalf of the Government, and in response the Redemptorist rule was formally submitted for State approval. From the point of view of the aged founder, the result was disastrous. The rule was approved, indeed, but in a fundamentally modified form (known in the controversies which followed as the 'Regolamento'), which set at naught many of the most essential features of the constitutions as hitherto observed, and which practically reduced it from the status of a religious Order to that of a mere pious association. Liguori, who was now 85, decrepit, deaf, and almost blind, was induced to sign the Regolamento, and it was for the time adopted in the Neapolitan dominions, but the Redemptorists belonging to the houses founded within the States of the Church energetically protested against the acceptance of any such caricature of their rule. The Holy See pronounced in their favour, and the unfortunate schism thus caused in the Order had not been healed when, on 1 Aug. 1787, the saint died at Nocera dei Pagani. His death, together with the outburst of popular enthusiasm which it evoked and the marvellous events that followed, brought about a happier state of feeling. The Government of Charles III. in Oct. 1790 approved the original Redemptorist rule, and in Aug. 1791, under papal sanction, the different houses of the Order were once more reconciled with each other. From this time forward, and especially after the subsidence of the disturbances caused by the French Revolution and the Napoleonic wars, the development of the Order was rapid. In 1786 the first Redemptorist house north of the Alps was founded at Warsaw by Clement Hofbauer, afterwards beatified. From there the Congregation gradually spread to Austria and through Europe, while a beginning was made in the United States in 1832 and in England in 1843. The Redemptorists have since made foundations in Ireland (1851), Kinnoull, near Perth, in Scotland (1869), in Brazil, Dutch Guiana, the Congo, Australia, New Zealand, and many other distant countries. At present the Order numbers rather over 4000 members, half of whom are priests, the rest lay-brothers and students preparing for ordination. The strict ultramontane views distinctive of the followers of St. Alfonso di Liguori have often brought them into disfavour with State officials, and, like the Jesuits, they have several times been banished from different European countries. Still no serious attempt has been made to connect them with any kind of political intrigue. The Redemptorists have remained steadily faithful to their primary work of giving missions and retreats, especially among the poor and uninstructed, and the severe rule of the Order has suffered no relaxation.

Alfonso di Liguori was beatified in 1816, canonized in 1839, and declared 'Doctor of the Universal Church' by Pius IX. in 1871. The terms of this last pronouncement, though somewhat vague, may be held to constitute a guarantee of orthodoxy for the saint's writings, at least when taken as a whole. Moreover, it may fairly be inferred from the language used that he is commended for holding a golden mean in his moral teaching between a Jansenistic rigorism on the one hand and dangerous laxity on the other. A full bibliography of Liguori's writings may be found in Berthe, Eng. tr., ii. 766 ff. Two works especially in this long catalogue have been subjected to much adverse criticism. Against the *Le Glorie di Maria*, first published at Naples in 1750, and since translated into every European language, many objections have been raised on the ground of its alleged extravagant 'Mariolatry' (see, *e.g.*, E. B. Pusey, *Eirenicon*, Oxford, 1865, *passim*). But it is to be remembered, as Newman points out, that 'St. Alfonso wrote for Neapolitans, whom he knew, and whom we do not know' (see the whole context in J. H. Newman, *Letter to Pusey on the Eirenicon*, London, 1866, p. 103 ff.). The character and traditions of the people are very different from ours, and he was writing to protest against what he considered to be a veiled attack on that simple and childlike devotion to the Blessed Virgin which he shared, and which is a very important factor in the religion of his countrymen. It is, however, the *Theologia Moralis* that more than anything else has been made the object of fierce invective. Liguori originally (*i.e.* in 1748) published his views on moral questions in the form of a commentary on a well-known text-book for students, the *Medulla* of the Jesuit Hermann Busenbaum. But the second edition in two volumes (Naples, 1753 and 1755) appeared as an original work, and the author continued to revise and enlarge it as the successive issues were exhausted. The eighth edition, which was printed in 1779, was the last to receive his personal attention. Seeing that not only has Alfonso been declared a doctor of the Church, but that earlier authoritative decrees in 1803 and 1831 pronounced that there was 'nothing worthy of censure' in his writings (on this cf. Newman, *History of my Religious Opinions*, note G, p. 353), and that all his opinions might safely be followed by confessors, it is fair to conclude that by the theology of Liguori the moral teaching of the Roman Church must stand or fall. But, while we admit this, it must be said that few indeed of the exoteric critics who have inveighed against his teaching have taken the trouble to understand it. It is easy to denounce the 'shocking laxity' of this or that isolated proposition set out, often inaccurately, and always apart from the context, as, *e.g.*, in the notorious pamphlet of Robert Grassmann (*Auszüge aus der Moraltheologie*, etc.), but the man who does this is most commonly a publicist who knows nothing of ethical systems and who has never considered the difficulties which follow from the acceptance of a contrary principle. Nothing can produce a better impression than to lay down the rule that under no possible circumstances must the truth be departed from, but those who most positively commit themselves to this are also those who have never attempted to think out the extremely difficult problems which arise in practical life, and who have never attempted to square their own conduct by any consistent principle.

They believe, as Newman well says, 'that on a great or cruel occasion a man cannot help telling a lie, and that he would not be a man did he not tell it, but still it is wrong and he ought not to do it, and he must trust that the sin will be forgiven him, though he goes about to commit it. It is a frailty, and had better not be anticipated, and not thought of again after "it is once over."'

Now Liguori, like all his fellow-bishops, believed that for those whose duty it was to hear confessions and instruct their flock it was necessary that these and other moral questions should be thought out. Moreover, it must be said, in answer to such criticisms as those of R. Grassmann and those contained in art. CASUISTRY (vol. iii. p. 240), that priests administer a code of law in the tribunal penance and, like lawyers, doctors, and magistrates, they have to acquaint themselves with technicalities which, in the case of certain offences, often involve unsavoury details quite unfit for public discussion.

One of the special grounds of reproach against Liguori's moral system is his adoption or defence of probabilism (*q.v.*). This charge is only partially justified and would be repudiated by all his own disciples. The principle which he enunciated, at least in his later years, was that of 'equiprobabilism' (*q.v.*). The difference between this and probabilism, rightly explained, is not very momentous, and many modern writers on the subject, especially the theologians of the Jesuit school, have maintained that St. Alfonso's views diverged but slightly from those of approved probabilists. According to the probabilist system, starting with the admitted axiom that a doubtful law does not bind (*lex dubia non obligat*), a man is not held in conscience to obey as long as there is a sound probability against the law—as long as, *e.g.*, in a matter of extrinsic testimony, where doctors disagree, one unexceptionable authority teaches that a particular precept has no binding force. The probabiliorists, on the other hand, held that, unless the authorities who maintained the binding force of the law or precept were notably less weighty than those who excused from it, such a precept could not be set aside without sin. Between these rival views comes that of Liguori, who held that, when the reasons or authorities were equally balanced for and against the law, then a man without peril to his soul was free to use his liberty.

'A doubtful law does not bind. But when two opposite opinions are equally or nearly equally probable, you have a strict doubt as to the existence of the law. Therefore the law, being only doubtfully promulgated, has no binding force. Therefore it is true that you can follow an equally probable opinion in favour of liberty' (Berthe, Eng. tr., ii. 143).

A critical and definitive edition of the *Theologia Moralis*, equipped with adequate notes, has only recently been brought to completion: *Theologia Moralis S. Alphonsi Mariæ de Ligorio*, ed. Leonardi Gaudé, 4 vols., Rome, 1905–12. The editor in his preface gives a satisfactory explanation of the inaccuracy of so many of the saint's quotations as printed in the current editions.

LITERATURE.—The fullest life of St. Alfonso di Liguori is that by A. Berthe, 2 vols., Paris, 1900, Eng. tr., H. Castle, 2 vols., Dublin, 1905 (the translation has been subjected to careful revision and is in many respects superior to the original). Other noteworthy biographies are those of A. Tannoia, *Della Vita ed istituto del' venerabile Alfonso Maria Liguori*, 3 vols., Naples, 1798–1802 (a valuable source written by a devoted disciple of the saint). See also C. Villecourt, *Vie et institut de S. Alphonse Marie de Liguori*, 4 vols., Tournai, 1863; K. Dilgskron, *Leben des heil. Bischofs und Kirchenlehrers Alfonsus Maria de Liguori*, Regensburg, 1887; A. Capecelatro, *La Vita di S. Alfonso Maria de Liguori*, Rome, 1879. A good account of the Order with full bibliography will be found in M. Heimbucher, *Die Orden und Kongregationen der kathol. Kirche*[3], Paderborn, 1908, iii. 313–333.

On the Probabilist and Equiprobabilist controversy see the anonymous *Vindiciæ Alphonsianæ*[2], Brussels, 1874, and *Vindiciæ Ballerinianæ*, Bruges, 1873; J. de Caigny, *Apologetica de Aequiprobabilismo Alphonsiano*, do. 1894, and *De genuino Probabilismo licito*, do. 1904; J. Arendt, *Crisis Aequiprobabilismi*, Brussels, 1902; J. Wouters, *De Minusprobabilismo*, Paris, 1905; A. Lehmkuhl, *Probabilismus Vindicatus*, Freiburg, 1906. A severe indictment of the moral teaching of St. Alfonso di Liguori will be found in A. Harnack, *Lehrbuch der Dogmengeschichte*[3], Freiburg, 1898, iii. 591, 644 ff.; P. von Hoensbroech, *Die ultramontane Moral*, Berlin, 1902; J. J. I. Döllinger and F. H. Reusch, *Geschichte der Moralstreitigkeiten*, Munich, 1889, and the pamphlet of R. Grassmann, *Auszüge aus der Moraltheologie des heil. Alphons v. Liguori*, Stettin, 1895, which has been widely distributed as a controversial tract. In reply see, *inter alia*, J. H. Newman, *History of my Religious Opinions*, London, 1865, pp. 273 ff. and 348 ff.; A. Keller, *St. Alphons v. Liguori oder Robert Grassmann?*, Wiesbaden, 1901; 'Pilatus,' *Was ist Wahrheit?*, do. 1902, and *Quos Ego*[2], do. 1903; F. ter Haar, *Das Decret des Papstes Innocenz XI. über den Probabilismus*, Paderborn, 1904; V. Cathrein, *Moralphilosophie*[3], Freiburg, 1899, i. 397 ff.; H. Ryder, *Catholic Controversy*[10], London, 1890.

H. THURSTON.

LIGURIAN RELIGION.

—So little is certainly known of the early history and geographical distribution of the Ligurians that any attempt to give a general account of their religion is impossible. Some of the deities that were worshipped in Roman times in the Ligurian area strictly so called may be mentioned. The most noteworthy are those closely attached to a particular spot, such as Mars Cemenelus (*CIL* v. 7871), sometimes worshipped without the first name, and clearly connected with the town of Cemenelum; and Bormanus, who was probably, like his namesake in the north of Gallia Transpadana, from whom the modern town of Bormio takes its name, a god of hot springs, and who gave the name to the Lucus Bormani on the coast to the east of (Album) Intimelium, the modern Ventimiglia. Not less local was the worship of Mars Leucimalacus at Pedo (*ib.* 7862), possibly an apple-ripening deity, the dedication to whom was made on some festival of waggoners or muleteers (*plostralibus*). Local, too, was the cult of the Matronæ Vediantiæ, where the plural is interesting, also honoured at Cemenelum in the district of the Vediantii. The worship of Matronæ with some local epithet or epithets was fairly common in N. Italy, sometimes combined with Genii, as in an inscription from Tremezzina on Lake Como (*ib.* 5277), generally with a local epithet, as Deruonnæ (*ib.* 5791, found at Milan) or Vcellasicæ Concanaunæ (*ib.* 5584, found at Corbetta, north of Milan). They are often joined with Jupiter Optimus Maximus, and sometimes themselves called Iunones—a plural form which never appears in pure Latin inscriptions. It would be exceedingly unsafe, without other evidence, to see in this a trace of any polygamous strain in the Ligurian conception of Olympus; a nearer parallel is the (presumably) generalizing plural in such animistic figures as Nymphæ, Fauni, or the 'Clouds' and 'Dawns' of the Tabula Agnonensis (see ITALY [ANCIENT]); or the Angitiæ of the Marsians—not to speak of the Parcæ of Græco-Roman fable or the Σεμναί at Athens.

Other Ligurian examples of these 'Great Mothers' will be found in the Index to *CIL* (p. 1180). The other deities of the locality are all of common occurrence in Italian communities.

On the important question of the ethnic character and connexions of the Ligures, reference must be made to *EBr*[11], art. 'Ligurians,' and the authorities there cited. If, and in so far as, the view of W. Ridgeway ('Who were the Romans?' *Brit. Acad. Trans.* iii. [1907] 42, with the comments of the present writer, *ib.*) may be accepted as sound, the early history of Ligurian religion would be the same thing as that of the pre-Tuscan population of Western Italy, in particular of the Aurunci and other early dwellers on the soil of what afterwards was Latium (see ITALY [ANCIENT], especially the paragraph on the archaic cult of Aricia).

R. S. CONWAY.

LINGAYATS.

—The Lingayats are a religious community in India, numbering nearly three millions at the census of 1911, of whom more than half are found in the southern districts of the Bombay Presidency. In the Bombay districts of Belgaum and Bijapur one-third of the population is Lingayat, and in the adjacent district of Dharwar they constitute nearly 50 per cent of the total. Beyond the limits of the Bombay Presidency, Lingayats are numerous in the Mysore and Hyderabad States. They also form an important element in the population of the north-west corner of the Madras Presidency.[1]

1. Description.—The Lingayats, who are also known as Lingawants, Lingangis, Śivabhaktas, and Viraśaivas, derive their name from the Skr. word *liṅga*, the phallic emblem, with the affix *āyta*, and are 'the people who bear the *liṅga*' habitually. Their name literally describes them; for the true Lingayat wears on his body a small silver box containing a stone phallus, which is the symbol of his faith, and the loss of which is equivalent to spiritual death. The emblem is worn by both sexes. The men carry the box on a red silk scarf or a thread tied round the neck, while the women wear it inside their costume, on a neck-string. When working, the male wearer sometimes shifts it to his left arm.

The Lingayats are Dravidian, that is to say, they belong to a stock that was established in India before the arrival of the so-called Aryans. They are dark in complexion, in common with the races of Southern India, and speak Kanarese, a Dravidian language. They have been not inaptly described as a peaceable race of Hindu puritans, though it may be questioned how far their rejection of many of the chief dogmas of Brāhmanic Hinduism leaves them the right to be styled Hindus at all. Of the Brāhmanic triad—Brahmā, Viṣṇu, and Śiva—they acknowledge only the god Śiva, whose emblem, the *liṅga*, they bear on their persons. They reverence the Vedas, but disregard the later commentaries on which the Brāhmans rely. Originally they seem to have been the product of one of the numerous reformations in India that have been

[1] The census of 1911 gives the following figures for Lingayats: Bombay Presidency, 729,431; Mysore, 1,339,248; Madras Presidency, 134,592; total India, 2,976,293.

aimed against the supremacy and doctrines of the Brāhmans, whose selfish exploitation of the lower castes has frequently led to the rise of new sects essentially anti-Brāhmanic in origin. It seems clear that, in its inception, Lingayatism not only rested largely on a denial of the Brāhman claim to supremacy over all other castes, but attempted to abolish all caste distinctions. All wearers of the *liṅga* were proclaimed equal in the eyes of God. The traditional Lingayat teacher, Basava, proclaimed all men holy in proportion as they are temples of the great spirit, and thus, in his view, all men are born equal. The denial of the supremacy of the Brāhmans, coupled with the assertion of the essential equality of all men, constituted a vital departure from the doctrines of orthodox Hinduism. Other important innovations were: the prohibition of child-marriage; the removal of all restriction on widows remarrying; the burial, instead of burning, of the dead; and the abolition of the chief Hindu rites for the removal of ceremonial impurity. The founders of the religion could scarcely have forged more potent weapons for severing the bonds between their proselytes and the followers of the doctrines preached by contemporary Brāhmanic Hinduism.

The reader must not assume that this brief description of the fundamental doctrines of a religious movement which dates from the 12th cent. A.D. conveys an accurate picture of the prevalent Lingayatism of the present day. In connexion with the attitude originally assumed towards caste distinctions, there has been a very noticeable departure from Basava's teaching. The origin of caste in India is as yet a subject requiring much elucidation. In its development no mean influence must be allotted to function, religion, and political boundaries. Nor can differences of race have failed materially to assist the formation of Indian society on its present basis. One of the most interesting phenomena connected with the evolution of modern caste is the working of a religious reformation in which caste finds no place on the previously existing social structure of caste units. If caste is largely a manifestation of deep-rooted prejudices tending to raise and preserve barriers between the social intercourse of different sections of the human race, it would seem not unnatural to expect that it would tend to reassert itself within the fold of an essentially casteless religion so soon as the enthusiasm of the founders had spent itself; and it is not unlikely that the mere fact of converts having joined the movement at an early stage in its history would generate a claim to social precedence over the later converts, and thus in time reconstitute the old caste barrier that the reformers spent themselves in endeavouring to destroy. One of the most interesting pages in the history of caste evolution, therefore, must be that which deals with the evolution of caste inside the fold of a religious community originally formed on a non-caste basis. A remarkable instance of such evolution will be found in the history of Lingayatism. The Lingayats of the present day are divided into three well-defined groups, including numerous true castes, of which a description will be found in the section dealing with their social organization (see p. 72). With the rise of caste distinctions, numerous other changes occurred in the nature of the Lingayat religion. The *ayyas* or *jaṅgams*, the priests of the community, devised in time a ritual and ceremonies in which the influence of the rival Brāhman aristocracy can freely be traced. The more important of these ceremonies are described in § 4 below. But it is essential to a thorough understanding of the nature of Lingayatism that the most important ceremony of all, known as the *aṣṭavarṇa*, or the eightfold sacrament, should be understood by the reader. It is commonly asserted nowadays by prominent members of the Lingayat community that the true test of a Lingayat is the right to receive the full *aṣṭavarṇa*, and that the possession of a few of these eight rites only does not entitle the possessor to be styled a member of the community. The contention seems scarcely in harmony with the popular usage of the term 'Lingayat.'

The *aṣṭavarṇa* consists of eight rites known as

1. Guru.	5. Mantra.
2. Liṅga.	6. Jaṅgam.
3. Vibhūti.	7. Tīrth.
4. Rudrākṣa.	8. Prasād.

On the birth of a Lingayat the parents send for the *guru*, or spiritual adviser, of the family, who is the representative of one of the five *āchāryas*, or holy men, from whom the father claims descent. The *guru* binds the *liṅga* on the child, besmears it with *vibhūti* (ashes), places a garland of *rudrākṣa* (seeds of the bastard cedar) round its neck, and teaches it the mystic *mantra*, or prayer, known as *Namaḥ Śivāya—i.e.* 'Obeisance to the god Śiva.' The child being incapable of acquiring a knowledge of the sacred text at this early stage of its existence, the prayer is merely recited in its ear by the *guru*. The child has then to be presented to the god Śiva in the person of a *jaṅgam*, or Lingayat priest, who is summoned for this purpose. On his arrival the parents wash his feet, and the water in which the feet are washed is described as the *tīrtha* or *charaṇatīrtha* of Śiva. This water is next poured over the *liṅga* attached to the infant. The *jaṅgam* is fed, and a portion of the food from the dish is placed in the child's mouth. This final ceremony is known as *prasād*. Occasionally the double characters of *guru* and *jaṅgam* are combined in one person. When the child attains the age of eight or ten, the ceremony is repeated with slight modifications.

It will be seen that this eightfold ceremony forms a very concise test of a Lingayat's religious status, and may be not unfitly compared to the rites of baptism and confirmation which are outward and visible signs of admission to the Catholic Church. But not all Christians are confirmed, and in the same way not all members of the Lingayat community undergo the full ceremony of initiation. It would probably be safer to apply the term 'Lingayat' to all wearers of the *liṅga*, whether they are entitled to the full *aṣṭavarṇa* on birth or conversion, or to a few only of the eight sacraments. In so doing, the lower orders, from a social standpoint, of the Lingayat community will not be excluded, as they would otherwise be, from the fold.

Lingayats are not permitted to touch meat or to drink any kind of liquor. The greater number of them are either occupied in agriculture or are traders. They are generally reputed to be peaceful and law-abiding; but at times they are capable of dividing into violent factions with such rancour and hostility that the dispute culminates in riots, and occasionally in murder. Among the educated members of the community there is a strong spirit of rivalry with the Brāhmans, whose intellect and capacity have secured them a preponderating share of Government appointments. Except for these defects, the community may be described as steady and industrious, devoted to honest toil, whether in professional employment or occupied in trading or the cultivation of the soil.

2. History.—Until the recent publication of two inscriptions, which have been deciphered and edited by J. F. Fleet, and throw an entirely new light on the probable origin of the Lingayat religion, the movement in favour of this special form of Śiva-worship was commonly supposed to have been set on foot by the great Lingayat saint, Basava, in the latter half of the 12th century. The acts and doctrines of Basava and of his nephew Channabasava are set forth in two *purāṇas*, or sacred books, named, after them, the *Basavapurāṇa* (ed. Poona, 1905) and the *Channabasavapurāṇa* (ed. Mangalore, 1851). But these works were not written until some centuries had elapsed since the death of the saints; and it seems certain that the substratum of fact which they contain had by that time become so overlaid with tradition and miraculous occurrences as to render them of little historical value. The *Basavapurāṇa* describes Basava as the son of Brāhman parents, Madiraja and Madalambika, residents of Bagevadi, usually held to be the town of that name in the Bijapur district of the Bombay Presidency. Basava is the Kanarese name for 'bull,' an animal sacred to Śiva, and thus a connexion is traced between Basava and the god Śiva. At the age of eight, Basava refused to be invested with the sacred thread of the twice-born caste, to which he belonged by birth, declaring himself a worshipper of Śiva, and stating that he had come to destroy the distinctions of caste. By his knowledge of the Śaiva scriptures he attracted the attention of his uncle Baladeva, then prime minister to the king of Kalyan, Bijjala. Baladeva gave him his daughter Gangadevi in marriage. Subsequently Bijjala, a Kalachurya by race, who usurped the Chalukyan kingdom of Kalyana in the middle of the 12th cent., installed Basava as his prime minister, and gave him his younger sister Nilalochana to wife. The *purāṇas* further recount the birth of Channabasava from Basava's unmarried sister Nagalambika, by the working of the spirit of the god Śiva. The myth in connexion with this miraculous conception is interesting. Basava, while engaged in prayer, saw an ant emerge from the ground with a small seed in its mouth. He took the seed to his home, where his sister swallowed it and became pregnant. The issue of this unique conception was Channabasava. Uncle and nephew both preached the new doctrines, and in so doing encountered the hostility of the Jains, whom they ruthlessly persecuted. A revolution, the outcome of these religious factions, led to the assassination of king Bijjala and to the flight of Basava and his nephew. Basava is said to have been finally absorbed into the *liṅga* at Kudal Sangameśwar, and Channabasava to have lost his life at Ulvi in North Kanara, a district in the Bombay Presidency. An annual pilgrimage of Lingayats to the shrine of the latter at Ulvi takes place to this day.

Two important inscriptions bearing on these traditions of the origin of the Lingayats deserve consideration. The first was discovered at the village of Managoli, a few miles from Bagevadi, the traditional birthplace of Basava. This record (as also many others) shows that king Bijjala gained the kingdom of Kalyan in A.D. 1156. It also states that a certain Basava was the builder of the temple in which the inscription was first put, and that Madiraja was *mahāprabhu*, or head of the village, when the grants in aid of the temple were made. Basava is further described as the grandson of Revadasa and son of Chandiraja, and as a man of great sanctity and virtue. The second inscription was found at Ablur in the Dharwar district of the Bombay Presidency, and belongs to about A.D. 1200. It relates the fortunes of a certain Ekantada-Ramayya, an ardent worshipper of the god Śiva. Ramayya came into conflict with the Jains, and defeated them, both in dispute and, the inscription says, by performing a miracle—we may venture to say, by arranging matters so that he seemed to perform it—which consisted in cutting off his own head and having it restored to him, safe and sound, by the grace of Śiva, seven days later. All this came to the notice of King Bijjala, who summoned Ramayya into his presence. And Ramayya, making his cause good before the king, won his support, and was presented with gifts of lands for the temple founded by him at Ablur in the new faith. The incidents related of Ramayya are placed shortly before A.D. 1162, so that he would have been a contemporary of Basava. No mention, however, of the latter or of his nephew is found in this record.

If we accept the contemporary inscriptions as more entitled to credit than the tradition overlaid with myth recorded at a later date, it seems clear that both Basava and Ekantada-Ramayya were reformers who had much to do with the rise of the Lingayat doctrine, and that the event is to be placed in the 12th century. Lingayat scholars of the present day, indeed, claim a far earlier date for the origin of their faith. But their contention that its origin is contemporaneous with that of Brāhmanic Hinduism has yet to be established by adequate evidence. The best opinion seems to be that of Fleet, who considers that there is no doubt that the present Lingayat sect is more or less a development of the gild (mentioned in many inscriptions) of the 500 Swamis of Aihole, a village in the Bijapur district, the protectors of the Vira-Bananju religion, who were always more or less strictly Śaivas, but, with a free-mindedness which is not now common, patronized also Buddhism. The movement, however, in which the 500 Swamis of Aihole joined seems certainly to have originated with Ekantada-Ramayya at Ablur. And probably the prevalent tradition of the present day, that Basava was the originator of it and the founder of the community, must only be attributed to his having quickly become acquainted with the new development of Śaivism started by Ramayya, and to his having taken a leading part in encouraging and propagating it in circumstances which rendered him more conspicuous than the real founder. Basava happened to be a member of the body of village elders at Managoli, and so to occupy a recognizable position in local matters, administrative as well as religious. Consequently, it seems likely that, when the first literary account of the rise of Lingayatism came to be written, which was unquestionably an appreciable time after the event, his name had survived, to the exclusion of Ramayya's. Accordingly, the writer of that account was unable to tell us anything particular about Ramayya, beyond duly recording the miracle performed by him, and attributed the movement entirely to Basava, assigning to him an assistant, his nephew Channabasava, who is perhaps only a mythical person. But it must be also admitted that the early history of the movement may be capable of further elucidation, and that the present-day claims of the leading Lingayats for a very early origin for their religion, though lacking the support of historical evidence, have this much to rely on, that it is essentially probable that the Dravidian races of Southern India, whose primitive deities were absorbed by the Aryan invaders into the personality of their god Śiva, always leant towards the special worship of Śiva to the exclusion of the other members of the Brāhmanic triad, and combined with this preference a dislike of Brāhmanic ritual and caste ascendancy which is the real substratum of the movement ending in the recognition of Lingayatism.

In dismissing the question of the origin of the Lingayat religion, it seems desirable to give an instance of the claims advanced by learned members of the community for a greater antiquity for their religion than historical evidence would afford it. Mr. Karibasavashastri, Professor of Sanskrit and Kanarese in the State College of Mysore, contends that the Śaiva sect of Hindus has always been divided into two groups, the one comprising the wearers of the *liṅga*, and the other those who do not wear it. The former he designates Viraśaiva, and declares that the Viraśaivas consist of Brāhman, Kṣatriya, Vaiśya, and Śūdra, the fourfold caste division of Manu. Quoting from the 17th chapter of the *Parameśvar āgama*, he declares that the Viraśaiva Brāhmans are also known as Śuddha Viraśaivas, Viraśaiva kings as Marga Viraśaivas, Viraśaiva Vaiśyas as Miśra Viraśaivas, and the Śūdras of the community as Anteve Viraśaivas. In his opinion, the duties and penances imposed on the first of these classes are (1) the *aṣṭavarṇa* (see p. 70), (2) penances and bodily emaciation, (3) the worship of Śiva without sacrifice, (4) the recital of the Vedas. He further asserts that the Hindu *aśramas*, or conditions of life of *brahmachārī*, *gṛhastha*, and *sannyāsī*, *i.e.* student, householder, and ascetic, are binding on Viraśaivas, and quotes, from various Sanskrit works, texts in support of this view. He furnishes a mythical account of the origin of Lingayats at the time of the creation of the world. The importance of this summary of his views lies in the fact that it is completely typical of the claims that many members of the Lingayat community have recently commenced to advance to be included, in a sense, within the fold of orthodox Hinduism, with the mistaken notion of thereby improving their social standing. They endeavour to divide themselves into Manu's fourfold caste scheme of Brāhman, Kṣatriya, Vaiśya, and Śūdra, regardless of the fact that theirs is in origin a non-caste religion, and that Manu's scheme, which can only with great inaccuracy be applied to the more orthodox Hindu castes, is totally unsuited to the Lingayats. A sign of this movement towards Brāhmanic Hinduism among Lingayats is to be found in the organized attempt made by certain Lingayats at recent censuses to enter themselves as Viraśaiva Brāhmans; and it seems probable that these claims to a great antiquity for their religion and for a caste scheme based on Manu's model are chiefly significant as signs of the social ambitions of the educated members, who are jealous of the precedence of the Brāhmans.

3. Social organization.—The results of investigations undertaken in the Bombay Presidency in 1900 by committees of Lingayat gentlemen entrusted with the duty of preparing a classification of the numerous social subdivisions of the Lingayat community tend to show that the relation of these various groups to each other is one of some complexity. Broadly speaking, Lingayats appear to consist of three groups of subdivisions.

(1) The first, which for convenience may be named 'Panchamsalis with full *aṣṭavarṇa* rites' (see p. 70 above), contains the priests of the community, known as *ayyas* or *jaṅgams*, and the leading trader castes, or *banjigs*. It is probable that this group is the nearest approximation to the original converts, who, it will be remembered, could interdine and intermarry without restriction. The seven subdivisions of this group may still dine together, but for purposes of marriage the subdivisions rank one above the other, and it is permissible for a bridegroom of one subdivision to take a bride only from the divisions below his. The reverse process, namely, of a bride marrying a youth of a lower division, is strictly forbidden. Members of the lower subdivisions of this group may rise to the higher by performing certain rites and ceremonies. The marrying of a boy to a girl beneath him in social rank and of a girl to a boy above her is part of a system of isogamy and hypergamy, and is not at all uncommon in many Indian castes. It is a probable speculation that the early converts in course of time came to rank themselves as superior to the more recent converts of the community, and the growth of this feeling would lead, in harmony with the ideas that prevail in all societies, to the early converts declining to wed their daughters to the newcomers, though they would accept brides from the latter as socially inferior, if only slightly so. The Panchamsalis, as they may be called for lack of a better name, are all entitled to the *aṣṭavarṇa* rites, and rank socially above the remaining groups. In *BG* xxiii. 218 they are described as 'Pure Lingayats.'

(2) The next group is that of the 'non-Panchamsalis with *aṣṭavarṇa* rites.' This group contains over 70 subdivisions, which are functional groups, such as weavers, oil-pressers, bricklayers, dyers, cultivators, shepherds, and the like. It seems probable that they represent converts of a much later date than those whom we have styled Panchamsalis, and were never permitted to interdine or intermarry with the latter. In this group each subdivision is self-contained in regard to marriage; that is to say, a *jāḍar*, or weaver, may marry only a *jāḍar* girl, a *bādig*, or carpenter, may marry only a *bādig* girl, and so on, resembling in this respect the ordinary Hindu castes, which are usually endogamous. Members of one subdivision may not pass to another. The names of the subdivisions are commonly indicative of the calling of the members, and it is of special interest to note here how the barriers erected by specialization of function have proved too strong for the original communal theories of equality which the Lingayats of early days adopted.

It is interesting to observe that considerable diversity of practice exists in connexion with the relations of the subdivisions of this group to the parent Hindu castes from which they separated to become Lingayats. In most cases it is found that, when a portion of an original Hindu caste has been converted to Lingayatism, both intermarriage and interdining with the unconverted members are finally abandoned, and the caste is broken into two divisions, of which one is to be recognized by the members wearing the *liṅga*, and the other by their wearing the sacred thread of the twice-born. But in some instances—*e.g.*, the Jeers of the Belgaum district—the Lingayat members continue to take brides from the non-Lingayat section, though they will not marry their daughters to them; it is usual to invest the bride with the *liṅga* at the marriage ceremony, thus formally receiving her into the Lingayat community. In other cases the Lingayat and non-Lingayat sections live side by side and dine together at caste functions, intermarriage being forbidden. In this case, however, the former call in a *jaṅgam* to perform their religious ceremonies, and the latter employ a Brāhman. The more typical case seems to be that of a caste subdivision given in the Indian Census Report (*Bombay Census Report*, 1901, ch. viii. p. 182). In the last century a Lingayat priest of Ujjini converted a number of weavers in the village of Tuminkatti, Dharwar district, Bombay. These converts abandoned all social intercourse with their former caste brethren, and took their place as a new subdivision in the non-Panchamsali group under the name of Kurvinaras.

This second group of subdivisions, therefore, differs essentially from the Panchamsalis, though the members also have the *aṣṭavarṇa* rites. It is described in *BG* under the name of 'Affiliated Lingayats.'

(3) The third group of subdivisions is the 'non-Panchamsalis without *aṣṭavarṇa* rites.' It contains washermen, tanners, shoemakers, fishermen, etc., which would rank as unclean castes among Brāhmanic Hindus. It is the practice among Lingayats of the present day to deny that the members of this third group are entitled to be classed as Lingayats at all. They maintain that, since the possession of the full *aṣṭavarṇa* rites is the mark of a Lingayat, these lower divisions, who at most can claim three or four of the eight sacraments, are only the followers or servants of Lingayats. The contention is not unreasonable; yet it seems that these lower orders would be styled Lingayats by the other Hindus of the neighbourhood, and would describe themselves as such. A classification of the Lingayat community would not there-

fore be complete unless they were included. On this point the evidence of J. A. Dubois is of interest. He writes:

'If even a Pariah joins the sect he is considered in no way inferior to a Brahmin. Wherever the *lingam* is found, there, they say, is the throne of the deity, without distinction of class or rank' (*Hindu Manners, Customs, and Ceremonies*[3], p. 117).

Lingayats of this description marry only within their subdivision. They are described as 'Half-Lingayats' in *BG*.

Within the subdivisions just described smaller groups are found, known as exogamous sections, that is to say, groups of which the members are held to be so closely connected that, like blood-relations, they must marry outside their section. Little accurate information is available regarding the nature and origin of these sections; but it appears that in the higher ranks they are named after five Lingayat sages, Nandi, Bhṛṅgi, Vīra, Vṛṣa, and Skanda, and in this respect closely resemble the ordinary Brāhmanic *gotras* (*q.v.*). The Lingayats do not allow the children of brothers to intermarry, nor may sisters' children marry together. Marriage with the children of a paternal uncle or maternal aunt is similarly forbidden. A man may marry his sister's daughter; but, if the sister be a younger sister, such a marriage is looked on with disfavour. Marriage is both infant and adult. Sexual licence is neither recognized nor tolerated, but is punished, if need be, by excommunication. Polygamy is permitted, but is usual only when the first wife fails to bear a son. The disputes that arise on social or religious questions are settled by the *pañchāyat*, or committee of five elders, an appeal lying to the head of the *maṭh*, or religious house. These *maṭhs* are found scattered over the tract of country in which Lingayats predominate; but there are five of special sanctity and importance, namely, at Ujjini, Śrīśaila, Kollepaka, Balehalli, and Benares. From these, decisions on vexed questions of doctrine and ritual issue from time to time.

4. Beliefs and customs.—It has been seen that the Lingayats are believers in the god Śiva, the third person of the Hindu triad, signifying the creative and destructive forces in the universe. Thence they derive the phallus, or *liṅga*, emblematic of reproduction, and the sacred bull, Nandi or Basava, found in all their temples, and in all probability the emblem of strength. The ceremonies in vogue at birth, betrothal, marriage, and death have been accurately described by R. C. Carr in his monograph on the Lingayat community (Madras Government Press, 1906), and are given below.

One principal Lingayat ceremony known as the *aṣṭavarṇa*, or eightfold sacrament, has been already referred to in some detail (p. 70 above). The essentially Lingayat beliefs and ceremonies, such as the wearing of the *liṅga*, the worship of the *jaṅgam*, and the administration of *aṣṭavarṇa* rites, are, however, as is usual in India, constantly mingled with many commonplace Hindu beliefs and customs. It is a common practice in India for Hindus to worship at the shrine of Musalmān *pīrs*, or saints, and in the same way Lingayats will combine the worship of the special objects prescribed by Basava with the worship of purely Hindu deities such as Hanuman, Ganapati, Yellamma, Maruti, and many others. The investigations hitherto conducted do not clearly show how far Lingayat and Hindu ritual are liable to be combined; but it can be confidently predicted that the lower orders of the community, who still keep in touch with the unconverted section of the caste to which, professionally speaking, they belong, will be found to adhere in many instances to the beliefs and customs of their unconverted fellow castemen, despite the teaching and influence of the *jaṅgams*.

The specially Lingayat ceremonies described by Carr are:

(1) *Birth.*—It is customary for the female relatives attending a confinement to bathe both mother and child. On the second or third day boiled turmeric and water is applied to the mother, and a ceremony known as *viralu*, or the worship of the afterbirth, is performed. The propitiation of the afterbirth by the offering of food, *nīm* leaves, turmeric, and a coco-nut, is considered necessary for the safe suckling of the child. When the child receives the *tīrth*, or water in which the *jaṅgam's* feet have been washed (see above, p. 70[b]), the mother also partakes of it.

(2) *Betrothal.*—For a betrothal the bridegroom's family come to the bride's house on an auspicious day in company with a *jaṅgam*. They bring a woman's cloth, a jacket, two coco-nuts, five pieces of turmeric, five limes, and betel-leaf and areca-nut. They also bring flowers for the *sūsaka* (a cap of flowers made for the bride), gold and silver ornaments, and sugar and betel-nut for distribution to guests. The bride puts on the new clothes with the ornaments and flowers, and sits on a folded blanket on which fantastic devices have been made with rice. Some married women fill her lap with coco-nuts and other things brought by the bridegroom's party. Music is played, and the women sing. Five of them pick up the rice on the blanket and gently drop it on to the bride's knees, shoulders, and head. They do this three times with both hands; sugar and betel are then distributed, and one of the bride's family proclaims the fact that the bride has been given to the bridegroom. One of the bridegroom's family then states that the bride is accepted. That night the bride's family feed the visitors on sweet things; dishes made of hot or pungent things are strictly prohibited.

(3) *Marriage.*—The marriage ceremony occupies from one to four days, according to circumstances. In the case of a four-day marriage, the first day is spent in worshipping ancestors. On the second day rice and oil are sent to the local *maṭh*, or religious house, and oil alone to the relatives. New pots are brought with much shouting, and deposited in the god's room. A marriage booth is erected, and the bridegroom sits under it side by side with a married female relative, and goes through a performance which is called *surige*. An enclosure is made round them with cotton thread passed ten times round four earthen pitchers placed at the four corners. Five married women come with boiled water and wash off the oil and turmeric with which the bride and the bridegroom and his companions have been anointed. The matrons then clothe them with the new clothes offered to the ancestors on the first day. After some ceremonial the thread forming the enclosure is removed and given to a *jaṅgam*. The *surige* being now over, the bridegroom and his relative are taken back to the god's room. The bride and her relative are then taken to the *pandal*, and another *surige* is gone through. When this is over, the bride is taken to her room and is decorated with flowers. At the same time the bridegroom is decorated in the god's room, and, mounting on a bullock, goes to the village temple, where he offers a coco-nut. A chaplet of flowers called *bāsiṅga* is tied to his forehead, and he returns to the house. In the god's room a *pañchkalaś*, consisting of five metal vases with betel and ashes, has been arranged, one vase being placed at each corner of a square and one in the middle. By each *kalaś* is a coco-nut, a date fruit, a betel-leaf, an areca-nut, and one pice tied in a handkerchief. A cotton thread is passed round the square, and round the centre *kalaś* another thread, one end of which is held by the family *guru* and the other by the bridegroom, who sits opposite to him. The *guru* wears a ring

made of *kuśa* grass on the big toe of his right foot. The bride sits on the left-hand side of the bridegroom, and the *guru* ties their right and left hands respectively with *kuśa* grass. The joined hands of the bride and bridegroom are washed, and *bilva* (*Ægle marmelos*) leaves and flowers are offered. The officiating priest then consecrates the neck ornament and the thread, ties the latter on the wrists of the joined hands, and gives the former to the bridegroom, who ties it round the bride's neck, repeating some words after the priest.

The tying of the *tāli* is the binding portion of the ceremony. Before the *tāli* is given to the bridegroom, it is passed round the assembly to be touched by all and blessed. As soon as the bridegroom ties it on the bride, all those present throw over the pair a shower of rice. The bridegroom places some cummin seed and *jāgri*, or unrefined sugar, on the bride's head, and the bride does the same to the bridegroom. Small quantities of these articles are tied in a corner of the cloth of each, and the cloths are then knotted together. The bride worships the bridegroom's feet, and he throws rice on her head. The newly married couple offer fruits to five *jaṅgams*, and present them with five pice. The relatives worship the bride and bridegroom, wash their feet, and offer presents, and the proceedings of the day terminate.

On the third day, friends and relatives are fed. On the fourth day, bride and bridegroom ride in procession through the village on the same bullock, the bride in front. On returning to the house they throw scented powder at each other, and the guests join in the fun. Then follows the wedding breakfast, to which only the near relatives are admitted. The married couple worship *jaṅgams* and the elders, and take off the consecration thread from their wrists and tie it at the doorway. The five matrons who have assisted are given presents and dismissed, and the marriage is now complete.

In a one-day marriage the above ceremonies are crowded into the short time allotted.

The remarriage of widows was one of the points on which Basava insisted, and was probably one of the biggest bones of contention with the Brāhmans. Widow remarriage is allowed at the present day, but the authorities at Ujjini see fit to disregard it. They say that among *jaṅgams* it is prohibited, and that among the other classes of Lingayats it is the growth of custom.

(4) *Death.*—The dead are buried in a sitting posture facing towards the north; but an exception is made in the case of unmarried people, who are buried in a reclining position.

Before the sick man dies, the ceremony called *vibhūti-velai* is performed. He is given a bath, and is made to drink holy water in which the *jaṅgam's* feet have been washed. He is made to give the *jaṅgam* a handkerchief with *vibhūti* (ashes), *rudrākṣa* (seeds of the bastard cedar), *dakṣiṇa* (coin), and *tāmbūla* (betel-leaf). This is followed by a meal, of which all the *jaṅgams* present and the relatives and friends of the patient partake. It appears to be immaterial whether the patient is still alive or not. It is stated that, if the invalid survives this ceremony, he must take to the jungles and disappear; but in practice this is not observed. The death party resembles in some respects an Irish 'wake,' though the latter does not commence until the deceased is well on his way to the next world.

After death the corpse is placed in a sitting posture, and the *jaṅgam*, who has received the offering before death, places his left hand on the right thigh of the body. The people present worship the corpse, and the usual distribution of coins and betel to *jaṅgams* follows. The body is then carried in a *vimān*, or bamboo chair, to the burial-ground. The grave should be a cube of 9 feet dimensions, with a niche on one side in which the corpse is to sit. The *liṅga* is untied and placed in the left hand, *bilva* leaves and *vibhūti* are placed at the side, the body is wrapped in an orange-coloured cloth, and the grave is filled in. A *jaṅgam* stands on the grave, and, after receiving the usual *douceur*, shouts out the name of the deceased, and says that he has gone to Kailāsa, or heaven.

Memorial ceremonies are contrary to Lingayat tenets; but in this, as in other matters, the influence of the Brāhmans appears, and among some sections an annual ceremony is performed. The performance of *śrāddha*, or the funeral ceremonies common to other Hindus, is unknown. Dubois tells us that a Lingayat is no sooner buried than he is forgotten.

'The point in the creed of the Sivaites which appears to me to be most remarkable is their entire rejection of that fundamental principle of the Hindu religion, *marujanma*, or metempsychosis' (p. 116).

From this it would follow that they do not believe in ghosts. But there is a generally accepted idea that evil spirits sometimes take possession of females. This may be a rude way of expressing the fact that the gentle sex is 'uncertain, coy, and hard to please.' Although the ceremony of *śrāddha* is unknown, once in a year on the new moon day of the month Bhadrapada or in Aswina, they offer clothes and food to (*a*) ancestors in general, (*b*) childless ancestors, and (*c*) men who have died a violent death.

Among Lingayats widow remarriage is common, and divorce is permissible. The ordinary law of Hindus is followed in regard to inheritance. Lingayats regard their *jaṅgams*, or priests, as incarnations of Siva, and will bathe their *liṅgas* in the water in which the *jaṅgam* has washed his feet and thus rendered holy. They have numerous superstitions regarding good and bad omens. Thus, it is lucky to meet a deer or a dog going from right to left, whereas the same animals passing from left to right will bring ill luck (monograph on Lingayats by R. C. Carr). They do not observe the pollution periods of the Hindus, and their indifference to the ordinary Hindu purification ceremonies is notorious (Dubois, pt. i. ch. ix.).

Members of other religious communities who wish to become Lingayats are called on to undergo a three days' ceremony of purification. On the first day they allow their face and head to be shaved, and bathe in the products of the cow, which alone they may feed on and drink that day. The second day they bathe in water in which the feet of a *jaṅgam* have been washed, and which is therefore holy water. They eat sugar and drink milk. On the third day they take a bath described as *pañchāmṛt*, *i.e.* they apply to the head and body a paste made up of plantains, cow's milk, clarified butter, curds, and honey, and wash it off with water; they again drink the *tīrth*, or water in which the feet of a *jaṅgam* have been washed, and are then invested with the *liṅga*, after which they are allowed to dine with Lingayats, and are considered members of the community. Women undergo the same ceremony, except the head-shaving.

5. General remarks.—It will be gathered from the foregoing sketch of the origin and present-day social organization and customs of the Lingayats that the community is virtually an original casteless section in process of reversion to a congeries of castes holding a common religion. It has been seen how, in the 12th cent., a movement was set on foot and spread abroad by two Brāhmans, Ekantada-Ramayya and Basava, devotees of Siva, to abolish the ceremonies and restrictions that fettered the intercourse between the different ranks of orthodox Hindu society of the period, and to establish a community on a basis of the equality of its members, irrespective of sex, by means of the purifying worship of the one god Śiva. It seems clear that the movement found special favour in the eyes of the Jain traders of the period, who would have ranked, as Vaiśyas, below both Brāhman priest and Kṣatriya warrior under the Hindu scheme of social precedence. The community encountered the hostility of the Jains, who remained unconverted, but clung tenaciously to its simple faith in the worship of Śiva, and in his emblem, the *liṅga*. We must assume the probability that the Brāhman converts, of whose existence we possess historical evidence, tended by degrees to assert for themselves social precedence as *ayyas* or *jaṅgams*, *i.e.* the priests of the community, for which position their knowledge and descent would give them special fitness. In time, indeed, they came to be regarded as the very incarnations of the god Śiva, and thus they were holy, imparting holiness in a special degree to the water in which they had bathed their feet, known as *tīrth*, so that it plays a prominent part to this day in the Lingayat ceremonies. Once the original notion of universal equality of rank had yielded to the priests a precedence incompatible with such equality, the way was prepared for the introduction of further social gradations, and the older members of the community commenced to claim over the later converts a precedence modelled on that which the priests had established against them. In such a manner the essential doctrine of equality became completely undermined, and in the end gave place to certain rites and ceremonies as the test of Lingayat orthodoxy. Thus, when the more recent cases of caste conversion occurred, a section of a Hindu caste became Lingayat, not, as the founders of the religion would have wished, by being admitted to a footing of equality on the common ground of the worship of Śiva and of his emblem the *liṅga*, but by investiture through certain rites and ceremonies with the *liṅga*, retaining their distinctive social status as a functional caste, with which other Lingayats would neither marry nor dine. It must be admitted that in the case of most of the Lingayat subdivisions the *jaṅgam* will take food in the house of the members, but here all trace of the original equality ceases; and the Lingayats of to-day present the curious and interesting spectacle of a religious sect broken in the course of centuries into social fragments, of which the older sections remain essentially sectarian, and the more recent in origin possess the typical attributes of ordinary Hindu castes. As in the case of Christianity in some parts of India, the social barriers of caste have proved too strong for the communal basis of the orthodox religion.

LITERATURE.—J. F. Fleet, *Epigraphia Indica*, v. (1899), also art. in *IA* xxx. (1901); C. P. Brown, 'Essay on the Creed, Customs, and Literature of the Jangams,' in *Madras Journal of Literature and Science*, ser. i. vol. xi. (1840); J. A. Dubois, *Hindu Manners, Customs, and Ceremonies*[3], Oxford, 1906; B. L. Rice, *Manual of Mysore and Coorg*, i. (1895); *BG*, 'Bijapur and Dharwar,' 1880; *Census of India*, 1901, ix., 'Bombay'; R. C. Carr, *Lingayats*, Madras, 1906; R. G. Bhandarkar, *GIAP* iii. 6 (1913), pp. 131-140.

R. E. ENTHOVEN.

gLING CHOS.—The *gLing chos* (*gLing*-mythology), or *gLing glu* (*gLing*-song),[1] is the mythology contained in Tibetan folk-lore, and is perhaps the most ancient religion of that country. It is distinguished from the ancient mythology of countries such as Finland and Russia by the fact that it has not to be pieced together from fragmentary allusions scattered through the whole range of Tibetan folk-lore, but can be gathered from complete hymnals and catechisms, in which the *gLing chos* has been preserved for us almost untouched.

1. Is the gLing chos the ancient religion of West Tibet only or of the whole of Tibet?—Although the present writer's materials were collected exclusively in West Tibet, it is probable that the *gLing chos* was the ancient religion of the whole country. (1) We are informed by a lāma of Tashilhunpo (in Central Tibet) that an endless variety of versions of the Kesar-saga (not the Kesar-epic, which belongs to the subject of Lāmaism) are current, just as is the case in Ladākh (Western Tibet), where each village has one or even more versions of its own. (2) In the legends of Milaraspa there are embodied several *gLing glu*.[1] Milaraspa seems to have been extremely clever in building a bridge from the *gLing chos* to Lāmaism. He was a native of Eastern Tibet, Khang chen åbyung lngā (or the Kanchanjanga) being his native country. But, even if the *gLing chos* can be proved to be, territorially, a real Tibetan religion, the question still remains whether it is the original property of the Tibetan (Indo-Chinese) race or belongs to the Mon and Bedha population, who are the principal preservers of it at the present day, and who are not of Indo-Chinese, but possibly of Aryan and Mundari, stock.

2. Cosmology of the gLing chos.—In all the sources mentioned below, in the Literature, three large realms are spoken of:

(1) *sTang lha*, heaven (literally, 'the upper gods,' or 'the gods above').—A king reigns in sTang lha called sKyer rdzong snyanpo.[2] He is also called dBangpo rgyabzhin, and åBum khri rgyalpo. The name of his wife, the queen of heaven, is bKur dman rgyalmo, Ane bkur dmanmo, or åBum khri rgyalmo. They have three sons, Don yod, Don ldan, and Don grub. The youngest is the most prominent figure. 'Lightning flashes from his sword out of the middle of black clouds.' Don grub descends to the earth and becomes king Kesar of gLing. According to one theory, thunder seems to be caused by the walking of the gods, and, according to another, it is the groaning of the dragon-shaped *åbrug*, dwelling in the dark clouds, when it is assailed by Kesar with his sword of lightning. Three daughters of the king of heaven are also mentioned.

The life of the gods is an idealized form of man's life. They constitute a State, with king, ministers, servants, and subjects. They abide in perfect happiness, and live, free from illness, to a good old age. They tend, apparently on the earth, certain goats known as *lha ra*. These they must defend against the devil bDud. Kesar later on discovers many of the *lha ra* in the latter's realm. The king and the queen often change their shape. The former becomes a white bird or a yak, and the latter takes the shape of a woman, a *dzo* (hybrid between a cow and a yak), a golden or turquoise fly, or a dove.

(2) *Bar btsan*, the earth (literally, 'the firm place in the middle').—Other names are *mi yul*, 'land of men,' and *gLing*, 'the continent.' The principal deity of this earth is mother Skyabs bdun (or Skyabs mdun). It is probable that she is identical with brTanma, the goddess of the earth (H. A. Jäschke, *Tibetan-English Dictionary*, London, 1881). She rides a horse called bTsan rta dmar chung. Of her subjects, the human race, we do not hear much in the saga. The

[1] The term *gLing chos* was first employed by the present writer. Among natives of Tibet the name *gLing glu* ('songs of *gLing*') is in more general use. In a hymnal discovered in Upper Kanāwār the words *Lha chos* and *Bon chos* are used for this type of religion.

[1] Some of these *gLing glu* will be found in B. Laufer's 'Zwei Legenden des Milaraspa,' in *ARW* iv. [1901] 100-123, *nga ni ngar seng dkarmoi bu*, etc.; 131-143, *seng ågangsla ågyingba spar mi åkhyag*, etc.; 194-211, *dbus ribo mchog rab mchod rtenla*, etc.

[2] This is the actual pronunciation. In literature the name is spelt *brgya sbyin* (Satakratu or Indra).

eighteen *agus* (see below) take the part of human beings.

(3) *Yog klu*, the under world (literally, 'the *nāgas* below').—Like sTang lha, Yog klu is also a State. There is a king called lJogspo (probably lCogpo is meant), with his servants and his subjects, who are remarkable for the large number of their children. The *klumo*, or *nāginī* (female *nāgas*), are famous for their beauty, and Kesar is warned not to fall in love with them. For this reason, at the present day, the Ladākhi women still desire to look like *klumo*, and wear the *perag* or *berag*, a leather strap set with turquoises. This *perag* represents a snake growing out of the neck of a human body, which, according to Indian Buddhist art, is the characteristic mark of *nāgas*.

3. The colours of these realms.—The most original system of colours seems to be contained in the Sheh version of the Kesar-saga. According to it, the colour of sTang lha is white—perhaps the colour of light; Bar btsan is red—perhaps on account of the reddish colour of the ground;[1] and Yog klu is blue—this may be due to the deep blue colour of many Tibetan lakes. The *klu* generally live in the water.

According to the Lower Ladākhi version of the Kesar-saga, the colour system is as follows: sTang lha is white; Bar btsan is red; and Yog klu is black. A still more advanced stage is represented in the Mongolian version (which is without doubt based on that of Tibet). Here sTang lha is white; Bar btsan is yellow; and Yog klu is black. The change from red to yellow has probably something to do with Tsong-kha-pa and his reformation of Lāmaism.

4. The devil bDud.—Occasionally, to the three realms of the world a fourth is added, that of the devil bDud, and then all the three realms become united in opposition to this new realm. The colour of the devil and of his realm is black (Sheh version) or violet (Lower Ladākhi version). It is situated in the north. The devil tries to carry away the goats of the gods. He is in possession of a beautiful castle, great treasures, and a girl who is kept in a cage. Near his castle is the well of milk and nectar. In size, appetite, and stupidity he closely resembles the giants of European mythology and folk-lore. There seems to be a close connexion between Yog klu and the devil's realm, as they both appear to go back to similar ideas. But gradually the devil developed into a morally detestable character, while the *klu* did not. Other names of the devil bDud are åDre lha btsan bog, Curulugu, Srinpo ('ogre'), and sDigpa ('sinful').

Of a very similar nature is agu Za. He is probably a mountain- or cloud-giant. He devours not only Kesar, but also sun and moon.

5. The seven and the eighteen agus.—Next to Kesar, the greatest heroes of the Kesar-saga are the eighteen *agus*. Kesar is their leader, and together with him they form a group of nineteen beings, in whom the present writer is inclined to see personifications of the twelve months plus the seven days of the week. Just as India had a group of seven *ādityas* before there were twelve, we find occasionally a group of seven *agus* who act by themselves, the others being forgotten. There is a female *agu* among the group of seven, and there is always a traitor among the *agus*. They are described as having non-human heads on human bodies, thus being similar in shape to the Chinese representations of the zodiac. The list of the eighteen is as follows:

1. Pasang ldan ru skyes, with a goat's head.
2. Anggar rtsangspo, with a lizard's head.
3. Khrai mgo khrai thung, with a falcon's head.
4. Kha rgan [d]gani, with a white beard.
5. sKya rgodpo, with a soup-spoon for a head.
6. zLaba bzangpo, with a moon for a head.
7. mDā dpon gongma, with an arrow-blade for a head.
8. Ala jong gol, with the sole of a boot for a head.
9. åBu dmar lam bstan, with a worm's head.
10. Shelgyi buzhung, with a concave mirror for a head.
11. [d]Gani gongba, with a collar for a head.
12. Lag lag rings, with a hand for a head.
13. rKang rKang rings, with a foot for a head.
14. Bong nag ldumbu, with a donkey's head.
15. bKā blon ldanpa, with a man's head.
16. dPalle rgodpo, with an old man's head.
17. rNa γyu rna åthsal, with a turquoise for a head.
18. zLaba dkarpo, with a white shell for a head.

The following is the list of the seven *agus*: (1) dPalle, (2) [d]Gani, (3) Gongma buthsa, (4) lTaba miggi rab, (5) rNa γyu rna åthsal, (6) mDa dpon gongma, (7) dPalmoi astag.

Both lists are from the Lower Ladākhi version. Certain names will be found to differ in other villages. It looks as if there were not much hope of finding the clue to this ancient zodiac.

6. The Lokapālas.—There is some likelihood that the *gLing chos* has always had deities for each of the four cardinal points. It is quite possible that the Indian Amoghasiddha, Vajrasattva, Ratnasambhava, and Amitābha were deities of the four quarters before they became Dhyānibuddhas. In close correspondence with them we find in the *gLing chos* the following deities of the four quarters: Don yod grubpa, North; rDorje sems dpa, East; Rinchen byung ldan, South; sNangba mthā yas, West. It is not necessary to assume that these deities were introduced from India together with Buddhism. It is more likely that the names represent an instance of mutual influence between pre-Buddhist Tibetan and Indian mythology. The name Don grub, which corresponds exactly to the Indian Siddhārtha, was not necessarily introduced with Buddhism. Siddhārtha was a common name in India long before Buddha's time, and may belong to a deity similar to Don grub and Don yod grubpa of Tibet. There are also four 'kings' of the four quarters, who correspond more closely to their Indian equivalents, and may therefore have been received from India; but even these have nothing to do with Buddhism. Like the deities mentioned above, they belong to the four quarters, and to nothing else in the *gLing chos*.

7. The Tree of the World.—It is called the 'king-willow,' or the 'far-spreading willow.' It has its roots in Yog klu, its middle part in Bar btsan, and its top in sTang lha. It has six branches, and on each branch a bird with a nest and an egg. On the first branch there is the huge bird Khyung with a golden egg; on the second, the wild eagle with a turquoise egg; on the third, the bird 'white-head' with a pearl-white egg; on the fourth, the eagle 'white-kidney' with a silver egg; on the fifth, a snow-pheasant with a coral egg; and, on the sixth, the white falcon with an iron egg.

8. Outline of the Kesar-saga.—

(1) *Prologue to the saga: the creation of the earth.*—The 'forefather and his wife' sow some seed which grows into a huge tree, the fruits of which are gathered into a barn. There the fruits become changed into worms, which eat one another until one huge worm is left. This worm becomes the child Dong γsum mila. The child kills an ogre with nine heads, and builds the world (gLing) out of its body in seven days. Dong γsum mila is married to eighteen girls, to whom are born the eighteen *agus*. The *agus*, eager to gain riches, start for the castle Pachi dpal dong. Agu dPalle arrives there first of all, receives the riches, and hears the prophecy about what will happen in the course of the Kesar story.

(2) *Birth of Kesar.*—Agu dPalle assists the king of heaven in his fight with the devil, in the shape either of yaks or of birds. He is allowed to ask a boon, and asks that one of the three sons of the king of heaven may be sent to the earth as king. All the sons are asked, and Don grub, who is the ablest in spite of his youth, decides to go. He dies in heaven, and is reborn on earth to Gog bzang lhamo. (The name *Kesar* or *Kyesar* is spelt in full *skye γsar*, and is said to have been given with reference to this story; it means the 'reborn one'.) The conception arises from Gog bzang lhamo's eating a hailstone, and the child is born

[1] The word *dmarpo*, 'red,' is also used for 'brown.' Cf. the traditional interpretation of the word 'Adam.'

through the ribs. It is of a most ugly shape, but at pleasure exchanges this for a beautiful shape, with sun and moon as attributes. The traitor among the *agus* makes some unsuccessful attempts to kill the child, and has to suffer himself. Together with Kesar, sun and moon and all kinds of animals are born.

(3) *Kesar's marriage to åBruguma.*—Kesar meets åBruguma on a plain where she is gathering roots. There are a great number of stories as to how he teases her. åBruguma is to be married to the traitor among the *agus*, but Kesar wins her through his skill in games. Her parents are disgusted when they see him in his ugly shape, and treat him with contempt. He runs away, and åBruguma has to seek him. She is pleased to find him in his beautiful shape, but at once he throws it off and sends hail and rain. Her parents say that their daughter will be given to him who brings the skin of the huge yak Riri (this yak looks almost like a cloud), and who will bring a wing of the bird Nyima khyung byung (this bird looks almost like the sun). The *agus* try; but only Kesar succeeds. Now he is accepted as son-in-law, and the wedding is celebrated. (Here Kesar is praised even as the inventor of firearms.)

(4) *Kesar's victory over the giant of the north.*—After religious preparations Kesar decides to start for the north to kill the devil. He finds it hard to have to leave åBruguma, and allows her to accompany him, but the queen of heaven sends her back. In the castle of the devil he finds a girl in an iron cage, whom he delivers. They have an enjoyable time together until the devil returns. Before his arrival Kesar is hidden in a pit which is dug inside the room in a miraculous way. Although the devil smells the presence of a human being, and although his book of magic assures him of it, he is soon persuaded of the contrary by the girl, and goes to sleep. Then Kesar is dug out again and kills the devil. The girl gives Kesar the food and drink of forgetfulness, and in consequence of this he forgets åBruguma, the land of gLing, and everything.

(5) *åBruguma abducted by the king of Hor.*—Because Kesar does not return, the king of Hor starts to carry off åBruguma. The traitor among the *agus* sits on the throne of *gLing*, and the other *agus* offer only feeble resistance. The most plucky among the *agus* is the youngest, åBu dmar lam bstan. åBruguma herself goes to fight, but is sent back with ridicule. She has to submit and become the wife of the king of Hor. Still she refuses to leave the land of gLing unless the king of Hor solves three difficult problems. Then åBruguma hides herself in a stable, but she is discovered and carried away. She begins to love the king of Hor. åBu dmar lam bstan makes a successful attempt to retake her, but he is killed through the treachery of åBruguma and the traitor among the *agus*. (This is the *Siegfried* story.) Agu dPalle sends two storks with a message towards the north to Kesar. He leaves the north and soon reaches the land of gLing. The horse arrives there before him, and together with the horse's adventure spring sets in.

(6) *Defeat of the king of Hor.*—The road to Hor, with its many obstacles, is described. First Kesar is led by a fox, then he gains the service of a dwarf. There is the door of rocks which opens and closes of its own accord; there are the stones flying about between heaven and earth; and the watchmen of Hor, who are killed in the same manner as Samson killed the Philistines in the hall. Kesar arrives in the shape of a beggar, and pretends to be the son of the smith of Hor. He is accepted after some difficulties and learns the trade of the smith. At a tournament he shows his superior power, and gains the victory in every contest. He is therefore sent with a force against the approaching *agus* of gLing. On this occasion he drowns all his followers from Hor, and sends the *agus* home again. He compels the smith to assist him in the fabrication of an iron chain, which is to be thrown on to the top of the castle of Hor. When it is finished, Kesar climbs to the top of the castle by means of the chain, kills the king of Hor, and regains åBruguma. On their way back to gLing, åBruguma's children, whom she had borne to the king of Hor, are offered to the door of rocks to induce it to open. In gLing, åBruguma is first punished for her treachery, then she is restored to her former position, and another wedding is celebrated.

(7) *Kesar's journey to China.*—(The Tibetan word for China—*rgya nag*—means 'the black expanse.') Kesar practises sorcery until the castle of the king of China falls to pieces and the king of China becomes ill. Kesar is entreated to go to China and heal the king. He sends the traitor *agu*, Khrai thung, in his place. Then he starts himself. The journey is one chain of obstacles (ice and snow, hills, lakes, an ogre and an ogress, etc.). All are overcome, and on Kesar's approach the king of China becomes better. Now he refuses to keep his word, and give Kesar his daughter (γYui dkon mchogmo). But the girl runs away with Kesar. He is, however, induced to go back again. Then the Chinese throw him into a pit with three dragons, which he does not mind much. He escapes in the shape of a fly, goes back to gLing, and smites the land of China with leprosy (snow apparently). The traitor among the *agus* has meanwhile gone back to gLing, turned åBruguma out of the castle, and seized the throne. He is punished, and Kesar lives in happiness with his two wives. The leprosy in China is stopped by another journey made by Kesar to that country.

(8) *Epilogue to the Kesar-saga: the story of Kesar's boy.*—Kesar and åBruguma have a boy called γSerri buzhung (or Shelli buzhung). He is married to Pimo (or Phyimo?) γSerralcan, but the ogre dPallepa carries this girl off. γSerri buzhung starts to seek her, and takes service at the ogre's castle. He is soon recognized, because the dogs, horses, and other domestic animals increase in an extraordinary way under his care. Before the ogres have succeeded in killing him, they are invited by Pimo γSerralcan to a feast. On this occasion the girl places nine frying pans, in which the lives (hearts) of the nine ogres dwell, outside the door. γSerri buzhung shoots with his arrow through eight of them, and thus eight ogres are killed. Then he runs away with Pimo γSerralcan and all the other girls of the ogres. dPallepa pursues him, but is destroyed with his army. Then the wedding is celebrated.

9. Is the Kesar-saga a myth of the seasons?—This was the present writer's idea from the first. As he was, however, assailed by several critics on account of it, he did his best to abandon it. But, when editing the 'Lower Ladākhi version of the Kesar-saga' for the *Bibliotheca Indica*, he was driven back to his former position. At any rate, he cannot help believing that myths of the seasons (mixed up, perhaps, with other materials) are contained in the Kesar-saga. Only a few instances may be noted: sun and moon are attributes of Kesar's beautiful shape, rain and hail of his ugly shape; he wields the sword of lightning 'in the middle of black clouds'; there is a full description of spring given on the occasion of Kesar's return to gLing (see above, § 8 (5)); the *agus* seem to point to an ancient zodiac; winter is apparently compared to leprosy; together with Kesar's departure (probably in winter) the male animals leave the female ones, but leave them with the hope of new offspring; Kesar's enemies are powers of darkness; the giant of the north; the king of Hor, also in the north; China is 'the black expanse.'

10. Relationship to other mythologies.—As has become evident, there are great similarities between the *gLing chos* and the mythologies of various Aryan nations. This, however, does not mean much, for even the mythologies of North American Indian tribes have much in common with European mythologies. But we must call attention to one particularly striking incident. The story of the Tibetan hero with the vulnerable spot, åBu dmar lam bstan, who is Kesar's representative, is very similar to the German story of *Siegfried*. The similarities are the following: both heroes have the vulnerable spot on the shoulder; both wear invisible caps; both are killed when drinking water; with both of them the vulnerable spot is pointed out by a woman who belongs to the side of the hero. All this is remarkable, because the corresponding Greek story, for instance, is greatly at variance with both of them, although there is an ethnic relationship between the Greeks and the Teutons.

11. gLing chos and Lāmaism.—It is not at all impossible that the *gLing chos* should have exercised an influence on Lāmaism. The following are a few instances. (1) With regard to the colours, white, red, and blue, there is a certain correspondence between the realms of heaven, earth, and under world on one side, and sPyan ras γzigs, åJam dbyangs, and Phyag rdor on the other. But with regard to their characters it is difficult to see a closer agreement. The three *mchod rten* of three different colours, white, red, and blue, seem originally to represent the three realms of the *gLing chos*, but are at the present time explained as having been erected in honour of the three Bodhisattvas. If this explanation is really true, it remains a strange fact that the *mchod rten* in the middle was always painted red, and not yellow; for yellow is the correct colour of åJam dbyangs. Thus the custom of erecting three *mchod rten* of three different colours seems to have its roots in the *gLing chos*, and in the Kesar-saga we often hear of the existence of three *lha tho* of the same colours, the prototypes of these *mchod rten* of the present day. (2) The story of Srong-btsan Gam-po with his two wives, the green and the white sGrolma, may have been influenced by the story of Kesar with his two wives. Thus åBruguma is addressed, 'Oh, thou milk-white fairy!' and Kesar's bride from China is called γYui dkon mchogmo, the turquoise goddess. Kesar is even called, in historical works, a suitor to the white sGrolma. (3) There can be hardly any doubt that the system of colours as we find it in the *gLing chos* has influenced the pantheon of Lāmaism with its white, red, blue, green, yellow, and golden-faced occupants. Still, it cannot account for all the different shades of colours. Some of them were probably introduced from India. (4) Most of the deities of the *gLing chos*, dBangpo rgyabzhin included, have been incorporated into the pantheon of Lāmaism, where they have to be satisfied with an inferior rank.

12. gLing chos and Bon chos.—The *gLing chos* was perhaps not such a pure religion of nature as it appears to have been from the preceding pages. It probably had its dark side of superstitions and sorcery. This dark side seems to have had its development down to the present day in the garb of the *Bon chos*.

13. Sacred numbers in the gLing chos.—Holy numbers in the *gLing chos* are 3, 7, 9, and 18. But it is remarkable that, whilst the first three of these numbers are quoted without a following number, the 18 is often followed up by 19; *e.g.*, 'They digged a pit of 18, 19 yards,' 'There appeared 18, 19 priests.' The 19 is favoured apparently as the sum of 12+7, the months of the year plus the days of the week.

14. Animism in the gLing chos.—Here we may mention the following personifications: *sKyeser*, the wind; *sbang char zilbu*, the rain; *sengge dkarmo γyu ralcan*, the glacier; *bya Khyung dkrung nyima*, (apparently) the sun; *byamo dkarmo*, the moon; *bya so mig dmar*, the morning-star; *γYan*, spirits living in rocks and trees. It is remarkable that several of these personifications are mentioned together with the representatives of the animal world. Some of such representatives are: *nyamo γser mig*, for fishes; *bya rgyal rgodpo*, for birds; *rKyang byung kha dkar*, for horses; *ȧBrong byung rogpo*, for yaks.

15. Festivals of the gLing chos.—(1) The *Lo γsar*, or New Year's festival. It is the festival of lamps and lights. Pencil-cedars are used for the decoration of houses. There are horse-races, and a goat is offered before a white *lha tho* (altar of the *gLing chos*). The heart is torn out of the living animal and offered to the *lha*. In the monasteries mask-dances are held, which were probably intended originally to show the victory of the coming spring over the demons of winter. Only at Hemis do the mask-dances take place in June, perhaps as a last remnant of a former festival to celebrate the highest point reached by the sun. (2) *Storma phangces*. This is the spring festival of driving out winter. At Khalatse a clay figure of human shape is carried outside the village and destroyed there. At other places the spirits of winter and disease are banished into magic squares of sticks and strings (*dosmo*) and destroyed outside the village. (3) The Kesar-festival. The festival is called 'Kesar-festival' only in Upper Kanāwār. In Ladākh it is called *mDā phangces*, 'arrow-shooting.' It is celebrated in spring. The *gLing glu* is played and sung; and the boys amuse themselves with arrow-shooting. There are processions round the fields to bless them, the *lha tho* (altars) are decorated with fresh twigs, and pencil-cedars are burnt. (4) The *Srub lha*, or harvest festival. In Skyurbuchan the boys dance with poles covered with fragrant alpine flowers. Offerings of grain are carried to the monasteries. The dates of all these festivals are fixed by the lāmas, and the lāmas take part in them.

16. The names of the gLing chos.—In the course of this article some of the names of the *gLing chos* are given with their English translation. The author has not ventured to translate all these names, because scholars are at variance with regard to the meanings of certain of them. In the names of the eighteen *agus* there is always contained the distinguishing mark of the *agu* which forms his head; thus in no. 2, *rtsangspo* means 'lizard'; in no. 4, *kha rgan* means 'old mouth,' *i.e.* a mouth surrounded by a white beard; in no. 1, *ru skyes* means 'horn-producer,' or goat. As for the group of seven *agus*, which has much in common with the heroes of such folk-lore as, *e.g.*, 'Sechse kommen durch die ganze Welt,' in the name of no. 4 the ability to see clearly is indicated; in the name of no. 5, the ability to hear clearly; in no. 6, to shoot well. There are certain names occurring in the *gLing chos* which are not of Tibetan origin: thus in the word *sengge* in the name sengge dkarmo γyu ralcan, 'white lioness with the turquoise locks,' the personification of the glacier has something to do with the Indian word *siṁha*. In the name of the smith Hemis, who teaches Kesar, the first part *hem* seems to be the Indian word *hima*, 'snow.' We find the word *hem* in the sense of 'snow' also in the name Hembabs, which means 'snow-falling,' and such Indian words as *rākṣasa*, 'monster,' Sītārām, Sītā and Rāma, and Indra occur occasionally in the *gLing chos*—which shows what an important part India has played in the shaping of certain tales of this ancient religion.

LITERATURE.—It must be admitted that all the following publications are one man's work. They have all passed through the present author's hands. It may, however, be pointed out that in no case did he write down the texts to the dictation of a native; he always employed natives to record them from the dictation of such other natives as were famous for their knowledge of this ancient literature.

(i.) Kesar-saga: 'Der Frühlings- und Wintermythus der Kesarsage,' in *Mémoires de la société finno-ougrienne*, Helsingfors, 1902, 'The Spring-myth of the Kesarsaga,' in *IA* xxxi. [1902], 'A Lower Ladakhi Version of the Kesarsaga,' in *Bibliotheca Indica*, 1908.

(ii.) Hymnals: 'A Ladakhi Bonpo Hymnal' (more correctly, 'The gLing glu of Phyang'), in *IA* xxx. [1901] 359 ff.; 'gLing glu of Khalatse,' contained in *Ladakhi Songs*, Leh, Kaśmīr, 1899–1903, nos. xxi.–xxx.; 'The Paladins of the Kesarsaga,' in *JRASBo* ii. [1906] 467–490, iii. [1907] 67–77.

(iii.) Catechisms: 'The Ladakhi Pre-Buddhist Marriage Ritual' in *IA* xxx. [1901] 131 ff.; *Die Trinklieder von Khalatse* (Tibetan text only, ed. A. H. Francke, Leipzig, 1903); *Das Hochzeitsritual von Tagmacig* (Tibetan text only, ed. A. H. Francke, reprinted from an old MS discovered at Tagmacig, 1904).

A. H. FRANCKE.

LION.—See ANIMALS.

LITANY.—A litany, according to the modern use of the word, may be described as a devotion consisting of a number of short petitions or invocations, to each of which a response is made by the people. It may be either said or sung, it may be processional or stationary, it may be liturgical, *i.e.* connected with the celebration of the Holy Eucharist, or independent, and it may be for regular use or used only on special occasions. Processional psalmody which is not of the responsive form is not now usually called a litany, but at one time the word was applied to anything sung in procession. The modern use of the term is the result of a long and somewhat complicated history. It is especially necessary to trace the growth of two forms of devotion which were originally distinct, but which have coalesced to form the modern litany. These are the liturgical responsive prayer and the procession.

1. Earliest use of the word.—The word λιτανεία is not common in classical Greek, and it seems to be used in the quite general sense of a supplication. The earliest mention of the word in connexion with Christian services appears to be by Basil (*c.* A.D. 375; *Ep.* ccvii. 'ad Cler. Neocæs.' [*Opera*, iii. 311 D]).

Objections had been raised to some innovations which Basil had made. 'These things were not,' the objector says, 'in the days of the great Gregory' (*i.e.* Gregory Thaumaturgus, *c.* 254). 'Neither,' replies Basil, 'were the litanies which you now use. And I do not say this by way of accusing you; for I would that you all should live in tears, and in continual repentance.'

These litanies were, therefore, penitential devotions of some kind, but there is nothing to indicate their precise character. The word *rogatio* was used in a similar general sense in the West.

2. The liturgical litany.—The earliest description of Eucharistic worship is that contained in the *Apologies* of Justin Martyr (A.D. 148). Here common prayers are spoken of 'for ourselves . . . and for all others in every place,' immediately before the Kiss of Peace and the Offertory, and therefore after the lessons and homily (*Apol.* i. 65). Whether these already took the form of the later litany there is nothing to show, and the response 'Kyrie Eleison' is not yet mentioned. And there is no further detailed information about the form of service until the liturgies which date from about the end of the 4th century. Here, however, the liturgical litany is found in the form which it has preserved in the Eastern Church ever since. It consists of a number of short petitions offered by the deacon, to each of which the people respond 'Kyrie Eleison,' and the most usual place for it is after the Gospel, but this is not invariable. Some litany of this kind appears to be almost universal in the Eastern liturgies. Many examples will be found in Brightman (*Liturgies Eastern and Western*, esp. pp. 4, 471, 521 for the most ancient forms, all belonging to the 4th cent.). The usual name for these devotions in the East is not λιτανεία, but ἐκτενή (lit. 'stretched out,' *i.e.* the earnest prayer), or συναπτή ('continuous'). There is nothing to show when Kyrie Eleison was first used in the services of the Church, but as its use is almost universal in the Eastern liturgies it must have been very early, and the expression is so natural, and would be so easily suggested by passages of the OT, that no explanation of its introduction is necessary. It was also in use among the heathen, as was pointed out by Claude de Vert (*Explication simple, littérale et historique des cérémonies de l'église*, Paris, 1706–13, i. 94; cf. Epictetus, *Diss. ab Arriano digestæ*, ii. 7). The *Peregrinatio Silviæ* (ed. G. F. Gamurrini, Rome, 1888, p. 47) mentions the Kyrie as the response made at Jerusalem to the deacon's list of names, and it appears in the litanies mentioned above as belonging to the 4th century.

3. The liturgical litany in the West.—It is probable that the Western liturgies originally contained litanies closely similar to those of the East. This was certainly the case, as far as can be judged from their scanty remains, with the liturgies of the Gallican (or non-Roman) type. The extant forms bear the closest resemblance to the Eastern litanies, and may in some cases be translations from the Greek (see some examples in L. Duchesne, *Christian Worship*[3], pp. 198–201; F. E. Warren, *Liturgy and Ritual of the Celtic Church*, p. 229). There is little doubt that there was originally a litany of the same character in the Roman liturgy also, and that the Kyries at the beginning of Mass are a relic of it. There is also another place in the service which should be noted. After the Gospel the priest says 'Oremus,' but no prayer or response follows; and this was so at least as long ago as the 8th cent., as appears from the Ordines Romani. Some prayers had evidently fallen out of the service even at that early date, and these were undoubtedly the Prayers of the Faithful, which occur in this place in the Eastern liturgies, and which are still preserved in the Roman rite in the prayers used on Good Friday. Probably these prayers dropped out of use because they were transferred, in substance at least, to the litany which came at the beginning of the service. St. Gregory the Great (*Ep.* ix. 12), when speaking of the use of the Kyrie, mentions other devotions that accompanied it, and which were no doubt a litany. In the present service only the Kyrie remains, and this is curious because the Kyrie was probably an addition made to the original litany from the East, so that it would seem that the original prayers have disappeared, while the exotic response has remained. There is nothing to show when the Kyrie was first used in Rome. It was not used, as in the East, as the regular response to the petitions, but at the beginning and end of the service, and it was alternated with Christe Eleison, which was never used in the East. Gregory says:

'We have neither said nor do we say Kyrie Eleison as it is said among the Greeks, because in Grecian countries all say it together, but with us it is said by the clerks and the people respond; and Christe Eleison is said as many times, and this is not said at all among the Greeks' (*loc. cit.*).

The Kyrie was, therefore, in use in Rome in Gregory's time, but for how long before that we do not know. The Council of Vaison (c. iii. [A.D. 519]), in ordering its use in the province of Arles, implies that it had been introduced into Italy at a not very distant date. The rest of the liturgical litany disappeared, as has been said, from the Roman service at some unknown date, but that the Kyrie was still regarded as part of a litany is shown by the fact that in the 8th cent. the Kyrie was omitted when there was a processional litany to the church. The natural conclusion of the introductory litany, whether processional or not, was the prayer in which the Bishop 'collected' the petitions of the people, and which was therefore called Collectio or Collecta. But, as the Kyrie was omitted when there was a procession, the collect on these occasions was the first thing that was said after the people reached the church, and hence ritualists came to regard it as the prayer 'ad Collectam plebis'—when the people are gathered together. Thus there arose a double derivation of the word 'collect' (*q.v.*).

4. Processions in the East.—During the centuries of persecution it was not likely that forms of devotion so conspicuous as processions would be used by Christians. The first historical mention of them appears to be in A.D. 398, in connexion with the Arian controversy. The Arians, not being allowed to hold their assemblies in the city of Constantinople, used to meet in the public squares during the night, and to march out at dawn to their places of worship, singing antiphonally. Fearing lest the orthodox should be attracted by this ceremonial, St. John Chrysostom instituted counter-processions on a more magnificent scale, in which silver crosses and lights given by the empress Eudoxia were carried. These particular processions were prohibited by the emperor in consequence of the disorders which they caused, but the custom of using processions, especially in times of emergency, continued. Socrates mentions a legend to the effect that the antiphonal singing used at such times had its origin in a vision of Ignatius of Antioch, the third bishop from St. Peter, in which he saw angels singing responsive hymns to the Holy Trinity (*HE* vi. 8; Soz. *HE* viii. 8). These occasional processions were, however, quite distinct from the litany in the Eucharist.

5. Processions in the West.—Processions became common in the Western Church at about the same time as in the East, but their origin appears to have been independent. They were probably at first transformations of pagan processions. The Roman festival of the Robigalia, intended to secure the crops from blight, was kept on the 25th of April, and the procession called the Litania Major, which took place on the same day, St. Mark's Day, seems to be a direct descendant of this. Even the actual routes of the heathen and the Christian processions were nearly the same. The institution of the Greater Litany of St. Mark's Day has been generally ascribed to Gregory I., but it was probably earlier, and perhaps dates from the pontificate of Liberius (352–366). The litany ordered by Gregory on St. Mark's Eve, A.D. 490, in order to avert a pestilence, seems to have been distinct from the Litania Major. Another ancient Roman festival, the Ambarvalia, was observed on three successive days in the month of May, and also had the fertility of the fields as its object. There is here a close resemblance to the Rogation processions on the three days before Ascension Day. These are said to have been instituted by Mamertus, bishop of Vienne (*c.* 470), on the occasion of various public disasters (Sid. Apoll. *Ep.* v. 14, vii. 1; Gregory of Tours, *Hist. Franc.* ii. 34); but such processions had probably been practised at an earlier date, and were only revived on this occasion. These rogations or litanies, called Litaniæ Minores to distinguish them from those of St. Mark's Day, spread rapidly through Gaul, and were adopted and reorganized at Rome by Leo III. (795–816). Both the Greater and the Lesser Litanies were ordered to be used in England at the Council of Cloveshoe (A.D. 747 [A. W. Haddan and W. Stubbs, *Councils and Ecclesiastical Documents relating to Great Britain and Ireland*, Oxford, 1869–71, iii. 368]). It may be noted that in the decree of this council, and elsewhere, *rogatio* and *litania* are regarded as equivalent terms ('lætaniæ, id est, rogationes'), and also that the terms seem to include all the devotions connected with those days. There is no allusion to responsive prayer, and the only reference to processions is a mention of relics being carried about. The words 'litany' and 'rogation' were still used in quite a comprehensive sense.

6. Mediæval litanies.—Hitherto the liturgical litanies in the Mass and processions have been regarded as distinct. But it is easy to see how they would coalesce. Various kinds of singing have always been used in processions, but that particular form of responsorial singing in which the people answer with an unvarying refrain was so naturally adapted for processional use, owing to the ease with which the refrain could be taken up by a moving crowd, that litanies of the type of the Eucharistic ectene came to be very commonly used in processions not only in the Mass, but on all sorts of occasions. And so the word 'litany' came to mean a form of prayer with a response, either processional or stationary, and either regular or occasional. As the processional use was the most conspicuous and popular, the word 'procession' came to be used as almost an equivalent term, and the book which contained the mediæval litanies was called the Processional. The litanies in most common use also assumed a regular structure. They consisted, as a rule, of the following parts: (1) the Kyrie Eleison, alternated with Christe Eleison; (2) a number of invocations of saints by name, with the response 'Ora pro nobis'; (3) a series of short prayers against various evils, called Deprecations, with the response 'Libera nos Domine'; (4) prayers on behalf of various people and for various objects, called the Supplications, with the response 'Audi nos Domine'; (5) the Agnus and the Kyrie, and a collect. Such litanies became very popular, and Cardinal Baronius estimated in 1601 that there were then 80 different forms in use. The invocations of the saints just mentioned formed a conspicuous part of most of these litanies. It is not clear when these invocations were first introduced; it was certainly before the 8th cent.; they are to be found in the Stowe Missal, and in a litany which probably belongs to the 8th cent. printed in Warren, *Lit. Celt. Ch.* (p. 179), but they may be much older. Some of the later litanies became little more than a string of invocations. It has been suggested that these lists of saints originally grew out of a heathen formula recited by the Pontifex Maximus, but there appears to be little or no evidence for this.

It has been noted that litanies, in the sense of responsive prayers, were often, though not necessarily, sung in procession, and so were commonly called processions. On the other hand, devotions sung in procession were often called litanies even though they were not responsive prayers. Psalms and anthems were also frequently used. For instance, Bede says (*HE* i. 25) that at the first meeting of St. Augustine with king Ethelbert the missionaries approached the king in procession, bearing the image of our Lord upon the Cross, and singing litanies; and then he specifies what they sang, and it was clearly an anthem, and not a litany in the usual modern sense. Again, the processions before High Mass on Sundays became, during the Middle Ages, a very popular and conspicuous devotion, but the psalmody was not usually in form a litany. In the 8th cent. at Rome it was so, or it was regarded as such; for, when there was a procession, as has been mentioned, the Kyrie at the beginning of Mass was omitted. Later on the Kyries became a fixed part of the service, and the processional psalmody took a different form. From the 12th cent., however, there was a tendency to use the term 'procession' of whatever was sung in procession, and to confine the term 'litany' to the Kyries, the Greater and Lesser Litanies of St. Mark's Day and the Rogation Days, and other similar forms.

7. Litanies in the Roman Church.—As has been mentioned, a large number of litanies came into use in the later Middle Ages. But by a decree of the Holy Office, dated 6 Sept. 1601, Clement VIII. forbade the use of any litany except that usually known as the Litany of the Saints, which had been included in the liturgical books. The Litany of Loreto had already been sanctioned in 1587. All others were forbidden to be used without the approbation of the Congregation of Rites. It is probable that this decree was never very strictly enforced, but it was renewed in 1727 and in 1821. A decree, however, of the Congregation of Rites, dated 23 April 1860, allowed the private use of litanies sanctioned by the Ordinary. The Litany of the Blessed Virgin or of Loreto mentioned above was probably used in some form at a very early date at Loreto, but in its present form it perhaps dates from the early 15th cent., and the earliest printed copy known belongs to the year 1576. Another popular litany was that of the Most Holy Name of Jesus. This was perhaps also composed in the early 15th century. It was not included in the decree of 1601, but later on it received some sanction from the Congregation of Rites, and it was finally allowed by Pius IX. in 1852 for certain dioceses, and for universal use by Leo XIII. in 1886. The Litany of the Sacred Heart was sanctioned in 1899.

8. The Anglican litany.—As the procession was a popular form of devotion, it was natural that it should be one of the first parts of the public services to be translated into English. The *Prymers* of the 15th cent., books of devotion for lay people, commonly contain a litany in English. The form now used in the English Church appeared in 1544, and it is no doubt the work of Cranmer, and perhaps the happiest example of his literary style. The occasion of its production was given by public calamities. In 1543 the harvest was bad, and Henry VIII. wrote to Cranmer to desire that 'rogations and processions' should be made. In the following year there was war with France and Scotland, so that the English Litany was produced in similar circumstances to those of the early litanies mentioned above. It was, however, also intended for regular use, and was printed in the *Prymer* of 1545 and in the first English *Book of*

Common Prayer of 1549. This litany was constructed with great care, and several sources were used. The chief portion was taken from the Sarum Rogationtide litany, and the main structure of this was adhered to, but the invocations of the saints were greatly shortened, being reduced to three clauses, which were themselves omitted in the First Prayer Book. Passages were also introduced from a Sarum litany for the dying, called Commendatio Animæ (also omitted in the First Prayer Book), and a considerable part of the Supplications was taken from a mediæval German litany which was revised by Luther in 1529, and published in German and Latin. This litany was included in the *Consultatio* of Archbishop Hermann of Cologne, and so came to England, and it was used for the litany in Marshall's *Prymer* of 1535. It must be noted that the English litany falls into two main sections: the first ends with the collect that follows the Lord's Prayer—a collect being the natural ending of a litany. What follows is a translation of suffrages which were added to the Sarum litany in time of war. The reason for their insertion was no doubt that war was going on in 1544, but they were appropriate for use at other times, and were retained. These suffrages are preceded by the antiphon and Psalm verse which began the Sarum Procession on Rogation Monday. Unfortunately, the accidental omission of the Amen at the end of the collect has led to the ridiculous custom of using the antiphon ('O Lord, arise, help us') as a sort of response to the collect. Until 1661 the conclusions of most of the collects were not printed in the *Book of Common Prayer*; in the revision of that year the Amens were printed, but most of the endings were omitted by mistake.

Although in his adaptation of the old litanies Cranmer added little or nothing of his own, he made a noticeable change in the rhythm: the old petitions were short and simple; Cranmer, either with a view to compression or, more probably, because he preferred sonorous periods, grouped several petitions together, and enriched them with epithets and synonyms. For instance, the Deprecations of the Sarum litany begin thus:

'From all evil—Deliver us, Lord.
From the crafts of the devil—Deliver us, Lord.
From thy wrath—Deliver us, Lord.
From everlasting damnation—Deliver us, Lord.'

In the new version this becomes:

'From all evil and mischief; from sin, from the crafts and assaults of the devil; from thy wrath, and from everlasting damnation—Good Lord, deliver us.'

At about the same time Cranmer intended to translate other processional hymns, such as 'Salve Festa Dies,' for he wrote to Henry VIII. in 1545 to say that he had done so. The attempt was probably relinquished because he became aware that he did not write so skilfully in verse as he did in prose.

The English litany has remained substantially unchanged since its first appearance in 1544. In 1549 the invocations of the saints were omitted, and in 1559 a petition about 'the tyranny of the Bishop of Rome.' 'The grace of our Lord' was added at the end in the same year. In 1661 the words 'and rebellion,' 'and schism,' were added, and 'Bishops, Pastors, and Ministers of the Church' was changed to 'Bishops, Priests, and Deacons.' The collection of collects at the end of the litany was altered more than once, and most of them were removed to other places in the *Book of Common Prayer*.

This litany was intended to be used for all the purposes for which the ancient litanies were employed. It was issued for occasional use at a time of distress, and it was sung in procession in the usual manner. Later on royal injunctions ordered it to be sung kneeling before Mass, and this became the usual, but not universal, practice. The present rubric allows either the stationary or the processional use. It was also related to the Rogationtide processions, being derived mainly from them, and it took the place of the Eastern ectene as a preparation for Mass. It was ordered from the first to be said on Wednesdays and Fridays, the ancient 'Station' days, on which especially Mass was anciently said, and, although its use on Sundays was not specified in the rubric until 1552, this was probably taken for granted from the first. Unfortunately, this special characteristic of the litany as a preparation for Mass was obscured later on, partly by the placing of the 'Grace' at the end, and partly by the rubric of 1661, which directs it to be said 'after Morning Prayer.' This made no practical difference so long as Matins, Litany, and Mass continued to be said in their natural order, but in recent years it has caused the litany to be regarded as a sort of appendage to Matins, and in many churches has led to its being altogether separated from the Mass.

9. Lutheran litanies.—As has been mentioned above, Luther published a revision of a mediæval litany in German and Latin in 1529. The original edition does not appear to be extant, but the litany was printed in the Psalm-books, and it was used in both languages for some time. The use of the Latin form seems to have died out in the 17th cent., and the German form, although it continued to be used on various occasions in North Germany, never became a popular form of devotion. The Calvinistic bodies objected to this form of service altogether, and the litany was one of the parts of the English *Book of Common Prayer* which were most disliked by the Puritans.

LITERATURE.—For Eastern litanies see F. E. Brightman, *Liturgies Eastern and Western*, Oxford, 1896. For Western litanies, F. E. Warren, *Liturgy and Ritual of the Celtic Church*, do. 1881; C. Wordsworth, *Ceremonies and Processions of . . . Salisbury*, Cambridge, 1901; *Sarum Processional* (ed. W. G. Henderson), Leeds, 1882; *York Processional*, Surtees Society, London, 1875; E. Hoskins, *Sarum and York Primers*, London, 1901; H. Littlehales, *The Prymer*, do. 1895; *Ordines Romani*, in Migne, *PL* lxxviii. 937 ff. For the Kyrie, E. Bishop, 'Kyrie Eleison,' in *Downside Review*, Dec. 1899 and March 1900; S. Bäumer, *Gesch. des Breviers*, Freiburg im Br., 1895, esp. pp. 128, 154. For a history of the litany, F. Procter and W. H. Frere, *New History of the Book of Common Prayer*, London, 1901; L. Pullan, *History of the Book of Common Prayer*, do. 1900; J. H. Blunt, *Annotated Book of Common Prayer*, rev. ed., do. 1895; L. Duchesne, *Christian Worship*³, do. 1903.

J. H. MAUDE.

LITERATURE.

LITERATURE (American).—The literature of the aborigines of America may conveniently be treated under two topics, viz. purely autochthonous literary expression, and works produced under Caucasian influence.

1. Autochthonous literature.—This group includes songs, orations, stories, legends and myths, rituals and possibly dramas, and chronicles. The sources of this literature are mainly oral tradition, though this tradition is fortified in many cases by mnemonic records, the most curious of which are the *quipus*—knotted and coloured cords—employed by the Peruvians. Petroglyphs and pictographs were wide-spread, and reached a considerable development in the direction of abstract symbolism, while among the Mayas, Aztecs, and other Mexican tribes they clearly gained the stage of hieroglyphic writing. Little progress has been made, however, towards the decipherment of the Mexican codices, except perhaps with respect to calendric computations, while the pictographic records of other Indian peoples depend for their interpretation upon individual initiation into the meanings intended. Such records as we have, therefore, are mainly transcriptions from oral expression.

American Indian songs are so intimately connected with American Indian music that they will be treated under art. MUSIC (American). Similarly, American Indian rituals, which are largely composed of cycles of songs and chants, will be treated under SECRET SOCIETIES (American) and PRAYER (American). Oratory was an art of prime importance among the many tribes who conducted their internal affairs by means of councils where the spoken word decided tribal policies. Gravity of mien and strict decorum characterized the orator, but his expression was often intensely passionate, and there is abundant testimony from white hearers to the power and eloquence of American Indian oratory, of which many fragments are preserved in scattered reports. More systematic records have been made of myths and legends, which are often documents of considerable length and no mean artistry. Their comparative stability of form under oral transmission may be studied in records of identical myths taken from different tribes (*e.g.*, the three versions of the 'Iroquoian Cosmology,' recorded by J. N. B. Hewitt, *21 RBEW* [1899–1900]). Legends of a historical character (as, *e.g.*, the legend of Hiawatha) give place in some tribes to conscious chronicles, or year-counts (see esp. G. Mallery, *10 RBEW* [1888–89], ch. x.; J. Mooney, *17 RBEW* [1895–96], 'Calendar History of the Kiowa'). Mooney (*19 RBEW* [1897–98], 'Myths of the Cherokee') classifies Cherokee myths as sacred myths, animal stories, local legends, and historical traditions. He traces many animal stories that have passed as of Negro origin to American Indian sources (notably the 'Brer Rabbit' stories of Joel Chandler Harris), and it is certain that the American Indians possessed tales designed for entertainment, often of a humorous character, as well as others intended for edification.

The artistic quality of which American Indian expression is capable may be suggested by a few examples. A. C. Fletcher (*27 RBEW* [1905–06], p. 431) records an Omaha song of four verses (or, with repetitions, seven), which she translates:

'No one has found a way to avoid death, to pass around it; those old men who have met it, who have reached the place where death stands waiting, have not pointed out a way to circumvent it. Death is difficult to face!'

This song is set to a moving native melody, which has been harmonized by Harvey Worthington Loomis ('Lyrics of the Red Man,' Newton Center, Mass., 1903, vol. ii. no. 2).

An impressive example of Indian eloquence is the speech of Smohalla recorded by Mooney (*14 RBEW* [1892–93], p. 720 f.), uttered in reply to the white commissioner's request that the Wanapum settle down to agriculture. The following is a fragment of Smohalla's peroration:

'You ask me to plough the ground! Shall I take a knife and tear my mother's bosom? Then when I die she will not take me to her bosom to rest.

You ask me to dig for stone! Shall I dig under her skin for her bones? Then when I die I cannot enter her body to be born again.

You ask me to cut grass and make hay and sell it, and be rich like white men! But how dare I cut off my mother's hair?'

In the Iroquoian creation myth, there is a somewhat subtle humour in the account of the fall of Ataentsic, the demiurgic Titaness, from the Sky-world to the chaos of nether waters:

'So now, verily, her body continued to fall. Her body was falling some time before it emerged. Now, she was surprised, seemingly, that there was light below, of a blue color. She looked, and there seemed to be a lake at the spot toward which she was falling. There was nowhere any earth. There she saw many ducks on the lake, whereon they, being waterfowl of all their kinds, floated severally about. Without interruption the body of the woman-being continued to fall.

Now, at that time the waterfowl called the Loon shouted, saying: "Do ye look, a woman-being is coming in the depths of the water, her body is floating up hither." They said: "Verily, it is even so." Now, verily, in a short time the waterfowl called Bittern said: "It is true that ye believe that her body is floating up from the depths of the water. Do ye, however, look upward." All looked upward, and all, moreover, said: "Verily, it is true"' (*21 RBEW*, p. 179 f.).

With this may be contrasted a fragment of the Navaho myth of the creation of the sun (*8 RBEW* [1886–87], pp. 275–277), which is not without a touch of grandeur:

'The people then said, "Let us stretch the world"; so the twelve men at each point expanded the world. The sun continued to rise as the world expanded, and began to shine with less heat, but when it reached the meridian the heat became great and the people suffered much. They crawled everywhere to find shade. Then the voice of Darkness went four times around the world telling the men at the cardinal points to go on expanding the world. "I want all this trouble stopped," said Darkness; "the people are suffering and all is burning; you must continue stretching."'

The more civilized Indian peoples of Mexico, Central America, and Peru show a corresponding advance in formal literary composition. The Aztec rituals recorded by B. Sahagun (*Historia general de las cosas de Nueva España*, Mexico, 1829) are dignified and ornate, and often imbued with a sombre and haunting beauty. The assembled lore of these more advanced peoples must have comprised a considerable body of legends, chronicles, oracles, spells, calendric computations, laws, etc., judging from the fragments which are preserved, while the existence of a secular artistic literature is probable. Brinton is of the opinion that the Central Americans possessed an autochthonous dramatic art (see *Library of Aboriginal American Literature*, no. iii., 'The Güegüence, a Comedy Ballet in the Nahuatl-Spanish Dialect of Nicaragua,' Philadelphia, 1883); and Clements Markham regards the 'Ollantay' as an example of a pre-Spanish dramatic literature (see Markham, *The Incas of Peru*, London, 1910, which contains a translation of this drama). For this literature of the semi-civilized nations see the artt. ANDEANS, CHILAN BALAM, DRAMA (American), POPOL VUH.

2. Literature produced under white influence.—This class consists of (1) works in the native languages, and (2) works by American Indian authors in European languages. (1) Works of the first type include translations of the Bible and other works by white missionaries and teachers, and native records of native ideas made after a system of writing had been acquired. Of the latter, perhaps the most notable instance is the Cherokee literature in the native alphabet invented by Sequoya. A large number of periodicals—some under native, some under missionary, editorship, some in the native tongues exclusively, some part English, some wholly English—have appeared or are now appearing for the expression of American Indian ideas. For the growing body of aboriginal records—chiefly myths, rites, and chronicles—appearing in the *Reports of the American Bureau of Ethnology* and elsewhere special modifications of the Roman alphabetic signs have been invented and systematized for the expression of the native tongues.

(2) A certain number of Indians or part-Indians have distinguished themselves in their literary mastery of European tongues. The names of Garcilasso de la Vega, Inca-Spanish in blood, and of Fernando de Alva Ixtlilxochitl, descendant of the caciques of Tezcuco, are notable as authorities for the native customs and histories of Peru and

Mexico respectively. To these might be added the names of Tezozomac, Chimalpahin Quauhtlehuanitzin, Nakuk Pech, and Fernando Hernandez Arana Xahila, Mexican and Central American post-conquest chroniclers of native history (see respectively E. K. Kingsborough, *Antiquities of Mexico*, ix., 'Cronica Mexicana'; R. Siméon, *Annales de San Anton Munon Chimalpahin Quauhtlehuanitzin*, Paris, 1889; D. G. Brinton, *Library of Aboriginal American Literature*, i., 'The Maya Chronicles,' vi. 'The Annals of the Cakchiquels'). In N. America, George Copway (Kagigegabo, 1818–63) was the author of several books, dealing chiefly with his own people, the Ojibwa, while Charles A. Eastman (Ohiyesa, b. 1858) is the author of essays and stories portraying the native life and ideals of his Siouan kinsfolk.

LITERATURE.—Bibliographical details are given in the *Handbook of American Indians, Bull. 30* of the American Bureau of Ethnology, Washington, 1907–10, under 'Books in Indian Languages,' 'Bible Translations,' 'Dictionaries,' 'Periodicals'; see also 'Copway,' 'Eastman,' 'Sequoya.' Scattered through the *Reports* and *Bulletins* of the Bureau are many texts and translations of myths, songs, and rites; the files of the *JAFL* are rich in similar material. Other collections of importance include E. K. Kingsborough, *Antiquities of Mexico*, 9 vols., London, 1830–48; D. G. Brinton, *Library of Aboriginal American Literature*, 8 vols., Philadelphia, 1882–90; J. G. Icazbalceta, *Nueva Colección de documentos para la Historia de México*, 5 vols., Mexico, 1886–92; E. Seler, *Gesammelte Abhandlungen zur amerikanischen Sprach- und Altertumskunde*, 3 vols., Berlin, 1902–08. Yearly increasing material is to be found in the *Comptes rendus du Congrès international des Américanistes*, Paris, etc.; the *Memoirs* and *Papers of the Peabody Museum*, Cambridge, Mass.; the *Memoirs of the American Museum of Natural History*, New York; the *Memoirs of the American Folklore Society*, New York; the *Publications of the Field Columbian Museum*, Chicago; *of the University of California*, Berkeley, Cal.; *of the University of Pennsylvania Museum*, Philadelphia; the *Contributions of Columbia University*, New York, etc. Of the nature of bibliographical guides are H. H. Bancroft, *Native Races of the Pacific Coast*, New York, 1875, vol. i. p. xvii ff., 'Authorities quoted' (cf. also vol. iii. 'Myths and Languages'); Justin Winsor, *Narrative and Critical History of America*, Boston, 1886–89, vol. i. 'Biographical Appendix'; *The Literature of American History*, ed. J. N. Larned, Boston, 1902; L. Farrand, *The Basis of American History, 1500–1900*, New York, 1904, pp. 272–289; H. Beuchat, *Manuel d'archéologie américaine*, Paris, 1912. See 'Literature' under artt. ANDEANS, CHILAN BALAM, MUSIC (American), POPOL VUH.

H. B. ALEXANDER.

LITERATURE (Babylonian).—Our knowledge of Babylonian-Assyrian literature has been gained chiefly by excavations. Only a few monuments are extant on rocks, among them the famous bilingual inscriptions of the Achæmenian kings, from the study of which the decipherment of the Babylonian script and language started. The statues of kings and deities, the colossi of bulls and lions, slabs, prismoids, cylinders, and various smaller objects of art inscribed with Babylonian legends are, as far as hitherto disinterred, not very numerous in comparison with the thousands of clay tablets which served the ancient Babylonian and Assyrian priests to record the deeds of the rulers of those Empires, to chronicle their historical events, to fix the common prayers, incantations, and religious rites, to place the outcomes of their superstitious belief in certain systems, and to transmit very ancient myths and legends to posterity.

As a matter of fact, these documents are not throughout conceived in the Semitic tongue of Babylonia. It is now well known that in the third millennium before our era the fertile alluvial plain of the twin rivers enclosing Mesopotamia, the Euphrates and the Tigris, was inhabited by a non-Semitic race called the Sumerians, and to them must be attributed the primitive culture of that country, the building of its earliest cities, the first works of art in Western Asia, and the invention of the cuneiform script, the development of which out of a picture writing can still be traced. At what time Semitic, *i.e.* Babylonian, tribes invaded Sumerian territory, and how the process of amalgamation between the two races developed, cannot as yet be ascertained. It may be fairly assumed, however, that at the time of the Babylonian king Ḫammurabi, who replaced the various feudal governments of his predecessors by a vast Babylonian Empire under one sceptre (*c.* 2000 B.C.), that process had come to a standstill, and subsequently the Sumerian literature was gradually superseded by that of the Babylonian-Assyrians. As, however, the religious hymns and psalms composed by the Sumerian writers were adopted by the Semites, forming part of their liturgy and subsequently translated by the priests into their native tongue, Sumerian was studied as a sacred language by the Babylonians and Assyrians, and its literature was carefully preserved and handed down to posterity, just as in mediæval and modern times the Latin language is treated and used as the language of the Church.

Sumerian literature is dealt with in this art. in so far as it forms part of the Babylonian-Assyrian incorporated therein. Babylonian literature actually begins in the time of Ḫammurabi, whose inscriptions (with one exception) and whose famous collection of laws (see LAW [Babylonian and Assyrian]) are conceived in pure Semitic Babylonian. Before entering into a detailed enumeration of the various branches of that literature, attention must also be called to the fact that the difference between the Babylonian and the Assyrian languages consists merely in dialectic varieties, so that Babylonian and Assyrian literature, practically speaking, are to be considered as identical, and are differentiated only by the respective time of their origin during one of the great monarchies of Western Asia—the Old Babylonian Empire, the Assyrian Empire, and the Neo-Babylonian Empire.

The history of the ancient East can now be authentically reconstructed from the historical inscriptions of the Babylonian-Assyrian literature. To the great kings of those monarchies the gaining of immortality by means of a careful tradition of their exploits, their successful campaigns, and building operations appeared most desirable, and so they caused the records of those deeds to be inscribed on a number of clay prisms, on cylinders and tablets, and on the animal colossi at the entrances of their palaces. The great extent of such texts is illustrated by a recently discovered tablet, on which the events of a single year (714 B.C.) are recorded so minutely that an English translation of the text would fill five columns of the London *Times*. Long prayers supplement the historical contents of these inscriptions, interspersed with the enumeration of the titles and abilities, virtues and religiousness, of the royal personages therein glorified. As a rule, the contents are arranged according to the years of reign or the campaigns, in chronological order, followed by an account of the building operations and, in some cases, of the hunting matches of the respective kings, while, at the end of the inscriptions, the blessing of the great gods is invoked upon a successor preserving the document, and their wrath upon its destroyer. To the historical documents must also be assigned the branch of the epistolary literature dealing with public affairs. It is from an extended correspondence between Ḫammurabi and one of his highest officials that an exact knowledge of the reign of the first Semitic ruler in the united Babylonian kingdom is gained — his personal care for the welfare of his vast dominion, the building of cornhouses and dykes under his auspices, the regulation of the temple-taxes, and the use of intercalary months by order of the crown. Of no less importance are the documents of a correspondence carried on in the middle of the second millennium between the Pharaohs of Egypt, then rulers of the whole civilized world, and the kings of Western Asia, including Palestine, the Phœnician ports, and the island of Cyprus, which have become generally known as the Tell el-Amarna find. Letters, proclamations, petitions, accounts of building operations, and short notes accompanying requisites for war were in constant use down to the end of the Neo-Babylonian Empire, and are of a historical value similar to that of the royal inscriptions mentioned above and various so-called 'epigraphs' which were added to the numerous bas-reliefs on the walls of the palaces, illustrating the kings' campaigns and other achievements.

Babylonian-Assyrian literature in the narrower sense of the word has become known chiefly from the documents preserved in a great Royal Library founded at Nineveh by Ashurbanipal, the last great king of the Assyrian Empire, who reigned from 668 to 626 B.C. and was called Sardanapalos by the Greek writers. This Library, generally known as the Kouyunjik Collection, the various portions of which have been secured since the middle of last century for the Trustees of the British Museum by Sir Henry Rawlinson and other English scholars, consists of copies and translations of ancient Babylonian and Sumerian works, and deals with every branch of wisdom and learning then appreciated by the Assyrian priests, who, by command of their royal patron, collected and catalogued, revised and re-copied, the various texts which had been gathered from the oldest cities and temple archives of the whole land. Recent excavations have in some instances also brought to light a number of hymns and prayers, certain omen-texts, and a few astrological inscriptions which must be attributed to an earlier period than that of Ashurbanipal, and apparently belonged to the mass of original documents from which the copies in the Library were made; and the same may be said of certain collections of the Neo-Babylonian time, in which, again, copies from the Kouyunjik Collection have been found. An exact idea of the literary achievements of the Babylonian-Assyrians, however, can be formed only by a perusal of the contents of the Library itself. Such a perusal yields the following results.

Apart from the epistolary literature, a few drafts for royal inscriptions, and numerous commercial texts—the last extending from early Babylonian times down to the beginning of our own era—Assyrian literature was devoted chiefly to superstitious belief, to religious rites and ceremonies, incantations and prayers, and, in close connexion with both branches, to medicine, astrology, and philology.

A large proportion of the documents here concerned deal with the appearance and actions of various animals, and it has been justly remarked that in these inscriptions survivals may be seen of a very ancient animal-cult—reminding one of certain parallels in Egypt—which in later times seems to have been superseded by an exquisitely astral religion. Closely connected with these animal omens are the numerous and systematically arranged texts bearing on monstrosities and other unusual features of births, as well as the large collections of documents dealing with the inspection of the liver of an immolated wether. The movements of various birds, the actions of dogs and pigs, the hissing of a snake, and the invasion of locusts were especially observed for the compilation of such omen-texts. Another means of divination used by the Babylonians was pure water, into which a small quantity of sesame-oil was poured, so as to produce the well-known interference-colours, re-discovered by Newton, and certain structures of rings and bubbles, from which the events of the future were predicted. The link between these forecasts and the religious texts must be sought in the medical prescriptions, which were laid down and redacted into a kind of pharmacopœia. Various diseases, arranged according to the limbs and members attacked, are enumerated in these collections, and the draughts, decoctions, and other therapeutics are described in detail. Mental disorder was attributed to the influence of evil spirits, and on this account the medical texts are frequently interspersed with incantation formulæ which otherwise constitute a class of literature by themselves. Three or four 'series' of tablets containing such incantation-texts, accompanied by directions for the respective ceremonies, have become known to us. They are chiefly directed against the pernicious actions of witches and sorcerers, supposed to be neutralized by destroying the images of these witches, mostly by burning. In the majority of cases the text of these incantations is in the interlinear bilingual style, *i.e.* in Assyrian and Sumerian; and in several instances it can be proved that the Sumerian original has been taken over from ancient sources, portions of which still exist. On the other hand, it can hardly be denied that the Semitic Assyrian priests themselves also composed such interlinear texts, using the Sumerian language, then long extinct, in much the same way as mediæval monks used Latin. Moreover, even pure Sumerian texts without an interlinear Assyrian version are preserved in Ashurbanipal's Library—a fact from which it may be concluded that such incantations even at his time were recited in the old sacred language. And the same holds good of the psalms, litanies, and other forms of prayers which are written either in Sumerian only or accompanied, in Assyrian times, by a Semitic version. Whilst the incantation-texts, however, are mostly preserved as parts of certain literary compositions or 'series,' the prayers and similar religious documents stand for the most part isolated, and only by their style can they be recognized as belonging to various classes. Of such, the prayers called after 'the lifting of the hand,' the hymns exhibiting a parallelism of members, the litanies addressed to certain deities, and the compositions showing acrostics may be mentioned as specimens.

Of special interest among the religious texts are the legends and myths, of which a number of 'series' have been discovered. A few of them, as, *e.g.*, the Babylonian Creation Legend and the Deluge Story, both of which have parallels in the OT, can be proved to reach as far back as the Old Babylonian period. It cannot be ascertained at present, however, at what time the account of the Deluge was incorporated in a great national epic, the so-called Gilgamesh Epic, which is founded on astral religion and seems to refer to the life in the nether world. Similarly the 'Descent of the goddess Ishtar to Hades,' an isolated poem preserved in Ashurbanipal's Library only, appears to depict nature's death in the autumn and its resuscitation in the spring, and the story of Nergal, the lord of tombs, and his consort, the goddess Erishkigal, likewise contains a description of the abode of the dead. Immortality was not granted to mankind, as we learn from another myth, the story of a pious man called Adapa, who, being misled by chance, refused to partake of the food of life and the water of life, which were offered to him in heaven.

As has already been remarked, it may be concluded from the Gilgamesh Epic and from other mythological texts that in the Assyrian time at least an astral religion was reigning in the valley of the Euphrates and Tigris. This appears to be borne out by another branch of Babylonian-Assyrian literature, viz. the astrological texts. A large composition, comprising at least 70 tablets, is devoted to observations of the movements of the celestial bodies, including atmospheric phenomena, such as thunder-storms, hurricanes, and earthquakes, and to the forecasts taken from such observations and referring to the welfare of the king, the devastation of temples and palaces, the growth of vegetation, and the increase of cattle and other animals. As early as in the 7th cent. B.C. these astrological documents were paralleled by purely astronomical texts, dealing with the heliacal risings and the culminations of luminous fixed stars and constellations, while of the Neo-Babylonian time documents with astronomical observations and calculations have been found which bear witness to the highly developed faculties of the later Babylonians for determining the velocity of the sun and moon, the length of the year, and the revolution of the five planets then known.

An equally high standard was attained by the Babylonian and Assyrian priests in grammar and lexicography. Those sacred Sumerian incantation-texts, hymns, and prayers must have early prompted the protectors of religious traditions to collect helps for studying the extinct sacred tongue, and in course of time such investigations necessarily involved a study of the Semitic native language of those priests as well. Paradigms of verb-forms, lists of synonymous words, and, above all, large collections of Sumerian ideographs explained according to their pronunciation and meaning have thus been handed down. And the numerous lists of names of animals, stones, plants, and wooden objects, of stars, temples, and deities, afford a clear insight into the wisdom and work of the philologists, by whom the oldest colleges on earth were founded and literary tradition was first carried on.

Babylonian literature was deeply influenced, as has been shown, by its older Sumerian sister, and the Assyrians, in developing it, seem to have played a rôle similar to that played in later centuries by the Syrians who conveyed Greek learning to the nearer East. On the other hand, the cuneiform Babylonian script spread all over Western Asia, and the Hittite and Mitanni nations, the Chaldic tribes, and the Canaanites appear to have adopted it in one or other form, and certainly became familiar to some extent with the literary documents of the Babylonian people. Babylonian legends found their way to the ancestors of the Israelite tribes, and similar Babylonian documents were studied in the middle of the second millennium by the learned priests of the Egyptian Pharaohs. Finally, the late Assyrian omen and astrological texts wandered to the East as far as China, left remarkable traces in the Indian literature, and were transmitted to Greece, where actual translations of such texts have been found. In this way also Babylonian literature has in the last instance influenced Christianity, and has left its marks throughout mediæval times down to the present day.

LITERATURE.—L. W. King, *A History of Sumer and Akkad*, London, 1910; E. A. W. Budge and L. W. King, *Annals of the Kings of Assyria*, do. 1902; J. A. Knudtzon, *Die El-Amarna-Tafeln*, Leipzig, 1907–14; J. Kohler and A. Ungnad, *Assyrische Rechtsurkunden*, do. 1913; C. Bezold, *Ninive und Babylon*³, Bielefeld and Leipzig, 1909; J. Hunger, *Babylonische Tieromina*, Berlin, 1909; F. Küchler, *Beiträge zur Kenntnis der assyrisch-babylonischen Medizin*, Leipzig, 1904; M. Jastrow, *Die Religion Babyloniens und Assyriens*, Giessen, 1902–13; F. X. Kugler, *Sternkunde und Sterndienst in Babel*, Münster, 1907–14; C. Bezold and F. Boll, *Reflexe astrolog. Keilinschriften bei griech. Schriftstellern*, Heidelberg, 1911; R. W. Rogers, *Cuneiform Parallels to the OT*, New York, 1912.

C. BEZOLD.

LITERATURE (Buddhist).—The sacred canon of Buddhism has been handed down in two forms. One, written in Pāli and preserved in Ceylon, Burma, and Siam, contains the doctrine of the older school, the Hīnayāna ('Little Vehicle'; see art. HĪNAYĀNA), the chief aim of which is to attain *arhat*-ship or the release of the individual from suffering. It is the canon of one sect only. The other, the Sanskrit canon, which is later, is not extant in any complete example, but is known only from fragments found during recent years in Central Asia by M. A. Stein, A. Grünwedel, and A. von le Coq, partly also from quotations in other Buddhist Sanskrit texts, as well as from Chinese and Tibetan translations. The chief texts of the Sanskrit Mūla-sarvāstivādins, who belonged to the older Buddhism, were translated from Sanskrit into Chinese in the years A.D. 700–712. This canon agrees largely with the Pāli canon both in wording and in arrangement. But there are also various divergences. These are to be explained by the descent of both from a common original in the Māgadhī dialect, from which the Pāli canon was derived in one part of the country, and the Sanskrit canon, later, in another. While the other sects had no complete canon, each regarded as specially sacred one or more texts, which either incorporated parts of or replaced a theoretically acknowledged canon. The great bulk of these Sanskrit Buddhists belonged to the new school of the Mahāyāna ('Great Vehicle'; see art. MAHĀYĀNA), the chief aim of which was the attainment of the condition of a Bodhisattva, or future Buddha, who brings *nirvāṇa* within the reach of the entire human race.

The forms of Buddhism preserved in Pāli and in Sanskrit have commonly been called 'Southern' and 'Northern' respectively because the former prevails in Ceylon, Burma, and Siam, and the latter in Nepāl, Tibet, China, and Japan. The distinction thus made is misleading, since all Buddhist canonical literature arose in the North of India. The Pāli canon contains no reference to the South, and the term 'Northern' confuses sects by the erroneous implication that it excludes the older school of the Hīnayāna. It is, therefore, more appropriate to speak of 'Pāli Buddhism' and 'Sanskrit Buddhism.'

The languages in which the two canons were composed require to be more precisely defined. Pāli is the sacred language common to the Buddhists of Ceylon, Burma, Siam, and Cambodia, but Pāli MSS are written in the four different alphabets of those countries, while it has become the regular practice to print European editions of Pāli texts in Roman characters. The Pāli language in which the texts have been handed down cannot be identical with the dialect in which the canon of the 3rd cent. B.C. was composed; the latter could only have been the language of Magadha (Bihār), in which Buddha first preached and which must have been used by the monks of Pāṭaliputra who put together the canon. Traces of such a Māgadhī canon may be found in the Pāli texts. In this connexion it is noteworthy that the titles of the canonical texts enumerated in Aśoka's Bairat inscription appear in a Māgadhī form. But Pāli differs from the Māgadhī which is known to us from inscriptions, literary works, and grammarians. Nor is it identical with any other dialect. It is, in fact, an exclusively Buddhist literary language, which, like other literary languages, is the result of a mixture of dialects. Its basis is, however, in all likelihood Māgadhī—a conclusion supported by the tradition that even identifies Māgadhī and Pāli. The language of the other canon is either correct Sanskrit or a Middle Indian dialect which, approximating to Sanskrit, is best termed 'mixed Sanskrit' (formerly as a rule called the 'Gāthā dialect').

No work of Buddhist literature goes back to Buddha's time. But much contained in the canon may very well hand down the words spoken by the Master, such as the famous sermon of Benares, especially if we consider the tenacity of the verbal memory in Indian oral tradition.

Almost the whole of the oldest Buddhist literature consists of short collections containing speeches, sayings, poems, tales, or rules of conduct, which are combined into larger collections, called *piṭaka*, or 'basket,' in a manner somewhat analogous to the formation of the *saṁhitā* of the Vedas (cf. HYMNS [Vedic]). Three such aggregate collections, called the *Tipiṭaka*, form the Pāli canon.

The canon as constituted in Aśoka's reign must have undergone appreciable changes between then and the time when it was fixed in the 1st cent. B.C. in Ceylon. But thenceforward it has been handed down with great care. Some modifications, indeed, must have taken place even after the 1st cent., because it is otherwise difficult to account for the numerous contradictions appearing in the canon. Taken as a whole, however, the Pāli *Tipiṭaka* may be regarded as not very different from the Māgadhī canon of the 3rd cent. B.C. For the quotations occurring in the Aśoka inscriptions diverge only slightly from the extant text, while the titles of seven texts mentioned in one of these inscriptions are partly identical with, and partly similar to, those which are found in the extant *Sutta-piṭaka*. Moreover, the sculptures and inscriptions of the monuments at Sāñchī and Bhārhut (*c.* 200 B.C.) afford corroborative evidence of the existence of a collection not unlike the extant *Sutta-piṭaka*. But the earliest direct evidence that the *Tipiṭaka* as a whole had already assumed its present form is furnished by the *Milinda-pañha*, which dates from the 1st cent. A.D. The age and authenticity of the Pāli tradition are confirmed by the Sanskrit canon, which, as already stated, is so closely allied to it as necessarily to be derived from the same original.

The texts which the sacred literature comprises will now be summarily described in regard to their chief contents.

I. *THE PĀLI CANON*.—**1. Vinaya-piṭaka.**—The first of the three main divisions is the *Vinaya-piṭaka*, the 'Basket of Discipline,' which supplies the regulations for the management of the Order (*saṅgha*), and for the conduct of the daily life of monks and nuns. It includes rules for reception into the Order, for the periodical confession of sins, for life during the rainy season, for housing, clothing, medicinal remedies, and legal procedure in cases of schism. Here and there are also to be found stories, some of which contain the oldest fragments of the Buddha legend, while others are valuable for the light that they throw on the daily life of ancient India.

2. Sutta-piṭaka.—The second 'basket' is the *Sutta-piṭaka*, our best source for the *dhamma*, or religion of Buddha and his earliest disciples. It contains, in prose and verse, the most important products of Buddhist literature grouped in five minor collections named *nikāyas*. The first four of these consist of *suttas*, or 'lectures,' being either speeches of Buddha or dialogues in prose occasionally interspersed with verses. These four are cognate and homogeneous in character. For a number of *suttas* reappear in two or more of them; there is no difference in the doctrines that they contain; and they all show a similar mode of discussion, probably preserving a reminiscence of Buddha's actual method as good as that which the Platonic dialogues preserve of Socrates' method. One of the features of the method of argument in these *suttas* is the very extensive use of parables and similes, which, though lacking in cogency, are valuable as throwing much light on the daily life of the artisans, cultivators, and merchants of the day. Since each of these *nikāyas* contains old along with more recent elements of a similar character, there is no reason to doubt that all of them were formed into collections about the same time.

(*a*) The *Dīgha-nikāya*, or 'Collection of long lectures,' consists of 34 *suttas*, each of which deals fully with one or more points of Buddhist doctrine. The very first, entitled *Brahmajāla-sutta*, or 'Lecture on the Brāhman net,' is of very great importance for the history not only of Buddhism, but of the whole religious life of ancient India. The Buddha enumerates a large number of the occupations of Brāhmans and ascetics from which the Buddhist monk should refrain. The second, the *Sāmaññaphala-sutta*, or 'Lecture on the reward of asceticism,' furnishes valuable information about the views of a number of non-Buddhistic teachers and founders of sects. The *Ambaṭṭha-sutta* illustrates the history of caste and Buddha's attitude to that system. The *Kūṭadanta-sutta*, 'Lecture on the sharp tooth (of the Brāhmans),' displays the relations between Brāhmanism and Buddhism, while the *Tevijja-sutta*, 'Lecture on the followers of the three Vedas,' contrasts the Brāhman cult with Buddhist ideals. The fundamental doctrine of Buddhism is treated in the *Mahānidāna-sutta*, or 'Great lecture on causation.' One of the most noteworthy texts of the Pāli canon is the *Sigālovāda-sutta*, or 'Admonition of Sigāla,' describing fully the duties of the Buddhist layman. But the most important text in the *Dīgha-nikāya* is the *Mahāparinibbāna-sutta*, or 'Great lecture on the complete Nirvāṇa,' a continuous account of the last days of Buddha. It is one of the oldest parts of the *Tipiṭaka*, as supplying the earliest beginnings of a biography of Buddha. It does not, however, all date from the same period, for in some passages Buddha appears entirely as a human being, while in others he is represented as a demi-god or magician. This text resembles the Gospels more than any other in the *Tipiṭaka*. On the other hand, the very title of the *Mahāpadāna-sutta*, or 'Great lecture on the miracles (of Buddha),' indicates its lateness. It already contains the dogma of six Buddhas as precursors of Gautama, and presupposes the whole Buddha legend.

(*b*) The *Majjhima-nikāya*, or 'Collection of (lectures of) middle (length),' consists of 152 sermons and dialogues dealing with almost all points of Buddhist religion. Thus Buddha is represented as admitting that a man may obtain *nirvāṇa* even without being a monk, or may commit suicide if he acts solely for the purpose of obtaining release; and as refuting the claim of Brāhmans to be the only pure caste and asserting the purity of all four castes. These *suttas* throw light not only on the life of Buddhist monks, but on such matters as Brāhman sacrifices, various forms of asceticism, and the relation of Buddha to the Jains, as well as superstitious, social, and legal conditions prevailing at the time. The difference in age of the *suttas* is indicated by the fact that here too Buddha sometimes appears as a purely human character and sometimes as a miracle-worker.

(*c*) Of the 56 divisions into which the *Saṁyutta-nikāya*, or 'Collection of combined lectures,' is divided the last is most noteworthy, as treating of the four truths (*sachcha*), and containing the famous *Dhamma-chakka-ppavattana-sutta*, the 'Lecture on setting in motion the wheel of the law,' usually described as the 'Sermon of Benares.' Of the *suttas* in one of its sections some contain a large admixture of stanzas, while others consist entirely of verse forming short ballads of great poetic merit.

(*d*) The *Aṅguttara-nikāya*, or 'Collection of lectures arranged according to increasing number,' consists of over 2300 *suttas* in 11 sections, so arranged that in the first are treated objects of which there is only one kind, in the second those of which there are two kinds, and so on. Thus, the second deals with the two kinds of Buddhas. In this collection are found a large number of *suttas* and stanzas which occur in other texts of the canon, and which here even sometimes appear as quotations. This alone points to a late date. But internal evidence also shows that it was composed at a time when Buddha was already regarded as an omniscient demi-god, if not an actual deity.

(*e*) The *Khudda-nikāya*, or 'Collection of small pieces,' is a late compilation added after the previous ones were complete. Its contents date from very different times; for, while several of its parts belong to the latest stratum of the Pāli canon, some go back to the earliest period. It is composed for the most part in verse, and, in fact, contains all the most important works of Buddhist Indian poetry. Of the works which it embraces the following may be mentioned. The *Khudda-pāṭha*, or 'Short reader,' comprises nine brief texts to be used by the novice or as prayers in the Buddhist cult. The first is the Buddhist creed; the second gives the ten commandments enjoined on monks; and the ninth is the fine *Metta-sutta*, in which kindness towards all creatures is praised as the true Buddhist cult. The *Dhamma-pada*, or 'Words of religion,' the most familiar and longest known work of Buddhist literature, is an anthology of maxims chiefly expressing the ethical doctrines of Buddhism. More than one-half of its 423 stanzas are found in other texts of the Pāli canon. The *Udāna*, or 'Solemn utterances,' consisting of old verses and prose stories (probably later additions), is a glorification of the Buddhist ideal of life and of the endless bliss of *nirvāṇa*. The *Itivuttaka*, or 'Sayings of Buddha,' is composed in prose and verse used in such a way that the same idea is expressed in both. Very often the verse simply repeats the statement of the preceding prose. The oldest parts of the work probably date from the time of Buddha himself. The *Sutta-nipāta* is a collection of poetical *suttas*, many of which, as shown by internal evidence, must go back to the beginnings of Buddhism, and have arisen at least among the first disciples of Buddha. They are important as supplying information about the original doctrine of Buddha, besides representing an early, though not the earliest, stage of the Buddha legend. The *Thera-gāthā* and *Therī-gāthā*, or 'Songs of monks and nuns,' are poems of great literary merit exalting mental calm as the religious ideal, and describing the value of Buddhist ethical doctrine from personal experience. It is quite possible that here may be included poems composed by some of the earliest disciples of Buddha, but several are much later, since they represent a Buddha cult like that of the Mahāyāna. The *Jātaka* is a book consisting of about 550 stories of former 'births' of Buddha in the character of a Bodhisattva, or future Buddha. It consists partly of poetry and partly of prose, but only the verse portions have canonical value. For a discussion of the work see art. JĀTAKA.

3. **Abhidhamma-pitaka.**—The *Abhidhamma-piṭaka*, or 'Basket of higher religion,' treats of the same subject as the *Sutta-piṭaka*, differing from that collection only in being more scholastic. It is composed chiefly in the form of question and answer, like a catechism. The starting-point of this collection appears to have been the *Sutta-piṭaka*, one of the texts of which, the *Aṅguttara-nikāya*, may be regarded as its precursor. Its first beginnings seem to have been certain lists called *mātikās*, which are already mentioned in the *Vinaya-piṭaka*.

While the Pāli canon (apart from additions) was entirely composed in India, the non-canonical literature was the work of monks in Ceylon. There is only one important exception, the *Milinda-pañha*, which must have been written in the north-west of India. It represents a dialogue supposed to have taken place between a Buddhist teacher and Menander (Milinda), the Greek king who from about 125 to 95 B.C. ruled over the Indus territory, Gujarāt, and the valley of the Ganges. The author, whose name is unknown, must have lived at a time when the memory of this king was still fresh. As the Greek domination came to an end soon after Menander, he could hardly have been remembered for more than a century. That the original portion of the work, books ii. and iii. with parts of i., is thus as old as the beginning of our era is supported by the fact that it bears comparison with the very best dialogues in the *Sutta-nipāta*. Books iv.–vii., besides differing in character from the rest, are wanting in the Chinese translation made between A.D. 317 and 420. These and the other spurious parts are the work of learned monks in Ceylon.

II. *SANSKRIT BUDDHIST LITERATURE.*—While one ancient sect created the Pāli canon, various later sects produced a Buddhist literature in pure or mixed Sanskrit, of which many extensive works have been preserved, though others are known only through Tibetan and Chinese translations. The great bulk of this Buddhist Sanskrit literature belongs to, or has been greatly influenced by, the later Mahāyāna school. That school, though acknowledging that the *Theravāda*, or 'Doctrine of the Elders,' went back to Buddha, regarded it as inadequate, because it made *nirvāṇa* attainable to the few only through the life of a monk. In order to bring salvation to all humanity, the Mahāyāna taught that every man could aim at being born as a Bodhisattva (*q.v.*); and any ordinary man, even a Pariah, could attain salvation by the practice of virtue and by devotion to Buddha. The Buddhas are now regarded as divine beings from the beginning, their earthly life and their *nirvāṇa* being nothing but an illusion. The Buddhas preceding Gautama, instead of being six, are now believed to be thousands or even thousands of millions in number; and an innumerable host of Bodhisattvas is revered as having for the salvation of mankind refrained from entering *nirvāṇa*. Under the influence of Hinduism a new mythology grew up in which a number of Hindu deities were added to the Buddhas and Bodhisattvas, and a much stronger devotion to Buddha, analogous to that of the Brāhman *Bhagavad-Gītā* (*q.v.*) to Kṛṣṇa. Brāhman doctrine influenced the development of Mahāyānism on the philosophical side also. For, while the old Buddhism denied the existence of the ego only, the Mahāyāna doctrine also denied the existence of everything (expressed by the formula *sarvaṁ śūnyam*, 'everything is void'), either as complete nihilism or as ideal nihilism (*vijñāna-vāda*, or 'doctrine' that nothing exists except 'in consciousness').

1. **Hīnayāna.**—The large realist sect of the Sarvāstivādins ('followers of the doctrine that everything is'), besides having an extensive literature, possessed a Sanskrit canon, of which, however, only fragmentary parts of the *Udāna-varga*, *Dharmapada*, and *Ekottarāgama* (corresponding to the Pāli *Udāna*, *Dhammapada*, and *Aṅguttara-nikāya*) have as yet been discovered. The *Mahāvastu*, or 'Book of great events,' is a text of the Lokottaravādins ('followers of the doctrine' that the Buddhas are 'supernatural beings'), a subdivision of the old schismatic sect, the Mahāsāṅghikas, or 'adherents of the great community.' Its chief content is a miraculous biography of Buddha, written in mixed Sanskrit. It is of great importance as containing many old versions of texts that also occur in the Pāli canon, such as the 'Sermon of Benares' and a section of the *Dhammapada*. About half of it consists of *jātakas*, many of which do not occur in Pāli. Though belonging to the Hīnayāna, it contains much that is akin to the Mahāyāna, as that the adoration of Buddha is alone sufficient for the attainment of *nirvāṇa*. There is, however, only a slight admixture of regular Mahāyāna doctrine, and nothing of Mahāyāna mythology. Some of the elements which it contains point to the 4th cent. A.D., but the nucleus of the book probably dates from the 2nd cent. B.C. (see MAHĀVASTU).

The *Lalita-vistara*, or 'Detailed account of the play (of Buddha),' though it seems to have originally been a Buddha biography of the Sarvāstivādins, has been extended in the sense of the Mahāyāna, of which it bears all the characteristics. It is a continuous narrative in Sanskrit prose, with long metrical pieces in 'mixed Sanskrit.' Containing old and new elements side by side, it is valuable for the development of the Buddha legend from its earliest beginnings to the deification of Buddha as a god above all gods.

The *Buddha-charita*, or 'Life of Buddha,' is an epic composed in pure Sanskrit. It is the work of Aśvaghoṣa (*q.v.*), a genuine poet, who, as one of the pioneers of the Mahāyāna and a contemporary of Kaniṣka, must have composed it about A.D. 100. Originally a Brāhman, he joined the Sarvāstivādin sect, but laid great stress on devotion to Buddha. His epic, however, contains no pronounced Mahāyāna doctrine.

Another work of the same school, dating probably from the 4th cent. A.D., is the *Jātaka-mālā*, or 'Garland of birth stories,' by Āryaśūra. It is composed in a mixture of verse and prose, conforming to the style of classical Sanskrit literature. It contains 34 *jātakas*, illustrating the *pāramitās*, or 'perfections,' of a Bodhisattva, and nearly all occurring in the Pāli Jātaka Book.

Cognate with the preceding works are a number of collections of *avadānas*, or 'stories of great deeds,' being practically *jātakas* in which the hero is a Bodhisattva (not Buddha). The older ones still belong to the Hīnayāna, though attaching special importance to the veneration of Buddha. Such is the *Avadāna-śataka*, or 'Century of great deeds,' which, dating probably from the 2nd cent. A.D., contains pieces from the Sanskrit canon of the Sarvāstivādins, and nothing connected with the cult of Bodhisattvas or with Mahāyāna mythology. Dating from about a century later, but including very old texts, is the *Divyāvadāna*, or 'Heavenly *avadānas*,' which often mentions the Sanskrit canon and quotes individual canonical texts, besides having several legends in common with the Pāli canon. Most of the stories are written in good simple Sanskrit with occasional *gāthās*, but others show the elaborate metres and long compounds of the artificial classical style.

2. Mahāyāna.—The Mahāyāna, not representing a homogeneous sect, possesses no canon. But there are nine *dharmas*, or 'religious texts,' which, composed at different times and belonging to different sects, are also called *Vaipulya sūtras*. The most important and most characteristic work of the Mahāyāna school is the *Saddharma-puṇḍarīka*, or 'Lotus of good religion.' It contains matter of different date represented by Sanskrit prose and by *gāthās* in 'mixed Sanskrit.' Its original form dates perhaps from about A.D. 200. Śākyamuni is here no longer a man, the mendicant of the Pāli *suttas*, but a god above all gods, who has lived for countless ages and will live for ever. His doctrine is that every one can become a Buddha who has heard the preaching of Buddha, performed meritorious works, and led a moral life. Even those who adore relics, erect *stūpas*, or make Buddha images obtain the highest enlightenment (see LOTUS OF THE TRUE LAW).

A whole *sūtra*, the *Kāraṇḍa-vyūha*, akin in language and style to the later Hindu *purāṇas*, is devoted to the exaltation of Avalokiteśvara, the 'Lord who looks down' with compassion on all beings, here the typical Bodhisattva who, in the exercise of infinite pity, refuses Buddhahood till all beings are saved. The yearning for salvation has probably never been more powerfully expressed than in the figure of Avalokiteśvara (*q.v.*). The cult of this Bodhisattva is known to have been in existence before A.D. 400. More mythological is the *Sukhāvatī-vyūha* (*c.* A.D. 100), or 'Detailed account of the Land of Bliss,' which is devoted to the praise of the Buddha Amitābha ('of unmeasured splendour'). The *Gaṇḍa-vyūha* (a still unpublished *dharma*) celebrates the Bodhisattva Mañjuśrī (*q.v.*), who occupies a prominent position in Mahāyāna cult and art.

Other Mahāyāna *sūtras* are of a philosophic and dogmatic character. The *Laṅkāvatāra-sūtra* (a *dharma*) describes a visit paid to the demon Rāvaṇa in Ceylon by Buddha, who answers a number of questions about religion according to the doctrines of the Yogāchāra school (founded by Asaṅga). The tenets of a number of philosophical schools are also discussed here. The *Daśabhūmīśvara* (a *dharma*) represents a lecture by Buddha in Indra's heaven, about the ten stages by which Buddhahood is to be reached. It dates from before A.D. 400, when it was translated into Chinese. The *Samādhi-rāja* (a *dharma*), or 'King of meditations,' is a dialogue in which Buddha shows how a Bodhisattva can attain the highest enlightenment by various stages of contemplation. The *Suvarṇa-prabhāsa* (a *dharma*), dating from not later than the 6th cent. A.D., is partly philosophical, partly legendary, and partly ritualistic in its contents. The Hindu goddesses Sarasvatī and Mahādevī are introduced, and magical formulæ and Tantra practices are dealt with. The *Rāṣṭra-pāla-sūtra* (before A.D. 600), besides containing Buddha's description of the qualities of a Bodhisattva, introduces a number of *jātakas*. Its main interest lies in its prophecy of the future decay of religion; for its realistic descriptions must largely reflect the lax morality of the Buddhist monks of the 6th century. The most important of all the *sūtras* of the Mahāyāna are the *Prajñā-pāramitās*, or *sūtras* on the 'perfection of wisdom.' They deal with the six perfections of a Bodhisattva, but especially with the highest, *prajñā*, 'wisdom,' the knowledge of the doctrine of nothingness, which denies not only being, but also not-being. The doctrine of the Mahāyāna *sūtras* was systematized by Nāgārjuna, originally a Brāhman who flourished about A.D. 200 and founded the Mādhyamika school, one of the main branches of the Mahāyāna. In order to remove the otherwise insoluble contradictions of complete nihilism, he lays down in his Mādhyamika *sūtras* that the doctrine of Buddha rests on two kinds of truth. The one is the conventional truth of everyday life (in which the higher truth is latent), and the other is truth in the highest sense. It is only through the lower that the higher truth can be taught, and it is only through the latter that *nirvāṇa* can be attained. This distinction resembles that between the higher and the lower knowledge in the Vedānta system of the Brāhmans (see MADHYAMAKA, MĀDHYAMIKAS).

Nāgārjuna cannot be regarded as the originator of the Mahāyāna doctrine itself. There must have been teachers and texts of that doctrine more than a century before his time; for Mahāyāna texts were translated into Chinese in the 3rd cent. A.D., and the Gandhāra type of Buddhist art, which represents the Mahāyāna doctrine, came into being about the beginning of our era.

Asaṅga (*q.v.*), the eldest of the three sons of a Brāhman from Peshāwar, probably flourished in the first half of the 4th century. Originally an adherent of the Sarvāstivāda school, he became the main exponent of the Mahāyānist Yogāchāra school, which recognizes existence in consciousness (*vijñāna*) only, denying the reality of the phenomenal world. The only absolute entity is truth (*bodhi*), which is manifested in the Buddhas, and which is attainable solely by those who practise *yoga* in ten stages. *Yoga* (*q.v.*) was thus brought into systematic connexion with the Mahāyāna doctrine. Asaṅga expounds the tenets of this school in his *Mahāyāna-Sūtrālaṁkāra*, a work consisting of memorial verses (*kārikās*) in various metres and a commentary written by himself. Asaṅga's brother, Vasubandhu, one of the most important figures in Buddhist literature, distinguished for profound learning and great powers of independent philosophic thought, is remarkable as having written authoritative works representing both the great divisions of Buddhism. His most important work, belonging to his earlier and Hīnayāna period, was his *Abhidharma-kośa*, which deals with ethics, psychology, and metaphysics, but is known only through a Sanskrit commentary and Chinese and Tibetan translations. In later life he was converted by his brother Asaṅga to the Mahāyāna doctrine, when he composed a number of commentaries on various Mahāyāna *sūtras*, which have, however, been preserved in Chinese and Tibetan translations only. The most important of the later Mahāyānists was Śāntideva, who probably lived in the 7th cent. and was the author of two works. The first, *Śikṣā-samuchchaya*, or 'Summary of the Doctrine,' is a manual of the Mahāyāna teaching, consisting of memorial verses (*kārikās*) and a commentary. The other is the *Bodhicharyāvatāra*, or 'Entry into the practice of enlightenment,' a religious poem of great literary merit, inculcating the pursuit of the highest moral perfection. The aim in both works is the attainment of enlightenment as a Bodhisattva by means of infinite compassion and the veneration of Buddhas, the highest wisdom being the belief in nothingness (*śūnyatā*).

An indication of the decay of Buddhism in India is the approximation of its later literature to that of Hinduism. Thus the Mahāyāna *sūtras* show striking resemblances to the Brāhmanic *purāṇas*, containing, like these, *māhātmyas*, or glorifications of particular localities, and *stotras*, or hymns addressed to various deities. There are also separate *stotras*, like those addressed to Viṣṇu and Śiva; many of them glorify the goddess Tārā, the female counterpart of the Bodhisattva Avalokiteśvara.

A further sign of degeneracy is the increasingly important position which the *dhāraṇīs*, or 'spells,' begin to occupy in Mahāyānist literature. They appear to have existed from the 3rd cent. A.D. They were probably in their earliest form intelligible *sūtras* containing Buddhist doctrine, but unintelligible mystic syllables gradually began to prevail as the 'kernel' of magic powers. Finally, under the influence of the Śaivite *tantras* they became pure gibberish and entered as essential elements into the Buddhist *tantras*.

The *Tantras* (*q.v.*), which probably date from the 9th to the 11th cent., and are composed in barbarous Sanskrit, represent the final stage in the degradation of Indian Buddhism. They are treatises partly concerned with ritual (*kriyā-tantra*) or rules of conduct (*charyā-tantra*), partly with the esoteric doctrine of the Yogīs (*yoga-tantra*). The former class is a revival of the old Brāhman ritual of the *Gṛhyasūtras*, and the mystical syllables contained in them are addressed not only to Buddhas and Bodhisattvas, but also to Śaivite deities. Most of the *tantras*, however, are connected with *yoga*, starting from the mysticism of the Mādhyamika and the Yogāchāra schools. The *yogī* here aims at the highest knowledge of nothingness (*śūnyatā*), not only by asceticism and meditation, but by magical rites, hypnotism, and other expedients. The teaching and practice of this *yoga* are a mixture of mysticism, sorcery, and erotics, accompanied by disgusting orgies. Nothing of Buddhism remains in them, for they differ in no respect, except in being described as 'promulgated by Buddha,' from the Śaivite *tantras*, inculcating as they do the worship of the *liṅga* and Śaivite gods, and introducing numerous female deities into their cult.

LITERATURE.—H. Kern, *Manual of Indian Buddhism*, Strassburg, 1896, pp. 1–8; L. de la Vallée Poussin, *Bouddhisme: Études et matériaux*, Brussels, 1897; T. W. Rhys Davids, *Buddhism*, London, 1904, Lect. ii., *Buddhist India*, do. 1903, chs. ix.–xi.; M. Winternitz, *Gesch. der ind. Litteratur*, vol. ii. pt. i. 'Die buddh. Litteratur,' Leipzig, 1913 (contains very full bibliographical notes on editions, translations, books, and articles on questions of detail—*e.g.*, on the history and authenticity of the Pāli canon, p. 1).

A. A. MACDONELL.

LITERATURE (Chinese).—The vast mass of Chinese literature is divided by Chinese scholars into four classes—classics, histories, writings of philosophers, and belles lettres. The term *king*, translated 'classic,' means originally the warp of a web, and by metaphorical extension comes to mean what is invariable, a rule. The Chinese classics are, therefore, those books which are regarded by the Chinese as canonical. Taoism and Buddhism as well as Confucianism have their classics; but in speaking of the Chinese classics one has in view the books of the Confucian canon only. If we speak of them as 'sacred,' we expose ourselves to misleading associations. We do, indeed, meet with the phrase *Sheng King* as designating the Confucian canon, where *Sheng* is the word which is used in Christian literature to express the idea of holiness. Originally, however, it refers to perfection of wisdom ('sage,' 'sagely'), and does not of itself suggest any relation to the divine. Of the perfect Sage it is said:

> 'He is seen, and the people all reverence him; he speaks, and the people all believe him; he acts, and the people all are pleased with him' (*Doct. of the Mean*, xxxi. 3).

The authority of the classics is due not to any special inspiration, but to their connexion with sages or sagely men who possessed this ideal development of human nature. Degrees of authority are recognized; Mencius, *e.g.*, in some of his pronouncements is held to have fallen short of the perfect balance of Confucius. In so far as education was founded on and almost confined to the classics, their influence has been enormous. Less legitimately their connexion with the sages has given them a pre-eminent share in that reverence, passing into superstition, with which all written and printed paper is regarded by the Chinese. Among the commentators on the classics, Chu Hsi (A.D. 1130–1200) has long been considered to be the standard of orthodoxy. The number of books embraced in the Confucian canon has varied. The Imperial edition of the T'ang dynasty included thirteen books. The present canon, taken in the strictest sense, includes the Five Classics and the Four Books.

1. The 'Five Classics.'—(1) *I King*, '*The Book of Changes*.'—The germ of this is the Eight Trigrams, further elaborated into sixty-four, alleged to have been copied by Fu Hsi, a legendary ruler of early China, from the back of a mysterious creature which appeared from the waters of the Yellow River. The diagrams are combinations of whole and broken lines, and are supposed to correspond to the powers of nature—heaven, earth, fire, water, etc. Wen Wang added to the diagrams his 'Definitions'; Chou Kung supplemented these with his 'Observations'; and, finally, Confucius added 'Ten Chapters of Commentary,' and the classic was complete. As being the joint work of these four sages, it enjoys a great reputation. It is a compound of obscure and fanciful speculation and of a system of divination. But with regard to its meaning and its origin, whether it is native to China or may be connected with Babylonia or elsewhere, various opinions have been held by scholars.

(2) *Shu King*, '*The Book of Historical Documents*.'—We read of a canon of one hundred

historical documents, ascribed on inadequate evidence to Confucius, with a preface the Confucian authorship of which is even more doubtful. What now exists is this preface and fifty-eight books of documents, the tradition of which is traced back to two scholars, Fu Sheng and An Kuo. The twenty-five books which rest on the sole authority of the latter are gravely suspect. The whole collection of documents, which by no means forms a continuous history, falls into five divisions—the books of T'ang, of Yü, of Hsia, of Shang, and of Chou. The earliest documents refer to a period about 2000 B.C., the latest to 627 or 624 B.C. Whatever be the admixture of legendary matter, the documents are of much historical interest. As a record of early moral and religious ideas their value is also great. The political ideal is a benevolent autocracy, and sovereignty is conferred or withdrawn according to the righteous judgment of God, who raises up the instruments of His providence.

(3) *Shi King*, '*The Book of Odes.*'—This comprises three hundred and five odes, with the titles only of six more, traditionally said to have been selected by Confucius from the numerous pieces extant in his time. This account greatly exaggerates his share in the making of the classic. Confucius attached great educational value to the odes. He claims that their design is summed up in this : 'Have no depraved thoughts'; but, while they are free from indecencies, a number of them spring from irregular passion. The subject-matter of the odes is various—praise of virtuous kings and ministers, and of chaste and submissive wives; longing for absent friends, and the joy of reunion; the griefs of neglected officers and forsaken wives; complaints of injustice, remonstrances with careless or wicked rulers; celebration of State banquets and sacrifices. The odes are not arranged in chronological order, but in four classes: (1) 'Lessons from the States,' 15 books of odes from various feudal States; (2) 'Minor Odes of the Kingdom,' 8 books; (3) 'Greater Odes of the Kingdom,' 3 books; and (4) 'Odes of the Temple and the Altar,' 3 books. The earliest odes date from the Shang dynasty (1765-1122 B.C.), and the latest from the time of King Ting (605-585 B.C.) of the Chou dynasty. Much can be gathered from the odes illustrating early Chinese civilization.

(4) *Li Ki*, '*Collection of Treatises on the Rules of Propriety or Ceremonial Usages.*'—Of the 'Three Rituals,' the *I Li*, the *Chou Li*, and the *Li Ki*, the last only has a place among the Five Classics. It is a collection condensed from a larger group of documents in the 1st cent. B.C., and augmented and finally fixed in the 2nd cent. A.D. The various treatises, which are not arranged in any logical order, cover a great variety of subjects—birth, capping, marriage, death, mourning, sacrifices, education, and intercourse between persons of different grades and ages. There is much wearisome detail, but it is from this classic that we learn the genius of the Chinese race as embodied in religious and social usages.

(5) *Ch'un Ch'iu*, '*Annals.*'—*Ch'un Ch'iu*, lit. 'Spring and Autumn,' a common name for annals, is the only one of the Five Classics ascribed to Confucius himself; but it falls so far short of Mencius's eulogy of the *Ch'un Ch'iu* which he knew that doubt—not supported by other evidence—has been expressed as to whether our *Ch'un Ch'iu* is indeed the Sage's work. It seems to be founded on, and may be merely transcribed from, the annals of Lu, Confucius's native State. It is an absolutely bald record of such things as the beginnings of the seasons, State-covenants, wars, deaths of persons in high estate, and extraordinary events. The notices of eclipses are important as affording chronological data. The record runs from 721 B.C. to the 14th year of Duke Ai, when Confucius's work ends, and is supplemented by his disciples up to the time of his death, 16th year of Duke Ai (478 B.C.). Even Chinese scholars admit that the record is not impartial, and is guilty of concealing the truth. An unfortunate cloud thus rests on the character of its author. The best known commentary on the *Ch'un Ch'iu* is the *Tso Chuan*, which supplements it in a lively style and carries the record to 467 B.C., with one entry of a slightly later date.

2. The 'Four Books.'—(1) *Lun Yü*, '*Analects.*'—These were probably compiled by Confucian scholars of the second generation. Conversations with Confucius and disconnected sayings of his, mostly quite brief, form the staple of the work; but bk. 19 contains sayings of disciples only, and these occur also in other books. The main themes are ethics and government. In spite of the general failure even to seek after righteousness, it is maintained that human nature is made for virtue, which is a life-long task. For the attaining of virtue there is sufficient strength, if only it is exerted. Hence the importance of moral culture, though some may be incapable of it. The ideal man (Chun Tzŭ) is depicted, and such topics as filial piety, friendship, and perfect virtue are discussed. 'Reciprocity'—not to do to others what one would not have done to oneself—is the highest moral rule. There is intentional reticence on extramundane matters. In politics the moral ends of government are emphasized, as is also the influence of a virtuous ruler over his subjects. Bk. 10 contains many particulars as to Confucius's deportment and habits. More important are the scattered estimates of Confucius by himself.

(2) *Ta Hsüeh*, '*The Great Learning*,' is so called with reference either to the importance of its matter or to the maturer age of its students. The text appears to be fragmentary. In one recension it forms a section of the *Li Ki*; but as usually printed it is arranged by Chu Hsi, though without authority, into text by Confucius and comment by Tsêng Tzŭ. The book professes to trace the development of morality from investigation of things, through extension of knowledge, sincerity of the thoughts, and rectification of the heart, up to cultivation of the person (which is the central idea); and then on to regulation of the family and tranquillizing of the empire. The work, though not without some excellent moral ideas, falls far short of its promise.

(3) *Chung Yung*, '*The Doctrine of the Mean*' (probably rather '*Equilibrium and Harmony*'), is ascribed to K'ung Chi, grandson of Confucius, commonly known as Tzŭ Ssŭ. This treatise, like the *Ta Hsüeh*, forms a section of the *Li Ki*. Human nature, as given by heaven, is the source of morality. In its original state it is 'equilibrium'; as developed into right action it is 'harmony.' The beginnings of this development lie at hand in ordinary duties and virtues, particularly in 'reciprocity,' which is here developed positively (=the Golden Rule; cf. *ERE* vi. 311b). Such development of nature is exhibited in the sages. When it is so developed that fact and ideal coalesce, we have 'sincerity.' Some have this sincerity by innate endowment; some attain to it by moral instruction. It is the *summum bonum*, and has a transforming influence on things and men. Confucius is eulogized extravagantly, though perhaps not precisely identified with the ideal man who is the equal of heaven.

(4) *Mencius* (371-288 B.C.).—Seven books of his teaching remain, which are credibly ascribed to Mencius himself in collaboration with his disciples. The main topics are ethics and politics. Human nature is made for righteousness. This original constitution is the child-heart which good

men preserve. Mencius maintains the disinterested nature of the affections, and asserts as according to nature the subordination of the passions to moral control. Nature in ordinary men and in the sages is one and the same, but for its development ceaseless effort is required. The 'passion nature' is not to be suppressed but disciplined. If nature does not evince its goodness, it is only as a hill constantly grazed on appears bare of verdure. Untoward circumstances should be regarded as divine discipline. Repentance so purges a man that he may even worship God. Mencius's views on politics are mostly developed in conversation with contemporary rulers, with whom he uses, on the whole, an admirable frankness. Government should be benevolent and righteous. Such a government inevitably prospers. Its main concerns are agriculture and education. Above all, the people, who are of the first importance in a State, must have a stable livelihood. If a monarch be utterly unworthy, it is not rebellion to depose him; but this must be done in accordance with the decree of heaven revealing itself in the popular mind. Mencius acutely criticizes the heretical views of his time. In IV. ii. 26 he recommends observation of phenomena as the source of knowledge. His style is lively, the illustrations abundant and mostly apt, and the dialectic keen. He has popularized and given a tone of his own to the doctrines of Confucius, to which his work is the most interesting approach.

LITERATURE.—For the English student the most accessible works are J. Legge's ed. of the *Chinese Classics*, Hongkong, 1861-72, and the volumes of his translations in *SBE* iii.^{2} [1899], xvi. [1882], xxvii. [1885], xxviii. [1885]. In W. A. P. Martin, *Hanlin Papers*, 2nd ser., Shanghai, 1894, there is a chapter on 'Chinese Ideas on the Inspiration of their Sacred Books.' For a more general view of Chinese literature one may refer to A. Wylie, *Notes on Chinese Literature*, London, 1867; H. A. Giles, *A History of Chinese Literature*, do. 1901; W. Grube, *Gesch. des chines. Litteratur*^{2}, Leipzig, 1909.

P. J. MACLAGAN.

LITERATURE (Dravidian).—Dravidian literature is the record of the best of the thought of those peoples of S. India who speak languages designated by Kumārila Bhaṭṭa, in the 7th cent. of our era, as Āndhra Drāviḍa. The four principal literary Dravidian languages are now Telugu, Tamil, Kanarese, and Malayālam. According to the Census Report of 1911, Telugu is spoken by 23½ millions of people, Tamil by a little over 19 millions, Kanarese by 10½ millions, and Malayālam by 6⅔ millions. That the Sanskrit-speaking Aryans were acquainted with S. India at an early period is evident from the mention of the Āndhras by the grammarian Pāṇini (probably *c.* 350 B.C.), but Aryan immigration into the South came at so late a period that the southern Dravidian languages retained, with but few exceptions, their own characteristic grammatical structure. Their vocabulary was, however, enlarged by the inclusion of Sanskrit technical terms and words or their corruptions. So widely did this Aryan influence on the literature of the South spread in course of time that J. Vinson says:

> 'Not one Telugu, Kanarese, or Tamil book now in existence is independent of Sanskrit. . . . Writing was not applied to vernacular languages before the 4th century. It was the Aryan Brāhmans or Jains or Buddhists who first having learned the vernaculars used them for literary purposes and then taught the natives to write and compose works. The preliminary or Jain period must have lasted two or three centuries' (*Siddhānta Dipika*, August 1908).

The southern inscriptions of Aśoka show that writing must have been familiar to the people by the 3rd cent. B.C. The present southern scripts are, however, all derived from the Āndhra alphabets of about the 4th cent. of our era. Telugu and Kanarese alphabets date from the 5th cent., while the oldest Tamil cursive writing comes from the 7th century. Previous to any writing or written records the folk-songs of the people, their moral aphorisms as well as their lyric outbursts of love and war, set as they were to music, were handed down by memory from generation to generation. P. Sundaram Pillai states that more than 19,000 lines of the hymns of the early poet Sambandhar, not later in date than the 7th cent., are still extant:

> 'Most of them appear to have been uttered impromptu, and all of them being lyrical are set to music. The original tunes are now mostly forgotten. They were lost in the later airs introduced by Aryan musicians of the north' (*Some Milestones in the History of Tamil Literature*, p. 5).

The intruding Aryan influence so blended with the indigenous Dravidian element that the Aryan lute (*viṇā*) completely ousted the primitive Dravidian musical instrument (*yāl*), no reliable description of which remains on record. Similarly, the old grammars and the grammars of the Pāṇinian and Āndhra school of grammarians have been superseded by the now standard authority for all classic compositions, the *Nan Nūl*, composed by a southern Jain grammarian, Pavanandi, about the beginning of the 13th century. The *Nan Nūl* lays down the rule that 'to reject the old and obsolete usage and to adopt new and modern usage is not an error but a yielding to the necessities of time and circumstance' (G. U. Pope, *Third Tamil Grammar*, Madras, 1859, Rule 462, 'Nan Nūl'). Notwithstanding this salutary rule, Dravidian prose and poetry are considered worthy of commendation by the learned only when they are as different from the spoken vernaculars as Anglo-Saxon is from modern English. The more they hold themselves aloof from the colloquial language of the time and people, and the more they are swathed in archaisms, the more they merit the praise of *paṇḍits.* The earliest, and therefore the purest, Dravidian literature, as freest from Aryan influences, lies enshrined in works dating from about the 2nd cent. of our era. Collections known as the *Ten Classical Poems* are assigned to a very early date; these were succeeded by *Eight Compilations* of various authors. Eighteen shorter stanzas, including the moral aphorisms of the *Kural* of Tiruvalluvar, followed, and the four hundred quatrains of the *Nālaḍiyār*, said to have been composed by a Jain poet of about the 8th century. The latter quatrains show strong Aryan influences, dealing as they do with the ordinary topics of Indian metaphysics—the pain of existence, transmigration of the soul, and release therefrom. Some of the quatrains are mere translations from such Sanskrit epics as the *Mahābhārata*. Pope, who translated and annotated the *Nālaḍiyār* in a scholarly edition, described it as 'The Bible of the Cultivators of the Soil.' Its style, however, is so classical that no cultivator of the soil could understand the meaning of the verses unless explained to him in the language that he is accustomed to speak. The moral epigrams of the *Kural* and *Nālaḍiyār*, in couplets and quatrains, have been acclaimed as the highest achievements of Dravidian literature. Pope (*Kural*, p. xiv) truly says of the *Kural* (and the same applies to the *Nālaḍiyār*) that a line 'is often little else than a string of crude forms artfully fitted together.' Style such as this, framed on Sanskrit corrupt compounds, can hardly claim the title of literature, however epigrammatic or moral the underlying and hidden thought may be. The *Nālaḍiyār* is, nevertheless, well suited to fill its present rôle as a literary puzzle for Tamil students at the Madras University, or for Honours candidates at other Universities.

To the same period, from the 2nd cent. to the 10th cent., are ascribed the chief versified Tamil romances—the *Maṇi Mekhalai*, the *Śilapp'adhikāram*, and the most perfectly constructed and the most untranslatable, on account of its open erotic sentiment, of all Tamil romances, the

Jivakachintamaṇi. These poems, amid a surrounding of love and romance, give a vivid view of early Jain and Buddhist life in S. India and reliable accounts of the doctrines of the Jain and Buddhist faiths. They still await translation into English to make them available for historical purposes. No translation could possibly convey the peculiar charm of the stately and leisured style of the original, its melodious and harmonic sequences of sound, and the subtlety of its quaint and involved conceits of metaphor. J. Vinson (*Manuel de la langue tamoule*, p. xlv) has given a valuable and balanced judgment respecting the comparative value of the best of Dravidian literature.

'Malgré tout, cependant, la littérature tamoule est secondaire. A part peut-être les recueils de sentences morales, il n'est pas un poème de quelque importance dont une traduction complète puisse être lue sans fatigue par des Européens. Ses descriptions y sont diffuses, monotones, pleines de mauvais goût et d'exaggérations choquantes, conformes d'ailleurs à un type uniforme donné. Ses poèmes d'amour ne sont pas plus variés, et les poèmes de guerre se ressemblent tous; ce sont proprement des jeux d'esprit, des amplifications de rhétorique sur une formule générale et sur un canevas minutieusement réglé. L'invention et l'imagination ne peuvent s'y exercer que sur les détails, sur les expressions, sur la mesure, sur la forme extérieure en un mot.'

This Aryan influence on the religious literature (see DRAVIDIANS [South India]) and even on the indigenous folk-songs of the people has had the result that without a previous knowledge of Sanskrit much is almost unintelligible. According to C. E. Gover (*Folk-Songs of Southern India*, p. 14), who gathered together folk-songs from the varied peoples of S. India,

'the foreign element progressed till almost the whole written literature of the country became Brahmanic. Indigenous poetry fell into undeserved contempt or, where that was not possible, was edited so unscrupulously that the original was hidden under a load of corruption.'

This Aryan influence so permeated the whole spirit and vitality of indigenous literature that Appakavi, a grammarian of the 17th cent., contemptuously declared that Telugu adaptations from the Sanskrit were merely for the use of women and Śūdras. The distinguished Dravidian scholar, G. V. Rāmamūrti, who quotes the above in his *Memorandum on Modern Telugu* (Madras, 1913, p. 3), further states that, should a Brāhman read the *Rāmāyaṇa* for religious merit, he reads the Sanskrit original and not a Telugu adaptation. The same writer, who is an ardent advocate for a reformed pure Dravidian literature freed from Sanskrit corruptions, states only the truth when he says:

'A Sanskrit original, whether it is the Rāmāyaṇa or Mahābhārata, is much simpler in style and language than a translation of it' (*op. cit.* p. 6).

Nevertheless, the simple peasant values these Telugu, Tamil, Kanarese, or Malayālam imitations of, or adaptations from, the Sanskrit poems, epics, and *purāṇas*. Read as they are by professional reciters under the village tree during the long star-lit evenings, they hold the simple folk in spellbound wonder and awe as they listen to a running translation and commentary in the current vernacular. They teach the village folk the simple story of life, of the rewards and joys of those who had faith in the gods and thereby gained salvation through the grace of the deity, of the triumph of good over evil, and, above all, the loved stories of wifely devotion and patient suffering under unmerited calamities.

LITERATURE.—R. Caldwell, *A Comparative Grammar of the Dravidian Languages*[2], London, 1875; C. E. Gover, *The Folk-Songs of Southern India*, do. 1872; V. Kanakasabhai, *The Tamils Eighteen Hundred Years ago*, Madras, 1904; G. U. Pope, trr. of *Kural*, London, 1886, *Nālaḍiyār*, Oxford, 1893, *Tiru Vāchakam*, do. 1900; M. Śēshagiri Sāstri, *Essay in Tamil Literature*, Madras, 1897; P. Sundaram Pillai, *Some Milestones in the History of Tamil Literature*, do. 1895; S. C. Chitty, *The Tamil Plutarch*, Jaffna, 1859.

R. W. FRAZER.

LITERATURE (Egyptian).

—The great bulk of extant Egyptian sacred literature may be grouped in three divisions: (1) the Pyramid Texts; (2) the *Book of the Dead*, with its related group of books, the *Book of Am Duat* (or of knowing that which is in the under world), the *Book of Breathings*, the *Book of Gates*, etc.; and (3) miscellaneous writings, embracing a number of hymns to various gods, Ra, Osiris, Hāpi, Amen, such writings as the *Lamentations*, and the *Festival Songs of Isis and Nephthys* and the *Litanies of Seker*, and a number of legends concerning the gods and their relations to mankind.

1. The Pyramid Texts.—These constitute by far the most important body of Egyptian sacred writings known to us, not only because they exhibit the religious beliefs of the nation at a very early period in its history, but also because the remains of primitive traditions embedded in them enable some of the Egyptian beliefs to be traced back even to pre-historic times, and because the development manifest in the later versions of them shows how gradual but important changes were happening in Egyptian religious belief within a definite period.

The great pyramids of the IVth dyn. kings have no interior inscriptions, and it was supposed that this was true of all other pyramids also, until in 1880 Mariette's workmen at Saqqarah managed to effect an entrance to the pyramid of Pepy I. of the VIth dyn., and later on to that of Merenra of the same line, and found that both contained lengthy hieroglyphic inscriptions, hewn in the stone and coloured green. Eventually inscriptions were found in five pyramids, of which the oldest is that of Unas of the Vth dyn., and the others are those of Teta, Pepy I., Merenra, and Pepy II., all of the VIth dynasty. The inscriptions thus cover a period of about 150 years, from 2625 to 2475 B.C., or, on Petrie's Sinai dating, from about 4210 B.C. onwards. Immediately after their discovery the texts were edited by Maspero, and the attention devoted to them has been steadily increasing. The best edition at present available is that of Sethe (*Die altägyptischen Pyramidentexte*, Leipzig, 1908–10).

These texts are, then, the oldest body of religious literature extant in the world, and a great deal of the material embodied in them carries us back to very much earlier times than their own sufficiently early date, referring to primitive customs and conditions of life which had long been extinct by the time of the Vth and VIth dynasties. The later versions show traces of editing, which has been undertaken in order to meet the new developments of religious thought arising in a period of 150 years. Broadly speaking, the object of these writings is to secure blessedness in the after life to the king on the walls of whose tomb they are inscribed; for there is as yet no trace of any idea that the immortality postulated for the Pharaoh may be also the property of the common people. The whole contents of the texts are directed towards the one purpose of securing entrance to the abodes of bliss for the dead king, and unification with the gods when his entrance is secured. These contents fall under the following divisions: (1) funerary ritual and ritual of mortuary offerings, (2) magical charms, (3) ancient ritual of worship, (4) ancient hymns, (5) fragments of ancient myths, and (6) prayers on behalf of the dead king.

The material is arranged in sections, each of which is headed by the words 'Utter (or recite) the words.' Of these sections the pyramid of Unas contains 228, and the other pyramids make up the number to 714. The amount of material is thus considerable, as may be judged from the fact that in Sethe's edition it fills two quarto volumes with over 1000 pages of text. It is arranged in the most haphazard manner possible, the scribes responsible for the different versions having made (as usual in Egyptian religious writings) not the slightest attempt to group together the various types of matter enumerated above. The hymns scattered through the collection already exhibit a familiar poetical arrangement, in the form of couplets showing parallelism in the ordering of words and thoughts; and the texts are not devoid of a certain wild and rude power of imagination which entitles them to rank as literature. Thus, when the dead king rises to the vault of the heavens,

> 'Clouds darken the sky,
> The Stars rain down,
> The Bows [a constellation] stagger,
> The bones of the hell-hounds tremble,
> The gatekeepers are silent
> When they see king Unas
> Dawning as a soul.'

And there is some power of fancy in the passage which pictures the king, after he has passed the lily-lake and drawn near to the gates of heaven, being challenged by voice after voice, out of the world of the dead, 'Whence comest thou, son of my father?' until, at last, when answer has been duly made to all the challengers, they fall silent, and the dead Pharaoh enters unopposed upon his heavenly kingdom.

The life of blessedness which the Pyramid Texts contemplate has already ceased to be that which we may take to be the earliest form of the Egyptian conception of the life after death—that of sojourn at and about the tomb. The deceased king's realm is in the sky, and, moreover, in the east of the sky —this in absolute contradiction to later belief, which always placed the abode of the blessed dead in the west. In the sky the king may develop either of two destinies: he may become a star, or he may be associated with Ra, the sun-god, finally becoming identified with him. These two destinies no doubt represent two different strata of earlier belief, which have been slumped together according to the regular Egyptian custom of associating incompatibles without attempting to reconcile them.

The earliest form of belief represented in the texts is solar; the deceased is constantly identified with Ra, and the Osirian belief is referred to in terms which show that it was held to be incompatible with, or even hostile to, the solar form. Certain prayers are designed to protect the pyramid and its temple against the intrusion of Osiris; and other passages show that 'to the devotee of the Solar faith, Osiris once represented the realm and the dominion of death, to which the follower of Re was not delivered up' (Breasted, *Development of Religion and Thought in Ancient Egypt*, p. 140). Gradually, however, and, as the texts show, even within the Pyramid Age, the Osirian faith began to assert its power and to appropriate part of the place which the solar religion had formerly occupied. In doing so the Osirian conception of the life after death, originally one of an under world, becomes more or less solarized, and the two faiths interpenetrate to some extent; but, on the whole, the Pyramid Texts present us with the picture of the gradual assertion of superiority on the part of the Osirian faith over the earlier solar creed. It would appear that in this transformation we witness the triumph of popular over State religion, as it is evident that, to start with, the solar faith was the State theology, while the cult of Osiris was always a popular form of religion.

On the whole, there is no more interesting body of religious literature in the world than this, the most ancient of all, and its interest is due, not to its own intrinsic value alone, but also to the fact that it takes us nearer than any other religious writing to the primitive ideas of mankind as to the modes of life in the world after death. Passages such as those which describe how the dead king in the other world lassoes and disembowels the gods, cooking them in his kettle, and eating them,

> 'Their great ones for his morning meal,
> Their middle-sized ones for his evening meal,
> Their little ones for his night meal,'

so that 'their magic is in his belly,' have their own value as literature for the wild power and vigour of imagination which they reveal; but they are still more valuable as survivals of a period when the Egyptian, whom we have never seen save in the decent, ordered civilization of the dynastic period, was actually an unregenerate savage, with beliefs on the same intellectual level as those of other uncivilized races.

2. The Book of the Dead.—Next in importance to the Pyramid Texts comes the collection of sacred writings which has for long been regarded as representative of Egyptian religious literature, and is most widely known by the totally erroneous title of *The Book of the Dead*. The only justification for the use of this title is that the texts more or less regularly used in the collection were, like the Pyramid Texts, entirely designed for the advantage of deceased persons in the other world. The Egyptians themselves called the collection 'The Chapters of Pert em Ḥru,' or 'The Coming Forth by Day' (or 'Ascending by Day'), a title whose significance is somewhat obscure, though the contents of the chapters suggest that it may have something to do with the powers which the knowledge of them conferred upon the deceased to go in and out from his tomb, and to live an unfettered life in the other world. Concerning the early history of the *Book of the Dead* we have no certain information. In fact, there is practically no literature extant from the period between the VIth and the XIth dyn. to show the development of religious thought. In the middle kingdom, however, under the XIth and XIIth dynasties, there begins to appear a series of texts which are regarded by some as an early recension of the *Book of the Dead*. These texts are written no longer on the walls of tombs, but on the inner surface of the cedar coffins in which the well-to-do people of the period are buried. They are generally written in black ink, and are ornamented with coloured borders representing the usual funerary offerings to the deceased. About one-half of the material thus preserved is taken from the Pyramid Texts, the other half consisting of material which is met with later in the genuine *Book of the Dead*; so that, really, the inscriptions of this period occupy a middle position between the old texts, whose object was the service of the king alone, and the later book, which was a popular compilation intended for the use of all and sundry. It might be useful, therefore, to distinguish these Middle Kingdom texts by some such title as that of 'Coffin Texts,' which Breasted employs to denote them. The writing of these texts is marked by the same carelessness and inaccuracy which characterize the later versions of the *Book of the Dead*. The scribe's sole object was to cover the prescribed surfaces as rapidly as possible; it was never expected that his work would be seen again, and consequently he took the least possible trouble with it. In one instance the same chapter is repeated five times over in a single coffin. Apparently the thought that by his carelessness he might be prejudicing the safety of his patron in the other world did not worry the Egyptian scribe.

The Coffin Texts are intermediate in character, as in time, between the Pyramid Texts and the *Book of the Dead*. The old solar ideas of the Pyramid Texts are still present; but the Osirianizing process, already begun, has been carried a stage further, and now we have indications of the intrusion of the essentially Osirian idea of an under world into the old solar idea of a celestial heaven. Breasted epigrammatically sums up the dip of the balance in the Coffin Texts towards the Osirian side by the remark that in the Pyramid Texts Osiris was lifted skyward, while in the Coffin Texts Ra is dragged earthward (p. 277). The idea of a Western Elysium, in contradistinction to the solar idea of an Eastern one, begins to appear, and the character of the Elysium begins to approximate to that of the Sekhet Aaru, 'Field of Bulrushes,' as found in the *Book of the Dead.* Thus one of the chapters of the Coffin Texts is concerned with 'Building a House for a Man in the Nether World, digging a Pool, and planting Fruit trees.' Already the Coffin Texts exhibit instances of the desire, which reaches full development later, of furnishing the deceased with words of power to enable him to assume various transformations. Various texts enable him to transform himself into 'the blazing eye of Horus,' into an '*ekhet*-bird,' or into 'the servant at the table of Hathor'; and along with this development comes another which reaches an extraordinary pitch in the *Book of the Dead*—that of charms to protect the deceased against the dangers of the under world. Thus there are charms for 'preventing the head of a man from being taken from him,' for repulsing serpents and crocodiles, for preventing a man from being obliged to walk head downwards, and so forth. This kind of rubbish, towards which the Egyptian mind had an extraordinary inclination, increases steadily in amount until the really valuable morality of the *Book of the Dead* is almost choked under its senseless bulk.

The *Book of the Dead*, properly so called, makes its appearance with the New Empire in the 16th and following centuries B.C., under the XVIIIth and XIXth dynasties. The change from inscriptions on tomb-walls to inscriptions on the inner surfaces of coffins is now followed by a further change: the texts which form the new compilation for the use of the dead are now written on rolls of papyrus, and placed in the coffin. The various versions extant from the XVIIIth to the XXIInd dyn. have mainly been derived from tombs near Thebes, and therefore the *Book of the Dead* of this period is known as the Theban Recension. It cannot be too clearly understood that there never was a standard text, or anything even remotely approaching to such a thing. Probably no two papyri agree as to the number of chapters, or the contents of them, and the divergencies are extraordinarily great. The size and content of the so-called *Book of the Dead* which was buried with any particular man depended entirely upon the power or the will of his friends to purchase a satisfactory copy for him or the reverse. The poor man has a meagre roll a few feet in length, containing a pitiful selection of a few of the more important chapters; the rich man may have a sumptuous version from 60 to 100 ft. in length and containing anything up to 120 or 130 chapters. In the XVIIIth dyn. the scribes began to ornament the text with designs in black outline, known as vignettes. Little by little the practice developed, and in the XIXth dyn. the illustrated papyrus had become the rule. The illustrations are often beautiful pieces of illumination, and sometimes attention has been given to them at the expense of the text.

In the most notable papyri of the XXIst dyn. the development of the artistic work continues at the expense of the text, which has become very corrupt, and also begins to contain passages which are not found in the older versions. This tendency is accentuated in the XXIInd dyn. papyri, which contain sections that, strictly speaking, have no connexion with the *Book of the Dead.* And from this time onwards there is a falling off in the versions, until a time is reached when no copies of the book seem to have been written. This period coincides with the decline of the power of the priests of Amen-Rā.

In the XXVIth dyn., however, the book takes a new lease of life. It now appears to have been reduced to some sort of order, to have been, in fact, edited and systematized. The result of this editing is the Saïte Recension. It contains four chapters which have no counterparts in the earlier versions.

In the Ptolemaic period we have a version which is best represented by the Turin Papyrus, from which Lepsius prepared his well-known edition. It is the longest extant collection of texts, containing nominally 165 chapters—some of them, however, are really vignettes, and others duplicates, the number of actual chapters being 153.

Meanwhile a number of short religious works had been compiled, containing what at this period was deemed to be most essential in the old versions of the book, and these are more commonly found in the end of the Ptolemaic period than the full version. These are known as the *Shai-en-Sensen* ('Book of Breathings'); they contain no hymns, no addresses to the gods—nothing, in fact, which does not directly refer to the life of the deceased in the world beyond. They may be regarded as an epitome of all that the Egyptian hoped to obtain in the spirit world.

In the Roman period there are still found small rolls of papyrus inscribed with statements referring to the happiness of the deceased in the next world; and even in the early centuries of the Christian era the knowledge and use of the book were not quite extinct, for selections from it are found on coffins as late as the 2nd century.

If we take into consideration the fragmentary versions in use as late as the 2nd cent. A.D., the actually extant documents of Egyptian religion, the Pyramid and Coffin Texts, and the *Book of the Dead*, cover a period of practically 3000 years on the most limited system of dating; and, allowing for the fact that even in the earliest texts theological ideas are to a great extent developed and stereotyped, we shall probably not exceed reasonable limits in saying that these documents represent the theological development of at least 5000 years. Petrie's system of dating would, of course, considerably extend this period.

The object of the *Book of the Dead* was simply and solely to secure for deceased persons eternal life and all the advantages which the Egyptian considered desirable in the world beyond the grave (cf. art. DEATH AND DISPOSAL OF THE DEAD [Egyptian]). There are chapters the knowledge of which was intended to preserve the body from decay or the ravages of certain animals—*e.g.*, ch. xxvi., 'Of driving away Apshait' (the beetle or cockroach), and ch. xlv., 'Of not suffering corruption in the under world'; chapters providing charms against the serpent Apepi, the serpent Rerek, and the crocodile that comes to take away the charm from the deceased; chapters 'Of not letting a man be burnt or scalded in the under world,' and 'Of not eating filth or drinking filthy water in the under world,' and so forth.

Generally speaking, it may be said of these chapters, and of many others of similar import, that they are somewhat melancholy reading. Allowance has, of course, to be made for the fact that they are full of allusions to a mythology the knowledge of which has almost absolutely perished, and that these allusions may have been full of signification to the Egyptian, though they are meaningless to us. It seems, however, that very early the sense of a number of the references had already been lost, as there are several chapters which contain glosses on the various allusions, and these glosses do not always agree. Very often the chapters do not rise above the level of mere vulgar incantation. Sometimes they consist simply of an endless series of names supposed to have magical power; sometimes they are merely ludicrous—*e.g.*, ch. xxxiii., 'Of repulsing serpents in the under world':

'Hail, thou serpent Rerek, advance not hither! Behold Seb and Shu. Stand still now, and thou shalt eat the rat which is an abominable thing unto Rā, and thou shalt crunch the bones of a filthy cat.'

The most important chapter of the book is cxxv., which embodies the Egyptian conception of the judgment of the dead. It consists of three parts: the introduction, the famous 'Negative Confession,' and a concluding text, and is fully discussed in artt. CONFESSION (Egyptian), and ETHICS AND MORALITY (Egyptian).

The fundamental religious idea of the Egyptian mind was that of immortality, and it is to the Pyramid Texts and the *Book of the Dead* that we owe our knowledge of the extraordinary development which this idea had reached in Egypt at the earliest historical period, of the wonderful persistency with which it was maintained and worked out into almost endless detail, and, most of all, of the strange resemblances which the Egyptian conception of resurrection and immortal life presents to the Christian conception. The *Book of the Dead* is not to be taken as in any sense a complete statement of Egyptian belief—a thing which as yet is conspicuously lacking. The name sometimes given to it, 'The Egyptian Bible,' is a total misnomer. But in the working out of its central theme it affords unquestionable evidence of the fact that the conception of immortality and resurrection held by the ancient Egyptian was such as no other religious system of antiquity ever approached.

Little is told us of whether any intercourse was expected in the other world with the souls of those who had been known on earth, but chs. lii., cx., and clxxxix. at least indicate that the deceased looked forward to recognizing and being protected by the spirits of his father and mother.

The other sacred books related to the *Book of the Dead* may be briefly dismissed.

The *Book of the Overthrowing of Apepi* contains fifteen chapters treating of the various methods of destroying this enemy of souls in the under world. Its material is largely borrowed from the *Book of the Dead* (Papyrus of Nesi-Amsu, British Museum).

The *Book of Knowing that which is in the Duat* contains a description of the twelve parts of the under world through which the bark of the sun journeyed during the hours of night. It tells the names of these divisions, of the gates and gods belonging to each, and states the advantages to be derived from a knowledge of these names.

The *Book of Breathings* is largely a compilation from the *Book of the Dead*, and in the later periods was buried with the dead, being placed under the left arm, near the heart.

3. Miscellaneous writings.—Under this heading are to be included numerous hymns of Rā, Osiris, Hāpi, Ptah, and other gods (cf. art. HYMNS [Egyptian]); the *Festival Songs of Isis and Nephthys*; the *Litanies of Seker*; the *Lamentations of Isis and Nephthys*, and other similar works.

The *Festival Songs* and *Lamentations* are poems dealing with the Osirian myth, and supposed to be recited by the two goddesses with a view to effecting the resurrection of the dead Osiris. The ancient *Legends of the Gods* and their relations to mankind are found in inscriptions in several tombs (notably in the tomb of Seti I.) and in various papyri, and have been frequently translated.

In addition there are certain books which do not strictly come under the heading of 'sacred,' but have yet a semi-religious character. Among them may be mentioned the *Precepts of Ptah-hetep*, *of Gemnikai*, *of Ani*, and *of Khensu-hetep*, writings essentially of the same character as the book of Proverbs, while the *Lay of the Harper* (or *Song of King Antef*) may be compared with Ecclesiastes, and a remarkable comment on the social and moral condition of the land in the Middle Kingdom is found in the *Admonitions of Ipuwer*.

LITERATURE.—i. *PYRAMID TEXTS.*—Versions: G. Maspero, *Les Inscriptions des pyramides de Saqqarah*, Paris, 1894; K. Sethe, *Die altägyptischen Pyramidentexte*, Leipzig, 1908–10. Examples of the texts are given by E. A. W. Budge, *Egyptian Religion*, London, 1908, and *Literature of the Egyptians*, do. 1914. The best summary of their contents and appreciation of their importance is found in J. H. Breasted, *Development of Religion and Thought in Ancient Egypt*, do. 1912.

ii. *THE BOOK OF THE DEAD.*—Versions: Coffin Texts, P. Lacau, 'Textes religieux,' *RTr* xxvi. [1904]–xxvii. [1905], xxviii. [1906]–xxxiii. [1911]; R. Lepsius, *Aelteste Texte des Todtenbuchs*, Berlin, 1867; S. Birch, *Egyptian Texts of the Earliest Period from the Coffin of Amamu*, London, 1886; Budge, *Facsimiles of Egyptian Hieratic Papyri in the British Museum*, do. 1911.

BOOK OF THE DEAD PROPER.—Versions: E. Naville, *Das ägyp. Todtenbuch*, Berlin, 1886; Lepsius, *Turin Papyrus*, Leipzig, 1842; Birch, tr. of the Turin Papyrus in C. C. J. Bunsen, *Egypt's Place in Universal History*, Eng. tr., v., London, 1867; Budge, *The Book of the Dead*, do. 1898 (contains also a translation of the *Book of Breathings*); Maspero, hieroglyphic transcript with Fr. tr. of abridged version of the *Book of the Dead*, in *Les Momies royales de Déir-el-Bahari*, Paris, 1886.

iii. *MISCELLANEOUS WRITINGS.*—For hymns, etc., cf. Literature in art. HYMNS (Egyptian). A good popular rendering of the *Legends of the Gods* is found in M. A. Murray, *Ancient Egyptian Legends*, London, 1913. The *Admonitions of Ipuwer* have been rendered by A. H. Gardiner, *The Admonitions of an Egyptian Sage*, Leipzig, 1909.

iv. *GENERAL REFERENCES.*—A. Erman, *Handbook of Egyp. Religion*, Eng. tr., London, 1907; A. Wiedemann, *Rel. of the Anc. Egyptians*, Eng. tr., do. 1897; P. Le Page Renouf, *Origin and Growth of Rel. of Anc. Egypt*[4] (*HL*), do. 1897; G. Steindorff, *Rel. of the Anc. Egyptians*, Eng. tr., do. 1905; Naville, *The Old Egyptian Faith*, Eng. tr., do. 1909; G. A. Reisner, *The Egyptian Conception of Immortality*, do. 1912; A. H. Sayce, *The Rel. of Anc. Egypt*[2], Edinburgh, 1913.

J. BAIKIE.

LITERATURE (Indian Vernacular).—The literature of the modern vernaculars of India may be divided into two main classes—that written under Musalmān, and that written under Hindu, influence. The former dates from the Mughul conquest, and was composed mainly in the Urdū form of Hindōstānī. Up to the introduction of printing at the beginning of the 19th cent. it was nearly all in verse and was confessedly written on Persian models and in Persian metres. The earliest works date from the 16th cent. A.D., but the standard of composition was set by Walī of Aurangābād in the Deccan, who flourished at the end of the 17th cent., and who is known as 'the Father of *Reḵta*,' *Reḵta* being the technical name for the form of Hindōstānī used by these poets. From the Deccan the taste for this literature spread to Delhi, where Walī found numerous successors, and thence to Lucknow. The most celebrated of the Delhi poets were Rafī'u's-Saudā, best known for his satires, and Mīr Taqī, famed for the purity of the language in which his *Ghazals* and *Mathnavīs* were expressed. Both these flourished in the 18th century. Among the Lucknow poets the most celebrated was Mīr Ḥasan (18th cent.). Hindōstānī prose hardly existed as literature till the foundation of the College of Fort William in Calcutta at the commencement of the 19th century. It began with the preparation of text-books for students at the College, and since then has had a prosperous existence. It has been specially successful in the department of fiction. The novels of such authors as Ratan Nāth Sarshār and 'Abdu'l Ḥalīm Sharar are worthy of a wider circle of readers than that to which they are condemned by the language in which they are written.

Although the above literature grew up under Musalmān auspices, its language has been successfully adopted by many educated Hindus, some of whom are looked upon at the present day as masters of an exceptionally pure style.

The beginnings of Hindu literature in the modern vernaculars were religious. In the North, up to about the 16th cent. A.D., the language of religion was Sanskrit, but, in the South, vernaculars were employed at a much earlier period. There is a great collection of Śaivite texts in Tamil, said to go back to the 2nd or 3rd century. The more important of them are described in the art. DRAVIDIANS (South India). To these can be added a long list of Vaiṣṇavite works in the same language dating from before the time of Rāmānuja (12th cent.). The most noteworthy of these are referred to by A. Govindāchārya in two papers in the *JRAS* (1910, p. 565 ff., and 1911, p. 935 ff.). The Dravidian doctors employed both Sanskrit and Tamil for their writings. As a rule, it may be said that the Vaḍagalais, or Northern Tamils, wrote in Sanskrit, while the Teṅgalais, or Southerners, wrote in Tamil (cf. Govindāchārya, in *JRAS*, 1912, p. 714).

In Northern India vernacular religious literature is of enormous extent and, considered merely as literature, of great merit. It owes its origin to the spread of the Vaiṣṇavite Bhakti-Mārga under Rāmānanda and his followers (see art. BHAKTI-MĀRGA, vol. ii. p. 539 ff., esp. 546). All the great writers of this early period belonged to humble ranks of life, and were not Sanskrit scholars. Each therefore wrote in his own vernacular.

'The greatest of all the moderns, Tulsī Dās, although a Brāhman by caste, was abandoned by his parents at birth, and was picked up and educated by a wandering ascetic. Kabīr was a weaver, and Dādū a humble cotton-carder. Nāmdēv, the founder of Marāṭhā poetry, was a tailor, and his most famous successor, Tukārām, a struggling Śūdra shopkeeper. Tiruvalluvar, the brightest star in the South Indian firmament, was a Pariah, the lowest of the low; and Vēmana, the most admired of Telugu writers, was an untaught peasant.'[1]

In Northern India this *bhakti*-literature falls into two groups—that devoted to Rāmachandra, and that devoted to Kṛṣṇa (Krishna). In both cases it includes not only devotional works, but all branches of literature ancillary thereto.

In the art. BHAKTI-MĀRGA (vol. ii. p. 543) it has been pointed out that the foundation of the religion is the belief in the fatherhood of God. This is more especially true as regards that literature in which Rāmachandra is regarded as the most perfect presentation of the Deity, and on this idea is based some of the most lofty poetry that India, ancient or modern, has produced. In the Ganges valley, Kabīr (15th cent.) preached the doctrine in wise and pithy sayings that are still household words in Hindōstān. An offshoot from his teaching was the Sikh religion, whose sacred book, the *Ādi Granth*, is a collection of hymns by various authors formed by degrees in the course of the 16th century (see artt. GRANTH, SIKHS). Both Kabīr and Nānak (the founder of Sikhism) were more or less sectarian in their teaching. A greater man than either, but the founder of no sect, was the famous poet Tulsī Dās (16th–17th cent.), the author of the religious epic entitled the *Rāma-charita-mānasa*, or 'Lake of the Gestes of Rāma,' and of at least eleven other important works. His influence down to the present day over the people of Hindōstān cannot be overrated. Tulsī Dās was a native of Awadh (Oudh), and this country was the scene of Rāmachandra's early life and of his latest years. The poet, therefore, wrote in the Awadhī dialect of Eastern Hindī, and this form of speech has ever since, in the Ganges valley, been the only one employed for celebrating the deeds of Rāmachandra, and, indeed, for epic poetry of every description.

[1] G. A. Grierson, in *IGI* ii. 415.

In Hindōstān proper, numerous followers and imitators of Tulsī Dās have narrated the story of Rāmachandra, and the same subject has also, though to a less extent, attracted writers in other parts of India. In Bengali there is the 16th cent. *Rāmāyaṇa* of Kīrttibās Ojhā, which is still recited at village festivals. In Marāṭhī, the learned Mōrōpant wrote several poems dealing with Rāma, but the favourite deity of this language is Kṛṣṇa. In the south of India we have a Tamil *Rāmāyaṇa* written by Kamban in the 11th cent., a Malayālam *Rāma-charita* of the 13th or 14th cent., and a Kanarese *Rāmāyaṇa* by Kumāra Vālmīki, said to be one of the oldest works in that language.

The literature based on the presentation of Kṛṣṇa as the Deity differs from the Rāma-literature in one important particular. The love of God is represented, not as that of a father to his child, but as that of a man for a maid. The soul's devotion to the Deity is pictured by the self-abandonment to Kṛṣṇa of his queen Rādhā, and all the hot blood of Oriental passion is encouraged to pour forth one mighty torrent of prayer and praise to the divine Lover. The whole idea is based on sexual relations; and, though the mystics who first wrote of it did so in all purity of conscience, in later years it developed into erotic poetry of a character too gross for description.

It is natural that most of the literature of this school should take a lyric form. According to tradition, Kṛṣṇa's earlier exploits centred round the town of Mathurā, and it was from this locality that his worship in the Ganges valley spread to other parts of Northern India. Hence, just as the Rāma-literature is couched in Awadhī, so the Kṛṣṇa-literature of Hindōstān is mainly recorded in the Braj Bhākhā dialect spoken round Mathurā. Its most famous writer was Sūr Dās (16th cent.), the blind bard of Āgrā. His *Sūra-sāgara*, or 'The Ocean (of songs) of Sūr Dās,' and the epic of Tulsī Dās are considered to have exhausted between them all the possibilities of Indian poetry—no later poet could write anything original. In spite of this dictum, one later writer in Braj Bhākhā, Bihārī Lāl of Jaipur (17th cent.), composed the *Sat Saī*, or 'Seven Centuries' of verses, a collection of seven hundred masterpieces in dainty miniature painting of scenes or incidents in the life of Kṛṣṇa. Numerous other writers connected with this phase of religion followed Sūr Dās in the Ganges valley. In Bihār, to the east, he was preceded by Vidyāpati Ṭhākur (15th cent.), who, however, wrote in his own language, an old form of Bihārī. He was the first of the old master-singers of Eastern India, and was followed and imitated by Chaitanya and other religious lyric poets in Bengali. Assam, further east, and, in the west, Rājpūtānā, Kashmīr, Gujarāt, and the Marāṭhā country have all been prolific in this style of composition, the most famous writers being Mīrā Bāī, the queen poetess of Mēwāṛ (15th cent.), and Tukārām (17th cent.) the Marāṭhā. In the south of India we have the great Tamil hymnology, the *Nālāyira-prabandham*, some of the contents of which are said to date from the 12th cent., and, in Telugu, the *Bhāgavata* of Bammera Pōtarāja, which ranks as a classic. There are also several works in Kanarese.

Reference has already been made to the Śaivite literature of S. India. There is a considerable literature devoted to Śiva in the north. The best known is that of Bengal, where the worship of Durgā, the *śakti*, or energic power of Śiva, is very popular. There were numerous writers who dealt with the worship of this goddess. The most admired is probably Mukundarāma Chakravartī (17th cent.), author of the *Śrīmanta Saudāgar*, or 'Adventures of the Merchant Śrīmanta,' and the *Chaṇḍī*, a poem in praise of the goddess Durgā. Extracts from the latter have been translated into English verse by E. B. Cowell (*JASBe* lxxi. [1902], extra no.). There is also a considerable Śaivite literature in Kashmīr. This directly deals with Śiva, rather than with his *śakti*, and is more in agreement with the Śaivite writings of the South described in the art. DRAVIDIANS (S. India).

A few lines must be devoted to the non-religious vernacular literature of India. Of great importance are the bardic chronicles of Rājpūtānā, Gujarāt, and the Marāṭhā country. The name of the earliest and most famous of these, the *Prithīrāj Rāsau* of Chand Bardāī (12th cent.), is familiar to students of J. Tod's *Rajasthan* (London, 1829–32, frequently reprinted), in which the poem is freely quoted. A semi-historical work, the *Padumāwati* of Malik Muḥammad, is an epic poem in Awadhī of considerable merit.

The technical study of poetics gave rise to a large literature, to a certain extent ancillary to the literature of religion. Its most famous writer in Northern India was Keśav Dās of Bundelkhaṇḍ (16th cent.), who wrote in Braj Bhākhā.

The introduction of printing into India has given an immense impetus to the writing of books. It is impossible to deal with the results of this great increase in the mass of reading matter, good and bad; it must suffice to say that, so far as Hindu literature is concerned, it has tended more and more to follow English models. The only writer in the vernacular who has gained a high reputation in both Europe and Asia on the grounds of originality and imagination is the modern Bengali poet Rabīndra Nāth Tagore.

LITERATURE.—The only work attempting to deal with the vernacular literature of India as a whole is R. W. Frazer, *A Literary History of India*, London, 1898; G. A. Grierson, in *IGI*, vol. ii. (Oxford, 1908), ch. xi., may also be consulted. Brief and incomplete accounts of the literatures of most of the literary languages of S. India have appeared in such periodicals as *IA* and in prefaces to grammars and dictionaries. For Marāṭhī literature the English student can find the most accessible account in the preface to J. T. Molesworth, *Marāṭhī Dictionary*², Bombay, 1857. For Bengali see Dinesh Chandra Sen, *History of Bengali Language and Literature*, Calcutta, 1911, the philological parts of which should be used with caution, and a valuable collection of selections from Bengali literature entitled *Vaṅga Sāhitya Parichaya*, Calcutta, 1914. For N. India generally cf. G. A. Grierson, *The Modern Vernacular Literature of Hindūstān*, Calcutta, 1889; the dates in this are frequently taken from native sources, and are not always to be relied upon. See also C. J. Lyall, art. 'Hindōstānī Literature,' *EBr*¹¹ xiii. 483 ff.; and Gaṇeśa Vihārī Miśra, Śyāma Vihārī Miśra, and Śukadeva Vihārī Miśra, *Miśrabandhu-vinōda* (Hindī), in course of publication, pt. i., Khaṇḍwā and Allāhābād, 1913.

G. A. GRIERSON.

LITERATURE (Jewish).—The term 'Jewish literature' is used to cover those writings of the Jewish people which were composed after the completion of the Biblical (OT) canon, and which are devoted to the discussion or exposition of Judaism—its teachings, its history, and its documentary sources—and designed primarily for Jewish readers. This definition excludes all such works of Jewish authorship as, though written in Hebrew and meant for Jewish readers, deal with matters of general learning or literature.

I. *THE TRANSITION FROM ORAL TRADITION TO WRITTEN RECORDS.*—Between the completion of the Hebrew canon and the rise of Jewish literature there is an interval of several hundred years, and the reason why the literary activity of the Jews was so long in abeyance is that they regarded it as unlawful to commit their teachings to writing. The Scripture, as the Book *par excellence*, could suffer no other book to approach it; all supplementary doctrine must be imparted orally (תורה שבעל פה); 'to set down the oral teaching in writing is forbidden.' Thus even the Biblical Apocrypha were regarded as ספרים חיצונים, 'extraneous books.' The idea that the production of new works was unlawful must have been prevalent by the time of the elder Sirach, and hence his collection of proverbs could not be received into the canon; an author who wished to reach the public by a book had to publish it under some ancient and venerable name, such as Daniel. That the Alexandrian Jews were at that time displaying a remarkable literary fertility did not affect the Jewish authorities in Palestine at all, for the works of the former were written in Greek, and could, therefore, make no claim to canonicity. Thus all the creations of the Jewish mind in this epoch remained unwritten; translations of the Bible, prayers, academic and popular instruction, the development of law and custom, of ethics and religion—all these were carried on by oral instruction only. Apart from letters and fugitive notes relating chiefly to ancient pedigrees,[1] there is only a single document that has come down from ancient times in a written form, viz. the roll of festivals (מְגִלַּת תַּעֲנִית), a list of joyous memorial days of the Jewish nation (Jth 8⁶, *χαρμοσυναὶ οἴκου Ἰσραήλ*)—that remarkable Aramaic calendar which stands as a monument of Jewish national pride, though it is extant only in a revised form with relatively late scholia (*JE* viii. 427 f.).

It would appear that as regards the Haggādā the interdict upon written communication was somewhat relaxed soon after the fall of the Jewish State, while as regards the Hălākhā it was still rigidly observed (Bab. *Giṭṭîn*, 60*b*). The first complete literary product of post-Biblical Judaism is the Mishnā, which was redacted *c.* A.D. 200 by R. Judah Nāśî. Whether the Mishnā was at once committed to writing is a question which is still—as it has been for a thousand years—a subject of controversy among scholars; and, while there are ostensible indications of its having been in written form from the first, yet our reliable sources rather support the hypothesis that at the time of its redaction and even for centuries afterwards it was still transmitted in a purely oral form (*JE* viii. 614). By the time we reach the redaction of the Babylonian Talmud, however (*c.* A.D. 500), the ancient prohibition must at length have been set aside, the change being necessitated, indeed, by the exigencies of the period—the repeated interference of the State in forbidding the continuance of the seminaries in their traditional ways—and also by the enormous growth of the material, which had now become too great a load for the human memory. In view of these facts, the last of the Amôrâîm and the Sabôrâîm found it necessary to break with the past by committing the Talmud to writing, and they thereby cleared the ground for the growth of a Jewish literature. Once the ban against writing had thus been lifted from the Hălākhā—that important domain where the interdict had been observed most rigorously—Jewish scholars formed the resolution, hesitatingly at first, but with time ever the more confidently, to write down and make more generally known the facts of their people's life and doctrine.

II. *LITERARY PERIODS.*—Jewish literature, in the fifteen centuries of its development, has passed through a variety of phases. To the period from *c.* A.D. 500 to 1000 we must assign its initial stages, in which the various branches of literature had to be evolved and wrought into form. While formerly knowledge of every kind was contained and indiscriminately massed together in the Talmud, special departments were now gradually disengaged from the mass, and were dealt with in monographs and more or less systematically. To the Gāôn Sa'adya b. Joseph (A.D. 892–942; see art. SA'ADYA) belongs

[1] Cf. Joel Müller, *Briefe und Responsen aus der vorgaonäischen jüdischen Literatur*, Berlin, 1886.

the distinction of having been the first to treat of the most widely varied branches of Jewish theology in special works, and thus to have laboured as a pioneer, so that he has been rightly named 'the chief of the speakers in every place.' From A.D. 1000 to 1200 Jewish literature passed through its mediæval period of fertility in two ramifications, viz. a Hispano-Arabic, which displays a powerful tendency to scientific thoroughness and systematization, and a Franco-German, which in more characteristic fashion further elaborated the traditional materials of knowledge. The period from 1200 to 1500 was one of decline, and from 1500 to 1750 one of profound decadence, during which the literary activity of the Jews was mainly confined to Poland and the East; but, from the advent of Moses Mendelssohn ([*q.v.*] 1729–86), Jewish literature, now in contact with the spirit of European culture, experienced a fresh revival which, mainly under the influence of Leopold Zunz (1794–1886), developed into a scientific treatment of Judaism, *i.e.* a methodical and critical discussion of the thought expressed in the Jewish teachings and evolved from the Jewish mind, and has since found expression in numerous works, not only in Hebrew, but in all the languages of Europe. We cannot here trace Jewish literature throughout its various epochs and in all its phases; it must suffice to examine the chief departments in which it was specially active, to indicate the tendencies that asserted themselves in it, and to search for the reasons that led to the success of this or that particular work. A characteristic feature of Jewish literature, as contrasted with the literatures of other peoples, is that it is not so much the work of individual authors as the collective product of the spirit of entire epochs. In many cases, too, it is ill preserved—a result of the fact that it was not studied by the learned only, but spread among all classes; and, further, that it did not merely serve an intellectual interest, but also provided for a religious need, and was in consequence often disseminated and transmitted by untrained hands, in a form very different from what was originally intended.

III. *THE SEVERAL DEPARTMENTS OF JEWISH LITERATURE.*— Jewish literature in its entire range **may** be conveniently brought under the following categories, with which we shall deal in order: (1) Scripture study and investigation of the Hebrew language; (2) works relating to the Talmud; (3) historical literature; (4) systematic theology; and (5) liturgical and secular poetry.

1. Scripture study and investigation of the Hebrew language.—Jewish literature is first of all, as it was originally, exegesis of Scripture—Biblical study in the broadest sense of the term. Targum and Midrash constitute its earliest forms, and perhaps the two were originally one, for the Targum was of the nature of paraphrase, and thus involved a kind of exegesis. Traces of the old, non-literal rendering of the Scriptures are found in the so-called Palestinian Targums—the Targum of Jonathan and the Fragmentary Targum. For the Pentateuch, however, the rendering to which Aquila first gave the name of the Targum of Onqelos, and which assumed its definitive form in the Babylonian schools of the 3rd cent. A.D., became the standard of authority; it was recited in the synagogue, and was generally regarded by the Jews as *the* Targum. For the Prophets, again, the acknowledged standard was the so-called Targum of Jonathan—not much later in date than that of Onqelos; while here, too, the other Palestinian Targums fell into the background. For the Hagiographa there was in the period of the Talmud no recognized Targum at all, and the renderings which we now possess were separately executed in the course of centuries, some of them,

indeed, not having been completed till after A.D. 1000 (cf. *JE* xii. 57 ff.). 'Midrash' (*q.v.*) denotes exposition of Scripture, and was at first attached to the particular passages explained; but in the Bible itself we find the word used in the sense of a reproduction of older narratives (2 Ch 24²⁷; cf. 13²²). The Midrash was of a twofold character; from the text of Scripture it evolved laws—the Hălăkhā—or else deduced moral and religious teachings, adding stories and parables—the Haggādā. The Hălăkhic Midrash was compiled chiefly in the schools of R. Ishmael ben Elisha (early 2nd cent. A.D.) and R. 'Aqîbă (see art. AḲIBA BEN JOSEPH), and the latter school continued to be regarded as authoritative; the work of both schools, however, being in the mass subsequently lost, has come down to us in mere fragments; and it is only recently that we have been able, with the help of the *Midrash haġ-Gādhôl*, a compilation of the 13th cent., written in Yemen, to piece the remains together, and obtain an approximate idea of the form of the ancient Midrashîm. The Haggādic Midrash is of vast extent; much of it is included in the Talmud, but it is found also in special collections. Leaving out of account the immense number of smaller Midrashîm (*JE* viii. 572 ff.), we may distinguish the following great compilations: the Midrash Rabbă or Midrash Rabbôth to the Pentateuch and the Five Meġillôth, to Esther, Ruth, Song of Solomon, Lamentations, and Ecclesiastes, the Tanḥūmā to the Pentateuch, and the Midrash- to the Psalms, Proverbs, and Samuel; but, while all these continuously follow the order of their respective texts, the Peṣiqtā collections deal only with selected portions of the Tôrăh or of the Prophets, for use at festivals or on special Sabbaths. Mention should also be made of the two great Midrashic compilations known respectively as the *Yalqūṭ Shim'ônî*, which probably took shape in Germany during the 12th cent. A.D., and embraces the entire Bible, and the *Midrash haġ-Gādhôl* of Yemen already referred to, which is confined to the Pentateuch (*ib.* 557 ff.). The Haggādic Midrash has been brought within the reach of contemporary scholarship by the monumental works of Wilhelm Bacher, *Die Agada der babylonischen Amoräer*, Strassburg, 1878, *Die Agada der Tannaiten*, do. 1890, 1902, and *Die Agada der palästin. Amoräer*, do. 1892–99.

The Midrash frequently gives simple explanations of the words and meaning of the Scripture text, but this is by no means its primary interest; in the main it is concerned with religious and devotional ends. Jewish scholarship did not evolve a rational exegesis of its own—exegesis in the scientific sense—till the time of Sa'adya, who was a pioneer and wrote independent commentaries upon, as also a translation of, the whole Bible. In his excursuses he, too, writes with a religious purpose; but, on the whole, his chief concern is the rationalistic, grammatical, and lexical exposition of Scripture. The movement which he initiated owes its further development in the main to European scholars. In Europe there arose two great exegetical schools, one in Spain, the other in Northern France. The Spanish school was largely influenced by Arabic learning, and its most prominent representative was Abraham ibn Ezra (1093–1168), whose works superseded those of all his predecessors (cf. *JE* vi. 520 ff., and art. IBN EZRA, § 1). His commentaries had an extraordinary popularity; they have come down to us in various MS copies, and were appended to the first printed editions of the Bible. The Northern French school, again, while it certainly lacked the scientific bent, the philological foundation, and the general culture of the Spanish, yet by its devoted study of the Biblical text and its sympathy with the spirit of the written word did a large amount of highly meritorious and exemplary work for the discovery of the verbal sense. It failed to gain recognition in its ripest representatives, who—particularly Samuel b. Meir (*c.* 1085–*c.* 1174)—have, in fact, been re-discovered by modern scholarship; but the favourite and most widely circulated commentary of the Middle Ages was the work of Solomon b. Isaac of Troyes, called Rashi (1040–1105), who combined the old method of the Midrash with the effort to ascertain the plain meaning; and consequently, though he certainly gives the dry details of exegesis, we also find in his work passages of an attractive and edifying character. His commentary eclipsed all others in general esteem; from the outset to the present day it has been widely read, and has formed a subject of study by itself; while in the course of centuries it has drawn to itself over a hundred special commentaries, and ranks in the popular mind as 'the commentary' κατ ἐξοχήν (cf. *JE* x. 324 ff.). A blending of the characteristic tendencies of the Spanish and Northern French schools appears among the scholars of Provence, from whose group sprang David Kimḥi (1160–1235; cf. *JE* vii. 494 f.), whose exegetical works on the Prophets and the Hagiographa were specially prized. The re-discovery of the predecessors and successors of the exegetes named, as also the historical evaluation of the entire literature of the period, has been the work of modern scholarship. In Kimḥi's commentaries we find a new type of exegesis—the philosophical, which soon passed into the mystical. Of the works that favour this type, those especially which were able to bring their more stubborn materials into a popular and generally accessible form attained a great vogue. These include the long-popular commentaries of Don Isaac Abarbanel (1437–1508; cf. *JE* i. 126), and also those of the so-called Bîûrists (*JE* iii. 232), dating from the age immediately after Moses Mendelssohn. On the whole field of exegetical literature cf. *JE* iii. 162–176.

Closely associated with the exegesis of Scripture were the works dealing with Hebrew philology. Linguistic study among the Jews was but rarely regarded as an end in itself, but, as the science of the language in which the Scripture was written, was pursued mainly as an adjunct to Biblical investigation. The literary treatment of Hebrew grammar and lexicography was systematically prosecuted by the Hispano-Arabic school, the masterly works of which, however, were composed in Arabic, and accordingly, even when translated into Hebrew, attracted but little notice; the philological writings of Judah b. David Hayyuj (b. *c.* 950; *JE* vi. 277 f.) and Abū al-Walīd Marwān ibn Jānāh (early 11th cent.; *ib.* vi. 534 ff.), important as they are, were re-discovered only recently. The works of Abraham ibn Ezra enjoyed an enormous vogue, as did also, and even in a still greater degree, the grammar and dictionary of David Kimḥi, which have in many quarters retained their pre-eminence until recent times. From the 15th cent., however, a marked decline in linguistic studies began; in proportion as mysticism prevailed, interest in the exact investigation of Hebrew fell away; the works of Elijah Levita (1468–1549; cf. *JE* viii. 46) attracted much less notice in Jewish than in Christian circles. Philology remained in a state of neglect until it was restored to its rightful position by the Mendelssohnian group; the manuals of J. L. Ben-Ze'eb (1764–1811; *JE* ii. 681 ff.) were widely studied until they were superseded by more modern and more competent works. The revival of Hebrew philology was due in a very special degree to the pioneer work of S. D. Luzzatto (1800–65; cf. *JE* viii. 224 ff.). Luzzatto was at the same time the first Jewish scholar for centuries who combined the study of the language with the exegesis of Scripture, and may also be regarded as the most eminent independent representative of Biblical literature among the Jews of last century. With the name of Luzzatto that of Abraham Geiger (1810–74) deserves to be specially associated. Speaking generally, we may say that the Biblical science of the Jews during last century was profoundly influenced by the contemporary critical works of Christian scholars in the same field.

2. Works relating to the Talmud.—The Talmud came to be the most important, the most comprehensive, and the most highly esteemed branch of Jewish literature; it is in a sense bound up with Biblical study, as its germs are found in the Midrash, and as it purports to be nothing more than an exposition of and a complement to the Scriptures. It consists of two parts, the Mishnā and its elucidation, the latter being the Talmud in the narrower sense; the term Gᵉmārā, which is usually applied to the second part, is of relatively late origin, and was introduced into the text by the clerical censorship. Our use of the expression 'the Talmud' involves a presumption due to the facts of historical development; for, although there is but one Mishnā, there are two commentaries upon it—one of Palestinian, the other of Babylonian, origin. In the process of historical development, however, the seminaries of Palestine were early dissolved, while those of Babylonia maintained their position, and succeeded in establishing the regulative supremacy of their views and decisions. The result was that, although in the earlier period the Palestinian scholars were held in great honour, and their decisions sought in all important questions, eventually the scholars of Babylonia came to be the sole recognized authorities. In the age of the Gᵉônîm (*c.* 600–1040) the Babylonian Talmud had secured so high a place in general esteem that its Palestinian counterpart was virtually forgotten; and when, about the year 1000, the latter was once more brought to mind, consolation for its long neglect was sought in the pretext that the decisions of the Palestinian scholars had been known to the Babylonians, and had been duly taken into consideration by them. In consequence, the Palestinian Talmud remained in comparative obscurity; it was not studied to anything like the same extent as the Babylonian, nor did it find a single commentator during the entire mediæval period; moreover, its text suffered such gross deterioration that we can now scarcely hope to see it restored even to a semblance of its original form. It should be noted, however, that a few Hălākhic collections from Palestine, the so-called Minor Tractates, were appended to the Babylonian Talmud, and were studied in conjunction with it, thus becoming a factor in the further development of religious practice and religious law. The two Talmuds are not related to the Mishnā in the same way; in the Palestinian Talmud we have the commentary to forty Mishnaic Tractates, belonging to the first four Orders; in the Babylonian we have thirty-six only, principally from the second, third, fourth, and fifth Orders, while of the first and sixth Orders only one tractate in each is dealt with.

As the Talmud, until the dawn of the modern epoch, occupied the central place in Jewish learning, and formed the supreme standard of religious thought and practice among the Jews, it became the nucleus of an enormous literature, which, in connexion with its more outstanding representatives, may be summarized in the following divisions.

(*a*) *Explanatory works.*—For so intricate a work as the Talmud, explanation was indispensable; its own expositions were frequently very brief, and the links of connexion could be supplied only by those who had been initiated into the peculiar mode of its dialectic; moreover, the language of the Jews, like their general conditions of life, underwent in process of time radical changes, and was no longer the same as was presupposed in the Talmud. The need of explanation was felt at an early date, and soon, indeed, explanatory notes seem to have been attached to the text and transmitted with it; thus we find writers of the 10th cent. quoting *verbatim* from comments dating from the 6th.[1] On the other hand, what we may call an expository literature was not evolved till a much later day, for it was the Gᵉônîm of the 10th cent. who first felt constrained to supply written comments—first of all in the form of explanations of words; and these, again, were the germs of the comprehensive dictionaries, of which the most celebrated was the *'Ārûkh* of Nathan b. Jeḥiel of Rome († 1106; cf. *JE* ix. 180 ff.). The first commentaries in the ordinary sense, however, were produced in N. Africa *c.* A.D. 1000; besides explaining words, they gave short notes elucidating the context. The most important of these N. African commentaries is that of R. Ḥananel b. Ḥushiel of Kairwan (990–1050; cf. *JE* vi. 205). In Spain little progress was made in the composition of commentaries, although it was in that country that the most influential Mishnā commentary of the Middle Ages was composed, viz. that of Moses Maimonides ([*q.v.*] 1135–1204; cf. *JE* ix. 73 ff.), written originally in Arabic, but afterwards translated into Hebrew, and from the time that it was first printed (1492) to the present day regularly embodied in editions of the Mishnā or the Talmud. The most notable contributions to the exposition of the Talmud were produced in Germany and France. Talmudic learning, carrying with it the earliest commentaries, spread by way of Italy to Germany. R. Gershom b. Judah, 'the Light of the Exile' († 1040; cf. *JE* v. 638 f.), who taught in Mainz, gave the impulse to a new method of Talmudic exposition. His school not only dealt in the most thorough manner with details, but attached great importance to bringing out the connexion of thought; and from that school emanated the most notable of all commentaries on the Talmud, that of Rashi mentioned above. Its greatness lies in the fact that its author, with the self-restraint of genius, surrenders his mind wholly to the text, suppressing his own opinions, and bent only upon discovering and exhibiting the thought of the original writer. Rashi never introduces superfluous matter; nor, again, does he ever gloss over a difficulty; he either gives a solution of it or modestly confesses that he has none to suggest. The work came to be used as an indispensable auxiliary to the study of the Talmud; it superseded all previous commentaries, and threw all the later into the shade. While much of the expository literature of that age was buried in oblivion until the modern period, Rashi's work was frequently conjoined with the MSS of the Talmud, and it has been bound up with the printed editions from the first; even at the present day, indeed, it is regarded as an essential adjunct to the study of the Talmud, and no less as a work on the whole unrivalled in its method. The French schools sought to supplement Rashi; they occasionally felt the need of a more dialectical mode of exposition, and thought that the text of the Talmud should be furnished with decisions of the questions proposed and with references to practical life; and, finding none of these things in Rashi's work, they wrote supplementary notes, *tôsāfôth*, which, however, did not run continuously with the text, but here and there supplied comments of the desiderated type upon particular passages. Of these Tôsāfists numerous schools arose in Germany and France during the 12th and 13th centuries; the works which they produced were much studied in the Middle Ages, and afterwards, from the time when the Talmud was first printed in its entirety (Venice, 1520), a number of them, selected for purposes of study, were issued in conjunction with it (cf. *JE* xii. 202 ff.). A peculiar development of the expository literature appears in the so-called 'novels' (*ḥiddûshîm*), which, taking their pattern from the works of Naḥmanides (1194–*c.* 1270) and Solomon b. Adreth (1235–1310), continued to be produced for hundreds of years from the 13th cent.; they were really commentaries in the form of treatises on entire sections of the Talmud. Talmudic commentaries finally degenerated into mere empty dialectic, and this was specially the case in Germany and Poland from the 15th century.

As regards the Palestinian Talmud, the Middle Ages scarcely produced a single commentator, and the modern period not even one, who deals with it from beginning to end. The best known and most widely circulated commentaries to it are the *Qŏrbān hā-'Ēdhā* of David Fränkel, the teacher of Moses Mendelssohn, and the *Pnē Môshe* of Moses Margolioth (*c.* 1700). For the literature of the commentaries see *JE* xii. 28 ff.

(*b*) *Compendia.*—While the Talmud was regarded as the standard to which all religious institutions must conform and by which all questions of law must be solved, it was, nevertheless, but ill adapted to facilitate consultation for the decisions that were often required in practical life. Apart from the fact that it was a work of vast compass, such as scarcely a single individual could completely master, it confined itself almost wholly to the discussion of the questions which it raised, and hardly ever gave a decision as to which of the opinions which it presented should be regarded as authoritative. Further, its matter is not always systematically arranged; it frequently passes abruptly from one theme to another, so that its discussions of a single question have often to be sought for and examined in widely separate places. In order to remedy these defects, Yehudai, Gāôn in Sura, had (*c.* A.D. 750) drawn up a compendium of *hălākhôth*, which was subsequently revised, enlarged, and, as the *Hălākhôth Gᵉdhôlôth*, given a place in the religious literature by Simon Qayyara (*c.* 850), from whose time it has been taken into account as a basis for all decisions (cf. *JE* vii. 461 ff.). The *Hălākhôth Gᵉdhôlôth* often follows the Talmud's own order, and, while abridging its discussions, it reproduces them with verbal accuracy, and in such a way as to make the final question quite clear. The same method was adopted by Isaac b. Jacob Alfasi (1013–1103), whose work was diligently studied, and was likewise used as a basis for decisions. This type of synoptical abridgment of the Talmud became the work of a special school, mainly in Spain, where it was cultivated by many scholars—and with outstanding success by Asher b. Jeḥiel († 1327), a native of Germany, who took Alfasi's text as his groundwork, and added to it numerous notes from the Tôsāfists; his compendium is generally given in the printed editions of the Talmud.

Another mode of epitomizing the matter of the Talmud was to arrange it under the 'Six hundred and thirteen commandments and prohibitions,' an arrangement which is first found as an introduction to the *Hălākhôth Gᵉdhôlôth*, and was subsequently often reproduced in comprehensive forms. The most important work of this class is the *Sēfer ham-Miṣwôth* of Moses Maimonides, which, originally written in Arabic, was several times translated into Hebrew, and found many opponents and many imitators (cf. *JE* iv. 181 ff.).

The most important and practically most serviceable type of compendium, however, was the 'Code' in the narrower sense of the word. Here, too, Maimonides stands supreme; his *Mishnē Tôrāh*, written in Hebrew *c.* A.D. 1180, is the most systematic book in all Jewish literature; with masterly skill he arranges the entire material of the Talmud according to subjects, groups it in paragraphs, and succeeds in presenting it in such a way that the reader can at once find his bearings. Each section of the work opens with a clear statement of its subject, and then proceeds from the less to the more significant, from details to essentials, all being set forth so lucidly that the solution of any particular problem can be found without delay. The book met with the approbation which it so well merited—though it likewise encountered opposition, not only because of the bold and unprejudiced views advanced by the author in the theological sections, but also—what chiefly concerns us here—because of its very structure. Codification was a process that was never greatly favoured among the Jews, who were disposed to fear that it might supersede the study of the sources; and with regard to the work in question, consisting as it did of abstractly formulated paragraphs, and giving no references to sources or to the learned champions of particular views, they thought it well to guard specially against that danger. Nevertheless, the admirable structure of the *Mishnē Tôrāh*, and the veneration in which its author was held, made it a standard work; and the writings designed to elucidate or criticize it constitute a literary aggregate of vast proportions.

Maimonides, in importing the entire material of the Talmud into his Code, took no account of the question whether it still applied to the conditions of his age; thus, *e.g.*, he dealt also with the laws regarding the Temple, the sacrifices, etc. About the year 1340, however, Jacob b. Asher drew up a new code, entitled *Arbā'ā Ṭûrîm*, in which he passed by such subjects as were no longer of practical significance, and took cognizance of views and decisions that had meanwhile come to the front; moreover, unlike Maimonides, he dealt with the various themes in treatises, not in separate paragraphs, and, in particular, he gave expression to the views of scholars who had lived in the centuries immediately preceding. The *Arbā'ā Ṭûrîm* came to be a work of the utmost significance in the following period. Joseph Qaro (1488–1575; cf. *JE* iii. 585 ff., and art. QARO, JOSEPH) wrote a voluminous commentary to it, the *Bēth Yôsēf*, from which he afterwards compiled an abstract entitled *Shûlḥān 'Ārûkh*. The *Shûlḥān 'Ārûkh* follows the arrangement of the *Arbā'ā Ṭûrîm*, and, like that work, is divided into four parts. It deals only with the laws that had been in force from the fall of the Temple, but it departs from its model and reverts to the method of Maimonides in giving rules only, short paragraphs, and in making no reference to its sources or to the advocates of particular views. In systematizing power and candour of thought, however, Joseph Qaro is signally inferior to Maimonides; he was strongly influenced by the mystical tendency in the theology of the period of decadence. The *Shûlḥān 'Ārûkh* was at first slighted, being regarded as a mere 'book for the ignorant,' and its eventual fame was due to its critics, who gave expression to their opposing views in commentaries and supplements to it. To begin with, Moses Isserles (1520–73; cf. *JE* vi. 678 ff.) published a series of supplements to the *Bēth Yôsēf* under the title of *Darkhē Môshe*, and afterwards re-issued them as glosses to the *Shûlḥān 'Ārûkh*; here, on the basis of the Talmudic tradition then dominant in Germany, he frequently modified the decisions of Qaro. It was in this supplemented form that the *Shûlḥān 'Ārûkh* was thereafter regularly given to the public, but it did not win full recognition till about 1650, by which date each of its four parts had already formed the text of celebrated commentaries; these, however, were not of the nature of expositions, but were rather supplements, and often, indeed, in direct opposition to their text. Thus at length it gained an acknowledged position, yet never without encountering resistance; and even in those circles of Jewish life where in principle it served as a norm there were countless departures from it in matters of detail. On the literature of the compendia cf., further, *JE* vii. 635 ff.

(*c*) *Responses.*—A combination of the two forms of Talmudic literature dealt with in the foregoing is found in the *Shᵉ'ēlôth ū-Tᵉshûbhôth* ('Questions and Answers'), which contain explanations, decisions of particular cases, etc. The literary interchange of views regarding Talmudic problems began very early,

[1] Cf. N. Brüll, *Jahrbücher für jüd. Gesch. und Litt.*, ii. (Frankfort, 1876) 43.

and an active correspondence by letter had been carried on between the teachers of the Talmud in Palestine and those in Babylonia. In proportion as the Jews became more and more dispersed, correspondence became more and more necessary; and from the time of the G^{e}ônîm there was a large increase in the number of responses; from that period itself, indeed, no fewer than fifteen more or less voluminous collections of responses have been preserved. Nor, when the centre of Jewish life was transferred to Europe in the Middle Ages, did the interchange of opinions diminish either in extent or in vigour. Thousands of opinions and legal pronouncements by certain eminent Rabbis of mediæval times have been preserved, and were in the mass consulted as an important source of information. The number of works embodying such responses is so enormous that we must be content to mention only the most extensive and the most generally consulted: from the Middle Ages we have those of Meir b. Baruch of Rothenburg (1220–93), Naḥmanides (1194–*c.* 1270), and Solomon b. Adreth (1235–1310), and that of Isaac b. Sheshet (1320–1408), all belonging to Spain; from the dawn of the modern period, those of Israel Isserlein († 1460) and Joseph Kolon (*c.* 1450), as also that of David ibn Abu Simra († *c.* 1570); and from more recent times those of Ezekiel Laudau († 1793) and Moses Sofer († 1839). On the literature of the responses cf. also *JE* xi. 240 ff.

(*d*) *Systematic works.*—Mention must be made, lastly, of that branch of the literature which deals with the problems of the Talmud in a methodical and systematic way—a mode of treatment but little regarded in the earlier period, and, indeed, never strenuously applied till modern times. The earliest work aiming at systematic treatment is the *Sēder Tannāîm w^{e}-Ămôrāîm*, dating from the 9th cent.; the next works of the kind to appear were the *M^{e}bhô hat-Talmūdh* of 'Samuel ibn Nagdila' (extant only in one part, which, however, is printed in all editions of the Talmud) and the *Maftēaḥ* of Nissim b. Jacob, both of the 11th century Of great importance in a methodological respect, again, are the introductions which Maimonides issued as prolegomena to his commentary on the Mishnā and several of its divisions. Later works worthy of mention are the *Sēfer hak-Krîthûth* of Samson of Chinon (*c.* 1300) and the *Hălîkhôth 'Ôlām* of Joshua ha-Levi of Tlemsen (*c.* 1450); the latter has drawn around it numerous commentaries, and has often been reprinted. A new epoch in these aspects of Talmudic study was ushered in by S. J. L. Rapoport (1790–1867; cf. *JE* x. 322 f.), who, in various Hebrew periodicals, as also in his dictionary, the *'Ĕrekh Millîn*, dealt with the problems of the Talmud in a scientific way, at once systematic and critical. The course marked out by Rapoport has been followed by Z. Frankel (1801–75; *ib.* v. 482 ff.) in his *Darkhē ham-Mishnā* and his *M^{e}bhô hā-Y^{e}rūshalmî*, Abraham Geiger (1810–74; *ib.* v. 584 ff.) in numerous treatises in his magazines, and I. H. Weiss (1815–1905; *ib.* xii. 495 ff.) in the historical work named below.

3. **Historical literature.**—The post-Biblical historiography of the Jews took its rise as an element in the systematic treatment of the Talmud. The majority of the earlier works in this field were written chiefly with the object of re-constructing the chain of tradition and of determining as accurately as possible the genealogies of eminent families and the chronicle of learned men. The germs of Jewish historical literature are found in the Talmud itself, and these furnished the pattern for the earliest developments. The chronology of the course of history from the Creation to the destruction of the Second Temple is given in the *Sēder 'Ôlām*, the nucleus of which was the work of Jose b. Ḥalafta (*c.* A.D. 160). An annalistic work, though dealing only with the family of the exilarchs, is found in the *Sēder 'Ôlām Zūṭā*, a genealogical register, which cannot have been drawn up before the 7th cent. A.D., and which assumes a disparaging attitude towards the exilarchs of the day. The biographical annals of scholarship, again, are represented by the *Sēder Tannāîm w^{e}-Ămôrāîm* (*c.* 880), and the *Epistle of Sherira* (987), the latter being our principal source for the period between A.D. 500 and 1000. To the same class belongs also the *Sēfer haq-Qabbālā*, composed in 1161 by Abraham b. David of Toledo, who is chiefly concerned to exhibit the continuity of learned tradition down to his own times; for, though he gives somewhat more detailed information regarding the Jews in Spain of the two preceding centuries, yet even there his manifest purpose is to trace the development of learning and recognized authority. The work of Abraham Zakuto, who was for a time a professor of astronomy and chronology in Salamanca, but after the expulsion of the Jews from Spain settled in the East, was upon similar lines; his *Sēfer Yūḥăsîn* (1504) contains a detailed study of most of the Talmudic authorities, and also a chronology brought down to his own day. For centuries this work was known only in a form containing a series of supplements, and was first made accessible in its original shape in 1857. Jeḥiel Heilprin, of Minsk, wrote his *Sēder had-Dôrôth* (*c.* 1700) solely for the purpose of supplementing the data of Zakuto and bringing the Rabbinical genealogies down to his own times.

A further incentive to the writing of history was provided by the peculiar fortunes of the Jewish people, and in particular by the sufferings and persecutions which they had to endure almost without intermission during the Middle Ages. These oppressions are chronicled in a vast number of fragmentary records, both in prose and in poetry, but there are very few connected and continuous accounts. We shall enumerate here only the more extensive compilations of this type still extant. A narrative of the persecutions which harassed the Jews, chiefly in the Rhine country, in connexion with the Crusades is given by A. Neubauer and M. Stern in their *Hebräische Berichte über die Judenverfolgungen während der Kreuzzüge*, Berlin, 1892. In those days of incessant persecution it was the practice to read (*commemorare*) in the synagogues the roll of those who had perished as martyrs; so-called memorial books were drawn up in the various communities, and were constantly added to. The most comprehensive of these books was published by S. Salfeld under the title *Das Martyrologium des Nürnberger Memorbuches*, Berlin, 1898. The earliest connected account of the persecutions was composed by the noted astronomer Judah ibn Verga († *c.* 1485), whose *Shēbheṭ Y^{e}hūdhāh* was supplemented by a younger relative named Solomon and another writer named Joseph, and published in its enlarged form. The best-known account of the Jewish martyrdoms in the Middle Ages is from the hand of the physician Joseph hak-Kôhēn, who lived in the 16th cent., and resided in various Italian cities; his *'Ēmeq hab-Bākhā* describes with accuracy and graphic power the persecutions and banishments suffered by the Jews from the destruction of the Second Temple. A strange combination of martyrology and the history of learning is found in Gedaliah ibn Yaḥya's *Shalsheleth haq-Qabbālā* (*c.* 1550), which, although much of it was shown at an early date to be untrue and even incredible, enjoyed an extraordinary popularity, and was again and again issued in printed editions.

The Jewish scholars of the Middle Ages had little aptitude for intelligently grasping or portraying their people's history. The *Book of Josippon*, a reproduction of the Latin Hegesippus (cf. *ERE* vii. 578[b]) in fluent Hebrew, composed in Italy in the 10th cent., stood long alone; by reason of its vivid and interesting style it has always been held in great esteem, and has been not only frequently edited in Hebrew, but also translated into many other languages. Even more rarely, if possible, do we find mediæval Jewish writers attempting to write profane history in Hebrew. A work of later date deserving of mention is Joseph hak-Kôhēn's *Chronicle of the Kings of France and Turkey*, written in 1553, while, a few decades afterwards, David Gans († 1613, in Prague) published, in his *Ṣemaḥ Dāwîdh* (Prague, 1592), records, first of Jewish, and then of universal, history from their respective beginnings to his own time; this work appeared also in a Latin translation. In general, however, Jewish writers restricted themselves to the composition of popular narratives of particular episodes.

It was not until comparatively recent times, indeed, that Jewish history was treated in a coherent and orderly manner. In 1820 I. M. Jost began the publication of a history of the Jews in many volumes and in various forms, in which he was primarily concerned to recount the political fortunes of his people, discussing their sociological development in an appendix. Leopold Zunz, while he wrote nothing of the nature of a systematic work on Jewish history, furnished in his *Zur Geschichte und Literatur* (Berlin, 1845) copious materials for all branches of that history, and suggestions as to the method of treating them. The best-known and most widely circulated work of this class, the *Geschichte der Juden* by H. Graetz (2nd ed., Leipzig, 1853–70), aims chiefly at exhibiting the development of the religion and literature of the Jews in relation to their political position and the martyrdoms suffered by them, while A. Geiger's *Das Judentum und seine Geschichte* (Breslau, 1871) deals solely with their religious development. I. H. Weiss, in his Heb. *Dôr Dôr wᵉ-Dŏrshāw* (Vienna, 1871–91), is likewise concerned only with the development of Judaism on its spiritual side. On the historical literature cf. also M. Steinschneider, *Die Gesch.-Literatur der Juden*, i. (Frankfort, 1905), and art. 'Historiography' in *JE* vi. 423 ff.

An important source of information regarding the history of the Jews in the Middle Ages is found in the copious narratives of the numerous Jewish travellers and wayfarers. The most important of such books of travel is the *Massā'ôth* of Benjamin of Tudela, who (*c.* 1165) made a journey from Spain to the East and back, and noted down in a racy style 'all that he had seen or heard.' In the edition of the *Massā'ôth* prepared by A. Asher (London, 1840), Zunz has given a detailed account of the geographical literature of the Jews ii. 230 ff.).

4. Systematic theology.—A great part of the Talmud and the Midrashîm is devoted to the religious and moral teachings of Judaism; the Haggādā in particular is concerned mainly with the problems of theology—with dogmatic and ethical ideas. No more than the Bible itself, however, does the Talmudic literature give a systematic presentation of theological doctrine. It was, in fact, only under the influence of Muslim theology that Jewish writers first essayed to deal systematically with the doctrinal fabric of their religion, and to support it by arguments. Their works were, to begin with, written in Arabic, but were soon all translated into Hebrew—largely through the efforts of the family of Ibn Tibbon, in Lunel—and in this form given to the Jewish world. The earliest speculative theologian among the Jews was Sa'adya Gāôn, who, in his *Ĕmūnôth wᵉ-Dē'ôth*, written in 933, sought to bring the doctrinal teachings of Judaism into relation with contemporary philosophy. Baḥya b. Joseph (first half of 11th cent.; *JE* ii. 446 ff.) won an extraordinary success with his *Ḥôbhôth hal-Lᵉbhābhôth*, which treats chiefly of the moral teachings of Judaism; the book was read far and wide, and was in its day perhaps the most popular work of general philosophical literature among the Jews. Judah Halevi (*JE* vii. 346 ff.; see also art. HALEVI), in his *Kuzari*, renounced philosophy altogether, and based theology exclusively upon the revealed faith and the experience of the Jewish people; the work, by reason of its poetic mode of treatment in the style of the Platonic Dialogues, enjoyed a great vogue. By far the most eminent work in this field, however, is the *Môreh Nᵉbhūkhîm* of Moses Maimonides, which, like his *Mishnē Tôrāh* mentioned above, is distinguished at once for its rigorously systematic structure and for the keenness and independence of its thought. Although the book, with its free handling of Jewish doctrine, aroused hostility on many sides, and was even publicly burned at the instance of Jewish accusers, yet in influence it stands supreme; all later study of Jewish philosophy revolves around the *Môreh*, and the most outstanding Jewish thinkers, such as Spinoza, Moses Mendelssohn (*qq.v.*), and Solomon Maimon, found in it the incentive to the construction of their own systems. The *Môreh* marks the culminating point of Jewish philosophical literature in the Middle Ages. Of writers belonging to the time after Maimonides we mention only Levi ben Gershon ([*q.v.*] *c.* 1350; *JE* viii. 26 ff.), who, with his *Milḥāmôth Ădhônāi*, was the first to make a stand against the authority of Aristotle; Ḥasdai Crescas (*c.* 1400; *ib.* iv. 350 ff.), whose *Ôr Ădhônāi* was drawn upon by Spinoza as an important source; and Joseph Albo (*c.* 1415; *ib.* i. 324 ff.), whose *'Ikkārîm* was an enormously popular book.

The period after Maimonides was, however, on the whole one of profound decadence in philosophical studies, which were, in fact, regarded as positively unlawful. The enlightened philosophy of Maimonides brought forth a counterpoise in the composition of the Qabbālā (see ḲABBĀLĀ), a peculiar medley of speculative ideas and curious fancies which was put forward as an esoteric doctrine of ancient origin, and sought to attach itself to the earliest authorities; its representatives, indeed, did not scruple even to disseminate writings purporting to be the work of the most venerable personages, including Moses and the Patriarchs. The most notable book of such speculative secret doctrine was the *Zôhār*, which was put into circulation *c.* 1300 by Moses de Leon, and passed off as the work of Simeon b. Yoḥai, a writer of the 2nd cent. A.D. It takes the form of a commentary to the Pentateuch, but is interspersed with many systematic dissertations, which bear special names, and are perhaps later insertions. The *Zôhār* was regarded with the utmost reverence; it was designated a divine book, and was ranked higher than the Talmud or even the Bible itself; its real origin was brought to light only in recent times. The name of Isaac Luria († 1572) marks a further stage in the development of the mystical literature. While Luria himself wrote nothing, his pupils promulgated his teachings in a vast number of biographies of their master, of commentaries to the Bible and the book of prayer, and of legal and ethical works. Likewise Ḥasîdism (cf. *ERE* vii. 606ᵇ), the last phase of Jewish mysticism, gave birth to countless works of the kind indicated above; but, as all of them reproduce the ideas of their respective schools in a most unsystematic and incoherent way, it is very difficult to describe them in terms of literary science.

It was not until comparatively recent times that Jewish theology again assumed a rationalistic character. The turning-point was marked by Mendelssohn's *Jerusalem* (Berlin, 1783), and thereafter, under the influence of Kant, Hegel, and Schelling, Jewish thought brought forth various systems, not one of which, however, can be said to have come into general favour. The modern Judaism of Western countries, in fact, has been powerfully influenced by the prevailing philosophy of the age. Of the latest works dealing with Jewish theology we would mention only K. Kohler, *Grundriss einer systematischen Theologie des Judentums*, Leipzig, 1910, and S. Schechter, *Some Aspects of Rabbinic Theology*, London, 1909.

The ideas embedded in the theological literature were given to the wider Jewish public by means of popular writings, including not only the many widely circulated discourses (*Dᵉrāshôth*), but also numerous books of morals, which, it is true, laid more emphasis upon ethics than upon the speculative verification of the faith. The most excellent of the books of morals produced in the Middle Ages is the *Sēfer Ḥăsîdhîm* of Judah b. Samuel of

Regensburg († 1217; *JE* vii. 356 ff.), a work of high ethical value, which, though not free from the superstition of its time, is pervaded by an admirable spirit of piety and an earnest desire to foster the mutual love of men. The books of morals were in many cases translated into the language of the country in which they arose, and they form a large part of the Judæo-German, Judæo-Spanish, and Judæo-Arabic literatures. From the time of their composition they have had an enormous currency, and even at the present day the most widely read and systematic work on Judaism is the *Ethik des Judentums* of M. Lazarus (Frankfort, 1898, 1911).

The theology of the Jews also involved the work of pointing out the lines of demarcation between their own religion and other creeds. The Jews, who from an early period formed but a sparse minority among the adherents of other faiths, had abundant occasion for such procedure. As might be expected, all their writings which deal with theological matters are concerned also with apologetics and polemics, but the systematic treatment of the questions at issue was a relatively late development. The works in this field which were given to the public and still survive are but few in number; from fear of the dominant religion, indeed, they were often suppressed, or at any rate not issued in printed form.[1] Jewish polemical works consist either of explanations of Biblical passages which had been interpreted in a Christological or Muhammadan sense, or of systematic treatises on the cardinal doctrines of Christianity or Islām. Of writings directed against Christianity the *Tôl^edhôth Y^eshū* (on which see *ERE* vii. 552[a]) was not used so much by Jews themselves as by Christian controversialists. Of Jewish polemical works that created a considerable stir, mention may be made of the *Niṣṣāḥôn* of Lipman-Mühlhausen, a resident of Prague (*c.* 1400), who in that work brought forward three hundred and forty-six passages of the OT as telling against Christianity, and the *Ḥizzūq Ĕmūnā*, in which Isaac Troki, the Qaraite, made a systematic attack upon Christian doctrine (*c.* 1580). Both of these works were translated into various languages, and many attempts were made to refute them by Christian theologians. On the polemical literature cf., further, *JE* x. 102 ff.

A considerable amount of varied polemical activity was likewise directed against the Qaraites and other Jewish sects, but for the most part it finds expression incidentally in more general writings, and we are unable to specify any monograph of importance in this smaller field.

5. Liturgical and secular poetry.—The worship of God supplied the most powerful impulse to the post-Biblical development of Hebrew poetry, which, now termed *pīyyūṭ*, was revived with a view to enriching the liturgy. All instruction in and laudation of Jewish history and religion, which in the olden time had been the work of the preacher, fell, from *c.* A.D. 600, to the function of the *paiṭān*. It was under the influence of the Arabs that Jewish religious poetry sprang into life, and it was from them that it borrowed its artistic forms, but it required first of all to mould the Hebrew language to its designs—a process which, after long-sustained efforts, was at length brought to full realization in Spain. The most distinguished *paiṭān* of the Middle Ages was Eleazar b. Jacob haq-Qalîr, who lived probably *c.* A.D. 750 in Palestine; he composed over two hundred well-known poems, which have found a place in the Jewish prayer-books of nearly all countries, though we must note the exception of Spain, which had its own eminent figures in this field, and where mediæval Hebrew poetry attained its highest level between 1040 and 1140. The most outstanding names here are those of Solomon ibn Gabirol, Moses and Abraham ibn Ezra, and Judah Halevi (*qq.v.*). Poems by these writers are found in all prayer-books, but such compositions form only a small part of their poetic work; they also wrote voluminous 'divans,' which, it is true, soon fell into oblivion, and were rediscovered only in recent times; a number of them still await publication. On the *pīyyūṭ* cf. *JE* x. 65 ff.

While liturgical poetry occupied the place of supreme regard, other branches of the poetic art were by no means neglected. Of these the most widely cultivated was the didactic, which was turned to account in every department of knowledge. The *pīyyūṭ* itself sometimes assumed a didactic form; but, in addition, we find disquisitions in verse relating to the calendar, philology, and Biblical study, the Hălākhā, the laws of religion, Talmudic jurisprudence, philosophy and polemics, history, medicine, astronomy, etc., and poems in all these branches of study are extant in large numbers (cf. *JE* x. 98 f.). Of more importance, as being more closely in touch with the poetic spirit, is Jewish lyric poetry. The religious poetry, once more, was to a great extent lyrical. But the earliest development of the lyric in the ordinary sense, *i.e.* the poetry that finds its themes in love, wine, war, patriotism, etc., took place in Spain, where the supreme master of this form was Moses ibn Ezra, where Judah Halevi won renown by his occasional poems and his poetical descriptions of nature, and where Abraham ibn Ezra and Judah al-Ḥarizi (early 13th cent.) found recognition as keen satirists. The greatest Jewish secular poet, however, was Immanuel b. Solomon, of Rome—the contemporary, perhaps a personal friend, of Dante—who combined Oriental fantasy with Italian erotics, and gave expression to them in highly polished Hebrew verse, writing, indeed, with such audacious abandon that the *Shūlḥān 'Arūkh* forbade the reading of the poet's *Maḥberôth* on the Sabbath, while even in our own time Graetz has accused him of having profaned the Hebrew muse. Another lyric writer worthy of mention is Israel Nagara (*c.* 1570), who, while he sings of God and of Israel, works upon a basis of love-songs and their melodies, and writes with such intensity of passion and such daring anthropomorphism that he too incurred the censure of the Rabbis. Moses Ḥayyim Luzzatto (1707–47) deserves mention as a writer of great emotional power, and as the first who composed epic poetry in the Hebrew language.

Jewish poetry, like Jewish literature in general, passed through a long period of barrenness, which lasted, indeed, until it was vitalized by the modern renascence of intellectual interests. The majority of the more distinguished poets of the present age are of Russian origin, the most eminent of all being Judah Loeb Gordon (1831–92; cf. *JE* vi. 47 f.), whose achievement, however, lies more in the field of satire than in that of the lyric. Of living poets special reference is due to H. N. Bialik, whose lyric poetry has justly met with the highest appreciation, and whose compositions have already been translated into nearly every European language. The last few decades have witnessed the rise of a copious Hebrew literature of general interest.

LITERATURE.—J. W. Etheridge, *Jerusalem and Tiberias; Sora and Cordova: Religious and Scholastic Learning of the Jews*, London, 1856; M. Steinschneider, *Jewish Literature from the Eighth to the Eighteenth Century*, Eng. tr., do. 1857; D. Cassel, *Lehrbuch der jüdischen Geschichte und Litteratur*, Leipzig, 1879, [2]Berlin, 1896, Eng. tr., *Manual of Jewish History and Literature*, London, 1883; G. Karpeles, *Geschichte der jüdischen Literatur*, Berlin, 1886, [2]1909, *Ein Blick in die jüdische Literatur*, Prague, 1895, *Jewish Literature and other*

[1] Writings connected with the long controversy between Judaism and Christianity were collected by J. B. de Rossi in his *Bibliotheca Judaica Antichristiana*, Parma, 1800, while Steinschneider has compiled a work entitled *Polemische und apologetische Literatur in arabischer Sprache zwischen Muslimen, Christen und Juden*, Leipzig, 1877.

Essays, Philadelphia and London, 1895; I. Abrahams, *A Short History of Jewish Literature*, London, 1906; S. Levy, 'Is there a Jewish Literature?' in *JQR* xv. [1903] 583-603; J. Jacobs, art. 'Bibliography' in *JE* iii. [1902] 199-201; I. Davidson, art. 'Literature, Hebrew,' *ib.* viii. [1904] 108-112.

I. ELBOGEN.

LITERATURE (Pahlavi). — Pahlavi ('Parthian,' *i.e.* 'heroic, belonging to heroic times'), or Middle Persian, literature dates, so far as its contributions to religion are concerned, from the 8th to the 11th cent. of our era; and its chief value in this regard is the elucidation of Zoroastrianism and Manichæanism (*qq.v.*), since it explains and supplements the data contained in the Avesta (*q.v.*) and adds materially to the scanty documents of Manichæan literature, besides giving fragmentary renderings of Christian texts. The religious material in Middle Persian falls into three categories: translations of Avesta texts, original compositions on Zoroastrian religious subjects, and Manichæan and Christian literature.

1. Translations of Avesta texts.—These translations are combined with running commentaries, sometimes of considerable length; but they are handicapped by failing to understand the original, especially in its grammatical relations, since the inflected type of the Avesta language had yielded, long before the composition of any Middle Persian of which we have any indication, to the analytic type present in Pahlavi, whose grammar differs only in unimportant details from that of Modern Persian and other modern Indo-Iranian dialects. At the same time, the Middle Persian translations of the Avesta possess a real value and must be considered in any attempt to decipher the meaning of the Avesta original, particularly in view of the allusions, etc., preserved by Iranian tradition (see, further, art. INTERPRETATION [Vedic and Avesta]). The principal Pahlavi translations are of the *Yasna*, *Vīsparad*, and *Vendīdād* (most conveniently ed. F. Spiegel, *Avesta*, Vienna, 1853–58; L. H. Mills, *The Ancient MS of the Yasna, with its Pahlavi Tr.* (A.D. *1323*), *generally quoted as J2*, Oxford, 1893, and *Gathas*, Leipzig, 1892–1913 [also with Sanskrit and Modern Persian versions, and Eng. tr.]; the *Vendīdād* separately by D. P. Sanjana, Bombay, 1895, and H. Jamasp and M. M. Ganderia, do. 1907), *Nyāyišns* (ed. [also with Sanskrit, Persian, and Gujarātī versions, and Eng. tr.] M. N. Dhalla, New York, 1908),[1] *Yašt* i. (ed. K. Salemann, in *Travaux du 3e congrès des orientalistes*, Petrograd, 1879, ii. 493–592), vi., vii., xi. (ed. J. Darmesteter, *Études orient.*, Paris, 1883, ii. 286–288, 292–294, 333–339; a complete ed. is promised by Dhalla), *Nīrangistān* (ed. D. P. Sanjana, Bombay, 1894; tr. of Avesta portion by Darmesteter, *Zend-Avesta*, Paris, 1892–93, iii. 78–148, and *SBE* iv.[2] [1895] 304–368), *Aogemadaēcā* (ed. and tr. W. Geiger, Erlangen, 1878), and *Hāḍōxt Nask* (ed. and tr. Hoshangji Jamaspji Asa and M. Haug, in their *Ardā Vīrāf*, Bombay, 1872–74, also tr. Darmesteter, *Zend-Avesta*, ii. 648–658, and *SBE* xxiii. [1883] 311–323). In addition, Pahlavi versions of *Yt.* ii., xiv., and xxiv., and of the *Āfrīnakāns* and *Sīh rōcaks*, are known to exist in MS.[2]

[1] Translations of the Pahlavi version of *Ys.* xxx. and lvii. have been made by H. Hübschmann (*Ein zoroastr. Lied*, Munich, 1872, and *SMA*, phil.-hist. Classe, 1873, pp. 651–664), of xi. by W. Bang (*Bull. de l'Acad. roy. de Belgique*, xviii. [1889] 247–260), of xxviii.-xxxii. 1 by M. Haug (*Essays on the Sacred Language, Writings, and Religion of the Parsis*^{4}, London, 1907, pp. 338–354), of ix. by M. B. Davar (Leipzig, 1904), and of *Vend.* i. by W. Geiger (Erlangen, 1877), of i., xviii.-xx. by Haug (*op. cit.* 355–393), and of xvii. by P. Horn (*ZDMG* xliii. [1889] 32–41).

[2] The authenticity of the *Vijirkarṭ-ī-Dīnīk* (ed. Peshotan, Bombay, 1848) is too dubious to be considered here. The book, of which the writer knows only two copies (in the Staatbibliothek, Munich, and in the library of A. V. W. Jackson, Columbia University), has been suppressed by the Parsis as unauthentic (cf. on it West, *GIrP* ii. 89 f.; C. Bartholomae, *Indogerman. Forschungen*, xi. [1900] 119–131, xii. [1901] 92–101).

2. Texts on Zoroastrian religious subjects.—Of these the longest and most important is the *Dīnkarṭ* ('Acts of the Religion'), dating from the 9th cent., and forming 'a large collection of information regarding the doctrines, customs, traditions, history, and literature of the Mazda-worshipping religion' (E. W. West, *GIrP* ii. 91). The first two books have been lost, and the ninth ends abruptly. The *Dīnkarṭ* is the chief source for a knowledge of Zoroastrian philosophy in the Sasanid period, and it also contains much legendary material of value, such as the traditions concerning Zoroaster (tr. West, *SBE* xlvii. [1897] 3–130), while two books, viii.–ix. (tr. West, *ib.* xxxvii. [1892] 3–397), contain summaries of the Avesta, including accounts of those large portions which are no longer extant. The text, which is of exceptional difficulty, has been edited by D. M. Madan (Bombay, 1911), and, with English and Gujarātī paraphrases, by Peshotan Behramji and Darab Peshotan Sanjana (do. 1874 ff.; vol. xiii. carries the work through *Dīnk.* vii. 2). The ***Bundahišn*** treats of Zoroastrian cosmogony, cosmology, and eschatology. It is found in two recensions: a shorter (ed. and tr. F. Justi, Leipzig, 1868; tr. West, *SBE* v. [1880] 3–151) and a longer—the so-called Great, or Iranian, *Bundahišn* (ed. T. D. Anklesaria, Bombay, 1908; summary of contents in *GIrP* ii. 100–102; tr. of portions by Darmesteter, *Zend-Avesta*, i. 267 f., ii. 305-322, 398–402; by J. J. Modi, *Asiatic Papers*, Bombay, 1905, pp. 225-234; and by E. Blochet, *RHR* xxxii. [1895] 99 ff., 217 ff.).

Eschatology forms the general subject of the *Arṭā-ī-Vīrāf Nāmak*, which sets forth, in describing the journey of Arṭā-ī-Vīrāf through heaven and hell, the future life of both righteous and wicked (ed. Hoshangji and Haug, Bombay, 1872–74). Here belong also the *Bahman Yašt*, which purports to be Ahura Mazda's revelation to Zoroaster of the future vicissitudes of the Iranian nation and religion (ed. K. A. Noshervan, Poona, 1899; tr. West, *SBE* v. 191–235); and the *Maṭan-ī-Šāh Vāhrām-ī-Varjāvand* ('Coming of King Vāhrām-ī-Varjāvand'), on the expulsion of the Arabs from Persia (ed. Jamaspji Minocheherji Jamasp-Asana, *Pahlavi Texts contained in the Codex MK*, Bombay, 1897-1913, p. 160 f.).

The principal Pahlavi texts of a purely general religious character are the following: *Māṭīgān-ī-Haft Amšaspand* ('Particulars of the seven Amesha Spentas'); *Stāyišn-ī Sīh-Rōcak* ('Praise of the Thirty Days'), which 'praises and invokes Aūharmazd as the creator of each of the thirty sacred beings whose names are applied to the days of the month, and whose attributes are detailed and blessed in succession' (West, *GIrP* ii. 108); *Stāyišn-ī-Drōn*, a laudation of the *drōn*, or sacred cake; *Ḥaqīqat-ī-Rōjhā* ('Statement of the Days'), stating what actions are suitable on each of the days of the month; *Māṭīgān-ī Māh Fravartīn Rōj Xūrdāt*, enumerating the marvellous events that have occurred on the sixth day of the first month from the beginning to the end of the world (ed. Jamaspji, *op. cit.*, pp. 102–108; tr. K. J. Jāmāsp Asānā, *Cama Memorial Volume*, Bombay, 1900, pp. 122–129); *Māṭīgān-ī-Sīh-Rōj*, containing material similar to the *Ḥaqīqat*, but in fuller detail (tr. D. P. Sanjana, *Next-of-kin Marriages in old Irân*, London, 1888, pp. 105–116); *Dārūk-ī-Xūrsandīh*, giving the components (contentment, perseverance, etc.) which are to be pounded with 'the pestle of reverence,' and taken daily at dawn with the spoon of prayer (ed. Jamaspji, *op. cit.*, p. 154); *Cīm-ī-Drōn* ('Meaning of the Sacred Cake'), dealing with the symbolism and consecration of the *drōn; Paṭēṭ-ī-Xūṭ*, a long formula for the confession of one's sins; a number of *Āfrīns* ('Benedictions'); the *Āšīrvād*, or marriage benediction; *Namāz-ī-Aūharmazd*, a laudation of Ahura Mazda (ed. and tr. E. Sachau, *SWAW* lxvii. [1871] 828–833; also tr. Darmesteter, *Une Prière judéo-persane*, Paris, 1891); and *Nām-stāyišnīh*, a laudation of the name and attributes of Ahura Mazda.

Second only to the *Dīnkarṭ* as a source for knowledge of the religious philosophy of the Sasanid Zoroastrians (and, like the larger work, doubtless embodying a large amount of older material) is what may be termed *responsa* literature. This treats of all sorts of matters on which questions might arise. One of the most important works of this type is the *Dāṭistān-ī-Dīnīk*, the 'Religious Opinions' of Mānūščihar, high priest of Pārs and Kirmān, in reply to the questions raised by Mitrō-Xūršēṭ and others (tr. West, *SBE* xviii. [1882] 3–276; the first 15 questions ed. D. P. Sanjana, Bombay, 1897); with this is connected a long and important Pahlavi *Rivāyat* (ed. Bamanji Nasarvanji Dhabhar, Bombay, 1913), while the same Mānūščihar wrote, in 881, three epistles on ritual problems (ed. Dhabhar, Bombay, 1912, tr. West, *SBE* xviii. 279–366), his brother, Zāṭ-Sparam, also being the author of a noteworthy religious treatise (tr. West, *SBE* v. 155–186, xlvii. 133–170, xxxvii. 401–405). Of equal importance with the *Dāṭistān-ī-Dīnīk* is the *Dīnā-ī-Maīnōg-i-Xraṭ* ('Opinions of the Spirit of Wisdom'), of which only a portion (ed. F. C. Andreas, Kiel, 1882) survives in Pahlavi, though the complete work is found in Pāzand and Sanskrit (ed. West, Stuttgart, 1871, tr. West, *SBE* xxiv. [1885] 3–113). The *Pursišnīhā* ('Questions') are chiefly answered by quotations from Avesta texts (the latter ed. and tr. Darmesteter, *Zend-Avesta*, iii. 53–77, *SBE* iv.[2] 276–299), and another noteworthy collection of *responsa* (as yet unedited) is contained in the *Rivāyat-ī-Hēmēṭ-ī-Ašavahištān*. Here, too, belongs, roughly speaking, the *Šāyast-lā-Šāyast* ('Proper and Improper'), whose contents 'are of a very varied character, but sins and good works, precautions to avoid impurities, details of ceremonies and customs, the mystic signification of the Gathas, and praise of the sacred beings are the principal subjects discussed' (West, *GIrP* ii. 107; tr. West, *SBE* v. 239–406). In this category may also be ranked the *Māṭīgān-ī-Yōšt-ī-Fryāno*, narrating how the righteous Yōsht answered the 33 questions of the wizard Axt, who was thus destroyed, whereas he had previously killed all who had failed to solve his queries—the Iranian version of the story of the sphinx (ed. and tr. Hoshangji and Haug, in their *Ardā Vīrāf*; also tr. A. Barthélemy, *Une Légende iranienne*, Paris, 1889). Controversial literature is represented by the *Māṭīgān-ī gujastak Abālīš*, recounting the disputation between the heretic Abālīš and Aṭūr-Farnbag (who began the compilation of the *Dīnkarṭ*) before the khalīf al-Ma'mūn about 825 (ed. and tr. Barthélemy, Paris, 1887).

Yet another important type of Pahlavi literature is that of didactic admonitions. To this class belong the *Pand-nāmak-ī-Zaratušt* (not the Prophet, but probably the son of Āṭūrpāṭ-ī-Māraspandān; ed. and tr. P. B. Sanjana, in his *Ganje-Shāyagān*, Bombay, 1885); *Andarj-ī-Xūsrō-ī-Kavāṭān*, purporting to be the dying counsels of Chosroes to his people (ed. and tr. Sanjana, *op. cit.*; also tr. L. C. Casartelli, *BOR* i. [1887] 97–101, and Salemann, *Mélanges asiat. tirés du bull. de l'acad. imp. des sciences de St. Pétersbourg*, ix. [1887] 242–253); *Andarj-ī-Āṭūrpāṭ-ī-Māraspandān*, being the advice of Āṭūrpāṭ to his son Zaratusht (perhaps the person mentioned just above; ed. and tr. Sanjana, *op. cit.*; also tr. C. de Harlez, *Muséon*, vi. [1887] 66–78); *Pand-nāmak-ī-Vajōrg-Mitrō-ī-Būxtakān* (ed. and tr. Sanjana, *op. cit.*); *Five Dispositions for Priests and Ten Admonitions for Laymen* (ed. Jamaspji, *op. cit.* 129–131); *Characteristics of a Happy Man* (ed. Jamaspji, *op. cit.* 162–167); *Vācak aēcand-ī-Āṭūrpāṭ-ī-Māraspandān*, the dying counsel of Āṭūrpāṭ (ed. Jamaspji, *op. cit.* 144–153); *Andarj-ī-Aōšnar-ī-dānāk, Injunctions to Beh-dīns, Admonitions to Mazdayasnians,* and *Sayings of Aṭūr-Farnbag and Baxt-Āfrīṭ* (these as yet unedited).

3. Manichæan and Christian literature.—Until comparatively recently it was supposed that Pahlavi literature was exclusively Zoroastrian; but the discoveries made in Central Asia by M. A. Stein, A. Grünwedel, A. von Le Coq, and P. Pelliot have revealed a new province of extreme interest and value. The decipherment of the MSS found by these explorers has only begun. Here it must suffice to say that we already possess Pahlavi versions of somewhat extensive portions of Manichæan literature—a fact the more important since this religion had hitherto been known only from the writings of its enemies. The most important collection of these texts thus far is that of F. W. K. Müller (with German translation, 'Handschriften-Reste in Estrangelo-Schrift aus Turfan,' *ABAW*, 1904; revised ed. C. Salemann, 'Manichaeische Studien, i.,' *Mém. de l'acad. imp. des sciences de St. Pétersbourg*, viii. 10 [1908]; Müller, 'Doppelblatt aus einem manich. Hymnenbuch,' *ABAW*, 1913). In the closely allied Soghdian dialect are numerous fragments of a version of the NT, perhaps from the 9th or 10th cent. (Müller, 'NT Bruchstücke in sog. Sprache,' *SBAW*, 1907, pp. 260–270; 'Sog. Texte, i.,' *ABAW*, 1913; cf. L. H. Gray, *ExpT* xxv. [1913] 59–61).

4. Pāzand and Sanskrit versions.—The special problems of the Pahlavi language cannot be discussed here (see F. Spiegel, *Gram. der Huzvâresch Sprache*, Vienna, 1851; P. B. Sanjana, *Gram. of the Pahlvi Lang.*, Bombay, 1871; C. de Harlez, *Manuel du Pehlevi*, Paris, 1880; Darmesteter, *Études iran.*, do. 1883; Salemann, 'Mittelpersisch,' *GIrP* I. i. [1901] 249–332; E. Blochet, *Études de gram. pehlvie*, Paris, n.d. [1905]); it must suffice to say that, when the Semitic words (or logograms) in Pahlavi are written in Iranian (e.g., *šāhān šāh*, 'king of kings,' instead of *malkāān malkā*), the language is termed Pāzand (Spiegel, *Gram. der Pârsisprache*, Leipzig, 1851). Many Pahlavi texts already listed are found in Pāzand as well. The great majority of the religious writings of this type, except the important *Sikand gūmānīg-Vijār* ('Doubt-dispelling Explanation'), probably dating from the latter part of the 9th cent. (ed. Hoshang and West, Bombay, 1887; tr. West, *SBE* xxiv. 117–251), and the *Jāmāsp-nāmak* (ed. J. J. Modi, Bombay, 1903), have been edited by E. K. Antiā (*Pâzend Texts*, Bombay, 1909). The *Sikand gūmānīg-Vijār* defends the doctrine of dualism, and in this connexion polemizes in very interesting fashion against Judaism, Christianity, Manichæanism, and—necessarily quite guardedly—Muhammadanism (cf. artt. JESUS CHRIST IN ZOROASTRIANISM, JEWS IN ZOROASTRIANISM); the *Jāmāsp-nāmak* gives a summary of Iranian cosmology, history, and future fortunes of the Iranian religion. Among the texts edited by Antiā are *doās* (benedictions recited on various occasions), *nīrangs* (charms, often of much ethnographical interest; for examples see Modi, *Anthropological Papers*, Bombay, 1911, pp. 48, 125–129; K. E. Kanga, in *Cama Mem. Vol.*, 142–145), *patēṭs* (confessions); and of texts not included in this collection mention may be made of *A Father instructing his Son* and *Andarj-ī-dānāk Marṭ*.

A number of Pahlavi (and Avesta) treatises are found in Sanskrit as well as in Pahlavi and Pāzand versions. Many of these are given in editions of Pahlavi texts enumerated above, but we must also note the ed. of Neriosangh's version of the *Yasna* by Spiegel (Leipzig, 1861) and the series of *Collected*

Sanskrit Writings of the Parsis, ed. S. D. Bharucha (Bombay, 1906 ff.).

5. Parsi-Persian literature.—Apart from Persian translations of Avesta and Pahlavi texts, there is a large amount of Zoroastrian literature in Persian, which, for the most part, still awaits study. The *Zartušt-nāmah*, dating from the 12th cent., which is now accessible in original and translation by F. Rosenberg (Petrograd, 1904), gives a legendary biography of Zoroaster. Another work of importance is the *Ṣad-dar* ('Hundred Gates'), which discusses a hundred subjects of note in Zoroastrianism. Two of its three recensions have been translated into English (West, *SBE* xxiv. 255–361) and Latin (T. Hyde, *Hist. religionis veterum Persarum*, Oxford, 1700, pp. 433–488). A different work, although along the same general lines, is the *Ṣad-darband-ī-Huš* (or *Ṣad-dar Bundahišn*; ed. B. N. Dhabhar, Bombay, 1909). Of worth for a study of the methods of Zoroastrian polemic against Muhammadanism is the *'Ulamā-i-Islām*, which is found in two recensions, the shorter of which has been edited and translated (ed. J. Mohl, *Fragmens relatifs à la religion de Zoroastre*, Paris, 1829; tr. J. Vullers, *Fragmente über die Religion des Zoroaster*, Bonn, 1831; Blochet, *RHR* xxxvii. [1898] 23–49). A particularly valuable collection of Parsi-Persian literature is contained in the MS Bu 29, belonging to the University of Bombay, the second volume of which has been edited by M. N. Unvālā (not yet published) and analyzed by Rosenberg (*Notices de litt. parsie*, Petrograd, 1909). It contains a large number of *Rivāyats* (religious traditions) and letters on the most diverse subjects—ritual, cosmogony, eschatology, etc.—the longer recension of the *'Ulamā-i-Islām* (pp. 72–80), the *Aḥkām-i-Jāmāsp* (containing the horoscopes of Zoroaster, Moses, Alexander the Great, Christ, Mazdak, etc., as well as cosmology and eschatology, pp. 111-130), *Vaṣf-i-Amšāsfandān* (attributes of the Amesha Spentas, pp. 164–192), *Āghāz-i-dāstān Mazdak va-Šāh Nūšīrvān 'Ādil* (on the heresiarch Mazdak, pp. 214–230), six parables connected with the Barlaam cycle (pp. 305–327; cf. art. JOSAPHAT, BARLAAM AND), and questions asked of Zoroaster by Jāmāsp (pp. 417–422). Among other Parsi-Persian texts, not yet edited, may be mentioned a *Discussion on Dualism* between a Zoroastrian priest and a Muhammadan, and the *Saugand-nāmah*, or 'Book of Oaths.'

The interesting secular works in Pahlavi, Pāzand, and Parsi-Persian, such as geographical matter, social rules, and tales, do not come within the sphere of religion.

Finally, it may be mentioned that translations of the Avesta have been made not only into Persian (for specimens see, in addition to works cited above, Darmesteter, *Études iran.* ii. 262 ff.), but also, from the 15th cent., into Gujarātī, the vernacular of the Indian Zoroastrians (see the Prolegomena to K. Geldner's ed. of the Avesta, Stuttgart, 1896, pp. vii–xi; Darmesteter, *Zend-Avesta*, i. p. xlii); and the modern religious literature of the Parsis is chiefly written either in Gujarātī or in English.

LITERATURE.—F. Spiegel, *Traditionelle Lit. der Parsen*, Vienna, 1860; E. W. West, 'Pahlavi Lit.,' *GIrP* ii. (Strassburg, 1904) 75–129; E. Wilhelm and K. B. Patel, *Cat. of Books on Irānian Lit. published in Europe and India*, Bombay, 1901, and the former scholar's annual report on 'Perser' in *Jahresberichte der Geschichtswissenschaft*.

LOUIS H. GRAY.

LITERATURE (Vedic and Classical Sanskrit).—**1. The language.**—The name 'Sanskrit' (*saṁskṛta*, 'adorned,' 'perfected,' perfect passive participle of the verb *saṁ-skar*, 'to adorn,' from *saṁ*, 'together,' and *kar*, 'to make') is ordinarily applied to the whole ancient and sacred language of India. It belongs more properly to that dialect which may be defined more exactly as Classical Sanskrit, the language which was treated by the Hindu grammarians, Pāṇini and his followers. For more than 2000 years, until the present day, this language has led a more or less artificial life. Like the Latin of the Middle Ages, it was, and is, even to-day, to a very marked extent, the means of communication and literary expression of the priestly, learned, and cultivated classes. The more popular speech upon which it was based is known as *bhāṣā* ('speech,' from *bhāṣ*, 'to speak'), of which there is no direct record. Sanskrit is distinguished more obviously from the phonetically later, decayed dialects, Prākrit and Pāli, the second of the two being the language of the canonical writings of the Southern Buddhists. The relation of the Prākrit and Pāli dialects to Sanskrit is closely analogous to the relation of the Romance languages to Latin. On the other hand, Sanskrit is distinguished, although much less sharply, from the oldest forms of Indian speech, preserved in the canonical and wholly religious literature of the Veda (Skr. *veda*, 'knowledge,' from *vid*, 'to know,' connected with Gr. Ϝοῖδα 'I know,' Lat. *videre*, Old Bulgarian *vědě*, 'I know,' Gothic *wait*, 'I know,' Old High German *wizzan*, Germ. *wissen*, Eng. *wit*, 'to know'). These forms of speech are in their turn by no means free from important dialectic, stylistic, and chronological differences; yet they are comprised under the name Vedic (or, less properly, Vedic Sanskrit), which is thus distinguished from the language of Pāṇini and its forerunner, the language of the Epics, whose proper designation is Sanskrit, or Classical Sanskrit.

Vedic differs from Sanskrit about as much as the Greek of Homer does from Attic Greek. The Vedic apparatus of grammatical forms is much richer and less definitely fixed than that of Sanskrit. The latter has lost much of the wealth of form of the earlier language, without, as a rule, supplying the proper substitutes for the lost materials. Many case-forms and verbal forms of Vedic have disappeared in Sanskrit. The subjunctive is lost; a single Sanskrit infinitive takes the place of about a dozen very interesting Vedic infinitives. Sanskrit also gave up the most important heirloom which the Hindu language has handed down from pre-historic times, namely, the Vedic system of accentuation. In the last forty years the recorded Vedic accents have proved to be of paramount importance in the history of the Indo-European languages. Vedic, however, notwithstanding its somewhat unsettled wealth of form and its archaic character, is not a strictly popular dialect, but a more or less artificial 'high speech,' handed down through generations by families of priestly singers. Thus both Vedic and Sanskrit, as is indeed the case more or less wherever a literature has sprung up, were in a sense caste languages, built upon popular idioms. The grammatical regulation of Sanskrit at the hands of Pāṇini and his followers, however, went beyond any academic attempts to regulate speech recorded elsewhere in the history of civilization.

Older forms lying behind the Vedic language are reconstructed by the aid of Comparative Philology. The Vedic people were immigrants to India; they came from the great Iranian region on the other side of the Himālaya mountains. The comparison of Vedic (and to a less extent Sanskrit) with the oldest forms of Iranian speech, the language of the Avesta and the cuneiform inscriptions of the Achæmenian Persian kings, yields the rather startling result that these languages are collectively mere dialects of one and the same older idiom. This is known as the Indo-Iranian or Aryan (in the narrower, and proper, sense) language. The reconstructed Aryan language differs less from the language of the Veda than Classical Sanskrit does from Prākrit and Pāli. The language of the Iranian Avesta is so much like that of the Veda that entire passages of either literature may be converted into good specimens of the other by merely eliminating the special sound changes which each has evolved in the course of its separate existence. And the literary style, the metres, and above all the mythology of Veda and Avesta are closely enough allied to make the study of either to some extent directly dependent upon the other. In fact, the spiritual monuments of the Avesta as well as the stone monuments of the Achæmenian kings became intelligible chiefly by the aid of the Vedic language. Since the revival of classical learning there has been no event of such importance in the history of culture as the discovery of Sanskrit in the latter part of the 18th century. There is at present no domain of historical or linguistic science untouched by the influence of Sanskrit studies. The study of this language gave access to the primitive Indo-European period, and originated the science of Comparative Philology in all its bearings. Linguistic Science, Comparative Mythology, Science of Religion, Comparative Jurisprudence, and other important fields of historical and philosophical study either owe their very existence to the discovery of Sanskrit or were profoundly influenced by its study.

2. The Veda as a whole.—The word 'Veda' is the collective designation of the ancient sacred literature of India, or of individual books belonging to that literature. At an unknown date, which is at the present time conventionally averaged up as 1500 B.C., but which may be considerably earlier, Aryan tribes (clans, *viś*, from which is derived the later name of the third, or agricultural, caste, Vāiśya) began to migrate from the Iranian highlands on the north of the Hindu Kush mountains into the north-west of India, the plains of the river Indus and its tributaries. The non-Aryan aborigines, called Dasyu, in distinction from Ārya (whence the word 'Aryan'), the name of the conquerors, were easily subdued. The conquest was followed by gradual amalgamation of the fairer-skinned conquerors with the dark aborigines. The result was a not altogether primitive, semi-pastoral civilization, in which cities, kings, and priestly schools rivalled the interests connected with cattle-raising and agriculture. From the start we are confronted with a poetical literature, primitive on the whole, and more particularly exhibiting its crudeness when compared with Classical Sanskrit literature, yet lacking neither in refinement and beauty of thought nor in skill in the handling of language and metre. That this product was not entirely originated on Indian soil follows from the above-mentioned close connexion with the earliest forms of Persian literature. Vedic literature in its first intention is throughout religious. It includes hymns, prayers, and sacerdotal formulæ offered by priests to the gods in behalf of lay sacrificers; charms for witchcraft and medicine, manipulated by magicians and medicine-men; expositions of the sacrifice, illustrated by legends, in the manner of the Jewish Talmud; higher speculations, philosophic, psycho-physical, cosmic, and theosophic, gradually growing up in connexion with and out of the simpler beliefs; and, finally, rules for conduct in everyday life, at home and abroad. This is the Veda as a whole.

At the base of this entire literature of more than 100 books, not all of which have as yet been unearthed or published, lie four varieties of metrical and formulaic compositions known as the four Vedas in the narrower sense. These are the Rigveda, the Yajurveda, the Sāmaveda, and the Atharvaveda. These four names come from a somewhat later time; they do not coincide exactly with the earlier names, nor do they correspond completely with the contents of the texts themselves. The earlier names are *ṛchaḥ*, 'stanzas of praise,' *yajūṁṣi*, 'liturgical stanzas and formulæ,' *sāmāni*, 'melodies,' and *atharvāṅgirasaḥ*, 'blessings and curses.' The collection which goes by the name of Rigveda contains not only 'stanzas of praise,' but also 'blessings and curses,' as well as most of the stanzas which form the basis of the *sāman*-melodies of the Sāmaveda. The Atharvaveda contains *ṛchaḥ* and *yajūṁṣi*, as well as blessings and curses. The Yajurveda also contains many blessings in addition to its main topic, the liturgy. The Sāmaveda is merely a collection of a certain kind of 'stanzas of praise' which are derived with some variants and additions from the Rigveda, but are here set to music which is indicated by musical notations.

3. The Rigveda.—The *Rigveda* is on the whole the most important as well as the oldest of the four collections. A little over 1000 hymns, equalling in bulk the surviving poems of Homer, are arranged in ten books, called *maṇḍalas*, or 'circles.' Six of them (ii.–vii.), the so-called 'family books,' form the nucleus of the collection. Each of these is the work of a different *ṛṣi*, 'seer,' or rather a family of poets, traditionally descended from such a *ṛṣi*, as may be gathered from certain statements in the hymns themselves. The eighth book and the first fifty hymns of the first book, belonging to the family of Kaṇva, are often arranged strophically in groups of two or three stanzas. These form the bulk of those stanzas which are sung to melodies in the Sāmaveda. The hymns of the ninth book are addressed directly to the deified plant *soma*, and the liquor pressed from it, in order that it may be sacrificed to the gods. The remainder of the first book and the entire tenth book are more miscellaneous in character and problematic as to arrangement. On the whole they are of later origin and from a different sphere. Their themes are partly foreign to the narrower purpose of the *ṛchaḥ*; witchcraft hymns of a more popular character and theosophic hymns appear in considerable numbers. The poems of the former class reappear, usually with variants, in the Atharvaveda.

On the whole the Rigveda is a collection of priestly hymns addressed to the gods of the Vedic pantheon (see VEDIC RELIGION) during sacrifice. This sacrifice consisted of oblations of intoxicating *soma*, pressed from the 'mountain-born' *soma*-plant, which reappears in the Zoroastrian Avesta under the name *haoma* (*q.v.*), and was therefore the sacred sacrificial fluid of the Indo-Iranians, or Aryans. In addition, melted butter (*ghṛta*, or *ghī*) was poured into the fire, personified as the god Agni (Lat. *ignis*), who performs the function of messenger of the gods (Aṅgiras). The ritual of the Veda is to a considerable extent pre-historic, and advanced in character—by no means as simple as was once supposed. But it is much less elaborate than that of the Yajurveda and the Brāhmaṇas (see below). The chief interest of the Rigveda lies in the gods themselves and in the myths and legends narrated or alluded to in the course of their invocation. The mythology represents an earlier, clearer stage of thought than is to be found in any other parallel literature. Above all, it is sufficiently primitive in conception to show clearly the processes of personification by which the phenomena of nature developed into gods (anthropomorphosis). The original nature of the Vedic gods, however, is not always clear, not as clear as was once confidently assumed to be the case. The analysis of their character is a chapter of Vedic philology as difficult as it is important. In any case enough is known to justify the statement that the keynote of Rigvedic thought is the nature myth.

4. The Yajurveda.—The *Yajurveda* represents the exceeding growth of ritualism or sacerdotalism. Its *yajūṁṣi*, 'liturgical stanzas and formulæ,' are in the main, though not wholly, of a later time. They are partly metrical and partly prose. The materials of the Rigveda are freely adapted, with secondary changes of expression, and without regard to the original purpose and order of their composition. The main object is no longer devotion to the gods themselves; the sacrifice has become the centre of thought: its mystic power is conceived to be a thing *per se*, and its every detail has swollen into all-importance. A crowd of priests (seventeen is the largest number) conduct a vast, complicated, and painstaking ceremonial, full of symbolic meaning even in its smallest minutiæ. From the moment when the priests seat themselves on the sacrificial ground, strewn with sacred grass, and proceed to mark out the altars (*vedi*) on which the sacred fires are built every act has its stanza or formula, and every utensil is blessed with its own fitting blessing. Every flaw is elaborately expiated. These formulæ are conceived no longer as prayers that may, or may not, succeed, but as inherently coercive magic. If the priest chants a formula for rain while pouring some sacrificial fluid, rain shall and must come; if he makes an oblation accompanied by the curse of an enemy, that enemy is surely destroyed. In fact, and in brief, the Yajurveda means the deification of the sacrifice in its every detail of act and word.

5. The Sāmaveda.—The *Sāmaveda* is the least clear of all the Vedas as regards its purpose and origin. Its stanzas, or rather groups of stanzas, are known as *sāmāni*, 'melodies.' The *sāman*-stanzas are preserved in three forms: (1) in the Rigveda, as ordinary poetry, accented in the same way as other Vedic poetry; (2) in the Sāmaveda itself in a form called *ārchika*, a kind of libretto composed of a special collection of stanzas, most of which, though not all, occur also in the Rigveda (see above); here also there is a system of accents, peculiar in its notation, but apparently with reference to the unsung *sāmans*; (3) in the third *sāman*-version, the *gānas*, or song-books, we find the real sung *sāmans*; here not only the text but the musical notes are given. Still this is not yet a complete *sāman*. In the middle of the sung stanzas exclamatory syllables are interspersed—the so-called *stobhas*, such as *oṁ*, *hau*, *hai*, *hoyi*, or *hiṁ*; and at the end of the stanzas certain concluding syllables—the so-called *nidhanas*, such as *atha*, *ā*, *iṁ*, and *sāt*. The Sāmaveda is devoted chiefly to the worship of Indra, who is a blustering, braggadocio god and who has to befuddle himself with *soma* in order to slay demons. It seems likely, therefore, that the *sāmans* are the civilized version of savage shamanism (the resemblance between the two words, however, is accidental), an attempt to influence the natural order of things by shouts and exhortations. It is well understood that the Brāhmans were in the habit of blending their own hieratic practices and conceptions with the practices which they found among the people. The *sāman*-melodies and the exclamations interspersed among the words of the text may therefore be the substitute for the self-exciting shouts of the shaman priests of an earlier time.

6. The Atharvaveda.—The oldest name of the Atharvaveda is *atharvāṅgirasaḥ*, a compound formed of the names of two semi-mythic families of priests, the Atharvans and Aṅgirases. At a very early time the former term was regarded as synonymous with 'holy charms,' or 'blessings,' the latter with 'witchcraft charms,' or 'curses.' In addition to this name, and the more conventional name Atharvaveda, there are two other names, practically restricted to the ritual texts of this Veda: *bhṛgvaṅgirasaḥ*, that is, 'Bhṛgus and Aṅgirases,' in which the Bhṛgus, another ancient family of fire-priests, take the place of the Atharvans; and *Brahmaveda*, probably 'Veda of the Brahma, or holy religion in general.' As regards the latter name, it must be remembered that the Atharvaveda contains a large number of theosophic hymns which deal with the *brahma* in the sense of the Neo-Platonic λόγος, as a kind of pantheistic personification of holy thought and its pious utterance. The Atharvaveda is a collection of 730 hymns, containing some 6000 stanzas.

7. The Vedic schools.—The redactions or collections of these four Vedas are known as *Saṁhitās*; each of them is handed down in various schools, branches, or recensions, called *charaṇa*, *śākhā*, or *bheda*, the term *śākhā*, or 'branch,' being the most familiar of the three. These 'branches' represent a given Veda in forms differing not a little from one another. The school differences of the Rigveda are unimportant, except as they extend also to the Brāhmaṇas and Sūtras of that Veda (see below). There are two Sāmaveda redactions, those of the schools of the Kauthumas and the Rāṇāyanīyas. A very persistent tradition ascribes nine schools to the Atharvaveda; the Saṁhitās of two of these, the Śaunakīyas and Paippalādas, are published, the latter in an interesting chromo-photographic reproduction of the unique manuscript of that text preserved in the library of the University of Tübingen. The Yajurveda, especially, is handed down in recensions that differ from one another very widely. There is in the first place the broad division into White Yajurveda and Black Yajurveda. The most important difference between these two is that the Black Yajurveda schools intermingle their stanzas and formulæ with the prose exposition of the Brāhmaṇa (see below), whereas the White Yajurveda schools present their Brāhmaṇa in separate works. The White Yajurveda belongs to the school of the Vājasaneyins, and is subdivided into the Mādhyaṁdina and Kāṇva recensions. The important schools of the Black Yajurveda are the Taittirīyas, Maitrāyaṇīyas, Kaṭhas, and Kapiṣṭhalas. Sometimes these schools have definite geographical locations. For example, the Kaṭhas and Kapiṣṭhalas were located, at the time when the Greeks became acquainted with India, in the Panjāb and in Kashmīr. The Maitrāyaṇīyas appear at one time to have occupied the region around the lower course of the river Narmadā; the Taittirīyas, at least in modern times, are at home in the south of India, the Deccan.

8. The Brāhmaṇas.—The poetic stanzas and the ritualistic formulæ of the Vedas collectively go by the name of *mantra*, 'pious utterance,' or 'hymn.' These were followed at a later period by a very different literary type, namely, the theological treatises called *brāhmaṇa*, the Hindu analogon to the Hebrew Talmud. The Brāhmaṇas are exegetical and commentative, bulky expositions of the sacrificial ceremonial, describing its minute details, discussing its value or reason, speculating upon its origin, and illustrating its potency by ancient legends. Apart from the light which these texts throw upon the sacerdotalism of ancient India, they are important because they are written in connected prose—the earliest in the entire domain of Indo-European speech. They are especially important for syntax: in this respect they represent the oldest Indian stage even better than the Rigveda, owing to the restrictions imposed upon the latter by its poetic form. The Brāhmaṇas also were composed in schools, or recensions: the various Brāhmaṇa recensions of one and the same Veda differ at times even more widely than the Saṁhitās of the *mantras*. Thus the Rigveda has two Brāhmaṇas, the *Aitareya* and the *Kauṣītakin*, or *Śāṅkhāyana*. The Brāhmaṇa matter of the Black Yajurvedas is given together with the *mantras* of that class (see above); on the other hand, the White Yajurveda treats its Brāhmaṇa matter separately, and with extraordinary fullness, in the famous *Śatapatha Brāhmaṇa*, the 'Brāhmaṇa of a Hundred Paths,' so called because it consists of a hundred lectures. Next to the Rigveda and Atharvaveda Saṁhitās this work is the most important production in the whole range of Vedic literature. Two Brāhmaṇas belonging to independent recensions of the Sāmaveda have been preserved entire, that of the Tāṇḍins, usually designated as *Pañchaviṁśa Brāhmaṇa*, and that of the Talavakāras or Jaiminīyas. To the Atharvaveda is attached the very late and secondary *Gopatha Brāhmaṇa*; its contents harmonize so little with the spirit of the Atharvan hymns that it seems likely to have been produced in imitation of the 'school' conditions in the other Vedas.

9. The Āraṇyakas and Upaniṣads.—A later development of the Brāhmaṇas is the *Āraṇyakas*, or 'Forest Treatises.' Their later character is indicated both by the position which they occupy at the end of the Brāhmaṇas and by their partly theosophical character. The name 'Forest Treatise' is not altogether clear. Either these works were recited by hermits living in the forest, or, owing to the superior sanctity of their contents, they were taught by teacher to pupil in the solitude of the forest rather than in the profaner atmosphere of the town or village. The two important Āraṇyakas are the *Aitareya* and the *Taittirīya*, belonging to the two Vedic schools of that name. The chief interest of the Āraṇyakas is that they form in contents and tone a transition to the Upaniṣads, the older of which are either embedded in them or form their concluding portions (see artt. ĀRAṆYAKAS, UPANIṢADS).

10. The Śrauta-Sūtras, or manuals of the Vedic ritual.—Both *mantra* and *brāhmaṇa* are regarded as revealed (*śruti*, or 'revelation'); the rest of Vedic literature as tradition (*smṛti*), derived from holy men of old. This literature has a characteristic style of its own, being handed down in the form of brief rules, or *sūtras*, whence it is familiarly known as Sūtra literature, or the Sūtras. They are, in the main, of three classes, each of which is, again, associated with a particular Vedic school, reaching back, as a rule, to the school distinctions of the Saṁhitās and the Brāhmaṇas. The first class of Sūtras are the Śrauta or Kalpa Sūtras, which may be translated 'Sūtras of the Vedic Ritual.' They are brief mnemonic rule-books compiled, with the help of oral tradition, from the Brāhmaṇas. They are technical guides to the Vedic sacrifice, distinguished from the diffusive Brāhmaṇas, where the ritual acts are interrupted by explanation and illustrative legend. To the Rigveda belong two Śrauta Sūtras, corresponding to its two Brāhmaṇa schools: the *Āśvalāyana* to the *Aitareya Brāhmaṇa*, and the *Śāṅkhāyana* or *Kauṣītakin* to the Brāhmaṇa of the same name. To the White Yajurveda belongs the Śrauta Sūtra of Kātyāyana, closely adhering to the *Śatapatha Brāhmaṇa*. There are no fewer than six Śrauta Sūtras belonging to the Black Yajurveda, but only three of them are published, or in the course of publication, those of Āpastamba and Baudhāyana, belonging to the schools of the Taittirīyas, and the Mānava, belonging to the school of the Maitrāyaṇīyas. The Sāmaveda has two Śrautas, those of Lāṭyāyana and Drāhyāyaṇa, belonging respectively to its two schools of the Kauthumas and the Rāṇāyanīyas; the Atharvaveda has the late and inferior *Vaitāna*.

11. The Gṛhya Sūtras, or 'House Books.'—Of decidedly greater, indeed of universal, interest is the second class of Sūtras, the *Gṛhya Sūtras*, or 'House Books.' These are treatises on home life, which deal systematically and piously with the events in the everyday existence of the individual and his family. Though composed at a comparatively late Vedic period, they contain practices and prayers of great antiquity, and supplement most effectively the contents of the Atharvaveda. From the moment of birth, indeed from the time of conception, to the time when the body is consigned to the funeral pyre, they exhibit the ordinary plain Hindu in the aspect of a devout and virtuous adherent of the gods. All the important events of life are sacramental, decked out in practices often of great charm and usually full of symbolic meaning. For ethnology and the history of human ideas the 'House Books' are of unexcelled importance. These manuals are also distributed among the four Vedas and their schools, each of which is theoretically entitled to one of them. More than a dozen are now known to scholars. The Rigveda has the *Gṛhya Sūtras* of its two schools, that of Āśvalāyana and Śāṅkhāyana; the White Yajurveda that of Pāraskara; the Black Yajurveda a large number, as those of the Āpastamba, Baudhāyana, Hiraṇyakeśin, Mānava, and Kaṭha schools; the Sāmaveda has the Gobhila, Khādira, and Jaiminīya. To the Atharvaveda belongs the unique *Kauśika Sūtra*, which, in addition to the domestic ritual, deals with the magical and medicinal practices that specially belong to that Veda.

12. The Dharma Sūtras, or 'Law Books.'—The third class of Sūtras are the *Dharma Sūtras*, or 'Law Books.' They also deal to some extent with the customs of everyday life, but are engaged for the most part with secular and religious law. In one department of law, that of expiation, these Sūtras root in the Vedic hymns themselves. A considerable number of expiatory hymns and stanzas, clearly of the same stock as the law of expiation, are found in Vedic texts, especially the Atharvaveda and the *Taittirīya Āraṇyaka*. The Law Sūtras, in their turn also, are either directly attached to the body of canonical writings of a certain Vedic school or are shown by inner criteria to have originated within such a school. The oldest Law Sūtras are those of the Āpastamba and Baudhāyana, belonging to the Black Yajurveda schools of that name; the Gautama belonging to the Sāmaveda; the Viṣṇu belonging to the Kaṭha school of the Black Yajurveda; and the Vāsiṣṭha of less certain associations. The earliest metrical law-books, the so-called *Dharmaśāstras*, written in Classical Sanskrit, seem also to be based on lost Sūtra collections of definite Vedic schools. The most famous of these, the *Mānava Dharmaśāstra*, or 'Law Book of Manu' (see LAW [Hindu]), may be founded upon a lost *Dharma Sūtra* of the Mānava or Maitrāyaṇīya school of the Black Yajurveda, while the briefer 'Law Book of Yājñavalkya' is unmistakably connected with some school of the White Yajurveda.

English readers may obtain ready insight into the contents of Vedic literature in all its important aspects through the series of translations edited by Max Müller in *SBE* (Oxford, 1879 ff.). Parts of the Rigveda are translated by Müller himself (vol. xxxii.) and H. Oldenberg (vol. xlvi.); the Atharvaveda by M. Bloomfield (vol. xlii.); the *Śatapatha Brāhmaṇa* by J. Eggeling (vols. xii. xxvi. xli. xliii. and xliv.); seven of the *Gṛhya Sūtras* by Oldenberg (vols. xxix. and xxx.); the older *Dharma Sūtras* by G. Bühler and J. Jolly (vols. ii. vii. and xiv.); and the Law Book of Manu by Bühler (vol. xxv.).

13. Vedic and Sanskrit literature contrasted.—

The form and style of Sanskrit literature differ a good deal from those of the Vedas. As regards the language, it is to be noted that prose in Vedic times was developed to a tolerably high pitch in the Yajurvedas, Brāhmaṇas, and Upaniṣads; in Sanskrit, apart from the strained scientific language (*sūtra*) of philosophy or grammar, or the diffuse and inorganic style of the commentators, prose is rare. It presents itself in genuine literature only in fables, fairy tales, romances, and partly in the drama. Nor has this prose improved in literary and stylistic quality, as compared with the earlier variety. On the contrary, it has become more and more clumsy and hobbling, full of long awkward compounds, gerunds, constructions in the passive voice where the active would do, and other artificialities. As regards the poetic medium of Classical Sanskrit, it also differs from the Veda. The bulk of Sanskrit poetry, especially the Epic, is composed in the *śloka* metre, a development of the Vedic *anuṣṭubh* metre of four octosyllabic lines of essentially iambic cadence. But numerous other metres, usually built up on Vedic prototypes, have become steadily more elaborate and strict than their old originals; in the main they have also become more artistic and beautiful.

Notwithstanding the wonderfully unbroken continuity of Hindu writings, the spirit of Sanskrit literature also differs greatly from the Vedic. The chief distinction between the two periods is that the Veda is essentially a religious collection, whereas Sanskrit literature is, with rare exceptions, such as the *Bhagavad-Gītā*, or the metrical Law Śāstras, profane. In the Veda lyric poetry as well as legendary and expository prose are in the service of prayer and sacrifice; in Sanskrit epic, lyric, didactic, and dramatic forms are all for the purpose of literary delectation and æsthetic or moral instruction. In Sanskrit literature, moreover, with the exception of the grand compilations of the *Mahābhārata* and the *Purāṇas*, the authors are generally definite persons, more or less well-known, whereas the Vedic writings go back to families of poets or schools of religious learning, the individual authors being almost invariably submerged.

14. Epic literature.—Sanskrit literature may be divided into epic, lyric, dramatic, didactic, narrative, and scientific. In epic poetry there is the important distinction between the freer, narrative epic called *itihāsa* (*q.v.*), 'story,' or *purāṇa*, 'ancient legend,' and the artistic or artificial epic called *kāvya*, 'poetic product.' The great epic, the *Mahābhārata*, is by far the most important representative of the former kind. Of somewhat similar free style are the eighteen *Purāṇas* (see below), of much later date than the *Mahābhārata*. The beginnings of the artistic style are seen in the other great Hindu epic, the *Rāmāyaṇa*. But the finished style of the *kāvya* is not evolved until the time of Kālidāsa about the 6th cent. A.D.

The *Mahābhārata*, or 'Great Bhārata Story,' the greatest of Hindu epics, is a huge authorless compilation for which tradition has devised the name Vyāsa, 'Redaction,' as author. It is written for the most part in the epic metre, the *śloka*, and contains altogether about 100,000 stanzas of four lines each, about eight times the length of the Homeric poems.

The kernel story of the epic, which is interrupted by many episodes, or interwoven narratives, tells how the ancient and wicked dynasty of the Kurus was overthrown by the pious Pañchālas and Pāṇḍus. At a gambling-match depicted in the most vivid language, Duryodhana, the king of the Kurus, cheats the Pāṇḍu princes, robs them of their kingdom, and exiles them for thirteen years. But this is only the preparation for the final war, or eighteen days' battle, between the opposing royal houses and their allies. In this the Kurus are finally overthrown and destroyed. The heroic story is not only interrupted by episodes, but is in general made the pivot around which philosophical (religious) and ethical discussions of great length revolve. Thus the work has assumed the place in Hindu literature of an encyclopædia of moral and religious instruction.

A *Bhārata* and a *Mahābhārata* are mentioned as early as the 'House-Books' (see above) of the later Vedic literature, but all dates assigned to the original simpler epic which preceded the encyclopædic poems in its finished form are mere guesses, except that it obtained its essentially present form in the 4th or 5th cent. of our era.

Among the episodes of the *Mahābhārata*, the *Bhagavad-Gītā*, 'The Song of the Divine One,' or 'Song Celestial,' is pre-eminent. It is in some respects the most interesting and important book in post-Vedic literature.

When the rival armies of the Kurus and the Pāṇḍus are drawn up against each other, Arjuna, the leader of the Pāṇḍus, stoutest of heroes, hesitates to enter upon the slaughter. Then Kṛṣṇa, one of the incarnations of Viṣṇu, acting as Arjuna's charioteer, silences his scruples by pointing out that action, which is the performance of duty, is the obligation of man in the world, although, finally, abstracted devotion to the Supreme Spirit alone leads to salvation. The poem is conceived in the spirit of eclectic Hindu theosophy or philosophy. At the bottom is the Sāṅkhya doctrine of dual matter and spirit, but this is tinged with monistic Vedāntist pantheism (see BHAGAVAD-GĪTĀ).

It is not likely that the poem formed part of the original 'Bhārata Story,' but there is no information as to its date and authorship. The *Mahābhārata* has been translated into English prose at the expense of Pratāpa Chandra Rāy (Calcutta, 1895), and by M. N. Dutt (do. 1895).

15. The Rāmāyaṇa.—The *Rāmāyaṇa*, the second of the great epics, is in the main the work of a single author, Vālmīki. Though all parts are not from the same hand, and though it is not entirely free from digressions, it tells a connected story of great interest in epic diction of the highest order. It is to this day the favourite poem of the Hindus. The central figures are Rāma and his devoted wife Sītā; the main event the conquest of Laṅkā (probably Ceylon).

Daśaratha, the mighty king of Oudh (Ayodhyā), having grown old, decides upon Rāma, his oldest son, as his successor, but his intriguing second queen, Kaikeyī, succeeds in changing his mind in favour of her son Bharata. Rāma, banished for fourteen years, retires with Sītā to the forest. Upon the death of Daśaratha, his son Bharata refuses to usurp Rāma's throne, but seeks him out in the forest in order to conduct him back to the throne in his capital city. Rāma in turn refuses to cross his father's decision; he offers his gold-embroidered shoes as a token of his resignation of the throne. But Bharata, on returning, places the shoes upon the throne, and holds over them the yellow parasol, the sign of royalty; he himself stands by and acts as the king's plenipotentiary. In the meantime Rāma makes it his business to fight the demons who molest the ascetics of the forest in their holy practices. Rāvaṇa, the king of the demons, who lives in Laṅkā, revengefully kidnaps Sītā. Then Rāma forms an alliance with Hanuman and Sugrīva, the kings of the monkeys, who build for him a wonderful bridge across from the mainland to Laṅkā. Rāma slays Rāvaṇa, is reunited with Sītā, returns home, and, conjointly with Bharata, rules his happy people, so that the golden age has come again upon the earth.

The story, notwithstanding the fact that it presents itself outwardly as a heroic legend, lies under the suspicion of containing one or more mythic roots. Certainly in the Veda Sītā is the personified furrow of the field, the beautiful wife of Indra or Parjanya (see VEDIC RELIGION). Hence Rāma certainly continues the qualities of Indra, the slayer of demons. The story also seems to typify the advance of Brāhmanical civilization southward towards Ceylon.

The *Rāmāyaṇa* consists of seven books, in about 24,000 stanzas. It exists in three recensions, which differ one from the other in their readings, the order of the stanzas, and in having each more or less lengthy passages that are wanting in the others. The best known and most popular recension has been translated by the Anglo-Indian scholar R. T. H. Griffith in five volumes (Benares, 1870–75).

16. The Purāṇas.—Somewhat related in character to the great epics are the *Purāṇas*, eighteen in number. They are later poetic works of mixed cosmogonic, epic, and didactic character. The word *purāṇa* occurs frequently in the prose texts of the Veda as a designation of the Veda's own cosmogonic and legendary lore; the name is also applied to the *Mahābhārata*. In its most distinctive sense the word refers to a class of writings which certainly do not date before the 6th cent. A.D. The existing *Purāṇas* seem to be sectarian religious manuals for the people, written in the interest of either the worshippers of Viṣṇu or those of Śiva. Though the fundamental later Hindu triad—Brahmā, Viṣṇu, and Śiva—is recognized, nevertheless the Vaiṣṇavite *Kūrma Purāṇa* does not hesitate to say: 'Viṣṇu is the divinity of the gods, Śiva of the devils.' To Brahmā all alike refer only in a perfunctory fashion. According to ancient tradition, the ideal *Purāṇa* is divided into five parts: (1) primary creation, or cosmogony; (2) secondary creation, or the destruction and rebuilding of the worlds; (3) genealogy of the gods and patriarchs; (4) *manvantaras*, or periods of reigns of the Manu; (5) the history of the dynasties of kings. Though no extant *Purāṇa* is so divided, yet their subject-matter roughly follows that order. The entire type of composition is of secondary importance; it borrows its themes very largely from the epic literature, and represents religious belief, practices, and legends in an exaggerated, fantastic, often disordered fashion (see PURĀṆAS).

17. The 'artistic epics.'—The Hindus consider six *kāvyas*, or 'artistic epics,' entitled to the epithet 'great' (*mahā-kāvya*). But their artistic, or, better, artificial, character removes them in reality from the sphere of genuine epic; they are interesting on account of their wealth of descriptive power and delicacy of illustration; they are deficient in the portrayal of strong character or stirring action. Moreover, they are commingled more and more with lyric, erotic, and didactic elements, as well as with bombast and play on words. Nevertheless, no less a person than Kālidāsa, the universal poet and dramatist, is the author of the two best known artistic epics, the *Kumārasaṁbhava*, or 'Birth of the War God,' and the *Raghuvaṁśa*, or 'Race of Raghu.' The former consists of seventeen cantos, the first seven of which are devoted to the courtship and wedding of the deities Śiva and Pārvatī, the parents of the youthful god of war. The real theme of the poem appears only towards the end, in the account of the destruction of the demon Tāraka, the object for which the god of war was born. The *Raghuvaṁśa*, in nineteen cantos, describes in the first nine the life of Rāma, together with that of his dynasty. Then in the next six cantos comes the story of Rāma himself, the same theme as that of the *Rāmāyaṇa*. The remaining cantos deal with the twenty-four kings who ruled as Rāma's successors in Ayodhyā. The remaining *kāvyas* deal for the most part with themes from the *Mahābhārata* and *Rāmāyaṇa*.

18. Lyric poetry.—Every form of artistic Sanskrit literature, whether epic, dramatic, or confessedly lyric, has a strong lyric cast. At the bottom these three kinds, in the Hindu poet's hands, are but thematically differentiated forms of the same poetic endowment. Ornate figures of speech, luxuriant richness of colouring, carried into literary composition from the gorgeous climate, flora, and fauna of India, subtle detail-painting of every sensation and emotion—these are the common characteristics of Hindu artistic poetry. Lyric poetry can hardly do more than emphasize or specialize these conditions, yet it has its individual traits, the most important of which is the refined elaboration of the single strophe, in distinction from continuous composition. In form and name these strophes are infinitely elaborated and varied. In no other literature have poets endeavoured so strongly to harmonize the sentiment of a stanza with its metrical expression. The most elaborate continuous lyrics of India are the *Meghadūta*, or 'Cloud Messenger,' and the *Ṛtusaṁhāra*, or 'Cycle of Seasons,' both by Kālidāsa.

The theme of the former is a message sent by a *yakṣa*, or elf, exiled from heaven. The messenger is a passing cloud which shall report to the *yakṣa's* wife, as she tosses lovelorn upon her couch through the watches of the night, the longing of her exiled husband. May the cloud, after delivering his message, return with reassuring news, and never himself be separated from his lightning spouse. The 'Cycle of Seasons' is famous for its descriptions of India's tropical nature, matched all along with the corresponding human moods and emotions.

The bulk of lyrical poetry, however, is in single miniature stanzas, which suggest strongly the didactic sententious proverb poetry which the Hindus also cultivated with great success. In fact the most famous collection of such stanzas, that of Bhartṛhari, consists of lyric, didactic, and philosophic poems. Bhartṛhari, who lived in the 7th cent. A.D., is perhaps the most remarkable Hindu poet next to Kālidāsa.

His stanzas, 300 in number, are divided into three centuries—the 'Century of Love,' the 'Century of Wisdom,' and the 'Century of Resignation.' There is no action in these stanzas Ever and again, within the narrow frame of a single stanza, the poet pictures the world of him for whom the wide universe is summed up in woman, from whose glowing eyes there is no escape. But, after singing woman's praise in every key, he finally declares that he has become an altered man. Youth has gone by; his thoughts, freed from infatuation, are all for contemplation in the forest, and the whole world he accounts but as a wisp of straw.

The second master of the erotic stanza is Amaru, author of the *Amaruśataka*, or 'Century of Amaru.' He also is a master at depicting all the moods of love: bliss and dejection, anger and devotion. None of the Indian lyrists treats love from the romantic or ideal point of view; it is always sensuous love. But a certain delicacy of feeling and expression, as well as a sensitive appreciation of those qualities of love which attract irresistibly, only finally to repel, lifts their stanzas above the coarse or commonplace. It is Hindu 'minne-song,' flavoured with the universal, though rather theoretical, Hindu pessimism.

19. Didactic poetry.—Even in erotic lyrics the Hindu's deep-seated inclination towards speculation and reflexion is evident. This has not only been the basis of that which is best and highest in their religion and philosophy, but it has assumed shape in another important product of their literature, the gnomic, didactic, sententious stanza, which may be called the 'Proverb.' O. von Böhtlingk (*Ind. Sprüche*, Petrograd, 1870–73) collected from all Sanskrit literature some 8000 of these stanzas. They begin with the *Mahābhārata*, and are particularly common in the moral envoys of the fable literature. Their keynote is again the vanity of human life, and the superlative happiness that awaits resignation. The mental calm of the saintly anchorite who lives free from all desires in the stillness of the forest is the resolving chord of human unrest. But for him who remains in the world there is also a kind of salvation, namely, virtue. When a man dies and leaves all behind him, his good works alone accompany him on his journey into the next life (metempsychosis). Hence the practical value of virtue almost overrides the pessimistic view of the vanity of all human action. These gnomic stanzas are gathered up into collections such as the *Śānti-śataka*, or 'Century of Tranquillity,' or the *Moha-mudgara*, or 'Hammer of Folly'; but the ethical saw is really at home in the fables of the *Pañchatantra* and *Hitopadeśa*. These works are paralleled by Buddhist compositions (see below). In fact, a Buddhist collection of this sort, the *Dhammapada*, or 'Way of the Law,' contains perhaps the most beautiful and profound words of wisdom in all Hindu literature.

20. The drama.—The drama is one of the latest

yet one of the most interesting products of Sanskrit literature. With all the uncertainty of literary dates in India there is no good reason to assume for this class of works a date earlier than the 5th or 6th cent. of our era. Certain Vedic hymns in dialogue are all that the early periods of Hindu literature suggest as a possible partial, yet very doubtful, basis for the drama. The Sanskrit word for 'drama' is *nāṭaka*, from the root *naṭ*, *nart*, 'to dance' (whence '*nautch* girls,' etc.). The word therefore means literally 'ballet.' It is not doubtful that dances contributed something to the development of the drama. In various religious ceremonies of earlier times dancing played a part; at a later time the cult of Śiva and Viṣṇu, and especially of Śiva's incarnation Kṛṣṇa, was accompanied by pantomimic dances. These pantomimes reproduced the heroic deeds of these gods, and were accompanied by songs. Popular representations of this sort, the so-called *yātras*, have survived to the present day in Bengal. They are not unlike the mystery-play of the Christian Middle Ages, and their modern continuation, the passion-play. The god Kṛṣṇa and Rādhā, his love, are the main characters, but there are also friends, rivals, and enemies of Rādhā. The *yātras*, a mixture of music, dancing, song, and improvised dialogue, while unquestionably in some way connected with the origin of the drama, are nevertheless separated by a very wide gap from the finished product of the *nāṭaka* as it appears in such works as the *Śakuntalā* of Kālidāsa, or the *Mṛchchhakaṭikā*, 'Clay Cart,' of Śūdraka.

It is still a moot question whether Western (Greek) influence, particularly the New Attic Comedy of Menander (as reflected in Plautus and Terence), has not in some measure contributed to the shaping of the Hindu drama. It is known that Greek actors followed Alexander the Great through Asia, and that they celebrated his victories with dramatic performances. After the death of Alexander Greek kings continued to rule in North-Western India. Brisk commerce was carried on between the west coast of India and Alexandria, the later centre of Greek literary and artistic life. Greek art and Greek astronomy certainly exercised strong influence upon Hindu art and science. The chief points of resemblance between the Hindu drama and the Greek comedy are as follows. The Hindu drama is divided into acts (from one to ten), separated by varying periods of time; the acts proper are preceded by a prologue spoken by the stage manager (*sūtradhāra*). The stage was a simple rostrum, not shut off from the auditorium by a curtain, but, on the contrary, the curtain was in the background of the stage; it was called *yavanikā*—that is, 'Greek curtain' (ἰωνική). The characters of the Hindu drama resemble in some respects those of the Attic comedy. There are courtesans and parasites, braggarts and cunning servants. Especially the standard comic figure of the Hindu drama, the *vidūṣaka*, the unromantic friend of the hero, compares well with the go-between, the *servus currens*, of the Græco-Roman comedy. The *vidūṣaka* is a hunch-backed, bald dwarf of halting gait, the clown of the piece. Though a Brāhman by birth, with maliciously humorous intent, he does not speak Sanskrit, but the popular dialect, Prākrit, like the women and the inferior personages of the drama. He plays the unfeeling realist, intent upon every form of bodily comfort, especially a good dinner, to the hero's sentimental flowery romanticism. Although it is just possible that one or the other feature of the Hindu drama may be due to outside influence, the inner matter is certainly national and Indic. The themes are, for the most part, those of the heroic legend in the epics, or they move in the sphere of actually existing Hindu courts. The themes, at any rate, are not different from those of other Hindu literature. They show no foreign admixtures. It must not be forgotten that certain general coincidences between the drama and the theatre of different peoples are due to common psychological traits; hence genuine historical connexion in such matters requires the most exacting proof.

The chief dramatic writer is Kālidāsa, the incomparable Hindu poet, master at the same time of epic and lyric poetry (see above). Three dramas are ascribed to him: the *Śakuntalā*, the *Urvaśī*, and *Mālavikāgnimitra*, or 'Mālavikā and Agnimitra.' From a time somewhat earlier than Kālidāsa comes the drama *Mṛchchhakaṭikā*, the 'Clay Cart,' said to have been composed by king Śūdraka, who is praised ecstatically as its author in the prologue of the play. Similarly, during the 7th cent. A.D., a king named Harṣa is said to have composed three existing dramas: the *Ratnāvalī*, or 'String of Pearls'; the *Nāgānanda*, whose hero is a Buddhist, and whose prologue is in praise of Buddha; and the *Priyadarśikā*. From the 8th cent. A.D. date the dramas of Bhavabhūti, a South Indian poet, the most distinguished dramatist next to Kālidāsa and Śūdraka. His most celebrated compositions are the *Mālatīmādhava*, or 'Mālatī and Mādhava'; and the two dramas *Mahāvīracharita* and *Uttararāmacharita*, both of which deal with Rāma, the hero of the *Rāmāyaṇa*. Finally may be mentioned Viśākhadatta, the author of the *Mudrārākṣasa*, the 'Seal of the Minister Rākṣasa,' a drama of political intrigue, whose composition also dates from the 8th century.

'Action is the body of the drama'—such is the dictum of the Hindu theorists. Precisely what we should call dramatic action is not the prominent quality of the greatest dramatist of them all, Kālidāsa. His dramas are rather distinguished by tenderness of feeling and delicacy of touch. They are lyric rather than dramatic. The action is slow, the passions profound but not elemental. The deepest feelings are portrayed in delicate forms which never approach violence or coarseness, but, on the contrary, are over-nice. At the height of the situation, perhaps in profound misery, the hero and the heroine still find time to institute comparisons between their own feelings and the phenomena of nature. There is indeed a plethora in them all of mango-trees and *śirīṣa*-blossoms, of creepers and lotus, of *bimba*-lips, of gazelles, flamingoes, and multi-coloured parrots. But we must bear in mind the climate of India, and its almost frenzied flora and fauna; then this excess will seem less extravagant. Kālidāsa's dramas are always artistic and finished, and their beauty strongly suggests the genius of Goethe. The single Hindu drama which calls to mind a real modern drama is the 'Clay Cart,' ascribed to king Śūdraka, whose persons, diction, and action, more than those of any other Hindu play, remind one of Shakespeare (see DRAMA [Indian]).

21. Fables and stories. — No department of Hindu literature is more interesting to the student of comparative literature than that of the fables and fairy tales. There is scarcely a single motive of the European fable collections that does not appear in the Hindu collections. The study of the migrations and relations of fables and fairy tales was first elevated to the position of a science by Theodor Benfey in his work on the *Pañchatantra* (Leipzig, 1859). On the other hand, the proverbs and instructions which are woven into the fables present the best and most practical picture of Hindu ethics. The most important and extensive collection of fables and tales is Buddhistic, being written in Pāli. This collection is designated as the *Jātakas*, which seems to mean 'Birth Stories.' Buddha is made to appear in every one of them as the wise or successful person or animal of the fable; he himself points the moral (see JĀTAKA). The two most important Sanskrit collections are the *Pañchatantra* and the *Hitopadeśa*. The *Pañchatantra*, or 'Five Books,' the most celebrated Sanskrit book of this sort, existed at least as early as the first half of the 6th cent. A.D., since it was translated by order of king Khusrū Anūshirvān (531–579) into Pahlavi, the literary Persian language of that time. It thence passed into Arabic, Greek, Persian, Turkish, Syriac, Hebrew, Latin, and German; and from German into other European languages. The name 'Pañchatantra' is probably not original, but took the place of 'Karaṭaka and Damanaka,' or some similar title, derived from the names of the two jackals prominent in the first book. This may be surmised, because the title of the Syriac version is 'Kalīlag and Damnag,' of the Arabic version 'Kalīlah and Dimnah.' Both the *Pañchatantra* and the *Hitopadeśa*, or 'Salutary Instruction,' were originally intended as manuals for the instruction of kings in domestic and foreign policy. The *Hitopadeśa*, said to have been composed by Nārāyaṇa, states that it is an excerpt from the *Pañchatantra* and 'other books.'

The most famous collection of fairy tales is the very extensive *Kathāsaritsāgara*, or 'Ocean of Rivers of Stories,' composed by the Kashmirian poet Somadeva, about A.D. 1070. This is in verse; three much shorter collections are in prose. The *Śukasaptati*, or 'Seventy Stories of the Parrot,' tells how a wife whose husband is away, and who is inclined to solace herself with other men, is for seventy nights cleverly entertained and deterred by the story-telling parrot, until her husband returns. The *Vetāla-pañchaviṁśati*, or 'Twenty-five Tales of the Vampire,' is known to English readers under the name of 'Vikram and the Vampire.' The fourth collection is the *Siṁhāsana-dvātriṁśikā*, or 'Thirty-two Stories of the Lion-seat' (throne), in which the throne of king Vikrama tells the stories. A noteworthy feature of the Sanskrit collections of fairy tales, as well as of the fables, is the insertion of a number of different stories within the frame of a single narrative. This style was borrowed by other Oriental peoples, the most familiar instance being the *Arabian Nights*. A few prose romances of more independent character may be mentioned in this connexion. The *Daśakumāra-charita*, or 'Adventures of the Ten Princes,' a story of common life and a very corrupt society, reminds one of the *Simplicissimus* of Grimmelshausen. Its author is Daṇḍin, and it probably dates from the 6th cent. A.D. The *Vāsavadattā* by Subandhu, and the *Kādambarī* by Bāṇa, are highly artificial romances; the latter narrates, in stilted language and long compounds, the sentimental love-story of an ineffably noble prince and the equally ineffably beautiful and virtuous fairy princess Kādambarī. These works are known as *charita*, 'narrative'; the same name is also used for chronicles or quasi-historical literature of inferior grade. The nearest approach to history, in our sense of the word, is the *Rājataraṅgiṇī*, or the Chronicle of Kashmīr, by Kalhaṇa, from the middle of the 12th cent. A.D.

22. Scientific literature.—India abounds in all forms of scientific literature, written in tolerably good Sanskrit, even to the present day. One of the characteristics of the Hindu mind is that it never drew the line between literary creation and scientific presentation, so that it is not easy to mark off from one another *belles lettres* and scientific literature. The ancient legal books of the Veda (see above) continue in the more modern poetical

Dharmaśāstras and *Smṛtis*. Of these the Law Books of Manu and Yājñavalkya (see above) are the most famous examples; Manu specially enjoys great authority to this day. Rooted in the Upaniṣads are the *sūtras*, or rules, of the six systems of Hindu philosophy, and their abundant expositions. Grammar, etymology, lexicography, prosody, rhetoric, music, and architecture all own a technical literature of wide scope and importance, and the treatment of most of these shows a surprising tendency to assume metrical form. The earliest works of an etymological and phonetic character are the Vedic glosses of Yāska, the so-called *Naighaṇṭukas* and the *Nirukta*, and the *Prātiśākhyas*, or phonetic treatises pertaining to the treatment of a Vedic text in a given school or *śākhā* (see above). Later, but far more important, is the *Grammar* of Pāṇini, one of the greatest grammarians of all times, and his commentators Kātyāyana and Patañjali. Mathematics and astronomy were cultivated from very early times; the so-called Arabic numerals came to the Arabs from India, and were designated by them as Hindu numerals. Indian medical science must have begun to develop before the beginning of the Christian era, for one of its chief authors, Charaka, was the head physician of king Kaniṣka in the 1st cent. A.D. The germs of Hindu medical science reach back to the Atharvaveda. The Bower Manuscript, one of the oldest of Sanskrit manuscripts (probably 5th cent. A.D.), contains passages which agree verbally with the works of Suśruta and Charaka, the leading authorities on this subject.

LITERATURE.—The most convenient sketch for English readers is A. A. Macdonell's thoroughly competent *History of Sanskrit Literature*, one of the volumes of 'Short Histories of the Literatures of the World,' edited by Edmund Gosse (London, 1900). The bibliographical notes at the end of the book are a safe guide to more extensive study. Readable and popular in style is R. W. Frazer's *Literary History of India* (London, 1898). Max Müller's *History of Ancient Sanskrit Literature*[2] (London, 1860) deals only with the Vedic period, and was important in its day, but is now antiquated. A. Weber's *History of Indian Literature* (from the German by T. Zachariae, London, 1878) is a learned and technical work, not at all adapted to the wants of the general reader; it represents the state of knowledge of a quarter of a century ago. The German work of L. v. Schröder, *Indiens Literatur und Cultur* (Leipzig, 1887), contains a fuller, very instructive, and readable account of Hindu literature; copious translations and digests of the texts themselves render this work very helpful. The more recent treatises are H. Oldenberg, *Die Literatur des alten Indiens* (Stuttgart, 1903), and V. Henry, *Les Littératures de l'Inde* (Paris, 1904), both excellent treatises, having in view more particularly æsthetic valuation of Hindu literature. Still more recently there have appeared three parts of M. Winternitz's *Geschichte der indischen Litteratur* (Leipzig, 1908 ff.), a most satisfactory and instructive book. The *GIAP*, commenced under the editorship of G. Bühler, and continued after his death by F. Kielhorn and others (Strassburg, 1896 ff.), covers the entire domain of Indo-Aryan antiquity, and contains authoritative information concerning many points and problems of Sanskrit literature.

MAURICE BLOOMFIELD.

LITHUANIANS AND LETTS.—**1. Ethnography.**—The Lithuanians and the Letts belong to the Aryan family of peoples, and together with the Borussians or Old Prussians, who became extinct in the 17th cent., form a distinct ethnological group. This group, now generally called the 'Baltic,' had already ramified into its several divisions in its pre-historic period, and its unity is now seen only in certain common elements of popular tradition and in the sphere of language—as regards which, however, the Lithuanians exhibit a much more archaic type than the Letts. The original home of the Lithu-Lettish or Baltic race was probably the basin of the lower Niemen, and, as that district is virtually coterminous with the Lithuania of to-day, while the Letts are found in Courland, the adjacent Prussian littoral, the southern half of Livonia, and Polish Livonia in the government of Vitebsk, it would appear that the Lettish branch had reached its present location by migrating to the originally Finnish districts of Courland and Livonia, and that, on the other hand, the Lithuanians remained fast upon their ancestral soil.

Numerically, neither member of the group is of great account, nor is it likely that either was ever important. The Lithuanians number some one and a half million, about 120,000 of them being in Prussia; the Letts less rather than more—the estimates varying from 1,200,000 to 2,000,000. In a physical respect both branches are mixed, though the mixture has been in no way detrimental to them, since many individual Lithuanians and Letts still exhibit all the distinctive marks of pure Aryan descent, while the rest, men and women alike, are generally self-reliant and sympathetic, well-formed, and often even handsome.

2. Political history.—The historical fortunes of the two peoples have run in quite distinct courses. (*a*) *Lithuanian.*—The history of the Lithuanians opens in the 11th cent. with prolonged frontier wars with Russia, from which, however, they emerged so successfully, and with their integrity still so far complete, that one of their princes, Mendowg (recognized by Pope Innocent IV. as king of Lithuania), actually contemplated the founding of a united Lithu-Russian State. This design, however, was frustrated by Mendowg's death (1263) and by internal embroilments. Nevertheless, it was at length brought to realization by the government of the Grand-duke Gedymin († 1341); and then, under the leadership of his sons, Olgierd (whom his brothers recognized as sovereign Grand-duke) and Keistut, the young nation succeeded in extending its sway from the Baltic to the Euxine, and from the Polish Bug to the Ugra and the Oka, though it did not include the western districts (Nadrauen, Schalauen, and Sudauen), which the Teutonic Knights had brought under their control during the years 1274–83.

At the death of Olgierd, in 1377, his place was taken by his favourite son, Jagiello, who, however, soon quarrelled with Keistut († 1382) and with his son Witaut, the outcome of the dissension being that the latter became the real lord of Lithuania, although nominally the sovereignty of Jagiello was not thereby infringed. Jagiello had shortly before (1386) married Hedwig, queen of Poland, thus opening the way for a political alliance between Lithuania and Poland which seriously threatened the independence of the former. Witaut strained every nerve and took all available measures to avert this danger. Not only did he seek to promote the independence of his country in a political sense, but he also endeavoured, by working for a union between the Greek and Roman communions within its borders, to make it ecclesiastically self-dependent. While these endeavours proved to be in vain, they won him the confidence of the Utraquist Hussites in such measure that upon the death of King Wenceslaus they offered him the Bohemian crown, and it was only the unpropitious political conditions of the time that prevented his acceptance of it. He was now all the more ready to assume the crown of Lithuania, which, indeed, the Emperor Sigismund, with a view to the complete severance of that country from Poland, had thrice offered him already. Here, again, however, Witaut was disappointed, as Poland intercepted the passage of the party which was conveying the crown to him, and he died shortly afterwards (1430)—four years before Jagiello, who, as Queen Hedwig's consort, had at her death (1399) become king of Poland.

In the succeeding period the Lithuanians repeatedly took occasion to assert their independence in relation to Poland, but this did not prevent the principality of Olgierd from gradually becoming a Polish feudatory. Witaut himself had been repeatedly compelled by the necessities of war and by external troubles to make concessions to Poland, and his successors, under the increasing pressure of the steadily growing power and rapacity of Moscow, were forced in even larger measure to purchase the help of Poland by ever closer fusion with that State. These rulers, moreover, almost without exception bore the name of Jagiello, and united in their individual persons the Grand-dukedom of Lithuania and the crown of Poland. The eventual result was the incorporation of the two countries in a single political organism whose fortunes were controlled by a common Diet. The incorporating union was effected at the Diet of Lublin in 1569.

(*b*) *Lettish.*—At the very outset of Lettish history we find the merchants of Lübeck taking steps to find an outlet for their commerce in the district of the Lower Dvina, and they were followed by German missionaries, who there founded the earliest Christian settlements. While these attempts at colonization were not at once greatly successful, they had, nevertheless, the effect of making Livonia known to the West, and of directing against that heathen land the enthusiasm for war against unbelievers which in that period of the Crusades dominated the thought of Christendom. It was owing to this enthusiasm that Albert, canon of Bremen († 1229), was able to secure a permanent footing in Livonia (1200), and as its bishop—supported as he was by constant immigration from Germany and by the Livonian Order of the Sword (founded in 1202)—to establish there a German colonial State, which was recognized in 1207 as a frontier-district of the Empire. Its suzerainty was shared by Albert and the Order in such a way as to make the power of the bishop preponderant; but this position of matters was fundamentally altered when, in 1237, the Livonian Order was merged in the Order of the Teutonic Knights, the latter thus adding the domain of the former to its own. Taking as its model the Prussian State, in which it alone held the reins of sovereign authority—the bishops themselves being subordinate to it—the Teutonic Order sought to curb the episcopal power among the Letts, and it was all the more successful in this policy as it managed to subjugate the hitherto unconquered heathen districts. The process of subjugation, so far as the Lettish provinces, Livonia and Courland, were concerned, was virtually completed by 1290. The Order, nevertheless, did not thereby win repose, but had constantly to take the field against unfriendly neighbours, and, as the fortune of war was on the whole unfavourable to it, while its powers were sapped by internal dissensions, and the secularization of its Prussian territory in 1525 isolated its Livonian domain, its authority in the latter also was at length completely shattered. In 1562 Livonia became a Polish province, while Courland, as a hereditary feudal duchy of Poland, came into the power of the last Master of the Livonian part of the Order, Gotthard Kettler. Finally, both provinces became subject to Russia.

3. Ecclesiastical history.—Thus, while the Western Lithuanians and the Letts came under German control in the 13th cent., the whole of Eastern—now Russian—Lithuania was brought into close relations with Poland a century later, and accordingly, as was to be expected, the two divisions came to diverge widely from each other, not only as regards their language, but also in the moral, and most of all in the religious, sphere. Eastern Lithuania, which at the time of Keistut's death was almost entirely pagan, was thrown open to Christianity by Jagiello, who himself had embraced that faith at his marriage with Hedwig, and strove with all the zeal of a new convert to propagate it among his own people of Lithuania; they became more and more closely bound to Poland, and the Church of the Polish Court and the Polish State soon gained complete spiritual authority among them. In this way Russian Lithuania became a Roman Catholic country, and such, except to a very small extent, it has always remained; its non-catholic population consists only of a small number of Lutherans, who were won to that communion through efforts directed from Courland, and of some 40,000 adherents of the Reformed Confession, whose forefathers were induced to renounce Roman Catholicism under the influence of Prince Nicholas Czarny Radziwill. The ecclesiastical history of the Western Lithuanians and the Letts took a different course. As in the Prussian territory of the Teutonic Knights, which under the Grand-Master Margrave Albert of Brandenburg became a secular Protestant duchy in 1525, so in Livonia and Courland the Lutheran teaching was enthusiastically welcomed, and, in fact, won universal acceptance in both provinces. Most of the inhabitants remained faithful to it, so that Protestantism is to-day almost universal among the Letts. The only exceptions are found in localities where Roman Catholicism was able to gain a footing under the protection of Poland, or where proselytes have been won by the Russian State Church.

4. Early religion.—The religion which prevailed among the Lithuanians and Letts prior to the introduction of Christianity was a developed nature-cult. Besides the worship of woods and waters, of trees, stocks, and stones, of fire and household snakes, we find a belief in the personality of the heavenly bodies, especially the sun, as also in the existence of divine beings who control all created things. Pre-eminent among these divine beings was 'God,' designated by the primitive Aryan name *dĕwas* (Lat. *deus*). He was regarded generally as the highest supramundane power, but sometimes, like θεός in Homer, he was a distinct mythological figure, and as such probably identical with Perkúnas (Lett. Pérkohns), the thunder-god, who presided over the heavenly bodies, and was regarded as armed. An ancient folk-song tells that, when the moon was unfaithful to his wife, the sun, and became enamoured of the morning star, Perkúnas cut him in pieces with a sword. According to Lithuanian belief, Perkúnas's aunt washed the wearied and dust-covered sun, who was once called the daughter of God, and who herself had sons and daughters; in popular songs these play a great part as mystic powers, but are always represented as human in all respects. We hear frequently also of the 'children of God,' and it would seem that the mythological imagination did not distinguish between the latter and the 'children of the sun.' The sun, nevertheless, was not regarded as the wife of *dĕwas* (or of Perkúnas), as appears not only from what has been said, but also from a Lettish folk-song which tells how, when Perkúnas set out to find a wife beyond the sea, he was attended by the sun, bearing a dowry-chest. The Letts, again, believed that Perkúnas was a polygamist, and in another of their folk-songs he is said to have as many wives 'as the oak has leaves,' though none of them plays an independent part in the mythology.

We need have no hesitation in assuming that the ancient religion of the Lithuanians and of the Letts alike recognized the existence of other divine beings, and the way in which these are associated shows that they originated in the observation of nature and human life. But, with the exception of Láime, the goddess of fortune, none of them comes down to us under a common Lithu-Lettish name, and we must be the more cautious in connecting such beings with the ancient religion because many of the divine names of the Lithu-Lettish mythology rest upon the misconceptions or fabrications of later times. There is adequate evidence, however, for an early belief in a number of demonic beings, such as the *laumes* ('fairies') and the *pũkis* ('goblin,' 'flying dragon'), and it is equally certain that the Lithu-Lettish religion was dominated from primitive times by the conception of a devil (Lith. Wélnias; Lett. Welns). While that conception never became perfectly distinct, it nevertheless formed so definite an antithesis to the idea of 'God' that we cannot doubt the presence of a dualistic element in the Baltic cult.

Corresponding to the belief in demonic beings, superstition of a more general kind was, and still is, very prevalent. It manifests itself in a belief in witches (*rãgana*, 'seeress'), in the practice of casting lots (Lith. *bùrti*; Lett. *burt*), in notions regarding countless occurrences of daily life, and not least in the idea that the spirits of the dead (Lith. *wēlēs*; Lett. *welji*) continue to move about among the living—an idea that is undoubtedly very ancient, as it is attested not only by distinct historical evidence, but also by certain features in folk-song (as, *e.g.*, the notion that disembodied spirits marry), and, above all, by graves dating from heathen times, which often contain the remains of both rider and horse, and are furnished with weapons and implements, thus pointing conclusively to the belief that the dead continue to exist in a condition not unlike that of their earthly life. As the majority of these graves contain skeletons, not ashes, they likewise show that the Lithu-Lettish peoples believed in the resurrection of the body. As to the situation of the Lithu-Lettish abode of the dead, there seems to have been no general agreement, some data suggesting the sky, others a nether world. In various localities we find traces of a doctrine of metempsychosis.

Whether the cult had a special class of priests cannot be made out. It had certainly no temples in the proper sense, and the 'ædes sacræ' of which we hear should probably be regarded as slight erections in which fire was kept burning. Sacrifices were common, and were offered not only by way of petition and thanksgiving, but also as propitiations; to judge from the Lettish designation, *ſeedi* ('blossoms'), the offerings would seem to have consisted originally of flowers and fruits, but we have historical evidence that there were from the first other kinds of sacrificial gifts, while, if not among the Letts, yet among the Lithuanians and Borussians, we find traces even of the practice of human immolation.

5. Sociological features.—Our data regarding the political and social conditions, the prevailing sentiments and morals, of the ancient Lithuanians and Letts are not sufficient to enable us to give a full and clear account of their civilization. With varying degrees of certainty, however, we may make the following statements regarding their mode of life: they were efficient in war, and were divided into numerous clans or cantons governed by chieftains; they lived by tillage, cattle-rearing, and hunting, and practised all manner of handicraft and trading; they lived in separate homesteads, and their family life was of the patriarchal type; marriage was based upon the purchase and capture of brides, and, while the wife was subject to the husband, she held a place of high honour among her children; finally, both peoples had a remarkable liking for song, but did not possess the art of writing.

6. Literary development.—One result of the lack of writing is that the Lithuanians and Letts have absolutely no literary remains from heathen times. It was, in fact, only when the Christian Church began to make use of texts written in the native languages—long after the invention of printing—that literary documents were at length produced. A Lithuanian and a Lettish translation of the Lutheran Catechism—the former by Martin Mosvidius, subsequently a clergyman, and published in 1547, the latter by various clergymen belonging to Courland, in 1586—a Lithuanian version of a Roman Catholic catechism by a canon named Michael Daukša (1595), and a work translated by a protestant Lithuanian nobleman named Pitkiewicz (1598), are the earliest known writings in the Lithu-Lettish languages. Like most of this earlier literary work, the further development of Lithu-Lettish literature was long due to clergymen, and thus, naturally enough, that literature, even when it is not of a distinctively religious character, is in its earlier stages largely pervaded by Christian feeling and moral earnestness. Among the Letts the most outstanding figure of the earlier secular literature was Pastor G. F. Stender (1714–96); among the Lithuanians, Pastor Christian Donalitius (1714–80), the distinguished author of a poem entitled 'The Seasons.' As contrasted with this earlier stage, contemporary secular literature is entirely modern in its point of view, as it not only bears the impress of the social revolutions of last century, but is informed by the spirit of a national consciousness, and aims at the independence and enlightenment of the Lithuanian and Lettish peoples. This progressive movement, which proceeded at first but slowly, has within recent decades become very vigorous, and alike in the field of politics and in that of letters has produced great, if not always good, results. Not a little of the poetic production of Lithuanian and Lettish writers is well worth the attention of foreign readers. Yet even the best of it is not to be compared in poetic quality with the lyrical survivals of the earlier eras, falling far short of the beauty of many Lithuanian folk-songs (*dainos*), and also of the charm of the countless Lettish lyrics in quatrains (*dſeesmas*).

LITERATURE.—*Scriptores rerum prussicarum*, 5 vols., Leipzig, 1861–74; A. Guagnini, *Sarmatiæ Europeæ descriptio*, Speyer, 1581; A. Bezzenberger, *Litauische Forschungen*, Göttingen, 1882; A. Leskien and K. Brugmann, *Litauische Volkslieder und Märchen*, Strassburg, 1882; G. H. F. Nesselmann, *Litauische Volkslieder*, Berlin, 1853; A. Mierzyński, *Źródła mytologii litewskiej*, Warsaw, 1892–96; A. Bielenstein, *Tausend lettische Rätsel*, Mitau, 1881; K. Baron—H. Wissendorff, *Latwju dainas*, Petrograd, 1894 ff.; V. Andreyanov, *Lettische Volkslieder und Mythen*, Halle, 1896; A., E., and H. Bielenstein, *Stud. auf dem Gebiete der lettischen Archäologie, Ethnographie und Mythologie*, Riga, 1896; W. Mannhardt, 'Die lettischen Sonnenmythen,' in *ZE* vii. [1875]; M. Praetorius, *Deliciæ prussicæ, oder preussische Schaubühne*, ed. (in extracts) W. Pierson, Berlin, 1871; A. Bezzenberger, 'Litauische Literatur,' and E. Wolter, 'Lettische Literatur,' in *Kultur der Gegenwart*, i. 9, Leipzig, 1908; R. Trautmann, *Die altpreuss. Sprachdenkmäler*, Göttingen, 1910. A list of Lithu-Lettish deities, with reference to early literature, is given by F. Solmsen, in H. Usener, *Götternamen*, Bonn, 1896.

A. BEZZENBERGER.

LITTLE VEHICLE.—See HĪNAYĀNA.

LITURGIES.—See WORSHIP.

LOCKE.—

1. Chief dates in his life.—John Locke was born on 29th August 1632, at Wrington, Somersetshire. Brought up at home till the age of fourteen, he was then sent to Westminster school, from which he passed in 1652 to Christ Church, Oxford. He found little satisfaction in the scholastic kind of training then in vogue at Oxford, and, although, after his election to a Senior Studentship at Christ Church in 1659, he held lectureships in Greek and Rhetoric, his interests eventually turned more to scientific and medical studies. His connexion with medical practice happened in 1666 to bring him into contact with Lord Ashley, afterwards Earl of Shaftesbury, who figured so prominently in the politics of Charles II.'s reign; and the meeting had an important influence on Locke's life. In the following year Locke went to London to act in the double capacity of confidential adviser to Shaftesbury himself and tutor to his son, while he was also engaged in political work and held some appointments. Shaftesbury was dismissed from office in 1673, and in 1675 Locke had to go to France for his health. He remained abroad for four years, staying chiefly at Montpellier and Paris, but in 1679 returned to England to assist Shaftesbury once more. The two years that intervened before the statesman's fall and flight were stormy, and, though Locke had disapproved and probably kept clear of the final plots, he thought it prudent in 1683 to betake himself to Holland, nor did he return until the Revolution had made it safe to do so in 1689. The two years 1689–90 saw the publication of the great *Essay* and two others of his principal works, and thus constitute a sort of literary epoch in his life. From 1691 onwards he lived more in retirement, and chiefly in the family of Sir Francis Masham, at Oates, in Essex. He was in great favour with the new government, and for four years (1696–1700) held the well-paid appointment of a Commissioner of Trade. Failing health compelled his retirement from this office. His death took place at Oates on 28th October 1704.

2. Characteristics as a thinker and writer.—'Perhaps no philosopher since Aristotle has represented the spirit and opinions of an age so completely as Locke represents philosophy and all that depends upon philosophic thought, in the 18th cent.—especially in Britain and France' (A. C. Fraser, *Locke*, Preface). Locke's claim to be regarded as thus representative may be based alike on the variety of the subjects on which he wrote—philosophy, education, politics, religion—and on the aims and qualities of his thinking. In all directions he exhibits the merits and the defects which are attributed to the period. He is impatient of authority and of 'the jargon of the schools,' seeks to put aside preconceptions and see the truth of things clearly for himself, believes firmly that 'reason must be our last judge and guide in everything,' and desires sincerely to pursue truth only and for its own sake. On the other hand, he has no adequate knowledge or appreciation of the heritage of the past, accepts current assumptions, distinctions, and doctrines without seeing any need to test them, tends to bring 'reason' down to the level of reflective common sense, and is quite ready to acquiesce in a very humble estimate of its reach as a human faculty. Moreover, although Locke was so eminently representative and exercised an immense influence on European thought, he cannot be ranked very high as a philosophic thinker. His thinking, though patient, laborious, and candid, is fatally deficient in the two qualities of thoroughness and system. The deficiency is partly explained, no doubt, by his occupation with practical affairs, which interfered with continuous philosophical pursuits, and partly, too, by the directly practical aims of much of his writing; but this practicalness of his aims is itself characteristic. Locke's 'discontinued way of writing' goes also to explain his great fault as a writer—the endless repetitions with which he wearies his readers. In the 'Epistle to the Reader' with which he prefaced the *Essay*, he admits frankly that he has not been at great pains to correct the fault, and at times he certainly seems to let his pen run on almost as it pleases. But his faults are not unconnected with real virtues—his intentness upon expressing his whole thought fully and clearly, his desire to drive home his point and to gain the full assent of the reader. When he writes with any care, his plain style is as excellent as it is appropriate, and, when he is moved to earnestness, he writes with force and real impressiveness. His faults are seen at their worst in his controversial writings. Although he professes his eagerness to be shown his errors, he seems in point of fact to have been rather impatient of criticism. He is too much taken up with exposing the misunderstandings and misrepresentations of which his critics have been guilty to try to penetrate to the real motives of their criticisms. Hence his replies do not carry us much further, while even as polemics they have their defects. For, although Locke can be very effective both in direct retort and in irony, he is too apt to weaken his case, not merely by over-elaboration, but also by an insistence on the letter of his own and his critics' statements which the reader feels to be petty and unprofitable.

3. The 'Essay concerning Human Understanding' (1690).—In the prefatory 'Epistle to the Reader' Locke tells us how he was started upon the line of inquiry which resulted, after some twenty years of interrupted labour, in the publication of the *Essay*. He was discoursing with a few friends on a subject which he does not specify, but which we know from another source to have been 'the principles of morality and revealed religion' (see Fraser's ed. i. p. xvii). The baffling character of the difficulties which arose in the course of the discussion caused Locke to ask himself whether, before entering upon such subjects, it was not rather 'necessary to examine our own abilities, and see what objects our understandings were, or were not, fitted to deal with.' He took up the task of this examination, and found it expand far beyond his first expectations. The aim of his whole inquiry, however, remained the same throughout, viz. that determination of the certainty, extent, and degrees of human knowledge which is the theme of bk. iv. of the *Essay*, and to which all the rest of the work is subservient.

But before this theme could be dealt with effectively certain preliminary matters had to be cleared up. To know is to have ideas about things—this at least, whatever more. If, then, we are to arrive at right conclusions about the scope of knowledge, we had best begin by examining this medium in which alone it exists; *i.e.*, we had better try to take stock of our ideas,[1] and see how we come by them. To Locke it was plain that we come by them only through experience. To convince the reader that our knowledge and our ideas have no other source, Locke devotes bk. i. of the *Essay* to showing that there are no 'innate' principles or ideas, unless we understand the term 'innate' in some sense which makes the assertion of such innate knowledge either insignificant or misleading. If there are no such innate ideas, then we must look to experience and experience only for the origin of all our ideas, and must try to trace them back, one and all, to their source therein. It is easy to underestimate the importance of Locke's teaching on this point, but it really constitutes one of his claims to be regarded as the founder of modern psychology.

Yet it was hardly as a psychologist that Locke himself was interested in the source and origin of our ideas; it was rather because he thought that, by seeing how, and at what point, our ideas emerge or are formed in the course of experience, we should be better able to measure the knowledge which we get by means of them. We should know, in short, what the actual experience is from which the ideas are derived, and on which, therefore, the knowledge which we have by means of the ideas is based. The results of Locke's stocktaking of our ideas in bk. ii. can be here only summarized.

He finds that all our ideas may be traced back to two great sources: sensation, which gives us the ideas involved in our knowledge of the external world, and 'reflexion,' which is the perception of the operations of our own mind, and which gives us ideas such as those of reasoning, believing, willing. The ideas derived from (one or both of) these sources may be either simple—such as the ideas of yellow, thinking, pleasure, unity—or complex. The complex ideas are subdivided (ii. ch. xii.) into ideas of modes, substances, and relations. By 'modes' are meant 'such complex ideas which, however compounded, contain not in them the supposition of subsisting by themselves, but are considered as dependences on, or affections of substances: such as are the ideas signified by the words triangle, gratitude, murder.' They may be either simple (=unmixed) or mixed, according as they are merely variations or combinations of one simple idea, or, on the other hand, involve different simple ideas; *e.g.*, the different numbers are simple modes of number or unity, whereas ideas like gratitude and murder are mixed modes. Under the above heads Locke proceeds to survey and examine the most important ideas or classes of ideas that enter into our knowledge. The classification is open to criticism in various ways, but where it principally fails Locke is in dealing with the more abstract and general categories, such as existence, power, unity, substance. The first three of these are said in ch. vii. to be simple ideas derived both from sensation and from reflexion. But it is obvious that they are not really comparable with simple ideas like yellow or hot; they are not sensible qualities. Locke himself speaks of the ideas of existence and unity as 'suggested to' the understanding by objects, and in ch. xxi. the idea of power seems to be reached by a process in which inference, as well as direct experience, plays a part. The general idea of substance seems in like manner to be a result of inference, if we are to give that name to a process and a result which Locke describes in terms so halting and dubious that it is not surprising that his critic Stillingfleet took offence at them. The mind, we are told (ch. xxiii. § 1 f.), takes notice that its simple ideas go constantly together in groups (the qualities that make up a single thing), and, 'not imagining how these simple ideas can subsist by themselves, we accustom ourselves to suppose some substratum wherein they do subsist, and from which they do result; which therefore we call substance. So that if any one will examine himself concerning his notion of substance in general, he will find he has no other idea of it at all, but only a supposition of he knows not what support of such qualities, which are capable of producing simple ideas in us.'

It was the ambiguous position of ideas like power and substance that gave an opening for Hume's sceptical criticism. Throughout the long analysis of ideas which occupies bk. ii. the modern reader, accustomed to a more precise demarcation of the provinces of logic, psychology, and metaphysics, is perplexed by the difficulty of giving any one consistent interpretation of Locke's procedure. The analysis is not simply a logical dissection of ideas into their simplest constituents. Yet it is too much influenced by the point of view of logical analysis to be a truly genetic or psychological account of the growth of our ideas. Finally, both interests are crossed by the further interest in the knowledge-value of our ideas, though the last point of view takes us over to the theme of bk. iv. Thus the discussion of primary and secondary qualities in ch. viii., and the discussions of power, substance, and identity in the chapters so named, are as definitely concerned with the knowledge-value of our ideas, and with the nature of the realities known by means of them, as any part of bk. iv.

In bk. iii. ('Of Words') Locke applies his analysis of ideas to the interpretation of the words by which we express them. The most striking feature of the book is the way in which the distinction of real and nominal essence is applied to the names which signify mixed modes (*e.g.*, moral ideas) and substances respectively. When we define man as a rational animal, we lay down a certain abstract idea, or combination of abstract ideas, by reference to which our application of the term 'man' is determined. This abstract idea is the 'nominal essence' of

[1] The term 'idea' is used by Locke in a very wide sense 'for whatsoever is the object of the understanding when a man thinks.' The equivalent in modern psychology is a term like J. Ward's 'presentation.'

man. The nominal essence, then, is for Locke nothing more than the statement of the meaning in which we intend to use the general name, whereas the 'real essence' of a thing is the real being or inner constitution of the thing itself. Now in Locke's view the ideas of mixed modes are ideas which we ourselves frame or put together at our own discretion. Therefore, so far as they are concerned, nominal and real essence coincide, and there is nothing, unless the complexity or vagueness of the ideas in question, to prevent us from stating their essence exactly and completely. But in the case of substances we are dealing with things which have a real essence, and, since in Locke's view their real essence is not known to us, we have in their case no guarantee that the distinctions which we draw by means of our abstract ideas or nominal essences will truly represent the real lines of division among the things themselves. In fact, by introducing the notion of essence at all we are assuming that there is a real division of things into species, and this assumption is liable at any point to turn out untrue. The lines of division which we suppose to exist may be found to break down. Hence Locke concludes that in the case of substances our general names express merely the nominal essence. 'The boundaries of species are made by men,' though, of course, we are guided in making them by those superficial resemblances among things which nature presents to our view.

In bk. iv. we come at last to those conclusions regarding the nature and extent of knowledge—or, where knowledge fails, of probability or probable judgment—to which the rest of the work had been subsidiary. Knowledge is defined by Locke as 'the perception of the connexion of and agreement, or disagreement and repugnancy of any of our ideas.' And of such agreement and disagreement he distinguishes four sorts: (1) identity or diversity (*e.g.*, 'blue is different from yellow'), (2) relation (*e.g.*, geometrical equality), (3) co-existence (of attributes in a subject or substance), and (4) real existence 'agreeing to any idea' (*e.g.*, 'God is'). Further, our knowledge of the agreement and disagreement of our ideas has different degrees of evidence. It may be (*a*) immediate or intuitive—and all certainty goes back to such intuition—or (*b*) demonstrative, *i.e.* reached by a series of steps, and therefore in Locke's view not quite so clear as immediate intuition, even though each step has, or ought to have, intuitive evidence. Lastly (*c*), there is 'sensitive knowledge,' our knowledge of the particular existence of external things when they are actually affecting our senses. The last degree of knowledge Locke regards as inferior to the other two, though not open to serious doubt. Whatever falls short of these degrees of evidence is matter, not of knowledge, but at the most of probability. From these preliminary determinations Locke proceeds to a series of discussions in which three problems are intertwined in a way that is rather confusing to the reader: (1) the problem how far we can have knowledge which is real in the sense of being authentic or valid, and not a mere imagination, (2) the problem how far this real knowledge is also general or universal, (3) the problem how far knowledge which is real in the first sense is also real in the further sense of being a knowledge of real existence, *i.e.* a knowledge of things which have a substantive existence or reality. The clue to Locke's answer to all three problems lies in the sharp opposition which he makes between our knowledge, *e.g.*, of mixed modes, where we are dealing with (complex) ideas which are 'archetypes of the mind's own making,' and our knowledge of substances and of real existence, where our ideas refer to archetypes beyond themselves. In the former case our knowledge (of relations among our ideas) can be at once real (in the first sense) and general, because it makes no further claim to be a knowledge of real existence (of things) or co-existence (of attributes in things). In the latter case our knowledge makes this further claim, and is therefore far more restricted. Our knowledge of the properties of a triangle or of the wrongness of murder is real and general, even though no perfect triangle could be drawn or no murder had ever been committed. But our knowledge of real existence and co-existence can never be thus general. As regards real existence, we have, according to Locke, an intuitive knowledge of our own existence, a demonstrative knowledge of God's existence, and a sensitive knowledge of that of external things. But it is to be observed that this knowledge is a knowledge of existence and not of substance, for on Locke's view we do not know the inner nature either of spiritual or of material substance. In fact, he offended his orthodox readers by suggesting that, while we may believe, we cannot know, that the soul (of man) is immaterial. The inner nature (or real essence) of material bodies he assumes to consist in a certain atomic constitution; and, since he regards this as inaccessible to our knowledge, he denies the possibility of physical 'science,' in the strict sense of the term 'science.' Such 'knowledge' as we have of material bodies is only of the co-existence of their superficial properties, and does not go beyond probability, though it may be extended and improved by experiment.

The subsequent development of philosophy and science has made many of Locke's positions seem strange to us. Our confidence in physical science is far greater, our reliance on abstract demonstrations of 'the existence of a God' far less than his. Above all, we have to be more careful about the relation of 'ideas' to real existence and less ready to separate and unite them alternately as suits our convenience. The weaknesses of Locke's compromise between common sense and philosophy have been made so abundantly evident by later criticism that it is hard to be fair to his real merits. And yet it is to the suggestiveness of his treatment of the problems of knowledge that later criticism owes the advance that it has made on his positions.

4. Ethics and politics.—Locke's contributions to ethics are scanty and of little value, unless we credit to ethics the discussion of free will contained in the chapter on power (bk. ii. ch. xxi.). Certainly this discussion, in spite of the perplexities which Locke candidly reveals to the reader, is full of interest and instruction alike for the moralist and for the psychologist. But in ethics proper his notion that morality is no less capable of demonstration than mathematics is an eccentricity, which can be explained only by his theoretical views about our knowledge of mixed modes. It certainly matches ill with his doctrine of moral obligation, which recognizes no higher motives than those of pleasure and pain, reward and punishment.

Nowhere are the features of Locke's thought displayed more characteristically than in his political doctrine. Published early in 1690, the *Two Treatises of Government* had a direct reference to current politics. The first was a refutation of Filmer's plea for the unlimited (paternal or hereditary) right of kings, the second a defence of the Revolution. Concerned only about the right of the people to resist oppressive and arbitrary rule, Locke is more than usually careless about thoroughness and system. He accepts with easy credulity the literal truth of a social compact, with the subsidiary doctrines of a state of nature, natural rights of the individual, and tacit consent of the individual to submit to the established government. In one and the same sentence (bk. ii. ch. xiii. § 149) he tells us that in a constituted commonwealth 'there can be but one supreme power, which is the legislative,' yet that 'the legislative being only a fiduciary power to act for certain ends, there remains still in the people a supreme power to remove or alter the legislative, when they find the legislative act contrary to the trust reposed in them.' He tells us (xi. § 134) that the legislative is 'sacred and unalterable in the hands where the community have once placed it,' yet admits that, as a result of historical changes, the legislative may cease to be representative and may therefore stand in urgent need of reform (xiii. § 157). And then, to complete the reader's confusion, he assigns the task of reforming the legislative to that royal prerogative whose arbitrary exercise he elsewhere denounces. In view of such incoherences we must be content to take Locke's treatise primarily as a pamphlet for his own time; it has at all events more historical than theoretical importance.

5. Toleration.—Locke's writings upon toleration serve as a link between his political and his religious doctrines. In 1689 he published in Holland a Latin *Epistola de Tolerantia*, which was translated into English in the same year. Criticisms (attributed to one Jonas Proast of Queen's College, Oxford) drew from Locke *A Second Letter concerning Toleration* and *A Third Letter for Toleration* in 1690 and 1692 respectively, and twelve years later he had even begun a fourth, of which, however, only a fragment was written. The original letter is a businesslike piece of argument, the second is longer, the third is very long and very tedious. Locke can see nothing at all in his critic's arguments, and it must indeed be admitted that the position which the critic had chosen to defend was anything but strong—viz. that, in the case of those who will not embrace the true religion, the magistrate ought to employ force, in the shape of moderate penalties, to compel them to consider the error of their ways. Against this position Locke shows again and again that compulsion can produce only outward conformity, not inward conviction, that what was punished was therefore really dissent and not 'want of consideration,' that any end which justified moderate penalties would equally justify the severest persecution where moderate penalties failed, that 'the true religion' must for practical purposes mean the magistrate's own religion, and that the arguments by which the critic sought to escape from these conclusions were either circular or question-begging. The practical force of Locke's argument lies in this, that the sincerity of religious dissent makes compulsion futile, while the actual divisions among Christian sects make it presumptuous. Philosophically these considerations were reinforced and explained by his view that in matters of religion there is no certain (or demonstrative) knowledge, and that we must be content with 'a persuasion of our own minds, short of knowledge' (*Works*[11], vi. 144). But he had also laid down clearly in the first letter the religious ground that it is 'in the inward and full persuasion of the mind' that 'all the life and power of true religion consists' (p. 11). 'I cannot be saved by a religion that I distrust, and by a worship that I abhor' (p. 28).

It can hardly be said, however, that the constructive argument of the original letter is in itself satisfactory. It is based on Locke's narrow conception of the State as concerned with little but the security of life and property, and as limited in its functions by the supposed consent of the individual. His argument is qualified, too, in ways which make its consistency doubtful. Thus it refuses toleration to atheists, because 'promises, covenants, and oaths, which are the bonds of human society, can have no hold upon an atheist' (p. 47), and, in effect, to Roman Catholics, because their religion requires them to submit themselves to a 'foreign jurisdiction' (p. 46). And this refusal does not square very well with that '*absolute liberty, . . . equal and impartial liberty*,' which, the reader was assured at the outset, '*is the thing that we stand in need of*.' Locke wants to separate sharply and completely the spheres of the civil power and the Church. As he denies to the magistrate any right to prescribe articles of faith or forms of worship, so he condemns those who 'upon pretence of religion' arrogate to themselves any peculiar authority in civil concernments: 'I say these have no right to be tolerated by the magistrate' (p. 46). But it seems strange that, with the recent history of his own country in view, he should not have recognized that an assertion of authority in civil concernments was almost certain to be made by the dominant religious sect, whatever it might be. The magistrate who was not to tolerate such ecclesiastical pretensions would hardly be able to avoid meddling in matters of religion. Nor was it to be expected that any religious sect, whether Catholic or Puritan, which was firmly convinced that it alone taught the true way of life and that its rivals were spreading pernicious errors would quietly acquiesce in its exclusion from the use and the control of the civil power. As in other cases, so here, Locke's argument makes a great show of robust common sense, but does not go very deep, and involves large tacit assumptions.

6. Religion.—One of these assumptions, no doubt, was that latitudinarianism of his own religious views which found expression later in his *Reasonableness of Christianity* (1695). In that work he seeks to show, by a great array of Scriptural evidence, that the one and only gospel-article of faith is this, that Jesus is the Messiah, the promised Saviour. To believe this, to repent of our sins, to endeavour after a sincere obedience to the Saviour's commandments—these and these only are the conditions required to make any one a Christian, these and these only are the true 'fundamentals' of the Christian religion, viz. those 'which are to be found in the preaching of our Saviour and his apostles.' Locke anticipates the objection that belief, on the strength of reported miracles, in the statement that Jesus is the promised Messiah is merely a historical, and not a saving, faith; but it can hardly be said that he sees the real force of the objection. He speaks, it is true, of the 'oblation of a heart, fixed with dependence on, and affection to God' as 'the foundation of true devotion, and life of all religion,' and describes faith as 'a stedfast reliance on the goodness and faithfulness of God' (*Works*[11], vii. 129, 131), but he does not explain sufficiently how this religious faith arises out of the historical belief. He insists on the inability of plain people, 'the day-labourers and tradesmen, the spinsters and dairy-maids,' to follow abstract reasonings, and on the consequent necessity for an authoritative religion and morality. 'The greatest part cannot know, and therefore they must believe' (p. 146). But whether such an appeal to authority would find its most natural satisfaction in Locke's simplified Christianity, or is even quite consistent with it, is not so clear. Among other advantages of an authoritative revelation he speaks of the support which it affords to morality, and he leaves us in no doubt as to the kind of support he has in view.

> 'The philosophers, indeed, showed the beauty of virtue; they set her off so, as drew men's eyes and approbation to her; but leaving her unendowed, very few were willing to espouse her. The generality could not refuse her their esteem and commendation; but still turned their backs on her, and forsook her, as a match not for their turn. But now there being put into the scales on her side "an exceeding and immortal weight of glory"; interest is come about to her, and virtue now is visibly the most enriching purchase, and by much the best bargain' (p. 150).

It has to be remembered, however, that appeals to self-interest—'the favourite passion,' as Butler calls it—were characteristic of the age.

7. Education.—Locke's views on this subject are contained in his *Thoughts concerning Education* (1693) and the posthumous *Conduct of the Understanding*. The latter connects directly with the *Essay*, and was originally designed to form a chapter of it. It has been highly praised, but, like other writings on the general education of the intellect, seems often to be elaborating truths of a somewhat obvious kind. Perhaps its main value, after all, lies in the ample illustration which it affords of Locke's own intellectual attitude and temper of mind. The other work makes a much more definite contribution to the art of education. The limited and practical aim of the *Thoughts* is emphasized by Locke himself, viz. to set forth 'how a young Gentleman should be brought up from his infancy.' As a medical man he does not disdain to give detailed advice as to bodily health and training. The characteristic feature, however —and the conspicuous merit—of the book is the paramount importance which it gives to the training of character.

'That which every Gentleman . . . desires for his Son, besides the Estate he leaves him, is contained (I suppose) in these four Things, Virtue, Wisdom, Breeding, and Learning' (§ 134).

The order expresses Locke's deliberate estimate of the relative importance of the qualities named, and this estimate governs his treatment of the subject consistently throughout the book. No reader of the *Thoughts* is likely ever to confuse education with instruction. So, too, in the case of intellectual education itself, Locke insists, in his *Conduct of the Understanding*, that the business of education 'in respect of knowledge, is not, as I think, to perfect a learner in all or any one of the sciences, but to give his mind that freedom, that disposition, and those habits, that may enable him to attain any part of knowledge he shall apply himself to' (§ 12). A writer who goes carefully into details must, of course, expose himself to criticism. Locke's advice as to bodily training is in some points certainly not such as medical authority would now approve, and some of his views on moral training are at any rate open to question. But there can be little question about this, that Locke is at his best in dealing with such matters. His fresh and independent view of his subject, his steady insistence on character as all-important, his own kindliness and affection for young people, and his practical common sense combine to make him an admirable exponent of the spirit in which the educator should go about his work.

LITERATURE.—The best ed. of Locke's works is, according to A. C. Fraser, that of E. Law, 4 vols., London, 1777. The references in the art. are to *Works*[11], 10 vols., do. 1812. The *Essay* has been edited by Fraser, 2 vols., Oxford, 1894. The chief *Life* is that of H. R. Fox Bourne, 2 vols., London, 1876. There are short accounts of Locke's life and philosophy by Fraser, Edinburgh, 1890, T. Fowler, London, 1880, and S. Alexander, do. 1908; and E. Fechtner's *John Locke: ein Bild aus den geistigen Kämpfen Englands im 17ten Jahrhundert*, Stuttgart, 1898, is a work of similar character. In addition to the histories of philosophy, the chapters on Locke in the following works may be referred to: R. Adamson, *The Development of Modern Philosophy*, Edinburgh, 1903, i.; Leslie Stephen, *Hist. of English Thought in the 18th Century*[3], London, 1902, both vols.; *The Cambridge History of English Literature*, Cambridge, 1907-12, viii. ch. xiv. (W. R. Sorley). Of more special works those of G. von Hertling (*John Locke und die Schule von Cambridge*, Freiburg, 1892), G. Geil (*Über die Abhängigkeit Locke's von Descartes*, Strassburg, 1887), and R. Sommer (*Locke's Verhältnis zu Descartes*, Berlin, 1887) deal with the difficult question of Locke's relation to his predecessors; that of E. Martinak (*Die Logik John Locke's*, Halle, 1894) with the philosophy proper.

H. BARKER.

LOCKS AND KEYS.

LOCKS AND KEYS.—Before the invention of bolts or, later, of locks and keys, a variety of devices were in use to secure safety. Many peoples at a low level of culture live in shelters or huts, one or more sides of which are quite open (Tasmanians, Seminoles, Indians of Guiana, etc.), and others live in a house only for occasional purposes—sleeping, birth, sickness, death, etc.[1]—so that there is no need of a fastening. But in other instances, even where no doors exist, attempts are made to render the entrance secure. The huts of the Eskimos are approached by a narrow winding passage along which one must creep on all fours. Kumi villages are stockaded, and the door is approached by a winding passage trebly stockaded.[1] In Fiji, the Caroline Islands, Kiwai Island, among the Indians of the Chaco and of Guiana, and in various parts of Africa the doorway is made very low or very narrow, or is merely a small aperture at some height from the ground (cf. Pr 17[19]).[2]

Sometimes the doorway is closed merely with a couple of large plantain leaves or palm leaves plaited into basket work, or with a branch of a coco-nut (Solomon Islands, Roro-speaking tribes of N. Guinea),[3] or with a *portière* (ancient Peru),[4] or with a kind of blind or mat which can be raised or lowered as desired (Uaupes, Samoa, Tonga, Tlascala, New Mexico).[5] To this might be fastened pieces of metal or shell which clattered and so gave warning when any one entered (Tlascala), or, as in New Britain, a rattle was hung in the doorway, so that any one entering at night might strike his head against it and warn the inmates.[6] In Benin, where locks were known (§ 1), a cord running through a staple, and attached to a block of wood, served to keep the door closed.[7] Or, again, a wooden screen is slid across the entrance—a kind of primitive door (Cross River, Kitimbiriu, ancient Mexico, Efik and Ekoi, Bageshu).[8] This is secured by thongs (Baganda, Melanesia [but the tying can be done from without through an opening made for the purpose]),[9] by props or a wedge (African tribes, Zuñis [stone slabs held in position by props]),[10] or by bars (Mexico, Upper Congo, Grebos, Dayaks, wild Malay tribes, Zuñis).[11] In some instances such doorways or doors are further protected by charms or fetishes which will work evil on any one trying to enter. These are analogous to the protectives placed at a keyhole to prevent fairies, spirits, etc., from entering through them (§ 3 (*c*)).[12] As knotted strings or thongs served for tents, so they were also sometimes used to fasten doors. In Babylonia and Egypt seals sometimes served the purpose of locks and keys, but bolts were also used, and over those of the temple of Šamaš in Babylonia libations of oil were poured as well as over other parts of the door

1 E. Casalis, *Les Bassoutos*, Paris, 1859, p. 132.

1 T. H. Lewin, *Wild Races of S.E. India*, London, 1870, p. 222.

2 T. Williams, *Fiji and the Fijians*, London, 1858, i. 82; F. W. Christian, *The Caroline Islands*, do. 1899, p. 140; J. Chalmers, *JAI* xxxiii. [1903] 118; E. Nordenskiöld, *Indianerleben*, Leipzig, 1912, p. 40; H. M. Stanley, *Through the Dark Continent*, London, 1878, ii. 134 [Uregga]; E. Holub, *Seven Years in S. Africa*, do. 1881, i. 97 [Koranna]; E. F. Im Thurn, *Among the Indians of Guiana*, do. 1883, p. 206.

3 H. B. Guppy, *The Solomon Islands and their Natives*, London, 1887, p. 59; C. G. Seligmann, *The Melanesians of British New Guinea*, Cambridge, 1910, p. 198.

4 H. Beuchat, *Manuel d'arch. américaine*, Paris, 1912, p. 638.

5 A. R. Wallace, *Travels on the Amazon and the Rio Negro*, London, 1853, p. 491; G. Turner, *Nineteen Years in Polynesia*, do. 1861, p. 256; W. Ellis, *Polynes. Researches*[2], do. 1832, i. 176; W. Mariner, *Account of the Natives of the Tonga Islands*[3], do. 1818, ii. 267; Waitz-Gerland, *Anthrop. der Naturvölker*, iv. [Leipzig, 1864] 94; *NR* i. 486.

6 Beuchat, p. 638; G. Brown, *Melanesians and Polynesians*, London, 1910, p. 24.

7 H. Ling Roth, *Great Benin*, London, 1903, p. 189.

8 C. Partridge, *Cross River Natives*, London, 1905, p. 176; H. H. Johnston, *Kilima-Njaro Expedition*, do. 1886, p. 140; *NR* ii. 573; J. Parkinson, *JRAI* xxxvii. [1907] 262; J. Roscoe, *JRAI* xxxix. [1909] 194.

9 J. Roscoe, *The Baganda*, London, 1911, pp. 368, 375; R. H. Codrington, *The Melanesians*, Oxford, 1891, p. 298.

10 E. Gottschling, *JAI* xxxv. [1905] 369 [Bawenda]; E. Torday and T. A. Joyce, *ib.* 407 [Ba-Mbala], xxxvi. [1906] 43 [Ba-Yaka]; J. Roscoe, *JRAI* xxxix. 194 [Bageshu]; *23 RBEW* [1904], p. 350.

11 *NR* ii. 573; J. H. Weeks, *JRAI* xxxix. 110; H. H. Johnston, *Liberia*, London, 1906, ii. 1006–08; S. St. John, *Forests of the Far East*, do. 1862, ii. 10; N. Annandale and H. C. Robinson, *Fasciculi Malayenses*, do. 1903–06, p. 45; *8 RBEW* [1891], p. 183; *16 RBEW* [1897], p. 164 f.

12 Partridge, *op. cit.* p. 176; A. Werner, *Nat. of Brit. Cent. Africa*, London, 1906, p. 80 f.; H. A. Junod, *Life of a S. Afr. Tribe*, Neuchâtel, 1913, p. 446; Torday and Joyce, *JAI* xxxv. 407; P. Sébillot, *Le Folk-lore de France*, Paris, 1904–07, i. 142.

(cf. § 3 (*d*)). A conqueror in Egypt sealed the doors of the temple of Rā after having bolted them.[1]

1. Primitive locks and keys.—In some of the instances cited above a bar set against the movable door from within and held in place by various means is found. Doors and gates swinging on hinges were also held with bars of wood, bronze, or iron, set across from one doorpost to the other, the ends being set in holes in these (Dt 3[5], Neh 7[3], Is 45[2], Jg 16[3]), or with bars and bolts (Neh 3[3], Babylonia, Egypt). In Homer, *Il.* xii. 455 ff., two bars are pushed out from square holes in the doorposts and meet in dovetailed fashion in the centre. A bolt or wedge keeps them in position. The primitive bolt, at first of wood, then of metal, slid into a staple on the doorpost.[2] Where folding doors were used, probably a vertical bolt above or below held one leaf, and a horizontal bolt fixed both in the centre. The bolt might be shot backwards or forwards by means of a cord from outside, secured to a catch by a series of knots. Or such a cord might lift a latch, the bar of which turned on a wooden pin.[3] Before the use of locks and keys a simple method of sliding a bolt was used in Greece as well as in central and northern Europe, in the shape of a bent hook or sickle-shaped rod. This was passed through a hole in the door and caught in a hole in the bolt or on a projecting knob. Such 'keys' have been found in archæological remains. A similar key about 2 ft. long made of iron with a brass handle ornamented with ring money, and known as the chief's door-key, is in use in N. Nigeria.[4] Another method was to hold the bolt in place by means of a peg also worked from outside by means of a string. A further development, implying the use of a key, consisted in using pegs which fell from an upright into corresponding sockets in the bolt. These pegs might be lifted in different ways according to the type of lock in use. In one type two pegs fell into notches in the bolt when it was pushed home, and held it in place. To raise these a T-shaped key was used.[5] It was pushed vertically through a hole in the door, given a quarter turn, bringing the arms into a horizontal position, and then pulled slightly back so that the returns of the T fitted into holes in the pegs, which could now be raised. The bolt was then pulled back by means of a string.[6] In the second type a number of small pegs drop into holes in the bolt and are then flush with its lower surface. The key consists of a rod bent at a right angle with teeth fitted variously upon the shorter piece. When inserted below the bolt, the teeth raise the pegs flush with its upper surface, and the bolt can then be pushed back by the key. Innumerable varieties of this type of lock are known, and the key is probably that known as 'Laconian' with three teeth, the invention of which was attributed to the Laconians. Locks and keys of this type were used in Egypt, among the Romans (often of an elaborate pattern), Greeks, Scandinavians, and possibly the Celts.[1] Both of these locks are of the 'tumbler' type, as is also the third, the tumbler being 'a bolt of a bolt.' In this the pins drop into holes in the bolt, which is hollow, until they are flush with the upper side of the hollowed-out part. The key consisted of a strip of wood or metal fitted with upright teeth corresponding in size and position with the pegs. It was inserted into the hollow of the bolt and raised the pegs, so that the bolt could be pulled back. In this case the key, which is sometimes of very large size, was put through a hole in the door large enough to let the hand pass through with it. But in some cases the lock was fixed on the outside. This type of lock was used in Egypt (perhaps not earlier than Roman times), and is still common there, in Oriental countries generally from early times—Syria, Arabia, Palestine—in Scandinavia, in Scotland, where it is still found in remote parts of the W. Highlands, among the Negroes of Jamaica, in British Guiana (where it may have been introduced by settlers), and among the Zuñis (perhaps of Mormon origin).[2]

The first of these types is supposed to be the kind of lock which Penelope opens in *Odyssey*, xxi. 46 ff.[3] Diels, however, regards the strap as fastening the bolt from outside. Penelope unloosens it (probably it was tied by a secret knot); then through a hole in the door she inserts a bar of metal bent twice at a right angle; its end strikes on a knob fixed on the bolt and pushes it out of its staple. If there were two bolts, both, connected together, could be shot at once.[4] A large key of this kind is often represented on monuments as a hieratic survival, carried by priestesses.[5] It is akin to the sickle-shaped key already described. In Benin a key and bolt working somewhat on this principle are in use. The bolt has a knob; the key is a metal rod, to the end of which is attached another piece bent twice at a right angle; at the other end is a ring-shaped handle. This key is inserted through a hole in the door, the keyhole being at a height above the bolt corresponding to the size of the key. The end of the key impinges on the knob, and, when a turn is given to it, the bolt is slid along. The bolts in the king's palace were of carved ivory.[6] Locks and keys more or less of this type, but of wood, are used by the Wamba of British Central Africa. The key has teeth of 2 or 3 inches in length. When it is turned, it moves a wooden bolt into place. Possibly these are of Portuguese origin.[7] Original native locks are made by the Hausa, and are traded among other tribes.[8] Du Chaillu refers to native locks used for chests and doors in Goumbi, Equatorial Africa, but does not describe them.[9] Among savage tribes generally civilized influences are introducing the use of European or American locks and padlocks—*e.g.*, among the Baronga and elsewhere in Africa.[10]

1 M. Jastrow, *Rel. of Bab. and Assyria*, Boston, 1898, p. 665; J. G. Wilkinson, *Manners and Customs*, London, 1878, i. 353; Herod. ii. 128.

2 *16 RBEW* [1897], p. 164 f.; D. Macdonald, *Africana*, London, 1882, i. 149 (door barred on outside when owner is at work in the fields); Daremberg-Saglio, *s.v.* 'Janua,' col. 607 (Etruria, outside bar); Perrot-Chipiez, vi. 188, 281; Hom. *Il.* xxiv. 453 f., 567, etc.

3 *8 RBEW*, pp. 183, 187.

4 O. Schrader, *Reallexikon der indogerm. Altertumskunde*, Strassburg, 1901, p. 725; Brit. Museum *Guide to Early Iron Age*, London, 1905, p. 125; the Nigerian key is in the Ethnographical section of National Museum, Edinburgh.

5 Or, as in the Faroe Islands, a key has teeth which fit into notches in the pegs when slipped in horizontally. The pegs are then raised vertically.

6 Brit. Mus. *Guide to Exhib. illustrating Greek and Roman Life*, London, 1908, p. 162 f.; H. Diels, *Parmenides' Lehrgedicht*, p. 131. A key of this type (still used in Norway) might be inserted into holes in the bolt (which had no pegs), and could then push it either way (A. H. L. F. Pitt-Rivers, *On the Development and Distribution of Primitive Locks and Keys*, p. 14).

1 Aristoph. *Thesm.* 421 ff.; Diels, p. 144; Wilkinson, i. 354; Brit. Mus. *Guide to . . . Gr. and Rom. Life*, p. 162 f. A key of this type might consist simply of a bent rod to lift one peg. This kind is used in Egypt, Persia, India, Turkey, etc. (Pitt-Rivers, p. 9).

2 Pitt-Rivers, *passim*; Diels, p. 141; Daremberg-Saglio, *s.v.* 'Sera'; H. Syer Cuming, *Journ. Brit. Arch. Assoc.* xii. [1856] 118, 120; T. Wells, *ib.* xiii. [1857] 335 f.; E. W. Lane, *Mod. Egyptians*, London, 1895, p. 27; A. Russell, *Natural History of Aleppo*², London, 1794, i. 21 f.; C. M. Doughty, *Arabia Deserta*, do. 1888, i. 143; *8 RBEW*, p. 187; Wilkinson, i. 354 f.; Egyptian and Roman specimens in Brit. Museum.

3 See reconstruction in Brit. Mus. *Guide to . . . Gr. and Rom. Life*, p. 102; Diels, p. 131.

4 See reconstruction in Diels, p. 135 f.; Daremberg-Saglio, *svv.* 'Sera' and 'Janua.'

5 Diels, p. 123 f.; Daremberg-Saglio. *locc. citt.*

6 H. Ling Roth, *Great Benin*, pp. 87–89 (specimen in Brit. Museum).

7 H. H. Johnston, *Brit. Cent. Africa*, London, 1897, p. 459.

8 T. E. Bowdich, *Mission to Ashantee*, London, 1819, p. 306.

9 P. B. du Chaillu, *Explorations in Equatorial Africa*, London, 1861, p. 254.

10 Junod, *op. cit.* p. 92; du Chaillu, p. 254 f.

In another type, used mainly in padlocks, the key thrust into the lock compresses springs, thus permitting the shackle to be withdrawn. Such padlocks were used in Egypt, and are still known in W. Africa (possibly of Egyptian origin). They were also used by the Romans, and are still extant in China and India (the so-called puzzle padlocks).[1] The Romans had flat keys for raising latches, similar to those in use to-day.[2] Both the Greeks and Romans knew the lock with wards through which the key passes, thus moving the bolt backwards or forwards. Keys of a simple type to suit such locks are represented on vases.[3] More elaborate keys are often small and form a part of finger-rings, the key lying flat upon the finger. False keys were also used by Roman robbers.[4]

While locks of the primitive types here described were used in different parts of Europe and are indeed still used in remote districts, the ward system, with obstacles to prevent any but the proper key from turning the bolt, was much used during the Middle Ages. The principle of the tumbler lock was applied to locks during the 18th century. Roman keys terminated in a flat or perforated handle; others were of an open lozenge, ovate, or round shape. Until the 13th cent. keys had little ornamentation. In the 13th to 15th centuries they terminated in a lozenge, trefoil, or quatrefoil. After this, and especially in the 16th cent., they had elaborate decoration and became works of art. The bows terminating the stems were filled with ornament, the stem itself was ornamented or took the form of an animal or human figure, or stem and bow took the form of a crucifix. Even the webs were sometimes ornamented.[5]

2. The key as symbol.—The importance of the key, as that by which doors guarding treasure, stores, etc., might be closed or opened, was marked in ancient times. This doubtless originated in the period when locks and keys of a primitive type were first invented and their value made plain to all.

(*a*) Frequently the wife as *Hausfrau* bears the household keys symbolically. She is the key-bearer for her husband. Among the Romans the newly-married wife was given the keys of the store-rooms. The divorced wife had to surrender the keys; hence the formula in the Twelve Tables signifying divorce—'claves ademit, exegit.' The wife who separated from her husband sent him back the keys—'claves remisit.'[6] Among the Teutons and Scandinavians the bride was decked with keys at her girdle. Here also at divorce she had to give up the keys, and 'taking away' or 'giving up the keys' became a formula of divorce.[7] Among the Gauls a widow placed keys and girdle on the corpse of the dead husband as a sign of renunciation in participation of goods—a custom found elsewhere, and also signifying that the widow was free of obligation.[8] Slaves carried keys of various parts of the house, and the janitor bore the house-key. In the Christian Church the church-treasurer who carried the keys of the treasury was known as *claviger*.[9] In Is 22^{22} 'laying the key of the house of David upon his shoulder' signifies transference of the supremacy of the kingdom, and the imagery is taken from the large keys opening tumbler locks carried on the shoulder in the East. In Equatorial Africa, as chests containing treasure are a synonym for property, and as they are kept locked with either native or American locks, the more keys a man has the richer he is. Hence keys in large numbers are worn as a symbol of wealth.[1]

(*b*) Since many divinities were key-bearers, their priestesses (not usually their priests) also bore keys symbolically, signifying that the divine powers were theirs, or that they were guardians of the sanctuary of the gods. Priestesses are often represented carrying on their shoulder a large key of the rectangular type, already alluded to as an archaic survival; a key represented on a grave-stone signifies the burial-place of a priestess.[2] Iphigenia is called *κληδοῦχος* ('key-bearer') of Artemis, and Io *κληδοῦχος* of Hera.[3] Cassandra bore the keys of Hecate, and in the mysteries of the goddess the priestess was *κλειδοφόρος*, while the priestess of Ceres *κατωμαδίαν δ' ἔχε κλαΐδα*.[4]

(*c*) As has been shown in the art. DOOR (vol. iv. p. 851^{b}), heaven and the under world were believed to be regions or abodes with doors and gates. These doors and gates had bars and bolts as well as locks. In Babylonian mythology Marduk made gates to the heavens and attached secure bolts to them. Šamaš is said to open the bolt of the bright heaven, and to Ištar's supremacy is said to belong the opening of the lock of heaven. Hades with its seven gates has also bolts. Over these dust is scattered, and Ištar threatens to break the bolts when she descends there.[5] The gates of Pluto's realm are closed with iron bars and keys.[6] The Hebrews had similar conceptions. Sheôl has bars (Job 17^{16}; cf. Ps 107^{16}); Hades and the Abyss have locks and keys (Rev 1^{18} 9^{1} 20^{1}). These conceptions were still retained in Christian belief, and nothing is more dramatic in the legends or theology of the *Descensus* than Christ's breaking the bars and bolts of Hades. Similarly in Mandæan mythology the regions of the dark worlds have gates with bolts and with locks and keys differing from all other locks and keys.[7] So also earth, sea, the world, etc., have locks and keys. The Assyrian Ninib holds the lock of heaven and earth, and opens the deep, and Ea unlocks fountains.[8] Cybele is represented with a key—that of earth, which is shut in winter and opened in spring. Eros has keys of sea and earth as well as of heaven, and Proteus has the keys of the ocean (*πόντου κλῇδας*).[9] The Egyptian Sarapis has keys of earth and sea.[10] In Hebrew thought the sea has doors and bars, and the earth has bars.[11] In Breton folk-lore is found the curious idea that menhirs are keys of the sea. Should they be lifted, the sea would rush in. They are also keys of hell.[12] Fairyland likewise has its doors with locks and keys, and the key is sometimes given to a favoured mortal in order that he may obtain treasure.[13]

(*d*) It is not surprising, therefore, that some gods were represented with keys, those of the region which they guarded or which was sacred to them, or that the key became a symbol of power—the power which was represented in the opening or

1 Cuming, *op. cit.* p. 118 f.; Wells, *op. cit.* p. 336; Pitt-Rivers, p. 26. Specimens are to be seen in most ethnological collections.

2 Brit. Mus. *Guide to . . . Gr. and Rom. Life*, p. 163 f.

3 Diels, p. 145 ff.

4 Sallust, *Bellum Jugurth.* 12.

5 Cuming, *op. cit.* p. 123 ff.; Wells, *op. cit.* p. 337 f.; Brit. Mus. *Guide to Mediæval Room*, London, 1907, p. 183.

6 Cicero, *Philipp.* ii. 28; Ambrose, *Ep.* 68 (*PL* xvi. 938); Ducange, *s.v.* 'Claves remittere.'

7 J. Grimm, *Deutsche Rechtsalterthümer*³, Göttingen, 1881, p. 176.

8 Grimm, *Teut. Myth.* tr. J. S. Stallybrass, London, 1882–88, p. 1757, *Kleinere Schriften*, Berlin, 1882, vi. 180.

9 Ducange, *s.v.* 'Claviger.'

1 Du Chaillu, p. 254 f.

2 Diels, p. 123 ff.

3 Eur. *Iph. in Taur.* 131; Æsch. *Suppl.* 299.

4 Eur. *Troad.* 256 f.; Daremberg-Saglio, iii. 49; Callimachus, *Hymn to Ceres*, 45; cf. 55.

5 M. Jastrow, *Rel. of Bab. and Assyria*, pp. 301, 311, 428, 435, 566, 569.

6 R. Wünsch, *Defixionum Tabellæ Atticæ*, Berlin, 1897, iii. b.

7 W. Brandt, *Mandäische Schriften*, Göttingen, 1893, pp. 154, 161 f.

8 Jastrow, pp. 214, 237.

9 Servius, *ad Æn.* x. 252; C. G. Schwarz, *De Diis Clavigeris*, p. 23; *Orph. Hymn.* xxv. 1.

10 Schwarz, p. 18.

11 Job 38^{10}, Jon 2^{6}.

12 Sébillot, i. 418, 421.

13 *Ib.* i. 474, ii. 123.

closing of the doors of that region to allow or prevent entrance or egress. This was more especially marked in Greek and Roman mythology, in which certain of the divinities bear the title κλειδοῦχος, *claviger*. Janus, as god of doors, is said to have been represented 'cum clavi et virga' in left and right hands—the key and the rod of the Roman doorkeeper. He sits guarding the gates of heaven with the Hours. At morning the doors of heaven are opened to let out the day, and they are shut again at night. Even more universally he was κλειδοῦχος, since all things—heaven, sea, clouds, and earth—were opened by his hand.[1] Portunus, another god of doors, probably of barns and stores, also carried keys, and perhaps some ritual act was performed with keys on the Portunalia.[2] Divinities of towns carried the keys of the town—*e.g.*, Athene is κλειδοῦχος of the town of Athens.[3] According to Parmenides, Dike carries the keys of the doors of day and night, *i.e.* of heaven, and removes the bar from the door when necessary.[4] So Helios, who comes forth from the doors of the sky, is said in the *Hymn* of Proclus (i. 2) to have keys. The same conceptions are found in Mithraic circles, perhaps partly taken over from these classical models. The Kronos of Mithraic belief carries a key in his right hand or one in each hand, or, like Janus, a key and a rod. These are the keys of the doors of heaven, by which souls enter or pass out to birth. He was addressed as 'the lord who fastens the fiery bars of heaven.'[5]

Divinities associated with the under world carry its keys. Hecate usually holds the keys of Hades on monuments or images of the goddess, and is also described as possessing them. She is even called 'the Lady bearing the keys of the Universe.'[6] In Caria every fourth year the procession of the key (κλειδὸς πομπή) was celebrated in her honour—a festival which lasted for several days. Pausanias (V. xx. 1) describes Pluto as having keys of Hades, which is closed by him so that none can go out thence. In the magic papyri and elsewhere other divinities bear the keys of Hades —Persephone, Æacus, Anubis—and here we enter the region of mingled classical, Oriental, and Egyptian beliefs which were popular after the decay of the Greek and Roman State religions.[7]

(*e*) Generally speaking, possession of the keys signifies power over the regions the locks of the doors of which these keys open. As heaven and Hades were regarded as towns or States with walls and gates, so they had locks and keys. The keys are entrusted to their respective guardian divinities, who have the power of opening or closing the gates. To those who were worthy of heaven its door was opened; to those who merited hell its door was opened. Once in, there was generally no egress. In Jewish thought Michael is said to hold the keys of the kingdom of heaven (3 Bar 11^2, cf. 4 Bar 9^5, Eth. version, where he holds open the gates of righteousness till the righteous enter in).

The power of the keys as associated with St. Peter is treated of in the art. BINDING AND LOOSING. Here it is sufficient to say that the idea of his being dowered with the keys of the kingdom of heaven is sufficiently obvious. The picture is still that of a State or town with gates. St. Peter, as κλειδοῦχος, can open to those worthy of the kingdom and its rewards, or can keep the door locked against the unworthy. But it should be observed that, while generally righteousness, obedience to divine law, was the condition of future reward, not only in Christianity but in other religions, there were other methods of compelling the opening of the gates of heaven. We find this in Mithraism, in Gnosticism, perhaps in the popular Christianity which was so much mingled with Gnosticism and paganism, and in the syncretistic magico-religious groups of the period. In these, submission to rites and ceremonies—*e.g.*, of baptism, purification, and communion—possession of amulets, knowledge of the right pass-words or the names of the demonic or divine guardians of the gates of the heaven, were all so many keys with which the soul could unlock the gates and pass onwards or compel the κλειδοῦχοι to unlock them.[1]

(*f*) The name 'key' might be given to anything which had the power of opening or disclosing. Rabbinic lore spoke of three keys which were given to no third party—the keys of the womb or of child-birth, of rain, and of resurrection of the dead.[2] As to the first of these, it is still a divine power which works in conception and birth, opening the womb, and we may compare the phrase of Aristophanes regarding Hera, that she guards the keys of marriage (κλῇδας γάμου φυλάττει), or that of Pindar when he says of Peitho that she bears the secret keys which open the way to the sanctities of love.[3] But the thought underlying this is seen in the erotic slang of many languages, which describes the male organ as 'key' and the female organ as 'lock.' The consummation of marriage by their means was a sacred act, consecrated to certain divinities. Similarly any book of secret knowledge or of mysteries or γνῶσις might be called a 'key.' It contained the means of unlocking mysteries, of opening the way to truth. The book of rites of the Paulicians is called *The Key of Truth*, and some of the magical texts current in the syncretistic groups already referred to bore the name 'Key.' The name is applied also to any book which purports to explain various matters, or even to literal translations of classical or foreign works; hence withholding 'the key of knowledge' of which Christ speaks (Lk 11^{52}) means debarring men from the knowledge of moral or spiritual truth which would give them entrance to the Kingdom of God. In the Coptic Gnostic documents Christ Himself is called 'the Key.'

As a symbol the key occurs in heraldry. It is found in the arms of the pope, of various bishoprics, of cities, of private families. It also occurs in the names and signs of shops and inns, and is here of ecclesiastical derivation—the Cross-keys, the Golden Key, etc. Keys, and especially that of the forbidden chamber, are prominent in folk-tales of the Bluebeard group (MacCulloch, *CF*, London, 1905, p. 306 ff.).

3. Locks and keys in magic.—The importance attaching to locks and keys gave them a place in various magical rites, while their being made of metal adds to their value, since metal of itself has magical power (see CHANGELING, vol. iii. p. 359^b; FAIRY, vol. v. p. 684; METALS AND MINERALS).

(*a*) As locks and keys make fast or open, bind or loose, so they are sometimes considered to have a sympathetic effect upon dwellers in the house—*e.g.*, at a birth or at death. It is a common custom to open all the locks at a confinement, lest the delivery should be hindered through their remaining fast, and so to lighten the labour. With this may be compared the Roman custom of presenting the woman with a key as a portent of an easy delivery. In Sweden in difficult labour the midwife asks the woman whether she has prayed to the Virgin for her key to open the womb. If not, the midwife

[1] Ovid, *Fasti*, i. 99, 117 ff.; Macrobius, I. ix. 7.
[2] W. W. Fowler, *Roman Festivals*, London, 1899, p. 203.
[3] Aristoph. *Thesm.* 1139.
[4] Diels, p. 29 f.
[5] F. Cumont, *Textes et monum. figurés rel. aux mystères de Mithra*, Brussels, 1895–99, i. 83 f. and plates; A. Dieterich, *Eine Mithrasliturgie*, Leipzig, 1903, p. 8.
[6] *Orph. Hymn*, i. 7.
[7] W. Köhler, *ARW* viii. [1905] 222 f.

[1] See, *e.g.*, *Pistis Sophia*, and *Book of Jeu*, *passim*; Origen, *c. Celsum*, vi. 31; Dieterich, *Mithrasliturgie*, p. 10 f.; Cumont, *Textes*, i. 41; J. A. MacCulloch, 'Ascent of the Soul,' *Irish Church Quarterly*, 1912, p. 122 f.
[2] A. Wünsche, *Neue Beiträge zur Erläut. der Evangelien aus Talmud und Midrasch*, Göttingen, 1878, p. 195.
[3] Aristoph. *Thesm.* 976; Pindar, *Pyth.* ix. 39.

says the prayer, the woman repeating it after her.[1]

If a witch was present at a wedding and snapped a padlock to at the benediction, dropping it into water, she caused the marriage to be unfruitful, until the padlock was recovered. This belief is found in Germany and, in a similar way, in Greece.[2]

On similar grounds the soul cannot leave the body of a dying person as long as any locks or bolts in the house are fastened; these are therefore unlocked or unfastened and the house-doors are opened.[3]

In all these we have instances of sympathetic magic—what is done to the lock is *ipso facto* done to the living person. They correspond to the world-wide use of knots (*q.v.*) and bindings in magic.

(*b*) In many cases the key itself, probably as a symbol of power, is used as an amulet or has magical virtues. Already among the ancient Greeks and Etruscans this use was found (see *ERE* vol. iii. p. 436[b]). In Italy small keys blessed by the priest are called 'keys of the Holy Spirit,' and are worn by infants as a preservative against convulsions. There, as well as in Portugal, Greece and the islands, Germany, and other places, the key is a frequent amulet against the evil eye. It may form one of the charms attached to the *cimaruta*, or sprig of rue, or may be a single amulet elaborately worked. Sometimes it is phallic, the handle being so shaped.[4] In Jerusalem necklaces from which charms depend are worn, and among the latter are a lock and key.[5] In China a common amulet given to an only son in order 'to lock him to life' is a silver lock. The father collects cash from a hundred heads of families and exchanges it for silver; of this a native padlock is made, and it is used to fasten a silver chain or ring round the boy's neck.[6] In Korea the neck ring lock is also a charm. For a girl it is a real lock of silver with a bar across the top (the bolt), and the key at the side. For a woman it is a mere symbol of the lock. On it is the inscription, 'Longevity, riches, and all you wish.'[7] With these practices may be compared an incident in a Danish *Märchen*: the hero gets a key as a christening gift, and it brings him luck.[8] In Norway a large old iron key is used against dwarf-struck cattle. It is hung over the stall, and is supposed to heal them. Such keys are supposed to have been forged by dwarfs (cf. the use of elf-shot, FAIRY, § 6).[9] An ancient method of warding off hail from a field was to hang keys around it—perhaps by way of locking the field in from harm, or merely as charms against the hail.[10] In Transylvania a lock is carried in the seed-bag in order to keep birds from the corn.[11] A key, partly for its own virtues, partly because it is of iron, is commonly placed in a cradle to prevent fairies from changing the baby.[12]

[1] F. Liebrecht, *Zur Volkskunde*, Heilbronn, 1879, p. 360; Festus, *s.v.* 'Clavis.'

[2] Grimm, *Teut. Myth.*, pp. 1073, 1175; J. C. Lawson, *Modern Greek Folklore*, Cambridge, 1910, p. 17.

[3] T. F. Thiselton-Dyer, *English Folk-Lore*, London, 1878, p. 228; *Choice Notes from Notes and Queries*, do. 1859, p. 117; cf. Scott, *Guy Mannering*, ch. 27, 'And wha ever heard o' a door being barred when a man was in the dead-thraw?—how d'ye think the spirit was to get awa' through bolts and bars like thae?'

[4] *FL* xvi. [1905] 142 f., xix. [1908] 218, 221, 223, 469; Cuming, *loc. cit.* p. 127; cf. also, for additional data, EVIL EYE, vol. v. p. 614[a].

[5] *FL* xv. [1904] 191.

[6] N. B. Dennys, *The Folklore of China*, London, 1876, p. 55; *FL* xvi. 369; Cuming, *loc. cit.*

[7] *FL* xiv. [1903] 114, 294 f.

[8] *FLR* iii. [1880–81] 214.

[9] *FL* xx. [1909] 323; cf. 315.

[10] Cf. *ERE* iii. 436[b].

[11] *GB*[3], pt. ii., *Taboo and the Perils of the Soul*, London, 1911, p. 308.

[12] E. S. Hartland, *Science of Fairy Tales*, London, 1891, p. 97.

In the island of Zacynthos a key is placed on the breast of a corpse, because, being of iron, it will scare away evil spirits, though the popular explanation is that it will open the gate of paradise.[1] According to a belief in Poitou, when a werwolf is struck between the eyes with a key, the enchantment ends, and the human form is resumed.[2]

(*c*) Another magical use is that of the Bible and key. A large key, sometimes an ancient or hereditary key, is placed flat between the leaves of a Bible, which is then closed and bound with cord. The handle of the key projects and is held in the hand or on the fingers of one or two persons, while some formula is being said. At the psychological moment it twists and turns, thus indicating whatever is desired to be discovered. This has superseded earlier methods—*e.g.*, with a sieve—but Reginald Scot already mentions the use of a psalter and key. (1) They are used as a cure for nose-bleeding. Here the patient turns the Bible and key round, while the wise man repeats a charm. Then the latter removes the key and places it down the patient's back, while the patient holds the Bible. This is supposed to cure the bleeding entirely. The latter part of the charm is often used, but seldom now in a magical way. A similar use of Bible and key is for the purpose of 'unwitching' a patient.[3] (2) It is also used in divination, usually to discover a thief or a witch. The names of the suspected persons are repeated with the formula, 'Turn Bible, turn round the key, turn, key, turn, and show the name to me.' At the right name the key twists and the Bible drops from the hand. Within recent years such a use is known to have actually led to an arrest.[4] The Bible and key (or the key alone) are used in E. Anglia to divine with, and also to help a vessel entering or leaving port. To assist it to enter port, the key is turned towards oneself, and, to leave port, away from oneself.[5]

(*d*) The keyhole, as an opening by which fairies, spirits, and the like may enter the house, is often magically protected. Thus in the Sporades it is stopped with a skein of flax to prevent vampires from entering. They would require to count all the threads in the skein before doing so. In Cyprus, on locking up, the cross is signed with the key over the keyhole.[6] In Germany the keyhole is stopped up in order to outwit the *Mar* ('nightmare') which enters thereby.[7] In Egypt it is customary to say, 'In the name of God, the Compassionate, the Merciful,' when locking a door, as a protection against genii. The door cannot then be opened by them.[8] In Aude a vase of water was placed before the keyhole to prevent visits from a spirit, and in Savoy a watch-glass. The spirit broke the latter and then left in disgust.[9] Stables, cow-houses, etc., are sometimes protected by tying charms to the key—usually a perforated stone (the key-stone which keeps off the demon Mara) and a horn.[10] In Babylonia demons were said to slip into houses through bolts, etc., 'gliding "like snakes,"' and it may have been to prevent this that libations were poured over these (§ 1; for other precautions taken see DOOR, vol. iv. p. 849[b]).[11]

[1] J. C. Lawson, pp. 109, 112.

[2] F. Pluquet, *Contes populaires*[2], Rouen, 1834, p. 15.

[3] *FL* xvi. 169 f. (Wye valley), 172.

[4] *FL* xv. 93 (Jamaica); *FLJ* ii. [1884] 156 f., 380 f. (England); W. Henderson, *Folk-Lore of Northern Counties*, London [1879], p. 232 f.; Grimm, p. 1109 (Germany). An alleged use of the Bible and key as an 'incantation' in a case tried at Runcorn Sessions is referred to in the *Evening Dispatch*, Edinburgh, May 19, 1914.

[5] *FL* iv. [1893] 391.

[6] *FL* x. [1899] 175, 365.

[7] K. Simrock, *Handbuch der deutschen Mythol.*, Bonn, 1864, p. 457.

[8] E. W. Lane, *Modern Egyptians*, p. 235.

[9] Sébillot, i. 142.

[10] Cuming, *loc. cit.* p. 129.

[11] Jastrow, p. 265.

(e) Keys were sometimes thrown into holy wells as a propitiatory offering to the spirit or guardian of the well, as at Criccieth on Easter morning.[1]

4. The key-flower.—Mediæval legend and later story had much to say regarding certain mysterious flowers which could either make locks fly open or cause a rock door in a mountain to swing open and so admit the seeker to obtain treasure hidden there. The flower was blue, red, or white, and was known as the 'wonder-flower' or 'key-flower' (*Schlüsselblume*); similar properties were also ascribed to the *Springwurzel*, or 'explosive root,' usually obtained from a woodpecker whose nest had been closed up with a wooden bung. She flies off to seek the root, returns with it, and applies it to the bung, which is forced out with a loud noise. It is then taken by the treasure-seeker, who uses it as the flower is used in other instances.[2] Ælian and Pliny know of this legend, but speak of a plant, and the latter elsewhere refers to a herb by which all things closed can be opened.[3] This is the *shāmîr* of Rabbinic legend, a kind of worm or a stone in possession of a moor-hen.[4] In connexion with these stories of mountain treasures obtained by the wonder-flower, there are usually mysterious white ladies who guard them, and who, like the *Hausfrau*, carry a bunch of keys which also give access to the treasure.[5] There is a German belief that where the rainbow touches the earth a golden key falls, which gives its name to the flower.[6] In the story of 'Alī Bābā, the rock door opens when the mysterious word *Sesame* is spoken. The word may have stood in an earlier version for the herb *sesamum*, but in other instances the use of magical words makes locks and bars open—*e.g.*, those of the Egyptian under world—while even in tales of enchantresses from New Guinea the use of the words, 'Oh, rock be cleft,' and 'Oh, rock be closed,' causes a rock door to open and shut.[7] In the lives of saints a not uncommon miracle is to unlock a door when the key is lost. They touch the lock with the hand, or their mere presence causes the door to open. In other instances they pass through closed doors, as modern mediums have claimed to do.[8] Probably the *point d'appui* of these saintly miracles is Ac 12[10].

LITERATURE.—J. Romilly Allen, *Proc. Scott. Soc. Ant.*, n.s., ii. [1879–80] 149–162; J. Chubb, *On the Construction of Locks and Keys*, London, 1850; H. Syer Cuming, 'History of Keys,' *Journal of the Brit. Arch. Assoc.*, xii. [London, 1856] 117–129; Daremberg-Saglio, *s.vv.* 'Janua,' 'Sera'; H. Diels (ed.), *Parmenides' Lehergedicht, mit einem Anhang über griech. Türen und Schlösser*, Berlin, 1897; J. E. Mayer, *Der Schlosser*, Regensburg, 1913; H. Havard, *La Serrurerie*, vol. ix. of *Les Arts de l'ameublement*, Paris, 1891–97; E. Higgin, 'Sketch of Hist. of Ancient Door Fastenings,' *Hist. Soc. of Lanc. and Cheshire*, Liverpool, 1850; W. Köhler, 'Die Schlüssel des Petrus,' *ARW* viii. [Leipzig, 1905]; F. Liger, *La Ferronnerie ancienne et moderne*, ii., Paris, 1875; L. I. Molinus, 'De Clavibus Veterum,' in A. H. de Sallengre, *Novus Thesaurus Antiq. Roman.*, The Hague, 1716–24, vol. iii.; A. H. L. Fox Pitt-Rivers, *On the Development and Distribution of Primitive Locks and Keys*, London, 1883; C. G. Schwarz, *De Diis Clavigeris*, Altdorf, 1728; C. Tomlinson, *On the Construction of Locks*, London, 1853.

J. A. MACCULLOCH.

LOCUST

LOCUST.—1. Introductory.—The Latin word *locusta* first denoted certain crustaceans—*e.g.*, the lobster—and the English word 'lobster' is itself a corrupt adaptation of the Latin *locusta*. Dialectically 'locust' denotes the cockchafer and the cicada. A certain resemblance to the lobster seems to have brought the English meaning of 'locust' back to the insect.[1]

Various species of different genera have been endemic plagues in N. Africa and the Levant from ancient times. In recent years S. Africa and Australia have suffered severely. Mediæval lore, continuing the Biblical traditions and many Oriental tales, and also making the most of some inroads into Central Europe, elevated the locust into a fabulous monster. The Romans and Greeks had similar fancies; Pliny, *e.g.*, speaks of Indian locusts three feet long, with legs of such hardness that they were used as saws.[2] Arabian legend created a body of myth about the insect. The locust addressed Muhammad thus:

> 'We are the army of the Great God; we produce ninety-nine eggs; if the hundred were completed, we should consume the whole world and all that is in it.'

At various dates Italy, Russia, Transylvania, Poland, France, and Spain were visited by swarms, and the accounts given vie in exaggeration. But in the East from Africa to N. India they have been and are still a dangerous pest to agriculture, as the example of Cyprus shows.

The insect chiefly referred to in historical accounts is *Schistocerca peregrina*, formerly classified as *Acridium peregrinum*. *Pachytylus migratorius*, formerly *Œdipoda migratoria*, also appears in the Levant. They belong to the family *Acridiidæ*, not the *Locustidæ*, and are the only Old World species, the others being American.[3] The locustid insects of entomologists are the European grasshoppers. The OT has nine different names; it is improbable that these refer to different species. That most often employed is *arbeh* (*e.g.*, Ex 10[4-15]), probably connected with *rābāh*, 'multiply.'[4]

The *larva*, not the perfect insect, is the destructive form. This blackish *larva*, which moves by hopping, resembles the *imago* very closely, but the wings are immature. The perfect insect walks until after a sixth change, when it is able to fly. Three to four inches in length, the *larva*, as it advances to the *imago*, passes from black to brown and green.

While we must distinguish the absolutely destructive *larvæ* from the relatively harmless winged insects, some accounts of the flights of the latter are essential, having produced so great an impression on the popular imagination. It is curious that only modern observers have described the march of the *larvæ*, as terrible in its completeness of destruction as that of the white 'ants' of Africa. But possibly such OT writers as Joel were familiar with the phenomenon, however vaguely they may refer to it. As will be seen from the account cited, it is far more impressive than the flight.

2. The locust flight.—Darwin's account has a typical value:

> '. . . a ragged cloud of a dark reddish-brown colour. At first we thought that it was smoke from some great fire on the plains; but we soon found that it was a swarm of locusts. They were flying . . . at a rate of ten or fifteen miles an hour. The main body filled the air from a height of twenty feet, to that, as it appeared, of two or three thousand above the ground.' The sound was 'like a strong breeze passing through the rigging of a ship. . . . They were not, however,

---

1 J. Rhys, *Celtic Folk-Lore*, Oxford, 1901, p. 364.
2 Grimm, pp. 971 ff., 1596 f.; E. H. Meyer, *Mythol. der Germanen*, Strassburg, 1903, p. 430; W. Mannhardt, *Germ. Mythen*, Berlin, 1858, p. 153; *FL* xvi. 143; Sébillot, iii. 469, 476.
3 Ælian, *Hist. Anim.* iii. 26; Pliny, *HN* x. 18, xxvi. 4.
4 S. Baring-Gould, *Curious Myths*, London, 1877, p. 386 ff.; L. Blau, in *JE* xi. [1905] 229 f.
5 Grimm, p. 963 ff.
6 Simrock, p. 32.
7 C. G. Seligmann, *Melanesians of British New Guinea*, pp. 399 f., 402.
8 J. J. von Görres, *Die christliche Mystik*, Regensburg, 1836–42, bk. iv. ch. 25.

1 *OED*, *s.vv.* 'Lobster' and 'Locust.' Old Cornish has *legast*, and Fr. *langouste*; cf. *Trin. Coll. Hom.* 127 (1200 A.D.): 'wilde hunie and languste his mete.' The word appears to mean originally the 'springer' (the 'grass-*hopper*'; cf. also Fr. *sauterelle*; *sauter*), and to be connected with Gr. ληκάω, Lettish *lèkt*, 'leap, spring' (A. Walde, *Lat. etymolog. Wörterbuch*[2], Heidelberg, 1910, p. 438 f.). The Boers term their 'locust' *voetganger*; this is the larva called by the Portuguese *saltona*, or 'jumper,' and by the Italians *cavalletta*, with which Germ. *Heupferd* may be compared. Jl 2[4] and Rev 9[7] repeat this analogy of form and movement with the horse.
2 *HN* xxxv. (29).
3 A. E. Shipley, art. 'Locust' in *EBi*; L. Gautier, art. 'Locust' in *DCG*.
4 G. E. Post, art. 'Locust' in *HDB*.

so thick together, but that they could escape a stick waved backwards and forwards.'[1]

Another account, from the Levant, states:

'Their swarms fill the air, darkening the sky, and the noise of their wings resembles the pattering of a heavy rain . . . towards nightfall they light . . . they often break the branches of the trees . . . the swarm invariably resumes its flight as soon as the sun has warmed it a little . . . it has not time to destroy all the vegetation.'[2]

In 1889 a swarm over the Red Sea occupied 2000 square miles; its weight was calculated at 42,850 millions of tons.[3]

Munro, writing of locusts in S. Africa, states that, when driven by a storm into the sea, they may 'lie on the beach as a bank from three to four feet thick and from fifty to one hundred miles in length, and the stench from the corruption of their bodies, it is affirmed, is sensibly perceived for a hundred and fifty miles inland.'[4] He describes the movements of the flying locusts as 'curious, interesting, and pretty.'

All observers agree with the Psalmist (Ps 109[23]) that locust swarms follow the course of the wind.

'To a certain extent' the flying insects 'do injure here and there . . . but they do not destroy everything before them, like the army of the larval stage or jumpers.'[5]

3. The locust march.—After the flight the females lay their eggs in the soil, each ovisac containing about a hundred eggs.

'When the tiny creatures issue from their nest . . . the very dust of the ground which was so still before, now seems to waken into life. They begin to move by a process of twisting or rolling over one another, so that for the first few days they receive the name of twisters (South Africa). Within eight or ten days, however, they can jump four or six inches, and at the age of three or four weeks a new characteristic makes its appearance. A desire to explore manifests itself, and in a surprising manner. The whole company moves in a body in one general direction, and more or less in a straight line, as if by one common instinct, without apparently having any recognised leader or commander.'[6]

Marching thus over the country, they eat everything that comes in their way, even the bark of trees; they enter houses and 'eat the very clothes and curtains at the windows'; they even eat the wool off the sheep; and, 'last stage of all that ends this strange, eventful history,' they will eat one another. When the *voetgangers* are on their way, they resemble and receive from the Boers the name of an 'army on the march.'[7]

'It is in this marching stage that the *voetgangers* do enormous damage and eat every edible thing in their path, and completely destroy the work of the husbandman. They are unlike the flying company of locusts, which only levy toll here and there, but these, when they pass, leave nothing.'[8] 'The black larvæ,' says Post, referring to Palestine, 'now spread like a pall over the land, eating every green thing, even stripping the bark off the trees.'[9]

The Syrians beat pans, shout, and fire guns to drive off a swarm. When they have settled, they are gathered in sacks. The government enforces a *per capita* contribution of eggs, or offers a price for them by weight. When the *larvæ* hatch out, in fifteen or twenty days, trenches are dug in their pathway, or fires are built.[10] The only successful method of exterminating locusts was adopted in Cyprus in 1881. Since 1600 the island had been a wilderness. Matthei, conversant with the habits of the *larvæ*, erected an insurmountable wall of calico and leather round the main area. Unable to pass the smooth leather, the locusts fell into the trench dug beneath. At the same time 1300 tons of eggs were destroyed. The plague has been obsolete ever since.

4. Superstition and metaphor. — Among the Dravidians of Mirzapur, when locusts threaten the gardens, the natives catch one, decorate its head with red lead (in accordance with ceremonial custom), salaam to it, and let it go. The whole swarm is then believed to depart.[11]

Similarly in Syria, when caterpillars invaded a vineyard or field, 'the virgins were gathered, and one of the caterpillars was taken and a girl made its mother. Then they bewailed and buried it. Thereafter they conducted the "mother" to the place where the caterpillars were, consoling her, in order that all the caterpillars might leave the garden.'[1]

It is not unlikely that the 'caterpillars' mentioned in this account are the locust *larvæ*. The conciliatory method of expelling pests and vermin is adduced by Frazer to explain such titles of Greek deities as Locust Apollo, Locust Hercules, and Mouse Apollo.[2]

Such worships 'were originally addressed, not to the high gods as the protectors of mankind, but to the baleful things themselves, the mice, locusts, mildew, and so forth, with the intention of flattering and soothing them, of disarming their malignity, and of persuading them to spare their worshippers.'[3]

In Hebrew literature, and thence to a certain extent in European, the locust is a symbol of destructive agencies.[4] The OT also employs it to illustrate number and combination.[5]

5. Locusts as food.—Since the time of Herodotus[6] the use of locusts as food has been known. Thomson limits it to the Bedawīn of the frontier, and observes:

'Locusts are always spoken of as a very inferior article of food, and regarded by most with disgust—to be eaten only by the very poorest people.'[7]

They are roasted and eaten with butter, after the head, legs, and wings have been removed. They are also dried and then beaten into a powder, as a substitute for flour.[8] According to Burckhardt, they were roasted and kept in sacks with salt. He adds that the Bedawīn never used them as a dish, but would take a handful when hungry.[9] Van Lennep states that they resemble shrimps in flavour. Horses and camels are often fed with them, and they are exposed for sale in the markets of Baghdād, Medīna, and Damascus.[10]

The Law forbade Israel to eat 'creeping' things; 'yet may ye eat of all winged creeping things that go upon all four, which have legs above their feet to leap withal upon the earth.'[11] This exception includes the locust. The gospel account of locusts forming part of the diet of John the Baptist is accepted by most writers.[12] But Cheyne argues in favour of the ancient tradition that the ἀκρίδες are the beans or pods of the carob tree. This is a definite meaning of the words ἀκρίς and 'locust,' and the latter is even applied to the similar bean of the cassia tree. The resemblance between the insect and the bean is the reason for the identity of name. The carob beans are the 'husks' referred to as food for swine in the parable of the Prodigal Son,[13] and they are still sold for food in Syria.[14] In mediæval literature these beans are St. John's bread. In ancient Palestine there was a proverb, 'Israel needs carob beans to do repentance.'[15] They were a type of the food of the poor, and the connexion is between poverty and repentance, the

1 *Journal of Researches*[2], London, 1845, p. 317.
2 G. E. Post, *loc. cit.*
3 A. E. Shipley, *loc. cit.*
4 Æneas Munro, *The Locust Plague and its Suppression*, London, 1900, p. 30.
5 *Ib.* p. 36.
6 *Ib.* p. 55 f.
7 Post, *loc. cit.*; cf. Munro, p. 57 f.
8 Munro, p. 59.
9 Post, *loc. cit.*; cf. Munro, p. 59.
10 Post, *loc. cit.*
11 W. Crooke, *PR*, London, 1896, ii. 303.

1 From the Canons of Jacob of Edessa, quoted by J. G. Frazer, *GB*[3], pt. v., *Spirits of the Corn and of the Wild*, London, 1912, ii. 279 f.
2 *Ib.* ii. 282 f.; Strabo, XIII. i. 64; Paus. I. xxiv. 8; Eustathius, on Homer, *Il.* i. 39, p. 34; cf. also O. Gruppe, *Griech. Mythol. und Religionsgesch.*, Munich, 1906, p. 1229.
3 Frazer, *op. cit.* p. 282.
4 Cf. Rev 9[3-11]; B. Disraeli, *Endymion*, I. xxxi. 288: 'The white ant can destroy fleets and cities, and the locusts erase a province.'
5 Jg 6[5] 7[12], Pr 30[27].
6 iv. 172.
7 W. M. Thomson, *The Land and the Book*, London, 1883, ii. 301.
8 Post, *loc. cit.*; H. J. Van Lennep, *Bible Lands*, London, 1875, p. 319; W. R. Wilson, *Travels in Egypt and the Holy Land*[2], do. 1824, p. 330; S. R. Driver, *Joel and Amos*, Cambridge, 1897, p. 82 ff.
9 J. L. Burckhardt, *Travels in Syria and the Holy Land*, London, 1822, p. 238 f.
10 Van Lennep, *loc. cit.*
11 Lv 11[21].
12 Mt 3[4], Mk 1[6] ἀκρίδες.
13 Lk 15[16]; T. K. Cheyne, art 'Husks' in *EBi*.
14 H. B. Tristram, *Nat. Hist. of the Bible*[10], London, 1911, p. 361. They form a constituent of Thorley's 'food for cattle.' English dealers call the pods 'locusts.' The hard brown seeds were formerly used by jewellers to weigh gold and silver, hence the word 'carat.' 'Carob' is the Arabic and Persian name for the tree, *Ceratonia siliqua* (Cheyne, *loc. cit.*).
15 *Wayyiqrā Rabbā*, 35.

Baptist being essentially the prophet of repentance.[1] It is impossible to decide a detail which is itself perhaps legendary. But its typical value is great; and, as such, the carob bean proverb leaves little doubt in identification. Treating the detail as historical fact, we reach the same conclusion in favour of Cheyne's view, for this reason, that, while the carob, like all leguminous food, is highly sustaining (the Levantines have always made such food their staple diet), the nutritious value of the insect locust is extremely small, and insufficient, with honey, to support life.

LITERATURE.—This is fully given in the article, excepting J. H. Fabre, *Souvenirs entomologiques*, Paris, 1879 ff., vi. 196–212, 248–297.

A. E. CRAWLEY.

LOGIC.—I. *DEFINITION.*—Exceptional difficulties lie in the way of a general description of logic, because the definite increment of knowledge which is undertaken by primary sciences is not claimed here in a sense that is comparable. In logic we merely 're-traverse familiar ground, and survey it by unfamiliar processes. We do not, except accidentally, so much as widen our mental horizon' (B. Bosanquet, *Essentials of Logic*, p. 2). And exceptional pains are necessary in explaining how unfamiliar processes which reveal no unfamiliar objects amount to knowledge and science. A knowledge of knowledge cannot be proposed with quite the same assurance as a knowledge of space, matter, organization, and history, or even beauty or goodness. Some writers have proposed an art, rather than a science or even a philosophy; and others, a science of a special kind of mental process, or a philosophy reflecting on special relations of our personality to the universe. Mansel collects the following varied descriptions of the subject (Introd. to Aldrich, *Artis Logicæ Compendium*[4], p. lviii).

Logic is a part of philosophy (the Stoics). It is not a part, but an instrument (Peripatetics). It is both a part and an instrument (Academics). It is both a science and an art (Petrus Hispanus and others). It is neither science nor art, but an instrumental habit (Greek commentators). It is a science and not an art (Albertus Magnus and others). It is an art and not a science (Ramus and others). It is the science of argumentation (the Arabians), of the operations of the mind so far as they are dirigible by laws (Aquinas), of the syllogism (Scotus), of the direction of the cognitive faculty to the knowledge of truth (C. Wolff), of the universal and necessary laws of thought without distinction of its objects (Kant), of the processes of the understanding concerned in the estimation of evidence (J. S. Mill). It is the art of thinking (P. Gassendi, Arnauld), of reasoning (J. Le Clerc, R. Whately, and others), of the right use of reason (J. Clauberg, Watts), of dissertation (Ramus), of teaching (Melanchthon), of directing the mind to any object (George Bentham), of forming instruments for the direction of the mind (Burgersdyck, R. Sanderson, Aldrich).

Underneath such summary phrases as 'laws of thought' and 'forms of knowledge,' which have become common in the more modern definitions, there still lie very varied suggestions as to scope and method. The following are influential examples:

'A collection of precepts or rules for thinking, grounded on a scientific investigation of the requisites of valid thought' (Mill, *Exam. of Sir W. Hamilton's Philosophy*[5], London, 1878, p. 462).

'If we analyse the mental phænomena with the view of discovering . . . the Laws by which our faculties are governed, to the end that we may obtain a criterion by which to judge or to explain their procedures and manifestations . . . we have a science which we may call the Nomology of Mind. . . . Pure Logic is only an articulate development of the various modes in which they [the primary conditions of the possibility of valid thought] are applied' . . . the laws of thought as thought (Hamilton, *Lectures*, Edinb. and London, 1859–60, i. 122, iii. 12, 78 f.).

The forms and laws of thought 'are those subjective modes of the connection of our thoughts which are necessary to us, if we are by thinking to know the objective truth' (Lotze, *Outlines of Logic*, Eng. tr., Boston, 1892, p. 6).

'The conditions under which thought can arrive at propositions which are certain and universally valid . . . and the rules to be followed accordingly' (C. von Sigwart, *Logic*, Eng. tr., London, 1895, § 1).

'The doctrine of the regulative laws, on whose observance rests the realization of the idea of truth in the theoretical activity of man' (Ueberweg, *System of Logic and Hist. of Logical Doctrines*, Eng. tr., London, 1871, § 3).

[1] Cheyne, art. 'Husks' in *EBi.*

'The subject-matter of Logic is Knowledge, *qua* Knowledge, or the form of knowledge; that is, the properties which are possessed by objects or ideas in so far as they are members of a world of knowledge . . . the characteristics by which the various phases of the one intellectual function are fitted for their place in the intellectual totality which constitutes knowledge' (Bosanquet, *Essentials of Logic*, p. 44, *Logic*, i. 3).

These definitions with one consent repudiate the relativity, or volitional limitation, which is suggested by the title 'art'; but the responsibilities which must fall on a professed science they acknowledge only with some qualification. Mill does not propose any 'scientific investigation' which is not already sponsored by psychology. Hamilton attenuates the specific guarantee by relying on conditions that are 'primary.' The others appear to undertake something further, but with the same risks as are attendant on speculative philosophy. Ueberweg expressly relies on 'universal laws of existence' borrowed from metaphysics, and 'laws of the life of the mind,' from psychology, for 'auxiliary axioms' (§ 2). In order that we may avoid the responsibility of assuming that the 'unfamiliar processes' of which Bosanquet speaks are 'knowledge' in the same sense as our more natural scientific processes are, and that logical doctrine consists of 'theses to be proved' and 'axioms to be applied,' as Ueberweg claims (§§ 1, 4), comparable with these in significance, we might define logic as the art of raising the natural scientific processes into explicit self-consciousness. The special labour of logical studies, in any case, is to be undertaken with a view to what psychologists describe as 'acquaintance with,' rather than 'knowledge about,' our natural processes.

'Without logic, the mind of man can admirably energise, admirably reason; but without it, does not know itself through and through; and ignores one of the fairest and most fruitful of its faculties. Logic brings to the mind self-acquaintance. Such is its use, and it cannot have any other' (Barthélemy Saint-Hilaire, *De la Logique d'Aristote*, p. xlii).

We might also require of any doctrine which claims to be logical that it shall be (1) reflective, as distinct from assertive, in its significance, (2) teleological or purposive in its principle, (3) *a priori* or independent in its authority, (4) theoretical rather than practical in its limitations, and (5) disciplinary, not objective, in its motive.

1. Reflexion.—Reflective contents belong to various kinds of philosophical doctrine. In logical doctrine they recover the reference to personality which has been discarded from scientific, and place an 'I know' where otherwise would be a 'So it is.' This reference is the ground for classifying logic with the sciences specially grouped as mental, as in Hamilton's scheme (*Lectures*, vol. i. ch. 7), or as an 'integral part of philosophy' (Ueberweg, § 6); and it forbids such arrangements as those made by A. Bain and H. Spencer, where, at least in part, it stands first in the series of natural sciences arranged in the order of abstractness. For logic is what it is, not because it leaves out of consideration the spatial and other aspects of reality which natural sciences accept, but because it accepts something which they reject, and so changes the significance of a scientific statement, in scholastic phrase 'a first intention,' into a 'reflective idea,' or 'second intention.'

2. Purpose.—Knowledge is a form of life, and, like other forms, cannot be explained by detailing its constituent energies or organs, without assuming a finality for the whole. For descriptive purposes we can say that 'the idea of complete knowledge is the motive power of theoretical effort' (Sigwart, § 62, 6); or, to mark off the occasion for logical study, that 'the *fundamental fact* which underlies all logical reflection . . . is that we make a *distinction, from the point of view of value, between the true and the false*' (W. Windelband, in *Encyclopædia of the Philosophical Sciences*, Eng. tr., i. 11); or, in co-ordinating cognitive life with other moments of cosmic existence, that 'the "value" which is the object of philosophical Logic is logical reality and fact itself' (B. Croce, *ib.* p. 203). Logical consciousness reinforces this finality, though the doctrine is essentially neither description of the experience nor discrimination of the faculty nor perspective of the event, but expression of the aim.

3. **Independence.**—In analogy with Kant's celebrated criticism of knowledge, that it all begins with experience, but does not all spring from experience, we can say that logical consciousness begins with knowledge, but does not spring from it, or wait for a licence from it in the same way that empirical science has to wait for its special data. Even the borrowings from psychology and metaphysics are not for the purpose of conferring authority on logic, but are methodical devices for making it precise, for 'unfolding an inward conviction,' as Butler claimed to do in regard to conscience. The logical rule is neither more nor less authoritative than the example, provided it is understood discriminatively. 'If any man stumbles at the fact that when we want to think about thought we must, in so doing, already follow the norms of right thinking—there is no arguing with him' (Windelband, *loc. cit.* i. 25). All we can do is, in the words of Kant, to 'make the rule followed by the understanding a separate object of thought' (*Logic*, Introd. § i.).

4. **Theory.**—Cognition gives us the control of nature; and the reflective faculty, the control of self. But logic is the expression of the reflective faculty so far, and so far only, as the self is cognitive and there is conscience in science. It is indifferent to the manifestations of personality in feeling or action, and even in so much of cognition as escapes control.

5. **Discipline.**—Thus the motive of logic is not furnished by the world of objects, but by the aims of personality; if an art, it is a cognitive art, if a science, a disciplinary science; and it is sustained by our solicitude for intellectual self-government. The historical beginnings of logical theory are to be found in those racial dispositions and social conditions which gave occasion for the deliberate control of our trains of thought. In India it appears to have originated with rules in ceremonial deliberation:

'From the Brahmanic decisions on disputed points arising in the course of sacrifice . . . collected in exegetical and philosophic aphorisms . . . Gotama [probably later than the 5th cent. B.C.] evolved a system' (Bodas, *Tarka-Saṅgraha of Annambhaṭṭa*, Introd. p. 29).

And with Gotama the inwardness of logical concern has outworn its ceremonial form.

'The end proposed is the escaping from liability to transmigration, and the attainment of tranquil and eternally uninterrupted beatitude' (*Aphorisms*, tr. J. R. Ballantyne, Introd. p. 5).

In Greece it originated with canons of public debate and scientific instruction: the propaganda of plausibility by the Sophists, the challenges to the complacency of popular beliefs issued by Socrates, the polemics of Zeno.

Some of Aristotle's predecessors, he records, 'had given rhetorical, others interrogative, discourses to learn—since they imagined that they should instruct their pupils by delivering, not [logical] art, but the effects of art' (*Soph. Elenchi*, ch. 34). The art which he constructed deepened, like Gotama's, into pure reflexion and self-communion, for 'dialectic [the art of discussion], being investigative, holds the way to the principles of all methodical thought' (*Topics*, i. ch. 2, *Soph. Elenchi*, ch. 2).

But in the Greek, unlike the Hindu, logical illumination, reflexion fastened upon conviction at the point where individual intelligence merged in the intelligence of humanity at large—just as in Greek ethics the good of the individual merges in that of the State. The Greek forms of proposition and syllogism seem to symbolize a world of intellects, where a common record of conviction can be maintained amid determinations of experience and foresight varying and changing with the individuals; the Greek analysis of demonstrative science idealizes the inner coherence of such a record, whereby it dominates the individual intellect, while the Greek dialectic is the interplay through which vitality, welling from the latter, streams into the record.

The motive of logic being disciplinary, its method must be adjusted to the intellectual forces which are permanently constitutive of civilization; and its general scope cannot change to the extent to which other sciences change, where any advance may open up new vistas of inquiry. Kant is able to say:

'Since Aristotle's time Logic has not gained much in extent, as indeed its nature forbids that it should. But it may gain in respect of accuracy, definiteness and distinctness. . . . Aristotle has omitted no essential point of the understanding; we have only to become more accurate, methodical and orderly' (*Logic*, Introd. § ii.).

Nevertheless, it must share the vicissitudes in fortune of civilization as a whole. And the more influential of these, since Aristotle, have been the limit set on the range of free judgment during mediæval centuries, the value set upon personality by modern religion and philosophy, and the accelerating progress of physical sciences in the most recent times—three influences which have some connexion with a certain exaggeration in value which has fallen upon the three Aristotelian departments of doctrine successively in scholastic, modern, and recent years, and has transformed at least the dialectic almost beyond recognition. For the contrasts and controversies between the historic schools are questions of emphasis and balance in what might be called the 'dimensions' of logical discipline, to borrow a conception from geometry; or in the fundamental 'ideas' used in forming our conceptions, to borrow from Whewell's philosophy of all scientific discovery whatever.

In almost every science 'controversies' have 'turned upon the possible relations of Ideas, much more than upon the actual relations of Facts' (*Philosophy of Discovery*, p. 255).

The dimensions or ideas in which the historic schools have formed conceptions for logical value may be distinguished as explicitness, consistency, relevance, and system.

II. *PRINCIPLES.*—Parallel with what Whewell says as to the progress of physical science—

it 'consists in reducing the objects and events of the universe to a conformity with Ideas which we have in our own minds—the Ideas, for instance, of Space, Force, Substance [Number, Composition], and the like . . . the Idealization of Facts' (*ib.* p. 385)—

we may expect for logic also that

'an exhaustive solution of the great aggregate of logical problems can only grow up out of the union of all the different methods of treatment to which Logic has been subjected in virtue of the inner essential manifoldness of its nature' (Windelband, *loc. cit.* i. 9).

But the different 'methods' must be such as are grounded, if not 'in the systematic continuity of a philosophical theory of knowledge,' as Windelband requires, still in the unity of dimensions in consciousness of logical value. The 'principles' of logic must be these dimensions.

1. **Explicitness.**—The earliest of such dimensions to be utilized in the formation of logical conceptions was that of explicitness. We must be conscious of the definite germinal organization within our judgments or inferences, whenever occasion arises to make them deliberate. Hamilton proposes as 'the only postulate of Logic which requires an articulate announcement . . . to be allowed to state explicitly in language all that is implicitly contained in thought' (*Lectures*, iii. 114). And Gotama inaugurated the history of the science by detailing sixteen conceptions for our guidance in the analysis of this 'content,' as 'standards of right notion.'

'Proof [*i.e.* the faculty of a right notion]; the object of a right notion; doubt; motive; familiar fact; scholastic tenet; syllogism; hypothetical confutation; ascertainment; discussion; controversial wrangle; cavil; semblance of a reason; perversion; futility; and unfitness to be argued with—from knowing the truth in regard to these [sixteen things], there is the attainment of supreme good' (*Aphorisms*, tr. Ballantyne, § 1. 1).

Most of these topics appear to represent 'stages in dialectic or in the process of clearing up knowledge by discussion' (Adamson, *History of Logic*, p. 166; cf. Saint-Hilaire, p. xxx). But logic in the long course of its development has always made use of a method dialectical in this sense, which should not hide from us a more inward motive and significance. While it was as yet only tradition, no other method was practicable; and, even when it became literary, the practical utility of the method preserved it alongside of interpretations that were more spiritual. The alliance of the two methods was assumed in the reforms and elaborations made by Dignāga about A.D. 500.

'Demonstration and refutation together with their fallacies are useful in arguing with others; and Perception and Inference, together with their fallacies, are useful for self-understanding; seeing this, I compile this Śāstra' (*Nyāya-praveśa*, quoted in Vidyābhūṣaṇa, *Hindu Mediæval Logic*, p. 89).

The Aristotelian exposition of the same alliance was turned to forensic uses by Cicero, to academic uses by the scholastics, and to educational uses by the many modern and the now contemporary authors who choose to teach a science of argument, as the medium for an implied science of knowledge.

The conceptions of explicitness suggested to a modern mind by Gotama's sixteen standards and the explanations which he and his commentators append to them would be such as follow. In placing a logical value upon any given judgment, we must bring into consciousness (1) the extent to which our cognitive faculties are committed to it, perceptually, inferentially, conceptually, or interpretatively; 'that I shall die' is inferential, the 'recognition of a sign'; (2) the genus of truth or reality which is thus assumed as accessible to the faculty, or 'fit to supply a right notion'—a topic similar to that of the 'category' in modern logic, or, in Whewell, the 'idea'; (3) the question, or predetermination of a void in the system of our knowledge, which brings faculty and reality into the relation—the problematic phase in the development of a judgment, such as fails us in truism or is perverted in paradox; (4) the emotive root which makes a thought worth thinking or even a science worth creating; for 'truth implies a reference to purpose as well as to reality' (W. R. Boyce Gibson and A. Klein, *Problem of Logic*, London, 1908, p. 2); 'that I shall die' is significant only for the businesses of life; 'that I shall not altogether die,' for the counsels of moral perfectness; (5) and (6) the sureness and definiteness which fact and dogmatic or conceptual principle bring with them to their function in inference; (7) the scheme of their co-operation in the inferential syntheses; there must be (*a*) the probandum, defined by doubt and motive; (*b*) the reason, appealing to a sign; (*c*) the example, verifying a principle of signification; (*d*) the application, investing the reason with the significance of the example; and (*e*) the conclusion, establishing the probandum as a significate. 'Shall I not die, seeing that I am but human, as my fathers died because they were human? For I am as human as they, and consequently I, too, must die.' It is the transition from the problematic to the assertory phase of thought that sunders the application and conclusion from the reason and probandum—a transition which disappears in all the Western schemes of explicitness, because it disappears in proofs and static formulations, as distinct from the processes, of knowledge. The remainder of the sixteen topics are adjustments imposed on a conviction by its entrance into an environment of other convictions on the same question, by its encounter with convictions current in the world of other persons, and by the entrance of its motive into a system of other motives within our manifold practical nature, an organism where cognition, after all, is only one of the forces constituting its life.

2. Consistency.—Under the more complex social and intellectual conditions of life in Greece, the logical consciousness became more sensitive to the contact of individual thinking with this 'static formulation' of knowledge. And the 'idea' most essential for forming conceptions suitable to the spiritual emergency is that of consistency. It is not the consistency between thought and thought which in modern times became the ideal of Hamilton and the 'subjectively formal' logicians, but that which makes possible the allegiance of individual intellects, with varying perceptions, memories, and premonitions, to common formulations of knowledge.

(*a*) *Interpretative.*—In recent psychology the paradoxical tenet is held that, while a 'permanently existing idea' appearing in consciousness 'at periodical intervals' is a mythological entity, yet 'the mind can always intend . . . to think the same' (W. James, *Text-book of Psychology*, London, 1892, chs. xi. and xiv.). Similarly, we may say that, while a judgment identical in many minds is mythological, varying acts of judgment may give allegiance to the same super-personal truth, and join in the same inferential trend. It is such truth and trend, and not any range of individual experience and foresight, that allow Aristotle to postulate 'the proposition of the same thing about the same thing' (*de Interpretatione*, vi. 1), and the continuation of the same section within the same collection, of actual or possible facts (*Pr. Anal.* I. i. 5–8). The actual variability within this mythical identity is veiled by the indefiniteness of the form of proposition named 'particular'; and the actual poverty of human foresight, by the 'universal' proposition, distributing possibilities, as though on a mere chart, to an infinite range. That 'some men die willingly' cannot be the same thought for you and for me, and that 'all men die' is beyond the intellectual concern of either of us. Yet we consent that death is not the supreme terror, and we foresee it widespread as far as our imaginations can have any concern. Aristotle's *Prior Analytics* must be interpreted as dealing with this situation, and as rendering into varieties of syllogistic form the ways in which formulated thought can tolerate the limitations of actual thought, and the reservations under which it must reject them.

'The first book of the *Prior Analytics*, after a brief statement of the nature of the proposition and of the fundamental law of predication, proceeds to analyse (1) the various kinds, figures, or modes of syllogism; (2) the means by which syllogisms are formed; (3) the reduction of various imperfect forms of argument to the perfect syllogistic type. . . . The second book . . . deals with the theory afterwards called that of *Consequence*, with circular reasoning, with the possibility and consequences of syllogisms formed by converting parts of the original argument, with certain modes of indirect argument and fallacy, and concluding with brief handling of induction, paradigm, enthymeme, argument from signs, probabilities,' etc. (Adamson, *History of Logic*, p. 40).

Such topics are the main teaching of academic logic to-day, in spite of criticisms renewed from generation to generation. It must be that the more adverse critics are preoccupied with the interest of some other direction of consistency than the Aristotelian, or with some dimension of logical value other than consistency. To their interests it may seem paradoxical that a professed theory of mental process should resolve this into linguistic elements—argument, syllogism, proposition, name (T. Case, *EBr*[11], art. 'Logic'); and unphilosophical that all the important distinctions should rest on the mere denotation of terms (Hamilton); and a mistaken subtlety to classify moods into figures, according to order of terms (Kant); and puerile that inductive conceptions should be referred to their own list of instances (Bacon); and an error that syllogism is an estimate of evidence (Mill); and a usurpation that the formalities of deduction should be limited to syllogistic, and to propositions with two terms only, and to terms that are classes rather than objective relations, and to the logical relation only of inclusion and exclusion (L. Couturat, in *Encyc. Philos. Sciences*, i. 167–169).

(*b*) *Conceptual.*—A second direction in which consistency may be sought is between the thought of the moment and an identity or permanency of personal knowledge, hardly distinguishable from 'meaning the same,' as described in psychology, but quite distinguishable from the impersonal truth or universally human trend assumed by Aristotle.

The mythological world of the super-personal is replaced by an equally mythological content of the personal microcosm, a static conceptual structure to which our ever variable thoughts conform. The 'subjectively formal' or 'conceptual' logic is the canonic for the stability of this. It originated with Kant's discrimination between the section of his *Critique of the Pure Understanding* which he named 'Transcendental Logic,' where the 'forms' of knowledge appear as contributions of the mind to the constitution of its objects, and the 'General Logic,' where 'forms' are relations of cognitions to each other (*Critique*, bk. ii. Introd. § 2, *Logic*, Introd. § 1). Once more, then, as in the Hindu discipline, knowledge is referred to personality; but personality comes back not as an isolated centre of motive interest, to be disciplined for its high destiny, but as a realm of mere abstracts, namely cognitions outside the world of natural sciences, yet factitiously evolved through the course of transcendental reflexion. Kant himself, not forgetful of this origin, found in knowledge a dimension of 'relevance' as well as one of consistency. In the living thought he found an interplay corresponding to the petrified formations of the transcendental 'object.' And, while accepting the law of non-contradiction as the principle of such inference as is merely possible, he added a law of reason and consequence, for the cogency of any actual inference (*Logic*, Introd. § 71); and in applying this second law we encounter transcendental distinctions, such as between 'logical' or *a priori* universals and 'quasi-logical' or inductive. And the neo-Kantian school of logicians better their instruction by re-introducing the detailed conceptions of intellectual synthesis framed in transcendental logic. To others, however, still following the disciplinary motive, and unconcerned with the origin of the new realm commended to them for study, the only dimension recognizable independently of every physical or primary object, in which cognitions could be related to each other, appeared to be consistency.

'The stricter followers of the Kantian logical idea, *e.g.*, Mansel and Spalding, recognise, as sole principles which can be said to be involved universally in the action of thought, the laws of identity, non-contradiction, and excluded middle, and in their hands logic becomes merely the systematic statement of these laws, and the exposition of the conditions which they impose upon notions, judgments, and reasonings' (Adamson, p. 15).

(*c*) *Symbolic.*—More recently, a third direction in which consistency might be followed has been taken, which seems to presuppose, if not the factitious abstracts of transcendental logic, yet still the reflective valuations of general logic. Given these, it furnishes a 'clearer, more precise, and more plastic expression' of them, and formulæ of equivalence between them. Algebra renders a similar service to arithmetic, but without raising any doubt as to the scientific priority of the latter. Symbolic logic is at least a discipline in consistency when we make logical reflexions. Whether it is also a direct discipline in scientific knowledge, as the older formal logic is, and so may supersede or absorb it, is as yet controversially obscure.

But on every logic of consistency, however judiciously its pretensions may be restrained, one critical comment may be made:

'I do not deny the scientific convenience of considering this limited portion of Logic apart from the rest . . . but the smaller Logic, which only concerns itself with the conditions of consistency, ought to be, at least finally, studied as part of the greater, which embraces all the general conditions of the ascertainment of truth' (Mill, *Exam. of Sir W. Hamilton's Philosophy*[5], p. 477).

3. Relevance.—The larger logic was inaugurated by Aristotle through the addition of his *Posterior Analytics* to the *Prior*.

'No demonstrative proposition [*e.g.*, about numbers or lines] is taken as referring to "any number you may know of," or "any straight line you may know of," but to the entire subject—to every possible number or line' (*Post. Anal.* i. 1).

Relevance is that in 'the things we know of' which, when we 'possess or receive a demonstration,' relieves us from the need of similarly 'knowing of' the 'entire subject.' It is what Bosanquet describes as 'an inmost character' of the content of knowledge, 'as revealed by the structural relations in which it is found capable of standing' (*Essentials*, p. 49). Aristotle conceives relevance as embodied in 'universals.' Mediæval Hindu logicians (Dignāga, Divākara [*c.* A.D. 530], and Nandi [*c.* A.D. 800]) taught the intervention of 'secondary ideas' or 'abstract conceptions' in the process of inference, and authorized a 'syllogism for self' in which this dispensed with the analogy between 'example' and 'application' still required in the 'syllogism for instruction.' But Aristotle elevated this secondary idea into an authoritative 'principle,' dominating our knowledge, whether personal or racial. The authority was conferred by the faculty of reason.

'From experience, or from the entire universal which is retained in the soul, the single unit apart from the manifold of sense, which is identical in all particular cases, comes the elementary principle of art and science. . . . Reason would seem to be the faculty which has the primary principles as its objects' (*Post. Anal.* ii. 19).

The universal as a principle assures applications that might escape the 'secondary idea.' 'Man is mortal,' therefore 'I, too, must be mortal,' although men instinctively may 'think all men mortal but themselves.' The inevitability was not objective, as Plato's metaphysics might imply, but inferential.

'It does not follow, if demonstration is to exist, that there must be Ideas, or a Unity outside the many individual things, but it does follow that some unity must be truly predicable of the many' (*Post. Anal.* i. 11).

The predicable unities appear in judgment as predicates that are 'genera' and 'definitions,' and as subjects that are 'second substances'; and in demonstration as the 'essences' of the things which we seek to explain, the 'nature' of the things whose destiny we wish to foretell, the 'reasons' for what we experience, and the 'causes' for what we infer. And, although these conceptions in the dimension of relevance still influence the texts of modern logic, philosophical progress has disclaimed the static, self-sufficing constitution, which seems to spring arbitrarily from the fiat of reason. The achievements of reason must themselves become conscious under the guidance of logical conceptions more liberal, such as 'conditions of a rule' (Kant), 'laws of connexion' between attributes (Mill), 'coherence' of conceptual 'content' (Lotze), or 'identity' of relational 'system' (Bosanquet). Two distinct operations of reason must be traced: that which explains the comparative complexity of universals whose constituents are available at will, and that which explains the selection of constituents from the passive sequences of experience.

(*a*) *Deductive.*—The definite logic of the first begins with Descartes, and that of the second with Bacon. The interest of modern mathematical science supplied to Descartes the 'doubt' and 'motive,' to use Hindu logical conceptions, which brought to an end the Aristotelian superstition of 'second substances,' and suggested a scheme of rational constructiveness, proceeding from what Lotze afterwards named 'first universals' to a vast Platonic hierarchy, the 'world of ideas.'

'Those natures which we call composite are known by us, either because experience shows us what they are, or because we ourselves are responsible for their composition' (Rule xii.). . . . 'There are but few pure and simple essences . . . existing *per se*, not as depending on any others' (Rule vi.); essences which 'cannot be analysed by the mind into others more distinctly known' (Rule xii.). . . . 'Intuition is the undoubting conception of an unclouded and attentive mind; . . . it is more certain than deduction itself, in that it is simpler. . . . For example, 2 and 2 amount to the same as 3 and 1' (Rule iii.). . . . Deduction proceeds 'by the continuous and uninterrupted action of a mind that has a clear vision of each step in the process' (*ib.*). 'It is presented to us [as a complete movement] by intuition when it is simple and clear. . . . We give it the name of enumeration or induction [when it is complex], because it cannot then be grasped as a whole at the same time by the mind, and its certainty depends to some extent on the memory' (Rule xi.; Descartes, *Works*, tr. E. S. Haldane and G. R. T. Ross, vol. i., Cambridge, 1911, pp. 7–43).

(*b*) *Inductive.*—It was a parallel but slower development of the scientific spirit, in observation and experiment, that inspired a complementary scheme of rational insight as to 'how experience shows the natures that are composite.' The field for unclouded intuition is here fenced off by the indefinite multiplicity of constituents in an actual experiential situation, and, however few and simple may be the 'ultimate essences,' the steps in their synthesis are beyond either complete intuitive penetration or memory. All that Hindu logic had here achieved was to classify the 'constant associations' between sign and significate. According to Nandi, the 'signs' are either positive or negative, perceptible or imperceptible; and are related to their significates (*a*) constitutively, (*b*) as resultants, (*c*) causally, or (*d*) by concrete order, of priority, subsequence, or simultaneity (Vidyābhūṣaṇa, p. 30 f.). Aristotle, in his *Topics*, when not prepossessed by the conception of second substances, reads more deeply into the indices of relevancy, suggesting comparative analysis of instances that are exceptional towards each other or contrary in their consequences, or are negative, reverse, privative, or relational to each other, or are homogeneous in whole or part, or vary methodically in quantity, time, place, or other relation. But these broken lights still left darkness of principle over the plans of manifestation for an 'essence' or 'nature,' and how reason finds them. It is inductive principle which Bacon appears to have been first in conceiving. The Baconian conception is:

'Observation presents to us complex natures which are the results of simpler, more general forms or causes. . . . The form which is sought can be detected only by examination of cases in which the given complex effect is present, in which it is absent, and in which it appears in different degrees or amounts; . . . a process of exclusion or elimination. . . . The method of exclusion can never be perfectly carried out; but all additional aids have significance only as supplying in part the place of exhaustive enumeration' (Adamson, p. 90).

Thus, were our experience divinely given on the perfect plan of reason, we should, in the words of Descartes, 'know what these natures are,' though we ourselves are not 'responsible for their composition.' J. S. Mill articulated the principle of exclusion or elimination in five experiential methods, with symbols and canons, and explained their cogency on the broad empiricist basis which his complete survey of logical doctrines is intended to commend and defend. But the ideal plan for the manifestation of universals in experience is as much the work of *a priori* reason as is the unclouded vision of synthetic essences described by Descartes, while the march of merely experiential sequences eternally withholds that definiteness and exhaustiveness of constituents which might thus unveil the pure tissue of relevancy. The neo-Kantian logicians can accept the canons of elimination as living expressions of the aspirations of thought, in such an intellectual nature as displays the 'categories of relation,' substantiality, causality, and reciprocity. But the rationalization of any given experiential sequence must be approached through a further dimension of logical value—that of system. In this we may conceive the 'additional aids' which transform aspiration into accomplished science. Relevance is a selective principle, system a comprehensive.

4. System.—A conviction which cannot be a stable truth through sheer restrictions of internal relevancy may have value through its membership of a world of other convictions—other convictions not defined by the same question, as in the Hindu system of standards, but by questions in all degrees of kinship to it.

(*a*) *Dialectical.*—Aristotle's *Topics* marks out a sphere where such value may be traced by expressly excluding both the harmony of personal investigation with super-personal truth and the open vision of truth through reason.

'The purpose of this treatise is to find a method which will qualify us as disputants in regard to every kind of subject, where the start of the inference is from probable judgments, and which will instruct us how to avoid stultifying ourselves when we ourselves sustain an argument. . . . We call probable what appears true to all men, or to the majority, or to the wise, and, among the wise, to all, to the greater number, or to the most distinguished and authoritative' (*Topics*, i. 1).

The wide ramifications of relationship of any conviction to the remainder of knowledge are suggested by a variety of incidental methods or 'auxiliary aids' to insight.

'The organa by which we find materials for syllogisms and inductions are . . . collection of opinion from various sources, resolution of ambiguities in meaning, discrimination between species and genera, assimilation of things to each other or in their relation to other things' (*Topics*, i. 13).

(*b*) *Methodological.*—In the modern era a more systematic study of system was begun by the *Novum Organum* of Bacon, the methodological reflexions of scientists themselves, and the theories of explanation, as distinguished from eliminative induction, and of approximate generalization, probability, and operations subsidiary to induction, resumed in detail by Mill. But the methods so formulated seem to be episodes in the consciousness of a more comprehensive development in the organization of our ideas. We continuously reform and refine our tentative concepts to meet the exigence of newly experienced facts (see artt. CONCEPT and INFERENCE). And in this process we both accept limitations from, and contribute pulsations to, a progressive sum of cognitive life. The logic of system frames conceptions of the limitation and the contribution, such as the colligation of facts by superinduction of conceptual schemata (Whewell), the depth to which concepts interpenetrate judgment or blur the purity of inferential synthesis (Lotze), the inversion of dependence in our thought between principle and application (Jevons), and the relation of approximation between science and final truth (F. Enriques). In the dimension of system, 'truth can only be tested by more of itself' (Bosanquet, *Logic*, ii. 267).

LITERATURE.—No bibliography of logic with any approach to completeness appears to have been attempted. J. M. Baldwin, *DPhP*, vol. iii. pt. 2 (New York, 1905), and the *Catalogue of Venn Collection, Univ. Lib.*, Cambridge, 1889, are the most useful. Reference is advisable to the following selection of representative authorities, besides such as have been quoted.

(1) *History, scope, and utility.*—C. Prantl, *Geschichte der Logik im Abendlande*[2], 2 vols., Leipzig, 1885 (the fullest history down to the Middle Ages); F. Harms, *Geschichte der Logik*, Berlin, 1881; A. Frank, *Esquisse d'une histoire de la logique*, Paris, 1838; P. Janet and G. Séailles, *Histoire de la philosophie*, pt. 2, do. 1887; R. Adamson, *A Short History of Logic*, London, 1911; W. Whewell, *On the Philosophy of Discovery*, do. 1860; *EBr*[11], art. 'Logic'; *Encyclopædia of the Philosophical Sciences*, Eng. tr., London, 1913, vol. i.

(2) *Hindu.*—F. Max Müller, *Six Systems of Indian Philosophy*, London, 1899; S. Suguira, *Hindu Logic as preserved in China and Japan*, Philadelphia, 1900; J. R. Ballantyne,

Aphorisms of the Nyâya Philosophy, Allahabad, 1850; M. R. Bodas, *Tarka-Saṅgraha of Annambhaṭṭa*, Bombay, 1897; S. C. Vidyābhūṣaṇa, *Hindu Mediæval Logic*, Calcutta, 1912.

(3) *Greek*.—A. Trendelenburg, *Logische Untersuchungen*², Leipzig, 1862; G. Grote, *Aristotle*², London, 1872–79, 1880; J. Barthélemy Saint-Hilaire, *De la Logique d'Aristote*, Paris, 1838; Porphyry; Cicero, *Topics*.

(4) *Mediæval*.—Works of Boethius, Avicenna, Aquinas, Duns Scotus, Ramus, etc.; V. Cousin, *Ouvrages inédits d'Abélard*, Paris, 1836 (with valuable historical introduction).

(5) *Modern*.—A. Arnauld and P. Nicole, *Logic, or the Art of Thinking; being the Port-Royal Logic*, tr. T. S. Baynes⁷, Edinburgh, 1872; F. Bacon, *Novum Organum*, 1620; T. Hobbes, *Computation* (*Works*, i.), London, 1839–45; E. B. de Condillac, *La Logique*, new ed., Paris, 1811; F. Burgersdyck, *Institutionum logic. libri duo*, Cambridge, 1680; H. Aldrich, *Artis Logicæ Compendium*⁴, ed. H. L. Mansel, Oxford, 1862; W. Hamilton, *Lectures on Metaphysics and Logic*, London, 1859–60, iii. and iv.; H. L. Mansel, *Prolegomena Logica*², do. 1860; J. S. Mill, *System of Logic*⁸, do. 1872; A. de Morgan, *Formal Logic*, do. 1847; G. Boole, *Investigation of the Laws of Thought*, do. 1854; F. E. Beneke, *System der Logik*, Berlin, 1842; G. W. F. Hegel, *Logic*, Eng. tr.², Oxford, 1894; M. W. Drobisch, *Neue Darstellung der Logik*⁵, Hamburg, 1887; H. Ulrici, *System der Logik*, Leipzig, 1852; L. George, *Die Logik als Wissenschaftslehre*, Berlin, 1868.

(6) *Recent*.—(*a*) Formal and symbolic: W. S. Jevons, *Studies in Deductive Logic*, London, 1880; J. N. Keynes, *Studies and Exercises in Formal Logic*⁴, do. 1906; J. Venn, *Symbolic Logic*², do. 1894; A. T. Shearman, *Development of Symbolic Logic*, do. 1906, *Scope of Formal Logic*, do. 1911; E. Schroeder, *Vorlesungen über der Algebra der Logik*, Leipzig, 1890–95; B. A. W. Russell and A. N. Whitehead, *Principia Mathematica*, pt. i., Cambridge, 1910–13.

(*b*) Critical or philosophical: T. H. Green, *Lectures on Logic* (*Works*, iii., London, 1886); F. H. Bradley, *Principles of Logic*, do. 1883; L. T. Hobhouse, *Theory of Knowledge*, do. 1896; J. Dewey, *Studies in Logical Theory*, Chicago, 1903; J. Bergmann, *Die Grundprobleme der Logik*², Berlin, 1895; E. Husserl, *Logische Untersuchungen*², Halle, 1913.

(*c*) Systems: F. Ueberweg, *System der Logik und Geschichte der log. Lehren*, Bonn, 1868, Eng. tr., London, 1871; R. H. Lotze, *System der Philosophie*², Leipzig, 1880–84; B. Bosanquet, *Essentials of Logic*, London, 1895, *Logic*², Oxford, 1911; J. Veitch, *Institutes of Logic*, Edinburgh, 1885; J. Venn, *Principles of Empirical or Inductive Logic*², London, 1900; W. Wundt, *Logik*², Stuttgart, 1893–95.

(*d*) Methodological: W. L. Davidson, *Logic of Definition*, London, 1885; A. Sidgwick, *Fallacies*, do. 1883, *Process of Argument*, do. 1893, *Distinction and the Criticism of Beliefs*, do. 1892, *Use of Words in Reasoning*, do. 1901, *The Application of Logic*, do. 1910; J. Venn, *The Logic of Chance*³, do. 1888; W. S. Jevons, *Principles of Science*, do. 1874; K. Pearson, *Grammar of Science*², do. 1900; H. Poincaré, *Science and Method*, Eng. tr., do. 1914.

For a summary of substantive logical doctrine see artt. BELIEF (Logical), CONCEPT, INFERENCE, JUDGMENT (Logical), and METHOD (Logical).

J. BROUGH.

LOGIC (Buddhist).—Buddhists have been called the real founders of the mediæval logic and logical literature of India, a position which they share to a great extent with the Jains.

> 'At about A.D. 400 began an epoch when they [Jains and Buddhists] seriously took up the problems of logic, and all the text-books on the Jaina and Buddhist systems of logic date at or after that time. Ujjainī in Malwa and Valabhi in Guzerat, . . . Patna and Drāviḍa [the Deccan],' were the principal seats of Jainist logical activity. 'The Nyāyāvatāra, by Siddhasena Divākara, dated about 533 A.D., was the first systematic work on the Jaina Logic.'[1]

The earliest seat of Buddhist mediæval logic is said to have been in Gandhāra (about Peshawar) on the Panjāb frontier, till the invading Huns dispersed all scholarly life. Only such literature survived as had been transported in translations to China and Tibet. There were, however, other schools at Ayodhyā (Oudh) and in the Deccan. From the latter school one systematic work of the 7th cent. A.D. has survived in Sanskrit: the *Nyāyabindu* of Dharmakīrti, and its commentary by Dharmottara.[2]

This ascription of the rise of logical studies in mediæval India to Jain and Buddhist culture is tantamount to saying that systematic treatment of the nature and regulation of reasoned knowledge as such first took shape when Indian culture was practically Buddhist and Jainist. That systematic treatment was more critical and exegetical than constructive. It is clear from the Buddhist scriptures, and also, so far as any work has yet been done upon them, from the Jain scriptures, that an unwritten and unelaborated body of normative principles and methods of thought had long existed in India. The early mediæval logics are exegeses, expounding and elaborating the logical categories applied in earlier works. These categories included classifications of knowledge, doctrines of terms and propositions, methods of induction, fallacies, and, possibly, in the Jain classics, syllogism. Of the methods and categories themselves the early works say little or nothing. Those works are the expression of the greater or constructive stage of the Buddhist and Jain movements. The Buddhist scriptures are often critical; but they criticize the traditions which they found holding the field, rather than the principles and methods of deduction and induction of their day.

Two passages in the Suttas afford an apparent exception to this assertion. In these, certain matters are declared to be 'not in the sphere of *takka*,' rendered by Rhys Davids and R. Otto Franke 'mere logic'[1] (*tarka-śāstra*, or 'rules of thought,' is one of the technical Indian terms for logic). And logic-mongers (*takkino*) and pedants (*vīmaṁsino*), failing to grasp them, are said to arrive at fantastic theories.[2] Again, in prescribing a pragmatic criterion of the merits of a religious doctrine, the Buddha is said to have excluded such criteria as authority, tradition, etc., and both *takkahetu* and *nayahetu*.[3] These, again, belong to the oldest technical terms for logic, *hetu* ('condition,' 'cause,' 'inference') and *naya* ('method') practically covering all reasoned thinking in both Jainist and Buddhist books.[4] This depreciation of ratiocinative method, combined with misconceptions of the orthodox theory of knowledge in early Buddhism, has given rise to the mistaken view that Buddhists rejected both logical method and the validity of any knowledge established by it.[5] But a careful consideration of the two *Suttas* quoted above, in the light of the sober intellectual method prevailing in the great majority of the *Suttas*, brings us to a very different conclusion. In the latter passage the soundness of any ethical doctrine or gospel is held to be rightly tested, not by metaphysical dialectic, but by a utilitarian calculus. In the former passage the 'logic' that is condemned as inadequate is such as often finds condemnation among ourselves, when we 'feel' rather than discern that deductions are being made from outworn, outgrown terms, from wrong data, from words ambiguously used. Only a culture which has a logic of recreated inductions will condemn such misuse of deduction as 'mere logic.' It is one of the penalties induced by such effete reasoning that the noble formulation of right thinking should, in popular usage, incur reproach, as if it had failed in general.

The Buddhist *Sutta* and *Abhidhamma Piṭakas* afford unmistakable evidence of (1) the existence of a current logical doctrine, (2) misuse of the same by dialecticians or 'sophists,' deducing from confused terms and wrong premisses, and (3) a constant faith in the appeal to judgment and argument, *i.e.* to logical faculty, and to logical principles. The *Suttas*, or discourses, were in great part addressed to relatively immature minds—to the 'man in the street' and to the average *bhikkhu* or *sekha* (learner in the Order). But the proportion of discourses filled with categorical assertions is very small. Most of them seek to capture the listener by argument. No sentence occurs oftener than *Taṁ kissa hetu?*, 'What is the reason of that?' The prevailing method of the Buddha in his replies to

1 S. C. Vidyābhūṣaṇa, *History of the Mediæval School of Indian Logic*, Calcutta, 1909, p. xviii.

2 Ed. P. Peterson, in the *Bibliotheca Indica*, Calcutta, 1890.

1 *Dīgha Nikāya*, i. 12; Rhys Davids, *Dialogues of the Buddha*, Oxford, 1899–1910, i. 26; R. O. Franke, *Dīgha Nikāya in Auswahl übersetzt*, Göttingen, 1914, p. 21.

2 *Dīgha Nikāya*, p. 16.

3 *Aṅguttara Nikāya*, i. 189.

4 Vidyābhūṣaṇa, *op. cit.* p. 4.

5 Cf., *e.g.*, *ib.* p. 59.

interlocutors is one of gentle 'reasonableness' (to adopt Matthew Arnold's rendering of ἐπιείκεια). And *nyāya* (*ñāya*), 'knowledge,' 'science,' which is the title-word in the oldest Indian logical works,[1] is used synonymously with *satya* (*sachcha*), 'truth,' as forming, with *dhamma* ('right' or 'norm') and *kusala* ('good'), the threefold foundation on which the perfect man should be established.[2] In the somewhat later collection called *Abhidhamma Piṭaka*, where doctrines, put forward *ad hominem* in the *Suttas*, are more abstractly expounded by way of question and answer, logical method is more systematically applied. The import of a great number of terms is set out, usually in dichotomic division, but sometimes in the distinctively Indian method of presenting the by us so-called Laws of Thought, thus: Is A B? If not, is A not-B? If not, is A both B and not-B? If not, is A neither B nor not-B (in other words, is A a chimæra)? The expositions, again, are sometimes exercises in converted propositions, sometimes arguments in hypothetical propositions. The books entitled *Yamaka* and *Kathāvatthu*,[3] respectively, consist entirely of these exercises and arguments. No definite exercise in, or allusion to, syllogism has been found in the *Piṭakas*, although it figures prominently in the earliest Buddhist and Jain treatises on logic. Nor, indeed, do the paired words *pamāṇa* ('immediate knowledge,' 'perception') and *anumāna* ('mediate knowledge,' 'inference') apparently occur in the *Piṭakas* as the indispensable logical terms which they subsequently became.[4] Nevertheless, the *Suttas* and the *Abhidhamma* books taken together, with all the legendary and illustrative matter discounted, present so varied an appeal to the intellect of their age that it is not surprising if one result of the paramountcy of Buddhist culture was to yield a harvest, not only of psychological, but also of logical, analysis and systematization. A still greater field of material for the history of logic will possibly be opened up when (1) the original Jain scriptures are all edited, and (2) the Chinese and Tibetan translations of Buddhist Sanskrit treatises on logic, as well as (3) the orthodox Theravāda philosophical works in Sinhalese and Burmese MSS, become accessible. A comparison of the conclusions gleaned from these sources, and from the Pāli materials as yet accessible, with the concepts of European logic will prove of deeper philosophical importance than may appear likely to those who see in logic only an academic exercise. By intellectual procedure, according to the norms of which logic is the interpreter rather than the dictator, the human mind has grasped the most general data of experience inductively and deductively. And that procedure has centred round certain concepts here, round other concepts there. The difference in emphasis thus produced tends to become absolute, hindering both mutual understanding and also thereby a positive, general advance in philosophy. The system, for instance, of definition by genus and species, of division by dichotomy only, of subsuming the particular under the more general, admirable as it has proved in all quantitative analysis, may prove a hindrance in estimating qualitative values in æsthetic and spiritual inquiry. The Buddhist scriptures did not keep rigidly to these (peculiarly Greek) lines in their analyses. They did not always, or emphatically, see things as decomposable substances, in wholes and particulars. Their founder disliked generalizing. 'I am not,' he is made to say, 'a generalizer, I am a particularizer.'[1] True, they expressed organic phenomena in terms of *khandha*, 'aggregate.' But *khandhas*, for them, were not 'things that *are*,' but 'happenings and ceasings,' 'risings and fallings.' They may be said to have seen things more as intercrossing force-rays, each abscissa or confluence of which gave occasion for a general term. Hence their definitions consist in the laying together of mutually intercrossing, overlapping, or partially coinciding notions.

Centuries later we find Buddhaghoṣa and Buddhadatta adopting consistently a fourfold scheme for the definition of psychological and ethical terms, viz. by salient character(s), essential properties, resulting phenomena, and proximate cause.[2] This method survives in a classic work centuries younger, but is no longer prominently used.[3]

To revert to the laws of thought—the way in which Indian logic presented the second and third of these (Contradiction and Excluded Middle) has been mentioned. But the first (Identity) was virtually traversed, in Buddhist thought, by the fundamental law of *anichcha* (*anitya*), 'impermanence' (*i.e.* incessant change). By this law A is never A for more than a moment, but is after that not A, but, as it were, A_1, A_2, A_3 . . . And, just as Aristotle rated as mere 'vegetable' the mind that rejected the (Greek) laws of thought, so for the Buddhists there was no intelligent or accurate thinking on any basis which ignored this law of impermanence. The other great tenets that 'all (life) is subject to ill,' and that 'all is without soul or substance,' are, in fact, corollaries of it.

The only general principle of thought put forward in Europe which harmonizes with Buddhist axioms is that 'Principle or Law of Sufficient Reason' for which certain logicians, notably Leibniz, claimed equal rank with the three named above, namely, that 'nothing happens without a reason why it should be so rather than otherwise.' This comes very near to the *idap-pachchayatā* ('this is conditioned by that') of Buddhist causality. And, generally speaking, it is in the logic of causation or of induction that we first notice the resemblances between Buddhist and European logic rather than the differences. The ancient formula of cause—'that being present, this becomes; from the arising of that, this arises; that being absent, this does not become; from the cessation of that, this ceases'[4]—is the nearest approach to our logical schemata that we find in the *Piṭakas*. And the mediæval elaboration of the principle so formulated—that 'its essential mark is the condition of the happening of a phenomenon[5] on the occurrence of its sole invariable antecedent phenomenon'—is well in tune with our more modern logic of induction.

LITERATURE.—This is given in the footnotes. Of the two important early classics, the *Milinda-pañha* (see MILINDA) and the *Netti-pakaraṇa*, the former argues mainly by analogy, while the latter uses only the first and last of Buddhaghoṣa's four heads given above.

C. A. F. RHYS DAVIDS.

LOGIC (Indian).—See NYĀYA.

LOGOS.—The Greek word λόγος has no exact equivalent in any other language. Just as Goethe's *Faust*, when translating the first verse of the Fourth Gospel into German, tries in succession and rejects *Wort*, *Sinn*, *Kraft*, and finally decides upon *That*, so Latin theology wavered between *Verbum*, *Sermo*, and *Ratio* before accepting

[1] Vidyābhūṣaṇa, p. 1.
[2] Cf. *Saṁyutta Nikāya*, v. 19, with i. 189; Rhys Davids, *Dialogues*, ii. 167 (*ñāya* is rendered 'system'). The formula of causation is repeatedly called Aryan (*i.e.* Buddhist) *ñāya*.
[3] Ed. for *PTS*, 1911-13, 1894-97. The *PTS* is publishing a translation of the latter work in 1915.
[4] *Pamāṇa* is used only for 'measure,' 'estimate'; *anumāna* apparently does not occur at all.

[1] Not an *ekaṁsavāda*, but a *vibhajjavāda* (*Majjhima Nikāya*, ii. 197). The Theravāda, or mother school, were long known as Vibhajjavādins.
[2] *Atthasālinī* (*PTS*, 1897), 109, *passim*; *Abhidhammāvatāra* (*PTS*, 1915), 2, *passim*.
[3] *Abhidhammatthasaṅgaha* ('Compendium of Philosophy'), probably 12th cent. A.D., p. 212 f. (*PTS*, 1884, tr. 1910).
[4] *Majjhima Nikāya*, ii. 32; *Saṁyutta Nikāya*, ii. 28, etc.
[5] *Abhidhammatthasaṅgaha*, p. 187.

Verbum, the least satisfactory, perhaps, of the three. The word has a history both in Greek philosophy and in Jewish Alexandrian theology. But, whereas in Greek philosophy the word means the divine Reason regarded as immanent in the cosmic process, the authors of the Septuagint use it to translate the Hebrew *Memra* and its poetic synonyms, which mean primarily the spoken word of the Deity.[1] Hellenized Jewish thought attempted to fuse these two originally distinct meanings; and so arose the Christian use of the word as a name for the second Person of the Trinity, incarnated in Jesus of Nazareth. It will be convenient to consider in succession the growth of the idea in Greek philosophy, in Jewish-Alexandrian theology (the use of *Memra* in the Hebrew sacred literature hardly belongs to our subject), and in Christian theology.

1. In Greek philosophy.—The history of the Logos-idea begins with Heraclitus of Ephesus (*c.* 535–475 B.C.), who, as F. M. Cornford has rightly maintained,[2] represents a mystical reaction against the materialism of the Ionian philosophers. For him the visible world is a symbolic system which half conceals and half reveals the reality. This truth or reality is the divine soul of the world, whose life is manifested in the endless cycle of birth and death, of becoming, change, decay, and renewal. There is *one* Logos, the same throughout the world, which is itself homogeneous and one. This wisdom we may win by searching within ourselves; 'it is open to all men to know themselves and be wise.' The divine soul is 'Nature,' the cosmic process; it is God; it is *ψυχή*, the life-principle; it is Logos, the divine law, or will of God. 'All human laws are fed by the one divine law. It prevails as much as it will, and is sufficient and more than sufficient for all things.' This Logos is the immanent reason of the world; 'it existeth from all time; yet men are unaware of it, both before they hear it and while they listen to it.' The Logos, like Wordsworth's 'Duty,' keeps the stars in their courses. It is the hidden harmony which underlies the discords and antagonisms of existence. There is no trace in Heraclitus of a transcendent God, whose reason or will the Logos could be. The system is rather a form of pantheism, with a strong mystical element. In Anaxagoras, however, the Logos, or *νοῦς* (he preferred the latter term), is intermediate between God and the world, being the regulating principle of the universe, the divine intelligence. In Plato, though he was the founder of a philosophy in which the Logos-idea was to find a congenial home, there is but little that bears directly on our subject. The world, he says in the *Timæus* (p. 29 f.), is created by a fusion of mind and necessity; it is itself a living and rational organism, the 'only-begotten (*μονογενής*) son of God,' itself a God, and the 'express image' (*εἰκών*) of the Highest.

In Stoicism the philosophy of Heraclitus received a new life and fresh developments. Like Heraclitus, the Stoics regarded Fire as the primordial substance, the material principle of the divine. Endowed with inherent productive activity, it is the 'seminal Reason' (*λόγος σπερματικός*) of the world, which manifests itself in all the phenomena of nature. These phenomena, or, rather, the active principles which create them, are often called *λόγοι σπερματικοί*, in the plural. Christian writers like Justin Martyr laid hold of this doctrine to connect Greek philosophy with their own religion. Every man, Justin taught, at his birth participates in the universal Reason, which he identifies with the Johannine Logos which 'lighteth every man.' Accordingly, he argues,[1] heathens like Heraclitus and Socrates, in so far as they lived *μετὰ λόγου*, may be claimed as Christians, and may be saved. The seminal Logos of the Stoics, when spoken of as a single Power, is God Himself as the organic principle of the cosmic process, which He directs to a rational and moral end. This power is not present in all creatures equally; only man participates in it so fully that he may be regarded as a real effluence of the Deity. The Stoics distinguished between the *λόγος ἐνδιάθετος*, the potential, unmanifested Reason, and the *λόγος προφορικός*, the thought of God expressed in action. This distinction led to a new emphasis being laid on the other meaning of *λόγος*, as 'word' or 'speech'; and in this way Stoicism made it easier for Jewish philosophy to identify the Greek *λόγος* with the half-personified 'Word of Jahweh.' Words and thoughts, according to the Stoics, were the very same things regarded under different aspects. The same *λόγος* which is Thought as long as it resides in the breast is Word as soon as it comes forth. The distinction between *ἐνδιάθετος* and *προφορικός*, often used by Philo and the Greek Christian Fathers, is really identical with that drawn by Aristotle between *ὁ ἔξω λόγος* and *ὁ ἐν τῇ ψυχῇ*.[2] Christian writers found another fruitful idea in the Stoic doctrine that, since the one Logos is present in many human souls, men may have communion with each other through their participation in the same Logos. The Logos-Christ might be explained Stoically as the indwelling revealer of the Father, with whom He is one; as the vital principle of the universe; as the way, the truth, and the life; as the inspirer of the highest morality; and, last, but not least, as the living bond of union between the various members of His 'body.' The world, for Stoicism, is simple and unique (*εἷς καὶ μονογενής*); it is a living creature (*οὐσία ἔμψυχος*). The Spirit (*πνεῦμα*) goes through all things, formless itself, but the creator of forms. The Logos, as World-Idea, is also single and simple (*εἷς καὶ ἁπλοῦς*), though it assumes manifold forms in its plastic self-unfolding. It is identified with Fate (*εἱμαρμένη*); and Stobæus says:

> 'Fate is the *λόγος* of the *κόσμος*, or the *λόγος* of those things in the universe which are directed by providence (*πρόνοια*). Chrysippus, however, instead of Logos uses Truth, Cause, Nature, Necessity, and other words' (*Ecl.* i. 130).

The question whether Stoicism identified God with the Logos is not easy to answer. E. Zeller is probably right in saying that the logic of Stoicism was rigidly pantheistic—it was a form of naturalistic monism: *Deus sive Natura*. Origen says that the Stoics and the Platonists both call the world God; but for Stoicism the world is the supreme God, for the Platonists only God in the second place. But the opponents of Stoicism are too harsh when they say that the Stoics bring in God only in order to be in the fashion. It was their religious need that made them bring Him in. Perhaps they could not consistently find room for any God above the Logos, but in fact they did ascribe to the Deity more personal attributes than could properly belong to their Logos. They were certainly able to feel enthusiastic devotion to the Logos as the principle of law and righteousness. This is shown by the famous hymn of Cleanthes:

> 'Thee it is lawful for all mortals to address. For we are Thine offspring, and alone of living creatures that live and walk the earth moulded in the image of the All. Therefore I will ever sing Thee, and celebrate Thy power. All this universe, rolling round the earth, obeys Thee, and follows willingly Thy command. . . . O King most high, nothing is done without Thee, neither in heaven nor on earth nor on the sea, except what the wicked do in their foolishness. Thou makest order out of disorder, and things that strive find in Thee a friend; for Thou hast fitted together good and evil into one, and hast established one Reason (*λόγον*) that lasts for ever. But the wicked fly from Thy law, unhappy ones, and though they desire to possess what

[1] Cf. E. Hatch and H. A. Redpath, *Concordance to the Septuagint*, Oxford, 1892–1906, pp. 881–887.
[2] *From Religion to Philosophy*, London, 1912, p. 184 f.

[1] *Apol.* i. 46. [2] *Anal. Post.* i. 10. 76.

is good, yet they see not, neither do they hear, the universal law of God. . . . But O God, giver of all things, who dwellest in dark clouds and rulest over the thunder, deliver men from their foolishness. Scatter it from their souls, and grant them to obtain wisdom, for by wisdom dost Thou rightly govern all things ; that, being honoured, we may repay Thee with honour, singing Thy works without ceasing, as we ought to do. For there is no greater thing than this, for mortal men or for gods, to sing rightly the praise of universal law (λόγον).'

In fact, this conception of a germinative principle of Reason which manifests itself in the universe, and especially in the minds of human beings as members of a universal community, prepared the soil on which a world-religion might grow. And at the same time the individual was brought into a closer relation with the divine than had been contemplated in any earlier system of Greek philosophy.

2. In Jewish-Alexandrian theology. — Hebrew thought about the 'Word of the Lord' does not enter the subject of the present article until the tendency arose to personify the self-revealing activity of Jahweh. The earlier books of the OT connect the operations of the *Memra* with three ideas—creation, providence, and revelation. God spake the word, and the worlds were made ; then at once His spirit, or breath, gives life to what the Word creates, and renews the face of the earth. The protecting care of God for the chosen people is attributed by the Jewish commentaries to the *Memra*. Besides this, the 'Word of the Lord' inspires prophecy and imparts the Law. The tendency to personify the activities of Jahweh is seen in the expressions used about the Angel, the Name, the Glory, and, above all, the Wisdom of God. Similar language about the Word is found in the frequent phrase 'the Word of the Lord came unto me,' and in such passages as Ps 147^{15}, Is $55^{10f.}$ 2^{1}, Ps 33^{4}, Jer 23^{29}. Nevertheless, the personification is throughout poetical rather than metaphysical, except in writers completely under Greek influence. On the whole, in the later books the conception of Wisdom tends to displace that of Word—a change which really brings the Jewish idea nearer to the Greek. 'Wisdom' in Job is the hidden purpose which God is working out in man's existence—the grand secret of life known only to God. In Proverbs Wisdom is the cardinal virtue; she stands at the corners of the streets, and invites men to walk in her ways. God created or prepared her before the world was made ; she was by His side when He planned the scheme of the world-order ; she was daily His delight, rejoicing always before Him. Therefore He assures those who listen to her of life, blessedness, and the favour of God. In Ecclesiastes, Ecclesiasticus, and Wisdom of Solomon we find a further development of Jewish thought in the direction of Greek philosophy. Ecclesiastes presents us with a pessimistic philosophy quite alien from Judaism and strongly influenced by Stoicism, though the trend is masked by numerous interpolations. Ecclesiasticus is more Jewish in sentiment ; 'Wisdom' has found her chief expression in the books of the Law. The book called Wisdom of Solomon is the work of an orthodox Jew, who has no sympathy with the views of Ecclesiastes, and resents their attribution to Solomon ; but his doctrine of the divine Wisdom is strongly coloured by Stoical and Platonic ideas. Wisdom is immanent in God, belonging to the divine essence, and yet existing in *quasi*-independence side by side with God. Wisdom was the active agent in the creation of the world, selecting among the divine ideas those which were to be actualized in the created universe. She is an emanation from God, pervading all things, and passing 'more rapidly than any motion' among them, without contracting any impurity by her contact with matter. In the human spirit she is the teacher not only of every virtue and of all theological knowledge, but of all the human arts and sciences. The identification of 'Wisdom' with the Greek Logos is almost explicitly made, as is the identification of Wisdom with the Holy Spirit of God. This book, in fact, marks a transition from the OT doctrine to that of Philo, and is of much importance in the history of Jewish-Alexandrian theology.

Philo not only blends Greek and Jewish ideas about the Logos; he achieves a syncretism of divergent Greek conceptions. His Logos is a combination of the Platonic ideas and Stoic universal causality. He takes over the main Stoical conception, but detaches it from materialism, and tries to harmonize it with the Platonic theory that visible things are only types of realities laid up in the intelligible world. His Logos is much like Plato's idea of the Good, except that it is regarded as creatively active. Philo found this conception useful, because he wished to conceive of the divine activity Hellenically, without ceasing to believe in the OT Jahweh. Jewish thought had been in danger of separating the Creator so completely from His creation as to produce an intolerable dualism. This tendency had been mitigated by poetical personification. Philo fixed these poetical symbols, and turned them from poetry to metaphysics by identifying the *Memra* with the Stoical Logos Platonized. In opposition to the earlier Jewish idea of the Word, Philo's Logos is an intermediary between God and the world ; He is the principle of revelation. Philo is fertile in forms of expression to convey the relation of this principle of revelation to the Godhead and to man respectively. In the former aspect, the Logos is declared to be the first-born Son of God, the first of the angels ; in the latter, He is the Man who is the immediate image of God, the prototypal Man in whose image all other men are created. The Logos dwells with God as His vice-gerent ; He is the eldest son of God, and Wisdom is His mother. In other places He is identified with Wisdom. Again, He is the Idea of Ideas, the whole mind of God going out of itself in creation. He represents the world before God as High Priest, Intercessor, Paraclete. He is the Shekinah, or glory of God ; but also the darkness or shadow of God, since the creature half conceals and half reveals the Creator. He is the intelligible world, the archetypal universe of the Platonists, and the real life of the world that we know. In man He operates as the higher reason. If we ask whether the Logos is an aspect of the divine nature or an individual being, we get answers which are hard to reconcile. The rational part of the soul exhibits the type of the Logos, the 'second Deity' ; no mortal could be formed in the likeness of the supreme Father of the world, or ever brought into comparison with Him. But elsewhere the Logos appears to be only an attribute of God. As an orthodox Jew (or one who wished to pass for orthodox), Philo cannot have thought of affirming two divine agents. And yet the Platonic doctrine of a transcendent unknowable God required a divine vice-gerent, while the Stoic Logos had been an independent immanent world-principle, very different from the Hebrew Jahweh. The amalgamation of these divergent philosophies in Philo is rather external and superficial. The Philonic Logos is a dynamic principle, but also a cosmic principle, who accounts for the existence of the world. Occasionally Philo seems to suggest that the Logos is 'the God of us the imperfect,' as if from the highest point of view the Logos were only an appearance of the Absolute. So in a thoroughly Plotinian passage he says :

'God appears in His unity when the soul, being perfectly purified and having transcended all multiplicity, not only the multiplicity of numbers but even the dyad which is nearest to unity, passes on to the unity which is unmingled, simple, and complete in itself' (*de Abrahamo*, 24).

But this is not a common line of speculation in Philo.

In the NT the technical use of the word Logos is found in the Fourth Gospel (unless we should add 1 Jn $1^{1f.}$ and Rev 19^{13}) only. But it is important to observe that St. Paul, especially in his later Epistles, gives us almost the whole of the Logos-doctrine which we read in the Prologue to the Fourth Gospel. The conception of Christ as a cosmic principle is even more emphasized in Colossians than in the Gospel. When we read of the Pauline Christ that He is the image (*εἰκών*) of God, that in Him the Pleroma of the Godhead dwells in bodily form, that He was the agent in creation, and the immanent Spirit 'through whom are all things,' that He pre-existed in the form of God, that He is the first-born of all creation, in whom and through whom and to whom are all things, that all things are summed up in Him, that He is all and in all, that His reign is co-extensive with the world's history, that He is life-giving Spirit, abiding in the souls of His disciples, forming Himself in them, and transforming them into His likeness, enlightening them and uniting them in one body with Himself, it does not seem that a candid criticism can deny that all the elements of a complete Logos-theology are to be found in the Pauline Epistles. Without assuming any direct influence of Philo, which is perhaps improbable, it is unquestionable that the Jewish-Alexandrian Logos-philosophy had a great and increasing influence upon St. Paul's doctrine of the Person of Christ. In proportion as the apocalyptic Messianism which we find in Thessalonians lost its importance for him, he approximated more and more to the type of Christology which we associate with the name of St. John. It must not be supposed that this statement stands or falls with the authenticity of Colossians and Ephesians. The Epistles to the Corinthians contain similar language.

The large obligations of the author of the Fourth Gospel to the Philonian school cannot reasonably be denied, though they have often been questioned. It is clear from the tone of the Prologue that Philo's conception of the Logos, or something akin to it, was already familiar to those for whom the Evangelist wrote. No explanation of the word Logos is given; and almost every verse in the Prologue might be paralleled from Philo. Technical terms from Philo (*σφραγίς* and *παράκλητος* are examples) abound in the Gospel. Indeed, the whole treatment adopted by the Evangelist presupposes the Jewish-Alexandrian philosophy of religion, and would be unintelligible without it. Nevertheless, it is true that the identification of the historical Jesus with the Logos, and of the Jewish Messiah with the Logos, makes a great difference. Philo had never thought of identifying the Logos with the Messiah—a figure in whom he took very little interest. The chief differences (which have often been exaggerated) between the Philonian and Johannine Logos are these: (1) the Evangelist defines far more clearly the relation of the Logos to God, as a second Person in the Godhead, distinct, though eternally inseparable from the Father; (2) the notion of God the Father as a transcendent unapproachable Being, to be known only through an intermediary, is foreign to the Gospel, in which God the Father acts directly upon the world; it is in consequence of the activity thus attributed to God the Father that the *creative* function of the Logos loses its interest and is not referred to after the Prologue; (3) in the Gospel the conception of the Logos is more dynamic than in Philo; the Logos-Christ is the complete revelation of the *character* of God rather than of His nature; the revelation of the Divine as self-sacrificing love is an idea not to be found in Philo; it follows that the conception of *life*, which implies growth, change, and development, has an importance for the Evangelist which it could not have for Philo; (4) could Philo have accepted the Incarnation? The difference between the two writers here has often been magnified by orthodox critics. Philo believed in theophanies, and could have easily accepted a docetic theory of the Incarnation. The Fourth Evangelist is no docetist; but for him too the Incarnation was primarily a *revelation*. The Johannine Christ became flesh that we might 'behold his glory,' and learn what could only thus be taught. But a real Incarnation of the Logos would no doubt have been inconceivable to Philo, for whom no historical event seems to have any importance as such.

The Logos-doctrine of the Prologue may be briefly summarized as follows. From all eternity, before time began, the Logos *was*. He is supra-temporal, not simply the Spirit of the World. He did not become personal either at the Creation or at the Incarnation.[1] The Logos was 'turned toward' (*πρός*) God. The preposition indicates the closest union, with a sort of transcendental subordination. The Father alone is the *πηγὴ θεότητος*. The opening words of the Prologue do not (with Meyer, Weiss, etc.) refer to the exaltation of Christ, but to His eternal relationship to the Father. Deification was to the Jews blasphemy, to the Greeks a light thing. The Evangelist shows that the principles of distinction and deeper unity are in God Himself. 'All things came into being through the Logos,' who is the mediate Agent in creation.[2] 'Apart from him nothing came into being. That which has come into being was, in him, life.' Bossuet, following Augustine, comments rightly:

> 'Everything, even inanimate things, were life in the eternal Word, by his idea and eternal thought.'

The Logos is the light of men *as life*; that is to say, revelation is vital and dynamic. God reveals Himself as vital law to be obeyed and lived. The cosmic process, including, of course, the spiritual history of mankind and of the individual, is the sole field of revelation. 'The light shineth in darkness.' As the first step in the first creation was to divide the light from the darkness, so the new creation effects the same division in the moral and spiritual sphere. 'And the darkness arrested (?) it not.'[3]

'This is the genuine light, which lighteth every man as it comes into the world.' 'He was (always) in the world, and the world knew him not.'[4] 'And the Logos became flesh and tabernacled among us.' Here (v.[14]) the Evangelist mentions the Incarnation for the first time. The Logos, who from all eternity was fully divine (*θεός*), became flesh (assumed visible humanity) at a certain time.

It is not easy to say whether the Evangelist conceived of the Logos existing *before* the Incarnation as 'true man from all eternity';[5] but 3^{13} and 6^{62} (cf. 1 Co 15^{47}) suggest that he did. It is certainly in accordance with Johannine ideas to hold that the Incarnation, and the Passion as the sacrament of the divine self-sacrifice, were part of the counsels of God from all eternity. The Logos before the Incarnation was, according to this thought, Man *ἐνδιάθετος*, though not *προφορικός*. The Prologue thus leads up to the Incarnation of the Logos,

1 There was nothing strange in this doctrine. The book of Proverbs (8^{23}) had asserted the same of Wisdom: 'I was set up from everlasting, from the beginning, or ever the earth was.'

2 This is also Philonic; cf. *de Cherub.* 35: *εὑρήσεις γὰρ αἴτιον μὲν αὐτοῦ [τοῦ κόσμου] τὸν θεόν, ὑφ' οὗ γέγονεν, ὕλην δὲ τὰ τέσσαρα στοιχεῖα, ἐξ ὧν συνεκράθη, ὄργανον δὲ λόγον θεοῦ, δι' οὗ κατεσκευάσθη.*

3 So Origen took *κατέλαβεν*, probably rightly.

4 This is exactly what Heraclitus also says about the Logos.

5 T. H. Green, *Works*, London, 1885–88, iii. 208 f.

which is the theme of the whole Gospel, though the historical form precludes any further discussion of the subject on its philosophical side. The incidents are selected for their symbolical and illustrative value, and the whole tendency of the treatise is quietly to transmute local and temporal ideas about the Incarnation into a more universal and spiritual form. The highest form of faith, he more than hints, is that which can dispense with ocular evidence. The ascended Christ can be 'touched' more readily than was possible when the Logos had His tabernacle among men.

3. In Christian theology.—The doctrine of the Logos has a very important place in the theology of the early Christian Church. It was the answer of orthodox Catholicism to various theories of the Person of Christ which at that time seemed plausible—theories which made Jesus a phantom, or an emanation, or a demi-god. Heretical thought, down to and including Arianism, tended to rank Christ with the imaginary intermediate Spirits which formed a hierarchy between the supreme God and humanity. The Johannine Logos-doctrine was a barrier against all such theories. The Apostolic Fathers do not supply much material. Ignatius calls Christ λόγος ἀπὸ σιγῆς προελθών,[1] which has a Gnostic ring, since Valentinus was soon to make Logos and Zoe the offspring of Bythos and Sigē. Hermas identifies the Son with the Law of God, just as Philo identifies Law and Logos. In the Acts of John the Logos-conception is separated from the man Jesus, so that Christ with His disciples can sing the praises of the Logos. And in ch. 13 the Voice teaches: 'This cross of light is sometimes called by me Logos, sometimes Jesus, sometimes Christ, sometimes νοῦς,' etc. In Montanism (*q.v.*) this notion of the Logos as a σύγκρασις of divine attributes was maintained. The anti-Montanist 'Alogi' represented a reaction against this tendency. They were 'feeble reptiles' (ἑρπετὸν ἀσθενές), according to Epiphanius. This was a time of unrestrained theosophical speculation, in which an attempt was made to throw into the Logos-conception a mass of heterogeneous elements—Jewish, Greek, and Oriental. The Fourth Gospel had a very steadying effect, when it was accepted as canonical; and so had the writings of the Apologists—Justin, Tatian, Theophilus, and Athenagoras. The Apologists were theological conservatives. They wished to preserve traditional Christianity, with its doctrine of revelation and its reverence for the OT. They do not philosophize for their co-religionists; they talk about the Logos to show the pagans that Christianity is in agreement with 'the best thought of our time,' just as our clergy talk about evolution.

The philosophy which the Apologists mainly wished to conciliate was Stoicism, which in the 2nd cent. was much stronger than Platonism.[2] So Justin argues that Christ is the 'Spermatic Logos,' the Reason of God, at first immaterial in the Father's bosom, then sent forth as the spoken word for creation and revelation. All men are made in the image of the Logos; and 'those who believe in Christ are men in whom the divine seed, which is the Logos, dwells.' Tatian[3] gives us a Stoic-Christian cosmology. The Logos was first δυνάμει, not ἐνεργείᾳ, residing in the bosom of the Father. Then, by the will of the Father, He came forth, and the worlds were made. The Logos is the ἀρχή in relation to the creatures. Theophilus[4] employs the Stoic terms ἐνδιάθετος and προφορικός, and gives in outline a systematic Logos-doctrine.

[1] *Magn.* 8.
[2] Non-Christian Platonism never attached much importance to the Logos; the word for them had a different meaning; their 'Second Person' was Νοῦς.
[3] *Orat.* 5.
[4] ii. 10.

Athenagoras[1] maintains that the Logos did not first acquire a personal existence in connexion with creation. Minucius Felix[2] equates the Christian Trinity with *Mens, Ratio, Spiritus*. This is to be noted, because later, under Platonic influence, a principle above Νοῦς (*Mens*) was asserted, and this, with Christian speculative mystics, was naturally identified with the Father, with the result that Νοῦς was now equated with the Logos, and *Ratio* (the will and thought of God transmuted into vital law) had to be awkwardly assigned to the Holy Ghost. This led to confusion. The Alexandrians continued to call the Father Νοῦς, feeling probably that the Neo-Platonic Absolute in no way corresponds to the Christian God the Father. Thus they introduced a distinction resembling that between the Godhead and God in Eckhart; a sublimated conception of Νοῦς was introduced between the Absolute and the Logos.

In Clement of Alexandria the Logos-doctrine is a doctrine of Immanence. The world is an organic whole, moving on to some exalted destiny in the harmony of the divine order. Humanity has its life and being in Christ. The Incarnation is no abrupt break in the continuity of man's moral history. Christ was in the world before He came in the flesh, and was preparing the world for His visible advent. Hence the prophecies of the Incarnation enter into the organic process of human history. The history of man's redemption is, for Clement, the education of the human race under its divine 'Instructor.' As Instructor, the Logos has always been present in the world; He spoke through Moses, and through Greek philosophy. He even gave the sun and moon to be worshipped, that men might rise from the lower worship to the higher.[3]

> 'He is the Saviour of all, some with the consciousness of what he is to them, others not as yet; some as friends, others as faithful servants, others hardly even as servants' (*Strom.* vii. 2).

Salvation is not a physical process, but a moral growth through union with God; knowledge is not merely speculation, but a growing sympathy and insight into the character of God and His laws. The union of the Logos with God is so intimate that we cannot hold (with the Gnostics and some Platonists) that the Father is *passive* in the work of redemption. The Incarnation is in itself the Atonement by which God reconciles the world to Himself. For Clement, as for other Greek theologians, there is properly only one dogma—the Incarnation.

For Origen's Logos-doctrine see art. ALEXANDRIAN THEOLOGY, vol. i. p. 316.

There were two schools which opposed the Logos-theology—the rationalistic Unitarians, who regarded the 'divinity' of Christ as a mere power bestowed on Him by God, and emphasized the humanitarian aspect of His Person, and the modalistic Monarchians, such as Praxeas, Noetus, and Sabellius. These maintained the old alliance with Stoicism, after the Catholics had adopted Neo-Platonism as their mistress in philosophy (see, further, art. MONARCHIANISM). Hippolytus's anti-Sabellian treatises show the line of argument used by the orthodox—a position which was later regarded as not wholly satisfactory. Methodius,[4] a Platonist but not an Origenist, argues that the Incarnation was the necessary complement of the Creation, the imperfection of Adam being natural. There is a double development—in the race and in the individual, both due to the immanent Logos. The κένωσις is perpetually re-enacted in spiritual experience. Macarius[5] teaches the same doctrine: in each believer a Christ is born.

[1] 10. [2] *Oct.* v. 10. [3] *Strom.* vi. 14.
[4] *S. Conviv.* iii. 5. [5] *Hom.* iv. 8 f.

The Arian controversy drove orthodoxy into something like a compromise with modalism. The test-word ὁμοούσιος gave the Monarchians most of what they wanted, and its adoption soon ended the hostility of this school. The Arian Christology is of no philosophical value; and its great opponent Athanasius, though he writes much about the Logos, does not add anything significant to the doctrine. It was, in fact, no longer thoroughly acceptable to the Catholics. The word λόγος was not allowed to appear in the Nicæan symbol; and the Synod of Sirmium (A.D. 451) condemned the doctrine of the λόγος ἐνδιάθετος and προφορικός. Other terminology, and to some extent other ideas, displaced it. It was never acclimatized in the Latin-speaking countries.

The Logos-doctrine has an obvious affinity with mysticism, and with types of religion which emphasize the divine immanence. It was revived by Eckhart in the Middle Ages, and has been a living article of faith with religious idealists, Christian Platonists, and speculative theists. It belongs to a permanent and very important type of religious thought, and can never lose its value, though there are now many who (like Max Müller) are ardent supporters of the Logos-idea in religious philosophy, while they cannot accept the Johannine identification of the Logos with a historical individual.

For an evolution in Indian philosophy somewhat similar to the development of the Logos-doctrine see art. VĀCH.

LITERATURE.—A. Aall, *Der Logos: Gesch. seiner Entwickelung in der griech. Philosophie und der christl. Litteratur*, 2 vols., Leipzig, 1896–99; J. Réville, *La Doctrine du Logos dans le quatr. évang. et dans les œuvres de Philon*, Paris, 1881; A. Harnack, *Dogmengesch.*, Freiburg im Br., 1893, Eng. tr., London, 1894–99; A. V. G. Allen, *Continuity of Christian Thought*, London, 1884; W. R. Inge, *Personal Idealism and Mysticism*, do. 1907; T. Simon, *Der Logos*, Leipzig, 1902.

W. R. INGE.

LOKĀYATA.

LOKĀYATA.—This word, which denotes properly 'belonging to the world of sense,' is the Indian name for the materialistic system whose adherents are termed Lokāyatikas or Laukāyatikas, or more usually Chārvākas, from the name of the founder of their doctrinal system. There are clear indications of the presence in India, as early as pre-Buddhistic times, of teachers of a pure materialism;[1] and undoubtedly these theories have had numerous adherents in India from that period onwards to the present day.

Although two authorities[2] bear witness to the former existence of text-books of materialism, viz. the *Bhāguri* and the *Sūtras* of Bṛhaspati, the mythical founder of the system, yet materialistic doctrines have never gained any further place in the literature of India. In order to understand these theories, therefore, we can only have recourse to a few passages of the *Mahābhārata*, to the polemic which was carried on against materialism in the text-books of the other philosophical schools, and to the doctrines of King Error in the philosophical drama *Prabodhachandrodaya*. This last was composed in the 11th or 12th cent. A.D., and aims at setting forth in allegorical style the superiority of Brāhmanical orthodoxy to all other theories of the universe. The principal source of our knowledge, however, is the first chapter of the *Sarvadarśanasaṅgraha*,[3] a compendium of all the philosophical systems of India, composed in the 14th cent. of our era by Mādhavāchārya, the celebrated teacher of the Vedānta, in which the doctrines of Indian materialism are set forth in the greatest detail. Mādhavāchārya begins his exposition with an expression of regret that the majority of the men of his day follow the materialism represented by Chārvāka.

The Lokāyata allows only perception as a means of knowledge, and rejects inference. It recognizes as the sole reality the four elements, *i.e.* matter, and teaches that, when a body is formed by the combination of the elements, the spirit also comes into existence, just like the intoxicating quality from the mixture of special materials. With the destruction of the body the spirit returns again to nothingness. The soul, therefore, is only the body *plus* the attribute of intelligence, since the existence of a soul distinct from the body cannot be established by perception. Supersensuous things are, of course, also wholly denied, and are dismissed at times with a mere jest. Hell is earthly pain, due to earthly causes. The Supreme Being is the king of the country of whose existence the whole world affords tangible proof. Emancipation is the dissolution of the body. The post-operative force of merit and demerit, which, according to the belief of all other Indian schools, determines the lot of each individual down to the smallest details, has no existence for the Lokāyatika, because this conception is reached only by inference. To the objection of an orthodox philosopher, that those who reject this controlling force in the universe leave the various phenomena of the latter without a cause, the materialist replies that the essential nature of things is the cause from which the phenomena proceed.

On the practical side this system exhibits itself as the crudest Eudæmonism; for it represents the gratification of the senses as the sole desirable good. The objection that sensual pleasures cannot be the highest aim for mankind, since these are always mingled with more or less pain, is met by the remark that it is for us to secure by prudence enjoyment as little alloyed as possible with pain, and to shun as far as is in our power the suffering inseparably connected with pleasure. The man who would have fish must take their skin and bones, and he who wants rice cannot exclude the husks from his bargain. Let him not then from fear of the pain renounce the pleasure which we instinctively feel to be congenial to our nature.

The Vedas are declared to be the idle prating of knaves, characterized by the three faults of untruthfulness, internal contradiction, and useless repetition; and the professors of Vedic science deceivers, whose doctrines are mutually destructive. To the Chārvākas the ritual of the Brāhmans is a fraud, and the costly and laborious sacrifices are useful only for providing with a livelihood the cunning fellows who carry them out. 'If an animal sacrificed at the Jyotiṣṭoma (the original form of the *soma* offering) rises to heaven, why does not the sacrificer prefer to slay his own father?' No wonder that in the view of the orthodox Hindu the doctrine of the Chārvākas is the worst of all heresies.

It is natural to conjecture that the Lokāyata system was based by its founder upon deeper principles, and developed upon more serious philosophical lines than the information which has come to us from their opponents allows us to understand. The conjecture, however, cannot be established.

LITERATURE.—J. Muir, *JRAS* xix. [1862] 299 ff.; A. Hillebrandt, 'Materialisten und Skeptiker' in *Alt-Indien, Kulturgeschichtliche Skizzen*, Breslau, 1899, p. 168 ff.; F. Max Müller, *Six Systems of Ind. Philosophy*, London, 1899, pp. 86, 97 ff.

R. GARBE.

LOKOTTARAVĀDINS.—See BODHISATTVA.

LOLLARDS.—See WYCLIF.

[1] See especially *Brahmajāla Sutta*, ed. P. Grimblot, *Sept Suttas pâlis*, Paris, 1876, and tr. D. J. Gogerly, *Ceylon Buddhism*, ed. A. S. Bishop, Colombo, 1908, pp. 401–472.

[2] Patañjali's *Mahābhāṣya*, vii. 3. 45; cf. A. Weber, *Indische Studien*, xiii. [1873] 343 f.; Bhāskarāchārya on *Brahmasūtra*, iii. 3. 53; cf. H. T. Colebrooke, *Miscellaneous Essays*[2], London. 1873, i. 429.

[3] Tr. E. B. Cowell and A. E. Gough[2], London, 1894.

LONGSUFFERING.—Longsuffering is alike a divine attribute and a human virtue. In both its uses its meaning is well represented by 'longanimity,' formerly a word of frequent occurrence, and not altogether obsolete.

The earliest example of 'longanimity' quoted in the *OED* (vi. 417) is from a 1450 tr. of *de Imitatione*, I. xiii. 14: 'Thou shalt overcome them [temptations] better litel and litel by pacience and longanimyte'; the most recent citation of the word is from the *Spectator*, 11th Jan. 1890: 'His longanimity under the foolishness of the young woman is really marvellous.'

The literal meaning of the Greek word (μακρόθυμος) of which 'longsuffering' is the translation is 'long-tempered,' the opposite of our familiar expression 'short-tempered' (cf. Germ. *Langmütigkeit*).

In three OT passages (Ex 34^{6}, Nu 14^{18}, Ps 86^{15}) the RV substitutes a more literal rendering of the Hebrew phrase (אֶרֶךְ אַפַּיִם, 'length of face')—'slow to anger'—for the AV 'longsuffering.' In many passages (Neh 9^{17}, Ps 103^{8} 145^{8}, Jer 15^{15}, Jl 2^{13}, Jon 4^{2}, Na 1^{3}) the two translations are interchangeable.

'Longsuffering or slowness to anger is the glory of man as it is the glory of God' (R. C. Trench, *Sermons preached in Westminster Abbey*, London, 1861, xxx. 349).

That the two expressions are synonymous in many contexts is evident from the retention in the RV of 'longsuffering' in Jer 15^{15} 'Avenge me of my persecutors; take me not away in thy longsuffering.' The former sentence seems decisive in favour of the interpretation which regards the divine longsuffering as displayed towards the persecutors and not towards the prophet.

'The petition shews how great was the peril in which the prophet perceived himself to stand: he believes that if God delay to strike down his adversaries, that longsuffering will be fatal to his own life' (C. J. Ball, *The Prophecies of Jeremiah*, London, 1890, p. 321).

A similar ambiguity arises in the interpretation of Lk 18^{7}; AV translates καὶ μακροθυμεῖ ἐπ' αὐτοῖς, 'though he bear long with them'; but RV 'and he is longsuffering over them.' A. Plummer (*ICC*[2], Edinburgh, 1898, *in loc.*) grants that ἐπ' αὐτοῖς may refer to the enemies of the elect, but prefers to understand it to apply to the elect. The meaning, then, would be: 'And shall not God deliver His elect who cry day and night to Him, while He is slow to act for them?' But the analogy of Jer 15^{15} (cf. Sir 35^{22}) suggests that the main thought is of God's patient forbearance with those who are at once His enemies and the oppressors of His chosen ones. J. Moffatt renders: 'And will not God see justice done to his elect who cry to him by day and night? Will he be tolerant to their opponents? I tell you, he will quickly see justice done to his elect!' (*The New Testament: A New Translation*, London, 1913).

The uncertainty in regard to the interpretation of the above and other passages may serve to emphasize what Plummer rightly insists upon, namely, that, although μακροθυμεῖ usually means 'is slow to anger,' yet 'it sometimes means "to be slow, be backward, tarry," and is almost synonymous with βραδύνω. . . . So also μακροθυμία may mean "slow persistency" as well as "slowness to anger." Comp. 1 Mac. viii. 4' (*op. cit.* p. 414).

The EV recognizes this wider meaning, and regards 'longsuffering' as equivalent to 'patience' in He 6^{12} and Ja 5^{10}. The corresponding verb is applied in Ja 5^{7} to the husbandman's patient waiting for the harvest. But 'patience' is more frequently the translation of ὑπομονή, 'the temper which does not easily succumb under suffering,' while 'μακροθυμία is the self-restraint which does not hastily retaliate a wrong' (J. B. Lightfoot, *Saint Paul's Epistles to the Colossians and to Philemon*, London, 1879, on Col 1^{11}).

To the 'longsuffering' of God reference is made in Lk 18^{7}, Ro 2^{4} 9^{22}, 1 P 3^{20}, 2 P 3^{9}, and to the 'longsuffering' of Jesus Christ in 1 Ti 1^{16} and probably 2 P 3^{15}. In Ro 2^{4} 'forbearance' (ἀνοχή) is linked with 'longsuffering.'

The distinction between these two words is that 'the ἀνοχή is temporary, transient: we may say that, like our word "truce," it asserts its own temporary, transient character. . . . This, it may be urged, is true of μακροθυμία no less. . . . But as much does not lie in the word; we may conceive of a μακροθυμία though it would be worthy of little honour, which should never be exhausted; while ἀνοχή implies its own merely provisional character' (R. C. Trench, *Synonyms of the New Testament*[11], London, 1890, p. 199).

As a moral attribute of God, 'longsuffering' is a manifestation of His grace. In 'the riches of His goodness' He waits long and patiently for the sinner's repentance (Ro 2^{4}), and in loving-kindness He tolerates those who deserve His wrath (Ro 9^{22}).

Yet '*patience and long-suffering* point not merely to the suspension of punishment, but to the love which never tires till it has exhausted its last resource. Owing to the contrast between the apparent impotence of long-suffering, and supreme moral omnipotence, this is an attribute which excites special reverence' (T. Haering, *The Christian Faith*, London, 1913, ii. 492 f.).

'Longsuffering,' as a Christian grace, is a 'fruit of the Spirit' (Gal 5^{22}). Though a passive virtue, it is the manifestation in human character of spiritual power received in answer to prayer from Him by whom believers are 'strengthened with all power, according to the might of his glory, unto all patience and longsuffering with joy' (Col 1^{11}). In his earnest prayers that Christians may be adorned with this grace, St. Paul asks that they may have the mind of Christ, for he obtained mercy, that in him, as chief of sinners, 'Jesus Christ might shew forth all his longsuffering, for an ensample of them which should hereafter believe on him unto eternal life' (1 Ti 1^{16}). In 1 Co 13^{4} 'longsuffering' is said to be an attribute of the 'love' by which we are made partakers of the divine nature. Tertullian (*de Patientia*, 12) and other Fathers 'explain it to mean greatness of soul or magnanimity,' but μακροθυμία differs from μεγαλοψυχία, the 'high-mindedness' of Aristotle:

'*First*, it is not a consciousness of greatness, but a largeness of conception. *Second*, it is not the loftiness of spirit that great men alone possess, but a moral and godly frame of mind to be exhibited in the life of every Christian. *Third*, it is not a noble pride that stands aloof, but an interested spectator of life's sufferings, though not an active combatant in the strife' (T. C. Edwards, *A Commentary on the First Epistle to the Corinthians*[2], London, 1885, p. 343).

In the *Apocrypha and Pseudepigrapha of the Old Testament* (ed. R. H. Charles, Oxford, 1913), *inter alia* the following instructive examples of the use of 'longsuffering' are found:

Test. Dan 2^{1}: 'Unless ye keep yourselves from the spirit of lying and of anger, and love truth and longsuffering, ye shall perish.'

Test. Gad 4^{7}: 'The spirit of love worketh together with the law of God in longsuffering unto the salvation of men.'

Test. Jos. 17^{2}: 'With longsuffering hide ye one another's faults.'

Pirḳê Ābôth 4^{1}: 'Who is mighty? He who controlleth his evil disposition; as it is said: "Better is the longsuffering than the mighty, and he that ruleth his spirit than he that taketh a city."'

LITERATURE.—The word 'longsuffering' is best studied with the aid of commentaries on the passages in which μακροθυμία occurs. There is an instructive and comprehensive article in *ExpT* xii. [1900–01] 330 ff.; the following bibliography is given: H. Cremer, *Bibl. Theol. Lexicon*[3], Edinburgh, 1880, p. 288 ff.; J. Taylor, *Works*, London, 1848, iv. 483 ff.; R. W. Dale, *Week-Day Sermons*, do. 1883, p. 38 ff.; F. Temple, *Rugby Sermons*, do. 1861, iii. 173 ff.; C. J. Vaughan, *University and Other Sermons*, do. 1897, p. 230 ff.; A. Maclaren, *Paul's Prayer and Other Sermons*, do. 1893, p. 217 ff. See also J. Hastings, art. 'Longsuffering' in *HDB* iii. 136; H. C. Lees, art. 'Long-suffering,' in *DCG* ii. 53 f.

J. G. TASKER.

LORD'S DAY.—See SUNDAY.

LORD'S PRAYER.—See PRAYER (Christian).

LORD'S SUPPER.—See EUCHARIST.

LORETO.—For many centuries the little town of Loreto, situated some 15 miles from Ancona on a hill commanding a view of the Adriatic, has been a notable place of pilgrimage. Montaigne, who visited it in 1580, and who apparently believed in the miracles of healing supposed to be wrought there, describes the town as 'containing few inhabitants except those who serve the needs of the religious devotees' (*Journal of Travels*, Eng. tr., London, 1903, ii. 196–209). The great basilica, the dome of which is visible from afar, was begun in 1468, completed in 1538, and has since received many additions and modifications. Of its artistic glories an excellent account is given in A. Colasanti (*Loreto*, Bergamo, 1910). But the basilica was built only to enclose and enshrine a tiny edifice known as 'la Santa Casa,' which is the real object of pilgrimage. The Holy House is believed to rest on the surface of the ground without foundations, and this fact seems to be authentic. It measures roughly 31 ft. by 13, and its walls are built of hewn stones, from their shape and colour often mistaken for brick, but externally they are hidden from view by a casing of marble richly adorned with sculptures. An ancient statue[1] of wood, of Byzantine inspiration, representing the Madonna and Child, now voluminously draped and also crowned, occupies a niche inside the little house at some height from the floor, and beneath it stands an altar at which Mass is said. Countless *ex votos* are suspended all around, but these probably represent only a small part of the rich gifts which belonged to the shrine before Napoleon rifled it in 1797. On that occasion the statue itself was carried off and taken to Paris, but in 1801 the First Consul returned it to the niche that it had formerly occupied. The words 'Hic Verbum caro factum est' sculptured above it indicate the shrine's official claim to the veneration of the faithful, but the story is more fully told in a Latin inscription set up in the basilica by Pope Clement VIII. in 1595, the approved English rendering of which runs as follows:

'Christian Pilgrim, you have before your eyes the Holy House of Loreto, venerable throughout the world on account of the Divine mysteries accomplished in it and the glorious miracles herein wrought. It is here that the most holy Mary, Mother of God, was born; here that she was saluted by the angel; here that the eternal Word of God was made flesh. Angels conveyed this house from Palestine to the town Tersato in Illyria in the year of salvation 1291 in the pontificate of Nicholas IV. Three years later, in the beginning of the pontificate of Boniface VIII., it was carried again by the ministry of angels and placed in a wood near this hill, in the vicinity of Recanati in the Marches of Ancona, where, having changed its station thrice in the course of a year, at length, by the will of God, it took up its permanent position on this spot three hundred years ago. Ever since that time both the extraordinary nature of the event having called forth the admiring wonder of the neighbouring people, and the fame of the miracles wrought in this sanctuary having spread far and wide, this Holy House, whose walls do not rest on any foundation and yet remain solid and uninjured after so many centuries, has been held in reverence by all nations.'

This statement lays little stress upon what is perhaps the most surprising feature of the legend, viz. the triple change of site after the arrival of the Holy House upon the shores of the Adriatic. Pietro di Giorgio Tolomei, best known, from his native town of Teramo, as 'Teramanus,' who between 1465 and 1473 drafted the earliest version of the translation story that has been preserved to us (the document has been discussed with great critical acumen by Hüffer in his *Loreto*, i. 33–66), explains that, because the Santa Casa was not sufficiently honoured where it was first deposited, near Fiume in Illyria, it was carried thence by angels across the Adriatic to a wood at Recanati belonging to the 'Lady Loretha'; hence the name which has since attached to the shrine ('inde accepit tunc ista ecclesia nomen "sancta Maria de Loretha" ab illa domina que erat illius silve domina et patrona'). Here, however, there was such a concourse of pilgrims that the wood was infested with robbers and murderers.

'For this reason,' the *Relatio Teramani* goes on, 'the Holy House was once more taken up by the hands of angels, and it was carried to the Mount of the Two Brothers, and on this same mount by the hands of angels it was set down. The which brothers, on account of the immense revenue and gain of money and other things, fell straightway into grievous discord and strife. Wherefore the angels, in the same manner as before, carried it away from the said place on the mount and brought it to a spot in the public road and there they made it fast.'

The legend also relates how the Blessed Virgin in 1296 appeared in his sleep to a certain man who was devout to her, and in this way made known the whole story. Thereupon sixteen good men and true journeyed to the Holy Land to measure the foundations of the Holy House at Nazareth. They discovered that these exactly agreed with the dimensions of the Santa Casa, and also that a stone tablet commemorated the disappearance of the little building which had formerly been venerated there. Furthermore, in the time of Teramanus himself two old men came forward and each testified that his grandfather's grandfather had confirmed from personal knowledge the account of the translation.

This was the story which, with further amplifications, added in the 16th cent., was believed from about the year 1470 to the present day. Although such antiquarian writers as M. Leopardi and G. A. Vogel betrayed their misgivings, they did not venture to throw doubts upon the substantial truth of the narrative. It was only in 1906 that U. Chevalier, following in the wake of the less elaborate criticisms of H. Grisar (at the International Catholic Congress of Munich in 1897), A. Boudinhon (in *Revue du clergé français*, xxii. [1900] 241), and L. de Feis (*La Santa Casa di Nazareth*, Florence, 1905), published a systematic refutation of the whole legend (*Notre-Dame de Lorette*). Since then an energetic and often acrimonious controversy has been carried on, both in magazine articles and in separate books, between the assailants and defenders of the legend; but, even among the organs of Roman Catholic opinion, the more weighty and critical reviews without exception have all ranged themselves on the side of Chevalier.

Apart from the intrinsic improbabilities of the legend itself, two lines of argument have been pressed home by the critics with irresistible force. The first, mainly negative, lays stress upon the fact that a shrine of Our Lady had existed at Loreto a century before the date of the supposed translation, that nothing whatever is heard of this translation until the middle of the 15th cent., and that, even when first spoken of, the accounts of the transportation by angels do not suggest that it was the house of the Holy Family at Nazareth which was so transported. Curiously enough—and this is a point which all the many writers on the subject seem to have missed—the earliest known mention of a miraculous translation by angels occurs in the narrative of an English pilgrim, William Wey, one of the original fellows of Eton College. His account, which is probably not of later date than 1462, runs as follows:

'Also twelve miles from Ancona and three miles from Recanati, is a hamlet which is called Loreto, where there is now a stone chapel of Blessed Mary which of old was built by St. Helen in the Holy Land. But because the most Blessed Mary was not honoured there, the chapel was lifted up by the angels, the most Blessed Mary sitting upon it, and was carried away from the Holy Land to Alretum, while the country-folk and shepherds looked on at the angels bearing it and setting it down in the place where it now is; where the most Blessed Virgin Mary is held in great honour' (*Wey's Pilgrimage*, Roxburghe Club, London, 1857, p. 54).

It will be noticed at once that the building transported is not the actual Holy House of Nazareth, but a chapel built by St. Helen. On the

1 Adolfo Venturi (see Hüffer, *Loreto*, i. 41, n.) assigns it to the early years of the 14th cent.; but it seems to be mentioned in documents of the year 1313, and other authorities attribute it to the 13th or even the 12th century. The legend declares it to have been carved by St. Luke the Evangelist.

other hand, the first papal document which gives any indication of the special sanctity attaching to the Loreto shrine is the bull of Paul II. in 1470, which speaks thus:

'Desiring to show our veneration for the church of Blessed Mary of Loreto, miraculously founded in honour of the same most holy Virgin outside the walls of Recanati, in which, as the statements of persons worthy of credit attest, and as all the faithful may ascertain for themselves, an image of the glorious Virgin, through the wondrous mercy of God, has been deposited, attended by a troop of angels, and to which (church) by reason of the countless stupendous miracles which the Most High through her intercession has worked for all who devoutly have recourse to her and humbly implore her patronage,' etc.

Here again not the least suggestion is conveyed that the building, even if believed to exist miraculously without foundations, was the actual house of the Holy Family of Nazareth. On the other hand, the terms of this notice lend great probability to the opinion, supported by Hüffer and others, that it was the statue, showing, as we have noticed, Byzantine characteristics, and consequently known to have come from a distance, that was at first supposed to have been brought to Loreto by the hands of angels. Then the fact that the chapel had no proper foundations seems to have given rise to the further development that the whole building had been miraculously transported from the East. And, finally, a reason was found for this exceptional providence by assuming that the building was none other than the actual Holy House of Nazareth. Considerable support is lent to this hypothesis of a gradual evolution of the legend by a curious parallel in the case of a chapel not far from Siena. The story is told first by A. Fortunio in his *Cronichetta del Monte San Savino* (Florence, 1583, pp. 9–11). In the year 1116 a little wayside chapel of the Blessed Virgin at Asciano belonged to a certain lord, who at his death left it to his two sons. They quarrelled over the division of the offerings and were on the point of fighting a duel when, during the night, the angels took the chapel up and bore it to a place about 14 miles off, called Colle di Vertighe, near Monte San Savino. G. B. Mittarelli, a really serious and critical antiquary of the 18th cent. (see his *Annales Camaldulenses*, Venice, 1755–73, iii. 89–92), bears witness to the existence of the chapel in his time and also to its great antiquity. Here again, just as at Loreto, the chapel was without foundations, and a great church had been erected over the smaller building to protect and enshrine it. Whether the Loreto legend or that of the Colle di Vertighe is really the older it is difficult to decide. In the case of Loreto the negative evidence tending to show that in the beginning no idea existed of the chapel having come from Nazareth is emphasized by the large number of documents of the 14th and 15th centuries which have been unearthed concerning it. It is incredible, as Hüffer shows in his very patient discussion, that the supremely sacred character of the building could have been ignored, as it is, in almost all of them, if men had then believed that this was actually the Holy House in which God had become incarnate.

The second line of argument, developed by Chevalier and other critics, claims to show that at Nazareth itself nothing was known to have happened in 1291, when the Holy House is supposed to have been transported westwards; no pilgrims comment on the disappearance of a shrine which was known to have been visited by their predecessors in the 12th and 13th centuries, nor do the accounts of what was venerated at Nazareth as the abode of the Holy Family apply in the least to such an edifice as we now see at Loreto. It may be noticed also that the measurements and proportions of the chapel of the English shrine of Our Lady of Walsingham, which happen to have been accurately preserved to us, do not agree with those of the Santa Casa, while, according to legend, the Walsingham chapel reproduced exactly the dimensions of the Holy House as measured by a pilgrim about the year 1060.

By the time of Pope Julius II. the legend of the Santa Casa had fully established itself in popular favour and it is incorporated in a bull of 1507, but with the qualification 'ut pie creditur et fama est.' In 1518 Leo X. identifies himself with the whole marvellous story 'ut fide dignorum comprobatum est testimonio,' and it must have been shortly after this that Thomas Duchtie or Doughtie of Musselburgh made his pilgrimage to the Holy Land and brought back that image of the Italian shrine for which he afterwards built a chapel on the land now occupied by Loreto School. Other pontiffs, notably Sixtus V. and in modern times Pius IX. and Leo XIII., adopted the tradition without any question, and Innocent XII. permitted the celebration of a special feast of the translation of the Holy House with a 'proper' Mass and Office. In the latter part of the 16th cent. the story of the miraculous translation was everywhere accepted, and the local traditions of Nazareth itself were modified to suit it. It should, however, be remembered that none of these papal bulls or other similar acts of ecclesiastical authority is regarded in the Roman Church as having any dogmatic force, and consequently all Roman Catholics are free to accept or reject the legend according to their own judgment of the historical evidence. The defenders of the tradition still lay stress upon an alleged scientific examination of the materials, particularly the stone of which the Santa Casa is built, and it is claimed that experts have declared that such materials are not found in Italy, but only in the neighbourhood of Nazareth (see D. Bartolini, *Sopra la Santa Casa di Loreto*, Rome, 1861). But these experiments were carried out in 1857, and it may be doubted whether their conclusions can be regarded as rigidly scientific. Let us also notice that the frescoes at Gubbio and in one or two other places, said to be of early date and representing angels carrying a house (the date and details are nearly always matters of controversy), cannot be assumed to refer of necessity to the Loreto legend. It is clear from the Monte San Savino chronicle quoted above that there was at least one rival tradition of the same kind in circulation. These frescoes, then, cannot be appealed to as a conclusive argument in favour of the early date of the Loreto story in particular.

LITERATURE.—The vast bibliography of the subject has been very fully, though not quite exhaustively, dealt with by J. Faurax, *Bibliographie lorétaine*, Tournai, 1913, and also by G. Hüffer, *Loreto* (see below), pp. 5–8; only a selection of books and articles can be mentioned here. The text of the early writers who elaborated the legend into the form which ultimately prevailed, viz. Teramanus, Jerome Angelita, Raphael Riera, and Horazio Tursellini, will be found printed at length in the voluminous work of P. V. Martorelli, *Teatro istorico della S. Casa Nazarena*, 3 vols., Rome, 1732–35. Besides this, we may note, among older works, the important treatises of G. A. Vogel, *de Ecclesiis recanatensi et lauretana earumque episcopis commentarius*, 2 vols., Recanati, published in 1859, though written in 1806, and M. Leopardi, *La Santa Casa di Loreto*, Lugano, 1841. Both these works give proof of much research among municipal archives and other MS sources. In the modern controversy, after U. Chevalier, *Notre-Dame de Lorette*, Paris, 1906, by far the most important contribution to the subject is that of G. Hüffer, *Loreto: eine geschichtskritische Untersuchung der Frage des heiligen Hauses*, Münster, 1913 (so far only one volume, but a second promised). See also A. Boudinhon, *La Question de Lorette*, Paris, 1910; C. Bouffard, *La Vérité sur le fait de Lorette*, do. 1910, and *The Month*, July 1912.

Of the various attempts made to reply to Chevalier's criticisms we may note A. Eschbach, *La Vérité sur le fait de Lorette*, Paris, 1910; F. Thomas, *La Santa Casa dans l'histoire*, Lyons, 1909; L. Poisat, *Lorette au xiiie siècle*, Arras, 1906; M. Faloci Pulignani, *La Santa Casa di Loreto secondo un affresco di Gubbio*, Rome, 1907; I. Rinieri, *La Santa Casa di Loreto*, 3 vols., Turin, 1911; G. Kresser, in *Theolog. praktische Quartalschrift*, Linz, 1907, pp. 795–820, and 1911, pp. 508–

526; cf. also *Theologische Quartalschrift*, Tübingen, 1909, pp. 212-248, 477-490.

On Loreto at Musselburgh see L. Barbé, *Byways of Scottish History*, London, 1912, pp. 141-152.

For a further bibliography see U. Chevalier, *Répertoire des sources hist. du moyen âge, topo-bibliographie*, Montbéliard, 1894-1903, cols. 1746-1749.

HERBERT THURSTON.

LOTS.—See DIVINATION.

LOTUS (Egyptian).—**I. Name.**—First we must dismiss entirely the modern botanical name 'lotus.' '*Lotus Arabicus* is a small leguminous plant resembling a vetch' (*Proc. Roy. Soc.* lxvii. [1900] 225). As plants more or less confused together, being all water-lilies, and popularly called 'lotus,' there may be specified (1) rose lotus (*Nelumbium speciosum*), distinguished by imbricated petals on the bud; (2) white lotus (*Nymphæa lotus*), distinguished by ribbed petals on the bud, rounded when opened; and (3) blue lotus (*Nymphæa cærulea*), distinguished by smooth, pointed petals. The two *Nymphæa* lotuses cross, and any intermediate form may occur naturally.

(1) *Rose lotus.*—This is at present an Indian plant unknown in Egypt, except as a cultivated rarity. It was known in Roman times, being found in the cemetery at Hawara (W. M. F. Petrie, *Hawara*, London, 1890, p. 52), and described by Athenæus:

'Lotus grows in the marshes . . . one like that of the rose, and it is the garlands woven of the flowers of this colour which are properly called the garlands of Antinous; but the other kind is called the lotus garland, being of a blue colour' (xv. 21).

It was known earlier to Herodotus:

'There are also other lilies like roses that grow in the river, the fruit of which is contained in a separate pod . . . in this there are many berries fit to be eaten' (ii. 92).

There does not seem to be any proof that this plant was indigenous, nor that any instance of it was represented in Egypt. It cannot, therefore, be reckoned as of importance in religion or art. Various instances have been alleged, but incorrectly. Loret states that the lotus-flower supporting Horus is a rose lotus; but the petals are equal-ended and striped as white lotus. He also states it to be on the head of Nefertum; but that flower appears rather to be a *Nymphæa*. He agrees that it is not shown on monuments. The capital found at Memphis (Petrie, *Palace of Apries*, London, 1909, xviii.), like other early capitals, is white lotus, and not rose.

(2) *White lotus.*—This is characterized by the sepals and petals being ovoid with rounded ends. It is frequent in canal scenes of the early kingdom; as a capital at Memphis (Petrie, *Palace of Apries*, xviii.); as figures of capitals (Zowyet el-Meyityn, VIth dyn.; El-Bersheh, XIIth dyn.: see E. Prisse d'Avennes, *Hist. de l'art égyptien*, Paris, 1879); as a garland (P. E. Newberry and F. Ll. Griffith, *El Bersheh*, London, 1895) it was placed upon the mummies of Aahmes, Amenhetep I., and Rameses II. It is represented as the flower upon which Horus is seated, shown by the strong ribbing of the sepals (R. V. Lanzone, *Dizionario di mitologia egizia*, Turin, 1886, ccxiv. 1). This figure is entirely of late date, 8th cent. B.C. and onward. Loret attributes this to the rose lotus; but J. G. Wilkinson emphatically states that it is the blue lotus (*Manners and Customs of Ancient Egyptians*, London, 1878, iii. 132 f.); the ribbing would indicate that it is, as a matter of fact, the white lotus.

(3) *Blue lotus.*—This is the most usual lotus-flower of all periods, with straight-edged pointed petals. It is found commonly in the tombs, and is the origin of the regular lotus-capitals. The Egyptian names of these flowers are variously equated. Loret puts the *neheb*, *nekheb*, or *nesheb* to the rose lotus, *seshni* to the white lotus, and *serpet* to the blue lotus. But we have seen that probably the rose lotus was a Persian importation, and could not therefore have a usual name dating from the VIth dyn. (Papyrus, i. col. 440). Now Loret gives Arab authority for the *sushan* being a blue flower (*Flore phar.*, p. 116), and the *khazam* (which in the *Scalæ=soshem*) being also blue. It seems probable that *seshni* is the blue lotus. The seeds of all three lotus-plants were eaten (Herod. ii. 92), and *seshni* was gathered in the IInd dyn. (see a seal in Petrie, *Royal Tombs*, London, 1901, ii., xxi. 171). If *seshni* were blue, probably the commonest name *nesheb* is the white lotus. The name *serpet* is more fully spelled out like a Syrian word, as *sairpata*. It seems obviously connected with *sirpād* of Is 55[13], where it stands in antithesis to myrtle, and is therefore probably a bush rather than a herb or water-plant. It does not appear to have any connexion with a lotus.

2. Meaning.—Though the lotus is so abundant naturally in Egypt, and so incessantly represented in decoration, yet it seems to have singularly little contact with the religion or writing. Its use as a vocal sign is rare and of late period, and before that it appears only as a determinative of the names of such plants. It is never associated with any early god. Nefertum, who wears the flower on his head, is a late deity, the figure first occurring in the XIXth dyn. (A. Mariette, *Abydos*, Paris, 1869-80, i. 38c), where also is a portable shrine with the lotus-flower of the god, clearly the blue lotus. Usually he is not represented till the Greek period. Horus, who appears seated on the lotus-flower, is so represented only in the Ethiopian and later ages (G. Colonna-Ceccaldi, *Monuments antiques de Chypre*, etc., Paris, 1882, pl. viii.; G. A. Hoskins, *Visit to the Great Oasis of the Libyan Desert*, London, 1837, pl. vi. base). As Wilkinson says of the lotus, 'there is no evidence of its having been sacred, much less an object of worship' (iii. 133).

LITERATURE.—The principal books are V. Loret, *La Flore pharaonique*[2], Paris, 1892, for the botany; G. Foucart, *Histoire de l'ordre lotiform*, do. 1897, for Egyptian architecture; W. H. Goodyear, *Grammar of the Lotus*, London, 1891, for general art connexions, but overstrained.

W. M. FLINDERS PETRIE.

LOTUS (Indian).—To the Indian taste the lotus has always been the fairest flower: it has enjoyed an unparalleled popularity throughout the length and breadth of India from the earliest times down to the present day, as is shown by its predominance in literature and art. Beginning to be mentioned in the oldest Veda, it plays a prominent part in the mythology of Brāhmanism. To the later Sanskrit poets it is the emblem of beauty to which they constantly compare the faces of their heroines. The lotus, moreover, enters into Indian art of all ages and all religions as a conspicuous decorative element. It appears thus on the oldest architectural monuments of Buddhism as well as later on those of Jainism and Hinduism all over India. With the spread of Buddhism to the countries of the Farther East, its use as an ornament in religious art has extended as far as Japan.

I. In literature.—The lotus is already named in the Rigveda and is mentioned with increasing frequency in the later Saṁhitās. Two varieties occur in the Rigveda. The *puṇḍarīka* (later known as a white variety of the *Nelumbium speciosum*) is once referred to (X. cxlii. 8) as a water-plant. In the Atharvaveda (X. viii. 43) the human heart is compared with this lotus, and the *Pañchaviṁśa Brāhmaṇa* (XVIII. ix. 6) speaks of its flower as 'born of the light of the constellations.' The Taittirīya recension (I. viii. 2. 1) of the Black Yajurveda mentions a garland of such lotuses (*puṇḍari-srajā*). The blue variety named *puṣkara* occurs several times in the Rigveda (VI. xvi. 3, VII. xxxiii. 11, VIII. lxxii. 11) and still oftener in the later Vedas. In the former it is alluded to as growing in lakes. Here also the term seems to be applied to the bowl of the sacrificial ladle, presumably on account of resemblance in shape; it is certainly so applied in the *Aitareya Brāhmaṇa*. That this variety of the flower also was early used for personal adornment is shown by the fact that the Aśvins, the youthful twin gods of the morning, are described (X. clxxxiv. 2) as wearing a garland of blue lotuses (*puṣkara-sraj*). Another kind of lotus, the *kumuda*, is mentioned, together with its various edible parts, in the Atharvaveda (IV. xxxiv. 3). The flower meant is doubtless the white edible lotus (*Nymphæa esculenta*), denoted by this name in later times.

In the *Brāhmaṇas* the lotus first appears associated with the Creator Prajāpati in cosmogonic myths. Thus the *Taittirīya Brāhmaṇa* (I. i. 3. 5 ff.) tells how Prajāpati, desiring to evolve the universe, which in the beginning was fluid, saw a lotus-leaf (*puṣkara-parṇa*) standing erect out of the water. Thinking that it must rest on something, he dived in the form of a boar, and, finding the earth below, broke off a fragment, rose with it to the surface, and spread it out on the leaf. Again, the *Taittirīya Āraṇyaka* (I. xxiii. 1) relates that, when the universe was still fluid, Prajāpati alone was produced on a lotus-leaf.

Later, in the epic poetry of the *Mahābhārata*, the Creator, under the name of Brahmā, is described as having sprung from the lotus that grew out of Viṣṇu's navel, when that deity lay absorbed in meditation. Hence one of the epithets of Brahmā is 'lotus-born' (*abja-ja, abja-yoni*, etc.). The lotus is thus also connected with Viṣṇu, one of whose names is accordingly *padma-nābha*, 'lotus-naveled.' It is further associated with Viṣṇu's wife Lakṣmī, goddess of fortune and beauty, in the *Mahābhārata*, where the myth is related that from Viṣṇu's forehead sprang a lotus, out of which came Śrī (another name of the goddess), and where one of Lakṣmī's epithets is *padmā*, 'lotus-hued.' The *Mahābhārata*, in its account of Mount Kailāsa, the abode of Kubera, the god of wealth, describes his lake Nalinī and his river Mandākinī as covered with golden lotuses.

2. In art.—As regards its application in religious art, the lotus figures, with the rise of that art in India, on all the Buddhist monuments which came into being in different parts of the country from about 200 B.C. onwards. In its simplest form the expanded lotus is very frequent as a circular ornament in the sculptures at Sānchī, Bhārhut, Amarāvatī, and Bodh Gayā, as well as in the rock-cut Buddhist temples of Western India, being introduced a as medallion on pillars, panels, and ceilings. Very elaborately carved half-lotuses sometimes appear used thus, or, in Ceylon, as so-called moonstones—semi-circular stone slabs at the foot of staircases. Lotuses growing on stalks also occur in the sculptures of Gandhāra and of Mathurā, and often figure in elaborate floral designs on the pillars of Sānchī or the panels of Amarāvatī.

The lotus is further found from the earliest times conventionalized either as a seat or as a pedestal on which divine or sacred beings rest in a sitting or standing posture. The oldest and most striking example of this use is exhibited in the figure of the Hindu goddess Lakṣmī in the Buddhist sculptures at Udayagiri, at Bhārhut, and especially at Sānchī, where it is frequently repeated on the gateways of the Great Stūpa. She is portrayed sitting or standing on a lotus and holding up in each hand a lotus-flower which is watered by two elephants from pots raised aloft by their trunks. This ancient type is found all over India at the present day; it even occurs among the old sculptures at Polonnaruwa in Ceylon.

After Buddha began to be represented in sculpture, from about the beginning of our era, his image constantly appears sitting cross-legged on a lotus seat, occasionally also standing on a lotus pedestal. In this form it occurs, for instance, at Rājgīr in Behār, in the Kaṇheri caves near Bombay, and often in the Gandhāra monuments of the North-West. From the latter region this type spread beyond the confines of India, reappearing in Nepāl, Burma, China, and Japan. Even when the seat is not actually the flower itself, two, three, or four lotuses are, in the Gandhāra sculptures, carved on its front. Such lotuses are even found delineated on a footstool on which Gautama rests his feet instead of sitting cross-legged. The number of the petals of such lotuses varies from four to six.

The use of the lotus seat has been extended to images of *bodhisattvas* not only in India but in Buddhist countries beyond its borders. Thus Mañjuśrī is represented sitting in this way not only at Sārnāth, near Benares, but also in Java and Tibet. In a modern Tibetan picture Maitreya is depicted on a lotus seat, and the figure of a Persian *bodhisattva* sitting on a seat adorned with lotuses and painted on a wooden panel was discovered by M. A. Stein during his first expedition to Central Asia. Even in China the *bodhisattva* Avalokiteśvara occurs sitting on a lotus seat, and in Nepāl also as standing on a lotus pedestal. The lotus is otherwise intimately connected with this *bodhisattva*; for he is represented as born from a lotus, and he regularly holds a lotus in his hand, whence is derived his epithet of Padmapāṇi, 'lotus-handed.' To him, moreover, refers the Buddhist formula *Oṁ maṇi padme Hūṁ* ('Yea! O jewel in the lotus! Amen'), which at the present day is the most sacred prayer of the Buddhists in Tibet (see art. JEWEL [Buddhist], § 7). The persistence of this application of the lotus is indicated by the fact that it often appears not only in modern Indian brass images of Hindu gods, but even in seated portraits of Mahārājas of the 19th century.

The lotus seat and pedestal have an almost universal application in connexion with the figures of Hindu mythology. Thus Brahmā appears seated on Viṣṇu's navel lotus. The three great gods of the Hindu triad, Brahmā, Śiva, and Viṣṇu, with their respective wives, Sarasvatī, Pārvatī, and Lakṣmī, as well as Agni, god of fire, Pāvana, god of wind, Ganeśa, god of wisdom, Viṣṇu's incarnation Rāma, and the demon Rāvaṇa, are all found represented on a lotus seat. Viṣṇu, in addition, regularly holds a lotus in one of his four hands. A lotus pedestal also serves as a stand for images of the god Indra, of Viṣṇu and nearly all his incarnations, and of the sun-god Sūrya; in Ceylon also of Śiva and Pārvatī, as well as of Kubera, god of wealth, and in Tibet of Sarasvatī, goddess of learning.

Similarly, in the ancient Jain sculptures found at Mathurā the lotus constantly occurs as a medallion or in more elaborate floral decoration. It also appears as the symbol of the sixth Jina, or Saint. At the present day it is worshipped generally by the Hindus in India, and even by low caste Muhammadans in some parts of the country. See also art. FLOWERS, vol. vi. p. 54[a].

LITERATURE.—R. Schmidt, 'Der Lotus in der Sanskrit-Literatur,' *ZDMG* lxvii. [1913] 462–70; A. A. Macdonell and A. B. Keith, *Vedic Index of Names and Subjects*, London, 1912, i. 163, 536, ii. 9; J. Muir, *Original Sanskrit Texts*, i.[2], do. 1872, pp. 31 f., 53; V. Fausböll, *Indian Mythology*, do. 1903; Vincent A. Smith, *A History of Fine Art in India and Ceylon*, Oxford, 1911, 'The Coinage of the Early or Imperial Gupta Dynasty of Northern India,' *JRAS*, 1889, p. 81 and pl. i. 15 (goddess on lotus seat), *Catalogue of the Coins in the Indian Museum, Calcutta*, Oxford, 1906, pl. xvi. 2, 8, 10; A. Grünwedel, *Buddhist Art in India*, Eng. tr., London, 1901, *Mythologie des Buddhismus in Tibet und der Mongolei*, Leipzig, 1900, *passim*; J. G. Smither, *Architectural Remains, Anura-*

dhapura, Ceylon, etc., London, 1894, pl. lvii.; A. Foucher, *L'Art du Gandhāra*, Paris, 1905; L. de Milloué, *Bod-Youl ou Tibet*, do. 1906, p. 186; S. W. Bushell, *Chinese Art*, London, 1904–06, i. 46, 110 (lotus sacred to Buddhism), ii. 78; R. F. Johnston, *Buddhist China*, do. 1913, frontispiece and illustrations opposite pp. 30, 98, 194, 280, 296; R. Pischel, *Leben und Lehre des Buddha*, Leipzig, 1906, p. 97 f.; H. C. Warren, *Buddhism in Translations* [3], Cambridge, Mass., 1900; *Jātakas*, Eng. tr., Index volume, Cambridge, 1913, *s.v.* 'Lotus'; E. Moor, *Hindu Pantheon*, London, 1810; G. C. M. Birdwood, *Industrial Arts of India*, do. 1880, p. 130, plates A, C, D, E, F, I, K; E. B. Havell, *Ideals of Indian Art*, do. 1911, p. 154; G. Watt, *Indian Art at Delhi*, Calcutta, 1903, p. 92; V. A. Smith, *Jaina Stūpa*, Allahabad, 1901, plates xxiv., liii.–lxiv., lxxiii.–lxxvi.; *NINQ* iv. [1894–95] § 289; T. A. Gopinātha Rao, *Elements of Hindu Iconography*, Madras, 1914, Index, *s.v.* 'Padmāsana.'

A. A. MACDONELL.

3. In Buddhism.—The symbolism of the lotus-flower (*padma, puṇḍarīka, utpala*) was borrowed by the Buddhists directly from the parent religion Brāhmanism. Primarily, the lotus-flower appears to have symbolized for the Aryans from very remote times the idea of superhuman or divine birth; and, secondarily, the creative force and immortality. The traditional Indian and Buddhist explanation of it is that the glorious lotus-flower appears to spring not from the sordid earth but from the surface of the water, and is always pure and unsullied, no matter how impure may be the water of the lake. It thus expresses the idea of supernatural birth, and the emergence of the first created object from the primordial waters of chaos; hence also the flower was regarded as the matrix of the Hindu creator himself, Nārāyaṇa, and his later form as the god Brahmā, who are respectively figured and described as reclining and seated upon a lotus-flower. As an emblem of divine purity, the lotus-flower is instanced in the pre-Buddhist Vaiṣṇavite *Bhagavad-Gītā* (*SBE* viii.[2] [1898] 64, xxxvi. [1894] 189); and this was possibly its signification when it was first applied to the historical Buddha, Śākyamuni.

As an emblem of divine birth, the lotus is the commonest of motives in Buddhist art and literature, as has been noted above (§ 2). In the Buddhist paradise of Sukhāvatī, the goal of popular Mahāyāna Buddhists, where no women exist, every one is born as a god upon a lotus-flower (*Saddharma-puṇḍarīka* [*SBE* xxi. (1884) 389, xlix. (1894) pt. ii. pp. x, 62]), and there are lotus-flowers of *maṇi*-gems (*SBE* xlix. pt. ii. 36). The Western notion of the beatitude of 'lotus-eating' is possibly a memory of this old tradition of divine existence.

A form of this myth of divine lotus-birth is probably the myth which invests Buddha with the miraculous power of imprinting the image of a lotus-flower on the earth at every step that he took. The references to this are innumerable in the Pāli canon; but in the book which the present writer has shown to be manifestly the earliest of all the books of that canon, the *Mahāpadāna Suttanta* (*JRAS* 1914, p. 663 f.), the account of the infant Buddha's first seven steps makes no mention of the lotus-flower imprints which appear in the later versions.

The lotus was especially identified with the sun. This association rested doubtless upon the natural observation that the flower opened when the sun rose and closed at sunset, so as to suggest to the primitive mind the idea that the flower might be the residence of the sun during its nocturnal passage through the under world, or that it might be the re-vivifier, resurrector, or regenerator of the fresh or refreshened sun of the next day. Its very large multi-rayed flowers would also contribute to this association. It is probably from its association with the sun that we find the lotus-flower in the Gandhāra sculptures, and often subsequently, taking the place on Buddha's footprints of the 'wheeled disk of the sun with its thousand spokes.' This possibly was the source of the lotus-marked footprints.

The device of a lotus-flower in the hand seems to have symbolized not merely divine birth but the possession of life everlasting, and the preservation and procreation of life. Such was it with the Aryan queen of heaven, the Brāhmanist goddess Śrī, and her derivative, the Buddhist Tārā, both of whom have the title 'Garlanded by Lotuses' (Tantra, *Rgyud*, xv. 4). In the mystical Vedic, pre-Buddhist *Śatapatha Brāhmaṇa* the lotus was a symbol of the womb (*SBE* xli. [1894] 215); and, as we have seen, it appears to have this sense in the famous *Oṁ maṇi padme Hūṁ* formula (see JEWEL [Buddhist], § 7). Probably, therefore, such a meaning may be in part implied in the lotus held in the hand of Avalokita, the consort of Tārā, to whom that formula is now specially addressed. In the hand of Maitreya, the next coming Buddha, and other divine *bodhisattvas* of Gandhāra, the lotus in the hand, however, may have had a metaphysical significance and have denoted the preservation of the life of the law and the re-vivifying of the same. It was possibly in this sense as cherishers of the law that we find that a lotus-flower adorns the hands of many of the images of Buddhas and *bodhisattvas* who do not specially possess the attribute of a lotus held in the hand (see list below).

The gods and goddesses of Buddhism who hold a lotus in their hand are here enumerated; this lotus, with the object which it carries, forms one of the chief conventional attributes of the particular divinity.

The simple lotus, one of the three kinds specified above, is the especial mark of Tārā, Avalokita, Padmapāṇi, and, occasionally, Maitreya. The lotus surmounted by a sword is an attribute of Amoghapāśa, Khagarbha, Siṁhanāda, Tārā, Padmapāṇyavalokita, and Maitreya; surmounted by a thunderbolt (*vajra*), it is an attribute of Mañjuśrī and mild Vajrapāṇi (*Śānta*); surmounted by a book, it is an attribute of Mañjuśrī and Prajñā Pāramitā; surmounted by a jewel, it denotes Kṣitigarbha and Ekajāta; by a sun, Samantabhadra. Among Tibetan saints the lotus is the especial emblem of the founder of the Order of Lāmas, Padmakara, 'the Lotus-born'; and Tsong-kha-pa, the founder of the Yellow-Hat reformed sect, the Gelug, has two, one on either side of him.

Images of divine symbols, such as the seven treasures (see JEWEL [Buddhist]), are figured usually upon lotus-flowers.

In Buddhist mythology the 'lotus' gives its name to two out of the twenty-four 'previous' Buddhas of the Pāli canon, namely Paduma (properly Padma) and Padumuttara, and to several *nāga* demigods, Padma, Padmottara, and Puṇḍarīka; also to several of the Buddhist hells, namely Paduma, Mahāpaduma, and Puṇḍarīka (*Sutta Nipāta* [*SBE* x. pt. ii. 121]; these appear to be named from the flower-shaped boils which torment the inmates therein). It is also used to denominate the highest number known to Buddhist computators, namely $10{,}000{,}000^{17}$, or 1 followed by 119 ciphers, which is called a *padma* or, in Pāli, *paduma*, whilst the white lotus, *puṇḍarīka*, gives $10{,}000{,}000^{16}$, or 1 followed by 112 ciphers (R. C. Childers, *Dict. of the Pāli Language*, London, 1875, pp. 315, 392).

The white lotus, *puṇḍarīka*, gives its name to one of the great canonical texts of Mahāyānist Buddhism, the *Saddharmapuṇḍarīka*, or 'Lotus of the True Law.' This is a theistic development of the Buddha-theory which represents Sākyamuni as the supreme god of the universe and the possessor of everlasting life. See following article.

LITERATURE.—This is sufficiently quoted throughout.

L. A. WADDELL.

LOTUS OF THE TRUE LAW.—No book gives a more accurate idea of the literature of the Great Vehicle or Mahāyāna (*q.v.*) than the *Saddharmapuṇḍarīka*, or *Lotus of the True Law*; and none gives a better impression of the character of the changes undergone by Buddhism in certain surroundings, from its beginnings down to the earliest times of the Christian era.

1. The Buddha in the Lotus.—In the ancient Pāli documents Śākyamuni is a man, a simple mortal, and he moves in a historical background. In the *Lotus* he is a sublime being, eternal or almost eternal, who unveils in a phantasmagoric setting the 'divinity,' *i.e.* the divine splendour and the majestic power, which Buddhists now attribute to the Buddhas; he is a god as Hindus and Buddhists understand the word—that is to say, he manifests himself especially by mythological performances, although he is a stranger to all notions of creation or of immanence. Such a being has no history; therefore, as Kern says (*SBE* xxi. p. ix), the *Lotus* is a sort of 'dramatic performance, an undeveloped mystery play. . . . It consists of a series of dialogues, brightened by the magic effects of a would-be supernatural scenery.'

Among the most characteristic episodes we may mention the silence which Śākyamuni maintains for thousands of centuries, lengthening out his divine tongue into the most distant worlds;[1] the appearance of the *stūpa* of a deceased Buddha, who had been in Nirvāṇa for a long time, but who wished to hear the *Lotus* (xi.);[2] the appearance of innumerable saints and Buddhas eager to hear the teaching of the Master, and coming from all the worlds. By means of Kern's excellent translation (*SBE* xxi.) we can appreciate the character of the 'sublime' and the 'supernatural' attributed by the Great Vehicle to the Buddha.

Although completely divine, Śākyamuni is not God in the *Lotus*. He is Buddha 'from the beginning'; he is the father of the worlds, the father of the future Buddhas and saints, the universal providence. In order to save human beings and to lead them to Nirvāṇa he appears in a human form which is illusory; he is born, teaches, and enters Nirvāṇa—at least as far as ordinary men can see; but in reality, while illusory Śākyamunis are appearing in this world, the true Śākyamuni reigns on a divine 'Mountain of vultures,'[3] surrounded by future Buddhas,[4] and imparting to them the true teaching, the true law. It is this true Śākyamuni that the *Lotus* shows.

Nevertheless, as we said, this god is not God. There is not a single word in the *Lotus* which is not capable of an orthodox, *i.e.* 'atheist,' interpretation. Śākyamuni may be styled Svayambhū,[5] 'who is by himself,' because, like all the Buddhas, he became Buddha without receiving the teaching from another. He is Buddha 'from the beginning';[6] but, just as the *Lotus* mentions a Buddha who will one day replace Śākyamuni, so we must believe that Śākyamuni is Buddha 'from the beginning of this cosmic age.' We know, moreover, that Brahmā himself

[1] The development of the tongue, capable of covering the whole face, is one of the signs of the 'great man' in the ancient sources.

[2] Contrary, evidently, to all Buddhist dogmas. The being 'who has attained Nirvāṇa' is 'invisible to gods and men,' since he is annihilated or has entered into eternal rest. The appearance of 'deceased Buddhas' in the *Lotus* is probably, therefore, only a case of the magical or deceptive power (*māyā*) of Śākyamuni.

[3] A hill near Rājagṛha, which was turned by the neo-Buddhists into a heavenly mountain.

[4] See art. BODHISATTVA.

[5] This is a name of Brahmā. The *Svayambhūpurāṇa* is a glorification of the Buddha of Nepāl (S. Lévi, *Le Népal*, Paris, 1905).

[6] Cf. this expression with the one described in art. MAÑJUŚRĪ. Mañjuśrī is 'the Buddha of the beginning, the middle, and the end,' therefore the Eternal and also the Absolute—quite different from Śākyamuni in the *Lotus*.

is not, properly speaking, eternal. Besides, Śākyamuni is not the only Buddha; other Buddhas reign and teach at the same time as he, his equals in nature, although not necessarily in merits, glory, or activity as a saviour; every Buddha has his own 'field.'[1] If he is the father of the world, it is not because he creates human beings; it is because by his teaching he is the father of the saints or future Buddhas.

So much for speculation. In practice, in the religious sentiment that the *Lotus* assumes, Śākyamuni is really God, providence, and reward of the saints.

2. The doctrine of salvation in the Lotus.—According to the *Lotus*, the saints of the Little Vehicle (see art. ARHAT), or Hīnayāna (*q.v.*), do not attain Nirvāṇa; they believe that they will not be re-born, but they are re-born to receive the true doctrine from the heavenly Buddhas. Deliverance cannot be obtained except by first becoming a Buddha; and for that purpose it is necessary to enter the Vehicle of the future Buddhas (see art. BODHISATTVA).[2] This doctrine is set forth in various parables, the most famous of which is that of 'The Prodigal Child' (iv.); it is not without a somewhat distant resemblance to the Gospel parable.

'It is . . . as if a certain man went away from his father and betook himself to some other place. He lives there in foreign parts for many years, twenty or thirty or forty or fifty. In course of time the one (the father) becomes a great man; the other (the son) is poor; in seeking a livelihood . . . he roams in all directions and goes to some place, whereas his father removes to another country.' The father is vexed at having no son; but one day, when, sitting at the gate of his palace, he is dealing with the affairs of millions of sovereigns [*aurei*, *suvarṇa*], he sees his son, poor and tattered. The son thinks, 'Unexpectedly have I here fallen in with a king or grandee. People like me have nothing to do here; let me go; in the street of the poor I am likely to find food and clothing without much difficulty. Let me no longer tarry at this place, lest I be taken to do forced labour or incur some other injury.' The father orders his son to be brought to him; but, before revealing his birth to him, he employs him for some years at all kinds of work, first at the meanest kind, and then at the most important. The father treats his son with paternal kindness, but the son, although he manages all his father's property, lives in a thatched cottage, and believes himself poor. At last, when his education is completed, he learns the truth. In the same way we are the sons of the Buddha, and the Buddha says to us to-day, 'You are my sons.' But, like the poor man, we had no idea of our dignity, of our mission as future Buddhas. Thus the Buddha has made us reflect on inferior doctrines; we have applied ourselves to them, seeking as payment for our day's work only Nirvāṇa, and finding that it is already ours. Meanwhile the Buddha has made us dispensers of the knowledge of the Buddhas, and we have preached it without desiring it for ourselves. At last the Buddha has revealed to us that this knowledge is to be ours, and that we are to become Buddhas like him.

3. Episodes.—Although the former part of the book (see below, § 4) is almost entirely devoted to Śākyamuni, chs. xxi.–xxvi. glorify several Bodhisattvas. We may mention the ἀριστεία of Avalokita (xxvi.), which is one of the most widely read works in China (see art. AVALOKITEŚVARA); the myth of the 'healer king,' Bhaiṣajyarāja (xxii.), a Bodhisattva who sets fire to his gigantic body for the salvation of human beings, and who is none other than the sun. In the Chinese Great Vehicle the practice of burning the skull is connected with this myth. In submitting to this cruel rite, the monk fulfils the duty of self-sacrifice incumbent on future Buddhas (J. J. M. de Groot, *Code du Mahāyāna en Chine*, pp. 50, 217, 227). The history of Sadāparibhūta, 'the always subdued one,' 'the always despised one' (xix.), exemplifies 'the superiority of simple-mindedness and pure-heartedness to worldly wisdom and scepticism' (Kern, in *SBE* xxi. p. xxxi). We should not have a right idea of the *Lotus* if we did not mention the glorification of the *dhāraṇīs*, or magical

[1] See art. MAHĀVASTU for the plurality of Buddhas and ĀDIBUDDHA for the stages in the divinization of the Buddhas.

[2] With this idea is connected the theory of the double teaching of Buddha—provisional teaching (Little Vehicle) and true teaching (Great Vehicle).

formulæ (xxi.), and the glorification of the *Lotus* itself (xx.): 'He who writes this book, or causes it to be written, obtains infinite merit,' etc. We know that, in the *Milinda*, a Pāli book of the Little Vehicle, all that is required to obtain a divine re-birth is to think of Buddha when dying (*SBE* xxv. [1890] 124); with more reason, in the Great Vehicle, the tendencies of *bhakti* predominate (see art. BHAKTI-MĀRGA).

4. Date of the Lotus.—The *Lotus* was translated into Chinese for the first time in A.D. 255; but this ancient translation is lost. The next one (286) contains chs. xxi.-xxvi., which criticism proves to have been added afterwards, the former ch. xxi. becoming ch. xxvii. On the other hand, the former chapters include verses (*gāthās*) and explanations in prose (the latter more recent). Kern therefore thinks that 'several centuries' separate the primitive redaction from the one which was certainly in existence before 286. Winternitz is not so generous, and places the original about the year 200. The present writer is inclined to favour an earlier date: the *sūtras* of Amitābha were translated into Chinese in 148-170, and show a Buddhology as developed as the *Lotus*. It is difficult to identify the Bodhisattvas of the Gandhāra sculpture, except Maitreya, but there is little doubt that this sculpture also shows the quasi-divinization of Buddhas and future Buddhas.

LITERATURE.—Skr. text, ed. H. Kern and B. Nanjio, Petrograd, 1908-09, Fr. tr. by E. Burnouf, Paris, 1852, Eng. tr. by H. Kern (*SBE* xxi. [1884]); the two translations are accompanied by introductions and notes (Burnouf, *Introduction à l'histoire du bouddhisme indien*, Paris, 1845, pp. 29, 60); M. Winternitz, *Gesch. der ind. Litteratur*, ii. (Leipzig, 1913) 230; works on Japanese Buddhism, especially R. Fujishima, *Bouddhisme japonais*, Paris, 1888; J. J. M. de Groot, *Code du Mahāyāna en Chine*, Amsterdam, 1893, pp. 50, 217, 227.

L. DE LA VALLÉE POUSSIN.

LOTZE.—1. General philosophical position.—Among German philosophers of the period which opens with the triumphant advance of natural science about the middle of last century, the most eminent name is undoubtedly that of Rudolf Hermann Lotze. Lotze's significance lies, above all, in his having instituted and constructed an all-embracing theory of the universe which does full justice to the claims of modern science, and at the same time conserves whatever was of real value in the results of the great idealistic movement of German philosophy in the preceding period; it was Lotze, in fact, who first directed those results to genuinely fruitful issues. To him belongs, moreover, the distinction of having stated and discussed the problems of thought with such outstanding clearness, force, and thoroughness that even in the most perplexing questions the reader is stimulated to form his own conclusions, or at least enabled to realize the difficulties that stand in the way of a definite result. The several philosophical sciences, accordingly, are indebted to Lotze's tireless intellectual labours for an effective and permanent furtherance and enrichment in numerous directions; and, indeed, it cannot be said that the results of his work have as yet been exhausted, or have been worked out in due measure by the general mind.

2. Life and works.—Lotze's early life falls within the period dominated by the thought and sentiment of Romanticism. Born on the 21st of May 1817 at Bautzen in Lusatia, he was grounded in classical study at the gymnasium of Zittau. Even as a boy he displayed that combination of critical acumen and lofty idealistic thought which characterized his riper years, and in a number of poems composed when he was about sixteen, and given to the public among his posthumous papers, we can clearly trace the rudiments of the comprehensive views which he subsequently elaborated; they reveal a maturity which amazes us in one so young. In 1834 he entered upon his academic course at the University of Leipzig, where he devoted himself to the study of medicine, and so came into practical touch with scientific pursuits and with the exact methods of contemporary natural science. Simultaneously, however, he sought to satisfy his philosophical and æsthetic aspirations by the study of German idealism, and to this end attended the lectures of Chr. Weisse. What he won from his University studies was, above all, the conviction that the mechanical mode of interpreting nature must be extended also to the organic, animate sphere, and that the current uncritical doctrine of 'vital force' must be banished from the scientific field (cf. his dissertation, *De futuræ biologiæ principiis philosophicis*, Leipzig, 1838); and this challenge to vitalism continued to be one of the leading features of his critical activity until his view at length won general acceptance.

After practising for a time as a doctor in Zittau, Lotze qualified as a Dozent both in the medical and in the philosophical faculty of the University of Leipzig (1839), and from that time to his call to Göttingen in 1844 he not only laboured successfully as an academic teacher (he had become a Professor Extraordinarius in 1842), but manifested a remarkable fertility as an author. In 1841 he published the first of his greater philosophical works, the *Metaphysik*, in which he stood forth as an independent thinker who had struck out upon fresh paths, though at the same time the powerful impetus which he had received from Hegel and Herbart is clearly traceable in the work. The distinctive feature of the *Metaphysik* is in constant presentation of the idea that that which truly exists—the ultimate root of reality—is to be found only in what by virtue of its unconditional value deserves to exist in this supreme sense. This line of thought, reminding us of Platonism and the Platonic insistence upon the supremacy of the Idea of the Good, finds pointed, if somewhat paradoxical, expression in the concluding statement of the book, viz. that the beginning of metaphysics lies not in itself, but in ethics. In 1842 Lotze issued a second work of importance, his *Allgemeine Pathologie und Therapie als mechanische Naturwissenschaften*. Here he attempts to apply without reservation the mechanical theory of things to the field of organic life, where the scientifically inadequate and, indeed, inadmissible idea of vital force had so long been resorted to; to that idea he likewise devoted a special article entitled 'Leben, Lebenskraft,' in R. Wagner's *Handwörterbuch der Physiologie* (Göttingen, 1843). In 1843 he also completed his *Logic*, in which he works on independent and often fresh lines, and strenuously emphasizes the 'spontaneity' of our thought-processes. His leading psychological views he wrought out at some length in another article in Wagner's *Handwörterbuch*, viz. 'Seele und Seelenleben' (1846), the most notable features of which were its doctrine of the substantial unity of the soul as a real entity and its unequivocal opposition to the materialistic views then forcing their way into psychology. His opinions in the field of æsthetics he set forth in a treatise entitled *Über den Begriff der Schönheit* (1845), which was soon followed by his *Über die Bedingungen der Kunstschönheit* (1847)—both appearing in the *Göttinger Studien*.

His *Allgemeine Physiologie des körperlichen Lebens* (1851) and *Medizinische Psychologie* (1852) develop the fundamental ideas of the *Pathologie*, seeking to examine more closely the validity of the procedure by which the mechanical method is extended to the organic sphere, as also to the psychological, and to define the necessary limits of that application. It is worthy of note that here

Lotze, in opposition to the parallelistic theory, quite definitely champions the hypothesis of a causal connexion between body and soul; and to this he adhered all his life. As regards the relation between the physical organism and the soul, in fact, he holds that the former is simply a system by which external stimuli are enabled to make a due impression upon the latter, and by which, again, the impulses of the soul are brought to bear upon the external world. The life of the soul is thus by no means a mere copy of the bodily life; the truth is rather that the soul governs the body, and makes it subservient to its own higher ends.

From 1856 to 1864 appeared the three volumes of Lotze's great work, *Mikrokosmus* (Eng. tr., 2 vols., Edinburgh, 1885), in which he set forth his philosophical system as a whole. His previous treatises, devoted almost entirely to a consideration of the basis of human life in nature, are here supplemented by a profound treatment of human life as expressed in history and the forms of civilization, and the work culminates in a survey of the universe from the standpoint of the philosophy of religion. The *Mikrokosmus* as a whole is dominated by the purpose in which Lotze's life-work in relation to his age took definite shape—to show how absolutely universal in its application, and at the same time how subordinate in its significance, is the function performed by mechanism in the structure of the world. It is in reality the philosophical problem of the age that Lotze here undertakes to solve; he makes it his task to refute the assumption that the modern mechanical science of nature demands as a necessary consequence a materialistic conception of the world; and his conclusion is that mechanism is simply the aggregate of the means by which the higher ideal element in the world can realize itself, and thus must not be allowed to rank as the ultimate reality. Hence, in particular, such mechanism does not conflict with that freedom of individual volition which we must postulate on moral grounds; the case is rather that it is to be conceived as simply the necessary condition of the efficient action of the autonomous will—as the mode of its self-realization. And just as little does this mechanism imply that the real world is a mere automaton, having its action fixed as by clock-work; on the contrary, the essential ground of the concatenation and process of the world is found by Lotze in the Infinite, which in the last resort can be conceived only as a living and all-embracing deity.

Lotze's next work of importance was his *Geschichte der Aesthetik in Deutschland* (1868). This work comprises (1) a history of the general points of view, dealing in the main with the æsthetics of Kant and of German idealism, but also treating of Herbart's views, and making reference to the fresh perspectives opened by the experimental method of Fechner; (2) a history of the fundamental æsthetic conceptions—'the agreeable in sensation,' 'the pleasing element in intuition,' and 'the beautiful in reflexion'; and, finally, (3) a history of the theories of art as developed in the various provinces of æsthetics.

In 1874 and 1879 respectively he published his larger *Logik* and *Metaphysik* (Eng. tr. of both, ed. B. Bosanquet, 2 vols., Oxford, 1884; *Metaphysics*², 2 vols., do. 1887, *Logic*², 2 vols., do. 1888) as the first two volumes of the *System der Philosophie* with which he hoped to crown his life-work. The third part, which was to have treated of ethics, æsthetics, and the philosophy of religion, was never completed. Lotze died in July 1881, shortly after taking up work in the University of Berlin, to which he had been called in the spring of that year. For the aspects of his final theory of the world, the composition of which in system he could not finish, we are therefore dependent upon his earlier works, especially the *Mikrokosmus*. Much valuable additional material on many points is to be obtained from the dictated portions of his lectures, edited by E. Rehnisch (9 vols., Leipzig, 1881 ff., Eng. tr., ed. G. T. Ladd, *Lotze's Outlines of Philosophy*, 6 parts, Boston, 1884–87).

3. Philosophical teaching.—The scientific foundation of Lotze's philosophy lies in his investigations of metaphysics; his chief interest is the problem of the causal connexion of things, and he arrives at a most characteristic solution of it. As the starting-point of his inquiries he takes the fundamental postulate of all natural science, viz. the assumption of a universal law of causal connexion operative among the elements of reality; or, to speak more precisely, he is concerned with the problem of 'transitive action' (*transeuntes Wirken*), *i.e.* the question how a change that occurs in an object A can be connected by a universal law with a change that takes place in a separately existing object B. In Lotze's view the fact of such connexion leaves us no option but to discard the theory that separate objects have an independent existence, and to regard all elements of reality as comprehended in a universal unity of being, in the Infinite, so that what was at first conceived as a 'transitive action' between separate substances passes into the conception of an immanent operation within a single substantial entity, the 'world-ground.' This Infinite, if it is to supply a real basis for the facts in question, cannot in the last resort be thought of otherwise than as analogous to our own spiritual being, though, of course, as raised to an incomparably higher power and freed from the limitations necessarily inherent in human nature as a finite thing. Ultimately, therefore, the world-ground is defined as an infinite spiritual being, or deity, the entire process of things being conceived as immanent in this deity, and as integrated and sustained by the unity of its being.

Lotze then proceeds to deal in a thorough-going way with the idea that this world-ground or deity forms the one ultimate basis of the existence and interpretation of all things. The elements of the real are all merely dependent parts or modifications of the Infinite; at a later period Lotze preferred to call them its 'actions.' Such actions of the Infinite he divides into two classes: first, the particles of the material world, or the atoms, which he speaks of as the 'elementary actions of the one world-ground,' but as 'actions always maintained in uniformity by it'; and, secondly, souls, the actions not always [so] maintained, but emerging at distinct points of the world-process, and for a section of that process generating a not previously present centre of 'internalization' (*Verinnerlichung*). Outside of and prior to the activity of the Infinite, however, there are no universal laws operative *per se*, nor any so-called eternal truths; there is no independently valid 'law of occurrence' (*Recht des Geschehens*) or of existence; 'law' and 'truth,' indeed, simply express the mode of realization by which the Infinite chooses to effect its will, and their validity depends absolutely upon the will of the Infinite, and lasts only so long as that will remains one with itself—a self-identity which, however, must be regarded not as a metaphysical necessity, but as a consequence of the ethical nature of the world-ground or deity, in the sense of the latter's 'fidelity to itself.'

Further, a vital constituent in Lotze's theory of the universe as originally formulated was the idea of the animate nature of all reality. The ultimate elements of the real he at first regarded as spiritual entities, as of kindred nature with the Leibnizian monads. He was led to take this view mainly by æsthetic motives, as also by the conviction that a purely material reality could have no independent existence. But, as he gradually wrought out his doctrine of the Infinite, the divine world-ground, his hypothesis of the animate nature of reality was more and more dispensed with, becoming ever the less necessary as what it had been designed to supply was equally well and, indeed, even better supplied by the fundamental position to which he latterly attained. He came at length to the above-mentioned conception of the material elements of reality as the mere 'actions of the Infinite,' maintained in a condition of uniformity, and thus differentiated in the clearest possible way from souls. Souls themselves, however, were likewise conceived as 'actions of the world-ground,' but as specially distinguished by their admirable and at bottom inexplicable capacity of feeling and knowing themselves as the active centres of an out-flowing life (*Met.* p. 601 f.). Some writers are of opinion that this view involves a denial of the doctrine of free will—a doctrine which Lotze always distinctly insists upon as an essential element in his theory of the universe, and for the sake of which he rejects, *e.g.*, the pantheism of Spinoza, notwithstanding the profound relationship between that theory and his own. Obviously, therefore, Lotze himself did not believe that his conception of souls as actions of the Infinite in any way implied the surrender of human freedom; but it is nevertheless true that he refers to the subject only in certain religio-philosophical reflexions, and never deals adequately with the crux which undoubtedly shows itself at this point, so that in his metaphysical construction he has left here a problem still unsolved.

Taken all in all, however, since the development of Lotze's thought is never guided by a purely systematic interest, but, on the contrary, takes the fullest possible account of experience, his philosophy presents a conception of the universe which is distinguished by a marvellous unity and completeness.

LITERATURE.—Of the more important works dealing with the life and philosophy of Lotze, the following may be named: E. Pfleiderer, *Lotze's philosophische Weltanschauung nach ihren Grundzügen*², Berlin, 1884; O. Caspari, *Hermann Lotze in seiner Stellung zu der durch Kant begründeten neuesten Geschichte der Philosophie*², Breslau, 1894; E. von Hartmann, *Lotze's Philosophie*, Leipzig, 1888; E. Rehnisch, 'Zur Biographie Hermann Lotze's' (see in Lotze's *Grundzüge der Aesthetik*, at the beginning), and 'Hermann Lotze' in *Neues Lausitzisches Magazin*, lxxvii. [1901]; R. Falckenberg, *Hermann Lotze*, Stuttgart, 1901 (*Frommanns Klassiker der Philosophie*, vol. xii.), and art. 'Lotze' in *Allgemeine deutsche Biographie*, suppl. vol. lii. [1907]; M. Wentscher, *Hermann Lotze*, i., Heidelberg, 1913. For further lit. cf. *DPhP* iii. [1905] 347-350.

M. WENTSCHER.

LOURDES.—Lourdes, a small town in the extreme south of France (diocese of Tarbes, department of Hautes Pyrénées), has become known as a place of pilgrimage only since 1858. In view of the insinuation that the development of this shrine represents a conscious design on the part of the Roman Catholic clergy to exploit pious credulity in the interest of the then newly defined dogma of the Immaculate Conception, it is worth while to point out that in 1858 and for some years afterwards Lourdes was one of the least accessible spots in the country. The nearest railway was at Bayonne, 80 miles off, and the road through Lourdes led nowhere except to some little-frequented health-resorts in the Pyrenees. If there were any question of deliberately organizing a fraud to impress the world, the choice of such a site would be inexplicable. Whatever judgment may be formed as to the nature of the phenomena of healing now witnessed at Lourdes, a careful study of the evidence regarding the manifestations which first brought the shrine into notice tends unmistakably to establish the good faith of all the persons primarily concerned. The history of the grotto of Lourdes is briefly this.

About mid-day on Thursday, 11th Feb. 1858, three little girls went to gather wood on the banks of the Gave. One of them, Bernadette Soubirous, a delicate child of 14, who looked much younger and who then could neither read nor write, was left behind by her companions. She was standing on a narrow strip of ground between the river and a low cliff known as the Massabieille, in which was a shallow cave or grotto with a sort of niche in the rock above it. Her attention was roused by such a rustling of the leaves as is caused by a sudden breeze, and, looking in front of her, she saw standing in the niche the figure of a beautiful young lady clothed in white and with a rosary in her hands. The figure made the sign of the cross, and the child, after doing the same, began to say her rosary. When the rosary was finished, the apparition smilingly saluted the child, and disappeared. This was the first of a series of similar apparitions of which a few details are given below. It is to be noted that, contrary to the usual experience of such visionaries, Bernadette had no clear intuition as to the identity of the heavenly visitant. Joan of Arc recognized her 'voices'—St. Michael, St. Catherine, etc.—from the first, but this was not the case here. 'A girl in white no bigger than myself' was her first description of the apparition (Cros, *Notre-Dame de Lourdes*, p. 16). The townsfolk, when they heard the tale, conjectured that she might have seen a soul from purgatory who came to ask for prayers, and, accordingly, when Bernadette went to the grotto a second time three days after, she took holy water with her and threw it at the apparition for fear the figure which she saw might be some delusion of the evil one, but the lady only smiled. Even after the sixth apparition Bernadette described her mysterious visitant in her patois as *aquéro*, *i.e.* 'it' (cf. Spanish *aquello*= *ecce illud*), and sometimes also as *un petito damizélo* (*une petite demoiselle*; cf. Cros, pp. 42, 302). The vision was at all times restricted to Bernadette alone; no one else saw anything or pretended to see anything—a fact which is in marked contrast to such cases as those of Marie Magontier at Le Pontinet in the Dordogne in 1889 (see L. Marillier, *Proc. Society for Psychical Research*, vii. [1891] 100 ff.) or that of Knock in Ireland in 1879-80 (see M. F. Cusack, *The Apparitions at Knock*, London, 1880). On the other hand, the child herself usually fell into a state of trance in which her features were completely transfigured, and Dr. Dozous, who went at first out of curiosity as a sceptical scientist in search of experience, testifies that the flame of a candle playing upon her hand for many minutes neither roused her from her trance nor left any trace of burning upon the skin. Bernadette, as early as 21st Feb., was subjected to the severest cross-examination by the commissary of police, M. Jacomet, and by the Procureur Impérial, M. Dutour, both of whom threatened her and her parents with punishment if she persisted. Still later, on 28th Feb., she was severely cautioned by M. Rives, the Juge d'Instruction, her proceedings at the grotto were closely watched by gendarmes, and she met with a severe rebuff, more than once repeated, from the curé, Abbé Peyramale, to whom the apparition had directed her to address herself. None the less, though timid by nature, she was never in the least shaken in her account of what she had seen, nor was she cowed by threats of punishment. Not one of the many formidable persons who cross-questioned her detected any signs either of unbecoming boldness or eagerness for notoriety or of a hysterical temperament. There is a large amount of contemporary evidence upon the point in the works of Cros, Estrade, and Dozous. As early as 27th March 1858, three physicians, appointed by the Prefect of the Department, who was anxious to suppress these manifestations, made a medical examination of Bernadette. In their report, dated 31st March (before the apparitions had come to an end), which is still preserved, the whole story of the early apparitions is recapitulated as the doctors heard it from Bernadette's own lips, and it is interesting to note its complete agreement with the account given by her many years later. Of mental disease or of any moral obliquity which would suggest the probability of conscious fraud the doctors found no trace. 'There is nothing,' they say, 'to show that Bernadette wished to impose upon the public.' On the other hand, nothing in the report suggests that the medical examiners themselves placed any faith in the story of the apparitions. They think that Bernadette was the innocent subject of a hallucination, and, while calling attention to her naturally impressionable character, they point out a certain development in the intensity of the trance with which the apparitions were normally accompanied. For the rest, they report that the child was delicate but perfectly sane and healthy-minded, and they offer no kind of suggestion that she should be put under restraint (Cros, p. 143).

It is interesting to contrast this report, which was fully justified by Bernadette's subsequent history, with the very unsatisfactory career of the two children who were witnesses of the alleged apparitions of the Blessed Virgin at La Salette in 1846, or again with Marillier's account of Marie Magontier, the child *voyante* of Le Pontinet, already referred to:

'I have no doubt,' says Marillier, 'so far as I am concerned, of the reality of her visions. In my opinion she certainly saw the Virgin in the crack of the wall. . . . She is no doubt subject to hallucinations; but at the same time she is ill-balanced and heavily weighted with the burden of heredity. She is the daughter of a father who was epileptic and of a mother who was doubtless insane, and she has the bearing, the character—in a word all the appearance of one suffering from hereditary degeneration. She is filled too with the morbid self-love and the enormous vanity so common among the degenerated' (*Proc. Soc. Psych. Research*, vii. 107).

According to the testimony of a number of persons who, much to the child's distress, pursued her with questions as to what she had seen, none of these undesirable characteristics was present in Bernadette Soubirous. Traps were laid to induce her to take money for herself or her parents, but her simplicity and good sense defeated them all. Though below the average in intelligence, she learned afterwards to read and write at the convent school, and until 1866 she remained engaged in humble occupations at Lourdes. She never saw the apparition again after 16th July 1858, though she visited the grotto frequently. In 1866 she became a nun at Nevers and remained there discharging the duties of infirmarian and sacristan, as far as her delicate health permitted, until her death in 1879. It is noteworthy that, though her body at the time of death was covered with tumours and sores, it was found, when the remains were officially examined in 1909, thirty years afterwards, entire and free from corruption (see Carrère, *Histoire de Notre-Dame de Lourdes*, p. 243).

With regard to the apparitions of the year 1858, it is to be noted that Bernadette always described the vision as one of ravishing beauty, and as living, moving, and speaking to her. The recorded words —for there seem to have been others which the child felt that she was bidden to keep secret as relating only to herself—are comparatively few. Though Bernadette several times asked the lady, as she had been bidden to do, to disclose her name, the apparition down to the sixteenth vision—that on March 25th—only smiled in reply. The dates and utterances of the series of apparitions are thus commemorated in an inscription upon marble which is erected near the grotto:

'Dates of the eighteen apparitions and words of the Blessed Virgin in the year of grace 1858. In the hollow of the rock, where the statue is now seen, the Blessed Virgin appeared to Bernadette Soubirous eighteen times—the 11th and the 14th of February, each day with two exceptions from Feb. 18th until March 4th, and on March 25th, April 7th, and July 16th. The Blessed Virgin said to the child on Feb. 18th: "Will you do me the favour (*me faire la grâce*) of coming here daily for a fortnight?" "I do not promise to make you happy in this world but in the next." "I want many people to come." The Virgin said to her during the fortnight: "You will pray for sinners, you will kiss the earth for sinners. Penitence, Penitence, Penitence." "Go tell the priests to cause a chapel to be built.' "I want people to come here in procession." "Go and drink of the fountain and wash yourself in it." "Go and eat of that grass which is there." On March 25th the Virgin said: "I am the Immaculate Conception."'

One point claims to be especially noted. These visions did not come to Bernadette at command. On two important occasions, as the inscription notices, she failed to see the apparition, viz. on 22nd Feb. and 3rd March, when she herself certainly expected to do so and when a large crowd —in the latter case some 4000 people, many of whom had spent the night upon the spot—had come long distances to assist at the manifestation. But, as sensible critics remarked even then, this arbitrary behaviour of the mysterious lady was a point in favour of the genuineness of the vision. 'If the child had simply invented the apparition,' said one of them, 'what was there to prevent its happening to-day, just as it happened yesterday?' (Cros, p. 121).

But what has given permanent significance to these occurrences was the discovery of the spring the healing virtues of which now bring hundreds of thousands of pilgrims to Lourdes from every part of the world. At the ninth apparition, on 25th Feb., the crowd of four or five hundred people who were watching Bernadette saw her rise and walk towards the grotto and then back again, moving to and fro in apparent perplexity. Finally she stooped down and began to scratch up the ground with her hand. A puddle formed, and the child then drank some of the dirty water and daubed her face with it and also ate a few blades of the grass which was growing in the same spot. Many of the spectators took this for proof that the poor girl had really gone out of her mind. Afterwards Bernadette explained that the Lady had bidden her drink of the spring, but, as she could find no spring, she had followed the apparition's directions in scraping up the ground as described. It seems absolutely certain that at that period the existence of any spring at this place was quite unknown to the inhabitants of Lourdes. By the next morning the trickle had grown to the thickness of a finger, a few days later it was like a child's arm, and since then and down to the present time it yields a quantity of water equal to 122,000 litres, or about 27,000 gallons, a day. This is the miraculous water which is the reputed source of so many miracles. The wonders of healing began almost at once, and several of them were juridically investigated by a commission appointed by the bishop of Tarbes, which occupied itself with the inquiry from Nov. 1858 to the end of 1861. It is to be noted, and the fact is proved by contemporary reports made to Baron Massy, the Prefect of Hautes Pyrénées, and to M. Rouland, the Minister of Worship, that for some months the clergy did all in their power to discourage these manifestations. They fully acquiesced when the Government erected obstructions barring access to the grotto, but the evidence of the cures that had taken place eventually bore down official opposition, and in Jan. 1862 the bishop of Tarbes, acting upon the advice of the Commission which he had appointed, issued a decree declaring that 'the apparitions (of the Blessed Virgin) have all the characteristics of truth and that the faithful are justified in believing them to be true.' Since then further ecclesiastical approbation has been given both to the apparitions and to the miracles of Lourdes in many ways, both direct and indirect, by the authority of the Holy See.

Any adequate discussion of the marvellous cures which take place at Lourdes must raise the whole question of the possibility of miracles. For Roman Catholics both the possibility and the continuance of a dispensation by which the Divine Omnipotence suspends at times the operation of natural causes are fundamental dogmas of the faith. Given the hypothesis that miracles may occur and do occur, it is difficult to imagine any facts more wonderful, either from the inveterate and organic nature of the diseases healed or from the abundance of the evidence with which the cures are attested, than the miracles worked at Lourdes. For those who wish to examine the subject for themselves no better or more convenient examples offer than the cures with which Emile Zola was brought into contact during his visit to Lourdes, and which he has introduced under fictitious names into his novel which bears that title.

Clémentine Trouvé (called in the novel Sophie Couteau) was cured instantaneously of a periostic fistula of the most aggravated kind which, down to the moment of her bathing in the piscina, was suppurating freely. Marie Lemarchand (*alias* Elise Rouquet) was also instantaneously healed. This was a most repulsive case of lupus, in which the face had been so eaten away as almost to lose the semblance of a human countenance. The evidence quoted by Bertrin in his last edition (*Histoire*, p. 363 f.) shows that seventeen years after the cure Marie Lemarchand was a healthy married woman with five children. Mme. Gordet (in the novel Mlle. de Guersaint) had been an invalid suffering from a complexus of most painful disorders, including tumour and phlegmon, for more than twelve years. The doctors declared that the only possible remedy lay in a dangerous operation, but she also was instantaneously cured in the piscina. In the case of Marie Lebranchu (Zola's La Gavotte), who was suffering from a tuberculous affection and had reached the very last stage of consumption, Zola supposes in his novel that the patient, after a temporary rally owing to the excitement of the pilgrimage, relapses soon after and falls a victim to the old disease which had never really relaxed its hold. In point of fact, the real Marie Lebranchu was in the enjoyment of vigorous health in 1908, fourteen years after the date of her cure (see for all these Bertrin, *Histoire*, who in his last edition has followed these cases up to the latest available date).

But examples of such cures are almost innumerable, and they may perhaps be most conveniently studied, especially by medical readers, in F. de Grandmaison's *Vingt Guérisons à Lourdes*, who gives an admirable choice of specially selected examples. It is not, of course, for one moment disputed that modern psychotherapeutics, and especially suggestion, have accomplished many marvels, but the instantaneousness of the cure, as witnessed more particularly in such cases as those of Pierre de Rudder, Mme. Rouchel, Gabriel Gargam, etc., can in no way be paralleled by any of Charcot's experiments at the Saltpétrière or elsewhere. Again, there are the extraordinary cases of the healing of quite young children, as, *e.g.*, the two-year-old infant of Dr. Aumaître of Nantes, born with a club-foot and instantaneously cured at Lourdes, of which a remarkable account is given in the *Annales des sciences psychiques* (1907, p. 858 f.). It may be confidently affirmed that the more carefully the evidence is studied, the more certain it becomes that the words 'suggestion' and, still less, 'hysteria' are not capable of accounting for the phenomena witnessed at Lourdes. In the preface to a booklet on Lourdes published by R. H. Benson a few months before his death, the writer describes his meeting with 'a famous French scientist—to whom we owe one of the greatest discoveries of modern times—who has made a special study of Lourdes and its phenomena.' The conclusions of this scientist, which, as Benson says, are particularly interesting because 'he is not himself at present a practising Catholic,' were formulated by him as follows:

'(1) That no scientific hypothesis up to the present accounts satisfactorily for the phenomena. Upon his saying this to me,' adds Benson, 'I breathed the word "suggestion," and his answer was to laugh in my face and to tell me, practically, that this is the most ludicrous hypothesis of all.

(2) That, so far as he can see, the one thing necessary for such cures as he himself has witnessed or verified, is the atmosphere of prayer. Where this rises to intensity the number of cures rises with it; where this sinks, the cures sink too.

(3) That he is inclined to think that there is a transference of vitalizing force either from the energetic faith of the sufferer or from that of the bystanders. He instanced an example in which his wife, herself a qualified physician, took part. She held in her arms a child aged two and a half years, blind from birth, during a procession of the Blessed Sacrament. As the monstrance came opposite, tears began to stream from the child's eyes, hitherto closed. When it had passed, the child's eyes were open and seeing. This Madame tested by dangling her bracelet before the child who immediately clutched at it, but from the fact that she had never learned to calculate distance, at first failed to seize it. At the close of the procession, the lady, who herself related to me the story, was conscious of an extraordinary exhaustion, for which there was no ordinary explanation.'

In a lecture given by Benson in June 1914 he stated publicly that the scientist here referred to was no other than Prof. Alexis Carrel, whose marvellous experiments in the transplanting of living tissue have constituted the great sensation of recent biological research. Indeed, signs are multiplying on all hands that in the less conservative circles of the medical profession the brusque dismissal of the phenomena of Lourdes as matters already classified and fully accounted for is going out of favour. This change of attitude was emphasized not long since by the action of the medical faculty of the University of Lyons. A lady doctor, Jeanne Bon, presented a *Thèse sur quelques guérisons de Lourdes* (Paris, 1912). This University thesis was officially approved, and certain of the professors superintended its composition. It was only at the last moment that the jury took fright and found a pretext for conferring the doctorate upon the candidate in virtue of some different title. The author in her thesis maintains that genuine cases of tuberculosis, in which laboratory experiment has established the fact that pseudo-tuberculous hysteria was not in question, have been spontaneously cured at Lourdes, and that these cures are effected under conditions of extreme rapidity which conspicuously mark them off from other spontaneous cures of consumption as generally observed. Finally, it should be noticed that, in contrast to the cures of Christian Science and many other faith-healing organizations, the fullest medical investigation is welcomed at Lourdes. Medical men of all creeds are invited to attend at the Bureau des Constatations, to which a permanent medical staff is attached, and every facility for observation is afforded to all scientific inquirers. Patients who believe themselves to have been miraculously healed or benefited are urged to bring their medical certificates and to attend personally at the Bureau that the case may be properly investigated, and efforts are also made to induce them to return after an interval of a year or more to afford the staff of the Bureau an opportunity of inquiring into the permanence of the cure.

LITERATURE.—Many of the earlier books on Lourdes, notably that of H. Lasserre, *Notre-Dame-de-Lourdes*, Paris, 1868, which has been translated into many languages and of which numerous editions have been published, are lacking in accuracy or in the medical knowledge desirable in the treatment of such a subject. The best general work is undoubtedly that of G. Bertrin, *Histoire critique des événements de Lourdes*, 37th thousand, Paris, 1912 (the Eng. tr., *Lourdes: A History of its Apparitions and Cures*, London, 1908, is unfortunately incomplete, lacking most of the documents printed in the Appendixes). Other valuable works are: F. de Grandmaison, *Vingt Guérisons à Lourdes discutées médicalement*, Paris, 1912; A. Vourch, *Quelques Cas de guérisons de Lourdes et la foi qui guérit; étude médicale*[2], do. 1913; A. Gemelli, *La Lotta contro Lourdes*, Florence, 1912, *Ciò che rispondono gli Avversari di*

Lourdes, do. 1912; Dr. Boissarie, *Lourdes: histoire médicale*, Paris, 1891, *L'Œuvre de Lourdes*, do. 1908, *Les grandes Guérisons de Lourdes*, do. 1901–13; J. Jörgensen, *Lourdes*, Eng. tr., London, 1914; R. H. Benson, *Lourdes*, do. 1914; J. P. Baustert, *Lourdes und die Gegner vor dem Forum der Wissenschaft*, Rindschleiden, 1913; A. Castelein, *Le Surnaturel dans les apparitions et dans les guérisons de Lourdes*, Paris, 1911. An interesting early account of Lourdes in English may be found in D. S. Lawlor, *Pilgrimages in the Pyrenees and the Landes*, London, 1870, pp. 296–448.

With regard to Bernadette Soubirous and the early history of the shrine see esp. L.J. M. Cros, *Notre-Dame de Lourdes*, Paris, 1901 (a summary of the historical portion of this work may be found in *The Month*, Sept. 1910); J. B. Estrade, *Les Apparitions de Lourdes*, Tours, 1899; Dr. Dozous, *La Grotte de Lourdes, sa fontaine, ses guérisons*, Paris, 1885; S. Carrère, *Histoire de Notre-Dame de Lourdes*, do. 1912; M. Reynès Monlaur, *La Vision de Bernadette*, do. 1914. Two valuable articles by F. de Grandmaison, defending Bernadette on medical grounds from the charge of hysteria and hallucination, may be found in the *Revue pratique d'apologétique*, xvi. [1913]. There is also a large number of books and articles which discuss the phenomena of Lourdes in a critical or hostile spirit, among others, J. Rouby, *La Vérité sur Lourdes*, Paris, 1911; H. Baraduc, *La Force curatrice à Lourdes et la psychologie du miracle*, do. 1907; J. Bonjour, 'Les Guérisons miraculeuses,' in *Revue de psychothérapie*, June and July 1913; a discussion of the whole question of faith-healing by several English physicians and surgeons in *Brit. Med. Journal*, June 18th, 1910; an art. by F. W. Myers and his brother A. T. Myers in the *Proceedings of the Society for Psychical Research*, ix. [1894]; and a similar discussion by M. Mangin, 'Les Guérisons de Lourdes,' in *Annales des Sciences Psychiques*, xvii. [1902] 815–866. Two periodicals, the *Annales de Lourdes* and the *Journal de la Grotte*, provide information regarding the reputed miracles and other incidents occurring during the pilgrimage to the shrine. A bibliography of earlier books on Lourdes will be found in L. Clugnet, *Bibliographie du culte local de la Vierge Marie* (France, Province d'Auch), pt. iii., Paris, 1903.

HERBERT THURSTON.

LOVE.

LOVE (Psychological and Ethical).—**1. The psychology of love.**—Love, as a complex psychical experience, may be classed as a 'sentiment' or 'passion,' the term 'passion' being here understood not as an explosive emotional outburst, but as a deep and steadfast enthusiasm. Whether we prefer to call love a sentiment or a passion will depend on the point of view from which we regard it. 'Sentiment' and 'passion' stand alike for stable and complex organizations of the emotional life, but, whereas the term 'sentiment' implies a higher intellectual development and greater refinement and subtlety of emotional feeling, the characteristic feature of a passion as distinct from a sentiment is its forcefulness. A passion is an emotional complex of a predominantly forceful kind.

A passion has been defined by A. F. Shand as 'an organized system of emotions and desires.'[1] When, as in the life of the lower animals, emotional impulses are independently active, they may still exercise some mutual restraint: a dog summoned from the pursuit of a cat by his master's whistle no longer feels the pure joy of the chase, for the fear of his master's displeasure tends to neutralize the joy. But such restraint is external and contingent: it does not suggest self-restraint. Where, however, the various emotions of the soul have found an object on which they can concentrate their desire or their aversion, or have become devoted to an idea about which they cluster and develop, a system of self-restraint grows up within the emotions.

> 'In every passion there is a system of self-control regulating more or less efficiently the intensity and behaviour of its emotions.'[2]

A mother loves her child. She may tend to be jealous if an aunt or a nurse wins too much the child's affection. But, if her love for the child is genuine, she is grateful for the kindness shown to the child, and the jealousy is inwardly controlled. Or she may yearn to shield him from every danger, but will surrender him despite her fears to the inevitable perils of hardy growth. Here emotions of solicitude, fear, and selfless surrender, like those of jealousy and gratitude on the former supposition, all feel the dominance of the steady, disinterested love, and, as they feel it, tend to pass into harmony with one another.

1 See art. 'M. Ribot's Theory of the Passions,' in *Mind*, new ser., xvi. [1907] 489.
2 *Ib.* 488.

A passion is not only organized emotion; it is also organized desire. For our emotions have their instinctive impulses, and these, when checked, tend to rise into conscious desires, into conative tendencies often urging in conflicting directions. Now it is of the very nature of a steadfast passion such as love to allow these desires and emotions place only as forms and expressions of itself; hence we find operative within the system a constant transforming influence. The emotions lose their primitive explosiveness and violence, for these disintegrating tendencies are incompatible with the centralizing, integrating work of the passion itself. As the spirit of this dominant passion circulates through all its members, exclusivenesses fall away, suspicion turns to interest, fear to respect, anger into the championship of just causes. The very form of the passion changes its character as the passion assumes mastery over the life. At first a concentrated persistency, as though set on an *idée fixe*, it relaxes and differentiates itself as the various emotions and desires become adjusted to its needs and demands, and become vehicles for its expression. The power of mere persistency passes into that of organized effectiveness. It is then a stable power, with its roots deep sunk in the vital affections and impulses; it has acquired the genuine stability which comes from organization and self-control.

As an organizing agency a passion will be functional at each point of its system, expressing itself as circumstance requires, now through this emotion or desire, now through that.

> 'In the love of an object, there is pleasure in presence and desire in absence; hope or despondency in anticipation; fear in the expectation of its loss, injury, or destruction; surprise or astonishment in its unexpected changes; anger when the course of our interest is opposed or frustrated; elation when we triumph over obstacles; satisfaction or disappointment in attaining our desire; regret in the loss, injury, or destruction of the object; joy in its restoration or improvement, and admiration for its superior quality or excellence.'[1]

From the foregoing it will be clear that, when we speak of the passion of love, we have in mind something very different from any mere passionate emotion. We have in mind a system of organized

1 Art. 'Character and the Emotions,' in *Mind*, new ser., v. [1896] 217 f.

emotions and desires which, by very reason of its systematic character and the principle which unifies it, is stable, regulative, inclusive, and instinct with a profound rationality.

For the normal development of love the fundamental condition is that there shall be joy in the object.[1] If there is this, the rest will follow; if there is not this, love is doomed from the outset.

The emotion of joy is characteristically spontaneous, expansive, vital. Its very expression bears witness to this.

'In joy the features dilate, the eye-brows are arched, the countenance opens out, the voice is louder and fuller, the gesture more ample and vivacious. The heart and lungs dilate, and the brain works more easily and more rapidly. There is increase of mental animation and of sympathetic feeling and goodwill in all that is said and done. In a word the expression of joy is the expression of liberty and therefore of liberality.'[2]

It may also become the fundamental expression of love. And the condition for this is that this expansive emotion, whose primitive bias is to go out of itself, shall fasten round some object and give it an intrinsic value, a value for its own sake. To have a joy in anything for its own sake is the primary essential for the development of love. Indeed it is this valuation of the object for its own sake, so essential to joy as to love, that is the mark distinguishing joy from pleasure. I am pleased with an object when it gratifies some interest of mine or some instinctive impulse. It gives me pleasure because it fulfils my need. It is a pleasure in relation to my sensibility or to my activity. And we speak correctly of the pleasures of sense and of movement. But joy is not self-centred like pleasure. No doubt there is pleasure in it, for all our emotions are toned by pleasure or pain, but such pleasure is but the pleasure of the joy. There is also a self-enlargement in joy, but this is not of its essence. The joy itself attaches not to the subject but to the object, and to have joy in an object is to value it for its own sake. Joy is thus an active disinterestedness, and its instinctive impulse is not only to maintain its object, but to surrender itself to it and rest freely in it as in something of intrinsic value and promise.

To have joy in an object is to respect its individuality. This is implied in the very idea of delighting in it for its own sake. To have joy in what is real is to subordinate individual opinion wholeheartedly to the truth of the matter; to have joy in what is beautiful is to trust to the inspiration of beauty and not to the contrivance of artifice. The interests of the object dictate at each step the line of advance.

And yet, essential as joy is to the development of love, it is not the whole of love, for love includes not only joy, but sorrow, and it includes these as co-operative and interpenetrative emotions. The joy of presence is followed by the sorrow of absence, and this sorrow at absence, possessing the imagination, has a selective and idealizing influence. We remember and dwell on those aspects of the object that tend to endear it and make it appear still more worthy of our joy and devotion, so that, when the object is restored, our joy in it is deepened and strengthened by these new insights won through sorrow. Thus sorrow and joy co-operate in the strengthening of the passion of love. But of the two emotions joy is dominant, sorrow 'recessive.' For sorrow is ever a search for a lost joy, whereas joy is not a search for a lost sorrow. Moreover, were it not for the joy in retrospect and prospect which is operative in and through sorrow, sorrow would have a contracting and depressing influence over life.

Love, then, is more than its dominant emotion, joy; more than any mere synthesis of joy and sorrow and their respective impulses. It is the inclusive passion and, in this supreme sense, the master-passion.

Love and belief.—Belief, following W. James's famous definition, is the sense of reality; or, if we wish to distinguish belief from faith, the intellectual from the intuitional aspects of spiritual sensibility, we might say that faith is the sense of reality, belief the sense of truth. Peirce, in his 'Illustrations of the Logic of Science' (*Popular Science Monthly*, xii. [1877], 289 f.), defines belief somewhat differently, but with similar purport, as the goal of thought and the starting-point of action. It is essentially the self-confidence that comes from having reached beyond doubt, and in its place built up settled habits or rules of action, the assurance that one is ready to meet the contingencies of life in any direction. At root this view identifies belief with the sense of power, power being here conceived as the reality with which our life is invested when doubt passes over into belief. To have a sense of power is to believe in one's self, to be ready to set one's own personal mark on whatever one touches; in a word, to hold, in James's phrase, that the *fons et origo* of all reality is ourselves.

Now, if we turn from belief so understood to love, and ask what the passion of love has to tell us about reality, we find that for love the supremely real thing is not itself, but its object. Clearly, if belief and love are to meet harmoniously, the sense of the reality and significance of self so essential to the belief that means power must be identical with that sense of the reality and supreme worth of its object which is so essential to love. Our joy in the object must be one with our belief in ourselves.

This requirement leaves us with the question: What must the nature of that object be which we can intimately identify with our own selves? It must be at least personal, or we could not identify ourselves with it. Moreover, the view that we take of the nature of our own personality must be of such a kind that we can conceive it as identified with this personal object without being lost or absorbed in it. If the self is lost in its object, the sense of power, the belief, will also go, and there will be no reconciliation of belief and love. Thus, if belief is to be love's belief, if faith is to be love's faith, the object of love must be such that communion with it heightens our sense of personality and makes us more truly ourselves than we were before.

But, it may be objected, when I really love anything, is it not one of the most satisfying features of this experience that I get away from myself? How can I surrender myself to the call of the great starry spaces of ether or of spirit and yet continue to be impressed with the importance of my own individuality?

The question goes to the root of all ethical inquiry. It compels us to recognize that there is something which we currently call our individuality, which is yet too weak to subsist in the presence of what is really sublime in the universe and in history. This individuality, which grapples itself to a finite body and shrinks from all the great things, from the infinite, from sacrifice and from death, how is it possible to conceive any organized sentiment or passion fulfilling itself within the limits of such being as this? Sooner or later it must strike its roots home into deeper personal ground. Only a self which has these roots of the infinite about its heart can ever ask the question out of which the true science of self emerges. Only in this infinite self can the will to love and the will to power prove no longer tendencies that are mutually destructive.

[1] Cf. A. F. Shand, *op. cit.* p. 495 f.

[2] A. Fouillée, *La Psychologie des idées-forces*, Paris, 1893, i. 155.

2. The ethics of love.—We have spoken of love as a sentiment or passion. We have spoken of it also as a power. We might go one step further back and speak of it as an instinctive power or an instinct, as a deep-rooted conative tendency shaped and determined in connexion with the supreme end of the preservation of life, *i.e.* of natural or spiritual existence whether in the individual or in the race. There is indeed good ground for claiming love as an instinct, provided we do not forget the fundamentally conative character of all instinctive behaviour, or insist that instinct shall from the outset have at its disposal some mechanism through which it operates. There is no such mechanism in the passion for the ideal, and yet this passion has the originality and fundamental force of an instinct. But this is not the place to attempt a systematic vindication of the independence of the spiritual life. It will be enough if we assume as the fundamental postulate of ethical science that the life animated by the ideals of truth, beauty, and right is not a mere derivative from the natural life of the body, but, as a *φυτὸν οὐκ ἔγγειον ἀλλ' οὐράνιον*, in Plato's memorable phrase[1]—a heavenly and not an earthly plant—has independent instincts of its own, instincts of spiritual self-preservation, instinctive passions for the ideal and the heroic, and that the instinctive passion *par excellence* is love.

Virtue is love.—When love is conceived in this ultimate way as the creative power of a new life, it is legitimate to look upon it as the supreme virtue. By virtue we understand the special power (*δύναμις*) and special excellence (*ἀρετή*) which enable us to live the best life. Now the question 'What is virtue?' received in the ancient world a great variety of answers; but of these, three stand out as of conspicuous interest and importance. Taken together they show a progressive deepening of the conception of virtue, so that the last of the three answers, properly interpreted, is not only the maturest, but also the most inclusive answer of the three. Of these three solutions—(1) Virtue is knowledge (Socrates), (2) Virtue is the habit of right willing (Aristotle), (3) Virtue is love (the solution of Christian ethics)—the second supersedes and includes the first, and the third supersedes and includes the second. With Aristotle virtue is primarily a matter of habit and not of mere rational insight; none the less the habit of right choosing, in which virtue essentially consists, is guided by the practical reason; for to choose rightly is in all things to choose the mean, and the practical reason alone can show where the mean lies. Thus with Aristotle we reach a more inclusive conception of virtue than that given by Socrates. The Aristotelian conception is a substitute for the Socratic only in the sense that it is a deepening or transcending of it. The Socratic 'reason' is taken up into the Aristotelian 'will' and made to function in its service. Similarly the definition 'Virtue is love' does not supersede the Aristotelian definition. It simply deepens, and by so doing develops and reorganizes it. To do justice to the value of habit we must look deeper than the habit. Moral habits grow from their instinctive foundations, not automatically, but through the enthusiasm which we put into the task of their formation. Hence, when we say 'Virtue is love,' we are far indeed from denying that it involves habits of right willing. We simply emphasize the motive power which is at the root of the formation of all habits of right willing. If enthusiasm for what is good fails to express itself in decisions and habits, it is no virtue; it is no more than the capacity for virtue.

But it is especially in relation to the varied emotions and impulses, to 'whatever stirs this mortal frame,' that love stands out as the great transforming and inclusive agency, and therefore as the ultimate virtue of the spiritual life, of the life which aims at a universal or common good. Working through the emotion of anger, it is the root of moral indignation and of justice;[1] through that of fear, it makes the object loved the object whose hurt is feared. It regenerates the self-regarding sentiments, transferring their affection from the atomic, private ego to the personal and inclusive self; the competition of others, directed as it is against the merely individual self, is no longer felt as an injustice to one's true personality and therefore excites neither envy nor ill-will.

'There is no remedy but love,' writes Goethe, 'against great superiorities of others.'[2]

Nor can the inclusiveness of true love tolerate the exclusive passion of jealousy. Moreover, with the complete passing of exclusiveness not only jealousy, but pride also, is transfigured, for love is not truly inclusive until it shows itself as ready to be grateful as it is to be generous, as ready to receive as to give. Love again is inseparable from reverence, and as such is the great security of true personal dignity. The negative element is never absent from love's sense of its own freedom. Inclusiveness does not mean loss of distinction between self and not-self. Intimacy with a friend through love means increased respect for his or her personality. There is thus in all love an element of reverence which guarantees that as intimacy grows so also does the value set upon personality. Again, we reverence the object of our love because we have a joy in it for its own sake, as an end in itself, and this joy is rooted in our sense of its reality, and most intimately associated also with the sense of our own reality. Belief or faith, an emotional belief in the intrinsic value of its object, is therefore essential to love, for faith is just this sense of personal reality.[3] Once again—and this is a central point—love is the source and also the very substance of moral volition. For by 'will' we mean the whole personality as active in deliberation, decision, and resolute conduct. And, when the whole personality is volitionally active in this broader sense of the term, and this activity is motived by the idea of a common good, then we seem justified in affirming that the power which vitalizes such activity, and the moral excellence which characterizes it—in a word, its virtue—is love. Finally, love is essential to knowledge, so that, if virtue is knowledge, it is for that very reason, and still more fundamentally, love. Love, at the root of our thinking, inspires the tendency to abandon ourselves to our object and identify ourselves with it. This has the effect of facilitating concentration and whole-hearted interest; the power of cleaving to a problem through thick and thin comes with the devotion of love. The best reason is love's reason, the reason born of sympathetic insight.

'Sympathy is the general principle of moral knowledge,' and the reason is that 'it furnishes the most reliable and efficacious intellectual standpoint.'[4] 'Quickened sympathy means liberality of intelligence and enlightened understanding.'[5] Or, again, 'genuine moral knowledge involves the affection and the resolute will as well as the intelligence. We cannot know the varied elements of value in the lives of others and in the possi-

[1] *Timæus*, 90 A.

[1] Cf. W. McDougall, *An Introduction to Social Psychology*, p. 73.

[2] Quoted by Hegel in *The Logic of the Encyclopædia*; see W. Wallace's tr., Oxford, 1892, p. 256.

[3] Cf. W. James, *Principles of Psychology*, London, 1891, ch. xxi.; also J. R. Seeley, *Ecce Homo*, do. 1865, ch. vi.

[4] J. Dewey and J. H. Tufts, *Ethics*, London, 1909, p. 335; cf. also G. Stanley Hall, *Adolescence*, ii. 136: 'Even knowledge at its best is a form of love. Interest is intellectual love, and one of the best tests of education is the number, intensity, and distribution of interests. . . . Even philosophy is not the possession, but the love and wooing of wisdom.'

[5] Dewey-Tufts, p. 389.

bilities of our own, save as our affections are strong. Every narrowing of love, every encroachment of egoism, means just so much blindness to the good.'[1]

So Plato, as we see in the *Republic*, connects the philosophical element in human nature very intimately with that which 'makes him fond of what he understands, and again makes him want to understand what he is attracted to,' for 'the understanding and the attraction go together.'[2] Indeed the very word 'philosophy' implies this.

But there is still one question to be faced if the inclusiveness of love as a virtue is not to be misconceived. There is such a thing as love's hate, for the lover of good is the hater of evil.[3] Hence, so long as evil actually exists, love must exclude it with all the force of its being. Now, in order that evil may actually exist, it must graft itself on to the good. For evil is a source of disintegration, and nothing can be wholly evil without being wholly disintegrated. Plato points out, in the first book of the *Republic*, that it is only in virtue of there being honour among thieves that the gang can subsist at all. Evil, in fact, can subsist in actuality only in virtue of the good which it possesses and enslaves. Hence, if love, through successive redemptions of all the elements of good contained in things evil, becomes inclusive of *all* good, evil as an actuality must cease to be. We cannot, indeed, think of it as annihilated, but we can conceive it as depressed to an infra-actual level of reality. At best it could survive as a real possibility of evil, real, that is, in relation to the will. As an actuality it would have vanished from the world. Then, and not till then, will love be inclusive of evil as of all else. For, though love cannot include actual evil, it must include at all times the possibility of evil, seeing that the possibility of evil is implied in the possibility of good, and all moral choice is ultimately a choice between possible evil and possible good. Hence, when evil shall have been reduced to the status of a real possibility, it will cease to lie outside love. Love will then be all-inclusive.

LITERATURE.—A. F. Shand, 'Character and the Emotions,' *Mind*, new ser., v. [London, 1896], 'M. Ribot's Theory of the Passions,' *ib.*, new ser., xvi. [1907], *The Foundations of Character*, do. 1914, and in G. F. Stout, *Groundwork of Psychology*, London and New York, 1903, ch. xvi. 'The Sources of Tender Emotion'; W. McDougall, *An Introduction to Social Psychology*, London, 1908; G. Stanley Hall, *Adolescence*, 2 vols., New York, 1904; W. R. Boyce Gibson, *God with us*, London, 1909, ch. viii.

For a more general treatment of the problem of love see F. M. Cornford, 'Olympian and Mystic Doctrines of Eros,' in *From Religion to Philosophy*, London, 1912; Plato, *Symposium*; Spinoza, *Ethics*, and *Short Treatise*, bk. ii. ch. v.; H. Jones, *Browning as a Philosophical and Religious Teacher*³, Glasgow, 1896, ch. vi. Cf. also R. L. Nettleship, in *Philosophical Remains*², London, 1901, pp. 37, 81, 85, 91 f.; for some living remarks on the meaning of love, F. von Hügel, *The Mystical Element of Religion*, London and New York, 1908, Index, *s.v.*; Rabindranath Tagore, *Sādhanā: The Realisation of Life*, London, 1913. On the problem of the relation of love to suffering see A. G. Hogg, *Karma and Redemption*, Madras and Colombo, 1909, and also J. P. S. R. Gibson, art. 'Karma and the Problem of Unmerited Suffering,' in *Church Missionary Review*, lxiv. [1913] 537. See also the standard works on Christian ethics. On the problem of sexual ethics see G. Stanley Hall, *Adolescence*, and F. W. Förster, *Marriage and the Sex Problem*, tr. Meyrick Booth, London, 1913. On the application of love as an educational principle see F. W. Förster, *Jugendlehre*, Zürich, 1904, and *Schule und Charakter*, do. 1908.

W. R. BOYCE GIBSON.

LOVE (Primitive).—The passion or emotion of love is as difficult to define as life itself, and probably for the same reasons. The following statements are useful:

'Simple et primitif comme toutes les forces colossales, l'amour paraît pourtant formé des éléments de toutes les passions humaines.'[4] Again, in its 'fully developed form the passion which unites the sexes is perhaps the most compound of all human feelings. Mr. Spencer thus sums up the masterly analysis he has given of it:—"Round the physical feeling forming the nucleus of the whole, are gathered the feelings produced by personal beauty, that constituting simple attachment, those of reverence, of love, of approbation, of self-esteem, of property, of love of freedom, of sympathy. These, all greatly exalted, and severally tending to reflect their excitements on one another, unite to form the mental state we call love."'[1]

Mantegazza, speaking of it as a colossal force, and Spencer, in his reference to exaltation, rightly emphasize the most remarkable characteristic of sexual love. This is the temporary raising of the individual to a higher power, the intensifying of all his capacities. A woman of the people said: 'When I am not in love, I am nothing.' Nietzsche has eloquently described this result:

'One seems to oneself transfigured, stronger, richer, more complete; one *is* more complete. . . . It is not merely that it changes the feeling of values; the lover *is* worth more.'[2]

For Plato love was a 'divine madness'; he was thinking of its automatism, its sweeping away of reason and even consciousness. It was perhaps this aspect that led Schopenhauer and others to condemn it as an illusion. But 'love is only a delusion in so far as the whole of life is a delusion, and if we accept the fact of life, it is unphilosophical to refuse to accept the fact of love.'[3] Ellis defines love 'in the sexual sense' as 'a synthesis of sexual emotion (in the primitive and uncoloured sense) and friendship.'[4] It is a minimum definition.

There is no doubt that the various forms of love—sexual, parental, fraternal, filial, and social—are kindred emotions. Their relative intensity decreases from the sexual to the social, but, as this decreases, extension increases, and more and more persons may be embraced. It is unnecessary to do more than mention the sociological truth that in all its forms love plays a part in society only less important than that of the instinct to live. It brings together the primal elements of the family, it keeps the family together, and it unites in a certain fellow-feeling all members of a race or nation.

I. *SEXUAL LOVE.*—Especially in its sexual grade, love has certainly during the progress of civilization become not only more refined and complex but more intense.[5] This is shown by a comparison with modern savages. Not only is the impulse weak, but the physical development is inferior, and consequently the difficulty of obtaining sexual erethism is great.[6] A social result of this last condition is the orgy, a method of periodic artificial excitement (see below). Jealousy is frequently absent, among the Central Australians to a remarkable degree.

'Amongst the Australian natives with whom we have come in contact, the feeling of sexual jealousy is not developed to anything like the extent to which it would appear to be in many other savage tribes.'[7]

Jealousy, however, seems to have little or no connexion with sympathetic love, but to be entirely concerned with animal instinct and the sense of property, and many savages show jealousy to as remarkable a degree as the Central Australians show its absence.

The question remains, and it is important for the study of the origin of the family, whether primitive love was merely organic desire. *A priori* it is conceivable that the family could have been established, monogamy made the type of marriage, and

[1] Dewey-Tufts, p. 423.
[2] R. L. Nettleship, *Lectures on the Republic of Plato*, London, 1897, p. 157 f.
[3] *i.e.* moral evil, or sin, not suffering, sorrow, or pain.
[4] P. Mantegazza, *Physiologie du plaisir*, Paris, 1886, p. 243.

[1] E. Westermarck, *MI* ii. 192, quoting Spencer, *Principles of Psychology*, i. 488.
[2] F. Nietzsche, *Der Wille zur Macht*, Leipzig, 1911, iii. 235. The neuro-muscular effects in man are curiously paralleled in animals not only by intensified activity, but by morphological developments; 'it produces new weapons, pigments, colours and forms, . . . new rhythms, a new seductive music' (Havelock Ellis, *Sex in Relation to Society* [*Studies in the Psychology of Sex*, 6 vols., Philadelphia, 1897–1910, vol. vi.], p. 179).
[3] Ellis, p. 139. [4] *Ib.* p. 133.
[5] Ellis, *Analysis of the Sexual Impulse in Man* (*Studies in the Psychology of Sex*, vol. iii.), p. 220 f.; Westermarck, *History of Human Marriage*³, London, 1901, p. 546.
[6] Ellis, *Sexual Impulse*, pp. 211, 209.
[7] Spencer-Gillen[a], p. 99 f.

more or less permanent unions fixed in social habit, merely by the operation of animal instincts. Similar results of the same causes are sufficient in the case of the animal world to preserve the race and render it efficient.

The accounts available vary from pessimistic denial of anything but reproductive impulse to fulsome predication of refined and romantic emotion. The contrast illustrates the difficulty of penetrating to the psychical processes or even the social feelings of the lower races.

The Australian bride is generally dragged from home to the man to whom she is allotted. But 'love' may come after marriage from kind treatment.[1] It is pointed out that 'love' must be assumed in Australian marriages by elopement, which was a recognized form of marriage.[2]

The Papuan language possesses no word for 'love.'[3] The Hos have no word for it: but 'they feel it all the same.'[4] The Paharias are said to form 'romantic' attachments.[5]

An observer remarks even of the Arabs that 'the passion of love is, indeed, much talked of by the inhabitants of towns; but I doubt whether anything is meant by them more than the grossest animal desire.'[6]

This statement is probably too sweeping, as also is the statement that the Bible contains no reference to romantic love.[7] Love-songs are rare among the lower races,[8] probably a mere result of the imperfect development of literature. But Polynesian peoples are adept at love-poetry,[9] which may be regarded as proving some degree of an emotional refinement, or rather irradiation, of the passion of love. At the other extreme, physical contact, it has been remarked that kissing and caressing are rare among savages, except towards young children.[10]

Yet among the Eskimo 'young couples are frequently seen rubbing noses, their favourite mark of affection, with an air of tenderness.'[11]

Suicide, which is fairly frequent among the lower races, is often prompted by unrequited passion.[12] But there are many trivial reasons for suicide which indicate merely a rudimentary development of character, and special conditions of social structure must also be considered. It may be regarded as a general rule that love, of any degree or character, is not an essential basis of marriage. Among the majority of early tribes marriage is a matter of arrangement; spouses are allotted by the relatives, often in infancy. In many cases such 'betrothed' couples are prohibited from all association until marriage takes place. That love, however, may be a basis of permanent marriage is another matter. It is probably as essential as the needs of the offspring. Marriage by arrangement and 'the marriage of convenience' were often contracted among the Greeks and Romans. They were frequent in mediæval Europe, and occur in modern civilization. But it is certain that social developments during the last century have involved a general adoption of the principle that marriage should be based on previous mutual attachment.

In the majority of early societies the two sexes are strictly separated, at least after puberty. Such a condition precludes much sympathy between youths and maidens when marriage is to be undertaken. This segregation sometimes extends to married life; in other words, there is a development of sex-clannishness, due either to natural inclination or to a certain subjection of women. Hence it is not surprising that among peoples like those of Eastern Africa it is regarded as disgraceful in a wife to show affection for her husband.[1] Among most rude peoples the man treats the woman with more or less roughness. This is to some extent the case in barbarism and among the lower classes of civilized society.[2] The ancient Greeks, Chinese, Hindus, and Muslims represent that stage of culture in which woman is a slave, a prisoner, or both. Notions of female inferiority combine with a sense of property and of proprietary jealousy, and polygamy in some cases is a contributory factor.

The conditions indicated above show that love in 'primitive' society had little chance of development except in and after marriage. 'Love comes after marriage' is a proverb used by Plutarch and by the Eskimo savage; it is common all over the world. What is termed 'romantic' love is rare, even in the highest societies, when the married state has been established for some time. Conjugal love is more affection than passion, and affection depends on intellectual and moral sympathy; community of interests, habitual association, and mutual care of children contribute to the complete character of the emotion. These factors also are sufficient to produce permanence in marriage and to bind the family together. It is therefore unnecessary to call in the aid of teleology in general, or natural selection in particular, to explain the origin of the family. Nor is it possible to argue that 'love has played little or no part in the institution of the family'[3] (see below, § 1). The cannibal Niam-niam are said by a good observer to show an affection for their wives which is 'unparalleled,'[4] and similar statements have been made of many savage peoples.[5]

It is a justifiable conclusion that conjugal love was real, though elementary. Combined with occasional rough treatment, it was still genuine affection, based on sympathy as well as on the sexual impulse.[6] Similarly, of primitive love in general it may be concluded that it possessed the same elements, in a less developed state and capacity, as modern love in its best manifestations. We need not accept either the frequent denials of any form of love or the attribution of 'chivalrous' love to Bushmen and Congo savages.[7] Lastly, in estimating the evidence of observers, it must be remembered that their diagnoses of love are not based on one invariable scientific definition of the emotion.

1. Development of conjugal love.—The extension of the elementary sexual impulse into conjugal affection with its complex associations should be regarded as, sociologically, the most important feature in the natural history of love. This emotion seems to have developed sufficiently in primitive society to assist in breaking down collective methods of mating, which apparently (as in Central Australia) were often liable to be induced by the hard conditions of savage life. The hypothesis is frequently put forward that the family and social organization are essentially antagonistic. But the pacific way in which they work together in existing races, both civilized and barbarous, and

1 R. Brough Smyth, *Aborigines of Victoria*, London, 1878, i. p. xxiv.
2 B. Malinowski, *The Family among the Australian Aborigines*, London, 1913, p. 83.
3 C. W. Abel, *Savage Life in New Guinea*, London, 1902, p. 42.
4 E. T. Dalton, *Descriptive Ethnology of Bengal*, Calcutta, 1872, p. 206.
5 *Ib.* p. 273.
6 Westermarck, *Hum. Marr.*3, p. 360.
7 The statement is that of H. T. Finck, *Romantic Love and Personal Beauty*, London, 1887, p. 110.
8 Westermarck, *Hum. Marr.*3, p. 357; Ellis, *Sexual Impulse*, p. 212.
9 G. Turner, *Samoa*, London, 1884, p. 98; see also *ERE* vii. 740a.
10 Ellis, *loc. cit.*, quoting authorities.
11 G. F. Lyon, *Voyage of Discovery*, London, 1824, p. 353.
12 Westermarck, *Hum. Marr.*3, pp. 358, 502.

1 W. Munzinger, *Ostafrikanische Studien*, Schaffhausen, 1864, p. 325.
2 J. Dawson, *Australian Aborigines*, Melbourne, 1881, p. 37; Malinowski, p. 83; *MI* i. 657.
3 As A. J. Todd, *The Primitive Family*, New York, 1913, p. 19.
4 G. Schweinfurth, *The Heart of Africa*, London, 1873, i. 510.
5 Westermarck, *Hum. Marr.*3, p. 502.
6 See F. Bonney, in *JAI* xiii. [1883] 130; Malinowski, p. 88.
7 As cited by Westermarck, *Hum. Marr.*3, p. 358. See on the whole subject *MI* i. 532.

also the fact that crude types of social organization have been broken up by the family, strongly oppose this partial view.

It is right to notice that a time came 'when the conditions of life became favourable to an expansion of the early family, when the chief obstacle to a gregarious life—scarcity of food—was overcome.'[1] But before that there was a different type of gregariousness, which, so far as it went, did possess elements antagonistic to conjugal affection, at least. It is probable that increased security of subsistence assisted the growth of this emotion and strengthened thereby the family bonds. Westermarck has argued:

'Where the generative power is restricted to a certain season—a peculiarity which primitive man seems to have shared with other mammals—it cannot be the sexual instinct that causes the prolonged union of the sexes, nor can I conceive any other egoistic motive that could account for this habit. Considering that the union lasts till after the birth of the offspring and that it is accompanied with parental care, I conclude that it is for the benefit of the young that male and female continue to live together. The tie which joins them seems, therefore, like parental affection, to be an instinct developed through natural selection. The tendency to feel some attachment to a being which has been the cause of pleasure . . . is undoubtedly at the bottom of this instinct. Such a feeling may originally have induced the sexes to remain united and the male to protect the female even after the sexual desire was gratified; and if procuring great advantage to the species in the struggle for existence, conjugal attachment would naturally have developed into a specific characteristic.'[2]

This is an important statement and calls for consideration. In the first place, the assumption that even the earliest palæolithic men were capable only of periodic impulse is insecurely based. That a more or less regular capacity did ultimately develop from a periodic is a different matter. Secondly, even admitting the above-mentioned view, no account is taken of the phenomena of habit. Habit is the essential factor to-day, and must always have been, in the development of conjugal affection from the primary incidence of the sexual emotion. And here habit is reinforced by many associations, one of which is the care of children. Another, itself a strong emotion, is the proprietary feeling, strengthened by habit. Even the rudest savage woman feels a right of property in 'her man,' however badly he treats her. Again, the invocation of 'natural selection' is, when analyzed, merely rhetorical. Westermarck admits that the sexual impulse is 'at the bottom' of conjugal affection and prolonged union, but he here ignores improved environment. Neither of these factors can, except by a metaphor, be identified with the agents or machinery of 'natural selection.'

The fact is that improvement of conditions and development of nerve and intelligence have been accompanied by an increase both in emotions and in their control; the emotion of love in all its grades has been no exception. To apply the doctrine of the survival of the fittest to such a development within the species is a misapplication of Darwinism, or, rather, an unnecessary extension of the doctrine.

2. Development of sexual love.—In order to estimate aright not only the course of development, but the character, of modern love in its typical form, it is necessary to note some further elements—in particular, complementary elements—in the love of man and woman. Male love is active and dominant; female love is passive and subservient.

'In men it is possible to trace a tendency to inflict pain, or the simulacrum of pain, on the women they love; it is still easier to trace in woman a delight in experiencing physical pain when inflicted by a lover, and an eagerness to accept subjection to his will. Such a tendency is certainly normal.'[3]

Hence various aspects of married life and of courtship:

'Among the Slavs of the lower class the wives feel hurt if they are not beaten by their husbands; the peasant women in some parts of Hungary do not think they are loved by their husbands until they have received the first box on the ear; among the Italian Camorrists a wife who is not beaten by her husband regards him as a fool.'[1] 'In courtship, animal and human alike, the male plays the more active, the female the more passive part. During the season of love the males even of the most timid animal species engage in desperate combats with each other for the possession of the females, and there can be no doubt that our primeval human ancestors had, in the same way, to fight for their wives; even now this kind of courtship is far from being unknown among savages. Moreover, the male pursues and tries to capture the female, and she, after some resistance, finally surrenders herself to him. The sexual impulse of the male is thus connected with a desire to win the female, and the sexual impulse of the female with a desire to be pursued and won by the male. In the female sex there is consequently an instinctive appreciation of manly strength and courage.'[2]

A connected result of male superiority in strength, activity, and courage is the element of protection in male love, and of trust on the side of the female. The pugnacity observed in the males, both of animals and of wild men, is one aspect of the general increase of capacity effected by passion. The intimate psychology of love reveals not only an impulse for union, but an association in the male psychosis with an impulse for destruction, and even for devouring. Love often uses the language of eating. The natural modesty and coyness of the female play an important part both in stimulating the love of the male and in refining it. 'La pudeur,' says Guyau, 'a civilisé l'amour.'[3] Connected with these differences is the relative slowness of the growth of love in woman; it proceeds by long circuiting. In men its growth is relatively rapid, and its duration generally less. Love, again, is 'only an episode in a man's life, whereas for a woman it is the whole of her life.'[4]

Biologically, courtship is a stimulus of love, a means of producing tumescence. Owing to the differences of secondary characters noted above, the love of the male is expressed chiefly in acts of courtship, that of the female in receiving them. If the preservation of love in a permanent union is analyzed, it will be found that it depends on a more or less continuous process of courtship.

A remarkable development of sexual love was made by the early Christians. This was the practice of close but chaste unions between the virgins and young men (see art. CHASTITY). The poetic or romantic exploitation of love to which the custom led (as is shown by the literature) was perhaps the only sociological result. It is possible that this became a tradition and thus influenced the mediæval valuation and practice of chivalrous love. 'For a mediæval knight the chief object of life was love.' It became a formal cult, and theoretically was defined as 'the chaste union of two hearts by virtue wrought.'[5] Dante's love for Beatrice is the highest type of the practice. Its essential condition was that the passion should be hopeless and should not be consummated in marriage. But, as with a similar ideal of love in ancient Greece, so in this case, the reality was generally immoral. The lady as a rule was the wife of another, and adultery was frequent.

In European civilization to-day the factor of intellectual and moral sympathy in love has become more pronounced with the greater freedom and higher education of women. Sympathy strengthens affection, and affection strengthens sympathy. The element of equal friendship in love has been greatly increased, and thus, curiously, in spite of the levelling which has taken place to some extent in class-distinctions, has made love between members of different social spheres more rare.

A 'gentleman' to-day 'seldom falls in love with a peasant

[1] *MI* i. 113.
[2] *Ib.* ii. 191, citing also *Hum. Marr.*[3], ch. ii.
[3] Ellis, *Sexual Impulse*, p. 74.

[1] Ellis, *Sexual Impulse*, p. 66 f.
[2] *MI* i. 657.
[3] See Ellis, *Evolution of Modesty* (*Studies in the Psychology of Sex*, vol. i.), p. 1; Stanley Hall, in *AJPs* ix. [1897] 31.
[4] *MI* ii. 440.
[5] *Ib.* ii. 432 f.

girl, or an artizan with a "lady."'[1] Again, 'to a cultivated mind youth and beauty are by no means the only attractions of a woman; and civilisation has made female beauty more durable.'[2]

Meanwhile, the importance in marriage of compatibility, physical and psychical, is becoming more and more recognized by the law.

3. Social habits.—(*a*) *Restrictions on love.*—The majority of primitive peoples impose restrictions on the physical gratification of love except in the marriage relation. This tendency thus harmonizes with the biological law that mating is the final cause of love. But an errant tendency is inevitable, and many peoples have permitted it, with a proviso. Thus, 'the Jakuts see nothing immoral in free love, provided only that nobody suffers material loss by it.'[3] In many of these cases the temporary possession of a lover is regarded as a test of complete womanhood, and in most of them the practice actually serves as a kind of trial-marriage. The case is very different in civilization.

(*b*) *The law of parity.*—A social and a biological tendency act as complementary factors, the one discouraging and the other encouraging love between biological similars. The one tendency is expressed in the remarkable rules of exogamy;[4] the other, which may or may not be connected, is the tendency for those persons to be mutually attracted who are of the same grade of pigmentation. It has long been a popular belief that fair persons are attracted by dark, and *vice versa*; even that short persons are attracted by tall, and *vice versa.* A. Bain speaks of 'the charm of disparity.'

'But da Vinci affirmed clearly and repeatedly the charm of parity . . . Men fall in love with and marry those who resemble themselves.'[5]

Modern investigations have established this conclusion.[6]

One of these began from 'the popular notion that married people end by resembling each other.' The explanation was that they began by so doing. On the other hand, persons are not attracted to members of the opposite sex 'who are strikingly unlike themselves in pigmentary characters.' 'With this feeling may perhaps be associated the feeling, certainly very widely felt, that one would not like to marry a person of foreign, even though closely allied, race.'[7] But the barriers between widely different races are occasionally broken by love.

(*c*) *Seasonal love.*—Among primitive peoples there is a constant practice of what may be termed the periodic love-feast. Types of these are to be found among the Central Australians and the Dravidians of India. Certain festivals of mediæval Europe have been classed in the same category, with little foundation.[8] A prevalent deduction from these 'periods of licence' was that the morals of savages were degraded and licentious. But a closer study of savages makes it certain that their existence is 'just as little a prolonged debauch as a prolonged idyll' (as was the still earlier view, instituted by Rousseau).[9] A more recent deduction was that among the earliest men and the lowest modern savages pairing took place only in spring and at harvest.[10] The festivals in question would be 'survivals' of a primitive pairing-season. Among mammal and other animals (though not domestic), a periodic rut is general, though not universal. A doubtful statement has been made of so relatively a high type of people as the Cambodians that they exhibit a rut twice a year.[11] It

1 Westermarck, *Hum. Marr.*³, p. 362.
2 *MI* ii. 391.
3 *Ib.* ii. 423; see also W. G. Sumner, in *JAI* xxxi. [1901] 96.
4 There is some evidence that love is rare between persons brought up together from childhood (*MI* ii. 375).
5 Ellis, *Sexual Selection in Man* (*Studies in the Psychology of Sex*, vol. iv.), p. 195.
6 *Ib.* pp. 201, 203.
7 *Ib.* p. 198.
8 Ellis, *Sex in Relation to Society*, p. 218 f.; Spencer-Gillen[b], ch. xii.
9 Ellis, *Sexual Impulse*, p. 209.
10 The hypothesis of Max Kulischer, *ZE* viii. [1876] 152 ff.
11 Mondière, *s.v.* 'Cambodgiens' in *Dictionnaire des sciences anthropologiques*, Paris, 1884-86.

is a fact that spring and harvest are among savages, barbarians, and modern peasants regular seasons both for general festivity and for special development of the sexual feelings. The reason may be partly biological, partly climatic, and partly connected with the food-supply. The probable conclusion is that, the conditions being favourable for any sort of expansion and perhaps specially so for amorous expression—an increase in the sexual impulse during these periods is established for modern peoples — the opportunity is taken by societies, which express themselves only socially, to stimulate their normally feeble sexuality and to obtain organic relief.[1]

The principle of dramatization, which is at the root of magical ceremony, may be noted in love-charms, of which all folk-custom, from the Australian to the European, has a store, and in a large class of primitive marriage ceremonies, which generally typify union. The latter are organized love-charms.[2]

The connexion between love and religion is of the same nature as the connexion between love and art and life generally.

'Very much of what is best in religion, art, and life, owes its charm to the progressively widening irradiation of sexual feeling.'[3]

4. Homosexual love.—Sexual love between individuals of the same sex is a not infrequent abnormality. 'It probably occurs, at least sporadically, among every race of mankind,'[4] and in post-Homeric Greece it became, so far as the male sex was concerned, almost a 'national institution.'[5] Cases of congenital perversion are very rare; habit and environment have been largely overlooked by investigators.[6] The majority of barbarian and civilized peoples have condemned the habit; in mediæval Europe it seems to have been regarded as connected with witchcraft and heresy.[7]

II. *NON-SEXUAL LOVE.*—**1. Parental love.**—As in the case of conjugal love, observation of primitive peoples is contradictory; but it is certain that maternal affection is universal, and paternal affection, though less intense, and often defective, is normal in the human race.[8]

According to Aristotle, parents love their children as being portions of themselves.[9] Espinas regards this love as a modified love of self or property.[10] A. Bain, however, derived parental love from the 'intense pleasure in the embrace of the young.'[11] But, as Westermarck notes, 'if the satisfaction in animal contact were at the bottom of the maternal feeling, conjugal affection ought by far to surpass it in intensity; and yet, among the lower races at least, the case is exactly the reverse, conjugal affection being vastly inferior in degree to a mother's love of her child.' He adds: 'It seems much more likely that parents like to touch their children because they love them, than that they love them because they touch them.'[12] According to Herbert Spencer, parental love is 'essentially love of the weak or helpless.'[13] Westermarck observes that 'when the young are born in a state of utter helplessness somebody must take care of them, or the species cannot survive, or, rather, such a species could never have come into existence. The maternal instinct may thus be assumed to owe its origin to the survival of the fittest, to the natural selection of useful spontaneous variations.'[14] But, as stated above, it is unnecessary to regard these instincts as cases of natural selection.

2. Filial love.—'Children's love of their parents is generally much weaker than the parents' love of their children. . . . No individual is born with filial love.' But 'under normal circumstances the infant from an early age displays some attachment to its parents,' especially to the mother. It is 'not affection pure and simple, it is affection mingled with regard for the physical and mental superiority of the parent.'[15]

1 Ellis, *Sex in Relation to Society* ('The Orgy'), pp. 127 ff., 147, 218 ff.
2 See A. E. Crawley, *Mystic Rose*, London, 1902, p. 318.
3 Stanley Hall, in *AJPs* ix. 31.
4 *MI* ii. 456.
5 *Ib.* p. 463.
6 *Ib.* p. 468.
7 *Ib.* p. 489.
8 *Ib.* i. 529, 531.
9 *Eth. Nic.* VIII. xii. 2.
10 A. Espinas, *Des Sociétés animales*², Paris, 1879, p. 444.
11 *Emotions and the Will*³, London, 1880, p. 140.
12 *MI* ii. 187.
13 *Principles of Psychology*³, London, 1881, ii. 623 f.
14 *MI* ii. 187, 190 f.
15 *Ib.* ii. 194.

Conversely, parental and, still more so, paternal affection includes a regard for weakness and helplessness. Filial love is proved to be normal in primitive races; as with other forms of love, it is both less intense and less complex than in civilization.

3. Fraternal and social love.—All peoples exhibit 'altruism of the fraternal type, binding together children of the same parents, relatives more remotely allied, and, generally, members of the same social unit.'[1] In primitive tribes social organization is the outcome of social needs, and a real social affection and friendly sympathy are proved. As before, Westermarck applies the doctrine of natural selection to this development.[2] With progress in culture social affection becomes a marked feature of religious and ethical practice and theory. Noteworthy examples are the doctrine and duty of charity,[3] in Christianity idealized by the Founder's love for all mankind and by the theory of brotherly love, and the Oriental systems, such as the *ahiṁsā* of Hindu religions.

The philosophical literature which exploits the idea of love is enormous. Plato developed the view that love is the creator of beauty, though beauty must have an objective element. Greek, Christian, and mediæval thinkers developed the connexion between love and faith, love of good and love of God. The *amor intellectualis Dei* of Spinoza is paralleled by many Oriental theories of contemplation. Throughout, love in religion stands midway between the philosophical and the human conceptions.

III. *LOVE-GODS.* — Deities embodying the abstract notion of love are hardly developed until the higher stages of barbarism are reached, but some points may be noted in the previous evolution. Animistic thought may produce, by a process of normal 'hallucination,' the belief that evil spirits, at a later stage various neutral or good spirits, behave as lovers of human beings. The peoples of the Dutch East Indies believe that evil spirits take the shape of handsome men and love their women.[4] Primitive psychology, by analogical reasoning, explains love as made of fire (the Malay notion[5]), or the state of love as one of possession. The latter animistic view is connected with any departure from the normal; the new character of the individual is regarded as due to the entrance of a spirit. The West Africans attribute love to possession by the god Legba, or Elegbra. Dreams of love are explained in the same way as in mediæval Europe with its ideas of the *incubus* and *succuba*.[6] Such a deity might develop, as others to be cited might have or actually have developed, into a deity 'of Love.' But, as usual, a deity has an indirect connexion only with this or that emotion. Many peoples, like the Finns,[7] have regarded love as a form of insanity (a variety of possession). It is doubtful whether the description of this or that deity as 'patron of love' has any more definite meaning than an indirect connexion, such as is usually the case with 'possession.' The Finns regarded the god of evil as the patron of love.[8] The Yoruba 'patroness of love,' Odudua, is 'worshipped' at erotic feasts.[9] Her connexion with love is probably indirect only. Such a connexion is frequent in the case of 'deities of fertility.' The Scandinavian Freyja, goddess of love and fruitfulness, seems to have been synthesized with Frigg, goddess of marriage.[1] Among the early Semites the Baal (like any local fetish of a hunting, pastoral, or agricultural tribe) was a source of fertility and a 'heaven-god,' and his wife, the Baalat, was therefore a goddess of fertility and of heaven. Some process, as yet uncertain, developed from this the figure of Ishtar, Astarte, Ashtoreth, worshipped at Erech as the goddess of love, and identified with Nana, the Sumerian goddess of the planet Venus (see artt. BAAL, ASHTART). The Heavenly Aphrodite of the Greeks is derived from this figure.[2] It is possible that the Hindu god of love and desire, Kāma, was developed in connexion with some such festival as the spring *Vasanta* of 'prosperity and love,' which is primitive in character, though his figure is a direct personification of an emotion.[3] A connexion is often made in early thought between love and the moon—possibly a case of the regular attribution of fertilizing power to the satellite. The serpent is occasionally connected with myths of the origin of love, and demons take the serpent-form in order to prosecute amours, or change from the human to the serpent-form on discovery.[4] The arrows of love, in folklore and poetry, seem to be due to an obvious analogy from the incidence of the emotion. Metaphor, throughout the world, speaks of the effect of love as a wound.

LITERATURE.—The more important authorities are given in the article.

A. E. CRAWLEY.

1 *MI* ii. 194 f.
2 *Ib.* ii. 197.
3 *Ib.* i. 559.
4 J. G. F. Riedel, *De sluik- en kroesharige rassen tusschen Selebes en Papua*, The Hague, 1886, pp. 252, 271, 340, 439
5 Crawley, *Mystic Rose*, p. 198.
6 A. B. Ellis, *The Ewe-speaking Peoples*, London, 1890, p. 44, *The Yoruba-speaking Peoples*, do. 1894, p. 67.
7 J. M. Crawford, *Kalevala*, New York, 1889, xxiii.
8 Todd, *The Primitive Family*, p. 19, citing Crawford.
9 Ellis, *Yoruba-speaking Peoples*, p. 43.

1 J. Grimm, *Teutonic Mythology* (tr. J. S. Stallybrass, London, 1882–88), i. 303.
2 J. G. Frazer, *Pausanias*, London, 1898, ii. 128 ff.; L. W. King, *Babylonian Religion and Mythology*, do. 1899, p. 24. See Herod. i. 199; Jer 7[18] 44[17ff].
3 E. W. Hopkins, *Religions of India*, Boston, 1895, pp. 154, 156, 452, 455.
4 Crawley, *Mystic Rose*, p. 193.

LOVE (American).—The psychology and social habits of the aboriginal American peoples are, on the whole, in line with those of other races at equivalent stages of development. But they exhibit one or two distinctive features. As an instance of the usual conflicting results of observations, there is Morgan's statement that the 'refined passion of love is unknown to the North American,'[5] and that of Catlin, that the N. Americans are not 'behind us' in conjugal, filial, and paternal affection.[6] An accidental case of difference, not due to observers, is the remarkable fact that the Nahuas possessed no word for love, while Quichua, the ancient language of Peru, had six hundred combinations of the word meaning 'to love.' Observation of this fact has led to an interesting analysis by Brinton of the expression of the idea in N. American dialects. He distinguishes four methods of linguistic reaction to the emotion of love: (1) inarticulate cries, (2) assertions of identity and union, (3) assertions of sympathy and similarity (2 and 3 are clearly not distinct), and (4) assertions of a desire. It is noted that the Mayas possessed a radical word for the joy of love, which was purely psychical in significance.[7] 'Romantic affection' is predicated, as usual, by certain observers.[8] It is clear that the Americans compared favourably with other races in the combination of love with female chastity, and in the filial and social forms of altruism. It is, for instance, stated that the Central Americans at the time of the Spanish invasion were remarkable for their brotherly love and charity to the needy. The Naudowessies

5 L. H. Morgan, *Systems of Consanguinity and Affinity*, London, 1870, p. 207.
6 G. Catlin, *Manners, Customs, and Condition of the N. Amer. Indians*[3], London, 1842, i. 121.
7 D. G. Brinton, 'The Conception of Love in some American Languages,' in *Proceedings of the American Philosophical Society*, xxiii. [1886] 546.
8 G. Gibbs, in *Contrib. N.A. Ethnol.* i. [1877], quoted by E. Westermarck, *Hum. Marr.*[3], London, 1901, p. 503 f.

(Dakota), Californians, and Eskimos, among others, are mentioned as being exemplary in their regard for aged parents;[1] but their care for children, though marked, is not above the standard of contemporary races.[2] In short, they exhibit a slightly more highly developed stage of the social form of affection. It is worth noting that all observers attribute to the Northern Indians a measure of chivalrous feeling.

One abnormality, namely, homosexual love between individuals of the male sex, was curiously prevalent; it is sufficient to refer to the remarkable list of authorities adduced by Westermarck.[3] It is possible that the military tone of N. American life—and the practice was chiefly characteristic of the Northern aborigines—was a predominant factor, as in the cases of the Fijians and ancient Greeks.

The personification of love in the figure of a deity and the worship of erotic forces are perhaps less conspicuous, as might be expected, than in other societies. The Nahua peoples celebrated, it is said, 'a month of love,' during which many young girls were sacrificed in honour of the goddesses Xochiquetzal, Xochitecatl, and Tlazolteotl, who were patronesses of sexual love.[4] But the Central American deities, with the exception of the leading members of the pantheon, were extremely vague personalities; it is generally doubtful whether two names refer to one deity or two, and it is still more problematical what forces or properties the divine names represented. But the name Tlazolteotl seems to have a definite connexion with love, though we cannot, with Camargo, regard her absolutely as 'the Mexican deity of love.'

'Her home,' he states, 'was in the ninth heaven, in a pleasant garden, watered by innumerable fountains, where she passed her time spinning and weaving rich stuffs, in the midst of delights, ministered to by the inferior deities. No man was able to approach her, but she had in her service a crowd of dwarfs, buffoons, and hunchbacks, who diverted her with their songs and dances. . . . So beautiful was she painted that no woman in the world could equal her . . . whoever had been touched by one of the flowers that grew in the beautiful garden of Xochiquetzal [*sic*] should love to the end, should love faithfully.'[5] She not only inspired and provoked acts of love, but was able to hear confessions and to give absolution.

The last detail has been emphasized by Spence,[6] in connexion with the meaning of her name, to reduce the goddess to the status of a Mexican Cloacina. But, in spite of the priestly rhetoric of her description, there is enough in its latter portion to establish her as a deity of love, though probably illicit. Brasseur de Bourbourg regarded a volcanic symbol and Boturini Benaduci the high god Tezcatlipoca, as deities of love, without any foundation.[7] Equally unfounded, except in the sense of indirect connexion, are the cases of the moon (especially among the most northerly peoples) and of fire.[8] The N. Americans are slightly behind their contemporaries in the development of deities of love.

LITERATURE.—This is given in the article.

A. E. CRAWLEY.

LOVE (Buddhist).—The way in which early Buddhist literature takes account of the emotion of love is many-sided. It cannot adequately be settled, as some have tried to settle it, by a treatment that is too abstract or, again, too specialized. The hunger for unity or simplification leads some historians to assign to every departure in religious or philosophical thought one fundamental or leading idea—a view that may be attained by closing the vision to all but a few considerations. No great teacher ever discoursed systematically, or even mainly, on one subject. And it is as misleading to say, of early or any Buddhism, that love is its 'ground-thought' as to substitute any other single emotion, idea, or aspiration in place of love. A glance at the scheme drawn up by the present writer of how, and with what frequency, or other emphasis, such things are envisaged in the saints' anthology of early Buddhism[1] should suffice to give pause to such generalizations. There it is shown that the inner, or upper, circle of adherents to what was first known as the Sāsana (rule, order), or Dhamma (norm, doctrine), of the followers of the Sākyas' son found, in the goal that they had reached, not a unison, but a diversity of aspects. And it is hardly wise for interpreters of another age and tradition to contradict them.

Further, Buddhism was a movement set on foot with a view to the needs and ideals not solely, or even mainly, of the academy or the cell, but of 'all sorts and conditions of men,' in so far as these were represented among dwellers between Himālaya and Ganges. Its doctrines were not promulgated only among a chosen few; its teachers went afield without delay, waiting in the groves by village and city to converse with all and any who came to hear. It is true that its ideals, like those of Christianity, stretched far beyond and away from the range of notions and wishes common among average errant mortals. But there was that in the one movement, as in the other, which availed to draw to it the hearts of the many as well as the aspirations of the few. And among the needs and the emotions covered by the word 'love,' the teachers of Buddhism and the compilers of its sacred literature met and dealt with every variety of channel, and every degree of refinement or the reverse. We may, for clearness of reference, set out those channels of normal love as follows: (1) parental, especially mother-love; (2) filial love; (3) fraternal and kin love; (4) friendship; (5) sex love; (6) love of a superior for an inferior; (7) love of an inferior for a superior; and (8) æsthetic and ideal love. It is easy to see that other emotions are blended with these, wherever they are found, but it is no less true that the word 'love' is much used for each one of the eight.

As a doctrine based with great and very frequent emphasis on the generally current fundamental principles of morality, or social conduct (such as the veto on murder, theft, loose sex-morality, harmful speech, and intemperance), Buddhism had homilies and a benediction for all channels of love so practised as to draw men together in mutual goodwill and domestic and social happiness. These are scattered about the *Nikāyas* (collections of *Suttas*, or discourses). But the homily to Siṅgāla[2] is the most comprehensive in its scope. The Buddha is represented as interrupting the open-air morning orisons of a young layman. The latter is rendering homage to the four quarters of the firmament, the nadir, and the zenith, presumably to the several devas—the 'four great rājas' and others—who presided over them, though they are not mentioned. The layman performs these rites out of loyalty to his dead father's wishes. The Buddha substitutes for these objects of worship six objects of devotion and service as more desirable, viz. the devotion of children to parents and of parents to children, that of learners to teachers and conversely, that of husband to wife and conversely, that of friend to friend, that of master

[1] *MI* i. 531, 534, 600, 603.
[2] *Ib.* i. 403 ff., 531.
[3] *Ib.* ii. 456 ff.
[4] H. H. Bancroft, *NR* ii. 336 f., quoting J. de Torquemada, *Monarquia Indiana*, Madrid, 1723, ii. 280, 299, and C. E. Brasseur de Bourbourg, *Hist. des nations civilisées du Mexique et de l'Amérique céntrale*, Paris, 1857-59, iii. 530, ii. 462 f.
[5] D. M. Camargo, in *Nouvelles Annales des Voyages*, xcix. [Paris, 1843] 132 f., quoted in *NR* iii. 377 f.
[6] L. Spence, *Myths of Mexico and Peru*, London, 1913, p. 380.
[7] *NR* iii. 505, 507.
[8] D. G. Brinton, *Myths of the New World*, New York, 1868, pp. 132, 146.

[1] *Psalms of the Early Buddhists*, London, 1910-13, pt. i. p. xxxvii, pt. ii. p. 420.
[2] *Dīgha Nikāya*, iii., xxxi.

to servant and conversely, and that of layman to recluse or Brāhman and conversely. The practical forms which these six several modes of devotion or worship should take are simply and concisely described. For our present purpose it is chiefly interesting to note that they are prescribed not as mere duties or moral acts, but rather as ways of giving expression to a spirit of 'compassion' felt by the agent. Thus not only should parents in five ways take compassion on (*anu-kampanti*, lit. 'vibrate towards or after') their children, and teachers in five other ways take compassion on their pupils, but wives, in yet other five ways, should take compassion on their husbands, friends and colleagues, in yet other five ways, should take compassion on any honourable man (*kulaputta*; this would refer pointedly to Siṅgāla and his companions), in yet other five ways servants should take compassion on their master, and in yet other six ways recluses and Brāhmans should take compassion on the laity. The corresponding term in the other six cases of reciprocated service—*e.g.*, of children to parents, husbands to wives, etc.—is 'ministering to,' or 'waiting upon.' And the choice of these two Pāli words, differing as they do from those that we should find in a similar European catalogue, is interesting. The former word—to show, take, feel 'compassion'—while it is here applied, for instance, to the devotion of the good servant, is very often used in the *Suttas* for the supreme instance of the reciprocal devotion—that of a superior for inferiors—to wit, the compassion moving a Buddha to spend himself 'for the welfare, the happiness of many folk, for the good . . . of gods and men,'[1] and 'to live perpetually moved towards the welfare of all that lives and breathes.'[2] It was this spirit that he prescribed for those whom he sent forth as missionaries.[3] For all these six forms of mutual service or devotion a Christian catalogue would probably use the word 'love,' however much the sources and outlets of the emotion so termed are shown to differ. The fact that the Buddhist catalogue does not bring in its ethics to supplement, or flow from, Siṅgāla's religious beliefs, but supersedes the latter by the former, and, again, the fact that it substitutes the 'divine emotion' of compassion and the practical devotion of ministry for our more familiar and pregnant 'love' show us the need that there is for caution in making affirmations about love in Buddhism. It may help us further towards some, or away from other, conclusions if we examine in brief detail some of these forms as met with in the five *Nikāyas*.

1. Parental love.—The typical form of intense and self-surrendering devotion is that of mother-love, just as the type of overwhelming sorrow is that of the bereaved mother.[4] The wise man should cleave to a genuine friend—a watchful, loyal, sagacious, sympathizing friend — as the mother is devoted to her child.[5] And not only to his friends:

> 'E'en as a mother watcheth o'er her child,
> Her only child, even with life itself,
> So let us for all creatures, great or small,
> Develop such a boundless heart and mind,
> Ay, let us practise love for all the world,
> Upward and downward, yea, before, behind,
> Uncramped, free from ill-will and enmity.'[6]

This simile is quite in keeping with the chosen term 'being moved, *or* vibrating towards,' or 'compassion,' since mother-love contains so large an element of passionate, protecting pity.

1 *Dīgha Nikāya*, iii. 211, etc.
2 *Aṅguttara Nikāya*, iv. 208, etc.
3 *Mahāvagga*, i. 10 (*SBE* xiii. [1881] 112); cf. *Aṅguttara Nikāya*, iv. 150.
4 C. A. F. Rhys Davids, *Psalms of the Early Buddhists*, pt. i. p. xxvii.
5 *Dīgha Nikāya*, iii. 188.
6 *Khuddaka Pāṭha* (*PTS*, 1915), p. 8.

2. Sex love.—No case is found of a woman seeking death or religion through the death not of her child, but of her husband. *Satī* does not appear in Buddhist literature. The anthology mentioned above has one case, vouched for by the Commentary only, of a man leaving the world because of his young wife's death from snake-bite.[1] And women are recorded, in text and commentary, as having left the world because their husbands had forsaken it for religion. The power of sex to enthrall is fully acknowledged,[2] as is that of sex-repulsion.[3] But there was no one ancient and moving 'Canticle' of sex-love calling for spiritualized annexation to the Buddhist books, such as we possess in the legacy left by Hebrew Scriptures to the Christian apostles. No allegory of the 'compassion' of a Buddha for his adherents is found in the pretty love-song of the *Sutta* called 'The Questions of Sakka.'[4] Conjugal love—a blend of sex-feeling, parent-feeling, and friendship—finds beautiful expression in old Indian literature, but in poems that are younger than early Buddhist books. This is possibly the outcome of a social evolution—an evolution which a century or two of Buddhist ethics as to the right devotion in husband and wife may have done much to bring about. It may be noted in this connexion that the Aśokan rock and pillar edicts, although they are now and then didactic on family relations, are silent as to conjugal life. Again, it is perhaps a pathetic touch in the Anthologies that shows woman at her best ready for the comradeship, but man blind to it. Mahā-Kassapa, who headed the Order at the Buddha's death, and Bhaddā Kapilānī, famed as a preacher, were, by commentarial tradition, husband and wife, and not in their final birth only. They left the world by mutual agreement, having gone through the form of marriage to please their kin. She, in the poems attributed to her, glories in her ex-husband's gifts and in their 'spiritual friendship' and common vision of the truth. His much longer poem reveals him as both the anchorite and the friend of mankind, even of the outcast, but has no word concerning her.[5] It is conceivable that the larger, more heterogeneous group composing the family in ancient India may have hindered the evolution of the conjugal relation. According to the sidelights thrown by the *Suttas* on domestic life, a girl left her home to enter the house not of her husband, but of her father-in-law.[6] She became more or less the servant of him and his wife as well as of her husband. Reference also is occasionally found to a second wife:

> 'Woeful when sharing home with hostile wife.'[7]

3. Love towards the Buddha.—Filial love alone is the form wherein early Buddhist devotees gave expression to their feeling for the founder of their rule and doctrine. They confessed themselves not seldom as the 'own mouth-born' sons and daughters of the Buddha[8]—a sentiment which, in the later commentarial records, finds an echo in these children being termed severally 'my son,' etc., by the Master.[9] Yet, so far as the present writer knows, none of the usual terms for love or affection is applied to him, and certainly no one is spoken of as loving him by 'taking compassion upon' him. He, as father, teacher, 'recluse,' is ministered to or waited upon; it is he who 'takes compassion' on children, disciples, and laity. Honour, worship, or homage, faith or confidence, and the term *pasanna*, which may be rendered 'resting in,'

1 Rhys Davids, *Psalms*, ii. 34. 2 *Aṅguttara Nikāya*, i. 1.
3 Rhys Davids, *Psalms*, i. 159 f., and several *Suttas*.
4 T. W. Rhys Davids, *Dialogues of the Buddha*, London, 1899-1910, ii. 301.
5 Rhys Davids, *Psalms*, i. 49, ii. 359 f.
6 *Majjhima Nikāya*, i. 186; Rhys Davids, *Psalms*, i. 159 f.
7 Rhys Davids, *Psalms*, i. 108, 163.
8 *Ib.* pt. i. p. xxxii, pt. ii. p. 50, and *passim*.
9 *Dhammapada Commentary*, i. 21, 430, etc.

'satisfied with'—such are the expressions for the emotion felt, but not 'love.' The Indian words for love were not sufficiently elastic to cover this relation—a relation which was not the less deep and genuine, whether it was expressed in terms of the self-surrendering devotion of a believing and adoring 'heart' or of the intellectual love of the philosophic mind:

> 'I see him with my mind as 't were mine eyes,
> By night, by day, incessant, watching ever.
> I reverence him while waiting for the morn.
> And thus methinks I'm ever with him dwelling.
> . . . .
> Truly my mind with him is joined, O brāhman.'[1]

The emancipating force of his teaching drew the imagination:

> 'So I, leaving the men of vision cramped,
> Come as the swan flies to the mighty sea.'[2]

And the charm or majesty of his presence drew by way of sense:

> 'O wondrous fair the All-enlightened shines
> . . . .
> Like a great storm-cloud in the summer sky,
> Thou on thy followers pourest precious rain,
> . . . . noble of aspect, whose skin
> Resembleth gold, say, what is friar's life
> To thee with presence so supremely fair?'[3]

This adoration for his person is usually accepted, but not always:

> 'Long have I wished, lord,' said the devoted Vakkali on his deathbed, 'to draw near to behold the Exalted One, but now is there no more strength left in me to come!' 'Let be, Vakkali, what hast thou to do with seeing this poor frame of me? He who seeth the Norm, he it is that seeth me; he that seeth me is he who seeth the Norm.'[4]

And indeed it was the conviction that, in this man of the long and tireless ministry, carried out purely from sweet compassion for the sons of men, such wisdom and goodness, charm and power, were combined as to banish, while and where he lived, the need for superhuman objects of worship from his followers, and which, long after he had passed away, aided the theological evolutions of Mahāyānism—the conception, namely, of Mañjuśrī, and Avalokiteśvara, wisdom and compassion personified. And Maitreya or Metteyya, the future Buddha, has been conceived as one who will revive the spirit of lovingkindness among men.[5]

4. Love towards deities.—For deity, or the deities of its age, early Buddhism finds no need of adoring devotion. No deities in our sense of the word exist for it. All *devas* are more like our conception of angels, beings differing from mankind only in degree and in quality of physical and mental characteristics. They inhabited other more or less adjacent worlds or spheres. On earth were nature-spirits or fairies, usually termed *devatā* (lit. 'deity'). All were to be treated with goodwill and friendliness, but nothing further. They were believed to have the power of communicating with man, and are found rebuking and admonishing the lax or lazy recluse. But in the case of the chosen few—a Buddha and his Arahants—it is the *devas* who render homage and minister to the man, not the reverse.[6]

5. Ideal love.—The emotion of ideal love, though it was not reserved for any personified deity in Buddhism, and though it played largely round the person of the founder, was not otherwise atrophied. It never appears as associated with the whole of that cosmodicy which, for the more intellectual Buddhists, takes the place of a theodicy. Devotion bestowed on a 'cosmic mechanism,'[7] not planned by divine wisdom, and involving for each and all so much unspeakable suffering, was not to be looked for. But the Norm, as doctrine and as a part of that cosmos, in Pāli *dhamma* and

[1] *Sutta Nipāta*, verses 1142, 1144.
[2] *Ib.* 1134.
[3] Rhys Davids, *Psalms*, ii. 403, 311.
[4] *Saṁyutta Nikāya*, iii. 119 f.
[5] T. W. Rhys Davids, *Buddhism*[22], London, 1910, p. 200.
[6] *e.g.*, Rhys Davids, *Psalms*, ii. 274, 389.
[7] H. Oldenberg, *Buddha*[6], Stuttgart, 1914, p. 367.

dhammatā, constituted for the intelligent adherent a source of austere affection (*rati*). Admiration for *dhammatā* is a refrain in the Brethren's anthology,[1] and the expression 'love for the Norm' (*dhammagatā rati*) is met with; *e.g.* (here called 'the Ideal'):

> 'Is his love set on the Ideal,
> . . . . . .
> Other loves that Love surpasseth.'[2]

The same emotion is aroused by the idea of Nirvāṇa (*nibbānābhirati*, a stronger form of *rati*):

> 'All my heart's love is to Nibbāna given,'[3]

and by that of the Sāsana, or 'religion,' 'rule' (*sāsanarati*).[4]

6. Friendship.—'Goodwill and friendliness' (*avyāpāda, adosa, mettā*) express, better perhaps than the overburdened word 'love,' that expanded sentiment of amity to all living things which the average man can cherish only for personal friend or comrade. The cultivation of amity (*caritas*), pity, sympathetic gladness, and equanimity formed a sort of sublimated or higher *sīla*, or code of morals, the first three of them forming a development of that 'vibrating towards,' or compassion, which is so essential an attitude in Buddhist ethics. It is to these that the Elder Revata refers in defending himself against the charge that he lived in the woods to receive stolen goods:

> 'Since I went forth from home to homeless life,
> Ne'er have I harboured conscious wish or plan
> Un-Ariyan or linked with enmity.
> Ne'er mine the quest, all this long interval:—
> "Let's smite our fellow-creatures, let us slay,
> Let them be brought to pain and misery!"
> Nay, love I do avow, made infinite,
> Well trained, by orderly progression grown,
> Even as by the Buddha it is taught.
> With all am I a friend, comrade to all,
> And to all creatures kind and merciful;
> A heart of amity I cultivate,
> And ever in goodwill is my delight.
> A heart that cannot drift or fluctuate
> I make my joy; the sentiments sublime
> That evil men do shun I cultivate.'[5]

If, as certain writers think, we should refrain from applying so warm-blooded a term as 'love' to *mettā*, 'amity,' this may be justified, perhaps, on etymological grounds, and on the ground that Buddhism sets itself against passionate feeling. But it cannot be justified either by lukewarmness in the exordiums to practise *mettā* and sympathy with pain or joy or by sluggishness in the carrying out of these virtues by leading Buddhists.

It would be hard to find in ancient literature any exordium so aglow with 'goodwill towards men' as that of the so-called Four Brahma-vihāras, *i.e.* Best Dispositions, or Four Infinitudes:

> 'Suffusing, tender and compassionate, such an one with the rays of our loving (or sympathizing) thought, and from him forthgoing suffusing this and that quarter, the whole world with loving consciousness far-reaching, . . . beyond measure;'[6]

or, again, as that of the emancipation of mind through 'amity':

> 'All the means that can be used as bases for right doing . . . are outshone in radiance and glory by this, which takes all those up into itself.'[7]

If this be amity only, we can let love stand aside!

There is no specific and positive injunction to 'love your enemies,' but this is only because the true spirit of the Dhamma would label no fellow-creatures as enemies. All were either to be 'ministered unto' with honour or to be taken compassion upon in that spirit of grave tenderness for the burden of ill on earth—and in the heavens too—which is Buddhism at its emotional best. 'Conquer the wrathful by mildness, . . . the stingy by giving, the liar by truth!'[8] is the prescribed line of action.

7. Altruism.—Among the channels for catholic altruistic sentiment, however termed, the giving of

[1] Rhys Davids, *Psalms*, ii. 29, n. 2.
[2] *Ib.* ii. 297.
[3] *Ib.* i. 166.
[4] *Ib.* i. 187.
[5] *Ib.* ii. 280.
[6] *Majjhima Nikāya*, i. 129.
[7] *Itivuttaka*, 19–21.
[8] *Dhammapada*, 223.

worldly, and the giving of spiritual, goods, Buddhist missionary labours from the earliest days are well known, and, from Aśoka's days, are matters of history. The *Sutta* describing a conversation between the Master and Puṇṇa of the Sunāparantas—a *bhikkhu* whose labours were crowned with martyrdom—is typical of the incorrigible unfaltering 'amity' of the missionary spirit.[1] Of the other kind of giving, while *dāna*, 'liberality,' is recommended, especially as a pious and profitable return to the dispensers of spiritual gifts, the absence of any systematic inculcation of 'charity,' or poor relief, is noticeable. There were poor folk and beggars, for the ideal king is described as giving largely to such.[2] But the fact that the religious 'friar' was termed almsman (*bhikkhu*), and took his place as a beggar among beggars (save that he never 'begged,' but only passed by), seems to indicate that the practice of charity at the door and in kind was a matter of course, not calling for special exhortation. Royal donors gave their charity in almshalls at each city gate.

A noteworthy feature in the developments of secedent Buddhism is the expansion, in eschatological hypotheses, of the altruistic spirit so strongly fostered, for life on earth, by the original teaching. In the early Dhamma concentrative self-training receives relatively more emphasis than any exercise in the expansion of emotional imagination. But in the altruistic patience and faith of the Bodhisattva ideal we see the mother-germ reaching a sublimity unattained in the poetic idealism of any other creed.

LITERATURE.—In addition to works cited in footnotes, see T. W. Rhys Davids, *Early Buddhism*, London, 1910, p. 60 f.; R. Pischel, *Leben und Lehre des Buddha*, Leipzig, 1906, p. 78 f., criticized in H. Oldenberg, 'Der Buddhismus und die christliche Liebe,' *Aus dem alten Indien*, Berlin, 1910, p. 1 f.

C. A. F. RHYS DAVIDS.

LOVE (Celtic).—**1. Gauls.**—The Celts do not appear to have had at any time in their history any special god or goddess of love. In later times the numerous goddesses of fertility often possess the attributes of love-patrons; and it is, therefore, probable that this conception was identified with them, if at any time it formed a special subject of worship among the Celts. We have, for example, among the goddesses of ancient Gaul one who is equated with Diana, but who possesses at the same time some of the characteristics of Venus (G. Grupp, *Kultur der alten Kelten und Germanen*, Munich, 1905, p. 160). It is possible, then, that there was a tendency among the primitive Celts to assign love-attributes to some of their deities. Thus, we are not yet certain of the form of cult addressed to the *Matres*, who were the special patrons of women, presiding at child-birth; but it was without doubt a kind of love-worship, especially that of motherhood, since these goddesses are usually represented with a child in their arms. In Christian times these wooden figures, blackened with age, were often mistaken for those of the Virgin, and, under the name of *Vierges noires*, were given a place of honour in the churches (J. A. MacCulloch, *The Rel. of the Anc. Celts*, Edinburgh, 1911, p. 45 f.; cf. also *ERE* iii. 280). Another class of divinities called *Virgines* were also closely associated with the *Matres*—in fact, this title may have been but an appellative of the latter. They were served by priestesses, whose existence has been explained by the hypothesis that many Celtic divinities were at first female, and were, therefore, served by women possessed of the tribal lore (*ib.* 317). Strabo (IV. iv. 6), copying from Pytheas, who visited the western seaboard of France about 322 B.C., gives an account of the mystic rites practised by some Samnite women who inhabited a small island in the ocean near the mouth of the Loire; and, though Strabo calls these rites Bacchic, it is very probable that they were connected with some form of love-worship.

In the betrothal rites of the founders of Marseilles there appear to be indications of the existence of a love-god. We are told that the daughter of the king, after a splendid repast, entered the room with a full cup in her hand, and extended it, by chance or otherwise, to a stranger. The father sanctioned it at once, declaring that it was a god who wished it (Aristotle, quoted by Athenæus, xiii. 36 [p. 576]). According to Plutarch (*Amatorius*, xxii., *de Mulierum virtutibus*, xx.), it was customary among the Asiatic Celts for the betrothal to take place before the altar of the goddess, who, in the case which he cites, happened to be Artemis. It is impossible to say how far those rites were influenced by the customs of the Greeks.

In spite of the miserable condition to which women were reduced among the Gauls, they were renowned for their devotion and fidelity to their husbands (see ETHICS AND MORALITY [Celtic], I. 2). Yet by the 4th cent. A.D., if we may accept the statement of the Emperor Julian (*Orat.* ii., text and tr. W. C. Wright, London, 1913, i. 218 f.; also *Ep.* 19; G. Dottin, *Manuel pour servir à l'étude de l'antiquité celtique*, Paris, 1906, p. 141), a sad change had taken place in the character of the Celtic women, especially among the Eastern Gauls.

Julian relates that the Celts took the Rhine as a judge of the fidelity of their wives. When a child was born, the father placed it on a shield and set it on the river. If the child was legitimate, it floated on the surface of the water; but if, on the contrary, it was illegitimate, it was swallowed up by the waves. We are uncertain, however, whether the tribes referred to were Celtic or German. The love-motive also existed without doubt in the cult of the Earth, the great mother of gods and men, but to what extent it is impossible to say (cf. C. Jullian, *Histoire de la Gaule*, Paris, 1908, ii. 123).

2. Irish.—In his well-known hymn St. Patrick prayed against the 'spells of women, smiths, and druids' (W. O. E. Windisch, *Irische Texte*, Leipzig, 1880 ff., i. 56). The women to whom the saint refers were probably those of the *side*, who rejoiced in eternal youth and beauty, and whose capacity for love was so great that they would go forth themselves to woo and win mortals. Once the spell was cast, not even the greatest hero could resist. The important rôle played by these divine women in Irish mythology is revealed in the account of the adventures of Connla, where even the powerful magic of druidism fails to remove the spell.

Connla, walking on the hills of Usnech in company with his father Cond, who was supreme king of Ireland from A.D. *c.* 122 to *c.* 157, saw a beautiful damsel approaching. She was attired in a strange garb; and, when Connla asked her whence she came, she replied: 'We are the great *sid*, hence we are called the people of the *side*,' *i.e.* of the mound or hillock. The father wished to know with whom his son was speaking, so the damsel informed him that she had come to invite Connla, whom she loved, to the Mag Mell, 'Plain of Delight,' where dwelt King Boadag. 'Come with me,' she cried, 'Connla the Red, of the spreckled neck, flame-red, a yellow crown awaits thee; thy figure shall not wither, nor its youth nor its beauty till the dreadful judgment.' Cond then bade Corán the druid, who, like the others, heard but did not see the damsel, chant a magic song against her. She departed, but not before throwing Connla an apple, which was his sole sustenance for a month, and yet nothing diminished from it. After a while longing seized Connla for the damsel, and at the end of a month he beheld her again, when she addressed him thus: 'It is no lofty seat on which Connla sits among the short-lived mortals awaiting fearful death. The ever-living beings (*bii bithbi*) invite thee. Thou art a favourite of the men of Tethra, for they see thee every day in the assemblies of thy father's house among thy dear friends.' Again the king urged the druid to chant against her, but she made answer: 'O Cond of the Hundred Battles, druidism is not loved, little has it progressed to honour on the Great Strand. A just man [probably an allusion to St. Patrick inserted in the saga] will come with a great following; and his law will destroy the incantations of druids from passing the lips of black, lying demons.' She then told Connla of another land, in which was no race save only women and maidens. When she had ended, Connla gave a bound into her ship of glass, and they sailed away. From that day to this they have never been seen, and no one knows whither they went (for the text of this saga see Windisch, *Irish Grammar*, tr. N. Moore, Cambridge, 1882, pp.

[1] *Majjhima*, iii. 267 f.

[2] Rhys Davids, *Dialogues*, i. 177.

134-136; Fr. tr. in d'Arbois de Jubainville, *L'Épopée celtique en Irlande*, Paris, 1892, pp. 384-390; and a summary in K. Meyer and A. Nutt, *Voyage of Bran*, London, 1895-97, i. 145 f.).

Oengus, the beautiful, sometimes called Mac Ind Óc, 'Son of the Young Ones' (*i.e.* of Dagda and Boand), is also a god of growth and fertility who possesses in a marked degree the attributes of a god of love. He has been called the Eros of the Gaels, because he was patron of Diarmaid, beloved of women, and because his kisses became birds which whispered thoughts of love to youths and maidens.

The love-motive occurs very frequently in the stories of the Tuatha Dé Danann, the youth and beauty of whose women were supposed to be unfading (S. H. O'Grady, *Silva Gadelica*, London, 1892, ii. 203). One of the earliest concerns Eri, sister of Bres, who was son of the Fomorian Elatha.

The love-motive is equally prominent in the Voyages of Bran and Maelduin, which are close parallels to the adventures of Connla. In both of these stories the happy mortal is allowed to visit Elysium, which he finds to consist of an island inhabited by an amorous queen, who gladly welcomes the mortal visitor and is equally reluctant to let him depart.

A most interesting example of the development of the primitive love-theme is found in 'Cúchulainn's Sick Bed.'

This saga relates that one day Cúchulainn was struck with a horse switch by two strange women, one of whom was attired in green and the other in red, and in consequence of this blow he lay till the end of the year without speaking to any one. Then came a stranger who sang verses promising health and strength to the hero, if he would accept the invitation of the daughters of Aed Abrat, to one of whom, Fann, it would give heartfelt joy to be espoused to Cúchulainn. Fann, daughter of Manannán mac Lir, who had been abandoned by her husband, had conceived a great affection for Cúchulainn, and the stranger, whose name was Líban, had been sent by her own husband, Labraid of the Quick Hand on the Sword, to tell Cúchulainn that, if he would come and fight against Labraid's enemies, he should have Fann as his wife. After sending his charioteer Lóeg to visit the Plain of Delight, the great hero accepted the invitation and went to overthrow the opponents of Labraid. After remaining a month with Fann, he returned to Ireland, promising to meet her again at a trysting place. Emer, his wife, having heard of this, went with fifty maidens, all armed with knives, to attack the lovers, and, when Fann saw them, she appealed to Cúchulainn for protection, which he promised. He was then bitterly upbraided by Emer for having disgraced her before all the women of Erin. Once they were together in dignity, and they might be so again if he desired. Cúchulainn took pity on her; and a contest then arose between the two women for the possession of the hero. The fairy queen finally yielded to the mortal, saying:

'Woe! to give love to a person,
If he does not take notice of it;
It is better to be turned away
Unless one is loved as one loves.'

When Manannán became aware of this, he came east to seek Fann, and no one could see him but Fann alone. He gave her choice to remain with Cúchulainn or go with him. She answered: 'There is, by our word, one of you whom I would rather follow than the other, but it is with you I shall go, for Cúchulainn has abandoned me—thou too hast no worthy queen, but Cúchulainn has' (d'Arbois de Jubainville, *Épopée celtique*, pp. 170-216; Nutt and Meyer, i. 153-157; ed. Windisch, i. 205-227).

Without multiplying examples, it is obvious that the woman is usually the aggressive figure in Irish mythology. In Christian times where beliefs revealing the pagan love-theme have survived, the method of procedure is different, the man pursuing the woman, often against her wishes. Thus, when King Fiachna was fighting against the Scots and in great danger of his life, a stranger appeared to his wife, announcing that he would save her husband's life if she would consent to yield herself to him. She agreed with reluctance; and the child born of this union was the 7th cent. King Mongán, of whom the annalist says: 'Every one knows that his real father was Manannán' (*Leabhar na hUidhre*, facsimile reprint, Dublin, 1870, p. 133[a], 19).

In the Cúchulainn cycle the love-motive is usually one of wild lust; and, as these stories doubtless reflect, to a great extent, the condition of society at the beginning of the Christian era, we can form from them an idea of the status of woman at that period. In his analysis of the *Táin*, the great epic of Ireland—which depicts to a great extent the morals of Connaught—H. Zimmer has pointed out that Medb, the heroine of the expedition, had been the wife of Conchobar, but, having abandoned him, married in succession two chiefs of the same name, Ailill, the second of whom is her husband at the beginning of the account ('Der kulturgeschichtliche Hintergrund in den Erzählungen der alten irischen Heldensage,' *SBAW*, 1911, pp. 174-227).

An idea of the unusual prominence of the love-motive in the early Irish saga can be formed from the list of titles given in d'Arbois de Jubainville's *Essai d'un catalogue de la littérature épique de l'Irlande* (Paris, 1883).

Thus on pp. 34-37 there are twelve stories bearing the title *aithed*, or 'elopement,' among the more important of which are *Aithed Blatnaite, ingine Puill, maic Fhidaig, re Coinchulainn*, or 'Elopement of Blatnat, daughter of Pall, son of Fidach, to Cúchulainn' (cf. G. Keating, *Hist. of Ireland*, tr. J. O'Mahony, New York, 1866, pp. 282-284); *Aithed Derdrenn re maccaib Usnig*, or 'Elopement of Derdriu to the sons of Usnech,' identical with *Longes mac n-Usnig*, or 'Exile of the Sons of Usnech (ed. Windisch, i. 67-82); and *Aithed Grainne re Diarmait*, or 'Elopement of Grainne to Diarmait' (*Book of Lecan*, fol. 181; Brit. Mus., Harley MSS, 5280, fol. 25). In addition to *Cath na Suirghe* and *Cath Tochmarca*, 'Battle of the Demand in Marriage' (d'Arbois de Jubainville, p. 82 f.), there are six sagas bearing the title *compert*, or 'conception' (92-94), of which the most famous are *Compert Conchobair*, or 'Conception of Conchobar' (*LL* 106), and *Compert Conculainn*, or 'Conception of Cúchulainn' (Windisch, pp. 134-145, 324 f.). *Eachtra an Phalais Dhroidhachtamhuil*, or 'Adventures of the Enchanted Palace' (d'Arbois de Jubainville, p. 124), is concerned entirely with love, as is also *Óen-ét a-mnas Ailella*, or 'Single Jealousy of Ailill' (178). There are five stories with the title of *serc*, or 'love' (205 f.), of which *Serc Fhinn go criocaib Lochand*, or 'Love of Finn in Norway,' deserves to be mentioned (Roy. Ir. Acad., Ossianic MS, 1789-1818). As for those with the title of *tochmarc*, or 'demand in marriage,' there are at least twenty (224-231). Of these, mention may be made of *Tochmarc Becfola* (ed. and tr. B. O'Looney, *Proceedings of the Royal Irish Academy*, i. [1870] 174-183), *Tochmarc Emere la Coinculainn*, or 'Demand in Marriage of Emer by Cúchulainn' (Windisch, p. 324 f.), *Tochmarc Etaine* (*ib.* 117-133), etc.

3. Welsh.—In Brythonic mythology the naturalism common to the Irish sagas has been greatly refined, and magic, especially in the form of the love-potion, assumes greater prominence. The nearest approach to a goddess of love is found in Branwen, 'White Bosom,' daughter of a sea-god, who has been called the 'Venus of the northern sea' (C. I. Elton, *Origins of English History*,[2] London, 1890, p. 291). She was in all probability a goddess of fertility, but reappears as Brangwaine in romance, giving a love-potion to Tristram, which in itself is perhaps a reminiscence of her former attributes as a goddess of love. Dôn, the Welsh equivalent of Danu, was also perhaps a goddess of fertility, and had for her children Gwydion, Gilvæthwy, Amæthon, Govannon, and Arianrhod (MacCulloch, p. 103). All these divinities play a more or less important part in the story of Gilvæthwy's illicit love for Goewin, the 'foot-holder' of Math in the *Mabinogion*.

Resorting to magic, Gwydion succeeded in obtaining for Math from the court of Pryderi certain swine sent him by Arawn, king of Annwfn, for the purpose of aiding him in his love affair. The trick was discovered, and a battle ensued, in which Gwydion slew Pryderi by enchantment. Having discovered that Gilvæthwy had seduced Goewin, Math transformed him and Gwydion successively into deer, swine, and wolves. It is also implied that Gwydion was the lover of his own sister Arianrhod, by whom he had two children. MacCulloch suggests (p. 106) that these are mythic reflexions of a time when such unions, perhaps only in royal houses, were permissible. Arianrhod, on her part, while being the mistress of her brother, pretends to be a virgin and refuses to acknowledge her children.

The more or less universal type of the treacherous wife is found in the story of the unfaithful dawn-goddess, Blodenwedd, who discovers the secret of her husband's life and then places him at the mercy of her lover (T. W. Rolleston, *Myths and Legends of the Celtic Race*, London, 1911, p. 383).

In the Welsh romances the element of love, due principally to foreign influences, assumes the aspect of woman-worship. This new attitude towards love is already apparent in Kulhwch and Olwen, which is comparatively an ancient tale, and is further developed in later stories like Peredur and The Lady of the Fountain (see A. Nutt, *Celtic and Mediæval Romance*, London, 1899). It is the main symptom of the extent to which, in comparison with the Irish, Welsh literature had lost its pure Celtic strain (Rolleston, p. 345 f.). The relations between the sexes in Wales have already been discussed in ETHICS AND MORALITY (Celtic), III. 1-7.

LITERATURE.—This has been sufficiently indicated in the article.

JOHN LAWRENCE GERIG.

LOVE (Chinese).—The importance of love as an ethical principle is recognized by Chinese moralists. This can be made sufficiently evident from the classical books.

When asked about benevolence (*jên*), Confucius replied: 'It is to love all men' (*Anal.* xii. 22). 'Jên is the characteristic element of humanity, and the great exercise of it is in loving relatives' (*Doct. of Mean*, xx. 5). 'The benevolent embrace all in their love; but what they consider of the greatest importance is to cultivate an earnest affection for the virtuous' (Mencius, VII. i. 45).

From these passages it appears that the general affection of love is modified in accordance with the claims of kinship and virtue. The ethical nature of true love is further brought out in such sayings as these:

'The Master said, "It is only the truly virtuous man who can love or who can hate others"' (*Anal.* iv. 3). 'The Master said, "Can there be love which does not lead to strictness with its object?"' (*ib.* xiv. 8).

The importance of love as an ethical principle may also be seen in what is said of 'reciprocity' (*shu*). This is '*jên* in action, to put oneself in another's place.' Primacy is given to it as the rule of life (*Anal.* xv. 23). It is not merely 'Not to do to another what I would not have done to myself,' but, more positively, 'To serve my father as I would require my son to serve me . . . to set the example in behaving to a friend as I would require him to behave to me' (*Doct. of Mean*, xiii. 3). In the Confucian ethic, however, the exercise of love is limited by retributive justice.

'Some one said, "What do you say concerning the principle that injury should be recompensed with kindness?" The Master said, "With what then will you recompense kindness? Recompense injury with justice, and recompense kindness with kindness"' (*Anal.* xiv. 36).

Specially interesting in connexion with the place of love in Chinese ethics is the philosopher Micius and his doctrine of universal love, as the bond of a perfect social state. The Confucian ethic has its religious counterpart in the classical representation of Shang-ti as benevolent and righteous (cf. art. GOD [Chinese]).

Of love in the narrower sense as between the sexes, neither its more romantic aspects nor its depravations are unreflected in Chinese literature from the *Shi King* and *Shu King* down to present-day novels. In view of too evident grossness of thought and life, one is surprised to find the religious sphere so clean. There is, *e.g.*, polytheistic superstition, but no grossness in the religious worship reflected in the classics, though it is true that regrettable features appear in popular superstition —spiritual beings may be attracted by the fair looks of maidens and call them to the other world to be their wives; prostitutes may worship a goddess of their own.

According to E. H. Parker (*Studies in Chinese Religion*, London, 1910, p. 7), 'there is a considerable amount of disguised linga worship, especially in the south of China.' He adds, 'In any case, prayers for children, offered up by women, are common enough in every province.'

Such prayers are in themselves innocent, but in some cases the accompanying ritual worship of the idol invoked is somewhat suspect, and is shy of publicity. Still it is substantially true that there is in China no deification of vice or any public practice of immoral rites.

LITERATURE.—In the classical religion and ethics, see the relevant vols. of *SBE*; and E. Faber, *Mencius*, Shanghai, 1897. For examples of popular superstition cf. H. C. Du Bose, *The Dragon, Image, and Demon*, London, 1886, chs. 19, 21.

P. J. MACLAGAN.

LOVE (Christian and New Testament).—I. **Divine love.**—The highest and most satisfying faith which the human mind has attained, or can attain, is formulated in the sublimely simple confession, 'God is love' (1 Jn 4[8. 16]). This is interpreted as meaning not only that God, self-conscious and moral, creates, sustains, and orders all things in love, but that love is His very essence; and the spiritual conflict of the ages has been, and is, waged against the forces opposing this first principle of religion and ethics, the acceptance or rejection of which leads logically to optimism or pessimism. A few expressions of the belief that eternal love subsists at the heart of all things, and manifests itself through them, may be chosen as typical.

'Let me tell you why the Creator made the universe. He was good . . . and desired that all things should be as like Himself as possible' (Plato, *Tim.* 29 E). 'The Lord is good to all; and his tender mercies are over all his works' (Ps 145[9]). 'For thou lovest all things that are, and abhorrest none of the things which thou didst make; for never wouldst thou have formed anything if thou didst hate it' (Wis 11[24]). 'And we know that to them that love God all things work together for good' (Ro 8[28]). 'O tender God, if Thou art so loving in Thy creatures, how fair and lovely must Thou be in Thyself' (Suso, quoted by W. R. Inge, *Christian Mysticism*[3], London, 1913, p. 302). For lovers of Nature Wordsworth expresses the conviction that nothing

'Shall e'er prevail against us, or disturb
Our cheerful faith, that all which we behold
Is full of blessings' (*Tintern Abbey*, 132 ff.).

There is no dubiety in R. C. Trench's large utterance:

. . . 'We and all men move
Under a canopy of love,
As broad as the blue sky above'
(*The Kingdom of God*, 4-6);

or in Browning's *cri du cœur*:

'God! Thou art love! I build my faith on that'
(*Paracelsus*, v. 51).

And in Carlyle's words there is at least a wistful longing to believe:

'O Nature! . . . Art not thou the "Living Garment of God"? . . . Is it, in very deed, He, then, that ever speaks through thee; that lives and loves in thee, that lives and loves in me?' (*Sartor Resartus*, 'The Everlasting Yea').

It is common knowledge, however, that this splendid creed of three syllables is not only severely tested but strenuously contested. The notion that love is the ultimate reality of things—that transcendent love is Creator and Lord of the world, and immanent love the life which pulsates through it, the Spirit ceaselessly operant in Nature and humanity—is pronounced by many to be a delusion and a snare. One of the champions of popular free-thought thus emphatically expresses himself:

'That God is love is a very lofty, poetical and gratifying conception, but it is open to one fatal objection—it is not true' (R. Blatchford, *God and My Neighbour*, London, 1907, p. 23).

One of the leaders of philosophic thought confesses that in the loss of this faith 'we are confronted by one of the great tragedies of life' (J. M. E. MacTaggart, *Some Dogmas of Religion*, London, 1906, p. 297). So manifest and repellent is the blending of good and evil in human lives that Swinburne makes the chorus of one of his dramas sing:

'The high gods . . .
. . . wrought with weeping and laughter,
And fashioned with loathing and love . . .
The holy spirit of man'
(*Atalanta in Calydon* [*Poems*, London, 1904, iv. 259]).

The bitter pagan belief, that the gods take the same pleasure in the sufferings of mankind as cruel children in the torture of flies, still has its adherents, finding expression, for example, in Thomas Hardy's pessimistic dictum, 'The President of the Immortals (in Æschylean phrase) had ended his sport with Tess.' Some critics of the world-order do not hesitate to declare that 'for all the Sin wherewith the Face of Man is blacken'd' God needs to take as well as give man's forgiveness (Omar Khayyām, quatrain lviii.). Worst of all, science hesitates to say that God is love. The belief so dear to the heart of Linnæus, that the phenomena of Nature bear witness to the benevolence of the Creator, is supposed to have received a staggering, if not a fatal, blow from the principle of evolution, so that no comforting rod or staff, but only a broken reed, appears to be left in the hand of the man

'Who trusted God was love indeed
And love Creation's final law—
Tho' Nature, red in tooth and claw
With ravine, shriek'd against his creed'
(Tennyson, *In Memoriam*, lvi.).

Confident assertions on the one side and the other help at least to make the issue clear, while they may also suggest that strong feeling is apt to be generated in the attempt to solve the problem of problems. Every man admits 'the one absolute certainty that he is ever in the presence of one Infinite and Eternal Energy, from which all things proceed' (H. Spencer, *Ecclesiastical Institutions*, London, 1885, p. 843). The question is whether that Energy is controlled by love, or, rather, is identical with love—whether the All-Great is the All-Loving.

(*a*) What answer comes from the heart of Nature? That a struggle for existence, with a resultant survival of the fittest and extinction of the unfit, has gone on through geological ages and is still going on is one of the demonstrated truths which modern science has added to the sum of knowledge. And many evolutionists find it difficult, if not impossible, to imagine a God of love ordaining and witnessing that secular conflict. But do they fairly interpret the struggle? The indictment against Nature which was frequently heard in the early and somewhat hysterical days of the evolution doctrine is now generally admitted to have been based upon half truths. Unqualified assertions that 'nature is one with rapine,' that any little wood is 'a world of plunder and prey' (Tennyson, *Maud*, IV. iv.), that 'the cosmic process has no sort of relation to moral ends' (T. H. Huxley, *Collected Essays*, London, 1898, p. 83; cf. 197), that all progress is attained by the methods of the gladiatorial show or the battle-field, are seen to be almost a libel. For the whole range of life upon the earth—vegetal, animal, social—bears witness to something quite different from hatred and strife. The two main activities of all living things are nutrition and reproduction, and, while the object of nutrition is to secure the life of the individual, the object of reproduction is to secure the life of the species. If one great factor of evolution is concerned with self-assertion, another is concerned with self-sacrifice, and it is not too much to assert that the world is not only an abode of the strong, but a home of the loving.

'Nature has more to say than "Every one for himself." There has been a selection of the other-regarding, of the self-sacrificing, of the gentle, of the loving' (J. A. Thomson, *The Bible of Nature*, Edinburgh, 1908, p. 179).

If Rousseau erred in closing his mind to everything but the love, peace, and harmony of Nature, we are equally at fault if we find in her nothing but discord and cruelty.

'Love is not a late arrival, an after-thought, with Creation. It is not a novelty of a romantic civilization. It is not a pious word of religion. Its roots began to grow with the first cell of life that budded on this earth.' It is 'the supreme factor in the Evolution of the world. . . . The Struggle for the Life of Others is the physiological name for the greatest word of ethics —Other-ism, Altruism, Love' (H. Drummond, *The Ascent of Man*, London, 1894, pp. 276–281). 'The principles of morality have their roots in the deepest foundations of the universe,' and 'the cosmic process is ethical in the profoundest sense' (John Fiske, *Through Nature to God*, London, 1899, p. 79).

If, then, creative evolution is God's theophany—His method of unfolding His purpose and revealing Himself—the facts of the case, on a wide and impartial survey, go far to prove that His central energy, or ruling motive, and therefore His true Name, is Love. And to Divine overtures of love the human heart cannot fail to respond. Viewing the world as mysteriously 'full of God's reflex,' Charles Kingsley exclaims, 'I feel a gush of enthusiasm towards God' (*Charles Kingsley: His Letters and Memories of his Life*, London, 1877, i. 56).

It must be admitted, however, that there is another side. Nature's physical and vital forces do not all inspire confidence, making us 'very sure of God' and ready to acclaim the sentiment, 'All's right with the world.' There are times when it is not easy to 'rise from Nature up to Nature's God,' or to maintain that He has done all things well. The facts that disturb one's faith in the benevolence of the Creator are too many and too conspicuous to be ignored. The life of the forest and the jungle is not all idyllic. The wolf does not lie down with the lamb, nor the lion eat straw like the ox. The tiger and the tarantula are no less real than the fawn and the dove. It is impossible to forget Nature's ruthlessness to the unfit or her savage outbreaks of fire and flood and tempest. Over against Natura Benigna we have always to set Natura Maligna, as T. Watts-Dunton does in a group of sonnets (*The Coming of Love*). And the existence of positive evil in the world has driven not a few observers, especially those who have been victims, to the conclusion that God, whether personal or impersonal, is no more than an irresistible and inexorable Force, indifferent to pain, regardless of life, and therefore to be dreaded, hated, or scorned, rather than trusted and loved. This is the view which lends a tragic pathos to the *Prometheus Vinctus*, the book of Job, and other literature of religious doubt.

With the best 'will to believe,' many a man cannot wholeheartedly affirm that 'the Variety of Creatures . . . is so many Sounds and Voices, Preachers and Trumpets, giving Glory and Praise and Thanksgiving to that Deity of Love, which gives Life to all Nature and Creature' (William Law, *The Spirit of Love* [*Works*, London, 1892–93, viii. 35]).

At the best the evidence is conflicting. Nature speaks with two voices. We can never be quite sure whether she is a kind mother or a cruel stepmother. Love is not seen at a glance to be her primal law. The men of science who decipher the testimony of the rocks do not feel constrained to proclaim with one accord that God is good, and, though they may comfort themselves with the reflexion that in Nature's infinite book of secrecy only a little has been read, and acknowledge that there is no religion without mystery, yet the inquiring spirit of man is troubled. Devout but open-eyed spectators of the world-drama are sometimes 'perplexed in the extreme.' They feel as if Nature were betraying the heart that truly loves her.

'God is love, transcendent, all-pervading! We do not get *this* faith from Nature or the world. If we look at Nature alone, full of perfection and imperfection, she tells that God is disease, murder and rapine' (H. T. Tennyson, *Alfred Lord Tennyson; A Memoir*, London, 1897, i. 314).

And, if 'to be wroth with those we love doth work like madness in the brain,' it is the crowning sorrow to doubt the God whose lovingkindness is better than life (Ps 63^3).

(*b*) But the God who speaks ambiguously through Nature reveals Himself also through humanity. He has His dwelling 'in the mind of man' (Wordsworth, *Tintern Abbey*, 99). Here it must not be forgotten that the isolation of the human species from the rest of the sentient creation is now known to be unscientific. This fact only makes the growth of ethical ideas and ideals the more wonderful. The basis of society is the family, and the cosmic process which has brought into existence the conscious personal relation between mother and child cannot be said to be indifferent to ethical ends; rather it may be held to exist for the sake of such ends. While Huxley is right enough in maintaining (L. Huxley, *Life and Letters of Thomas*

Henry Huxley, London, 1900, ii. 268) that moral purpose, in the strict sense, is 'an article of exclusive human manufacture,' he is wrong in denying it a place in the cosmic process. Human nature is an integral part of nature. If Nature is personified, human life is her crowning achievement.

The development of 'the moral sentiments, the moral law, devotion to unselfish ends, disinterested love, nobility of soul—these are Nature's most highly wrought products, latest in coming to maturity; they are the consummation, towards which all earlier prophecy has pointed' (J. Fiske, *op. cit.* p. 130).

Now, these constitutive elements of the moral life are the root and ground of that assurance of Divine love which must be regarded in the first instance as an instinct or intuition of loving hearts. The writer of the Song of Songs makes a Hebrew maiden, inspired by her passion of holy love, exclaim: 'For love is strong as death . . . the flashes thereof are flashes of fire, a very flame of the Lord' (8^6). This means not only that the pure love which glows and burns in the human breast is a fire kindled and cherished by God, but that it is an emanation from, and in quality identical with, His own uncreated flame of love. He 'never is dishonoured in the spark He gave us from his fire of fires' (Browning, *Any Wife to Any Husband*, iv.). Follow the gleam, and it leads to God. The natural is seen to be supernatural. 'The spirit of man is the lamp of the Lord' (Pr 20^{27}). The prophet Hosea, made wise by a patient love outwearing mortal sin in his own home, had the truth flashed upon his mind that a human affection which bears, hopes, believes, endures all things, and never fails, is explicable only as a radiation from the love of God, a revelation of the heart of the Eternal. His own ideal conduct in the supreme moral crisis of his life sensitized his mind to receive a new and true image of the Absolute. His forgiving pity, his redeeming love, his confidence in the ultimate triumph of good, gave him an unerring insight into the controlling principle of the Divine character. Love, he sees, is paramount in heaven and earth, and justice is its instrument. Love is therefore the *Leitmotiv* of his prophecy, his master-key to the mysteries of religion and history. He dares to make his own *confessio amantis* the preface to a stupendous love-tale, of which the scene is the world and the hero is God. He represents Israel's patient Divine Friend as saying, 'I delight in love, and not in sacrifice. When Israel was a child, then I loved him. . . . I drew them with cords of a man, with bands of love' (6^6 $11^{1.4}$; cf. 3^1 14^4). Later prophets and lawgivers reiterate Hosea's teaching in many beautiful forms—'I have loved thee with an everlasting love: therefore have I continued lovingkindness unto thee' (Jer 31^3). 'He will rest in his love, he will joy over thee with singing' (Zeph 3^{17}; cf. Dt 4^{37} 7^{18} 10^{15}, Is 48^{14} 63^9). 'But it is not too much to say that the entire faith and theology of later Israel grew out of Hosea, that all its characteristic views and ideas are first to be found in his book' (C. H. Cornill, *The Prophets of Israel*[4], Chicago, 1899, p. 53).

(*c*) Jesus linked His gospel with the prophecy of Hosea by repeatedly quoting the words 'I will have mercy and not (ritual) sacrifice' (Mt 9^{13} 12^7). No one was so swift as He to discover the evidences of Divine love in Nature. The beauty of flowers, the ways of birds, the benediction of the rain, the glory of clouds, and the splendour of the sun in its strength spoke to Him of a goodness that was over all and in all. He sanctioned the religious use of Nature. He assumed that God is omnipresent in the external world. But that was not His whole message. Nature's goodness was not His evangel. Least of all did He worship Nature.

'Know, man hath all which Nature hath, but more,
And in that *more* lie all his hopes of good'
(M. Arnold, *To an Independent Preacher*, 5 f. [*Poet. Works*, London, 1890, p. 5]).

And it is the spirit of the Ideal Man—His personal expression in word and deed—that constitutes mankind's surest evidence of the love of God. In His compassion for the multitudes, His tenderness to sinners, His hope for the vilest, His yearning to bring back the lost, His forgiveness of those who 'know not what they do,' He is the Revealer of God. He changes Israel's Lord of Hosts into mankind's 'Our Father.' The writer of the Fourth Gospel represents Him as saying, 'He that hath seen me hath seen the Father' (Jn 14^9), and the love of God which is in Christ Jesus our Lord is a fact which science must reverently accept. Christ is indeed the crown of evolution, fulfilling not only the spiritual ideals of Israel, but the æonian ethical strivings of Nature.

'Our first reason, then, for believing that God is Love, is the authority of Jesus Christ—His declaration and manifestation of the fact as God incarnate. That is to say, all the cumulative and complex proofs of Christianity are proofs to us of this fact, which simply is the kernel of Christianity. If Christianity is true, God is Love' (J. R. Illingworth, *Christian Character*, London, 1904, p. 87).

(*d*) The apostles always interpret Divine love in the light of Christ's sacrifice. The love which inspired the early Church was more than that of the Father who makes His sun to shine on the evil and on the good. It was that of the Father who withheld not His own Son, but delivered Him up for us all; that of the Son who laid down His life for the sin of the world. In the NT the identification of Divine love with atonement is axiomatic. 'Herein is love'—in a Divine initiative which provided a propitiation for sin (1 Jn 4^{10}). Personal faith centres in 'him that loveth us, and loosed us from our sins by his blood' (Rev 1^5), in 'the Son of God, who loved me and gave himself for me' (Gal 2^{20}). It was His Spirit of sacrifice that conquered the intellect as well as the heart of the ancient world. His age-long empire is the expression, not of the love of power, but of the power of love. He can never cease to be hailed as

'Strong Son of God, immortal Love.'

2. Human love.—Great and true conceptions of love have not been confined to any single nation. In the Greek classics love is often something much higher, purer, and nobler than sensual passion or natural desire. This fact appears clearly in the cosmogonic myths. The Eros of Hesiod is not 'erotic' in the later sense of the word. His Love is the fairest of the gods, who rules over the minds and councils of gods and men, the great uniting power, who brings order and harmony among the conflicting elements of Chaos. To the lofty mind of Plato love is the sympathy of affinities, the instinctive rushing together of kindred souls, the harmony of spirits, not without such a touch of natural feeling as strengthens without dishonouring the union. And the Stoics laid the foundation of a noble ethic in their conception of the brotherhood of men, regarded as akin to God, or even as children of one great Father.

'For we,' says the *Hymn* of Cleanthes, 'are Thine offspring, alone of mortal things that live and walk the earth moulded in the image of the All' (cf. Ac 17^{28}).

But Christianity raises love to a higher mood, smites it with a new ardour, purifies it by the touch of God, making the natural love of man and woman sacramentally holy, and changing the bitterest foe into a potential friend as 'the brother for whom Christ died.' The very vocabulary of love is changed, Eros, a word too often profaned, giving place to Agape. The natural elements of conjugal love, real and imperious enough, but consecrated now to the highest uses, have superadded to them the intimate communion of heart and soul. The genius of love is seen to be sacrifice, which has its source and sanction in God's eternal self-giving.

'Thrice blest whose lives are faithful prayers,
Whose loves in higher love endure'
(Tennyson, *In Memoriam*, xxxii.).

Only of such lives can it be safely said that 'love is an unerring light, and joy its own security' (Wordsworth, *Ode to Duty*, 19 f.). The strongest affection decays unless it is rooted in idealism. The house of life cannot be built on the shifting sand of passion. Love faints and fails unless it is braced by the sense of duty. Lovelace's hero, going to the wars, says to Lucasta:

'I could not love thee, dear, so much,
Loved I not honour more.'

It is always the 'higher love'—patriotism, the passion for liberty, the enthusiasm of humanity, the zeal for God's Kingdom, any one of which may claim love's final sacrifice—that gives the affections of the home a purity and an intensity never dreamed of in the life of pampered individualism. When Christ says, 'He that loveth father or mother . . . son or daughter, more than me is not worthy of me,' He is calling men to the ideal life, which includes whatsoever things are pure and lovely and of good report. 'We needs must love the highest when we see it' (Tennyson, *Guinevere*, *ad fin.*).

The truth is that the heart's deepest instinct—its passionate 'amoris desiderium'—cannot be satisfied with an earthly affection. The Hebrew poet speaks for the human race when he says that, as the hart pants for the water brooks, so his soul pants after God, thirsts for the living God (Ps 42[1. 2]).

'The most philosophical students of love from Plato and Plotinus to Augustine and Dante have felt that it demands, in the last resort, an infinite object and an infinite response' (Illingworth, p. 88).

Modern science has immeasurably widened man's mental horizon, and the vaster the material world becomes the greater is the spirit's unrest in its cage of sense. It suffers from 'the malady of the ideal,' and is restless till it rests in God. The deepest thoughts of a nation are expressed by its artists and poets. Rossetti painted human love languishing for fullness of life, but evermore fearing death. Watts painted divine love leading life *per aspera ad astra*. Tennyson protests that his love would be half-dead to know that it must die (*In Memoriam*, xxxv.), while his faith in immortality stays itself on his deathless love of a friend.

'Peace, let it be! for I loved him, and love him for ever: the dead are not dead but alive' (*Vastness*, *ad fin.*).

At the close of life his supreme wish was to

'learn that Love, which is, and was
My Father, and my Brother, and my God!'
(*Doubt and Prayer*, 7 f.).

Browning repeats in a hundred forms his reasoned conviction that

'There is no good of life but love—but love!
What else looks good, is some shade flung from love—
Love gilds it, gives it worth'
(*In a Balcony* [*Works*, London, 1885, p. 17]).

And he is certain that love cannot be quenched by death.

'No: love which, on earth, amid all the shows of it,
Has ever been seen the sole good of life in it,
The love, ever growing there, spite of the strife in it,
Shall arise, made perfect, from death's repose of it'
(*Christmas Eve*, v. 97–100).

If love is thus proved to be the essential character alike of God and of the sons of God, this result profoundly affects all human relationships. (*a*) True intercourse with God Himself is a fellowship of love. To be right with Him is to have the heart of a lover or a child. Though the OT breathes many passionate longings for such an intercourse, the NT alone exemplifies it in its perfection. The bare notion of such a divine fellowship was strange to the Gentile, whose relation to the object of his worship was always cold and distant. Jesus lived in uninterrupted filial communion with His Father, teaching His followers to do the same. It is their high privilege to keep themselves in the love of God (Jude [21]), and so to have His love shed abroad in their hearts by the Holy Spirit given to them (Ro 5[5]).

(*b*) The knowledge of God can be attained only through love. In love's lore a 'dry light' helps but little. Theology at its best, like 'divine philosophy,' is always charged with feeling. 'Pectus facit theologum.' Selfishness absolutely disqualifies the student of divine things. God reveals Himself to those who tread, like Himself, the 'love-way'—the path of lowly service. 'Even as the eye,' said Plotinus, 'could not behold the sun unless it were itself sunlike, so neither could the soul behold God if it were not Godlike' (*Ennead*, I. vi. 9). Not to sympathize is not to understand. Love is the great hierophant of the mysteries of God. He that willeth to do the will of God shall not doubt His highest teaching (Jn 7[17]); but he that loveth not his brother whom he hath seen, and therefore cannot love God whom he hath not seen (1 Jn 4[20]), has lost 'the key of knowledge' (Lk 11[52]).

(*c*) The ideal society consists of persons animated and united by the spirit of love, each seeking the good of all and all of each. The programme of Christianity is the renewal of human life and the reconstruction of human society, on the basis of the faith that 'God is love.' While hatred has a fatal power of division, love is the bond of perfectness (Col 3[14]). Human associations are strong and stable in proportion as they are welded together by that brotherly love which is the law of the kingdom of heaven.

'Love rules the court, the camp, the grove,
And men below, and saints above;
For love is heaven, and heaven is love'
(Scott, *Lay of the Last Minstrel*, III. ii. 5–7).

(*d*) As man's chief good, love is a task as well as a gift—an *Aufgabe* as well as a *Gabe*. It is not a passive sentiment or an involuntary emotion. The verb 'to love' has an imperative mood, which the greatest lawgivers—Jesus as well as Moses—frequently use. To this extent Christianity as well as Judaism is legalistic. The practice of love is the highest exercise of freedom. 'The love of the will' is no less real than that of the heart (Illingworth, p. 101). Love's rise and progress are dependent on a continuous effort, and the more perfect it becomes the more does it embody the inmost desires and strongest impulses of the soul. It is more than good-nature, which is no satisfactory basis for ethics; more than good intentions, which are proverbially delusive; it is a good will—which, according to Kant, is the one absolutely good thing in the universe.

(*e*) All duties spring ultimately from the one duty of love. It is more than a poetic fancy, it is a literal fact, that, 'as every lovely hue is light, so every grace is love.' Augustine describes virtue as the unfolding of love—'Virtus est ordo amoris'—and in reference to the cardinal virtues he says:

'I would not hesitate to define these four virtues which make such an impression upon our minds that they are in every man's mouth: temperance is love surrendering itself wholly to Him who is its object; courage is love bearing all things gladly for the sake of Him who is its object; justice is love serving only Him who is its object, and therefore rightly ruling; prudence is love making wise distinctions between what hinders and what helps itself' (*de Moribus*, i. 15 [25]).

The law of love is called the royal law (νόμος βασιλικός, Ja 2[8]), because, being supreme in dignity and power among the principles which control human action, it brings all the others into subjection to itself.

'All thoughts, all passions, all delights,
Whatever stirs this mortal frame,
All are but ministers of Love,
And feed his sacred flame' (Coleridge, *Love*, 1–4).

(*f*) And love is perfected when even its most laborious duties are performed with gladness. It is true that 'tasks in hours of insight will'd can be through hours of gloom fulfill'd' (M. Arnold, *Morality*, 5 f. [*Poet. Works*, p. 256]). But the moral life needs the heart to aid the will. It never flourishes long if its roots are left dry. Its strength and fruitfulness are always traceable to hidden springs of affection. Schiller was justified in complaining that Kant made too much of the categorical imperative and too little of the æsthetic side of morality —the beauty of holiness. Duty is not perfectly done unless a great love makes the yoke easy and the burden light. Under this potent influence, each of a thousand thoughtful deeds becomes a 'labour of love' (κόπος τῆς ἀγάπης, 1 Th 1[3]). Ferdinand in *The Tempest* (III. i. 7) says that the mistress whom he serves makes his 'labours pleasures,' and Jacob's seven years seemed to him but so many days because of his love (Gn 29[20]). Moral education advances rapidly when a man can say from the heart, 'To do Thy will, O Lord, I take delight.' It is not enough that morality be 'touched' by emotion; it needs to be transfused with the spirit and transfigured by the glory of love.

'No heart is pure that is not passionate; no virtue is safe that is not enthusiastic' (J. R. Seeley, *Ecce Homo*[3], London, 1866, p. 8).

It thus becomes evident that, before the activities of love can be spontaneous, a man's very nature must be changed. 'Every one that loveth is born of God' (1 Jn 4[7]). That which is natural, the self-life, is first, and afterwards that which is spiritual, the life of self-renunciation. And nothing changes the natural into the spiritual like the contemplation of the sacrifice of Christ.

'Thou hast no power nor may'st conceive of Mine,
But love I gave thee, with Myself to love,
And thou must love Me who have died for thee!'
(Browning, *An Epistle*, *ad fin.*).

Many have found it possible to conceive for Christ 'an attachment the closeness of which no words can describe' (Seeley, p. 187). To cherish a love for Him is to love His Kingdom, which ideally embraces the whole human race. Where the AV reads 'We love him, because he first loved us,' the RV has 'We love, because he first loved us' (1 Jn 4[19]), which may be rightly interpreted, 'We love the Son of Man and, for His sake, every son of man.' Christ's constraining love is at once the impulse and standard of all Christian love—'that ye should love one another, as I have loved you' (Jn 15[12]). Judaism supplied the law of love (Dt 6[5], Lv 19[18]), Christianity supplies the power—the grace which came by Jesus Christ (Jn 1[17]). It seems *a priori* impossible to love the world that hates us, but it is morally impossible not to love the world which God has so loved. Faith works by love (Gal 5[6]), and works miracles.

'The gospel . . . desires the text "Love thy neighbour as thyself" to be taken quite literally. . . . Is, then, this demand reasonable, and is its fulfilment possible? The coolly reasoning, common-sense intellect answers "No," a thousand times over. . . . The gospel replies to this *No* with a decided, quiet *Yes*' (W. Bousset, *The Faith of a Modern Protestant*, London, 1909, p. 77 f.).

While, however, all finite love flows from God's infinite love, it is not always conscious of its source. It may well up pure and strong in a heart which has never been able by searching to find out God. And it is none the less acceptable to God though He is not yet its object. This truth is exquisitely expressed in Leigh Hunt's poem of 'Abou Ben Adhem,' who, though not yet one of those who love the Lord, has it revealed to him that, because he loves his fellowmen, his name stands first among those whom love of God has blessed. And it is expressed more authoritatively in Mt 25, where our Lord proclaims that deeds done in love to the least of His brethren are accepted as done to Himself. Those who do them are unconscious Christians. Their merit, of which they are astonished to hear, is real, and their reward, which they never sought, is sure.

'For they love goodness, and to love goodness is in fact to love God. . . . While, therefore, the unbelief of men who lead good lives must always cause regret to the Christian, the goodness of their lives need not perplex him, as being implicitly due to the same cause which has for himself become explicit' (Illingworth, p. 102).

George Herbert calls sin and love the 'two vast, spacious things' which it behoves every man to measure (*The Agonie*, 4). The one seems, but the other is, infinite. And the stronger subdues the weaker. Where sin abounds, grace—which is Divine love in its redeeming energy—superabounds (Ro 5[20]). And all hope for the world lies in the fact that a God of holy love is, through His Spirit in His children, for ever wrestling with its sin.

'Is not God now i' the world His power first made?
Is not His love at issue still with sin,
Visibly when a wrong is done on earth?'
(Browning, *A Death in the Desert*, 211 ff.).

Augustine uses a still finer figure than that of the arena. He speaks of 'the glory of love . . . alive but yet frostbound. The root is alive, but the branches are almost dry. There is a heart of love within, and within are leaves and fruits; but they are waiting for a summer' (*In Epist. Joannis ad Parth.* v. 10). The leaves of the tree are for the healing of nations torn by passions of hatred. And, with eyes opened by eating of the fruit, men find their *Paradiso* in letting their desire and will be turned,

'Even as a wheel that equally is moved,
By the Love that moves the sun and the other stars'
(Dante, *Par.* xxxiii. 144 f.).

LITERATURE.—In addition to books named in the article, see E. Westermarck, *The Origin and Development of the Moral Ideas*, London, 1906; L. T. Hobhouse, *Morals in Evolution*, do. 1906; H. H. Wendt, *The Teaching of Jesus*, Edinburgh, 1892; W. Beyschlag, *NT Theology*, do. 1895; E. Sartorius, *The Doctrine of Divine Love*, do. 1884; G. B. Stevens, *The Theology of the NT*, do. 1899; J. Seth, *A Study of Ethical Principles*[3], Edinburgh and London, 1898; J. C. Murray, *A Handbook of Christian Ethics*, Edinburgh, 1908; T. B. Strong, *Christian Ethics*, London, 1896; T. von Haering, *The Ethics of the Christian Life*, do. 1909; R. Law, *The Tests of Life*, Edinburgh, 1909; F. W. Robertson, *Sermons*, iv., London, 1874, p. 222 f.; R. F. Horton, *The Trinity*, do. 1901, p. 133 f.

JAMES STRAHAN.

LOVE (Greek).—I. *GODS OF LOVE*.—**1. Introductory.**—Gods of love, whether co-ordinate with, or actually in opposition to, deities presiding over marriage and fertility, are products of a relatively late development. Doubtless, too, the moment of gratification gave rise to certain 'momentary gods,' and served to fix their permanent influence in the cultus; this group will include Aphrodite Πρᾶξις in Megara (Paus. I. xliii. 6), Aphrodite Πόρνη in Abydos (Athen. xiii. 572 C; cf. R. Meister, *Griechische Dial.*, Göttingen, 1882-89, ii. 230), Aphrodite Μιγωνῖτις in Gythium (Paus. III. xxii. 1), and Aphrodite Περιβασώ in Argos (Hesych. *s.v.*; Nicand. frag. 23 [Schneider]). In Provence the phallic demon Τέρπων was dedicated to her service (*IG* xiv. 2424), and the comic poet Plato (i. 648 [Kock]) enumerates a group of kindred figures in her retinue. Another special goddess is the Ῥαψώ of an inscription from Phalerum (J. N. Svoronos, *Das athen. Nationalmuseum*, ii. [1903] 495), whose character may be deduced from the epithets δολοπλόκος and Μαχανῖτις (Paus. VIII. xxxi. 6) applied to Aphrodite. With this single exception, however, Aphrodite is everywhere the most prominent figure.

2. Aphrodite.—Aphrodite was originally by no means merely a goddess of love; on the contrary, she also presided over the development of female life from the period of youth, and a relic of this conception survives in the story that she nurtured the daughters of Pandareus (Hom. *Od.* xx. 68). At marriages sacrifices were offered to her in conjunction with Hera and the Charites (*Etymologicum Magnum*, 220, 54) or else to her alone (in Hermione [Paus. II. xxxiv. 11]); in Sparta the bride's mother made a sacrifice to Aphrodite Hera (*ib.* III. xiii. 9). Aristophanes (*Nub.* 52, *Lysistr.* 2) speaks of Aphrodite Κωλιάς as specifically the goddess of women; and the Γενετυλλίδες, the goddesses of birth, belong to her circle (schol. to Aristoph. *Thesmoph.* 130, *Lysistr.* 2; Hesych. *s.v.*). In an epigram of Theocritus (no. 13; cf. U. von Wilamowitz-Möllendorff, *Textgesch. der Bukoliker*, Berlin, 1906, p. 118) a woman of Cos thanks her for the fruits of her marriage. The prayers of widows for a second husband were directed to her (Naupactus [Paus. X. xxxviii. 12]); in Sparta she was entreated to retard the coming of old age (*ib.* III. xviii. 1; *Carm. Pop.* frag. 2 [Bergk]).

In addition to these functions, however, she promoted increase and growth in the larger world of nature, as appears from such epithets as Δωρῖτις (Cnidus [Paus. I. i. 3]) and Εὐδωσώ (Syracuse [Hesych. *s.v.*]), which can hardly apply exclusively to the δῶρα Κύπριδος. To her, as the goddess of fertility, the goat was sacred, and she rides upon it (A. Furtwängler, *SMA*, 1899, ii. 590 ff.; P. Gardner, *Mélanges Perrot*, Paris, 1902, p. 121 ff.).[1] Moreover, sacrifices of swine were offered to her, as to Demeter, at the festival of the Ὑστήρια in Argos (Athen. iii. 96 A; the name of the festival is ancient, as is shown by the mode of its formation; cf. Ἀνθεσ-τήρια); as also in Cos (W. Dittenberger, *Sylloge inscrip. Græc.*^{2}, Leipzig, 1898, p. 621), Thessaly, and Pamphylia (Strabo, ix. 438).[2] And, just as goddesses of the field and of fertility, like the Charites and the Horæ (*qq.v.*), were often represented as triads, so we find three Aphrodites in one temple at Thebes (Paus. IX. xvi. 3), and also—probably derived therefrom—in Megalopolis (*ib.* VIII. xxxii. 2).[3] In this broader capacity she was worshipped along with Zeus, as was Dione (who in Homer is her mother) in Dodona (*ib.* III. xii. 11; *IG* xii. 5. 220, where the names of Aphrodite and Zeus Ἀφροδίσιος occupy the first place in a dedication; *ib.* 551 *additam.*). Her association with Hermes is, no doubt, to be understood in the same way (Paus. VIII. xxxi. 3; *IG* xii. 5. 273; C. Michel, *Recueil d'inscr. grecques*, Brussels, 1896–1900, nos. 832, 33; *Ancient Greek Inscriptions in the British Museum*, London, 1874–93, iv. 796; F. Hiller von Gaertringen, *Inschriften von Priene*, Berlin, 1906, no. 183). To her as the tutelary goddess of the meadow and of fertility, of the prosperity of man and beast, pertain also the dedications made to Aphrodite—probably as thanksgiving for εὐετηρία—by those who were leaving office, as found in Halicarnassus (*Ancient Inscr. in the Brit. Mus.*, iv. 901), Cos (*IG* xii. 5. 552), Paros (*ib.* xii. 5. 220), Megara (*ib.* vii. 41), Acræ in Sicily (*ib.* xiv. 208 ff.), and elsewhere. As the protectress of a whole people she is called Πάνδημος (cf. *CGS* ii. 658), and in this capacity she was actually accorded a πομπή at Athens (*IG* ii. Suppl. 314*c*). She invites human beings generally, not merely the sexes, and is thus called Ἑταίρα (Wilamowitz-Möllendorff, in G. Wentzel, Ἐπικλήσεις Θεῶν, Göttingen, 1890, p. 4) and Ἅρμα (Plut. *Amat.* xxiii., though a reference to marriage is also possible here).

Then the sinister aspect of her character as an earth-goddess is likewise duly brought out; she bears the epithets Ἐρινύς (Hesych. *s.v.*) and Μελαινίς (Paus. II. ii. 4; Athen. xiii. 588 C; Paus. VIII. vi. 5, IX. xxvii. 5), as does Demeter in Arcadia; in Thessaly there was a festival of Aphrodite Ἀνοσία or Ἀνδροφόνος (Nilsson, p. 378), which, it is true, seems to have had a reference to female love; probably Περσιθέα (Hesych. *s.v.*) is also to be interpreted by this conception. According to an ancient theogony, she, together with the Erinyes and the Moiræ, is descended from Kronos (schol. Soph. *Œd. Col.* 42). A kindred figure is the Nemesis of Rhamnus (Phot. *s.v.* Ῥαμνουσία Νέμεσις; cf. Wilamowitz-Möllendorff, *Antigonos von Karystos*, Berlin, 1881, p. 10), while in Smyrna, again, we find two Νεμέσεις (*CGS* ii. 595 B, C; interpreted by F. G. Welcker, *Griechische Götterlehre*, Leipzig, 1857–63, iii. 34).

In Aphrodite was merged another goddess, the pre-Hellenic Ariadne or Ariagne; the result is most clearly seen in Delos, where she acquires the name Hagne (*BCH* vii. [1883] 308), and in Amathus, where a festival in which the two sexes exchanged garments was celebrated in the grove of Aphrodite Ariadne (Nilsson, p. 369). Then in Cyprus we find a goddess of Spring named Aphrodite θεὰ Ϝηρπό(μ)πα (R. Meister, *SSGW*, 1910, p. 247), who appears again in Crete as Ἄνθεια (Hesych. *s.v.*), and in Pamphylia, where her priestesses are called ἀνθηφόροι (*CIG* ii. 2821 f.). Certain glosses of Hesychius (*s.vv.* θύλλα and ἀοῖα) which bring her into relation with the May-pole have likewise to do with this aspect of her character. In Amathus she is thought of as androgynous under the name of Ἀφρόδιτος (Hesych. *s.v.*); in Phæstus, similarly, we find the androgynous dæmon Leucippus (Nilsson, p. 270). It is usually supposed that the Aphrodite cult of this district was derived from the worship of Astarte, and that it spread thence over Greece (most recently Nilsson, p. 362; cf. also *ERE* ii. 118^a). It has already been noted, however, that the Aphrodite cult of the Greek motherland presents certain features which cannot be explained as importations. There is also the fact that androgynous forms are unknown as regards Astarte (W. Baudissin, *PRE*^{3} ii. 156), and that such are shown to be Hellenic by the figure of Leucippus and the festival of Ariadne in Amathus. The epithet Ἀνίκατος, borne by the goddess in Cyprus (*SSGW*, 1910, p. 245), is certainly met with elsewhere only as an attribute of Oriental goddesses (O. Weinreich, *Ath. Mitt. des deut. archäolog. Instituts*, xxxvii. [1912] 29, note 1), but the name ἄμαχος θεός (Soph. *Ant.* 800) suggests that it was peculiarly congruous with Greek sentiment. Moreover, E. Sittig (*De Græcorum nominibus theophoris*, Halle, 1911, p. 105) has noted that there are in Cyprus no Phœnician theophoric names formed with 'Astarte.' It is true that in the ancient Greek tradition likewise there are only 'comparative,' but no theophoric, names derived from that of the goddess of love,[1] but the same holds good as regards Eros (*ib.* p. 110). In view of the early relation between Cyprus and Arcadia, it is of great importance to note that her birth-place was transferred not only to Cyprus or Cythera, but also to the River Ladon (Hesych. *s.v.* Λαδωγενής). On the other hand, it is not to be denied that the figure of Aphrodite shows a considerable admixture of Oriental features. Such are certainly the ritual prostitution of Paphos and Corinth (Nilsson, pp. 365, 376), the worship of Aphrodite Οὐρανία (*CGS* ii. 629), and perhaps the fact that her image was armed (*ib.* 654). Her relation to Ares, which is frequently ascribed to epic influence, has not been satisfactorily explained (cf. K. Tümpel, *Fleckeisen's Jahrb.*, Suppl. xi. [1880] 641). Another doubtful point is the Hellenic origin of Aphrodite Εὔπλοια, the goddess of navigation (H. Usener, *Legenden der heiligen Pelagia*, Bonn, 1879, xx.); she may quite well have been evolved from the goddess of Spring, who was brought across the sea from Cyprus (cf. Theognis, 1275 ff.). On the other hand, we must certainly assign a Semitic

[1] Gardner's attempt to find an Oriental origin for this feature is rendered abortive by the fact that the goat has no place in the Astarte cult; similarly Furtwängler's efforts to interpret Aphrodite Ἐπιτραγία as a goddess of light are futile, as the aureole with which she is occasionally portrayed merely implies that at a later period she was identified with Οὐρανία.

[2] Farnell (*CGS* ii. 646) and M. P. Nilsson (*Griechische Feste*, Leipzig, 1906, p. 386) are undoubtedly wrong in seeking to trace in all these instances a connexion with Adonis; such a connexion finds no support in tradition, and, so far as the Argive festival is concerned, is contravened by the fact that there was no State cult of Adonis in Greece.

[3] Cf. H. Usener, in *Rhein. Museum*, lviii. [1903] 205, where he points out that the distinguishing names given by Pausanias must be of late origin.

[1] Even Ἀφρόδιτος (*IG* vii. 585) and Ἐπαφρόδιτος are 'comparatives'; there is no Ἐπαφροδίσιος at all.

origin (see W. R. Smith, *Rel. Sem.*[2], London, 1894, p. 471) to the sacrifice of an *ovis pellita* to Aphrodite in Cyprus.[1] The worship of Aphrodite was also influenced by foreign deities in other districts; on the Black Sea there was an Οὐρανία of Scythian origin (Herod. iv. 59, 67), the lady of Apaturon (B. Latischev, *Inscrip. Pont. Eux.*, Petrograd, 1885–90, ii. 19).

The function of the goddess was in historical times narrowed down to that merely of the protectress of love. It is only as such, with the exception already noticed, that she is recognized in the Ionic epic, and it is therefore worthy of remark that her cult was introduced into Smyrna (Tac. *Ann.* iii. 63) and Ephesus (Michel, *Recueil*, 839 A 5, B 25) by means of oracles. Even at a later period theophoric names formed from 'Aphrodite' rarely occur in Ionia proper (Sittig, p. 108). Her temples in that region were almost all devoted to the goddess of love. In this capacity, too, she absorbed Peitho, who had originally an independent cult (in Sikyon [Paus. II. vii. 7]), but subsequently became sometimes an epithet (*IG* ix. 2. 236), sometimes an attendant, of Aphrodite (Weizsäcker, in Roscher, iii. 1797), as is aptly shown by the figure of Farnesina (*Mon. dell' Inst.* xii. [1885] 21). She usually appears as the goddess of female love, although the Aphrodite Αργυννίς of Bœotia (Phanocl. *ap.* Clem. Alex. *Protr.* ii. 38 [*PG* viii. 17]; Athen. xiii. 603 D; Steph. Byz. *s.v.* 'Αργύννιον) seems to have had to do with παιδικὸς ἔρως, as is certainly true of the Aphrodite Σκοτία of Phæstus (*Etym. Mag.* 543, 49; in Crete the boys were called σκότιοι [schol. to Eur. *Alc.* 989]). As Aphrodite was brought into relation with the evening star in the myth of Phaon-Phaethon (Wilamowitz-Möllendorff, *Hermes*, xviii. [1883] 416 ff.; *Sappho und Simonides*, Berlin, 1913, p. 33 f.), it is easy to see why maidens should murmur their love-pangs to the moon-goddess (schol. to Theocr. ii. 10; Hesych. *s.v.* οὐρανία αἴξ), just as in the Erotic Fragment (6) the lover invokes the stars and the συνερῶσα νύξ.

3. Eros.—Besides Aphrodite the only Greek love-deity of real importance is Eros. He too had a more general function as a deity of procreation, viz. in Thespiæ, where he was worshipped as a stone fetish (Paus. IX. xxvii. 1), as also probably in Parion, in Laconian Leuktra (*ib.* III. xxvi. 5), and in the sex-cult of the Lycomids (*ib.* IX. xxvii. 2; cf. Furtwängler, *Jahrb. des deut. archäolog. Instituts*, vi. [1892] 116 f.). In Elis he is represented beside the Charites, and to the right of them (Paus. VI. xxiv. 7), *i.e.* as their leader, like Hermes elsewhere. From his procreative aspect arose the cosmic character which he bears in Hesiod and among the Orphics. In consequence of the obvious derivation of his name, however, he remained all along the god of sensual desire. His cult had only a narrow range. In Laconia and Crete sacrifices were offered to him before a battle (Athen. xiii. 561 C), and the connexion between these and pæderasty has been explained by E. Bethe (*Rhein. Mus.* lxii. [1907] 445). We are told also that in the Academy he had an altar which was supposed to have been erected in the period of the Pisistratidæ (Athen. xiii. 609 D; Plut. *Sol.* 1), but Euripides (*Hipp.* 538) asserts that offerings were never paid to him at all. In literature and art his figure was always a mutable one, and he is the subject of no clear-cut myth (J. Boehlau, *Philolog.* lx. [1901] 321, and cf. O. Waser, in Pauly-Wissowa, vi. 487). Alcman (frag. 38 [Bergk[4]]) calls him a boy; Anacreon sometimes obviously regards him as a youth (frags. 2, 47), while in other passages (*e.g.*, frag. 62) one may well doubt whether he thinks of him as a personal deity at all. But this indefiniteness of outline, which persists throughout the subsequent period, is counterbalanced by the magnificence of the associated conception. While Sappho (frag. 1) naively prays to Aphrodite, who inflicts and removes the pains of love, Æschylus (frag. 44 [Nauck[2]]) extols the might of that craving which pervades all that lives, and depicts the shattering effects of ἀπερωπὸς ἔρως (*Choeph.* 599); and the other two great tragedians give expression to similar ideas regarding the destructive and enravishing power of Ἔρως (Soph. *Ant.* 781; Eur. *Hipp.* 525, 1268, *Iph. Aul.* 543). Thereafter philosophical speculation seizes upon the conception, and exalts it to heights before undreamed of. Plato (*Conviv.* 187 D), playing upon the etymology of the words, contrasts Οὐρανία and Πάνδημος as sacred and profane love—a contrast having no foundation in their essential meaning, but dominating their usage for the future.

4. Later developments.—In the sphere of common life the deities of love declined as the practice of hetærism gained ground. In this period the 'Αφροδίσια became a characteristically hetæristic festival (Nilsson, p. 374). Besides Eros we now find Ἵμερος and Πόθος, 'Longing' and 'Fulfilment' (Paus. I. xliii. 6; on the meaning of Πόθος cf. Wilamowitz-Möllendorff on Bion's *Adonis*, v. 58), and in other districts 'Αντέρως (Paus. I. xxx. 1, VI. xxiii. 3, 5). The earlier tradition still makes itself felt in the verses in which the bearded Eros of Simias (*Bucolici Græci*, ed. U. von Wilamowitz-Möllendorff, Oxford, 1905, p. 147) describes his powers, but coincidently, from the period of the vase paintings ornamented with gold, a multitude of dallying Erotes find their way into art and literature, as shown by the epigrams of the Anthology and the paintings found in Pompeii. Among the Hellenistic societies the Aphrodisiasts were largely represented (F. Poland, *Griechisches Vereinswesen*, Leipzig, 1909, p. 189 ff.), though it is true that there were among them numerous foreign (Syriac) cults. The high favour enjoyed by Adonis also served to revive the worship of Aphrodite; the deities of love in general now reached their highest vogue, and it is in this period that we first meet with theophoric names derived from Aphrodite, though no doubt—with but few exceptions—in the lower ranks of society (Sittig, p. 108). Aphrodite and Eros are no longer deities of the procreative impulse, but are the guardian spirits of love in the modern sentimental sense. It is worthy of note that unhappy lovers now frequent the supposed tomb of Rhadine and Leontichos, the heroine and hero of the romance of Stesichorus (Paus. VII. v. 13). Syncretism once more laid hold of the figure of the love-goddess, and combined it with that of the healing mother of the gods (*IG* iii. 136), while the recollection of her larger function survives in the literary tradition, as appears in the Proem of Lucretius, and as reveals itself also, immediately before the collapse of the ancient religion, in the *Pervigilium Veneris* (*Anth. Lat.* i. 144 [Riese and Bücheler])—the last memorial of antiquity to the goddess whose influence pervades the universe.

LITERATURE.—The more important works have been cited in the course of the article. The reader may also consult: W. H. Engel, *Kypros*, Berlin, 1841, ii. (materials); A. Enmann, 'Kypros und der Ursprung des Aphroditekults,' in *Mém. de l'Acad. Imp. de St. Pétersbourg*, xxxiv. [1886] p. xiii; L. Preller and C. Robert, *Griechische Mythologie*[4], Berlin, 1887–94, i. 345, 501; W. H. Roscher, art. 'Aphrodite,' in Roscher; A. Furtwängler, art. 'Eros,' *ib.*; P. Weizsäcker, art. 'Peitho,' *ib.*; K. Tümpel, art. 'Aphrodite,' in Pauly-Wissowa (to be used with caution); O. Waser, art. 'Eros,' *ib.*

KURT LATTE.

II. *ETHICAL IDEAS.*—**1. The Homeric age.**—It remains to examine what ideas concerning the

[1] The πρόβατον κωδίῳ ἐσκεπασμένον (Joh. Lydus, *de Mens.* iv. 65) is doubtless to be understood in this sense; cf. J. Marquardt, *Privatleben der Römer*[2], Leipzig, 1886, p. 476.

emotion of love and its ethical value were characteristic of the Greeks; and the survey will reveal considerable develpoment in consequence of political and social movements, together with a certain variety of contemporary opinions in the most important eras. The charming pictures of domestic affection which are to be found in the Homeric poems, such as the parting of Hector and Andromache (*Il.* vi. 370 ff.) or the meeting of Odysseus and Penelope (*Od.* xxiii. 85 ff.), and even occasional comments like 'there is nothing mightier and better than when husband and wife keep house with united hearts' (*Od.* vi. 182 ff.), and the tenderness of the allusion to the soft voices of the youth and maiden while they are courting each other (*Il.* xxii. 128), reflect a condition of society in which wedded love was highly prized. This was the natural outcome of the respect with which women were treated, and of the comparatively high degree of liberty which they enjoyed.

2. Post-Homeric development. — The causes which led to the disappearance of the Achæan monarchies are imperfectly known to us (see art. KING [Greek and Roman]), and the evidence available does not enable us to trace the course of the changes which lowered women in public estimation by depriving them of their earlier freedom. But signs of their depreciation may be observed even in the utilitarian precepts of Hesiod regarding marriage (*Works and Days*, 700 ff.); and the same tone pervades the invective of Semonides of Amorgos (frag. 7), whose pattern wife is the offspring of the busy bee blessing with material increase the gathered store of her mate (line 83 ff.). It is remarkable that the same simile is employed by Ischomachus in describing to his wife the duties which he expects her to perform (Xen. *Œcon.* vii. 32), and the whole of the training prescribed in Xenophon's dialogue (*op. cit.* vii.-x.), as well as casual allusions to domestic happiness, shows that the Attic ideal was satisfied by the loyalty of a careful and thrifty housewife (Lys. i. 7). In historical times an ordinary Greek marriage was so entirely prompted by motives of convenience that we read without surprise the typical sentiment of the Athenian orator:

'While we keep a mistress to gratify our pleasure and a concubine to minister to our daily needs, we marry a wife to raise legitimate issue and to have our property carefully preserved' ([Dem.] lix. 122).

3. Sappho.—It must not be supposed that in the meantime the passionate outpourings of the lover failed to find adequate expression in literature. In this respect the poems of Sappho occupy so peculiar a position that an attempt must be made to define it. Sappho, a poetess of such eminence as to have been accounted the rival of Homer and to have earned the title of the tenth Muse (*Anth. Pal.* VII. xiv. 15; cf. Strabo, p. 617), owed most of her reputation to the fervour of her love-poems. Yet in estimating their tendency we encounter unusual difficulty, partly because, notwithstanding the additions made in recent years, only scanty fragments of her writings survive, and partly because comic poets and later gossip-mongers have shrouded her name in unmerited scandal. It is generally admitted that the story of her unrequited love for Phaon and of her despairing leap from the Leucadian rock are fictions due, perhaps, to a misunderstanding of her own words (U. von Wilamowitz-Möllendorff, *Sappho und Simonides*, Berlin, 1913, pp. 24-40). The grosser suspicions, such as those indicated by Seneca in his reference (*Ep.* lxxxviii. 37) to the discussion of Didymus 'an Sappho publica fuerit,' are not to be supported by such doubtful evidence as frag. 52, and are contradicted no less by the soundest part of the tradition, which represents her as a wife and a mother (Suid. *s.v.* Σαπφώ; cf. Sappho, frag. 85), than by the sincerity and freedom of her genuine utterances. The psychological problem presented by frags. 1 and 2 and Berlin frags. 2 and 5 is to understand how the yearning affection inspired by the loss or departure of one of her girl friends came to be expressed in terms usually reserved for the rapturous emotions of sexual love. The solution, so far as the evidence permits us to form a definite conclusion, is to be sought in the character of a remarkable personality. If Sappho was the inspiring genius of a society of beautiful and high-born maidens, who sought at her hands instruction in the poetic art (frag. 136), and with whom she lived on terms of intimate affection, there was no reason why she should not, with a different intention, have anticipated the behaviour of Socrates to his young disciples, by giving utterance to her whole-hearted devotion in the language of passionate love. The parallel was drawn in antiquity by Maximus Tyrius (xxiv. 9), who was, doubtless, not the first to suggest it; and in modern times the good name of Sappho has been defended by F. G. Welcker (*Kleine Schriften*, Göttingen, 1816, ii. 80-144) and, more recently, by von Wilamowitz-Möllendorff (*op. cit.* pp. 17-78).

4. Tragic and other poets.—The poetic treatment of love was usually confined, as, *e.g.*, by Mimnermus and Anacreon, to its sensual aspect, and it is clear from the history of the tragic stage that a serious preoccupation with the causes, symptoms, or effects of love was considered unworthy of a poet who aspired to be true to his calling. Hence Aristophanes (*Ran.* 1043 f.), in the character of Æschylus, attacked the degeneracy of Euripides in exhibiting on the stage the lust of Phædra and Stheneboea, whereas the elder poet had never been guilty of describing a woman in love. The unfairness of this criticism is sufficiently demonstrated by the nobility of the female portraits to be found in the extant plays; but it is particularly important to observe that here, as in some other respects, Euripides was the herald of a new development in imaginative literature of which the climax has probably been reached in the extraordinary popularity of the romantic novel during the last hundred years. To this we shall presently return. If we exclude certain features in the psychological studies of Euripides, however, the dominant conception of love figured its victims as entirely passive, since love was an over-mastering force which, entering into a man's body, permeated it so completely that he was no longer able to control his impulses. Love was a particular phase of possession by a demonic being as popularly conceived (cf. Plut. *Amat.* xviii. p. 763 A), and was consequently described as a disease (Soph. *Trach.* 544) or a madness (Eur. frag. 161). The medium which conveyed the mysterious influence was the faculty of sight (Æsch. *Ag.* 427 f.; Thuc. II. xliii. 1; Arist. *Eth. Nic.* ix. 5. 1167*a* 4). The lover's glance was a physical emanation from the eye, which, making its way straight to the eye of the beloved object, was met in its course by the responsive gaze speeding as fast towards the lover (Soph. frag. 433; Heliod. iii. 7; Plut. *Quæst. Conv.* V. vii. 2, p. 681 B). The shaft of light then came to be regarded as a weapon (βέλος, τόξευμα) which inflicted a wound upon its victim (see *ClR* xxiii. [1909] 255 ff., where copious illustration is given). But the love-god had his wings as well as his bow and arrow (Eur. *Hipp.* 530 ff.). For, by another figure, every violent transport of emotion, including poetic inspiration (Pind. *Isthm.* v. 64) and fear (Apoll. Rhod. iv. 23), as well as frenzy (Eur. *Bacch.* 332) and love (Plat. *Phædr.* 246 D, etc.), was represented in the guise of soaring wings, as if under such influences the agent were lifted out of his normal sphere into a higher region by some supernatural force. Sophocles, in a famous fragment (frag. 855 N.²), characterizes the love-goddess, here a personification of the passion itself, in the following words:

'Love is not love alone, but is called by many names; it is Death, it is immortal Might, it is raging Frenzy, it is vehement Desire, it is Lamentation; in Love is all activity, all peace, all that prompts to violence.'

Over and over again stress is laid upon the irresistible power of Love: he is the mightiest of all the gods (Eur. frags. 269, 430; Menand. frag. 235, iii. 67 K., frag. 449, iii. 129 K.); and not one of them (Soph. *Trach.* 443), not even Zeus himself (Eur. frag. 684; Menand. frag. 209, iii. 60 K.), can withstand his attack.

'He is not wise,' says Deianira in the *Trachiniæ* (441 f.), 'who stands forth to contend with Love, like a boxer at close quarters.'

It is not difficult to imagine the result of this assumption upon the attitude of the average Athenian citizen. The celebrated ἱερόδουλοι of the Corinthian Aphrodite (cf. Pind. frag. 122 and art. HIERODOULOI [Græco-Roman]) help to explain the absence of moral reproach directed against the notorious ἑταῖραι of Athens. Resistance to the onset of Love is no less reprehensible than it is futile (Eur. frag. 340), though excessive indulgence is as much to be deprecated as entire abstinence (Eur. frag. 428). Such self-control as was exhibited by Agesilaus in refraining, despite the violence of his passion, from accepting the kiss offered by a beautiful Persian boy (Xen. *Ages.* v. 4 f.) was so rare that the historian felt it to be altogether marvellous.

5. Pæderasty. — The passage last quoted confronts us with that form of the love-passion, the love of boys, which has come to be known as 'Greek love,' and has tarnished the whole fabric of Greek morality. There is no trace of this custom to be found in the Homeric poems; for the assertion of such relations having existed between Achilles and Patroclus is not, so far as we can tell, earlier than Æschylus (frag. 136 [*Tragicorum Græcorum Fragmenta*², Leipzig, 1889, p. 44]). But there is no doubt of its antiquity, at any rate, among the Dorian branch of the Greek race. This is established by the evidence of certain Theraic inscriptions (*Inscriptiones Græcæ insularum maris Ægæi*, ed. F. Hiller von Gaertringen, iii. [1904] 536 f.); by the relation between the εἰσπνήλας and ἀΐτας in the disciplinary system of Spartan training (Plut. *Lyc.* xvii. f.; Ælian, *Var. Hist.* iii. 10, 12); and by the curious custom of the Cretans, according to which the lover carried off his favourite by a show of force, and was more or less seriously resisted according to his supposed merit (Strabo, pp. 483, 484). The inveteracy of the habit may be attributed to its long descent from a primitive period when continuous military service involved a scarcity of women (Bethe, in *Rhein. Mus.* lxii. 438 ff.). Moreover, it is fair to admit that the results of such companionship were by no means invariably bad.

T. Gomperz has well remarked that 'the sentiment in question appeared in as many, if not more, varieties and gradations, than the love of women at the present day. Here, as elsewhere, a noble scion was often grafted upon a savage stock. Devotion, enthusiastic, intense, ideal, was not infrequently the fruit of these attachments, the sensual origin of which was entirely forgotten' (*Greek Thinkers*, Eng. tr., London, 1901-12, ii. 380).

Such an elevation of sentiment is the easier to understand if we bear in mind the continually increasing segregation of the sexes to which reference has already been made, and which, owing to the natural craving for sympathy and affection, left a gap to be otherwise filled. Widely spread as the evil undoubtedly was,[1] there were many—probably an increasing number—who were keenly alive to its disgrace. But sentiment varied among different communities, and, as compared with Athens, Thebes and Elis were subject to an unenviable notoriety in this respect (Xen. *Symp.* viii. 34; Plat. *Symp.* 182 D).

6. Philosophic love. — Such was the state of society when the teaching of Socrates began to open a new era in the progress of morality. By putting sexual desires more or less on the level of the other bodily wants (Xen. *Mem.* IV. v. 9, *Symp.* iv. 38), Socrates scarcely advanced beyond the prudential standpoint of the ordinary person. But his character, so completely vindicated by Alcibiades in the *Symposium* (215 A ff.), was free from any suspicion of vice; and, though he sometimes ironically pretended to be enamoured of beauty (Xen. *Mem.* VI. i. 2, *Symp.* iv. 27), and actually described himself as the lover of his younger companions and pupils (Xen. *Symp.* viii. 2), yet he energetically repressed the erotic tendencies of his associates (Xen. *Mem.* I. ii. 29, I. iii. 8), and required that a spurious love should be converted into a true friendship aiming solely at the moral improvement of the beloved object (Xen. *Symp.* viii. 27). Plato developed his master's teaching on this subject by connecting it with the innermost core of his philosophical system, and, in the dialogues *Symposium* and *Phædrus*, he expounded with matchless literary skill his doctrine respecting the true nature and purpose of love. The argument in the *Phædrus* (250 A) starts from the hypothesis of the immortality and pre-existence of the soul, which in its ante-natal state was associated with the eternal verities of the ideal world. Now, the ideas of Justice and Temperance are scarcely visible in their earthly counterfeits, and their apprehension is difficult and seldom attained. But Beauty is always so conspicuous that its phenomenal representation attracts at once the admiration even of those who are strangers to the mysteries of wisdom, and are engrossed in their mortal surroundings. Thus souls from which the glories of the images once beheld have faded by contact with earthly clogs, so far from being sanctified and inspired by the sight of beautiful forms, are stirred only with fleshly desire. But it is different with the lover who is also a philosopher, and his progress is described in the lecture of Diotima reported by Socrates in the *Symposium* (pp. 210, 211). The true lover, by contemplating the beauty of the beloved object, is immediately reminded of absolute Beauty itself. With his personal admiration for his beloved freed from the trammels of bodily fetters, he sees even more keenly the beauty of mind and character of which the outward form is only the reflexion. Presently he perceives the common kinship of beauty wherever it is manifested in action or thought, and learns that its complete apprehension is the task of a single science. Lastly, passing entirely from the individual to the universal, his soul is so greatly purified as to become re-united with the idea of Beauty itself, which is the ultimate source of all beautiful persons and things belonging to the phenomenal world. Such is the significance of τὸ ὀρθῶς παιδεραστεῖν (*Symp.* 211 B), or τὸ παιδεραστεῖν μετὰ φιλοσοφίας (*Phædr.* 249 A).[1] Plato's philosophy left its mark upon subsequent ethical speculation, but was too much exalted to affect the opinion of the ordinary citizen. Aristotle distinguished perfect friendship between good men based upon character from the spurious friendship of lover and beloved aiming at pleasure or utility (*Eth. Nic.* viii. 4. 1157*a* 1 ff.). Whereas the Epicureans entirely rejected love as a violent impulse attended by frenzy and distraction (Epic.

[1] The free use of the word παιδικά in this relation is itself significant.

[1] J. Burnet has recently undertaken to show that the whole of the doctrine commonly attributed to Plato was actually propagated by Socrates (*Greek Philosophy*, i., 'Thales to Plato,' London, 1914, p. 140). It is obviously impossible to discuss the question here.

frag. 483 [Usener]), the Stoics followed closely in Plato's footsteps by recommending it to the Wise Man as an attempt to produce friendship with youths who displayed in their beauty a capacity for virtue (Diog. Laert. vii. 129; Stob. *Ecl.* ii. p. 115, 1 [Wachsmuth]; Cic. *Tusc.* iv. 70, etc.). Plotinus, as might be expected, adopted the rules laid down in the *Symposium* as a means of approach to the supra-rational and transcendent First Being (Porphyr. *Vit. Plotin.* xxiii.). On the other hand, Plutarch, whose dialogue entitled ἐρωτικός aimed at reconciling conflicting views by a return to the commonsense point of view, while he was largely influenced by Platonic imagery, vindicated the claim of woman as the proper object of a divinely inspired passion (21, p. 766 E ff.). We even find Plato condemned altogether as unworthy of serious attention by such writers as Dionysius of Halicarnassus (*de Admir. vi dicendi in Demosth.*, p. 1027), Athenæus (508 D), and Heraclitus, the author of the Homeric Allegories (76, p. 101, 19).

7. Romantic love.—In the meantime we are able to trace the growth in Greek literature of the romantic love-story in which the hero and heroine, who have fallen in love at first sight, after a series of adventures are at last happily united. The realistic treatment by Euripides of certain tragic subjects was undoubtedly one of the causes which contributed to the appearance of the domestic drama known as the New Comedy. Among the stock elements in the plots of Menander and his rivals we find the intrigue of the son of a rich citizen with a slave-girl who often proves to have been originally a free-born Athenian exposed by or otherwise lost to her parents; the overreaching of an unsympathetic parent or a rascally pander by the cunning of a devoted slave or parasite; and the ultimate reconciliation of all parties, leading to the marriage of the happy lovers. But pathos and sentiment were entirely alien to the cold atmosphere and artificial mechanism of these plays. A new tone—that of sympathy with the fortunes of the lovers—asserted itself for the first time in some of the masterpieces of Alexandrian literature. Whether this was merely the result of the diffusion of the Hellenic spirit outside the confines of the city communities through the countries which then constituted the civilized world, or more specifically of closer acquaintance with popular Eastern tales such as that of Abradates and Panthea in Xenophon (*Cyrop.* v. i. 3, vi. i. 31 ff., iv. 2–11, vii. i. 29–32, iii. 2–16; see J. P. Mahaffy, *Greek Life and Thought*², London, 1896, p. 254; E. Rohde, *Der griechische Roman*², p. 583 ff.), it is impossible now to determine. The vigour of Alexandrian love-poetry receives its best illustration in the third book of Apollonius's *Argonautica*, where the growth of Medea's passion for Jason, the conflicting interests prompting her to struggle against it, and her final submission to an irresistible emotion are depicted with poetic power of a very high order. There is no doubt that Vergil made Apollonius his chief model when constructing the well-known episode of the loves of Dido and Æneas. Another example was the love-story of Acontius and Cydippe described by Callimachus in the course of a digression in the *Ætia*, the conclusion of which has recently been discovered in one of the Oxyrhynchus Papyri (no. 1011 [=vii. [1910] 15 ff.]). The various features which became common to the writers of these romantic narratives have been summarized (A. Couat, *La Poésie alexandrine sous les trois Ptolémées*, Paris, 1882, pp. 140–160; J. P. Mahaffy, *op. cit.* p. 256 ff.) as follows: (1) the minute portraiture of the personal beauty of the lovers; (2) the sudden interposition of the love-god at their first meeting; (3) the record of the misfortunes obstructing the fulfilment of their wishes; (4) the description of the pangs of thwarted love; and (5) the importance attached to the preservation of the virgin purity of the heroine amidst all her trials and dangers until her final reunion with the hero. It is unnecessary to follow in detail the influence exerted by the art of Callimachus and Philetas upon Latin poetry, and especially upon the works of Catullus, Propertius, and Ovid; but mention should be made of the Μιλησιακά of Aristides, which had an extensive circulation in the Roman era (Ovid, *Trist.* ii. 413; Lucian, *Am.* i.). This was a collection of erotic tales put together in the 2nd cent. B.C., whose general character may be inferred from Petronius, Apuleius's *Metamorphoses*, and Lucian's *Asinus*. The work of Parthenius dedicated to Cornelius Gallus was different in both scope and purpose: it consisted of excerpts relating to the misfortunes of lovers and drawn from various historians and poets. The characteristic features of the romantic love-story enumerated above were closely followed by the later romance-writers (ἐρωτικοί; cf. art. FICTION [Primitive] (*j*)), who were the direct inheritors of the Alexandrian tradition and became extremely popular in the Middle Ages (I. Bekker, *Anecd. Græca*, Berlin, 1814, p. 1082). The best of these novels was the *Æthiopica* of Heliodorus (3rd cent. A.D.), who was preceded by Xenophon, the author of the *Ephesiaca*, and followed by Achilles Tatius (*Leucippe and Clitophon*) and Chariton (*Chæreas and Callirrhoe*). The *Daphnis and Chloe* of Longus was constructed according to the same plan, but under the influence of the pastoral *Idylls* of Theocritus. To these names should be added the fictitious love-letters of Alciphron and Aristænetus, which aimed at restoring the Attic flavour of the New Comedy.

LITERATURE.—Several of the authorities consulted have been indicated above. Certain portions of the subject-matter are covered by E. Bethe, 'Die dorische Knabenliebe,' *Rhein. Mus.* lxii. [1907] 438 ff.; E. Rohde, *Der griechische Roman*², Leipzig, 1900. For the ethical development in general, see the authorities quoted under ETHICS AND MORALITY (Greek), and especially L. Schmidt, *Die Ethik der alten Griechen*, Berlin, 1888, i. 204–208; J. Denis, *Histoire des théories et des idées morales dans l'antiquité*², Paris, 1879, ii. 122–154.

A. C. PEARSON.

LOVE (Jewish).—The dictionaries define love as 'a feeling of strong personal attachment, induced by that which delights or commands admiration.' The subdivisions of this sentiment comprise the impulses of attachment, due to sexual instinct, or the mutual affections of man and woman; the impulses which direct the mutual affections of members of one family, parents and children, brothers and other relatives; the attachment that springs from sympathetic sentiments of people with harmonious character, friendship; and, finally, the various metaphorical usages of the word, as the love for moral and intellectual ideals. To the last class belongs the religious concept of love for God, while the particular Biblical conception of God's love for Israel is closely related to the idea of paternal affection.

1. Sexual love.—Love for woman as an irresistible impulse is most strongly represented in Canticles in the words:

'Love is strong as death; jealousy is cruel as the grave: the flashes thereof are flashes of fire, a very flame of the Lord. Many waters cannot quench love, neither can the floods drown it: if a man would give all the substance of his house for love, he would utterly be contemned' ($8^{6f.}$).

The passion of sexual instinct which must be elevated by a feeling of love is repeatedly referred to in the same book ($2^{6f.}$ 3^{5} $5^{6.8}$ $8^{3f.}$; see also $1^{3f.7}$ $2^{4f.}$ $3^{1-4.5.10}$ 7^{7}), and sensuous life of the low physical type is often mentioned either directly (Pr 7^{18}) or as the most natural metaphor for reprehensible inclinations (Hos 3^{1}). The Biblical stories give us repeated instances of the power of sexual passion, as in the case of Samson (Jg 14^{16} $16^{4.15}$), where the demonic power of woman over man leads man to ruin. Similar is the case of Shechem (Gn 34), though in his case the love for Dinah is not of the strictly carnal nature which characterizes the relation between Samson and Delilah. The love of King Solomon for many strange women—a prototype of the baneful influence of the harem on politics in the Orient—is given in the Bible (1 K 11[1]) as the cause of the downfall of the wisest of kings. The Rabbis consistently prove from this story that it is impossible for any man to guard against the influence of woman, and use this fact as support for the theological doctrine that law is unchangeable; for even Solomon, who thought he was wise enough to be safe from having his heart turned away by women (Dt 17[17]), fell a victim to their influence (*Ex. Rabbā*, ch. vi., *Tanḥūmā*, *Ex.*, ed. S. Buber, Wilna, 1885, p. 18).

With equal force sexual passion is described in the case of Amnon, raping his stepsister Tamar (2 S 13), when, after the gratification of the brutal impulse, Amnon's passion turns into hatred and disgust (v.[15]), a story which has a remarkable parallel in Max Halbe's tragedy *Jugend* (Berlin, 1893). The term 'love' is also used with regard to other physical pleasures, as love for delicacies (Gn 27[4]).

2. **Matrimonial and parental love.**—The higher conception of matrimonial love as an attachment which elevates sexual relationship, just as the latter without such relationship is degrading, is often referred to both in principle and in illustrative story. The case of Jacob, who was willing to work seven years in order to gain Rachel, and the remark that those seven years passed by like 'a few days' (Gn 29[20]), as well as the hope of Leah that the birth of her third son would make Jacob love her (v.[34]), show that ideal matrimonial relations are to be governed by spiritual affection. Thus the marriage of Isaac and Rebekah, arranged by their parents, ripens into love (Gn 24[67]). A further stage to the relation of Jacob and Leah is that of Elkanah and Hannah (1 S 1[8]), where the husband tries to console his wife, longing for the blessing of children, by saying, 'Am I not better to thee than ten sons?' David is spurred by the love of Michal to do great acts of valour (18[28])—a conception of life akin to that of troubadour times. Even in the story of Esther the king's love for the queen (Est 2[17]), while in many ways showing the characteristics of an Oriental despot, willing to give half of his kingdom away in order to gratify the whim of an odalisk, is presented as an attachment seizing the king with the force of a sudden passion. Such passion is referred to in the case of a captive of war, and the law requiring that she be allowed time to become assimilated to her environment is dictated by a delicate understanding of womanly feelings (Dt 21[10-14]). The placing of duty above personal feeling underlies the law for the conduct of a man who has two wives, one of whom is beloved, and the other hated (vv.[15-17]). It is worthy of note that Rabbinical apologetics explains the love as a tribute of piety and hatred as being 'hated by God' (*Sifrē*, ed. M. Friedmann, Vienna, 1864, p. 113). At the same time Rabbinic ethics derives from this law a condemnation of polygamy as leading to domestic trouble (*ib.*). In a warning against sexual licence the author of Proverbs advises (5[19]) devotion to 'the loving hind and the pleasant doe'; and the author of Ecclesiastes gives as a recipe for happiness the advice:

> 'Live joyfully with the wife whom thou lovest all the days of the life of thy vanity . . . for that is thy portion in life' (9[9]).

It is significant that such advice was put in the mouth of King Solomon. In full harmony with this conception of domestic felicity, as the highest ideal of life, are many Rabbinical statements.

> 'Of him who loves his wife like himself and honours her more than himself, Scripture (Job 5[24]) says: "Thou shalt know that thy tent is in peace"' (*Yᵉbhāmôth*, 62*b*).

Closely related to this conception of love is the love of children, so often referred to in the OT, and already implied in the many passages praising the happiness derived from the possession of children (Ps 127[3-5] 128[3], Pr 17[6]) and the misfortune of not having children, as in the case of Rachel, who would rather die than live without them (Gn 30[1]), and in the similar case of Hannah (1 S 1). The love of Jacob for Joseph, because 'he was the son of his old age' (Gn 37[3f.]), and the love for Benjamin, who, in addition to being a son of his father's old age, was the only one left of his mother (44[20]), are so naturally presented that they show the psychological continuity of human nature. The same feature of truly human life is seen in the story of Jacob and Esau, where the father loves the daring hunter Esau, while Rebekah feels more affection for Jacob, the young man of domestic habits (25[28]). Such affection does not rest in the blood, but is often stronger in persons attracted by congenial feelings. There is hardly in the whole world's literature a nobler expression of devotion than the words spoken by Ruth to Naomi (Ru 1[16f.]), and the words of felicitation spoken to Naomi on the birth of Ruth's son, that Ruth's love for her is greater than that of seven sons (4[15]), are felt by the reader of to-day as a profound truth, just as they were at the time when they were written. A similar feeling of affinity is that of the faithful servant, of which the law takes cognizance in the case of a slave who would rather stay in the house of his master than go free (Dt 15[16], Ex 21[5]).

3. **Friendship and wider love.**—The love of friends is naturally presented in comparison with that arising from sexual and blood relationship. David says of Jonathan: 'Thy love to me was wonderful, passing the love of women' (2 S 1[26]). A true friend is one 'that sticketh closer than a brother' (Pr 18[24]). False friends who fail in the hour of need are often referred to (Ezk 16[33. 36f.] 23[5. 9], Hos 2[9. 12. 15], La 1[19], Ps 109[4f.]). The happiness that friendship brings in poverty is contrasted with abundance and hatred (Pr 15[17]). In correct interpretation of this experience the Rabbis speak of the natural friendship of the ostracized for each other, naming the proselytes, slaves, and ravens (Talm. *Pᵉsāḥîm*, 113*b*). As specimen of the highest love the Rabbis give the case of David and Jonathan (1 S 20[17]), and contrast it with that of Amnon and Tamar, showing that the first, because unselfish, lasted, while the second, being based on carnal passion, could not last (*Ābhôth*, v. 16).

Love, as not limited to friends, but extended to all mankind, is a principle the priority of which Jewish and Christian theologians have been contesting with one another. On the Jewish side it was claimed that the command, 'Thou shalt love thy neighbour as thyself' (Lv 19[18]), is universal. As proof for this conception it was adduced that the commandment of love in the same chapter is extended to the stranger, 'for ye were strangers in the land of Egypt' (v.[34]),[1] and that, therefore, it expresses implicitly the idea of Hillel (*q.v.*)—a teacher of the 1st cent. B.C.—'What is hateful unto thee do not unto thy neighbour; this is the whole Torah, and all the rest is its commentary' (Talm. *Shabbath*, 31*a*). It is claimed that in the same sense Rabbi Aqîbā, a teacher of the 2nd cent., said: '"Love thy neighbour as thyself" is a great principle[2] in the Torah' (*Sifrā*, *Qᵉdhôshîm*, ch. 4; *Yᵉrūshalmī Nᵉdhārîm*, x. 3). Christianity, on the other hand, claims that Jesus, in the parable of the Good Samaritan (Lk 10[30-37]), was the first to answer the question, Who is my neighbour?, in

[1] See also Dt 10[18]. [2] Or the fundamental principle.

the universalistic sense.[1] One might introduce the argument that the Rabbis interpret the commandment, 'Love thy neighbour as thyself,' as teaching a humane method of execution, evidently implying that even the criminal remains our neighbour (Talm. *Pes.* 75*a*). The Hebrew word *ôhēbh* ('lover') for friend is also used in the social sense, as in the case of Hiram and David (1 K 5^{15} [EV 5^{1}]).

True love is tested by the sincerity which will not hesitate to rebuke and which will accept rebuke (Pr 9^{8}), but, on the other hand, loving friendship will overlook faults (10^{12} 17^{9}). In the same sense the Talmud reports that Johanan ben Nūrî praised his companion Rabbi Aqîbā for having loved him more each time that their teacher chastised him on the ground of a charge made by Johanan (*Arākhîn*, 16*b*). For this reason controversy on religious questions between father and son, teacher and disciple, will promote their mutual love (*Qîddûshîn*, 30*b*). At the same time it is commanded to suppress hostile feelings. In Talmudic casuistry the question is asked, What precedes, if a man see at the same time his enemy's and his friend's ox or ass lying under his burden (Ex 23^{5})? The answer is given that he must first help his enemy 'in order that he train himself in subduing passion' (*Bābhā M^{e}ṣî'ā*, 32*b*). Love is also used in the plain social sense, as when it is said that 'breakfast removes jealousy and brings love' (*ib.* 107*b*). The making of friends is true greatness. He is a strong man who can turn his enemy into a friend (*Ābhôth R. Nāthān*, ch. 23). Just as true friendship is praised and recommended, so false friendship is condemned. The Rabbis warn man to keep at a distance from high officials, for 'they pose as lovers, when they have use for you, and will not assist you in the time of distress' (*Ābhôth*, ii. 3). The utilitarian point of view in friendship is presented in the case of Canaan who—so the Talmud says—admonished his sons to love one another, but at the same time to love all vices (*P^{e}sāḥîm*, 113*b*). On the other hand, it is cited as an expression of true love, when Rabbi Judah han-Nāsî, while the spiritual head of the Jewish community, repealed his own decision in a legal case when he heard that Rabbi Jose had decided differently.

4. Metaphorical uses.—Love in the metaphorical sense is used very frequently in connexion with wisdom, especially in the introduction to Proverbs (4^{6} 8^{17}); see also the counterpart of loving folly or hating wisdom (1^{22} 8^{36}). As true wisdom is identical with the Torah, we find the love of the Torah (Ps 119$^{97. 163}$) and of God's commandments (vv.$^{47f. 159}$) monotonously repeated in the long Psalm, which evidently is the work of an early Pharisee who anticipates the ideal presented in the sayings of the Fathers:

'Turn it [the Torah] over and turn it over, for everything is in it, speculate over it, grow old and grey with it, and never depart from it, for there is no higher conception of life than this' (*Ābhôth*, v. 22).

This conception is repeated innumerable times in theory and story. In commenting on the passage, 'This day thou art become the people of the Lord thy God' (Dt 27^{9}), the Rabbis say:

'Israel had indeed become God's people forty years previously, but Scripture wishes to say that to one who studies the Torah earnestly, it becomes new every day' (*B^{e}rākhôth*, 63*b*).

As an example of such devotion Joshua is quoted (*M^{e}nāḥôth*, 99*b*), to whom God said, not in the sense of a commandment, but in the sense of a blessing, that the Torah should not depart out of his mouth (Jos 1^{8}).

The love of instruction—in Hebrew synonymous with reproof (Pr 12^{1})—wisdom (29^{3}), purity of heart (22^{11}), righteousness (Ps 45^{7}), and kindness (Mic 6^{8}) are characteristic traits of the pious, just as to love their opposites is characteristic of the wicked (Ps 52$^{5f.}$). The injunction of Micah (6^{8}) to do justice, to love mercy, and to walk humbly with God is presented by a Rabbi of the 4th cent. as the sum-total of 'the 613 commandments of the Torah' (*Makkôth*, 24*a*). The true disciple of Aaron is, according to Hillel, 'he that loves peace and pursues it' (*Ābhôth*, i. 12; cf. Ps 34^{14}). To Rabbinic theology ethical conduct and ritualistic conformity are equally divine commands (*ib.* ii. 1), and therefore the righteous is he who practises God's laws without regard to material advantage. Moses took care of Joseph's remains (Ex 13^{19}) while the Israelites were busy trying to secure the booty of the drowned Egyptians, which shows how he loved God's commandments (*Sôṭāh*, 13*a*), for to bury the dead is the highest of the cardinal virtues (see To 1$^{17-19}$ 2$^{3ff.}$, Mt 8^{21}, Lk 9^{59}). Fulfilling God's commandments at a great personal sacrifice is another proof of love. The legend reports that Rabbi Gamaliel bought a palm-branch at a thousand drachmæ to fulfil the divine commandment (Lv 23^{40}) even while on board a ship (*Sukkāh*, 41*b*). A similar story of a great number of ducats paid for an *ethrôg* (citron used on the same occasion) is told by L. Münz, *Rabbi Eleasar genannt Schemen Rokeach*, Trèves, 1895, p. 115. God's sanctuary, as a place where only the righteous may set their foot (Ps 15^{1}), is also an object of love for the righteous (26^{8}). In a eudæmonistic sense love is advised for the practical pursuits of life in the Rabbinic saying:

'Love M^{e}lākhāh [work in the sense of man's occupation], avoid office and seek not the acquaintance of those in power' (*Ābhôth*, i. 10).

As devotion to practical pursuits, love is mentioned in the case of king Uzziah, who is praised as one who 'loved husbandry' (2 Ch 26^{10}). Perhaps the obscure passage in Ec 5^{9} is to be interpreted in this sense of a king who is devoted 'to the field.' The popularity of a king is referred to as love in 1 S 18^{16}. As a love of the ruler for the people the Rabbis define the devotion to public improvements in the case of Joshua, who is said to have built roads and erected public buildings (*'Ērūbhîn*, 22*b*). Time-serving is implicitly condemned in those who 'love the rich, while the poor is hated by his own neighbour' (Pr 14^{20}). Prophets who seek their own material advantage are denounced as 'watchmen loving to slumber' (Is 56^{10}), and the people steeped in materialism are said to 'love cakes of raisin' (Hos 3^{1}).

A special theological aspect of love in the metaphorical sense is the use of the word as referring to the mutual relation of God and Israel, both in Biblical and in Rabbinical literature. The traditional liturgy speaks very often of God's love for Israel in giving it His commandments, especially Sabbath and holy days, and this love is often referred to in the Bible as the love of a father for his children, as that of a loving husband, and especially as that of a bridegroom (Dt 7$^{8. 13}$ 23^{7}, 1 K 10^{9}, 2 Ch 2^{11} 9^{8}, Is 43^{4} 63^{9}, Hos 3^{1} 9^{15} 11^{1} 14^{4}, Mal 1^{2} 2^{11}). Inasmuch as Israel is ordained to maintain the heritage of Abraham to do justice (Gn 18^{19}), God loves justice and righteousness (Ps 33^{5} 37^{28} 146^{8}, Is 61^{8}) and hates him 'that loveth violence' (Ps 11^{5}). As Zion stands for the embodiment of all that is noble, God loves Mount Zion (78^{68}); and, as Israel's patriarchs were the living representatives of this ideal, God loves them and, for their sake, their descendants (Dt 4^{37}). Just as Israel is not selected by God for His power, but for His righteousness (Dt 7^{8} 10^{15}; cf. Pr 15^{9}), so He loves the humble (Is 66^{2}) and His symbol, the stranger (Dt 10^{18}). Prosperity is not a sign of God's love, and affliction is not a sign of His hatred, for the Lord often 'correcteth him that he loveth' (Pr 3^{12}; see Job 5^{17}). Yet prosperity is

[1] M. Lazarus, *Die Ethik des Judentums*, Frankfort, 1898, pp. 144–183.

repeatedly quoted as a token of God's love, as in the case of Solomon (2 S 12[24]). In a satirical sense the correctional value of suffering is referred to in a Talmudic story.

R. Ḥănînā calls on his friend R. Johanan who is ill, and asks him whether he loves his sufferings. Johanan answers: 'Neither the sufferings nor their reward' (*Bᵉrākhôth*, 5*b*).

The case of king Manasseh (2 Ch 33[12f.]) is quoted as proof that suffering ought to be received with love (*Sanhedrîn*, 101*b*).

As a fundamental doctrine R. Aqîbā presents the principle that God loved mankind, for He created man in His image; He loved Israel, for He called them His children; and, furthermore, Israel is beloved by God, for He gave them a most precious gift, His Torah (*Ābhôth*, iii. 14). R. Aqîbā evidently wishes to grade God's love as the love of mankind in general, of Israel in particular, and of the law-observant Israelite as the best beloved. God, according to Rabbinic ethics, loves especially the humble and peaceful (*Bᵉrākhôth*, 17*a*), and more generally him who is beloved by his fellow-men (*Ābhôth*, iii. 10). Modesty is the best means to gain God's love.

'I love you, says God to Israel, because, when I elevate you, you humble yourselves, for Abraham called himself "dust and ashes" (Gn 18[27]), and Moses said of himself and Aaron: "What are we?" (Ex 16[8]), and David called himself: "I am a worm, and no man" (Ps 22[6])' (*Ḥullin*, 89*a*).

God loves, says the Talmud in a different passage (*Pᵉsāhîm*, 113*b*), him who is calm, temperate, and humble, but hates him who is a hypocrite, who does not offer testimony when he knows something of the case, and who sees his neighbour commit a wrong and testifies, although he is the sole witness (gossip). Most probably in the sense of condemning luxury in the building of synagogues R. Ḥisdā, who lived in Babylonia in the 3rd cent., says, commenting on Ps 87[2]:

'God loves the gates, ornamented with the Hălākāh [play on words: *ṣiyūn*, 'heap of stones,' and Ṣiyôn] more than all synagogues and schoolhouses' (*Bᵉrākhôth*, 8*a*).

It is consistent with this principle that the true Israelite who is beloved of God is in the sense of St. Paul (Ro 2[28]) the spiritual Israelite, and therefore the heathen who came to Hillel to be converted, and desired to be assured that he might become high priest, was satisfied when he heard that 'the stranger who comes with his staff and wallet has the same rights as the Israelites who are called God's children' (*Shabbāth*, 31*b*). Israel is beloved by God, for the *Shᵉkhînāh* accompanies them wherever they are exiled (*Mᵉgillāh*, 29*a*). A distinctly polemical idea is found in the statement of R. Jose, who says: 'God loves Israel so that they need no mediator' (*Yômā*, 52*a*), probably an antithesis to the statement in the Gospel of John (3[16] 14[6]). Yet the Rabbinic theologians considered also a miracle a proof of divine love (*Ḥăgîgāh*, 26*b*; *Ta'ănîth*, 20*a*).

The correlate term to God's love for Israel is Israel's love for God. It is enjoined as a duty in Dt 6[5], and this section is the principal part of the daily morning and evening devotion, thus practically enjoining the doctrine of Jesus (Mt 22[37f.]), which makes this the principal commandment. The injunction to love God is typical of the Deuteronomic code (5[10] 7[9] 10[12] and often) and of the Psalms, where the pious are called lovers of God, of His salvation, or of His righteousness (5[11] 31[23] 40[16] 97[10] 119[132] etc.). To those who love Him God will do good (Ex 20[6], Dn 9[4], Neh 1[5] 13[26], Mal 1[2]), and therefore Abraham (Is 41[8], 2 Ch 20[7]) and Solomon (1 K 3[3]) are called lovers of God, and Jehoshaphat is reproved for loving God's enemies (2 Ch 19[2]), whom the pious must hate (Ps 139[21f.]).

An important theological discussion, leading back to the early days of Christianity, is carried on in the Talmud between R. Eliezer and R. Joshua, whether the piety of Job is to be found in his love or in his fear of God (*Sôṭāh*, 27*b*). The love of God is characterized in the Talmud by man's conduct, which sheds lustre on his religion (*Yômā*, 86*a*). As Zion stands for Israel's ideal, the pious are those who love Zion (Ps 122[6]) and the wicked those who love strange gods, often presented by the metaphor of adultery and sinful love (Is 57[8], Jer 2[25] 8[2], Ezk 16[16], Hos 2[17] 4[18]). From a practical point of view the Talmudists say that one who marries his daughter to a Rabbi (*Kᵉthūbhôth*, 111*b*), or one who studies the Torah with no expectation of worldly glory (*Nᵉdhārîm* 62*a*), loves God. A special sign of the love of God is submission to His decrees, as in the case of Hananiah ben Hezekiah and his school, who wrote down 'the scroll of the fasts' (a chronicle of Israel's misfortunes) because they rejoiced at the tribulations, thus exemplifying the spirit of Job, who served God out of love.

See, further, 'Semitic and Egyptian' section below, §§ 2, 4.

LITERATURE.—In addition to the Jewish sources quoted in the article, see E. Grünebaum, 'Der Grundzug und dessen Entwicklung der Liebe im Judenthume,' in A. Geiger's *Wiss. Zeitschr. für jüd. Theol.*, ii. [1836] 285, iii. [1837] 59, 180; M. Lazarus, *The Ethics of Judaism*, ii., Philadelphia, 1901; S. Schechter, *Studies in Judaism*, 2nd ser., London, 1908, 'Saints and Saintliness,' pp. 148–181; K. Kohler, art. 'Love,' in *JE* viii. [1904] 188–190. Cf. also art. CONSCIENCE (Jewish); M. Joseph, 'Jewish Ethics,' in *Religious Systems of the World*, London, 1901, pp. 695–708.

G. DEUTSCH.

LOVE (Muhammadan).—Although in the Qur'ān the vengeance and wrath of Allāh are more forcibly depicted than His mercy and love, any one reading the successive revelations in chronological order, as far as possible, will observe that the latter conception was gradually gaining ground from the hour when the Prophet's struggle for recognition began to the day when his victory was no longer doubtful. The epithet *wadūd* ('loving') is applied to Allāh in a *sūra* of the oldest Mecca period (lxxxv. 14); but, with this exception, and a few others dating from the period immediately before the Prophet's migration, all the Qur'ānic references to divine love occur in those chapters which were revealed at Medina. It is likely that his settlement in a city where he could not fail to be brought into contact with Christian ideas cooperated with the happy change in his fortunes and caused him to emphasize the milder aspects of Allāh in a corresponding degree. Of these references, which are about thirty in number, most are brief statements that God loves various classes of men—*e.g.*, the beneficent, the patient, those who trust in Him, fight for Him, keep themselves pure, and so on—and that He does not love various other classes, such as the transgressors, the proud, and the unjust. Muhammad denies the claim of the Jews and Christians to be the children and, in a peculiar sense, the beloved of Allāh (v. 21). Man's love of God is mentioned in three passages: some men take idols which they love as much as they love Allāh, but the faithful love Allāh more than anything else (ii. 160); those who love God must follow His Prophet, then God will love and forgive them (iii. 29); if any of the faithful apostatize, Allāh will fill their places with men whom He loves and who love Him (v. 59).

Many traditions ascribed to the Prophet on the subject of divine love go far beyond the somewhat arid and perfunctory allusions in the Qur'ān, but there is no reason to suppose that they are genuine. They belong to the mystical doctrine which developed under Christian influence in the 2nd cent. of Islām, and which in the course of time established itself, as a guiding and inspiring principle, at the centre of Muhammadanism. The following examples are often cited by Ṣūfī authors:

'When God loves a man, his sins hurt him not; and one who repents of sin is even as one who is without sin' (*Qūt al-qulūb*, Cairo, 1310 A.H., ii. 50. 15).

God said: 'False are they who pretend to love Me, but when the night covers them sleep and forget Me. Does not every lover love to be alone with his beloved? Lo, I am near to those whom I love. I hearken to their secret thoughts and prayers, and I am the witness of their moaning and lamentation' (*ib.* ii. 60. 22).

God said: 'My servant draws nigh unto Me by works of devotion, and I love him; and when I love him, I am the ear by which he hears and the eye by which he sees and the tongue by which he speaks' (cf. al-Qushayrī, *Risāla*, Cairo, 1318 A.H., 169, penult; there are several versions of this tradition).

It is obvious that the doctrine of divine love will assume different forms according to the relative orthodoxy of its exponents. We often find it linked with mysticism of an ascetic or devotional type, while in other cases it accompanies a thorough-going pantheism, or occupies various points between those extremes. The subject is exhaustively treated by Ghazālī in bk. vi. of his *Iḥyā* (Būlāq, 1289 A.H., iv. 280–349). Only a brief abstract can be given here, but this will suffice to show the scope and development of the doctrine as it is set forth in the most popular and authoritative encyclopædia of Muhammadan ethics.

Love (*ḥubb*) is the natural desire for that which gives pleasure; when that desire grows intense, it is called 'passion' (*'ishq*). Each of the bodily senses takes pleasure in different objects. Similarly, the spiritual sense, whose organ is the heart (*qalb*), has its own objects of pleasure which are imperceptible to the bodily senses. Ghazālī enumerates five chief causes of love: (1) *Self-interest.* Every one desires to preserve his life or to make it as perfect as possible. Therefore men hate death and seek wealth, children, etc. (2) *Beneficence.* Men love those who benefit them. This is indirectly a species of self-love. (3) *Disinterested love of good.* Sometimes a good man is loved for his own sake, not for any advantage that may be derived from him. (4) *Love of beauty* (moral or spiritual), when the whole pleasure which it gives consists in the perception of it. (5) *Spiritual affinity.* Ghazālī then proceeds to demonstrate that all these motives have their ultimate source in God, who is the sole object of true and perfect love, although love of God necessarily includes love of the Prophet and the saints. The strongest and rarest motive, he says, is spiritual affinity. Man is called to an *imitatio Dei* in respect of certain attributes, according to the tradition, 'Form yourselves on the moral nature of God' (*takhallaqū bi-akhlāq Allāh*). He becomes near to God through his acquisition of knowledge, benevolence, compassion, and other virtues. But, underlying this, there exists between God and man a real and intimate relation, of which Ghazālī speaks with the utmost caution as an ineffable mystery which is revealed to theosophists. It is indicated by the verse of the Qur'ān where God says that He breathed His spirit into man, by the divine command given to the angels to worship Adam, and by the tradition that God created man in His own image.

Every human sense and faculty seeks a particular end, which constitutes its pleasure. The spiritual faculty—it is described by different names, *e.g.*, reason, faith, illumination, insight—seeks to know the essences of all things. God is the highest object of knowledge; therefore knowledge of God is the highest pleasure. The gnostic (*'ārif*) inevitably loves that which he knows and contemplates; and his love increases in the same degree as his knowledge. Both spring up together in his heart when he has purged it of worldly desires and sensuous impressions. What he longs for is perfect contemplation and perfect knowledge. The former, though it is not attainable in the world of phenomena, may be enjoyed in the beatific vision hereafter, but perfect knowledge of the Infinite Reality can never be reached either in this world or in the next. Consequently the gnostic's longing (*shawq*) is everlasting; even in the bliss of union with God he moves unconsciously towards an unrealizable perfection.

Having defined love as the soul's desire for that which gives it pleasure, Ghazālī points out that the term is metaphorical in its application to God, who wants nothing and regards nothing except His essence and His essential attributes. When it is said that God loves certain men, the intended meaning may be expressed as follows: God raises the veil from their hearts in order that they may behold Him spiritually, and enables them to draw nigh unto Him, and has eternally willed that they should so draw nigh by means of works of devotion, which are the cause of their becoming pure within, and of the raising of the veil from their hearts, and of their attaining to the rank of nearness to God. All these are acts of favour, involving no change in the divine perfection, but inwardly transforming the person who is the object of them. How shall a man know that God loves him? Ghazālī answers this question by enumerating the signs which characterize the lovers of God, since their love of Him is the best proof that He loves them. The true lover yearns to meet God and therefore desires death, or, if he be unwilling to die, it is because he feels that he is not yet ripe for the heavenly vision; he is assiduous in worship and good works, for disobedience cannot co-exist with perfect love; he loves recollection (*dhikr*) of God, and he loves the Qur'ān, which is the Word of God, and the Prophet and his fellow Muslims and all God's creatures, yet he has no joy but in solitary communion with his Beloved, knowing that the more he loves God in this world the greater will be his bliss in the world to come. Some long for paradise, and they shall enter it, but God will give Himself only to those who have fixed their desires on Him. According to Ghazālī, true love always contains an element of fear: the lover dreads lest God should turn away from him or deprive him of contemplation, not on account of such sins as are committed by ordinary men, but to punish him for the hidden deceit (*al-makr al-khafī*) of insincerity, spiritual pride, preoccupation with spiritual delights, and similar offences against divine love, from which no one except the firmly grounded theosophist is secure.

In his concluding chapters Ghazālī explains the meaning of two terms, *uns* and *riḍā*, which denote states connected with the fruition of mystical love. *Uns* is the joy of immediate contemplation of the divine beauty without regard to any possibility that the present experience may be transcended at some future time. Such persons flee from intercourse with mankind, and when they appear in the company of others they are really alone. God allows them to address Him familiarly and to use a freedom of speech that would be considered blasphemous in any one less enraptured. *Riḍā* ('satisfaction') signifies willing acquiescence in whatever God has ordained. The lover cheerfully accepts tribulation and suffering at the hands of men, because he sees that God is the only real agent, and that all good and evil is divinely decreed. Ghazālī shows that prayer is not incompatible with *riḍā*. He also refutes those who use the doctrine of *riḍā* as an argument in favour of antinomianism.

In more advanced and pantheistic forms of Ṣūfīism the term 'love' becomes a symbol for the soul's aspiration to attain *fanā*, *i.e.* to lose itself in union with God. Especially do the Islāmic mystical poets exhaust all the resources of erotic imagery in order to describe the subtleties of a passion that is wholly pure and spiritual; though sometimes the same style may be deliberately adopted as a mask for other sentiments or as an artistic device. The selflessness associated with the highest types of human love makes it an apt emblem of the ecstasy in which the mystic passes away from consciousness of his individuality and lives only in the eternal and universal. The following lines by Ḥallāj are often quoted:

'I am He whom I love, and He whom I love is I;
We are two souls dwelling in one body.
When thou seest me, thou seest Him,
And when thou seest Him, thou seest us both'
(L. Massignon, *Kitāb al-Ṭawāsīn*, Paris, 1912, p. 134).

As the true lover thinks only of his beloved, so the true mystic thinks of nothing but God. Such meditation, however concentrated it may be, cannot in itself produce love, which is a divine gift of rapture beyond the reach of learning; it is the inevitable effect of love, not its cause. By emancipated Ṣūfīs the word 'love' is constantly employed to denote the essential spirit of all religion as contrasted with particular creeds, the ardent inward feeling of adoration as distinguished from ritual ceremonies and forms of worship. Love is the harmonizing and unifying element that transcends sectarian differences.

'Because He that is praised is, in fact, One,
In this respect all religions are one religion'
(Jalāl ad-din Rūmī, *Masnavi*, abridged tr., by E. H. Whinfield, p. 139).

'None of the two and seventy sects with mine
Agrees, nor any faith but Love Divine.
Saint, sinner, true believer, infidel,
All aim at Thee: away with name and sign!'
('Omar Khayyām, ed. E. H. Whinfield, London, 1901, no. 287 [translated by R. A. Nicholson]).

Thus the value of religious systems, including Islām itself, is only relative, and depends on their power to inspire love. Acts of devotion inspired by any other motive are worthless. There is no paradise except union with the Beloved, and no hell except separation from Him. These doctrines lead many Ṣūfīs into a position that practically coincides with free thought. On the other hand, if love of God stands in sharp antithesis to conventional religion, it is equally opposed to logic, philosophy, and every form of intellectual activity. Real knowledge does not come through the mind; it is a divine revelation that flashes upon the hearts of those whom God loves. Possessing 'the light of certainty,' the lover wants no evidence for his faith, and scorns the demonstrative arguments of the theologian.

LITERATURE.—A. von Kremer, *Gesch. der herrschenden Ideen des Islams*, Leipzig, 1868, pp. 79-89; E. H. Whinfield, Introduction to his abridged translation of the *Masnavi* of Jalāl ad-dīn Rūmī, 2nd ed., London, 1898; I. Goldziher, *Vorlesungen über den Islam*, Heidelberg, 1910, pp. 157 ff., 170 ff.; D. S. Margoliouth, *The Early Development of Mohammedanism*, London, 1914, p. 175 ff.; R. A. Nicholson, *The Mystics of Islam*, London, 1914, pp. 102–119; see also art. ṢŪFIS, where further references will be found.

REYNOLD A. NICHOLSON.

LOVE (Roman).—Nothing is more significant of the practical character and the prosaic morality of the early Roman than his attitude towards love. In the earliest known period of Roman religion, the so-called 'religion of Numa,' we do not find a single trace of any deity connected with love. Now, inasmuch as all phases of life had their representatives in the world of the gods, the conclusion would seem to be inevitable that, while there was, of course, natural affection, there was no pronounced development of sentiment, along either moral or immoral lines. Immoral expression was checked by that extraordinary self-restraint which characterized a people who were instinctively conserving all their energies for future conflicts; and expression along moral lines was discouraged by the severely practical view of marriage merely as an institution for the propagation of the race. So far as we are able to tell, therefore, we have in the case of the early Romans a people without any deity of love. In the course of Rome's development she was destined to receive a goddess who was eventually to represent in her world all that the Greeks included under the concept of Aphrodite. This goddess was known as Venus, and was, from about the year 300 B.C. onwards, identified with Aphrodite; but she did not exist in Rome before Servius Tullius, for we have absolutely no trace of her in the 'calendar of Numa.' On the other hand, the name *Venus* seems Latin, and it is certainly Italic and not Greek;[1] and the fact that, when the Romans learned of Aphrodite, they called her by this name seems to indicate that she was known to them before Aphrodite was, and that there was sufficient resemblance between her and Aphrodite to make an identification possible. Our first task, therefore, is to find what is known about Venus in the period before Aphrodite arrived. All books on Roman religion, except a few of the most recent ones, are full of information about an Italic, a Latin, and even a very early Roman Venus. It is our duty first to examine these statements.

1. The question of the Italic Venus.—In general the assertion is made that in very early times there was present throughout Italy the cult of a goddess who was called Venus. But a closer examination shows that many of the facts adduced to prove this statement are of very doubtful value. (1) It has been repeatedly said that this goddess of gardens was especially worshipped in Campania, that, in other words, she is the Venus so famous at Pompeii, the *Venus Pompeiana*. But this is false, for the Venus Pompeiana is the Venus whom the veterans of Sulla brought to Pompeii when they were settled there, the goddess of the *Colonia Veneria Cornelia*, a combination of Venus-Aphrodite and Felicitas (see below, § 3). Her cult, therefore, does not antedate the first cent. before Christ. (2) We hear of the worship among the Oscans of a goddess akin to Venus, a certain *Herentas* (mentioned in three Oscan inscriptions: two from Herculaneum [R. von Planta, *Gramm. der oskisch-umbrischen Dialekte*, Strassburg, 1892–97, ii. 510], and one from Corfinium [*ib.* ii. 546]). In one of these inscriptions Herentas has the cognomen *herukinai* (= *Erucinæ*, *i.e.* the Aphrodite of Mount Eryx in Sicily). This proves, therefore, that the goddess resembled Aphrodite; it tells nothing of Venus, so far as any early Italic cult is concerned.[1] (3) We are in a similar position regarding *Frutis*, for whom we have two passages: Cassius Hemina, quoted by Solinus, ii. 14, who tells us that in the country of the Laurentes Æneas dedicated the statue of Aphrodite, which he had brought from Sicily, to 'Mother Venus who is called Frutis'; and Paulus, in the excerpt from Festus (p. 90), who says that the temple of Venus Frutis was called *Frutinal*. But these passages show merely that an otherwise unknown goddess Frutis[2] was identified with Aphrodite, and again nothing is gained for the old Italic Venus. (4) There are, however, traces of a very early Venus cult at Lavinium and Ardea. Strabo (p. 232) tells us that Lavinium had a temple of Venus which was the common property of all the Latin cities (*i.e.* the Latin league), and that it was in charge of priests from Ardea; further, that near Ardea itself there was a shrine of Venus, which served as a meeting-place for the Latins. These statements must be taken at their full value, in spite of the fact that suspicions readily suggest themselves. It is suspicious, for instance, that Pliny (*HN* iii. 56) and Pomponius Mela (ii. 4) refer to a place in this region as Aphrodisium—an unfortunate name for an old Latin cult. Following the ordinarily sound principle that on solemn occasions the Romans often made sacrifice at the mother-city of a Roman cult, Wissowa tries to prove (*Religion und Kultus der Römer*², p. 289) that Ardea was the source of the Venus-cult in Rome, because in 217 B.C. the Decemviri (later Quindecimviri), who had charge of the Sibylline books, commanded the Romans to sacrifice to Venus at Ardea (Livy, XXII. i. 19). The Roman cult may well have come from Ardea, but this reference scarcely proves it, for the sacrifice was made under Greek auspices, and the connexion of Ardea and Rome in the Æneas-legend was likely to suggest such an act, merely as one step in the metamorphosis of the Æneas-legend into a State dogma, which was taking place during the 3rd cent. B.C.

2. Traces in Rome of the early worship of Venus.—If a search for early traces of an Italic Venus is not very rewarding, an attempt to discover early traces in Rome itself is still less so. The three old cults of Venus ordinarily quoted are Venus Cloacina, Venus Libitina, and Venus Murcia, all of them old, but not one of them originally or at any time officially connected with Venus. (1) *Venus Cloacina*. Cloacina was the goddess of the *cloaca*, and possessed a shrine on the north side of the Forum, near the Comitium, at a point where the Cloaca Maxima entered the Forum.[3] No ancient writer refers to her as Venus Cloacina until Pliny (*HN* xv. 119, and, depending on him, Servius, *ad Æn.* i. 720) makes Cloacina a cognomen of Venus. Starting from this, a passage in Obsequens (8, from the year 178 B.C.), where he speaks of a fire in the Forum as having absolutely destroyed the temple of Venus, has been interpreted to mean a temple of Venus Cloacina. On the contrary, the presence of an old Venus-temple near this point may have been the origin of the false association of ideas.[4] (2) *Venus Libitina*. The old Roman goddess Libitina, whose cult was connected with the burial of the dead,

[1] On the word see especially A. Walde, *Lat. etymolog. Wörterbuch*², Heidelberg, 1910, p. 818 f.

[1] On the etymology of the name see Walde, p. 369.

[2] For etymology see Walde, pp. 321, 870.

[3] Cf., on the recently discovered remains of this sanctuary, D. Vaglieri, *Bull. arch. com.* xxviii. [1900] 61; C. Huelsen, *Röm. Mitt.* xvii. [1902] 45, note, xx. [1905] 62 f., *Roman Forum*, Eng. tr., Rome, 1906, p. 132.

[4] On Cloacina cf. Plaut. *Curc.* 471; Livy, III. xlviii. 5; Pliny, xv. 119; Obseq. 8 [62]; for her image on a coin see H. Cohen, *Description historique des monnaies de la république romaine*, Paris, 1857, 'Mussidia,' 6, 7; cf. H. Dressel, *Wiener Studien*, xxiv. [1902] 418 ff.

and whose sacred grove on the Esquiline was the headquarters of the undertaking establishments of Rome, had originally no connexion with Venus. Later she was popularly confused with Venus, forming Venus Libitina—a combination which never existed in the actual cult. It is easy to see two or three things which led to this: the presence eventually of a temple of Venus not far from the shrine of Libitina; the association of Aphrodite with graves, and her cognomen ἐπιτυμβία; lastly, Venus's own cognomen *Lubentina*, or *Libentina*, which was readily confused with Libitina.[1] (3) *Venus Murcia.* Murcia was an old Roman goddess, whose nature was entirely forgotten in the closing centuries of the Republic, but whose name was kept alive by association with a shrine (*sacellum*) in the valley of the Circus Maximus on the Aventine side. The locality was known as *ad Murciæ* or, later, as *Murcia vallis.* Subsequent generations, trying to find who Murcia was, connected her with *Murtia, Murtea, Myrtea*, and so thought that they had found in her a cognomen of Venus, the goddess of the myrtle.[2]

Little thus remains of an old Venus-cult in Rome, except the temple near the shrine of Libitina, which need not be older than the 3rd cent. B.C. We have seen, therefore, that there are very slight traces of early Italic Venus-worship, and still slighter ones of specifically Roman worship. The existence of the Italic name Venus, by which Aphrodite was known at her introduction into Rome, compels us to presuppose some sort of an Italic deity with that name, who was known and worshipped before the coming of Aphrodite. There is another possibility, which we venture merely to suggest, namely, that we have in Venus a case which resembles in part the case of Hercules and Castor-Pollux, and in part that of Mercury. Like Hercules and Castor-Pollux, she may have been originally a Greek deity, who moved up through Italy, and became nationalized into a Latin cult at Ardea, just as Hercules was at Tibur and Castor-Pollux at Tusculum. On the other hand, the name may have been derived, like that of Mercury, from the translation into Latin of an explanatory cognomen. But, whether Venus was from the beginning a Latinized form of Aphrodite or an original Italic goddess later identified with Aphrodite, one clue to her character is afforded us in the fact that, when the directly Greek Aphrodite came (and, of course, she came before the Æneas-legend), it was especially her function as a goddess of gardens that appealed to the Romans. This function, secondary in Greece, seems to have been primary in Rome.[3]

3. The coming of Aphrodite.—We do not know exactly when or how the Aphrodite-cult came into Rome—probably not at first by order of the Sibylline books. She came, however, before the Æneas-legend, though, of course, Aphrodite and Æneas were subsequently inseparably connected. The first datable temple is in 295 B.C., and the first official proclamation of the Æneas-dogma by the State was in the year 282 B.C. Naturally Aphrodite was known before 295 B.C., and the Æneas-legend had been circulated privately before it was publicly proclaimed. The two oldest temples of Venus-Aphrodite in Rome were the one in the grove of Libitina, the date of whose foundation is unknown, but was probably in the 3rd cent. B.C., and the one founded in 295 B.C. near the Circus Maximus. The dedication day of both these temples was August 19th, which was also the festival of the *holitores*, or kitchen-gardeners (Varro, *de Ling. Lat.* vi. 20)—a proof of the emphasis laid upon Aphrodite's function as goddess of gardens. The temple of 295 B.C. was, however, in its origin connected with Venus-Aphrodite as a goddess of love rather than of gardens, for it was built by the ædile, Q. Fabius Gurges, from the fines obtained from the punishment of women taken in adultery (Livy, X. xxxi. 9). During the First Punic War the Romans became acquainted with the cult of Aphrodite on Mount Eryx in Sicily; during the Second Punic War, in the year 217, this goddess, under the name of Venus Erycina, was formally introduced into Rome at the command of the Sibylline books, and given a temple on the Capitoline. A generation later, in 181 B.C., another temple[1] of Venus Erycina was built outside the Porta Collina. But, though Aphrodite may have come in first as the goddess of gardens, this deity of Mount Eryx was pre-eminently a goddess of love, with a pronounced accent upon illegitimate love. A reaction was inevitable, and about the beginning of the 2nd cent. B.C. an altar was erected to Venus Verticordia (Ἀφροδίτη Ἀποστροφία [cf. Paus. IX. xvi. 3; L. Preller and C. Robert, *Gr. Myth.*, Berlin, 1894, i. 368]), who 'turns the heart back' from evil passions (cf. Val. Max. VIII. xv. 12; Pliny, *HN* vii. 120; Solin. i. 126). In 114 B.C. a temple was erected to this same goddess (Ovid, *Fasti*, iv. 133 ff.; Obseq. 37; cf. Oros. V. xv. 22) as an atonement for a prodigy which showed the anger of the gods on account of the unchastity of three Vestal virgins. We do not know where this temple was (Servius, *ad Æn.* viii. 636, wrongly places it in the valley of the Circus Maximus, confusing it with Murcia). Thus by the end of the 2nd cent. B.C. Rome was equipped with two forms of the worship of the goddess of love—the Venus of Mount Eryx, representing licentious love, and the Venus Verticordia, domestic affection. Finally, during the last century of the Republic, Venus assumed three more forms. First, under the leadership of the dictator Sulla, who translated his name *Felix* into ἐπαφρόδιτος and devoted himself especially to the worship of Aphrodite, we have the rise of the cult of Venus Felix, a combination of Venus and Felicitas. This is the Venus Pompeiana (cf. *CIL* iv. 26, 538, 1520, 2457) of whom we find so many pictures at Pompeii; secondly, we have Venus Victrix, for whom, in company with Felicitas, Pompey erected a temple in connexion with his theatre, in 55 B.C.; and lastly comes the Venus Genetrix of Julius Cæsar, the mother of the Julian house, for whom the dictator built a temple in the middle of his Forum (46 B.C.). Thus the tradition was established that Venus was the especial protectress of the Imperial house—a tradition which must have influenced Hadrian in the building of his magnificent temple of Venus and Roma (on the site of the present church of S. Francesca Romana), in A.D. 135.

It is scarcely necessary to add that Amor, Cupid, etc., are merely the Latin translations of the names of Greek gods of love, and that they are confined in Rome entirely to poetry and art, and were never the recipients of an actual cult.

Thus we have seen that, so far as we are able to tell, Rome began life without any deities of love; that her first genuine goddess of love was the

[1] On Libitina cf. Dion. Hal. iv. 15; Plut. *Quæst. Rom.* 23; Ascon. *in Milon.* 34; *CIL* vi. 9974, 10022.

[2] On Murcia cf. Varro, *de Ling. Lat.* v. 154; Livy, I. xxxiii. 5; Pliny, xv. 36; Fest. p. 148; Serv. *ad Æn.* viii. 636.

[3] On Aphrodite as the garden-goddess cf. the cult-name Ἀνθεία (Hesych. *s.v.*); the gardens at Paphos, ἱεροκηπίς (Strab. p. 683); the Urania ἐν Κήποις in Athens (Paus. I. xix. 2); and the Aphrodite ἐν καλάμοις at Samos (Strab. p. 343; Athen. xiii. 572 F). On Venus as garden-goddess in Rome cf. Nævius, quoted by Paulus, p. 58, where Venus=*holera*, 'vegetables'; Plaut. *Men.* 371 (cf. Pliny, *HN* xix. 50); Varro, *de Re Rust.* I. i. 6; Fest. p. 265; *CIL* iv. 2776; and the frequent references in *CIL* vi. to the Venus Hortorum Sallustianorum; cf. Huelsen, *Röm. Mitt.* iv. [1889] 270 ff.

[1] This temple is not to be confused with the Venus Hortorum Sallustianorum (*e.g.*, *CIL* vi. 122), which R. Lanciani thought he had located (*Bull. arch. com.* xvi. [1888] 3 ff.; cf. Huelsen, *Röm. Mitt.* iv. 270 ff.).

Greek Aphrodite; that even here the Greek ideas of Venus Erycina were offensive to her feelings, so that a corrective was sought and found in Venus Verticordia; that in the last century of her Republic three of her great rulers paid homage to Venus as their especial protectress; and, finally, that the example of Julius Cæsar's cult of Venus Genetrix elevated Venus into the goddess of the Imperial household during a large part of the Imperial period which followed.

LITERATURE.—On Venus in general: G. Wissowa, *Religion und Kultus der Römer*[2], Munich, 1912, pp. 234–239; W. W. Fowler, *Roman Festivals*, London, 1899, pp. 67, 68, 69, 85, 86; E. Aust, *Rel. der Römer*, Münster, 1899; J. Marquardt, *Röm. Staatsverwaltung*, ed. Wissowa, Leipzig, 1885, iii. 374 f.; L. Preller, *Röm. Mythol.*, ed. H. Jordan, Berlin, 1881–83, i. 434–450 (good, but out of date). In addition to the special references given above, see, for Herentas, Wissowa, in Roscher, i. 2298; for Cloacina, Wissowa, in Pauly-Wissowa, iv. 60 f.; H. Steuding, in Roscher, i. 913; O. Gilbert, *Gesch. und Topog. der Stadt Rom im Altertum*, Leipzig, 1883–85, i. 338 (to be used with caution); for Libitina, Wissowa, in Roscher, ii. 2034 ff.; Gilbert, i. 176; for Murcia, Wissowa, in Roscher, ii. 3231 ff.; Gilbert, i. 71.

JESSE BENEDICT CARTER.

LOVE (Semitic and Egyptian).—**1. Among the primitive Semites.**—No written records or oral traditions have come down to us from that remote time when the forefathers of the several branches of the Semitic race dwelt together in the desert of Central Arabia. Our knowledge of that period is derived solely by the comparative method of research, which assumes that common elements in the life, thought, and language of the later Semites are an inheritance from their early ancestors. The love-songs of the Babylonians, the Egyptians, the Hebrews, and the Arabs disclose many common features that we may unhesitatingly assume to have belonged to primitive Semitic thought.

The poems of the pre-Muhammadan Arabs in particular have preserved the ancient type with remarkable fidelity. For generations this poetry was transmitted by oral tradition, but in the second, or the third, century of Islām the songs were collected and written out by the grammarians. The most important collections are the *Ḥamāsa*, which contains 884 songs, or fragments; the *Mu'allaḳāt*, or seven most famous poems; the *Mufaḍḍalīyāt*, a collection of thirty odes, the *Dīwāns*, or collected poems, of Labīd; and the *Kitāb al-Aghānī*, which contains the traditions in regard to the lives of the poets and the circumstances of the composition of their songs.

Love is the emotion that finds most frequent expression in the old Arab poetry. Every *ḳaṣīda*, or ode, begins normally with an account of the poet's affection for some woman and his grief at separation from her, and continues with a description of the way in which he solaces himself for her loss by war, or by adventure on his fleet camel or horse. The *ḳiṭ'a*, or fragment, the other main type of Arabic lyric, is often merely a portion of an ode. Where it is an independent composition, it usually has love for its theme. The seven *Mu'allaḳāt* are all love poems, and the 124 songs of the fourth division of the *Ḥamāsa* all treat of this subject.

These poems show that, although Arabian society had already passed into the patriarchal stage in the pre-Muhammadan period, yet many traces of a primitive matriarchal organization still survived (see *ERE* ii. 116[b]). The greatest liberty existed in the relations between the sexes; and women were free not only to choose their husbands, but even to receive in their tents lovers of other tribes. During the winter the rainfall was sufficient to cover the great steppes of the Nejd with scanty verdure, and to replenish the springs that dried up in summer. Then the tribes forsook their permanent headquarters by the perennial springs, and wandered far and wide over the plains. The clans were brought into new temporary relations, and their men and women had the opportunity to become mutually acquainted. The result was numerous inter-tribal attachments.

The poets relate how they first met their lady-loves, and were captivated by their charms. Imra al-Ḳais hid the clothes of 'Unaiza while she was bathing, and would not return them until she promised to carry him home with her on her camel. Duraid fell in love with al-Ḥansa, herself a poetess, while, scantily clad, she was anointing a sick camel with pitch. Under such circumstances it is not surprising that the bards were able to describe the charms of their mistresses with as great detail as those of a favourite she-camel. Large parts of the poems are devoted to word-pictures of the beloved that are as circumstantial as the praises of the 'fairest among women' in the Song of Songs. As among the modern Orientals, fatness and heavy perfumes are specially admired in women. When an attachment was established, the poet made secret visits by night to the tent of his inamorata. If she were a maiden, she went out with him into the solitude of the desert, dragging a heavy garment behind her to obliterate the footprints in the sand (*Mu'allaḳa* of Imra al-Ḳais, 28 ff.). If she were a mother, she remained in her tent, receiving his caresses with one hand, while with the other she stilled her babe (*ib.* 18). The poet protested his devotion and fidelity, and besought her to cease coquetry, and give him her love; and, he assures us, his entreaties were not in vain. Often the lady belonged to a hostile tribe, and such visits were accomplished only by stealing past the sentries at the risk of life (see *ERE* ii. 116[a]). The poems are full of accounts of such love-adventures, and Imra al-Ḳais even boasted to 'Unaiza of the number of women that he had loved in the past (*op. cit.* 7, 18).

All this came to an end with the cessation of the winter rains and the drying up of the springs and the pasture. Then the tribes moved away to their distant homes, and the lovers were separated.

The poets tell us how they visited the spot where the tent of the beloved had stood and found it deserted. They called to mind the happy hours that they had once spent there, and shed bitter tears, and refused to be comforted. All the poems of the *Mu'allaḳāt* begin with this theme, and they show rare beauty and pathos in its treatment.

Love of family and friends also finds frequent expression in the old Arab poetry, particularly in the laments, one of the most numerous and most beautiful products of the lyric art.

This passion, like all strong human emotions, was ascribed to the direct influence of a divinity. Possibly in the earliest times a special dæmon presided over love in distinction from the powers that presided over reproduction and birth. Traces remain of an old Arabian god Wadd, *i.e.* 'love' (see J. Wellhausen, *Reste arabischen Heidentums*[2], Berlin, 1897, pp. 14–18; *ERE* i. 662). Little is known about his character, but he may be a personification of love similar to other Semitic gods such as Gîl, 'joy,' and Paḥad, 'fear' (Gn 31[42. 53]). His erotic character is evident from a verse of Nābigha preserved by Ibn Ḥabīb and cited by Wellhausen (p. 17):

'Farewell Wadd, for sporting with women is no longer permitted us, since religion is now taken seriously' (*i.e.* since the introduction of Islām).

However this may be, it is certain that, long before the separation of the Semitic races, the function of inspiring love had been assigned to the great mother-goddess 'Ashtar, the giver of springs and the producer of life in all realms of the organic world. Under the varied forms that this divinity assumed in different Semitic lands she was everywhere the goddess of love. The love that she inspired was not merely sexual, but also maternal, paternal, fraternal, and social. In the ancient Arab poetry she is occasionally mentioned by the titles al-Lāt, 'the goddess,' and al-'Uzzā, 'the strong,' and the infrequency with which she appears is almost certainly due to Muslim substitution of Allāh for al-Lāt. In other Semitic literatures she is constantly described and invoked as the awakener of love (see ASHTART, vol. ii. p. 115 f.; ATARGATIS, *ib.* 165 f.; ISHTAR, vol. vii. p. 430).

This goddess was the chief divinity of the Semites in their primitive matriarchal stage of social organization. She was the analogue of the human matriarch, free in her love, the fruitful mother of her clan, and its leader in peace and in war. In her supremacy there was a potentiality of monotheism peculiar to the Semites; and it is a fact of deep importance for the growth of the religion of Israel that its starting-point in primitive Semitic religion was not the deification of nature, but the deification of maternal love. In the cult of the mother-goddess there existed in germ the message of the Prophets that God is most truly revealed in unselfish human love, and the message of the gospel that the supreme revelation of God is the perfect love of Jesus Christ.

2. Among the Hebraic Semites.—When the matriarchal form of society gradually gave place to the patriarchal, it was no longer natural to think of the chief deity of the tribe as a mother, but rather as a father. Two things might then happen to the old mother-goddess 'Ashtar. (1) She might be degraded to the position of consort of one or more male gods. This was the step taken in Babylonia, Syria, Canaan, and most other parts of the Semitic world. It involved a surrender of the incipient monotheism that was characteristic of primitive Semitic religion, and an adoption of polytheism. It also involved an over-emphasis of the sexual element in the conception of deity. (2) 'Ashtar might change her sex and become a father-god. Thus the monotheistic tendency of primitive Semitism would be preserved, and the paternal element would be blended with the maternal in the conception of the tribal god. This was what happened in the branch of the Semitic race to which the Hebrews belonged. In S. Arabia, Abyssinia, and Moab, 'Ashtar changed her sex and became the masculine 'Athtar (='Ashtar) who retained feminine characteristics (see *ERE* ii. 115ᵇ; cf. also vii. 429ᵇ). In Ammon and Edom also the tribal god was masculine and had apparently no feminine associate. Jahweh was originally a god of this sort. He was the father of His people, who united maternal characteristics with paternal, and who reigned without a consort. This is a phenomenon of great interest in the development of Hebrew monotheism. By it sexual dualism, the curse of other Semitic religions, was avoided, and at the same time maternal tenderness was retained as a fundamental element in the conception of the deity.

3. Among the ancient Egyptians.—Our knowledge of love and gods of love among the Egyptians is derived partly from the pictures and inscriptions on the monuments, and partly from occasional references in the elegant literature, but mainly from collections of popular love-songs. The chief of these are the London MS (Harris 500), which dates from about 1400 B.C.; the Turin MS, which dates from about 1200 B.C.; the Gizeh ostracon, from about 1350 B.C.; and the Paris fragment, which may be a copy of an original of the Middle Empire. These were first published by C. W. Goodwin, *TSBA* iii. [1874] 380, and G. Maspero, *JA*, 8th ser., i. [1883] 5; and in a much more correct edition and translation by W. M. Müller, *Die Liebespoesie der alten Ägypter*. They contain true folk-poetry, free from the artificialities and tediousness of the conventional Egyptian classics and of the ordinary Oriental literature, and in their simplicity and directness they make a strong appeal to modern taste and interest. The poems in these MSS show the same loose arrangement that is seen in the Hebrew Song of Songs.

The Egyptians belonged to the Hamitic stock, which was closely related to the Semitic; and from the earliest times they were mixed with infusions of Semitic population. It is not surprising, therefore, that their conceptions of love were similar to those of the ancient Semites. In the earliest times they seem to have been organized matriarchally (see A. Erman, *Life in Anc. Egypt*, Eng. tr., London, 1894, p. 155), and at this time their marriage was exogamous; but with the adoption of agriculture they passed over to a patriarchal organization and endogamous marriage. In order to retain their small farms in the family, marriage with a sister, or half-sister, became a common practice, just as among the Hebrews and settled Arabs marriage with a cousin on the father's side was usual (*ib.* p. 154). Hence in the poems the regular name for 'lover' is 'brother,' or 'sister,' as in the Song of Songs the 'fairest among women' is called 'sister,' *i.e.* 'kinswoman.'

In spite of the patriarchal endogamous organization of society, the ancient freedom of the matriarchal exogamous organization was still accorded the Egyptian women, as among the pre-Muhammadan Arabs. The liberty of the Egyptian women was without a parallel in the ancient world, and is rivalled by only a few of the most progressive modern communities. In every respect, legally and socially, they were on an equality with men. In sexual relations they were as independent as their brothers. They were free to marry the men of their choice, and a case is on record of a daughter who threatened to starve herself if she were not permitted to marry as she pleased. Under these conditions the danger of sexual licence was as great on the part of the women as on that of the men (*e.g.*, Potiphar's wife, Gn 39); at the same time an honest, equal love was attained between men and women that has not since been possible until modern times.

An interesting result of this independence was that women wooed men as often as men wooed women. In the love-poems the 'sister' speaks more frequently than the 'brother.' The maiden is sent out by her mother to catch wild fowl in nets, but she confesses that she has been so distracted by thoughts of her beloved that she has caught nothing all day (Müller, *Liebespoesie*, p. 22). She invites her beloved to walk with her in the park between Memphis and Heliopolis, and runs to meet him with her hair decked with flowers and a flower fan in her hand (*ib.* 29); she invites him to hunt with her in the green marshes that are full of birds and flowers (*ib.* 20); she takes him bathing with her, and lets him see her charms through a dress of fine diaphanous linen (*ib.* 41). When he does not respond quickly enough to her advances, she plies him with wine until he becomes more yielding (*ib.* 39); and, when this means fails, she resorts to love-philtres, though she knows that this is punishable by beating with rods (*ib.* 17). She asks him why he does not take her to cook for him, since she is so lonely without him (*ib.* 23). When she has won his love, she describes her transports of joy, and tells how she silences his every excuse for leaving her (*ib.* 14). She chides the dove (the bird of 'Ashtar) for disturbing the meeting with her lover by its cooing (*ib.* 24). When he has left her, she walks in the garden, and every flower tells her something about him (*ib.* 26). The fig offers its shelter to her as a trysting place (*ib.* 39), the pomegranate threatens to tell her secret (*ib.* 39), the sycamore promises not to reveal what it has seen (*ib.* 40). Sometimes, as in other lands, the lover does not come when he is expected; then the maiden mourns for him, suspects that he has stayed with another girl, and hopes that he may make the new love as miserable as he has herself (*ib.* 25). Sometimes the 'sister' is cast off by her 'brother'; then she raises a bitter lament, and prays the gods to restore him to her (*ib.* 23).

The 'brother' also expresses his emotions, although less often than the 'sister.' Unlike the Semites, the Egyptians did not admire fatness, but preferred a girlish, undeveloped figure. Their beauties had a fair complexion, large dark eyes, whose expressiveness was enhanced by pointing the edges of the lids with stibium, masses of jet black hair, red lips, white teeth, quantities of jewellery, particularly earrings, garlands of flowers on the head and around the neck, and, above all, plenty of heavy perfumery. The poems dwell on the 'scent' of the beloved more often than on any other feature (cf. Ca 1³). The 'brother' is smitten by the charms of his 'sister' (Müller, pp. 16, 44); her love fills him as honey mixes with water, or as a strong spice penetrates a perfume (*ib.* 15); he is ensnared by her locks, as a wild goose is caught in a net (*ib.* 16); he is sick from love, and cannot be cured until she comes to him (*ib.* 18). When he goes on a pilgrimage to a temple, he can think of nothing better to ask of the gods than a meeting with her, and he begs each of them to give her his favourite flower to adorn her for his coming (*ib.* 18). He longs to be her slave, to be scolded or beaten by her, if only he may be with her (*ib.* 19), her handmaid, that he may see her lovely form, her washerman, that he may smell the perfume of her garments, her ring, that he may be ever on her hand (*ib.* 43). He swims a river full of crocodiles in order to meet her, and is filled with ecstasy when he sees her (*ib.* 42). Her kiss intoxicates him like beer (*ib.* 42).

In connexion with these poems a number of gods, such as Ptah, Sekhmet, Nefer-Atum, and Amon (*ib.* 18, 23), are invoked to favour one's suit; but the proper divinity of love was Pet, 'the sky,' who, under the forms of Nut, Neith, Bast, Hathor, and a variety of other local names, was the chief Egyptian goddess. She was conceived either as a celestial cow, whose belly formed the dome of the sky, or as a woman raised up from the embrace of her brother-husband, the earth-god Keb. Under the form of Hathor, 'abode of the sun,' at Denderah she attained the greatest glory, and became one of the chief divinities of the empire. Here she was depicted as a benevolent-faced woman with the ears of a cow, or with a head-dress consisting of the horns of a cow enclosing the solar disk (see *ERE* vii. 430^{a}). Since she was originally a sky-goddess, her function as love-goddess must be regarded as secondary, and as due to Semitic influence. The Semites who settled in Egypt in the earliest period found in her characteristics as mother and as cow the nearest counterpart to their own mother-goddess 'Ashtar, and accordingly attributed to her all the erotic qualities of the latter. Thus she early became the Egyptian form of 'Ashtar, and the two goddesses were regarded as identical both by the Asiatic Semites and by the Egyptians. The Canaanite 'Ashtart was depicted with the attributes of Hathor, and Hathor with the attributes of 'Ashtart. During the XIXth dynasty 'Ashtart received extensive worship in Egypt under her own name, or under the epithet of Ḳadesh (see *ERE* iii. 182^{a}, 184^{b}).

4. Among the Hebrews.—We know that love-poetry existed among the ancient Hebrews from such incidental allusions as Am 6^{5}, Is 5^{1} 23^{16}, but specimens of these compositions have as a rule been excluded from the books of the OT. Only the Song of Songs, thanks probably to an allegorical exegesis, has found a place in the sacred canon. This is to be regarded as a collection of folk-songs, similar to those found in modern Palestine, which were sung at weddings in the villages round about Jerusalem. As such it is an invaluable source of information in regard to the Hebrew conception of love. The collection as a whole dates from the Persian or Greek period, but its individual songs may have a much greater antiquity. Besides these primary sources, we have numerous incidental references to love in the other books of the Bible.

The earlier writings of the OT show that women enjoyed much of the freedom that existed among the primitive Arabs and the Egyptians. They dared to love even before they had been wooed (1 S 18^{20}), and they were allowed to express their choice in marriage (Gn 24^{58}). In the Song of Songs the woman is fully as ardent as the man.

The same passionate intensity that existed among the primitive Semites was found also among the Hebrews. The Song of Songs bears a close resemblance to the love-poetry of the ancient Arabs and of the Egyptians. It describes the physical charms of the beloved with the same sensuous detail (*e.g.* 4$^{1-15}$ 7$^{1-7}$ 5$^{10-16}$), and it praises the joy of love with an ardour that is surpassed by no other literature ancient or modern (*e.g.*, 1$^{2.\ 4}$ 2$^{3-5}$ 4$^{9.\ 10.\ 16}$ 5^{1} 7^{10}–8^{4}). This erotic tendency led the early Israelites into all sorts of sexual excesses. Polygamy, concubinage, and prostitution remained unchecked down to a late time, and brought no disgrace to either man or woman. Married women were required to be chaste, but no limits were set to the licence of the men. Love led often to crimes of violence (Gn 34^{2}, 2 S 11. 13); but, on the other hand, it also produced beautiful instances of self-sacrificing devotion (Gn 24^{67} 29^{20}, Hos 3^{1}) and of persistent, though unrequited, love (Gn 29$^{18.\ 32}$). The OT shows also numerous cases of strong paternal love (Gn 25^{28} 37^{3}, 2 S 12$^{15-17}$ 18^{33}), and the love of David and Jonathan stands out conspicuously as the most perfect friendship in all literature (1 S 18^{1} 20^{17}, 2 S 1^{26}).

With all these forms of love Jahweh, the God of Israel, was closely connected in the early Hebrew consciousness. There is strong evidence that He was originally the tribal god of the Kenites who dwelt at Mount Sinai, and that He first became the God of Israel through the work of Moses. Among the Kenites He can have had no consort, for otherwise she would have been adopted by Israel at the same time when He was accepted; but in the old Hebrew religion we find no trace of any such goddess. Jahweh must, accordingly, have belonged to the class of Semitic gods that have been considered above (2), namely, mother-goddesses that were transformed into father-gods in consequence of the transition from the matriarchal to the patriarchal form of society. As such He united with paternal characteristics all the maternal characteristics of the ancient Semitic chief goddess 'Ashtar. (1) He was a god who manifested Himself in life-giving springs (*ERE* ii. 285^{b}). (2) He was the producer of vegetation, and sacred trees stood in His sanctuaries (*ERE* ii. 286). (3) He was the creator of animals; the Passover was celebrated in acknowledgment of His gift of the young of the flock, though these were still known as *'ashtarôth* (Dt 7^{13} 28$^{4.\ 18}$). (4) He presided over sexual love; circumcision, a primitive Semitic rite of preparation for marriage, was the special badge of loyalty to Him (Ex 4$^{24f.}$, Gn 34). In swearing by Him the hand was placed 'under the thigh' (Gn 24$^{2.\ 9}$ 47^{29}). The *ăshērā*, the symbol of the mother-goddess, stood originally beside His altar (2 K 13^{6} 18^{4} 21^{7} 23$^{6.\ 15}$). The *qᵉdhēshîm* and *qᵉdhēshôth*, or temple-prostitutes (see art. HIERODOULOI [Semitic and Egyptian]), were connected with His temples in pre-prophetic times, and did not disappear until after the Deuteronomic reformation (1 K 14^{24} 22^{46}, 2 K 23^{7}, Hos 4^{14}, Dt 23^{18}). (5) He was the giver of children (Gn 21^{1} 30$^{2.\ 22}$, 1 S 1^{20}). His most characteristic blessing was 'be fruitful and multiply' (Gn 1^{22} etc.). A plausible etymology of His name is that it means 'He who causes to live,' *i.e.*, gives children and the young of the flocks and herds. To Him as the giver of offspring the first-born of animals and the first-born child were originally sacrificed, as to the mother-goddess 'Ashtar (Ex 22^{30} 34^{19} 22^{29}, Ezk 20$^{24-26.\ 31}$). (6) He showed maternal love in His care of His people (Hos 11$^{1-4}$, Is 49^{15} 63^{9}). (7) He was the moral governor of His people (Ex 21–23. 34). (8) He gave oracles for the guidance of His people (1 S 14$^{18-20.\ 36-42}$ 28^{6} 30^{7}). (9) Like the old mother-goddess, He was a god of war, who fought for the defence of His children (Ex 15$^{3f.}$ 17^{16}, Jg 5^{23}, 2 S 5^{24}, Dt 23^{14}). (10) By a natural association of thought He was also, like 'Ashtar, a storm-god, who came in the thunder-cloud to fight for His people (Jos 10^{11}, Jg 5$^{4f.}$, 1 S 12^{17}, Ps 18). (11) He was the destroyer as well as the giver of life (Gn 7. 12^{17}, 2 S 24^{13}). For the analogies of these traits in 'Ashtar-Ishtar see *ERE* ii. 115 f., vii. 429–431. These facts seem to show that the Kenite Jahweh was the old Semitic goddess of love and fertility who had been transformed into a father. These maternal traits were never wholly lost in the later development of the religion of Israel.

The message of Moses, that Jahweh, the God of the Kenites, had taken pity on Israel and had determined to rescue it from the bondage in Egypt, laid an altogether new emphasis upon the love of this god. His affection for Israel was not necessary, like that of a parent for a child, but was free and moral, like that of a husband for a wife. Henceforth the redeeming love of Jahweh in the deliverance from Egypt and in the gift of the land of Canaan became the keynote of the religion of Israel. From His people He demanded exclusive worship and a love for Him like His love for them. As early as the Song of Deborah His worshippers are called His 'lovers' (Jg 5^{31}). It is clear also that from the first Jahweh demanded a kindness to fellow-Israelites similar to that which He had shown when He delivered the nation from bondage. Thus for Israel Jahweh became the God of love in an ethical sense that had not yet appeared in any other Semitic religion.

After the conquest of Canaan Israel was confronted with the problem of the relation of Jahweh to the gods of Canaan. This problem was solved by the identification of Jahweh with the *bᵉʿālîm* and other male divinities of the land, so that their sanctuaries and rites became His, and they ceased to exist by being absorbed into Him (*ERE* ii. 291^{b}). With 'Ashtart, 'Anath, and other goddesses the case was different. They could not be identified with Him, and He had no consort with whom they could be combined; consequently they remained His rivals with whom He waged war to the death. In all the pre-Exilic literature Jahweh is never once said to inspire sexual love, although this was certainly one of His primitive functions, apparently because this was regarded as the work of His rival 'Ashtart. Everything connected with the sexual life and with birth rendered one 'unclean,' that is, 'tabu' from participating in the worship of Jahweh, because of the association with the hated mother-goddess; yet, with curious inconsistency, Jahweh was still regarded as the giver of children.

In the Prophets from Hosea onwards the moral love of Jahweh that had appeared already in the Mosaic religion received fresh emphasis. In his love for his wife Hosea saw 'the beginning of Jahweh's speaking' unto him (Hos 1^{2}). When she forsook him for her lovers and plunged into the depths of degradation, he found that he could not give her up, and, when the opportunity came to buy her as a slave and to take her back to his home, he eagerly embraced it (3^{1-3}). Through this experience of unselfish love in himself he received his vision of the love of Jahweh for Israel. Jahweh had taken Israel as His bride at the time of the Exodus and had loved her ever since with unfailing fidelity; she had forsaken Him for the *bᵉʿālîm* of Canaan, yet He could not give her up. He must send her into exile to reform her, yet He would not cease to love her; and, when she repented, He would restore her. This message of Hosea is echoed by all the other pre-Exilic prophets, and finds its noblest expression in the words of Jer 31^{3}, 'I have loved thee with an everlasting love.' It is the recognition that in unselfish human love the truest revelation of the character of God is found.

In return for His love Jahweh demanded the undivided love of Israel. This teaching found its classical expression in Dt 6^{5}, 'Thou shalt love Jahweh thy God with all thy heart, and with all thy soul, and with all thy might.' The recognition of Jahweh's love for Israel carried with it the realization that He required love in the Israelite's treatment of fellow-Israelites. This thought runs through all the pre-Exilic prophets, and is finally summed up by the Holiness Code (*c.* 600 B.C.) in the words, 'Thou shalt love thy neighbour (*i.e.* fellow-Israelite) as thyself' (Lv 19^{18}). Even the alien residing in Israel was to be treated kindly (Dt 10^{19}, Lv $19^{33f.}$), but the extension of such treatment to the foreigner was not yet imagined (Dt 14^{21} 15^{3}, Lv $25^{44f.}$). The interpretation of Jahweh's love in the terms of wedded love reacted also upon the conception of marriage. In the post-Exilic period monogamy became the rule, prostitution was condemned, and men were urged to cleave in fidelity to the wives of their youth (Pr 5^{3-23} 9^{13-18} 31^{10-31}). This higher ideal of marriage is nobly expressed in Ca $8^{6f.}$: 'Love is as strong as death, passion as insatiable as Sheol. The flashes thereof are flashes of fire, a very flame of Jahweh. Many waters cannot quench love, neither can the floods drown it. If a man should give all his possessions in exchange for it, would any one despise him?' Here wedded love is regarded as more precious than all worldly possessions, and as a flame kindled by Jahweh Himself in the soul. An utterance of such purity and profundity concerning love is not found in the whole range of classical literature.

Jesus took up the prophetic conception of the love of God for Israel, and clarified and intensified it by teaching that love was not merely an attribute, but the very essence of the divine nature. The Prophets said, 'God has love'; Jesus taught, 'God is love' (1 Jn 4^{16}). He also declared the universality of God's love, which had not yet been grasped by the Prophets (Jn 3^{16}). He reaffirmed the old commandments, 'Thou shalt love Jahweh thy God with all thy heart,' and 'Thou shalt love thy neighbour as thyself,' and gave them new meaning by His juxtaposition of them, through which love to man became the supreme expression of love to God, and by His new interpretation of 'neighbour' as meaning every fellow-man (Mk $12^{30f.}$, Lk 10^{25-37}). He recognized that in Himself God's love to man and man's love to God and to man were perfectly manifested, and therefore He proclaimed Himself as the supreme revealer of God and the reconciler between God and man.

See, further, 'Jewish' section above.

LITERATURE.—F. Rückert, *Hamâsa*, Stuttgart, 1846; W. Ahlwardt, *Über Poesie und Poetik der Araber*, Gotha, 1856; T. Nöldeke, *Beiträge zur Kenntniss der Poesie der alten Araber*, Hanover, 1864; C. J. Lyall, *Translations of Ancient Arabic Poetry*, London, 1885; F. E. Johnson, *The Seven Poems Suspended in the Temple at Mecca*, do. 1894; W. M. Müller, *Die Liebespoesie der alten Ägypter*, Leipzig, 1899; G. H. Dalman, *Palästinischer Diwân*, do. 1901: E. Littmann, *Neuarabische Volkspoesie*, Göttingen, 1902; P. Haupt, *Biblische Liebeslieder*, Leipzig, 1907 (full bibliography on the Song of Songs).

LEWIS BAYLES PATON.

LOVE-FEAST.—See AGAPE.

LOYALTY.—1. Derivation and definition.—The connexion between the common meaning of this word and its derivation is obscure enough to suggest that a clearer apprehension of its significance may be gained by considering its probable origin. 'Loyalty' is the Anglicized form of the French *loyauté*; its base is *loi*, and corresponds to the English 'law' and the Latin *lex* (stem *leg*). French has also *légalité* and English 'legality,' the late Latin abstract term being adopted without change either of meaning or of form.

Now *loi* in French, and more particularly in the derivative *loyal*, means in respect of its denotation much more than 'law' in the limited sense of a definite written code. It is a generic term, and stands for that which ought to be obeyed; its source may be the will of an acknowledged ruler or ruling class, or it may be popular consent, or it may be personal agreement, whether by contract or by voluntary allegiance. It stands, moreover, for the law of nature and the dictates of reason and conscience, more especially and imperatively if these are conceived in terms of religion as manifestations of the Divine command. Law to the ancient Hebrew of the last few centuries before our era meant this last, and, in so far as it evoked his sentiment of loyalty, it meant little else. To every man the object of his loyalty is as *loi*, or 'law,' in the sense of our inquiry—the authority whose claim on his allegiance he, as a true man, admits. Furthermore, in the natural exercise of his quality, the loyal man applies it to all persons and groups of persons in whom he recognizes any claim of bounden duty or faithful service.

But not only is the range of application wide; the claim for loyal service goes very deep: it is the service of those who desire to serve, and to do so up to the limit of their ability. The law is to be within them, written on their hearts, as the Scripture says, and incorporate in their will. The whole of Ps 119 is, indeed, an expression of the loyalist spirit in application to the Divine law. The devotion expressed by this loyalist in religion is entire; the Divine law is conceived as not perfectly apprehended by him, but he sets no limit to his desire to fulfil it to the end. It is by this note of unlimited purpose, upheld by faith and chastened by humility, that the loyalty of the Psalmist stands out in contrast to the spirit of precise legality, limited by the letter of the law and its tradition, that marked certain developments of a later era. This distinction between the loyalist and the legalist may be found in all times and all places. It applies to allegiance of every kind, whether it be to the supreme law however conceived, or to human ordinance by ancient tradition, modern statute, authoritative utterance of prophet or king, the word of a leader, the rule of a commander. There is the legalist who does what he is told, breaks no rules; he keeps faith to the word that is written and can be read. There is the loyalist who does this but can by the very nature of the spirit that is in him be counted on for more, who puts his whole mind into his duty, who forms his spirit in accordance with the spirit of the purpose to be served.

Loyalty, then, may be defined as the quality of character which issues in free devoted service to the appointed person or the appointed cause. Thus the perfectly loyal person is certain to obey, to serve, despite all obstacles, at all costs, to the best of his ability. And the best of his ability implies that he uses all means to make himself efficient in knowledge and skill and in understanding the requirements laid upon him. The perfect loyalist of story corresponds to this description. We always find him carrying out his instructions—which are his *loi*—with zealous care to undertake them so that, by fulfilling them in the spirit as well as in the letter, the purpose may be accomplished even should the letter fail. He has to be intelligent, alert, resourceful—not merely obedient to precise instructions given—and these qualities he needs the more in proportion to the importance and difficulty of his task. It follows that the development of perfect loyalty throughout a company requires that the duties should be accurately apportioned in accordance with the abilities of each member. It requires also that opportunities for the training and exercise of latent abilities should be given to all. This ideal does, in fact, appear, both in pagan heroic story and in mediæval romance, as characterizing bands of pre-Christian heroes and bands of Christian knights.[1] The unwritten law—not mere personal law, but a pact of comradeship—that bound the Round Table knights to mutual loyalty, and to the king above all, is a notable case in point. The two chief cycles of Irish Gaelic story are noteworthy also in this connexion. Later comes the age of chivalry with its blossom of romantic lore. Fealty and loyalty are main dramatic motives in all these.

2. Loyalty and fealty.—'Fealty,' from Latin *fidelitas*, 'faithfulness,' has an equivalent in all the Romance languages, and so has 'legality.' But loyalty was neither of these. English adopts the French *loyal* to mean 'law-fulfilling' in the sense of the Sermon on the Mount, and distinguishes it from 'lawful,' or 'legal,' which means allowable, and from 'law-abiding,' which connotes submissiveness to the law, the passive quality of the orderly citizen. German translates by specialization and slight change of significance, using such words as *Untertanentreue* (fidelity in a subordinate) and *Vaterlandstreue* (fidelity to the Fatherland); the quality, of course, exists in many diverse applications, and, though fidelity or fealty is not identical with loyalty, the one characteristic is apt to be accompanied by the other. Loyalty connotes a certain specialization of good faith and faithfulness towards the person, principle, ideal, or covenant in respect of which it is expressed; it lays stress on this obligation of specialized fealty rather than on any wider duty of humane comradeship and general goodwill. Nevertheless, there is close affinity between those qualities, the deeper motives of which so widely overlap. The good comrade who, in time of danger or trouble, takes up his responsibilities with settled mind and faithfully sustains them is apt for loyal service wherever his allegiance is given. This is often understood to be given when it is not as a fact, in which case we have either the sturdy rebel or the disloyal man.

The giving of allegiance is in effect a vow to serve; the standard case of loyalty coincides, therefore, with the standard case of fealty in which a pledge of service is given, as, for instance, by oath of allegiance to a king, by marriage vows between two persons, or by acclamation—and vote—in tribal assemblies, when law was promulgated and accepted thus. The standard cases are the same, but in the development of thought the two ideas differ. Loyalty specializes in respect of the object of service, fealty in respect of faith to the pledge. Of these the latter is the more necessary for virtuous character, and so it has been judged by the common sense of mankind, as the testimony of language shows. So long as men were either free or under strict rule, they were simply required either to keep their covenants in the former case or to do what they were told in the latter; faith and obedience were their primal social virtues. The conception of religion, for instance, as consisting in a covenant with the god, was a distinct advance on its conception as a slave service by which he was to be propitiated. The Bible as a whole contains the story of man's progress in religion from the slave service of the bondsman, through covenant, to the free man's willing recognition of a law which it is at once his bounden duty and his delight to obey, and thence to conformity of mind with the Divine purpose for mankind and thus to 'the glorious liberty of the sons of God.' Here we have the specific evolution of loyalty in its highest application, as at once the supreme duty, the supreme delight, and the social virtue of man. On a much smaller scale of motive and in a murkier atmosphere we might trace it in application to finite secular affairs.

3. Personal honour expressed in devotion to social ends.—The free development of fealty by self-discipline to social ends, and of loyalty as a particular case, may be studied in the literature of chivalry and romance. The practice of knightly vows, however, is much older and pre-Christian; so far as records go, it was specially characteristic of the people and the social conditions reflected in Celtic hero lore. The champion of the Gaelic stories is essentially a free man, free of feudal and —except for the spirit that binds him—free of tribal bonds. Social affection binds him too, but honour is his only law. The young hero from his

[1] Thomas Malory, *Morte d'Arthur*; see also the Celtic originals in the Welsh *Mabinogion*

childhood is educated carefully in all manly accomplishments, and in all social courtesies, including respect for women, children, and grey hairs. He emerges from his tutelage free, comradelike, and courteous, a strong individual. But this is not all. Not the least important part of his education is the contribution which he makes to the formation of his character by laying bonds or obligations (in the Gaelic *geis*) on himself that he will or will not do certain things. The obligation never to refuse assistance to a woman frequently occurs, and may supply occasion for the turning-point of the story. Others are of the nature of obligations to a king, leader, or comrade, or to all the members of a band. King Arthur and his Round Table come to mind, or, for those who know Gaelic story, Fionn and the band of heroes whose story has been a fund of moral instruction for western Irish children to this day. Some stories turn on a conflict of two loyalties, each claiming dominion over the loyal soul. The discussion of such difficult situations, however, is not in terms of loyalty, but in terms of keeping faith; in a certain typical case where the vows appear to be of equal weight the decision is given on grounds of common sense quite modern in complexion, whether one agrees with them or not.

This practice of self-made vows in the social interest has, no doubt, been a principal factor of moral education, in its best form of self-discipline for the sake of service, among the peoples of N.W. Europe, where mild forms of government by loose tribal organization of free men prevailed. Faith to a self-made vow covers all cases of voluntary allegiance, and so, as the feudal system was established throughout Europe, it availed itself instinctively of this free man's social virtue by the institution of the oath of fealty from the feudal subordinate to his over-lord. At this point loyalty emerges; fealty and respect for authority maintain each the other and are fused. Fealty, however, is not exhausted in the compound. It remains as the quality of faith to the pledge once given, the central virtue of the self-respecting hero who cannot be false to his word. Carried to the point of fulfilment in spirit, rather than merely in letter, this implies not being false to the reasonable expectations involved in mutual understandings between his fellows and himself. The ideal of the honourable man signifies all this. Such a one is 'loyal,' or 'leal,' so far as his conduct goes, but in his motive he is primarily 'feal.' It may be that only he himself is aware of the difference. As a rule, no doubt, the motives are mixed, but it seems probable that in many, or indeed most, cases either one or the other is the backbone of the composite characteristic. If so, it is important that in the education of each person sufficient demand should be made on the leading trait to evoke it strongly, and sufficient social opportunity given to direct its practical expression in terms of the other—the faithful soul realizing itself in service to others, the loyal spirit fulfilling its service by self-reliant intelligence and steadfast faith.

4. Political loyalty and its object in feudal and modern times.—Loyalty connotes attachment to some definite authority which has a right to be served. The growth of the feudal system in Europe was favourable to the special personal turn which its application took. The political problem was the organization of many small groups into one large inclusive group, or nation, especially for purposes of defence against some common foe. The moral strength of such a national organism consisted largely in the series of loyalties from man to master that bound each to his feudal superior, from the lowest vassal upwards to the supreme over-lord or king. Each primary group was sufficiently small, and grouped round a leader sufficiently well known, to bring out men's normal instincts to follow their chief, to cleave to him truly, to give him allegiance, acclaim him lord, and be his men. This is loyalty of the most picturesque and primitive type, steeped, moreover, in a high mood to which religious enthusiasm is akin. What the man was to the lord, the lord was to his over-lord, and so the national system was linked up unit by unit into larger units all under the supreme over-lordship of the king. The system of loyalties, as signified in this actual system of political allegiances, would in the perfect State have likewise been linked up, all loyalty centring in the king. When the kings of France succeeded in making all the under-feudatories take the oath direct to the king, they established themselves as the centre beyond all doubt. Under absolute personal government the king stands for *la loi*; his will—bound more or less by his coronation oath—is the standard and subject-matter of service due; his under-lords are subordinates commissioned to use their subordinates as his servants in so far as he may require.

The reality, to be sure, was never so systematic, and bred many other qualities, bad and good, besides its modicum of high-toned loyalty. It is, however, certain that such a system would profit by encouragement given to so useful a quality. Thus the situation was favourable to much praise of loyalty as a prime virtue in the mouths of the upper classes and, for this and other better reasons, in the mouths of their dependents—poets and men of letters generally, lawyers and all who had to do with the executive government, whether on the national or on the local scale.

As feudalism declined, or was broken up, the source of authority gradually defined itself anew as duplex in form: (1) the king administering the realm in accordance with the law, and (2) Parliament, *i.e.* the *élite* of the nation, Lords and Commons, wielding sole power by joint action with the king to change the law. The Lords were, in the first instance, the true peers of the king—the displaced feudal lords—and the old sentiment of feudal loyalty continued for long to be expected more or less by them and conceded less or more. As local magnates of one sort or another, they have in this country had a prolonged and honourable reign. In France they disappeared from view politically, as did the king himself, at the Revolution, and as later did the pseudo-king or emperor in 1870. England is still in process of change as regards the sentiment of the rural masses towards the aristocratic classes; but certainly it is no longer necessary to consider loyalty as a sentiment greatly affecting the relations between ordinary people and the Parliamentary peers who are lords of the soil. No historic sentiment of the kind attaches personally to the elect of the people in the House of Commons. Each commands the loyalty of his own supporters in his own constituency, so long as he and they are in general agreement on political issues. But he is not in any sense *la loi* to them, except in so far as he adopts, and with sufficient ability expounds, those principles of national policy which are common to them and him. Their feeling to him is rather that of fealty—not the maximum of fealty—than of loyalty: they support him so long as he continues to support that policy with which they continue to agree. Personal loyalties, of course, emerge, but they are not in the nature of the case. There is a very real loyalty, however, to 'the party' as a whole—either party—and to the leader of the party, also, more especially when he is an outstanding figure satisfactory to the moral sense, arresting to the imagination, strong and of a good courage.

But for the civilized world of Europe in general little importance in the first instance attached to

Parliament in any form as an object of loyalty. The king and the law emerge from the feudal system as claimants by moral right on the service of men. The sphere of service to which loyalty properly applies lies beyond and includes the sphere of duties and restrictions enforced under fear of punishment. Loyal service to the king included, as of course, loyal obedience to the law; but loyalty, no doubt, was more consciously directed to the king and fused with a sentiment rising to passionate personal devotion. The Bourbons in France and the Stuarts in England assumed themselves to be kings by Divine right after the manner of the Roman emperors—in effect, claimed all loyalty, and from many obtained it, as due to the king. The revolt in England took its stand on the law as binding on the will of kings, and claimed restitution of the people's rights as guaranteed by ancient charter. The English Revolution of the 17th cent. was, in effect, not a revolution but a restoration of the ancient constitution, cleared, however, of feudal complications, the great Whig families standing with the common people, and the Royalists, who more especially esteemed themselves as loyalists, with the defeated dynasty. In due course there emerged from the welter of pitiful plots and gallant endeavour on the one hand, and conflicting interests around the court *de facto* on the other, the British Constitution—or rather its first edition—with all its 20th cent. characteristics latent, and sure to develop, in it.

Here it is, a sufficiently complex object of loyal regard:

(1) The law of the land as the one authority which *all* must obey; and all commands by persons in office must be in accordance with it.

(2) King, Lords, and Commons making one Parliament; and these three only, and by consent of each, can change that law, order taxation, or decree the appropriation of the revenue to the uses of the Executive Government.

(3) The King and his ministers, by whose advice all his decrees are made, whom he appoints by the established custom of the constitution from the leaders of the political party which commands a majority in the House of Commons; the maintenance of this custom is guaranteed by the Commons' hold on the Power of the Purse.[1]

So there emerged slowly in England the modern State, which has emerged elsewhere more suddenly and with less of the attractive complexity of detail which links it with its own historic past. This is what stands for *la loi* to the modern Englishman. As an object of loyalty it has advantages over some other examples of the 'Mixed State.' Not only is the British Constitution built as it is in order to preserve intact the ancient liberties of the people, but it has been built, bit after bit, by the very act of maintaining them. It is apt, therefore, to excite a high degree of enthusiasm in the minds of all those who care about history, all those who lay store by the liberties of the people and the powers of the House of Commons. To them the members of that House, and especially the two front benches, whichever party is in power, constitute the political aristocracy, in the fine Platonic sense. If they are loyal citizens, they will be loyal in the full sense to their own front bench, and law-abiding to the other front bench if it happens to be in power. In stormy times, when great principles, on one or other or both sides, are at stake, the adherents of the party likely to be defeated steady their minds to bear the shock by a very real loyalty, pitched finely in the more abstract key of devotion to the Crown and Constitution, whatever betide. This sentiment is effectively upheld by the consciousness of historic continuity throughout all changes, each having been effected by self-evolution within the Constitution itself; the King's prerogatives that have come under the power of the Commons have done so by the King's consent; the House of Lords, too, in 1911, submitted to the limitation of its veto.

5. Grades and modes of loyal sentiment in modern life.—Among persons outside the large circle who take deep interest in political problems the sentiment of political loyalty is probably in many cases practically non-existent, or at least very shallow, except, indeed, when roused by some real or imaginary national danger. This, no doubt, is the reason why some newspapers bristle with intimations of national danger when, a general election being at hand, it seems necessary to awaken the latent patriotism of voters. Of the others—the great majority, it may be hoped—there are those to whom the ideal of the nation to be served, in some small way or other as one can, makes a constant appeal as steady as that of his lord to the devoted henchman. For some this social service lies entirely outside the sphere of State control; for others it consists in service under, or co-operation with, the State. In all cases it is better done by those who understand the ways of the public administration as it is related to their work, so that they may use it to better effect by working loyally with it. State Insurance, Old Age Pensions, and recent legislation for the benefit of children are cases in point; voluntary workers disposed to loyal co-operation can do much. No form of loyalty is more honourable than this.

Quiet, non-political people, whose sphere of work or leisure does not impinge at all on public affairs, do very often, nevertheless, take a keen interest in the doings of the State and have a certain loyalty for King and Constitution, or King and Country, which, though not productive of any service, is quite real in its way. Without party-bias for the most part, they are proud of the whole complex system under which they live, with preferences in attachment, it may be, to one or other constituent in it. This class includes all 'armchair politicians' except that large section of 'armchair political critics.' There is the 'philosophic radical,' watching for signs of the social millennium in the House of Commons. There is the Tory gentleman of 'the good old school,' who has not lost faith in the future, and still sees the Constitution as he would wish to see it. There is the genuine Royalist, who anticipates great things in the future, of which he seldom speaks, from the character and ability of the Royal family, and believes generally that events are moving steadily in the direction of absolute monarchy, world-wide and British, a century or so hence. Others there are, without any preconceptions as to an absolute best towards which we are tending, who have a comfortable loyalty for things as they are. These, if they have votes, tend to support the ministry of the day. Their existence is one reason why it is better in general, when the sands are running out, for the ministry to dissolve than to resign.

6. Loyalty in the public services.—Persons who are in the service of the State are, of course, the servants of the Executive. Efficient service according to agreement, reticence in confidential matters, and abstinence from public comment on the policy either of the ministry they serve or of the opposition they may have to serve—these make up the obvious minimum of their bounden duty. To reach the maximum two things are needed: (1) zeal in the service because it is the service, and (2) self-identification with the instructions under which they work, or loyal adherence to the leader under whom they serve. Under adverse circumstances

[1] Since the battle of the Constitution had been fought to a large extent on the people's claim to be taxed only by their own consent, given by a majority of their elected representatives in the House of Commons, it was inevitable that the Power of the Purse should be stoutly claimed and rigorously retained by the Commons; and from this it followed, by the logic of events, that no ministry could remain in power that did not command the confidence of the Lower House.

these conditions may fail to be possible in whole or part; in that case the loyal temper still shows itself by putting the best face upon the matter and keeping silence.

It is in the military and naval services more particularly that the idea of service, as to the king direct, counts for most. Here we are back to primitive requirements. The soldier is under bond to risk his life at the word of command. Respect for this word is vital to his character—respect without limits—and this, in the last resort, is self-devotion unto death. The good soldier's loyalty, no doubt, is often fealty pure and simple, as, *e.g.*, it certainly is when he has naturally no sentimental tie to the service in which he finds himself. Normally, however, we may take it to be a compound mixed in various proportions, into which enter loyal attachments to his sovereign, his country, his leader, his comrades, and the flag he follows, the last being a symbol of all these things and of his own self-respect as bound to stand or fall by them.

7. Problems arising from the complexity of the modern State.—Casual reference has been made above to non-political loyalty as between friends, lovers, kindred, and the members of a voluntary group or a natural social order. Clearly this is not the primary application of the word, but the tendency to use it in this, rather than in the political, sense appears to be on the increase. This is due, no doubt, to that confusion of ideas as to the political object of loyalty consequent on the complexity of the modern State. Angry politicians are apt to use the word 'disloyal' rashly to denote persons who differ from themselves as to the right balance of power in the State and the focus, consequently, of right loyalty. Thus claims have sometimes been made in the name of loyalty to right of attack on the lawfully constituted State, as, *e.g.*, in the case of constitutional reform to which a minority strongly objects. This implies confusion of ideas between the State in some special sense—*e.g.*, apart from the principle of development which it contains—and the State as it is, including its provision of a sovereign authority empowered by law and precedent to make changes in all things, including itself. A somewhat wilful confusion of ideas to the opposite effect is also possible between hostility to the *personnel* and policy of the ministry of the day, which is the normal motive-force that sways the political pendulum, and disloyalty to the sovereign Parliament which happens to be led by that ministry, and the majority of which takes responsibility for its doings. The complex character of the modern State lends itself to such confusion of feeling in times of stress and change. Every attempt at large reform divides the citizens into two camps, each vowing loyalty to its own ideal of the State in some particular. This is party loyalty, which is quite consistent, as the inner circles fully understand, with perfect loyalty to the actual State as by law established—that self-conserving, self-developing organization of King, Lords, and Commons with which we are all familiar. An attractive focus for the loyal sentiment of the simple or careless citizen, who makes no attempt to join issue in the political dialectic, is provided by the presence in the trio of the hereditary monarch in his uplifted place, holding his supreme veto to be used only on the side of the majority in the House of Commons, subject to the delaying powers of the House of Lords. The number of persons in Britain whose sole effective loyalty centres in attachment to the Crown is probably large; it counts doubtless for much also in the British colonies.

8. The focus of loyalty in republican nations.—In republican States this focus is supplied—so far as it is supplied at all—by a more vivid consciousness of the organized nation as a self-governing whole, the ark of whose covenant is the Constitution. The ideal of the republic as the lode-star of loyal sentiment is highly developed in France. The French mind has perhaps a natural genius for the concrete ideal, as indeed is perhaps implied by its turn of speech in favour of thought—eloquent thought—by means of generic terms that fire the imagination. In the United States of America loyal affection is rather to the composite nation in reference to all its interests, each more or less on its own—a wonderful 'Union' of diverse elements, run by a carefully planned political machine, which would do its work much better if all the citizens in every section were more enthusiastic in serving it according to their lights. The ideal of the Republic as an organization of free citizens for purposes of self-government seems to have lost for a time something of its pristine freshness and attractive force. At any rate, it is of the United States rather than of the United States Republic that many Americans think as the focus of their political loyalty. This much may be said in their defence. The good of the nation is, of course, in all cases the ultimate end of the political art, and the final object, therefore, of that sentiment which reveres as its proximate end the national institutions.

9. The ideal of loyalty.—To be loyal is to be much more than law-abiding. Whether the object be a person to whom we owe duty or affection, the community of persons to which we belong, the institutions under which we live, the service to which we are pledged, or the law—human or divine—by which we ought to regulate our conduct, the loyal man is distinguished from the law-abiding man as one who serves with his whole heart and mind, making of himself a veritable organ of expression for the purpose, or the master, or the mandate, under which he serves. No voluntary sins of commission, omission, or ignorance does he permit himself. We realize him at his time of special effort in a passion of service, every faculty awake and urgent to achieve his end. And in the intervals of passivity his mind is clear and steady—stayed, as it were, on his whole nature as a rock. Self-training to this effect in any school of wholesome service must work like a leaven on character as a whole. Even under questionable conditions of service it goes far, as all experience of public service shows, to make a man. But it must be remembered that, without either a morally attractive cause or wise and sympathetic leadership, the loyal sentiment which is the motive of self-training is not adequately evoked.

History and literature abound in examples. Three lines of thought, independent of each other and contrasted, may be distinguished in their logical order here.

(*a*) *The heroic romance of Western Europe*, developing through the centuries from its original sources in Classic, Celtic, and Norse or Germanic lore, deals largely in loyalties within the smaller social sphere, intimate, personal, and glorified by affection. Patriotic loyalty in this dawn of the civilized world has little to do with government, but is steeped in a vivid idealism; the race-life and the home-land are seen as of infinite value, objects in effect of religious faith, worthy of devotion through all suffering unto death. These are the primitive loyalties—to kindred, friendship, race, and land. Nor is the spirit which forms them dead; it does not die so long as a race either vaguely or clearly believes in itself as having a part of some kind in the fulfilment of human destiny. This is why the history of any nation true to itself is capable of being treated as the development of an ideal implicit from the first.

(*b*) For the ideal of personal virtue relative to civic institutions, and for the fundamental theory of the State even as we know it to-day, we go back to the Greeks, and specially to *Plato in The Republic and The Laws.* It is his conception of the individual soul in relation to the State that concerns us here. The ideal of the State, as he teaches, should be built up within the soul. Thus —wedding his thought to our inquiry—we may say that the soul of the loyal citizen is trained, or trains itself, into accordance with the ideals realized in the constitution of the State. Thus he exceeds the law-abiding, and is the loyal, man. Further, it is implied in Plato's thought that of those who have political power the loyal ones are they who cultivate their philosophic aptitude to perfect the ideal of the State in the soul, in order that they may labour to develop the organization of the real State and bring it into harmony with the ideal.

This obviously is what the sincere modern statesman does, or thinks he is doing. It is a necessary part of his loyalty that he should spare no pains to do it. Moreover, in the modern self-governing State, every enfranchised citizen shares this duty.

(*c*) Finally, we find in *post-Exilic Judaism* the supreme example of a people held together by allegiance to the law—the law embodied in a written code that he who runs may read. The Davidic monarchy had come to an end; the high priest held the supreme office as chief ruler in the little theocratic State. But from the time that Ezra had read in the ears of the people all the words of the book of the law which he had brought from Babylon,[1] the Jew who was faithful and pious felt that the law was above the priesthood and that he was to obey it and understand it for himself. Externally the Jewish people had many masters after this; internally—in his own mind—each pious Jew spent all his loyal sentiment on the law of his God. This was no short commandment, but the whole law, dealing with conduct in all social relations and with ceremonial ordinances in considerable detail. The Jew who loyally obeyed the law was, in quiet times—except for taxation—to all intents and purposes a free man. The ideal of his State in its essentials was built up in the mind of the properly instructed Jew; if a professing Jew, he obeyed, whether grudgingly, willingly, or loyally, *i.e.* with his whole heart seeking to understand and to obey more perfectly. In that perfect inward obedience his freedom was realized, though it was not his quest. The Psalms and the Prophets abound in expressions of this loyalist spirit applied to the Supreme Law:

'Teach me, O Lord, the way of thy statutes;
And I will keep it unto the end.
Give me understanding, and I shall keep thy law;
Yea, I shall observe it with my whole heart' (Ps 119[33ff.]).

So runs the Psalmist's typical prayer, and it continues in the same strain, asking for help to go in the path, to incline his heart aright, to turn away his heart from vanity, to establish God's word unto His servant. In NT times, when the elaborated legalism of the latter-day Pharisees prevailed, the great Master Teacher set over against it the true doctrine of loyal observance, the fulfilment of the law by being the kind of person who expresses its purpose naturally in all his acts. 'I am not come to destroy, but to fulfil' (Mt 5[17]). 'A good man out of the good treasure of his heart bringeth forth that which is good' (Lk 6[45]). And later, St. Paul, following the same line of thought, attains to the vision of the 'liberty of the sons of God' (Ro 8[21]). Thus the cycle of reason on the highest as on all lower planes is complete, from the free man's fealty through loyalty to the higher liberty of devoted service to the ideal in his soul.

LITERATURE.—Little of note appears to have been written dealing directly with this subject. (1) It enters into the history of the development of the State more especially as a serviceable motive-force in the mediæval growth of the feudal system: see *Cambridge Mediæval History*, ii. [1913], ch. xx., 'Foundations of Society' (Origins of Feudalism), and F. Warre Cornish, *Chivalry*, London, 1901; *Essays on Romance and Chivalry*, do. 1870, containing reprints from Hallam and Sir Walter Scott, are also interesting. (2) The primitive ideal of heroic character to which the political virtue corresponds may be studied in Celtic and Teutonic hero lore and in their later developments, (*a*) under the influence of mediæval chivalry, and (*b*) in recent years. Sufficient exemplification will be found in *Völsunga Saga* and *Grettir the Strong*, tr. E. Magnusson and W. Morris, *Three Northern Love Stories*, London, 1875; E. Hull, *Cuchulain, the Hound of Ulster*, do. 1911; T. W. Rolleston, *The High Deeds of Finn*, do. 1910; T. Malory, *Morte d'Arthur*, ed. do. 1894, and its primitive prototype, the Welsh *Mabinogion*, tr. Lady Charlotte Guest, do. 1877.

S. BRYANT.

LOYOLA.—St. Ignatius Loyola, the founder of the Jesuits (*q.v.*), was the youngest of the eight sons of Don Beltrán Yañez de Oñez y Loyola. The name Lopez de Ricalde, by which Ignatius is often designated (so, *e.g.*, in *AS* and in the British Museum Catalogue), is a simple blunder, due originally to the carelessness of a notary. He was born in the house, or *casa*, of Loyola near Azpeitia in the Basque province of Guipuzcoa. The year of his birth is disputed. Astrain (*Hist. de la Compañia de Jesús*, i. 3 ff.), the best modern authority, assigns it to 1491, but others have thought 1495 more probable (cf. Tacchi Venturi, in *Civiltà Cattolica*, 21st July 1900). The name Ignatius, by which Loyola is now generally known, was not that which he himself used in his youth. Down to 1537 Inigo (not, however, Iñígo, as Astrain prints it) was his invariable signature, but he then began to use sometimes Ignacio, sometimes Inigo, and after 1542 Inigo hardly occurs at all. It seems certain, though early biographers intent on edification have glossed over the fact, that the future ascetic passed an unbridled youth, following the course which was then almost inevitable for all who adopted the career of arms (Astrain, i. 12–16). But at the siege of Pampeluna in 1521 he was dangerously wounded by a cannon-ball, and in a long convalescence which followed he gave himself up to reading the lives of Christ and the Saints, with the result that, after many inward conflicts, he determined to make a complete change in his own way of living. As soon as he was able to travel, he journeyed to the monastery of Monserrat, made a very devout confession, and, after a sort of vigil of arms, divested himself of his knightly attire and went forth to beg his bread. He then took refuge for nearly a year in a cavern near Manresa. The life that he led in this retreat was one of terrible self-maceration, marked by tempestuous inward trials of which he has left a relatively full account in the autobiography. It was during his stay at Manresa that he drew out at least the broad outlines of that manual of ascetical discipline so widely famed under the name of the *Book of the Spiritual Exercises*. There seems no reason to claim such originality for this system of spiritual training as to exclude the influence of earlier ascetical writers like Garcia de Cisneros of Monserrat (see J. M. Besse, in *Revue des questions historiques*, lxi. [Paris, 1897] 22–51) and especially Gerard de Zutphen and Johannes Mauburnus, Brothers of the Common Life; but, as Watrigant has shown, the combination of these materials into one instrument employed for a clearly recognized and uniformly consistent purpose is entirely the work of Ignatius,

[1] 'The law of thy God which is in thine hand' it is called in the decree of the great king Artaxerxes (Ezr 7[14]).

and bears the imprint of his eminently practical mind.

It must always be remembered that the *Spiritual Exercises* is not a book intended merely for reading and reflexion, but a manual of training to be put into practice. In this it differs *toto cœlo* from such a work as À Kempis's *Imitation of Christ*, and it would be as vain to expect literary graces in the *Exercises* as in a proposition of Euclid. After some preliminary considerations on the end of man, the exercitant is directed, during a week or ten days and always under the advice of a competent spiritual guide, to occupy his mind with the recollection of his past sins and of the punishment which they have deserved, and to cultivate a sense of shame and sorrow, bringing external adjuncts to bear to deepen the impression—*e.g.*, by depriving himself of light, warmth, unnecessary food, and all intercourse with his fellows. After this preliminary discipline, he is introduced to the study of the life of Jesus Christ, who is set before him in two powerful military parables as a chieftain appealing for volunteers to aid Him in the task of reconquering the world from the dominion of sin and the devil. It is easy to see that Loyola's thought had been powerfully influenced by the still vivid remembrance of the struggle to rescue the soil of Spain from the yoke of the infidel. The meditations of this 'second week' of the *Exercises* are estimated to occupy another ten days. By this time it is assumed that the well-disposed exercitant will have been brought to the point of resolving to leave all things and follow Christ if God should make it plain that He was calling him to a life of humiliation and self-sacrifice. A formal election of a state of life is introduced, accordingly, at this stage, and the two remaining 'weeks' of the *Exercises* are intended to confirm the choice so made. In the third week the exercitant is bidden to use much bodily penance and to meditate upon the Passion of Christ; in the fourth he is directed to allow the body its meed of rest and refreshment, while the mind is occupied with consoling thoughts derived from the consideration of the Resurrection of our Saviour and the remembrance of the joys of heaven.

It was natural that one who laid so much stress upon the study of our Lord's life upon earth should feel the need of coming as closely as possible into contact with the scenes of those events with which his mind was filled. Accordingly, in Feb. 1523 Ignatius set out on a pilgrimage to Jerusalem, living on alms and, to a large extent, travelling on foot. He passed through Rome and Venice, and thence sailed to the Holy Land, so that almost a year elapsed before he found himself back in Barcelona. That he was specially called to labour 'for the greater glory of God' had by this time become a deep conviction, but the precise manner in which he was to further the work of Christ on earth does not seem to have been made clear to him until many years later (see F. Van Ortroy, 'Manrèse et les origines de la Compagnie de Jésus,' in *Analecta Bollandiana*, xxvii. [1908] 393–418). Still, he seems to have realized, at least vaguely, that to become an efficient instrument for good he required a better education than he then possessed. Thus we find him at the age of 33 learning the rudiments of Latin with the school-children of Barcelona (1524–26), and thence proceeding to the Universities of Alcalá and Salamanca (1526–28). A personality like that of Loyola was bound to influence men wherever he went, and it is not altogether surprising that he fell under the suspicion of the Inquisition, on account of the disciples who gathered round him and who imitated in some measure his own austerity of life. At first he seems to have been careless of what men said of him, conscious of his own integrity; but later he found that these suspicions hampered his influence for good, and he went out of his way to court and even to insist upon a judicial inquiry. The proceedings before the Inquisition, so far as they have been preserved, are printed in the *Scripta de Sancto Ignatio*, i. 580–629. Partly on account of the hindrances to his work for souls which these suspicions engendered, partly, it would seem, in the hope of finding companions more in harmony with his ideals than any whom he had yet met (see Fouqueray, *Histoire*, i. 7 f.), Ignatius, in Feb. 1528, made his way to the University of Paris. There at the Collège de Montaigu and afterwards at that of Sainte-Barbe he pursued his studies for the priesthood. At Sainte-Barbe he must, at least occasionally, have encountered Calvin, who had studied there himself and still visited it in 1533. For his support Ignatius, owing in part to his unselfish generosity to his countrymen, had to depend upon alms, and during the begging expeditions made in the vacation season to that end he visited London, Bruges, and Antwerp. Contradictions and persecutions in abundance were also still his portion, but in Paris he found at last what his heart had always craved—a group of companions capable of sympathizing in his high ideals, and of an intellectual force which lent real weight to any cause which they undertook. The story of his conquest of Francis Xavier by the constant repetition of the words 'What doth it profit a man if he gain the whole world and suffer the loss of his own soul?' is well known. An even earlier recruit was Peter Le Fèvre, whose position in the University was already an influential one. To them were added James Laynez, Francis Salmeron, Simon Rodriguez, and Nicholas Bobadilla. Laynez and Salmeron were destined to play a great part as theologians in the Council of Trent. Laynez was also to be Loyola's successor as second General of the Society. But even in 1534, when on 15th Aug. these friends met together in the chapel of St. Denys at Montmartre, and at the mass of Le Fèvre, who was so far the only priest amongst them, took vows of poverty and chastity (Astrain, i. 79), there seems to have been as yet no clear design of founding a religious Order. The third vow, which they added to the other two, pledged them only to make the attempt to undertake apostolic work in the Holy Land; but if, after a year's waiting, it was found impossible to obtain passage thither, in that case they were to place themselves at the disposition of the pope, for any work that he might assign them. This it was that actually happened. In the middle of 1537 war broke out between the Sultān Sulaimān and the Venetian Republic. There was no longer any possibility of obtaining a passage to the Holy Land. The little band of companions waited the prescribed year, and meanwhile Ignatius himself was ordained priest at Venice (24th June 1537), and he and his companions spent the interval in serving in the hospitals and in apostolic work in many different Italian towns. Eventually it was decided that they ought to address themselves to the pope, then Paul III., and, in spite of contradictions, they had a most favourable reception. It was apparently only at this time that the desirability of organization as a formally recognized religious society living under obedience seemed to take shape in their minds. It was characteristic of Ignatius that he always attached much more importance to the inward spirit than to the written letter. Even after he had recognized the fact that in order to perpetuate their work they must be bound together in some regular institute, he was reluctant to provide written constitutions. But the various stages in the development of the Order now followed rapidly. Already in 1537 the companions had found it necessary to give themselves a collective name, and they agreed that, if interrogated, they should describe themselves as belonging to the 'Company of Jesus' (Astrain, i. 89). When they had found favour with the pope, the scheme of a definite religious institute (*formula instituti*) was drafted, and approved in the bull *Regimini militantis ecclesiæ*, 27th Sept. 1540. On 4th April 1541 Ignatius, in spite of his own reluctance, was elected superior, and from that date until 1550 he busied himself at Rome in compiling constitutions. The spread of the Society was extraordinarily rapid, and, as the twelve volumes of his correspondence attest, the official business connected with his office of General steadily increased day by day until his death on 31st July 1556. Ignatius was interested, and he considered it the duty of his subjects to be interested, in every form of religious work which was for the greater glory of God. Although the Society of Jesus was the backbone of the Counter-Reformation movement, it would be a mistake to regard the Order as having been instituted with the conscious design of counteracting the religious teaching of Luther and Calvin. The central idea, which is found alike in the *Exercises* and in numberless passages of the *Constitutions*, and which may be taken as the dominant conception of the whole Ignatian spirituality, was the desire to assist in and carry on the work of rescue and sanctification for which Jesus Christ had come on earth. Loyola was not in any way a man of brilliant intellectual gifts, but he possessed clear judgment and indomitable energy; and, contrary to the idea so often formed of his religious descendants, he was by the testimony of all who knew him a man who was absolutely fearless and straightforward in all his relations with others. He was beatified in 1609 and canonized in 1622.

LITERATURE.—The first place among the sources for the life of Ignatius Loyola must always be given to the so-called 'Autobiography,' dictated by the Saint to Luis Gonzalez de Camara. A Latin version is printed in *AS*, 31st July, vii., but a more accurate text in the original, partly Spanish and partly Italian, has been provided in the *Monumenta Ignatiana, Scripta de S. Ignatio* (i. 31–98), which form part of the great collection of *Monumenta Historica Societatis Jesu* (Madrid, 1894 ff.), edited by the Spanish Jesuits. In fact, the whole contents of the *Monumenta Ignatiana*, which include a critical ed., in 12 vols., of Loyola's own letters and official documents, are of first-rate importance. An Eng. tr. of the *Autobiography* (by E. M. Rix), with notes, appeared under the title *The Testament of Ignatius Loyola*, London, 1900. See also J. Susta, 'Ignatius von Loyola's Selbstbiographie,' in *Mitteilungen des Inst. für österr. Geschichtsforschung*, xxvi. [1905] 45–106. A vast number of papers and letters which bear upon the history of Ignatius and his first companions may be found in the other volumes of the *Monumenta Historica Soc. Jesu*. The biography of Ignatius by Pedro Ribadeneira, which appeared originally in more than one redaction—the first at Naples, in 1572—is also re-edited in *AS*, *loc. cit.* A young disciple of the saint, who knew him and lived with him, Ribadeneira is an important authority. Translations of this life have been published in French and many other languages. Of the 17th cent. biographies of Loyola by far the most valuable is that of D. Bartoli, who had important original materials at his command. The best available ed. is in French, with supplementary notes, by L. Michel (Bartoli, *Histoire de S. Ignace de Loyola*, 2 vols., Lille, 1893). Of other lives the best are C. Genelli, *Das Leben des heil. Ignatius von Loyola*, Innsbruck, 1848, Eng. tr.[2], London, 1881; 'Stewart Rose,' *Life of St. Ignatius Loyola*[3], London, 1891; F. Thompson, *Life of St. Ignatius*, do. 1910. An excellent short sketch is that of H. Joly (*St. Ignace de Loyola*[5], Paris, 1904, Eng. tr., London, 1899). But by far the most trustworthy source of information among modern works is to be found in A. Astrain, *Historia de la Compañía de Jesús*, i., Madrid, 1902, this volume being entirely devoted to the period of the life of Ignatius. It may be supplemented for French affairs by H. Fouqueray, *Histoire de la Compagnie de Jésus en France*, i., Paris, 1910; and for those of Italy by P. Tacchi Venturi, *Storia della Compagnia di Gesù in Italia*, i., Rome, 1909. See also J. Creixell, *San Ignacio en Barcelona*, Barcelona, 1906.

Few of those who have studied the life of Loyola from an antagonistic or Protestant standpoint seem to have taken the trouble to acquaint themselves accurately even with the facts of his career. The best is perhaps E. Gothein, *Ignatius von Loyola und die Gegenreformation*, Halle, 1895, but on this see *Analecta Bollandiana*, xv. [1896] 449–454. Even more fantastic is H. Müller, *Les Origines de la Compagnie de Jésus*, Paris, 1898, on which cf. *The Month*, xciv. [1899] 516–526. Some valuable materials and criticisms are, however, contained in the work, very hostile in tone, of the ex-Jesuit M. Mir, *Historia interna documentada de la Compañía de Jesús*, Madrid, 1913. Other points of criticism are dealt with by B. Duhr, *Jesuitenfabeln*[4], Freiburg i. B., 1904; H. Stoeckius, *Forschungen zur Lebensordnung der Gesellschaft Jesu im 16ten Jahrhundert*, Munich, 1910 ff.

The only works of St. Ignatius besides his letters are the *Spiritual Exercises* and the *Constitutions of the Society of Jesus*. A facsimile of the 'autograph' of the Spanish original of the *Ejercicios Espirituales* was published in Rome in 1908; innumerable other editions, including several English translations, have been published in every language. The most illuminating discussion of the genesis of the *Exercises* is supplied by H. Watrigant, *La Genèse des Exercices de S. Ignace*, Amiens, 1897. As to the *Constitutions*, a facsimile of the original Spanish text has appeared, *Constituciones de la Compañía de Jesús, reproduccion fototípica*, Rome, 1898, with valuable illustrative material.

HERBERT THURSTON.

LUCIAN.—See ANTIOCHENE THEOLOGY.

LUCK.—See CALENDAR, CHARMS AND AMULETS, DIVINATION.

LUCRETIUS.—Titus Lucretius Carus was a Roman poet (99 [?]–55 B.C.) who, in the last century of the republic, accepted the philosophy of Epicurus, and expounded it to his countrymen in a noble didactic poem, entitled *de Rerum Natura*.

1. Life and writings. — Little is known of Lucretius except a notice in Jerome's additions to the Eusebian chronicle, under the year of Abraham 1923 (=94 B.C.):

'Titus Lucretius poeta nascitur. Postea amatorio poculo in furorem versus, cum aliquot libros per intervalla insaniæ conscripsisset, quos postea Cicero emendavit, propria se manu interfecit anno ætatis quadragesimo quarto.'

This strange story of madness and suicide, which Tennyson has made familiar, is no doubt derived ultimately from Suetonius, *de Vir. Illust.*, and, if it comes from such an antiquary, probably has a basis of fact (cf. Lachmann on i. 922, p. 63 of his ed.; Munro[4], ii. 1 ff.; Sellar, *Roman Poets of the Republic*, p. 283 ff.). But there is an error of four or five years either in the birth year or in the age assigned to the poet, most likely in the former. According to Donatus (*Vit. Verg.*), Lucretius died on 15th October 55 B.C., and not, as Jerome's figures would imply, in 51 or 50 B.C. This is confirmed by the earliest extant mention of the poem in a letter of Cicero to his brother Quintus (*ad Quint. fr.*, II. ix. 4). This letter, written early in 54 B.C., presupposes the publication of the poem and, presumably, the poet's death. For on internal evidence alone most scholars agree that *de Rerum Natura*, like Vergil's *Æneid*, never received a final revision from the author's hand; certain passages, especially in the last three books, seem to be afterthoughts or additions imperfectly adjusted to their context. In the dearth of external testimony, something may be gleaned from the poem itself. It seems clear that the author was a Roman noble, well acquainted with the luxury of the time (ii. 24–28, iv. 75 ff., 973, 1121) and with the rivalry and ambition of political life (ii. 11 ff., 40 ff., v. 1120 ff.). Strongly impressed by the crime and bloodshed of the civil wars (i. 29 f., 40–43, iii. 70–74, v. 999 ff.), he deliberately chose, almost alone among the Romans, a contemplative life (i. 922 ff., ii. 1 ff., iii. 1 ff.). Further, we see that he possessed a poet's clear, minute, exact observation with a poet's love of nature and delight in open-air scenes (i. 280 ff., 305, 326, 404 ff., ii. 144–149, 323–332, 342 ff., 349 ff., 361 ff., 374 ff., 766 f., iv. 220, 575, v. 256, 991 ff., vi. 256–261, 472), that he had unbounded reverence for Epicurus, both as a scientific discoverer and as a moral reformer (iii. 9–30, v. 1 ff., vi. 1 ff.), that Democritus and Empedocles were also objects of respectful admiration (i. 729–733, iii. 371, 1039), and that he never mentions the Stoics or the Socratic Schools, although sometimes alluding to their doctrines, 'quod quidam fingunt' (i. 371; cf. 690 ff., 1083, ii. 167–176). He dedicated the work to Memmius, the patron of Catullus, who was prætor in 58 B.C., and at that time an opponent of Cæsar. He addresses Memmius as an equal; the Lucretii belong to a gens distinguished in the early annals of Rome, and the cognomen Carus is said to be attested by an inscription. The author's purpose in writing a philosophical treatise in verse is clearly explained (i. 54 ff., esp. 106–145, 922–950, iv. 1–25). His aim is genuinely scientific—to gain our assent to certain propositions concerning the atomic theory (bks. i. and ii.) and its applications to the relations of mind and body (bk. iii.), the wraiths or images whence he deduces the popular belief in the future life (bk. iv.), the origin of our world, of civilization, and of language (bk. v.), and the phenomena of sky or earth which are supposed to come from the vengeance of the gods, such as thunder, tempests, earthquakes, and volcanoes (bk. vi.). He admits that the system which he advocates is unpopular (iv. 18 ff.), and fears that Memmius will some day fall away (i. 102 ff.). He therefore provides an antidote. Poetry is the honey at the edge of the cup which shall make palatable the medicine of truth. It is no less obvious that the sympathy evoked in the reader, the effect upon his imagination, is bound up with the philosophic poet's soaring frenzy ('furor arduus'; Statius, *Sil.* II. vii. 76). A philosophical argument is ill-adapted for hexameter verse, but the mental power and perseverance displayed in so arduous an undertaking call for unstinted admiration. The difficulties of his task spur the poet on, and to overcome them so far as may be is at once his merit and his delight. His grasp of his subject with all its perplexities and problems bespeaks a logical mind, and he is eminently successful in discovering and marshalling whole groups of particular facts which lead up to and illustrate a general principle (i. 159–214, 265–328, ii. 333–380, 581–699), in the use of analogies, and in vividly picturing the consequences of hypotheses (i. 215–264, 968 ff., 988–995). It has been conjectured that the poet followed the larger epitome of Epicurean doctrine mentioned by Diogenes Laertius (x. 39 f., 73 [Giussani, i. 10]). Whether this is so or his choice and arrangement of topics are dictated by his own immediate purpose must remain an open question. In any case the idolatry of the disciple and his close study of the master's writings (iii. 10) afford a reasonable certainty that he introduced no innovations in substance, although the exposition, with its flights of imagination, its flashes of feeling, and its insight, is all his own. In what follows attention is directed to those parts of the system only where Lucretius fills a gap in the scanty outlines left by Epicurus himself or gives a fuller treatment of particular doctrines (see EPICUREANS).

2. **Atomic theory.**—Lucretius begins by advancing the two propositions (1) that nothing can arise out of nothing, and (2) that nothing can be annihilated, which he proves separately from the order and regularity of the processes of nature, as especially seen in the generation of the species of organic life. The obvious objection that we cannot see the particles dispersed when a thing is destroyed is met with a series of analogies from the potent invisible agencies at work in the world. The existence of empty space (vacuum or void) is then proved from the impossibility of otherwise accounting for motion, which all the facts of experience confirm. The opposite view, that the world is a plenum, is next refuted mainly by the consideration that condensation and expansion no less than motion imply the existence of a vacuum. Next, the existence of any *tertium quid* other than body and empty space is denied. All other nameable things, even time itself, must be regarded as the qualities (whether essential properties or transient accidents) of these two forms of reality. Body is then divided into simple and composite, according as it is or is not conjoined with void. The composite are what we call things (*res genitæ*), the simple bodies are atoms (*materies, corpora genitalia, semina rerum, principia, elementa*, or simply *corpora*). To postulate the existence of atoms is to deny the infinite divisibility of matter. And here again Lucretius employs his favourite negative procedure, following out the consequences of infinite divisibility to absolute annihilation, which he has proved impossible. Infinite divisibility would be incompatible with the natural laws (*fœdera naturæ*) which regulate the production of things and the permanence of organic species; for, unless the constituent atoms of things are unchangeable, there will be no uniformity of nature, and it will be uncertain what can and what cannot arise.

Summing up these arguments and collecting what is said elsewhere in the poem, we arrive at the following conception: an atom is a little hard kernel of matter, quite solid and therefore immutable and indestructible (since heat, cold, and moisture, the destroyers of the composite things about us, cannot enter where no void exists). Each atom is a distinct individual ('solida pollentia simplicitate'); it is perfectly elastic; it has minimal parts, of which, however, it is not compounded, for they have no independent existence; hence it has size, shape, and weight, but no secondary qualities, no colour or temperature, no sound, flavour, or smell, no sentience, the different qualities of composite things being due to the variety of atomic shapes, which, though very great, is not infinite.

After refuting the divergent views of Heraclitus, Empedocles, and Anaxagoras (i. 635–920), Lucretius proves by a variety of arguments that both matter and space are infinite, and refutes the opposing view that all things tend to the centre of the universe and the assumption of antipodes which it involves. He subsequently deduces from infinite space and infinite matter an infinite number of worlds, which come into being, grow to maturity, and ultimately perish (ii. 1023–1174).

3. **Clinamen or swerving.**—Atoms are in constant motion. They move through space (1) by their own inherent motion, and (2) in consequence of collision. Some atoms of intricate shape form after collision a close union, thus giving rise to the things we call hard; others rebound to greater distances and thus form softer substances; others, again, do not unite at all, but wander freely through space. It is next shown how by imperceptible motions (*motus intestini*) atomic groups or molecules increase in complexity and size until they reach the limits of visibility, like motes in the sunbeam (ii. 125–141). It will help us to understand the relation between these internal atomic movements and the motion of the group of atoms as a whole, if we take Giussani's admirable illustration (i. 111 ff.): as a swarm of insects moves slowly through the air in one direction, the individual insects of which it is composed are executing all manner of far more rapid movements, some of them in divergent or even opposite directions. The first motion of atoms, always through empty space, is inconceivably rapid and uniformly in the same downward direction; the apparent upward motion of some sensible things is shown to be not inconsistent with this. But at quite uncertain times and places atoms, travelling downwards by their own weight, and therefore in parallel lines, swerve a very little from the perpendicular. The least possible change of inclination must be assumed, although it is imperceptible to the senses. Otherwise atoms would never collide, so as to unite and give birth to things, for in empty space, where there is no resisting medium, heavy and

light atoms fall with equal velocity, so that the heavier would not overtake the lighter. There is a further proof of this in the consciousness of spontaneous initiative, the power by which each living creature goes forward whither the will leads, the something which struggles and resists when we move involuntarily under compulsion (ii. 216–293). For our spontaneous movements originate in sole atoms, and their existence at all can be explained only by assuming a certain indeterminism or contingency in the movements of such sole atoms. Thus the mind does not feel an internal necessity in all its actions, nor is all motion linked together in an unending chain of cause and effect (as the Stoics maintained), but atoms initiate motion, breaking through the decrees of fate. It will be seen that the postulate of uniformity—the decrees of nature which govern the birth and growth of organic species—to which appeal is so often made in the poem, is subject to certain limitations of which our information is imperfect. This being the case, it is not altogether strange that, while M. J. Guyau deduces from the *clinamen* universal contingency in the Epicurean scheme of nature, T. Gomperz and Usener incline to regard it as no more than a consistent determinism in opposition to Stoic fatalism (Giussani, i. 125–167).

4. Isonomy.—The atomic motions which go on now are the same as they have always been and always will be. What they have produced they will again produce; for, the sum of matter being constant, there can be no complete change of conditions and no change in the order of nature. The main distinction is between motions which tend to foster birth and growth and those which tend to destroy, whether the aggregate formed be inanimate or an organism. The forces of production and destruction alternately prevail (ii. 1105–1140), but are so evenly balanced that, if we look to the whole universe, the result is equilibrium, as in an indecisive battle (ii. 569–580, v. 380–415). This principle of equable distribution is best known from Cicero, *de Nat. Deor.* I. xix. 50, but undoubtedly it was familiar to Lucretius. Combined with the infinity of atoms of every shape, it guarantees that fixity and perpetuation of species to which he so often appeals as a fact. That in an infinite universe the possible is also the real is the premiss underlying some of the astronomical portions of the poem (cf. v. 526–533).

5. Psychology.—The poet undertakes to prove that the soul is as much an actual part of a man as the hand or foot, and has therefore to refute the theory once current and last represented by Aristoxenus (iii. 130–132) that it is a harmony or immaterial relation subsisting between corporeal elements or parts of the body. Though a single nature, it consists of two parts, mind (*animus*, *mens*) and vital principle (*anima*), the seat of feeling, the former lodged in the breast, the latter diffused all over the frame. The single nature which mind and feeling unite to form is, like everything else, material—an atomic aggregate formed of the very finest atoms of (1) wind, (2) heat, (3) air, and (4) a nameless something in which sensation begins. The preponderance of one or other element in the single substance compounded of the four explains the diversity of character and the variety of the emotional states in animals and men. Soul and body, like mind and vital principle, form one whole, so constituted that neither can exist without the other (iii. 94–416), and this is enforced by twenty-eight arguments against the immortality of the soul (iii. 417–829), whence it follows that man's fear of death is unreasonable. The impassioned discourse on death in which these conclusions are driven home (iii. 830–1094), while sharing the defect of all attempts to 'make fear dig its own false tomb,' is yet by its moral earnestness and depth of feeling one of the most impressive passages in literature.

The atomist theory of perception is developed at great length in bk. iv. Images or films (εἴδωλα) are continually parting from the surface of things and streaming off in all directions, but we see them only when and where we turn our eyes to them. An image pushes before it the air between it and the eye. This air sweeps through the pupil and thus enables us to judge the distance of the object seen. This takes place almost instantaneously; we do not see the images singly, but there is a continuous stream of them whenever an object is seen (iv. 239–258). The theory of images is applied to those cases where the senses seem to be mistaken. The square tower at a distance looks round, because the images are blunted in their long journey through the air. In this and similar instances the eyes are not deceived. What they see they rightly see; it is the mind that errs in the inference which it draws. The error lies in the opinion which the mind superinduces upon what the senses really perceive. The sceptic contradicts himself. For how does he know that nothing can be known? By what criterion does he distinguish knowing from not knowing? The senses are true, all equally true, for each has a distinct power and faculty of its own which the others cannot challenge or convict of error, nor is a single sense at one time more certain than at another. Reasoning, since it depends upon the senses, must be false if they are false, and with the overthrow of reason life itself would be impossible (iv. 469–521). The mind, too, receives its impressions from images, but these images are finer than those by which we see, hear, taste, and smell. Moreover, they do not all come directly from the surface of actual objects; sometimes images from several distinct things unite, as a centaur, or they may be spontaneously formed by atoms in the air. In sleep, when senses and memory are inactive, images still find their way to the mind, wraiths or ghosts of the departed being one special kind. Dream images appear to move because some are coming, some going, in continuous succession, so that they appear to be the same in different postures. In the least sensible time many times are latent in which images can appear. Unless attention is directed to them, they pass unheeded. This explains why we think of what we will, and different men have different thoughts.

6. Cosmogony.—The working of the causes which produce, build up, and ultimately destroy worlds such as ours is described in outline as a corollary to the doctrine of the infinity of matter and space (ii. 1023–1174). The details are filled up in bk. v. The world is not eternal, as some philosophers held. Lucretius starts by proving that it is mortal, *i.e.* had a beginning and will have an end (v. 91–109, 235–415). It must be dissoluble, for it is neither impenetrable like the atom nor intangible like space, nor, like the sum of reality, can it be said to have nothing outside it into which it could pass and out of which destructive forces may come. Our world began with a chaotic jumble of discordant atoms. By the escape of the lighter atoms from the heavier this mass broke up into horizontal layers, ether at the top over air, air over the other two elements, water and earth, the sea being nothing but the moisture squeezed out as the earth condensed. In the infancy of the earth and of the world, vegetation began with herbs and bushes, and then tall trees shot up; animal life followed, first birds, then quadrupeds, last of all man, all sprung from the earth—not from the sea—and nourished by Mother Earth. The existing species are a survival out of a far greater number which the earth first tried to produce. The monstrous births perished because they could not grow up and continue their kind. Many species must have died off, because they lacked natural weapons of defence or could not be utilized and protected by man. But the union of two incompatible natures in the fabled creations—centaurs, chimæras, mermaids—is impossible. At no time did they exist (v. 878–924). This account mainly follows Democritus, but in the primeval monsters the influence of Empedocles is discernible.

7. **Anthropology.**—Civilized society is the product of a long course of development. The sketch of man's gradual advance from primitive savagery (v. 925–1457) is not without interest and value even in the present day when so much fresh material has been accumulated and is continually enlarged. Men at first were hardier and more like the brutes than now. Knowing nothing of tillage, they lived on acorns or berries, without fire, clothes, or houses, without law, government, or marriage. Their foes were the beasts, from whose fury they suffered. Civilization began with the use of huts and skins and the ties of family life. Then came compacts with neighbours for friendship and alliance; and then speech, a natural impulse quickened by need, not due to any single inventor. The next step was the discovery of fire from lightning or the friction of branches. Further improvements led to the building of cities, the allotment of lands, and the discovery of gold. With the origin of political life is linked the origin of religion. Another important discovery was the use of metals, especially iron and copper, which were accidentally discovered when the burning of woods caused the ore to run. Hence came improvements in warfare, the extension of agriculture, and the invention of weaving. The art of music followed. When a knowledge of all the useful crafts had thus been attained, progress was complete.

8. **Religion.**—The popular faith, with its whole apparatus of prayers, vows, offerings, and divination, had been rejected not only by Epicurus, but by almost all philosophers since the feud between poetry and philosophy began with Xenophanes and Heraclitus. Lucretius is bitterly hostile; his indignation at the evil wrought by religion glows throughout the poem as fiercely as in the famous description of the sacrifice of Iphigenia (i. 80–101). But it is not merely popular superstition that he condemns; he is equally opposed to the philosophic monotheism or pantheism of Plato and the Stoics, and, in fact, to whatever is meant by the term 'natural theology.' The negative propositions which he maintains are all-important. (1) There is no purpose in nature; the argument from design is disallowed in advance; adaptation is the product of experience.

> 'Nil ideo quoniam natumst in corpore ut uti
> possemus; sed quod natumst, id procreat usum' (iv. 834 f.).

The bodily organs were not given in order to be used. On the contrary, the eye preceded seeing, and man had a tongue before he could speak. Thus the activity of the senses is explained on mechanical principles without assuming final causes, and a similar explanation holds for all other activities, nourishment by food, and growth, walking and locomotion generally, sleep and dreams. Hence (2) there is no divine providence. The course of nature is not sustained by a divine power working for the good of mankind. The flaws in the world ('tanta stat prædita culpa') at once and for ever dispose of that hypothesis (ii. 165–181; cf. v. 195–234). Hence, too, (3) the world is not divine. So far is it from being conscious and intelligent that it is the most fitting example of what we mean by insensible and inanimate (v. 110–145). (4) The world was not created by the gods. What could induce them to take such trouble inconsistent with their majesty? Or, supposing them willing to create, whence came their notion or preconception (πρόληψις) of man before he existed (v. 181–186)? On the contrary, the world and all that is therein was gradually formed by mere natural causes through the fortuitous concourse of some part of an infinity of atoms in some part of infinite space (ii. 991 ff., v. 187–194).

But negative criticism is not all. On the positive side the existence of gods is proved by the agreement of all nations, although the fables and legends told of them (ii. 600 ff.) must be rejected. The gods are blessed and immortal. They need nothing of mankind, bestow no favours, take no vengeance (ii. 646–652). Their abodes, which in fineness of structure correspond to the impalpable nature of the divine body, too delicate for our sense to perceive, are in the *intermundia* (a word not used by the poet), or lucid interspaces between the worlds. They touch nothing that is tangible for us, since that cannot touch which cannot admit of being touched in turn (v. 148–152). There is a significant reference (iii. 819–823) to the conditions under which alone immortality is possible, namely the absence of destructive forces or their being kept at bay, or being held in equilibrium by conserving forces (see Giussani, i. 239). Not content with proclaiming the true doctrine, Lucretius goes on to explain how the false arose. The belief in gods arose from the images seen by the mind in waking hours and still more in sleep. The shapes thus seen were of more than mortal size, beauty, and strength. As these shapes were ever present, and as their might appeared so great, men deemed them to be immortal and blessed, and placed their abodes in the heavens because the unexplained wonders of the heavens had already excited awe. Thus all things were handed over to the gods, and the course of nature was supposed to be governed by their nod. This fatal error sprang from the instinctive fear which associates with divine vengeance the calamity and ruin wrought by storms and earthquakes (v. 1161–1240). Lucretius more than once exults at the overthrow of this delusion (i. 62–69, ii. 1090–1104, iii. 14–30). On the other hand, it is obvious that he has gone too far in his concessions to anthropomorphism. The criticism which he successfully applies to the incongruous creations of legend, centaurs, and chimæras would, on his own grounds, be just as valid against the blessed immortals. The superhuman beings whom he reverences as gods are simply the Homeric divinities purified, refined, and rationalized.

9. **Ethics.**—In a poem professedly dealing with physics we hardly expect to find a systematic treatment of ethics, yet there are enough short notices or digressions in which the subject appears (ii. 16–61, 172 ff., iii. 14–16, 459 ff., 978–1023, v. 9–51, vi. 9–41) to establish the author's complete agreement with the teaching of Epicurus. The end is pleasure—in other words, to secure that pain hold aloof from the body, and that the mind, exempt from cares and fears, feel its own true joy (ii. 16–19). Whoever has been born must want to continue in life so long as fond pleasure shall keep him (v. 177 f.). Gratification of desires which, though natural, are not necessary affords no true happiness. The tortures of conscience make a hell upon earth. Tantalus and Sisyphus and the like are types of men tormented in this life by various lusts and passions. The pangs of remorse are emphasized as well as the constant apprehension that, though the wrong-doer has hitherto eluded gods and men, he cannot keep his secret for ever (v. 1156 f.). Epicurus is extolled as the saviour who, seeing the miserable condition of mankind, partly from ignorance, and partly from mistaken fear of the gods and of death, proclaimed those truths which

alone can bring salvation: that death is nothing to us, that the gods do not interfere with the course of nature, that the world is a fortuitous and temporary concourse of atoms, and man himself a still more ephemeral combination in that world. These are the doctrines which, he thinks, will redeem mankind. But, while master and disciple are perfectly agreed in the literal acceptance of these propositions, there is a marked difference in the spirit of their teaching. Starting with the proposition 'There is no joy but calm,' Epicurus deduces his ideal of a simple, almost ascetic life of intellectual enjoyment, spent in the society of congenial friends. By a life thus regulated according to circumstances he sought to attain the maximum of pleasure. Lucretius, too, advocates an austere hedonism; the pleasure which is the universal law and condition of existence is not indulgence, but peace and a pure heart (v. 18). From all who would live worthily he demands fortitude, renunciation, and unswerving loyalty to truth. No ancient writer was more profoundly impressed with the mystery of existence, and the ills that flesh is heir to. He assailed the foundations of belief with fanatical zeal which rises, one might almost say, to the intensity of religion. Under this aspect, his earnestness has its counterparts in the *Divina Commedia* or *Paradise Lost.*

LITERATURE.—Editions by C. Lachmann (Berlin, 1850, [4]1871), H. A. J. Munro (Cambridge, 1864, [4]1886), F. Bockemüller (Stade, 1873), C. Giussani (Turin, 1896–98), supplemented by *Note Lucreziane*, do. 1900, W. A. Merrill (New York, 1907), also bk. iii. by R. Heinze (Leipzig, 1897); H. Lotze, in *Philol.* vii. [1852] 696–732; P. Montée, *Etude sur Lucrèce*, Paris, 1860; A. J. Reisacker, *Der Todesgedanke bei den Griechen . . . mit besonderer Rücksicht auf Epicur und den röm. Dichter Lucrez*, Trèves, 1862; C. Martha, *Le Poème de Lucrèce; morale, religion, science*, Paris, 1869; F. A. Lange, *Gesch. des Materialismus*, Iserlohn, 1866, [3]1876, pp. 1–25, 70–121, Eng. tr. by E .C. Thomas, London, 1877–81, chs. i., iv., and v., pp. 3–36, 93–158; H. Usener, 'Zur latein. Literaturgesch.' in *Rhein. Mus.* xxii. [1867] 444–445, xxiii. [1868] 678–680 [*Kleine Schriften*, ii., Leipzig, 1913, nos. xii. and xix.]; A. Bästlein, *Quid Lucretius debuerit Empedocli Agrigentino*, Schleusingen, 1875; J. Veitch, *Lucretius and the Atomic Theory*, London, 1875; J. Woltjer, *Lucretii Philosophia cum fontibus comparata*, Groningen, 1877; J. B. Royer, *Essai sur les arguments du matérialisme dans Lucrèce*, Paris, 1883; J. Masson, *The Atomic Theory of Lucretius contrasted with modern Doctrines of Atoms and Evolution*, London, 1884, *Lucretius, Epicurean and Poet*, do. 1907, and a complementary vol., 1909; J. Bernays, *Gesammelte Abhandlungen*, Berlin, 1885, ii. 1–67 [notes on bk. i. 1–685]; W. Y. Sellar, *The Roman Poets of the Republic*[3], Oxford, 1889 [chs. xi.–xiv.]; J. Mussehl, *De Lucretiani libri primi condicione ac retractatione*, Berlin, 1912. Translations by Munro, new ed. Bohn's Classical Library, London, 1908, and by C. Bailey, Oxford, 1910.

R. D. HICKS.

LUGH.—See CELTS, FESTIVALS AND FASTS (Celtic).

LULLISTS.—Among the figures of the 13th cent. none is more picturesque, none more representative of the great forces, spiritual and mental, of the age than Raymond Lull, 'The Illuminated Doctor,' logician, philosopher, scientist, poet, missionary, and martyr. He was born at Palma, in Majorca, in 1236, when the first spiritual enthusiasm of the Franciscan movement was dying away. During his boyhood the spiritual Franciscans were making desperate, but vain, efforts to maintain the simplicity of the original vow of poverty which had been the joy of their founder. Human nature made it inevitable, however lamentable, that an Order should possess property. Another deviation from the singleness of mind of St. Francis was, happily, inevitable also. During his life a brother was not allowed to possess a book, and learning seemed as alien as riches. But true devotion cannot be permanently content without the offering of the realms of mind as well as of soul and body. Thus we find in the lives of Roger Bacon and Raymond Lull, members of Franciscan Orders of the next generation, an enthusiasm for learning linked with an enthusiasm for Christ as intense as that of Brother Giles and Sister Clare. These are the figures whom we find toiling amid the dim foundations of the great Palace of Science, blackened by the suspicion of the narrow-minded orthodox, strenuously maintaining the nobility of the offering of science, knowledge, and thought at the foot of the Cross. They were fervent lovers of Christ who stood at the parting of the ways of Scholasticism, still recognizing and using its words and its processes, but adding the facts and inferences of a dawning science of Nature. Their lives were enthusiastic fulfilments of the command, 'Thou shalt love the Lord thy God *with all thy mind.*'

Lull was seneschal of the household of James II. of Majorca, and till the age of thirty he lived the ordinary life of a libertine noble. Suddenly conscience was aroused, and in his chamber, as he was writing love poems, he beheld the vision of Christ on the Cross, and heard Him say, 'Oh Raymond, follow me henceforth.' Then came the agony of conviction and the determination to forsake the world and follow Christ entirely. Two aims at once filled his life—to gain martyrdom, and to convert to Christianity the Saracens around. He would use no carnal weapons; he would go to the Holy Father and to Christian kings, and induce them to endow colleges for the learning of the languages of the unbelievers. For himself he would write a book so irrefutable as to ensure the conversion of Saracen, Jew, and heretic to the Catholic faith. A sermon on the renunciation of St. Francis of Assisi completed his resolution; he left wife and children with sufficient for the necessities of life, sold all else, and went forth in coarsest attire to the new life. He kept a cell for himself on Mount Randa, and there during nearly ten years he sought to fit himself for his work. By the advice of his friends he chose this solitary study in preference to the University of Paris, the centre of the intellectual life of Europe. He learnt Arabic from a Saracen whom he bought as a slave, and narrowly escaped being murdered when this infuriated Muslim realized the object of his study. The crown of his long preparation came when eight days of profound meditation were succeeded by an illumination which Lull himself always claimed as a direct divine inspiration. Under this impulse he wrote the *Ars Magna*, the first of the great works associated with his name. By its methods he felt sure that the truths of Christianity could be so irrefragably stated that the infidels could not possibly refuse acceptance of them. Nothing is more striking in the subsequent history of the philosopher and his followers than the absolute conviction, which they all shared, of the direct divine origin of the mode of reasoning here initiated. The assertion is crystallized in the title 'The Illuminated Doctor' by which he is always known among succeeding generations of Lullists. The woodcuts adorning the great folios in which Salzinger has issued his works all represent the divine beam of light shining down upon him. Enthusiastic disciples confidently appeal to the logical power of the processes as more than possible to unaided human intellect. The unbiased judgment of our own day fails to discover the same immense value or power.

It may be briefly characterized as a mechanical method by which all possible subjects may be subjected to all manner of questions, and thus a complete category of statements may be obtained. The apparatus in its original form is a number of concentric circles divided into compartments denoted by letters of the alphabet. These letters denote in different circles different ideas. Thus we have in one nine subjects: God, Angel, Heaven, Man, the Imaginative, the Sensitive, the Negative, the Elementary, the Instrumental. In another circle we have nine predicates: Goodness, Magnitude, Duration, Power, Wisdom, Will, Virtue, Truth, Glory. In another we have nine questions: Whether? What? Whence? Why? How large? Of what kind? When? Where? How? One of these circles is fixed, the others rotate, and we thus obtain a complete series of combinations, first of questions and then of statements. The precise form of the mechanism varies; in some works we have triangles of various colours intersecting each other; in others we have a tree with roots, trunk, branches, twigs, each labelled with some term contracting from the universal to the special. Letters vary in meaning with the apparatus. But in every case the general idea is the codifying of every possible statement on all subjects. The method, intended first solely as a Christian apologetic, was speedily found to be as applicable to other subjects, and among the numerous works assigned to Lull are many in which the *Ars* is applied to Medicine, Chemistry, Mathematics, Physics, and Astronomy.

Lull commenced at once to use his new weapon with all the enthusiasm of the direct emissary of God. He gave a series of lectures on its application at the Universities of Montpellier and Paris and in the monasteries of France, Italy, and Spain. The failure of his persuasions to induce monarchs or pontiff to develop fresh enterprise for the conversion of the Saracen led Lull himself, at the age of fifty-six, to land as a missionary in Tunis, there confidently expecting to win all to Christianity through his reasoning. Imprisonment and expulsion did not check his zeal; we find him ardently continuing his work wherever there were Muslims or heretics. His own islands, Cyprus, and Armenia certainly saw many converts, and the ban of death did not prevent his returning twice to Africa. The assertions of his much wider travel need further proof.

Lull's scheme for colleges for the study of missionary languages bore fruit for a time in a foundation by his own king, in 1276, of a college for Arabic at Miramar in Majorca, but it was not until the Council of Vienne, in 1311, that papal authority was given for schools for Hebrew, Greek, Arabic, and Chaldee in the Roman Curia, Oxford, Bologna, Salamanca, and Paris. It is interesting thus to realize that in Lull's enthusiasm we have the germ of the Hebrew professorships at our English Universities, as well as the broader ideas of missionary education which he and Roger Bacon alike impressed upon the Church. The same instinct which sent Lull to talk to Saracens in Arabic led him to overleap the limits of tradition and to write many of his works, both devotional and logical, in his native Catalan. He was a pioneer in that movement which, by entrusting to vernacular languages thoughts hitherto imprisoned in the Latin of the learned, gave a new dignity to national speech and a new impulse to the development of the common people: his great religious romance *Blanquerna* was written in Latin, Arabic, and Catalan; his ecstatic hymns entitled *Hours of the Virgin*, with many others of his works, in Catalan alone.

Round Raymond Lull there has gathered a misty halo of romance and unorthodoxy through his incursions into the world of alchemy. His Franciscan supporters are eager to free him from this charge, which has repeatedly brought him within danger of the censure of the Church. He is stated to have learnt from Arnauld of Villeneuve the secret of the philosopher's stone. There is a tradition, exceedingly doubtful but not entirely discredited, of a visit to England to make gold for Edward II. in return for his help against the unbelievers. Certain it is that a number of works on alchemy are assigned to his name which were obviously not written by him. It is proved that on Lull has been fixed the discredit of certain works on magic by another Raymond of Tarrega, a renegade converted Jew, which were condemned by Pope Gregory XI. But we must remember that alchemy was the beginning of natural science, that the early alchemists were religious men who commenced their works in the name of the Trinity, and that the man who believed that he had discovered a universal transmuter of the elements of thought might not unnaturally aim at a universal transmuter of the elements of matter. Lull's dominating idea was that there is one great principle running through the universe, since it is the expression of one divine mind. Scattered among his acknowledged works are repeated references showing that he thought much on alchemy, though he did not expect impossibilities from it. We can well believe that he wrote as well as thought on the subject. Indeed, Roger Bacon (*de Emendandis Scientiis*, bk. iii.) refers to the fact of such writing.

The last period of Lull's life revealed a foe within the Church against which he fought unceasingly. Round the name of Averroes (Ibn Rushd, † 1198; see AVERROES, AVERROISM), the Arab interpreter of Aristotle, had been gathering the thoughts and theories of Muslim, Jewish, and Scholastic successors, diverging gradually into the banishment of the Deity beyond the reach of prayer or care for the individual, the denial of individual immortality, and ultimately even asserting the identity of the soul of all men. Averroism thus, while using the name of a single devout Muslim, was really the composite deposit of a century of more or less sceptical thought; through Maimonides (*q.v.*) and Michael Scot it gained the ear of a section of Scholasticism and won over as votaries many in the University of Paris, the intellectual focus of the world. In attempting to save its orthodoxy it asserted that what might be true in faith might be false in philosophy. This was the special heresy against which Lull spent his life; the authorities at Paris eagerly sought his assistance in combating the heresy which threatened to capture the whole University. The contest was so keen that Lull himself was obliged repeatedly to obtain certificates of his own orthodoxy. At the Council of Vienne Lull worked hard, though apparently without success, to secure an edict forbidding the teaching of Averroism in Christian schools. It lingered for a couple of centuries longer, more and more tending to materialism and finding its chief sphere in the medical school of Padua. Lullism always provided its strongest foes.

When nearly eighty years of age, Lull set off on another missionary journey to Africa; his fervid exhortation roused the fury of the Muslim mob, and he was stoned to death at Bugia on June 30, 1315, thus gaining the coveted crown of martyrdom. The body was carried to Palma and was there interred amidst the laments of his nation.

The immense mental activity of Lull left a vast number of works, many of which have never been printed. Salzinger in his great (incomplete) edition (1721–48) gives a list of 205 treatises as undoubted, besides 93 others more or less probably assigned to his name. Perroquet (1667) names 488, and states that several authors of weight assign no fewer than 4000 to his pen. A large number of enthusiastic pupils, gathered from the lecture-halls of Paris and of the Franciscan monasteries, continued and applied his methods, and in many places Lullist schools grew up side by side with the older-established Thomists and Scotists. The aim of the Lullists was to apply a logical method to the proof of doctrines of the faith, to fight Averroism, and to fit men for missionary work. Enthusiasm for his methods was the special characteristic of the followers of the great enthusiast. This enthusiasm was speedily met by a bitter opposition. It is almost certain that Lull had been a member of the third Order of St. Francis. Rivalry between the great religious Orders, however, belittled his growing fame. The Dominican Eymeric, Inquisitor-General in Aragon (1320–99), initiated the campaign by an accusation of heresy in 500 passages taken from Lull's works. Franciscan apologists assert that Eymeric was a disbeliever in the doctrine of the Immaculate Conception, which was the special enthusiasm of the University of Paris and was warmly advocated by Lullists, and that this was the seed plot of Eymeric's opposition. The Inquisitor asserted that 200 Lullist errors had been condemned by Gregory XI. in 1376. This bull has never been found, though the papal archives have again and again been searched, and N. de Pax (1519) and L. Wadding († 1657), the annalist of the Franciscans, have made out their case that Eymeric invented it, or forged it, or confused it deliberately or accidentally with the condemnation of the works of Raymond of Tarrega, already referred to (most conveniently accessible in *AS*, June, vii. 618–623). Eymeric was degraded and subsequently sent by King John of Aragon into exile; Lullism was declared sane and wholesome in 1386 by the Inquisitor Emangaudius at Barcelona.

In 1483 Ferdinand the Catholic founded the University of Majorca, with a 'studium generale' for the study of Lull's method. Naturally it is the native island of the founder that has been most devoted to the propagation of his philosophy and has fiercely fought for its recognition. But its fortunes have varied elsewhere. In the University of Paris at times students were officially warned against its study, but about the year 1515 it attained great glory there under the inspiring teaching of Bernard de Lavinheta. Its doctrines were again and again assailed as unorthodox, and as earnestly defended. A favourable sentence was obtained from the Council of Trent and from the Inquisition at Madrid. But its foes procured the inclusion of Lull's works on the Index Expurgatorius under Paul IV. They were finally removed from the Index in 1594. The hold of Lullism on the University of Palma continued into the 18th century. In 1635 Urban VIII. ordered that its scholars during their last two years of study should daily hear lectures on the *Ars*. In 1673 Maria Anna of Austria issued an edict assigning precedence to Lullists even over scholars senior to themselves. Objections, insufficient to prevent Lull's beatification, have obstructed his canonization, though the process recounting the miracles at his tomb was presented by the bishop of Majorca in 1612. The principal charges were due to unguarded utterances that seem to ignore the necessity of faith and to bring the truths of religion within the powers of human reason. Others considered the processes of the *Ars* mere word-chopping. Later apologists like Perroquet confess that sciolists made it their boast that by this method they could speak on any subject, to any length, at a moment's notice, and Perroquet laments the undeserved obloquy which such charlatans have brought on their master (*Vie*, p. 118 f.). The specimens given of the method explain why it has now passed away. Ps 20 and Wis 6 are expounded by Perroquet as samples. We find a careful analysis of the subjects and predicates of each verse, and an exhaustive statement of their combination —the whole producing a somewhat commonplace expository commentary. Lull has become the national saint of the Balearic Isles. Here the enthusiasm never died, but the philosophic method gradually merged itself in an enthusiasm for the memory of the saint and a national pride in collecting and publishing the Catalan poems and imaginative works on which Lull's fame will finally rest. The Lullists of to-day are a number of patriotic and cultured men who are proud of their national literature and its great exponent.

LITERATURE.—*AS*, June, vii. [1867] 581–676 (30th day), gives life, and history of the disputes on orthodoxy; I. Salzinger, *Opera Raymundi Lullii*, Mainz, 1721–48, vols. i.–vi., ix., x.; A. Perroquet, *Apologie de la vie et des œuvres du bienheureux Raymond Lulle*, Vendôme, 1667; K. Prantl, *Geschichte der Logik*, Leipzig, 1867 (vol. iii. deals with Lull's system); A. Helfferich, *Raymund Lull und die Anfänge der catalonischen Literatur*, Berlin, 1858, deals with his place in literature. Modern lives are M. André, *Le Bienheureux Raymond Lulle*, Paris, 1900 (edifying but uncritical); S. M. Zwemer, *Raymund Lull, First Missionary to the Moslems*, New York, 1902; and W. T. A. Barber, *Raymond Lull the Illuminated Doctor*, London, 1903. For further bibliography see U. Chevalier, *Répertoire des sources hist. du moyen âge, bio-bibliographie*, new ed., Paris, 1905–07, cols. 3891–3893.

W. T. A. BARBER.

LUMBINĪ.—A pleasaunce, or small wood, mentioned in Pāli records as the birthplace of the Buddha. It is now occupied by the shrine of Rummindēī in Nepāl, approximately in 83° 20′ E. long., 27° 29′ N. lat., about four miles north of the frontier between the British possessions and the Nepālese Tarai, and half a mile west of the river Tilār.[1]

The references to it so far traced in the N. Indian Pāli books are only three. One is in an old ballad, containing the prophecy of the aged Asita about the infant Buddha, this Asita story being the Buddhist counterpart of the Christian story of Simeon. The ballad is certainly one of the very oldest extant Buddhist documents, and must be earlier than 400 B.C. It is now included in the anthology called the *Sutta Nipāta*, and it states at verse 683 that the child was born in the village of Lumbinī (*Lumbineyye gāme*). The other two references are in the *Kathā Vatthu*, composed in the middle of the 3rd cent. B.C. by Tissa, son of Moggali. In that work (ed. A. C. Taylor for *PTS*, London, 1894–97, pp. 97 and 559) it is stated that 'the Exalted One' was born at Lumbinī (*Lumbiniyā jāto*).

Our next information is the inscription found on a pillar in Dec. 1896. The pillar had been known for years to be standing at the foot of the small hill on which the tiny shrine is situated, but the fact that the *graffiti* on the exposed part of it were mediæval and unimportant, combined with the difficulties resulting from its being in foreign territory, caused it to be neglected until 1896. When it was then uncovered, the top of an inscription was discovered three feet beneath the soil. The inscription is in old Pāli letters, and in a dialect which the present writer would call Kosalī —a dialect so nearly allied to the literary Pāli of the canon that other scholars prefer to call it Pāli. The translation is as follows:

'The beloved of the gods, King Piyadası (that is, Aśoka), has come in person and paid reverence; and to celebrate the fact that the Buddha, the Sākiya sage, was born here, has had a stone horse (?) made and put up on a stone pillar; and because the Honourable One was born here has remitted the tax of one-eighth on Lumbinī village (that is, parish).'

There are slight differences in the translations by various other scholars, but not as to the double insistence on the fact that the Buddha was born at the spot where the pillar was erected.[2] The letters are beautifully clear, each being nearly an inch in height. When the present writer made a copy of them in 1900, though they had then been three years exposed to the light, they seemed almost as if freshly cut. In the dim light of the cell above, containing the shrine, can be discerned a bas-relief representing the birth-scene. But the Brāhman who claims the right to the petty income arising from the pence of the peasantry refuses any proper examination of it. So far as a cursory inspection permits of a decision, it seems to be much later than the inscription.

A legend in the *Divyāvadāna*[3] purports to give

[1] See V. A. Smith, in *JRAS*, 1902, p. 143.

[2] See A. Führer, *Buddha Sakyamuni's Birthplace*, Allāhābād, 1907; G. Bühler, in *Epigraphia Indica*, v. [1898]; R. Pischel, *SBAW*, 1903, p. 724 ff.; A. Barth, *Journal des Savants*, 1897, p. 73.

[3] Ed. E. B. Cowell and R. A. Neil, Cambridge, 1886, p. 389.

the conversation between Aśoka and his guide Upagupta on the occasion of the visit recorded in the inscription. Perhaps the tradition that Upagupta, very possibly another name of the author of the *Kathā Vatthu*, accompanied him is historical. The work in question is in Buddhist Sanskrit; and, though its date is unknown, it must be at least five centuries later than Aśoka, who spoke, of course, the language of his inscription, and would not have understood the words here put into his mouth.

Still later are certain references in the Pāli commentaries written at Kāñchīpuram[1] or Anurādhapura[2] (*qq.v.*). In order to explain how the birth took place in a grove, they say that the mother, on the way to be delivered among her own people, was taken with the pains of delivery half-way between Kapilavatthu, her husband's home, and Devadaha, her father's home. This is quite probable; but, on the other hand, it may have been suggested by the meagre facts recorded in the ancient books. Neither the Buddhist Sanskrit writers nor the Pāli commentators could have understood the long-buried inscription, even had they known of its existence.

It is very interesting to see that this spot, so deeply revered by all Buddhists, should have retained its original name through so many centuries of neglect and desertion. Watters says that 'according to some accounts' it had been named Lumbinī after a great Koliyan lady who had dedicated it to public use.[3] This is quite probable. There are other instances of a similar kind; but, unfortunately, Watters gives neither name nor date of any of the Chinese books to which he refers. But we know that both Sākiyas and Koliyas found difficulty in pronouncing the trilled *r*. Perhaps this was true of all Kosala. The inscription at Lumbinī, for instance, has *lāja* for *rāja*; and Lumbinī itself is often written in Pāli MSS with a dotted L, which may represent an untrilled *r*. Thus Rummindeī stands for Lumbinī Devi, the goddess of Lumbinī. But that goddess was not really a goddess at all, nor even Lumbinī, but only the mother of the Buddha. We have no evidence as to when or how the transformation took place. And in face of the stubborn opposition of the Nepālese Government, and of the Brāhman who has taken possession of the shrine, there is very little hope of any further excavation at the site to throw light on this question, or to explain the divergent statements of Chinese writers as to what they saw at the place.[4]

LITERATURE.—See the sources cited in the article, and cf. also art. KAPILAVASTU.

T. W. RHYS DAVIDS.

LUNACY.—See INSANITY.

LUSHAIS.—The Lushais are a composite community, consisting of those groups which were absorbed and reduced to a more or less complete unity by the skill and sagacity of the Thangur chiefs of the Lushai clan in the last century. They practise *jhuming*, a form of cultivation which involves constant moves from one site to another. In this fact is found a reason for some at least of their peculiar characteristics.

Each village is a separate State ruled by its own chief, who usually belongs to the Sailo clan, whose talent for government has made them the masters of nearly the whole of the area now known as the Lushai Hills. The sons, as they reached maturity, were provided with a wife and followers, and were sent forth to found new villages. The youngest son was the heir general. Elders assist the chief in the village administration, and each village possesses, in addition to the council of elders, officers to settle where the *jhums* are to be made, a village crier, a blacksmith, and a wise man, *puithiam* (lit. 'much knower'). The population of a Lushai village consists of members of different clans and tribes brought under the unifying influence of their subordination to the Thangur chiefs. Their religion, therefore, exhibits traces of a mixed origin; there are features in it which recall some of the more notable characteristics of the systems of their congeners, east as well as in the more distant north, all of whom speak cognate dialects.

The Creator is a spirit called Pathian, beneficent, but with little concern in the affairs of men. Subordinate to Pathian is a spirit Khuavang, whose appearance to men causes illness. He is also spoken of as a personal genius—an idea which is still further elaborated in the belief in the *mivengtu*, the watchers of men. Each man has two souls, *thlarao*, the one wise and the other foolish. One *mivengtu* is good and the other evil. The *huai* are demons inhabiting water and land, are all bad, and are the causes of all sickness and misfortune; the *lashi* are spirits who are concerned only with wild animals, whom they control; the spirits of the dead need constant propitiation and receive offerings of firstfruits. Each clan has a spirit, or clan deity, *sakhua*, to whom a special chant is addressed by the *puithiam* (who must be a member of the clan), and identity of chants and ritual is a sure proof of membership of the clan.

The rites performed for the purpose of address to some definite spiritual being may be separated from the rites which seem to be efficacious without the intervention or mediacy of any definite spiritual being. The *sakhua* chants recorded by Shakespear are accompanied by sacrifices of a sow. The sacrifices to *huai*, supposed to frequent houses and villages, are various, now a pig, now a cock, and sometimes a goat being offered. Three sacrifices should be performed after marriage. Dreams afford an indication of the necessity for the performance of one of those rites. Temporary tabus, closely akin to those so common in the Nāga area, are part of the necessary liturgy. The ritual for appeasing the *huai* of the woods and waters is not dissimilar, but some of the most efficacious rites are the patent of certain clans. The villages close their gates on the occasion of an epidemic of cholera, so as to exclude all visitors from the infected area, and frighten away the demon causing the sickness by erecting a rough gate across the road leading to the distressed villages, which they man with straw figures of armed men; they suspend from the gateway the portions of the dog sacrificed in these emergencies, which are reserved for the demon—as a rule, the extremities with the heart, liver, and entrails. Some of the birth-rites are addressed to *huais*, while others are seemingly of almost automatic efficacy. In the second category of rites are those which are performed to bring back a straying soul (for men sometimes lose one of their souls), to produce children, to afford protection against sickness, to secure good hunting and to ascertain the luck of the intended chase, to benefit the crops, to obtain power over the spirits of animals and men killed in this world, and to secure freedom from the ghost of the slaughtered enemy. The series of five feasts which affect the future life in important ways are religious rites of a specially interesting nature. Most of the rites are accompanied by a regulation requiring that the social group concerned, be it a household or a whole village, shall abstain from all but the most

[1] Com. on *Therīgāthā*, p. 1.
[2] *Majjhima Com.*, *JRAS*, 1895, p. 767; *Jātaka Com.* i. 52, 54.
[3] T. Watters, *On Yuan Chwāng's Travels in India*, ed. T. W. Rhys Davids and S. W. Bushell, London, 1905, ii. 15.
[4] See Watters, *op. cit.*

necessary work, and shall not leave the prescribed area. The blacksmith's forge possesses sanctity, and is a place where persons who have accidentally come into contact with any noxious influence may take sanctuary and be purified. The priesthood consists of the *puithiam* and the members of special clans. Any one can acquire by purchase the *hlā*, songs or charms which form the stock-in-trade of the *puithiam*, whose success must depend largely on luck and on short memories of his failures.

The first man, Pūpawla, or the ancestor Pawla, possibly in revenge for his death, stands armed with bow and pellets at the entrance to the spirit world. Except the *thāngchhuah*, *i.e.* those who have performed the series of five rites (fasts, as they are sometimes called) in this world, none can escape his aim. Yet he spares still-born children or those who die young, for he heeds their plea that, had they lived, they too might have performed the due ritual and so been free to enter with the *thāngchhuah* into Pielrāl, where all is pleasant. Those whom Pawla wounds go to Mithi khua. Their wounds swell painfully for three years, and for a like period the scar remains. Thereafter they die again, are born as butterflies, and then die again, to reappear as dew on the ground; as dew they enter the loins of a man, and are reborn as human children. In addition to the personal advantages of the *thāngchhuah* rites, the man may take his wife with him to Pielrāl, whence there is no return to reincarnation, and he may wear certain special clothes, build a verandah at the back of his house, enjoy a window in his house, and put an additional shelf near his bed.

The Lushais are a superstitious people, and believe firmly in witchcraft; not very long ago, to test the efficacy of the belief that the victim of witchcraft would surely recover if he could but taste the liver of the wizard, they killed three whole families who were thought to be bewitching an aged chieftainess, cut the livers of the wizards out, and carried them back, only to find that the old lady had died in their absence. Naturally *le voisin ennemi* is an expert at the black art, but their neighbours return the compliment to them in full.

Certain persons, especially women, can put themselves into a trance (*zawl*) and communicate with Khuavang, from whom they acquire information as to the particular sacrifice required to cure the sick. The process of divination employed on these occasions requires the use of an egg and a shallow basket of rice, in which appears the footprint of the animal to be sacrificed. Possession by the spirit of a wild animal (*khawring*) is contagious and hereditary, and takes the form of passing from the hostess to another woman, who speaks with the voice of the original hostess. The belief in the power of men to assume the form of a tiger is common.

LITERATURE.—T. H. Lewin, *The Hill Tracts of Chittagong*, Calcutta, 1869; J. Shakespear, *The Lushei Kuki Clans*, London, 1912.

T. C. HODSON.

LUSTRATION.—See PURIFICATION.

LUTHER.—**I. Life.**—The career of Martin Luther naturally divides into three periods—the first, of preparation (1483-1517); the second, of protest (1517-21); the third, of construction (1521-46). He was born at Eisleben in Saxony on 10th Nov. 1483. His birthplace was only the temporary home of his parents. They had come thither from Moehra, the real home of the family, some 80 miles to the south-west. The father, as an older son, had no share in the paternal estate, and was, therefore, in straitened circumstances, until, by his daily labour in the copper mines, and by economy and thrift, he became proprietor of mines and furnaces, and an influential member of the community. Both as a child in his home and in his early school days, Luther knew what the struggle with poverty meant. As he advanced, his father was at last able to provide him with the means for a liberal education. Both his father, John Luther, and his mother, Margaretta Ziegler of Eisenach, were deeply religious, and subjected him to a discipline, continued in the schools to which he was first sent, that was legalistic rather than evangelical. His childhood was spent at Mansfeld. His elementary training was received chiefly at Eisenach, among his mother's relatives, and his University course at Erfurt, an institution which, at his entrance in 1501, was over 100 years old, and the most numerously attended of the German Universities. Intended by his father for the legal profession, he devoted his first years at Erfurt to classical literature and philosophy. While he read with absorbing interest the Latin classics, and derived from them the benefit of a wider horizon and a deeper acquaintance with human nature, it is a great exaggeration to affirm, as some recent writers have done, that they made him more of a humanist than a theologian; for he read them with a critical eye, and reacted against the excessive devotion to the purely formal that dominated the humanistic school. His teachers in philosophy were nominalists, who introduced him to Occam, Biel, and Gerson, and instilled a critical disposition towards the current scholasticism. Attaining A.B. in 1502, and A.M. in 1505, he reluctantly began the study of Law, for which he had little taste. His dissatisfaction with the calling into which his father was forcing him was intensified by spiritual conflicts, brought to a crisis by the sudden death of a friend by his side—whether by a bolt of lightning or by assassination can scarcely be determined—and by his own narrow escape in the storm that is said to have destroyed his friend. In obedience to a vow made in the moment of peril, he turned his back upon the world two weeks later, and entered the cloister of the Augustinian hermits at Erfurt (17th July 1505). Purity of life, deep moral earnestness, devotion to the study of the Holy Scriptures, and ability as preachers distinguished the Saxon Augustinians; but it is incorrect to infer from their name any special interest in Augustine's doctrine of sin and grace. With all the intensity of his nature the young novice devoted himself to the scrupulous observance of every detail of the requirements of the Order, and rose rapidly in the esteem of his brethren and superiors. He found edifying spiritual advisers in an aged monk whose name has not been preserved, and especially in John Staupitz, his Vicar General. Some of his modern critics accuse him of morbid conscientiousness and needless scrupulosity in his conceptions of truth and duty. The rules of the Order came to him with all the claims of divine commands, which he could not decline to observe in all their strictness without, in his belief, sinning against God. Nor could he be satisfied with anything less than certainty with respect to his relations to God. It matters little that, as has been recently urged, in some of his earlier discourses, composed while he was still a monk, as, *e.g.*, in the lately discovered lectures on the Epistle to the Romans, evangelical statements can be found foreshadowing his future position. For it is no uncommon circumstance for writers advancing towards a conclusion, amid many vacillations, not fully to grasp the meaning of their own words.[1] In 1507 he was ordained to the

[1] Cf. Otto Scheel, *Die Entwicklung Luthers bis zum Abschluss der Vorlesung über den Römerbrief*, Leipzig, 1910.

priesthood, and his father, with a large retinue of personal friends, honoured the occasion of his first celebration of the Mass; but that, even then, the breach between father and son was not completely healed appeared at the meal which followed, when the former in his blunt way reminded the clergy that obedience to parents is a command from which no dispensation could be given, and that what they esteemed a call from God might be nothing more than a delusion of Satan. Selected by Staupitz in Nov. 1508 as instructor in Philosophy in the University of Wittenberg, founded only six years before, Luther was delighted, when, four months later, as a Bachelor of Theology, it was his privilege to lecture also on the Holy Scriptures. Recalled the succeeding autumn to Erfurt, he was assigned the task of lecturing on the *Sentences* of Peter Lombard. Two years later (1511) he was sent to Rome to represent Staupitz in regard to certain business affairs of the Order. This visit was of the highest moment to Luther's subsequent career. His most recent Roman Catholic biographer, Grisar, candidly says that the Rome which he visited was the Rome of the then ruling Julius II. and his predecessor, Alexander VI.—Rome glorified by art, but the deeply degenerate Rome of the popes of the consummation of the Renaissance.[1] He was grieved by the many abuses forced on his attention; and, notwithstanding the credulity with which, as he afterwards acknowledged, he accepted much of what he there saw and heard, the hold which the papal name and authority had had upon him was greatly weakened. The story of his experience on Pilate's Staircase rests solely on the testimony published after his death by his son Paul. Rapid promotion followed, as a testimonial to the success of his mission. Receiving the degree of Doctor of Theology at the age of twenty-nine (1512), he accepted it as a special call 'to explain the Scriptures to all the world,' and broke the traditional modes of instruction by his method of lecturing. Although he retains the 'four-fold sense' of Scripture, he lays the chief stress upon finding allusions to Christ in all the prophecies of the OT, and interprets the Psalter by the gospel of the NT. From the OT books he turned to the NT, treating successively Romans, Galatians, and Hebrews. From the nominalists, Occam and Gerson, he had turned to Augustine, and from Augustine more and more to Paul. The mystical writer, John Tauler, and the anonymous author of *The German Theology* had a decided formative influence. His time, however, was largely absorbed by administrative duties. In 1515 he was appointed Vicar, with the oversight of eleven monasteries.

It was in the midst of these duties that he became involved in the controversy concerning indulgences (*q.v.*). The doctrine of indulgences was rooted in the denial of the completeness of the satisfaction for sins made by Christ. This satisfaction, it was taught, had value for original sin, and, beyond it, was made for actual sins only by commuting the penalty from one that was infinite, and beyond man's power to afford, to one that is finite and within his limitations, either in this world or in that which is to come. Penitence, it was further taught, consisted of contrition, confession, and satisfaction, made by the penitent. Such satisfactions could be made only for such sins as were recognized by the sinner. But, as in this life the knowledge of many sins escapes the notice of even the most faithful, purgatory was provided, where satisfactions could be rendered for sins unrepented of at death. Relief from such satisfactions would be found, however, in the fund of the superfluous merits of the saints acquired by their works

[1] H. Grisar, *Luther*, i. 41.

of supererogation—a fund upon which the Church, through its head on earth, could draw, so as to grant indulgence by the payment of an equivalent. Heretofore, no more had been claimed for a letter of indulgence than an abbreviation of the pains of purgatory for those who had already departed. As the granting of these letters afforded large revenue, abuses constantly grew. It was the most convenient and effective way of raising funds for Church purposes, with percentage allotted to the agents who collected them. The luxurious habits of Leo X. and especially the completion of St. Peter's church at Rome rendered this expedient very serviceable at this time. Albrecht of Brandenburg, Archbishop and Margrave, had contracted to collect fees from this source, with the stipulation that he retain one half. He commissioned as one of his agents John Tetzel, a Dominican monk and emotional preacher, who, by his appeals to the terror of his hearers, created great popular commotion wherever he appeared, and urged them to purchase his wares. It would not be difficult to accumulate from Roman Catholic writers abundant censure of the course of Tetzel. For more than a year Luther, entirely ignorant of the connexion which both Albrecht and the pope himself had with Tetzel's traffic, had been uttering protests at a distance; but, as Tetzel drew nearer Wittenberg, the revelations made to Luther as a spiritual guide in the confessional compelled him first to appeal repeatedly to his ecclesiastical superiors, and, finally, when these appeals were fruitless, to publish his Ninety-five Theses for an academic discussion in the University. The effect which they produced, as well as the publicity which they received, was beyond all expectation. While in these Theses he strikes boldly and remorselessly at the very roots of the abuse, he is evidently still feeling his way, and has not entirely freed himself from some positions that were afterwards very forcibly repudiated.

There were formal answers the next year by John Eck and Silvester Prierias, which called forth responses, with characteristic vigour, from Luther. There was a barren conference with Cardinal Cajetan at Augsburg (Sept. 1518), and another with Miltitz at Altenburg (Jan. 1519), followed by the Leipzig Disputation (beginning 23rd June), in which, after Eck and Carlstadt had argued for days, Luther's debate with Eck began (4th July) on Church authority, significant because of the advance shown by Luther upon anything that he had previously declared, in the maintenance of the fallibility of Councils, and the censure of the Council of Constance for condemning Hus. The aid offered from the camps of humanism Luther not only declined, but repelled, as he wished to make it clear that his protest rested upon entirely different grounds from theirs. The year 1520 is noted for three monumental treatises, two polemical, one irenic and constructive. Of the former, the first was his famous 'Appeal to the Christian Nobility,' which might appropriately bear the title, 'The Responsibility and Duty of the Laity in Spiritual Affairs,' and the second, 'The Babylonian Captivity,' a scathing criticism of the sacramental system of the Roman Church. The latter, 'The Liberty of the Christian Man,' has evoked the following tribute from one of his most prominent modern critics:

> 'One cannot help asking how the same hand which delighted to shatter as with a sledge-hammer all that had hitherto been held sacred and venerable, could also touch so tenderly the chords of divine love' (Janssen, *Gesch. des deutschen Volkes*, Eng. tr., iii. 239).

The bull of excommunication promulgated by the pope on 15th June 1520 did not reach Wittenberg until four months later, and was formally burned by Luther before the students of the

University (10th Dec. 1520). On 16th and 17th April 1521 Luther appeared before the Emperor, Charles V., at the Diet of Worms, and declared that he could not recant. There were too many political complications involved to enable the Emperor to act promptly against him, and before such action could be taken the Elector of Saxony, as a precaution, had Luther arrested, while returning from the Diet, and carried to the Wartburg, overlooking Eisenach, where he remained in retirement until the following spring.

The isolation of those ten months afforded opportunity to review his work at a distance from the scene, to mature his convictions by the close and uninterrupted study of Scripture, to form some plans for the future, and to begin his most important work, the translation of the Bible into German. The NT was translated, from the second edition of the Greek Testament of Erasmus, within three months from the time when it was begun. The translation was brought with him when he returned to Wittenberg from his exile (6th March 1522), and appeared the succeeding September. The translation of the OT was a much more difficult undertaking, in which he had the assistance of Melanchthon, Aurogallus, Roerer, Foerster, and others, and was published in parts, until in 1532 the entire Bible appeared complete, followed by the Apocrypha two years later.

On his return to Wittenberg the character of his labours was much changed. He had at once to meet with decision the radical reaction against Rome, which had resorted in some cases to revolutionary, and in others to precipitate, measures. Three days after his return he began a series of eight sermons, preaching daily, into which he threw all his energy to check their excesses and, against them, to define the principles for which he had been contending. The reformation of the churches in districts no longer under the dominion of the old Church now became necessary, to prevent them from being misled by the confusion that had been introduced, and in order, by a re-organization, to build them upon solid evangelical foundations. Henceforth, while the polemic against Rome did not cease, and almost equal energy was directed against the opposite extreme, he was occupied largely with constructive work—the visitation of churches, the preparation of Church constitutions, the re-organization of schools, the revision of the liturgy, the writing of catechisms, the composition of hymns, and the publishing of popular sermons, not only for private edification, but especially as models for the inadequately prepared preachers, besides his lectures to his classes and incessant correspondence and conferences—until, from sheer exhaustion, he fell a victim to disease, while acting as a mediator between the counts of Mansfeld, and died in his native town of Eisleben (16th Feb. 1546). Among the more important events of this later period of his life are his marriage with Catherine von Bora (1525); the Marburg colloquy with Zwingli (Oct. 1529); his second period of isolation, at the castle of Coburg, during the Diet of Augsburg (1530); his conferences in 1535 with representatives of the English Church, which had an important influence on the English Reformation and its literary monuments; the Wittenberg Concord of 1536 with Bucer and other representatives of the Reformed Church; and the Schmalkald Articles of 1537. Probably the point that has occasioned most heated discussion was his relation to the bigamy of Philip of Hesse in 1540 (see W. W. Rockwell, *Die Doppelehe des Landgrafen Philipp von Hessen*, Marburg, 1904).

2. Appreciation.—The greatness of Luther lies largely in the versatility of his gifts and the readiness with which he could call them into service. Intensity, concentration, earnestness, directness, and action are constantly present. Beneath his efforts there is always some important practical end. His scholarship has a higher end than mere love of learning. He availed himself of the weapons of humanism, so far as he could use them, without being in any sense a humanist. He had lectured for years on philosophy, only to repudiate both the Greeks and the scholastics. His writings abound in numerous historical allusions, without suggesting that he ever could be rated as a historical investigator. It is rather his experience as a Christian that is ever leading him the more deeply into the treasures of Holy Scripture, to find therein the solution of the problems of human life.

As a professor he was neither a scientific exegete nor a systematic theologian. He cut loose from all scholastic formulæ and methods. While he could not entirely escape from the influence of mediævalism, he was in constant antagonism to its authority. Even in the class-room he was a great preacher, stimulating the thought and life of his pupils, instead of retailing stereotyped definitions. His lectures were almost entirely confined to particular books of the Bible, which he expounded with great freedom of manner.

As an author, it is in his form rather than his matter that he reflects the present moment. Eminently conservative and slow to reach a conclusion, when once he has reached it he writes in an intense glow of feeling; words crowd one upon the other with great rapidity of thought, and with wealth of illustration often of the most homely character. He never has difficulty in making his meaning intelligible. He can write with equal ease as a scholar or for the plainest of the people. He loves paradoxes. He concentrates his attention so intensely on the particular form of the subject before him as to make no qualifications in order to forestall possible incorrect inferences or misrepresentations. The whole, real Luther can be read only by placing side by side his declarations under varying circumstances, and against opponents that widely differ. Few writers, therefore, can be so readily perverted by partisans. His language is not infrequently rough, and his allusions such as were in keeping with the rude age in which he lived.

He was master of the art of translation. Not verbal exactness, but the precise reproduction of the very shade of meaning of the original in the language of the simplest people of a later age, was his aim. His German Bible is a modern book, which at last fixed the form and became the standard of modern German. His hymns are paraphrases of Scripture, or free renderings of the old Latin hymns of the Church. His sermons are most frequently expositions of long passages of Scripture, and grow naturally out of the text, as applied to contemporary circumstances and conditions; and hence generally reflect that with which his attention at the time was chiefly occupied. They have come to us mostly as taken down in shorthand by some of his hearers, and not in finished form from his own pen.

His contributions to the re-organization of churches are embodied not only in documents that bear his name, but also in those of his co-labourers, Melanchthon, Bugenhagen, and others, who applied the principles which he laid down, and acted with his constant co-operation and advice. He was the advocate of liberal culture, the study of the Greek and Latin classics, the education of women, and free public libraries. So far was he from precipitate and revolutionary methods of reform that he proceeded with the greatest caution, upholding what had been fixed and approved by long usage, until a break with the past was no longer avoidable, but, when the critical moment came, always acting with promptness and decision. His aim was not even a restoration of Scriptural models, but the continuance of whatever in life, worship, and organization was not contrary to Scripture. External union was approved only as it was the expression of a preceding inner unity. Agreement as to the faith of the gospel was the condition of all attempts at Church union, which he esteemed valuable only as the servant of faith; hence the faith was never to be adjusted to the supposed expediencies of union.

As a theologian, his chief effort, on the negative side, was to free theology from its bondage to philosophy, and to return to the simplicity of Scripture. He was dissatisfied with technical theological terms, because of their inadequacy, even when the elements of truth which they contained restrained him from abandoning them. He was not without a historical sense and a reverence for antiquity, provided that it was subjected to the tests of Holy Scripture. Scripture was not to be interpreted by the Fathers, but the Fathers were to be judged by their agreement or disagreement with Scripture. It was his especial privilege to have entered into the spirit of St. Paul as none before him, not even Augustine. Luther's theology is Pauline theology, in the language of modern times. It begins and ends with the revelation of God in Jesus Christ. Christology is the key to all knowledge of the nature and attributes of God and the doctrine of the Trinity. Christ is the interpreter of Scripture. All doctrines are to be considered in their relation to Christ. With Augustine, he taught the organic union of all men in Adam, and the organic union of all sins in original sin. Original sin is emphasized rather as the corrupt state resulting from the Fall than as the act itself whence this state proceeds—a state of spiritual death, from which man can neither of himself escape nor contribute towards his deliverance. The Incarnation presupposes man's sin. God became man in order, by His sufferings and death, to provide redemption. In the personal union, as the result of incarnation, the integrity of both natures is preserved, the divine inseparably pervading and energizing the human; the human bringing the possibility of suffering, and the divine sustaining and imparting to the human its infinite efficacy. The humiliation (*kenosis* [*q.v.*]) is not of the divine nature, but of the divine person in His human nature. Hence humiliation is not synonymous with incarnation, but is only a determination of the human nature, glorified from the very first moment of its union with the divine. Redemption is made for all men and all sins, although not received and realized by all. The doctrine of predestination, he insists, should always be treated as a supplement to Christology, since what God has predetermined concerning our salvation from eternity He has revealed in the gospel, and, therefore, the gospel itself exhibits the contents of God's eternal decree concerning salvation. The blessings of salvation, to be realized, must be appropriated by faith; but this faith is God's gift. Man cannot believe in Christ, or come to Him, by his own reason or strength. It is the office of the Holy Spirit alone to bring man to Christ and Christ to man, to call, enlighten, and regenerate. If man is saved, it is entirely by the work of the Holy Spirit in applying redemption through Christ; if he is lost, it is entirely by his own persistent resistance of the offers of divine grace. There are no degrees in justification; it is perfect and complete, however weak the faith that apprehends it, since the righteousness which it imparts is the perfect righteousness of Christ. If regarded as forgiveness, where the least sin is forgiven, all are forgiven, and where the least sin is unforgiven, none are forgiven. But justification is more even than forgiveness. Christ and man have exchanged places; so that, while all the guilt of man is assumed by Christ, all the righteousness of Christ is transferred to man. Hence the confidence of man before God. Faith kindles love. As an active principle, faith not only receives what God offers, but also, through the new powers imparted with justification, exercises itself in obedience towards God, and in efforts for the good of man.

'It is as impossible to separate works from faith, as it is to separate heat and light from fire' (*Introduction to the Epistle to the Romans*, 1522 [*Works*, Erlangen ed., lxiii. 124 f.]). This passage has called forth the unqualified commendation of the Roman Catholic theologian, J. A. Moehler, although he incorrectly adds that it is 'in the most amiable contradiction with the Lutheran theory of justification' (*Symbolik*[8], Mainz, 1872, i. 163, tr. J. B. Robertson, London, 1843, i. 185).

Furthermore, the Holy Spirit comes to men only in and through the Word and Sacraments, through the word of the Law, producing sorrow for sin, and through the gospel, *i.e.*, the promise of the forgiveness of sins producing faith. The office of the Sacraments is to individualize the general promise of the gospel. The chief thing in baptism is not the water, but the Word, which, in and with the water, is applied to the person baptized. The chief thing in the Lord's Supper is not the bodily eating and drinking, but the assurance, 'Given and shed for you,' which is declared to the guests, and sealed by the elements and the heavenly mystery that they offer. Since, wherever this Word is preached, whether orally or visibly in the Sacraments, the Holy Spirit is active, Word and Sacraments become marks, designating where at least some truly believing children of God are to be found; *i.e.*, they indicate the presence of the Church, which otherwise is a matter of faith, as the Creed confesses: 'I *believe* in the Holy Catholic Church, the communion of saints.' The direct relation of each individual to Christ, unmediated by any other agency than Word and Sacrament, creates the spiritual priesthood of believers, and obliterates the distinction between an order of priests and laymen. The ministry of the gospel is not a priesthood, but an office of the Church for the administration of Word and Sacraments, in which administration ministers are only the executives of the congregation, and, through the congregation, of Christ Himself, who has called and ordained them. Distinctions of rank among ministers are not admissible by divine law, but may be very advantageous when agreed upon simply according to human law. Uniformity of Church government and ceremonies is unnecessary, however desirable it may be as a matter of expediency. The Church has no power but that of the Word. Even in regard to those matters where the Word of God allows no freedom, we have no right to attempt to constrain others by any other means than by the preaching of the Word.

'I will preach and talk and write against these things, but no one will I attempt to force' (*Eight Sermons preached at Wittenberg, Lent, 1523* [*Works*, Erlangen ed., xxviii. 219]). 'The Word that has created the heavens and the earth must do this, or it will be left undone' (*ib.*).

The dualism in ethics that pervaded the mediæval religionism, according to which there is an inherent antagonism between the spiritual and the material, the heavenly and the earthly, entirely disappears in Luther. The separation caused by sin is removed by redemption and regeneration, and the spiritual now pervades the material, the heavenly the earthly. Hence the believer is not only a spiritual priest, but also a spiritual king, and lord over all things; and his chastened enjoyment of them belongs to that gratitude which he owes the Redeemer who has provided them for him. Nevertheless, while by faith lord over all, by love he is servant of all, and obeys God's law from an inner necessity of his regenerated nature (cf. C. E. Luthardt, *Die Ethik Luthers in ihren Grundzügen*, Leipzig, 1867, *Geschichte der christlichen Ethik*, do. 1893, vol. ii.).

Probably with only one exception in all history, no one has been so much praised or so bitterly and incessantly attacked as Luther. The discussion of his life and deeds is constantly renewed with all the interest of almost contemporaneous occurrences. His voluminous works, many of them reaching us through the notes of others instead of from the pen of the author himself, the memoranda of friends who jotted down from memory fragments of his conversations in the bosom of his family, his most confidential letters to his most intimate associates, humorous and satirical as well as serious, afford an inexhaustible mine for students of successive generations. Researches in archives heretofore closed and in libraries where they have lain unnoticed are bringing to light MSS of decided historical importance. Thus, in the last year of last century, his lectures on the Epistle to the Romans,[1] for which scholars had long been looking, were found in so public a place as the Berlin Library, shortly after a student's notes of the same lectures had been discovered in the Vatican, and succeeding only by a little over ten years the discovery of lectures on the Psalms, belonging also to his formative period. New biographies from both friends and opponents, as well as from those who profess to apply with rigid impartiality the highest standards of historical criticism, succeed each other with a frequency that is remarkable when it is remembered that he has been dead for over three centuries and a half, showing clearly that the last word has not been said on many questions that he started, and that cannot be answered without a thorough study of his own presentations.

LITERATURE.—(*a*) Of the more recent Roman Catholic critics of Luther and his work, the following may be mentioned: **J. Janssen**, *Geschichte des deutschen Volkes seit dem Ausgang des Mittelalters*, 8 vols., Freiburg im Br., 1879–94, Eng. tr., 16 vols., London, 1896–1911; **H. S. Denifle**, *Luther und Luthertum*^{2}, 2 vols., Mainz, 1906; **H. Grisar**, *Luther*, 3 vols., Freiburg im Br., 1911–12.

(*b*) Among the replies called forth are the following: **J. Köstlin**, *Luther und J. Janssen, der deutsche Reformator und ein ultramontaner Historiker*^{2}, Halle, 1883; **R. Seeberg**, *Luther und Luthertum in der neuesten katholischen Beleuchtung*, Leipzig, 1904; **T. Kolde**, *P. Denifle, seine Beschimpfung Luthers*, do. 1904; **J. Haussleiter**, *Luther im röm. Urteile*, do. 1904; **W. Köhler**, *Ein Wort zu Denifle's Luther*, Tübingen, 1904; **G. Kawerau**, *Luther in kath. Beleuchtung, Glossen zu H. Grisar's Luther*, Leipzig, 1911. The results are condensed in: **W. Walther**, *Für Luther wider Rom*, Halle, 1906 (an exhaustive answer to the polemics of Janssen, G. G. Evers, and Denifle); and **H. Boehmer**, *Luther im Lichte der neueren Forschung*^{3}, Leipzig, 1914.

(*c*) The collected works of Luther have been comprised in seven editions of varying excellence and completeness: the Wittenberg (1539–58); the Jena (1555–58); the Altenburg (1561–64); the Leipzig (1729–40); J. G. Walch (1740–53), of which the St. Louis (1880–1910) is a thoroughly revised reprint; the Erlangen (beginning in 1826); the Weimar, the fullest and edited with greatest critical accuracy, under the patronage of the German Emperor. It was begun in 1883, and is still far from completion. For details concerning these editions see *PRE*^{3}, art. 'Luther.' A very convenient edition of select works, edited with critical care and with introductions, is that of G. Buchwald, G. Kawerau, J. Köstlin, M. Rade, and E. Schneider, 8 vols., with 2 supplementary vols., 3rd ed., Berlin, 1905. Of greater scientific value is **O. Clemen**, *Luther's Werke in Auswahl*, 4 vols., Bonn, 1912–14.

(*d*) The list of biographies begins with that of **Melanchthon**, published the year after Luther's death, in the introduction to the second Latin volume of the Wittenberg edition of Luther's works. Mention may be made of the following: **M. Meurer**, Leipzig, 1843, ^{3}1870; **J. Köstlin**^{5}, ed. G. Kawerau, Berlin, 1903; **T. Kolde**, Gotha, 1884–93; **M. Rade**, Neustadt, 1887; **A. Hausrath**, Berlin, 1904; and the English biographies of **C. Beard**, London, 1889; **H. E. Jacobs**, New York, 1898; **T. M. Lindsay**, Edinburgh, 1900, and esp. in his *History of the Reformation*, i., do. 1907; **H. Preserved Smith**, London, 1911; **A. C. McGiffert**, do. 1911. A very condensed, but most excellent and suggestive, classification of biographers and other writers on Luther, according to schools, is the work of Boehmer, above cited, pp. 7–27. For a critical study of Luther's theology see the treatises on that title by **T. Harnack**, Erlangen, 1862–67, and **J. Köstlin**, Stuttgart, 1863, Eng. tr. of 2nd German edition (1883) by C. E. Hay, Philadelphia, 1897.

HENRY E. JACOBS.

LUTHERANISM.—Notwithstanding the protests which Luther himself raised against it, the term 'Lutheran' was soon applied in the 16th cent. to the principles of which he was the chief advocate. However necessary plans for Church organization became when the attempt was made forcibly to suppress his protests, it had never been Luther's aim either to found a new Church or even within the historically existing Church to carry out any elaborately pre-arranged form of re-organization. Nor was the initiative for such re-organization taken by Luther or by those theologians who were most closely associated with him, but either by the radical extremists whom he repudiated or by the Protestant rulers, who justly realized that the churches in their realms could not be left without some form of administration.

Lutheranism starts with the assertion of the responsibility of the individual conscience to God alone in all matters of faith and life. But, in maintaining this position, it does not proclaim pure individualism, since the conscience is always bound by the Word of God, and that Word is not to be interpreted arbitrarily, but by comparing spiritual things with spiritual. In its treatment of the doctrine of the Church, the emphasis rests not so much upon the external institution, with a well-defined organization and codes of ecclesiastical laws, as upon the association of truly Christian people, maintained by their communion in the one faith of the gospel, through the activity of one and the same Spirit within their hearts and minds. The appeal, accordingly, is never made to the authority of any outward visible organization, but to the individual conscience. All Church power inheres in the Word of God.

'This power is exercised only by teaching or preaching the Gospel, and administering the Sacraments' (*Augsburg Confession*, art. xxviii.).

The Church has no sword but that of the Spirit with which to enforce obedience. Nevertheless, as for the administration of Word and Sacraments, external association, as well as the internal communion of believers with each other, is necessary; the external Church must always be maintained, but the form of its organization must be determined by the circumstances in which the Church is placed, the preservation of the pure Word and Sacraments being the first consideration. The preference is always on the side of that which has been historically approved, a break in the existing order being justified only when such order cannot be maintained without impairing fidelity to God's Word. It was not by any concerted action among Lutherans, nor with any thought of a united Lutheran Church, that the Church constitutions of the Reformation period were formulated, but they were prepared in various countries and provinces according to the peculiar needs of each. Externally, there were many Lutheran churches, but no one Lutheran Church. The very first word of the first article of the Augsburg Confession ('ecclesiæ apud nos') declares this. There was, however, an external bond in their common confession. This confession, properly speaking, is no particular historical document, however widely accepted among Lutherans, but the enunciation of those Scriptural principles for which the Lutheran Church peculiarly stands. Such confession, however, has found concrete expression in certain classical historical agreements that have greater or less recognition. It is not the Confession of Faith, but the faith of the Confession, that determines the Lutheranism of any individual teacher

[1] Critically edited and published, with historical introduction, by J. Ficker, *Luther's Vorlesungen über den Römerbrief*, 2 vols., Leipzig, 1908.

or Church body. Where the doctrines of the Confessions are held and confessed, even though the Confessions themselves be not subscribed, or even known, the Lutheran character of the teaching is established; while, on the other hand, where the contents of the Confessions are not cordially received, as a matter of faith, *i.e.* as derived from God's Word, and there is no subscription to such Confessions with qualifications expressed or with mental reservations, the test is not met. A real Confession of Faith is not so much a law as the joyful declaration of Christian freemen of the liberty that they have attained in Christ, and of the limits within which this liberty is to be found and exercised (cf. art. CONFESSIONS, vol. iii. p. 845).

What are known historically as the Lutheran Confessions are not attempts to summarize the doctrines of the Holy Scriptures, as are various other Confessions in Christendom that are, in reality, systems of doctrine. The confessional development of Lutheranism has proceeded on the principle that Holy Scripture is its own interpreter, and needs no formal explanation by Church authority, unless the meaning of Scripture be involved in serious controversies that greatly agitate the Church and call for the careful guarding of the purity of the gospel from those who would pervert it. Articles of faith that have not been attacked or misrepresented need no confessional treatment. A Confession, from this view, should never be an exhaustive presentation of the Church's faith, but there should be a readiness, as new controversies arise, to meet them with the same weapons and in the same spirit with which preceding controverted points have been treated. Hence the Augsburg Confession closes with the words:

'If anything further be desired, we are ready, God willing, to present ampler information according to the Scriptures.'

The Lutheran Confessions have thus been determined by certain practical ends in view at several crises in the experience of the churches that call themselves Lutheran.

Of these Confessions, the two Catechisms (cf. art. CATECHISMS [Lutheran], vol. iii. p. 253 ff.), both written by Luther in 1529, are handbooks of elementary religious instruction rather than theological documents. The four theological Confessions are: the unaltered Augsburg Confession, the Apology of the Augsburg Confession, the Schmalkald Articles, and the Formula of Concord. The first of these chronologically, as well as by general recognition, the Augsburg Confession, was prepared by Melanchthon for presentation at the Diet of Augsburg in 1530. It is an irenic document, emphasizing the points of agreement with the Roman Church, in the hope that some way might yet be found to avoid a break in the Western Church. The term 'unaltered' is used to distinguish the Confession presented at Augsburg from unauthorized revisions made by Melanchthon personally in 1540 and 1542, in the interests of a nearer approach to the Reformed. The fact that the term 'unaltered' may not strictly belong to even the best text—since the original copies placed in the hands of the Emperor Charles V. have both been lost, and Melanchthon was compelled to reproduce the Confession from the very full notes of himself and his colleagues for publication the succeeding spring—does not justify the rejection of the distinction historically fixed between the two types of the Confession. The Apology of the Augsburg Confession (1531) is a full and learned defence, also written by Melanchthon against the criticisms contained in 'The Confutation of the Augsburg Confession' by the Roman theologians at Augsburg. The Schmalkald Articles (1537), prepared by Luther, with a long Appendix by Melanchthon, mark a stage in the controversy with Rome when the differences were no longer reconcilable. The Formula of Concord (1577) gives a decision concerning controversies among Lutherans, as the other Confessions had treated those which had assailed them from without (see, further, art. CONFESSIONS, § 13).

Differences between Luther and Melanchthon were intensified among their followers. These differences, due primarily to differences of temperament, training, and religious experience, caused no personal rupture between them. Melanchthon, gentle, timid, and sensitive, loved the retirement and occupations of the study, and shrank from conflict. Far more of a humanist than Luther, he was swept by the force of events, and, much to his regret, from classical studies into the current of theological discussions. He had passed through no such inner spiritual conflicts as had Luther. Accordingly, he excelled in the sphere of the formal rather than of the material. No one could give such accurate and graceful literary expression to Luther's thoughts. But, when Luther's influence was removed, he was not only vacillating, but dominated by two principles, viz. a much higher regard than Luther for patristic authority, and a greater concern for the external peace and the impressiveness of the Church's government. He was frequently involved in negotiations with respect to Church politics, which compromised his position, and brought into prominence his great contrast with Luther in this particular. Notwithstanding his sharp arraignment of scholastic methods in the first edition of his *Loci Communes* (1521), he soon manifested a bent towards the principles which he had repudiated, placed undue importance upon the philosophy of Aristotle, and became the founder of Lutheran scholasticism. The perpetuation of these two types of thought has caused not only differences in regard to the attitude of their adherents to individual Confessions, but also a stricter or a laxer standard of Confessional subscription. The Formula of Concord is a formal repudiation of Melanchthonianism in its divergence from Luther.

Of the two principles of Protestantism, the formal and the material, it has often been observed that Lutheranism lays greater stress upon the material—'Justification by Faith alone'—than upon the formal—'The Sole Authority of the Holy Scriptures.' While, in fact, the two are never separated, the Scriptures are regarded as the absolute norm of revealed truth rather than as a magazine or receptacle in which the truth is stored. For it must not be forgotten that the gospel itself was proclaimed orally before it was committed to writing, and was no less the power of God unto salvation where thus preached, or where taught by those who had heard it from the first ear-witnesses, than when read on the printed page. Nor can the Scriptures be correctly apprehended except as in regeneration a new spiritual sense is imparted.

'When even the most able and learned men upon earth read or hear the Gospel of the Son of God, and the promise of eternal salvation, they cannot, from their own powers, perceive, apprehend, understand or believe and regard it true, but the more diligence and earnestness they employ to comprehend with their reason these spiritual things, the less they understand or believe, and before they become enlightened, or taught of the Holy Ghost, they regard this only as foolishness or fictions, 1 Cor. 2. 14' (Formula of Concord, pt. ii. ch. ii. § 9, Eng tr., H. E. Jacobs, *Book of Concord*, p. 553).

The true interpretation of Scripture is to be found only as the relation of each part to Christ as the centre is correctly apprehended, and this is possible only by the regenerated man.

While protesting against all ecclesiastical authority that arrays itself against Holy Scripture, Lutheranism lays great stress upon the continuous witness to the truth of the gospel, given through the Holy Spirit, as this truth is applied and developed from age to age in believing personalities. Such believers, according to its teaching, constitute the inner spiritual organism of the Church. In this respect its doctrine is in contrast with that of Rome, on the one hand, which lays so much importance upon the decisions of the externally organized Church, and that of the Reformed, on the other, which is apt to isolate the individual from his historical relations and the mediation of those through whom Word and Sacraments reach him. The same principle obtains in its conception of the relation of the Holy Spirit to Word and Sacraments, since, besides being a source of revealed truth, it regards the Word as a real means of grace through which alone the Spirit calls, illuminates, regenerates, and sanctifies; and the Sacraments as efficacious instrumentalities by which the promise of the gospel concerning the forgiveness of sins and the grace of God is individualized.

Like all ideals, those of Lutheranism suffer various modifications as embodied in a concrete form in external organizations. The union of Church and State in European lands has not only prevented the principles of Lutheranism from being applied in entire consistency to practice, but has also often interjected adjustments of theory and policy foreign to both its spirit and its teaching. As in the time of the Reformation, so at all times since, there have been those whose intense conservatism has shown the presence of a Romanizing, or whose greater freedom that of a Reformed, tendency. Indifferentism, Unionism, Mysticism, and Rationalism have had their learned advocates among those claiming the Lutheran name, and within Church organizations known as Lutheran, just as the Christian Church has much within it for which Christianity is not responsible.

LITERATURE.—For the study of the subject the Lutheran Confessions are indispensable. The best ed. is that of J. T. Mueller, Stuttgart, 1848, [10]Gütersloh, 1907, containing in parallel columns the official German and Latin texts, with exhaustive scholarly introductions and minute index, Eng. tr., ed. H. E. Jacobs, Philadelphia, 1882–83, 2 vols., vol. i. containing the Confessions, vol. ii. introductions and documents; condensed ed., containing Confessions alone, do. 1911.

Next in importance for an intelligent acquaintance with Lutheranism is Martin Chemnitz, *Examen Concilii Tridentini*, Frankfort, 1565–73, and many other edd. (far more than a thorough criticism of the Decrees and Canons of Trent; it is a very full discussion also of the constructive principles of Lutheranism in doctrine, ethics, liturgics, polity, and pastoral theology); see also G. L. Plitt, *Einleitung in die Augustana*, Erlangen, 1867; F. H. R. Frank, *Die Theologie der Concordienformel*, do. 1858–65; P. Tschackert, *Die Entstehung der lutherischen und reformierten Kirchenlehre*, Göttingen, 1910; F. Uhlhorn, *Geschichte der deutsch-lutherischen Kirche*, Leipzig, 1911; C. P. Krauth, *The Conservative Reformation and its Theology*, Philadelphia, 1871; T. E. Schmauk and C. T. Benze, *The Confessional Principle and the Confessions of the Lutheran Church*, do. 1911; treatises on Symbolics by G. B. Winer, Leipzig, 1824, [4]1882, Eng. tr., Edinburgh, 1871; H. E. F. Guericke[3], Leipzig, 1861; R. Hofmann, do. 1857; G. F. Oehler, Tübingen, 1876; K. H. G. von Scheele, Gotha, 1881; F. A. Philippi, Gütersloh, 1883, and E. F. K. Mueller, Leipzig, 1896; *Lutheran Cyclopedia*, ed. Jacobs and J. A. W. Haas, New York, 1899; *PRE*[3], *passim*; *Bureau of the Census, Special Reports*, 'Religious Bodies, 1906,' Washington, 1910, ii. 340–404.

HENRY E. JACOBS.

LUXURY.—I. **Historical aspects of luxury.**—One of the incentives towards social progress is the desire to procure a surplus after the needs of a mere physical existence have been met. Somewhere within the limits of this surplus is that portion of it which constitutes expenditure upon luxuries. What exactly is to be termed luxury depends to a large extent on the situation and condition of a community, and, in a somewhat less degree, upon its standard of life.

Once a tribe managed to procure a sufficient food supply to maintain itself, any increase rendered possible an unproductive consumption of the excess in the form of feasting, and under these circumstances a rude form of luxury would have been evolved. Thus a primitive type of luxury must have come into existence in pre-historic times. In the early civilizations luxury made its appearance in well-defined and striking forms. In Egypt, Nineveh, and Babylon, and at Tyre and Sidon, the primary tendency towards decoration and display appears to have shown itself in relation to religious observances, and, closely connected with this, there was the pomp of the royal family, where, as in Egypt, it claimed divine authority. But the example of the supreme ruler extended sooner or later to the governing classes, and in this way luxurious expenditure by individuals manifested itself. The chief gratifications sought were the pleasures of the table in eating and drinking, of personal adornment (both in dress and by the use of costly perfumes), of buildings and monuments (such as the Pyramids), or of dwellings and their appurtenances (as, for instance, the hanging gardens of Babylon). Among the Greeks there were traces of luxury in the heroic age, such as rich armour and dresses, and artistic ivory work, but it was at Athens after the defeat of the Persians (490–480 B.C.) and in the time of Pericles († 429 B.C.) that sumptuous expenditure became a characteristic both of the State and of the individual citizens. Public festivals were conducted on a scale of great magnificence, while the erection of public buildings was carried on at an outlay which was very great for the times. What differentiates the luxury of the Greeks from that of the Eastern nations was the artistic aspect of the movement. On the Acropolis there was the Pinacotheca beautified by the frescoes of the painter Polygnotus, near which stood the immense statue of Athene Promachos, the work of Pheidias, and beyond was the Parthenon, also embellished by the sculpture of Pheidias. With the rapid increase of wealth private expenditure increased; vases for household use became more decorative, and dress was more ornate. The conquests of Alexander the Great (336–323 B.C.) introduced the somewhat crude display of the Eastern nations, and, to a large extent, degraded the externals of social life. In Rome luxury became marked after the Punic Wars. Gladiatorial games had been introduced in 264 B.C., and by 186 B.C. lions and panthers were brought long distances at great cost to stimulate the lust for sensation which was being shown by the people. Rich citizens began to spend profusely on food and table appliances—anchovies were brought from Pontus and wine from Greece. As the power of Rome grew, luxury increased, till it culminated under the Empire. Augustus claimed to have erected 408 marble pillars, and to have provided 8000 gladiators and 3000 wild beasts for the arena. Ostentation developed into the excesses of Caligula and Nero, which were copied by private individuals according to their means. In the Byzantine Empire luxury was, if possible, greater than at Rome; it was certainly more decadent. If at Athens art had glorified luxury, at Constantinople luxury debased art; the Byzantine style has almost become synonymous with over-elaboration and tasteless display. Even before the Renaissance luxury had become remarkable in Italy, more particularly at Florence; afterwards it developed and produced a by-product in the encouragement of art and commerce. The more generous expenditure of the upper classes in France during the reign of Philip IV. (1285–1314) was met by his attempted sumptuary legislation regulating dress. In England Edward III. considered that extravagance was diminishing the taxable resources of the country, and, in order to prevent the evil, the statute 'de Cibariis Utendis' was passed in 1336, by which the courses of meals were limited to two, except on the principal feast-days, when three were permitted. In 1363 a further act was passed against outrageous and excessive apparel, while in 1463 there was a more detailed sumptuary law. The inflow of precious metals to Europe after the discovery of America, followed by the extension of foreign trade, increased the stock of several classes of goods which previously had been excessively rare and costly. Hence commodities which had been of great value became relatively less expensive. The improved organization of industry facilitated production, so that Adam Smith was able to point to the fact that the most common artificer's accommodation exceeded that of many an African king, 'the absolute master of the lives and liberties of ten thousand naked savages' (*Wealth of Nations*, bk. i. ch. i.). Sumptuary legislation in England may be said to have ended with the Tudors. Mercantilism, in its encouragement of manufactures, tended to permit the production of luxuries for exportation. The growth of foreign trade enabled seafaring nations to participate in it and in the re-exporting of rare and costly goods. Accordingly, though there remained a sturdy body of opinion against luxuries generally, and more especially against those luxuries brought from foreign countries, sumptuary laws ceased to be observed in England. In Scotland, on the other hand, as late as 1681 the Scots Parliament prohibited the importation of a long list of foreign commodities which were held to be 'superfluous.' The industrial revolution followed by the acceptance of the doctrine of *laissez-faire* (*q.v.*) made the State less disposed to interfere with private expenditure unless upon moral or social grounds, as, for instance, in the regulation of wines and spirits. In the 19th cent. the principle of the taxation of luxuries came to be more and more recognized, partly on the ground of restraining the consumer from a species of consumption which was hurtful to himself (*e.g.*, taxation of spirits), partly as raising revenue from what were admitted to be superfluities, and thereby collecting revenue from classes who would not pay taxes otherwise (*e.g.*, tea and sugar taxes). A few taxes may be regarded as having a sumptuary element, such as the tax on armorial bearings or those on male servants and on motor cars.

2. The economic questions arising out of the existence of luxury.—Social observers who approach the problem of luxury from the historical side are inclined to urge against it that it has been the cause of the fall of great empires. Frequently, if not invariably, luxury has been a symptom of decadence, but a closer analysis tends to show that the moral weakness had already shown itself, and, as it increased, it manifested itself in public and private extravagance, while extravagance again gave fresh impetus to the forces of political and social disintegration. In these cases it is clear that the evil lay in the abuse of luxury.

Some of the most powerful economic motives are to be found in the desire of men to realize an idea or scheme of life which seems to them an improvement on their present one. Once their mere bodily wants are satisfied, their further desires may be called luxuries. This, however, is not strictly accurate. In a great number of occupations the worker who is able to satisfy the former wants only would not be efficient. Therefore one must extend the meaning of the term 'necessaries' so as to include in it all those things which are required for efficiency. What is consumed beyond that point may well be described as consisting of luxuries. It follows that the term 'luxury' must be understood in relation to time, place, and the general circumstances. It is easy to determine whether any specific commodity is a luxury to a given individual in regard to whom the necessary data are known; the problem becomes much more difficult in the case of a whole community. Certain forms of expenditure, as a rule, do not aid efficiency, and these can usually be classed under the head of luxurious outlay; certain others, again, are usually incurred with the object of conferring distinction on the spender, and, where such can be isolated, they fall into the same class. For the rest, all that is possible is to note with care what happens in the majority of cases in order to ascertain whether a certain type of expenditure is necessary or a luxury.

In the case of individual expenditure, luxury can arise only where there is a surplus beyond physical needs. If that expenditure is so directed as to cut into the margin required for efficiency, then inroads are being made into future income-earning power. But, after full provision has been made for efficiency, there is yet another claim on the surplus—namely, that for the accumulation of capital. It is this claim that has led many economists to condemn luxury. Expenditure on luxury repays or restores the capital which was temporarily locked up in the commodities consumed as luxuries. Therefore such expenditure cannot leave production much larger than it had been before the goods were purchased.[1] Wealth which becomes capital is also consumed, but in such consumption it becomes an instrument for further production. Thus that part of the surplus which is used as capital is more fruitful as regards production than the other portion which, in the phraseology of J. S. Mill (*Principles of Political Economy*, London, 1886, bk. i. ch. iii.), is consumed unproductively.

Consumption of luxuries has other consequences which are partly economic, but which are also of considerable social and ethical importance. Expenditure on superfluities has a tendency towards a relaxation of concentrated effort. In extreme cases it weakens the moral fibre and opens the way to dangerous excesses. It not only tends to injure the person whose life is luxurious, but reacts on others by the force of example. Thus there is a contest in the fixing of the prevailing standard of living between luxury and a wise and discriminating frugality. Even in periods of national and individual prodigality there were always moralists who pleaded for a simple life, and it is the relative degree of support which either class of precepts attracts that fixes whether a particular age or a particular class can be described as luxurious or not.

In the view of luxury that has been adopted the central point is the fixing of the standard of expenditure which is required for full efficiency. As society progresses and as further resources become available, it becomes possible for a community to increase enjoyments which are largely immaterial. The enjoyment of art is a case in point. If progress is conceived in a wide sense, the highest culture becomes an element in national efficiency. Accordingly, in a wealthy nation, where the inequalities of incomes are not too great, a condition is possible where the dividing line between luxuries and the necessities for efficiency is drawn at a much higher point than in another community which is less fortunately situated. And the higher standard of living can become a step towards further advance in civilization. But, at the same time, there is a somewhat insidious danger—namely, that consumption which was begun as conducive to efficiency may be continued much beyond that point. By becoming luxurious, it reacts on efficiency, and in the end results in a check instead of an increase in progress.

[1] The matter is stated this way to allow for the possibility that the producer of the luxury may save a portion of the profit which he has realized from its sale. Such savings would be available for new production

LITERATURE.—[B. Mandeville,] *The Fable of the Bees*[4], London, 1725; I. Pinto, *Essai sur le luxe*, Amsterdam, 1762; David Hume, *Essays and Treatises*, Dublin, 1779 (pt. ii. 'Of Commerce, of Refinement in the Arts'); G. M. B[utel] D[umont], *Théorie du luxe, ou traité dans lequel on entreprend d'établir que le luxe est un ressort non seulement utile, mais même indispensablement nécessaire à la prospérité des états*, London and Paris, 1771; F. Fénelon, *Les Aventures de Télémaque*, Paris, 1699 (bk. xxii.); K. H. Rau, 'Ueber den Luxus,' in *Lehrbuch der polit. Oekonomie*, Leipzig, 1876–78; H. Baudrillart, *Histoire du luxe privé et public depuis l'antiquité jusqu' à nos jours*, 4 vols., Paris, 1878–80; W. Roscher, 'Ueber den Luxus,' in *Ansichten der Volkswirtschaft aus dem geschichtlichen Standpunkte*, Leipzig, 1861; Voltaire, *Le Mondain* (1736), and *Défense du Mondain ou l'apologie du luxe* (1737); H. Sidgwick, 'Luxury,' in *IJE* v. (Philadelphia, 1895); E. J. Urwick, *Luxury and the Waste of Life*, London, 1908; Werner Sombart, *Luxus und Kapitalismus*, Munich, 1913.

W. R. SCOTT.

LYCANTHROPY.—The word 'lycanthropy' is used in two senses. (1) It may indicate merely a form of madness in which the patient imagines that he is an animal, especially a wolf, and acts as such. This disease was common in antiquity, and especially in the Middle Ages, doubtless as a result of the wide-spread belief that transformation into animal form was possible (§ 3). (2) It indicates the popular belief that on occasion a human being can actually transform himself, or be transformed, into a wolf or some other animal. In this form he slays and eats men. But, if wounded while in his wolf form, it is found that a corresponding wound exists on the human body from which the transformation has taken place. When wounded or killed, the werwolf's human form is restored. While the wolf transformation is that which is or was most common in Europe, it is by no means the only one. For this superstition is practically world-wide, and everywhere it is generally the fiercest and most dreaded animals whose shapes are taken. The wolf transformation has been most usual in all parts of Europe and in N. Asia from early times, but in the North of Europe the bear form is also general, and in modern Greece the boar. In Abyssinia and E. Africa the hyena form is taken; in other parts of Africa the hyena, leopard, lion, and sometimes the shark, crocodile, or even the elephant. In India and other parts of Western Asia the tiger form is usual; in Borneo and Shoa the tiger or leopard; in China and Japan the tiger, fox, etc. In N. America the wolf form is mostly found; in S. America the jaguar. But, while in regions where such wild animals have become extinct the old tales are still told, now other less harmful animal forms are believed to be taken by witches or sorcerers—*e.g.*, those of the cat, hare, etc.—and in these animal shapes considerable mischief is supposed to be done, while the idea of the wound being continuous in the animal and human shapes ('repercussion,' see § 5) also prevails.

'Lycanthropy' is derived from λύκος, 'wolf,' and ἄνθρωπος, 'man,' the Gr. form being λυκάνθρωπος (cf. κυνάνθρωπος, 'dog-man'). The common English name is 'werwolf,' lit. 'man-wolf,' A.S. *werewulf*, O.H.G. *weriwulf*, Norman *guarwolf* (*wer*, 'man'; cf. O. Ir. *fer*, Lat. *vir*, and cf. 'wergild'). The French name for werwolf is *loup-garou*. In this case *garou* has been thought to be a corruption of *wer* and *loup*, but this is uncertain. The old French romances contain the forms *warouls, warous, vairous, vairals*. *Bisclaveret* for *bleiz-garou* (*bleiz*='wolf') occurs in the *Lai* of Marie de France (§ 1). The Slavic names are O. Ch. Slav. *vlŭkodlakŭ*, Slovenian *volkodlak*, Bulgarian *vŭlkolak*, Polish *wilkolak*, White Russ. *volkolak*, Russ. *volkulakŭ*, etc. The Serbian *vukodlak*, however, means 'vampire'; hence, probably, modern Gr. βρουκόλακας, βουρκόλακας, 'vampire,' though occasionally 'werwolf.' The Slavic form means literally 'wolf-haired,' or 'wolf-skinned.'

The wolf has long been regarded with superstitious awe. An old belief in Europe is to the effect that, if a wolf sees a man before being seen by him, the man is deprived of sight or hearing, or goes mad or dies (cf. Pliny, *HN* viii. 24; Verg. *Ecl.* ix. 53; Theocr. *Id.* xiv. 22; J. C. Lawson, *Modern Greek Folklore*, Cambridge, 1910, p. 10). J. Cardan (*de Subtilitate*, Lyons, 1554, p. 17) says that there is something in the eye of a wolf contrary to man, by which the breath is stopped, and consequently the voice. In European folklore the wolf is usually a creature of the devil (cf. the wolf-shape of Ahriman; see O. Dähnhardt, *Natursagen: eine Sammlung . . . Fabeln und Legenden*, i., Berlin, 1907, p. 146 f.).

It is obvious that lycanthropy, in so far as it involves an actual belief in shape-shifting, is connected with the wider belief in transformation into animal form, which is of universal occurrence. Men, especially medicine-men, claim or are believed to possess this power, as well as that of transforming others; it is also ascribed to the gods, spirits, demons, and ghosts of the dead, as well as to animals, which sometimes assume human form, as some of the following paragraphs will show (see METAMORPHOSIS). But the actual origins of the belief are probably to be sought elsewhere (see § 3).

1. Extent of the superstition.—In one form or another the werwolf superstition is world-wide.

It was known to the *ancient Greeks*. In Æsop the thief who pretends to be a wolf says that when he has yawned three times he will become a wolf. Circe changed men to wolves, etc., by means of drugs. The superstition is also found embedded in the myths pertaining to the cult of Zeus Lycæus, the Wolf Zeus. Lycaon, king of Arcadia, was said to have been changed into a wolf when he sacrificed a child on the altar of Zeus Lycæus.[1] In other versions of the myth Zeus came disguised as a labourer, and the sons of Lycaon slew a child and mixed its flesh with the sacrificial food set before the guest. Zeus then changed them to wolves, or slew them and transformed their father.[2] These myths probably arose from werwolf stories current in Arcadia, a district where wolves abounded. The stories took two forms.

In one it was said that at the yearly sacrifice on Mt. Lycæus he who at the sacrificial feast ate the flesh of the human victim mixed with that of animal victims became a wolf for ten years—a fate which is said to have befallen Demænetus, who afterwards became a victor in the Olympic games. If he abstained during that period from human flesh, he regained his human form.[3] In another version lots were drawn by the members of a certain family, and he on whom the lot fell was led to a lake, where he stripped and, hanging his clothes on an oak, plunged in and swam across. Emerging on the other side, he became a wolf and herded with wolves for nine years. In this case also, if he did not eat human flesh he regained his own form at the end of that time.[4]

Perhaps such stories, based on an existing werwolf belief, may have been connected with the ritual of the cult of the wolf-god, if the priests wore a wolf-skin and ate part of a human victim. This ritual wearing of a wolf-skin occurred in the cult of Apollo Soranus on Mt. Soracte, where the gild of worshippers, the Hirpi Sorani, or 'wolves of Soranus,' apparently wore skins of wolves and acted as wolves. Possibly the cult was totemistic in origin, and the Hirpi were members of a wolf clan.[5]

In *modern Greece* the old belief in lycanthropy still exists, either as such or in other forms. The name βρουκόλακας is applied in Thessaly and Epirus to those who fall into a trance or catalepsy, while their souls enter wolves and raven for blood,[6] or who in a state of somnambulism bite and tear man and beast. Stories exist of the *vrykolakas* being wounded, while next day a man is found with a similar wound, and he confesses to being a *vrykolakas*.[7] More usually, however, this word signifies a vampire in Greece. In Southern Greece the name λυκάνθρωποι is applied to men known in other parts as Karkantzari or, more usually, Kallikant-

[1] Paus. viii. 2.
[2] Lycophron, 481; Hyginus, *Fab.* 176.
[3] Plato, *Rep.* viii. 15, p. 565 D; Paus. viii. 2; Pliny, *HN* viii. 22.
[4] Paus. vi. 8; Pliny, *HN* viii. 22; cf. Augustine, *de Civ. Dei*, xviii. 17.
[5] See W. R. Smith, *Rel. Sem.*[2], p. 209; L. R. Farnell, *CGS* i. 41, who thinks that Lycaon 'may darkly figure the god himself'; cf. also O. Gruppe, *Griech. Mythol. und Religionsgesch.*, Munich, 1906, p. 805 f.
[6] *PC*[3] i. 313; C. Robert, *Les Slaves de Turquie*, Paris, 1844, i. 69.
[7] Lawson, p. 379 f.

zari. The Kallikantzari are beings of monstrous form, hurtful and evil, who destroy men and carry off women, and sometimes make a meal of their prey.[1] Lawson considers that the Kallikantzari represent the ancient Centaurs, whom he regards as a Pelasgic tribe of Centauri credited by the Achæans with shape-shifting. Some connexion also exists between them and the mummers of the Dionysia who represented the satyrs and Sileni. They appear and are feared from Christmas to Epiphany—the period of the Kalends when such mumming took place. In some districts, however, the Kallikantzari are equivalent to werwolves, and are regarded as men transformed into monstrous shapes, or seized with recurrent bestial madness at this period. This is attributed, *e.g.*, to the mountaineers of E. Eubœa. This madness may be congenital—*e.g.*, children born between Christmas and Twelfth Night are supposed to have a taste for human flesh. Lawson regards this as a modification of the original Kallikantzari belief caused by the werwolf superstition or by actual forms of insanity.[2] The name λυκοκάντζαροι is given to the Kallikantzari in Messenia and Crete, and in Macedonia they are called λύκοι. To escape these beings the house must be carefully closed at all openings; but a brave man may bind them with a straw rope. Various apotropæic and propitiatory rites are also in use to keep off these dreaded beings, who are 'a species of werewolves, akin to the Wild Boar and the Vrykolakas.'[3] Wicked Turks gradually turn into wild boars before death, and rush through the land on all fours, attacking wayfarers or trying to get into houses. After forty days such a being goes to the mountains, remaining there as a wild beast, but still wearing on its foot the ring which the man wore on his hand (cf. the Abyssinian *buda*, below).[4] The Bulgarians have a similar belief, but with them the transformation of the Turk takes place after death.[5] In Albania the *liouvgat* is a dead Turk with huge talons, wandering in his shroud, devouring what he finds, and strangling men.[6] Here the vampire superstition is approached (§ 4). In the Cyclades witches are thought to turn into birds at will. They are called στρίγλαι, and are akin to the Harpies.[7]

The *Romans* also knew of lycanthropy, and called those who changed their form *versipelles*, 'turn-skins.'[8] Vergil describes how by magic herbs Mœris became a wolf, and Propertius speaks of spells which have the same effect.[9] But the most detailed account is found in Petronius.

Niceros tells how his soldier friend stripped off his clothes and addressed himself to the stars. Then he 'circumminxit vestimenta,' and all at once became a wolf, which ran howling into the woods. Niceros next heard from a widow whom he visited that a wolf had been worrying her cattle, and had been wounded in the neck. On his return home he found his friend bleeding at the neck, and knew then that he was a *versipellis*.[10] This is a typical and early version of the werwolf story.

In more modern times the superstition survives in *Italy*. Straparola tells how Fortunio received from a wolf the power of changing to wolf form, and the superstition is also referred to by Basile. At the present day in Naples the werwolf, who is a man cursed by being born on Christmas night, is known by having long nails, and runs on all fours, but retains the human form, and tries to bite. If blood is drawn from him, his madness ceases. This is a case of lycanthropy in its medical sense.[1] More akin to the true werwolf superstition is the general belief that witches can turn into black cats and do much harm, especially to children. In one case a woman caught such a cat and clipped its hair, whereupon it turned into the witch.[2]

1 G. F. Abbott, *Macedonian Folklore*, Cambridge, 1903, pp. 73 f., 93; W. H. D. Rouse, *FL* x. [1899] 174 f.; J. Rennell Rodd, *Customs and Lore of Modern Greece*, London, 1892, p. 197 f.; Lawson, p. 190 ff.

2 Lawson, pp. 208, 254.

3 Abbott, pp. 73 f., 93; Rouse, *FL* x. 174 f.; Rodd, p. 197 f.

4 Abbott, p. 215 f. 5 *Ib.* p. 216.

6 A. Dozon, *Contes albanais*, Paris, 1881; J. G. v. Hahn, *Albanes. Studien*, Jena, 1854, i. 16 f.

7 J. T. Bent, *The Cyclades*, London, 1885, p. 388.

8 Pliny, *HN* viii. 22.

9 Verg. *Ecl.* viii. 95 f.; Prop. iv. 5.

10 Petron. *Sat.* 61.

Among the *Semites* lycanthropy was not unknown, but recorded instances of the belief are few. Among the Ṣeïʿar in Ḥaḍramaut part of the tribe could change into ravening werwolves in time of drought, others into vultures or kites.[3] The Arabs also regarded some men as having the nature of a hyena, and said that, if a thousand men were shut up with one of these and a hyena came, it would go at once to him.[4]

The belief among the *Celts* is illustrated by a story told by Giraldus Cambrensis.

An Irish priest was met by a wolf in Meath and desired to come and see his dying wife. They were natives of Ossory, whose people had been cursed for their wickedness by St. Natalis, and were compelled to take two by two a wolf-shape for seven years, returning to their own form at the end of that time. The priest was persuaded to give the she-wolf the sacrament, for the other turned her skin down a little, showing that she was an old woman. Giraldus says that he was asked to give his advice on this case at the synod of Meath two years after, and that it was referred to the pope.[5]

A citation in the *Book of Ballymote* (140*b*) says that the 'descendants of the wolf' in Ossory had the power of changing themselves and going forth to devour people. St. Patrick is also said to have cursed a certain 'race' in Ireland so that they and their descendants are wolves at a certain time every seventh year, or for seven years on end.[6] These may be explanatory legends about older wolf-totem clans, later accused of lycanthropy—an already current superstition—when totemism was requiring an explanation, as in the case of the wolf-clan in Arcadia. To the same category may be referred the statements of early English travellers in Ireland to the effect that the Irish took wolves as godfathers, prayed to them to do them no ill, and used their teeth as amulets. Lycanthropy ran in families, and here also it may point to an older totem clan. Laignech Fáelad and his family could take a wolf-shape at will and kill the herds, and Laignech was called Fáelad because he was the first of them to go as a wolf.[7] In Irish and Welsh *Märchen* transformation to wolf-form of children by a stepmother or of a husband by a wife is not uncommon.[8] Giraldus already refers to the belief that hags in Wales, Ireland, and Scotland can change to hares and suck cattle for their milk, but, with St. Augustine, regards this supposed change as a delusion of the senses.[9] This belief is thus contemporary with that in lycanthropy, but long survived it. Later Celtic witches—Irish, Welsh, Manx, Scots—usually turn into hares or cats, less often into dogs, weasels, ravens, porpoises, whales, etc., for the purpose of doing mischief. In Donegal the change is said to be effected by a hair rope made of a stallion's mane and by the recital of charms. In some cases the transformation is confined to certain families. Such witch animals can be shot only with a silver bullet. When followed up, the woman has resumed her true form and is found to have a corresponding wound. A miller in Cork who saw a number of

1 *FL* viii. [1897] 9.

2 *Ib.* viii. 3; C. G. Leland, *Etruscan Roman Remains*, London, 1892, pp. 203, 222.

3 W. R. Smith, *Rel. Sem.*⁴, p. 88.

4 W. R. Smith, *Kinship and Marriage in Arabia*, new ed., London, 1903, p. 232.

5 *Top. Hib.* ii. 19.

6 W. Stokes, *RCel* ii. [1873] 202; *FL* v. [1894] 310 f.

7 E. Windisch and W. Stokes, *Irische Texte*, Leipzig, 1880 ff., iii. 377, 421.

8 P. Kennedy, *Legendary Fictions of the Irish Celts*, London, 1886, p. 267; W. Larminie, *W. Irish Folk Tales*, London, 1894, p. 11.

9 *Top. Hib.* ii. 19.

cats attacking his flour threw his knife at them and cut off the leg of one. Next morning he found his daughter with her hand cut off, and concluded that she was a witch. Hares are usually thought to be unlucky, and are suspected of being witches in disguise. The ancient Welsh laws already speak of their magical character, regarding them as companions of witches, who often assumed their shape.[1]

The *Slavic* werwolf belief is referred to under DEMONS AND SPIRITS (Slavic), vol. iv. p. 624[a]. Possibly the Neuri, mentioned by Herodotus (iv. 105), were a Slavic people (cf. E. H. Minns, *Scythians and Greeks*, Cambridge, 1913, p. 102 f.). The Scythians and Greeks said that every year each Neurian became a wolf for a few days and was then restored to human shape. Among the Magyars witches and wizards assume the form of horses, cats, etc. If the former are caught and shod or the latter injured, they are found next morning in human form with iron shoes on hands and feet or seriously wounded.[2] Hertz notes the sinister character of the belief through its connexion with that in the vampire, the names for both being interchangeable.[3]

The Serbians think that the *vukodlak* have annual gatherings, when they hang their wolf-skins on trees. Should such a skin be taken and burnt, the owner retains human form. A girdle of human skin laid across a threshold by a witch in a house where a wedding is taking place will cause all who step over it to become wolves. In three years' time, if the witch covers them with skins with the hair turned outwards, they resume their human form. This is a Polish belief. In White Russia the werwolf is sometimes a man transformed by the devil, and, contrary to the usual belief, he is harmless, but is driven to wander from place to place.[4]

In a Polish story a wolf seizes a girl at a merry-making and carries her off to the forest. Years after, one of the peasants meets his long-lost brother, who confesses that he was the wolf changed by sorcery, that he had carried off the girl, who had died of grief, and that then he was consumed with rage against all men and killed as many as he could. He had come to see his home once more, but must resume his wolf-form immediately, which he did.[5] In another case a peasant, released from his wolf shape, returned home to find his wife married again. He cried, 'Why am I no longer a wolf that I might punish this woman?' Immediately he was re-transformed, and killed his wife and child. The neighbours came and slew the wolf, when the body was seen to be that of a man.[6]

Olaus Magnus says that at Christmas many werwolves collect and try to enter houses to drink in the cellars. Between Lithuania, Samogitia, and Livonia is the wall of an old castle whither thousands of werwolves come to try their skill at leaping. The unsuccessful one is beaten by one of the captains or by the devil. The method of the transformation was to drink to one in a cup of ale and mumble certain words. Then he could assume or lay aside the wolf form when he pleased. The Livonian werwolves collected at Christmas, and crossed a river which had the power of changing them to wolves, like the lake in Arcadia. They resumed their human shape at the end of twelve days. In Livonia a servant whose power as a werwolf was disputed went to the cellar and soon after came out as a wolf. The dogs bit out one of its eyes, and next day the man appeared with one eye.[7]

In *Scandinavia* and *Germany* the superstition was well known, and here the wolf, and in the former also the bear, were animals into whose form the transmigration took place. Boniface, Archbishop of Mayence in the 8th cent., mentions the belief.[1] The change was caused by a man himself—*e.g.*, by donning a wolf-skin (*úlfhamr*, hence the name 'skin-changer'; cf. Lat. *versipellis*), or a wolf-girdle, or a girdle of human skin; or it might be forced upon him—*e.g.*, by throwing such a skin or girdle at him, or by shaking a wolf-skin glove at him. The girdle had sometimes magic signs on it, and was held in place by a buckle with seven catches. When the buckle was broken off, the transformation ceased. In such cases the man was a wolf or bear by night, and a man by day; or he assumed the animal form for nine days, or even for three, seven, or nine years, the eyes alone retaining a human appearance. He howled and devoured like the actual animal. Such persons were said to be *eigi einhamr*, 'not of one form,' or *hamramr*, *hamhleypa*, 'changing form.' In some instances the gift of transformation was imparted by trolls. Burchard of Worms speaks of certain *Parcæ* who at birth can cause that the child may later transform himself into a wolf or any other form.[2] In later times Finns, Lapps, or Russians were thought by Scandinavians to have the power of changing others to wolves or to bears at will,[3] and were therefore disliked. The belief was apparently much mingled with and probably influenced by the fact that wild warriors and outlaws—*e.g.*, the *berserkr*—wore wolf-skins or bear-skins over their armour or clad themselves in these, while they were often victims of ungovernable passion and acted as if they were animals.[4] This is illustrated in the earliest Scandinavian instance of the werwolf belief—that contained in the *Volsunga Saga* (chs. 5–8).

King Volsung had ten sons and a daughter, Signy, who was married to King Siggeir. Siggeir later slew Volsung and bound his sons in the stocks. There nine of them were devoured by an old she-wolf—the mother of Siggeir, who had taken this form. Through Signy's craft the tenth son, Sigmund, overcame this werwolf and went into hiding. Signy exchanged form with a sorceress, and had a son by Sigmund, called Sinfiötli. He and Sigmund took to a wandering life and, on one occasion, came to a house where two men were sleeping, with wolf-skins hanging above them. For nine days they were wolves and on the tenth day came out of their skins. Sigmund and Sinfiötli donned the skins and became wolves, and each went his way, after agreeing that neither should attack more than seven men without howling for the other. In the sequel Sinfiötli slew eleven men without Sigmund's aid. The latter, hearing of this, flew at his throat and wounded him. When he was healed and the day had come for doffing their wolf-skins, they agreed to lay them aside for ever, and burned them in the fire. Of this wild tale Baring-Gould (p. 38) has said that it is 'divested of its improbability, if we regard these skins as worn over their armour.' While this is true, and while *vargr*, 'wolf,' means also 'outlaw,' the story is an important witness to the belief itself, as is seen from the words of Goðmund to Sinfiötli, 'Thou thyself hast eaten wolves' meat and murdered thy brother. Thou hast often sucked wounds with cold mouth, and slunk, loathsome to all men, into the dens of wild beasts' (Vigfusson-Powell, i. 136).

In another wild tale from the *History of Hrolf Kraka*, Björn was transformed into a bear by his stepmother, who shook a wolf-skin glove at him. He lived as a bear and killed many of his father's sheep, but by night he always became a man, until he was hunted and slain (Sir W. Scott, *Minstrelsy*, London, 1839, p. 354).

---

1 *FLJ* i. [1883] 53, 87, ii. [1884] 258; *FL* viii. [1897] 17; W. Gregor, *Folk-Lore of N.E. of Scotland*, London, 1881, p. 128; D. Hyde, *Beside the Fire*, do. 1890, p. 128; S. Hibbert-Ware, *Descr. of Shetland Islands*, Edinburgh, 1822, p. 599; J. G. Dalyell, *Darker Superstitions of Scotland*, Glasgow, 1835, pp. 50, 53; J. Rhŷs, *Celtic Folklore*, Oxford, 1901, i. 294 f., 309, 326; J. A. MacCulloch, *Misty Isle of Skye*, Edinburgh, 1905, p. 240; C. I. Elton, *Origins of English History*, London, 1882, p. 297; J. G. Campbell, *Witchcraft and Second Sight in the Highlands and Islands of Scotland*, Glasgow, 1902, p. 6.

2 *FLJ* i. 354.

3 *Der Werwolf*, p. 113.

4 S. Baring-Gould, *The Book of Were-wolves*, p. 115 f.; J. Grimm, *Teut. Myth.* p. 1095.

5 Hertz, p. 118.

6 *Ib.*

7 Olaus Magnus, *Hist. of the Goths*, London, 1658, p. 193 f.; M. F. Bourquelot, 'Recherches sur la lycanthropie,' *Mém. de la soc. des ant. de France*, new ser., ix. 235. For further references to the Slavic werwolf see G. Krek, *Einleitung in die slav. Literaturgesch.*[2], Graz, 1887, p. 410; and, for Lithuanian material, A. Bezzenberger, *Litauische Forschungen*, Göttingen, 1882, p. 67 f.

1 *Sermo* xv. 'de Abren. Diaboli' (*PL* lxxxix. 870–872).

2 Baring-Gould, p. 56.

3 Grimm, *Teut. Myth.* p. 1097; B. Thorpe, *Northern Mythology*, London, 1851–52, ii. 18 f., 93 f.; G. W. Dasent, *Popular Tales from the Norse*[3], do. 1888, p. lxi f.; Vigfusson-Powell, *Corpus Poet. Boreale*, Oxford, 1883, i. 425; P. D. C. de la Saussaye, *Rel. of the Teutons*, Boston, 1902, p. 298. See also *ERE* iv. 632.

4 Cf. Vigfusson-Powell, i. 425; Baring-Gould, p. 36 f.

The poet Ari has a curious tale of two 'skin-changers,' Dubhthach and Storwolf. The former took the form of a bull, the latter of a bear. They fought, and next day were found in bed badly bruised.

Modern collections of Scandinavian and German *Märchen* contain many werwolf stories.

In one Swedish tale a cottager was transformed by a Vargamor or Wolf Crone (Troll-wife), because he had not crossed himself when felling a tree. Years after, he appeared at his house, and recovered his true form when his wife gave him food.[1] In a Danish tale a man, when in his wife's company, noticed that the time of the accustomed change drew near. He bade her strike with her apron at anything which came to her. Soon after a wolf attacked her; she struck at it, and the wolf bit a piece of the apron and disappeared. Presently the man came, carrying the piece, and explained that now he was free from the curse.[2] In a N. German tale a reaper saw his neighbour gird himself with a strap and become a wolf.[3] In another a woman told her husband to throw his hat at any wild beast which came. When she appeared as a wolf among the hay-makers, a boy stabbed her with a pitchfork. The wolf changed back to the woman, who was found to be dead.[4] A Dutch story tells how a man shot with an arrow a wolf which was attacking a girl, and that the arrow stuck in the wound. Next day he heard that a strange serving-man was dying with an arrow sticking in his side. He went to see him, and found his own arrow, whereupon the man confessed that he was a werwolf.[5] In a Flemish tale a shepherd received a wolf-skin from the devil, by which he became a wolf at night. If the skin was burned, he himself would suffer as if his own skin were being burned, but would be freed from this curse. In the sequel his master succeeded in releasing him in this way.[6]

In many modern tales and also in mediæval witchcraft belief the transformation of the witch was usually into a cat, dog, hare, or duck (the bird of Freya, great mother of the witches), and these, when wounded, became the woman with a similar wound in her body. Spina says that such cat-women ate the brain of a cat and rubbed themselves with the flesh of a newly-born child which had been offered to Satan.[7]

In *England* and *Scotland* werwolf stories are scanty, but there are traces of the superstition in early literature. The word *werwulf* in the sense of 'robber' occurs in the *Laws* of Canute, and it is also found in later ballads and poems. Gervase of Tilbury refers to the existence of men called *gerulfos* in Wales, *werwolf* in England, who change their form at the change of the moon. William of Malmesbury also alludes to the superstition.

A well-known old English poem, translated from a 12th cent. French poem, is that of *William and the Werwolf*, in which the king of Spain's son, changed to wolf form by his stepmother, rescues the king of Sicily's child, whom his uncle wishes to murder. The story relates how the wolf cared for the boy, his further adventures, and the eventual re-transformation of the wolf to his human form.[8] Drayton, in his *Mooncalf* (ii. 504), tells of a man who found that by gathering a certain herb at a certain hour with appropriate spells, and eating it, he would be changed into a wolf. Having done this, he committed much havoc on sheep, etc. When he attacked an ass which was a man so transformed, the latter assumed his rightful shape and caused the people to slay the lycanthrope.

If tales of werwolves are scanty, there are innumerable tales and traditions of witches changing to hares, cats, dogs, and the like in order to do harm. No charge is more common in the 16th and 17th cent. witch trials, and frequently the belief is found, as in the case of the werwolf, that such a wer-animal can be hurt only by a silver bullet. In some instances wounding causes the witch to assume her true shape, when she is found with a corresponding wound.[9]

In *France* the earliest literary version of the belief is found in the *Lai du Bisclaveret* of Marie de France (13th cent.).

A knight went from time to time to the forest, then the haunt of many werwolves, undressed, and became a wolf. He told his wife the secret, and she obtained his clothes on one of these occasions, after which he had to remain in wolf form. As a wolf he retained human wisdom, and eventually, through the king's command, his clothes and consequently his own form were restored to him, but not before he had revenged himself on his unfaithful wife.

This story is found in other literary versions—*e.g.*, the *Roman de Renard* of the Clerk of Troies (14th cent.), in the *Lai de Melion* (ed. F. Michel, Paris, 1832), in the story of *Arthur and Gorlagon*, and elsewhere. These are all literary versions of a folk-tale.[1] The legend of St. Ronan in mediæval Brittany told how he had taken the form of a werwolf and had eaten children.[2]

Gervase of Tilbury, in his *Otia Imperialia*, tells of a certain Pontio de Capitolio, who out of despair became a werwolf in Auvergne, ate children, and wounded older people. A carpenter hacked off one of his feet, and at once he resumed his human form, and acknowledged that the loss of his foot was his salvation.

The belief survived in modern times. In Normandy the werwolf was a godless man or one under a curse, who for four or seven years must nightly assume wolf-shape and submit to castigation by the devil.[3] In Berry those who, by a pact with the devil, at the cross-roads, at midnight, become *loups-garous* can be wounded only by a ball which has been blessed or has had the Lord's Prayer or Ave Maria said over it five times. Once wounded, they take human form, and the spell which attached them to Satan is broken.[4] In Brittany, towards the end of the 18th cent., sorcerers were supposed to take the form of wolves or clothe themselves with a wolf's skin when going to the Sabbat.[5] In many parts of France every *flûteur* is supposed to lead wolves, himself sometimes changed into a wolf, whereby he is placed beyond the power of shot. He directs the wolves where to go for hunting.[6] In Périgord sons of priests must rush to a fountain at full moon and plunge into it. They emerge, clad in a goat-skin, which the devil has given them, and rush about on all fours, attacking men and animals. They resume human form by plunging again into the fountain at daybreak.[7] This recalls the Arcadian and Livonian beliefs (see above). Numerous stories relate how a *châtelaine*, transformed into a wolf, cat, etc., has a paw cut off, and is afterwards found in bed with one hand lacking.[8] In a Breton tale a werwolf hid his wolf-skin in an oven. Sympathetic magic established a link between skin and owner, so that whatever was done to the skin happened to him. A fire was lit in the oven, and the owner of the skin soon began to leap about, crying, 'I burn, I burn.'[9]

In *Portugal* a seventh son, where there were no girls, was thought to belong to the devil and to become a werwolf—a belief found also in the Azores.[10]

Cervantes, in his *Persiles y Sigismunda* (ch. 8), relates how an enchantress made advances to Rutilio, who repelled her. She turned into a wolf. He stuck his knife into her breast, and as she fell her human form came back to her.

Passing now to *Asia*, clear evidence of the belief is found in *Armenia*. Sinful women are sometimes forced by a spirit to don a wolf-skin and become wolves for seven years. Soon the wolf nature

1 Thorpe, ii. 96. 2 *Ib.* ii. 168.
3 *Ib.* iii. 27. 4 *Ib.* iii. 76.
5 *Ib.* iii. 201. 6 Hertz, p. 68.
7 F. B. de Spina, *Quæstio de Strigibus*, ch. 20, in *Malleorum Quarundam Maleficarum*, Frankfort, 1582; Grimm, p. 1097; Hertz, p. 71 f.; Thorpe, ii. 191 f.
8 ed. F. Madden, London, 1832, Roxburghe Club.
9 Rhŷs, i. 326; Dalyell, pp. 50, 53, 560; J. Napier, *Folklore*, Paisley, 1879, pp. 70, 118; A. E. Bray, *Borders of the Tamar and the Tavy*, new ed., London, 1879, ii. 112; A. and J. Lang, *Highways and Byways on the Border*, London, 1913, pp. 183, 277.

1 For *Arthur and Gorlagon* see *FL* xv. [1904] 50 ff. Gorlagon was changed to a wolf by being struck with the thin end of a sapling which grew up on the night he was born. For the folk-tale see 'Prince Wolf'—a Danish version—*FLR* iii. [1880] 225 f., and a Norse version in Dasent, no. 36. In both the husband remains a wolf or bear through the wife breaking a tabu, and has originally been transformed by a stepmother.
2 *RCel* xxiv. [1904] 324.
3 A. Bosquet, *La Normandie romanesque et merveilleuse*, Paris, 1845, ch. 12; Hertz, p. 108.
4 Bourquelot, p. 247.
5 La Tour d'Auvergne-Corret, *Origines gauloises*[2], Paris, 1794, p. 39.
6 P. Sébillot, *Folk-lore de France*, i., Paris, 1907, p. 284 f.; cf. A. Dumas' story, *The Wolf-Leader*.
7 Sébillot, i. 205. 8 *Ib.* iv. 304.
9 *RCel* i. [1870] 420.
10 *FL* xiv. [1903] 142; cf. *FLR* iii. 143.

grows in them. They devour their children, then those of relatives, then children of strangers. Doors and locks fly open before them by night. In the morning the skin is doffed. If the skin is found and burned, then the woman suffers fearful agony and vanishes in smoke.[1] In Asia Minor generally werwolves are feared especially at Christmas and in Holy Week.

In *India*, where the tiger is the fiercest creature known, its form is supposed to be adopted. Already in the *Satapatha Brāhmana* the monomaniac is said to be consecrated to the man-tiger.[2] In most instances the Hindus attribute the power of shape-shifting to the aboriginal tribes. Numerous stories are current regarding men with the power of becoming wer-tigers—*e.g.*, among the Khonds (with whom, by the aid of a god, one of a man's four souls becomes a *mleepa* tiger), the Lushais, Kukis, etc.[3]

Dalton describes how a Kol, tried for murder, maintained that his victim was a wer-tiger, which he had followed to the man's house after it had killed his wife. The relatives of the victim had admitted that they had suspected him of such power and had handed him over to the prisoner, who slew him.[4]

Sometimes the eating of a root is believed to produce the change.[5] Occasionally the witch assumes the form of a badger and carries off children.[6] Witches also ride about on tigers or in the water on crocodiles, dishevelled, with glaring eyes, and heads turned round. Wizards also have tigers as familiars, or, as a Thana belief has it, mediums are possessed by a tiger-spirit.[7] The souls of those slain by tigers are believed to pass into tigers to slay and devour in their turn, or to sit on the heads of tigers and direct them to their prey, calling out in a human voice so as to attract the unwary.[8]

In *Indonesia* the wer-tiger is very commonly believed in among the Malays, Dayaks, etc. Sometimes the power of transformation is thought to be confined to one tribe, as in Sumatra to the Korinchi Malays. There are many tales of men leaving their garments in a thicket, whence a tiger has presently emerged, or in human form vomiting feathers of fowls eaten when in their tiger form. A wer-tiger slain was found to have gold-plating in its teeth, as the man who assumed tiger form had. The Lavas of Burma are also regarded as wer-tigers. While the wer-tiger is generally very dangerous, in Java it is believed to guard plantations against pigs, and the change is effected by spells, charms, fasting, etc. In Malaysia the medicine-man is sometimes possessed by a tiger-spirit, and acts as a tiger when exorcizing a spirit from a sick man.[9]

A gruesome Malay story of a Semang who became a tiger (*Si Ridong*, 'He of the hairy face'—a euphemism), and sucked blood rather than ate flesh, is told by H. Clifford. The tiger burst into a hut where several people were collected. One of them was able to reach a shelf near the roof, and from there he saw how the tiger killed them all and drank deep draughts of blood. One girl he first played with as a cat with a mouse, and all night he tossed the bodies about and tore them, disappearing at dawn.[10] Another story tells how the transformation was seen taking place. A bride saw her Korinchi husband returning home as a tiger, which thrust its head above the top rung of the entrance ladder. 'It palpitated and changed, and the face of the husband came up through the face of the beast.' Later this wer-tiger was caught in a trap, but escaped, when it was tracked to the house. There the man was said to be sick, and soon after he and his sons disappeared. The story was reported to the District officer, and such a transformation is 'to the native mind a fact, not a mere belief.'[1]

The tiger familiar spirit is also possessed by certain men, and after their death their spirits appear as tigers, or the medicine-man has subject to him an actual tiger which is immortal (Benua of Johore).[2] The soul of a dead wizard enters the body of a tiger, and the corpse is left in the forest for seven days until the change is effected.[3] A curious Malay belief concerns the fold in which tigers possessed of human souls are penned. Periodical attacks of fierceness come on them, when they break bounds and go after their prey. Passing through one door, they become men, and on returning through another door they become tigers again. Their chief is always in human form, and enters the bodies of sorcerers when they invoke the tiger spirit.[4] The transformation into tiger form is effected in different ways: by sympathetic magic—*e.g.*, donning a *sarong* (yellow with black stripes) and repeating charms—by offerings to evil spirits, by charms, or by a mysterious poison which is supposed to affect the soul; or the power is conceived as hereditary. Among the Semang the medicine-man lights incense and invokes a spirit. Presently fur and a tail appear on him, as he himself believes, and he goes about for twelve days destroying cattle. Then he returns home and is sick, vomiting bones. During the twelve days his wife must always keep the fire burning and burn incense, else he would disappear. Such a wer-tiger cannot be shot, as it disappears so quickly.[5] Various beliefs are held regarding the transformation among the Malays—the whole body takes part in it, or merely the soul substance, the body remaining at home.

Among the wild Malays of the Patani States there is a belief in *badi*, or mischief, which remains by a body after death and devours the *semangat* or, sometimes, the liver of passers-by. Birds and beasts also have *badi* or, in the case of tigers, leopards, and jungle-cats, *pegrung* or *begrob*; and, if a man is affected by this, he goes mad, and either imitates the actions of the creature or is subject to an abnormal growth resembling one natural to it.[6]

In Lombok the crocodile form is assumed by certain men in order to destroy their enemies, and many strange stories are told of them. This form is also taken among the Klemantans, one group of whom claim the crocodile as a relative. One man found his skin become rough, his feet like a crocodile's, and a tail forming, until he was completely transformed. He made his relatives swear that they would never kill a crocodile. Many people saw him in his crocodile form.[7]

In *China* there are various wer-animals—tiger, wolf, dog, fox, etc. The change is usually a bodily one, but an ethereal human double may pass into an animal either before or after death. There are many literary notices of such transformations.

An early instance is mentioned in a document of the 2nd cent. B.C., in which, after the crisis of an illness, a man changed to a tiger and killed his brother.[8]

Such transformations are often ascribed to delirious patients, and, if the patient does not kill a man, he may return to human form. This suggests a popular confusion between the fancies of insanity

---

1 A. F. L. M. von Haxthausen, *Transcaucasia*, London, 1854, p. 359; cf. *ERE* i. 800.
2 *SBE* xliv. [1900] 414.
3 *FL* xx. [1909] 411 f.; Tylor, *PC*³ i. 309.
4 E. T. Dalton, *Descriptive Ethnol. of Bengal*, Calcutta, 1872, p. 290.
5 Crooke, *PR* ii. 216. 6 *Ib.* ii. 264. 7 *Ib.* ii. 267.
8 T. W. Webber, *Forests of Upper India*, London, 1902, p. 27; *ERE* iii. 314ᵃ; cf. *PR* ii. 211.
9 W. W. Skeat, *Malay Magic*, London, 1900, pp. 160 f., 436 f.; A. Bastian, *Die Völker des östlichen Asien*, Leipzig, 1866, i. 119; J. Knebel, in *Tijdschrift van nederl. Ind.* xii. [1899] 570; for Cambodia see *ERE* iii. 158ᵃ.
10 H. Clifford, *In Court and Kampong*, London, 1897, p. 198 f.

1 Clifford, pp. 65, 67.
2 H. Ling Roth, *Natives of Sarawak and Borneo*, London, 1896, i. 205; *Journ. Ind. Arch.* i. [1847] 276 f.
3 See *ERE* i. 530ᵃ. 4 Skeat, p. 157 f.
5 *Ib.* p. 161; N. W. Thomas, *FL* xvii. [1906] 262; Skeat-Blagden, *Pagan Races of the Malay Peninsula*, London, 1906, ii. 227.
6 N. Annandale and H. C. Robinson, *Fasciculi Malayenses*, London, 1903–06, pt. i. pp. 100 f., 104.
7 A. R. Wallace, *Malay Archipelago*, London, 1869, i. 161; C. Hose and W. McDougall, *Pagan Tribes of Borneo*, do. 1912, ii. 81 f.
8 J. J. M. de Groot, *Rel. System of China*, Leyden, 1892 ff., iv. 160.

and actual belief in the power of shape-shifting. Sometimes the transformation is ascribed to a community of aborigines, and is effected by magical means. In other cases the cause may be divine displeasure because of the neglect of religious duties. Here the victim goes mad and turns into a tiger. In one such instance he is covered with a spotted skin by the god, as in European cases, where a wolf-skin is used. Stories of transformation by wearing a tiger-skin are said to abound in China.

A 14th cent. writer tells how he saw a man slowly becoming covered with hair like a tiger, his body adorned with spots and stripes. During the night he ate a hog.[1]

Other cases of this kind are of frequent occurrence. Wer-tigers and tigresses are sometimes favourably disposed and give presents. This is especially the case with wer-tigresses on behalf of those who excite their love.[2]

The wolf transformation is also known.

In one case a peasant was attacked by a wolf and cut off its paw. By the traces of the blood he followed it to a house, where an old man was found lacking a hand. He was killed, and in dying took the form of a wolf. Before his period of transformation he had been long ill, and, after being healed, had disappeared. In another instance a youth after an illness acquired the power of sending forth his soul in the form of a wolf, and devoured children—obviously a case of hallucinatory insanity combined with cannibalism, as in European instances.

Other tales of this kind are current.

An old woman finds her body being covered with hair and a tail forming, after which she becomes a wolf, and escapes, though sometimes she returns to see her family. In another instance a man weds a woman who is really a wolf, as also are her servants, and he is devoured by her.[3] In a 4th cent. work all wolves are said to be transformed to men after the five-hundredth year of their age.[4]

Other wer-animals are also known—*e.g.*, the dog, though here, as in the case of the fox, perhaps it is the animal that takes human form. In one instance men who are beaten become dogs; and a dog-man who was stabbed changed to a dog when dying.[5]

In China the fox superstition is a kind of inverted werwolf belief, especially in N. China. The wer-foxes dwell in the debatable land between earth and Hades, and can take human form at will—most frequently that of a young and pretty girl—but they may be detected by the possession of tails. Spirits of the dead may occupy the bodies of such foxes and revenge injuries on the living. Some legends show that the fox lives in graves and borrows human form from a corpse by instilling into himself the soul-substance. Wer-foxes can do either good or ill to men, but are grateful to those who are kind to them. Foxes in male form live with women, in female form with men; in either case a morbid erotic state is produced, resembling that caused by the mediæval *incubi* and *succubæ*. When killed in human form, all that remains is the body of a fox. Their animal form also appears spontaneously in sleep, or when they are overcome by wine, of which they are very fond. Sometimes they enter and occupy a house invisibly, acting exactly like the *Poltergeist*.[6]

It is also believed that witches can take the form of the fox, cat, or hare.[7] The tiger-ghost is also believed in.

'When he wishes to eat people he puts off his clothes and is changed into a striped tiger. He then advances with a great roar, and the traveller is instantly torn to pieces.'[8]

Tigers are said to make slaves of the souls of men devoured by them. These souls go before them to point out traps or to act as beaters,[9] as in the similar Indian belief.

1 De Groot, iv. 172 f.

2 L. Wieger, *Folk-lore chinois moderne*, Sienhsien, 1909, pp. 11, 62 f.; de Groot, iv. 156 ff.

3 Wieger, pp. 126 ff., 142.

4 De Groot, iv. 182.

5 *Ib.* p. 124 f.

6 H. A. Giles, *Strange Stories from a Chinese Studio*, London, 1880, i. 32, 85, 163, 182; N. B. Dennys, *Folk-Lore of China*, do. 1876, pp. 61, 70; Wieger, pp. 11, 111, and *passim*; de Groot, iv. 188 f.

7 Dennys, p. 90.

8 *Ib.* p. 91.

9 Wieger, p. 11.

The wer-fox superstition is found in *Japan*, but was not introduced there until the 11th century. There are different kinds of foxes. The wild fox, Nogitsune, can take any form, or become invisible, but its reflexion in water is always that of a fox. The Ninko fox can also take various forms, especially that of a pretty girl, in which shape it will even marry a man.[1] These foxes also possess men, or live in their houses, bringing luck if well treated, but they are dangerous if ill-treated. Some Samurai families are believed to own foxes, which steal for them or torment their enemies. Foxes to whom some kindness has been shown, either in their own or in human form, reward the doer of it with money, etc., part of which turns to grass. Often the house in which the fox lives is illusory and cannot be found again (see FAIRY, vol. v. p. 679). Men possessed by foxes run about yelping and eat only what foxes eat, but the possessing goblin-fox may be exorcized.[2]

The same fox-belief exists among the Ainus, and with them the fox has both good and evil powers, and can cause death. Foxes also exhume and eat corpses. But the same powers of transformation to human form are ascribed to the horse, mole, crow, etc. The spirit of the bear, dog, otter, and especially the cat, can enter into and bewitch a man as a punishment; the victim eats as a cat, wastes away, and dies mewing like a cat. This may occur when a man has killed a cat. To prevent possession by its spirit, he must eat part of it.[3] The Eskimos and some American Indian tribes also possess the fox superstition.[4]

The wer-animal superstition is found in *Africa* in connexion with a variety of savage beasts. All over N. Africa it is believed that the *jinn* can take animal forms—wolf, jackal, lion, serpent, scorpion. This is also true of the *ghūls*, who appear as men or animals, and feed on dead bodies, or kill and eat living men.[5] More akin to the werwolf superstition is the belief that twin children go out at night as cats, their bodies meanwhile remaining at home as if dead. If they are beaten by any one, they tell this to their parents next day.[6] Among the Berbers witnesses maintain that they have seen girls, when born, change into ogresses, who throw themselves on men until they are strangled.[7] Among the Abyssinians there is a wide-spread belief in the *budas*, who change into hyenas and kill and devour. They are distinguished from ordinary hyenas by greater malice. The *budas* are sorcerers; and blacksmiths, found mainly among the Falashas and Agaos, are supposed to be *budas*. Hyenas have been killed with earrings in their ears, and these are believed to be *budas*, though it has been thought that sorcerers put earrings in the ears of young hyenas to bolster up this superstition. The *budas* have a king in the neighbourhood of Abbolo to whom they bring offerings of corpses daily. As blacksmiths are a hereditary folk, their sorcery is also hereditary, but a *buda* confers the gift on his children by a mysterious decoction of herbs. Cases of transformation are believed to have been actually witnessed. In one such case

1 Cf. the Baluchistān belief that the black bear 'takes the form of a beautiful woman at night, and hugs men to death if they are not wary' (M. L. Dames, *FL* xiii. [1902] 265).

2 A. B. Mitford, *Tales of Old Japan*, London, 1871, *passim*; L. Hearn, *Glimpses of Unfamiliar Japan*, do. 1894, i. 312 ff.; B. H. Chamberlain, *Things Japanese*, do. 1890, *s.v.* 'Fox'; see also *ERE* iv. 610b.

3 J. Batchelor, *The Ainu and their Folklore*, London, 1901, *passim*, *The Ainu of Japan*, do. 1892, *passim*; B. H. Chamberlain, *Aino Folk-Tales*, do. 1888, p. 22.

4 Dennys, p. 96; H. J. Rink, *Tales and Traditions of the Eskimo*, Edinburgh, 1875, p. 144.

5 E. W. Lane, *Arabian Society in Middle Ages*, London, 1883, pp. 34, 42.

6 Lady Duff Gordon, *Last Letters*, London, 1875, cited in Dennys, p. 90 f.

7 R. Basset, *Contes populaires berbères*, Paris, 1888, iii., iv.

the *buda* sprinkled ashes over his shoulders, and the change began. Besides killing men and drinking their blood, the *buda* takes possession of his victim, entering his body by a look, or when he is eating, or in illness. The victim becomes more or less insane, laughing like a hyena, then falling into a trance, when the *buda* speaks through him, often telling who he is and why he thus personates the patient. Sometimes the victim tries to get into the forest, where the *buda* is supposed to devour him. The *buda* is kept off by the wearing of amulets, by which also he can be exorcized. He can also transform his victims into animals, and sometimes digs up corpses to eat them. This is also done by actual hyenas.[1]

The belief in the wer-hyena occurs from the Sūdan to Tanganyika, and is perhaps strengthened by the fact that wizards at their meetings howl and caper like hyenas, eat horrible food, and commit excesses the sight of which makes the onlooker mad. Even in the daytime their glance causes a deadly sickness. Certain tribes in the Sūdan are supposed to possess this power of transformation, but it is dangerous to shoot them. One of them who was shot was seen to enter the hut of a wizard, who died soon after. The man who shot him soon followed him to the grave.[2] Generally among the black races the usual animals, besides the hyena, are the lion, leopard, and crocodile. In Nubia old women are called hyenas, and are believed to enter the bodies of these animals by night.[3] In the Sūdan the hyena shape is supposed to be assumed at an ant's nest. The Awemba wizards receive power to become wild beasts from spirits called *vibanda*.[4] The Wanyamwesi of E. Africa think that sorcerers can transform themselves into animals in order to injure their enemies.[5] In E. Central Africa witches kill men, and in the form of hyenas try to get at the graves of their victims in order to eat their flesh.[6] The Akikuyu tell of a man, who, after his marriage, went to the wilds and lived like a hyena on dead bodies. Returning home, he ate his child. His brothers killed him, but the woman's second husband also became a hyena and ate her and his child.[7] In British Central Africa the bewitcher (*mfiti*) can turn himself into a hyena, leopard, crocodile, etc. He then digs up dead bodies and eats them. Sometimes the change takes place after death, and, if the creature kills people, some method of appeasing it is adopted. The wer-hyena is thought by the Makanga to have a wife who at night opens the door of the *kraal* to admit him and then runs off with him to feast. In one case, when a goat was carried off, tracks of a hyena and of human feet were seen together.[8] Among the Tumbuka of Central Africa certain women wander about smeared with white clay, and are believed to have the power of changing into lions.[9] In W. Africa the Yoruba think that the wer-hyenas assume their animal shape at night to prey on cattle and sheep, and, if possible, on human beings, who are sometimes compelled to go out to them when they utter certain howls.[1] In Loanda the belief existed that the chief could change himself to a lion, kill some one, and then resume his own form.[2] The Ibos believe that a man's spirit can leave his body and enter into an animal. This is called *ishi anu*, 'to turn animal,' and it is done by means of a drug. If the animal is killed, the man dies; if wounded, his body is covered with boils.[3] Wilson says of sorcerers in Guinea that they can turn into leopards and change their enemies into elephants, in which form they kill them.[4] In Senegambia a sorcerer who changes to an evil animal is kept off by means of salt; or, when transformed, he leaves his skin behind him. If it is rubbed with salt, he suffers, and comes to beg that the grains of salt be removed.[5] In W. Africa generally the power of certain persons to change into leopards or to send their souls into leopards, which are then guided by the human possessor to kill such persons as are obnoxious to them, is very commonly believed in. The person so changed is called *uvengwa*, and cannot be killed. Many persons actually believe that they have thus metamorphosed themselves and done harm. Other animals—lion, panther, crocodile, or shark—are occasionally made use of.[6] One family, living at the mouth of the Congo, can change into leopards, but, if once they lap blood, they remain leopards for ever, exactly as in the case of the Arcadian werwolves.[7] In Calabar a man may become a rat, bat, or owl, etc. In this form he throws his victim into a deep sleep. He then resumes his human form, and sucks his blood, and the victim falls sick and dies. After burial, the body is taken by witches from the grave for a cannibal feast. A witch continues to have this power after death, and may still be called to cannibal feasts or summoned to aid living witches. In old days witches laid aside their skins to assume animal form. If such skins were found, pepper was rubbed into them, so that the witches could not resume them. They were thus caught, and burnt to death, care being taken to destroy the heart, in which the witch power resided.[8] In equatorial Africa the wer-leopard is also much dreaded.[9] The whole belief in such transformations is much mixed up with the existence of leopard societies, the members of which disguise themselves in leopard-skins and commit murders.

In S. Africa similar beliefs are common. The lion form is assumed by wizards on the Zambesi by means of drinking a certain liquid. They kill men and animals.[10] In N. Rhodesia even educated natives believe in the power of certain men to become evil wer-lions or leopards through magic. This is combined with a belief that the soul of the chief is transformed at death into a lion. It comes as a cub from his grave and is told to be good, but by means of a test it may be discovered to be an evil wer-lion.[11] The Barotse credit certain persons,

[1] N. Pearce, *Life and Adventures of N. Pearce . . . with Coffin's Visit to Gondar*, ed. J. J. Halls, London, 1831, i. 287; H. Salt, *Voyage to Abyssinia*, do. 1814, p. 427; W. C. Plowden, *Travels in Abyssinia*, do. 1868, pp. 116 ff., 262; M. Parkyns, *Life in Abyssinia*², do. 1868, p. 300 ff.; cf. *ERE* i. 57ª.

[2] W. Schneider, *Die Religion der afrikan. Naturvölker*, Münster, 1891, p. 236.

[3] D. Macdonald, *Africana*, London, 1882, i. 227.

[4] J. H. W. Sheane, *JAI* xxxvi. [1906] 155.

[5] R. H. Nassau, *Fetichism in W. Africa*, London, 1904, p. 231.

[6] Macdonald, i. 107.

[7] W. S. and K. Routledge, *With a Prehistoric People*, London, 1910, p. 326.

[8] A. Werner, *Natives of Brit. Cent. Africa*, London, 1906, pp. 84 ff., 241.

[9] W. A. Elmslie, *Among the Wild Ngoni*, London, 1899, p. 74.

[1] A. B. Ellis, *The Yoruba-speaking Peoples*, London, 1894, p. 122.

[2] D. Livingstone, *Missionary Travels*, London, 1857, p. 642.

[3] J. Parkinson, *JAI* xxxvi. 314.

[4] J. L. Wilson, *W. Africa*, London, 1856, p. 398.

[5] L. J. B. Bérenger-Féraud, *Contes populaires de la Sénégambie*, Paris, 1886, p. 236.

[6] R. E. Dennett, *Folklore of the Fjort*, London, 1898, pp. 5, 10; Nassau, pp. 70, 201 f.; M. H. Kingsley, *Travels in W. Africa*, London, 1897, p. 542; Wilson, pp. 161, 398; *AE* xvii. [1905] 99.

[7] A. Bastian, *Die deutsche Exped. an der Loango-Küste*, Jena, 1874–75, ii. 248.

[8] J. K. Macgregor, 'Some Calabar Beliefs,' *United Free Church Miss. Record*, Edinburgh, 1914, p. 223 f.; Nassau (p. 123) says that wizards go forth to the Sabbat in their spirit-bodies. If any one rubs the real bodies with pepper, they cannot re-enter them, but must die.

[9] P. B. du Chaillu, *Wild Life under the Equator*, London, 1869, p. 254.

[10] D. and C. Livingstone, *Expedition to the Zambesi*, London, 1865, p. 159.

[11] C. Gouldsbury and H. Sheane, *Great Plateau of N. Rhodesia*, London, 1911, pp. 133, 200.

both living and dead, with power to change to an animal—hyena, lion, serpent, or alligator—and to do harm to men or cattle.[1] Among the Baronga a secret society exists the members of which send out their spirit-bodies or go out bodily at night to devour human flesh. They leave their shadow, or the appearance of themselves, behind, but this is in reality a wild animal with which the person has chosen to identify himself. If this appearance is stabbed, a hyena rushes howling from the hut, and the real man falls through the roof with a similar wound. Such persons enter huts, take the true self of the occupant, and eat him. Only his shadow is left, and he dies next morning. Some think that such wizards are not aware of their night work. Those who have long practised it, however, are aware. Perhaps the basis of the whole idea is to be found in the dream-conceptions of hysterical subjects.[2] The Basuto also believe in wer-animals, *māhilithoumes*, men who turn temporarily into animals and kill and eat human beings. They have the tradition of the introduction of sorcery through a queen who could call troops of wolves, monkeys, etc., to her nocturnal gatherings—a belief not unlike that of the wolf-leader in France.[3] The Hottentots believe in the power of changing to lion shape and killing men or animals. This is illustrated by a story bearing some resemblance to European werwolf tales.

A Hottentot and a Bushwoman travelling saw some horses. He bade her turn into a lion and kill one, as he knew her to possess this power. Hair appeared on her neck, her nails became claws, her features altered, and she bounded off as a lion, the man in turn climbing a tree until she re-assumed her human form.[4]

The Bushmen believed that sorcerers could assume the form of jackals, etc., and, conversely, that the lion could take human form.[5]

Similar beliefs exist among the Negroes of America, carried thence by their forefathers from Africa. In Missouri the Negroes think some cats are devils, *i.e.* witches in disguise.[6] The Voodoo is credited with the power of changing to a black wolf, dog, cat, owl, or bat at night. To stop this the human or the animal skin must be found and salted. This assumes a real change of skin.[7]

With all the *N. American Indian* tribes it was believed that wizards and witches could take the form of wolves, foxes, bears, owls, bats, or snakes —a belief which was probably strengthened by the wizards wearing skins of animals and imitating their howls, etc.[8]

The Nishinam had a legend of a medicine-man who was seized with a spasm and went on all fours. His nails grew long and sharp, a tail grew on him, hair covered his body, and he became a bear. This transformation lasted until the spasm passed.[9]

A belief similar to that of the Chinese fox superstition exists, as with the Narraganset, and the Tlaxcalans believed in a wer-dog. The Musquakies have curious tales about trees which appear as human beings, each bearing the marks of injuries done to the other, and of an old man who, denying that he was a bear, is proved to have taken that form by the fact that his tracks and those of the bear both have traces of grease. He is therefore killed because he has 'a devil in his nose.'[10] Lafitau tells of wizards who, having taken the form of birds and been wounded, are found to have identical wounds, while the magical bolts with which the birds were shot are found in their bodies. The Chippewa sorcerer for a fee will turn into an animal and inflict injuries on the person described to him.[1]

In a Chippewa story a boy left by his father in charge of his elder brother and sister is neglected and eats the leavings of wolves. These pity him, and he follows them. The brother one day heard a child's voice crying, 'I am turning into a wolf,' followed by a howl. Then he saw the boy half turned into a wolf. As he watched, the change became complete, and with the words, 'I am a wolf,' the werwolf disappeared.[2]

Among the higher American Indian peoples similar beliefs prevailed. Maya sorcerers could turn into dogs, pigs, etc., and their glance was death to a victim; and in Guatemala the name of the priests was derived from the fact that they could take animal forms. In Yucatan sorcerers claimed to have such powers, and one in dying confessed to a priest that he had often so transformed himself.[3] Among the Tarahumare Indians of Mexico, if a sorcerer sees a bear, he will beg an Indian not to shoot it, as it is he, or, if an owl screeches, he will say, 'It is I who am calling.'[4] The European belief in the transformation of witches into cats was carried to America.[5]

Following the belief into *S. America*, we find that the Abipone *keebet*, or priest, was believed to turn himself into an invisible tiger which could not be killed. When a *keebet* threatened to transform himself and began to roar like a tiger, the onlookers fled, believing that the change was actually taking place.[6] The people of Guiana believe in the *kenaima*, a being who can send forth his spirit to injure or cause wasting disease, or place it in the body of any animal—jaguar, serpent, bird, or insect—which follows up the victim and slays him. His spirit may also enter a man in the form of a caterpillar, and cause disease. Such a caterpillar is often withdrawn from a patient's body by a *peaiman*, or doctor, and killed, but the spirit escapes, so that the *kenaima* does not die. The animal in which the *kenaima* usually places his spirit is the jaguar or tiger—the *kenaima*-tiger —which it puzzles an Indian to kill. A certain small bird is also much feared as a *kenaima*-bird; this is shot and every scrap of it carefully burned, so that there may be one enemy the less. Certain *peaimen* are thought to have the power of sending their spirit into an animal.[7] The wer-jaguar is believed in by many of the tribes.

A Tucuman story tells how a man saw his brother take three grains of salt, spread a jaguar-skin on the ground, and dance round it, when he became a jaguar. Much horrified, he later obtained the skin and burned it. Returning home, he found his brother dying, but was asked by him to procure a piece of the skin. He did so, and the dying man threw it over his shoulders, and became a jaguar, which fled into the forest. In this case bullets merely rebounded from the wer-animal. In a Paraguay story the man becomes a man-eating jaguar by falling prone, and is re-transformed by reversing the process. Once he was wounded by a youth, who followed him up and killed him in his den, which was filled with human bones.[8] In another tale from the Paraguayan Chaco two men who visited a village when the men were absent decamped when they heard from the women that they would soon return. When the men returned, they said that the visitors were jaguars, who had come to deceive and destroy them, and they had seen the marks

1 L. Decle, *Three Years in Savage Africa*, London, 1898, p. 75; Livingstone, p. 642.
2 H. A. Junod, *The Life of a S. African Tribe*, Neuchâtel, 1913, pp. 462, 466 f.
3 E. Jacottet, *Contes pop. des Ba-Soutos*, Paris, 1895, p. 110 f.; E. Casalis, *Les Bassoutos*, do. 1860, p. 289; T. Arbousset and F. Daumas, *Exploratory Tour*, Cape Town, 1846, p. 12.
4 T. Hahn, *Tsuni-Goam*, London, 1881, p. 108; W. H. I. Bleek, *Reynard the Fox in S. Africa*, do. 1864, p. 57.
5 Bleek, *Bushman Folk-lore*, London, 1875, pp. 15, 40.
6 Leland, p. 221. 7 *Ib.*, citing M. A. Owen.
8 R. M. Dorman, *Origin of Primitive Superstitions*, Philadelphia, 1881, p. 248 ff.
9 *NR* iii. 546.
10 M. A. Owen, *Folk-lore of the Musquakie Indians*, London, 1904, pp. 6, 89 f.

1 *14 RBEW* [1896], p. 151.
2 H. R. Schoolcraft, *History . . . of the Indian Tribes*, Philadelphia, 1853–57, ii. 232.
3 *NR* ii. 797; D. G. Brinton, *Lib. of Aborig. Amer. Lit.*, Philadelphia, 1882–87, vi. 46; *FLJ* i. 249.
4 C. Lumholtz, *Unknown Mexico*, London, 1903, i. 325.
5 S. A. Drake, *New England Legends*, Boston, 1884, p. 260.
6 M. Dobrizhoffer, *Account of the Abipones*, London, 1822, ii. 77.
7 E. F. Im Thurn, *Among the Indians of Guiana*, London, 1883, pp. 328 f., 332 ff., 349; W. H. Brett, *Ind. Tribes of Guiana*, do. 1868, p. 368.
8 A. H. Keane, *Man, Past and Present*, Cambridge, 1899, p. 380 f., citing *Anales de la Soc. Científica Argentina*, xli. [1896] 321.

of their claws near the village. They were then pursued and killed.[1]

Among the *Melanesians* in Banks Islands the nearest analogy to the werwolf is the *talamaur*, the soul of a person which leaves the body to eat a corpse. A woman threatened to do this. Watch was kept, and, when a noise was heard near the corpse, the watchers threw a stone and hit something. Next day the woman was found to have a bruise on her arm caused by the stone which hit her soul.[2] In Lepers' Island wizards transform themselves into blow-flies and cause sickness to their victim, or into a shark and eat enemies. In Aurora magicians take the form of sharks, owls, and eagles.[3] A story from this island illustrates the belief.

Tarkeke devoured men by turning into a fish, or entering a fish or a kind of magic image of a fish. His son found this image and got into it, when it went out to sea. Tarkeke then went after the boy and punished him.[4]

In the examples quoted it is interesting to note in how many ways the change is thought to be effected. In many instances—Scandinavian, German, Slavic, French, Chinese, and the Tucumans of S. America—it is by donning an animal skin or girdle (see GIRDLE), presumably after removing the clothing, as this is a necessary preliminary in other methods. Eating a drug or root or rubbing the body with a salve or oil is found in ancient Italy, the Netherlands, England, India, Indonesia (where also a poison infecting the soul is thought to be the cause of the change), and in Africa, and in many cases tried judicially in Europe. Charms, spells, and other magical methods also effected the change in Celtic, Slavic, Chinese, Indonesian, Cambodian, and other instances, and no doubt the use of spells accompanied the other means referred to. The power might be given by the devil (Russian), or by spirits (Awemba), or the change might be caused in a man by a witch. It might be the effect of a divine or saintly punishment or other curse (ancient Greece, China, Celts of Ireland, Normandy); or it might be the result of eating human flesh (ancient Greece), or of making use of some particular action —swimming (ancient Greece, Périgord), falling prone (Paraguay), yawning (ancient Greece); or it might be the natural gift of a seventh son (Portugal), or of one born on Christmas night (Naples) or between Christmas and Twelfth-night (Greece).

In some cases the power is ascribed to a special tribe or to a people living in a special district—Arcadians, Korinchi Malays, aboriginal tribes in China, Ṣei'ar of Ḥadramaut. This has perhaps an equivalent in the appearance of epidemics of lycanthropy in certain places, so common in the Middle Ages and later.

Very often it is said that, when the wer-animal is wounded or killed, the human form comes back spontaneously. This is found in many European instances, and also inversely in that of the fox and dog superstition in China.

In general, where the animal skin may be separated from the man, there is still a sympathetic relation between it and him. Thus, if it is burned (Flemish, Breton, American, S. American instances), or rubbed with salt or pepper (Senegambia, Calabar, Negroes of America), he suffers terribly and may die, as in the case of the *lamboyo* in Celebes (below, p. 218 f.). On the other hand, this may release him from being a werwolf, as in the case of other men under enchantment who lose their beast nature when the skin is burned. Conversely, the seal or mermaid wife recovers it when she discovers her skin.

[1] W. B. Grubb, *A Church in the Wilds*, London, 1914, p. 61, where also a story of a woman who married a jaguar is given.

[2] R. H. Codrington, *The Melanesians*, Oxford, 1891, p. 222; see also ABORIGINES.

[3] *Ib.* p. 207.

[4] *Ib.* p. 407 f.

While in Europe the man who is a werwolf is known by his eyebrows growing together over his nose, or by a small wolf's tail growing between his shoulder-blades, in Indonesia the man-tiger as a man lacks heels or the furrow of the upper lip, or is marked by twisted feet or by peculiar actions.[1]

There are various methods of curing or ending the transformation. Burning the skin and wounding have already been mentioned. Another method was for the witch to cover the werwolf with a skin with hair turned outwards (Serbia). In the case of wounding, some special methods are referred to—the werwolf had to be scratched above the nose so as to extract three drops of blood (Brittany), and in Germany stabbed on the brow three times with a knife or pitchfork. The effusion of blood as a cure here corresponds to the drawing of blood from a witch as a well-known means of destroying her power. Naming the werwolf by his baptismal name and reproaching him were also effective.[2] In one story cited above the wife shakes her apron at her husband and so restores him. In Cambodia the werwolf is deprived of his power if struck with a hook on the shoulder.[3]

2. Lycanthropy as a theological doctrine.—Throughout the Middle Ages, but more emphatically in the 16th and 17th centuries, theologians turned their attention to lycanthropy as a branch of sorcery. The general doctrine was that by the help of Satan sorcerers could transform themselves into noxious animals, particularly wolves, for purposes inimical to others. Innumerable theologians expressed these views, and many treatises were written on the subject, while it was also discussed in general works on the evils of sorcery. Of these theologians J. Bodin is one of the best examples; in his *De Magorum Demonomania* (Frankfort, 1603) he maintains the reality and certainty of the transformation. Theological opinion thus coincided with popular superstition, and many of the instances cited as proofs are little better than the popular tales referred to above—*e.g.*, where a wolf is wounded and a human being is found with a similar wound soon after. The severest measures were therefore taken against lycanthropes, especially on the part of the Inquisition, and this authoritative announcement of the reality of the transformation added to the popular terrorism. People easily imagined the truth of the charges brought against those charged with them, or came forward as witnesses of the alleged facts. Indeed, the prisoners themselves often maintained their truth, showing that insanity and hallucination had much to do with the matter (§ 3). The peculiarly heinous aspect of the crime is seen in this: H. Boguet, a judge who tried many cases and who wrote many works against sorcery, drew up a code in 1601 in which he stated that, while sorcerers should be first strangled and then burned, the *loups-garous* should be burned alive.[4] The belief in sorcery as well as the theological animus against it often led to epidemics of sorcery; the people in a district, *e.g.*, became terrorized by the idea that all around them were sorcerers, or many persons, half crazy, maintained this regarding themselves. At the beginning of the 16th cent. in Lombardy, during such an epidemic, witches were freely accused of having changed into cats and entered houses to suck the blood of children.[5] Reports of many trials of reputed lycanthropes are still extant, and afford sad evidence of human credulity.

[1] Grimm, pp. 1097, 1630; de Groot, iv. 167, 170; Thorpe, ii. 169.

[2] Thorpe, ii. 169; O. Hovorka and A. Kronfeld, *Vergleichende Volksmedizin*, Stuttgart, 1908–09, i. 450; Hertz, p. 61.

[3] See *ERE* iii. 158ᵃ.

[4] See the code in J. Garinet, *Hist. de la magie en France*, Paris, 1818, p. 302.

[5] Bourquelot, p. 246.

In 1521 Pierre Burgot and Michel Verdun were tried by the prior of the Dominicans of Poligny, in the diocese of Besançon. The former alleged that years before, when his cattle had strayed, a black cavalier had brought them together after he had agreed to give himself to his master, the devil. Later Verdun taught him at the Sabbat how to become a werwolf by rubbing himself with a certain ointment. Then he saw himself with four paws and his body covered with hair, while he was able to run like the wind. Verdun also transformed himself in the same way; the ointment had been obtained from his demon master. In the form of wolves they killed several children, sucked their blood, and ate part of their flesh, finding it excellent. Burgot also said that he had sexual relations with wolves. Both men were burned alive at Besançon.[1] In the same year, before the same court, three sorcerers were executed for the same crime. One of them had been wounded as a wolf by a hunter, who, following the trail, came to a hut, where he found him having his wound dressed by his wife. These lycanthropes are represented in a painting in the chapel of the Dominicans.[2] A curious case is that of Gilles Garnier, a hermit of Lyons, who, finding his solitude irksome, had taken a female companion. They had several children and lived in great misery. In 1572 a wolf terrorized the district, and the bodies of several children were found half devoured. A boy was attacked by the wolf, but his cries attracted attention. Garnier was found near the body, and at his trial before the Parlement of Dôle avowed that he was the wolf, that he had sold himself to the devil, and had obtained the power of transformation by the use of an ointment. He had killed and eaten the children, the woman also sharing in the ghastly meal. He also was burned alive.[3]

In Auvergne in 1588 the wife of a gentleman was burned alive as a werwolf. Her husband had asked a hunter to bring him some game. The hunter was attacked by a wolf, and cut off one of its paws. On his return to the château he drew the paw from his bag, when it was seen to be the hand of a woman, with a ring on the finger which the gentleman recognized as his wife's. Suspecting her, he went in search of her, and found that she had lost a hand. On her confession that she was the wolf, she was condemned.[4]

Henri Boguet, grand judge of the ecclesiastical court of St. Claude (1569–1616), was most active against sorcerers, and, according to Voltaire, boasted of having put to death more than 600 lycanthropes. His *Discours exécrable des sorciers* (Lyons, 1602) contains many instances of alleged lycanthropy, with the confessions of those accused. He believed firmly in the possibility of the transformation, whether by rubbing with an ointment or otherwise, some chapters of his work dealing specially with this subject. It is remarkable also, as showing the state of feeling at the time, that on 3rd Dec. 1573 the Parlement of Franche-Comté gave a ruling for the pursuit of *loups-garous*.[5]

Towards the end of the 16th cent. Pierre Stumf was executed at Bibburg, in the diocese of Cologne, on his own confession of having lived with a *succuba*, who gave him a girdle by which he could become a wolf, not only in his own sight, but in that of others. He had killed and eaten fifteen children in his wolf form, and had tried to eat two of his daughters-in-law.[6]

The beginning of the 17th cent. was marked by new epidemics of lycanthropy, and hundreds of executions took place.

In 1603 Jean Grenier, a boy of 14, alleged before the judge of Roche-Chalans that he was a werwolf, as a result of a demoniacal gift, and that he had eaten some children. He also accused his father of being a werwolf and possessing a wolf's skin, and another man, Pierre la Thillaire, of having his skin and ointment. The conduct of the boy in court showed that he was insane, and he was detained in a convent. Nevertheless the charge was continued against the two men. The youth was visited in his convent by De Lancre in 1610, who found that he could run on all fours with ease, and that his method of eating was disgusting. He still persisted in his delusion of being a werwolf.[7]

In 1604 at Lausanne five persons were burned as werwolves. A peasant of Cressi had cursed his child and, as a result, five sorceresses in the form of wolves had carried him off to the devil, who sucked his blood. The sorceresses then cut him up, boiled him in a cauldron, and made an ointment of his flesh.[8]

These will suffice as examples of the trials and executions for alleged lycanthropy which were so numerous at this period. Not the least noteworthy fact in the whole sordid business is that some of the writers on the subject show the most extraordinary credulity regarding the cases. Petrus Marmorius, in his *De Sortilegiis*, maintained that he had seen the change of men into wolves in Savoy.[1] Bourdin, procureur général of the king, assured Bodin that there had been sent to him from Belgium the *procès*, signed by judge and witnesses, regarding a wolf shot in the thigh with an arrow. Soon after a man was found in bed with the arrow in a wound, and, when it was drawn out, it was recognized for his own by the person who had shot the wolf.[2] Other cases are related in which cats attacked a man, who wounded them. Women were then found in bed with similar wounds, and they were at once believed to be the cats in question.[3] While the whole was generally attributed to diabolical influence, there were different ways of accounting for it. Some writers thought that there was a real transformation,[4] or that the devil clothed the men with an actual wolf-skin[5] or with one condensed out of air.[6] Others, however, thought that the devil wrought by fantasy or by means of unguents on the man or on the onlookers, so that they imagined that the man or woman was an animal, while he or she was similarly deluded.[7] Others, again, suggested that the devil caused the person in sleep to imagine that he was a wolf, and that he actually did the deeds of which he dreamed.[8] This is akin to the theory of St. Augustine, who refused to believe that the demons could actually change man's corporeal substance. In sleep or trance the man's 'fantasm' went from him and might appear to others in corporeal, animal form, while to the unconscious man himself it might then appear that he was in such a form and acting in accordance.[9] The effect of such drugs as stramonium caused hallucinations of riding through the air and of transformation, such as witches confessed to, and this may have been the food given by women to others in Italy so that they believed themselves beasts of burden.[10] Such a drug might occasionally be responsible for lycanthropic hallucination. Still others, more rational, regarded lycanthropes as lunatics who imagined themselves wolves. The last is probably the true solution of the whole matter.

3. Lycanthropy as a form of mental aberration.—Both in earlier times and even in the period when severe sentences were being passed against alleged werwolves, the existence of a diseased mental condition in which the patient imagined himself to be an animal—a form of melancholia with delirium—was clearly recognized by some. The popular belief in werwolves was not accepted by scientific writers in antiquity. Herodotus (iv. 104) would not be persuaded of the alleged transformation of the Neurians. Pausanias, admitting the transformation of Lycaon as a divine punishment, refused to believe in the recurrent transformations in Arcadia. Pliny (*HN* viii. 34) was equally incredulous. Medical writers regarded lycanthropy as a form of mental derangement. Of these, Marcellus of Side wrote a poem in which he treats lycanthropy in this fashion. The poem has not survived, but a prose version, abridged, by Ætius exists.

1 Bodin, p. 235.
2 J. Français, *L'Eglise et la sorcellerie*, Paris, 1910, p. 119.
3 Bodin, p. 234.
4 Garinet, p. 149.
5 Bourquelot, p. 245.
6 M. A. Del Rio, *Disquis. Magicarum Libri Sex*, Louvain, 1599, lib. ii. qu. 18.
7 P. de Lancre, *Tableau de l'inconstance des mauvais anges et démons*, Paris, 1613, p. 252.
8 Bourquelot, p. 245.

1 Bodin, p. 237.
2 *Ib.* p. 236.
3 Instances in Bodin, p. 236 f.; cf. De Spina, ii. 549.
4 Bodin, p. 245, and *passim*.
5 D. Sennert, *Opera Omnia*, Lyons, 1666, ii. 393 f.
6 De Spina, ii. 582.
7 J. de Nynauld, *De la Lycanthropie*, ch. i.; De Spina, ii. 500, 581 f.; B. de Chauvincourt, *Discours de la lycanthropie*, *passim*.
8 J. Wier, *De Præstigiis Dæmonum*³, Basel, 1566, *passim*.
9 *De Civ. Dei*, xviii. 17 f.
10 Cf. R. Reuss, *La Sorcellerie*, Paris, 1871, p. 133 f.; E. Parish, *Hallucinations and Illusions*, London, 1897, p. 40 f.; Leland, p. 207.

According to Marcellus, those afflicted by the lupine or canine madness go out at night in February, imitating wolves or dogs, and lurk among tombs. He gives the signs by which they may be known—pale face, tearless eyes, dry tongue, burning thirst, etc. He also suggests various remedies for this disease, which he regards as a form of melancholia.[1] Greek physicians knew also the κυνάνθρωπος, the man who imagined himself to be a dog.[2]

The existence of such a form of madness was known to the Semites, as the account of Nebuchadrezzar (Dn 4[33]) shows.[3] Several 16th and 17th cent. writers regard lycanthropy as a form of madness. Of these Wier is the best known, though he still believed in demoniacal influence. According to him, those who believed themselves wolves were really troubled in their minds by the devil, so that in sleep they imagined that they had actually perpetrated the actions of which they accused themselves. He also cites the passage of Marcellus just referred to.[4] J. de Nynauld, a doctor who wrote on lycanthropy, thought that the lycanthropes were deluded by the devil, or that he actually gave them unguents, liquids, or powders, by which their sense impressions were affected. There were, however, natural lycanthropes, persons afflicted with *folie louvière*. He denies any actual transformation,[5] such as was insisted on by Bodin. The possibility of persons, more or less imbecile, living in a wild state in the forests, or even found among wild animals, such as wolves, was also suggested by some later writers.[6] Modern alienists take the view that lycanthropy was a form of insanity, often endemic. The patient suffers from a degradation of the personality, and imagines that he is a beast. The disease was common in the Middle Ages, because people then believed such a transformation possible. Now such melancholia with delirium is rare, because this belief hardly survives in Europe. Sporadic cases, however, are still known; in one instance the patient imagined that he was a wolf, and ate raw meat.[7]

Some of the instances cited in the previous sections may be best explained as cases of insanity of the type described. Cf. the Greek βρουκόλακας and the human Kallikantzari, the Malay instances of men with *badi*, several Chinese examples, the Japanese belief in fox-possession, the Ainu belief in possession by various animals, the Abyssinian belief in possession by a *buda*, the Nishinam man possessed by a bear, as well as various European instances. In all these the imitation of the possessing animal is noticeable, and the additional accounts of the growth of hair, claws, etc., may be imaginary, or may be exaggerated accounts of abnormal growth of hair or nails in cases of such insanity (cf. Nebuchadrezzar) or of hypertrichosis in general.[8] The instances of medicine-men pretending to become animals, and of the witnesses actually believing that they see hair and claws growing on them, are perhaps exploitations of this diseased condition.

Further examples of possession from all stages of culture are worth citing.

1 Ætius, bk. vi. cap. 11; W. H. Roscher, 'Das von der Kynanthropie handelnde Fragment des Marcellus von Side,' *ASG*, philol.-hist. Classe, xvii. [Leipzig, 1896] no. 3; cf. R. Burton, *Anatomy of Melancholy*, London, 1836, p. 88 f.

2 Galen, x. 502.

3 Some theologians thought that there was a real change, others that it was imaginary, and others that his soul had passed into the body of a beast.

4 Wier, pp. 241 f., 446 f., 453 f.

5 De Nynauld, ch. i. For other writers who took the view that madness was the cause of lycanthropy see Bourquelot, p. 268. Voltaire appears to regard the demoniacs of Scripture, who wandered among the tombs, as lycanthropes, who also had that habit (*Essai sur les Mœurs*, in *Œuvres*, Paris, 1819, xiii. 195).

6 *e.g.*, L. F. Calmeil, *De la Folie*, Paris, 1845, i. 74; Reuss, p. 143.

7 D. Hack Tuke, *Dict. of Psychol. Medicine*, London, 1892, i. 434, ii. 752; L. Bianchi, *A Text-Book of Psychiatry*, do. 1906, pp. 323, 597, 689; cf. Bourquelot, p. 260 f.

8 See A. F. Le Double and F. Houssay, *Les Velus*, Paris, 1912, p. 170, and *passim*.

A. Werner, writing of the tribes of British Central Africa (among whom the possibility of transformation is firmly believed in), tells of a man who had a strong feeling at times that he was a lion, and was impelled, as a lion, to kill and mutilate. He would watch by the wayside, leap out, and stab his victim, and was undoubtedly insane. Other men believed that they were similarly transformed.[1] A boy was burned in Ashango-land because he confessed that he had changed into a leopard and murdered two men—a case not unlike certain occurring in the 16th century.[2] Some men of the Garo hill tribes are afflicted occasionally by a temporary delirium, in which they walk like tigers and shun society. This is known among these tribes as 'transformation into a tiger,' and is supposed to be caused by the application of a medicine to the forehead. Those who thus suffer do not know what has happened when they return to their senses.[3] Certain demoniacs among the Goṇḍs are believed to be possessed by the tiger-god, and will fall on a kid and devour it alive.[4] In the Malay peninsula so real is the belief in the wer-tiger that boys play a game based on the belief. In this one boy is hypnotized, and the others run off, imitating cries of fowls. Then he rises, pursues, scratches, and bites any whom he catches, or climbs trees in his assumed character. Any one who finds himself at his mercy may break the spell by calling out his real name (cf. the European werwolf instances parallel to this)—probably because this was pre-suggested to him. He is supposed to be temporarily possessed by a spirit, but it is obvious that this is on a par with actual cases of insanity, and that the boy might easily become insane, imagining himself to be a tiger. The game is also played in Sumatra and Java, where other animals are also imitated.[5] Among the Dayaks men who eat forbidden flesh are liable to penalties. They will run about the woods naked, imitating a deer, if they have eaten deer's flesh.[6] In Annam an adept who wishes to ask something from the tiger-god prays it to incarnate itself in him. He falls on all fours, growls, eats raw meat, and breaks with his teeth the vessel which contains it. When he is calmed down, he is rubbed with alcohol so that he may come to himself.[7]

Most of these cases from low levels of civilization are obviously temporary cases of insanity, actual or assumed, explained in terms of current belief regarding shape-shifting, etc. They suggest that, even among savages, with whom the general shape-shifting belief is very strong, insanity may, partially at least, have suggested actual wer-animal ideas.

In Europe, during the period when the werwolf superstition was most prevalent, the belief in the possibility of transformation and in the power of the devil over men deluded by him was generally too strong to allow of the truth of the matter being understood. Nevertheless some alleged werwolves were clearly seen to be lunatics and treated as such.

The case of Jacques Rollet, arrested as a werwolf at Condé in 1598, is an example. Two wolves were seen devouring a child's body, while a third rushed off into a neighbouring field. There a man of wild appearance was found, who claimed to be the wolf and maintained that the two wolves were his brother and cousin, and that they had killed and devoured the child. His answers at his trial were contradictory, but he clearly believed that he sometimes became a wolf by means of an ointment. His life was one of great poverty and misery, and it is not impossible that he had killed the child and devoured part of it, and that his ghastly meal was interrupted by wolves. He was sentenced to death, but the Parlement of Paris annulled the sentence and sent him to a hospital.[8] In another case related by Lercheimer, he describes how he visited an alleged werwolf in prison. He was really a lunatic, but maintained that at Easter, through the power of his master, the devil, he became a wolf, took off his chains, and flew out of the prison window. This man would have been burned alive, but Lercheimer obtained his release.[9] In a third case, at Pavia in 1541, a man maintained that he was a wolf and had killed several persons, and that he differed from other wolves merely in the fact that their skin was covered with hair, while his hair was between his skin and his flesh. He was given over to the doctors for treatment, but died soon after.[10] In more modern times such cases are sporadic. Gurney recounts that of a young man at Corfu who in a state of maniacal frenzy imitated a serpent, crawling

1 Werner, p. 86 f.; cf. H. H. Johnston, *Brit. Cent. Africa*, London, 1897, p. 439.

2 P. B. du Chaillu, *Journey to Ashango-land*, London, 1867, p. 52.

3 R. G. Latham, *Descriptive Ethnology*, London, 1859, i. 110.

4 Dalton, p. 280.

5 *FL* xxi. [1910] 371 f.; Skeat, *Malay Magic*, p. 498 f. (imitation of a pole-cat); *FL* xxii. [1911] 240.

6 *FL* xxii. 239; Ling Roth, i. 296.

7 Paul Giran, *Magie et religion annamites*, Paris, 1912, p. 231.

8 P. de Lancre, *L'Incrédulité et mescréance du sortilège*, Paris, 1622, p. 785 f.

9 A. Lercheimer, *Souvenirs de magie*, Strassburg, 1586, p. 120; cf. the case of Baronga transformation and flight, § I. It may be based on dream experiences and hallucinations, as this obviously was.

10 Wier, p. 453; cf. the curious description of a mad lycanthrope in Webster's *Duchess of Malfi*, act v. sc. 2.

about, hissing, and also howling like a dog.[1] In another instance, treated by Morel in the asylum at Maréville, the patient had the delusion that he was a wolf, and ate raw meat.[2]

It is obvious that in facts like these lies one explanation of the origin of the belief in lycanthropy. The unfortunate victims of melancholia with such delusions, imitating in their frenzy the cries and actions of various animals, must have suggested, both in primitive and in later times, certain aspects of the shape-shifting dogma, especially that of the werwolf. And, where the people believed in the possibility of such transformation, it was easy for them to think that such persons, when actually seen imitating the actions of an animal, were really in that animal's shape. Examples of this hallucination have already been given from among the Abipones and the Abyssinians. The frightful prevalence of this mania during the later Middle Ages and in the 16th and 17th centuries may be explained by the miserable conditions under which thousands of the peasantry lived, constantly on the verge of starvation, by their pre-conceived ideas, and by the terrorism to which so many were reduced by the wide-spread demonology, with its sinister shapes of fear and horror as well as its peculiarly vile conceptions of both cruelty and sensuality.[3] Nor is it impossible that half-insane persons, suffering constantly from hunger, may have killed and eaten human victims, whether under the delusion that they were wolves or not.[4] Necrophagy is not unknown in the annals of mental science,[5] and no crime was more commonly attributed both to werwolves and to witches at the Sabbat, and also alleged by them, than the eating of human flesh. This crime was doubtless largely hallucinatory, but it may have had a foundation in fact. Such persons may have actually covered themselves with a wolf-skin in order to terrify their victims more completely.[6] Among savages, sorcerers and medicine-men have traded on the existing delusion or dementia, and have claimed the power of transformation, as many of the above instances show. This is the case with Abipone sorcerers, and another instance is found among the Chippewa and other American Indian tribes, with whom sorcerers dress in the skin of an animal, and imitate its howls and gestures, until the spectators believe in the reality of the transformation.[7] Nicaraguan sorcerers were much feared for their supposed power of assuming animal forms. To strengthen this belief, they disguised themselves in the skins of animals.[8] In such cases, where an exact imitation of the animal's howls or movements was gone through, credulity would aid the deception, and, as the sorcerer pulled off the skin, he would be thought to have resumed his human form. Mediæval and later sorcerers doubtless also exploited the current delusion in these and other ways. This would account for such cases of the change being witnessed as have already been cited.

The constantly recurring idea that the animal change is for a certain period, so many days or years, and the statement that the person knows when the change is about to come, are also strongly suggestive of periodical or recurrent attacks of insanity.

In several of the above instances, where the change occurs through the donning of an animal's skin, there may be a trace of the fact that insane persons with lycanthropic delusions did actually heighten the delusion by wearing a skin, as perhaps in the case of the *berserkr*. In the Irish instance mentioned by Giraldus, the human body is visible underneath the skin. As far as the popular belief was concerned, in many cases the clothing was first removed. This may point to what actually occurred before the animal skin was put on. But it may be the relic of an older belief that the human skin was first removed; cf. the Voodoo instance (above, § 1, p. 213[a]).

[1] E. Gurney, F. W. H. Myers, and F. Podmore, *Phantasms of the Living*, London, 1886, ii. 121.

[2] Hack Tuke, *op. cit.*

[3] Cf. the horrible accounts of orgies at the Sabbat in documents of the period.

[4] Cf. the Galician case of 1849 cited by Baring-Gould, p. 238 ff.; Bourquelot, p. 255.

[5] Français, p. 262 f.

[6] Voltaire suggests as one explanation of lycanthropy a joke played by a young peasant who covered himself with a wolf-skin to frighten old women and so to gain the reputation of a werwolf (*Dict. philosoph.*, *s.v.* 'Enchantment'). The alleged necrophagy by witches is already found in Apuleius.

[7] Dorman, p. 248.

[8] *NR* iii. 496.

Perhaps the werwolf belief was also aided by such phenomena as imbecile children, brutalized, and having animal appetites. These 'wild boys' were often believed to have been stolen by animals—the bear, the wolf—and to have been brought up and suckled by them. While many stories about such children are not authentic, there are some cases in which boys were actually found in the dens of wolves in India. They could not stand upright, went on all fours, ate raw meat, and tore clothes into shreds. Various theories have been suggested to explain their having been thus brought up, but, if some cases are authentic in wolf-haunted districts in India, there may have been instances from time to time in similar districts in Europe. This would in part explain the numerous folk-stories about children suckled by animals—*e.g.*, that of Romulus and Remus.[1] The cases are of the kind described as 'idiocy by deprivation,' and, if such children survived, they would hardly differ from the insane persons who imagined they were wolves, went on all fours, and ate raw flesh.[2]

The case is parallel to that of women carried off by baboons or orang-outangs, which has doubtless some foundation in fact (see *CF*, p. 277).

4. Werwolf and vampire.—While both werwolf and vampire have a liking for human flesh and blood, there is a marked difference between them. The werwolf is a living person assuming animal form for the sake of gratifying his desire. The vampire, on the other hand, is a resuscitated corpse, which rises from the grave to prey on the living, the reasons for the resuscitation being of various kinds (see VAMPIRE). But here and there links of connexion exist. Thus in Germany, Serbia, and modern Greece it is thought that the man who was a werwolf in life becomes a vampire after death. Hence the werwolf was burned, not buried, lest he should do mischief.[3] Again, the dead sometimes appear as werwolves. King John Lackland was said to be a werwolf after his death, on the evidence of a monk of Worcester.[4] In Normandy within the last century priests watched at the grave to be sure of the good conduct of the deceased. If they saw that some lost person was about to become a werwolf, they cut off his head and threw it into the river.[5] A ghost may also appear as a wolf, like the wolf of Anspach in 1684, which was the ghost of a dead Burgomeister.[6] This corresponds to the Malay belief that ghosts of dead wizards enter the bodies of tigers, unless the son of the wizard by certain rites attracts his father's spirit to himself.[7] Similar beliefs have already been noted among the Slavs, Benua, Chinese, natives of British Central Africa, Rhodesians, etc. (§ 1). In New Zealand lizards were feared because the souls of those whose death-rites had been neglected became malignant and entered such creatures. They then gnawed the entrails of living men.[8] Demons and

[1] J. A. MacCulloch, *CF*, p. 277; E. B. Tylor, 'Wild Men and Beast Children,' *Anthrop. Review*, i. [1863] 21 f.; V. Ball, *JAI* ix. [1880] 465; *PR*[2] ii. 153. For a recent instance of a wild girl found at Nainital, see *Morning Post*, July 27, 1914, and other newspapers of same date. Cf. also R. Kipling's *Jungle Books*.

[2] E. B. Sherlock, *The Feeble-minded*, London, 1911, p. 166.

[3] Hertz, pp. 88, 122, 128.

[4] *Ib.* p. 110.

[5] Sébillot, iv. 240.

[6] Hertz, p. 88.

[7] T. J. Newbold, *British Settlements in Straits of Malacca*, London, 1839, ii. 387.

[8] E. Tregear, *JAI* xix. [1890] 120.

spirits of all kinds frequently take animal forms and act as the werwolf or vampire. Thus the French *lubin* was a spirit in the form of a wolf, which haunted churchyards to prey on the dead, like the Arabian *ghūl*, which takes the form of men or animals and eats corpses.[1] In Ethiopian lives of saints the king of the devils rides on a fire-breathing wolf and is followed by fiends in the form of wolves, while in Meroe the wicked are thought to be visited by evil spirits as wolves, jackals, etc.[2]

5. **The 'sending.'**—A phenomenon analogous to that of the werwolf is that of the 'sending'—a thing or animal, sometimes animated or even created by the sorcerer, or some part of the sorcerer himself (his soul, etc.) and sent out by him to annoy or injure people. Examples occur over a wide-spread area and at various levels of civilization. The 'sending' is a kind of familiar of the wizard. In S.E. Australia the lizard is such a wizard familiar and is sent out to do injury.[3] Among the Roro-speaking tribes of British New Guinea snakes and crocodiles are sent by sorcerers to kill. A fragment of the victim's garment is put beside the snake in a pot; then heat is applied to the pot, and the snake strikes at the fragment. Then it is let loose near where the victim passes, and attacks him because it recognizes the smell of the fragment on him. More magical is the method of the Bartle Bay sorceress, a 'sending' from whose body causes death. It leads a separate life from her after her death, or may pass to her daughter. At Gelaria this 'sending' is called *labuni*, and resembles a shadow. It leaves the woman's body when she is asleep, and causes disease by inserting bone or stone in the victim. Should any one see it, it turns into an animal, and then again takes its human form. At Collingwood Bay the 'sending' is called *farum*, and is like a limbless old woman. It turns to a mosquito and sucks the victim's blood, resuming human form at dawn.[4] In Banks Island, if any one eats a piece of a corpse, its ghost will go forth to harm a victim at the will of the eater. Here also and in the New Hebrides the *mae*, or sea-snake, acts as the familiar spirit of those who profess to have had intercourse with it.[5] Among the Malays and in Java insects and even horned deer are used as 'sendings.'[6] Among the Yoruba sorcerers use the owl as a 'sending,' and, should it be caught by the person whom it is intended to destroy, and its claws and wings broken, a similar injury is done to the sorcerer's limbs.[7] In the Cameroons a man selects a hippopotamus, leopard, elephant, gorilla, etc., as a friend, and the animal is then supposed to harm his enemies by stealth. But, if the animal dies or is slain, the man dies. Hence such animals are usually not hunted by fellow-tribesmen.[8] Matabele wizards dig up corpses, transform them into hyenas, and use them as messengers or steeds. A wounded hyena escaping into a *kraal* is thought to show that this is the dwelling of a wizard.[9] Baronga wizards send forth crocodiles, lions, snakes, etc., to kill or wound.[10] In Calabar each wizard has two owl messengers, or sends forth insects—stinging ants, beetles, etc.—into the house where he is to find his victim. Then he sends his *ikim*—a gourd—to examine the house. Insects and *ikim* report whether there is any dangerous *juju*, or medicine, in it.[1]

1 W. C. Hazlitt, *Faiths and Folklore*, London, 1905, p. 374; Hertz, p. 110; Lane, *Arabian Society*, p. 42.
2 E. A. W. Budge, *The Egyptian Sûdân*, London, 1907, i. 268.
3 A. W. Howitt, *JAI* xvi. [1887] 34.
4 C. G. Seligmann, *Melanesians of Brit. New Guinea*, Cambridge, 1910, pp. 282 f., 640–643.
5 Codrington, pp. 221 f., 188.
6 *FL* xiii. 157.
7 *Les Missions catholiques*, Lyons, 1884, p. 249.
8 J. G. Frazer, *Totemism and Exogamy*, London, 1910, ii. 596 f.
9 T. M. Thomas, *Eleven Years in Central S. Africa*, London, 1872, p. 293.
10 Junod, p. 466 f.

Bavili sorcerers will leopards and crocodiles to go and destroy, having obtained this power through a medicine rubbed into their eyes. Then the animal becomes visible to them, and they know that it is at their service.[2] In British Central Africa wizards can create lions, or sometimes inspire existing lions, to go forth and destroy.[3] Among the Bondei 'dolls' of Indian corn are animated by the sorcerer, and go forth to suck the blood of a victim, who turns sick and dies.[4] Zulu wizards send out owls and other animals, and Basutos crocodiles, to injure their victims. These are called their *amanxus*, 'attendants.'[5] The Eskimo *angakok* sends a *tupilak*—a seal made by him. Should the victim kill it, he loses all strength and becomes a cripple. This seal is made of bones of various animals, covered with turf and blood, and charmed into life by a magic song.[6] A Siberian shaman will send out a *ye-keela*, or witch-animal, to fight that of another shaman. The shaman whose *ye-keela* is worsted shares its fate. Lapland wizards sent flies and darts against their enemies, and also a kind of ball. The last was fatal to the victim as well as to any one who came in its way.[7] Witch-doctors among the Paraguay Indians send forth witch-beetles to enter their victims, and these beetles cause great terror when seen.[8] In Mexico, among the Tarahumare Indians sorcerers cause snakes, scorpions, toads, and centipedes to eat a man's heart so that he dies.[9] The Twanas explain sickness as caused by an evil animal sent by a sorcerer to eat away the patient's life.[10] In ancient Scandinavia it was believed that sorcerers could raise up a ghost or a corpse by their magic power and send it to do harm to an enemy.[11] The Indian, Benua, and Japanese examples of the animal familiar, cited above (§ 1), should also be noted.

Danish witches were believed to make a hare out of some wooden pegs and an old stocking, and send it to steal milk from cattle.[12] The Esthonians believed in magic packets made by wizards and sent forth to do all kinds of mischief—*e.g.*, to transform the victim.[13] Among the Celts the druids had the power, by singing spells over a wisp of straw and flinging it in their victim's face, to cause him to become mad, and all madness was attributed to such a 'sending.'[14]

Not dissimilar to this conception of the 'sending' is the belief entertained in Celebes regarding the wer-man. The Torajas believe that a man's spirit or inside, *lamboyo*, can go forth from him as a deer, pig, cat, ape, etc., while he is asleep at home. The *lamboyo* then assumes human form (this resembles the New Guinea *labuni*). Its victim is first made unconscious; then in human form the *lamboyo* cuts him up, eats the liver, and joins the body together again. Soon after the victim wakes,

1 Macgregor, p. 224.
2 R. E. Dennett, *FL* xvi. [1905] 391–393.
3 Johnston, p. 451.
4 G. Dale, *JAI* xxv. [1895] 223.
5 H. Callaway, *Religious System of the Amazulu*, Natal, 1884, p. 348; *JAI* xx. 115.
6 K. Rasmussen, *People of the Polar North*, London, 1908, p. 155; cf. F. Nansen, *Eskimo Life*, do. 1893, p. 285.
7 A. Calmet, *Les Apparitions*, new ed., Paris, 1751, i. 107.
8 W. B. Grubb, *An Unknown People in an Unknown Land*, London, 1911, p. 155 f.
9 Lumholtz, i. 315.
10 M. Eells, *Ten Years of Mission Work among the Indians*, Boston, 1886, p. 43.
11 Vigfusson-Powell, Introd. p. lxxvii; *FL* x. 460.
12 Thorpe, ii. 192; *FL* x. 460.
13 W. F. Kirby, *The Hero of Esthonia*, London, 1895, i. 208, 257, ii. 168.
14 E. O'Curry, *Manners and Customs of the Ancient Irish*, London, 1873, ii. 203.

he dies. Elsewhere in Celebes a man is thought to have three souls. One of these, the *tonoana*, leaves him in sleep and acts as a werwolf, but, if it is long away or is fatally hurt, the owner dies.

A wer-man in human shape arranged for a rendezvous with a woman. Her husband overheard, and followed the wer-man, whose bodily form was meanwhile at work. He struck the *lamboyo* or *tonoana*, which turned to a leaf. This he thrust into his bamboo tobacco box. Then, carrying it to the place where the man was at work, he placed it on the fire. The owner begged him not to do this. But he still kept it in the fire, whereupon the man fell dead.

In some cases this power of sending forth the soul is a natural gift, in others it is the result of contagion from another wer-man, or from anything with which he has been in contact. This contagion can be made to leave such a person in the form of snakes or worms by means of severe medical treatment. The wer-man is known by his long tongue and unsteady eyes, which are of a green colour. A wer-man, when discovered, is punished by death. In these instances the spirit is but little different from the 'sending' or familiar spirit. In some cases, however, it is thought that there is an actual bodily transformation, and here, if the animal is wounded, the man who has thus changed his form is similarly hurt when discovered, or dies.[1] Among the Oraons a witch sends out her soul as a cat, herself remaining insensible. Should it be injured in any way, she bears a similar wound.[2]

This likeness may be further extended to the kindred phenomena of the bush-soul and the *nagual*, both of which bear some resemblance to the 'sending' and to the *lamboyo* or *tonoana*. In Calabar the bush-soul is one of four souls possessed by every man. It lives in a pig, leopard, etc., unseen by its owner, but it must not be neglected by him, else the owner turns sick. Then the witch-doctor advises that an offering be made to it. If this appeases it, all is well. If not, the man dies. The witch-doctor can tell the man what sort of animal encloses his bush-soul. He then takes care that neither he nor any one else harms it, for, if it is shot or trapped, the man dies; *vice versa*, when the man dies, the bush-soul also dies.[3] Another observer, J. K. Macgregor, writes that the death of the bush-soul merely causes weakness to its owner. But it is possible for a man to purchase an extra bush-soul from a witch-doctor which is stronger than the other, and can be used for purposes of offence. He may command it to go and kill goats, if a leopard, or trample a farm, if a hippopotamus. If this soul dies, the owner also dies. The owner of a bush-soul can transform himself into the animal in which his bush-soul is.

A chief's son who had a hippopotamus for his bush-soul had been paying a visit to another chief, but sent away his canoe. Asked how he would cross the river, he replied, 'You will see.' He took the leaf of a coco-yam, placed it on the water, sat on it, and at once disappeared below the surface. Then he was seen to cross the river as a hippopotamus, and on the other side he became a man.

It should be observed also that a man's human soul, residing in himself, may leave his body through a medicine and take the souls of things that he desires out of a house. Then he materializes them, and the original articles fall to pieces.[4] In Northern Nigeria among the Angass a man is held to have a *karua* which enters him at birth, and another, its counterpart, which enters an animal. The death of the one causes the death of the other.[1] The whole belief in the bush-soul is not unlike the Roman belief in the genius. A man's health depended on that of his genius, which often resided in a snake. If that was killed, the man whose genius it was also died.[2]

The *nagual* belief is found in Central America. In this case a youth obtained his *nagual* by dreaming of an animal after a period of solitude and fasting. The *nagual*-animal is closely bound up with the man henceforward. When it dies, the man dies; when it is sick, he is sick. He has also the power of appearing as his *nagual*. Any wound caused on the animal form is then found on the man.[3] This resembles the belief in Motu, Melanesia. A lizard, snake, or stone, etc., is selected as a man's *tamaniu*. His life is bound up with it. If it dies, or gets broken, or lost, the owner dies.[4] As already seen, the *talamaur* may be the soul, and, if it is wounded, the body is found to have a similar wound. In an Eskimo story the spirit of a witch who has made a young man ill is wounded in the heel. At the same moment the witch dies in the next house.[5]

Between the werwolf superstition and the various beliefs cited in this section there are certain similarities. Of these that which recurs constantly is the belief in repercussion.

Injury to the 'sending' entails injury to the sorcerer (Yoruba, Eskimos, Siberia); injury to the animal friend entails injury to the owner (Cameroon); injury to the bush-soul, *nagual*, *tamaniu*, wer-soul, entails injury to the owner (Celebes, African instance, Oraons, Indians of Guiana); injury to the soul which takes the form of an animal entails injury to the owner; injury to the soul which enters an animal temporarily entails injury to the owner; injury to the soul absent from the body for some mischievous purpose entails injury to the owner (Eskimos, Melanesians); injury to the werwolf or other wer-animal entails injury to the man in his human form.[6]

The real point of connexion between all the beliefs is that something belonging to the man, some part of the man, or the man himself in another form is injured. The injury then, because of the vital connexion between the part and the whole, or thing owned and owner (sympathetic magic), is seen on the man himself. But it is not clear that, as Frazer supposes, the wide-spread belief in wer-animals may 'be found to resolve itself into a belief in the external soul.'[7] The wer-animal is, save in a very few instances (Khonds, Oraons, Malays, Chinese, Ibos and other W. African peoples, Indians of Guiana), the man himself transformed, not his soul. And, even where the owner of bush-soul or *nagual* is supposed to change himself into the animal containing it, or an animal of the kind, the transformation is a bodily one. The external soul, injury to which causes injury to the owner, is one thing; the wer-animal, which is really the man himself transformed, is another. But the same theory or belief in repercussion is applicable to both. It is not by any means certain that the instance on which Frazer bases his theory of the wer-animal and the external soul can support it. There is no evidence that, when the Nūtka novice is supposed to die and come to life

[1] A. C. Kruijt, 'De weerwolf bij de Toradja's van Midden-Celebes,' *Tijdschrift voor Indische taal-, land- en volkenkunde*, xii. [1899] 548 f.; J. Knebel, *ib.* 568 ff.; *GB*³, pt. vii., *Balder the Beautiful*, London, 1913, i. 311 ff.; N. W. Thomas, *EBr* xvii. 149; A. C. Kruijt, *Het Animisme*¹¹, The Hague, 1906, p. 109 f.

[2] P. Dehon, *Memoirs of the Asiatic Society of Bengal*, i. [1906] 141.

[3] M. H. Kingsley, *West Afr. Studies*, London, 1899, p. 208 f.; J. Parkinson, *Man*, vi. [1906] 121; Frazer, *Totemism and Exogamy*, ii. 594; cf. p. 598 for a similar belief among the Balong of Cameroon.

[4] Macgregor, p. 28; H. Goldie, *Calabar and its Mission*, Edinburgh, 1901, p. 51.

[1] Frazer, *Totemism and Exogamy*, ii. 598.

[2] Plutarch's *Romane Questions*, ed. F. B. Jevons, London, 1892, p. xlvii.

[3] T. Gage, *New Survey of the W. Indies*³, London, 1677, p. 334; A. de Herrera, *Gen. Hist. of Continent and Islands of America*, do. 1726, iv. 138; Brinton, 'Nagualism,' *Proc. Amer. Phil. Soc.*, xxxiii. [1894] 26 f.; Frazer, *Totemism and Exogamy*, iii. 443 f.

[4] Codrington, p. 251. [5] Rink, pp. 371 f., 458.

[6] An injury done to a fantasm or double is also found to be done to the actual person (see A. Lang, *Cock Lane and Common Sense*, London, 1894, p. 51); cf. the Zulu idea that the *imamba*, or dead chief in the form of a snake, can be killed but may come to life again with the mark of the wound still upon it (Callaway, p. 225).

[7] *Totemism and Exogamy*, ii. 599 f.

again before becoming a member of the wolf-society, he has exchanged souls with a wolf, so that both man and wolf are werwolves, or that there is anything here akin to the bush-soul.[1] Nor again is it clear, as N. W. Thomas maintains,[2] that lycanthropy is connected with nagualism rather than with transformation, or that the wer-animal was originally the familiar of the medicine-man. The comparatively few instances of the spirit going forth as a wer-animal suggest that we are here on the track of a different if analogous superstition to that of lycanthropy with its supposed bodily transformation. Again, the familiar is hardly a form of the man himself, as the werwolf is, but rather sometimes of part of the man, or it is his messenger, which the werwolf does not seem to be.

There may, however, be a connecting link if we regard the phenomena of lycanthropy as based on the hallucinatory dreams of insane persons, preoccupied with ideas of transformation. Where a medicine-man is supposed to send forth his spirit either in its own shape or in that of an animal, while he remains quiescent at home, this may also be suggested by a hallucinatory dream.

It seems better, therefore, to regard lycanthropy with its bodily transformation as distinct from the transformation of the outgoing spirit, and also from the 'sending,' messenger, or familiar. They are analogous beliefs, to which similar conceptions —*e.g.*, that of repercussion—have attached themselves. But they are in origin different. In the same way, though there is much in the fairy, demon, or witch superstitions which is common to all (see FAIRY), these are really distinct in origin.

6. Conclusion.—The wide diffusion of the werwolf superstition forms an excellent example of a universal belief being worked up into a superstition or story bearing a common likeness in different regions. Without the belief in shape-shifting the werwolf superstition could not have existed. But, this being granted, persons of diseased mind in all stages of civilization easily conceived themselves to be ferocious animals preying upon other human beings. The belief itself was easily exploited by interested persons—medicine-men, sorcerers, etc.; or some of these might themselves be half-crazed, as medicine-men often are through their austerities (see AUSTERITIES). In certain cases—*e.g.*, that of the Norse *berserkrs*—the insane fit was heightened by the wearing of animal-skins; or, in others, totemism, in its later stages, may have helped the form of the superstition, as in the Arcadian and some Irish Celtic examples.

LITERATURE.—Of the numerous works written on this subject in the 16th and 17th centuries, the following are the most important: B. de Chauvincourt, *Discours de la lycanthropie*, Paris, 1599; J. de Nynauld, *De la Lycanthropie*, Louvain, 1596; Wolfeshusius, *De Lycanthropis*, Leipzig, 1591. More modern works are: R. Andree, *Ethnographische Parallelen und Vergleiche*, Leipzig, 1889, pp. 62–80; S. Baring-Gould, *The Book of Were-wolves*, London, 1865; M. F. Bourquelot, 'Recherches sur la lycanthropie,' *Mémoires de la société des antiquaires de France*, new ser., ix. [1849] 193–262; J. Grimm, *Teutonic Mythology*, Eng. tr., London, 1882–88; W. Hertz, *Der Werwolf: Beitrag zur Sagengeschichte*, Stuttgart, 1862; R. Leubuscher, *Ueber die Wehrwölfe und Thierverwandlungen im Mittelalter*, Berlin, 1850; E. B. Tylor, *PC*³, London, 1891, i. 308 f.

J. A. MACCULLOCH.

LYING.—The English word 'lie' with its congeners and derivatives represents a concept which, if hard to define, is yet unique and irresolvable into any other. While it cannot be claimed either (*a*) that all persons are agreed as to what precisely constitutes a lie or lying, or (*b*) that anything like the same ethical significance has at all times and in all communities been attached to the practice generally understood to be denoted by the Teutonic word and by the words commonly regarded as its equivalents in other languages, yet in English at any rate this term, and in a somewhat less degree any word or periphrasis which is thought to be merely a covert alternative for it, is viewed and, by those to whom it is applied, is resented as conveying a reproach, or at least an opinion, generically different from any other. It would probably be conceded that nowhere has antipathy to lying and sensitiveness to the imputation of it reached a higher intensity than among ourselves; and a study of the import of the term in our own language may therefore be taken as in a manner typical and representative.

1. Sources of modern conception.—Historically the English lie has, if we may so speak, a fourfold pedigree—Saxon, Jewish, Græco-Latin, and Christian. It signifies, that is, a vice or vicious act, which derives its peculiar reputation partly from the language and sentiment of our pagan forefathers, partly from conceptions that find expression in the Hebrew Scriptures of the OT, partly from Greek and Roman thought and literature, and, as we shall contend, partly from the specific teachings of Christianity. If it be alleged against this analysis that our sensitive regard for veracity is rather of feudal origin, the objection, even if well-founded, is of no moment, that feature of feudal ethics being itself derived from some or all of the four sources enumerated.

(1) *Saxon.*—The presence in all the Teutonic languages of a substantially identical word of like meaning attests the perennial importance of the thing meant. To 'lie' is to say that which is not. And we cannot doubt that the tribesman who had the skill, and the heart, on occasion to do this undetected was held in different esteem from the man who could not or would not; whether in higher or in lower esteem, we cannot in the absence of adequate evidence be sure; that might perhaps depend on, and change with, the varying circumstances of the community.

(2) *Jewish.*—When at length on British soil the Anglo-Saxon invaders were gradually led to profess the Christian faith, that faith brought with it a moral code derived in unequal degrees from the three other sources named above, of which the most ancient and explicit was the Hebraic. Although the Decalogue contains no precept 'Thou shalt not lie,' the prohibition of 'false witness' reprobates the most frequent and injurious form of lying. Prophets and moralists enlarged the prohibition. 'The voice of the Lord crieth unto the city,' says Micah (6⁹), 'for the inhabitants thereof have spoken lies, and their tongue is deceitful in their mouth' (6^{12}; cf. Is 30^9 59^{13}, Jer 23^{14}); 'Lying lips are an abomination unto the Lord' (Pr 12^{22}); 'A righteous man hateth lying' (13^4; cf. Ps 119^{163}). Especially guilty are 'false prophets' who in the name of the Lord 'prophesy lies . . . a lying vision . . . a thing of nought, and the deceit of their own heart' (Jer 14^{14}; cf. Zec 13^3).

(3) *Græco-Latin.* — Meanwhile early Hellenic sentiment viewed lying without horror; virtually, as craft, it had in Hermes a patron-god. Perjury, however, was deemed perilous, incurring the wrath of Zeus. Subsequently, as witness the gnomic poets,[1] civic morality coupled veracity with justice as laudable (cf. Plato, *Rep.* i. 331 B); and Sophocles proclaimed the ugliness of falsehood:

'Honourable (καλόν) it nowise is to speak lies; though when the truth brings a man dire destruction, 'tis pardonable to say even what is not honourable' (frag. 323).

Finally, philosophy pronounced falsehood intrinsically vicious. Plato (*Rep.* ii. 382 A, 389 B–D), while permitting his 'guardians' to use it, now and again, medicinally and officially 'for the benefit of the State,' bids them punish it rigorously in private individuals as 'a practice pernicious and subversive

[1] *Totemism and Exogamy*, ii. 599, iii. 549, *GB*³, pt. vii., *Balder the Beautiful*, ii. 270 f.
[2] *EBr*¹¹ xvii. 149, *Man*, ii. [1902] 117.

[1] *e.g.* Mimnermus, frag. 8: 'With thee and me be truth, most just of all things.'

of the commonwealth,' and in his latest work (*Laws*, 730 B f.) extols truth as 'foremost of all good things'; for the truthful man is 'trustworthy, whereas he who loves wilful falsehood is untrustworthy (ἄπιστος), and he who loves involuntary falsehood is foolish.' Aristotle (*Eth. Nic.* iv. 7. 6) deems 'lying' (τὸ ψεῦδος) essentially 'mean (φαῦλον) and blameworthy.' The 'truth-lover' (φιλαλήθης) stands in notable contrast with him who rejoices in falsehood (ὁ τῷ ψεύδει αὐτῷ χαίρων), a type of character distinct from him who lies for the sake of gain or glory (*ib.* § 12). In Stoicism the viciousness of falsehood, although not expressly affirmed, is tacitly assumed. Thus ideal good is in effect defined by Seneca (*Ep.* lxvi. 6) as 'a mind set on truth.'[1] To the consistent Stoic acceptance of unverified 'opinion' as a substitute for truth or real knowledge would be equivalent to inveracity. Altogether, Greek philosophy had energetically discountenanced the art of lying, and, when Latinized, had found an ally in old-fashioned Roman prejudice against wilful untruth.

(4) *Christian.*—The NT endorsed and deepened the injunctions of Jewish theology and Gentile ethics. 'Lie not one to another,' writes St. Paul to the Colossians (3^9); the Christian is to forgo all 'lying,' and this for the new and characteristically Christian reason that 'we are members one of another' (Eph 4^{25}). And with this Pauline monition the warnings of the Apocalypse agree. Into the heavenly city no 'liar' may enter (Rev 21^7); outcast thence is 'every one that loveth and maketh a lie' (22^{15}), where nothing is lost to the ethics of truth if by 'lie' be meant idol or counterfeit god; that, theologically, *is* the typical lie—idolatry falsifying man's conception of the divine attributes and therewith the standard of truth. In the Synoptic Gospels 'hypocrisy' (Mt 23^{28}, Lk 12^1) would appear to express what in St. John is called simply 'lying' (ψεῦδος), of which 'the devil' (Jn 8^{44}) is first cause. Thus for Christianity the spirit of lying is opposed to the spirit of truth as darkness is to light. It is antagonistic to God and incompatible with fellowship in the Church of Christ. And this abhorrence of lying as deadly sin, though too often grievously violated in nominal Christendom, has endured throughout the centuries, permeates our finest literature, and is reflected in the life and conduct of many a plain, honest man to-day.

2. Philosophical theories.—Theology and custom-morality apart, moral philosophers of different schools condemn lying on different grounds; the intuitionist as intrinsically repugnant to 'right reason' or 'moral sense' or 'conscience,' the eudæmonist or perfectionist because it impairs well-being and self-development, the utilitarian because, on the whole, if not in every instance, it would tend to the diminution of the sum-total of pleasure experienced. Whether the utilitarian sanction is well-founded in fact may be questioned. It is arguable that the wide acceptance of utilitarian ethics has been attended by an increased indifference to truth. Whereas lying is demonstrably contrary to other ideals—universal benevolence, perfection, or the beautiful—there is no guarantee that truth-seeking will bring either to the individual or to the community a surplus of pleasure, or that more pleasure may not be secured by an admixture of well-timed falsehood. But, even if utilitarian theory could demonstrate the all but universal inexpediency of lying, such calculative disapproval of it as hedonistically impolitic is not the same thing as hating a lie for its own sake. It is this that would seem to be ethically the point of main consequence, distinguishing man from man—the presence or absence of a deep aversion to lying as such. Of less real importance is the much debated question, too complex to summarize here, of exceptional contingencies in which, notwithstanding that aversion, it may be right to speak falsely, just as killing is sometimes right. But we may consider whether lies can be classified, and attempt a more exact determination of the essential constituents of lying.

3. Analysis and classification of lying.—The aim of a lie is to misrepresent facts, or purpose, or feeling. To be a liar is to do this habitually and wilfully. Of each particular lie the motive is normally some gain foreseen or conjectured as attainable by deceiving somebody as to (1) what has happened, (2) what one purposes, or (3) how one feels. In popular usage the term 'lie' is apt to be limited to the first kind. But I lie no less really, if (2) I promise what I have no intention of doing, or if (3), being glad, I feign sorrow. This is sometimes overlooked or even denied. With regard to declarations of purpose, it is rightly urged that unforeseen circumstances alter cases, and to promise what one may eventually see reason not to perform is no falsehood. But it *is* lying, if at the time of speaking I have not the intention professed; or if I deliberately, but insincerely, protest that in no circumstances will I change my mind; or if, having changed it, I allow those concerned to go on believing my purpose to be unchanged. The last is a very common form of falsehood. Similarly, as regards feeling, many people who would be ashamed to state that they had seen what they had not seen, make no scruple about pretending goodwill towards persons for whom they have none, with the object sometimes of getting general credit for a kindness of heart which is not theirs, sometimes of misleading the victims of their dissimulation.

Not all deceit, however, is lying. For, although the essence of lying is intent to deceive, there must be also, to constitute a lie, either (*a*) untrue words, or (*b*) such reticence as in the context (of speech or action) amounts to false statement—*e.g.*, if I say 'He gave me twenty pounds,' when in fact he gave me fifty (cf. Ac 5^8), or if I adopt and publish as my own an essay largely written by another man. To lie is, as Kant well says, 'to communicate one's thoughts to another through words which (intentionally) contain the opposite of that which the speaker thinks.'[1] It matters not whether the false belief is created by positive affirmation or by omission of words necessary to the establishment of a true belief.

Allegory is not falsehood, provided it is designed and adapted to embody truth. It was because early Greek mythology did not in Plato's judgment fulfil this condition that he regarded allegorizing interpretations of it as in no way bettering the case for Homer and Hesiod (*Rep.* ii. 378 D). As with allegory, so with all fiction. Stage-plays and novels exhibit in the form of 'stories' events that are not history, present or past, and yet mislead nobody. A 'story' is a lie, then, only when it falsely disowns its fictitious origin. Even pseudonymous authorship does not necessarily involve falsehood. Not all illusion is deception. Daniel is dramatically as legitimate as Hamlet or Coriolanus. But the pope who, to intimidate a Frankish king and practising on his credulity, sent him a private letter purporting to come from St. Peter was no dramatist, but a forger; and forgery is falsehood. It is doubtful whether equivocation, where a statement is equally susceptible of two meanings, one false and one true, should, because calculated to deceive, be accounted lying. As an isolated act, it probably should not. But the man who habitually

[1] 'Animus vera intuens, peritus fugiendorum ac petendorum, non ex opinione, sed ex natura pretia rebus imponens.'

[1] E. Caird, *Critical Philosophy of Kant*, Glasgow, 1889, ii. 337.

equivocates is an untruthful man. Under the head of equivocation may fairly be brought many of those partially deceptive utterances which are sometimes, but unconvincingly, defended as mere social conventions on a par with the customary phraseology of address and other 'common forms of speech generally understood.'[1] If, *e.g.*, in declining an unwelcome invitation I express regret at being unable to accept it, the defence that this is a usual and well-understood way of notifying my intention, while disguising the motive, is inadequate. But, supposing I do regret the disappointment which my refusal may cause or the circumstances which render the invitation unacceptable, the phrase employed is equivocal rather than actually false. If, instead of declining, I profess 'pleasure in accepting' the invitation, the pleasure need not be wholly fictitious; for it is in my power by an effort of goodwill (*a*) to feel pleasure in accepting, and not refusing, the civility offered, and (*b*) to find altruistic pleasure in a visit not naturally attractive. By thus *choosing* to be pleased, a man determines on the side of truth what would have been equivocation. Even where there is an actual element of falsehood, we recognize degrees of insincerity. A statement which in the main reveals the speaker's purpose, feeling, or knowledge of fact, but disguises some detail, is not in the same degree vicious as an entirely misleading utterance, unless, of course, the point misrepresented is the most essential, in which case the saying may be exemplified that 'the worst lies are half truths.' Yet we cannot altogether reject the widely spread view of 'common sense,' that a direct lie stands on a different footing from any indirect device whether of hiding the truth (*suppressio veri*) or of creating a false impression (*suggestio falsi*). There is a common understanding that, when we speak, we do not state what we know to be untrue. Socially regarded, then, a direct lie is a graver breach of faith, and a worse blow to mutual confidence, than any statement, however evasive, which does not actually violate this understanding.

4. Conclusion.—On the whole, the main difference between ancient and 'modern' views of inveracity is that in the latter censure is directed primarily on discrepance between statement and thought rather than on the divergence from reality of a spoken, or unuttered, proposition. 'Modern' morality tends to be severe upon misstatements, apparently wilful, of particular facts, but is strangely lenient wherever 'ignorance' can be pleaded—as if ignorance was not often wilful, or reckless, indifference to truth. Many persons will habitually declare as fact anything that they do not positively know to be untrue, and, when convicted of error, take no shame to themselves. They 'thought' it was so. To Plato such untrue 'thought' or 'lie in the soul' appeared more manifestly evil than any spoken lie; and, though Christianity, supervening, emphasized the distinction between wilful sin and intellectual error, there is nothing in the NT to justify, and the Johannine writings abundantly discountenance, the 'modern' view aforesaid, which indeed rests upon nothing better than the assumption that we are entitled to ignore truth, if not to pervert it. In practice the former habit leads on to the latter. Having once entertained and echoed some untruthful allegation, a man will often shut his ears to all disproof and pervert other facts in support of it. Again, if 'lying' proper implies some kind of utterance, the wider concept of 'falsehood' includes (*a*) self-deception, and (*b*) the unuttered lie cherished in the heart and potent to vitiate judgments whether of fact or of value. The dishonest-minded man frequently propagates untruth without any formal or positive lying. If he thus on technical grounds escapes being designated a liar, he yet comes within Aristotle's description of 'the man who delights in falsehood as such.' Doubtless this permanent disposition is acquired only through repeated indulgence in lying for the sake of some particular gain. If it is seldom attained, an intermediate stage is very frequent. Many men and women rarely tell the truth, regarding it as something too precious to give away!

The relation of inveracity to 'that most excellent of all virtuous principles, the active principle of benevolence,' emerges in Butler's 'Dissertation of the Nature of Virtue.' Linking 'falsehood' as a cardinal vice with 'injustice' and 'unprovoked violence,' Butler holds that 'veracity as well as justice is to be our rule of life'; by these our benevolence must be conditioned.

Of the view which condemns lying as violation of a man's duty to himself, the typical exponent is Kant, who stigmatizes a lie as 'an annihilation of the dignity of man,' and deprecates argument from the injury done by the liar to others as confusing 'the duty of truth with the duty of beneficence' (Caird, ii. 384). On the other hand, the best English moralists of the past century, notably Sidgwick and Martineau, take a wider and at the same time a more discriminating view of the nature and harmfulness of falsehood.

LITERATURE.—In addition to the authorities quoted in the art. see H. Sidgwick, *Methods of Ethics*⁷, London, 1907, bk. iii. ch. vii. (from the intuitional standpoint), bk. iv. ch. iii. (from the utilitarian standpoint); J. Martineau, *Types of Ethical Theory*², Oxford, 1886, section on 'Veracity' (pt. ii. bk. i. ch. 6, § 12); T. H. Green, *Prolegomena to Ethics*, do. 1883, p. 344 f.; J. S. Mackenzie, *Manual of Ethics*, London, 1897, pp. 189, 319 f.; H. Rashdall, *Theory of Good and Evil*, Oxford, 1907, i. 90, 192–196. For the attitude of non-Christian peoples towards lying see *MI*, ch. xxx. f.

J. M. SCHULHOF.

[1] J. Butler, *Analogy*, Dissertation ii. 'Of the Nature of Virtue' (*ad fin.*) (ed. J. H. Bernard, London, 1900, p. 295).

M

MA'ARRI.—

1. Life.—Abu'l-'Alā Aḥmad ibn 'Abdallāh ibn Sulaimān al-Ma'arri, the celebrated Muhammadan poet and man of letters, was born in A.D. 973 at Ma'arra (Ma'arrat al-Nu'mān), a prosperous Syrian town situated about 20 miles south of Aleppo. At an early age he became almost completely blind in consequence of an attack of smallpox, but so extraordinary was his power of memory that this misfortune did not seriously interfere with the literary studies to which he afterwards devoted himself. It would seem that at first he intended to make poetry his profession. The sums gained by writing panegyrics were often immense, and may well have tempted an ambitious youth with the example of Mutanabbī before him. Abu'l-'Alā, however, declares that his poems were not written for hire. Probably this is true in the sense that he soon abandoned a career which, lucrative as it might be, entailed dependence on the precarious favours of patronage and was destructive of every feeling of self-respect. From the age of 20 to 35 he remained at Ma'arra, a poor and comparatively unknown scholar, supported by a small annual pension paid from a trust-fund. During this time he composed the greater part of the collection of poems entitled *Siqṭ al-zand* ('Sparks from the Tinder'), in which the influence of Mutanabbī is apparent. With the object of seeking a wider field for his talents, he left Ma'arra in A.D. 1008 and journeyed to Baghdād, where he was well received by the learned men; but, instead of settling there, as he had planned, he departed after a stay of eighteen months, and, on returning home, announced his intention to retire from the world. Though, according to his own statement, it was lack of means and the news of his mother's illness that caused him to quit the capital, there seems to be little doubt that he took this step on account of an indignity which he suffered at the hands of a powerful noble whom he was so imprudent as to offend. The remainder of his life was passed in teaching and writing. His picture of himself as a misanthropic recluse conveys a false impression. From Baghdād he returned with a reputation that not only made him the first man in his native town, but also brought disciples from all parts to hear him discourse on Arabic philology and literature. He had many friends, and his letters to them show 'a kindly interest both in men and things' (*The Letters of Abu'l-'Alā*, ed. Margoliouth, Introd. p. xxx). He complains of his poverty, but the Persian poet Nāṣir-i Khusrau, who visited Ma'arra in A.D. 1047, describes him as very rich (*Safar-nāmah*, ed. C. Schefer, Paris, 1881, p. 10= p. 35 of the Fr. tr.). Ma'arrī died in A.D. 1058.

2. **Writings.**—Besides the *Siqṭ al-zand*, already mentioned, Ma'arrī is the author of another and far more remarkable volume of poetry, entitled *Luzūm mā lam yalzam*, in reference to a technical peculiarity of rhyme, and generally known as the *Luzūmiyyāt*. These poems, written after his visit to Baghdād, contain religious, moral, and philosophical reflexions and deal with a great variety of topics. The prevailing tone is pessimistic and sceptical, but many passages occur in which Ma'arrī speaks as an orthodox Muslim. The *Risālat al-ghufrān* (described and partially translated by the present writer in *JRAS*, 1900, pp. 637–720, and 1902, pp. 75–101, 337–362, 813–847; ed. Cairo, 1907) takes the form of an epistle addressed to 'Alī ibn Manṣūr of Aleppo, who is better known by the name of Ibn al-Qāriḥ. In this Lucianic work Ibn al-Qāriḥ is imagined to have entered paradise, where he holds a series of conversations with pre-Islāmic poets, and the author discusses the opinions of the leading Muhammadan freethinkers (*zanādiqa*). His *Letters*, composed in an elaborately artificial and allusive style, have been edited, with Eng. tr., by D. S. Margoliouth. The long list of his minor works, of which only a few are extant, includes a supposed imitation of the Qur'ān, entitled *Al-fuṣūl wa 'l-ghāyāt*. Ma'arrī is said to have boasted that, if it were 'polished by the tongues of four centuries of readers,' it would bear comparison with the original (see references in I. Goldziher, *Muhamm. Studien*, Halle, 1889–90, ii. 403); but this appears to be an invention. What he attempted was probably a parody of Qur'ānic style rather than a deliberate challenge to the dogma of *i'jāz*, which claims for the Qur'ān a miraculous and inimitable perfection.

3. **Doctrines.** — It is difficult to give a clear account of Ma'arrī's religious and philosophical beliefs. Not only are they, to a large extent, negative in character, but the evidence derived from some passages in his writings is counterbalanced by other passages which, if they stood alone, would lead us to the opposite conclusion. These contradictions are most strikingly exemplified in his attitude towards Islām. Any one who wished to prove him orthodox might quote from the *Luzūmiyyāt* numerous instances in which the poet unequivocally accepts nearly all the chief Muhammadan doctrines, yet his pages are full of denials, doubts, and criticisms which, though cautiously expressed, show a strong anti-Islāmic tendency, and will convince any impartial reader that the charge of heresy brought against him by certain of his contemporaries was not unjustified. Several explanations of the inconsistency have been offered. The question is important, since whatever solution we adopt must affect our estimate of Ma'arrī. Can it be assumed that he is equally sincere when he writes as a pious Muslim and when he preaches the gospel of rationalism? That seems incredible, except on the hypothesis that Ma'arrī, while doubting the divine origin of Islām, also distrusted the human intellect, and hesitated to cut himself loose from the faith in which he was bred. Such an explanation, however, does not accord with his confident and emphatic appeal to reason as the highest authority. The following quotations from the Cairo ed. of the *Luzūmiyyāt* (A.D. 1891) illustrate his views on this point.

'Reason is the most precious gift thou hast received' (i. 151. 1). 'Traditions have come down to us which, if they be genuine, possess great importance; but they are weakly attested. Consult Reason and pay no heed to anything else. Reason is the best adviser in the world' (i. 288. 8 f.). 'Be guided by Reason and do whatever it deems good' (i. 394. 8). 'My Reason is indignant that I should lay it aside in order to follow Shāfi'ī and Mālik' (ii. 150. 3). 'O Reason, 'tis thou that speakest the truth. Perish the fool who invents traditions or expounds them!' (ii. 196. 4).

Those who hold that Ma'arrī's orthodox utterances do not express what he wholly or partly believed, but were designed to mask his real convictions and to serve as a defence against any dangerous attack, are attributing to him a course of action that he himself openly professes.

'Society compels me to play the hypocrite' (ii. 139. 4). 'I raise my voice to pronounce absurdities, but I only whisper the truth' (ii. 36. 13). 'Conceal thy thoughts even from the friend at thy side' (i. 272. 1).

His opinions were of a sort that could not be communicated without some disguise; and this necessity, which he disliked (cf. ii. 34. 2), is the source of many superficial contradictions in his writings. The suggestion that his ideas were dictated and controlled by the complex form of rhyme which he uses throughout the *Luzūmiyyāt* is inadequate as a general explanation of the facts, although it may cover part of them. Something also should be allowed for the influence of an Islāmic atmosphere and tradition upon the language of the poems, an influence to which, perhaps, their author at times consciously surrendered himself.

While Ma'arrī adopted certain ascetic practices and held certain religious and moral beliefs, his genius was essentially critical, sceptical, more apt to destroy than to construct. He could think for himself, but lacked the power of developing and combining his speculations. Unable to find rest in any religious or philosophical system, he fell into a fatalistic pessimism tempered, as not seldom happens in such cases, by a good deal of active benevolence. He claims to unfold to his readers the secret thoughts of mankind (i. 230. 15), and it is true that his poems reveal the inmost spirit of contemporary Muhammadan culture in its many-sided aspects. We are here concerned only with his main points of view and with the opinions and beliefs to which he was led by reflecting on the problems of life. For the sake of convenience the subject may be classified under a few general heads.

(*a*) *Scepticism.* — In several passages of the *Luzūmiyyāt* Ma'arrī discusses the origin and nature of religion. He ignores, although he does not formally deny, the theory of divine revelation. Religion, as he sees it, is a matter of inheritance and habit.

'They live as their fathers lived before them, and bequeath their religion mechanically, just as they found it' (i. 248. 13). 'In all thy affairs thou art satisfied with blind conformity, even when thou sayest, "God is One"' (i. 252. 2).

He disapproves of conformity (*taqlīd*), not because it is opposed to genuine faith, but on the ground that it is irrational.

'It is not reason that makes men religious: they are taught religion by their next of kin' (ii. 403. 13); cf. the celebrated verses (ii. 201. 7 ff.): 'The Muslims are mistaken and the Christians are on the wrong road, | And the Jews are all astray and the Magians are in error. | Mankind fall into two classes—the intelligent | Without religion, and the religious without intelligence.'

The whole fabric of popular religion is raised on fear, fraud, and greed (i. 251. last line, 65. 9, ii. 196. 5). The poet characterizes the great world-systems as a mass of forged traditions and doctrines which not only are repugnant to reason but have undergone vital alteration at the hands of their own adherents (ii. 20. 15, 196. 3, 404. 2, 409. 9). All of them are tainted with falsehood; no community possesses the truth (*hudā*) entire (ii. 177. 10). Ma'arrī does not shrink from applying this principle to Islām, though here, as has been remarked above, he speaks with two voices and avoids positive statements of disbelief. In the case of other religions his criticism is less restrained; thus, referring to the Crucifixion, he says (ii. 409. 7 ff.):

'If what they [the Christians] say concerning Jesus is true, where was His father? How did He abandon His son to His enemies? Or do they suppose that they defeated Him?'

He disbelieves in miracles (ii. 252. 11), augury

(i. 104. 3, 327. 10), and astrology (i. 254. 1, ii. 330. 2). On these matters he had been able to reach a definite conclusion, but he was rarely so fortunate. Experience assured him that human knowledge is a leap in the dark.

'There is no certainty; my utmost effort results only in opinion and conjecture' (ii. 23. 14). 'Colocynth does not know what gave it its bitterness, nor honey why it is sweet. Ye asked me, but I had no power to answer you: any one who pretends to know is a liar' (i. 103. 6).

All his metaphysical speculations close on the note of agnosticism.

'Some men assert that nothing really exists, but have they proved that there is neither misery nor happiness? We oppose them in this controversy, and God knows which of us is farther from the truth' (ii. 281. 1).

As regards the question of a future life, he admits that the soul may perhaps be immortal (ii. 171. 7). No one can tell whither it goes (i. 225. 7, 248. 6). It is a subtle thing, and, although it is confined in the body, the intellect cannot perceive it; will it be conscious of what befalls it hereafter? (i. 211. 6). If mind accompanies it, it may have memory of its life in this world (i. 140. 6). The doctrine of metempsychosis is not corroborated by reason (ii. 171. 9 ff.). In other passages, however, he alludes to an infinite cycle of dissolution and re-composition, of death and re-birth, as the destiny of all living beings (ii. 169. 13 ff.).

(*b*) *Pessimism.*—Amidst the welter of doubt from which he struggled in vain to escape Ma'arrī found one undeniable fact, namely, death (i. 256. 6, 291. 1 f.). Wherever he looked, he saw the cruel hand of Fate dragging all to destruction (ii. 146. 13). The life of man is a journey to the tomb (ii. 81. last line), a bridge between two deaths (i. 308. 12), a disease which only death can cure (i. 182. 3), a long torment (i. 69. penult.). Contemplating the futile pain of existence, he exclaims:

'May I never rise from the dead! I take no delight in living, though my fame is spread afar' (i. 426. 9 f.; cf. i. 374. 17).

Of such a view of life celibacy is the logical consequence, nor in this case could the poet be accused of preaching what he did not practise (ii. 359. 7 ff.). He held that procreation is a sin (i. 45. 3 ff., ii. 299. 4). No one has the right to increase the sum of suffering by bringing children into the world (i. 349. 13):

'If you wish to be kind to your sons, leave them in your loins' (i. 397. last line).

Children are burdens (i. 289. 12), and a man's son is his worst foe (i. 400. 2; cf. i. 45. 3 ff.). Fathers should provide husbands for their daughters, but should warn their sons not to marry (i. 216. 10). Ma'arrī depicts the universal misery and wickedness of mankind in terms that no satirist has surpassed. The world is a sea of raging passions which drive us to and fro until we are engulfed (i. 49. 6); it is like a carcass, and we are the dogs barking around it (i. 224. 9).

'When you come back to realities, every human being is wretched' (ii. 20. 7).

He repeats again and again that human nature is radically evil (i. 50. 8, 94. 3, 353. 11 f., 403. 5).

'Better than the best of them is a rock which commits no wrong and tells no lies' (i. 95. 12).

Good is soon burnt out, but evil smoulders for a long time (i. 270. 11 f.). The proportion of good in the world is exceedingly small (i. 315. 3). Fate, not free will, is the cause of men's wickedness, and the crow cannot change its colour (i. 311. 6 ff.).

'Do not seek to reform a world whose righteousness God never ordained' (i. 110. 3).

It follows that no human actions incur blame or deserve praise, and the poet says in one place (ii. 79. 10 f.) that only religious scruples prevented him from accepting this doctrine. Elsewhere he denies that men sin under compulsion (i. 354. 8, ii. 254. 3).

'They are unjust to each other, but the Creator of injustice is certainly just' (ii. 280. 6).

While castigating his neighbours and contemporaries, Ma'arrī does not spare himself (i. 48. 7). His pessimism extends to the future:

'If this age is bad, the next will be worse' (ii. 171. 17).

(*c*) *Asceticism.*—He earnestly desired to withdraw from a society of knaves and hypocrites and a world of bitter illusions.

'Would that I were a savage in the desert, idly smelling the spring flowers!' (ii. 28. 14). 'Be a hermit as far as possible, for one who speaks the truth is a bore to his friends' (i. 66. 1). 'The happiest man in the world is an ascetic who dies childless' (i. 212. 3).

But the value of asceticism depends on the motives by which it is inspired: the humble father of a family is superior to the ostentatious pietist (i. 208. 17 ff.). Ma'arrī seems to have learned at Baghdād, if not during his earlier travels, some peculiar doctrines and practices of Indian origin, connected more particularly with the Jains. He thinks it wrong to kill animals for food or to hurt them in any way, and therefore excludes from his diet not only meat, but also eggs, milk, and honey (i. 232. 9 ff., ii. 169. 9, 210. 13, 264. 13, 373. 9; cf. *JRAS*, 1902, p. 313 ff.). In his opinion there is greater virtue in letting go a captured flea than in giving alms to a beggar (i. 212. 9). He praises the Indian custom of burning the dead instead of burying them, and adduces practical arguments in favour of cremation (i. 235. 5 ff., 418. 20 f., ii. 407. 3). The religious enthusiasm of the Indian ascetics who throw themselves alive into the flames fills him with admiration (i. 260. 6 ff., ii. 253. 5 f.). Characteristically enough, he alleges as a reason for abstaining from wine the fact that the forbidden beverage is destructive to the intellect (ii. 312. 14, 361. 11).

(*d*) *Religion and ethics.*—Though Ma'arrī believed the whole conception of religion as a supernatural revelation to be false, he was nevertheless a firm monotheist (i. 47. 12, 279. 12, 281. 4 f.). Reason, he says, assures us of the existence of an eternal Creator (i. 249. 9), whom he seems to have identified with an omnipotent, all-encompassing Fate. Whether his idea of God is truly expressed by the orthodox phrases which he employs may be left an open question. At all events, his religious beliefs were based on intellectual conviction, not on traditional authority (i. 128. 8, 129. last line, 358. 15).

'Truth is not to be found in the Pentateuch: follow thy reason and do what it deems good' (i. 394. 8 f.).

Religion, as he defines it, is fear of God, renunciation of pleasures, and avoidance of sin (i. 315. 12, 361. 17, ii. 298. 12, 329. 12), but also embraces the obligation of dealing justly with every one (i. 103. 11). He asserts that all acts and forms of worship are useless without obedience to the unwritten moral law which is prescribed by reason and conscience. It is evident that he regarded this law as supreme and self-sufficing, for he never made the pilgrimage to Mecca nor did he take part in the public prayers (i. 100. 8). Virtue consists not in fasting and praying and wearing ascetic garb, but in abandoning wickedness and purging the breast of malice and envy (i. 285. 13 f.). That man is ignorant of true piety who, when he has an opportunity of satisfying his desires, does not abstain (ii. 159. 13 f.). A trivial wrong to one's neighbour will be more severely punished hereafter than neglect to fast or pray (ii. 294. 9). Ma'arrī had no sympathy with religious or sectarian prejudice.

He observes that, 'when a religion is established, its adherents contemn and revile all other creeds' (ii. 405. last line), but his own opinion is that a Christian priest may do one more good than a Muslim preacher (ii. 93. 7). 'Were it not for the radical hatred implanted in human nature, churches and mosques would have risen side by side' (ii. 82. 5).

Worldly ambition causes theologians to write controversial books full of vain words and endless analogies (i. 249. 5 ff.).

'Ask pardon of God and pay no heed to what is said by Abu'l-Hudhail and Ibn Kallāb' (i. 131. 5).

While refusing to acknowledge any authority that is less than divine, the poet finds the source and sanction of his freedom in the reason with which God has endowed him.

'Serve God Himself, not His servants, for religion enslaves and reason emancipates' (i. 326. 13).

Though man is naturally evil, the mind can acquire virtue (i. 241. 4). Virtue must be sought and practised for its own sake without desire of praise from men or hope of reward from God : it is a consolation for the woes of this life (ii. 341. 15 f. ; cf. i. 142. 5, 312. 10, 333. 10, 437. 7). Humility should go hand in hand with charity.

'Do as you would be done by' (ii. 87. 7). 'Show kindness to the poor and never despise them for receiving your bounty' (i. 175. 11). 'Forget your good deeds' (i. 349. 15). 'Forgive your neighbours, but be merciless to yourself' (i. 360. 13).

Slaves ought to be treated kindly, also animals and birds (ii. 25. 16 f., 31. 4). If Ma'arrī says some hard things about women, he is far from being a misogynist, and he makes handsome amends when he declares that a good wife is man's first paradise (i. 356. 12). He regards polygamy as unjust to the wife and calamitous for the husband, but his views on the education of women must have seemed to his Muslim readers curiously old-fashioned (i. 62. 12 ff., 192. 2 ff., ii. 235. 1 ff.).

LITERATURE.—The most complete biography of Ma'arrī is contained in D. S. Margoliouth's ed. of the *Letters*, Oxford, 1898, Introd., and the best general survey of his religious and philosophical opinions in A. von Kremer, 'Ueber die philosophischen Gedichte des Abul-'Alâ Ma'arry,' *SWAW*, phil.-hist. Classe, cxvii. 6 [1889]. See also, in addition to the works cited in the art., C. Rieu, *De Abu-'l-Alæ Poetæ Arabici vita et carminibus*, Bonn, 1843 ; A. von Kremer, *Culturgeschichte des Orients unter den Chalifen*, Vienna, 1875–77, ii. 386–396, also in *ZDMG* xxix. [1875] 304–312, xxx. [1876] 40–52, xxxi. [1877] 471–483, xxxviii. [1884] 498–529 ; D. S. Margoliouth, 'Abu'l-'Alā al-Ma'arrī's Correspondence on Vegetarianism,' *JRAS*, 1902, pp. 289–332 ; R. A. Nicholson, *A Literary History of the Arabs*, London, 1907, pp. 313–324 ; H. Baerlein, *The Diwan of Abu 'l-Alā*, do. 1908, *Abu 'l-Alā the Syrian*, do. 1914 ; C. Brockelmann, *Gesch. der arab. Litteratur*, Weimar and Berlin, 1898–1902, i. 254 f.

REYNOLD A. NICHOLSON.

MACEDONIANISM.—**1. Introduction.**—In the closing years of the 4th and the first half of the 5th cent. the Arians, Eunomians, and Macedonians were regarded as the most important heretical groups deriving their origin from the Arian controversies. Three laws of Theodosius, dating from A.D. 383 and 384 (*Cod. Theod.* XVI. v. 11–13), are in the main directed against them, and the latest of these speaks of the three heretical designations as 'inter sacræ religionis officia pro suis erroribus famosa nomina.' About three years afterwards Jerome (*in Eph.* ii. [on 4[5f.]], ed. D. Vallarsi, Venice, 1766–72, vii. 1, p. 610 C=*PL* xxvi. 528) and, as far down as 450, Nestorius (*Liber Heraclidis*, tr. F. Nau, Paris, 1910, p. 148) link together the names of Arius, Macedonius, and Eunomius in a similar way. Didymus of Alexandria, in his *de Trinitate*—a work which is not distinctly named in Jerome's *Catalogue of Authors* (ch. 109), and which, therefore, cannot have been written long before A.D. 392, and may even be of later date—regards the Arians, Eunomians, and Macedonians, whom he sometimes conjoins (ii. 11 [*PG* xxxix. 661 B], ii. 12 [*ib.* 673 B and 688 B]), as the most outstanding adversaries of orthodoxy. Augustine (*c.* 402) brings them before us as the non-Catholics of the East (*de Unit. eccl.* I. iii. 6 [*PL* xliii. 395]) ; in 415 Jerome describes them in similar terms (*Ep.* cxxxiii., 'ad Ctesiphontem' 11 [Vall. i. 2, p. 1040 B=*PL* xxii. 1159]) ; and Socrates (*c.* 440) recognizes them as the heretical sects of his time (*HE* I. vi. 41, V. xx. 1). As regards the heresy *τῶν Εὐνομιανῶν, εἴτουν Ἀνομοίων, καὶ τὴν τῶν Ἀρειανῶν, εἴτουν Εὐδοξιανῶν* (Council of Constantinople in 381 ; J. D. Mansi, *Sacrorum conciliorum . . . collectio*, Venice, 1759–98, iii. 560), we are so well informed that in dealing with them we can start from their date of origin. In the case of the Macedonians, however, the position is less favourable. It will therefore be advisable, first of all, to determine the characteristic standpoint of the Macedonians who, towards the close of the 4th and in the first half of the 5th cent., formed a definite sect distinct from the orthodox Church.

2. Sources for the history of the Macedonians from c. 383 to 450.—As sources for our inquiry we have, besides the historians of the 5th cent., the following works : (*a*) the *de Trinitate* of Didymus mentioned above (*PG* xxxix. 269–992) ; (*b*) the third of the five pseudo-Athanasian dialogues, *de Trinitate* (*ib.* xxviii. 1201–1249 : Διάλογος Γ' *περὶ τῆς ἁγίας Τριάδος, ἐν ᾧ αἱρετικοῦ φρονοῦντος τὰ τοῦ Πνευματομάχου Μακεδονίου ἀντίθεσις πρὸς* Ὀρθόδοξον) ; (*c*) the two pseudo-Athanasian *Dialogi contra Macedonianos* (*PG* xxviii. 1291–1330, and 1330–1338) ; and (*d*) the fragmentarily preserved *Sermones Arianorum*, printed in Migne (*PL* xiii. 593–630) from A. Mai's *editio princeps* (*Veterum scriptorum nova collectio*, Rome, 1825–38, III. ii. 208 ff.). Of these four sources, the *Sermones Arianorum*, which seem to have been composed *c.* 400, or some years later, in the Latin-speaking portion of the Balkan Peninsula, are of little service for our purpose ; but what they say regarding the teaching of the Macedonians rests, to some extent at least, on what 'Soziphanes [of whom otherwise we know nothing], princeps eorum, scripsit' (613 C). As regards Didymus, *de Trinitate*, and the two sets of dialogues enumerated above, the present writer, in a recent paper ('Zwei macedonianische Dialoge,' in *Sitzungsberichte der Königlich Preussischen Akademie der Wissenschaften*, xix. [1914] 526–551), seeks to show (1) that in Did. *de Trin.* we find no fewer than thirty-one fragments (printed and numbered *loc. cit.* pp. 526–534) of a learned dialogue of Macedonian origin, written between *c.* 381 and the date of Didymus's work ; (2) that this dialogue was known to and used by the author of the third of the five *Dialogi de Trinitate*, who wrote, as it would seem, in the period between the date of Did. *de Trin.* (*c.* 392) and the Nestorian controversy (*c.* 430), and that many sections of this third dialogue have probably been taken—verbatim, more or less—from the said Macedonian dialogue ; (3) that the first of the two *Dialogi contra Macedonianos* is of prior date to Did. *de Trin.*, and that its preliminary disquisitions (i.–viii. [pp. 1292–1301]) enable us to reconstruct a *second* dialogue of Macedonian origin, considerably shorter than that mentioned in (1) above, and written between A.D. 381 and *c.* 390 (printed as no. 32 in Loofs, 'Zwei maced. Dialoge,' p. 536 f.). With these data at our disposal we are in a position to sketch the teaching of the Macedonians to a great extent from their own writings, and, in order to bring out this point clearly, we shall in the following paragraphs, when quoting from the two Macedonian dialogues in question, give the number of the relevant fragment as found in the present writer's paper cited above.

3. Doctrine of the Macedonians in the same period.—The leading doctrine of the Macedonians is found in the thesis characterized by their opponents as 'Pneumatomachian,' viz. that the Holy Spirit is not to be designated Θεός (frag. 32, lines 1–8, *Dial. c. Maced.* i. 1 [p. 1292 A] ; frag. 29, Did. *de Trin.* III. xxxvi. [p. 965 B]). The development of this thesis on its negative side seems to have been conditioned among the Macedonians by the antithetic positions of the Nicæno-Constantinopolitan Creed : the Macedonians disputed the *κυριολογεῖσθαι* of the Holy Spirit (frag. 32, ll. 8–12, *Dial. c. Maced.* i. 3 [p. 1293 B]), His *ζωοποιεῖν* (frag. 16, Did. *de Trin.* II. vii. 3 [p. 573 A]), and His προσκυνητέον εἶναι (frag. 32, ll. 13–33, *Dial. c. Maced.* i. 4 [p. 1293 C, D]; frag. 12, Did. *de Trin.* II. vi. 18 [p. 545 B, C]; frag. 22, *ib.* II. x. [p. 641 B]). Only τῷ ὀνόματι τῷ τοῦ Πνεύματος συναριθμεῖται [*sc.* τῇ Τριάδι] (frag. 32, ll. 33–35, *Dial. c. Maced.* i. 6 [p. 1297 C]). On the positive side it was urged that in 1 Ti 5[21] St. Paul does not mention the Holy Spirit ὡς συντάξας δῆθεν τοῖς ἀγγέλοις (frag. 14, Did. *de Trin.* II. vi. 19 [p. 548 B, C]; cf. frag. 18, *ib.* II. vii. 8 [p. 581 D]: κατάγεται . . . τὸ Ἅγιον Πνεῦμα εἰς ἀγγέλου φύσιν); the angels, too, are ἅγιοι καὶ πνεύματα τοῦ Θεοῦ (frag. 4, *ib.* II. iv. [p. 481 B]). The Holy Spirit, however, was not regarded as merely one of the angels; He was described as Θεοῦ μὲν ἥττων τῇ φύσει, ἀγγέλων δὲ κρείττων, μέσην τινὰ φύσιν καὶ τάξιν εἰληχός (frag. 17, *ib.* II. vii. 3 [p. 576 B]). Nor is it only orthodox writers who on these grounds ascribe to the Macedonians the doctrine that the Holy Spirit is a created being, for we find it stated also in the *Sermones Arianorum* that 'Macedoniani Spiritum Sanctum iussu Patris per Filium creatum defendunt, et nuntium et ministrum Patris eum esse prædicant, sicut et nos' (*PL* xiii. 611 A). The Macedonians themselves sought rather to disguise their position here; for, although they were willing to admit that the Spirit was included among the πάντα of Jn 1[3]: πάντα δι' αὐτοῦ (*i.e.* διὰ τοῦ Λόγου) ἐγένετο (frag. 32, ll. 44–46, *Dial. c. Maced.* i. 8 [p. 1300 C]; frag. 27, Did. *de Trin.* III. xxxii. [p. 957 B]), they expressly denied that He should on that account be described as τῶν κτισμάτων ἕν (*loc. cit.*: οὐ κοινοποιεῖται τοῖς πᾶσι μοναδικὸν ὂν τὸ Ἅγιον Πνεῦμα; cf. frag. 20, Did. *de Trin.* II. viii. 1 [p. 617 C]: οὔτε εἰς θεικὴν ἀξίαν ἀνάγουσι τὸ Πνεῦμα, οὔτε εἰς τὴν τῶν λοιπῶν φύσιν καθέλκουσιν). Even so, however, they do not advance beyond the Arian doctrine of the Spirit, as the *Sermones Arianorum* likewise assert that 'Spiritus Sanctus . . . melior et maior ceteris omnibus in tertio loco . . . *singularis* atque solus in sua singularitate dinoscitur' (*PL* xiii. 601 A).

In their interpretation of the Scripture texts on which the orthodox writers based their doctrine of the Spirit, the Macedonians proceeded partly on grounds of purely grammatical exegesis—*e.g.*, frag. 32, l. 12, *Dial. c. Maced.* i. 3 (p. 1293 B): περὶ τοῦ Κυρίου λέγει [*sc.* Paul, in 2 Co 3[17]] ὅτι ὁ κύριος τὸ Πνεῦμα; and partly on arguments of textual criticism—*e.g.*, that in Ro 8[11] we should read διὰ τὸ ἐνοικοῦν αὐτοῦ Πνεῦμα, as the one or two MSS with διὰ τοῦ ἐνοικοῦντος, κτλ. in the hands of the orthodox had been tampered with (frag. 25, Did. *de Trin.* II. xi. [p. 664 C]; cf. *Dial. de Trin.* iii. 20 [p. 1233 B, C]), while in Ph 3[3] the correct reading was πνεύματι Θεῷ not Θεοῦ (frag. 25, Did. *loc. cit.* 664 B, etc.; cf. frag. 25, ll. 9–13, Did. *loc. cit.* and *Dial. de Trin.* iii. 26 [p. 1244 B, C]); partly, again, they applied the principle that οὐ χρὴ ὁμωνυμίαις ἢ συνωνυμίαις ἢ ὁμοιολεξίαις προσέχειν (frag. 3, Did. *de Trin.* II. iii. [p. 476 A]), or that τὰ ἀλληγορικῶς ἢ προσηγορικῶς ἢ μεταφορικῶς ἢ ὁμωνύμως λεγόμενα οὐ χρὴ εἰς δόγματος ἀκρίβειαν παραλαμβάνειν (frag. 23*a*, *ib.* II. x. [p. 645 A]). It seems clear that the last of these devices was largely adopted by the Macedonians (cf. the ὁμωνύμως also in frag. 9, Did. II. vi. 4 [p. 516 C], and frag. 19, l. 19, *ib.* II. viii. 1 [p. 605 B]). A view held by the learned, and supposed—wrongly, as the present writer thinks—to have the support of Augustine (*PL* xlii. 39), viz. that certain Macedonians regarded the Spirit as a δύναμις ἀνυπόστατος (cf. J. A. Mingarelli's note [83] on Did. *de Trin.* I. xviii. = *PG* xxxix. 357, n. 83), cannot be verified directly from Macedonian sources. It appears to lack probability, and seems to the present writer to have no better support than the casual and forced interpretations of orthodox controversialists (Did. *de Trin.* II. viii. 1 [p. 620 A]), or the misinterpretation of certain passages in which the Macedonians distinguished between the Πνεῦμα Ἅγιον and the spiritual power of God inseparable from God Himself (*Dial. de Trin.* iii. 23 [p. 1240 A]; *Dial. c. Maced.* i. 20 [p. 1328 B, C]; cf. Did. *de Spiritu Sancto*, xxiii. [*PG* xxxix. 1053 A]).

As regards the Christology of the Macedonians, we have, as far as the present writer knows, only a single statement emanating directly from the Macedonian side, and unfortunately it cannot be detached with certainty from its context. In the *Sermones Arianorum* we read as follows:

'Macedoniani post hæc omnia [there is, unhappily, a lacuna in what precedes] corrigunt se et dicunt: Filium similem per omnia et in omnibus Deo Patri esse dicimus; his autem qui dicunt esse differentiam inter lumen natum et inter lumen non natum, non communicamus, quia nullam differentiam esse inter deum natum et inter Deum non natum dicimus; *æquales honore, æquales virtute* Soziphanes, princeps eorum, scripsit' (*PL* xiii. 613 B, C).

Is it only the words here italicized that are ascribed to Soziphanes, or are we to regard the whole statement, *i.e.* also the affirmation of the doctrine ὅμοιος κατὰ πάντα (and therefore κατὰ οὐσίαν), as a formulation due to him or some other Macedonian? Be this as it may, the present writer has now—formerly he advocated a different view (cf. *PRE*[3] xii. 47)—no doubt that the sect of the Macedonians (and it is of the sect only that we are meanwhile speaking) were Homoiousian, not Homoousian, in their mode of thought. This is, in fact, distinctly stated—even if we leave out of account the passage just quoted from the *Sermones Arianorum*—by Didymus (*de Trin.* I. xxxiv. [p. 437 A]: ὁμοιούσιον . . . καὶ οὐχὶ ὁμοούσιον λέγοντες), by the author of the *Dial. de Trin.* (iii. 1 [p. 1204 C]: ἡμεῖς [οἱ Μακεδονιανοί] . . . ὁμοιούσιον λέγομεν καὶ οὐχ ὁμοούσιον), and by the writer of the *Dial. c. Maced.* (ii. [p. 1336 B, C]); and there are good grounds (cf. Loofs, 'Zwei maced. Dialoge,' p. 549 f.) for supposing that the passage in *Dial. de Trin.* iii. 16 (κἂν ἓν τούτων δείξῃς, γίνομαι ὁμοουσιαστής [p. 1228 A]) is borrowed from the longer Macedonian dialogue. There is in addition the fact that the so-called Confession of Lucian (Athanasius, *de Synodis*, xxiii. [*PG* xxvi. 721 B]), which the Macedonians, to judge from their own utterances (cf. Loofs, 'Zwei maced. Dialoge,' p. 550 f.), would seem to have regarded as *their* confession, does not contain the Homoousia. The present writer has therefore no doubt that the Macedonians of the closing years of the 4th cent. and the first half of the 5th cent. were Homoiousians in their mode of thought. Statements to the contrary are found only among Western writers who did not know the facts (Augustine, *de Hæres.* lii.: 'de Patre et Filio recte sentiunt, quod unius sint eiusdemque substantiæ'; also Philastrius [see below]), or among Arians and Eunomians, who regarded the Homoiousia as no less objectionable than the Homoousia (*Sermones Arianorum* [*PL* xiii. 611 A]: 'de Patre et Filio convenit illis'; on Philostorgius cf. J. Bidez, in the pref. to his ed., Leipzig, 1913, p. cxxiv f.). Moreover, in circles where the Homoousian orthodoxy of the later Nicæans differentiated the τρεῖς ὑποστάσεις in an almost polytheistic fashion (*Dial. de Trin.* iii. 6 [p. 1212 A] = *Dial. c. Maced.* i. 18 [p. 1320]), the distinction between the Homoiousian and the Homoousian way of thinking was so slight that even the author of the *Dial. c. Maced.*, who was acquainted with the Homoiousian teaching of the sect (ii. [pp. 1329 C, 1336 C]), could represent the Macedonian as saying to the orthodox: περὶ μὲν τοῦ Υἱοῦ καλῶς λέγεις (i. 20 [p. 1325 C]). As regards their Christology in the narrower sense, it need only be observed that, according to the *Dial. c. Maced.* (ii. [pp. 1329 C, 1333 C]), the Macedonians, like the Arians, denied that the Υἱὸς σαρκωθείς, or Υἱὸς ἐνηνθρωπηκώς, had a human soul.

4. The relation between these Macedonians and the Homoiousians of the 4th century.—What we know of the teachings of the Macedonians in the period between A.D. *c.* 381 and *c.* 430 (cf. § 3) would make it necessary to assume (even if we had no direct information on the point) that the sect was historically connected with the Homoiousian or semi-Arian party. In point of fact, however—even apart from Rufinus, Socrates, and Sozomen, whom meanwhile we leave out of account (cf. § 5, below)—that connexion can be traced in the older sources. Jerome, who, when referring (*c.* 380) in his *Chronicle* (*ad ann.* 342 [ed. R. Helm, Leipzig, 1913, p. 235 h]) to the installation of Macedonius as bishop of Constantinople, does not fail to add, 'a quo nunc hæresis Macedoniana,' regards the Homoiousian doctrine alone as the 'Macedonianum dogma' (*ad ann.* 364 [*ib.* p. 243 d]); and in the famous twenty-four anathemas of Damasus (A.D. 380 [?]), given by Theodoret (*HE* v. 11 [ed. L. Parmentier, Leipzig, 1911, p. 298; in Latin, *PL* xiii. 359 A; cf. Parmentier, p. lxxxii]), all that is said of the Μακεδονιανοί is:

οἵτινες ἐκ τῆς Ἀρείου ῥίζης καταγόμενοι οὐχὶ τὴν ἀσέβειαν ἀλλὰ τὴν προσηγορίαν ἐνήλλαξαν.

Further, Auxentius of Dorostorum writes (*c.* A.D. 383) of Ulfilas as follows:

'Omoeusion autem dissipabat, quia . . . Filium similem esse Patri suo non secundum Macedonianam fraudulentam pravitatem dicebat' (ed. F. Kauffmann, *Aus der Schule des Wulfila* (= *Texte und Untersuchungen zur altgerman. Religionsgesch.*, i., Strassburg, 1899, p. 74; cf. p. 17).

By *c.* 380, however, the 'Macedonianum dogma' embraced also the Pneumatomachian thesis. The Ἡμιαριανοί, ἤγουν Πνευματομάχοι, who were condemned by the Synod of Constantinople (381, can. 1; Mansi, iii. 559), were, like the Pneumatomachian Semiariani of Philastrius (*Hær.* lxvii.; *Corpus hæres.*, ed. F. Oehler, Berlin, 1856, i. 66), indubitably, in part at least, the same as the Macedonians of Jerome. Nicetas likewise, hardly before 381, speaks distinctly of the 'Macedoniani vel eorum in hac curiositate participes' as those 'qui quæstionem de Spiritu induxerunt' (*de Spir.* v. 2 (*PL* lii. 853 B]). As the anathemas of Damasus in their opening words impugn Pneumatomachian ideas—though without applying any heretical designation—we may probably infer that Damasus was acquainted with the doctrine of the Spirit held by the Arians, Eunomians, and Macedonians. And the reason that Auxentius does not mention the Macedonian doctrine of the Spirit is that, like Ulfilas, he had nothing to criticize in the so-called Pneumatomachian ideas.[1] For, like Origen, all the theologians who in the Arian controversy rejected the Homoousia of the Son affirmed by the Nicene Creed—Eusebians, Arians, Homoiousians, and Eunomians—regarded the Spirit as a κτίσμα subordinate to the Son. Even the Nicene Creed itself did not proscribe that view; all that it says regarding the Spirit is: καὶ [πιστεύομεν] εἰς τὸ Ἅγιον Πνεῦμα. Moreover, its partisans were at first concerned to assail only the Logos-doctrine of their opponents. At the earliest it was in the *Epistles to Serapion* (*PG* xxvi. 529–676), written by Athanasius during his exile from 9th Feb. 356 to 21st Feb. 362, that that theologian contended also for the Homoousia of the Spirit. The opponents of whom Serapion had informed him, and against whom these Epistles were directed—ἐξελθόντες ἀπὸ τῶν Ἀρειανῶν διὰ τὴν κατὰ τοῦ Υἱοῦ τοῦ Θεοῦ βλασφημίαν, φρονοῦντες δὲ κατὰ τοῦ Ἁγίου Πνεύματος καὶ λέγοντες αὐτὸ μὴ μόνον κτίσμα, ἀλλὰ καὶ τῶν λειτουργικῶν πνευμάτων ἓν αὐτὸ εἶναι (*Ep.* i. 1 [p. 529 f.])—were obviously the precursors of the Macedonians of the 5th century. This is shown by the demonstrable similarity between the *Dialogues* of Didymus and the *Epistles to Serapion* in many of their ideas, although the former is, no doubt, dependent upon the latter (cf., *e.g.*, *ad Serap.* i. 10 [pp. 556 C and 557 A] with Did. *de Trin.* II. vi. 19 [p. 548 B, C]). Not only do the opponents of Athanasius as well as those of Didymus make use of 1 Ti 5^{21} as a 'dictum probans' (*Ep. ad Serap.* i. 10; Did. *loc. cit.*; cf. also Basilius, *de Spir. Sancto*, xiii. 29 [*PG* xxxii. 117 C])—here Didymus may well have borrowed from Athanasius—but we find also that Am 4^{13} (κτίζων τὸ πνεῦμα) and Zec 4^{5} (ὁ ἄγγελος ὁ λαλῶν ἐν ἐμοί) are appealed to by the opponents of Athanasius (*Ep.* i. 9 [p. 552 B, C], i. 11 [p. 557 B]) as well as by the Macedonians of the 5th cent. (*Dial. de Trin.* iii. 26 [p. 1244 B, C] and 23 [p. 1237 C]). Above all, we have the fact that the mockery poured by Athanasius upon the τρόποι recognized by his adversaries (*Ep.* i. 7 [p. 548 B])—whom he stigmatizes as τροπικοί (*ib.* 21 [p. 580 D], 32 [p. 605 A])—recalls that Macedonian practice of resorting to ὁμωνυμίαις, συνωνυμίαις, etc., to which Didymus draws attention.

It is surprising, however, that Athanasius here makes no mention of Macedonius; as a matter of fact, he names no exponent of the doctrine which he criticizes.[1] Nor even later, when, as a result of the attitude assumed by Athanasius, of the anathema uttered by the Alexandrian Synod of A.D. 362 against all who regarded the Holy Spirit as a κτίσμα (Athan. *ad Ant.* iii. [*PG* xxvi. 800 A]), and of the acceptance of that doctrine by Meletius of Antioch at an Antiochian Synod of A.D. 363 (Mansi, iii. 366 f.), many had become interested in the Pneumatomachian question, do we hear anything, to begin with, about Macedonius himself. Neither Basil of Cæsarea, who in 372 went definitely over to the anti-Pneumatomachian side, and for that as for other reasons quarrelled with his friend Eustathius of Sebaste in the following year, and who composed his *de Spiritu Sancto* (*PG* xxxii. 67–218) in 375, nor Epiphanius, who, writing in 376, inserts the Πνευματομάχοι in his catalogue of heretics (*Hær.* lxxiv.), mentions Macedonius by name. Epiphanius, without giving any name at all, is content to characterize the Pneumatomachians as ἀπὸ τῶν Ἡμιαρείων καὶ Ὀρθοδόξων τινές; Basil, in his *de Spiritu Sancto*, likewise gives no name; but two years later (377) he states that Eustathius is the πρωτοστάτης τῆς τῶν Πνευματομάχων αἱρέσεως (*Ep.* cclxiii. 3 [p. 980 B]; on the attitude of Eustathius towards the doctrine of the Spirit as a created being cf. Soc. *HE* II. xlv. 6). In view of these facts, we must ask what was the connexion between the Macedonians and their nominal head.

5. Macedonius and the Macedonians.—This question leads us to a consideration of the life of Macedonius. It will not be necessary to discuss here the difficulties regarding the date and circumstances of his elevation to the episcopal throne of Constantinople (on these matters the present writer may perhaps refer to his art. 'Macedonius,' in *PRE*[3], and to E. Schwartz, 'Zur Geschichte des Athanasius,' ix., in *GGN*, hist.-phil. Klasse, 1911, p. 476 ff.).[2] Here we need merely state that Macedonius, who,

[1] The words 'contra Pneumatomachos' in Auxentius, lxi. (ed. Kauffmann, p. 75), rest upon a false reading and a false conjecture; cf. K. Müller, *Ulfilas Ende*, Leipzig, 1914, p. 88 ff.

[1] The bishops Acacius of Cæsarea and Patrophilus of Scythopolis, to whom he alludes in *Ep. ad Serap.* iv. 7 [p. 648 B], were Arian Homoians.

[2] Although V. Schultze (*Altchristl. Städte und Landschaften: I. Konstantinopel*, Leipzig, 1913, p. 45, note) regards the present writer's labours on this subject as inferior to what was done nearly twenty years earlier by Franz Fischer ('De patriarcharum Constantinopolitanorum catalogis et de chronologia octo primorum patriarcharum,' in *Commentationes philologicæ Jenenses*, iii. [1884] 263–333), yet the present writer cannot withdraw his objection in principle to what he regards as an unscientific mode of using Socrates and Sozomen (*PRE*[3] xii. 43; cf. xviii. 486), and to Schultze's and Fischer's over-exaltation of their merits.

according to Socrates (II. vi.), had as an aged deacon (τῇ ἡλικίᾳ γέρων) contested the see of Constantinople with Paul upon the death of Alexander (installed, in all likelihood, while Constantine was still reigning), found himself in secure possession of the see after what the present writer (*SK*, 1909, p. 294) regards as the final deposition of Paul in 342. He had been raised to the dignity by the anti-Nicene party, and, as regards his theological position, must have belonged to it, although, as the presbyter of Paul, he must have been in ecclesiastical communion with the latter (Athan. *Hist. Ar.* vii. [*PG* xxv. 701 A]). This does not necessarily imply that he had been an 'Arian'; for the later Homoiousians also belonged, till A.D. 358, to the 'Eusebian' group of the opposition, and even at the event which ushers in the rise of the Homoiousians, Macedonius, as documentary evidence shows, is found in that group: the Epistle of George of Laodicea, written in 358, and preserved by Sozomen (IV. xiii. 2 f.), names him first among the persons addressed. Epiphanius (*Hær.* lxxiii. 23 and 27 [ed. D. Petavius, Paris, 1622, 870 D and 875 C=*PG* xlii. 445 A, 456 B]) recognizes him as one of the Homoiousian party which was (from 358) opposed to the Acacians, the later Homoians, just as his presbyter, Marathonius, subsequently[1] bishop of Nicomedia, and Eleusius, whom he made bishop of Cyzicus (Soc. II. xxxviii. 4; Soz. IV. xx. 2), were partisans of Basil of Ancyra and Eustathius of Sebaste.[2] At the Synod of Seleucia (359) he was associated with Eleusius and the other Homoiousians in supporting Basil against the Acacians (Soz. IV. xxii. 7 ff.), and, like Basil, Eleusius, Eustathius, and other Homoiousians—as, indeed, the most prominent of them all—he was deposed by the Acacians at the end of the year 359 or in January 360 (Jer. *Chron. ad ann.* 359 [ed. Helm, p. 241 h]; Philostorg. v. 1 [ed. Bidez, p. 66; cf. p. 224]; Soc. II. xlii. 3; Soz. IV. xxiv. 3). He then retired, according to Sozomen (IV. xxvi. 1), to a place in the vicinity of Constantinople, and died there. He cannot have very long survived his deposition, as he does not appear in the important movements of his party after 364. In the interval between his deposition and his death, according to Socrates (II. xlv. 1–3) and Sozomen (IV. xxvii. 1, 2),[3] he founded a new party. Socrates states that (by letter? [see below]) he called upon his associates Sophronius (of Pompeiopolis) and Eleusius (of Cyzicus) to adhere for the future to the Antiochian formula recognized at Seleucia, *i.e.* the Confession of Lucian (cf. C. P. Caspari, *Alte und neue Quellen*, Christiania, 1879, p. 42 f.). Sozomen (IV. xxvii. 1) is more explicit:

> εἰσηγεῖτο δὲ τὸν Υἱὸν Θεὸν εἶναι, κατὰ πάντα τε καὶ κατ' οὐσίαν ὅμοιον τῷ Πατρί· τὸ δὲ Ἅγιον Πνεῦμα ἄμοιρον τῶν αὐτῶν πρεσβείων ἀπεφαίνετο, διάκονον καὶ ὑπηρέτην καλῶν καὶ ὅσα περὶ τῶν θείων ἀγγέλων λέγων τις, οὐκ ἂν ἁμάρτοι.

Rufinus (*HE* i. 25 [ed. T. Mommsen, Leipzig, 1908, p. 990]) somewhat earlier makes a similar statement. The tradition is nevertheless untenable. It refers in reality to the earliest public appearance of the Homoiousians, not of the Macedonians, and it displays even less knowledge of the actual beginnings of the Homoiousian party some two years previously than does Philostorgius (iv. 9 [p. 62]). Then, in the further course of the narratives of Socrates and Sozomen, the term 'Macedonians' becomes, in conformity with that report, the regular designation of the Homoiousians generally. Thus the 'Macedonians,' in the reign of Valens, draw closer to the orthodox party; they accept the ὁμοούσιον; they come to an understanding with Pope Liberius, and, especially in Constantinople, live in religious communion with the orthodox (cf. esp. Soz. VII. ii. 2), until at length (cf. *ib.* 3), after the death of Valens, they once more stand forth as a party by themselves. But, had the Homoiousians been in reality universally designated Macedonians, as Socrates and Sozomen assume, we should certainly have found some evidence of the fact in Athanasius and the Cappadocians. One is prompted to ask, nevertheless, whether the statement of Sozomen (V. xiv. 1), viz. that during Julian's reign οἱ ἀμφὶ Μακεδόνιον, ὧν ἦν Ἐλεύσιος καὶ Εὐστάθιος καὶ Σωφρόνιος, ἤδη εἰς τὸ προφανὲς Μακεδονιανοὶ καλεῖσθαι ἀρξάμενοι, can possibly be based upon mere error. We are compelled to assume that, just as in Antioch, after the installation of Euzoius, the loyal adherents of Meletius came to be called 'Meletians,' so in Constantinople the followers of the deposed Macedonius who did not attach themselves to the church of Eudoxius, his successor (Soz. IV. xxvii. 7, VIII. i. 7), were presently designated 'Macedonians.' The connexion between Macedonius and the later 'Macedonians' would thus simply be that the latter gained accessions from the Homoiousian circles of which the adherents of Macedonius, as dwellers in the metropolis, formed the best-known group in the Balkan Peninsula. This solution of the historical problem—a solution which surrenders the literal significance of the name 'Macedonians'—is certainly a possible one. For it was in the neighbourhood of Constantinople—on the Hellespont, in Bithynia, and in Thrace—that the 'Macedonians' were most numerous (Soz. IV. xxvii. 2; Soc. II. xlv. 8, IV. iv. 5); and it is from Constantinople and its neighbourhood that, with a single exception (Damasus), our oldest authorities for the use of the name (Jerome, Auxentius, Nicetas) are derived, while both Socrates (cf. V. xxiv. 9) and Sozomen (cf. II. iii. 10) wrote largely under the influence of the same local tradition. In view of the active intercourse between Rome and Constantinople, the single exception of Damasus does not mean much. Rufinus, again, may have gained his information from Jerome through literary channels (cf. Jer. *Chron. ad ann.* 364 [ed. Helm, p. 243 d] with Ruf. *HE* i. 25 [p. 990]) as well as by personal contact; and Didymus had relations with both. Moreover, the random use of the name 'Macedonians' is confirmed by the fact that, according to Socrates (II. xlv. 4) and Sozomen (IV. xxvii. 5), the Macedonians were also called 'Marathonians'; and Sozomen (*loc. cit.*) even expresses the opinion that, in view of the personal and material support for which the party were indebted to Marathonius, the name was not inappropriate.

Still, it is quite intelligible that K. Holl (*ZKG* xxv. 388 f.), especially in view of the witness of Didymus, should put forward the question whether the connexion between Macedonius and the Macedonians was not, after all, of a more substantial character. The present writer is, however, of opinion that the information possessed by Didymus is less than Holl makes out. Didymus seems, *e.g.*, to have regarded Marathonius as the successor of Macedonius (*de Trin.* II. x. [p. 633 A]: Ἀρειανῶν τῶν χειροτονησάντων τὸν αἱρεσιάρχην ὑμῶν Μακεδόνιον καὶ μετ' αὐτὸν Μαραθώνιον); and if, as the present writer thinks possible (cf. 'Zwei maced. Dialoge,' p. 544), the person addressed in *de Trin.* II. viii. 1 (p. 613 C) is not the author of the Macedonian dialogue, but, by a figure of rhetoric (cf. frag. 17, Did. *de Trin.* II. vii. 3 [p. 576 A]), Macedonius himself, then the information given in *de Trin.* II. viii. 1, viz. that Macedonius was made bishop by the

[1] Cf. Tillemont, *Mémoires*, Venice ed., vi. 397, 770.

[2] On Eleusius, cf. Epiph. *loc. cit.*; on both, Philostorgius, viii. 17 (ed. Bidez, p. 115).

[3] It may be remarked that these two Church historians differ noticeably in their judgment of Macedonius; for, while Socrates simply disparages him, Sozomen betrays a certain admiration of the monastic ideals which he shared with Marathonius (cf. Soz. IV. xxvii. 3 ff.).

Arians, but was previously a deacon of the orthodox Church, supplements that given in II. x. only by the latter—and, indeed, correct (cf. Soc. II. vi. 3)—statement. Nor is it inconceivable that Didymus obtained the name 'Macedonians' and his information regarding Macedonius from the Macedonian dialogue used by him. Yet the correspondence between what that dialogue tells us regarding the Macedonian teaching and what Athanasius must have known when he wrote his *Epistles to Serapion* is striking. Can it have been the case that the above-mentioned summons of Macedonius to Eleusius and Sophronius, referred to by Socrates (II. xlv. 2), was contained in a letter, and that this letter had come into Serapion's hands? This would explain how the Alexandrians had obtained information regarding the Macedonians at a relatively early stage; it would explain the information possessed by Didymus regarding the *αἱρεσιάρχης Μακεδόνιος*, and also the account given by Socrates (and Sozomen) of the origin of the Homoiousian party. The hypothesis is not impossible; for the first letter of Athanasius to Serapion may quite well have been written as late as A.D. 361. The point, however, cannot be decided in the present state of our knowledge.

6. The persistence or recrudescence of Homoiousianism among the Macedonians.—There is still another question to be considered. Athanasius was aware that those who were known to Serapion as opposed to the Deity of the Holy Spirit felt themselves repelled by the Arian 'blasphemy' against the Son (*Ep. ad Serap.* i. 1 [p. 529 f.]), and that they were detested by the Arians (*ib.* i. 32 [p. 605 B]; this fits in remarkably well with the situation from the beginning of A.D. 360). Somewhat later the Homoiousians ('Macedonians'), as a result of negotiations with Liberius at a synod held at Tyana in 367, passed completely over to the side of the Nicene Creed (Basil, *Ep.* ccxliv. 5 [*PG* xxxii. 917 D]; Soz. VI. xii. 2 f.; cf. Sabinus, *ap.* Soc. IV. xii. 11). Thereafter, as we read (Soc. V. iv. 1; Soz. VII. ii. 2), the 'Macedonians,' who at that time had neither a church nor a bishop in Constantinople (Soz. IV. xxvii. 6, VIII. i. 7), maintained ecclesiastical communion with the Homoousians. Thus the question arises how it came about that the later Macedonian doctrine was Homoiousian. Basil (*Ep.* ccxliv. 9 [*PG* xxxii. 924 B]) tells us that, at a synod held at Cyzicus in A.D. 376—otherwise unknown to us (Loofs, *Eustathius*, p. 17 f.)—Eustathius of Sebaste, the *πρωτοστάτης τῆς τῶν Πνευματομάχων αἱρέσεως* (cf. § 4), subscribed a formula which, together with Pneumatomachian clauses, contained statements pointing away from the Nicene Creed to the Homoiousion (*τὸ ὁμοούσιον κατασιγάσαντες τὸ κατ' οὐσίαν ὅμοιον νῦν ἐπιφέρουσι*), and that from 375 he had drawn closer, ecclesiastically, to the Homoiousian court-bishops (Basil, *Ep.* ccxliv. 7 [p. 921 A, B]; cf. 5 [p. 920 A], ccli. 3 [p. 936 B]; cf. Loofs, *Eustathius*, p. 76 ff.); Basil is of opinion that the fundamental Arian tendency of Eustathius had once more manifested itself (*Ep.* cxxx. 1 [p. 564 A]). Was this reversion of Eustathius to the Homoiousion—an act that (as he merely suppresses, without overtly rejecting, the Homoousion) did not as such altogether exclude recognition of the Nicene Creed [1]—a decisive factor in the later position of the Macedonians? Our sources do not enable us to answer the question. But to the present writer it seems beyond doubt that what is here said of Eustathius lends support to an account of similar purport given by Sozomen (VII. ii. 3), and less fully by Socrates (V. iv. 2 f.), regarding a synod held at Antioch in Caria (378). These historians record that, when, after the death of Valens (9th Aug. 378), the Emperor Gratian enacted a law (not now extant) conferring freedom of worship upon all religious parties except the Manichæans, the Photinians, and the Eunomians (Soc. V. ii. 1; Soz. VII. i. 3), the Macedonians seceded again from the Homoousians, with whom they had hitherto been in communion, abandoning the Nicene Creed, and asserting their preference for the *ὁμοιούσιος* as against the *ὁμοούσιος*. From that time a section of the Macedonians (Homoiousians) had continued to exist as a distinct party (*ἰδίᾳ ἐκκλησίαζον*), while another, breaking away from the latter, had united themselves all the more closely to the Homoousians. These statements are not altogether free from difficulties. The present writer would not lay stress upon the fact that the notice in Soz. IV. xxvii. 6 (cf. the words *οὐ γὰρ συνεχώρουν, κτλ.*), which obviously refers to this re-appearance of the Macedonians, points to the reign of Arcadius,[1] as the notice in question is manifestly erroneous. Here, indeed, Sozomen seems to have wrongly interpreted the statement of his authority (Sabinus), which he renders verbatim in VIII. i. 7.[2] May it not be the case, however, that in Soz. VI. xii. 4 we have a doublet of VII. ii. 3, clearly derived from Sabinus, and providing fresh difficulties? In VI. xii. 4 likewise we read of a synod in the Carian Antioch, where, in opposition to the Homoousion, the Confession of Lucian was made the standard; this synod, however, was held subsequently to the synod of Tyana (367), and in opposition to those members of the Homoiousian party who had gone over to the Homoousion. The present writer must admit that he finds this 'doublet'—if it is a doublet—a disturbing element. Still, it is possible that, as H. Valesius (*Adnot.* to Soz. VI. xii. 4) assumes, there were two Homoiousian synods at Antioch in Caria (A.D. 368 and 378); and, in fact, if the bishop of that city was an intransigent Homoiousian, there is much to be said for the theory. If we accept it, we must regard it as probable that the second of these synods likewise gave its adherence to the Confession of Lucian, which, as we have seen, was so highly esteemed by the Macedonians. It is in the period succeeding that date that we find the later Macedonians. For Macedonianism was simply the Homoiousianism which, on account of the doctrine of the Spirit, broke away from the Homoiousians adhering to the Nicene Creed. The fact that Epiphanius had also heard of certain Pneumatomachians who were orthodox as regards their Christology (see above) proves nothing to the contrary, since that author wrote at a time prior to the synod of Antioch; nor is our statement refuted by the fact that Gregory of Nazianzus, in a Whitsuntide sermon of the year 381, addressed the Pneumatomachians as *περὶ τὸν Υἱὸν ὑγιαίνοντες* (*Or.* xli. 8 [*PG* xxxvi. 440 B]). Gregory had as valid grounds for this friendly judgment as had the Orthodox when, shortly afterwards, at the synod of 381, they reminded the thirty-six Pneumatomachians who attended under the leadership of Eleusius of their negotiations with Liberius (Soc. V. viii. 7; Soz. VII. vii. 4).

The breach which had been started by the rupture between Eustathius and Basil, and by the synods of Cyzicus and Antioch in Caria, was rendered absolute by the Council of 381. The Pneumatomachians withdrew from the Council, and were condemned by it (cf. § 4). The amicable overtures made at the instance of Theodosius I. to the Arians, Eunomians, and Macedonians at

[1] Cf. Loofs, *Eustathius*, p. 78, with note 2, where, however, the defection of Eustathius from the Nicene Creed is not sufficiently recognized.

[1] J. Bidez has kindly informed the author of this art. that all the MSS read Ἀρκαδίου.

[2] *μέχρι τῆς ἐχομένης βασιλείας*. If the source here is referring mainly to the time of Valens, this would point to Gratian's reign.

Constantinople in 383—Eleusius being once more the representative of the last-named group (Soc. V. x. 24; Soz. VII. xii. 9)—were unsuccessful in winning the sect back to the Church. The Macedonians, undisturbed by the laws against heretics passed in 383 and 384 (cf. Soc. V. xx. 4; see above, § 1), still remained a distinct group apart from the Church, but how far beyond A.D. 450 they maintained their position the present writer cannot say.

LITERATURE.—In addition to the Histories of Dogma and the more general works dealing with the Arian controversy, the following may be consulted with advantage: L. S. Le Nain de Tillemont, *Mémoires pour servir à l'histoire ecclésiastique*, ed. Venice, 1732–39; G. H. Goetze, 'Dissertatio historica de Macedonianis,' in J. Vogt, *Bibliotheca historiæ hæresiologicæ*, i. 1, Hamburg, 1723, pp. 165–199; *Damasi papæ opera*, ed. A. M. Merenda, Rome, 1754 (*PL* xiii. 109–442); F. Loofs, *Eustathius von Sebaste*, Halle, 1898; J. Gummerus, *Die homöusianische Partei bis zum Tode des Konstantius*, Leipzig, 1900; T. Schermann, *Die Gottheit des heil. Geistes nach den griechischen Vätern des vierten Jahrhunderts*, Freiburg i. B., 1901; F. Loofs, art. 'Macedonius,' in *PRE*³ xii. 41–48; K. Holl, in *ZKG* xxv. [1904] 388 f.; V. Schultze, *Altchristliche Städte und Landschaften: I. Konstantinopel (324–450)*, Leipzig, 1913; F. Loofs, 'Zwei macedonianische Dialoge,' *Sitzungsberichte der Königlich Preussischen Akademie der Wissenschaften*, xix. [1914] 526–551.

F. LOOFS.

MADAGASCAR.—The religion of the Malagasy is extremely simple. They believe in one god, whom they call Zanahary, 'creator of all things'; but this god, being essentially good and, consequently, incapable of doing evil, is more or less neglected. His attributes are vague, and there is, properly speaking, no cult connected with him. Indeed, with the exception of sorcerers, there are in Madagascar no individuals or classes of individuals connected officially with any religion or cult.

1. Ancestor-worship.—The shades of ancestors, however—for all the Malagasy believe in a future life—are the objects of profound veneration, and inspire their worshippers with extraordinary awe. They are credited with all power of good and evil over the living, whom they visit from time to time. A dead husband, *e.g.*, will sometimes pay a visit to his widow, and in this case the birth of posthumous children is considered perfectly legitimate. Offerings are made to ancestors, generally of a small piece of ox-flesh and a few drops of rum, which are taken to the grave of the ancestor whose favours are sought.

2. Sorcery and fetishism.—The Malagasy do not believe in death from natural causes, except in the very rare case of extreme old age. Their idea is that death is always the effect of witchcraft or evil spells cast by sorcerers, and they are, therefore, careful to collect all hair-cuttings, nail-parings, etc., in case a sorcerer should find them and use them to work evil on their owner. The Sakalava kings were always accompanied by a servant whose sole charge was to gather up the earth upon which they had spat.

Diviners or sorcerers play a very important part in the life of the Malagasy. The natives believe that they are in communication with the spirits of the dead and can cure disease, foretell the future, discern whether the outcome of any enterprise will be favourable and what is the most suitable moment for undertaking it, indicate lucky and unlucky days, and warn against what is forbidden (*fady*). The Malagasy never embark upon any important undertaking without first consulting the sorcerer, who makes use of *sikidy*—a ceremony in which a handful of seed is spread out on a cloth, according to well-defined rules, so as to form sixteen figures, which are then interpreted with the aid of a code. The *sikidy*, which was introduced, or at least very frequently employed, by the Antimorona, has been in general use throughout the island for a long time.

The sorcerers, who are called *mpanazary*, *ombiasa*, *masina*, etc., according to the different provinces, have as one of their occupations—and that not the least lucrative—the manufacture of amulets or talismans (*ody*), which generally consist of small pieces of carved wood, bulls' horns ornamented with glass beads, or crocodiles' teeth. The horns and teeth are usually filled with earth or sand and various small objects such as gilt nails, iron-filings, and so on. After invoking the god and sprinkling the talisman with grease, the sorcerer, for a consideration, hands it over to the purchaser, who then hangs it round his neck. The result is supposed to be that the wearer is successful in all his undertakings, fortunate in love, immune from gun-shots or crocodile bites, and so on. The natives have the most implicit faith in these *ody*.

The Merina introduced the worship of national fetishes, which were very similar to the foregoing. These fetishes were regarded as royal personages, and had a special residence with officiating servants. The oldest and most famous of them was Kelimalaza.

3. Fady.—In almost every case there is some *fady* connected with these amulets and fetishes—*i.e.*, it is forbidden to do certain things and to eat certain foods. If this prohibition is not rigidly respected, the *ody* loses all its virtue and is useless. The *fady*, which occurs throughout the whole of Madagascar, is extremely curious, and recalls the tabu of the Oceanians. There are some places which are regarded as *fady* for every one, while others are *fady* only for certain families or even for certain individuals. There are *fady* days, when no one should begin anything new or start on a journey. If a child is born on one of these unlucky days, it is killed—or, rather, it was until quite recently, especially in the southern parts of the island—because it is supposed to bring evil upon its family. There are also *fady* words, *i.e.* words which must not be pronounced; naturally, these are fast disappearing from the language. As an example of this we have the words which went to make up the names of the Sakalava kings, the use of which was prohibited after their death. These *fady* are really of a religious nature; their aim is to appease the wrath of spirits and otherwise gain their favour.

4. Human sacrifice.—Human sacrifice has now been abolished in Madagascar, but it is not very long since it was the custom, when a Sakalava king was shaving for the first time, to dip the razor for this important operation in the blood of some famous old chief killed for the occasion. This ceremony was still in vogue when the king of Ménabé, Toera, who met his death in the attack on the village of Ambiky by the French troops in 1897, reached the age of manhood. Not many years ago, in accordance with an ancient custom practised in S. and W. Madagascar, the favourite wife of a great Mahafaly chief was killed on his grave, that he might not be alone in the other world; four of his servants were also put to death and their bodies laid under those of the chief and his wife, so that they might not touch the ground.

5. Crimes and punishments.—The Malagasy have no moral code. Their religion seems to authorize anything and everything, and the only recognized sin is failure to observe the external formalities of worship; such a sin of omission may be absolved by the penitent's making a small offering to the god.

Before the conquest of Madagascar by the French, justice was of an extremely summary nature (except in the case of the Merina, who had a code of laws modelled on European codes), based simply upon traditional use and wont.

Justice was meted out by the king or the village chief, and in certain tribes—*e.g.*, the Betsileo—by an assembly of the leading men of the tribe. The *lex talionis* was in universal use. The principal crimes were cow-stealing, failure to pay debts, and —the greatest crime of all—sorcery, which was always punished by death.

6. Ordeals and oaths.—In cases of doubt, recourse was had to trial by ordeal. The poison test, or *tanghin*, which has made so many victims among the Hova, is one of the best-known methods, and another test consisted in making the accused cross a river infested with crocodiles, or an arm of the sea where sharks abounded, these animals being supposed to eat the guilty and to do no harm to the innocent.

Another interesting practice is the 'water-oath.'

Into a bowl half full of water are put a bullet, some powder, earth from a sacred spot—*e.g.*, the tombs of the old kings of Imerina—and especially a bit of gold. The accused, or the two litigants in a law-suit, drink this water, vowing their good faith during the process; and all the ills that flesh is heir to are supposed to fall on those who swear falsely.

There is another ceremony similar to this—the 'blood-oath,' or *fatidra*—by which two persons promise each other mutual aid and protection throughout their lives, and enter into a voluntary relationship more intimate and binding than real blood-relationship.

To the contents of the bowl described above are added a few drops of each individual's blood, drawn from a slight cut made on his breast. While each holds in his hand the shaft of his spear or the ramrod of his gun, with the points dipped in the bowl, an orator announces the news of this fraternal union to their ancestors in an eloquent speech, and calls upon God to inflict the most severe punishment if either of them fails to keep his oath (cf., further, art. BROTHERHOOD [Artificial], § 13).

7. Exorcism.—The Malagasy have a peculiar ceremony which shows their belief in demoniacal possession and exorcism. Its aim is to cure certain maladies, and also to render thanks to God for the cure effected. This is practised chiefly in the west and south of the island, and is termed *bilo*[1] or *salamanga*. Those who are submitted to treatment of this kind are supposed to be possessed of a devil, which must be expelled.

The patient is led out of the village to a large open space where a platform 10 or 12 ft. high, with a primitive ladder leading up to it, is erected for the occasion. At the foot of this platform all the inhabitants of the neighbourhood are grouped on one side, and the cattle belonging to the invalid or his family on the other. When he arrives, dancing and singing begin, and there are great libations of *toaka* (rum), large quantities of which must be consumed by the patient. The unfortunate man is then led into the middle of the cattle, where he has to point out with a stick two oxen, one of which acts as a kind of scape-animal and is sacred to the man's parents, who treat it with every kindness, while the other is immediately sacrificed and eaten by the spectators. The patient, drunk with alcohol, noise, and the heat of the sun, has then to climb up to the platform—an operation not altogether free from risk. If he reaches the top without much help, God is supposed to be favourable to him and he will get better; if not, his case is hopeless. Once he is safely established on the mat covering the top of the platform, a woman, who has had to remain in a state of absolute chastity for twenty-four hours previously, gives him food which she has cooked specially for him, particularly newly-killed ox-flesh. If he eats it, or even pretends to do so, that is a sure sign of his speedy recovery to health and long life. The tumult of singing and shouting then begins again with redoubled energy. The sick man is left lying there, several feet above the ground, sometimes for a very long time, while those who have assisted at the ceremony intoxicate themselves with rum and gorge themselves with meat. He is then carried back with great pomp to his dwelling, where, nine times out of ten, he succumbs to the effects of his treatment.

8. Death and disposal of the dead.—Among the most characteristic customs of the Malagasy are those connected with burial of the dead. The funeral rites are not the same throughout the whole island; some peoples hide their cemeteries in the heart of the forest, among hills and rocks, in desert places, or anywhere far from the sight and sound of man; others, again, bury their dead by the side of the high road or right in the midst of human dwellings. The former, who are terrified at death and everything connected with it, are mainly found among the coast tribes, except in the south-east, where the people are of Arab origin. The latter, who like to live within sight of their last resting-place, belong to the centre of the island, and consist chiefly of the Merina, Betsileo, and other tribes civilized by the Malays.

The eastern tribes put the dead body in the hollowed-out trunk of a tree, closed with a badly-fitting lid in the form of a roof, and this improvised coffin they lay either on the ground or on a small platform in the middle of a palisade roofed over with branches and leaves.

The Antankarana make their cemeteries in the natural grottoes or rock-caves found in the numerous small islands along the coast or in the limestone mountains of the north, and here again the coffins, with beautifully carved lids, are simply laid on the ground. Some Betsileo and Bara families follow the same custom, and bury their dead in the hollows and caves which abound on the higher reaches of their mountains.

The other natives of the island bury their dead beneath the ground. The western and southern tribes—the Sakalava, the Mahafaly, the Antandroy, and most of the Bara—cover their graves with a heap of loose stones in the form of a long parallelepiped, while some Sakalava families surround their tombs with posts carved in different shapes (human beings, birds, crocodiles, etc.), which recall certain cemeteries of Oceania.

The Merina custom is to hollow out a mortuary chamber, above which they usually build a small house for those of noble birth, and for the Hova, or freemen, a small rectangular wall, where they gather together stones and blocks or fragments of quartz, with a raised stone at one end. The head is generally turned to the east.

All the Malagasy have the same idea of the impurity of a dead body and its power to communicate uncleanness to others. A funeral procession must never pass in front of the king or anywhere near his residence, and it must also avoid the neighbourhood of sacred stones. Those who have taken any part in a burial ceremony must cleanse themselves before going home.

As may be gathered from the prevalence of ancestor-worship, all the Malagasy without exception stand in awe of the dead, and desire above all things to be buried in the family tomb. When a Malagasy (in particular a Merina) dies away from home, his urgent wish is that his relatives should come, no matter how long after his death it may be, and carry his bones back to his native land. This desire is respected in almost all cases, and even to-day it is no rare thing to meet little processions of Hova carrying back the mortal remains of a member of their family wrapped in a white cloth hung on a long bamboo pole. In many cases they go as far as four or five weeks' journey from Tananarivo. When the body cannot be recovered, the pillow or mattress of the deceased is buried in his stead, or a stone or a post is erected to his memory at the side of the road or near his native village.

In Madagascar mourners cut their hair short and keep it dishevelled; they wear coarse dirty clothes, and are not allowed to wash or look in a mirror, even if they possess one—they must appear as unkempt as possible so as to keep other people at a distance. On the death, or—as the phrase goes in Madagascar, where ordinary everyday words would never be used in connexion with such high and exalted personages as kings—on the 'departure,' of a sovereign, a number of sumptuary

[1] The Arabic word for 'devil' is *Iblīs*, and from this the Malagasy have formed *bilo*, which is the name both for the evil spirit and for the ceremony of exorcizing it.

laws came into force which had to be strictly obeyed, if one did not wish to run the risk of being considered responsible for the death of the king and of being subjected to capital punishment as a sorcerer. The following are some of the restrictions enforced on the death of Radama I. (1810–28): all the inhabitants of the kingdom, with the exception of the heir to the throne, had to shave their heads, sleep on the ground instead of in beds, use neither chairs nor tables, pass each other without greeting in the street, neither play any musical instrument nor sing, have no fire or light at night, do no work except in the fields, refuse to be carried in a palanquin, use no mirror, go about bare-headed, wear no fine clothes, and, in the case of women, keep the shoulders bare. As in the East, white, not black as in Europe, is the colour of mourning.

Several Malagasy tribes—*e.g.*, the Betsileo and the Antankarana—have the peculiar and repugnant custom of not burying their dead immediately after death; frequently they even wait till decomposition has set in; and in many cases the putrid liquid is collected and set apart. Their funeral watches are naturally far from agreeable, and, to be able to live at all in the midst of the nauseating odours, the relatives and friends of the dead man drink rum all the time and burn quantities of incense, suet, and even leather. This custom, which is of Oceanic origin, comes from the desire not to bury any putrescible or impure matter along with the bones. Even the tribes which do not have this practice generally have two burial ceremonies—one consisting in simply burying the dead, and the other taking place some years after, when nothing but the skeleton remains, and when the body is finally placed in the family tomb. Sometimes, as in Imerina, the body is put into the family vault at once, but it is wrapped round with several silk *lambas* and is not placed in a coffin. Later, at a certain specified time, the ceremony of the *mamadika* takes place. This consists in changing the soiled *lambas*, and the Merina say then that they turn the bodies on their other side so that they may not get tired of lying in one position.

Funerals in Madagascar are always the occasion of feasts in honour of the dead. The richer the man is and the more cattle he possesses, the more brilliant are the orgies that are indulged in. Shots are fired and bulls are killed, the flesh being eaten at the funeral feast, and the head and horns being placed with great ceremony on the tomb of the deceased. Rum flows like water, and as long as there is anything left to eat or drink the feast continues; the funeral festivities of great and noble personages have been known to last for months.

LITERATURE.—R. Baron, 'A Hova Custom with regard to People at the Point of Death,' in *Antanànarivo Annual*, 1892, p. 502; C. Benevent, 'Conception de la mort chez les Malgaches,' in *Rev. de Madagascar*, 1901, pp. 637–648; E. Besson, 'Rites funéraires en usage chez les Betsiléos,' in *L'Anthropologie*, v. [1894] 674–682 (with illustrations); W. E. Cousins, 'The Ancient Theism of the Hova and the Names of God,' in *Antanànarivo Annual*, 1875, pp. 5–11; E. de Flacourt, *Hist. de la grande île de Madagascar*, Paris, 1658; A. Grandidier, 'Des rites funéraires chez les Malgaches,' in *REth* v. [1886] 213–232; G. Grandidier, *Madagascar au début du xxe siècle* (Ethnographie), Paris, 1902, pp. 217–292; A. and G. Grandidier, *Hist. physique, naturelle et politique de Madagascar*, 4 vols., in course of publication, i., do. 1908, ii., 1914, iii., 1915; De la Vaissière, *Vingt Ans à Madagascar*, do. 1885; J. B. Piolet, *Madagascar: sa description, ses habitants*, do. 1895; J. Sibree, 'Carving and Sculpture and Burial Memorials amongst the Betsileo,' in *Antanànarivo Annual*, 1876, pp. 65–71, 'A Sakalava Custom,' *ib.*, 1879, p. 16, *The Great African Island*, London, 1880; *Guide de l'immigrant à Madagascar*, Paris, 1899; and, for a complete list of works on the religion of Madagascar, see G. Grandidier, *Bibliographie de Madagascar*, 2 vols., Paris, 1905–06.

G. GRANDIDIER.

MĀDHVAS, MADHVĀCHĀRĪS.

—The Mādhvas or Madhvāchārīs are an Indian sect, one of the four *sampradāyas*,[1] or churches, of the Vaiṣṇava Bhakti-mārga (see art. BHAKTI-MĀRGA, vol. ii. p. 545). It has usually been stated that this sect represents an attempt to form a compromise or alliance between Śaivas and Vaiṣṇavas,[2] but an examination of the authoritative documents of the faith shows that this is far from the truth. It is therefore advisable to include in this article an account of the life of the founder of the religion, and of the legends connected with his coming.

The authorities on which the following account is based are: (1) the *Maṇimañjarī* (quoted as *Mm.*), which deals with the religious history of India down to the birth of Madhva, the founder of the sect; (2) the *Madhvavijaya* (*Mv.*), which deals with the life of Madhva himself; both these works are in Sanskrit, and are written by one Nārāyaṇa, who was the son of Trivikrama, an actual disciple of Madhva; (3) the *Vāyustuti* of the above Trivikrama; and (4) C. N. Krishnaswami Aiyer's *Śrī Madhwa and Madhwaism* (K.), which includes a summary in English of (1) and (2).

1. Accounts of the founder.—The basis of the Mādhva religion is, first, that Viṣṇu is the Brāhman of the *Upaniṣads*; and, secondly, that, whenever he becomes incarnate, he always has his son, Vāyu, the air-god, as his friend and helper. Accordingly, the first four *sargas*, or chapters, of *Mm.*, after describing the order of creation, give detailed accounts of the Rāma and Kṛṣṇa incarnations, Rāma's great friend and ally being Hanumat, the son of Vāyu, and Kṛṣṇa's ally being, not Arjuna, as we might expect, but Bhīma (cf. *Mv.* i. 41), one of the five heroes of the *Mahābhārata*, and also a son of the air-god. In both of these cases the sonship is looked upon as equivalent to incarnation. In the *Mahābhārata* Bhīma is described as having performed many glorious feats, and as having conquered many terrible demons; but in Mādhva theology these are all ignored save one, which, compared with the others, is, in the epic, of quite minor importance. In the *Vana-parvan* (*Mahābh.* iii. 11,661 ff.) it is related that Bhīma attacked certain Yakṣas or Rākṣasas belonging to the country beyond the Himālaya, and killed their leader, Maṇimat. Maṇimat had formerly offered a filthy insult to the Indian sage Agastya (the apostle of southern India), and had been cursed by him to be slain by a mortal. Such stress is laid upon this story by the Mādhvas that they maintain that the version, as we have it now in the *Mahābhārata*, was, with the sanction of Vyāsa, the author of the epic, rewritten and completed by Madhva himself (K. p. 42).

The narrative of the events in the Kaliyuga, or present age of the world, commences in the 5th *sarga* of *Mm.* At first, the knowledge of the Vedas, as taught by Kṛṣṇa and Bhīma (*Mm.* v. 1), reigns supreme. Then the Asuras conspire to spread false doctrines. The demon Śakuni, urged by Chāṇakya, the son of Lokāyata, points out that other heresies, such as those of the Chārvākas, Jains, and Pāśupatas, had all failed (9–15). Therefore Maṇimat, who alone had sufficient skill, must become incarnate as a Brāhmaṇa ascetic, and must destroy the Vedānta, under cover of explaining it (15 ff.). Maṇimat is dispatched with instructions to abolish the Vedas and Purāṇas, to ridicule the theory that Viṣṇu has *guṇas*, or qualities, and to establish the identity of the soul with Brāhman (19 ff.).

Here (29) the story digresses to tell how at that time the whole earth was under the sway of Buddhism, and to describe the efforts of Śabara and Kumārila to refute it by the aid of the *Pūrva-Mīmāṁsā* system of philosophy. The 6th *sarga* continues this, narrating the successes of Kumārila and the rise of the rival Prābhākara school.

At this stage of affairs Maṇimat is born as a widow's bastard (*Mm.* vi. 6; *Mv.* i. 46). He is hence named Saṁkara.[3] He is

[1] It is called the *Brahma-saṁpradāya* because it is said to have been first communicated by Viṣṇu to Brahmān, who spread it through the world with the help of his brother, Vāyu. See below.

[2] *e.g.*, by Wilson, *Religious Sects of the Hindus*, p. 149.

[3] The Mādhva books uniformly change the great Saṁkara's name to Saṁkara. The object is plain. Saṁkara means

brought up in great poverty, and (as a slap at the monism subsequently taught by him) it is related that in his boyhood he could count only one thing at a time, never being able to see a second (*Mm.* vi. 10). He is taken to Saurāṣṭra, where, under the patronage of Śiva, he quickly masters the sacred books (14). He then goes from teacher to teacher, but is turned off by them for his heretical views. He invents his doctrine, described as *śūnya-mārga* and *nirguṇatva*, and is hailed by the demons as their saviour (24). On their advice he joins the Buddhists and teaches Buddhism under cover of Vedāntism. He makes the Vedas without meaning, and equates Brāhman with nothingness (*śūnyatva*) (46). He becomes a Śākta, and messenger of Bhairavī, who confers upon him a magic spell (51).

The 7th *sārga* describes further disgraceful events in Saṁkara's life. He seduces the wife of his Brāhmaṇa host (1 ff.). He makes converts by magic arts. He falls sick and dies. His last words are instructions to his disciples to uproot the learned Satyaprajña, the last of the great teachers of the true Vedic doctrine.

In the 8th *sarga* we have the doings of Saṁkara's followers. They persecute their opponents, burning down monasteries, destroying cattle-pens, and by magic arts killing women and children (2). They forcibly convert one of their chief opponents, Prājñatīrtha, and compel him and his disciples to adopt the *māyā*-system (5). These, however, still secretly adhere to the true religion, and, after consulting Satyaprajña, determine to cause one disciple to become thoroughly learned in the *māyā*-system, who should start a line of disciples, outwardly Māyins, but really devoted to Hari (*i.e.* Viṣṇu). In this line of disciples came, in due course, Achyutaprekṣa. In his time the Lord, *i.e.* Vāyu, became incarnate as Madhva, in the house of Madhyageha, and studied under Achyutaprekṣa (34 ff.). The book ends with a brief account of Madhva's work, specially mentioning that he composed a commentary on the Vedānta Sūtras utterly destroying that made by the thief Maṇimat-Saṁkara.

It thus appears that Madhva, like Bhīma, was an incarnation of Vāyu, who came to the earth to destroy the followers of Śaṁkara and all their teaching, that the true religion was delivered to the present age by Kṛṣṇa and Bhīma, that it was upheld by Kumārila in the *Pūrva-Mīmāṁsā*, and that it was revived by Madhva. Śaṁkara's *māyā*-system was declared to be only Buddhism in disguise (*prachchhanna-Bauddha* [*Mv.* i. 51]). There is no trace whatever of any attempt to reconcile the Śaiva teaching of Śaṁkara with Vaiṣṇavism. Here also must be mentioned one other doctrine of Mādhvism not referred to above, but of considerable importance—that salvation can be obtained only through Vāyu (*i.e.* in the present age, through Madhva), and through no one else (K. p. 68).

In *Mv.* the first *sarga* sums up briefly the contents of *Mm.*, special stress being again laid on the Maṇimat story (i. 39), and on Bhīma's close connexion with Kṛṣṇa (41). The incarnation of Vāyu is plainly stated in ii. 24. The rest of the work is a prolix account of Madhva's life, too long to analyze here. The main facts are as follows: Madhyageha Bhaṭṭa, Madhva's father (*Mv.* ii. 9, 14), was a Brāhmaṇa living at Rajatapīṭha[1] (6), close to the modern Uḍipi, a town on the sea-coast of the present district of S. Kanara, and about 40 miles due west of Sringeri, then, and still, the head-quarters of the Smārta followers of Śaṁkarāchārya.

The ancient name of the country now comprising the Districts of Dhārwār and N. and S. Kanara, together with the western portion of the State of Mysore, was Tuluva, the modern Tulū, and it is here that the Mādhvas have always been strong. No census figures are available for their number, but a very rough estimate of the materials available leads us to put it at something like 70,000. Elsewhere they are very few.[2]

After the usual natal rites, the boy was named Vāsudeva, but in later years he was known as Madhva. The most probable date of his birth is the Śaka year 1119 (=A.D. 1197), but some authorities put it as late as A.D. 1238.[1] Numerous tales are told of his youthful exploits and of miracles that will be referred to below. His prowess in physical exercises was recognized by his schoolfellows, who nicknamed him 'Bhīma' (*Mv.* iii. 42–48). When he grew up, he became a pupil of the Achyutaprekṣa already referred to (*Mv.* iv. 6), and in due course, amidst a burst of prophecy from the assembled crowd, received initiation under the name of Pūrṇabodha or Pūrṇaprajña (33). He continued his studies under Achyutaprekṣa in the Ananteśvara monastery at Uḍipi, and finally received from him the name of Ānandatīrtha (*Mv.* v. 2), the title adopted by him in future as his pen-name. All this time, it must be remembered, he was studying the Vedānta, according to the *māyā*-school of Śaṁkara.

After further study, he made a tour through southern India, having in the meantime developed his own system of dualism in opposition to the monism of Śaṁkara. He journeyed along, disputing with the doctors in each town, his most important combat being at Anantapura (the modern Trivandrum) with the head of the Śāṁkara monastery at Sringeri (*Mv.* v. 36). Here there seems to have been a drawn battle. The combatants parted in enmity, and thenceforth began the deadly hatred that ever after existed between the followers of the two systems. Madhva had to take refuge for four months at Rāmeśvara (v. 41 ff.), after which he returned to Uḍipi. The result of this first tour was to establish Madhva as the leader of a new sect and to widen the breach between him and the authorities at Sringeri (K. p. 32).

After some years of further study at Uḍipi, during which (K. p. 33) he seems to have completed his commentary on the *Vedānta Sūtras*, Madhva started on his second tour, this time through northern India. He at length reached Hardwār. Here, after fasting and meditation, he left his followers and went off alone into the heart of the Himālaya, where he is said to have stayed with Vyāsa, the compiler of the *Mahābhārata* (*Mv.* vii. 16 ff.). Vyāsa encouraged him to return to India and there to publish his commentary (viii. 44 ff.). He accordingly went back to Hardwār, where he widely proclaimed his doctrine, and 'ground opposing commentaries and false systems to dust' (ix. 6 ff.). He made a leisurely return to Uḍipi, converting more than one eminent Śaṁkarite on the way (ix. 17), and finally converted his own teacher, Achyutaprekṣa (ix. 35).

There now began a period of persecution (*Mv.* xii. and xiii.), in which the Śaṁkarites, led by the head of the Sringeri monastery, did all that they could to destroy the new teacher and his followers. They even went so far as to carry off Madhva's entire library, and it was restored only through the interposition of the local prince, Jaya Siṁha of Viṣṇumaṅgala. It was shortly after this that Madhva converted Trivikrama (xiii. 50 ff., xv. 64), the father of the author of *Mm.* and *Mv.* In his last years Madhva again toured to the North, and is said to have rejoined Vyāsa, in whose company he still remains awaiting the conclusion of the present age. His final journey is described in *Mv.* xvi. The date of his death was probably Śaka 1198 (=A.D. 1276), when he was 79 years old.[2] Thirty-seven different works are attributed to him, of which the most important are his commentaries on the *Vedānta Sūtras* and on the *Bhagavad-Gītā*, and his commentary on the *Mahābhārata*, entitled the *Mahābhārata-tātparya-nirṇaya.*

'auspicious,' but Saṁkara 'misbegotten' or 'rubbish.' The whole account is a ferocious libel on the founder of the system which it opposes.

[1] Probably identical with the ancient town and still existing village of Kalyāṇapura (*IGI* xiv. [1908] 314).

[2] It is, however, important to note that the Vaiṣṇavism of Bengal, founded by Chaitanya (*q.v.*), is an offshoot of Mādhvism (see Pratāpa-Siṁha, *Bhakta-kalpadruma*, Lucknow, 1884, p. 46).

[1] See Subba Rau, *Bhagavad-Gītā*, p. xi ff.; cf. Bhandarkar, *Vaiṣṇavism, Śaivism, and Minor Religious Systems*, p. 59.

[2] See Bhandarkar, p. 59. A list of the thirty-seven works attributed to him is given in Bhandarkar's *Report on the Search for Sanskrit MSS in the Bombay Presidency for 1882–83*, Bombay, 1884, p. 207.

2. Doctrines of the sect.—Mādhvism rejects not only the monism of Saṁkara but also the *Viśiṣṭādvaita*, or qualified monism, of Rāmānuja (see art. BHAKTI-MĀRGA, vol. ii. p. 545). Its followers call themselves Sad-Vaiṣṇavas to distinguish themselves from the Śrī-Vaiṣṇava followers of the latter. The basis of the whole philosophical system is *dvaita*, or dualism. By this is not meant the dualism of spirit and matter, or that of good and evil, but the distinction between the independent Supreme Being (*Paramātman*) and the dependent principle of life (*jīvātman*). There are five real and eternal distinctions (*pañchabheda*), viz. (*a*) between God and the individual soul, (*b*) between God and matter, (*c*) between the soul and matter, (*d*) between one soul and another, and (*e*) between one particle of matter and another. The account of the order of creation given in *Mm.* i. 2 ff. closely follows the well-known Sāṅkhya-Yoga system, as modified by the Purāṇas, and need not detain us. Viṣṇu, Nārāyaṇa, or Parō Bhagavān, not Brāhman, is the name given to the Supreme Being. He is endowed with all auspicious qualities (*guṇa*), and has a consort, Lakṣmī, distinct from, but dependent on, him. By her he has two sons, Brahmān, the Creator, and the Vāyu mentioned above, who is the Saviour of mankind. *Mokṣa*, or salvation, consists in release from transmigration and eternal residence in the abode of Nārāyaṇa. Souls (*jīva*) are innumerable, and each is eternal, has a separate existence, and is subject to transmigration. They fall into three groups, viz. (*a*) the lesser gods, the *pitṛs*, *ṛṣis*, kings, and a few other select classes of the good; these are destined to salvation; (*b*) those who are neither sufficiently good to belong to the first class nor sufficiently bad for the third; these are destined to perpetual transmigration (*saṁsāra*); and (*c*) demons, etc., and sinners, especially followers of the *māyā*-doctrine and other heretics who reject Vāyu; these are destined to eternal hell. Again, it must be noted that there is no salvation, except through Vāyu, *i.e.*, in the present age, through Madhva. It is also noteworthy that in this religion the idea of eternal bliss, or *mokṣa*, is balanced by the idea of an eternal hell—a logical symmetry that is missing in the other religions of Madhva's time.

The natural soul is characterized by ignorance (*avidyā*), and this ignorance is dispelled, and salvation is obtained, by right knowledge of God. This knowledge is obtainable by souls of the first class, and eighteen means are described as necessary for its attainment. Such are distaste of this world (*vairāgya*), equanimity (*śama*), attendance on a *guru*, or religious teacher, *bhakti* directed to God, due performance of rites and ceremonies (cf. the *Pūrva-Mīmāṁsā*), reprobation of false doctrines, worship (*upāsanā*), and so on.[1]

Service to Viṣṇu (*i.e.* to God) is expressed in three ways: (*a*) by stigmatization, or branding (*aṅkana*) the body with the symbols of Viṣṇu; (*b*) by giving his names to sons and others (*nāmakaraṇa*); and (*c*) by worship (*bhajana*) with word, act, and thought. Worship with word consists in (1) veracity, (2) usefulness, (3) kindliness, (4) sacred study; with act, in (5) almsgiving, (6) defence, (7) protection; with thought, in (8) mercy, (9) longing, and (10) faith. Worship is the dedication to Nārāyaṇa (*i.e.* God) of each of these as it is realized.[2]

The custom of branding symbols of Viṣṇu on the shoulders and breast is not peculiar to the followers of Madhva, being also adopted by the Śrī-Vaiṣṇavas; but among the Mādhvas, instead of being occasional, it is universal, and is declared to be necessary according to the *śāstras*. All classes, whether monks or lay, are branded. The chief of each *maṭh*, or

[1] The complete list is given by Bhandarkar, p. 60 f.

[2] *Sarva-darśana-saṁgraha*, tr. p. 91.

monastery, tours among the faithful, and every time he makes his visitation the laity undergo the ceremony (K. p. 40). The sectarian marks, common to monks and laity, are, besides these brands, two white perpendicular lines on the forehead, made with *gopī-chandana* earth, and joined at the root of the nose. Between them is a straight black line made with incense-charcoal, and terminating in a spot of turmeric. Madhva did not allow bloody sacrifices. The old sacrifices were retained, but he enjoined the substitution of a fictitious lamb made of rice-meal as the victim, instead of a lamb of flesh and blood.[1] Mādhvism is also remarkable for the extreme lengths to which fasting of great rigour is carried out. The life of an orthodox Mādhva is one continuous round of fasts, and, according to one writer, this has had an injurious effect on the average physique of the members of the sect (K. p. 70). A full account of these fasts will be found in the *BG* xxii. 72 ff.

The chief *maṭh*, or monastery, of the sect is at Uḍipi, and is said to have been founded by Madhva himself. He also founded two others at Madhyatala and Subrahmanya respectively—both, like Uḍipi, in the coast district of Mangalor—and gave a *svāmin*, or head, to each of the three. The main settlement he divided into eight sub-monasteries, to each of which he also gave a *svāmin*. Each of these eight *svāmins* conducts the worship of Kṛṣṇa at the head monastery in his turn, his term of office lasting for two years. The change (*paryāya*) of *svāmins* thus takes place every second year, when the sun enters the sign of Makara, or Capricorn, early in January. It is the occasion of a great fair and festival. The succession of chief pontiffs is recorded in the *BG* xxii. (p. 59), and the thirty-fifth pontiff was living in 1883. There are now eighteen subsects, of which ten are the followers of the ten *svāmins* appointed by Madhva and five were started by his four immediate successors. Only two, and these still more modern, refuse to acknowledge the authority of the head pontiff at Uḍipi. The most salient doctrinal difference depends on the interpretation of the word *bhajana*, or worship, and even this is of small importance (K. p. 60).

3. Influence of Christianity.—In the art. BHAKTI-MĀRGA (vol. ii. p. 548) it was pointed out that the southern Indian reformers had probably been to a certain extent influenced by the Christianity then existing in their neighbourhood.[2] The apparent influence of Christianity is especially noteworthy in Mādhvism. Madhva's birthplace was either in the ancient city of Kalyāṇapura or close to it. Kalyāṇapura has always been reputed as one of the earliest Christian settlements in India, and here, so long ago as the 6th cent. A.D., Cosmas Indicopleustes (p. 178 f. [*PG* lxxxviii. 169]) found a bishop who was appointed from Persia.[3] These Christians were Nestorians (Garbe, p. 155). No stress need be laid on most of the childish miracles attributed to Madhva in *Mv.*, because they are such as are attributed to the infancy of many religious teachers; but some of the legends deserve

[1] It will be remembered that Madhva is said to have revised the *Mahābhārata*, and in this connexion it should be noted that in the southern recension of the epic, after XII. cccxliv. 20, six verses have been inserted in which it is directed that animals of flour should be used at sacrifices.

[2] The present writer takes this opportunity of withdrawing the remark made in *ERE* ii. 548[b] that Alopen had visited the court of Śilāditya. See *JRAS*, 1913, p. 144.

[3] A. Burnell, *IA* ii. [1873] 274 ff., iii. [1874] 310 ff.; cf. R. Garbe, *Indien und das Christentum*, Tübingen, 1914, p. 151 ff. The passage in Cosmas is not quoted in J. W. McCrindle's *Ancient India*, Calcutta, 1877. Garbe (p. 152) considers it probable that the Kalliana of Cosmas was another Kalyāṇa farther north and near Bombay, but it seems to the present writer that the wording of Cosmas connects Kalliana so closely with Male (Malabar) that it must be the town near Uḍipi. Garbe himself appears to accept this in his note on p. 273.

a passing notice. Thus, before Madhva appeared on earth, at a festive gathering at the temple at Uḍipi the spirit of Ananteśvara (Viṣṇu) came upon a Brāhmaṇa and made him a messenger of good news to proclaim that the kingdom of heaven was at hand (K. p. 13). After the child had been presented in the temple at Uḍipi, as his parents were taking him through a forest, a *graha*, or evil spirit, opposed their way, but departed on being rebuked by the divine child (K. p. 16; *Mv.* ii. 32 ff.). When the child was five years old, his parents missed him, and after an anxious search of three days found him at Uḍipi, in the temple of Ananteśvara, teaching gods and men to worship Viṣṇu according to the *śāstras* (K. p. 16; *Mv.* iii. 1 ff.). On his southern tour Madhva multiplied food in a wilderness, to meet the needs of his followers (K. p. 27; *Mv.* v. 32). On one of his northern tours he walked across water 'without wetting his clothes' (K. p. 35; *Mv.* x. 27), and on another occasion he stilled an angry sea by his look (K. p. 48; *Mv.* xvi. 11). The substitution at sacrifices of a lamb of rice for a lamb of flesh and blood also offers a striking analogy, but, as K. p. 68 points out, it may with equal probability be ascribed to Jain influence. Under any circumstances, considering the fact that Madhva was born and brought up in the neighbourhood of Christians and that the doctrine of *bhakti* is common to all forms of Vaiṣṇavism and to Christianity, there is considerable probability that at least some of these legends grew up under Christian influence. Still more striking, however, is the central article of Mādhva belief that Vāyu is the son of the Supreme God, Viṣṇu, and that salvation can be obtained only through him. This is evidently an idea borrowed from Christianity, quite possibly promulgated as a rival to the central doctrine of that faith.

4. Traces of Manichæism.—In the two papers already quoted, Burnell points out that Persian immigrants were welcomed in this part of India long after the time of Cosmas, and that before the beginning of the 9th cent. A.D. they had acquired sovereign rights over their original settlement of Maṇigrāma, by a grant from the *perumal*, or local chief. Burnell goes on to suggest that these Persians were Manichæans, and that the name of their settlement meant 'Manes- (Mani-) town,' not 'Jewel-town,' as the compound would ordinarily mean in Sanskrit. Burnell's theory was attacked in the same journal and, according to Garbe (p. 152), completely controverted by R. Collins. To the present writer it seems that, in the discussion, Collins failed in his main point—the meaning of 'Maṇi' in 'Maṇi-grāma'—and that Burnell's suggestion, though certainly not proved, may possibly contain more elements of truth than Garbe was prepared to admit.[1] It seems that Burnell's suggestion that 'Maṇi' refers to Manes receives some confirmation from the Maṇimat theory of the Mādhvas. It is intelligible that Bhīma should be selected as the hero, but it is unintelligible why the altogether unimportant Maṇimat of the epic should be selected as the origin of the arch-heretic Śaṁkara. Bhīma killed many much more noteworthy demons, who would have served Madhva's purpose better; but so small a part does Maṇimat, the demon from beyond the Himālaya, play in the epic[2] that Madhva had, according to the legend, actually to get Vyāsa's permission to re-write the story, so as to make it complete. It must, on the other hand, be admitted that there is little resemblance between Manichæism and Śaṁkara's theology. The former is dualist and the latter is monist. But Mani's dualism taught the existence of two beings—light and darkness. Light had God at its head, and darkness had no god at its head. There is a certain resemblance between this and Śaṁkara's Brāhman obscured by *māyā*. At any rate, it is possible that Madhva, who (K. p. 36) could speak the language of the Mlechchhas (foreigners), may have become acquainted with Manichæism, and may have associated it in this way with Śaṁkara's theory of *māyā*. The question deserves more investigation than has hitherto been given to it.

LITERATURE.—The *Maṇimañjarī* and the *Madhvavijaya* have been already mentioned. Several editions of these have been published in India. A useful summary of Mādhva doctrines will be found on p. 16 ff. of the *Sakalāchārya-mata-saṁgraha*, an anonymous work published in the Benares Sanskrit Series in 1907. A fuller account will be found in Padmanābhasūri, *Madhvasiddhānta-sāra*, Bombay, 1883, quoted by Bhandarkar, p. 59. Finally, there is Mādhvāchārya, *Sarva-darśana-saṁgraha*, of which many editions have been published in India. Of this there is an Eng. tr. by E. B. Cowell and A. E. Gough (2nd ed., London, 1894). The system of Purṇaprajña, *i.e.* Madhva, will be found in ch. v. p. 87 ff. of the translation.

As for works in English, the earliest account of the Mādhvas is contained in 'Account of the Marda Gooroos, collected while Major Mackenzie was at Hurryhurr, 24th August 1800,' printed on p. 33 ff. of the 'Characters' in the *Asiatic Annual Register* for 1804 (London, 1806). We next have H. H. Wilson, *Sketch of the Religious Sects of the Hindus*, reprinted from vols. xvi. and xvii. of *Asiatic Researches*, London, 1861, i. 139 ff. A useful little book is C. N. Krishnaswami Aiyer, *Śrī Madhwa and Madhwaism*, Madras, no date. This has been freely utilized in the foregoing pages. See also the following: R. G. Bhandarkar, *Vaiṣṇavism, Śaivism and Minor Religious Systems* (=*GIAP* iii. 6), Strassburg, 1913, p. 57 ff.; *BG*, vol. xxii., 'Dhārwar,' Bombay, 1884, p. 56 ff. (full account of the history, religion, and customs of the Mādhvas of the present day); and G. Venkobo Rao, 'A Sketch of the Hist. of the Madhwa Acharyas,' beginning in *IA* xliii. [1914] 233 (refers to C. M. Padmanābhāchārya, *Life of Madhvāchārya*).

For an authentic account of Madhva's doctrines see S. Subba Rau, *The Vedanta-sutras, with the Commentary by Sri Madhwacharya, a complete Translation*, Madras, 1904, *The Bhagavad-Gita, Translation and Commentaries in English according to Sri Madhwacharya's Bhashyas*, do. 1906. Both of those are in English. The preface of the latter contains a life of Madhva from the orthodox point of view; cf. also P. Ramachandra Rao, *The Brahma Sútras: Construed literally according to the Commentary of Sri Madhavácharya* (Sanskrit text), Kumbakonam, 1902.

G. A. GRIERSON.

MADHYAMAKA, MĀDHYAMIKAS.—

Madhyamaka is the name of a system of Buddhist philosophy, 'the system of the middle way,' 'the system of the Mean' (μέσον); the adherents of this system are called Mādhyamikas.

1. Nāgārjuna.—The work upon which the Madhyamaka philosophy is based, the *Mūlamadhyamakakārikā*, still survives, and tradition is agreed in ascribing it to Nāgārjuna; numerous commentaries have been written upon it: Nāgārjuna's own, the *Akutobhaya*; those of Buddhapālita and Chandrakīrti, which seem to give a faithful rendering of the author's meaning; and that of Bhāvaviveka, which transmits his personal views. There are two branches of Madhyamaka, but the difference between them has not been studied, and seems to consist in a mere divergence in the method of demonstration.

All this literature is, or will soon be, accessible in the editions of the originals or in translations.[1] The *Mūlamadhyamaka* is probably the authentic work of Nāgārjuna, who flourished about the middle of the 2nd cent. A.D. We knew that this mysterious and miraculous person was the putative father of the Great Vehicle, or Mahāyāna (*q.v.*), and, in particular, the revealer of the *sūtras* of the *Prajñāpāramitā*, the teaching of which is akin to that of the Madhyamaka. It is even possible that several *sūtras* of the Great Vehicle were written with the sole purpose of stating the theories of the Madhyamaka philosophy under the guise of 'words of

[1] The following are the references to the whole controversy. Garbe (*loc. cit.*) refers only to one of Collins's communications, and does not notice any of Burnell's replies: *IA* ii. 273 (Burnell), iii. 308 (Burnell), iv. [1875] 153 (Collins), 181 (Burnell), 311 (Collins), v. [1876] 25 (Burnell).

[2] For the references see S. Sörensen, *Index to the Names in the Mahabharata*, London, 1904 ff., p. 464.

[1] See Literature at end of article.

the Buddha.' It is difficult to determine what part Nāgārjuna took in the redaction of the *sūtras*, but respect for tradition would lead us to believe that his share was a large one. In any case, the Madhyamaka school must be held responsible for a considerable proportion of the Great Vehicle. All this must be assigned, probably, to the early centuries of the Christian era, from the first onwards.

2. The Madhyamaka system and its antecedents.—It is not difficult to show the place occupied by the Madhyamaka in the development of Buddhist philosophy from its beginning, and such a historical sketch is indispensable to a definition of the system itself.

The Buddha had given his revelation as a 'path,' or a 'way' (*magga, paṭipadā*), and had qualified this path by 'middle' (*majjhima = madhyama*), doubtless, as has been often said, because he repudiated two 'extremes' (*anta*)—an exaggerated asceticism (*tapas*), and an easy secular life (*sukhallikā*). But he had also condemned other 'extremes,' viz. contradictory theories, such as: 'Everything exists,' 'nothing exists'; 'The person who feels is the same thing as sensation,' 'the person who feels is a different thing from sensation'; 'The Buddha exists after death,' 'the Buddha does not exist after death'; and some texts—few, but explicit—prove that, at the time of the redaction of the Pāli *Nikāyas*, 'middle way' meant a 'way between certain negations and affirmations.' This way is simply the philosophy of the *dharmas* and of the negation of the individual (*pudgala*, 'τὶς'), which is almost exactly the philosophy of the Canon, and finds, from the very first, clear and skilful expression in the theory of dependent origination (*paṭichchasamuppāda*, *pratityasamutpāda*).

The Canon teaches that there is no individual (*pudgala*), one and permanent, of whom we can say that he is identical with sensation or different from it, or that he survives or fails to survive the destruction of the body. The individual does not exist in himself (*pudgala-nairātmya*); he is merely a mass of *dharmas* following one another in unbroken succession, cause and effect.

But what is meant by *dharma*? This word, as Max Müller said,[1] is difficult to translate, though easy to understand. Man is a collection, a 'series' of *dharmas*; every thought, every volition, every sensation, is a *dharma*. His body is composed of material *dharmas*. Sound, colour, smell, whatever can be struck or touched, is composed of material *dharmas*. The organs of sense and intellect (*mana, indriya*) are *dharmas* of subtle matter. Concupiscence, hatred, and delusion are mental *dharmas*, 'co-ordinated with thought.'

The *dharmas* are 'realities,' things which actually exist, and nothing exists but these elementary realities, which are all doomed to destruction; some—*e.g.*, the mental *dharmas* and the *dharmas* forming the successive instants of the existence of a flame—perish moment by moment, while others sometimes last for a long time.

Just as a waggon is nothing but the collection of the parts of a waggon, so man is simply the collection of the elementary realities, material and spiritual, which constitute his pseudo-individuality. Apart from *dharmas*, man and waggon have only an ideal existence—an existence of designation (*prajñāpti*), as the Buddhists say.

It will be observed that none of these elementary realities exists in isolation, but that every *dharma* combines with other *dharmas* to form a more or less solid complex. The four chief elements (*mahābhūta*) combine in the formation of every material thing. Anger presupposes, besides delusion, an elaborate complex of intellectual *dharmas*—contact, sensations, ideas, and intellections; and this intellectual complex presupposes, at least as a rule, a physical complex—body, sense-organs, heat, vital organ, not to mention former actions to be rewarded, which are sometimes regarded as subtle matter.

All *dharma* is intimately bound up with its causes and effects; its essential nature is to be an effect and to be a cause; it is a moment in continuous time. Every thought has as determining causes (*pratyaya*) a great number of *dharmas* more or less exterior to itself (object of vision, visual organ, etc.), but its cause, properly so called (*hetu*), is the thought immediately preceding it—just as every moment of the duration of a flame depends, of course, upon the oil, the wick, etc., yet is, as a matter of fact, the continuation of the preceding moment of the flame. The Buddhists were quick to see that flame and thought are made up of 'instants' of flame and thought succeeding each other moment by moment. Extending this observation, they formulated the general theory that 'the *dharmas* perish the very moment they are born.' They perish without any other cause of destruction than their very birth or their nature; they are not merely 'transitory' (*anitya*), as the Buddha said; they are 'momentary' (*kṣaṇika*) (cf. art. IDENTITY [Buddhist]). There can be no distinction between a stone and a human being: they are both collections, more or less complex, of *dharmas*, which do not last. The collections last by constituting series, because the *dharmas* renew themselves—always the same in the case of the stone, often very different in the case of the living being. In the course of an existence our vital organs, sense-organs, etc., renew themselves without any essential modification; volition, on the contrary, creates *dharmas*—retribution, etc.—which are different from volition itself. Volition is controlled by judgment; and, when judgment is illumined by the law of the Buddha (*yoniśo manasikāra*), 'supramundane' (*lokottara*) actions become possible, and these destroy passions, desire, action, and retribution, and make for the realization of *nirvāṇa*, that is to say, the collection of mental *dharmas* begins to become impoverished and finally disappears; desire is no longer present to give life to it. Such is the philosophy of ancient Buddhism, and it can be summed up in two words: *pudgalanairātmya*, the unreality of the individual, and *dharmānityatva* or *dharmakṣaṇikatva*, the transitory or momentary character of the *dharmas*.

This philosophy satisfied Buddhists for a long time. But it did not satisfy the Madhyamaka school, who put a more rigorous interpretation upon the word 'void,' so often applied by the Buddha to everything in general, and held that this philosophy is in its nature not free from the two 'extremes' of perpetual duration and annihilation (*śaśvata, uchchheda*), seeing that it inevitably regards *nirvāṇa* as the annihilation of a series of thoughts. The Madhyamaka school claims to find the true 'middle way' by declaring, not only the unreality of the individual (*pudgalanairātmya*), but also the unreality of the *dharmas* themselves; it denies the existence not only of the being who suffers, but also of pain. 'Everything is void.'

Nāgārjuna and his school seem to hesitate between two positions.

i. Everything takes place as if things and living beings were composed of substantial *dharmas*, and, to arrive at *nirvāṇa*, the methods defined by the ancients must be followed: eliminate the *dharmas* which generate new *dharmas* because they are associated with desire; and insert, in the complex series that constitutes our being, the *dharmas* of the knowledge that destroys desire, and so arrest the renewal of the *dharmas*. Yet we do not put

[1] *SBE* x. [1898] 31.

an end to existence by this method, for existence is void of reality in itself, since the *dharmas* do not exist substantially; we put an end to a *processus* of 'void' (*śūnya*) *dharmas* which renew themselves in 'void' *dharmas*. It is important to know this, for the only knowledge that can arrest the renewal of unreal *dharmas* is knowledge of their radical and fundamental unreality.

The ancients saw that the essential nature (*dharmatā*) of things (*dharma*) is to be produced by concurrent causes (*pratītyasamutpanna*), 'dependently originated.' The Madhyamaka school observes that 'what is produced by causes is not produced in itself, does not exist in itself.' The essential nature of things consists in not being produced in themselves, in being void of all substantial reality—*i.e.* in 'vacuity' (*śūnyatā*). This term 'vacuity' has been variously understood. For some it is 'nothingness'; for others it is a permanent principle, transcendent and undefinable, immanent in transient and illusory things. It would be a long and difficult task to explain the mystical significance that it has in certain Buddhist books; we know that it ends by being confused with the term *vajra*, 'thunder-bolt, diamond, male organ.' One thing is beyond all doubt: for the Madhyamaka, 'vacuity' is neither nothingness nor a transcendent-immanent principle, but the very nature of what exists; 'things are not void because of vacuity' (*śūnyatayā*)—conceived as exterior to things—'but because they are void,' and they are 'void' because they are produced by causes. 'Vacuity' means 'production by causes,' and is only an abstraction, a mere word; 'void' means 'produced by causes.'

Existence (*saṁsāra*), therefore, is a complex *processus* of *dharmas* which have no reason in themselves for existing and which cannot exist substantially by reason of their causes, *i.e.* former *dharmas* which do not exist by themselves. The following formula explains this clearly: *dharmas* resembling delusions of magic or reflexions in a mirror (*māyopama, pratibimbopama*)—we might say 'contingent' *dharmas*—give birth to *dharmas* that are equally illusory. Like begets like.

The objection of the realist against the Madhyamaka is, therefore, fruitless: 'If everything is void, then existence and *nirvāṇa*, impurity and purity, ignorance and wisdom, are the same thing; and the path of salvation does not exist.'

Nāgārjuna himself formulates this difficulty, and answers it. Existence is the continuous production of phenomena not substantial but actually existent, because they are existent by the only existence that there is—void existence, or existence produced by causes. *Nirvāṇa* is the end of the production of these phenomena. Impurity is attachment to phenomena conceived as pleasant; purity is complete detachment from phenomena. Ignorance is a clinging to the substantiality of phenomena, which induces attachment; wisdom is real truth, knowledge of the vacuity of things.

Nāgārjuna, Chandrakīrti, and Śāntideva very often took this point of view, which is quite within the logic of Buddhism and not unreasonable. But, in order to give a true picture of the Madhyamaka as it is, we must add that our teachers often go much further.

ii. Just as their criticism destroys all ideas of experience and religion—the notion of movement, of time, of 'passion' (since the connexion between the passionate man and passion 'does not bear investigation')—it also destroys the notion of causality; not only do the *dharmas* not exist substantially; they do not exist at all, either in reality or apparently. They are like the daughter of a barren woman, like the beauty of the daughter of a barren woman: this beauty evidently does not exist except in so far as it may be described; but, in reality, the object described, the description, and the person describing are all similarly non-existent.

Absolute truth, which is, properly speaking, 'knowledge of a Buddha,' is a 'not-knowledge'; it is midway between affirmation and negation. The *dharmas* are like the hairs that a monk with diseased eyes thinks he sees in his almsbowl; he does not see them, for the knowledge which he has of them does not exist any more than its object. This is proved by the fact that a man with undiseased eyes has no thought about these hairs at all; he neither denies nor affirms their existence, because he knows them in their true nature (which is 'void') by not knowing them. The legitimate conclusion of this system is formulated in our sources: 'Absolute truth is silence.'

LITERATURE.—i. *BRĀHMANICAL AND JAIN SOURCES.*—*Sarvadarśanasaṁgraha*; Śaṅkara on the *Brahmasūtras* (*Muséon*, new series, iii. ff. [1902 ff.]). ii. *BUDDHIST SANSKRIT SOURCES.*—*Mūlamadhyamakakārikā*, with Chandrakīrti's commentary, *Prasannapādā* (*Bibl. Buddhica*, iv. [Petrograd, 1903–12]); *Madhyamakāvatāra* (Tibetan tr., *Bibl. Buddhica*, ix. [do. 1907 ff.], Fr. tr., *Muséon*, viii. ff. [1907 ff.]); Nāgārjuna, *Akutobhaya*, Germ. tr., after the Tibetan and Chinese, by M. Walleser, Heidelberg, 1911–12; *Bodhicharyāvatāra*, ch. ix. (*Bibl. Indica*, Calcutta, 1901 ff.), Fr. tr., *Introduction à la pratique des futurs Bouddhas*, Paris, 1907. iii. *TIBETAN SOURCES* (history and doctrines of the school).—Mañjughoṣahāsavajra, *Siddhānta* (summary in W. Wassilieff, *Buddhismus*, Petrograd, 1860, p. 326 ff.); Tāranātha, *Gesch. des Buddhismus*, tr. A. Schiefner, Petrograd, 1869, *passim*. iv. *EUROPEAN ACCOUNTS.*—L. A. Waddell, *The Buddhism of Tibet*, London, 1895, pp. 11, 124; H. Kern, *Manual of Indian Buddhism*, Strassburg, 1896, p. 126; D. T. Suzuki, *Outlines of Mahāyāna Buddhism*, London, 1907, pp. 21, 62, etc.; L. de la Vallée Poussin, *Bouddhisme: Opinions sur l'hist. de la dogmatique*, Paris, 1909, p. 191; M. Winternitz, *Gesch. der ind. Litteratur*, ii. (Leipzig, 1913) 250.

L. DE LA VALLÉE POUSSIN.

MADRAS AND COORG.—In the Government Census for 1911 the vast majority of the population in the Madras Presidency are classed as Hindus. Out of a total population of 41,870,160 in the Presidency and the small Feudatory States included in it, the Hindus number 37,230,034. The rest of the population are classified as follows: Musalmāns, 2,764,467; Christians, 1,208,515; Animists, 638,466; Jains, 27,005; Buddhists, 697; Parsis, 489; Brāhma Samāj, 374; Jews, 71; while 42 are classed simply as 'others.'

1. Christianity.—The most progressive of all these religious bodies is the Christian. Excluding the 40,928 European and Anglo-Indian Christians, whose numbers do not largely vary from decade to decade, we find that the Indian Christians have increased during the decade from 1901 to 1911 by 168,964, or 17 per cent—a rate more than double that of the increase in the total population, and one which compares favourably with an increase of 8 per cent among Hindus, and 11 per cent among Muhammadans.

The main cause of this increase in the Christian population is the movement among the out-castes of Hindu society towards Christianity that has been in progress in S. India for the last sixty years. Conversions to Christianity from the higher castes of Hindus or from the Musalmāns have been comparatively rare. On the other hand, the out-castes are being gathered into the Christian Church in the village districts in increasingly large numbers, especially among the Telugus in the northern part of the Presidency. The causes that have led to this great movement are mainly social. The out-castes are the hereditary slaves or serfs of their Hindu masters, and have been kept for many generations in a state of abject poverty and utter ignorance. They have seen in the Christian Church the hope and possibility of new life, and for the last half century have been crowding into it in thousands. The great force behind the movement, therefore, is a natural human craving for life and freedom. At the same time, there is also a strong spiritual element in the movement. In almost every district where it is in progress it has owed either its origin or its power to a few men and women of true spirituality, and the fact that a large number of the converts have to endure a very bitter persecution when they first join the Christian Church is in itself an indication that the movement is due to something higher than a mere desire for immediate temporal gain. This great movement is bound to have a very striking influence in the future, not only upon the Christian Church itself, but also upon the religious life and thought of India as a whole. A great Christian Church is steadily and rapidly rising up in India from the lowest stratum of Hindu society. The conscience of educated Hindus is becoming awakened to the injustice and the social evils inherent in the caste system. Slowly and surely the work of the Christian Church is preparing the way for a great economic, social, and religious revolution throughout the length and breadth of India.

2. Hinduism.—Hinduism in the Madras Presidency does not differ greatly as regards either its doctrines or its customs from Hinduism in other parts of India. One striking difference observable between the Hinduism of S. India and that of N. India is the predominance of the Brāhmans in the South, but this difference is social and political rather than religious. The Vedāntist philosophy and the monism of Śaṅkara are more widely held in the South than in the North, mainly owing to the fact that Muhammadanism, with its clear teaching on the unity and transcendence of God, has had far less influence there than in N. India. The stern and gloomy worship of Śiva, the Destroyer, which has absorbed into itself many elements of the old animistic cults, is the predominant form of Hinduism; but the worship of Viṣṇu, the Preserver, in all his manifold incarnations, has a large number of devotees, and has a special attraction for the lower castes of Śūdras whom it has admitted more freely to its temples than the rival cult of Siva.

3. Animism.—The prevalence of animism in the Madras Presidency is very inadequately represented by the small number of people (638,466) classed as animists in the Government Census. The large majority of the Hindus in the villages, with the exception of the Brāhmans, even when they are devotees of Viṣṇu and Śiva, are also animists worshipping the village deities, the Grāma-Devatās, as they are called in the vernacular, and a host of spirits, good, bad, and indifferent. The worship of these village deities forms an important part of the conglomerate of religious beliefs, customs, and ceremonies which are often classed together under the term Hinduism. In almost every village and town of S. India may be seen a shrine or symbol of the Grāma-Devatā, who is periodically worshipped and propitiated. As a rule, the shrine of the village deity is far less imposing than the Brāhmanical temples in the neighbourhood; very often it is nothing more than a small enclosure with a few rough stones in the centre, and often there is no shrine at all; but still, when calamity overtakes the village, when pestilence, famine, or cattle-disease makes its appearance, it is to the village deity that the whole body of the villagers turn for protection. Śiva and Viṣṇu may be more dignified beings, but the village deity is regarded as a more present help in trouble, and is more intimately concerned with the happiness and prosperity of the villagers. In the animal sacrifices offered to these deities the treatment of the blood, which is sometimes drunk by the worshippers, sometimes sprinkled upon their bodies, sometimes sprinkled on the houses or the gate-way of the village, and sometimes mixed with boiled rice and sprinkled all round the village site, and also the sacrificial feast upon the flesh of the victim, connect the sacrifices to the Grāma-Devatā in India very closely with the primitive systems of animal-sacrifice which are found all over the world. Traces of human sacrifice, too, are often found in connexion with these cults. In Mysore the present writer came across a ceremony called 'the human sacrifice ceremony,' in which the man who represents the victim, instead of being killed, is simply touched with a bunch of coco-nut flowers. Lewis Rice states that similar traces of human sacrifice are found among the Coorgs in the hill country to the west of the Mysore State, whose religion is anti-Brāhmanical and consists of the worship of ancestors and demons. With reference to the worship of Grāma-Devatās among them, he says that, as among other Dravidian mountain tribes, so also in Coorg, the tradition relates that human sacrifices were offered in former times to secure the favour of their Grāma-Devatās, who are supposed to protect the villages from all evil influences. At the present day a he-goat or a cock is often sacrificed instead of a man.

The special features which broadly distinguish the worship of the village deities in S. India from that of Śiva and Viṣṇu are three. (1) The fact that the village deities, with very few exceptions, are female. In the Tamil country, it is true, almost all the village goddesses have male attendants, who are supposed to guard the shrine and to carry out the commands of the goddesses; and one male deity, Iyenar, has a shrine to himself, and is regarded as the night watchman of the village. In the Telugu country there is a being called Potu-Razu, who figures sometimes as the brother and sometimes as the husband of village goddesses, and sometimes as an attendant. But, with the exception of Iyenar and one or two other deities, all the male deities are so distinctly subordinate to the goddesses that they do not contravene the general principle that village deities are female and not male. (2) The fact that the village deities are almost universally worshipped with animal sacrifices. Buffaloes, sheep, goats, pigs, and fowls are freely offered to them, sometimes in thousands. In the Tamil country this custom is modified by the influence of Brāhmanism, which has imbued the villagers with the idea that the shedding of blood is low and irreligious. The animal sacrifices are regarded, therefore, as offered to the male attendants of the goddess and not to the goddess herself. (3) The fact that the Pujaris, *i.e.* the men who perform the worship and officiate as priests, are not Brāhmans, but are drawn from the Śūdra castes or sometimes from the out-castes. On the other hand, in the temples of Śiva and Viṣṇu, the officiating priests are Brāhmans, no animal sacrifices are ever offered, and the principal deities are male and not female. The origin of these cults is lost in antiquity; they are certainly pre-Aryan, but have been more or less modified in various parts of S. India by Brāhmanical influence. Some details of the ceremonies used in them seem to point back to a totemistic stage of religion; some of the deities are obviously agricultural, others are the spirits of women who have died in childbirth or of men or women who have died by violent deaths, others are connected with disease and pestilence, especially cholera and smallpox; many of the deities are of quite recent origin, and it is easy to observe a deity in the making even at the present day.

Snake-worship and tree-worship are also widely prevalent throughout S. India and have become incorporated in popular Hinduism. Almost every village has its sacred *pipal* tree, representing a female, and a *margossa* tree, representing a male, planted close to each other. These two trees are married with the same ceremonies as human beings. In every house of one section of the Brāhmans (called Mādhvas [*q.v.*] or Raojis) there is a *tulasi* plant (sacred to Viṣṇu). The snake is closely connected with the worship both of Viṣṇu and of Śiva. A cobra forms the *vāhana* (sacred vehicle) on which Viṣṇu rides, and Śiva is always represented with a cobra in his hand. At the entrance of almost every village of S. India there are figures of the cobra carved on stone in bas-relief erected on raised platforms for the adoration of the public. Brāhmans and Sūdras alike make offerings at these shrines. The living serpent is very generally worshipped, and few Hindus will consent to kill one. If a cobra takes up its abode in the thatched roof of the house or in one of the walls of the compound, it is not only left undisturbed, but is fed with milk. A woman is often the priest in the worship both of trees and of serpents, and women are the chief worshippers, mainly for the purpose of obtaining offspring.

On the W. Coast in Malabar snake-worship is especially prevalent. Some families are supposed to be consecrated to the snake deity, and to exercise a peculiar influence over the deadly cobras which are reputed to swarm in their houses and crawl in and out among the members of the family without ever doing them any injury.

Demonolatry is very prevalent, especially in the Southern part of the Tamil country, and devil-dancing, performed by a class of men who are supposed to have supernatural powers over the devils, forms a weird feature of the religion of the Tamil villagers. Some diseases, especially nervous maladies, are supposed to be the result of possession by an evil spirit. Devils innumerable surround the village—water-devils, cow-devils, horse-devils, and buffalo-devils—who are always ready to pounce down upon the unhappy villager. The poor people who are supposed to be possessed by these devils are often put to terrible tortures by the exorcist. Red-hot iron needles are sometimes stuck all over their bodies, or they are bound hand and foot and then beaten with sticks.

The innumerable superstitions connected with popular Hinduism are excellently described by Edgar Thurston in his *Omens and Superstitions of Southern India.*

LITERATURE.—*Census Reports*, 1901 and 1911, 'Madras'; E. Thurston, *Omens and Superstitions of Southern India*, London, 1912; H. Whitehead, *The Village Deities of Southern India*, *Bulletin of Madras Government Museum*, v. [1907] no. 3, reprinted, London, 1915; J. A. Dubois, *Hindu Manners, Customs, and Ceremonies*³, tr. H. K. Beauchamp, Oxford, 1906.

H. WHITEHEAD.

MADURA.—Madura is the name of an important District in S. India—280 to 380 miles south of the town of Madras. Its capital, Madura, had a population of 134,130 in 1911, and is situated 10° N. lat. by 78° E. longitude. It is a prosperous town among whose progressive people are found about 50,000 weavers. Yet, apart from government and railway works and the Scottish spinning mill, there is hardly one horse power of steam used in the whole community—by which it may be known that modern prosperity in the East is not necessarily connected with the use of most modern industrial appliances and forces.

Madura is a town of considerable antiquity. It was known to Ptolemy (VII. i. 89, VIII. xxvi. 17) as Μόδουρα, and was the centre of the ancient Pāṇḍya kingdom whose fame spread westward through the Greeks and Romans even before the advent of the Christian era. Even to-day ancient Roman coins are occasionally discovered in the town and surrounding regions.

Madura has long been designated 'the Athens of S. India'; the ancient and famed Madura College was the source and inspiration of Tamil classical literature for centuries. Many of its most popular legends gather round its poet-saints, the narrative of whose struggles and conflicts is a perennial source of delight to the people.

But it is its great Mīnākṣī temple that is the source of its pride and the centre of its life. The town is built around its sacred precincts, all the main streets running parallel to the four walls of the temple. This temple has a past which runs far beyond history into the misty realm of legend and myth.

The first historical reference is to its partial destruction by Malik Kāfūr, the famous general of the Mughal emperor, 'Alā-ud-dīn, in 1310. He destroyed its outer wall and fourteen high towers, and left little but the inner shrines, which were saved only by an opportune dissension among the vandals.

Perhaps all that now exists of this architectural pride of S. India (except the inner shrines and contiguous courts) is not older than the 16th cent. and is largely the gift of kings of the Nayaken dynasty, by far the most prominent of whom was Tirumala Naik (1623–59).

S. Indian temples are the most spacious in the world. The Madura shrine is the third in size, but is the first in architectural excellence, best in its upkeep, and most thoroughly devoted to its religious purposes. Its outer walls, which are 25 ft. high, form almost a square (830 ft. by 730 ft.) and enclose an area of about 14 acres. Each wall is surmounted at its centre by a richly embellished *gopura*, or tower, which is about 150 ft. high. These towers are the landmarks of the country around.

Granite is almost exclusively the material used in the temple, even the roof being of granite slabs. Its monolithic pillars are legion, and nearly all of them are elaborately carved, some exhibiting marvellous patience and skill. The 'Hall of a Thousand Pillars' (correctly speaking, its pillars are only 985 in number) is the culmination of its architectural claims. Of this J. Fergusson writes:

> Its 'sculptures surpass those of any other hall of its class I am acquainted with . . . but it is not their number but their marvellous elaboration that makes it the wonder of the place' (*Hist. of Indian and Eastern Architecture*², i. 392).

This hall is eclipsed, perhaps, by only one other, the so-called Choultry, or Puthu Maṇḍapam, which is outside and to the east of the temple proper and is the most imposing of all sacred edifices in S. India. It was erected by Tirumala Naik about 250 years ago, is 330 ft. by 105 ft., and is supported by 124 richly sculptured pillars 20 ft. high. It is a worthy granite monument to one of the great kings of S. India. The whole temple is distinctly Hindu in its architecture—a style in which the arch is entirely absent and densely pillared halls predominate. Its many *gopuras* are pyramidal in form, and are a striking development of the ancient *stūpa*, or pagoda, of Buddhism.

The temple is one of the most distinguished fanes of Śaivism, representing that type of the Brāhmanic cult which first appealed to and was adopted by the Dravidian people of S. India. Because this is the more austere form of Hinduism, it is more closely allied than the mild Vaiṣṇavism to the cruel demonolatry of the aboriginal people of that region. This temple and its worship also admirably illustrate the habit of the Brāhmanic propaganda, which never antagonized a new and contiguous faith, but rather fraternized with it, then adopted its leading features, and finally absorbed it entirely. Śiva's representative in this shrine is Sokkaliṅgam or Sundareśvara. The first name is Dravidian, revealing the non-Brāhmanic or non-Aryan origin of the god who was adopted from the pantheon of the Dravidian cult to that of the Aryan. Later, this S. India manifestation of Siva popularized the northern faith among the people of Madura by marrying the most dreaded demoness of that region, Mīnākṣī. The latter, doubtless, was an ancient queen who was slain in war, and was soon exalted to the highest place in the Dravidian pantheon. By this marriage the Aryan cult of the north was wedded to the supreme faith of the south, and the great annual marriage-festival of the temple celebrates and perpetuates the union of the two diverse cults in that region. In that most popular festival there is another interesting feature: Mīnākṣī is said to be the sister of Alahan, a popular Vaiṣṇava demon-deity a few miles from Madura, and this brother comes to attend the wedding ceremonies of his sister at Madura; but, unfortunately, he arrives a day late, and is so incensed by the fact that he will not enter the city or temple; his idol is thus kept for three days on the outskirts of the town, during which period all the people, both Saivites and Vaiṣṇavites, fraternize together and bring their offerings to the aggrieved god. Thus, upon this occasion, we find the three cults of that region, Saivism, Vaiṣṇavism, and demonolatry, most strikingly brought together.

In many ways the worship of this famous Hindu temple reveals a fact which outsiders can understand only with much difficulty. In a certain way, all the Dravidian people are a part of Hinduism and are loyal to that faith. But it is a Hinduism which is completely impregnated with Dravidian and animistic ideas. The worship of the Aryan deities in S. India is a pleasing pastime; but the people are still obsessed with the fear of their myriad demons, and find their chief religious concern in appeasing them in the many demon shrines which are found in every town and village. Even Kālī, the chief consort of Siva, who also finds a prominent place in this temple, is so Dravidianized and demonized with a bloodthirsty passion that no one can separate her from the many Dravidian *ammans*, or demonesses, who haunt that region and terrorize the whole community.

It is thus that we learn what the amorphous thing called Hinduism is in S. India. In outward form it poses as an Aryan cult, but in its inner spirit it reveals the pervasive animistic genius which has characterized the Dravidian mind and heart from time immemorial. The Aryan has given to the religion its outer form and *éclat*; but the Dravidian has retained and conveyed into it all the animism which his ancestors entertained and practised. It is largely the spirit of the south robed in the garb of the north. The Madura temple furnishes one of the best illustrations of this animistic type of Hinduism.

LITERATURE.—J. Fergusson, *Hist. of Indian and Eastern Architecture*,[2] London, 1910; W. Francis, *District Gazetteer*, Madras, 1906; M. Monier-Williams, *Hinduism*, London, 1877; A. Barth, *The Religions of India*, do. 1882; E. W. Hopkins, *The Religions of India*, do. 1896.

J. P. JONES.

MÆNADS.—The character of the Mænads was long a subject upon which the most mistaken ideas prevailed. The accounts of them given by poets, mythographers, and historians were all mingled together, and were, moreover, mixed up indiscriminately with the representations of the cult of Dionysus in art, while, again, these artistic products were not submitted to any process of critical analysis. Thus arose the conception of a wildly fantastic religious service celebrated by delirious women in nearly all parts of Greece and Asia Minor. The first to reduce the literary and artistic data to order, and to give a clear impression of the development and character of the Dionysus-cult, was A. Rapp, in his 'Die Mänade im griechischen Kultus, in der Kunst und Poesie' (*Rhein. Mus.* xxvii. [1872] 1–22, 562–611; cf. Roscher, ii. 2243–2283). Then at length the powerful movement introduced into Greece by the new deity, and the influence of that movement upon the spiritual life of the people, were exhaustively delineated by E. Rohde (*Psyche*[4], Tübingen, 1907, ii. 5 ff.). The researches of the folklorists among other peoples have also brought to light interesting parallels to the ancient Dionysian cult and customs; but great caution must be exercised with regard to the ideas of 'vegetation deities,' 'spirits of fertility,' etc., to which the modern tendency to trace analogies everywhere has given rise (cf., *e.g.*, O. Gruppe, *Griechische Mythologie und Religionsgeschichte*, Munich, 1906, p. 905 f.).

Dionysus, the lord of the Mænads, of the 'Bacchæ,' so named after him, was, as is now universally recognized, and as was already known to Aristarchus, not originally a Greek deity, but was derived from Thrace (cf. Herod. v. 7, and the notes of W. W. How and J. Wells, London, 1912), where he was worshipped under the name of Sabos or Sabazios (schol. Aristoph. *Vespæ*, 9 ff.). It is true that Sabazios is also spoken of as a Phrygian deity (reff. in Rohde, ii. 7, note 3), but, as the Thracians and the Phrygians were, in the judgment of the ancients, closely related peoples, we need not be surprised that the worship of the Phrygian national goddess Cybele should show so many points of contact with the forms of the Thracian cult of Dionysus. The latter was a non-Greek cult which was celebrated upon the mountain heights of Thrace in the winter of every alternate year (and in Greece, therefore, subsequently called the τριετηρίς). At these celebrations women danced in wild frenzy amid the glare of torches, whirling dizzily to the clangour of rude music—the clashing of bronze vessels, the hollow roll of large drums (cf. CYBELE), the shrill whistling of flutes—and with loud shouts of εὖ οἶ (which afterwards became *euhoe*, *evoe*, and finally *evoë*). These raving creatures (μαινάδες; used generically as early as Hom. *Il.* xxii. 460), with their dishevelled hair streaming in the wind, were clothed in long flowing βασσάραι (whence they were also called Βασσαρίδες), over which they wore the νεβρίς (cf. Æsch. frag. 64, and the pictorial representations), and in their hands they carried serpents (animals sacred to Sabazios [Theophr. *Char.* xxx. 4; cf. the πομπή of Ptolemy II. in Athenæus, 198 C, etc.]), daggers, or thyrsi. In their religious frenzy they threw themselves upon the sacrificial animals, tearing them in pieces with their teeth (Eur. *Bacch.* 736 ff., etc.; but cf. the singular explanation of the practice in Gruppe, p. 731 f.). In these riotous scenes the fumes of wine played no part; the women used no strong drink to stimulate their frenzy, but, on the contrary, were able to work themselves into such a condition of over-excitement as would bring about the ecstatic state. Their delirium was regarded as a means of compelling their god to appear (Eur. *Bacch.* 141 ff., 306 f.; Paus. VI. xxvi. 1: καὶ τὸν θεὸν σφισιν ἐπιφοιτᾶν ἐς τῶν Θυίων τὴν ἑορτὴν λέγουσιν). A notable analogy to these practices is found in the leaping of the Perchtas in the Tyrol; here, on Shrove Tuesday (cf. art. CARNIVAL, vol. iii. p. 225 ff., esp. p. 228[a]), the Perchtas (so named, like the Bacchæ, after the deity whom they thus honour) work themselves into a frenzy. Their raving is carried to such a pitch that at length they think that they actually see Percht herself in their midst, and it is even said that she has sometimes mangled her worshippers (F. A. Voigt, in Roscher, i. 1041 f.).

This tumultuous cult, whose votaries were also called Κλώδωνες and Μιμαλλόνες, maintained itself till later times; even Queen Olympias, the mother of Alexander the Great, was devoted to the wild practices of the Thracian religion, and her tame snakes, which would suddenly wriggle out from amongst the ivy or from the sacred winnowing-fans, not seldom startled the court of Philip (Plut. *Alex.* 2). In that form, however, the cult certainly met with opposition as it spread through Greece. What mythology tells us, now of Lycurgus and the struggle which he made against Dionysus and his τιθῆναι (so Hom. *Il.* vi. 132 ff.; concrete details regarding the τιθῆναι are lacking), as of Pentheus, and now of the Minyads and the Prœtids, shows at least that at some time the Bacchus cult had once or oftener encountered enemies in various districts to which it spread. Its complete triumph throughout almost the whole of Greece is, of course, a commonplace of history. The new religion, with its outlandish features, came to be so thoroughly naturalized that its alien origin was almost forgotten: Herodotus speaks (iv. 79) of the Bacchic frenzy as a peculiarly Hellenic characteristic in contrast to the practices of other lands; the Spartan Mænads, the δύσμαιναι, raved upon the heights of Taygetus (reff., *e.g.*, in Rohde, ii. 45, note 2); and Galen (*de Antid.* 8, vol. xiv. 45 [Kühn]) could speak of snake-rending as still practised at the Bacchic festivals.

But the educative power of Delphi was now at work, and Apollo exercised his softening influence upon the raging Bacchus. It was with very different rites that the women performed their worship of Bacchus on Mt. Parnassus. Here, every two years, about the time of the shortest day, the Thyiads 'awaked' Λικνίτης, the god who lies in the sacred winnowing-fan (Plut. *de Is. et Osir.* xxxv.); here (Rapp, *Rhein. Mus.* xxvii. 5) a caste of priestesses was employed, who attended to the rites of this winter festival on Parnassus. With such rites, too, the Attic Thyiads celebrated at similar intervals the orgies of the god at Delphi. Thus the celebration had now to do not with Dionysus only, but with Apollo as well (Paus. x. xxxii. 7). Of this cult, whose Bacchic ecstasy had been refined by Apollonian moderation, we find a picture in the celebrated chorus of the *Antigone* of Sophocles (1126 ff.), which tells indeed of the torch-swinging Θυῖαι and of their dancing by night upon Parnassus, but does not speak of the mad fury of the Thracian observance—the reason being that in the precincts of Delphi this element no longer had a place. Then Euripides, who, in contemplating the unrestrained frenzy imported from the North, broadened and enriched that poetic sense which understands all, produced a permanent memorial of the thrillingly graceful activities of the Mænads. In his *Bacchæ* the actual and the poetic run naturally into each other. Here the enthusiastic troops of women, crowned with wreaths of ivy and smilax, garbed in the many-coloured νεβρίς, and holding the thyrsus in their hands, plunge madly through the mountains, and fall to the ground in the fullness of their rapture; while, again, they rush to the slaughter of the goats, the ground flows with milk and wine, and the stroke of the thyrsus upon the rock causes a spring to break forth; ferocious animals are on a friendly footing with the Mænads, who offer the breast to fawns and young wolves, while ill-disposed men flee before the hurtling thyrsus (*Bacch.*, *passim*).

Investigators have had great difficulties also with the portrayal of the Bacchus cult in art. In this field, too, it was necessary to disengage the mythological aspects from the presentation of the real. As a whole, it is only the general impression to be found here that corresponds to the literary account. On the artistic side it is pre-eminently the Attic vases that merit consideration. On the earlier specimens of these we see the orgiastic dancing of women to the cadence of flutes; later additions are the swinging of torches, the beating of drums, and the head thrown back upon the shoulders. According to the more recent explanation, the celebration thus represented is the Lenæa, the festival of the raving women (λῆναι), which had been brought from Bœotia (on all this cf. A. Frickenhaus, *Lenäenvasen* [*Programm zum Winckelmannsfeste der archäolog. Gesellsch.* lxxii.], Berlin, 1912). With these designs are mingled others showing a distinct background of mythology, and here we also find names of the Mænads, such as Μαι[νάς], Θηρώ, etc. (cf. C. Fränkel, *Satyr- und Bakchennamen auf Vasenbildern*, Halle, 1912). Then later art brought the depictment of that furious, almost hysterical, ecstasy to its most vigorous expression, and even extended it, most unnaturally, to the uncouth satyrs; this intense expression of feeling is seen in its finest form in the Mænads of Scopas (M. Treu, in *Mélanges Perrot*, Paris, 1902, p. 317 ff.). Nearly everywhere in art, however, the representation of the Mænads is an expression of early religious emotion, and the vase-paintings designedly set forth the strict reserve of the Bacchæ in contrast to the loose merry-making of the satyrs. The introduction of the Bacchic procession, with its troops of men and women rolling wantonly along, and the transformation of the primitive festival, attended by females only, into a turbulent orgy were the work of the superficial art of the Hellenistic age.

LITERATURE.—This has been sufficiently indicated in the article.

J. GEFFCKEN.

MAGADHA.—Magadha, an ancient kingdom in India, was the scene of the greater part of Buddha's preaching and the last stronghold of his faith in India. It was equivalent to the modern districts of Patna, Gayā, and Shāhābād in S. Bihār. The name Bihār itself, which is now that of a vast district, is evidence of the predominance of Buddhism in these lands, for it was originally the name of a town with a celebrated Buddhist monastery (Skr. *vihāra*). Buddha was not born in Magadha, but in the country to the north of it, at the grove of Lumbinī (*q.v.*), near Kapilavastu (*q.v.*), the Śākya capital in the Nepālese Tarāi. Magadha was the home and the nucleus of two of the greatest Indian empires, the Maurya and the Gupta. It is celebrated in Sanskrit literature as one of the richest, most fertile, and best irrigated districts in India. As the home of Buddhism and Jainism, it is full of archæological remains of the greatest religious interest.

Its earliest capital was a very ancient hill fortress named Girivraja (Pāli Giribbaja), built, according to tradition, by an architect named Mahāgovinda; its place was taken in the 6th cent. B.C. by the better known Rājagṛha (Pāli Rājagaha), built at the foot of hills on which Girivraja stood; Rājagṛha is the modern Rājgēr, which, however, stands about a mile to the south. Its walls still exist, and are probably the oldest stone buildings in India. Rājagṛha had reached its zenith about Buddha's time, soon after which it began to decline with the growth of Pāṭaliputra (the modern Patna). The modern town of Gayā, although now a place of pilgrimage for Hindus, has no ancient religious associations; 7 miles to the south, however, are the remains of Bodh (Buddh) Gayā (see GAYĀ, vol. vi. p. 181 ff.), one of the most interesting sites in India, where Gautama Śākyamuni finally attained enlightenment (*bodhi*). To the south of Gayā is the hill of Dhongra, the Prāgbodhi (Po-lo-ki-pu-ti) of Hiuen Tsiang, with a cave in which Buddha once rested. Punāwān, 14 miles east of Gayā, is rich in Buddhist sculptures; to the south of it is Hasrā hill, which has been identified with the Kukkuṭapādagiri of the Chinese pilgrims.

A. Cunningham, however, recognizes the latter in Kurkihār, which lies some miles to the north. Gunerī, Dharawat, and Kavadal are all rich in Buddhist remains, the last-named with a colossal stone image of Buddha. Jetian, or Jakhtiban, is the Yaṣṭivana ('bamboo-forest') of Buddha's wanderings; near it at Tapoban are the hot springs, visited by Hiuen Tsiang, at which Buddha bathed. In this neighbourhood the Chinese pilgrim visited a cave with a stone which had been used by Indra and Brahmā for pounding sandalwood to anoint Buddha's body. In the side of Baibhār hill, near Rājgēr, was the Sattapaṇṇi cave in which the first Buddhist synod met in 543 B.C.; according to Cunningham,[1] this cave is the modern Son Bhāndār cave on the southern side of the hill. On the adjacent hill of Ratnāgiri is the *pipal*-tree cave of Fa-Hian in which Buddha used to meditate after his meals. On the top of this hill there still is a small Jain temple; Ratnāgiri is the Pandao of the Pāli chroniclers and the Ṛṣigiri of the *Mahābhārata*. The extensive ruins at the modern Baragaon are the ancient Nālandā (*q.v.*), the greatest centre of Buddhist learning in ancient India. Near Giriak on the Panchāna river a bathing festival is held annually to commemorate Kṛṣṇa's crossing of the river here on his way to challenge Jarāsandha. Sasaran, Monghyr, and Shergarh are rich in relics of Muhammadan architecture. At Sītāmarhi is a cave with which a legend of Sītā is associated. The annual bathing festival of Sonpur, held in November at the junction of the Gandak and the Ganges, is one of the oldest and most popular in India; it was here that Viṣṇu rescued the elephant from the crocodile, and here Rāma built a temple. At Afsar there is a fine sculpture of the *varāha* (boar) *avatār* of Viṣṇu.

LITERATURE.—T. W. Rhys Davids, *Buddhist India*², London, 1905; A. Cunningham, *Ancient Geography of India*, do. 1871; J. Legge, *Travels of Fa-hien*, Oxford, 1886; T. W. Watters, *On Yuan Chwang's Travels*, London, 1904–05; *IGI*, *passim*.

J. ALLAN.

MAGAS.—See SAURAS AND MAGAS.

MAGH.—Magh, or, popularly, Mugh, Mugg, is the designation of a group of Indo-Chinese tribes, numbering 128,545 at the Census of 1911, and practically all confined to Bengal. The derivation of the name is uncertain. A. P. Phayre (*Hist. of Burma*, London, 1884, p. 47; cf. H. Yule and A. C. Burnell, *Hobson-Jobson*², do. 1903, p. 594) connects it with Magadha, the ancient name of modern Bihār, while L. Vivien de St. Martin (J. W. McCrindle, *Ancient India as described by Megasthenes and Arrian*, Calcutta, 1877, p. 133, note), identified the Magh with the Maccocalingæ of Pliny (*HN* VI. xxi. 8).

'All Maghs are Buddhists of the Southern school, and regard the Northern Buddhists of Tibet as wholly unorthodox. The wilder sections of the Thongchas, however, retain some vestiges of an earlier animistic faith, which bids them sacrifice cattle, goats, and swine, and make offerings of rice, fruits, and flowers to the spirits of hill and river. Among the Maramagris, on the other hand, the tendency is to follow after modern Hinduism, particularly in its Tantric developments, and to add the gross worship of Siva and Durga to the simple observances prescribed by their own communion. It thus comes to pass that while the Buddhist *Phungyis* or *Rdolis* are the recognized priests of all the tribes, considerable respect is shown to Brahmans, who are frequently employed to determine auspicious days for particular actions, and to assist in the worship of the Hindu gods. Among the Thongchas old women often devote themselves to the service of religion, and although not charged with special ceremonial functions, are regarded as in some sense priestesses, and are called by the distinctive name *lerdama*' (H. H. Risley, *TC*, Calcutta, 1891, ii. 33).

The people thus described are the Khyoungtha of the hill tracts of Chittagong, who, as T. H. Lewin states (*Hill Tracts of Chittagong*, Calcutta, 1869, p. 37, *Wild Races of S.-E. India*, London, 1870, p. 95), are known to the Bengalis of the plains as 'Hill Mugh,' and are to be carefully distinguished from the true Maghs of the Chittagong District, otherwise called Rājbansī, who are the offspring of Bengali women by Burmans, when the latter possessed Chittagong. They supply the famous Magh cooks, well known in Calcutta and other parts of Bengal. The true Khyoungtha are Buddhists and believe in the doctrine of metempsychosis or transmigration of souls; but their Buddhist worship is of a simple character—the presence of a priest is not indispensable; prayers are made and offerings of flowers, food, etc., are placed before the shrine of Gautama by the people themselves. Many villages have no priest, except wandering friars, who are not so much ministers of religion as recipients of alms. Each village has a temple (*khiong*), a bamboo structure built under the shade of some trees, inside which, on a small raised platform of bamboos, stands an image of Gautama, made either of gilded wood or of alabaster, the figure being in a sitting posture, with a pagoda-shaped headdress indicative of superior power. Before it the village girls lay offerings of flowers and rice every morning, and, at the same time, bring the daily food of any priest or wayfarer who may be resting there. By the side of the image hangs a small stand of bells, which each villager, after removing his turban and bowing to the semblance of the Teacher, rings to announce his presence. Each one prays for himself, except that now and again a father may be seen leading his young son by the hand and teaching him how to pray. Each year, before the commencement of the burning of the jungle for the purpose of sowing their crops, the boys are clothed in yellow robes of the priesthood, have their heads shaved, and go through a rite before a priest which seems to be an assumption on their part of religious responsibilities. Women do not participate in this rite; but it is common for a man to perform it two or three times during his life. If a relative is sick, or he himself has escaped any danger, he performs the ceremony as a supplication or as an acknowledgment of the mercies which he has received.

LITERATURE.—The authorities are quoted in the article.

W. CROOKE.

MAGI.—I. The name (Gr. Μάγος, Lat. *Magus*, from Old Pers. *Magu*) is familiar to us from the classical writers, and from two appearances in the NT. It meets us first on the Behistān Inscription of Darius, where the king describes (*Bh.* [Pers. text] i. 35 ff.) the usurpation of 'Gaumata the Magus' (*Gaumāta tya Maguš*) and his own successful plot against him, by which he restored the Achæmenian dynasty to its ancient throne. There is nothing in the inscription to show what *Magu* meant, and we must fall back on our Greek sources, Herodotus first, and the rest *longo intervallo*. In Herod. i. 101 we are told that Ἀριζαντοί, Μάγοι, and four others were Μήδων γένεα. The six names were explained as Aryan caste-titles by J. Oppert long ago (*Le Peuple et la langue des Mèdes*, Paris, 1879, p. 7), and again, on different lines, by A. J. Carnoy (*Muséon*, new ser., ix. [1908] 121 ff.); the tolerable certainty that five are Aryan makes a strong presumption that Μάγος must be interpreted from the same language group.

The etymology, however, must be left undecided. Putting aside some attempts of Semitists to claim it, we have at least two plausible accounts from the Indo-European side. Carnoy (*loc. cit.*) compares μηχανή and Μαχάων with the meaning 'helper, healer,' while Moulton (*The Thinker*, ii. [1892] 491; see his *Early Zoroastrianism*, pp. 428–430) connects Gothic *magus*, O. Ir. *mug*—a connexion which Carnoy accepts, but in a different sense. The Gothic word translates τέκνον once, and παῖς (='servant') elsewhere. The latter meaning is that of the Irish word; we may probably compare the development of our 'maid' and local uses of 'boy.' That 'boy' is the primitive meaning is confirmed by the Later Avestan *maγava*, 'unmarried.' The significant fact that *moγu* (=O. Pers. *magu*) occurs only once in the Avesta, and that in a prose passage (*Ys.* lxv. 7)

[1] *Ancient Geography of India*, p. 463.

obviously late, speaks for the meaning 'servant'; the Magi were thus the leading tribe of the aboriginal population, enslaved or reduced to political subjection by the invading Aryans. But the whole history of the word is open to great uncertainty. The authority of T. Nöldeke and C. Bezold (*ap.* C. Bartholomae, *Altiran. Wörterbuch*, Strassburg, 1904, p. 1111) may be referred to against the Semitic claim.

2. While the Magi were thus a distinct caste of Medians, and apparently the recognized leaders of the subject population in the time of Aryan (Persian) dominion, there is no reason for doubt that their ascendancy was essentially religious, like that of the Brāhmans in India. Darius writes of his repairing temples which the Magus had destroyed (*Bh.* [Pers. text] i. 63–66), and so far the inscription favours the existence of a marked difference of religion—of course, its scanty reference does not definitely prove anything one way or another. But the testimony of Herodotus and all later classical writers is so unanimous and precise that we need no other. It would appear that, having failed in their bold bid for political supremacy, as leaders of the people against Aryan invaders, they began to build up power upon their popular vogue as shamans. It was easy to insinuate themselves into the open place of priest in the unreformed Iranian nature-worship, as described most accurately by Herodotus (i. 131 ff.); they had only to emphasize certain clear points of resemblance between their own religion and that of the Aryans, veneration of the sun and of fire being the chief. There is one important detail of ritual in which we can with high probability trace an appearance of Magianism separate from Aryan connexions at a very early date. Ezk $8^{16f.}$ describes, as the greatest of three 'abominations' that had brought Jahweh's wrath on Jerusalem, the sun-worship of men in eastward position, who 'put the branch to the nose.' To hold a bough before the face in solar cultus is a natural action; its special interest for us lies in its coincidence with the Parsi use of the *barsom* (*q.v.*), a bunch of tamarisk twigs held by the priest before his face in worship. The name, and the peculiar use of the verb 'spread' to describe the preparation of the instrument, alike take us to something quite different—the Aryan carpet of stalks of tender grass (Herod. i. 132) on which the offering was laid (Skr. *barhiṣ*, Av. *baresman*). We may infer that the Magi adapted the Aryan use to their own by prescribing that a bunch of the sacred stalks should be picked up from the ground and held reverentially before the face.

3. This notice enables us to trace the Magi in a separate activity as far back as 591 B.C., when they seem to have secured proselytes in Judæa. This is quite in keeping with what we know of them. Their contemporary appearance in Babylon is probably attested by Jer $39^{3.13}$, where 'the Rab-Mag' appears among Nebuchadrezzar's officers (for alternative views of Rab-Mag see the *Oxford Lexicon* and *EBi*, *s.v.*). H. Zimmern and H. Winckler (*KAT*³, 416) explain the Rab-Mag's name, Nergal-sharezer, as 'Nergal, protect the king'; and in their account of Nergal they expressly compare Ahriman, who in the Later Avesta has features which could be very easily connected with Babylon. The head of a caste of exorcists, who by their charms can keep the Satan from harming the king, is wholly in place at court. We compare at once the apotropæic functions of the Magi in Plutarch, *de Is. et Osir.* 46. We may add to this small but important peculiarity several other traits by which the Magi may be distinguished from the Persians in religion, whether in the earlier or the later stages of what we now call Parsiism. First come two conspicuous features recognized from the first by Greek writers as Magian and not Persian: (1) their exposure of the bodies of the dead to birds and carrion dogs was distinguished by Herodotus (i. 140) from the Persian custom of burial after encasing in wax. It has pronounced aboriginal affinities, and was neither Semitic nor (almost certainly) Aryan. Coupled with this was (2) their insistence on next-of-kin marriage, which they belauded extravagantly for its accumulations of merit. It was never accepted by the Persians, and never found its way into the Avesta (see on this Moulton, p. 205 f.), first appearing in the Pahlavi writings of the Sasanian age as a precept of developed Parsiism. But modern Parsiism repudiates it with the utmost emphasis, and its scholars attempt the heroic but impossible task of denying that their predecessors meant anything of the kind (see art. MARRIAGE [Iranian], § **2**). (3) The very name of *magic* attests the strength of their association, in the mind of antiquity, with an accomplishment altogether ignored in the Avesta, and never countenanced in Parsiism. Equally ignored is (4) *oneiromancy*. The Magi were renowned for their skill in divining by dreams; but the very word for dream occurs only once in the Later Avesta (*Yt.* xiii. 104), and there is no hint that dreams were ever studied. Closely linked with this is (5) *astrology*, with which the Magi were traditionally credited. But the Avesta, while it has plenty of star-lore, and some mythology, has never a hint of ideas belonging to astrological conceptions. A curious point under this head is the inconsistent views of the planets held in the later Parsi Scriptures (the Avesta has nothing one way or the other). On one side there is the official view that planets were malign; on the other we find them named by the names of the good *yazatas*, including Ormazd himself. These names are simply equivalents for the Babylonian terms, like those which we ourselves have taken over through the later Greeks and the Romans, so that the date is post-Avestan. But it seems probable that the Magi put the planets into the creation of Ahriman because of their irregular motion, while the Parsis generally believed in their beneficence. There is the same kind of discrepancy in (6) the views of *mountains*, which in Aryan and Semitic mythology alike were venerated as divine, but by the Magi were treated as blots on the symmetry of creation, to be smoothed out when the Regeneration came. It will be seen that most of these peculiar traits, by which we may distinguish the Magi from the people whose religion they adopted and adapted, are incompatible with either Aryan or Semitic affiliation, or at least do not suggest the one or the other. It seems a fair inference that they were aboriginal Medians, who, like the Elamites, belonged to neither of the two great races which divided Nearer Asia between them. To what stock they belonged we may not be able to say. L. H. Gray (*ExpT* xxv. [1914] 257) points out that there were Magas in India, about whom we hear in the *Bhaviṣya Purāṇa* and the *Bṛhatsaṁhitā*; he thinks that these were probably Magians, accepting the general view of them which has been outlined above, and he believes them to be immigrants to India from Persia.[1]

It must be premised that the foregoing view of the ethnography of the Magi and their religious origins is to some extent new, and has not yet had the benefit of full discussion. The extent of approval expressed by L. C. Casartelli (*Manchester Guardian*, Dec. 23, 1913) and L. H. Gray (*loc. cit.*) encourages the writer to epitomize here the thesis set forth in his *Early Zoroastrianism*, chs. vi. and vii. (cf. also K. Geldner, in *ThLZ* xxxix. [1914] 290).

4. Pursuing this thesis further, we are led to credit the Magi with all that is fairly called 'dualistic' in Parsiism. There is nothing really

[1] It may be noted that a Skr. *Maga* cannot be directly equated with Iranian *Magu*; but *Magu* may be borrowed as a foreign word with altered declension (the form *Magu* also occurs in the *Bhav. Pur.*). This would imply an Iranian origin, which suits our theory. See, on the Magas, art. SAURAS AND MAGAS.

dualistic in Zarathushtra's *Gāthās*. The very name of Ahriman (*angra mainyu*, 'enemy spirit'; see art. AHRIMAN) occurs only once there (*Ys.* xlv. 2), as a casual epithet and not a fixed title. The good and evil spirits make their choice in the beginning, but there is never any real question as to the issue of the strife between them; one whose perpetual counsel is 'Resist the devil and he will flee' can never be called a dualist. But the Magi, on Plutarch's express testimony, offered sacrifices to Ahriman.[1] The practice is entirely absent from the Avesta—a fact that does not discredit Plutarch, but only shows the survival of distinct usages among the Magi, whose genius is well suited by the mechanical division of the world into creations of Ormazd and creations of Ahriman. This is practically absent from the *Gāthās*, and even from the *Yashts*, where a pure Iranian nature-worship shows small sign of influence from Zarathushtra on the one hand or the Magi on the other. The prose Avesta (excluding the early *Gāthā haptanghaitī*)—which by the loss of metre and the presence of much dubious grammar proclaims itself composed in a virtually dead language—is full of this dualism. Even words have to be distributed between the two camps; different terms are used for the head, hand, voice, etc., of an Ormazd-worshipper and those of an Ahrimanian. Every *yazata* has a demoniacal opponent; but we note that the balancing is imperfectly completed, and that the fiends are often of manifestly late origin and vague functions, so that we should suppose the work of correlation to have been rather half-heartedly undertaken as a concession to theory. The type of dualism implied suggests affinity with that which apparently called forth the declaration of Is 45^7. The presence of such a system in Babylonia during the Exile suits our view of the Magi as shamans exercising influence far beyond their own land of Media; and the presumption adds something to the case for recognizing the Rab-Mag as an ἀρχίμαγος. We may observe that, if Jahwism emphatically denied this dualistic assigning of darkness to an evil demiurge, Zarathushtra himself was no less clear in his claim that Mazda made the night as well as the day (*Ys.* xliv. 5).

5. We are reduced mainly to conjecture when we ask what was the Magian eschatology. That death must be abolished if Ormazd is at last to conquer Ahriman—*pouru-mahrka*, 'many-slaying,' according to his standing Avestan epithet—seems a natural inference from their first principles. We know, further, that they pictured a regenerate world in which such unsymmetrical features as mountains would disappear, and the earth would become a 'slopeless plain.' But how far they pressed their form of the doctrine of immortality we have no means of knowing. Our early Greek witness, Theopompus, according to an important statement of Diogenes,[2] declared that the Magi taught the future resurrection of men to a deathless existence. This excellent 4th cent. authority may, of course, be describing only the doctrine of Persian religion in his own time, when the Magi were its long-established priests. But the extract apparently connects this immortality with a doctrine that looks rather characteristic of the Magi themselves. The *locus classicus* in Plutarch, already quoted, is ordinarily taken as silent as to any doctrine of a resurrection among the Magi. But E. Böklen (*Die Verwandtschaft der jüdisch-christl. mit der pars. Eschatologie*, Göttingen, 1902, p. 102 ff.) argues that in Plutarch's quotation from Theopompus[1] we should translate 'Hades is to be deserted,' which agrees with the other accounts of the testimony of Theopompus. The absence of any doctrine of immortality in Tobit can hardly be regarded (as in Moulton, p. 416) as a contributory argument. For, whether the book is rightly or wrongly held (as by Moulton, ch. vii. and p. 332 ff., and D. C. Simpson in the Oxford Apocrypha) as containing a Median folk-story re-written by a Jew, we must admit that the adapter was not likely to include that element unless he agreed with it, which, if the date was early, he would not do. It is clear that, if Zarathushtra's eschatology came before Jews during the Exile only in an adaptation determined by Magian ideas, it was very little likely to attract the thinkers of Israel. The common belief that the rise of the doctrine of immortality in post-Exilic Judaism owed some real stimulus to Persian influence becomes less and less probable as the history of early Zoroastrianism is investigated more thoroughly.

6. Such, then, in outline were the Magi as a sacred tribe, so far as our information allows us to isolate them for separate portraiture. Most of what we hear of them naturally belongs rather to the religious system upon which they fastened so tenaciously. As early as the travels of Herodotus, they had compensated for their failure to regain political ascendancy by making themselves indispensable to the ritual of Persian religion. It involved, as we have seen, considerable suppression of beliefs and usages traditional among themselves. These they continued to practise in their own community, with or without attempts at propaganda. They could easily use general similarities between their religion and that of the native Iranians so as to prove to the latter their fitness to serve their altars; and the people to whom they ministered, including a large proportion of their own kin, would be slower to realize how much change the proselytes were bringing to the religion which they so zealously adopted.

7. Later developments of Magianism belong to the history of Zoroastrianism as established under the Sasanian dynasty. It only remains here to add a few words about the Magi as they figure in the Nativity story of our First Gospel. To discuss the historic credibility of that story, or the various theories that have been devised to explain the star, must be left to the Dictionaries of the Bible. Here it suffices to connect the foremost traits of the Magi, as described above, with points in the story of Mt 2. That these Μάγοι ἀπὸ ἀνατολῶν answer to the picture as experts in dream-interpretation and in star-lore is clear. It is noteworthy, therefore, that Mt 2, so far as its testimony goes, isolates the Magi from Persian religion, which, as we saw, has practically no room for either (see art. FRAVASHI, *ad fin.*). This constitutes within its limits a rather striking witness, when we remember how little we are able to discover about the Magi as apart from the religion with which even four centuries earlier they were almost completely identified. Naturally we must not be tempted to make too much of evidence so limited in its range.

LITERATURE.—Greek and Latin *loci classici* are collected in A. Rapp's two papers, *ZDMG* xix. [1865] 1–89 and xx. [1866] 49–140. Those which affect Zoroaster are conveniently printed together in A. V. W. Jackson, *Zoroaster, the Prophet of Ancient Iran*, New York, 1899. The account here given depends largely on the writer's full discussion of the whole subject in *Early Zoroastrianism* (*HL*), London, 1913.

JAMES HOPE MOULTON.

[1] *de Is. et Osir.* 46: 'Zoroaster the Magus . . . taught them to sacrifice to the other [Areimanios] offerings for averting ill, and things of gloom.' The blood of a wolf is specially mentioned. Cf. the Mithraic dedication *DEO ARIMANIO*.

[2] Diog. Laert. *Prooem.* 9, ὃς (sc. Theopompus) καὶ ἀναβιώσεσθαι κατὰ τοὺς Μάγους φησὶ τοὺς ἀνθρώπους καὶ ἔσεσθαι ἀθανάτους. See Moulton, pp. 405, 415 f., for a full discussion.

[1] *de Is. et Osir.* 47: τέλος δ' ἀπολείπεσθαι τὸν Ἅιδην, καὶ τοὺς μὲν ἀνθρώπους εὐδαίμονας ἔσεσθαι, μήτε τροφῆς δεομένους μήτε σκιὰν ποιοῦντας, κτλ. Hades has been usually taken as a name for Ahriman, but this almost demands the alteration of ἀπολείπεσθαι.

MAGIC.

MAGIC (Introductory).—**1. History of the term and problem of its definition.**—In any general treatment of the subject of magic the problem of its definition must occupy the chief place, seeing that it constitutes a veritable storm-centre in the anthropological literature of the present day. As so often happens when a word belonging to the common language, and used in vague and conflicting ways, is taken over by science that it may correspond to some precise concept, theorists interested in different and more or less incompatible concepts claim exclusive rights over the same technical term; so that, if they are at all equally matched, the term becomes for the time being ambiguous, *i.e.*, it answers to more concepts than one. Something of this kind has occurred in regard to the word 'magic.' It may be instructive, then, to begin with a glance at its meaning as a popular expression. It is, of course, the lineal descendant of the Gr. μαγεία and the Lat. *magia*, which in their strictest sense refer simply to the religion, learning, and occult practices of the Persian Magi, or priests of the sect of Zoroaster, in the form in which they became known to the West (see art. MAGI). Such matters, however, being both foreign and ill-understood, would naturally be more or less suspect. Hence the word tends from the first to carry with it the unfavourable associations summed up in the notion of witchcraft (see, for instance, Hesychius, *s.v.* γόης, which he identifies with μάγος, and Pliny, *HN* xxx. 11; and for further references cf. H. Hubert, in Daremberg-Saglio, *s.v.* 'Magia'). These associations the equivalent words in the various languages of modern Europe have never lost. Bacon's attempt to rehabilitate *magia* as natural science in its operative aspect (*de Augmentis scientiarum*, iii. *ad fin.*) proved quite abortive. Thus it comes about that the modern anthropologist in attributing 'magic' to a given people can hardly do so without at the same time implying that it is something inferior and bad—something that, however prevalent it may be, belongs to the lower levels or even to the pathology of mind and society. A survey of representative views on the subject will bring out the fact that, in this respect at least, most, if not all, theories tend to be at one.

2. Representative views.—As far back as 1870 E. B. Tylor laid it down that the 'confusion of objective with subjective connexion, . . . so uniform in principle, though so various in details, . . . may be applied to explain one branch after another of the arts of the sorcerer and diviner, till it almost seems as though we were coming near the end of his list, and might set down practices not based on this mental process, as exceptions to a general rule' (*Researches into the Early Hist. of Mankind*, p. 129). He adds that the same state of mind will account for tabus, many of the food-prejudices of the savage, for instance, depending on the belief that the qualities of the eaten pass into the eater (*ib.* p. 133). Such an attitude of mind he characterizes as one of 'gross superstition and delusion' (*ib.* p. 119), even while allowing that at a stage of development when human life 'was more like a long dream' such a system of error was perfectly 'intelligible' (*ib.* 139 f.). He pursues the same line of explanation in his later work, *Primitive Culture*, where magic is described as 'occult science,' *i.e.* a 'pseudo-science' (3rd ed., i. 112, 119). 'The principal key to the understanding of occult science is to consider it as based on the association of ideas, a faculty which lies at the very foundation of human reason, but in no small degree of human unreason also' (i. 115 f.). He adds a disquisition on the futility of magic arts, in which he maintains that 'in the whole monstrous farrago' there is practically no truth or value whatever (i. 133). Meanwhile, he holds that the laws of mind are as unchanging as the laws of chemical combination, so that 'the thing that has been will be' (i. 159). The 'symbolic magic' of the savage and modern spiritualism are alike hurtful superstitions born of fallacies to which the human mind is naturally prone (see ch. iv., *passim*, esp. *ad fin.*).

J. G. Frazer (*The Golden Bough*) maintains a position which in most respects is identical with that of Tylor. In the first edition (1890) he credits primitive man with two views of the world that exist side by side, the one view being that it is worked by personal beings acting on impulses and motives like his own, the other view amounting in germ to the conception of nature as a series of events occurring in an invariable order without the intervention of personal agency. The latter is the view involved in sympathetic magic (GB^1 i. 9), though the savage acts on it, not only in magic art, but in much of the business of daily life (*ib.* 31). In the second edition (1900) Frazer lays far more stress on the 'fundamental distinction and even opposition of principle between magic and religion,' being influenced especially by the theories of H. Oldenberg (*Die Religion des Veda*, Berlin, 1894), F. B. Jevons (*Introduction to the History of Religion*, London, 1896), and A. C. Lyall (*Asiatic Studies*, 1st ser., London, 1899). More than that, he is now disposed to affirm that, 'in the evolution of thought, magic, as representing a lower intellectual stratum, has probably everywhere preceded religion' (GB^2 i. p. xvi). He still represents magic as 'next of kin to science,' since the two have in common the 'general assumption of a succession of events determined by law.' Magic is nevertheless only 'the bastard sister of science.'

'All magic is necessarily false and barren; for were it ever to become true and fruitful, it would no longer be magic but science.'

All cases of sympathetic magic resolve themselves on analysis into mistaken applications of the laws of the association of ideas by similarity and contiguity.

'Legitimately applied' these same principles 'yield science; illegitimately applied they yield magic' (*ib.* p. 62).

Religion, on the other hand, 'is opposed in principle both to magic and to science,' since its fundamental assumption is that the course of nature and of human life is controlled by personal beings superior to man. Towards such beings conciliation must be employed, whereas to exert mechanical control is the object of magic and science, though the former often essays to control spirits, treating them, however, exactly as if they were inanimate agents (*ib.* p. 63 f.). Finally, the human race are assumed to have passed through an 'intellectual phase,' in which they 'attempted to force the great powers of nature to do their pleasure,' and had not yet thought of courting their favour by offerings and prayer. Such an 'age of magic' finally gave place to an 'age of religion' only because mankind at length were led by experience to a 'tardy recognition of the inherent falsehood and barrenness of magic,' whereupon the more thoughtful part of them cast about for a truer theory of nature (*ib.* pp. 73, 75). In the third edition (1911) these main theses are retained, but the following scheme of the principal branches of magic (taken over from *Lectures on the Early History of the Kingship*, ch. ii.) is added, in accordance with the view that magic is simply misapplied association of ideas:

- **Sympathetic Magic** (*Law of Sympathy*)
  - **Homœopathic Magic** (*Law of Similarity*)
  - **Contagious Magic** (*Law of Contact*),

while 'the whole erroneous system, both theoretical and practical,' which answers to the name of magic is classified under aspects according to the following tabular form:

- **Magic**
  - **Theoretical** (Magic as a pseudo-science)
  - **Practical** (Magic as a pseudo-art)
    - **Positive Magic** or **Sorcery**
    - **Negative Magic** or **Tabu.**

(See *GB*³, pt. i., *The Magic Art*, i. 54 and 113.)

The view that tabu is a negative magic did not appear in earlier editions of *The Golden Bough.* Frazer holds that, if not the whole doctrine of tabu, at all events a large part of it, would seem to be but a special application of sympathetic magic, with its two great laws of similarity and contact (*ib.* i. 111 n.).

E. S. Hartland (*Ritual and Belief*, London, 1914) enters on a full discussion of 'The Relations of Religion and Magic' (p. 26 ff.). He insists at the outset that they spring from a common root.

'I venture to suggest that in man's emotional response to his environment, in his interpretation in the terms of personality of the objects which encountered his attention, and in their investiture by him with potentiality, atmosphere, *orenda, mana*—call it by what name you will—we have the common root of magic and religion' (p. 66).

Correspondingly, magician and priest are differentiated from a common type, namely, the medicine-man.

'Roughly and provisionally it may be said that the professional magician is he who in the course of the evolution of society, by birth, by purchase, or by study and practice in the conventional methods, has acquired the most powerful *orenda.* Similarly, the professional priest is he who in these ways, or by prayer and fasting, has obtained the favour of the imaginary personages believed to influence or control the affairs of men—who has, in a word, possessed himself of their *orenda.* The union of these two professions in one person is not adventitious; it is probably fundamental' (p. 95 f.).

Hartland, while thus differing from Frazer on the question of origin, is disposed in other respects to follow the latter's method of delimiting magic and religion.

Magic 'conveys the notion of power, by whatsoever means acquired, wielded by the magician as his own, and not as that of a higher being whose coöperation is only obtained by supplication and self-abasement' (p. 86).

On his view prayers and sacrifices are magical processes just in so far as a constraining power is attributed to them; and he asks, 'Have analogous beliefs in the magical powers of a rite even yet disappeared from Christianity?' (p. 87).

Religion, on the other hand, is 'confined to cultual systems, whose objects, so far as they are personal, are endowed with free will, are to be approached with true worship, and may or may not grant the prayers of their suppliants. . . . Where the object is impersonal, or is but vaguely personal, it is none the less treated with reverence and submission, as something transcending man; it is the object of an emotional attitude, actively directed towards it. The object thus, even where it is not personal, tends to become so' (p. 88).

A. Lehmann of Copenhagen (*Aberglaube und Zauberei von den ältesten Zeiten an bis in die Gegenwart*, Stuttgart, 1898) defines superstition (*Aberglaube*) as any belief which either fails to obtain authorization from a given religion or stands in contradiction with the scientific conception of nature prevailing at a given time. Correspondingly, magic or sorcery (*Magie oder Zauberei*) is any practice which is engendered by superstition, or is explained in terms of superstitious notions (p. 6 f.). By insisting on the essential relativity of these two ideas he claims to have avoided many difficulties that puzzled former inquirers. For instance, if it be asked how magic is to be distinguished from miracle, the reply is that it is all a question of standpoint, Aaron performing miracles while his Egyptian rivals are mere magicians (p. 9). For the rest, he finds two more or less independent theories to be equally at the back of magical practice, namely, the spiritist, which relies on the intermediation of personal agents, and the occultist, which calls into play mysterious powers of nature (p. 314).

H. Hubert and M. Mauss ('Esquisse d'une théorie générale de la magie,' in *ASoc* vii. [1904]) start from the conception of rites. Rites are traditional acts that are efficacious in a non-mechanical way, thus involving the notion of *mana* (*q.v.*), or wonder-working power (p. 14; cf. p. 138). Such a notion underlies the idea of the sacred as implied in a religious rite like sacrifice. A magical rite, though non-religious, involves ideas of the same order (p. 2 f.). The differentia of magical rites consists in the fact that they do not form part of an organized cult, and therefore tend to be regarded by the society concerned as illicit (p. 19). Thus religion and magic tend to stand to one another as two poles representing severally the social and the anti-social ways of trafficking with the miraculous. Finally, magic, as being always the outcast of society, becomes charged with all the effects of decomposition and rejection, and so is gradually differentiated from religion more and more. This very ingenious and weighty study of magic, to which a short sketch cannot pretend to do justice, is made, it must be remembered, from a strictly sociological standpoint, and throughout regards magic and religion not as phases of mind, but as social institutions, having as such a reality of their own determinable in terms of form and function.

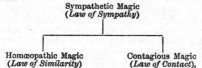

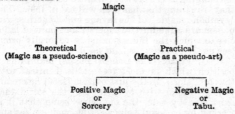

Arnold van Gennep (*Les Rites de passage*, Paris, 1909) treats the magico-religious as an indivisible whole, distinguishing only between the theoretical and the practical activities which it comprises, and assigning the term 'religion' to the former and 'magic' to the latter. It is essential, in his view, to insist on the indissolubility of the relation between the theoretical and the practical sides, since the theory divorced from the practice passes into metaphysic, while the practice founded on another theory becomes science. For the rest, the mysterious forces which are the objects of magico-religious theory may be conceived equally well under an impersonal or a personal form; and, correspondingly, magico-religious practice, whether it issue in positive acts or in abstentions—viz. in the observance of tabus—may seek to deal with things either directly or indirectly through personal agents having power over the things, while the mechanism of association by similarity and contact is involved in both cases alike. The theory is stated (p. 18) in tabular form as follows:

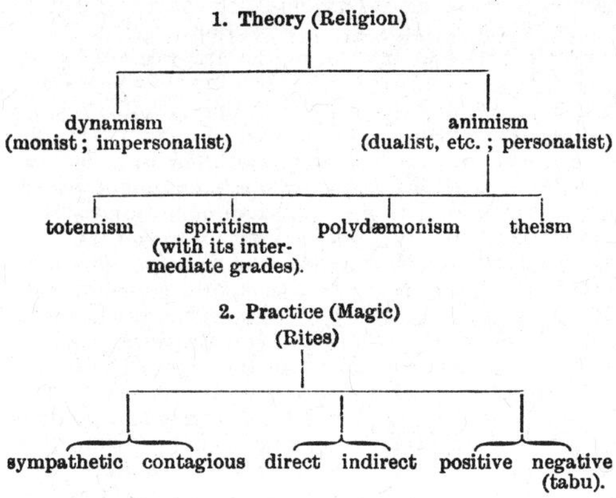
1. Theory (Religion)
dynamism
(monist; impersonalist)
animism
(dualist, etc.; personalist)
totemism
spiritism
(with its inter-
mediate grades).
polydæmonism
theism
2. Practice (Magic)
(Rites)
sympathetic
contagious
direct
indirect
positive
negative
(tabu).

Wilhelm Wundt (*Völkerpsychologie*, vol. ii. pts. ii. and iii., Leipzig, 1907–09) makes myth or belief the ultimate source of cult or ritual, since the latter is but the former put into practice. There is but one mythical idea at the back of all rites, namely, the idea of soul; and from it are generated in succession three forms of cult, magic, fetishism, and totemism, which by reaction cause the idea of soul to develop correspondingly. To deal only with the first of these, magic in its primary form consists in the supposed direct action of soul on soul, as when the evil eye is feared, while the secondary form consists in supposed action from a distance, when the soul-influence makes itself felt indirectly by means of a symbol (ii. 46 f.). Thus Wundt is entirely opposed to the Frazerian theory that magic implies a theory of natural causation on the part of the savage. On his view, while ordinary events are accepted as a matter of course, extraordinary events, demanding as they do a theory that will account for them, are at first ascribed to the soul-power or will of a man, and later (when the stage of magic is transcended) to that of a magnified man, or god, similar soul-power or will being ascribed to inanimate objects and to animals at the intermediate stages of fetishism and totemism.

Here perforce must end the survey of representative views, those selected for examination at least exemplifying the wide diversity of the notions which it is sought for purposes of science to impose on a highly plastic, since popular, term. Now the purely verbal side of the question need not be a source of trouble. If the things are envisaged distinctly, the words may be trusted to look after themselves. Thus in the present case there are evidently different concepts answering to separate aspects of human life; and it will be sufficient for the present purpose if these aspects are discriminated, so that terminology may be given the chance of adjusting itself to the facts.

3. Magic as a general name for rudimentary cult.—On any theory of the evolution of religion which represents it as a single movement falling into distinguishable stages, there will always be a first stage of minimum development immediately preceded by a stage of what Bacon would call *absentia in proximo*—a 'pre-religious' stage, as it might be termed. Now, since the word 'magic' tends to bear an unfavourable sense, nothing is more natural than to dub magical whatever fails to come up to the evolutionary standard which religion is more or less arbitrarily taken to embody. It hardly matters whether, after the manner of Frazer, an age of magic is held to have preceded the age of religion, or whether, in the style of Wundt, magic is identified with the lowest form of religion. In either case magic answers to something to which is assigned an unfavourable, because inferior, place in the evolutionary scale as compared with religion at its most characteristic. Anthropological science, however, is becoming increasingly chary of constructing any such scale on lines so simple and so drastic. Human evolution is a tissue of many interlacing strands; and, again, the savage of to-day is no older or earlier than the civilized man, so that typological and historical primitiveness cannot be identified offhand. At most, then, it is with the help of psychological and sociological considerations of a general type that a primordial stage of mind and society can be theoretically posited, out of which determinate religion may be shown to have emerged by some sort of subsequent process. Such general considerations suggest that, just as Jourdain talked prose before he realized the fact, so the primeval savage acted before he thought about his action. Correspondingly, therefore, in the sphere of nascent religion there must have been a stage of cult or ritual (if so it may be termed), the product of sheer unreflective habit, which preceded the growth of ideas concerning the how and why of what was being done. Certain recurrent situations in the social life—and, as for the individual life, it is wholly subordinate to the social so long as mere gregariousness prevails—induce states of emotional intensity. The emotions must find a vent somehow. This they do either through activities directed to practical ends, such as hunting, fighting, and love-making; or else through secondary activities such as are not immediately practical in their object but serve simply as outlets of superfluous energy, such as the dances that simply play at hunting, fighting, or love-making. In either case habit entwines with the activities in question all sorts of more or less functionless accidents; and the presence of these unaccountable details helps to make the whole performance seem mysterious to the performers and still more so to the civilized onlooker. When the activity is of the directly practical kind, say, hunting, whereas the tracking, the killing of the game, and so on, explain themselves, the accompanying observances enjoined by custom which do not explain themselves so readily—for instance, wearing such and such a garb, uttering certain words, and the like—may well seem to call for justification even to the unthinking savage, who will at least translate his sense of the value of custom into the vague doctrine that there is 'power' in these things, that they 'work.' When, on the other hand, the activities belong to those of the secondary type which are not immediately practical, constituting 'protreptic' rites, as they might be termed, which, while affording emotional relief, act likewise on the whole as preparations for the business of life—very much as play does, in the case of the young—then accretions in the way of accidental features due to custom are likely to be more pronounced, inasmuch as there is no discipline of hard fact to impose bounds on the action. Meanwhile, in proportion as these secondary activities conform to the same stimuli as the primary activities of which they are the by-product, as, for instance, when the hunting interest overflows into a pantomimic rehearsal of the chase, they will wear an imitative appearance, though in reality being 'repercussions' rather than imitations. When, however, an *ex post facto* justification of them becomes necessary, it is quite natural that the doctrine that they have 'power' should implicate the belief that their seemingly imitative character has something to do with their efficacy. It is putting the cart before the horse to say, as Frazer seems to do, that the belief that 'like produces like,' or what not, generates symbolic ritual. It is, on the contrary, symbolic ritual—*i.e.* a ritual that involves a more or less realistic reproduction of some practical activity—that generates the doctrine of 'sympathetic' causation in one or another of its forms. As a matter of fact, the so-called symbolic rites usually include all manner of details the mimetic bearing of which is at least not obvious; and the generalization that an 'age of magic' indulges in rites which are symbolic and sympathetic through and through is reached by picking out the abstract element of imitativeness which runs through primitive cult (and to no small extent through the more 'advanced' types of cult as well), and ignoring everything that is like nothing but itself, yet forms just as persistent a part of the approved ritual. If, then, we are going to use the word 'magic' loosely as a name for rudimentary or unreflective cult in general, let us at least identify the magical quality, not with the imitativeness, which is a secondary feature, but with the customariness, which is the real source of the value attaching to these non-utilitarian accompaniments of the more exciting moments of the practical life —these 'superstitious' practices, as the civilized onlooker ranks them. For the rest, in so far as these relatively unideated discharges of the social energy need any supporting doctrine, they would seem to find it, not in any philosophy about like producing like, and so on—ideas that appear quite late in the history of thought—but in vague notions of the *mana* type (see MANA). In other words, the savage comforts himself with no theory of *how* these ritual practices work, but is content to feel and know *that* they work—that, despite all appearances to the contrary (since their non-utilitarian character may be supposed to become gradually manifest), they have power and efficacy in them or behind them. It is just this faith in their efficacy that distinguishes nascently religious practices from such as are merely æsthetic. The former are so closely related to the practical activities that a sense of their contributory value runs through them, and they thus suggest and foreshadow practice in all sorts of ways that make for hope, courage, and confidence, whereas æsthetic enjoyment, though possessing a recreative function, does not thus point beyond itself. It remains only to ask whether 'magic' is a suitable word for the designation of the most rudimentary type of cult. On the whole, it would seem a pity for the evolutionist to apply a term redolent of disparagement to what on his view is a genuine phase of the serious life as lived under certain conditions of culture. It is far less question-begging to predicate religion throughout (unless, indeed, one is prepared to follow van Gennep, and predicate magic throughout as well as a general name for the practical side of religion—which is surely an abuse of language). The science of comparative religion, if it is to do its work properly, must impartially embrace the cults of all mankind in its survey.

An observation may be added for the benefit of the field-worker, who, as a rule, has to take over his classificatory apparatus ready-made from the hands of the theorist. If such an one has learnt to identify magic with the sympathetic principle or with those early forms of cult in which this principle appears to predominate, he will be inclined to label his collections of specific ceremonies 'hunting magic,' 'productive magic' (a term often used to describe rites of the *intichiuma* type, which bear on the increase of food-animals and plants), 'agricultural magic,' and so on. But it is just as easy to speak of hunting and agricultural 'rites' or 'ritual'; and it is much more likely to lead to an unprejudiced description of all the relevant facts, whether they be of the sympathetic order or not. So, again, tabus are better treated as a part of ritual, namely, as observances of negative prescriptions, which will invariably be found to form one context with sundry other positive prescriptions; to make them a part of magic is neither necessary nor even natural according to the ordinary usage of speech. It may even be said to be now a recognized working principle that the first-hand observer should class all magico-religious phenomena under one general heading, and leave the theorists to determine how far, and along what lines, the differentiation of the magical and religious elements involved in the complex needs to be pushed (see *Notes and Queries on Anthropology*[4], issued by the Royal Anthrop. Institute, London, 1912, section on 'The Study of Magico-Religious Facts,' p. 251 f.).

4. **Magic as a name for the black art and allied developments.**—The view which has just been discussed and deprecated, that identifies magic with rudimentary cult as a whole, may be said to draw a horizontal line between magic and the later and more evolved products of the same tendencies which rudimentary cult embodies. The other view, which will now be examined, differs altogether from the former in that it draws a perpendicular line between magic and certain contemporaneous but rival growths which may be broadly classed under the two heads of religion and science. This point comes out very clearly in Lehmann's definition, which correlates magic with superstition as practice with theory, and in turn makes superstition co-extensive with such ideas as stand to the accepted religious and scientific beliefs of a given time in a relation of more or less direct conflict and contradiction.

(*a*) *Magic as the rival of religion.*—Starting once more from the fact that the word 'magic' tends to stand for something bad, we realize at once that it is possible to treat magic as a general name for all the bad kinds of trafficking with the occult and supra-sensible in vogue in a given society, while, conversely, religion may be taken to comprehend all the good kinds of such trafficking. Obviously the power of bringing wonders to pass is a two-edged sword, since surprising things may happen for weal and for woe, while, again, immoral as well as moral persons may seek benefit from miracle. It is, indeed, eminently characteristic of ideas of the *mana* type that they are, from a moral point of view, ambiguous and two-sided, covering all manifestations of the efficacy of rites, whether they be beneficent or maleficent in their intention (see MANA). Now it is easy to see how rites of an ill-intentioned kind will come to be practised and will have efficacy imputed to them. Hate, greed, and the other types of anti-social attitude being more or less endemic at all levels of society, they are bound to find expression in habitual activities that assume the character of mystic rites in proportion as they abound in accretions and in secondary activities of the expletive order, such as cursing in set phrases or destroying an absent enemy in pantomime. Moreover, the very fear which hate and malice awake in the breasts of those against whom they are directed is enough to create an atmosphere in which the natural seeds of black magic cannot but germinate freely. The almost universal dread of the evil eye illustrates very well how the responsibility for the existence of a belief in sorcery often rests with the credulous victim just as much as, or more than, with the alleged aggressor. Anthropological literature is full of striking examples of the tendency which W. E. Roth (*North Queensland Ethnography*, Bulletin no. 5, Brisbane, 1903, p. 28) calls *thanatomania*, namely, the suggestibility leading sooner or later to death on the part of one who satisfies himself that he is doomed. Roth has had personal experience as a medical man of five or six such cases among the Queensland natives. Thus it comes about that, by an extension of the same line of thought, 'evil magic' becomes the stock explanation offered for any form of accident or mysterious disease.

'An individual becomes incapacitated through some chronic and painful illness which does not answer to the various aboriginal methods of treatment or materia medica: the illness weighs upon his mind, and after a time he becomes more and more confirmed in his conviction that someone has been "pointing" the *munguni* (death-bone) at him—*i.e.* that a "bone," pebble, flint, etc., has been put inside him and his blood removed' (W. E. Roth, *Ethnological Studies among the North-West-Central Queensland Aborigines*, Brisbane, 1897, p. 154).

Indeed, it has often been observed that the savage scarcely recognizes the fact of 'natural' death, so ready is he to impute the event to the sinister arts of some particular individual or at least to the machinations of persons unknown (cf. art. LIFE AND DEATH [Primitive], § 7). From these vaguer attributions of ill-will to one's neighbours it is but a step to the conception of an evil magic independent of the will and intention of any person at all. Various more or less impersonal forms of evil —such as the *arungquiltha* of the Arunta (Spencer-Gillen[a], London, 1899, p. 548 n.), the *otgon* of the Hurons (J. N. B. Hewitt, *Am. Anthropologist*, new ser., iv. [1902] 37 n.), or the *badi* of the Malays (W. W. Skeat, *Malay Magic*, London, 1900, p. 94) —are regarded as malignant and destructive agencies in their own right, very much as one thinks of the plague or the influenza. In short, there is always more or less of black magic 'in the air' for the panic-ridden savage. For this reason, and seeing also how much the healer of diseases and, again, the witch-finder do to foster the evil reputation of the magician by their highly-coloured accounts of the dreadful arts which it is their professional privilege to be able to counteract, one might almost be tempted to declare that the sorcerer is a mere bogey, the creation of abject fear wedded to ignorance and credulity. But this would be to go too far. There seems good evidence that in Australia men and even women, despite the fact that black magic practised within the group is normally held to be punishable by death, wreak their vengeance in this way on their private enemies. Roth's own black servant, a mere layman, actually dared to point the bone at a native doctor, the latter dying about a fortnight later (*N. Queensland Ethnography*, Bull. no. 5, p. 30). At most, then, it may be surmised that for every case of genuine guilt there are far more false accusations; and, in short, generally, in every witch-haunted society, whether it be native Australia or 17th cent. England, that the proofs of witchcraft mainly rest on an argument from effect to cause.

As for love-magic, it may not seem at first sight to have the anti-social character of the magic of hate; but, if closely observed, it will be found on the whole to minister to hardly less disreputable purposes. Thus among the Arunta of Central Australia such magic is chiefly resorted to in order to bring about a runaway match. It is true that, according to native ideas, it is merely a case of one tribal husband trying to entice the woman away from another tribal husband, so that, as Spencer and Gillen say, 'it is a breach of manners but not of custom' ([a], p. 544). Even so, however, it would seem to be extremely liable to lead to a general fight within the group, or between one local group and another, so that its anti-social tendency is bound in the long run to become tolerably manifest.

So much for what are perhaps the clearest instances of types of ritual acts generated by passions and desires which society is bound to try to suppress in the interest of its own self-preservation. Such rites can be placed in a more or less determinate class by themselves, whereas over against this class can be set in contrast another class of rites, entirely similar as regards the general nature of their mechanism, but embodying motives of a kind held to be socially salutary. Broadly speaking, all public rites have this common quality of being licit and reputable, since the fact that they are the recognized custom of the community is taken as a sufficient guarantee that they exist for the furtherance of the common weal. Thus the totemic ceremonies of the Central Australians, the object of which is the increase of the food-animals and plants, occupy exactly the same place in the life of the people as is filled by the rites of the Church in a Christian country. Hence E. Durkheim (*Les Formes élémentaires de la vie religieuse*, Paris, 1912) takes the totemic system of Australia as the typical instance of an elementary religion, whereas Frazer, adopting what has been termed the horizontal line of division between magic and religion, would assign these totemic rites wholesale to the age of magic. Indeed, no better instance could be cited to illustrate the incompatibility between the horizontal and the perpendicular methods of viewing magic and religion in their relation to each other. While, then, for the simpler societies at all events, public rites always rank as good and licit, does it follow that private rites as such will tend to be regarded as bad and illicit? According to Robertson Smith (*The Religion of the Semites*², London, 1894, p. 263 f.), it well-nigh amounts to this:

'It was the community, and not the individual, that was sure of the permanent and unfailing help of its deity. It was a national not a personal providence that was taught by ancient religion. So much was this the case that in purely personal concerns the ancients were very apt to turn, not to the recognised religion of the family or of the state, but to magical superstitions. . . . Not only did these magical superstitions lie outside religion, but in all well-ordered states they were regarded as illicit. A man had no right to enter into private relations with supernatural powers that might help him at the expense of the community to which he belonged. In his relations to the unseen he was bound always to think and act with and for the community, and not for himself alone.'

Granting, however, that in the small undifferentiated society private enterprise is suspect, we must recognize that, as the division of labour develops and the individual asserts himself more and more, the law is increasingly ready to sanction, or at least condone, the use of ritual forms for securing personal ends, such as the protection of property by tabu-marks having the force of conditional curses (see P. Huvelin, 'Magie et droit individuel,' in *ASoc* x. [1907] 1 f.; and cf. M. Mauss and M. H. Beuchat, *ib.* ix. [1906] 117, on the magico-religious significance of the Eskimo property-marks). For the rest, there will always be in every society a number of ceremonial practices to which a certain amount of magico-religious value attaches that fall most naturally under the category of folk-lore, having no place in the official cult, yet being too insignificant to call for much notice favourable or unfavourable, and, on the whole, tending to be despised rather than condemned. In short, for certain purposes of science it is best to treat all magico-religious rites as generically akin, even while making due allowance for their tendency to group themselves round the opposite pole of beneficence and maleficence, of social service and individual greed or spite. More especially is this so when the interest passes from intent to content, from motive to mechanism. Social and anti-social rites are hardly distinguishable in respect of their external forms at the stage of the most rudimentary culture. Thus the agents bear the closest resemblance to each other, the sorcerer and priest often meeting in the person of the medicine-man. The rites are of the same general pattern, whether they be manual or oral. Lastly, the ideas that are bound up with the rites conform to a common type, now to that of *mana* and now to that of spirit (cf. Huvelin, *op. cit.* p. 2). After all, it is no wonder that differentiation should hardly have begun, seeing that, so long as society is represented by an aggregate of small groups living in a state of perpetual discord, what would be evil if practised on a friend becomes good the moment it is directed against the people just across the way. Or, again, society may halt as it were between two ethical opinions, with the result that ritual practices of contradictory intent may obtain something like equal toleration ; the moral status of love-magic was especially ambiguous, so that, for instance, among the Kurnai tribe of Victoria, where marriage by elopement verges on the position of a recognized institution, 'while there were medicine-men who assisted those who wished to elope, there were other medicine-men who aided the pursuing kindred to discover them' (A. W. Howitt, *The Native Tribes of S.E. Australia*, London, 1904, p. 277). Once more the medicine-man in his capacity of tribal head-man may use his supernatural power to punish offenders against the laws of the group, such as the novice who behaves improperly at the initiation ceremonies, or the man who attacks another by means of evil magic ; but he will likewise in his private capacity use his power against his enemies, and will even bring to bear on them the power of Daramulun, the great anthropomorphic god of the mysteries, the very embodiment of all that is most religious in the eyes of the tribe (Howitt, pp. 543, 382). Clearly, then, it is not to the simpler and more undifferentiated societies that we must look for an accurate evaluation of the purposes embodied in rites, leading sooner or later to their organization in rival systems that henceforth to some extent develop independently. Organization and system, however, are terms that perhaps are hardly applicable even to the later developments of black magic. It is religion that has all the organization to itself, because public approval affords it every chance of free expansion. Magic, on the other hand, as the enemy of organized cult and, indeed, of the social organization as a whole, must lurk in dark places, and grows not by internal systematization, but merely as does a rubbish-heap, by the casual accumulation of degraded and disintegrated rites of all kinds. At most it may affect a certain definiteness of form by imitating religious ritual in a spirit of blasphemous parody, as in the case of the 'black mass.' On the whole, however, it is utterly deficient on the side of theory, and consists simply in a congeries of practices which by perversion and distortion have lost most of the meaning that they once had. Only in this sense, then, do they rest on the principle of compulsion as opposed to conciliation, that, being mere rites, lacking the support of any consistent scheme of thought, they have to depend for their validity on the bare fact that they appear to work. Religion, on the other hand, though never wholly escaping the tendency to impute value and efficacy to its ritual as such, is free to develop an ethical conception of the godhead in which the action of mere power is gradually converted into that of a power that makes for righteousness, and is therefore to be moved and conciliated not by rites but by righteous conduct.

(*b*) *Magic as the rival of science.*—The view advanced by Frazer to the effect that the fundamental conception of magic is identical with that of modern science (*GB*[3], pt. i., *The Magic Art*, i. 220) will hardly bear close inspection. The magician surely does not postulate 'that the same causes will always produce the same effects.' On the contrary, his art is based on the supposed possibility of miracle—on what might be termed super-causation as contrasted with normal causation. In other words, he seeks to help out ordinary action by means of an increment of power borrowed from a supra-sensible source. This is what Tylor means by characterizing magic as 'occult science.' It makes a fatal difference if, after the manner of Frazer, this qualification be omitted. Magic thus stands in far closer affinity with religion than with science, inasmuch as religion and magic equally consist in dealings with the supra-sensible and differ not as regards the means employed but simply as regards the ends pursued, since the one tries to bring blessings to pass by means of miracle, and the other to bring curses. On the other hand, at no known stage of his evolution does the existence of man consist in one continuous round of mystic practices. It is mainly at the crisis, periodic or occasional, in the social and individual life that the need to draw on unseen sources of support is felt. In the intervals the workaday world of actions, guided by the routine of sense-perception, stands in the foreground of attention ; and this is the world in which science in the sense of natural science has always been at home. Chipping a flint so as to produce a cutting edge is nascent science, whereas bringing up a quartz-crystal mysteriously from one's inside is a magico-religious proceeding belonging to quite another order of experience. A considerable part at any rate of modern science has originated in technical processes of a directly utilitarian and 'lay' character. Thus European geometry would seem to be the outcome of the art of the 'cord-fasteners' who measured out the land in Egypt after each inundation of the Nile (cf. J. Burnet, *Early Greek Philosophy*[2], London, 1908, p. 24). It cannot be denied, however, that, so long as their occult character be recognized, certain developments of the magico-religious way of thinking may be held to correspond to sciences or pseudo-sciences, inasmuch as they severally represent a body of organized lore intended on the whole for the furtherance of secular and purely technical ends. Of these the most characteristic types are faith-healing and divination (*qq.v.*). Faith-healing is in its most typical form a direct counterblast to sorcery, which is in essence a faith-hurting. White magic and black magic determine to a large extent each other's form, since the natural procedure of the healer is first to establish by his diagnosis what exactly the wicked magician has done, and then by dramatic reversal of the action to undo it. Indeed, as has already been suggested, witchcraft is in no small part a pure invention on the part of leechcraft. To bring about a faith-cure it is essential to show that what is wrong is something that will answer to the proposed method of putting it right ; and what more plain than that medicine-man may checkmate medicine-man, diamond cut diamond ? Meanwhile, the occult science of the faith-healer is not the only form of medical science known to the savage. On the contrary, it may be more or less sharply distinguished from the ordinary folk-medicine, towards which it stands in a certain attitude of rivalry.

Thus Roth, who, as a medical man, went very carefully into the various methods of dealing with disease that prevailed among the aborigines of North Queensland, shows that 'no "doctors" attend specially on the sick, the charge of all such being left to individual caprice, *e.g.*, a woman looks after her husband, a mother after her child. Nor do they specially prescribe, the knowledge—where known to all—of the therapeutical value of any plant, of massage, etc., being common to the tribe' (*N. Queensland Ethn.*, Bull. 5, p. 29). It is only when the ordinary treatment fails that the aid of the medicine-man is called in (*ib.*).

Among the specifics in common use among the natives observed by him, Roth enumerates more than forty different plants, for some of which at least genuine remedial properties can be claimed. Again, ligatures, bleeding, massage, poultices and fomentations, dressings for cuts, the use of splints for fractures, and so on, are 'lay' methods of treatment which rest on a basis of what we too would be ready to recognize as 'science,' *i.e.* a more or less organized common sense. At the same time, the lay mind is likewise addicted to what the modern doctors would regard as pure superstition, such as reliance on charms, amulets, the sucking-string, etc. But at any rate the atmosphere of mystery with which the professional faith-healer surrounds the exercise of his craft is absent from these applications of communal lore to the ills of life. Further, the professional enters into competition with the layman in order to demonstrate how superior his wonder-working is to the humdrum procedure of the ordinary folk-medicine.

Thus Roth specially notes that 'among the Boulia blacks, there are indications of a desire on the part of the medicine-men to claim a share in the cure, with a corresponding reward.' The common cure for snake-bite being a vapour-bath, which apparently answers very well, the medicine-man undertakes to help it out by operating on the snake. 'The doctor himself goes to the place where the accident happened, is shown where the snake lies hid, digs it out, and lets it glide away a few feet before commencing to pelt it with stones. During this process the snake gradually diminishes in size, and gradually becomes harmless, when it is carried back to camp, where the medicine-man, turning its skin half-way inside out while still alive, throws it into water, and so makes an end of it. It is needless to say that no layman is allowed to witness any part of this procedure' (*ib.* p. 42).

It only remains to add, in fairness to the medicine-man, that a reputation for magic in the sense of a more or less bad and anti-social kind of wonder-working is thrust upon him by the very fact that he is a professional and hence has the public against him, according to the principle that whatever is private in rude society is suspect. As Huvelin points out, so long as society remains undifferentiated, all custom rests on the common belief and wears a religious character, so that every manifestation of individuality is destitute of sanction, when it does not actually amount to a crime. Hence, when social organization begins to come into existence through the division of labour, individual activity is obliged to disguise itself under a cloak of religious forms, which gives the professional an ambiguous character, not only in the eyes of others, but even in his own eyes, since others suspect, while he himself is obscurely conscious, that powers and practices which originally came into being for the public service are being exploited for private ends (Huvelin, p. 46). Whether it be the professional doctor or the professional smith, his right to be a specialist has been purchased at the cost of seeming, and being, something of a humbug.

Passing to the subject of divination, we have an even clearer case of a pseudo-science, since, whereas faith-healing has been to a certain extent purged of its supernaturalism and incorporated into modern medicine, divination has no part or lot in the science of to-day, unless we detect its aftermath in the accepted postulate that the goal of science is prediction. On the other hand, divination has in certain of its developments all the appearance of science so far as concerns the organization of its principles and the directly practical character of its aims. Thus Babylonian divination, the literature of which is particularly rich, reveals an amazing wealth of lore involving the most elaborate classifications of omens resting on a wide basis of genuine observation. It is also to be noticed that here the practice of the art depending on this body of would-be knowledge was thoroughly respectable, being, in fact, a branch or department of the official religion (see DIVINATION [Assyro-Babylonian]). It is not, in fact, until it migrates into Europe that Babylonian astrology is differentiated from astronomy, and the opposition between the two becomes apparent. Again, at a lower stage of social evolution divination can fill the place of science in so far as it calls out the reasoning powers of the mind and supplies some sort of intellectual gymnastic. Thus H. A. Junod, a missionary, who gives an admirable account of the use of the divinatory bones among the Thonga of S. Africa, spent many hours with his native teachers trying to acquire the principles of this system of theirs which they call 'The Word,' and vaunt to be superior to the missionary's Bible:

'So I had an opportunity of reaching the depths of the Bantu mind, that mind which has perhaps invented nothing more elaborate and more magical than the divinatory system. Of course no sensible person would for a moment believe in the objective value of these practices. Astralogomancy has no more real worth than Cheiromancy, Necromancy, and all the other "mancies." But I am obliged to confess that the Thonga system is far more clever than any other which I have met with, and that it admirably answers to the wants of the Natives, as it comprehends all the elements of their life, photographs them, so to speak, in such a way that indications and directions can be obtained for all possible cases' (*The Life of a South African Tribe*, Neuchâtel, 1913, ii. 494).

It remains to show how science in the modern sense has managed to shake itself free of its rivals, the pseudo-sciences. As far as relates to what has been called 'the European epoch of the human mind,' the mother of science is undoubtedly ancient Greece. There the human spirit shook itself free of the domination of the magico-religious, thanks to its interest in the things of this world.

'Between Homer and Herodotus, Greek Reason has come into the world. . . . Man has become the measure of all things; and things are worth observing and recording . . . according as they do, or do not, amplify human knowledge already acquired, or prompt or guide human attempts to classify and interpret them. In this high meaning of the word all Greek records are utilitarian, relative to an end in view: and this end is ever anthropocentric, it is nothing less, but it is also nothing more, than the Good Life, the Wellbeing of Mankind' (J. L. Myres, in *Anthropology and the Classics*, ed. Marett, Oxford, 1908, p. 123).

There is no violent breaking with the old-world rituals and the associated beliefs; but colonization, trade, and the progress of the industrial arts beget a secular frame of mind which dismisses theological prejudices in so far as they conflict with technical improvements.

'All ailments are from God,' writes Hippocrates, 'no one of them being more divine than another, or more human either, but all alike from God. But each of such things has a process of growth, and nothing comes into being without a process of growth.' Wherefore he turns without more ado to the study of these physical causes (cf. Myres, *loc. cit.* p. 140).

Meanwhile, in philosophy, which at first understands by 'nature' something eminently supernatural in its potency for making wonders happen, there gradually develops a scientific tradition by the side of a mystic tradition, the former of which affirms the reality of the many things of the sense, world as against the reality of the one transcendental world-soul conceived by the latter (cf. F. M. Cornford, *From Religion to Philosophy*, London, 1912, p. 144 f.). The former view culminates in the atomism of Democritus, which has prevailed in the sphere of physical science until recent times. Now this whole scientific movement is opposed in spirit to magic and religion alike. It contradicts the whole tenor of the magico-religious type of procedure whether by manual or by oral rites, and hence cannot be identified or equated, after the fashion of Frazer, with magic regarded as equivalent to the earliest phase of cult in general. Nor, again, has it any real affinity with black magic or any parallel development, save in so far as all technical processes undertaken by experts are at first more or less suspect as private exploitations, as has already been explained. Natural science by association with the productive arts has taken into its hands the entire control of the mechanical and material sphere of human life, and within this sphere will brook no rival. In the moral sphere, on the other hand, it shows no signs of making headway against the claim of religion to be the supreme authority. Meanwhile, neither science nor religion can afford to tolerate the anti-social and immoral person, the man who tries to make a living out of the credulity and idle fears of weak humanity. In practice, however, both find it hard to distinguish between the delinquent and the innovator, so that the line between evil magic and charlatanry, on the one hand, and mere heterodoxy, on the other, tends to be even now of a somewhat fluctuating kind. As for black magic, it has almost disappeared from view in civilized society. As the folklorist knows, however, a permanent possibility of demoralizing superstition lurks in human nature, and only education in regard to both physical facts and moral truths can keep the monster down.

LITERATURE.—The subject has a vast literature, more especially seeing that, according to one definition of the term, magic covers all the ruder forms of cult. The following works are in various ways authoritative: E. B. Tylor, *Researches into the Early History of Mankind*[2], London, 1870, ch. vi., *PC*[3], do. 1891, ch. iv., art. 'Magic,' in *EBr*[9]; J. G. Frazer, *GB*[3], pt. i., *The Magic Art*, do. 1911 (see also earlier edd.), *Lectures on the Early History of the Kingship*, do. 1905; A. C. Lyall, *Asiatic Studies*, 1st ser., do. 1899, p. 99 ff.; F. B. Jevons, *Introduction to the History of Religion*, do. 1896, 'The Definition of Magic,' *Sociological Review*, i. [1908] 105 ff.; *Trans. of 3rd Internat. Cong. of Religions*, i. [Oxford, 1908] 71 f., *Introduction to the Study of Comparative Rel.*, New York, 1908, p. 70 f.; R. R. Marett, *The Threshold of Religion*[2], London, 1914, essay ii.; L. T. Hobhouse, *Morals in Evolution*, do. 1906, [2]1914, ii.; A. Lang, *Magic and Religion*, do. 1901; A. C. Haddon, *Magic and Fetishism*, do. 1906; W. E. Roth, *North Queensland Ethnography*, Bull. no. 5, 'Superstition, Magic, and Medicine,' Brisbane, 1903; W. R. Halliday, 'The Force of Initiative in Magical Conflict,' in *FL* xxi. [1910] 147 ff.; E. S. Hartland, *Ritual and Belief*, London, 1914; W. W. Skeat, *Malay Magic*, do. 1900; I. King, *The Development of Religion*, do. 1910; E. S. Ames, *The Psychology of Religious Experience*, do. 1910; J. H. Leuba, *A Psychological Study of Religion*, New York, 1912; H. Hubert and M. Mauss, 'Esquisse d'une théorie générale de la magie,' *ASoc* vii. [1904], *Mélanges d'histoire des religions*, Paris, 1909; P. Huvelin, 'Magie et droit individuel,' *ASoc* x. [1907]; H. Hubert, art. 'Magia,' in Daremberg-Saglio, vi.; A. van Gennep, *Les Rites de passage*, Paris, 1909, p. 17 f.; K. T. Preuss, 'Der Ursprung der Religion und Kunst,' in *Globus*, lxxxvi. [1904]; H. Oldenberg, *Die Religion des Veda*, Berlin, 1894; W. Wundt, *Völkerpsychologie*, vol. ii. pt. ii., Leipzig, 1907; J. Ennemoser, *Geschichte der Magie*, Munich, 1844; A. Lehmann, *Aberglaube und Zauberei*, Stuttgart, 1908.

R. R. MARETT.

MAGIC (Arabian and Muslim).—The word used in Arabic for this notion is *sihr*, connected with the verb meaning 'to produce illusion' on the eyes (*Qur'ān*, vii. 113); it seems, therefore, to be in origin the causative of the verb *ḥāra*, 'to be bewildered,' and is explained by the verb 'to frighten' (*istarhaba*), whence the whole phrase resembles μαγεύων καὶ ἐξιστάνων in Ac 8[9]. It is probable that the Hebrew *shaḥar*, used twice by Isaiah for 'conjure away,' is identical, and the Armenian *skhroumn*, 'marvel,' may be borrowed from this word. The passage in the Qur'ān which contains most information on the subject is ii. 96, where it is stated that the *siḥr* was revealed to the two angels in Babel, Hārūt and Mārūt, who taught it to mankind, without concealing the fact that they were tempting them; the *siḥr* showed how to separate a man from his wife, *i.e.* was the contrary of a love-philtre. Isaiah (47[11]) connects the *shaḥar* with Babylon, which, according to classical writers also, was the headquarters of magic:

> 'Tunc Babylon Persea licet, secretaque Memphis
> Omne vetustorum solvat penetrale Magorum'
> (Lucan, *Pharsalia*, vi. 449 f.).

Hārūt and Mārūt seem from their names to be Aramaic personifications of mischief and rebellion, with which their recorded operation corresponds.

In the Qur'ān, as might be expected, it is not clear whether the results of *siḥr* are always subjective only or may be objective; and some commentators think both possible. When, therefore, a miracle is branded as *siḥr*, it may be regarded either as an optical illusion or as an illicit process due to the employment of demons; it is true that Solomon employed them (according to the Qur'ān), but this may have been a prophetic privilege. And a theological difficulty arises from the statement that *siḥr* was revealed to two angels, as what is revealed ought not to be evil. The orthodox view is that magic can be objective; but some Mu'tazilite doctors and some members of the Shāfi'ite and Ḥanifite schools took the other view; and even those who believed that it was objective thought that it could affect accidents only, and could not transmute substances.

The practice was forbidden, and, indeed, under penalty of death; Mālik held that one convicted of sorcery should not even be given the option of repentance, whereas Shāfi'ī confined the death-sentence to the case where examination of the accused proved him to be guilty of unbelief (Qasṭallānī, *Commentary on the Mawāhib Laduniyyah*, Cairo, 1278, vii. 116). Acquisition of the theory was, however, permissible, and, according to some, a duty incumbent on certain members of the community, as protection against those who practised the art.

The recognition by Islām of the existence of *jinn* furnished a basis for the belief in magic, to which, however, the attitude of the educated and of serious writers is about the same in most countries; it is not ordinarily recognized as an agent in the course of events, yet may well be admitted into tales of wonder and delight, whereas the superstitious may resort to it for a variety of needs.

It figures on one occasion in the biography of the Prophet, when an illness was brought upon him by a Jew named Labīd ben al-A'sam; according to one account, the latter obtained possession of some hair left on the Prophet's comb, which he hid with some other objects in a well; according to others, the object hidden was a string with a number of knots upon it. The latter version is doubtless suggested by the penultimate *sūra* of the Qur'ān, which is a spell against eclipses and women who breathe or spit on knots. The practices against which these spells are directed are similar to, if not identical with, those which are enumerated by classical writers (*e.g.*, Lucan, vi. 460 ff.). Others, of which the *Arabian Nights* offers ample illustration, also have analogies in the literature of classical antiquity; the transformation of men into animals by a witch's potion is found as early as the *Odyssey*. In Arabic there is a special word for this process, *maskh*.

Ḥājī Khalīfah (*Lexicon bibliograph. et encyclopæd.*, ed. G. Flügel, London, 1835–58, iii. 584) classifies the various magical methods as follows:

> The Indian consists in purification of the soul; the Nabatæan in the employment of spells at suitable times; the Greek in compelling the service of the spirits of the spheres and the stars; that of the Hebrews, Copts, and Arabs in mentioning names of unknown meaning—this method being a variety of that by incantation, those who employ it professing thereby to press into their service the angels who have power over the *jinn*. This last expression recalls Lucan's
>
> 'habent haec carmina certum
> Imperiosa deum, qui mundum cogere, quicquid
> Cogitur ipse potest' (vi. 497 ff.).

The classification cannot be maintained, though it is possible that the tendency in the case of the different nations corresponded roughly with the methods assigned; thus doubtless the theory that ascetic practice won command over the gods was carried to greater lengths by the Indians than elsewhere, whereas the theory of mysterious words may be particularly Jewish, and the Hermetic magic specially astrological; ordinarily, however, all these ideas are confused or combined.

The difference emphasized by Lucan between authorized and unauthorized occultism ('si quid tacitum, sed fas erat' and 'detestanda deis saevorum arcana magorum') was fully recognized in the Islāmic State, which had its official astrologers while it condemned the black art. Since, however, what was required from the former was prediction of the future, the distinction could not be maintained with the desirable clearness.

Ṭabarī records (*History*, ed. M. J. de Goeje, Leyden, 1879–1901, iii. 1463) how the highly respected astrologer, 'Ali ben Yaḥyā, in the year 247, was reading out to the khalīf a book of predictions (*malāḥim*), when he came across the statement that the tenth khalīf would be slain in his own reception-room; he had to alter the text in consequence. Much the same is recorded by him in the case of an unauthorized lad, who possessed 'the Book of the Empire' (*Kitāb al-daulah*), where there was a prophecy that the khalīf Mahdī would last ten years. Since such a prophecy would mean certain death to any one who was discovered to be in possession of it, the word 'forty' was substituted for 'ten' in the book, and with such skill that no one could detect the interpolation (iii. 497). In the year 284 (Ṭabarī, iii. 2179) an unknown person haunted the palace of the khalīf Mu'taḍid, who summoned 'the lunatics and the conjurers' to detect him; the conjurers were to get control of the demon in possession of one of the lunatics, who would then give the necessary information. The behaviour of the lunatics, however, so much alarmed the khalīf that he dismissed them all with gratuities before anything could be done.

Similarly, there is a distinction between the normal or legitimate spell and that which would be condemned by the orthodox, though here, too, clearness is wanting. The child's amulet called *tamīmah* is regarded as normal. About the magical employment of Qur'ānic verses there seem to be differences of opinion. The historian Sakhāwī (*Tibr Masbūk*, Cairo, 1896, p. 218) records a controversy about the *ḥafīẓat Ramaḍān*, certain verses which, if written on the last Friday in Ramaḍān, will secure the house which contains them from burning and the ship whereon they are inscribed from being wrecked; the historian's teacher wished for government interference with their inscription, but the practice was too widely spread to admit of this. In the *Maqāmahs* of Ḥarīrī the impostor succeeds with the spells which he composes; in one case the magic lies in the eloquence of the composition, whereas in the other (for facilitating childbirth) the work is really done by a drug with which he happens to be acquainted.

In the *Arabian Nights* the magician is frequently a Moor (*Maghribī*), and the association of magic with those regions is not extinct; the most elaborate treatise which we possess on Islāmic magic is E. Doutté's *Magie et religion dans l'Afrique du Nord* (Algiers, 1909). Women and negroes also play a considerable rôle. In the tradition the art has a tendency to be connected with Israelites, as we have seen in the case of the Prophet.

According to Mas'ūdī (*Murūj al-dhahab*, ed. and tr. B. de Meynard and P. de Courteille, Paris, 1861–77, iv. 266), one of the complaints against Uthmān, the third khalīf, was that he had shown insufficient firmness in dealing with the case of a Jew, named Batrunī, who had performed some marvellous exploits in the mosque of Kūfa; 'he caused a mighty king mounted on a horse to ride in the court, he then turned himself into a camel, then produced a phantom ass, which passed through him, then he beheaded a man, and by another stroke with his sword put him together again'; a pious spectator beheaded the Jew, who probably was a conjurer, and performed some feats which the narrators have exaggerated.

Written spells which are brought to Europe from Islāmic countries are often in Hebrew or contain Hebrew words.

The limits which separate the practices condemned by the Prophet from those which he approved are again very narrow; thus in the authoritative collection of traditions by Muslim (Cairo, 1290, ii. 180–183) evidence is adduced to show that Muhammad sanctioned the employment of spells or magical prayers for treatment of the evil eye, snake-poison, and disease generally; the expert who employed the Qur'ānic texts for this purpose might even charge a fee, out of which the Prophet would accept a royalty. The word *ruqyah* is employed for charms of this kind, and in the case of snakes it would seem, from a story told by Jāḥiẓ (*Zoology*, Cairo, 1906, iv. 134), that their effectiveness depended on the loudness of the charmer's voice.

The name for collections of oracles is, as has been seen, *Malāḥim*, and this word is applied to those prophetical works wherein the future is regularly read (*e.g.*, the Book of Daniel), as well as to less authoritative books. Others were of the sort known as *Consulting-books*, *i.e.* tables whence the future could be divined by certain modes of combining the words, letters, or figures which make them up. It is likely that the primitive practices which constitute the magicians' chief stock-in-trade, and are common to many countries, are handed on by oral tradition, and to be learned only from the persons who perform them or from travellers who have made careful observations (*e.g.*, E. W. Lane, *Manners and Customs of the Modern Egyptians*, London, 1895).

LITERATURE.—The authorities are quoted in the article. Cf., further, DIVINATION (Muslim), CHARMS AND AMULETS (Muhammadan).

D. S. MARGOLIOUTH.

MAGIC (Babylonian).—For the purpose of this article we may regard the term 'magic' as connoting practices which have their origin in the belief that man is able by their exercise to control the unseen powers and force them to act in accordance with his own will. Without attempting to discuss the vexed question of the relationship of magic to religion (see 'Introductory' section above), we may say that this generally accepted use of the term has great advantages for the classification of material. And it corresponds, moreover, to a distinct contrast in attitude towards the supernatural. Magic may be said to be present wherever power over the unseen is believed to be inherent in the ritual, whereas, according to the religious concept, the seat of power is regarded as resting outside the sphere of man's deliberate control. When the term is used in this sense, it must be admitted that a great body of the religious beliefs and practices of the Babylonians and Assyrians should be more accurately described as falling under the category of magic.

It is true that, when reading some of the Babylonian religious compositions, one is struck by the resemblance which many of the phrases bear to ethical passages in the Hebrew Psalms and prophetical writings. Quoted apart from their context, such passages suggest an extraordinarily high standard of morality and great depth of feeling. But it is dangerous to judge any literature merely by extracts or anthologies; and, when studied in their own surroundings, they are at once seen to have a background that is largely magical rather than moral. To take a single example, the Babylonian penitential psalms and many of the prayers to the gods show that the Babylonians had a very keen sense of sin. The contrition and misery of the penitent are expressed with great beauty of metaphor; but it is essential to examine the precise meaning of the words employed, and not to read extraneous associations into them. In this connexion it is important to realize that the moral character of sin which we find emphasized in the Hebrew prophets is quite foreign to the Babylonian conception. In almost the whole of their religious literature the expressions 'sin,' 'sickness,' and 'possession by evil spirits' are employed as pure synonyms; they denote merely an evil state of the body. In fact, all sickness and disease were believed to be due to the attacks of evil spirits, under whose power or influence the sufferer had fallen, whether by his own act or through the machinations of a hostile sorcerer or sorceress. Such spirits and powers of evil were legion, and were ever on the look-out to inflict bodily harm on men. They might be ghosts of the dead, or gruesome spirits half-human and half-demon, or, lastly, fiends and devils of a nature corresponding to, but lower than, that of the gods.

The sole object of the magical texts was to enable the priests to control and exorcize these demons, or to break in some way the malign influence which they exerted upon their victim. And, in order to be successful, it was of the utmost importance that the spirit or evil influence which affected the sick man should be mentioned by name. To this end the magician repeated long lists of ghosts and devils, any one of which might be the cause of the sickness. Thanks to this practice, we know a great deal about the Babylonian demons and their characteristics. In order to illustrate the manner of their attack, and how dissociated this was from any moral offence on their victim's part, it will suffice to refer briefly to one class of spirits, the ghosts of the dead. These spirits were the ghosts of dead people which, for some reason or other, could not find rest, but wandered as spectres over the earth. After death the spirits of men and women who died in the ordinary course of nature and were buried were believed to enter the under world, where they eked out a miserable existence with the help of offerings and libations paid to them by their descendants and relatives upon earth. But, if the offerings were not made, or if the corpse was left unburied, the spirit might wander unsatisfied. Other ghosts were the spirits of those who died violent or unnatural deaths, or who departed this life before completing certain natural functions—such as the ghosts of women who died in childbed. As a rule, such spirits haunted ruins or desolate places, and, if a man wandered there, they might seize on him and plague him. A spirit of this sort could also fasten himself on any one who had been in any way connected with him in this life, by the sharing of food with him or by the mere act of eating, drinking, or dressing in his company. From these instances it will be seen that a man was liable, through no fault of his own, to supernatural attack, and precisely similar results were believed to follow both ceremonial and moral offences. To touch the chair or bed of a person already affected by such evil influence or ban was, according to the texts, quite as dangerous as committing a moral offence, such as theft, adultery, or murder, and the resulting condition of sickness or misfortune was the same.

In order to escape the ban and cure his sickness or misfortune, the sufferer had recourse to the magician, who, by his knowledge of magical words, prayers, and ritual, could invoke the help of the great gods, and so gain control over the demon itself, or, in cases induced by human intervention, over the hostile sorcerer or sorceress who had cast the spell. In a large class of texts prepared for the use of the magician their purely magical character is sufficiently apparent from their contents. In others, where the contents refer more to the condition of the sufferer than to the possible causes of his misfortune or the means to relieve it, the essentially magical character of the compositions may sometimes be detected in notes or 'rubrics' which give directions for their due recital and for the performance of accompanying rites and ceremonies. For the rites prescribed often have an intimate connexion with the subject-matter of the prayer or incantation. Sometimes the offerings and the accompanying rites have, to our eyes, only a vague relationship to the character of the god or goddess addressed. But in other compositions the media employed for the magic are specifically named in the recitative, or liturgical, portion of the text. In fact, a study of the rubrics makes it clear that many present a certain general resemblance in giving directions for the recital of the main text over something which is mentioned in the accompanying formulæ. The relationship between text and ritual may be illustrated by the following group of rubrics from the Eighth Tablet of the *Maḳlû* series, col. iii. lines 8–22, which give directions for the due recital of incantations on the Sixth Tablet of the series and the performance of accompanying rites.

'(*a*) The incantation (beginning): "Thou art good, who in a pure place art born!" over a good offering shalt thou recite, and upon the fumigation-bowl, which is at the head of the bed, shalt thou place it.

(*b*) The incantation (beginning): "Come my sorceress or my enchantress!" over a *nulukhkha*-plant shalt thou recite, and upon the fumigation-bowl, which is at the head of the bed, shalt thou place it; (and) with an upper-garment shalt thou envelop the bed.

(*c*) The incantation (beginning): "Come my sorcerer or my enchantress!" over twelve pieces of *sha'irru*-wood shalt thou recite, and upon the fumigation-bowl, which is at the head of the bed, shalt thou place them.

(*d*) The incantation (beginning): "Come my sorceress, my witch, whose paths are over all the world!" over two caged locusts shalt thou recite, and to the right of the door and to the left of the door of the enchanted man shalt thou set them.

(*e*) The incantation (beginning): "Come my sorceress, my witch!" over a stone from the mountain shalt thou recite, and in the court (of the house) shalt thou lay it.

(*f*) The objects for ceremonial burning (*ḳutari*), which belong to the incantation (beginning): "Ellil my head," all that are described as potent against bans, shalt thou heap together and make to go up in smoke. The incantation (beginning): "Ellil my head," shalt thou recite.'

The connexion between these rites and the corresponding sections of the liturgical, or recitative, portions of the composition is clear. For example, the incantation referred to in section (*b*) corresponds to *Maḳlû* vi. 102–109, which twice refers to the *nulukhkha*-plant (cf. 108 f.); that in (*c*) corresponds to *Maḳlû* vi. 110–117, and the *sha'irru*-wood is referred to in line 115 of the text, which should read: 'At the head of my bed will I place twelve pieces of *sha'irru*-wood'; that in (*d*) is *Maḳlû* vi. 118–126, and the two locusts are symbolical of the two 'gods of the watch' who will slay the sorceress (cf. 123 ff.).

This rite of the locusts, which may be regarded as typical of a great body of Babylonian ritual, will be seen, when examined, to be an obvious example of sympathetic magic. The locusts were set, one on each side of the sick man's door, to represent Lugal-girra and Meslamtaea, who, as 'gods of the watch,' would be ready to pounce upon the sorceress and slay her. The magic would work and the gods would act at the second recital of the incantation.

In many of the rites and ceremonies the use of fire was essential, and it would seem that, after the recital of the correct formulæ, the destruction of the objects collected by the magician for that purpose synchronized with the destruction or removal of the evil influence under which the patient suffered. The rites sometimes required substances of some value or rarity, such as fragments of gold or precious stones; and it is probable that, except for powerful or wealthy clients, the magician would make the same fragments do again and again. But the objects used by the magician also included plants, pieces of wood, various sorts of seeds, vegetables, dates, palm-spathes, sheep-skin, wool, etc.—all perishable substances which could easily be consumed. And in their case the sympathetic connexion between the destruction of the ban and that of the object is obvious. That this is the correct explanation of this whole class of ritual is clear from a singularly instructive sub-section, in which the employment of images is prescribed in place of unfashioned natural objects or substances. The images were to be fashioned in human form, to represent the hostile sorcerer or sorceress, and the destruction of these by fire, to the recital of the correct formulæ, was obviously believed to synchronize with the destruction of the hostile person whose figure had been imitated. These images could be made of wax, honey, bitumen, sesame-seed, and the like—all perishable and common substances. When metal was employed, we may assume that the mere passing through the fire was sufficient for the purposes of the magic. Evidence of the great part played by fire in Babylonian magic may be seen in the titles of the two chief magical works, *Shurpu* and *Maḳlû*, both of which signify 'burning,' and in the great number of prayers and incantations addressed to the fire-god.

In one particularly interesting class of magical rites the relationship which was constituted by the magician between the hostile influence and the object destroyed may be clearly traced. Here the magician is engaged in exorcizing a demon from his patient, and, having gained control by the necessary formulæ, he transfers him to some object which may be destroyed or rendered harmless. In one such case the medium is a pot of water, which is then broken and the water spilt; in another a clay image is fastened to the patient's body and afterwards removed; or the body of a pig might be spread upon the sick man, and afterwards thrown out of the house. In these cases we have a physical transference of the hostile power from the sick man to the object employed. In other rites, such as the knotting of cords, the weaving and unweaving of coloured threads, and the like, it is not clear how far the physical action was believed to exercise a direct influence. It is possible that we should explain such rites on the principle of imitation, which is the basis of sympathetic magic.

But it must be confessed that with regard to a considerable section of the ritual we are still not in a position to follow the underlying trains of thought. The large class of so-called medical prescriptions were, no doubt, essentially magical, and, although in some instances the substances prescribed may have actually had curative effects, the associations which led to their employment by the Babylonians are still obscure.

Most of our knowledge of Babylonian magic is derived from purely textual sources, for we have recovered but few amulets, in which we may be said to deal with magic in a concrete form. It is true that we possess a few plague-tablets, inscribed with a text relating to the plague-god, and intended to be hung up in houses to keep off the plague; we have also recovered the figures and heads of demons, sometimes inscribed with incantations; and these, too, were doubtless employed in propitiation or defence. But the only magical apparatus, in the strict sense of the term, that has come down to us may be seen in certain rectangular plaques of cast metal, moulded on the face with the figure of a sick man lying on a couch, attended by the magicians or exorcizers, and surrounded by various hostile demons and protecting spirits or their emblems, which are arranged in horizontal registers. On the back is the large figure of a demon in relief, with his head usually protruding above the top of the plaque. From the subject of the reliefs it is clear that the plaques are to be classified under the general heading of sympathetic magic, but the precise manner in which they were employed by the magician in cases of sickness is not certain. Another class of objects, consisting of little clay figures of deities or birds, which were buried below the pavement in the main doorways of a temple or a palace, may be treated as magical in their supposed effects, but they fall rather under the special heading of foundation-deposits. It may be added that the magical beliefs and practices of the Babylonians survived their racial disappearance, and, largely through Jewish, Syriac, and Mandaic channels, contributed in no small degree to the great and composite body of mediæval magic.

LITERATURE.—General treatises on Babylonian magic will be found in M. Jastrow, *Die Religion Babyloniens und Assyriens*, ii., Giessen, 1910; A. H. Sayce, *The Religions of Ancient Egypt and Babylonia* (Gifford Lectures), Edinburgh, 1902; C. Fossey, *La Magie assyrienne*, Paris, 1902; R. C. Thompson, *Semitic Magic*, London, 1908; R. W. Rogers, *The Religion of Babylonia and Assyria*, New York and London, 1908; and J. Morgenstern, *The Doctrine of Sin in the Babylonian Religion* (=*MVG* x. 3 [1905]). For edd., with trr., of the principal magical works see K. L. Tallqvist, *Die assyrische Beschwörungsserie Maqlû*, Leipzig, 1894; H. Zimmern, *Die Beschwörungstafeln Šurpu*, do. 1896, and *Ritualtafeln für den Wahrsager, Beschwörer, und Sänger*, do. 1901; L. W. King, *Babylonian Magic and Sorcery*, London, 1896; Thompson, *The Devils and Evil Spirits of Babylonia*, do. 1903–04; and S. Langdon, *Sumerian and Babylonian Psalms*, Paris, 1909. Full references to other published texts (up to 1910) are given in Jastrow, *op. cit.*; and for subsequent references, the bibliographies in *ZA*, *AJSL*, or the Babylonian sections of the *Orient. Bibliographie* may be consulted. For the plague-tablet amulets see King, in *ZA* xi. [1896] 50 ff.; and for the magical plaques for the cure of the sick see K. Frank, *Babylonische Beschwörungsreliefs*, Leipzig, 1908. For the latest discussion of the survival of Babylonian magical practices, cf. J. A. Montgomery, *Aramaic Incantation Texts from Nippur*, Philadelphia, 1913, p. 106 ff.

L. W. KING.

MAGIC (Buddhist).—If we rightly understand the real character of Buddhism, what Buddhism ought to be according to its cardinal tenets, there is no possible connexion between Buddhism and magic. The only aim of the Buddhist monk is '*nirvāṇa* to be attained in this life,' *i.e.* absolute freedom from passion in order to reach freedom from rebirth, *i.e.* eternal, blissful *nirvāṇa*. All the machinery of intellectual and moral life is organized with a view to this. Buddhism does not deny that there are good (*kuśala*) acts that ripen into happiness in a future life (*svarga*, 'paradise'),[1] but monks consider them not only as of no avail for, but even as obstacles to, *nirvāṇa*. Ascetic and religious acts (*śilavrata*, *tapas*, *pūjā*) have no place in the training for *nirvāṇa*, and it is a very grave and delusive heresy to lay stress upon them. *A fortiori*, in contrast with Vedism and Brāhmanism, Buddhism ignores all the magical theories connected with sacrifice, worship, or asceticism as a means of salvation. As far as every-day or trivial magic is concerned, its efficiency is acknowledged, but Buddhists are strictly forbidden to practise it; all kinds of magical arts and performances—even of a benevolent nature—are regarded as pernicious.[2]

But 'historic Buddhism' is not, in every respect, what Buddhism ought to be. Buddhists are Hindus, 'regular' Hindus; and no large religious body has ever been found that was always scrupulously faithful to the true spirit of its creed, the more so as the Buddhist creed implies a superhuman disinterestedness and a non-Oriental disregard for any kind of superstition.

1. **Ṛddhi.**—There is a large category of 'superhuman' activities, which to some extent would be understood by Europeans as magical, and which are 'very good Buddhism.' We mean *ṛddhi* (Pāli *iddhi*)—in the words of Rhys Davids, 'mystic wonder,' 'wondrous gift,' 'magic power,' a mastery (*prabhāva*), which is only the exercise of a power acquired by pious works, by penance, and also by 'formulæ,' and especially by contemplation.

There is nothing 'preternatural' in the *ṛddhi*, and the natural character of the 'miracles' performed by *ṛddhi* is clearly shown in the following passage of the *Milinda-pañha*: '"There are persons who can go with this four-element-made body to

[1] These are 'mundane' (*laukika*) good acts, in contrast with 'supramundane' (*lokottara*), those which lead to *nirvāṇa*, *i.e.* the volitions concerned with 'trances' (*dhyāna*) and other 'concentrations' (*samādhi*).

[2] On the position of the Buddha with regard to magic see T. W. Rhys Davids, *Dialogues of the Buddha*, i. (*SBB* ii., London, 1899) 273.

Uttara-kuru [see art. BLEST, ABODE OF THE (Buddhist)], or to the Brahma world . . ." "But how can they?" "Do you admit having ever jumped three or six feet of ground?" "Yes, I do; I can jump twelve feet." "But how?" "I cause this idea to arise: 'There will I alight!' With the genesis of this idea, my body becomes buoyant to me." "Just so does a monk, who has *iddhi* and mastery over his thought, travel through the air."'[1]

The man whose thought is concentrated has indeed a great power over his body; but this power is not different, in nature, from the power of an ordinary man.

Birds are, by nature, endowed with magic power, as is proved by the fact that they go through the air. Their *ṛddhi* is 'born from the ripening of acts,' *i.e.*, the special character of some of their acts in a former birth endows them with this special 'superhuman' faculty. Gods are, of course, magicians; they go through the air, they create at their will palaces and pleasures (*bhoga*). Sovereign kings or world-emperors (*chakravartin* [*q.v.*]), too, are magicians by nature. Ordinary men obtain momentary magic power by many devices, and are 'superhuman' at some time and for some object.[2]

As a matter of fact, Buddha was looked upon by his followers—as he was by the unbelievers—as a great magician; and it is recognized by all Buddhists that magic power is one of the natural possessions of the saints, since they are holy men, just like the *yogīs* of old and the modern *faqīrs*. Magic power ranks therefore with the divine eye, the divine ear, the knowledge of the thought of others, the knowledge of former births, the knowledge of the disappearing of passions, *i.e.* with the most desirable gifts of saintship. And it is no mean eulogy of Maudgalyāyana that he is styled 'the best of the Buddha's disciples with regard to magic.'

It is evident that the admission of the reality of *ṛddhi* is beset with many dangers. Buddhists were, accordingly, strictly forbidden to boast of possessing superhuman faculties; that was one of the gravest sins.

There is nothing specially Buddhist in the manifestations of *ṛddhi*. Buddha's disciples win success in the phantasmagorial shows which have long been familiar to Hindu romancers and dreamers:

'Being one, he becomes many, or having become many, becomes one again; he becomes invisible or visible; he goes, feeling no obstruction, to the other side of a wall or rampart or hill, as if through air; he penetrates up and down through solid ground, as if through air; he walks on water . . .; he travels cross-legged in the sky; even the sun and the moon, so mighty though they be, does he touch and feel with his hand; he reaches in the body even up to the heaven of Brahmā. . . .'[3]

Stories of miraculous exhibitions intended to convert the incredulous are frequent. Buddha and his disciples willingly condescend to give 'signs.'

When the Tibetan writer Tāranātha narrates the mediæval miraculous tournaments between the Buddhist and Brāhmanist scholars, which often conclude with the Buddhist victory and the conversion of kings, he only testifies the continuance of an old tradition. But—and this restriction is of paramount import—even when narrating miracles, the old texts add that miracles, by themselves, prove nothing; the unbelievers, conquered by the more powerful magic of Buddha, used to say: 'Gautama'—the 'mundane' name of the Buddha, and the one used by unbelievers—'Gautama is the magician (*māyāvin*); every thousandth year there appears in the world a great magician who eats or enjoys the world' (*Abhidharmakośa*); or, in the words of the *Kevaddhasutta*: 'Well, Sir! there is a certain charm called the gandhāra-charm. It is by the efficacy thereof that he performs all this.'[4]

There is in the *Bodhisattvabhūmi*, a text-book of the Vijñānavādins (by Asaṅga, 4th–5th cent. A.D.?), a complete survey of the magical power of the *bodhisattvas*. It is said to be twofold: *pāriṇāmikī ṛddhi*, power of transformation, when a *bodhisattva* modifies the nature of an existing thing; and *nairmāṇikī*, power of creation, when he creates some thing or some person. The 'created persons' (*nirmita, nirmitaka*) are frequently mentioned in the Mahāyāna works; but they are not unknown in the Hīnayāna, both Pāli and Sanskrit. Elaborate theories on the *nirmitakas* are to be found in the *Abhidharma* treatises of the Sarvāstivādins (*Lokaprajñāpti*, 1st cent. A.D.), which embody the views of the Sanskrit Hīnayāna; and in the *Abhidharmakośa* (ch. vi.), where the creative power of Buddha and of the gods (*nirmāṇarati*, etc.) is discussed.[1]

2. Paritta.—Another very orthodox form of magic is *parittā*, or *rakkhā*, 'guard,' 'safeguard.' It plays an important part in Siṁhalese Buddhism under the name of *pirit* (Spence Hardy, *Eastern Monachism*, London, 1850, p. 240, *Manual of Buddhism*², do. 1880, p. 47; D. J. Gogerly, *Ceylon Buddhism*, ed. A. S. Bishop, Colombo, 1908, pp. 327–393). Good examples are found in Pāli literature.

Taking refuge in the three 'jewels' (*ratna, ratana*), Buddha, the *Dharma*, and the *Saṅgha*, forms a charm called '*sutta* of the jewels,' which is very efficacious against illness:

'Whatever spirits have come together here, either belonging to the earth or living in the air, let all spirits be happy, and then listen attentively to what is said. Therefore, O spirits, do ye all pay attention, show kindness to the human race who both day and night bring their offerings; therefore protect them strenuously. Whatever wealth there be here or in the other world, or whatever excellent jewel in the heavens, it is certainly not equal to Tathāgata. . . . By this truth may there be salvation.' In the same way: 'Nothing is equal to the *Dharma*, to the *Saṅgha*!'[2]

So also, in the Peacock *Jātaka*, sun-worship ('the only king, the one who beholds, the light of the world') is connected with that of the Buddhas:

'I worship thee, golden and luminous being! May I spend this day under thy care! Homage to the omniscient sages! May they protect me! Homage to the Buddhas and to the illumination, to the delivered and to the deliverance! . . .'

When Śākyamuni was a large golden peacock, he recited this half-solar, half-Buddhist prayer morning and evening, and consequently avoided all dangers. And, as the peacock is the born enemy of serpents, the '*sutta* (or 'charm') of the peacock' is used as a preventive and as a cure for serpent-bites.[3]

In these examples the magical character is not very prominent: there is nothing pagan in the formulæ, which are, above all, acts of Buddhist faith; there is nothing mechanical, nothing really magical, in the efficacy ascribed to the *pirit*. The non-Buddhist gods are clearly subordinated to the Buddha: it is almost a dogma that the Buddha converted gods and demons;[4] and it is quite reasonable to believe that they will grant their favour to the disciples of Buddha. It is believed also that benevolence (*maitrī*) possesses a power in itself (*maitrībala*), which is capable of protecting the benevolent person against all the attacks of the wicked; in order to avoid serpent-bites, it is not a bad plan to sleep on a raised bed, but the right method is to declare to all the tribes of serpents that they are being enveloped in a universal sentiment of benevolence.[5] This magic of bene-

[1] C. A. F. Rhys Davids, *Buddhist Psychology*, London, 1914, p. 161; see also pp. 127, 190, 199; *SBE* xxxv. [1890] 129 f. Magic power (*ṛddhi*) is sometimes only a momentary possession; cf. the story of a disciple who, when crossing a river, concentrates his mind, and, accordingly, walks on water; but, being distracted, he sinks (*Jātaka* 190).

[2] On the ten kinds of *iddhi* see *Paṭisambhidāmagga* (London, 1907), ii. 205. The *iddhi* 'born from spells' or 'made of spells' (*vijjāmaya*) is the worst.

[3] See 'Sāmaññaphalasutta,' *Dialogues of the Buddha*, i. 88, and *Mahāvyutpatti*, § 14 f. (*Bibl. Buddhica*, xiii., Petrograd, 1911).

[4] *Dialogues of the Buddha*, i. 278.

[1] A summary of the *Bodhisattvabhūmi* has been published by C. Bendall and the present writer in *Muséon*, vi. [1905] 38–52, vii. [1906] 213–230. A summary of the *Lokaprajñāpti* is being published as an Appendix in *Cosmologie bouddhique, troisième chapitre de l'Abhidharmakośa*, London, 1915.

[2] 'Ratanasutta' (*Sutta-Nipāta*, ii. 1); Rhys Davids, *SBE* xxxv. 213; art. JEWEL (Buddhist), § 9.

[3] *Morajātaka*, *Jātaka*, ed. V. Fausböll, London, 1877–97, ii. 33.

[4] It is a dogma for the Sarvāstivādins (see A. Csoma and L. Feer, 'Analyse du Kandjour,' *AMG* ii. [1881] 167). The Pāli sources admit that there are still wicked gods (*Dīgha*, xxxii.).

[5] See *Chullavagga*, vi. 2. 3, and v. 6. 1 (*SBE* xx. [1885] 163 f., 75 f.).

volence is the most noteworthy invention of Buddhism in connexion with the subject which we are discussing.

3. Hindu influences.—All practices tainted with magic or superstition, from the most trivial to the most serious, are strictly forbidden: astrology, divination, charms, incantations—in a word, all that any one may accomplish with the help of certain secret recipes and a technical method. Holy men, in ancient as in modern India, priests or sorcerers, had only too much opportunity for making huge profits by giving horoscopes and practising white or black magic. The Buddha—the first Order—was anxious that the monks should be sheltered from this temptation, and drew up a long list of 'wrong means of livelihood,' of low arts, that were strictly prohibited. The Brāhmans also made an effort to distinguish themselves from sorcerers.

Among these 'low arts' we may mention specially:

'Arranging a lucky day for marriages; using charms to make people lucky or unlucky, to procure abortion, to bring on dumbness, deafness, to keep a man's jaw fixed; obtaining oracular answers by means of the magic mirror, or through a girl possessed; bringing forth flames from one's mouth; causing virility; making a man impotent; invoking Siri (Śrī), the goddess of luck; worship of sun,' etc.[1]

Whatever precautions the Order took to avoid all paganism and superstition, there is, nevertheless, a Buddhist magic. It was impossible to guard against Hindu infiltrations. At no time could people have been completely ignorant of the sun or the inferior deities; a day came when the infiltrations became 'streams,' when paganism—gods, rites, theurgies—under a thin Buddhist veneer, took its place in sacred literature. Of course, we find popular magic always condemned in principle (love-rites, elixir of life, etc.). What is more serious, official worship and mysticism are permeated with Hindu elements, heavily laden with magic; this is, properly speaking, what is called Tantrism (*q.v.*).

Among the earliest of these infiltrations we may mention: (1) in some very orthodox books of the Mahāyāna, the great value attached to the sacred texts, to the *sūtras*, the mere reading of which effaces sin; (2) the great value attached to sacred names (*e.g.*, the name of Amitābha): devotion turns to superstition pure and simple; (3) the name replaced or strengthened by mystic formulæ (see AVALOKITEŚVARA), represented, when carried to an extreme, by the Tibetan 'prayer-wheel'; it has been noticed that, in the *Lotus of the True Law* (*q.v.*), in which there is no mention of a female deity, the formulas are made from feminine vocatives: these invocations or litanies are undoubtedly borrowed from rituals; (4) the coming of a day when the rituals received the consecration of literature, and were put at the service of the great work of identifying the faithful with the Buddhas (Tantrism).

LITERATURE.—R. C. Childers, *Dictionary of the Pali Language*, London, 1875, *s.vv.* 'Iddhi,' 'Parittā'; M. Winternitz, *SBE* i. [1910], *s.vv.* 'Iddhi,' 'Magic,' 'Miracles'; *Jātaka*, Eng. tr., ed. E. B. Cowell, Cambridge, 1895–1913, vii. *s.vv.* 'Magic,' 'Miracles'; L. de la Vallée Poussin, *Bouddhisme*, Paris, 1909, p. 362 f.

L. DE LA VALLÉE POUSSIN.

MAGIC (Celtic).

1. Wielders of magic.—Magical rites resembling those used by other races abound in Celtic paganism. They were performed by the gods, the Tuatha Dé Danann being later regarded as supernal wizards, by kings (a reminiscence, perhaps, of the origin of the kingship in the magic-wielding class), and by all members of society, but, above all, by the druids as the official magical class. There is evidence that they had ousted women as the earlier magic-wielding persons. The rites of agriculture and the possession of much primitive lore having been first of all in the hands of women, and these rites being largely magical, they were *par excellence* magicians. With the gradual encroachment of man on woman's domain, with the growing supremacy of gods over goddesses, men became also greater magicians. But women still professed magic, and their claims were never forgotten. The so-called 'druidesses' of the later empire, the priestesses of Sena, and the virgin guardians of Brigit's fire were magic-wielders. The 'spells of women' were feared even by St. Patrick, as they had been in earlier times by Connla's father,[1] and in the Irish texts women as magicians, performing all magical rites ascribed to druids, are much in evidence. But their magic was, so to speak, non-official; hence, when the druids were overthrown, they still retained their powers, and much mediæval witchcraft is directly connected with them. Women, as the earliest, remained also the latest, magicians, though in time they were proscribed and persecuted. On the other hand, many of the druidic magical rites were later ascribed to the *filid*, or poets, and also to Christian saints. Whatever view may be taken of the origin of the druids, it is certain that the Celts believed firmly in magic, and did not require to learn the superstition in any of its branches from the races which they conquered.

For the druids as magicians in Gaul and Ireland see DRUIDS, § 7. Their prominence is seen in the fact that in later Celtic literature 'druid' is the equivalent of *magus*, 'magician,' as in the lives of Celtic saints *magi* = 'druids,' while in saga and folk-tale 'druidism' = magic.

2. Elemental magic.—The druids, who claimed to have created the elements, claimed also to rule them. They could cover the dry land with the sea to destroy their victims;[2] they produced enchanted mists in which to hide people or places; they changed day into night, or caused blinding snow-storms. These feats are ascribed to them even in the lives of early Celtic saints.[3] They caused showers of fire to fall upon enemies during battle.[4] In other cases they dried up all the rivers and wells in an enemy's country by means of spells, though the druids of the latter caused water to flow again by shooting an arrow into the ground.[5] They even claimed to remove mountains and dash them against an opposing host.[6] Druids accompanied the warring hosts of Erin, and these marvels usually occurred on such occasions, the rival magicians striving to outdo each other. These and other powers—*e.g.*, rain-making—were later claimed by wizards (*tempestarii*) and witches in Christian times over the Celtic area. Rain-making was usually associated with a sacred well, whither the people went in procession, probably with an image of a divinity, which was sprinkled with the water; in some instances it was sufficient to beat the water with branches, sprinkle it on stones, or throw it in the air. In certain cases the Church took over this rite by making it a part of an elaborate ritual, including a procession with an image of a saint, the priest officiating and saying prayers.[7] But in pagan times the presence of a druid was probably essential. The control of the elements by *tempestarii*, which was denounced by the Church, was directly borrowed from druidic magic. Until comparatively recent times the

[1] See Rhys Davids, *Dialogues of the Buddha*, i. 23 f.—a collection of interesting documents on the ancient life of India.

[1] W. O. E. Windisch, *Irische Texte*, Leipzig, 1880 ff., i. 56; H. d'Arbois de Jubainville, *L'Épopée celtique en Irlande*, Paris, 1892, p. 387.

[2] D'Arbois, p. 277.

[3] W. Stokes, *Three Middle-Irish Homilies*, Calcutta, 1877, p. 24.

[4] *RCel* xii. [1891] 83; d'Arbois de Jubainville, p. 424.

[5] E. O'Curry, *Lectures on the MS Materials of Ancient Irish Hist.*, Dublin, 1861, p. 271 f.

[6] *RCel* xii. 81.

[7] L. F. A. Maury, *Croyances et légendes du moyen âge*, Paris, 1896, p. 14; P. Sébillot, *Folk-lore de France*, do. 1904–07, i. 101, ii. 224 f.; L. J. B. Bérenger-Féraud, *Superstitions et survivances*, do. 1896, iii. 169, 190.

priest in rural French parishes was believed capable of causing rain in time of drought, or of averting tempests.[1]

3. Magic affecting human beings.—The druids could make themselves or others invisible, and this was also done by Celtic saints.[2] A spell used for this purpose, or by which the person using it appeared in another form to his enemy and so escaped, as well as the effect produced, was called *fœth fiada* ('the wild beast's cry'). By it he and his followers appeared as deer to their foes.[3] The power of such an incantation is still spoken of in remote parts of the W. Highlands.[4] Still more common was the power of shape-shifting, which was also ascribed to women. The evidence of Irish texts shows that the druid could take any shape, or invest others with it, while the same power is also ascribed to divinities.

The children of Ler became swans through the arts of their step-mother, the daughter of the god Bodb Derg, while Oisin's mother became a fawn through the power of the druid Fear Doirche (P. W. Joyce, *Old Celtic Romances*2, London, 1894, p. 1ff.; P. Kennedy, *Legendary Fictions of the Irish Celts*, do. 1866, p. 235). The priestesses of Sena could take any shape (Pomp. Mela, iii. 6), and many tales of goddesses or women assuming the shape of birds are found in the sagas. In some instances the belief is evidently connected with totemism, explaining a tabu upon eating certain animals by saying that they were human beings transformed.

'Riming' people to death—a practice used by the *filid* as well as by the druids—was connected with the power of the spoken word, though it may also be connected with the actual power of violent emotion to affect the body. It was usually the result of a satire spoken in verse to the victim; black, red, and white blotches arose on the face, and were followed, sooner or later, by decay or death. The satire was probably a magical spell, and the fear of such a spell brought about the result automatically. Coirpre pronounced the first satire in Ireland upon Bres, king of the Fomorians, and many other instances occur in the texts.[5] To the power of the satire was attributed a quelling force over nature itself.[6] A magical sleep was also produced in different ways. Sometimes it was done by music, which produced first laughter, then tears, then sleep. These three results are uniformly ascribed to music in Irish saga; they were brought about by Dagda's harp, as well as by the songs of the *filid*.[7] All this probably reflects the power of music upon primitive minds, especially since it is so frequently connected with religious or magical dances and orgiastic rites, in which the motion and the music produce delirium, then exhaustion. But it may also suggest the soothing power of music. Similar magical sleep was caused by the music of divine visitants (see BLEST, ABODE OF THE [Celtic], §§ 2, 6). In other cases sleep was produced by a 'drink of oblivion,' probably some narcotic made from herbs;[8] but sometimes the effect was curious, as when Cúchulainn, by the drink given him by the druids, was made to forget his fairy mistress, and his wife to forget her jealousy.[9] Another 'druidic sleep,' in which the victim is made to forget or is rendered motionless, and occasionally in that state is caused to tell secrets, is of frequent occurrence, and is suggestive of hypnotism, the powers of which are well known to savage medicine-men, and may quite well have been employed by the druids.[10] The power of 'glamour' produced by

[1] Bérenger-Féraud, iii. 218; *GB*3, pt. i., *The Magic Art*, London, 1911, i. 232.
[2] D'Arbois de Jubainville, p. 387.
[3] Windisch, i. 52; Stokes, *Tripartite Life of St. Patrick*, London, 1887, p. 38.
[4] A. Carmichael, *Carmina Gadelica*, Edinburgh, 1900, ii. 25.
[5] *RCel* xii. 71; O'Curry, p. 248.
[6] Windisch, *Die altir. Heldensage, Táin bó Cúalnge*, Leipzig, 1905, line 5467.
[7] *RCel* xii. 109; O'Curry, p. 255.
[8] Joyce, p. 279.
[9] Windisch, *Ir. Texte*, i. 226.
[10] Joyce, p. 88; *RCel* xxiii. [1902] 394.

magicians, by which stones or trees seemed to be armed men and were attacked by the victim, is also strongly suggestive of hypnotic influence. It may, however, be merely the record of actual hallucinatory cases, since the 'glamour' in which the modern Celt believes is little else than hallucination. The druid could also turn a man into a lunatic by throwing a wisp of straw at his face after saying a spell over it.[1] Even more primitive was the method of killing a person by throwing a spear into his shadow,[2] or of making an image of him and sticking pins into it or placing it in running water, so that he might suffer or waste away. This image is the *corp creadh*, still known and used in remote Celtic regions.

4. The Airbe Druad, or 'Druid's hedge,' was an invisible magic barrier made by the magician round an army, probably by circumambulating it sunwise and singing spells. Its effect was that the ranks could not be broken, but, if any one was bold enough to break through, its power was gone, though the act usually cost the trespasser his life.[3]

5. Magical rites connected with stones and trees.—The cult of stones and the belief that sepulchral stones were the abode of the ghosts of the dead probably gave rise to many magical rites, the origin of which must be sought in remote times. Many of these are still practised, and the method used throws light upon the earlier pagan customs. These are of a magico-erotic nature, and, like similar rites among savages, are founded on the belief that the ghost can cause fruitfulness, or perhaps may incarnate himself in the barren woman who performs the rite. The woman sits on the stone, or slides down it, or thrusts her head or body through a hole in one of the stones of a dolmen. Pregnant women do the same to ensure an easy delivery, or unmarried girls to procure a husband.[4] Similar practices are used in connexion with boulders or stones which are not sepulchral, and probably these were anterior to the use of megalithic monuments. In these cases the rocks were believed to be the abode of spirits, or perhaps manifestations of the power of the Earth divinity, who gave vitality or fruitfulness to those performing the rites. A small offering was usually left on the stone.[5] Such practices may already have been used by the Celts, though they necessarily adapted them to existing stones and monuments in the lands conquered by them. Other practices were the passing of sick persons three times through a holed dolmen or a weather-worn hole in a rock, to obtain strength and healing.[6] In other cases a slit was made in an oak or ash sapling, through which the patient was passed, and the slit was then carefully closed and bound. The underlying idea is complex. The spirit of tree or stone was expected to cause healing, or there was a transference of the disease to either, or perhaps there was some idea of a new birth with renewed strength to the re-born.[7]

Certain magical stones had the power of producing rain or wind when turned with appropriate rites, or in other cases the water in which stones of a fetish kind had been dipped procured healing when it was drunk—a method used by St. Columba.[8] Other magical rites with stones were used in cursing an enemy.

[1] O'Curry, *Manners and Customs of the Ancient Irish*, London, 1873, ii. 203.
[2] *RCel* xv. [1894] 444.
[3] Stokes, *Lives of Irish Saints*, Oxford, 1890, p. xxviii.
[4] Bérenger-Féraud, i. 529 ff.; T. A. Trollope, *A Summer in Brittany*, London, 1840, ii. 229; W. C. Borlase, *The Dolmens of Ireland*, do. 1897, iii. 841.
[5] Sébillot, i. 334 f.
[6] Bérenger-Féraud, i. 529, ii. 367.
[7] *L'Anthropologie*, iv. [Paris, 1893] 33; F. T. Elworthy, *The Evil Eye*, London, 1895, pp. 69, 106.
[8] Adamnan, *Vita S. Columbæ*, ii. 34; J. A. MacCulloch, *The Misty Isle of Skye*, Edinburgh, 1905, p. 249.

6. Celtic saints and magic.—Much of the magic of the druids was popularly ascribed to the saints who combated them—with this difference, that their power was held to come from God. In the *Lives* of Celtic saints we find them opposing druids with their own weapons—neutralizing their magic, controlling the elements, producing rain, rendering themselves invisible, producing marvellous supplies of food, and causing transformation or confusion through their curses. The popular belief in magic could not be eradicated, and they who now filled the place of the ancient priesthood were freely dowered by the people and by their biographers with the ancient powers.

See also CHARMS AND AMULETS (Celtic).

LITERATURE.—J. A. MacCulloch, *The Religion of the Ancient Celts*, Edinburgh, 1911; S. Reinach, *Cultes, mythes, et religions*, Paris, 1905-12, *passim*.

J. A. MACCULLOCH.

MAGIC (Chinese).—Magic in all its forms is a subject which has always fascinated the Chinese mind. The literature which deals with the theory and practice of magic is enormous; and, if much of this literature is wearisome to the modern reader on account of the childish credulity of its authors and the extravagance of their speculations, it is nevertheless worthy of more patient scrutiny and analysis than it has yet received from anthropologists and students of folklore, or even from serious students of Chinese life and character. In this article we cannot do more than touch the fringe of a subject which derives much of its interest from the fact that a belief in magic is still a living force in the China of to-day.

There are many early references to a class of sorcerers or witches known as *wu*. This name is often applied to male as well as female witches, though the more correct designation of the former is *chi*. The term *chi* is rarely found outside the old books, but the term *wu* (usually in some such combination as *wu-p'o*, which means 'witch-wife') has persisted throughout the ages, and is still in common use. In pre-Confucian days the *wu* held a recognized position in the social organization of the country. They were entrusted even in the courts of kings with certain quasi-sacerdotal functions, and in public ceremonials they had stated duties to perform in connexion with divination and exorcism. Judging from the somewhat meagre accounts which we possess, we may suspect that the rites observed by the *wu* were in many respects identical with those practised to this day by the shamans of Central Asia and Siberia (see BURIATS, SHAMANISM). Their methods included mimetic dancing, drum-beating, chanting of mystic formulæ, and trance-mediumship, and their efforts were directed towards the foretelling of the future, the conjuration of spirits, and (in general) the invocation of good influences and the expulsion of evil. In the course of ages their position gradually deteriorated. This was largely the result of the rise of Confucian culture, which always aimed at reducing every non-Confucian ideal and practice to a position of inferiority; but it was also due to the fact that many of the magical notions and methods of the *wu* fraternity were taken up and systematized by the Taoists. This is one of the reasons why the popular Taoism of modern times concerns itself with magic and sorcery to an extent which seems quite unwarranted by early Taoist philosophy, and why the illiterate village witches and fortune-tellers of the present day usually profess to act in co-operation with one or more of the innumerable Taoist deities, in spite of the fact that they are the sole surviving representatives of the ancient *wu*, whose name they still bear.

There is reason to believe, however, that besides the officially-recognized *wu* there were always numerous 'free-lance' witches who carried on a lucrative business among the superstitious multitudes, and whose connexion with the State-cult or predominant religion of the time was little more than nominal. It was probably sorcerers of this type that were aimed at in certain anti-witchcraft regulations (reminding us of Plato's *Laws*, xi. 933) which we find in the *Li Ki*—the canonical 'Book of Rites.'

'Those who gave false reports about spirits, about seasons and days, about consultings of the tortoise-shell and stalks, so as to perplex the multitudes: these were put to death' (*SBE* xxvii. 237 f.). It may be added that the same fate befell inventors of 'wonderful contrivances and extraordinary implements,' because such things raised 'doubts among the multitude' (*ib.*).

But it seems that even the official *wu* were not always free from peril, for the very fact that they were supposed to have a mysterious controlling power over the forces of nature rendered them liable to terrible punishment if those forces seemed to be showing hostility to mankind.

In the year 683 B.C., *e.g.*, there was a disastrous drought, and a certain reigning duke expressed his intention of dealing with the situation by burning two persons—an emaciated or deformed man and a witch. Evidently this was a familiar practice in such emergencies, and the reason why special mention was made of it in this particular case was that, owing to the remonstrances of the duke's minister—who seems to have been far in advance of his time in his attitude towards popular superstitions—the barbarous custom was not carried out.[1] From a similar story which refers to the reign of Duke Mu (409-377 B.C.) it appears that the practice had been modified to the extent that the witch and deformed man were no longer burned alive, but were merely exposed to the scorching heat of the sun.[2]

One explanation of these customs is that by burning a deformed or emaciated man, or by exposing him to the sun, the pity of the heavenly powers would be aroused and rain would be sent to alleviate the wretched man's sufferings; and that the same happy result would follow the burning or exposure of a witch, because a witch was a person who was able to compel spirits to descend to earth. A sounder explanation is based on the belief in the supposed interaction of the principles of *yang* and *yin*—the male and female, or active and passive, forces, which by their alternating pulsations or activities give rise to all natural phenomena. In time of drought the *yang* principle shows excessive activity and disturbs the harmony of nature's processes; steps must be taken, therefore, to redress the balance of forces. The intricacies of the *yin-yang* theory are necessarily bewildering to a Western reader until he has acquired some knowledge of the principles of *feng-shui* (*q.v.*); but it is this pseudo-philosophy—belief in which is slowly decaying in China, but is still far from extinct—that supplies some of the most important hypotheses on which the edifice of Chinese magic has been erected.

No doubt it was only in extremely serious cases of drought that the witches were tortured or put to death. The regular method of obtaining their assistance in rain-making was to send them out, under the guidance of their official leader, the *ssŭ-wu*, to perform a ritual dance.[3] The dancing of the witches formed part of the ordinary ritual observed on the occasion of the official rain-sacrifices; and, if we may judge from similar practices in other parts of the world, the dancing partook of the nature of mimetic magic.[4] It was

[1] See *Tso Chuan*, in Legge's *Chinese Classics*, vol. v. pt. i. p. 179 f.

[2] See *SBE* xxvii. 201. It has been suspected by commentators that the two stories refer to the same historical incident.

[3] *Chou Li* (Biot's tr., ii. 102).

[4] The ceremonial dancing of ancient China was not always magical. There were six dances officially recognized under the Chou dynasty, of which only one (the *huang*) had anything to do with rain-making. Ceremonial dancing is not yet extinct in China, for it still forms part of the ritual proceedings at the Confucian sacrifices. For an interesting account of the ancient Chinese dances see H. A. Giles, *Adversaria Sinica*, Shanghai, 1906, p. 119 f.

accompanied by music; and, if there is any truth in such ancient legends as that of King Mu (whose reign ended in 947 B.C.), we may suspect that music preceded dancing as a means of producing rain. We are told that the method adopted by that monarch for putting an end to an excessive drought was to play magic music on his flute.

Many of the observances still carried out at the popular festivals in China are undoubtedly of a magical character, and are intended to regulate the rainfall, to expel disease and misfortune, to ensure good harvests, and to attract good luck. Communal magic of this kind is sometimes official in character, as in the case of the spring-welcoming ceremonies presided over by the local district-magistrates; but for the most part the rites are conducted by the villagers themselves, under the guidance of their own clan-committees (*hui-shou*), or headmen. Ceremonies which at one time were doubtless carried out with punctilious care and with something like religious awe have in many cases become mere village games and pastimes of which the original significance has been partially or wholly lost. Such are the lantern-dances and stilt-walking of the children of N. China at the full moon of the first month of the year. Few of those who take part in such merry-makings understand that by the skilful manipulation of their paper lanterns they are supposed to be helping and encouraging the moon to go successfully through her phases; that in getting up before dawn on a certain day and cooking a dumpling which 'rises' they are assisting nature to stimulate the dormant activities of animals and vegetation; and that in walking on stilts over ground destined to produce a crop of grain they are helping the wheat and millet to grow to their full height. It is perhaps a significant fact (when we remember the important part played by women in fertility-magic in other parts of the world) that many of the men and boys who take part in these festival-ceremonies are clothed for the occasion in women's garments.

Magical notions are also traceable in numerous simple acts which practically every family performs with a view to the well-being of its own members. Such are the hanging of certain plants above the doorway on certain days, the entwining of red threads in the queues of children to protect them from the demons of disease, and the affixing of pieces of scarlet cloth to the scrub-oak bushes to ensure the protection of the shrubs and the silkworms against hurtful insects and noxious influences. At the New Year it is customary to cover the outsides of doors and windows with paper scrolls containing sage mottoes, quotations from classical and other literature, and words expressive of virtuous aims or suggestive of material prosperity. These scrolls may fairly be regarded as magic charms which will not only prevent evil from entering the house, but will attract the influences which make for good fortune and happiness. Many of the usages connected with death and burial, the ceremonial summoning of ancestral spirits, and the tabuing of personal names are also essentially magical, though their intimate connexion with religious beliefs and observances makes it difficult to decide where magic ends and religion begins.

In China, as elsewhere, magic arts are practised for private and personal as well as for public and family purposes, and many persons who know of no normal method whereby they may bring about the fulfilment of their desires are glad to seek the aid of magicians and witches. The witches of China have had many illustrious clients. One of them was the T'ang emperor Hsüan Tsung, who ordered certain Taoist necromancers to summon before him the shade of his dead consort, the beautiful Yang Kuei-fei. Very similar stories are told of the emperor Wu of the Han dynasty and the emperor Hsiao-Wu of the earlier Sung dynasty. As for the self-styled 'First Emperor,' who reigned in the 3rd cent. B.C., the assistance of witches and necromancers in his case was unnecessary, for he—like the king Solomon of Muhammadan legend—was himself a king of magicians.[1] Returning to more recent times, we find that the great empress-dowager, who died in 1908, put implicit faith for a time in the magical attainments of the 'Boxers'; and, though the 'Sacred Edict' of the emperor K'ang-hsi bids men abjure all kinds of heterodox teachings and practices, among which the arts of magic are included, and though in quite recent years proclamations have been issued warning the people not to allow themselves to be deluded by witches and soothsayers, it is beyond question that a belief in the reality of magic is by no means confined to the ignorant peasantry.

The official attitude towards 'black magic' (to use the convenient Western term) is clearly demonstrated in the anti-witchcraft clauses of the Penal Code of the late Manchu dynasty. The punishments inflicted on persons convicted of this crime were extremely severe, though it is only fair to add (in the words of a scholarly student of the subject) that 'the pages of Chinese history have never been stained by such a mad epidemic of witch-killing as disgraced Europe and America in the seventeenth century.'[2]

As recently as the summer of 1914 an alleged case of 'black magic' occurred in the territory of Wei-hai-wei, at present administered by Great Britain.

The inhabitants of a certain village approached one of the British Courts with a petition in which they complained that a fellow-villager had been practising magic with disastrous results to their little community. It was stated that he had quarrelled with the village headman, and had foretold the headman's death. 'And sure enough,' they said, 'the headman died, though there was nothing whatever the matter with him.' Two or three other enemies of the accused subsequently died in the same mysterious way; and, to crown all, a villager, on going to the shrine of the guardian-spirit of the village, discovered there a slip of paper on which were written, in the accused's handwriting, the names of various people with whom he was known to be on bad terms. This discovery created a panic among the villagers, who took it for granted that the list comprised the names of all those unfortunate persons whom the wizard had condemned to a speedy death. They therefore seized him and brought him before the writer of this article, who in his magisterial capacity had to perform the somewhat delicate task of differentiating between real and imaginary wrongs and grievances.

From the point of view of the student of magic, the special interest of this particular case centres in the unexpected part played by the tutelary deity of the village. Here, it would appear, we have an instructive example of the intermingling of religion and magic, and the junction seems to have been brought about in this way. One of the principal functions of the *t'u-ti*, or village deity, is to receive the spirits of the newly dead and to act as their spiritual friend and guardian.[3] Each village has its own little shrine dedicated to the local deity, and this shrine usually stands by the roadside a short distance outside the village. When a villager dies, the members of his family go in procession to the *t'u-ti* shrine to make a formal announcement of the death, in order that the deity may make arrangements for the proper reception of the dead man's spirit. Now, at first sight, there seems to be no obvious reason why an

[1] For some of the stories of his magical exploits, which included the transfixing of the sun with a needle in order that uninterrupted daylight might be secured for the building of the Great Wall, see R. F. Johnston, *Lion and Dragon in Northern China*, London, 1910, p. 20 f.

[2] E. T. Williams, in a paper on 'Witchcraft in the Chinese Penal Code,' *JRAS* (North China Branch) xxxviii. [1907] 95.

[3] For a full discussion of the *t'u-ti* and his functions see Johnston, p. [illegible]1[illegible]

expert in black magic who wishes to bring about the death of his enemies should expect the *t'u-ti*—who is regarded as friendly to men and interested in their welfare—to give him help and countenance in carrying out his nefarious designs against their lives. What, then, is the magician's object in placing a list of the names of his intended victims on the little stone altar of the village *t'u-ti*? The theory seems to be that, when the *t'u-ti* perceives the list of names, he will assume that the persons bearing those names are already dead, and will make preparations in the under world for the reception of their souls. These preparations will act with a powerful attractive force upon the souls concerned, and will create in them an irresistible inclination to sever their connexion with their respective bodies. The non-arrival in the under world of the spirits of persons whose death had already been announced in a formal manner would cause bewilderment to the well-meaning *t'u-ti*, and might perhaps arouse his wrath; and, as it is strongly advisable, in the interests of the community in general, to 'save the face' of the *t'u-ti* and maintain friendly relations with him, the only reasonable course for the spirits in question to adopt is to bow to the inevitable and acquiesce in the premature loss of their physical bodies.

Magical and semi-religious theories of this kind are hardly likely to find Western parallels; but many of the ordinary magical practices of the Chinese are strikingly similar to some of those forms of sympathetic and mimetic magic with which we are familiar in Europe.

The great artist Ku K'ai-chih (4th cent. of our era), one of whose paintings is among the most treasured artistic possessions of the British Museum, was himself a graduate in magic. When spurned by the girl whom he loved, he drew her portrait, and in the place where the heart should be he stuck a thorn. Thereupon the girl, who knew nothing of the portrait and the thorn, began to suffer pain in the region of the heart, and next time her lover paid his addresses to her she did not scorn him. The artist then withdrew the thorn from the portrait, and, though the pain in the damsel's heart promptly disappeared, her love for him remained.

That many of the poets and artists of China have been credited with a knowledge of magic is no matter for surprise when we know how frequently their passionate love of wild nature brought them into contact with the Buddhist and Taoist saints and hermits, whose favourite dwelling-places have always been the caves and forests and ravines of the mysterious mountains. These mountain-dwelling ascetics have been for ages regarded as the discoverers and guardians of occult secrets of various kinds, and, though their disciples and biographers endowed them with faculties which they never possessed and which the best of them never pretended to possess, it is highly probable that there were some who, in the course of their own heart-searchings and their solitary communings with nature, not only made valuable discoveries as to the properties of plants and herbs, but were also successful pioneers in various untrodden fields of psychology and mysticism. To some extent, at least, the popular belief in their supernormal capacities and attainments was justified.

When Buddhism first came to China, and for some centuries afterwards, the relations between Buddhists and Taoists were often strained to breaking point. The victories of the Buddhists—if we may credit the Buddhist historians and biographers—were often brought about by miraculous occurrences which non-Buddhists would perhaps describe as magic if not as mere conjuring tricks. It is difficult, perhaps, in some cases, to draw a distinction between miracles and magic. A miracle, as E. S. Hartland remarks, is 'legitimate magic,' while magic is 'a forbidden miracle.'[1] However this may be, many of the marvellous doings attributed to Buddhist monks and hermits bear a close resemblance to those recorded of Christian saints. But we know from the earliest Buddhist scriptures that the brethren were not encouraged to perform miracles, and it was certainly not by the help of miracles or of magic that the Buddhists achieved their most substantial successes in China. The Taoists, however, did not scruple to ally themselves with various forms of magic and sorcery, and it is their fatal readiness to meet the popular demand for signs and wonders that is largely answerable for their present degeneration (see TAOISM).

If we had space to deal with matters of detail, it would be necessary to describe the various magical uses made of plants and animals and also of manufactured articles such as metal mirrors and weapons. An authority has stated (see *EBr*[11] xviii. 577) that magic mirrors are mentioned in Chinese literature of the 9th cent.; but they are mentioned and their uses fully described much earlier than that. The curious book known as *Pao P'o-tzŭ*, which was written by the famous wizard Ko Hung in the 4th cent. of our era, contains full accounts of how to detect the presence of evil spirits and other dangerous beings by the use of magic mirrors. The belief once prevalent in the British Isles that a witch could turn herself into a hare is paralleled by the Far Eastern belief (still extremely common in China) that demon-witches can assume the form of foxes and other beasts.[2] A book could be filled with the magical notions and theories which in China are based on the habits and peculiarities of animals. Even insects are not exempt from the necessity of making a contribution to the treasury of magical lore. There is in China a destructive little insect known to Europeans as the silver-fish (*Lepisma saccharina*), which is a most unwelcome visitor to libraries. It is believed that, if one of these insects gets into a Taoist classic and eats the two characters *shên-hsien* ('spiritual-immortal'), its silvery body will become five-coloured. If the coloured insect be subsequently caught and eaten, the man who eats it will have the happiness of attaining the goal of Taoist ambition—he will overcome death and develop into a spiritual being. As to trees, plants, and herbs, large numbers are believed to possess some magical property or to be adaptable to magical uses. The cypress, pine, and similar trees are supposed to be conducive to immortality, and, when we learn that a noted hermit was in the habit of sleeping on a bed of pine-needles, we may be sure that this was not done merely as a means of mortifying the flesh.[3] The willow is much used as a rain-charm. In times of drought in Shansi and neighbouring provinces adults and children may be seen going about with willow-wreaths on their heads. The peach-tree is famous for its magical properties, and for this reason peach-twigs and peach-blossom are frequently mentioned in Chinese fairy-lore. The use of peachwood for the exorcism of evil spirits is very ancient, for the brandishing of peach-wands was part of the recognized procedure of the professional *wu* at royal courts under the Chou kings and probably at a much earlier date.

That large and important subdivision of Chinese magic which concerns itself with charms and amulets and divination is dealt with elsewhere (see Literature below). Here it must suffice to mention that the principal purveyor of charms is

1 *Ritual and Belief*, London, 1914, p. 81.

2 For a full discussion of all forms of zoanthropy see de Groot, *Religious System of China*, iv. 156 f.; see also art. LYCANTHROPY.

3 See Johnston, *Buddhist China*, London, 1913, p. 245, and *Lion and Dragon in Northern China*, pp. 262 f., 375–384.

the 'Celestial Master' — usually described by Europeans as 'the Taoist pope'—who lives among the Dragon-Tiger Mountains in the province of Kiangsi. The practice of divination is also largely in the hands of Taoist specialists and *wu-p'o*; but Confucianism has always had under its patronage the complex systems of divination which are based on that abstruse classic the *I King*, or 'Book of Changes' (*SBE* xvi.). There is a grass known as *shih-ts'ao* which grows on the grave of Confucius and is carefully gathered and put up into packets. The stiff dried stalks of this plant are believed to retain some of the *ling*, or spiritual efficacy, which lies latent in the sacred soil, and they are or were highly valued for divining purposes. During recent years a very interesting discovery of 'oracle bones' and tortoise-shell fragments was made in the province of Honan. They are believed (mainly on the evidence of the archaic script) to belong to the 12th cent. B.C., though certain authorities assign some of them to a somewhat later period. An inspection of these fragments throws a most welcome light on the classical and post-classical references to the ancient methods of 'fortune-telling.'[1]

Divination by the tortoise-shell and by the dried stalks of certain plants 'were the methods by which the ancient sage kings made the people believe in seasons and days, revere spiritual beings, stand in awe of their laws and orders; the methods (also) by which they made them determine their perplexities and settle their misgivings' (*Li Ki*, I. i. 5. 27 [*SBE* xxvii. 94]).

The forms of magic which are or were popularly supposed to be associated with astrology and palmistry, and with automatic writing, telepathy, clairvoyance, and 'possession' by gods or demons, are all familiar to the people of China; and there is good reason to believe that any society for 'psychic research' which showed itself enterprising enough to conduct some patient investigations on Chinese soil would be rewarded by interesting and perhaps valuable results.

LITERATURE.—The subject of magic and allied topics is exhaustively dealt with in J. J. M. de Groot, *The Religious System of China*, Leyden, 1892 ff., esp. vols. v. and vi. E. Biot's Fr. tr. of the *Chou Li* (*Le Tcheou-Li*, Paris, 1851) should be consulted for information regarding the official standing and functions of the *wu* (see esp. ii. 76–104). There are many references to sorcery and magic—some of them shrewdly critical—in Wang Ch'ung, *Lun Hêng*, an Eng. tr. of which (by A. Forke) has appeared in two parts (pt. i., London, 1907; pt. ii., Berlin, 1911). In J. Legge, *Chinese Classics*, Hongkong, 1861–72, and *SBE* xvi. [1882], xxvii. [1885], xxviii. [1885], xxxix. [1891], and xl. [1891], English readers will find all the references to magic which occur in the canonical literature mentioned in the above article. Students of the subject will also do well to consult H. Doré, *Recherches sur les superstitions en Chine*, Shanghai, 1911 (*Variétés sinologiques*, no. 32), and L. Wieger, *Folklore chinois moderne*, Paris, 1909. From a more popular point of view the subject of Chinese magic has been dealt with in N. B. Dennys, *Folklore of China*, London, 1876, and F. H. Balfour, *Leaves from my Chinese Scrapbook*, do. 1887. Interesting sidelights on popular notions of magic can be gathered from the collection of stories known as the *Liao Chai*, tr. H. A. Giles, under the title of *Strange Stories from a Chinese Studio*, London, 1880, new ed., Shanghai, 1908. The Chinese literature dealing with the subject from every conceivable point of view is voluminous, and hitherto only fragments of it have been translated. Good Chinese bibliographies will be found in the works of de Groot, Doré, and Wieger referred to.

See also artt. DEMONS AND SPIRITS (Chinese), CHARMS AND AMULETS (Buddhist), DIVINATION (Buddhist), FENG-SHUI, FESTIVALS AND FASTS (Chinese), CALENDAR (Chinese), FORTUNE (Chinese), COMMUNION WITH THE DEAD (Chinese), COMMUNION WITH DEITY (Chinese).

R. F. JOHNSTON.

MAGIC (Egyptian).—**I. The Egyptian view of magic.**—If the Egyptians had been more self-analytic than they actually were, they might, from their own point of view, have described all their actions as either ordinary or magical. By ordinary actions would have been understood all those simple ways of coping with inanimate things and living beings which were suggested by habit, mother wit, or acquired skill. But, when inanimate matter proved recalcitrant, and living creatures were unmoved by requests, prayers, commands, promises, or threats, there still remained, in their opinion, a method of achieving their ends by means of an art that they called *ḥike'* (Coptic ϩⲓⲕ). There is direct traditional authority for translating this very ancient term by the English word 'magic' (μαγεύων, μαγίαι, Ac 8[9. 11]), and the examination of the hieroglyphic and hieratic examples of its use proves it to correspond fairly well to what we understand by 'magical power.' Wherever mysterious, miraculous knowledge was required to effect a purpose, that was *ḥike'*; *ḥike'* was something different from the techniques and practices of everyday life, since it postulated special powers in its user, and always made a greater or less demand upon faith.

2. Magic and religion.—For our traditional Western thought magic and religion are always more or less consciously contrasted with one another, whence students have often unwarrantably assumed that the two are radically heterogeneous, and that they represent successive strata in the mental development of mankind. Some investigators argue that magic is the earlier and ruder product (*e.g.*, Frazer), while others (*e.g.*, Erman) hold it to be a debased corruption of the nobler phenomenon of religion. So far as Egypt is concerned, there cannot be the slightest doubt that *ḥike'* was part and parcel of the same *Weltanschauung* as created the religion which it deeply interpenetrated. Before defining 'magic' and 'religion' for Egyptological purposes—and we must insist on our right to frame our own definitions within the limits prescribed by the current, untechnical meaning of these terms—it will be profitable to make a rapid survey of the facts to be distributed between the two provinces.

It is with active relations that we are here concerned, and with doctrines only in so far as they are involved in the same. There are three classes of being that are affected, namely the living, the dead, and the gods. Perhaps the most remarkable characteristic of the Egyptians' view of the universe is the thoroughgoing and impartial logic with which they drew the consequences of their belief that the gods and the dead were beings of like nature with themselves, subject to human appetites and needs, and amenable to the same methods of persuasion or compulsion. Hence the principal duty of the priests was to keep those whom they served provided with food and drink, and to maintain their houses in good order; the analogy with the domestic services demanded by the living was fully conscious, for the priests of the gods and the dead were called 'the servants of the god' (*ḥm-nṯr*) and 'the servants of the departed spirit' (*ḥm-k'*) respectively, even as the temple was called 'the house of the god' (*ḥ'-t nṯr*) and the tomb (or an essential portion of it) 'the house of the departed spirit' (*ḥ'-t k'*). Again, the Egyptians could seek help of their gods and dead in the same naive and unsophisticated way as one man sought help of another—*e.g.*, by prayer, by questioning (asking for an oracle), and by writing letters (for letters to the dead, see art. LIFE AND DEATH [Egyptian], § 9). But in their own everyday life, as seen above (§ 1), the Egyptians resorted, when all else failed, to mysterious, uncanny arts (*ḥike'*) to achieve various difficult aims; the method employed was not simply coercion, but coercion of an abnormal and special kind. It would have been strange if the practice of *ḥike'* had been restricted to the narrow circle of the living, when the living shared with the gods and the dead all their other modes of intercourse. In point of fact, it was *ḥike'* more than anything else that welded together the seen and the unseen worlds. The self-protective rites of the living, as we shall have abundant occasion to see, are full of trafficking with the gods and the dead. But the gods and the dead themselves had a use for the miraculous power called *ḥike'*; Thōth and Isis were famous adepts of the art (below, § 10), and in a demotic story the dead priest Neneferkaptah deeply resents the attempt to rob him of a book of incantations that had been buried with him in his tomb (F. Ll. Griffith, *Stories of the High Priests of Memphis*, Oxford, 1900, p. 30 f.). Nothing could better prove the wide range of *ḥike'* than to observe its transference from secular to funerary or divine employments and *vice versa*. In the *Pyramid Texts* and the *Book of the Dead*, compilations intended to ensure the well-being of the departed, one may often come across spells that must originally have been composed for earthly use—spells directed against the bites of snakes (e.g., *Die altägyp. Pyramidentexte*, ed. K. Sethe, Leipzig, 1908, §§ 246, 247) or of crocodiles (e.g., *Book of the Dead*, tr. E. A. W. Budge, London, 1908, chs. xxxi., xxxii.), for example; even erotic charms may be found inscribed on coffins (cf. H. Schack-Schackenburg,

[1] See, *e.g.*, various passages in the *I King*, *Shu King*, *Li Ki*, and *Chou Li*. A recent account of the new discovery is to be found in *JRAS* (North China Branch) xlv. [1914] 65 f.

Zweiwegebuch, Leipzig, 1903, pl. 16. 11–13). Conversely, the *Book of Overthrowing Apophis* (Budge, *Egyptian Hieratic Papyri*, London, 1910) was a liturgy intended for daily recitation in the temple of Amen-rēʻ at Thebes, Apophis being the mythical snake that was supposed to be the eternal foe of the sun-god Rēʻ; the rubrics of this book nevertheless declare that it will prove of the greatest advantage to the private individual who recites it in the presence of the god. It may be added that the word *ḥike'* is quite common in all parts of the *Book of the Dead*, as well as in such temple rituals as the *Book of Overthrowing Apophis* just mentioned.

It may therefore be taken as proved that *ḥike'* was as intimately associated with the presumed existence of the gods and the dead as it was with the real existence of the living. But, further than this, a greater or less element of *ḥike'* may have been inherent in all the dealings between men on the one side and the gods and the dead on the other. The two last classes of being were, after all, creatures of a world apart, elusive in their nature and hard to reach by ordinary, matter-of-fact means. The very idea of their existence puts a strain upon the imagination, and for this reason set forms of words, indicative of an effort to break down mystical barriers, had to accompany even such simple deeds of homage as the presentation of food-offerings. In other terms, the gods and the dead could hardly be approached save by the medium of what is known as 'ritual,' and the attribute which distinguishes ritual from ordinary performances may have been just that attribute which the Egyptians called *ḥike'*. The point is not susceptible of absolute proof, for it was naturally only in the more extreme cases, where the sense of mystery and miracle-working had to be emphasized, that the term *ḥike'* was actually applied; but the view that *ḥike'* underlies all ritual is favoured by the close resemblance between the divine and funerary rites, on the one hand, and the rites performed for human benefit (self-protective and similar rites), on the other. The formulæ of the *Book of the Dead* differ neither in form nor in substance from the incantations which the Egyptians used to heal their own maladies; and the same general similarity also runs through the daily liturgies of the temples and the tombs (see A. Moret, *Le Rituel du culte divin journalier en Egypte*, Paris, 1902).

From the Egyptian point of view we may say that there was no such thing as 'religion'; there was only *ḥīke'*, the nearest English equivalent of which is 'magical power.' The universe being populated by three homogeneous groups of beings—the gods, the dead, and living human persons—their actions, whether within a single group or as between one group and another, were either ordinary or uncanny (*ḥīke'*). But the gods and the dead were somewhat uncanny themselves, so that all dealings with them or performed by them were more or less *ḥīke'*. It was only when men treated them ordinarily, and as man to man, that this quality of *ḥīke'* was reduced to a minimum, as in the case of spontaneous prayer and the letters to the dead—in fact, just in those rare instances where the solemn phraseology of ritual was avoided.

3. Magic defined for Egyptological purposes as privata religio.—We shall hardly be able to avoid rendering *ḥīke'* in English by the words 'magic' or 'magical power'; but, if the Egyptian conception of *ḥīke'* be taken as the criterion of what is magical and what is not, we shall have little or no use for the word 'religion,' and a multitude of facts which the common parlance would more naturally describe as 'religious' will fall under the head of 'magic.' It is advisable, therefore, in defining 'magic' for Egyptological purposes, to strike a compromise between the Egyptian connotation of *ḥīke'* and the English connotation of 'magic.' Taking our cue from the former, we shall restrict the sense of 'magic' to those actions which clearly have the implications of mystery and the miraculous; at the same time we shall attempt to maintain the distinction between magic and religion, or, rather, between magic and other kinds of religious acts. It is fully in accordance with the practice of Egyptologists, instinctively adopted but inconsistently carried out, to contrast 'magic' with the 'cult of the dead' and the 'cult of the gods,' as referring exclusively to those rites which deliberately and in the first instance aimed at the advantage of living human beings, the cults of the dead and of the gods being in this division implicitly classed together as 'religion.' Magical actions may therefore, for our purposes, be defined as those actions which men performed for their own benefit or for the benefit of other living men, and which demanded certain miraculous powers for their performance. Warning must be given against two misconceptions: in the first place, it must be clearly understood that the gods and the dead may, as indeed they usually do, enter into the *dramatis personæ* of the magical rite; the principle of division is not *de quibus* but *cui bono*; in the second place, magic as thus defined did not differ essentially in its mechanism from the cults of the dead and of the gods, nor was it necessarily regarded with feelings of moral reprobation.

For a similar definition see A. H. Gardiner, 'Notes on Egyptian Magic,' in *Trans. Third Internat. Congr. Hist. Rel.*, Oxford, 1908, i. 208–210. Erman (*Ägyptische Religion*[2], Berlin, 1909), though forming a very different estimate of magic from that here adopted, accepts the same tripartite division of the active aspect of religion into *Götterkultus*, *Totenkultus*, and *Zauberei*. Magic as thus defined has a whole native literature of its own: various hieratic papyri in Leyden, Turin, London, Berlin, Cairo, Rome, Vienna, and elsewhere, mostly dating from the New Kingdom; several similar papyri of the Middle Kingdom, in the Ramesseum find of 1896, still unpublished and in the writer's hands; numerous ostraca in various collections. Besides these must be named the medico-magical papyri (see art. DISEASE AND MEDICINE [Egyptian]), and the so-called *Cippi of Horus*, of which the type is the *Metternich Stele* (ed. W. Golenischeff, Leipzig, 1877).

The abstract concept of *ḥīke'* is once or twice found deified, apparently in something like the restricted meaning assigned to 'magic' in this section. Two physicians of the Old Kingdom bear, besides the honorific title 'priest of Horus in Hundred-town,' also that of 'priest of Ḥīke'' (A. Mariette, *Les Mastabas de l'ancien empire*, Paris, 1889, p. 96; R. Lepsius, *Denkmäler*, Berlin, 1849–58, ii. 91a).

The deified concept of Ḥīke' is figured in the form of a man in some sculptures of the Vth dyn. (L. Borchardt, *Das Grabdenkmal des Königs Sahure'*, Leipzig, 1913, ii. pl. 20), and is of occasional occurrence also in the texts (*ib.* p. 99). A funerary incantation whereby it was sought to confer upon the deceased the powers of Ḥīke' himself has recently come to light (P. Lacau, *Textes religieux*, Paris, 1910, no. lxxviii.); here Ḥīke' is described as a creation of the sun-god in primordial times, when as yet nothing else existed.

4. The purposes of magic.—In theory the domain of magic was as wide as men's desires themselves, magical art supplying all those things that were not procurable by simpler means. Our existing materials, which illustrate only a limited number of purposes, are probably very one-sided. The Egyptians believed, or feigned to believe, that their wizards could work all kinds of wonders; in a late tale a charm is made to bring the viceroy of Ethiopia up to Egypt, to the place where Pharaoh dwells, where he is to be beaten with five hundred blows of the stick, and returned to the land of Ethiopia again, 'all in six hours thither' (Griffith, *Stories of the High Priests*, p. 59). It is said to have been related at the court of Cheops how one magician fashioned a crocodile of wax that devoured an adulterer, how another parted the waters of a lake into which a jewel had accidentally fallen, and how a third cut off a goose's head and replaced it in a twinkling (Erman, *Die Märchen des Papyrus Westcar*, Berlin, 1891, i. 8 f.). The magical contest of Moses with Jannes and Jambres (Ex 7^{8-13}, 2 Ti 3^{8}) is thus quite Egyptian in spirit. Passing from such fabulous reports to practical magic, we may classify the attested uses under a comparatively small number of heads:

i. *DEFENSIVE.*—How important this class was may be judged from the fact that in a general panegyric of God as creator He is said to have 'made magical spells for men for defence against things that happened' (*Pap. Petersburg 1116 A* [ed. Golenischeff, Petrograd, 1913], line 136 f.).

(1) *Prophylactic.*—To avert death, W. Pleyte and F. Rossi, *Papyrus de Turin*, Leyden, 1869–76, pl. 120 f.; W. M. F. Petrie, *Gizeh and Rifeh*, London, 1907, pl. 27 c; against scorpions, *Pap. Turin*, 134; *Pap. Leyden 349*; against lions, hyænas, and 'all long-tailed animals that eat flesh and drink blood,' *Le Papyrus magique Harris* (ed. F. J. Chabas, Châlon-sur-Saône, 1861; also Budge, *Egyptian Hieratic Papyri*), verso B; against crocodiles and other dangers of the river, such as drowning, *ib.* recto; against snakes, L. Stern, *Papyrus Ebers*, Leipzig, 1875, pl. 97. 17.

(2) *Preventive.*—'To prevent a woman from conceiving,' *Ramesseum medical*, unpublished; 'to prevent rats from devouring the grain in a barn,' *Ebers*, 98. 6.

(3) *Counter-charms.*—'To lay a spell (*ḫ;' s;*) on him whom one fears,' *Louvre, Hier. Ostr.* 694, no. 1; 'to banish magic from the body' (prescription of drugs), *Ebers*, 34. 2, 7, 10; against a complaint named 'the artifice of spells,' *Ebers*, 88. 13. A book containing 'formulæ for repelling the evil eye' (ⲉⲓⲉⲣ-ⲃⲱⲛ; cf. also *Pap. Anast.* iii. 5. 4) was preserved in the Library of Edfu (*ZÄ* ix. [1871] 44).

(4) *Curative.*—Spell to cure scorpion-stings, *Pap. Turin*, 31 +77; headache, *Pap. Leyden 348*, verso 2. 9; burns, *Ebers*, 69. 3, 6; *Pap. Leyden 348*, recto 3. 1; to ease pain, *Ebers*, 30. 6. For the relations of magic and medicine see below, § 8.

(5) *Psychological.*—'A book for repelling fear which comes to befall a man by night or day, from front or behind,' *Pap. Leyden 348*, recto 2. 1.

ii. *PRODUCTIVE.*—(1) *Obstetric.*—To facilitate birth, Erman, *Zaubersprüche für Mutter und Kind*, Berlin, 1901, pl. 5. 8, 6. 8; *Pap. Leyden 348*, recto 12. 6; 'to bring milk to a woman who is nursing a child' (prescription only), *Ebers*, 97. 10; 'to keep a child warm,' *Zaubersprüche*, verso 2. 2.

(2) *Weather-charms.*—'Thou shalt perform these ceremonies when a storm rages in the east of heaven, or when Rē' sets in the West, to prevent storm-clouds in the east of heaven. . . . Thou shalt perform these ceremonies many times against bad weather, that the sun may shine, and Apophis be overthrown in truth' (*Book of Overthrowing Apophis*, 23. 14 f.).

(3) *Love-charms.*—A spell to secure sexual enjoyment, secondarily used for funerary purposes, has been alluded to in § 2. Erotic charms must have been frequent, but those that are known are of late date; in demotic, see F. Ll. Griffith and H. Thompson, *Demotic Magical Papyrus*, London, 1904, p. 14; in Greek, C. Wessely, *Griechische Zauberpapyrus*, Vienna, 1888, lines 296 f. and 1877 f.

(4) *General.*—'He who recites this book is blessed every day; he hungers not, thirsts not, lacks not clothes, and is not melancholy. He does not enter into the law-court, nor does judgment go forth against him. But if he enters the law-court, he goes forth vindicated, praise being given to him like a god. Nor does his popularity depart from him' (*Pap. Leyden 347*, 12. 10–12).

iii. *PROGNOSTIC.*—Many cases that fall under this head are on the border-line between magic and the techniques of ordinary life.

(1) *Obstetric.*—To know whether a child will live, *Ebers*, 97. 13; to know whether a woman will give birth, W. Wreszinski, *Medizinischer Papyrus des Berliner Museums*, Leipzig, 1909, verso 1. 3, 7, 9, etc.

(2) *Divination.*—A number of magical modes of divination are detailed in the *Demotic Magical Papyrus*, ed. Griffith-Thompson (see p. 14), but these instances do not seem to be of ancient origin. Oracle-seeking does not come under the head of magic, as here defined.

(3) *Soothsaying.*—In the tale of Unamūn (*RTAP* xxi. [1899] 81) there is related a case of a young man being 'seized by the god' and giving a solemn warning while in this condition.

(4) *Prophecy* may perhaps be brought within the sphere of magic, as it postulates supernatural power in its human mouthpiece, and usually involves the welfare of human beings. There is only one very ancient book of predictive prophecies, in a Petrograd papyrus (see A. H. Gardiner, *Journal of Egyptian Archæology*, i. [1914] 100 f.).

There seems to be no Pharaonic evidence for horoscopes, ordeals, and other forms of prognostic magic.

iv. *MALEVOLENT.*—See next section. Cursing and oaths (conditional self-curses) are magical in quality, but cannot be dealt with in this article.

5. Magic and law.—The Egyptians themselves seem to have made no distinction between 'black magic' and 'white magic,' but, when magical arts were used for wicked purposes and to injure others, they naturally came within the category of legal offences.

Thus papyri of the XIXth dyn. (*Les Papyrus Lee et Rollin*, published by T. Devéria, *Œuvres et fragments* [*Bibliothèque égyptologique*, v.], Paris, 1897, ii. 97 ff.) record the case of two harem-conspirators, one of whom 'made magical writings to lead astray and work mischief, and made certain gods of wax and certain medicines to weaken the limbs of men,' while the other procured 'writings for giving himself fearfulness and majesty,' and made 'men of wax and writings in order that they might be introduced into the harem . . . so as to lead astray the one faction and so as to bewitch the rest.' Both these criminals were condemned to death.

6. The magical rite.—A characteristic example of a magical spell, translated *in extenso* from the original, will give a truer impression of the methods of Egyptian magic than any amount of mere description.

'Flow out, thou poison, come forth upon the ground. Horus conjures thee, he cuts thee off, he spits thee out, and thou risest not up but fallest down. Thou art weak and not strong, a coward and dost not fight, blind and dost not see. Thou liftest not thy face. Thou art turned back and findest not thy way. Thou mournest and dost not rejoice. Thou creepest away and dost not appear. So speaketh Horus, efficacious of magic! The poison which was rejoicing, the hearts of multitudes grieve for it; Horus has slain it by his magic. He who mourned is in joy. Stand up, thou who wast prostrate, Horus has restored thee to life. He who came as one carried is gone forth of himself; Horus has overcome his bites. All men, when they behold Rē', praise the son of Osiris. Turn back, thou snake, conjured is thy poison which was in any limb of N the son of M. Behold, the magic of Horus is powerful against thee. Flow out, thou poison, come forth upon the ground.

To be recited over a hawk with the two feathers on its head, being made of isy-wood and painted. Open its mouth and offer to it bread and beer and incense. Place it on the face of one suffering from the bite of any snake and recite from beginning to end. It will repel the poison. A successful specific' (*Pap. Turin*, 131. 1–8=*Metternich Stele*, 3–8).

7. Analysis of the magical rite.—Except in certain border-line cases (prognostics, medical treatment, etc.), the magical rite is always twofold and comprises (1) an oral rite, consisting of certain words to be recited, and (2) a manual rite, consisting of certain actions to be performed. These two portions must be discussed in detail.

(1) *The oral rite.*—The task that lay before the magician usually involved a struggle with some difficulty, which might consequently be regarded as a hostile and aggressive force. This force is not always completely personified, but more often than not it is treated personally, being commanded, persuaded, cajoled, warned, threatened, or cursed, just like a human being.

A leading idea in defensive magic, which embraces no small part of our material, is that of 'possession.' The possible antagonists are often enumerated in a long rigmarole—*e.g.*, 'the assaults of a god, the assaults of a goddess, the assaults of a male pain, the assaults of a female pain, the assaults of a dead man, or the assaults of a dead woman,' etc. (*Ebers*, 30. 13); 'enemy male or female, dead man male or female, adversary male or female' (*Pap. Turin*, 122. 5). Any god could doubtless attack human beings, but savage or malicious deities, like Seth, the murderer of Osiris, or Sakhmet, the 'lady of pestilence' (*nb-t 'idw*), were doubtless most to be feared. The dead were specially to be feared; nor was it only those dead who were unhappy or unburied that might torment the living, for the magician sometimes warns them that their tombs are endangered (*Zaubersprüche*, recto 8. 7–9; *Pap. Turin*, 124. 12–13). The possessing spirit was particularly likely to be of foreign origin, a negress or an Asiatic woman (*Zaubersprüche*, recto 2. 7–8); and it was wont to come secretly, 'arriving in darkness, gliding in, its nose backwards and its face turned' (*ib.* 1. 9 f.). Its mode of taking possession is, as a rule, vague; the 'demon' (*i;ḫ*, Boheiric ⲓϩ) doubtless often dwelt 'with' or in the afflicted one (*Bekhten Stele*, 11. 19=Budge, *Egyptian Reading Book*, London, 1888, p. 27 f.), but sometimes it merely injected some kind of poison, such as its semen, urine, or the like (*Pap. Leyden 348*, verso 6. 6 f.; cf. especially the word '*ō'e*' in *Ebers*, 24. 14, 34. 10, etc.). Or else, again, the hostile power might attack with arrows (*Pap. Leyden 346*, 1. 5). The evil influences were most easily ejected through the excretions of the body, such as the sweat or urine (*Zaubersprüche*, recto 2. 8–10); or they might come out in the form of winds (*Pap. Leyden 348*, verso 12. 9). All the members of the body were subject to attacks of the kind, whence their frequent enumeration in magical texts (see below); here they are not seldom called upon to 'open their mouths and vomit forth what is in them' (*Pap. Leyden 345*, recto G 2. 2. 14–3. 1).

The malignant force was sometimes merely informed of its defeat:

'Thou flyest before the sorcerer, before the servant of Horus, as soon as he mentions the name of Horus, or the name of Seth, the lord of heaven. He raiseth his scimitar, and smiteth thy forearm and thy throat. Thou failest upon the ground on which thy loin-cloth is spread, and there thou gropest in quest of thy heart. So dost thou die, and the report goes forth to the house of Rē' that Horus has conquered the disease' (*Pap. Leyden 345*, recto G 3. 12–4. 1).

Sometimes the magician frustrates the aims of the enemy by a simple veto:

'Dost thou come to kiss this child? I suffer thee not to kiss it' (*Zaubersprüche*, recto 2. 1).

Elsewhere, as in the example quoted in § 6, the poison is bidden to flow forth upon the earth. Warnings frequently supplemented and reinforced such commands, as:

'Fall not upon his tongue; it is a serpent at the mouth of its hole' (*Zaubersprüche*, recto 3. 11, in the midst of a long series of similar phrases).

Commands and warnings failing in their effect, a more persuasive means is tried:

'Come, lay thee down, departing to the place where thy

beauteous women are, on whose hair is myrrh, and fresh incense on their shoulders' (*Zaubersprüche*, recto 3. 5–6).

Or else the demon is made to understand that in delaying to obey the magician he holds the whole order of nature in suspense:

'Rē' waits for thee in order to shine, and Atum to set, that thou mayest quit the arm of N son of M. The chief of the Westerners waits for thee in order to enter in triumphant, that thou mayest quit the arm of N son of M' (*Pap. Leyden 345*, verso G 4. 2–4).

In the last resort curses are employed:

'Every god curses thee, every goddess curses thee. . . . The [great] Ennead curses thee, the little Ennead curses thee' (*Pap. Leyden 343*, verso 1. 1–3).

It often happens, indeed almost in every spell, that gods are summoned to the sorcerer's aid. They are invoked with salutations and praise:

'Hail to thee, Horus, thou that art in the town of Hundreds, thou sharp-horned one, who shootest at the mark. . . . I come to thee, I praise thy beauty; destroy thou the evil that is in my limbs' (*Pap. Leyden 347*, 3. 10–13).

A trait characteristic of Egyptian magic, noted already by Iamblichus (ed. G. Parthey, Berlin, 1857, p. 245), is the threatening tone often adopted towards the gods; examples are very common:[1]

'On the night that the wife of Horus (Selkis, the scorpion goddess) shall bite thee, I suffer not the Nile to beat upon its bank, I suffer not the sun to shine upon the earth, I suffer not the seed to grow, I suffer not cakes to be made, I suffer not jugs of beer to be brewed for the 365 gods, who are hungry by both day and night—on that night of the burial of Osiris' (*Pap. Turin*, 137. 1–4).

The most daring menace of all is the following:

'I will throw fire into Busiris and burn up Osiris' (*Pap. Turin*, 135. 10; cf. *Ebers*, 30. 8).

On such occasions the magician is apt to disclaim his responsibility:

'It is not I who say it, it is not I who repeat it; it is Isis who says it, it is Isis who repeats it' (*Pap. Leyden 348*, recto 11. 7; *Pap. Turin*, 136. 8–9; *Pap. mag. Harris*, 9. 11).

Elsewhere the gods are referred to in the third person, and the more numerous they are, the more efficacious the rite is likely to be. Thus, when the limbs of the body are enumerated,[2] it often happens that each separate limb is identified with, or said to belong to, some special deity; and the list ends with the words,

'There is no limb of his without a god' (*Pap. Leyden 348*, verso 6. 2).

Origen (*c. Celsum*, viii. 58) asserts that the Egyptians divided the human body into thirty-six parts, and placed each one of them under the charge of a god; 'and so,' he says, 'invoking these, they heal the diseases of the limbs.' The divine names mentioned by Origen are those of the gods of the decans, or ten-day periods.

The magician often speaks of himself in the first person, but sometimes identifies himself with a particular god whose assistance he desires—*e.g.*,

'I am Rē' in this his mysterious name "He-who-was-in-the-Nun," shooting his arrows against his foes' (*Pap. Leyden 347*, 4. 11 f.)—

or else with some god who, like the person for whom the rite is performed, had once been menaced by some imminent danger:

'Avaunt thou, for I am Horus; retire thou, for I am the son of Osiris. The magic of my mother (Isis) is the protection of my limbs' (*Hearst medical Papyrus*, 11. 4 f.)

At other times he merely claims to be 'the servant of Horus' (*Pap. Leyden 345*, verso F 1; *Pap. Turin*, 134. 1.).

Often a mythical precedent was alluded to or narrated at length, and the mere mention of a parallel case seems to have been considered a useful expedient for ensuring the success of the rite. Thus the magician declares:

'I will banish all bad and evil things which come to fall upon N the son of M, even as Rē' saved himself from his enemies, even as Khnum saved himself from Sobk, even as Horus saved himself from Seth, and even as Thōth saved himself from Be'bō'' (*Pap. Turin*, 118. 9–10).

[1] For similar examples from the funerary books see H. Grapow, *ZÄ* xlix. [1911] 48–54.

[2] See Erman's remarks, *Zaubersprüche*, p. 23.

More often the point of the narrative is merely implied; in the following short incantation against burns even the names of the interlocutors, namely a messenger and Isis, are omitted:

'"Thy son Horus has been burnt in the desert." "Is water there?" "There is no water there." "There is water in my mouth, and a Nile between my legs; I am come to quench the fire"' (*Ebers*, 69. 3–4; see H. Schäfer, in *ZÄ* xxxvi. [1898] 129–131).

Many valuable fragments of myths have been preserved to us by this means.

Especially frequent are tales that turn upon the revelation of the true name of a god; a well-known instance is the story of how Isis devised a stratagem by which the sun-god Rē' should be compelled to divulge his name; this she brought about by causing him to receive a snake-bite which none could cure save herself (*Pap. Turin*, 131–133). Less well known is the narrative of the attempts made by Seth to provoke Horus into betraying his real name, which would have given the mischievous god power over his nephew; Horus, however, invents various absurd names, and so manages to elude his wicked uncle (*Pap. Turin*, 134 f.).

The importance of *names* in Egyptian magic was very considerable; the knowledge of names gave control, whether for good or for evil. It was not a rare proverb that 'a man lives who is conjured by his name' (*Pap. Turin*, 133. 6, 11, 134. 7, 9, etc.). Thus to be familiar with the names of the epagomenal days (*Pap. Leyden 346*, 2. 6) was a safe method of protecting oneself against their perils. This is a topic that might be greatly elaborated (see art. NAMES [Egyptian]).

Closely akin to the question of the importance of names is that of the importance of *language*. Certain formulæ were supposed to possess particular efficacy, such as the words 'Protection behind, a protection that comes, a protection!' (*Zaubersprüche*, recto 9. 2). The magical potency of anything depends in a large degree on its mysteriousness, and it is therefore but little wonder that cabbalistic gibberish (*Pap. mag. Harris*, verso C) and foreign spells were held in high esteem (*Der Londoner medizinische Papyrus*, ed. W. Wreszinski, Leipzig, 1912, nos. 27, 28, 32, the last being in the Kefti language).

The significance attached to names and language is an aspect of the doctrine of *sympathy*, by far the most fertile conception of all those underlying the magical rite. This doctrine holds that things that have once been associated in any way remain henceforth connected and almost interchangeable for practical purposes; its chief varieties are (1) the principle of *contagion*, which affirms that things that belong together or have once been in contact continue to influence one another even when separated; and (2) the principle of *homœopathy*, according to which like has special power to affect like. These and other forms of sympathetic magic not so easily classified are of constant recurrence in the Egyptian magical books, both in the oral and in the manual rites; the recital of mythical precedents also clearly comes under this head. The very idea of the oral rite is an instance of homœopathic magic, for language may be said to imitate and image the things which it expresses, and in so far verbal references to a desired effect may have been considered instrumental in producing it.

Sympathetic magic takes curious forms at times; one or two instances may be singled out. In connexion with the importance of language reference may be made to the significance of puns. A magician says:

'I make a charm for him against thee of *'afai*-plant, which does injury, of onions, which destroy thee, and of honey, which is sweet to men and sour to the dead' (*Zaubersprüche*, recto 2. 4).

The virtues here ascribed to the *'afai*-plant and to honey are of obscure origin, but the destructive property of onions is clearly due to the fact that the Egyptian word for onions was *ḥădg* (the vowel is merely guessed), while 'to destroy' was *ḥŏdg*. In order to tell whether a new-born infant would live or not, its first articulate cries were to be noted:

'If it says *ny*, that means it will live; if it says *mbi*, that means it will die' (*Ebers*, 97. 13);

the sound *mbi* resembles the emphatic Egyptian expression for 'no' (see *ZÄ* xliv. [1907] 132).

A widely different example of the supposed influence of like upon like is illustrated by the following words, addressed to a demon that is causing sickness:

'Thy head has no power over his head, thy arms have no power over his arms, thy legs have no power over his legs' (A. H. Gardiner, J. G. Milne, and H. Thompson, *Theban Ostraca*, London, 1913, p. 14 f.).

A conditional curse that runs upon similar lines may also be quoted:

'He who is deaf to this decree, may Osiris pursue him, may Isis pursue his wife, and Horus pursue his children' (H. Sottas, *Préservation de la propriété funéraire*, Paris, 1913, p. 128).

The mystical potency attaching to certain *numbers* doubtless originated in associations of thought that to us are obscure. The number seven, in Egyptian magic, was regarded as particularly efficacious. Thus we find references to the seven Hathors (*Pap. med. Berlin*, 21. 8; *Pap. Turin*, 137. 12; cf. αἱ ἑπτὰ Τύχαι τοῦ οὐρανοῦ [A. Dieterich, *Eine Mithrasliturgie*[2], Leipzig, 1910, p. 71]):

'The seven daughters of Rēʿ,' who 'stand and weep and make seven knots in their seven tunics' (*Pap. Turin*, 135. 12 f.);

and, similarly, we read of

'the seven hawks who are in front of the barque of Rēʿ' (*ib.* 136. 3).

Oral rites have occasionally to be recited seven times (*ib.* 138. 9, 10), but the more usual number is four (*Pap. Leyden 348*, verso 3. 3, 5, 4. 10, etc.; *Pap. mag. Harris*, 7. 4), a number doubtless associated with the 'four pillars of heaven' (οἱ τέσσαρες στυλίσκοι [Dieterich, p. 71]), or, as we should say, the four cardinal points.

A characteristic feature of the oral rite is its complexity. This is shown in various ways, and not least in the love manifested for enumerations. Reference has been made to the long lists of parts of the body, and to the formulæ naming all the possible enemies from whom attacks are to be feared. Similarly, lists are found of the various ways in which a man might meet his death (*Pap. Turin*, 120-121; Petrie, *Gizeh and Rifeh*, pl. 27 c), and of the various excretions through which the demon might transmit his baneful influence (*Pap. Leyden 348*, verso 6. 6 f.). This *quasi*-legal tautology is to be explained partly by the desire to cover all eventualities, and partly by the necessity of compelling respect for the learning and skill of the magician.

(2) *The manual rite*.—(*a*) *Active elements*.—The employment of *images* played an important part in the manual side of magic. Sometimes it is the hostile power to be destroyed that is thus counterfeited and done to death; so, in the *Book of Overthrowing Apophis*, the words of the oral rite are

'to be recited over an Apophis made of wax or drawn on a new sheet of papyrus and thrown into the fire' (26. 20; cf. 22. 6).

More often the object imitated represented a means of effecting the purpose of the rite.

Thus in a spell to assist child-birth there was made 'a dwarf of clay to be placed on the forehead of the woman who is giving birth' (*Pap. Leyden 348*, recto 12. 6).

Miniature hands, seals, and crocodiles were powerful to ward off evil, doubtless by slaying it, sealing it up, or devouring it (*Zaubersprüche*, verso 2. 4; cf. *ZÄ* xxxix. [1901] 87). A great number of the *amulets* found in such abundance in Egyptian tombs were of a magical nature, all, indeed, except those whose purpose was exclusively funerary. Like the images mentioned above, amulets can, if explicable at all, always be interpreted by the principle of sympathetic magic in one or other of its various forms (see Petrie, *Amulets*, London, 1914).

The materials of which such images and amulets should be made are nearly always specified, and it is evident that this was considered a matter of vital importance. Here we meet with a new aspect of sympathetic magic, namely the doctrine of *properties*; every plant, stone, metal, and colour possessed its own peculiar virtue, which prompted its use in the diverse cases. Wax and clay were very commonly employed, and perhaps not only because they were easy of manipulation; their plasticity may have been thought symbolic of a wide adaptability. Aetiological myths assign a divine origin to various substances; thus the bees that supply the wax are said to have sprung from tears shed by Rēʿ (*Pap. Salt 825*, 2. 5-6, [unpublished]), and the cedar-tree emanated from the sweat of Osiris (*ZÄ* xlvii. [1910] 71).

Images were not immediately potent of themselves, but had to be charged with magical power in one way or another. The oral rite is usually recited over them (*dd mdw ḥr*, *passim*), and this transitory and intangible kind of contact seems to have ensured their continuous efficacy.

In a fabulous story the magician Hor, the son of Pa-neshe, made a litter with four bearers and 'pronounced writing upon them, gave them breath of respiration, and made them live' (Griffith, *Stories of the High Priests*, p. 59).

Elsewhere the ceremony of 'opening the mouth,' familiar from the funerary ritual, was performed over the magical figure (*Pap. Turin*, 131. 7), and offerings and incense were presented to it in token of its now animate condition (*ib.*; *Pap. Leyden 346*, 2. 3). Drawings upon papyrus or rag were treated in exactly the same way, and seem to have been equally effective (*Pap. Leyden 346*, *ib.*; *Pap. Turin*, 31 + 77. 3); or the figures of the gods whose help was invoked could be sketched on the patient's hand, and licked off by some one (*Pap. Turin*, *ib.*). At times the mediating image could be dispensed with; the magician pronounced his spell, and then spat on the diseased limb (*Ebers*, 30. 17).

Magically charged amulets, images, or beads were often attached to the person whom they were designed to protect or heal; some kind of contact was a prime necessity of Egyptian magic; *e.g.*, we read of spells that were fastened to the left foot (*Pap. Leyden 348*, verso 4. 3); but the neck was naturally the spot where most charms were worn (*Zaubersprüche*, recto 1. 3, 8. 3, and *passim*). The string or strip of rag employed for this purpose was usually tied into magical knots (*q.v.*), seven being the favourite number. Such knotted strings have often been found and are to be seen in many collections (Erman, *Zaubersprüche*, p. 31). In other lands than Egypt the idea of the magical knot is frequently to 'bind' the hostile force; but, though references to binding demons can be found in Egyptian magical texts (*Pap. mag. Harris*, verso A 6), it is not in connexion with knots. One view that seems to have been taken of knots is that they were obstacles, as, *e.g.*, in the following words put into the mouth of a magician:

'If the poison pass these seven knots, which Horus has made on his body, I will not allow the sun to shine,' etc. (*Pap. Turin*, 135. 8).

Particularly interesting is a spell where twelve gods were invoked.

These were drawn 'on a rag of fine linen to be tied into twelve knots. Offer to them bread, beer, and burnt incense. To be placed on the neck of a man' (*Pap. Leyden 346*, 2. 3).

Here evidently each knot was put under the guardianship of a special deity, and thus formed a divinely protected barrier between the malign influence and its possible victim.

Imitative or significant actions were frequently performed with the apparatus of the magical rite; we have seen how a waxen image of Apophis was thrown into the fire and so destroyed, and similar cases could be multiplied.

At this point may be mentioned the composite stelæ known as *Cippi of Horus*; these are of comparatively late date (Saite period and after), and are covered with magical texts of the kind described above, and with sculptured figures, chief among which is the figure of Horus with his feet on two crocodiles. Such stelæ seem to have been placed in buildings for their protection, and especially to rid them of snakes and scorpions (see Golenischeff, *Metternichstele*; G. Daressy, *Textes et dessins magiques*, Cairo, 1903).

(*b*) *Negative or precautionary elements.*—Magical rites could not be performed at any time and under any conditions, but strict rules and restrictions had to be observed. Of these some, like the injunction to the magician to stand 'with his face to the East' (*Pap. Leyden 347*, 12. 10), are of so many different types that they elude classification. *Times and seasons*, like everything else in ancient Egypt, had their own specific properties; some days were lucky and others unlucky, in part at least through mythological associations (for such calendars on papyrus see art. CALENDAR [Egyptian], § 2). Such considerations had to be taken into special account where magical rites were concerned, and perhaps more attention was paid to the question of time than is indicated in the brief instructions usually given as to the performance of the manual rites.

Of one spell we learn that it had to be recited 'at eventide, when the sun is setting' (*Zaubersprüche*, verso 3. 7); in another case seven knots have to be tied, 'one in the morning, and another in the evening, until seven knots are complete' (*Zaubersprüche*, verso 3. 3).

Magical rites were also in demand for safeguarding men against dangerous periods of the year. As in ancient Mexico (*GB*[3], pt. iv., *Osiris, Attis, and Adonis*[2], London, 1914, ii. 28, n. 3), the intercalary days, in Egypt known as the five epagomenal days, were fraught with exceptional risks, against which enchantments were employed (*Pap. Leyden 346*); the user of these had to refrain from all work during the period in question (*ib.* 3. 4).

Purity was requisite in him who would be benefited by magic (*Book of Overthrowing Apophis*, 24. 19, etc.), just as ch. lxiv. of the *Book of the Dead* was ordained to be recited by 'one pure and clean, not having eaten venison or fish, and not having been near women.' In another place the user of a spell is charged to purify himself for nine days, and his servants are to do the same (E. Naville, 'Destruction des hommes,' line 79, in *TSBA* iv. [1876] 16).

Secrecy was essential in dealing with magic. In reference to a spell written on a strip of fine linen the warning is given that 'it is not to be looked at' (*Pap. Leyden 348*, recto 2. 7); of another it is said that it must not be used for any one except him for whom it was prescribed (*ib.* verso 8. 6). For similar instructions in the *Book of the Dead* see J. Baillet, *Idées morales dans l'Egypte antique*, Blois, 1912, pp. 72–75.

8. Magic and medicine.—Magical spells are often recommended on account of their proven efficacy; 'a true remedy on many occasions' is a formula extremely frequent in the magical papyri (*e.g.*, *Pap. Leyden 347*, 13. 2–3). This appeal to experience indicates a desire to justify magic as a science, and hints at the possibility of a real science arising out of it. There cannot be the slightest doubt that Egyptian medicine is the direct offspring of Egyptian magic, and that it never became really emancipated from its parent.[1] The medical books are seldom free from incantations, and the magical papyri are leavened with medical prescriptions (e.g., *Zaubersprüche*, recto 7. 2). In the selection of drugs the doctrine of properties undoubtedly played a great part, though the defectiveness of our evidence and the fact that medicine was in process of becoming an empirical science tend to conceal this from our observation. It is no argument against the thesis here supported that many of the herbs and drugs prescribed were actually, and were known to be, wholesome. In the first place, magic itself is not necessarily irrational in its methods, and, in the second place, even the utility of many wholesome things like onions was based upon essentially magical conceptions (see above, § 7 (1)). The exotic and abhorrent nature of many drugs cannot conceivably be explained except as due to superstitious reasons; how else could one account for the use of 'the bones of an oxyrhynchus-fish' (*Ebers*, 6. 3), or 'the urine of a male ass that has begotten another' (Griffith, *Petrie Papyri*, London, 1898, pl. 5, l. 18)? It is significant that the latter medicament occurs in a treatise on midwifery and kindred topics. One can often make a shrewd guess at the meaning of a prescription. To cure a complaint called 'the working of charms' (*ḥmt-s'*) the following is prescribed:

'A large beetle (*ḫprr*), whose head and wings have been cut off. To be burnt and put into fat, and then applied' (*Ebers*, 88. 13).

The point of this must surely be that, the word for beetle being derived from the verb *khōper* (*ḫpr*), 'to become,' a mutilated beetle would symbolize the frustrated achievement of a purpose; the purpose here to be frustrated was 'the working of charms.'

It must not be imagined that there was no distinction between a medical prescription and a magical rite. The former consisted mainly, if not wholly, of what may be considered as a specialized development of the manual rite, namely, the enumeration of drugs and directions for their use. The diagnosis, which is ushered in by the words 'so shalt thou say' (*dd-ḥrk*), and which sometimes precedes the list of drugs, may owe its origin to the oral rite of magic—just as the magician sometimes declares that he knows the name of the enemy. A difference is made in the medical papyri between an 'incantation' (*shīnet*) and a 'remedy' (*pakhret*); the latter is, in the main, an enumeration of drugs. In the same way the physician (*sunu*) was not quite the same thing as the magician; the physician might be a layman, while the magician was a priest (below, § 9).

That even in the 'remedy' (*pakhret*) magical ideas were latent may be proved by some additional evidence. The following is explicit enough:

'*Formula for drinking a remedy*: Welcome, remedy, welcome, which destroyest the trouble in this my heart and in these my limbs. The magic (*ḥike'*) of Horus is victorious in the remedy' (*pakhret*) (*Ebers*, 2. 1–2).

We also find formulæ to be recited in applying remedies generally (*Ebers*, 1. 1–11), in using the medicine-measures (*Pap. med. Hearst*, 13. 14), in using animal fat (*ib.* 14. 4), and so forth. These formulæ seem intended to supply the place of the incantations of which most medical prescriptions have purged themselves; their reintroduction was a reactionary step.

Where, then, does medicine begin and magic end? There is no definite boundary-line. Medicine may be said to begin when incantations are no longer used. At that point medicine becomes a technique, though using means which it does not understand, and which, if it pauses to give ex-

[1] The writer thus agrees with the views of E. Thrämer (in art. HEALTH AND GODS OF HEALING [Greek]) against F. von Oefele and H. Schneider.

planations, it explains by superstitious reasons. So far as medicine was practised without a sense of mystery and without making appeals to faith, it was a technique of ordinary life like any other; but, wherever there was consciousness of its exceptional, occult nature, it might be said to lapse back into the domain of magic. Egyptian medicine was at its best in diagnosis and in its physiological speculations; the *materia medica*, on the other hand, remained permanently under the influence of magical conceptions.

9. The magician.—A Greek alchemistic treatise quoted by Maspero (*PSBA* xiii. [1891] 502) exactly defines the difference between the physician (*sunu*) and the practitioner of magic. The former exercises his craft ἀπὸ βιβλίου . . . μηχανικῶς, 'mechanically and by book,' while the latter is a 'priest' (ἱερεύς), 'acting through his own religious feeling' (διὰ τῆς ἰδίας δεισιδαιμονίας ποιῶν). There appears to be no common word for 'magician' (*s;w*, 'charmer,' *e.g.*, in *Ebers*, 99. 3, is very rare), and magicians certainly formed no caste of their own. It is in accordance with the homogeneity of religion and magic emphasized above (§ 2) that the priests should have been the chief repositaries of magical knowledge, and particularly those priests whose function it was to be versed in the sacred writings. The subjects of many of the books kept in the library of the temple of Edfu cannot be described otherwise than as magical (see H. Brugsch, *Aegyptologie*, Leipzig, 1889–90, p. 156; cf. Clem. Alex. *Strom.* vi. 268). The 'lector-priest' (*chrai-ḥab*) is specially named as empowered to perform cures (*Pap. med. Berlin*, 8. 10), as having discovered incantations (*Pap. med. London*, 8. 12), and as being endowed with the gift of prophecy (*Pap. Petersburg 1116 B*, recto 9); and the wonder-workers at the court of Cheops in the tale were all 'chief lectors' (see Erman, *Märchen des Papyrus Westcar*, i. 21). A passage in the *Ebers Papyrus* (99. 2) singles out the 'priests of Sakhmet' (*w'ēb Sakhmet*) for special mention as skilled members of the magico-medical profession; this is because Sakhmet was a baleful goddess who manifested her wrath in inflicting disease; her priests were likely to know best how to cope with her. Priests, doctors, and sacred scribes alike received the final touches to their education at colleges called 'the house of life' (*per-'onkh*); of these we know but little.

A 'chief physician' of the time of Darius describes how he was summoned by Pharaoh to restore the *per-'onkh* (in Sais) 'because His Majesty knew the value of this (*i.e.* the medical) art' (*ZÄ* xxxvii. [1899] 74). There was a *per-'onkh* at Abydos, apparently attached to the temple (*Louvre A 93*=*ZÄ* xxxii. [1894] 119). The word ἱερογραμματεῖς in the bilingual decrees is rendered in the demotic as 'scribes of the house of life' (see Griffith, *Rylands Papyri*, Manchester, 1909, p. 81, n. 13, *Stories of the High Priests*, p. 19). Magic could be learnt at the *per-'onkh* (*ib.*; *Pap. mag. Harris*, 6. 10).

On the whole, we receive the impression that less importance was attached in Egypt than in other lands to the personality of the magician; his powers might in some cases be due to special gifts, but, broadly speaking, the belief in magic was a tribute to knowledge, and not to the supernatural powers of certain men. The instructions appended to magical incantations usually presuppose that private individuals could use them for their own profit if only they observed the right precautions. Thus the magician's presence was not essential, and his authority lay solely in the fact that he was the possessor of magical knowledge; the epithet 'knower of things' (*rakh ikhet*) was commonly applied to him (*Bekhten Stele*, 11; *Ebers*, 1. 9). This point is well brought out in a passage describing the all-wisdom of the Pharaoh Amōsis:

'An unique king, whom Sothis taught, praised of the goddess of writing; the reverence of Thōth is beside him, and he gives to him knowledge of things, so that he guides scribes according to the true rule. He is one great of *ḥike*'' (Sethe, *Urkunden*, iv. [Leipzig, 1906] 19 f.).

10. Celebrities in magic.—Egyptian-wise, we will begin with the gods. Thōth was the most powerful of all magicians; in the end this qualification of his gave rise to the fame of Hermes Trismegistos (*q.v.*; see Griffith, *Stories of the High Priests*, p. 58). The skill of Thōth as a magician is associated with his reputation as the inventor of hieroglyphs and the sciences of astronomy and mathematics; in the myth of Osiris he played the part of 'physician of the eye of Horus' (*Pap. med. Hearst*, 14. 6). Isis enjoyed great fame as a sorceress, mainly on account of the charms which she devised to protect her infant son Horus (*Pap. Turin*, 31+77. 6; *Ebers*, 1. 12 and *passim*). Horus himself was not devoid of magical ability, though it was mainly in his skill in warding off attacks that this was displayed; the Horus of Letopolis is described as the 'chief physician in the house of Rē'' (*Pap. Turin*, 124. 5). The eye of the sun-god, which was subsequently called the eye of Horus and identified with the Uræus-snake on the forehead of Rē' and of the Pharaohs, the earthly representatives of Rē', finally becoming synonymous with the crown of Lower Egypt, was a mighty goddess, Uto or Buto by name; she is often referred to as Wēret-ḥīke', 'she who is great of magic' (Sethe, *Untersuchungen zur Gesch. und Altertumskunde Aegyptens*, v. [Leipzig, 1912] 128).

According to Manetho, King Athothis of the Ist dyn. practised medicine and composed anatomical books. Under King Zoser of the IIIrd dyn. lived the wise Imhotep, whose skill as a doctor led to his identification by the Greeks with Asclepius; like Amenhotpe, son of Hepu, a famous man of the reign of Amenophis III. (XVIIIth dyn.), Imhotep was in late times worshipped as a god (see art. HEROES AND HERO-GODS [Egyptian], II. 2). The prince Hardedef, a son of Cheops, was similarly noted for his deep learning and wise utterances; he was the reputed discoverer of various books of *ḥīke'* incorporated in the *Book of the Dead* (see Erman, *Märchen des Papyrus Westcar*, i. 18). Another royal prince, who was high priest of Ptah, became the hero of many tales in which he appears as a great magician; this was Khamwēse, one of the innumerable progeny of Ramesses II. (see Griffith, *Stories of the High Priests*, p. 2 f.). In the later Greek and patristic literature reference is made to various Egyptian magicians of note, Sochos, Psenosiris, and, above all, Nectanebo, the last native Pharaoh, who plays an important part in the legend of Alexander the Great.

11. The nature of Egyptian magic.—The magical rite, as described in § 7, was by no means wholly irrational in its methods; indeed, granting its premisses, namely the existence of gods and demons, the theory of possession, the principles of sympathy, and the doctrine of properties, its manner of setting to work was perfectly logical and businesslike. Here, at first sight, we are face to face with a paradox; the essence of *ḥīke'* we stated to reside in its opposition to the mechanism of ordinary action (§ 1), yet now the methods of magic are declared to be simple and straightforward. The fact is that no explanation of the magical rite is afforded by the consideration of its parts either severally or collectively; its explanation can be sought only in the concept of *ḥīke'*, which is a thing apart from, and, as it were, superimposed upon, the methods and premisses of the magical rite, a sort of pervading vital principle making this what it is.[1] Without the concept of *ḥīke'* the magical rite would doubtless have seemed to the Egyptians no more than what to us it appears to be, a puerile, though not wholly meaningless,

[1] For the proof of this assertion see H. Hubert and M. Mauss, 'Esquisse d'une théorie générale de la magie,' in *ASoc* vii. [1902–03], esp. pp. 97–108.

combination of words and pantomime. There was perhaps once a period when even the most gifted were utterly ignorant of the limitations of their own power and that of the world outside; they saw forces which they treated personally in all kinds of external phenomena, and the law of sympathy seemed to them very good logic indeed. In this hypothetical period magic and science were undifferentiated. Later on, a distinction became gradually discernible between the simple techniques of ordinary life and the less successful or, at least, less trustworthy means by which men sought to achieve more difficult aims, and the notion of *ḥike'*, or magical power, was precipitated. *Ḥike'* gathered round itself just those less matter-of-fact preconceptions which were found unserviceable in ordinary life, and these became its methods. Now, the simple techniques are always able to detect, amid the complex environment in which acts are necessarily performed, the actual determining factor in their results; not so *ḥike'*, which is therefore apt to regard the whole complex environment as essential to the achievement of its purposes. This is the reason for the meticulous attention that *ḥike'* pays to detail, the set form of words to be recited, the restrictions as to time and place, the purity of the officiant, etc. The more restricted the domain of *ḥike'* became and the less successful it was, the greater the necessity which it felt of insisting on its own inherent efficaciousness, and of diverting attention from its methods; hence its love of secrecy, and its use of mystic, incomprehensible jargon to enhance the impression of the wisdom lying behind it. In this context mention must be made of two more ways in which it was sought to obtain credit for *ḥike'*, namely the appeal to antiquity and the appeal to authority.

Such and such a rite was 'found at nightfall in the forecourt of the temple of Coptos as a secret of this goddess (Isis) by a lector of that fane; the earth was in darkness, but the moon shone upon this book, illuminating it on every side. It was brought as a wonder to King Cheops' (*Pap. med. London*, 8. 11–13).

The papyrus from which this quotation comes was written in the time of Amenophis III., more than a thousand years after the reign of Cheops. A mythical origin is assigned to other spells.

One was said to have been 'invented by Geb on his own behalf' (*Pap. med. Hearst*, 5. 11); while others were devised by Nut or Isis on behalf of Rē' (*ib.* 5. 13, 15).

A more reputable way of appraising the value of a magical rite was by appealing to the test of experience; it is often claimed for a particular spell that it has been successful on many occasions (see above, § 8). Where the claim has proved justifiable, or where it has seemed sufficiently so for the rite to pass into general use, the more mysterious elements rapidly disappear, and the rite becomes an ordinary technique; so in the case of medicine and, it may be here added, of legal oaths.[1] Nothing can better illuminate the nature of *ḥike'* than the alterations which it undergoes in the course of its transformation into some ordinary technique.

LITERATURE.—This has been indicated in the body of the article. Of general treatises may be named E. A. W. Budge, *Egyptian Magic*², London, 1901; A. Erman, *Ägyptische Religion*², Berlin, 1909, ch. vii.; A. Moret, *La Magie dans l'Egypte ancienne* (*Bibliothèque de vulgarisation du Musée Guimet*, xx.), Paris, 1907; A. Wiedemann, *Magie und Zauberei im alten Ägypten* (*Der alte Orient*, vol. vi., pt. iv.), Leipzig, 1905.

ALAN H. GARDINER.

MAGIC (Greek and Roman).—I. *INTRODUCTORY.*—It is practically impossible to extract anything from the great mass of magic theory and practice as certainly the particular contribution of any given people. There is no system of human thought which, in its unchanging essential principles, is more primitive and, for that very reason, more cosmopolitan, more literally devoid of distinguishable national traits, than magic. Anything which might be considered indigenous is usually secondary as well as comparatively unimportant, and, in any case, can rarely be identified with certainty. This is especially true of the two great nations of classical antiquity. Here, as elsewhere, magic was believed and practised by the common man, and even the literary record of magic theory and practice begins with Homer and continues with increasing volume and particularity until the latest times. But, rich as they are, the records of classical magic are too incomplete and the possibility of filling the lacunæ is too remote to warrant us in hoping that a search for the indigenous would meet with any success. We shall therefore omit all reference to this aspect of our subject. For this reason, too, as well as on account of the intimate cultural relations between Greece and Rome, it seems best to deal with the two nations as one.

1. **Magic and religion.**—From more than one point of view the civilization of classical antiquity is still quite justified in challenging comparison with that of any other period in history. No civilization has shown such remarkable ability to observe, reflect, organize, and create in so many great departments of human thought and action. And yet among all the higher civilizations of the world there is none in which magic—of all things the most relentlessly and essentially primitive—had such an abiding influence, none in which men had such a perennial interest in the subject, none in which the progress of magic from the lore of the farmer to the lucubrations of the philosopher is more clearly marked and more profusely illustrated.

The paradox, however, is only apparent. Owing to its exaggerated conservatism, the religion of both nations always remained amazingly primitive, so primitive that it was always impossible to distinguish it from magic on the basis of any essential details of ceremonial or of the generalizations from which they were derived. Even the doctrine of incantation, with all the conclusions for which it is ultimately responsible, was never distinctive of the one as opposed to the other. It is obvious, therefore, that the Greeks and Romans were always in the position of their primitive ancestors—they were utterly unable to differentiate clearly between magic and their religion on the basis of this or of any other criterion which, when seriously applied, would have left their religion unimpaired, and at the same time would have transformed their once redoubtable magic into an interesting but harmless fossil. Their only course was to cling to the ancient distinction of official recognition.

According to this distinction, 'religion is prescribed, official, an organized cult. Magic is prohibited, secret; at most it is permitted, without being prescribed' (N. W. Thomas, *EBr*¹¹ xvii. 305, summarizing H. Hubert).

Magic cannot be distinguished from religion by the doctrine of sympathy, or by any supposed necessary sequence of cause and effect, or even by its maleficent character. Religion, then, is the orthodox, magic is heterodox, it being understood, of course, that for the Greeks and Romans the criterion of orthodoxy was the official recognition of their own State. The god must be officially recognized by the State, and his ceremonial must be the one prescribed by the official experts of the State. Other gods, and therefore their ceremonials, are heterodox. Even orthodox gods must be approached only by prescribed ceremonials.

This Græco-Roman retention of the primitive distinction between magic and religion is our only guide in establishing meaning and coherence in

[1] Legal oaths are, of course, a fairly effectual way of guaranteeing truthfulness; but less because the implied curse is feared than because perjury is a criminal offence.

the bewildering array of phenomena with which we have to deal. For instance, it will be seen at once that the only effect of this criterion, so far as magic itself is concerned, is, so to speak, to define its social position. It does not necessarily destroy or even impair the belief in the reality and power of magic as such; on the contrary, from the very nature of the distinction, it takes them both for granted. Hence the persistence of magic in a civilization otherwise so advanced as was that of classical antiquity.

We must assume this test of orthodoxy, *e.g.*, in the case of Cato's cure for a sprained hip (*de Agr.* 160). By any other test it is patently magic; but Cato did not consider it magic, or he would not have recommended it. It was orthodox, *i.e.*, it was Roman, it had an immemorial tradition in the Roman countryside; at the most, it had become secularized. By the same test the old Roman ritual for calling out and appropriating the gods of a conquered city (Macrob. III. ix. 7) is religion, and the operation known as 'calling down the moon' is magic. Again, the same criterion is responsible for the well-known method of raising the heterodox to the orthodox by official recognition. This device of naturalizing foreign cults and thereby embracing within the sphere of their influence heaven and hell as well as humanity, is several times illustrated in the religious history of the Romans.[1]

All foreign religions, therefore, were classified as magic. The foreign cult, as such, was occasionally despised, but quite as often it was thought to be full of terrible possibilities in the way of mysterious knowledge. This was especially the case if its possessors were an older nation or a nation far away in space or time. Despite their native good sense, the Greeks were much impressed by the pretentious wisdom of the East, as after them were the Romans by the complicated mummeries of the Etruscans. Nations living far away, particularly those who live at or near the place where the sun rises from the under world in the morning or goes down into it at night, are notable for their knowledge of magic. Under such circumstances as these whole nations may be endowed by nature with magic power, especially for some given thing. Remoteness in time is, if anything, a more powerful factor than remoteness in space. When a faith has been superseded, it thereby becomes magic. In Italy the term *la vecchia religione* is known to be used as a synonym for 'magic.' So the elder and alien race is apt to be looked upon, especially by those who superseded it in the same country, as a race of formidable magicians—so formidable, in fact, and, by reason of their antiquity, so much nearer the days of the gods, that they themselves are sometimes believed to have been of supernatural origin. But they are still heterodox, they belong to the old order of things, they are more or less allied to the Lords of Misrule.

One of the most characteristic features of magic is a direct result of this persistent association of the heterodox and the foreign. From the very first, there is no magician like the one from foreign parts (Theocr. ii. 162 and often), no magic like the imported brand. Helen's nepenthe (Hom. *Od.* iv. 219), as the poet is careful to tell us, was 'Egyptian'; the very word 'magic' suggests the influence of Persia; and to the end of the Empire the native practitioner had no vogue as compared with that of his rival who was, or pretended to be, from Egypt, Chaldæa, Colchis, India, or any other place but Rome.

It is true, of course, that 'magic is prohibited, secret; at the most, not prescribed.' But, so far as classical antiquity is concerned, these distinctions seem to be secondary and derivative. Magic was prohibited because it was heterodox. The Romans, in particular, disliked secret rites of any sort, above all, foreign rites with *mysteria*, like those Greek cults so much affected by the Greeks themselves. If the Greeks objected to the secrecy of magic, it could only have been because magic itself was heterodox. So far, then, as secrecy was felt to characterize magic as opposed to religion, the ultimate source of the distinction in Greece as well as in Rome was the criterion of orthodoxy. To the same criterion is due the fact that, as a rule, men turned to magic for the things which they could not or would not ask of religion. Nor, of course, was magic necessarily maleficent; on the contrary, it might be distinctly otherwise. So long as orthodoxy was the test, magic was magic whether it happened to be white or black—and this, of course, explains why the Roman law never made any attempt to distinguish between the two.

2. Magic and legislation.—The general reputation of magic at all times was due to the same criterion; it was always illicit, it was always distrusted, it always had a bad name. And when the law stepped in—as it did at an early date in both Greece and Rome—the orthodox and the legal, the heterodox and the illegal, became synonymous terms. Magic was then criminal, and punished accordingly. The history of magic before the law began at an early period, but, so far, at least, as Greece is concerned, our records are too incomplete to give a very satisfactory idea of the question. In Greece, however, as in Rome, it concerned itself most seriously with the matter of strange religions—a burning question as soon as communication with the outside world became more intimate and extensive; still more in Rome when, owing to rapid expansion after the Second Punic War, alien beliefs and rituals came pouring in from every side. From the Decemviri to Theodosius and beyond, the Roman laws against magic were affirmed and reaffirmed, the domain of magic was at once particularized and extended, new laws were frequently passed, and the jurisprudence of the subject grew steadily in volume and importance. And, so far as the legal aspect of magic is concerned, it may be emphasized anew that, whether in Greece or in Rome, the ultimate foundation and guide of procedure was always the old criterion of orthodoxy. It is clear, for instance, that the characteristic tendency of the law to extend its scope was both suggested and guided by this criterion. It was particularly useful whenever the law felt obliged to take cognizance of some system of activity more or less mental that was 'good in parts'— such, *e.g.*, as divination (*q.v.*), which stands on the border line between magic and religion, or alchemy (*q.v.*), which hovers in like manner between magic and science, or, again, certain types of mysticism (*q.v.*), which were more or less an amalgam of magic and logical thinking. In every case what was to be considered legal and what illegal was determined by official recognition. Above all, the inclusion of foreign rites and religions within the legal concept of magic was an obvious and entirely logical deduction from the test of orthodoxy. Not only so, but by the same test it was equally obvious that precisely those foreign rites were the most serious question in magic. How, *e.g.*, shall we define the legal status of the native religions of the provinces? The final solution was again entirely logical. The Emperor was the civil and religious representative of the State. He was therefore entitled to investigate them and to make such use of them as seemed proper. But this privilege was his alone, and only by virtue of his office. In the hands of private individuals it was

[1] E. Schmidt, 'Kultübertragungen,' in *RVV* viii. 2 [1909].

considered dangerous, and no doubt it was largely for this reason that magic was so rigorously proscribed and its illegality so sedulously kept alive.[1]

The recorded history of Roman legislation on the subject of foreign rites begins with the *cause célèbre* of its type, the *Senatus consultum de Bacchanalibus* in 186 B.C. (Livy, xxxix. 8–19),[2] in connexion with which it was ordered that all books of divination and magic should be destroyed. The history of Roman legislation on the subject of magic, whether directed against specific practices or against the art as a whole, begins with the Decemviri (*Leges XII. Tab.* viii. 8*a*).[3] Notable in later days was the *Lex Cornelia de Sicariis et Veneficis* in 82 B.C.[4] Dio Cassius (xlix. 43) tells us that in 32 B.C. the triumvirs, Octavius, Antony, and Lepidus, banished the magicians and *astrologi*, and refers (lii. 36) to a speech by Mæcenas against foreign religions and secret societies for purposes of magic. In A.D. 16 Tiberius banished the magicians and *mathematici*, and in the same reign L. Pituanius was thrown from the Tarpeian Rock and P. Marcius was executed 'more prisco' outside the Porta Esquilina (Tac. *Ann.* ii. 32), and Mamercus Scaurus committed suicide to escape a suit for magic (*ib.* vi. 29). Under Nero, Servilia, the young daughter of Soranus, was accused of selling part of her dowry to procure the means to save her father's life by magic rites (*ib.* xvi. 31). The prescriptions of Tiberius were renewed by Claudius (*ib.* xii. 52) and Vitellius (Suet. *Vitell.* 14), and the end of official paganism was marked by the laws of Diocletian against the *malefici*, *Manichæi*, and *mathematici* (*Coll.* xv. iii. 1 [Huschke]). Sometimes the law prescribed special and severe punishments, and how far the law itself had extended by the 3rd cent. A.D. may be seen from the *Sententiæ* of Iulius Paullus[5] on the *Lex Cornelia de Sicariis*:

'Qui abortionis aut amatorium poculum dant, etsi id dolo non faciant, tamen mali exempli res est, humiliores in metallum, honestiores in insulam amissa parte bonorum relegantur; quod si ex hoc mulier aut homo perierit, summo supplicio adficiuntur. Qui sacra impia nocturnave ut quem obcantarent, defigerent, obligarent, fecerint faciendave curaverint, aut cruci suffiguntur aut bestiis obiiciuntur. Qui hominem immolaverint exve eius sanguine litaverint, fanum templumve polluerint bestiis obiiciuntur, vel si honestiores sint capite puniuntur. Magicæ artis conscios summo supplicio adfici placuit, id est, bestiis obiici aut cruci suffigi. Ipsi autem magi vivi exuruntur. Libros magicæ artis apud se neminem habere licet; et penes quoscumque reperti sint, bonis ademptis ambustis his publice honestiores in insulam deportantur, humiliores capite puniuntur. Non tantum huius artis professio, sed etiam scientia prohibita est.' See also the *Cod. Theodos.* ix. 16, xvi. 10; *Cod. Iustin.* ix. 18.

Doubtless the object of the law was or, at least, ought to have been merely to punish the abuse of magic (Plato, *Legg.* 933 D), but it went much further than that. All the old laws were revived and reinforced by new legislation as soon as, under Constantine, Christianity succeeded paganism as the official religion of the Empire. Of course, the moment the change was effected Christianity became the plaintiff and paganism the defendant in the ancient process of Religion *v.* Magic. It was Christianity now that was responsible for the welfare of the State in this world. But, among other things, Christianity differed essentially from paganism in the fact that it had also a keen interest in the welfare of every member of the State in the world to come. Between the two, the new representative of orthodoxy—in the hands of those who do not understand or appreciate its message and meaning, the most intolerant of all religions—thought fit to proceed against its predecessor with a zeal worthy of a better cause and a rigour that amounted to persecution.[1]

The practice of the courts naturally went hand in hand with the law and was regulated by it. The charge of magic in one form or another was always a cause of action. It was perhaps most common in cases in which our plea is 'undue influence.' In Greek testamentary law, *e.g.*, this plea was specified either as ὑπὸ φαρμάκων or as γυναικὶ πειθόμενος (*i.e.*, 'drugs,' in the ancient sense of the word, or 'persuaded by one's wife').

The best known case of this kind is the one brought against Apuleius, the famous rhetor and author of the 2nd cent. A.D., by the relatives of the impressionable old widow, Pudentilla, whom he had just married. The charge was that he had won her affections by magic, and specified practices were alleged.[2] The legal basis of the action was perhaps ultimately the *Lex Cornelia de Sicariis et Veneficis* passed by Sulla in 82 B.C. The defendant conducted his own case and won it by a speech, the *de Magia*, which still survives and is a valuable contribution to our knowledge of magic in that period. It must be said, however, that for the most part the great rhetor does not touch upon the real point at issue.

Considering the comparative frequency of such litigation in everyday life, we can understand with what interest the Athenian audience listened to the famous scene in the *Andromache* of Euripides in which she is charged by Hermione, the wife of Neoptolemus, with winning his affections by the use of philtres. Her dignified and stinging reply,

'Not of my philtres thy lord hateth thee,
But that thy nature is no mate for his.
That is the love-charm: woman, 'tis not beauty
That witcheth bridegrooms, nay, but nobleness'
(205 ff.; tr. A. S. Way, *Tragedies*, London, 1894–98),

is doubtless the poet's own protest against the folly of such a charge. But, if one may judge from cases still occasionally reported in the daily press, it is a charge which, old as it is, will never cease to be preferred in one form or another.

3. Derivation and definition.—All the words for 'magic' in Greek and Latin record some real or supposed fact in the history of the subject or else indicate that some particular manifestation of it was sufficiently prominent to stand for the whole.

The ordinary Greek words for 'magic' are μαγεία, γοητεία, and φαρμακεία. The last two are old and popular. The γοήτης, according to the derivation offered by the Greeks themselves —ἀπὸ τῶν γοῶν καὶ τῶν θρήνων τῶν ἐν τοῖς τάφοις γινομένων— was specifically a necromancer in the original sense of that word, *i.e.*, like the Witch of Endor, he called up the dead (νεκυομαντεία)—a thing which in all ages has been one of the most important specialties of the magic art. It is true that the derivation just quoted is on the face of it equally descriptive of professional mourners, and, as Hubert observes,[3] the two occupations are not incompatible. The γοήτης may very well have been both. But, as we shall see below, the old etymologist is not thinking of mourners; he is giving a very good description of a special and particular type of magic with which he himself was doubtless quite familiar. The γοήτης was, no doubt, much feared by the population in general, but he was also more or less a roadside charlatan, and in other respects the associations with a person of his type were such that of the three ordinary names of 'magic,' γοητεία appears always to have been the most distinctly pejorative. The prominence of φαρμακεία in this connexion is due to the primitive idea that the action of any drug (φάρμακον)—using that word in its most extended application—is due to magic power. In its original sense φαρμακεία means the science which deals with the magic properties of plants and simples. Hence the φαρμακός—in all countries the primitive ancestor of the doctor, the apothecary, and the toxicologist (amateur or professional)—was the magician whose specialty was this particular branch of the subject, and the φάρμακον, *i.e.* the 'drug' which he prepared, was a magic charm. As such, the efficacy of the φάρμακον is enhanced, if not actually conditioned, by the incantation which generally is associated with some stage of its history. In most cases, too, it must be discovered, prepared, or given under certain conditions or in a certain way. Of course, its effect may be helpful or harmful according to the intentions of the giver. Hence the secondary use of the word in the sense of either a 'poison' or a 'remedy.' Homer himself generally distinguishes by the use of an adjective (*Od.* iv. 230). The origin and use of μαγεία (Lat. *magia*), from which, through the substantivized adjective (τέχνη μαγική, *ars magica*), our own word is derived, are an

[1] T. Mommsen, 'Religionsfrevel nach römischen Recht,' in H. von Sybel's *Hist. Zeitschr.* lxiv. [1890] 389–429, reprinted in *Gesammelte Schriften*, Berlin, 1905 ff., iii. 389–422.

[2] C. G. Bruns, *Fontes iuris romani antiqui*[6], Freiburg, 1893, p. 160.

[3] *Ib.* p. 30.

[4] *Ib.* p. 93.

[5] Collected by P. E. Huschke, *Corpus iurisprudentiæ anteiustinianæ*[6], Leipzig, 1908–11, v. xxiii. 14 ff., vol. ii. p. 149 f.

[1] Maury, *La Magie et l'astrologie*, p. 106 ff.

[2] A. Abt, 'Die Apologie des Apuleius von Madaura und die antike Zauberei,' in *RVV* iv. 2 [1908] pp. 75–344.

[3] In Daremberg-Saglio, *s.v.* 'Magia,' p. 1499.

excellent illustration of the Greek and Roman attitude towards an alien faith to which allusion has already been made. In its original and restricted sense μαγεία meant nothing more than the religion of the Persian Magi (so, *e.g.*, Plato, *Alcib. I.* 122 A). It is well known that this faith, which was imported to Greece by the Magi (*q.v.*), takes rank as one of the great religions of the world. But it was imported, and had no official standing; even though impressive, it was unauthorized. Between these two facts μαγεία became a general term for 'magic' as early, at least, as the 4th cent. B.C., as we see from Theophrastus, *Hist. Plant.* ix. 17, and, perhaps, Aristotle, frag. 36[1] (though this is only an indirect quotation by Diog. Laert. *procem.* vi. 8), and thereafter retained no apparent traces of its specific and pretentious origin. Μαγεία is perhaps the most colourless of the three words; γοητεία, except when it returns to its original and distinctive use, is a pejorative term for magic in general; φαρμακεία, when used generically, is possibly fuller than the others of vague and dreadful associations; but otherwise there seems to have been no great difference between them in current speech. Hesychius, *e.g.*, defines γοητεία by μαγεία, and for Porphyrius the general term for 'magic' is γοητεία (pejorative) and whatever may be detached from it is religion. The Mystics (*e.g.*, Porphyr. *de Abstinentia*, ii. 40) differentiated theoretically the use of these words; they distinguish between good magic and bad magic, and enter into all sorts of subtle speculations regarding the hierarchy of demons through whose aid the good or the bad magic, as the case may be, is able to accomplish its purpose. The Alexandrian school of philosophers undertook to draw a distinction between γοητεία and the particularly pretentious *theurgia* of later days. But Augustine (*de Civ. Dei*, x. 9) is too much of a practical, clear-headed Roman not to see the essential weakness of the entire theory. The worship of God, he says, is a matter of 'simplici fide atque fiducia pietatis, non incantationibus et carminibus nefariæ curiositatis arte compositis, quam vel magian vel detestabiliori nomine goetian vel honorabiliori theurgian vocant, qui quasi conantur ista decernere et illicitis artibus deditos alios damnabiles, quos et maleficos vulgus appellat (hos enim ad goetian pertinere dicunt), alios autem laudabiles videri volunt, quibus theurgian deputant; cum sint utrique ritibus fallacibus dæmonum obstricti sub nominibus angelorum.' In other words, Christianity is orthodox; therefore all else is heterodox, *i.e.* magic. And, whatever we call it, however we disguise it, magic is—magic. This, of course, is nothing more or less than our familiar old criterion of orthodoxy, unimpaired and unaltered by the fact that Christianity instead of paganism happens to be the official and legal standard of comparison. For the Romans themselves—at least, after the 1st cent. A.D.—the difference between the *maleficus*, the *veneficus*, the *saga*, and the *magus* was only difference of degree.[2]

Pliny's opinion (*HN* xxx. 2) is that magic began with medicine, and that the chief causes of further growth were the admixture of religion and astrology (*ars mathematica*)—all with intent to deceive. In the same way magic is extended to alchemy and divination (Tert. *de Idol.* 9, *de Cultu Fem.* 1 f., etc.). Hubert rightly observes[3] that, in spite of the fact that the Chaldæi and the plain magicians are in the same class, a sharp distinction should be made between astrology and magic. The business of astrology is to foretell the very things which it is the business of magic to prevent or, at least, to modify. If, therefore, magic enters into astrology, it is for that purpose (*Pap. Paris*, 2891, 2901, 2910). Hubert does acknowledge, however, that the astrologer's ceremonial in consulting the stars derives no small part of its efficacy from the fact that it has so much in common with the incantations of magic. We might, perhaps, add that the whole 'science' of astrology is based upon a type of reasoning so primitive, so nearly akin to that upon which magic itself is based, that one might be excused for failing to see sometimes where magic begins and astrology ends. There was at least one large and especially popular class of astrologers about whom there could be no doubt: the so-called Ἰατρομαθηματικοί, or astrological quacks, whose entire practice was founded on speculations regarding the mystic properties and powers of mere numbers. The Roman legislators were quite justified in believing that, if there was any distinction between this theory and the theory of magic incantation, it was a distinction without a difference.

It is also quite true, as Hubert insists, that alchemy should be reckoned *per se* as a science. We might add, however, that alchemy never had a chance to be reckoned *per se*. Not until it assumed the *alias* of chemistry was it able to escape from its old associations with magic (see ALCHEMY).

It has already been noted that divination, even by the old criterion of official sanction, occupies a more or less indeterminate position between magic and religion. Indeed, μαντεία and magic are so thoroughly commingled that even in antique parlance the one is often merely a synonym for the other.[1] In others a fairly sharp distinction is supplied by official sanction. *Nekyomantia*, for instance, was religious if used in a family cult, *i.e.*, it was presumed that a man has the right to call up his own ancestors if he pleases. By a somewhat similar presumption it was also sanctioned in the cult of the heroes.[2] Under any other circumstances it is not only magic, but one of the most formidable and characteristic operations of magic. The same distinction holds good in another very important and extensive branch of divination, one in which every one was interested and which all the schools of philosophy, especially the Stoics, investigated and discussed at great length—the source, valuation, and interpretation of dreams (ὀνειροκρισία; see DREAMS AND SLEEP, vol. v. p. 30 f., and cf. Artemidorus, *Onirocritica*, a curious treatise of the 2nd cent. A.D. which still survives). The method officially sanctioned for securing true and prophetic dreams (ὀνειροπομπία, ὀνειραιτησία) was *incubatio*, but the magic papyri (esp. the *Pap. Lugd. Batav.*, Leyden, 1843–85, v., vi.) are full of ὀνειραιτητικά, formulæ and charms for obtaining such dreams. Hubert would also include within the sphere of magic such practices as divination *per sortes* with verses of Homer, Vergil, or the Scriptures, φαρμακομαντεία (Athen. vi. 80 [261 F]) and, in general, any ceremonial for purposes of divination which implies the use of magic rites in our sense of the word. By that criterion, of course, we should agree with Hubert that divination in private cults was strongly tinged with magic. The same was true even of official divination, although this was when the oracles were revived in the 2nd cent. and was for historical reasons. In all these cases, however, magic was distinguished from religion by the usual criterion of official sanction.

II. *MYTHOLOGICAL PERIOD.*—Until the age of Pericles the history of our subject is largely confined to what Hubert calls the 'mythology' of magic. This is partly due to the fact that our record is so fragmentary and that what survives belongs to types less likely to be concerned with such a subject. But it is fairly certain that not far from the time of Pericles magic itself rapidly assumed greater importance in the everyday life of the nation. By that time the average man's faith in the old gods was rapidly diminishing; and among the factors contributing to the growth and spread of magic and kindred ideas in any people the decay of orthodox belief is by no means the last to be considered.

1. **The magicians.**—Among mythical magicians, the Telchines (or Telchinæ), the Dactyli, the Curetes—and in connexion with the Curetes the Corybantes (see KOURETES AND KORYBANTES)—hold a position which amply illustrates the fundamental ideas about magic already mentioned. The first three were reckoned the primitive pre-Hellenic inhabitants of Greek lands—the Telchines, of Rhodes (Strabo, p. 472; Diod. Sic. v. 55, though here, as with the others, there is a tendency to confusion in names and places of origin); the Dactyli, of Cretan or Phrygian Ida (Strabo, p. 355; Apoll. Rhod. i. 1129); and the

[1] ed. V. Rose, Leipzig, 1886.
[2] T. Mommsen, *Röm. Strafrecht*, Leipzig, 1899, p. 639 ff.
[3] *Op. cit.* p. 1495.

[1] C. A. Lobeck, *Aglaophamus*, Königsberg, 1829, p. 632.
[2] *Ib.* p. 236; L. Deubner, *De Incubatione*, Leipzig, 1900, p. 6.

Curetes, of Acarnania.[1] As such, they were all regarded as servants of the gods and, indeed, as themselves more or less divine; and, in some cases, they actually had a cult.[2] Even the Telchines, a synonym of spitefulness in the folklore of Greece, were in their time founders of cults (Diod. Sic. v. 55; cf. Paus. IX. xix. 5). But they all belong to the old order, they are all heterodox, they are all classed as γοήτεις (Nonn. xiv. 36 f.; Strabo, p. 601).[3] Indeed, the Telchines are inimical to the gods and spiteful towards men. They use the water of the Styx in their charms (Nonnus, *Dionys.* xiv. 36); they are malignant sorcerers, who wither the plants, ruin the crops, and make barren the domestic animals.

Most notable is the position of these clans in the history of the arts. As the Cyclopes were the servants of Hephæstus, so these semi-divine corporations of smiths were the first workers in iron and copper, gold and silver; in fact, they were the inventors of metallurgy. Hence the Telchines in particular are aptly compared by W. Pape[4] to the *Kobolde* of Germanic mythology. These clans of demoniac master magicians know all the secrets of nature. The Dactyli were masters of music and of the healing art. They taught Orpheus (Diod. Sic. v. 64) and, long afterwards, Pythagoras. Paionius, Iasius, Akesidas, the three great physicians of the epic, are all Dactyli. Later, they were regarded as inventors of the famous *Ephesia Grammata* (Clem. Alex. *Strom.* i. 15 [*PG* viii. 781]). The Centaurs Chiron and Nessus are also masters of the healing art. The gift of prophecy, though naturally common to all by reason of their magic powers, is especially associated with the Curetes. Among all nations the most notable symptom of the power to prophesy is an ecstatic state of mind. The assumed origin and pattern of the Corybantic worship, the best known and most widely spread cult of this nature among the Greeks and Romans, was the wild noise and clatter of the armed dance of the Curetes around the baby Zeus—really a primitive spell, an ἀποτροπαῖον, to keep the child from harm (see KOURETES AND KORYBANTES).

The great individual magicians of Greek mythology are Prometheus (Apoll. Rhod. iii. 845; Val. Flac. vii. 356), Agamedes,[5] Melampus (Apollod. II. ii. 2), Œnone (*ib.* III. xii. 6), Pasiphae (*ib.* III. xv. 1), Agamede or Perimede (Roscher, *s.vv.*; Theocr. ii. 16 and schol.), Circe (Roscher, ii. 1193), and Medea (*ib. s.v.*). The special, though not the exclusive, interest of all is φαρμακεία. Prometheus, the wise and kindly Titan, belongs to the old régime. Melampus comes from Thessaly, the distant land of magicians. All the rest (except Œnone, and even she is a water-nymph) are in some way connected with the sun or—which amounts to the same thing—with the sea or the moon. Agamedes is the grandson of Poseidon. The rest are descendants of Helios. Agamede is also the beloved of Poseidon. The greatest of all are Circe and Medea—both of the seed of Helios and Poseidon, both from Colchis, the distant land where the sun-god himself rises at dawn from the ocean stream.

Circe.—In the Homeric account—the most marvellously correct and sympathetic portrayal in all literature of her curious, abnormal, not quite human type—Circe dwells far away in the mystic and trackless seas. Cruel, but no more consciously cruel than the child who separates some luckless fly from its wings, this φαρμακίς, whose special power is metamorphosis, amuses herself with enticing such wandering mariners as come within her reach to drink magic potions which straightway turn them into swine. Like any other queen of the mermaids, Circe is unmoral rather than immoral. Nothing could be more in harmony with her type than her first meeting with Odysseus and their subsequent life together, or than the fact that, in the long run and all things considered, the Wanderer never had a more disinterested friend among women.

Medea.—Medea is a relative of Circe and, like Circe, was sometimes worshipped as a goddess (Hes. *Theog.* 956 ff.; Alcman, cited by Athenag. *Legat. pro Christ.* 14); in fact, the Romans identified her with Angitia and the Bona Dea (Macrob. I. xii.; Serv. on *Æn.* vii. 750). Of all mythical magicians she is most distinctly the sorceress, and her powers as such are the most varied and terrible. As Hubert says,[1] she is evidently the most highly developed personality in a group of homonyms. It was therefore the constant tendency of tradition to make her the originator of rites and charms which previously had no definite pedigree at all or were attributed to some more obscure rival. At all events, in song and story, in the long annals of magic itself, there never has been a sorceress to compare with Medea. Medea, the beautiful and awful Colchian, as awful as her mistress the goddess of the crossways, Medea παμφάρμακος, daughter of Æetes and granddaughter of the sun-god, is still the arch-enchantress of all the Occident. She is first and foremost a φαρμακίς. It is therefore particularly, though not exclusively, from her knowledge of φάρμακα that her power is derived. Her box of magic simples is often mentioned (Apoll. Rhod. iii. 802, iv. 25), and in art she is often represented as holding it in her hand. Her charms are innumerable.[2] She can restore youth, bestow invulnerability, lull the dragon of the golden fleece to slumber, quiet the storms, make the rivers pause in their courses, call down the moon from heaven, etc. Indeed, Apollonius's description (iv. 1665–72) of her procedure when, from the deck of the Argo, she cast the evil eye on the giant Talus far away on the cliffs of Crete and brought him down to his death is enough to chill one's blood. But Medea is also beneficent, and K. Seeliger (in Roscher) even suggests that this was really her primitive character. She heals the wounds of the Argonauts, cures Heracles of his madness, frees the Corinthians from a famine, and is even a prophetess.

Even in the fancy of the unlettered her memory never fades. On the contrary, the popular tradition of her continued to grow in its own way (Tib. I. ii. 51, note, ed. K. F. Smith, New York, 1913). Special feats of magic were supposed to have been her invention (*e.g.*, Paus. II. xii. 1), and, as the line just cited from Tibullus suggests, we may be sure that the *libri*

> 'carminum valentium
> Refixa coelo devocare sidera'

of Canidia to which Horace refers (*Epod.* xvii. 4) contained more than one charm claimed to be Medea's own. So, too, the magic plants and simples for which Thessaly was so famous were supposed to have sprung up in the first place from the box of charms lost by Medea as she was passing over that land with her winged dragons (schol. Aristoph. *Nubes*, 749; Aristides, i. p. 76 [Dindorf]). Her fame in the written word is unique. We are obliged to agree that she never lived among men; she was merely a child of popular fancy and the foster-child of a long line of literary artists few of whom were men of transcendent genius; and yet she emerges as perhaps the most wonderful woman in all classical antiquity. Poets, historians, orators, philosophers, even unimpressionable grammarians

[1] Roscher, ii. 1588. [2] *Ib.* ii. 1611.
[3] Lobeck, p. 1181 ff.
[4] *Wörterbuch der griech. Eigennamen*³, Brunswick, 1875, *s.v.* Τελχίν.
[5] Deubner, p. 18, n. 7.

[1] *Op. cit.* p. 1498.
[2] Roscher, ii. 2483, for list and references.

and commentators—few fail to mention her. Ovid never escaped from her spell. From Homer to the last feeble echoes of rhetoric, and again in the renaissance of the modern world, hers is a dominant personality, and the story of her love and her lover, her betrayal and her terrible revenge, has never grown old or lost its interest and charm.

As we might guess, Medea is the typical Græco-Roman enchantress. Her connexion with Hecate, her methods of discovering, securing, preparing, and administering her φάρμακα, and the large preponderance of φαρμακεία itself in her theory and practice of magic are all typical of every other enchantress both in literature and in life from Homer to the end of the classical world.

2. Their methods.—Φάρμακα are either to be swallowed or to be applied outwardly as salves or plasters. The distinction is medical, but it is also Homeric, and applies equally well to magic at any time. Circe uses a salve to restore her victims to human shape (*Od.* x. 391 f.); Medea uses another to render Jason invulnerable (Apoll. Rhod. iii. 1041 ff.), and still another—in the form of an aspersion—to put the dragon to sleep (*ib.* iv. 156); in the old Lesbian folk-tale Aphrodite gave Phaon a box of salve which, when applied as directed, gave him youth and surpassing beauty (Ælian, *Var. Hist.* xii. 18; Serv. on *Æn.* iii. 279; Palæphat. 49; Lucian, *Dial. Mort.* ix. 2; Roscher, *s.v.* 'Phaon'). The shirt of Nessus and the robe of Creusa belong to the same type. Pamphila (Apul. *Met.* iii. 21) went so far as to have a box filled with little caskets, each containing a special salve for a given metamorphosis.

Quite as ancient and characteristic is the φάρμακον taken as a drink. So Helen, herself a sorceress, administered her Egyptian nepenthe (*Od.* iv. 220–232); so Circe effected all her transformations (*ib.* x. 237); so Medea performed some of her feats. And here, again, the method is typical of later times. One branch of it—the use of φίλτρα or *pocula amatoria*, *i.e.* drinks to inspire love—is perhaps the commonest and most characteristic feature of all ancient magic. It is to be noted here that in Circe's case the process is not completed until she touches the victim with her ῥάβδος, or magic wand. In art Medea is frequently represented with a wand; with a wand Athene makes Odysseus look young again (*Od.* xvi. 172); so Hermes overpowers our senses (*Il.* xxiv. 343; *Od.* v. 47); and, as every one knows, to this day no magician's outfit, even if he is nothing more than an ordinary sleight-of-hand performer, is complete without this ancient and dramatic accessory. The use of the wand seems to be an application of the doctrine of sympathy. It facilitates the transfer of the magician's power to the object upon which he wishes to exert it. But in all cases the wand is a help rather than an actual necessity. Except, perhaps, in the case of the gods just mentioned, who, as such, are too powerful to need it, the really essential thing is the φάρμακον, and, as we have seen, the Græco-Roman theory of magic presupposes that Circe had already prepared her φάρμακα to the accompaniment of the proper charm, and that Helen's nepenthe had been similarly treated either by herself or by the specialists from whom she had procured it.

The same rules hold good for φαρμακεία in the art of healing. The sons of Autolycus bind up the wound of Odysseus, and stop the flow of blood with an ἐπαοιδή (*Od.* xix. 457); the divine physician, Asclepius, follows the same methods (Pind. *Pyth.* iii. 52; cf. iv. 217; schol. *Isthm.* vi. 53; cf. Soph. *Œd. Col.* 1194 [Jebb]), and at all times the use of incantation with a remedy was so characteristic that one of our richest sources for the study of φαρμακεία as magic is the works of the physicians from Hippocrates to Marcellus. Not that men like Hippocrates and Galen were much impressed by the magic of medicine; but their patients were, and any good doctor learns that his most powerful allies are the patient's own determination to recover and his belief that he is going to succeed. In popular medicine, of course, the survival of magic is much more marked. Here, too, the practice of pre-Periclean times is typical. The case of Iphiclus (Apollod. I. ix. 12; Roscher, ii. 306) is an excellent example.

For ten years Iphiclus could have no children. At last he consulted Melampus the seer. Melampus, whose specialty, like that of Mopsus the Argonaut (Apoll. Rhod. iii. 916 ff.), was the language of birds, consulted the vulture. The vulture said that ten years before, while castrating rams, Iphiclus had threatened his father Phylacus with the knife. It was then discovered that the knife had at that time, and presumably by Phylacus himself, been struck into the tree with which the life and well-being of Iphiclus were bound up,[1] and that it had stuck there ever since. The knife was removed, the rust scraped off and prepared as a φάρμακον, and, when Iphiclus had taken it as prescribed, he immediately recovered his powers. Similarly, the wound of Telephus could be cured only by the rust on the spear of Achilles by which the wound had originally been inflicted. The principle is, of course, frequently illustrated in the later history of Græco-Roman magic, and still survives in our own homely saying that 'the hair of the dog cures his bite.'

Other branches of magic referred to in this period are equally typical. According to Homer (*Od.* x. 516 ff.), Odysseus learned from Circe how to call up the dead, and the ceremonial of *nekyomantia*, as the poet pictures it, always remained practically the same. Indeed the antics of Empedocles, as described by Diog. Laert. (viii. 59, 62 ff.), show clearly that the type of the γοήτης became finally fixed at a very early period. Again, the bag of winds given by Æolus to Odysseus (*Od.* x. 16 ff.) repeats the symbolism of wind and weather magic in all times and countries.[2] The same is true of the primitive rustic magic attributed to the Telchines. Finally, the love-charm known as 'drawing down the moon' was certainly familiar long before the time of Sophron, who, according to Suidas, was a contemporary of Xerxes. Presumably this charm was from the first looked upon as the special property of the Thessalian witches. At all events, the idea was firmly fixed in the time of Aristophanes (*Nubes*, 749) and was never afterwards forgotten.

III. *FOREIGN INFLUENCES.*—We have seen that, in conformity with the law of distance in time or space or both, the early Greeks attributed special magic powers to their alien predecessors, the Telchines, Dactyli, and Curetes—apparently, too, the Pelasgi—and that unusual activity and ability in magic were attributed to what at the time were felt to be such distant countries as Colchis, Egypt, Thessaly, and even the Islands. As time went on and the horizon of the known world became correspondingly wider, such local centres became *pari passu* more and more distant, and the strange tribes of the African deserts, the mysterious nations of the Far East, and the still more mysterious peoples of the Far North took their turn as redoubtable magicians.

But the primacy always remained with Thessaly. In the time of Aristophanes as in the time of Apuleius, Thessaly was *par excellence* the realm of magic and magicians. The literature is full of it, and evidently the literature was in this respect a faithful reflexion of average opinion in the world at large. Numberless passages might be cited to show that in the Athens of Pericles, as long afterwards in the Rome of Augustus, the average professional enchantress found it 'good business' to advertise herself as a 'genuine Thessalian.'

Orphism.—Thrace too, though Pliny (*HN* xxx.

[1] W. Mannhardt, *Antike Wald- und Feldkulte*, Berlin, 1877, p. 30 ff.

[2] *GB*[3], pt. i., *The Magic Art*, London, 1911, i. 319 ff.

1 f.) denies it, was another famous locality for magic. But Thracian magic, as Hubert warns us,[1] was really another name for Orphic magic. Now Orphism itself was not essentially magic; on the contrary, it was not only a religious movement but a religious movement of the most momentous importance in the spiritual development of classical antiquity and ultimately of the entire Western world (see ORPHISM). But it was heterodox and, therefore, 'magic.' This seems to be the first great and definite example within historical times of the impingement of a strange religion on Greek orthodoxy. Aristophanes and his fellow poets make all manner of fun of the Orphics, and such a passage as Euripides, *Cyclops*, 639 ff. (cf. Plato, *Rep.* 364 E), shows that Orpheus, like Musæus, had already become an inventor of magic, a sort of protomagician and doctor.[2] Finally, Orpheus the magician, as he appeared to the popular mind of the 5th cent. B.C., became a character of great importance in the mystic magic of later days,[3] the rites of the Orphics were associated with those of the Chaldæi, the Ophitæ claimed Orpheus as their founder, and he was even made one of the founders of astrology and alchemy. Indeed, as Hubert says,[4] it is often difficult to distinguish between Orphic texts and magic texts. Further confusion was caused by the lustral ceremonies peculiar to Orphism, and to the association of Orpheus with the cult of Selene and Hecate. So far as the average man was concerned, the distinction between the ἀγύρται and the μάντεις and the unattached priests of Orphism (Plato, *Rep.* 364 B; Theophr. *Char.* xxx. [xvi.])[5] was practically negligible. The standing charge against them was their emphasis on *mysteria*. But Orphism itself suffered from the fact that, being a strange religion, it was at once classed as mere magic. As such, it had no standing and inevitably began to deteriorate. It justified more and more its new name of ordinary magic, and its adherents assumed more and more the habits and point of view of ordinary magicians. On the other hand, ordinary magic was enriched and enlarged, as usual, by contact with new principles and methods of procedure. Here, of course, we have one important reason for the incomparable wealth and variety of Græco-Roman magic.

The Magi.—But of all these foreign influences on native magic the religion of the Persians, *i.e.* of the Magi, was perhaps the most important. At any rate, in the ordinary opinion of later times it was the type of all such influence in general. An almost immediate result, *e.g.*, of absorption by its native rival was the designation of the new combination as μαγεία. As we have seen, this was not later than the middle of the 4th cent. B.C.; we are therefore safe in assuming that by that time the Greeks had already drawn the inevitable corollary, afterwards generally accepted, that the original fountain-head of the new combination was Zoroaster, the Persian. The intrusion of Zoroaster upon magic is characteristically reflected in the later history of the subject. Thus, as it was popularly believed in the ancient world that great scholars and sages—especially if, like Pythagoras, Epimenides, Democritus, and even Plato, they had also travelled in foreign parts and had been vouchsafed the ineffable mysteries of the Oriental religions—were thereby mighty magicians, if not actually the first to reveal their wondrous art to the world at large (Val. Max. VIII. vii. 7, ext. 2; Solinus, 3; *HN* xxx. 3 f., xxiv. 156 ff., xxv. 13 ff.; Plut. *Sympos.* viii. 8; Aul. Gell. x. 12; Apul. *de Mag.* 27, 31; Diog. Laert. ix. 7; Lucian, *Necyomantia*, 6; Apoll. Tyan. *Ep.* xvi), we now hear that Pythagoras was a pupil of Zoroaster; indeed, we are told still later that he was also a pupil of Zaratas the Chaldæan (Lobeck, *Aglaophamus*, p. 471). Democritus broke into the tomb of Dardanus in order to secure the wondrous MSS buried with the defunct; and others say that, after being initiated by the Persian Osthanes, he became one of the fountain-heads of the tradition of alchemy.

Of these Persian sages associated with the tradition of Græco-Roman magic the most famous was Osthanes (*HN* xxx. 8, etc.). His special prominence was partly due to the belief that he had committed to writing all the voluminous and unutterably precious but, until his time, entirely oral tradition of ancient magic (*ib.*). The first book on medical magic was attributed to him (*ib.* xxviii. 6), and also certain apocryphal books on alchemy.[1] Of all the authors on magic he is the most frequently referred to, and his name may be found cited as an important authority in 'dream-books' still for sale.

As we shall see, all this foreign influence on magic was much discussed by the philosophers (Diog. Laert. *procem.* 1). One of the most notable contributions must have been the so-called Μαγικός, usually attributed to Aristotle (*Frag. Aristot.*, ed. Rose, frag. 32 ff.). Suidas (*s.v.* 'Antisthenes') does well to doubt Aristotelian authorship, for the symptomatically childish statements referred to it are eminently uncharacteristic of that residuary legatee of Hellenic thought, the hard-headed and highly intellectual Stagyrite.

IV. *ITALIC MAGIC.*—The traditional history of Italic magic is not so well attested, but the assumption that, generally speaking, it was quite the same as that of Greece is fully supported by such testimony as survives. The first Roman reference to magic is the law of the Twelve Tables ('QVI FRVGES EXCANTASSIT. . . . NEVE ALIENAM SEGETEM PELLEXERIS)[2] which forbids the transference—by magic—of the crops growing in other people's fields to your own. This primitive and universal explanation of the reason why the wheat-ears in your neighbour's field are full of grain and yours are not never died out among the Romans. It is illustrated by Pliny's typical anecdote of one Furius Chresimus (*HN* xviii. 41), and as late as the 6th cent. A.D. we are told by Agobardus of Lyons, *de Grandine et Tonitruis*, 2 (*PL* civ. 148), that in his time the belief was current that the witches had formed a sort of trust and were transporting all the crops in air-ships to a land with the significant name of 'Magonia.'

A certain amount of magic of this primitive type is preserved by the Elder Cato (*de Agr.* 70 f., 73, 96, 102, 127, 156–160) and Varro (*de Re Rust.* I. ii. 27) and is more or less discernible in later authors (*e.g.*, *HN* xi. 5, xxviii. 4; Sen. *Quæst. Nat.* iv. 7; Serv. on *Ecl.* viii. 99; Aug. *de Civ. Dei*, viii. 10; Pallad. i. 35). It will be observed that the only difference here between magic and religion is that religion is officially sanctioned, while magic is not. The effect of the law of the Twelve Tables is simply to establish this distinction from the legal point of view.

Divination, as usual, occupies a more or less indefinite position between religion and magic. Hence *nekyomantia* was practised to a certain extent by private individuals, and Cicero's accusation of Vatinius (*in Vatin.* vi. 14) is not so extraordinary as it sounds.

1 *Op. cit.* p. 1499.
2 For formulæ attributed to Orpheus see E. Abel, *Orphica*, Leipzig, 1885; R. Wünsch, *Rhein. Mus.* lv. [1900] 78.
3 *Orphica*, 974 ff.; *Lithica*, 50; A. Dieterich, *Abraxas*, Leipzig, 1891.
4 *Op. cit.* p. 1499.
5 Lobeck, p. 625.

1 M. Berthelot and E. Ruelle, *Collection des anciens alchimistes grecs*, Paris, 1888, ii.
2 Bruns, p. 30.

The usual term for a magician is *maleficus*, but the word does not occur in the law until Diocletian.[1] *Veneficium* is the generic name for any magic ceremony, whether legal or illegal, and *veneficus* or *venefica* as the epithet of a magician is used in the same way. The *magus* in Cicero's time was still more or less associated with his Persian origin, but with the first year of Tiberius[2] he comes under the ban of the law, and after Trajan's time the word was applied to any one who practised illegal magic (*Cod. Theodos.* ix. 16. 4; *Cod. Iustin.* ix. 18. 7). *Saga*, 'wise woman,' is probably one of the oldest words for a 'witch' in the language, and the fact that it also means a 'bawd' is a sufficient indication of the *saga's* social position as well as of her specific functions as a magician. She is one of the standard characters of the Roman elegy. *Striges* (*strigæ*, Petron. 63; Ital. *streghe*), lit. 'screech owls,' was a name for witches which records the popular Roman explanation of vampires.

As the Greeks looked upon Thessaly, so the old Romans appear to have looked upon Etruria, as a land of magic and magicians. Among other accomplishments, the Etrurians knew how to call up the dead, bring on rain, and discover hidden springs (Wissowa, in Pauly-Wissowa, *s.v.* 'Aquilex'). So, too, such ancient and mysterious peoples as the Sabines, Marsi, and Pæligni were particularly famous for certain magic powers (Verg. *Æn.* vii. 758; Hor. *Epod.* v. 76, xvii. 29, 60, *Sat.* I. ix. 29 f.; *HN* xxi. 78; Ovid, *Fasti*, vi. 141 f.). The Romans saved the Etruscan *haruspicina* at an early date by naturalizing it. Cato (*de Agr.* v. 4) classes it with the rituals of the *augures*, *harioli*, and *Chaldæi* as a matter which any solid farmer would do well to avoid; but, although he himself was doubtless unaware of it, his own charm for a sprained hip has a suspiciously foreign sound. Even then Roman magic had been exposed for some time to the influx of foreign religions which set in soon after the Second Punic War; the overpowering influence of Hellenism began still earlier; and, as we have seen, Greek magic itself had been thoroughly commingled and overlaid with foreign elements. Finally, our principal Roman source for the details of magic practice is the poets—and the poets confine themselves for the most part to the Greek tradition. The result is that after Cato's time we are dealing not so much with Greek magic or Roman magic as with the magic of the Græco-Roman Empire.

Before referring to the ancient literature connected with this subject—originally enormous and still formidable—it should be observed that no small amount of magic of a certain type had already passed into the category of what Hubert aptly calls 'magie éternelle,'[3] *i.e.* magic too old to have a definite origin, and so common that the fact that it was ever magic at all has long since been forgotten—in short, magic that has been secularized and is reckoned merely so much scientific knowledge already acquired. This explains why Pliny, a hard-headed Roman who had no use whatever for what he would define as magic, is for us a principal source for those magic formulæ and incantations which long usage had made a part of medicine and the various sciences with which he deals. And to a greater or less extent similar material may be found in any other ancient authority who deals with the same matters. One of the most important themes of Græco-Roman science was the tradition of the given subject. Perhaps this explains the curious fact that in the course of time the very word φυσικός itself acquired the secondary meaning of 'magic.'

For these as well as for other reasons already given, few sources are so valuable to the student of Græco-Roman magic as the ancient treatises concerned with medicine, especially if, like Pliny, the author is an inveterate collector of useful information, or if, like the *de Medicamentis* of Marcellus, the book is intended for home use. One of the most notable and characteristic developments of antiquity, especially during and after the Alexandrian age, was the extent to which every conceivable subject of a scientific or *quasi*-scientific nature was treated as literature, particularly as a theme for verse. In such cases whatever magic there was in the subject was rarely forgotten. Valuable sources for the magic of medicine, therefore, are the *Theriaca* and *Alexipharmaca* of Nicander (even more famous were the lost poems on the same subject by Æmilius Macer) and the long passage on snakes in Lucan, ix. 607–937, which doubtless owed much to Macer. Particularly valuable, too, are those writers who deal with some homelier branch of medicine, such as the art of the veterinary—like Palladius and the authors of *Hippiatrica* and the *Mulomedicina*. Especially notable among physicians are Ætius of Amida, Theophanes Nonnus, and Alexander of Tralles, but, above all, Cyranides and Dioscurides. Scribonius Largus and Serenus Sammonicus also might be considered. In short, any ancient doctor, however wise or learned, is likely to contribute something to medical magic.

The writers on agriculture and kindred themes (*e.g.*, Cato, Varro, Columella, the author of the *Geoponica*, Gargilius Martialis), the writers on botany, beginning with Theophrastus (*Historia Plantarum*), the naturalists, and the writers of φυσικά, like Neptunalius, are valuable. The same is true of antiquarians like Gellius and Macrobius, of the Paradoxographi, of the Agrimensores, and of the Parœmiographi. In short, omitting for the present that large and important class of writers who deal with the subject merely as a literary asset, any ancient author, no matter what his theme may be, is likely to contribute something to our knowledge of contemporary magic.

It is the philosophers, however, especially the philosophers of a certain type, who are most intimately associated with the most remarkable phase in the history of our subject. We have already seen at how early a date the spiritual life of antiquity began to feel the impact of foreign ideas and systems. The Orphics, the Magi, the worship of Mithra, the Assyrians, the Babylonians, the Phœnicians, the Egyptians, the Hebrews—these are merely the most important. And the process was facilitated to an indefinite extent by the conquests of Alexander, as it was again later by the extension of Roman power to whatever seemed worth while in the way of territory. Laws were passed and, as we have seen, were severely enforced. But they appear to have been practically powerless. The classical world was a babel of creeds, and in the time of Augustus the great capital was alive with a dozen different kinds of magicians, from the lowly *saga* to the impressive *Chaldæus*. As yet the average man of birth and education was not, as one might say, dangerously affected by these different varieties of heterodoxy; but already powerful disintegrating influences had long been at work. As early as three hundred years before Augustus, the great tide of mysticism and related ideas was already rising. Orphism was prominent in it. But Orphism (and, for that matter, any other specific creed that one might name) was perhaps quite as much a symptom as a cause. Spiritual unrest was world-wide. Men needed new wine, and the old bottles could not contain it. The craving which for generations had been more or less vague grew in volume and intensity, and finally reached its acme not far from the beginning of the 2nd cent. of our era. There were creeds then—like those of Isis and Mithra—that would seem to have just missed becoming great religions of the future. There were men, too, in that period—*e.g.*, Apollonius of Tyana and the Peregrinus of Lucian—who were philosophers of the contemporary type,

[1] Mommsen, *Strafrecht*, p. 640, n. 3.
[2] *Ib.* p. 640, n. 7.
[3] *Op. cit.* p. 1501.

and posed as the more or less inspired founders of creeds—all charlatans, of course, but not entirely so; and it is not altogether inconceivable that the names of some of these men might have gone ringing through the ages instead of being merely an object of occasional scholastic contemplation.

Mysticism.—The unusual prominence of magic in this period is symptomatic and due to a number of causes. There was, of course, the ignorant lower class, who always believe in magic. But there was also a higher class, fairly well educated—heavily recruited in a period like this—who had lost their faith in orthodoxy, but who lacked the character to seek the truth elsewhere and the continuity of purpose to attain it. They preferred to give themselves up to whatever promised the incredible—in a way sufficiently dramatic and interesting to gratify the taste for novelty. Under such circumstances there is always another class ready to cater to this form of intellectual and spiritual dissipation. Both these classes—the willing deceivers and the willingly deceived—are pictured to the life in Lucian's admirable skit, the *Philopseudes*, *i.e.* 'Liars for the love of it.' A few, of course, ridiculed the whole matter; the most notable example is Lucian himself, who has been well named 'the Voltaire of antiquity.' Others undertook to demolish magic by argument; chief among these were the Sceptics, the Cynics, and the Epicureans, *i.e.* those who did not believe in orthodoxy, and therefore, by our familiar criterion, were not logically driven to accept the reality of heterodoxy. Finally, however, there were also others—especially the Gnostics and the Alexandrian school of philosophy—who, after honest and conscientious investigation, became responsible for the most remarkable development of magic in Græco-Roman times. This is the magic of mysticism in its various forms. Among the most important authorities for this aspect of the Alexandrian school are Porphyrius (*de Abstinentia* and *de Mysteriis*) and Proclus (*de Sacrificio et Magia*). The theory, as Hubert observes,[1] is one in which the philosophical and the religious elements are still imperfectly differentiated. It is a synthesis of all the known methods of acting on the powers of the supernatural world. It is halfway between religion and ordinary magic, and capable of moving in either direction. The philosophers, of course, emphasized the religious character of the combination, but, as Augustine (*loc. cit.*) saw, and as Porphyrius himself acknowledged (quoted by Eus. *Præp. Evang.* v. 10), they could make no satisfactory distinction between *goetia*, *magia*, and *theurgia*. Their principal criterion was the character and intentions of the individual performing the given ceremony—a criterion hard to apply and of no real value in itself. Their *theurgia* became dissociated from religion; its position in society, like that of the *theurgia* of the old Egyptians, was not such as to give it the character of a religion; in fact, even without it the Alexandrian philosophy had all the outward appearance of magic. The attack on Apuleius was supported more by the various initiations of which he was so proud and the sanctity of the traditions which he invoked than by any specific acts of magic with which he was charged. *Theurgia* did afterwards enter religion, but it entered by the Gnostics, not by the philosophers—and this only in so far as the Gnostics who transformed it into a cult were recognized as a religious organization. So, too, the cult of Mithra gave a religious character to theories and ceremonials that in Pliny's time (*HN* xxx. 17 f.) were described as magic. On the other hand, it was always difficult to distinguish between the Ophitæ and the regular associations of magicians.[2]

[1] *Op. cit.* p. 1501. [2] Dieterich, p. 149.

Theurgical philosophy was violently attacked by the Sceptics, Epicureans, and Cynics (Philostr. *Apoll. Tyan.* vii. 39). Among the most important works were the Κατὰ Μάγων of the Epicurean Celsus (probably the adversary of Origen, and the one to whom Lucian dedicated his *Pseudomantis*), and the Γοήτων Φωρά of the Cynic Œnomaus. The Πρὸς Μαθηματικούς of Sextus Empiricus still survives, and it is unusually dreary reading. Like Lucian (*e.g.*, in his *Alexander seu Pseudomantis*, *Demonax*, *Philopseudes*, etc.), they attacked not only magic, but everything marvellous in either religion or mythology. Lucian feels that the wandering priests of the Syrian goddess are no better than any other magicians. All magic is a mere pretence, all magicians are hypocrites, rascals, and charlatans, whose object is to play on the credulity of the average man.

The Christians.—The attitude of the Christians, as we have seen, was different. According to Origen, Celsus had no right to deny the reality of magic; Augustine was quite certain that the rites used for summoning demons were efficacious (*de Civ. Dei*, xxi. 6); and, indeed, the Church Fathers in general are far from denying the existence and power of magic (Epiph. *Hær.* xxxiv. 1; Tert. *Apol.* 35, *de Anima*, 57; Eus. *Præp. Evang.* v. 14), especially in those early days when it seemed necessary to make the sharpest possible distinction between the Christians and the Gnostics. All heretics in general and Gnostics in particular were magicians and their faith was magic (Iren. *Hær.* i. 13 ff.; Justin Martyr, *Apol.* i. 26). Paganism in any form was magic. For the Alexandrian *theurgi* the difference between gods and demons was merely a difference in degree; for the Christians there was an absolute opposition between the two: God was good, all the demons were evil; the pagan gods were all demons, therefore all the pagan gods were evil. Any and all marvels which did not happen to be orthodox were the work of the demons.

It will be seen that this is really the familiar old distinction between the orthodox and the heterodox, with a much greater emphasis on the secondary conclusion, also ancient, that the one was good and the other evil, *per se*. And the same old distinction carried with it the same old assumption that the one was just as real as the other. The Christians never seem to have realized any more than did their pagan forefathers that the difference between their gods and other people's gods might conceivably be the difference between gods who are and gods who never were. The only way to deal with the pagan gods was to classify them as evil demons (Tatian, *Orat.* viii.). They were just as real as ever; the marvels and prodigies attributed to them were just as real and just as readily believed as ever; it was merely insisted that the same had been wrought with intent to deceive. The 'idols' still nodded and gave signs from time to time, just as they had always done; but that was a *magica operatio* wrought by the demons of the old religion (Iren. *Hær.* v. 28. 2; Eus. *HE* ix. 3). The persistence of this old prodigy of nodding, etc., is an interesting proof that the Christians still clung to the old pagan idea, more or less generally entertained by the less educated class, that the gods actually inhabited their statues. Many a priceless example of ancient art has been destroyed for this reason, and the idea still survives in the famous mediæval story of the 'Ring of Venus.'

Of particular interest to the student of magic of this strange period are such surviving treatises as the *Poimandres* of Hermes Trismegistus, *Asclepius sive Dialogus Hermetis Trismegisti*, the *Hieroglyphica* of Horapollon, and the astrological works of Nechepso and Petosiris.[1] The literature of the magic oracles belongs to astrology as well as to magic. Another important source is the *Tabellæ Devotionis*, so many of which have come to light in recent years.[2]

The magic papyri.—But most important of all are the magic papyri which continue to turn up from time to time in Egypt. Hubert[3] gives the list of those published down to 1904; for later finds and their discussion, the reader is referred to Von Christ (*op. cit.*), L. Mitteis and U. Wilcken, *Papyruskunde* (Leipzig, 1912), the *Archiv für Papyrusforschung*, and the occasional reports in Bursian's *Jahresbericht des klassischen Altertums*.

The magic papyri belong for the most part to the period between A.D. 300 and 500. Their discovery is peculiarly fortunate in view of the fact that they belong to a type which came under the ban of the law, and which some of the later emperors, notably Diocletian, made sedulous efforts to destroy. They are not original and independent works, but merely handbooks of magic, and, as might be expected, the editorial tradition is very poor. There are often different versions of the same thing; sometimes the hymn or formula in one version will be considerably abbreviated as compared with the same hymn or formula in another version; again, certain habitual formulæ are often merely indicated. It is therefore extremely difficult to reconstruct any complete and trustworthy text of this type.

The authorities habitually quoted and the sources, so far as we can trace them, seem in some respects to bear out Pliny's statements in his account (*HN* xxx. 1 ff.) of the growth and development of magic. Pliny distinguishes three principal sources of ancient magic: (1) the Persian school, founded by Zoroaster; his 2,000,000 verses on this important subject (note the childish exaggeration characteristic of this sphere) were revealed and explained to the Greeks by Osthanes. Pythagoras, Empedocles, and Democritus belonged to this school, and also certain ancient Medes, Babylonians, and Assyrians. Democritus explained the magic books of Dardanus, which he had found in his tomb; they were written in Phœnician. (2) The second is the Jewish school, descended from Moses, Iamnes, and Iotapes (*Pap. Mag.* p. 755; Apul. *de Mag.* 9; Ex 7^{10-12}), and (3) the third is a Cypriote school.

It will be observed that Pliny makes no reference to the Egyptian school, which was particularly important and which, of course, is often mentioned in the papyri themselves. One of the most important authorities in magic alchemy is Maria, the Jewess, but the papyri also refer to real philosophers like Thales, Anaxagoras, Heraclitus, and Diogenes. The genuine magicians, *i.e.* the contemporary or recent authorities, are generally referred to under such names as Zosimus, Synesius, Olympiodorus, Pelagius, and Iamblichus. Now and then we find such curious and characteristic documents as a letter of the magician Nephotes to Psammetichus, a charm of Solomon, or a letter of Pitys, the Thessalian, to Osthanes. This gives some idea of the attitude of the Alexandrian magicians towards the tradition which they followed.

It is no longer possible to trace the Persian, druidical, and Brāhmanical elements in this strange compound. Assyro-Chaldæan influence must have been strong, but it appears to have been indirect. Jewish influence, on the contrary, was both strong and direct, the magic papyri being strongly affected by Judaism. Jewish magicians were in evidence, and they doubtless encouraged the impression that they were the only depositories of the genuine tradition of real magic. But, as Hubert remarks,[1] they brought no organized system to bear upon the Græco-Roman type, but merely introduced certain powerful elements of magic. Especially important here was the Bible, which was presented in Egyptian by way of the Hermetic tradition, after being translated from Greek, and furnished part of the more or less peculiar mythology of magic at this time. Their god, as we should expect, is frequently mentioned in incantations, especially the different forms of his name (Aoth, Abaoth, Arbathiao, Abriao, Adonai, etc.). Especially frequent, too, are the names of Moses, Abraham, Jacob, Solomon, and the various archangels. F. G. Kenyon[2] has explained 'Abraxas' as a corruption of the Hebrew benediction *hab-bᵉrākhāh dābhᵉrāh*, 'pronounce the blessing,' which still survives in the magic of modern times as the familiar 'abracadabra.' Hebrew words more or less corrupted are frequent in the papyri, and Christian influence is also evident; it followed in the wake of Judaism, and, though naturally not so strong, is of the same general type.

But one of the most remarkable contributions of all is that of Egypt, as we might expect of a country so ancient, so full of pretentious wisdom, with a language so utterly strange, and an alphabet which to the ordinary outsider seemed so hopelessly complicated and mysterious. The last two qualifications alone—both sovereign for charms—are enough to establish the reputation of any country as a land of magic and magicians. It may be observed, however, that, unlike the Jews, the Egyptians contributed a complete, organized system of magic to the combination. The fact that, as we learn from the *Book of the Dead*,[3] a magician could be prosecuted shows that the old Egyptians had long since separated magic from religion by the familiar criterion of official recognition. So far as the Greeks and Romans are concerned, the great name here is Hermes Trismegistus. He is not only the principal vehicle and interpreter of Egyptian magic, but, as we have seen, the Hermetic tradition is quite as powerful in the articulate presentation of the Hebrew contributions.

All these foreign influences on the theory and practice of Græco-Roman magic of this later period are more or less clearly traceable in the magic papyri. But it is to be observed that they are never clearly differentiated. Isis, *e.g.*, reveals the wonderful art of magic to Horus. This is all well enough; Horus was one of the family. But Isis learned all her magic from one of the Hebrew archangels. It is equally surprising to see Sabaoth approached with Greek rites. Often special efficacy is gained by issuing a sort of general call to all the pantheon or—which, thanks to the doctrine of sympathy, amounts to the same thing—by adding to one god the names of the most revered gods in a number of nationalities. Magic naturally turns to the foreign religions. It also believes that the plural is more redoubtable than the singular. Hence the more or less chaotic pantheon of magic, especially in its more advanced stages, the symptomatic tendency to multiplication and mixture for purposes of power, which reflects to a certain extent the fact that magic is an outlaw, that it is not subject to official control, and that it has no assured position in the body politic.

V. *THEORY OF MAGIC.*—The procedures of magic, especially of magic so highly developed as was that of Greece and Rome, are, at first sight, bewilderingly complex. But the main ideas, the essential principles from which they all derive and upon which they

[1] See W. von Christ, *Gesch. der griech. Litteratur*⁵, Munich, 1908, § 820, for editions, etc.
[2] See esp. W. S. Fox, 'The Johns Hopkins Tabellæ Defixionis,' *AJPh*, Suppl. to vol. xxxiii. [1912] and references.
[3] *Op. cit.* p. 1503 ff.

[1] *Op. cit.* p. 1513.
[2] *Greek Papyri in the Brit. Museum*, London, 1893 ff., i. 63.
[3] ed. E. A. W. Budge, London, 1899, p. cli.

are all founded, are simple, universal, and eternal. The fundamental purpose of magic is to compel by supernatural means; the primary object and supposed result of every charm is some form of constraint. Possession or obsession (κάτοχος) is a constraint, any form of metamorphosis (such, *e.g.*, as lycanthropy) is a constraint, *fascinatio* in all its numerous forms is a constraint. The ancients habitually associate the processes of magic with the ideas of binding, tying up, nailing down, and their opposites. A magic act is a κατάδεσμος, a κατάδεσις, a *defixio*, a *devinctio*; the removal of its effect is an ἀνάλυσις, a *solutio*, and the corresponding verbs are, *e.g.*, καταδέω, *defigo*, λύω, *solvo*. The language of charms and the details of ritual are largely suggested and guided by some form of this fundamental idea. One sees it most clearly in such symbolic acts as the tying of knots, the driving of nails, and the binding of images.

'The object of every magic act is to put beings or things into or take them out of a state in which certain movements, certain changes, certain phenomena must infallibly ensue. A character or condition is either produced or suppressed, a spell is either imposed or removed.'[1]

1. **The doctrine of sympathy.**—One of the great fundamental principles of magic art is the doctrine of sympathy; but, while the doctrine of sympathy explains much, it should not be forced to explain all. This would be expecting too much of such a phenomenon as magic, in spite of the fact that its deductions are, in their way, so amazingly logical. It is also true that magic is supposed to work in two different ways; it either reaches its object independently and directly and acts at once, as it were, automatically, or—and this was the prevailing theory of the Greeks and Romans—it reaches its object indirectly through the agency of some intervening power to whom its behests are addressed and by whom they are executed. The distinction is important and enlightening; but here, again, we must not apply it too rigidly. There are cases in which the characteristic features of both methods are more or less traceable. We must not expect too much of the magician; he is not always a clear thinker, and he has an inveterate habit of calling all known powers to his aid, whether they happen to be logically related or not.

The doctrine of sympathy is most clearly seen in the direct method. The simplest and most common form among the Greeks and Romans is that in which the magic power possessed or acquired by a given thing works upon the desired object by contact. The virtue of the amulet (see CHARMS AND AMULETS) is shared by the person who wears it, the virtue of philtres and φάρμακα of any kind is appropriated by those who take them as directed. It may be observed, however, that even here, so far as the Greeks and Romans were concerned, the supernatural power had already intervened in the preparation of the given article; and the magician's characteristic method of pluralizing for power is naively illustrated by the rule that in preparing a φάρμακον one should combine ingredients which individually are capable of producing the desired effect. The reasoning is evident. The large use of magic of this type, *i.e.* φαρμακεία, helps to explain the magician's particular interest in the properties of plants and simples. For a similar reason the alchemist is particularly interested in the properties of stones and gems; some of them are sovereign for certain diseases, if ground up and taken inwardly with the appropriate ceremonial. Primitive medicine is a fearsome adventure for the patient. In rare cases the *mana* inheres in the object as such, but this is generally a secondary conclusion. As a rule, the *mana* is acquired, or merely accidental. Some objects are only conductors of *mana*—which explains why they can be used for apparently contradictory purposes. Other staple ingredients in a large number of charms—such as honey, flour, rain-water, etc.—have lost their original significance. Objects are selected according to the usual rules—some real or fancied resemblance, especially the association with some god, etc. A certain thing, *e.g.*, is yellow, therefore it is good for jaundice. Such odd names for plants as 'Jove's Beard' or 'Venus' Ears' record associations with gods, and were doubtless originally secret. The place from which an object comes is often a decisive factor: articles found in the public baths were magic. The Christians considered certain filthy animals magic because they were associated with the devil. Certain names of plants and minerals are magic because they correspond to the planets.[1] Sometimes the decision is made from etymology, true or false; the *reseda* owes its power to its name only (*HN* xxvii. 131). The virtue of lead for certain purposes is due to the fact that it is heavy or cold or indestructible, etc.

One of the most important applications of the doctrine of sympathy is the use of symbolism.[2] As we have already seen, symbolism is even more characteristic of magic than it is of religion. Hubert[3] defines two methods. In the one, which is particularly dramatic, the person or thing upon which we wish our magic to act is represented by a substitute. The most notable example of this class is the use of clay and waxen puppets. The second consists in prefiguring the desired action and result (Tib. I. vi. 53 f.; Soph. *Aias*, 1175)—

e.g., apply a stone to a wart (contact and sympathy), throw the stone away (symbolism), and the wart goes with it. Or, if you have a pain in the stomach, apply the stomach of a frog to the part affected, and your pain becomes his pain, etc. (*HN* xxii. 149; Marcellus, xxvii. 123).

The same idea of contact and sympathy creates the familiar rule of magic homœopathy, that the cause of a given thing is also its remedy.

But, so far as magic is concerned, perhaps the most momentous deduction from the doctrine of sympathy is the rule that the part may stand for the whole, that the two are inseparably connected; the part is able to draw the whole to itself, if aided by magic. What Vergil called the *exuviæ* of Æneas had a special function and a special significance in the pretended *solutio amoris* of the unhappy Dido (*Æn.* iv. 494 ff.). Without assuming the active co-operation of this principle, we cannot appreciate the true inwardness of the most striking performances of magic in classical antiquity. If, for instance, a magician can secure bones of the dead, he has a special and powerful means of calling up the dead to whom those bones originally belonged (Tib. I. ii. 46)—which is one important reason why witches were so often accused of haunting the graveyards (Hor. *Sat.* i. 8; Lucan, vi. 530), and in primitive times the principal reason why the corpse was so carefully watched until it was safe in the grave (Petron. 63; Apul. *Met.* ii. 21). So, too, if we wish to reach the living, it is very important to possess a lock of their hair, the parings of their nails, a garment, or anything nearly or remotely associated with them. Nothing is more intimately and entirely part and parcel of a thing than its real name. 'Rome,' it is said (Tib. I. ii. 57 f., with the present writer's note; Macrob. III. ix. 2; *HN* xxviii. 18, iii. 65; Plut. *Quæst. Rom.* 61 [p. 279 A]; Serv. on *Æn.* i. 277; Solinus, 1; Lydus, *de Mens.* iv. 73), is only the *alias* of the great city with world dominion. The true name, *i.e.* the name which would have enabled her enemies to conjure against her with magic, was a religious secret. So the clay or waxen image may be comparatively harmless until it has been

[1] Hubert, *op. cit.* p. 1506.

[1] Dieterich, p. 171 ff.
[2] See esp. *GB*[3], pt. i., *The Magic Art*, i. ch. 3.
[3] *Op. cit.* p. 1507.

ceremonially named with the true name of the person whom it is meant to represent.[1]

Names are not the only words which are an integral part of the things which they represent. A similar relation exists between the verb, or the sentence, and the action described by it. Hence, of course, the theory of incantation as opposed to that of prayer in the modern sense. From this point of view the lines of Euripides (*Hippol.* 478 f.),

εἰσὶν δ' ἐπῳδαὶ καὶ λόγοι θελκτήριοι·
φανήσεταί τι τῆσδε φάρμακον νόσου,

echoed by Horace (*Epist.* I. i. 34 f.) in

'Sunt verba et voces quibus hunc lenire dolorem
Possis et magnam morbi deponere partem,'

are true not only of magic theory in general, but of the Græco-Roman conception of magic in particular. Incantation is rarely, if ever, absent from some stage of the act. The influence of the indirect method is seen even more clearly in the fact that sympathy is often created by the incantation which accompanies the act (*e.g.*, *HN* xxvi. 93). In the exorcism of disease the incantation is often sufficient in itself. Again, a mere verbal comparison is sufficient, especially if accompanied by a gesture.

'Salvum sit quod tango!' ejaculates Trimalchio piously (Petron. 63), to avoid possible consequences when he touches his friend's arm to illustrate where and how the unfortunate character in his story was touched by the witch.

Given, therefore, the right words in the right order and pronounced in the right way, the desired result must ensue. But which words? Ancient formulæ connected with or naming the appropriate gods are, of course, valuable, but in many cases nothing can compare with ancient words in an utterly incomprehensible tongue. The most famous example in antiquity was the so-called *Ephesia Grammata* attributed to the Dactyli.[2]

But it is by no means necessary that an incantation should consist of what, even in the most general sense, could be termed articulate speech of any sort. Mere music, *e.g.*, as such is distinctly magic. The great musicians of mythology—Amphion, Orpheus, Väinämöinen, etc.—are always magicians. We no longer attribute the power of music to magic in the literal sense, but primitive man can hardly be blamed for doing so. The ancient doctors made a considerable use of music in their practice, and we ourselves have learned that it is sometimes distinctly beneficial in certain obstinate nervous disorders of long standing.

Here, however, our particular concern is with a class of sounds which are anything but musical, but which are mentioned again in the literature of the Empire as being especially powerful and efficacious in magic incantations. Lucan, vi. 686 ff., tells us that all the sounds of nature were imitated by such an expert as Erichtho, and does not fail to add his usual and characteristic catalogue. But Lucan is too anxious to tell us all he has read in his uncle's library to be of any great value in a matter like this. Whatever they afterwards may have become, we can be sure that these phenomena were simpler and more specific, that they were probably inspired by some aspect of the doctrine of sympathy, and used for a special purpose.

The Romans habitually describe them by *stridor* and *stridere*. The sounds to which these words are applied are many, and vary from the filing of a saw to the creaking of a door and the shrilling of a locust. But they are all alike in being inarticulate, high-pitched, and disagreeable. The obvious and instructive parallel is the primitive Greek γοητεία. The γόητες were specifically necromancers and, as we saw above (p. 271^{b}), they were supposed to have received their name from the most notable peculiarity of their magic, viz. 'from their wailing and crying among the tombs.' So, long afterwards, in Græco-Roman times the charms described by *stridor* and *stridere* are very characteristic of *nekyomantia*. If so, and we can hardly doubt it, the inarticulate magic charms connoted by these two words should be just those described as 'wailing and crying among the tombs,' and their purpose should be to call up the dead. Such being the case, the two most common and characteristic uses of *stridor* and *stridere* outside the sphere of magic itself are illuminating. (1) One of these is that squeaking and gibbering of the dead to which the ancients so often refer:

'Ecce inter tumulos atque ossa carentia bustis Umbrarum facies diro stridore minantur' (Petron. cxxii. 137); 'auribus incertum feralis strideat umbra' (Lucan, vi. 628; cf. Stat. *Theb.* vii. 770; Sil. Ital. xiii. 600; Claudian, *in Ruf.* i. 126; Ovid, *Fasti*, v. 458; Verg. *Æn.* vi. 492 f.; Hom. *Od.* xxiv. 5; and Hor. *Sat.* I. viii. 40 f.).

By the doctrine, therefore, of sympathy the *stridores* of the necromancers were an imitation of the wailing and crying of the dead, and owed their efficacy to that reason. (2) *Stridor* is regularly used to describe the hoot of the *strix*, or screech-owl—that long-drawn, shuddering scream that suggests nothing so much as the wail of the banshee, the moaning of souls that can find no rest, the ominous cry of the βιαιοθάνατοι, questing ghosts of those who died before their time (see HECATE'S SUPPERS). No wonder the *strix* is the most remarkable and ill-omened bird in classical folklore. Owls, disembodied spirits, or necromancers calling up those spirits—so far as the cry alone was concerned, how was one to be sure which was which? As a matter of fact, all three were more or less inextricably confused with each other, and there can be no doubt that the cry had much to do with the situation. The *strix* is associated with all sorts of witchcraft in antiquity, but especially and above all with vampirism in its various forms (see the present writer's note on Tib. I. v. 42). The classics are rich in examples of the type which happens to be more familiar to us, especially in the erotic sphere. The return of Protesilaus is a case in point (Roscher, *s.v.*), also the story of the Lamia (Philostr. *Apoll. Tyan.* iv. 25) immortalized by Keats, and the simple and touching tale told by Phlegon of Tralles (*Mirab.* 1) which is the prototype of Schiller's 'Braut von Korinth' and Gautier's 'Morte Amoureuse.'

But witches can turn owls whenever they like, and they do so regularly, when their object is some form of necromancy.

Ovid, *Amor.* I. viii. 13–18, speaking of Dipsas, the redoubtable saga with eyes of different colours ('pupula duplex'),[1] says:

'Hanc ego nocturnas versam volitare per umbras
Suspicor et pluma corpus anile tegi;
Suspicor, et famast; oculis quoque pupula duplex
Fulminat et gemino lumen ab orbe micat;
Evocat antiquis proavos atavosque sepulcris
Et solidam longo carmine findit humum.'

But the ever present and most gruesome side of this idea, as of magic in general, is the sexual side. Most frequently the witch is like Pamphila in Apuleius (*Met.* iii. 21). She assumes the form of a *strix* to fly to her lover; she never comes to him as a human and normal woman. The fires of hell are in her eyes, the fires of hell are in her veins, the taste of blood and death is on her lips. She is the erotic vampire—the *succuba*, as she was called in the Middle Ages—who haunts her victim in his dreams and little by little draws to herself the very marrow in his bones. Hence it is that the Græco-Roman screech-owl, who, even at her best, as Pliny substantially says (*HN* x. 34), seems to make no effort to look or act like a well-meaning and self-respecting fowl of the air, belongs quite as

[1] E. Rohde, *Psyche*⁴, Tübingen, 1907, p. 61; often in the papyri.

[2] See E. Kuhnert, in Pauly-Wissowa, v. 2771–2773, and references.

[1] See K. F. Smith, in *Studies in Honor of B. L. Gildersleeve*, Baltimore, 1902, p. 287.

much to the kingdom of dreams as to the kingdom of birds. How can one be sure in any given instance whether the *strix* is a real *strix* or a witch in the form of one (Ovid, *Fasti*, vi. 141)? Indeed, as early as Plautus (*Pseud.* 820; cf. Propert. IV. v. 17) *striges* already meant 'witches' as well as 'screech-owls,' and this designation of what is evidently the Roman parallel of the old Greek γοήτεις records a popular belief which showed no tendency to diminish in later days.

2. Sources of magic power. — Our surviving testimony is insufficient to give us a very clear idea how the powers of the classical magician were defined or from what sources they were supposed to be derived. For the Egyptians, as Hubert[1] remarks, the magician was like the priest in being closely associated, if not actually identified, with the god whose power he was utilizing,[2] and perhaps in the ultimate issue this is everywhere the explanation of his power. Particularly notable was the development of this principle among the Alexandrian *theurgi*. Here, of course, the characteristic Græco-Roman preference for the indirect method afforded a favourable soil, but, without doubt, the chief factor was the direct influence of the Egyptian theory just mentioned.

But, granted that he does identify himself with the god, how does he compass it? Is it a gift, or does he acquire it, and, if so, how? The *theurgi* emphasized the theory that it was acquired, and the methods recommended indicate in themselves the effort to raise magic to the level of a religio-philosophical system permeated with the ideas and ceremonials characteristic of mysticism. Asceticism was recommended, but, above all, the magician must be an adept. Such persons may have a revelation coming to them more or less directly by way of the fallen angels or the archangels (Tert. *de Idol.* 9 f., *Apol.* 35). Indeed, Maria the Jewess was instructed by God Himself.[3] Gods, kings, great philosophers, and sages of old loom large in this aspect of later magic. The 'Book of Moses'[4] gives us a good idea of the complicated ceremonial through which the candidate was supposed to pass in order to arrive at the perfection desired. There were purifications, sacrificial rites, invocations, and, to crown all, a revelation of the Κοσμοποιία (how the universe was made and the secrets thereof). This puts the adept in relation not with certain specific gods, as appears to have been the idea of the Egyptian prototype, but with the stars and planets, *i.e.* the universal powers. The magician, especially the magician-alchemist, derives his power from the acquaintance with the forces of nature. He has established *rapport* with the universe; and, as there is also *rapport* between all the parts of the universe, he has extended his power over the entire universe as a whole. This, of course, is the old doctrine of sympathy on a particularly grand and impressive scale. The result of the ceremony is that the magician, the *theurgus*, is himself no longer a man, but a god.[5]

This is a conception calculated to appeal to any man whose imagination is still in working order, but it does not emerge clearly in ordinary magic. It belongs rather to mystic magic, which was the special development of serious souls, some of them really great, who believed that this path would lead them to the undiscovered secrets of life, death, and immortality. To speak in terms of the average man and of the history of the art as a whole, the ideas which determined the powers of the magician were much the same as those which dictated the choice of a magic object or the construction of a charm, and which, in fact, are fundamental in the art of magic as a whole. Generally speaking, magic is a gift and, as such, it is often due to some accident of birth or to some special privilege. In some cases it is inalienable; again, it can be outgrown or easily lost. Children, *e.g.*, merely as such, sometimes possess it.[1] Virginity has always been considered an important condition of the power to prophesy (*Geopon.* XI. ii. 4; Plut. *de Defectu Orac.* 46).[2] The idea seems to be that the seeress is, as it were, married to the god and that infidelity to him is punished by loss of the power which he gave her. The entire world seems to be agreed that women, simply as women, are peculiarly gifted in this direction (Demosth. *c. Aristog.* i. 17; Aristoph. *Nubes*, 749; Lucian, *Dial. Deor.* xx. 10, *Dial. Meretric.* i. 2, iv. 4, *Bis Accus.* 21). We have already seen how important they are in the mythology of Greek magic, and this is true of all magic. They are less prominent in the magic of the mystics and their brethren, but this is itself symptomatic of the ideals and pretensions of the movement. In the genuine, traditional, immemorial magic of everyday life in Greece and Rome they never lost their importance. As a φαρμακίς, Medea was typical of her sex. The knowledge and practice of φαρμακεία as a branch of magic were always more or less confined to women.

The distant, the foreign, the strange, the unusual, even the horrible, are all important factors. 'Magic' is a primitive name for anything abnormal. Those who come from distant countries, especially if, like the Brāhmans (Philostr. *Apoll. Tyan.* iii.), they are also the priests of strange and remote religions, are magicians. Hence, on the principle of 'omne ignotum pro magnifico,' there are distant countries in which all the inhabitants are magicians or possess the evil eye or some such uncanny gift. Any person with the evil eye is a magician; so, too, the ventriloquist (schol. Aristoph. *Vespæ*, 1014; Plato, *Soph.* 252 C; Plut. *de Defectu Orac.* 9). Anything abnormal about one's birth or pedigree is likely to give one magic powers. Persons born with a caul have the gift of prophecy. The child of incest, especially of deliberate incest, is bound to be a magician. This was harped on continually in the witch trials of the Middle Ages, but it is also prominent in ancient tradition, especially in connexion with the Magi themselves (Catullus, xc.; Xanthus, frag. 28 [*FHG* i. 43]; Sotion, *ap.* Diog. Laert. *proœm.* 7; Strabo, p. 735). Sometimes whole peoples, clans, or families are supposed to be magicians (Herod. iv. 105);[3] some—*e.g.*, the Thibii (*HN* vii. 17)—owe it to the possession of the evil eye; others have some particular specialty.

The Ophiogenes, the Psylli, the Marsi, etc. (*ib.* xxviii. 30, vii. 13–15), can kill snakes simply by breathing on them, or can cure snake-bites merely by touching the wound with their hands. A certain family in Corinth could calm tempests (Hesych. and Suidas, *s.v.* ἀνεμοκοῖται), and so on. Many similar statements made by Alexandrian authors and others now lost are preserved by Pliny (*HN*, esp. bks. vii. and xxviii.).

In the majority of such cases the ability is more or less vaguely conceived of as inborn, in others it is a secret transmitted from generation to generation. But, whether inborn or imparted, magic is a secret. Indeed, initiates were sworn to secrecy in the later days among the mystics.

3. The powers invoked.—But the most characteristic feature of Greek and Roman magic is the universal prevalence of the indirect method and its influence on the development of the art. So far as Greece and Rome were concerned, the theory of demons—those spirits to whose action practically every phenomenon is due—was as characteristic of the world at large as it was of Plato and his

[1] *Op. cit.* p. 1509.
[2] Dieterich, p. 136.
[3] Berthelot, ii. 80.
[4] W. Kroll, 'De Oraculis Chaldaicis,' in *Breslauer philol. Abhandl.*, vii. 1 [1894], p. 56.
[5] Dieterich, p. 136, n. 1.

[1] Abt, *op. cit.* pp. 245, 262.
[2] See E. Fehrle, 'Die kultische Keuschheit im Altertum,' in *RVV* vi. [1910].
[3] Cf. Lobeck, p. 1196.

followers (Plut. *de Defectu Orac.* 10). Diseases were caused by specific demons, panic was caused by Pan; such figures as the Erinyes, Nemesis, Pœna, Empusa, the Μοῖραι, Ἀνάγκαι, and Βασκοσύναι are not only popular but very old. There are even demons whose only function is to execute the commands of the magic tablets deposited in the baths, and there are others who are merely ἀπόρροιαι, or emanations. The efficacy, *e.g.*, of the ἴυγξ demands, as Hubert observes,[1] the creation of a demon or of a special god[2]—a curious but characteristic retention of the primitive view that nothing in this world can happen or be except by the individual exertion in every case of conscious, energizing will.

The magician may find it necessary or advisable to consider other spirits besides the specific agents of the phenomenon in question. He cannot be sure of success beforehand. He may make mistakes, and a mistake in a ceremonial is fatal. And, even if everything is correct, the ceremony may be entirely upset by something unexpected and unforeseen. In addition, therefore, to the specific energizing demon, he considers it prudent to summon to his aid such other powers as he can command. He calls on some appropriate god, *e.g.*, to send him the necessary energizing demon, or he summons the spirit to whom the efficacy of the rite itself is due; hence the theory of the 'familiar,' the magician's own 'demoniac factotum,' which assumed such importance in the Middle Ages.

The object, therefore, of magic was to act upon and use the supernatural powers either as energizing spirits or as auxiliaries. Some of these powers occur only in the tradition of magic itself, but the large majority are common to both magic and religion. Most important here are the demons. Plato himself (Suidas, *s.v.* μαγεία), as well as the average man, attributed to them the success of any magic rite.[3] The magic charms of the later period are full of invocations to demons—demons of all kinds and descriptions and exercising every imaginable function, but all of varying degrees of inferiority to the great gods. In fact, as time goes on, the realm of the supernatural assumes more and more the aspect of an Oriental despotism with a thoroughly organized bureaucratic government, all in the hands of demons. There are secretaries and under-secretaries, guards, doorkeepers, messengers —a regular hierarchy of demoniac officials, whose rank and functions are established and fixed with meticulous exactness. The only private citizens in this government are the ordinary human man and the occasional person with 'influence,' *i.e.* the magician; and it is curious to see how soon and easily the latter assumes the methods and attitude of the influential citizen who lives under a similar government in this world. If he wishes to reach the ear of the all-highest at the other end of the line, he addresses the demon of lowest rank, the message is transmitted through the appropriate channels, and in time he gets his answer. Indeed, as in all such governments, the first demoniac underling may be so nearly human and, therefore, so much in sympathy with the magician himself as to take a really personal and lively interest in furthering the matter in hand. All this question of rank and functions was carefully discussed by Proclus and Porphyrius (*de Mysteriis Ægyp.*), and, in fact, the prominence of it is particularly characteristic of their school and period. This school, it may be observed, made a distinction between good demons and bad demons, attributing the errors of γοητεία to the latter. The demons were identified with the Jewish angels in their function of divine messengers, and even the old pagan gods, reduced to the rank of demons, became messengers of the universal deity (Aug. *de Civ. Dei*, ix. 19), while the archangels, Michael, Gabriel, etc., take rank with the *archontes* of the Gnostics as tutelary gods of the planets (W. Anz, *TU* xv. [Leipzig, 1897] *passim*). With Christianity the old gods became demons, and all were considered evil. But magic, the conservative of conservatives, never gave them up, though all of them now without distinction were in the service of the devil.

One of the most important classes of demons connected with magic are the spirits of the dead, the νεκυδαίμονες, especially those who, like the βιαιοθάνατοι, died violent deaths or otherwise before their time, or never received proper burial, and therefore cannot rest in their graves.[1] The heroes, so to speak, have a somewhat higher social position, but they too are important in magic.[2]

A notable peculiarity of paganism as contrasted with its successor was the inability to make a sharp distinction between gods and demons. The obvious criterion would be power or disposition. Neither were trustworthy. Some demons were greater than some gods, and some gods were as unmistakably malignant as some demons were beneficent. The demons, therefore, were not the only powers to whom the magician addressed himself. The gods themselves practised magic (Apollod. I. ii. 1, III. vi. 8); indeed, Pindar says (*Pyth.* iv. 213 ff.) that it was Aphrodite herself who taught Jason how to 'draw down the moon'; and so the magician would naturally turn to them (Apul. *de Mag.* 31). The preference is, of course, for the *di inferi*—Hades, Demeter, Persephone, Baubo, the Praxidikai, the Erinyes, Gaia, Cybele, especially those who, like Hecate, Selene, and Hermes, habitually pass back and forth between the two worlds.

The greatest of all, the goddess *par excellence* of magic and magicians throughout antiquity, is Hecate-Selene,[3] the Dea Triformis of the crossways, and the queen of the ghosts, who sweeps through the night followed by her dreadful train of questing spirits. Her power is universal, but she is specially connected with the magic of love, metamorphosis, and φάρμακα. The most famous and dramatic incantations of antiquity are associated with her. The *lunulæ*, the ἴυγξ, the *selenitis*, the redoubtable *spuma lunaris*, and the *rhombus* are only a few magic objects and properties directly associated with her. The schol. on Apoll. Rhod. iii. 478 even informs us that Circe was her daughter. At all events, Medea was her priestess, Musæus was called her son, etc. Next to her, perhaps, especially in the magic papyri, comes Hermes Chthonius, often confused with Hermes Trismegistus (Diog. Laert. *prooem.* 7; Porphyr. *de Abstin.* ii. 16).[4]

But the Κύριοι Θεοί, the great gods, are also addressed, and not only the great gods of foreign races —which we should expect—but those of Greece and Rome. This habit, however, belongs more prominently to the babel of the later period. Here the habit of calling on a number of gods at once, or of reinforcing the name of some Greek god with the names of all the strange gods of foreign lands who are supposed to be identical with him, or of using Ἰάω as the name of the god of gods, or Ἰάω, in the feminine, to sum up, as it were, all the aspects of divinity, or of combining gods in the hermaphroditic form for the same purpose—all these are so many illustrations of the magician's inveterate habit of pluralizing for power. The result is, of course, that the divinities lose all personality and, as Hubert says, 'become mere factors of a divine total.'[5] Nothing was left but the name, and even

[1] *Op. cit.* p. 1511.
[2] Kroll, *op. cit.* p. 39.
[3] J. Tambornino, 'De Antiquorum Dæmonismo,' in *RVV* vii. [1909], *passim.*

[1] E. Riess, in *Rhein. Mus.* xlviii. [1893] 307 ff.
[2] Deubner, p. 29.
[3] Abt, *op. cit.* p. 197 ff.
[4] Deubner, p. 21 n.
[5] *Op. cit.* p. 1513.

this was more or less concealed or defaced in the magician's characteristic effort to get at the true name, the name of power for the now somewhat vague supernatural force which he wished to utilize. Having the name and also the image of the god, he could use the force for anything desired, it being understood, of course, that such accompanying ceremonials had been performed as were appropriate for realizing the mystic presence of the god.

4. Rites and ceremonies.—Thanks to this habit of pluralizing for power, of summoning from every direction all kinds of strange and, therefore, particularly irresponsible forces, a magic ceremony was even more complex than a religious ceremony. Especially notable in all ages is the number of conditions and precautions which have to be observed. This is characteristic of any cult in which the theory of incantation still survives. Under such circumstances the immediate conclusion always is that religion is a perilous pursuit. Any man who approaches gods with an invocation so worded and presented that it is a command which must be obeyed knows that he is handling an edged tool able to cut both ways. The gods resent the imperative, especially from an inferior, and will destroy him if they can. The Roman account of the death of old king Tullus shows how dangerous it was in their opinion—even in religion, much more in magic—for an amateur to start the complicated machinery of invocation. There was an old Greek saying that 'the witch who draws down the moon finally draws it down on herself.' The saying reflects the general idea, afterwards so strongly emphasized in the Middle Ages, that the magician, of all people, is foredoomed to something like the fate of Tullus Hostilius in the end. The Greek is also apt as a specific illustration. It was generally held that of all charms one of the most difficult and dangerous was 'drawing down the moon'—so dangerous, in fact, that the magician deemed it wise to arm himself in advance with a protective counter-charm against the very power whom he was about to invoke. The Διαβολὴ πρὸς Σελήνην preserved in the *Papyrus Paris*, line 3622 ff., is an interesting example of what was considered efficacious against the wrath and vengeance of Πότνια Σελάνα, 'Our Lady Moon'—a suggestive forerunner of the 'magic circle' of which we hear so much in the more pretentious magic of the Middle Ages.

The magician must also observe certain rules, likewise characteristic of religion, which, to a large extent, are suggested by the nature of the powers with whom he has to deal.[1] He, or the person in whose interest the charm is being performed, or both, must be in such a condition that contact with the spirits evoked shall be without danger. Regulations vary, but among the most common are ἁγνεία, 'purity,' ablutions at stated intervals, anointings with oil, avoidance of certain foods (esp. fish), fasting, temporary chastity[2] (cf. Tib. II. i. 11 f.; the regular *secubitus* so often referred to by the elegiac poets, etc.). More rigorous and more numerous are the conditions attending the performance of the rite itself, and most important is the observance of nudity or its ceremonial equivalent.[3] The costume must be flowing, *i.e.* without knots or fastenings of any kind, or it must be coarse, or of linen, and in the last case, either white or white with purple streamers (the ceremonial significance of colours has already been referred to).[4] Having gone through the preliminary purifications and donned the appropriate raiment, the operator must then consider the attitude to assume. This

[1] Deubner, p. 20 ff.; T. Wächter, in *RVV* ix. 1 [1910].
[2] Cf. Fehrle, *loc. cit.*
[3] J. Heckenbach, 'De Nuditate sacra sacrisque vinculis,' in *RVV* ix. 3 [1911].
[4] See Abt, *op. cit.* p. 148, n. 3, for literature on this point.

is vital. In most cases there are gestures which cannot be omitted.[1] Equally important is the magician's own state of mind. He must have faith, he must put all his soul into the accomplishment of the rite (Gargilius Martialis, 19).

The time at which the rite should be performed is also very important. This is largely determined by the habits and associations of the god to be addressed, and is an immediate deduction from the law of sympathy. For magic in general, but in particular for all magic connected with Selene-Hecate, sunset and the few minutes just before sunrise are very favourable; so, too, any phase of the moon, but, above all, the new and full moon. The stars and planets for the most part became important only after astrology gave greater precision to the sort of influence supposed to be exerted by each. As a matter of course, night is a better time than day.[2]

The place is quite as important as the time, and the choice of it is again a direct deduction from the law of sympathy, as regards either the god to be addressed or the person to be affected. Roads, streets, boundaries, and the threshold are all sacred in both magic and religion. The cross-roads suggest Hecate, the graveyard *nekyomantia*. Both are favourite spots so far as the magician is concerned.

Finally, as we have just seen, there are ceremonies which the operator does not venture to perform unless he is armed with some sort of protective charm against the god whom he is addressing, or against any one who might interrupt the ceremony, or against the effect of possible counter-charms.

The best and clearest description of the ceremony, properly speaking, is given by Hubert.[3] It involves the use of two kinds of rites. The purpose of the one is to accomplish the object itself of the ceremony by a logical application of the principles of magic action; the object of the other is to manufacture or, at least, to assure the presence of the actual magic power sufficient to work in the way prepared and thus to accomplish the purpose desired. In other words, to state it in terms of modern electrical science—the theory of which is curiously near to that of magic—he must construct the proper machinery and establish the proper connexions; then, before turning on the power, he must see to it that the power is really there.

The first class of rites, the machinery and connexions, calls for the use of a certain number of objects or parts which, in the end, generally come to be considered magic in themselves. One of the most common and dramatic is the magic wand, which is really a conductor of the magician's *mana*. The divining rod,[4] though used in a different way and for a different purpose, derived its efficacy from a similar conception. The Etruscans used it in searching for hidden springs (Daremberg-Saglio, *s.v.* 'Aquilex'), and, as the writer of this article can testify from personal observation, as late as twenty years ago a similar method for discovering the best place in which to dig a well was still used occasionally in the American countryside. In addition to the magic wand and the divining rod, we have the apparatus of *dactylomantia* (Amm. Marc. XXIX. i. 29 ff.), the lamps in *lychnomantia*, the basins of water in *lecanomantia*, keys in their symbolic use, cymbals, the various substances referred to above, threads of different colours, portions of the dead, the ἴυγξ (Pind. *Pyth.* iv. 213, and often), the famous *rhombus*, *turbo*, or *vertigo*, *i.e.* the 'witches' wheel,' the rotation of which, by imitation and sympathy, was sovereign to influence the will of the person whom one wished to gain, etc.

[1] Deubner, p. 36, for examples.
[2] Abt, *op. cit.* p. 292 ff.
[3] *Op. cit.* p. 1516 ff.
[4] The examples of its use in classical literature are collected by E. Norden, *Jahrb. für Phil.*, Suppl. Bd. xviii. [1894] 317 ff., 319 n.

All these end by being considered magic in themselves, but, in view of what has been said, it will be seen that this idea is secondary. Their real function and purpose was to facilitate or render possible the action of magic power and, at least originally, they were chosen from that point of view.

Sometimes the ceremonial proper needs the assistance of some rite whose object is to put the person interested in a state to receive the benefit of the action desired. A case in point is the ceremonial of *incubatio*.[1] The purpose of *incubatio* is to surround a person with the appropriate conditions to secure for him the true and prophetic dream which he desires. Conditions are, as often, dictated by the law of sympathy. And, except that the nature of dreams was never quite clear to the ancients—and perhaps will never be quite clear to any one—the nameless theorists and thinkers by whom these conditions were first discovered and formulated appear to have been quite familiar with the results of J. Börner's famous dissertation afterwards incorporated and extended in W. H. Roscher's *Ephialtes: eine pathologisch-mythologische Abhandlung über die Alpträume und Alpdämonen des klassischen Altertums*, Leipzig, 1901.[2] Börner showed that, among other things, in a healthy person nightmare is usually due to partial suffocation caused by burying one's head in the pillow, coverlet, etc., that the rapidity with which the nightmare, the *incubus*, appears to approach the dreamer is always measured by the rate of suffocation, but, above all, that the appearance of the *incubus* itself is to a surprising extent determined by the sleeper's surroundings, especially by the material and texture of his coverings. Such being the case, though L. Laistner[3] goes too far in his theory that the *Uralptraum*, the primeval nightmare, is the father of all mythology, we may at least suspect with Roscher that Pan's legs were the inevitable result of the style of bed-quilts used by his primeval worshippers (cf. Latinus's method of securing an interview with Faunus in Verg. *Æn.* vii. 81 ff.), and, for that matter, that the *incubi*, *succubæ*, *striges*, and all their monstrous brood must have entered this world in the first place by the Ivory Gate. If so, it is certain that some of our most cherished legends, our best and most thrilling stories, and our finest poetry are literally the stuff that dreams are made of.

But of all magic operations none is more common and characteristic, more dramatic and impressive, or a better illustration of the doctrine of sympathy than the casting of spells (cf. Heliodorus, xi. 14, and the examples noted below). The special feature of this operation is due to the theory that, if the person whom we wish to reach with our magic is absent or far away, his place may be filled by a puppet, or some symbolical substitute for him. If, then, the ceremonial is appropriate, whatever we do to the puppet will be exactly repeated, literally or symbolically, as desired, on the person whom the puppet represents. Consecration of the one is immediately followed by consecration of the other (Verg. *Ecl.* viii. 74 f.), binding of the one by the desired condition symbolized by it in the other, running needles into the heart of the one by some effect on the other symbolized by such a process—as, *e.g.*, wasting away to death with no apparent cause (Ovid, *Amor.* III. vii. 29 f., *Heroid.* vi. 21, and often). Sometimes one figure may stand for an indefinite number, as in the spells of Nectanebo (pseudo-Callisthenes, i. 1). One may cast a spell on spirits as well as mortals by this means (Eus. *Præp. Evang.* v. 12 ff.). Hence we have cases in which two puppets are used, one representing the person to be acted upon, the other the spirit by whom the action is to be performed (Hor. *Sat.* I. viii. 25 f.).[1] Occasionally even three figures appear to have been used (schol. Bern. on Verg. *Ecl.* viii. 75). Often they were hollow, and their power was enhanced by putting written incantations inside. As a rule, these puppets must be made of clay or wax, but occasionally other substances were just as rigorously prescribed. Eusebius (*loc. cit.*) speaks of such an image of Hecate made of pulverized lizards and the roots of rue. A sheet of metal or even of paper upon which the figure has been traced is often considered sufficient.[2] The value and philosophy of *exuviæ* have already been mentioned. But one may use such arbitrary substitutes as the body of a bird, a sprig of myrtle or of rue, etc.[3] Indeed, as we have already seen, the name is sufficient in itself. On the same principle, a written incantation placed in a tomb has the same effect as would a puppet[4] (Apul. *Met.* i. 10, *de. Mag.* 53).

The verbal portions of a magic rite are of the highest importance. In many cases they are the operator's instructions to the intervening demon in order that he may make no mistake as to the meaning and object of the symbolic rite. The puppet is inscribed with the name of the person whom it represents, and sometimes this is accompanied by a written statement of what is to happen to him. So, when one gathers a medicinal plant, one should be careful to utter the name of the patient who is to be benefited by it. Again, in constructing a *devotio*, one should specify in order each and every part in which it is desired that the proposed victim shall suffer.[5]

The indirect method is also directly responsible for the conclusion that incantations are a special help to the operator in the accomplishment of his second great task—the creation of magic power. Hence the use of the magic hymns and litanies, the object of which is to ensure the presence and active participation of the appropriate spirit, to indicate his duty, and, if necessary, to frighten him into doing it.[6]

We have seen how various objects, plants, simples, etc., originally selected as facilitating in some way magic *rapport*, finally came to be considered magic in themselves. Names and incantations underwent precisely the same secondary development. From being a means to an end they became magic *per se*. The further conclusion was then drawn that their power might be indefinitely increased by frequent repetition, by lengthening certain syllables to an extraordinary extent, by abstracting certain syllables and decorating them with affixes and suffixes, by rearranging them in different combinations, and especially by disposing them so as to form certain figures.[7] Examples still surviving are 'abracadabra,' and 'sator arepo tenet opera rotas' (see *Thesaurus Ling. Lat.*, *s.v.* 'Arepo'). The *Ephesia Grammata* belong to the same type (Porphyr. *de Myster.* vii. 4). Mystery and power were further enhanced by the use of magic alphabets, by certain sacred inks, and so on. Numbers pass through the same experience and acquire the same magic power *per se*—*e.g.*, there are seven planets. If, therefore, we wish to invoke them, there is nothing so compelling as the pronunciation of the seven vowels or a sevenfold repetition of a ceremony,

[1] L. Deubner's *De Incubatione*, Leipzig, 1904, is the standard work on this subject.
[2] Cf. *AJPh* xxii. [1901] 233.
[3] *Rätsel der Sphinx*, Berlin, 1889.

[1] Cf. Riess, *op. cit.* p. 908.
[2] R. Wünsch, *Sethianische Verfluchungstafeln*, Leipzig, 1898.
[3] G. Knaack, *Rhein. Mus.* xlix. [1894] 310.
[4] For clay and waxen images see Abt, *op. cit.* p. 153 ff., and L. Fahz, in *RVV* ii. [1905] 125 ff.
[5] See esp. Fox, *op. cit.*
[6] Dieterich, p. 63; K. Dilthey, *Rhein. Mus.* xxvii. [1872] 375–419.
[7] K. Wessely, in *Wiener Studien*, viii. [1886] 184.

gesture, or word (Eus. *Præp. Evang.* v. 14). Odd numbers have always been significant (Verg. *Ecl.* viii. 75, and often), three and multiples of three are sacred to Hecate, and certain special numbers like four, ninety-nine, etc., have a special importance.

In magic as in religion the object of sacrificial rites is to ensure the actual presence of the gods invoked. And here again the indirect method suggests that these rites are of material assistance to the operator in acquiring the desired power (Theocr. ii. 3, 10, 159). In the choice of what shall be sacrificed in any given instance the usage of magic as a rule does not differ materially from that of religion. This, of course, is quite natural. As a rule, the gods addressed are common to both and of equal importance in both; in fact, it is perhaps safe to guess that, so far as sacrifice is concerned, the usage of magic and religion is a common inheritance. For example, the notable preference of magic for black victims is not distinctive of magic. It simply means that, in accordance with the naive analogy set forth, for instance, in the old hexameter quoted by Eusebius (*Præp. Evang.* iv. 9)—

Φαιδρὰ μὲν οὐρανίοις, χθονίοις δ' ἐναλίγκια χροιῇ,

'dark victims to the powers of darkness, light to the powers of light—

the gods to whom magic habitually addresses itself are the gods of the under world. So wine,[1] honey, milk, perfumes, meal (Theocr. ii. 18, 33), certain cakes dear to these same gods, a cock to Hermes, a white dove to Aphrodite, etc.—all common to both religion and magic—are frequently employed. The use of blood is defined by Hubert as a sacrificial rite; it is at any rate—as in Sallust's account of the oath administered by Catiline to his fellow-conspirators—a striking illustration of the law of sympathy (Lucan, vi. 544). The sacrifice of human beings, especially of little children, even of the unborn babe torn from its mother, is a standing charge against magic in all ages (Hor. *Epod.* v.; Philostr. *Apoll. Tyan.* viii. 5),[2] and, for that matter, against any heretical sect with secret rites. The Christians in their time were charged with such abnormalities as infant-sacrifice and promiscuous incest at their meetings—precisely the same charges which, a millennium later, they themselves preferred with wearisome regularity during their long persecution of witchcraft, especially in connexion with the 'witches' Sabbath.' In most cases the charge of human sacrifice is as conventional as it is untrue; but it would be unsafe to deny it *in toto*. We can hardly expect such an outlaw, such a striver for extraordinary effects, as magic to abstain altogether from what was quite regular in the religion of more than one savage race, and which—in accordance with the familiar theory that extraordinary occasions demand extraordinary sacrifices—has been known to occur more than once at some grave crisis in the religious life of nations which, comparatively speaking, occupied a much higher plane of civilization. Finally, it may be noted that, as was the case with the incantations, names of the gods, etc., mentioned above, the things sacrificed, whatever they were, soon passed into the secondary stage of being considered magic *per se*.

One important aspect of our ceremony—quite as important in religion as it was in magic—remains to be considered. As we have seen, the operator must be careful to follow certain prescribed rules in order to get into the necessary and intimate spiritual relation with the gods whom he is addressing, and, therefore, with the sacrifice which he is conducting. The relation is abnormal and distinctly perilous. To get out of it safely is, therefore, quite as important as to get into it safely; prescribed rules are as necessary for the one as for the other. The object of these rules is to end the ceremony, to limit the effects of it so far as the operator is concerned, to make it safe and possible for him to return to the conditions of everyday life. Above all, the remains of the sacrifice, unless he wishes to preserve them to produce some lasting effect (as, *e.g.*, in a *devotio*), must be disposed of ceremonially. One may deposit them at some prescribed spot sacred to the god to whom the sacrifice itself was offered. The καθάρματα, for instance, the ceremonial remains of the sacrifice to Hecate (see HECATE'S SUPPERS), were deposited at the cross-ways. The more usual method was to eliminate them ceremonially by burning them, burying them, or throwing them into running water or the sea (Verg. *Ecl.* viii. 102, with the notes of Conington and Forbiger). The Μαντεία Κρονική (*Pap. Paris.* 3095) shows that, at least in some cases, the ceremony closed with a prayer to the god in which he was invited kindly but firmly to go back to where he belonged:

Ἀπέλθε, δέσποτα, κόσμου προπατήρ, καὶ χώρησον εἰς τοὺς ἰδίους τόπους, ἵνα συντηρηθῇ τὸ πᾶν. Ἵλεως ἡμῖν, κύριε.

It will be seen, therefore, as Hubert observes,[1] that among the Greeks and Romans the standard ceremony of magic and the standard ceremony of religion, so far as their essential elements were concerned, were practically the same, even to the point of using the same names for these elements. Furthermore, with some comparatively slight exceptions, the gods of magic are equally important in religion, and, on the whole, they are treated with the same reverence. As we have seen, some of the abnormalities of magic are just as characteristic of religion, and they are generally due to the fact that, at the time when these abnormalities occur, both are specially concerned with the infernal gods. The worship of these gods, whether in religion or in magic, is visibly influenced by the universal idea that the under world is the reverse of ours. It is dark, silent, barren, loveless, childless, eventless, stationary—a complete contrast to the world above, a contrast regularly symbolized in rituals to the dead and their gods by such things as the use of the left hand instead of the right. It is, no doubt, this ancient idea of reversed conditions in Hades that suggested the most striking feature of the famous 'Black Mass' as practised by the early Christian magicians (Iren. *Hær.* I. xiii. 2). The normal 'White Mass' is addressed to heaven; if we reverse it, *i.e.* if we read it backwards, we address it to hell. But the Christian magician, in so far as he was a Christian, was bound to assume that his Black Mass was a wicked and impious rite. Hence the inevitable deduction was soon established that, the more wicked and impious magic could be, the greater and more terrible its power. For the magician of Græco-Roman paganism there seems to have been no such parodying of religious rites—above all, no such deliberate and malignant desecration of things considered divine as that of which we hear so much in mediæval magic and which appeared again in the modern cult of Satanism (*q.v.*), as described some years since by Jules Bois[2] and as utilized for purposes of fiction by J. K. Huysmans.[3]

Summary.—In so far as there was any real and essential difference between magic and religion in Græco-Roman paganism, the ultimate cause of it was largely, if not entirely, the steady maintenance of the ancient distinction of official recognition as defined and explained at the beginning of

1 K. Kircher, 'Die sakrale Bedeutung des Weines im Altertum,' in *RVV* viii. [1910].
2 See also J. Grimm, *Teutonic Mythology*, tr. J. S. Stallybrass, London, 1882–88, pp. 44–46, 1300 f.

1 *Op. cit.* p. 1520. 2 *Le Satanisme et la magie*, Paris, 1891.
3 *La-bas*, Paris, 1891; cf. also G. Legué, *La Messe noire*, do. 1903.

this article. It is the business of magic, as long as it remains magic, to speak only in the imperative. It must, therefore, retain and emphasize those primitive doctrines—notably the doctrine of sympathy in all its forms—which are supposed to enable it to use the imperative successfully in addressing the gods. It is also the business of magic, partly because it is an outlaw and bound to assert its importance in order to live, to promise extraordinary, if not impossible, things—among them, things which the social and legal restraints of religion would not allow it to promise. In the course of its long and exceptionally brilliant history classical magic promises practically everything from a cure for warts to a receipt for personal immortality—all tried and true. Magic, therefore, was obliged not only to retain but to develop in every possible way those primitive aids to its imperative. It pluralized for power. And religion had done the same. But magic was an outlaw, it had no position in society, it was free to range at will, to gather into one portentous plural strange and terrible gods from the four corners of the earth, to combine them with the native gods, to re-arrange, re-interpret, disguise, mutilate, etc., in the ways described. In the long run, as we have seen, the pantheon of Græco-Roman magic was a pandemonium, and confusion worse confounded, in which the only relating principle seems to be the fact that the doctrine of sympathy in all its forms has been pushed to its uttermost limits.

To the very end magic was obsessed by the old imperative and, therefore, by the time-honoured means for securing it. When it rose in the social scale, it merely learned to be pretentious. Even when it had been adopted, so to speak, by some distinguished family like the mystics, had changed its name, and had been carefully educated and refined, it was still haunted by the old ideas, and generally ended by infecting with them its benefactors and teachers.

The same may be said of the contemporary development of popular magic. Our great authority here is the magic papyri. They all come from Egypt and are much affected by local influences; but, among other things, they show that, under the circumstances, the old rule of official recognition was eminently wise. In the civilization of Greece and Rome magic was given a rare, a unique, opportunity to make the most of itself. But, whether it improved the opportunity or not, the final result, as we see it in the papyri, is a striking illustration of its besetting sins. If it had clung to the native gods, as religion was forced to do, it is conceivable that, even with the heavy handicap of the imperative and its attendant vices, magic might have risen to comparative respectability. But its weaknesses were encouraged rather than checked. By the 2nd cent. the number of strange religions available, not to mention the semi-detached religious theories, had increased to an indefinite extent. The result was that from being a thing which, at least, could appeal to the imagination and the æsthetic sense, it steadily degenerated into utter absurdity as pretentious and complicated as it was dreary and commonplace.

But, fortunately for us, Græco-Roman magic in its best days was the familiar possession of all classes in a highly intellectual and highly imaginative people. Men of Ovid's calibre and training may not have believed in it to any extent, but there never was a time when magic as such became unfamiliar to any one. Even the major operations of magic were always being performed somewhere, and, as we have seen, the charge of magic was always kept alive in the courts. Hermione was far from being the only jealous woman to soothe her wounded pride by accusing her successful rival of resorting to philtres. The charge was quite as characteristic of the Augustan age as it could ever have been of Homer's time (Tib. I. v. 41; Propert. IV. vii. 72). Nor was the charge by any means always unfounded. *Pocula amatoria* were a regular specialty of the *lena*, or go-between, and they actually were so frequently administered that the average man generally assumed that they were responsible for certain lingering diseases, especially certain mental or nervous abnormalities, for which he could see no apparent cause. Examples in point are the traditional account of the death of Lucretius and the contemporary explanation of the vagaries and perversions of Caligula's tempestuous brain (Jerome, *Chron. Euseb.*, 1924; Sueton. *Calig.* 50).

VI. *MAGIC IN LITERATURE.*—The more or less familiar presence of magic not only in folklore and legend, but also in ordinary everyday life, is reflected to an extraordinary extent in the written word. It is continually turning up in the arts, sciences, and professions, in law, religion, and philosophical discussion, in history, anecdote, and any other record of everyday life past or present. All this, however, is characteristic of any people among whom magic still survives as an active force, and it appeals for the most part only to such persons as the special investigator and the historian of manners and customs. But the most characteristic and interesting aspect of Græco-Roman magic is the deliberate exploitation of it in the interests of conscious literary art. One is inclined to assume, and perhaps justly, that this was particularly notable of such periods as the Hellenistic age, the time of Augustus and his immediate successors, and the Sophistic revival of the 2nd century. This use of magic was especially characteristic of poetry and of such types of prose as that of the highly rhetorical and semi-Romantic historians of the Alexandrian age, the Paradoxographers, the writers of *novelle* and tales of marvel, even the practice debates of the rhetorical schools, and, in later times, the throng of professional declaimers for whom those schools were ultimately responsible. But this aspect of classical magic is far from being a matter merely of period and department. On the contrary, nothing is more characteristic of it than the extent and variety, as well as the unbroken continuity, of its use in practically every department of artistic literature. No one could be more thoroughly alive to its æsthetic possibilities than was Homer himself, and he created a tradition of its literary use which not even the semi-Oriental and unutterably dreary fooleries of the papyri were able entirely to destroy.

In an article like this it is impossible as well as inadvisable to attempt a thoroughgoing investigation of the debt of creative literature to magic in antiquity. We must content ourselves with a passing reference to a few of those magic operations which are most frequently mentioned, and which by reason of their dramatic possibilities are best suited to the purposes of literary art.

One of the most notable of these is *nekyomantia*, calling up the dead to ask them questions. *Nekyomantia* is rarely absent from that catalogue of magic feats with which so many of the Roman poets seem impelled to supply us (Tib. I. ii. 42, and note). They also mention even more frequently three other feats which are particularly awesome, but for which the modern reader, at least, can see no adequate reason until it dawns upon him that they are merely a useful, though by no means necessary, preparation for *nekyomantia*. These are producing earthquakes, splitting the ground, and making the rivers either stand still or run backwards. The magician uses his earthquake to split the ground; the behaviour of the rivers is merely a consequence of the quake. He splits the ground so that the ghosts can hear his incantation (*i.e.* be reached and affected by it) and then can come straight up to him from Hades (Sen. *Œdip.* 571; Lucan, vi. 728). As we have seen, the literary use of *nekyomantia* begins with the famous passage of the *Odyssey* (xi. 24 ff.). The essential details of the ceremonial as Homer describes it were always the same not only in literary tradition but in actual life. Doubtless, Lucan felt that his own long and lurid description of Erichtho's special performance for the benefit of Sextus Pompeius before the battle of Thapsus (vi. 728 ff.) was the masterpiece of its kind. And so it is. It would be hard to find a more glaring illustration of what can happen to literature in an age when a furious lust for effect is not restrained by any principles of rhetorical self-control or common sense. *Nekyomantia* had a long and brilliant tradition in the drama. Examples still surviving are Æschylus, *Persæ* (the ghost of Darius), and Seneca, *Œdipus*, 560 ff. Indeed, ghosts were as common, it would appear, in the ancient as in the Elizabethan drama. Κλίμακες Χαρωνεῖοι, 'Charon's step-ladder,' was the popular name for the regular staircase by which the ghosts appeared on the stage as if from the world below. *Nekyomantia* was also quite as characteristic of comedy. In the later days of the Roman Republic Decimus Laberius wrote a mime entitled *Necyomantia*, and we know that this and similar themes were characteristic of the mime as developed by Philistion and his immediate successors during and after the Augustan age. Brilliant examples in the satirical sphere are Horace, *Sat.* I. viii., and Lucian's *Necyomantia.*

If we choose to emphasize the literary influence as such of the Homeric *Nekyia*, we can say that it is responsible for one of the most notable developments in classical literature. This is the theme of the Descent into Hades. The Homeric passage is directly responsible for the 6th book of the *Æneid* and its numerous echoes in epic and narrative poetry both ancient and modern. Nor was epic the only department to be affected. The theme was a favourite in the Old Comedy of Athens, although, as it happens, the *Frogs* of Aristophanes is the only example now surviving. The same is true of the satirists and popular philosophers of the Alexandrian and Hellenistic ages. It was characteristic of their didactic methods to appropriate for their own purposes the traditional forms and themes of literary art, and one of the most notable was the Κατάβασις εἰς Ἅιδου, which practically became conventionalized as a *mise-en-scène* for the presentation of doctrines and opinions. Allied to it are such examples as Horace, *Sat.* II. v., Seneca, *Apocolocyntosis*, such works of Lucian as the *Dialogues of the Dead*, and Claudian's attacks on Eutropius. The *Epicharmus* of Ennius and probably certain of the lost satires of Lucilius and Varro were illustrations. The poet Sotades used it to a notable extent.

But, while *nekyomantia* is the most prominent and pervasive aspect of literary magic, the most famous and picturesque was the love-charm known as 'drawing down the moon.'[1] It is first mentioned in surviving literature by Aristophanes, *Nubes*, 750, again and again by later writers, and still survives, it is said, in modern Greece. It was the theme of no fewer than four masterpieces: a lost mime of Sophron in the time of Xerxes, the lost *Thettale* of Menander (*HN* xxx. 7), the second *Idyl* of Theocritus (founded on Sophron), and the eighth *Eclogue* of Vergil (founded on Theocritus). Certainly, too, Lucian, *Philopseudes*, 14 ff., is a masterpiece of its kind. The atmosphere reflects to the life that aspect of the 2nd cent. which suggests the modern *milieu* in which theosophy, spiritualism, and kindred ideas are wont to grow luxuriantly.

In this passage of Lucian we have the 'Professor's' story of how his disciple, Glaukias, was saved by the great 'Hyperborean' magician. It seems that Glaukias, a rich young orphan whose father had been dead about a year, fell fairly ill with love for the disdainful Chrysis—a genuine prototype of Jemmy Grove and cruel Barbara Allen. His condition became so serious that the 'Professor,' as he says, 'felt it his duty' to secure the services of the great Hyperborean. Four minæ had to be paid in advance—to supply the necessary sacrifices—and sixteen more if the operation was successful. By way of preliminary—which showed that the specialist was not only a great man but also a just and scrupulously conscientious man—he insisted on having an elaborate rite of *nekyomantia*, to call up the boy's late lamented father and ask his consent. The old gentleman was furious at first, but finally told them to proceed. A dramatic description of the ensuing ceremony follows—how the moon came down, how Hecate came up, how the ghosts flocked around, how, at the psychological moment, the distinguished operator 'told the sort of little figure of Cupid which he had fashioned out of clay to go and fetch Chrysis.' Away flew the tiny thing at once. A few minutes later there comes a knock on Glaukias's door, in rushes Chrysis, throws her arms around him, ὡς ἂν ἐμμανέστατα ἐρῶσα ('like a girl utterly crazy with love'), and there she stays till cockcrow! Then up rose the moon to heaven, down sank Hecate to Hades, and all the ghosts disappeared.

But the 'Professor's' listener is not duly impressed. Besides, he knows the girl. He doesn't see the use, he says, of calling on one Hyperborean magician, one goddess, and one clay ambassador to unite in overcoming the disdain of a girl who, as every one knows, is ready to follow a man to the North Pole and beyond for twenty drachmæ.

Such books as the *Metamorphoses* of Ovid and the lost poem of the same name by his predecessor, Nicander, show that change of form was quite as characteristic of classical mythology and folklore as of the *Thousand and One Nights.* Transformation was Circe's specialty, and the Homeric account of her methods (*Od.* x. 212 ff.) has always remained the most famous literary account of the performance. Apart from the Homeric passage, the most vivid and circumstantial accounts of transformation by magic are those in which Apuleius (*Met.* iii. 21 ff.) and Lucian (*Asinus* [the common source of both was the lost romance of Lucius of Patras]) tell how the witch, Pamphile, made an owl of herself, and how, immediately afterwards, Fotis, her maid, made an ass of Lucius. But, as a rule, magic as such is not prominent in metamorphosis as a literary theme. This is, of course, quite natural; for in this particular feat the dramatic point is the transformation scene, and all else is likely to be subordinated, even in those cases where the transformation is confessedly due to magic. Vergil's sorceress, *e.g.*, says that she has seen the werwolf transformation with her own eyes and that it was done by magic:

'Has herbas atque hæc Ponto mihi lecta venena
Ipse dedit Moeris (nascuntur plurima Ponto);
His ego sæpe lupum fieri et se condere silvis
Moerim' (*Ecl.* viii. 95 ff.).

But in all the famous werwolf stories of antiquity,[1] as in most of the stories told by Ovid, the magic element is either absent, ignored, or referred to so slightly that it calls for no special notice here. Magic command of the wind and weather is often mentioned, and nothing in the way of magic was more common in everyday life, but the one famous passage is that in which Æolus gives the bag of winds to Odysseus (*Od.* x. 19 ff.). Also unique—and terrible—is the spell of the evil eye cast by Medea upon the giant Talus (Apoll. Rhod. iv. 1652 ff.). Ovid (*Met.* vii. 160 ff.) gives a full and dramatic description of her charm for renewing the youth of Jason's father, Æson. More famous was her pretence of doing the same favour for the aged Pelias at the instance of his daughters (Apollod. I. ix. 27; Hygin. *Fab.* 24; Macrob. V. xix. 9 f.). This was the theme of the lost Ῥιζοτόμοι

[1] W. H. Roscher, *Selene und Verwandtes*, Leipzig, 1903, with a plate reproducing a vase-painting of the process; M. Sutphen, in *Studies in Honor of B. L. Gildersleeve*, p. 315.

[1] J. Heckenbach, *op. cit.* p. 36; Kirby Flower Smith, *JHC*, 1893, *Publicat. Modern Lang. Assoc. of Amer.*, 1894.

of Sophocles. Indeed, the lost plays of the Greek tragic poets would have been a wonderful field for the study of the use of magic for literary purposes.[1]

Creusa's robe was a famous theme. Euripides (*Medea*, 1156 ff.) merely described the awful effect of it upon the wearer; Seneca (*Medea*, 740 ff.), the preparation of it. Which is the more artistic and effective may easily be seen by comparison.

On the other hand, there are types of magic in which it is precisely the preliminaries, the things which witches do because they have something terrible in prospect, that are full of dramatic possibilities. This is especially true of *nekyomantia*. As we have seen, the necromancers are always eager to get mortal remains in order to be better able to call up their late owners. Striking examples are Trimalchio's story in Petron. 63, and the dramatic experience of Thelyphron as told by him after dinner in Apuleius, *Met.* ii. 21 ff. So, speaking in terms of magic theory, the dreadful scene of Horace, *Epod.* v., was only a means to an end; the object of the witches was to secure the strongest possible love-charm. The liver is the seat of desire (Hor. *Odes*, IV. i. 12); therefore the liver is sovereign in a charm to produce desire. Now, when a savage wants snake-poison for his arrows, he irritates the snake for some time before he kills it, so that it may secrete more poison and that the poison may be more virulent. So, here, the idea is that the more the liver feels desire, so much the more it actually accumulates desire, as it were, and stores it up within. If, therefore, we can secure a liver still containing a maximum of desire so accumulated, we have a charm of maximum power for arousing desire in others. Hence, in this scene, the poor child who has been kidnapped by the witches for that purpose, is buried to the neck and left to die of a prolonged agonizingly intense desire for food and drink, which is deliberately aggravated as much as possible by always keeping food and drink before his eyes. After the child was dead, his liver was removed, and, upon being prepared with the appropriate ceremonial, became a love-charm of superhuman power, a φίλτρον secured in a special way for a special purpose.

The gathering of herbs is another preliminary of φαρμακεία, which was fully appreciated for its dramatic possibilities. In literature the process is regularly associated with Medea (Apoll. Rhod. iii. 843 ff.; Valer. Flaccus, vii. 323 ff.; Ovid, *Met.* vii. 224 ff.; special emphasis was probably laid on this by Sophocles in his Ῥιζοτόμοι). She went out at night and by the light of the full moon cut her plants with a brazen sickle[2] held in her left hand and behind her back, *i.e.* ἀμεταστρεπτί (see HECATE'S SUPPERS).

So far as philtres are concerned, the most notable contribution to literature is what might be called the case of Beauty *v.* Magic in the court of Love.[3] Its first appearance is in the scene between Hermione and Andromache (Eur. *Androm.* 205 ff.), to which attention has already been called. The subsequent tradition of the question at issue is a striking and characteristic illustration of the methods and development of ancient literary art. The topic was announced from the stage, discussed in the boudoir, argued in the schools of philosophy, enlarged upon in the schools of rhetoric (Menander, frag. 646 K.; Afran. 378 R.; Lucret. iv. 1278 ff.; Tib. I. v. 43, viii. 23; Ovid, *Med. Fac.* 35 ff., *Ars Amandi*, i. 299 ff.). At some time in the unrecorded past it was given a new turn and made the basis of a properly illustrative and sprightly anecdote in which the appropriately magnanimous mother of a great conqueror—any great conqueror will do—was in the position of Hermione, but possessed the wisdom of Andromache. In Plutarch, *Conj. præc.* 23, the position is held by the mother of Alexander; the sands of Egypt have lately disclosed the fact that in Satyrus, *loc. cit.*, it was held by the mother of Darius. Others may yet appear.

But for any one who is at all interested in the development of magic for literary purposes the *Metamorphoses* of Apuleius is a veritable treasure-house. Those who have studied this unique book generally gain the impression that its author is a past master in the art of telling a tale of magic. Two examples may be given by way of illustration.

The first (*Met.* i. 11 ff.) is told by Aristomenes, and might be called 'The Witches' Revenge.' While travelling about Thessaly a short time previously, Aristomenes ran across one Socrates, an old friend whom he had not seen for several years. The man was a monument of rags, squalor, and wretchedness; he was also in a constant state of abject terror. He had drifted into a *liaison* with a famous but elderly witch named Meroe, and, in fact, had been living with her, more or less per-force, for a number of years. Now he was trying to run away. Aristomenes decided to help his friend to flee the country. He took a room at the inn, made him presentable with a bath and some clothes, the two ate a heavy dinner, accompanied by too much wine, and retired early so as to be off betimes in the morning. Aristomenes barred the doors, and for greater safety pushed up his trundle-bed against them. Socrates fell asleep at once and snored loudly, but Aristomenes lay awake for hours. At last, about the third watch, just as he had dropped off into a doze, there was a horrible noise, the doors flew open and, indeed, came to the floor with such a crash that the bed with Aristomenes still in it was turned upside down. Then in walked Meroe and her sister, Panthia, the one carrying a leathern bottle, the other a sponge and a naked sword, and gathered about Socrates, who was still plunged in his magic slumber. Aristomenes could see all this from beneath his trundle-bed and hoped he had escaped observation, but in vain. Meroe was anxious to kill him at once with the sword, but Panthia thought it better to tear him limb from limb. 'No,' said Meroe, changing her mind, 'let him live, so that, when the time comes, he may cover his friend with a little earth.' With that Socrates' head was drawn to one side, and Meroe drove the sword into his neck just behind the left collar-bone. Then she plunged her arm into the gaping wound, and plucked his heart out. Meanwhile she caught all the blood in her bottle so skilfully that not one betraying drop escaped. When this was done, Panthia pushed her sponge into the wound, with the words:

'Sponge, sponge, born o' the main,
Haste ye, haste ye back again!
When you reach the river-side,
In the water slip and slide;
Water, water, flowing fast,
Bears you onward home at last.'

Then, after heaping nameless insults on Aristomenes, the two women left the room, the doors flew back in place, the bolts shot to (a regular occurrence in witchcraft; cf. Apoll. Rhod. iv. 41 ff.), and all was as before—all but the murdered friend. How was Aristomenes to explain that in the morning? He tried to escape, but the porter was obdurate and even suspicious. Then he went back in despair and attempted to hang himself from the window-frame. But the rope broke, and, what made it more horrible, he fell on the corpse—whereat the corpse leaped up in high dudgeon at being so rudely disturbed. After all, it had only been a dreadful nightmare, a warning against too much eating and drinking late in the day. Next morning the friends set out, and, when it was time, proceeded to take their breakfast beside a stream under the shade of a tree. Socrates was as pale as wax, but he ate heartily, and then, at the suggestion of Aristomenes, knelt down on the bank of the stream to drink. As he leaned over, his neck gaped open, and a sponge, followed by a few drops of blood, dropped out, fell into the water, and was swept away. In a moment he was dead. So then and there Aristomenes dug a shallow grave and 'covered his friend with a little earth.'

The second story (*Met.* ii. 32 ff.) is unique as a satirically exaggerated illustration of what can be accomplished by the doctrine of sympathy when it is really given a fair chance. During his stay at Hypata young Lucius, the protagonist of the book, was entertained by his father's old friend, Milo. The rest of the family consisted of Milo's wife, Pamphila, who was a redoubtable sorceress, and Fotis, a beautiful slave-girl, with whom Lucius immediately fell in love. One night he went out to a dinner-party, and by the time he started for home it was very late and very dark—and the wine had been very strong. Just as he reached the door, the dim shapes of two great burly figures jostled up against him on either side. Thinking they were thieves, he leaped back, whipped out his sword, and ran them both through. He was barely awake the next morning, with a vague but awful memory of what had happened, when all the magistrates appeared, full of fear and office, and arrested him for murder.

The trial scene, which begins at once, is a masterpiece. It

[1] Abt, *op. cit.* p. 173 ff.

[2] *Ib.* p. 159.

[3] Kirby Flower Smith, 'Note on Satyros, Life of Euripides, Oxyr. Pap. 9, 157-8,' *AJPh* xxxiv. [1913] 62-73.

all seemed like a nightmare to the prisoner at the bar, and his impressions are fully shared by the reader. What surprised him—and it surprises us too—was that the trial was held in the amphitheatre. Stranger yet, every seat was taken, and people had even climbed up on the pillars to get a better view. After the trial had gone on for hours, some one suggested that the prisoner must have had accomplices, and that he be put to the torture and made to name them. At this point the poor old mother of the two murdered ones came forward, and insisted that the unfeeling assassin be compelled to look upon his innocent victims. The corpses were brought in, lying side by side, and decently covered with a cloth. Lucius was forced, much against his will, to raise the cloth, and discovered not two stalwart men cold in death, but two wine-skins—horribly gashed by his ruthless falchion blade, but unmistakably wine-skins. A huge roar of laughter went up from the crowd. Mystified, but relieved, Lucius was escorted home in triumph. The day, he was told, was the regular festival of Risus, the goddess of laughter. His own contribution on this particular occasion had been so original and successful that the city had unanimously voted him a bronze equestrian statue. Lucius was still mystified and, indeed, somewhat resentful. As soon, however, as Fotis had the opportunity, she let him into the secret.

As Pamphila was passing the barber's shop the day before the 'murder,' she had caught sight of a blonde youth from Bœotia who was in the chair having his hair cut. She fell in love with him then and there, and went straight home and began preparing a charm to draw him to her. The necessary preliminary, of course, was the possession of something belonging to him. 'So,' as Fotis says in substance, 'I was sent out to steal a lock of his hair. But the barber caught me before I could get away, and our reputation in town is so bad that he made me give up the hair, which I had hidden in my dress. I was in despair. But on the way home I passed a shop in which a man was clipping the hair off some wine-skins. So, to save a beating, I picked up some of the yellowest locks I could find, and managed to palm them off on my mistress for the real thing. She took them, and began her charm about the time you started for the dinner-party. The charm worked only too well. The robbers whom you met and slew at our door were the original owners of those locks—two passionate wine-skins struggling madly to get at their love and melt at her feet. And so it comes that "non homicidam nunc, sed utricidam amplecterer" ("the lover now in my arms is after all not a homicide, but a jugicide").'

But nothing, perhaps, is a clearer proof of the prominence of magic in everyday life than the fact that, as H. Reich has abundantly shown,[1] the favourite and most characteristic habitat of magic as a literary asset is the most popular type of drama in the ancient world. This is the *mimus* (see DRAMA [Roman], vol. iv. p. 904). Transformations of men and animals were frequent; all kinds of charms were performed; the effects of all kinds of powerful magic were represented. Witches, warlocks, magicians, prophets, ghosts, demons, popular divinities, Empusa, Mormo, Incubo, Anna Perenna, Ephialtes, etc., were all favourite characters. The play went on in fairyland quite as often as on the Imperial streets or in the Imperial country-side. And sometimes, no doubt, it was hard to tell which was which. And yet the *mimus* was realistic—the very name insists upon it. But the investigation of Græco-Roman magic emphasizes the undoubted fact that, after all, the realism of antiquity was not, and never could be, our realism. The native gifts of imagination and fancy were too enduring, the native inheritance of mythology and folklore was too rich and interesting, to allow it. Magic was one of those vices of intellectual youth which the Græco-Roman world never quite outgrew. But intellectual youth also has its virtues; and these two great Aryan races of the Mediterranean basin, in some other respects as well, retained to the last their unique and priceless gift of never really growing old.

LITERATURE.—This is given for the most part in the text. The best and most complete discussion of the subject is given by H. Hubert, in Daremberg-Saglio, *s.v.* 'Magia.' L. F. A. Maury, *La Magie et l'astrologie dans l'antiquité et au moyen âge*, Paris, 1860, is still valuable as a general survey. R. Heim, 'Incantamenta magica Græca Latina,' *Jahrb. für class. Philol.*, Suppl. Band xix. [1893] pp. 463–576, collects and discusses the actual texts of surviving charms and incantations. Particularly valuable for special topics is the *Religionsgeschichtliche Versuche und Vorarbeitungen* (*RVV*), ed. R. Wünsch and L. Deubner, Giessen, now in its 15th volume.

KIRBY FLOWER SMITH.

[1] *Der Mimus*, Berlin, 1903.

MAGIC (Indian).—I. *HINDU*.—Indian magic is essentially the profession of certain castes, though magical rites may be practised by laymen and magical properties are attributed to countless objects. The caste which is peculiarly devoted to magic as a vocation is that of the Yogīs, which is primarily Hindu but has Muhammadan elements affiliated to it. The Yogī claims to hold the material world in fee by the magical powers which he has acquired through the performance of religious austerities, but this claim soon degenerates into superstition of the worst type, and the Yogī in reality is little better than a common swindler, posing as a *faqīr*. Thus, in the tale of the magic boat, the gift of it comes from a *sādhu*, or religious mendicant.[1] Brāhmans, however, possess much magical lore, though the practice of magic is not a Brāhmanical function and the sections which make a profession of it tend to form sub-castes. The Brāhmans are said to have secret books on the subject which contain over 50 *jotias*, or figures, consisting partly of numbers and partly of mystic symbols, cabalistic words, and geometrical figures not unknown to free-masonry; these are used for all kinds of purposes, including the causing of abortion, success in gambling, etc.,[2] as well as to ensure easy parturition.[3]

The Yogīs in particular claim power to transmute base metals into silver and gold—a claim which enables them (and those who personate them) to reap a great harvest from the credulous.

This power is said to have been discovered by the Yogī Dīna Nāth, who, passing one day by a money-changer's shop, saw a boy with a heap of copper coins before him and asked for some in alms. The boy replied that they belonged to his father, but offered him some of his own food. Touched by his generosity and honesty, the Yogī prayed to Viṣṇu for power to reward the boy, bade him collect all the copper coin he could find in his father's house, and then, melting it down, recited *mantras*, or charms, and sprinkled a magic powder over it, whereby it was changed into pure gold. This occurred in the time of Sulṭān Altamsh (A.D. 1210–36), who witnessed Dīna Nāth's performance of a similar feat, and in commemoration of it had gold *mohars* struck with Dīna Nāth's name on them as well as his own. These Dīna Nāthī *mohars* are said to be still found. The secret of the *mantras* and the powder has been handed down, but is known only to the initiated.

1. Occasions.—Magical rites are practised at weddings, during pregnancy, at birth to procure offspring and ensure its safety and to determine and predict its sex, and to resuscitate the dead.

(1) *Marriage.*—The magic practised at a wedding is often symbolical. For example, just as naked women plough the soil in times of scarcity to ensure a crop, so at weddings a Telugu bridegroom of the Balija caste performs a mimic ploughing ceremony, stirring up earth in a basket with a stick or miniature plough.[4] Similar rites are in vogue among the Palli,[5] Kamma,[6] Sambadavan,[7] and Toṭṭiyan.[8] The Kamma bride carries seedlings in her lap, apparently to be planted by the groom. Among the Kāpu a milk-post of *Odina Wodier* is set up, and, if it takes root and flourishes, it is a happy omen.[9] An Unni bride plants a jasmine shoot, whose flowers she should present to the deity.[10] The parting of the bride's hair with a thorn is probably an imitation of the ploughing rite.[11]

The Indian conceptions that all life is one, and that life is something tangible or material, come out in several rites. Thus, at the beginning of a wedding, the Beḍar scatter rice and gram (*dhāl*)

[1] *NINQ* v. [1895] § 69. [2] *PNQ* i. [1883] § 686.
[3] *Ib.* § 1017.
[4] E. Thurston, *Castes and Tribes of Southern India*, Madras, 1909, i. 144. The full rite is of interest.
[5] *Ib.* vi. 20. [6] *Ib.* iii. 103. [7] *Ib.* vi. 355.
[8] *Ib.* vii. 193. [9] *Ib.* iii. 235.
[10] *Ib.* vii. 226. The milk-post is sometimes made of twigs of other trees—*e.g.*, among the Agamuḍaiyan it is made of three kinds of tree, typifying Brahmā, Viṣṇu, and Śiva (*ib.* i. 14).
[11] *BG* xxiii. [1884] 45.

seed on some white-ant earth near five pots filled with water. By the time the wedding is concluded, these seeds have sprouted and are culled by the pair, taken to the village well, and cast into it—obviously to ensure their fertility.[1] An Iḍaiyan couple sow nine kinds of grain in seven trays,[2] and the Māla groom digs with his knife a few furrows, which his bride fills with grain and waters after he has covered it up.[3] Apparently the widespread custom of pounding grain at weddings has a similar origin. This is done by five women, *e.g.*, in Bombay.[4]

The grindstone is also used among the Bhondāri in Madras; the bridegroom stands on it, while women bring a mill-stone and powder three kinds of grain with it; then he sits on the dais, and a number of married women each touch seven times with a grinding-stone an areca nut placed on his head.[5] A Beḍar couple are invited by the Brāhman priest to stand on a grinding-mill placed beneath the *pandal*.[6]

Among the Agamuḍaiyan a grinding-stone and a roller, representing the god Śiva and the goddess Śakti, are placed in the north-east corner at the actual wedding, and at their side pans containing nine kinds of seedlings are set. Seven pots are arranged in a row between the stone and a branched lamp, and married women bring water from seven streams and pour it into a pot in front of the lamp.[7] The grinding-stone is also used in Bombay.[8]

The future offspring of the union is symbolized among the Komaṭi by a doll which is rocked in a cradle, but both the prospective parents profess lack of leisure to look after it.[9] The Parivāram use a stone rolling-pin to represent the child, which the husband hands over to the wife, who accepts it as 'the milk is ready.'[10] The Konga Vellāla bridegroom takes some fruit and a pestle to a stone, which he worships. It is supposed to represent the Kongu king whose sanction to every marriage used to be necessary, and the pestle represents the villagers; but the fruit is not explained, and the myth is probably ætiological.[11] A newly-married Beḍar or Boya couple sit on a pestle, and are anointed after rice has been showered over them.[12] In Bombay the rice-powder is used to personate the baby.[13]

Fertility can also be communicated to a bride by placing a child in her lap, and fruit is an effective substitute for one.[14] On the same principle women whose husbands are alive are admitted to take part in marriage rites,[15] more especially if they have sons living; whereas widows and those whose children have died should be excluded, at least from the more significant rites.[16] Similarly, widowers are excluded from certain functions.[17] Unmarried girls may, however, take the place of married women; *e.g.*, among the Badaga, married women or virgins, preferably the bridegroom's sisters, go to a stream in procession to bring water for cooking purposes in decorated new pots.[18]

Water as a source of fertility also plays a great part in wedding rites. Thus bathing is an essential part of the ritual for both parties at weddings, and visits to a well or stream are very common. The use of pots full of water is to be explained in the same way. Thus among the Alitkar of Bombay a couple already married bring pots from a potter's house to that of each party to the marriage, and after an elaborate rite the boy pours water from a jar. A jar also plays a prominent part in other rites, including a widow's re-marriage.[1]

1 Thurston, i. 205. 2 *Ib.* ii. 359. 3 *Ib.* iv. 364.
4 *BG* ix. pt. i. [1901] 159. 5 Thurston, i. 233.
6 *Ib.* 201. 7 *Ib.* 13.
8 *BG* xviii. pt. i. [1885] 124. 9 Thurston, iii. 333.
10 *Ib.* vi. 158. 11 *Ib.* iii. 420.
12 *Ib.* i. 202. 13 *BG* xviii. pt. i. 216.
14 *Ib.* xii. [1880] 117, xviii. pt. i. 217, xx. [1884] 132.
15 *Ib.* xv. pt. i. [1883] 161. 16 Thurston, i. 33.
17 *Ib.* 107. 18 *Ib.* 104 f.

Fish being an emblem of fertility, they are often caught by the bridal pair—*e.g.*, among the Gudigāra of Madras;[2] the Holeya let the fish go after kissing them.[3] But the Kṣatriya, in Madras, only pretend to catch them,[4] as do the Nambūtiri Brāhmans.[5]

The potter's wheel, symbolical of the creative power which fashions the earth as it fashions clay, is also in evidence at weddings. The clay is formed into a revolving lump, like a *liṅga*, and wheel and clay together bear a strong resemblance to the conjunction of *liṅga* and *yoni*.[6]

The Pole-star (Dhruva in northern India) is called Arundhatī in Madras, and, as the wife of the *ṛṣi* Vasiṣṭha, is pointed out to the bride as the model of conjugal fidelity.[7]

(2) *Birth.*—Magical rites to procure children are very usual. A typical rite, often resorted to by barren women, consists in burning down seven houses. In Madras a Koyī woman sometimes throws a cock down in front of the cloth on which portraits of ancestors are sewn, and makes obeisance to it,[8] and this cures her sterility. Bathing is also a cure for this misfortune, especially bathing over a corpse.

In the Andamans a pregnant woman sows seed.[9] Pregnancy, moreover, involves peculiar risks necessitating the protection of magic[10] and the avoidance of various acts, such as stepping over the heel-ropes of a horse,[11] which might apparently cause protracted labour, or crossing a running stream, which would result in miscarriage—a common belief in the Panjāb. In Travancore tamarind juice is dropped into a pregnant woman's mouth to cast out devils.[12]

When his wife's first pregnancy is announced, a Kota husband in Madras lets his hair grow long and leaves his finger nails uncut, and on the child's birth he is under pollution till he sees the next crescent moon.[13] A Mukkuvan husband also lets his hair grow until the third day after the birth. A coco-nut, betel leaves, and areca nuts are laid at the place where he sits to be shaved, and the coco-nut is smashed to pieces by one of his own sept.[14] A Nambūtiri Brāhman also remains unshorn while any of his wives are pregnant.[15]

Pre-natal divination to ascertain and magic to determine the child's sex are also common. Thus the Cheruman in Madras employ devil-drivers, who seat the woman in front of a tent-like structure with a coco-nut-palm flower in her lap. When cut open, the fruits predict the child's sex, the birth of twins, and the child's expectation of life or death. The goddess Kālī is supposed to be present in the tent, and prayer is offered to her to cast out the devil from the woman's body.[16]

Another rite which is believed to influence the child's sex is the so-called *sīmanta* of the Śūdras in Madras. In a first pregnancy, water or human milk is poured over the woman's back by her husband's sister.[17]

To ensure that the child shall be a male the *puṁsavana* is performed in the third month of pregnancy, the wife fasting that day until she is fed by her husband with a grain of corn and two beans symbolizing the male organ. Sometimes curd is poured over them before she swallows them, and she also pours juice of a grass into her right nostril.[18]

1 Draft Monograph No. 52, *Ethnographical Survey of Bombay*, 1907.
2 Thurston, ii. 306. 3 *Ib.* 330. 4 *Ib.* iv. 87.
5 *Ib.* v. 203. 6 *Ib.* iv. 191. 7 *Ib.* i. 15, 108, 143.
8 *Ib.* iv. 63. 9 *Census Report*, 1901, i. 206.
10 *BG* ix. pt. i. 31, 161. 11 *NINQ* ii. [1892] § 136.
12 *Census Report*, 1901, i. 331; cf. Thurston, ii. 416.
13 Thurston, iv. 23. 14 *Ib.* v. 115. 15 *Ib.* 169.
16 *Ib.* ii. 73 f. 17 *Ib.* vi. 102. 18 *Ib.* v. 211, 213.

Quite distinct from this Brāhmanical rite is one observed in the seventh month in Travancore.

The woman goes to the foot of a tamarind tree, where she receives a thread seven yards long. This she entwines round a tree, and, if it breaks, either she or her child will soon die. Next day the thread is unwound, and her husband gives her a handful of tamarind leaves. On re-entering the house, he also gives her tamarind juice to drink, pouring it through his hands into hers. The priestess employed in this rite then pours oil on her navel, and from the manner of its fall divines the child's sex. As she drinks the juice, the woman leans against a cutting from a mango, which is then planted; and, if it fails to strike root, the child is doomed to adversity.[1]

Among the polyandrous Kammālan the woman's brother gives her rice gruel mixed with juices of the tamarind, mango, and *Hibiscus*.[2]

In protracted labour the washings of a brick from the fort of Chākabu or Chakrabhyu Amīn near Pehoa are potent, or it suffices to draw a plan of the fort and drink the water into which the picture has been washed off.[3] The origin of this rite is obscure. The 'fort of Chākabu' is a game played by children: they make a maze on paper, and one child finds his way through it with a pencil. A dot within represents the treasure which it is supposed to contain. Vaiṣṇavas of the Vallabha *sampradāya*, or school, often make their *ārti* in this shape.[4]

Difficult labour is dealt with in parts of Madras by calling in a woman who has had an 'easy time'; she presents the patient with betel, etc., and, if that fails, a line of persons drawn up pass water from hand to hand until it reaches the woman who had the 'easy time,' and she gives some of it to the sufferer. Here the luck or quality of the one woman is transmitted to the other.

In one caste, the Mālas of the Telugu country, who are Pariahs, the placenta is put in a pot in which are *nīm* leaves and the whole is buried, lest a dog or other animal should carry it off, which would make the child a wanderer.[5]

(3) *Death*.—A magical rite of resuscitation is practised by the Dāsaris, a class of priests who minister to Śūdras, in Madras. If a Dāsari is offended, he will revenge himself by self-mutilation or even by cutting off his own head. News of this is miraculously carried to all his caste-fellows, and, when collected, they display their magical powers by frying fish which come to life again on being placed in water, by joining together limes cut in two, and, finally, by bringing the suicide to life again. The rite can fail only if the victim's wife is in pollution or when the rite is not carried out reverently.[6]

2. Agents.—First-born children have power to stop rain. Muslims say that they can do so by stripping naked and standing on their heads, heels in the air. In Calcutta they need only make a candle of cloth and burn it.[7] A first-born son leaning against anything will, it is believed in S. India, attract a thunder-bolt to it.[8] Girls born in the asterism of Mūla are believed in S. India to place their mother-in-law in a corner, *i.e.*, make her a widow, and so such a girl, if her mother is not already a widow, finds difficulty in securing a husband.[9]

Just as charms are made out of various natural substances, so such substances often possess magical powers. The acacia is inhabited by a *jinn*, but its wood is unlucky only if used to make or mend a bed; no one will be able to sleep on it. Here the spirit in the tree appears to endue it with magical properties; a man who conveys himself in servitude to the spirit of this tree will get all that he wants, but only at the risk of his life. For twenty-one days he must take a pot full of water daily to the jungle, and on his way back cast half of it upon a particular tree; on the twenty-first night he will be irresistibly drawn towards it; the devil will appear to him, and, if he escapes death, he will get all that he wants as the price of his bondage.[1] The tree called *barkhar* (*Celtis caucasia*) has magical properties; any one cutting it down or tampering with it loses all his hair and becomes very ill. It yields a milk which raises blisters, and even to sit in its shade, while it is exuding it, has that effect. Indeed it is dangerous to sit in its shade at any time. This belief is current in the Murree Hills, in the Panjāb, but in that very part the Gūjars use amulets of *batkar* (its usual Indian name) to ward off the evil eye (*naẓar*) from both men and cattle, and its fruit is also much relished.[2]

To cure scorpion bite the insect should at once be caught and burnt, and the smoke allowed to touch the bite.[3] To cure *saya*, or consumption, in a child (said to be due to enchantment caused by ashes taken from a burning place and thrown over or near the child) the parents should give away salt equal to the child's weight.[4] Toothache is cured by a magical rite which consists in spreading sand over a clean piece of board and writing on it the first six letters of the Arabic alphabet. The patient then holds his aching tooth between his thumb and index finger, and touches each letter in turn with a pointed instrument. When he reaches the sixth letter, if not before, he will be cured. At each he should be asked if he is cured, and, when he says that he is, he should be asked how long he wishes for relief. He should reply 'two years,' as that is the limit of the charm's efficacy.[5]

After a bad dream, a Gāro, in Assam, collects a reed-like grass and is beaten with it by a priest, who repeats certain exorcisms. Then they carry a cock to the nearest stream, kill it, and let its blood fall into a toy boat; the boat is launched, and as it starts the dreamer bathes in the water. The prayers, the chastisement, and the sacrifice appease the spirits, and the boat is allowed to carry off the ill-luck.[6]

On the first day of sowing sugar-cane, sweetened rice is brought to the field, and women smear the outside of the vessel with it, after which it is given to the labourers. Next morning a woman puts on a necklace and walks round the field, winding thread on a spindle. This custom is falling into disuse.[7]

Magic squares are in vogue among Hindus. Thus one which totals 90 lengthways cures quartan ague; one totalling 100 every way causes excess of milk in cows and women and of *ghi* in a churn; one totalling 130 every way will, if worn round one's neck or in one's *pagṛī* (turban), bring any person under one's power;[8] and one totalling 15 each way brings luck and is commonly found on shops. Squares totalling 55 and 20 each way should be placed under one's seat to ensure success at play.[9]

1 Thurston, ii. 416. This rite cannot be said to correspond to the *puṁsavana*, which is intended to influence the sex of the child.
2 *Ib.* iii. 131.
3 *Karnāl Settlement Report*, 1883, p. 154; A. Cunningham, *Archæological Survey Reports*, Calcutta, 1871, ii. 223.
4 *NINQ* v. § 642.
5 Thurston, iv. 369 f.
6 *Ib.* 382.
7 *PNQ* i. §§ 116, 463.
8 *NINQ* i. [1891] § 378.
9 *Ib.* § 379.

1 *NINQ* iv. [1894] § 797.
2 *PNQ* ii. [1884] § 272, and *Selection Calcutta Review*, viii. [1896] 124 (*Calcutta Review*, lxxv. [1882] 290). In the latter R. C. Temple identifies the *bhar* with the Skr. *vaṭa*, or banyan-tree, but describes the *batkar* as a low thorny shrub of the *zizyphus*, or jujube, family, the fruit of which is the 'fruit of paradise' in Arabic poetry—on which account the tree is much prized in Tripoli and Tunis.
3 *NINQ* i. § 563.
4 *Ib.* § 561.
5 *Ib.* § 370.
6 A. Playfair, *The Garos*, London, 1909, p. 115 f.
7 *Karnāl Settlement Report*, p. 181.
8 *PNQ* i. § 462.
9 *Ib.* § 537.

The power of magic is so great that by mere assertion of its potency a *bīr*, or demon, may be brought into subjection.

Fast the whole of a ninth lunar day falling on a Friday, and in the evening eat sweet rice milk. At 8 p.m. don red clothes perfumed, and make a circle of red lead on the ground. Sit in its centre with four cardamons, some catechu, betel-nuts, and eight cloves. Light a lamp fed with clarified butter and say: 'Incantation can break down the stars' 5000 times—and a demon will be at your service.[1]

II. *ISLĀM*.—Muhammadans classify magic as high (*'ulwī*), divine (*raḥmānī*), low (*siflī*), and satanic (*shaiṭānī*). In divine magic perfection consists in knowledge of the greatest of God's names—the *ism-al-a'ẓam*, which is imparted only to the elect, and by which the dead can be raised. But God's other names, and those of Muhammad and of the good *jinn*, are also efficacious, and written charms are composed of them or of passages from the Qur'ān, as well as of mysterious combinations of numbers, diagrams, and figures. Satanic magic is condemned by all good Muslims. It depends on Satan's aid and that of the evil *jinn*, who ascend to the lowest heaven and hear the angels so that they can assist magicians. Enchantment (*al-siḥr*) is a branch of this magic; but, as it has been studied with good intent and with the aid of good *jinn*, there is a science of enchantment which may be regarded as lawful. Enchantment results in death, paralysis, affliction with irresistible passion, possession, or metamorphosis. Metamorphosis is effected by spells or invocations to the *jinn* accompanied by the sprinkling of dust or water on the object to be transformed. Against enchantment and other evils a talisman (*ṭilism*), *i.e.* mystical characters, astrological or otherwise magical, or a seal or image on which they are engraved, is effective. When rubbed, it calls up its servants.

Divination (*al-kihāna*), which is also practised by the aid of Shaiṭān, is obtained by magic, by invoked names, and by burning perfumes. Its forms are: *ḍarb al-mandal*, inscribing the enchanter's circle,[2] *ḍarb al-raml*, the moving of sand, *'ilm al-nujūm*, astrology,[3] and *al-zijr*, or augury from beast and bird.[4]

The Imām Zamānī rupee is said to be dedicated to that *imām*, and is worn by Muhammadans on the right arm when starting on a journey.[5]

The names of 'Alī and the *imāms* are used in magical squares according to the *abjad*, or letter-value system of computation. Notices of the custom are not uncommon in Indo-Persian histories as having been practised on the Mughal court-ladies.[6]

Islāmic medicine is acquainted with the olive of Bani-Isrā'īl, a stone found on the banks of the Indus. It is black with a little red and yellow, or olive-coloured with small white lines, and is used only for sprinkling over wounds and stings by Muslims. Hindus are said to worship it as a god, and to the Persians it is known as the *sang-i-Yāhū*, or 'stone of Jahweh,' or the *ḥajar al-Hunūd*, or 'stone of the Hindus,' in Arabia. Jasper (in Pers. *yashm*, Arab. *ḥajar al-bashaf*, or 'hard stone'), when olive, green-yellow, or opaque green, is used in charms; and, when white, in medicine. The hair of a child will never turn white if a piece of it be tied on his neck at birth. If a piece is tied on the right wrist, he will be immune to witchcraft and the evil eye. Tied to a woman's thigh, it ensures painless labour; and, if by the light of *lailat al-qādir* (the night when Muhammad spake with God) a man be sketched over it and the picture worn over the head, the wearer will be safe from wounds in battle.[1]

III. *MAGIC AND RELIGION*.—It has been held by many scholars that in ancient India the confusion of magic and religion was rife, just as it survived among other peoples that had risen to higher levels of culture. H. Oldenberg[2] regards the sacrificial ritual of the earliest known period as pervaded with primitive magic, and he tells us that the rites celebrated at marriage, initiation, and the anointment of a king are complete models of magic of every kind, and that the forms employed are of the highest antiquity. Sylvain Lévi[3] observes of the sacrifices prescribed in the *Brāhmaṇas* that they have all the characteristics of a magical operation, effective by its own energy, independent of the divinities, and capable of producing evil as well as good; it is only distinguishable from magic in that it is regular and obligatory, so that both matters are treated in the same works. Thus the *Sāmavidhāna Brāhmaṇa* is a hand-book of incantations and sorcery, as is the *Adbhuta Brāhmaṇa* portion of the *Ṣaḍviṁśa Brāhmaṇa*. M. Bloomfield[4] also holds that witchcraft became intimately blended with the holiest Vedic rites, the broad current of popular superstitions having penetrated into the higher religion of the Brāhman priests who were unable and possibly unwilling to cleanse it from the mass of folk-belief which surrounded it. W. Caland,[5] in his introduction to the *Kauśika Sūtra*, enlarges on the agreement between the magic ritual of the old Vedas and the shamanism of the so-called savage. Indeed, some authorities would derive Brāhman from *brahman*, 'a magic spell,' so that, if they are right, the Brāhman would seem to have been a magician before he was a priest.[6]

On the other hand, J. G. Frazer[7] also points out how in India, from the earliest times down to the present day, the real religion of the common folk appears always to have been a belief in a vast multitude of spirits of whom many, if not most, are mischievous and harmful. This belief subsists under the great religions, like Brāhmanism, Buddhism, and Islām, which may come and go; and in support of this thesis he cites Oldenberg for the Vedic and Monier Williams for the modern periods. It is to this deep-seated and universal belief in the existence of spirits, which fill all created matter—the sky, the earth, trees, beasts, the earthly waters and clouds—that many, if not all, magical practices are to be ascribed, at least in their inception. At every stage of a ritual sacrifice, *e.g.*, spirits have to be appeased, and the very stake to which a willing victim is tethered for the sacrifice must be cut, shaped, and erected

1 *NINQ* v. § 214.

2 *Mandal* is doubtless from the Gr. *μάνδαλον*, and not connected with Skr. *maṇḍala*, a circuit or group of villages. The *μάνδαλον* was a kind of drum used to conjure up demons; hence an enchanter's circle.

3 It was taught by the two fallen angels Hārūt and Mārūt, who became enamoured of the songstress Zuhra, who ascended to the sky and mingled her splendour with the star Zuhra (Venus).

4 H. Wilberforce Clarke, *Divān-i-Ḥāfiẓ*, Calcutta, 1891, ii. 616 f., citing the *Mishkāt-al-Maṣābīḥ*, ii. 394, 384, 385, 388, and *Mirāt al-zamān*, i. 1. For a charm to divine which of two rivals will prevail see the *Sirāj al-raml* by Maulavī Roshan 'Alī and the *Miṣdāq al-raml* by Muḥammad 'Aṭṭār Māl Lahorī, Lucknow, cited in *Divān-i-Ḥāfiẓ*, ii. 831. It consists in writing the two names in *abjad*, and dividing by nine. Then, if both the quotients be odd or even, the lesser in number will conquer; if both are equal, the lesser in age; and, if one be odd, the other even, the greater in number will prevail.

5 *NINQ* i. § 695.

6 *PNQ* i. § 686.

1 *PNQ* ii. § 17, quoting from the *Makhzan al-Adwiyāt*, or 'Treasury of Medicine,' of Muḥammad Ḥusain of Delhi, 1761, published by Newal Kishore, Cawnpore and Lucknow.

2 *Die Religion des Veda*, Berlin, 1894, pp. 59, 177 (for particular examples of the blending of magical with religious ritual in ancient India see pp. 311 f., 369 f., 476 f., and 522 f.).

3 *La Doctrine du sacrifice dans les Brāhmanas*, Paris, 1898, p. 129.

4 *Hymns of the Atharva-Veda* (*SBE* xlii. [1897] p. xlv f.).

5 *Altindisches Zauberritual*, Amsterdam, 1900, p. ix.

6 O. Schrader, *Reallexikon der indogermanischen Altertumskunde*, Strassburg, 1901, p. 637 f.

7 *GB*³, pt. i., *The Magic Art*, London, 1913, i. 228 f., pt. vi., *The Scapegoat*, do. 1913, p. 89 ff., citing Oldenberg, p. 39 f., and Monier Williams, *Religious Thought and Life in India*, do. 1883, p. 210 f.

with the most minute precautions against their sinister influences. Every point in sacrificial ritual is symbolical, but the guiding principle in it is not magical, but religious. By the part of the stake which is dug in the sacrificer gains the lower world of the fathers, by its middle part that of men, and by its top the world of the gods. But this winning of the three worlds is conditional on his success in averting the onslaughts of evil spirits. In the whole ritual of animal-sacrifice at the stake (*yūpa*), as prescribed by the *Śatapatha Brāhmaṇa*, there is no trace of magic or of magical practices.[1]

A question of minor interest is whether Indian magic was derived from or has influenced that of Arabia and the Nearer East. The Skr. word *śilpā*, 'black magic,' may be the original form of *siflī*, or, conversely, the Arab word *siflī* may have been Sanskritized as *śilpā*. A typical rite in *śilpā* illustrates the spiritual basis of belief in magic. When performed with the object of destroying an enemy, it is known as *chel*, or *ghāṭ*, in the United Provinces. A vessel is filled with iron nails, knives, etc., and sent by certain incantations through the air until it descends on the victim's head and kills him. But, if a river intervenes, a sacrifice to the spirit called *ghaṭbai* (lit. 'ferryman'), which is supposed to guard the river, must be made to induce him to let the vessel cross.[2] Thus black magic has to reckon with the spirits, however it works and whatever its origin.

LITERATURE.—i. The Hindu literature is vast, but mostly unpublished. It comprises many treatises on special topics—*e.g.*, the *Kashtauli* (?) *Sukdeoji*, a Gurmukhi MS, contains only magic squares for all kinds of ailments.[3] It commences with the Atharvaveda, upon which and other texts is based Alfred Hillebrandt, *Ritual-Litteratur: Vedische Opfer und Zauber* (=*GIAP* iii. 2), Strassburg, 1897.

ii. The Shī'a Muhammadans, who are prone to occultism, have six books on magic: the *Ja'afar Jāma*, *Safīnat al-nijāt*, *Tuḥfat al-'awām*, *Mahaj al-da'wāt*, *Mukārim al-ikhlāq*, and *Anwār i-Na'māniya*. The Sunnis also have books on magic: such are the *Mujarrabāt-i-Dīrbī* and the *Naqsh-i-Sulaimān*.[4]

H. A. ROSE.

MAGIC (Iranian).—**1. Religion and magic.**—Although religion and magic are two essentially different things, the interpenetration of the two is fairly common; but nowhere are they so intricately commingled as in Mazdeism.

First of all, a clear line of demarcation has to be traced between the real doctrine of Zoroaster, as it is expounded in the *Gāthās*, and the Later Avesta.

In the Gāthic hymns we find a religion of a highly moral character. It admits of no deity besides Ahura Mazda except personified moral entities, and it expressly undertakes a struggle against the lower beliefs and the magical practices of the people of the time. The cult of the *daēvas* in general and the nocturnal orgiastic sacrifices in which *haoma* (*q.v.*) was drunk by the worshippers were specially condemned.[5]

The Later Avesta also anathematizes the sorcerers (*yātu*) and witches (*pairika*), but many of the beliefs and practices which Zoroaster had associated with them have found their way back into religion. The whole subject is rendered all the more intricate by the fact that a coherent system has been formed from a combination of the superior elements of the Zoroastrian creed (sophisticated to a great extent by adaptation to a lower standard of religious thought) and the popular and inferior beliefs of the Iranian people, including much that is in origin magical. As is well known, this is the system called dualism (*q.v.*). It is based on the assumption that there are two cosmic elements, the one created by Ahura Mazda, the real god, and the other by his adversary, Angra Mainyu. Every creature of the wise lord is good, but all that has been created by his foe is evil. Each creator has thus communicated to his creatures his own specific nature and power. His creatures both share in their lord's natural and supernatural power and must assist him in the incessant struggle which is going on between the good and the evil spirit—a contest which will not be settled before the end of this world.

It follows that good creatures have a power over evil ones and evil over good. Of course, we may imagine that a good being, when he neutralizes the evil deeds of his opponent, acts, after all, as a depository of his creator's power; but in practice it is as though he had a real and effective power of his own against demons.

A good work is an act of war, capable of helping effectively towards the triumph of good over evil and having, therefore, an efficacy of its own to conjure and oppose the noxious activity of evil creatures such as evil spirits; and this is very much like the efficacy ascribed to magical rites. The only difference between such an activity and magic is that, with the latter, material interests are generally at stake, whereas, in the majority of Mazdean religious acts, the concern is mostly supra-terrestrial, being the religious purity of the faithful (*ašavan*) as a preparation for the future happiness of the blest. The contrary state, the impurity of the imps of the *druj* (*dregvants*), has to be destroyed.

2. Purification.—For the Zoroastrian the normal means of getting rid of an impurity acquired by sin is to outweigh it by merit[1]—a process which, of course, is far from being magical. Sin, however, being in Iranian eyes not only a breach of order which has to be repaired by repentance and good works, but a positive product of the evil spirits, of the evil creation, produces a substantial, though invisible, pollution—a moral disease like a bodily illness—and death likewise results from some mysterious contrivance of the originators of all evil. A material means of removing that pollution is therefore requisitioned, just as a remedy by its beneficial properties, as a piece of good creation, cures an ordinary disease. The power of purifying man from impurity belongs in the highest degree to water—an eminently good element of Mazda's creation. Besides water, other substances—e.g., *gaomaēza* (urine of cattle)—are supposed to have great power to purify. The rites of purification by means of these substances are strictly fixed, as in a magical proceeding: the priest has to sprinkle every part of the body in a definite order, beginning with the head, till the *druj* is expelled from the left toes, which are the last refuge of the evil spirit. Dogs have a specially powerful wholesome influence. More intricate ceremonies tending to the same result existed besides this relatively simple one—*e.g.*, the great purification of the nine nights (Pahl. *barašnūm nū šaba*) expounded in *Vend.* ix.; the ground is prepared, holes are dug, and furrows are drawn, according to a strict ritual; *gaomaēza* is put into the holes, the patient rubs the ground, and is sprinkled with water and perfumes by means of a spoon and a stick of a fixed size, etc. The proceeding cannot, however, be completely identified with magic, because, however material the concept of purity may have been in the thought of the Iranian people at that time, it was, after all, a duty not confined to human interests in this world, because the activity of the purifying substances and acts derives from an essentially beneficent power, whereas the counter-spells, although tending to

[1] J. P. Vogel, 'The Sacrificial Posts of Isapur,' in *Archæological Survey Report for 1910–11*, Calcutta, 1914, p. 44 f.

[2] *NINQ* i. § 351. [3] *PNQ* ii. § 901. [4] *Ib.* i. § 686.

[5] Moulton, *Early Zoroastrianism*, p. 71 f.

[1] Moulton, p. 144.

neutralize noxious influences, are regarded as possessing a power of the same kind as the one which they oppose, and, lastly, because the rites, in spite of their magical tendencies, are devoid of all mystery. They are a public and accepted procedure, assumed—wrongly, of course—to date back to the Prophet's teaching, and forming part of the sacred struggle of good against evil. Man is supposed to make use of the weapons which Mazda has put into his hands for a contest in which he is serving the lord's interests. Nevertheless, it is clear that a real degeneration towards magic has taken place in these ceremonies, and also that many an ancient magical prescription for averting evils may have been introduced. This process is analogous to that which we observe in Mazdaism from Zoroaster to the Later Avesta period.

Moral beings, like the *amesha spentas* ([*q.v.*] justice, good spirit, piety, etc.), have been turned into—or, rather, identified with—the genii of fire, cattle, earth, etc., and Sraosha, 'obedience,' has become a good spirit protecting men during the night against demons and sorcerers, having the cock and the dog as his assistants in this task (*Bund.* xix. 33).[1]

3. Sacrifice.—Of sacrifice we may say much the same as of purifications. Neither to the Indians nor to the Iranians was the sacrifice properly a magical act. Oldenberg[2] is quite right when he says that sacrifice is in Vedic times a gift to the god, which, in the mind of the sacrificer, is to influence the intentions of the deity, not by way of compulsion, but by securing his powerful goodwill. This conception, however, was likely to degenerate, and did. Indra and Agni are sometimes described as being mastered by the sacrificer.

Agni, the fire, is regarded as a miniature of the sun, the great fire, and, by kindling fire, one gets the sun to rise. Indeed, the *Śatapatha Brāhmaṇa*[3] says that the sun would not rise if the fire-sacrifice did not take place. A similar process can be traced in Irān, where the sacrifice is given its place in the general cosmic conflict, so that it

'is more than an act of worship; it is an act of assistance to the gods. Gods, like men, need food and drink to be strong; like men, they need praise and encouragement to be of good cheer. When not strengthened by the sacrifice, they fly helpless before their foes.'[4]

Sacrifice has thus a value of its own independently of the will of the gods. It is an act of war, helping God in His struggle against the evil creation, so much so that gods also have to practise cult:

'Aūharmazd performed the spiritual Yazišn ceremony with the archangels (*ameshōspendān*) in the Rapītvīn Gāh, and in the Yazišn he supplied every means for overcoming the adversary.'[5]

The value of sacrifice in itself is also to be discerned in the fact that it produces merits independently of the piety and attention of the sacrificer. If he does not obtain them for himself, they are not lost, but are collected in a store (*ganj*) of merits.[6] The sacrifice of the *haoma* (=Ind. *soma*), although itself not really magical in principle, was specially prone to develop in that direction. The *haoma*=*soma*, in the thought of the proto-Aryans, was a plant wherein resided an extraordinary strength of life capable of giving immortality to the gods, who were supposed to live on it like the Homeric gods on ἀμβροσία, and of giving a superexaltation of life to man, in whom it caused intoxication. As was said above, the *haoma* orgiastic sacrifice had been banished from Gāthic religion in company with the magical procedure of the *daēva*-worshippers. In the post-Gāthic period we see it reappear, but it has been deprived of its savage character and turned into a mystical drink.[1] Not only was it supposed to confer a greater intensity of human life, but it was regarded as a highly beneficial spirit, imparting to man also the gift of spiritual life and a title to the supra-terrestrial reward.[2] It led to a division into two *haomas*.[3] The one, the actual plant, was the yellow *haoma*, the other, supra-terrestrial, called the white *haoma*, was identified with the tree *gaokerena* (Pahl. *gōkarṭ*) 'that stands in the middle of the sea *Vouru-Kaša* . . . that is called "the All-healer" and on which rest the seeds of all plants.'[4] It is by drinking the *gaokerena* that men on the day of the resurrection will become immortal. For that reason it was customary to put a drop of *haoma* on the lips of a dying Zoroastrian. *Haoma*, having been made the principle of all life and fecundity, was supposed to receive its healing power from Vohu Manah, and to be the son of Ahura Mazda. This mysterious power of the drink of life is an approach to magic, although it is extended to domains to which healing and vivifying power cannot normally attain—*e.g.*, the gift of swiftness to horses in races, of healthy children to pregnant women, and of bridegrooms to girls. Moreover, it is, in the traditions of the Indo-Iranians, closely connected with a mystical bird which took the *soma*=*haoma* from the place where it lay hidden and brought it to gods and men.[5] The Avesta speaks of the bird Saēna, which is the Sīmurgh of the Persians, who make him play the same part as the bird Vārengana in *Yt.* xiv. 35 f.—a part which is completely magical.[6]

'Get thee a feather of the wide-feathered bird Vārengana, Oh Spitama Zarathushtra. With that feather thou shalt rub thy body; with that feather thou shalt curse back thine enemy. He who hath a bone of the mighty bird or a feather of the mighty bird gaineth (divine) favour. No one, (however) magnificent, smiteth him or turneth him to flight; he first gaineth homage, he first (gaineth) glory; the feather of the bird of birds bestoweth help.'

Thus we have here to do with a real amulet.

4. Spells.—If the sacrifice is apt to degenerate into a magical rite, prayer may become a spell. The message of Zoroaster to man is a *manthra*, a noble word which properly means 'utterance,' 'word,' 'ordinance,' but has in the Later Avesta the meaning of 'spell' and, indeed, the sermons of the Prophet, instead of being a subject for meditation, are chanted in a dialect obsolete for ages, and have degenerated into mere spells, the exact pronunciation of their words achieving what their author sought by pure life and diligence in a noble calling.[7] The finest Mazdean prayers, such as the *Ahuna Vairya* ([*q.v.*] Pārsī, *honovar*)—a kind of profession of faith—have stiffened into a mechanical repetition of formulæ, and have acquired an infinite power of their own, so much so that they become a weapon for the Creator Himself. The *Bundahišn* (i. 21) narrates how Aūharmazd, having recited the *Ahunavar* and uttered its twenty-one words, confounded the evil spirit and secured the victory over him, in the first days of creation. The power of the same prayer and of some others is also expounded in *Vend.* xix. (cf. also *Yt.* xvii. 20). Recited as many times as is prescribed on every occasion, they help as a spell the purification of man, which is

[1] L. C. Casartelli, *Philosophie religieuse du Mazdéisme*, Paris, 1884, § 106.
[2] H. Oldenberg, *Religion des Veda*, Berlin, 1894, p. 304 f.
[3] II. iii. 15 (Oldenberg, p. 110); *SBE* xii. [1882] 328.
[4] Moulton, p. 417, note.
[5] *Bund.* ii. 9, tr. West, *SBE* v. [1880] 14.
[6] Casartelli, § 250. The *Yazišn* is the ritual reading of the *Yasna*.

[1] Moulton, p. 72 f.
[2] C. P. Tiele, *Godsdienst in de Oudheid*, Amsterdam, 1895–1901, ii. 222.
[3] Casartelli, § 173. [4] *Yt.* xii. 17.
[5] So Odin as an eagle carries away the mead. The victor Kṛśānu was supposed to have shot off a feather of the eagle (Oldenberg, p. 247).
[6] Art. CHARMS AND AMULETS (Iranian), vol. iii. p. 448.
[7] Moulton, p. 153.

primarily attained by the marvellous power of the substances and ceremonies mentioned above.

No wonder, therefore, if the *manthra* is mentioned as a regular means of curing diseases. *Vend.* xx. distinguishes healing by plants, by the knife, and by the *manthra*, the last being the most powerful. A series of formulæ is to be found there for repelling both diseases and evil beings. The prayer contained in *Vend.* xx. 11 is supposed to be peculiarly powerful. It is directed to Airyaman, the healing god *par excellence*. *Vend.* xxi. 18–23 is also a spell against all kinds of diseases, consisting of some fragments of other parts of the *Vendīdād* and of some very well known prayers. These are the means that Airyaman has at his disposal for curing the 99,999 diseases created by Angra Mainyu for the bane of mankind (*Vend.* xxii.). Airyaman is an old Indo-Iranian god: in the Veda he is an *āditya* (Aryaman) who is generally found in company with Varuna and Mitra. He is a beneficent and helpful god, but in Persia he has been narrowed down to the character of a healing god. He survives in Parsiism as the *īzad* of heaven, but, in his quality of healing god, he is replaced by Farīdūn (=Thraētaona), who, having killed the dragon Azi Dahāka, is supposed to be a powerful enemy to the works of evil spirits. The Iranians knew, moreover, of a healing fruit, which, according to *Bund.* iii. 18, Ahura Mazda pounded up before his coming to the ox, 'so that its damage and discomfort from the calamity (*zanišn*) might be less.'[1] On the same footing as the *manthra* for healing diseases must, of course, be put the numerous incantations and mystical formulæ for removing the pollution inflicted upon anything which has come into contact with a corpse. *Vend.* viii. 14 ff., *e.g.*, explains that a road whereon the dead bodies of dogs or men have been carried cannot be traversed again by men or flocks, till the yellow dog with four eyes or the white dog with yellow ears has gone three times across it and an *ātharvan* has gone along it, saying aloud the fiend-smiting words of the *honovar*. *Vend.* vii. 28 ff. contains the method of purifying wood which has been in contact with a corpse, and formulæ for all kinds of good elements infected by the same pollution (cf. *Vend.* x., xi., etc.). In such cases the *Gāthās* had become a mere spell (cf. *Vend.* x. 1 ff.). The reason of this custom with regard to corpses is originally a magical one, which has been fitted into the general Mazdean system. It is the old conviction of mankind that death, like illness, cannot occur without the maleficent intervention of some spirit, which has therefore to be averted. For a Mazdean to die was to pass into the power of the *druj* Nasu. Hence it was necessary to minimize the evil produced by this demon by protecting all good beings and substances from its power and freeing, as soon as possible, the beings or substances that had fallen into its hands. The intervention of maleficent beings and the utility of spells were felt in many other circumstances—*e.g.*, in the case of a woman on the eve of child-birth (*Vend.* xxi. 8, 12, 16), or when some accident occurred to cattle.[2]

5. Fire.—Among the elements which have to be kept carefully from any pollution, fire occupies a prominent position. It is well known that among the Parsis it enjoys a veneration which is not far from being superstitious. Here, the process is not a degenerative one, but rather the elevation of an elementary and, to a great extent, magical belief which is common to many nations, but which is specially Indo-Iranian (cf. art. FIRE, FIRE-GODS, § 6 f.). Fire is the great purifier, which illuminates the night, keeps off bitter cold and wild beasts, and, as such, is the great enemy of demons and the friend and ally of man. It repels diseases, and it plays an important part in the proceeding of Indian magic, as is expounded in the Atharvaveda[1]—a name which is taken from the *atharvans*, who were originally priests of fire. The Iranian myth of Ātar's victory over the serpent Azi Dahāka (*Yt.* xix. 45 ff.) belongs to the same order of thought. Indeed, fire, in the conception of the Persian *ātharvan*, keeps closer to its original part, inasmuch as it does not become, as in India, the agent which conveys to the gods the substances of sacrifice. It remains the great averter of everything impure, and must on no account be put in contact with anything that is not pure, least of all with corpses or with anything coming from the body. It has become an earthly form of the eternal, infinite, godly light, the purest offspring of the good spirit, the purest part of his pure creation,[2] the weapon of Ahura (*Ys.* li. 9). It is the principle of all life, in men as well as in plants, the son of Ahura Mazda.[3] We can distinguish several forms of it, among which the *bahrām* fire is the most sacred. It is supposed to be an emanation on earth from the fire above and the most powerful protection of the land against foes and fiends.[4] It took its name from Verethraghna (Skr. *vṛtrahan*), in Indian myth the genius of victory and the slayer of the demon Vṛtra.

6. Influence of stars.—Astrology, as is well known, was the chief concern of the Magi, as the ancients describe them to us; but there is abundant evidence that this element of activity was not of Iranian origin. The proto-Aryan element of astrolatry was extremely small, in contrast with Babylonian religion.[5] We have, however, the cult of Tištrya, the star (Sirius) which was regarded as a good genius that brought rain after having slain the drought demon Apaoša (*Yt.* viii. 20 ff.). It is a very good genius which, at the dawn of creation and before man was created, destroyed the noxious creatures by an effusion of beneficent waters. It would be an exaggeration to treat as real magic such beliefs concerning the part of Tištrya as we find in the Avesta. There is reason to believe, however, that in some parts of Persia rain spells were in use. The *Great Bundahišn* says:

> 'The plague created against Saīstān is abundance of witchcraft; and that character appears from this, that all people from that place practise astrology: those wizards produce . . snow, hail, spiders, and locusts.'[6]

On the other hand, it was a current belief among Iranians that planets had a malign influence; but this does not oblige us to admit that they had any belief in the influences of stars upon men's fate (cf. art. FATE [Iranian]).

7. Recent superstitions.—Among the superstitions prevalent among the Parsis and the Muhammadan Persians many customs, no doubt, go back to old Mazdean practices or, more probably, to popular beliefs which persisted beside the official creed.

The great power assigned, among the old Mazdeans, to plants in general, and in particular to some specially marvellous ones, as well as the extensive practice, among the Babylonian Magi,[7] of natural or magical treatment of diseases by herbs, probably explains the important part played by plants in the superstitious customs attached to the ancient Persian festivals as described by Persian writers[8]—*e.g.*, rubbing with olive oil on the day of Naūrūz as a riddance from sorrows during the new year, eating a pomegranate on the feast of Mihr (Mithra) to avert dangers, hitting

[1] *SBE* v. 18.
[2] W. Geiger, *Ostīrānische Kultur*, Erlangen, 1882, p. 332.

[1] V. Henry, *Magie dans l'Inde*, Paris, 1904, pp. 4, 186, 233.
[2] Darmesteter, *SBE* iv.[2] [1895] p. lxxvi.
[3] Tiele, p. 303; cf. M. N. Dhalla, *Zoroastrian Theology*, New York, 1914, pp. 42 f., 134–137.
[4] Darmesteter, p. lxiv.
[5] Moulton, p. 210.
[6] Moulton, p. 209.
[7] Pliny, *HN* xxx. 6.
[8] Decourdemanche, *RTP* xxiii. 209.

an eating animal with an orange on the day of Ādar in November as a way of securing happiness, giving garlic to one's friends on the Gōš rūz (14th Dec.), and boiling herbs on the same day, in order to get rid of demons, fumigation with liquorice on the day of Dī-mihr rūz in order to avoid starvation or misery, eating apples and daffodils on the same day in order to secure success in one's enterprises, placing betel, walnuts, etc., on a pregnant woman's bosom, to make her fertile,[1] etc.

The power of fire against evil beings is illustrated by the lighting of a fire on the night of the Bahmān (Vohu Manah) festival (10th Jan.). This fire, on which perfumes were thrown, was lit under the image of the genius in order to repel wild beasts. During the whole night it was guarded by standing Persians.[2] Anquetil du Perron reports that on 15 Spendarmaț the Parsis used to hold a spell, written on a sheet of paper, in the smoke of a fire, in which they had put pieces of horn from an animal killed on the festival of Mihr, cotton seed, resin, and garlic, in order to remove the *dēvs* (*daēva*) from their houses.[3] The magic for rain has survived in the custom of pouring out water on 30th Jan. in order to obtain rain during the year.[4]

In the last days of the Persian year the souls of the departed are said to come and pay a visit to their relatives, who prepare a sumptuous meal for them. The souls—or, rather, the *fravashis* (*q.v.*)—are supposed to gaze at the food and smell it.[5] This also, no doubt, is a survival of the beliefs concerning the *fravashis*.

The use of the Gāthic hymns and of the chief Zoroastrian prayers as spells against diseases or against the evil eye is current to this day among the representatives of the Mazdean faith.

'In order to avert the influence of the evil eye or to cure a child of some disease, a parent will occasionally hire the mobeds . . . to read from the Yasna, the Yashts, or the Khordah Avesta; and when women are childless, they will sometimes pay to have the Vendîdâd Sadah recited by the priests, in order that the curse of sterility may be removed.'[6]

J. J. Modi knows of charms for diseases of the eye[7] or for avoiding pollution from contact with all that comes from the human body—*e.g.*, hair or nails.[8] Amulets are also used for the same purpose.[9]

LITERATURE.—There is no special book on Iranian magic. The general bibliography on Mazdaism has to be consulted, especially the translation of the Avesta by J. Darmesteter (*AMG*, Paris, 1892-93); J. H. Moulton, *Early Zoroastrianism*, London, 1913. For spells and charms see literature at end of art. CHARMS AND AMULETS (Iranian). For Parsis cf. J. A. Decourdemanche, in *RTP* xxiii. [1908] 209 ff.; D. Menant, *Les Parsis*, Paris, 1898.

A. J. CARNOY.

MAGIC (Japanese).—Japanese magic is such a vast subject that, if we were to treat it systematically, with all its logical divisions and subdivisions, it would be almost impossible to give even a bare index to the volume that would have to be written to describe it. We shall, therefore, dismiss everything that springs from foreign influences, and even in Japanese magic proper we shall ignore the general classifications under which the innumerable details supplied by the rich literature of the country might be arranged. We shall confine our attention to emphasizing the essential point, viz. the existence of magic in the very heart of the national religion, in the most authentic documents of pure Shinto.

For this purpose we must apply chiefly to the ancient rituals (*norito*) collected in the *Engishiki* in the 10th cent., although several of these—and precisely those that contain most of the magical element—were certainly composed at a much earlier date, even before the most ancient mythico-historical works, the *Kojiki* and the *Nihongi*, which were written in the 8th century. By glancing over the most typical of these *norito*, and explaining them with the help of certain related passages in the *Kojiki* and the *Nihongi* or in other equally ancient sources, rather than by abstract classifications, we shall gain a vivid idea of what Japanese magic was in its most ancient and most original form.

The old rituals seem to have been not so much prayers as magical formulæ, solemn incantations, and we shall see that at the same time they were enveloped in powerful rites by which the magician priests of primitive Japan conquered their gods.

This magical spirit appears at the very beginning of the collection, in the 1st ritual, *Toshigohi no Matsuri*, which was said every year at seed-time to obtain a good harvest. The chief priest (*nakatomi*), who recited it in the name of the emperor, addressed the gods in these words:

'I believe in the presence of the sovereign gods of the Harvest. If the sovereign gods will bestow in many-bundled ears and in luxuriant ears the late-ripening harvest which they will bestow, the late-ripening harvest which will be produced by the dripping of foam from the arms and by drawing the mud together between the opposing thighs, then I will fulfil their praises by setting up the firstfruits in a thousand ears and many hundred ears, raising high the sake-jars, filling and ranging in rows the bellies of the sake-jars, in juice and in ear.'

Other offerings are then enumerated, among which we notice a white horse, a white pig, and a white cock. Now, a 9th cent. document, the *Kogoshūi*, gives the legendary origin of this detail: Mi-toshi no Kami, 'the god of the august harvest,' had cast his curse on the rice fields; but the diviners obtained from him, by the gift of these same white animals, the secret of a magical process which enabled them to save the imperilled crop. The ritual is, therefore, based on a history of magic. The main point to remember from this first text, however, is the conditional character of the offerings which are to obtain the desired result. The same precaution is found again, in the same words, towards the end of this document, where the officiant invokes the gods who preside over the departure of the waters on which irrigation depends. This ritual, therefore, is not so much a prayer as a contract, a matter-of-fact agreement, by which the gods receive in advance the remuneration promised in exchange for the services expected from them, and thus find themselves morally compelled to render them. We accordingly see at the very beginning the familiar nature of the relations between these very human gods and the priestly magicians who exploit their power.

In the 2nd ritual, *Kasuga Matsuri*, we again find this idea of the bond which must unite the offerings with the services rendered; for it is 'in consequence' of these offerings that the gods are asked to protect the sovereign and his court. We may also observe that, of the four gods worshipped in the temple of Kasuga, the first two, Take-mika-dzuchi and Futsu-nushi, were represented by magical swords (cf. *Kojiki*, tr. B. H. Chamberlain, 2nd ed., Tokyo, 1906, p. 36), and that the other two, Koyané and his wife, are connected with the famous eclipse in which that god, by his 'powerful ritual words,' helped to bring back the sun-goddess (*Kojiki*, 64).

There is the same spirit in the 3rd ritual, *Hirose Oho-imi no Matsuri*, devoted to the goddess of food.

1 Menant, *Les Parsis*, p. 116.
2 Decourdemanche, p. 214.
3 Menant, p. 108.
4 Decourdemanche, p. 215.
5 *Ib.*; Menant, p. 106.
6 A. V. W. Jackson, *Persia Past and Present*, New York, 1906, p. 378 f.; Khudayar Sheriyar, in *Sir Jamsetjee Jejeebhoy Madressa Jubilee Vol.*, Bombay, 1914, p. 299 f.
7 J. J. Modi, 'Charms or Amulets for some Diseases of the Eye,' *JASB* iii. [1894] 333–345 (reprinted in Modi's *Anthropological Papers*, Bombay [1911], pp. 43–50).
8 Modi, 'Two Iranian Incantations,' *JASB* viii. [1909] 557–572 (reprinted in *Anthropological Papers*, pp. 340–354).
9 Modi, 'Nirang-i-Jashan-i-Burzigarân' and 'An Avesta Amulet for Contracting Friendship,' *JASB* v. [1900] 398–405, 418–425 (reprinted in *Anthropological Papers*, pp. 122–139).

Her worshippers make a bargain with her; while bringing her various offerings, they promise her others if the harvest is very abundant.

The 4th ritual, *Tatsuta no Kaze no Kami no Matsuri*, is just as characteristic, and, moreover, relates its own legendary origin. For several years unknown gods have bungled all the crops, and the diviners have not been able to discover who these gods are. Then the sovereign himself 'deigns to conjure them,' and they reveal themselves to him in a dream. They are 'Heaven's Pillar's augustness and Country's Pillar's augustness,' the gods of the winds who maintain the order of the world. They require certain offerings, the founding of a temple at Tatsuta, and a liturgy, by means of which they 'will bless and ripen the things produced by the great People of the region under heaven, firstly the five sorts of grain, down to the least leaf of the herbs.' Here it is the gods who state their conditions. The people hasten to fulfil them 'without omission,' but evidently the recollection of past calamities has left some mistrust, for, when making the present offerings, they announce future gifts for the autumn: if, between now and then, the gods have deigned not to send 'bad winds and rough waters,' but to 'ripen and bless' the harvest, they will grant them the firstfruits of it. This will be their small commission.

We shall pass over the 5th, 6th, and 7th rituals, which are not so interesting, and come to the 8th, *Ohotono-Hogahi*, *i.e.* 'Luck-bringer of the Great Palace.' This title itself indicates the magical character of the document, and, in fact, we find the ritual defined in its own text in the words, *ama tsu kusushi ihahi-goto*, 'the celestial magical protective words.' It is a formula the recitation of which wards off all calamity from the palace, as an amulet would do; this is shown by the importance ascribed to the perfect regularity of the words pronounced; for, in another passage, certain 'corrector'-gods (*naho*) are begged to rectify all the omissions that they may have seen or heard in the rites or the words of the ceremony. This ceremony itself throws abundant light on the magical character of the ritual of which it was a part. We have a description of it in the *Gi-shiki* of the 9th cent. (see E. Satow, in *TASJ*, vol. ix. pt. ii. [1881] p. 192 f.). A priestly retinue, in which we distinguish chiefly the *nakatomi*, the *imibe* ('abstaining priests'), and the vestals, goes through the palace in every direction; and in different places, from the great audience-hall to the bath-room, even to the emperor's privy, the vestals sprinkle rice and *sake*, while the *imibe* hang precious stones on the four corners of the rooms visited by them. We observe here an application of the custom, called *sammai*, which consisted in scattering rice to ward off evil spirits. Whatever is the reason of this custom—whether it is simply a bait thrown to the demons or perhaps a symbolical use of grains whose shape represents one of the aspects of the generative power, of the vital force which combats illness and death—the rite in question was very frequently practised in Japanese magic. Rice was scattered inside the hut in which a woman was about to be confined; in the divination at cross-roads (*tsuji-ura*; see art. DIVINATION [Japanese]), a boundary was sometimes marked on the road, where rice was also strewn, in order to take afterwards as an oracle the words spoken by the first passer-by who crossed this bewitched line; and an old legend tells how, when the son of the gods descended from heaven to Mount Takachiho, grains of rice were thrown at random in the air to disperse the darkness from the sky. Just the same is the magical use of jewels to combat evil influences. Through the whole of Japanese mythology there is the sparkle of jewels, some of which are talismans—jewels which, at the time of an eclipse, the gods suspended to the highest branches of the sacred *cleyera*, and whose brilliance recalled the sun (*Kojiki*, 64); jewels which, in another famous story, enabled their possessor to make the tide flow or ebb at his will (*ib.* 150); jewels which even aimed at resuscitating the dead, as we shall see below. We can, therefore, easily understand the magical rôle of the red jewels which, paraded in the imperial apartments, caused the dark threats of the invisible everywhere to retire before their brightness. Still another point to be remarked is that, according to the description cited, the *imibe* recite the ritual 'in a low voice.' Polynesian sorcerers also said their prayers in a low singing, perhaps even hissing, tone, similar to the hissing, whispering voice which they attributed to their gods; and even in Japan, in the divination by the harp (*koto-ura*), one of the practices of the officiant was a complicated whistle. All this magical atmosphere which surrounds the ritual suits its text very well. It points out, first of all, the propitiatory rites which the *imibe* have accomplished in hewing down the trees intended for the construction of the palace. Then it recalls the mythical recollections which assure beforehand the efficacy of the formula recited. Then the protector-gods of the palace are entreated to ward off certain calamities, several of which—*e.g.*, serpent-bites, or the droppings of birds falling through the smoke-hole in the roof—are ritual 'offences.' Lastly, in the same way as it invokes the corrector-gods for every possible omission, the text insists on this fact—that the 'innumerable strings of luck-bringing grains' have been made by sacred jewellers 'taking care to avoid all pollution and to observe perfect cleanness.' The care in all these details shows the magical importance attached to each of the rites of the ceremony, and to the most insignificant words of the incantation.

We shall omit the 9th ritual, *Mikado Matsuri*, 'Festival of the Sublime Gates,' devoted to the gods who guard the entrance of the palace against the evil influences of the 'crooked' gods (*maga*), and come to the 10th, which is much more important. This is the 'Ritual of the Great Purification' (*Oho-harahi*). This ritual was recited by the chief of the *nakatomi*, at the end of the 6th and the 12th months, to blot out all the transgressions, both moral and ritual, that the whole people had committed in the interval. The choice of these dates is in itself significant: the summer ceremony recalls the lustrations formerly practised on the Eve of St. John in different countries of Europe, and the ceremony at the end of the year corresponds with the need of renewal experienced by the majority of men at this time, and which, in Japan, still takes the popular form of a dramatized exorcism called *tsuina*, 'expulsion of the demons.' The Great Purification included various rites; but the ritual is often mentioned as if it itself formed the whole ceremony—which proves the magical power ascribed to the words recited. This ritual begins by stating clearly that it is the emperor who 'deigns to purify and wash away' (*harahi-tamahi kiyome-tamafu*) the offences committed—from which we see that the gods who, a little later, are to be invoked to intervene really play a part inferior to that of the emperor, and act only, so to speak, at his command. The right of absolution which he exercises thus arises from the general sovereignty conferred 'respectfully' upon him by the celestial gods at the beginning of the dynasty, as the continuation of the text immediately recalls. Then follows the enumeration of ritual crimes, voluntary or not, which are to be effaced (see Revon, *Anthologie de la littérature japonaise*, Paris, 1910, p. 28 f.). We may select from this list at least two offences connected with our subject. The one is the 'planting of wands' (*kushi-sashi*) in rice-fields, probably with incantations—a process which an ancient native interpretation explains as the erecting of magic boundaries on the field of which one claims to be proprietor, though perhaps it is an example of pointed wands secretly stuck into the mud to hurt the bare feet of a neighbour, just as, among the Malays, a person in flight retarded the pursuit of his adversaries by this means. The other offence (*maji-mono seru tsumi*) is the 'performing of witchcraft,' either in a general way (cf. *Kojiki*, 326 f.) or in particular against a neighbour's animals (if we connect this passage with the expression *kemono-tafushi*, 'to kill animals,' which precedes it). In any case the Chinese character employed shows that it is a question of black magic; and that is why the *norito*, although it is itself a magical text, does not hesitate to condemn it. The ritual afterwards shows that, when these faults are committed, the great *nakatomi* has to prepare some twigs in a certain way, doubtless intended to form a sort of purificatory broom, then to recite 'the powerful ritual words of the celestial ritual' (*ama tsu norito no futo norito-goto*). The native commentators tried for a long time to find out to what mysterious incantation this passage could possibly allude, without seeing that it simply referred to the *norito* itself. This is the 'celestial' ritual which the gods revealed on high to the ancestor of the emperors, and whose 'powerful words' his descendant causes to be repeated—an expression intended to recall the intrinsic virtue of this formula. When the high priest recites it thus, according to the text of the ritual itself, the gods of heaven and earth will approach to listen, and all offences will disappear, being swept off, carried away to the ocean by the goddess of the torrents, swallowed by the goddess of the sea-currents, driven to the nether regions by the god whose breath chases before it all impurities, and there they will be seized at last by a subterranean deity who will banish them for ever. Clearly these deities are only the four wheels of the machine which the emperor sets in motion by the hand of the great *nakatomi*, the magician who knows the sacred words which even the gods obey. As for the rest, to make more certain, they bring a horse whose erect ears will incite these gods to listen attentively, just as the crowing cocks, the lighted fire—all these magical processes of the myth of the eclipse (*Kojiki*, 63-65)—would recall the sun, or as, in another account of the old Shinto annals (*Nihongi*, tr. W. G. Aston, London, 1896, i. 106), one had only to whistle to raise the wind. Then an order is given to the *urabe* ('diviners') to throw into the river the expiatory offerings, to which a mysterious sympathy unites the sins themselves, which will disappear along with the objects to which they have been attached. The ritual finishes, therefore, with a last example of the magic which has inspired the whole of it.

We may mention the 11th ritual along with this one. It is an invocation which the hereditary scholars of Yamato pronounced immediately before the ceremony of the Great Purification, and in which they presented the emperor with a silver-gilt human effigy, which would play the part of scapegoat by removing calamities from him, and a gilded sword on which he breathed before it was taken from him, with the same intention of driving away, after this magical transfer, both the sins committed and their material support.

Another ritual which is plainly magical is the 12th, the title of which, *Ho-shidzume*, 'Appeasing of the Fire,' shows that its purpose was not to worship the god of fire, but to banish him from the palace. As in the 10th ritual, the text first recalls the celestial revelation which has confided to the emperor the 'powerful words' by means of which he is superior to this god. Then it recounts the atrocious crime of this 'child with the wicked heart,' who caused his mother's death by burning her when she gave him birth (cf. *Kojiki*, 32-33); and tells how Izanami herself, cursing this son who had caused her death, came up from the nether regions to give birth to the water-goddess, the gourd, the river-plant, and the princess of the clay mountains, four divine things whose magical use against fire she immediately taught. Then, in order that this wicked god 'may deign not to be terribly lively in the palace of the august sovereign,' he is loaded with offerings, which have the effect of captivating and subduing him. This ritual was accompanied by rites which consisted mainly in the lighting of a fire by the *urabe* in the four outside corners of the precincts of the palace, with the primitive apparatus (*hi-kiri-usu*) of which a specimen may be seen in the University Museum, Oxford.

The 13th ritual, *Michi-ahe*, also aimed at employing certain gods to combat others. Those who were invoked on this occasion were three gods of roads and cross-roads, whose phallic character caused them to be looked upon as 'preventive gods' (*sahe no kami*) against the epidemics sent by the demons. The ritual begins by reminding these protector-gods, without great reverence, that their duties were inaugurated in heaven itself, where they already served the son of the gods. It then dictates to them what they must do:

'Whenever from the Root-country, the Bottom-country, there may come savage and unfriendly beings, consort not and parley not with them, but if they go below, keep watch below, if they go above, keep watch above, protecting us against pollution with a night guarding and a day guarding.'

In return they are presented with offerings, which they are to enjoy while defending the great roads 'like a multitudinous assemblage of rocks,' and, finally, the celebrant insists once more on the 'powerful words' of his formula.

The next ritual, the 14th, was devoted to the *Oho-nihe*, 'Great Offering of Food.' Before eating the new rice of the year, the ancient Japanese performed a ceremony called *Nihi-name*, 'new tasting,' which had a propitiatory purpose towards the spirit of the rice (Uga no Mi-tama). The *Oho-nihe* was a more solemn *Nihi-name*, celebrated some time after the accession of the emperors, and constituting a sort of religious coronation for them. The ritual relating to this festival contains nothing very curious in itself; but it is interesting to find that the very complicated ceremony with which it was connected included a long series of preparations, in which magic occupied a large place, just as in the essential part of the festival, when the emperor in person, surrounded by ladies of honour who repeated a mysterious formula, shared in the repast which he had just offered to the gods.

The 15th ritual is another document whose magical value appears as soon as it is placed in its psychological surroundings. It is entitled *Mi-tama shidzumuru*, which shows that its purpose was 'to appease the august spirit,' *i.e.* the spirit of the emperor. It was a case of keeping the imperial soul in his body, of recalling it if it seemed to wish to escape—in a word, of renewing magically the vital force of the sovereign for the coming year and thus prolonging his life. This is the meaning of the ceremony called *Chinkonsaï*, which was celebrated at the end of the year in the sanctuary of the priests of the court (see *Nihongi*, ii. 373). Now, the gloss identifies this festival with an ancient ceremony called *Mi-tama furishiki*, 'shaking of the august jewels,' which again plunges us into deep magic. The *Kiujiki* (ii. 2) says, in fact, that, when the sun-goddess gave the investiture to the ancestor of the emperors, she bestowed upon him ten precious treasures:

'one mirror of the offing, one mirror of the shore, one eight-hands-breadth sword, one jewel of birth, one jewel of return from death, one perfect jewel, one jewel road-returning [evil things by the road they came], one serpent-scarf, one bee-scarf, and scarf of various things.' She added: 'In case of illness, shake these treasures and repeat to them the words: *Hi, fu, mi, yo, itsu, mu, nana, ya, kokono, tari*, and shake them *yura-yura* (onomatopœia). If thou doest so the dead will certainly return to life.'

The objects enumerated by the sun-goddess are talismans, several of which occur in the most ancient Japanese mythology (see *Kojiki*, 86, 150, 324, etc.). As for the incantation, it represents simply the series of numbers from one to ten, which demonstrates its intrinsic power, independent of the meaning of the words. We know, besides, that the same incantation was recited at this festival by young sacerdotal virgins (*mi-kamu-ko*), who performed the sacred *kagura*, in imitation of the dance of Uzume in the eclipse myth (*Kojiki*, 64–65), while a *nakatomi* knotted threads, which were clearly meant to retain the imperial soul, and which he shut up in a closed vessel.

We shall omit rituals 16 to 24, which refer exclusively to the offices of the temples of Ise; it will be sufficient to mention in this group the formula of the 23rd ritual, for the installing of a princess as vestal:

'The offering of a sacred princess of the blood imperial to serve as the deities' staff, having first, according to custom, observed the rules of religious purity for three years, is to the end that thou mayst cause the Sovereign Grandchild to live peacefully and firmly as long as Heaven and Earth, the Sun and the Moon may last. I, the Great Nakatomi, holding the dread spear by the middle, with deepest awe pronounce this dedication of her by the Mikado to the end that she may serve as an august staff.'

We have here evidently a survival of the 'abstainer' of primitive Japan, whose asceticism assured on pain of death the good fortune and health of the village, in the same way as here the sacrifice of the imperial virgin is to guarantee the happiness and long life of the sovereign (cf. art. ASCETICISM [Japanese]).

The 25th ritual, of a more general interest, is entitled: *Tatari-gami wo utsushi-tatematsuru norito*, 'Ritual for the Respectful Removal of the Gods who send Plagues.' In the 13th ritual the gods of roads were made to intervene against these wicked gods; now they themselves are directly addressed. It is, therefore, a real formula of exorcism. The text begins by recalling how the supreme council of the celestial gods, wishing to 'pacify' the country before the descent of the future emperor, sent Futsu-nushi and Take-mika-dzuchi, who triumphed over the terrestrial gods and 'silenced the rocks, trees, and the least leaf of herbs likewise that had spoken.' After this warning, undisguised and all the more plain because, according to the ritual, the wicked gods know well, 'by virtue of their divinity, the things which were begun in the Plain of high heaven,' numerous gifts are made to them to win them over—and not only the usual offerings of cloths, fish, game, vegetables, rice, and *sake*, but also, in a naive form,

'as a thing to see plain in, a mirror; as things to play with, beads; as things to shoot off with, a bow and arrows; as a thing to strike and cut with, a sword; as a thing which gallops out, a horse.'

Lastly, after having thus loaded them with numerous toys and abundant dainties, which they beg them to accept 'with clear hearts, as peaceful offerings and sufficient offerings,' they earnestly ask these 'sovereign gods' to be good enough,

'without deigning to be turbulent, deigning to be fierce, and deigning to hurt, to remove out to the wide and clean places of the mountain-streams, and by virtue of their divinity to be tranquil.'

Passing in silence a less interesting ritual (the 26th), we come at length to the last document of the collection, the 27th ritual, which is called *Idzumo no kuni no miyakko no kamu yogoto*, 'The Divine Words of Good Fortune of the Chiefs of the Country of Idzumo.' These local chiefs, after having lost their civil sway, had preserved their religious power. It is they who to this day in this old province hand down the primitive fire-kindler which their legendary ancestor, the god Ame-no-hohi, had received from the sun-goddess herself, and which each chief priest of Idzumo bequeaths to his successor by the ceremony called *Hi-tsugi*, 'perpetuation of fire.' In this ritual the *miyakko* first announces that he will recite the formula, after many ritual preparations, to bring happiness to the reign of the 'visible god,' *i.e.* the sovereign. He then relates how Ame-no-hohi and, later, other celestial ambassadors were sent to earth to prepare for the descent of the son of the gods; how Ohona-mochi, the divine king of Idzumo, who achieved the 'making of the country' with the help of a stranger magician, and who was the first to found a government in this important region of the archipelago, was persuaded by the celestial envoys to abandon his temporal rule to the son of the gods; how he then divided his souls, by a curious application of the Japanese idea which allows the possible separation of the multiple souls of man, attaching his 'gentle spirit' (*nigi-tama*) to a fetish-mirror which he caused to be placed in a temple of Yamato, while his 'rough spirit' (*ara-tama*) went to rest in the great temple of Idzumo; and how at length Ame-no-hohi received from above the command to bless the sovereign henceforth, that his life might be long, healthy, and happy (cf. *Kojiki*, 54, 58, 113–124). It is while carrying out this command that the descendant of Ame-no-hohi intervenes, as he himself declares. He brings to the emperor 'divine treasures,' whose magical rôle—fortunately for us—he clearly defines. There are, first of all, sixty jewels, white, red, and green.

'These white jewels are the great august white hairs [to which your Majesty will reach]; the red jewels are the august, healthful, ruddy countenance; and the green-estuary jewels are the harmonious fitness with which your Majesty will establish far and wide, as with a broad sword-blade, his lasting great august reign over the Great-eight-island-country which he governs.'

We have here, therefore, a typical case of the action of like upon like, which is one of the essential doctrines of primitive man, and which, in the present case, attaches to the different jewels a power corresponding to their colour. The formula continues by other applications of this principle of imitative magic:

'As this white horse plants firmly his fore-hoofs and his hind-hoofs, so will the pillars of the Great Palace be set firmly on the upper rocks and frozen firmly on the lower rocks; the pricking up of his ears is a sign that your Majesty will, with ears ever more erect, rule the Under-Heaven,' etc.

It is possible that at some time these rites may have become symbols; but it is impossible not to recognize in them, especially at the beginning, practices inspired by that primitive logic which has always and everywhere constructed magic on the same universal principles.

Ancient Shinto, therefore, as it appears to us in its most authentic liturgies, is a religion in which the magical element still prevails over the religious sentiment. The rituals are essentially magical formulæ, addressed to magician gods (as is demonstrated by all their mythical exploits) by magician-priests (the *nakatomi*, the *imibe*, and the *urabe*), and encircled in magical rites. Magic is, therefore, at the base of the national cult of the Japanese, and it appears there with all the characteristics familiar to the student of comparative religion.

To finish with a vivid illustration, which, after the necessarily short descriptions given above, will show this magic in application in a typical and exact case, we shall choose as an example sorcery, as it was practised in the most ancient times. The following is the curious account of the subject given in the *Kojiki* (326 f.):

'The Deity of Idzushi [the country of the 'sacred stones'] had a daughter, whose name was the Deity Maiden-of-Idzushi. So eighty Deities wished to obtain this Maiden-of-Idzushi in marriage, but none of them could do so. Hereupon there were two Deities, brothers, of whom the elder was called the Youth-of-the-Glow-on-the-Autumn-Mountains, and the younger was named the Youth-of-the-Haze-on-the-Spring-Mountains. So the elder brother said to the younger brother: "Though I beg for the Maiden-of-Idzushi, I cannot obtain her in marriage. Wilt thou be able to obtain her?" He answered, saying: "I will easily obtain her." Then the elder brother said: "If thou shalt obtain this maiden, I will take off my upper and lower garments, and distil liquor in a jar of my own height, and prepare all the things of the mountains and of the rivers, in payment of the wager." Then the younger brother told his mother everything that the elder brother had said. Forthwith the mother, having taken wistaria-fibre, wove and sewed in the space of a single night an upper garment and trousers, and also socks and boots, and likewise made a bow and arrows, and clothed him in this upper garment, trousers, etc., made him take the bow and arrows, and sent him to the maiden's house, where both his apparel and the bow and arrows all turned into wistaria-blossoms. Thereupon the Youth-of-the-Haze-on-the-Spring-Mountains hung up the bow and arrows in the maiden's privy. Then, when the Maiden-of-Idzushi, thinking the blossoms strange, brought them, he followed behind the maiden into the house, and forthwith wedded her. So she gave birth to one child. Then he spoke to his elder brother, saying: "I have obtained the Maiden-of-Idzushi." Thereupon the elder brother, vexed that the younger brother should have wedded her, did not pay the things he had wagered. Then when the younger brother complained to his mother, his august parent replied, saying: "During my august life the Deities indeed are to be well imitated; it must be because he imitates mortal men that he does not pay those things." Forthwith, in her anger with her elder child, she took a one-jointed bamboo from an island in the River Idzushi, and made a coarse basket with eight holes, and took stones from the river, and mixing them with brine [*shiho*, in the sense of 'hard salt'], wrapped them in the leaves of the bamboo and caused this curse (*tokohi*) to be spoken [by her younger son]: "Like unto the becoming green of these bamboo-leaves, do thou become green and wither! Again, like unto the flowing and ebbing of this brine [again the word *shiho*, but here with the meaning of 'sea-water'], do thou flow and ebb! Again, like unto the sinking of these stones, do thou sink and be prostrate!" Having caused this curse to be spoken, she placed the basket over the smoke [apparently on the hearth of the elder son]. Therefore the elder brother dried up, withered, sickened, and lay prostrate for the space of eight years. So on the elder brother entreating his august parent with lamentations and tears, she forthwith caused the curse to be reversed. Thereupon his body was pacified. This is the origin of the term "a divine wager-payment."'

In this text we have a case of original sorcery, founded on sympathetic magic (a conception so well expressed by the Japanese word for 'magic,' *majinahi*, which conveys the idea of 'to mix'), but before the time when the progress of the arts and foreign influences could have given the idea of exercising sorceries on the effigy of an enemy. (For this later development see, *e.g.*, the popular ballad of Shuntoku Maru, in *TASJ*, vol. xxii. pt. iii. [1894] pp. 294–308.) We are, therefore, in the presence of a thoroughly Japanese rite, whose ancient character is shown by its very obscurity, and which cannot be understood unless it is replaced in the midst of the primitive beliefs from which it came. First of all, the mother provides herself with the mysterious bamboo on which the life of her elder son is to depend. Purposely she does not gather it in any chance place; she takes it from an island—which already connects that object with the aquatic element. With this bamboo she weaves a basket, in which she takes care to leave eight holes, which will be the eight openings by which eight years of misfortune are to enter for the victim. In this basket she places river-pebbles, which, even more than the bamboo, come from the water. But it is from fresh water that they have come; and the nature of the rite demands that they should assume a maritime character. They are, therefore, put among brine; by this union the assimilation is made, and the sorcery can be accomplished. The only thing that remains to be done is to pronounce the formula whose powerful words will act on all these things. The victim will wither like the leaves of bamboo, in the same way as, in another legend (*Kojiki*, 238), the magical imprecation (*ukebi*) of a chief had made a great oak-tree suddenly decay; or, better still, in the same way as, by the effect of a general malediction, man, formerly immortal, was condemned to die as the flowers of the cherry-tree fade (*Kojiki*, 140–142). Then, as the high water falls back, the guilty one will be abased. Lastly, he will be seen foundering as a stone sinks when disappearing under the waves. This curse pronounced, the basket of perdition is placed in the smoke of the hearth; the green leaves become black; the threat is executed. Yet in the end the mother's heart hears the repentance of her son. She reverses the curse, *i.e.*, the terrible magical formula is this time pronounced backwards (cf. *Kojiki*, 238), and immediately the body of the young man is 'pacified'; he returns to health, to life.

In this sorcery the most curious point is that which is connected with the sea element. The fate of the young man is, in fact, connected with the ebbing of the tide. We have here an interesting illustration, among the insular Japanese, of the belief so wide-spread among primitive races, according to which a mysterious harmony exists between the life of man and the flowing and ebbing of the sea. In this belief, it is when the sea is flowing in that one is born, becomes strong, prospers; it is when it is ebbing that one loses his energy, falls ill, and dies. The Japanese sorceress, the depositary of primitive traditions, is well aware of this secret agreement. She knows that, even far from the seashore, an artificial connexion can be formed between these two manifestations of a single force. Consequently she brings into connexion with the salt element these river-pebbles, into which the consecrated words will bring the very existence of her son; and the cursed one is immediately delivered up to the enchantment of the waters; he becomes like a pebble on the beach, the tide carries him away, drags him towards the brightnesses of life, then lets him fall back and roll in darkness and death. This story of witchcraft has, therefore, given us at one and the same time a typical case of Japanese magic and a new proof of the strange unity observable even in the most curious beliefs of humanity in general.

LITERATURE.—This has been cited in the article.

M. REVON.

MAGIC (Jewish). —The attitude assumed by Judaism towards everything not sanctioned by its own monotheistic teaching has also affected the practice which may be called 'magic,' and it thus becomes necessary, first of all, to obtain as clear a definition as documents of the OT and Jewish tradition allow as to what is to be understood by the term.

It must at once be pointed out that divination and charms (see DIVINATION [Jewish] and CHARMS AND AMULETS [Jewish]) are not part of Jewish magic, which, properly speaking, corresponds most closely to 'witchcraft.' The difference between witchcraft and other forms of magic is that the magician has nothing whatsoever to do with forecasting the future or with preventing any occurrence that is sure to happen in the ordinary course of nature. He has nothing to do primarily with spells or incantations, nor is the writing of any formula an indispensable condition for magic. Magic can only be 'performed'; no magic is effective unless it is the result of some 'operation'; the magician must 'act' in one way or another in order to accomplish his purpose; and herein lies the profound difference between magic and any other form of superstition—preventing and altering the regular operations of nature. The magician is not helping things to fruition; on the contrary, he seeks to subvert the regular course of events. He is expected, if possible, to obscure the sun and moon, to bring the dead to life, to change human beings into animal shapes or *vice versa*; he is to produce fruit in winter, and, in fact, to do everything that is contrary to the regular laws of nature. The magician will kill, he will create strife—his activity will always be an evil one. He is not expected to do good; he will be the agent for vengeance, hatred, and everything that makes for strife, death, and destruction. But he cannot carry out his intention without an 'operation'; he must 'do' something in order to bring about the desired result. Unlike the diviner, who is guided by certain signs and omens, which he is able to understand and combine, so that he can read the future in the events of the present, and unlike the charmer, who can only undo the magician's evil work by certain spells, songs, formulæ, and written amulets, the magician must perform a whole set of ceremonies quite independent of signs, omens, and spells. It is a new definition that is here offered, which, by circumscribing much more narrowly the field of superstition, is an endeavour to give to magic its real meaning. The magician's work, again, is not expected to be of a permanent character; it is temporary, and it can be undone by other means, or by other magicians who know the secret of the action and the means by which it has been achieved. In order, then, to disturb the laws of nature, to transform existing things, to shape and mould new creatures, the magician requires the help of superhuman powers. This is the very root and basis of magical art; the magician must be able to command the services of spiritual powers—demons, gods, or ghosts—malignant in their disposition and willing to do mischief.

Jewish magic presupposes the existence of such spirits, and occupies the borderland between orthodoxy and heresy, between Judaism and paganism. It is an art that lives in the twilight between truth and falsehood; and the line of demarcation shifts according to the change of theological views in the course of development and transition. It depends also upon the nature of those spirits and upon the theological attitude towards them—whether they are considered as forces opposed to God or as mere negative forces that are also creatures of God and yet unwilling, by their own innate wickedness, to do good. The conception of a rebellious angel who has been cast down from the heavenly heights because of his arrogance and insubordination does not enter into the sphere of Jewish magic, nor, with rare exceptions, have the gods of other nations become evil spirits subservient to the wish of the magician and willing to do his behest.

The Hebrew term for 'magic' is *keshef*, which, like all technical expressions connected with superstition, is of obscure origin; though many attempts have been made to elucidate its primitive meaning, not one has yet proved satisfactory. The primitive meaning of *keshef*, in the view of the present writer, is apparently 'hidden,' 'obscure,' 'a thing done in a secret manner,' which is the very essence of magic. The performance is a secret one, and even those who are allowed to witness it are slow to understand its meaning. The word *keshef*, with its various derivatives, occurs twelve times in the Bible. It is to be noted that all the references in the Pentateuch are to Egypt, while of the references in the Prophetical writings some are to Assyria as well as to Palestine itself. In 2 Ch 33^{6} Manasseh is described as having practised witchcraft as well as other forbidden things (cf. also Mal 3^{5}); the wizards of Egypt are mentioned in Ex 7^{11} 22^{18}; in Babylon there is only one allusion to them, in Dn 2^{2}.

The LXX translates *keshef* by φάρμακον, which does not mean 'poison,' but, as in later Greek, a 'spell' cast by a magician. *Keshef* has remained the technical term in Hebrew literature. Witchcraft is called *kishshūf* in the Mishna and Talmud, and no words have been more widely used, and yet with a very definite meaning attached to them, than *kishshūf* and *m*ᵉ*khashshēf*, nor is there any doubt that the real meaning of this 'magic' is exactly witchcraft. It is clearly stated (*Sanh.* vii. 4, 11) that only he is to be called a magician who produces a real act, but not the man who produces an optical illusion, a kind of jugglery.

The fact that witchcraft is mentioned in connexion with Egypt (exclusively, in the Pentateuch, and occasionally, in other passages in the Bible) shows the probable source of the magical art known and practised in Bible times. The Egyptian *m*ᵉ*khashsh*ᵉ*fīm* in Ex 7^{11} 22^{18} perform precisely the acts defined above as the work of the magicians; they endeavour to change the order of nature. No details are given regarding the operation of the magician in the Bible; but from Is 47$^{9.12}$, Mic 5^{12}, Mal 3^{5}, Nah 3^{4}, Jer 27^{9}, and 2 K 9^{22} it is clear that, in the eyes of the prophets, the work of sorcery was tantamount to idolatry and to lewdness, possibly through the performance of some action by the magician. That some of the witches performed such acts in a state of absolute nakedness is an attested fact throughout the history of magic, and it is possible that the prophets had this in view when in speaking of witches they placed them on the same plane as harlots. It is noteworthy that the witch, and not the wizard, is mentioned in Ex 22^{18}, Dt 18^{10}. The sin of the *m*ᵉ*khashshēfāh* must have been so heinous that the law punished it with death. Witchcraft must, therefore, have been connected with idolatry (Mic 5$^{11f.}$); it was characterized as an 'abomination' (Dt 18^{10}), and was also described as *z*ᵉ*nūnīm*, 'lewdness' (Nah 3^{4}, 2 K 9^{22}).

The scanty references in the OT, which show that the practice could not have been wide-spread in Bible times, become clear in the light of the tradition of Rabbinical literature. We learn to know through what powers the magicians were able to carry on their operations; the spirits become, as it were, more materialized.

The existence of demons is not denied; on the contrary, they are universally acknowledged, possibly through the influence of Babylon, and the Jewish belief of the period endeavours to account for them in a world created by God (see DEMONS AND SPIRITS [Hebrew] and DEMONS AND SPIRITS [Jewish]).

According to the *Pirḳē Abhôth*, v. 9 (cf. C. Taylor, *Sayings of the Jewish Fathers*², Cambridge, 1897, *ad loc.*) and *Gen. Rab.* 7, *mazzīkīm* were created by God Himself at the close of the sixth day; but, as the Sabbath supervened before their creation had been completed, they remained half human, half spirit. They are not fallen angels, nor are they ancient heathen gods, but intermediate between angel and man, and mostly of an evil inclination.

How they are to be used—*i.e.* the art of witchcraft—has been taught to man by two angels who have forfeited all rights to the bliss of heaven. According to a legend found in the *Book of Enoch*, the *Chronicles of Jerahmeel* (tr. M. Gaster, London, 1899), and other Jewish Haggadic collections, the two angels Uzza and Azael, who showed their discontent at the creation of Adam, and afterwards were sent by God, at their own request, to see whether they could withstand temptation, both fell in love with a woman and were punished by God. One of them hangs head downwards from heaven, and the other is chained behind the dark mountains; it was the latter who taught women the arts of witchcraft and cosmetics (*Jerahmeel*, ch.

25, and notes, p. lxxiii).[1] The Kenites, the descendants of Cain, were the pupils of these angels, and, according to the *Book of Jubilees*, corrupted the descendants of Seth and brought about the Flood. According to another tradition, the *mazzîḳîm* and *shēdhîm* were the children of Adam and Lîlîth, the *shēdhāh* who leads the procession of *shēdhîm*, and who, during the one hundred years that Adam was separated from Eve, consorted with him (*Zôhār*, i. 176; cf. *ERE* iv. 614[a]). Lîlîth plays a great rôle in magical literature; she later becomes the demon who kills infants at birth and, together with her companions, is constantly mentioned in Aramaic inscriptions on magical bowls from Assyria and Babylon (see below). The demons are both male and female, and they also endeavour to consort with human beings—a conception from which arises the belief in *incubi* and *succubæ*—and it is through these demons that the magician is believed to be able to carry on his work.

In apocryphal and legendary literature we get a clearer glimpse of the beliefs prevalent among the Jews concerning magic and magical operations. Faith in demons and demoniacal powers seems to have been established by that time; at any rate, these beliefs are far more in evidence, and do not seem to be seriously contested. The character of these spiritual potencies is somewhat indefinite, except in the *Book of Enoch*, where, as we have seen, angels who had fallen in love with human women use such powers as instruments for deception and sorcery. In the book of Tobit another side of this belief is shown in which we may begin to see a differentiation between a white magic, or a magic tolerated by Judaism, and that kind of magic which ranked as pure paganism, and which probably would fall under the category of the witchcraft for which the death penalty was prescribed by law. Here we find the angel Raphael himself helping, by means of fumigation, to counteract the work of a demon who, falling in love with Sarah, had become an *incubus*, and would, therefore, kill any one who intended to approach her. The spirit thus exorcized was Asmodæus, who is recognized in the later demoniacal hierarchy as the king of the evil powers.[2] The position of Beliar, or Belial (the name given also in Samaritan tradition to the evil spirit who deceived Eve), is, in the *Ascension of Isaiah* and other apocryphal writings, not so clearly defined, but in any case he is an evil spirit approximating to the character of Satan in the book of Job (cf. BELIAL, BELIAR).

To obtain the assistance and help of these powers, certain means had to be devised: gifts or sacrifices were made in order to win them over and gain control over them. Maimonides,[3] in interpreting Dt 32[17], 'they sacrificed to *shēdhîm*,' says that the gift most acceptable to the evil spirits was blood, and that their willing help was obtained by giving them the blood of the sacrifice as food; the magician must partake of the blood, thus sharing the food of the evil spirits, so as to become their associate. To this sacrifice, which was not limited to the shedding and partaking of blood, other ceremonies had to be added, all best understood as sacrifices; just as the fumigation or burning of incense in the temple is an offering to God, so fumigation and the burning of incense must be understood primarily as gifts very acceptable to the spirits, who are not sufficiently materialized to enjoy material food (cf. the Biblical parallelism of magic with idolatry, noted above). In addition there was the lighting of candles and the use of a knife with a black handle which is mentioned by Rashi to *Sanh.* 101*a*, and which can be understood only as a symbolical sacrificial knife. Philtres must be served in glass bowls (*Bābhā meṣîʿā*, 2*a*). Fasting and other ceremonies are all intended to propitiate the evil spirit, and this is what made magic and magical operations objectionable to Jews and an 'abomination' to Judaism. Yet Rabbis made allowance for weaknesses of human nature and, except on rare occasions, avoided rigorous measures against witchcraft. But when necessary they did not shrink from them. During the first centuries of the Christian era the whole of what might be termed the civilized world—Egypt, Babylon, Greece, and Rome—stood under the absolute sway of belief in evil spirits. It was partly Babylonian tradition that ascribed every form of evil and harm to the action of the *shēdhîm* and *mazzîḳîm* and produced a large literature of invocations and magical formulæ for harm and for protection, and partly the Egyptian tradition of magical operations and ceremonies of a mystical and magical character. During Talmudic times it seems to have been believed that some *shēdhîm* were harmless, and, though they were looked upon as evilly inclined and malignant, a friendly intercourse with them does not appear to have been considered contrary to Jewish law. Thus a Rabbi once assisted in a dispute between two *shēdhîm*, in which one who had taken unlawful possession of a place belonging to the other was vanquished and a few drops of blood were found floating on the well where they dwelt (*Levit. Rab.* 24); but, on the other hand, Abaya saw a seven-headed monster coming out of a well and killed it.[1] The attitude of the Rabbis was justifiable so long as it did not lead to real idolatry.

The belief in the power of the Ineffable Name (see CHARMS AND AMULETS [Jewish], NAMES [Jewish]) was as old as any belief in witchcraft. As soon as the existence of evil spirits could not be denied, they also were given mysterious names, and it was held that, the moment the magician possessed the secret of their names, he could win their assistance, provided it was not contrary to the will of God. Legend says (*Pal. Targ.* to Gn 25[1ff.]) that among the first who obtained mastery over these demons and the knowledge how to deal with them for their own purposes were the children of Abraham by his wife Keturah, to whom he had imparted the knowledge of the mystical names of the demons (the names of the unclean). It was through the names of these evil spirits that 'the prophet of the heathen,' as Balaam is called, was able to perform his witchcraft and was expected to harm the Israelites. He was considered to be the greatest magician of old, and, according to *Pal. Targ.* to Nu 25[1], he taught the daughters of Moab to practise sorcery and witchcraft and thus entice the young men to idolatry and immorality, which brought the plague upon Israel. It is also said that Balaam tried to escape by flying in the air, but Phinehas, through the Holy Name, was able to fly higher and smite him. The magicians in Egypt who unsuccessfully withstood Moses were Jannes and Jambres (so already in *Pal. Targ.* to Ex 1), well known in apocryphal literature as the great magicians at the court of Pharaoh (cf. also 2 Ti 3[8]). According to the Samaritan *Apocrypha of Moses*, the sorcerer who predicted the birth of Moses was a certain Palti. The Samaritans trace the origin of sorcery and witchcraft to the 'Book of Signs' given to Adam before he left Paradise; but in Jewish and Christian

[1] For an Egyptian parallel to this legend ascribing the origin of magical art to the teaching of an angel who had fallen in love with a woman see M. Berthelot, *Collection des anciens alchimistes grecs*, Paris, 1887-88, i. 31.

[2] Later the host of *shēdhîm* had other rulers and princes besides Asmodæus (cf. Jerus. *Sheḳ.* v. 49*b*, *Gen. Rab.* 20, *Levit. Rab.* 5, and later Midrashic compilations).

[3] *Guide*, iii. 56.

[1] This is one of the earliest mentions of a seven-headed dragon, which plays such an important rôle in fairy-tales.

apocryphal literature it is the 'Book of Adam,' or the 'Book of Rāzîēl,' a title afterwards given to a handbook of practical *ḳabbālā* full of such mystical names of angels, rulers, princes, stars, planets, and sublunar worlds. Still less could the Rabbis object to belief in power over these demons when they remembered that even the Temple in Jerusalem was said to have been built by Solomon with the assistance of the *shēdhîm*—a legend which rests on a peculiar interpretation of the word *shiddāh*, occurring in Ec 2[8]. So firm was the later belief in Solomon's power over the *shēdhîm*—and whatever was allowed to Solomon could not be refused to any other Jew—that Josephus has preserved to us (*Ant.* VIII. ii. 5) the tradition of Eleazar, who came before the Roman emperor Vespasian, and was able to drive away an evil spirit by using the ring of Solomon and certain herbs.

In the Solomonic cycle Asmodæus is mentioned as their king, and Lîlîth, Mahalat, and Agaron are also described later as leaders of evil spirits, while even a demon Meridianus has been evolved out of Ps 91[6]. Once the grouping of spirits was conceded, numbers came from various quarters to swell the host. Among these we find reference, in the Talmud, to the princes or rulers over oil and eggs,[1] rulers over the thumb or, rather, thumbnail, and over crystal—all shining objects used, no doubt, for crystal-gazing (*q.v.*). It was a time of syncretism, in which everything that helped either to do or to avert evil was eagerly sought by the credulous. The work of the magician was wrapped in obscurity; his books were kept secret, and his operations were accessible only to the adept, whence much of the practical operation is almost lost to us. What has survived is, with few exceptions, the accompanying formulæ by which these various spirits and invisible powers were invoked or subdued either for evil, as in most cases, or for good. In the Greek magical papyri some fragments of the formulæ are extant, but very little of the operations. Much more seems to have been preserved in the Hebrew *Sword of Moses* (ed. and tr. Gaster, *JRAS*, 1896, pp. 149-198), of extreme antiquity, and in some MSS of practical *ḳabbālā*, or practical occultism, mostly in the possession of the present writer (one of the prescriptions in these is given below). A large number of bowls, many of them dating from the first centuries of the Christian era, have been found in Babylonia with Hebrew and Syriac inscriptions, these vessels being used by the ancient magicians for the purpose of making the incantation or conjuration written on them effective. The inscriptions in question contain whole lists of demons and spirits who are in the service of the magician or whose power he is expected to check. A large number of them have been published by J. A. Montgomery (*Aramaic Incantation Texts from Nippur*, Philadelphia, 1913), and one (no. 32) may here be reproduced as showing the state of mind and the beliefs of the people. The translation is independent and differs somewhat from that given by Montgomery.

'This bowl is prepared for the sealing of the house and the wife and the children of Dīnōi, son of Ispandarmēd, that the Terrifier (fright) and evil Dreams may depart from him. The bowl I lifted up and I have watered (drained) it, an operation like that which was established by Rab Joshua bar Peraḥyah, who wrote against them—a ban against all Demons and Devils and Satans and Lîlîths and curses which are in the house of Dīnōi, son of Ispandarmēd. Again: he wrote against them a ban which is for all time, in the name of ATMDG, Atātōt Atōt, within T, Atōt Atōt, the name a scroll within a scroll. Through which are subjected heaven and earth and the mountains; and through which the heights are raised (lifted) up; and through which are fettered the magician, Demons and Devils and Satans and Lîlîths and curses; and through which he passed over from this world and climbed above you to the height (of heaven) and learned all counter-charms for hurt and for healing to bring you forth from the house of Dīnōi, son of Ispandarmēd, and from everything that belongs to him. I have dismissed you by the ban, and it is bound and sealed and countersealed, even as ancient lines (of writing) which do not fail and men of old who were not surrounded (tied). . . . Again: bound and sealed and countersealed is this ban in the name of YHYHYHYHYH, YHYH, YHYH, A. (Amen), Amen, Amen, Selah.

Sealed and protected are the house and dwelling of Dīnōi, son of Ispandarmēd, from the Terrifier (fright) and evil Dreams and the Curse. And sealed and protected be [his wife and son] from the Terrifier and evil Dreams and Curses and Vows and . . . Hallela. Amen.'

This inscription has been selected because it contains the name of the famous Joshua (Jesus) b. Peraḥyah who was so important a figure in the time of John Hyrcanus at the end of the 2nd cent. B.C. He was the teacher and friend of R. Simeon b. Sheṭaḥ, whose dealings with the witches of Ashkelon are mentioned below. In the apocryphal stories about Jesus a noteworthy part is assigned to this Joshua b. Peraḥyah, who had fled to Egypt, where he was believed to have learned the art both of working and of combating magic.

The Jerus. *Talm.* (*Sanh.* vii. 19, fol. 25*d*) tells a curious legend concerning this same R. Joshua, who is made the contemporary of R. Eleazar and R. Gamaliel. These three came to a place where they found a young man whose manhood had been taken away by a witch. R. Joshua sowed flax seeds on the table, and they sprouted in an instant and grew up. Out of the midst a woman with dishevelled hair suddenly appeared—the witch. R. Joshua seized her and ordered her to loosen the spell, but she refused, whereupon he threatened to divulge her name. She then answered that she could not undo the spell, because the things had been thrown into the sea. R. Joshua then ordered the angel of the sea to throw them up, and thus the young man was restored to health, and later became the father of R. Judah b. Bethera.

In the light of the Babylonian bowls, it is not improbable that this is a story of Joshua b. Peraḥyah, but, as nothing was known of his magical powers, it was transferred later to another Rabbi also named Joshua.

The Rabbis had no doubt as to the origin of witchcraft: it came from Egypt. According to *Ḳiddūshîn*, 49*b*, ten measures of witchcraft have come down into the world, nine of which have gone to Egypt, while one has spread throughout the rest of the world. The Talmud names one or two witches who are said to have practised in Jerusalem, among them being Yôḥnā, the daughter of Reṭîbî (*Sôṭāh*, 22*a*), famous as a witch affecting childbirth.

One day, whilst she was assisting a woman in travail, a neighbour came into her house. Hearing a noise in a vessel like that of a child in the womb, she lifted the cover; the noise ceased, and the woman was easily delivered. Hence it was recognized that Yôḥnā was a witch.[1]

Evidence of the Egyptian origin of witchcraft and of its purely temporary character—as is shown by the fact that, if put to the proper test, it vanishes—is seen in the Talmudic story of Ze'ērî.

He bought an ass in Alexandria, but, when he attempted to cross the river on it, it turned into a plank the instant it touched the stream, for no witchcraft can withstand running water. All who saw him laughed at his discomfiture, but he recovered the money which he had paid for the ass. Another Rabbi, Jannai, being offered a drink of water, poured some of the liquid on the ground, whereupon the rest turned into scorpions. He then compelled the witch to drink and she was transformed into an ass, on which he rode into the market. There another witch, recognizing her, broke the spell, and the Rabbi was then seen to have the witch for his steed (*Sanh.* 67*b*).

As soon as magical operations came to be regarded as idolatry, sterner measures were taken, one of the foremost opponents of magic being R. Simeon b. Sheṭah (*Sanh.* 44*b*, and Rashi, *ad loc.*), who lived in the time of King Jannæus and Queen Alexandra (1st cent. B.C.). He went to Ashkelon, where, with the assistance of eighty pupils, he caught eighty witches actually practising their magic arts, and he hanged them all in one day.

[1] The rulers of the egg must mean those who obtained an insight into the work of the spirits or mastery over them through looking intently into the yolk of an opened egg (*Sanh.* 67*b*).

[1] This idea of a witch who holds the soul, or the eyes, or the heart in close imprisonment in certain vessels which, when broken (the contents being restored to the owner), restore life, health, and sight occurs frequently in fairy-tales and is derived from Egyptian tradition.

The details are of much interest, for they show a complete continuity of practice from that day onward. The women procured food and drink in a miraculous manner, and in the midst of their feasting did not disdain to invite the Rabbi's pupils to share in their banquet. Each of the young men then took one of the witches in his arms and lifted her from the ground, whereby she lost her magical power, the reason given for this procedure being that no harm could befall a witch as long as she touched the earth.

It was, however, found necessary to bring some order into the chaos of magic, for the Rabbis could not transgress a clear prescription of the Bible, and a sin which was punished with death could not be passed over lightly. On the other hand, what was a deadly sin for the followers of one creed might be tolerated by those following another; a heathen might be allowed to be a magician and not fall under the ban of the Law, while a Jew was strictly forbidden to follow such practices, and, *vice versa*, a Jew might be considered a magician by the followers of another creed. To a Jew all heathen practices and even religious ceremonies might be magic, and the Rabbis, therefore, divided magic into three categories. First, the death penalty by stoning (Lv 20^{27}) was inflicted only on those who practised magic and performed magical operations. The second class consisted of those who merely acted as jugglers or produced optical illusions, and who were warned not to indulge in such practices, but were not punished. A third type of magic was that by which operations and identical results obtained by the Holy Name were not only tolerated, but actually sanctioned. A difference was thus made between the use of the names of the unclean spirits (magic) and the names of the clean ones (*ḳabbālā*). By the former are meant demons and spirits, by the latter angelic powers. At the same time mastery over demoniacal beings might be obtained through the mediation of heavenly powers.

Thus, when R. Simeon b. Yoḥai and other sages went to Rome, they caused a demon, ben Teמalîôn, to enter the emperor's daughter; and, when they arrived at the city, they were able to cure her by expelling the spirit (briefly told in *Meʿilāh*, fol. 17, *a–b*, enlarged form in A. Jellinek, *Bēt ha-Midrasch*, Vienna, 1853–78, vi. 128–130; also Rashi, *ad loc.*; Gaster, *Exempla of the Rabbis*, London, 1896, no. 19; M. Seligsohn, in *JE* xi. 360 f.).

Thus was established a compromise which was facilitated by the manifold meanings attached to the word *rūaḥ*, 'spirit,' used even in the Bible for both a good and an evil spirit coming forth from the Lord, possessing man and departing from him. So strong was the belief in the harm which such evil spirits could produce that, as far back as the time of the Mishna, a light might be extinguished on the Sabbath if an evil spirit was feared (*Mishn. Shab.* ii. 5); and in the Bible *rūaḥ* is already occasionally applied to evil spirits, demons, and devils (Jg 9^{23}, 1 S $16^{14-16.\ 23}$ 18^{10}, 1 K $22^{22f.}$, Zec 13^{2}).

Despite the stern attitude taken by the Rabbis, magic flourished among the Jews, for the adepts of this science often deluded themselves as to the true character of their art. Not only did they continue their forbidden practices and their operations for evoking spirits and subduing demons, but in their formulæ they introduced names of spirits and demons gathered from every form of warring creed and ancient tradition, and gods and spirits long dead and forgotten were retained in magical practices and invocations. Gnostic, Babylonian, and Egyptian names, and even such appellations as Soter, Alpha, Omega, and Evangelion are found side by side with Ṣebhāôth and Shaddai. Actual specimens of these conjurations are very rare, for the magician would never disclose his mode of operation, but the following example (taken from the present writer's Cod. no. 443, fol. 13*b*) is characteristic of the peculiar mixture of names and powers used by the magician.

'And they are called "the princes of bdellium." Take bdellium and write upon it with olive oil[1] 'AUNGIL (or) AUNGILEIA;[2] and take a boy seven years old and anoint his hand from the top of the thumb to the end of the finger; and put the bdellium into his hand in the anointed place and seize his hand; and you shall sit upon a three-legged stool and put the boy between your loins so that his ear shall be against your mouth and you shall turn your face towards the sun and say in his ear: "Aungil, I adjure thee in the name of the Lord God, God of Truth, God, Keeper of the Hosts, ALPHA, AIDU,[3] that thou shalt send from thee three angels." Then the boy will see (a figure) like (that of) a man; and say (the charm) twice more, and he will see two (figures); and the boy shall say unto them: "Your coming be in peace!" And then tell the boy to ask of them that which you wish. And if they will not answer him, the boy shall adjure them, and say: "KASPAR, KELEI, 'EMAR (or) BLEITEISAR,[4] the master and I adjure (you) with a second adjuration that you tell me that thing or who has committed that theft." And know that he who wishes to do this must do it on a clear, cloudless day, and in winter time at mid-day.'

The most remarkable product of this type of syncretism is the *Sēfer Maftēaḥ Shlᵉômôh* ('Key of Solomon'), a complete facsimile of which has been edited by H. Gollancz (Oxford, 1914).

No legal command could eradicate so deep-seated a belief as that in magic and magician, and, though it is true that it was forbidden, almost on pain of death, to become a pupil of a magician (*amgūshî*) (*Shab.* 75*b*), yet his help might be invoked to break a spell in the case of a man who had become seriously ill through witchcraft. This was done almost to modern times (*Ṭūr, Yôreh dēʿāh*, § 179, and the commentary of R. Joseph Ḳaro [see QARO, JOSEPH], *ad loc.*).

Belief in magic received an additional impetus through the mysterious teachings of the *Zôhār*, which, from the 14th cent., held almost unbroken sway over the mind of the majority of the Jews. In it the Talmudic legends concerning the existence and activity of the *shēdhîm* are repeated and amplified, and a hierarchy of demons was established corresponding to the heavenly hierarchy. Halls of the nether world and their demon rulers are fully described in the *Zôhār* (Ex. 246*b*–268*a*) and exorcism of the *shēdh* or any evil spirit was recognized as within the power of every man fully versed in mystical lore and in the mystical names of God. Many a tale is told of such expulsion of demons by holy and pious men, such as Heliodorus in Catania in the 8th cent. (L. Zunz, *Zur Gesch. und Lit.*, Berlin, 1845, p. 486); and others are mentioned by Manasseh in his *Nishmat Ḥayîm* (Amsterdam, 1652), bk. iii., which is full of information concerning belief in demons and the power of the pious to master them and use them for their own purpose. Even the scholarly and learned Rabbis of the 17th cent. clung to the belief, while in the legendary lore of the Middle Ages such men as Maimonides (*q.v.*), Ibn Ezra (*q.v.*), R. Judah the Pious, Rashi, and Naḥmanides (*q.v.*) were all credited with magical powers, and many a legend is told of their operations. Rabbi Jehiel of Paris has even found a place in Victor Hugo's *Notre Dame de Paris* as a wonder-working Rabbi, and no less famous was R. Loeb of Prague (17th cent.), who was regarded as a great magician and was credited with having a clay famulus that was able to perform wonderful deeds, since it had under its tongue a plate on which a mysterious name had been engraved. The Baʿal Shēm († 1760), who founded the sect of the Ḥasîdhîm, had many encounters with the *shēdhîm*, as described in his biography (*Shibḥē Baʿal Shem Ṭob*, Berdichev, 1815 ff.), and a collection of miraculous deeds performed by him and after him by wonder-working Rabbis of the Ḥasîdhîm as detailed in the *Kᵉhal Ḥasîdhîm* (Lemberg, 1864); nor should we forget the legendary contest, de-

[1] S. Daiches, *Bab. Oil Magic in the Talmud and in the Later Jewish Literature*, London, 1913.

[2] Εὐαγγέλιον.

[3] Ὤμεγα (?).

[4] The three kings from the East, Kaspar, Melchior, and Baltazar—a curious invocation in the mouth of a Jewish magician. It is evident, from the corrupted form of the names, that the copyist did not understand what he was writing.

scribed in an anonymous chapbook, between a bishop magician and a red Jew, who had come from beyond the waters of the mysterious river Sambaṭyôn, for upon the issue of the struggle depended the life of the Jewish communities in Germany. To this very day the Jews in Syria perform such magical operations as fumigation, libations, and offerings of oil, bread, and lighted candles, which are put in the four corners of an empty house to propitiate the *shēdhîm* before the people venture to enter the dwelling and make the proper dedication. Gradually, however, the belief in the *shēdhîm* is waning, and the literature of practical *ḳabbālā* is slowly but steadily being discarded. Indeed, much of Jewish magic to-day is, in reality, little more than a concession to ignorance. When a Rabbi was asked why the aid of a magician may be invoked in case of serious illness, he replied, according to Joseph Ḳaro (commentary on *Tūr, Yôreh Dēʿāh*, ch. 179), that, although there was no basis of fact for the procedure, such an appeal might soothe and comfort the patient, and therefore he saw no objection to it. This is practically the answer which is given in modern times when the people are asked why they continue to believe in the harm done by demons, and in magical operations intended to propitiate them and to obtain relief and safety. It is merely a temporary comfort to those who are loath to give up old beliefs which are now recognized as vain imaginations.

LITERATURE.—In addition to the books mentioned in the text see the Literature at artt. CHARMS AND AMULETS (Jewish), DIVINATION (Jewish), and BIRTH (Jewish). M. GASTER.

MAGIC (Slavic).—The Slavic countries are a peculiarly rich field for the study of folk-lore, as they were not Christianized until the 10th cent., remained isolated from Western influences, and have conserved their written traditions.

On the vast uplands of the northern steppes man's relations to nature were characteristic. The Greeks, in their narrow, diversified, hilly country, developed a corresponding mythology, varied and beautiful; the modern Western European, a city-dweller, turns to nature in a romantic manner, semi-religiously idolizing what is to him unwonted and fresh. But to the Slav peasant nature was business, his everyday surrounding, beside which nothing else existed. He was rather unimaginative and quite ignorant. Whilst the Norsemen and the Greeks created mythologies out of natural phenomena, the Slav, in the drear monotony of his plains, fell into neither the deep religious fatalism of the Scandinavians nor the bright imagery of the Greeks; he simply saw that the sun ripened and the sun scorched; that the earth was moist and fertile or parched and frozen; that he was environed by unknown powers to be obeyed or to be subdued; he addressed prayers and incantations to them in a prosaic, almost rationalist, attitude of mind, without adoration, with merely a recognition of inevitable dependence. His spells and invocations (the bastard descendants of heathen rites) were unsound science, but good rationalism. A. N. Rambaud[1] says that the primitive Slavs adored matter and never felt the incentive to personify, idealize, or philosophize it; perhaps it was a mere acceptance of necessity.

The Pomeranian Slavs, the only Slavs who had access to the sea, had a very elaborate ritual, and worshipped many-headed images in temples, not in groves, like the other Slavs. Their greatest oracles and pilgrimages were in the isle of Rügen; these pagan shrines were destroyed by Valdemar I. of Denmark in 1168.

The recollection of this sacred island has strongly influenced Slav myth and magic. The word Rügen is derived from the same root as the English 'rough,' and is called in Early Russian Ruyán. Now the word Buyán comes from a synonymous root, and looks like a translation of the Teutonic name Rügen; and it is thus a safe and probable theory to identify the fabulous island of Buyán with the historical shrine of Rügen—all the more so as the mysterious stone Alátyr is thought perhaps to mean amber, which was an article of Baltic commerce.

When Christianity had effaced the old Slavic nature-gods, the need for which they stood still remained—that of dealing with nature, coaxing and dominating her, and mastering her secrets. Fragments of the old ritual, degenerating into incomprehensible patter, continued to be used at the old sacred haunts, but these incantations were clandestine; though the beings invoked were believed in, they were considered illicit or hellish; heathendom had changed into magic.

Every village had its magician or witch-doctor. These practitioners certainly possessed great knowledge of healing, as herbalists and masseurs; but, where all nature consists of discontinuous miracles, such cures had to be accompanied with the ritual that was calculated to conciliate the powers and convince the patient.

The Russian sorcerer lived alone; he had learnt the magic formulæ, and had been instructed by the woodsprites (*leši*), the goblin of the hearth (*domovóy*), the fairies of the fields and the water (*polevóy, vodyanóy*). Such practitioners are known by many names—*e.g.*, *znákhar*, *kóldun*, *kudésnik*, *vedún*, *vorožéy*, etc.; the women-witches are called *vedĭma*; and to them more extraordinary powers are attributed. These magicians hand down their wisdom to their youngest children—a custom signifying that this magical knowledge was derived from non-Aryan peoples, and taken over by the Aryan conquerors.

It is said that the *znákhar* has physical marks —a troubled eye, a grey complexion—that he mutters, has a hoarse voice, and so on. Unless he communicates once a year, earth will not receive his body, and then he wanders after death as a vampire, sucking others' blood. Witches are credited with the power of flying, and are supposed to have marvellous muscular strength and a spotted skin. They are said to forgather in the gusts and whirls of snow at cross-roads; a pious man should cross himself when he comes upon such whirling columns, for in them the witches dance. If a knife be thrust into such a column, it will drop to the ground blood-stained; and it then becomes an implement for sorcery—*e.g.*, a man crossed in love may use its broad blade to wipe out the track of his maiden in the snow.

The wizard is believed to have terrible powers; among the Galician Rusins, *e.g.*, if the *znákhar* inserts a knife under the threshold of his intended victim's dwelling, the victim is snatched away by a whirlwind, and detained until the knife is removed.

The magical formulæ are very curious. They are framed for every occasion of need; and, to be efficacious, they must be spoken in one breath without any departure from the text—only thus can the powers of nature be quelled, and the wizard be the lord of creation. The following is the text of a charm against lead, copper, and iron bullets:

'In the lofty chamber, at the river mouth, beyond the river Vólga, a fair maiden stands, stands and decks herself, commends herself to valorous folk, glories in deeds of war. In her right hand she holds bullets of lead, in her left bullets of copper, on her feet bullets of iron. Do thou, fair maiden, ward off the guns of the Turks, the Tatars, the Germans, the Circassians, the Russians, the Mordvins, of all tribes and foes;

[1] *La Russie épique*, Paris, 1876, p. 215.

smite with thy invisible might the hostile weapons. If they shall shoot from their guns, may their bullets not hit, but strike the moist earth, the open field. May I be whole and uninjured in this war, and my steed whole and uninjured, and my dress stouter than armour. I close my decree with a lock, and I hurl the key into the Ocean-sea, on the burning stone Alátyr. And, as it is not to the sea to dry, as the stone may not be seen, the keys not be reached, so may I not be hit by bullets for all my life.'

A charm against fever runs as follows:

'On the Mountains of Athon there is an oak, and under the oak thirteen sages with the Sage Pafnúti. To them there go twelve maidens, fair, with simple tresses, and simple belts. And the Sage Pafnúti with the thirteen sages says: "Who are these who have come to us?"—And the twelve maidens say: "We are the daughters of King Herod, we journey across the earth to freeze up bones and torture the body." And the Sage Pafnúti spake to his sages: "Break off three rods, and we will beat them on for three dawns and three gloamings." The twelve maidens besought the thirteen sages with the Sage Pafnúti; but in vain. And the sages began beating them, saying: "Hail, ye twelve maidens! Be ye turned into water-sprites, and weakened, and live in the chilled water; nor enter the world, nor afflict bones, nor torture bodies." The maidens fled into the cold water as water-sprites,' etc.

These charms contain weird mixtures of legend: beyond the sea of Khvalynsk (probably the Baltic), on the isle of Buyán, on the mystic stone Alátyr, or on a sacred oak magical maidens sit; or there is a mighty sword, a man with a huge bow, a gigantic raven, or a castle with seven locked gates. In fact, the epic portion of the incantations is a medley of all the ancient myths, the one common feature being the locality of the island, and, occasionally, distinct recollections of the ritual practised at Rügen by the Pomeranian Slavs in the 12th century. These incantations also contain, as necessary parts, an invocation in which the 'servant of God,' the suppliant, states his request, and a conclusion, such as 'my word is strong,' 'a seal on my words,' to ratify, as it were, and assert the mastery over nature ensured by the spell.

Incantations must be pronounced in the traditional manner and at the right time and spot—*e.g.*, on midsummer's day, facing east, on the threshold, etc., during the offices at church (to contrive murder, a candle should be held upside down during the hearing of Mass). The professional enchanter expresses his desires forcibly and effectually to the natural powers whom he has under his sway, by means of formulæ which are a farrago of ancient Finnish magic, Aryan folklore, and Christian apocalypse. The incantations contain words of action, such as 'I stand up,' 'I wash myself,' 'I shroud myself in the clouds,' 'I surround myself with the crowded stars'; and the expression creates an illusion of the reality of the action.

Among the incantations against toothache, one invokes the dawn-goddess to cover the aching teeth with her veil against the attacks of the fiend Limar; the epic part goes on:

'In the field there is a hare, in the sea there is a stone, in the depths there is Limar.'

Another invokes the horned moon to cure the affliction. A third invokes, literally in the same breath, the Christian saints Martha, Mary, and Pegalea, and the water-demon. A fourth runs as follows:

'I go neither on the road nor on the street, but on empty lanes by copses and canals. I meet a hare. Hare, where are your teeth? Give me yours, take mine. I go neither on a road nor a path, but in the dark forest, a grey wood. I meet a dusky wolf. Wolf, dusky wolf, where are your teeth? I will give you mine, give me yours. I go neither on earth nor on water, but on the open plain, the flowery mead. I meet an old woman. Old woman, where are your teeth? Take out your wolf-like teeth, take out my falling teeth.'

In an incantation to stay the flow of blood the *znákhar* squeezes the wound and recites three times in a breath:

'In the Ocean-sea, on the Isle of Buyán a fair maiden was weaving silk; she did not leave off weaving silk; the blood ceased flowing.'

Again, in another formula, the Holy Virgin is depicted, like Svantovít, one of the principal gods worshipped at Rügen by the Pomeranian Slavs, or St. George, as riding across the golden bridge on her horse—an unmistakable reminiscence of the chariot of the sun on the rainbow.

There are charms to lull a child to sleep, and these sometimes invoke mysterious beings—Kriks, Plaks, and Šcekotuna—as well as the dawn, coupled with the names of Christian saints.

To save a man from drunkenness a worm is taken out of an empty wine-cask, dried, and then steeped anew in wine, whilst this formula is recited:

'Lord of the sea-depths! Carry the mettlesome heart of thy servant out of the shifting sands, the burning stones; breed in him a winged brood.'

The following examples illustrate the lyrical quality occasionally found in these strange compositions, especially in some of the spring invocations:

'Thou, Heaven, hearest, thou, Heaven, seest what I wish to accomplish on the body of thy servant X. [There follow four words unintelligible. An unintelligible patter is sometimes found, which looks very like a tradition of a lost language.] Thou Moon, turn away the servant of God from wine; thou little Sun, bring peace to the servant of God from wine. Ye bright stars, do ye assemble in the wedding-cup! But in my cup be there water from the mountain-well! Ye stars, do ye wean X, the servant of God, from wine. My word is potent.'

'Thou bright Moon, come into my net! But in my net there is neither bottom nor cover! Thou generous Sun, approach my door, my courtyard, but in my courtyard there are neither men nor beasts.'

The field of Slav magic is too vast and intricate for adequate treatment in these few words. The varied superstitions have been voluminously compiled by Sakharov and his generation; but it should be particularly noted that there are extant songs of witches in a meaningless gibberish, which some philologist might very possibly interpret and so assign definitively some origin to part of the magic ritual, at any rate, of Russia.

In the 18th cent. Russian magic became specifically demonological. An infernal hierarchy was foisted upon it with anti-ecclesiastical ritual. These late charms impress the reader as being identically artificial, like the imitative ballads of the same period; in form they copy the mediæval spells.

Summary.—The history and decline of Russian magic, it would appear, traced the following course. The primitive vague and inchoate nature-worship of the Slav Aryans was profoundly influenced and deflected by the subject races of the Finns, Čuds, and other Turanian races, who became typical magicians and had mystic powers ascribed to them. The elaborate ritual of the Pomeranian Slavs originated in a greater intermixture of race, and, when suppressed, was soon forgotten; but it lingered on in tradition and folk-lore, in the incomprehensible patter of the spells, and especially in the legend of the isle of Buyán and the stone Alátyr.

As Christianity spread, the ancient gods of thunder, spring, and progeny, the sun and moon, etc., were duly canonized, whilst the pagan soul and the pagan adoration of nature remained the same, and the festivals were held, often on the same day in the same place, and with similar ceremonies.

In the second mediæval stage, merged in and with the incantation are village science and medicine, village nature-poetry, and primitive *religio loci.* The specialization of the medicine-man, the healer, the priest, and the minstrel came with advancing civilization, the herbalist degenerating into the magician and enchanter. Post-mediævally, a formal demonology arose, a positive anti-Christianity, artificial, sporadic, and short-lived.

LITERATURE.—F. Saklovity, *Volkhvy i Vorozei*, Petrograd, 1889, no. 6; A. A. Kotlyárevski, *Pogrebalnye obyčai u drevnikh Slavyan*, do. 1884; V. Yagic, *Národopisný Českoslovanský Vjesník*, Prague, 1906; I. I. Sreznevski, *Svyatilišča i obryady yazyčeskago bogosluzenia drevnikh Slavyan*, Kharkov, 1846; S. M. Soloviev, 'Očerk nravov i yazyčeskoy religii Slavyán,' *Arkhiv ist. yur. sved. Kalačova*, Kn. 7; P. J. Safarik, *Slawische Alterthümer*, Germ. tr. Leipzig, 1843–44; L. Niederle, *O povodu drevnych Slovian*, Prague, 1896, *Slovanské starozitnosti.*, do. 1902 ff.; Borozdin and Anickov, *Ist. Russkoy Literatury*, Petrograd, 1876; A. S. Famintsyn, *Bozestva drevnikh Slavyan*, do. 1884; I. P. Sakharov, *Skazaniya russkago naroda*, do. 1836; P. Milyukov, *Religiya Slavyan*, do. 1896.

L. A. MAGNUS.

MAGIC (Teutonic).—In all ages and in all localities the belief in magic is found to have sprung from the same roots: panvitalism, *i.e.* the conception of nature as alive in every part; the incapacity of primitive man to distinguish persons or things from their names or representations; the belief in the transferability of the powers of nature and of human souls; and the dread of soul-spirits and demons, as also of such hostile persons as were believed to be in league with these supernatural existences. We need not wonder, therefore, if the means by which the various peoples of the earth have sought to defend themselves from all sinister influences of the kind should likewise show a large degree of uniformity. Naturally the most effective mode of securing immunity from the machinations of magic was to counteract them, if possible, by a magic still more potent. From the earliest times the amulet and the spell have been specially resorted to as protective expedients. While the former, however, was employed exclusively as a prophylactic, the magic formula was used in the practice of other kinds of the occult art, whether its design was beneficent or the reverse.

With reference to the ideas and customs associated with the belief in magic, the Teutons formed no exception to the general rule. Among them, as among other races, are found the belief in the soul and the various forms of superstition developed from and dependent upon it. The souls of the departed were believed to pervade and animate all nature; they could assume at will human or animal forms, and bring good or evil fortune to men. From the soul of the sorceress came the powers of the witch whose devices could work injury upon other human beings. Many of the nature-demons, whose place of origin was the physical environment, were regarded as being endowed with magical powers. Among the Germans, likewise, the practices of soothsaying and magic were intimately connected with the belief in soul-spirits. The prophetic faculty was attributed to women as well as men. In the north of Europe the *Völven* had a great reputation as prophetesses and sorceresses. The practice of magic was on the whole more fully developed among the Northern Teutons than in Germany, being fostered in the former case by the shamanism of the neighbouring Finns, a people famous over the entire North for their magic. The most powerful and formidable sorceresses mentioned by the Norse sagas belong, for the most part, to the Finnish race, which, again, in its religion, its demonology, and its magic, is very closely allied to the ancient Sumerian peoples. It is possible that many elements in the magic and demonology of the Northern Teutons were borrowed from the Finns. At all events, the practice of resorting to the latter people in order to acquire their magic arts became so prevalent that at a later time the Christian Church found it necessary to enact laws prohibiting it. But this was not the only channel by which the Teutons became acquainted with the magical ideas and usages of foreign, and especially of the Roman, Greek, and Oriental, peoples. The Northern Teutons visited the Mediterranean Sea both as Vikings and as peaceful merchants, while the Southern Teutons were the near neighbours of the Romans, and were sometimes in their pay as mercenaries. In point of fact, however, the occult art and its adepts are found among the Teutons from the outset. Here, just as on Greek and Roman soil, the idea prevailed that it was possible to work changes in the nature of objects simply by the magical virtues of the spoken and written word or of the symbol. The magic utterance and the magic rune—the engraved talismanic symbol—were used for the most varied purposes. According to the *Ynglinga Saga*, runes and spells owed their origin to Oðin, while the rune-master of the *Hávamál* knows the right method of engraving the characters, as well as the songs which effect cures, restrain enemies, render weapons harmless, quench fires, subdue winds and waves, call up the dead, and awaken a maiden's love, though the words of the songs are not given. Other magic songs are referred to in the *Sigrdrífumál*. That a similar profusion of magic songs was to be found among the Southern Teutons is shown by the *Homilia de sacrilegiis*, which came into existence in the Southern Frankish kingdom under the Merovingians. Alike in the North and in the South these songs were in great part employed as expedients for the cure of disease in man and beast; nor is this to be wondered at when we remember that disease itself was regarded as due to demons and malefic magic. Magic alone, in fact, could undo the work of magic.

Now, the articles exclusively employed for the purpose of influencing the magical properties of things were amulets and ligatures. There was not the slightest misgiving as to the efficacy of the appropriate amulet. Discoveries in tombs furnish ample information regarding the objects specially in request as amulets among the Teutons. Thus, for the protection of the dead, belemnites, amber rings, stone arrow-heads, and hook crosses were laid in the grave along with the body. Amulets were also fashioned out of all kinds of objects bearing figures and drawings, while a special vogue was enjoyed by the so-called *bracteates*, which were imitated from Roman coins, and brought to the North in the early centuries of our era. These were mostly of gold. The images of the gods which served as amulets likewise date from the period of Roman influence.

When the missionaries of the Roman Church introduced the Christian religion among the Teutonic tribes, they found ideas and practices quite similar to what had prevailed in pagan Rome and its provinces. Accordingly, they sought to apply the same procedure as had been previously resorted to, *i.e.*, they incorporated the deities of the pagan Teutons into the system of demons whose existence the Church recognized, while they forbade all worship of them, as also the practice of magic in general, and inflicted severe penalties upon the disobedient. From the early centuries of the Church's history, synods and councils had found it necessary to forbid even the priests to pander to the people's craving for amulets, written spells, adjurations, and magic potions; and, as late as the 8th cent., clergy in Thuringia, the missionary district of St. Boniface, were making amulets of small cards inscribed with Biblical verses of supposed protective or remedial powers, and hung from the neck by a cord, just as if they had been pieces of amber or agate. The use of incantations was also vigorously assailed from the pulpit, while other ecclesiastical enactments against amulets and spells are found among the rules for penance and in the ecclesiastical or Christian codes. Among the various collections of penitential regulations—which, it is true, prohibit many non-Teutonic superstitions—a peculiar place is occupied by those of the Anglo-Saxons, as the Frankish regulations are in great measure verbally dependent upon them. They warn against 'divinationes,' 'auguria,' 'somnia,' 'mathematici,' 'emissores tempestatum,' and especially against 'incantationes diabolicæ,' 'filacteria,' and 'ligaturæ.' As yet excommunication was the extreme penalty for transgression. The Venerable Bede (*HE* iv. 27) relates that, during a time of pestilence and high mortality, recourse was had to adjurations and spells. The abbot Regino of Prüm has incorporated an entire series of the decrees of councils dealing with the subject in his work *de Synodalibus Causis* (A.D. 906; *PL* cxxxii. 187 ff.), and from that work much has been borrowed by Burchard of Worms, who wrote about the beginning of the 11th century (*PL* cxl. 537 ff.).

That similar ideas and usages were still flourishing in England at this period is shown by Ælfric's *Passio S. Bartholomei Apostoli*, with its injunction that no one shall seek to regain health by using a ligature of medicinal herbs or praising a herb in a 'magic song.' The ecclesiastical ordinances of Eadgar and the Northumbrian priests' laws contain regulations to the same effect. Among the Northern Teutons likewise canon law directed its mandates against superstition and magic.

Till well on in the 16th cent. synods and councils of the Church were constantly under the necessity of dealing with the use of spells and amulets and the evils arising from them. Thus can. 9 of a papal bull enacts for the Lateran Council of 1514 that *sortilegia* made by invoking demons, by incantations, or by other superstitious practices are unlawful. Clerics who offend are to be punished at the discretion of their superiors, and laymen are to be excommunicated or visited with civil penalties.

In dealing with such offences, the national codes of the various Teutonic peoples do not show the same unanimity as the Church. The Teutonic nations that came into existence on Roman territory found it necessary to base their legislation against magic directly upon the ordinances of Roman law. The earliest Teutonic code, the *lex Visigothorum*, enacted (bk. vi. tit. 2, 4) that those who 'quibusdam incantationibus' bring hailstorms upon the fields and the vineyards 'ducentenis flagellis publice verberentur et decalvati deformiter decem convicinas possessiones circuire cogantur inviti.' Rotharis, king of the Longobardi, sternly prohibited the belief in cannibal witches. Among the Germans, as among all other races, the feeling prevailed that one who practised malefic magic must at all costs be got rid of, whether by expulsion from the tribe or by death. But, on the other hand, we have a variety of testimony from Northern Europe which seems to show that the practice of magic was not in all circumstances deemed criminal.

In the civil law of the Anglo-Saxons, from the 7th cent. onwards, we find penal enactments against superstition and magic, and in particular against the employment of spells and amulets. The laws of Alfred the Great dealing with magic are founded mainly on the Biblical denunciations of the practice. Of similar character are the legal ordinances directed against the occult art among the Northern Teutons. The older Icelandic canon law of the 12th cent. ordains that those who tamper with incantations or witchcraft shall be punished by banishment.

The evil against which the enactments of the Teutonic codes were mainly directed was malefic magic (*maleficium*). Until the 8th cent. we find no similar enactments against other superstitions which eventually gathered round the belief in witchcraft. But the belief in the existence of cannibal witches and in witches' flights was explicitly forbidden by ecclesiastical and civil legislation, though Ivo of Chartres (*c.* A.D. 1100) thought it possible that witches exerted some influence upon the sexual functions. The Church, however, notwithstanding all its exertions, was by no means successful in ridding the people of their magic beliefs and practices. Both continued to flourish abundantly in the department of medicine, thanks to the recrudescence of the old neo-Platonic—in reality, the Babylono-Egyptian—doctrine of demons. At an early period medicine had become the monopoly of the cloister; the demons of disease were exorcized by the priest; and to relics, to the rosary, and to the 'Agnus Dei' were ascribed the greatest virtues. Those who in sickness and trouble applied to the priests were treated by means of the amulet and the incantation, so that as late as the 16th cent.—at a time, that is, when a medical profession in the proper sense existed—adjurations were still resorted to by doctors.

The attitude of the Church towards the belief in magic was twofold. On the one hand, it accepted magic as an indisputable reality. On the other hand, it ranged itself with the civil legislation in an uncompromising opposition to certain dangerous popular superstitions. But in the 13th cent. came a momentous change in the Church's standpoint. The doctrine of Satan was now made the basis of the doctrine of magic and witchcraft. The nightly journeys of witches, the transformation of human beings into animals, the sexual intercourse of men with female demons, and the operation of sorcery in the sexual functions—all these things were now accepted as facts not to be gainsaid. Then in the 14th cent. the two currents of heresy and sorcery, which had hitherto run side by side, became amalgamated with each other, and merged in the belief in witchcraft. While among the Teutonic tribes the practice of magic had hitherto been penalized—to speak strictly—only because of the mischief which it might work, in the 13th cent. the civil legislatures in Germany likewise resolved upon a new policy. The Old Saxon code (*Sachsenspiegel*) sent those who practised magic of any kind to the stake, and its example was followed by other municipal and territorial codes. In spite of the rigour of the Inquisition, it is true, the earlier penal law (which threatened with excommunication the users of incantations, amulets, or other magic devices) was still pleaded for by the councils and by certain outstanding men among the clergy. But the Inquisition at length silenced every stricture against its competence to deal with magic. By the civil legislation of the 16th cent. those who dealt in magic and soothsaying were punished mainly by fines; the death-penalty was scarcely ever mooted. On the other hand, the Hamburg criminal code of 1508 enacts that the punishment of malefic magic shall be death by fire, and this clause was taken over by the Imperial legislation —the 'peinliche Gerichtsordnung Kaiser Karls V.'—while we find that the criminal code of the Electorate of Saxony (1572) sentenced witches to death by fire, and its example was followed by the legislation of the several States. The persecution of witches was gradually introduced into the various territories of Germany during the second half of the 16th century. In England the earliest processes of this kind seem to have been trials for real or alleged attacks upon the person of the sovereign, as from the reign of Henry VI. But in England the laws against witchcraft were in general much more lenient than was commonly the case on the Continent. Witch-persecution in England dates from about the middle of the 16th cent.; in Scotland cases are found as early as the beginning of that century. With regard to Sweden, we are not in a position to say whether witches were burned before or during the Thirty Years' War. These measures, however, were incapable of extirpating the belief in magic—just as the Reformation itself failed to destroy it, though the delusion certainly received a telling blow from the Reformers. As to the question whether sorcery has a foundation in fact, the Reformers themselves shared the ideas of their age, and the final deathblow to the belief in witchcraft and sorcery was administered by the reconstituted sciences of modern times.

Even in the earliest ages a clear line of demarcation was drawn between lawful and unlawful magic. The latter was treated by all races with the utmost rigour, and not seldom punished with death. Among the Teutons, as elsewhere, incantations and amulets were utilized as a means of securing protection and profit to the individual and his belongings, and also to work injury upon others, and their possessions. The magic spells of the Teutons may therefore be arranged in two main divisions, according to the purposes that they were intended to serve: (1) magic formulæ supposed to secure protection and advantage; (2) magic formulæ intended to injure others. But, as the subject itself suggests, the former class may be further divided according to the effects which the spells were intended to produce. Their object might be either (*a*) to drive away an existent evil, to 'exorcize' it, or (*b*) to avert a possible evil by means of a 'blessing.' This dichotomy of the first main group, however, will not be found exhaustive, and it is necessary to mark off another subdivision. Magic formulæ were used not only for the purpose of dislodging present and averting future evils, but also as a means of inducing spirits to throw light upon the future, and upon hidden things generally. In so far as this (*c*) prophetic magic (as it may be called) had often to do with things which lay in the future, it comes into close touch with the class of magic formulæ designed to prevent possible evil. But, while the received spells can for the most part be assigned to one or other of these four *genera*, many particular species may be differentiated within the larger groups. The number of different varieties will in general correspond to that of the various purposes which the formulæ were meant to serve.

Magic can be overcome only by counter-magic; such was at one time the universal postulate of the occult art. In primitive times, however, all sorcery consisted in words and symbols, generally conjoined with actions. Thus, with reference to the Germans, Tacitus (*Germ.* x.) states that, when the deity was consulted by means of the lot, the priests held aloft the magic wand engraved with symbols, muttering incantations the while. Sundry Anglo-Saxon spells specify the appropriate action to be performed. Thus the incantation for bewitched soil gives precise directions regarding the requisite symbolic actions and sacrificial usages. For the formula against the machinations of witches the instruction runs: 'wið færstice feferfuige and seo reade netele, ðe þurh ærn inwyxð, and wegbrade: wyll in buteran'; then at the end, 'nim þonne þæt sæx, ado on wætan.' But word and action had already been frequently employed independently of each other, and it is not surprising that the word came to be used apart from all accessaries or symbolic actions. The Teutonic conviction that magical effects could be directly produced by the spoken word must doubtless have found expression in the particular form of the spell. But the simplest —and hence, no doubt, the oldest—vehicle of direct influence is the express command, and, accordingly, such command must have formed the nucleus of the Teutonic incantation. Two examples of Teutonic spells may be given here. The first is a formula from the 9th–10th cent., which has come down to us bearing the title 'contra vermes' (C. von Müllenhoff and W. Scherer, *Denkmäler deutscher Poesie und Prosa*[3], i. [1892] 17):

'Gang ût, nesso, mid nigun nessiklînon
ût fana themo marge an that bên,
fan themo bêne an that flêsg,
ût fan themo flêsge an thia hûd,
ût fan thera hûd an thesa strâla,
drohtîn, uuerthe sô!'

With this may be associated the Anglo-Saxon 'blessing of bees,' the 'wyð ymbe,' from a Cambridge MS of the 11th century. After a direction regarding a magical action, and a verse explanatory thereof, it continues (C. W. M. Grein and R. P. Wülcker, *Bibliothek der angelsächs. Poesie*, i. [1883] 319 f.):

'Sitte ge, sigewif, sigað to eorþan!
næfre ge wilde to wudu fleogan!
Beo ge swaagemindige mines godes,
swa bið manna gehwilc metes and eþeles.'

It is quite conceivable that spells of this kind should exist independently, and unattached to any preliminary narrative. This has been observed also by Schröder in his article 'Über das Spell' (*ZDA* xxxvii. 259):

'Probable as it is that at a certain stage of civilization the action of the *galdr*, *i.e.* the spell in the proper sense, or of certain species of it, was produced in connexion with the narration of a particular mythical incident, yet there is not the slightest doubt that in other periods the epic narrative and the magic formula are disjoined, and may each maintain a separate existence.'

Besides these adjurations strictly so called, which were complete in themselves, and which may be regarded as the earliest Teutonic spells, there comes down to us from the same age another species—that in which an epic narrative is prefixed to the formula proper.

The classical examples of this type are the two Merseburg incantations, and the Anglo-Saxon spell against the practices of the witch is constructed on similar lines. The substance of the introductory portion—the narrative—is generally borrowed from mythology. The procedure was to relate some incident traditionally associated with an effect identical with or similar to that which the formula was meant to produce. It was not necessary to say in so many words that the spell should now operate with like efficacy; the bare recitation of the story invested the formula with all the potency required. But this dependence of the formula upon the narrative certainly indicates a change of view regarding the power of the formula. The performer has lost his earlier reliance on his own capacity, and this must, accordingly, be reinforced from without.

While this epic type of spell is often referred to as the primitive Teutonic form, the facts would seem to imply its secondary character, though its root may indeed lie in paganism, but in any case the recitation of a short narrative before the actual formula is not peculiar to the Teutons—let alone the Western Teutons—this form of spell being traceable among other races and in much more remote times. It was certainly known to the Romans and the Hindus. But, as a matter of fact, there is evidence to show that it was not even a distinctively Indogermanic usage, since it is found also among the Babylonians and the Egyptians. An Egyptian papyrus of the XXth dynasty (now in Turin), for instance, contains a spell which in its whole design shows a striking resemblance to the Merseburg incantation for fracture of the leg. In the Babylonian and Egyptian spells, too, precisely as in the Teutonic, the scene of the narrative part is always laid in the mythological sphere. In view of the vast influence exercised by the Oriental, and especially the Babylonian and Egyptian, magical ideas upon the nations of the West, it is a tempting conjecture that Oriental models may have been largely instrumental in propagating the narrative spell among the Indogermanic peoples of Europe —first of all in the Greek and Roman area, and then derivatively in the Teutonic. At all events, the theory that the Teutons had a primitive type of spell consisting of a prose narrative followed by a rhythmical formula, as adopted by Schröder (*loc. cit.*), is beside the purpose. The primordial element was certainly the formula, the narrative being added later; and, as we have seen, each could be used by itself alone. We find, moreover, that in Christian times quite different introductions were combined with the real nucleus of the spell. We must therefore think of each part as distinct in itself, and in no degree the less so because in the recitation 'saying and singing' came alternately. In all probability the spells were simply muttered in an undertone; there is a large mass of evidence —and not from Teutonic sources only—pointing to this mode of recital.

Thus the missionaries who came to evangelize the Teutonic tribes found two types of indigenous incantations, viz. the purely imperative and the narrative. As the Church was unable to put an end to heathen customs and practices, or the use of magic formulæ, it adopted the policy of assimilating everything that could in any way be reconciled with its own views, hoping that by the device of clothing the objectionable thing in a Christian garb, it might succeed in eradicating the superstitions of the heathen. It likewise endeavoured to transform the ancient formulæ, and here probably its first, as also its most urgent, task was to eliminate the heathen characters from the narrative spells and put Christian ones in their place. These new formulæ were generally composed in verse, and were embellished with rhyme. Their narrative portions exhibited Biblical characters, such as Jesus, Mary, the apostles, and others, in perfectly appropriate situations—a fact which in itself conclusively shows that the spells in question originated in ecclesiastical circles. Such imitations of heathen formulæ composed by the clergy are relatively numerous, and date for the most part from the 11th and 12th centuries.

From this narrative species of Christian spell, again, was in part evolved a new type. This took the form of a comparison or allegory, and its rubric ran thus: 'As such and such a result was brought about then, so let it be produced now.' Very few of the surviving spells of this type are in metrical form; the great majority are in prose.

A further form of blessing, for the use and diffusion of which the clergy must again be regarded as mainly responsible, derives its origin from the special Roman Catholic ceremonies known as the sacramentals. New formulæ were formed on the pattern of the 'exorcisms,' 'benedictions,' and 'consecrations,' or these were simply translated into the vernacular. This species is probably not older than the 13th century.

Mention must also be made of a type of magic formula in regard to which the monks played merely an intermediate rôle. This group consists mainly of formulæ handed down in ancient medical writings. The design of most of these is the cure of disease, but adjurations for use in digging up medicinal plants were also transmitted in this way. These formulæ were, of course, mostly in the Latin language. Their potency lay mainly in phrases and letters—magic words and characters largely of Eastern origin, being derived from Babylonian, Egyptian, and Jewish magic. This group, accordingly, comprises the most ancient type of spell, which, it is to be observed, always exhibits an unintelligible jumble of words. From the earliest times, indeed, this very unintelligibility was the indispensable condition of the efficacy of the spell. From the 13th cent., however, we must take account also of another contributory source of the superstition which is concerned with words and letters—and, it may be added, numbers also. This was the religious philosophy of the Jews, as set forth in the works of the Ḳabbālā (*q.v.*).

These leading types will suffice to classify the great majority of magic formulæ, and even the hybrid, composite, and other derivative varieties which inevitably made their appearance in the course of centuries. But the prime factor in such secondary formations was doubtless oral tradition, to the action of which a large proportion of the spells would certainly be subject at some stage of their development. The learned formulæ of the Church are usually of considerable length, and in their full form would have relatively little vogue among the common people. From these larger spells, accordingly, certain typical portions were excerpted, and then used independently. The popular mind laid the main emphasis upon the nucleus of the spell—the formula proper; and examples of this type become numerous from the 16th century. In these the strict parallelism of the earlier ecclesiastical blessings is to some extent abandoned. It was now considered sufficient to say: 'As surely as this act has taken place, so surely may this effect ensue.' Sometimes, in fact, the place of the parallel is taken by the antithesis. It became the practice, further, to draw upon still more remote quarters for the conclusion of the blessing, and to introduce formulæ which in themselves had formerly done duty as blessings, so that the formulæ of blessing, being supplemented by invocations of God and multiplied petitions, often actually approximated to the character of prayer itself.

When we consider the mass of Teutonic formulæ —even with the 16th cent. as the ulterior limit—in relation to the purposes which they were meant to serve, we see that the multiplicity of forms mentioned in the *Hávamál*, the *Sigrdrifumál*, and the *Homilia de sacrilegiis* is by no means an exaggeration. Adjurations against disease certainly constitute the largest class. Many maladies were believed to be due to malignant demons and unfriendly magicians, and were therefore combated by the magic formula. But the same means was employed in dealing with diseases about the origin of which there was no uncertainty. The remedies employed in such cases were supposed to acquire peculiar efficacy by having a spell uttered over them.

Nor was it human beings only who in their distresses were benefited by spells. As had been believed from the earliest times, protection was equally indispensable for the lower creatures most closely associated with human life, viz. the domestic animals. In their case also, therefore, magic formulæ were used to ward off disease and other evils. The dog, and especially the shepherd's dog, was protected in this way from the dangers to which it was exposed from wild beasts. People were very specially concerned, however, to guard against the bite of mad dogs. A certain blessing, 'ad pullos de nido,' was supposed to help the growth of chickens. The purpose of the somewhat numerous 'bee-blessings' was to keep the insects from swarming.

There was, besides, a multitude of adjurations for animals other than the domestic. People tried to rid their houses of flies, mice, and rats by appeal to the power of the formula; wolves were adjured not to hurt the cattle in the fields; serpents, to be easily caught. The bite of the serpent was averted by spells, and by means of adjurations the reptiles were induced to yield up the potent ophite stone, and to be obedient to all commands. The tooth and the right forepaw of the badger acted as charms against all kinds of injury, and with the shoulder of a toad a man could win the love of whomsoever he chose.

In the therapeutics of ancient and mediæval times an important place was assigned to medicinal herbs. It was of vital moment, however, that these herbs should still retain their supposed virtues after being plucked, and certain magical formulæ were believed to ensure this. The practice was to adjure either the whole world of herbs, or a definite number of them (cf. the Anglo-Saxon 'nine-herb spell'), or, again, some particular herb. But still further manifestations of the potency of herbs could be elicited. They could be made to secure the traveller against fatigue, to act as a defence against weapons, and to protect the cattle from sorcery and the crops from hailstorms. They could also help one to win love, to open locks, to ascertain truth, and to read both the future and the past.

Then the magic formulæ served to protect men not only against disease, but also against the malice of their fellows and the threat of misfortune. By their aid a person sought to safeguard himself—especially when on a journey—against the artifice of his enemies, to blunt their weapons, and to free himself from prison. By the same means he could defend himself against malefic magic, and against the bewitching of his food and drink. Other formulæ possessed the power of procuring friendship, love, and favour, and of gaining justice before a legal tribunal. Wives sought, through the medium of magic, to turn the harshness of their husbands into love. An astute merchant of the 16th cent. would even try by a spell to induce people to buy up his stock of stale wares.

Human life was thus surrounded by a rampart of spells, and property likewise was in similar fashion made proof against evil influences. Houses were secured by spells against burglary and fire, and corn in the granaries was kept from decay. If anything was lost or stolen, the magic formula could restore it, and even lead to the discovery of the thief. The same means were also used to protect, and to increase, the fruits of gardens and fields.

The number of extant magic formulæ designed to work harm is quite insignificant—a circumstance which is, no doubt, due to the rigorous treatment meted out from the earliest times to the practice of malefic magic. Such hurtful spells might be used by the malicious to sow dissension between old friends, to change the love of a married couple into hatred, to bring every conceivable disaster upon another, and even to overwhelm with destruction all that he possessed.

LITERATURE.—i. *HISTORY, FORM, AND SPECIES OF THE MAGIC FORMULÆ.*—J. Abercromby, 'Magic Songs of the Finns,' in *FL* i. [1890] 17 ff.; E. Baluze, *Capitularia regum Francorum*, Paris, 1780, ii.; A. Boretius and V. Krause, *Capitularia regum Francorum*, Hanover, 1883–87, i.; H. Brunner, *Deutsche Rechtsgeschichte*, i.[2], Leipzig, 1906; C. P. Caspari, *Homilia de sacrilegiis*, Christiania, 1886; J. Diefenbach, *Der Zauberglaube des 16ten Jahrh.*, Mainz, 1900; O. Ebermann, *Blut- und Wundsegen, in ihrer Entwicklung dargestellt*, Berlin, 1903 (=*Palaestra*, xxiv.); E. Friedberg, *Aus deutschen Bussbüchern*, Halle, 1868; J. Grimm, *Teutonic Mythology*, tr. J. S. Stallybrass, London, 1882–88, *Deutsche Rechtsaltertümer*[4], Leipzig, 1899; *Handbuch der Gesch. der Medizin*, ed. M. Neuburger and J. Pagel, Jena, 1901–05, i.; J. Hansen, *Quellen und Untersuchungen zur Gesch. der Hexenwahns*, Bonn, 1901; M. Höfler, 'Krankheitsdämonen,' in *ARW* ii. [1899], *Deutsches Krankheitsnamenbuch*, Munich, 1899; O. von Hovorka and A. Kronfeld, *Vergleichende Volksmedizin*, Stuttgart, 1908–09, ii.; A. John, *Sitte, Brauch, und Volksglaube im deutschen Westböhmen*, Prague, 1905; F. Jostes, 'Volksaberglauben im 15ten Jahrh.,' in *Zeitschr. für vaterl. Gesch. und Altertumskunde Westfalens*, xlvii. [1889]; J. M. Kemble, *The Saxons in England*, 2 vols., London, 1849; H. C. Lea, *Hist. of the Inquisition of the Middle Ages*, New York and London, 1908–11; F. Liebermann, *Die Gesetze der Angelsachsen*, Halle, 1903; K. Maurer, *Die Bekehrung des norweg. Stammes*, Munich, 1855–56, ii.; E. H. Meyer, *Mythologie der Germanen*, Strassburg, 1903; E. Mogk, *Germanische Mythologie*[2], do. 1898, 'Die Menschenopfer bei den Germanen,' in *ASG*, 1909; O. Montelius, *Kulturgeschichte Schwedens*, Leipzig, 1906; *MGH* i., iii.; H. Pfannenschmid, *German. Erntefeste*, Hanover, 1878; R. Schmid, *Die Gesetze der Angelsachsen*[2], Leipzig, 1858; A. E. Schönbach, 'Studien zur Gesch. der altdeutschen Predigt,' ii., in *SWAW* cxlii. [1900] vii.; R. Schröder, *Lehrbuch der deutschen Rechtsgesch.*[5], Leipzig, 1907; H. Schurtz, 'Amulette und Zaubermittel,' in *AA* xxii. [1894]; B. Thorpe, *The Homilies of the Anglo-Saxon Church*, i., London, 1844; K. Weinhold, 'Die altdeutschen Verwünschungsformeln,' in *SBAW*, 1895, ii.; W. E. Wilda, *Das Strafrecht der Germanen*, Halle, 1842; A. Wuttke, *Der deutsche Volksaberglaube der Gegenwart*[3], Berlin, 1900; I. von Zingerle, 'Johannissegen und Gertrudenminne,' in *SWAW* xl. [1862].

ii. *COLLECTIONS OF MAGIC FORMULÆ.*—H. Bang, *Norske Hexeformularer og magiske Opskrifter*, Christiania, 1901 f.; K. Bartsch, *Sagen, Märchen, und Gebräuche aus Mecklenburg*, Vienna, 1879–80; J. Brand and W. C. Hazlitt, *Popular Antiquities*[2], London, 1870; G. Chaucer, *The Miller's Tale, The Tale of the Man of Lawe* (*Works*, ed. W. W. Skeat, Oxford, 1894–97); T. O. Cockayne, *Leechdoms, Wortcunning, and Starcraft of Early England*, London, 1864–66; W. Dorow, *Denkmäler alter Sprache und Kunst*, Berlin, 1823–24; H. Oesterley, *Niederdeut. Dichtung im Mittelalter*, Dresden, 1871; F. W. Schuster, *Siebenbürgisch-sächsische Volkslieder*, Hermannstadt, 1865; E. Steinmeyer and E. Sievers, *Die althochd. Glossen*, iv., Berlin, 1898; E. Wadstein, *Kleinere altsächs. Sprachdenkmäler*, Norden, 1899; T. Wright and J. O. Halliwell, *Reliquiæ antiquæ*, London, 1841–43.

F. HÄLSIG.

MAGIC (Vedic).—**1. Definition.**—The sphere of cult and ritual has two aspects in Vedic literature—religion and magic. The former (see art. VEDIC RELIGION) represents the relation of man to the gods and lesser divine beings. Its object is to cultivate their goodwill by means of hymns as well as sacrifice, and thus to induce them to bestow in return the benefits which man desires. The essential character of Vedic religion, therefore, is propitiatory and persuasive. Magic, on the other hand, endeavours to gain its ends by influencing the course of events, without the intervention of divine beings, by means of spells and ritual. Its essential character is, therefore, coercive. Both aim at the same result, but in different ways. Religion achieves its purpose indirectly by inclining the will of a powerful ally through prayer and gifts, for instance, to destroy an enemy; magic does so directly by operating with the impersonal (and imaginary) causal connexion between the means which it employs and the effect to be attained, as burning the effigy of an enemy in order to burn the enemy himself. Its practice was in part auspicious and beneficent, as the ritual for the obtaining of offspring or luck, of rain or victory, but it was largely maleficent in the interest of individuals and not of the community, and, therefore, as being dangerous, was condemned by the priesthood, except in so far as it was applied by themselves.

2. Literary sources.—The sphere of religion, as considered apart from magic, is chiefly represented by the earliest product of Indian literature, the Rigveda, which consists almost entirely of hymns addressed to various gods, in which their greatness and their deeds are praised and all kinds of welfare are prayed for, and which are intended to accompany the ritual of the Soma sacrifice (cf. art. HYMNS [Vedic], § 7 f.). Only a dozen of its 1028 hymns are concerned with magic, about one half of them being auspicious, the rest maleficent in character. As to any magical rites connected with the sacrifice, the Rigveda gives us no information. On the other hand, magic is the main and essential subject-matter of the Atharvaveda (art. HYMNS [Vedic], § 11); it is a collection of metrical spells, largely to be accompanied by ceremonies aiming at the welfare of the magician or the injury of his enemies. The Yajurveda (art. HYMNS [Vedic], § 13) occupies an intermediate position between these two Vedas as regards magic. In its original part, which consists of prose formulæ, the gods are only secondary, bearing a kind of mechanical relation to the sacrificial ceremonial with which these formulæ are associated, and which they follow in its minutest details. Its character is thus of a magical rather than a religious type. The great development, in this period, of an intricate ritual and the concentration of sacerdotal thought on its perfect performance had led to the new conception that sacrifice was not meant to propitiate the gods, but directly to control the natural course of things.

The prose theological works called Brāhmaṇas,

which represent the next stage of Vedic literature, being concerned with explaining and interpreting the details of the ritual, supply much information regarding the magical notions and observances with which the sacrificial ceremonial was permeated. The Upaniṣads, though a continuation of the Brāhmaṇas, are philosophical rather than religious, but their speculations on the nature of *brahman* and on the supernatural powers acquired by knowledge and asceticism are charged with magical notions.

The final phase of Vedic literature, which comes down to *c.* 200 B.C., is represented by the Sūtras. These concise manuals, especially those dealing with domestic life (*gṛhya*), and to a less extent those concerned with customary law (*dharma*), show how the observances of everyday life were saturated with magical beliefs and practices (cf. also art. LITERATURE [Vedic and Classical Sanskrit], §§ 8-12).

3. Importance of the subject.—A knowledge of Vedic magic is obviously important to the investigator of magic in general, for here we have magical material, bearing on every aspect of human life, which began to be recorded well over 3000 years ago, and which can, from that time onwards, be historically studied in continuous successive literary stages, extending over more than 1000 years. Such facilities are afforded by no other ancient literature as regards either the antiquity or the quantity and quality of the evidence afforded. The material in Vedic literature does not require to be laboriously gathered together from scanty and scattered references, as is necessary elsewhere. It is here supplied not only in great abundance, but, for the most part, in an easily accessible collected form. Its aid is, moreover, essential to the student of Indian religion: without it he would arrive at erroneous or exaggerated conclusions as to the purity and advanced character of the beliefs and practices of that religion in its earliest form.

4. Sacrifice and magic.—Considering that in the Rigveda we have a collection of prayers, and in the Atharvaveda one of spells, are we justified in supposing that the spheres of religion and of magic were already separated in the Vedic period? By no means. It is, indeed, certain that the sacrificial invocation had by that time assumed a literary type, and that the hymns of a magical character found in the Rigveda are very few and late. It must, however, be borne in mind that the prayers of the Rigveda, being addressed to the great gods, offered few opportunities for references to magical practices, while the ritual which the hymns of the Rigveda were intended to accompany, and which is fully described in other Vedic texts, is, though carried out by the sacrificial priests, from beginning to end saturated with magical observances. Again, where there is a group of ceremonies directed to the accomplishment of a particular purpose and, therefore, favourable to a greater prominence of the magical element, such as the wedding and funeral rites, we meet with quite a network of magical usages bearing the stamp of extreme antiquity. It is thus impossible to suppose that the sacrificial priests of the Rigveda, the composers of the old hymns, should have occupied an isolated position, untouched by magical practices derived from a much earlier age and afterwards continued throughout the priestly literature of later times. In fact, a close examination of the hymns of the Rigveda actually affords evidence that even in them the belief in magical power independent of the gods is to be found. Thus in one hymn (X. xcviii.) the sacrificing priest Devāpi begins with the intention of appealing to the gods for rain, but then himself brings down the waters by the magical powers of his sacrificial art: 'the sage Devāpi sat down to the duty of Hotṛ priest, familiar with the goodwill of the gods; he then poured down from the sea above to the sea below the heavenly waters of rain' (V. v.). Every page of the Brāhmaṇas and of the ritual Sūtras shows that the whole sacrificial ceremonial was overgrown with the notion that the sacrifice exercised power over gods and, going beyond them, could directly influence things and events without their intervention. An incipient form of this notion already appears in the Rigveda, where exaggerated sacrificial powers are in several passages mythically attributed to ancient priests; *e.g.*, 'with mighty spells the Fathers found the hidden light and produced the dawn' (VII. lxxvi. 4); 'the Fathers adorned the sky with stars, like a black steed with pearls; they placed darkness in night and light in day' (X. lxviii. 11); 'with their kindled fire the Aṅgirases (ancient priests) found the cows and steeds hidden by (the demon) Paṇi' (I. lxxxiii. 4); they 'by their rite caused the sun to mount the sky' (X. lxii. 3); '(the ancient fire priest) Atharvan by sacrifices first prepared the paths; then the sun, the guardian of ordinances, was born' (I. lxxxiii. 5). The ancient priest Viśvāmitra, by directly invoking the rivers, made them fordable for the tribe of the Bharatas (III. xxxiii. 1-12). The composers of all such passages must have attributed to the sacrifice in their own day the powers which they thus projected into the past.

An examination of the ritual literature shows that the dividing line between a sacrificial act, which is meant to propitiate the gods, and a magical act, which is intended to control the course of things, is by no means always definite, but that the two are often intermingled. Thus the morning sacrifice at sunrise, of which we read in the Rigveda (*e.g.*, IV. li. 7), when the fire is kindled and an offering is made to the fire-god, in the *Śatapatha Brāhmaṇa* (II. iii. 1. 5) assumes a magical character, the fire being kindled to produce sunrise: 'By offering before sunrise he (the sacrificer) makes him (the sun) to be born: he would not rise, if he were not to sacrifice in it (the fire).' A similar view seems already to be expressed in a verse of the Rigveda: 'Let us kindle thee, O Agni, that thy wondrous brand may shine in heaven' (V. vi. 4). Again, there are several passages in the Rigveda (*e.g.*, IX. xlix. 1, xcvii. 17, cvi. 9, cviii. 9 f.) in which the Soma ritual is spoken of in the magical character of producing rain direct, without influencing the goodwill of the gods that shed rain.

The blending of a sacrificial and a magic rite may be of two kinds. A ceremony which is primarily sacrificial may assume a magical character by the nature of the object which is offered for the attainment of a special purpose.

There can be little doubt that only food eaten by man originally constituted the sacrifice offered to the gods in fire. On the Vedic sacrificial ground there was, by the side of the fire, the litter of grass (*barhis*) on which the gods were conceived as sitting to receive the offering. On the conclusion of the ceremony the *barhis* was thrown into the fire, originally, no doubt, to render it innocuous after, by the divine presence, it had become dangerous to profane contact. To the *barhis* corresponds, in the ancient Persian ritual, the *baresman* (a bundle of twigs; see art. BARSOM) on which the sacrificial offerings were placed, and which was the seat of the gods. This indicates that the oblation in fire was an Indo-Aryan innovation, and that the burning of the *barhis* not improbably formed the transition to the fire-sacrifice.

The ritual literature furnishes innumerable examples of sacrifice receiving a magical turn by the employment or addition of a non-eatable substance; as when a man wishing for cattle offers the dung of a couple of calves (*Gobhila Gṛhyasūtra*, IV. ix. 13 f.); or when poison is added to an offering in order to destroy ants (*Kauśika Sūtra*, cxvi.). On the other hand, objects suitable for direct magical manipulation could easily be turned into an offering by those habituated to the sacrificial idea in order to invest magical acts with the garb of sacrifice. Thus the burning of injurious substances would become a sacrifice; for instance, arrow tips might be offered in order to destroy an enemy (*ib.* xlvii. 44). In this way the sacrifice came to assume the rôle of driving away demons; of helping a woman to overcome her rivals; of enabling a prince to conquer his enemies or to return from exile; and of producing many other magical results. The gradual mixture of the religious and the magical in the direction of the latter led the whole system of sacrifice to assume this character in the later Vedic period.

Various causes contributed to this result. The belief in the divine presence at the sacrifice, and in the mysterious success produced by the sacrifice, encouraged an increasing application of magical practices as the ceremonial system became more elaborate. Secondary observances of the sacrificial ritual might already have belonged to the sphere of magic from the beginning. Efforts to explain accidental features of the ceremonial would lead to the discovery of effects allied to magic. Priests would also foster belief in the magical power of sacrifice in order to secure their own indispensableness. The magical tendency would be increased by the mixture of prayer and spell; if in the prayer accompanying the sacrifice the magical effects of a spell were assumed, such effects would naturally be attributed to the sacrifice also.

5. Predominantly magical ritual. — There are several groups of rites which, though belonging to the sphere of sacrifice, are predominantly magical in character. They are partly connected with family and partly with public life. The most important of these are:

(1) *The wedding ceremony.*—What little worship of the gods is found in this group of rites is almost restricted to the cult of Agni, the domestic god, who was constituted a witness of the marriage, and who, in the form of the domestic fire, was to accompany the young pair through life. On the other hand, the ceremony was surrounded by magical acts, of which the following were the principal. The bride's hand was grasped that she might be delivered into the power of her husband. She stepped on a stone to acquire firmness. She took seven steps with him in order to establish friendship. She ate the sacrificial food with him to create community of life. When she reached her husband's house, she sat down on a red bull's hide to ensure fertility. The son of a woman who had borne only living male children was placed on her lap in order to fulfil the hope of healthy male progeny. Later, during pregnancy, a magical powder was placed in her nose to secure the birth of a son.

(2) *Initiation.*—Of the various religious ceremonies which were performed during boyhood, and which display the same predominantly magical character, the chief was that of initiation (*upanayana*). This, though not mentioned in the Rigveda, goes back to pre-historic times, as is shown by the parallel Avestic ceremony, and is the Vedic transformation of a rite by which, on the attainment of puberty, a boy was received into the community of men. In India it was regarded as a second birth, as being the entry into a new life, when the boy was introduced to a religious teacher with a view to Vedic study. The outward signs of the initiation are the girdle, which is wound three times round the pupil's waist, and the sacred cord, worn over the left shoulder and under the right arm, with which he is invested. The ceremony includes a number of observances and involves various tabus in regard to food, some of which will be mentioned below (see also VEDIC RELIGION, § 6 *h*, and cf. INITIATION [Hindu]).

(3) *Public rites.*—The public ceremonies of Vedic times were performed on behalf not of the clan or tribe as such, but of an individual, who in these cases was the king. The most prominent of them, aiming at the attainment of certain definite purposes, are magical in their main elements. At the royal consecration (*abhiṣeka* [*q.v.*]) the king sits on a throne made of wood from the *udumbara* fig-tree, which to the Indian was the embodiment of all nourishment. The seat was covered with a tiger-skin, the emblem of invincible strength. The contents of a cup made of *udumbara* wood, filled with butter, honey, and rain-water, were poured over the king in order to communicate to him their strength and abundance. The royal inauguration (*rājasūya*) is a further series of rites, chiefly of a symbolical character (cf. 12 (*b*)) intended to ensure a successful reign. A still more imposing ceremony was the Vājapeya, the two main features of which, a conventional race and another symbolic observance, have a magic purpose (12 (*b*); cf., further, art. ABHIṢEKA). Finally, the horse sacrifice (*aśvamedha* [*q.v.*]) was the highest sacrificial expression of regal power, which was undertaken for the fulfilment of all the most ambitious wishes of the king, and in which the victim indicated the desire to transfer the swift might of the horse to the sacrificing monarch.

6. Priest and magician.—The magician of prehistoric ages, who manipulated only the lower ritual concerned with demons and natural forces, had long before the time of the Rigveda (at least as early as the Indo-European period) developed into the priest, who dealt with a higher cult in which he invoked and sacrificed to gods. In the later Vedic period of the Yajurveda, however, we find the priest to a considerable extent reverting to the rôle of a magician; for he now constantly appears, independently of the gods, driving away evil spirits or influencing the powers of nature by the use of spells and other expedients of sorcery. In various lesser rites the priest acts quite in the style of prehistoric times. Thus he makes the bride step on a stone to ensure steadfastness; he causes fish to be eaten for the attainment of speed; he produces an imitation of rain that it may actually rain—here he is not a servant of the gods, but a magician. Yet even in the earliest period, that of the Rigveda, the sacrificial priest was a magician as well (though by no means necessarily the only magician, for both here and later references are made to sorcerers whose magic is directed against the sacrificial priest). It cannot be supposed that even the most advanced minds among the priests regarded prayer and sacrifice as the only means of securing welfare, while rejecting magic as an ineffective and reprehensible superstition. Magic was still to some extent used by those who had occasion to apply it, as is apparent from the character of some hymns of the Rigveda which, although late, form part of its canonical text. But not the employment of every form of magic was approved nor the practice of magic as a profession, doubtless because alliance with evil spirits and the use of maleficent magic were liable to injure the community. This is sufficiently clear from the words of the author of a passage of the Rigveda: 'May I die to-day if I am a sorcerer (*yātudhāna*), or if I have harassed any man's life; then may he lose his ten sons who falsely calls me "sorcerer"; he who calls me, that am no sorcerer, a practiser of sorcery, or who, being a demon, says that he is pure, may Indra strike him with his mighty weapon, may he sink down below every creature' (VII. civ. 15 f.). It was because the Atharvaveda contained a body of maleficent spells that it did not attain to canonical recognition till after it had become associated with the sacrificial cult by the addition to its text of numerous hymns borrowed from the Rigveda. On the other hand, in the Atharvaveda itself (*e.g.*, V. viii., VII. lxx.) magic is expressly approved when directed against the sacrifice offered by an enemy; and the ritual texts are full of directions for the sacrificer who wishes to destroy his enemy, in particular, when he desires to give his sacrifice a magical turn for the purpose of inflicting injury. The post-Vedic *Code of Manu* even contains the express statement (xi. 33) that the magic spells of the Atharvaveda are the Brāhman's weapon, which he may use without hesitation against his foes. In the Upaniṣads the magician-priest has become a philosopher who has passed from the path of ritual (*karma*) to that of knowledge (*jñāna*); but his mode of thought is still full of traits derived not only from sacrificial, but from magic lore. Of such a nature are his conceptions of the world-soul (*brahman* [*q.v.*]) and of the identity with it of the individual soul (*ātman* [*q.v.*]), as well as his speculations on the sacred syllable *om* (analogous in sense to 'amen'). Such, too, is his doctrine of *karma* (*q.v.*) as an impersonal power which, free from any divine influence, rules future existences with inexorable force. The same mental attitude is indicated by his approval of the grotesque and forcible exercises of Yoga, which is an inextricable blend of philosophy and magic. By the aid of Yoga he believed himself capable of acquiring the ability to make himself minute and invisible, to increase his size infinitely, to multiply his body, to remember his former existences, and so forth.

7. Asceticism and magic. — There is evidence that from the earliest Vedic period ascetic practices (*tapas*, lit. 'heat'), primarily exposure to heat, but including other forms of self-mortification, such as fasting, abstinence, and silence, were regarded as a means of attaining various supernatural powers resulting from the ecstatic condition induced by them. Thus the Rigveda says (X. cxxxvi. 2) of those who are in such a frenzied condition that 'the gods have entered into them.' A poet of the same Veda tells (VIII. lix. 6) how, in a vision produced by austerity (*tapas*), he saw the old creations of ancient sages, the first sacrificers, in the remotest past of the human race. There are many other Vedic passages ascribing similar powers: dream is born from the soul filled with austerity (Atharvaveda, XIX. lvi. 5); speech born of austerity penetrates to the gods (*Taittirīya Āraṇyaka*, V. vi. 7); he who has practised great austerity reaches the sun (Rigveda, X. cliv. 2); after practising austerity Indra won heaven (X. clxvii. 1); the magical power of austerity peculiar to the Brāhman will bring calamity on the man who injures him (X. cix. 4). Austerity confers the power to produce the mightiest creations: the goddess Aṣṭakā, performing austerity, produced the greatness of Indra (Atharvaveda, III. x. 12); the seers were born of austerity (XI. i. 26, XVIII. ii. 15, 18). In many passages of the Brāhmaṇas the creator Prajāpati is described as gaining by the practice of austerity the power to evolve out of himself the worlds and all living creatures; and in one place (*Śatapatha Brāhmaṇa*, X. iv. 4. 2) he appears as practising such asceticism that from all his pores came forth lights, which are the stars. The Brāhmaṇas also tell how various mythical beings attained by austerity to a high degree of enlightenment that revealed to them some secret of sacrificial lore. It is for such magical effects that austerity is required as an essential element in the preparation for various particularly holy sacrificial rites. Thus the Soma sacrifice is preceded by a consecration (*dīkṣā*) of the sacrificer in which he practises austerity lasting, according to some authorities (*ib.* XIII. i. 7. 2), till complete physical exhaustion ensues.

8. Magical conditions and agencies.—Magical effect is largely, if not altogether, based on contact (very often impalpable), which has to be brought about if the agency is beneficial to oneself, or to be prevented if the agency is injurious to oneself. The result desired is attained by the use of spells and rites of various kinds. The place selected for the practice of magic, except when it is an element of the sacrificial ceremonial, is generally a lonely one. A cemetery, the seat of flesh-eating demons, is a specially suitable place for its operations. A cross-road is a favourite locality to divest oneself of evil influences. A secluded part of a house, a shed, and solitary spots in field or forest are also used. The time at which many operations of hostile magic take place is night; but that of others depends on their circumstances or their purpose. Direction is an important element. Thus the south is the home of demons and *manes*; hence performers of rites connected with them must face that point of the compass. In auspicious rites walking and other kinds of movement are directed from left to right, following the course of the sun, while in funeral and other uncanny ceremonies the direction is invariably reversed, the performers moving from north to south.

(*a*) *Spirits and demons.*—Some of the lesser spirits are concerned only with one activity, such as presiding over the fields and helping at harvest; others, with Arbudi at their head, are invoked to spread terror and death among enemies on the field of battle (Atharvaveda, XI. ix. 1 ff.). The characteristic of most of the rest is to cause damage and destruction in the sphere of human life. These demons are usually called by the generic name of *rakṣas*, *yātu*, or *piśācha*, though many of them also have individual designations. Their appearance is for the most part human, though often with some kind of deformity; but they not infrequently have an animal or bird shape, such as that of a dog, wolf, owl, or vulture. They also appear in assumed figures, human or animal; thus at funeral rites they intrude in the form of the souls of the ancestors to whom the offering is made; and they approach women in various disguises. The sorcerer himself (as well as the spirits serving him) might assume animal form and thus injure his enemies. Belief in such transformation is already expressed in the Rigveda, where hostile magicians are spoken of as becoming birds and flying about at night (VII. civ. 18). Setting demons in motion is regarded as letting them loose against an enemy. Thus in the Rigveda (X. ciii. 12) the demon of disease Apvā is let loose against a hostile army with the spell: 'Go forth, Apvā, to confuse their minds, to seize their limbs; attack them; burn them with thy heat in their hearts; let the foe fall into deep darkness.' Such spells might be accompanied by magical acts, such as letting loose a white-footed ewe, in which the power of disease was supposed to be embodied, against the hostile army.

Evil spirits are thought to be everywhere—in the sea, in the air, but most of all in human dwellings; otherwise they especially infest the place where four roads meet. The time of their activity is chiefly evening and night; at night they seek to kill the sacrificer who has undergone consecration (*dīkṣā*). But they are particularly active during the night of new moon. Their usual mode of attack (mentioned in both the Rigveda [VIII. xlix. 20] and the Atharvaveda [V. xxix. 6–8, VII. lxxvi. 4]) is to enter into a man, especially through the mouth; they then eat his flesh, suck his marrow, drink his blood, and create disease of every kind; they also cause madness and take away the power of speech. They are chiefly dangerous on the most important occasions of domestic life—at births, weddings, and funerals. One of the main objects of their attack is the sacrifice: the Rigveda speaks (VII. civ. 21) of the Yātus that seize the sacrificial food, and the Atharvaveda contains (VII. lxx. 1 f.) the spell of a magician desiring to destroy the sacrifice of an enemy through the wiles of a demon. Hence the sacrificial ceremonial is, from beginning to end, accompanied by formulæ directed to defence against demons. These evil spirits, moreover, do harm to man's property, drinking the milk of his cows, eating the flesh of his horses, and damaging his dwellings. In short, every moment of life, every act, every possession is assailed by hosts of invisible foes, the allies of human workers of calamity.

(*b*) *Injurious substances.*—Closely allied to these demoniac enemies are the numerous substances—the most general expression for which in the Vedic language is *tanū*, or 'body'—which, conceived chiefly as impersonal, though sometimes still tinged with personality, perhaps represent an advance of thought. Hence the boundary-line between personal demons and impersonal agencies is not fixed; thus the term *pāpman*, 'evil power,' as a masculine is used in the former, as a neuter in the latter sense. Nor are even injurious creatures like snakes, ants, and worms clearly distinguished from evil spirits, being often spoken of as demons to be driven away. Examples of impalpable agencies are the 'substance' of disease, of hunger and thirst, of guilt, even of such abstractions as sonlessness; or the intangible influence proceeding from auspicious or baneful stars and from the waning or waxing of the moon. These are supposed to fly about in the air and to affect man by various forms of contact. The sphere of magical operations is greatly extended by the belief that, if a 'substance' or power is embodied in any creature or object—*e.g.*, irresistible strength in a tiger—that power is inherent in all its parts and in all that is connected with it. Such a power, therefore, resides not only in the flesh of an animal, but in its skin, horn, hair, and so on. Again, the essence of water dwells in aquatic plants like the *avakā* (*Blyxa octandra*), and in aquatic animals like the frog; the nature of the boar is present in the soil that is torn up by its tusks; the force of lightning is latent in a splint of wood from a tree that has been struck; the virtue of one's native land exists in a clod taken from it; a man is connected with the earth by his footprints; even an image or a name is conceived as containing a part of the essence of the beings or things which they represent or name. As all such powers are communicable by contact, the whole sacrificial ritual is full of rules as to the persons or things which the performers are to touch, for thus the beneficial power of the sacrifice is transferred to them. For instance, the skins of various animals communicate the characteristic quality attributed to them: one who seats himself on the hide of a bull acquires fertility; on that of a black antelope, sanctity; on that of a he-goat, plenty; on that of a tiger, invincible power.

9. Magical procedure.—The operations of magic are mainly directed against hostile agencies, either by preventing their contact with the operator or by bringing about their contact with an enemy. Auspicious rites, besides being much less numerous, are often only another aspect of offensive magic, and will, therefore, be treated under the various types of action, partly auspicious and partly hostile, employed in magical ceremonies (§ 12).

10. Defensive magic. — This type of magic, though consisting in warding off injurious powers, is not always expressed in the form of hostility when demons are concerned; it may then be attended by a certain amount of propitiation. Thus in the Atharvaveda (I. xii. 2) deterrent homage is paid to a demon of disease: 'Thee, lurking in each limb with burning, we, paying homage, would worship with oblation'; lightning is similarly addressed (I. xiii. 2): 'Homage to thee, child of the height, whence thou gatherest heat; be merciful to ourselves; do kindness to our offspring'; also instruments and ministers of death: 'To those weapons of thine, O Death, be homage; homage to thy benediction, homage to thy malediction; homage to thy favour, O Death; this homage to thy disfavour' (VI. xiii. i. 2). Again, sacrifices to demons are often mentioned (*Baudhāyana Dharmasūtra*, II. i. 32); and in the general sacrificial cult they receive their share, which, however, consists only of inferior offerings, such as blood and offal. Hostile words or actions are often accompanied by spells expressive of homage. *Hiraṇyakeśin Gṛhyasūtra* contains a direction (I. xvi. 20 f.) that a brand burning at both ends should be thrown at a jackal (regarded as possessed by the evil powers of death), and that the animal should at the same time be worshipped with the Vedic verse, 'Thou art mighty, thou carriest away.' In a rite concerned with serpents the reptiles are addressed with homage, while the intention to destroy them is also expressed (*Sarpabali*, xi.). A ceremonial intended to ward off ants (*Kauśika Sūtra*, cxvi.) begins with propitiatory offerings and spells; but, if these fail, they are followed with a poisoned oblation surrounded by symbols of hostility and accompanied by an invocation of the gods to destroy their eggs and progeny. Propitiation, however, plays but a very subordinate part in this type of magic.

i. PREVENTIVE MAGIC.—On the principle that prevention is better than cure the procedure of defensive magic is largely prophylactic, everything being avoided that might attract injurious powers. The precautions taken are of the following kinds.

(1) *Avoidance of contact.*—The touch of beings in which maleficent spirits or substances were supposed to dwell was eschewed. Thus to touch the mother during the ten days of impurity after childbirth was regarded as dangerous; and the stones used in erecting an altar for Nirṛti, the goddess of dissolution, were put in their place without being directly handled. The access of injurious powers through other senses was similarly avoided. Thus listening to impure sounds involved risk. Precautions were taken not to see impure or dangerous persons or things; the sight of offerings to the dead or to the uncanny god Rudra was to be avoided; and those who were departing from a place where inauspicious ceremonies had been performed, such as those concerned with the dead, with demons, with the goddess Nirṛti or the god Rudra, abstained from looking back. On occasions when evil spirits were likely to be in the neighbourhood care was taken to prevent their coming too near. Thus a bundle of twigs was tied to the corpse on the way to the burning ground in order to efface the footsteps and so hide the path from the demons; and the sacrificial fire of the departed, having by his decease become a seat of death-bringing powers, was removed by some aperture other than the door.

(2) *Fasting.* — One of the chief precautionary measures against the attacks of hostile powers was abstention from food, in order to prevent them from entering the body. It is, therefore, a leading element in the preliminary consecration (*dīkṣā*) for the Soma sacrifice. With reference to this, one of the Sūtras remarks (*Āpastamba Śrautasūtra*, X. xiv. 9): 'When an initiated man (*dīkṣita*) grows thin, he becomes purified for the sacrifice.' A special form of fasting was the avoidance of particular kinds of food. Thus the performer of the new and full moon sacrifice had, on the eve of the ceremony, to refrain from eating either flesh or the kind of food which he was going to offer on the following day. The teacher who has invested a pupil with the sacred cord may not eat flesh for a night and a day; while the student himself has to refrain from eating salted food and drinking milk for three days after the ceremony; he must also abstain from food altogether for three days, or a day and a night, before he enters upon a particularly holy part of his Vedic course. A newly married couple must, during the first three nights following the wedding ceremony, avoid all salted or pungent food. The efficacy of fasting is illustrated by the precept (*Gobhila Gṛhyasūtra*, IV. vi. 13) that one who desires to gain a hundred cart-loads of gold should observe the vow of fasting during one fortnight.

(3) *Abstinence.*—Another safeguard is the practice of chastity. This is enjoined for three nights after the wedding ceremony in order to ward off the attacks of demons that destroy offspring. It is observed by the performer of the new and full moon sacrifice on the night before the rite takes place; for a day and a night by the teacher who initiates a pupil; for twelve nights by the offerer of the Śabalī sacrifice; during the course of the Dīkṣā by him who undergoes that consecration; and by the Vedic student during the whole period of his apprenticeship.

(4) *Asceticism.*—This expedient appears in various forms. One of them is exposure to heat; it is an element in the Dīkṣā ceremony, a special formula being quoted for use when the initiated man breaks into perspiration. Sleeping on the ground is prescribed, during the same length of time as abstinence for the newly married couple, the Vedic student, and the performers of the Dīkṣā consecration, of the new and full moon ceremony, and of the Śabalī sacrifice. As a safeguard against demons dangerous to the sleeper, watching through the night is enjoined during the Dīkṣā ceremony, and on the eve of setting up the sacrificial fires and of the new and full moon sacrifice. Silence is to be observed by the sacrificer undergoing the Dīkṣā consecration, by the man about to set up the three

sacrificial fires, and by the Vedic student on various occasions. Holding the breath, which was regarded as an important form of asceticism, appears, for instance, in a rite during the funeral ceremony. It may here be added that austerities of various kinds had to be undergone by one preparing to cure epilepsy, before he was qualified to perform the magical ceremonies intended to effect the recovery of the patient.

(5) *Concealment.*—Another means of guarding against the attacks of hostile powers was concealment of one's person or of its parts, as seclusion in a shed and covering the head during the observances of the Dīkṣā ceremony; or putting on garments to make oneself unrecognizable; or hiding the hair of the head and beard or nails cut off at sacramental rites, such as the initiation of the Vedic student (cf. § 8 (*b*)).

(6) *Amulets.*—Charms worn on the body were frequently employed both for the negative purpose of warding off evil influences from one's person (amulets) and for the positive purpose of attracting prosperity (talismans). Sometimes the same charm serves both purposes; thus the pearl destroys demons, disease, and poverty, and at the same time bestows welfare and long life. Amulets were for the most part made of wood, but also of various other substances. Their efficacy is regarded as dependent on the particular power of repulsion inherent in them, and is not infrequently spoken of as imparted by the gods. They are called god-born, are said to have been given by gods to men, to have been strengthened by the gods, or to have had their power communicated to them by the gods, who co-operate with them; the gods themselves are described as having once been successful by the power residing in them; by amulets Indra overcame the demons (Atharvaveda, X. iii. 11). Their potency sometimes emanates from their names. An amulet derived from the *varaṇa* tree (*Cratæva Roxburghii*) destroys enemies because, according to the meaning attributed to the name (*ib.* X. iii. 5), it drives off (*vārayati*). An amulet made of this wood is thus addressed in the Atharvaveda (X. iii. 14, 11): 'As the wind and the fire consume the trees, the lords of the forest, so do thou consume my rivals; this *varaṇa* upon my breast, the kingly, divine tree, shall smite asunder my foes, as Indra the demons.' One of the amulets most frequently mentioned in the Atharvaveda is that made from the *jaṅgiḍa* tree, which protects from diseases and demons. Again, a long hymn of the same Veda (VIII. v.) dwells on the aggressive powers of an amulet fashioned from the wood of the *sraktya* tree, which destroys foes, demons, and sorceries. Cf., further, art. CHARMS AND AMULETS (Vedic).

ii. REMEDIAL MAGIC.—Magical operations are performed not only to ward off maleficent powers that are threatening, but also to expel them after they have taken possession of their victim in the form of diseases or ailments. The Atharvaveda is full of spells directed against these. Many such incantations make no mention of any concrete remedies with which their use was accompanied; but the evidence of the Sūtras shows that these incantations, at least very often, formed part of a magical rite in which concrete remedies were an element. Examples of simple spells for the cure of diseases are the following: 'As the rays of the sun swiftly fly to a distance, thus do thou, O cough, fly forth along the flood of the sea' (VI. cv. 3); and 'The disease that racks and wastes thy limbs, and the sickness in thy heart, has flown as an eagle to the far distance, overcome by my charm' (V. xxx. 9). Curative spells are, however, more usually accompanied by the express employment of material objects, chiefly plants. The hymns of the Atharvaveda abound in references to such remedies. These represent the earliest beginnings of medical lore in India. The border-line between magic and primitive science here is not always definite, for in some cases the plant used with the spell may have been an actual cure for a particular disease, while in other cases its application was purely magical, as that of the herbs used to promote the growth of hair on bald heads (these were doubtless as ineffective as the hair-restorers of modern times). The following are two charms from the Atharvaveda intended for this particular cure: 'That hair of thine which drops off, and that which is broken root and all, upon it do I sprinkle the all-healing herb' (VI. cxxxvi. 3); 'Make firm their roots, draw out their ends, expand their middle, O herb! may thy hairs grow as reeds, may they cluster black about thy head!' (VI. cxxxvii. 3). The Atharvaveda contains many spells in which the *kuṣṭha* plant (probably *Costus speciosus* or *arabicus*) is invoked to drive out fever; two of its hymns (I. xxiii. f.) are meant to cure leprosy by the use of a dark plant; one (VII. lvi.) operates with a herb that destroys snake poison, and another (VI. xvi.) with a plant against ophthalmia. Fractures are cured by the plant *arundhatī* (IV. xii.), and wounds by the use of the peppercorn (VI. cix.). The use of ointment is associated with one hymn of the Atharvaveda (IV. ix.), of which this is one of the spells: 'From him over whose every limb and every joint thou passest, O salve, thou dost, as a mighty intercepter, drive away disease.' Water not infrequently appears as a magical remedy, and its general curative powers are thus expressed by the following spell of the Atharvaveda (VI. xci. 3): 'The waters verily are healing, the waters chase away disease, the waters cure all ailments; may they prepare a remedy for thee.' It also cures individual diseases, as excessive bodily discharges: 'The spring water yonder which runs down from the mountains, that do I render healing for thee, in order that thou mayest contain a potent remedy' (II. iii. 1); or heart-disease: 'From the Himavat mountains they flow forth, in the Indus is their gathering place: may the waters, indeed, grant me that cure for heart-ache' (VI. xxiv. 1). *Pāraskara Gṛhyasūtra* (III. vi. 2) describes how water is used in a magic operation for the cure of headache: the performer moistened his hands and passed them over the eyebrows of the sufferer with the spell: 'From the eyes, from the ears, from the whiskers, from the chin, from the forehead I drive away this disease of the head.' Another remedy is the horn of an antelope, used against a hereditary disease named *kṣetriya*: 'Upon the head of the nimble antelope a remedy grows! He has driven the *kṣetriya* in all directions by means of the horn' (Atharvaveda, III. vii. 1).

II. Offensive magic.—Aggressive operations against maleficent powers cannot always be distinguished, especially in regard to demons, from that form of defensive magic which is directed to warding off their attacks. Hence the expedients adopted are to some extent the same for both purposes.

i. MEANS EMPLOYED.—(1) *Fire.*—Fire was one of the chief direct means of driving away demons and all hostile sorcery. Thus in the Rigveda Agni, the god of fire, is frequently invoked (I. xii. 5, xxxvi. 20) with such verses as: 'Burn, O Agni, against the sorcerers; always burn down the sorcerers and the allies of the demons.' This use of fire, probably the earliest in cult, though overlaid with its later and much more extensive sacrificial application, still survives in the Vedic ritual. Thus a special fire called the 'lying-in fire' (*sūtikāgni*) is introduced into the lying-in chamber (*sūtikā-gṛha*). Of this fire the author of one of the domestic Sūtras remarks (*Hiraṇyakeśin Gṛhyasūtra*, II. iii. 6 f.):

'Sacred rites, except fumigation, are not performed with it; he fumigates the child with small grains mixed with mustard seeds'; he then adds a number of spells to drive away various demons that prowl through the village at night, that drink out of skulls; Agni is invoked to burn their lungs, hearts, livers, and eyes. At the sacramental ceremony of cutting the child's hair a fire is kindled while a number of auspicious verses are recited; as nothing is said of its application to sacrificial purposes, it was presumably meant to ward off demons. Of similar significance were the fire employed at the investiture of the Brāhman student, behind which both he and his teacher step, and that kindled when the pupil entered upon his course of Vedic study. That this was the significance of the fire beside which the Soma sacrificer watched during the night in the Dīkṣā ceremony is certain, because it is expressly said (*Taittirīya Saṃhitā*, VI. i. 4. 6) that Agni is here appointed 'for the destruction of the demons.' It can hardly be doubted that in the great sacrificial ritual of the three fires the southern fire was understood to have the magical power of dispelling demons, for the south is the direction from which the souls of the dead and the injurious spirits allied to them approach. In the funeral ritual a brand was taken from the southern fire and laid down pointing to the south, while a formula was pronounced in which Agni was invoked to drive away all demons that, assuming manifold forms, might venture near. At the conclusion of the funeral ceremony a fire was used by the survivors for the purpose of warding off the powers that cause death. Fire was also on various occasions carried round what was to be protected against the attacks of evil spirits. Thus a brand lighted at both ends was moved round the funeral offering; and a firebrand was also borne by the priest round the victim, the post, and other accessaries of the animal sacrifice.

(2) *Water*.—Water is another efficacious means of repelling hostile agencies, as is indicated by the statement (*Maitrāyaṇī Saṃhitā*, IV. viii. 5) that 'the demons do not cross the waters.' We have already noted some examples of the use of water in curing diseases and ailments. Water is further regarded as a chief means of removing possession by evil spirits. At the birth ceremony water is supposed to wash away all injurious powers from the new-born child. A purifying bath is prescribed before entering on various ceremonies, as the Dīkṣā, to remove supernatural substances that might be inimical to their success. Thus the bride and bridegroom take a bath or perform ablutions before the wedding ceremony. In rites of expiation especially, bathing and washing play an important part. Various ceremonies also conclude with a bath in order to obviate the risk of taking back into ordinary life the magical influence inherent in the rite. Such is the case at the end of the Dīkṣā, when clothes and implements used during the ceremony are also laid aside. The significance of the bath taken by the Brāhman student at the end of his apprenticeship is similar. There is, further, a rule that after the utterance of spells addressed to uncanny beings, such as the dead, demons, or Rudra, one should purify oneself with water from the contact with those beings which has thus been incurred. The urine of cows was specially esteemed as a means of purification, being perhaps at the same time regarded as communicating the abundant nutritive power inherent in the animal. As long as a magical condition is meant to continue, bathing or washing is avoided; hence dirt is the characteristic of one who, by means of asceticism (*tapas*), aims at acquiring special magical power.

(3) *Plants*.—We have already seen that plants were frequently used along with spells as a magical cure of disease. Cognate to this medicinal employment is the application of herbs to the purpose of securing the love of a man or a woman, and of promoting or destroying virility; of both these classes of charms the Atharvaveda contains many examples. But they are also resorted to for other objects. Thus some are employed against demons and sorcerers, others to counteract curses, and several are associated with battle-charms. Aquatic plants, together with frogs, as representing water, are combined with spells to quench fire. Bdellium (*guggulu*), the fragrant exudation of a tree, frequently occurs in the ritual as, by its odour, driving away demons of disease or frustrating a curse.

(4) *Stones, etc.*—In the wedding ceremony, as we have seen, the bride stepped on a stone to ensure steadfastness. A stone, as representing a dividing mountain, was regarded as a means of keeping off evil spirits, and with this intention it was employed in the funeral ritual to separate the living from the dead, where also a clod of earth taken from a boundary was similarly used. In the same ceremony a mat was laid down while the formula, 'This is put between against calamity,' was pronounced (*Kauśika Sūtra*, lxxxvi. 14). A wooden fence was placed round the sacrificial fire, the purpose being 'to strike away the demons' (*Taittirīya Saṃhitā*, II. vi. 6. 2).

(5) *Lead*.—This metal was frequently employed in magical operations, as, *e.g.*, in wiping off dangerous substances. The Atharvaveda contains a hymn (I. xvi.) in which lead was used against demons and sorcerers, this being one of its spells: 'If thou slayest our cow, if our horse or our domestic, we pierce thee with lead, so that thou shalt not slay our heroes.'

(6) *Weapons and staves*.—These appear on various occasions as a protection against demons. Thus a man who woos a bride is accompanied by one armed with a bow and arrows. At the wedding ceremony little staves are shot into the air, with the formula: 'I pierce the eye of the demons that prowl around the bride who approaches the fire' (*Mānava Gṛhyasūtra*, I. x.). At the royal inauguration the priest beats the king with a staff, saying, 'We beat evil away from thee' (*Kātyāyana Śrautasūtra*, XV. vii. 6). The staff is a part of the ritual equipment in the Dīkṣā ceremony, its significance here being explained by the *Śatapatha Brāhmaṇa* (III. ii. 1. 32) thus: 'The staff is a thunder-bolt to drive away the demons.' The Vedic student, as peculiarly liable to the attacks of evil spirits, is provided with a staff at the rite of investiture. This he must always carry, never allowing any one to pass between it and himself; he parts with it only at the end of his apprenticeship, when he casts it away into water, along with his girdle and other sacred objects. On entering the next stage of religious life the Brāhman receives a new staff made of a different wood, the purpose of which is sufficiently expressed by the spells employed at the accompanying rite: 'Protect me from all powers of destruction on all sides,' and 'Destroy all hosts of enemies on every side' (*Hiraṇyakeśin Gṛhyasūtra*, I. xi. 8). A wooden implement shaped like a sword, technically called *sphya*, and very variously applied in sacrificial rites, has evidently the significance of a demon-repelling weapon. At the sacrifice to the dead the *sphya* is passed over the altar with the words, 'Smitten away are the devils and demons that sit on the altar' (*Śāṅkhāyana Śrautasūtra*, IV. iv. 2).

ii. MAGICAL ACTION.—Certain types of action are regarded as producing a magical effect in various rites. They may be grouped as follows.

(*a*) *Hostile*.—(1) To make a *noise* is believed to be an efficacious means of driving away demons. At the solstitial festival drums were beaten in order to scare evil spirits, which were deemed to be especially powerful at the time of the shortest day. A gong was sounded at the ritual for exorcizing the demon of epilepsy. At the funeral ceremony a din was produced by shattering pots.

(2) A frequent method of removing injurious influences is to *wipe* them *off*. Thus lead or a black thread of wool was used as an aid in the process. In particular, the *apāmārga* (*Achyranthes aspera*) plant (popularly interpreted to mean 'wiping out') was most variously employed in this sense. The Atharvaveda contains several hymns with which the plant is applied, the following being one of the spells in which this action is expressed (IV. xviii. 8): 'Having wiped out all sorcerers, and all grudging demons, with thee, O Apāmārga, we wipe all that evil out.' The *Śatapatha Brāhmaṇa* remarks (V. ii. 4. 14) that by the aid of this plant the gods wiped away fiends and demons. Among other magical applications of this action may be noted the requirement that one who has seen an evil dream should wipe his face.

(3) Another means of getting rid of demons or injurious powers is to *shake*, *cast*, or *strip* them *off*. The black antelope skin used at a sacrifice is shaken out with the words, 'Shaken away is the demon; shaken away are the goblins' (*Vājasaneyi Saṃhitā*, i. 14). After feeding the souls of the dead, the officiant shakes the hem of his garment in order to remove the souls that may be clinging to it. At the conclusion of the funeral ceremony, the bundle of twigs, used to efface the footsteps of death, is thrown away for fear of the dangerous substance which it may have derived from those footprints. For similar reasons clothes worn at uncanny rites, such as funerals, are cast aside. Injurious substances are deemed to be stripped off by passing through some aperture the person to whom they adhere. This notion is found even in the Rigveda (VIII. lxxx. 7), where Indra is said to have cured the girl Apālā, who suffered from skin disease, by drawing her through an opening in a car. It is doubtless a survival of this form of purification when, in the wedding ceremony, the aperture of the yoke of a car is placed on the head of the bride.

The removal of injurious substances is not always a mere riddance, but is often also a transference to remote places or to other objects animate or inanimate. The Rigveda and the Atharvaveda contain several formulæ or spells to relegate evil agencies to particular places or persons in the far distance. Thus hostile magic is expelled beyond the ninety streams (Atharvaveda, VIII. v. 9, x. i. 16); the disease Takman (a sort of fever) is sent away to far-off peoples, such as the Gandharians and the Magadhas (*ib.* v. xxii. 14); evil deed and evil dream are banished to the divine being Trita Āptya in the remotest distance (Rigveda, VIII. xlvii. 13–17). Injurious agencies are also transferred to others at particularly uncanny spots, especially crossroads. A garment containing certain impurities is removed to a forest, suspended from a tree, or hung over a post, to which its dangerous influence is conveyed, and thus rendered innocuous (Atharvaveda, XIV. ii. 49 f.). Snake-poison is removed to a firebrand, which, being then thrown at a snake, returns the danger to its source (*Kauśika Sūtra*, xxix. 6). Fever is transferred to a frog as an antidote representing water (Atharvaveda, VII. cxvi. 2); while jaundice is conducted in a homœopathic manner to a yellow bird (*ib.* I. xxii. 4).

(*b*) *Auspicious*.—(1) A very prominent part is played by *eating* in the communication of beneficial influences; contact with injurious substances, which would, of course, be equally well effected by eating, is avoided by fasting (cf. § 10. i. (2)). The Vedic ritual contains innumerable examples of the magical power conveyed by the eating of sacrificial food. The eating of the food is regarded as communicating the blessing embodied in it; and in the most various forms the view appears that the sacrificial substance conveys the special kind of power implied in a particular sacrifice. Thus, when the religious teacher initiates his pupil, he gives him the remnant of the offering with the formula, 'May Agni place his wisdom in thee.' On the occasion of the ploughing festival a mixture of the milk of a cow that has a calf of the same colour and dung, bdellium, and salt is eaten. At the ceremony for the obtaining of male offspring the wife has to eat a barleycorn and two grains of mustard seed (or two beans), one of which has been laid on each side of it (as symbolizing a male being). The act of two or more persons eating together establishes a community between them; at the wedding ceremonial the bride and the bridegroom eat together, and at the royal inauguration the king and the priest.

Based on the idea that an animal, when eaten, communicates its special characteristics to the eater is the correspondence in sex, colour, and other qualities between the victim and the god to whom it is offered. To Indra a bull or (less often) a buffalo, to which he is often compared, is sacrificed; to the Aśvins, twin gods of the morning, a reddish he-goat, for 'of reddish colour, as it were, are the Aśvins' (*Śatapatha Brāhmaṇa*, v. v. 4. 1); to the goddess Sarasvatī a ewe of certain qualities; to Agni, with his column of dark smoke, a he-goat with a black throat; to the Sun and to Yama (god of death), two he-goats, one white, the other black. A cognate magical correspondence appears in the offering of a black victim in a rite for the obtaining of rain: 'It is black, for this is the nature of rain; with that which is its nature he wins rain' (*Taittirīya Saṃhitā*, II. i. 8. 5). When the destruction of enemies is intended, a blood-red victim is offered by priests dressed in red and wearing red turbans.

(2) There are several ceremonies in which *anointing* is applied for the attainment of auspicious ends. In the Dīkṣā rite the sacrificer is anointed with fresh butter to give him unimpaired vigour and sound sight. In the animal sacrifice the stake is anointed with clarified butter for the purpose of bringing blessings to the sacrificer. At the royal inauguration the king is anointed with a mixture of butter, honey, rain-water, and other ingredients, which communicate to him the powers and abundance inherent in them. At the same ceremony the king anoints himself with the fluid contained in the horn of a black antelope and refrains for a year from cutting his hair, which has been moistened by it. At the Sautrāmaṇī rite, an expiatory part of the Soma sacrifice, the priest consecrates the king by sprinkling him with the fat gravy of the sacrificial animals: 'With the essence of cattle, with the highest kind of food, he thus sprinkles him' (*Śatapatha Brāhmaṇa*, XII. viii. 3. 12).

(3) *Charms*, made for the most part of wood, but also of other materials, were frequently attached to parts of the body for various auspicious purposes. A talisman made of wood from the *parṇa*-tree (*Butea frondosa*) was worn in order to strengthen royal power (Atharvaveda, III. v.); a bridegroom, while reciting a hymn of the Atharvaveda, fastened to his little finger, by means of a thread coloured with lac, a talisman made of liquorice wood to secure the love of his bride (*Kauśika Sūtra*, lxxvi. 8 f.); at the full moon ceremony the sacrificer tied on his person talismans made of lac, together with all sorts of herbs, for the attainment of prosperity; while sowing seed, the husbandman put on a talisman of barley. The Vedic student who, at the conclusion of his apprenticeship, has taken the purifying bath ties a pellet of *badara* (*Zizyphus jujuba*) wood to his left hand and fastens a pellet of gold to his neck; he then attaches two earrings to the skirt of his garment, and finally inserts them in his ears. A talisman of gold secures long life: 'He who wears it dies of old age,' in the words of the Atharvaveda (XIX. xxvi. 1). To ensure conception a woman puts on a bracelet with the spell, 'An acquirer of offspring and wealth this bracelet has become' (VI. lxxxi. 1).

(*c*) *Indifferent*.—(1) *Burying* was a frequent secret method of conducting magical substances to others, generally with hostile intent. The Atharvaveda is full of spells expressing fear of magic buried in sacrificial straw, or fields, or wells, or cemeteries. Objects belonging to a woman who is to be injured—a garland, hair, a twig for cleaning the teeth—together with other things productive of misfortune are placed between three stones in a mortar (a symbol of crushing) and buried. The luck of a person thus attacked might be restored by digging up the objects, while an auspicious spell was uttered. The *Śatapatha Brāhmaṇa* relates (III. v. 4. 2 f.) a myth how the demons buried charms in order to overcome the gods; but the latter, by digging them up, made them inoperative. The Soma sacrifice even contains a ceremony the express purpose of which is to dig up the magical objects buried by rivals or enemies. This idea of burying things sometimes has an auspicious intention, as when a mixture of milk, dung, bdellium, and salt is buried in order to promote the welfare of cattle (*Kauśika Sūtra*, xix. 19).

(2) The action of *looking* at an object may be either beneficial or injurious. It has the former effect, *e.g.*, when the sacrificer says (*Vājasaneyi Saṃhita*, v. 34) to the priest, 'Look at me with the eye of Mitra' (the sun-god); or when a guest addresses the sweet food that is offered to him, saying, 'With Mitra's eye I regard thee' (*Aśvalāyana Gṛhyasūtra*, I. xxiv. 14). But the evil eye (*q.v.*), *e.g.* of the serpent, brings disaster on him towards whom it is directed. At the wedding ceremony the bridegroom secures himself against the evil eye of the bride by anointing her eyes and saying, 'Look not with an evil eye, bring not death to thy husband' (*Pāraskara Gṛhyasūtra*, i. 4; *Śāṅkhāyana Gṛhyasūtra*, i. 16). In the Atharvaveda (IV. ix. 6) ointment is conjured against the evil eye with the spell, 'From the evil eye of the enemy protect us, O salve'; the *jaṅgiḍa*-tree is invoked against the evil eye of the hostile-minded (XIX. xxxv. 3); and a certain plant is employed with the spell, 'Of the enemy who bewitches with his eye we hew off the ribs' (II. vii. 5; cf. XIX. xlv. 1). On the other hand, the evil effect produced by an inauspicious object on him who sees it is shown by innumerable directions enjoining avoidance of such sights. Thus the Vedic student who, at the conclusion of his apprenticeship, has taken his purifying bath must not look at an enemy, a malefactor, a corpse-bearer, or ordure. For similar reasons, one returning to the sacrificial ground should not look round after performing an inauspicious ceremony, such as an offering to the goddess Nirṛti or a rite for the slaughter of demons.

(3) The action of *circumambulation*, which occurs very frequently in the Vedic ceremonial, is regarded as having a magically auspicious effect when the performer walks round an object in sunwise fashion by keeping his right hand towards it (*pradakṣiṇā*). Both living and inanimate things are three times circumambulated in this manner; *e.g.*, priests thus walk round other priests or the victim, and the wives of the king walk round the dead sacrificial horse. Sacrificial altars and temples, the ground where a house is built, as well as houses (as a protection against serpents), are circumambulated. This rite is especially often performed with the sacrificial fire, as at the wedding ceremony and at the initiation of the Vedic student. Water is circumambulated at a wedding, as also a new house, while water is at the same time sprinkled round it. When the ceremony is inauspicious, the direction is reversed, the left hand being kept towards the object. This is done especially in funeral rites at the burying ground and at cross-roads. Thus the mourners walk three times round the unlucky fire deposited where four roads meet, with their left sides towards it, beating their left thighs with their left hands. When a patient is to be cured of snake-bite, the priest walks round him to the left. When a servant who is disposed to run away is asleep, his master, making water into the horn of a living animal, walks three times round him to the left, sprinkling the water round him with the spell, 'From the mountain on which thou wast born, from thy mother, from thy sister, from thy parents, and thy brother, from thy friends I sever thee' (*Pāraskara Gṛhyasūtra*, III. vii. 2). Movement both in the auspicious and in the reverse direction is not restricted to walking. Thus in the sacrifice to the dead the officiant grasps a water jar with his left hand and pours out its contents from right to left; he also holds the ladle in his left and deposits the offering on the grass in the same direction (cf., further, art. CIRCUMAMBULATION).

12. Sympathetic magic.—A special type of magic is that which has been called 'sympathetic,' being the influence exercised on a remote being or phenomenon by means of a telepathic connexion between it and what is manipulated by the magician. It may be either beneficent or injurious.

(*a*) *Effigies.*—An image is frequently made and operated on for the purpose of producing a similar effect on the victim. Thus an enemy is destroyed by piercing the heart of his clay effigy with an arrow, or by transfixing his shadow. His death is also produced by melting a wax figure of him over the fire, or by killing or burning a chameleon as representing him. The elephants, horses, soldiers, and chariots of a hostile army are imitated in dough, and sacrificed piece by piece so as to bring about its destruction. The magician annihilates worms by stamping on or burning twenty-one roots of the *uṣīra* plant, while he pronounces the spell, 'I split with the stone the head of all worms male and female; I burn their faces with fire' (Atharvaveda, V. xxiii. 13). In order to exterminate the field vermin called *tarda*, a single *tarda*, as representing the whole class, is buried head downwards, its mouth being tied with a hair so as to prevent its eating grain (*Kauśika Sūtra*, l. 19). With a view to smashing the limbs of evil spirits pegs are driven into the ground. One who pounds the Soma-shoots for sacrifice directs the blows against his enemy by fixing his thoughts on him during the operation.

The sympathetic connexion is sometimes very remote, as when implements or materials are used in which a particular power is regarded as inherent. Thus an exiled prince receives food rendered magical by being cooked with wood that has grown from the stump of a tree, symbolizing the restoration of fallen fortunes. At a ceremony for the removal of troublesome ants a sacrificial ladle of *bādhaka* wood is employed simply because the name of the tree means 'remover.' At a rite to destroy demons the dipping spoon is made of wood from the *palāśa* (*Butea frondosa*) tree as representing the magical spell (*brahman*), which is a slayer of demons. When the sacrifice for the restoration of an exiled prince is performed, earth and other material from his native country are employed. At a sacrifice for victory in battle, soil torn up by a boar is taken for the altar (*vedi*), with a view to communicating the fierceness of that animal to the combatants on behalf of whom the offering is made.

(*b*) *Imitative processes.*—The higher cult concerned with the three sacrificial fires abounds with rites in which the desired effect is produced by an imitation of the event or phenomenon. Thus the kindling of the sacrificial fire in the morning develops into a magical rite to make the sun rise; and the dripping of the Soma-juice through the purifying sieve becomes a rain charm. At the ceremony of the royal inauguration, the conventional chariot race in which the king wins is meant to gain for him speed and victorious might. On various occasions in the ritual a game of dice is played; this has clearly the magical purpose of securing luck and gain for the sacrificer. At the solstitial ceremony an Āryan and a Śūdra (representing a white and a black man) engage in a struggle for the possession of a circular white skin, the former ultimately wresting it from the latter; the magical aim of this performance is the liberation of the sun from the powers of darkness. In the same ceremony, as well as at the Soma and the horse sacrifice, there are certain sexual observances the obvious purpose of which is to produce fertility in women. A good example of the imitative method is the procedure meant to deflect a river into another channel. The new course is first watered; it is then planted with reeds; and, finally, representatives of water, such as a frog and the aquatic plant *avakā*, are deposited on it; the imitation is believed to produce the reality.

(1) This type of magic is very frequently found in the particular form of *rain-making*. Such is the purpose when, at the solstitial festival, a cowhide is pierced with arrows—probably an imitation of the myth of Indra's release of the waters by piercing the rain-clouds (which frequently appear as cows in the Rigveda). On the same occasion girls dance round a fire with jars full of water which they pour out, while they sing a song calling upon the cows to bathe. At the ceremony of piling the fire-altar jars of water are emptied on the ground, on which rain is thus said to be shed, and grain is sown on the spot. When an otter is thrown into the water, rain falls in abundance; or, if any one desires rain, he casts herbs into the water, submerges them, and then lets them float away.

(2) A modified form of sympathetic magic is *divination*, the aim of which is to find out what is hidden or future, largely from the occult correspondence between the representation and the reality. Dreams and sacrificial and funeral rites are the most significant representations; these can be interpreted by spiritual persons who possess inner illumination, strengthened by the power of asceticism and other magical means. From the direction taken by a cow at a particular point in the ritual it may be inferred that the sacrificer will attain his purpose. If at a certain sacrifice the fire flames up brightly, the sacrificer will obtain twelve villages; if the smoke rises, he will obtain at least three. The fire kindled in a special way between two armies about to fight prognosticates the result of the battle by the direction of the smoke. The observer who, at a funeral, notes which of the three sacred fires catches the corpse first can tell whether the soul of the deceased is in heaven, in air, or on earth.

The following examples of divination are of a more general type. If one wishes to know whether an unborn child will be a male, the son of a Brāhman must touch a member of the mother; supposing the member has a masculine name, the child will be a boy. When it is desired to ascertain whether a girl will make a good wife, she is bidden to choose between various clods taken partly from auspicious soil (as that of a furrow or a cowshed), partly from an unlucky spot (as a cemetery or cross-roads); her choice betokens her character and her future. A special form of prognostication is the foretelling of weather by old Brāhmans from the smoke of dung.

Mixed with the knowledge of the future obtainable from a symbolic process is that derived from gods or spirits, by interpreting the movement, the flight, or the cry of animals or birds specially connected with gods or spirits, such as the wolf and hyæna, the owl, crow, pigeon, and vulture. Thus, in one of the two hymns of the Rigveda concerned with augury, the bird crying in the region of the Fathers (the south) is invoked to bring auspicious tidings (II. xlii. 2). Again, in one of the Sūtras, the owl 'that flies to the abode of the gods' is addressed with the words, 'Flying round the village from left to right, portend to us luck by thy cry, O owl' (*Hiranyakeśin Gṛhyasūtra*, I. xvii. 1. 3). The direction from which the wooer will come is indicated by the flight of crows after the performance of the rite for obtaining a husband for a girl. Such omens seem to be a later development, resulting from the simplification of the symbolical method of divination by isolating a single feature of a complex process.

13. Oral magic.—Magical formulæ are usually accompanied by some ritual act; but the spoken word in the form of a spell, a curse, or an oath also has a magical effect by itself.

(*a*) *The spell.*—The spell has generally a metrical form, being sometimes an old religious verse degraded to magical use. Though the formula is magical in application, it is in form often a mixture of prayer and spell, the gods being mentioned or invoked in it; *e.g.*, 'Between the two rows of Agni Vaiśvānara's teeth do I place him that plans to injure us when we are not planning to injure him' (Atharvaveda, IV. xxxvi. 2; cf. XVI. vii. 3); 'Thy ninety-nine spirits, O Night, shall help and protect us' (XIX. xlvii. 3–5). It is, indeed, characteristic of the hymns of the Atharvaveda to contain the names of numerous deities, while the panegyrics of the Rigveda are addressed to one only; *e.g.*, 'Heaven and Earth have anointed me; Mitra has anointed me here; may Bṛhaspati anoint me; may Savitṛ anoint me' (VII. xxx. 1). The magician very usually threatens or commands in his own person; *e.g.*, 'I plague the demons as the tiger the cattle-owners; as dogs that have seen a lion, they find not a refuge' (IV. xxxvi. 6); 'As the lightning ever irresistibly smites the tree, so would I to-day beat the gamesters with my dice' (VII. l. 1); 'Swift as the wind be thou, O steed, when yoked to the car; at Indra's urging go, swift as the mind; the Maruts shall harness thee; Tvaṣṭṛ shall place fleetness in thy feet' (VI. xcii. 1). But he also often mentions in his spell a parallel case, in order to effect his purpose, like the symbolical process in sympathetic magic; *e.g.*, 'With the light with which the gods, having cooked porridge for the Brāhmans, ascended to heaven, to the world of the pious, with that would we go to the world of the pious, ascending to the light, to the highest firmament' (XI. i. 37); 'As one pays off a sixteenth, an eighth, or an entire debt, thus we transfer every evil dream to our enemy' (VI. xlvi. 3); 'As the rising sun robs the stars of their brilliance, so I rob of their strength all the men and women hostile to me' (VII. xiii. 1); 'The cows have lain down in their resting-place; the bird has flown to its nest; the mountains have stood in their site; I have made the two kidneys stand in their station' (VII. xcvi. 1). A frequent feature of spells, in order to make sure of striking the injurious spirit, the seat of evil, or whatever else is aimed at, is the enumeration of a whole series of possibilities; *e.g.*, 'Out of eyes, nose, ears, brain, neck, back, arms I drive the disease' (II. xxxiii. 1 f.). If, however the demon is known, this knowledge is emphasized as bestowing magical power over him; *e.g.*, 'This is thy name; we know thy birth; this thy father, this thy mother.'

On the most varied occasions spells are uttered without any accompanying rite. The application of one that may be pronounced by a man on entering a court of justice is thus described (*Pāraskara Gṛhyasūtra*, III. xiii. 6): 'If he should think, "This person will do evil to me," he addresses him with the words, "I take away the speech in thy mouth, I take away the speech in thy heart; wherever thy speech is, I take it away; what I say is true: fall down inferior to me."' Spells are also uttered, *e.g.*, when a man mounts an elephant, a camel, a horse, a chariot, when he comes to cross-roads, when he swims across a river, and in many other situations.

A formula sometimes consists of two or three words, or even of one word. If a man has spoken what is unworthy of the sacrifice, he has only to murmur 'Adoration to Viṣṇu' as an expiation. The daily repetition of the single sacred syllable *bhūḥ* averts death from him who utters it; 'he has nothing to fear from serious diseases or from sorcery' (*Gobhila Gṛhyasūtra*, IV. vi. 1). Again, the mere mechanical repetition of a prayer meant for a totally different purpose may have a magical effect. Thus, the celebrated Gāyatrī verse of the Rigveda (III. lxii. 10)—'We would attain that excellent glory of Savitṛ the god, that he may stimulate our prayers'—if muttered 3000 times, frees a man from the sin of accepting unlawful presents. Even the formulaic use of a stereotyped dialogue secures the desired result. Thus, when the rite of parting the hair of a woman is performed, the husband asks her, 'What dost thou see?' 'Offspring,' she replies.

(*b*) *The curse*.—A special form of the magically effective spoken word is the curse. The earliest examples of it in Vedic literature are mythological. In the Yajurveda (*Taittirīya Saṃhitā*, II. vi. 6. 1) Agni curses the fish for betraying his hiding-place in the waters, predicting that men shall kill it by means of various artifices: 'Hence men kill fish with various artifices, for they are cursed.' In *Tāṇḍya Brāhmaṇa* (VI. v. 11) the gods curse the trees with the threat that they shall be cut down with an axe the handle of which is made from themselves. That the employment of actual curses was also common in early Vedic times is obvious, and is confirmed by the occurrence of many spells intended to counteract them or to make them recoil on him who utters them. The Atharvaveda contains several such; *e.g.*, 'Avoid us, O curse, as a burning fire a lake; strike him that curses us, as the lightning of heaven the tree' (VI. xxxvii. 2); 'Let the curse go to the curser, we crush the ribs of the hostile eye-conjurer' (II. vii. 5; cf. V. xiv. 5, X. i. 5). Plants, such as the *apāmārga*, are invoked to free from the calamity consequent on a curse. The *Śatapatha Brāhmaṇa* contains several passages showing the potency attributed to curses. Thus it is there said (II. i. 4. 19, III. ii. 1. 9) that, 'if any one were to curse him, saying, "May the sacrifice turn away from him," then he would indeed be liable to fare thus'; 'Were any one to curse him, saying, "He shall either become demented or fall down headlong," then that would indeed come to pass.' It is there also said that he who curses a Brāhman possessed of certain knowledge leaves this world bereft of his strength and the result of his good deeds. In other Sūtras those who raise their hand to pronounce a curse are said to be one of the seven kinds of assassin (*Viṣṇu-smṛti*, v. 191).

(*c*) *The oath*.—This is really a curse directed against oneself, as is indicated by the verb *śap*, which in the active means 'to curse,' but in the middle 'to curse oneself,' 'to swear.' It calls down on oneself and one's belongings loss of life or possessions in this world and the next as a penalty for telling an untruth or breaking one's word. Thus, in the ceremony of royal inauguration the priest causes the king to swear the following oath (*Aitareya Brāhmaṇa*, viii. 15): 'All the merit of my sacrifices and gifts from the day of my birth to the day of my death, my position, my good deeds, my life, my offspring shall belong to thee, if I deceive thee.' If the oath is broken, the punishment ensues; *e.g.*, the Yajurveda (*Taittirīya Saṃhitā*, II. iii. 5. 1) relates how, when the moon-god did not keep the oath which he had sworn to the Creator Prajāpati, he was attacked by the disease of consumption.

LITERATURE.—i. *TEXTS*.—(*a*) *Vedas*.—For edd. and trr. see HYMNS (Vedic), vol. vii. p. 58, and add: *Taittirīya Saṃhitā*, tr. A. B. Keith, Cambridge, Mass., 1915. (*b*) *Brāhmaṇas*.—For edd. see A. A. Macdonell, *Hist. of Sanskrit Literature*, London, 1900 (bibl. notes on ch. viii.). Trr.: *Aitareya Brāhmaṇa*, by M. Haug, Bombay, 1863; *Aitareya Āraṇyaka*, by A. B. Keith, Oxford, 1909; *Śāṅkhāyana Āraṇyaka*, by Keith, London, 1908; *Jaiminīya*, or *Talavakāra, Brāhmaṇa*, by H. Oertel, in *JAOS* xvi. [1894]; *Śatapatha Brāhmaṇa*, by J. Eggeling, in *SBE* xii. [1882], xxvi. [1885], xli. [1894], xliii. [1897], xliv. [1900]. (*c*) *Upaniṣads*.—For edd. see Macdonell, *op. cit.* (bibl. notes on ch. viii.). Trr. of several Upaniṣads by F. Max Müller, *SBE*, vols. i. [1879] and xv. [1884]; P. Deussen, *Sechzig Upanishad's des Veda*, Leipzig, 1897; *Chhāndogya Upaniṣad*, O. Böhtlingk, do. 1889; *Bṛhadāraṇyaka Upaniṣad*, Böhtlingk, do. 1889. (*d*) *Sūtras*.—For edd. see Macdonell, *op. cit.* (bibl. notes on ch. ix.). Trr. of Sūtras on domestic (*gṛhya*) rites (*Śāṅkhāyana, Āśvalāyana, Pāraskara, Khādira, Gobhila, Hiraṇyakeśin, Āpastamba*), by H. Oldenberg, in *SBE* xxix. [1886], xxx. [1892]; of Sūtras on customary law (*dharma*), *SBE* ii. [1879], xiv. [1882], by G. Bühler (*Āpastamba, Baudhāyana, Gautama, Vasiṣṭha*, the latter two being called Śāstras, or 'Codes'). The most important parts of the *Kauśika Sūtra* (belonging to the Atharvaveda) have been translated into German by W. Caland under the title of *Altindisches Zauberritual*, Amsterdam, 1900.

ii. *GENERAL WORKS*.—A. Bergaigne, *La Religion védique*, Paris, 1878–83; H. Oldenberg, *Die Religion des Veda*, Berlin, 1894; A. Hillebrandt, *Ritual-Litteratur: Vedische Opfer und Zauber*, Strassburg, 1897; V. Henry, *La Magie dans l'Inde antique*², Paris, 1909; cf. also A. A. Macdonell, *Vedic Mythology*, Strassburg, 1897; H. Oldenberg, *Die Lehre der Upanishaden und die Anfänge des Buddhismus*, Göttingen, 1915; and M. Winternitz, *SBE* l. [1910] 'A General Index.'

iii. *MONOGRAPHS*.—A. Weber, *Omina und Portenta*, Berlin, 1859, *Über den Vājapeya*, do. 1892, *Rājasūya, über die Königsweihe*, do. 1893, *Indische Studien*, esp. vols. x. xiii. xvii., Leipzig, 1868, 1873, 1885; A. Hillebrandt, *Das altindische Neu- und Vollmondsopfer*, Jena, 1880, *Die Sonnwendfeste in Alt-Indien*, Erlangen, 1889; R. Lindner, *Die Dīkṣā*, Leipzig, 1878; J. Schwab, *Das altindische Thieropfer*, do. 1886; M. Winternitz *Der Sarpabali*, Vienna, 1888, *Das altindische Hochzeitsrituell*, do. 1892; W. Caland, *Über Todtenverehrung bei einigen der indogermanischen Völker*, Amsterdam, 1888, *Altindischer Ahnencult*, Leyden, 1893, *Die altindischen Todten- und Bestattungsgebräuche*, Amsterdam, 1896, *Altindische Zauberei (Wunschopfer)*, do. 1908.

A. A. MACDONELL.

MAGICAL CIRCLE.

MAGICAL CIRCLE.—For the 'operation' of 'conjuring' spirits the mediæval sorcerer sat in the centre of a circle described on the ground. This formed a spiritual barrier, protecting him from ghostly attacks, while enabling him to question his 'familiars' or other spirits from a coign of supernatural vantage.

'Circuli sunt munimenta quaedam quae operantes a malis spiritibus reddunt tutos.'[1]

The concepts of circle, circular, and encircling lend themselves naturally to dramatic ceremonialism, and ideas of continuity, finality, and eternity have been appropriately expressed by circular symbolism.

In Scandinavian mythology a serpent engirdles the earth. Popilius Lænas, delivering an ultimatum from the Senate of Rome to King Antiochus, drew with his staff a circle round himself in which he awaited the reply.[2]

The circular form of certain shrines and religious structures may involve some symbolism, possibly astrological. According to the Talmud, a round house and a three-cornered house do not become unclean—*e.g.*, from the contagion of leprosy—whereas a square house does.[3] Possibly the sacred number 3 renders the three-cornered house immune; possibly, again, the three corners represent the points of supernatural weapons.[4] In the case of the round house the idea may be that nothing can cling to its smooth outline.

The circle as a supernatural protective barrier has several analogies in primitive custom, and variations of form involve corresponding variations of meaning. Throughout, from the earliest examples to the latest, importance is usually attached to the material or the instrument with which the circle is traced.

Among the Shuswap Indians the bed of a mourner is surrounded by thorn-bushes, the object being to ward off the ghost of the dead person.[5] The Bellacoola Indians, also of British Columbia, have a similar practice. Besides surrounding the bed with thorns, mourners cleanse their bodies while standing in a square formed by thorn-bushes, as a protection against the ghost.[6] Here the mystic *zareba* depends not on its shape but on its completeness in the geometrical sense.

Water and fire, excellent bulwarks both in human warfare and in spiritual conflict, and, possibly for this reason, among others, regarded as supreme cleansers, are often used to avert evil influences.

The Laotians had a custom of keeping a fire burning in a circle around the bed of a mother for some weeks after child-birth. In Abyssinia the bed was surrounded by blazing herbs, while the mother herself was held in the circle by 'stout young fellows.'[7] In a moving or dynamic form the fiery circle was used for the same purpose in Scotland. Morning and night fire was carried

1 G. C. Horst, *Zauber-Bibliothek*, Mainz, 1822, iii. 70.
2 Livy, xlv. 12; Cicero, *Phil.* viii. 8. 23; Vell. Pat. i. 10.
3 R. C. Thompson, *Semitic Magic*, London, 1908, pp. 186, 189.
4 This seems to be one notion in the use of the pentagram or pentacle (see Thompson, *locc. citt.*).
5 *GB*³, pt. ii., *Taboo and the Perils of the Soul*, London, 1911, p. 142, quoting F. Boas.
6 *Ib.*, pt. vii., *Balder the Beautiful*, London, 1913, ii. 174.
7 J. G. Frazer, in *JAI* xv. [1886] 84 f.

round the mother till she was churched, and round the child till it was christened. In some parts of Scotland a fir-candle was whirled three times round the bed where mother and child lay.[1]

It has been suggested that in some such cases the idea was to prevent the soul in its critical state from leaving the body, but the greater proportion of cases certainly depend on the idea of protecting the patient from external evil, though the fire-treatment of childbed may have originated simply in a primitive clinical intention of producing comfort or obviating complications.

In China candles are kept alight round the coffin to 'give light to the spirit,' or to light him on his way.[2] The Caribs burned a fire round the grave.[3] A Chinese charm consists in laying a circle of ashes round the dead man; it is supposed to resuscitate him.[4] The Romans carried water or fire round mourners on their return from the funeral.[5]

The curious custom of circumambulation as a mark of honour was practised by Hindus, Greeks, and Celts.

In ancient India, walking round a person three times to the right (sunwise) was a ceremony of honour,[6] as it was among the Gauls and Celts.[7] The ancient Indians walked round the funeral pyre, as Achilles drove round the pyre of Patroclus [8] (see art. CIRCUMAMBULATION). The ancient Indians also practised the rite as a cure for a sick person.[9] Possibly the idea of protecting a person with a mobile, living ring is behind the honorific variety.

In Nias a candidate for the priesthood consorts with spirits in the mountains; when he returns home, he splits a young tree and creeps through the fissure, 'in the belief that any spirit which may still be clinging to him will thus be left sticking to the tree.'[10] Highlanders of Scotland used to send their sheep through hoops of rowan to 'ward off the witches.'[11] Similar customs are found in N. Europe and England as cures for sickness.[12]

The Lapps wore a brass ring on the right arm by way of protection against the ghost of the dead person.[13]

Frazer instances superstitions about rings—arm or finger rings—suggesting that the idea is to keep the soul in the body. For this purpose magic cords are tied round wrist, ankle, or body among various peoples.[14]

'To keep the soul in or the demons out' is a question where convergence of practice is natural. In ancient India the medical magician encircled the bed of a woman at child-birth with black pebbles to ward off demons.[15] This is in line with primitive practices mentioned above, but a suggestion of V. Henry possibly connects it with Babylonian magic: he finds in old Indian magic traces of the double pentacle, or Solomon's Seal, the famous constituent of the mediæval magical circle, consisting of two equal and equilateral triangles, cutting each other so that the resulting segments are equal. The underlying idea may be that the points of the star pierce the invisible enemies.[16] The Indian data alone show a connexion, by means of this astrological element, with the Semitic, and it is from the Semitic practice that the magical circle of mediæval Europe, along with a considerable body of astrological magic, was developed. This is a remarkable case of permeation from one source. Semitic magic and its conquest of Europe may be described, not altogether fancifully, as a left-handed compliment to Semitic religion and the conquest of Europe by the Bible.

The Babylonian texts continually refer to the *usurtu*, which Thompson justly identifies as 'the prototype' of the magical circle, possessing the properties of a 'ban.'

1 Frazer, in *JAI* xv. 85, note.
2 J. Doolittle, *Social Life of the Chinese*, New York, 1867, i. 126.
3 Frazer, in *JAI* xv. 91, note.
4 J. J. M. de Groot, *The Religious System of China*, Leyden, 1892 ff., vi. 952.
5 Servius, on Virgil, *Æn.* vi. 228.
6 *SBE* ii. [1897] 25, vii. [1900] 236 f.
7 J. Rhŷs, *Celtic Heathendom*², London, 1892, p. 567.
8 *SBE* xvii. [1882] 299.
9 *Ib.* xlii. [1897] 425.
10 *GB*³, pt. ii., *Taboo*, p. 175.
11 *Ib.* p. 184 f.
12 *Ib.* pp. 180, 184 f.
13 *Ib.* p. 314.
14 *Ib.* p. 315 f.
15 V. Henry, *La Magie dans l'Inde antique*², Paris, 1909, p. 142.
16 *Ib.* p. 93.

The *ašipu*-priest recited over the sick an incantation: '(The man) of Ea am I, . . . the messenger of Marduk am I, . . . the circle of Ea is in my hand.'[1]

In more detail, the sick person was safeguarded by an enchanted circle (of the nature of a tabu-mark) made with flour or other material, 'as a kind of *haram* through which no spirit could break.' The priest first performed a ceremony of atonement, in which a kid was sacrificed. He flung the kid away, and then described the circle. 'Enclose the man with kusurra (flour), flour of lime, surround the shut gate right and left. The ban is loosed.'[2] A mixture of meal and lime seems to be intended; both substances possessed virtue. The 'flour of Nisaba (the corn-god)' was the 'ban of the great gods.'[3] In another ceremony, before the god Nergal, the priest described with lime a circle round seven winged figures,[4] and in yet another flour and water were used for drawing the circle.[5] Here Thompson compares the mediæval use of the Host as a protection against vampires and witches. The Babylonians described the mixture as the 'net of the corn-god.' Similarly the Jews of Jerusalem employed the virtues of food against evil influences, scattering a mixture of food round the bed of a sick person.[6] A Semitic parallel to the idea of stripping off evil by passing through a ring, or arch, or other circumscribed opening is found in a cure for headache, which consisted in making a circle round a desert-plant with meal, plucking it up before sunrise, and tying it on the head. When the plant was removed, the headache disappeared simultaneously. On the same principle an ailing limb was cured by tying round it a charmed thread, and then casting this away, along with the sickness.[7]

The development of magic, white and black, in Europe, and its remarkable exploitation, lasting till well after the scientific period had begun,[8] were bound up with Semitic animism, or rather dæmonism, if the distinction may be observed. The causes producing a state of culture in which every man of science was a necromancer and conjurer of spirits do not concern us here, but the invariable employment of the magical circle for the conjuration of spirits is typical of the culture of those ages. The primitive Babylonian practice was now divorced from medical magic. As applied to the evocation of elemental demons, whose aid was invoked for alchemical research or prophecy or evil magic against individuals, its main purpose was to protect the sorcerer from the dangerous servants whom he called up.[9] At the same time the geometrical possibilities of the circle appealed to the mathematical instincts of the scholar, and geometry perhaps owes something to magical experiments upon the circle. Kabbalistic lore was also called upon for the exploitation of names and numbers of power, to be inscribed in the circle. Here begins the positive virtue of the circle, which, in connexion with the universal concepts of the figure, made it something more than a protective barrier. It became rather a mystic focus of power, and had at least the merit of concentrating the alchemist's or astrologer's thoughts. Lastly, the astrological elements of the zodiacal system were applied to it, and it thus became an intermediary between chemistry and astronomy, as the focus to which were attracted the infernal and supernal powers alike.

The Arabic and Hebrew developments of magic in the early centuries of the Middle Ages are obscure. The account given by Psellus of a *Hecatinus circulus*, Ἑκατινὸς στρόφαλος, calls for notice, though its meaning is confused. He writes:

'Hecate's circle is a golden sphere, enclosing a sapphire in the centre, turned by a thong of bull's hide, and having characters through the whole of it. They made conjurations by turning this; and they are wont to call such things ἴυγγες, whether they have a spherical or triangular or any other shape whatsoever. Shaking these, they uttered unintelligible or beastlike sounds, laughing, and striking the bronze. It accordingly teaches the operation of the rite, or the motion of such a circle, as possessing secret power. And it is called "Hecate's" as being dedicated to Hecate; and Hecate is a divinity among the Chaldæans.'[10]

1 Thompson, p. xxiii.
2 Thompson, p. lvii, quoting P. Haupt, *Akkad. und sumer. Keilschrifttexte*, Leipzig, 1881–82, xi. ii.
3 *Ib.* p. lix.
4 *Ib.* p. lviii.
5 *Ib.* p. 123.
6 *Ib.* p. 102.
7 *Ib.* p. 165.
8 See F. Barrett, *Magus*, London, 1801, *passim*, for proof that magic was practised at the end of the 18th century.
9 *Ib.* ii. 105; the circles 'are certain fortresses.'
10 *Expositio oraculorum Chaldaicorum* (*PG* cxxii. 1133).

This account may be simply confusing the Babylonian magical circle with the Greek magical wheel (ἴυγξ, *torquilla*); but, just as the mediæval circle was made material and portable in the form of metal amulets and talismans, so it is possible that Græco-Chaldæan superstition may have developed the circle into a wheel like the ἴυγξ. The fact that such 'wheels' were sometimes triangular or of other shapes is an interesting hint in the direction of the pentagrams and other figures with which the mediæval circles were filled. Psellus notes that the object of the *invocatio* was oracular, the idea, no doubt, being to evoke spirits for the purpose of forcing them to predict future events. As for the Greek wheel on which the ἴυγξ, wryneck, was tied, there is considerable doubt as to its nature.[1]

The magical circle of mediæval occultism had innumerable varieties, according to the purpose, the time, and the species of spirit to be invoked; and it also varied according to the predilections of the operator. The following may be considered typical examples of the method of description and formulæ of blessing and of invocation. The magician, after purifying himself, collected his paraphernalia, including his magic wand, blessed candles and holy water, magical sword or knife, and so forth, and traced the circle, usually 9 ft. in diameter,[2] with his wand or sword. He then blessed the circle, a typical blessing being:

'In the name of the holy, blessed, and glorious Trinity, proceed we to our work in these mysteries to accomplish that which we desire; we therefore, in the names aforesaid, consecrate this piece of ground for our defence, so that no spirit whatsoever shall be able to break these boundaries, neither be able to cause injury nor detriment to any of us here assembled; but that they may be compelled to stand before this circle, and answer truly our demands.'[3]

More elaborate formulæ include such terms as:

'Sanctify unto myself the circumference of nine feet about me, . . . from the East, Glavrab, from the West, Garron, from the North, Cabon, from the South, Berith.'[4]

Good spirits seem to have been invoked but rarely; necromancy was also rare, though two forms of this were used, one in which the body and the other in which the 'shadow' of the dead was conjured. Evil spirits of power were the usual object of conjuration, and extraordinary precautions were taken in the process.[5]

'Now, if any one would call any evil spirit to the circle he must first consider and know his nature and to which of the planets it agrees and what offices are distributed unto him from the planet. This being known, let there be first sought out a place fit and convenient and proper for his invocation according to the nature of the planet and the quality of the offices of the same spirit as near as it can be done; as if their power be over the sea, rivers or floods, then let the place be the sea-shore, and so of the rest. Then chuse a convenient time for the quality of the air (being serene, quiet, clear, and fitting for the spirits to assume bodies). . . . Let the circle be made at the place elected, as well for the defence of the invocant as the confirmation of the spirit. And in the circle write the divine general names and all those things which do yield defence to us; and with them those divine names which do rule his planet, and the offices of the spirit himself; likewise write therein the names of the good spirits which bear rule in the time you do this and are able to bind and constrain that spirit which we intend to call.

We may add characters and pentacles[6] . . . frame an angular figure with the inscription of such convenient numbers as are congruent amongst themselves to our work. . . . Further, we are to be provided with lights, perfumes, unguents and medicines, compounded according to the nature of the spirit and planet which agree with the spirit by reason of their natural and celestial virtue . . . holy and consecrated things necessary not only for the defence of the invocant and his companions, but also serving for bonds to bind and constrain the spirits; such as holy papers, lamens,[7] pictures, pentacles, swords, sceptres, garments of convenient colour and matter. Then let the exorcist (*sic*) and his companions enter the circle.'[1] If, after a prayer to God and an invocation, the spirit refuses to appear, 'reiterate the same three times, from stronger to stronger, using contumelies, cursings, punishments, suspension from his power and office, and the like.' If the spirit make a doubtful assertion, it must be tested by oath; the operator stretches his sword out of the circle and swears the spirit by laying his hand on the sword.[2]

At last, when the operation is beginning to have effect, 'there will appear infinite visions, apparitions, phantasms, etc., beating of drums, and the sound of all kinds of musical instruments; which is done by the spirits, that with the terror they might force some of the companions out of the circle.' At this point, 'holding the pentacle in his hand let him [the operator] say, Avoid hence these iniquities.'[3] The spirit invoked would now normally appear.

A plain circle was the exception. In some, two diameters were drawn in the form of a cross,[4] but, as a rule, the circle included a pentagram or combination of pentagrams. Two intersecting pentagrams, viz. two equilateral and equal triangles cutting each other so that their segments are equal, constituted Solomon's Seal;[5] this seems to have been often regarded as more efficacious than the circle itself. These triangles were described before the circle, a frequent method being to draw a 9 ft. square, then the diagonals, and then the circle round the square.[6] An inner circle was described at a distance of a foot from the outer, and between these were inscribed various 'names of power,' or injunctions to the spirits, Alpha, Omega, On Adonai, El-Zebaoth, Tetragrammaton, Elohim, Jahweh; 'I forbid thee, Lucifer, to enter within this circle,' 'Obey me, Frimost,' being examples of these.[7] The mystic combination *Agla* was a favourite. Dove's blood, especially that of a white dove, was sometimes used for writing these names and formulæ.[8] The circle, figures, and names might be described with holy water, charcoal, or consecrated chalk; when the magical knife was used for the drawing, the lines were sprinkled with holy water. This knife, which also served to frighten the spirits,[9] should have a black handle of sheep's horn, and the steel should have been tempered in the blood of a black cat and the juice of hemlock. For more important operations, especially in black magic, as when using the 'great kabbalistic circle,' the tracing should be done with the magical stone Ematille.[10] A curious refinement was a gate in the circumference, by which the operator and his associates might go out and in; on leaving the circle, they closed the gate by inscribing names and pentacles.[11] The more elaborate circles were filled with names and kabbalistic figures and 'characters.'[12] Candles and vervain crowns were placed within the circle, and the operator had with him gold or silver coins to fling to the spirit when evoked, the 'seals' to be shown to the spirit, and talismans, generally made of coloured satin embroidered with silver. Incense was burned within the circle, or it was perfumed with musk, and holy water was sprinkled over it. When the preparations were complete, the operator and his associates stood or sat in the centre of the circle, often in small circles marking their places, and the operator began his invocation of the spirit required.[13]

The 'great kabbalistic circle' was made with strips of the skin of a sacrificed kid. These were

[1] Cf. O. Gruppe, *Griech. Myth. und Religionsgesch.*, Munich, 1906, pp. 851 f., 897.
[2] Barrett, ii. 106.
[3] Thompson, p. lx; Barrett, ii. 106.
[4] A. E. Waite, *Occult Sciences*, London, 1891, p. 47.
[5] Barrett, ii. 69 f.
[6] Pentacle (properly = pentagram) is used of any talisman with figures (not necessarily angular) incised or embroidered within a circle.
[7] Linen or vellum plaques inscribed with figures.

[1] Barrett, ii. 99 f.
[2] *Ib.* ii. 101 f.
[3] *Ib.* ii. 114.
[4] Horst, ii. 103.
[5] A. E. Waite, *The Book of Ceremonial Magic*, London, 1911, p. 221; Barrett, ii. 109.
[6] Waite, *Occult Sciences*, p. 46.
[7] Waite, *Ceremonial Magic*, p. 286; Horst, ii. 103; Barrett, ii. 110.
[8] *Ib.*
[9] Waite, *Ceremonial Magic*, pp. 280, 322, 286, 154, 156.
[10] *Ib.* p. 244; Waite, *Occult Sciences*, p. 60.
[11] Waite, *Ceremonial Magic*, p. 82.
[12] *Ib.* p. 185 f.
[13] *Ib.* pp. 244, 225, 124 ff., 321.

fixed in the ground or floor by nails. Five concentric circles, close together, formed a strong protective circumference. A triangle took the place of the pentagram, and three small circles were described for the stations of the operator and assistants.[1]

The elaboration of geometrical design and astrological figures within the circle was connected with its positive efficacy for conjuration and control of the spirit. Thus Giordano Bruno writes:

'O! quanta virtus est intersecutionibus circulorum et quam sensibus hominum occulta! Cum caput Draconis in Sagittario exstiterit, diacedio lapide posito in aqua, naturaliter spiritus ad dandum responsa veniunt.'[2]

Consultation of the stars and seasons was essential.

'Oportet in constituendo circulo considerare quo tempore anni, qua hora circulum facias, quos spiritus advocare velis, cui stellae et regioni praesint, et quas functiones habeant.'[3]

For summoning chance spirits or seeing visions generally, a circle was made (probably at cross-roads) and perfumed, and the operator had to walk round its circumference, east to west, till he was giddy.[4] For necromancy the churchyard was an appropriate site.[5] The operator wore elaborate vestments, and was anointed with holy oil.

The circle was invariably obliterated on the conclusion of the operation.[6] A similar practice of destroying the traces of magical rites is regular throughout the history of magic, even in primitive culture.

The talismans, pentacles, or seals, used freely by the magician, depended largely upon the magical circle which was described round them. Here, as in the large operating circle, the more concentric circles, the more potent the efficacy. Against the attacks of spirits they were very powerful, 'presiding with wonderful influence.'[7] They were exhibited to the spirit on its appearance; by their means the operator bound the spirit, and was able to prevent it from departing 'without a licence.' The issue of the licence was an important detail; if it was omitted, the death of the operator might result.[8] The first virtue of a seal was from the star under whose influence it was, and, accordingly, it would be made of gold, if the planet were the sun, of iron, if the planet were Mars.[9] Seals 'of the names of God' were most powerful. Others had the names of angels, such as Raphael, Michael, Gabriel, inscribed between two concentric circles. Those which may be distinguished as pentacles proper had a Solomon's Seal surrounded by a circle.[10] The most usual form had enclosed within the circle the 'table' of a planet. These tables, it is interesting to note, were 'magical squares' in the mathematical sense (see below). Each planet, and each of the other forces, had its own magical squares.[11] The Seal had an obverse and a reverse, and was the size of a large medallion.[12] In connexion with the pentagram, this figure was a synonym for health. It was also developed into a continuous figure, by combining two, resulting in five, not six, points.[13]

The 'characters' of spirits were taken by the operator within his circle. These were in a book, which, when completed, was consecrated in a triangle described just outside the circle.[14] When a spirit appeared, it was asked to place its hands on its 'character' and swear.[15]

Mediæval amulets for general use were frequently stamped with the magical circle in its numerous varieties, as also were talismans of various make. The latter were effective, as a rule, only in co-operation with a ring engraved with 'characters.' This was worn on the finger, and the talisman on the arm or body.[1] The magician's wand was sometimes pliant and could be made into a circle, the ends being joined by a gold chain.[2] Described on parchment, the magical circle served as a basis for astrological calculations. This use was prevalent wherever Arabic culture penetrated. Thus, in Malaysia at the present time the circle is employed for all kinds of divination. To select a lucky day for a journey or business, a circle enclosing a heptacle is used, but every alternate day is skipped, the lines of the continuous heptacle running from, *e.g.*, Sunday to Tuesday, Thursday, Saturday, Monday, Wednesday, Friday, Sunday, and so on.[3] This heptacle is an ingenious development of the double pentacle. Magic squares of three or five numbers enclosed in a circle are less frequently used. Another form of divinatory circle has only radii from the centre. Colours emphasize the various parts of these circles.[4]

As a mathematical curiosity, the so-called magical circle is a development from the magical square, known since the earliest Arabic science. The latter is a square divided into smaller squares in each of which a number is written, and so arranged that the sum of the numbers in any row, horizontal, vertical, or diagonal, is always the same. The magical circle, or circle of circles, has numbers in concentric circles with radial divisions, possessing the same property as the rows in the magical square.[5]

LITERATURE.—In critical literature, R. C. Thompson, *Semitic Magic*, London, 1908, and G. C. Horst, *Zauber-Bibliothek*, Mainz, 1822, are the best of a very few. Francis Barrett, himself an adept, remains the most useful of the uncritical exponents, in his *Magus*, London, 1801.

A. E. CRAWLEY.

MAGYARS.—See HUNGARIANS.

MAHĀBAN (Skr. *mahā*, 'great,' *vana*, Hindī *ban*, 'forest').—A sacred town in the Mathurā District of the United Provinces and Oudh, on the left bank of the river Jumnā; lat. 27° 27′ N., long. 70° 45′ E.; famous as the scene of the adventures of Kṛṣṇa as a child.

Here and at Gokul (*q.v.*), as might have been anticipated, the places where the young god was attacked by the witch Pūtanā, where he played his pranks in the dairy and was saved from the falling wooden mortar, and where he overcame the demons Tṛṇāvarta and Śakaṭa are now shown. Mahāban was, in reality, only the water-side suburb of Gokul, which has now appropriated much of its sanctity, possibly because Mahāban never recovered from its sack by Maḥmūd of Ghaznī in A.D. 1017 (H. M. Elliot, *Hist. of India*, London, 1867–77, ii. 458, 460). In the fort are found fragments of Buddhist sculptures, and it is believed that Mahāban was the site of some of the Buddhist monasteries which, in the time of the Chinese pilgrim Fa-Hian, stood on both banks of the river. The existing temples are modern and mean. Only one is of any importance, that dedicated to Mathurānāth, Kṛṣṇa as lord of Mathurā. The most interesting building, however, is that known as Assī Khambhā, 'the eighty pillars,' which also has the name Chhaṭhī Pālnā, so called because women come here to be purified on the sixth day (*chhaṭhī*) after child-birth, and here the cradle (*pālnā*) of the infant god is exhibited. In its original form it seems to have been a Buddhist building, afterwards used for Hindu ceremonial, and finally converted into a Muhammadan mosque.

1 Waite, *Occult Sciences*, p. 60, *Ceremonial Magic*, p. 243 ff.
2 *De Monade*, 139, quoted in Horst, iii. 70.
3 *Ib.*
4 Barrett, ii. 95; see also 91.
5 *Ib.* ii. 69.
6 Waite, *Occult Sciences*, p. 48.
7 Barrett, ii. 109.
8 *Ib.* ii. 115 f.; Horst, iii. 98 ff., 142, 161.
9 Barrett, i. 88, 174.
10 *Ib.* i. 88, ii. 41, 80, 109.
11 *Ib.* i. 143, 174.
12 *Ib.* ii. 41.
13 *Ib.* ii. 66, 41.
14 *Ib.* ii. 90 f.
15 *Ib.* ii. 66 f., 90.

1 Waite, *Ceremonial Magic*, p. 124 ff.
2 *Ib.* p. 130.
3 W. W. Skeat, *Malay Magic*, London, 1900, p. 558.
4 *Ib.* pp. 555, 560.
5 C. A. M. Fennell, in *EBr*[11], *s.v.*

The style of the colonnades closely resembles that of the more famous building of the same class near the Quṭb Minār at Delhī (*q.v.*), and both buildings have been ascribed to the same age, the close of the 12th cent. A.D. The most remarkable feature in this building is that one half of the southern end consists of the shrine of a Hindu temple almost undisturbed, with the original roof still in position.

LITERATURE.—The history, legends, and architecture of the place have been fully described by F. S. Growse, *Mathurā*[3], Allahabad, 1883, p. 272 ff., and A. Führer, *Monumental Antiquities and Inscriptions in the North-West Provinces and Oudh*, do. 1891, p. 103 f.; *IGI* xvi. [1908] 427 f.

W. CROOKE.

MAHĀBHĀRATA.—The *Mahābhārata* is an epic poem of India in eighteen books, containing altogether about 400,000 verses of eight and eleven syllables each, although these verses are united into stanzas (called *śloka* and *triṣṭubh*) of four verses each, so that the Hindus call it a poem of a lakh (100,000) of stanzas. The books are of very unequal length, varying from a few hundred to several thousand stanzas, and there is also a supplementary book—the *Harivaṁśa*—of 16,000 stanzas. The matter of the poem is partly narrative and partly didactic. The epic proper contains about 20,000 stanzas embedded in and embellished by moral, political, religious, and metaphysical dissertations, the whole forming a heterogeneous mass of tale and teaching, which gradually accumulated around the epic kernel. As a tale the *Mahābhārata* ('Great Bharata' story) represents in its oldest form the *purāṇa*, or ancient tale, in distinction from the *kāvya*, or studied, elegant poem, of which the other epic, called the *Rāmāyaṇa* (*q.v.*), is the representative. It is probably older in its oldest parts than the *Rāmāyaṇa*, and yet in its entirety much later. It belongs rather to western ('Midland') India, while the *Rāmāyaṇa* belongs to the east. It celebrates Kṛṣṇa as representative of Viṣṇu on earth, while the *Rāmāyaṇa* celebrates Rāma. Finally, it has not the unity of the *Rāmāyaṇa*, nor was it written by one poet, as was the *Rāmāyaṇa*. According to a tradition still extant in the work itself, the *Mahābhārata* at first contained only 8800 stanzas and was subsequently increased to 24,000, after which it was again enlarged by the addition of numerous episodes till it reached its present size. The chief individual characters in the poem are known in part in ancient literature, but not the popular characters, the heroes of the winning side in the story as now extant. The war waged was between the old and the new; the date of the poem as it stands cannot, therefore, be that of the antique characters of the Brāhmanic age. As a whole, the poem dates from about the 2nd cent. B.C., extending to the 2nd cent. A.D., or, with the margin allowed by some scholars, its period extends from 400 B.C. to A.D. 400, this representing the centuries during which the whole poem was developed into its present shape. The additions since A.D. 400 must have been slight, though it is possible that one of the most probable references to Christianity in the poem, contained in the story of the White Island (xii. 335–339), was among such 'latest additions.' The material wrought into the poem is in part older than the poem itself, probably by centuries, especially the narrative and didactic episodes, some of which seem to be of Buddhistic origin. But the mass of the poem is greater than the epic narrative itself, and this mass, being largely didactic, led to the theory that the epic was originally didactic only, the narrative of human conquest being utilized as a frame on which to hang interminable sermons. This theory, put forth by Dahlmann, was further burdened with the thesis that the encyclopædic epic dated from pre-Buddhistic times and was the work of one author; but neither this most improbable hypothesis nor the basic theory—to wit, that the epic proper was merely ancillary to the didactic mass—has obtained general recognition. It is merely the exaggeration of a truth not denied by any one, viz. that moral and narrative poetry have always been more or less commingled in India. If the hypothesis of Dahlmann could be established, it would, of course, tend to show that Buddhism had been very much over-rated as an originator of ethical teaching. Very simple critical tests show, however, that no such great antiquity can be assigned to the *Mahābhārata*; the metre alone proves that it belongs to a period much later than that of Buddhistic beginnings. The epic is first mentioned in the *Gṛhyasūtras*, withal not the earliest (*Āśvalāyana Gṛhyasūtra*, iii. 4), to which there is no cogent reason to ascribe an antiquity greater than the 3rd cent. B.C., and it is not impossible that even this reference may be interpolated. In the 2nd cent. A.D. the Greeks refer to an Indian Homer (Dio Chrysostom, *Orat.* liii. 6), and this perhaps implies the supposititious author or compiler Vyāsa, to whose activity the Hindus give the name of authorship of the epic, as they say that Vyāsa compiled or arranged the Vedas—a story without any historical importance. Not more successful has been the counter-theory of Holtzmann, who holds that the epic was much later than the Christian era. He would date the *Mahābhārata* from the 5th to the 9th cent. A.D., and thinks that the story as we have it is an inversion of an older epic, in which not the Pāṇḍus but the Kurus were the characters originally besung by some earlier poet, and that it is due to the retention of older material that sins ascribed to the Pāṇḍus and their ally Kṛṣṇa have been kept in the poem of to-day. This theory also has failed to find recognition, in part because it ignores the weight of inscriptional evidence, which shows that, half a millennium before the *Mahābhārata*, according to this theory, had been completed, it was already of the size it is now.

The completed *Mahābhārata* represents an age well acquainted with foreign nations, even Greeks, Scythians, Persians, and Chinese being occasionally referred to in it (*e.g.*, v. 19); it represents also a time of empire, when, however exaggerated, the conquest of all India was regarded as quite a possible feat. It shows a superficial knowledge of the extreme north and south and a very intimate knowledge of Middle India. Castes are recognized as orders of society naturally, or, rather, divinely, established (*e.g.*, xii. 72, 297). Heterodox beliefs are freely discussed; outlandish morals are gravely reproved (*e.g.*, viii. 45). *Satī* is approved, but is not regarded as imperative; the ethical standard is high. Buddhist remains and Hindu temples are mentioned (*e.g.*, iii. 190). Different epochs have amalgamated their beliefs in regard to the gods. In one episode the Vedic gods are paramount; in another the authority of Brahmā is supreme; elsewhere Viṣṇu is the one great god, or Śiva alone is God and Viṣṇu is his representative. Only one late passage recognizes the Trimūrti, or triad of Brahmā, Viṣṇu, and Śiva, as three forms of one god (iii. 272).

The *Mahābhārata* begins with an Introduction, or Book of Beginnings, which tells how the childhood of the heroes was passed and gives their origin, and also, incidentally, the origin of gods and men in general. For the story, it may be compressed into the following statements. Two brothers, Dhṛtarāṣṭra and Pāṇḍu, are educated by their uncle Bhīṣma. The former brother grows up and marries a western woman, Gāndhārī, who has a hundred sons, called Kurus. Pāṇḍu has two wives, one of whom, Mādrī, commits *satī* at his death; the other, Pṛthā or Kuntī, survives Pāṇḍu and brings up his five children, called the Pāṇḍus, who are really sons of the gods, whom Kuntī and Mādrī had invoked. These sons are Yudhiṣṭhira (son of the god Dharma, or Right), Bhīma (son of the wind-god), Arjuna (the chief hero of the epic, son of Indra), and the twins Nakula and Sahadeva (sons of the Aśvins, or Dioskouroi). After this Introduction, which, like most childhood-recitals, is in general late, comes the 'Sabhā,' the title of the second *parvan* (book), taken from the assembly in the gaming-hall (*sabhā*), where the epic drama begins. At Hastināpur (about 60 miles north of Delhi) the Kurus hold an assembly, to which they have invited the Pāṇḍus, who, after various adventures, had built a town at Indraprastha (near Delhi). The Kurus intended to cheat the Pāṇḍus out of their kingdom by a game of dice, since they were afraid of the waxing power of their cousins. Yudhiṣṭhira plays away all his wealth and kingdom, and finally his brothers and himself. Then he plays Kṛṣṇā, the daughter of Drupada, polyandrous wife of the five brothers, and loses her. Once more he plays, all that he has lost against a term of exile, and on losing again he and his brothers and wife are driven ignominiously forth to live for twelve years in the forest. The third book is called 'Vana' ('Forest'), and narrates the life of the exiles. It is a storehouse of legend and tales, such as the story of Sāvitrī, and that of Nala and Damayantī, told to relieve the tedium of exile. The fourth book receives its name 'Virāṭa' from the name of the king with whom the Pāṇḍus take refuge at the close of the twelfth year. They stay in town collecting allies and assisting Virāṭa against attacks by the Kurus. They are at first disguised, and incidents of court life form the main part of this book, which is obviously, in its details, a late part of the epic. The fifth book is called 'Udyoga' ('Preparation for War'). Kṛṣṇa (Viṣṇu) is now enlisted upon the side of the Pāṇḍus, as, with her brother's consent, Arjuna has married his sister after eloping with her. The following four books are named from the leaders in the battle which now takes place, 'Bhīṣma,' 'Droṇa,' 'Karṇa,' and 'Śalya.' Bhīṣma and Droṇa are the uncle and teacher respectively of the cousins now at war. Into the 'Bhīṣma Parvan,' at the beginning of the battle, is inserted the long poem called *Bhagavad-Gītā* (*q.v.*). This book ends with the fall of Bhīṣma, and Droṇa then assumes the leadership of the Kurus. Numerous encounters are described with wearisome iteration, and Śiva is lauded as the great One God. Karṇa, the half-brother of the Pāṇḍus, son of the sun-god, had been insulted by the refusal of Kṛṣṇā to recognize him as a worthy knight when she chose her husband, and had taken part with the Kurus against his brothers. He now leads them into battle, but is slain by Arjuna. This leads to the 'Śalya Parvan' (ninth book), in which Śalya is made leader of the Kurus; but, with the exception of a few warriors, they are all routed and slain, and the chief Kuru prince is killed (after the battle) by Bhīma. The tenth book is called 'Sauptika' ('Night-Attack'), and describes how the surviving Kurus make an attack by night on the camp of the victors, killing all the army except the Pāṇḍus themselves. It is followed by a short book called 'Strī' ('Women'), which gives an account of the lamentation of women over their dead. The war is now over; but Bhīṣma has miraculously survived, and in the long didactic books called 'Śānti' and 'Anuśāsana' he is resurrected to preach religion and philosophy, and give rules of ethical behaviour. Yudhiṣṭhira is crowned emperor, and in the fourteenth book, called 'Āśvamedhika' ('Horse-Sacrifice'), he performs the horse-sacrifice, which is the sign of undisputed lordship (see art. AŚVAMEDHA). Into this book is inserted (16–51) the *Anugītā*, a poem imitative of the *Bhagavad-Gītā*. The fifteenth book, called 'Āśramavāsika' ('Hermitage'), takes up the life of Dhṛtarāṣṭra and his queen, who, with Kuntī, the Pāṇḍus' mother, retire into the woods, where they are burned. The sixteenth book, called 'Mausala' ('Club-Battle'), tells of the death of Kṛṣṇa and his brother Baladeva, and the fate of their city Dvārakā, which was flooded by the sea. The family of Kṛṣṇa, the Yadus (Yādavas), are cursed by a Brāhman, and destroy each other. The seventeenth book, 'Mahāprasthānika' ('Great Renunciation'), tells how the Pāṇḍus give up their kingdom and climb to heaven by way of the northern mountains; this is supplemented by the last book of the epic proper, called 'Svargārohaṇa' ('Ascent to Heaven'), describing the journey. To this is later added the *Harivaṁśa* ('Genealogy of Viṣṇu'), a long account in three sections of the life and family of Kṛṣṇa as a form of Viṣṇu. It has, in part, the characteristics of a Purāṇa (*q.v.*), and is, without doubt, a subsequent addition, dating perhaps from the 2nd cent. of our era, though generally regarded as still later.

The *Mahābhārata* may be viewed as a rich store of philosophical and religious lore as well as a tale, and as embodying important geographical and historical data. It undoubtedly reflects some real contest, which may have taken place about a millennium before our era. It extols the lunar race (the other epic, the *Rāmāyaṇa*, extols the solar race), and derives the heroes from kings who descended from Soma, the moon-god, himself the son of the seer Atri. Budha, son of Soma, had as wife Ilā, a daughter of Ikṣvāku of the solar line. Their son was Purūravas, whose son, Āyus, was the father of Nahuṣa, the father of Yayāti, from whom came Pūru and Yadu, the ancestors of all the lunar race, Yadu being the ancestor of Kṛṣṇa, and Pūru being the ancestor of Bharata and Kuru, whose descendant, Śāntanu, was the father of Bhīṣma (above) by the goddess Gaṅgā (the river Ganges). Śāntanu's wife, Satyavatī, was also the mother of Vyāsa and of Vichitravīrya, who died without children; but Vyāsa raised up children for him, and these were Dhṛtarāṣṭra and Pāṇḍu. If these legends be reconstructed historically with the aid of the Purāṇic lists of kings, they show that a real historical background is reflected in the maze of myth. The polyandry of the Pāṇḍus is a trait of certain hill-tribes, and is not unknown on the plains; it is undoubtedly a genuine bit of tradition which serves to mark the Pāṇḍus as a ruder race than the old and long-respected Kurus.

An attempt to group the participants in the great war according to their place of origin has been made by F. E. Pargiter (*JRAS*, 1908, pp. 309–336, and 1910, pp. 1–56), who seeks in this examination to determine whether the theory of successive invasions leaving inner and outer rings of Aryans in India can be substantiated thereby; but the result seems to leave considerable doubt as to such invasions having left traces in the poem, though the theory of successive invasions may be substantiated on other grounds. The didactic teaching of the epic is not confined to any one part of the work, and from a general view of this teaching it is evident that a later pantheistic system has become amalgamated with the dualistic doctrines of the Sāṅkhya philosophy in its later theistic tendency as represented by the Yoga. This mixed system is represented not only in the *Bhagavad-Gītā*, but in the *Anugītā* and in the philosophical chapters of the twelfth and thirteenth books. The outcome of the systematic speculation is in accord with the teaching of the Vedānta, but the terminology and basic ideas are those of the

Sāṅkhya system throughout. The chief interest of the religious doctrine lies in the insistence upon the loving devotion of the worshipper and the saving grace of the supreme spirit (see BHAKTI-MĀRGA). Kṛṣṇa as a form of Viṣṇu is not revered (as later) in his child-form, nor is anything made of his being the lover of milk-maids, though both traits are recognized. They come out strongly in the *Harivaṁśa* and later Purāṇas, and it is perhaps not unjustifiable to conclude that they did not form part of the worship as originally adopted into Brāhmanism.

Directly opposed to Kṛṣṇa-Viṣṇuism is the Śiva-cult also found in the epic, as already indicated. This cult appears to have been set against that of the Kṛṣṇa-worshippers by the more orthodox upholders of Brāhmanism, although neither Śiva nor Kṛṣṇa was a Vedic god. But Śiva had long been recognized as a form of the Vedic Rudra, and, though probably at first a popular god, like Kṛṣṇa, he was already accepted by the Brāhman priests. The parts of the poem exalting Śiva as All-god or as the One God are not early; on the contrary, they bear the marks of later composition and the trait now so familiar, that of phallus-worship, appears only in a few late passages. As this aspect cannot be in itself a late feature, it must have acquired the seal of respectability only by degrees, being probably repugnant to the orthodox priests of Brahmā. The special sectarian cults or forms of cults as advocated in the Purāṇas are unknown in the epic. The cult of Viṣṇu is that of the pantheistic All-god; the cult of Śiva is that of the only One God. But, with the opposing claims of each sect, each god gradually assumes the distinctive attributes of the other. Viṣṇu is the one theistic god and Śiva is the pantheistic All-god. Each in turn claims to be maker, preserver, and destroyer; and Brahmā also, though originally creator-god, becomes destroyer as well, till all three, the sectarian Kṛṣṇa-Viṣṇu and Śiva and the older Brahmā of Brāhmanism, coalesce into the 'one god with three forms,' or, as the Hindu says, 'three gods and one form.' Besides these great gods it is noteworthy that a revival of sun-worship leads to strange exaltation of the sun as supreme god (but only in late passages), probably because of the identification of Viṣṇu with the sun on the one hand and the later Persian sun-worship on the other; for, though the epic was probably rounded out to its present size by the 2nd cent. of our era and was virtually complete in all probability as an epic two or three centuries before (by 100 B.C.), yet numerous episodes and laudatory hymns have been added at all times, as may be seen by the manifold additions in the recently published southern text of the epic, which contains thousands of verses in great part of this character (in part, narrative). Of such sort also are the hymns to Durgā and probably also the exaltation of Skanda as the great army-leader of the gods, raised far above his earlier conception. All these later additions are of priestly sectarian origin. The original lay of the Bharata war may also have been of priestly rather than of popular origin, though 'hero-lauds' sung by hired minstrels are not unknown in early literature. But it was part of the business of the king's chaplain to recite laudations in his honour, and it is not impossible that some chaplain of the epic kings may have expanded the theme, for not only the king living but 'dead kings and their glory' formed the topic of lays and eulogies. The completed *Mahābhārata* was intended for recital, but this was in dramatic form, so that even to this day it is acted as well as recited by the purveyors of amusement at country fairs.

LITERATURE.—M. Monier-Williams, *Indian Wisdom*, London, 1876; J. Dahlmann, *Das Mahābhārata als Epos und Rechtsbuch*, Berlin, 1895, *Genesis des Mahābhārata*, do. 1899; Adolf Holtzmann, *Das Mahābhārata*, Kiel, 1892–95; C. V. Vaidya, *The Mahābhārata: a Criticism*, Bombay, 1904; R. Garbe, *Die Bhagavadgītā*, Leipzig, 1905. See also for general analysis and extracts: J. Muir, *Original Sanskrit Texts*, London, 1858–72; A. Weber, *Indische Literaturgeschichte*, Berlin, 1876; A. A. Macdonell, *History of Sanskrit Literature*, London, 1900; M. Winternitz, *Gesch. der indischen Litteratur*[2], Leipzig, 1909, i.; L. von Schroeder, *Indiens Literatur und Cultur*, do. 1887; for special studies see E. Washburn Hopkins, *The Great Epic of India*, New York, 1901, and *Epic Mythology*, Strassburg, in press. A. M. Pizzagalli, *Nāstika, Cārvāka e Lokāyatika*, Pisa, 1907, and *La Cosmogonia di Bhṛgu*, Milan, 1910, has contributed useful studies of epic problems. Otto Strauss, *Ethische Probleme aus dem Mahābhārata*, Florence, 1912, gives a careful survey of the didactic material regarding the better life on earth. H. Jacobi, *Mahābhārata*, Bonn, 1903, provides a table of contents, index, and concordance. V. Fausböll, *Indian Mythology according to the Mahābhārata in Outline*, London, 1903, furnishes a good epitome of epic mythology. See also S. Sörensen, *Index to the Names in the Mahabharata*, do., 1904 ff. A critical ed. of the *Mahābhārata* is still a *desideratum*. The best edd. are, for the Northern text, Bombay, 1890, and for the Southern, do. 1906–11; the only complete trr. are by Protap Chandra Roy, Calcutta, 1884–96, and Manmatha Natt Dutt, do. 1895–1905.

E. WASHBURN HOPKINS.

MAHĀBODHI.—See GAYĀ.

MAHĀR, MHĀR, MEHRĀ.—One of the menial or depressed castes of W. India and the Deccan, numbering 3,342,680 at the Census of 1911. Their name is very doubtfully connected by G. Oppert (*Orig. Inhabitants of Bhāratavarṣa or India*, London, 1893, p. 28 ff.) with that of the ancient Indian Malla; and, according to J. Wilson (*Indian Caste*, Bombay, 1877, ii. 48), they gave their name to the country of Mahārāṣṭra, from which the Marāṭhās take their title. They are practically all Hindus by religion. Another caste, the Ḍheḍ or Ḍheṛ, is sometimes included with them, and, if not identical, they are allied, with the Holeyā menials of the Madras Presidency (E. Thurston, *Castes and Tribes of S. India*, Madras, 1909, ii. 329 ff.).

In the Central Provinces 'the Mahārs say they are descended from Mahāmuni, who was a foundling picked up by the goddess Pārvatī on the banks of the Ganges. At that time beef had not become a forbidden food; and when the divine cow, Tripād Gāyatri, died, the gods determined to cook and eat her body, and Mahāmuni was set to watch the pot boiling. He was as inattentive as King Alfred, and a piece of flesh fell out of the pot. Not wishing to return the dirty piece to the pot, Mahāmuni ate it; but the gods discovered the delinquency and doomed him and his descendants to live on the flesh of dead cows' (R. V. Russell, *Central Provinces Ethnographic Survey*, pt. ix., Allahabad, 1911, p. 84; cf. E. J. Kitts, *Census Report, Berar*, 1881, p. 114 n.).

Their religion is of the primitive animistic type, with a veneer of Hinduism. In the Khāndesh District they keep the regular Hindu fasts and feasts, and worship the popular gods of that country—Viṣṇu, or Viṭhobā; Śiva as Khaṇḍobā; Mahāsobā, an evil spirit who abides in an unhewn stone smeared with red lead; Bhairoba, or Śiva in his terrible Bhairava form; and the Mother-goddess in the form of Āī Bhavānī, whose image they keep in their houses. Besides these they worship snakes and the spirits of their dead ancestors (*BG* xii. [1880] 118 f., xvii. [1884] 172 ff.). At a temple in Kāṭhiāwār the Dheḍs worship what is really an image of Viṣṇu reposing on his serpent Śeṣa as Hānī, who is said to have been a deified woman of the caste. Women who are unable to nurse their babies and owners of cows which give a scanty supply of milk vow to wash this image in milk if their milk be increased (*BG* xiii. [1884] 415).

In the Central Provinces 'the great body of the caste worship the ordinary deities Devī, Hanumān, Dūlhā Deo, and others, though, of course, they are not allowed to enter Hindu temples. They principally observe the Holī and Dasahrā festivals and the days of the new and full moon. On the festival of Nāgpanchmī they make an image of a snake with flour and sugar and eat it. At the sacred Ambāla tank at Rāmtek the Mahārs have a special bathing-ghāt set apart for them, and they may enter the citadel and go as far as the lowest step leading up to the temples: here they worship the god and think that he accepts their offerings. They are thus permitted to traverse the outer enclosures of the citadel, which are also sacred. In Wārdha the Mahārs may not touch the shrines of Mahādeo, but must stand before them with their hands joined. They may sometimes deposit offerings with their own hands on those of Bhimsen, originally a Goṇḍ god, and Mātā Devī, the goddess of smallpox.'

In Berār they worship a curious collection of deities, among whom are included the archangels Gabriel, Azrael, Michael, and Anādin, all of whom, they say, come from Pāndharpur. In Berār the worship of these archangels was probably borrowed from the Muhammadans; but in Gujarāt it was apparently taken from Christianity.

'It seems that the attraction which outside faiths exercise on the Mahārs is the hope held out of ameliorating the social degradation under which they labour, itself an outcome of the Hindu theory of caste. Hence they turn to Islām or to what is probably a degraded version of the Christian story because these religions do not recognise caste, and hold out a promise to the Mahār of equality with his co-religionists, and in the case of Christianity of a recompense in the world to come for the sufferings which he has to endure in this one. Similarly the Mahārs are the warmest adherents of the Muhammadan saint Sheikh Farīd, and flock to the fairs held in his honour at Girār in Wārdha and Pratāpgaṛh in Bhandāra, where he is supposed to have slain a couple of giants' (Russell, p. 90 ff.).

LITERATURE.—Besides the authorities quoted in the art. see *Census Report, Central Provinces*, 1901, i. 182, *Bombay*, 1911, i. 287; A. Baines, *Ethnography* [=*GIAP* ii. 5], Strassburg, 1912, p. 76 f.

W. CROOKE.

MAHATMA.—See THEOSOPHY.

MAHĀVASTU.—The *Mahāvastu*, one of the most noteworthy books of Buddhist antiquity, is a huge confused compilation of legends 'on the origins of Buddhism, on the persons of its founder [up to the gift of the *jetavana*] and his first disciples—in a word, on that *ensemble* which, with infinite varieties of detail, crossed and ramified in every way, is the common property of all Buddhists.' Besides all this, it includes a gnomic treasure, which is also traditional, an enormous mass of *jātakas* ('birth-stories') and tales, certain dogmatic speculations (see below, § 3), interminable lists of Buddhas—'needless digressions, mere padding—two, three, four accounts and more of the same episode, from different sources, sometimes contradictory, sometimes following one another, sometimes scattered through the book, dovetailed into one another, dismembered, lacerated.'[1]

The interest attaching to the *Mahāvastu* is of many kinds: (1) it is a book of *vinaya* ('discipline') of one of the ancient sects, and its history, so far as it can be traced, is instructive; (2) it is a vast repertory of legend and folklore, which, when compared with Pāli literature, supplies innumerable documents on the nature and primitive state of Buddhist tradition; (3) the *Mahāvastu*, from the point of view of dogmatic ideas, marks a period or a transition stage between the Hīnayāna and the Mahāyāna; and (4) its language, too, deserves attention.

1. History and contents.—The *Mahāvastu*, or, according to the colophon (which is open to suspicion), *Mahāvastv-avadāna*, claims to be a part of the *Vinayapiṭaka*, of the 'recitation' (*i.e.* the canon) of the Lokottaravādin Mahāsāṅghikas of the Madhyadeśa.

(1) The Mahāsāṅghikas are one of the old sects or branches of the Order, the other branch being that of the Sthaviras or Theras (see SECTS [Buddhist]); from the beginning it probably had special rules of *vinaya*, or 'discipline.' (2) The expression Lokottaravādin, 'believer in the supernatural character of the *bodhisattva*' (see below, § 3, and art. BODHISATTVA), indicates a dogmatic school. It is possible that there were Mahāsāṅghikas who were not Lokottaravādins. It would not be difficult to eliminate from the *Mahāvastu* the passages which have a Lokottaravādin tendency. (3) The Madhyadeśa, or 'middle country,' of the Buddhists comprises N. India, Magadha, Kośala, and Videha; but there were Mahāsāṅghikas outside of the Madhyadeśa, notably the Pūrvaśailas and the Aparaśailas, who were also Lokottaravādins.

In order to understand the word *mahāvastu* and to see how the *Mahāvastu*, in which discipline takes only a very small place, can belong to the section on 'discipline,' it is necessary to go far back.

The disciplinary literature (*Vinaya*) was from the beginning composed of two parts: (1) the formula of confession (*prātimokṣa*, *pāṭimokkha*), a list and classification of grave and venial faults, to which an explanatory and historical commentary was soon added: on what occasion such and such a prohibition was made by the Master; in the Sarvāstivādin school this commentary is called *Vibhāga*, in the school of the Pāli language *Vibhaṅga*; and (2) the statutes of the Order, a collection of the texts (*karmavākya*, *kammavācha*) relating to ecclesiastical acts (ordination, fortnightly confession, etc.) and of rules referring to ordination, confession, the cenobitic life during the rainy season, to parishes, medicines, beds, and schisms. These texts and rules were also embedded in a historical commentary. In the Pāli canon they are divided into two sections (*khandhaka*), in two chapters or books (*vagga*)—the 'Great Vagga' and the 'Little Vagga' (*Mahāvagga* and *Chullavagga*), the latter being devoted to subsidiary questions. There is the same division in the canon of the Sarvāstivādins, under different titles: the *Kṣudrakavastu* (*vastu*, 'thing,' 'topic,' 'point of discipline or doctrine,' 'story'), corresponding to the *Chullavagga*, and the *Vinayavastu*, which, although it does not bear the title 'Great,' corresponds to the *Mahāvagga*.

One of the characteristics of the *Mahāvagga* (and the *Vinayavastu*) is that, especially in its first part, it assumes the form of history. It contains a short epitome of the origin of the Order, which is perfectly justified as an introduction to the *vastu* of ordination: it was in a book of discipline that the most ancient writers, for want of a better planned library, deemed it expedient to place some pages from the life of the Buddha—his illumination, his first sermon, etc. The editors of the *Vinayavastu* (which is, as we have said, the *Mahāvagga* of the Sarvāstivādins), who came long afterwards, took far more liberties: in the first ten chapters their work preserves the character of a historical treatment of monastic discipline; but the last chapter (devoted in principle and in title, like the corresponding chapter of the *Mahāvagga*, to the internal strife of the Order) contains not only a fresh statement of the biographical elements of the first chapter, but also the history of Śākyamuni from the beginning of time, related in a continuous account down to the schismatic intrigues of Devadatta; a list of the *chakravartin* kings, the creation of the universe and life of primitive men, and the history of the Śākyas (ancestors of Śākyamuni); legends of the birth of Śākyamuni, his education, his departure, his mortifications, etc.—a *summa* of ancient traditions among which are to be found documents which have an independent existence in the Pāli canon (*e.g.*, the *Ajaññasutta*). Of the five hundred pages in the eleventh chapter of the *Vinayavastu*, little more than forty are devoted to the schism which gives its name to the chapter, and which, in all probability, was at first its only *vastu*, its one subject. In a word, the *Vinayavastu*, as a whole, is a faithful replica of the *Mahāvagga*; but it shows a very wide use of interpolation.

It is different with the *Mahāvastu*, and the manifest contradiction between the title and the contents raises a delicate question. Such a title

[1] Barth, *Journal des Savants*, 1899, pp. 463, 623.

implies that the book was, like the *Mahāvagga* and the *Vinayavastu*, meant to be a history of disciplinary rules. As a matter of fact, of thirteen hundred pages about twenty treat of discipline (especially at the beginning, two lines on ordination), and certain parallelisms with the *Mahāvagga* cannot be mistaken; *e.g.*, there is 'a series of stories in the *Mahāvastu*, in the Pāli *Mahāvagga*, and in the Tibetan *Vinaya* which hold together, and really seem faintly to reproduce a common prototype' (Barth, *loc. cit.* p. 464). But, on the whole, the *Mahāvastu* is a collection of legends without any connexion with discipline.

One can easily understand how a primitive *Mahāvastu*, a historical treatment of discipline, would be fed (Barth says *nourri*) by a mass of heterogeneous materials, differing in date and character, which, by their inorganic or chaotic accumulation, would explain all that non-disciplinary literature which forms ninety-nine hundredths of the present *Mahāvastu*. This task of enlarging and of 'feeding' was carried on in all the Buddhist sects, for a longer or shorter time, with more or less moderation; and what is true of the literary units is still more true of the canonical collections. Although we at present know nothing about the library of the Mahāsāṅghikas, we may suppose that it had no shelves in which the *jātakas, suttas*, and stanzas would be arranged. The only course was to gather together in the *Mahāvastu* all that seemed precious.[1] The development of the *Mahāvastu*, therefore, if it had remained to any extent a history of discipline, and if some pieces of the framework of the *Mahāvagga* were perceptible, would seem quite simple. Must it be admitted that the last compilers of the *Mahāvastu* systematically cut away the elements of *vinaya* already sunk in the legendary mass? Or that, in the fearful disorder in which the literature of the *Mahāsaṅgha* was weltering, these elements fell into oblivion? Or that the *Mahāvastu* was never in any respect, except its title, a replica of the *Mahāvagga*? The three hypotheses seem equally inadmissible.

Some light is perhaps afforded by the history of the *Divyāvadāna*. E. Huber (and after him S. Lévi[2]) has proved that this book is, above all, a collection of anecdotes and legends taken from the *Vinaya* of the Sarvāstivādins. The extracts have not always been made very consistently, and some fragments of *vinaya* proper—disciplinary rules—are to be found in the *Divyāvadāna*. The history of the *Mahāvastu* is probably similar. The colophon gives it the name of *Mahāvastv-avadāna*: is this to be translated 'the narrative part of the *Mahāvastu*'? In the Pāli *Vaggas* the various episodes are linked to the history of the *Vinaya* by explicit references or allusions; these, without exception, are wanting in the *Mahāvastu*: 'So those same episodes which in the *Mahāvagga* and the *Chullavagga* are more or less prolix and discursive chapters of a treatise on discipline are here mere narratives, which end by making the *Mahāvastu* a book of stories.'[3]

However this may be, 'the materials which have entered into the composition of the *Mahāvastu* are of widely different ages; . . . the source of the compilation is certainly ancient, since it forms part of the canon of one of the ancient schools. It must be admitted, therefore, that it took a long time to be formed, for it is certain that it was not completed until very late.' The mention of astrologers under a Western name (*horāpāṭhaka*) and that of the writings of the Chinese and of the Huns, Peliyakṣa (Felix ?), Ujjhebhaka (Uzbek ?), indicate the 4th or 5th century. At that date, however, 'the persistence, in the prose, of the ecclesiastical jargon, which will be discussed below [§ 4], is an astonishing fact.'[4] We must, therefore, admit late interpolations and carry the date of the compilation a little further back. In order to realize the character of this compilation, it must be noticed that 'the editors do not allow themselves to invent anything, and do not dare even to correct the most flagrant contradictions.'[1]

1 See the Introductions and notes of E. Senart, and cf. Barth, *Journal des Savants*, 1899, p. 623 f.
2 *T'oung-pao*, II. viii. [1907] 105 ff.
3 Barth, *loc. cit.* p. 529.
4 *Ib.* p. 629.

2. Comparison with Pāli canon.—There are numerous parallel passages in the *Mahāvastu* and Pāli literature. Minayeff, Oldenberg, above all Senart and Barth, and, lastly, Windisch, have called attention to many, but not to all. Differences which seem to be marks of sect are rare. We are able to study the unsettled state of Buddhist tradition and the infinite diversity of arrangement and treatment of the same materials.

'In these examples, the amount of similarity is of all degrees, from simple community of subject and vague resemblance to complete identity. The latter, however, is rarely attained, and never for long. . . . The similarity, especially in the verses, is to a large extent an exterior one; it is shown in mode of expression, in general assonance, in words more than in matter, in sounds more than in words; the stanza is the same, when the meaning is sometimes quite different, like an egg of which nothing remains but the shell. . . . They all go back to one original. . . . The probabilities are not always in favour of the Pāli edition. But for the *ensemble* of the fragments as well as for the detail of their rendering, it is the Pāli that is the best on the whole and that gives the best representation of the original version.'[2]

It is well known that all the comparisons set up between the Pāli canon and the other canons arrive at the same conclusion. The Pāli writings were fixed and codified first.

3. Relation to Mahāyāna and Hīnayāna.—The *Mahāvastu* may be said to form the bridge between the Old Vehicle and the New. As is seen in art. MAHĀYĀNA, the two Vehicles are not incompatible, and the book may present certain characteristics peculiar to the Great Vehicle while remaining unacquainted with the others.

(1) The 'Buddhology' of the *Mahāvastu* marks a stage between the conception of Buddha as a simple mortal (Little Vehicle) and that of Buddha as a quasi-eternal god sending illusory images down to this world (Great Vehicle). The Buddha of the *Mahāvastu* is a superman. He feels neither hunger nor thirst; he lives in ignorance of carnal desires; his wife remains a virgin. It is from consideration for humanity, in order to conform to the customs of the world (*lokānuvartanā*), that he behaves as a man, or that he gives to men the false impression that he is behaving as a man. In technical terms, he is *lokottara*, 'superior to the world.'[3]

(2) The infinite multiplication of Buddhas in the past and in the present is also a characteristic of Mahāyānist tendency. It must be noticed, however, that the Sarvāstivādins, who are reputed to be free from Mahāyānism, allow that several Buddhas may co-exist, though in different universes, or 'fields of Buddha.'

(3) Much more marked is the tendency of one of the chapters of the *Mahāvastu*, entitled *Daśabhūmika*, 'the book of the ten *bhūmis*'—successive steps by which the future Buddhas have to mount up to the state of Buddha.

'It is to the beings who aspire resolutely to the condition of Buddha that the *Daśabhūmika* ought to be set forth . . . for they will believe; the others will only cavil' (i. 193).

The *Mahāvastu*, therefore, has incorporated a book which is addressed, in so many words, to the men who wish to become, not *arhats*, but Buddhas, *i.e.* to the men who enter the Vehicle of the future Buddhas, the Mahāyāna.[4]

1 Barth, *loc. cit.* p. 624.
2 *Ib.* p. 627.
3 The text says that his body is *manomaya*, 'mind-made.' This expression has been discussed by E. Senart and A. Barth (see art. BODHISATTVA). According to the *Abhidharmakośa*, it means, not 'mental body,' 'body formed of mind,' but 'body created by the mind,' without intervention of seed and blood. Such is the body of the creatures called *aupapāduka*, 'apparitional,' one of whose characteristics is that, on dying, they leave no trace.
4 Several other instances of Mahāyānist tendency are discussed by Senart and Barth (*loc. cit.* p. 526). Different interpretations may be suggested from that of these two scholars for

On the other hand, Amitābha, Avalokita, Mañjuśrī, the *dhāraṇīs* ('spell'), and the *śūnyatā* ('voidness')—and, we may add, *karuṇā* ('compassion')—are unknown in the *Mahāvastu*, which remains 'a book of the Hīnayāna in its mythological and legendary part,' as Barth remarks (p. 527), and which is really Mahāyānist only in the considerable interpolation of the *Daśabhūmika*.[1]

4. Language.—The ancient religious literatures of India—with the exception of the Brāhmanic—were written in popular and spoken dialects. In course of time these dialects became 'fixed languages,' subject to rules. This happened with the Jains (*ardhamāgadhī*), and with the church which was afterwards that of Ceylon (Pāli). The Buddhist school of the Sarvāstivādins adopted Sanskrit, and Sanskritized both the ancient nomenclature and the traditional texts in prose and in verse. The language of the Mahāsāṅghika school remained 'in an unsettled state: it was neither Sanskrit nor Pāli, nor any of the known Prākrits, but an arbitrary and unstable mixture of all these.'

It is a literary language, says Senart, 'and it is certain that it was no longer [*i.e.* at the time of the compilation of the *Mahāvastu*] a spoken language, and not less certain that, for several centuries before and after that time, inscriptions and books were written in much the same way. But, in the *Mahāvastu*, is it still a language? At bottom, there is undoubtedly the substance of a real idiom, akin to that of the most ancient inscriptions and to that which has come to us so admirably fixed in the Pāli texts,' but this idiom remained without grammar and without orthography, and, especially in the prose, 'it was indefinitely open to the influence of Sanskrit.'[2]

Such is the language of the *Mahāvastu* in the present state of the text—more Prākrit in the poetry than in the prose, and extremely interesting for the linguistic history of India. This language has received the name of 'language of the *Gāthās*,' because it was first studied in the books of the Great Vehicle, the prose parts of which are in Sanskrit or quasi-Sanskrit, and the verses or stanzas (*gāthās*) in this peculiar jargon. This difference of treatment does not exist in the *Mahāvastu*, in which the Sanskritisms seem to be unconscious.

LITERATURE.—E. Senart, *Le Mahâvastu* (Skr. text, introduction, and commentary), i.–iii., Paris, 1882–97; A. Barth, *RHR* xi. [1885] 160, xlii. [1900] 51, and *Journal des Savants*, 1899, pp. 459, 517, 623; E. Windisch, 'Die Komposition des Mahāvastu,' *ASG*, phil.-hist. Klasse, xxvii. [1909] 467–511; M. Winternitz, *Gesch. der ind. Litteratur*, II. i. (Leipzig, 1913) 187. The remarks of P. Minayeff and H. Oldenberg are quoted by Barth.

L. DE LA VALLÉE POUSSIN.

MAHĀVĪRA.—See ĀJĪVIKAS.

MAHĀYĀNA.—I. *DEFINITION AND DESCRIPTION.*—1. In order to define Mahāyāna, we must first notice certain characteristics of the Hīnayāna.

Buddha has said that, as salt is the only flavour of the sea, the only flavour (*rasa*) of his doctrine, the true doctrine or religion (*saddharma*), is the flavour of deliverance (*mokṣa, mukti*), or of *nirvāṇa*. Buddhism, therefore, can be looked on as a path (*mārga, pratipad*) leading to *nirvāṇa*, as a supramundane (*lokottara*) path leading to the end of the

two passages in which they think they discern references to the two sects of the Mahāyāna—the Yogāchāras and the Mādhyamikas. (1) *Yogāchāra*, in *Mahāvastu*, i. 120, means simply 'he who practises *yoga*, "contemplation."' It is by this name that the *Abhidharma* (ch. vi. *ad init.*) designates the ascetic who practises 'meditation of the horrible' (*aśubhabhāvanā*, contemplation of the corpse, etc.), the *smṛtyupasthānas*, etc. (2) As regards the 'middle path' described in iii. 448, it is certainly Mādhyamika, but it is also 'canonical' (*Saṁyuttanikāya*).

[1] We know that one of the chief books of the Mahāyāna is called *Daśabhūmika* (tr. into Chinese, A.D. 265–316). The Yogāchāras claim it as patronizing their doctrine, because it teaches that 'all things are only thought' (*chitta*)—a theory which does not appear in the *Daśabhūmika* of the *Mahāvastu*. The *bhūmis* of the two works have been compared in art. BODHISATTVA. The scholars of the Mahāyāna argue from the fact that the theory of the *bhūmis* is taught in the *Mahāvastu*, a Hīnayāna book.

[2] Barth, p. 459.

constant succession of re-births (*saṁsāra punarbhava*) which constitutes the 'world' (*loka*) or existence (*bhavaloka*), or as a vehicle (*yāna*) conveying those who mount it to the same goal, 'the town of *nirvāṇa*, the island of *nirvāṇa*.'

The first metaphor has been adopted by primitive Buddhism; the second one by the new Buddhism. The adherents of this later Buddhism found fault with the earlier Buddhism; and, accordingly, while styling their own creed *mahāyāna* ('great vehicle'), true, great, and profound (*gambhīra*) doctrine of salvation, they characterized the creed of their predecessors as *hīnayāna* ('little vehicle'), an inferior, imperfect, inefficient doctrine of salvation. Another name for the older Buddhism, a more polite one, is *śrāvakayāna*; in the old scriptures the disciples of the Buddha who have entered the path are called *śrāvaka* ('disciples,' 'auditors,' or 'preachers' of the Law), or *āryaśrāvaka* ('noble disciples,' 'true disciples'). The term *śrāvakayāna* conveys the idea that the old doctrine is nevertheless an efficient means of salvation. Moreover, it marks a contrast between the two Buddhist creeds; for the adherents of the new Buddhism style themselves *bodhisattva* (future Buddhas) and employ the term *bodhisattvayāna* ('vehicle that conveys the *bodhisattvas*') as a synonym of Mahāyāna.

(1) The Hīnayāna asserts that salvation can be quickly gained; it is a vehicle drawn by deer (*mṛgaratha*). It professes to lead, when duly practised, to *nirvāṇa* in this existence (*dṛṣṭadharma*). One has to become an *arhat*, *i.e.* a *jīvanmukta* (*q.v.*), a man freed even in this life. In fact, the *arhat* has already obtained *nirvāṇa*, the *nirvāṇa* called *sopadhiśeṣa*, the liberation from desire and lust, the machinery of life continuing automatically until it runs down. When dying, he says: 'I have nothing more to do. I shall not be re-born here again,' and he enters into *nirupadhiśeṣa nirvāṇa*, 'absolute *nirvāṇa*.'

It is mysticism, but a perfectly coherent mysticism. It involves no elements that are foreign to the end which it has in view, viz. the destruction of desire or thirst, the suppression of all activity (*karman*) liable to induce a new existence. It consists essentially in contemplation (*darśana* = 'sight') and meditation (*bhāvanā*) on the four truths: everything is painful, etc. These four truths may be summarized in a philosophical dogma: what we call the 'soul,' or the 'ego,' is only a complex of incongruous, transitory elements (*skandhas*), which endures by means of desire (or thirst) alone; and an ethical dogma: desire can be rooted out and the consequences of action can be suppressed by meditations which emancipate and deliver from existence.

(2) This method of salvation (the method of supramundane meditations) cannot be practised except by a person who observes, and has observed for some time, 'morality'—*i.e.* the laws that make an action or a thought good (see art. KARMA)—and, what is very important, a person who practises continence (or the religious life *brahmacharya*) as a Buddhist monk.

(3) Although the Buddha is neither a god nor a supernatural being, he is nevertheless very different from the other saints. The saints, like the Buddha, have attained *nirvāṇa* in this life, because they have attained *bodhi* ('illumination'); but it was the Buddha who discovered the truths of salvation which potentially contain *bodhi*, and who showed the 'path'; and he was able to do so because in the course of his innumerable existences, with a view to saving human beings, he had accumulated good works and acquired infinite knowledge.

(4) The cult of the Buddha is not distinguished by what is properly called 'devotion' (*bhakti*)—

this sentiment implies a living god—though the *Abhidharmakośa* employs the term. Veneration of relics, *stūpas*, etc., is useful and recommended; it is good, it is helpful, as penance (*tapas*) is, but it is not essential.

(5) Ancient Buddhism is not merely a vehicle of *nirvāṇa*; it also teaches how to be re-born in heaven, in the world of Brahmā.

Three Vehicles are usually distinguished: (1) the Vehicle of the Śrāvakas, (2) the Vehicle of the Pratyekabuddhas, (3) the Vehicle of the *bodhisattvas*. The first two together constitute the Little Vehicle, the third the Great Vehicle (see E. Burnouf, *Le Lotus de la bonne loi*, Paris, 1852, pp. 52, 315, 369; H. Kern, *SBE* xxi. [1884] 80, *Manual of Indian Buddhism*, p. 61; *Dharmasaṁgraha*, ed. F. Max Müller and H. Wenzel, Oxford, 1885, p. 2, and sources cited on p. 35; E. J. Eitel, *Handbook of Chinese Buddhism*[2], London, 1888, *s.v.* 'Triyāna'; cf. *Buddhavaṁsa* [*PTS*, London, 1882], Commentary, p. x f., where the Śrāvaka-Pratyekabuddhas are opposed to the Samyaksambuddhas). There is no difference between the Vehicle of the Śrāvakas and that of the Pratyekabuddhas; both arrive at the same *bodhi*, or illumination, and the same *nirvāṇa*; but, while the Śrāvakas appear at a time when the Law of the Buddha is known, and profit by the teaching of others, the Pratyekabuddhas attain to *bodhi* themselves at a time when the Law of the Buddha has disappeared; while the Śrāvakas preach (*śrāvayanti*; *śrāvaka*, translated 'hearer,' means rather 'preacher' [see *SBE* xxi., *Saddharmapuṇḍarīka*, iv. 53]), the Pratyekabuddhas do not convert except by miracles. There are still other differences, but they are of no importance to the Vehicle of salvation (see *Abhidharmakośabhāṣya*, ch. iii., Fr. tr., London, 1915, p. 103 and notes; Chandrakīrti, *Madhyamakāvatāra* (Fr. tr., *Muséon*, new ser., viii. [1907] 2 ff., quoting literary authorities). It is natural, then, for the Vehicle of the Śrāvakas and the Vehicle of the Pratyekabuddhas to be fused in the Little Vehicle (Hīnayāna [*q.v.*]).

2. Great Vehicle.—The new Buddhism adopts the name of *mahāyāna* ('great vehicle'). The word *yāna* ('vehicle') is used to express the same idea as that conveyed by the 'supramundane path' (*lokottaramārga*), the 'path leading to *nirvāṇa*.' But, as we shall see, there are various kinds of Mahāyāna, and this fact explains the diversity of definitions and the evident difficulty in which early writers—*e.g.*, the Chinese pilgrims—found themselves when they tried to explain the difference between the Little and the Great Vehicle.

The Great Vehicle consists of (1) the practice of the virtues (*pāramitās*) of a *bodhisattva* or future Buddha (i.e. *pāramitāyāna* [*°naya*] or *bodhisattvayāna*); by it one becomes a Buddha (*buddhayāna*); (2) the wisdom or knowledge of vacuity (*prajñāyāna* or *jñānamārga*); (3) devotion; it is the path of devotion (*bhaktimārga*).

(1) *Career of the bodhisattva.*—The books which profess to belong to the Great Vehicle (*Mahāyānasūtras*) tend to assert that *nirvāṇa* cannot be attained by the ancient method. To obtain deliverance from desire, ignorance, and existence it is necessary to practise all the virtues and acquire all the knowledge of the Buddhas, to enter on the career of a future Buddha (*bodhisattvacharyā*) and pursue it for centuries. Instead of 'Great Vehicle,' it may therefore be called 'Vehicle of the future Buddhas' (*bodhisattvayāna*), or 'Method of the perfect virtues, charity, patience, etc.' (*pāramitānaya*).

Now the Buddha Śākyamuni, during his former existences, has always lived in the world. It is possible, therefore, to enter the 'Vehicle of the future Buddhas' although married. Nothing, however, prevents monks from making the 'vow to become Buddhas'; by this vow they mount the 'Vehicle of the future Buddhas,' but by their monastic observances they belong to the 'old Buddhism,' and form part of one of the disciplinary schools of the Śrāvakas. Young laymen often take the vows of monks, and, after acquiring merit in this way for a time, renounce them in order to take the vows of a future Buddha.

(2) *Vacuity.*—The books that treat of philosophy explain that the ancient dogma, 'The soul is nothing but a complex of transitory elements (*skandha*),' is perfectly accurate, but unsatisfying; they would add that these elements themselves do not exist in themselves, but are 'void' (*śūnya*). (For the two ways of understanding vacuity, and the two schools of the Great Vehicle, see artt. MADHYAMAKA and VIJÑĀNAVĀDINS.) The doctrine of vacuity (*śūnyatāvāda*) is the second characteristic of the Great Vehicle. But a layman or a monk can perform the 'vow to become a Buddha' without thinking out the doctrine of vacuity. The 'theologians' themselves declare that, as the beginning of the saintly career is entirely devoted to charity, it is not good to give too much thought to philosophy, *i.e.* to universal nothingness. On the other hand, an adept of the Little Vehicle who does not believe in the necessity of becoming a Buddha may adhere to the doctrine of vacuity and become imbued with it, in order to attain *nirvāṇa* as an *arhat*, *i.e.* in this present life. Some texts even explain that, if the doctrine of vacuity is really indispensable to the attainment of *nirvāṇa*, it is sufficient, without the career of the future Buddha.

(3) *Devotion.*—A third characteristic of the Great Vehicle is the worship of the Buddhas and 'future Buddhas' of high rank (see art. BODHISATTVA). The Buddhas are great gods, almost eternal, who sit upon thrones in heavens surrounded by saints, and send 'magic bodies' down to earth to save men. The worship of the Buddhas may exist independently of any desire to become oneself a Buddha and independently of philosophic speculation.[1] There is therefore a Great Vehicle that is merely devotional: (*a*) the Buddha (Amitābha, *e.g.*) is a god in the full meaning of the word, eternal or almost so (Amitābha, 'infinite splendour,' is sometimes called Amitāyus, 'infinite life'); (*b*) the only concern of the faithful is to be re-born in the paradise of this god, 'the blissful world' (Sukhāvatī), the western paradise, by the grace of the god and with the help of the holy saints Avalokita, etc.[2]

This Mahāyāna, purely devotional and with monotheistic tendencies, is not a 'Vehicle of future Buddhas.' In the books discussing it (*Sukhāvatīvyūha*, etc.) there is practically no reference to *nirvāṇa*. This Vehicle is a Buddhist form of the Hindu *bhakti*, or devotion. *Bhakti* must be accompanied by highly orthodox acts of worship, which are recommended in the Hīnayāna: worship of *stūpas*, *maṇḍalas* in honour of the Buddha, abstinence from food before worshipping Buddha, etc. But the Mahāyānist *bhakti* is laden with litanies and formulæ; it declares that rites efface sin, and attributes salutary virtue to the reading of the *sūtras* and the repetition of the name of the Buddhas—which is not quite orthodox.

It is to be noticed that the worship of Buddhas, Tārās, etc., is compatible with the strict orthodoxy of the Hīnayāna, as has been remarked in regard to Java, which is very idolatrous and yet attached to the Hīnayāna.[3]

3. Vedāntic and Tāntric Vehicle.—The Mahāyāna, as analyzed above, is, from the philosophical point of view, a phenomenalist system, and, from the religious and mythological point of view, polytheism with monarchical and devotional tendencies. From early times phenomenalism and polytheism led to conceptions of immanence and monism.[4] In the days of Asaṅga (A.D. 4th cent.) men believed in an Ādibuddha (*q.v.*) who would play the part of Brahmā in his various aspects as Brahmā, or Kṛṣṇa divine, or Kṛṣṇa incarnate. These speculations upon immanence and emanation, which often mingle with the doctrines of the Mahāyāna proper,

[1] For the combination of the cult of the Buddhas and compassion, or charity, with meditation on vacuity, see art. BODHISATTVA.

[2] See artt. AMITĀYUS; BLEST, ABODE OF THE (Buddhist); cf. Matsumoto Bunzaburō, *Gokuraku jōdo ron* ('Study of the Pure-Land Sukhāvatī'), Tokyo, 1909, and *Miroku jōdo run* ('Study of the Pure-Land of Maitreya'), do. 1911 (Fr. tr., M. N. Péri, in *Bull. de l'Ecole franç. d'Extrême-Orient*, xi. [1911] 439 ff.).

[3] A. Barth, 'Le pèlerin chinois I-tsing,' in *Journal des Savants*, 1898; cf. the remark of Winternitz, *Geschichte*, ii. 157, on the Buddha in Buddhaghoṣa: 'eine Art Halbgott wie in den Mahāyānasūtra.'

[4] See Poussin, *Bouddhisme, Opinions sur la dogmatique*, p. 391; also his papers on the three bodies of a Buddha and allied subjects in *JRAS*, 1910, p. 129, and *Muséon*, new ser., xiv. [1913] 257; cf. D. T. Suzuki, *Outlines of Mahāyāna Buddhism*, London, 1907.

are the basis of the 'Vehicle of formulæ' (*mantrayāna*), the 'diamond method' (*vajranaya*), also called the 'Tāntric Vehicle' (*tantrayāna*). This Vehicle is Vedānta in Buddhist disguise as regards its doctrine, and Śaivite and pagan as regards its mythological representations and its rites. Its goal is the condition of a Buddha, its doctrine that (1) every being is, in his inmost nature, a Buddha, and (2) every being can, by meditation, spells, (*sādhana*), and theurgic practices of all kinds (often erotic), 'realize' this Buddha nature at little expense (see TANTRISM).

4. Is the Mahāyāna the only Vehicle?—This is an interesting question and worthy of our attention. Do the Mahāyāna teachers regard the Mahāyāna as the only Vehicle of salvation? I-tsing's remarks may be accepted as giving the general opinion:

'These two systems [Mahāyāna and Hīnayāna] are perfectly in accordance with the noble doctrine [of the Buddha] . . . Both equally conform to truth and lead us to Nirvâna.'[1]

But the scholastic literature and the *Mahāyāna-sūtras* of course give different and often narrower views. Maitreya-Asaṅga says that 'the meditation (*dhyāna*) of the Hīnayāna, though impure, leads to salvation';[2] but for Śāntideva the Hīnayāna is of only relative truth, and its followers are upon a path that has no issue;[3] Chandrakīrti sees no virtue in the Hīnayāna except its teaching of 'vacuity' (see MADHYAMAKA): there are old *sūtras* which proclaim vacuity (*śūnyatāpratisamyukta*); in an extreme case *arhat*ship and *nirvāṇa* may be attained by meditation on these *sūtras*[4]—in an extreme case, we say, because the follower of the Hīnayāna has no part in the spiritual aids that are reserved for the future Buddha; he does not have the great 'means' (*upāya*) of salvation, compassion, great compassion (*mahākaruṇā*), *i.e.* the desire and the vow to save all creatures; the possession of wisdom (*prajñā*) is unavailing, since he lacks the great 'means' of remission of sins and elimination of passion. In fact, there is only one Vehicle, as the *Lotus of the True Law* (*q.v.*) and several *sūtras* teach very clearly. The only way to salvation is to become a Buddha. But this demands a long career; so the Buddha has shown men a nearer goal, the *nirvāṇa* of the *arhat*, that they may not lose heart—like a caravan-leader who creates a magic town in the midst of the forest, far from the end of the journey, that the travellers may think they are near their destination, and take heart to advance.[5] 'The men who mount the Vehicle of the Śrāvakas cannot obtain deliverance by the Vehicle of the Śrāvakas'; embracing a false *nirvāṇa*, they are like a lover who embraces his mistress's corpse; they have, however, advanced nearer to the true *nirvāṇa*. At death, they falsely think that they have attained deliverance and exemption from re-birth; they are re-born, for they are not yet delivered, but they are re-born beyond the world (*tridhātu*), in the 'pure realm' (*anāsravadhātu*), in lotuses which open their petals to the rays of Amitābha and other Buddhas. There they learn the true Vehicle, make the *bodhi* vow, and enter, through numerous lives, upon the career of a future Buddha.[6]

The Chinese texts studied by J. J. M. de Groot (*Code du Mahāyāna en Chine*, Amsterdam, 1893, p. 94) reduce the Hīnayāna to the observation of monastic rules, taking no notice, either purposely or through ignorance, of all the Noble Path and meditation on the truths. They say that the Little Vehicle, thus understood, leads to re-birth in the very inferior paradises of the world of Kāma (see COSMOGONY AND COSMOLOGY [Buddhist]); it is therefore a Vehicle that leads to the gods (*devayāna*, according to de Groot's translation), and not a Vehicle of salvation.

5. Speculative doctrines of the Mahāyāna.—These are examined in the artt. MADHYAMAKA and VIJÑĀNAVĀDINS, which discuss the two chief philosophic schools of the Great Vehicle. The doctrines connected with the 'career of the future Buddha' (*bodhisattvacharyā*) are treated in art. BODHISATTVA. Many details might be added on the technique of meditations; but the works on this subject (*Abhisamayālaṁkārāloka*, *Bodhisattvabhūmi*) have not been published, and present very serious difficulties.

6. Discipline (Vinaya) of the Mahāyāna.—The Indian schools of devotion (*bhakti*) are often not strict as regards morality and discipline. There existed, accordingly, lax Mahāyāna, inclining to Tantrism, which preached salvation and the remission of sins by the recitation of formulæ, etc., independently of rules of conduct.

But there is also a rigid Mahāyānist 'monachism,' sometimes adhering to the ancient *Vinayas*, sometimes introducing new ones.

(1) The *Ākāśagarbhasūtra* says:

'If a Bodhisattva [*i.e.* an adept of the Great Vehicle] begins to think: "The Bodhisattva does not require to study the law which forms part of the Hīnayāna; he need not make it a rule for himself. What is the use of accepting this rule? What is the use of this rule?"—if he thinks in this way, he is guilty of error, and renders himself very culpable.'

Śāntideva speaks in the same strain:

'The adept of the Great Vehicle will never give his hearers the vain hope of acquiring purity by simply reading the books of the Great Vehicle, and reciting formulas, while abandoning the rules of conduct.'[1]

One fully realizes I-tsing's statement:

'Which of the eighteen schools [of the Hīnayāna] should be grouped with the Mahâyâna or with the Hînayâna is not determined. . . . Both [Mahāyāna and Hīnayāna] adopt one and the same discipline (Vinaya).'[2]

Monks and convents practising the strict monastic observance of the ancient *Vinayas* adopted the dogmas and worship of the Mahāyāna; Yuan Chwang therefore mentions monks who were 'Mahāyānists of the Sthavira-school and all perfect in Vinaya observance.'[3] It has been supposed that the *Vinaya* of the ancient Mahāsāṅghika sect was the most popular in Mahāyānist convents, because it was in a Mahāyānist convent that Fa Hian found the Mahāsāṅghika *Vinaya*,[4] because the Mahāsāṅghikas seem to have been the forerunners of the Mahāyāna.[5]

(2) The Mahāyāna apparently introduced into the discipline some new rules concerning the use of milk and meat. The Sarvāstivādins (Hīnayāna) allowed the use of meat under certain conditions; the Mahāyānists condemned it. I-tsing tells a touching story of a young Mahāyānist, Chittavarman, who was refused ordination in a Hīnayāna convent until he renounced, in tears, his principles of diet.[6]

Sooner or later, however, the Mahāyāna created a new *Vinaya* for itself—a *Vinaya* that was independent of the ancient *Vinayas*, that had a different purpose in view and that could be, and was often

[1] *A Record of the Buddhist Religion*, tr. J. Takakusu, Oxford, 1896, p. 15.
[2] *Sūtrālaṁkāra*, xvi. 50.
[3] *Bodhicharyāvatāra*, iv. 7, ix. 49.
[4] *Madhyamakāvatāra*, 19; *Bodhicharyāvatāra*, *locc. citt.*
[5] See Poussin, *Bouddhisme, Opinions sur la dogmatique*, pp. 313–320; *Lotus of the True Law*, tr. Kern (*SBE* xxi.), p. 181; *Madhyamakāvatāra* (*Bibl. Budd.*, Petrograd, 1912), p. 402, and source cited.
[6] *Abhisamayālaṁkāraloka*, p. 166 of Poussin's MS, on *Aṣṭasāhasrikā*, xxxiv. 3, who cites the *Laṅkāvatāra*, the *Ratnamegha*, Nāgārjuna, etc.

[1] *Śikṣāsamuchchaya*, p. 61; *Bodhicharyāvatāra*, tr. L. de la Vallée Poussin, *Introd. à la pratique des futurs Bouddhas*, Paris, 1907, ch. v.
[2] *Op. cit.* p. 14.
[3] T. Watters, *On Yuan Chwang's Travels in India, 629–645*, London, 1904–05, i. 227, ii. 136, 188, 199, 234, 248.
[4] A. Rémusat, *Foe-koue-ki*, Paris, 1836, p. 318; J. Legge, *Travels of Fa-hien*, Oxford, 1886, p. 98.
[5] See the *Mahāvastu*; the 'basket of magic formulæ' (*Vidyādharapiṭaka*) said to be a part of the Mahāsāṅghika canon; Kern, *Manual*, p. 4; S. Julien, *Voyages des pèlerins bouddhistes*, Paris, 1853–58, i. 158, iii. 37.
[6] I-tsing, *Mémoires*, etc., tr. E. Chavannes, Paris, 1894, p. 48; Julien, *Voyages*, i. 50; Watters, *Yuan Chwang*, i. 55, 57, 79, ii. 173, 192; I-tsing, tr. Takakusu, p. 43.

expected to be, used together with the ancient *Vinayas*. The ancient *Vinayas* were for the use of monks; the Mahāyāna *Vinaya* is the 'Vinaya of the future Buddhas,' or, more exactly, 'of incipient future Buddhas' (*ādikarmika bodhisattva*). (*a*) It was while making the vow to become a Buddha that Śākyamuni, prostrating himself at the feet of a Buddha, became a 'future Buddha'; this vow is valid, not only for present existence, but also for numerous future existences; like the vows of a *bhikṣu* (see KARMA), it creates 'discipline' (*saṁvara*), the obligation and, to a certain extent, the 'grace' (the moral power) to perform certain duties. We have no longer a Buddha in our midst to receive such a vow from us; we must be content to take the 'discipline of a son of Buddha' (*sugatātmajasaṁvara*) before a qualified person (*sāṁvarika*), or, in the absence of such, before all the Buddhas of the quarters.[1] (*b*) The future Buddha must practise the perfect virtues (*pāramitās*); theologians have therefore to explain how he is to fulfil the virtues of giving, energy, and meditation. (*c*) He commits errors; he must know how to confess them, before whom (*i.e.* Buddhas of confession), and how to obtain pardon. (*d*) The ancient devotional practices, worship of *stūpas*, etc., are not sufficient for devotees of Avalokita, Amitābha, and Tārā; fixed rules of worship must therefore be made.[2]

We have no exact information regarding the oldest forms of the *Vinaya* for *bodhisattvas*. But documents which give an accurate idea of the rules of life of the Mahāyānist monk will be found in the *Brahmajālasūtra* (tr. de Groot, *Code du Mahāyāna en Chine*), and in the 'Daily Manual of the Shaman' (S. Beal, *A Catena of Buddhist Scriptures*, London, 1871, p. 239). The ritual of the office in honour of Avalokita (Beal, *Catena*, p. 398) indicates the nature of the cult.

(3) The Mahāyānist monks belonged to one of the Hīnayāna schools, and fulfilled the obligations of future Buddhas[3] in addition to those of their own school. Later, there were monks who adhered solely to the monastic code of the Mahāyāna (the type given in de Groot, *Code du Mahāyāna en Chine*), which became a complete code in itself, a conglomeration of different *Vinayas*. Finally, it is always possible for a monk to renounce his vows and return to the world; the Great Vehicle favoured this tendency inasmuch as it had a special 'code of the future Buddha' for the use of married people.[4] It is understood, however, that ordination to future Buddhahood can be granted only to persons who are at least Upāsakas, 'devotees,' who have taken the three refuges and are ritually bound by the five vows (not to kill, etc.).[5]

(4) The relative importance of duties for monks who are at the same time 'future Buddhas' is not always clear. I-tsing declares that he is not writing 'concerning those who claim to follow the practice of a Bodhisattva rather than the Vinaya rules.'[6] Śāntideva cites an extreme case—the story of the monk who had practised continence for a long time (84,000 years) consenting to satisfy the desires of a woman so that he might fulfil the requirement of benevolence and kindness that is the essential law of future Buddhas.[1] For them the sins of hatred are very serious, while the sins of desire are venial. The very spirit of the Mahāyāna, therefore, may perhaps be responsible for the singular development of Kashmīr monasticism, viz. married monks.[2]

II. *HISTORY AND ORIGINS OF MAHĀYĀNA DOCTRINES.*—As we have seen, the Mahāyāna differed from the ancient Vehicle in three points: (1) the substitution of the 'career of a future Buddha' for the 'conquest of the quality of *arhat*'; in other words, the substitution of the *bodhisattva*, who might be a layman, for the *bhikṣu*, 'monk'; (2) the creation of a new ontological theory, 'the doctrine of the void' (*śūnyatā*) or of 'the non-existence in themselves of the constituent elements of things and of the human ego' (*dharmanairātmya*), superimposed upon the doctrine of 'the non-existence in itself of the human ego' (*pudgalanairātmya*); and (3) the transformation of the Buddhas into great mythological gods, almost eternal; the deification of 'future Buddhas' as helping providences; and, by a parallel development, the practice of devotion (*bhakti*) towards these 'great beings' (*mahāsattva*) instead of the respect and meditation practised by the ancients towards the Buddha; what was formerly venerated in the Buddha, what men 'took refuge in' (*śaraṇagamana*) when taking refuge in the Buddha, was the complex of the moral and intellectual qualities in virtue of which a certain person is Buddha. To admire and meditate on these qualities is an excellent means of gaining morality, tranquillity, *nirvāṇa*. The Mahāyānist addresses himself to living, gracious, paternal gods.

There are, therefore, three formative elements in the Mahāyāna; and its history means the history of the development and inter-relation of these three elements. This comprises three distinct histories; for, though the three elements are sometimes united, they are often separate; and, though their development has been parallel, or almost so, they have no connexion from the logical point of view. We may safely attempt to give the scheme the evolutionary curve of these three elements, but it is very difficult to give chronological dates or precise details in the evolution.

1. Career of the bodhisattva.—Ancient Buddhism holds that Buddhas are very rare, but the Mahāyāna invites all who desire salvation to enter on the career of a future Buddha. This is a fundamental change from the dogmatic point of view, and involves a corresponding change in morale: in short, the monk believed that the quickest way to reach *nirvāṇa* was by meditation; he worked entirely 'for himself' (*svārtham*); the activity of the future Buddha, on the contrary, is, above all, altruistic (*parārtham*).

Our literary evidence on the stages of this transformation is unsatisfactory. On the other hand, it is easy to guess the motives behind it. The following factors are of great importance.

(1) The ideal of ancient Buddhism, the *arhat* useless to others and an utter egoist, to the extent of insensibility, appeared mean when compared to the Buddha, the being of compassion and pity. Hence the 'saint for himself,' the 'delivered while

[1] See *Bodhisattvabhūmi*, i. 10, fol. 62, and the fragments of the *Bodhisattvaprātimokṣa* (B. Nanjio, *Catalogue of the Chinese Translation of the Buddhist Tripiṭaka*, Oxford, 1883, nos. 1096–1098), quoted in *Śikṣāsamuchchaya*, p. 11. On the vow of the future Buddha see Śrījñāna, *Bodhipathapradīpa* (*JBTS* i. [1893] 39), and art. BODHISATTVA, vol. ii. pp. 746, 748 f. The *Bhadracharīpraṇidhāna* has been published by Watanebe, Strassburg, 1912. The *Vinayas* of the Mahāyāna were first placed under the patronage of Upāli (*Upālipariprchchha*); later they were more completely cut off from the tradition of the Hīnayāna.

[2] See, *e.g.*, *Ādikarmapradīpa*, in Poussin, *Bouddhisme*, Paris, 1898.

[3] De Groot, *Code du Mahāyāna en Chine*, p. 8.

[4] Kern, *Hist. du bouddhisme dans l'Inde*, ii. 34, following B. H. Hodgson, *Essays on the Languages, Literature, and Religion of Nepal and Tibet*, London, 1874, p. 145.

[5] Śrījñāna, *Bodhipathapradīpa*, tr. Sarat Chandra Dās, in *JBTS* i. 47.

[6] Cf. Takakusu's tr., p. 197.

[1] *Śikṣāsamuchchaya*, p. 167.

[2] See M. A. Stein, *Kalhaṇa's Rājataraṅgiṇī, a Chronicle of the Kings of Kaśmīr*, London, 1900, p. 74: 'In one half of the monastery she placed those Bhikṣus whose conduct conformed to the precepts; and in the other half those who, being in possession of wives, children, cattle and property, deserved blame for their life as householders' (on the date see Introd. p. 81). Cf. Hodgson, *Essays*, p. 52, and various predictions of the *Mahāyānasūtras* as to the decadence of Buddhist law.

still alive,' so long the dream of India, was no longer held in honour. The creation of the type of the Buddha, the hero of charity, saving the world at the cost of so many lives consecrated to the world, reveals tendencies in ancient Buddhism towards the doctrine of the 'career of the *bodhisattva*' open to all.[1]

(2) The question arose, further, whether the *arhat* actually obtains *nirvāṇa*. Formerly the *arhat* was required to show, not only 'morality,' 'harmlessness,' but also 'feelings of benevolence' for the mass of human creatures, as it is only just to mention, but his 'equipment of merit' appeared somewhat slight, and we may suppose that men were even then tempted to ask whether his 'equipment of knowledge' was sufficient. Metaphysics and psychology had made progress. Many existences are necessary, they may have said, to obtain 'knowledge' sufficient for deliverance; just as, in order to achieve deliverance from desire, love of self, and love of existence, the first necessity is devotion to others.

(3) It is possible, also, that faith in *nirvāṇa* was shaken, or that, not knowing exactly what *nirvāṇa* was, men were somewhat afraid of it, and devoted their attention rather to the acquisition of celestial powers and the bliss of the Buddhas (now transformed into very happy and long-lived personages) (see below, 3).

The *Daśabhūmika*, a very technical work on the 'career of the future Buddhas,' was translated into Chinese between A.D. 265 and 316; the *Mahāvastu* (*q.v.*), of much earlier origin, gives a lengthy account of the stages or degrees (*bhūmi*) of this career. According to Chandrakīrti (*Madhyamakāvatāra*), the Hīnayāna knows nothing of the 'Vehicle of the future Buddhas,' which is the characteristic trait of the Mahāyāna.

2. Vacuity.—We have more extensive information on the philosophic doctrine. Here we are dealing with a development rather than with a transformation: (1) the principles of analysis and speculative annihilation applied by ancient Buddhism to the ego and the great unities (the body, the chariot) were now applied to the *dharmas* ('elements of things'), the minute elementary realities constituting the ego and the great unities; this is the Mādhyamika system (see art. MADHYAMAKA); and (2) the ancient idealist tendencies were developed which saw in thought the cause of all: 'All that we are is the result of what we have thought; it is founded on our thoughts, it is made up of our thoughts' (*Dhammapada*, i. [*SBE* x. (1898) 3]). Hence the conclusion that matter does not exist; thought alone exists.[2]

The two philosophical schools of the Mahāyāna (Mādhyamikas and Vijñānavādins) are both in line with the most ancient tradition. Nāgārjuna, the great master of the former, is placed in the 2nd cent. A.D.; but there is a great deal of Mādhyamika philosophy in the Pāli canon,[3] and the *sūtras* of the *Prajñāpāramitā*, where this philosophy is predominant, are ancient.[4] Chandrakīrti establishes the fact that the true doctrine of the void was known to the Hīnayāna, or, to be more exact, that the Buddha had already taught this doctrine in his first revelation, in the *sūtras* of the Hīnayāna. But, it will be asked, if this Vehicle, the Vehicle of the Śrāvakas, teaches the non-existence in themselves of the elements of the ego (*dharmanairātmya*), where is the need of the Mahāyāna? The Mahāyāna, replies Chandrakīrti, teaches not only the *dharmanairātmya*, but also the stages of the career of the future Buddha, the perfect virtues (*pāramitā*), the resolutions or vows to save all creatures, the application of merit to the acquisition of the quality of Buddha, the great compassion (*Mādhyamakāvatāra*, tr. in *Muséon*, new ser., viii. 272), whence the Mahāyāna was necessary.

3. Devotion.—As regards the deification of Buddhas and worship of Buddhas and *bodhisattvas*, we have a sure date in the Chinese translation (between A.D. 148 and 170) of the *Sukhāvatīvyūha*, the book in which the monotheistic religion of Amitābha (see above, I. 2. (3)) is formulated.[1] The Gandhāra monuments, the exact date of which is not known, but which can hardly be later than the 1st cent. A.D., take us back even further than the earliest date of the Chinese translation. They show, or at least may be held to show, the worship of the *bodhisattvas* associated with that of the Buddhas.[2]

On the other hand, we know from the documents of the Hīnayāna that the worship of the Buddha is of great antiquity. In the art. ĀDIBUDDHA the present writer has mentioned some of these documents, and (although he no longer sees in certain passages the quasi-deification of the Buddha which he saw in 1908) they show that the Buddhists, or at least certain Buddhists, came to the conclusion that Śākyamuni did not descend in person to the earth, but was content to send his image (cf. DOCETISM [Buddhist]). This is, in substance, the teaching of the Great Vehicle on Buddha—the Buddha almost eternal and saving beings by means of magical creations. Scholars who admit the authenticity of the *Kathāvatthu* as a whole are compelled to locate this belief before the time of Aśoka. Without believing in the authenticity of this very composite book, the present writer would willingly admit that the deification of the Buddha and his 'almost' eternity belong to a period long before the formal documents.

It is almost certain, too, that this transformation of the Buddha may be explained by the natural evolution of the Buddhist dogma on Hindu soil. The resemblance between the Buddha reigning peacefully in a paradise and sending images of himself down to this world, on the one hand, and Kṛṣṇa, gladdening beings in his own world (Goloka) and appearing in a human form, on the other, is striking, and contains a valuable lesson.

Nevertheless, it must be noted that, although Śākyamuni plays an important rôle in the *Lotus of the True Law* and in the Mahāyānist literature of which he is the revealer, he does not seem to have such a leading part in the religions of the Great Vehicle. In the first rank are Maitreya,[3] the future Buddha, more living than Śākyamuni, and especially personages of obscure origin, Avalokiteśvara (see art. AVALOKITEŚVARA), Amitābha,[4] Vairochana, Vajrapāṇi, and many others, whose Buddhist character is not very marked.

Several scholars, moreover (and no mean ones), regard the origin of the devotion to the Buddhas as a real 'puzzle' (Max Müller), and believe that it is to be found in the influence of the 'barbarians,' notably the Mazdæans—an influence which was exercised especially in Northern India, the Panjāb, and Kashmir, where religious statuary reached such high development. The pre-historic mythology of the Great Vehicle is veiled in obscurity, and future researches may perhaps confirm this hypothesis; but the comparisons to which attention has been called up to the present have little value and do not prove that Amitābha is an Ahura Mazda or an Apollo disguised. In any case it is useless to explain the worship of the Buddhas by the influence of Greek sculptors who, it is believed, were the first to make images of Buddhas. The whole 'theology' of the

1 The *Chariyāpiṭaka*, not one of the most ancient books, is the first in Pāli literature to mention the doctrine of the *pāramitās*, 'perfect virtues' necessary for making a Buddha, 'a doctrine that plays no part in the older books' (Rhys Davids, *Buddhist India*, London, 1903, p. 177). The doctrine of the *bodhisattva*, the theory of his charity, merits, etc., is relatively highly developed in the *Abhidharmakośa* and its sources (Sanskrit Buddhism of the Hīnayāna).

2 But its existence is not *paramārthika*, 'absolute'; it is only *saṁvyavahārika*, 'contingent,' as will be seen in art. VIJÑĀNAVĀDINS.

3 H. Oldenberg (*Buddha*[6], Stuttgart, 1914, p. 323) disagrees with the present writer on this point.

4 The *Prajñāpāramitā* was translated into Chinese between A.D. 147 and 164. We are told that the Pūrvaśailas and the Aparaśailas possessed a *Prajñā* in Prākrit (Wassilieff, *Buddhismus*, p. 291), which is quite possible. They were Lokottaravādins (see art. BODHISATTVA, vol. ii. p. 742[b]). But what is the date of this *Prajñā*?

1 See the tr. of Max Müller and Takakusu in *SBE* xlix. (1894).

2 See A. Foucher, *L'Art gréco-bouddhique*, ii., who treats of the difficult identification of the icons of Gandhāra and their date.

3 *Bull. de l'Ecole franç. d'Extrême-Orient*, xi. 442.

4 See Poussin, *Bouddhisme, Opinions sur la dogmatique*, p. 266.

religion of Amitābha is Indian; the belief in the providence of Amitābha and of Avalokita, the belief in their saving grace, has very little in common with ancient Buddhism, but is excellent Kṛṣṇaism. The paradise of the west (Sukhāvatī), and the name of Amitābha, 'infinite light,' which probably are in reality 'solar,' have not up to the present been sufficiently studied and explained. The idea of multiple universes, however, each ruled by a Buddha, is very authentic Buddhism (sec, *e.g.*, the *Mahāvastu*).

III. *HISTORY OF THE SCRIPTURES OF THE MAHĀYĀNA.*[1]—1. **Controversy on the authenticity of the books and legends concerning them.**—We know that the books of the Hīnayāna appeared surrounded with a very definite ecclesiastical history. Whatever may be the value to modern scholars of the tradition referring to the Councils (*e.g.*, R. O. Franke, *Dīghanikāya*, Göttingen, 1913, p. xlii), the Buddhists of the Mahāyāna and of the Hīnayāna admitted the authenticity, in the strict sense, of the ancient canon. But the adherents of the Hīnayāna did not recognize the books of the Mahāyāna for the simple reason that these books were unknown in ecclesiastical history:

'This is the word of the Buddha which is found in the Sūtra, which appears in the Vinaya, which is in harmony with religion, with Truth (*dharmatā*).'[2]

This old text of the *Dīgha* is, according to them, the condemnation of the Mahāyāna, which not only is not authentic, but is even full of heretical novelties.

The most weighty argument of the Mahāyānists is the speculative argument. The Mahāyāna, they say, is in harmony with the *dharmatā*; it is the only vehicle of *nirvāṇa*. The Hīnayāna is indeed authentic, but the Buddha taught it only as provisional truth, taking into consideration the weakness of mind of his hearers. Besides, if the doctrine of the Mahāyāna is not found in your *sūtras*, it is found in ours; if you do not admit our *sūtras*, we admit them. But, the Hīnayānists reply, our *sūtras* are authentic since you admit them; yours are not authentic, and that is why we reject them. To this the Mahāyānists answer that there are far more reasons for admitting the *sūtras* of the Mahāyāna, since they are the true path to salvation.[3]

The Mahāyānists further maintain that the Mahāyāna is not new, and that the Hīnayānist tradition shows that the Mahāyāna is authentic. (1) The *Saṁyuttanikāya* (ii. 17 and iii. 142) proves that even in the Hīnayāna the Buddha taught the non-existence in themselves of the elements of the ego (see above, II. 2; *Madhyamakāvatāra*, p. 22). (2) The doctrine of the multiple teaching of the Master, of his 'accommodation to the ideas of the world' (*lokānuvartana*), is taught in the Canon of the Pūrvaśailas, a sect of the Hīnayāna (*Madhyamakāvatāra*, Fr. tr., *Muséon*, new ser., xi. [1910] 134); which is also (3) said to have possessed the *sūtras* of the *Prajñāpāramitā* edited in Prākrit. This sect, however, is strict in the matter of doctrine, since it orders the expulsion of those who do not understand the 'reserved questions' (see art. AGNOSTICISM [Buddhist], vol. i. p. 221[b]; *Madhyamakāvatāra*, p. 251). (4) The *Mahāvastu* (a book of the Hīnayāna) teaches the stages in the career of a *bodhisattva* and the perfect virtues.[4]

1 For a description and analysis of the literature of the Great Vehicle see Wassilieff, *Buddhismus*, pp. 157–207, and Winternitz, *Gesch. der. ind. Litteratur*, ii. 187–250; see also Winternitz on the *Lalitavistara* and the *Mahāvastu*—works which belong to both Vehicles. Among translations see 'The Lotus of the True Law,' *SBE* xxi., 'The Sukhāvatī, etc.,' *SBE* xlix.

2 *Dīgha*, ii. 124; Mañjughoṣahāsavajra, *Siddhānta*, i. 128b; *Sūtrālaṁkara*, ed. S. Lévi, Paris, 1907, i. 20.

3 See *Bodhicharyāvatāra*, ix. 42 f., Fr. tr., *Introduction à la pratique des futurs Bouddhas*, p. 120; *Sūtrālaṁkāra*, i.; Poussin, *Bouddhisme, Opinions sur la dogmatique*, p. 137 f.

4 Arguments 3 and 4 are given in the Tibetan work, the *Siddhānta* of Mañjughoṣahāsavajra, p. 128[b], in the Urga ed., tr. by Wassilieff in *Buddhismus*, p. 264 (291). The connexion of the Mahāyāna with the Mahāsāṅghika school, of which the Pūrvaśailas are a branch, is beyond doubt; but the antiquity of the doctrine of this school is rather doubtful.

If the whole of the Mahāyāna was not known to the ancients, it was because the doctrines were too sublime to be understood by the compilers of the Hīnayāna. But it was the Buddha who taught them, and they were heard by the *bodhisattvas* Samantabhadra, Mañjughoṣa, Guhyeśvara, Vajrapāṇi, and Maitreya. In fact, immediately after having obtained illumination, the Buddha preached to the gods (in the heaven of the Thirty-three) and to the *bodhisattvas* (J. Edkins, *Chinese Buddhism*, London, 1880, p. 18; A. Foucher, *Iconographie bouddhique*, p. 86).

The *bodhisattvas*, throughout the course of the ages, have revealed the Mahāyāna to men; Mañjuśrī took the form of a *bhikṣu* and, it is said, made known the *Prajñāpāramitā* in 80,000 articles (Tāranātha, tr. A. Schiefner, Petrograd, 1869, p. 58). It was Maitreya, the future Buddha, who explained the *Prajñāpāramitā* to Asaṅga, and who is the author of the treatises of the Vijñānavādin school (*Muséon*, vi. [1905] 145, xv. [1914] 42). According to a Japanese tradition, interesting as an example although without historical value, Mañjuśrī and Maitreya had published the Mahāyāna in the year 116 of Nirvāṇa: 'If these books had not existed before, whence would they have been obtained?'—a very childish argument.[1] This Mahāyāna is said to have been completed in 200 of Nirvāṇa, notably by the publication of the *Avataṁsaka* (=*Gaṇḍavyūha*). All these revelations took place before Nāgārjuna (R. Fujishima, *Le Bouddhisme japonais*, Paris, 1888, p. 54).

Nevertheless, it is to Nāgārjuna that our most trustworthy documents give the honour of the revelation of the Mahāyāna. The *Laṅkāvatāra* and a *Mahāmeghasūtra*[2] put into the mouth of the Buddha words like the following:

'Four centuries after my *nirvāṇa* this Ānanda will be the *bhikṣu* called Nāga; he will teach the Great Vehicle.'

It is said that Nāgārjuna obtained the *Prajñāpāramitās* or the *Avataṁsaka* from the Nāgas (Wassilieff, *Buddhismus*, p. 118 f.). We cannot give an account of all the legends referring to the revelation of the books of the Mahāyāna (see Tāranātha, p. 61 f.); what has already been said will give a sufficient idea of the beliefs that arose in the Buddhist world concerning the origin of these books. Apart from a few ardent partisans of the Hīnayāna, all Buddhists readily believed all that appeared as the 'word of Buddha.'

2. **Criticism of the legends and conjectures.**—The library of the Mahāyāna consists of two parts, which the Tibetans have carefully distinguished: first, the *sūtras*, divine works, uttered by Bhagavat himself, which are arranged in the *Kanjūr* (=*bka hgyur*, 'word of the Master'); and, secondly, the commentaries on the *sūtras* and the treatises (*śāstras*) properly so called, human works, the greater number of which were written by the scholars to whom tradition ascribes them; all this literature forms part of the *Tanjūr* (*bstan hgyur*, 'instruction, scholasticism'). This distinction has not always a historical value. Many *sūtras* are frankly scholastic works, and it is probable that some of them are later than the signed treatises whose doctrine they contain and authorize.[3]

We know that Asaṅga wrote five treatises which he gave as a revelation of Maitreya. Although revealed, these treatises are included as part of the *Tanjūr*, because in form they are not *sūtras*, but mere treatises (*kārikās*, mnemonic verses, with a

1 Maitreya-Asaṅga believes (*Sūtrālaṁkāra*, i. 7) that the two Vehicles are contemporaneous.

2 See *Madhyamakāvatāra*, p. 76; Fujishima, pp. 32, 55; for the prophecies of Laṅkā, which are wanting in the first Chinese version, see Max Müller, *India, What can it teach us?*, London, 1883, p. 298 f.

3 We must confine ourselves to a few remarks here. This subject will depend for a long time yet upon monographs.

prose commentary). Presented with the formula, 'Thus have I heard. Bhagavat was on the Mount of Vultures, surrounded by thousands of Bodhisattvas . . .,' they might have made good *sūtras*. There is therefore some truth in the legends which we were discussing above: the scholars of the Mahāyāna forged the *sūtras* in order to publish their philosophic doctrines, to glorify their chosen saints, to authorize their beliefs in the saviour Amitābha, and so on. In the same way, whether at the same time, earlier, or later, the thaumaturges and the magicians first made collections of magical formulæ and then compiled the *Tantras*, attributed to demi-gods or semi-demons, whom they were believed to evoke. The work of editing and compiling the *Sādhanas* (magic rituals) and the *Tantras* took a very long time—Tāranātha abounds in really historic stories on this subject—and the Mahāyāna probably developed by similar processes.

The scholastic character of the *Laṅkāvatāra* is very definite. This *sūtra* implies the existence of a strong Vijñānavādin doctrine; it is full of controversy. The *Daśabhūmika*, which, augmented by résumés in verse, became transformed into the *Daśabhūmīśvara*, sets forth a theory of the ten stages of the future Buddha which is quite in the manner of a 'treatise.' One of these *sūtras*, invoked by Chandrakīrti to confirm a Mādhyamika formula, seems to have been written according to the same formula (see *Madhyamakavṛtti*, p. 249). Careful study will probably prove the close connexion between the *sūtras* and the treatises.

What exactly was the rôle of Nāgārjuna in the elaboration of this literature? It is thus defined by Kern:

'Nāgārjuna may have been one of the most talented and influential leaders of the movement rather than its originator. . . . An influential person, the first eminent leader of a school imbued with Hinduism and the methods of Indian scholastic philosophy.' He then became 'a comprehensive name of the activity of Mahāyānism in the first phase of its onward course' (*Manual*, pp. 6, 123).

Nāgārjuna's importance lies in having discovered the doctrine of the 'void,' which showed the inferiority of the ancient Vehicle. His name is inseparable from the *Prajñāpāramitā*. It may well be that Nāgārjuna, being the author of the treatises which are the scholastic working-out of the principles of the *Prajñāpāramitā*, is of some account in the redaction of the *Prajñāpāramitās*, the revelation of which tradition attributes to him.

There are many ancient materials in the *sūtras* of the Mahāyāna.

'Not a few elements of the Mahāyānist scriptures are taken bodily from the Tripiṭaka, with such omissions and additions as deemed necessary' (Kern, *loc. cit.*).

Whole passages, *e.g.*, of the *Lalitavistara*, recur almost word for word in the Pāli scriptures. The work that H. Oldenberg has done for the *Divyāvadāna* and E. Windisch for the *Mahāvastu*[1]—in comparing these two works of the Sanskrit Hīnayāna with the Pāli canon—might be done with advantage for several *sūtras* of the Mahāyāna. The comparison would also be very fruitful between the Mahāyāna and the Sanskrit Hīnayāna. The *Abhidharma* of the Sarvāstivādins (Hīnayāna) is accepted by the Mādhyamikas (Mahāyāna); the Sautrāntikas (Hīnayāna) have opened the door to the Vijñānavādins (Mahāyāna); the *Daśabhūmika* (Mahāyāna), we may believe, depends on the *Mahāvastu* (Hīnayāna); the scholars of the Mahāyāna know and quote the Hīnayāna.[2] When they invent, preaching vacuity or the career of a *bodhisattva*, they make use of old models, reason in the manner of the *Abhidhārmikas* and the Brāhmans, and model the career of the *bodhisattva* on the path of the *arhat*, and the new meditations on the canonical meditations.

1 Oldenberg, *Trans. of the 5th Intern. Congress of Orientalists*, Berlin, 1881–82, ii. 107–122, 'Studien zur Gesch. der buddh. Kanon,' *GGN*, 1912, p. 155; Windisch, *Die Komposition des Mahāvastu, ein Beitrag zur Quellenkunde des Buddhismus*, Leipzig, 1909, and also *Māra und Buddha*, do. 1895, and *Buddha's Geburt*, do. 1908.

2 Cf., *e.g.*, the theory of the 'meritorious material gifts' (*aupādhikapuṇyakriyāvastu*) in *Aṅguttara*, ii. 54, in *Abhidharmakośa*, iv. 113 f. (Skr. Hīnayāna), in *Āryaratnarāśisūtra*, cited in *Sikṣāsamuchchaya*, p. 138 and *Madhyamakavṛtti*, p. 309.

LITERATURE.—The sources mentioned in artt. ĀDIBUDDHA, BODHISATTVA, MADHYAMAKA, MAÑJUŚRĪ, VIJÑĀNAVĀDINS; H. Kern, *Geschiedenis van het Buddhisme in Indie*, Haarlem, 1882–84, Fr. tr., *Hist. du Bouddhisme dans l'Inde*, Paris, 1901, *Manual of Indian Buddhism*, Strassburg, 1896; W. Wassilieff, *Der Buddhismus*, Petrograd, 1860; L. de la Vallée Poussin, *Bouddhisme, Études et matériaux*, London, 1898, *Bouddhisme, Opinions sur l'hist. de la dogmatique*, do. 1909; M. Winternitz, *Gesch. der ind. Litteratur*, ii., Leipzig, 1913. For the iconography of the Mahāyāna: A. Foucher, *Étude sur l'iconographie bouddhique*, 2 vols., Paris, 1899–1905, *L'Art gréco-bouddhique du Gandhāra*, 2 vols. do. 1905–15; A. Grünwedel, *Buddhist Art in India*, Eng. tr., ed. J. Burgess, London, 1901, *Mythologie du Bouddhisme au Tibet*, Leipzig, 1900.

L. DE LA VALLÉE POUSSIN.

MAHDĪ.—The title Mahdī was first associated with 'Alī's son Muhammad b. al-Ḥanafiyyah, and, apparently, given him by the adventurer Mukhtār b. Abī 'Ubaid, who, after the death of Ḥusain at Kerbela, ostensibly championed the claims of this personage to the khalīfate. The word is ordinarily interpreted 'the divinely guided,' from a verb which frequently occurs in the Qur'ān in the corresponding sense, though this particular derivative is not found there; yet this explanation did not give universal satisfaction, and several others were current (see Yāqūt, *Geographical Dictionary*, ed. F. Wüstenfeld, Leipzig, 1866–73, iv. 693. 4). Mukhtār clearly used it as analogous to a title attached to the name of 'Alī, calling him 'the Mahdī, son of the Waṣī' (Ṭabarī, *Chronicle*, ed. Leyden, 1879–1901, ii. 534), where the latter title means 'the legatee,' *i.e.* he to whom the Prophet had bequeathed the sovereignty; it is, however, often interpreted as 'the trustee.' It is doubtful whether this Muhammad used it himself, as a letter purporting to be from him, in which it is prefixed to his name, was condemned as spurious by one of his correspondents on that account (Ṭabarī, ii. 611 [66 A.H.]). After the death of 'Alī's two sons by Fāṭima, the Prophet's daughter, it would seem that some Muslims were ready to recognize the claim of this Muhammad, 'Alī's son by another wife, to the sovereignty, but he himself acted with extreme caution in the matter of asserting it; he was, however, imprisoned for a time by the partisans of 'Abdallāh b. Zubair, who endeavoured to wrest the throne from the Umayyads; but, when their supremacy was restored, he accepted a governorship, and appears to have ended peacefully. Some uncertainty existed with regard to both the time and place of his death, and a sect arose called the Kaisāniyyah, who declared that he remained alive in his supposed tomb in Mt. Raḍwa, whence he would one day emerge; and the poet of this sect, the Sayyid Ḥimyarī, fully expected this occurrence, though the Mahdī had disappeared for sixty years (*Aghānī*, Cairo, 1285, viii. 32). The poet Kuthayyir asserts that his reappearance had been foretold by Ka'b al-Aḥbār († 34 A.H.), whose name is often mentioned in connexion with matter drawn from the Jewish Scriptures. This prophecy may well owe its origin to that of the return of Elijah; but how the Mahdī came to be substituted for that prophet is not clear; if the reference to Ka'b be genuine, we should gather that the word had been used before Mukhtār's time with a religious import. The poet further asserts that this Mahdī's book was studied by the Kaisānis in Mecca; but such a work must assuredly have been a forgery.

With this personage the idea of an awaited deliverer is first connected in Islām, and this notion is expressed by the name Mahdī, to which the participle 'expected' (*muntaẓar*) is sometimes attached. The various pretenders from the house of Alī received the title—*e.g.*, Zaid (after whom the Zaidīs are called); he was defeated and killed in the year 122 A.H., and his body was afterwards crucified. An Umayyad satirist said that he had never before seen a Mahdī hanging on a tree (Mas'ūdī, ed. and tr. C. Barbier de Meynard and Pavet de Courteille, *Les Prairies d'or*, Paris, 1861–77, v. 471). When the pretender Muhammad b. 'Abdallāh first made his appearance, the people of Medīna cried out: 'The Mahdī has come forth' (Ṭabarī, iii. 159 [A.H. 144]). It was to be expected that prophecies of the appearance of such a personage should be attributed to the Prophet Muhammad, and such were current, though of questioned authenticity, the best, according to Muṭahhar b. Ṭāhir, who wrote about 325 A.H. (*Le Livre de la création et de l'histoire*, ed. C. Huart, Paris, 1899–1903, ii. 161), being

'The world shall not pass away until my nation be governed by one of my house whose name agrees with mine.'

This tradition is also found in the collection of Tirmidhī († 279; ed. Cairo, 1292, ii. 36), where it is followed by another in which the Mahdī is mentioned:

'We were afraid of some trouble occurring after the Prophet's death, so we asked him, and he said: In my nation there is the Mahdī who shall come forth; he shall live five (or seven or nine) years; a man shall come unto him and say, "O Mahdī, give me!"; and the Mahdī shall pile into his lap as much as he can carry.'

The author of this fiction appears to have interpreted the word as 'the giver,' which should rather be Muhdī. Somewhat more information is to be found in the contemporary collection by Ibn Mājah († 273; Cairo, 1313, ii. 269): the tradition just given is repeated with some variations, indicating that under the Mahdī men would enjoy greater blessings than they had ever experienced; to it is prefixed one to the effect that certain persons with black standards (*i.e.* the 'Abbāsids) would come from the East,

'who shall ask for good and not be given it, and shall fight and be victorious and be offered what they asked and not accept it until they hand it [the sovereignty] to one of my house who shall fill it with justice as they filled it with injustice.'

Another tradition states that the Mahdī is to be a descendant of Fāṭima; another gives as the list of lords of paradise the following members of the family: the Prophet, his uncle Ḥamzah, his cousins 'Alī and Ja'far, and his grandsons Ḥasan and Ḥusain and the Mahdī. The last is:

'Men shall come forth from the East, and shall prepare the way for the Mahdī.'

It seems clear that the authors of these fictions had somehow heard of an expected Mahdī, and made up traditions calculated either to encourage the munificence of princes or to win adherents for some political party. Muṭahhar adds another, that the only Mahdī to be awaited was 'Īsā b. Maryam, *i.e.* the Christian Saviour; and, since orthodox Islām looks forward to His returning to judge the world—according to the law of Muhammad—it is not quite easy to find room for another Deliverer. One of the etymologies suggested for the name, viz. the man of the *mahd*, 'cradle,' favours this view, the reference being to Qur'ān, xix. 30 ff., where Christ speaks 'in the cradle.'

There is little reason for supposing that the Prophet Muhammad contemplated the appearance of a Mahdī, however interpreted; but the outbreak of the civil wars within a generation after his death, and the perturbed condition of Islām which followed, led to the adoption of the idea from Jews or Christians, who look forward respectively to the appearance and reappearance of the Messiah; why the title Mahdī should have been adopted for the expected Deliverer is, as has been seen, an unsolved puzzle. To the etymologies suggested we should be inclined to add one more, viz. from *hadā* in the sense 'to give,' making the word mean 'He to whom has been given,' as in Mt 28[18] the Risen Saviour says, ἐδόθη μοι πᾶσα ἐξουσία ἐν οὐρανῷ καὶ ἐπὶ γῆς, and a similar interpretation was current for the name Shîlôh in Gn 49[10], 'until Shiloh come,' viz. *shel-lô*, 'whose is.' Thus the Shī'ite author of the *Fakhrī* (ed. W. Ahlwardt, Gotha, 1860, p. 58), speaking of the Mahdī Zaid (executed in 122 A.H.), curses those who deprived him of his 'right.' However this may be, the function of the expected Mahdī was, in the first place, to fill the world with justice in lieu of injustice, which often meant the abolition of unauthorized practices and the enforcement of orthodox doctrine and conduct; in the second, to achieve the conversion of the world to Islām, and often this was identified with the taking of Constantinople. Some, however, were satisfied with a partial execution of this programme; and among persons who had been accepted as the Mahdī by various writers up to his time Muṭahhar (*loc. cit.*) mentions 'Alī himself, the pious Umayyad 'Omar II., and the 'Abbāsid al-Mahdī, who reigned A.D. 775–785.

About the signs whereby the Mahdī was to be recognized when he appeared there were differences of opinion; a common theory was that he should have the name Muhammad and the patronymic Abu'l-Qāsim, and that he should belong to the Prophet's house; yet not all demanded the fulfilment of these (not very difficult) conditions. To all—save the few who suppose that the Mahdī has come already—he is ὁ ἐρχόμενος, 'he that shall come'; and, on the whole, the Sunnī view is that his appearance will be that of an ordinary man whose career is that of a reformer and conqueror, while the Shī'ite view is that he is in hiding somewhere, and has been concealing himself for an unlimited period. In our times there were in the Sūdān two Mahdīs simultaneously, representing these different opinions. The line between the two is not quite easy to draw, except where some definitely historical personage is expected to reappear; for it has been found possible to adopt the theory that the Mahdī is some one in hiding, without any suggestion of supernatural concealment. In more than one case of a successful revolution the victory has been won by a commander in the name of an obscure individual, who has been brought forward only when success has been assured. Thus the author of the *Fakhrī* (p. 171), describing the rise of the 'Abbāsids, remarks that, while the Khurāsānites under the brilliant leadership of Abū Muslim were fighting for the *imām* Ibrāhīm (representative of the 'Abbāsids), he was himself in retirement somewhere in Syria or Arabia, attending to his devotions and the affairs of his family, the greater number of his adherents being unable 'to distinguish between his name and his person,' *i.e.* knowing nothing at all about him.

The rise of Mahdīs from time to time, then, was due to the disordered state of Islām in normal circumstances, but also to the wide-spread sentiment that the sovereign should be a descendant of either the Prophet or 'Alī, for with some communities the latter was regarded as the more important personage, and indeed the master whom the former betrayed (see Yāqūt, *Dictionary of Learned Men*, ed. D. S. Margoliouth, London, 1913 ff., i. 302). The pretenders of the house of 'Alī were repeatedly supposed by their adherents to have escaped death, notwithstanding their ostensible execution, and the Shī'a sects were to a certain extent divided by their loyalty to different pretenders whose return they expected. Such pretenders were Muhammad b. 'Abdallāh, executed 145 A.H., whose return was awaited by some of the Jārūdiyyah sect; Yaḥyā b. 'Umar, executed

250 A.H., expected to return by others of the same sect; Muhammad b. al-Qāsim, who revolted in the year 219, was captured, but escaped and disappeared; and Mūsā b. Ja'far, who died of poison in Baghdād in 186 A.H. Several others are mentioned with these by Ibn Ḥazm (*Kitab al-Fiṣal*, Cairo, 1321, iv. 179 f.). The sect called Qat'iyyah got their name from making sure of the death of this Mūsā b. Ja'far, without having ascertained it (Mas'ūdī, *Tanbīh*, ed. M. J. de Goeje, Leyden, 1894, p. 232). Believers in the continued existence of Muhammad b. al-Qāsim were to be found in the time of Mas'ūdī (332 A.H.; *Prairies d'or*, vii. 117) in the district of Kūfah, in the mountains of Ṭabaristān and the Dailam, and the districts of Khurāsān. The person ordinarily acknowledged to be the 'expected Mahdī' is Muhammad b. Ḥasan al-'Askarī, whose father died 260 A.H. There was, however, great doubt as to the age of this Muhammad at the time of his father's death, some denying that he ever came into existence, and all agreeing that he could have been only a few years old at the time. Shahrastānī locates him in Sāmarra (ed. W. Cureton, London, 1842–46, p. 128); but at some time in the 7th or 8th cent. A.H. he appears to have taken up his abode at Ḥillah. The traveller Ibn Baṭūṭa († 780 A.H.; ed. and tr. C. Defrémery and R. B. Sanguinetti, Paris, 1853–58, ii. 98) gives a weird account of the ceremonies which he found there, and which seem to be relics of some pagan cult.

'There is a mosque with its door covered by a silken curtain, called the sanctuary of "the Lord of the Age." Each afternoon a hundred of the inhabitants come out of their houses armed with drawn swords; going to the governor, they obtain from him a horse with saddle and bridle, or else a mule; beating drums and playing musical instruments, they then proceed, fifty of them in front of the charger and fifty behind. Others arrange themselves on either side. Coming to the mosque that has been named, they halt before its door, and say: "Bismillah, O Lord of the Age, come forth. Mischief is rampant, and wrong abundant; this is the time for thee to come forth, that God may distinguish by thee between the true and the false." This they continue till the prayer of sunset, playing their musical instruments the whole time.'

Ibn Khaldūn, a contemporary of Ibn Baṭūṭa, who has no high opinion of his veracity, tells the same story, with some variation. According to him, the people of Ḥillah hold that their Mahdī entered a cellar in their habitation, and every night they appear with a mount before the entrance to this cellar, and keep calling him to come out, from the prayer of sunset until the stars are all shining (*Prolegomena*, Beirut, 1900, p. 199). It is surprising that in the *Ta'rīkh-i-Guzīdah* (compiled 730 A.H., ed. E. G. Browne, London, 1910, p. 208) the connexion of this Mahdī with Ḥillah appears to be unknown.

'In his ninth year he disappeared in Sāmarra, and was never seen since; the people of the Shī'ah, however, believe that he is the Mahdī of the end of the world, is still alive, and will come forth when the time arrives.'

Probably even the revised version of Ibn Baṭūṭa's story requires further redaction.

The majority of the Mahdīs have thus played a larger rôle in the imagination than in reality; there have, however, been cases wherein the character has been assumed with very considerable and even permanent success. The first capital of the Fāṭimids in Africa was called Mahdiyyah after the Mahdī who founded the dynasty (297 A.H. = A.D. 909). The conquests which prepared the way for his sovereignty were all achieved by an agent, who had ultimately to produce the person to whom he had preached allegiance; and, according to the statements of his enemies, the person produced was an impostor, suddenly called to play the part, the real Mahdī having perished on his way to Africa. According to an author of weight (Niẓām al-Mulk, † 485; see C. Schefer, *Chrestomathie persane*, Paris, 1883–85, i. 165), the propaganda of this sect began at least a century before, and proselytes to whom the mysteries had been communicated were forbidden to divulge them until the Mahdī appeared. Probably with this community (in theory at least) the Mahdī, called also, as has been seen, 'the Lord of the Age,' was the legitimate occupant of the Fāṭimid throne; when the sovereign al-Ḥākim disappeared, doubtless through assassination, his continued existence and future reappearance became the dogmas of a sect.

Another Mahdī whose efforts resulted in the foundation of a dynasty was Ibn Tūmart (*q.v.*; † 524 = A.D. 1130), who started the empire of the Almohads. Of this personage there is an unusually full and interesting biography by Ibn Khallikān (tr. W. M. de Slane, Paris, 1843–71, iii. 205 ff.), which is doubtless somewhat coloured by prejudice. He appears to have started genuinely as a religious and moral reformer, and to have taken the title Mahdī when opposition and danger induced him to draw the sword; he is likely then to have been influenced by the prophecy of the appearance of such a reformer, which, as we have seen, had already found its way into an authoritative collection of traditions. The pedigree which brought him into connexion with 'Alī may well be an invention later than his time, and as such his biographer appears to regard it. Some stories told by Ibn Khallikān are characteristic of such adventurers, though not perhaps true in this case; he got access to the *Book of Jafr*, in which 'Alī had prophesied all that was to occur till the end of time (see art. DIVINATION [Muslim]), whence he obtained the letters which formed the name of the person destined to be his chief helper and successor, with a description of his appearance. In order to be armed with a miracle, he persuaded a learned associate to feign illiteracy and ignorance of correct Arabic; one day this person claimed to have learned the Qur'ān by heart in a dream, and this miracle convinced the most stubborn; the confederate then proclaimed Ibn Tūmart the Mahdī, whereas he had previously been called *imām*. According to Ibn Khaldūn (*History*, Cairo, 1284, vi. 229), the only heresy of which he could be convicted was his agreeing with the Imāmiyyah sect that the sovereign was infallible. In his treatment of opponents he appears to have been as ruthless and intolerant as any religious leader; but a singular feature of his career as a Muhammadan saint was that, besides asceticism in diet, he observed strict chastity. His creed, which has been published (*Majmū' at al-rasā'il*, Cairo, 1328, p. 44 ff.), does not appear to differ from the orthodox *kalām*.

The prophecy of a Mahdī assumed special importance at the commencement of the century preceding the first millennium of Islām, especially in India. According to the details collected by H. Blochmann (*Āīn-i-Akbarī*, i. [Calcutta, 1873] p. iv ff.), the Mahdist movement started in Badakhshān, where one Sayyid Muhammad Nūrbakhsh gained numerous adherents, defied the Afghān government, was defeated, and fled to 'Irāq, where he maintained himself till the end of his life. In India it assumed a definite form through the action of Mīr Sayyid Muhammad of Jaunpur, who found an adherent in Gujarāt in Sultan Maḥmūd I. Apparently this personage was, like Ibn Tūmart in his early days, a preacher and reformer, whose doctrines gave offence, and who was forced to leave one place after another. Ultimately he decided that the burden of Mahdī-ship was too heavy for him to bear, and that, if he returned home, he would recant; he died in 911 (= 1505) at Farah in Baluchistān, where his tomb became a place of pilgrimage. An interesting account of another Indian Mahdī of this century is given by the historian Badā'ūnī in his *Muntakhab al-Tawārīkh* (tr. G. Ranking, Calcutta, 1898, p. 507 ff.). This person was named Shaikh 'Alā'ī, and was born in Baiāna in Hindustan. To the same place there came one Miyān 'Abdallāh, who had come under the influence of Muhammad of Jaunpur.

'He adopted the manners of a Mahdī [which would seem to have been settled by Ibn Tūmart, for they consisted in extreme asceticism]; making his dwelling in the corner of a grove far from the haunts of men, on the borders of a tank, he used to cast water on his head; and when the times of prayer came round, he used to gather together certain of the labourers who had to pass that way, and compel them to form an assembly for prayer, with such a degree of asceticism that, if he met any man disinclined for the meeting, he would give him a few coins and encourage him.'

Shaikh 'Alā'ī was much impressed by this example.

He too, 'trampling under foot his self-esteem and conceit, devoted himself to the poor of his neighbourhood, and, entering the valley of self-renunciation and abnegation, he bestowed all his worldly possessions, even to his books, upon the poor.'

He became a disciple of Miyān 'Abdallāh; the two formed a community of ascetic socialists or communists, consisting of three hundred householders, who, abandoning all other source of gain and traffic, agriculture, and skilled labour, spent their time with them. In spite of their asceticism, they were in the habit of keeping arms and implements of war always with them as a protection against their enemies, but also in order to interfere with any proceeding in the city or the market of which they disapproved.

'They would go and call the offenders to account by main force, admitting no investigation by the governor, and on most occasions they got the best of it.'

After a time the place came to be too hot for Shaikh 'Alā'ī, who, along with his followers, whose numbers had now reached six or seven hundred heads of families, migrated to Khawāṣpur, near Jodhpur; but here, too, he interfered seriously with the government of the place, and he was compelled to go back to Baiāna, accompanied by his disciples. Islam-Shāh had by this time obtained possession of Agra, and he summoned Shaikh 'Alā'ī to his court, whither the Mahdī proceeded with a party of select companions fully armed; according to the chronicler, the Shaikh nearly effected Islam-Shāh's conversion to his views, but he was presently expelled and sent to the Deccan. Meanwhile, his former teacher and associate had started a sect of his own, which with some difficulty was suppressed by the authorities; and the Shaikh 'Alā'ī was himself ere long summoned again to Agra, and requested to abandon his claims to the Mahdī-ship; refusing to do this, he was tortured to death. His followers, however, were numerous, and increased, and were known as the Mahdawīs; they were persecuted, but not exterminated, in the reign of Akbar.

Blochmann observes that these Indian Mahdīs were men of considerable eloquence, who by their preaching obtained great influence over the populace, and that they regularly came into conflict with the authorized expounders of the law at the Muhammadan courts. Badā'ūnī takes evident pleasure in narrating how Shaikh 'Alā'ī triumphed over the official theologians who were employed to argue with him. They endeavoured to bring the practice of their co-religionists into harmony with the strict principles enjoined by the Sunnī codes, and especially to banish practices which had been borrowed from their pagan neighbours.

The Mahdī who acquired the greatest fame in Europe was the personage whose enterprise led to the Anglo-Egyptian conquest of the Sūdān. The best account of the early stages of the movement is given by F. R. Wingate in *Mahdiism and the Egyptian Sudan* (London, 1891). After the strong hands of Zubair Pasha, Samuel Baker, and General Gordon had been withdrawn from the Sūdān, that country was subject to violent oppression, and the 'broad basis of the Mahdi's appeal was the injustice and cruelty of every sort which sprang up the moment Gordon's wholesome discipline was withdrawn' (p. 12). Muhammad Aḥmad, who took this title, was born at Dongola in 1848 of a family of boat-builders; at the age of 22 he was already a shaikh with a great reputation for sanctity, and became a powerful preacher; he denounced the iniquities of the Egyptians, and laid stress on the promised appearance of a Mahdī, with whom he presently identified himself, and, indeed, in the Shī'ite sense; he claimed to be the twelfth *imām*, the son of Ḥasan 'Askarī. His claims were first recognized in 1881 at Abba Island, 150 miles south of Khartum, when a band of men declared him their appointed leader, and he communicated to them the secret that he was the Mahdī. News of his 'issuing forth' having come to Khartum, the governor sent to have him arrested; but he declined to obey, and, when troops were sent to enforce the order, he succeeded in annihilating them. He evidently possessed some skill both as an organizer and as a military leader, for he soon enrolled among his followers tribe after tribe of Sūdānese, and proceeded from victory to victory until, at his death on June 22, 1885, shortly after the historic fall of Khartum, his empire extended from lat. 5 to 21 S., and from long. 23 to 38 E. of Greenwich. Wingate suggests as an epitome of Mahdīism the sentence 'Your money or your life'; in practice it was an enforced communism, maintained by plunder, divided arbitrarily by the Mahdī. Success also appears to have made of the Mahdī a coarse voluptuary. Like some of his predecessors, he seems to have aimed at reproducing what were supposed to be the conditions of early Islām, and to have insisted on a sort of asceticism; his followers were advised to go on foot, or at any rate to ride asses and not horses, except in war. Further, they were told to reduce expenditure on weddings. These ascetic tendencies were indicated by the name which his followers assumed, Darwīsh ('poor'), for which at a later period the Mahdī substituted the appellation Anṣār ('helpers'), which had been given by the Prophet Muhammad to his entertainers in Medīna. The Mahdī himself clearly aimed at reproducing the career of the Prophet, since he had a *hijrah*, or 'migration,' viz. from Abba, where he first came forward, to Masat in the Nuba mountains; and he assigned four chairs to persons representing the eminent associates of the Prophet who became the first successors. The chair of Abū Bakr, the first khalīf, was filled by 'Abdallāh al-Ta'aishī, who afterwards became famous as the Mahdī's successor, or *khalīf*, and is said to have suggested the rôle of Mahdī first to Zubair Pasha and then to Muhammad Aḥmad (*Muqtaṭif*, xxiv. [1900] 5).

The asceticism of the Mahdī, like that of the Wahhābīs, included the tabu of tobacco, the smoking of which it regarded as a greater offence than the drinking of wine; in his early days he showed leanings towards Ṣūfiism, and would gladly have obtained recognition from the head of the Sanūsīs; this being refused, he abolished all 'orders' except his own.

After the fall of Khartum the Sūdān was gradually evacuated by the Anglo-Egyptian government, and the *khalīf* extended the Mahdī's empire by fire and sword till it reached the bounds of Egypt; in 1896 the reconquest of the country began, and this was achieved at the battle of Omdurman (Sept. 22, 1898). The new State had achieved nothing but devastation and destruction.

The success of the Sūdānese Mahdī encouraged many others to play the part. It seems that the title 'al-Mahdī' in the case of the head of the Sanūsī community was originally a proper name; its holder, however, gave it the familiar application, and even claimed to have on his body the 'seal of prophecy,' *i.e.* the nævus between the shoulders which had indicated the office to which Muhammad was born (the Sūdānese Mahdī also bore a mark, but it was a mole on his right cheek). In the oracle which foretold his appearance the beginning of the 13th Islāmic cent. (1301 = 1883) was specified as the date. His theories will be found in the art. SANŪSĪS. He was rarely seen by strangers himself, having a 'double,' Sī Aḥmad b. Biskrī, who resembled him very closely, to play the part before them. In 1884 he enjoined the Muslims to pay no attention to the Sūdānese pretender, who was merely 'an impostor and a liar.' In 1888, when an appeal was made to the Sultan of Borgo to assist in the suppression of Mahdīism by revolutionaries in the Sūdān, the Sanūsī Mahdī, to whom the matter was referred, advised the Sultan to abstain from interference with Sūdānese affairs and fight with the *khalīf* only if himself attacked.

The measures taken by the Protectorate of Nigeria in recent years to regulate taxation, emancipate slaves, and introduce other reforms led to the rise of numerous Mahdīs ; between the years 1900 and 1905 there were a dozen in Sokoto, and as many in the other provinces. In 1905 Mahdīs arose simultaneously in Saturu, Bauchi, and Kontagara. Most of these were caught, tried, and executed, the government regarding such severity as necessary for the preservation of order. In 1907 there was one Mahdī at Bima in Bauchi, 'but the situation was in general satisfactory' (*Revue du monde musulman*, iv. [1908] 144).

While the tradition, which, as we have seen, has been admitted into some authoritative works, is likely to produce aspirants to the Mahdī-ship from time to time, it is probable that the general introduction of good and stable government will render their appearance constantly rarer and their adherents fewer. To the question whether there were any relics of Mahdīism in the Sūdān, the Cairene journal *Muqtaṭif* as early as 1902 (xxvii. 1126) replied that the introduction of security and justice in place of the long reign of terror which that system had produced had effectually destroyed its traces.

LITERATURE.—The authorities have been cited throughout the article.   D. S. MARGOLIOUTH.

MAIMONIDES.—1. Life.—Maimonides (Moses ben Maimon), Talmudist, philosopher, and physician, born at Cordova, 30th March 1135, died at Cairo, 13th Dec. 1204, is known in Jewish literature as 'Rambam' (the letters r, m, b, m being the initials of Rabbi Moses ben Maimon) and in Arabic literature as Abū 'Imrān Mūsā ben Maimūn ibn 'Abd Allāh. His native city falling into the hands of the Almohads, Maimonides, when yet a lad of thirteen, was compelled either to leave or to embrace Islām. He, together with his father, chose the former course, and settled at Fez. Here they led for a time the double life of Muslim and Jew. But, the Muslim authorities growing suspicious of their *bona fides*, father and son determined to leave Fez. Accordingly, in April 1165, they boarded a vessel bound for Palestine. Acre was reached after a month's stormy voyage, and after a short stay there they went on to Jerusalem ; but, as Palestine had just been the scene of the Second Crusade, and the Jews there were few in number and poor in goods as well as in culture, Maimonides fixed upon Egypt as a more congenial centre. A home was made in Fostat, a suburb of Cairo. Soon after their arrival here, both the father and the brother of Maimonides died, and, becoming financially reduced in consequence, Maimonides took up the practice of medicine as a means of livelihood.

After several years of obscure practice he became court physician to Saladin, pursuing his Rabbinical and philosophical studies undaunted while following out the exacting duties of his profession. The eminent position which he has ever held in Jewish estimation is expressed in the popular Jewish saying, 'From Moses to Moses[1] there was none like Moses.'

2. Works.—Maimonides' works can be classified under the following heads.

i. PHILOSOPHY AND THEOLOGY.—(*a*) *Dalālat-al-Hairīn* ('Guide of the Perplexed'), known in Heb. as *Môrēh Nᵉbhūkhīm.* The Heb. tr. was effected in 1204 by Samuel ibn Tibbōn, and another and less popular Heb. tr. was made by the celebrated Hebrew poet Al-Ḥarizi in the 13th century. The Lat. tr. by the younger Buxtorf (Basel, 1629) is based on the Heb. of Ibn Tibbōn. Salomon Munk published a Fr. tr. of the Arabic original entitled *Guide des égarés* (3 vols., Paris, 1856–66), and there are two Ital. trr. of the whole work and several Germ. trr. of parts. An Eng. rendering of pt. iii. was brought out by J. Townley (London, 1827) under the title of *The Reasons of the Laws of Moses.* The standard Eng. ed. with commentary and introduction is that of M. Friedländer.

(*b*) A work on the terms used in logic entitled *Maḳālah fi-Ṣina'at al-Manṭiḳ,* popularly known in its Heb. tr. (by Moses ibn Tibbōn) as *Millôth Higgāyôn.* Sebastian Münster published a Lat. tr. (Basel, 1527). There are two Germ. renderings, and the most noteworthy Heb. commentary is that of Moses Mendelssohn.

(*c*) *Maḳālah fi al-Tauḥīd,* on the unity of God, known in Heb. as *Ma'ǎmar hay-Yiḥūdh.*

ii. COMMENTARIES ON TALMUD AND MISHNAH.—(*a*) Commentary on the Mishnah known in Arabic as *Sirāj* ('Light'). The component parts of the work were translated into Heb. by various mediæval scholars. W. Surenhusius rendered the Heb. into Lat., and E. Pococke published parts with a Lat. tr. (Oxford, 1654). The section known as 'The Eight Chapters' (*Shᵉmôneh Perāḳīm*) was edited with an excellent Germ. tr. and valuable annotations by M. Wolf (Leipzig, 1863). A new ed. with a very good Eng. tr. and notes is that of Gorfinkle (Columbia University Press, 1912). Various edd. of small sections have been brought out by other scholars ; and there is much that still awaits the light.

(*b*) *Kitāb al-Farā'id,* rendered into Heb. under the title of *Sēfer Ham-Miṣwôth* by Ibn Tibbōn. Moses Bloch brought out a complete ed. with a Fr. tr. (Paris, 1888), entitled *Le Livre des préceptes.* [The book might also appropriately be classified under iii.]

iii. HALĀKHĀ OR CODIFICATION OF RABBINIC LAWS.—*Mishneh Tōrāh* ('Repetition of the Law'), known also as 'The Strong Hand' (*Yād hā-ḥazāḳāh*). It is divided into fourteen component books, and was written by the author in Hebrew. Extracts were translated into English by H. Bernard and E. Soloweyczik in 1863. The work is of gigantic proportions, and was meant to be an easily intelligible compendium of Jewish ritual law.

iv. LETTERS AND OCCASIONAL ESSAYS.—(*a*) *Iggereth hash-Shᵉmādh* ('Letter on Conversion'), written in Arab. and translated anonymously into Hebrew. It deals with the subject of forced conversions. Maimonides maintains that a Jew who outwardly through compulsion professes to embrace Islām does not thereby forfeit his claim to be considered a righteous Jew. But the authenticity of the 'Letter' has been doubted by scholars.

(*b*) *Iggereth Tēman* ('Letter to Tēman,' *i.e.* Yemen), written in Arab. and translated into Heb. by Ibn Tibbōn and others. The Jews of Yemen are given advice as to how to conduct themselves in times of religious persecution.

(*c*) *Ma'ǎmar Tᵉḥiyyôth ham-Mētim* ('Essays on the Resurrection of the Dead'), written in Arab., translated into Heb. by Ibn Tibbōn and also by Al-Ḥarizi (see Steinschneider, *Hebräische Uebersetzungen,* p. 431). He maintains a spiritual view of resurrection as opposed to the largely prevalent material view of the resurrection of a united body and soul.

(*d*) 'Letter to the men of Marseilles,' written in Arab. and translated into Heb. by Ibn Tibbōn, a discussion on astronomy and astrology, in which Maimonides upholds the truth of the former, but rejects belief in the potency of the stars.

(*e*) 'Letter to Rabbi Jonathan of Lunel,' in which Maimonides, while replying to certain queries on ritual topics, discloses much of his private and personal life. A similar note is struck in a letter to Ibn Tibbōn (translated into Eng. from the Heb. by H. Adler, in the *Miscellany of Hebrew Literature,* i., 1872).

v. MEDICINE AND ASTRONOMY.—(*a*) An essay on the Jewish calendar, called *Sēfer Ḥibbūr* (written at the age of twenty-three), composed in Arab. and translated into Heb. by an anonymous writer, to be found in the collection *Ḳôbhēṣ Tᵉshūbhôth hā-Rambam* (Leipzig, 1859).

(*b*) Various minor works on detailed points in medicine. These were all written in Arab., and were translated into Heb. by Jews of the Middle Ages. There are also Lat., Fr., Germ., and Span. trr. of several.

vi. RESPONSA.—Maimonides' correspondence embraced nearly all the Jewish communities of the Middle Ages. They were translated at an early date into Heb., and comprise the collection known as *Ḳôbhēṣ Tᵉshūbhôth hā-Rambam.*

3. Place in philosophy.—Maimonides holds a

[1] *i.e.* Moses Mendelssohn (*q.v.*).

significant place both in Jewish and in general philosophy, his importance in these respects resting mainly on his three larger works—the 'Guide of the Perplexed,' the *Sīrāj*, or Commentary on the Mishnah, and the *Mishneh Tôrāh*. The most essentially 'Jewish' of the three is the *Mishneh Tôrāh*. It is an elaborate text-book of 'law' as understood by Jewish orthodox tradition, its sources being the Bible, the Talmud, and the whole Rabbinical literature previous to Maimonides. What prompted the author to write it was the fact that the Talmud and the Rabbinical literature generally are a large, unwieldy, unsystematized mass of opinions and rules, laws, counsels, prescriptions, permissions, and prohibitions, with no vestige of any attempts at logical classification and arrangement; so that, unless a Jew possesses a complete mastery of those intricacies, he is puzzled to know what is, and what is not, Judaism as laid down by the Rabbis and sanctioned by orthodox tradition. Maimonides felt the necessity of aiding Jews in this cardinal respect. Judaism appeared to him to be in danger of losing itself in mazes of its own invention; he therefore planned a work in which both the letter and the spirit of the Talmud should reappear in a simple, orderly, and systematic guise. All the controversies, disputations, and doubtful points in the original are omitted. The faithful Jew who wishes to know the settled Rabbinical view on any subject of ritual or belief need no longer wade for the information through oceans of unnecessary details. It is given him in definite, clear-cut, and brief language. As can be understood, this good service rendered to Judaism was not without an admixture of evil. Talmudic law, once flexible, became rigid. Maimonides, by aiming at laying down opinions which were to be the norm of all future religious practice and belief, was felt to have exercised a too arbitrary dogmatism. He made development impossible and chained Judaism to the letter, instead of leaving it free to the eternally unfolding life of the spirit. The numerous attacks—very often virulent and abusive—which were hurled against him both in life and after death on account of this dogmatism, and on kindred grounds, constitute a substantial chapter in Jewish mediæval history. On the other hand, the book was well received in many Jewish communities, though the hope of the author that it would one day become the authoritative code for all Israel was never realized.

In the making of 'codes' or 'compendia' of Jewish law, Maimonides had both predecessors and successors. But his work stands out from all these in two commanding respects: (*a*) a greater variety of subject, a broader interpretation of the scope of Judaism as a system both of 'law' and of 'theology'; (*b*) the metaphysical [Aristotelian] colouring pervading his treatment of religion and ethics, as well as the addition of dissertations on such subjects as the calendar, idolatry, and free will. He was no mere codifier in the sense that others were. His was the genius of the literary artist working out his own original conception of divine truth as understood by the Jew. Hence, whereas to-day resort is had to other codes only when enlightenment is sought on points of strict 'legalism' or strictly orthodox ritual—what is forbidden and what is not forbidden by the 613 precepts of the *Tôrāh*—the code of Maimonides is a source of edification to the theological student generally, quite irrespective of its relation to the Jewish life. The first of the fourteen books comprising the *Mishneh Tôrāh* is entitled 'Maddā'' ('Knowledge'). Maimonides feels that, before a man can be ordered to worship God, he should first be informed of what God really is; so he sets out with proofs of the existence of God, of the impossibility of a plurality of gods, of the impossibility of a world without God, of the various grades of animate and inanimate existence—angels, 'spheres,' men, plants, minerals (introducing, of course, the 'four elements,' viz. earth, air, fire, water). He shows how all these have their places in the cosmos, and how all reveal God in their several ways and degrees. In the framework of such a treatment he discusses the Rabbinic views of prayer, divine worship, Sabbath, feasts and fasts, repentance, and the whole host of ethical and civil prescriptions which the Talmudic Rabbis had deduced from Scripture and had laid down for observance by the Jewish commonwealth. It is all done in a way which shows that, while Maimonides defended what he considered the eternal sanctity of 'ceremonial,' he was too spiritual, too mystical a thinker to omit giving due prominence to the ethical and spiritual aspects of Judaism—the aspects which justify and transfigure the rest.

The *Sīrāj*, or Commentary on the Mishnah, has not as yet had full justice done to it by scholars and students. It has been in many senses overshadowed by the more popular commentary of Obadiah Bertinoro, an Italian Rabbi of the 15th century. But there can be no doubt that, with the growing modern recognition of the necessity of studying the Rabbinical literature on strictly scientific lines, the *Sīrāj* will yet come into its own.

The object of Maimonides was to enable the layman to understand the Mishnah—its technical phraseology as well as its general drift—without the necessity of working through the involved disquisitions of the Talmud. The Talmud is *par excellence* the commentary on the Mishnah, but its elaborations and criticisms of the Mishnah, instead of throwing light on the latter, often render the darkness all the greater. Further, Maimonides was of opinion—and critical study shows that he was right—that the Talmudic masters did not always understand the Mishnah, because their extraneous knowledge was faulty. He therefore planned a work in which the student would be able to see the Mishnah as it essentially is and irrespective of the Talmudic glosses. Not that Maimonides ignores these glosses. He incorporates them—and largely too—in the commentary. But he sometimes adopts an independent view; and this is just one of the facts that make his work serve as a really valuable introduction to the study of the Talmud. It is also very valuable for the many long dissertations which it contains on points in theology, philosophy, history, and exegesis. Thus, commenting on Mishnah xi. in the Treatise *Sanhedrīn* on the words 'All Israelites have a portion in the world to come,' he is led to write a treatise on the Jewish creed, in which he draws up the famous 'Thirteen Principles of Faith' (for which see *ERE* iv. 246[a]), being the first 'Rabbanite' (*i.e.* as opposed to 'Ḳaraite') Jew to ask the Synagogue to accept a set, formulated creed of Judaism. For this he was severely criticized by a famous 15th cent. Jewish philosopher, Ḥisdai Crescas, in his *Ôr Ădhônai* ('Light of the Lord'). But, as subsequent history proves, there was no necessity for attaching any really serious importance to these 'Thirteen Principles of Faith,' seeing that the Synagogue at no time did, and even at the present time does not, attach any canonical validity to them. In all probability Maimonides promulgated them with no dogmatic intent. They are useful as a literary monument of the often-forgotten fact that Judaism emphasizes inward belief as well as outward conduct.

Another remarkable excursus is that known as

'The Eight Chapters.' Just as Philo attempted to expound the OT on the basis of Plato, so Maimonides here attempts to present Judaism in the dress of Aristotle. Rabbinical ethics are viewed through Greek spectacles, and Aristotle's doctrine of 'the mean' (μεσότης) is shown to underlie the sacred moral truths of Judaism.

'This perfect Law does not teach us to subject the body to useless and uncalled-for tortures. On the contrary, its aim and intention is that man according to the dictates of nature should pursue the path of moderation, eat and drink moderately and according to his means' (opening words of ch. iv.).

Adopting this standpoint and with the aid of the Aristotelian psychology, Maimonides shows how the Jew's path to ethical perfection lies only through the adoption of the mean. With all its Greek colouring, the spirit and teaching of the book are thoroughly Hebraic. OT and Talmud contain the highest wisdom and are man's surest guide to God.

Maimonides' greatest contribution to metaphysics, however, is his 'Guide of the Perplexed.' It is designed, as he himself says, 'for thinkers whose studies have brought them into collision with religion,' for men who 'have studied philosophy and have acquired sound knowledge, and who, while firm in religious matters, are perplexed and bewildered on account of the ambiguous and figurative expressions employed in the holy writings.' Thus the book is not meant to convince the unbeliever, but, rather, to correct the believer. His introductory motto is, 'Ye who have gone astray in the field of the holy Law, come hither and follow the path which I have prepared. The unclean and the fool shall not pass over it.'

The object of the book is to provide a working harmony between reason and faith. But whose conception of reason does Maimonides take as the standard? No one but Aristotle's. What is faith to Maimonides? Belief in the Torah, which is for all time the one true embodiment of the divine word. There is no contradiction between divine revelation as entrusted to the Jews and the metaphysical truths given to the world by the brains of the philosophers. For not only is it a fact that both in the last resort emanate from God, but it has also to be borne in mind (so argued Maimonides) that the prophets of the OT received a twofold divine message. Besides the message which is manifest to us in their written prophecies, they received oral revelations of a philosophical kind. The written prophecies are really instinct with these oral philosophies; and Scripture enshrines, in ways and degrees which can be detected only by the student of philosophy, a body of metaphysical truth. As the average Jew, through the dulling effect of the repeated persecution of his race, fails to grasp this metaphysical truth, Maimonides conceived it his duty to devote the major portion of the first book of the 'Guide' to an exhaustive examination of the anthropomorphic expressions occurring in the Scriptures in order that the reader should thereby learn the first and fundamental tenet of all metaphysic, viz. that God is incorporeal, and that all the Scriptural passages which talk of 'the eye' or 'the hand' or 'the foot' of God, or which describe divine movements such as 'passing,' 'dwelling,' 'coming,' 'standing,' etc., must be understood allegorically, seeing that they express transcendental metaphysical truths about the deity. But there is another leading consideration. What about the Scriptural 'attributes' of God? Is not the misunderstanding of these liable to lead to an infringement of both the incorporeality and the unity of God? Maimonides saw real danger here, and, therefore, after a severe examination of the meanings and inter-relations of the different attributes of God, he proves the inapplicability of them all to God. All that can be predicated of God is that He exists. God is indefinable. Even to assert, as Scripture repeatedly does, His unity, power, wisdom, eternity, will, is inadmissible. But how, then, can we justify Scripture? By assuming, he says, that, owing to the poverty of language, these terms must be understood as describing not a positive quality but a negative of its opposite. Hence to say that 'God is one' is merely tantamount to saying that God is not a plurality. Hence the deity can be described only by negative attributes; and, since the number of these is infinite, the positive essence of the deity must for ever lie outside human comprehension. But, despite all this, the deity is unquestionably active in the universe; He is the creator of the cosmos, and the traces of divine design are everywhere obvious. How are these divine relations with the universe to be understood? Before grappling seriously with this subject, Maimonides enters into an acute criticism of the views of the Mutakallimūn, or philosophers of the *kalām* (*q.v.*). As against Aristotle, who maintained the eternity of the universe, these Arabian philosophers defended the *creatio ex nihilo*. Maimonides, while as a Jew differing on this fundamental point from his teacher Aristotle, agreed with the Mutakallimīm, but differed from the latter again on several other fundamental propositions of theirs. Maimonides' originality of mind as well as his fearless liberality of spirit in the investigation of religious truth can be clearly gauged in this connexion. He rejects, as has just been said, the propositions of the Mutakallimīm—but only as propositions, *i.e.* theories or methods of proof. For he accepts their results. He believed, just as much as they believed, not only in the *creatio ex nihilo*, but also in the existence, incorporeality, and unity of God. On the other hand, while opposing Aristotle on the question of the *creatio ex nihilo*, he practically employs the whole paraphernalia of the Aristotelian cosmology in order to prove the *creatio ex nihilo*. The latter came about through the work of a Primal Cause, who is identical with the Creator alluded to in the Scriptures. From this Primal Cause there emanate the intellects of the spheres (these 'intellects' are identified with the angels of Holy Writ). All changes on earth are due to the revolutions of the spheres, which have souls and are endowed with intellect. God created the universe by producing first the intellects of the spheres, which give to the spheres the faculties of existence and motion and are thus the *fons et origo* of the entire universe. It is of deepest interest to both the theologian and the mystic to note in this connexion the quaint Maimonidean exegesis of Gn 1 (*Ma'ăsĕh Berēshîth*) and Ezk 1 (*Ma'ăsĕh Merkābhāh*). His whole theory of emanation (*hashpā'ā*) is a wonderful combination of what are usually regarded as two diametrically opposite frames of mind, viz. rationalism and mysticism.

Aristotle believed in the eternity of matter. Maimonides argues against this at great length in pt. ii. of the 'Guide,' in favour of the *creatio ex nihilo*—not that he believed that the latter thesis was really provable from Scripture, but because he felt it a necessary peg on which to hang the essentially Jewish doctrines of miracles, revelation, and prophecy. On the latter subject his views are strikingly original but highly debatable. There is a strong element of passive ecstasy in prophecy. The prophet is wholly the passive instrument in the divine hand. Imagination is an essential element in all prophecy. Prophecy is an impulse descending from the Active Intellect to man's intellect and imagination. Can any man become a prophet? No, because, while it is in the power of many a man to bring himself to the high pitch of moral and intellectual perfection which prophecy necessitates, another factor is still required. This factor consists in a special vouchsafing of the divine will, *i.e.* divine inspiration. A man may be intellectually and morally perfect, but may be unable to prophesy, because prophecy arises, in the last resort, only at the call of a divine *fiat*; and the *fiat* is arbitrary.

Maimonides' subsequent discussions on the nature and origin of evil, on belief in divine providence and man's free will (in which he strikingly discusses the central problem in the book of Job), on the purpose of the Biblical precepts, on the meanings of the Biblical narratives, on the stages by which man comes to hold real communion with the divine—all these are treated with a fullness of knowledge which makes them a contribution to general as well as to Jewish theology. A vein of unvarying optimism permeates his teachings on sin and evil. Evil has no positive existence, but is merely the absence of good, just in the same sense as sickness denotes the absence of the possession of health, or poverty the absence of sufficiency, or folly the absence of normal wisdom. In support of the argument he quotes Gn 1^{31}, 'And God saw every thing that he had made, and, behold, it was very good,' the Midrashic comment upon which is, 'No evil thing descends from above' (*Bᵉrēshîth Rabbā*, xviii. 9). Divine providence extends to individual human beings, but not to animals, plants, or minerals. Here Maimonides differs from Aristotle, who held that Providence took no account of particulars, because His knowledge was limited to universals. Scriptural passages are quoted in refutation of Aristotle's views. Can free will be reconciled with the fact of divine omniscience, seeing that the latter must imply predestination? Numerous passages from Scripture are quoted in illustration of the difficulty of the problem. Maimonides bases his answer on the words of Is 55^8, 'My thoughts are not your thoughts, neither are your ways my ways.' God's knowledge is unique; and the great mistake that men always make is that they persist in thinking and speaking of God's knowledge in the same senses as they think and speak of man's. It is identical with His essence, and is independent of existence or of time—past, present, and future are all the same to God.

The object of the divine precepts is 'to give man true knowledge or to remove wrong knowledge, or to give a correct ordering of life or to remove oppression, or to give a training in good morals or to exhort against bad morals.' Man's final consummation of 'knowing' God can come about only after man has perfected himself, not only inwardly, but in all his external relations to society, to the State, to the world. Maimonides discusses every precept of the Torah with the object of showing how their rightful understanding and practice lead to this goal. By an ingenious adaptation of Scripture he shows that the reason why God 'led the people about, by the way of the wilderness by the Red sea' (Ex 13^{18}), instead of leading them straight to the Promised Land, was in order to give them the necessary preliminary training in the endurance of hardship, in the cultivation of courage in face of danger, and in all the social and martial qualities which a self-governing nation needs. Even so, says he, is it with man. Before he can live on the high level of knowing God, he must live on the lower level of an obedience to all the divine precepts which are the training-ground for his more exalted rôle. 'Knowing' God and 'loving' God are identical.

Maimonides influenced all succeeding generations of Jewish thought by his introduction of what we nowadays call 'the scientific spirit' into the study of Judaism. Henceforward an anthropomorphic conception of God became impossible. God is spirit, and the worship of Him—based as this is on the carrying out of the 'laws' of the OT as interpreted by the Rabbis—is not a series of mechanical performances, but a movement of the human spirit towards its divine source. Man's intellect is his greatest asset. Hence Judaism, rightly understood, can never really become fossilized, seeing that the application of the intellect to it cannot but result in a continuous chain of development in consonance with the changing phases of human thought as time goes on. Although much of the substance of the 'Guide' is now obsolete, its encouragement to a freedom of spirit in the handling of religious problems will always, unlike the dogmatism of the *Mishneh Tôrāh*, make its appeal to the thinker and the moralist. Maimonides the liberal philosopher will live on long after Maimonides the dogmatic ritualist is forgotten.

The influence of Maimonides on general European thought has not yet been adequately appraised. The Latin translations of the 'Guide' in the 13th cent. affected the great Franciscan, Alexander of Hales, as well as his contemporary, William of Auvergne. The great Christian scholastics, Albertus Magnus and Duns Scotus, drew inspiration from its pages. Thomas Aquinas's whole theological system is permeated with the theological view-points of Maimonides. What debt, if any, Spinoza's philosophy owes to him is a moot point, but that the reading of the 'Guide' influenced Spinoza's mode of life is certain.

LITERATURE.—The *editio princeps* of the *Mishneh Tôrāh* is undated, and the place of publication is unknown. Numerous subsequent edd. are those of Soncino, 1490; Constantinople, 1590; Amsterdam, 1702; Heb. and Eng., H. H. Bernard, Cambridge, 1832; Heb. and Germ., Vienna, 1889; Eng., J. W. Peppercorne, London, 1838, 1863. The *editio princeps* of the 'Guide of the Perplexed' appeared first without place or date; then in Heb., Venice, 1551; Berlin, 1791; in Lat., Paris, 1520; Basel, 1629; in Germ., Krotoschin, 1839; in Arab. and Fr., S. Munk, 3 vols., Paris, 1856–66; Ital., Leghorn, 1879–81; Eng., 3 vols., M. Friedländer, London, 1885, 2nd ed. in 1 vol., do. 1904. The commentary on the Mishnah was first published at Naples, 1492, and is accessible in the Lat. tr. of W. Surenhusius, in his *Mishna*, Amsterdam, 1698–1703.

On the life and works of Maimonides, the following should be consulted: Peter Beer, *Leben und Wirken des Maimonides*, Prague, 1834; A. Geiger, *Moses ben Maimun*, Breslau, 1850; I. M. Jost, *Israelitische Annalen*, Frankfort, 1839, p. 308, ed. 1840, p. 32, *Allg. Gesch.*, Berlin, 1832, iv. 116, and *Gesch. des Judenthums*, Leipzig, 1857–59, ii. 430; S. Munk, *Notice sur Joseph ben Jahoudah*, Paris, 1842, and in *Archives Israél.*, do. 1851, p. 319; S. B. Scheyer, *Das psychologische System des Maimonides*, Frankfort, 1845; A. Benisch, *Two Lectures on the Life and Writings of Maimonides*, London, 1847; A. Bukofzer, *Maimonides im Kampf mit seinen neuesten Biographen*, Berlin, 1844; F. Lebrecht, 'Ueber die Apostasie des Maimonides,' in *Magazin für Literatur des In- und Auslandes*, do. 1844, no. 62; F. Wüstenfeld, *Gesch. der arabischen Aerzte*, Göttingen, 1882, p. 110; E. Carmoly, *Histoire des médecins juifs*, Brussels, 1844, p. 52; M. Steinschneider, *Cat. Lib. Heb. in Bib. Bodl.*, Berlin, 1852–60, cols. 1861–1942, *Hebräische Uebersetzungen*, do. 1893, *passim*, *Die arabische Literatur der Juden*, Frankfort, 1902, § 158, and 'Sammlung Gedichten über Maimonides,' in *Kôbheṣ 'al-Yādh*, Berlin, 1885 and 1886; I. H. Weiss, *Bēth Talmūdh*, i., Vienna, 1881, no. 6; M. Joël, *Die Religionsphilosophie des Moses ben Maimon*, Breslau, 1859; D. Kaufmann, *Die Geschichte der Attributenlehre*, Gotha, 1877, p. 363; S. Rubin, *Spinoza und Maimonides*, Vienna, 1868; M. Eisler, *Vorlesungen über die jüdischen Philosophen des Mittelalters*, do. 1870; D. Rosin, *Die Ethik des Maimonides*, Breslau, 1876; W. Bacher, *Die Bibelexegese Moses Maimûni's*, Strassburg, 1897; H. Kahan, *Hat Moses Maimonides dem Krypto-Mohammedanismus gehuldigt?*, Berlin, 1899; A. Berliner, 'Zur Ehrenrettung des Maimonides,' in *Israelit. Monatsschrift*, do. 1901, no. 6; L. Dünner, *Die älteste astronomische Schrift des Maimonides*, Würzburg, 1902; W. Bacher, M. Brann, D. Simonson, J. Guttmann, *Moses ben Maimon: sein Leben, seine Werke und sein Einfluss*, Leipzig, 1908; L. M. Simmons, *Maimonides and Islam*, London, 1888; K. Pearson, 'Maimonides and Spinoza,' in *Mind*, viii. [1883] 338; J. Guttmann, *Die Scholastik des dreizehnten Jahrhunderts*, Breslau, 1902, p. 10; I. Friedländer, *Der Sprachgebrauch des Maimonides*, i., 'Arabisch-deutsch. Lexikon,' Frankfort, 1902; D. Yellin and I. Abrahams, *Maimonides*, London, 1903; H. Graetz, *Geschichte der Juden*, vi. 310, Eng. tr., iii. chs. xiii.–xv., London, 1892, Heb. tr. by S. P. Rabbinowitz, Warsaw, 1890–98; 'Moses ben Maimon,' in *JE* ix. 73 ff.;

'Maimonides,' in *PRE*³ xii. 80–84; Louis-Germain Lévy, *La Métaphysique de Maïmonide*, Dijon, 1905, and 'Maimonide,' in *Collection des grands philosophes*, Paris, 1911; J. Münz, *Moses ben Maimon: sein Leben und seine Werke*, Frankfort, 1912; J. I. Gorfinkle, *The Eight Chapters of Maimonides on Ethics*, New York, 1912.

J. ABELSON.

MAJHWĀR, MĀNJHĪ.—A non-Aryan tribe numbering, Majhwār 14,210, Mānjhī 4933, according to the Census of 1911, and found in the United Provinces of Agra and Oudh, Bengal, Central Provinces, Berār, and Assam. The name is usually derived from Skr. *madhya*, in the sense of 'headman,' and ethnologically they are closely connected with the Goṇds and Kharwārs (*qq.v.*).

In the United Provinces the Majhwār possess a well-marked system of totemistic exogamous divisions, some being named from trees, animals, or birds, each of which is held sacred and not injured or eaten by the members of the division who take their name from it. The tribal legend describes the rescue of their forefathers by a tortoise; they therefore worship the tortoise, and will not injure or kill it. Their death rites recognize the survival of the soul after death, and they take measures to prevent the return of the malignant spirits of the dead, particularly those who have died by accident or in some tragic way. But some of the ancestral spirits are supposed to be re-incarnated in their descendants, or in a calf which is taken care of and not used in ploughing. At marriages a fowl and spirituous liquor are offered to ancestors, and in their honour the *patārī*, or tribal priest, offers a fire sacrifice (*homa*). Among the special tribal deities of the Majhwār may be mentioned Dulhā Deo, the spirit of a bridegroom who in the olden days perished in a specially tragic way. As is the case with the cognate tribes, there is, in their beliefs, a clear distinction between those who live more or less within the range of Hindu influence and those who are less exposed to it. The former worship, under the title of Mahādeva, 'the great god'—a name of Śiva—a deity who seems to be identical with Baṛā Deo, 'the great god' of the Goṇds, both of whom are believed to use the ox as a 'vehicle' (*vāhana*). This cult has a basis of phallicism, which is more clearly seen in the worship of Lingo or Lingal (Skr. *liṅga*, the phallic symbol). The *patārī*, at his periodical visits to his parishioners, worships Mahādeva by rattling a number of iron rings fixed on a staff. The collective village-gods are impersonated by a male deity Dih (Pers. *dih*, 'the village'), whose name at least is of modern origin, while his female counterpart is known as the Deohārin (Hindī *deuhrā*, Skr. *devagṛha*, 'house of the gods'), so named because she occupies the village-shrine, a mass of rude stones piled under a sacred tree, usually the *sāl* (*Shorea robusta*). More advanced members of the tribe identify her with the Hindu Devī. The shrine contains a water vessel, over which a red flag is hung, and the seat of the deity is a little mud platform on which offerings are laid and a fire sacrifice is performed. The officiant at these rites is the *baigā* (*q.v.*), the village medicine-man, who holds a goat or fowl facing the east and sacrifices it by cutting off the head and allowing a little blood to drop on the platform. The worshipper, his friends, and the priest then and there cook and eat the flesh. No blood sacrifice is offered to ancestors, but flesh cooked by the wife of the eldest son (perhaps a survival of mother-right) is offered in the family kitchen, where the honoured dead are supposed to live. When they eat they throw a little food on the ground for the earth-goddess. Women may be present at the worship of the higher gods, but not at that of the village-deities. They also propitiate a number of demons or evil spirits, such as Turkin, the ghost of a Turk or Muhammadan woman, and her consort Barwat, who rule all the mountain-spirits of the neighbourhood. Other spirits inhabit streams and water-pools, and with these are joined the snake-gods—the Nāg and his consort, the Nāgin. A special tribal rite is the worship of the sacred *karama* tree (*Nauclea parvifolia*), which is ceremonially cut down and brought into the village, where the people dance round it to the beating of drums. The rite is probably, like similar rites in other parts of the world described by J. G. Frazer (*GB*³, pt. i., *The Magic Art*, London, 1911, i. 247 ff.), a form of symbolical or imitative magic to promote the fall of rain and the fertility of the people, their crops, and cattle (W. Crooke, *PR*² ii. 94 ff.). Only the more Hinduized members of the tribe employ Brāhmans, the real priests being the *patārī* and *baigā*, who are usually drawn from the more primitive allied tribes, which are believed to preserve unimpaired the knowledge of the local cults. Fetishism, so called, appears in the reverence for the sacred chain (*gurdā*) hung in the village shrine, with which hysterical girls are beaten in order to drive out the evil spirit supposed to cause such attacks. The belief in witchcraft, the evil eye, and omens is wide-spread.

LITERATURE.—W. Crooke, *Tribes and Castes of the North-Western Provinces and Oudh*, Calcutta, 1896, iii. 413 ff.

W. CROOKE.

MĀL, MĀLĒ, MĀL PAHĀRIĀ.—A non-Aryan tribe, containing various groups, numbering, Māl 2,135,329, Māl Pahāriā 54,069, at the Census of 1911, and found in the greatest numbers in Madras, Haidarābād, and Bengal.

The inter-relations of the North and South groups have not been clearly ascertained, but they seem to be, to a large extent, pure Dravidians, and those in the Rājmahāl Hills in Bengal are closely allied to the Orāons (*q.v.*). The Māl, a cultivating caste in W. and Central Bengal, are mainly Hindus, and few vestiges of primitive beliefs can be traced among them. The snake-goddess, Manasā, is their special guardian, and they also worship the local village-deities. The earliest account of their religion in the Rājmahāl Hills is that by Shaw, which has been supplemented by Risley and Dalton.

'At the head of their system stands the Sun called Dharmer Gosain, and represented by a roughly-hewn post set up in front of each house. He is worshipped with offerings of fowls, goats, sindur [red lead], and oil at the commencement of the harvest season, and at other times when any misfortune befalls the family. When people are gathered together for this purpose, the village headman, who acts as priest, goes round the congregation with an egg in his hand, and recites the names of certain spirits. He then throws away the egg, apparently as a propitiatory offering, and enjoins the spirits to hold aloof and abstain from troubling the sacrifice' (Risley, *TC*, ii. 57).

Shaw describes various gods inferior in rank to the sun-god. Whenever a tiger, smallpox, or any other plague attacks the village, Ruksey or Raksī is supposed to desire that a shrine should be raised for him. Accordingly the *demāno*, or tribal priest, is directed to search for the god. He gets a branch of the *sīdī* tree, and gum benjamin is burned, which he smells. He is thus enabled to point out a place where he directs the people to dig, and the god, in the shape of a sacred black stone, is discovered. The *mānjhī*, or headman, then sets out in search of a large tree, under the shade of which he places the stone, and encloses it with a stone fence and hedge. A fowl and a goat are sacrificed, and the headman or some other worthy person does worship to the god and then retires (*Asiatic Res.* iv. 46 f.). This god at the present day is the tutelary deity of strong drink, who is worshipped by the headman before he begins to distil liquor from the fresh crop of *mahuā* (*Bassia latifolia*) (Risley, ii. 57). Chal, or Chalnad, presides over a group of villages, but he is not worshipped until some plague attacks the people, when the *demāno* dreams that a shrine should be raised, and the god, when found in the shape of a stone, is placed under a *mukmum* tree near the village, the stone undergoing no change in form from the chisel (*Asiatic Res.* iv. 48 f.). Goats and pigs are usually offered to him, but the triennial sacrifice of a cow, mentioned by Shaw, seems now to have fallen into disuse (Risley, ii. 58).

The first worship performed by young men is offered to Pāū Gośāīn, god of the road, but it is not undertaken till some accident has induced the worshipper to consult an exorcist, who decides whether a sacrifice will be acceptable.

On the day of thanksgiving at harvest he proceeds to a high road, and clears a space under the shade of a young *bel* tree (*Ægle marmelos*), in the centre of which he plants a branch of the *mukmum* tree. Round it he makes marks with red paint and, laying some rice and an egg decorated with three streaks of vermilion near the sacred branch, he invokes the god of the highway to protect him on his journeys. A cock is sacrificed, some of the blood being dropped on the branch, and the offering is cooked and eaten by the worshipper and his friends. The rite concludes with the breaking of the egg, and is never repeated unless the person concerned should meet with an accident in travelling (*Asiatic Res.* iv. 51 f.).

At present the offering prescribed for the god is a white goat, and the sacrifice is very expensive, owing to the large amount of rice-beer which must be offered to the god and then drunk by the assembled worshippers (Risley, i. 58).

'The tutelary deity of the village, spoken of by Lieutenant Shaw under the name of Dwára Gosain [god of the doorway], is now called Bára-Dwári, because he is supposed to live in a temple with twelve doors. The whole village worship him in the month of Mágh [Jan.–Feb.]. Colonel Dalton suggests that this god may perhaps be the same as the Oraon Dárá. Kul Gosain, "the Ceres of the mountaineers," and Autga, the god of hunting, appear not to be known at the present day. Gumo Gosain, or the god of the pillar, is represented in every household by the wooden post (*gumo*) which supports the main rafters of the roof. On this the blood of a slain goat is sprinkled to propitiate the spirits of ancestors. The fact that this god is common to the Málés and Mál Pahárias, and is worshipped by both in the same way, seems to tell strongly in favour of the common origin of the two tribes. As in Lieutenant Shaw's time Chamda Gosain still ranks high among the tribe, and demands offerings on a larger scale than any other god' (Risley, ii. 58).

At the present day the priests of the tribe are said to be the *demānos*, who were originally diviners; but it is declared that generally the *demāno* does not officiate as priest, but merely directs the village headman, head of the household, or other influential person chosen for the occasion (*ib.*).

The religion of the Māl Pahāriās is of much the same type. Their chief god is the sun, who is addressed as Gośāīn, 'Lord,' and to whom an offering of rice is presented and then given to a goat, which is decapitated by a blow from behind. The meat is cooked, and served up at a feast, of which the neighbours partake. The head alone, which is regarded as sacred food (*prasād*), is carefully reserved for the members of the family. Next in honour to the sun are Dhartī Mātā, Mother Earth; her servant or, as some say, her sister, Garāmī; and Singhbāhinī, 'she who rides on a tiger,' who rules tigers, snakes, scorpions, and all manner of noisome beasts. The tribe also performs the *karama* rite, dancing round the sacred tree (see MAJHWĀR). Chordānū, 'the thief demon,' is a malevolent spirit, who must be propitiated by sacrifice and the offering of the firstfruits of the crop, which, as usual, are under tabu (J. G. Frazer, *GB*[3], pt. v., *Spirits of the Corn and of the Wild*, London, 1912, ii. 48 ff.). To Mahādānā eggs are the appropriate offering. Gūmo Gośāīn, the house pillar, represents the *lares* of the household, and every village has its own tutelary deity, which lives in a *sāl* tree (*Shorea robusta*). This is periodically daubed with red lead, and may on no account be cut down.

LITERATURE.—T. Shaw, 'On the Inhabitants of the Hills near Rájamahall,' in *Asiatic Researches*, iv. [London, 1798] 31 ff.; H. H. Risley, *Tribes and Castes of Bengal*, Calcutta, 1891, ii. 45 ff., 51 ff., 66 ff.; E. T. Dalton, *Descriptive Ethnology of Bengal*, do. 1872, pp. 138 ff., 263 ff.; a popular account of the Pahāriās, mainly based on the above authorities, will be found in F. B. Bradley-Birt, *The Story of an Indian Upland*, London, 1905, pp. 7 ff., 287 ff.

W. CROOKE.

MALABAR JEWS.

—See JEWS IN COCHIN (MALABAR).

MALAY ARCHIPELAGO.

—The religious beliefs and customs of the natives of the numerous isles of the Malay Archipelago, all of them belonging to the great Malayo-Polynesian family,[1] were certainly in the main identical, but, owing to historical facts and foreign influences, by far the greater part of the population have forsaken their ancestral creed. The native population, with insignificant exceptions, of Java and Sumatra, except most Battak, profess Muhammadanism, as do the Macassars, Buginese, Mandarese, Bimanese, and some other tribes of the West and North coast of Celebes, and of Borneo; the small islands of Ternate and Tidore are also peopled by Muhammadans. The Balinese in Bali and Lombok are Saivites, with a sprinkling of Buddhists, whereas the Sassaks of Lombok are followers of Islām. Christianity is the prevailing religion in Amboina, the Minahassa, the Sangir, and Talaut Islands, and has an increasing number of adherents among the Battak, Torajas, Sawunese, and Rottinese; Roman Catholic natives are chiefly found in the Eastern part of Flores. Some small communities of converts to Christianity are also found in Java.

1. Animism.—The religion of the pagan tribes of the Archipelago is what is generally denoted as animism. In speaking of the beliefs prevailing in the Malay Peninsula Skeat rightly says:

'The root-idea seems to be an all-pervading Animism, involving a certain common vital principle (*sĕmangat*) in Man and Nature, which, for want of a more suitable word, has been here called the Soul. The application of this general theory of the universe to the requirements of the individual man constitutes the Magic Art, which, as conceived by the Malays, may be said to consist of the methods by which this Soul, whether in gods, men, animals, vegetables, minerals, or what not, may be influenced, captured, subdued, or in some way made subject to the will of the magician.'[2]

All this applies to the pagan Indonesians, and, in many respects, also to the natives who have adopted another religion and, in their own opinion, are sincerely attached to it.

Sumangat, with dialectic variations, is the general word with the Malays also in Indonesia for 'soul,' 'vital force,' penetrating the whole body, but distinct from the latter, so that it can leave the body temporarily, *e.g.*, in dreams, and finally at death. The Macassars and Buginese use the same word, *sumanga*, *sumangĕ* with the same meaning. The Battak use the term *tĕndi*, *tondi* for exactly the same idea; and the Dayaks have *hambaruan*, *amirue*, *amiroi*, *blua*, and other dialectic variations of the same word. With the Torajas in Central Celebes the usual term is *tanoana*, properly 'homunculus'; another expression is *wayo*, or *limbayo*, *i.e.* 'shadow' (Jav. *wayang*, Mal. *bayang*). When the soul temporarily leaves the body, it assumes the form of a homunculus or an animal. A man whose soul thus goes forth in order to feed upon the souls of others appears in the shape of a deer, pig, crocodile, monkey, buffalo, or cat. Like many other Indonesians, the Torajas believe that there are witches who can separate their head and entrails from their body in order to suck the blood of sleeping persons. Such beings may be compared with the Mal. *penanggalans*, 'vampires.'

1 With the doubtful exception of the people of Ternate Tidore, Halmahera (Gilolo).

2 *Malay Magic*, London, 1900, p. 579 f.

The word for 'soul' in Nias is *noso*, which, like Skr. *prāṇa* and Gr. πνεῦμα, is properly the 'breath of life,' and then 'life,' 'vitality.' The same may be said of *ñawa* (Jav., Mal. etc.). There are several other Indonesian words for 'soul'—*e.g.*, Tontembuan *imukur*, *nimukur*, Sangir *himukudĕ*, Bentenan *himukur*, Ponosakan *dimukur*.

The common belief is that not only men, but also animals, vegetables, and minerals have a soul. The Ngaju Dayaks make a distinction between *hambaruan* and *gana*, the former belonging to men, animals, rice, and money, the latter to slaves, some trees, and things. The *gana*, like the *hambaruan*, can leave its abode and appear in the shape of a human being to men in dreams.

The soul leaves the body at death, and returns to its origin, the creator, or passes, directly or indirectly, into another human body, an animal, or a plant. The residuum of the individual, however, continues a shadowy existence as spirit. Such a spirit of the dead is called *liau* among the Ngaju Dayaks, and *diau*, *andiau*, among the Olo Dusun. It is commonly believed that the *liau* goes forthwith to Lewu liau, the spirit land, which it often leaves to roam in the woods or haunt its burial-place. During that time it is often harmful to the survivors, particularly by causing disease.

The common word for 'spirit' in Battak is *begu*, Nias *beghu*, which not only denotes the spirit of the departed, in which case we may translate it by 'ghost,' 'spectre,' but is applied also to superhuman beings, demons, and gods. The Torajas use the term *anga* for the spirit of the dead, and, in particular, *anitu* for the spirits of chieftains and heroes. This word *anitu*, or *nitu*, so wide-spread throughout the whole area of the Malayo-Polynesians, in Formosa, the Philippines, and the isles of the Pacific, is the common term for the ghosts of ancestors in the Moluccas, Timor, and Rotti. The Rottinese use it also for demons, whereas the Hill Torajas apply it to their gods, who, in fact, are deified ancestors. In general it is difficult to distinguish the ghosts of the departed from the spirits of higher beings or gods, but among some Torajas, who use the term *lamoa*, we find that a distinction is made between higher and lower *lamoas*.

According to R. H. Codrington (*The Melanesians*, Oxford, 1891, p. 124 f.), 'it must not be supposed that every ghost becomes an object of worship. A man in danger may call upon his father, his grandfather, or his uncle; his nearness of kin is sufficient ground for it. The ghost who is to be worshipped is the spirit of a man who in his lifetime had *mana* in him.'

The same may be said with reference to the people in the Malay Archipelago, and not the heathen exclusively. The ghosts of different kinds are not equal in power. The Karo Battak hold the ghosts of stillborn children in particular awe, making little houses for them, and honouring them with offerings. The inhabitants of the Luang Sermata Isles believe that the ghosts of those who have died a violent death are most powerful and zealous to help their kinsfolk. In Halmahera the ghosts of persons killed in war or by accident are called *dilikè* in Galelarese, *dilikini* in Tobelorese. They are more powerful than other ghosts, protecting the living, especially in battle,[1] and are worshipped in the village temple. The Torajas also honour the ghosts of those who have fallen in battle.

To another category of ghosts belongs the protecting genius of places, regarded as the founder of a village or the common ancestor of the population. In Java every village honours the ghost of its founder, the *tjakal desa*, with frequent offerings. The tutelary deity of a place is called *ḍanghyang*, *i.e.* 'the god'; as the name implies, he is not a ghost, but a supernatural being. The worship of the reputed founder of a settlement is very common in the Moluccas. The Galelarese call the genius of a village and the forefather of its people *wongé*.

The Indonesians in general live in constant dread of innumerable ghosts, who are mostly malignant, and therefore must be propitiated by offerings or warded off by other means. Most feared is the *pontianak*, a word which with slight variations recurs in the whole archipelago, the Malay Peninsula, and the Philippines. The *pontianak* is the reputed ghost of a woman who has died in childbirth and, out of jealousy, penetrates the bodies of pregnant women to kill the unborn children. Usually she is thought to have the shape of a bird,[1] but to be invisible when she approaches her victim. In the archipelago the customary prophylactic against her insidious attempt is to suspend the thorny branches of a certain lemon-tree, the fruits of which are also employed as a means of repelling ghosts (for other means see Kruijt, *Het Animisme*, pp. 245–251).

All sorts of diseases are ascribed to the baleful influence both of ghosts and of other spirits. Especially in Nias we find several names of *beghus* who are held responsible for the appearance of different diseases and evils. It is no wonder that the people employ every means in their power to cure sickness or to prevent threatening attacks. In apprehension of the danger which may accrue from the dead, the Malays take care that the dead body is so treated that the ghost may not return. With many tribes one of the symbolical means of doing this is to scatter ashes, as if to blind the ghost.[2] The relatives of a deceased person have to undergo a longer or shorter period of mourning, during which they must wear the conventional mourning dress, observe certain restrictions in the use of food and drink, and refrain from amusements. At the end of this period it is customary for some tribes to offer human sacrifices, the ruling idea responsible for this custom apparently being that the ghost ought to be given a companion by way of propitiation.

It is commonly believed that the ghosts of the dead remain for some time in the neighbourhood of their former dwelling, whence the custom of erecting a hut in which to place the necessary offerings. With some Indonesians it is usual to prepare a bed of state for the ghost during the first days after the death. Even the Christians of Amboina and the Sangir Isles believe that the dead man pays a visit to his former home on the third day.

The ghosts continue to wander and meet with all sorts of difficulties before finally reaching the realm of the dead, which is situated somewhere in the West. When they are supposed to have arrived there, a great commemorative feast is arranged, such as the *tiwah*[3] of the Ngaju Dayaks and the *tengke* and the *mompemate* of the Western Bare'e Torajas.[4] For the ceremonies of the feast among the Dayaks of Sarawak see Ling Roth, *The Natives of Sarawak*, i. 208–210.

In the primitive belief of the less civilized Indonesians there is a bond of connexion between a dead man and his body, chiefly his bones. It is usually the skull that is used as a medium for

[1] For further particulars see M. J. van Baarda, *Woordenlijst van het Galelareesch-hollandsch*, p. 98; A. Hueting, *Tobèloreesch-hollandsch Woordenboek*, The Hague, 1908, p. 61.

[1] But cf. Skeat, p. 325 f.

[2] See, for other peculiar action, Kruijt, pp. 251–268, and cf. Skeat, p. 325.

[3] Described in Hardeland, *Dajacksch-deutsches Wörterbuch*, p. 608 ff.

[4] Described in Adriani-Kruijt, *De Bare'e-sprekende Toradjas*, p. 117.

communication. It is preserved with great piety, honoured with offerings, and worshipped. Not seldom a magic power is ascribed to parts of the body, which thus come to be in reality miracle-working relics. Another medium of communication is found in idols representing the deified ancestors; these are held to be inspired after due initiation. Such images are very numerous in Nias, where they are called *adu*, and occur also in Ceram and in some parts of Borneo. The Battak have no idols of particular ancestors, but keep two puppets in their houses, one male, the other female, called Silaon ('the primeval ones'), or Debata idup ('deities of life'). They seem to represent the primordial couple from whom mankind is sprung. Among the Ngaju Dayaks puppets called *hampatong* represent the ghost (*gana*) of the slaves of the deceased at the *tiwah*, but the term has also the more general meaning of 'puppet.' The Toraja tribes, on the other hand, except the To Lage and To Onda'e, have no images, but wooden masks (*pemia*). Stones are also objects of worship, as well as certain earthen pots or urns, which are regarded as sacred and inspired.

2. **Shamanism.**—The belief that persons, during madness, epilepsy, and sometimes abnormal states of mind, are possessed by spirits has led to attempts to reproduce the same phenomenal conditions in order to get into contact with spirits to learn from them what medicines to apply or how to act in matters of importance. The medium through whom the spirits manifest themselves is the shaman, who is brought into a state of mental abnormality by artificial means, the rites employed for this purpose being multifarious among the peoples of Indonesia, but, in general, similar to what we find elsewhere—*e.g.*, among the Buriats (*q.v.*).

The Battak distinguish the shaman (*sibaso*) from the priest (*datu*). Though their functions are not seldom analogous, there is this difference between them: the former acts unconsciously, under inspiration, whereas the latter gives his decision, based upon his knowledge of the books of his craft, in full consciousness. With the Dayak tribes it is a priest or priestess who acts as medium. The *dayong* of the Kayans is a priestess who sends her own soul to bring back the soul (*blua*) of a sick person, or to conjure up the ghost of the dead. The *manang*, a word properly meaning 'one who exercises power,' is with the Sea Dayaks the man who is able to meet and converse with spirits. The same character belongs to the *walian, belian, basir*, or *dayang* of other Dayaks. Such persons are more properly medicine-men than priests or shamans. Yet it is true that in doing their work they occasionally show signs of ecstasy caused by their being inspired. A peculiar kind of shamanism, which, however, is of foreign origin, is found in Halmahera.[1]

3. **Fetishism.**—Various substances are supposed to conceal a powerful soul within themselves. They are therefore held sacred and worshipped in one way or another in the hope that by their power some desired object may be attained. All over the archipelago we find the use of so-called thunder-stones, chiefly as a means of gaining invulnerability in battle or as a preservative against lightning. Not less common is the belief in the wonderful effects attending the possession of the bezoar.[2] A high sacredness is attached to stones of a certain uncommon shape, especially in the eastern isles of the archipelago. In Timor the finder of such a stone, considered to be the abode of a spirit, puts it on a sacred place (*voho*) and brings sacrifices to it. It looks as if such a sacred stone is a rude form of idol, for idols also are inhabited by the deity. Various other fetishes are used as amulets, and a prophylactic fetish called *matakau* is in common use. It consists of a collection of leaves and sticks, which are hung in fruit trees to repel thieves. With the Torajas and Dayaks the suspended materials are mostly of a sympathetic character.

4. **Mythology.**—In general it may be said that the pagan Indonesians recognize the existence of real gods, and that the supreme god is the creator, more or less directly, of the world and the preserver of it, and punishes the transgressors of his laws. In the Moluccas and the South-Eastern Isles the supreme deity is generally known under the name of Upu Lero (with dialectic variations). The word means 'Lord Sun'—a sufficient proof of his origin. Upu Lero may be identified with Upu Langi, *i.e.* 'Lord Heaven.' The earth is a female deity, and represents the female principle, who, in the West monsoon, is impregnated and fructified by the male principle, Lord Sun-Heaven. Similarly, the Torajas recognize two supreme powers: Ilai, 'the Man,' and Indara, 'the Maiden'; these formed men, but not animals or plants. In the Minahassa Muntumuntu is the sun and lawgiver. In the confused mythological lore of Nias we find Lowa Langi represented as the creator of men, though he himself is not primordial, but came forth from the bud of a tree. His counterpart is Lature, the chief of the evil spirits, who, curiously enough, is said to have his seat in the sun; he is the master of all that is perishable. The highest god of the Toba Battak is Ompu mula jadi na bolan, 'the Great Lord Origin of the Creation'; and his subordinates are the three gods Debata na tolu: Batara guru, Soripada, and Mangala bulan. The use of the somewhat corrupt Sanskrit words is sufficient proof of foreign influence, but the name of the highest god is original. Bhaṭara Guru is a title of Śiva among the Śaivites in ancient Java. Among the Karo Battak he is the highest god; and likewise among the Macassars and Buginese in former times. The Sanskrit word *bhaṭṭāra*, in some more or less changed form, is found in many Indonesian languages in the sense of 'god' or 'divine being.' So the Ngaju Dayaks call the creator Mahatara, but also Hatalla or Mahatalla, borrowed from Arabic *Allāh ta'ālā*; and the same name is used by the Manyan Dayaks. With the Sea Dayaks *pĕtara* or *bĕtara* is a name for higher beings. Thoroughly original is the word for the supreme being in Halmahera, viz. Galelarese *Giki-moi*, Tobelorese *Gikiri-moi*, the 'First Being.' The moon plays a considerable part in the myths, but not in the cult; but there are traces that formerly it was otherwise. In the belief of the people of Babar Rarawolai, the war-god, has his seat in the moon, with nine female ministers.

The host of minor deities or demi-gods is so great that only a few classes can be mentioned here. The *sangiangs* of the Ngaju Dayaks are benevolent demi-gods related to men. The most powerful of them is Tempon telon; his principal function is to conduct the ghosts to the land of spirits. The *djatas* (from Skr. *devatā*) are water-gods, whose ministers are the crocodiles. The water-spirits are called *taghazangarofa* in Nias. The *hantus* and *hantuens* of the Ngaju Dayaks are malignant spirits, or demons, whereas the *antu* is considered by the Sarawak Dayaks to be a helpful spirit. The belief that demons make their appearance in the shape of snakes, dogs, pigs, crocodiles, tortoises, and men is very general. The Kayans have a great number of gods—*e.g.*, a god of war, three gods of life, a god of storms and thunder, of fire,

[1] See van Baarda, *s.v.* 'Djini.'

[2] For the ideas of the Malays in the Peninsula see Skeat, pp. 195-197, 275; see also following article.

of harvest, of the waters, and of insanity, and the gods who conduct ghosts to the subterranean world. Above all these gods or demons stands Laki Tenangan, whose wife is Doh Tenangan, the patroness of women. Laki Tenangan is identical with Pa Silong of the Klemantans, and Bali Pony-long of the Kenyahs.

5. Nature-worship.—Nature-worship in its widest sense finds its expression in the sacred character of mountains, volcanoes, seas, and rivers, all of them being inhabited and ruled by super-human powers.

LITERATURE.—The following is only a selection from the writings relative to the subject. **N. Adriani and A. C. Kruijt**, *De Bare'e-sprekende Toradjas van Midden-Celebes*, Batavia, 1912; **M. J. van Baarda**, *Woordenlijst van het Galelareesch-hollandsch*, The Hague, 1895; **J. von Brenner**, *Besuch bei den Kannibalen Sumatras*, Würzburg, 1894; **C. Brooke**, *Ten Years in Sarawak*, London, 1866; **L. N. H. A. Chatelin**, 'Godsdienst en bijgeloof der Niassers,' *Tijdschrift van het Bataviaasch Genootschap van Kunsten en Wetenschappen*, xxvi. [1880]; **J. A. Fehr**, *Der Niasser im Leben und Sterben*, Barmen, 1901; **W. H. Furness**, *The Home-Life of Borneo Head-hunters*, Philadelphia, 1902; **N. Graafland**, *De Minahassa*, Rotterdam, 1867–69; **H. J. Grijzen**, 'Mededeelingen omtrent Beloe of Midden Timor,' *Verhandelingen van het Bataviaasch Genootschap van Kunsten en Wetenschappen*, xliv. [1904]; **B. Hagen**, 'Beiträge zur Kenntniss der Battareligion,' *Tijdschr. van het Batav. Genootsch.*, xxviii. [1883]; **A. Hardeland**, *Dajacksch-deutsches Wörterbuch*, Amsterdam, 1858; **J. L. van Hasselt**, *Volksbeschrijving van Midden-Sumatra*, Leyden, 1881–82; **G. Heijmering**, 'Zeden en gewoonten op het eiland Timor,' *Tijdschrift voor Nederlandsch Indië*, 1844; **H. A. van Hien**, *De Javaansche geestenwereld*, Semarang, 1896; **G. W. W. C. van Hoëvell**, 'De Aroe eilanden,' *Tijdschr. van het Batav. Genootsch.*, xxxiii. [1890], 'De Kei eilanden,' *ib.*, 'De Leti eilanden,' *ib.*, 'De Tenimber en Timorlaoet eilanden,' *ib.*; **C. Hose and W. McDougall**, *The Pagan Tribes of Borneo*, London, 1912; **J. P. Kleiweg de Zwaan**, *Die Insel Nias bei Sumatra*, *Die Heilkunde der Niasser*, The Hague, 1913; **F. Kramer**, 'Der Götzendienst der Niasser,' *Tijdschr. van het Batav. Genootsch.*, xxxiii. [1890]; **A. C. Kruijt**, *Het animisme in den indischen Archipel*, The Hague, 1906; **H. Ling Roth**, *The Natives of Sarawak and British North Borneo*, London, 1896; **B. F. Matthes**, 'Over de bissoes of heidensche priesters en priesteressen der Boeginezen,' *Verslagen en Mededeelingen der Kon. Akademie van Wetenschappen*, vii. [Amsterdam, 1872]; **J. H. Neumann**, 'De Begoe in de godsdienstige begrippen der Karo-Bataks in de Doessoen,' *Mededeelingen van wege het Nederlandsch Zendelinggenootschap*, xlvi. [Rotterdam, 1903], 'De tĕndi in verband met Si Dajang,' *ib.*, xlviii. [1904]; **A. W. Nieuwenhuis**, *In Central Borneo*, Leyden, 1900, *Quer durch Borneo*, do. 1904–07; **C. M. Pleyte**, *Bataksche Vertellingen*, Utrecht, 1894; **J. G. F. Riedel**, *De sluik- en kroesharige rassen tusschen Selebes en Papua*, The Hague, 1886, 'Das Toumbuluhsche Pantheon,' *Abhandlungen und Berichte des ethnographischen Museums*, Dresden, 1892–93; **W. Schmidt**, 'Grundlinien einer Vergleichung der Religionen und Mythologien der austronesischen Völker,' *DWAW*, 1910; **H. Sundermann**, 'Die Olon Maanjan und die Missionsarbeit unter denselben,' *Allgemeine Missionszeitschrift*, xi. [Berlin, 1884]; **J. W. Thomas**, *Drei Jahre in Südnias*, Barmen, 1892: **J. L. van der Toorn**, 'Het animisme bij den Minangkabauer,' *Bijdragen tot de Taal-, Land- en Volkenkunde van Nederlandsch Indië*, v. 5 [The Hague, 1890]; **S. W. Tromp**, 'Ein Dajakfeest,' *ib.*; **P. J. Veth**, *Borneo's Wester-Afdeeling*, Zalt-Bommel, 1854–56; **J. Warneck**, 'Der batakscbe Ahnen- und Geisterkult,' *Allgem. Missionszeitschr.*, xxxi. [1904]; **P. te Wechel**, 'Erinnerungen aus den Ost- und West-Dusun-Ländern (Borneo),' *AE* xxii. [1914]; **L. C. Westenenk**, 'De Mocalang- en Sekadan Dajaks,' *Tijdschr. van het Batav. Genootsch.*, xxxix. [1897]; **C. J. Westenberg**, 'Aanteekeningen omtrent de godsdienstige begrippen der Karo-Bataks,' *Bijd. tot de Taal-, Land- en Volkenkunde van Nederlandsch Indië*, v. 7 [1892]; **G. A. Wilken**, *Het animisme bij de volken van den Indischen Archipel*, i., Amsterdam, 1884, ii., Leyden, 1885, 'Het shamanisme bij de volken van den Indischen Archipel,' *Bijd. tot de Taal-, Land- en Volkenkunde van Nederlandsch Indië*, v. 2 [1887]; 'De betrekking tusschen menschen-, dieren- en plantenleven naar het volksgeloof,' *Ind. Gids*, 1884, ii.; **N. P. Wilken**, 'De godsdienst en godsdienstplegtigheden der Alfoeren in de Minahassa,' *Tijdschr. voor Nederlandsch Indië*, 1849, ii.

H. KERN.

MALAY PENINSULA.—1. Geography.—

The Malay Peninsula, a long scimitar-shaped piece of land, stretches from Burma and Siam to Singapore. Its length from the northernmost extremity to the southern confines of Johor, immediately to the north of the island of Singapore, is rather under 1000 miles; its breadth varies from 35 miles to less than 200 miles at the broadest part. The result is that the peninsula, though distinctly a part of the mainland, is insular in character rather than continental. At a comparatively late geological period its southern half was indeed actually insular, being at this time joined to the island of Sumatra, and entirely separated from the northern portion. The line of division ran, somewhat roughly, from Singora on the one side to Perlis on the other, and it may be observed that at the very point where this line traverses the peninsula a marked change in the flora and distinct ethnographical differences occur. The lower and more properly Malayan portion of the peninsula is separated from that to the north by a low divide. The backbone of the peninsula is formed by ranges, mainly of granite formation, the source of numerous rivers and streams which drain the country. The ranges are steep and precipitous, rising to 7000 or 8000 ft. and containing stanniferous and sporadic auriferous deposits. The wild aborigines make their homes chiefly on the foot-hills, but they are also found on the main mountain complex to a height of upwards of 3000 feet. The upland valleys are narrow and covered with dense jungle. They offer little attraction to any but the scattered aboriginal population who still find shelter in their fastnesses and, in some districts, to the Chinese miners. Further towards the coast the valleys become larger and more fertile, and their loamy soils have long been cultivated by the Malays, and in recent years by numerous European planters. As the rivers reach the sea on either side, the soil tends to become more and more a clayey or sandy alluvium. Often the rivers are tidal for a great many miles inland. On the east coast, for some four months of every year, the steady beat of the China monsoon seals all the river-mouths with a sandy bar, and during the height of this monsoon all trade is effectually prevented. On the west coast the land is sheltered, as if by a colossal breakwater, by the neighbouring island of Sumatra. Here muddy mangrove flats are found, but with magnificent expanses of sandy beach at intervals. The light breezes that prevail have led to the evolution of quite different types of boats and canoes from those on the China Sea. The peninsula is rich in tin ore. It produces an amount estimated, roughly, at three-quarters of the entire world's supply. The revenue derived from this industry has been ably applied by the governments of the native States to their development. Out of this income a railway has been built from Penang to Singapore, another is under construction round the main mountain mass on the east coast, and will be continued to meet the Siamese railways from Bangkok, while the railway from Penang is also to be extended to meet the same railway system. Together with a most excellent road system, second to none in the East, these modern means of transport have changed entirely the old conditions of life, and have brought this part of British Malaya, in one generation, into vital contact with our own economic world. Besides the mining industry there are now large agricultural industries dealing with rubber and coco-nuts. In the main these industries are worked by a non-indigenous population from China and the south of India, for whose sustenance large supplies of rice are imported annually. The British possessions consist of the islands of Penang and Singapore, and of three small strips of land: Province Wellesley opposite Penang, and the Dindings and Malacca between Penang and Singapore. The Federated Malay States of Perak, Selangor, and Nĕgri Sembīlan on the Straits of Malacca, and Pahang, on the China Sea, form a compact core dominating the centre of this part of the peninsula. To the north of the Federated Malay States are the States of Perlis and Kedah on the west coast, and of Kelantan and

Trengganu on the east coast, all of which have recently been taken under British protection, and also the State of Patani, which is under Siamese suzerainty. To the south of the Federated Malay States lies the State of Johor, also now under British protection. It is common to speak of the units of the British sphere as British Malaya, a term which formerly included our far greater possessions in Sumatra and the densely populous island of Java. Occasionally the term is more accurately extended to include the island of Labuan, British N. Borneo, a British possession, and the protectorates of Brunei and Sarawak also represent British interests in Malaya, though the conditions there differ materially from those in the peninsula and ought to be considered with the archipelago.

2. Ethnological affinities and history. — The ethnological affinities of the area of which the Malay Peninsula forms a part, as well as of the adjacent areas, are still obscure in many respects. In so far as they have yet been elucidated by ethnological investigations and an examination of historical records, they bear out conclusions deducible from the geographical data. The Malay Peninsula itself would appear from very early times to have served as a causeway for migrations from the Asiatic continent, while the protected character of the waterway on the west side, and the richness of this part of the peninsula in minerals and other products, have favoured its economic development, and made it not only attractive to higher civilizations, as the study of its entire history shows, but also a rendezvous of merchants and workers from many far-separated countries. At the present day not the least important element in the population consists of a congeries of alien races, Chinese from the southern provinces of China, Canton, Fu-kien, and the island of Hainan, Tamils from S. India and Ceylon, and, in a lesser degree, Sikhs, Panjābīs, and Paṭhāns from N. India, and Javanese and Malays from all parts of the Eastern archipelago. In the north of the peninsula isolated outposts of Siamese have pushed for a considerable distance over the Kraw Divide, overstepping the ancient ethnological boundary of the peninsula. Old, forts can be traced in the Patani valley and for some way down the Perak valley, the defences of which were strengthened with a hedge of thorny bamboo, which is not indigenous in this region. On the Upper Perak valley and in a few places further south there are distinct traces of Siamese influence in comparatively recent times.

(*a*) *Malays.*—The peculiar importance of the native religions of the region here discussed is due to the fact that they exhibit a clearly-defined series of superimposed ceremonial strata, native (*i.e.* aboriginal of at least two different types, and Malayan) Indian and Islāmic. The most recent ethnological investigations confirm the view that the native population consists of the descendants of immigrants of a comparatively recent date, superimposed upon a more ancient stratum consisting, to a great extent, if not entirely, of aboriginal races. The Malays proper belong to the modified Southern Mongoloid group of peoples found in Formosa, Sumatra, Java, and throughout a great part of the Malay Archipelago. When the Palĕmbang emigrants first began to arrive from Sumatra, about 900 to 1000 years ago, introducing a Hinduized civilization into the peninsula, it is probable that they found some Indo-Chinese race of superior culture already in possession. This is suggested by certain features of the aboriginal dialects, and by other considerations.

It is of great importance to note that some of the Sumatran settlers, who followed, after some centuries, the earlier Palĕmbang colonists, are still in the matriarchal stage as distinct from other Sumatran settlers, by whom customs of a patriarchal type are followed. In the Malayan phrase, the people of the Nĕgri Sembīlan 'follow the '*adat pĕrpateh*,' which may be described as '*Pĕrpateh* custom,' whereas the other Malays of the peninsula 'follow the '*adat Tĕmenggong*' ('custom of the *Tĕmenggong*'), these two contrasted bodies of custom being based on mother-right and father-right respectively.

These Sumatran settlers, who were agriculturists, amalgamated with the aborigines, at any rate in some districts—*e.g.*, in the State called Nĕgri Sembīlan—but the conversion of the Malays from tolerant Hinduism to Muhammadanism from the late 14th to the 16th cent. began to drive the aborigines into the jungles and hill fastnesses of the interior. Since that time Sunnī Muhammadanism of the Shāfi'ite school has remained (as in Java) the official religion of the peninsula, although among the less educated of the Malays it is the merest veneer covering a vast body of practices and beliefs which can be traced either to the influences of Hinduism or to primitive shamanistic beliefs, such as are still held by the aborigines. Malay Islāmism is nevertheless still fervent.

It may be remarked that the Malay Peninsula belongs, geographically and ethnographically, to Indo-China, a name which well expresses the fact that, with hardly any exception, the congeries of races inhabiting the peninsula from time immemorial represent strata of races belonging to one or other of the two chief families of nations in various parts of Asia, viz. a Mongoloid and a non-Mongoloid, both terms being used broadly. Belonging to the latter family we have (1) Indonesians (defined by A. H. Keane[1] as the pre-Malay 'Caucasic' element, of which the Veddas and Korumba, and one at least of the Australian aboriginal races, are typical), often called 'Dravidian' (though, like 'Malayo-Polynesian,' this term should strictly be confined to linguistic affinities); on the other hand, we find, as representatives of the same great family, (2) a more highly developed or specialized type, possibly the tall brown-skinned Polynesian. These two main Indonesian types are said to be represented in the peninsula, the pre-Malay 'Caucasic' element of the Korumba-Vedda type, by the aboriginal Sakai, centred in S.E. Perak and N.W. Pahang (cf. one of the basic elements in the Malay language),[2] while to the pre-Malay Oceanic 'Caucasians' (of the Polynesian or Maori type) belong the taller east coast 'Malays' of Kelantan and part of Patani. The latter may be described as very tall, somewhat fleshy, large-limbed men, with light brown or cinnamon-coloured skins, straight or wavy black, sometimes nearly curly, hair, and regular, sometimes almost European, features.

Again, the great Mongolian family of nations is represented both by the Siamese (or Thai) in the northern portion of the peninsula and by the Malays themselves in the southern part, the Malays proper being perhaps best regarded as a highly specialized offshoot of the southern or 'Oceanic' Mongoloid race, immediately immigrant from central and southern Sumatra. They have long, lank, bluish-black, straight hair, of circular section, and are almost beardless, with skin of a dark yellow-brown or olive hue (or the 'colour of newly-fallen leaves'); they are round-headed (brachycephalic), and often have more or less wide

[1] *Man Past and Present*, Cambridge, 1899, p. 231.

[2] R. O. Winstedt, *Malay Grammar*, Oxford, 1913, p. 12. 'This connexion was first definitely asserted by Prof. Schmidt of Mödling, Austria, and is now generally accepted; it establishes an ultimate prehistoric relationship between Malay and the languages of the aborigines in the Peninsula' (*ib.*).

and flattened noses, and somewhat thick ears, and on the average are about 1·61 m. in height. The women are usually much shorter than the men. Both sexes have rather short, often almost stumpy, feet, with toes that are to some extent prehensile; they will walk up a thin sloping pole leading to a raised platform or house-floor by gripping it with the hands and at the same time holding it between the great toe and remaining toes of each foot. Their joints are remarkably fine and small; the dagger-ring of a well-developed old-style rebel chief, which was worn on his fore-finger, was too small for an average-sized little finger of a European. A jungle Malay can commonly perform certain feats with his limbs that are impossible to a European unless he has been specially trained as an acrobat.

In Sumatra the race was moulded by Indian influences into a comparatively civilized condition before they crossed to the peninsula. When they arrived, they found the country occupied by the three pagan races (see below, (*b*)), whom they drove before them into the fastnesses of the mountainous and jungle-clad interior. It is thought that they also found some branch of the Môn-Khmer or Môn[1] races holding the coast-line and other points of vantage, and thus occupying almost the same relation towards the aboriginal races as the Malays do at the present day, and that they then partly absorbed the Môns, by thinning them of their women, and partly drove them into the jungle. This episode is, however, a lost chapter in the history of the peninsula, although some such theory seems evidently necessary in order to account for all the actually extant conditions.

The Malays proper are but partially civilized, a graft upon a savage stock, allied not only to the Central and Southern Sumatrans and Indonesians, but also perhaps ultimately to the Chams of Champa.[2] See CAMBODIA, CHAMS.

The hereditary savagery of the Malay nature, for many years after the introduction of the British Residential system (introduced to curb the turbulent Malay Rajas, who were fostering piracy), continually broke out, the commonest form in which it showed itself being perhaps the *âmok*, the national Malay method of committing suicide, until the gradual strengthening of the right arm of British law made it too risky to indulge in, when by degrees it became unfashionable. Other striking evidence of the high-strung excitability of the Malay temperament is still to be seen in the form of the mysterious disease called *latah* (corresponding to what has been called 'arctic hysteria'), which also has not yet been thoroughly investigated.

(*b*) *Aborigines.*—Various theories have been put forward as to the ethnological character of the several wild races which form the substratum of the population. It was held by the older ethnologists that they belonged to a homogeneous group—a Negrito race modified by admixture with the Malay population. This is what has been termed the 'Pan-Negrito' theory of A. de Quatrefages, N. von Miklucho-Maclay, and others. This hypothesis, however, has proved untenable, and the result of later researches has established the fact that at least three[1] types are to be found among these primitive tribes. Of these tribes two, at least (the Semang and Sakai), can be found in a relatively pure state, though only in very limited areas, and the third (the Jakun) is probably nowhere really pure. Admixture between the three has taken place in varying degrees throughout the peninsula, and the only satisfactory procedure anthropologically is to compare each tribe with the pure, unmixed standard or standards to which it is most closely related. By no other method can any really useful conclusions be reached, or, indeed, the drawing of the most fallacious inferences avoided.

(1) *Semang.*—The Semang are a nomad Negrito race — comparable with the Negrito (Pygmy) peoples of Central Africa, and probably most closely connected with the Andamanese, whose group of islands lies off the Burmese coast at its southward end—belonging to a primitive group of peoples found to a greater or less extent as a relic of the aboriginal population as far as New Guinea and the Philippines, although it is remarkable that no traces of any such race have yet been quite proved in Borneo midway between these two Negrito centres. The physical characters of these people are short stature (1·491 mm. male, 1·408 female), brachycephaly, skin varying from dark copper or chocolate to shiny black, hair woolly, nose broad, lips everted, beard scanty. They extend from Patani to Kedah, and from Kedah to Mid-Perak and N. Pahang.

In view of the fact that the Semang (or, as they are called on the east coast of the peninsula, Pangan) are so frequently described as being of Negro character—'like African negroes seen through the reverse end of a field-glass'[2]—it cannot be too strongly stated that this is a mistake. At the utmost, it may be conjectured, with W. H. Flower, that they represent, with the true Pygmies, an original undeveloped stock from which the Papuans, like the Negroes, may have branched off. But even for this theory there are many difficulties, and it cannot be said to have been in any way established. Hence the Negrito and the Negro must be regarded as totally different races—the former having short or round heads and the latter being long-headed.

(2) *Sakai.*—The Sakai were at one time regarded as Semang admixed with Malay, but are now clearly differentiated as a separate and independent type[3] most nearly akin to the Dravidian group of peoples. They are taller than the Semang (average height 1·504 mm. male, 1·437 female), dolichocephalic, skin very variable, light to dark brown, hair wavy, nose fine and small, cheek-bones broad, mouth small, lower lip full and projecting, beard as a rule non-existent. The habitat of the purest Sakai is S.E. Perak and N.W. Pahang.

(3) *Jakun.*—The Jakun are a mixed group inhabiting especially the south of the peninsula, probably everywhere blended, to a varying extent, with Semang and Sakai. This fact is the more remarkable since a relatively important element running throughout all the aboriginal dialects in

[1] Pronounced 'Mown.' The Môns, or Talaing, are remnants of an old pre-Malay ('Caucasic') race which once covered the whole of lower Burma. The Talaing language is the oldest literary vernacular of Indo-China, and is fast dying out, though it is the original tongue upon which the Burmese alphabet and religion were modelled, and in which were composed the Môn inscriptions, which go back to about the 11th cent. of our era.

[2] The Cham dialect has in recent years been shown to contain Malay elements (E. Aymonier and A. Cabaton, *Dictionnaire čam-français*, Paris, 1906). One of the most peculiar customs (though in this case non-Malay) attributed to the Chams is that the women ask the men in marriage.

[1] Wilkinson has recently suggested that five aboriginal race types should be recognized. When, therefore, the new elements, such as would be required in order to form the two proposed new types, have been differentiated, and these elements are all shown not to be referable to either one or the other of the three types already identified, the problem will have reached a further stage of development. Certainly, as there are still some unexplained points, it is probable that some further racial element may eventually be isolated (see *F.M.S. Govt. Papers on Malay Subjects: Aboriginal Tribes*, 1910).

[2] Hugh Clifford, *In Court and Kampong*, London, 1897, p. 172. But this is a microscopic slip for an author who has done as much as any other ten men to familiarize the English public with the peoples of Malaya.

[3] This all-important differentiation was first clearly established by R. Martin; see his *magnum opus*, *Inlandstämme der malayischen Halbinsel*, Leipzig, 1905.

varying degrees consists of some Malayo-Polynesian tongue, the vocabulary of which shows affinities with the Malayan languages of the Far Eastern Archipelago, unlike modern (peninsular) or standard Malay. The reason for this is not apparent, unless we may conjecture that at some remote period a race whose national speech was of this Malayo-Polynesian type prevailed in the peninsula. The Jakun may be classified as consisting of at least three related groups, blended as above. In so far as they are of Malayan type, they should be to that extent regarded as aboriginal Malays. In physical character they are a little taller than the Sakai, the head is brachycephalic, the skin dark coppery, hair long, straight, and smooth, nose thick, flat, and short; the eyes show little tendency to obliquity, and the mouth is large and broad, with well-formed lips. The Jakun proper are divided by the Malays into Hill Tribes (Orang or Jakun Bukit) and Sea Jakun (Orang Laut).

The surest test in regard to these tribes is the hair-character; hence we may distinguish the three main racial groups as ulotrichi ('woolly-haired'), cymotrichi ('wavy-haired'), and lissotrichi ('smooth-haired').

There has undoubtedly been a considerable admixture between all the wild tribes, but, owing in particular to their being still pagans, it is improbable that they have been materially affected by intermingling with the Malays, since nothing could be rarer than that a Malay woman should demean herself by marrying a heathen husband. The case is rather the other way about, since a Malay marrying a woman of the wild tribes would see that his children were brought up as Muhammadans, while in many districts, especially in Kedah, the adoption of the Muhammadan religion by a large portion of the aboriginal Semang element has caused them to be reckoned as part of the recognized Malay population.

3. **Culture.**—(*a*) *Malays.*—Apart from such tendencies as have already been mentioned, the Malay character may be regarded as a softened and more civilized form of the Mongol, since under ordinary circumstances he may be relied upon to show himself a peaceable, quiet, civil, and loyal subject, though he still retains much of his old proud sensitiveness, and in inland districts he is still reserved in his ways of life, and to some extent suspicious of strangers. In countries where he is less trammelled by civilization, the Malay is frequently of a bold and even savage character and makes an excellent soldier; there should, therefore, be no doubt that with training he would soon develop first-rate soldierly qualities. His alleged laziness is due in part to his natural reserve, which allows more pushing races to outstrip him, and in part to the simplicity of his life, and to the absence of any spur to industry in a land where the climate supplies out of its own superabundance the greater part of his few simple wants—a land which to him is a veritable 'island of fruits,' of 'bowery hollows crowned with summer sea.' It must be remembered, too, that before the advent of the British the employment by his rulers of the *krah* or *corvée* system, as well as the wide prevalence of debt-slavery, made it difficult for the average Malay to reap the reward of his labour.

Among the institutions of the Malay race which it shares more or less with other races in the same region are the use of sea-canoes (*prahus*,[1] once associated with piracy), the building of houses on piles (inland as well as on the border of tidal rivers), the use of the blowpipe with poison-tipped darts (now practically confined to the aborigines), and the *kris*, the *sarong* (the national Malay plaid skirt-like garment, closely corresponding to the kilt of our own Highlanders, though worn somewhat longer on the western seaboard of the peninsula), the filing, gold-plating, and blackening of the teeth (now all but completely obsolete customs), the use of the *balei*, or council-hall (now confined to Rajas), and a strong belief in animism. In spite of being animists at heart, however, the Malays are not infrequently more or less bigoted Muhammadans, being in this respect at the very antipodes to the Battak of Sumatra, who have a literature of their own, and who are still to some extent inclined to be cannibals.

The Malay traditions and romances contain distinct references to human sacrifices, which would appear to have lasted until the advent of the British. The men show mechanical skill of a high order, and would probably respond readily to a more advanced training especially in engineering. Many are still adept in manual arts, notably in those belonging to the jungle and the sea.

The material culture of the Malay is of the insular Malayan (chiefly Sumatran) character. It has never been influenced by Hinduism to such an extent as, for instance, the culture of Java (as exemplified in the architecture of Borobudur and other famous temples of ancient date in that island). The Malays are skilled and artistic craftsmen in certain arts, though in others they are somewhat conspicuously backward. Their textile work reaches a high standard, and they display considerable ingenuity in their weaving processes and in combining their dyed threads to produce elaborate and often intricate patterns, among which a variety of check patterns predominate. In metal-work, especially in the working of silver, their taste is, under favourable circumstances, less florid than the Indian and less coarse than the Chinese. In ornamenting metal and damascening, in inlaying, and especially in niello-work, their work, both in design and in technique, is excellent of its kind. Distinction in such branches of metallurgy as the manufacture of blades for their krisses, and other weapons, is rare, though not non-existent; a high degree of skill in the adornment of the hilts of weapons and the sheaths in which they are kept is appreciably common. They pay special attention to the manufacture of waved kris-blades, and their damascene-work is a technical process of considerable elaboration, the more so because the proportions and even, in some cases, the ornamentation of the blade are determined by an elaborate set of rules governing the dimensions and intended properties of the various portions. These rules are not entirely technical, though compliance with them requires some degree of technical skill, but are in part magical, and designed to secure excellence in the blade and success in its employment. Similar rules are sometimes applied in a lesser degree to the *parang* (woodman's knife). Metal casting by the *cire perdue* process is known and employed not only for copper but also for white metal or *tutenague* (sometimes popularly called 'tooth and egg' metal). Coins (round cash) were formerly cast on the east coast in the form of 'cash-trees,' from which the cash were snipped off, and before the British entered the country the superfluous tin was run into ingots shaped like elephants, crocodiles, cocks, etc., which were used as currency.[1] Time was reckoned by water-clock (as in India and Ceylon and also, it may be mentioned, in ancient Britain). Thus for the mains at cock-fights in Kedah it was kept by means of a

[1] These *prahus*, being roomy boats paddled by large numbers of men, and of extremely shallow draught, could habitually elude pursuit by men-of-wars' boats by slipping over the innumerable river-bars of the peninsula, and escaping into the network of salt-water creeks. It was not till the second half of the 19th cent. that the *prahu* was vanquished by the paddle-wheel.

[1] R. C. Temple, *The Obsolete Tin Currency and Money of the Federated Malay States*, Mazgaon, 1914 (reprinted from *IA*).

perforated half coco-nut shell set afloat in a water-bucket, and timed to sink in a definite period. Pottery is made both with and without the wheel, and also by moulding in a split trunk, but in a few places only, and is often crude; on the west, in some cases, Indian influence is traceable, the types being both graceful and artistic. In some cases hæmatite, which turns black on firing, is used as a varnish. The wide-spread use of bamboo and the palm-spathe bucket as a receptacle is, no doubt, responsible for the lack of a more extended development of fictile ware, in spite of the great abundance of clays suitable for porcelain. On the east coast generally, and less commonly on the west, mat-making is a fine art; at Malacca highly artistic baskets are made of twisted strips of pandanus. The woodwork of the Malays, as shown in the ornamentation of household utensils, as well as on the structural side of house and boat manufacture and furniture, is excellent, though as regards mere ornament it is decidedly scanty—the heart-breaking effect of the superficial Muhammadan veneer which has been imposed on the Malays from without. The further from such influences, the commoner such ornament becomes, and the better its quality. The Malays are especially ingenious in adapting means to ends and in conforming to the conditions of their surroundings; their houses are well adapted to the conditions of life of a jungle-dwelling race, whilst the seaworthy qualities of the Malay *prahu*, or sailing-boat, bear witness to the reputation of the Malay as a sailor.[1]

(*b*) *Aborigines.*—The culture of the wild tribes presents generally many features of similarity. The inland tribes are still nomads to some extent, existing largely by hunting, fishing, and the produce of their search for fruits and roots of the jungle. But most of them practise a primitive agriculture, sowing in a rude way small patches of rice or millet; their method of cultivating their half-wild orchard-trees, which grow as well in the jungle as elsewhere, is limited to throwing away in certain patches of the jungle the seeds or stones of the fruit they have eaten. The Sea Jakun are especially skilled in all devices for securing a livelihood along the foreshore, while the jungle tribes give evidence of a high degree of ingenuity in slaying and snaring their game by hunting and trapping.

The Semang are the most nomadic of the pagan tribes, though they are now taking to agriculture. Their typical clothing consists of a girdle of leaves or barkcloth, or, on festal occasions, a belt of shining black strings, made of the rhizomorph of a toadstool. Their typical habitations are of a primitive character, consisting of mere lairs, or rock-shelters, or of simple round or rectangular leaf-shelters planted on the ground or in trees. Those of a more developed type are large enough to shelter a whole tribe, each individual having a separate fire and bamboo sleeping-place. Frequently the head is more or less shaved and the teeth are filed to form a concave surface, possibly in accordance with a once usual Malay custom. They do not circumcise or (as a rule) chew betel, nor do they tatu or scarify the body. They have no boats, but use bamboo rafts on the river-reaches. Their most distinctive weapon is the bow with poisoned arrows; in fact, among the pagan tribes, the bow is, in the present writer's opinion, good *prima facie* evidence of Semang admixture; the northern Sakai, who also possess it, have most likely borrowed it from the Semang. Almost all, however, now also employ the bamboo blowpipe, of a different type from that of the Sakai, the idea of which has been copied, in all probability, from their Sakai neighbours.

The Semang have no organized body of chiefs, but each tribe has a single head-man. The tribes are organized in villages, each under a chief, to whom disputes are referred. Quarrels between villages were settled by meetings of these chiefs. Complete equality exists as between individuals, and all property is held in common. Crime is rare, and punishable generally by fines.

The Sakai, a mountain race, are still largely nomadic. Their habitations consist of tree huts and temporary shelters; their clothing is a loin-cloth of tree-bark, though they also decorate themselves on occasion with a girdle of leaves. They tatu the face and practise scarification and body-painting, and sometimes wear a porcupine quill or a metal ring through the nasal septum. Their distinctive weapon is the bamboo blowpipe. Agriculture is of a very primitive type, the principal implement being a digging-stick. They use neither boats nor rafts. The ornamentation of their implements, more especially the blowpipe and quiver, is considerably more artistic than that of the other aboriginal races.

Their social order, like that of the Semang, is of a primitive type; the only functionary is the *pĕnghulu* (Mal. 'head-man'),[1] who has every right over his tribe. Except when enforcing his position, however, he is only the equal of his fellow tribesmen. The office is hereditary, but, failing a direct heir, the *pĕnghulu* may appoint his successor during his lifetime. In their laws the penalty of death is reserved for murder, the relatives of the victim being the executioners. Cases of this kind are rare. For theft, also rare, the punishment is exclusion from the tribe. For other crimes the delinquent makes compensation, or pays a fine. Individual property does not exist, its place being taken by family property. The family as a unit cultivates the land, and the produce is shared between the members. The limits of the family property are designated by the *pĕnghulu*, and abandoned land may not be taken up without his consent.

A more highly developed social order exists among the Jakun, or aboriginal Malayans, as represented, *e.g.*, by the Southern Sakai, who show strong Malayan influences.

The Jakun are still to some extent a community of hunters, although among the Land Jakun agriculture is practised, more especially rice-planting. Their clothing resembles that of the Malays, but is scantier. They sometimes file their teeth to a point. Their typical weapon is a blowpipe of bamboo, or, as in Kuantan, uniquely made of two half cylinders of wood fitted together for the purpose—corresponding exactly to a form of blowpipe used in Peru. They have no bows. They use spears and cutlasses; in some cases they also carry sword and kris like the Malays. They live in huts built on piles and use 'dug-out' boats of hollowed tree-trunks, but on the river only, not on the sea. They still use face- and body-paint, but do not tatu or scarify the face. Their marriage customs include, like those of the Malays, 'bride-purchase,' the ceremony of eating together, and, in addition, the bride-chase, which takes place round a large bell-shaped mound, constructed for the occasion, or an ant-hill or tree, if the tribe is a land one, or in a dug-out canoe—the form which it took among the sea-gypsies (Orang Laut). Their social organization is of a distinctly higher type than that of either Semang or Sakai. The chief of their tribe, the *batin*, is the head of a group of villages, and has certain subordinate officers

[1] See H. Warington Smyth, 'Boats and Boat-building in the Malay Peninsula,' in *Journal of the Soc. of Arts*, 1902 (reprinted in *IA* xxxv. [1906] 97 ff.).

[1] *Pĕnghulu* = Mal. 'head-man' (from obs. Mal. *hulu* or *ulu*, 'head'). On the other hand, *pelima* or *pĕnglima* = Mal. 'hand-man' (from obs. Mal. *lima*, 'hand'), *i.e.* executive officer.

who represent or act for him upon occasion. Thus, among the Besisi of Langat, the *batin* is the arbiter of all disputes referred to him by the sub-chiefs, besides being the priest at marriages, the magician in cases of illness or disaster, and the judge whose duty it is to punish wrong-doing. His substitute is the *jinang*. Their subordinate, known as the *pĕnghulu balai*, has charge of the tribal feasts and councils, whilst the *jukrah* (probably=Mal. *jurukrah*, or 'corvée officer') is the summoner of the tribe; the *pĕnglima* is the *batin's* executive officer. Among the Benua each *batin* has authority within his own jurisdiction, but difficult or unusual cases are referred to a council composed of all the *batins*. In this division of the Jakun, as indeed among all, crime against personal property is rare, and is expiated by payment of fines in the form of coarse Chinese plates or saucers. One half of the fine goes to the *batin* and one half to the injured person. The office of *batin* descends, as a rule, from father to son, except among the Johor Jakun, where the eldest son has to be accepted by the tribe, and, if his brothers as well as himself are rejected, a stranger to the family is elected. If suitable, the sons of minor officials would be appointed by the *batin* to succeed their father. The inheritance of property was generally from father to children, but varied from tribe to tribe in the proportion assigned to sons and daughters or to wife and other relatives. Property held by a man before marriage among the Mantra was assigned on his death to his parents, brothers, and sisters.

4. **Languages.**—(*a*) *Malay.*—The Malay language belongs to the Malayo-Polynesian family, related forms of which occur sporadically over an amazingly vast insular area, extending from Formosa in the North to New Zealand in the South, and from Madagascar in the West to Easter Island in the Eastern Pacific.[1] Malay itself has, moreover, very considerable importance as a *lingua franca* over a great part of the same region. In recent years a connexion has been sought between the Malayo-Polynesian family of languages and a family of 'Austro-Asiatic' languages, including S.E. Asia, Muṇḍā (Central India), Khāsī (Assam), Mōn, or Talaing, and Khmer, or Cambodian (Indo-China), Nicobarese, and the aboriginal dialects of the Malay Peninsula; 'this connexion is now generally accepted.'[2] This fact would actually link up the Malayan language in prehistoric times with the corresponding element in the Sakai and Semang dialects of the peninsula. This theory is entirely the work of Schmidt; but C. O. Blagden's work[3] in tabulating the various elements in these aboriginal dialects first made this identification possible.

The Malay tongue, by which the standard speech of the peninsula and E.C. Sumatra is meant, is of an agglutinative character, the roots being, as a rule, unchanged, and new words being formed by means of affixes, infixes, and reduplication. The roots are mostly dissyllabic, and the derived words frequently very numerous, while any harsh juxtaposition of consonants is avoided, by means of either assimilation or dissimilation, following certain recognized euphonic rules.

From a phonetic point of view, Malay shows a remarkably small, almost a minute, number of changes during the last four centuries. At an earlier period it had, however, become morphologically simplified, analysis showing the development of the modern affix system out of an earlier and more restricted substratum of similar particles common to Malay itself and to the islands of the archipelago.[4]

The oldest foreign loan-words in Malay are Sanskrit, and include words for religious, moral, and intellectual ideas, with some astronomical, mathematical, and botanical terms, a court vocabulary, and a large number of everyday words.[5]

The plural is theoretically formed by reduplication, though, as a rule, in the vernacular speech no difference is made between plural and singular. Reduplication is, however, also employed to express a metaphorical meaning. Thus we have *orang*, 'person' or 'man' (whence *orang-utan*, 'man of the woods' or 'wild man'), but *orang-orang*, 'pupil of the eye' (corresponding to what are called, in Elizabethan literature, 'children,' or 'babies of the eye'); *kuching*, 'cat,' but *kuching-kuching*, 'biceps muscle' (from the play of the muscle; the Romans, by a curious antithetical metaphor, compared it to a little mouse—*musculus*). Similar metaphorical reduplications give us *kuda*, 'horse,' but *kuda-kuda*, 'wooden horse' or support (as in our own towel-horse); and *tupai*, 'squirrel,' but *tupai-tupai*, 'belaying pin' (on a mast, which is compared to a squirrel running up a tree).

With regard to the difficult question of the penultimate accent, Winstedt[1] (with H. van der Wall and Gerth van Wijk) has recently (1913) come to the conclusion that the stress falls, even in standard Malay, upon the penultimate syllable, both in the case of simple words and in words that are mere derivatives. In this he is probably correct, although it is far from being in accordance with the usually received opinion.

The Malay parts of speech frequently fail to coincide with our own: a root-word or radical, *e.g.*, may often be used either as a substantive or as an adjective, with complete indifference, and the same remark holds true of substantive and verb. Words which logically would have priority take precedence of those which should not do so. Thus the actual subject or thing talked about, having prior importance logically, precedes any word which is merely qualificatory; also the normal sentence-order is subject, verb, object. There is no inflexion for gender, number, or case, and the syntax is as simple as that of 'pidgin English.' Thus it has been accurately remarked that the lines,

'Little boy, box of paints,
Licked his toy, joined the Saints,'

would be verbose to a Malay, who would express it as follows:

'Little boy, box paint[s],
Lick[ed] toy, join[ed] Saint[s].'[2]

Similarly an up-country European traveller who happened to inquire whether there would be time for him to reach a neighbouring village before nightfall might be puzzled to receive by way of reply the mysterious monosyllabic 'Can' or 'Dark' (as the case might be), the meaning in the first case being that he could safely reckon on doing so, and in the second that night would fall before he reached his destination.

Malay may, therefore, be thought of—if such an expression may be allowed—as a kind of 'shorthand speech'—a fact which is the more remarkable because in the written literary language it often reaches the opposite extreme of exuberant verbosity.

The dialects of Malay are many and varied, but the three that are of most importance to the present subject are: (*a*) the dialect of Kelantan and Patani, (*b*) the dialect spoken in Nĕgri Sembilan (*i.e.* especially in Naning and Rembau), and (*c*) the Riau-Johor dialect (spoken in Selangor, Perak, Pahang, etc.). Of these the first is that which especially shows survivals from the Malayo-Polynesian tongue, to which reference was made above. This correspondence, moreover, is fairly close, as can be seen from the Maori *rua*=Malay *dua* ('two'); Maori *ika*=Malay *ikan* ('fish'); cf. even the Easter Island *mate*=Malay *mati* ('dead'); Malagasy *vulana*=Malay *bulan* ('moon'); Formosan *pidlak*=Malay *perak* ('silver').[3] Even New Guinea dialects (usually supposed to be free from Malay) contain some words of evident Malay origin. In view of other evidence, it seems permissible to believe that this particular Malay dialect of the east coast of the peninsula forms a much-needed link between standard Malay and the nearest Malayo-Polynesian languages, and, further, that it was from this precise district on the continental seaboard of south-eastern Asia that this Malayan dialect spread throughout the Polynesian islands. The corresponding social links are (*a*) their very similar kin-systems and (*b*) the general use of tabu.

(*b*) *Aboriginal dialects.*—The languages of the wild tribes are split up into a number of dialects, each confined to a relatively small area. They are rapidly disappearing, especially in the southern districts of the peninsula, their place being taken by Malay as the wild tribes become more nearly assimilated with Malays in status and culture under modern conditions. Setting aside purely local and unimportant differences, the linguistic material, scanty as it is in most cases, has been classified into three main groups, which may be referred to three principal types or standards: (i.) typical Semang dialects, best represented by the speech of the aborigines in central Kedah and the adjoining State of Raman; (ii.) typical Sakai dialects, the best specimens coming from south-eastern Perak and the adjoining district of Pahang; and (iii.) in the southern part of the peninsula, the Jakun dialects, which may be classed together as Jakun or Malayan in spite of the fact that they contain a large number of Sakai words, because the great bulk of their words are Malayan and not Sakai, although they do not afford material so favourable for clear type-differentiation as is found among the Sakai and Semang. Both in phonology and in vocabulary the Sakai and Semang show considerable divergence, but between the strongly contrasted type-dialects are intermediate variations, the linguistic evidence thus supporting the ethnological data in pointing to contact and admixture.

Roughly speaking, the dialects fall into groups which correspond, though not accurately, with the anthropological varieties of the aboriginal races, at least in the case of Sakai and Semang.

Of the affinities of the aboriginal languages and the elements which have entered into their composition something has already been said. It is clear that all the dialects as now spoken contain a considerable number of purely Malay words, more or less modified in pronunciation by the borrowers. In addition to these loan-words, however, which are easily identifiable, there is a considerable element remaining which is not traceable to standard Malay. The latter element, of which we have already spoken, was not developed within the peninsula, and this and the Malayo-Polynesian factor in the aboriginal dialects which is akin to the insular Malay spoken in the Malay Archipelago together make up what is perhaps the largest component in the languages of the aborigines. A third and still

[1] For illustration of this astonishingly wide range see below, p. 353[b].
[2] See above, p. 349, n. 2.
[3] W. W. Skeat and C. O. Blagden, *Pagan Races of the Malay Peninsula*, London, 1906, vol. ii. ch. iv. 'Language.'
[4] Winstedt, p. 12.
[5] W. Maxwell, *Malay Grammar*, London, 1888, Introd.

[1] P. 31. [2] Winstedt, p. 173. [3] See above, p. 353[a].

more interesting element has been proved to show a very close affinity with the Môn-Khmer or Môn dialects of western Indo-China. The identifications, though certain and numerous and even striking, are rather disappointing, if considered as a vocabulary percentage. Sidney Ray himself once remarked to the present writer: 'What is the use of our assuming [as certain scholars had done] that the Sakai dialects are identifiable with Môn, when all that has been identified is about 20 per cent of the entire vocabulary? The question is, what is the remaining 80 per cent?'

To reply, we must study attentively both the Semang and Sakai syntax structure and a considerable percentage of the vocabulary, and especially, as regards Sakai, the phonology; the modern Jakun dialects are of no less importance. In each group there remains an unidentified element. Semang embodies a number of words which are confined to the Negritos and which are completely *sui generis*. It is clear that the Semang dialects did not originally belong to the Môn-Annam group. These words relate to matters of everyday life, and presumably they represent the old original dialects of the Negritos. Relationship with Andamanese has been suggested, but remains completely hypothetical; for hardly a single word of Semang is recognizable in the Andaman dialects, and this fact is one of the many and great puzzles of the Semang problem. For the unidentified element in Sakai no suggestion as to origin has been made, though it is possible that many of the uncertain words may yet be traced not to a Malayan but to a Môn-Annam origin. In the case of the Jakun it is pointed out that some of the words of unknown origin occur in Semang, but not in Sakai, but they are hardly of sufficient number to support the view that Jakun dialects were originally allied to Semang; on the contrary, a large number of Jakun words are certainly allied to Sakai, and Wilkinson, treating as Jakun certain southern Sakai dialects, seeks to eliminate Blagden's linguistic Jakun, but leaves unexplained both Kĕnāboi and the common element in which Mantri, Beduanda, and Jakun differ from every other known language.

5. Religion: greater gods.—(*a*) *Malay.*—The official Malay religion, as has already been stated, is Muhammadanism, but the popular beliefs and ritual afford abundant proof, which is supported by the historical evidence, that this religion has been superimposed upon some form of Hinduism, which itself, when introduced into the country, superseded an earlier and more primitive type of belief, of shamanistic character. Folklore, charm-books, and romances go to show that the greater gods of the Malay pantheon—so far as their names go—are borrowed Hindu divinities, while the lesser gods and spirits are native to the Malay religious system, incorporated in and modified by the higher religions, but not entirely forgotten.

Taking first the Hindu divinities, we find Viṣṇu, the preserver, Brahmā, the creator, Batāra Guru[1] (Śiva), Kala,[2] and Seri[3] simultaneously invoked by the magician. Of the greater divinities Batāra Guru is, in the minds of the Malays, unquestionably the most important; in other words, the Malays were of the Śaivite sect of Brāhmanism. In the *Hikayat Sang Samba*, the Malay version of the *Bhaumakāvya*, Batāra Guru appears as the supreme god Śiva, with Brahmā and Viṣṇu as subordinate deities. He alone has the Water of Life which resuscitates slaughtered heroes. The Malay magician will, on occasion, boldly declare that he was the all-powerful spirit who held the place of Allāh before the advent of Muhammadanism, a spirit so powerful that he 'could restore the dead to life'; and that to him all prayers were addressed at that period. It may be noted that most of the theological terms in use among the Malays are of Sanskrit origin, and that the titles Sang-yang ('the deity') and Batāra are used mostly of the older Hindu divinities. The Malays, however, in adopting the Sanskrit title of Guru, seem to have transferred it to a hunting-god, whom they identify in certain localities with the 'Spectre,' or 'Demon Huntsman,' though pure Hinduism would certainly not have recognized hunting (one of the deadly sins of that religion) as a pursuit fit for one of their deities. Further, the Malays distinguish between a good and a bad side of Batāra Guru's character, which may point back to the combination into one of what were originally two distinct personalities, Batāra Guru and Kala. Thus the Malay Kala holds as his only definite sphere of influence the foreshore, a strip intermediate between the land-sphere of Batāra Guru and the dominion of a third deity called 'Grand-Sire Long-Claws' (Toh Panjang Kuku). This attempt to divide the spheres of land and sea must again be attributed solely to the Malays, as Hindu mythology knows nothing of the sea. It is clear, therefore, that in the greater deities of the Malayan pantheon we may, after all, recognize Malayan deities simply re-named after the gods of the Hindus. The Batāra Guru of the sea is identified by some magicians with Si Raya, and occasionally with the god of mid-currents (Mambang Tali Harus). Sickness is sometimes ascribed to him, but it is not usually so fatal as illness induced by the malice of the Demon Huntsman, and fishermen and seafarers, on the other hand, obtain from him many benefits. The only other deities of importance are the White Divinity, who dwells in the sun, the Black Divinity, who dwells in the moon, and the Yellow Divinity, who dwells in the sunset; the last is considered most dangerous to children, and Malayan parents always endeavour to keep their children within doors at sunset and during the twilight in order to avoid his malignant influence.

[1] *Guru*=spiritual guide. Batāra is Skr. *bhaṭṭāra*, 'highly honourable'; in Jav. (Manjapahit) and Sej. Mal. it='king.'

[2] Skr. *kāla*, 'black,' an epithet of Śiva.

[3] Skr. Śrī, goddess of good fortune and wife of Viṣṇu.

(*b*) *Pagan races.*—In view of the still inadequate evidence of the beliefs of the pagan tribes in relation to a supreme deity, it is necessary to exercise some caution in making any statement as to their ideas upon the subject. On the other hand, it is at least safe to remark that any one who, as the result of mere worrying by questions, commits himself to the statement that any of these pagan races have no such beliefs whatever proves merely that his own methods of investigation are at fault in these matters.

It appears, moreover, clear that the Semang and Jakun, and possibly also the Sakai, are at present in the stage of development, common to most primitive peoples, in which the supreme deity belongs to the realm of mythology rather than of religion proper. Since he stands more or less aloof from the affairs of this world and the next, and possesses no cult, his claims to recognition are set aside in favour of spirits more closely in touch with mundane affairs, whose powers for good and evil are constantly capable of exercise and who at every turn must be propitiated. Among the Semang there is clear evidence for a belief in the existence of such a being, combined with a crude dualism based upon natural phenomena.

According to one account, Tā' Pönn ('Grandfather Pönn') is a powerful but benevolent being described as the maker of the world. He was, in fact, described to the present writer by the Semang of Kedah as being 'like a Malay Raja; there was *nobody above him*.' He is the moon's husband and lives with Āg-Āg, the crow who is the sun's husband, in the eastern heavens. Tā' Pönn has four children, two male and two female. His mother Yāk is the old Earth-mother, and lives underground in the middle of the earth. He has a great enemy, Kakuh, who lives in the west. He is dangerous and very black. That is why the east is bright and the west dark. The heavens are in three tiers, the highest of which is called Kakuh, and which are defended against unauthorized intrusion by a giant coco-nut monkey, who drives away any one found trying to enter the heavens.

The naturalistic dualism of this account is obvious; from his place of abode, and from his having the moon as his consort, we may perhaps conclude that Tā' Pönn is a spirit of the rising sun. In addition it has been maintained that the Semang recognize two other superior deities, Kari, a thunder-god, the supreme creator, ruler, and judge, and Ple, a related but subordinate divinity, who, under Kari, created earth and man. The evidence, however, is too slender for dogmatic statement, and the point still awaits the collection of further material.

The religion of the Sakai is more shamanistic in character than that of the Semang, and, if any corresponding belief exists among them, as has been maintained, it is overshadowed by the cults of demons, ghosts, and spirits. The Jakun afford more certain evidence of a belief in a supreme deity, although their conceptions at the best are vague and shadowy. The Mantri say that Tuhan Di-Bawah, lord of the under world, created the earth and dwells beneath it, supporting everything above him by his power. The Benua believe in one god, Pirman,[1] who dwells above the sky and is invisible. He made the world and everything that is visible. The greater part of the Jakun of Johor know and acknowledge a supreme being whom they call by the Malayo-Arabic name of Tuhan Allāh; the grotesquely slight influence, however, that is really exercised by Muhammadanism on the wild races of the Malayan jungles is best evidenced by the statement of those tribes who believe that Muhammad, the prophet of God, is the wife of the supreme deity.

6. Lesser gods, spirits, and ghosts.—(*a*) *Malay.*—Subordinate to the great gods are lesser gods or spirits whose place in Malay mythology is due to Muhammadan influences; their inferiority may in part be due to the law that the gods of the autochthones are usually considered by an invader more powerful than his own deities. These lesser gods and spirits are the *jin*, or genii. The Malays, to a certain extent, show a tendency to identify them with the spirits of the older Hindu religion, but only the Black King of the Genii (Sang Gala[2] Raja) appears to rise on occasion to the level of the great divinities, when he is regarded as a manifestation of Batāra Guru in his destructive aspect as Śiva, or Kala, though later he came to be considered a separate personality. This would also explain the difficult problems of how the Black and White Genii come to be regarded as brothers, the latter being identified with Mahārāja Deva, 'great king of the gods.' The genii are also subdivided into good and faithful (*jin islām*) and bad (*jin kāfir*), this nomenclature being obviously a Muslim accretion. In addition to these subdivisions they are also regarded as attached to special objects—*e.g.*, the powerful *jin* of the royal musical instruments. The genii are able to do infinite harm to mortals, and choose as their dwelling-places hollows in the hills, solitary places in the forests, dead epiphytes on trees, etc. They are sometimes said to derive from the dissolution of various parts of the anatomy of the world-snake Sakatimuna, the first great failure at man's creation.

The Malays have also adopted into their popular religion the Muhammadan belief in angels (Azrael, Michael, and Gabriel), prophets (Solomon, David, and Joseph), and chiefs, four in number penned in the four corners of the earth.

Ghosts and spirits are known by the generic name of *hantu*. Of these there are many varieties. *Hantu kubor* are grave-demons who, with the spirits of murdered men, prey upon the living whenever they see an opportunity; *hantu ribut* is the storm-fiend; *hantu ayer* and *hantu laut* are water- and sea-spirits; *hantu rimba*, deep forest demons; *hantu běrok*, the baboon-demon; *hantu bělian*, the tiger-demon; and *hantu songkei*, the 'loosening' demon, who interferes with rope-snares and traps for wild animals. In addition there are giants and 'tall' demons (*bota*, *gasi-gasi*, and *hantu tinggi*) as well as 'good people' (*bidadari* or *pěri*), who are of foreign origin; echo[3] spirits (*orang bunyian*), spirits of whom little is known except that they are good fairies and very easily cheated; blood-sucking demons of various kinds, mostly birth-spirits (these last being certainly among the ghastliest conceptions of humanity); and others such as the *hantu kopek*, which is the equivalent of our own nightmare.

(*b*) *Pagan races.*—Except in one or two cases, little has been recorded concerning the beliefs of the pagan tribes relating to the spirits or demons. Those which most afflict the Sakai of Ulu-Bertam are the 'tiger-spirit,' the 'jungle-spirit,' and the 'river- or water-spirit.' Against these charms and simples can prevail. Against the tree-spirit, however, who slays his victims before any one can help, there is no protection. The Sakai of Selangor had a ceremony at which they sat and blew bamboo pipes and sang to the demons.

The spirits in which the Běsisi believe include the wind-demon (*jin angin*), who lives on a white rock near Tanjong Tuan (Cape Rachado); the demonic legion (*jin sa-ribu*), who dwell in the earth and, when possible, feed upon human beings; and the garrotting demon (*jin sa-rapat*), who lives in the uplands. Certain trees are the embodiment of spirits, notably the gutta, eagle wood, and camphor trees, and this idea is extended to inert objects—*e.g.*, canoes, treasure-jars, and stone implements. Chipping a jar kills its spirit.

The Demon Huntsman (*hantu si buru*) is ten ft. high, and his face is very hairy. From nightfall onwards during the full of the moon he hunts the wild boar and the *sambhar*-deer. Although he is highly dangerous to mankind, many have made friends with him, and, when they have invoked him, he has cured them of their illness. Other spirits are the river-spirit, the demon of fatal birth-sickness, and the tomb-demon, which, in one of its manifestations, plunders graves in the form of wild beasts, such as deer and tigers.

7. The soul.—(*a*) *Malay.*—In Malay beliefs the *sěmangat* ('human soul') is a thin, unsubstantial mannikin, temporarily absent from the body in sleep, trance, or disease, and permanently departed after death. It is about the size of the thumb and invisible, but is supposed to correspond in shape, proportion, and complexion to its embodiment; it can fly quickly from place to place, and it is often, perhaps metaphorically, addressed as a bird. In mental attributes it is quasi-human and may possess, independently of its corporeal owner, personal consciousness and volition. It has been alleged that the *sěmangat* cannot be the 'soul' because it is believed to quit the body and wander about during sleep, and that it must therefore be a spirit of vitality. But this very same reasoning would show that it cannot be a spirit of vitality. What is actually meant here by 'soul,' however, is the native (and our own mediæval) idea of the soul, which is something very different from the soul of our modern idealistic Christianity. The latter might indeed almost be described, in comparison with its mediæval prototype, as a 'super-soul,' and it is only the more primitive idea of the soul in which we are here interested.

In charms it is addressed as having a house, usually, though not necessarily, identified with its embodiment (the body of its owner). As the *sěmangat* is separable from the body, it follows that, if called in the right way, it may be made to follow—a powerful weapon in the hands of an enemy or lover who possesses the requisite magical powers. When abducted, it may be imprisoned in a lump of earth, a cloth, or a wax mannikin. The lump of earth should have been in contact with the victim's body—*e.g.*, with the sole of the naked foot. An escaping or swooning *sěmangat* may be recalled to the owner's body; hence the form of certain kinds of medical treatment. In the older charms

[1] But this name (=*Firmān*, 'Word of God') is clearly borrowed, like Allāh, from Muslim sources.
[2] Possibly Skr. *śaṅkara*, 'beneficent,' an epithet of Śiva.
[3] Or 'hidden.'

the *sĕmangat* is distinctly referred to as being sevenfold, and, as a similar multiple division is found elsewhere among savages (*PC*[4] i. 391 f.),[1] this may be taken as original, although seven is a somewhat favourite number in Malay magic.

The belief in the existence of *sĕmangats* does not confine them to human beings. Animal, vegetable, and mineral *sĕmangats* are clearly recognized. While in the case of animals the *sĕmangat* is a counterpart, on a reduced scale, of its embodiment, in the vegetable and mineral kingdoms the tree *sĕmangat* or the ore *sĕmangat* is usually an animal, whereas the rice *sĕmangat* is treated as resembling a human infant. The *sĕmangat* of the eaglewood tree, *e.g.*, takes the form of a bird, the tin-ore *sĕmangat* that of a buffalo, the gold-ore *sĕmangat* that of a deer, and so forth. A box or a treasure-jar may also have a *sĕmangat* until chipped or broken, when the *sĕmangat* escapes from it. An interesting variation has been said to occur on the east coast of the peninsula, where the *sĕmangat* of a particular kind of boat is called by a special name, *mayor*, as opposed to the usual soul-name, *sĕmangat*.[2] But there is no trace of this form on the west coast or apparently in other parts of the peninsula.

This creed is no empty belief inoperative in daily life. It forms the basis of the Malay's mental attitude and practice in all dealings with the animal, vegetable, and mineral kingdoms.

Although Malay animism is consistent and complete in extending the belief in the *sĕmangat* to all nature, animate and inanimate, side by side with the purely animistic belief there is abundant evidence of a special Circe-like theory attributing animals, birds, fishes, reptiles, and trees to an (accursed) human origin. The elephant, tiger, bear, deer, crocodile, solid-crested hornbill, and stick-insect are examples. Evidence of such anthropomorphic ideas is to be found not only in the folklore but in many magical ceremonies and charms of Malaya (on the *sĕmangat* see, further, INDONESIANS).

(*b*) *Pagan races.*—Of the conception of the *sĕmangat* held by the pagan tribes very little is known, and, lacking definite statement, their beliefs must be inferred from their methods of burial and treatment of the dead and their views of the life after death.

According to the eastern Semang (Pangan) of Kelantan, each man has a *sĕmangat* shaped exactly like himself, but 'red like blood' and 'no bigger than a grain of maize.' It was passed on by the mother to her child. After death the *sĕmangats* of the wise proceed to a paradise in the west in which grow fruit-trees. To reach it they cross a bridge consisting of the trunk of a colossal tree. At the end of the bridge sits a hideous demon, and such of the Semang as are scared by him fall into a vast boiling lake beneath, in which they swim for three years until the Lord of the Paradise of Fruit-Trees lets down his great toe for them to clutch, and in this contemptuous fashion pulls them out. The old and wise men for this reason were buried in trees, so that they could fly over the demon's head. The western Semang believed that only the medicine-men went to the Land of Fruit; the lay members of the tribe crossed the sea to a land of screw-pines and thatch-palms, wherein was the hole into which the sun fell at night. If they had committed any bad action, they started by the same road, but turned north to a land which had two months of day and one month of night. Among the Sakai it has been

[1] See also W. W. Skeat, *Malay Magic*, London, 1900, pp. 50, 411, etc. It is surprising to find among Malays this sevenfold division of Plato himself.

[2] N. Annandale, 'The Theory of Souls among the Malays of the Malay Peninsula,' *JRAS*, Straits Branch, v. 3 [1909].

said that *sĕmangats* proceed to a Hades (*Nĕrāka*[1]) where they are washed clean by one 'Granny Long-Breasts,' and made to walk across a boiling cauldron on the sharp edge of a chopper. Bad *sĕmangats* fall in, good ones escape to an Island of Fruit, where they wait until a friend comes to show them the way to the 'Husks of the Clouds.'

The Mantri possess peculiarly positive faith in the continued existence of the *sĕmangat* after death. It leaves the body and is carried by Bayang Lasa either to Ngangnari or to Fruit Island (*Pulau Buah*), far away in the region of the setting sun, where all *sĕmangats* dwell in harmony, marry, and have children. Those who die a violent death go to Red Land (*Tanah Merah*), a desert place and barren, repairing thence to Fruit Island to get their nourishment. The Benua, on the other hand, believe that after death the *sĕmangat* dissolves into nothingness again, having been fashioned from air by Pirman. Notwithstanding this, they hold that the *sĕmangats* of medicine-men, while their animate bodies remain behind, are conveyed or carried to heaven in music.

8. Animism.—Although it would in any case be justifiable to regard the attitude of the Malays towards the *kĕrāmat*, or holy place, as a survival from an earlier stage of religious belief on the analogy of similar ideas among more primitive peoples, there is, in addition, abundant evidence to support the view that not only Muhammadanism, but also the popular ideas traceable to a modified Hinduism, are superimposed upon a form of religion in which animism was the predominant factor. A belief in spirits pervades the whole of the every-day life of the bulk of the people. The position and importance of the medicine-man or magician (*pawang* and *bomor*), the language of the innumerable charms recited on any and every conceivable occasion, and the ceremonies which accompany any and every action or undertaking—even in some cases the most trivial—would in themselves point to this particular conclusion, even if we lacked the evidence supplied by the statements of the Malays themselves with regard to their object and meaning. Important proof of this connexion is furnished by the relations of the Malays with animals, with trees, and with the crops, and especially by their remarkable beliefs with regard to mining.

(*a*) *Animals.*—To nearly all animals, but especially to the larger, the Malays attribute anthropomorphic traits and, in some cases, superhuman powers. The elephant and tiger, *e.g.*, are believed to possess cities or districts in which they assume human form and live in houses. According to a legend which comes from Labu in Selangor, a man tracked an elephant to her home and married her in human form. She resumed her animal form when, on returning to his country against her express directions, he gave her food which included certain young tree-shoots. The tiger, which is an object of especial fear, is believed to be a demon in the form of a beast; in the legendary 'Tiger Village' the roofs of the houses are thatched with human hair, men's bones are the rafters, and men's skins the hut-walls. The original tiger was a boy found in the forest who changed into a tiger when beaten with many stripes by his schoolmaster. The latter placed a ban upon him to compel him to 'ask for' his prey. The tiger therefore uses divination by leaves (of certain forest trees) to ascertain whether his petition for a victim has been granted. It may be added that he is also believed to doctor his wounds with leaf-poultices. The belief in wer-tigers is one of the most deeply ingrained of Malay superstitions, but the power to become such a being is believed to belong especially

[1] Skr. *naraka*, 'hell.'

to one tribe of Sumatrans, the Korinchi Malays, of whom there are a number living in the peninsula. In one case a dead wer-tiger was identified by his possessing a gold tooth derived from his human original (see LYCANTHROPY). Both ghost-elephants and ghost-tigers are strongly believed in. They are distinguished by having one shrunken foot, are harmless, and are the tutelary spirits of certain regions of sacred localities. The most famous ghost-tigers of the peninsula dwelt on Mount Ophir (4000 ft.), near Malacca; in Selangor they were the guardians of a shrine on the summit of the Jugra Hill. The latter were formerly reputed to be the pets of the princess of Malacca; thus the two stories were connected. The princess is said by local report to have established herself on Mount Ophir at the time of the Portuguese invasion, and still visits the hill in Selangor, accompanied by a handsome tiger, though herself invisible. When a tiger was killed, a public reception was accorded to him in the nearest village, at which he was treated as a powerful war-chief or champion, and was entertained by an exhibition of dancing and fencing. Both claws and whiskers of the tiger are greatly valued as charms; the latter are sometimes twisted up with a man's moustache, to strike terror into his enemies, and the former are imitated in the tiger's claw knives worn on their fingers by the men who pretend to be wer-tigers.

Equally significant are the stories and beliefs connected with the mouse-deer or chevrotain. This animal occupies the place of Brer Rabbit in Malay folklore;[1] it figures in numberless proverbial sayings and romances, and is honoured by the title of Mentri Bĕlūkar, 'the Vizier of the (secondary) Forest-growth.' In the fire-getting ceremony it is said to ask for fire wherewith to 'singe its mother-in-law's feathers' (a bird).

Hunting dogs are continually addressed as if they were human beings. It is, however, believed that it is unlucky to see them in the jungle, unless the person meeting them barks after the manner of a wild dog before they have time to do so. Cats, in addition to possessing supernatural powers (*e.g.*, in the rain-making ceremony), are lucky because they wish for the prosperity of their owners. On the other hand, cat-killers, when in purgatory, will be required to cut and carry coco-nut logs to the number of hairs on the cat's body, wherefore cats are not 'killed,' but only set adrift on rafts to perish of hunger.[2]

The flesh of swine is now regarded as unclean by the modern (Muhammadan) Malay, but there are indications that this was not always the case; thus a wild pig's paunch is required in a Malay recipe for turning brass into gold; the wild pig, moreover, is hunted and eaten with avidity by the wild jungle tribes, as is still the case in N. Borneo and other parts of the Malayan region. It may also be noted that the flesh of the buffalo is preferred to that of the ox, and the former is used, and not the latter, for sacrificial feasts—a fact which suggests an obscure survival of Hindu belief. The earth itself is supported on the horn of a gigantic wild buffalo.

The attitude of the Malays towards wild animals and their belief in their magical powers are further indicated by the fact that in hunting and trapping no skill can avail unless it is itself supported by magic, by special charms supplied by the medicine-man, and by formulæ to be repeated in setting the traps and snares or when actually engaged in hunting operations, either to ensure success or to serve as a protection. Like the Siamese elephant-wizard, the Malay deer-wizard himself must first enter the toils before a hunt begins, in order to influence the deer magically to enter the deer-snares. If this were omitted, the ropes would fail to hold the deer, nor would the deer enter. The marks on the legs of the *sambhar* deer (*rusa*) are due to ulcers on the legs of its human original.

Fish and other inhabitants of the water, like land animals, are regarded as having human or superhuman qualities, and, when catching them, the Malays have to perform ceremonies to overcome their spiritual nature and magical powers. The crocodile, *e.g.*, is, according to one account, a boy who fell from his mother's arms into the water. The various species of fish also have their special origin; one kind is said to be originally a cat, another a monkey, another a human being drowned in the river, and so forth. The Norse myth of the rivers sprung from the teats of the cow Auðhumla is recalled by a Perak story of a large specimen of the mudfish called *aruan*. Many magical or semi-magical beliefs cling round the crocodile. In many of the rivers certain crocodiles are regarded as the sacred embodiment of dead chiefs, and are free from molestation. When hunting these reptiles, the Malays repeat charms and take precautions to secure capture by symbolic actions such as striking the water with the canoe-paddle in imitation of the crocodile's tail; or, when eating curry, by gulping down three lumps of rice successively in the way in which it is hoped the reptile will take the bait; or (by avoidance) by not taking the bones of curry-meats for fear that the wooden cross-piece buried in the bait will fail to hold the crocodile.

An elaborate ceremony precedes and accompanies a fishing expedition. It includes notification by three loud cries to the land-spirits that offerings, consisting of rice, betel, parts of a goat sacrificed for the purpose, cigarettes, etc., hung up on a tree in a sacrificial tray, await their acceptance, and the offering of two similar trays, one in shallow water and one, containing the goat's head, at the seaward end of the fishing stakes. Miscellaneous offerings from a basket are scattered while the boat is rowed out to the stakes, and, when they are reached, saffron-coloured and parched rice is scattered on the water, while the 'neutralizing rice-paste' ceremony is performed on the stakes and the boats. A number of tabus, such as seven days' refraining from sexual indulgence, the avoidance of bathing without a bathing-cloth, or of taking an umbrella into the fishing-boats, or of climbing the fishing-stakes with boots on, are strictly enforced. The use of a tabu language by the fishermen is also *de rigueur*.

Among the wild tribes similar beliefs are entertained, but in particular they look upon animals as the embodiment of their illustrious dead. The elephant, the largest and most important of the animals, is the one into which the *sĕmangats* of Semang chiefs are supposed to migrate. In consequence, it has euphemistic and propitiatory names. The same applies to the tiger. Monkeys, snakes, and birds play an important part in Semang mythology, while among insects the stick-insect is the most important. The list of animals to which the *sĕmangats* of chiefs are supposed by the Bĕsisi to migrate is extended beyond beasts of prey, including deer and pigs as well as tigers and crocodiles. Among the Mantri the tigers are the slaves of the wizard, or *poyang*, and are supposed to be immortal, while the Jakun believe that, if a tiger meets them in their path, it is a man who has sold himself to the evil spirit in order that in such a form he may wreak vengeance on his enemy or give play to his malignity. The amount of *un*-natural history associated with animals is, indeed, quite remarkable for a race whose jungle knowledge is so complete as it is among real up-country Malays. The case of the large caterpillar which is believed to metamorphose into a squirrel is typical.

(*b*) *Birds.*—Ideas of various kinds, mostly animistic or anthropomorphic in character, are very generally associated with birds by the Malays. As a rule, nocturnal birds are ill-omened. If one species of owl alights near a house and hoots, it is said that

[1] W. W. Skeat, *Fables and Folktales from an Eastern Forest*, Cambridge, 1901, Introd. p. xiii.
[2] Clifford, p. 47.

there will soon be a 'tearing of cloth' for a shroud. If the *băberek*, a nocturnal bird which flies in flocks (a goat-sucker or night-jar), is heard, the peasant brings out a wooden platter, beats it with a knife, and calls out, 'Great-grandfather, bring us their hearts,' in the hope of deluding the spirits into the belief that he forms one of the train of the Spectre Huntsman (*hantu pĕmburu*) which these birds accompany, and must therefore not be attacked by them.

The argus pheasant (*kuang*) is said in Perak to have been metamorphosed from a woman; the female, moreover, is believed to reproduce its kind by swallowing the male bird alive. In Selangor it is believed that a hornbill was transformed from the murderer of an old man, another variety (*rhinoplax*) to have been a man who slew his own mother-in-law. The *toh katampi* (a variety of horned owl) is believed to enter the fowl-house and there live on the intestines of fowls, which it extracts during life by means of a charm. The luck-bird—a small white bird about the size of a canary—if caught and placed in a rice-bin, ensures a good harvest to its owner; a ground-dove, kept in a house, is a prophylactic against fire. If any one is fortunate enough to secure the nest of a kind of heron, or *ruwak-ruwak*, it confers upon him the power of invisibility. But the list of birds to which it has been recorded that the Malays attach peculiar ideas and significance may be said to be limited only by the varieties indigenous to the peninsula.

In fowling, as in hunting, sympathetic magic plays a prominent part, while every operation has its appropriate charm for repetition. In catching wild pigeons, constant reference is made to their *sĕmangats*, and the aid of the *pawang* is required to perform the 'neutralizing rice-paste' ceremony in the space in front of the conical snarer's hut, enclosed for the purpose, which is known as King Solomon's Court-yard, or to recite a charm over the long bamboo decoy-tube or pigeon-call. During the operation great care is taken that no part of the snarer's paraphernalia is called by its proper name (which might be understood by the pigeon); everything is called by some euphemism—*e.g.*, 'the Magic Prince' (for the name of the hut) and 'Prince Distraction' (instead of the word 'pigeon-call').

(*c*) *Vegetation.*—The Malayan beliefs in relation to trees and other forms of vegetation follow to a great degree, if not entirely, their concepts in relation to animals. It is not clear that they hold that all trees have a *sĕmangat*, but it is certain that some trees, such as the durian, the coco-nut-palm, the trees producing eagle-wood, camphor, and gutta-percha, and others are supposed to possess *sĕmangats*. This belief extends even to dead and seasoned wood, as is shown by the invocation addressed to the timbers used in the ceremony of launching a boat—a ceremony which is frequently represented in Malay romances as taking place (as formerly in Fiji) over human rollers. In earlier days the men used to try to frighten the durian groves into bearing by threats addressed to them verbally. The medicine-man struck the trunk of an unfruitful tree seven times with a hatchet and threatened to fell it if it did not bear. The toddy collector said to the coco-nut-palm: 'Thus I bend your neck and roll up your hair; and here is my ivory toddy-knife to help the washing of your face.'[1] The malacca cane is regarded from the same animistic point of view, and it is believed that a cane with a long joint will protect the owner from harm by snakes and animals, as well as bring him good luck in everything. In Selangor the stick-insect is supposed to be the embodiment of the malacca cane-spirit. In felling a *tualang* tree (apparently not a specific tree, but a generic term for all trees containing a bees' nest)—a matter in which great reluctance is shown—it is necessary to obtain the services of a *pawang* to drive away demons by charms and incantations. In the course of the incantation the heads of two white fowls are cut off and the blood is sprinkled upon the tree-trunks. The lime is another tree of which the spirit is the object of a special cult; it is revered and looked upon as their chief patron by the theatrical players of Penang. In searching for the diseased and perfumed wood known as *gharu*, or eagle-wood, the services of a *pawang* are required to burn incense and repeat the appropriate charms. According to one account, the *pawang* uses a shelter near the selected tree (which is indicated by a low whispering or singing in the tree), and then repeats a charm which induces the *gharu*-spirit to appear to him, generally in a dream, and to inform him of the kind of sacrifice required. When the tree has been felled, any one passing between the trunk and the stump will die immediately. The *pawang* uses and carries with him a piece of eagle-wood, the *gharu mĕrupa* (or shaped eagle-wood), which possesses a natural resemblance to some animal or bird. This is believed to contain the *sĕmangat* of the eagle-wood and to assist in the search for that product. Similar beliefs are entertained, and similar ritual is followed, in the collection of camphor and gutta-percha. It is interesting to note that in the collection of camphor a special language must be used, *pantang kapur*, which, so far as known, is Malay in part only. A portion of any food eaten during the search for camphor must be thrown into the jungle for the *bisan*, or camphor-spirit.

Many rules followed in planting the crops are based upon sympathetic magic and animism. In the first place, the propitious season for each operation must be indicated by the *pawang*. Sugar-cane must be planted at noon; this makes it sweeter by drying up the juice and leaving the saccharine matter. Maize should be planted with a full stomach, a thick stick, and thick dibble; this will swell the maize ear. Plantains should be planted after the evening meal, as they fill out better; sweet potatoes, to ensure their having plenty of 'eyes' when they begin to sprout, should be set when the night is starry.

Of all agricultural pursuits, however, the cultivation of rice exhibits most completely the animistic ideas which underlie the relation of the Malays to nature. At every stage of the procedure precautions are taken to ensure the well-being and prosperity of the rice-soul, upon which the success of the cultivation depends.

The time of the sowing is determined by the *pawang*; prayers are read over a portion of the seed at the mosque (replacing an earlier ceremony at the holy place, or *kĕrămat*); in sowing, the mother-seed is placed in a specially-prepared bed in one corner of the nursery-plot before the rest of the seed is scattered. When the rice is ready, it is transplanted with proper propitiatory ceremonies, and occasionally, say once in three or four years, these were accompanied by a ceremony—a sort of mock combat (*singketa*)—to drive off evil spirits. When the rice is ready for reaping, in order to begin the harvest, the reapers must first obtain the *pawang's* permission. The first operation was to take the *sĕmangat* out of all the plots, and before cutting the rice it was usual to sprinkle it with the neutralizing rice-paste. From the spot where the rice is finest and where there are seven joints to the stalk, seven stems are clipped ceremonially to be the *sĕmangat* of the rice-crop. Another handful is tied by the *pawang* in the centre with a strip of a special variety of sugar-cane, to be the mother of the rice-crop of the year following. This mother-sheaf should be reaped last, preferably by the wife of the owner. The *sĕmangat* was made into the shape of an infant dressed in swaddling clothes, placed in a basket with a Malay umbrella to shade it from the sun, and laid on a new sleeping-mat, with pillows at its head, in the house of the owner. For three days the people in the house must observe certain tabus; *e.g.*, rice, salt, oil, money, etc., must not leave the house, perfect quiet must be observed, hair must not be cut, and so forth. These tabus were practically identical with those imposed in the case of the birth of children. For three days after the taking of the *sĕmangat* the

[1] Skeat, *Malay Magic*, p. 217.

mother-sheaf was treated as a young mother; *i.e.*, young shoots of trees were pounded and scattered over it every evening, and on the evening of the third day coco-nut pulp and goat-flowers mixed with sugar were eaten and a little ejected from the mouth on to the sheaf—an analogue of the salad administered to a mother. A woman, when entering the clearing, must kiss the stalks, saying, 'Come, come,[1] soul of my child,' as if embracing one of her own infants. Ultimately the rice obtained from the *sĕmangat* (representing the child) and from the sheaf (representing the mother) are mixed and placed in the receptacle in which rice is stored, together with a wreath of the straw of the first ceremonial pounding of the *padi*, the ears first pounded being those cut immediately after the taking of the *sĕmangat*. Some is mixed with next year's seed, and some is used to make the *tĕpong tawar*.[2]

From all that has been said it will be clear that the gist of the Malayan harvest ceremony consists in the attempt to simulate, on behalf of the vegetative rice-crop, a lucky birth as of a human infant, in the hopes that this mock-ceremony may stimulate the productive powers of the rice-plant for the following harvest.

(*d*) *Mining.*—In the western States of the peninsula tin-mining was, and still is, the most important industry. Although mining is now carried on chiefly by Chinese, the ceremonies in use at the opening of a mine are purely Malayan. Formerly a lucrative and highly important post was that of mining wizard; some of these magicians were believed to possess the power of bringing ore to a place where it did not exist, and of turning into grains of sand, or of sterilizing, such ore as existed. The ore itself was regarded as endued not only with vitality, but also with the power of functional increase. Sometimes it was said to resemble a buffalo, and in this shape could travel to and fro underground. The gold-spirit in one case (at Raub in Pahang) was believed to take the form of a golden roe-deer—an idea obviously based on the imaginary shape of some large nugget. Beyond tin, gold, and possibly a little silver and galena, no metals are worked in the peninsula.

The natives, however, have a great reverence for iron. The Lump of Iron in the royal regalia, when placed in water, is the most solemn and binding oath known to those who use it, and it is referred to in the most terrible denunciations of the Malay wizard; a long iron nail guards the newborn child and the rice-soul; betel-nut scissors (also of iron) or a dagger protect a corpse from evil contact, and a Malay in the jungle often plants his knife-blade edgewise to the source in a stream before he drinks, in order to drive away any chance demons. Bezoar-stones and stone implements alike are said to be endowed with magical properties and powers; a unique east-coast belief regards the latter as arising out of the ground, and not, as almost everywhere else in the world, as being hurled down from the sky in the form of thunderbolts.

The objects of the charms employed by the mining wizards seem to be to clear the jungle of evil spirits, to banish evil spirits from the ground before starting excavations, to propitiate the local spirits and induce the tin-ore to show itself when the tin-bearing stratum is reached, and to persuade the spirits to partake of a banquet spread for them in a receptacle intended to represent a royal hall of audience. The spiritual 'audience chamber' is usually two or three feet square and furnished with offerings similar to those normally placed on the sacrificial tray, with certain articles, such as sugar-cane, plantains, yams, etc., supposed to be specially characteristic of the food eaten by miners. The chief tabu is the killing of any sort of living creature within the mine, except in case of sacrifice, when a white buffalo may be slain upon the brink of the mine, the head being buried and small portions representative of each part being deposited in the 'audience chamber.' Other tabus are the wearing of a sarong, burying the skin of any beast in the mine, wearing shoes, and even carrying an umbrella; the last is particularly offensive to the spirits, since it is the insignia of Malay royalty. A special language has to be used in so far as certain words are concerned. No animal or thing not itself allowed in the mine (such as an elephant, tiger, or cat), nor even lime-fruit, may be mentioned by any but this substituted title. Nor may any one assume the attitude or dress (a black coat) worn by the wizard in building the altar for the preliminary sacrifice, in performing the magical ceremonies, or in uttering the invocations (such as the attitude of standing with both hands on the hips or behind the back), nor may even the wizard himself assume them on any ordinary occasion.

(*e*) *Water.*—The Malays have been a seafaring race from time immemorial, and the rivers were also of great importance to them before the making of roads. It was by the rivers that they first penetrated the country; the old Malay settlements are all on river-banks, and the streams are still the chief source of supply for irrigating the rice-fields. To both river and sea many superstitions and legends are attached. Their animistic notions include belief in water-spirits, against whom precautions are taken for the protection of their boats. It was formerly the custom to fasten a bunch of sugar-palm twigs to the top of the mast to prevent the water-spirit from settling on the mast-head. The sea-spirits are invoked to point out shoals, etc., and sometimes in rapids or other difficult places offerings are made to the spirits of the rivers. The tidal wave (bore or eagre) on a river was formerly held to be caused by the passing of a fluvial monster, which ascends the river; one of these (on the bore ceasing) was described to the present writer as having been killed by being knocked on the head with a stick. Eredia (A.D. 1613) says that the Malays attribute such bores to souls of the dead who are passing the ocean in *cafilas* from one region to another, *i.e.* from the Golden Chersonese to the river Ganges. Ordinary river-floods (which were distinguished as male and female) were thought to be caused by similar agency.

9. Cosmology and natural phenomena.—(*a*) *Malay.*—In Malay folklore the theory of creation is that light emanating from the supreme being became the ocean, from which ascended foam and vapour. The earth and sea were then formed, each of seven tiers, the earth resting on the surface of the water from east to west, the mountains of the Caucasus being regarded as a chain put round the earth to keep it stable on the face of the waters. Beyond them is spread a vast plain, the sand and earth of which are of gold and musk, the stones rubies and emeralds, the vegetation of odoriferous flowers. Besides the Caucasus, which are known to the Malays as Bukit Kof ('Hills of Kāf'), and are of immense importance in popular lore, there is a great central mountain called Maha Meru, which is sometimes identified by Malays with a hill in Sumatra. Another version of the Creation, in part obviously due to Muslim influence, describes how God, the eldest magician, pre-existing by Himself, created the pillar of the Ka'ba[1] of which the four branches form the four corners of the earth, and the world-snake, Sakatimuna, which was killed by Gabriel and broke asunder, the head and fore part shooting up to heaven, the tail part penetrating downwards beneath the earth. The description of this serpent (whose name suggests an Indian origin)

[1] Lit. 'Cluck, cluck,' the call commonly addressed to domestic fowls.

[2] 'Neutralizing rice-paste' (see above).

[1] Lit. 'cube' (the cube-shaped sanctuary of the Black Stone at Mecca). For the Ka'ba see MECCA.

is remarkably anthropomorphic; in fact, it is a serpent in little more than name.

It was usually believed that the world was of oval shape and revolves on its axis four times in the year, and that the sun was a body of fire moving round the earth and producing the alternations of day and night. Some at least imagined the firmament to consist of a perforated stone or rock, the stars being caused by the light which streams through these apertures. Further, the earth is declared to be carried by a colossal buffalo on the tip of its horns—an obvious Malay parallel to the world-elephant in the *Rāmāyaṇa* and the boar-incarnation of Viṣṇu. When one horn gets tired, the buffalo tosses up the earth and catches it on the other horn, the concussion thus produced being the cause of earthquakes. This buffalo stands on an island in the nether ocean, or on a giant tortoise (according to some versions), or on the monstrous fish called Nun (Arab. 'fish'). The universe is girt round by a huge serpent which feeds upon its own tail. Peculiarly Malay, on the other hand, is the idea of the tides, which, it is said, are caused by the movements of a colossal crab that twice a day leaves and re-enters its cave at the foot of the world-tree Pauh Janggi (the sea-coco-nut-palm), which grows on a sunken rock or quicksand in the 'Navel' or Central Whirlpool of the Ocean (*pusat tasek*). The sun's name in Malay is Mata-hari, which means 'eye of day,' but on the east coast it is held to be a horse which is conducted in procession through the heavens by angels during the day, and led back again at night-time to the point whence it started.

Eclipses of the sun and moon are considered to be due to the devouring of these bodies by a gigantic dragon (Rāhu), or, according to some, a god. Malays, like the Chinese and other more primitive races, endeavour to save the sun and moon by making a vigorous noise to drive away the destroyer. The spots on the moon represent an inverted banyan tree, under which sits an old hunchback, plaiting strands of tree-bark, or, as some say, spinning cotton. As soon as his task is finished, he will angle for everything on the earth's surface. The line has not yet been completed because a rat gnaws through it despite the vigilance of the old man's cat, which is always watching. It should be added that the Malay phrase, *bulan bunting pĕlandok* ('the moon is great with the mouse-deer'), is doubtless explainable by the fact that in Sanskrit mythology the spots on the moon are thought to be a hare or antelope, which, being hard pressed by a hunter, appealed to the moon for protection and was taken up by her into her arms; the phrase is often used when she is three-quarters full.

Landslips in the hills during the rains, being often accompanied by floods, are said to be due to dragons breaking forth from the hills, where they have been doing penance, on their way to the sea. Rocks and waterfalls of unusual appearance are believed to owe their origin to demons. A rainbow, if only a small portion of the end is visible, betokens the death of a Raja, if it appears in the west. The treasure which lies where the foot of the rainbow touches the earth has never yet been found, as 'no one can ever arrive at the place' where it touches. The rainbow itself is often taken to be a snake and is sometimes said to be seen drinking (*ular minum*). On the east coast it is sometimes said to be the head and entrails of a horse or a bullock which comes down to earth to drink. There is a house on the east coast of the peninsula in which a water-jar (*tĕmpayan*) had been drained dry by a rainbow.

Sunset is a time of danger, since then all evil spirits have power, while the name applied to the yellow glow of the last rays of the sun (*mambang kuning*, 'the yellow deity') is a term associated with terror. In Perak children are called in at sunset to save them from this danger, and women often chew and spit out at seven points, as they walk round the house at sunset, *kunyet tĕrus*, an evil-smelling root much disliked by evil demons. Pulau Tioman, an island south-east of Pahang, is believed to be actually the body of a dragon, or *nāga*. The Malay who told this to the present writer said that a long while ago an English Government vessel was passing this island, when her crew, catching sight of the then existing three points of the dragon's crest on the summit of the island, fired, breaking them off, and that the vessel itself sank afterwards. There are now said to be a number of people living on it, none of whom is allowed to make the least use of vinegar; if any vinegar is spilt, an earthquake follows, because the island is in reality the monstrous body of an enormous dragon.

(*b*) *Pagan races*.—The Semang endow both sun and moon with human form, both being female. Like the Japanese, who have been credited by some authors with Malayan affinities, they associate the sun with a crow (Ag-Ag), whom they assert to be the husband of that luminary, whereas the husband of the moon is Tā' Pönn (see above, p. 354b). When the sun sets, it falls into a cavern, which some Semang identify with a species of Hades. Eclipses are caused by a huge dragon, or serpent, which tries to swallow the luminary; in the case of the moon, the Semang assert that the serpent is the moon's mother-in-law, who has assumed this form and is trying to embrace it—an act which is clearly regarded by the Semang with loathing and abhorrence. The rainbow is a huge python, or serpent, and the spots where it touches the earth are feverish and bad to live near. During a storm of thunder and lightning the Semang draw a few drops of blood in a bamboo internode and throw it skywards. As the ghosts of wicked tribesmen fly up to the heavens, this is intended to propitiate them and persuade them to return. Sometimes, however, it is believed that the spirits go downwards and become water-spirits. In this case part of the blood is thrown towards the sky and part groundwards (Pangan).

Thunderbolts are supposed to be hurled as the result of undue familiarity towards a mother-in-law. An unusual explanation of thunder and lightning from Kedah is that the latter phenomenon is the flashing of the top-cords of dead medicine-men. The thunder is the hum of the tops themselves when revolving.

The Kedah Semang hold that heaven consists of three tiers or layers: the highest is filled with fruit-trees which bear luxuriantly all the year round, and is inhabited by the greater personages of Semang mythology; the second also contains fruit-trees, but is defended against unauthorized pillagers by a gigantic baboon who pelts any such would-be assailants with 'false durian-fruit' (the produce of a wild fruit-tree);[1] the third has nothing but the low brooding clouds which bring sickness to humanity.

Of Sakai beliefs little that is typical has been recorded, such information as is available witnessing to a close resemblance to Semang beliefs. Rā-hū' (obviously the Indo-Malay Rāhu), a being resembling a dragon, tries to swallow the sun and moon, but is driven away by the beating of drums and bamboo clappers. Kĕlang Bĕlok, a world-eagle, at one time destroyed all human beings except a boy and a girl. With a magic knife the boy slew the

[1] This fruit is sometimes called by Malays the 'Ha-ha' fruit, from the belief that demons, on flying up to inspect it, see that it is not the real durian-fruit, and indulge in loud peals of sardonic laughter

eagle, and from this pair all mankind are descended. The Sakai are said to indulge in ceremonial exorcism of the spirits of thunder, and it is believed that the forces of nature assist the souls of certain evil spirits or demons, which cause them to harm people, though the forces themselves are not demons. The earth is a thin crust resting on the nether ocean, and the heavens possess several layers, or tiers; the inhabitants of the uppermost are said to include a female deity who has to wash the sin-blackened souls in hot water.

The Blandas of Selangor say that the earth was originally the shape of a flat long betel-box (*sōdok-sōdok*), the nether ocean had the form of a globular tobacco-box (*lōpak-lōpak*), and the heavens were round and over-arching like an umbrella. The Blandas' account of paradise resembles that of the Bĕsisi. The latter hold that the souls of the good (or wise) pass away to the Island of Fruit-Trees, which they identify apparently with the moon, an eclipse being the work of a spirit that wishes to annihilate their spirit ancestors, the moon's inhabitants. This Island of Fruit-Trees is reached by crossing a fallen tree-trunk which serves as a bridge, and from which the wicked fall into a lake or boiling cauldron. This happens only to those who allow themselves to be frightened by a big dog which sits at the parting of the ways by which the souls must go. The magicians of the tribe are reputed to be able to visit paradise and bring back fruit with them. Gaffer Engkoh dwells in the moon, which he reached by a ladder now broken, and protects from wild animals dead souls who visit the Island of Fruit-Trees.

The Mantri have not, to any extent, acquired Malay traditions as regards the form, character, and motion of the sun, moon, stars, etc. The dark spots in the moon they believe, however, to be a tree beneath which sits the moon-man Moyang Bertang, an enemy of mankind, who is constantly making nooses with which to catch them—a task which he is prevented from accomplishing by mice, who continually gnaw through the strings. Eclipses are not attributed to a snake or a dragon, but to a devouring evil spirit. The sky is a great [? inverted] copper pot, suspended over the earth by a string, and around its edge the earth is constantly sending up sprouts which would join the stars if an old man did not cut and eat them. In addition the Mantri have a version of the sun-rope belief, viz. an idea that the sun is a woman tied by a string which her lord is always pulling, while the stars are the moon's children. The sun once had as many children as the moon, but, having been tricked by the latter into eating them, now pursues the moon, and, when he succeeds in biting her, causes an eclipse to happen. This explains why the moon hides her children by day.

In the beliefs of the Benua Jakun the world is globular in shape and enclosed in the sky. Farthest north and south are the extremities of a great beam, the north being twenty days' journey from Boko, where there was a great hill from which the north winds issued. The sun and moon move round the earth, producing darkness and light alternately.

10. Origin of man.—(*a*) *Malay.*—What is now the most usual account of the creation of man, from the four elements of earth, air, fire, and water, appears to be a Malayized version of the Muhammadan story. Adam was formed from the heart of the earth by the angel Azrael, not without strenuous opposition and protests from the earth itself. A common feature of Malayan romances and legends, which also appears in Japanese folklore, and is probably to be attributed to an Indian origin, describes the supernatural origin of human beings in the interior of some vegetable product, as, *e.g.*, in the story of a giant bamboo, which continually sent forth fresh shoots as it was cut down, and in which King Daśaratha, according to the story in *Sri Rama* (the Malay version of the *Rāmāyaṇa*), found the princess, or, again, in the tradition of the discovery of Teh Purba in the river-foam.

(*b*) *Pagan races.*—The Semang story of the origin of the human race is that the first woman, seeing that all other animals had children, was desirous of having offspring of her own, but did not know how to obtain them. She and her husband took to carrying a brace of fire-logs under their arm-pits by way of make-believe. But one day the coco-nut monkey (B'ro), on noticing what they were doing, gave them advice, as a result of which they had four children, two boys and two girls. These married and had children of their own, but the ring-dove (*tĕkukor*) warned the children of the first generation that they had united within the forbidden degrees, and advised them to separate and 'marry other people,' in which case their children might intermarry without impropriety.

Among the Mantri the story of their origin forms an incident in a group of myths connected with Mĕrtang, the first medicine-man, and his younger brother, Blö, who came from a place called 'Rising Land' (Tanah Bangun) in the sky and returned there after a sojourn on earth. They were the children of two people called 'Drop of Water' (Ayer Să-Titik) and 'Handful of Earth' (Tanah Să-Kĕpal), the latter being their mother. Mĕrtang took his youngest sister to wife, and from them the Mantri are descended. Blö married the other sister, but had no offspring. When men increased in numbers to an alarming extent, To' Entah (or 'Lord-knows-who'), the first *batin*, a son of Mĕrtang, drew his father's attention to the circumstance. Mĕrtang wished things to remain as they were, but Blö suggested that 'men ought rather to die, after the fashion of the banana, which itself expires, although its young scions survive.' Thus it was decided, and so the old now die, although they leave their children behind them. According to another version, the Mantri are descended from two white apes (*ungka putih*) who sent their young ones down into the plains, whereupon they developed so rapidly that they and their descendants became men. Yet another version says that men came down from heaven in a ship built by God, which floated upon the waters of the earth. The story of the princess found in the bamboo also occurs among the Mantri. She married the son of the first Raja, and she and her husband both live invisible to this very day.

Benua tradition says that a man and woman were created by Pirman when he formed the world. When the Lulumut mountains, the oldest land, rose out of the water, a ship of *pulai*[1] wood, completely enclosed, in which the man and woman were contained, was left floating on the surface of the water. After the ship ceased to move, they nibbled their way out, and from this pair men are descended. As the male child was born from the right leg and the female from the left, children of the same womb cannot marry. The Jakun say that God created a man and woman in heaven who came down to earth in the State of Johor.

11. Personality; the body and personal possessions.—Malays, in common with all peoples of a primitive civilization, have implicit faith in the magical possibilities of personality and of intimate personal possessions. This is very clearly shown in the beliefs relating to the spiritual or magical powers of the Rajas, the theory of the king as the divine man being strongly held and consistently adhered to. It is alleged that the Malay king originally had the right to slay any one at pleasure,

[1] ***Alstonia scholaris***, which furnishes the Malay substitute for cork.

without being guilty of a crime and without any inconvenient questions being asked him. Not only is his body sacred, but that sanctity extends to the royal regalia, which no one may touch, or even make models of, without incurring the risk of a grave illness, possibly even death itself. Any one who infringes the royal tabus, offends the royal person, or wrongfully makes use of the royal insignia or privileges will be struck down by the divine (quasi-electric) discharge of the royal sanctity (*daulat*). In the Malay romances the kings are credited with all the attributes of inferior gods; they are usually invulnerable and gifted with miraculous powers, such as that of transforming themselves, returning to life, and resuscitating the lives of others. As a divine man the Malay king possesses a number of prerogatives which enter into almost every act of life and effectually set him apart from ordinary men. One of these is the sole use of white for the royal umbrella, and the use of yellow cloth (the white umbrella, once the royal emblem throughout Indo-China, has now been abandoned for yellow). Linguistic tabus are also employed with reference to the king, such words as *santap*, 'to eat,' *bĕrādu*, 'to sleep,' *gĕring*, 'to be sick,' being substituted for the usual Malay words when reference is made to the royal person. At the Malay king's death his name is dropped and he is called Marhum,[1] the deceased, with the addition of a phrase descriptive of some prominent, and often uncomplimentary or grotesque, event of his lifetime. One of the most important and significant beliefs connected with the king is that which attributes to him a personal influence over the works of nature, such as the growth of the crops and the bearing of fruit-trees. This also, in a minor measure, applies to his delegates, and in modern times has even been extended to European officials employed in the government of the country.

In a lesser degree the magical property upon which the regal sanctity is based is a quality of the ordinary individual, though usually inversely in the sense that it is susceptible to evil influence, or, in the case of parts of the body, capable of conveying evil to the owner. The head is still, to some extent, regarded as sacrosanct. In cases of assault greater penalty is exacted for an injury to the head than for that to any other part of the person. Great circumspection is employed in cutting the hair; sometimes it is never shorn; more often it is not cut during a special period—*e.g.*, after the birth of a child. Often a boy's head is shaved after birth with the exception of one lock in the centre of the head, which is allowed to grow until he begins to grow up, or even, in consequence of some parental vow, until he attains the period of puberty or marriage. These customs may be due to the sanctity of the head, or possibly to the idea that magic may be brought to bear upon the former owner of the hair by means of that which has been cut off. For this reason both hair-clippings and nail-parings are carefully disposed of, while they are invariably mentioned as part of the ingredients of the well-known wax mannikin still believed to be most effective in bringing about the illness or death of an enemy. To the same category belongs the practice of kneading up with the substance of a mannikin the eyebrows or saliva of the intended victim, or soil taken from his footprint.

12. Holy places.—Notwithstanding the existence of the mosque as the centre of religious life, there is in every small district a sacred place, or 'high place' (*kĕrāmat*),[2] at which vows are paid on special occasions. Such spots are invested with a high degree of sanctity. In theory they are the burial-places of holy men, the early apostles of the Muhammadan faith, or the first founders of the village, and persons of local celebrity; but, as a matter of fact, in many if not in most cases, they belong to an earlier state of belief than such an origin would imply. Many of these *kĕrāmat* are not graves at all, but fall into the category of those holy places which the Malays themselves, when asked to interpret them, explain as being 'spirit places' (*kĕrāmat jin*). For instance, the *kĕrāmat* of Nakhoda ('shipmaster') Ḥusain on Bukit Nyalas, near the Johol frontier, consists of a group of rocks exhibiting no sign of any kind of burial. This (orthodox) *jin* presides over rain and streams and all kinds of water. Incense is burnt here to prevent floods and to get sufficient water for irrigation. It is probable that the name is a later accretion and the rite a relic of the worship of the spirit of streams of water. In another place the *kĕrāmat* is a tree with a protuberance on the trunk. This swelling is closely connected with the harvest; it increases in good years and in bad decreases.

In Klang there is a famous wishing-rock, called Batu Tre, to which the Mantri have resorted from time immemorial. A similar rock is situated on the top of Gunong Berembun ('Berembun Crag'), while other mountain summits also have similar wishing-places, each possessing its good spirit. The suppliant who visits these places carries with him a couple of white fowls and samples of various articles of food in a tray, which is suspended from a tree or placed on the highest peak of the summit. After his wishes have been silently addressed to the spirit of the mountain, the petitioner sets a meal prepared on the spot for the purpose.

It may be noted, however, that such sacred places were not recognized by the Semang, possibly owing to their nomadic habits. The Sakai and Jakun appear to have set apart certain sites for the purpose of burning incense and registering vows, and they had, in addition to these shrines, medicine-huts, either solitary cells in the depths of the forest, in which the medicine-man kept a selection of his charms and spells, or diminutive shelters which screened him and his patients during the ceremony of exorcism.

13. Rites: prayer and sacrifice.—In the case of both prayer and sacrifice, the Malay standpoint is entirely materialistic. The prayer is invariably a request for material advantage; its efficacy is increased by repetition. Sacrifice, as is shown by the language of the charm, is, or was originally, regarded as a simple gift. There is evidence, however, of the progression from this point of view to that of homage, and, finally, to that of self-abnegation. The spirit or deity is invited to eat or drink of the offerings placed before him. An intermediate stage between the gift and the idea of homage is marked by the use of substitutes and a sacrifice of parts for the whole. For instance, in the instruction of the magician, 'if the deity demands a human sacrifice, a cock may be substituted'[1]—a statement which points, moreover, to the former prevalence of human sacrifices. In one case a more explicit declaration was made to the present writer, who was told that for a man a buffalo could be substituted, for a buffalo a goat, for a goat a cock, for a cock an egg—a statement which explains the frequent use of an egg in Malay sacrifices. The idea of abnegation among the Malays appears to be confined to votal ceremonies or vows in which the votary's offering is not regulated by custom, but there is often a tacit understanding that he will sacrifice something of value to himself.

The chief rites performed on various occasions, to which reference is made below in connexion with special beliefs, are: (*a*) rites performed at

[1] Arab. *marḥūm*, 'one who has found [divine] mercy.'
[2] From Arab. *karāmah*, 'respect,' 'veneration,' 'miracle.'

[1] Skeat, *Malay Magic*, p. 211; cf. p. 144, note.

shrines; (*b*) the rite of burning the incense; (*c*) the scattering of the sacrificial rice; and (*d*) the application of the neutralizing rice-paste.

(*a*) The principal elements of the rites performed at shrines are the burning of incense, the offering of *nasi kunyit* (yellow-stained rice), and the killing of he-goats. The worshippers partake of the flesh of the goats and, in some cases at least, of the yellow rice, while the white ('soul') cloth, five cubits in length, which is laid on the shrine now becomes the property of the mosque attendant (*bilal*), though formerly it doubtless went to the *pawang*.

(*b*) The burning of incense is the commonest form of burnt sacrifice. An invocation is sometimes addressed to the spirit of the incense, urging it 'to pervade the seven tiers of the earth and the seven tiers of heaven respectively,'[1] so as to ensure that the offering reaches the nostrils of the gods. Omens are drawn from the way in which the smoke rises.

(*c*) The scattering of the sacrificial rice is performed with four varieties of rice-grain (parched, washed, saffron-stained, and a special kind called 'glutinous rice,' or *pulut*). The parched rice is generally used for scattering on the sacrificial tray after banana-leaves have been spread over it. The saffron-stained and the washed rice are sprinkled on the persons to be benefited, or upon the ground or house-floor, while the glutinous rice is generally used for feasts at high places.

(*d*) Lustration is accomplished by fire or water. Of the former the best examples are the fumigation of infants and the roasting of the mother after child-birth. One form of lustration by water is an integral portion of a large class of ceremonies, such as those relating to building, fishing, agriculture, marriage, etc. It is called *tĕpong tawar*, or the 'neutralizing rice-paste' (really rice-flour water). It consists in the application, by dabbing, painting, or sprinkling, of a thin paste (made by mixing the rice-flour with water, taken up in a leaf-brush or sprinkler) on the objects which it is intended to protect or neutralize. The brush is made of bunches of five, seven, or nine leaves of certain plants bound with fibrous strings of shredded tree-bark or creeper. The materials and combinations vary, of course, with the object and occasion of the ceremony (whether, *e.g.*, for a marriage, for blessing the fishing-stakes, or for taking the rice-soul). Short rhythmic charms were often used to accompany the rites, but were not repeated audibly.

Developments of the idea of lustration by water are to be found in the bathing of the mother and child after birth and the washing of the floor on similar occasions, the ablution of the sick, of the bride and bridegroom, and of corpses, and the annual bathing expeditions which purify the bathers and protect them from evil. Fasting in the form of religious penance is now seldom practised, but used in former days to be undertaken to secure a state of exaltation, to induce visions, or to acquire supernatural powers. The fast always took place in a solitary place, usually on the summit of a lofty hill or mountain. Such fasts did not imply complete abstinence; a small modicum of rice was allowed daily, with the result that they might be prolonged almost indefinitely.

14. Magic and the medicine-man.—(*a*) *Malay*.—Although the office of the medicine-man, or magician (*pawang*), is falling into abeyance in towns, it was at one time of great importance; and this is still the case to a large extent in country places. The *pawang* is the accredited intermediary between men and spirits, and, although he has no connexion with the Muhammadan religion, without him no village community would be complete. The office is often hereditary, or at least confined to the members of one family. Certain properties, such as a peculiar kind of head-dress, are, as it were, the regalia or official insignia, and are handed down from one generation to another. The functions of the medicine-man are many and diverse. Few of the operations of life can be undertaken without his intervention. In fishing, trapping, and hunting, in the gathering of jungle produce, in agricultural matters, such as sowing, reaping, irrigation, and clearing the jungle, in prospecting for minerals of all kinds, in every crisis of life—birth, adolescence, and marriage—of sickness, death, and burial, his aid is invoked to decide the propitious moment for action, to prescribe the ritual, and to carry out the rites. Not the least important of his powers in former days was that of controlling the weather—traces of which are still preserved in Malay weather charms. For his services in these matters he receives a small payment.

For the most part the *pawang's* instructions consist of prohibitions, or *pantang*; *e.g.*, it is *pantang* in some places to work in the rice-fields on

[1] Skeat, *Malay Magic*, p. 75.

the fourteenth and fifteenth days of the lunar months; certain instruments are proscribed: in the interior a reaping-hook may not be used for cutting the *padi*, or at least the *tuai* (a small instrument consisting of a crescent-shaped blade, set transversely in a slip of bamboo, which will cut only one or two heads of rice at a time) must be used to begin the reaping. By these prohibitions, it may be concluded, the *pawang* preserves the traditional method of an older *régime*—*e.g.*, in enforcing an adherence to the custom of the fixed maximum prices for the sale of rice and other articles within the village, infraction of which entails a bad harvest.

The *pawang* is sometimes supposed to keep a familiar spirit which is hereditary in the family, enabling him to deal summarily with wild spirits of a noxious character, and also to bewitch and thus to punish people who are bold enough to dispute his authority. Such punishment is usually inflicted by a 'sending,' or 'pointing,' one form of which consisted in pointing a kris in the direction of the intended victim, the point of the dagger beginning to drip blood as soon as the charm began to work. Another form consists in burning the point of the cordiform top of a newly opened bunch of bananas growing on the tree; this causes excruciating agony; then the *pawang* cuts off the top and the victim dies vomiting blood, his heart having fallen out of its proper position. The Malay witch also commonly keeps a familiar, which may have as its embodiment a night-owl, a badger, etc.

In certain respects, it is important to note, the magician stands on the same footing as the divine man or king; *e.g.*, he possesses a regalia which is called by the same name (*kabĕsăran*) as the insignia of royalty, he may (at least in some cases) use the royal colour, and he may, like the king himself, enforce the ceremonial use and disuse of certain words and phrases. Probably both offices are held to be dangerous. Other powers and attributes of the medicine-man which may be mentioned are his ability to act as a spirit-medium and to give oracles in trances, and his practice of austerities and observation of chastity for the time being. His use of mesmerism is not yet recorded, but motor automatism certainly occurs.[1]

Although the office of magician is hereditary, the power may be acquired by certain recognized methods. One of these is to raise and meet face to face the ghost of a recently murdered man or of an infant, by means of incantations and fumigations performed at the grave-side.

The Malays themselves make some distinctions between the *pawang* and the *bomor*, the latter being the medicine-man who is concerned especially with the curing of diseases. The two terms are, however, sometimes used as if they were interchangeable. The basic principles of the medical man's art are identical with those of the *pawang*; they depend upon a belief in spirits, and the aim of his treatment is either to propitiate or to overcome their influence.

The *bomor's* procedure in dealing with disease falls under two clearly distinguished headings. First comes the ceremonial inspection or diagnosis, when the character of the therapeutic treatment is determined by divination, by means of omens from the smoke of burning incense, by the position of coins thrown into a water-jar, or by the aspect of parched rice floating on the water's surface.

The therapeutic rites are various in character:

(1) *Propitiatory ceremonies*, the most popular of which is the use of the sacrificial tray called *anchak*, a small frame of bamboo or wood decorated with a fringe of plaited coco-nut-leaf, on which offerings of food are laid for the spirits to eat when it has been hung in a suitable spot outside the house

[1] Skeat, *Malay Magic*, pp. 466-468.

As an alternative method models of certain objects are placed upon the tray, the evil spirits are invited to enter them, and the tray is then got rid of by being hung up in the jungle or set adrift on the sea or nearest river.

(2) *Neutralizing ceremonies*—the use of counter-charms to neutralize the active principle of poisons, extended by the medicine-men to cure all cases where any evil principle (even a familiar spirit) is believed to have entered a sick person's body. The ceremony of applying such charms usually consists in mixing powder from a grated bezoar-stone or celt with water and drinking it after reciting the incantation.

(3) *Expulsory ceremonies*—rites intended to expel from the patient's body all kinds of evil influences or principles, such as may have entered him on his touching a dead animal or bird, or from meeting the 'Wild Huntsman.' The evil principle known as *badi* attaches to everything that has life, including inert objects such as trees, and even stones and minerals, which, in the Malay view, are animate. Of these evil principles or 'mischiefs' there are one hundred and ninety, or, according to some, one hundred and ninety-three. To 'cast out the mischief,' the patient is stroked down with a brush (made of certain prescribed leaves and plant-sprays) which has been dipped in water in which woods have been grated or pieces of scrap-iron allowed to soak, or else he is rubbed with limes, appropriate charms being recited in either case. In another form of the ceremony the 'mischief' is driven from the body along a red thread, which the patient holds in his hand, until it reaches certain dough images of birds, beasts, and fishes, placed upon the *anchak*. A 'disease-boat,' sometimes a mere raft, is also used as a vehicle for the spirits and set afloat on sea or river. The evil may also be expelled by a long and elaborate ceremony in which a protective spirit, such as the tiger- or elephant-spirit, may be summoned. In such cases the spirit, seizing upon the medicine-man, who, while in a state of possession, simulates the movements of the animal-spirit summoned, expels the evil by its superior spiritual powers.

(4) *Revivificatory ceremonies*—ceremonies to recall the sick person's *sĕmangat*. In one such rite dough is rolled into a human figure, which is laid upon five cubits of white cloth. Rice is scattered, incense burned, and a charm recited to induce the *sĕmangat* to enter the dough image and be transferred thence to the soul-cloth, and thence to the patient. Similar ceremonies are used to prevent the *sĕmangat* of a swooning person from escaping.

(*b*) *Pagan races*.—The *bĕlian* (shaman, or medicine-man) is the most important member of the tribe among the Semang. In normal circumstances the chiefs or head-men are always *bĕlians* of more or less reputation. They obey certain prohibitions which do not affect ordinary members of the tribe: they may not eat the flesh of domestic animals, like the goat or buffalo, and that of domestic fowls but rarely. They receive a special form of burial, traditionally regarded as specially honourable, consisting of a rude shelter built in a tree, in which are placed a modicum of food and water, a jungle-knife, etc. It is believed that they are able to proceed to paradise in trances and to drive out devils. They alone know the love-charms that never fail, and can slay men by 'sendings' at a distance of several days' journey. They alone have the power to change themselves into wer-tigers, and at their death their *sĕmangat* passes into the body of an elephant, tiger, or rhinoceros. When the latter dies, they proceed to paradise.

Not merely are diseases caused by demons, but they *are* demons, and have to be exorcized as such. They are abstracted sympathetically from the body by pulling up sapling stumps at or near the place where the disease is believed to have entered the patient. The affected part is rubbed with earth taken from the hole in which the root grew; chewed betel is ejected on the body (in imitation of the Malay medicine-man), and the hurling of dead saplings into the wood, so that the evil spirits may be cast out likewise, ends the ceremony.

'Sendings' or 'pointings' are achieved by a minute dart or splinter of bamboo about two inches long, which is laid on the right palm and is ordered to go forth and slay the victim. This dart or sliver flies through the air and, reaching the victim, pierces his heart and kills him. Sometimes a taper formed of wax from a deserted bees' comb is burned at the same time. Such 'sendings' were said by the Semang to be effective at 'a distance of probably two days' journey.'

The Mantri believe that all diseases are caused either by the spells of bad men or by spirits. Among the latter are the smallpox demon, which the Mantri avoid even mentioning by name; the dropsical demon (*hantu kĕmbong*), which haunts the abodes of men and afflicts them with pains in the stomach and head; the Demon Huntsman (the *hantu si buru* of Malayan origin), who dwells in lakes or pools, is black, and has three dogs which he will cause to chase a man in the forest; if they catch him, they will drink his blood. In every stream, in the ground, in trees, and in caves and crevices of rocks dwell malignant demons who cause disease or mischief to men in various ways, as by sucking their blood and thus causing their death. When a person is wounded, the *hantu pari* fastens on the lesion and causes the blood to flow by sucking. The Berembun tribes believe that diseases are inflicted by the spirits of the rivers (*hantu sungei*), which are evil and feed on the human *sĕmangat*.

The Mantri magician's most noted form of 'sending' is the *tūju*, or pointing ceremony, which is achieved by the use of wax from an abandoned bees' nest.

When a wind blows in the direction of the victim, the magician takes a vessel of water and a lighted candle or two, and mutters an incantation while 'gazing' into the water. When he discerns the image of his intended victim in the water, he throws the wax into the air, and the wind instantaneously carries it to his victim. The latter feels as if struck by some unseen assailant, and is immediately seized by sickness, which may result in death, should the strength of the spell be great enough.

This attack may be averted if the victim has surrounded himself by counter-spells or charms of a prophylactic character. These may not only ward off the blow, but may even prevent the magician from seeing the image of the victim in the water. Amulets are much used as prophylactics against those diseases which are most frequently attributed to 'sendings,' but which may also be due to unsatisfied cravings (*sākit pūnan*).

Among the Benua Jakun the magicians are an order combining the offices of priest, physician, and sorcerer. They and the Bĕsisi medicine-men are much dreaded by the Malays, who believe them (as autochthones) to be more powerful than their own magicians, especially, *e.g.*, in matters in which the performance of the Bĕsisi *bĕrsawai* ceremony is likely to be effective. Not only can the medicine-men cure, but they can inflict disease and death-sickness. This is usually effected by the 'pointing,' or *tūju*, ceremony. Even tigers are subject to these medicine-men, and every magician of repute is believed to have one in constant attendance. In curing disease, incantations are accompanied by the music of the *gĕlondang*, a long bamboo struck by sticks, which are always made of wood of the *mĕrawan* tree. Conjurations are addressed to Jiwa-jiwa (=Mal.-Skr. *deva-deva*), who resides in heaven and alone can approach Pirman. The incantations last all night for one, two, three, or four nights, until the medicine-man announces that he has received the medicine or that the deity is inexorable. The Berembun tribes, like the Malays, attribute the magician's powers to his command over spirits. Every shaman has disciples, who accompany him when he visits the sick. These pupils alone enter the small hut of leaves erected near the house in which the medicine-man performs his incantations, these being continued until the wizard is possessed by the spirit. The latter then answers the medicine-man's questions respecting the mode of treating the diseased person. The Jakun of Madek (Johor) believed that the great magicians (*poyang bĕsar*) of the tribe could reach heaven itself, and that they could disappear without dying, or else, on sickening for death, by arranging to have incense burned over them for two days after their apparent decease, they could return to life again.

A ceremony of exorcism known as *sĕoi*, or, more commonly, as *sawai*, is employed by the Bĕsisi in case of illness or when an answer is required to a question concerning the welfare of an individual.

The ceremony takes place in a hut in complete darkness. After incantations accompanied by the rhythmic drumming of bamboo 'stampers' on the central beam of the floor, the spirit descends upon one member of the company, who answers any questions put to him while he is in a state of trance or possession. In the case of illness the magician erects a small leaf-chamber or cell (*balai bumbun*) near the walls of the hut, in which he conceals himself while the ceremony progresses.

The Blandas employ spells and exorcisms to cast out disease and evil spirits. Spirits of tigers, elephants, and monkeys are summoned to enter the magician's body, and the sick man is then brushed with leaves seven times downwards from head to foot while a charm is repeated. In the blood-throwing charm water is used, and a charm against the Wild Huntsman is also recited.

15. **Birth ceremonies and beliefs.**—(*a*) *Malay.*—There are four spirits, or, rather, demons, which are specially feared by the Malays in relation to child-birth. The *bajang*, a demon which appears in the form of a civet-cat, is evoked by incantation over the grave of a still-born child. It may, however, be inherited, and its possessor can send illness, usually in the form of convulsions or delirium, to an enemy. It is especially inimical to children, who are sometimes made to wear a black silk string armlet as a protection against its attacks. The *langsuir*, a woman who has died in child-birth, becomes a flying demon, or banshee, who, through a hole in the back of her neck, sucks the blood of children. It is believed that these demons have on occasion become wives and mothers, but, when allowed to dance at village merrymakings, they will assume their original form and fly off again into the forest. The *pontianak* is the still-born daughter of a *langsuir*. As a precaution intended to prevent the dead mother or still-born child from originating these mischiefs, the *langsuir* and *pontianak* are buried with glass beads in the mouth (to prevent them from shrieking), an egg under each armpit (to prevent them from waving their arms in flight), and needles in the palm of each hand (to prevent them from opening and shutting their hands in flying). The *pontianak* appears under the form of a species of night-owl. The *pĕnanggalan*, a colossal flying head with hair matted by clots of blood, a species of monstrous vampire or banshee that sucks the blood of children, sits on the roof-tree, or endeavours to force its way through the floor, whenever a child is born, to attack the infant. In addition to these four spirits specifically connected with child-birth, there are the familiar two, called *polong* and *pĕlĕsit*, which also give rise to anxiety at this time, though they do not confine their activities to new-born children. The *polong* originates from the blood of a murdered man which has been placed in a bottle and over which certain incantations have been recited. It is described as a diminutive female figure about as large as the top joint of the little finger, and is usually preceded by the *pĕlĕsit*, its pet or favourite, which, in the form of a cricket, searches for a victim and enters his body, when found, tail foremost. The *pĕlĕsit* is obtained by exhuming the body of a first-born child, a first-born mother's offspring, which has been dead for less than forty days, and burying the child's tongue, with incantations, in a spot where three cross-roads meet. It has been noticed that these demons belong to the category of familiar spirits who are sent to attack their victims by an owner, and, as such, are sharply distinguished from the more primitive animistic ideas relating to disease, etc., which are held by the Bomor.

In regard to the observances at and after child-birth, it is usual to engage the midwife (*bidan*) in the seventh month by sending her a copper vessel containing four or five areca-nuts, three or four packets of betel-leaf, tobacco, and so forth, all of which the *bidan* charms and then empties upon the floor for the purpose of taking the omens. She then chews some of the betel-leaf and ascertains the child's horoscope. At the appointed time she chooses the luckiest place in the house for the child to be born, by dropping an adze-blade, point downwards, first in one place and then in another, until it sticks upright in the ground (under the usual Malay pile-dwelling). Beneath this spot, under the raised floor of the house, are fastened a bunch of prickly screw-pine leaves, the 'acid' egg-plant, or *brinjaul*, and a *lĕkar jantan* (rattan stand for a cooking-pot) as a snare for and protection against any evil spirit (who will, it is believed, prick himself with the former and catch his head in the latter as in a noose). Demons so caught have been pecked to death by the fowls. A tray covered with husked uncooked rice and two mats with several thicknesses of sarong between are prepared for the child's reception. As soon as the new-born infant is laid upon this, it is formally adopted by the father, who (nowadays) breathes into its ear a Muhammadan formula. Mother and child are purified by bathing in warm water containing various kinds of leaves, with areca palm-blossoms. The child is then swaddled. Mother and child are next marked, especially the latter, as a precaution against convulsions and straining, and also, in the case of both, by way of protection against evil spirits. For this ceremony chips of wood from the thin end of the threshold, from the house-ladder, or from the house furniture, in combination with a coat of garlic, a coat of an onion, assafœtida, a rattan pot-stand, and fibre taken from the monkey-face of an unfertile coco-nut, are collected and burned, and the ashes are mixed with a little betel-water. The proper charm is repeated, and, the forefinger having been dipped in the mixture, the centre of the child's forehead is marked—if a boy, with an arrow-shaped mark; if a girl, with a cross, and also with daubs on nose, cheeks, chin, and shoulders. The mother is marked with a line from breast to breast and on the end of the nose also. The evil one will then, it is thought, take woman and child to be his own (who are supposed to be similarly marked) and refrain from harming them. In addition, if the child is a girl, the eyebrows are shaved, and a curve is drawn in their place, extending from the root of the nose to the ear. If the head is considered to be 'too long' (the Malays being on the whole a round-headed race), a yam-leaf cap is made to compress it.

Other ceremonies affecting the child are the administering of the 'mouth-opener,' the rite of giving the first drink from half a green coco-nut, followed by the laying of a gold and a silver and an amalgam ring on its lips, and by fumigating it before it is laid for the first time in the swing-cot, which takes the place of the Malayan cradle. The cot is protected by a funnel-shaped bunch of leaves of the *brinjaul* and other materials, including the casing of the charred torch used at the severing of the umbilical cord, a spice-block, and a trap against blood-sucking demons, made of a *parang*-blade, a coco-nut scraper, and a rattan pot-stand. This trap hangs under the bunch of leaves. The spice-block is explained as being a substitute for the child itself; it is laid in the cot during the first part of the fumigation ceremony, and for the first seven days, whenever the child is taken from the cot, the block must replace it. The naming ceremony takes place usually within the first week, and the first head-shaving and nail-cutting a few days later. Of the naming ceremonies the most characteristic is represented by the east-coast practice of writing seven different names on as many separate banana-fruits, and then allowing the infant to choose between them.

The most characteristically Malayan custom connected with child-birth is that which requires the mother to 'ascend the roasting-place' (*naik saleian*) daily. A rough couch is prepared for her on a small platform, beneath which a large fire is lighted, and upon this bed she has to recline two or three times a day, and that, moreover, for an hour or two together. Sometimes heated hearth-stones wrapped in rags are applied to her stomach. This is said to continue for the whole period of the forty-four days of convalescence. In some cases the 'roasting' was carried out with such rigour as to cause aberration of mind or even the death of the unfortunate patient. At the end of the forty-fourth day a purificatory ceremony takes place, wherein the floor is smeared with rice cosmetic and scratched over by the claws of a fowl held tightly in the grasp of the cleanser. At about the same period, of the fortieth day, the child (in Perak) is presented to the river-spirits, being made to stand with one foot on a couple of coco-nuts and the other on a fowl (both of which have been deposited in the water). A boy then, if the infant is a boy, is sent up-stream to catch a fish with a casting-net; if a girl, a girl acts as the fisher. In Upper Perak the baby himself, with a number of other young children, is caught in the net; he will then never want for fish to feed on.[1]

During the forty-four days' period there are many food prohibitions—*e.g.*, any foods which, from the Malay point of view, are lowering, such as certain vegetable foods, things which irritate the skin or cause faintness, sugar (except coco-nut sugar), coco-nuts themselves, and chillies are prohibited.

Both before and after child-birth many prohibitions are laid not only on the wife, but also on her husband. The latter may not shave his head or cut his hair until after the child's birth; he may not sit in or obstruct the doorway. Any untoward act may cause deformity: a child was born with only a thumb, forefinger, and little finger on the left hand owing to the father having, just previously to the child's birth, killed a crab with a cutlass. In fact, it was at one time prohibited for him to cut the throat of a buffalo or a fowl preparatory to cooking it, or even to take any life whatever. In Perak any log marked by, or distorted in growth by, a parasite, if used in building the house, would cause deformity, protract delivery, and endanger the life of both mother and infant.

(*b*) *Pagan races.*—Superstitions and practices connected with birth, so far as known among the pagan tribes, or, rather, among those pagan tribes for whom Malayan origin and affinities are here claimed, strongly confirm the view that the popular beliefs of the more highly civilized natives of the peninsula are essentially primitive in character. The practice of roasting the mother, *e.g.*, of course on a quite minor scale, is found among the Jakun, Běsisi, and Mantri, while among the Blandas the charms used at birth are directed against the demons, the *langhui* (Malay *langsuir*), *polong*, and *pontianak*—identical, at least in name, with those of the Malays. Another incantation is repeated at the moment of removing the caul as a charm against the caul-demon, which licks up the blood of the sufferer. The Sakai bury the umbilicus and placenta under human habitations so that the rain may not beat upon them and turn them into birth-demons.

It must be stated, however, that our knowledge of the birth customs of the pagan tribes is by no means adequate, and the whole subject awaits further investigation. In one account of the Semang, for instance, it was alleged that their birth customs were based upon a belief in a bird-soul which was carried by the expectant mother in a bamboo receptacle; but, although the conception of the *sěmangat* as a bird is certainly familiar to the Malays, this statement still awaits confirmation among the wild tribesmen. Both Sakai and Jakun make use of the services of a *sage-femme*, who, among the former, has a special hut used by the women of the tribe for purposes of confinement.

The Běsisi decorate the mother's mosquito-curtains with the leaf-hangings used on all important ceremonial occasions, while among the Mantri a cup of water is charmed during labour and administered to the mother. The sap of certain leaves is given to the child, and a charm is repeated. A name, which is retained until marriage, is given to the child at the moment when the umbilical cord is severed. The Benua Jakun fastened round the neck of the child at birth a string to which pieces of turmeric, and so forth, were attached. The Jakun also observed a number of food prohibitions: while the children were unable to walk, the parents abstained from certain fish and animal foods, the latter including fowls and eggs, deer of all kinds, tortoises, and lizards.

16. Adolescence and maturity customs. — (*a*) *Malay.*—Of the purely Malay ceremonies at adolescence the most important are the filing of the teeth and the cutting of the first locks of hair—the latter, of course, only when, owing to some vow of the parents, the 'first head-shaving' operation has been postponed until marriage.

Tooth-filing is done by a professional tooth-wizard (*pawang gigi*). Neutralizing rice-paste, charms, and the scattering of the several kinds of sacrificial rice and rings of precious metal are employed by the *pawang* in order to avert the 'mischief' (*badi*) from his instrument, as well as from the teeth of the patient. The medicine-man's eyes are considered to be especially endangered by the *badi* emanating from the teeth, while an unskilled performer may cause much pain to the patient if he does not know thoroughly how to 'neutralize' the evil.

The rings of precious metal which are pressed against the patient's teeth as part of the rite of extracting the *badi* are also used in the hair-cutting ceremony. The bride's hair is arranged in seven long tresses hanging down her back below the veil which, on this occasion, shrouds her head; to each of these is attached a ring of precious metal, and then each tress of hair, on being cut, is allowed to fall with the attached ring into a coco-nut vessel (ornamented for the purpose with a chevron edge), which is half full of fresh coco-nut milk. For this ceremony also the proceedings are opened by the aspersion of the bride with the neutralizing rice-water, some of it being also sprinkled on the palm of her left hand, by those who take part in the ceremony.

The ear-boring ceremony appears to have fallen into abeyance, though in some of the Malay States a special kind of large, round, ornamental ear-ring, or ear-stud, is still the mark of virginity. Significantly, the ear-studs of a virgin bride are tied on to the ear-lobes of a widow who remarries, the latter being regarded, so to speak, as a sort of 'merry widow,' and being, in fact, actually called jeeringly 'the widow adorned' (*janda běr-hiyas*). Ear-boring is now usually performed when the child is quite an infant.

Circumcision is practised, the instrument being traditionally a knife of bamboo, but in all the mere accessaries of the practice it seems to be entirely a non-Muhammadan rite. Especially in the Northern States it is accompanied by such a wealth of irrelevant detail as to suggest that it has been grafted upon an ancient festival (probably the tonsure ceremony) belonging to an older faith than that of Islām.[1]

It is accompanied by the usual purificatory rites, and the ceremony is made the occasion for a banquet, at which the boy is dressed like a pilgrim and stained with henna like a bridegroom, after which the customary gifts are offered. In Perak he is then taken aside and robed in rich raiment, his mouth filled with the sacrificial saffron-stained rice, and his body sprinkled with the purifying rice-dust. After this, two coconuts and two small packets of rice are slowly rolled over him from head to foot. A hen is then placed 'on his chest to pick up grains of the yellow rice from his mouth. This is done to drive away ill-luck.'[2] The boy's teeth are next tapped with a stone by the operator, and, after feasting, a procession to the river follows, the object of which is to propitiate the water-spirit. The boy then has his top-knot shorn off and returns to the house for the actual circumcision, during which he takes his seat either on a sack of rice or on the stem of a banana. In the procession the youths are sometimes carried on men's shoulders, sometimes (east coast) in a litter shaped like some strange bird or mythical animal.

The girls' ceremony is much simpler, much more private: it was formerly accompanied by ear-boring and tooth-filing, and by staining the teeth 'black as a borer-bee's wing.' Large round ear-studs were also formerly assumed by girls at this period, as emblems of maidenhood; but, though these are still sometimes worn on the east coast, they are now assumed, on the west coast, only at the wedding ceremony in preparation for the rite of discarding them a few days later.[3]

In the same part of the peninsula (east coast) the ceremony is not called, as on the west coast, 'entering into Islām,' but, most significantly, ***masok jawi***,

[1] R. J. Wilkinson, in *Papers on Malay Subjects* [printed for the F.M.S. Government], 1908, 'Life and Customs,' pt. i. p. 5.

[1] Cf. Wilkinson, p. 68. [2] *Ib.* p. 17 f. [3] *Ib.* p. 19.

which means literally 'admission into the body of the Malay people'—the most usual meaning of *jawi* being the vernacular, or 'Malay,' language. Yet another term for the ceremony in these parts was 'purification' (*chuchi tūboh*, literally 'cleansing of the person')—a phrase which is also applied in the same parts of the country to marriage.

(*b*) *Pagan races.*—Of the various operations with which it is usual among primitive peoples to mark the attainment of maturity, neither incision nor circumcision is practised by the wild tribes except, in the case of the former, among the Sembrong and Jakun of the Batu Pahat in Johor, and the Benua, and, in the case of the latter, as elsewhere, only where Muhammadan influence has penetrated. It may, in fact, be said that the rite is virtually synonymous with conversion to Islām, and that it may be taken as the broad dividing-line between Muhammadanism and mere pagandom. Nor, with the exception of a single record from the Perak Sakai, is there any tatuing in the strict sense of the expression. Scarification, however, is found among both Semang and Sakai, but not among the Jakun, and, judging both from distribution and from frequency, there is good reason to believe that the custom originated among the Sakai, and was introduced, though only to a limited degree, among the Semang. The scarification consists of divergent lines on the cheek from the nose towards the ear, produced by the scratches of a thorn or edge of a sugar-cane leaf, charcoal being rubbed into these scratches by way of pigment. Body-painting is of wider distribution, and is to be seen among Semang, Sakai, and Jakun, but more especially among the Sakai. The colours used are black, white, red, and occasionally yellow. The designs are decorative and magical rather than tribal. Perforation of the nasal septum with the wearing of a nose-bar or porcupine's quill also appears to be more especially a Sakai practice. Boring the ears, however, is, as a ceremony, practically universal, whilst the ceremonial filing and blackening of the teeth may belong rather to the Malayan order of ideas. It occurs among the Semang of Kedah and Kelantan, but is there undoubtedly borrowed from the Malays of the neighbouring country.

The shaving of the head, with the exception of a top-knot, which is temporarily removed at puberty, is found among the Semang, but, though also found with differences among the Malays, is most likely a native custom of the wild Negritos, as it is also found among their Andamanese kindred.

17. Betrothal and marriage.—(*a*) *Malay.*—Negotiations for marriage and the ceremony of betrothal are carried out by representatives of the families implicated. The betrothal is a simple affair, consisting chiefly of the offering of betel-leaf by the representatives of the prospective bridegroom and its acceptance by the bride's parents, the two parties meeting in a 'family circle,' at which the offer used originally to be made, and the reply given, in rhyming stanzas. The term of the engagement is then settled. The amount of the marriage settlement is fixed by custom at two *bharas* of dollars ($22, about £2, 6s.) in Selangor, or $31·25 (about £3, 5s.) in Perak, etc. The sum is not usually mentioned unless a modification of this arrangement is to be made. A breach on the part of the bride's parents involves forfeiture of double the marriage portion. The affianced pair avoid one another, but there is a regular system of exchange of presents, those given by the girl being deposited in exquisitely woven baskets made in the shape of birds or fishes. It should be added that the Malay name of the ceremony in the peninsula, *bĕrpinang*, is an interesting parallel to the splitting of the betel-nut (*pinang*), which is the symbolical act of betrothal to this day among the Dayaks of Borneo.

The actual marriage ceremonies cover a period of four days, beginning with the work of decorating both houses, which includes the erection of a dais, with two standard candlesticks, often 6 ft. high, before the door of the bride's chamber. The arrangement of the dais (*pĕlammin*) is of extreme importance, since the number of big white (or in case of a Raja, yellow) pillows used indicates, according to a rigid code of etiquette, the rank of the contracting parties. The whole of the dais is covered with a mosquito-curtain, and the walls of the chamber are adorned with striped or 'rainbow' hangings (*kain pĕlangi*), while the ceiling is decked with an awning or 'heaven' (*langit-langit*).

The basic forms of the rite, which were those of a royal wedding, include the so-called 'bride-price,' the food-sharing ceremony, and the approximation of the dress of the bride (who on this occasion wears trousers) to that of her husband (who wears a skirt). It is this fact that, as A. E. Crawley[1] has explained, helps to account for the apparent resemblance to royal ceremonies that may be noticed in so many Malay customs. The idea seems partly to disguise the subjects of the ceremony in order to avert the possible danger attaching to what is certainly regarded as a critical occasion, and partly to promote a more perfect union between the pair by means of (1) a pledge passing between them (*i.e.* the 'bride-price') as well as by (2) the sharing of a meal together, and (3) the obliteration (so far as may be practicable) of the distinctions of sex. The pretence of kingship by which the bridegroom is made to wear the bracelets, chain, neck-ornament (and, if we may go by the analogy of Malay funeral custom, even the kris) is simply, therefore, an attempt to secure a really effective disguise for the party in danger. The shaving of the bride's forehead may be similarly explained, since the bridegroom is also shaved. Although these are all likewise usages of royalty, it is wrong to regard them merely as a species of social self-advertisement; they are really the paraphernalia worn by all persons of the Malayan race on certain critical occasions,[2] in order to banish the spirits of evil and thus to avert mischief and danger. Till recent years the ceremonies over the greater part of the peninsula were almost entirely non-Muhammadan, and often took place in country districts without the intervention of any mosque official whatever. Lustrations followed, and on the east coast processions in monstrous or bird-shaped litters.

In certain details the wedding ceremonial has now become Muhammadanized in character; among these is to be included, most probably, the staining of the fingers of the bride and bridegroom with henna. The henna-staining at first is done in seclusion ('by stealth'), the initial public appearance of the married couple at their respective dwellings occurring on the second night, when ceremonial rice-water is sprinkled, offerings of rice made to each of the parties, and the 'henna dance' (*tari hinei*) performed; on the fourth day the procession of the bridegroom to the house of the bride's parents takes place. Here, on his arrival, his progress was in former days occasionally opposed by a mimic conflict (*mĕlawa*), which terminated only on his payment of a small fine or ransom to these (for the nonce) self-constituted 'authorities.' This part of the ceremony, which used to be explained as an example of the so-called 'marriage by capture,' is now taken to be merely an expression of the antagonism between the sexes. In some cases a rope or piece of red cloth barred the way, and a stout resistance was offered until the bridegroom had paid the fine demanded. Even then admission to the house had to be made against the resistance of women of the bride's party. The simple marriage service—a mere bald statement of the fact and of its acceptance by the groom—is now performed by the *imām* (Muhammadan priest) in the presence of the bridegroom only. It is said that, according to the old custom, the ceremony took place on the day before the procession. The groom

[1] *The Mystic Rose*, London, 1902, p. 336, quoting the Malay ceremony.

[2] Not specially in connexion with kingship.

is then taken to the bride, and both are seated ceremonially side by side (*bĕrsanding*)[1] on the dais and partake of rice, each feeding the other from a specially-prepared receptacle (*nasi sĕtakōna*=Skr. *aṣṭakoṇa*, 'octangle')—an octagonal erection of three tiers which holds the 'rice of the presence' (*nasi adap-adap*), coloured eggs (*tĕlor joran*), etc., and stands before the *pĕlammin*. The eggs, which have coloured streamers, and represent a fruit, with flower and leaf, are given to the guests as wedding favours. On the third day of the lustrations which follow the marriage the ceremony of bathing for good fortune takes place in the evening. Later, at night, a bonfire was formerly lit outside the house and the groom 'stolen,' *i.e.* carried off to his parents. He was escorted back to his house next day, and a water-fight with syringes (called 'water-bows') took place (sometimes in a specially-erected pavilion) between the friends of the two parties. After this the bride and bridegroom each pulled one of the ends of a slip-knot made of a young coconut frond, and the bridegroom broke through threads wound seven times round himself and the bride; in some cases (Patani) the threads were severed by burning. Seven days after the concluding feast-day the rite of the 'discarding of the ear-rings'—the emblems of the bride's maidenhood—takes place. For two years the bridegroom may be expected to remain under the roof of his mother-in-law. It has been remarked that in the 'bridal rice' (*nasi bĕr-astăkōna*), in the 'bridal thread' (*bĕnang pancharōna*), and in the 'bathing pavilion' (*balai pancha-pĕrsāda*) we have not only Indian customs, but Indian names.[2]

In addition to this regular form of marriage with the consent of the girls' parents, the Malays recognized another form of marriage when the parents were notoriously unwilling, the essential feature being that the would-be bridegroom, fully armed, must force his way to the women's apartment and secure the person of his bride, or prevent her from escaping. If the parents should then give their consent, the customary payments were doubled. This procedure was known as the *panjat angkara*.

In a second and more peaceful form, the *panjat 'adat* (once frequently employed by Malayan Rajas), the groom did not break into the house himself, but sent his kris, accompanied by a message that he was ready with the dower, doubled in accordance with custom. If the kris was returned (*e.g.*, on an unfavourable answer), the parents must send back with it a double dower.

W. E. Maxwell gave both these forms of marriage as being recognized by Malay custom.[3] Wilkinson, however, assenting to the second, regards the first as a mere *crime passionel*.[4]

The marriage ceremony is called in most parts of the peninsula by terms which are obviously of Arabic or Persian origin; on the east coast, however, where Muslim influence is less strong, it is often termed, significantly, by a Malay word denoting 'purification.' Like their Polynesian co-linguists, certain Malays (*e.g.*, Nĕgri Sembīlan) forbid the marriage of two brothers' (or sisters') son and daughter, but not that of a brother's son and a sister's daughter.

(*b*) *Pagan races*.—Among the pagan tribes the essential feature in the marriage ceremony is a ritual purchase and a repast shared between bride and bridegroom. Among the Semang the price consisted of the blade of a chopper (*parang*), presented by the bridegroom to the bride's parents, and a coiled girdle of great length, said to be manufactured from the rootlets of the sugar-palm, given to the bride. This act of purchase, so long as it was performed before witnesses, was in itself binding. The Semang, as a rule, were monogamists, and conjugal infidelity was strongly discountenanced, the immemorial penalty being death, which would now be commuted for a heavy fine. Among the Perak Sakai the nuptial present was, as among the Semang, a knife or yam-tubers.

According to one account, the bride and bridegroom attended at the house of the chief, who, after an inquiry as to their prospects, declared the man and wife united. Another account states that the relatives of both parties assembled at the bride's house, and that the two betrothed persons ate rice out of the same dish together. The little finger of the man's right hand was joined to the little finger of the left hand of the woman, and they were pronounced husband and wife by the elders of the settlement.

The Sakai occasionally, but rarely, took more than one wife. Death or a fine was the penalty for infidelity.

The Jakun ceremony embodied several features of peculiar interest and importance.

In addition to the nuptial presents for the bride and her parents—beads, white cloth, etc.—the husband was expected to provide a hut, cooking-pots and pans, and other household requirements. Either party or both were questioned as to their ability to carry out the duties of their future state, the requirements in the case of the man being proficiency in the use of the blowpipe, ability to fell trees or to climb after fruit in the jungle, and even ability to smoke a native cigarette. The *batin* (head-man of the tribe), as a rule, was present and pronounced the parties husband and wife at the end of the ceremonies. Among the Bĕsisi of Selangor the head-man then gave the bride and bridegroom a new name. According to one account, among the Selangor Sakai, the smoking of a native cigarette was substituted for the common meal. The Mantri bride and bridegroom presented a love-token of betel-leaf to one another before the feast, at which they ate together from the same plate. The most distinctive feature, however, in the Jakun marriage was the use made of a conical or, rather, bell-shaped mound of earth (sometimes an actual ant-heap) decorated with natural and artificial 'flowers,' the latter being representations of the solar disk with rays, etc., and other ornaments; around this mound the bride was pursued by the bridegroom, in some cases three, in others seven, times; if he succeeded in catching her, they were declared to be married. Among the Bĕsisi of Kuala Langat (Selangor) the bridegroom was conducted before the present writer seven times round this mound at a walking pace, and the bride once, before they partook of a common repast, consisting of a dish of rice and drink from a bowl of water which had both been placed on top of the mound (*būsut*). This was, of course, a survival of the mound-race ceremony. In one form of this rite among the Mantri there was no mound, but the pursuit took place round a circle of varying size; in the case of the Benua of Pahang, a fire was substituted. In the case of some Jakun tribes of Johor, in the middle of a dance the bride ran into the forest, and was followed by the bridegroom. The counterpart of this ceremony among the Land-Tribes (Orang Darat) was, it is important to note, among the Sea-Tribes (Orang Laut) of Johor a ceremony in which the bride had to be pursued by the bridegroom for a given distance on the river, in canoes.

Monogamy was generally, though not invariably, the rule. Although marriage was recognized as strictly binding by the Bĕsisi and other Jakun, yet at their drinking carnival (*main jo'oh*), which took place at the end of the rice-harvest, they were allowed to exchange their wives promiscuously.

18. Burial customs and mourning.—(*a*) *Malay*.—The Malays are not among those races who fear, but rather among those who pay respect to, the ghost of the departed.

After death the body is shrouded in sarongs and laid on the back, with hands crossed on the breast, on a mattress which, in turn, rests on a new mat of pandanus. A pair of scissors used in the preparation of betel-leaf is placed on the chest, the explanation being that, should a cat by any accident come in contact with, or brush against, the body, the touch of iron will prevent the corpse from returning to life, as once happened. Cats are always expelled from the house while it contains a dead body, and the corpse is watched day and night in case evil should come near it. The preparation of the body for the grave includes ceremonial washings, which should be performed while it rests on the outstretched legs of four people (members of the family) sitting on the floor. Failing volunteers for this office, banana-stems are used as rollers. A final washing of 'nine waters' is performed by the *imām* (if accessible), 'three scoops' of water being scattered to the right, three to the left, and three over the body from head to foot. The orifices, including the ears, eyes, and nose, are plugged with cotton, and the corpse is wrapped in a white cotton shroud, the selvedge of which is torn off and used to bind up the body at the breast, hips, knees, head, and feet, the shroud having been fastened with the 'five knots.' The corpse is then placed on the mattress in the position which it is to occupy in the grave, lying, that is, on the right side with the head to the north, and face looking towards Mecca (westward). When the relatives give the last kiss before the shroud is fastened, they must be careful that no tears fall on the face, as these might disturb the deceased's spirit. The position of the body in the grave depends upon the kind of coffin used. If it is a single-plank bier (*pāpan sa'kĕping*), the body is placed in a recess at the left side of the grave, and the plank is fixed in a sloping position with pickets closing the aperture, so that the plank itself may neither touch the body nor allow the earth to fall upon it. Another kind of receptacle

1 'Wherever the old Palembang (Sumatra) tradition exists—in Pahang, Johor, Riau, Malacca, Selangor, and Perak—the enthronement or *bersanding* varies very little. But if we leave the Palembang area and cross into Patani, the ceremony is different, the regalia are different. We see before us the ghost of the ancient Northern Courts and of the old and high civilizations that have been crushed out of existence by the Siamese' (Wilkinson, p. 70).

2 Wilkinson, p. 64.

3 *Ap.* Skeat, *Malay Magic*, p. 394.

4 P. 28.

(the *kăranda*), a plain oblong box, is placed in the middle of the grave-pit. The *long*—made either of two planks united along one edge in the form of a gable with bulging sides or of three planks fastened together like the sides of a box without bottom—is placed over a trench in the middle of the grave which contains the body. While the grave is being filled in by the bystanders, the diggers, who must not leave the grave until the operation is completed, fend off the earth from the body with small hurdles. A relative fashions two small (temporary) grave-posts of wood, one of which is placed over the head and one over the waist, to both of which strips of white cloth (as signs of recent death) are fastened. The *imām*, after pouring libations on the grave, and scattering shredded blossoms of scented flowers, reads the *talkin* ('exhortation') amid profound silence. The reason given for this silence is that the dead man is supposed to open his shroud, the fastenings of which have been loosened for the purpose, and, feeling that its border has no selvedge, thus first becomes cognizant of the fact that he has died, beyond any possibility of doubt. He then sits up to listen to the preacher, supporting himself on his elbow until, at the end of the reading, he falls back really lifeless. The mourners, led by the *imām*, then recite the *tahalil*, the Muslim profession of faith, one hundred times, beginning very slowly and increasing their speed at regular periods (finally at an extremely rapid rate), after which they return to share in a feast given by the head of the household ; before they leave, however, the contributions collected in the alms-bowl which stands near have been divided among all present. Feasts follow on the third, seventh, and fourteenth days, and, in the case of the wealthy, on the fortieth and hundredth days, and on the anniversary. Then the grave is made up, and a framework of planks is placed round it to keep the earth of the grave-mound banked up properly. In the case of a chief, a small hut or shelter is often erected over the grave, and this the writer has sometimes seen furnished actually with a mosquito-curtain.

No special sign of mourning is worn, but the sarongs in which the corpse is wrapped and the pall must be as costly as possible, consistently with the rank and wealth of the deceased person.

In the formerly Malayan district of Singgora, north of Patani, various forms of exposure of the dead frequently took place until recently, when the Siamese Government prohibited the custom with great strictness. One of these consisted in suspending the corpse in a cigar-shaped receptacle or wrapper between a couple of trees in the jungle, at a height of about 8 ft. from the ground. Another consisted in depositing the body of the deceased person (placed at an angle) in a large rectangular box, supported on lofty posts — a method which is of exceptional interest, since it may be linked up with the custom of burial in a chest on high posts, still practised in Borneo. The remarkable point about these forms of tree-burial, or corpse-exposure, is that they were in both cases explained by the people who employed them as being reserved for any one who had died a 'bad' death, the idea being apparently that ordinary interment or cremation would not suffice in such an instance to bring peace to the *sĕmangat*. The Patani Malays also had once a similar custom—casting out to be eaten by dogs and vultures the bodies of those who had died a bad death. Yet from the statements of mediæval Chinese writers (*e.g.*, Ying Yai Sheng Lan, A.D. 1416), though quoted by Wilkinson,[1] it is clear that such exposure, from the analogy of ancient Java, was in no way limited to bad deaths, but was an honourable and pious form of burial offered even by the children of a family to their parents, so that it falls into line, in this regard, with the funeral customs of modern Tibet, where dead relatives are dismembered and given to the dogs and vultures. It would, on the other hand, perhaps readily come about that such methods should be regarded as barbarous and even 'wicked,' when the country was settled by a people to whom such forms of burial were alien.

A third remarkable method was practised by the so-called 'white Prâms' of the Malayo-Siamese region, who had a small cemetery in Patalung, wherein their dead were deposited in a sitting position.

(*b*) *Pagan races.*—Among the pagan tribes the burial customs exhibit considerable variation, but they are especially significant as revealing the attitude of the various groups towards death, and particularly towards the spirits of the departed. The Semang appear to have no special fear of the dead, although they do exhort their deceased friends to think of the spirits of their departed ancestors and not to trouble the living. The Sakai, on the other hand, appear to have great terror of the spirits of the dead, and it is usual for them not merely to desert the house in which any one has died, but to abandon the whole clearing, even if the crops are standing. The Jakun are distinguished from both the Semang and the Sakai by the tender care which they show for their dead relatives.

[1] P. 67.

The Semang method of interment is simple.

Among the Kedah Semang the grave is usually surrounded by a low fence of palm-leaves, and the two bamboos upon which the body was carried to the grave are laid upon it. The corpse is placed on its side, with the head and knees to the right, on a mat or rough platform of twigs, and a screen of sticks, driven diagonally into the side of the grave and roofed with palm-leaves, prevents any earth from falling on it. The legs are drawn up, probably, as the grave is only 5 ft. long, for the sake of mere convenience. Three coco-nut shells containing rice are placed in the grave-pit at the head and sides, and a coco-nut shell at the foot holding water.

It is probable that at one time the Negritos (Semang) practised tree-burial. The bodies of their medicine-men may still occasionally be exposed in trees in the forest—this being a more honourable form of burial. Among the Malays a tradition is current that the Semang used once upon a time to devour their dead. It is unnecessary to place any credence in this statement; its importance lies in the fact that it probably alludes to the existence at one time of a custom analogous to that of the Andaman Islanders, who disinter and dismember their dead after a certain interval.

Of Sakai methods of burial little is known with certainty, the reason being apparently the fact that they threw the bodies of their dead into the jungle, or simply left them to rot away in their primitive hut-shelters. It is certain that they have always shown the utmost abhorrence and terror of the dead, abandoning their huts—and even clearings with growing crops—when a death had happened in their encampment. A modified form or survival of platform-burial is found among the so-called Sakai of Selangor (Ulu Langat), by whom the body was exposed on a platform in front of the house for twenty-four hours.

Jakun (or Malayan) ritual and practice are more elaborate than those of the Semang, and in the solicitude shown for the welfare of the departed imply an entirely different mental attitude towards death from that of the Sakai and the Semang. In many respects there is close affinity with Malay customs.

The body is carefully washed and prepared for the grave. It is covered with white cloth, and laid on a mat, which, in turn, is placed upon a tree-bark wrapper. This tree-bark is then lashed round the body and used for carrying it to the grave-side. Frequently the blade of a chopper (*parang*) is laid on the breast of the departed. The Orang Bukit cut a hole in one of the cloths in order that the corpse may 'breathe' more fully. It is customary also for them to make crosses on the palms of the hand and soles of the feet with a yellowish root which, on being bruised, leaves a stain behind it. By these marks the deceased person recognizes, on waking in the other world, that he or she is really lifeless. At the grave the tree-bark wrapper is removed, and the body is laid on its back, or sometimes facing east if an adult, west if a child (Mantri). A gable-like covering, in accordance with the Malay custom, is formed from pickets covered with tree-bark or a sloping plank (this being also a Malay usage) to keep the earth from striking the body. The Orang Bukit (Hill Men) place a dish of boiled rice at the feet for the spirits, and one at the middle for the departed. It is commonly the custom to lay in the grave some or all of the property of the deceased, usually articles most distinctive of the daily duties of the sexes. An extremely interesting practice among the Bĕsisi consists in their erecting, a yard or two away from the foot of the grave, a small triangular hut thatched with a big fan palm-leaf made to lean against it, fitted with a stick-ladder by which the ghost may climb up. In the hut are placed models of domestic and other utensils and implements, again distinctive of sex, betel-shoots, seed-rice, and fish, acid fruits, water, and sugar. When the grave has been filled in, the seed-rice is scattered on the mound and about the grave in order to provide the ghost, when the grain has grown up and ripened, with suitable nourishment. Among these people it was also the custom for two men to stand one on each side of the grave and simultaneously to let fall two choppers, horizontally crossed, upon the mould at about the spot where the breast would be, this being done in order to 'fix the ghost in the grave' and to 'prevent it from harassing the living.' The Mantri broke a blowpipe (no doubt that of the deceased) and scattered the fragments on the grave-mound. At each end of the mound the Jakun commonly placed wooden tomb-posts bound with white cloth similar to those used by the Malays, and, again like the Malays, they enclosed the grave, when made up, with a framework of wooden planking.

The feeling for the welfare of the dead which is expressed among the Bĕsisi by the seed-rice sown over the grave is also responsible for the depositing of a number of offerings at or near the place of interment. The Bĕsisi themselves plant yams, sweet potatoes, etc., near by, while on the grave of a *jukrah* ('tribal chief') described by D. F. A. Hervey (*JRAS*, Straits Branch, no. 8 [1882], p. 119), were sticks to serve as ladders for the soul to climb up, coco-nut shells, a torch in a stand, and a cooking-pan, as well as the basket in which firewood is usually carried. This grave was also provided with a trench in which the dead man could paddle his canoe—apparently a link with boat-burial. Among the Berembun a bamboo was placed upright near the face of a child, with one end projecting from the ground—undoubtedly a survival of an earlier custom of feeding the corpse through the bamboo, as is still done by the Dayaks of Borneo. It was not uncommon for a fire to be lighted near the grave for three days, while the Sabimba visited the grave on the third and seventh days and one month after interment. The Jakun sometimes, though not usually, abandoned the house and clearing after a death; usually, however, this took place after a month's interval.

19. Omens, divination, and ordeals. — Astrological calculations based upon the supposed values of times and seasons or the properties of numbers are largely employed in divinatory ritual. Exhaustive tables of unlucky and lucky times and seasons have been compiled by the Malays, but are proved to have been largely translated from Indian or Arabic sources. The oldest and best known of the 'magic squares' founded upon these systems is that known as the 'five times' (*kătīka līma*), in which the day is divided into five parts, while five days form a cycle, the name of a Hindu divinity being assigned to each division. Mystic values are also attached to certain colours in connexion with these divisions. Another scheme is based upon the seven heavenly bodies, the divisions being, correspondingly, seven in number. Malayan astrological knowledge and the signs of the zodiac upon which the various systems are founded appear to be largely Arabic in character, though there can be little doubt that the original home of this lore was Babylonia (or Chaldæa), and some part of it may have come in through Indo-Persian channels. The division of the month into *rĕjangs*, thirty in number, each with a separate symbol, is based upon the twenty-eight *nakṣatras*, or lunar mansions, of the Hindus, rather than upon the *anwā* of the Arabs. The Malays are especially partial to the magic square, which generally takes the form of the magic square once used in Europe, but sometimes works conversely—the latter being, no doubt, the older native form proper to the Malays of the peninsula. As has been remarked, the Malays introduce both coloured squares and the names of five of the greater Hindu deities. Besides these squares, many other magic figures—pentacles, compass-figures, and the like—are much used by Malay diviners.

In interpreting omens from dreams the method usually employed is that the initial letter of the thing dreamed of determines the character of the omen. *T* is very unlucky, *N* indicates sorrow, *H* a visitor from a distance, and so on. In another system an almost entirely arbitrary interpretation is put upon the subject-matter of the dream, or, at most, it is interpreted by analogy. In a third method, however, the nature of the thing dreamed does actually suggest its interpretation, with the proviso that so-called 'direct' dreams come only on the eve of a Friday, whereas on other days the dream works backwards.

It may be added that the doctrine of luck plays a most important part in what may be called Malay 'natural religion.' By certain signs and indications not only human beings but also birds and animals are either credited with the possession of luck or believed to be invested with the power of bringing it to others; in a fine passage the Malay deer-wizard chants as follows:

'From the seven Hills and the seven Valleys
Comes the intense barking of my Hounds.
My Hounds are *Hounds of Luck*,
Not Luck that is adventitious,
But Luck incarnate with their bodies.'[1]

Even inert objects, such as krisses and other weapons, may be brimful of luck, or otherwise.

(*a*) *Malay*.—Omens and divinations play a part of paramount importance in every department of life's activities in Malaya. Equal significance is attached to signs deduced from the acts of men and those taken from the events of nature.

Among the acts of men may be mentioned sneezing, which is held to be fortunate, since it tends to drive away the demons of disease. Yawning, on the other hand, when audible, is a bad sign; but, if the yawning is silent and happens when the stomach is craving for food, it implies that the craving will soon be satisfied. It is unlucky for a child to lie on its face or kick its feet together in the air; this is a sign of the approaching death of one or other of its parents.

The evil eye is much feared, and praise of children is conveyed in a roundabout way to avoid ill-fortune.

Among omens drawn from natural events, the following may be mentioned.

A star in apparent proximity to the moon portends an approaching wedding. The entrance of an animal which does not usually frequent the house denotes ill-fortune; to be barked at by a wild jungle-dog is a fatal portent; a wild bird entering the house should be caught carefully and smeared with oil and then released in the open air, a formula being recited which bids it fly away with all the ill-luck or misfortune of the household. Omens are taken from the flight and cries of certain birds, such as the night-owl, night-jar, or *caprimulgus*, the crow, and certain kinds of wild dove, as well as from a bird called the 'rice's husband.'

Such prognostics are drawn from entirely fortuitous events, but they may also be the natural reply to actions initiated by the inquirer. In such cases we have the rite of divination properly so-called (*tīlek*=Skr. *tilaka*, 'mark').

One form of divination is effected by means of a lemon which, after offerings have been made and certain ceremonies performed, is suspended with incantations over a brazier by seven strands of coloured silk thread, the fruit being itself thrust through by a needle. The motions of the suspended lemon answer questions in the negative or affirmative, and will discover a thief by indicating which of a number of names written on paper is that of the guilty man. The mirrored surface of water held in the palm of the hand, or saliva, or a bowl filled with water and covered with a cloth upon which the names of suspected persons are successively placed is employed to discover those who may have been guilty of stealing. In the last-named case, two men each place a finger in the bowl, which begins to turn when the name of the culprit is placed upon the cloth above it. Another method is the use by the medicine-man of a divining-rod composed of one, three, or more rattan-stems, inscribed with magical devices, and connected at the base or butt-end, which vibrate when the thief approaches; these rods may also be used for treasure- or water-finding, as by our own 'dowsers,' and also even for exorcizing demons.

It is noteworthy that the Malays attribute the arts of the diviner to animals as well as to men; thus the tiger is said to employ divination when it wishes to secure a human victim, just as tigers are believed to poultice themselves with *ūbat tāsak* (the medicament applied to the newly circumcised) when wounded.

An important and solemn ordeal was that by diving. This required the consent of the Sultan, and could be conducted only in the presence of the four great (west coast) chieftains.

In the case of a dispute, each of the adversaries in defence of his own case writes a solemn statement. After certain formal preliminaries, this document is enclosed in a bamboo sheath or covering. One of these bamboo receptacles is given to each of the two

[1] Skeat, *Malay Magic*, p. 182.

adversaries, who are escorted to the river and placed up to their necks in the water. A bamboo pole is then made to rest upon their heads and, at a given signal, they are both pressed downwards. Each remains under the water as long as he can, but, as soon as one of the two gives in and appears above the surface, his tube is snatched from him. The winner is led back, his bamboo opened, and the result declared to the bystanders.

(*b*) *Pagan races.*—The savage Malays of Malacca also paid much attention to omens when a new clearing was to be made, and charms were used to expel the jungle spirits. The Mantri, in choosing a new locality for a clearing, paid strict attention to the attitude of the spirits toward his undertaking as signified by the dreams of the party. To dream of being chased by a dog or an enemy, entering water, or being flooded out was an evil omen; to dream of felling or climbing trees, of ascending trees, or of growing plants was of good import.

Divination among the Sakai, so far as records go, is practically non-existent. Among the Jakun it is employed as a part of their medical diagnosis, but, whether used as a part of a tribal or group ceremony or by the medicine-man alone, it falls more properly under the category of exorcism.

20. Charms, amulets, and talismans. — (*a*) *Malay.*—Not only does the Malay attempt to foresee the coming of evil, but he endeavours to ward it off by charms and talismans. Charms in the shape of invocations are extremely numerous, and are addressed to every conceivable form of spirit on every conceivable occasion. But, in addition, free use is made of charms of a more material character. Examples of this class include a length of the *sămambu* (Malacca cane) with a joint equal to the height of the owner, which protects him from snakes and animals; so, too, the 'coco-nut pearl' (apparently a form of 'tabasheer'), the 'eyeless coco-nut' (which confers invulnerability by 'sympathy'), the 'dragon's blood' rattan or cane, the tiger's whiskers and claws, and many others are all, for various reasons, much sought after by warriors. Some of these are directly effective, others work only by influencing the volition of another mind, as in the case of love-charms, charms for securing conjugal fidelity, and so forth. In most cases the charm consists of a short Arabic or Malay and Arabic prayer or a few magical letters or figures inscribed on paper or cloth and worn on the person. One important use of a charm is to enable the devotee of this magic to abduct the *sĕmangat* of a person from his (or her) body, for the purpose either of benefiting the operator or of harming the intended victim. There is a variety of methods of attaining these objects. In some the charm works without contact; in others contact is necessary. Although there is considerable variety, the principle in all cases is the same, and is based upon the Malay theory of the *sĕmangat*. Thus, *e.g.*, soil is taken from the intended victim's footprint and treated ceremonially by wrapping in red, black, and yellow cloth; and this, when suspended from the centre of the magician's mosquito-curtain, becomes the embodiment of his victim's *sĕmangat*. As such it is switched with seven strokes three times a day for three days and then buried in the middle of a path where the victim is bound to pass; on doing so, he becomes distracted. Wood scraped from the floor where he has been sitting, parings of his nails, and clippings of his hair are utilized in various ways; sometimes they are kneaded into a wax figure, which is either transfixed with a thorn in the member that the enchanter desires to injure or burned to ensure the victim's complete destruction.

Of the various methods of abducting the *sĕmangat* without contact, the simplest is to go out when the sun clears or when the newly-risen moon glows red, and, standing with the big toe of the right foot resting on the big toe of the left, make a trumpet of the right hand, and recite the appropriate charm thrice over. At the end of each recital, blow through the hollowed fist, using it as a trumpet. The words of the charm, 'I loose my shaft,' suggest a 'sending,' analogous to that of the medicine-man. Other methods are to beat one's own shadow, to hang a seven-fruited lime-branch from the top of one's mosquito-net on three successive nights, to wave the end of one's head-cloth in the direction of the moon seven times for three successive nights, and so forth, the appropriate charm in each instance being, of course, recited.

With their customary logical thoroughness, the Malays attribute the use of charms and amulets in some cases to wild animals, and even to reptiles. The wild boar, *e.g.*, is believed to possess a talisman of extraordinary power called *rantei babi*, 'the wild boar's chain,' which is hung up on a neighbouring bush by the animal whilst he is occupied in wallowing, and which can therefore sometimes be stolen by a lucky native. Another talisman carried by the boar for defensive purposes is the *kulum babi*, 'boar's sucking stone'; the two together made a wild boar invulnerable. A similar 'lucky stone' was sometimes worn by serpents. Any magically potent object is called *ber-tuah*.

(*b*) *Pagan races.*—Amulets and talismans are common among the wild tribes. Coins are strung on necklaces to serve as 'medicine,' and necklaces of tufts of squirrels' tails, teeth of apes, wild pigs, and monkeys, and bones of birds and animals, as well as the bristles, teeth, and claws of tigers, were first worn, as among the Malays, quite as much for magical purposes as for ornament. The Mantri strung pieces of turmeric on strings of *artocarpus* bark, and these were worn round the neck, wrists, or waist as prophylactics against demons, bad winds, and, generally, all kinds of evils. They also placed great reliance on the efficacy of spells to render them invulnerable. Semang women wear armlets of *pālas* (*Licuala peltata*) leaf, and men wear similar ornaments of the 'rock vein' (*urat batu*) fungus. It appears that among these tribes, as elsewhere, much of their personal adornment was intended to protect them against evil from the spirits by which they were on all sides surrounded. The elaborate patterns of the combs of the Semang and half-breed Sakai-Semang women were similarly designed to ward off accidents and disease, and the copper bracelets, rings, and other objects worn by the Sakai were in effect talismans which preserved the wearer from ill-health and misfortune. The Semang, when wearing the Malay sarong, frequently still retain underneath it the primitive string girdle of 'rock-vein' fungus, possibly from habit, but more probably for magical reasons.

The most important class of charms or talismans employed by the wild tribes is undoubtedly the ornamental geometrical patterns with which they adorn various objects of common use. These designs are intricate and have as yet been adequately studied and elucidated only to a small extent. So much, however, is clear: the pattern, as a rule, is symbolical of the use to which the object on which it appears is to be put, and its aim is to secure the successful attainment of that object. Exception to this rule may be made in the case of the women's combs and other articles, the patterns on which are intended to ward off disease, the attacks of reptiles, animals, and noxious insects, and other accidents. The difficulty of comprehending and interpreting these designs is increased by the fact that, in the usual fashion of primitive artists, the wild tribes make a part stand for the whole. The slots of deer on a bamboo quiver, *e.g.*, represent the whole animals, which, it is hoped, will be induced, by being represented as approaching towards certain wild jungle-fruits beloved of the deer, to visit a particular feeding-ground, when they can be the more easily marked down and captured. The articles decorated in this manner with magical intent include, in addition to the Semang combs, large bamboo tubes used as quivers for darts and arrows, the last being covered with patterns intended to secure success in hunting. Other articles similarly adorned are 'stampers' (*i.e.* bamboos struck on the ground during magical ceremonies, amulets against disease, insect pests, drought, etc.). Besides these they decorate bamboo rice-dibbers, poison receptacles, tobacco receptacles, blowpipes, arrows, nose-sticks, etc., mats and wallets (Sakai and Jakun, not Semang), bark-cloth (with painting only), and the human body, the last not only with painting, but also with tatuing and scarification (likewise especially among the Sakai).

LITERATURE.—This is cited throughout the article. Especial use has been made of W. W. Skeat, *Malay Magic*, London, 1900; and Skeat and C. O. Blagden, *Pagan Races of the Malay Peninsula*, do. 1906 (with full bibliography).

W. W. SKEAT.

MALE PRINCIPLE.—See PHALLISM, SEX.

MĀLIK IBN ANAS.

—Mālik ibn Anas, the founder of the Mālikite school, was born in the month of Rabīʿ al-Awwal A.H. 95 (A.D. Nov. 713). He was of pure Arabic stock, being descended from Dhū Aṣbaʿ al-Ḥārith, who belonged to one of the tribes of Yaman. When still a youth, he had already acquired a full knowledge of the Qurān, the *ḥadīth* (tradition), and other Muslim sciences, and soon he was held in reverence as a great authority in these matters.

During his long career Mālik ibn Anas resided in his birthplace Medīna as a *muftī* and teacher of Muslim law. Like many men who have spent their lives in study, he has not left much for his biographers to record. His chief work was the so-called *Muwaṭṭaʾ* (lit. 'The Beaten Path'), the basis of the whole Mālikite system of Muslim law. This book is not a mere collection of traditions. It deals not only with the sayings of the Prophet but also with the opinions of several famous *faqīhs* in Medīna and with Mālik's personal views on various matters of canon law. It is often alleged that Mālik rejected every kind of reasoning by means of argument and kept exclusively to the literal sense of the sacred texts. But the contents of the *Muwaṭṭaʾ* prove the contrary. According to his later biographers, Mālik repented of this in his old age. It is told that, when he sat down in his last illness and wept, he was asked: 'What makes thee weep?' He answered: 'Who has more reason to weep than I? By Allāh, I should wish I had been flogged and reflogged for every question of law on which I pronounced an opinion founded on my own fallible judgment!'

The text of the *Muwaṭṭaʾ* is handed on by Mālik's disciples in different versions. The best known is the text of Yaḥyā al-Maṣmūdī, which was printed with the commentary of Muhammad al-Zarqānī in 4 vols. at Cairo (1863). Another version is that of Muhammad al-Shaibānī, the famous disciple of Abū Ḥanīfa, who studied three years in Medīna (printed at Lucknow, 1879).

It seems that the opinions of Mālik ibn Anas were not always in agreement with the views of the government. In the year A.H. 145 (A.D. 762), as some persons had accused him of declaring that he did not consider the oath of allegiance to the 'Abbāsid khalīfs as binding, he was even flogged and treated in a most scandalous manner. After this cruel punishment, however, he rose still higher in public estimation in Medīna, where he died on the 10th of the month Rabīʿ al-Awwal, A.H. 179 (A.D. 3rd June 795).

Mālik ibn Anas enjoys the reputation throughout the whole Muslim world of being one of the greatest *faqīhs* and traditionalists of Islām. At the present day his school is still dominant in the west of the Muslim territory, in the French and Italian possessions (Morocco, Algiers, Tunis, Tripoli), and in many other parts of Africa.

LITERATURE.—Ibn Khallikān, *Biographical Dictionary*, tr. M. de Slane, Paris, 1843–71, ii. 545–549; I. Goldziher, *Muhammedanische Studien*, Halle, 1889–90, ii. 213–226; C. Snouck Hurgronje's review of I. Goldziher's *Die Zâhiriten* in *LOPh* i. [1884] 419; C. Brockelmann, *Geschichte der arabischen Litteratur*, Weimar and Berlin, 1898–1902, i. 175 f.; A. von Kremer, *Culturgeschichte des Orients*, Vienna, 1875–77, i. 477–479; T. Nöldeke, *Orientalische Skizzen*, Berlin, 1892, p. 129; *The Kitāb al-Ansāb* of al-Samʿānī with an introduction by D. S. Margoliouth, Leyden and London, 1912, p. 41; F. Wüstenfeld, *Genealogische Tabellen der arabischen Stämme und Familien*, Göttingen, 1852, ii. 'Die jemenischen Stämme,' Tabelle 3.

TH. W. JUYNBOLL.

MALTHUSIANISM.

—Some economic and social investigations seem to be haunted by an evil fate. The subject with which they are concerned seizes popular attention for a time, and the results of the inquiry come to be represented in a form which is little more than a travesty of the original meaning and intentions. One of the most remarkable instances of this tendency is to be found in the reception accorded to the work of Thomas Robert Malthus (1766–1834) on *Population*. Popular interest in his work grew much more rapidly than the time or the capacity for assimilating it, and he was criticized by many who had not read his books. He was accused in his own day of being an enemy of the human species, and of being guilty not merely of heterodoxy but also of atheism. It was said that 'the insults the theory of Malthus levels at God, and the injuries it meditates inflicting upon man, will be endured by neither' (M. T. Sadler, *Law of Population*, i. 15). Further, the principles of population enunciated by Malthus have been expanded and developed in several directions by subsequent writers; and all these views are described roughly by the vague and comprehensive term 'Malthusianism,' which means little more than the consideration of the relation between increase of population and the available food supply. Malthusianism, in fact, has no more definite meaning than 'Smithianismus' in Germany.

It would be a mistake to consider that Malthus was the first economist who treated of population. The Mercantilists had explicitly advocated 'populousness' as an important condition of national wealth, and their views had influenced social legislation and poor-law administration in England during the 18th century. In 1776 Adam Smith had mentioned that 'every species of animals naturally multiplies in proportion to the means of their subsistence, and no species can ever multiply beyond it' (*Wealth of Nations*, bk. i. ch. viii. [ed. J. E. T. Rogers, Oxford, 1869, i. 84]), but it was not till almost the end of the century that Malthus selected the subject of population for separate treatment. It is true that more than a century earlier William Petty had published several essays relating to the numbers of the people, but his point of view was entirely statistical, whereas that of Malthus was directly related to the conditions of progress. In a sense the work of Malthus was begun to oppose the theories of William Godwin, who had published his book on *Political Justice* in 1793 and his *Enquirer* in 1797. Godwin had been influenced by Condorcet and other writers of the era of the French Revolution, and he advocated human perfectibility by means of a gradual equalizing of wealth, under which condition there would be a sufficiency for the reasonable wants of all. In time the peaceful influence of truth would render force and even government unnecessary, so that a state of human perfection was possible on earth. Godwin's views formed a common topic of discussion among those who were interested in political science. One such conversation was destined to have important results. It took place between Malthus and his father. The latter, Daniel Malthus—a friend of Voltaire and the literary executor of Rousseau—was favourably disposed towards Godwin's views, while the son had doubts, which he afterwards placed in writing. The treatise which resulted was his *Essay on Population*, published anonymously in 1798.

Malthus believed that a fatal objection to the thesis of Godwin and other writers who maintained the same view was to be found in the relation of population to the means of subsistence. Population, when unchecked, doubles itself every twenty-five years; the means of subsistence, under circumstances the most favourable to human industry, could not possibly be made to increase faster than in an arithmetical ratio; *i.e.*, the progression for population, if unchecked, would be 1, 2, 4, 8, 16, 32, 64, 128, 256, while that of subsistence could not exceed 1, 2, 3, 4, 5, 6, 7, 8, 9. Population had not increased in a geometrical ratio, owing to the checks imposed upon it by misery and vice, the former being certain and the latter probable. Society as a whole makes 'a constant effort towards an increase of population,' with the result that there is a constant tendency towards distress among the lower classes (*Essay*, 1798, p. 29). As against Godwin, Malthus pointed to the grim spectres of famine, war, pestilence, and evil-living as the necessary limitations to the natural increase of mankind—either positively by reducing a redundant population, or negatively by the dread of these evils. The first edition of the *Essay* can be understood only by remembering the controversial purpose out of which it arose. In opposition to the optimism of Godwin and his sympathizers it overestimates the darkness of the situation. An attempt was made to correct this in the second edition (1803), which is practically a new book. The treatise of 1798 was in the main the critique of a Utopia from the point of view of the support of a growing population; that of 1803 was a scientific examination of the principle of population, as far as possible in isolation from other phenomena. There was, however, a greater change than that of external form; the two progressions remain, but the exposition of the checks to increase of numbers is worded differently. Misery and vice become subordinate to what Malthus terms 'moral restraint.' This new characteristic anticipates, and so prevents, a pressure on the means of subsistence; and, where it is observed, actual misery, as a result of population, need not arise. Moral restraint is, strictly speaking, 'moral' only in so far as it is exclusive of 'irregular gratifications'; its main characteristic is rather that of rational prudence, based on man's 'reasoning faculties which enable him to calculate distant consequences' (*Essay*, 1803, pp. 9, 11), such as his capacity to support a large family without lowering a suitable standard of life. Hence moral restraint operates in the direction of postponing early marriages as well as irregular connexions. It means, in fact, as J. Bonar puts it, simply continence (*Malthus and his Work*, p. 53).

Much of the popularity of the principles of Malthus may have been due to his summing up the foundations of his theory in a formula which is capable of being apprehended easily and remembered, especially as the geometrical and arithmetical ratios seem to provide the certainty of a mathematical demonstration. But the formula suffers from a false simplicity; the first important objection is that Malthus founds his argument upon two alleged necessities which he claims as co-ordinate, but it is clear that a supply of food is much the more urgent need. The celibate must be fed if he is to live. It follows that the tendency towards increase of population is a conditional one, and hence any ratio which is established at a given time is susceptible of alteration, irrespective of changes in the quantity of food. Malthus often speaks as if population must increase up to the limits of the means of subsistence; but since his day there have been cases of countries where increased resources have been followed, not by an increase in population, but by an improvement in the general standard of living. The arithmetical ratio, as the maximum possible increase in the production of food, was never formally and fully proved by Malthus; indeed, his sections on the state of population in America (*Essay*, 1798, p. 20) partially contradict his view of the ratio. Moreover, not only the production of food but its consumption must also be taken into account. Economies in consumption without loss of efficiency would enable a larger population to be maintained by the same supply. The whole statement of Malthus regarding agriculture in his earlier editions is embarrassed by his ignorance of the Principle of Diminishing Returns; some of his expressions almost suggest it, but he makes no real use of this law. This theorem, which was stated clearly by West in 1815, soon changed the manner in which the population question was formulated. Torrens, James Mill, and McCulloch understood Diminishing Returns not so much as a theoretical tendency, but as a condition of the working of the extractive industries in practice. Accordingly, in spite of improved methods of production, they thought that the increase of population drove agriculturists to cultivate more and more inferior soils, so that a larger and larger proportion of the world's labour would be required for providing the necessaries of life. J. S. Mill stated this point of view concisely when he wrote: 'It is in vain to say, that all mouths which the increase of mankind calls into existence, bring with them hands. The new mouths require as much food as the old ones, and the hands do not produce as much' (*Principles*, bk. i. ch. xiii. § 2). Mill, like the rest of the Classical School, regarded Diminishing Returns as a 'law' which could be suspended only temporarily by the disturbing influence of improvements. The present disposition of economists is to consider Diminishing Returns as a tendency which is subject to frequent counteraction. The difference of outlook removes some of the gloom which settled on the population question during the 'dismal' era of economics in the first half of the 19th century. The real influence of Malthus survives in a much modified form, on the one side in the responsibilities of parents in being able to provide for their offspring, on the other in a ceaseless effort to effect improvements in the productive arts, particularly in those connected with the provision of the world's food supply.

It is scarcely necessary to add that the doctrines and practices of 'Neo-Malthusianism,' or the voluntary restriction of the birth-rate, form no part of Malthus's own teachings and would doubtless have been indignantly repudiated by him.

LITERATURE.—W. Godwin, *Enquiry concerning Political Justice*, 2 vols., London, 1793, *The Enquirer: Reflections on Education, Manners and Literature*, do. 1797; T. R. Malthus, *An Essay on the Principle of Population as it affects the Future Improvement of Society; with Remarks on the Speculations of Mr. Godwin, M. Condorcet, and other Writers*, do. 1798, *Essay on the Principle of Population, or a View of its past and present Effect on human Happiness, with an Inquiry into our Prospects respecting the future Removal or Mitigation of the Evils which it occasions*, do. 1803 (2nd ed.), 3rd ed. 1806, 4th ed. 1807, 5th ed. 1817, *An Inquiry into the Nature and Progress of Rent, and the Principles by which it is regulated*, do. 1815; E. West, *An Essay on the Application of Capital to Land, with Observations showing the Impolicy of any great Restriction of the*

Importation of Corn, and that the Bounty of 1688 did not lower the Price of it, do. 1815; N. W. Senior, *Two Lectures on Population, to which is added a Correspondence between the Author and Mr. Malthus*, do. 1829; M. T. Sadler, *The Law of Population*, do. 1830; Robert Torrens, *An Essay on the Production of Wealth, with an Appendix in which the Principles of Political Economy are applied to the actual Circumstances of this Country*, do. 1821; James Mill, *Elements of Political Economy*, do. 1821; J. R. McCulloch, *Principles of Political Economy with a Sketch of the Rise and Progress of the Science*, Edinburgh, 1825; J. S. Mill, *Principles of Political Economy, with some of their Applications to Social Philosophy*, London, 1848; J. Bonar, *Malthus and his Work*, do. 1885, *Philosophy and Political Economy*, do. 1893, *Malthus—Parallel Chapters from the first and second Editions of the Essay on Population*, Economic Classics Series, New York, 1893; V. Lebrecht, *Il Malthusismo e i problemi sociali*, Turin, 1893; E. Leser, *Malthus, drei Schriften über Getreidezölle*, Leipzig, 1896; J. Bonar, 'Malthus,' in *Dictionary of Political Economy*, London, 1900; E. Cannan, *A History of the Theories of Production and Distribution in English Political Economy*[2], do. 1903; C. E. Strangeland, *Pre-Malthusian Doctrines of Population, a Study in the History of Economic Theory*, New York, 1906.

W. R. SCOTT.

MALŪK DĀSĪS.—The Malūk Dāsīs form a small Vaiṣṇava sect of northern India. It is an offshoot of the Rāmānandīs (see *ERE* ii. 546), and is named after its founder, Malūk Dās, a trader by occupation, who lived in the reign of the Emperor Aurangzīb (latter half of the 17th cent. A.D.). He is said to have been born at Kaṛā, in the present District of Allāhābād, where there is a shrine in his honour and a monastery of his followers. The neighbouring village of Sirāthū is said to have been granted to him by the emperor.

The main point that differentiates Malūk Dāsīs from other Rāmānandīs is the fact that their teachers, like their founder, are laymen. Wilson adds that there is also a shorter streak of red in the sectarian mark on their foreheads.[1] Like other Rāmānandīs, they worship the Rāma incarnation of Viṣṇu. Wilson mentions six other monasteries of the sect in the Ganges valley, and also one of great repute at Jagannāth, in Orissa, where Malūk Dās is said to have died.

So far as the present writer is aware, none of Malūk Dās's works have been published. He is said to have written a poem called the *Daśa Ratna*, or 'Ten Jewels.' Two lately discovered works of his are the *Bhakta-vatsala*, dealing with Kṛṣṇa's regard for devotees, and the *Ratna-khāna*, a dissertation on the soul and God,[2] and he is also the reputed author of many well-known detached verses and apothegms. One of his verses is probably the stanza that is best known and most often quoted in the north of India, and offers a striking resemblance to the leading thought of Mt 6[26]. According to Hindu belief, the *ajagara*, or python, is unable to hunt for its food. It can only lie with its mouth open to wait for what will walk into it. The verse runs as follows:

Ajagara karai na chākarī Pañchhī karai na kāma,
Dāsa Malūka kahi gaē Sabha-kā dātā Rāma,

'The python doth no service, nor hath the fowl of the air a duty to perform (to earn its living);
Quoth Malūk Dās, for all doth Rāma provide their daily bread.'

LITERATURE.—Jīvarāma, *Śrī Rasikaprakāśa Bhaktamāla*, Bankipur, 1887 (section 19 deals with Malūk Dās, and the commentary gives some legends about him); H. H. Wilson, *Sketch of the Religious Sects of the Hindus*, London, 1861–62, i. 100–102; F. S. Growse, *Mathurā: A District Memoir*, Allāhābād, 1880, p. 212; *Gazetteer of the Allahabad District*, 1911, pp. 250, 301; R. G. Bhandarkar, 'Vaiṣṇavism, Śaivism and Minor Religious Systems' (=*GIAP* iii. 6), Strassburg, 1913, p. 74.

G. A. GRIERSON.

MAMMON.—The word occurs three times in Lk 16 among the somewhat disconnected Logia that follow the parable of the Unjust Steward (16[9. 11. 13]), the last of which, 'Ye cannot serve God and mammon,' is found also in Mt 6[24]. It is a transliteration of the Gr. μαμμωνᾶς, a form which, with μμ, appears in TR, with Latin Vulgate, six Old Latin, and a few Greek minuscules. The correct Greek, however, is μαμωνᾶς, which is found in RV, with all Greek uncials, and most minuscules, as well as in the Complutensian and the first two editions of Erasmus; but the influence of the Vulgate led to the appearance of *mm* in the later editions of Erasmus and in AV (for further details as to spelling see E. Nestle, in *EBi*).

The word is not Greek, nor is it found in the Hebrew Bible. It is a hellenized form of the Aram. מָמוֹן, which means 'money,' 'riches,' 'worldly goods.' Wyclif and Purvey translated the word by 'riches' ('richessis'), but Tindal followed the Vulgate in transliterating the word, and so did all later English versions, except Geneva.

1. Derivation.—The Aramaic form מָמוֹן (*stat. emph.* מָמוֹנָא) follows a well recognized form of nominal inf. מִקְטַל, but scholars are divided as to what is the verbal root.

(1) J. Drusius (quoted in J. Buxtorf, *Lexicon Chaldaicum*, Basel, 1640, *s.v.*) and Dalman (in *PRE*[3] xii. 153) derive the word from אָמַן, *i.e.* מָמוֹן = מָאמוֹן, which would mean 'that on which man trusts,' or, as Dalman prefers, 'that which brings man into safety.' (2) Jastrow (*Talmud Dictionary*, p. 794[b]) derives it from המה; and thus מָמוֹן = מַהְמוֹן 'that which one accumulates.' (3) Levy (*Neuhebräisches und chaldäisches Wörterbuch*, iii. 138) considers מנן = מָנָה, 'to distribute,' to be the root, and thus our word means 'that which is distributed.' (4) W. Gesenius (*Thesaurus linguæ Hebreæ et Chaldææ*, Leipzig, 1829, ii. 552), as if μαμμωνᾶς were the true form, derives it from טָמַן, 'hide,' whence מַטְמוֹן = מָמוֹן, 'that which one hides or treasures' (Gn 43[23], Job 3[21], Pr 2[4], Is 45[3], Jer 41[8]). However much the learned may now differ as to the derivation, it seems certain to the present writer that the Syriac versions all derived the word from אָמַן, and that they assumed a paronomasia to exist between our word מָמוֹנָא and מְהֵימַן (pass. part. of אָמַן), which means 'faithful' or 'trustworthy,' thus: 'He that is trustworthy in little is trustworthy also in much; and he that is not trustworthy in little is not trustworthy in much. If ye have not been trustworthy (מְהֵימְנָא) in the unrighteous mammon (מָמוֹנָא), who will entrust (מְהֵימַן) to you the true?' But, since the verb אמן is as common in Galilæan Aramaic as in Syriac, may we not go further, and say that the paronomasia was probably intended by our Lord in the original Aramaic?

2. Usage.—The trade of the world, before the time of Alexander, had long been in the hands of Phœnicians and Aramæans; and we have evidence that in both languages *mamon* was the word for 'money.' As to the former, it occurs on Phœnician inscriptions on tombstones; and Augustine, in two passages (*de Serm. in Monte*, II. xiv. 47, and *Quæst. Evang.* ii. 34), states that the Punic word for *lucrum* ('wealth') is *mammona*. Its Aramaic usage is also abundantly attested. Jerome (*Ep.* cxxi. 6) affirms:

'Non Hebræorum sed Syrorum lingua, mammona divitiæ nuncupantur.'

Irenæus (III. viii. 1) attests its use

'secundum Iudaicam loquelam, qua et Samaritæ utuntur.'

The Aramaic Targums often contain the word: *e.g.*, Pr 3[9], 'Honour the Lord with thy *māmôn*'; Is 55[1], 'O ye that wish to learn . . . come and learn without price and without *māmôn*'; Jg 5[19], 'They accepted no *māmôn* of silver'; in Ex 18[21] the ideal judges are those 'who hate the receiving of *māmôn*.' In the Aramaic sections of the Palestine Talmud the same story is told twice (*Nāzir*, v. 3; *Berākhôth*, vii. 2) of 300 poor Nazirites who came for purification. R. Simeon asked King Jannæus to give half the cost, but it turned out that the king paid all

[1] *Religious Sects*, i. 101.
[2] See *Report on the Search for Hindī Manuscripts for 1904*, Allāhābād, 1907, p. 60, and *for 1909–11*, do. 1914, p. 271.

the money (*māmôn*) and the Rabbi's half was his knowledge of Tôrāh. *Bᵉrākh.* 61*b* says:

'There are men whose money (*māmôn*) is dearer to them than their own body.'

There is also a classification in lawsuits between those which concern money (דִּינֵי מָמוֹן) and those which concern the person (דִּינֵי נְפָשׁוֹת). This is found often in the Talmud and also in *Jerus. Targ.* to Dt 1^{18}. The pre-Christian usage of our word even in Hebrew is shown from Sir 31^{8}, 'Blessed is he . . . that has not yet gone after *māmôn*.' The translators of LXX show themselves acquainted with the word, for in Ps 36 (EV 37^{3}) they misread אֱמוּנָה as מָמוֹן, 'Thou shalt dwell in the land and be fed on its wealth'; and in *Pirqē Ābhôth* (ii. 16) we have a 'saying' of R. Jose: 'Let the property (מָמוֹן) of thy friend be as precious to thee as thy own.'

The very phrase 'mammon of unrighteousness' is quite common in Jewish literature; in the pre-Christian *Book of Enoch* the wicked say:

'Our soul is satiated with unrighteous mammon, but this does not prevent our descending into the flame of the pains of Sheol' (63^{10}).

The phrase מָמוֹן דִּשְׁקַר is a well recognized phrase in the Targums for 'money earned through deceit or fraud.' The crime of Samuel's sons was that 'they turned after mammon of fraud' (1 S 8^{3}; cf. also Pr 15^{27}, Is 33^{15}, Ezk 22^{27}, Hos 5^{11}).

3. Exegesis.—(1) In Lk 16^{9}, 'Make to yourselves friends by means of the mammon of unrighteousness,' the difficulty is: to whom was Christ speaking? Lightfoot (*Horæ Hebraicæ*, iii. 159 ff.), A. B. Bruce (*Expositors' Greek Testament*, i. [1897] 586 f.), and Merx (*Die Evangelien Marcus und Lucas*, p. 328 f.) hold that He was speaking to the Pharisees and publicans to whom ch. 15 was spoken (15^{3}), and who were still in the crowd (16^{14}). It was certainly more suitable for them than for the Twelve, who had not much 'mammon' of any kind; and, if so, the phrase has the same meaning here as in Jewish literature—'money ill gotten,' 'money gained by fraud.' Thus the advice which Jesus gives to the Pharisees is that they should make restitution to God by deeds of benevolence. Christ's advice is, says Merx (p. 328), 'Ye who have acquired money unrighteously and cannot refund it, use this wealth in making friends for yourselves,' as Zacchæus, when converted, volunteered to give half his goods to the poor.

'The counsel is to use wealth in doing kindness to the poor, . . . only care must be taken not to *continue* to get money by unrighteousness in order to have wherewith to do charitable deeds' (Bruce, *loc. cit.*).

The alternative view, that the words are said to the Twelve, and that *μαμωνᾶ τῆς ἀδικίας* is the evil stamp placed on all wealth, 'because great wealth is seldom gained or employed without injustice,' is forcefully presented by Moffatt, in *DCG* ii. 106 f.

(2) In Lk 16^{11} we have a contrast between *τὸ ἄδικον μαμωνᾶς* and *τὸ ἀληθινὸν μαμωνᾶς*, which seems to turn on a second meaning of שְׁקַר. In the original Aramaic, שְׁקַר means (*a*) 'deceit,' 'fraud,' and (*b*) 'nothingness,' 'illusion,' 'vanity.' We believe that *ἀληθινός*, here as elsewhere in NT, means 'real,' 'permanent,' 'belonging to the spiritual world,' in contrast with the present life of illusion and vanity, where 'the things that are seen are ephemeral' (2 Co 4^{18}). We surmise, then, that מָמוֹנָא דִּשְׁקַר would, in the original Aramaic, appear in both v.^{9} and v.^{11}; but in v.^{9} שְׁקַר means 'deceit,' 'fraud,' while in v.^{11} it means 'illusion,' 'vanity,' and thus presents a contrast to the 'true,' the 'real,' 'spiritual' riches. Our Greek translation, of course, obliterates or ignores the distinction between the two meanings of שְׁקַר.

(3) In Lk 16^{13}, 'Ye cannot serve God and mammon,' the emphasis is on 'serve' (*δουλεύειν*). No man can at the same time be the *δοῦλος* of God and of worldly wealth. The ordinate pursuit of wealth is not condemned. It is the undivided concentration of mind—the surrender of body and soul to money-getting—that is censured, as being incompatible with whole-hearted devotion to God and to His service. Mammon is personified as the object of undivided attention and service, as in Ro 16^{18} Paul speaks of those who 'serve' their own sensual nature (*δουλεύουσιν . . . τῇ ἑαυτῶν κοιλίᾳ*), and as in Col 3^{5} he utters a warning against 'covetousness, inasmuch as it is idolatry,' *i.e.*, wealth so easily erects itself into an idol, which woos men's affections from God and makes men averse to giving cheerfully what they acquire. Here and in Lk 16^{13} there is, no doubt, a personification of wealth, as also in Tertullian (*adv. Marc.* iv. 33).[1] When Milton, therefore, speaks of Mammon as one of the fallen angels in hell, 'the least erected Spirit that fell from heaven,' who even in heaven was

'admiring more
The riches of Heav'n's pavement, trodd'n gold,
Than aught, divine or holy, else enjoyed
In vision beatific'

(*Par. Lost*, i. 678 ff.; cf. also ii. 228),

we have, perhaps, not so much the flight of the poet's imagination as an indication of his familiarity with apocryphal lore. The phrase 'mammon-worship' has been made familiar by Carlyle (*Past and Present*, bk. iii. 2, bk. iv. 4, 8, etc.), and is, no doubt, useful in emphasizing strenuously the warning of Jesus, 'Ye cannot serve God and mammon.'

LITERATURE.—A. Merx, *Die Evangelien Marcus und Lucas*, Berlin, 1905; J. Lightfoot, *Horæ Hebraicæ*, ed. R. Gandell, Oxford, 1859, iii.; T. Zahn, *Einleitung in das NT*³, Leipzig, 1906, i. 11 f.; A. Meyer, *Jesu Muttersprache*, Freiburg and Leipzig, 1896, p. 51 n.; the commentaries on Mt 6 and Lk 16; Jacob Levy, *Neuhebräisches und chaldäisches Wörterbuch*, Leipzig, 1876–89; and Marcus Jastrow, *Talmud Dictionary*, London and New York, 1903; W. H. Bennett, in *HDB*; J. Moffatt, in *DCG*; E. Nestle, in *EBi*; G. Dalman, in *PRE*³.

J. T. MARSHALL.

MAN.—See ANTHROPOLOGY, ETHNOLOGY, EVOLUTION, PSYCHOLOGY, SOCIOLOGY, etc.

MAN, ISLE OF.—See CELTS.

MANA.—*Mana* is a native term belonging to the Pacific region, but, for the purposes of the science of comparative religion, serves likewise as a category of world-wide application. The local sense will be found to stand in close relation to the scientific, despite the fact that the latter represents but the generalized content of various concepts prevailing in different ethnic areas and presumably of more or less independent origin.

1. Local meaning of mana.—'The word,' says R. H. Codrington (*The Melanesians*, p. 119 n.), 'is common I believe to the whole Pacific, and people have tried very hard to describe what it is in different regions. I think I know what our people mean by it, and that meaning seems to me to cover all that I hear about it elsewhere.' For the twofold reason that Codrington's account has in no respect been impugned by later observations, and that it is the classical source from which the scientific use of the term *mana* is derived, it will mainly be followed here, though one must bear in mind that it deals primarily with the Melanesian usage, whereas there is reason to suppose that the actual word is an importation from Polynesia. It will be convenient to consider the *mana* of the Pacific region under two aspects: (*a*) theoretical, comprising the native view of what it is, how it is

[1] W. Taylor Smith calls the attention of the present writer to a passage in the 'Passio Sancti Bartholomæi Apostoli,' in *Acta Apostolorum Apocrypha*, ed. R. A. Lipsius and M. Bonnet, Leipzig, 1891–1903, pt. ii. vol. i. p. 156: 'Vidit (Satanas) se exclusum, et alterum sibi angelum apostolicum, qui Mamona dicitur, sociavit, et protulit immensa pondera auri argenti gemmarum et omnem gloriam quæ est in hoc sæculo et dixit ei: Hæc omnia tibi dabo si adoraveris me.'

manifested, where it resides, and whence it comes; and (*b*) practical, involving the methods by which it is sought to turn the supposed fact of its existence to human advantage.

(*a*) *Theoretical aspect.* — *Mana* is defined by Codrington thus:

'It is a power or influence, not physical, and in a way supernatural; but it shews itself in physical force, or in any kind of power or excellence which a man possesses. This *mana* is not fixed in anything, and can be conveyed in almost anything; but spirits, whether disembodied souls or supernatural beings, have it and can impart it; and it essentially belongs to personal beings to originate it, though it may act through the medium of water, or a stone, or a bone' (p. 119 n.). Or, again, he describes it as 'a force altogether distinct from physical power, which acts in all kinds of ways for good and evil, and which it is of the greatest advantage to possess or control' (p. 118 n.).

In this account three points are specially to be noted: (1) that the power or excellence for which *mana* stands is 'in a way supernatural,' namely, in so far as it is 'what works to effect everything which is beyond the ordinary power of men, outside the common processes of nature' (p. 118); (2) that, even if it be in itself impersonal, resembling a contagion, or such a force as electricity, in that it can have a material object for its vehicle, 'it essentially belongs to personal beings to originate it'; (3) that it 'acts in all kinds of ways for good and evil,' or, in other words, may be used 'to benefit or to afflict friends and enemies' (p. 200), and is thus indiscriminately at the service of religion or of the black art. So much for the nature attributed to *mana*—which, be it noted, is noun, adjective, or verb, since it is equally a property, quality, or state. It may next be shown how such an attribution is a result of experience and sometimes even of experiment.

'If a man has been successful in fighting, it has not been his natural strength of arm, quickness of eye, or readiness of resource that has won success; he has certainly got the *mana* of a spirit or of some deceased warrior to empower him, conveyed in an amulet of a stone round his neck, or a tuft of leaves in his belt, in a tooth hung upon a finger of his bow hand, or in the form of words with which he brings supernatural assistance to his side. If a man's pigs multiply, and his gardens are productive, it is not because he is industrious and looks after his property, but because of the stones full of *mana* for pigs and yams that he possesses. Of course a yam naturally grows when planted, that is well known, but it will not be very large unless *mana* comes into play; a canoe will not be swift unless *mana* be brought to bear upon it, a net will not catch many fish, nor an arrow inflict a mortal wound' (p. 120).

Moreover, in this matter the native mind proceeds logically enough by the method of hypothesis and verification.

'A man comes by chance upon a stone which takes his fancy; its shape is singular, it is like something, it is certainly not a common stone, there must be *mana* in it. So he argues with himself and he puts it to the proof; he lays it at the root of a tree to the fruit of which it has a certain resemblance, or he buries it in the ground when he plants his garden; an abundant crop on the tree or in the garden shews that he is right, the stone is *mana*, has that power in it' (p. 119).

Hypothesis and verification even lurk behind the forms of prayer.

Thus at Florida, one of the Solomon Islands, a fisherman addresses Daula, a *tindalo*, or ghost, connected with the frigate-bird, in these words: 'If thou art powerful, *mana*, O Daula, put a fish or two into this net and let them die there.' If he makes a good catch, he thereupon exclaims, 'Powerful, *mana*, is the *tindalo* of the net' (p. 146).

Again, the heir of a famous chief must live up to the reputation of his predecessor, or society decides that the *mana* has departed (p. 52).

For instance, a man claimed to have received from the ghost of a late chief, a very great man, a stone for producing pigs together with the *mana* chant for working the stone; the people were ready enough to believe this, but the stone proved unproductive of pigs, and so the departed chief had no spiritual successor (p. 57).

To pass on to the question who or what may act as a host or vehicle of *mana*, it is plain from the foregoing examples that it may reside (though always conditionally and, as it were, by favour) either in a man or in a thing. For a man to have *mana* and to be great are convertible terms.

'To rise from step to step [in the *Suqe*, *i.e.* secret society or club] money is wanted, and food and pigs; no one can get these unless he has *mana* for it; therefore as *mana* gets a man on in the *Suqe*, so every one high in the *Suqe* is certainly a man with *mana*, and a man of authority, a great man, one who may be called a chief' (p. 103; cf. p. 115). In the after-life, too, 'the ghost who is to be worshipped is the spirit of a man who in his lifetime had *mana* in him; the souls of common men are the common herd of ghosts, nobodies alike before and after death. The supernatural power abiding in the powerful living man abides in his ghost after death, with increased vigour and more ease of movement' (p. 125).

As for the *mana* associated with inanimate things, the following example will show how it may come to be attributed.

'If a man came upon a large stone with a number of small ones beneath it, lying like a sow among her litter, he was sure that to offer money upon it would bring pigs,' and such a stone would be thought to have *mana* (pp. 181, 183).

Moreover, the *mana* (herein, as has been said, resembling a contagion, or such a force as electricity) may be transmitted by one thing to another.

Thus, to make sunshine, certain leaves are held over a fire, and a song is sung to give *mana* to the fire, which gives *mana* to the leaves, so that, when the latter are hung high upon a tree, the wind may blow abroad the *mana* derived from the fire, and sunshine may result (p. 200 f.).

In other cases, the *mana* is seen to lend itself not only to transmission, but likewise to a sort of accumulation.

To make rain, leaves that are *mana* for this purpose are caused to ferment so that a steam charged with *mana* may rise up to make clouds, and at the same time a stone that is *mana* for rain is placed among them to assist the process (p. 201).

It remains to notice the native theory of the ultimate source of *mana*. It has already been noted that, according to Codrington, 'it essentially belongs to personal beings to originate it' (p. 119 n.)—namely, to a dead man's ghost, a spirit (which was incorporeal from the first), or a living man (p. 151). The claim of the living man to originate *mana* is, however, somewhat doubtful, inasmuch as, if a man has *mana*, it resides in his 'spiritual part,' which after death becomes a ghost, while, for the rest, it is permissible only to say that a man has *mana*, not that he is *mana*, as can be said of a ghost or spirit (p. 191). In short, the native theorist would seem to have arrived at the view that *mana*, being something supernatural (to use Codrington's own term), must ultimately come from pre-eminently supernatural personalities such as ghosts or spirits. The existence of such a view, however, need not blind us to the fact that it is the man who does great things in his lifetime that is after death supposed to be a ghost with *mana*, a fighting man's ghost, for instance, being known specifically as a *keramo*, or ghost of killing, and hence much prized as a spiritual ally who can give *mana* (p. 133). Similarly, it is because the stone with little stones round it is like a sow among her litter that it is credited with *mana*; and the doctrine that it belongs to spirits (p. 183) is, clearly, but an explanatory after-thought. Thus neither animism (in Tylor's sense of 'the belief in spiritual beings') nor even animatism (the attribution of life and personality) would seem to be essentially involved in the naive experience of the wonder-working thing, whatever be the last word of native theory on the subject.

It must be allowed, however, that, if *mana* does not necessarily imply personality in the case of the thing with *mana*, it is none the less perfectly capable of co-existing with it, as in the case of the living man with *mana*; and, being itself something indwelling, comes to be intimately associated with the indwelling 'spiritual part.' In this way *mana* and its derivatives have come in various Polynesian dialects to supply all that is needed in the way of a psychological vocabulary, standing not merely for 'heart' and 'belly,' but for the 'interior man' and all therein comprised, namely, 'desire,' 'love,' 'wish,' and 'feelings' generally, as also 'thought' and 'belief,' and even in some sense 'conscience' and 'soul' (see E. Tregear, *Maori-Polynesian Comparative Dictionary*, *s.v.* 'Mana'). Even if, however, *mana* thus in certain contexts almost amounts to what we term 'personality,' it must be remembered that, according to the native view, such personality is transmissible (just as we are liable to think of a man's—say, an artist's—personality as attaching to his work), so that the *mana* as the realized personality of a powerful individual may be operative through the medium of what he makes or owns or leaves behind him at death.

(*b*) *Practical aspect.*—Codrington roundly declares that 'all Melanesian religion' consists in getting *mana* for oneself or getting it used for one's benefit—all religion, that is, so far as religious practices go (p. 119 n.). As he shows by numerous examples, to obtain *mana* is the object to which all prayers and sacrifices are directed. Or, again, as can be gathered from Tregear's *Dictionary*, *mana* may be used to express the performance of miracles, the exertion of a gift of healing, the interpretation of omens, an act of prophecy, in short, all the manifestations of a wonder-working beneficence which a religious man may aspire to set in motion. On the other hand, *mana* is a two-edged sword which may just as readily be employed in the service of maleficence. Those who have the *mana* to produce wind or calm, sunshine or rain, are wont 'to turn it either way as it is made worth their while to turn it' (Codrington, p. 200). Healing medicine and poison are alike *mana* (*ib.* pp. 198, 308). As Tregear's citation of phrases shows, accident and misfortune, cursing and intimidation, involve the exercise of *mana* no less than does any and every form of blessing. In short, all traffickings with the unseen and occult, whether licit or illicit, involve *mana*; and, just as electrical energy may be exploited alike in the public service and with criminal intent, so *mana* lends itself to the manipulation of the expert, be his motive moral or the reverse. Further, whatever is *mana* is likewise, in a complementary aspect, 'not to be lightly approached,' or, as we find it convenient for comparative purposes to say, 'tabu,' though, in Melanesia at all events, the word *tambu* (=*tabu*, *tapu*) has a rather different sense, implying human sanction and prohibition, the sacredness involving a supernatural sanction being rendered rather by *rongo*, or, where it is held to be especially severe, by *buto* (*ib.* p. 215; cf. pp. 190, 31). Whatever has magico-religious value in any degree is treated with more or less of awe, not to say fear, because in a corresponding degree it has supernatural power which it is liable to exercise on the unwary with such effects as usually attend the careless handling of something extremely potent. In sheer self-protection, then, the profane, that is to say, ordinary folk in their ordinary manner of life, observe a number of tabus towards the person or thing that is *mana*. Meanwhile, conversely, such tabu may be looked upon as helping to keep the holy person or thing inviolate, or guarding the *mana* from desecrating influences that will somehow spoil its efficacy.

2. Scientific meaning of mana.—It remains to determine what *mana* may appropriately mean when used as a class-name of world-wide application. Just as *tabu* has been turned into a general category standing for any prohibition resting on a magico-religious sanction, despite the fact that in Melanesia another shade of meaning apparently attaches to the term, so *mana* has of late obtained a wide currency as a general name for the power attributed to sacred persons and things, and is so used without reference to the particular associations which may have gathered round the word in this or that part of the Pacific region. Thus, even if it be true, as Codrington's somewhat guarded account leads one to suspect, that in Melanesia *mana* has been more or less successfully incorporated in an animistic system, so that its ultimate source is usually supposed to be a ghost or spirit, that is no reason why, for the general purposes of comparative science, *mana* should not be taken to cover all cases of magico-religious efficacy, whether the efficacy be conceived as automatic or derived, *i.e.*, as proceeding immediately from the nature of the sacred person or thing, or mediately because a ghost or spirit has put it into the person or thing in question. Meanwhile, the simplest way of ascertaining what modifications, if any, need to be imported into the local meaning of *mana* in order that the term may be employed generically, so as to cover analogous ideas hailing from a variety of other cultural areas, will be to review sundry examples of such kindred notions.

(1) *Orenda.*—This word is Iroquoian, belonging more especially to the Huron dialect, and apparently has the literal sense of 'chant' or 'song,' whence it comes to stand for the mystic power put forth by means of a magic song or in any other magico-religious way. Thus we are near the original meaning when we find 'one who exerts his *orenda*' as the regular expression for a soothsayer, or hear of the *orenda* of the cicada, which is known as the 'maize-ripener' because, if it sings in the early morning, a hot day follows. Not only the soothsayer, however, but the mighty hunter likewise, or he who succeeds in a game of skill or of chance, is credited with great *orenda*, though, if the hunter fails, or the gambler is worsted, then his *orenda* has been thwarted by the greater *orenda* of the game or of the rival player (J. N. B. Hewitt, *American Anthropologist*, new ser., iv. [1902] 38 f.). Indeed, everybody and everything would seem to have *orenda* in some degree, the world being regarded as a sort of battle-ground where unequal forces are matched against each other, and the strongest obtains his desire ('he is arrayed in his *orenda*' is the regular way of expressing 'he hopes' [*ib.* p. 39]), while the weaker must submit ('he lays down his *orenda*' is equivalent to 'he prays' [*ib.* p. 40]). Whether it implies personality may be doubted; for, whereas at one end of the scale it is associated with personal activities such as singing, charming, praying, hoping, and so forth, and sometimes almost amounts to 'intelligence,' as when it is said of a shy animal that 'its *orenda* is acute' (*ib.* p. 39), at the other end of the scale we find it attributed freely to trees, plants, stones, meteors, water, a cloud, a storm, or again to medicine, to a ceremony, and so forth (*ib.* pp. 33, 41, etc.). Sometimes *orenda* seems to come near to what we should term will-power, and doubtless such will-power is freely attributed to what we consider to be inanimate objects, as when 'it is making its *orenda*' is said indifferently of an animal in a rage or of a storm brewing. But sometimes the *orenda* would seem to act automatically and independently of the wills of those who seek to bring it into action, as when the condolence ceremony, whereby a sort of figurative resurrection is accorded to a dead chief, has to be performed in winter lest its association with death should exert an evil *orenda* on the crops (*ib.* p. 34). For the rest, *orenda* may work either for good or for evil, though a separate word *otgon* may be used to denote the specifically bad kind of *orenda*, and is actually displacing the more general term, as if the malign aspect of its manifestations made the more lasting impression on the tribal mind (*ib.* p. 37 n.). See, further, art. ORENDA.

(2) *Wakan.*—This Siouan word is strictly parallel to *orenda*, and stands for all 'power which makes or brings to pass.' It may come near to the idea of will-power, as in the Omaha act of

wa-zhin-dhe-dhe, the 'sending of power' by singing to an absent friend engaged in war, or in the chase, or in a game of skill. On the other hand, menstrual blood is *wakan* (whence the nudity charm described by H. R. Schoolcraft, *Indian Tribes*, Philadelphia, 1853-57, v. 70 [see A. C. Fletcher, *Proc. Amer. Assoc. for Adv. of Science*, 1897, p. 326]). In short, the term may be applied indifferently to a shaman, to sun, moon, thunder, to animals and trees, to fetishes and ceremonial objects of all sorts, and, in fact, to anything that exhibits wonder-working power (cf. W J McGee, *15 RBEW* [1897] 182).

(3) *Manitu.* — Here once more we have an Algonquian word that is generically identical in meaning with *orenda* or *wakan*. It is primarily an impersonal substantive; for in the Algonquian dialect a rigid distinction of gender is made between things with life and things without life; and, when *manitu* stands for a virtue or property, the form expressive of inanimate gender is used, though, 'when the property becomes identified with objects in nature, the gender becomes obscure and confused' (W. Jones, *AJFL* xviii. [1905] 183 f.). The following account by an Indian of the Fox tribe of the beneficent effects of the sweat-lodge brings out very clearly the non-personal nature of the force set in motion by a man for his personal betterment; he might almost as well be describing an electric bath.

'Often one will cut oneself over the arms and legs . . . it is done to open up many passages for the *manitou* to pass into the body. The *manitou* comes from its place of abode in the stone. It becomes aroused by the heat of the fire, . . . proceeds out of the stone when the water is sprinkled upon it, . . . and in the steam it enters the body, . . . and imparts some of its nature to the body. That is why one feels so well after having been in the sweat-lodge' (*ib.* p. 183 f.).

See, further, art. MANITU.

(4) *Hasina.*—This word is used in Madagascar to express the power or virtue which makes a thing unusually good and effective, such as the efficacy of a remedy, the power of a prophecy to come true, the virtue residing in an amulet or in a spell, the sanctity of holy persons and things, and so on. *Hasina* belongs in a high degree to the king, seeing that he is born in a family which has it, and is strengthened by the ceremonies of people having it, such as sorcerers and his own relatives. Hence his *hasina*, being highly contagious, is apt to cause his subjects to fall ill and die, if they but touch him. He dare not even speak to them, save through an intermediary. Meanwhile it is his duty to guard his *hasina* intact for the public good, so that A. van Gennep is probably right in regarding such a tabu as that which prohibits the subject from entering the court of the palace with his hat on his head as a *fady* (= tabu) *de conservation* (*Tabou et totémisme à Madagascar*, p. 17). Indeed, the native theory of kingship turns entirely on this notion of *hasina*. Thus, at the king's enthronement, the monarch-elect stands on a sacred stone charged with *hasina* and cries aloud to the people, 'Have I, have I, have I the power?', to which they reply, 'The power is thine' (*ib.* p. 82). Taxes paid to the king are called *hasina*, being derived from firstfruits and hence inherently sacred, in fact, a tithe. Even when the king is dead, his body transmits its *hasina* to the place of the grave, which is henceforward sacred (*ib.* p. 104). It may even be, as van Gennep suggests, that the royal practice of strict endogamy, which was carried as far as sister-marriage, was due to the desire to keep the *hasina* in the family (*ib.* p. 162). *Hasina* is, however, by no means the exclusive property of the king. Nobles have it too, but in less degree. Even common men have some, and the very animals, trees, and stones have their share likewise. *Hasina*, in short, is relative. If I plant something in my field, I put into it some of my *hasina*. Another man will therefore respect it, unless he feel his *hasina* to be greater, in which case he can receive no harm (*ib.* p. 18). Meanwhile I shall do well to fortify myself by protecting my property with amulets full of *hasina*, these often amounting to veritable boundary-stones (*ib.* p. 186). For the rest, whatever is sacred has *hasina* and for this reason is likewise *fady*, or tabu, so that, for instance, the stranger who has *hasina*, and is therefore *fady*, must be received with rites of admission the object of which is *détabouer*, 'to remove the tabu' (*ib.* pp. 40, 46).

(5) *Baraka.*—This is the term used in Morocco to describe the holiness attributed to 'saints,' male or female, as well as to places and natural objects, which are, however, thought of as deriving their holiness from the saint. The name *sîyid* (*i.e.* *sayyid*), 'saint,' is meanwhile bestowed impartially on person or place, implying a certain 'confusion of categories' (E. Westermarck, in *Anthrop. Essays presented to Tylor*, London, 1907, p. 368). To secure that the power shall be exercised in his favour, the Arab puts a conditional curse ('*ār*) upon the saint by throwing a stone on the cairn marking his tomb, or by tying a rag near by. The most efficient conductor of such a curse is, however, the blood shed in a sacrifice, for the blood contains *baraka*, supernatural energy, in itself, and hence lends potency on its own account to the curse with which it is loaded (*ib.* p. 365). *Baraka* is, however, by no means necessarily noxious (as it is when it provides the sting of a curse); for it stands equally for the blessing, *l'-baraka del 'īd*, 'the benign virtue of the feast,' which flows from the sacrificial meal, and is further distributed among the worshippers by a man clothed in the victim's skin (Westermarck, *MI* i. 445). Or, to take another example, the *baraka* inherent in the Moorish bride 'implies not only beneficial energy, but also a seed of evil or an element of danger,' so that people partake of her dried fruit to rid themselves of evil on account of her *baraka*, even while they regard a gift from her as bringing a blessing, and likewise suppose her *baraka* to give efficacy to the ceremonies practised with a view to producing rain for the good of the crops (Westermarck, *Marriage Ceremonies in Morocco*, London, 1914, p. 360 ff.).

(6) *Manngur.*—This word among the Kabi tribe of Queensland is used to express the 'vitality' with which the doctor is full and whereby he effects his miracles. He is also known as *muru muru*, 'the man full of life' (*murubarnan*, 'to live'). The force that pervades him is conceived, hylomorphically, as a number of those magic crystals which are so much in evidence when he engages in his acts of healing. As a native witness put it, 'always pebbles in his inside are. In the hand bones, calves, head, nails' (J. Mathew, *Eaglehawk and Crow*, London, 1899, p. 191). These pebbles enter the patient, so that he in turn becomes *manngur bathin*, 'full of vitality.' Or, conversely, the *muru muru*, the man full of life, sucks out the pebbles which some other ill-disposed person has put into the victim, so that the latter recovers, the potency resident in the pebbles being thus equally capable of killing or curing according to the intention of the powerful man who has control of them (*ib.* p. 191 f.). Or the medicine-man may relieve his patient by drawing out the evil by means of a rope, and such a rope he obtains from Dhakkan, the rainbow, who is himself *manngurugur* (superlative of *manngur*), superlatively potent (*ib.* p. 192).

These examples, which might be multiplied indefinitely, will suffice to show that there is a widespread tendency on the part of the peoples of the lower culture to isolate in thought and invest with a more or less independent being of its own the power whereby a holy person or thing proves his or its holiness by means of action supremely efficacious, whether for good or for evil. Modern anthropology lays great stress on this notion of the savage (whether it be conceived and expressed by him with full explicitness or not), because it appears to stand for something which lies at the very centre of what he feels, thinks, and does in regard to the supernatural and unseen. Whether it is more or less central and fundamental than the notion of spirit is a question that need not be raised here. In any case it would be quite beside the mark to seek to assign exact relations of logical priority and posteriority to these two ideas, seeing that savage doctrine is tolerant of confusion, not to say downright contradiction, and uses the one or the other conception alternatively or in manifold conjunction as a particular situation may seem to suggest.

Here, then, it will be more profitable to indicate shortly what general purposes of theory are served by reference to the group of ideas for which *mana* may by convention be allowed to stand when used in its scientific as distinguished from its purely local sense. In the first place, *mana* usefully calls attention to the element which magic and religion have in common. Among savages my religion corresponds roughly to whatever system of rites is resorted to by the community in general for self-preservation in the face of all the dangers, real or imaginary, that beset them. If you are a member of another tribe in perpetual strife with mine, I am not disinterested enough to attribute to you any religion worth speaking of, even if your rites bear the closest family resemblance to mine; but rather incline to pay you the compliment of supposing you to wield a most malignant magic, in proportion as I feel respect for your power of getting the better of me. It is a case of me and my gods against you and your devils. Gods or devils, however, they have power alike, and to the stronger power, whichever it be, the victory goes. Similarly, within the tribe a particular individual may have recourse to mystic rites to help a public cause or to help himself in a way of which the public approves, or contrariwise in order to wreak his private spite on his neighbour. In the former case he is behaving piously, in the latter he shows himself a wizard and deserves to die the death; but in either case indifferently a wonder-working power is set in motion. *Mana*, then, as representing what may be broadly described as the element of the miraculous, enables theory to treat the magico-religious as a unity in difference, the unity consisting in wonder-working power and the difference in the social or anti-social use to which it is put by the rival systems. In the second place, *mana*, taken together with *tabu*, provides a minimum definition of the magico-religious, such a delimitation coinciding accurately with the distinction which the savage both in theory and in practice draws between the world of the supernatural and the world of the workaday and ordinary. Whatever else it may be as well, and however diverse the characters it may otherwise wear, the magico-religious in all its manifestations is always hedged round with respect because of the potency inherent in it. *Tabu* and *mana* always imply each other, so that either can stand by itself for the whole two-sided notion. Thus *tapu* (=*tabu*) was 'a general name for the system of religion' in Hawaii (Tregear, *s.v.* 'Tapu'). Conversely, *wakan*, a word of the *mana* type, is translated by McGee 'mystery,' because the notions of 'power,' 'sacred,' 'ancient,' 'grandeur,' 'animate,' 'immortal' all fall alike within the wide circle of its implications (*15 RBEW*, p. 183). *Mana*, however taken by itself offers the more adequate characterization of the nature of the magico-religious, since it reveals the positive ground of the negative attitude of fear and shrinking which *tabu* involves. It only remains to add that, having by means of such terms expressed the generic characters of the class of objects to which magic and religion relate, the anthropologist is merely on the threshold of his task, and must go on to distinguish by means of fresh terms of narrower connotation the specific types in which this class abounds. Thirdly, *mana* is well suited to express that aspect of the magico-religious or sacred in which it appears as a transmissible force or influence. Thus van Gennep shows the notion of *hasina*, which is of the *mana* type, to be closely bound up with that of *tohina*, contagion (*Tabou et totémisme*, p. 17). The idea of spirit, on the other hand, does not lend itself so readily to the representation of such transmissibility or infectiousness on the part of what is sacred, except where some sort of dual personality is manifested, as in the case of what is known as 'inspiration.' Meanwhile the passing on of sacredness between one person and another, one thing and another, or a person and a thing in either direction, is a constant feature of primitive belief, corresponding as it does to that play of association to which the uncritical mind is prone, more especially when rendered suggestible by emotional excitement. Thus, in the Melanesian charm for sunshine, the operator's desire, as expressed in his song, starts a train of actions—the lighting of a fire, then the placing of leaves therein to warm them, then the hanging of the leaves upon a tree to impart their warmth to the wind; and the whole process is interpreted in terms of the transmissibility of *mana*, from the song to the fire, the fire to the leaves, the leaves to the wind, the wind to the sun, in strict accordance with the associational flow of the interest (cf. Codrington, *Melanesians*, p. 201). Lastly, *mana* is the term best suited to express magico-religious value as realized in and through ritual; and ritual, as Robertson Smith has shown once for all, comes before belief in order of importance for the peoples of the lower culture. If *mana* is, regarded in itself, an impersonal and quasi-mechanical force operating on its own account, even though personal beings may have set it in motion, this is largely because a more or less automatic efficacy is imputed to ritual as such. Whereas the reason and conscious design that are immanent in the ritual are at most but dimly apprehended, the rite itself, on the other hand, stands out clearly as something that can be seen and enacted, and thus acquires independent value. Whatever it may exactly mean, at all events it works. Thus the ideas of *mana* and of ritualistic control go very closely together, the former being little else than a projection of the latter into the world of objects, which are thought of as so many foci in a system of partly co-operating and partly conflicting controls. And so it is also with the civilized man's notion of luck, which is a genuine, though degraded, member of the *mana* group of conceptions. Those who still hold to a belief in luck are precisely those who likewise believe in the possibility of controlling it.

LITERATURE.—For the local use of the word *mana* the *locus classicus* is R. H. Codrington, *The Melanesians*, Oxford, 1891. Cf. also E. Tregear, *Maori-Polynesian Comparative Dictionary*, Wellington, N.Z., 1891, *s.v.* 'Mana.' For the kindred words, *orenda*, *wakan*, etc., see the references given above A. van Gennep, *Tabou et totémisme à Madagascar*, Paris, 1904, deals with *hasina* in strict relation to the local context, yet in a broad way that suggests interesting applications to general theory. On the scientific use of the term see various essays, the earliest going back to 1899, by R. R. Marett, reprinted in *The Threshold of Religion*[2], London, 1914. In 1904 Marett, in 'From Spell to Prayer,' *ib.*, and H. Hubert and M. Mauss, in *A Soc.* vii., independently made *mana* the basis of a theory of magic. See also I. King, *The Development of Religion*, New York, 1910, and J. H. Leuba, *A Psychological Study of Religion*, do. 1912. Important papers dealing with the subject from various points of view are E. S. Hartland, *Address to Section H, British Association*, York, 1906, and *Address to Section I, 3rd Internat. Congress for the Hist. of Religions*, Oxford, 1908; A. O. Lovejoy, *The Monist*, xvi. [1906] no. 3; V. Gronbech, 'Soul or Mana,' *4th Internat. Congress for the Hist. of Religions*, Leyden, 1912; P. Saintyves, *La Force magique*, Paris, 1914. Important books illustrating the theoretical applications of the idea of *mana* are L. Lévy-Bruhl, *Les Fonctions mentales dans les sociétés inférieures*, Paris, 1909; E. Durkheim, *Les Formes élémentaires de la vie religieuse*, do. 1912; J. E. Harrison, *Themis*, Cambridge, 1912.

R. R. MARETT.

MANCHURIA.—See SHAMANISM.

MANDÆANS.—**1. Introduction.**[1]—The Mandæans claim our interest not only as being a separate surviving branch of the Semitic stock, but also on account of their religion, their language, and their sacred literature. Besides the records of their religious teaching and their religious poetry, that literature includes fragmentary remains and revisions of ancient Gnostic speculation and myth. Adherents of the Mandæan faith, either as larger communities or as distinct family groups, were to be found some forty years ago—and may perhaps still be found—in cities and smaller market-towns on the lower Euphrates, the lower Tigris, and the rivers which water the eastern 'Irāq al-'arabī and the adjacent Persian province of Khūzistān (Arabistān). It is, indeed, necessary for them to live in the neighbourhood of rivers, since immersion in flowing water is an essential, and certainly the most characteristic, feature of their religious practice.

As far back as our records carry us, we find them subsisting in very humble conditions, earning their living as tradesmen—carpenters, smiths, locksmiths, goldsmiths—or as shopkeepers. Upon their priests rested the duty of preparing and directing the public religious ceremonials, which were few and by no means sumptuous, as well as that of performing certain rites on behalf of individual members of the community. At these functions it was their regular task to recite a number of extracts from the sacred books. In the Mandæan religion, as in others, such recitations take the place of the incantations that are no longer permitted, and in conjunction with the religious rites they serve to effect or to ensure the salvation of the soul.

From the time when the Mandæans began the serious collection of their religious texts—their mythological and legendary documents may also be regarded as revelations—the transcribing of their sacred books, and even a monetary contribution to the expense of such labour, ranked among them as a work which could purge from sin; hence not merely priests, but also a considerable number of laymen, possessed copies. Some of these were obtained by Christian missionaries from their converts, and others were bought, with the result that since the middle of the 17th cent. not a few Mandæan MSS have found their way into European libraries. The books are composed in a distinct Semitic idiom, and written in a special script.

2. Mandæan writings.—The most valuable, from the historical point of view, and—at least in the main—the most ancient portions of Mandæan literature are collected in the voluminous *Sidrâ rabbâ* ('Great Book') or *Genzâ* ('Thesaurus'), which is divided into a right and a left part.[2] This consists largely of theological, mythological, ethical, and historical treatises, which are interspersed with revelations, prayers, and hymns. All these components, so varied in their matter, may be called 'tractates,' though only by way of having a uniform term by which they may be enumerated and cited. From the introductory 'blessings,' which occur some twenty times, and from postscripts, we may infer that the sixty-four pieces, with three collections of hymns, were gradually incorporated in the 'Thesaurus,' now singly, now in groups. Originally each tractate was independent, though in the very first three or four separate writings have been brought together. The last tractate of the Right is the 'King's book,' which contains a survey of cosmic events as they appeared to a Mandæan who expected the end of the world to take place one hundred and fifty years after the foundation of the Arabic sovereignty, and assigned to that sovereignty a duration of only seventy-one years; hence the tractate must have been composed in the early years of the 8th cent. A.D. The short tractate, xix. R, speaks of Mahamat the Arab (Muhammad) as one who had lived at least from two to three generations in the past. To the much more important i. and ii. R, however, notices referring to Muhammad have been attached only at the end, the redactors of these tractates evidently thinking that they must fill out the historical sketch; no other tractate exhibits any knowledge of Muhammad or any trace of his teaching. As regards the narrative tractates, we can distinguish between those of more and those of less importance, the latter having taken their materials or their themes from the former. In some we find fragments interpolated from older works not now extant, while not a few are a mere patchwork of remnants of what they originally contained. When all has been said, it cannot be doubted that these documents of the *Genzâ* which speak authoritatively of Mandæan thought and sentiment were composed prior to Muhammad's day, and such later redaction—often far from competent—as they have undergone was the work of Mandæan priests who were concerned to transmit in some form to future generations the greatest possible amount of their ancestral literature. The formal nucleus or focus of the entire collection is a manifesto of the Mandæan priesthood to the community (xxvii. R; cf. *MR*, supplement A).

Like the *Genzâ*, the *Sidrâ d'Yahyâ* ('The Book of John'), or *Drâšê d'malkê* ('Recitations of the Kings'), more rarely designated *Drâšê d'Yahyâ* ('Recitations of John'),[1] is also a collection of tractates, many of which have come down in an incomplete, or at least in a corrupt, textual form. A considerable number of them relate to the experiences and the teachings of John the Baptist. The book also contains narratives (*e.g.*, one about the 'fisher of souls'), instructions in conversational form, etc. The diction is still good, but the legend of the baptizer of the Jordan, who is mentioned only once in the *Genzâ*, where he is described as a truly wise and devout prophet, is here brought down to the sphere of popular taste, and expounded with entertaining stories. The older form of his name, 'Yôhannâ,' is superseded by the Arabic 'Yahyâ' (cf. § 40), and from these facts we infer that the contents of this collection are of considerably later origin than those of the great 'Thesaurus.'

The *Qolastâ* is a volume containing the liturgies for the annual baptismal festival and the service

[1] In this art. the abbreviations *MR* and *MS* indicate respectively the present writer's *Mandäische Religion* and *Mandäische Schriften*, cited at the end of the Literature.

[2] A transcription of a complete MS with a list of variants from three others, executed by H. Petermann, was published in lithographic form as *Thesaurus sive liber magnus*, Leipzig, 1867. We shall cite from this ed., using the letters R and L for the right and left parts respectively, while the accompanying figures will indicate the page and line. The right-hand pages are for the living, the left-hand for the dead.

[1] ed. M. Lidzbarski, *Das Johannesbuch der Mandäer*, i., Giessen, 1905; a second vol., with tr., is promised for 1915.

for the dead (*masseqtâ*).[1] Its poetical sections, which are intended to be recited as hymns or prayers, are worthy to stand beside the songs in the *Genzâ*, though they are possibly not so ancient. The liturgical directions attached to them are certainly of much later origin, being the work of writers who were not familiar with the pure form of the Mandæan language. The same statement holds good of the two sections of the *Marriage Ritual*, which has not yet been printed, though there are MSS of it in Oxford.

To the liturgical rubrics of the two works just mentioned corresponds the *Dîvân* preserved in the Bibliothèque Nationale in Paris. The name *dîvân* is given by the Mandæans to a work written on one long strip of paper. The Paris example is 136 × 6 cm., and gives the procedure for the expiation of ceremonial offences (cf. T. Nöldeke, *Mandäische Grammatik*, p. xxiv). Another *Dîvân*, now in the Vatican Library, is 7·6 metres in length, and consists of a series of sketches representing the halting-places through which the soul of a deceased Mandæan must pass in its ascent (cf. § 28), and, at its destination, the scales and the throne of Abatûr. Its numerous figures have been drawn mainly with ruler and compass, and might be the work of a child's hand, while some parts of the text found between or at the side of the figures have been rendered illegible by stains and dilapidation of the paper. The Latin notes added by Ignatius a Jesu to explain the figures sometimes do not agree at all with the original text, and at certain points there is convincing evidence that the missionary could not read a word of the Mandæan language. It would appear that he had the work explained to him by one of his converts, but that he frequently failed to understand his informant, and made fresh errors in writing his notes.[2]

Another Mandæan work, one main division of which bears the title *Asfar malwâšê* ('Book of the zodiacal Constellations'), is found in the Royal Library of Berlin.

According to Nöldeke (*loc. cit.*), 'it is a compilation, containing all sorts of astrological material of very diverse date, and translated in part from Arabic and Persian; portions of it are of Jewish origin.'

Mention should also be made of the recently discovered earthenware bowls with Mandæan inscriptions intended to avert a curse or an evil spell.[3] They furnish melancholy evidence of the complete decay of Mandæan theology.

3. The Mandæan language.—The idiom in which this literature is composed is recognized by Nöldeke as of importance for the study of the Semitic languages; it is the form of Aramaic which developed in lower Babylonia, and its nearest congener is the special dialect of the *Talmûd Babhlî* (*i.e.* the Aramaic of Upper Babylonia). The script (see below, § 19) has the advantage of expressing the vowel-sounds by letters, and does not require diacritical signs. A correct interpretation of the texts—at least so far as they are accurately written and in good preservation—has been made possible by the grammar which Nöldeke has drawn up from them (*Mandäische Grammatik*).

4. Translations.—Ignatius a Jesu, who, as a missionary in Baṣra in the 17th cent., was in close contact with Mandæans for nearly thirty years, simply says that he had some knowledge of their language, while his successor, Angelus a S. Josepho, thought himself able to furnish the key to their writings. The material extracted by the learned Maronite, Abraham Echellensis, from three Mandæan books, and given to the public in a work printed in 1660 at Rome, that scholar had doubtless succeeded in reading with the assistance of Mandæan converts then resident in Rome (cf. *MR*, p. 5 f.). From the same period come three renderings of the supposed Mandæan baptismal formula, but these show how utterly bewildered the translators were even with the first line of the Mandæan books, for it is in reality their introductory formula. Later essays in translation, the most notable of which were the arbitrarily conjectural version by M. Norberg and the more careful but still very erroneous studies of G. W. Lorsbach, are considered in some detail in *MS*, pp. xiv–xix. In the latter half of the 19th cent. it also transpired that there was no such traditional interpretation as scholars had expected to find in the hands of the Mandæan priests (cf. *MR*, pp. 7–20). The specimens of translation offered by H. Petermann simply repeat the errors of Norberg (*ib.* pp. 99, 186, 214, 234).

Even with Nöldeke's *Grammar* at our disposal, there are still serious obstacles to a complete translation of the Mandæan writings. These contain a large number of expressions which we can interpret only conjecturally or else not at all; some appear to be Persian in origin, but there are also a number of genuine Aramaic words whose usage in other dialects does not suit their Mandæan context, while in other cases the context does not clearly show which modification of meaning has been developed from their etymological root. In some instances, again, it is obvious that words and phrases have acquired a theological or ritual sense which is not clearly determinable. All this, however, has to do with matters of detail; the course of thought and most of the constituent elements lie within the scope of literal reproduction. H. Pognon (*opp. citt.*) has taken the utmost care in establishing the renderings of the inscriptions, and has also, in connexion with them, translated numerous passages in the *Genzâ* and the *Qolastâ*—though he, too, has made mistakes. The same may be said of *MS*.

5. Interest of the Mandæan texts.—The largest and most interesting portion of the Mandæan writings is liturgical and mythological in character. The myths relate to the origin and nature of the world of the gods and that of men, and also to the religious history of mankind. They are not derived from conceptions of nature, nor did they originate in the popular mind, but were constructed in accordance with theological views. The scientific gains which this vein of liturgy and myth seems to promise—and it is the prospect of such gains that draws us to the study of the Mandæan texts—are in the main as follows: (*a*) enlightenment regarding the meaning of the Mandæan rites; (*b*) a tenable view of the origin and early history of the Mandæan religion; and (*c*) an advancement of our knowledge regarding the character of Oriental Gnosis and its religious bearings.

6. General contents of the Sidrâ rabbâ, or Genzâ.—In seeking to solve the riddle presented by the Mandæans and their writings, we must begin with a critical examination of the oldest portions of their literature. We shall, therefore, first direct our attention to the matter found in the *Genzâ*. There we find a teeming world fabricated by religious and theological fantasy. Gods and demons, or beings of like nature, come before us with actions and utterances which, almost without exception, relate to the creation of the world, the

[1] A copy, beautifully transcribed and ed., with variant readings, by J. Euting, was published as *Qolasta oder Gesänge und Lehren von der Taufe und dem Ausgang* (erroneously, the original having, not מאפיקתא, 'exit,' but מאסיקתא, 'ascent') *der Seele*, Stuttgart, 1867.

[2] A photographic facsimile of this *Dîvân*, ed. J. Euting, was published at Strassburg, 1904.

[3] H. Pognon, *Une Incantation contre les génies malfaisants en Mandaïte*, Paris, 1893, and *Inscriptions mandaïtes des coupes de Khouabir*, do. 1897–99; cf. M. Lidzbarski, 'Mandäische Zaubertexte,' in *Ephemeris für semitische Epigraphik*, i. [1902] 89–106. A few Mandæan texts are to be found in J. A. Montgomery, *Aramaic Incantation Texts from Nippur*, Philadelphia, 1913.

founding of religions, and the destiny of the human soul. Not infrequently it seems as if one and the same being stood before us under different names, while in other texts the bearers of these names are found in company with one another; sometimes, again, a particular action is ascribed to beings of altogether diverse character, or, as the action of one and the same being, it is described and characterized with much variation in different texts. It would be impossible here to set forth or unravel all this, and we shall seek only to give a concise survey of the most important trains of thought and imagination to which the vast variety of the materials may be reduced.

7. Ancient Gnostic elements in the Genzâ.—The tractates that first claim our interest, as being probably the oldest, are those which exhibit polytheistic beliefs, or are at least ultimately based upon polytheistic views. Some of these open with speculations regarding the origin of all things, including the world of the gods, and to this group belong the sections in which emanational doctrines are set forth (cf. *MR*, p. 24 ff.). Here 'the Great Fruit,' from which innumerable other fruits have sprung,[1] and—as a personal divine being—'the Great Mânâ of Glory,' from whom, in like manner, other 'Great Mânâs' have arisen, are spoken of as primal entities. Beside the Great Mânâ we frequently find 'his counterpart,' 'the radiant ether' (*ayar zîwâ*), or 'the great ether of life' (*ayar rabbâ d'hayyâ*), who appears sometimes as a primitive being, sometimes as one of the first emanations; and the same holds good of 'the First Life,' also called 'the Great Life,' and of 'the Great Hidden First *Niṭuftâ*' (*i.e.* 'drop,' perhaps thought of as a sperm-drop). In all the sections of this type we read also of 'the great Jordan,' which is always represented as a river of white water, as 'the living water,' 'the gleaming and lustrous water.' It encircles the realm of the *ayar*, the world inhabited by the higher beings, and in its descent it is joined by innumerable other Jordans which water the *ayar*-realm; or, again, it traverses that realm as 'the great artery of life.' So unorganized is the system, however, that as early as the middle period of the *Genzâ* we find the personified figure of Wisdom making request for revelations as to the gradation of the higher beings according to their period and dignity (*MS*, p. 202 f.). Nor do the texts in question present us merely with diverse elaborations of a single underlying view, or with various attempts to reconstruct an imperfectly conceived system; on the contrary, they contain originally divergent conceptions of the origin of things—conceptions either fabricated or gathered from foreign sources by the Mandæan scholars themselves at a period before the transmitted texts were written. Of the authors of the *Genzâ* it is only the polytheistic group that have made use of these conceptions.

Of the narratives describing the creation of the terrestrial world, some still bear a relation to the theogonies, the relation being peculiarly close in the long and important tractate vi. R, which we may call the Mandæan Genesis. In this text 'the Life' calls 'the Second Life' into existence by a 'request to itself.' Then this 'Second Life' creates for itself a second celestial world, and among the spirits of this higher realm of second rank (the *'ûtrâs* of the Second Life) arises the idea of creating a third world, viz. our earth, with inhabitants who should know and worship only the Second Life, not the First. Then the Great Mânâ of Glory, in order to frustrate this design, calls into existence the Mandâ d'hayyê, who was to see that the First Life was worshipped also upon the earth.

1 According to Hippolytus, *Ref.* (=*Philosophoumena*) v. 9, vi. 37, viii. 8 (cf. x. 16), the Naassenes, Valentinus, and the Docetists had a similar idea (cf. *MR*, p. 187 ff.).

In the Mandæan dialect *mandâ* is a by-form of *maddâ* or *middâ*, a noun from the root ידע (cf. Nöldeke, *Mand. Gramm.*, p. 75), and *Mandâ d'hayyê* is equivalent to γνῶσις τῆς ζωῆς, 'the knowledge of life'—such a knowledge of life as gives one a portion in life. The term 'Mandæan' is a rendering of *mandâyâ*, γνωστικός.

8. The polytheistic strain in Mandæan theology.—While the Mandæan writers esteem the theological speculations of their books as mysterious and ancient revelations, in their own religious thinking they retain only the belief in 'the Great Life'—or simply 'the Life'—whom they regard as the deity of the world of light. They use the word *pîrâ* for the most part as equivalent to 'fruit' in the ordinary sense, and the term *ayar* (ultimately derived from Gr. ἀήρ) as denoting the air of the celestial world and the north wind associated with it. The word *mânâ* (usually='vessel,' 'instrument') is still found in a group of hymns (L 38–74) in which the soul of the Mandæan asserts its heritage in the higher world, declaring, 'I am a *mânâ* of the Great Life,' while occasionally an exalted celestial being is distinguished by the epithet 'pure *mânâ*.' At first the deity referred to as 'the Life' is still regarded as a plurality, being designated 'the Fathers,' and is thus conceived as a council of gods—though one that is small and always unanimous. Very soon, however, 'the Life' comes to be spoken of in the singular. In the polytheistic writers a number of other gods appear besides 'the Life'—not, indeed, as its subordinates, but inferior to it in power and prestige. These are not called 'gods'—among the Mandæans, in fact, that term was long restricted entirely to the false foreign deities (*MR*, supplement C)—but are referred to each by his proper name. The heavenly beings created for a special purpose are called *'ûtrâs* (lit. 'wealth'), as are also the countless angels who play a more ornamental part.

Far below the realm of *ayar* lies a world of darkness—'the black water' (*mayyâ syâwê*). We are nowhere told that the black water is merely a portion of the under world, or that it bounds or covers it, and yet the idea that the under world is in a liquid condition is quite irreconcilable with a large number of its features as presented in the narratives.

The creation of the earth which lies solid in the black water, and of the firmament expanded over it, is ascribed by the writers of this school to Ptahil (on whom cf. *MS*, p. 60 f., note). The characterization of this demiurge shows a remarkable degree of variation. Ptahil merely resembles the higher beings, and has arisen out of the black water; he acts only by permission, or, indeed, upon the authority, of 'the Life,' and with the means vouchsafed to him by the latter, but he oversteps his orders; or he has accepted the proffered help of the evil spirits. Again, he is in fault solely because he has not boldly resisted such an evil spirit, or, once more, he himself has committed no transgression, and it is only after he has duly performed his work that evil comes into the world.

The creation of man is wrought in part either by Ptahil or by the evil spirits, but is left incomplete, the soul and the finer organs, or at least the former, being still lacking. The soul—that which makes man live—is breathed into Adam by Mandâ d'hayyê, or else brought down from the treasure-house of 'the Life' and placed in Adam's body by one of the celestial beings. By this means, and also by the fact that the first man was at once enlightened regarding his origin and the true religion, the design of the subordinate spirits (those of the Second Life) to create a world whose inhabitants should belong to them and worship them alone was foiled.

The wicked spirits, however—of the *'ûtrâs* of the

Second Life nothing is said even in the 6th tractate —do not at once accept defeat. By magic they create all manner of noxious things—poison and corruption, predatory animals and serpents, devouring fire and earthquake, etc., as well as evil passions—and mingle them with the good creation. According to vi. R, the first to be deluded by the wicked ones was the son of the first man (*âdâm bar âdâm*); and Mandâ d'hayyê, or his representatives (Hibil, Šitil, 'Enôš), must once more appear to fortify and maintain mankind in the true faith. These evil spirits are the Rûhâ (Jud.-Aram. רוחא) and her children, viz. the spirits of the seven planets and of the twelve zodiacal signs. Prior to the creation of the earth her abode was the region overlying the black water, and from her and her sons all evil things have come into the world—demons, founders of false religions, teachers of heresy, and men of violence. The Rûhâ, who also bears the epithet of 'world-mother' or 'mother of the world,' bore these children to 'Ûr, the Mandæan devil, who was himself her son. He is a most villainous creature, and had to be laid under restraint before the earth and the firmament were created, the reason evidently being that the 'solidification' of the land in the black water would otherwise have been impossible. According to vi. R, it was Mandâ d'hayyê himself, according to viii. R, it was his son Hibil zîwâ, who cast 'Ûr to the ground, loaded him with chains, and set warders over him —or, on another view, immured him in 'Ûr's own dark realm. Detailed accounts of how these measures were carried out—mainly by magic and trickery—are found in the tractates cited; and viii. R (one of the later portions of the *Genzâ*) relates further, with reminiscences of Bab. myths, how the 'fathers' of 'Ûr, the lords of three deeper regions of the under world, were rendered harmless (complete tr. in *MS*, pp. 137–191).

9. Biblical matter in the tractates of the polytheistic earlier school.—The Rûhâ and her son 'Ûr, dwelling upon the surface of a watery expanse that existed before the creation of the solid land, and in some way interested in that work of creation, since their names are not Mandæan, but of Heb. origin, can be none other than the female רוח אלהים who, according to the opening words of the Heb. Genesis, 'brooded upon the face of the waters,' and the light (אוֹר),[1] which is said in the same passage to have been the first work of the creation. The Gnostic writer here adopts a theory according to which the light was born of the Rûhâ (of God), as were also, subsequently, the lights of the heavens. The word קרי, 'call,' as used for 'call into being,' can be traced to the Biblical Genesis, as well as the names of Âdâm and his wife Hawwâ, and, consequently, also that of their son Šitil (*i.e.* שֵׁת, lengthened in Mand. to שִׁיתִיל) and the names of the other two genii Hibil and 'Enôš. The exaltation of Abel (הבל), slain in his innocence, as Hibil zîwâ seems to the present writer to be of later origin (cf. § 14). The Heb. narrative of the Fall, in which knowledge is described as a forbidden fruit, is one that the Gnostic author could not use at all, since he must have regarded it as directly in conflict with the view that the knowledge of good and evil, of truth and error, was revealed to the first man immediately after he had received a soul from the higher worlds, and that that revelation marked the founding of the true religion.

In connexion with the account of the origin of the worlds and the true religion, the Mandæan Genesis refers to the false religions. It states that all of them, as well as the peoples who profess them, were called into existence by the planetary spirits, and that, in particular, Judaism was created by Šâmeš ('the sun'), 'whom all people call Adônai.' The writer does not mention Christianity by name, but in the place of Mercury he inserts the Messiah (*Mšîhâ*), of whose followers he says that they 'all accuse one another of lying,' and of himself that he had distorted the teaching of the true religion. This reference to the mutually conflicting teachings of the Christian Church (R 120. 7 ff.) comes doubtless from the hand of the Mandæan redactor.

10. Possible traces of a Gnosis entirely independent of Christianity.—In the texts relating to the cosmogony (and theogony) there is nothing to remind us of Christianity except the fact that the rivers which contain the 'living' water are each called 'Jordan.' Among the Mandæans the word *yardnâ* is used as an appellative; but, as it is not a native Mandæan formation, this usage is, no doubt, to be explained by the peculiar respect accorded to the chief river of Palestine by the Gnostics, whose writings had been appropriated or used by the Mandæans. There are certain facts which lend support to the opinion that the high honour paid to the river Jordan is of an older standing than the gospel narrative of John the Baptist and Jesus (cf. *MS*, p. 16 f., note; Brandt, *Elchasai*, p. 154); and upon this point depends the answer to the question whether the Mandæan documents show vestiges of a Gnosis that was not affected by Christianity, and was perhaps pre-Christian.

11. Jesus Christ as Mandâ d'hayyê.—Tractates bearing unmistakable signs of dependence upon a tradition of gospel history, and emanating, at the same time, from the polytheistic school, are found in ix. and xi. R. These two tractates stand out from the rest of the *Genzâ* in that they alone speak of the Mandâ d'hayyê as having appeared 'in Jerusalem and Judah,' or in company with Yôhannâ the Baptist at the Jordan, with a view to 'selecting' the believers in the true religion 'from amongst all peoples and families' (R 175. 10), while the proclamation of the true doctrine, which, according to the view otherwise universal among the Mandæans, was revealed in the days of Adam, is in these tractates utterly ignored. The Mandæans gave their sanction to the narratives without suspecting that they related to the Lord of Christian believers, and also without adjusting their own theological views to the contents. The appearance of the Mandâ d'hayyê among the Jews, or among a human race long in existence, is never again mentioned—so far, at least, as the *Genzâ* is concerned—by later Mandæan writers.

12. The monotheistic school, or doctrine, of the king of light.—With the polytheistic Gnosis described in the foregoing paragraphs Mandæan writers of, we would surmise, the 4th or 5th cent. A.D. conjoined a strictly monotheistic Gnosis, which, from its leading theme, we shall call the doctrine of the king of light. i. and xxv. R furnish a complete and almost unvitiated account of it.

'One is the lofty king of light in his kingdom'—lord of all heavenly beings, source of all good, creator of all forms, of infinite greatness and goodness, highly extolled by the 'kings' or 'angels' who stand before him and inhabit his paradise. Of distinctively Mandæan character are the features noted in 3. 11 ('he sits in the lofty north') and 6. 17 ('victims are not sacrificed before him), and the description given in 9. 8: 'The Jordans of the worlds of light are white waters, full, whiter than milk, cool and delectable. . . . And the 'ûtrâs and kings who drink do not taste of death'; their garments and crowns are things of splendour and light. A complete contrast to all this is seen in the realms of darkness, with their black waters, and with a king who, like the Manichæan devil, has the head of a lion, the body of a serpent, and the wings of an eagle; he is hideous and of terrific proportions; 'iron seethes in the exhalations of his mouth; the stone is burned up by his breath; when he lifts his eyes the mountains tremble; the plains quake at the whisper of his lips.' With all his demons he once projected an assault against the realm of light, but, coming to the border of his kingdom, he

[1] In the pronunciation of the word the Mandæans may quite well have made the mistake of substituting *û* for *ô*, just as they said *Yûhânâ* instead of *Yôhanâ*. On the initial ע cf. Nöldeke, *Mand. Gramm.* p. 7.

found no gate, no way, no means of ascending to the celestial heights. Then the lofty king of light calmed the agitated world by proclaiming that 'All the projects of the Daywâ ['demon'] come to naught, and his works have no continuance' (cf. *MR*, p. 43 f., *MS*, p. 231 f.).

According to the theology which finds expression here, the earth and the firmament, with all that they contain—stars, winds, fire, plants, animals, and human beings—were created by command of the king of light through the agency of an *'ûtrâ* named Gabriêl the Ambassador.

In the record of the mandate given to Gabriel the Mandæan redactor has interpolated a passage referring to the subjugation of the world of darkness (R 12. 8–12), but nothing is said of this subjugation in the account of the actual creation. The creation of man is briefly recorded as follows (13. 9): 'And the man Adam and his wife Hawwâ were fashioned, and the soul fell into the body.' Then (13. 11-15) 'the fire-angels came; they made submission to Adam; they came and worshipped before him, and changed not his word. One was the evil one, by whom wickedness was formed, who departed from the word of his lord; and the lord fettered him with a fetter.'

13. The moral code.—With this theological exposition in i. R and also in the parallel ii. R is associated a code of practice, which seems to be of identical origin, and which, at all events, has been transmitted (R 13–26; cf. *MS*, pp. 24–43) as a record of the doctrine of the king of light. Here, *e.g.*, we read:

'I say unto you, all who give heed to the name of God: In your standing and your sitting, in your going, coming, eating, drinking, resting, lying—in all your doings name and glorify the name of the lofty king of light.'

That the record in question is derived from a non-Mandæan original appears from its use of the term *alâhâ*, 'God,' and also from its repeated mention of 'the Saṭan,' and of 'Saṭans.' The laws relating to food are of special significance; they forbid the faithful to partake of the flesh of animals that have died otherwise than by slaughter, or to taste of blood, and of meats and drinks that have been prepared by heterodox hands. This portion of 'knowledge' (*maddâ*, R 13. 23), however, has likewise been moulded into conformity with the Mandæan faith, and distinctively Mandæan commandments have been inserted in it—those enjoining white clothing with girdle, immersion in a river, the Mandæan communion, the *masseqtâ* for the dead, and the washing of all foods, as well as those prohibiting lamentation for the dead and condemning fasting.

14. Judæo-Christian Gnosis in the doctrine of the king of light.—The monotheistic concept of the king of light, as set forth, with marked Parsi colouring, in the *Genzâ*, must be originally Jewish or Judæo-Christian. The present writer is of opinion that it reveals a Judæo-Christian Gnosis. From what was said above (§ 10), the mention of the 'Jordans' of the world of light must not be regarded as decisive evidence; but in the moral code (R 25. 20, 48. 9) we find the injunction:

'Arm yourselves with the weapon that is not of iron; let your weapon be Naṣaritism (*nâṣârûtâ*; variant *nâṣîrûtâ*) and the direct utterances of the place of light.'

In the *Genzâ* the terms Nâṣôrâyê and Mandâyê are used synonymously; according to the Mandæans, both terms apply, or, at least, should properly apply, to themselves alone. We know, however, that down to the end of the 4th cent. the former designation was specially used of the Jews who believed in Jesus, and that it is applied in the Qur'ān (ii. 59, 105, 107, 114, 129, 134, iii. 60, v. 17, 21, 56, 73, 85, ix. 30, xxii. 17) to the Christians generally. The injunction just quoted permits us to hazard the conjecture that the doctrine of the king of light was the source from which the Mandæans adopted the name Nâṣôrâyê.

No other unmistakable features of a specifically Christian character occur in the tractates of the school under notice. In the final sections of its two most notable documents (i. and ii. R), 'the Messiah, the prophet of the Jews,' is actually described as a leader among the wicked spirits who make the human race abandon the true religion. These sections, however, retain only the scantiest elements of the original doctrine of the king of light. Such residual elements might with most likelihood be found in the figures of Hibil zîwâ, who (like Mandâ d'hayyê in the polytheistic Gnosis) instructs the first man in all that is necessary for salvation, and 'Enôš-'ûtrâ, who in the course of the world's history comes forth to rehearse that instruction (R 29; cf. *MS*, p. 48).

15. 'Enôš and the cloud; Mšunê kuštâ.—The Mandæan 'Enôš (אנוש ,ענוש) rests upon an identification or fusion (due, possibly, to the author of the Judæo-Christian doctrine of the king of light) of the OT 'Enôsh (Gn 4[26]) with the Son of Man (*bar 'enāsh*) of Dn 7[13]. Abel, Seth, and Enoch—or, in their Mandæan form, Hibil, Šitil, and 'Enôš, three *'ûtrâs*—are associated with Adam as messengers of the true religion and as his auxiliaries. 'Enôš, however, comes forth again, appearing in Jerusalem at the same time as 'Išû-mšîḥâ (Jesus Messiah), who poses as a wonder-worker, and whom he unmasks as a deceiver; he performs miracles of healing (perhaps on the basis of Mt 11[5]), proclaims the true religion, causes three hundred and sixty (or three hundred and sixty-five) 'disciples' to go forth from Jerusalem, and ascends to 'the Life,' by whom (his father [here sing.]) he is charged to destroy the city, and does so in the form of a white eagle—corresponding to the white falcon in *Bundahišn*, xix. 23 (*SBE* v. [1880] 71 f.; cf. *MR*, p. 155 f.). In all these acts 'Enôš has at his disposal a cloud, in which he dwells; and from its matter he fashions the body in which he appears upon the earth as a man. This cloud is in its origin doubtless the cloud of the gospel narratives (Mk 9[7], Mt 17[5], Ac 1[9]), and this, again, probably has its source in the clouds of heaven which form the vehicle of the Son of Man in Daniel (7[13]; cf. 2 Es 13[2-4], Mt 26[64] etc.). In the closing period of the *Genzâ* literature the Mandæans began to depict the cloud of 'Enôš in conformity with the Parsi conception of the garden of Yima (see art. BLEST, ABODE OF THE [Persian]), and it then came to be conceived as a country floating above the earth—a realm called *mšunê kuštâ* from the 'righteous translated ones' who inhabit it (R 338 f.); the name recalls the Jewish traditions about the righteous ones (Enoch, Elijah, Isaiah) who were translated to heaven (cf. *MS*, p. 77, note).

16. The Christian Redeemer in the Genzâ.—From all this we seem to be entitled to infer that the Mandæans became acquainted, first of all, with the figure of Mandâ d'hayyê in the framework of a Gnosis working with polytheistic ideas, and appropriated it, and that they afterwards adopted the figure of 'Enôš from the Judæo-Christian doctrine of the king of light, while, at a still later date, they met with the Messiah Jesus in writings of another origin. The tractates or books in which they found the name last mentioned were, as regards their contents, more closely related to the gospel narrative than were their other sources, and in them the Christian Saviour was intimately connected with the Holy Spirit. Hence, as the Mandæan savants identified the Holy Spirit (*rûhâ d'qudšâ*) with the Rûhâ whom they had long known as an evil being, the mother of 'Ûr, they could not but regard 'Išû mšîḥâ likewise as belonging to the group of evil spirits. In the later sections of the *Genzâ* tractates which profess to relate the religious history of man—in other tractates the Messiah does not appear at all—He is usually surnamed the 'liar' or 'impostor,' on the ground, of course, that He sought to usurp the rôles of Mandâ d'hayyê and 'Enôš. Where the writers of these sections still employ the scheme of the earlier system, they assert that He is the planet Mercury, and, similarly, that Rûhâ is Venus, and that Adônai, the god of the Jews, is Šâmeš, the sun (on the Mandæan names of the planets cf. *MS*, p. 45). The observance of Sunday was not as yet a Mandæan practice, though it later became obligatory (R 56. 12; cf. *MR*, p. 90, and below, § 32).

An account of the baptism of Jesus in the Jordan is given in the *Sidrâ d'Yahyâ*, which, however, narrates the incident in the following way: the Baptist is at first unwilling to perform the ceremony, and does so only after he has received from heaven (Abatûr) the written mandate, 'Yahyâ, baptize the liar in the Jordan.'

17. The relation of the Mandæan religion to Judaism.—Besides the OT characters already mentioned, several others are named in certain sections of the *Genzâ*, but are of no importance in Mandæan theology. Virtually all of them are enumerated below.

It is curious to note that in one passage (L 18 f.) the promise is made to Adam that, 'on the great Day of Resurrection' he and all his race will rise again and be transported to his own land, while in the same tractate, immediately before, the soul of Adam is said, quite in keeping with the Mandæan view, to have ascended to the 'house of the Life.' The idea of a resurrection from the dead is altogether foreign to Mandæan theology, so that the passage about the promise must have been carelessly transferred from a Jewish or Christian-Gnostic work. The Jewish materials in the *Genzâ* were drawn, not directly from the OT, but from Aramaic sources, including some of a Gnostic character. The ark of Noah (Nû) ran ashore—as the Targums also tell—on the mountains of Qardû (Gordyæa, *i.e.* Kurdistan); Abraham and Moses were prophets of Rûhâ; King Solomon, like King Jamšîd in Iranian legend, held the demons in subjection until he ceased to give thanks to his Lord, and let himself be adored; the world-conflagration which had once annihilated the human race before the Deluge was kindled by 'the angel Daniel, to whom was given power over fire,' at the order of 'Ĕl-rabbâ and Rûhâ (*MR*, pp. 129 f., 123).[1]

The assumption that the Mandæans were originally a Jewish or Judæo-Christian sect (Hilgenfeld, Wellhausen) seems to be at variance with the following facts. Their knowledge of the most eminent names associated with the teachings of Judaism was not obtained from oral tradition; on the contrary, they found the names in written documents—found them, moreover, as foreign words, for they read them incorrectly. Thus they render the name of Moses as Mêšâ, Miriam as Miryai, Abraham as Abrahim, Israel as Usriêl, Jacob as Yaqif; Sabbath appears as *Šaftâ*, *malăkhê*, 'angels,' as *malkê*, 'kings,' and Benjamin actually as *bnê 'Amîn*, 'the sons of Amin.' The inevitable inference is that the Mandæans had been throughout complete strangers to the religious tradition of Judaism. The same may be said of Jewish religious life. In the entire Mandæan literature there is no evidence to show that the Mandæans ever observed the Sabbath, or practised circumcision, or turned towards Jerusalem in their prayers. Like the Essenes (*q.v.*), they rejected animal sacrifices, and believed that the soul was liberated from the body at death; but marriage—in the form of monogamy, though with a succession of wives—and the procreation of children were enjoined upon them as a religious duty; they had nothing like the organized communal life characteristic of the Essenes, while their views regarding the planets are quite inconsistent with such a practice as that of according an adoring salutation to the rising sun. A further point of importance is that in their prayers the Mandæans turned towards the north, where the exalted king of light sits upon the throne, while the common Jewish view (held also by Elkesai) is that the evil spirits and their chief Sammâêl (from *s^emăl*, 'the left,' *i.e.* the northern one) have their abode in that very region of the heavens.

18. Conjectures regarding the origin of the Mandæan religion.—The relation between the Mandæan teachings and Manichæism (*q.v.*) cannot be fully discussed here. The parallels have been collected by the present writer in *MS*, pp. 223-228 (cf. *Elchasai*, p. 142 f.), and to that list should be added the correspondence between a passage in the Manichæan narrative regarding the awaking of the first man to life (as quoted by Pognon, *Inscr. mand.*, p. 130 f., from Theodore bar-Khônî's *Book of Scholia*), and one in L 46 f. In the verifiable parallels the Mandæan versions seem to be secondary, and we must infer that both sides are indebted to the same group of sources. A large proportion of the material common to both is explained by the mass of Parsi ideas in the Judæo-Christian groundwork of the doctrine of the king of light on the one hand, and in the theology of Mânî on the other. Doubtless, too, the Mandæan redactors introduced into their tractates a number of fragments from Manichæan documents unknown to us (cf. *MR*, p. 198 f.). The religious teachings of the two faiths, however, were essentially distinct in character; the fundamental dualism of the Manichæan system—a doctrine that finds a soteriological design even in the creation of the world, and involves an ascetic mode of life—is far removed from the Mandæan view. It may also be noted that, according to a passage in the *Kitāb al-Fihrist* (ed. G. Flügel, Leipzig, 1871-72, p. 328, line 5), the father of Mânî, shortly before the latter's birth, joined the Mughtasila, a sect akin to the Mandæans; this point, however, need not be further discussed here (for fuller details cf. Brandt, *Elchasai*, p. 137).

On the other hand, we cannot place the slightest reliance upon bar-Khônî's statement (in Pognon, pp. 154 f., 224-227) that the sect of the Mandæans was founded in the land of Maišân by a beggar named Ado, of Adiabene: 'Companions came to him, and there they played on cymbals, as beggars are accustomed to do.' Some of the names of Ado's relatives, as given in the context, are also borne by well-known figures in the Mandæan religion, while most of the others would at least be quite suitable for such. Nöldeke is doubtless right in his conjecture that Ado is simply a corruption of Adam—ܐܕܘ from ܐܕܡ. Here, in fact, we recognize a blunder on the part of the heresiologist, due to his habit of regarding alien religions as sects, and tracing each to a distinct founder.[1]

The religious teaching of the Mandæans must, however, in the opinion of the present writer, be explained in other ways than those suggested by the theories discussed, and the view to which our critical examination of the *Genzâ* leads us will be found to do justice to all the data, and has at the same time the merit of simplicity; moreover, it derives some degree of support from what can be ascertained regarding the age of the Mandæan script.

19. Age of the Mandæan script.—Comparing the Mandæan written characters with the various alphabets collected by Julius Euting in his *Tabula scripturæ aramaicæ* (Strassburg, 1890; the work contains also the Pahlavi script), we find that, while they are somewhat like the characters employed in the Nabatæan inscriptions of Sinai, dating from the 2nd-5th centuries A.D., they

[1] The *Genzâ* refers also to the Iron Mountain (L 17. 5: *ṭûrâ d'parzlâ*), which, though not noticed in the OT, is mentioned in the Targum of Jonathan in connexion with the fixing of the eastern frontiers of Palestine in Nu 34^{3-11} (also in Josephus, *BJ* IV. viii. 2 [§ 454, ed. Niese]).

[1] On bar-Khônî's designation of the Mandæans as Dostæans see especially PRE^3 xii. 157, 159 f.

approximate more closely to those found in the inscriptions of El-Hajr, written in the 1st cent. A.D. (in these comparisons we must, of course, disregard the hair-strokes due to the cursive mode of writing). In particular, the circle by which the Mandæans represent א is closely matched by the corresponding characters in col. 53 of Euting's *Tabula*, and the א of an inscription at Baṣra, dated 17 B.C., is similar in form to the Greek minuscule σ.[1] Thus, as the Mandæan written character dates from about the beginning of the Christian era, and as there is no ground for supposing that the Mandæans had previously used a different alphabet, the rise of the Mandæan literature cannot well be dated earlier than the 1st cent. A.D.

20. The baptistic nature-religion.—The idea that the rivers descended from the celestial world by way of the mountains in the distant north and that their waters impart fresh energies to the pious who bathe in them—a naturistic element of belief retained by the Mandæans amid all the thoughts and fantasies subsequently acquired—was probably inherited from their ancestors. In explanation of that belief we would advance the conjecture that this Semitic people had not always lived among the lower courses of the rivers, but at an earlier period had dwelt in a locality much further north, and nearer the sources—in a district from which they could see, upon their northern horizon, huge mountains towering to the sky (cf. *MR*, pp. 69-72; *MS*, pp. 213-217). We scarcely need to explain how these facts would provide a basis for the belief in question, and we can easily understand, too, how a people, if driven from their native region and compelled to endure a miserable existence in their new abode, should seek, in conformity with the practice of their ancestors, *i.e.* by means of immersions, constantly repeated, to absorb the virtues which the river brought from the higher world to the low-lying plains. We do not claim, of course, that this is more than a surmise, yet we would draw attention to the fact that there are linguistic phenomena which might be adduced in its support. Thus the Syriac idiom used in Kurdistan and on Lake Urmia is found to agree with the Mandæan dialect in the formation of the infinitive and in not a few features of the pronoun —a fact which Nöldeke (p. xxvii) recognizes as 'of great importance.' If, however, we set the theory aside as over-hazardous, we must be content to suppose either that the very simple religious ceremony of ablution had prevailed from primitive times among the country people of Lower Babylonia or that by some means or another it had spread to that district from Syria (cf. Brandt, *Elchasai*, pp. 151, 154).

21. The adoption of Gnostic tractates.—The Mandæans, then—though not yet bearing that name—practising their religious ablutions, and sharing the general Semitic belief in demons, were living in Southern Babylonia at a time when the intermingling of religions had proceeded so far in the districts in which the Aramaic and Persian languages were spoken that it had at length evolved those creations of theological fantasy commonly called Gnostic, with which, however, we must here combine the Manichæan teachings and, in great part, the substance of the Pahlavi books (*Bundahišn*, etc.). The priests of this baptistic tribe were not, intellectually, sufficiently advanced to share in the reflective activity which strives to interpret the objects of faith and the influences of religion as cosmic entities and occurrences; nor had they much appreciation for explanations of the world-process by pre-suppositions which purported to guarantee future salvation to all who acted in accordance with them, although this salvation itself and its mythological elements, the ideas of the gods and all their imaginative embroidery, were quite of a kind to make a powerful impression upon them. In reality it was into the hands of a class whose learning was confined to a little reading and writing that 'Gnostic' tractates fell, and these texts, written in a foreign language, and, therefore, to be read only with difficulty—documents coming from afar, dealing with things of a remote past, and unveiling the world of the gods—wrought upon them with the force of oracles, revelations from above, records of a superhuman wisdom. Accordingly, the priests adopted the tractates as their own, translating them, of course —at first orally, no doubt—into their own dialect. Conceivably, indeed, it was the desire of having these precious revelations in their own language that prompted them to draw up an alphabet of their own; and it is also possible that it was the translators themselves, and not their descendants in a later generation, who came to believe that the documents were from the first meant for them and their people, that the contents had been revealed to their forefathers, and that the 'Mandâyê' addressed therein were none other than these ancestors and themselves.

22. The rise of Mandæan theology.—It seems beyond question that the earlier generations of Mandæans who had a knowledge of writing (covering, we should estimate, a period of at least two hundred years) treated all the texts in their possession—as far as the contents comported in some measure with their own religious sentiment—as records of revealed wisdom; in their backward intellectual condition, moreover, they could not fail to be impressed with matter so unfamiliar. In the work of translation, however, as well as later in transcribing and renewing dilapidated texts, they themselves learned the art of literary composition. Thus, if they found that these strange documents made no mention of, *e.g.*, 'the Jordan,' the bath of immersion, or anything else that they could have wished to discover in them, they added what was required, while fragments of defective MSS they either inserted into others or put into such order as they could devise. From translation they advanced to redaction, and from redaction to independent composition. Such, then, was the genesis of the Mandæan literature; it consists essentially of borrowed matter. The circumstance that very diverse cycles of conception had a place in this material stimulated the Mandæan scholars to attempt the task of combining one with another, and of mediating between the different views. This, again, explains the development of the Mandæan theology, and it also accounts for the confusion that prevails in it.

The Mandæans never had an orthodox system of theology. Their authors busied themselves with the motley materials that had accumulated in their minds only with a view to reproducing the narrative of the creation of the world and of the human race in a fresh and improved form; and the one central thought that guides all their efforts is the necessity of explaining the harsh lot of the devout Mandæan in his earthly circumstances, and of giving him the strongest possible assurance that his soul will return again to the bright and joyful realm which is its true home.

23. The religious beliefs of the Mandæan writers.—Amid all the conceptions and the varied views with which the Mandæan writers became familiar, and notwithstanding all the reverent interest with which they received the new materials, they never

[1] Nöldeke (*Mand. Gram.*, p. xxxiv) notes that the Mandæan script bears a fairly close relation to the earliest form of Pahlavi, especially the so-called Chaldæo-Pahlavi, but its conformity with the Nabatæan inscriptions mentioned above seems to the present writer much more striking.

surrendered the traditional religious practice of their people, although their ideas of the benefits to be derived from the bath of immersion underwent a process of refinement in conformity with the development of their theology.

From the heterogeneous Gnostic trains of thought by which these theologians were influenced there arose, in course of time, a distinctively Mandæan religious belief, which can be traced without difficulty in most sections of the *Genzâ* writings. The main features of that belief are as follows. Far above, beyond the heaven of the planets, there is a world full of light and splendour, where dwell the Life (as the supreme deity) and other divine beings, or where, according to another phase of doctrine, the 'exalted king of light,' surrounded by hosts of angels, sits enthroned. From that realm the soul of man derives its origin—the soul of Adam and the souls of his descendants in the Mandæan community. Far beneath, again, is the world of darkness with its black waters. Part of it has been 'thickened,' brought into a solid state; this is the earth inhabited by mankind. The earth has now the black water upon the south; upon the north it stretches over lofty mountains to the world of light; from that world the rivers descend by way of the mountains; and thus the Mandæans, by bathing in the 'living' water of the rivers, maintain their connexion with the higher realm. The souls of the devout dwell upon this earth as in a foreign land. Here, meanwhile, evil spirits reign, akin to the powers of darkness now immured—the deities of other peoples and other creeds—and it is they and their creatures or servants who make life a torment for the Mandæans. Hence the believer waits with earnest longing for his salvation, *i.e.* his deliverance from this earthly existence.[1] At the hour of death a divine being descends from the world of light, and, as the 'liberator,' takes the soul from the body, and bears it upwards through the celestial spheres to the world of light and of the Great Life.

24. The Mandæan typology.—The soul of the Mandæan, until the hour of its deliverance, is sustained by the symbolism of the ritual elaborated by the priests. Confessors of the true faith are plants of the world of light or of Mandâ d'hayyê (R 89 f., 220, 15 f., etc.), and they are summoned to their most important religious duty in the words *Pârûn yardnâ* (R 17. 20), 'Make the river sprout' or 'blossom' (*MR*, p. 99 f.; *MS*, p. 163, note). What is implied here is that the water streams from the world of eternal life and infuses life into those who bathe in it, so that they may be said to spring from the river like plants. They were also required, however, to mark their brow with the living water, and likewise drink of it (the draught is called 'gushing'), partake of a loaf (the loaf is termed *pehtâ*, 'opening,' 'unlocking'), etc.; and those who take part in these ceremonies have a share in the benign fountains of the better world—in the great baptism in the heavenly Jordan, in the gushing of radiance, in that treasure of the Light which is to be opened. The liturgical recitations (*drâšê*) were meant to represent the beams (*drafšê*) of splendour which would flow from the house of the Life to meet the soul as it sped upwards from the earth (*MS*, p. 49), etc. The ultimate ground of trust, however, was always the ceremony of immersion; thus in R 18. 13 we read:

'Your token is the token of the living water, by which you ascend to the place of the Light.'

At the ceremony of immersion—originally this itself was the sign—it was the practice, as early as the period of the *Genzâ*, to utter names, viz. those of the Great First Life (R 196. 8; or of the king of light, R 17 f.) and Mandâ d'hayyê (*MR*, p. 104 f.).

To their own rite of immersion, whether performed, as was usually the case, by the individual himself, or, as on feast-days, with the co-operation of a priest, or administered to children, the Mandæans applied the term *maṣbutâ* (מאצבותא, presumably for מאצבועתא; the odd pronunciation given by Siouffi, *masouatta* [French], could be approximately correct only for the plural form of the noun), a word which certainly comes from the Sem. verb צבע (the sound of ע is lost in Mand.), which the Mandæans use exclusively in connexion with the religious practice in question (cf. § 38). For Christian baptism, on the other hand, the writers of the *Genzâ* persistently employ the term used in the Syrian Church, *ma'môdîtâ* (מאמודיתא=ܡܥܡܘܕܝܬܐ) and the Afel forms of ܥܡܕ. They contemn and vilify the Christian ceremony because it is performed not in 'living,' but in (or with) 'cut-off' water.

25. Kušṭâ.—In the ethical and religious sections of the Mandæan literature much is said about *kušṭâ*, 'straightness,' 'rectitude,' 'veracity.' In the ritual the ceremony of immersion included a gesture called 'putting forth *kušṭâ*,' this being identical with what is described in several texts as a stretching out of the hand 'from the bath of immersion,' or (after the performance of some other religious duty) 'before Mandâ d'hayyê.' The gesture was made with the right hand, and it corresponds to the clasp of hands with which the soul would be welcomed by the Life and other great celestial beings when it reached the world of light. It was an outward manifestation of the upright mind and of loyal devotion. Further particulars regarding the religious ceremonies, which were constantly being increased and rendered more complex by the priests, will be found in § 33 below, and more fully in *MR*, pp. 96–120, 221–226.

26. Ceremonial purity.—In this period the idea of purity was recognized in the sense of a relation to the world of light so intimate that it carried with it exclusion from every object and condition antipathetic to it ('Hibil zîwâ, pure Mânâ'; L 116. 17, 'the Jordan of the Life, from which I have taken purity'). The laws already mentioned regarding food came to the Mandæans through the medium of the ethical code in the doctrine of the king of light, as did also the injunction that husbands and wives should 'wash themselves with water' after cohabitation, and women after menstruation. It was only later that the commandment of ablution was extended to many other occasions of life (Siouffi, cited in *MR*, p. 95 f.).

27. Prayers.—Among the Mandæans prayer was known as 'compassion,' or 'petition and praise.' According to the ethical code just mentioned, believers must rise to pray thrice in the day-time, and twice during the night, but in other texts, apparently of Judæo-Christian origin, the only prayers enjoined are one in the morning, one at the seventh hour of the day, and one before sunset, while in one passage (R 300) prayer in the night-time is actually forbidden. We read also of a 'man' who (like the archangel Michael among the Jews) receives the prayers, and stores or preserves them in the treasure-house of the Life (R 221 f., 300). In the later redaction of a regulation in the ethical code the believer is commanded to ask a blessing upon flesh-food before eating (R 68; cf. *MR*, p. 94). The priests drew up short forms of prayer for these ordinances; but for protection against distress and danger they regarded prayer in the proper sense as less effective than a long series of recitations from the ancient books.

28. The masseqtâ.—The ceremony termed *mas-*

[1] The Christian belief in a redemption from spiritual evil, from the dominion of Satan and the power of sin, is quite foreign to Mandæan thought.

seqtâ, 'mounting up,' 'ascent,' consists exclusively of such recitations, and is designed to help the souls of the departed if in their journey or flight to the better world they should be stopped by evil-disposed spirits or because of their own sins. The imagination of the Mandæans gave itself with zest to descriptions of this ascension and of the stations through which the soul must pass. Each station is pictured as a place where the adherents of a false religion, or various classes of sinful men, are kept in ward and punished, the term applied to such a place being *maṭrâ*, or *maṭṭartâ*, *i.e.* 'ward,' 'place of custody,' 'prison.' Some of the descriptions contain features taken from Parsi-Gnostic sources, as, *e.g.*, the 'gates' of the planets situated one above the other (mentioned as Mithraic in Origen, *c. Cels.* vi. 22; cf. *MS*, p. xii), or the guardian spirits who come to meet the soul, and—in the latest *Genzâ* texts—the tree of life, the balance in which the soul is weighed, the judge of the dead, etc. (*MR*, p. 195 f.; so, in the Vatican *Dîvân*, beasts of prey lie in wait for the soul). The souls of the devout pass all the wards without molestation, because, according to the tractates of the *Genzâ* which describe the ascension (x. R and iv. L), they give the 'name and sign' that they have 'taken from the waves of the water,' *i.e.* because they profess the Mandæan faith and thus show that they belong to the world of light. In place of this name and sign, however, the hymns of the *Genzâ* (about 120 pieces), all of which find their themes in the destiny of the soul, its imprisonment in the body, its release, and its journey home to the world of light, insist rather upon the necessity of good works; with these was probably associated a devout spirit (cf., *e.g.*, L 101. 3: 'I loved the Life, and Mandâ d'hayyê dwelt in my heart'). It is but seldom, however, that we find in these hymns even a few words referring to the religious practice of the Mandæans or to the 'Jordan.' The explanation of this curious fact we take to be as follows. The *masseqtâ* for the dead is in reality a Mandæan imitation of a corresponding ceremony in the Parsi religion. According to Parsi doctrine, the soul, after leaving the body, is received by its own good thoughts, words, and works—which assume the form of a beautiful maiden—and by them is led across the narrow Chinvat bridge, or guarded against other objects of fear. Now the hymns in the *Genzâ* are simply *masseqtâ* hymns, *i.e.*, they were composed for use in the Mandæan ceremony. They are the work of Mandæan writers, as cannot be doubted in view of the matter incorporated in them, but in composing them the writers must have let their thoughts be guided by the example of the Parsi ceremony and the Parsi texts.

29. Mandæan poetry.—Although the majority of the Mandæan hymns can lay little claim to real poetic merit, they show at least that the Mandæans did not deal with their religious knowledge on purely intellectual lines, but found in it a source of true emotion, and the spirit that inspires them seems to be one of sincere and genuine emotion. As a specimen of the *masseqtâ* hymns we give here one of the most pleasing (L 89 f.); it should be premised that the use of the expression 'my conflict' rests upon the idea that the soul is entangled in the body and in its earthly conditions generally —an entanglement that is dissolved at death.

1. 'How I rejoice! How my heart doth rejoice! How I rejoice on the day when my conflict is dissolved, and I go to the place of the Life.

I fly and I go. At the ward of Šâmeš ['the sun'] I arrived. I utter a call: "Who taketh me past the ward of Šâmeš?"

"Thy merit and thy works and thine alms and thy well-doing take thee past the ward of Šâmeš."'

Strophes 2, 3, 4, and 5 are all mere repetitions of the first, except that for Šâmeš they substitute respectively the moon, fire, the seven, and Rûhâ. The hymn then proceeds:

6. 'How I rejoice! How my heart doth rejoice! How I rejoice on the day when my conflict is dissolved, and I go to the place of the Life.

I fly and I go. I arrived at the water-brooks. As I arrived at the water-brooks, the radiant beam (? צוריר ויוא) came forth to meet me. He took me by my right hand and led me through the water-brooks. They [the celestial beings appointed for the purpose] brought splendour and clothed me with it; they brought their light and wrapped me round with it. Life reclined upon life, and found its own life; its own life it found.'

Here follow a few sentences composed of ancient formulæ; their construction and, in part, their sense are difficult to make out.

30. The Mandæans under Sasanian rule.—The Mandæans never played a part in the field of politics. As long as they were allowed to go about their daily tasks without interference, their frame of mind was one of entire content. They were in no sense a warlike people, and their whole history, as well as their literature, shows that they were able to offer only a weak resistance to persecution and attacks upon their religion.

Babylonia, in the period preceding its conquest by the Arabs, belonged to the empire of the Sasanians. We cannot say whether the Mandæan hatred of the Jews was kindled by documents embodying an anti-Jewish Gnosis; it may perhaps date from the first half-century of our era, when a number of rapacious Jewish satraps, as related by Josephus (*Ant.* XVIII. ix. 1 ff. [§ 310 ff., ed. Niese]), provoked the whole population to an outbreak against themselves and their compatriots.

The Sasanians persecuted the Manichæans and the Christians who adhered to Rome, but they spared the Nestorian Church, which was subject to the State, and the peaceable Mandæans. The latter, however, were sometimes ill-treated by Christian monks who went to them as missionaries. In the *Genzâ* (xvi. R) we find an account of the Roman Catholic clergy and worship, and (i. and ii. R) we are told that the attempts to convert the Mandæans were not always carried out 'with sweetness'—with discourses and promises—but were also supported by force. In that satrapy, doubtless, the Nestorian Church had at one time sufficient influence to have the soldiery employed on its behalf; and, accordingly, we read (R 28. 16):

'When He [the 'Saviour Jesus'] compels you, say, "We are thine"; but in your hearts acknowledge Him not, and deny not the word of your lord, the exalted king of light; for hidden things are not manifest to the lying Messiah.'

31. In the period of the Arabian invasion; migration.—Then (*c.* A.D. 650) came the incursion of the Muslim Arabs, and the collapse of the Sasanian empire. Certain late portions of the *Genzâ* make reference to the gate and the demons of the planet Mars, 'Nirig [Nergal] who is called the Arab 'Abdalâ.'

'The whole earth is made subject to his throne'; to his followers all things fall a prey; 'day after day they make war and shed blood, and are ever an oppression to the tribe of the souls, and to the great family of the Life'; 'and there are also many souls of the great family of the Life who go over to them, and deny the name of the Life. . . .' In their distress the devout Mandæans comforted themselves with the thought that the wicked 'Abdalā had fallen into one of the infernal prisons, where his followers take him to task, asking why they now suffer torments in the realm of darkness while 'the servants of the alien [*i.e.* Mandâ d'hayyê], against whom we drew the sword, mount up to the world of light' (*MR*, p. 162 f.).

It must have been about this period, in the 7th or 8th cent. A.D., that most of the Mandæans, having reached the limits of endurance, gave way before the Muslim Arabs, and migrated from Babylonia to the adjacent districts of Persia. It is possible that the minority, as found later on the Euphrates and the Tigris, had for a time ostensibly adopted Islām, or that they concealed themselves among the adjoining marshes.

32. Restoration of the cultus.—Tractate xxvii. R may be interpreted as a summons to a meeting of the Mandæan communities either on the banks of the rivers of Khūzistān or (after peace had been restored) in their old home; it is a manifesto in which 'we, the Tarmîdâs,' turn with prayer and adjuration to the Mandæans of both sexes to urge them to fulfil their religious duties. The people are to come on Sundays to the temple (lit. 'dwelling'; down to modern times it was nothing more than a small house with gabled roof), where, in becoming order, they are to stand praying behind the Tarmîdâs, to take part in the communion, etc. This tractate is unmistakably one of the very latest compositions in the *Genzâ*, and is a documentary witness to the rise of an ecclesiastical organization among the Mandæans. In earlier texts the term *tarmîdê* (for תלמידי), like the corresponding word *μαθηταί* in the NT, means simply 'believers'; but by this time it was the name which the priests applied to themselves. The institution of Sunday, as is shown by its designation as *habšabbâ* (ܚܕܒܫܒܐ; cf. Peshiṭta of Mt 28[1]), was adopted by the Mandæans from Syro-Christian usage, though, of course, through the medium of documents of whose origin they were ignorant. The manifesto urges the due observance of the day (*MR*, pp. 88, 90). The religious ceremonies enjoined are those of old: immersion, performed by the individual himself or applied by parents to children, the stretching forth of the right hand, and the partaking of communion-bread. Everything is as yet quite primitive, in harmony with the fact that the *tarmîdê*, 'priests,' are still hardly distinguishable from the *malfânê*, 'teachers,' reverence for whom had been enjoined in the moral code (cf. § 13).

33. Introduction of new ceremonies by the priests.—In the period that immediately followed the priests formed themselves into an organized body and gradually amplified the religious ceremonial with rites requiring the co-operation of an official celebrant, or, at least, elaborated such rites from the traditional usages, and conjoined them with the simple ceremonies of earlier times. Even towards the close of the period of the *Genzâ* as attested in the latest sections of that work (cf. *MR*, p. 104), we find, besides the rite of marking the forehead with water from the river, a sign made with oil; a certain mixture was prescribed, and was to be prepared and applied by the priests. The draught of 'living' water was duplicated, being taken once from the individual's own hand and once from the priest's bowl (*qanînâ*). The priesthood ventured even to institute, in addition to the ordinary communion-bread, a host of higher order, the 'superior *pehtâ*,' which was reserved for themselves and the Salmânâs (see below). They also instituted a sacrament for the dying (cf. *MR*, p. 82), and, in addition to the *masseqtâ* of the dead, one for the living. The latter was an eight days' ceremony, and conferred upon the person concerned the title of *šalmânâ ṭâbâ*, 'blessed perfect one,' as well as priestly rank; he was thenceforward regarded as dead to the world, and had to abstain from sexual intercourse. The ordinary immersions performed by the individual Mandæan as time and opportunity permitted—every day, morning and evening (Le-Gouz, *Voyage et observations*, p. 301), or only on Sundays and feast days, and the days preceding them (Siouffi, *La Religion des Soubbas*, p. 83)—could still be regularly performed without priestly assistance. About this time, however, an annual festival was introduced at which all the members of a community assembled upon the bank of a river. This celebration, conducted by a priest, included, in its first part, all the ceremonies requiring to be performed in the river and with river water; but here the priest, using his right hand, submerged the layman three times; thrice, too, he made the sign upon the recipient's forehead, and thrice, with his own hand, gave him water to drink (*Qolastâ*, fol. 9. 32 ff.). Further, the first immersion of children now assumed the form of a baptism administered by a priest with one or two assistants (for texts and references bearing upon these baptisms cf. *MR*, pp. 221–224).

34. Ceremonies wrongly interpreted by Europeans.—The assertion that the Mandæans worship the cross rests upon references in the *Narratio* of Ignatius a Jesu (p. 38), and is due to misapprehension. What actually takes place is that at great festivals a priest of higher rank sticks a few cane rods into the ground close together and crosswise, and that he renders homage to this symbol. The structure is termed 'beams of splendour,' and may thus be regarded as symbolizing the world of light.

Reports dating from the 17th cent. agree in stating that it was the practice of the Mandæans in Baṣra to sacrifice a fowl once a year, and Jean Thévenot writes that he himself had witnessed 'la sacrifice de la poule' on the 2nd of November 1665. Since, however, the Mandæan religion does not permit animal sacrifices, such statements refer in all likelihood to the fowl whose blood was used in preparing the special host mentioned above. According to Siouffi, the 'superior *pehtâ*' was made but once a year, and was in the form of baked wheaten cakes, each of which was sprinkled on both sides with four drops of sesame oil and four drops of the blood of a newly-killed pigeon. The dead bird was afterwards buried in the temple, presumably with a view to ratifying its slaughter as a sacred act. The act was thus in no sense a sacrifice, and it is so little in keeping with the fabric of the Mandæan cult that its institution can be characterized only as a gross blunder on the part of the priests.

35. The priestly hierarchy; an order of confession in the Persian settlement.—The priestly system included the following grades: pupils, who were in training from their fifth or seventh year; assistants employed in the sacred ceremonies; priests, who had to pass an examination and be ordained; and high priests, chosen by the ordinary priests from their own number. The name applied to an assistant (and perhaps also to a pupil) was *šgandâ* or *škandâ* (cf. *MS*, p. 169), and to a priest, *tarmîdâ*, while a high priest bore the Persian title of *ganzibrâ*, 'treasurer.' Each priest had his own dishes and table, and partook of food and drink apart from the others; but his wife, by a special consecration, might sit with him at meals. There are numerous data which seem to indicate that the clericalizing of the Mandæan cult was carried furthest in the Persian settlement. Besides the title of the high priest, the names of several articles of priestly attire (*rastâ*) are Persian words —*tâgâ, kanzalâ, pandâmâ*. The priest's seal-ring (Siouffi, 'le chaumiavar') bears the device, 'Name of Yâwar zîwâ'; had the inscription originated in Babylonia, it would have been 'Name of Mandâ d'hayyê.' Again, while the *Narratio* of Ignatius (p. 23) shows distinctly that the Mandæans of Baṣra knew nothing of the practice of confessing to a priest, Siouffi's informant, who appears to have studied in Persia, tells of a form of confession according to which the sinner, upon making a penitent acknowledgment of his sins, three times receives absolution for the same sin, *i.e.*, he is assured of the remission of future penalty; but after the third time further transgression can be expiated only by certain good works. The passage of the *Genzâ* to which appeal is made in support of this ordinance simply enjoins that the devout shall thrice 're-erect' apostates or transgressors before casting them out of the community.

36. Final redaction of the Genzâ writings.—Persian loan-words are found even in the oldest Mandæan texts, but names like Yâwar ('friend,' 'helper'), Sâm, and Bahrâm (Verethraghna) could hardly have come into vogue among the Mandæans except on Persian soil. When, accordingly, in many tractates we find these names taking the place of the undoubtedly more ancient Mandâ d'hayyê, and when we observe that in others, in passages where the bearer of that epithet is mentioned, it is added that he is also called Sâm, Yâwar, etc., it seems highly probable that most of the tractates in the *Genzâ* underwent their final redaction, *i.e.* attained their present form, in the Persian province.

37. Religious decadence; obsolescence of the language.—By the time when the 'Abbāsid khalīfs had established peace and order throughout their domains, the Mandæan religion had passed its zenith. The desire for knowledge and the spirit of enthusiasm were quenched; the theological activities that had been earnestly directed towards a solution of life's enigmas had spent themselves, and had given place—as in the writers of the *Drâšê d'malkê* and the *Sidrâ d'Yahyâ*—to placid dialectics and fable-making. The soul which knew that it had come forth from a better world and would again behold its primal abode was no longer a well-spring of sacred lyric; the Mandæan had, in fact, become familiarized with his faith, and was now anxious simply to bring his store of ancient hymns into order, to keep it intact, and to use it properly. It was in this period that the Mandæans gathered their writings into collections, and composed the liturgical directions or regulations comprised in the *Qolastâ*, the *Marriage Formulary*, and the Paris *Divân*. Moreover, living, as they now did, in isolated groups among peoples of other faiths, they gradually lost the use of their ancestral dialect, and Arabic, which had made its way into these districts, became their vernacular, though Mandæan still maintained its place in religious worship. In the process of organizing the ritual every ceremony came to be introduced and concluded with recitations from the sacred books; in the *masseqtâ*, indeed, the recitations constituted the main element, and, according to Siouffi, this ceremonial, designed to succour the departed, lasted for seven days. Since, however, the teachings of the *Genzâ* required all believers to engage in such recitations, the priests endeavoured, by instructing the young, to confer upon the laity the ability to read and, as far as possible, to understand the texts, although their own learning was doubtless almost wholly confined to a knowledge of the liturgy and a traditional understanding of their own language.

38. The Ṣābians of the Qur'ān; Mughtasila and Mandæans.—In the Qur'ān we find three passages (ii. 59, v. 73; cf. xxii. 17) in which the Jews, the Naṣaræans (Christians), and the Ṣābians are assured of religious toleration. The famous Muslim scholar al-Mas'ūdī, writing in the 10th cent., speaks of Chaldæan or Babylonian Ṣābians 'whose remnants live to-day in villages among the swamps between Wāsiṭ and Baṣra,' states that in their prayers they turn to the pole-star and Capricorn, and describes them as 'those who wear girdles' (S. de Sacy, *Notices et extraits*, VIII. i. [1810] 132 ff.). The Mandæans turned towards the north, and wore the girdle. Moreover, the *Kitāb al-Fihrist* (p. 340, l. 26) states that the Ṣābians of the marshes are the Mughtasila, a word meaning 'those who wash themselves,' and it also declares that they wash all their food—a practice which, so far at least as flesh-food is concerned, is also enjoined in the *Genzâ*. To these Mughtasila, however, the same writer ascribes a doctrine of dualism—a thing quite unknown in the Mandæan documents; and he also states that many of them still worship the stars, while, on the other hand, the guarantee of toleration in the Qur'ān assumes that the Ṣābians believe in One God (and in the Last Judgment). To account for these references to the Mughtasila there seem to be two alternative hypotheses at our disposal: we may suppose either that the Ṣābians of the marshes were descendants of that group of originally heathen baptists of Babylonia which did not share the religious development of the Mandæans, or that some of the Mandæans had taken refuge from the Arabs in the swamps (§ 31), and there, while adhering to their custom of bathing and washing, had adopted new and alien doctrines. For further particulars regarding the Mughtasila cf. art. ELKESAITES, vol. v. p. 268.

The passages in the Qur'ān and the name 'Ṣābians' would apply most approximately to the Mandæans. The Mandæans, in speaking of their practice of immersion, always employ forms of the verbal root צבע, as, *e.g.*, in R 286. 1: בנאיון ובנאתון צאביא, 'who immerse their sons and their daughters'; by their Arab neighbours they were termed Ṣubba down even to recent times, and in European accounts dating from the 17th cent. they were called 'Sabbi,' 'Sabbei,' 'Sabi,' 'Sabæi'—the termination being that of the Ital. or Lat. plural. The name may formerly have covered the Mughtasila as well, and the latter possibly also came under the references of the Qur'ān. As regards the Mandæans, we have already seen that, as an outcome of the doctrine of the king of light, they had become monotheists, and that they believed in a future retribution.

39. Ostensible Christianity of the Mandæans.—The toleration extended to the Ṣābians by no means secured for the Mandæans a condition of life satisfactory in every respect. In course of time—perhaps more than once—circumstances arose in which they thought it better to be regarded as Christians. As, however, besides the name of 'Mandâyê,' they had also adopted that by which the Christians were known, viz. 'Nâṣôrâyê'—in the *Genzâ* the latter is actually used more frequently than the former—it would demand no great effort on their part to say that they were Christians. If, *e.g.*, they no longer wished to be regarded as akin to the Ṣābians dwelling in the marshes, or if they hoped to evade a tax imposed specifically on the Ṣābians, they would probably assume the Christian name without misgiving. According to Ignatius a Jesu (*Narratio*, i., a chapter written by himself), the Mandæans of Baṣra believed that Muhammad had granted them a document guaranteeing their safety, but that his successors had not respected it. Ignatius also states that the Mandæans were formerly united with the Chaldæan Christians, but that, about one hundred and seventy years before his time, they had renounced the authority of the Babylonian patriarch and abandoned the name of 'Christians.' If we qualify this statement by saying that the Mandæan communities had at one time joined hands with the Church—though only for a while—it will be quite correct.

The Arabian writer, Ḥamza Iṣfahānī (belonging, like the two Arabian writers already cited, to the 10th cent.), affirms that the true Ṣābians, *i.e.* those whom the Qur'ān has in view, were heretical Christians, 'living between the desert and the swamps.' This opinion may have arisen from a fusion of vague reports about the Mandæans and the Mughtasila, and it might possibly be taken as indirect evidence that as early as the 10th cent. the Mandæans desired to be regarded as Christians. On the other hand, a Muslim might quite well think of all the Ṣābians, by reason of their baptistic practices, as belonging to the Christian body.

40. The Mandæans as 'Christians of St. John.'—The Portuguese monks through whose reports the existence of the Mandæans was first made known in Europe asserted that they were descended from the disciples of John the Baptist (cf. a letter from Pietro della Valle, dated June 1622), and from that time, in treatises and text-books of Church History, they have been referred to and regarded (on the ground of Ac 18^{25} $19^{1ff.}$) as Christiani S. Ioannis, 'Christians of St. John.' It was not without some support from their own side that this designation gained currency. A number of Mandæans who had transferred their allegiance to the Roman Catholic Church visited Rome in the period between 1652 and 1660, and Abraham Echellensis, who cultivated a most friendly intercourse with them in order to gain the fullest possible information regarding their characteristics and doctrine, was told by them that their people called themselves 'Naṣaræans of Yahyâ'—though in Arabic only, the qualifying phrase perhaps meaning that they did not call themselves so in their own religious language, or among themselves, but that they adopted the name only in their intercourse with people of a different faith; at all events the phrase implies that they did not speak of themselves as *kriṣṭiânê* (R 55. 14, 282. 12).

John the Baptist is mentioned in a single tractate only (cf. § 11), which long lay almost unnoticed by the Mandæans, but at length, when the final additions and a number of titles to the writings of the *Genzâ* came to be formulated (R 57. 23, 188. 26, 213. 10, 218. 23), a period opened in which the Mandæans turned to the figure of the Baptist with intense interest, and it is worthy of note that his old name Yôhannâ (which they pronounce Yûhânâ) was now expanded to Yahyâ-Yôhannâ, or was sometimes simply superseded by Yahyâ. Yahyâ is the Arabic form of the name—the form by which the Baptist is mentioned and highly extolled in the Qur'ān (iii. 34, vi. 85, xix. 13–15). May we not, therefore, venture to suppose that the reason why the writers of this period bring John into such prominence and make him a hero of their people was that they had already begun to refer to him, in the presence of the Muslim authorities, as the prophet of their religion? Henceforth they could claim, whenever and wherever they thought fit, to rank as 'Nâṣôrâyê d'Yahyâ'—a name which, to all except themselves, could mean nothing else than 'Christians of John.'

Finally, they are said actually to have introduced the name of Yahyâ-Yûhânâ into their baptismal formula, and to have done so, in fact, by speaking of the rite itself as having been instituted by God, by Mandâ d'hayyê, and by John (cf. *MR*, p. 225, on Siouffi's authority). This innovation would seem to be best explained as a result of the lesson constantly impressed upon the Mandæans by Roman Catholic missionaries during the 17th cent., viz. that their baptism was only the baptism of John mentioned in Ac 18^{25} 19^{3}, and as a counterstroke to the attempts to bring them within the Roman Catholic fold.

41. In the period of the Portuguese ascendancy in the Persian Gulf.—In the 16th cent. the Portuguese dominated the Indian Ocean, establishing themselves securely at Goa on the Indian and at Muscat on the Arabian coast, and in the harbours of Ceylon. They forced their way into the Persian Gulf, and on the coast of Persia made the island of Hormuz the base of their military forces; and with the pasha of the district of Baṣra they reached an agreement by which, in return for annual gifts, he permitted them to have a trading-station in Baṣra, and promised to protect it. The Portuguese soldiers and traders were everywhere followed by the Jesuits, who founded missions, and secured the government of such settlements as 'Christian territories' according to the regulations of the Inquisition. Thus Portuguese monks came to Baṣra, where they obtained a house and made one of its rooms into a church, their hope being to win for the Roman faith more particularly the schismatic (Nestorian and Armenian) Christians living in the district. Their attention, however, would soon be attracted by the Mandæans, for the number of the latter in Baṣra and its neighbourhood in the 17th cent. was still estimated at 14,000–15,000, while in the city itself they are said to have formed the majority of the population (Le-Gouz). Decades may have elapsed, however, before the monks learned that the 'Sabbi' held John the Baptist in honour and baptized their children, and so came to believe that this baptistic people were already semi-Christians, and needed only a little instruction in order to become good Catholics. The *Discursus* which Ignatius issued as a supplement to the *Narratio* provides the arguments to be employed in persuading the Mandæan priests; but the latter were not to be won over by such simple means. Thereupon the missionaries, bent upon gaining their end, induced the pasha to order the Sabbi, under threat of fines or bodily penalties, to attend the Roman Catholic place of worship and observe Sunday according to the Christian practice of resting from servile work on that day. In this way the work of conversion was set on foot, supported, however, by doles of food and clothing to the children of the poorer Mandæans.

About this time the Mandæan communities suffered a considerable loss from another cause. In the early years of the 17th cent. the Portuguese found that their commercial monopoly on the Persian coast was challenged, and by way of strengthening their powers of defence they resorted to the employment of mercenaries. To the Portuguese cantonments the Mandæans are said to have flocked in vast numbers from Baṣra, and, no doubt, from Persia also—people who, of course, had there barely managed to live. In their new capacity they were instructed in the Christian faith and received Christian baptism (Le-Gouz, della Valle).

The fortified inshore island of Hormuz, which commanded the entrance to the Persian Gulf, was invested by British merchantmen and the military forces of the 'Duke' of Shiraz in 1622, and surrendered on the 1st of May of that year. The prestige of the Portuguese was at an end; their missionaries withdrew from Baṣra, and the Mandæans once more enjoyed freedom in their religious services. Of the Christian converts some embraced Islām, while the rest reverted to their ancestral faith—'et ne s'en conserva pas quatre Chrétiens' (Le-Gouz).

42. In Baṣra in the time of Ignatius a Jesu.—The place of the Portuguese Jesuits was taken by an Italian mission of Discalced Carmelites under the leadership of Ignatius a Jesu. Within a few years Ignatius came to realize that great or lasting results would never be secured among the Mandæans while they lived in Persia, and he devised the plan of persuading them to emigrate to Christian territories. From the Portuguese viceroy in the Indian Ocean he obtained a guarantee that Mandæans who so desired would receive grants of land in the colonies under the viceregal authority, on condition that they would give their allegiance to the Roman Catholic Church. The offer of settlements in Ceylon was accepted by many who were eventually rejected because they insisted upon being allowed to take their priests with them and to remain loyal to their faith; but, notwithstanding this, a number of Mandæans were sent forth, such migrations having taken place, as has been ascertained by Assemani from documents of the *Congregatio de propaganda fide*, in the years 1629, 1633, 1646, and 1650. The whole affair, however, came to very little, and all that Ignatius himself says of it is that he had once sent to the viceroy of Goa a number of men who were to act as the spokesmen of their people, and also to look for suitable residences in Ceylon, and that at length other fifty Mandæans, some of them with their wives and children, had set out for Muscat. It may be remarked that between 1638 and 1658 the Portuguese were gradually expelled from Ceylon by the Dutch.

43. Numerical strength of the Mandæan communities in the 17th century.—Information regarding the numerical strength of the Mandæans and their diffusion in the contiguous provinces of Turkey and Persia—as found, probably, in the first half of the 17th cent.—is provided by a map published in Paris by Melchisedech Thévenot in 1663. This map, which, unfortunately, bears no date, embraces the area throughout which the Mandæan communities were scattered, and gives on its lower margin a list of the townships in which they were located and the number of families in each community. We find an aggregate of 3279 families living in 31 settlements. By far the largest figure, exactly 2000, is conjoined with Ḥuwaiza, in Persia;[1] next comes Ṭina with 500 families and Baṣra with 400, then one place with 50, two with 30, and others with numbers ranging from 2 to 20, while to four place-names a dotted line is attached, and to several others only a stroke. We shall thus hardly err in assuming a total of some 3400 families.

44. Reports of European travellers since 1650.—Ignatius a Jesu left Baṣra in 1650 or 1651, and the Christians no longer endeavoured to win the Mandæans for the Church. It is true that the mission-house was not abandoned, and that the banner of the Cross continued to wave from its roof, while the pasha still received his annual gift; but, when Jean Thévenot lodged there in 1665, he found that it was tenanted only by a single Italian monk, and that the church stood open for prayer not only to Europeans, but to Nestorian and Armenian Christians. Shortly afterwards, when the station had once more been brought into working order, its director, the Carmelite Archangelus a S. Theresia, was obliged to expend a considerable sum of money to procure Mandæan MSS for Robert Huntington, who lived in Aleppo from 1671 to 1681. The vendors were a couple of Mandæans, one of whom had to be assured upon oath that his co-religionists should never hear of the transaction, while the other had become a convert to Islām.

A long period then elapsed during which little or no information regarding the Mandæans reached Europe. Paragraphs devoted to them (and often referred to in encyclopædias) in J. Chardin, *Voyages*, etc. (Paris, 1686 ff.), and E. Kaempffer, *Amœnitatum*, etc., fasc. v. (Lemgow, 1712), simply repeat accounts previously published. In 1765 Carsten Niebuhr visited Baṣra and found that only a few 'Sabians' lived there; he had their alphabet transcribed for him by a smith. Naval Lieutenant Ormsby, the friend of J. R. Wellsted, stayed at Hiṭ for five days in 1833, and ascertained that the Mandæans had a community with a priest in that city, though neither there nor elsewhere could he learn anything about them but the most meagre details.

The first European to gain really fresh information regarding the Mandæans was the German Orientalist H. Petermann, who, in the spring of 1854, spent three months in Sūq eš-Šiyūkh on the Euphrates, learned the Mandæan language from the local high priest Yahyâ (-Bûlad), and in the latter's company was permitted to be present at a number of ceremonies, including the five days' baptismal festival. At length, however, a much greater addition to our knowledge was contributed by the information with which a grandson of this Yahyâ gratified the curiosity of N. Siouffi, French vice-consul at Baghdād, in 1875. The fullness and accuracy of the communications are explained by the fact that the informant, before embracing Christianity when about twenty-five, had received an education qualifying him to become a Mandæan priest, but it is necessary to state that his account of the Mandæan doctrines and legends was wholly dependent upon a late version, from which every difficulty had been expunged (cf. *MR*, pp. 17–19), and that he could describe the methods and customs of his people only in their most recent phases of development.

45. The Mandæans in the 19th century.—The books of Petermann and Siouffi contain observations from which we may learn how the Mandæans had fared in the long interval from the 17th cent., and it would seem that in this period, too, the vicissitudes of their ordinary life were due to suffering and want. About the year 1800 30 families in Shushter alone are said to have seceded to Islām, and 'many Mandæans' are reported to have done so about 1825. The great pestilence which ravaged Persia and Mesopotamia in 1831 carried off the entire priesthood with the exception of two *šgandâs*, and at some unspecified date the Mandæans forsook Baṣra owing to its deadly climate. In the vicinity of Ḥuwaiza only 25 families remained, all the rest having removed because the river (Ḳercha) had almost completely dried up. Sūq eš-Šiyūkh (which does not appear in the list subjoined to Thévenot's map), or rather the village of Ṣubbuye on the other side of the river, had become one of the main domiciles of the Mandæans (the 'Ṣubba'), and was named after them. The district, however, was ruled by a Bedawin *shaikh*, who so afflicted the village with chicanery and extortion that about 200 of the 260 families composing the local Mandæan community abandoned it in 1853 and removed to Ammāra on the Tigris, where the second largest community (about 100 families) had enjoyed a more favourable lot under Turkish rule. Petermann also mentions Qurna, at the confluence of the Euphrates and the Tigris, with 40 families, and Muhammara, on the Shaṭṭ al-'Arab below Baṣra, with 4, as well as the Persian towns of Dizful with 80, and Shushter with 34. He makes an aggregate of about 560 families, with 10 priests. Siouffi mentions other 11 settlements, 6 in Turkish and 5 in Persian territory, and his estimate of the total number of Mandæans is 4000, of whom 1500 were males. These two enumerations bring us to the years 1854 and 1875 respectively. Whether any Mandæan communities still exist the present writer is not in a position to say.

LITERATURE.—i. On the Ṣābians, Mughtasila, and Mandæans: D. Chwolsohn, *Die Ssabier und der Ssabismus*, Petrograd, 1856; G. Flügel, *Mani, seine Lehre und seine Schriften*, Leipzig, 1862, p. 133 ff.; W. Brandt, *Elchasai*, do. 1912, pp. 134–151 (gives information regarding the Arabic data, with translations, and discusses the question as to the origin of the Bab. practice of baptism).

ii. On the Mandæans in the 16th and 17th centuries: *Viaggi di Pietro della Valle il Pellegrino, La Persia*, Rome, 1658, pp. 412–414; P. F. Ignatius a Jesu and others, *Narratio Originis, Rituum, et Errorum Christianorum Sancti Joannis, Cui adiungitur Discursus per modum Dialogi in quo confutantur XXXIII Errores eiusdem Nationis*, Rome, 1652 (the bulk of the text consists of an earlier account which, with the *Discursus*, had probably been written during the time of the Portuguese mission, and afterwards amended and supplemented here and there by the Italian monks; to this Ignatius himself prefixed a new 'first chapter' in which he states his views of the Mandæans—a view differing from that given in the original first chapter, now the second—and he also inserted his notes regarding the *Dîvân*); F. de la Boullaye-

[1] According to a statement of Pietro della Valle, dating from 1622, the Mandæans in Persia lived principally in the district of Kamalawa, not far from Ḥuwaiza.

Le-Gouz, *Voyage et observations*, Paris, 1652, [2]Troyes and Paris, 1657, p. 291 ff. (chs. xliii.–xlix.); **Jean Thévenot**, *Suite du Voyage de Levant*, Paris, 1674 (posthumously), pp. 324–328; Melchisedech Thévenot, *Relations de divers voyages*, do. 1663–64 (large quarto, without continuous pagination), pt. i., 'Vera Delinatio Civitatis Bassoræ' (the map mentioned in § 43); Abraham Echellensis, *Eutychius patriarcha Alexandrinus vindicatus*, ii. ('De Origine nominis Papæ'), Rome, 1660, pp. 310–336.

iii. Works published in the 19th cent. and later: **J. R. Wellsted**, *Travels to the City of the Caliphs*, London, 1840, i. 316 f. (from notes of Lieut. Ormsby); **H. Petermann**, *Reisen im Orient*, 2 vols., Leipzig, 1860–61, ii. 83–137, 447–465; **N. Siouffi**, *Études sur la religion des Soubbas ou Sabéens, leurs dogmes, leurs mœurs*, Paris, 1880 (on pp. 198–204 will be found an extract relating to the Mandæans from the *Voyage en Russie*, etc., of J. M. Lycklama a Nijeholt, Amsterdam, 1872–75, on which cf. *MR*, p. 12, note); **T. Nöldeke**, *Mandäische Grammatik*, Halle, 1875, Introduction; cf. also his art. in *GGA*, 1869, pp. 481–501; **K. Kessler**, art. 'Mandæans,' in *EBr*[9], and 'Mandäer,' in *PRE*[3] (cf. *MR*, p. 230 f.); **M. Lidzbarski**, 'Uthra und Malakha,' in *Orientalische Studien, Theodor Nöldeke zum 70ten Geburtstag*, Giessen, 1906, pp. 537–545; **W. Brandt**, *Die mandäische Religion*, Leipzig, 1889, *Mandäische Schriften*, Göttingen, 1893.

W. BRANDT.

MANETHO.—This historian of Egypt was born at Sebennytus, the *Theb-Neteret* of the hieroglyphic inscriptions, and lived during the reigns of Ptolemy Lagi and Ptolemy Philadelphus. His name is probably the Gr. form of *Mā-en-Teḥuti*, 'Gift of Thōth'—equivalent to the Gr. Ἑρμόδωρος. The following works have been attributed to him, some of them on doubtful authority: (1) Αἰγυπτιακά, (2) Βίβλος Σώθεος, (3) Ἱερὰ Βίβλος, (4) Φυσικῶν ἐπιτομή, (5) Περὶ ἑορτῶν, (6) Περὶ ἀρχαισμοῦ καὶ εὐσεβείας, (7) Περὶ κατασκευῆς κυφίων. His reputation rests upon the Αἰγυπτιακά, a history of Egypt which he compiled at the request of Ptolemy Philadelphus. The first part of his work dealt with the mythological era in the history of Egypt, and the first eleven of the thirty historical dynasties; the second began with the XIIth dynasty, and ended with the XIXth; the third comprised dynasties XX.–XXX. The work was written in Greek, and has, unfortunately, perished, with the exception of the list of kings, which has been preserved in corrupt and incomplete forms by Julius Africanus, Eusebius, and George the Syncellus.

An examination of these king lists shows that in many particulars Julius Africanus and Eusebius do not agree in their rendering—*i.e.* in arrangement of the dynasties, in the lengths of the reigns, and in the total number of kings assigned to the various dynasties. According to Africanus, 561 kings reigned in about 5524 years, while, according to Eusebius, only about 361 kings reigned in 4480 or 4780 years. The version of Africanus is clearly the more accurate of the two, agreeing best with the monuments. It seems fairly certain that Africanus had access to the actual work of Manetho. The version of Eusebius was based on that of Africanus, and shows carelessness in the copying of both names and figures. It will thus be seen that the work of Manetho must be received with some caution, for his king lists have become very corrupt; and it is probable that the Christian writers who transmitted his system, being anxious to reconcile it with the accepted Biblical chronology, have curtailed his lists to some extent. Nevertheless Manetho's work remains the standard authority on Egyptian chronology, and upon it all attempts to restore that chronology must be based.

The chief original authorities with which his work may be compared are: (1) the Turin Royal Papyrus—lamentably mutilated, and badly restored; (2) the Tablet of Abydos, containing a list of 75 kings, dynasties I.–XIX.; (3) the Tablet of Ṣaqqārah—47 royal names in practically the same order as (2); and (4) the Tablet of Karnak, containing a list of 61 kings—the cartouches are not arranged chronologically. The lists of Manetho are much more complete than any of these, and it is to him that we owe the accepted distribution into dynasties.

Opinions differ widely as to the value of his historical work. A period in which he was regarded as a mere fabricator was succeeded by one in which his authority was considered practically unimpeachable. Thus Lenormant says:

'He is now the first of all authorities for the reconstruction of the ancient history of Egypt' (*Anc. Hist. of the East*, i. 201).

More modern authorities are sharply divided. Adverse opinion may be represented by Breasted's sweeping dictum:

'A late, careless and uncritical compilation, which can be proven wrong from the contemporary monuments in the vast majority of cases where such monuments have survived. Its dynastic totals are so absurdly high throughout that they are not worthy of a moment's credence, being often nearly or quite double the maximum drawn from contemporary monuments, and they will not stand the slightest criticism. Their accuracy is now maintained only by a small and constantly decreasing number of modern scholars' (*Hist. of Egypt*, p. 23).

This is so sweeping as to suggest bias at once; and, when it is remembered that an exactly opposite judgment is pronounced by authorities of such standing as Maspero and Flinders Petrie, its oracular tone becomes merely ridiculous. Maspero's verdict is as follows:

'The system of Manetho, in the state in which it has been handed down to us by epitomizers, has rendered, and continues to render, service to science; if it is not the actual history of Egypt, it is a sufficiently faithful substitute to warrant our not neglecting it when we wish to understand and reconstruct the sequence of events. His dynasties furnish the necessary framework for most of the events and revolutions, of which the monuments have preserved us a record' (*Dawn of Civilization*, p. 228).

Still more emphatically favourable is Petrie's judgment:

'An authority of the highest order. . . . The internal evidence is also strong for the care given to his work and its precision. . . . Manetho has been often accused of double reckoning, by stating two contemporary dynasties or kings separately. Every instance in which this has been supposed has broken down when examined in detail. Not a single case of overlapping periods can be proved against him. On the contrary, there are two excellent proofs of his care to avoid such errors' (*Researches in Sinai*, p. 171).

Possibly the truth may lie somewhere between the two extreme opinions, and Manetho may be neither so careless as Breasted alleges nor so immaculate as Petrie affirms. In any case, even his detractors cannot afford to do without him; for every reconstruction of the history of Egypt is based, and will continue to be based, on the dynastic framework which he has provided.

What system of dating we are to derive from his dynastic scheme and other sources is another question. Here also there is fundamental disagreement. As far back as 1580 B.C. there is practically no difference between the various schemes of dating, and Egyptian chronology may be looked upon as settled with only a few years' margin of error up to that point. Beyond that lies chaos. The Berlin school, represented by Meyer and Breasted, dates the beginning of the Ist dyn. at 3400 B.C., and that of the XIIth, fixed by astronomical data, at 2000 B.C. Wallis Budge, still clinging to Brugsch's system, gives 4400 B.C. for the Ist dyn. and 2400 B.C. for the XIIth. Petrie gives 5510 B.C. for the Ist dyn., and, using the same astronomical data as the Berlin school, 3459 B.C. for the XIIth. Here it is most unlikely that the truth lies between the two extremes, and Brugsch's *via media* seems to lead nowhere. The gigantic gap between Petrie's dates and those of Berlin is due to the fact that Petrie holds that the advocates of the shorter system have dropped a whole Sothic period of 1460 years out of their reckoning. If the astronomical foundation be sound, the truth must lie either with the shortest or with the longest system, and only further research can clear up the problem. Meanwhile the tendency has been somewhat in the direction of the Berlin system, which, according to Petrie, 'defies all the history and the collateral facts which support it' (*Ancient Egypt*, London, 1915, pt. i. p. 37); and Manetho's credit remains in suspense.

In addition to his service to chronology, Manetho has contributed, though only at second-hand, two interesting traditions of Egyptian history. These are preserved by Josephus (*c. Apion.* i. 26 f.), and give a somewhat nebulous account of the Hyksos invasion, and the narrative of the expulsion of a race of lepers and unclean persons, which may conceivably represent the Egyptian tradition of the Hebrew Exodus.

Manetho's chronological scheme is too long to be given in detail, but will be found, in part or in whole, in most of the Egyptian Histories—*e.g.*, completely in Budge, *Hist. of Egypt*, i. 130–140.

LITERATURE.—I. P. Cory, *Ancient Fragments*, London, 1832, pp. 94–181; F. Lenormant, *Ancient History of the East*, do. 1869, i. 196–201; J. Lieblein, *Recherches sur la chronologie égyptienne*, Christiania, 1873; C. C. J. Bunsen, *Egypt's Place in Universal History*, Eng. tr., London, 1848, i. 56–96; G. Maspero, *The Dawn of Civilization*, Eng. tr., do. 1894, pp. 225–230, 785–790; H. Brugsch, *Histoire d'Egypte*, Leipzig, 1859, i. 16–30, 287–293; W. M. F. Petrie, *History of Egypt*, London, 1894, i. 16–23, *Researches in Sinai*, do. 1906; E. A. W. Budge, *History of Egypt*, do. 1902, i. 111–161, *A Short History of the Egyptian People*, do. 1914; E. de Rougé, 'Examen de l'ouvrage de M. le Chevalier de Bunsen,' in *Annales de philosophie chrétienne*, xiii.–xvi. [1846–47]; J. H. Breasted, *History of Egypt*, London, 1906; R. M. Burrows, *The Discoveries in Crete*, do. 1908; H. R. Hall, *Ancient History of the Near East*, do. 1913.

JAMES BAIKIE.

MANICHÆISM.—I. Sources.—Manichæism, the religion of Mānī or Manes, is one of those systems which are usually classed together under the name of Gnosticism. The Manichæan religion arose in Babylonia about the middle of the 3rd cent. A.D., and during many generations exercised great influence both in the East and in the West. Of the literature of the Manichæans very little has survived. The fragments of Manichæan MSS which have lately been discovered in Central Asia present great difficulties of interpretation, so that, while they confirm much that was previously known, they do not enable us to form a connected idea of the subject.[1] The attempts which have been made in modern times to prove that some well-known books, in particular certain of the Apocryphal Gospels and Acts, are of Manichæan origin must be pronounced wholly unsuccessful. Hence our information respecting this religion is derived almost entirely from non-Manichæan authors, most of whom wrote with an avowedly hostile purpose. As our conclusions must depend largely on the relative importance which we attach to the various sources, it is necessary first to give some account of them. They fall into four main groups: (1) Oriental Christian sources, (2) Zoroastrian sources, (3) Western sources, (4) Muhammadan sources.

(1) *Oriental Christian.*—These have, in some respects, the greatest claim to consideration. The Aramaic-speaking Christians of Syria and Mesopotamia were in race, in language, and in general culture nearly akin to the primitive Manichæans, and had every opportunity of becoming well acquainted with the new religion. Unfortunately very little of their testimony has come down to us. Aphraates, in the first half of the 4th cent., the earliest Syriac author whose works have been preserved in any considerable quantity,[1] briefly alludes to Manichæism as a dangerous heresy:

> 'The children of darkness, the doctrine of the wicked Mānī, who dwell in darkness like serpents, and practise Chaldæism [*i.e.* astrology], the doctrine of Babel.'[2]

More information may be gathered from the works of a younger contemporary of Aphraates, the well-known Ephraim of Nisibis, commonly called Ephraim Syrus. References to Manichæism are found in several of his writings, especially in a series of five discourses, entitled *Letters to Hypatios*.[3] The treatise against Manichæism composed by Gabriel, bishop of Hormizdshēr, in the 6th cent., seems now to be lost.[4] Later Syriac writers, such as Theodore bar-Khōnī[5] and Barhebræus,[6] do not supply much that is of importance.

Among Oriental Christian authorities we must also reckon the Armenian writer Eznik of Kolb, who lived in the 5th cent.,[7] and Sa'īd ibn al-Biṭrīq, generally called Eutychius, who was Patriarch of Alexandria from A.D. 933 to 939.[8]

(2) *Zoroastrian.*—The evidence contained in Zoroastrian literature is, if anything, scantier than that which may be collected from the works of Oriental Christians; moreover, it is much more difficult to interpret, owing partly to the unsatisfactory condition of the text and partly to our imperfect acquaintance with the language. But the vehement condemnations of Manichæism which are found in Zoroastrian books bear witness at least to the dread with which the Persian priesthood regarded the rival faith.[9]

(3) *Western.*—Accounts by Greek and Latin authors exist in far greater quantity, but they are, from the nature of the case, much less trustworthy. Manichæism was so essentially Oriental (*i.e.* non-Hellenic) in its character that the Christians of the West would probably have had considerable difficulty in understanding it, even if they had been wholly impartial. That this was out of the question hardly needs to be stated. The strangeness of the system was doubtless an attraction to some minds, but those who are attracted by mere novelty are usually uncritical, while the attitude of uncom-

1 These fragments are written in various languages (Persian, Turkish, and Chinese). They have been published by F. W. K. Müller, 'Handschriften-Reste in Estrangelo-Schrift aus Turfan,' in *SBAW*, 1904, p. 348 ff., and in *ABAW*, 1904, 'Ein Doppelblatt aus einem manichäischen Hymnenbuch,' in *ABAW*, 1912 (republished separately, Berlin, 1913); A. von Le Coq, 'Ein manichäisch-uigurisches Fragment aus Idiqut-Schahri,' in *SBAW*, 1908, p. 398 ff., 'Ein christliches und ein manichäisches Manuskriptfragment in türkischer Sprache aus Turfan,' *ib.*, 1909, p. 1202 ff., 'Dr. Stein's Turkish Khuastuanift from Tun-Huang, being a Confession-prayer of the Manichæan Auditores,' in *JRAS*, 1911, p. 277 ff.; C. Salemann, *Ein Bruchstük manichäischen Schrifttums im asiatischen Museum*, Petrograd, 1904 (=*Mémoires de l'Académie Impériale des Sciences*, VIII. vi. 6), *Manichäische Studien*, i., do. 1908 (=*Mémoires*, VIII. viii. 10), *Manichæica*, i.–iv., do. 1907–12 (=*Bulletin de l'Académie impériale des Sciences*); E. Chavannes and P. Pelliot, 'Un traité manichéen retrouvé en Chine,' in *JA*, 1911 (republished, Paris, 1912).

1 On Aphraates see W. Wright, *Short History of Syriac Literature*, London, 1894, p. 32. The *Homilies* of Aphraates have been re-edited, with a Lat. tr., by I. Parisot (Paris, 1894).

2 *Hom.* iii. Why the Manichæans were accused of astrology will appear later on.

3 The first of these discourses and part of the second were published by J. J. Overbeck in his *Sancti Ephraemi Syri aliorumque opera selecta*, Oxford 1865, p. 21 ff. This portion of the second discourse was reprinted by K. Kessler (*Mani*, p. 268 ff.), with a very inaccurate Germ. tr. The remainder of the work, with the exception of some passages which are effaced in the MS, was first made known by C. W. Mitchell (*S. Ephraim's Prose Refutations*, i., London, 1912). In Ephraim's *Carmina Nisibena* (ed. G. Bickell, Leipzig, 1866), no. xlv., there is an interesting passage which doubtless refers to the Manichæans, though they are not expressly named: 'Fools in their perversity have forged a tale, how that the Darkness ventured to disturb the Light,' etc.

4 See Wright, *op. cit.* p. 120.

5 Theodore's account of Mānī has been published and translated by H. Pognon in his *Inscriptions mandaïtes des coupes de Khouabir*, Paris, 1897–99. It is borrowed in part from Epiphanius, and therefore cannot be regarded as purely Oriental. Cf. also F. Cumont, *La Cosmogonie manichéenne, d'après Theodore bar Khôni* (=*Recherches sur le Manichéisme*, i.), Brussels, 1908.

6 The testimony of Barhebræus is to be gathered partly from his Syr. *Ecclesiastical History*, partly from his Arab. *Compendium of the Dynasties*.

7 See V. Langlois, *Collection des historiens anciens et modernes de l'Arménie*, Paris, 1867–69, ii. 375 ff., and the tr. by J. M. Schmid, Vienna, 1900, p. 94 ff.

8 *Eutychii Annales*, ed. E. Pococke, Oxford, 1658–59, which contains the original Arab. text with a Lat. tr.

9 Perhaps the most important passage on this subject is that which E. W. West has translated in his *Pahlavi Texts*, iii. 243 ff. (*SBE* xxvi. [1885]). A Germ. tr. is given by Salemann, *Ein Bruchstük manichäischen Schrifttums im asiat. Museum*.

promising hostility, which was adopted by the great majority of Christian theologians, naturally proved even less favourable to accurate comprehension.

The foreign origin of Manichæism is duly emphasized by Eusebius in the brief notice which he devotes to this 'insane heresy.'[1] Alexander of Lycopolis, the author of a short tract against Manichæism,[2] was probably a contemporary of Eusebius. He deserves notice as being the only Western writer who treats the subject from a purely philosophical point of view; though he speaks of Christianity with a certain respect, it is doubtful whether he ever became a Christian. Of more importance is the testimony of a somewhat later controversialist, Titus, bishop of Bostra in Syria, who died about A.D. 370. In a geographical sense, Titus must be reckoned among Oriental Christians, but his *Treatise against the Manichæans*[3] proves him to have been thoroughly Western in his education and habits of thought, deeply imbued with Greek philosophy, in particular with Stoicism, and full of contempt for 'barbarians.' He distinctly states that he derived his information from a Manichæan book,[4] but he tells us nothing definite as to its authorship. His words, however, seem to imply that the book was not composed by the founder of Manichæism himself, for in quoting it he says, 'as is stated by the author who wrote down the doctrines of that maniac';[5] and, again, 'these are the very words used by him or else by one of his followers.'[6] He afterwards mentions a Manichæan work entitled *The Treasure*,[7] but whether this is identical with the book cited previously cannot be determined. In any case it is interesting to observe that, according to Titus, the Manichæans made every effort to conceal from outsiders the writings of their founder, apparently in obedience to his express orders.[8] Another fact, no less significant, is that Titus professes to have softened down the expressions which he found in his source: 'these are not the words used by him, but this is what he meant to say, translated into more decent language.'[9] In estimating the evidence supplied by Titus this tendency must be constantly borne in mind.

A more popular but a much less respectable authority is the *Acta Archelai*, a work which professes to record a disputation between Manes and Archelaus, bishop of Carchar[10] in Mesopotamia.

1 *HE* vii. 31.
2 ed. A. Brinkmann, Leipzig, 1895.
3 Of the four books into which this work is divided only the first two and the beginning of the third have been preserved in the original Gr.; but all four are extant in a Syr. tr., which must have been made very early, as it is contained in a Brit. Mus. MS written in A.D. 412. The Gr. text was first published by J. Basnage in 1725; the best edition is that of P. A. de Lagarde (Berlin, 1859), who also edited the Syr. version. It is to be noted that the Gr. text has a long insertion (printed as an Appendix by Lagarde, pp. 69–103) which is absent in the Syriac. In *SBAW*, 1894, p. 479 ff., August Brinkmann has endeavoured to prove that this piece is a fragment of a book against the Manichæans by Serapion of Thmuis, a friend of Athanasius.
4 αὐτῇ λέξει φησὶν ἡ παρ' αὐτοῖς βίβλος (bk. i. § 21); φησὶ γὰρ αὐτὸ τὸ γράμμα ἀφ' οὗ τὰ παρὰ τοῦ μανέντος παρεθήκαμεν (bk. i. § 22). The punning use of μανείς, μανία, etc.. in allusion to the name Manes, is extremely common.
5 ὥς γε ὁ τὰ τοῦ μανέντος συγγράφων φησίν (bk. i. § 21).
6 φησὶ δὲ πρὸς λέξιν αὐτὴν ἐκεῖνος ἢ ἕτερός τις τῶν ἀπ' ἐκείνου (bk. iii. § 4). Photius states that the source used by Titus was the work of a certain Addas: ἔδοξε μὲν κατὰ Μανιχαίων γράφειν, ἔγραψε δὲ μᾶλλον κατὰ τῶν Ἄδδου συγγραμμάτων (*PG* ciii. 288).
7 Syr. *sīmĕthā* (bk. iii. § 9). This is probably the work called θησαυρός by Epiphanius, and θησαυρὸς ζωῆς in the Greek *Formula of Abjuration*. Both al-Ya'qūbī and al-Bīrūnī ascribe to Mānī a book known as *Kanz-al-Iḥyā*, 'Treasure of Life-giving,' but it is to be noted that the list of Mānī's writings in the *Fihrist* (p. 336, line 8 ff.) does not include this title, although it mentions a *Sifr-al-Iḥyā*, 'Book of Life-giving.'
8 Bk. iii. § 9.
9 εἰ γὰρ καὶ μὴ τούτοις γε τοῖς ῥήμασιν, ἀλλά γε ταῦτα βούλεται λέγειν, ἅπερ εὐσχημονέστερον πάνυ γε πρὸς ἡμῶν εἴρηται (bk. i. § 17).
10 The name is doubtful. Possibly the author, or a later scribe, may have confused the two places Karkhā and Kashkar; the latter form agrees with that given by Epiphanius in his version of the story.

Here for the first time we meet with the remarkable theory that Manichæism originated, not with its reputed founder, but with a certain Scythianus, from whom the system was passed on to Manes. These *Acts* are extant in a Latin translation, made from a Greek text of which we possess some long fragments.[1] According to Jerome,[2] the book was originally composed by Archelaus himself in Syriac ('Syro sermone') and afterwards translated into Greek. But it has been clearly proved that Archelaus is not the author, and that the narrative is to a large extent, if not entirely, fictitious. Nevertheless, some modern writers have endeavoured to show that, though Jerome was mistaken in ascribing the *Acts* to Archelaus, he was right at least in believing them to have been composed in Syriac. The arguments which Kessler has advanced in support of this theory have been shown by T. Nöldeke to be worthless.[3] The author of the *Acts*, whoever he was, evidently possessed no accurate information about the country in which he placed the scene of his story. For example, he represents the river Strangas as the Western boundary of the Persian Empire—a notion which is derived from the Greek *Romance of Alexander the Great* (pseudo-Callisthenes), as Nöldeke points out. A writer who was capable of falling into such mistakes can scarcely be supposed to have had any definite knowledge as to the early history of Manichæism. Nevertheless, it is not surprising that his statements were readily believed by Western Christians. With some variations, the story contained in the *Acta Archelai* reappears in Epiphanius,[4] Socrates, Theodoret, and several later writers.

By far the most celebrated of the Western authorities on Manichæism is Augustine. At first sight it might seem that his testimony ought to outweigh all others that have been mentioned, for during nine years (from A.D. 373 to 382) he was a professed Manichæan. Among the works that he composed on the subject, after his conversion to Catholic Christianity, are the following: *Contra Epistolam Manichæi quam vocant Fundamenti, Contra Faustum, Contra Fortunatum, Contra Adimantum, Contra Secundinum, De Actis cum Felice Manichæo, De Genesi contra Manichæos, De Natura Boni, De Duabus Animabus, De Utilitate Credendi, De Moribus Ecclesiæ Catholicæ et de Moribus Manichæorum.* Many passages relating to Manichæism are to be found in his other writings, particularly in the *Confessions*. But, on the whole, the amount of positive knowledge which can be gathered from Augustine is much less than might have been expected. In the great majority of cases he confines himself to vague generalities, and, when he descends to particulars, his statements seem mostly to rest on hearsay. It may be doubted whether even his Manichæan informants were at all accurately acquainted with the history and writings of their founder. Faustus, whom Augustine represents as one of the ablest and most influential among the Manichæans, was a native of N. Africa, and it is therefore unlikely that he could read the sacred books of his religion in the original Aramaic. Nor have we any reason to believe that the other Manichæans with whom Augustine came in contact were better instructed.

One of the latest, but not the least important, of the Western sources is the Greek *Formula of Abjuration*,[5] which repentant heretics were required to pronounce before being admitted into the com-

1 See M. J. Routh, *Reliquiæ sacræ*², Oxford, 1846–48, v.
2 *De Vir. Illustr.*, no. lxxii
3 See *ZDMG* xliii. [1889] 535 ff., and xliv. [1890] 399.
4 See F. Oehler, *Corpus Hæreseologicum*, Berlin, 1856–61, II. ii. 398 ff.
5 See A. Gallandi, *Bibliotheca Patrum* 14 vols., Venice, 1765–88, xiv. 87 ff.

munion of the Byzantine Church. In its present shape this document cannot be older than the 9th century. It consists of a series of anathemas, directed partly against doctrines and partly against persons, put together without any definite plan. Some of the doctrines are undoubtedly Manichæan, but some emanate from other sects, and some appear to be gross misrepresentations. Yet, in spite of the uncritical manner in which it is compiled, the *Formula of Abjuration* contains a certain number of interesting facts.

(4) *Muhammadan.*—Evidence from Muhammadan literature does not begin before the 9th cent. of our era. Nevertheless, the Muhammadan accounts are, on the whole, the most instructive of all, much fuller than those by Oriental Christians and less misleading than those by Western writers. For this several causes may be assigned. In the first place, the Muhammadan scholars to whom we owe these descriptions wrote from a historical, rather than from a controversial, point of view. Moreover, some of them at least had access to very ancient and trustworthy sources of information; for Babylonia, the political centre of the Muhammadan Empire, was also the ecclesiastical centre of the Manichæan community, and, accordingly, in that country the text and the traditional interpretation of the Manichæan Scriptures were most likely to survive. It is true that after the Muhammadan conquest the Aramaic language gradually ceased to be spoken, but the knowledge of it never wholly died out, as we see in the case of the Christians and the Mandæans, who have retained their sacred books, in their respective Aramaic dialects, down to the present day.

Almost all Muhammadan historians who treat of pre-Muhammadan or early Muhammadan times take some notice of Manichæism, but the authors from whom we learn most on this subject are the following: (*a*) Ibn Wāḍiḥ, also called al-Ya'qūbī, who in A.D. 891 composed a *History of the World*;[1] (*b*) Muḥammad ibn Isḥāq, who probably lived about the end of the 10th cent. of our era, and is known as the author of the *Fihrist*, *i.e.* 'Catalogue,' a great storehouse of information respecting literary works of various kinds;[2] (*c*) al-Bīrūnī, who died A.D. 1048, one of the most learned men that the East ever produced, the author of a book on *Chronology*[3] and other important treatises; (*d*) al-Shahrastānī, who died A.D. 1153, the author of a work on religious and philosophical sects.[4] All these authors wrote in Arabic, although the last two were of Persian nationality.

The story of Mānī in the *Shāh-nāmah* of Firdausī, the well-known Persian epic poet, is almost entirely legendary, and the same may be said of nearly all the popular Muhammadan accounts, whether written in Persian or in Arabic.

2. The founder of Manichæism.—With regard to the history of the founder we are mainly dependent on Muhammadan writers, for the Western authorities either tell us nothing definite or else repeat, more or less faithfully, the legend contained in the *Acta Archelai*. The story there related is briefly as follows:

In the time of the Apostles there lived a man named Scythianus, who is described as coming 'from Scythia,' and also as being 'a Saracen by race' ('ex genere Saracenorum'). He settled in Egypt, where he became acquainted with 'the wisdom of the Egyptians,' and invented the religious system which was afterwards known as Manichæism. Finally he emigrated to Palestine, and, when he died, his writings passed into the hands of his sole disciple, a certain Terebinthus.[1] The latter betook himself to Babylonia, assumed the name of Budda, and endeavoured to propagate his master's teaching. But he, like Scythianus, gained only one disciple, who was an old woman. After a while he died, in consequence of a fall from the roof of a house, and the books which he had inherited from Scythianus became the property of the old woman, who, on her death, bequeathed them to a young man named Corbicius,[2] who had been her slave. Corbicius thereupon changed his name to Manes, studied the writings of Scythianus, and began to teach the doctrines which they contained, with many additions of his own. He gained three disciples, named Thomas, Addas, and Hermas. About this time the son of the Persian king fell ill, and Manes undertook to cure him; the prince, however, died, whereupon Manes was thrown into prison. He succeeded in escaping, but eventually fell into the hands of the king, by whose order he was flayed, and his corpse was hung up at the city gate.

It is needless to say that this narrative, as it stands, has no claim to be considered historical. Some details, in particular the account of the execution of Manes, are confirmed by more trustworthy authorities, but as to the main point—the existence of Scythianus and Terebinthus—no such confirmation is forthcoming. The assertion that Terebinthus took the name of Budda seems to be a confused reminiscence of the fact that Mānī represented the Indian Buddha as one of a series of prophets who had preceded him. But this, so far from tending to support the story as a whole, is rather an argument against it.

The accounts of the principal Muhammadan authorities may be briefly summarized thus:

Mānī,[3] the son of F-t-q,[4] was born in Babylonia[5] about A.D. 216.[6] His father was originally a heathen, and frequented an 'idol-temple' at or near Ctesiphon, the Persian capital, 'as other people were wont to do.' But shortly before the birth of Mānī he abandoned his former religion, and joined[7] the sect of the Mughtasila, *i.e.* 'those who practise ablutions.'[8] Mānī at an early age became convinced that he had received divine revelations, and that he was chosen to preach a new faith.[9]

---

1 ed. M. T. Houtsma, Leyden, 1883.

2 ed. G. Flügel, and published after his death by J. Rödiger and A. Müller, Leipzig, 1871–72. The section relating to Manichæism was published separately by Flügel, with a Germ. tr. and copious notes, under the title *Mani, seine Lehre und seine Schriften*, Leipzig, 1862. The author of the *Fihrist* is sometimes called al-Nadīm, but it is doubtful whether this name, or rather nickname, belonged to him or to one of his ancestors.

3 ed. E. Sachau, Leipzig, 1878, and tr. by him into Eng., *The Chronology of Ancient Nations*, London, 1879. Al-Bīrūnī is the Arab. form of the Pers. Bērūnī.

4 ed. W. Cureton, London, 1846, and tr. into Germ. by T. Haarbrücker, Halle, 1850–51.

---

1 As to this name the authorities vary.

2 This name also is uncertain.

3 So the name is written in Arab., and the adj. derived from it is usually *mānawī* (formed according to the ordinary rule in Arab.), but sometimes *manawī*, *manānī*, or *mānī*. In Syr. the name Mānī seems to have been pronounced as in Arab., although the Syr. spelling does not enable us to decide positively whether the first vowel was long or short. In the case of rare proper names the vowel-points added by later Syrian scribes have, of course, no authority. In Zoroastrian writings the name appears with a final aspirate, *Mānih* (adj. *mānīhīk*), and this aspirate accounts for the form Μανιχαῖος, *Manichæus*, which Gr. and Lat. writers often use, not only as an adj., but also as the equivalent of Μάνης, *Manes*. The origin and meaning of the name Mānī are unknown. But this very fact tends to show that it is a real name, not an honorific title like Christ or Buddha.

4 This is the form given in the *Fihrist*. The vowels are uncertain, but the consonants agree with those of Πατέκιος, who is expressly mentioned as the father of Manes in the Gr. *Formula of Abjuration*. It is well known that the Arabs have no sign for P, and use F or B instead. According to the *Fihrist*, F-t-q also bore the name of Bābak (=Pers. Pāpak), while al-Ya'qūbī calls him Ḥammād. The last name, which is purely Arabic, must be due to some mistake.

5 According to al-Bīrūnī, the birth-place of Mānī was a village called Mardīnū, on the upper part of the Kūthā canal, *i.e.* a little to the south of Baghdād.

6 The statement of al-Bīrūnī that Mānī was born in the year 527 of the era of Alexander (*i.e.* the Seleucid era) agrees very nearly with what we are told in the *Fihrist* as to the age of Mānī when he came forward as a public teacher.

7 G. T. Stokes, in *DCB*, *s.v.* 'Manes,' states that Mānī's father 'founded' this sect—an assertion for which there is no authority.

8 These details are given in the *Fihrist*, evidently from a Manichæan source. What was the precise form of heathenism which Mānī's father originally professed is not clear. The terms used in the *Fihrist* point to some local cult rather than to Zoroastrianism. The religion of the Mughtasila seems to have been a kind of Judaic Christianity mingled with heathen elements. It was not identical with that of the Mandæans in later times, though the two sects had much in common.

9 The narrative in the *Fihrist* clearly implies that Mānī did not derive his system from any human teacher. On the other hand, al-Bīrūnī describes Mānī as a 'disciple of Fādarūn,' and a similar statement appears in the well-known historical work of al-Mas'ūdī, who lived about a century before al-Bīrūnī, except that the name is there written somewhat differently (see Mas'ūdī, *Les Prairies d'or*, ed. C. Barbier de Meynard and Pavet

Before he was twenty-five years old he had privately gained a few disciples, but he began his public propaganda on the day when Shāpūr (=Sapor I.), the son of Ardashīr, was crowned king, *i.e.* March 20, A.D. 242.[1] He succeeded in securing the patronage of the king's brother Pērōz, and through him obtained access to the king himself.[2] In the course of his journeys he is said to have visited Central Asia, India, and China, but it does not appear that he ever penetrated into the Roman Empire. He composed numerous books and epistles in Aramaic, and at least one book in Persian, probably the work known as the *Shāpūraqān*, which, according to al-Bīrūnī, was written for king Shāpūr.[3] We learn from Ephraim Syrus that Mānī illustrated his writings with coloured pictures;[4] his fame as a painter survived for many centuries in the East. He is also said to have invented the peculiar alphabet which the Manichæans afterwards employed; it was a modification of the Syriac *Estrangĕlō* character, as the recently discovered fragments prove. Mānī was put to death by king Bahrām (or, according to the older pronunciation, Warahrān) I., who reigned from about A.D. 274 to 277.[5] Whether he was flayed alive, as al-Ya'qūbī and some other authorities state, is doubtful. His corpse, or, according to others, his skin stuffed with straw, was hung up, by order of the king, at the gate of Gundē-Shāpūr, an important city which lay a little to the east of the ancient Susa. In after times that gate was always known as 'the Mānī-gate.' The execution of Mānī was evidently due not so much to the personal caprice of the king as to the enmity of the Zoroastrian priesthood. At the same time the Persian government made a strenuous, but wholly fruitless, attempt to exterminate the adherents of the new religion.

3. The Manichæan system.—Manichæism, like other forms of Gnosticism, professes to be at the same time a religion and a philosophy, inasmuch as it not only sets up an ideal of holiness, but also undertakes to explain the constitution of the world. It is not, however, to be regarded as a philosophy in the ordinary European sense of the word. It attempts to arrive at philosophical truth by means of a method which, to us, appears wholly unphilosophical. Though the Manichæans confidently appealed to human reason and were always ready to defend their conclusions by argument, they did not pretend that those conclusions had been reached by abstract logic or by any kind of scientific induction; on the contrary, they claimed, no less than the primitive Christians, to be in possession of a direct revelation from God. Thus Mānī himself says, in a passage which al-Bīrūnī quotes from the *Shāpūraqān* (see above):

'Wisdom and deeds[6] have always from time to time been brought to mankind by the messengers of God. So in one age they have been brought by the messenger called Buddha to India, in another by Zarādusht [Zoroaster] to Persia, in another by Jesus to the West. Thereupon this revelation has come down, this prophecy in this last age, through me, Mānī, the messenger of the God of truth to Babylonia.'

Such was the claim put forward by Mānī. We have now to consider the substance of his teaching.

The Manichæan system is based upon the idea of the essential and eternal contrast between good and evil, between light and darkness. But it is not correct to say, as Western writers have frequently done, that Mānī identified good with spirit, and evil with matter (ὕλη). Whether he ever attained to the conception of matter may be doubted;[1] at all events, it is clear that he represented evil, or darkness, as something capable of thought and volition;[2] in other words, his dualism was of the imaginative, or poetical, not of the philosophical kind. The following is an abstract of the account given in the *Fihrist.*

Originally the light and the darkness bordered on one another, but were unmingled, the light being limitless above and the darkness limitless below. The light is identical with God, who is called 'the King of the Paradises of Light,' but the realm of light includes also an atmosphere and an earth which are co-eternal with the Godhead. Moreover, there are various other beings called gods,[3] who are subordinate to the King of the Paradises of Light. Out of the darkness arose Satan, the Primal Devil, who 'did not exist from all eternity, although the elements of which he is composed are eternal.' At first he wrought havoc in his own domain, and then invaded the kingdom of light.[4] 'When he saw the flashes of light, he conceived a hatred for them, shuddered, and rejoined his native elements.' He made a second attack, and the King of the Paradises of Light, in order to repel him, produced a being called the Primal Man, who went forth armed with a fivefold panoply—the breeze, the wind, the light, the water, and the fire. Satan, on the other hand, arrayed himself in the smoke, the consuming flame, the darkness, the scorching blast, and the cloud. After a long struggle Satan prevailed over the Primal Man. The heavenly powers then intervened and rescued the Primal Man, but the elements which formed his panoply became mingled with the elements of darkness. Out of this confused mass the heavenly powers fashioned the actual world which we inhabit. Not only all animal and vegetable organisms, but even objects which we regard as wholly inanimate, such as metals, contain portions of divine light. Hence the distinction which we are accustomed to make between natural and spiritual phenomena does not exist in Manichæism, since it represents all the processes of nature as part of a spiritual contest.[5] The visible universe is, in fact, a vast and complicated machine devised by God for the purpose of enabling the elements of light to effect their escape. When the light contained in the earth separates itself from the darkness, it ascends in the form of a pillar, called 'the pillar of glory,' first to the moon,[6] thence to the sun, and thence to the higher regions. This process continues until at length the final separation is brought about by a conflagration, which will last 1458 years. Thereafter the light will be secured for ever against the assaults of the darkness.

The most singular part of the Manichæan system is that which relates to the origin and history of mankind. Unfortunately, the statements of the *Fihrist* on this subject are fragmentary and full of obscurities, which the other sources do not enable us to explain in an altogether satisfactory manner. But it is clear at least that the first human beings, whom Mānī called Adam and Eve,[7] were represented as the offspring of devils, the object of the devils in producing them being to imprison, and so to keep in their own possession, a portion of the elements of light. The heavenly powers, in order to frustrate the purpose of the devils, sent Jesus (who is here regarded as a celestial being) to instruct Adam on the subject of 'the Paradises and the gods, Hell and the devils, the earth and the heaven, the sun and the moon,' and in particular to warn him against sensuality. As to the history of Adam and Eve many details are given, some of which have been borrowed from the OT, some perhaps from sources unknown to us, while some appear to be wholly fantastic.

de Courteille, Paris, 1861–77, ii. 167; also Flügel, *Mani*, p. 141). Who Fādarūn was we are not told; it is therefore vain to inquire whether he really existed, and, if so, whether Mānī had any connexion with him. The assertion of Barhebræus that Mānī was at one time a Christian, and even 'a presbyter,' rests upon no evidence whatever.

1 See T. Nöldeke, *Geschichte der Perser und Araber zur Zeit der Sasaniden*, Leyden, 1879, p. 412.

2 That king Shāpūr was ever converted to Manichæism, as al-Ya'qūbī states, is very improbable.

3 The fullest list of Mānī's writings is to be found in the *Fihrist* (p. 336 ff.). Unfortunately many of the titles are doubtful, and even those which are certain seldom give us any clue as to the nature of the contents.

4 See C. W. Mitchell, *op. cit.* i. 126 ff. of the Syr. text.

5 That Mānī was executed under Bahrām I. seems tolerably certain, though one historian (Theodore bar-Khōnī) places the event in the reign of Shāpūr, another (al-Dīnawarī) in the reign of Hurmuz (*i.e.* Hormizd I., about A.D. 273), and a third (Eutychius) in the reign of Bahrām II., the son and successor of Bahrām I. For the sake of readers unacquainted with Arab. it may be worth while to point out that in Sachau's tr. of al-Bīrūnī's *Chronology*, p. 191, line 17, the word 'Hurmuz' is a slip of the pen; the Arab. text says merely 'and *he* killed,' referring to Bahrām. By a curious coincidence there is an exactly similar mistake in H. Zotenberg's tr. of the corresponding passage in the history of al-Tha'ālibī (Paris, 1900), p. 503: 'Sâboûr fit aussi mettre à mort. . . . Cette action gagna à Sâboûr. . . .' Here again Bahrām is meant.

6 *i.e.* the theory and the practice of religion.

1 Alexander of Lycopolis (ed. Brinkmann, p. 5) observes that in the Manichæan system the term ὕλη is not used in the Platonic or the Aristotelian sense; accordingly Alexander defines the Manichæan ὕλη as 'motion without order' (ἡ ἄτακτος κίνησις).

2 According to al-Shahrastānī, some Manichæans held that the mingling of the darkness with the light had taken place 'blindly and by accident,' not as a result of volition. But this is obviously a later philosophical speculation.

3 The nature of these gods is not clearly defined; they are regarded as the offspring of the Supreme God.

4 It is instructive to compare this narrative with the parallel passage in Titus of Bostra, bk. i. § 17. For 'the Primal Devil' Titus substitutes ἡ ὕλη.

5 Thus, for instance, the rain is explained as due to the perspiration of devils (Titus of Bostra, bk. i. § 17).

6 The moon, as it waxes and wanes, is compared to a bucket which alternately fills and empties itself (*ib.*).

7 It is to be observed that Adam, 'the first man' (in Arabic *al-insān al-awwal*), is wholly distinct from 'the Primal Man' (*al-insān al-qadīm*).

As we learn from the passage of the *Shāpūraqān* quoted above, Mānī held that a series of divine revelations had been promulgated in the world by Buddha, Zoroaster, Jesus, and finally Mānī himself.[1] Al-Bīrūnī adds that Mānī, in another of his books, claimed to be 'the Paraclete (*al-Fāraqlīṭ*) announced by Christ,' and this we learn from other sources also, both Christian[2] and Muhammadan. As the Muhammadan authorities use the Greek word, it may be assumed that it was used by the Manichæans themselves, but we are not to conclude that Mānī knew Greek, still less that he had read the NT in the original. The term Paraclete was in common use among Aramaic-speaking Christians, from whom Mānī doubtless borrowed it. Precisely what meaning he attached to it is a question not easy to answer. From the statements in the *Fihrist* as to his parentage and birth we may infer with certainty that, though he laid claim to a divine commission, he did not profess to be more than a human being in the ordinary acceptation of the term.[3] And it is to be observed that in the *Shāpūraqān* the earlier prophets, including Jesus, are placed on a level with Mānī. This would seem to imply that they also were regarded as mere men. It is, therefore, not a little surprising to find that Christian authors, such as Titus of Bostra[4] and Augustine, frequently represent Mānī as holding a Docetic theory with regard to Jesus, namely, that He was not born of a woman and that His body was a phantom.[5] And the difficulty of ascertaining what was really the Manichæan doctrine on this point is still further increased by the statement in the *Fihrist* that Mānī pronounced Jesus to be a devil (*shaiṭān*).[6] The *Fihrist* informs us also (p. 336, line 10 ff.) that one of Mānī's works, *The Book of Secrets*, contained a chapter on 'the son of the widow, that is to say, according to Mānī, the crucified Messiah, whom the Jews crucified.' How the strange phrase 'the son of the widow' is to be explained, and how this passage is to be reconciled with that in which Jesus is said to have been called a devil, we have no means of determining. But, whatever the Manichæans may have believed as to the origin of the historical Jesus, the nature of His body, etc., it would

[1] The list of prophets given by al-Shahrastānī (i. 192) is longer, viz. Adam, Seth, Noah, Abraham, Buddha, Zoroaster, Christ, Paul—'then shall come the seal [*i.e.* the last] of the prophets to the land of the Arabs.' Whether this sentence is simply a Muhammadan interpolation, or a distorted form of some passage referring to Mānī, is uncertain.

[2] Christian writers, from Eusebius onwards, sometimes wrongly interpret this to mean that Mānī identified himself with the Holy Ghost. It is scarcely necessary to recall the fact that even in the NT the term *παράκλητος* is applied not only to the Holy Ghost but also to Christ (1 Jn 2^1). The statement of Titus of Bostra (bk. iii. § 1), Augustine, and other Christian writers, that Mānī called himself an 'Apostle of Jesus,' has been confirmed by one of the recently discovered fragments (F. W. K. Müller, M. 17). This title does not necessarily imply more than that Mānī believed his own teaching to be substantially identical with that of Jesus.

[3] The fact that in one of the fragments published by F. W. K. Müller (M. 311) Mānī is addressed as 'Mānī, son of the gods' (*Mānī yazdān frazēnd*), does not prove anything to the contrary, since the phrase may be understood in a purely spiritual sense.

[4] Bk. iv. § 33 ff., p. 145 of the Syr. text.

[5] As Baur remarks (*Das manich. Religionssystem*, p. 235), the Christian Fathers tell us at great length what Mānī denied with respect to the person of Christ, but they say scarcely anything about his positive teaching on the subject.

[6] *Fihrist*, p. 335, line 8; see Flügel, *Mani*, note 284. A more explicit statement is to be found in the treatise *De Fide contra Manichæos*, ascribed to Euodius, a friend of Augustine: 'Sic enim in Epistola Fundamenti dicit: Inimicus quippe qui eundem Salvatorem iustorum patrem crucifixisse se speravit ipse est crucifixus, quo tempore aliud actum est, atque aliud ostensum. Princeps itaque tenebrarum affixus est cruci, idemque spineam coronam portavit cum suis sociis, et vestem coccineam habuit, acetum etiam et fel bibit, quod quidam Dominum potasse arbitrati sunt, atque omnia quæ hic sustinere visus est, tenebrarum ducibus irrogata sunt, qui clavis etiam et lancea vulnerati sunt' (ch. 28 [*PL* xlii. 1147]). The fragment on the Crucifixion published by F. W. K. Müller (M. 18) unfortunately leaves the question open.

certainly appear that they denied the fact of His crucifixion. Hence, according to Augustine,[1] they were in the habit of contrasting the unreal sufferings of Christ with the real sufferings of Mānī, which they solemnly commemorated by an annual ceremony known as the *Βῆμα*. That the Muhammadan writers say very little on this Christological question may be due to the fact that here their own views happened to resemble those of the Manichæans.[2]

The teaching of Mānī as to the duties and ultimate destiny of individuals was in accordance with his theory of the universe as a whole. Since the visible world has as its aim the separation of the light from the darkness, practical religion must consist mainly in the furthering of this process. The divine element in man must be freed from its fetters in order that it may return to its heavenly source. With regard to this part of the Manichæan system much misconception has prevailed in the West, from the time of Augustine to the present day. The divine element in man is not to be identified absolutely with the soul, though the Manichæans sometimes used language which admitted of such an interpretation. Yet, if we examine the evidence carefully, it becomes clear that, when they spoke of the soul as divine, they meant only that it contained something divine; and even this was not asserted with respect to the soul of every individual.[3] Another misapprehension, due chiefly to Augustine's treatise *De Duabus Animabus*, is that man was represented as having two souls, one good and the other evil.[4] In reality the passages which are cited as proofs of this theory affirm only the existence of two opposite *tendencies* in man. And, just as the soul is not wholly good, so the body is not wholly evil; for, according to the *Fihrist* (p. 335, line 16 ff.), the Manichæans held that after the death of the righteous man the 'powers' contained in his body, namely, the water, the fire, and the breeze, have to be extracted by 'the sun, the moon, and the shining gods,' and then 'the *rest* of his body which is altogether darkness is cast into hell.'

But, although it was the duty of all Manichæans to take part in the liberation of the light from the darkness, their share in the great work naturally varied according to their several capacities. First of all, a broad distinction was made between the ordinary Manichæans, who were known as 'the Hearers' or 'the Combatants,' and the inner circle of teachers or ascetics, whom Western writers call 'the Elect' (*οἱ Ἐκλεκτοί*, *Electi*) and Muhammadans *al-Ṣiddīqūn*.[5] The Elect again were subdivided

[1] 'Cum sæpe a vobis quærerem illo tempore, quo vos audiebam, quæ causa esset, quod Pascha Domini plerumque nulla interdum a paucis tepidissima celebritate frequentaretur, nullis vigiliis, nullo prolixiore ieiunio indicto auditoribus, nullo denique festiviore apparatu; cum vestrum Bema, id est, diem quo Manichæus occisus est, quinque gradibus instructo tribunali et pretiosis linteis adornato ac in promptu posito et obiecto adorantibus, magnis honoribus prosequamini; hoc ergo cum quærerem, respondebatur eius diem passionis celebrandum esse, qui vere passus esset; Christum autem, qui natus non esset, neque veram sed simulatam carnem humanis oculis ostendisset, non pertulisse, sed finxisse passionem' (Augustine, *c. Epistolam Fundamenti*, viii.).

[2] It is well known that, according to the Qur'ān (iv. 156), Christ was never crucified; but, when His enemies sought to slay Him, He was removed from the earth and 'a likeness was made to appear to them.' This theory, it will be observed, does not imply any denial of the reality of Christ's body. That Muhammad borrowed the conception from the Manichæans is very improbable, but at all events there is a striking analogy.

[3] The souls of those who are finally lost seem to have been regarded as wholly evil. Thus we read in the *Fihrist* (p. 331, line 16 ff.) that Eve had two daughters, one of whom possessed an abundant measure of divine light and wisdom, whereas the other possessed none at all.

[4] See the very instructive discussion by Baur, p. 162 ff.

[5] This expression means in Arab. 'the veracious,' but, as Kessler has pointed out (*Mānī*, p. 318, note 4), it is here to be understood in the sense of its etymological equivalent in Syr.,

into several grades and formed an elaborate hierarchy, at the head of which stood the representative of Mānī himself. But the position of the Elect differed essentially from that of the Christian clergy, inasmuch as the Elect exercised no sacerdotal functions properly so called. Whether Mānī instituted anything of the nature of a sacrament is doubtful; in any case, if there were Manichæan sacraments, they cannot have occupied an important place in the system, since the Oriental authorities make no mention of them, unless, indeed, we apply the term 'sacrament' to such practices as prayer and fasting.[1] Hence the main characteristic of the Elect was not that they had the exclusive right, or power, to perform certain acts, but rather that they possessed a fuller knowledge of religion and abstained from certain things which were lawful to the rest of the community. This duty of abstention was called by the Manichæans 'the three seals,'[2] which Augustine more definitely characterizes as *signaculum oris*, *signaculum manuum*, and *signaculum sinus*.[3] The first 'seal' imposed restrictions with respect to food and speech, the second with respect to outward acts, the third with respect to thoughts and desires. Thus the Manichæan asceticism implied no thought of expiation; the idea that self-inflicted suffering atones for sin—an idea which has exercised so disastrous an influence in some sections of the Christian Church—was quite foreign to the religion of Mānī. The prohibitions which he issued are based upon the belief that certain acts, such as the destruction of life and the intercourse of the sexes, are essentially Satanic, and therefore retard the liberation of the light. In matters of detail the Manichæan code naturally appears arbitrary to us; it is evident that in drawing the line between what is 'Satanic' and what is not Mānī was guided much more by his fancy and by various casual associations than by any abstract logical principle. Thus, for instance, all Manichæans were forbidden to kill animals, but it would seem that the Hearers were permitted to eat flesh. The Elect abstained from both flesh and wine; they were also forbidden to pluck fruit or vegetables, so that the food on which they subsisted had to be supplied by the Hearers. Similarly the Hearers were allowed to marry and to engage in worldly avocations, whereas the Elect might neither marry nor acquire property, 'except food for one day and clothing for one year.'[4] It is remarkable that among the things most strictly prohibited were idolatry and magic.[5] As in nearly all Oriental religions, fasting played an important part. Sunday was observed as a fast-day by ordinary Manichæans, Monday by the Elect; there were also monthly and annual fasts. Of the prayers, which were recited several times in the day, the following specimens are given by the author of the *Fihrist* (p. 333, line 15 ff.):

'(1) Blessed is our Guide, the Paraclete, the Ambassador of Light, blessed are his guardian angels and adored are his shining hosts.

(2) Adored art thou, O shining one, Mānī our Guide, source of brightness, branch of life,[1] thou great tree which art wholly medicine.

(3) I prostrate myself and adore, with a pure heart and a truth-speaking tongue, the great God, the Father of Lights, the Essence of Lights, adored and blessed art Thou, all Thy majesty and Thy blessed worlds which Thou hast called;[2] he adoreth Thee who adoreth Thy hosts, Thy holy ones, Thy word, Thy majesty, and that which seemeth good to Thee, because Thou art the God who is all truth, life, and holiness.

(4) I adore and prostrate myself before all the gods, all the shining angels, all the lights, and all the hosts, who proceed from the great God.

(5) I prostrate myself and adore the great hosts and the shining gods who by their wisdom have pierced, expelled, and overcome the darkness.

(6) I prostrate myself and adore the Father of majesty, the Great, the Luminous. . . .'[3]

It will be noticed that these utterances contain not a single petition, no confession of sin, and no reference to the need of pardon. But we should not be justified in arguing that such conceptions were alien to the Manichæan system, for great stress seems to have been laid on repentance and the forgiveness of sin.[4] Since, however, the Manichæans did not admit the idea of a propitiatory sacrifice, their theory as to the forgiveness of sin necessarily differed from that which was accepted by the great majority of Christians. Precisely what Mānī himself taught on this subject we cannot hope to determine; but the view which appears to have been current among the Manichæans, at least as early as the 4th cent., was that repentance naturally leads to forgiveness, 'since man is not punished for sinning, but for failing to grieve over sin.'[5]

With respect to Mānī's doctrine of the future life we have somewhat fuller information. The division of mankind into three classes, the Elect, the Hearers, and the Wicked, is here specially emphasized. The Elect, immediately after death, ascend by means of 'the pillar of glory' to the moon, and thence are conveyed to paradise; the Hearers must pass through a long process of purification and of wandering to and fro, before they join the Elect; while the souls of the wicked roam about the world, in a condition of hopeless misery, until the final conflagration, and are then consigned for ever to the realm of darkness.[6]

4. The relation of Manichæism to other religions.—When we consider the complex nature of Mānī's teaching, it will not surprise us to find that very different opinions have been expressed as to its general character and its connexion with other religious systems. Until comparatively recent times it was the fashion to represent Manichæism, and Gnosticism generally, as a mere fantastic perversion of Christianity. When Zoroastrianism and Buddhism began to attract serious attention in Europe, the real or apparent resemblances between these religions and Manichæism naturally gave rise to the theory that Manichæism is a combination of Christian with Zoroastrian or

viz. *Zaddīqē*, 'the righteous,' which we may assume to have been the form employed by the Manichæans themselves (see C. W. Mitchell, *op. cit.* i. 30: 'A Manichæan who is called a *Zaddīqā*,' p. 127 ff.: 'Those idle women of the party of Mānī, those whom they call *Zaddīqāthā*'). Neither Kessler nor any previous writer seems to have noticed that from the same Syr. word is derived *zandīq*, or *zindīq*, 'heretic,' a term which was applied especially to the disciples of Mānī by the Persians of the Sasanian period, and afterwards by Muhammadans. Various other interpretations of this word have been proposed, but none that is at all plausible. The substitution of *nd* for *dd* is a phonetic change for which there are many analogies. That a term which was originally used as a title of honour should afterwards have acquired an opprobrious sense is likewise quite natural; cf. the Germ. *Ketzer*, from καθαρός. The Persian terms for the 'Hearers' and the 'Elect' respectively are Niyōshāgān and Vižīdagān.

[1] According to Augustine (*c. Fortunatum*, i.), the Elect were supposed to celebrate a kind of Eucharist in their secret meetings. But, as Augustine himself admits that he knew nothing definite on the subject, we cannot attach much importance to his testimony.

[2] *Fihrist*, p. 333, line 5; Flügel, *Mānī*, note 217.

[3] *De Moribus Manichæorum*, ii. 10.

[4] Al-Birūnī, *Chronology*, p. 208.

[5] The prohibition of idolatry is the first of the ten commandments which, according to the *Fihrist* (p. 333, line 10 ff.), all Manichæans were required to observe.

[1] For *ḥayā*, 'bashfulness,' we should no doubt read *ḥayāt*, 'life,' as Nöldeke has suggested.

[2] That is, apparently, 'called into existence'—the Arab. verb *da'ā* seems here to be a rendering of the Aram. *qĕrā*, on the use of which see H. Pognon, *Inscriptions mandaïtes*, p. 185, note 1.

[3] Here follows a short clause which is unintelligible.

[4] See Baur, p. 262, and the *Khuastuanift*, ed. A. von Le Coq (*JRAS*, 1911).

[5] 'Non enim punitur quia peccavit sed quia de peccato non doluit' are the words of the Manichæan Secundinus, cited by Augustine (*c. Secundinum*).

[6] *Fihrist*, p. 335. In this passage we find nothing which distinctly confirms the statement of Augustine that the souls of the Hearers and of the Wicked were believed to pass into plants and animals (*c. Faustum*, bk. v. 10, *de Hær.* xlvi.). At the same time the idea of metempsychosis is not definitely excluded.

Buddhist elements, but whether Christianity, Zoroastrianism, or Buddhism formed the basis of the system was a disputed point. During the last twenty years the prevalent tendency to explain everything in the ancient world as due to Babylonian influence has led to the belief that Manichæism and all other forms of Gnosticism are simply modifications of the old Babylonian religion.

But to those who impartially examine the sources none of these hypotheses will appear satisfactory. Whatever elements Mānī may have borrowed from older Oriental religions, it is clear that the fundamental principles of his system are neither Zoroastrian, Buddhist, nor Babylonian. The relation in which Manichæism stood to Christianity was undoubtedly closer, but to call Manichæism a Christian heresy would be misleading. The characteristics which Manichæism and other Gnostic systems share with primitive Christianity are not necessarily derived from any Christian source; they are, for the most part, products of a general movement which, as mankind outgrew the older religions, spread over the civilized world and assumed various forms, according to the special circumstances of each case. The general movement in question has been well described by H. Oldenberg as a shifting of the centre of gravity, in religious matters, from without to within.

'The antique conception of religion, as a sort of offensive and defensive alliance between man and God, a mutual agreement whereby the worshipper secured for himself prosperity, success, and victory over his enemies, gradually faded away, or sometimes was violently shattered, and in its place there arose a new kind of belief, which held out the hope, not of earthly enjoyment, triumph, and dominion, but rather of rest, peace, and redemption' (*Buddha*³, Berlin, 1897, p. 3).

In the time of Mānī the old heathenism was by no means extinct in Babylonia, though Zoroastrianism had become the religion of the State.[1] Moreover, large Jewish colonies had long been established in the country. Of the early history of the Christian Church in those regions next to nothing is known, but there can be no doubt that before the beginning of the 3rd cent. Christianity had taken root among the Aramaic-speaking population which occupied the Western provinces of the Parthian Empire. It is also tolerably certain that the Christians of Babylonia were divided into various parties, and that their beliefs sometimes diverged widely from the ordinary orthodox type.[2] In particular the sect founded by the Syrian Christian Bar-daiṣān (Bardesanes), who died in A.D. 222, seems to have had great influence. Ephraim Syrus goes so far as to call Bar-daiṣān 'the teacher of Mānī';[3] this is not meant to imply that Mānī was ever a Bardesanist, but merely that he adopted certain Bardesanist doctrines. In any case it is essential to realize that Manichæism arose in a country where several religions were competing with one another, and where, in consequence of this, various hybrid sects had been formed. Of such sects we have already had an example in the Mughtasila, the community to which Mānī's father attached himself.

The hostility of Mānī to popular paganism is sufficiently shown by his strict prohibition of idolatry. That he clearly distinguished between ordinary paganism and Zoroastrianism appears from his inclusion of Zoroaster among the messengers of God. He must, therefore, have regarded the Zoroastrianism of his own age as corrupt rather than as radically false; but how much he actually borrowed from it is a very difficult question. To suppose that Mānī's dualism was due mainly to Zoroastrian influence would be an unwarranted assumption; for, though both systems are rightly described as dualistic, they nevertheless differ profoundly. The aim of the Zoroastrian is to banish evil from the world; the aim of the Manichæan is to extract from the world that which is good. In this respect Manichæism has more in common with Buddhism than with Zoroastrianism; but from the fact that Mānī represented Buddha as the communicator of a divine revelation we must infer that Mānī's acquaintance with Buddhism was of a very vague kind. It is manifest, however, that in matters of detail he appropriated freely elements derived from very different quarters. Thus we can attach no great importance to his adoption of certain ancient Babylonian myths—*e.g.*, such as relate to the nature and movements of the heavenly bodies.[1] In like manner he borrowed narratives, directly or indirectly, from the OT, although his general attitude towards Judaism was one of decided opposition. That he refused to recognize Moses as a prophet is abundantly proved;[2] hence in Christian writings directed against Manichæism the defence of the OT generally occupies a prominent place. It is probable that Mānī's aversion to Judaism was largely due to his horror of a practice which Judaism notoriously has in common with popular paganism, namely, the sacrificing of animals.[3]

Towards Christianity he was much more favourably disposed. Whence he derived his information on the subject is indeed uncertain, for, though it seems probable that the greater part of the NT had been translated into Syriac some time before Mānī was born, we cannot safely assume that he had access to it. Hence his peculiar teaching as to the person and history of Christ, to which allusion has been made above, may be due in some measure not to perversion of the gospel narrative on his own part, but to the beliefs of his Christian informants. In any case it is clear that some of the most essential features of primitive Christianity, in particular the ascetic view of the present world, were thoroughly congenial to Mānī. But he had one great advantage over the Christians, namely, that he provided a much more secure dogmatic basis for asceticism than any previous teacher. The Christian ascetics, in condemning natural feelings and appetites, were constantly hampered by their theory of God as the Creator of the universe in general and of man in particular; the distinction which they were obliged to make between human nature as such and human nature in its present corrupt state gave rise to endless difficulties. On the other hand, the Manichæan dogma that humanity is of Satanic origin, however shocking it may be to modern sentiment, greatly simplified the problem. In this, as in some other points, Mānī displayed a boldness and originality of conception which entitle him to be regarded as a genius of the first order. To represent his system as a mere patchwork of older beliefs is therefore a total perversion of the facts.

5. History of the Manichæan community.—At the time of their founder's death the Manichæans were already a numerous and highly organized

[1] The theory that Zoroastrianism did not become the State religion till after the overthrow of the Parthian dynasty (about A.D. 224) rests on no trustworthy evidence.

[2] F. C. Burkitt's *Early Eastern Christianity* (London, 1904) relates chiefly to the Christianity of Edessa and its immediate neighbourhood; but much of what he says probably applies also to Babylonia.

[3] C. W. Mitchell, *op. cit.* p. 8.

[1] Astrological myths and speculations played a considerable part in some other Gnostic systems, notably in that of Bar-daiṣān.

[2] See, for instance, the beginning of the account of Manichæism in al-Shahrastānī (i. 188). The statement in the *Fihrist* (p. 335, line 5 ff.), that Mānī rejected the prophets generally, is an exaggeration based mainly on his treatment of Moses.

[3] In this respect, of course, Mānī did not differ from some of the early Christians. Thus the *Epistle to Diognetus*, which is usually regarded as a product of orthodox Christianity, speaks of animal sacrifices in terms of unqualified condemnation, and even in Rabbinical literature a tendency to disparage sacrifice occasionally shows itself.

sect, scattered over a great part of the Persian Empire and drawn from the ranks of various older religions. Some of them belonged to the Persian aristocracy; hence the bitterness with which the Zoroastrian priesthood opposed the new faith. Mānī's immediate successor, as head of the community, was a certain Sīs (Gr. Σισίννιος). For many centuries Babylonia continued to be the headquarters of the Manichæan organization, in spite of repeated persecutions on the part of the Persian government. Now and then there was a king sufficiently powerful and intelligent to restrain the intolerance of the priests, but as a rule the Manichæans were treated even worse than the Christians.[1] For this no political pretext could be alleged, since the Manichæans were politically inoffensive, whereas the Christians not infrequently brought persecution upon themselves by an ostentatious display of their philo-Byzantine sentiments. The principal result of these attempts to suppress Manichæism in Babylonia and Persia was that large numbers of Manichæans took refuge in Central Asia, where they carried on a successful propaganda among the Turkish tribes.

The precise date at which Manichæism began to spread in the Roman Empire is not certain, but it was undoubtedly well known there early in the 4th century. With respect to its prevalence in N. Africa, two or three generations later, Augustine furnishes ample evidence. The Christian emperors, as we might have expected, showed themselves no less intolerant towards Manichæism than the kings of Persia. In the persecution of the Manichæans Pope Leo I. played a specially prominent part. As to the later history of the Manichæans in Europe very little can be discovered with certainty, on account of the vagueness with which the term 'Manichæan' is used by Catholic writers. Thus the charge of Manichæism was brought against the Bogomils in the Byzantine Empire and the Albigenses (*q.v.*) in Provence, but how little these accusations prove may be gathered from the fact that even at the present day the religion of the Russian Molokanye has been described as a modified form of Manichæism.

On the overthrow of the Persian Empire by the Muhammadan Arabs, about the middle of the 7th cent., the followers of Mānī in the East enjoyed a period of comparative repose. Strictly speaking, they had no legal claim to toleration, for the Qur'ān, which expressly recognizes Jews, Christians, and Sabians[2] as capable of deserving the favour of God (ii. 59, v. 73), does not mention Manichæism. Nevertheless, it would appear that in the early days of the Muhammadan Empire no penalties were inflicted upon the Manichæans. The extreme simplicity of their cult, and in particular their abhorrence of idolatry, may for a while have served to protect them from molestation under Muhammadan rule. At length it began to be rumoured that some Muhammadans in high positions had secretly adopted Manichæism. In many cases these reports were certainly false; thus, for instance, the Khalīfa al-Walīd II. (A.D. 743–744), whom Muhammadan historians depict as a monster of impiety, is accused of having said that Mānī was the only prophet whom God ever sent into the world.[1] If al-Walīd really uttered these words, they would prove not that he was a Manichæan, but that he knew next to nothing of Manichæism. It is, however, impossible to deny that secret conversions to Manichæism actually took place among the literary classes. Apostasy from Islām is notoriously a capital offence according to Muhammadan law (see art. APOSTASY [Muhammadan]). Hence we cannot wonder that in the latter half of the 8th cent., when under the 'Abbāsid dynasty the spirit of religious intolerance became dominant in the Muhammadan world, a systematic attempt should have been made to extirpate Manichæism.[2] The organizer of this persecution was the Khalīfa al-Mahdī (A.D. 775–785), who instituted for the purpose a State Inquisitor, with the title of 'Inspector of the Zanādiqa.' The term *zanādiqa* (plural of *zindīq*)[3] was used primarily to denote the Manichæans, though Muhammadan writers often employ it vaguely in the sense of 'heretics' or 'atheists.'[4] That al-Mahdī did not make a very clear distinction between Manichæism and some other heresies may be inferred from a passage in which he is represented as elaborately justifying his policy of persecution;[5] the accusations here brought against the Manichæans include, *e.g.*, the practice of marriage with near relatives (*nikāḥ al-akhawāt wa-l-banāt*), which was characteristic of the Zoroastrians (see art. MARRIAGE [Iranian]), but seems to have been altogether foreign to Manichæism.

The religious policy of al-Mahdī was generally followed by his successors. The number of persons put to death on the charge of Manichæism certainly amounted to many thousands, while Christians and Jews, though subject to various disabilities, were usually tolerated. But, in spite of all, the religion of Mānī long survived even in the heart of the Muhammadan Empire. Some two centuries after al-Mahdī, the author of the *Fihrist* tells us (p. 337, line 26 ff.) that he had been acquainted with about 300 Manichæans in Baghdād alone. But the region in which they were most numerous was Central Asia. In the territory of the Turkish tribe Taghazghaz the majority of the population professed Manichæism; a Muhammadan traveller who visited that country describes it as flourishing and civilized.[6] When, in the reign of the Khalīfa al-Muqtadir (A.D. 908–932), the Muhammadan governor of Samarqand condemned to death a large number of Manichæans, they were saved, it is said, by the intervention of their co-religionist, the prince of the Taghazghaz.[7] This is the only known case in which Manichæism became the religion of a political community. We do not know how long this state of things continued, or when Manichæism finally died out; but we may conjecture that it was swept away, like many other beliefs and institutions, by the great Mongol invasion of the 13th century.

That the Manichæan community in the course

[1] The Persian officials, in dealing with persons suspected of Manichæism, sometimes adopted the curious method of requiring the accused to 'kill ants,' just as Christians, in the Roman Empire, were required to throw incense upon a heathen altar (see E. Rödiger, *Chrestomathia Syriaca*[2], Halle, 1868, p. 94).

[2] The Sabians (a name which, of course, has no connexion with that of the ancient Sabæans) seem to have been a sect, or possibly a group of sects, who existed in Arabia at the time of Muhammad. The disciples of Muhammad were at first called Sabians by the heathen Arabs, and in later ages the title of Sabians was falsely assumed by several religious communities, as a means of protection—*e.g.*, by the pagans of Ḥarrān, in Mesopotamia, and by the Manichæans of Samarqand, as we learn from al-Bīrūnī.

[1] *Kitāb-al-Aghānī*, vi. 135, last line.

[2] See the very interesting paper by I. Goldziher, 'Ṣāliḥ ibn 'Abd-al-Ḳuddûs und das Zindîḳthum während der Regierung des Chalifen al-Mahdî,' in *Trans. of the Ninth Intern. Congress of Orientalists*, London, 1893, ii. 104 ff. Goldziher is of opinion that the Manichæan propaganda under the early 'Abbāsids was somehow connected with the anti-Arabian movement of the Persian nationalists (the so-called *Shu'ūbīya*). Whether there is any truth in this view may be doubted, for Manichæism had nothing to do with nationality. At the same time it is not surprising that Muhammadans should often have confounded these wholly distinct tendencies.

[3] See p. 398[b], note 5.

[4] Thus from the statement in Ibn Qutaiba, *Kitāb-al-Ma'ārif* (ed. F. Wüstenfeld, Göttingen, 1850, p. 299), it is very unsafe to conclude, with G. Jacob (*Altarabisches Beduinenleben*[2], Berlin, 1897, p. 107), that there were Manichæans at Mecca in the time of Muhammad.

[5] Al-Ṭabarī, iii. 588.

[6] See Yāqūt's *Geographical Dictionary*, ed. Wüstenfeld, Leipzig, 1866–73, i. 840.

[7] *Fihrist*, p. 337; Flügel, *Mani*, p. 106.

of its long history was not altogether free from internal dissensions might have been safely assumed. But the positive information which we possess on this subject is very scanty. We learn from the *Fihrist* (p. 334, line 4 ff.) that at a date which is not specified, but in any case some time before the end of the 7th cent., a party among the Manichæans severed their connexion with the central authority established in Babylonia and set up an independent organization; whether this schism was due to dogmatic differences or to other causes it is impossible to say. A second division took place about the beginning of the 8th cent., when a branch-sect was formed and became known as the Miqlāṣīya, after the name of their leader Miqlāṣ. The majority of the Manichæans, who remained faithful to the head of the community, a certain Mihr, were thenceforth called the Mihrīya. The points in dispute between these parties seem to have been matters of discipline rather than of religious belief.

LITERATURE.—In modern times, the first serious attempt to investigate the subject was made by the French Protestant theologian I. de Beausobre in his colossal work, *Histoire critique de Manichée et du manichéisme*, Amsterdam, 1734–1739; in dealing with the sources he shows considerable acumen, but his book is ill-arranged and contains many irrelevant digressions. An admirable summary and examination of the evidence, so far as it was then available, will be found in the treatise of F. C. Baur, *Das manichäische Religionssystem nach den Quellen neu untersucht, und entwickelt*, Tübingen, 1831. Perhaps the best general account is F. Spiegel, *Erânische Alterthumskunde*, Leipzig, 1871–78, ii. 195–232. The works of K. Kessler—*Mani, Forschungen über die manichäische Religion*, i., Berlin, 1889, art. 'Mani, Manichäer,' in *PRE*[2] and *PRE*[3]—supply much valuable information, but they should be used with extreme caution; the author's speculations are often fantastic and his linguistic knowledge is very superficial. A. Harnack, art. 'Manichaeism,' in *EBr*[9] (revised by F. C. Conybeare in *EBr*[11]), is largely based upon Kessler. The same may be said of the work of E. Rochat, *Essai sur Mani et sa doctrine*, Geneva, 1897. Very important contributions to the study of the subject are contained in a series of monographs by F. Cumont and A. Kugener, entitled *Recherches sur le Manichéisme*, Brussels, 1908–1912.

A. A. BEVAN.

MANIPURIS.—Officially the Manipuris are Vaiṣṇavite Hindus. They cremate the dead, they receive the *mantra* from a recognized Hindu *guru* in many but not in all cases, they recognize Hindu festivals (but observe them a day late), they revere the cow, they are scrupulous in the matter of food, but, on the other hand, they do not practise child-marriage, they do not seclude their women, they permit divorce, they permit the remarriage of widows, they do not allow the supremacy of the Brāhman, and none of the ordinary definitions of caste applies to their social order. Knowledge of the Vaiṣṇavite doctrines is spreading with the spread of education, but they are still the most backward of all Hindu groups in Assam. With them Hinduism, adopted as the State religion by royal edict (*c.* A.D. 1705), is of social and political value in that it separates them from the ruder tribes inhabiting the hills and from the subordinate peoples of the valley. It provides the rites and ceremonies of everyday life. It is, so far as externals are concerned, the religion of the Meitheis. It exists side by side with the earlier faith to which in the hour of trial and trouble, be they Rāja or ryot, they turn unhesitatingly. The continued existence of this earlier faith in such vigour is a notable fact which enables the student of religious development in India to study at close quarters the process by which in Hinduism animism is tempered by metaphysics, and magic transformed by philosophy.

The historical records of Manipur, *Ningthaurol*, are valid documents for at least five centuries. It is a settled State far removed from savagery. At the present time the population consists of two main divisions—the Meitheis and the Lois. The Meitheis consist of seven clans, each divided into numerous families, the principal clan being that known as the Ningthauja, or Royal, clan. The name Meithei now borne by all the clans is thought to have been the name of the Ningthauja clan before its hegemony was completely established. The Lois, or the conquered people, are not admitted into the Meithei confederacy, but are of similar stock to the Meitheis, and the Meitheis worship the gods of these Loi villages as much as the Lois themselves. The Meithei confederacy is an endogamous group in theory, although in practice the issue of mixed marriages is admitted. The principal order of divine beings is the *ūmang lai*. There were originally, as recent research has shown, nine *ūmang lai*, or forest gods, with whom were associated seven *lairemas*, or goddesses. There are now 364 such deities. The gods married with mortals, and their issue were promoted to divine rank. The deities have different names in different places, and there are cases where Rājas have been deified after death. The creator deity is identified both with the chief of the gods and with the snake ancestor of the royal family. Other gods are identified with the clan deities of clans still existing. Yet others are members of a special group, whose function is to guard certain areas and who are therefore known either as *maikeingākpa*, watchers over or guardians of direction, or *lamlai*, gods of definite areas. Here there is obviously a combination of ideas dating back to the time when definite areas were occupied by local groups each possessing a group deity. Then among the *ūmang lai* is the rain-god, and last is the god of the household (Sena-mehi), who is occasionally said to be the son of one of the seven goddesses. The function of the *maikeingākpa* deities was to keep sickness from entering the State. Each family has a special deity, male or female, who is obviously in origin a deified ancestor, but the worship of some at least of these group deities is not now confined to members of the group. The seven goddesses bear titles describing their functions. From each of them is sprung one of the clans composing the Meithei confederacy. The earth, water, grass, rice, iron, fish, gold and silver, salt, cotton, fire, and the winds are sprung from these goddesses, either directly or from their daughters. Each of these deities has a *laipham*, or god's place, specially sacred to him or her. Some reside on hill-tops, but for the convenience of their worshippers have abodes in more accessible spots. Such *laipham* abound, notably on the ridges and passes, and are marked by heaps of stones and leaves. In the sacred groves near the villages of their special worshippers are houses for the deities, and these groves are sanctuaries for bird and beast. The gods play the national game of polo, and a stick and ball are kept for their use. In some cases they are represented by images or material objects. They also reside in the chief official of the group, village, or family which forms their special clientele. The principal ceremony in the worship of the *ūmang lai* is called the *laiharaoba*, literally 'pleasing the god.' In every case the god has to be enticed from running water. The ceremony rouses him from a state of quiescence into activity, as is shown by his entering into some selected worshipper. The god benefits directly by the rite, which gives him strength so that he becomes thereby more potent to aid his worshippers. The process of enticing the deity varies somewhat according to the deity, and is accompanied by numerous subsidiary rites, mainly in order to avert all evil influence. Special precautions have to be taken—*e.g.*, clean fire must be manufactured by means of a bamboo and a cane in cross friction. Dancing is a necessary accompaniment of the rite, which often includes the use of foul abuse—a feature which gives the god great pleasure. While the ceremony is in progress, social and sexual tabus, immediately paralleled by the customs of the hill-tribes, are strictly enforced, thus indicating that the purpose of the rite is to restore the solidarity of social life and to produce in the worshippers a sense of religious exaltation. The social divisions, resting on age and other lines of social cleavage, function separately on these interesting occasions. The offerings are in some cases such as render the active participation of professing Hindus a matter of some difficulty, but the difficulty is surmounted by substituting a Loi, a member, *i.e.*, of the non-Hindu section of the community, for the Hindu believer for and by whom and on whose behalf the rite is performed. The Hindu may salve his conscience by merely sniffing the savour of the sacrifice, unmindful of the fate of the Pīr Alīs of Bengal, who fell from orthodoxy by mischance in that manner. In general, the tendency would seem to be to substitute offerings of fruit and flowers for animal flesh. Human sacrifice was undoubtedly practised, probably at no very distant date.

The priests of the ancient order are designated *maibas* and *maibis*, and are recruited by the admission of those who become possessed by the deity at one of the high religious festivals. Inasmuch as sickness and disease are attributed to spiritual beings, the *maiba* is also the doctor of the community, but here there are specialists, and the practical knowledge of the *maibas* is far from despicable. The wide-spread belief in possession as a token and source of abnormal power and religious authority is beyond a doubt at the root of much that is important in Hindu doctrine. There is no evidence forthcoming as yet from Manipur to show that the priesthood is hereditary or that the members of the order, like *bhakats* and *jogīs*, are regarded as *jīvanmukta* (*q.v.*), or that their funeral rites differ from those of ordinary people. On its practical side the religion ministers to the simple needs of an agricultural community dependent on the regularity, adequacy, and seasonability of the rainfall for their subsistence. There are rites to secure rain and rites to stop excessive rain. Not the least interesting of the numerous rites to secure good fortune for the State is the annual selection of the *chāhitāba*, the person who gives his name to the year. Various means of divination are employed for the purpose of securing for this office a person who shall bring the good luck that is dependent on his personality.

Beliefs in evil spirits, who accompany animals and fish, and are ever hurtful to mankind, in beautiful sirens who lure young men and make them insane, in vampires, in witchcraft, in the power of trees and of tree-spirits to cure as to cause sickness, and in the maleficent activity of the ghosts of those who die by violence or of women who die in childbirth are also notable features of their organized religious system. The rites which are performed for the purpose of protection and exorcism in these cases are full of interesting detail, but in general outline resemble the rites performed elsewhere on a similar level of culture for similar purposes.

LITERATURE.—W. McCulloch, 'Account of the Valley of Munnipore,' *Selections from the Records of the Government of India* (Foreign Department), xxviii., Calcutta, 1859; T. C. Hodson, *The Meitheis*, London, 1908; J. Shakespear, 'The Religion of Manipur,' in *FL* xxiv. [1913] 409 ff.

T. C. HODSON.

MANITU.—*Manitu*, a word originally applied by the Eastern Algonquins to a spirit, is properly *anit*, 'spirit,' with the sign *m*, meaning any spirit or genius in the shamanistic devil-cult of the Indians, and also any *genius loci* without the implication of evil. In consequence of the teaching of the missionaries, the conception of one Great Spirit became current among the Indians, and this was expressed by the word *kit* or *keht* prefixed to *anit*; thus Keht-anit, or Kitanit (Kittanit), to which was again added the syllable *wit*, meaning a mode of existence; hence Kittanitowit, 'the existence (known as) the Great Anito,' the paraphrase of God as taught by the missionaries. That the Indians themselves had evolved no such conception is abundantly manifested by the absence in any American language of a word capable of expressing the idea of God, the words used in John Eliot's Bible (Cambridge, Mass., 1663) and employed by the Penobscot Indians, Kiehtan and Keitanitom, being merely variants of this artificial compound. As such the conception was introduced in opposition to a spirit variously called Hobbomoco, the Evil Spirit, or Malsum, 'the Wolf.' Another form of the latter appears to have been evolved in antithesis to a contracted form of Keitanitom, namely, Tan'tum, as opposed to Squantum, the Devil ('angry god'). *Manitu* is, then, a general word for any sort of a dæmonium, good or bad, and it has reached a higher significance by purely artificial means.

Nevertheless, the missionaries did not invent the idea of a good spirit, or of an evil spirit, or of a spirit-creator. What they did was to seize upon ideas already current in another form, fuse them, and present to the Indians the fusion (really confusion) as the embodiment of one unitary conception. The Indians believed that a spirit might be a good or good-natured power, and that he might be an inimical power, and they also believed that a certain ancestral spirit had always been favourably disposed towards his children, but it was far from the thought of the Algonquins that there was an ever good and supreme Great Spirit, creator and benefactor, opposed to a Great Spirit of Evil. Wherever such ideas are found, they reflect the thought inherited from forefathers who had been under Christian influence. Thus the Mandans painted upon one side of the tent a figure representing the Good Spirit and on the other side a figure representing the Evil Spirit, that they might be under the protection of both these powerful spirits; but this is merely the degradation of teaching originally strange to them. They recognized certain spirits who aided and certain spirits who opposed them, but not as in any case Great Spirits. They believed rather that the 'medicine-man' could control all spirits. Similarly, when the 'epic' of Kulóskap describes this god of the Passamaquoddies as the son of a divine unknown mother and antithetical to a twin evil spirit, as the principle of goodness opposed to a sort of Ahriman, it must be remembered that the Passamaquoddies have long been under higher religious guidance than that of their medicine-men. Even the 'vague faith in a Supreme Spirit' ascribed to them is derived from the same source. What is original is the conception of a superior being, who is father of the special tribe or race that revere him as leader and helper. In general it may be said that worship is not paid to any evil spirit as such, but also that worship is not paid to any good spirit as such.

The *manitu* is often confused with the *wakan* of western tribes. But the latter is often less a spirit than a power, like the *mana* (*q.v.*) of the Polynesians, which lies inherent in certain objects as well as in certain men. Its possession gives power, not, to the Indian's thought, a supernatural power, but a perfectly natural, although unusual, power. Between the two conceptions lies that of the ordinary *oke*, which at bottom is one with *wakan*, but is conceived as sometimes a spirit and sometimes a spiritual power. There is some corresponding word to be found in most of the languages of the American Indians, and every one of them connotes a power which may be called spiritual. Sometimes it is the purely shamanistic power contained in the medicine-bag, which is not really a medicine-bag at all, but a collection of objects of fetishistic nature, and sometimes it is a spirit, embodied or disembodied, such as the spirit of a waterfall, the spirit of thunder, the spirit of animals, etc. It is a mysterious force which may inhere in matter or may make itself felt as an expression of spirit. The powers of nature have it, generally winds, storms, productive earth, and animals all have it, though some in larger amount than others. Finally, men have it in certain cases. But there is no sharp distinction between this power and that found in spirits proper, where it becomes individualized. It is this very power that is the 'medicine' of the conjurer and nature-subduing priest. Whether it be called *manitu*, *oke* (*oki*), *wakan*, or even *ku* (in Maya form), it is always the same thing under a shifting terminology, except that among certain tribes it is more apt to be conceived as impersonal and among others as personal. *Manitu* is generally personal, *wakan* is generally impersonal, but the alternate use of either is not unusual. *Wakan* has been defined by Brinton (*Myths of the New World*, p. 45) as 'supernatural in its etymological sense,' in that it means in the forms current among the Iroquois and Dakotas, namely, *oke* and *wakan* respectively, something 'above,' and Brinton interprets this as *super* in the sense of supernatural. But it is more probable that the word means *super* in the sense of superior. These Iroquois and Dakota forms are etymologically allied, and a possible connexion with Sioux *oghee* may be admitted; but it would be unprofitable to attempt, with Brinton, to connect these terms with the above-mentioned *ku* of the Mayas. The 'Quaker' of the Powhatans is another form of the same word, the quaker gods being, however, not the higher but the lesser spirits. This word, like Tan'tum and Squantum above, is an adaptation from approximately corresponding Indian sounds (Quaker is *qui-oki*, 'small spirits') and contains the *oki* of the Iroquois and Algonquins, but it is not probable that it is one with the southern *huaca*, *ku*, etc. The Algonquin *oki* means a spirit of any sort—*e.g.*, the spirit of a body of water, or the spirit of winter—and expresses also the idea of a distinctly demoniac power ruling the winds, but not in a devilish manner; for, especially among the Hurons, the *oki* gives good fortune and regulates the winds for the benefit of the good Indian. It also implies a ghost, and in this respect differs from the conception of *anit* (*manitu*), though in other respects it is difficult to perceive any distinction between the *anit* (*manitu*) and the *oki*; perhaps, as appears from the geographical distribution of the two words, the *anit* was confined to the East, while the *oki* penetrated from the West to the Eastern tribes.

The *manitu* of greatest authority among the Algonquins was Michabo, and an analysis of this peculiar being shows that he was far from being a supreme spirit. Like many of the Indian spirits, he was a very superior animal, Michabo meaning 'great hare' (originally *manibozho*). This *manitu* was revered from the Northern line of the States to Virginia and from the East as far West as the Mississippi. He was represented as the originator of all the system of conjuring and exorcizing which makes the real science of the medicine-man; he ruled the winds and guarded his people, but was as often tricked and deceived as he in turn tricked and deceived; he was for the most part a humorous buffoon, whose exploits amused the Indians, as those of Brer Rabbit amuse the Negroes. On the other hand, he is referred to as 'the hare that made the moon,' and he is even said to have created the earth. But as creator he is not dignified, nor even serious. It is more natural to him to hunt, and, when autumn comes, to smoke his last pipe before turning in to sleep through the winter. It is the smoke of his last pipe that makes the haze in the air of autumn. That he originally came from the East, and, according to the earlier accounts, sends (not creates) the sun and moon out of the East, has led to the ingenious conjecture that Michabo has come from a confusion of *wabos*, 'hare,' with *wabi*, 'light' (Brinton, *Myths of the New World*, p. 165). There is the greatest confusion in the form of the name now known as Michabo, which appears as Missibizi and Messou as well as Nanibozho and Manibozho, apparently because the name was sometimes rendered *michi* ('great') and sometimes *manitu* ('spirit'), with *wabos*, 'hare.' That is, Michabo was thought of as the 'spirit-hare' or as the 'great hare,' and this 'hare,' according to Brinton, is a later Indian mistake for 'light.' Although the words are alike, and *wabi* means 'white' (*wapa* means the eastern light), yet nothing is more apt to lead one astray than reliance upon such etymological chances. We are, then, far from agreeing with Brinton when he says that 'beyond a doubt this is the compound in the names Michabo and Manibozho which therefore means the Great Light, the Spirit of Light, the Dawn' (*ib.* p. 166). Much as Brinton has done for American studies, he wrote under the dawn-myth influence of his day and probably laid more stress upon etymology than upon ethnology. The truth is that the 'great hare' is the interpretation best justified in accordance with Indian belief and tradition. Michabo was a demoniac animal of kindly disposition and endowed with a great magician's knowledge and cunning, which, however, could not keep him out of ludicrous difficulties. He was not a god, still less a god of goodness, but, as has been said of similar Indian spirits, a spirit of good-nature. He is the son of the wind, one of four brothers born at a birth, but he took command of them. As they were born North, South, East, and West, it seems as if he represented one of the four winds. Yet the early missionaries declared that he *and* the four winds were the chief Algonquin gods. As expressed in the account of the year 1616, Michabo and the four winds were the only gods that the Algonquins had at that time. Further, it must be remembered that Michabo is sometimes portrayed (as among the New Jersey Indians) as a devil, while at others he is represented as the 'ancestor'—a term which has often led to the false conclusion that believers in an ancestor-spirit must necessarily believe in a creator-god. Other tribes also have ancestral or at least specially revered animals, such as the bear, deer, and wolf of the Mohigans. None of the Western or Southern American Indians had the conception of a Creator-God, but many of them derived their stock from certain animals. To this class of animal-gods Michabo, the greatest *manitu* of the East, appears to belong. The history of the brothers is told in various forms in various tribes, and has been interpreted as additional evidence that, when there is a good and a bad brother, we have a fundamental dualism, which, however, is unsubstantiated by any close analysis even of the tales as handed down. In the Iroquois version there are two brothers, the Beautiful Spirit and the Ugly Spirit or Good Mind and Bad Mind, as interpreted by the missionaries. But these are in reality the two brothers, 'White' and 'Dark,' Ioskeha and Tawiskara, who contend with one another till White Spirit conquers and rules from the East. Both are grandchildren of the moon, but Ioskeha becomes 'father of mankind'—an expression which means that he is the ancestor of the Iroquois. He destroyed the frog, which had made earth a desert by swallowing all the water, and he learned the wisdom of the tortoise which supports the world, namely, how to make fire. Ioskeha gave this knowledge to man. Yet here the brother is not represented as an animal; it is a simple conflict of white and dark, or light and darkness, a culture-myth which the Algonquins kept in animal-form, while the Iroquois preserved or invented it without basing the myth upon anything save the natural antithesis of light and darkness (cf. art. DUALISM [American]). It is this myth that caused the belief in American Indian dualism to receive wide acceptance, as it was thus originally interpreted by Brébeuf in 1626.

As the word *manitu* has been widely used by ethnologists, it has naturally lost somewhat its original signification and at the same time has gained a new connotation, so that it has come to mean special forms of spirit-power more or less unknown to the Algonquins. Thus it has come to denote the personal guardian-spirit of certain Western tribes which has occasionally arisen out of the personal guardian of an individual. The mythical ancestor of a village at a certain period in his life retires into solitude, and after fasting and prayer is rewarded with the vision of a certain animal, which then becomes his totem. This is adopted by his clan; and, when the clan becomes part of a larger tribal organization, it still remains as the guardian of the clan, though with a marked tendency to become simply a totem-crest. The tutelary guardian-*manitu* thus becomes a mere symbol. Sometimes such crests become merely the property of certain families. The ancestors who received the totem-*manitu* received with it the powers or privileges still retained by the *protégés* of the spirits, who continue to appear to the young men of the tribe, and the possession of these secrets forms the basis for the secret societies widely spread among the Indians of the North-West. This is the 'individual totem' acquired by every youth at puberty, which, when the organization of the clan is in a decayed state, is no longer identical with that of the ancestor and is no longer inherited. The youth at this period wanders from his father's lodge and in a secluded spot fasts and cries to the spirits, inviting any one of them to become his spiritual patron (cf. art. COMMUNION WITH DEITY [American]). During this period, when he falls asleep, the first animal, bird, or reptile of which he dreams he considers to be the one designated by the Great Spirit of the tribe for his mysterious protector during life. He then returns home, kills such an animal as he has seen in his dream, and preserves its skin in his mystery-bag ('medicine-bag'). It is possible that the individual *manitu*, though in some cases a later development than the clan-totem, is in other cases, notably among the Eastern tribes, of independent origin and as antique as the totem-*manitu*. Even among the Eastern Algonquins the acquisition of a special *manitu*-spirit in animal form by the youth who fasts is not unknown.

LITERATURE.—G. Catlin, *The North American Indians*[3], London, 1842; D. G. Brinton, *Myths of the New World*, New York, 1868, *The American Race*, do. 1891; A. H. Keane, *Man, Past and Present*, Cambridge, 1899; *Relation de la nouvelle France pour l'an 1637* (and subsequent years); H. Webster, *Primitive Secret Societies*, New York, 1908. The earliest source of information is contained in the *Relations* of the early missionaries. Brinton and Webster (*opp. citt.*) give full bibliographies. The *Annual Reports* of the Bureau of American Ethnology should be consulted for modern conditions.

E. WASHBURN HOPKINS.

MAÑJUŚRĪ.—Like the majority of Buddhist 'gods,' Mañjuśrī is represented under various aspects: (1) in the Great Vehicle, or Mahāyāna (*q.v.*), properly so called, he is a *bodhisattva*, an entirely Buddhist personage in definition if not in origin (his origin is obscure; cf. AVALOKITEŚVARA); (2) in the 'Tāntric Vehicle,' which is of very early date and is not always distinguished from the Great Vehicle proper, Mañjuśrī becomes one of the names, and often the principal 'exponent,' of the Supreme Being; (3) the cult of Mañjuśrī, originating in India, took a peculiar development in China: it probably spread from China into Nepāl, where Mañjuśrī is the mythical giver of civilization.

1. As bodhisattva.—The most ancient of his numerous names is perhaps Mañjughoṣa, 'pleasant voice.' His usual epithet is *kumāra*, or *kumārabhūta*, 'young man,' 'royal prince';[1] this title, whatever its origin, means technically a *bodhisattva* at the stage when, having received consecration (*abhiṣeka*) as a prince, he is associated with the power of a Buddha and becomes his right arm (see BODHISATTVA, vol. ii. p. 748[a]). He is named in the first rank of *bodhisattvas*, before Avalokiteśvara, at the beginning of the *Lotus of the True Law* (translated into Chinese A.D. 147–186), where he is represented (ch. xi.) as a great converter. The 'scholastic' *sūtras* and devotional works give him as a type of *bodhisattva*, relate his vow, attribute to him moral counsel for the conduct of true believers of the Great Vehicle, and celebrate his power.[2] Legend associates him with the revelation of the books of the *Prajñāpāramitā*.[3] Revealer of the *Prajñā*, god of the Word, he is the patron of the Great Vehicle, of the 'second dispensation,' and becomes the god of wisdom, a personage of high importance. According to Fa-Hian (see J. Legge, *Fā-Hien, A Record of Buddhistic Kingdoms*, Oxford, 1886, p. 46), the followers of the Mahāyāna worshipped the *Prajñā*, Mañjuśrī, and Avalokiteśvara. We have many images of Mañjuśrī; the most ancient, with two arms, are those which make his characteristic mark the *Prajñā* carried upon a lotus.

2. As Tāntric god.—It is in the Tāntric section of the Tibetan scriptures (*Rgyud*, *Kanjur* as well as *Tanjur*) that Mañjuśrī takes an extraordinary development.[4] Half a dozen *Tantras* (*Kanjur*) bear his name; among them is 'The List of the true Names of Mañjuśrī Jñāna-sattva.'[5] The last term, 'Essence-of-knowledge (?),'[6] is opposed to the name *bodhi-sattva*, and is more dignified. We find it again in one of the numerous magic rituals devoted

[1] On this expression see H. Kern, in *SBE* xxi. [1884] 4; cf. *Saddharmapuṇḍarīka*, ed. H. Kern and B. Nanjio, Petrograd, 1908 ff., p. 66: 'A certain Buddha will live twelve cosmic ages, not counting the time he is *kumāra*.'

[2] Various legends are told of his former human lives, but they are not so developed as the legends relating to Maitreya. See (1) E. Chavannes, 'Le Sūtra de la paroi occidentale de l'inscription de Kiu-yong Koan,' in *Mélanges Harlez*, Leyden, 1896, p. 75 (this *sūtra* is a *dhāraṇī*, sacred to Vairochana, 'the Brilliant,' the Buddha to whom Mañjuśrī is sometimes subordinated); (2) the *Mañjuśrīguṇakṣetravyūha* (translated into Chinese A.D. 300), where Mañjuśrī tells how he took his *bodhisattva* vow: 'I do not wish to become a Buddha quickly, because I wish to remain to the last in this world to save its beings'; 'In all my existences I wish to follow the example of Akṣobhya and be a monk' (*Śikṣāsamuchchaya*, Petrograd, 1902, p. 13); (3) the *Mañjuśrīvikrīḍita* (translated into Chinese in 313), a book patronized by the Mādhyamikas, giving the story of the conversion of a light woman by Mañjuśrī in the guise of a handsome young man; the only real sin of the *bodhisattva* is the sin of hatred (*Śikṣāsamuchchaya*, p. 149). All these works are scholastic, as is the *Bodhipakṣanirdeśa*, an account by Mañjuśrī of the 'wings' (*pakṣa*) of illumination. The devotion to Mañjuśrī, the virtue of his name, which protects against all female birth, and his glorification as the hero (*śūra*) are to be noted. Mañjuśrī is one of the saviours and patrons invoked in the 'Stanzas of Good Practice' (*Bhadracharyāgāthā*), one of the classical texts used every day by the Buddhists of the Great Vehicle (*Śikṣāsamuchchaya*, pp. 297, 365; *Bodhicharyāvatāra* [*Introd. à la pratique des futurs Bouddhas*, Paris, 1907, p. 8 f.]).

[3] Tāranātha, *Gesch. des Buddhismus*, tr. A. Schiefner, Petrograd, 1869, p. 58.

[4] See P. Cordier, *Catalogue du fonds tibétain de la Bibliothèque nationale*, iii., Paris, 1810.

[5] *Nāmasaṁgīti*, ed. J. P. Minayeff, Petrograd, 1887.

[6] Probably this term has been invented on the model of *bodhisattva* for the purpose of implying something more sublime, and yet more mysterious, than the word *bodhisattva*. This heaping up of terms is characteristic.

by the *Tanjur* to Mañjuśrī: 'spell (*sādhana*) of the Ādibuddha, the Essence-of-knowledge Mañjuśrī,'[1] which begins as follows:

'Homage to the Buddha of the beginning, the middle, and the end, free from every stain of sin, a body immaculate by nature, primordial Buddha.'

Sādhanas (spells) are magical operations by means of which the worshipper brings a deity into his presence in order to identify himself with the deity—which is not difficult to accomplish, since every man is essentially nothing but deity, though particularized and stained. These operations include 'diagrams' (*maṇḍalas*), 'geometrical figures formed of squares and circles, more or less ornamented, and inscribed within each other, upon which is ranged an endless succession of deities' represented by magic syllables.[2] Mañjuśrī often occupies the centre of these *maṇḍalas*.

Tāntric gods have two aspects, a 'right hand' aspect and a 'left hand' (or erotic) aspect. Under the former Mañjuśrī is called 'Lord of speech of the ontological Universe' (Dharmadhātuvāgīśvara); under the latter he is 'Diamond-Love,' 'Thunderbolt-Love' (Vajrānaṅga).[3] His right-hand aspect is seen from the following:

'Qu'on s'identifie à Dharmadhātu-Vāgīśvara, qui a le corps tout blanc, quatre faces, huit bras: les cinq Bouddhas [who represent the five kinds of knowledge of which Mañjuśrī is the synthesis] ornent sa couronne de joyaux . . . les deux mains (originelles) font le geste de l'enseignement; les trois autres de droite tiennent le glaive, la flèche, la hache; les trois autres de gauche, le livre de la Prajñā.'[4]

Here, Foucher goes on to say, the book, the four arms (the eight is simply a multiple), and especially the four faces, suggest representations of Brahmā. Grünwedel remarks that Mañjuśrī and Brahmā share the favours of a common *śakti* (divine energy, feminine aspect, of a god), Sarasvatī.[5]

It is noteworthy also that the *Nāmasaṁgīti* (viii. 19) gives Brahmā among the names of Mañjuśrī. As soon as the Buddhas and *bodhisattvas* became 'gods,' they inevitably became gods after Hindu fashion: Avalokita has more likeness to Śiva, and Mañjuśrī to Brahmā. Mañjuśrī always occupies an important, and often the chief, place in Buddhist polytheism.

3. As developed in China.—E. Huber was the first to observe that the canon of one of the Buddhist schools of the Little Vehicle, or Hīnayāna (*q.v.*), contained traditions foreign to India—*e.g.*, the legend of a town of Khotan—and he wondered, therefore, whether 'this canon had not been considerably augmented and modified in Turkestan itself.'[6] It is now certain that 'Serindia'[7] and, later, China itself collaborated in the development of Buddhism. The story of Mañjuśrī, who, according to the Chinese pilgrim,[8] now dwells in China, who is represented in the miniatures of the Nepālese MSS as a god worshipped in China,[9] and who, according to the Nepālese tradition, came from China to Nepāl, is interesting from this point of view.[10]

LITERATURE.—This is sufficiently cited in the footnotes.

L. DE LA VALLÉE POUSSIN.

1 *Jñānasattvamañjuśrī-ādibuddha-sādhana* (*Rgyud-ḥgrel*, vol. 71) (according to a transcription by P. Cordier).

2 A. Foucher, *Catalogue des peintures népâlaises et tibétaines de la collection B. H. Hodgson*, Paris, 1897, p. 24.

3 On the word *vajra*, 'diamond,' 'adamant,' 'thunderbolt,' etc., see art. TANTRA.

4 Foucher, *Étude sur l'iconographie bouddhique*, ii. (Paris, 1905) 47.

5 *Ib.*; cf. also vol. i. (Paris, 1900) p. 114; A. Grünwedel, *Mythologie des Buddhismus*, Leipzig, 1900, p. 136; J. Burgess, *Arch. Survey of Western India*, London, 1876.

6 *Études de littérature bouddhique*, viii., 'La Destruction de Roruka' (*Bull. de l'Ecole franç. de l'Extrême-Orient*, vi. [1906] 335).

7 From the Pamir mountains to the Great Wall.

8 I-tsing, *A Record of the Buddhist Religion*, tr. J. Takakusu, Oxford, 1896, p. 169.

9 Foucher, *Étude sur l'iconographie*, ii. 42, 115.

10 Cf. S. Lévi, *Le Népal*, Paris, 1905-08, i. 330-347. Of ancient sources see B. H. Hodgson, *Essays on the Languages, Literature, and Religion of Nepal and Tibet*, London, 1874, and E. Burnouf, *Lotus de la Bonne Loi*, Paris, 1852.

MAN OF SIN.—See ANTICHRIST, ESCHATOLOGY.

MANTRAS.—See CHARMS AND AMULETS (Indian), MAGIC (Iranian).

MANU.—See LAW (Hindu).

MAORIS.—See POLYNESIA.

MĀRA.—It seems that during the so-called late Vedic period, new gods, gods of a new style, were created. They wear, on the one hand, an aspect which is popular and mythological, and, on the other, one which is sacerdotal and esoteric; they are the expression of a pantheistic and pessimistic philosophy; but they, nevertheless, appeal to devotion and worship. Brahmā-brahman is the most eminent among them. Kāla, 'Time,' creator and destroyer, Kāma, 'Desire,' a cosmical entity, and many others may be embodied in the figures of the popular pantheon. Our Brāhmanic information on these gods is, as a rule, scanty, and, in many cases, we are largely indebted to Buddhist or epic sources.

This is the case with Māra, who is not unknown in the Atharvaveda, that aristocratic compendium of demonology; he is an important figure in Buddhism, and the Upaniṣads show the elaboration of the ideas which constitute his frame in Buddhism.

The Atharvaveda joins together Yama, the old Āryan king of the dead, Mṛtyu, Death, Agha Māra, the evil slayer or hateful murderer, Nirṛtha, the destroyer, and Śarva, the prototype of Śiva (VI. xciii. 1). Elsewhere (XI. viii. 19) it mentions the 'deities called Misfortune, or Ill, or Evil' (*pāpmāno nāma devatāḥ*), and has deprecatory invocations (VI. xxvi. 1-2, cxiii. 2, XVII. i. 29) to Misfortune (*pāpman*). Māra, or Mṛtyu, is Death personified, the god who kills, and he has already acquired his Buddhist qualification *pāpman*, 'the evil one' (Pāli, *pāpiman*). With this dark figure may be identified Yama or Śarva, also a mythological god.

That is what we know of Māra from the oldest literature. He quickly acquired a metaphysical and moral significance. For the thinkers of the age of the Brāhmaṇas and of the Upaniṣads, who admit transmigration and are anxious to find the path to the other shore of transmigration, Māra, or Death, may be regarded as the sovereign of this subsolar universe: whoever obtains a passage beyond the sun reaches the realm of immortality. For the common people, the recurrence of birth and death is the rule; the sun is Death. The legend of Nachiketas in the *Kāṭhaka Upaniṣad* is of importance for the history of Death: a young Brāhman descends to Hades, and, unmoved by all promises of transient pleasures, wrings from Yama, the god of death, the secret of that which lies beyond death and the means of liberation from death, this only means being the knowledge of Brahman which confers immortality. H. Oldenberg rightly compares this Nachiketas-Yama legend with the Buddha-Māra legend. Buddha also rejects the offers of Māra in order to obtain the *summum bonum*; but, whereas Yama is benevolent and himself reveals the liberating truth to Nachiketas with only the habitual jealous reluctance of a god, Māra is the evil one, the tempter.[1]

In the Buddhist scriptures all these premisses are fully developed. Māra actually assumes the rôle of the sovereign of the world, both of men and of gods; god of death, he is also the god of the living, who are only the food of death; he is the god of re-birth. Māra is Kāma, 'Desire,' since desire is the *raison d'être* of birth and death; and, because

1 Oldenberg, *Buddha*, tr. Hoey, p. 54.

Buddha is the deliverer from death and birth, Māra is the personal enemy of Buddha and Buddhism, the evil one, the tempter of Buddha and Buddha's disciples.

The dogmatic position of Māra is clear in all our texts: Māra embodies desire, the universal fetterer, the sensual life both here and in the other world.

In scholasticism three Māras—*devaputra māra*, the deity Māra, *maraṇamāra*, Māra as death, and *kleśamāra*, Māra as vices and passions—are distinguished. In ancient times these Māras were confused. Māra is not an allegory in the Pāli stories of temptations; he is a demon; he is spoken of as Namuchi, a Vedic demon killed by Indra.

It follows that mythological features are not wanting, even in the oldest tales of the Pāli canon. They are not, however, predominant. We are actually confronted with the temptation of Buddha by Māra's daughters; but these daughters are Desire, Unrest, Pleasure (Taṇhā, Arati, and Rati). It has been said that these stories—the intervention of Māra in order to make the future Buddha abandon his austerities (a common topic in the *Mahābhārata*: gods grow jealous of the power acquired by penitents, and dispatch fair damsels to trouble their meditation), or in order to make Buddha reach *nirvāṇa* prematurely—are only poetical descriptions of the *crises de conscience* of Śākyamuni. This view is by far too rationalistic. Such stories, it may be, were looked upon in this light by some philosophers or 'modernists,' but it is safer to admit that the Buddhists believed in a divine enemy of the eternal welfare of men, and embodied this enemy in the traditional god of death. Mythical and folk-lore accretions, as well as scholastic concoctions, naturally follow from such a belief. Monks and nuns, especially when living in the 'hermitages,' knew that Māra could appear to them under any form, and ensnare them into philosophical discussions.

The Sanskrit sources, late when compared with the Pāli ones, but not insignificant even for the restitution of the passages which they have in common with Pāli, indulge in much more dramatic and would-be poetical descriptions of Māra's attacks upon Śākyamuni. Some episodes are entirely unknown in the *Tipiṭaka*, viz. the battle for the *bodhi*-tree, the possession of which, for the compilers of the *Lalitavistara*, seems to be almost identified with the possession of the *bodhi*, the Enlightenment, itself.

It has been pointed out that even in the Pāli canon the Māra-stories show a gradual development, and that the inventions to be found in the more modern biographies of Śākyamuni, the *Lalitavistara* and the *Buddhacharita*, mark a further point in this development. There is truth in this statement—the multiplication of Māra's daughters and their counter-attacks, a large part of the *mise en scène* of the *Lalitavistara*, are not archaic—but the course of the development is not necessarily a chronological one. Less or more mythological versions may be productions of the same age in different circles.

It appears that the Māra folklore has been more luxuriant than can be judged from the Pāli canon. Some bits of popular folklore which have found their way into the authorized literature may be regarded as fragments of a larger cycle. It is only by a mere chance that we know that Māra roams everywhere, 'in the visible shape of murky smokiness,'[1] to catch the souls of the dying.

It is worth while mentioning that Māra, who is often associated with Brahmā ('the world of men and gods with Brahmā and Māra'), has no fixed abode, no heaven of his own, in the official cosmology of the Sarvāstivādins (see art. COSMOGONY AND COSMOLOGY [Buddhist]).

[1] See C. A. F. Rhys Davids, *Buddhist Psychology*, London, 1914, p. 21; *Saṁyutta*, i. 222, iii. 124.

See art. TEMPTATION (Buddhist) for the comparison between the Buddhist stories of temptation and the Gospels.

LITERATURE.—E. Senart, *Essai sur la légende du Buddha*, Paris, 1882; E. Windisch, *Māra and Buddha*, Leipzig, 1895; H. Oldenberg, *Buddha*, tr. W. Hoey, London, 1882, pp. 54, 84; H. Kern, *Histoire du Bouddhisme dans l'Inde*, Fr. tr., G. Huet, 2 vols., Paris, 1901, i. 52, 73, 180, 219; L. de la Vallée Poussin, *Bouddhisme, Opinions sur l'histoire de la dogmatique*, do. 1909, p. 227; R. C. Childers, *Dict. of the Pāli Language*, London, 1875, *s.v.* 'Māro.'

Original sources, Vedic, Pāli, and Sanskrit, have been studied by Senart and Windisch.

L. DE LA VALLÉE POUSSIN.

MARCIONISM.

1. The founder.—According to the earliest and most reliable accounts, Marcion was a shipmaster (*nauclerus*, or ναύτης) of Pontus, and may have been a native of Sinope. The story[1] which makes him the son of a Christian bishop in that region, and declares that he was excommunicated by his father for corrupting a virgin, is, on the whole, improbable, and may have been based on a misunderstanding of some phrase about his corrupting the doctrinal purity of the Church. It is possible that he was born and bred a pagan, and was converted to Christianity about the time of his journey to Rome. But the fact that his system of doctrine is based entirely on the Jewish and Christian Scriptures makes it, on the whole, more probable that he spent his youth in a Christian atmosphere.

Marcion arrived in Rome in or near A.D. 140—'after the death of Hyginus,' according to Hippolytus (see Epiph. *Hær.* xlii.). Whether or not a recent convert, he at first became a zealous member of the Roman Church, to which, according to Tertullian (*de Præscr.* 30), he presented the sum of 200,000 sesterces. But before long trouble arose through his falling under the influence of the Syrian teacher Cerdo, who had a certain connexion with the Gnostics, and whose distinctive doctrine was that

> 'the God proclaimed by the law and the prophets was not the father of our Lord Jesus Christ. For the former was known, but the latter unknown; while the one also was righteous, but the other benevolent' (Iren. *Hær.* I. xxvii. 1).

It is easy to see how Cerdo's teaching would lead Marcion into uncomfortable relations with the orthodox Church; and it is not surprising to learn that his gift of money was returned to him, and that he was placed outside the pale. This took place about the year 144, and from that date the Marcionite propaganda must have been active, since Justin Martyr tells us in his *First Apology* (*c.* 150) that Marcion

> 'by the help of devils has caused many of every nation to speak blasphemies, and to deny that God is the maker of this universe, and to assert that some other being greater than He has done greater works' (xxvi.).

Tertullian, who was writing his *adversus Marcionem* in 207 or 208, places the activity of Marcion in the reign of Antoninus Pius ('sub Pio impius'). Irenæus (*loc. cit.*) says that Cerdo came to Rome in the episcopate of Hyginus (*c.* 137–141), and that his successor Marcion flourished under Anicetus (154–166). In view of the different statements, we may conclude that Marcion became active as a teacher some years before 150, and that his activity ended before or about the time of the death of Anicetus. For Marcion's own death no date can be definitely assigned.

2. The doctrine.—The teaching of Marcion may be reviewed under five heads: (*a*) theology proper, or the doctrine of God, (*b*) Christology, (*c*) criticism

[1] This account, which was unknown to Tertullian, may be traced through Epiphanius to Hippolytus. The Armenian version is thus given by Eznik (5th cent.): 'This Marcion was a native of Pontus, the son of a bishop. And having corrupted a virgin, he went into exile on account of his father's having expelled him from the Church. And going to Rome at that time to seek absolution (lit. penitence) and not obtaining it, he was irritated against the Faith' (*Against the Sects*, bk. iv.).

and exegesis of the Scriptures, (*d*) the application of religion to practical life, and (*e*) the ritual of worship.

(*a*) *Theology*.—In theology Marcion's main assertion was that the just God of the law and of the OT generally was other than and inferior to the God revealed in Jesus Christ, the chief attribute of the latter being goodness or loving-kindness. The idea of a dual godhead seems to have come from the Gnostics through Cerdo, and this fact may be connected with the (otherwise doubtful) statement by Clement of Alexandria (*Strom.* VII. xvii. 107) that Marcion, 'being contemporary with' Basilides and Valentinus, 'companied with them as an elder with younger men.' At all events, Marcion's theology differed from the Gnostic in excluding any doctrine of æons, and, indeed, any element which could not be derived from his interpretation of the Jewish and Christian Scriptures.[1] His teaching was not in any sense pagan. His lost work named the *Antitheses* contained the proofs of his theology, which were attained by placing utterances by and concerning God in the OT side by side with opposed statements by Jesus and Paul about God in the NT.

He further differed from the Gnostics by abstaining from any attempt at a completed speculative system. The contrasts which he drew out were final, and he did not seek to harmonize them in a higher principle; for him the two ἀρχαί were and remained completely separate, in spite of the moral superiority of the God of the NT. The logical weakness of the position is well shown by Tertullian. On the one hand, the introduction of number or plurality was inconsistent with the essence of true godhead; and, on the other, the interposition of the good God—'the Stranger'—in a world which had been created by and belonged to another was an obvious stumbling-block.

(*b*) *Christology*. — The mode of self-revelation employed by the good God was, according to Marcion, that 'in the 15th year of the reign of Tiberius He (*i.e.* Jesus Christ) came down to the Galilæan city of Capernaum'—to which Tertullian adds the explanation, 'of course meaning from the heaven of the Creator, to which He had previously descended from His own' (*adv. Marc.* iv. 7). The relation of Christ to the good God His Father does not seem to have been otherwise defined than by the idea of sonship. Of the human experience and suffering of Christ Marcion took a wholly Docetic view. Rejecting the Gospel accounts of a human birth, he represented the supposed sudden appearance of Christ in the year 29 as an entirely new phenomenon, without any root in the past history either of the people or of the human race. And, while he regarded the life of Christ on earth and His crucifixion as the means of salvation for men, he nevertheless believed that our Lord suffered only in appearance. On the other hand, he did accept the historical facts narrated in those portions of the Third Gospel (see below) which he believed to be genuine, and shared the belief of his time in other elements of the Christian creed; thus he laid great stress on our Lord's descent into Hades and His preaching to the men of former generations who were there confined.

Again, as he believed in two Gods, he also recognized two Christs. According to him, the Messianic prophecies of the OT were true predictions, referring, however, not to Jesus Christ but to another Messiah who was to appear later as the messenger of the just God of the OT. But his exposition of the work of this Messiah does not seem to have proceeded beyond applying to him the language of OT prophecy.

(*c*) *Criticism and exegesis of the Scriptures*.—In his dealing with the Scriptures Marcion combined a high estimate of the objective truth of the OT as a historical document with a startling and audacious subjective criticism of the NT. His mode of handling each was largely dictated by the necessities of his position. Convinced of the fundamental discrepancy between the theologies of the OT and of that which he regarded as the genuine kernel of the NT, he naturally laid stress on every narrative, discourse, or even verse in the Jewish Scriptures which seemed to him to set forth the Jewish as opposed to the Christian view. His treatment of the OT has at least one great merit—he rejected allegorical explanations such as were current among the Gnostics; he took the history literally, and laid full stress on its distinctive characteristics. In the NT, on the other hand, while he similarly preferred the literal to the allegorical explanation, he proceeded ruthlessly in the way of cutting out such books or portions of books as did not fit in with his view of the facts, and in re-editing the text to any extent on subjective grounds. As the Third Gospel seemed on the whole to suit best the requirements of his theology, he adopted this, though in a mutilated and much altered state, as the only reliable portion of the historical writings contained in the NT. To him Paul was the only true apostle of the Master, and he believed that the Third Gospel—which he did not call Luke's—had been written under Paul's supervision and expressed Paul's view of the life of Christ. The other Evangelists[1] he regarded as handing on a false Judaic tradition which had grown up among the Twelve, and he therefore rejected their works *in toto*. In the rest of the NT he accepted only ten Pauline Epistles, rejecting the Acts, the Pastoral Epistles of Paul, and the rest of the NT writings so far as known to him. And in the ten Epistles he used considerable freedom in rejecting or altering passages which conflicted with his views. An understanding of his detailed treatment of the NT can be best obtained by reading the fourth and fifth books of Tertullian's *adv. Marcionem*.

(*d*) *The application of religion to practical life*.—It is easy to see that, however arbitrary and subjective was Marcion's attitude in relation to the Christian tradition and its literature, his main interest in the matter was not speculative or theoretical, but religious and practical. This is shown by the fact that he attempted no higher synthesis, but allowed what seemed to him the irreconcilable opposition between the Creator and the NT God to continue until the end of time. To him the means of salvation was faith in Jesus Christ and in His Father. This faith was to issue in an ascetic life which despised and rejected the works of the Creator, so far as the conditions of human life allowed. Thus the celibate alone were admitted to baptism. A further consequence of this attitude was that Marcion denied the resurrection of the body; the salvation through Christ was for the soul and spirit only. The moral earnestness of the Marcionite community was proved both by the zeal of its propaganda and by the large number of its martyrs.

(*e*) *The ritual of worship*.—The aim of Marcion was to found not a school, but a church. Accordingly, in points of ritual he for the most part followed the usage of the orthodox Church, but admitted catechumens to the same privileges in Church worship as baptized persons, and forbade the use of wine in the eucharistic service. Some

[1] Marcion appears to have held the independent, though passive, existence of ὕλη, or matter. He certainly did not attribute to it the degree of activity which some of his followers did. In his view the Creator (*i.e.* the just God or God of the law) was the ruler of the whole material universe.

[1] There is no definite evidence as to whether Marcion knew the Fourth Gospel.

of the peculiarities of usage in the Eastern branch of the Marcionite church may be gathered from the statements of Eznik (bk. iv.):

'He allows not one baptism only, but three after (successive) transgressions, and in place of catechumens who have died he urges others to be baptized. And he has the boldness to direct women to administer baptism—which no one from the other sects has taken upon himself to do—but not to administer a second or a third baptism, nor (does he venture) to admit women to be priests,' etc.

Marcion's followers seem to have elevated him (at least virtually) to the rank of bishop, and the constitution of the sect was probably episcopal, though on this point we have not much information.

3. **Later developments.**—Among the followers of Marcion some, like Potitus and Basilicus, followed their master in recognizing two principles or divine beings; but some, like Apelles, held only one ultimate principle, the God of the NT, while others accepted three independent principles—the Good, the Just, and the Evil. Of these different teachers Apelles is the most interesting. Starting from the Marcionite opposition between the Creator and the NT God, he seems to have regarded the former as 'an opposing spirit' who owed his existence to the supreme God. The material world, in the view of Apelles as of Marcion, was created by this 'opposing spirit,' and so Apelles also taught an ascetic view of life. On the other hand, he rejected Marcion's Docetism, and held that Christ really felt and suffered in His earthly experience, although He did not possess a truly human nature in the orthodox sense. But he maintained that in the Crucifixion lay the hope of man's salvation.

The doctrines of Marcion were for a time widely spread both in the West—Rome and Italy—and in the East—Arabia, Syria, Armenia, Cyprus, Egypt, and perhaps even Persia. After sharing in the persecutions inflicted on the Church, particularly under Diocletian, the Marcionites seem to have enjoyed a short period of toleration early in the 4th cent., to judge from an inscription of A.D. 318–319 discovered a few miles south of Damascus, which records the existence of a village community of Marcionites. But their worship was soon prohibited by Constantine. In the West they seem early to have succumbed to the more powerful propaganda of Manichæism (*q.v.*), but in the East they may be judged to have exerted a stronger and more enduring influence. We infer from the attention given to them in the controversial works of Ephraim, and from the careful account of their doctrines left us by Eznik, an Armenian writer of the 5th cent., that they counted for much in Eastern Christendom. So late as the 10th cent. they are mentioned in Arabic by the *Fihrist*.

As the best illustration of the nature of Eastern Marcionism, we subjoin a literal translation of Eznik's Armenian account:

'Marcion wrongly introduces a strange element (lit. strangeness) in opposition to the God of the Law, positing with him also Hyle, by way of essence, and three heavens. In the one (they say) dwells the Stranger, and in the second the God of the Law, and in the third his armies; and in the earth Hyle, and they call her the Power of the Earth.

And he so orders the world and the creatures, as the law says. But he adds that in union with Hyle he made all that he made, and Hyle was as though a woman and a wedded wife. And after making the world, he went up together with his armies into heaven; and Hyle and her sons remained in the earth, and they each held authority—Hyle in the earth, and the God of the Law in heaven.

And the God of the Law, seeing that the world is beautiful, thought to make in it a man. And going down to Hyle in the earth, he said, "Give me of thy clay, and from myself I give spirit, and let us make a man according to our likeness." On Hyle giving him of her earth, he moulded it and breathed into it a spirit, and Adam became a living soul, and therefore was called Adam because he was made from clay. And moulding him and his wife, and putting them in the garden (as the law says), they continued giving him commands, and rejoiced in him as in a common son.

And (he says) the God of the Law, who was lord of the world, seeing that Adam is noble and worthy of ministration, pondered how he could steal him from Hyle and appropriate him to himself. Taking him aside, he said, "Adam, I am God, and there is no other, and beside me thou shalt have no other god. But if thou takest any other god beside me, know that thou shalt surely die." And when he said this to him and mentioned the name of death, Adam, struck with fear, began by degrees to separate himself from Hyle.

And Hyle, coming to give him commands according to custom, saw that Adam was not obeying her, but was purposely holding aloof and not coming near her. Then Hyle, amazed in her mind, knew that the Lord of Creatures had deceived her. She said, "From the source of the fountain its water is befouled. How is this? Before Adam is increased with offspring, he has stolen him by the name of his godhead from me. Since he hates me, and has not kept with me the covenant, I will make many gods, and will fill with them the whole world, that he may enquire who is God and not find out."

And she made (they say) many idols and named them gods and filled the world with them. And the name of God, that of the Lord of Creatures, was lost among the names of the many gods, and was not found anywhere. And his offspring was led astray by them and was not serving him, for Hyle claimed them all for herself, and did not suffer one of them to serve him. Then (they say) the Lord of Creatures was enraged, because they forsook him and obeyed Hyle; and one after another, who were departing from their bodies, he was casting in anger into Hell. And Adam he cast into Hell because of the tree, and so went on casting all into Hell, up to twenty-nine generations.

And (they say) the good and strange God, who was sitting in the third heaven, seeing that so many peoples perished and were tortured between the two deceivers, the Lord of Creatures and Hyle, was grieved for those fallen into the fire and tortured. He sent his son to go and save them, and to take the likeness of a servant and assume the form of a man among the sons of the God of the Law. "Heal," he said, "their lepers, and raise their dead to life, and open the eyes of their blind, and do among them great cures without price; until the Lord of Creatures see thee, and be jealous, and crucify thee. And then when thou diest, thou shalt go down into Hades, and bring them from thence; for Hades is not wont to admit life within it. And therefore thou goest up on the cross, that thou mayest become like the dead, and Hades may open its mouth to admit thee, and thou mayest enter into the midst of it and empty it."

And when he crucified him (they say), he went down into Hades and emptied it. And taking the souls in the midst of it, he led them into the third heaven to his Father. And the Lord of Creatures, being enraged, in anger tore his garment and the veil of his temple, and darkened his sun and clothed his world in blackness, and sat in grievous mourning.

Then Jesus, going down a second time in the form of his godhead to the Lord of Creatures, was entering into judgment with him about his death. And the Lord of the World, seeing the godhead of Jesus, knew that there is another God besides himself. And Jesus said to him, "I have a suit with thee, and let none be judge between us but thine own law which thou didst write." And when they produced the law, Jesus said to him, "Didst not thou write in thy law that whoso killeth shall die; and whoso sheddeth the blood of a righteous man, they shall shed his blood?" And he said, "I so wrote." And Jesus said to him, "Now give thyself into my hands, that I may kill thee and shed thy blood, as thou didst kill me and shed my blood, for I am indeed juster than thou, and have wrought many benefits in thy creation." And he began to reckon up the benefits which he had wrought in his creation.

And when the Lord of Creatures saw that he had conquered him, and knew not what to say because out of his own law he was condemned, and was finding no answer because he deserved death in return for his death, then falling to prayer he was beseeching him, "Because I have sinned and killed thee in ignorance, because I knew not that thou art a God, but reckoned thee a man, it is given thee as satisfaction for that to carry off where thou wilt all those who shall be willing to believe in thee." Then Jesus leaving him laid hold of Paul and revealed to him the purchase and sent him to preach that "We are bought with a price, and every one who believes in Jesus has been sold by the Just to the Good."

This is the beginning of the heresy of Marcion, besides many other worthless things. And this all do not know, but a few of them. And they hand on the teaching to one another orally. The Stranger (they say) has bought us with a price from the Lord of Creatures; but how or with what the purchase has been made, that not all of them know.'

LITERATURE.—A full list of authorities is supplied by A. Harnack, *Geschichte der altchristlichen Litteratur bis Eusebius*, Leipzig, 1893–1904, i. 191–200; and a shorter list by G. Krüger, in *PRE*³ xii. 266 f. The main ancient sources are Irenæus, Tertullian (esp. *adv. Marcionem* and *de Præscr. Hær.*), Clement of Alexandria, Origen, pseudo-Tertullian (*Carmen adv. Marcionem*), Adamantius, Ephraim, Epiphanius, Theodoret, and Eznik. An exhaustive account of Marcion's dealings with the NT will be found in T. Zahn, *Geschichte des NT Kanons*, Erlangen, 1888–92, i. 585–718.

N. McLEAN.

MARCUS AURELIUS ANTONINUS.—

1. **Early influences.**—By birth and training, alike on his father's and his mother's side, Marcus, son of Annius Verus, belonged to the official aristocracy of Rome. From boyhood he was inured to the

round of absorbing and ceremonious etiquettes which, under the régime of Hadrian, made up the official life of the capital. Through his uncle Antoninus, whom Hadrian appointed *Quatuor vir* for the administration of Italy, he was brought from childhood into personal touch with the Emperor himself, and the playful 'Verissimus' accorded to him by Hadrian re-appears even in the formal address of the Christian apologist.

Another influence, which he himself attributes to his mother's fostering care, sank deep into the fibre of his being. In the antique life of Rome, *religio*, dependence upon God, pervaded every turn and act; and from the simpler life of the home and farm the ancient pieties and rituals had never died away. Under Augustus the historic festivals and shrines, the ancient brotherhoods and colleges and gilds, of Salian priests, of Arval Brothers, of Vestal Virgins, and others were revived, and a profusion of new cults was introduced. Priesthoods became the dress of leadership and rank, and patriotism found articulate expression in the worship of the Emperor and in countless forms of mystery worship. To this religious complex Marcus was acclimatized from youth. At eight years old he was enrolled among the Salii, the most primitive of all the priestly colleges at Rome, and 'got all the forms and liturgies by heart.'[1] At sixteen, as *Præfectus feriarum Latinarum*, he solemnized the fête upon the Alban Mount; and besides the formal dignities of *Pont. Max.*, *XV vir Sacr. Fac.*, and *VII vir Epul.*, he wore the cowl of Master among the Arval Brotherhood. The prayer of the college is still extant which besought blessing for him and L. Verus in their conflict with the Marcomanni. At the outset of his great campaigns he purified the people with the solemn ritual of the *Lectisternium*; at Athens he was himself initiated in the Eleusinian mysteries; on the Danube he approved the casting of lions into the stream at the bidding of the Eastern magi. His Stoic monotheism lent itself to sympathy with cults of every kind, as witnesses to the divine power.

2. Life.—His boyhood was given to wholesome and studious disciplines. At Rome he fenced, played ball, and eschewed the mischievous excitements of the circus and the amphitheatre; at Lorium he rode, hunted, walked, and shared the glee of rural industries and festivals. The correspondence with Fronto, his master in rhetoric, shows rare docility of type. Boyish experiments in philosophy ended in complete conversion under the perusal of Ariston, the influence of Rusticus, and the charm of Epictetus.

His life falls into three sections: A.D. 121–138, boyhood, ending with his adoption in 138; 138–161, apprenticeship to rule, as Cæsar and lieutenant to his adoptive father, Antoninus; 161–180, Imperial rule, shared nominally in 161–169 with L. Verus, and from 177 with his son, Commodus.

Till 167, when the Danubian campaigns begin, the years are filled with unremitting administrative activities. The *Edictum perpetuum* of Salvius Julianus furnished the basis of the Pandects of Justinian; Gaius and Papinian immortalize the era, as master-builders among those who reared the great fabric of Roman law. Under the direction of Stoic principles the rigours of the *patria potestas*, the slave-owner, and the creditor were brought within control; protection was accorded to women, children, wards, minors, freedmen, slaves; educational and charitable endowments were multiplied; professorships were established at Universities; and medical service was organized for communities. Commerce, industries, and communications were liberally fostered by provision of roads, aqueducts, bridges, and havens, while in special crises, as of earthquake, fire, famine, or inundation, State aid was ungrudgingly extended. The collection and distribution of taxation were vigilantly supervised, and vast extension given to the forms and activities of local and municipal government. Wealth lavished its resources upon the provision of temples, baths, gardens, colonnades, and other embellishments of city life, while among all classes of the community gilds, colleges, and clubs, though kept under strict surveillance, multiplied to an almost incredible extent.

In his *dealings with the Christians*, Marcus followed the practice of his predecessors. First by Nero, then by the Flavian Emperors, especially Domitian, Christianity had been treated as a form of sacrilege (ἀσέβεια, ἀθέοτης) and treason, that lay outside the province or protection of law and entailed the penalty of death. Like rebellion or brigandage, it fell under the summary jurisdiction of the Emperor or his representative. Trajan, setting his face against professional or anonymous delation, and Hadrian, going still further in discouragement of malicious information or assault, did much to arrest active persecution; but Christianity continued to be a capital offence, and the forms of the Imperial cult furnished a standing test of complicity or disclaimer. Enforcement of the penalty rested with the Emperor's delegate, and was rarely exercised. But outbursts of personal hostility, of local prejudice, or of racial or religious jealousies might at any moment bring it into play. The progress of Imperial consolidation, and the rapid social developments of Christianity, both tended to enhance the seeming disaffection of Christians to Imperial unity. In Pliny the note of condescension and compassion softens contempt for the perverse superstition, which seemed to invite and almost compel persecution; in Marcus the accent of irritation becomes prominent; to him Christian defiance seemed like the melodramatic pose which induced Proteus Peregrinus, in the story of Lucian, to cast himself on the pyre as the finale of the Olympian festival. On the main merits of the case he shared, no doubt, the judgment of his compeers, the leading Hellenists of the time, and among them his own intimate associates. The persiflage of Lucian and the malignant disdain of Celsus do not stand alone; Fronto still credits the Christians with nameless crimes and immoralities; Ælius Aristides satirizes their mean and mischievous self-seeking; Galen quotes them as the type of impenetrable bigotry. The Emperor's political philosophy led him the same way. The Græco-Roman unity of Empire was the World-Cosmos finding realization in the communities of men; the highest and best hopes of the world were centring in that consummation of the civic bond about the person of the Emperor; and the self-willed isolation of the Christian was essential atheism, in its estrangement from the divine impulse immanent in man.

But, as a statesman, Marcus holds to the prescriptions of Imperial policy. The rescript, cited by Eusebius,[1] is plainly unauthentic, and belongs, if to any period, to that of Antoninus. Melito[2] himself discredits the persecuting edicts to which he refers, and bears witness to the clemency and philosophy of the Emperor in checking tumultuary acts of violence against the Christians. The decree, or rather rescript, uttered against 'demoralizing superstitions' may have been partly aimed at Christians; but the terms were general, and it was retained upon the statute-book under later Christian Emperors. Possibly under its terms Christians were sent to the mines of Sardinia, but

[1] *Capit.* 4.

[1] *HE* iv. 13. [2] In Eus. *HE* iv. 26. 5 f.

in point of fact the penal provisions—deportation for those of higher rank, and death for humbler offenders—would mitigate, not enhance, the penalty to which all avowed Christians stood liable. In their social organization the Christians remained as free as other sects. In Rome itself Church-membership and jurisdiction, episcopal authority, and literary activity advanced apace. Apologists, such as Justin, Melito, Athenagoras, one after another addressed their pleas to the Emperor in person; Tatian and Hermas retort scorn and invective on their antagonists. Christians served in the Imperial households and, as the story of the Thundering Legion proves, were numerous among the legionaries.

None the less, illogical as was the situation, the profession of Christianity remained under the Imperial ban, and Christians as such were judicially liable to death. In two of the most famous instances when the penalty was enforced, responsibility devolves directly on the Emperor. The first concerns Justin, apologist and martyr, who with six associates was brought before the bar of Rusticus, prefect of the city, on the charge of 'atheism and sacrilege'; each in succession adhered to the Christian confession, and, on refusing to abjure or to offer sacrifice, was ordered to execution. Marcus was at the time resident in Rome, and, no doubt, endorsed the sentence passed by the Stoic prefect, his close friend and ex-preceptor. Still more famous is the persecution recorded in that masterpiece of Christian martyrologies, the letter of the Christians of Lyons and Vienne to the sister churches in Asia and Phrygia.[1] The outbreak, rooted in racial, even more than religious, antipathies, was fanned to fever heat by the frenzies of the amphitheatre, where the Christians were subjected by the mob to hideous and revolting tortures and indignities. When order was restored, and the martyrs, rescued from the fury of the mob, were remanded to prison, their sentence was referred to the Emperor himself, whose ruling was that, if they still persisted in recalcitrance, the law must take its course. The incident was fresh in his mind when he wrote down his reflexion on Christian perversity and bravado.[2] In Asia too, and in Africa, sporadic acts of persecution took place, and martyrdom was judicially inflicted, though for the most part Christians were screened under the Imperial ægis from outbreaks of popular fanaticism or dislike. Of systematized persecution there was none, and to the Church historians and apologists of the next generation the era of the Antonines was an age of peace and toleration.

Marcus's latter years were clouded with calamities, public and personal. In 166 Italy was desolated by plague, from which it never recovered; in its track came famine, earthquakes, and inundations of unusual severity; then the yet more terrific inroad of barbarians, streaming across the Alps, and knocking at the gates of Aquileia. From that date onwards the legions of the West were locked in a life-and-death struggle with Marcomanni, Quadi, Jazyges, and other trans-Danubian hordes, sustained and carried to a triumphant conclusion only by the dogged and intrepid leadership of Marcus himself.

3. The 'Thoughts.'—From these ordeals the *Thoughts* emerge. They are not the exposition of a system, but a criticism of life; reflexions confided 'To Himself' in the hours of loneliness and interstices of strain; a retrospect and record of experience; a manual of duty and endurance. In them a soul communes with itself, examines motives, probes illusions, corrects or re-affirms conclusions, emits the sigh of weariness or the ejaculation of disgust, but perpetually renews resolve, unalterably clinging to the noblest hypothesis with which it was familiar. Beginning in almost random reminiscence, composition gave relief from strain, and became a substitute for company, and a pleasure for its own sake; and for Marcus Stoic principles so interpenetrated the whole fabric of conduct and creed that these self-communings shed clearer light upon the actualities of Roman Stoicism than the homilies of Seneca or the *Memorabilia* of Epictetus.

(1) *Logic.* —In his theory of knowledge and sensation he adheres closely to the terms of Epictetus. The φαντασίαι are in part sense-impressions proper, derived from things, in part impressions of aims, qualities, or attributes, moral or æsthetic, belonging to things, and conveyed to the reason. It is for reason to sit in judgment on them, determine their true content and value, and firmly maintain its own prerogative. In the one passage in which he formally discusses the doctrine of assent (συγκατάθεσις, v. 10) he drops the Stoic claim to final certitude—τὰ πράγματα ἀκατάληπτα. But there remains a tenacity of moral assurance which suffices for conduct of life. Reason as part of the divine immanence attains a coherence, a consistency, and strength which give the indefeasible assurance of truth.

(2) *Theory of being.*—In Stoic monism matter, form, and force are an inseparable unity. The life-power, self-determined from within, is embodied in the various forms of phenomenal and spiritual being. The variety of being is explained physically by the doctrine of τόνος, that is, of 'tension within the life-producing force,' present in ever-varying grades in all forms of existence, material or spiritual. In the successive grades of inorganic, vegetable, animal, and human life each variation represents a different degree or kind of tension in the informing πνεῦμα, or life-power. Cohesion, life, and reason are resultant phases of embodied spirit, varying in the same way as inorganic substances are seen to vary under processes of rarefaction or condensation. Ἕξις, 'hold,' or 'cohesion,' is the characteristic property of being in its inorganic forms, φύσις, 'growth-power,' of vegetable life (vi. 14), ψυχή of 'soul' realized in the animal phase (ix. 9, x. 33), while the higher grade of 'reason'—λόγος, co-extensive, it will be noted, with the faculty of speech—appears only at the stage attained by man. The higher tension always includes the properties of the lower, so that the higher order shares the attributes of the lower, but with its own *differentia* superadded. Thus man shares with the inferior orders ἕξις, φύσις, and ψυχή, but 'reason' is all his own.

Each type finds its guarantee of individuality and perpetuity in the seminal or generative principle, the σπερματικὸς λόγος, which defines and reproduces the type. This survives immutably, until its final re-absorption into the 'seminal principle' of the universe, the primal reservoir of life (iv. 14, 21, vi. 24). That of the universe at large contains and is likewise immanent in the countless individualized σπερματικοὶ λόγοι, which determine, conserve, and reproduce life in all the several orders of being through their 'productive capacities of realization, change, and phenomenal succession' (iv. 14, ix. 1).

(3) *Soul.*—Man, the microcosm, within his individual range, is the counterpart of the macrocosm, in which he dwells, and with which he reciprocates currents of sensation (αἴσθησις,), impulse (ὁρμή), emotion (πάθη), and reason (διάνοια, νοῦς). All these are activities and reactions of the soul, the counterpart and product of that cosmic soul which permeates and moves the universe. Soul is self-moved, within the range of those seminal principles

[1] Eus. *HE* v. 1.
[2] xi. 3.

from which it originated. As, in the individual, soul actualizes itself in physical energies, such as life, growth, sensation, and all bodily functions and appetites, in moral, such as impulse (ὁρμή), inclination (ὄρεξις), aversion (ἔκκλισις), will (προαίρεσις), or in intellectual, such as perception (φαντασίαι), judgment (ὑπόληψις, κατάληψις, πρόληψις), mind (νοῦς), or reason (διάνοια), so, too, the world-soul operates in energies no less diverse in operation, now as the natural forces that actuate all inorganic or organic life, *e.g.* heat, moisture, breath, contraction, expansion, or the like, now as the moral forces which we know as fate, destiny, necessity, the 'laws' of nature or of God, and now, again, as those purposive or reasoning powers which, as design, providence, Zeus, God, direct the plastic movement of the whole.

For Marcus these conclusions are the key which unlocks all problems of life and thought. No Stoic thinker applies this key more resolutely and consistently to the whole field of ethics, personal and social. Every action, every relation, is referred to the cosmic test; by it he construes all the accepted formulas of the school, and resolves their ambiguities.

(4) *Cosmic unity.*—Cosmic unity stands at the centre of his thought, the pole to which his moral compass continually turns. In its contemporary phase of microcosmic self-expression the unity of the cosmos was realized and reflected in that world-Empire of Rome whose vital activities centred in and radiated from Marcus himself. The Emperor was the indwelling god of the State, as earth was of the universe.

Unity is written large upon the face and in the heart of things. The idea that the world-order can result from chance, from the confused clash and welter of atoms, is impatiently dismissed. It would imply permanent confusion, moral and intellectual—a universe as unintelligible as intolerable. Beyond all possibility of mistake, materially and spiritually, the cosmos is a perfectly co-ordinated unity, 'one order made of all things, one God through all, one being, one law, one reason common to all things intelligent and live' (vii. 9), as is shown by the ramifying bond of ubiquitous design (συνάφεια εὔλογος, iv. 45) and that unfailing rapport between the constituent parts (συμπάθεια τῶν μερῶν, v. 26, ix. 9) which results from perfect interpenetration (κρᾶσις δι' ὅλων), and makes the whole inseparably one.

Design is everywhere apparent, in small and great—in all the processes of nature, in the adjustment of means to ends, in the social life of animals, in economy of materials, in the entire 'concatenation of the web.' Nature is a vast laboratory, in which there is no destruction and no waste, but processes of cyclic transmutation and repair. Divination, oracles, dreams, add their corroborative testimony to the providential plan that runs through all.

Without reserve Marcus embraces the Stoic explanation of reason immanent within the world, accounting for its unity, its order, and its constitution. The most general term employed for this pervading and directive reason is the unifying Logos, which the Stoic school derived from Heraclitus, 'the reason and the ordinance of the city and commonwealth most high' (ii. 16), the all-pervading, all-directing, all-perfecting principle and power which animates and operates in all that is. Less frequently it is called nature, or 'the nature of the whole' (vi. 9, x. 6, 7). But the preference is for terms which associate it with those analogies in human consciousness on which the whole conception is based. Marcus speaks not only of the world-mind and thought (νοῦς, διάνοια), world-soul and moral sense (ψυχή, ἡγεμονικόν), but also of world-impulse and world-sensation. The world, as a live whole and being (ἓν ζῷον, iv. 40, x. 1), throbs to one master purpose as truly as all the energies of man respond to the direction of the unitary sovereign self.

(5) *Unity of things.*—The unifying power, a common gravitation revealing itself in man as truth, beauty, and love, combines, constrains, and co-ordinates all to a common end (xii. 30). It finds its type or organ in the central sun.

> 'I am the eye with which the Universe
> Beholds itself and knows itself divine'
> (Shelley, *Hymn of Apollo*, vi. 1 f.).

But the splendid harmony invests common things and processes with an appeal and beauty of their own; they contribute to the advantage of the universe; they are notes, or discords, which swell the great accord. Not only the heavenly bodies in their orbits, sun and stars, rain and air, the hiving bees and nesting birds, the lustre of the emerald, and the bending of the corn, but even things unprepossessing in themselves—the cracks and crevices in bread-crust, the foam that flecks the wild boar's mouth—appeal to him who is in unison with nature, and touch hidden springs of answering admiration and desire.

> 'Earth is in love with rain, and holy æther loves—Yea, the world-order is in love with fashioning what is to be. To the world-order I profess Thy love is mine' (x. 21).

(6) *World-soul.*—The unity of the indwelling mind corresponding to personality in the individual man is commensurate with the scale of the universe, beneficent and rational in aim. Degrees of goodness and of value are part of the great scheme, but everywhere 'things lower are for the sake of things higher' (v. 16, 30, vii. 55, xi. 10, 18, etc.), and all is for the best.

(7) *Evil.*—The oneness of the cosmos is utilized to explain the mystery of evil. Seeming evil is good misapprehended or disguised. The course of nature is all good. 'It contains no evil, does no evil, and inflicts no hurt on anything.' Analyze the facts, suppress the hasty, ill-formed inference, and the evil ceases to exist, or changes its complexion (vi. 36, vii. 26). It is the discord that prepares and shapes the harmony; the coarse jest (as Chrysippus said) that gives the comedy its point (vi. 2). 'Nothing is hurtful to the part which helps the whole' (x. 6).

(8) *Providence.*—The mind of the universe is social, 'civic' (πολιτικός) in all its aims. Fate, destiny, necessity (μοῖρα, τὸ πεπρωμένον, τὸ εἱμαρμένον, ἀναγκή), overrule all things for good; man's freedom is accord with the movements of the universal Providence, the object of his reverence, trust, regard.

(9) *The round of being.*—Everywhere there is the recurrent transformation of elements, pursuing their continuous round. Change is nature's joy (ix. 35, iv. 36), the life of individuals, of nations, and of the universe at large. The 'passage up and down' repeats itself in history, upon the small scale and the great; always 'the same dramas, the self-same scenes reproduced; the court of Hadrian, the court of Antoninus, the court of Philip, Alexander, Crœsus; the same stock rôles, only with change of actors' (x. 27; cf. vi. 46). This is the depressing side of the Emperor's philosophy, the resignation from which he would not deign to extricate himself by self-deception.

(10) *Man a part of cosmos.*—Man is by nature an inherent part, a living and organic member—μέλος, not μέρος merely—of the whole. He draws from its organic life as vitally as the branch draws sap from the parent tree. His 'nature' is the nature of the universe; self-realization of that nature is an instinct and a call as primary as that of self-preservation, attained by deliberate co-operation with its designs and ends, by loyal following

of law and reason, by active citizenship in the world-commonwealth.

(11) *Virtue.*—Moral obligation is fulfilment of function, active acknowledgment of reciprocal relation to the whole. And this alone is able to minister interior content, 'life with the gods,' 'citizenship in heaven.' The soul—a particle of Zeus (v. 27), the good genius or the God within (iii. 4, 6, 16), the lord and law-giver (iv. 1, 12), the pilot reason (vii. 64), the fellow-citizen, the priest and minister of God—is the power within which makes for righteousness. The indwelling presence becomes almost that of the Holy Spirit in the Christian believer. Prayer is not merely communion with the inner self, but a true intercourse with God; the self-communings which the sage has left us are but part and sample of his habitual practice of the presence of God.

(12) *Littleness of man.*—Man is indeed part of the universe, but how immeasurably small a part—a morsel in the mighty sum, a moment between two infinities. Fame is as transient as it is brittle and precarious—a short-lived rattle of tongues, a bubble that bursts and vanishes (ii. 7, iii. 10, iv. 3, 19, viii. 20, etc.); gratitude is precarious and belated; virtue is its own and sole reward; it consists in mastery of the will, ability to uphold and satisfy the instincts of reason in fellowship with nature and God. If ever that is forbidden or debarred, then indeed God sounds the signal for retreat. Unmurmuring and undispleased, we quit the rank. The exodus is quick and easy—a 'bare bodkin' is enough. The play is ended (xii. 36); ring the curtain down. Death is the natural end of man's ephemeral endeavour. Whatever be its physical analysis, extinction, dispersion, or transmutation (xi. 3)—alternatives which are dispassionately considered—the dissolution of the material elements ends the present resultant; they take their place in other compounds, while the 'seminal principles,' or life-seeds, will either integrate new forms and activities of being or themselves be resumed into the central reservoir of the world-life.

(13) *Ethics.*—In ethics the eye is fixed upon the inner self, upon the duties, disciplines, and obligations proper to his own experience. But the Imperial position assumed gives breadth and elevation of view, and the fixed sincerity of the writer atones for lack of form, or method, or variety. The commonplaces or the paradoxes of Stoicism—the inseparateness of virtue, or the indefectibility of the wise—are not discussed at large. The more developed casuistry of later Stoicism, with its scheme of conditional duties (*officia*, or καθήκοντα), its recognition of preferential moral choice (in προηγμένα and ἀποπροηγμένα), its admission of relative moral values (κατ' ἀξίαν), its belief in 'proficiency' (προκοπή), or progressive growth in philosophic grace, is everywhere assumed, though seldom in scholastic phraseology. The philosopher is on the throne, and passion is outlived. Duties of inferiors, sins of the flesh, all vulgar vices of the tyrant or the profligate, even the licence and the luxuries of city life, are not in view. The whole attitude is one of strained, insistent obligation, wrought out in patience inexhaustible; men are the recipients, himself the dispenser, of benefits; in realization of the social tie, duties to equals and duties to inferiors monopolize the field. Against ingratitude nature has provided forbearance as an antidote. Of the four cardinal virtues courage seldom receives mention; truth is not protest or resolve, but that singleness of word and act, that quiet undeviating 'pursuit of the straight course,' which power and place make doubly difficult; justice comes urging, not the rights of the oppressed, but the obligations of the strong; as regards wisdom or self-control, it may be said that the whole book is an enlargement upon that theme. The moral perturbations which he dreads are those which beset power and place and privilege, such as impatience, discourtesy, distrust, officiousness, or such more delicate delinquencies as self-absorption in the press of current duties, the want of moral nerve or fixity of aim, or the indolence which, rushing to hasty conclusions, admits unwarranted impressions or desires. And beside the solid virtues and charities incumbent on the ruler are set the social graces which adorn the official and the gentleman—consideration, candour, modesty, attentive and intelligent perception, courtesy, tact, address in conversation; and the compass of morality is extended to such refinements as cheerfulness in leadership, belief in friends' affection, wise husbandry and just apportionment of powers, careful selection among competing claims, reserve of opportunities for self-examination and recreation of the inner life. Leisure as well as labour, thought as well as action, deportment as well as motive, are scrupulously moralized.

'Blame none,' 'Do not find fault,' 'To expect no one to do wrong is madness' (xi. 18), are maxims for the ruler rather than prescriptions of the teacher. 'Can the world go on without shameless people? Certainly not. Then do not ask for the impossible' (ix. 42). The supremacy of the ἡγεμονικόν—in Marcus the favourite and characteristic term for man's highest governing self—secures to man self-mastery and personal equilibrium in an unstable world; within his own circumference he becomes 'a sphere self-orbed,' proof against all assaults of circumstance, all enticements and deceits of sense, and all dominion of impulse, appetite, or feeling. To that extent he can identify himself, his will, with the sweep of the great cosmic current, and, at one with nature, reason, God, be wrapped in calm. To such an one all outer things become 'indifferent,' for 'no man can rob us of our will' (xi. 36). Man is a citadel, 'a promontory against which the billows dash continually; but it stands fast, till at its base the boiling breakers are lulled to rest' (iv. 49). This attitude of set endurance gradually moulds his moral as well as his physical lineaments to that resolved serenity which is engraved upon the stones of the Imperial arch, and abstention rather than action, isolation rather than corporate fellowship, becomes the keynote of morality. Towards this the influences all conspired—the austere renunciations of his creed; the mood of sombre, almost wilful, resignation; the solitude and destitution of the close. Before his eyes Latin literature breathed its last. The great equestrian statue, the memorial column, the reliefs of his triumphal arch, the apotheosis of Faustina, are the last triumphs of expiring art. Human fecundity was stricken with a strange paralysis of reproductive power; the very Campagna was changing to a depopulated waste. Religions, politics, literatures, and Rome herself were dying. In unmistakable letters the handwriting was blazed upon the wall, and he himself was ἔσχατος τοῦ γένους. With his death decline and fall set in, not on the Danube only, but throughout the whole Empire of the West. His end was like his life, a slow tenacious struggle with the inevitable. No longer able to eat or drink, he lay upon his couch, still exercising the habits of duty and authority; spoke passionately of the vanity of life; and with the words, 'Haec luctuosi belli opera sunt,' turned to his rest.

LITERATURE.—i. *TEXTS, ETC.*—*Text*: Gul. Xylander, Zürich, 1558; M. Casaubon, London, 1643; T. Gataker, Cambridge, 1652, [2] London, 1697; Tauchnitz ed., J. M. Schultz, Leipzig, 1829, etc.; Teubner ed., J. Stich, rec. H. Schenkl, do. 1913 (full conspectus of MS variants); Oxford ed., J. H. Leopold, Oxford, 1908 (with valuable digest of emendations). *Editions*: T. Gataker, Cambridge, 1652 ff. (far the most learned and copious);

H. Crossley, *Meditations*, bk. iv., London, 1882. *English translations*: M. Casaubon, London, 1634; J. Collier, do. 1701; Foulis ed., R. I(bbetson), Glasgow, 1742 ff.; J. Thomson, London, 1747; R. Graves, Bath, 1792; G. Long, London, 1862; G. H. Rendall, do. 1901; J. Jackson, Oxford, 1906.

ii. *HISTORICAL.*—Besides general Histories, E. E. Bryant, *Reign of Antoninus Pius*, Cambridge, 1895; W. W. Capes, *Age of the Antonines*, London, 1880; P. B. Watson, *Marcus Aurelius Antoninus*, do. 1884; and, besides general Church Histories, G. Boissier, *La Religion romaine d'Auguste aux Antonins*, Paris, 1874, *L'Opposition sous les Césars*2, do. 1885, *La Fin du paganisme*, do. 1891; S. Dill, *Roman Society from Nero to Marcus Aurelius*, London, 1904; T. R. Glover, *Conflict of Religions in Early Roman Empire*, do. 1909; E. Renan, *Marc-Aurèle*3, Paris, 1882; J. D. Peyrou, *Marc-Aurèle dans ses rapports avec le Christianisme*, do. 1897.

iii. *PHILOSOPHICAL AND BIOGRAPHICAL.*—General Histories of Philosophy; L. Alston, *Stoic and Christian in the 2nd Century*, London, 1906; E. V. Arnold, *Roman Stoicism*, Cambridge, 1911; M. Arnold, *Essays in Criticism*3, London, 1865; P. Barth, *Die Stoa*, Stuttgart, 1908; E. Bevan, *Stoics and Sceptics*, Oxford, 1913; A. Bonhöffer, *Epictet und die Stoa*, Stuttgart, 1890, *Die Ethik des Stoiker's Epictet*, do. 1894, *Epiktet und das Neue Testament*, Giessen, 1911; J. B. Brown, *Stoics and Saints*, Glasgow, 1893; F. W. Bussell, *Marcus Aurelius and the Later Stoics*, Edinburgh, 1910; W. W. Capes, *Stoicism*, London, 1880; W. L. Davidson, *The Stoic Creed*, Edinburgh, 1907; J. W. Draper, *History of the Intellectual Development of Europe*3, London, 1864; F. W. Farrar, *Seekers after God*, do. 1868; J. A. Farrer, *Paganism and Christianity*, do. 1891; C. H. Herford, *Stoics as Teachers*, Cambridge, 1882; M. Heinze, *Erkenntnislehre der Stoiker*, Leipzig, 1879; R. D. Hicks, *Stoic and Epicurean*, London, 1910; R. Hirzel, *Untersuchungen zu Cicero's philosoph. Schriften*, ii., Leipzig, 1882; T. Jordan, *Stoic Moralists in the First Two Centuries*, Dublin, 1880; M. Königsbeck, *De stoicismo Marci Antonini*, Königsberg, 1861; C. Martha, *Les Moralistes sous l'empire romain philosophes et poètes*, Paris, 1865; F. W. H. Myers, *Classical Essays*, London, 1883; Noël Desvergers, *Essai sur Marc Aurèle*, Paris, 1860; W. Pater, *Marius the Epicurean*, London, 1888; F. Ogereau, *Essai sur le système philosophique des stoïciens*, Paris, 1885; G. H. Rendall, *Marcus Aurelius Antoninus to Himself*, London, 1898; A. Schmekel, *Die Philosophie der mittleren Stoa*, Berlin, 1892; L. Stein, *Erkenntnistheorie der Stoa* (= *Psychologie*, ii.), do. 1888; E. de Suckau, *Étude sur Marc-Aurèle, sa vie et sa doctrine*, Paris, 1857.

iv. *LITERARY.*—M. D. Brock, *Studies in Fronto and his Age*, Cambridge, 1911; W. S. Teuffel, *Geschichte des röm. Literatur*, Leipzig, 1870, Eng. tr., London, 1873.

v. *ART.*—E. Petersen, A. von Domaszewski, and G. Calderini, *Die Marcus-Säule auf Piazza Colonna in Rom*, Munich, 1896; E. Strong, *Roman Sculpture, from Augustus to Constantine*, London, 1907.

G. H. RENDALL.

MARKET.—**1. Definition.**—The term 'market' may be defined as a periodic gathering of persons at an appointed place for the purpose of trading by way of exchange or purchase and sale, subject to the special regulations which law or custom may impose. The term 'fair' is frequently used in conjunction with the term 'market,' and has been defined as 'a greater species of market recurring at more distant intervals.' In either case, the essential element is the same—recurrence, namely, at a fixed time and at a fixed place.[1]

Provided that this element is present, any circumstances which bring men together can produce a market or a fair.[2] The occasion may be a religious festival,[3] a popular assembly,[4] the formation of a camp,[5] the temporary sojourn of a court at a royal residence,[6] the stay of a caravan at one of its customary halting-places,[7] the concourse at a saint's tomb,[8] the celebration of funeral games at the burial-place of a hero,[9] or the temporary cessation of hostilities between besieger and besieged.[10]

1 *EBr*11, *s.v.* 'Fair'; P. Huvelin, *Essai historique sur le droit des marchés et des foires*, Paris, 1897, p. 26 ff.

2 Huvelin, p. 36; see D. Crantz, *History of Greenland*, Eng. tr., London, 1820, i. 160.

3 See § 2 below. 4 See § 2 below.

5 J. M. Kemble, *The Saxons in England*, new ed., London, 1876, ii. 302.

6 Huvelin, p. 35.

7 Boyd Alexander, *From the Niger to the Nile*, London, 1907, ii. 4; F. Stüwe, *Die Handelzüge der Araber unter den Abbassiden durch Afrika, Asia, und Osteuropa*, Berlin, 1836, p. 34.

8 K. Rathgen, *Die Entstehung der Märkte in Deutschland*, Darmstadt, 1881, p. 7; Huvelin, p. 7.

9 E. O'Curry, *On the Manners and Customs of the Ancient Irish*, ed. W. K. Sullivan, London, 1873, i. p. cclv; cf. Huvelin, p. 138 ff.

10 See authorities in P. J. Hamilton-Grierson, *The Silent Trade*, Edinburgh, 1903, p. 59 f. See also § 4 below.

2. Geographical distribution of the market.—The institution of the market is not universal; in many parts of the world it is either altogether unknown or known only in its most rudimentary forms.[1] It has been pointed out that certain geographical conditions and certain racial characteristics are more favourable than others to its establishment and development. Thus, the markets of insular regions, especially those which are situated on the coast, are, in general, of little importance, perhaps because the necessity for an exchange of articles of diet hardly arises among populations whose economic status is the same, and whose daily needs are supplied by the bounty of nature seconded by their own exertions. In such regions the occasion for a market arises only where different economic conditions come into touch—where, *e.g.*, a tribe of fishermen have a tribe of agriculturists for neighbours.[2]

According to J. G. F. Riedel,[3] there are no market-places in Ceram; and, while we hear of the market in Java,[4] Sumatra,[5] and Borneo,[6] we are reminded by a high authority[7] that, in many of the islands inhabited by Malay peoples, the institution does not exist, or, if it does exist, is to be regarded as imported rather than as indigenous.

In New Guinea, markets are to be found in the German[8] as well as in the British portion of the island.[9] W. Ellis[10] supplies an account of those in Madagascar; and we have a few notices of Polynesian and Melanesian markets.[11]

The market thrives best where, in addition to favourable geographical conditions, the natural bent of the population is towards commercial pursuits, as in the case of the Negro and Bantu races.[12]

In N. America we find only few and scattered indications of the existence of the market;[13] and to the hunting tribes of S. America it is practically unknown; while among many of the peoples of Central America,[14] and especially in the old

1 As to native markets in Australia see art. GIFTS (Primitive and Savage), 6 (2).

2 R. Lasch, 'Das Marktwesen auf den primitiven Kulturstufen,' *Zeitschr. für Socialwissenschaft*, ix. [1906] 701.

3 *De sluik- en kroesharige rassen tusschen Selebes en Papua*, The Hague, 1886, p. 127.

4 T. S. Raffles, *The History of Java*, London, 1817, i. 198.

5 W. Marsden, *The History of Sumatra*, London, 1783, p. 308; F. Junghuhn, *Die Battaländer auf Sumatra*, Berlin, 1847, ii. 228 f. There seem to be no markets among the Gajos (C. Snouck Hurgronje, *Het Gajōland en zijne bewoners*, Batavia, 1903, p. 378 f.).

6 S. St. John, *Life in the Forests of the Far East*, London, 1862, ii. 85 f.

7 Lasch, p. 702 f.

8 B. Hagen, *Unter den Papua's*, Wiesbaden, 1899, pp. 217, 219.

9 A. C. Haddon, *Head-Hunters*, London, 1901, pp. 265, 269; cf. R. W. Williamson, *The Mafulu Mountain People of British New Guinea*, do. 1912, p. 232 f.

10 *History of Madagascar*, London, 1838, i. 332 ff.

11 We hear of the markets on the river Wairuku in Hawaii (W. Ellis, *Polynesian Researches*2, London, 1832–36, iv. 325), at Somu-Somu in the Fiji Group (C. Wilkes, *Narrative of the United States Exploring Expedition during the Years 1838–42*, London and Philadelphia, 1845, iii. 300 f.), in the Bismarck Archipelago (R. Thurnwald, 'Im Bismarckarchipel und auf den Salamoninseln,' *ZE* xlii. [1910] 119; G. Brown, *Melanesians and Polynesians*, London, 1910, p. 297; Hagen, p. 117 f.), and in New Caledonia (J. J. Atkinson, 'The Natives of New Caledonia,' *FL* xiv. [1903] 245; J. Moncelon, 'Réponse alinéa par alinéa pour les Neo-Calédoniens,' *BSAP* III. ix. [1886] 374).

12 Lasch, p. 702. The Boloki are a Bantu people, yet they have no markets (J. H. Weeks, *Among Congo Cannibals*, London, 1913, p. 114).

13 The principal market resorted to by the tribes on the coast near the Stikine river was held three or four times a year at a village about 60 miles from Lake Dease (G. Simpson, *Narrative of a Journey round the World during the Years 1841 and 1842*, London, 1847, i. 210). Markets are held by the Eskimo of Point Barrow and those of Demarcation Point (J. Simpson, 'Observations on the Western Esquimaux and the Country they inhabit,' in *Further Papers relating to the Arctic Expeditions, presented to both Houses of Parliament, 1855*, London, 1855, p. 936; see N. A. E. Nordenskiöld, *The Voyage of the Vega round Asia and Europe*, tr. A. Leslie, do. 1881, ii. 118 and note). Markets were also held at the Falls of the Columbia (M. Lewis and W. Clarke, *Travels to the Source of the Missouri River . . . in the Years 1804–06*, new ed., London, 1815, ii. 427), and at Prairie du Chien (J. Carver, *Travels through the Interior Parts of North America in the Years 1766–68*, London, 1778, p. 99).

14 Among the Toltecs (F. de A. Ixtlilxochitl, *Relaciones históricas*, in A. Aglio, *Antiquities of Mexico*, London, 1830–48, ix. 332) and the Chibchas (J. de Acosta, *Compendio histórico del descubrimiento . . . de la Nueva Granada*, Paris, 1848, p. 207), and in Yucatan (G. F. de Oviedo y Valdés, *História general y*

civilizations of Mexico[1] and Peru,[2] it formed an important element in the national life. In Arabia fairs and markets arose at places whither pilgrims were wont to repair.[3] The fairs at Ukāṭz,[4] Mujanna, and Dzul Majāz[5] were visited by the Prophet, and there were great markets at Senaa and Baṣra.[6] Not infrequently the resting-places of caravans are little markets, where the Bedāwi may lay aside his animosities and trade in peace.[7]

So, too, the religious festivals of Harar, Batne, and Mabug were the resort not only of pilgrims but of traders;[8] and the immense assemblage which gathered twice a year at the sacred tomb at Teuta, a city of the Delta, was devoted to commerce as well as to worship.[9]

The antiquity of the market in China is vouched for by the Book of Rites, which contains elaborate regulations for its conduct.[10] G. M. Curzon[11] speaks of the markets as the most picturesque and characteristic of Annamite spectacles; and the great feature of life in the Shan country is the bazaar, which is held on every fifth day in all the chief villages of the States.[12]

The Khāsis of Assam hold a market every four days.[13] Lasch[14] observes of India that, in early times, fairs and markets were to be found at the holy places frequented by pilgrims; and that the Rigveda and the *Laws of Manu* contain references to markets.

We know that markets were held on the boundaries of certain Greek States under the protection of θεοὶ ἀγοραῖοι,[15] and that an active commerce found its home in the sanctuaries of Olympia and Delphi; and Homer and Herodotus tell us of the market-places of foreign seafarers, and especially of those of Phœnician visitors.[16] In later times the institution of the market spread from Massilia, from the north of the Balkan Peninsula, and from the cities on the shores of the Euxine to the countries of the neighbouring barbarians.[1] In Latium the fairs were of great antiquity. In Rome and in Etruria they were associated with religious festivals; and the most important of the Italian fairs was held on the boundary which separated the Etruscan from the Sabine land at Soracte in the grove of Feronia.[2] In heathen times the religious festivals and popular gatherings of Norway and Sweden[3] and, in ancient Germany,[4] the tribal assemblies seem to have supplied occasions for the holding of markets.

So, too, in the past, the great markets of France, Germany, and England showed their close connexion with the observances of the Church.[5]

3. Origin of the market.—We have seen[6] that one of the earliest, if not the earliest, of the forms of commerce is that which has been called 'the silent trade.' Those who engage in it are strangers to one another and are consequently enemies. But, so long as it lasts, they observe a truce, which is safeguarded by a supernatural sanction. This sanction derives its force primarily from the sacredness of the relation between the traders, which the trade creates, and—in very many cases—in a degree hardly less considerable, from the sanctity of the place where the trade is carried on. This spot lies often within a border-land—a locality which is very generally regarded by primitive peoples as holy ground—and such a situation is frequently chosen not only because it possesses this characteristic, but because it is easily accessible. Goods set out on the seashore, on a river bank, or at a meeting of ways are likely to catch the eye of the passing trader; and, if he is satisfied with his exchange, he will return, as we are told, again and again, to the known place at the known time. In this strange custom is to be seen, in our opinion at least, the germ of the market.[7] Richard Lasch, however, in his admirable essay on the 'Primitive Market,'[8] urges two objections to this view. He contends that, in its beginnings, the market is, to a large extent, a provision market, mainly in the hands of women. He admits that, in certain cases, an exchange of articles of food may be transacted by the methods of the silent trade. A tribe of bushmen, *e.g.*, which has a tribe of agriculturists for neighbours may employ these methods in bartering game for bananas. In such a case the traders are men, not women. But to infer from such evidence that the market is derived directly

natural de las Indias, Madrid, 1853, xxvi. 27, xxxii. 3; J. Roman y Zamora, *Repúblicas de Indias*, in *Coleccion de libros raros ó curiosos que tratan de América*, do. 1897, i. 306), Vera Paz (J. Roman y Zamora, *loc. cit.*), Nicaragua (G. F. de Oviedo y Valdés, *Histoire de Nicaragua*, in H. Ternaux-Compans, *Voyages . . . pour servir à l'histoire de la découverte de l'Amérique*, Paris, 1840, xiv. 70), and on the Pearl Coast (B. de las Casas, *História de las Indias*, bk. i. ch. 171, in M. Fernandez de Navarrete, *Coleccion de documentos inéditos para la história de España*, Madrid, 1842-95, lxiii.).

1 J. de Torquemada, *Monarquia indiana*, Madrid, 1723, xiv. 14, 16, 23; B. de Sahagun, *Histoire générale des choses de la Nouvelle-Espagne*, tr. D. Jourdanet and R. Siméon, Paris, 1880, viii. 36; F. L. de Gomara, *Chronica de la Nueva España*, cap. lxxix., in A. G. Barcia, *Historiadores primitivos de las Indias Occidentales*, Madrid, 1749; *Carta de relacion de Fernando Cortés*, §§ xi., xxx., in Barcia, *op. cit.*; D. Duran, *História de las Indias de Nueva España*, ed. J. F. Ramirez, Mexico, 1867-80, i. 215 ff.; F. S. Clavigero, *História antigua de Megico*, tr. from Ital. by J. J. de Mora, London, 1826, i. 348 ff.

2 Garcilasso de la Vega, *First Part of the Royal Commentaries of the Yncas*, tr. C. R. Markham (Hakluyt Society), London, 1869-71, vi. 35, vii. 11; Pedro de Cieza de Leon, *Travels*, tr. C. R. Markham (Hakluyt Society), do. 1864, i. 390 ff.

3 A holy place of Hadramaut, which was neither a town nor a village, but merely a mosque near a saint's tomb, was visited on a certain day by pilgrims from every quarter, and became for the time being a great market, where all might trade in safety (L. W. C. van den Berg, *Le Hadhramout et les colonies arabes dans l'archipel indien*, Batavia, 1886, p. 14).

4 J. Wellhausen, *Reste arab. Heidentums*, Berlin, 1887, p. 85; W. Muir, *The Life of Mahomet and History of Islam to the Era of the Hegira*, London, 1858-61, ii. 1, 181.

5 Muir, ii. 181. 6 Stüwe, pp. 174, 179.

7 Stüwe, p. 34. The 'journeying canvas city' of the pilgrims to Mecca contained a market (*sūq*) within itself (C. M. Doughty, *Travels in Arabia Deserta*, Cambridge, 1888, i. 71, 205 ff.).

8 At Mabug the festival was celebrated in spring and autumn; and at the autumn festival at Batne, at the beginning of September, a great throng of traders congregated (F. C. Movers, *Das phönizische Alterthum*, Berlin, 1856, iii. 135 ff.; Amm. Marcell. xiv. 3. 3 (Batne); Pliny, *HN* xii. 40 (Harar).

9 A. H. L. Heeren, *Historical Researches into the Politics, Intercourse, and Trade of the Carthaginians, Ethiopians, and Egyptians*, Eng. tr., 2 vols., Oxford, 1832, i. 450.

10 *Le Tcheou-li, ou Rites des Tcheou*, tr. E. Biot, Paris, 1851, xiv.

11 'Journeys in French Indo-China,' *The Geographical Journal*, ii. [1893] 110.

12 C. E. D. Black, 'The Indian Surveys, 1893-94,' *The Geographical Journal*, vi. [1895] 30; R. G. Woodthorpe, 'Some Account of the Shans and Hill Tribes of the States on the Mekong,' *JAI* xxvi. [1896-97] 19.

13 J. D. Hooker, *Himalayan Journals*, London, 1854, ii. 277.

14 *Loc. cit.* p. 706. Lasch refers to H. Zimmer, *Altindisches Leben*, Berlin, 1879, p. 258, and to the *Laws of Manu*, viii. 201; see G. Bühler's tr. in *SBE* xxv. [Oxford, 1886], and J. Jolly, *Recht und Sitte* (=*GIAP* ii. 8), Strassburg, 1896, p. 110. See also A. H. L. Heeren, *Historical Researches into the Politics, Intercourse, and Trade of the Principal Nations of Antiquity*, Eng. tr., 3 vols., Oxford, 1833, iii. 373 ff. (Benares, Juggernaut, etc.).

15 Especially Hermes, Zeus, Artemis, and Athene (O. Gruppe, *Griech. Mythol. und Religionsgesch.*, Munich, 1906, pp. 1340, note 9, 414, note 7, 1118, 1282, note 1, 1142, note 3).

16 O. Schrader, *Linguistisch-historische Forschungen zur Handelsgeschichte und Warenkunde*, Jena, 1886, p. 35, *Reallex. der indogerm. Altertumskunde*, Strassburg, 1901, p. 522 f.; Hom. *Od.* xv. 415 ff.; Herod. i. 1. G. Grote (*A History of Greece*⁴, London, 1872, iii. 294, note) observes that both Velleius Paterculus (i. 8) and Justin (xiii. 5) refer to the Olympian festival as *mercatus*. See also Cic. *Tusc. Quæst.* v. 3.

1 Schrader, *Reallex.* p. 523.

2 T. Mommsen, *The History of Rome*, tr. W. P. Dickson, new ed., London, 1867, i. 203.

3 K. Lehmann, 'Kauffriede und Friedensschild,' in *Germanist. Abhandlungen zum 70ten Geburtstag K. von Maurers*, Göttingen, 1893, p. 50; S. Laing and R. B. Anderson, *The Heimskringla, or the Sagas of the Norse Kings, from the Icelandic of Snorre Sturlason*², London, 1889, i. 104; J. J. A. Worsaæ, *An Account of the Danes and Norwegians in England, Scotland, and Ireland*, do. 1852, pp. 100, 232.

4 Schrader, *Reallex.* p. 521 f. The Roman word *mercatus*, applied in the first instance to the trading of pedlars and hawkers in S. Germany and the Rhineland, was not used to designate the market as a place until the Germans had come to settle in towns. Thereafter, the word was adopted in almost all the Germanic languages as the expression for market (*ib.* p. 523; see Rathgen, p. 3 f.; S. Rietschel, *Markt und Stadt*, Leipzig, 1897, p. 33 ff.). Rathgen (p. 9) observes that, in Karolingian times, the institution of the market was fully developed.

5 See the works of Huvelin, Rathgen, and Rietschel cited above; C. Elton and B. F. C. Costelloe, 'Report on Charters and Records relating to the History of Fairs and Markets in the United Kingdom,' in *First Report of the Royal Commission on Market Rights and Tolls*, London, 1889, i. 5; C. Walford, *Fairs, Past and Present*, do. 1833.

6 See art. GIFTS (Primitive and Savage). As to the markets in ancient Ireland see § 14 below.

7 See Hamilton-Grierson, p. 28 ff., and 'The Boundary Stone and the Market Cross,' *Scottish Historical Review*, xii. [1914] 25 f. The view indicated above as to the origin of the market is held by H. Schurtz, *Das afrikanische Gewerbe*, Leipzig, 1900, p. 122 ff.; A. Sartorius von Waltershausen, 'Die Entstehung des Tauschhandels in Polynesien,' *Zeitschr. für Social- und Wirtschaftsgeschichte*, iv. [1895] 54 f.; M. Kulischer, 'Der Handel auf den primitiven Culturstufen,' *Zeitschr. für Völkerpsychologie und Sprachwissenschaft*, x. [1878] 380 ff.; cf. Huvelin, p. 10; O. Schrader, *Linguistisch-historische Forschungen*, pp. 11, 34, *Reallex.*, *s.vv.* 'Handel,' 'Markt.'

8 Pp. 623 ff., 700.

from the silent trade seems to Lasch to be wholly unwarranted. His second objection rests on the nature of the goods brought to market, which are, he says, for the most part perishable. They are produced constantly and they are in constant demand. Accordingly, market must follow market at a short interval, the times being fixed to suit the convenience of the traders. But the existence of such arrangements presupposes an exchange of views between those interested; and such an exchange involves a complete breach with the principles of the silent trade. The best way of dealing with arguments such as these is to turn to what evidence we have regarding the market in its beginnings. We shall find that it is attended by men only, and that, in some instances, it exhibits features which recall to us those of the silent trade.

S. Passarge,[1] *e.g.*, describes a market on the Benue to which a river tribe resorted for the purpose of exchanging fish and grain for the skins and game brought in by a tribe of bushmen. The former left a man in each canoe to hold it in readiness in case of a quarrel. Only men were present, and each man stood, weapons in hand, in front of his merchandise. On an alarm the bushmen sprang into the jungle, and the river-men took to their canoes. Insults were hurled, and arrows began to fly; and, in the end, after a few men had been killed on either side, each party returned home, satisfied with the day's work. Another example is supplied by Ellis's[2] account of the fair or market held in the island of Hawaii on the banks of the Wairuku river. The inhabitants of the different divisions[3] into which the island was parcelled out, although frequently at enmity, frequented this meeting-place for the purpose of exchanging the specialties of their respective districts. These consisted of mats, native cloth, dried fish, hogs, and tobacco. 'From bank to bank the traders shouted to each other and arranged the preliminaries of their bargains. From thence the articles were taken down to' a large square rock which stood in the middle of the stream. 'Here they were examined by the parties immediately concerned in the presence of the' king's 'collectors, who stood on each side of the rock, and were the general arbiters in the event of any dispute arising. To them also was committed the preservation of good order during the fair; and they, of course, received a suitable remuneration from the different parties.' Again, we are told[4] that at Somu-Somu, in the Fiji group, 'the market is held on a certain day in the square, where each deposits in a large heap what goods and wares he may have. Any one may then go and select from it what he wishes, and carry it away to his own heap; the other then has the privilege of going to the heap of the former and selecting what he considers to be an equivalent. This is all conducted without noise or confusion. If any disagreement takes place, the chief is there to settle it; but this is said rarely to happen.' It is reported of the Eskimo of Point Barrow that, in their intercourse with those of Demarcation Point, they 'seem to be very wary, as if they constantly keep in mind that they are the weaker party and in the country of strangers. They describe themselves as taking up a position opposite the place of barter on a small island to which they can retreat on any alarm, and cautiously advance from it making signs of friendship. They say that great distrust was formerly manifested on both sides by the way in which goods were snatched and concealed when a bargain was made; but in later years more women go, and they have dancing and amusements, though they never remain long enough to sleep there.'[5]

A very curious instance, in which women were the traders, and in which the method employed recalls that example of the silent trade mentioned by R. and J. Lander,[6] is recorded by Torquemada[7] in his account of the Mexican markets. He tells us that the Indian women made exchanges without a word being spoken. One held out the article of which she wished to dispose to another, who herself had something to barter. The latter took what was offered in her hand, and indicated by signs that it was worth very little in comparison with the value of her own article, and that something must be given in addition before she could consent to the exchange. If the addition required was made, the bargain was complete; if not, each retained her own property.

In these instances we have the mutual distrust, and, in some of them, traces of the strange methods, which marked the silent trade. Further, the evidence shows that, so long as the market may at any moment become a battle-field, it is, even where its business is confined to the exchange of provisions, entirely in the hands of men. So soon, however, as women can visit it in security, they assume the entire conduct of its traffic in articles of food, and the men attend only as guardians of its peace,[1] or confine themselves to dealing in the objects of their special concern, such as cattle and slaves.[2]

Two further observations may be made in reference to Lasch's arguments. In the first place, there are many instances in which perishable articles, such as fresh fruit and fresh meat, are exchanged by the methods of the silent trade.[3] In the second place, many cases can be cited in which the places where the silent trade is to be found in operation are matters of common knowledge.[4]

4. Situation of the market.—The primitive market was held, just as the silent trade was practised, at spots so situated as to secure the safety of the trader.[5]

Thus, a river separated those who resorted to the market on the Wairuku, the articles to be bartered being laid upon a flat rock in mid-stream.[6] In many instances the market is held within a border-land,[7] as in the Baluba country,[8] in Somaliland,[9] and in British New Guinea.[10] We have already mentioned the border markets of Greece and Rome;[11] and we are told that the frontiers of the Roman world formed a vast zone of markets.[12] In Usambara[13] and in some districts in British New Guinea[14] the markets are held on the borders of different districts; and the Batua markets[15] in the virgin forest and those of Angola[16] are generally equidistant from the nearest villages. Among the Akikúyu the site chosen for the market is an open space where the inhabitants of several districts can conveniently attend,[17] while in the Congo countries the market-places are often situated in an open country.[18] In both cases a hill-top is a favourite situation. Among the Gallas of the Western Abyssinian country markets are usually held on the top of a small hill, near some big farm[19]; in the Gazelle Peninsula, on plateaux, about an hour's journey from the coast[20]; and, among the Lapps, sometimes in open fields, and sometimes on the ice.[21] On the Lualaba,[22] at

1 *Adamaua*, Berlin, 1895, p. 360.

2 *Polyn. Res.*[2], iv. 324 f.

3 The tradition that, at one period, each division had its own king points to a time when each was a separate State (W. Ellis, *Narrative of a Tour through Hawaii or Owhyhee*, London, 1826, p. 116).

4 Wilkes, iii. 300 f.

5 J. Simpson, p. 936.

6 *Journal of an Expedition to explore the Course and Termination of the Niger*, London, 1832, iii. 161 ff. See art. GIFTS (Primitive and Savage).

7 xiv 23.

1 A. C. Haddon, p. 269; B. Hagen, p. 117; H. Clapperton, *Journal of a Second Expedition into the Interior of Africa from the Bight of Benin to Soccatoo*, London, 1829, pp. 149, 205.

2 P. Labat, *Voyage du chevalier des Marchais en Guinée, îles voisines, et à Cayénne, fait en 1725–27*, Paris, 1730, ii. 203, 208; see § 7 below.

3 Hamilton-Grierson, pp. 44–47, 51, 53; P. and F. Sarasin, *Reisen in Celebes*, Wiesbaden, 1905, ii. 275.

4 A. da Ca da Mosto, in *A General Collection of Voyages and Discoveries made by the Portuguese and the Spaniards during the 15th and 16th Centuries*, London, 1789, p. 57; W. W. Skeat and C. O. Blagden, *The Pagan Races of the Malay Peninsula*, do. 1906, i. 227.

5 Another method employed by traders for this purpose was that of exchanging hostages (*Voyages du chevalier Chardin en Perse et autres lieux de l'Orient*, ed. L. M. Langlès, Paris, 1811, i. 145 f.; cf. J. Bruce, *Travels to discover the Source of the Nile in the Years 1768–73*[2], Edinburgh, 1804, v. 401).

6 Ellis, *Polyn. Res.*[2], iv. 324 f.

7 As to the connexion of the market, the border-land, and the supernatural, see below, § 8.

8 H. von Wissmann, *My Second Journey through Equatorial Africa*, London, 1891, p. 125.

9 P. Paulitschke, *Ethnographie Nordost-Afrikas; die materielle Cultur der Danâkil, Galla und Somâl*, Berlin, 1893, p. 313.

10 Haddon, p. 269; M. Krieger, *Neu-Guinea*, Berlin, 1899, p. 329.

11 See above, § 2.

12 Rathgen, p. 3 f.; Huvelin, p. 343, note 6.

13 F. H. Lang, 'Die Waschambala,' *ap.* S. R. Steinmetz, *Rechtsverhältnisse von eingeborenen Völkern in Afrika und Ozeanien*, Berlin, 1903, p. 265. The markets are held in open spaces.

14 C. G. Seligmann, *The Melanesians of British New Guinea*, Cambridge, 1910, p. 204.

15 H. von Wissmann, L. Wolf, C. von François, H. Müller, *Im Innern Afrikas*, Leipzig, 1888, p. 259.

16 A. Bastian, *Afrikanische Reisen* (=*Ein Besuch in San Salvador, die Hauptstadt des Königreichs Congo*), Bremen, 1859, p. 116.

17 W. S. and K. Routledge, *With a Prehistoric People: the Akikúyu of British East Africa*, London, 1910, p. 105.

18 W. H. Bentley, *Life on the Congo*, London, 1887, p. 53.

19 C. W. Gwynn, 'Surveys on the proposed Sudan-Abyssinian Frontier,' *Geographical Journal*, xviii. [1901] 568.

20 Hagen, p. 117.

21 J. Scheffer, *The History of Lapland*, Oxford, 1674, p. 71. See also Regnard, *A Journey through Flanders*, in J. Pinkerton, *A General Collection of the best and most interesting Voyages and Travels in all Parts of the World*, London, 1808–14, i. 173: 'The church is called Chacasdes, and it is the place where the fair of the Laplanders during winter is held.'

22 V. L. Cameron, *Across Africa*, new ed., London, 1885, p. 288 f.

Mogelo,[1] at Andshira,[2] and among the Kabyles[3] markets are situated in uninhabited places, while in Benin the two great markets were held in large clearings, with only small villages adjacent.[4] At Malani, which consists of two villages, the market lies between them,[5] and a somewhat similar account is given of that at Abu-Gher.[6] In one of the districts of Bornu the market is generally held at some distance from the town,[7] and a like practice is frequently to be found elsewhere.[8] In some countries it is held near a principal town, as in Madagascar,[9] or in an open space near a village, as in German New Guinea,[10] or outside a town, as among the Western Mandingoes,[11] or between the town-wall and a river, as at the chief town of the Wymar country.[12] Markets are not infrequently held on islands. Thus, on the Gwosdew Islands an exchange takes place between natives of N. America and N. Asia;[13] and a fair, attended by the Chukchis and other nomad tribes, takes place annually on an island on the Anui River.[14] Markets are held on river-banks on the Niger[15] and on the Benue,[16] at points equidistant from the neighbouring villages, as on the Congo,[17] or at cross-roads, as on the Congo[18] and in Dahomey,[19] at spots easy of access by visitors from several districts, as in Somaliland,[20] on the sea-shore, as in New Caledonia[21] and among the ancient Northmen,[22] on the banks of great lakes, such as the Victoria Nyanza,[23] and, as at Guzzula, on a plain between mountains.[24]

Many of these situations point to a time when the fear of attack was prevalent; and Schurtz[25] suggests that the arrangement in the Mahee[26] country by which the weekly markets were held outside the walls, so that strangers might not enter the town, while the daily markets attended by the inhabitants were held within it, is a survival of the old state of things.

Where an established order exists, however, the market is generally held within the town.

Thus, at Koolfu and Zaria the market-place is within the walls;[27] and at Kanó it is situated on a neck of land stretching across a marsh, which nearly intersects the city.[1] The markets at Hang-Chau[2] and in the city of Mexico[3] were held in great squares within the town. Timbuctu may be cited as an instance of a town which had its beginnings in a temporary market.[4] In Java the markets are held under large trees on spots dedicated to the purpose from time immemorial.[5] In Silindong the market-places are generally at the foot of the hills, and are marked by old fig-trees.[6] In the Sherbro and its Hinterland the markets are always held under large trees;[7] and those on the upper Lualaba frequently take place on grassy mounds under the shade of great spreading trees.[8] In the chief town of Uganda,[9] at Loango,[10] at Paweea and Seka in the Mahee country,[11] among the Kabyles,[12] and in the Mekeo district of British New Guinea[13] the markets are held under the shelter of large trees; and a somewhat similar account is given of markets on the Congo.[14]

5. Day of the market.—In the Shan States and in Korea the market is held on every fifth day in all the chief villages.[15] This practice prevails throughout western Yun-nan,[16] and is found in Java[17] and Abeokuta,[18] at Igbegbe and Onitscha,[19] at Kong, and at Bobo,[20] in the Mekeo district of British New Guinea,[21] in ancient Mexico,[22] and in many other places.[23] At Ikoradu, on the lower Ogun, the market between the townsfolk and the bushfolk takes place every eight days,[24] and in the Banyeng country markets are generally held with an eight days' interval.[25] In regard to the markets on the caravan routes between Matadi and Leopoldville, a distinction must be kept in view between those held daily by the neighbouring villages for the caravans' supply and the weekly markets. The Fioti week is one of four days; but frequently the market is held every eighth day. In order to mark the week when there is no market, it is called *onduelo*, 'little,' 'insignificant.' On the Lower Congo each market bears the name of one of the days of the Fioti week, followed by the name of the village where it is held.[26] The Khāsis of Assam,[27] the Battak of Sumatra,[28] the tribes of the Lower Niger,[29] and the Akikúyu[30] hold a market every four days. On the Lualaba the

1 G. A. Haggenmacher, *Reise in Somali-Lande*, Gotha, 1874, Ergänzungsheft no. 47 zu *Petermann's Geogr. Mitth.*, 1876, p. 36; cf. W. Munzinger, *Ostafrikanische Studien*, Schaffhausen, 1864, p. 519.

2 O. Lenz, *Timbuktu*, Leipzig, 1884, i. 79.

3 A. Hanoteau and A. Letourneux, *La Kabylie et les coutumes kabyles*, Paris, 1872–73, ii. 77.

4 H. Ling Roth, *Great Benin*, Halifax, 1903, p. 134.

5 H. Barth, *Travels and Discoveries in North and Central Africa*, London, 1857–58, v. 377.

6 *Ib.* iii. 386 f.

7 Alexander, i. 268; cf. ii. 236. 'Most of the markets in this part of Bornu are held some way off the towns, partly no doubt to make them more central to the neighbouring villages, and partly because the people do not wish to have near their homes the many undesirable persons that a market always attracts' (*ib.* ii. 79).

8 Barth, ii. 168 (Gúmmel), iv. 292 (Dóre); Lenz, i. 154 (Fez).

9 W. Ellis, *Madagascar*, i. 333.

10 Hagen, p. 220. It is sometimes held within a village.

11 B. Anderson, *Journey to Mussardu, the Capital of the Western Mandingoes*, New York, 1870, pp. 104, 109.

12 *Ib.* p. 80.

13 F. von Wrangel, in K. C. von Baer and G. von Helmersen, *Beiträge zur Kenntniss des russischen Reichs*, Petrograd, 1839, i. 60.

14 W. H. Dall, *Alaska and its Resources*, Boston, 1870, p. 514 f.

15 W. Allen and T. R. H. Thomson, *A Narrative of the Expedition to the River Niger in 1841*, London, 1848, i. 398.

16 Passarge, p. 360.

17 Bastian, *Afrikanische Reisen*, p. 116.

18 *Ib.* p. 190 f.

19 J. Duncan, *Travels in Western Africa in 1845–46*, London, 1847, i. 289.

20 Paulitschke, p. 312.

21 Moncelon, p. 374.

22 Worsaæ, p. 100.

23 J. Roscoe, 'Further Notes on the Manners and Customs of the Baganda,' *JAI* xxxii. [1902] 80.

24 Leo Africanus, *The History and Description of Africa, done into English in the Year 1600 by John Pory*, London, 1896 (Hakluyt Society), ii. 283.

25 *Op. cit.* p. 116.

26 Duncan, i. 100. 'Where a town or city has two walls, the public market is held within the outer walls. This market is often attended by strangers from a great distance. The private market is invariably held within the walls' (*ib.* ii. 101). See Alexander's observations regarding the Bornu markets quoted above. A similar practice prevails in some of the towns of Adamaua (Passarge, p. 85). A. W. P. Verkerk Pistorius, in his *Studien over de inlandsche huishouding in de Padangsche Bovenlanden*, Zalt-Bommel, 1871, p. 13, observes that the market-place, situated on a large open space in the middle of the village, is called *perdameian*, or place of peace. But, when circumstances permit, the site chosen for the market is outside the village; and some markets are held on spots quite uninhabited.

27 Clapperton, pp. 135, 158.

1 D. Denham, H. Clapperton, and W. Oudney, *Travels and Discoveries in Northern and Central Africa in 1822–24*, London, 1826 (Capt. Clapperton's Narrative), p. 51.

2 H. Yule, *Book of Ser Marco Polo*[3], ed. H. Cordier, London, 1903, ii. 201 f.

3 See Cortés, §§ xi., xxx.; Gomara, § lxxix.; and the other authorities cited in § 2 above.

4 Lenz, ii. 148.

5 Raffles, i. 198.

6 Junghuhn, ii. 228 f.; C. B. H. von Rosenberg, *Der malayische Archipel*, Leipzig, 1878–79, p. 82; Pistorius, p. 13, quoted above; cf. Marsden, p. 309.

7 T. J. Alldridge, *The Sherbro and its Hinterland*, London, 1901, p. 216.

8 H. M. Stanley, *Through the Dark Continent*, London, 1878, ii. 167.

9 Roscoe, p. 79.

10 L. B. Proyart, *Histoire de Loango, Kakongo, et autres royaumes d'Afrique*, Paris, 1776, p. 159.

11 Duncan, ii. 56, 100.

12 Hanoteau-Letourneux, ii. 78. These markets are situated, if possible, near a water-course.

13 Seligmann, p. 314.

14 *Guide de la section de l'état indépendant du Congo à l'exposition de Bruxelles-Tervueren en 1897*, Brussels, 1897, p. 69.

15 Black, p. 30; Woodthorpe, p. 19; C. H. Hawes, *In the Uttermost East*, London, 1893, p. 8.

16 Yule, ii. 107, note 1.

17 J. B. Jukes, *Narrative of the Surveying Voyage of H.M.S. 'Fly,'* London, 1847, ii. 113; cf. Raffles, i. 198.

18 R. F. Burton, *Abeokuta and the Camaroons Mountains*, London, 1863, i. 71.

19 W. B. Baikie, *Narrative of an Exploring Voyage up the Kwóra and Bi'nue in 1854*, London, 1856, pp. 268, 297.

20 L. G. Binger, *Du Niger au Golfe de Guinée*, Paris, 1892, i. 318, 370.

21 Haddon, p. 265.

22 Gomara, § lxxix.; Clavigero, i. 348; Sahagun, iv. app.; Duran, ii. 216. There was also a daily market of less importance (Clavigero, *loc. cit.*).

23 See Schurtz, p. 117.

24 Burton, ii. 17.

25 F. Hutter, *Wanderungen und Forschungen im Nord-Hinterland von Kamerun*, Brunswick, 1902, p. 267.

26 *Guide de la section de l'état indépendant du Congo*, p. 69; A. J. Wauters, *L'État indépendant du Congo*, Brussels, 1899, p. 330; H. H. Johnston, *The River Congo*[4], London, 1895, p. 85 ff., who says: 'For the rest of the "week" or "fortnight" the market-place is void and desolate.'

27 Hooker, ii. 277.

28 Marsden, p. 308.

29 Allen and Thomson, i. 398; Baikie, p. 316.

30 W. S. and K. Routledge, p. 105.

market is held every fourth day, other markets being frequented in the interval.[1] At Ambas Bay the market takes place every third day.[2] There are daily markets at Loango,[3] at Kanó,[4] and at Mogelo.[5] The Bini have now eight days in their week; but formerly they had four only. On each day there is a market in or near Benin city.[6] Three markets a week are held at Kassa-Kanó;[7] and two a week at Marrakesh,[8] at Koolfu,[9] and at Banjaribuan.[10] Weekly markets are held in Morocco,[11] at Popalahun in the Sherbro,[12] in Lega-land,[13] among the Oromó,[14] among the Kabyles,[15] and at Passumah in the southern part of Sumatra.[16] In the Kuantan districts of Central Sumatra each market has its own special day of the week allotted to it.[17] In Silindong there is a daily market, but the place at which it is held varies from day to day.[18] In this last instance, and in many other cases,[19] the market takes place here to-day, there to-morrow, and in a different locality on each of the days following, until the round is completed. The order is fixed, and so the inhabitants of each district know where the market is to be held each day.

6. Hour of the market.—In Kúkawa, Maseña, Kanó, Sókoto, and Timbuctu, the market is held in the hottest hours of the day.[20] According to Clapperton,[21] the market at Kanó is crowded from sunrise to sunset. The Yo (Bornu) market begins about 9 a.m. and ends about 3 p.m.;[22] and the Congo markets commence towards 10 or 11 a.m. and cease at 3 or 4 p.m.[23] In some places in the neighbourhood of Harar the markets begin about noon;[24] and at Gire in Adamaua they are in full activity by that hour.[25] At Saria the busiest time of the market is from 2.30 p.m. to 5.30 p.m.,[26] and at Kulka in Bornu about 3 p.m.[27] In Tshambá the market is held in the late afternoon,[28] and at Coosoo[29] in Yoruba in the evening. It takes place at Aden two hours after sunset,[30] and at Bida and Ilorin[31] and in some parts of Malacca[32] in the night. On the upper Ubangi it is held from 8 to 10 in the morning.[33] On the Livingstone it is deserted after noon.[34] In the Padang district of Sumatra it is little frequented in the early morning, but by 10 o'clock it is full.[1] Markets in the early morning are less frequent, for the obvious reason that they interrupt the day's work of those who resort to them more than do markets held towards the close of the day, and also because those at a distance cannot attend them.[2]

7. Frequenters of the market; market-women.—H. H. Johnston[3] observes that both men and women make long journeys to sell their goods, the men always travelling furthest.

Among the Bondei, if the market be near, the woman goes and her husband supplies the goods. If it be at a distance, the husband generally goes alone.[4] At Whydah on the Gold Coast,[5] and among the Battak of Sumatra,[6] traffic in slaves was confined to the men. Among the Bakuba the men bring goats and palm-wine to market,[7] and in the Mandingoe markets they trade in cloth.[8] At Woodie the women sell milk and honey, fowls and herbs, while the men sell oxen, sheep, and slaves.[9] At the Harar markets the frequenters are grouped by sexes, *i.e.* according to the articles which they sell.[10]

In many instances the business of the market is entirely in the hands of women.

Thus, in the districts near Kilimanjaro, 'the women do all the trading, have regular markets, and will, on no account, allow a man to enter the market-place.'[11] At Koolfu, the principal town of Nupe, nine out of ten of those who resort to the daily market are women;[12] and the Foulahs or Fallatas leave the market in their hands.[13] A similar state of things is reported from many quarters.[14] It is of interest to observe in this connexion that, in the Congo area, when a thief is caught, his punishment—that of being stoned to death—is inflicted by the women.[15] In Nicaragua no male above puberty might enter the market-place of his own village to buy or sell. He might not even look at it from a distance. But men and women from other friendly or allied villages might go to it.[16] The women selling at the market of Brunei in Borneo are generally old slaves.[17] At Kuka in Bornu the principal slaves are generally the traders, while their masters loiter about, spear in hand.[18] The Oromó market people form a caste by themselves; they attend all the larger markets in person, and send their servants to the smaller ones.[19]

8. Religion and the market; the market peace.—The market peace is sacred; and this quality may be due to one cause or to a concurrence of

1 D. Livingstone, *Last Journals in Central Africa*, London, 1874, ii. 112.
2 Burton, ii. 35.
3 A. Bastian, *Die deutsche Expedition an die Loango-Küste*, Jena, 1874, ii. 81; Proyart, p. 159.
4 Denham, Clapperton, and Oudney (Capt. Clapperton's Narrative), p. 53.
5 Munzinger, p. 519.
6 R. E. Dennett, *At the Back of the Black Man's Mind*, London, 1906, p. 214.
7 Duncan, ii. 130.
8 Lenz, i. 256 (on Thursdays and Fridays).
9 Clapperton, p. 135. 10 Junghuhn, ii. 228.
11 Lenz, i. 79, 154, 203. 12 Alldridge, p. 215.
13 J. M. Schuver, *Reisen im oberen Nilgebiet* (Ergänzungsheft no. 72 zu *Petermann's Geogr. Mitth.*), Gotha, 1883, p. 17.
14 Paulitschke, p. 313. 15 Hanoteau-Letourneux, ii. 77.
16 Lasch, p. 765. 17 *Ib.*
18 Junghuhn, ii. 228; Marsden, p. 308.
19 *e.g.*, in Madagascar (Ellis, i. 332). Among the Akikúyu (W. S. and K. Routledge, p. 105) the date of the market every fourth day is fixed so as to avoid clashing with other markets in the district.
20 Barth, ii. 168.
21 Denham, Clapperton, and Oudney (Capt. Clapperton's Narrative), p. 53.
22 Alexander, ii. 79 f.
23 *Guide de la section de l'état indépendant du Congo*, p. 70.
24 Paulitschke, p. 314. 25 Passarge, p. 55.
26 P. Staudinger, *Im Herzen der Haussaländer*, Berlin, 1889, p. 210.
27 G. Rohlfs, *Land und Volk in Afrika*, Bremen, 1870, p. 77.
28 Schurtz, p. 118. 29 Lander, i. 137.
30 L. di Varthema, *Travels in Egypt*, London, 1863 (Hakluyt Society), p. 59.
31 A. F. Möckler-Ferryman, *Up the Niger*, London, 1892, pp. 159, 210.
32 In a Chinese account of Malacca it is said that 'women hold a market at night, but must finish at the second drum' (W. P. Groeneveldt, 'Notes on the Malay Archipelago and Malacca,' in *Miscellaneous Papers relating to Indo-China and the Indian Archipelago*, London, 1887, ser. ii. vol. i. p. 247).
33 Schurtz, p. 118. 34 Stanley, ii. 167.

1 Lasch, p. 768. 2 Schurtz, p. 118.
3 *British Central Africa*, London, 1897, p. 471.
4 G. Dale, 'An Account of the Principal Customs and Habits of the Natives inhabiting the Bondei Country,' *JAI* xxv. [1895-96] 204.
5 Labat, ii. 208. 6 Lasch, p. 707.
7 Von Wissmann, etc., *Im Innern Afrikas*, p. 249.
8 Anderson, p. 55.
9 Denham, Clapperton, and Oudney (Major Denham's Narrative), p. 53.
10 Paulitschke, p. 314. As to the division of labour according to sex in primitive times, see K. Bücher, *Die Entstehung der Volkswirtschaft*[4], Tübingen, 1904, p. 36; Schurtz, p. 122; J. G. Frazer, *GB*[3], pt. v., *The Spirits of the Corn and of the Wild*, London, 1912, i. 113 ff.
11 D. and C. Livingstone, *Narrative of an Expedition to the Zambesi and its Tributaries, 1858-64*, London, 1865, p. 192; cf. G. Volkens, *Der Kilimandscharo*, Berlin, 1897, p. 289.
12 Clapperton, p. 136. 13 *Ib.* p. 205.
14 Livingstone, *Last Journals*, ii. 112 (Nyañgwé); H. von Wissmann, *Unter deutscher Flagge: Quer durch Afrika von West nach Ost*, Berlin, 1889, p. 94 (Lubuku); Schurtz, p. 121 (Lower Congo; in the *Guide de la section de l'état indépendant du Congo*, p. 69, it is stated that the women traders are more numerous than the men traders; vegetables are always sold by the former); Denham, Clapperton, and Oudney (Major Denham's Narrative), p. 69 (Kuka, in Bornu); Anderson, p. 44 (Boporu, a market of the Western Mandingoes); Lander, i. 108 (Egga); J. J. Monteiro, *Angola and the River Congo*, London, 1875, ii. 25, 27; G. Merolla, *Voyage to Congo in 1682*, in Pinkerton, *Voyages*, xvi. 299 (Loanda); Burton, i. 131, 304 (Egbas); B. H. Chamberlain, 'The Luchu Islands and their Inhabitants,' *Geographical Journal*, v. [1895] 448 (Nafa); G. W. Lewes, 'Notes on New Guinea and its Inhabitants,' *Proceedings of the Royal Geographical Society*, new ser., ii. [1880] 611 (Hood Bay, New Guinea); Haddon, p. 269 (Mekeo District, British New Guinea); Curzon, p. 110 (Shan States); J. Bruce, iv. 303, 352, 474 (Abyssinia); H. O. Forbes, *A Naturalist's Wanderings in the Eastern Archipelago, 1878-83*, London, 1885, p. 463 (Timor); Raffles, i. 198 (Java); St. John, ii. 85 f. (Brunei, in Borneo); Moncelon, p. 374; Atkinson, p. 245 (New Caledonia); R. Thurnwald, p. 119 (Gazelle Peninsula and Admiralty Islands).
15 N. W. Thomas, 'The Market in African Law and Custom,' *Journal of the Society of Comparative Legislation*, new ser., ix. [1908] 100.
16 Oviedo, *Histoire de Nicaragua*, xiv. 70.
17 St. John, ii. 85 f.
18 Denham, Clapperton, and Oudney (Major Denham's Narrative), p. 70.
19 Paulitschke, p. 313.

several causes. It may be due to the nature of the relation between traders which the act of exchange creates, to the sacredness of the place where the trading takes place, to the consecration of the market at the time of its foundation,[1] or to the fact that the market is under the protection of a god,[2] or is associated with a religious festival.[3]

Large fairs, held at different points on the Niger, are professedly regarded as sacred ground, whatever wars there may be in the land; and, although this neutrality is not infrequently violated, still the traders return with remarkable pertinacity.[4] The Shilluks enticed the Khartum traders to their camp by a display of attractive merchandise, and then butchered them for their arms and ivory;[5] at the close of a Bakuba market the chief allowed his bodyguard to plunder the market-women;[6] and Livingstone speaks of a massacre of Manyuema market-women by Arab traders.[7] 'But,' he observes, 'they have great tenacity and hopefulness. An old established custom has great charms for them: and the market will again be attended, if no fresh outrage is committed.'[8]

Sometimes such violence kills the market.[9] 'To "revive" a "dead" market, there must be an assemblage of the local magnates; a pig or pigs must be furnished by the town to which the market belongs, and slaughtered, and divided up among the towns represented. Whenever possible, the culprit who caused the disturbance, or his substitute, if he is a wealthy man, is burned or buried alive; if other ways of killing are resorted to, his skull is fixed up on a post in the market-place to "strengthen the law."'[1]

The Congo markets, held at points equidistant from several villages, are neutral spots;[2] and the market at Mogelo, held within an enclosed space, is neutral.[3] Market-places on the banks of the Livingstone, at intervals of three or four miles, are resorted to by the aborigines of either bank, and are regarded as neutral ground;[4] and a similar privilege attaches to a fair held on the Lukalla, in the territory of the Kalosh,[5] and to a trading-place which lies deep in the forest at a point where the countries of the Baluba, the Babinde, and the Balunga touch.[6]

Dennett[7] says of the 'silent' markets of the Bavili that he has never known of their being abused; and in many places in the Philippines, especially in Mindanao, commerce is carried on at regular intervals on neutral ground by the method of the silent trade.[8]

During the last two months of one year and the first and seventh month of the following year, war was suspended throughout Arabia, and fairs were held;[9] at Guzzula there was a complete truce three days a week, when the markets were held, and for two months during the annual fair.[10] Again, at the great fair at Prairie du Chien hostile tradesmen abstained from all unfriendly acts;[11] and during the Batta markets hostilities are entirely suspended. 'Each man who possesses one carries his musket with a green bough in the muzzle as a token of peace, and afterwards, when he comes to the spot, following the example of the director or manager of the fair, discharges his loading into a mound of earth, in which, before his departure, he searches for his ball.'[12]

Among the Kabyles the market is a neutral ground placed under the *anaya* of its owners; and, while within their territory, all who frequent it are under their protection.[13] By the Rifis the market, with the roads leading to it, is regarded as safe from the exercise of private vengeance.[14] Women from different districts, even when those districts are engaged in actual hostilities, pass to and from the Lualaba markets unmolested;[15] and a like immunity is secured to the women of the Masai and Wachaga by agreement, although those tribes are mortal enemies.[16] A compact to the same effect holds good between the Masai and Wa-Kikúyu;[17] and at Nyangwé[18] and among the Somali[19] feuds are suspended during the passage of traders to and from market. This protection is afforded by the tribe where the form of society is tribal, by the king where it is monarchical, and by the king or the feudal lord where it is feudal.[20]

The history of the boundary-stone and of the market-cross is of great interest in this connexion. It has been pointed out[21] that the intimate relation of the market, the border-land, and the supernatural is illustrated by the characteristics of Hermes-Mercury. His symbol was an upright stone; and, as boundaries were marked by such

1 It is said that, at Stanley Pool, the establishment of a market was the occasion for the sacrifice of a slave (Costermans, 'Le District de Stanley Pool,' *Bulletin de la société d'études coloniales*, 1895, p. 62); and it seems not improbable that the object of this sacrifice was to convert the soul of the victim into a protecting demon (*PC*[4], London, 1903, i. 106; *GB*[3], pt. ii., *Taboo and the Perils of the Soul*, do. 1911, p. 90; F. Liebrecht, *Zur Volkskunde*, Heilbronn, 1879, p. 284 ff.; cf. A. Wuttke, *Der deutsche Volksaberglaube der Gegenwart*[3], Berlin, 1900, § 440, and R. Proctor, *The Story of the Laxdalers done into English*, London, 1903, ch. 17, where we read that Hrapp desired to be buried standing in the firehall doorway that he might look after his household gods; see also the story of the Philæni [Sall. *de Bell. Jugurth.* 79]). A. B. Ellis, *The Tshi-Speaking Peoples of the Gold Coast of West Africa*, London, 1887, p. 53, tells us that it was regarded as impossible for a hostile force to make its way into Elmina, if the body of a human victim were cut up and distributed round the outskirts of the town so as to enclose it. The victim, for which nowadays a sheep is substituted, was offered to a river-god. With this may be compared C. Coquilhat's statement (*Le Haut Congo*, Brussels, 1883, p. 85) that, among the Bayanzi, when an agreement has been made between two villages as to the price of victuals, it is solemnized by digging a ditch between them, and throwing into it a slave whose arms and legs have been broken, and to whom no one may give either meat or drink. Among the Bondei, when a market is founded, the witch-doctor sets up his *fingo* at every road which opens into it (Dale, *JAI* xxv. 231); and in the Congo countries a gun is buried on a like occasion, and an agreement made that no arms of any kind shall be introduced (Dennett, p. 48). Cf. also, in general, art. FOUNDATION, FOUNDATION-RITES.

2 M. H. Kingsley ('African Religion and Law,' in *National Review*, xxvii. [1897] 134) tells us of a W. African market-god who punishes the cheat and the thief; and among the Ewe-speaking peoples Aisan is the protector of markets and public places, performing the functions of the multitudinous gods of the Tshi-speaking peoples (A. B. Ellis, *The Ewe-Speaking Peoples of the Slave Coast of West Africa*, London, 1890, p. 52). See also Hamilton-Grierson, p. 53 and note 2. Lasch (p. 711) holds the view that the market-trees either are personifications of market-gods or serve as their abodes, and that, as a consequence, they are regarded as 'tabu,' or sacred. He bases his view upon the facts that, according to primitive conceptions, the market-place is holy ground, and the sanction which secures its peace is supernatural; but, while we admit these facts, we cannot regard them as in themselves justifying the inference which he draws from them.

3 See above, § 2. In the ancient North the market peace was a peace of God, when the market was held during a religious festival. When the king went to the frontier to settle boundary questions, and a trade arose, the peace was a host's peace (K. Lehmann, p. 50 f.). In Greece a special religious peace extended beyond the territory where the great festivals were celebrated, and secured the person and property of those who frequented them, even in their passage through a hostile district (Huvelin, p. 76 ff.; see above, § 2).

4 Allen and Thomson, i. 398.

5 G. Schweinfurth, *The Heart of Africa*, tr. E. E. Frewer, London, 1873, i. 101.

6 Von Wissmann, etc., *Im Innern Afrikas*, p. 250.

7 *Last Journals*, ii. 133 ff.

8 *Ib.* ii. 139. It is for this reason that sellers prefer to do their business at the market. If an offer is made, the reply is 'Come to the market' (*ib.* ii. 112, 132). The same view prevailed in Mexico (Torquemada, xiv. 16).

9 When the market has been 'killed,' all law is suspended, and crimes may be committed, the responsibility for which falls upon the family of the person in fault, until he has been delivered up (M. de Saegher, 'Les Coutumes des indigènes de l'état indépendant du Congo,' *Bulletin de la société d'études coloniales*, Brussels, 1894, p. 91).

1 W. H. Bentley, *Pioneering on the Congo*, London, 1900, i. 399.

2 Bastian, *Afrikanische Reisen*, p. 116.

3 Munzinger, p. 519.

4 Stanley, *Through the Dark Continent*, ii. 167. On the portion of the river called Lualaba the markets are neutral (Cameron, p. 288 f.; cf. Livingstone, *Last Journals*, ii. 56, 136).

5 Von Wissmann, *Second Journey*, p. 125.

6 Von Wissmann, etc., *Im Innern Afrikas*, p. 283.

7 *Op. cit.* p. 193.

8 A. E. Jenks, *The Bontoc Igorot*, Manila, 1905, p. 159; see F. Blumentritt, 'Ueber die Negritos von Mindanao oder die Mamanuas,' *AE* ix. [1896] 251. Blumentritt's informants say nothing of the method of the barter.

9 Muir, i. p. clvi.

10 Leo Africanus, ii. 282.

11 Carver, p. 99.

12 Marsden, p. 308. See, however, Hagen's account of the markets on the Tobah Lake to which the men and youths come armed (*Eine Reise nach dem Tobah See in Zentralsumatra*, in *Petermann's Geogr. Mitth.*, 1883, p. 173).

13 Hanoteau-Letourneux, ii. 80.

14 B. Meakin, *The Moors*, London, 1902, p. 402.

15 Livingstone, *Last Journals*, ii. 136.

16 J. Thomson, *Through Masái Land*, new ed., London, 1887, p. 93.

17 *Ib.* p. 177.

18 Cameron, p. 288.

19 Haggenmacher, p. 37. We may note E. F. im Thurn's statement (*Among the Indians of Guiana*, London, 1883, pp. 214, 271) that in British Guiana the trading Indians, who bring specialties of their own country for the purposes of exchange, are allowed to pass unharmed through the country of their enemies, by whom they are for the time being treated as fellow-tribesmen.

20 Elton and Costelloe, pp. 3, 28; Huvelin, pp. 223 ff., 360 ff.

21 H. S. Maine, *Village Communities in the East and West*, new ed., London, 1890, p. 192 f.; J. Lubbock, *The Origin of Civilisation and the Primitive Condition of Man*[6], do. 1902, p. 318 ff.

stones, he came to be regarded as the god of boundaries. In many cases the border-land consisted of tracts of neutral territory whither merchants repaired to exchange their wares; and thus the god of boundaries became the god of traders.[1] Now we are told that the ancient Germans used to raise poles at their public meetings, which were consecrated to the god of the public assembly.[2] These poles were, in all probability, erected upon a stone;[3] and it has been suggested that this 'truncus super lapidem,' replaced in later days by a stone column, is the prototype of which Irminsäulen, Rolandsäulen, *perrons*,[4] and many of the market-crosses of Scotland[5] are later forms. In view of the facts, it is tempting to conjecture that the stone which formed the base of the column, and which seems to have served as a seat of justice, was, in many cases at all events, a boundary-stone.[6]

In the Middle Ages the market-cross was not always fixed, but was raised at the commencement of the fair. It became fixed only when the temporary market became a permanent market, when the temporary peace became a permanent peace.[7]

In China an official notified the beginning and end of the market peace by hoisting and lowering a flag;[8] in British New Guinea a drum is beaten at the opening and closing of the market;[9] the trade between the people of the Rifi and the Spanish garrison whom they were besieging ceased on the ringing of a bell.[10]

Many instances might be cited of trading during a truce, followed by a resumption of hostilities as soon as the trading was over.[11]

9. The law of the market and its enforcement.—We have already seen[1] that acts of violence perpetrated upon the frequenters of a market may and probably will 'kill' it—for a time, at all events. The recognition of this fact appears to produce two results. In the first place, offences committed within the market are punished with exceptional severity, as imperilling its peace. In the second place, since offences committed outside of the market are not regarded as a danger to its peace, those who have committed them are in consequence not subjected to punishment so long as they are within it.

On the lower Congo every breach of the regulations of the market renders the culprit liable to death. He is 'either buried to his neck in a hole, in the centre of the market place, and his skull crushed by a heavy stone; or he is beaten to death with sticks, and his body is subsequently lashed to a pole, which is erected alongside a native path.'[2]

Bentley[3] tells us that in some of the Congo markets 'a man who brought a gun with him would be promptly buried alive, and the muzzle of his gun would be left protruding' as a warning to the rowdy elements in the fair. 'Sometimes a pile of firewood is ready to burn the culprit alive. On some markets no stick or knife may appear, a heavy fine being imposed in case of infraction.'

Among the Kabyles every offence committed in the market is punishable with death without trial. The crowd seize the offender and stone him without mercy. It is the strangers that execute the law. The tribesmen try to avoid these executions as they discredit the market.[4] At Berbera any one from the interior or the coast who by his conduct does serious injury to trade must pay the death penalty. Still, as such an execution occasions reprisals, it is avoided as far as possible.[5]

The fairs of ancient Ireland were regulated by strict rules, any breach of which was punished with death.[6]

In ancient Greece,[7] in ancient Norwegian and Danish law,[8] and in the France and Germany of the Middle Ages[9] a breach of the special peace of the market was dealt with more severely than was a breach of the common law.

In Mexico he who stole in the market was punished with death;[10] and he who was suspected of selling stolen goods, if he could not tell from whom he had received them, was condemned to death.[11]

As we have already indicated, there is evidence to show that, in many instances, those who had committed deeds of violence or contracted debt before coming to the market were safe from pursuit or arrest so long as it lasted and they remained within it.

Thus, among the Kabyles the avenger of blood who kills a man in the market suffers the same penalty as a common murderer;[12] and the same rule seems to have been observed at Berbera.[13] There, too, the trader who brought stolen goods to the market could not be proceeded against.[14] Those who resorted to the fairs of the Middle Ages were safe from prosecution or arrest for crimes committed or debts incurred beyond their bounds,[15] and enjoyed privileges, and were allowed relaxations

1 See also Schrader, *Ling.-hist. Forsch.*, pp. 97–100; Hamilton-Grierson, pp. 29, 60.

2 Goblet d'Alviella, *The Migration of Symbols*, Westminster, 1894, p. 116. This god was probably Thingsus, the Germanic equivalent of Zeus Agoraios (see note below); see, however, Mogk's art. GOD (Teutonic), vol. vi. p. 304[a]. According to Cæsar (*de Bell. Gall.* vi. 17), the Gauls worshipped a deity whom he identified with Mercury.

3 D'Alviella, p. 117.

4 D'Alviella (*Les Perrons de la Wallonie et les Market-Crosses de l'Écosse*, Brussels, 1914, pp. 27, 42, *The Migration of Symbols*, p. 103 ff.) indicates his agreement with the views of E. Monseur (*Supplément littéraire de l'indépendance belge*, 3rd May 1891). He observes that, before the diffusion of Christianity, the poles, to which we have referred, were at once the symbol of the god of assemblies (Thingsus, the equivalent of Zeus Agoraios) and of the autonomy of those assemblies. It is not improbable that, for the purpose of ornament, a representation of the god in the likeness of an armed man was attached to them or carved upon them; and that, when the meaning of these representations came to be forgotten, the popular imagination gave to them the name of the Paladin most popular at the time, and the Irminsäulen became Rolandsäulen. When the Church established herself among the barbarous peoples, the old columns continued in many places to serve as the rallying points of collective life. Sometimes they bore the emblem of Christianity; sometimes they were altered or transformed so as to symbolize something new or additional; and sometimes they were replaced by the crosses planted by the Church in sign of possession.

5 The resemblance which many of the market-crosses of Scotland bear to the *perron* has been pointed out by W. G. Black (*Glasgow Cross, with a Suggestion as to the Origin of Scottish Market-Crosses*, Glasgow and Edinburgh, 1913), and his suggestion as to their origin has been approved by d'Alviella in the later of his two works cited above. At p. 39 of this work d'Alviella figures certain of the Scottish crosses, and it is curious to observe how close is the similarity of some of them with the image of Hermes figured by him on p. 194 of *The Migration of Symbols*.

6 See Hamilton-Grierson, 'The Boundary Stone and the Market Cross,' *Scot. Hist. Rev.*, xii. 24 ff. As to the cult of the boundary in N. India see art. DRAVIDIANS (North India), § 33.

7 Huvelin, p. 354, note 4, where the authorities are cited. See also pp. 223 f., 350.

8 *Le Tcheou-li*, i. 309.

9 Haddon, p. 269.

10 N. Cotte, 'Mœurs politiques et sociales du Maroc; l'Administration . . . les Pirates du Riff,' *Revue contemporaine*, Paris, 15th Dec. 1857, p. 29 f.

11 Laing and Anderson, iii. 92 (Biarmaland); *NR* i. 723 (Mosquito Coast); C. F. P. von Martius, *Von dem Rechtszustande unter den Ureinwohnern Brasiliens*, Munich, 1832, p. 44; *The Captivity of Hans Stade of Hesse in A.D. 1547–55, among the Wild Tribes of Eastern Brazil*, ed. R. F. Burton, London, 1874 (Hakluyt Society), p. 88 (aborigines of Brazil); J. S. Polack, *New Zealand, being a Narrative of Travels and Adventures*, London, 1838, ii. 313; G. F. Angas, *Savage Life and Scenes in Australia and New Zealand*, do. 1847, ii. 61 f. (New Zealanders); N. Cotte, p. 29 f. (Rifis); C. Letourneau, *L'Evolution du commerce*, Paris, 1897, p. 76.

1 Above, § 8.

2 H. Ward, 'Ethnographical Notes relating to the Congo Tribes,' *JAI* xxiv. [1894–95] 290.

3 *Pioneering on the Congo*, i. 399. Among the Akikúyu no one may carry arms in or near a market (W. S. and K. Routledge, p. 106); and a similar regulation is in force at the fairs held at Sona and Quimalenço, near Bembe (Monteiro, i. 210). See also Schurtz, p. 119. In the largest town of the Wymar country, the sale of palm-wine at the market is forbidden (Anderson, p. 79; cf. T. J. Alldridge, 'Wanderings in the Hinterland of Sierra Leone,' *Geographical Journal*, iv. [1894] 131).

4 Hanoteau-Letourneux, ii. 81; cf. iii. 198.

5 Haggenmacher, p. 37.

6 O'Curry, i. p. cclvi.

7 Huvelin, p. 73.

8 W. E. Wilda, *Das Strafrecht der Germanen*, Halle, 1842, p. 237.

9 Huvelin, p. 227; E. Mayer, 'Zoll, Kaufmannschaft und Markt zwischen Rhein und Loire,' in *Germanist. Abhandlungen zum 70ten Geburtstag K. von Maurers*, p. 478 ff.; S. Rietschel, p. 204. As to the relation of the market peace to the king's peace see Huvelin, p. 349 ff.; Mayer, p. 482 ff.; and cf. W. Stubbs, *The Constitutional History of England*, Oxford, 1875, i. 179 ff.

10 Torquemada, xii. 5.

11 Sahagun, viii. 36.

12 Hanoteau-Letourneux, iii. 303.

13 Haggenmacher, p. 37.

14 *Ib.*

15 As to Scotland see *Laws and Customs of the Four Burghs*, quoted by Elton and Costelloe, i. 7, 99; as to Ireland see O'Curry, i. p. cclvi.; as to France and Germany see Huvelin, pp. 227, 445 ff.; L. Goldschmidt, *Handbuch des Handelsrechts*[3], Stuttgart, 1891, i. 228 f.

of the common law which attracted not only the merchant but those in search of pleasure.[1]

10. Administration and execution of the law of the market.—It has been observed[2] that, where the market lies within the territory of a tribe, its law is administered and executed in part by those who resort to it and in part by officials appointed by the tribe of the district. Where, however, it is held within the territory of a king, chief, or feudal lord,[3] it is his officers that act as police, and, in some instances, as judges.

In the Kabyle markets, *e.g.*, an official—the chief of the market, who belongs to the leading family of the tribe which owns it[4]—sees to the preservation of the peace, escorts those who fear attacks on the road, summarily expels the quarrelsome, and fines those who create disturbance.[5] He is concerned only with offences which affect the public, while civil and commercial disputes are referred to a marabout of the tribe.[6] At the same time, it is the strangers in the market that execute its law by stoning the delinquent.[7] Again, in the Berbera market, there is no supreme authority to whom the enforcement of the law is entrusted. Its execution is in the hands of the market chiefs. An assembly of those belonging to the district is sole judge in disputes; but the disputants need not abide by its decision. If they ignore it, they must leave the market.[8]

But where the market lies within the territory of a king, he or his officer sees to the maintenance of order.[9]

Thus, at a fair on the Lukalla, within the country of the Kalosh, 'the chief kept watch in his greatest pomp with half a dozen guards, in order that no dispute might disturb its peace. His companions were all well-known by the broad axe which they carried on their shoulders.'[10] Among the Baganda a chief appointed by the king performs similar duties;[11] and these are discharged at Wairuku by the king's collectors,[12] and among the Gallas by the local headman.[13]

At Maidugari—the largest market of Bornu—there is a market king who settles disputes between buyers and sellers; and the women choose a market queen for their protection, through whom they transact all their business.[14]

This last instance shows that, while, in some cases, the duties of the officers of the market are confined to the preservation of the peace,[15] they are, in many others, of a much more varied character.

Among the Waschambala the superintendent of the markets collects the dues and attends to matters of police.[16] At Wairuku the king's collectors are the general arbiters of disputes;[17] and throughout the country of the Gallas, on the western Abyssinian plateau, the market is held under the superintendence of the local headman, who decides all questions arising out of broken contracts.[18] At Whydah the chief constable of the market attends to its cleanliness;[19] and a high officer named Conagongla sees that the strings of beads which serve as money are composed of the proper number. Those which are deficient he confiscates for the king's benefit and for his own.[20] Among the Gallas the duties of direction of the market are exercised by an important official who is entrusted with the conduct of foreign trade and the supervision of the exchequer.[21] In the Congo markets there is, in most cases, a chief of the market, perhaps an old fetish-man, who regulates all disputes, and fines both the litigants so heavily that all are chary of invoking his assistance.[22] At Kanó the judge of the market sits all day to try disputes arising in the course of trade;[1] and in the Loango markets an official is charged with seeing that no deceptions are practised in the trade between natives and Europeans.[2]

The quality of articles brought to the market is, in general, a matter of consideration only when disputes arise.

The milk brought to the market of Jakoba, however, is daily subjected to examination;[3] and in Morocco an officer is appointed to inspect the provisions offered for sale.[4] He must constantly attend the markets and see that purchasers are not overcharged; and, in view of the plenty or scarcity of the goods exposed, he must fix the prices.[5] At Kanó the shaikh of the market fixes the prices;[6] and among the Bangala the price is fixed by the chiefs with reference to a standard.[7] At Mecca and Jidda a public officer fixes a maximum price to all victualling traders.[8] In some of the markets in Hawaii the chiefs regulated the prices;[9] and in ancient Mexico they were fixed by the superintendents of the market.[10] In China the officer placed over the market was charged not only with the maintenance of order, but with the supervision of weights and measures, and with the administration of justice in more important cases.[11] The Greek ἀγορανόμοι appear to have exercised similar functions in regard to the preservation of the peace and the use of weights and measures. They also fixed the hours of the market, and regulated its conduct generally.[12] The Roman ædile preserved order by means of his officers, and imposed fines upon the peace-breakers. He allotted their positions to the traders, and saw to the accuracy of weights and measures. To assure the *bona fides* of transactions within the markets was his special care, both by exposing frauds and by rejecting articles which were unfit for sale.[13] In the market of Tenoxtitlan ten or twelve judges sat in a house on the market-place to deal with cases as they arose and to see to the punishment of delinquents. There were also officers who went among the people, saw what was bought and sold, and broke any false measures which they found in use.[14] It was the duty of these officers to fix the prices and to prevent frauds.[15]

11. Market dues and their collection.—In some markets—*e.g.*, at Silindong—dues are not exacted.[16] Among the Hausa, while dues are levied, entrance into the town is free to the market people.[17] At Eetcho men can enter the market and trade without charge, but every woman must pay ten cowries to the government.[18]

When trade took place in the temple of the sun, the priest collected dues on behalf of the divinity.[19]

At a fair on the Lukalla, in Kashama's country, each district whose representatives were present must make a gift to the prince. Kashama, who performed a series of dances in the market, after each dance received their contributions from the market-women, who danced as they paid.[20] In the Bomma markets the king grants his protection and collects the dues;[21] and in the horse-market of Fez,[22] and at the market of Rabat,[23] an officer levies a small percentage on behalf of the government. At Adamaua,[24] and in Hawaii,[25] king's collectors are present in the markets; and in those of Usambara the superintendent (*mgelu*) takes a double handful of the market-women's pro-

1 Huvelin, p. 438; see below, § 14.
2 *Ib.* p. 343 ff.
3 As to the relative position of king and feudal lord in this matter see Huvelin, p. 347 ff.
4 Hanoteau-Letourneux, iii. 303.
5 *Ib.* ii. 80 ff. 6 *Ib.* 7 *Ib.*
8 Haggenmacher, p. 36 f. If a stranger is killed in the market, the traders leave until the blood-price has been paid to the heirs.
9 Huvelin (p. 346) refers, among others, to the nations of Islām, the Slavs, and the Magyars.
10 Von Wissmann, *Second Journey*, p. 125.
11 Roscoe, p. 79 f.
12 Ellis, *Polyn. Res.*2, iv. 324 ff. 13 Gwynn, p. 568.
14 Alexander, i. 268. A market queen presides over the markets of Asaba. She deals with offences, fixes prices, and collects dues (N. W. Thomas, *Anthropological Report on the Ibo-speaking Peoples of Nigeria*, pt. iv., 'Law and Custom of the Ibo of the Asaba District, S. Nigeria,' London, 1914, p. 187 f.; see Index, *s.v.* 'Ormu').
15 Duncan, ii. 115 (Quampanissa); W. S. and K. Routledge, p. 106 (Akikúyu); Anderson, p. 79 (Wymar country); G. Nachtigal, *Saharâ und Sûdân*, Berlin, 1879, i. 679 (Kuka); Leo Africanus, ii. 282 (Guzzula).
16 Lang, *Die Waschambala*, *ap.* Steinmetz, p. 266 (Usambara).
17 Ellis, *Polyn. Res.*2, iv. 324 ff. 18 Gwynn, p. 568.
19 Duncan, i. 120. According to Labat, ii. 203, this official, with four armed attendants, goes through the market, hearing complaints, dispensing summary justice, and selling thieves and troublers of the peace.
20 Labat, *loc. cit.* 21 Paulitschke, ii. 127.
22 H. H. Johnston, *The River Congo*4, p. 87.

1 C. H. Robinson, *Nigeria, Our Latest Protectorate*, London, 1900, p. 165.
2 Proyart, p. 124 f. Between the natives themselves fraud is unknown. A mother sends her six-year-old child, knowing that it will not be cheated. All the articles for sale are divided into parcels of the standard weight of equal value. There is no advantage in comparing those of one trader with those of another, the contents of each parcel being the same in quantity and quality (*ib.* p. 160).
3 Schurtz, p. 121, citing G. Rohlfs, in *Petermann's Geogr. Mitth.*, Ergänzungsheft no. 34, 1872, p. 56.
4 W. Lempriere, *A Tour from Gibraltar . . . over Mt. Atlas, to Morocco*, in Pinkerton, xv. 709.
5 *Ib.* p. 709.
6 Denham, Clapperton, and Oudney (Capt. Clapperton's Narrative), p. 51.
7 Coquilhat, p. 305 f.
8 J. L. Burckhardt, *Travels in Arabia*, London, 1829, p. 377.
9 W. Ellis, *Narrative of a Tour*, p. 390.
10 Sahagun, viii. 36.
11 *Le Tcheou-li*, xiv.; Huvelin, p. 53.
12 Authorities in Huvelin, p. 72 ff.
13 *Ib.* p. 113 ff.
14 Cortés, *Carta de Relacion*, § xxx., Gomara, § lxxix., Torquemada, xiv. 14, and Oviedo (*Historia General*, xxxii. 3) give a similar account of the administration of justice in the Yucatan markets; on those of Vera Paz see Roman y Zamora, i. 306, and on those of Nicaragua see Oviedo, *Histoire de Nicaragua*, in Ternaux-Compans, *Voyages*, xiv. 70.
15 Sahagun, viii. 36. 16 Junghuhn, ii. 229.
17 Staudinger, p. 527. 18 Lander, i. 165.
19 Theophrastus, *Hist. Plant.* ix. 4.
20 Von Wissmann, *Second Journey*, pp. 126, 129. We are reminded of the dances which accompanied trading in New Caledonia (Lambert, *Mœurs et superstitions des Néo-Calédoniens* [*Nouméa*], Paris, 1901, p. 157 ff.; Atkinson, p. 245).
21 Bastian, *Die deutsche Expedition*, ii. 79.
22 Lenz, i. 155. 23 *Ib.* i. 205. 24 Passarge, p. 87.
25 Ellis, *Polyn. Res.*2, iv. 324 f.

visions for the king, and levies a contribution for himself.[1] Among the Baganda a chief appointed by the king collects a tax upon every sale;[2] and at Quampanissa the people pay a tax on every article of food exposed for sale.[3] In the Loango markets the chief of police sees to the payment of the dues;[4] and at Kanó the shaikh of the market lets out the stalls at so much a month, the rent forming a part of the governor's revenue.[5] In China there are special market-dues, which are collected by a special officer.[6] In ancient Greece the ἀγορανόμοι collected dues, which were applied in the first instance to the needs of the market;[7] and in the markets of imperial Rome, and especially in those of the Middle Ages, a fully developed system of taxation obtained.[8] In the Mexican markets a fixed tribute was paid to the emperor, in return for which he granted his protection against thieves.[9]

In ancient India the king was entitled to market dues, which varied, according to circumstances, from a twentieth to a tenth of the value of the goods.[10] The frequenter of the Baluba market at Kabao must pay three cowries to the chief, whatever the value of his goods may be;[11] and in the Bondei market every person who brought articles for sale had to hand over one of each kind.[12] In the Aruwini district the dues amount to one-twentieth of the value of the goods brought to market;[13] at Nyangwé to a tenth or a sixth.[14] Those who expose goods in the Whydah market pay very heavy dues to the king of Dahomey,[15] while in the Hawaiian markets two-thirds of the proceeds of whatever the natives sold was demanded by the chief.[16]

12. The arrangements of the market-place.—Among the Lega-Gallas the markets are held only if the weather permits; for the climate is variable, and the market-places are wholly without shelter.[17] In the markets of Madagascar there are neither shops nor booths, the articles for sale being set out upon mats.[18] The markets on the Lualaba are held at uninhabited places, except at Nyangwé, where there are houses for traders and huts for slaves and porters.[19] When the caravans arrive at Berbera from the interior, booths and dwellings are erected; and, within a week, on what was previously a desert spot several hundred huts are ready for the strangers coming thither over sea.[20] At Sennâr the traders transact their business protected by temporary erections of boughs and mats;[21] and at Guzzula the wares are exposed in tents and shelters of boughs, where stranger merchants are entertained and housed,[22] while in some of the Sumatran markets huts are provided, where stranger merchants can display their merchandise, and pass the night for a mere trifle.[23]

At Maidugari, the largest market in Bornu, lines of sheds and stalls cover an extensive area;[24] similar erections are found in the markets at Tusáwa and Kátsena;[25] and Passarge[26] says of the markets in Adamaua that they contain numerous flat-roofed huts, which form a long street.

At Kinsay (Hang-Chau) the markets were held in great squares surrounded by shops, where all kinds of crafts were carried on and goods sold[27]—a description which recalls to us the accounts of the markets of ancient Mexico.[28]

In many markets the position assigned to the different traders depends on the nature of their wares,[29] the result being that, where those wares are traded in by one only of the sexes, a specific portion of the market is allotted to each sex.[30]

1 Lang, p. 265 f. Similarly, at the market of Bobo Dioulasou, a man carrying a gris-gris staff, accompanied by a drummer and a crowd of urchins, sets down his staff before each merchant ceremoniously, and, unopposed, helps himself, by means of a small calabash holding about a litre, from the merchant's calabash (Binger, i. 371).
2 Roscoe, *JAI* xxxii. 80.
3 Duncan, ii. 115.
4 Bastian, *Die deutsche Expedition*, ii. 40.
5 Denham, Clapperton, and Oudney (Capt. Clapperton's Narrative), p. 51.
6 Huvelin, p. 54.
7 *Ib.* p. 75.
8 *Ib.* pp. 103 ff., 578 ff.
9 Torquemada, xiv. 14.
10 Lasch, p. 775.
11 Von Wissmann, etc., *Im Innern Afrikas*, p. 250.
12 Dale, *JAI* xxv. 231.
13 Schurtz, p. 120.
14 *Ib.*
15 Duncan, i. 120.
16 Ellis, *Narrative of a Tour*, p. 390.
17 Schuver, p. 17.
18 Ellis, *Hist. of Madagascar*, i. 333.
19 Cameron, p. 288 f.
20 Haggenmacher, p. 36 f. These erections belong to the trader; and, when the market is over, they form a perquisite of the *abban* (protector).
21 Lasch, p. 776.
22 Leo Africanus, ii. 283.
23 Lasch, p. 776.
24 Alexander, i. 267.
25 Barth, ii. 21, 59.
26 Pp. 55, 234.
27 Yule, 201 f.
28 Cortés, § xxx.; Torquemada, xiv. 14; Sahagun, viii. 36.
29 Passarge, p. 85 f. (Adamaua); Haggenmacher, p. 39 (Berbera).
30 Paulitschke, i. 314.

In the markets of ancient Mexico each class of merchandise had its appointed place,[1] the more cumbrous kinds being stored in the neighbouring streets, or in floats on the canals;[2] in those of the Middle Ages what determined the trader's position was not only the character of his goods, but his nationality; and, in some cases, the latter was the sole determinant.[3]

13. Modes of bargaining in the market.—One of the most characteristic practices of the primitive trader is that of transacting business by means of a third person. Dall[4] tells us that the Aleuts never trade with one another directly; and we have suggested that some light is thrown upon the origin of this method by the instance of the exercise of the silent trade reported by Lander.[5] It is said that, among the natives of Australia, children are made *ngia-ngiampe* in order that they may act as the agents of their respective tribes in the business of barter;[6] and many cases may be cited in which the man who takes a stranger under his protection not only acts as his host, but assists him in buying and selling, and is generally responsible for his conduct.[7]

At Berbera each stranger must choose a protector (*abban*). He dare not trade without him, and must pay him one per cent on the value of every article which he brings into the market. The *abban* is his broker; he protects him against the extortions of the natives, and settles all disputes in which he may have become involved.[8] A similar account is given of the part played by the host at Dioulasou.[9] In Nigeria, whenever an article changes hands, the seller pays a commission to a third party, who is supposed to have facilitated the purchase.[10]

In the markets of many Asiatic countries a curious practice prevails by which traders, when bargaining in the presence of others from whom they wish to conceal their business, drive and conclude their bargains by touching the points of each other's fingers under a shawl without a word being spoken. It has been found in use at Mecca,[11] at Calicut,[12] among the Somali,[13] at Jidda,[14] at Pegu,[15] in Malacca,[16] in Mongolia,[17] and elsewhere.[18]

Torquemada[19] notes a curious practice which prevailed among the Indian women in the markets of ancient Mexico. They exchanged their wares without a word being spoken. The one party held out the article of which she wished to dispose; and the other, taking it in her hand, made signs that it was not a fair equivalent for what she proposed to give in exchange. If the first party refused to add anything, she ran the risk of losing her customer; if she added what was demanded, the bargain was concluded.

14. Methods of securing attendance at the market; its place in public and social life.—In some of the Congo countries it is penal for a woman to go to her farm on a market day.[20] To the desire to induce the stranger to come to market Heeren[21] ascribes certain Lydian and Babylonian regula-

1 Cortés, § xxx.; Torquemada, xiv. 14; Sahagun, viii. 36; Clavigero, i. 348; Gomara, § lxxix.
2 Clavigero, *loc. cit.*; Gomara, *loc. cit.*
3 Huvelin, p. 504 ff.; Elton and Costelloe, pp. 5, 22.
4 *Op. cit.* p. 394; cf. E. W. Nelson's account ('The Eskimo about Bering Strait,' *18 RBEW* [1899], pt. i. p. 359 f.) of the 'Asking' festival.
5 Art. GIFTS (Primitive and Savage), § 6 (11).
6 *Ib.* § 6 (2).
7 Art. STRANGERS, 2 (*b*). In ancient Germany the host in many cases was at once protector, broker, and interpreter (see C. Koehne, 'Markt-, Kaufmanns- und Handelsrecht in primitiven Culturverhältnissen,' *ZVRW* xi. [1895] 206 f.).
8 Haggenmacher, p. 36.
9 Binger, i. 372.
10 Robinson, p. 165.
11 Burckhardt, p. 191.
12 L. di Varthema, p. 108; Pyrard de Laval, *Voyage to the East Indies* . . ., London, 1887–90 (Hakluyt Society), ii. 178.
13 Haggenmacher, p. 37; see Paulitschke, i. 322.
14 Bruce, ii. 175.
15 Cæsar Frederick, *Voyages*, in R. Hakluyt, ***The Principal Navigations . . . of the English Nation***, London, 1598–1600, II. i. 239.
16 Groeneveldt, ser. ii. vol. i. p. 246.
17 E. R. Huc, ***Travels in Tartary, Thibet, China***, *1844–46*, London, 1852, ch. v.; see H. Yule, *Cathay and the Way Thither*, do. 1866 (Hakluyt Society), i. p. clvii.
18 See notes to Varthema and Pyrard de Laval; see also *PC*⁴ i. 246 note.
19 xiv. 23.
20 Bentley, i. 400. According to the ancient laws of India, in ancient Mexico, and during the Middle Ages, the market was the only place where it was permissible to sell movables. He who sold outside of it was regarded as an illicit trader, and he who bought from him as his accomplice (Lasch, p. 778; Torquemada, xiv. 16; Huvelin, p. 457 f.).
21 Heeren, ***Hist. Res. into the Politics, Intercourse, and Trade of the Principal Nations of Antiquity***, i. 105 f., ii. 199.

tions regarding the relations of foreigners with the women of the country; and we may assign to a like origin such customs as the temporary marriages of Central Asia, and similar usages there and elsewhere.[1]

In the Batta markets gaming, cock-fighting, and, in some cases, boat-racing form special attractions.[2] At the fair of Ukâtz transactions intertribal and communal were adjusted, truces were declared, evil-doers were proclaimed, and tribute was brought in. It was there that betrothals were arranged by parents, who brought their daughters with them, that poets produced their verses, and that great men, ambitious of reputation, sought to gain it by exercising a profuse hospitality.[3]

In Ireland the *aenach*, or fair, was 'an assembly of the people of every grade without distinction: it was the most common kind of large public meeting, and its main object was the celebration of games, athletic exercises, sports, and pastimes of all kinds.'[4] The most important of the *aenachs* were those of Tailltenn, Tlachtga, and Ushnagh.[5] The people of Leinster held a provincial *aenach* at Carman, or Wexford, once every three years, which began on 1st August and ended on the 6th.[6] 'Professors of every art, both the noble and the base arts, and non-professionals were there selling and exhibiting their compositions and their professional works to kings: and the rewards were given for every [work of] art that was just or lawful to be sold or exhibited or listened to.'[7] New laws were promulgated, old laws were rehearsed, peace was proclaimed. There was music, recitation of poetry, feats of arms, athletic sports, horse-racing, and juggling.[8]

In Madagascar the market is a place of public resort, and it is there that the public announcements of the sovereign are made.[1] In the Kabyle market feasts and fasts and all matters that affect the community are proclaimed. It is the place of news, gossip, and friendly intercourse, of plannings, and of plots.[2] The Papuan markets last all day, and are enlivened with feastings and dances;[3] and similar amusements accompany some of the Eskimo markets.[4] Those who resort to the Congo markets go not only to buy and sell, but to meet friends, to drink *malafou* and enjoy a gossip with them, to settle thorny questions, to hold palavers, to arrange disputes between clans and villages, to decide on war and peace, to bargain about the purchase of a wife, to describe slaves lost or stolen, and to give publicity to transactions such as the release of hostages or prisoners of war, or the payment of the price of blood. It is there that the man who is robbed gives information of the robbery, and that the creditor, if he cannot get payment, proclaims the infamy of the debtor. It is there, too, that ordeals are administered and criminals executed. Under the trees in its vicinity the drinkers of palm-wine, the politician, and the news-monger hold rendezvous.[5]

LITERATURE.—The authorities are cited in the course of the article; but special reference must be made to three works, to which the writer of the article owes a special debt: R. Lasch, 'Das Marktwesen auf den primitiven Kulturstufen,' *Zeitschrift für Socialwissenschaft*, ix. [1906] 619 ff., 700 ff., 764 ff.; P. Huvelin, *Essai historique sur le droit des marchés et des foires*, Paris, 1897; H. Schurtz, *Das afrikanische Gewerbe*, Leipzig, 1900.

P. J. HAMILTON-GRIERSON.

MARQUESAS.—See POLYNESIA.

MARRIAGE.

MARRIAGE (Introductory and Primitive).—Marriage has two main functions: it is the means adopted by human society for regulating the relations between the sexes; and it furnishes the mechanism by means of which the relation of a child to the community is determined. Owing to the preponderant importance which has been attached to the former function, the more strictly social functions of marriage have been largely overshadowed by its moral aspect, and it has not been sufficiently recognized that the function of marriage as the regulator of social relations may be of the most definite kind where the institution is of a very lax and indefinite order when regarded from the moral standpoint of civilized man.

The institution of marriage may be regarded as the central feature of all forms of human society with which we are acquainted. It stands in an especially close relation to the family—using this term for the group consisting of parents and children. This social group rests absolutely on the institution of marriage. Where marriage is monogamous, the group formed by the family will consist of the consorts and their children; where marriage is polygynous, it will consist of a man, his wives, and their children; while in polyandry, the family will consist of a woman, her husbands, and her children by those husbands or assigned to those husbands by social convention.

The institution of marriage also underlies the extended family, this term meaning the social group consisting of all persons related to one another either by consanguinity or by those social conventions which so often take its place (see art. KIN, KINSHIP). It is the marriages of the members of the extended family that immediately determine the limits and functions of this mode of social grouping.

The relation of the clan and other similar social groups to marriage is less simple. While marriage is the foundation of the family, it is possible that the clan-organization has grown out of a state of society in which individual marriage did not exist; but, whether this has been so or not, the clan-organization as it now exists is intimately related to marriage, this institution being the means by which descent, inheritance of property, succession to rank, and other social differentiations are regulated.

1. Regulation of marriage.—In all forms of

[1] E. Westermarck, *The History of Human Marriage*[2], London, 1894, pp. 73–75; Yule, *Book of Ser Marco Polo*, i. 144, 193, 210, 212, ii. 54, 56 f., 202, 204; A. H. Post, *Grundriss der ethnologischen Jurisprudenz*, Oldenburg and Leipzig, 1895, i. 28; E. Wilutzky, *Vorgeschichte des Rechts*, Berlin, 1903, i. 45 f.; K. Weinhold, *Altnordisches Leben*, do. 1856, p. 447; R. Sigismund, *Die Aromata in ihrer Bedeutung für Religion, Sitten, Gebräuche, Handel und Geographie des Altertums*, Leipzig, 1884, p. 141; W. Roscher, *System der Volkswirthschaft*[7], Stuttgart, 1899, iii. 83. In the charter of Bressieux in Dauphiné, A.D. 1288, it was provided as a special privilege '. . . et sint omnes in dictis nondinibus (sic) existentes quieti et immunes a crimine adulterii' (Huvelin, p. 438).

[2] Marsden, pp. 274, 380; Hagen, *Eine Reise nach dem Tobah See in Zentralsumatra*, p. 173. The gaming booths which are found in the most populous parts of Gajoland seem to be the only centres of trade (Snouck Hurgronje, p. 279).

[3] Wellhausen, pp. 85 f., 183. According to Burckhardt, p. 449, it was the custom among the Assyr. Arabs, before the Wahhābi conquest, to bring their marriageable daughters to market, and it was there only that the match was concluded.

[4] P. W. Joyce, *A Social History of Ancient Ireland*, London, 1903, ii. 438; see J. Rhys, *Lectures on the Origin and Growth of Religion as illustrated by Celtic Heathendom*, do. 1888, p. 409 f.

[5] Joyce, *loc. cit.*

[6] *Ib.* ii. 441.

[7] O'Curry, iii. 529, 531.

[8] *Ib.* i. pp. cclv, cclvi, cccxxvi, ii. 152.

[1] Ellis, *Hist. of Madagascar*, i. 332 f.

[2] Hanoteau-Letourneux, ii. 77 f.

[3] Hagen, *Unter den Papua's*, p. 219.

[4] J. Simpson, p. 396.

[5] *Guide de la section de l'état indépendant du Congo*, p. 69.

human society there are definite rules regulating whom the members of the community may and may not marry. These rules are of many different kinds, but they all fall under one or other of two main forms: regulation by kinship or genealogical relationship; and regulation by some form of social mechanism, consisting of clans or similar social groups. The rules may also be distinguished according as they prohibit or enjoin certain unions.

Among all those peoples who have the family as their main form of social grouping marriage is regulated solely by kinship, and the rules regulating marriage consist exclusively of prohibitions, forming the 'table of prohibited kindred and affinities.' Peoples whose social system is founded mainly on the clan or other similar mode of grouping do not, however, regulate their marriages solely by this mechanism, but this kind of regulation, in all cases of which we have any exact knowledge, is combined with the regulation of marriage by kinship, the two modes of regulation co-existing, and supplementing one another. Further, this double mode of regulation does not consist entirely of prohibitions, but, side by side with rules of prohibition, there are often definite rules which enjoin marriage with certain relatives.

The regulation of marriage associated with modes of social grouping assumes certain definite forms for which there are well-established terms, such as exogamy, endogamy, and hypergamy.

2. **Exogamy and endogamy.**—Much confusion has been produced in the use of these terms through the mistaken idea that the processes which they denote are opposed to one another, this being chiefly due to an error on the part of McLennan, who was the first to draw attention to the practice of exogamy. According to this writer, exogamy is a custom in which a person has to marry outside his tribe. There are a few cases on record, though even about these we need far more exact information than we possess, in which it seems that people have to marry outside their tribe or other similar social group, but in the vast majority of the cases for which the term 'exogamy' is used the exogamous social group is not the tribe, but that subdivision of the tribe for which the term 'clan' is generally employed. When we say that a community possesses the clan-organization, we mean that it is divided into a number of groups, the members of each of which must marry outside their own group. If they must marry into some other group of their own community, we have to do with the practice of endogamy, the community as a whole being endogamous, while the clan within the community is exogamous. From this it will follow that exogamy and endogamy are not antithetical processes, but, where both exist, supplement one another.

Endogamy in this sense is a relatively infrequent practice, being most fully developed in the caste system of India, in which the caste is the endogamous group and the *gotra* (*q.v.*) or other corresponding sub-group the exogamous unit (see art. CASTE). The social system of the Todas is another pure case of the division of endogamous social groups into exogamous clans. In other parts of the world obligatory endogamy is rare. There are many people who are isolated from their neighbours, either by physical or, still more frequently, by social conditions, such as constant warfare, who habitually marry within their own community, but their case differs fundamentally from that of the Hindu or Toda in that there is no definite prohibition of marriage within the community, and, if the opportunity arises, such marriages meet with no opposition. Even in Europe there are cases in which marriage within the village or other social group is so habitual and departure from this custom meets with such social reprobation that we come very near to true endogamy. It would seem that this tendency to endogamy is especially pronounced where the people of the village follow one occupation, and this association of endogamy with occupation is not only characteristic of the caste system of India, but is also found in one of the exceptional examples of obligatory endogamy, which occurs in Africa in the case of the smiths, who often form a social group kept separate, by having to marry within their own body, from the rest of the community to which they belong. It is noteworthy also that there is a definite tendency towards the association of endogamy and occupation in the cases of priesthood and royalty, and in some cases marriage within these classes is so strictly enjoined that it amounts to a form of endogamy.

The practice of exogamy occurs in many forms according to the nature of the social system of which it forms part. If the community is totemic, the exogamous social group will be the totemic clan. If the community is organized on a social or territorial base, the exogamous unit will be the village, the hamlet, or the quarter of a town. If the grouping rests on a belief in common descent, the exogamous group may take its name from the ancestor, this mode of organization differing from regulation by kinship in that the common ancestor is remote, and in some cases mythical or fictitious. In one frequent form of exogamy the whole community consists of two moieties, the men of one moiety marrying women of the other. The rule that two people with the same family name may not marry, which is found in China, may be regarded as another variety of exogamy. In Australia this mode of organization is modified so as to produce a complicated system consisting of social groups known as matrimonial classes.

3. **Australian matrimonial classes.**—These form a special variety of exogamous system in which a person has not only to marry outside his own class, but has to marry into another specified group. In one form, known as the four-class system, each moiety is composed of two sections, the marriages of members of one section of one moiety being limited to one section of the other. This system is associated with a peculiar mode of descent in which a child does not belong to the class of either father or mother, but to the other section of the moiety of one or other. In another form, known as the eight-class system, each of the four classes is composed of two sections, in which descent follows the same kind of rules as in the four-class system, but of a more complicated kind. This form of social organization has until recently been supposed to be unique, but A. R. Brown has shown[1] that it is nothing more than a systematization of the regulation of marriage by kinship which is generally associated with exogamous systems. In Melanesia there are probably similar groupings, though of a less definite kind than in Australia.

4. **Hypergamy.**—This name has been given to a peculiar form of the regulation of marriage, only known to occur in India, in which a woman must marry a man of a caste or sub-caste higher than her own. Where this custom is found, men and women of the same caste or sub-caste are sometimes also allowed to marry, but there is the strictest prohibition of the marriage of a woman with a man of a caste lower than her own.

5. **Regulation of marriage by kinship.**—Among peoples whose social system is based specially on the family and the nature of whose system of relationship shows that this mode of social organization has been of long duration, marriage is

[1] *JRAI* xliii. [1913] 143 ff.

regulated exclusively by genealogical relationship. Marriages with certain classes of relatives are forbidden and those with other classes allowed, while other marriages may not be strictly prohibited, though looked upon with more or less disfavour by the community, the chief example of this difference of attitude occurring in the case of first cousins. We do not know, however, of any such people among whom marriages with certain relatives are obligatory, or even so habitual as to stamp their presence on the nomenclature of relationship.

The regulation of marriage solely by relationship is not limited to peoples whose system of relationship is based on the family, but occurs also among many people who follow the classificatory system of relationship. It is found in many parts of Africa and America; it is characteristic of Polynesia, and occurs in some parts of Melanesia; while, as already mentioned, the matrimonial classes of Australia are only a specialized form of this mode of regulation. Among all these peoples, however, the results of this type of regulation differ widely from those already considered in that the restrictions apply to the very wide circle of relatives involved in the use of the classificatory system. Among such peoples we have not to do with the prohibition of marriage merely between brother and sister or between first cousins, but also between those whom we should call second and third cousins, or even more remote relatives. Sometimes the rule forbids marriage with a person with whom any kind of genealogical connexion, apart from relation by marriage, can be traced. More frequently the prohibition does not take this extreme form, but there are rules limiting the prohibition to certain classes of genealogical relationship, a frequent form of such limitation being the exclusion from the prohibition of those cases in which cousins are descended from persons of different sexes. Thus, among many peoples the marriage of the children of two brothers or of two sisters is strictly prohibited, but not only is the marriage of cousins who are the children of a brother and sister allowed, but, as will appear shortly, these relatives may be the natural consorts of one another. The people who thus regulate marriage exclusively by relationship have lost the clan-organization which their use of the classificatory system shows them to have once possessed. Even those who still possess this form of social organization do not rely solely upon it for the regulation of marriage, but marriages with many relatives are prohibited outside the circle of the exogamous group. Sometimes this prohibition takes the form that a man must not only seek a wife out of his own clan, but must avoid the clans of both father and mother, and perhaps the clans of all the grandparents. More often, however, the prohibitions rest more directly upon kinship, and do not involve all the members of the clans with which the man is related. Many gradations occur between people who regulate marriage solely by kinship and others among whom marriage is chiefly regulated by the clan-mechanism, but we know no people who have been carefully investigated and have been found to be wholly devoid of the mode of regulation by kinship.

6. Marriage with relatives.—Among many peoples, and especially among those who use the classificatory system of relationship, the regulation of marriage by kinship is not confined to prohibitions, but there are often definite regulations which make marriage with certain relatives the orthodox unions, and even in those cases in which such marriages occur but are not especially frequent the influence which they have had upon the nomenclature of relationship shows that they must once have been habitual. The influence upon systems of relationship is so definite that it is possible to infer from their nature the existence of forms of marriage in the past which are no longer in vogue, thus affording evidence which makes it possible to trace the past history of marriage.

(*a*) *Parent and child.*—We know of no people who allow marriage between mother and son. In many places, especially in Africa, a man may marry one of his father's wives, but in these cases his own mother is definitely excluded. Marriage between father and daughter is said to occur occasionally, though it is probable that in such cases the marriage is not that of a man with his own daughter, but with one whom he calls daughter in the classificatory sense. The marriage of a man with his brother's daughter would be a union of this kind, and such marriages certainly take place in some parts of Melanesia and in Australia.

(*b*) *Brother and sister.*—The case in which we have the most definite evidence for this form of marriage is that of royal families. Examples of the marriage of brother and sister are known from history in the royal families of Egypt and Persia, and occurred also among the Incas of Peru. In recent times the marriage of brother and sister is, or has been, the custom in Siam, Burma, Ceylon, Uganda, and the Hawaiian Islands. In the last case the highest kind of chief was one whose father and mother were own brother and sister, who were themselves the offspring of a similar union. In this case certainly, and probably in the others, this form of marriage is definitely forbidden to those of other than royal or chiefly rank, and the practice is due to the belief in the virtue of royal blood and the desire to keep this blood as pure as possible.

Marriage between brother and sister has occasionally been recorded as the general custom of a people. There are well-established cases where marriage is allowed between half-brother and half-sister, usually where they are the children of one father by different mothers, more rarely by one mother and different fathers. No other cases are well authenticated, and some records of the marriage of brother and sister, such as the case of the Veddas, are now known to be mistaken. In general, not only is this form of marriage prohibited, but its prohibition forms the central and most definite feature of the moral code; and this applies to the marriage not merely of own brother and sister, but of those relatives in the widest classificatory sense.

It has been supposed by Morgan and others that the marriage of brother and sister was once general among mankind, and that it formed a stage in the history of the institution of marriage, but this opinion is chiefly based on misinterpretation of the evidence. Thus, avoidance between brother and sister (see KIN, KINSHIP, III. 2) has been held to show the former presence of sexual relations between these relatives. This is probably correct; but in Melanesia, from which region some of our best examples of this form of avoidance come, the custom is almost certainly a relatively recent practice due to external influence.[1] In all cases where marriage or sexual relations are allowed between brother and sister, they are probably of late occurrence, due either to relaxation of morality, or to the working of special ideas, such as that of the virtue inherent in royal blood.

(*c*) *Cousins.*—It is necessary to distinguish here between the marriage of cousins in general and the marriage of those cousins, usually known as cross-cousins, who are descended from persons of different sex. The marriage of cousins in general is sometimes allowed and sometimes prohibited, this prohibition being a necessary consequence of the

[1] Rivers, *History of Melanesian Society*, Cambridge, 1914, ii. 153.

classing of all or some cousins with brothers and sisters in different forms of the classificatory system.

The marriage of cousins is frequent among Muhammadans, usually with the daughter of the father's brother, and here, as in other cases in which this form of marriage occurs sporadically, the motive is the desire to keep property within the family.

The most frequent form of marriage of cousins is that which takes place between cross-cousins, namely, cousins who are the children of brother and sister. In many places this marriage is not merely allowed, but is the orthodox union, and is so habitual that it determines the form of the system of relationship and gives a special character to the whole social system. All the peoples who are known to practise this form of marriage use the classificatory system of relationship; but usually the marriage is not between cross-cousins in the wide classificatory sense, but between the children of own brother and sister. In some communities these relatives are regarded as husband and wife without the need of any ceremony or other social arrangement, and still more frequently they apply to one another the terms used between husband and wife, even when they are not actually married to one another.

In the most frequent form of this union a man marries the daughter either of his mother's brother or of his father's sister, but occasionally his choice is limited to one or other of these relatives, the case which occurs the more frequently being that he may marry the daughter of his mother's brother but not of his father's sister. This form of marriage occurs among a few peoples of Australia, in several parts of Melanesia, including Fiji, and in India, especially in the south of the peninsula, though it was probably once more widely distributed.[1] It is also found among the Haida and a few other peoples of N. America, but has not yet been recorded from S. America. In Africa it has recently been found by Mrs. R. F. A. Hoernle among the Hottentots.

This type of marriage has usually been regarded as a secondary consequence of the dual organization of society, and has probably arisen in most, if not in all, cases out of this form of social organization. In Melanesia it has probably had as its immediate antecedent marriage with the father's sister or with the wife of the mother's brother, but elsewhere it seems to be actuated by the desire to keep property within the family.[2] In some parts of Australia the form taken by the matrimonial classes involves the marriage of second cousins, but we do not know how far such marriages occur between true second cousins or between more distant relatives. In some parts of the New Hebrides it is the custom to marry certain relatives whom we should class as first cousins once removed. Thus, a man may marry the daughter of his father's sister's son or daughter, the daughter of his mother's brother's daughter, or the daughter of his mother's mother's brother. One of these forms of marriage is especially frequent, viz. that with the daughter's daughter of the father's sister.

(*d*) *Uncle and niece.*—In general, marriage between these relatives is prohibited, but occasionally a man is allowed to marry his brother's daughter, and this marriage would seem to have sometimes been so habitual as to have influenced the system of relationship. This marriage occurs in northern Australia and in some parts of Melanesia. It has also been recorded elsewhere, and is allowed in some parts of Europe. Several peoples of S. India permit a man to marry his sister's daughter. In some cases it is only the daughter of an elder sister who may be married.

Another marriage which may be included under this heading is one occurring in Melanesia, in which a man marries the wife of his sister's son, or in which he and his sister's son have their wives in common.

(*e*) *Aunt and nephew.*—Marriage with the father's sister occurs sporadically in certain parts of Melanesia, and is a regular practice among some of the Déné peoples of N. America, and marriage with the mother's sister is said to occur among the Ossetes of the Caucasus. Marriage with the wife or widow of the mother's brother is still practised in many parts of Melanesia, and is shown by the nomenclature of relationship to have once been a common practice. This form of marriage also occurs among some of the Bantu peoples of Africa, and many systems of relationship of N. America have features which would be its natural result.

(*f*) *Grandparent and grandchild.*—In Pentecost Island in the New Hebrides it is, or has been, the custom to marry the daughter's daughter of the brother; and this marriage with one who, through the classificatory system, has the status of a granddaughter has imprinted itself so deeply on the nomenclature of relationship that it must once have been the habitual custom of the people. This form of marriage has also been recorded among the Dieri of Central Australia.

A form of marriage similar to that just described, in that a man marries a woman two generations below his own, occurs in Ambrim, adjacent to Pentecost Island. In this island a man marries the daughter of his sister's son. Still more widely distributed is marriage with the wife or widow of the father's father. The occurrence of this form of marriage was first inferred from the nature of the terminology of relationship in Fiji and in Bougainville Island in the Solomons, but the present writer has since found it in vogue in several islands of the New Hebrides, not only with some wife of the father's father, but with the actual grandmother.

We do not at present know of marriage between grandparents and grandchildren outside of Australasia, but there are features of some African systems of relationship which suggest its occurrence at present or in the past.

7. Polygamy.—The forms of marriage so far described are characterized by the social status of the partners to the union. The varieties now to be considered arise out of the number of the persons who enter into union. The term at the head of this section is most conveniently used as a generic term to include all such cases other than monogamy. Its different forms are polygyny, in which one man marries more than one woman; polyandry, in which one woman marries more than one man; and communal marriage, in which more than one man marries more than one woman.

8. Polygyny.—Though this form of marriage exists, or has existed, in every part of the world, it is very rarely, if ever, practised by all members of the community, but is the special privilege of the powerful and wealthy. Polygyny can be universal only among a people which obtains women by capture or some other means from outside its own community. Sometimes the practice is limited to chiefs, sometimes, where large payments for a wife are in vogue, it is only the wealthy who can marry more than one wife. Sometimes polygyny is the privilege of those who have shown their superiority to the rest of their community in some way, as in Eddystone Island in the Solomons, where a second wife is allowed to men who have taken ten heads in warfare.

[1] *JRAS*, 1907, p. 611.
[2] C. Hill-Tout, *British North America*, London, 1907, p. 145; F. J. Richards, *Man*, xiv. [1914] p. 194.

Polygynous unions differ considerably in the degree of social differentiation accompanying the union. The different wives may live together in one household, or each may have her own establishment. Sometimes one wife is superior to the rest, and her children differ from those of other wives in social status—a condition which passes insensibly into the distinction between marriage and concubinage (see below, § 11). Sometimes there are definite rules regulating the behaviour of the husband to the different wives.

The continent in which polygyny has reached its highest degree of development is Africa, in many parts of which the practice is so frequent and has so impressed itself upon the social organization that it has influenced the nomenclature of relationship, and special terms are used to distinguish from one another the children by the different wives of a polygynous marriage. Other regions where polygyny is well established are Australia and parts of Melanesia, where the polygyny forms part of an organized system of monopoly of the young women by the old men of the community.

It is sometimes the custom in polygyny that the wives shall be sisters, a man who marries a woman having the right to take her sisters also as they reach marriageable age.

9. Polyandry.—This custom is far less frequent than polygyny. At the present time its chief home is in India and its neighbourhood, and it also occurs in a definite form in the Marquesas Islands and among the Bahima and Baziba, Bantu peoples of Africa. In ancient times it has been recorded among the Arabs, Britons, Picts, and Guanches, but our information about these and many of the recently-recorded cases is not sufficient to show whether the condition was one of true polyandry or a variety of sexual communism. Even in India there is a distinct tendency for polyandry to be associated with polygyny, thus producing one form of communal marriage. Two varieties of polyandry are generally recognized, in one of which husbands are brothers, while in the other they are not necessarily related to one another. Following McLennan, these two forms are often called Tibetan and Nair (Nayar) respectively, but are better distinguished as fraternal and non-fraternal.

Both among the Todas and in Tibet and neighbouring regions, where polyandry exists in its purest form, it is of the fraternal variety. Usually the eldest son of a family marries, and, as his brothers grow up, they share his wife with him. Even if one of the younger brothers takes a wife among the Todas, she becomes also the wife of the other brothers. It is doubtful whether the recorded cases of non-fraternal polyandry should be regarded as polyandry at all. Among the Nayars, who furnished McLennan with his pattern of this form of polyandry, a girl goes through a form of marriage with a man, but then or later consorts with a number of men who need not be related to one another. It is a question, however, whether these men should not be regarded as cicisbei rather than husbands—a point difficult to decide, since the purely matrilineal institutions of the people make the fact of fatherhood of little social importance.

A variety of polyandry which may be distinguished is one which occurs among several peoples of India, in which a young boy marries a wife who consorts with the boy's father or maternal uncle or some other man. The wife's offspring are counted as the children of the boy-husband, and, when the boy reaches adult age, he will consort with the wife either of one of these children or of some other boy. The motive of the custom is said to be that the boy shall have a son to take him out of *Put* (hell). A similar practice has been recorded elsewhere, as among the Ostiaks and Ossetes. In Melanesia a man and his sister's son might share a wife or wives in common, but this was almost certainly part of a system of communal marriage, and it is probable that this is also the true nature of some or all of the other cases of this variety of polyandry. The polyandry of the Marquesas is peculiar in that the husbands are of different social status, one husband belonging to a more influential section of the community than the other.

We know very little of the social mechanism by means of which the status of the children is determined in cases of polyandry. In several cases it has been recorded that the children are assigned to the different husbands in order of age, but it is certainly not true of the Todas, who were once credited with this practice. Among this people there is no need for any special ascription of the children to the different husbands when these are brothers, owing to their common habitation and their common possession of property. It is only when the husbands are not brothers that the necessity arises, and then fatherhood is determined by means of a ceremony at the seventh month of pregnancy, the man who performs this ceremony becoming the father of the child for all social purposes.

We know little or nothing of the causes which have led to polyandry. Among the Todas and in the Marquesas Islands, and possibly elsewhere, polyandry is associated with female infanticide, and it has been supposed that the polyandry is a result of the scarcity of women so produced. It has also been supposed that polyandry has been the result of inequality in the proportion of the sexes, due to scarcity of the food-supply, this either producing a small proportion of female births owing to physiological causes or leading to the practice of infanticide.

It is noteworthy that the only definite example of polyandry recorded in Africa should occur among a pastoral people whose culture possesses several features closely resembling that of the Todas.

10. Communal or group-marriage.—The question whether this form of marriage exists has been the subject of a lively controversy between different schools of sociologists for many years. If we define this type of marriage as a union of more than one man with more than one woman, no one doubts that cases occur which conform to the definition. This form of union is found among the Todas, for instance, but there it seems to have arisen as a combination of polygyny with polyandry. It is when we pass from such cases to those in which large groups of men are held to be the husbands of large groups of women that doubt arises.

The solution of the problem turns largely on the sense in which we use the term 'marriage.' If this word be employed for relations between the sexes, there is no question that group-marriage does not merely exist, but is a widely distributed practice. If, on the other hand, marriage is regarded essentially as an institution by which the social status of children is determined, we are met by our very imperfect knowledge of the exact nature of the recorded cases from this point of view; and another difficulty is that of drawing the line between wife and concubine, between husband and cicisbeo.

The recorded case which seems most to deserve the name of group-marriage is that of the Ngarabana (Urabunna) of Central Australia. It is stated that, among this people, no man has exclusive rights over any woman, and that we have not to do with a confusion between wife and concubine appears from comparison with an adjoining people, the Dieri. The Dieri have a definite term for individual marriage, viz. *tippa-malku*; this exists side by side with the *pirrauru* relationship, which is certainly one in which a group of men and a group of women have the right to sexual relations with one another. The Ngarabana have consorts called *piraungaru*, who evidently correspond with the *pirrauru* of the Dieri, and the relations between the Ngarabana men and women who call one another *nupa* would, therefore, seem to correspond with the *tippa-malku* union of the Dieri, except that they are group-relationships, while the *tippa-malku* union occurs between individuals. The *tippa-malku* marriage, however, is associated with the custom of lending a wife, while men other than the husband have marital rights as part of the marriage ceremony. If the *tippa-malku* union is regarded as true marriage, it is difficult to withhold this name from the union between *nupa* which seems to correspond with it among the Ngarabana. In order to reach a positive decision on the matter, however, we should like to be more fully informed about the exact social relations which exist between children and the male partners in the different kinds of union.

In some parts of Melanesia there is an association of definite individual marriage with the occurrence of sexual relations between the group of men formed by the husband's brothers and the group of women formed by the wife's sisters. Since these groups consist of brothers and sisters in the classificatory sense, they may be of considerable size. This case is, now at any rate, confined to relations between the sexes, and it seems, therefore, better not to regard this as a form of group-marriage, but to speak of sexual communism associated with individual marriage.

Those cases may be similarly regarded in which all the members of a conventional brotherhood possess marital rights over the wives of other fellows. The most definite case of this kind of which we know is that recorded by C. G. Seligmann[1] among the Massim of New Guinea, in which all the members of a brotherhood who called one another *eriam* have marital rights over the wives of the *eriam*.

11. Concubinage and cicisbeism.—Reference has already been made to the difficulty of distinguishing these conditions from marriage. The most convenient use of the word 'concubine' would be to denote a woman with whom sexual relations are permitted, although the union does not involve fatherhood if there should be offspring. Similarly, the term cicisbeo would be most conveniently used of the male partner in a similar union. If the terms were used in this sense, the *pirrauru* and *piraungaru* of the Dieri and Ngarabana would be concubines or cicisbei. The distinction would be especially applicable in such a case as that of the Todas, whose *mokhthodvaiol* would be distinguished as cicisbei from the husbands proper, there being the important difference between the two that the *mokhthodvaiol* partnership is not subject to the law of endogamy which regulates the polyandrous marriage. The *mokhthodvaiol* also never obtains the status of father to his partner's children except in those rare cases in which, being of the same endogamous group as an expectant mother whose husband is dead or missing, he is called upon to perform the ceremony which determines fatherhood.

The difficulty in using the term 'concubine' in the sense thus proposed is that in some of the cases, such as those of the OT, in which the use of the term is fixed, concubinage carries with it the social relation of fatherhood, sometimes even with full rights of inheritance and succession (cf. art. CONCUBINAGE [Introductory]).

12. Marriage and sexual relations.—In this article marriage has been considered chiefly as a social institution by means of which the relations between parents and children become part of an organized social system. People among whom marriage is a social institution of the most definite kind may vary greatly in their attitude towards the sexual relations of married persons. All gradations can be found between peoples who regard any sexual relations other than those between husband and wife as a heinous offence and those who allow very great freedom in this respect. Of all the cases of which we have any knowledge, however, the extra-marital relations of married persons are subject to definite restrictions, the clue to the nature of these restrictions resting upon the conception of a wife as the personal property of her husband. Thus many peoples who will kill or make war upon the offender, if a wife is found to have transgressed, will nevertheless freely allow others access to their wives if their consent is asked, or will offer no objection if relations with other men form part of the saturnalia or other occasions when relaxation of the ordinary moral rules is allowed.

The chief modes of departure from marital chastity are exchange of wives, which is especially a feature of Australian society, and lending wives to guests, which occurs in many parts of the world. Allowing the use of a wife in return for money or other kind of compensation is more rare, and is often only a feature of the relaxation of morality which follows contact with external influence.

13. Sexual relations before marriage.—Peoples differ greatly in their attitude towards sexual relations before marriage. In general, pre-nuptial freedom is allowed to men, but great divergencies are found in the views held about female chastity before marriage. Among many people the pre-marital chastity of the wife is so highly valued that it may lead to such a practice as infibulation (cf. *ERE* iii. 668[a], 669[b]), and the testing of chastity may form an important part of the marriage ceremony, the failure of this test leading to annulment of the marriage or depriving the relatives of the woman of the bride-price or other benefits which they would otherwise obtain from the marriage.

Among other peoples freedom of sexual relations before marriage is regarded as a normal occurrence, and there may even be an organized system of payments for such relations, or prostitution in some form may be regarded as a regular preliminary to marriage, and those who have been successful in this career may be especially sought as brides. In other cases sexual relations before marriage may take place more or less freely, though they are not openly condoned. Among many peoples such sexual relations are allowed so long as they do not result in offspring, and often, as in many parts of Europe, the occurrence of pregnancy forms the usual preliminary to, and occasion for, marriage.

In addition to the forms of marriage dependent upon the social status of husband and wife and the numbers of partners who enter into union, other varieties can be distinguished according to the place of residence of the married persons, and the age at which the union takes place.

14. Patrilocal and matrilocal marriage.—These are terms respectively for cases in which the wife goes to live with her husband, and the husband goes to live at the home of his wife, the usual consequence being that in the one case the children

[1] *Melanesians of British New Guinea*, Cambridge, 1910, p. 473.

will belong to the locality of the father, and in the other to that of the mother. These two varieties of marriage have often been distinguished, especially by writers on Indian sociology, by means of the Siṁhalese words *deega* and *beena*, but the above terms, first proposed by N. W. Thomas, are now coming into general use. Intermediate cases between the patrilocal and matrilocal forms occur in which the man goes to live at his wife's home for a time, the case being closely related to that mode of obtaining a wife in which a man has, for a period of months or years, to serve the parents of the woman he hopes to obtain as a wife (cf. § 19).

Sometimes, as in the island of Tikopia, the visit to the wife's home is of so short a duration that it is probably only a survival in ceremony of a former condition of matrilocal marriage. Still another condition is that which occurs among the Arabs of the Anglo-Egyptian Sūdān, in which the wife returns to the home of her parents in order to give birth to her children.

15. Infant marriage.—It is necessary to distinguish between infant marriage and infant betrothal, though the line between the two is often indefinite. Children are often promised as husbands or wives when very young or even before they are born, but it is only when ceremonies are performed or transactions carried through which are of the same nature as those accompanying the marriage of adults that we ought to speak of infant marriage.

Even in this limited sense, infant marriage is a very widely distributed practice. It is especially prominent in India, where its combination with the prohibition of re-marriage of widows makes it a very important feature of social life. Infant marriage occurs as an established practice in Australia and Melanesia, but here, as in other parts of the world, the process is often one of betrothal rather than of marriage. Sometimes a girl married in infancy goes at once to live with her husband's people; in other cases she continues to live with her own parents until she is of age for the marriage to be consummated.

Infant marriage has probably had two chief causes. It is a means of promoting the chastity of the young, adopted by peoples who attach importance to chastity before marriage, and this is especially the case when the girl goes to live with her husband's parents, who are thus able to watch over their son's wife. It may also be the result of any social condition which makes it difficult to obtain a wife, such as scarcity of women due to infanticide or natural causes, or monopoly of women by one section of the community. A lowering of the age of marriage for these reasons only accentuates the difficulty in obtaining a wife, and the lowering of age thus tends to be progressive, producing, in course of time, the marriages in extreme infancy which are found among some peoples (cf. art. CHILD MARRIAGE [in India]).

16. Arrangement of marriage.—In the very rare cases in which the choice of a consort is absolutely free the arrangement of marriage is a simple matter, and the same is true of the condition which seems to occupy the other end of the scale, in which the marriage of a person is pre-determined by the social rules of the community, as in those cases in which a man has to marry a certain relative. Even, however, in cases in which the choice is largely free, it is often the custom to make use of an intermediary, or the transactions connected with the marriage are arranged by the relatives or friends of the partners in the proposed union.

An important difference in the nature of the process of courtship turns upon whether the initiative comes from man or woman. Among many peoples proposals of marriage should come from the women.

The part played by other persons in the arrangement of marriage largely turns upon the extent to which relatives and friends take part in the pecuniary transactions which so often accompany marriage; but in many communities the consent of certain relatives is necessary, quite apart from this. Among those peoples whose social system is based on the family it is the consent of the parents that is chiefly needed. Among other peoples the place of the parents in this respect may be taken by some other relative, such as the mother's brother or the father's sister. In some parts of Melanesia the consent of the father's sister is essential. She usually chooses a wife for her nephew, and has the power of vetoing his marriage if he should choose for himself.

17. Marriage by purchase.—In most parts of the world marriage is accompanied by pecuniary transactions. In some cases payments are made by the husband or his relatives to the relatives of the woman, this payment being usually known as the bride-price. In other cases payments are made by the relatives of the bride, these being usually known as a dower. In other cases again there are complicated transactions in which payments pass between the two parties, but often these are chiefly of a ceremonial nature, either existing alone or, more frequently, accompanying the transference of the bride-price or dower.

Sometimes the payments made for a wife or husband may be so large as to form a definite impediment to marriage. They tend to raise the age of marriage, or may even prevent some members of the community from marrying at all. In some cases, however, in which the payments seem to be very large the common ownership of property distributes the payments over a large circle, making them more practicable than would be the case if they had to be given by an individual person. Sometimes the payments are made in different stages which may correspond with betrothal and marriage, and sometimes they do not cease at marriage, but continue for some time afterwards, the birth of each child of the union being an occasion for them.

Among peoples who follow the custom of marrying certain relatives it sometimes happens that the payment for a wife is made only in those cases in which a man marries some other woman.

The most frequent mode of marriage by purchase takes the form of the bride-price; but in India, and in some parts of Europe, the dower or payment to the husband is the more usual custom.

18. Marriage by exchange.—The most definite case of this mode of contracting marriage is that in which a man gives his sister to the brother of his bride, and, since this custom usually occurs among peoples who use the classificatory system of relationship, it may lead to the exchange of women between groups of considerable size. The motive usually assigned for this form of marriage by those who practise it is that it does away with the necessity of paying for a wife; but there is some reason to suppose that in some cases the practice may have arisen out of, or be otherwise associated with, the cross-cousin marriage.

19. Marriage by service.—This kind of marriage, which has become well known through its occurrence in the OT, is probably not very common, and, as already mentioned (§ 14), passes insensibly into the matrilocal form of marriage.

20. Marriage by elopement. — Among many peoples elopement is so frequent and is so little objected to by the community that it may be regarded as a regular mode of contracting marriage. In some cases it would appear to be the result of restrictions upon marriage which have developed to such an extent as to have become irksome to the community. In the absence of any social mechanism for the abrogation of these restrictions it has become the custom to connive at their infraction by taking a lenient view of elopement. In Australia and some parts of Melanesia where elopement is frequent it may be the secondary consequence of the monopoly of women by the old men. In other cases it may be a means of escape from the obstacles to marriage due to the bride-price.

21. Marriage by capture.—This form of marriage has aroused great interest in consequence of the idea of McLennan that, at one period of the history of human society, it was the normal mode of obtaining a wife. The capture of wives is known to occur, and the marriage ceremonial of many parts of the world includes either a definite conflict for the possession of the bride or features which may be interpreted as survivals of this process. It is very doubtful, however, whether any people habitually obtain wives from without their tribe, though the Khonds of India are said to do so, and it is probable that the conflicts of wedding ceremonial are derived from other social processes, such as the custom of marrying relatives, which gave certain persons a vested interest in the women of their own community. The vogue of the cross-cousin marriage in southern India makes it probable that a conflict which takes place between the husband and his wife's cousin in some parts of Malabar is a survival of that form of marriage in which the cousin had a proscriptive right to the bride.

It is probable that many of the other customs which have been regarded as survivals of the capture of women from hostile tribes are rather the results of a social condition in which it was the custom that women should become the wives of certain members of their own community.

22. Trial marriage.—Unions to which this term has been applied have been recorded among many peoples, but many, if not most, of these cases should be regarded as trials before marriage rather than as examples of marriage in the sense in which the term is used in this article. Temporary unions are especially frequent where marriage is contracted with little or no ceremonial, and these cases shade off insensibly into trials before marriage on the one hand and into ease and frequency of divorce on the other. A union should be called a trial marriage only if there is a definite contract or ceremony entered upon with the condition that the union shall be annulled if it is unfruitful or if the parties to it wish to separate after a certain period.

23. Social functions of relatives by marriage.—Marriage brings the partners to it into definite social relations with large groups of persons in whom they had previously no special interest. Among some peoples, and especially among those who use the classificatory system of relationship, these social functions may take very definite and well-established forms. Prominent among those is the custom of avoidance (see KIN, KINSHIP, III. 9) between a married person and his or her parents-in-law. The restrictions on conduct are usually most pronounced in the case of a man and his wife's mother, and the avoidance in this case may be so strict that the two are not allowed to see one another or to be in the same house or even in the same village. A more frequent form of avoidance is that a man may not speak to his mother-in-law or may not speak to her familiarly, and still more frequent is the custom that he may not use her personal name, but must address her by the appropriate term of relationship. A similar mode of conduct often accompanies the relationship of a man to his wife's father, but usually the avoidance is less strict, and the avoidance between a woman and her husband's parents is also, in general, less rigid than that between her husband and her parents. In some places certainly, and probably everywhere, these customs of avoidance are definitely associated with the idea of the likelihood of sexual relations between those who avoid one another, but the occurrence of similar customs of avoidance between persons of the same sex shows that this is not the only explanation.

Similar customs of avoidance also occur between brothers- and sisters-in-law, using these terms in the classificatory sense; but they are usually less strict, and often limited to prohibition of the use of the personal name or of familiar conversation. Often these customs are combined with certain duties on the part of these relatives towards one another—duties which may be summed up as those of mutual helpfulness. This is especially the case with the relationship of brother-in-law. Sometimes the duty of helping one another goes so far that a man may use any of the property of his brother-in-law. Sometimes the men must defend one another in case of danger, while the presence of the relatives on different sides may put an end to a fight. Still another duty sometimes assigned to these relatives is that one must dig the grave or take the leading part in the funeral ceremonies of the other.

This combination of customs of avoidance with the obligation of mutual helpfulness may possibly be explained as having grown out of the relations which arise when marriages habitually take place between hostile peoples, or they may be the result of the marriages which form part of the process of fusion of two peoples.

24. Marriage ceremonial.—The rites accompanying marriage vary greatly in duration and complexity among different peoples. Sometimes they are so fragmentary that they can hardly be said to exist, while in other cases the ceremonial may consist of rites of the most diverse and elaborate kinds, prolonged over weeks or months. In the lower forms of culture the ceremonial of marriage is, in general, scanty, especially where it is the custom to marry relatives. Its greatest complexity, on the other hand, is reached in India, south-eastern Asia, and the Malay Archipelago, the elaboration in the last region being almost certainly the result of Hindu influence. It is possible to distinguish certain main varieties of ceremonial. Putting on one side feasting and adornment as the expression of æsthetic motives natural to any important event in social life, we find a number of ceremonies which are connected with the economic side of marriage. Such is the transmission of objects from the friends of one partner to those of the other which form the bride-price or dower. In some parts of the world, as in Melanesia, the transactions of this kind are numerous and complicated and form nearly the whole of the ceremonial. Sometimes, however, these transactions have aspects which suggest a religious character, especially in the customs of exchange which are so prominent in the ceremonies of Polynesia, Melanesia, and some N. American peoples.

Another group of ceremonies which may have a motive chiefly economic is the conflicts and other features which are probably indications of interference with vested interests affected by the marriage.

A large group of ceremonies consists of acts symbolic of features of marriage. Such are the joining of hands and the tying together of garments. Allied to these are the acts which seem to show the superior status of one or other partner to the union. Thus the superiority of the bridegroom may be symbolized by presenting him with a whip or by his boxing the bride's ears, and possibly tying the *tāli* in India and the use of the wedding ring of our own ceremony may have had a similar meaning. Elsewhere, as in Morocco, the bride may perform various acts, such as riding a pack-saddle, which are designed to give her power over her husband.

Similar to these are the many forms of rite in which bride and bridegroom eat together or march round a fire. Other rites, such as that of pouring rice or wheat on the head of the bride, probably have as their motive the desire to promote the fertility of the union, or to ensure an abundance of food for the household.

Another large group of rites seems to be connected with the idea that some danger is attendant upon entrance into the marriage state. It may be that rites of this kind at marriage form part of a general custom of performing ceremonies at any transition from one period of life to another—the 'rites de passage' of A. van Gennep.[1] Another motive may be the idea of the danger accompanying sexual intercourse to which so great an effect has been ascribed by Crawley.[2]

Among features dependent on ideas of this kind may be mentioned the prolonged period which often has to elapse before consummation of the marriage is allowed, and the frequent customs according to which husband and wife are not allowed to see one another before a certain stage in the ceremonial. The many rites of purification, the assumption of new garments, and such disguises as dressing in the clothes of the opposite sex may also be of this order. It is probable that some rites of marriage are designed to impart to others the spiritual sanctity which is supposed to attach to newly-married persons.

Many of the motives for ceremonial so far considered are of the kind usually supposed to underlie magic. Other features are definitely religious in that they involve specific appeal to some higher power. Such are definite rites of sacrifice and prayer, while the practice of divination to discover whether the higher powers are propitious also falls under this head.

Among most people of rude culture no part is taken by any person who can be regarded as a priest, but, as definite religious motives come to actuate the ritual, its performance tends to pass more and more into the hands of a class of persons especially set aside for the performance of this and other religious functions.

25. Marriage to inanimate objects.—In several parts of India it is the custom, under certain circumstances, that persons shall go through ceremonial marriages with such objects as a tree, a bunch of flowers, a dagger, a sword, or an arrow. One occasion for this kind of marriage is the entrance of a dancing-girl upon her career, the motive being apparently that, though the future occupation of the girl will render a husband superfluous, she shall, nevertheless, be married.

Another motive for this form of marriage is the belief in the unluckiness of certain numbers. Thus, to counteract the belief that a second marriage is unlucky, a widower may marry an inanimate object in order that his succeeding union with a woman shall be his third marriage. It is probable, also, that marriage to a tree may, in some cases, especially where this forms a part of the ordinary marriage ceremonial, depend upon a belief in the influence of the tree upon the offspring, possibly in the future reincarnation of an ancestor represented by, or whose representative is present in, the tree.

26. Marriage after death.—In some parts of India the body of a girl who dies unmarried is the subject of marriage rites, while the marriage of dead bachelors seems to have been a feature of ancient Aryan culture (*ERE* ii. 22). The Aryan practice seems to have been connected with the custom of killing the wife on the death of her husband, and to have had as its motive the desire to provide the man with a wife in the life after death. We do not know the motive for the modern Indian practice.

27. Widowhood.—In some parts of the world the re-marriage of widows is absolutely prohibited, and in others widows normally become the wives of certain relatives, while intermediate cases occur in which their marriage is allowed, but is not subject to any special rules. Among many peoples, especially in the case of chiefs and more influential members of the community, wives are killed as part of the funeral ceremonies of their husbands, and there is reason to suppose that there is a connexion between this practice and the total prohibition of re-marriage, particularly as the latter practice is often found in the neighbourhood of places where the killing of wives on the death of the husband is or has been practised. Two places where the association occurs are India and the Solomon Islands, and the connexion of the two practices is supported in the latter locality by the fact that widows undergo a period of seclusion after death, with features suggesting that the seclusion is intended to represent a ceremonial death. It would seem that the prohibition of re-marriage is adopted when the more extreme measure has been given up.

Several cases in which a widow normally marries certain relatives have already been mentioned. Sometimes, especially in Africa, a son takes his father's widow, excluding his own mother. Elsewhere a widow may be married by the sister's son, or the son's son, of the deceased husband; but the most widely distributed form of union of this kind is that known as the levirate, in which a wife is taken by the brother of the deceased husband.

28. The levirate.—The best known example of this practice is that recorded in the OT, in which the custom is limited to the case in which the dead husband has no children, the motive of the marriage being to raise up seed for the dead brother. The term is now used for any case in which a man marries his deceased brother's wife, and in most cases the Biblical limitation and motives are not present. The practice may be based on the idea that a wife is property to be taken by the brother with other goods, or it may form part of the duty of guardianship over the children of the brother and be designed to prevent the management of the children's property passing into the hands of a stranger whom the widow might otherwise marry.

In India, and in some parts of Melanesia, the practice of the levirate is subject to the limitation that the widow of a man may be married only by his younger brother, a man having no right over his younger brother's wife. It is not easy to see how this limitation can arise out of the motives for the practice already mentioned. It was supposed by McLennan that the levirate is a survival of polyandry, and it is possible that in these Indian and Melanesian cases the practice is derived from either polyandry or communal marriage, the limitation being connected with some social functions of the relationship between elder and younger brother of which at present we have no knowledge.

Though the OT motive does not wholly account for the custom of the levirate, it shows itself in

[1] *Rites de passage*, Paris, 1909.
[2] *The Mystic Rose*, London, 1902.

other forms among many peoples. In many parts of Africa a child born to a widow even many years after the death of her husband is held to be the child of that husband, and the Dinkas of the Anglo-Egyptian Sūdān have a custom according to which a widow without male offspring who is beyond the age of child-birth will purchase a girl and pay a man to beget children by this girl for her dead husband. Again, where there is a need for male offspring, especially to perform religious rites, a man without sons may call on his brother or some other man to beget children by his wife.

29. Re-marriage of widowers.—We know of no people who prohibit the re-marriage of widowers, and the chief point of interest in this subject is the difference of attitude towards marrying with the deceased wife's sister. It has already been mentioned that in polygynous unions it is often the custom to marry sisters, and among people who follow this custom and many others the wife's sister is the natural spouse of a widower. Other peoples prohibit this form of union. Among many of these peoples the wife's sister is regarded as a sister, a conventional relationship often shown in terminology, and the prohibition of marriage is definitely connected with this idea. It is an expression of the general reprobation of marriage between persons who stand in the relationship of brother and sister, even when this relationship has come about through some social convention, and when the use of the term is only metaphorical.

30. History of marriage. — Widely different views on this topic are at present current. On the one side are those who regard monogamy as the original state from which the other forms of marriage have developed; on the other are those who believe that monogamy has come into existence by a gradual process of evolution from an original condition of complete promiscuity through an intermediate stage of group-marriage. Lewis Morgan, who has been the chief advocate of an original state of promiscuity, based his opinion on evidence which we now know to be fallacious, and at present not only do we have no knowledge of any promiscuous people, but there is also no valid evidence that a condition of general promiscuity ever existed in the past.

The problem of group-marriage stands on a different footing. Whether the communistic unions of different parts of the world be regarded as marriage or not, there is no question that such unions exist, and there is much reason to believe that they have been more general in the past than they are at the present time. The nature of the classificatory system of relationship is most naturally explained by its origin in communistic conditions. Even if this view be accepted, however, it does not commit us to the position that this condition was once universal among mankind. It is possible that only some of the main varieties of mankind have been communistic. Still less does it follow that sexual communism was the primitive condition of mankind. No people now in existence can be regarded as primitive, or even as a sure representative of primitive conditions. Even if it be accepted that sexual communism was once widely distributed or even universal, it would remain possible, if not probable, that it is not a primitive condition, but only represents a stage in the evolution of human society. If, as there is much reason to believe, mankind originally lived in small groups, perhaps consisting only of parents and children, the original state would have been monogamy, and, if so, the wide prevalence of communistic forms of marriage must be ascribed to some factors which came into action as the social group increased in size. Even if the classificatory system be founded in communistic conditions, it has features, such as the clear recognition of generations, which are most naturally explained by its growth out of a still earlier condition in which the unions between the sexes were monogamous, or were restricted to such small groups of persons as to approximate to that condition.

LITERATURE.—L. H. Morgan, 'Systems of Consanguinity and Affinity of the Human Family,' in *Smithsonian Contributions to Knowledge*, xvii. (Washington, 1871), *Ancient Society*, London, 1877; J. F. McLennan, *Studies in Ancient History*, do. 1876–96; J. Kohler, *Zur Urgeschichte der Ehe*, Stuttgart, 1897; E. Grosse, *Die Formen der Familie und die Formen der Wirtschaft*, Freiburg and Leipzig, 1896; A. Giraud-Teulon, *Les Origines du mariage et de la famille*, Paris, 1884; C. Letourneau, *L'Évolution du mariage et de la famille*, do 1888; A. H. Post, *Grundriss der ethnolog. Jurisprudenz*, Oldenburg and Leipzig, 1894–95, i. 17–65, 139–156, 184 f., 273–327, 380 f., ii. 54–134; E. Westermarck, *Hist. of Human Marriage*, London, 1891, *Marriage Ceremonies in Morocco*, do. 1914; O. Schrader, *Reallex. der indogerm. Altertumskunde*, Strassburg, 1901, *s.vv.* 'Ehe,' 'Familie,' 'Heirat,' 'Verwandtenehe,' 'Zeugungshelfer,' etc., *Sprachvergleichung und Urgesch.*[3], Jena, 1907, ii. 303 ff.; G. E. Howard, *A Hist. of Matrimonial Institutions*, Chicago and London, 1904; H. Hirt, *Indogermanen*, Strassburg, 1905–07, p. 702 ff.; F. Bernhöft, *Verwandtschaftsnamen und Eheformen der nordamerikan. Volksstämme*, Rostock, 1889; N. W. Thomas, *Kinship Organisations and Group Marriage in Australia*, Cambridge, 1907; J. G. Frazer, *Totemism and Exogamy*, London, 1910; F. Müller-Lyer, *Formen der Ehe*, Munich, 1911; W. H. R. Rivers, *Kinship and Social Organisation*, London, 1914.

W. H. R. RIVERS.

MARRIAGE (Celtic). — **1. Gaul.** — Polygamy does not seem to have been customary in Gaul. In the only passage that we have on the subject (Cæsar, *de Bell. Gall.* vi. 19) the plural *uxores* is certainly due to the plural *viri*. At the time of Gaul's last struggle against the Romans every Gaul bound himself by a sacred oath neither to enter his house again nor to see his children, relatives, or wife (*uxorem*, vii. 66) until he had ridden twice through the enemy's lines. We know that, as in other places, the wife (*uxor*) brought a dowry, but the husband also added an equal amount taken from his own property.

On the death of either husband or wife, the survivor received both portions, along with the revenues accumulated after marriage (vi. 19). Marriage was often employed as a means of securing political alliances; thus Orgetorix gave his daughter to Dumnorix; and the latter had his mother wedded to a noble of the Bituriges, and married his sister and other female relatives into other cities (i. 3, 9, 18). The wife's position, then, was very much superior to that of a slave. Plutarch relates that, before the Gauls had crossed the Alps, the women reconciled the opposing parties after a terrible civil war, and ever afterwards the Celts continued to admit their wives to their council when deliberating on peace and war, and to let the disputes with their allies be ruled by their wives' judgment. An agreement was made, later, between Hannibal and the Celts that, if the Celts had any grievance against the Carthaginians, the Carthaginian generals would judge, and, if the Carthaginians had any complaints against the Celts, the case would be judged by the wives of the Celts (*de Mul. Virt.* 6; cf. Polyænus, vii. 50). The numerous stories handed down to us by the ancients about the women of the Celts—Chiomara (Polyb. xxii. 21), Camma (Plut. *de Mul. Virt.* 20), Eponina (Tac. *Hist.* iv. 67), Gyptis (Athen. xiii. 38; Justin, xliii. 3)—seem to prove that the Celtic wife was not the passive being that the wife has remained among most barbarous peoples. Cæsar, who often gives her the title of *materfamilias*, relates nevertheless that, when a *paterfamilias* of high birth was about to die, his relations assembled, and, if there was any suspicion in connexion with his death, they cross-examined his wife like a slave; if any delinquency was proved, they put her to death by fire and all kinds of torments. But there is really nothing more in this than the exercise of the power of life and death which the *paterfamilias* had over his wife as well as his children (vi. 19).

2. Ancient Britain and Ireland.—Among the ancient Britons the position of woman was quite different. The women were the common possession of ten or twelve husbands, especially of brothers, or of fathers and their sons; but the children born from these unions belonged to the man who had married the woman first (Cæsar, *de Bell. Gall.* v. 14). Women were common property also in Caledonia (Dio Cass. lxxvi. 12; cf. lxii. 6). In Ireland, it is stated, it was quite a natural thing for men to have intercourse with the wives of other men, with their mothers, or their sisters (Strabo, IV. v. 4; cf. Jerome, *in Jovin.* ii. 7), but we find a much more advanced social state among the Irish and Britons described in the ancient epics and the collections of laws and customs.

3. Mediæval Ireland.—In Ireland, although the wife might bring all her own personal belongings (*tinól*) with her, it was the husband first of all who provided a dowry (*tinnscra*) for his wife. This dowry consisted of metals (gold, silver, copper, brass), clothing, or cattle; sometimes it consisted in some condition to be fulfilled by the future husband. In fact, marriage was generally a sort of sale, for the laws stipulate that the wife's father has a right to the whole dowry for the first year, to two-thirds the second year, half the third year, and so on, his share decreasing until the twenty-first year, when the debt is cancelled; during all this time the wife has control of what remains of her dowry each year. As a rule, marriages were celebrated by preference on the first days of August, at the time of the Fair of Tailltenn, or in the month of November. Polygamy seems to have been practised, perhaps as an exception, a little before the Christian era. In any case, if it was very uncommon to have several wives of the free class, a king often had one or more concubines of a servile class in addition to his lawful wife (*cétmuinter*, 'first wife'). Kinship ties were not always an obstacle to marriage: Lugaid, king of Ireland, married his mother; and a king of Leinster had his two sisters as wives.

The rights of the woman after marriage depended largely on her personal status in the community. In cases of separation for serious offence or by mutual consent, the wife received either the part of her dowry that was left her or what she brought on her marriage-day; in dividing the property, all that she had acquired by work and manufactured articles was taken into account, and the very smallest details were controlled by law.

4. Mediæval Wales and Brittany.—The laws of Wales show in their archaic parts a similar social state. The woman brought with her a dowry (*agweddy*) equal to half of what her brother would have (*gwaddol*), and articles for her own use (*argyfreu*); she received from her husband a present proportionate to her position and payable on the morning after the consummation of the marriage (*cowyll*). The conditions of separation depended on how long the union had lasted. If it had continued for a period of seven years all but three days, the belongings were divided equally between the couple; but, if the wife left her husband before this time, and without good reason, she had no right to anything beyond her *cowyll*. Polygamy was forbidden. Fosterage seems to have been less wide-spread than in Ireland.

The Britons who emigrated from Great Britain to Armorica in the 9th cent. called the dowry given by the husband to the wife *enepuuert*, 'face-price.' It was often property in land. Cf. also artt. CHILDREN (Celtic), ETHICS AND MORALITY (Celtic), FOSTERAGE, II. 5-7.

LITERATURE.—H. d'Arbois de Jubainville, *Cours de littérature celtique*, vii., Paris, 1895, pp. 210–253; C. Jullian, *Histoire de la Gaule*, do. 1907, ii. 407–409; P. W. Joyce, *A Social History of Ancient Ireland*, London, 1902, ii. 1–19; J. Rhŷs and D. Brynmor-Jones, *The Welsh People*, do. 1902, pp. 207–214; Aneurin Owen, *Ancient Laws and Institutes of Wales*, do. 1841; *Ancient Laws and Institutes of Ireland*, Dublin, 1865–1901.

G. DOTTIN.

MARRIAGE (Christian).—**1. The Christian ideal.**—The NT does not profess to set forth any new law or theory of marriage. Our Lord's answer to the Pharisees who questioned Him on the subject of divorce (Mt 19^{3}, Mk 10^{2}) implies that the perfect ideal of marriage is sufficiently declared in the passage in Genesis which professes to record the original institution of the holy estate of matrimony (Gn $2^{18ff.}$). The teaching and legislation of the Christian Church on this subject may, therefore, from one point of view, be regarded as a series of attempts to define more clearly and fully what is implied in the words of the original institution, and to enforce in practice the careful observance of the principles therein involved.

It is, accordingly, not strange that the subject of marriage occupies a comparatively small space in the teachings of the NT, and is for the most part confined to general rules as to the behaviour of married people such as might very well have found a place in the teaching of any heathen philosopher.

In the Gospels we have no direct reference to marriage, with the exception of our Lord's deliverances on the subject of divorce, which probably represent sayings uttered on different occasions, but which are, at any rate, all to the same purport: divorce is in itself sinful and inconsistent with the original divine institution of marriage. In the Epistles we have a number of practical exhortations in which the duties of married persons are clearly declared. The supremacy of the husband as the head of the wife is recognized, and the duty of wifely obedience declared. Mutual love and consideration are urged with considerable insight, while the perfect unity of husband and wife as 'one flesh' is duly emphasized.[1]

The NT, in fact, deals with marriage as an established social institution as it deals with other established institutions, laying down broad general principles of conduct, and demanding faithfulness and uprightness in the discharge of all recognized duties.

It was not necessary for the first Christian teachers to condemn polygamy, for in both the Græco-Roman and the Jewish world in their time monogamy was the universal rule. Polygamy is not expressly forbidden in the OT, nor was it uncommon in ancient Israel; but the Jewish teachers of the post-Exilic period had come to recognize that it was not consistent with the spirit of the original institution, which plainly demands the union of one man and one woman in marriage. Extra-matrimonial connexions might not be seriously condemned in the Gentile world, but, for the begetting of legitimate children, it was the rule that there should be only one wife to one husband. While it is safe to say, however, that monogamy is assumed throughout the NT, there is perhaps only one passage which a lover of proof texts could quote as distinctly forbidding polygamy, viz. 1 Co 7^{2} 'Let each man have his own wife, and let each woman have her own husband.'

Yet, although the NT does not profess to put forth any new laws on the subject, it is most true that the religion of the gospel has done inestimable service, not only in restoring and preserving preci-

[1] The passages of the NT dealing directly with marriage are Mt 5^{31} 19^{3-12}, Mk 10^{2-12}, Lk 16^{18}, Mt 22^{23-30}, Mk 12^{19-25} Lk 20^{27-35} Ro 7^{1-4}, 1 Co 6^{16-18} 7 *passim*, Eph $5^{22ff.}$, Col $3^{18f.}$, 1 Ti $2^{11ff.}$ 5^{9-16}, He 13^{4}, 1 P 3^{1-8}.

ous principles which were being forgotten in an age of luxury and grievous moral laxity, but also in changing profoundly men's ideas of the marriage-relation and of its duties and responsibilities. This result is the direct outcome of the teaching of the NT.

(1) The spirit and teaching of the NT tend to put the mutual love of husband and wife in the foremost place. Marriage has been described as a provision for the propagation of the race and the proper bringing up of children. The NT recognizes the importance of the Christian household and the rightful education of Christian children, but does not describe this as the main object of marriage. Again, marriage has been regarded as a provision for the satisfaction of a natural desire and a restraint upon unbridled indulgence. St. Paul acknowledges that marriage serves this purpose, but does not give it any great prominence (1 Co 7[9ff.]). According to the book of Genesis, marriage was instituted, in the first instance, to satisfy the need of man's social nature. Because it was 'not good that the man should be alone,' because companionship with his fellows was necessary for the perfect development of his nature, marriage was instituted to provide him with the closest and most intimate form of companionship. Thus the words, 'The twain shall become one flesh,' imply much more than a merely carnal relationship—a thought which is instructively developed by St. Paul in Eph 5[22ff.]

(2) It is not too much to say that our whole conception of the marriage-relation has been changed, and changed for the better, by the high and honourable position accorded to women in the NT, and the general improvement in the status of woman which has been brought about under Christian influence, and which has not yet, perhaps, reached its final goal. A system in which 'there can be no male and female' (Gal 3[28]) so far as all blessings, privileges, and responsibilities are concerned, under which husband and wife are taught to remember that they are 'joint-heirs of the grace of life' (1 P 3[7]), must of necessity tend to elevate, and, if it may be so expressed, to equalize, the marriage-relation.

When St. Paul compares the marriage-bond to the union between Christ and the Church, he is, no doubt, making use of a very familiar idea frequently expressed by the OT prophets, and applying it to the Christian community. It is easy to see, however, that the substitution of Christ—our brother—for the awful Jahweh of the OT makes all the difference in the world, *the* essential difference, in fact, between the old world conception and that of the Christian Church. The ancient Romans had a high ideal of the sanctity of married life—an ideal which, as the very bitterness of the satirists proves, was not wholly lost in the terrible immorality of the times when Christianity made its appearance. Nevertheless, among Jews and Romans alike, as also, to a considerable extent, among the Greeks, the relation of the wife to the husband was, to all intents and purposes, that of a slave to her master. Under the gospel the superiority of the husband is more that of the parent to the child or, rather, of a protecting brother to a sister. It is sometimes asserted that the terms in which the supremacy of the husband and the duties of obedience and reverence on the wife's part are put forth in the NT are too strong to be in harmony with our ideas to-day, and that we have, in fact, passed beyond the point of view of the NT. If so, this very advance is the natural and necessary outcome of the gospel just as truly as the abolition of slavery—another social institution which is nowhere directly condemned in the NT. It may be argued on rational grounds that the natural characteristics of the sexes must involve a certain superiority and controlling power on the man's side in the nuptial relation; but such questions cannot be decided by the mere appeal to isolated texts of the Bible.

(3) The union of the sexes has been purified, and the happiness of the married relation secured, by the absolute prohibition of every kind of extra-matrimonial connexion. Such connexions were regarded with absolute indifference by the Greeks, and, in consequence, the temporary connexion with the ἑταίρα, or courtesan, came to be much more highly valued than the legitimate marriage, to the manifest injury of the home life and the status of the lawful wife. By the Romans, it may be said, such connexions, though not so lightly regarded as among the Greeks, were, on the whole, regarded with contemptuous indifference. Although the case was different, so far as the Jewish law was concerned, we cannot doubt that the Jews would be much influenced by the prevailing tone of thought in the Gentile world and would imbibe something of the very lax principles of morality current in their day. All such connexions are emphatically condemned in the NT, and it is expressly taught that the physical connexion of itself involves the obligation of the marriage-bond (see 1 Co 6[16]).

(4) The gospel emphatically condemned divorce as essentially sinful. In ancient Rome divorce was regarded as in some sense dishonourable, and therefore undesirable. For five hundred and twenty years it was boasted that divorce was unknown in Rome (Val. Max. ii. 1), and the very bitterness with which the satirists denounce the laxity of their time in this matter shows that the old idea has not yet been wholly lost. Nevertheless, it is only too evident that, in the time of luxury and advanced civilization in which the gospel was first preached, divorce was coming to be looked upon with the utmost indifference as a commonplace fact in ordinary social life.

The Jews had no doubt as to the lawfulness of divorce (cf. art. 'Divorce,' in *JE* iv. [1903] 624–628), and it is probable that Mt 19[3] most truly represents the form of their question to our Lord. They desired to have His opinion, not on the question of the lawfulness of divorce, but as to the causes for which divorce might be legitimately instituted. Our Lord's answer declares the essential sinfulness of divorce as inconsistent with the original institution of marriage.

(5) The teaching of St. Paul about marriage as the symbol or analogue of the mystical union of Christ with His Church (Eph 5[22-34]) has had a profound effect on Christian thought, elevating and purifying the conception of marriage. Marriage for the Christian is something more than the ordinary social institution; it is, above everything else, 'a holy estate.' Man and wife are no longer twain, but one flesh. This, as has already been pointed out, implies more than a merely physical union. How much more? It may be said that it implies a perfect union of love and affection, and entire community of aims and interests, as also of worldly possessions, and a perfect mutual understanding. This positivist explanation may perhaps seem sufficient to the modern mind; but it is easy to see that the comparison with the spiritual union between Christ and the Church might, to Hellenic readers, very naturally suggest something more, something in the nature of a metaphysical basis for the union of aims, affections, and interests. This basis may be conceived as a sort of mystic, or, possibly, psycho-physical bond, uniting the two spirits so as to form a kind of single personality. It is quite conceivable—we may even say that it is probable—that some such idea was in the

mind of the Apostle. The idea may not seem altogether absurd to a modern metaphysician; but, if it should seem inconceivable, we are not bound to defend the infallibility of St. Paul's metaphysics, and may be quite satisfied with the simple, positive, and practical view of the union.

It is, however, necessary to bear in mind that this idea of a mystic or psycho-physical bond formed in matrimony is, essentially, that sacramental view of marriage which was authoritatively defined in the Middle Ages, which is still the accepted doctrine of the Roman and Eastern churches, and which has had important practical consequences for Christian thought and Christian life.[1]

2. Marriage rites and ceremonies.—The history of the rites and ceremonies accompanying marriage belongs properly to the sphere of the Christian antiquarian; but, inasmuch as those rites and ceremonies have been the subject of mystical interpretation on the part of Christian theologians, and have thus acquired a certain religious significance, a brief notice of them may well find a place in the present article.

Marriage-celebrations in all times and in all countries have been either essentially religious functions or, at all events, accompanied by religious rites and ceremonies. The solemnization of marriage by a religious ceremony is, therefore, no new thing peculiar to the Christian Church. In fact, there is not a single feature in the marriage-services of the Christian communities that cannot be traced back to the *sponsalia*, or to the nuptial ceremonies, of the Roman Empire. On the other hand, the form of our Christian services, the ministerial benediction, and the clear expression of Christian doctrine in prayers and exhortations have helped to preserve a living sense of the peculiar sanctity of marriage as taught in the NT.

Marriage is, in the first place, an affair of the family. In the earliest period the Christian congregation regarded itself as a spiritual family, and the life and concerns of every member of the congregation were of intimate interest to the whole body. No member of the congregation ought to enter upon so important a step as the contract of matrimony without the advice and approval of the whole congregation. This is implied in the words of Ignatius:

πρέπει δὲ τοῖς γαμοῦσι καὶ ταῖς γαμουμέναις[2] μετὰ γνώμης τοῦ ἐπισκόπου τὴν ἕνωσιν ποιεῖσθαι, ἵνα ὁ γάμος ᾖ κατὰ κύριον καὶ μὴ κατ' ἐπιθυμίαν (*Ep. ad Polycarp.* v.).

It is inconceivable, therefore, that the celebration of marriage should not have been accompanied from the very first with suitable acts of Christian worship, or that the accustomed marriage-rites should not have been celebrated as a solemn religious function. With the expansion of the Church and the consequent weakening of the close bond of social union between members of the same congregation, the necessity for ecclesiastical sanction for marriage would be less strongly felt, and marriages might be contracted without any formal benediction.

The testimony of the Fathers, from the middle of the 3rd cent. onwards, shows that what we should now describe as civil marriages were not unknown, perhaps were not uncommon, but at the same time were strongly discountenanced by the Church. It is evident that the general feeling in the Church was very much the same as it is to-day. While a religious ceremony was not required as a condition of Christian communion, it was felt that the right and proper course was for all Christian people marrying honourably to seek the benediction of the Church upon their union.[1]

[1] Whenever the sacramental idea is referred to in this article, it may be taken that the idea herein explained is meant.

[2] J. B. Lightfoot prefers γαμούσαις.

From the 5th cent. onwards there can be little doubt that the celebration of marriage with ecclesiastical benediction was the almost universal custom. The inference which has sometimes been drawn from the fact that about A.D. 802 Charlemagne prohibited marriage without benediction (*Capit.* vii. 363) and that so late as A.D. 900 Leo the Philosopher issued a similar edict (*Novel.* 89), that purely civil marriages were very common up to the end of the 8th or 9th cent., is not borne out by anything that we know of those ages.

Nevertheless, marriage without benediction, though thus condemned by the civil law, was, if otherwise unobjectionable, regarded as valid in the Church up to the time of the Council of Trent. That Council (A.D. 1563, sess. xxiv.) decreed that henceforth no marriage should be considered valid unless celebrated by a priest in the presence of at least two other witnesses. The decree, indeed, clearly expresses the principle that the ceremony is not of the essence of the sacrament, the matter of which remains, as before, the consent of the parties; but it claims the right on the part of the Church to regulate the conditions under which a valid marriage can be celebrated. The decree holds good only in those countries in which the decrees of the Council have been published.

In the Eastern Churches the Confession of Peter Mogilas of Kieff (A.D. 1640), in which the priestly benediction, the accustomed formularies, and the invocation of the Holy Spirit are declared to be essentials of marriage, is regarded as authoritative.

The marriage-ceremonies in use all over the Christian world for hundreds of years past contain elements derived from two sources, viz. the *sponsalia*, the ancient ceremony of betrothal, and the *nuptiæ*, or marriage-ceremony proper. The solemn troth-plight, the joining of hands, and the giving and receiving of a ring or rings with certain gifts of money—the *arrhæ*, pledge of the dowry—were the principal features of the betrothal ceremony. The veiling of the bride, the crowning of the bride and bridegroom, the formal handing over of the bride by her parent or guardian to the care of the bridegroom, the solemn declaration of the completion of the contract, and the bringing home of the bride in triumphal procession to her future home were the accustomed nuptial ceremonies. The priestly benediction may perhaps be considered as the distinctively Christian addition to the ancient ceremonies, yet even this may have been simply a special sanctification of the ancient congratulations of the family; it is even possible that in the Christian service there was some attempt to recall the ancient *confarreatio*, which had by Christian times become practically obsolete, but which, with its accompaniment of sacrifice and solemn benedictions, was the only form recognized by Roman law for the celebration of an absolutely indissoluble marriage. The reference to the demand for ten witnesses in St. Ambrose[2] would naturally suggest the *confarreatio*. Old customs are often preserved in an imperfect fashion even when they have become obsolete (see MARRIAGE [Roman]).

[1] The following passages may be referred to as bearing out the view here presented: Clem. Alex. *Pæd.* iii. 11, *Strom.* iv. 20; Tert. *ad Uxor.* ii. 9, *de Pudic.* 4 (this passage is worth quoting in full: 'Ideo penes nos, occultae quoque coniunctiones, id est non prius apud ecclesiam professae, iuxta moechiam et fornicationem iudicari periclitantur. Nec inde consertae obtentu matrimonii crimen eludant'); Ambrose, *Ep.* xix. 7, condemning mixed marriages with unbelievers, which the Church censured, but could not wholly prevent in the earlier centuries; Synesius, bishop of Ptolemais, *Ep.* cx.; Basil, *Ep.* xvii., canon 69, etc.

[2] 'Nam si inter decem testes confectis sponsalibus, nuptiis consummatis, quaevis femina viro coniuncta mortali non sine magno periculo perpetrat adulterium' (*de Lapsu virginis consecratæ*, v.). This passage may, of course, simply refer to the old Roman custom by way of example.

There is no express evidence that the veiling of the bride formed part of the Roman ceremonies of betrothal; it seems rather to have been confined to the nuptials proper. In Tertullian's time, however, it was a betrothal ceremony amongst Christians, the bride continuing to wear the betrothal veil from the time of the betrothal to the wedding-day (Tert. *de Virg. velandis*, xi.).

A passage in Tertullian would seem to imply that the giving of a ring, though a harmless heathen custom, was not practised by Christians in his day (*de Idolol.* xvi.). This may have been the case with some of the stricter or more old-fashioned Christians, but the universal custom of the Church from the 4th cent. onwards would seem to show that the giving of the ring had always been generally practised.

The crowning of the bride and bridegroom was condemned by Tertullian as implying acknowledgment of heathen deities. Yet it continued to be commonly practised in the Western Church long after his day. In the Eastern Church it prevails to the present day, and is regarded as the most important part of the marriage-ceremony, marriage in the East being often described as 'the crowning.'

That *sponsalia* and actual nuptials were still regarded as distinct ceremonies, between which an interval of time might elapse, up to the middle of the 9th cent., is evident from the letter of Pope Nicholas I. to the Bulgarians (A.D. 865 [*PL* cxix. 980]), in which he treats of the marriage customs of the Western Church. It is, however, most probable that from much earlier times the two ceremonies had been generally combined in practice. Formal *sponsalia* were not required by Roman law, and were frequently omitted. In such cases it would be natural that the giving of the ring, the troth-plight, and other espousal ceremonies would take place at the actual marriage. The Anglican custom of celebrating the first part of the marriage-service in the body of the Church, while the concluding prayers and benediction are said at the altar, is a vestige of the ancient distinction between espousals and marriages.

3. Asceticism and marriage.—The idea that there is something necessarily impure and degrading in the union of the sexes in marriage, or that, at all events, marriage must be regarded as a somewhat grudging concession to human weakness, finds no place in the teaching of the NT. Notwithstanding the strict inculcation of the general principle of self-denial, there is nothing to suggest that the celibate or virgin state is in any way higher or holier than the estate of marriage. There is just one passage, in the Apocalypse of John (14^4), which, however interpreted, seems to imply a preference for the virgin state; otherwise the NT gives no support to the doctrine. If St. Paul prefers the unmarried state, it is on purely utilitarian grounds, because of the greater freedom from worldly cares enjoyed by the unmarried. If we may accept the Pastoral Epistles as his, or as expressing his mind, the Apostle thought it most desirable that younger widows should contract a second marriage. Yet, inasmuch as what we may call ascetic ideas were widely prevalent, not only among the Essenes (*q.v.*) in Judaism, but in certain circles in the heathen world, it is very likely that such ideas were to some extent prevalent in the Church from the very first. The awful prevalence of vice and immorality, the consequent demand for a resolute fight against those 'fleshly lusts which war against the soul,' and a sense of the strength of sensual desires and impulses would naturally create a feeling of repulsion against all forms of indulgence, even the most innocent, in those newly aroused to a desire for a new and higher life. It is not surprising, therefore, that from the middle of the 3rd cent. the ascetic view should have taken a firm hold on the Christian Church and should have speedily become the predominant and, in fact, universally accepted view. The rise of monasticism and the admiration aroused by the devotion of the monastics and also, from the middle of the 4th cent., the intensified worldliness of the now fashionable Church would naturally foster the growth of the ascetic ideal. The command, 'Love not the world' (1 Jn 2^{15}), had to find some new interpretation when the world was no longer a professedly heathen world, but a community of nominal Christians. The doctrine of the earlier Gnostics, Basilidians, Saturninians, Encratites, etc., and of the Manichæans, of the essential sinfulness of conjugal union was, of course, formally condemned, but in the extravagant laudations of virginity in the writings of St. Jerome, and even the more moderate utterances of St. Augustine, the disparagement of the married state sometimes approaches very closely to the views of those heretics. Throughout the Middle Ages the doctrine of the superiority of the virgin state firmly held its ground, and led to many extravagances. But the teaching of the NT and the constant witness of the Church served at all events as a safeguard against the worst results of the disparagement of marriage.

It was not until the Reformation of the 16th cent. that any serious attempt was made to vindicate the claims of healthy home life and happy marriage to a position of equality with the virgin state. In Luther's eyes all monastic vows were essentially sinful (*de Votis monasticis*, 1521), and, in general, the Reformers maintained a similar position. The question of the superiority of virginity became an essential point of controversy between the Roman Catholics and their opponents, and the Council of Trent (sess. 24, can. x.) condemned with anathema the doctrine of the equality of the married state with, or its superiority over, the state of celibacy.[1]

The objection to second marriages, which were discouraged by the Church and absolutely forbidden by the Montanists, was one result of the ascetic spirit. This we should now regard as a mere harmless eccentricity of no serious importance in the history of Christian thought; but it is far otherwise with another result of the ascetic movement—the enforcement of the celibacy of the clergy.

It is significant that it was in the course of the 3rd cent. that the question of the propriety of clerical marriage seems first to have become prominent. Hitherto the clergy, like other Christian men, might be married or not, according to their discretion. Those who held the essential superiority of the celibate life would naturally consider that the clergy, as especially belonging to the class of holy persons, should be unmarried. At all events, in the 3rd cent. it came to be recognized that, as each man should 'abide in that calling wherein he was called' (1 Co 7^{20}), the clergy should not contract marriage after their ordination. Decisions to this effect are found in the canons of some local synods, though the Council of Ancyra (A.D. 314) made an exception in the case of deacons, who, before ordination, should inform the bishop if they intend to marry. From this position it was a natural step to the view that after ordination clerics should cease to maintain conjugal relations with their wives—a view which could scarcely have been put forth except by a council of celibates. The Council of Elvira (Illiberis; A.D. 305) laid down this rule under penalty of deprivation. The ecumenical Council

[1] In some of his Homilies—*e.g. Hebrews*, serm. 4, *in Seraphim*, serm. 1—Chrysostom strongly asserts the equal blessedness of the married state. Jovinian, the opponent of St. Jerome, was a warm advocate of the same view, but the general consensus of Christian opinion was on the other side.

of Nicæa (A.D. 325) was restrained from passing a similar ordinance only by the emphatic protest of the Martyr Confessor Paphnutius, who pleaded earnestly in favour of the perfect sanctity of married life. From the close of the 4th cent. the principle that the clergy ought to be celibates was universally adopted in theory in the Western Church. Pope Siricius (A.D. 385) in his *Epistle to Himerius* (*PL* xiii. 1132 ff.), described by H. H. Milman[1] as 'the first authentic Decretal, the first letter of the Bishop of Rome, which became a law to the Western Church,' absolutely interdicted the marriage of the clergy. Nevertheless, all through the Middle Ages, despite the zealous efforts of men like Boniface I., St. Gregory the Great, St. Anselm, and St. Dunstan, despite papal edicts and decrees of councils, the marriage of the clergy continued to exist in every part of Europe. It was regarded in general with indifference, sometimes with approval, by the laity, and was zealously contended for as a right by the secular clergy. Even after the vigorous crusade of Hildebrand (1020–85), the 'scandal,' as it was considered, of 'clerical concubinage' maintained its existence here and there, though it was probably never after Hildebrand's time regarded with the same indifference as before.

In the Eastern Church the rule of celibacy has never been imposed on the inferior clergy. By the 6th Council of Constantinople (in Trullo; A.D. 680) the marriage of clerics after ordination was forbidden, but for those married before ordination, with the exception of the bishops, the continuance of conjugal relations was permitted; the wife of a bishop was compelled either to become a deaconess or to retire into a convent. For all practical purposes this remains the rule of the Eastern Churches to the present day, except that marriage is not merely permissible but compulsory for the parish priest, who must, however, be married before ordination. The bishops are chosen from the ranks of the monastics, so that no parish priest can look forward to promotion to the highest position in his Church.

4. Ecclesiastical law and Church discipline.—The Christian Church from the very beginning was constituted as an organized society or, at all events, as a closely connected congeries of societies claiming as a right and duty to exercise moral supervision and discipline over individual members. Church law and ecclesiastical jurisdiction are, then, no late outgrowth or corruption of primitive Christianity, but trace their origin to the earliest time, and even to the days of the Apostles. It was inevitable that in the Apostolic Age such questions connected with marriage should arise as would be considered suitable for the judgment of the community. In 1 Co 7 we have an interesting example of such questions and of the apostolic method of dealing with them. The saying of Ignatius as to the necessity of submitting a proposed marriage-contract for the approval of the bishop has already been quoted.

Nor is it at all surprising that matters connected with marriage should have, from the Apostolic Age until now, occupied an important place in ecclesiastical legislation. From the civil side, marriage is regarded as a legal contract which must be regulated for practical purposes by the State. From the Christian point of view, marriage is a holy estate which the Church may claim to regulate in the highest interests of religion and morality. Experience shows that there must ever be a possibility of conflict between the two jurisdictions, and that, consequently, difficulties in practice may often result.

'Aliae sunt leges Caesarum, aliae Christi; aliud Papianus aliud Paulus noster praecepit' (Jerome, *Ep.* lxxvii. 3).

But, while in theory it is very simple to say that the Christian must at all events give the 'leges Christi' the first place in his obedience, in practice he may often find himself confronted with the question whether a law or supposed law of the Church must really be received as a divine ordinance. So long as the Church was a small and uninfluential body in the heathen world, it did not much matter whether its regulations for the discipline of its members came into conflict with generally received opinions or not, and, as a general rule, in the earlier centuries Christians were content to abide by the rulings of their ecclesiastical authorities, though even then we have reason to believe that Church censures were sometimes defied or evaded when Christians wished to avail themselves of some legal right in opposition to the rule of the community. The case of mixed marriages with Jews or pagans, which often took place despite the ecclesiastical prohibitions, is an example in point.

In the Middle Ages the matter was settled by allowing marriage, for Christians at all events, to become entirely an affair of the Church. Much laxity of observance might prevail, and the lawless men of the mediæval period might often flout the wholesome restraints of the law; the princes of the Frankish, Teutonic, and other new nations might decline to abandon their ancient right to have a plurality of wives; but, none the less, it was fully recognized that the Church's jurisdiction in such matters ought to be respected as supreme. It is in the modern period, since the Reformation, that the question of the two jurisdictions and the proper relations of the one to the other has come into prominence and has given occasion to many practical difficulties arising from the conflict of two different ideals. The Reformers vindicated the claims of the State and of the civil magistrate as against the extravagant claims of the mediæval Church, holding that the laws of the Christian State must be regarded as Christian laws and must be obeyed, and that no law-abiding citizen should be subjected to Church censure or other social inconvenience for neglecting some ecclesiastical ordinance, so long as he did nothing illegal or dishonourable. It was, of course, understood that no law contrary to the teaching of the gospel should be obeyed. The Roman Catholic party, on the other hand, while in general admitting the duty of obedience to the law of the State, held that it was the province of the Church to define what should or should not be considered lawful in the matter of marriage. Both parties would agree that the object of all marriage laws should be to safeguard purity and morality, and would probably admit that the Church had no right to impose anything in opposition to the law of the State, unless it were in some sort necessary for that object; but the Reformers would by no means concede to their opponents that it was for the Church to impose any regulations which it pleased, whether in conformity with the laws of the State or not. The two questions which in modern times have given occasion to most difficulty have been the question of divorce and the question of the conditions of valid matrimony.

(*a*) *Divorce.*—Divorce, in the strict and proper acceptance of the term, means the complete rupture of the marriage-bond, the persons divorced being left free to marry again. Canonists and theologians, however, frequently apply the term to what is more properly called 'separation' or, when sanctioned by legal process, 'judicial separa-

[1] *Hist. of Latin Christianity*, London, 1872, i. 97; see also A. P. Stanley, *Lectures on the Hist. of the Eastern Church*, do. 1861, lectt. i. and v.; H. C. Romanoff, *Rites and Customs of the Greco-Russian Church*, do. 1868; Photius, *Nomocanon*, Paris, 1615.

tion,' in which the *vinculum* is not supposed to be broken and re-marriage is, therefore, not permissible. The latter is described as *divortium a mensa et thoro*, in contradistinction to the more complete *divortium a vinculo matrimonii.*

It has been universally admitted that adultery and, perhaps, some other grave offences justify the separation of man and wife. Such separation is, indeed, contrary to the high Christian ideal of marriage; but under the new dispensation, as under the old, it is necessary for the hardness of men's hearts in this imperfect world to make provision for occasional failures to attain the perfect ideal. But, while this is the case with regard to separation, there has been considerable difference of opinion on the more difficult question of divorce in the proper sense of the word. The broad general principle is that divorce is something which ought not to be, that it ought not even to be thought of as a possibility by Christian people. But is the broad general principle to be regarded as a law binding universally and unconditionally? If any exceptions are to be allowed, in what cases do they apply? Should man and woman stand on the same footing as regards the right to claim divorce? Should any difference be made between cases where both partners are professing Christians and those in which one is an unbeliever or a heretic? These and similar questions have from century to century occupied the attention of Christian teachers and legislators.

The teaching of our Lord on this subject, as it has come down to us, is found in four passages in the Synoptic Gospels, viz. Mt $5^{31f.}$ 19^{3-9}, Mk 10^{2-12}, and Lk 16^{18}. In Mark and Luke the prohibition of divorce and re-marriage is absolute and unqualified; in Matthew the qualifications 'saving for the cause of fornication,' 'except for fornication',[1] are added. Roman Catholic divines and those Anglicans who adopt the stricter view maintain that, as each Gospel must be taken in and by itself as authoritative, the passage in Mark must be accepted as the decisive rule for Christians, while the qualified statement in Matthew must be understood as merely giving sanction to separation 'a mensa et thoro' in case of adultery.

On the other hand, it is contended that the ordinary rules of exegesis require us to interpret the unqualified statements in Mark and Luke by the fuller and more balanced statement in Matthew, so that we must not take each Gospel as an independent entity, but must compare one with another to ascertain what Christ really taught. Moreover, it is contended that, when He spoke about divorce, our Lord must have had in mind the complete severance of the marriage-bond, since that was the only meaning His hearers could possibly attach to the word. It is pointed out that the sayings in Mark and Luke are simply ordinary examples of the method of the great Prophet, who was accustomed to set forth broad principles in an absolute and sometimes an extreme form, leaving it to His people to apply His teachings with all the necessary qualifications in the manner of legislation to their individual cases and needs. That this principle has always been recognized in the interpretation of the Sermon on the Mount without in the least detracting from the supreme value of that great utterance cannot well be denied. Our Lord as teacher was a prophet rather than a legislator. Hence it is maintained that the passage in Matthew may be taken as a fuller expression of the Lord's mind than the briefer passages in the other Gospels, that we have His express sanction for divorce in case of adultery, with consequent permission to marry again in the case of the innocent partner. It is not, of course,

1 παρεκτὸς λόγου πορνείας (5^{32}); μὴ ἐπὶ πορνείᾳ (19^{9}).

denied that, if the bond is broken, it is broken alike for both partners, but, as the guilty partner is, or has been, living in notorious sin, and can give no evidence of repentance except by abstaining altogether from marriage, such guilty partner must necessarily be refused the Church's benediction in the case of re-marriage. The latter principle has been invariably and universally accepted.

Although it is evident that adultery affects the marriage relation more closely than any other offence, yet it may fairly be said that there are other things which may make married life so intolerable, and the perfect ideal union so impossible, that, if divorce or separation be allowed at all, the grounds for such separation ought not in reason to be confined to the one offence of adultery. This difficulty was met by many of the Fathers by showing, on good Scriptural authority, that idolatry, covetousness, unnatural offences, etc., might rightly be classed under the heading of spiritual adultery. There is probably no more than a formal difference between this and the argument which appeals most forcibly to modern minds—that there are offences which make married life so intolerable that there can be no restoration of affection, that, where the tie of affection has been absolutely destroyed, the real *vinculum* has been ruptured, and that, therefore, such offences may rightly be put in the same category as conjugal infidelity in the strict sense of the word.[1]

The passages in the Synoptic Gospels have been treated as they stand in the NT without any reference to the results of modern criticism; it will be generally admitted that such treatment is justified in dealing with ethical or doctrinal questions. It must, however, be acknowledged that the recent higher criticism of the Synoptic Gospels has thrown a new light upon the matter and, to a certain extent, strengthened the case of those who condemn divorce absolutely. A large and increasing number of competent critics are of opinion that the qualification, 'except for the cause of fornication,' formed no part of our Lord's teaching (*e.g.*, A. B. Bruce, H. Weiss, H. H. Wendt, P. W. Schmiedel, B. W. Bacon, C. G. Montefiore), and that He forbade divorce simply and absolutely. The four passages are reduced to two. The passage Lk 16^{18}, probably derived from the source Q, may be regarded as the original and genuine form which has been edited by the first Evangelist in Mt 5^{32}. It is quite evident that Mt 19^{3-9} and Mk 10^{2-12} are but slightly different versions of the same conversation, while everything goes to show that the form in Mark is the original (see W. C. Allen, *ICC*, 'St. Matthew,'[3] Edinburgh, 1912, *ad loc.*).[2]

If the modern critical view is generally accepted, it will, no doubt, be admitted that the case of those who absolutely condemn divorce will be somewhat strengthened, but it is not likely that the existing state of opinion on the whole will be very much affected. The acceptance of the critical view will simply bring into greater prominence the fact that questions of this kind have never really been decided on grounds either of exegesis or of authority pure and simple, but that our interpretation of our Lord's teaching has always been guided by moral and theological considerations. The saving clauses, παρεκτὸς λόγου πορνείας and μὴ ἐπὶ πορνείᾳ, may be admitted to be early notes of interpretation added by the Church—a reminiscence, perhaps, of instruction actually received from the Lord—but those

1 Augustine frequently expressed the idea of the wider interpretation of 'fornication.' 'Si infidelitas fornicatio est, et idololatria infidelitas, et avaritia idololatria, non est dubitandum avaritiam fornicationem esse' (*de Serm. Domini*, I. xvi. 46). See also several passages to the same effect in the *de Conjugiis adulterinis*. In the *Retractationes* Augustine expresses doubt as to the legitimacy of this exegesis (i. 19). Passages from Hermas and Origen in which the idea is expressed are also cited (cf. Bingham, *Antiq.* XXII. v. 2).

2 W. C. Allen, though holding the critical view, yet protests, in letters to *The Guardian* (lxv. [1910] 920, 985, 1684 f., 1782), against making use of critical results to decide dogmatic questions, and justifies the use of the NT as received by the Church. J. Keble, in his pamphlet, 'An argument for not proceeding immediately to repeal the laws which treat the nuptial bond as indissoluble' (Oxford, 1857), attempted to defend the stricter view on the ground that the passages in Matthew were meant only for the Jews of Christ's own time, and were not to apply to Christians, for whom the absolute prohibitions were intended. This view does not seem to have met with much approval, and is not now advanced.

who plead for the right of divorce will still maintain that the interpretation was fully justified and quite on a level with many of our other interpretations of the Sermon on the Mount.

The only other passage in the NT where the subject of divorce is directly treated is 1 Co 7, where St. Paul appeals to our Lord's authority, repeating the general prohibition of divorce. There is nothing, however, to indicate that, when he speaks of a separation between wife and husband, he has the special case of conjugal infidelity before his mind. The presumption is rather the other way, and it would seem as if he were merely thinking of the case of separation for what we should describe as incompatibility of temper. The chief interest of this chapter centres in the rules and regulations laid down by the Apostle with reference to matters about which he could not appeal to any direct utterances of the Lord Jesus.

In the first place, he recognizes the possibility of separation 'a mensa et thoro' (v.[11]); if husband and wife are separated for any reason, they are to remain single or become reconciled to each other. Even though he were not actually considering the case of separation for conjugal infidelity, we may feel sure that, if he had done so, the Apostle would have approved of the counsel given in the *Shepherd* of Hermas.

The Jewish husband who divorced his wife was forbidden by the law to take her back; but it is characteristic of the gospel to give prominence to the possibility of repentance; and so Hermas charges the husband who has put away his unfaithful wife to remain unmarried (διὰ τὴν μετάνοιαν) so that the sinner might have an opportunity for repentance with consequent restoration (*Mand.* iv. 1).

In the second place, St. Paul deals with the case of a marriage between a Christian and an unbeliever—Jew or heathen. If it is desired that the union should continue, well and good; if not (v.[15]), a brother or sister is not under bondage in such a case, and, if the unbeliever dissolves the connexion, the Christian is free. This must be taken to mean free to marry again (cf. Ro 7[1ff.] for the use of the terms 'freedom' and 'bondage'). This passage was expressly cited in later times as the authority for the canon law of the Roman Church, which permits divorce by mutual consent in cases of mixed marriages between Christians and unbelievers (see Innocent III., *Decretales Gregorii*, iv. 19, 'de Divortiis,' ch. 7).

The canon law of the Roman Catholic Church unqualifiedly forbids divorce 'a vinculo matrimonii,' if both parties at the time of marriage had been baptized Christians. In the Eastern Churches, on the contrary, divorce is permitted, not only for adultery, but also for other serious causes, as, *e.g.*, high treason, designs by either party on the life of the other, insanity, leprosy, etc.; but no one is permitted to obtain a divorce more than once. In East and West alike, in the earlier period, and more especially after the ascetic movement became popular—*i.e.* after the middle of the 3rd cent.—the Fathers were strong in their denunciations of re-marriage, even in the case of an innocent partner. In some cases such unions were made the subject of ecclesiastical censure and at least temporary excommunication. Yet, while the civil laws permitted re-marriage, it is evident that all the eloquence of the Fathers could not entirely prevent it, and it is probable that the average lay opinion did not generally approve of the excessive rigidity of what we may call the ecclesiastical view. The Eastern Church, however, has, from the time of the removal of the seat of empire to Constantinople, been at all times more dependent on the civil power, and, as a natural consequence, more subject to the influence of lay opinion, than the Church of the West, where the power of the ecclesiastical authorities was more unfettered.

In the matter in hand this difference is very well illustrated in the 5th cent. by the moderation of the views of St. Basil, who refused to condemn re-marriage absolutely, though he could not approve of it, and of Lactantius, as compared with the Western teachers of the same period. Yet even up to the 12th cent., when the present canon law of the Roman Church was finally formulated, it is evident, from a careful study of the various decrees of synods and councils, that it was not possible in practice to enforce strictly the principle of the absolute indissolubility of marriage.

Re-marriage in certain cases is permitted implicitly or explicitly by the following Councils: Elvira (Illiberis, *c.* 305), Vannes (465), Agde (506), Orleans (533), Compiègne (756), and Bourges (1031); to these we may add the testimony of the *Penitential* of Theodore of Canterbury, drawn up for the guidance of the churches under his control, which in some respects perhaps goes to an extreme in making allowances for the weakness of human nature, but in which very considerable liberty is allowed in the matter of re-marriage.

Civil legislation from the time of Constantine to Justinian bears witness, indeed, to the growth of Christian influence in the attempts made to limit the grounds for divorce and, in general, to make divorce more difficult. Nevertheless, the law permitting divorce by mutual consent remained in force until the time of Justinian, while the grounds on which it might be obtained were numerous enough. Under the legislation of Theodosius the Second and Valentinian a wife might divorce her husband for (1) treason, (2) adultery, (3) homicide, (4) poisoning, (5) violating sepulchres, (6) forgery, (7) stealing from a church, (8) robbery, (9) cattle-stealing, (10) attempts on her life, (11) introducing immoral women into the house, and (12) common assault. A husband might divorce his wife for any of the above causes, and also for (13) dining with men not relatives without her husband's permission, (14) going from home at night without permission or reasonable cause, and (15) frequenting circus or theatre without permission; to which Justinian added (16) procuring abortion, and (17) mixed bathing.

It was very natural that the Reformers in the 16th cent. should call in question the rigid mediæval views on the subject of divorce, regarding them as an outcome of the claims of the ecclesiastical authorities to supreme jurisdiction, and as inspired by the spirit of asceticism. The Protestant and Reforming divines held that divorce with the permission of re-marriage was justified in the case of adultery and, generally speaking, of cruelty or prolonged desertion. In the 16th and 17th centuries the same view was generally expressed by Anglican teachers, even by those who, like J. Cosin and H. Hammond, are generally considered as belonging to the High school in theology.

The Reformers rejected the sacramental theory of marriage, and held that the words 'the twain shall become one flesh' signified no more than a very comprehensible union based on common interests and mutual affections. The doctrine that marriage could be dissolved only by death, since husband and wife could no more cease to be husband and wife than brother and sister to be brother and sister, seemed to them to be the natural outcome of the sacramental doctrine. This is not, indeed, wholly true; for it is quite possible to hold the sacramental view, or something very like the sacramental view, and yet to believe that grievous sin may rupture the mystic bond as really and completely as death itself. Still it is evident that rejection of the sacramental theory makes it easier to reject the strict doctrine of indissolubility.

In the next place, the Reformers maintained

that, since separation 'a mensa et thoro' was permitted, it was more conducive to morality and more in accordance with the teaching of 1 Co 7[9] that an innocent partner should be allowed the right of re-marriage than that temptations to a life of sin should be multiplied. Further, they pointed out that the strict enforcement of the canon law forbidding divorce had not succeeded in putting an end to the evil; that in the later period the multiplication of grounds on which marriage might be declared null and void *ab initio*, implying the consequent dissolution of perfectly honourable unions, had really made divorce easier and more common than before, and had become a grave scandal and the source of much immorality. Finally, with their profound reverence for the Scriptures of the OT, it was natural that the Reformers should urge that divorce could not in every case be morally wrong, since, if it were, it could never have been allowed by God under any circumstances. This last argument was put forward by John Milton with much power and eloquence in his *Doctrine and Discipline of Divorce* (1643). Probably no Christian writer has ever gone so far as Milton in advocating the utmost liberty for Christian men—he does not concede the liberty to women—in this matter. He is, indeed, willing to admit that 'what God has joined together man may not put asunder,' but he will by no means allow that a mere marriage contract or ceremony, though entered upon freely by mutual consent and duly consummated, must necessarily constitute such a joining together. Marriage is indissoluble only when there is complete and perfect unity of heart and soul between the partners. It may be safely said that the absurdities to which Milton's doctrines would lead if pushed to their logical conclusions are a sufficient refutation, nor does this work of his seem to have had much effect on English thought in his own or any succeeding age.

In most Roman Catholic countries civil legislation has conformed to the ecclesiastical ruling of the Council of Trent, and divorce has been forbidden. In Austria, however, it is permitted to those who are not members of the Roman Catholic Church. France is an exception. The *Code Napoléon* (1804–10) restricted the unlimited licence which had been permitted in the earlier years of the Revolution, but allowed divorce on various grounds, including 'mutual consent.' With the restoration of the monarchy (1816), the older law was again adopted and divorce was forbidden. It was not until 1884 that the provisions of the *Code Napoléon* were revived, with certain modifications, serious injuries or cruelty being admitted as sufficient cause, but divorce by mutual consent being forbidden.

In America the laws vary from one State to another. In S. Carolina and Maryland, originally Roman Catholic States, divorce is not permitted; in New York it is granted only on the ground of adultery; while in Maine and Dakota it may be granted on almost any pretext.

If the Report of the Commission appointed by Edward VI. (*Reformatio legum ecclesiasticarum*) had resulted in legislation, it is probable that the opinions of Cranmer, Bucer, and Peter Martyr in favour of divorce would have become part of the law both of the English Church and of the English State. With the king's death, however, the prospect of any alteration of the old law passed away. The Commission appointed to report on the case of the Marquis of Northampton, who, having obtained a separation under the ecclesiastical courts, desired to marry again, allowed the second marriage; but, as the marriage had already taken place while the Commission was sitting, its decision cannot be considered as absolutely unbiased. The Marquis, however, was advised to have his second marriage legalized by special Act of Parliament, and an Act to that effect was passed in 1548, but was repealed when Queen Mary came to the throne. This case is important, as it may be said to have ruled English practice until the passing of the Divorce Act of 1857. The canons of 1604 (can. 107) confirmed the authority of the ecclesiastical court to grant judicial separation, but only on condition that a definite pledge was given by the parties not to contract a second marriage. Divorce proper with privilege of re-marriage could be obtained only by special Act of Parliament. Between the time of the Reformation and the passing of the Divorce Act 317 cases had been dealt with by Act of Parliament in England and 146 in Scotland.

The Act of 1857 abolished the jurisdiction of the ecclesiastical courts in matrimonial cases, and established a civil court for the purpose. In England and Scotland divorce can now be obtained through the court without special legislation, but the law does not apply to Ireland, where an Act of Parliament is still necessary. In Scotland a wife may obtain a divorce on the ground of adultery alone, but in England cruelty or other serious offence on the husband's part must be proved in addition. In both countries a wife may be divorced on the ground of adultery alone.

In 1909 a Royal Commission was appointed to consider the whole question of the laws relating to divorce and separation. The Commission, after very careful investigations, extending over two years, published their report in Nov. 1912. No attempt has as yet been made, however—up to the middle of 1915—to give effect to their recommendations by way of legislation. On two points the commissioners were unanimous: if divorce is to be allowed, the method of procedure should be cheapened by the institution of special courts, so that the divorce should be made, not easy for any class, but as easy for the poor as for the rich; secondly, men and women should be placed on an equal footing, a wife being allowed to divorce her husband on the ground of adultery alone. The majority of the commissioners were in favour of extending the grounds on which divorce might be granted so as to cover cases of wilful desertion for at least three years, cruelty, incurable insanity after five years' confinement, and imprisonment under commuted death sentence; but a strong minority protested against this proposal, and claimed that divorce should be granted only in case of adultery.

The resolutions of the Lambeth Conference of 1888, in which this difficult practical question was fully discussed, may fairly be taken as representing the authoritative ruling of the Anglican Church as a whole at the present time.

'(1) Inasmuch as Our Lord's words expressly forbid divorce except in the case of fornication or adultery, the Christian Church cannot recognize divorce in any other than the excepted case, or give any sanction to the marriage of any person who has been divorced contrary to this law during the life of the other party.

(2) That in no case, during the lifetime of the innocent party in the case of a divorce for fornication or adultery, should the guilty party be regarded as a fit recipient of the blessing of the Church on marriage.

(3) That, recognizing the fact that there has always been a difference of opinion in the Church on the question whether Our Lord meant to forbid marriage to the innocent party in a divorce for adultery, the Conference recommends that the clergy should not be instructed to refuse the sacraments and other privileges of the Church to those who under civil sanction are thus married.' These resolutions were reaffirmed by the Conference of 1908, with an addition to the effect that 'when an innocent person has by means of a court of law divorced a spouse for adultery, and desires to enter into another contract of marriage, it is undesirable that such a contract should receive the blessing of the Church.'

The increase of wealth and luxury, and the growth of a spirit of self-indulgence so characteristic of the present age, together with the widely spread intellectual unrest, tend to encourage the demands for a wider extension of the facilities for divorce. Impatience of old-fashioned restraints and a certain loosening of old-established bonds are the natural characteristics of an age like ours. The deepened sense of the supreme importance of the spiritual union and companionship in marriage which Christianity has fostered makes the bond more irksome than ever where such union is supposed not to be ideal. Those who realize how much the stability and sanctity of home life depend on the unbroken firmness of the marriage-tie, and who recognize that the frequency of divorce must have a degrading effect upon individual character as well as on society in general, naturally regard with some anxiety the tendency in the present day to make divorce easier and more common. It is undoubtedly necessary for the Christian Church to make resolute protest against this tendency. It is, however, certain that the effects of nineteen centuries of Christian influence can never be wholly shaken off. We shall never again be able to regard divorce with the same easy indifference with which it was commonly regarded in the 1st cent. of our era. Christian influence will make itself felt on behalf of the Christian view of marriage, not in the modern world in the way of conciliar decrees and authoritative edicts, but by the weight of Christian public opinion guided by the principles of the NT.

(*b*) *Conditions of valid marriage.*—(1) *Equality of rank or condition* between the contracting parties, though required by Roman law, has never been regarded as essential in the Christian Church, however desirable in itself.

In Imperial times connexions were sometimes formed between slaves and free women, such connexions, though officially described as concubinage, being regarded as perfectly honourable and moral. It is not improbable that in the Christian Church, with the close relations of brotherhood prevailing between all classes and the excess of the number of free-born women over that of free-born men, such connexions would be by no means uncommon —the fact that they were socially recognized as creditable would, of course, have considerable weight. Some references which have come down to us seem to show that this was the case, and that such connexions were regarded by the Church as essentially marriages.

'Si quis habens uxorem fidelis concubinam habeat, non communicet. Caeterum qui non habet uxorem et pro uxore concubinam habet, a communione non repellatur tantum ut unius mulieris aut uxoris aut concubinae, ut ei placuerit, sit coniunctione contentus' (1st Council of Toledo [*c.* 400], can. 17). 'Christiano non dicam plurimas sed nec duas simul habere licitum est, nisi unam tantum aut uxorem aut certo loco uxoris si conjux deest concubinam' (Isidore, *ap.* Gratian, *Diss.* 4, quoted by Natalis Alexander, *Hist. Eccles.*, Lucca, 1734, i. 29).

(2) The question of *mixed marriages* between Christians and non-Christians was, as might have been expected, one of the earliest practical problems with which the Church was called upon to deal. It formed the subject of one of the queries proposed to St. Paul by his Corinthian converts. The Apostle's reply is clear enough so far as marriages contracted before conversion are concerned. A Christian ought to continue such a union so long as the unbelieving partner is willing that it should be so. The children born of such a marriage were holy, *i.e.* rightful subjects for Christian baptism. If the unbeliever decided to dissolve the union, 'the brother or the sister is not under bondage in such cases'—which must mean that the Christian would be at liberty to contract another marriage (see, for St. Paul's use of terms 'bondage' and 'freedom,' Ro $7^{1ff.}$). In 1 Co 7^{39} the Apostle declares that a Christian is at liberty to contract marriage 'only in the Lord.' The general principles laid down in this chapter have always been regarded as the primary authority on this matter, though there has been much controversy as to the practical application, and even as to the exact meaning, of his teaching. Do the words 'only in the Lord' mean that any marriage contracted between one already a Christian and an unbeliever is unlawful? Does 'in the Lord' mean only with a fellow-Christian, and, if so, must the words of St. Paul be taken as a positive command or merely as a counsel of prudence? On these questions St. Augustine expresses himself with some doubt and hesitation, but his opinion on the whole may be taken as expressing the general view of the Church in the preceding centuries. Mixed marriages with unbelievers were discouraged, and even declared, though with some hesitation, to be unlawful for Christians; yet such marriages could not be wholly prevented, nor was any penalty attached to them in the first three centuries, so far as appears. The Council of Elvira affords the earliest example of a specific penalty (five years' penance) being attached to such unions. From the beginning of the 6th cent. the decrees of councils are more numerous and more distinct, while the penalties are in general much more severe.

The civil law supported the ecclesiastical judgments, the Theodosian Code making such wedlock a capital offence. In the Middle Ages the question of the exact interpretation of the Apostle's permission to converts to separate from unbelievers was the subject of much controversy, the chief question being whether the separation should be the deliberate act of the unbeliever, or whether any circumstances making it impossible for the believer to remain 'sine contumelia creatoris' might not justify the separation. The question was decided, on the whole, in the broader sense, by Innocent III. (*de Divortiis*, 1198).

In early times marriage with heretics and schismatics was generally brought under the same condemnation as marriage with Jews or pagans. It is now, however, generally recognized both in the Eastern and in Roman Catholic communions that all marriages duly celebrated between baptized persons are valid and indissoluble, though in the case where one of the parties is a heretic or schismatic the other may be subjected to censure or penalty. Where the decrees of the Council of Trent have been published, however, this ruling does not free those contracting mixed marriages from considerable inconvenience, inasmuch as 'due celebration' is defined to be celebration in the presence of a priest in a Roman Catholic place of worship, the man being further obliged to guarantee that children born of the marriage shall be brought up in the Roman Catholic faith. Marriage otherwise celebrated is declared to be null and void. The publication of these decrees, for all practical purposes, in these countries by Pope Pius X. in the well known 'Ne temere' decree (1907) has given rise to much controversy. Roman Catholic divines defend the decrees on the ground that the Church has a right to make any regulations she pleases as to the conditions on which she shall recognize marriages, and that it is desirable to prevent mixed marriages as far as possible, and is, further, the duty of the Church to take care that the children of marriages blessed by her shall be brought up in the faith. Their opponents urge that it is inevitable that mixed marriages will sometimes occur in a large mixed community; that, when this is so, and a marriage is lawfully performed, the Church has no right to cast a slur on respectable persons who have, admittedly, been guilty of no immoral conduct; that to insist on a religious ceremony to which one party may object is to put undue pressure upon conscience, while to demand a pledge for the education in a particular way of children to be born is to override the law of the land and the natural rights of parents, and that such interference is unjustifiable.[1]

(3) *Kindred and affinity.*—It was a common complaint with the Reformers and those who sympathized with them that the multiplication of grounds of prohibition of marriage, the custom of papal dispensations in doubtful cases or cases of illegality, and the facility with which decrees of nullity of marriage could be obtained had created much uncertainty in the matter of marriage-relations and had been the source of grave scandals. This is forcibly expressed in the statute of Henry VIII. for the regulation of marriages (1533–34):

'Many persons, after long continuance together in matrimony without any allegation of either of the parties or any other at their marriage why the same matrimony should not be good, had been divorced contrary to God's law on the pretext of pre-contract or by reason of other prohibition than God's law permitteth. Marriages have been brought into such uncertainty thereby that no marriage could be so surely knit or bounden but it should lie in either of the parties' power to prove a pre-contract, a kindred and alliance, or a carnal knowledge to defeat the same.'

In the Roman Catholic Church three kinds of relationship are laid down as impediments to valid marriage, viz. blood-relationship or consanguinity, affinity or connexion by marriage, and spiritual affinity, as, *e.g.*, the connexion between godparent and godchild, or between two persons who are god-parents to the same child. In the Eastern Church the system is even more elaborate, and the grounds of prohibition more numerous than in the Western, while at the same time the custom of dispensation commonly practised in the West since the 8th cent. is unknown in the Eastern Church. In the East two brothers are not allowed to marry two sisters, and, in general, marriage between the members of two families debars the members of either from marriage with members of the other within the prescribed limits.

A different method of describing relationships prevails in the two branches of the Church. In the East uncle and nephew are related in the third degree, first cousins in the fourth, and so on; marriage is forbidden within the seventh degree of kindred or affinity, natural or spiritual. In the West first cousins are related in the second degree, second cousins in the fourth, and so on, marriage being forbidden—since the Lateran Council (1215)—within the fourth degree. This is in practice almost the same as the Eastern rule. The Lateran Council, however, abolished all prohibitions on the score of affinity within the second degree according to the Western reckoning. No trace of these somewhat burdensome restrictions is to be found before the 5th century. In the earlier centuries Christians would be familiar both with the Levitical Law of Holiness (=Lv 18) and with the ordinary Roman law, which were, to all intents and purposes, to the same effect—marriage being forbidden within the second degree according to the Western reckoning. It goes without saying that their marriages would be regulated according to the provisions of those codes.

The only question in connexion with this subject of prohibited degrees which excites interest or gives occasion to serious controversy at the present time is the much-vexed question of marriage with a deceased wife's sister. Such marriages have long been legal and customary in America, in the British colonies, and in several European countries. In England they were not unknown prior to 1835, though condemned by the canon law of the English Church. Such marriages were held by the civil courts to be perfectly valid and unimpeachable in law, unless voided by special legal process undertaken during the lifetime of the parties; but Lord Lyndhurst's Act in 1835 declared all such marriages within the prohibited degrees absolutely illegal. After many futile attempts, and in face of very strong opposition, an Act legalizing marriage with a deceased wife's sister in the United Kingdom was passed in 1908. A saving clause permits clergymen who have a conscientious objection to refuse to celebrate such marriages, but in the case of Bannister *v.* Thompson, in which proceedings were taken against a clergyman for refusing the Holy Communion to persons so married, it was decided that the clergy may not refuse the sacraments to persons legally married though within the prohibited degrees. Meanwhile the table of affinities in the Anglican Prayer-Book remains the law of the Church, and, in strictness, it would seem that the clergy are prohibited from celebrating a marriage between a widower and his deceased wife's sister, even if they do not feel themselves bound by the famous canons of 1604 to hold that such marriages are 'incestuous and unlawful and altogether null and void' (can. 99). The logical course might seem to be to revise the table of kindred and affinity, but to this a very influential body in the Anglican Church is strongly opposed. Those who object to these marriages do not now, as a general rule, claim that they are expressly prohibited in Lv 18, though attempts more or less ingenious have been made to prove that they are. It is held, however, that the general principle that near affinity is a bar to marriage is laid down in the Law of Holiness, that a greater number of cases of affinity than of consanguinity are cited in Lv 18, and that the case of the deceased wife's sister is so exactly parallel to that of marriage with a husband's brother that the same principle may be held to stand good. Further, it is said that the reference to the sin of the Canaanites (Lv 18^{27}) shows that the prohibitions are regarded as matters of universal moral obligation and not national enactments applicable only to the Israelites. Again, it is maintained that the healthy moral sentiment which makes us regard with loathing and repulsion such unions as those between brother and sister and uncle and niece should also prevail between those who are brought into such close relations of affection as brothers and sisters by marriage. The same sentiment ought to prevail, and anything which may tend to destroy it must be regarded as morally injurious and degrading. Those who hold the sacramental view of a mystic spiritual bond formed in marriage urge that this bond creates as close a relationship between a man and the members of his wife's family as exists between blood-relations. Finally, it is pointed out that marriage with a deceased wife's sister has been expressly forbidden by the Church, at all events since the 4th century. It is most inadvisable, therefore, it is said, to tamper with so long established a custom or, indeed, with any well-established custom in connexion with so delicate a subject as the marriage-relation. Such are the main arguments by which marriage with a deceased wife's sister may be opposed. It is now worth while to consider the arguments which have been brought forward on the other side.

It is very doubtful, it is urged, whether the Levitical law relating to a different state of civilization and specially intended for the people of Israel can be regarded as a moral law binding on Christians; but, even if it be accepted as such, not only is there no express prohibition of marriage with a deceased wife's sister, but, on the contrary, it is implied that such marriage is perfectly lawful (v.[18]). The Jews have never regarded such

[1] On the subject of mixed marriage in general see Decrees of Councils: Illiberis (305), Arles (314), Laodicea (*c.* 341), Agde (506), Orleans (533). See also *Cod. Theod.* iii., xvi.; *Decretum of Gratian*, c. 1–17, C. xxviii. q. 1 (A.D. 1139–42); Innocent III., *de Variis questionibus*, c. 1200; Augustine, *de Fide et operibus*, xix.

unions as forbidden, nor were they forbidden by the ancient Roman law. The very fact that an apostolic canon (date probably late in the 3rd cent.) forbids such marriages *to the clergy* shows that they were not generally regarded at that time as unlawful *per se*.

No injury has resulted, it is held, either to married life or to the general tone of social morality from the permission of such marriages in America and in the British colonies. It is evident from experience that such marriages are in very many cases desired, and in large centres of population among the poorer classes it is absolutely necessary as a safeguard to morality that they should be permitted. It is denied that any feeling of repulsion similar to that inspired by incestuous connexions exists, or ought to exist, in the case of one's wife's near relations. Affinity ought, in certain cases, to be a bar to marriage, but the true ground of prohibition in this case is what is known as *respectus parentelæ*. The marriage of a man with his step-daughter or with his nephew's widow is shocking to the moral sense because of the more or less paternal relationship involved in the connexion. According to old Eastern ideas, this relationship would also prevail between a woman and her deceased husband's brother, now become the head of the house. That marriage with a deceased husband's brother was not regarded with moral repulsion, in itself, is shown by the fact that it was commanded in the case of a man dying without children. There is no reason, therefore, for thinking that any other principle than that of the *respectus parentelæ* governs the prohibitions of marriage within certain degrees of affinity in Leviticus, while, in the evident total absence of any sense of repulsion against such unions among the majority of modern civilized people, no reason can be given why they should be forbidden. It is further urged that, even if the sacramental theory of marriage be accepted, since the mystic bond is dissolved by death, it may be fairly held that the connexions formed are no longer binding. That a great distinction is made between marriage with a deceased wife's sister and marriage with those closely connected by blood is evident from the fact that the Roman Church freely and frequently grants dispensations for the former, notwithstanding her high sacramental belief.

Some Anglicans, while not prepared to condemn marriage with a deceased wife's sister as absolutely wrong or immoral, yet consider it so undesirable that at least it should not receive the blessing of the Church by a marriage ceremony. Such an attitude has in most periods been taken up with regard to objectionable, but not absolutely forbidden, marriages. As pointed out above, it is the position taken by the Lambeth Conference with reference to the re-marriage of the innocent partner in a divorce case. It has, however, been said that such an attitude is not logical, and is at the same time unjust to Christian people. The majority of Christians have come to regard the nuptial benediction as almost, if not altogether, an essential of marriage and the right of every Christian. If members of the Church are committing no moral offence, they may reasonably claim the blessing of the Church upon their union; if they are entitled to receive the sacraments, it is held that it is unjust to cast such a slur upon them as is implied in a refusal to hallow their union.

5. Conclusion.—Poets and story-tellers have made the love and courtship which lead up to marriage a matter of such all-absorbing interest that married life itself may well seem, by comparison, to be utterly dull, prosaic, and uninteresting. At the same time, divines and canonists have generally directed attention to the sterner aspect of the matter, dwelling exclusively on restraints and prohibitions, and scanning with watchful suspicion every form of natural indulgence. Nevertheless, the Scriptural ideal of marriage has maintained its hold in the Christian world and has been a mighty influence for the sanctification of family life and the development of character.

From one point of view, marriage is a restraint—a healthy restriction imposed on unbridled licence and excessive indulgence; it brings with it duties and responsibilities which must tax our powers and energies to the utmost and call for the continued exercise of patience and self-denial. It is well that, in a matter of so much importance, so intimately connected with our social and moral welfare, the restraints and responsibilities should be clearly defined and earnestly enforced. But there is another point of view which is, after all, the higher and truer. In this, perhaps more clearly than in any other connexion, we are taught by the gospel that restraints are imposed and self-denial demanded, not for their own sakes, but as a means to truer and more abiding blessedness. Holy matrimony has been divinely instituted for man's good, and to be a source of blessing. In happy married life man is to find his truest and most lasting happiness, and to reach the fullest perfection of which his nature is capable.

LITERATURE.—Tertullian, *de Monogamia*, *de Virginibus velandis*, *ad Uxorem*, *de Pudicitia*, etc.; Augustine, *de Conjugiis adulterinis*, *de Fide et Operibus*, *Retractationes*. For conciliar decisions, early and mediæval, consult C. J. Hefele, *Conciliengeschichte*[2], Freiburg, 1873–90; for papal decrees see H. J. D. Denzinger, *Enchiridion*[11], Würzburg, 1911; for canon law, A. Friedberg and A. L. Richter, *Corpus juris canonici*, Leipzig, 1876–80; G. van Mastricht, *Historia juris ecclesiastici*, Halle, 1719; J. Johnson, *Collection of the Laws and Canons of the Church of England*, new ed., Oxford, 1850–51; Z. B. van Espen, *Jus ecclesiasticum universum*, Cologne, 1777; for general treatment of the subject, J. Bingham, *Antiquities of the Christian Church*, London, 1840, bks. 4, 5, 6, 22; H. Hammond, *On Divorces*, do. 1674; J. Cosin, *Works*, Oxford, 1843–55, iv.; H. C. Lea, *History of Sacerdotal Celibacy*[3], London, 1907; H. D. Evans, *Christian Doctrine of Marriage*, New York, 1870; T. D. Woolsey, *Divorce Legislation in the United States*, do. 1882; O. D. Watkins, *Holy Matrimony*, London, 1895; J. Milton, *The Doctrine and Discipline of Divorce*, published in convenient form with his other prose works, do. 1898; the works of E. Glasson (*Le Mariage civil et le divorce dans l'antiquité et dans les principales législations modernes de l'Europe*[2], Paris, 1880), G. Perrone (*De matrimonio christiano*, Lyons, 1840), and other Roman Catholic writers can be consulted in convenient form in J. P. Migne's *Theologiæ Cursus Completus* (Paris, 1840–45); artt. 'Marriage,' 'Divorce,' 'Sermon on the Mount,' etc., in *DCA*, *PRE*[3], etc.; in W. E. H. Lecky, *Hist. of European Morals*[9], London, 1890, and *Democracy and Liberty*, do. 1899, ii., the whole subject is discussed and much interesting information given, with reference to both the modern and the mediæval periods.

W. M. FOLEY.

MARRIAGE (Egyptian).—Amid the abundance of documents from ancient Egypt there is singularly little to enlighten us on this subject. No representation of the ceremonial or festivities of marriage has been recognized among tomb or temple scenes; the scenes of the divine marriage of Ammon with the queen mother at Luxor and Deir el-Bahri can hardly be quoted for illustrating the human rite. Written contracts of marriage are first found in the XXVIth dyn. (*c.* 600 B.C.), and first became common in the Ptolemaic period; and, notwithstanding the multitudes of relatives recorded in tombs and on stelæ, it is difficult to ascertain what degrees of consanguinity and how many wives were permitted or usual.

To secure hereditary rights in a community with matriarchal tendencies and where women held property, close endogamy might often be convenient. This would especially be the case with the Pharaohs, who claimed the distinction of divine descent, and to them would be permitted acts which could hardly be allowed to their subjects. A genealogical statement regarding the prince Nefermaat at the end of the IIIrd dyn., literally interpreted, would seem to show that he was the offspring of the union of King Seneferu with his eldest daughter (K. Sethe, in *ZÄ* l. [1912] 57), but a more probable interpretation of the same genealogy is given in Erman's *Aegypten*, p. 227, and by H. Sottas, in *REg* xiv. [1914] 150, making him grandson of Seneferu and son of his eldest daughter. There is plenty of evidence that later Pharaohs married their sisters or half-sisters (cf. Erman, p. 221); a case of a less exalted person doing so in the XXIInd dyn. (9th cent. B.C.) is noted by J. H. Breasted (*Ancient Records of Egypt*, Chicago, 1906–07, iv. 388). In the XXIst dyn. two marriages of uncle and niece in one family are pointed out by A. H. Gardiner (*ZÄ* xlviii. [1910] 50). The Ptolemys followed the precedent of the Pharaohs. In the Roman age marriage of half-sisters and full sisters occurred commonly in the families of cultivators of the soil and artizans (K. Wessely, *Karanis und Soknopaiu Nesos*, Vienna, 1902, p. 23; J. Nietzold, *Die Ehe in Aegypten zur ptolemäisch-römischen Zeit*, Leipzig, 1903, p. 12; the evidence there quoted comes from the Greek papyri of the Fayyum or Arsinoite nome, but A. S. Hunt assures the present writer that there is similar evidence also from Oxyrhynchus). The divine example of Osiris and Isis may have had special force at that period. In the First Story of Sethon Khamwêse (Ptolemaic period), the ancient Pharaoh's argument about his son Neferkeptah and his daughter Ahure seems to be that it would be impolitic, when there were only two children in the royal family, to risk the succession by marrying them together. His preference, following a family custom, would be to marry them to a son and a daughter of two of his generals in order to enlarge his family. At a banquet he questioned Ahure, and was won over by her wishes to the other plan; thereupon he commanded his chief steward to take the princess to her brother's house that same night with all necessary things; Pharaoh's whole household gave her presents, and Neferkeptah made a 'good day' and entertained them all on the marriage eve. This is the only account that we possess of an Egyptian betrothal or marriage that is not of the fairy-tale order, and it is noticeable that there is no mention in it of the writing of a contract, perhaps because this marriage was an affair within the family.

Marriage was no doubt entered on soon after puberty and the circumcision of the male, though evidence here is lacking. Müller (*Liebespoesie*, p. 3, note 5) quotes an instance at the end of the Ptolemaic period of the wife of a priest being married at twelve and a half years of age. Some of the ancient Egyptian stories offer examples of love-matches, but parents or guardians would naturally have had the first word in the disposal of young people.

Although several wives may be recorded on a man's tomb, there are few clear cases of more than one living at the same time except in the large *harīms* of royal wives and concubines (cf. Erman, p. 219). For all these questions see CIRCUMCISION (Egyptian), FAMILY (Egyptian), CONCUBINAGE, vol. iii. p. 811, CHILDREN (Egyptian); also ADULTERY (Egyptian), ETHICS AND MORALITY (Egyptian), vol. v. p. 481 f., § 9 f. Divorce is provided for in the late contracts mentioned above, sometimes on behalf of the man, sometimes of the woman, and writings of divorce are known (see LAW [Egyptian]). Of the treatment of widows nothing is known beyond that their defenceless state made them objects of help and pity to the just and charitable.

LITERATURE.—A. Erman, *Aegypten und ägyp. Leben*, Tübingen, 1885, p. 216 ff.; W. M. Müller, *Liebespoesie der alten Aegypter*, Leipzig, 1899, Introduction.

F. LL. GRIFFITH.

MARRIAGE (Greek).

1. General. — The Greeks, as a rule, seem to have entered upon marriage from religious or prudential motives rather than on sentimental grounds. The generation of children[1] was, in fact, the recognized main end of marriage, with which went also the desire to obtain a capable housekeeper.[2] This utilitarian motive lies at the root of that long conversation of Socrates and Ischomachos on household management which, as reported by Xenophon, is our most illuminating evidence on Greek married life in the 5th and 4th centuries B.C. (see esp. *Œc.* vii. 19 f.). The purely physical significance of marriage in relation to the State itself found, doubtless, its strongest and most logical recognition in Sparta, where wives were taken simply ἐπὶ τὸ τῆς τεκνώσεως ἔργον (Plut. *Comp. Lyc. cum Numa*, iv. 77), and their interchange for this object was both permitted and encouraged.[3] Yet even in Athens, as a result of the development of city life, in which women could not take any direct part (cf. the oft-quoted words ascribed to Pericles [Thuc. ii. 45]), marriage lost the delicate and romantic bloom which belongs to it in the Homeric poems.[4] Indeed the average Athenian woman must have been too ignorant to have been a helpmeet for her husband, intellectually or spiritually, at least in any but the lowest class of society. It would, however, be a mistake to regard the exaggerations of the comic poets, or the *chroniques scandaleuses* of the orators, as complete and faithful reflexions of the ideals and facts of the social life of their time. Nor, again, is it possible to deduce the precise degree of affection, respect, or influence actually enjoyed within the precincts of the home by the Athenian wife, from the regulations of the legal system of which she appears to be the passive victim. That the position of women and the conditions of married life in historical Greece exhibit a considerable variation, apparently for the worse, from the state of things depicted in the Epic is undeniable, however it may be explained; but it is an error to contrast the idealizations of Homer with the crudities of Attic law. The actual content of life, then as now, was just what the man and wife chose to make it.

Monogamy was the Hellenic rule, as among the Egyptians (Herod. ii. 92). Examples to the contrary, however, are not lacking; *e.g.*, in Sparta King Anaxandrides kept a double establishment (Herod. v. 40).[5] It is doubtless true enough that no definite law of Athens nor reference to any law asserting the principle can be adduced, and, on the other hand, that cases of bigamy occurred in Athens as elsewhere; but neither of these facts justifies the statement that Attic law simply took no account of polygamy one way or another.[6]

[1] ἐπὶ παίδων γνησίων σπόρῳ, or ἀρότῳ, betrothal formula given in Clem. Alex. *Strom.* ii. 23; cf. Menander, *Perik.* 435: ταύτην γνησίων παίδων ἐπ' ἀρότῳ σοι δίδωμι.

[2] Cf. the naive confession in Dem. lix. 122: τὰς μὲν γὰρ ἑταίρας ἡδονῆς ἕνεκ' ἔχομεν, τὰς δὲ παλλακὰς τῆς καθ' ἡμέραν θεραπείας τοῦ σώματος, τὰς δὲ γυναῖκας τοῦ παιδοποιεῖσθαι γνησίως καὶ τῶν ἔνδον φύλακα πίστην ἔχειν. See also Aristotle, *Eth. Nic.* viii. 12. 7: οἱ δ' ἄνθρωποι οὐ μόνον τῆς τεκνοποιίας χάριν συνοικοῦσιν, ἀλλὰ καὶ τῶν εἰς τὸν βίον.

[3] Xen. *Rep. Lac.* i. 8: εἰ δέ τις αὖ γυναικὶ μὲν συνοικεῖν μὴ βούλοιτο, τέκνων δὲ ἀξιολόγων ἐπιθυμοίη, καὶ τούτῳ νόμον ἐποίησεν, ἥντινα εὔτεκνον καὶ γενναίαν ὁρῴη, πείσαντα τὸν ἔχοντα, ἐκ ταύτης τεκνοποιεῖσθαι.

[4] Cf. the description of a perfect marriage, put into the mouth of Odysseus, in *Od.* vi. 182–185.

[5] In Herod. vi. 61, 'Αρίστωνι βασιλεύοντι ἐν Σπάρτῃ καὶ γήμαντι γυναῖκας δύο παῖδες οὐκ ἐγίνοντο, the brevity of the expression leaves it uncertain whether Ariston had two wives at once. In vi. 63 he divorces the second, to marry a third—from which, perhaps, he may be allowed the benefit of the doubt (cf. E. Meyer, *Gesch. des Alterthums*, Stuttgart, 1884–1901, ii. § 59 A). But the feature of Sparta was rather practical polyandry (Polyb. xii. 6).

[6] Cf. Hruza, *Polygamie und Pellikat*, p. 31: 'Das attische

That concubinage existed at Athens to a considerable extent cannot be doubted, owing to the influx of free women and their men-folk from the rest of Greece. Lysias mentions a law which authorizes an injured husband to slay with impunity an adulterer caught *flagrante delicto*, whether it be with his wife or with his concubine, though the latter are 'less valuable' than wives (Lys. i. 31 : καὶ ἐπὶ ταῖς παλλακαῖς ταῖς ἐλάττονος ἀξίαις τὴν αὐτὴν δίκην ἐπέθηκε). So also in a law of Drakon quoted by Dem. xxiii. 53 : ἢ ἐπὶ παλλακῇ ἣν ἂν ἐπ' ἐλευθέροις παισὶν ἔχῃ. These passages must cover free foreign women, from which class, as well as from that of slaves and freedwomen, the majority of παλλακαί at Athens doubtless came. It is clear, however, from Is. iii. 39, ἐπεὶ καὶ οἱ ἐπὶ παλλακίᾳ διδόντες τὰς ἑαυτῶν πάντες πρότερον διομολογοῦνται περὶ τῶν δοθησομένων ταῖς παλλακαῖς, and from other passages that native Athenian women (πολίτιδες, ἀσταί) also sometimes became ἑταῖραι and παλλακαί. No special laws touching the case of these and giving them privileges over foreign women living ἐν παλλακίᾳ with Athenian citizens can be produced. Hence the hypothesis[1] of the existence at Athens of a status of 'legitimate concubinage,' in which an Athenian citizen, already lawfully married, contracted another union with another Athenian woman, who was, like the wife, formally betrothed (ἐγγυητή) by her κύριος, her children being therefore legitimate, but who nevertheless was not a wife, falls to the ground, as being simply the assertion of legalized bigamy.

Here also should be mentioned Müller's theory[2]—that after the failure of the Sicilian expedition, probably in 411 B.C., changes were introduced into the Athenian marriage law with a view to increasing the number of citizens. His theory is that another form of union (*Nebenehe*) was set up by the side of regular marriage. Marriage in the proper sense could be contracted only with an Athenian woman, but the new legislation permitted a man to take, in addition to his Athenian wife, a partner who was neither γυνή nor παλλακή—a secondary wife, who had, in fact, no specific title. This *Nebenfrau*, or secondary wife, might be either an Athenian or a foreign woman; her children were citizens, but νόθοι, not being admitted to their father's φρατρία. If the father left no children by his real wife, theee νόθοι had full rights of inheritance, but had a claim only to νόθεια, a prescribed fraction of his estate, if he left legitimate issue by the real wife. This institution was abolished on the restoration of the democracy in 403 B.C.

2. Permissible marriages.—It was illegal for an Athenian citizen to marry a foreigner, the alien wife or husband being liable to be sold into slavery (law in Dem. lix. 16, dating perhaps only from the time of Pericles, 451 B.C. [cf. Plut. *Per.* 37], and revived in 403 B.C.). Such marriage, however, was legal if Athenian citizenship had been bestowed on the individual, or if he or she belonged to a community to which the Athenian assembly had granted rights of intermarriage (ἐπιγαμία); but, in spite of the law and its penalties, Athenians not infrequently did contract such marriages and smuggle their issue into their φρατρία. Legally, the issue of such marriages were illegitimate (νόθοι), like the issue of ἀνέγγυοι.[3]

Forbidden degrees were few, the practical working of the laws of inheritance and adoption (*qq.v.*) being to encourage marriage between near relatives, and even to enforce it. Marriage of cousins was common (cf. Dem. xliii. 74); union of uncle and niece was possible (cf. Lys. xxxii. 4; Is. iii. 74),[4] and even of aunt and nephew (case of Demosthenes, father of the orator, betrothing on his death-bed his prospective widow to his nephew [Dem. xxvii. 5]). A man might marry his half-sister by the same father, but seemingly not by the same mother.[5] There were, it seems, no other prohibited degrees of affinity, except between individuals in the direct line of descent or ascent (cf. Plat. *Laws*, 838); there is, however, some indication that law and public opinion were not in accord in this matter (Aristoph. *Frogs*, 1081).

It follows from the above that even considerable disparity of age cannot have been generally regarded as an obstacle to marriage. The elder Demosthenes arranged that his five-year-old daughter should marry his nephew ὅταν ἡλικίαν ἔχῃ, explained as signifying in ten years' time (Dem. xxvii. 5). The wife of Ischomachos was not fifteen years old at the time of her marriage (Xen. *Œc.* vii. 5). The relatively early age at which girls became nubile in the climate of Greece is to be remembered.[1] The Gortynian Code pronounces a girl nubile at twelve years of age; in Athens the lower limit was perhaps fourteen.[2] The husband must at least have passed his δοκιμασία, *i.e.*, he must be turned eighteen. It seems to have been the rule that the husband should be a good deal senior to the wife; and this was approved by the philosophers.[3] Inequality of social position was felt to be a more serious obstacle to marriage than mere disparity in age; but neither this sentiment itself nor the consequences of its violation are specially Athenian (cf. Aristoph. *Clouds*, 41 f.; Æsch. *Prom. Vinct.* 890: τὸ κηδεῦσαι καθ' ἑαυτὸν ἀριστεύει μακρῷ). The point lay in the fact that, in historical times, a wife brought a dowry with her, which sometimes had the effect of making her the dominant partner in the household.

3. Choice of wife.—In the selection of a partner neither bridegroom nor bride had much voice; the respective parents arranged the match—often with the aid of a match-maker (προμνήστρια). Moreover, the Athenian bridegroom had little opportunity of making his bride's acquaintance, or even of seeing her, before marriage, unless she was a near relative, owing to the strict conventions under which Athenian women in general lived—more strict, apparently, than those which obtained in the rest of Greece[4] (see art. FAMILY [Greek]).

4. Betrothal.—By Attic law betrothal (ἐγγύησις)[5] was the indispensable condition of valid marriage, except in the case of an 'heiress' (ἐπίκληρος), who was, of course, claimed before the Archon by the next-of-kin (cf. Is. vi. 14: ἢ ἐγγυηθεῖσαν κατὰ τὸν νόμον ἢ ἐπιδικασθεῖσαν; see art. INHERITANCE [Greek]). Failing the formal ceremony of ἐγγύησις, illegitimacy attached to the issue of the marriage. It was simply a contract made between the suitor (or his father or guardian) and the person who as κύριος had legal authority over the woman, viz. her father, full brother, paternal grandfather, or

Recht hat die Polygamie gewiss nicht ausdrücklich verboten, aber wahrscheinlich auch nicht geradezu erlaubt. Das Gesetz enthielt keine Bestimmung, und damit war der Willkür der Bürger freier Raum gegeben.' The law of Charondas of Thurii, inflicting loss of political rights on a man who gave his children a stepmother (Diod. xii. 12, 14), clearly implies universal monogamy (cf. Hruza, p. 56).

[1] See Buermann, 'Drei Studien,' etc. (=*Jahrbücher für cl. Philol.*, 1877–78, Supplementband ix. pp. 578 f., 638 f.); cf. R. Zimmermann, *De nothorum Athenis condicione*, Berlin, 1886.

[2] O. Müller, 'Untersuchungen,' etc. (=*Jahrbücher für cl. Philol.*, 1899, Supplementband xxv. p. 667 f.); cf. Wyse, *The Speeches of Isæus*, p. 280.

[3] Pollux, iii. 21: γνήσιὸς μὲν ὁ ἐκ γυναικὸς ἀστῆς καὶ γαμετῆς . . . νόθος δ' ὁ ἐκ ξένης ἢ παλλακίδος.

[4] At Sparta King Anaxandrides had his niece to wife (Herod. v. 39).

[5] Cf. Dem. lvii. 20: ἀδελφὴν γὰρ ὁ πάππος οὑμὸς ἔγημεν οὐχ ὁμομητρίαν, Paus. I. vii. 1: ὁ Πτολεμαῖος Ἀρσινόης ἀδελφῆς ἀμφοτέρωθεν ἐρασθεὶς ἔγημεν αὐτήν, Μακεδόσιν οὐδαμῶς ποιῶν νομιζόμενα, Αἰγυπτίοις μέντοι ὧν ἦρχεν, Plut. *Them.* 32: Μνησιπτολέμαν ἐκ τῆς ἐπιγαμηθείσης γενομένην Ἀρχέπτολις ὁ ἀδελφός, οὐκ ὢν ὁμομήτριος, ἔγημεν. Marriage of full brothers and sisters was, however, not outside the range of Greek ideas; cf. *Od.* x. 5 f. (sons and daughters of Aiolos)—on which a schol. remarks: ἀρχαῖον ἔθος τὸ συνοικίζειν ἀδελφούς. καὶ ὁ Ζεὺς ἀδελφῇ οὔσῃ συνοικεῖ τῇ Ἥρᾳ. Cf. also Paus. IV. ii. 3. According to Phil. Jud. *de Spec. Leg.* ii. 779, the Spartan law just reversed the Athenian. See Plat. *Rep.* v. 461 B, and H. Richards, in *ClR* iv. [1890] 6; Hruza, *Polygamie und Pellikat*, p. 159 f.

[1] Soranus, παθ. γυν. iv. 20: τὸ δὲ ἔμμηνον ἐπιφαίνεται τὸ πρῶτον περὶ τὸ τεσσαρεσδέκατον ἔτος κατὰ τὸ πλεῖστον ὅτε καὶ τὸ ἡβᾶν καὶ τὸ διογκοῦσθαι τοὺς μαστούς.

[2] Deduced from F. Blass's restoration of Aristotle, *Ath. Pol.* lvi. 7: μισθοῖ δὲ καὶ τοὺς οἴκους τῶν ὀρφανῶν καὶ τῶν ἐπικλ[ήρων, ἕως ἄν τις τετταρ]ακαιδεκέτις γένηται. For the early age at which girls were married at Troezen, see Arist. *Pol.* 1335*a*, with W. L. Newman's note (*The Politics of Aristotle*, iii. [Oxford, 1902] 464).

[3] Cf. Ar. *Pol.* 1335*a*: διὸ τὰς μὲν ἁρμόττει περὶ τὴν τῶν ὀκτωκαίδεκα ἐτῶν ἡλικίαν συζευγνύναι, τοὺς δ' ἑπτὰ καὶ τριάκοντα· ἐν τοσούτῳ γὰρ ἀκμάζουσί τε τοῖς σώμασι σύζευξις ἔσται, καὶ πρὸς τὴν παῦλαν τῆς τεκνοποιίας συγκαταβήσεται τοῖς χρόνοις εὐκαίρως. Sometimes, however, the husband was very young (cf. Dem. xl. 4: συνέβη γάρ μοι δεηθέντος τοῦ πατρὸς ὀκτωκαιδεκέτη γῆμαι). Hesiod (*Works and Days*, 695 f.) recommends a man to marry at about 30, the woman at 18 or 19. Plato, *Rep.* v. 460 E, says: ἆρ' οὖν σοι ξυνδοκεῖ μέτριος χρόνος ἀκμῆς τὰ εἴκοσιν ἔτη γυναικί, ἀνδρὶ δὲ τὰ τριάκοντα; cf. Solon, fr. 14.

[4] Hence the curious expression in Xen. *Œc.* vii. 10: ἐπεὶ ἤδη μοι χειροήθης ἦν καὶ ἐτετιθάσευτο, 'after she was accustomed to my hand, that is, was tamed,' used by Ischomachos of his girl-wife.

[5] The form ἐγγύησις is used by Isæus only in iii. 53: τὴν μαρτυρίαν περὶ τῆς ἐγγυήσεως τῆς γυναικός. Elsewhere he uses the form ἐγγύη (and so Dem. xlvi. 18; Plat. *Laws*, 774 E; Hyper. iii. (v.) 16). But modern writers have in general agreed to use the form ἐγγύησις in reference to betrothal, and so restrict the form ἐγγύη to signify 'pledge' or 'surety,' which is, in fact, its ordinary significance. The verb ἐγγυᾶν is used of the κύριος of the woman, ἐγγυᾶσθαι (mid.) of the suitor, and ἐγγυᾶσθαι (pass.) of the woman; but the last use is not common, its place being taken by periphrases with the noun ἐγγύη or the adj. ἐγγυητή (Wyse, on Isæus, iii. 4).

legally constituted guardian.[1] It was essentially a family ceremony (although regulated by law)[2] at which, besides the principals, relatives and other witnesses were present, in numbers corresponding to the social distinction of the parties (cf. Is. iii. 18: *ὁ μὲν γὰρ ἐγγυᾶν μέλλων εἰς τὸν τριτάλαντον οἶκον, ὥς φησι, τὴν ἀδελφήν, διαπραττόμενος τηλικαῦτα ἕνα μάρτυρα παρεῖναι αὐτῷ προσεποιήσατο*). Nothing, however, is said in any passage as to the presence of the woman, which certainly was not legally necessary, any more than her consent to the match; in point of law she was simply the object of a purely business arrangement or barter between her *κύριος* and the suitor. Of the formalities necessary or usual we know nothing. Herodotus, in his account of the wooing of Agariste of Sicyon, seems to preserve in part the verbal formula of the Athenian marriage-contract in the 5th cent. B.C.[3] It is strange that there is no allusion to any written record of the contract, at any rate at Athens, where, indeed, there was much laxity in this regard; but it is hard to believe that the proceedings were purely oral—more especially as it was at the *ἐγγύησις* that the dowry agreed upon was actually paid, or agreements entered into as to its future payment.[4]

It should be clear from the above that the use of the term 'betrothal' as a rendering of the Greek term *ἐγγύησις* (*ἐγγύη*) is simply by way of analogy and in default of a more appropriate word. For the essentials of a modern betrothal, namely (1) free consent of the woman, and (2) that the act takes place between the two individuals who so declare their will and intention, without any necessary intervention of third parties, are entirely lacking in the Athenian ceremony. The origin of the latter lies in the primitive marriage by purchase, and Athenian law did as a matter of fact select this primitive element, namely, the formal validity of the compact preparatory to the surrender (*ἔκδοσις*) of the woman, rather than the formalities of the consequent nuptials, as decisive in regard to the all-important question as to the legitimacy of the offspring. It does not appear that the wedding ceremonies and home-bringing of the bride had actually any legal significance, except as the natural and public consequences of the formal private contract; and, just because these were the natural and normally inevitable consequences, Athenian jury-courts, so far as our knowledge goes, were never called upon to decide at what precise moment the status of marriage became actual, or what was the precise juristic significance of the *γάμος* in which the suitor asserted the rights bestowed upon him by virtue of the marriage contract (*ἐγγύησις*).[5]

The question, therefore, which has been debated,[6] as to whether *ἐγγύησις* was an act of betrothal or affiancing preceding marriage, or was not rather the beginning of the married state itself—the first and most important of the ceremonies of the wedding-day, and actually constitutive of marriage *per se*—seems to receive its solution through purely historical considerations. Primarily and originally, the ceremony of *ἐγγύησις* was a literal putting of the woman by her *κύριος* into the hands of the suitor for price paid, the interval between the striking of the bargain and exercise of conjugal rights (*γάμος*) being filled by the leading home of the newly-purchased bride. This home-leading, being that part of the entire transaction which was of a striking and necessarily public character, came to possess ever increasing social significance, while at the same time it was the moment at which religion intervened to invest the ceremonies with its own special solemnities, whether of a prophylactic or of a prognostic sort. The whole mass of ceremonial, of infinite variety, and of very various degrees of consciously realized import, which constitutes the actual procedure of marriage, in its social and non-juristic sense, interesting and important as it is for the student of anthropology, can be given here only in barest outline.

5. Wedding ceremonies.—The Greek *γάμος* was essentially a religious ceremony (*τέλος*),[1] covering the deportation of the bride from her parents' house into that of her husband. The month Γαμηλιών (Jan.–Feb.) was generally selected, and Greek custom seems to have prescribed in general the winter season as proper for marriage; and the speculations of the philosophers were in accord (cf. Arist. *Pol.* iv. (vii.) 14=1335*a*: *τοῖς δὲ περὶ τὴν ὥραν χρόνοις ὡς οἱ πολλοὶ χρῶνται καλῶς καὶ νῦν, ὁρίσαντες χειμῶνος τὴν συναυλίαν ποιεῖσθαι ταύτην*). The bride dedicated to various deities (*θεοὶ γαμήλιοι*) her girlish toys and other gifts, and more especially her maiden tresses, now shorn (Pollux, iii. 38, says that before marriage girls offered their hair to Hera, Artemis, and the Fates; cf. Hesych. *s.v.* *γάμων ἔθη*).[2] The most important pre-nuptial ceremony was that of the bath (*λουτρὸν νυμφικόν*);[3] at Athens the water must be fetched from the Kallirrhoe (Thuc. ii. 15), tall water-jars of peculiar shape (*λουτροφόροι*) being used for the purpose—which it was also the custom to set up on the tomb of those dying before marriage.[4]

The order of the details of the nuptial ceremonies is not certainly known, and doubtless varied according to the locality. A feast was given in the house of the father of the bride, thus securing publicity of the event, for the guests were really witnesses (Dem. xxx. 21; Is. viii. 18).[5] Associated with this was the unveiling of the bride (the *ἀνακαλυπτήρια*).

[1] Cf. law quoted in Dem. xlvi. 18: *Ἣν ἂν ἐγγυήσῃ ἐπὶ δικαίοις δάμαρτα εἶναι ἢ πατὴρ ἢ ἀδελφὸς ὁμοπάτωρ ἢ πάππος ὁ πρὸς πατρός, ἐκ ταύτης εἶναι παῖδας γνησίους.*

[2] Cf. Hyper. iii. (v.) 16: *ἀλλὰ μὴν οὐκ ἀπέχρησε τῷ νομοθέτῃ τὸ ἐγγυηθῆναι τὴν γυναῖκα ὑπὸ τοῦ πατρὸς ἢ τοῦ ἀδελφοῦ, ἀλλ' ἔγραψε διαρρήδην ἐν τῷ νόμῳ, κτλ.*; Dem. xlvi. 18: *σκέψασθε τοίνυν καὶ τοὺς νόμους, παρ' ὧν κελεύουσι τὰς ἐγγύας ποιεῖσθαι, κτλ.*

[3] Herod. vi. 130: '*τῷ δὲ Ἀλκμέωνος Μεγακλέϊ ἐγγυῶ παῖδα τὴν ἐμὴν Ἀγαρίστην νόμοισι τοῖσι Ἀθηναίων.*' *φαμένου δὲ ἐγγυᾶσθαι Μεγακλέος ἐκεκύρωτο ὁ γάμος Κλεισθένεϊ.*

[4] Dem. xli. 6: *μάρτυρας παρέξομαι τοὺς παραγενομένους, ὅτ' ἠγγύα μοι Πολύευκτος τὴν θυγατέρα ἐπὶ τετταράκοντα μναῖς.* In the island of Myconos, in Macedonian times, public record was made of the amount of the dowry. See inscr. 817 in W. Dittenberger, *Syll.*², Leipzig, 1898–1901, where the entries are of the type *Σώστρατος τὴν θυγατέρα Ξάνθην ἐνηγγύησεν Ἐπαρχίδει καὶ προῖκα ἔδωκε χιλίας καὶ τριακοσίας δραχμάς . . . ἀργυρίου δὲ προσέθηκεν ἑκατὸν δραχμάς, ἐσθὴν δὲ τετιμημένην διακοσίων δραχμῶν.* See R. Dareste, B. Haussoullier, and T. Reinach, *Recueil des inscr. jurid. grecques*, i. [Paris, 1895] 48 f.

[5] Yet *ἐγγύησις* as such did not give either party an action for specific fulfilment (in spite of the assertion to the contrary by Partsch, *Griechisches Bürgschaftsrecht*, p. 49, relying upon Ælian, *Var. Hist.* vi. 4). Action for breach of promise of marriage was unknown in Athens. But, if the dowry had been paid, the *κύριος* of the woman could recover it with interest (Dem. xxvii. 17).

[6] Especially by Hruza, who sums up his position (*Ehebegr. nach att. Rechte*, p. 40) thus: 'Sie (*ἐγγύησις*) ist kein blos präparatorischer Akt, wie die Sponsalien, sondern die Ehebegründung selbst. Wäre die *ἐγγύησις* nur ein Verlöbnis, so müsste später noch die Ehe durch einen besonderen Akt begründet werden. Davon ist aber nichts überliefert.'

[1] Cf. Pollux, iii. 38: *καὶ τέλος ὁ γάμος ἐκαλεῖτο· καὶ τέλειοι οἱ γεγαμηκότες· διὰ τοῦτο καὶ Ἥρα τελεία, ἡ ζυγία.* The Danaids, who, in pseudo-Plato, *Axioch.* 573 E, are *ἀτελεῖς*, are *τῶν οὐ μεμυημένων* in Paus. x. xxxi. 9. The sacrifice preliminary to a wedding was called *προτέλεια*, and the first night was the *νὺξ μυστική*. Cf. J. E. Harrison, 'The Meaning of the Word *τελετή*,' in *ClR* xxviii. [1914] 36 f.

[2] Cf. Paus. II. xxxii. 1: *ἑκάστη παρθένος πλόκαμον ἀποκείρεταί οἱ* [*sc.* Hippolytos] *πρὸ γάμου, κειραμένη δὲ ἀνέθηκεν ἐς τὸν ναὸν φέρουσα*, at Troezen; I. xliii. 4: *καθέστηκε δὲ ταῖς κόραις χοὰς πρὸς τὸ τῆς Ἰφινόης μνῆμα προσφέρειν πρὸ γάμου καὶ ἀπάρχεσθαι τῶν τριχῶν*, at Megara; he compares the Delian custom (for which cf. Herod. iv. 34); II. xxxiii. 1: *κατεστήσατο δὲ καὶ ταῖς Τροιζηνίων παρθένοις ἀνατιθέναι πρὸ γάμου τὴν ζώνην τῇ Ἀθηνᾷ τῇ Ἀπατουρίᾳ.* See J. G. Frazer, *Pausanias's Descr. of Greece*, London, 1898, iii. 279 f. For the dedication of the girdle (*ζώνη*, or *μίτρα*) to Aphrodite, see Theocr. xxvii. 55; Mosch. ii. 73.

[3] In Troas the bride bathed in the river, saying *λαβέ μου, Σκάμανδρε, τὴν παρθενίαν* (Æschines, *Epist.* 16). See M. P. Nilsson, *Griechische Feste*, Leipzig, 1906, p. 366 f. We must be content here with bare reference to the strange survival, apparently, of pre-nuptial defloration, in the island of Naxos, to which allusion is made in the opening lines of the recently discovered frag. of the *Aitia* of Callimachos (*Oxyrh. Pap.* vii. [1910] 15 f.: *ἤδη καὶ κούρῳ παρθένος εὐνάσατο | τέθμιον ὡς ἐκέλευε προνύμφιον ὕπνον ἰαῦσαι | ἄρσενι τὴν τᾶλιν παιδὶ σὺν ἀμφιθαλεῖ*) about which much literature has gathered; see A. Puech, *REG* xxiii. [1910] 255 f.; D. R. Stuart, *Class. Philol.*, Chicago, vi. [1911] 302 f.; C. Bonner, *ib.* 402 f.; K. Kuiper, *REG* xxv. [1912] 318 f.

[4] Cf. Dem. xliv. 18: *τελευτᾷ τὸν βίον . . . ἄγαμος ὤν· τί τούτου σημεῖον; λυτροφόρος ἐφέστηκεν ἐπὶ τῷ τοῦ Ἀρχιάδου τάφῳ* (see also § 30); P. Wolters, 'Rotfigurige Lutrophoros,' in *Mitth. arch. Inst. Ath.* xvi. [1891] 371 f.

[5] Cf. the story of the unfortunate affair of Orgilaos at Delphi given in Plutarch, *Reip. gerend. præc.* 32; cf. Arist. *Pol.* vii. (v.) 4=1303*b*.

The procession accompanying the bride ἐφ' ἁμάξης to her new home took place in the evening, by torchlight, the Hymenaios song being meanwhile sung to the piping of flutes (see the description of the scene on the Shield of Achilles in *Il.* xviii. 491 f.). The bride was introduced to the hearth amid showers of dates, figs, and other sweetmeats (καταχύσματα).[1]

In Sparta a survival of the primitive capture of the bride lay in the custom of the bridegroom taking his bride from her mother's arms with simulated violence (Plut. *Lyc.* 15; Dion. Hal. ii. 30). For other survivals see M. P. Nilsson, 'Die Grundlagen des spartanischen Lebens,' in *Klio*, xii. [1912] 308 f.; E. Kessler, *Plutarchs Leben des Lykurgos*, Berlin, 1910.

6. **Bride-price.**—In primitive times, remarks Aristotle, men bought their wives (*Pol.* ii. 8 = 1268*b*; cf. Plato, *Laws*, 841 D). The Epic contains frequent mention of the bride-price (ἕδνα), normally calculated in oxen, paid by the suitor to the bride's father. It must sometimes have happened, even in very early times, and under a general system of marriage by purchase, that a father must give something to boot with his daughter in order to secure the desired son-in-law. The economic factor, the relation between population and food-supply, may have contributed largely to establish the custom of dower in place of the bride-price. In historical times, at any rate, the bride-price has been wholly replaced by the dowry given to and with the girl by her parents.

The Epic contains evidence of the transition stages. Of Andromache it is said that Hector took her from her father's house, 'having given bride-price untold' (*Il.* xxii. 472).[2] Of the slain Iphidamas it is said that he fell 'far from his bride, of whom he had known no joy, and much had he given for her' (*Il.* xi. 242 f.; he saw no return for his expenditure of 100 kine). In order to appease Achilles, Agamemnon offers to let him have a daughter of his free (*Il.* ix. 146 f.)—nay, more, to give a present with her (ἐγὼ δ' ἐπὶ μείλια δώσω | πολλὰ μάλ', ὅσσ' οὔπω τις ἑῇ ἐπέδωκε θυγατρί);[3] cf. *Od.* vii. 314, xx. 342.

Ultimately the ἕδνα come to be a dowry given by her parents to the bride—perhaps through a transition stage in which the bride-price received from the suitor was used wholly or in part to equip the bride and to furnish the feast.[4] In the *Odyssey* the two systems are both found; *e.g.*, in *Od.* ii. 53, Ἰκαρίου, ὥς κ' αὐτὸς ἐεδνώσαιτο θύγατρα, the meaning is 'give for the bride-price' (cf. *Od.* xvi. 77, 391 f., xix. 529); but in *Od.* i. 277 f. = *Od.* ii. 196 f., οἱ δὲ γάμον τεύξουσι καὶ ἀρτυνέουσιν ἔεδνα | πολλὰ μάλ', ὅσσα ἔοικε φίλης ἐπὶ παιδὸς ἕπεσθαι, a dowry given by the parents is meant, just as by Pindar and Euripides ἕδνον is used as equivalent to φερνή.[5]

7. **The dowry.**—In historical times, in Athens, the marriage settlement or dowry (προίξ, φερνή) was almost a criterion of honourable marriage as distinguished from concubinage; for the freedom of divorce allowed by Athenian law to the husband made the position of a portionless wife very precarious (cf. Is. iii. 28: κἂν ἀργύριον πολλῷ μᾶλλον ὁ ἐγγυῶν διωμολογήσατο ἔχειν αὐτὸν ἐπὶ τῇ γυναικί, ἵνα μὴ ἐπ' ἐκείνῳ γένοιτο ῥᾳδίως ἀπαλλάττεσθαι, ὁπότε βούλοιτο,

[1] The marriage was followed by some ceremony or act for which the technical and fixed phrase was γαμηλίαν ὑπὲρ τῆς γυναικὸς τοῖς φράτερσιν εἰσφέρειν (cf. Is. iii. 79, viii. 18; Dem. lvii. 43). This has been variously interpreted by both ancients and moderns as an introduction or enrolment of the wife among the members of her husband's φρατρία, or as a banquet, sacrifice, or donation (see Wyse, *Isæus*, p. 363).

[2] Cf. *Il.* xvi. 178, 190; *Od.* xi. 282. It is clear from *Od.* xv. 367 that the ἕδνα were given to the parents, not to the bride. Hence is explained the term used in *Il.* xviii. 593, παρθένοι ἀλφεσίβοιαι, 'realizing a high price in oxen' (see G. Murray, *Rise of the Greek Epic*², Oxford, 1911, p. 185 f.). In *Od.* viii. 318 f. there is talk of getting the price of a 'bad bargain' refunded. In *Il.* xiii. 366 Othryoneus receives Cassandra ἀνάεδνον, but gives service in war in lieu of bride-price.

[3] Leaf in his note on this passage prefers to see in it an example of an intermediate stage, in which the ἕδνα are given by the suitor to the bride herself, and may be increased by gifts from her parents, the word μείλια being the technical term for such additional gifts (cf. *Il.* xxii. 51). The example quoted from *Od.* vi. 159 as an illustration of this intermediate stage ('loading thee with gifts') is not in point, the meaning being 'prevail over other suitors with offers,' *sc.* to the parents of the girl.

[4] Such a transition stage would enable us to explain the difficult expression in *Il.* xiii. 382: (συνώμεθα) ἀμφὶ γάμῳ, ἐπεὶ οὔ τοι ἐεδνωταὶ κακοί εἰμεν, where ἐεδνωταί is by Leaf translated 'match-makers,' 'marriage-brokers,' or (Lang, Leaf, and Myers, tr., London, 1883) 'exacters of gifts of wooing.' It means 'one who makes a profit out of the ἕδνα.'

[5] See on this development P. Cauer, *Grundfragen der Homerkritik*², Leipzig, 1909, p. 286 f.

τῆς γυναικός). Instances, indeed, are found where no settlement was made; in the lower classes the amount must always have been trivial. Moreover, no legal obligation to provide a dowry can be proved for the father,[1] just as for brothers also the obligation to dower sisters suitably and not suffer them to grow old unmarried was moral, not legal (Lys. xiii. 45).[2]

The dowry did not become the husband's property, but he enjoyed the usufruct;[3] he was generally required to mortgage real estate as security (ἀποτίμημα) for its eventual repayment.[4] If the capital sum was not to be paid at once, either because the woman's κύριος had not enough ready money or because her husband could not give adequate security for the whole sum, interest upon the outstanding balance was paid to the husband according to agreement (Dem. xli. 6; *Inscr. jurid. grecques*, i. 133 f.). All these arrangements were made before witnesses (cf. Dem. xxx. 9, 21), but were not put in documentary form before an official and published, as at Myconos and Tenos; at Athens the permanent stone record of the mortgage was deemed sufficient safeguard of the rights of the parties. Naturally all this implied the necessity of keeping clearly distinct the property of husband and wife (cf. Dem. xlvii. 57, liii. 28); neither Athens nor, so far as our knowledge goes, the rest of Greece knows community of property between husband and wife, in spite of the recommendations of philosophers.[5] It is clear that the Athenian dowry system, which was probably that of Greece in general, tended to maintain the connexion of the wife with her father's family; the wife did not, as in early Rome, become once for all a member of her husband's family (Dion. Hal. ii. 25).

(*a*) *Amount of dowry.*—According to Plutarch,[6] a law of Solon limited the size of dowries at Athens; but this, if ever enforced, was certainly obsolete in the 4th cent. B.C., and was, in fact, virtually abrogated by the law fixing the minimum amount to be settled on a poor ἐπίκληρος by her next-of-kin—a law which equally passed as Solonian (Dem. xliii. 54). Hipponicus, the richest Athenian of his time, gave his daughter ten talents on her marriage with Alcibiades (Plut. *Alc.* 8). The father of Demosthenes the orator, with a property estimated at fourteen talents, gave a dowry of two talents (Dem. xxvii. 5). The orators contain mention of dowries ranging from ten *minæ* to more than 100 *minæ*. Athenian mortgage-pillars, set upon property pledged as security for the repayment of dowries, show sums ranging from 300 to 4500 *drachmæ* (6000 *drachmæ*, or 60 *minæ* = 1 talent); but it is not certain, under the circumstances, that these sums constitute the whole dowry. The register from Myconos (3rd cent. B.C.) shows amounts varying from 700 *drachmæ* to 14,000 *drachmæ* (*Inscr. jurid. grecques*, i. 48; Dittenberger, *Syll.*², 817). The widow of the rich banker Pasion received three talents (Dem. xlv. 28, 35:

[1] A father might settle a dowry on his daughter by will (Lys. xxxii. 6), but was not obliged to make this provision; failing which, a daughter had no legal claim on his estate. The Code of Gortyn is more liberal, giving daughters a legal claim to one-half of a brother's share, in lieu of a dowry—an already portioned daughter having no further claim. That is to say, at Gortyn there was legal obligation to dower. Ephoros, as quoted by Strabo, p. 482, φερνὴ δ' ἐστίν, ἂν ἀδελφοὶ ὦσι, τὸ ἥμισυ τῆς τοῦ ἀδελφοῦ μερίδος, attributes the Gortynian rule to Crete generally, and may be correct in so doing.

[2] The nearest male relative of a poor ἐπίκληρος or θῆττα was under legal obligation either to marry her himself or to portion her on a scale fixed by law (Is. i. 39; law in Dem. xliii. 54). Contempt of the law was possibly construed as κάκωσις ἐπικλήρων, involving partial ἀτιμία.

[3] Hence Euripides makes Medea complain that women have to buy a husband (*Med.* 230 f.).

[4] Harpocr. xxx. 15: Εἰώθεσαν δὲ οἱ τότε, εἰ γυναικὶ γαμουμένῃ δίδοιεν οἱ προσήκοντες, αἰτεῖν παρὰ τοῦ ἀνδρὸς ὥσπερ ἐνέχυρόν τι τῆς προικὸς ἄξιον, οἷον οἰκίαν ἢ χωρίον. A mortgage-stone (ὅρος) was set up on the pledged property, with an inscription of the following type: Ὅρος χωρίου καὶ οἰκίας ἀποτίμημα προικὸς Πυθοστράτει Μενάλκου Ἀναφλυστίου XXX (*i.e.* 3000 *drachmæ*; see E. S. Roberts and E. A. Gardner, *Introd. to Greek Epigraphy*, pt. ii., *The Inscr. of Attica*, Cambridge, 1905, p. 497; Dittenberger, *Syll.*², 818).

[5] Cf. Plut. *Præc. conj.* 20.

[6] Plut. *Sol.* 20. See the explanation given by G. Glotz, *La Solidarité de la famille dans le droit criminel en Grèce*, Paris, 1904, p. 330 f. Plato, in *Laws*, 742 C, lays down the principle γαμοῦντα δὲ καὶ ἐκδιδόντα μήτ' οὖν διδόναι μήτε δέχεσθαι προῖκα τὸ παράπαν μηδ' ἡντινοῦν (cf. 774 D). The νόμος περὶ τῆς προικός (Dem. xl. 19) has not been preserved.

προστιθεὶς προῖκα ὅσην οὐδεὶς τῶν ἐν τῇ πόλει φαίνεται; cf. Menander, Περικειρομένη, *Oxyrh. Pap.* ii. 211, line 40, where the father promises three talents dowry, to the lover's great content). Apparently there was at Athens no law on the subject, but in other places it was found necessary to fix a legal maximum in order to prevent extravagant dowries; *e.g.*, at Massalia the maximum was fixed at 100 χρυσοῖ, with an additional five χρυσοῖ for clothes, and five for ornaments (Strabo, p. 181). The aim of the Gortynian Code, in fixing a daughter's share in her father's estate, was probably rather to curtail dowries than to extend women's rights. The general tendency in the 4th cent., at any rate, was to give large dowries; and this in Sparta, as Aristotle remarks, was in part responsible for the concentration of property in the hands of women and their preponderant influence in the State (Arist. *Pol.* ii. 9=1270*a*: ἔστι δὲ καὶ τῶν γυναικῶν σχεδὸν τῆς πάσης χώρας τῶν πέντε μερῶν τὰ δύο, τῶν τ' ἐπικλήρων πολλῶν γινομένων, καὶ διὰ τὸ προῖκας διδόναι μεγάλας; cf. Plut. *Agis*, 4, 7).

(*b*) *Refund of dowry.*—In Athens the dowry usually consisted of a sum of money, rarely of real estate (cf. Plut. *Aristid.* 27).[1] The bride's trousseau, however, was in some cases valued and expressly reckoned in the dowry, so that its equivalent was recoverable from the husband—otherwise it was held to be a free gift of the κύριος, and was not recoverable (cf. Is. iii. 35, viii. 8; see note in Wyse, p. 314).

Whilst the union continued, the dowry could not be withdrawn; but, upon dissolution of marriage on the initiative of either party[2] or by mutual agreement, it must be refunded to the woman's κύριος. It is usually held, however, that in case of the wife's adultery restitution was not enforceable upon her repudiation; but there is no sufficient evidence of this exception.[3] The principles observed are: (1) rupture of union *inter vivos* compels restitution of the dowry, the existence of issue being immaterial; and (2) rupture by death of either party compels restitution, if there is no issue; if there is issue, the children benefit, except when the widow (mother) exercises her option of going back with her dowry to her father's house. Thus the dowry follows the wife, or goes to her children.[4]

The Code of Gortyn shows that there, as at Athens, the wife's dowry was not merged in the family estate, and it was forbidden to the husband to sell or mortgage her property; for in case of dissolution of marriage the wife returned to her own family, taking with her her dowry, together with half the increase thereof, and half the fruits of her own labour, as well as five *staters* if the husband was to blame for the separation. On the other hand, the interests of the husband's family were protected by the provision that he might not make any larger donation than 100 *staters* to his wife, nor might a son make a larger gift to his mother—the intention being the same in both cases, namely, to prevent absorption of the husband's estate by the wife, for all such gifts belonged to her absolutely. If her husband predeceased her, she might, if she chose to remarry, take her own property out of his estate into that of her second husband; the existence of issue was only so far material that, if there were children, she was limited to taking her dowry and such donation as her husband might have made within the legal limit aforesaid, and in the presence of three adult male witnesses. If there were no children, she might take, in addition to her dowry, half the fruits of her own labour, and half the produce in the house—the balance going to her dead husband's heirs-at-law. If she did not wish to remarry, her property remained in her own hands until she died, and then it was divided among her children; she enjoyed, therefore, a more independent position than the Athenian widow, whose property, in similar circumstances, passed into the hands of the eldest son as soon as he came of age.

Under the Gortynian Code, if the wife died before her husband, having had no children, her next-of-kin was entitled to recover her dowry, with the half of its fruits and half of the work of her hands; but, if the widower was left with children, he had the management and use of his dead wife's property until he died or remarried, in which cases it went to her children.[1]

8. Dissolution of marriage.—Dissolution of marriage in Athens was easily effected. The husband's power of repudiation was unfettered by any legal conditions or formalities. He simply sent the woman, with her dowry, back to her father's house. A prudent man would, as usual, summon witnesses, but need not do so (Lys. xiv. 28). When the wife sought a separation, she must lodge with the Archon τὸ τῆς ἀπολείψεως γράμμα (Plut. *Alc.* 8; Andoc. iv. 14: ἀπολιπεῖν, ἐλθοῦσαν πρὸς τὸν ἄρχοντα κατὰ τὸν νόμον); but nothing is known of the procedure. Against a wife proved guilty of adultery the husband was compelled by law to use his right of repudiation, condonation of the offence being visited with ἀτιμία (Dem. lix. 87). On the other hand, it is certain that adultery of the husband gave the wife no legal right of divorce,[2] and it is probable that it was not generally regarded as sufficient ground of separation.[3] It is evident that the possession of a dowry must have been a strong protection to the wife against a husband's caprice, and in many households must have made her virtually mistress of the situation.

Two special features call for remark in this connexion. It was competent for husband and wife to agree to a mutual dissolution of marriage in order that another more congenial union might be made. Thus Pericles so parted from his wife with her consent, to take Aspasia (Plut. *Per.* 24).[4] Again, the operation of the laws respecting heiresses (ἐπίκληροι) often, according to Is. iii. 64, severed husband and wife (see INHERITANCE [Greek], vol. vii. p. 304). The latter occasion of dissolution of marriage differs from the first-mentioned in that it came about as the result of an application to a court of law by the next-of-kin as claimant (ἐπιδικασία). In all other cases there is no sufficient evidence that any public legal procedure was in use, for even the wife's application to the Archon does not seem to have been more than an application or formal notice to him *in camera*. It is doubtful whether the δίκη ἀπολείψεως and the δίκη ἀποπέμψεως, which are said to have been available for husband and wife respectively, as if a sort of suit for restitution of conjugal rights, are not mere figments.[5]

1 Cf. Dittenberger, *Syll.*², 826: Ἡγησοῦς τῆς Κλεομόρτου θυγατρὸς προὶξ τὸ χωρίον (inscr. from Syros).

2 Dem. lix. 52: κατὰ τὸν νόμον ὃς κελεύει ἐὰν ἀποπέμπῃ τὴν γυναῖκα, ἀποδιδόναι τὴν προῖκα, ἐὰν δὲ μή, ἐπ' ἐννέα ὀβολοῖς τοκοφορεῖν καὶ σίτου εἰς ᾠδεῖον εἶναι δικάσασθαι ὑπὲρ τῆς γυναικὸς τῷ κυρίῳ, *i.e.*, alimony at the rate of 18 per cent interest upon the dowry was recoverable from a recalcitrant husband (cf. Is. iii. 8, 35, ii. 9).

3 Certainly not to be proved for Athens in the 4th cent. B.C., by inference from the Ephesian inscr. of the 2nd cent. (Dittenberger, *Syll.*², 510. 60): ἢ γήμαντες καὶ διαλυθέντες μὴ ἀποδεδώκασι τὰς φερνὰς οὔσας ἀποδότους κατὰ τὸν νόμον—even if that will prove anything at all (see T. Thalheim, *Lehrbuch der griech. Rechtsaltertümer*⁴, Freiburg i. B., 1895, p. 163).

4 Cf. L. Mitteis, *Reichsrecht und Volksrecht in den östl. Prov. des röm. Kaiserreichs*, Leipzig, 1891, p. 232: 'Die vom Vater bestellte Mitgift enthält eine Erbabfindung der Tochter'; cf. Plato, *Laws*, xi. 923 D, E: ὅτῳ δ' ἂν τῶν υἱέων ὑπάρχων οἶκος ᾖ, μὴ νέμειν τούτῳ τῶν χρημάτων, θυγατρί τε ὡσαύτως ᾗ μὲν ἂν ἐγγεγυημένος ὡς ἀνὴρ ἐσόμενος ᾖ, μὴ νέμειν· ᾗ δ' ἂν μή, νέμειν.

1 For comparison of the Gortynian regulations with the later regulations in the East ('jenem spätgriechischen Stadtrecht, welches man heute fälschlich als syrisches Rechtsbuch diagnosticirt,' p. 240) see Mitteis, p. 230 ff.

2 Athenian sentiment on this matter was very far removed from the position of Arist. *Œc.* i. 4=1344*a*: ὥσπερ ἱκέτιν καὶ ἀφ' ἑστίας ἠγμένην ὡς ἥκιστα δεῖ ἀδικεῖν· ἀδικία δὲ ἀνδρὸς αἱ θύραζε συνουσίαι γιγνόμεναι; cf. *Pol.* iv. (vii.) 16 = 1335*b*; Plato, *Laws*, 784 E. 'Dass die Ehe dem Manne keine Treupflicht auferlege, gehört zu den Grundmerkmalen der antiken Ehe gegenüber unseren Anschauungen und Rechtseinrichtungen' (Hruza, p. 20).

3 According to Herod. v. 39, at Sparta barrenness was good ground for divorce, at any rate for the royal house; cf. vi. 61.

4 Other examples: Dem. xxxvi. 28 f.; Is. ii. 6 f., 9: κἀκείνη τὸ μὲν πρῶτον οὐδ' ἠνέσχετο αὐτοῦ λέγοντος, προϊόντος δὲ τοῦ χρόνου μόλις ἐπείσθη· καὶ οὕτως ἐκδίδομεν αὐτήν; cf. the case of Protomachos who, becoming entitled to a rich heiress, persuaded his wife to agree to a dissolution and fresh marriage (Dem. lvii. 41). In Thurii, according to Diod. xii. 18, freedom of divorce was limited by a law forbidding the person to whom the divorce was due to marry one younger than the original partner.

5 The δίκη προικός or δίκη σίτου, suits brought by the woman's κύριος for the restitution of her dowry or payment of interest thereon, protected the woman's interests in respect of aliment. From this it follows that a woman who married without a dowry was in practically the same position as a παλλακή, and had no protection whatever against a husband's caprice short of actual violence to her person.

9. Widows.—The Athenian regulations concerning widows were as follows. If there were no children, born or adopted, the widow must return with her dowry to her father's house; she must, as a rule, if of suitable age, marry again in accordance with the wishes of her dead husband or those of her *κύριος* (Is. viii. 8). If there were children, she might remain in her husband's house, where she passed under the authority of her children's guardian, if they were still minors, and under that of her eldest son when he came of age—her dowry becoming the property of her children, subject to her right to support (Dem. xlii. 27, xlvi. 20). She might, however, return with her dowry to her father's house, and be given again in marriage (Dem. xl. 6 f.). The same option was open to her if, on her husband's death, she declared herself pregnant (Dem. xliii. 75), in which case it was the Archon's duty to protect her interests (Arist. *Ath. Pol.* 56. 7). It is clear that here again the existence of the dowry secured on mortgage put the final decision completely into the hands of the widow and her *κύριος*.

10. Marriage law in the papyri.—In Egypt, under the Ptolemys, Hellenic legal ideas and principles came in contact with those of another, in some respects more highly developed, type; later, both were influenced by the legal conceptions and practices of the Romans. In the Papyri we have, therefore, to distinguish between the enchorial marriage, in which the parties are Egyptians, and the Hellenic marriage, the regulations concerning which are partly derived from the older Greek law and partly developed under the influence of native models.

The technical term for marriage in the Papyri is *γάμος* or *συνοικίσιον*. Dissolution of marriage (and probably therefore entry upon marriage) is no longer a purely private act, but requires the lodging of an *ἀπογραφή* before an official (cf. what was required of the women in Athens, Dem. xxx. 17, 26; Is. iii. 78: *πρὸς ὁποῖον ἄρχοντα ἡ ἐγγυητὴ γυνὴ ἀπέλιπε τὸν ἄνδρα ἢ τὸν οἶκον αὐτοῦ*, as well as the intervention of *ἱεροθύται*.[1] The precise relation between the religious element thus imported into the transaction and the civil element represented by the *ἀπογραφή* and the marriage contract itself is by no means clear as yet.

The extant marriage-contracts exhibit, when taken together, the following elements. (1) Statement of the giving or receiving of the woman in marriage; *e.g.*, Mitteis-Wilcken, *Grundzüge*, ii. 317, n. 283: *λαμβάνει Ἡρακλείδης Δημητρίαν Κῴαν γυναῖκα γνησίαν παρὰ τοῦ πατρός*, as in the older Greek law (cf. Is. ix. 27: *ὅτε γὰρ ἐλάμβανε Θεόφραστος ὁ ἐμὸς πατὴρ τὴν ἐμὴν μητέρα παρὰ Ἱεροκλέους*).[2] (2) Acknowledgment of receipt of the *φερνή* brought by the woman. (3) Mutual marital obligations; the husband promised to support the wife and to treat her properly (*μὴ ὑβρίζειν μηδὲ κακουχεῖν*), and engaged not to repudiate her (*μὴ ἐκβαλεῖν*) or to be unfaithful (*μὴ εἰσάγεσθαι ἄλλην γυναῖκα μηδὲ παλλακὴν μηδὲ τεκνοποιεῖσθαι ἐξ ἄλλης γυναικός*); on her side the woman promised to remain at home day and night (*μηδ' ἀφήμερον μηδ' ἀπόκοιτον γενέσθαι*), to be faithful (*μηδ' ἄλλῳ ἀνδρὶ συνεῖναι*), and to look after their joint interests in the household (*μηδὲ φθείρειν τὸν κοινὸν οἶκον*). (4) The sanction of the mutual obligations; the husband guilty of breach of his promises must repay forthwith (*παραχρῆμα*) the dowry with addition of half its amount (*τὴν φερνὴν ἡμιόλιον*); the wife so guilty lost her dowry entirely. Apparently the ordinary courts settled disputes so arising. (5) Divorce on the man's side (*ἀποπομπή*) was tantamount to breach of his promise *μὴ ἐκβάλλειν*, and rendered him liable to the aforesaid penalty; separation on the woman's part (*ἀπαλλαγή*) was not regarded as breach of promise, but provision was made for repayment of the dowry within a stated time. That is to say, the husband had entirely lost that unfettered power of repudiation, under condition of simply refunding the dowry, which belonged to him under the older Hellenic law. On the other hand, the dowry retained here also the overwhelming importance which it had in Hellas.[3] Here also it was, if not a definite sum of money, valued and expressed as such, and the husband was liable only for refund of that stated amount—the principle being, as at Athens, that the wife's dowry should neither increase nor diminish (cf. the Code of Gortyn); from which it follows that the management of the dowry must have been in the hands of the husband, as was the case at Athens.

LITERATURE.—A. H. G. P. van den Es, *De iure familiarum apud Athenienses*, Leyden, 1864; A. Philippi, *Beiträge zu einer Geschichte des attischen Bürgerrechtes*, Berlin, 1870; H. Buermann, 'Drei Studien auf dem Gebiet des attischen Rechts,' in *Jahrbücher für cl. Philologie*, Supplementband ix. [1877–78]; E. Hruza, *Beiträge zur Gesch. des griech. und röm. Familienrechtes*, i. *Die Ehebegründung nach attischem Rechte*, Erlangen and Leipzig, 1892, ii. *Polygamie und Pellikat nach griech. Rechte*, do. 1894; O. Müller, 'Untersuchungen zur Gesch. des attischen Bürger- und Eherechts,' in *Jahrbücher für cl. Philologie*, Supplementband xxv. [1899]; W. Wyse, *The Speeches of Isæus, with critical and explan. Notes*, Cambridge, 1904; C. A. Savage, *The Athenian Family*, Baltimore, 1907; A. Ledl, 'Das attische Bürgerrecht und die Frauen, II.,' in *Wiener Studien*, xxx. [1908] 1–46; J. H. Lipsius, *Das attische Recht und Rechtsverfahren, unter Benutzung des attischen Prozesses von M. H. E. Meier und G. F. Schömann*, vol. ii. pt. 2, Leipzig, 1912; A. Brückner, 'Athenische Hochzeitsgeschenke,' in *Mittheil. des kais. deutsches arch. Inst., Athen.* Abt. xxxii. [1907]; L. Beauchet, *Hist. du droit privé de la rép. athénienne*, i. 'Le Droit de famille,' Paris, 1897; J. Partsch, *Griechisches Bürgschaftsrecht*, pt. i., Leipzig and Berlin, 1909; artt. in Daremberg-Saglio by E. Caillemer, and in Pauly-Wissowa; H. Lewy, *De civili condicione mulierum Græcarum*, Breslau, 1885; J. Kohler and E. Ziebarth, *Das Stadtrecht von Gortyn, und seine Beziehungen zum gemeingriechischen Rechte*, Göttingen, 1912; L. Mitteis and U. Wilcken, *Grundzüge und Chrestomathie der Papyruskunde*, vol. ii., in 2 parts, Leipzig and Berlin, 1912.

W. J. WOODHOUSE.

MARRIAGE (Hindu).—**1. General characteristics.**—The earlier Vedic texts, which may be said to cover the period down to the end of the 5th cent. B.C., present with practical uniformity the same account of the condition of marriage among the Hindu tribes whose life they depict. Among these tribes marriage was a union of man and woman, for all practical purposes indissoluble save by death, and normally monogamic except among the highest strata of the population. Marriages were contracted between persons of full age, and often by mutual consent; while there are clear traces of the payment of a bride-price for a wife, there is also proof of the giving of dowries by fathers or brothers in order to secure the marriage of daughters or sisters. Traces of marriage by capture are scanty and confined to the warrior class.

The position of the wife in these conditions of society was one of security and dignity. She was, indeed, under the complete control of her husband, though we do not know to what extent of personal restraint his power extended. But she was the mistress (*patnī*) of the household, as her husband was the master (*pati*). In the marriage-hymn of the Rigveda (X. lxxxv. 46) she is told to exercise authority over her father-in-law, and her husband's brothers and unmarried sisters. The case contemplated seems to be one in which the eldest son of a family marries at a time when his father, through decrepitude, has ceased to exercise full control over the family, and when, therefore, the wife of the eldest son becomes the mistress of the joint family. This is not inconsistent with the respect elsewhere mentioned as due from a daughter-in-law to her father-in-law, which doubtless applies to the case in which the father is still able to control his son and to exercise the rightful authority of the head of the house. The wife was also a participator in the sacred rites performed by her husband; but in this regard a certain deterioration of her position can be traced in the Vedic period, doubtless as the result of the growing importance of the priestly class and the rule that women could not be priests. This regulation seems to have been due to the view that women were impure as compared with men, and the same idea may have been at the root of the practice, which appears first in the *Śatapatha Brāhmaṇa* (I. ix. 2. 12), requiring a woman to eat after her husband, just

[1] For these see W. Otto, *Priester und Tempel im hellenistischen Ägypten*, 2 vols., Leipzig, 1908, i. 163 f., ii. 295 f.

[2] A curious exception in *Pap. Giss.* ii. 8 (*ἐξέδοτο ἑαυτὴν Ὀλυμπιὰς . . . γυναῖκα γαμετήν*), in which the woman, of Macedonian origin, gives herself away in marriage, may be a survival of native Macedonian law, which in this respect, therefore, must have resembled that of the Lydians, of whom Herodotus remarks with surprise that the women give themselves in marriage (i. 93: *ἐκδιδόασι δὲ αὐταὶ ἑωυτάς*—besides collecting their own dowries *σώματι ἐργαζόμεναι*).

[3] Mitteis-Wilcken, ii. 1. 219: 'Im Gerippe dieser Urkunden bildet die *φερνή* das Rückgrat, an welches alle anderen Bestimmungen sich nur anlehnen.'

as in Bengal at the present day a wife normally feeds on the remnants of her husband's meal.

Naturally enough, there were different views as to the character of women. A wife completes a husband and is half of his self, we are told (*Bṛhadāraṇyaka Upaniṣad*, I. iv. 17; *Śatapatha Brāhmaṇa*, V. ii. 1. 10), and her good qualities are frequently mentioned. On the other hand, the *Maitrāyaṇī Saṁhitā* (I. x. 11, III. vi. 3) describes woman as untruth and as connected with misfortune, and classifies her with dice and drink as the three chief evils. Elsewhere (*Taittirīya Saṁhitā*, VI. v. 8. 2) a good woman is ranked below even a bad man, and the *Kāṭhaka Saṁhitā* (xxxi. 1) alludes sarcastically to her ability to obtain things from her husband by cajolery at night.

The most important function of a wife was doubtless that of bringing into the world a son in order to perform the necessary funeral rites to his father and to continue the race. Adoption, indeed, was known as early as the Rigveda, but it was not popular (cf. art. ADOPTION [Hindu]), and lack of a son (*avīratā*) was regarded as the greatest of evils. On the other hand, the birth of a daughter was regarded as a misfortune; the *Aitareya Brāhmaṇa* (vii. 15) contrasts a daughter as misery (*kṛpaṇa*) with a son as a light in the highest heaven. But the view once widely held, that the Vedic Indians practised infanticide in the case of girls, has been disproved by O. von Böhtlingk.[1]

In political life women took no part; men alone went to the assembly. But, while the position of the wife in the sacrificial ritual was narrowed by the priests, there is evidence that women took part in the speculative activity which manifested itself in the 6th cent. B.C. in the *Upaniṣads*. We learn there not only of several women teachers, who may or may not have been married, but also of one of the two wives of the great sage Yājñavalkya, who shared her husband's intellectual activities.

In the *Gṛhyasūtras* and *Dharmasūtras*, which mark the end of the Vedic period proper, and which may be held to represent the views of the period from the 4th cent. B.C. onwards, in the epics (*c.* 200 B.C.–A.D. 200), in the *Arthaśāstra*, and in the *Kāmasūtra* we find in full force the tendencies which reveal themselves in the later classical literature, and can be observed in their development at the present day. Different types of marriage are now recognized and classified, being assigned to the different classes of the population. Marriages between people of full age are still allowed; thus the warrior class is permitted to marry by capture or to form love matches, while the *Kāmasūtra* permits love matches generally. Against these special cases must be set the general rule, which first appears as a counsel of perfection in the *Mānava* (I. vii. 8) and *Gobhila Gṛhyasūtras* (III. iv. 6), but which by the time of the later *Smṛtis*—*i.e.*, not later probably than the beginning of the Christian era—has won full acceptance, viz. that it was sinful on the part of a father[2] to allow his daughter to attain puberty without being married, and the girl herself fell to the condition of a Śūdra (*vṛṣalī*), marriage with whom involved degradation on the part of a husband. The date of marriage is placed earlier and earlier as the authority is later in date. Thus the *Smṛti* of Manu (ix. 94) fixes the ages of husband and wife at 30 and 12 or 24 and 8 respectively; the later work of Bṛhaspati (*ZDMG* xlvi. [1892] 416 f.) and the didactic portion of the *Mahābhārata* (XIII. xliv. 19) give the wife's age in these cases as 10 and 7 respectively, while yet later texts give 4 to 6 as the lower and 8 as the upper limit. There is abundant evidence that these dates were not merely theoretical: the old marriage-ceremonial, which included as its essential part the taking of the bride to her new home, whence the name of marriage (*vivāha*) was derived, was divided into two parts; the actual ceremony took place shortly after the betrothal (*vāgdāna*), but the taking of the bride to her husband's home was delayed until after puberty. The unmarried daughter (*kumārī*) living at home was distinguished from the married daughter (*suvāsinī* or *svavāsinī*), whose connexion with her parents was still recognized to the extent that, contrary to the rule that no mourning was observed for a married daughter, a brief period of mourning was prescribed in the event of her death before her departure from her old home. The early prevalence of the custom is also vouched for by the Greek authorities,[1] and was noted by al-Bīrūnī in the 11th cent. A.D.[2] At the present time, despite the efforts of reformers, it is still the prevailing practice among all Hindus who stand under the influence of the Brāhmans to marry their daughters before puberty, and the practice has spread even among Muhammadans.

The better side of such marriages is put before us in the *Hārīta Smṛti* (iii. 3). The wife is to devote her whole thought to her house and her husband, to prepare his food, eat what is left over by her husband and sons, wash the utensils, strew cow-dung on the floor, make the domestic offerings, embrace her husband's feet before going to rest, in the hot season fan him, support his head when he is weary, and so forth. On the other hand, to her falls the place of honour in the household, and she is undisputed mistress of her daughters and any other women living under her husband's roof. The description in the *Smṛti* is confirmed by the literature and by the practice of the present day. On the other hand, it must be noted that the intellectual achievements of women in India since the rule of early marriage became effective have not been in accord with the normal development which might have been expected from the state of society depicted in the *Upaniṣads*, and the heroines of the epic and the classical poetry are chosen, as a rule, from those women who, for some reason or other, have not fallen under the operation of the ordinary practice. There is also much evidence in the proverbial literature of the demerits which were attributed to women in general and wives in particular.

2. Forms of marriage.—In the Vedic period the normal form of marriage appears to have been one in which much was left to the choice of the two persons concerned. It is, at any rate, not proved that the father could control the marriage of either son or daughter of mature age, though doubtless parents often arranged marriages for their children. Of the practice of giving a bride-price there is clear evidence from the later *Saṁhitās*, but there is also clear evidence of the practice of a father and, in his absence, a brother giving a dowry to enable a daughter or sister to obtain a husband; or a daughter might be given to a priest in return for his assistance at some rite. There is also a trace of marriage by capture in the Rigveda, where we hear (I. cxii. 19, cxvii. 20, X. xxxix. 7, lxv. 12) of the carrying off by Vimada of the daughter of Purumitra, apparently with the good will of the maiden but against her father's desire. The normal marriage was duly celebrated at the house of the father of the bride, and its ceremonial, which is fully described in the *Gṛhyasūtras*, is marked by many features which have been found in the marriage-ritual of other Indo-European and non-Indo-European peoples. Of these practices the most

[1] *ZDMG* xliv. [1890] 494–496.

[2] In his default a brother, grandfather, maternal uncle, or mother, or an agnate or cognate, should act (Nārada, xii. 20–22).

[1] Hopkins, *JAOS* xiii. [1889] 343.

[2] *India*, tr. E. Sachau. London, 1888, ii. 154.

important and wide-spread were the solemn handing over of the maiden by her father (*kanyādāna*), the joining of the right hands of the bride and bridegroom (*pāṇigrahaṇa*), the recitation of Vedic formulæ, including a speech by the bridegroom to the bride asserting their unity, the offering of libations in the fire and the threefold circumambulation of the fire, the seven steps taken together by the wedded pair, and, finally, the taking away of the bride to her new home by the bridegroom. There is evidence in the later literature that these customs formed the kernel of the normal marriage-ceremonial throughout the Middle Ages, and much of the ritual is still observed at the present day.[1]

In the *Smṛti* literature eight forms of marriage are recognized and described, but with many differences in detail. In the case of Brāhmans Manu (iii. 24) recognizes as approved four forms: the *brāhma*, *daiva*, *ārṣa*, and *prājāpatya*. The characteristics of these forms are that in the first the father spontaneously offers his daughter to a suitable husband, in the second he gives her to a priest engaged in performing a rite for him, in the third the suitor gives a pair of oxen, and in the fourth the initiative in proposing the marriage comes from the bridegroom. The first and fourth forms, therefore, practically represent marriages by mutual consent and parental arrangement, while the second and third have traces of marriage by purchase, though the texts are careful to explain that the pair of oxen was not intended as a price (*śulka*), but was to be given to the daughter by her father as a mark of honour. It is perfectly clear, however, that the original sense of the custom was a purchase, and this fact is borne out by references in the older *Gṛhyasūtras* of Pāraskara (I. viii. 18) and Śāṅkhāyana (I. xiv. 16) to the practice of giving the father-in-law a hundred oxen with a waggon, and by the recognition in the *Gṛhyasūtras* of the Kāṭhaka and the Mānava schools (I. vii. 11) of a usage by which the bride-price was paid in money to the father.

Marriage by purchase was recognized among the warrior class; in the *Mahābhārata* (I. cxiii. 9 f.) we are told that Pāṇḍu paid the Madra king in gold, jewels, horses, elephants, ornaments, etc., for the hand of his sister, and that the purchase of women was the family practice of the king. Still more was the custom prevalent among the lower classes of the people. Manu admits (iii. 24) that some allowed the Vaiśyas and the Śūdras the *āsura* marriage, which was an open, out-and-out sale, though he condemns the practice *in toto*. But facts have prevailed over the objections of the Brāhmans to the sale of children, and even at the present day marriage by purchase is common enough in Bombay, Madras, and the Panjāb, and is the normal form in Assam. In Bengal it is restricted to the lower classes of the population, but there the practice of the purchase of bridegrooms prevails instead, the practice of child-marriage having placed a high price on eligible husbands.

In addition to the *āsura* form, the warrior class was allowed the *rākṣasa*, the *gāndharva*, and the *paiśācha* forms, though the last is condemned by Manu along with the *āsura* as altogether improper. The former type of marriage was marriage by capture in its simplest form, and its performance is related of many of the heroes of the epic, though the rape of women of high rank is elsewhere regarded as a capital offence. But, outside the epic, we hear little of this remarkable privilege of the warrior class, and this practice has left no survivals in modern India, though it is found among some primitive hill tribes, where it is of independent origin. Some, indeed, of the details of the marriage-ritual given in the *Gṛhyasūtras* have been interpreted in this sense, but the interpretation is neither necessary nor probable. The *gāndharva* rite, which some authorities recognize as applicable to all classes, and which the *Kāmasūtra* eulogizes as the best form of all, is described as a mutual union by desire, the classical example of which is that of King Duṣyanta and Śakuntalā. The *Kāmasūtra* recommends that its performance should be accompanied by the usual offerings in the fire and the circumambulation of the fire by the wedded pair, on the ground that the observance of these formalities would compel the parents of the bride to recognize the validity of the marriage. The *paiśācha*, which is variously described, was marriage with a girl when drunk or insane, and is not recognized as a legitimate form by some authorities, like Āpastamba and Vasiṣṭha.

For the Vaiśya and Śūdra the forms of marriage recognized were the *gāndharva* and the *āsura* with, according to some authorities, the *paiśācha*. In modern times the forms of marriage recognized are, even for Vaiśyas and Śūdras, either the *āsura* or the *brāhma*, under which term is understood a form of marriage containing the essentials of the first four forms of the *Smṛtis*.

The *Smṛtis* do not recognize a form of marriage which plays a great part in the epic—the *svayaṁvara*, or self-choice, a ceremony at which a princess chooses for herself a suitor at a great assembly held for the purpose. The act of choice might be preceded by a trial of strength on the part of the suitors, the victor being rewarded with the hand of the maiden, and, even when this formality was omitted, it is probable enough that the choice was only nominally free, and that the princess was guided by the will of her father or brothers. The only *svayaṁvara* which the *Smṛtis* mention is the right of a daughter in any class, if her father does not find her a husband, to seek one for herself; in this case the daughter ceases to have any right to any ornaments received from her own family, while the husband need not pay any bride-price, and is permitted to steal her away.

Only the first four forms of marriage are at all religious in character; the marriage hymn of the Rigveda (x. 85), which serves to provide verses for the normal form of marriage, deals with marriage in general and the prototype of all marriage in the form of the wedding of Soma, the moon, with Sūryā, the daughter of the sun. This legend is certainly recondite in character, and it is legitimate to deduce from this fact, and from the fact that the *Smṛtis* do not deal with the forms of marriage, that the religious ceremonial was not the essential or primitive part even of the higher forms of marriage.

3. Restrictions on marriage.—It is uncertain how far the modern rule of marriage, which permits alliance between members of the same caste only, was in vogue in the early Vedic period, when the distinction of castes (*jāti*) was only in process of evolution from the system of classes (*varṇa*). It is clear from the *Brāhmaṇas* that purity of descent was an important qualification for Brāhmanship, but cases are recorded (*e.g.*, *Aitareya Brāhmaṇa*, ii. 19) which show that the son of a Brāhman and a Śūdra wife might yet be a Brāhman, and that Brāhmans could marry the daughters of members of the warrior class. With this accords the evidence of the *Gṛhyasūtras* and *Dharmasūtras*, which recognize with a good deal of agreement the right of each class to marry women of the classes below them in the established order, Brāhman, Kṣatriya, and Vaiśya, and which differ seriously only on the validity of marriages with the Śūdra women. Arrian, probably on the authority of Megasthenes, records (*Indica*, xii. 8)

[1] See M. Winternitz, *Das altindische Hochzeitsrituell*, Vienna, 1892; A. Weber and E. Haas, *Indische Studien*, v. 177-411.

that marriages were not allowed between γένη—probably a reference to the castes which were certainly in existence by 300 B.C. The Buddhist texts[1] yield the same result, but they recognize that the king might marry where he would and make his son by any wife his heir-apparent. Manu still recognizes mixed marriages subject to the rule of hypergamy, but the later *Smṛtis* tend to rule them out as objectionable. The modern rule is strict against mixed marriages, confining the possibility of marriage to the modern castes; but the date when this practice finally prevailed is unknown, as even late texts repeat the permission for such marriages sanctioned by the older authorities, and the Kulin Brāhmans of Bengal still avail themselves of this now pecuniarily very valuable privilege.

Simultaneously with the growth of the prohibition of marriage within the caste were developed restrictions on marriage within the family. In one hymn in the Rigveda (x. 10) the marriage of brother and sister is expressly treated as improper, and there is no reason to suppose that this was an innovation, as suggested by Weber.[2] No other restriction is alluded to, and the *Śatapatha Brāhmaṇa* expressly refers (I. viii. 3. 6) to marriage as permitted in the third or fourth generation, the former being the rule, according to the commentator, among the Kāṇvas, the latter among the Saurāṣṭras, while the Dākṣiṇātyas, or people of the south, permitted marriage with the son of the father's sister or daughter of the mother's brother, but not, apparently, with the son of the father's brother or the daughter of the mother's sister. The *Gṛhyasūtras* and the *Dharmasūtras* in effect agree in prescribing that marriage should not take place between a man and a woman of the same *gotra* (*q.v.*) as his father, or a *sapiṇḍā* of his mother, and these terms extended at least to all relatives within five degrees on the mother's and seven on the father's side. Later texts add to the restrictions by extending the prohibitions in the case of the mother, and by forbidding unions with the daughter of a spiritual teacher or pupil. At the same time, concessions are made to local customs, and the practice of marriage of cousins in S. India is recognized by Baudhāyana (I. ii. 3). But the practice of marrying outside the *gotra*, a term of wide extension and indefinite sense, but covering all those of the same family name, is recorded by al-Bīrūnī,[3] and is the general rule at the present day throughout India—at any rate, among all the higher castes. The chief exceptions are found in S. India, where some tribes practise the opposite rule of endogamy.

In Rājputāna, among the Rājputs who claim to be descendants of the old warrior class, exogamy is closely connected in their history with the practice of marriage by capture; but there is no sufficient evidence for the view[4] that the development of the custom generally was connected with marriage by capture.

Of much less importance are the restrictions arising from the feeling that the eldest son and the eldest daughter should be married before the younger sons and daughters, a breach of this rule being merely a ground for a penance, and not a fatal bar to the validity of the marriage. The rule is, however, very old, being found in the *Yajurveda* (*Maitrāyaṇī Saṁhitā*, IV. i. 9), and recognized throughout the later literature. In the south members of Brāhman castes adopt the practice of a mock marriage of the elder brother with a branch of a tree in order to avoid the evil result of a breach of this rule by a younger brother.

1 R. Fick, *Die sociale Gliederung im nordöstlichen Indien zu Buddha's Zeit*, Kiel, 1897, pp. 36–40.
2 See Macdonell and Keith, *Vedic Index*, i. 475, n. 7.
3 Tr. Sachau, ii. 155.
4 See Jolly, *Recht und Sitte*, p. 63.

The bride should be a virgin, and the importance of this rule lies in the fact that it renders the re-marriage of widows difficult. In the Rigveda (VI. xlix. 8) there is some indication[1] that a woman might re-marry if her husband had disappeared and could not be found or heard of, and in the Atharvaveda (IX. v. 27 f.) mention is made of a spell to secure that a woman married twice may be united in the next world with her second, not her first, husband. The reference here may be to re-marriage in the case of an absent husband or one who had lost caste. The doctrine of Manu is that a woman should never be re-married, and that the marriage formulæ are intended only for maidens, but he admits one exception in the case of a woman whose husband dies before the completion of the marriage. Other authorities permit re-marriage in the case where a husband has disappeared, is dead, has entered a monastic order, is impotent, or has been expelled from his caste; but the authorities differ widely as to the length and condition of absence which entitle a woman to re-marriage. The son of a widow who has re-married (*paunarbhava*) is ranked by Manu and other authorities only among the second six of the twelve kinds of son admitted by Hindu law. But the dislike of re-marriage was one which developed gradually; the actual reprobation of such a son first occurs in Bṛhaspati (xxv. 41), and the forbidding of the re-marriage of a widow occurs only in the *Ādipurāṇa* and later works. The objections to such marriages in modern India are very strong among those castes which lay most stress on child-marriage, and, despite the legalizing of them by Act XV. of 1856, and efforts of social reformers, they are still disapproved by the higher castes.

In the case of a man, while impotence was recognized as a ground on which the wife might contract a new marriage, the marriage was not in itself null, and even mental derangement was not regarded as justifying re-marriage on the part of the wife.

4. Polygamy.—The practice of polygamy among the Vedic Indians is abundantly proved by direct references in the Rigveda and other texts, though in the main monogamy is recognized as normal. In the case of the king four wives are expressly mentioned—the *mahiṣī*, the first wedded, the *parivṛktī*, or discarded (apparently one who bore no son), the *vāvātā*, or favourite, and the *pālāgalī*, who is explained as the daughter of one of the court officials. The *mahiṣī* seems to have been the wife proper, though the others were evidently not mere concubines. In the *Arthaśāstra*, the *Smṛtis*, and the epic the rule is laid down that a man may have wives from his own caste and each of those below his, either including or excluding the Śūdra, and in such cases the wife of the same caste was the wife *par excellence* (*dharmapatnī*), with whom the husband performed his religious duties. The heroes and Brāhmans of the epic are frequently represented as having several wives, but one of them always ranks first, and, similarly, later in inscriptions one wife only is often mentioned with her husband. The rule of precedence among wives according to caste and, within the caste, to date of marriage might, however, be overridden by the husband, who could degrade a wife from her position as chief wife; in that case he was required to make her a present equivalent to that made to the new wife whom he was marrying. The modern rule permits the husband to contract as many marriages as he wishes without any need for justification or consent on the part of his existing wives.

1 R. Pischel and K. F. Geldner. *Vedische Studien*, Stuttgart, 1888–1901, i. 27.

In addition to wives proper, the *Smṛtis* recognize the existence of concubines (*dāsī, bhujiṣyā*), who were distinguished from wives by not being married in due form, and who could not in any case become their husband's heirs. They were, however, entitled to maintenance by his brothers as his heirs on his death, and intercourse with one of them was regarded as adultery. Similarly, at the present day the keeping of concubines by wealthy Hindus is a recognized usage.

The *Smṛtis* show some preference throughout for monogamy. Āpastamba (II. xi. 12) expressly disapproves the re-marriage of a man who has a wife living, and other authorities restrict the right to become the heir of a husband to the chief wife, who is the surviving half of her husband. In all religious observances the husband is to act with his chief wife only, and marriage is treated by Manu (ix. 101) as a pledge of mutual fidelity between husband and wife.

5. Polyandry.—While polygamy is recognized in the Vedic period, though chiefly among kings and important Brāhmans, there is no clear trace of polyandry, all the passages adduced from the Rigveda (x. lxxxv. 37 f.) and the Atharvaveda (XIV. i. 44, 52, 61, ii. 14, 17) admitting of more probable explanations. On the other hand, the heroes of the epic, the five Pāṇḍavas, are represented as marrying Draupadī and having her as wife in common—a fact which is elaborately explained and defended in the epic. This form of polyandry is recognized by Bṛhaspati (xxvii. 20) as practised in the south, and by Āpastamba (II. xxvii. 2) as an antiquated use. At the present day polyandry is still found among Brāhmans, Rājputs, and Śūdras alike in Kumaon, where children are shared by the brothers as by the Pāṇḍavas, and among hill tribes in the Panjāb, where the children are divided among the brothers. The reasons given for the practice are poverty and the desire to avoid division of property. Among the Jāṭs of the Panjāb the wife of the eldest brother has to serve often as the wife of the younger brothers also, and the practice is common in the case of the Himālayan tribes. The custom also prevails in the south among the Nairs of the Kanara country and the Todas of the Nīlgiris. The modern evidence comes mainly from Tibetan and Dravidian tribes, and there is no indication that the practice was ever widely spread among tribes of Aryan culture.

6. Divorce.—The characteristic quality of a Hindu marriage was that it was a union for life; in striking contrast to the Dravidian and Tibeto-Burman usages, marriages among Hindus were seldom broken by divorce. In the *Smṛti* literature,[1] however, cases are recognized in which divorce in the form of the contracting of a new marriage by the wife during her husband's lifetime is allowed, and the occasions for divorce (*tyāga*), *i.e.* abandoning a wife and leaving her without maintenance on the part of the husband, are set out. The abandonment of a faithful wife counts as a serious crime, which must be expiated by a severe penance, and which may involve expulsion from caste. Adultery affords a ground for divorce, and might in certain cases be punished with death, but, according to other authorities, it could be expiated by severe penances. Any serious offence against a husband might, according to Yājñavalkya (i. 72), be a ground of divorce, and Nārada (xii. 92, 93) gives as offences justifying such treatment attempts to murder, wasting property, or the procuring of abortion. In modern Hindu law divorce depends on local custom and, where allowed, is permitted only for adultery, but divorces are very common among all Dravidian tribes, which also allow freely re-marriage of wives in the case of the disappearance, long-continued absence, impotence, or loss of caste of their husbands.

[1] The *Kauṭilīya Arthaśāstra* (possibly 4th cent. B.C.) goes far in allowing divorce (III. ii. 59, iii. 59).

7. Position of widows.—In the funeral rites of the Rigveda the wife of the dead man is represented (x. xviii. 7 f.) as lying beside him on the pyre and as being summoned to leave the dead in order to be united with his brother, apparently as a bride. The passage clearly shows that the wife was not to be burned with the dead, but it unmistakably suggests the existence of an older custom to this effect, and the Atharvaveda (XVIII. iii. 1) refers to this as an old practice.[1] It was evidently not approved by the Brāhmans of the Vedic age, for it is not mentioned in the *sūtras*, and appears first in the late *Vaikhānasa Gṛhyasūtra* (vii. 2) and in interpolated passages of the *Viṣṇu Smṛti* (xxv. 14, xx. 39). The later *Smṛtis* approve it, but not without occasional dissent. In the epics it plays little part,[2] though one of Pāṇḍu's wives insisted on being burned with her husband (*Mahābhārata*, I. cxxv. 31); but in the later romances and historical works it is often mentioned, and as early as A.D. 509–510 an inscription is found to celebrate a *satī*. Forbidden in British India in 1829, it was observed in 1839 in the Panjāb at the death of Ranjit Singh, and in 1877 at that of the Mahārāja of Nepāl. The primitive character of the rite is shown by the fact that often other attendants perished with the queen or queens when the dead man was a prince. Normally the wife was burned with the dead man; if he died away from home, she might be burned alone (*anumaraṇa*), but the burning of a pregnant widow or one with a young child was forbidden, and the practice was normally more or less voluntary, except in the case of royal families, where reasons of policy doubtless reinforced considerations of religion in favour of burning.

In many cases death was doubtless regarded as preferable to the fate of a widow, whom the *Smṛtis* and modern usage, despite the efforts of reformers, condemn to a life of fasting, devotions to her dead husband, pilgrimages, and abstinence from any form of luxury, such as the use of a bed, ornaments, etc. If she had grown-up sons, she fell under their control; if not, under that of her husband's kin, who were bound to maintain her so long as she remained faithful to her late husband. The later texts also recognize her right to be heir to her husband, but only on condition that she remained unmarried—a disability which is not altered by Act XV. of 1856. The harshness of the rule is better realized when it is remembered that the practice of child-marriages enormously increases the number of widows.

In the Rigveda it seems to have been the practice for the wife of the dead man to be taken in marriage by his brother, whether or not the latter had a wife already. This, the natural interpretation of the funeral hymn (x. xviii. 8; cf. also xl. 2), is borne out by the fact that the modern usage in the Panjāb,[3] which has preserved much of ancient practice, is for a man to marry his brother's widow, with the result that many men have two wives. In the *sūtras*, however, this practice is whittled down to the permission given to the brother of the dead or, if there is no brother, a near kinsman to beget a son with the widow in order to continue the race of the dead man. Such a son, when of age, would inherit his father's property, which, until then, would be managed by his mother or by his real father, to

[1] A. Hillebrandt, *ZDMG* xl. [1886] 710, explains these passages quite differently; but his view can hardly be correct.
[2] H. Jacobi, *Das Rāmāyaṇa*, Bonn, 1893, p. 107 f.
[3] Cf. Bṛhaspati, xxvii. 20, ii. 31; *Arthaśāstra*, III. iv. 59.

whose estate also he might in certain cases succeed. By an extension of the principle the texts allow an impotent or ill man to appoint another during his life to beget a son for him, and in the epic the right to act in these cases is frequently recognized as specially appropriate for Brāhmans. But the general tendency of the later *Smṛtis* is more and more against the practice, which was subjected to increasing restrictions or absolutely forbidden, and in modern times the practice of appointment (*niyoga*) has been replaced by the more primitive form of actual marriage with a brother's widow.[1]

8. Marriage and morality.—Though fidelity on the part of both parties to a marriage was doubtless an ideal, there is abundant evidence throughout the literature that infidelity on the part of the husband was neither rare nor considered worthy of moral censure. In the case of the wife there is no doubt that in the *Smṛti* literature and in modern usage adultery is regarded as a serious offence which may in certain cases be punished by death. Some of the Vedic passages (*Taittirīya Saṁhitā*, v. vi. 8. 3; *Maitrāyaṇī Saṁhitā*, III. iv. 7) cited as showing tolerance of adultery are susceptible of other interpretations, but there remain the facts that a special ritual at the *Varuṇapraghāsa* is clearly intended to remove the ill-effects of adultery (*Maitrāyaṇī Saṁhitā*, I. x. 11; *Śatapatha Brāhmaṇa*, II. v. 2. 20), that the *Bṛhadāraṇyaka Upaniṣad* (VI. iv. 11) contains a spell to expiate adultery with the wife of a Brāhman, and that the *Bhāradvāja Gṛhyasūtra* (ii. 28) advises a husband how to proceed in the case of going on a journey if he desires his wife to have lovers in his absence. The romances and fable literature frequently allude to cases of infidelity, and the *Arthaśāstra* and the *Smṛtis* recognize as one kind of son the *gūḍhotpanna*, or secretly born, an illegitimate son who can, nevertheless, succeed to the property of his mother's lawful husband. Baudhāyana (II. iii. 34) and Āpastamba (II. xiii. 7) preserve a saying of a sage to the mythical king Janaka, referring to a time when the virtue of married women was lightly estimated, and the *Mahābhārata* refers (I. cxxii. 4 ff.) to a time when wives were used in common, a practice terminated by Śvetaketu. The lack of chastity of the women of the East is recorded by Bṛhaspati (ii. 30). Too much stress must not, however, be laid on these notices; the reference to the Eastern women may be an allusion to the loose marital relations in Tibet, and the references to the lax morality of previous times are made for the purpose of proving that the recognition of illegitimate sons then accorded was antiquated at the time of the texts.

9. Marriage and property.—The widow of the dead man, according to the *Nirukta* (iii. 4) and Baudhāyana (II. iii. 44–46), was denied the power of becoming an heir. Gautama (xxviii. 21 f.) mentions her in the list of heirs, but points out the alternative of the adoption of the practice of *niyoga* for providing the son in whose absence alone could the mother be heir. In Viṣṇu (xvii. 4) and Yājñavalkya (ii. 135) is first found the express mention of the widow as the next heir in the absence of male issue. But the extent of the right thus obtained is expressly limited by the texts: the widow could not give away, or mortgage, or sell the property thus inherited; she held it for her enjoyment for life, subject to continued chastity and to her not contracting a second marriage, but she held it under the control of her husband's kindred and with the limitation that it should return to them on her death.[2] If there were several widows, the chief wife seems to have been entitled alone to succeed as heir, but on her fell the duty of maintaining the other wives—a rule which is not recognized in modern Hindu law, where all the wives have an equal right of succession.

Distinct from the property obtained by inheritance was the *strīdhana* of the wife, which is mentioned by Gautama, but first described in detail in the *Arthaśāstra* (III. ii. 59) and by Viṣṇu (xvii. 18). It included any presents from parents, sons, brothers, or kinsmen, the marriage gifts, the bride-price when given by her father to her, and the fine paid by her husband in the case where she was degraded from her position as chief wife in favour of another. This property fell on her death to her daughters, if she had any; if not, apparently to her sons, who, according to some authorities, shared it with their sisters in any event; and, in the case of failure of all issue, to her husband only if she had been married according to one of the four superior forms of marriage; otherwise it went to her father. In some cases the unmarried daughter was preferred to the married in heirship to her mother. In the later *Kātyāyana Smṛti* (xx. 80 ff.) are found elaborate rules as to the power of a woman over her *strīdhana*. She was at liberty to dispose in any way of presents from living relatives, even if consisting of immovables; her husband could not use them without her consent. She was also entitled to receive from her sons any property promised by their father and not paid to her, while gifts to wives were encouraged, if not exceeding 2000 *paṇas* or consisting of immovables. On her death her property went back, in so far as it consisted of gifts from relatives, to those relatives; the rest went to any unmarried daughter, or, failing such, to her sons and married daughters, while, if she left no children, her property passed to her parents if she were married in one of the lower forms of marriage, and any landed property went to her brothers. The later texts and the commentators develop in much detail the doctrine of *strīdhana*, and the *Mitākṣarā* (a commentary on Yājñavalkya) argues that all property which women receive in any way falls under that head, and must obey the special laws of devolution of *strīdhana* proper. This is contrary to the earlier evidence, which expressly differentiates between *strīdhana* in the narrow sense and property inherited from a husband, earned by a woman's own exertions, or given by strangers, over which she can exercise power of disposal only with her husband's consent.

LITERATURE.—In addition to many notices scattered throughout the literature, the Hindu marriage of the end of the Vedic period and in the classical period is dealt with in the *Dharmasūtras* and in the *Smṛtis* with their commentaries, and in comprehensive treatises based on the *Smṛtis*. Of the *sūtra* texts, those of Āpastamba, Gautama, Vasiṣtha, and Baudhāyana have been translated by G. Bühler (*SBE* ii.[2] [1897] and xiv. [1882]). The *Smṛti* of Manu has also been translated by Bühler (*ib.* xxv. [1886]), and those of Viṣṇu, Nārada, and Bṛhaspati by J. Jolly (*ib.* vii. [1900] and xxxiii. [1889]). Yājñavalkya has been translated by A. Stenzler, Berlin, 1849. Of these Manu is the oldest, Yājñavalkya may be dated in the 4th cent. A.D., Nārada about A.D. 500, and Bṛhaspati about 600. Somewhat earlier than Bṛhaspati is Kātyāyana. Of the later texts the *Mitākṣarā* of Vijñāneśvara (c. A.D. 1100) is the most important, as having become authoritative throughout India except in Bengal. Of modern works, for the Vedic period the most important are: A. Weber, *Indische Studien*, Berlin and Leipzig, 1849–84, v. and x.; B. Delbrück, 'Die indogermanischen Verwandtschaftsnamen,' in *ASG* xxv. [1889] 381–606; H. Zimmer, *Altindisches Leben*, Berlin, 1879; and A. A. Macdonell and A. B. Keith, *Vedic Index*, London, 1912. For the epic a full account is contained in E. W. Hopkins, art. in *JAOS* xiii. [1889], and much material is also given by R. Schmidt, *Beiträge zur ind. Erotik*, Leipzig, 1902. The rules of the law-books and the modern law are dealt with in R. West and G. Bühler, *Digest of Hindu Law*[3], Bombay, 1884, and in J. D. Mayne, *Hindu Law and Usage*[3], Madras, 1883, and a summary of the whole subject with full citations and references to the literature is given by J. Jolly, in *Recht und Sitte*, Strassburg, 1896 (=*GIAP* ii. 8).

A. BERRIEDALE KEITH.

[1] Mayne, *Hindu Law and Usage*, § 69.
[2] Kātyāyana, xxiv. 55 ff.; Bṛhaspati, xxv. 46 ff.

MARRIAGE (Iranian).—**I. Zoroastrian.**—According to the sacred texts of Zoroastrianism, marriage is divinely favoured (*Vendīdād*, iv. 47; cf. artt. ASCETICISM [Persian], FAMILY [Persian]). The second happiest place in the world is that in which a righteous man sets up his household (*Vend.* iii. 2). In the *Gāthās* the pair who wed are urged to strive to live a life of righteousness and to help one another in good deeds (*Ys.* liii. 5).

Since marriage is regarded as almost a religious duty, Zoroastrians hold it a meritorious act to help their co-religionists to enter the wedded state, and such assistance may even serve to atone for sin (*Vend.* iv. 44, xiv. 15). It is by no means unusual, therefore, for Parsis to enjoin by will or by a trust that a certain amount of their wealth be expended in aiding poor brides to marry, and certain institutions, as the Parsi Pañchāyat of Bombay, provide special funds for this purpose.

The Parsi community in India has passed through so many vicissitudes that it is difficult to determine which of the various marriage customs of the Parsis were originally Zoroastrian, although it appears to be practically certain that the strictly religious portion comes under this category. At the very beginning of the *Aśirvād*, or blessing known as the *Paēvand-nāmah*, which is recited at the wedding ceremony, the officiating priest declares that the ceremony is 'according to the law and custom of the Mazdayasnian religion.'

According to the Avesta, both manhood and womanhood were attained at the age of 15 (*Ys.* ix. 5; *Yt.* viii. 13 f., xiv. 17; *Vend.* xiv. 15; *Bundahiśn*, iii. 19). Since in the Avesta we find maidens praying for suitable husbands (*Ys.* ix. 23;[1] *Yt.* v. 87), it would appear that child-marriage was not practised. The ritual recited at the marriage ceremony, bidding the pair to express their consent after 'truthful consideration,' points in the same direction. The present Parsi Marriage Act enjoins the age of 21 for males and 18 for females; if the contracting pair are below that age, the marriage certificate must be signed by their parents.

The marriage ceremony is preceded by several other rites. When the match is arranged, an auspicious day is fixed for the betrothal, such as the day of new moon, or the first (Hormuzd) or twentieth (Bāhram) day of the Parsi month. At times, especially in Mofussil (provincial) towns, the parties consult Hindu astrologers, who name one or more auspicious days for the betrothal, marriage, etc. The match is usually arranged by the parents, with the consent of their children; but often, at the present time, the contracting parties make their own choice with the approval of their parents. Mutual friends of the two families generally carry messages and bring about the match—a course recommended by the *Pand-nāmak-ī-Āturpāt-ī-Māraspandān* (xlii.) and attested in the *Śāh-nāmah* (tr. A. G. and E. Warner, London, 1905 ff., i. 177 ff., ii. 125, 86–88) by the marriages of the three sons of Farīdūn with the daughters of the king of Yemen, of Rustam with Tahmīnah, and of Kāūs with Sūdhābah. Until recently professional match-makers were not unknown, and they still exercise a certain amount of activity.

On the day of betrothal[2] the women of the groom's family visit the house of the bride and present silver coins to her, and the groom receives a similar present from the women of the bride's family. The older term for this ceremony, now called *adrāvvūn*, was *nām pādvūn*, 'to name' (from Pers. *nāmzad shudan*), since after the betrothal the bride receives in religious recitals of prayers for her the name of the groom, even though, by some mishap, marriage does not take place. An unbetrothed girl was said to be 'unnamed' (*nā kardah nām*). Betrothal is regarded as a solemn part of the marriage ceremony, the *miθra vīrō-maza*, or 'pledge of the magnitude of a man' (*Vend.* iv. 2, 4, 9, 15), being considered by the *Rivāyats* to mean a promise of marriage. At the present time the priests do not take an active part in the betrothal, except in Mofussil towns, where two priests—one for each family—formally ask the parents that the bride and groom respectively be given in marriage to each other. The priests took part in the *nāmzad* (betrothal) at Surat in the middle of the 18th cent. (Anquetil du Perron, *Zend-Avesta*, Paris, 1771, ii. 557 f.), when the two families met, and the groom's family priest, after prayer, placed the hand of one of the contracting parties in that of the other.

The betrothal is followed by the Divō, when a lamp (*divō*) is lit early in the morning, and the women of the two families interchange visits and gifts. This day is regarded as more important than the betrothal proper, because on it the dresses and wedding rings are usually presented. The Divō is followed by the Ādarni, when the dowry given by the bride's father is presented to the groom's family.[1] Presents are exchanged, chiefly from the bride's family, on several other days between betrothal and marriage.

An auspicious day, such as the day of new or full moon, is fixed for the marriage as for the betrothal. Tuesday and Wednesday are inauspicious.

In some families the astrologer's services are engaged before the marriage also. When matches are being arranged by mutual friends, the horoscopes of the intending bride and groom are submitted to him, to find whether the stars predict harmony between the pair. If this is not to be the case, the projected match is broken off.

In the morning or afternoon of the marriage day the bride and groom take a sacred bath—a custom which is mentioned in the *Śāh-nāmah* (ed. T. Macan, Calcutta, 1829, p. 1579), where Bahrām Gūr takes his Indian wife to the fire temple for that purpose. The religious portion of the wedding is usually performed shortly after sunset, perhaps to symbolize that, just as day and night unite and blend, so the wedded pair should be united in weal and woe.

The marriage is generally celebrated with much pomp, as was the case in ancient Irān, as recorded in the *Dīnkarṭ* (ed. P. B. Sanjana, Bombay, 1874 ff., ii. 97). The groom, wearing a white ceremonial robe and holding a shawl in his hand, sits among friends and relatives of his own sex in the compound. Around his neck he has a garland of flowers, and on his forehead is a vertical line of red pigment (*kuṅkun*). In colour this is held by some to represent in India an earlier custom of the sacrifice of animal life, and in shape to symbolize the brilliant, fructifying sun, whereas the round *kuṅkun* of the bride is supposed to be a symbol of the moon, which absorbs the rays of the sun.

A short time before the marriage, a procession, headed by the officiating priests, and often by a band of music, goes to the house of the bride, where the ceremony generally takes place. The men seat themselves in the compound, and the women in the house. At the door, the side posts of which—like those of the groom's house—are

[1] Geiger, *Ostīrān. Kultur*, p. 241, sees in this passage an allusion to the custom of asking the hand of the bride from her parent or guardian (cf. also *Vend.* xv. 9).

[2] A considerable time might elapse between betrothal and marriage (*Vend.* xv. 9; cf. Geiger, p. 242).

[1] In early times it was apparently more customary for the groom to give presents. The sum of 2000 silver dirhāms and 2 gold dīnārs, mentioned in the *Aśirvād*, seems to have been the average sum which a groom of moderate means was expected to provide for his bride. On the *Aśirvād*, with Pahlavi, Pāzand, and Skr. text and tr., see Shapurji Kavasji Hodivala, *Zarathushtra and his Contemporaries in the Rigveda*, Bombay, 1913, pp. 77–80.

marked with turmeric (whose yellow colour is held to symbolize the sun, and hence abundance and fertility), the groom is welcomed by his future mother-in-law, a fresh mark of *kuṅkun* is made on his forehead, and rice is made to adhere to it, and is also thrown over his head.

During the marriage ceremony the officiating priest again sprinkles rice over the bride and groom, and before the recital of the marriage blessing the pair throw a handful of rice on each other, some mothers making the couple eat a few grains of rice thus thrown.

An egg, a coco-nut, and a little tray of water are now passed three times round the groom's head and cast away, and in the course of the evening the women of the bride's family make the groom dip his hand in a water-jar, in which he leaves for them a silver coin. Formerly it was also the custom for the feet of the bride and groom to be washed after the marriage ceremony, but the adoption of English foot-gear has caused this to survive only in washing the tip of the boots.

After the groom has been thus welcomed at the door, he is made to cross the threshold without touching it, and with his right foot first, these precautions being observed also by the bride when she first enters her husband's house. Having entered the house, the groom awaits the bride, who sits on his left, the chairs being placed in the centre of the apartment. On stands beside the chairs are trays of rice to be thrown over the pair, and lighted candles, while beside the bride is a small vessel of *ghī* and molasses (typifying gentleness and sweetness); a servant stands before the pair, holding a burning censer in one hand and a little frankincense in the other. Beside each of the contracting parties stands a witness, usually the nearest kin, and generally married persons.

The following requisites are necessary for a regular marriage: (1) the marriage must be celebrated before an assembly of at least five persons who have been summoned for this special occasion; (2) the contracting parties are asked by the officiating priest whether they consent to be united in wedlock; (3) the hands of bride and groom are joined (*hāthvarō*, 'hand-fastening') and a symbolic knot also plays a prominent part in the ceremony; (4) the actual marriage ceremony is followed by a benediction accompanied by sprinkling with rice, etc.

Before being seated side by side, the bride and groom are made to sit opposite each other, separated by a piece of cloth as a curtain. The senior officiating priest now joins the right hands of the pair, and, with the recital of the *Yathā ahū vairyō*, a piece of cloth is passed round the chairs of both so as to form a circle, the ends of the cloth being tied together. With a repetition of the *Yathā ahū vairyō* the *hāthevarō* is then performed by fastening the right hands with twists of raw yarn, which is passed round the hands seven times, then seven times round the bridal pair, and, finally, an equal number of times round the knot in the encircling cloth. The fee for this ceremony is the perquisite of the family priests, even though the rite may be performed by other priests. The attendant next puts frankincense on the fire, and the curtain between the pair is dropped, while the bride and groom throw over each other a few grains of rice which they have held in their left hands. The one who first throws the rice is said to 'win,' and during the recital of the benedictions the priests also throw rice over the pair. They are now seated side by side.

The more strictly religious portion of the ceremony follows. Two priests stand before the pair, the elder of whom blesses them, praying that Ahura Mazda may grant them 'progeny of sons and grandsons, abundant means, strong friendship, bodily strength, long life, and an existence of 150 years.' He then asks the witness who stands beside the groom whether, on behalf of the bridegroom's family, he consents to the marriage 'in accordance with the rites and rules of the Mazdayasnians, promising to pay her [the bride] 2000 dirhāms of pure white silver and 2 dīnārs of real gold of Nīshāpūr coinage.' A similar question is asked of the witness for the bride's family, and then of the contracting parties, the questions being repeated thrice. Next follows the recital, by both the officiating priests, of the *Paēvand-nāmah* or *Aśīrvād* (tr. F. Spiegel, *Avesta übersetzt*, Leipzig, 1852–63, iii. 232–234, and, in great part, by the present writer, in Dosabhai Framji Karaka, *Hist. of the Parsis*, i. 182 ff.). The admonitions in the *Aśīrvād* are followed by a series of benedictions, in which Ahura Mazda is besought to grant to the wedded pair the moral and social virtues characterizing the *yazatas* (angels) who give their names to the thirty days of the month. Prayer is also made for other blessings, and that the bride and groom may be granted the virtues and qualities of the great heroes of ancient Irān, that they may live long, and have many children, etc. A portion of this address is repeated in Sanskrit—probably a reminiscence of the times of the earliest Parsi emigration to India, when it was desired to make the address intelligible to their Indian hosts.

The *Aśīrvād* is followed by another group of benedictions in Pāzand, this group being called the *Tan darustī* (ed. E. K. Antiā, *Pâzend Texts*, Bombay, 1909, p. 160 f., tr. Spiegel, *op. cit.* iii.).

The marriage ritual is repeated at midnight. From Anquetil du Perron (i., pt. i. 319, ii. 558, n. 5) this appears to be a reminiscence of the earlier Persian custom when, in Kirmān, the marriage ceremony was performed at midnight. This custom is not, however, universal.

A number of minor usages, not regarded in any way as part of the solemn ritual, are also observed, especially by women, in the Mofussil towns. The first of these, which, like the others of this class, is now observed more as a joke, is *chhedā chedi*, in which the nearest friends or relatives tie the skirt of the *jāmā*, or flowing dress, of the groom to that of the *sārī* of the bride; thus united, the pair go to the bridegroom's house. This is followed by foot-washing (cf. above), after which comes the *dahi kūmrō*, or making the newly-wedded pair partake of food consisting of *dapi* (curd) and rice from the same dish, each giving the other to eat. Another custom, now almost obsolete, is making the bride and groom play *eki beki* ('odd or even'). Each takes several rupees in the right hand and asks the other whether the number is odd (*eki*) or even (*beki*); if the opposite party guesses the number rightly, he or she is said to win. The underlying principle is probably similar to that of the rivalry of bride and groom to be the first to cast rice on the other, as already noted.

Marriage songs are sung frequently through the nuptial ceremony; and the whole concludes with a banquet, at which courses of fish (a symbol of good omen) and sweets are essential, but meat is forbidden, either out of deference to Hindu scruples or from motives of economy.

JIVANJI JAMSHEDJI MODI.

2. Next-of-kin marriage.—A problem of peculiar delicacy in connexion with Iranian marriage is the question of the *xvaētvadatha* (Pahlavi *xvētōkdas*), usually translated 'next-of-kin marriage.'[1] The modern Parsis maintain that this is a marriage

[1] The etymology of the word is apparently *xvaētu*, 'belonging to (esp. the community or sib)'—cognate with Lat. *suus*—and *vadatha*, 'marriage' (C. Bartholomae, *Altiran. Wörterb.*, Strassburg, 1904, col. 1860). For a less plausible etymology, based on native tradition (*Dīnkart*, iii. 82, tr. West, *SBE* xviii. 400), see Darmesteter, *Zend-Avesta*, i. 126 n.

between first cousins, and such is certainly its present connotation. The Greek and Latin writers, on the other hand, regarded *xvaētvadatha* as referring to marriages of parents with children and of uterine brothers and sisters; and in this view they are followed by the great majority of non-Parsi scholars of the present day.

The Avesta itself offers no data for the solution of the problem, and mentions *xvaētvadatha* only in five passages—all late.

The Mazdayasnian religion commands *xvaētvadatha* (*Ys.* xii. 9); in certain religious ceremonies a young man is to be chosen who has contracted it (*Visp.* iii. 3; cf. *Gāh* iv. 8); corpse-bearers may be purified, not only with the urine of cattle, but also with the mingled urine of a man and woman who have performed *xvaētvadatha* (*Vend.* viii. 13; no other human beings can produce this vehicle of purification); and Vīshtāspa is the protector, among others, of the youth who fulfils the requirement of *xvaētvadatha* (*Yt.* xxiv. 17). Bartholomae's claim (col. 1822) that Vīshtāspa's wife Hutaosa was also his sister, on the basis of *Yt.* xv. 35 f., can scarcely be deemed cogent (see Moulton, *Early Zoroastrianism*, p. 206 f.), in spite of the assertion of the late Pahlavi *Yāṭkār-ī-Zarīrān*, 48. The Pahlavi commentator on *Ys.* xlv. 4 clearly sees an allusion to *xvaētvadatha* between father and daughter, but the text does not sustain his exegesis.[1]

The evidence of the Greek and Latin writers is unambiguous as regards the nature of *xvaētvadatha*. That the royal house should practise the marriage of parents and children, or of brothers and sisters, is not inexplicable. It probably rests, at least in historic times, upon a desire to keep the royal blood absolutely pure, and finds a conspicuous illustration in the history of Egyptian dynasties.[2] Thus Cambyses married his sister, and, though Herodotus says (iii. 31) that before this ruler's time 'the Persians were not wont to cohabit with their sisters,' we are told that the notorious Parysatis urged her son Artaxerxes Longimanus to wed his sister Atossa (Plut. *Artax.* 23; cf. Euseb. *Præp. Evang.* vi. 275 C; for a less certain instance see Ctesias, *Pers.* 2), to whom her own brother Darius later offered marriage (Plut. *Artax.* 26). The Bactrian satrap Sysimithres married his mother (Quintus Curtius, VIII. ii. 19), and Terituchmes his sister (Ctesias, *Pers.* 54). The only case alleged in the Sasanian period was the marriage of Kavāṭ with his daughter Sambyke (Agathias, ii. 23). The custom is reported, however, not only of the royal family, but also of the Persians generally. Marital relations with mother, daughter, or sister are ascribed to them by Diogenes Laertius (*Proœm.* 7, ix. 83), Strabo (p. 735), Plutarch (*de Fort. Alex.* i. 5), Antisthenes (quoted by Athenæus, v. 63), Jerome (*in Jovin.* ii. 7), Clemens Alexandrinus (*Pæd.* i. 7), and Minucius Felix (*Octav.* 31). Philo states (*de Spec. Legg.*, p. 778 B) that children from union of mother and son were deemed particularly well-born, and Catullus says (lxxxiii. 3 f.) that 'magus ex matre et gnato gignatur oportet.'

This last quotation is of considerable significance in determining the real origin of a custom which excited horror among the classical authors. Xanthus Lydus, as cited by Clemens Alexandrinus (*Strom.* iii. 2, *ad fin.*), had, centuries before, recorded such marriages as peculiarly Magian, and Strabo (p. 1068) declared them to be an ancient usage (cf. also Sotion, cited by Diog. Laert. *Proœm.* 7). In the Sasanian period the Christian martyr Mihrāmgushnasp had, before his conversion, married his sister (G. Hoffmann, *Auszüge aus syr. Akten pers. Märtyrer*, Leipzig, 1880, p. 95); and, some two centuries later, the reformer of Magianism, Bah Afrīd, forbade his followers to marry their mothers, sisters, daughters, or nieces (al-Bīrūnī, *Chronology of Anc. Nations*, tr. E. Sachau, London, 1879, p. 194; al-Shahrastānī, *Religionspartheien und Philosophenschulen*, tr. T. Haarbrücker, Halle, 1850–51, i. 284; cf. also above, p. 401[b]). Yet there was a tradition, reported by Mas'ūdī (*Prairies d'or*, ed. and tr. Barbier de Meynard and Pavet de Courteille, Paris, 1861–77, ii. 145), that Farīdūn (the Thraētaona of the Avesta) begot a daughter by his granddaughter, another by his great-granddaughter, and so to the seventh generation (cf. also Justi, *Iran. Namenbuch*, Marburg, 1895, p. 192).

In the Pahlavi texts allusions to *xvētōkdas* are common. Observance of it is one of the surest signs of piety in the coming days of evil, *i.e.* the Arab conquest (*Bahman Yt.* ii. 57, 61); it expiates mortal sin and forms the one insuperable barrier to the attacks of Aēshm, the incarnation of Fury (*Šāyast lā-Šāyast*, viii. 18, xviii. 3 f.); it is especially obnoxious to demons, whose power it impairs (*Dīnkarṭ*, iii. 82); it is the second of the seven good works of religion, and its neglect the fourth of the thirty heinous sins, and it is the ninth of the thirty-three ways of gaining heaven (*Dīnā-ī Māīnōg-ī-Xraṭ*, iv. 4, xxxvi. 7, xxxvii. 12). It is even said to have been prescribed by Zarathushtra as the eighth of his ten admonitions to mankind (*Dīnkarṭ*, iii. 195; cf. *Selections of Zāṭ-Sparam*, xxiii. 13), and to arrange it is a work of merit (*Dāṭistān-ī Dīnīk*, lxxviii. 19). In a word, from it is to arise 'complete progress in the world . . . even unto the time of the renovation of the universe' (*ib.* lxxvii. 6 f.).

These Pahlavi texts, however, cast no light on the precise connotation of the term. Yet there are references in this literature which are the reverse of ambiguous. The Pahlavi synopsis of the 18th *fargarṭ* of the lost Avesta *Varaštmānsar Nask* clearly refers to the *xvētōkdas* of brother and sister (*Dīnkarṭ*, IX. xli. 27),[1] and that of the 21st *fargarṭ* of the lost *Bakŏ Nask* to the wedlock of father and daughter (*ib.* lxvii. 7, 9).[2] The most explicit statement is found in the account of a controversy between a Zoroastrian theologian and a Jewish objector, recorded in *Dīnkarṭ*, iii. 82 (tr. West, pp. 399–410):

'The consummation of the mutual assistance of men is Khvêtûkdas. . . . That union . . . is . . . that with near kinsfolk, and, among near kinsfolk, that with those next-of-kin; and the mutual connection of the three kinds of nearest kin—which are father and daughter, son and she who bore him, and brother and sister—is the most complete that I have considered.'

These three forms are illustrated, respectively, by the union between Ahura Mazda and his daughter Spenta Armaiti (cf. on *Ys.* xlv. 4, above; and on its probable origin as a cosmogonic myth of the ἱερὸς γάμος of Heaven and Earth, cf. L. H. Gray, *ARW* vii. [1904] 367), from which sprang the primeval being Gāyōmarṭ; by the return of some of the seed of the dying Gāyōmarṭ to Spenta Armaiti (cf. also *Bundahišn*, xv. 1; *Dāṭistān-ī-Dīnīk*, lxiv. 6; al-Bīrūnī, p. 107), resulting in the birth of the first human pair, Masyē and Masyāōī; and by their prolific union (cf. also *Dīnkarṭ*, VII. i. 10, *Dāṭistān-ī-Dīnīk*, xxxvii. 82, lxv., lxxvii. 4 f.).[3]

In the 8th chapter of a Pahlavi *Rivāyat*, probably

[1] See L. H. Mills, *Gâthâs*, Oxford, 1892–1913, p. 224 f.; West, *SBE* xviii. 392 f. The latter scholar dates the final revision of the Pahlavi version in the 6th century. For another possible, though uncertain, reference to the *xvaētvadatha* of Ahura Mazda and Spenta Armaiti, see *Dīnkarṭ*, IX. lx. 2–5. There is an unmistakable allusion to it in *Dīnkarṭ*, III. lxxxii. Darmesteter, *Zend-Avesta*, i. 344, n. 12, misunderstands the Pahlavi commentary on *Ys.* liii. 3 as containing a possible reference to *xvaētvadatha*; for the correct rendering see Mills, p. 376 f.

[2] For many other instances see F. Justi, *GIrP* ii. [1904] 437; E. Westermarck, *Hist. of Human Marriage*[2], London, 1894, pp. 290–295. Cf. also 'Egyptian' section above.

[1] The statement that Arṭā-ī-Vīrāf 'had seven sisters, and all these seven sisters were as wives of Vīrāf' (*Arṭā-ī-Vīrāf Nāmak*, ii. 1–3, 7–10; scarcely earlier than the 6th cent. A.D.) may be compared, but is not absolutely certain in meaning (West, p. 397 f.).

[2] So West, p. 397; later (*SBE* xxxvii. [1892] 382) he retranslates the passage so that *xvētōkdas* is not necessarily implied.

[3] Another stock argument for brother-and-sister marriage was found in the legend of the union of the primeval twins Yima and his sister (Pahlavi Yim and Yimak; see *Bund.* xxiii. 1, and West, *SBE* xviii. 418 f.), which is not mentioned in the extant Avesta, though it evidently dates from the Indo-Iranian period, since it forms the theme of Rigveda x. 10.

written between the Arab conquest of Persia and the 16th cent., found preceding the *Dāṭistān-ī-Dīnīk* in many MSS, there is a lengthy polemic in favour of *xvētōkdas*, there written *xvētōdāṭ* (ed. Bamanji Nasarvanji Dhabar, *Pahlavi Rivâyat accompanying the Dâdistân-î-Dînîk*, Bombay, 1913, pp. 9–21, tr. in extracts West, *SBE* xviii. 415–423). Defending it by the old examples of Ahura Mazda and Spenta Armaiti and of Masyē and Masyāōi, it declares that, when contracted with mother, daughter, or sister, *xvētōkdas* is superior in religious merit even to the ceremonial worship of Ahura Mazda, the replenishing of the sacred fire, or showing becoming reverence to a priest, and that it saves the most heinous sinner from hell.

When the millennium is about to dawn, 'all mankind will perform Khvêtûdâd, and every fiend will perish through the miracle and power of Khvêtûdâd.' The first time that a man practises it, 'a thousand demons will die, and two thousand wizards and witches . . . and when he goes near to it four times, it is known that the man and woman become perfect. . . . Whoever keeps one year in a marriage of Khvêtûdâd becomes just as though one-third of all this world . . . had been given by him . . . unto a righteous man. . . . And when he keeps four years in his marriage, and his [funeral] ritual is performed, it is known that his soul thereby goes unto the supreme heaven (garôdmân); and when the ritual is not performed, it goes thereby to the ordinary heaven (vahishtô).' The good deeds of those who observe *xvētōkdas* are a hundred times more efficacious than the same deeds performed by other pious men; and the penalty for dissuading from it is hell.

From certain passages in the same chapter it is very evident that *xvētōkdas* in the narrow sense here advocated was by no means pleasing to the Parsi community.

Thus, when Ahura Mazda and Zarathushtra held colloquy, 'Zaratûsht spoke thus: "Which duty and good work shall I do first?" Aûharmazd spoke thus: "Khvêtûdâd." . . . Zaratûsht spoke unto Aûharmazd thus: "In my eyes it is an evil (vadô) which is performed." . . . Aûharmazd spoke thus: "In my eyes, also, it is just as in thine; but "'—since nothing is so perfect that there is no evil mixed with it—'"it should not seem so"' (West, p. 423).

As early as the date of composition of *Dīnkarṭ*, iii. 82, however, there are indications that *xvētōkdas* had come to bear its present meaning of marriage of first cousins, and this is the teaching of more modern Parsi *Rivāyats* (West, pp. 404, 425 f.) and the practice of Zoroastrians at the present day.

The Parsi theory of the origin of *xvaētvadatha* is fairly clear. The *Dīnkarṭ* holds (iii. 82) that its basis was a desire to preserve purity of race, to increase the compatibility of husband and wife, and to increase the affection for children, which would be felt in redoubled measure for offspring so wholly of the same family. Another reason—doubtless well founded, especially after the Arab conquest—was that marriage outside the family might tend to religious laxity and even to perversion to another faith (*Rivāyat* viii., tr. West, p. 416 f.). As a matter of fact, however, these arguments are inadequate to explain the real origin, and the suggestion of Justi (*GIrP* ii. 435) that the source is to be found in Egypt (cf. 'Egyptian' section, above) is equally improbable.

There is no evidence that incestuous *xvaētvadatha* was known in the Avesta,[1] and it is not until Pahlavi writings of the 6th–9th centuries that it is unmistakably advocated (West, p. 427 f.). At the same time, the testimony of the Greek and Latin writers cannot be ignored; and, while we may grant, for the sake of argument, that in the later Sasanian period there was vital religious reason for incestuous *xvaētvadatha*, as set forth by the *Dīnkarṭ* and the *Rivāyat*, no such reason can be alleged for the Achæmenian and succeeding periods. It is clear, moreover, that incestuous *xvaētvadatha* was then not restricted to noble and royal families, but that it was also practised widely among the common people. On the other hand, the present writer knows at present of no cases in the historic (as distinguished from the legendary) period of Zoroastrianism, except the Sasanian royal instance mentioned above, and the marriage of Mihrām-gushnasp.

We must also note that incest was abhorrent to the Indian branch of the Indo-Iranian family (for the strong exogamy of India see J. Jolly, *Recht und Sitte* [=*GIAP* ii. 8], Strassburg, 1896, p. 62 f.).[1] Among the other Indo-European peoples the Greeks permitted marriage between uncles and nieces, nephews and aunts, and half-brothers and half-sisters on the paternal side (see 'Greek' section, above, § 2); the ancient Prussians and Lithuanians are said to have allowed marriage with any kinswoman except one's own mother (O. Schrader, *Reallex. der indogerm. Altertumskunde*, Strassburg, 1901, p. 909 f.); and equal licence is ascribed to the ancient Irish (cf. 'Celtic' section, above).

There remain, then, two hypotheses on the origin of incestuous *xvaētvadatha*. (*a*) It may be derived from a non-Indo-European people. This is the theory maintained by Moulton (pp. 204–208), who holds that the custom was Magian, and so neither Indo-European nor Semitic (cf. *ib.* chs. vi.–vii., and art. MAGI)—not Iranian at all. (*b*) Without denying or even criticizing Moulton's very plausible, even probable, theory, it may be suggested that the practice was genuinely Persian. In view of the extremely primitive character of the Balto-Slavic peoples, who have, not without reason, been claimed as those who have retained most truly the original type of Indo-European civilization (S. Feist, *Kultur . . . der Indogermanen*, Berlin, 1913, p. 478; O. Schrader, *Sprachvergleichung und Urgesch.*[3], Jena, 1907, ii. 129 f.; and art. ARYAN RELIGION, *passim*), the occurrence among them—as among the almost equally primitive ancient Irish—of what is practically identical with incestuous *xvaētvadatha* is certainly significant. On this hypothesis, Zarathushtra's reformation did away with *xvaētvadatha*, as with so much else of the older Iranism which his loftier teaching rejected; but, when the more ancient folk-religion returned, it restored *xvaētvadatha*, together with many other things that had been discarded. In the present state of our knowledge the writer does not attempt to decide between these hypotheses; he merely presents his own for what it may be worth.

Whatever the origin of incestuous *xvaētvadatha*—which is perhaps nothing but endogamy carried to its extreme—so much is clear: pure Zoroastrianism never knew it; it was practised by non-Zoroastrian Persians; it was advocated at least during the Sasanian and early Arab periods by a Magianized priesthood; it appears to have then been a theoretical ideal, prompted by the religious and political situation of the period, rather than an actual practice; it was constantly resisted (even as an ideal) by a large—and, doubtless, ever increasing—body of the faithful; it has disappeared. It had a certain justification during the days of Arab persecution, and Parsis should recognize this. It has been one of the cheap taunts of the type flung against every religion by the ignorant or malevolent outsider, and no Parsi can be reproached for sensitiveness on the subject. Yet it was at worst

[1] It is true that the Pahlavi summaries of lost Avesta texts affirm in them the presence of this type of *xvaētvadatha* (see above, p. 457b), but the baseless reading of *xvaētvadatha* into *Ys.* xlv. 4 by the Pahlavi commentator (above, p. 457a) hints that we cannot repose implicit confidence in the accuracy of these summaries.

[1] The instance of Yama and Yamī, already mentioned, does not militate against this; for in the hymn Rigveda x. 10 (on which see especially L. von Schröder, *Mysterium und Mimus im Rigveda*, Leipzig, 1908, p. 275 ff.) Yama manifests extreme reluctance to the union. The problem involved was the origin of the human race from a primeval pair of twins. The same remarks apply to the myth of Brahmā's union with his daughter, a cosmogonic myth comparable with the ἱερὸς γάμος of Ahura Mazda and Spenta Armaiti, noted above (cf. Rigveda, I. clxiv. 33, v. xlii. 13, x. lxi. 5 ff., and especially Muir, *Orig. Sanskrit Texts*, i.[2] [1872] 107–114, iv. [1873] 45–48).

merely a temporary excrescence, never a real tenet; and it was repudiated, no doubt, as intensely by Zarathushtra as by his modern followers.

3. Old Persian.—Concerning the specifically Old Persian marriage rites we possess only meagre information. Strabo tells us (p. 733) that marriages were performed at the beginning of the vernal equinox, and that before the bridegroom went to the nuptial couch he ate an apple or camel marrow, but nothing else during the whole day. We also learn from Arrian (*Anab.* VII. iv. 7) that a seat of honour (*θρόνος*) was provided for the groom, and that his prospective bride came 'after the cups had gone round' (*μετὰ τὸν πότον*), being welcomed by her husband with the giving of the right hand and a kiss. Naturally a banquet formed part of the wedding (Est 2[18]; Jos. *Ant.* XI. vi. 2).

To the Scythians (*q.v.*), at least some of whom were Iranians, the Greeks ascribed the practice of each man having free access to the wives of his fellow-tribesmen, although Herodotus (i. 216, iv. 104) restricts this to the Massagetæ and Agathyrsi. The latter were possibly Iranian (E. H. Minns, *Scythians and Greeks*, Cambridge, 1913, p. 102; cf. W. Tomaschek, in Pauly-Wissowa, i. 764 f.); the former are considered Iranian—their name is certainly so—by J. Marquart (*Untersuchungen zur Gesch. von Eran*, Göttingen and Leipzig, 1896–1905, ii. 77 f., 240, *Ērānšahr*, Berlin, 1901, p. 156), though this is doubted by Minns (p. 111), who, probably rightly, regards them as 'a mixed collection of tribes without an ethnic unity.' In any event, as he says (p. 93), this form of marriage (for other Indo-European instances of which see H. Hirt, *Indogermanen*, Strassburg, 1905–07, p. 703; Schrader, *Reallex.* p. 634) is probably non-Aryan.

See, further, art. FAMILY (Persian).

LITERATURE.—B. Brisson, *De regio Persarum principatu*, ed. J. H. Lederlin, Strassburg, 1710, pp. 157 f., 491–498; A. Rapp, *ZDMG* xx. [1866] 107–114; F. Spiegel, *Erân. Alterthumskunde*, Leipzig, 1871–78, iii. 677–681; W. Geiger, *Ostīrān. Kultur im Altertum*, Erlangen, 1882, pp. 240–249; F. Justi, *GIrP* ii. [1904] 434–437; Dosabhai Framji Karaka, *Hist. of the Parsis*, London, 1884, i. 170–188; Jivanji Jamshedji Modi, *Marriage Customs of the Parsees*, Bombay, 1900; Darab Peshotan Sanjana, *The Alleged Practice of Next-of-Kin Marriages in Old Irān*, London, 1888; L. C. Casartelli, *Philosophy of the Mazdayasnian Religion under the Sassanids*, Bombay, 1889, pp. 156–160, and *BOR* iii. [1889] 169–174, 200–204; J. Darmesteter, *Zend-Avesta*, Paris, 1892–93, i. 126–134; H. Hübschmann, *ZDMG* xliii. [1889] 300–312; E. W. West, 'The Meaning of Khvêtûk-das or Khvêtûdâd,' *SBE* xviii. [1882] 389–430; J. H. Moulton, *Early Zoroastrianism*, London, 1913, pp. 204–208; the *Patmānak-ī-Katak-xūtāīh*, or 'Marriage Contract,' is ed. by Jamaspji Minocheherji Jamasp-Asana, *Pahlavi Texts Contained in the Codex MK*, Bombay, 1897–1913, pp. 141–143, tr. *ib.* Introd. pp. 47–49.

LOUIS H. GRAY.

MARRIAGE (Japanese and Korean). — I. *JAPAN*. — From ancient times marriage and marriage regulations have been considered important by the Japanese people. Both ideas and legal regulations concerning marriage, however, seem to have passed through three distinct stages: (1) that of the age of the Taiho-ryo (A.D. 701–1192), much influenced by Chinese morals and laws; (2) that of feudalism (from the end of the 12th cent. to the Meiji era), moulded by *bushido*, Japanese knightly morality, to a much higher development; and (3) that of the period since the Restoration, characterized by Christian influences.

1. Consent of parties.—The chief point of difference between Japanese and Western marriage laws may be found in the family system. From the earliest times the Japanese people have been grouped in families as social units, to one of which every individual belongs, and in each family there is a head, who governs the rest. The authority of the head (*patria potestas*) has varied from age to age, but in general may be said to have been strong in ancient times and to have weakened in recent years. The family in the time of the Taiho-ryo was often very large, including over one hundred persons, but the numbers gradually decreased, until at present a family usually consists of only five or six individuals. Marriage under such a system not only brings changes in the status of the contracting parties, but also means the removal of a member of one group to another. In other words, marriage is an act between a man and a woman and also between two families. Therefore, when a marriage is to take place, not only the free contract of the parties is required, but also the consent of the heads of the two families.

From the time of the Taiho-ryo to that of the Meiji era, a marriage engagement was first made between the parents of the parties, and often the consent of the parties was not required, for filial obedience was considered one of the highest and noblest virtues. Lately, with the development of the idea of freedom, the point of view has somewhat changed; according to the regulations of the present civil code, it is necessary to have the free consent of the parties in addition to the consent of the parents. Moreover, when a man reaches the age of thirty and a woman that of twenty-five, the law no longer requires the consent of the parents for the sanction of marriage.

2. Caste.—While caste in the strict sense of the term never existed in Japan, by the Taiho-ryo a humble class, which was not allowed to intermarry with others, was recognized, and the child of such a marriage belonged to the humble class. During the feudal age the people were divided into lords, knights, and commoners including farmers, artisans, and merchants; and intermarriage required special permission. A marriage between members of the lordly class required sanction from the central government until 1871. According to the Taiho-ryo, Buddhist priestesses were not allowed to marry; and one who transgressed was sent to a far island or put to death; but this ban was abolished in 1872.

3. Age of consent.—At the time of the Taiho-ryo a male was allowed to marry at the age of 15 and a female at 13; but the present civil code requires the age of 17 for the male and 15 for the female. There has been no prohibition of marriage on account of old age.

4. Monogamy.—Old laws and customs in Japan forbade multiple marriages, but not concubinage. According to the Taiho-ryo, concubines occupied the position of relatives in the second degree, and no limitation was made as to their number. The child by a concubine held an inheritance right. The custom of concubinage was prevalent among the noble and rich, and society did not condemn it. Moreover, in the opinion of some, concubinage was considered necessary, with the existing family-system, in order to preserve the family line from possible extinction. In the Meiji era, however, through the influence of Christianity, the idea of monogamy became strong; and in 1882 concubinage ceased to be recognized by law, though the long-established custom still lingers to some extent.

5. Second marriage.—When a marriage contract has been dissolved by divorce or the death of one of the parties, a second marriage is permitted. In ancient times, however, the proverb 'A chaste woman never sees two men' had great force; and for a woman to refrain from re-marriage was regarded as a beautiful virtue. There were not a few women who cut off their hair, or became priestesses, or committed suicide, on hearing of the death of their husbands in battle. Such forms of devotion gradually declined; and the civil code does not forbid a woman to re-marry, merely requiring six months to elapse between the dissolution of the first marriage and the consummation of the second.

6. Marriage of adulterers.—A man and woman, either of whom has been divorced or sentenced to be divorced on account of adultery with the other, may not marry—a prohibition which has existed since the time of the Taiho-ryo. Social disapproval of such union is very severe; and, even when the husband or wife forgives and consents, the prohibition is binding and cannot be evaded, so that those found thus married are separated by law.

7. Marriage of relatives.—Marriage between near relatives in direct and collateral lines is forbidden for the sake of health and protection from degeneracy. The marriage of cousins, or of a widow or widower with a brother or sister of the deceased, is not prohibited; and such marriages are not rare.

8. Relation of husband and wife. — In olden times the rights of a husband were very far-reaching, and a wife who obeyed her husband absolutely was considered virtuous. Men were held in high regard, while women were not. Lately the position of woman has improved, but even yet, when a wife makes a contract, she has to get her husband's consent in many cases, and the wife's property is always under the supervision of her husband while they are married. In Japan a woman's private property is very limited; and those who possess property in addition to their dresses and ornaments are very few; for, according to the law of succession, all property is inherited by the eldest son, and only in the case of disinheritance or of there being no son by marriage or adoption can the woman inherit in regular succession. Thus, as a rule, the wife has no property, but is dependent upon her husband for support. Some change, therefore, must be made in the law of succession if the position of woman is to be materially raised.

9. Engagement and ceremony of marriage.—The customs as well as the laws of marriage in Japan have passed through a series of changes. In ancient times marriage by sale and marriage by capture were common; but from the time of the Taiho-ryo customs gradually became more refined. There is in Japan, however, no custom of direct personal engagement or of previous personal acquaintanceship. Such things would be regarded as disgraceful by all Japanese above the middle class, for a formal marriage is always arranged by a match-maker who renders service to the parties and parents. When consent is given and the engagement made, gifts are exchanged, and a marriage-contract is considered to have taken place. Then, upon an auspicious day, the wedding ceremony is performed, usually at the home of the bridegroom at night. The marriage intermediary, escorting the bride in her best attire, takes his seat at an appointed place, and the bride and bridegroom drink wine, exchanging cups nine times. This constitutes the entire ceremony, after which the bride and bridegroom are introduced to relatives and friends at a wedding dinner. No religious or legal form is required, except that, by the present civil code, notification must be made to a registrar in order that the marriage may be officially sanctioned. With the coming of Christianity marriages are increasingly performed in churches; and recently the custom has arisen of holding services at Shintō shrines. The law, however, requires no religious sanction, as it is only a civil marriage that is officially recognized.

10. Divorce.—Before the promulgation of the present civil code (1896–98), divorce, or, rather, repudiation, was very easily secured at the husband's will. No legal procedure was necessary beyond the husband's writ with his signature, but the law fixed seven causes, one of which must exist in order to make the *repudium* effective. Thus the power of the husband was somewhat curtailed; but only the husband could repudiate. The present code recognizes two forms of divorce: by mutual consent, and by judicial decree. The former requires only the mutual consent of the parties, while the latter requires an act of the court upon the contested request of one of the parties. This form of legal divorce must be for some one of certain causes recognized by law, and becomes operative only after judicial judgment has been given. Statistics for 1908 show the total number of marriages to have been 8,583,168 and of divorces 60,376, *i.e.* about 7 divorces out of 1000 marriages. Only judicial divorces, however, are given in statistics, and by far the greater number are by mutual consent.

11. Judicial separation.—This system does not exist in Japan.

II. *Korea.*—In Korea marriage is according to the old custom. Early marriage prevails, and government control has had but little effect, though upon several occasions laws have been issued, even setting the age for marriage at 20 for men and 16 for women. It is usual for a girl of 12 or 13 years to marry a boy of 10 or less. Wives are usually a few years older than their husbands. Second marriage is not prohibited, but is considered a disgrace by most; and those above the middle class never re-marry. Arrangements for marriage are made by fathers, grandfathers, or elder brothers and relatives in authority; and the wishes of those who are to be married are not taken into account. The ceremony is performed at the home of the bride, and it is not necessary to notify a civil officer. Only the husband can divorce, and the wife has no way of refusal. There is no system of divorce by consent, but by the new law, since annexation, a way has been opened for a wife to seek divorce. The number of marriages made in 1912 was 121,993, and that of divorces only 9058.

Literature.—Alice M. Bacon, *Japanese Girls and Women*, London, 1905; D. Kikuchi, *Japanese Education*, do. 1909, ch. xviii., 'Position of Women'; B. H. Chamberlain, *Things Japanese*[4], do. 1902; L. W. Küchler, 'Marriage in Japan,' in *TASJ* xiii. [1885], pt. i. pp. 114–137; Douglas Sladen, *A Japanese Marriage*, London, 1904; Inazo Nitobé, *The Japanese Nation*, London and New York, 1912.

T. Nakajima.

MARRIAGE (Jewish).—'Every man is bound to marry a wife in order to beget children, and he who fails of this duty is as one who sheds blood, diminishes the Image [of God], and causes the Divine Presence (*sh^ekhīnāh*) to depart from Israel'—thus runs the rule in the Code of Qaro (*Shūlḥān 'Ārūkh, Ebhen hā-'ezer*, i. 1). It is based on ancient Rabbinic (Tannaitic) prescription (*Y^ebhāmôth*, 63*b*, 64*a*), itself inferred from well-known Biblical texts (esp. Gn 9[6] combined with following verse), and it is emphasized by the somewhat later apophthegms: 'Whoever has no wife rests without blessing'; such a one 'is not called a man' (*ib.* 62*b*). Marriage was the means by which the human race imprinted on the generations the divine image; it, with the consequent domestic felicity, was the expression of true manhood. It was the basis of the social order, and thus its regulation was, in Rabbinic opinion, one of the chief differences between Jewish and primitive systems (cf. Maimonides, *Ishūth*, i.). The social obligation was strengthened by Messianic hopes: 'the son of David—*i.e.* the Messiah—will not come until all souls stored up for earthly life have been born' (*Y^ebh.* 62*a*). Though the purpose of marriage was the begetting of children, other aspects of marital life were fully appreciated (see art. Family [Jewish]; and cf. the quotations in M. Mielziner, *The Jewish Law of Marriage and Divorce*, New York, 1901, p. 18 f.; I. Abrahams, *Jewish Life in the Middle Ages*,

London, 1896, p. 114). Very profound is the Rabbinic view that man's *yēṣer* is in this instance the cause of good; but for his passions man would not build a house, nor marry a wife, nor beget children (*Genesis Rabbā*, ch. ix.). Man, in Rabbinic theology, is impelled by two *yēṣers* ('impulses,' 'inclinations'), one good and one evil, both of which are to be used in turning him to the love of God (*Sifrê* on Dt 6[5], *Mishnāh Berākhôth*, ix. 5). The bodily passions are not in themselves evil (cf. F. C. Porter, 'Yeçer Hara,' in Yale Bicentenary vol. of *Biblical and Semitic Studies*, New York, 1901, pp. 91–156, and M. Lazarus, *Ethics of Judaism*, Eng. tr., Philadelphia, 1901, ii. 79 ff.); Torah was the means by which the control of passion and its direction into holy ends were effected (cf. Maimonides, *Guide of the Perplexed*, iii. 33). The Rabbinic theory of marital intercourse is summed up ideally and, in a sense, mystically in the saying: 'Three are associated in every human being: God, father, and mother' (*Qiddûshîn*, 30*b*).

With regard to the authority of parents in arranging the marriages of their children while minors see *ERE* v. 742[a]. When the parties were adult, the consent of parents was not necessary to make a marriage valid (Maimonides, *Îshûth*, vii.), but, as Mielziner adds,

'In consequence of the high respect and veneration, however, in which father and mother have ever been held among Israelites, the cases of contracting marriages without the parents' consent fortunately belong to the rarest exceptions' (p. 69).

Early marriages, arranged by the parents, were long considered a valuable aid to morals. The legal age for valid marriage was the age of puberty, but the usual age of the bridegroom in Talmudic times was 18 to 20 (S. Krauss, *Talmudische Archäologie*, Leipzig, 1910–11, ii. 28). A Jewish court would often put pressure on a man over 20 to compel him to take a wife (*Ebhen hā-'ezer*, i. 2), but such pressure was not applied in the case of students, while (as the gloss *ad loc.* points out) in modern times all attempts at compulsory marriages have become obsolete. Curiously enough, no rule is stated with regard to the age of the bride. Girls were treated as marriageable from the beginning of their thirteenth year, and at various times very youthful marriages have prevailed (see Abrahams, ch. ix.). In recent times, while, on the whole, Jews probably marry at a somewhat earlier age than the general population, assimilation in social customs is modifying differences (statistics in *JE* viii. 339). The general impression prevails that Jews more frequently than others marry their cousins. Intermarriage between Jews and Christians has increased (statistics in *JE* vi. 612). No section of Jewish opinion favours marriages between parties who are not of the same religion, the difficulties of the education of the children and the disturbance of the home harmony being felt to offer strong objections. There is no bar, however, to the religious solemnization of a marriage with full Jewish rites in the case of proselytes to the synagogue.

The Biblical 'degrees' were maintained in later Jewish law, with certain extensions (*Yebh.* 21; Maimonides, *Îshûth*, i. 6; Mielziner, p. 37), the latter being partly theoretical prolongations of lineal ascendants and descendants; but in one case a 'new degree homogeneous to the Biblical was added'; for, 'while the Mosaic Law [Lv 18[14]] expressly forbids only the *father's* brother's wife, the Talmudic Law adds also the *mother's* brother's wife, and, besides, the father's uterine brother's wife' (Mielziner, p. 38). The Ḳaraites (see *ERE* vii. 663[a]) imposed still further rigours on the marriage law.

The general question of the relation between Jewish marriages and the civil law of England is historically and legally considered in the monograph of H. S. Q. Henriques, *Jewish Marriages and English Law*, London, 1909. It may in general be said that, while orthodox Jews maintain some disabilities not upheld by the law of the land, no Jews permit marriages which, though allowed by Jewish law, are forbidden by the civil law. Thus, though marriage with a deceased wife's sister is valid in Jewish law, such a marriage was never solemnized in England while English law disallowed it. So, too, though by Jewish law a man may marry his niece (though a woman may not marry her nephew), no such marriage would be performed by Jewish rites, since English law forbids such a union. But, where the Jewish law is more severe than the English, the severity is in most cases maintained, though the tendency in Jewish liberal organizations is toward equalizing Jewish custom with civil conditions. The orthodox Jews do not permit a *kôhēn*—*i.e.* one tracing descent from the ancient priestly family—to wed a divorced woman; nor would the re-marriage of a divorced person be solemnized by the orthodox synagogue unless a divorce had also been obtained from a *Bēth Dîn* (Jewish ecclesiastical court). On the other hand, the levirate marriage, which was no longer in general use (though a few instances are recorded) at the beginning of the Christian era (the Sadducean question in Mt 22[23] was probably theoretical), has now lost all vogue (*Ebhen hā-'ezer*, clxv., and commentaries; *JE* vi. 171). In the case of a childless widow the brother-in-law goes through the ceremony of *ḥălîṣāh* (Dt 25[7-10]), which frees her to marry a stranger (Mielziner, p. 54 f.; *JE* vi. 170 f., where the rite is illustrated). On the levirate marriage see, further, I. Mattuck, in *Studies in Jewish Literature*, Berlin, 1913, p. 210; on marriages between uncle and niece, S. Krauss, *ib.* p. 165.

Except for rare cases in countries where Muhammadan law prevails, monogamy is enforced by both law and custom among Jews, although neither Bible nor Talmud formally forbids polygamy (for the Talmudic evidence see Krauss, ii. 27). Only in the case of the levirate marriage did the Pentateuch actually ordain a second marriage, and, as has been mentioned above, the levirate marriage fell into disuse. That monogamy was the Biblical ideal is shown by Gn 2[24], Pr 31[10-31], and the whole tendency of the Song of Songs (cf. A. Harper, *Song of Solomon*, Cambridge, 1902, p. xxxiv); and the same conclusion must be drawn from the prophetic imagery in which marriage typifies the relation between the one God and the unique people Israel. Polygamy survived among the Jews into the Christian era (see references in *JE* viii. 658), but monogamy was then and thereafter the general rule. The difficulty was that, as the end of marriage was the begetting of children, childless marriages were no fulfilment of that end, and in case of the wife's sterility the older authorities were divided in view as to the relative advisability of insisting on divorce or of permitting a second simultaneous marriage (on this and several other questions of Jewish marriage and divorce, see the writer's evidence before the Divorce Commission); but by the beginning of the 11th cent. monogamy was made the binding and absolute rule for all western Jews (Abrahams, ch. vii.).

The ancient and mediæval preliminaries to marriage have, in modern times, lost much of their old significance. Betrothal (*ērûsîn* or *qiddûshîn*) in Rabbinic law was not a mere agreement or contract for a future marriage (*nissûîn*); though not involving the actual privileges or responsibilities of the married state, betrothal was so far the initiation of marriage that it could be terminated only by death or divorce.

'Faithlessness on the part of the betrothed female was treated as adultery. Without having been formally divorced, she could not enter a marriage contract with another person; if entered upon it was void' (Mielziner, p. 77; on the status of the betrothed woman in the 1st and 2nd centuries A.D., cf. A. Büchler, in *Festschrift zu Israel Lewy's 70ten Geburtstag*, Breslau, 1911, p. 110).

Since the 16th cent. the two ceremonies of betrothal and marriage have been performed on the same day, though in Talmudic times a year might intervene between them (*Mishnāh, Qiddūshîn*, v. 2). The legal betrothal was always preceded by an 'engagement' (*shiddūkhîn*), and this 'engagement' gradually replaced the older betrothal. Often a professional match-maker (*shādkhān*) was employed in the Middle Ages, and the custom is still in some vogue (Abrahams, p. 170 f.). The ceremonies of marriage now include the older betrothal and marriage rites. The essence of the marriage ceremony is the presentation by the bridegroom to the bride, in the presence of two witnesses, of an object of value, and the recital of the formula: 'Be thou consecrated unto me by this [ring] according to the law of Moses and Israel.' The marriage rite was and is invalid without the bride's consent —her consent is formally stated in the *kᵉthūbhāh* (see below); but, until recent times, she took a passive part in the ceremony, the formula being spoken by the man only. In some orthodox and in most liberal synagogues the bride's part is now more active. For the validity of a marriage the presence of a Rabbi is not essential, but such presence is usual, and so are other ceremonies: the use of a ring and a canopy (*ḥuppāh*), the breaking of a glass, the recital of the *kᵉthūbhāh*, and the repetition of the 'Seven Benedictions.'

The ring, now so usual in Jewish weddings, is not mentioned in the Talmud, but was introduced in the Gaonic age (A. Harkavy, *Tᵉshūbhôth hag-gᵉônîm*, Berlin, 1887, § 65), perhaps in the 7th century. The ring replaced the older gift of money or of an article of value; it must not contain gems (Abrahams, p. 183), and need not be of gold. Possibly the use of the ring was derived from Rome, just as the objection to marriages between Passover and Pentecost corresponds to the Roman prohibition of marriages in May (J. Landsberger, in *Jüd. Zeitschrift für Wissensch. und Leben*, vii. [1869] 81). In the Middle Ages Friday was a favourite day for Jewish marriages, though the Talmud objected to such a choice. Wednesday was also a common day for virgins, and Thursday for widows. In modern times there are no restrictions as to days of the week, except that marriages are not celebrated on Sabbaths or festivals. In the orthodox synagogues marriages are still not performed (except on specified dates) between Passover and Pentecost, nor on certain anniversaries of a mournful nature. During the marriage ceremony the ring is put on the forefinger of the bride's right hand; she afterwards removes it and places it on the customary finger of the left hand. Marriages are now frequently celebrated in the synagogue, though there is no loss of validity if the ceremony occurs elsewhere, as is widely the custom in America. The whole problem as to the place where Jewish marriages may be celebrated is treated by L. Löw in his *Gesammelte Schriften*, where many other Jewish marriage questions, historical, social, and legal, are also discussed (iii., Szegedin, 1893, pp. 13–334).

The bride and bridegroom usually stand under a *ḥuppāh*, or 'canopy,' during the marriage ceremony; the rite has been abrogated in some of the modern Jewish congregations. Originally the *ḥuppāh* was the marriage chamber, into which the bridal pair were conducted after a procession; but it is now merely symbolical, and consists of four upright posts covered by an awning of silk or tapestry (for details see Abrahams, p. 193; for illustrations, *JE* vi. 504 ff.). A regular preliminary of the ceremony is the signing by the bridegroom of the *kᵉthūbhāh* (lit. 'writing'), or marriage contract (for the ordinary wording see Mielziner, p. 87), which sets forth the amount payable to the wife in case of the husband's death or the wife's divorce, and in olden times often rehearsed the wife's dowry, in respect of which, as of the husband's settlement, the *kᵉthūbhāh* conferred on her an inalienable claim on her husband's property. The wife had considerable rights over her own property (see Mielziner, p. 104 f.), and the *kᵉthūbhāh* protected those rights, and also formed a potent restraint against rash divorces. Mielziner's statement (p. 89) that the *kᵉthūbhāh* is 'now almost entirely dispensed with,' refers only to certain American and other reform congregations; it is still retained in most Jewish marriages, though it has little legal significance in many countries. The *kᵉthūbhāh* is ancient, being perhaps referred to in To 7¹⁴; it is certainly as old as the beginning of the 1st cent. B.C. (*Kᵉthūbhôth*, 82*b*; Abrahams, p. 207, note 2; E. N. Adler, in *JE* vii. 474; for the earliest instance of the terms of the wife's jointure the reader may refer to L. Ginzberg, *Geonica*, New York, 1909, ii. 72). In Oriental lands the *kᵉthūbhāh* often included a solemn undertaking by the bridegroom to observe strictly the law of monogamy (see Abrahams, p. 120, and the document published by him in *Jews' College Jubilee Volume*, London, 1906, p. 101).

Of the many marriage customs which have prevailed in Jewish marriages one deserves special mention. The bridegroom breaks a glass, but the meaning of the rite is uncertain. Some have seen in it a symbolical allusion to the close of the ante-nuptial condition, but 'the most acceptable theory is that the custom arose from . . . a desire to keep even men's joys tempered by more serious thoughts, and on the other hand from the never-forgotten memory of the mourning for Zion' (see *Annotated Edition of the Authorised Daily Prayer Book*, London, 1914, p. ccxvii). The memory of Zion is frequently recalled in the Jewish wedding hymns and songs (on which see Abrahams, p. 188 f., and 'Hebrew Love Songs,' in *Book of Delight*, Philadelphia, 1912, p. 184 ff.). The same phenomenon is seen in the 'Seven Benedictions' cited below, where Jer 33¹⁰ᶠ· is effectively used. As regards the *memento mori* idea the following incident is recorded in the Talmud (*Bᵉrākhôth*, 30*b*):

'When the son of Rābbinā was married, the father saw that the Rabbis present were in an uproarious mood, so he took a costly vase of white crystal worth 400 zūzîm and broke it before them to curb their spirits.'

On the other hand, joyousness is the predominant note of Jewish weddings—a joyousness hallowed by the principle that the participation in such functions is a religious duty. The dowering of poor brides was an act of sanctified loving-kindness (*Shabbath*, 127*a*); and the assistance at wedding festivals was an element in pious life (*Pᵉsāḥîm*, 49*a*). Lyric praises of the bride were so regular a habit that we find quaint discussions as to the terms to be used in the eulogies (*Kᵉthūbôth*, 17*a*). On the subject of other wedding customs, both Oriental and Western, see Abrahams, chs. ix. and x.; *JE* viii. 340 ff.; Krauss, ii. 37; W. Rosenau, *Jewish Ceremonial Institutions and Customs*, Baltimore, 1912, ch. xi.

Most characteristic of the Jewish marriage ceremony are the Seven Benedictions, which are already quoted in the Talmud (*Kᵉthūbhôth*, 8). First comes the benediction over wine (on the use of wine in Jewish ceremonial see *Annotated Prayer Book*, p. cxxxix); then follows the praise of God as the creator of all things to His glory; after this eulogy of the creator of all comes the praise of Him as creator of man; and next the benedictions pass to the creation of woman, the memory of Zion, the bridal joy, and the hope of Israel's restoration. The current text is as follows (*Annotated Prayer Book*, p. 299):

'Blessed art thou, O Lord our God, King of the universe, who createst the fruit of the vine.

Blessed art thou, O Lord our God, King of the universe, who hast created all things to thy glory.

Blessed art thou, O Lord our God, King of the universe, Creator of man.

Blessed art thou, O Lord our God, King of the universe, who hast made man in thine image, after thy likeness, and hast prepared unto him, out of his very self, a perpetual fabric. Blessed art thou, O Lord, Creator of man.

May she who was barren (Zion) be exceeding glad and exult, when her children are gathered within her in joy. Blessed art thou, O Lord, who makest Zion joyful through her children.

O make these loved companions greatly to rejoice, even as of old thou didst gladden thy creature in the garden of Eden. Blessed art thou, O Lord, who makest bridegroom and bride to rejoice.

Blessed art thou, O Lord our God, King of the universe, who hast created joy and gladness, bridegroom and bride, mirth and exultation, pleasure and delight, love, brotherhood, peace and fellowship. Soon may there be heard in the cities of Judah, and in the streets of Jerusalem, the voice of joy and gladness, the voice of the bridegroom and the voice of the bride, the jubilant voice of bridegrooms from their canopies, and of youths from their feasts of song. Blessed art thou, O Lord, who makest the bridegroom to rejoice with the bride.'

Thus the married state is brought into relation with the story of creation and with Israel's Messianic hopes. The Seven Benedictions, which were recited during the grace at the wedding banquet as well as during the wedding ceremony, cover the whole of Israel's history. The popular maxim, 'Marriages are made in heaven,' was accepted as a commonplace truth by the Rabbis (Abrahams, *Book of Delight*, p. 172 ff.). The reverence for the wife was shown by the husband's recital every Friday eve of the eulogy of the virtuous woman from the last chapter of Proverbs. In many other ways the sanctity of wedded life was symbolized, both in its human aspects and as a type of perfect harmony with the divine scheme of creation.

LITERATURE.—This is cited in the course of the article.

I. ABRAHAMS.

MARRIAGE (Roman).—It is a comparatively easy task to describe the Roman idea and practice of marriage, if we confine our description to historical times; for there the evidence is fairly complete, and the state of society familiar to us. But the subject is complicated by its antiquities; and these cannot be wholly omitted, for they are interesting to a student of marriage systems, and they reflect the earlier conditions of Roman society from which the later practice descended. We shall begin, then, with these antiquities, and so clear away the main difficulties, which, however, cannot be fully explained in the present state of our knowledge.

1. Pre-historic.—There is some evidence, in the form of survivals in later procedure, that marriage by capture existed among the ancestors of the Latin race; but at what stage, whether among the people of the *terremare* in N. Italy or still further back, we cannot tell. The simulated rape of the bride at the *deductio* (see below), the parting of her hair with a spear, possibly the lifting her over the threshold of her husband's house, taken together with the legend of the rape of the Sabine women, may well suggest capture. True, each scrap of evidence may, if taken separately, be explained otherwise, but it must be allowed that the cumulative evidence is strong. On the other hand, capture implies exogamy, of which there was no trace in historical Rome; marriage was originally within the limits of the *gens* (Marquardt, *Privatalterthümer*, p. 29, notes 1 and 2); if, therefore, marriage by capture is to be assumed as an original practice of the race, it must have been so before the development of the *gens* as a social institution. But, if this early form of marriage is not provable for the Roman people, it is highly probable that the later form of marriage by purchase existed among them at one time, leaving its traces in the later *coemptio*, which, as we shall see, was a simulated transference of the bride by purchase from the *potestas* of her father to the 'hand' (*manus*) of her husband (for the possible connexion of the *dos* with marriage by purchase see Westermarck, *MI* ii. 384 ff.).

2. Early forms of marriage: confarreatio, coemptio, and usus.—In early Roman society we find three distinct forms or rules by which marriage could be effected. As to the historical interpretation of these there is endless dispute, but the object and conception of marriage as an institution are clear enough. The object of a *iustum matrimonium*, such as was the result of all of these methods, was beyond doubt to produce children capable of keeping up the religion (*sacra*) of the family, and also of serving the State in war and peace. Children of *concubitus*, *i.e.* cohabitation without marriage, were not so capable; they could not be Roman citizens, and could not represent either family or State in any capacity. The word which covered all legitimate forms of union was *connubium*; as Ulpian says, in the clearest exposition that we have of the subject (v. i. 2), 'iustum matrimonium est si inter eos qui nuptias contrahunt connubium sit.' *Connubium*, or *ius connubii*, is thus the right of contracting true or legal marriage, and belonged, as Gaius tells us (i. 56), to Roman citizens only, to Latins and foreigners only when it had been granted by the State. And, as marriage in this true sense meant the transference of the bride from one definite legal and religious position to another, from the *sacra* of one family to those of another (see FAMILY [Roman]), and from the *potestas* of one *paterfamilias* to the *manus* of another, it is obvious that the process was one of the utmost gravity both for the families concerned and for the State. The sense of this grave importance is best seen in what, rightly or wrongly, is generally believed to have been the oldest form of patrician marriage, which was applicable only to patrician families throughout Roman history—*confarreatio* or *farreum*, so named from the sacred cake of *far* (the old Italian wheat) used sacramentally in the rite.

Confarreatio stood alone as needing the presence of the Pontifex Maximus and the Flamen Dialis, the former, no doubt, representing in the Republican age the Rex of an earlier time (see Fowler, *Religious Experience of the Roman People*, London, 1911, p. 271), and the Flamen representing Juppiter, the deity of good faith in all alliances. When the preliminaries had been adjusted (*sponsalia*, *auspicia*, etc. [see below]) which were common to all *iusta matrimonia*, a cake of *far* was offered to Juppiter Farreus, and sacramentally shared by bride and bridegroom, in the presence of the Pontifex Maximus, the Flamen Dialis, and ten other witnesses. This number ten has given rise to much conjecture; but it is so common throughout Roman procedure that there need be no special significance in it (in Livy, xxxvii. 3, it apparently has a religious meaning, and so perhaps in *confarreatio*). A victim also was offered (to what deity is uncertain), the skin of which was stretched over two seats, on which the bride and bridegroom had to sit (for these and other details see Gaius, i. 112; Serv. *ad Æn.* iv. 103, 374, *Georg.* i. 31; Dion. Hal. ii. 25). The priests, it must be noted, do not perform the service, but witness it, giving this rite a peculiar solemnity which our authorities do not explain, probably because they did not understand it. Modern scholars and students of Roman law have usually thought of it as the real original form of marriage in the Roman State, which must be imagined as consisting entirely of patrician families; it survived into historical times only as a means of supplying persons duly qualified to fill the old priesthoods descended from that patrician State, viz. the Rex Sacrorum and the three Flamines maiores, Dialis, Martialis, and Quirinalis (see Gaius, i. 112). Of late, however, it has been suggested (by Cuq, *Institutions juridiques*, p. 215 ff., followed by Launspach, *State and Family in Early Rome*, p. 159 ff.) that it came into use only when the old custom of marrying within the *gens* was broken through, when the religious difficulty of transferring a bride from one *gens* to another called for special religious interference by the State. There is something to be said for this; but to the present writer it seems hardly sufficient to account for the sacramental character of the rite and the use of the skin of the victim. No ancient author says that this was the only form of patrician marriage; if it had been so, the Rex and the Flamen must have been constantly in requisition for weddings, more often than would be consistent with their other duties. But it is possible that *confarreatio* may have been a very special religious form, originating in the marriage of the Rex only, or in families forming an inner circle of aristocracy, from which the Rex might be chosen, and which would be likely or willing to supply children qualified to become *camilli patrimi et matrimi* in the service of the State (Serv. *ad Georg*. i. 31). It must be remembered that the patrician State itself had a history, and did not come into existence full-blown; the *confarreatio* probably represents an early form of it, but not exactly that which we have been accustomed to imagine.

There were two other ancient methods of transferring a bride from one family to another, from the *potestas* of her father to the *manus* of her husband; but it is to be noticed that neither of these was, strictly speaking, a marriage ceremony, and it is to be assumed that, when they were used, the real marriage rite was that described below under marriages which did not produce *conventio in manum.* In other words, the true marriage rite was, except in *confarreatio*, distinct from the act which transferred the bride from the *potestas* of her father to the *manus* of her husband, or to that of his father, if he were a *filiusfamilias* in the *potestas* of his father. Thus *coemptio*, the form by which, in the presence of five witnesses and a *libripens* (a form which could be used for other purposes besides marriage), the bride was made over to the *manus* of her husband by a symbolic purchase (Gaius, i. 113), looks as if it were a legal addition devised for some particular purpose, perhaps to enable the ordinary patrician family, which did not seek to produce children capable of filling the highest religious offices, to obtain by a single act the same legal results as in *confarreatio*. This is, indeed, a mere guess, and one among many, into which it is not necessary to go in this article.

The other method which produced *conventio in manum* took a whole year to complete the process; if a duly qualified pair lived together for an entire year without a break, *manus* followed of necessity by *præscriptio*; but by the XII Tables it was possible for the bride to escape this result by absenting herself yearly for three nights from her husband's house, by which means, in legal language, the *usucapio* would be barred (Gaius, i. 111). It is not unlikely that this was really the oldest form by which the husband could acquire *manus*, and the one most commonly in use. *Confarreatio* and *coemptio* both presuppose the existence of the law and religion of the State in full development, but *usus* may go much further back. *Usus* and *coemptio* are, however, alike in this, that they have a private and not a public character, and do not need the presence of priest or magistrate; it was easy, therefore, to pass them on to non-patricians, plebeians or Latins, when these attained *connubium*; but this could not be so with *confarreatio*, if, as we have assumed, the main object of the latter was at all times to produce children capable of holding the exclusively patrician religious offices.

In these three methods of marriage the union was accompanied by *manus*, though in the case of *usus* not till after a year had elapsed. *Usus*, indeed, shows us plainly that the Roman of early times did not think of marriage and *manus* as inseparable: for the bride must have been properly married under *usus*, if her children were to be Roman citizens, though for a year at least she was not under *manus*. We must also remember that, if the husband were not *sui iuris*, but a *filiusfamilias* under the *potestas* of his father, as must constantly have happened, the wife passed under the *manus*, not of her husband, but of his father. Quite early marriage and *manus* became separable both in thought and in fact; under the XII Tables, as we have seen, the wife was given the option of escaping a change of *manus* altogether, and this may be taken as proving that a tendency in this direction had shown itself much earlier. After that time, mainly, no doubt, from reasons of convenience connected with the family property, marriage without *manus* came to be almost universal. *Usus* died out altogether (Gaius, i. 111); *coemptio* survived as a legal expedient in certain cases (*e.g.*, *CIL* vi. 1527—the *Laudatio Turiæ*, line 14); and *confarreatio* became so irksome that its bonds had to be relaxed by Augustus in order to get a supply of candidates for the old patrician priesthoods (Gaius, i. 136; Tac. *Ann.* iii. 71, iv. 16; Sueton. *Aug.* 31). Yet marriage long continued to be as complete and binding a union as before, and we now have to see what made it so, by briefly examining the process as we know it in historical times.

3. The historic period.—(*a*) *Conditions of marriage.*—The necessary conditions of marriage were: (1) the families of both parties must possess the *ius connubii* (as explained above); (2) the parties must not be within the prohibited degrees of relationship (*cognatio*). Originally no *cognati* could marry who were within the seventh degree of relationship; *i.e.*, second cousins could not marry; this was, no doubt, a survival from a period in which families of three generations lived together under the same roof, and were therefore, by a well-known psychological law, unsuited for intermarriage (see E. Westermarck, *Hist. of Human Marriage*[2], London, 1894, p. 320 ff.). Traces of such large households are not wanting in Roman history (Val. Max. IV. iv. 8; Plut. *Crassus*, i., and *Cato the Elder*, xxiv.). But these strict rules were gradually relaxed, and from the time of the Punic wars it seems to have been possible for first cousins to marry (see Marquardt, *Privataltertümer*, p. 30, note). When the Emperor Claudius married his brother's daughter, he had to obtain a decree of the Senate for the purpose, and this licence, which was afterwards repealed, was not generally approved (Tac. *Ann.* xii. 6; Gaius, i. 62). (3) The consent of the parents was absolutely necessary, but not that of the parties themselves, who were often betrothed by their parents at a very early age; *e.g.*, Cicero betrothed his daughter when she was only ten years old (Fowler, *Social Life*, p. 140 f.). This was a survival of a practice still common in many parts of the world, where the maintenance of the family is a matter of supreme importance, and no time is to be lost in securing that children shall not remain unmarried. The betrothal (*sponsalia*), however, at Rome was a promise rather than a legal contract, and might be broken by consent if there was a strong dislike on the part of either boy or girl (see, however, Serv. Sulpicius, in Aul. Gell. iv. 4). The early betrothal serves to show us that the idea at the root of marriage was that of service to family and State, *i.e.* the procreation of children capable of such service, and that love and romance lay wholly outside it. Steady affection there might be and often was (Fowler, *Social Life*, pp. 141, 159 ff.); but the modern idea of passion with marriage as its consummation, which too often subsides and ends in divorce, was unknown at Rome. (4) As a last condition, we must note that bride and bridegroom must be of proper age, *i.e.*, they must have reached the age of puberty and laid aside the *toga prætexta* of childhood; this might happen at different ages, according to natural development, but the minimum age was 12 for a girl and 14 for a boy.

(*b*) *Ritual.*—If all these conditions were fulfilled, a day was fixed for the marriage which must be one of good omen; as with us, May was an unlucky month for this purpose, and so was the early part of June, while certain other *dies religiosi* were to be avoided (Fowler, *Rel. Exper.*, p. 38 ff.). At earliest dawn, according to ancient usage both public and private, the auspices were taken by the flight of birds; but by Cicero's time this seems to have dropped out, and the examination of the *exta* of a victim took its place, as a preliminary to the first step in the procedure, which was the declaration of consent by the parties, usually but not necessarily recorded on *tabulæ nuptiales*. Then the bride assumed the wedding dress, viz. the *flammeum*, or hood of red or yellow, and the *tunica recta* with a woollen girdle fastened with the *nodus herculeus*; this knot, we learn from Pliny (*HN* xxviii. 63), was also used for binding up wounds, and we may therefore suppose that it was a charm against various kinds of evil (cf., however, *ERE* vii. 749[a]). Her hair was parted into four separate locks with a spear-head (*hasta cœlibaris*), which may have been a survival from pre-historic marriage by capture; and under the *flammeum* she carried a bunch of herbs picked by her own hand (Festus, *s.v.* 'Corolla' [p. 56, Lindsay]). She was then ready for the actual marriage rite, which, as will now be seen, was a matter not only of secular contract, but of religious usage; it is occasionally called a *sacrum*, as in Lucan, *Phars.* ii. 350 (of the marriage of Cato): 'sacrisque deos admittere testes.'

(1) The first act of the ceremony was the *dextrarum iunctio*, a symbolic act of union, in which, under the guidance of a *pronuba*, who must be a matron only once married, the bride placed her right hand in the right hand of the bridegroom (Festus, p. 242 [p. 282, ed. Lindsay]). This act, and the sacrifice which seems to have followed, are represented on many monuments, of which accounts will be found in A. Rossbach, *Römische Hochzeits- und Ehedenkmäler*, Leipzig, 1871, *passim*; these are, however, all of very late date, and not easy to interpret. The *dextrarum iunctio* took place, so far as we can discern, either in the bride's house before the hearth or in front of some temple (Nonius, 531); but what temple this was we do not know, nor is it clear to what deity sacrifice was offered. On the monuments we see both cow and pig, which suggest Juno and Tellus (Varro, *de Re Rust.* II. iv. 9, refers to the pig as an Etruscan marriage victim). Possibly Tellus was the usual deity in early times (Fowler, *Rel. Exper.*, pp. 121, 138), and Juno later on; but Vergil combines the two in *Æn.* iv. 166. When the sacrifice had been offered by the pair, the persons present shouted 'Feliciter' by way of good omen, and the wedding-meal followed, and lasted till evening.

(2) The next act was the *deductio*, in which the bride was conducted to her new home—a beautiful ceremony, exquisitely described by Catullus in his 61st poem. She was taken, as it were by force, from the arms of her mother, and led in procession to the house of her husband by three boys, sons of living parents (*patrimi et matrimi*), pure and of good omen, one of whom carried a torch of whitethorn, while the other two held her by the hands; flute-players and torch-bearers went before, the mysterious and unexplained cry 'Talasse' was raised, and nuts were thrown to the youthful lookers-on. When the bride reached the house, she smeared the doorposts with oil and fat (of wolf or pig), and tied a thread of wool around them; probably these old customs were originally charms to avert evil (for wool see J. Pley, 'De Lanæ in antiquorum ritibus usu,' in *RVV* XI. ii. [Giessen, 1911] 82). She was then lifted over the threshold, perhaps as a last sign of simulated reluctance to be thus transplanted, and was received in her new home.

(3) This reception, the third act in the procedure, is obscure in its detail, but the general meaning is plain. It was called 'reception into community of fire and water' ('aqua et igne accipere'), *i.e.* into partnership in these necessities of human existence (E. Samter, *Familienfeste der Griechen und Römer*, Berlin, 1901, p. 18 ff.). We are also told that she brought with her three coins (*asses*), one of which she gave to her husband, one she laid on the hearth, and the third she threw down at the nearest *compitum* ('crossways' [Nonius, p. 852, Lindsay]). Here she seems to be making an offering to the genius of her husband, to the spirit of the hearth-fire, and to the Lar of the family's land allotment, who dwelt in a *sacellum* at the *compitum* (see Fowler, *Rel. Exper.*, p. 77). She was now in the *atrium*, at the end of which, opposite the door, the *lectus genialis* had been made ready. The morrow would find her a *materfamilias* sitting among her maids in that *atrium* or in the more private apartments behind it.

To help maintain the establishment which the marriage was to set up, she brought with her a *dos*, or dowry, which in strict law became the property of the husband (for modifications of this rule see art. 'Dos,' in Smith's *Dict. of Gr. and Rom. Antiquities*[2]). As Cuq well puts it (p. 231), her position of dignity in the house, and her title of *domina* as mistress of its slaves, would have been impaired if she entered it with empty hands and lived at the expense of her husband. The *dos* was also the means of securing to the children born of the marriage succession to their mother's property as well as to the *patrimonium* of the father.

The ritual which we have been examining plainly indicates that the Roman bride was to hold a much nobler position in the household than the Greek wife (see MARRIAGE [Greek]). She shared with her husband all the duties of the family, religious and secular; she lived in the *atrium*, and was never shut away in a woman's chamber. She took her meals with her husband; in all practical matters she was consulted, and only on questions political or intellectual was she expected to be silent.

'When she went out arrayed in the graceful stola matronalis, she was treated with respect, and the passers-by made way for her; but it is characteristic of her position that she did not as a rule leave the house without the knowledge of her husband, or without an escort' (Fowler, *Social Life*, p. 144).

The character induced and expressed by such a position is exemplified in the legendary Volumnia of the story of Coriolanus, in Cornelia the mother of the Gracchi, in Cæsar's mother Julia, and, among many others, in the perfect lady whose courage, good sense, and domestic virtues live for ever on the marble of the *Laudatio Turiæ* (*CIL* vi. 1527; Fowler, *Social Life*, p. 159 f.).

4. Divorce.—No doubt towards the end of the

Republic the type of womanly virtue just described was growing rare, owing to the gradual break-up of the old type of family life—the result of a moral degeneracy which even Augustus was unable effectually to check. This downward tendency is best seen in the history of divorce. Marriage by *confarreatio* had been practically indissoluble; we hear of *diffarreatio*, but it is said (Plut. *Quæst. Rom.* 50) to have been so awful a rite that we assume that it was used only for penal purposes. But the other forms of marriage, not being of the same mystical or sacramental character, did not present the same difficulty, and the legal formula of divorce is as old as the XII Tables, and therefore probably earlier than the 5th cent. B.C. ('claves adimere *or* exigere' [Cic. *Phil.* ii. 28; cf. above, p. 122[a]]). By the 2nd cent. marriage was becoming unpopular in high social circles, and divorce was becoming common (Fowler, *Social Life*, p. 147 ff.). In the Ciceronian age it was extraordinarily frequent; almost all the well-known ladies of that period were divorced at least once. Pompey, though a man of excellent character, was married five times, Cæsar four times, Cicero three times, and under the Empire the virtuous Pliny the Younger also three times. There was no difficulty in the operation of divorce; it was purely a private matter, and either party could send the other notice of it without any given reason or any complaint of misconduct. No remedy was found for a disorder so universal; and to the looseness of the marriage-tie, and the corresponding disregard of what had once been the chief object of marriage, must be ascribed in part at least the degeneracy of Rome and Italy in the first three centuries of the Empire (L. Friedländer, *Sittengeschichte Roms*[7], Leipzig, 1901, Eng. tr., London, 1908-13, i. 242 f.).

LITERATURE.—A. Rossbach, *Untersuchungen über die römische Ehe*, Stuttgart, 1853 (still the standard work); O. Karlowa, *Die Formen der röm. Ehe und Manus*, Bonn, 1868; art. 'Matrimonium,' in Daremberg-Saglio and Smith's *Dict. of Greek and Roman Antiquities*[2], London, 1875; J. Marquardt, *Privatalterthümer der Römer*, Leipzig, 1868, p. 27 f.; A. de Marchi, *Il Culto privato di Roma antica*, i. (Milan, 1896) 146 ff.; E. Cuq, *Institutions juridiques des Romains*, Paris, 1891, p. 204 ff.; C. W. L. Launspach, *State and Family in Early Rome*, London, 1908, ch. x.; W. Warde Fowler, *Social Life at Rome in the Age of Cicero*, do. 1908, ch. v. The most complete ancient authority is Gaius, i. 108 ff.

W. WARDE FOWLER.

MARRIAGE (Semitic). — Students of social evolution seem justified in holding that the family of primitive man was an intermediate development between those of the highest animals and the lowest living men. In the lowest known human societies the form of marriage is usually a temporary monogamy.[1] This temporary monogamy has been accompanied among most early men by a greater or less degree of sexual irregularity, and has varied according to economic circumstances and the bent of the people. So far as can be ascertained from the existing evidence, it underwent some interesting variations among the primitive Semites.

1. Primitive Semitic. — Among many savage or semi-savage peoples it is customary to allow unmarried girls complete sexual liberty. In such communities it might in time easily come to be thought that a woman who had exercised such liberty was more likely to bear children than one who had not. There is reason to believe that something like this prevailed among the primitive Semites, and that superstitious value attached to this exercise of liberty, for in many widely-scattered portions of the Semitic world it became a sacred duty for women to sacrifice their virtue by one or more acts of free love. It was thus, apparently, that the temporary *hierodouloi* originated (see HIERODOULOI [Semitic and Egyptian], vol. vi. p. 672 f.). Besides the existence of *hierodouloi* among the Semites, both temporary and permanent, there is also evidence of much sexual irregularity among them.

It is the working hypothesis of most Semitic scholars to-day that Arabia was the cradle-land of the Semitic people. Naturally, the peculiar desert and oasis environment of the Arabian peninsula left its impress on the Semitic family life. In the oases dates and fruit were raised, and some sustenance for the flocks was produced, but it was necessary to lead the flocks into the desert in search of pasturage. Whether, however, men lived in an oasis or wandered from place to place, women would always be needed to perform the duties of the household and the camp, that the men might be free to fight, either in defence or for plunder. There are two reasons for believing that the women were for the most part the sisters and mothers of the men, whether the clan was resident in one fertile spot or was nomadic: (1) Semitic marriage was notoriously temporary, and (2) kinship was reckoned through the mother.

That marriage was, on the whole, temporary seems probable from the frequency of divorce in Semitic lands, especially among the Arabs and Abyssinians (see below). The researches of W. Robertson Smith established as well as the evidence will permit that among the early Semites kinship was reckoned through the mother.[1] The reasons for this view are as follows. (1) The well-known Biblical phrase for relationship is 'bone of my bone and flesh of my flesh.' 'Flesh' (*bāsār*) is explained in Lv 25[49] by the general word for 'clan.' The Arabs attach great importance to a bond created by eating together; we must suppose, therefore, that the bond between those of the same womb and nurtured at the same breast would be more nearly of the same 'clan' and the same 'flesh' than any others. (2) The word *raḥim*, 'womb,' is the most general word for kinship, and points to a primitive kinship through the mother. (3) The custom called *'aqīqah*, by which a child is consecrated to the god of his father's tribe, cannot have been primitive, but must have sprung up in a state of transition to ensure the counting of the offspring to the father's side of the house. (4) Cases occur in the historical period in which a boy when grown attaches himself to his mother's tribe. The poet Zuhair is a case in point, and the Arabic antiquarians appear to have known that such cases were not uncommon. (5) The fear that sons would choose their mother's clans led men who were wealthy to marry within their own kin. (6) Kinship between a man and his maternal uncle is still considered closer than that between a man and his paternal uncle. (7) Joseph's sons born of his Egyptian wife were not regarded as members of Israel's clan until formally adopted by him (Gn 48[5f.]). (8) Tamar might legally have been the wife of her half-brother Amnon, the relation being on the father's side (2 S 13[13]). Such unions were known in Judah as late as the time of Ezekiel (Ezk 22[11]). Tabnith, king of Sidon, married his father's daughter,[2] and such marriages were known in Mecca. Since the marriage of those really regarded as brothers and sisters was abhorrent to the Semites, kinship must in these cases have been counted through the mother. (9) In the Arabic genealogical tables metronymic groups are still found. (10) In Aramaic inscriptions found at Hegra metronymic clans appear.[3] To this evidence may be added a few items gathered by other scholars. Nöldeke noted that among the Mandæans a man is described

[1] See E. Westermarck, *Hist. of Human Marriage*[2], London, 1894, pp. 14 f., 50; F. H. Giddings, *Principles of Sociology*, New York, 1898, pp. 264, 266.

[1] *Kinship and Marriage in Early Arabia*[2], p. 175 ff.; cf. also Barton, *Semitic Origins*, p. 51 f.

[2] *CIS* I. i. 3. ll. 13-15.

[3] *Ib.* II. i. 198. 209.

as the son of his mother, which indicates that kinship was reckoned through the mother.[1] F. E. Peiser pointed out that among the Babylonians a man could, if he chose, join the kindred of his wife, which is a relic of the same custom.[2] Wellhausen has observed that in the Pentateuch J counts descent through the mother, while P reckons it through the father.[3] Among some primitive peoples kinship is counted through the mother because they are ignorant of the part of the father in reproduction;[4] among others, as, *e.g.*, the Nairs of the Malabar coast, it is reckoned through the mother because a system of polyandry prevails. The wife has several husbands, no one of whom lives with her, but all of whom visit her occasionally, and it is not known which one of them may be the father of a child.[5] Which of these causes led to the Semitic system of female kinship? We have no evidence to show that the Semites were so ignorant of the processes of reproduction that paternity was unknown to them. On the other hand, there is considerable evidence indicating that at one time a type of polyandry somewhat similar to that of the Nairs prevailed among the early Semites.

In three of the *Mu'allaqāt* poems there are specific statements that the women whom the poets visited only occasionally were members of other clans, and that they often visited them at personal risk,[6] on account of the strained relations of the clans. The marriages of Samson (Jg 14, 16) were of this nature. Such marriages were often terminated by the migration of the tribes in different directions.[7] Ammianus Marcellinus was, no doubt, speaking of this type of marriage when he said that among the Arabs the bride presents her husband with a spear and a tent, and, if she chooses, withdraws after a certain day.[8] In this type of marriage kinship would necessarily be reckoned through the mother, and the fact that such alliances prevailed would be sufficient to account for the early Semitic custom of female kinship.

Such marriage conditions, while compelling the women to live with their brothers and sons rather than with their husbands, left them comparatively free from the masculine domination to which they were subjected after the rise of polygamy. Something of this freedom still survives in Arabia in parts of the peninsula like Oman and Hasa, which are not so dominated by Islām as the rest of it.[9]

The type of marriage which seems to have prevailed, at least in part, was a combination of polyandry and polygamy. Just as a woman might receive successive husbands, so the husbands also might have several wives in different clans. On the whole, however, the more numerous partners would seem to have been enjoyed by the women, for the practice of putting girl babies to death prevailed down to the time of Muhammad (see Qur'ān, xvi. 61, lxxxi. 8), so that women must have been fewer than men. Marriages of this early Semitic form were not always exogamous, for Imr-al-Qais boasts in his *Mu'allaqāt* that he followed one day the women of his tribe and spent a day in their company, and the Unaizah with whom he afterwards rode and whose fruit he boasts he repeatedly tasted was the daughter of his uncle.[10] In like manner Lailah, the woman celebrated in the poem

[1] *Monatsschrift*, xvi. [1884] 304.
[2] *MVG* i. [1896] 155.
[3] *GGN*, 1893, p. 478, n. 2.
[4] A. J. Todd, *The Primitive Family as an Educational Agency*, New York and London, 1913, p. 70 f.
[5] Letourneau, *Evolution of Marriage*, p. 311 f.
[6] See *Mu'allaqāt* of Labīd, 16–19; that of 'Antarah, 5–11; and that of Ḥārith, 1–9. That these were real marriages, and not mere amours, Smith has shown in *Kinship*², p. 87 f.
[7] Labīd, *loc. cit.*
[8] xiv. 4.
[9] J. R. Wellsted, *Travels in Arabia*, London, 1838, i. 351–354; W. G. Palgrave, *Central and Eastern Arabia*, do. 1866, ii. 177.
[10] See in F. A. Arnold's ed. of the *Mu'allaqāt* (Leipzig, 1850) the commentators' explanation of 11.

of 'Amr b. Kulthūm, was 'Amr's kinswoman.[1] Whether the marriages which occurred within the tribe were more permanent than the alliances which were made in other clans cannot be determined, but one would naturally suppose that they were. Out of these general conditions there developed a type of temporary marriage for a specified time —three nights or more—called *mut'ah* marriage, which continued till the time of Muhammad.[2]

Another type of polyandry, that called Tibetan, because first studied in Tibet, was the form of marriage in vogue at one time in the southern part of Arabia. In this form of marriage a whole family of brothers possess one wife in common. The most important witness to this type of marriage is Strabo, who says, in describing Arabia Felix:

> 'All the kindred have property in common, the eldest being lord; all have one wife, and it is first come first served, the man who enters to her leaving at the door the stick which it is customary for every one to carry; but the night she spends with the eldest. Hence all are brothers of all; they also have conjugal intercourse with mothers; an adulterer is punished with death; an adulterer is a man of another stock.'[3]

The reference to conjugal intercourse with mothers is probably not to be taken literally, but it is to be explained by Qur'ān, iv. 26, where it appears that men had married wives of their fathers.[4] In other respects the passage describes all the features of Tibetan polyandry. Its existence in that part of Arabia is also attested by epigraphic evidence.[5]

W. Robertson Smith collected considerable evidence to show that this type of polyandry was also known in N. Arabia.[6] His points are:

> (1) Bukhārī relates that two men made a covenant of brotherhood, which resulted in their sharing goods and wives—a fact which seems to betray a survival of a custom of fraternal polyandry. (2) In Arabic *kannah* means the wife of a son or brother, but is used also to denote one's own wife; in Hebrew *kallāh* means both betrothed and daughter-in-law, while in Syriac *kalāthā* means both bride and daughter-in-law. These facts can be most easily explained as remnants of fraternal polyandry. (3) The Arabic law that a man has the first right to the hand of his cousin, and the fact which the fourth *sūrah* and its attendant traditions attest, that, if a man died and left only female children, the father's male relatives inherited the property and married his daughters, are regarded as the results of a previously existing condition of fraternal polyandry. (4) The Qur'ān (iv. 23 ff.) forbids men to inherit women against their will, and forbids them to take their stepmothers in marriage 'except what is past.' This is regarded as evidence that down to the time of Muhammad these attendant circumstances of polyandry had continued, and that the Prophet did not dare to annul existing unions, though he forbade such marriages in future.

Wellhausen,[7] F. Buhl,[8] I. Benzinger,[9] and Barton[10] have also held that the existence of the levirate marriages in Israel was an outgrowth of fraternal polyandry. This has been contested by C. N. Starcke[11] and Westermarck,[12] but their arguments appear inconclusive. It is difficult to explain why one should ever have thought of counting the seed of one brother as that of one who had died, if there had not been a previous state of polyandry in which all brothers shared in the offspring. The levirate was known in Arabia,[13] in Abyssinia,[14] and in Israel.[15]

It would seem that fraternal polyandry of the Tibetan type may have been an intermediate stage between the less well regulated polyandry of an

[1] See *Mu'allaqāt*, 11, 13, 14.
[2] Smith, *Kinship*², p. 87 f.
[3] xvi. 4.
[4] Cf. W. R. Smith, in *JPh* ix. [1880] 86, n. 2.
[5] See E. Glaser, in the *Beilagen* of *Allgemeine Zeitung*, Munich, Dec. 6, 1897, and 'Die Polyandrie bei den Minäern,' in H. Winckler's *Altorientalische Forschungen*, II. i. [1898] 81–83.
[6] *Kinship*², p. 160 f.; cf. Barton, pp. 50, 65.
[7] Pp. 460 f., 474 f., 479 f.
[8] *Die socialen Verhältnisse der Israeliten*, p. 28 f.
[9] *Hebräische Archäologie*², Tübingen, 1907, p. 113.
[10] P. 67 f.
[11] *The Primitive Family*, London, 1889, pp. 141–160.
[12] Pp. 510–514.
[13] Smith, *Kinship*², p. 105.
[14] Letourneau, p. 265.
[15] Smith, *Kinship*², p. 92 f.

earlier time and the patriarchal form of marriage, which generally was prevailing at the time of Muhammad. W. R. Smith so regarded it. But, be this as it may, by the time of Muhammad there had come into vogue in Arabia a type of marriage in which the husband was practically the owner (*ba'al*) of the wife, and which is, consequently, known as *ba'al* marriage. In this type of marriage children belonged, of course, to the father's clan. Smith attributed the origin of the *ba'al* marriage to wars and to the consequent custom of marriage by capture. Marriages of this type might be either monogamous or polygamous, according to the caprice or the wealth of the husband. In much earlier times they had become the custom among the other Semites, who had migrated to lands more fertile than Arabia.

What form of marriage ceremony the early Semites had is largely a matter of conjecture. The type of marriages of which the early poets boast was probably without ceremony. A simple affinity or agreement between the parties sufficed.[1] This must often have been the case also with the later *mut'ah* marriages. After a marriage of this kind was recognized by the clan of the bride, a feast was celebrated for a week, during which there was much jollity of a type suited to the rough character of the civilization (see Jg 14[8f.]). As marriage became more permanent, somewhat similar festivals became the rule and have persisted in all parts of the Semitic world.

2. Babylonian and Assyrian.—There is little direct evidence of marriage and the position of women in Babylonia earlier than the time of Ḥammurabi (*c.* 2000 B.C.), though it is certain that the regulations embodied in his Code of laws are for the most part only the expression of customs that had then been of long duration.

The most conspicuous instance of the position of a married woman of the earlier time is that of Barnamtarra, wife of Lugalanda, Patesi of Lagash about 2825 B.C. From an archive of tablets discovered at Telloh, which contained the pay-rolls of the attendants of her palace, memoranda of her gifts to temples and festivals,[2] and even a record of her accouchement,[3] it appears that she held a position in Lagash analogous to that of a queen in a modern European country. One cannot say that her husband had no other consorts, but it is certain that her position and importance were shared by no others. Her freedom and prominence in the eyes of the public have few parallels in Babylonian history, and are in striking contrast to the insignificance of the women in the *ḥarīm* of Assurbanipal (668–626 B.C.), into which many princesses went, never to be heard of again.[4] Sammuramat, the wife of Adad-nirari IV. (810–782 B.C.), was prominent enough to be described as 'lady of the palace and its mistress.'[5] She is the nearest Mesopotamian parallel to Barnamtarra. In the light of later Babylonian laws, however, it is probable that Barnamtarra was the only wife of Lugalanda, and that he was, at least in theory, a monogamist. If this was true of the ruler, it would be true for most of the men of his kingdom.

For the period of the first dynasty of Babylon (2128–1924 B.C.) the Code of Ḥammurabi affords an authoritative source of information on marriage. The Code contains this regulation: 'If a man takes a wife and does not execute contracts for her, that woman is no wife' (§ 128). This is proof that in Babylonia marriage had passed from the less formal stage of early Semitic life, and had, in consequence of long legal development, become a matter of record. The marriage ceremony was incomplete without the signing of contracts. The law did not recognize anything like our modern 'common law' marriage. One reason for this was that the bride usually brought a dowry from her father's house, which the law safeguarded for her and her children. The husband also generally gave a bride-price to his father-in-law, which, upon certain conditions, reverted to him (§§ 138 f., 162–164). As Babylonian law dealt much in the evidence of written contracts, these were regarded as necessary to a legal marriage. The terms of the marriage, according to the Code, bore somewhat more heavily upon the woman than upon the man. True, if a man was caught defiling the wife of another, both he and she suffered capital punishment (§ 129); if he forced the betrothed of another, he was put to death and the woman went free (§ 130); but a woman, if only slanderously suspected of infidelity, was required to purge herself by the ordeal of throwing herself into the sacred river. The man, on the other hand, might have children by a concubine and suffer only the inconvenience of rearing the children (§ 137). If a man was taken captive, and there were means in his house to support his wife, she must remain true to him; if means were lacking, she was free to marry another (§ 133 f.). If she contracted such a marriage and bore children to her new husband and her former husband afterward gained his freedom and returned, she was bound to return to him, but the second husband retained his children (§ 135). If the husband's absence was due to desertion of his city, he had no claim on his wife on his return, if she had remarried (§ 136).

The Code assumes that marriages shall be monogamous, although it imposes on the father the duty of raising the children of his concubines. Nevertheless, it recognizes that in the case of women who had served as sacred servants in the temple (see HIERODOULOI [Semitic and Egyptian]), and had married late and were, accordingly, unlikely to bear children, and also in the case of wives who through sickness were rendered barren, he may take another (§§ 145–149). If the second wife is taken because of the chronic illness of the first, the first may, if she wishes, take her dowry and return to her father's house (§ 149). Slave concubinage was frequently practised, but a female slave who had borne her master children could not be sold (§§ 146 f., 171).

According to the Code, a man might divorce his wife, if he wished, but in that case he must make certain specified monetary settlements, which varied according to whether the wife had or had not borne him children (§ 137 f.). A woman might take the initiative in a divorce. If she did so, her husband could, if he wished, divorce her without alimony (§ 141). If the wife complained of ill-treatment, the life of the family was subjected to investigation. If her claim proved true, she could take her marriage portion and return to her father's house; if untrue, she was to be thrown into the river (§ 142 f.).

In the marriage contracts of the time of the Ist dynasty it appears that greater privileges of divorce were sometimes secured to the bride than the Code would have granted her. *E.g.*, a priest married, and his contract provided that, if he divorced his wife, he must return her dowry, and pay a half-*mana* as alimony.[1] Another contract, which seems to equalize the penalties for

[1] Smith, *Kinship*[2], p. 84.

[2] Published by V. A. Nikolsky, *Documents of Economic Accounts from the more ancient Chaldæan Epoch* [Russian], Petrograd, 1908; H. de Genouillac, *Tablettes sumériennes archaïques*, Paris, 1909; Allotte de la Fuye, *Documents présargoniques*, do. 1908–09; and M. I. Hussey, *Sumerian Tablets in the Harvard Semitic Museum*, pt. i., Leipzig and Cambridge, U.S.A., 1912.

[3] See Nikolsky, no. 209, and *RAssyr* ix. [1912] 144 f.

[4] Cf. *KB* ii. 168 f.

[5] Cf. *ib.* i. 193.

[1] See *Bab. Exp. of the Univ. of Pennsylvania*, vi.[2] [1909] 40.

divorce, provides that, if the husband divorces the wife, he shall be driven out to the oxen of the palace; if she divorces him, she shall be driven to the carriage-house of the palace.[1] Another contract provides for a divorce on the part of the man by payment of the usual alimony; on the part of the wife, on pain of having her hair cut off and being sold for money.[2] The latter was a less severe penalty than being thrown into the river. In general, however, the penalties for initiating divorce imposed upon the wife in the marriage contracts are as severe as those of the Code, though not always identical. In one case the wife is to be thrown from a tower;[3] in another, impaled.[4] Nevertheless, the penalty most often imposed is that mentioned in the Code.[5] One marriage, concerning which two documents bear witness,[6] records the wedding of two sisters by one man, but provides that the older shall be the chief wife, and that the other shall perform for her certain specified duties.

From the Neo-Babylonian and Persian periods several marriage contracts have come down to us.[7] The stipulations in them as to bride-price and dowry are in general the same as in those of the time of the Ist dynasty, but the conditions on which the parties may separate are generally omitted from the contracts of that period, although divorce did then occur.[8] In most of the marriage contracts the man acts for himself and arranges with the parents of the bride, though, if the husband is a minor, the parents make the arrangement for him. The bridegroom enjoyed in this respect more liberty of action than the bride. In Babylonia, as in the ceremony of the English Church, she had to be 'given away.'

We have no knowledge of ancient Babylonian marriage ceremonies further than that before marriage every woman had to act once as a temporary *hierodoulos* (see HIERODOULOI [Semitic and Egyptian], vol. vi. p. 674a).

3. Hebrew.—In the story of Samson there are, as noted above, some faint traces of that early Semitic type of marriage in which the wife belonged to a hostile clan, lived with her people, and was visited by her husband for longer or shorter periods. The stories of the Patriarchs reflect various phases of matrimonial development. The marriage of Jacob to the daughters of Laban indicates a type of marriage in which the husband resides in the wife's clan and the children are counted to her family, for Laban says: 'The daughters are my daughters, and the sons are my sons' (Gn 31[43]). Then Jacob broke away, and the children were counted to his stock. This narrative forms a transition from one system of kinship to the other. A number of survivals of the two matriarchal types of marriage just mentioned are found in the narratives of the OT; Shechem, *e.g.*, consented to circumcision to render himself acceptable to the clan of his proposed wife (Gn 34[15f.]). A number of instances also occur in which a son inherits his father's concubines: Ishbosheth regarded Saul's concubine as his own, and resented Abner's taking her (2 S 3[7]); Solomon for the same reason regarded Adonijah's desire to marry Abishag as treason (1 K 2[22]; cf. v.[15]); Reuben was denounced for endeavouring to anticipate the inheritance of his father's concubine during his parent's lifetime (Gn 35[22]). As noted above (§ 1), these are survivals of Semitic polyandrous marriages. Another survival was the levirate—a custom which required a brother to take the widow of a deceased brother and count the first fruit of the union as the child of the deceased (Dt 25[5f.], Gn 38[7-11], Ru 3, 4). The influence of these early forms of marriage is also seen in the great liberty enjoyed by women of the early period (see 1 S 25[18], 2 K 4[22]). In the stories of Abraham and Jacob the type of marriage is also reflected in which slave concubines may be given by a wife to a husband, for the sake of obtaining an offspring which the wife is unable to bear (see *Code of Ḥammurabi*, §§ 144, 146). The general type of marriage of which we have evidence in the Hebrew writings was, however, *ba'al* marriage, the regular Hebrew word for husband being *ba'al*, and that for a married women *be'ūlāh*, which means 'owned,' 'possessed.' Another evidence of this conception of marriage may be seen in Ex 20[17], where the wife is counted among a man's possessions. Among the poor, marriages were probably often monogamous, but there was no sentiment against polygamy, and it was often practised by the rich and powerful, as the large *ḥarīms* of David and Solomon abundantly show. Dt 21[15f.] presupposes that a man will also often have two wives. The law of Ex 21[7-11] takes it for granted that female slaves will become the concubines either of their owner or of his sons. A similar assumption underlies Dt 21[10-14].

The list of the degrees of kinship in which marriage was prohibited in Lv 18, 20, and Dt 27 belongs to the period of Judaism, which began with the Babylonian Exile. At no period were young people allowed to arrange matrimonial affairs for themselves; such arrangements were made by the parents (cf. Gn 21[21] 24[3] 28[1] 34[4] and Jg 14[2]). Down to about 650 B.C. a man could divorce his wife without any formalities whatever (see Hos 3[3] and 2 S 3[14]). This liberty was somewhat modified by the Deuteronomic Code, which provides (24[1ff.]) that, if a man wishes to divorce a wife, he must give her a written statement to that effect. It permits him to issue the divorce for any cause; she need only 'have found no favour in his eyes.' Apparently this law was designed to make divorce less easy than in earlier times, when no written statement was necessary; for, in an age when writing was not a usual accomplishment, it was quite an undertaking to get the document composed. In Judaism, however, this provision was held to justify frequent divorces.

The law of Deuteronomy permitted only the man to initiate divorce; it granted to the woman no corresponding power. It represents, no doubt, the usual custom among the Hebrews. One instance, however, is known in which a Hebrew bride secured by her marriage contract a similar liberty. Among the Jewish papyri discovered at Elephantine in Egypt a marriage contract was found, which contains this passage:

> 'If to-morrow or any later day Miphṭaḥyah shall stand up in the congregation and say, "I divorce As-Ḥor, my husband," the price of divorce shall be on her head. . . . If to-morrow or any later time As-Ḥor shall stand up in the congregation and say, "I divorce my wife, Miphṭaḥyah," her marriage settlement shall be forfeited,'[1] etc.

Whether other Jewish women at Elephantine were accustomed to gain this liberty by contract, or whether there were special reasons why it was secured to Miphṭaḥyah, we do not know, but in any event it is a significant modification of the OT status of women in such matters.

The Deuteronomic law defined two cases in which a man was for ever powerless to divorce a wife: if he had falsely charged his bride with not

1 *PSBA* xxix. [1907] 180 f.
2 *Bab. Exp. of the Univ. of Pennsylvania*, vi.2 48.
3 *Cuneiform Texts from Babylonian Tablets in the British Museum*, vi. 26a.
4 *Ib.* ii. 44.
5 B. Meissner, *Zum altbabylonischen Privatrecht*, Leipzig, 1893, pp. 89, 90; *Cuneiform Texts*, viii. 7b.
6 *Cuneiform Texts*, ii. 44; Meissner, p. 89.
7 See, *e.g.*, the cases cited in Kohler and Peiser, *Babylonisches Rechtsleben*, i. 7 f., ii. 7 f., iii. 10 f., iv. 11 f.
8 See *Babylonian and Assyrian Literature*, Aldine ed., New York, 1901, p. 270 f.

1 See A. H. Sayce and A. E. Cowley, *Aramaic Papyri Discovered at Assouan*, London, 1906, Papyrus G, i. 20 f. Papyrus C confirms the statement.

being a virgin, and if he had been forced to marry a woman whom he had violated (Dt 22$^{19f.\ 28f.}$).

The penalties for adultery bore more heavily on the woman than on the man, the only cases where they were equal being when the crime was committed with the wife or betrothed of another; then both the man and the woman were to be stoned (Dt 22$^{22-27}$). The point of view was that adultery with a married woman was an offence against her husband's property (cf. art. ADULTERY [Semitic]). The wife was accordingly compelled to be faithful, but no similar fidelity was exacted of him. So long as he did not violate the honour of those who were really or prospectively the wives of others, he was not punished, except that, if he violated a maiden, he might be compelled to take her as an additional wife. The penalty imposed on a wife or a betrothed maiden for adultery seems in the earlier time to have been burning (Gn 38^{24}), but was later changed to stoning (Dt 22$^{13f.\ 23f.}$). If a woman was simply suspected of adultery, she was tried by ordeal (Nu 5$^{11-31}$). As the ordeal consisted, however, in drinking water into which holy dust from the sanctuary floor had been thrown, it must generally have resulted in the release of the accused woman. The frequent denunciation of adultery on the part of the prophets would indicate that the penalties were not well enforced and that it was of frequent occurrence (2 S 11 and Hos 3 afford specific instances in which the penalty was not enforced).

4. Arabian. — The early Arabian marriage customs have been sufficiently treated above (§ 1); it remains to note how these customs were affected by Islām. By the time of the Prophet *ba'al* marriage had apparently become the normal type, and polygamy prevailed among the rich. The husband had full power over the wife and could enforce his authority by beating her (Qur'ān, iv. 38). Some survivals of customs which belonged to the earlier time were, as noted above, condemned by the Prophet (iv. 26). Before the time of Muhammad no limit had been set to the number of wives a man might possess. In the interest of moderation, Muhammad ordained that legal wives should be not more than four, but that a man might also enjoy as concubines as many slaves as he was able to possess (iv. 3, 29). The Prophet himself was allowed as many as he wished (xxxiii. 49). Marriage with one's mother, daughters, sisters, paternal and maternal aunts, nieces, mother-in-law, step-daughters, and daughters-in-law was prohibited (iv. 27). Marriages with foreign women were permitted, if the women were believers (lx. 10). Adultery was a crime for a woman, but apparently not for a man. Before the time of the Prophet an adulteress had been literally immured,[1] but Muhammad changed this to imprisonment in the house of the wronged husband (iv. 19). A slave girl was to receive half the penalty of the married woman (iv. 30). Divorce of a wife, as among the Hebrews, was possible to the husband at will. Before the time of Muhammad, the formula of divorce consisted of this sentence, which the husband pronounced to the wife: 'Thou art to me as my mother's back!' After this had been pronounced over her, it was considered as unnatural to approach her as it was to approach a real mother,[2] and so it was regarded as wrong to re-marry a divorced wife. Muhammad called this 'backing away' from wives (lviii. 2). He declared, however, that the utterance of this formula did not constitute a real relationship, and so permitted a man to marry a wife whom he had divorced (xxxiii. 4). A man might not divorce a woman who was pregnant, or who was nursing a child (lxv. 4, 6), but apart from this

[1] E. H. Palmer's *Qur'ān*, i.; *SBE* vi. [1900] 74, n. 1.
[2] Palmer, ii.; *SBE* ix. [1909] 138, n. 2.

condition a man and wife who did not agree might separate at any time (iv. 129), though liberal alimony was enjoined (iv. 24). It is assumed (xxxiii. 48) that men will frequently divorce their wives for mere whims after marriage, even before connubial relations have been established. Liberty of divorce has been freely exercised by the faithful both in ancient and in modern times.[1] Thus 'Alī, the son-in-law of the Prophet, married, including all that he married and divorced, more than two hundred women. Sometimes he included as many as four wives in one contract, and he would divorce four at one time and marry four others in their stead.[2] A certain Mughairah b. Sha'abah is said to have married eighty women in the course of his life,[3] and Muhammad al-Ṭayib, a dyer of Baghdād († 423 A.H.), is said to have married in all more than nine hundred women.[4] Palgrave relates that the Sultan of Qaṭar in E. Arabia married a new wife every month or fortnight, who was then divorced and placed on a pension.[5] C. M. Doughty tells how Zaid, his host, a petty shaikh, not only permitted his wife to be courted by another Arab, but offered to divorce her so that Doughty could marry her.[6]

Naturally a woman could not marry so many men, because she had not the right of divorce, and because she could have only one husband at a time; some of them, nevertheless, managed to have a surprising number. A certain Umm Kharijah of Yemen is said to have had upwards of forty husbands, and her son Kharijah did not know which one was his father.[7]

In parts of Arabia certain old marriage customs still survive in spite of Islām. Thus in Sunan and among the 'Asīr in S. Arabia marriage for a definite term still exists,[8] and a man who has a permanent wife may also take a temporary one. In Sunan the agreement is witnessed before the *qādī*, and so has the sanction of Islām. At the expiration of the contract, the couple may separate without the formality of a divorce; if they continue to live together, a new contract is necessary. Such marriages are still practised in Mecca at the time of the pilgrimage.[9] Marriage ceremonies among the Arabs vary greatly according to circumstances. Sometimes they consist of a feast,[10] sometimes of a civil contract before the *qādī*,[11] and sometimes there is no ceremony at all. The much married woman Umm Kharijah, mentioned above, is said to have reduced the contract to very simple terms. A man approached her and said to her, 'Betrothed?' and she replied, 'Married!' and was from that moment his lawful wife.[12]

5. Abyssinian.—Abyssinia is Christian, though its form of Christianity is the result of an arrested development. Marriages celebrated by the Church assume something of the permanent character of marriage in other Christian countries. Such marriages are solemnized by a priest, and the contracting parties partake of the Holy Communion. A candidate for holy orders is compelled to marry once, as in the Greek Church, but he cannot divorce his wife, and, if she dies, he may not marry again; one matrimonial venture alone is permitted to him.[13] Among the people religious marriages are not popular. All travellers agree that the Abyssinians prefer to be married by civil contract, as these

[1] See Wellhausen, *GGN*, 1893, p. 452 f.
[2] See Lane, *The Thousand and One Nights*, i. 318 f.
[3] *Ib.* [4] *Ib.* [5] ii. 232 f.
[6] *Arabia Deserta*, Cambridge, 1888, i. 320 f.
[7] See Lane, i. 318 f.
[8] Wilken, *Het matriarchaat bij de oude Arabieren*, p. 18; Black and Chrystal, *Lectures and Essays of William Robertson Smith*, p. 586 f.
[9] C. Snouck Hurgronje, *Mekka*, The Hague, 1888–89, ii. 5 f.
[10] See Doughty, *Arabia Deserta*, ed. New York, 1908, i. 128.
[11] Cf. Wilken, *loc. cit.* [12] So Lane, *loc. cit.*
[13] See Bent, *The Sacred City of the Ethiopians*, p. 3 f.

marriages may be dissolved at the desire of either party to the contract. This liberty is freely exercised. Wives are changed at will, by mutual agreement, a man divorcing his own and marrying the wife divorced by another.[1] Divorces do not necessarily dissolve friendly relations between those who separate; Parkyns visited a man whose divorced wife and her children lived in the same compound with him and his new wife and family.[2] It frequently happens that those who have been divorced and have each married others divorce their second spouses and are again reunited. If the separating couple have children, the children are divided. The eldest son falls to the mother, the eldest daughter to the father; if there is only one son, he goes with the mother; and, similarly, one daughter goes with the father; if the remaining children are unequal in number, they are divided by lot.[3]

In addition to these irregularities, there is also much concubinage in Abyssinia, as in other Semitic countries. The levirate exists there, and its compulsion operates not only when a brother dies, but when, as so often happens in African wars, he is emasculated, so as to be incapable of begetting children.[4]

These peculiarities of Abyssinian matrimonial life are clearly a survival from early Semitic conditions, and Christianity has never been able to eradicate them.

When a man desires to marry a girl, he applies directly to her parents or nearest relatives; when their consent is obtained, and the dower arranged, the affair is considered settled, the girl being given no voice in the matter. Civil marriages are celebrated by feasts much as in other Semitic lands, the bridegroom and his friends feasting by themselves, and the bride and her friends by themselves. After a day of festivity, the bride is carried to the house of her husband, and the marriage is accomplished. This formality is observed no matter how many times the bride may have been married before.

LITERATURE.—The literature has been fully cited in the notes, but the principal works may be here recapitulated. C. J. M. Letourneau, *The Evolution of Marriage*, New York, n.d.; E. W. Lane, *The Thousand and One Nights*, London, 1841, i. 318 f.; G. A. Wilken, *Het matriarchaat bij de oude Arabieren*, Amsterdam, 1884; J. Wellhausen, in *GGN*, 1893, pp. 435–480; W. R. Smith, *Kinship and Marriage in Early Arabia*², London, 1903; F. Buhl, *Die socialen Verhältnisse der Israeliten*, Berlin, 1899; G. A. Barton, *A Sketch of Semitic Origins, Social and Religious*, New York, 1902, ch. ii.; I. Benzinger, 'Marriage,' in *EBi* iii. 2942–2951; W. P. Paterson, 'Marriage,' in *HDB*, iii. 262–277; J. F. McLaughlin, 'Marriage,' in *JE* viii. 335 ff.; C. W. Emmet, 'Marriage,' in *SDB*, pp. 583–587; J. Kohler and F. E. Peiser, *Babylonisches Rechtsleben*, Leipzig, 1890–98; J. Kohler and A. Ungnad, *Hammurabi's Gesetz*, do. 1904–10, iii. 4–8; M. Schorr, *Urkunden des altbabylonischen Zivil- und Prozessrechts*, do. 1913, pp. 5–16; J. S. Black and G. Chrystal, *Lectures and Essays of William Robertson Smith*, London, 1912, p. 586 f.; J. C. Hotten, *Abyssinia and its People*, do. 1868, pp. 41 f., 45 f., 50; W. Winstanley, *A Visit to Abyssinia*, do. 1881, ii. 75 f.; J. T. Bent, *The Sacred City of the Ethiopians*, do. 1893, pp. 31–36; A. B. Wylde, *Modern Abyssinia*, do. 1901, pp. 161, 254.

GEORGE A. BARTON.

MARRIAGE (Slavic).—As early as the pagan period the family life of the Slavs was regulated by legal marriages, which were concluded in a solemn manner. Like other nations, the ancient Slavs had two forms of marriage: marriage by capture of a girl belonging to another family or tribe, and marriage by purchase. In the Christian period only the latter was sanctioned by the Church as a more civilized and noble form of marriage, whereas marriage by capture was prohibited and gradually disappeared. Nevertheless, a series of traditions and observances which visibly reflect traces of the old form of marriage by capture is preserved in the wedding ceremony. To these customs belongs, *e.g.*, that of stopping the bridegroom on his way to the house of his bride and that of shutting the door before the bridegroom and hiding the bride; and here may also be mentioned the habit of presenting a false bride to the bridegroom. In S. Russia the wedding-guests engage in symbolical fights, which may rightly be deemed a survival of the ancient marriage by capture. The companions of the bridegroom violently attack the house where the bride lives, while her kinsfolk defend it and repel the aggressors, but at last the two parties put an end to the hostilities and restore harmony by a peaceful negotiation. The Southern Slavs (the Jugoslavs) have preserved the custom of marriage by capture to the present time, and, where this form of marriage has died away, symbolical traditions have taken its place.

The wedding ceremonies celebrated by the different Slavic nations vary widely, but it is possible to discover in them some fundamental traits which are common to all Slavs, and which may be regarded as a survival of ancient times, while their antiquity is also confirmed by their accordance with the chief type of Indo-European wedding ceremony, as reconstructed by H. Hirt and O. Schrader.[1] Among all the Slavic peoples the first preliminaries to the ceremony proper are the 'wooing' and the marriage contract. The deputies of the bridegroom (*družba, svat, starosta, djever*, etc.) negotiate with the bride's father concerning the conditions of the marriage and arrange the precise date for the wedding ceremony. The ceremony begins with the crowning of the bride with a wreath variously arranged and more or less ornate; the bride and the bridegroom shake hands as a mark of their mutual consent, and pass three times round the table or the hearth. Thus the nuptial knot is formally tied, and the pair give each other various presents of symbolical meaning (rings, apples, wedding-shirts, etc.). Afterwards the bride is veiled and conducted in solemn procession to the house of the bridegroom, where a hearty reception is given her, and bread and honey are distributed among the guests, who cast upon the bride various fruits, such as corn, millet, peas, nuts, hops, rice (nowadays sweets), etc., to express their wish that she may bear many children. A similar meaning underlies the custom practised by some Slavic peoples of placing a child in the bride's lap when she arrives at her new home. It is customary, when she reaches the door of the bridegroom's house, to carry her over the threshold and to place her upon a fur, the hair of which is turned upwards. One of the most significant gifts which the wedding-guests bring to the couple is a cock and a black hen. In S. Russia the bride throws such a hen under the hearth, probably as a sacrifice for the domestic genii. A very important place in the wedding pastry is occupied by a large wheat cake, decorated with eggs, flowers, ribbons, and sweets, which is cut in pieces at the wedding feast and distributed among the guests. To the symbolic nuptial ceremonies belong, further, the untwisting or cutting of the bride's plaits and the covering of her hair with a cap-like scarf. There was a rule among the Slavs—which is still, for the most part, observed—which obliged unmarried women, for the sake of distinction, to wear their hair in long, loose plaits, while married women wore a cap. The bride's entrance upon the status of a married woman was symbolized by the ceremony just mentioned, which was performed in a closed room by the women present. Then the bride used to unloose the shoes of her bridegroom

[1] See Hotten, *Abyssinia and its People*, pp. 41, 45 f., 50; Winstanley, *A Visit to Abyssinia*, ii. 73 f.; Bent, p. 31 f.; and Wylde, *Modern Abyssinia*, pp. 161, 254.
[2] M. Parkyns, *Life in Abyssinia*, New York, 1854, p. 272 f.
[3] Hotten, p. 41.
[4] Letourneau, p. 265.

[1] H. Hirt, *Indogermanen*, pp. 436–447; O. Schrader, *Reallex. der indogerm. Altertumskunde*, Strassburg, 1901, pp. 353–362, *Sprachvergleichung und Urgesch.*³, ii. 318–322, 333–335.

to show her submission (sometimes she even received symbolical blows), and, after being clothed in new garments by the women and the 'best man,' she went to bed with her husband in the presence of the witnesses. After the nuptial night purification was performed in a clear stream or at a well; later on, this procedure was reduced to a mere sprinkling with water.

Besides these chief and almost fundamental ceremonies, the various Slavic peoples have other customs connected with the popular wedding, the details of which cannot be described at full length in this article. It is interesting, however, to notice that for a long time the people attached far greater importance to these domestic wedding ceremonies than to the rites prescribed by the Church. Historical documents testify that, even in the 16th and 17th centuries, not only the common people but also the more cultured classes regarded the ecclesiastical ceremony as a purely religious act without any legal significance. A marriage became legal only after the precise performance of all prescribed observances inherited from the ancestors and consecrated by the family tradition; and this conviction is still to be found among some of the Slavic nations.

LITERATURE.—G. Krek, *Einleitung in die slav. Literaturgesch.*[2], Graz, 1887, pp. 196–198, 363; F. S. Krauss, *Sitte und Brauch der Südslaven*, Vienna, 1885, pp. 331–465; O. Schrader, *Sprachvergleichung und Urgesch.*[3], Jena, 1906–07, ii. 322–332. All these contain references to works in Slavic languages, as does also H. Hirt, *Indogermanen*, Strassburg, 1905–07, p. 711 f. See, further, art. FAMILY (Teutonic and Balto-Slavic), § I, vol. v. p. 750.

J. MÁCHAL.

MARTINEAU.—James Martineau (1805–1900) was born in Norwich, April 21, 1805, the fourth son and seventh child of Thomas Martineau, a manufacturer of bombazine. Of Huguenot ancestry, he was also descended through his father's mother from John Meadows, one of the ejected ministers of 1662. After four years at the Norwich Grammar School he was placed under the care of Dr. Lant Carpenter at Bristol (1819–21), to whom he owed his 'spiritual rebirth.' His teacher was a pioneer in education, and combined instruction in the elements of science as well as psychology and moral philosophy with classical and mathematical training. Thus equipped, he was placed in machine-works at Derby, but relinquished his apprenticeship after a year (partly under the shock of a bereavement which 'turned him from an engineer into an evangelist' [speech at Nottingham, 1876; Carpenter, *James Martineau*, p. 24]), and in 1822 he entered Manchester College, York, as a student for the ministry. He had been brought up in the Unitarian theology of Priestley, and embraced his necessitarian pantheism with ardour, though at Bristol he had read Wilberforce and Hannah More, and was not without occasional misgivings concerning the freedom of the will. On the completion of his College course he took charge of Dr. Carpenter's school for a year (1827–28), and, after a short period of ministerial service in Dublin (1828–32), terminated through his refusal of the endowment known as the Regium Donum, he began his longest pastorate in Liverpool (1832–57). In 1840 he undertook the additional duty of Professor of Philosophy and Political Economy in Manchester New College, on its return from York to the city of its foundation. During the erection of the Hope St. Church by his congregation (1848–49) he spent fifteen months with his family in Germany, returning to resume his ministry. The transference of the College to London led to his settlement there in 1857, and from 1859 he also ministered in Little Portland St. Chapel till 1872, when a threatened failure of health led to his retirement. In the meantime he had succeeded to the Principalship of the College in 1869, which he held till June 1885.

For more than fifty years he had been actively engaged in literary work of many kinds. To the religious denomination of his birth and education he gave unstinted service, and his was the chief influence in transforming its fundamental theological conceptions, while in the wider field of philosophy he was the powerful antagonist of the empiricism and utilitarianism of the Mills, the monism of Spinoza, scientific materialism, and the agnostic philosophy of Spencer.

The Unitarians of Martineau's youth followed the tradition of Locke. Accepting the NT as the final authority in Christian doctrine, they recognized Jesus Christ as the Messiah, whose teachings were authenticated by miracles. To this interpretation Martineau remained faithful till after 1832. But further study of the Gospels confronted him with the predictions which implied the return of Jesus in the lifetime of His disciples to judge the world, and this begot an investigation into the significance of revelation which led him to declare in his first work, *The Rationale of Religious Inquiry* (1836), that 'no seeming inspiration can establish anything contrary to reason, that the last appeal in all researches into religious truth must be the judgments of the human mind' (p. 125). To work out this principle was to be one of the main occupations of his life. He followed the progress of German critical study; he was familiar with Paulus and Strauss; he adopted the general results of the Tübingen school, and became their earliest and most accomplished English exponent ('The Creed and Heresies of Early Christianity,' *Westminster Review*, 1853). By 1845 he had abandoned the apostolic authorship of the Fourth Gospel, and in the third edition of the *Rationale* (1845) he ceased to demand belief in the gospel miracles as essential for the Christian name. In the *Prospective Review* (1845–54) and its successor, the *National Review* (1855–64), he secured an organ for his theological and philosophical essays, while others not less brilliant appeared in the *Westminster*. Indefatigable in study, a constant teacher of the young, he devoted long courses of lectures to the exposition of the NT and the history of Christian doctrines, and in his last large treatise, *The Seat of Authority in Religion* (1890), he returned to his earliest theme. He re-examined the claims of the Roman Catholic Church, the infallibility of the Bible, and the historical significance of Christianity, and presented Jesus no longer as the Jewish Messiah, but as the 'prince of Saints,' revealing the highest possibilities of the soul. Looking back at ninety (1895), he wrote to William Knight:

> 'The substitution of Religion at *first-hand*, straight out of the immediate interaction between the soul and God, for religion at *second-hand*, fetched, by copying, out of anonymous traditions of the Eastern Mediterranean eighteen centuries ago, has been the really directing, though hardly conscious aim of my responsible years of life' (Carpenter, p. 540).

Martineau thus remained to the last a Unitarian in his interpretation of the Deity, and a Christian in his allegiance to Jesus Christ. But his position was often misunderstood, partly because of his sympathy with many aspects of traditional devotion, and partly because of his steadfast refusal to belong to a Unitarian *Church*. This was due to the discovery of the real nature of the foundation on which the majority of chapels occupied by Unitarians were held. Some of these had been founded in the 17th cent., others in the 18th, by the English Presbyterians, who, under the leadership of Baxter, had stood for 'catholicism against all parties,' and repudiated creeds of 'human imposition.' In dedicating their chapels 'for the worship of God by Protestant Dissenters' (sometimes specified as Presbyterians, sometimes as

Independents, sometimes as both together), they deliberately rejected all limiting doctrinal names. By slow processes of Scripture study many ministers and congregations gradually became Unitarian in theology. Attention was at length called to this issue, and a suit was instituted against the trustees of a charity in York founded by Lady Hewley, whose husband, Sir John Hewley (M.P. for York in the reign of Charles II.), had been a warm supporter of the Presbyterians. The decision (December 1833), which displaced the Unitarian trustees, was at once seen to imperil the tenure of all the chapels of similar foundation; and after long litigation the existing worshippers were secured in possession only by the Dissenters' Chapels Act (1844). The controversy had a lifelong effect on Martineau's views of the true basis of Church union. To the association of individuals for the promotion of Unitarian teaching he remained constant all his life. But he could not accept a theological name as a condition for religious fellowship. It was inevitably exclusive instead of catholic; it seemed to involve treachery to his spiritual ancestors; it barred the way to those very possibilities of change which had been the secret of the Unitarian advance. Deeply conscious of indebtedness to various schools of religious life, Martineau endeavoured (1868) to form a Free Christian Union, which was joined by representative men of every British Church, but was disbanded two years later. Subsequently he worked out a scheme for 'the National Church as a Federal Union' (*CR* li. [1887] 408 ff.), which proposed to abolish the Act of Uniformity, to release the Church of England from State control, and associate it with the other communions in a United English Christian Church. The plan aroused considerable academic interest, but the Bill in which it was embodied was never actually laid before Parliament.

From the time of his settlement in Liverpool, Martineau had been continuously engaged in teaching and writing, and his intercourse with the young was a prominent cause of the changed view of the moral consciousness which led to the reconstruction of his philosophy. Trained in the pantheistic necessitarianism of Priestley, he had lived under a habitual tension of obligation without realizing its significance. Many influences now contributed to give it new meaning. Wordsworth had long been his favourite poet; Plato called forth his admiration for 'the fair and good'; Coleridge and Carlyle revealed unsuspected deeps of thought and passion in human nature; Channing emphasized its freedom and dignity. In reviewing Bentham's 'Deontology' (*Monthly Repository*, 1834), while still placing the 'criterion of right' in the 'tendency of an action to promote the happiness of an agent,' he laid stress, against Bentham, on the reality and worth of the disinterested affections, and prepared the way for a wholly new set of moral values. The questions of his pupils, his persistent NT studies, and the hymns of the Wesleys opened new aspects of the inner life; and in the lecture on 'Moral Evil' in the Liverpool Controversy (1839) he formally abandoned the determinism of his youth. The change involved many modifications. He ceased to regard revelation as 'communicated truth'; it was effected through character; its organ was the conscience and the affections; its supreme historic type was seen in Christ as the image of the Father.

Reinforced by his reading of Kant, and in opposition on the one hand to the 'association' philosophy of James Mill, and on the other to the monistic schemes of Spinoza and Hegel, Martineau began to work out his new analysis of man's moral nature. The sphere of judgment was transferred from consequences without to springs of action within. In this inner world lay a multitude of appetites and energies, which were not all of equal rank. When they were examined side by side, some revealed themselves as higher, while others fell into a lower place; and this distinction of rank was irresolvable into any other element such as order, truth, beauty, sympathy, or reason. All moral estimates, therefore, were *preferential*; there was always an alternative before the mind, and the power to recognize these diverse values lay with conscience, which pronounced this better and that worse. This view was first expounded in the *Prospective* (1845), in an essay on Whewell's 'Elements of Morality,' and led to the definition: 'Every action is *right* which, in the presence of a lower principle, follows a higher; every action is wrong which, in the presence of a higher principle, follows a lower' (*Essays*, iii. 352). The year before, during a visit to Liverpool, Mrs. Carlyle had described Martineau as 'the victim of conscience.' He was to become the greatest English moralist since Butler. Here was the witness of Deity within; here the access of the soul to divine things; here the true ground for the conception which he was afterwards to define as 'the perennial Indwelling of God in Man and in the Universe.' Alongside this view of man's ethical constitution ran an exposition of our knowledge of the external world (in a review of J. D. Morell's *Historical and Critical View of the Speculative Philosophy of Europe in the Nineteenth Century*, London, 1846, in *Prospective*, 1846): 'The act of Perception gives us simultaneous knowledge of subject and object' (p. 562). Again and again in subsequent essays Martineau vindicated this 'natural dualism' against idealism on the one hand and pantheism on the other, and vigorously defended the veracity of our faculties. But perception involved more than passive consciousness; it was evoked by resistance and the effort needed to overcome it; besides the space-relation of the I and the not-I, a cause-relation was revealed in the same antithesis. In the strenuous conviction of personality which he derived from his ethical experience, Martineau found the true meaning of cause; its seat was in the personal power of the will, and this he boldly applied to the interpretation of the surrounding scene. The 'not-self' must be comprehended personally; its varied energies were but the manifestations of one living Will. Science, by the rising doctrine of the correlation of forces, might point to their ultimate identity. Martineau entrenched himself securely in his prophetic recognition of the part played by the same energy in the constitution of human nature. The relation of the soul to God was a moral relation. Known in the conscience, He was one; the manifoldness of the world, therefore, was only the veil of a hidden unity; and the foundations of theism were thus laid on the conception of God as cause of the universe and revealer of righteousness in man.

Such was the general scheme of the philosophy of religion which Martineau worked out with rich elaboration in the next forty years. His sojourn in Germany and his renewed studies in Plato and Hegel gave him a securer hold of great ontological conceptions. He described it afterwards as 'a new intellectual birth.' But he remained faithful to the English tradition of psychological method, and slowly built up the fabric of thought on the basis of self-knowledge. Again and again he sought to construct a table of the springs of action in the order of their relative worth. This was finally embodied in the first of his three large treatises, *Types of Ethical Theory* (2 vols., 1885). After reviewing 'unpsychological theories,' transcendental (Plato), immanental (Descartes, Malebranche, Spinoza), and physical (Comte), he expounded (vol. ii.) his own interpretation of the nature of moral authority. This involved a classification of the propensions, passions, affections, and sentiments, and an arrangement of them in a scale of values. The scheme thus wrought out of human experience was then contrasted with the hedonist ethics of the older utilitarians, and the modifications introduced by the idea of evolution. In emphasizing 'Hitches in the Evolutionary Deduction' he denied that laws of matter and motion could explain the genesis of consciousness, while the feeling of moral right and freedom involved another point of fresh departure. The section on 'Conscience developed into Social Consensus and Religion' further supplied hints which modified the stress of individualism in some of his earlier writings.

The stream of Essays had ceased for some years after the suspension of the *National Review* (1864); but an important address on *Religion as affected by Modern Materialism* (1874), suggested by John Tyndall's discourse to the British Association at Belfast, and its sequel, *Modern Materialism: its Attitude towards Theology* (1876), brought Martineau again prominently into the field of philosophical discussion. Two other addresses, *Ideal Substitutes for God* (1879) and *The Relation between Ethics and Religion* (1881), belonged to the period in which he was slowly completing the treatise modestly entitled *A Study of Religion* (2 vols., 1888). It opened with an investigation of the limits of human intelligence, a fresh defence of 'natural realism,' a plea for the objective reality of space and time, a reply to the empirical doctrine that we know nothing but phenomena, and a refutation of the agnosticism of Spencer. God had been presented at the outset as a 'divine Mind and Will ruling the Universe and holding Moral relations with mankind' (vol. i. p. 1); and the bases of theism in the doctrine of His sole causation in the natural order and His perfection in the moral order were re-established and supported with fresh illustration. The teleological conceptions which had been discarded in earlier revolt against Paley were now revived on a far wider scale, and the presence of rational ends was displayed with varied scientific knowledge in the vast process of evolution. Assuming the results of his analysis of human nature in the previous treatise, Martineau then argued that the principle of obligation implied the presence within us of a moral order in which God was disclosed as transcendently holy. The intelligent Purpose and the righteous Will were then identified; the place of pain and sin under such a rule was defined; and the theodicy concluded with a refutation of pantheism and a defence of human freedom. A final book carried the argument up to 'the Life to come.'

Martineau's last word on the grounds of belief and their illustration in the NT was uttered in *The Seat of Authority in Religion* already cited, in which the origins of Christianity were expounded with remarkable force and daring (1890). The work was less technical than its predecessors, and appealed to the wide circle of those who had found invaluable help in the author's devotional writings. In the *Endeavours after the Christian Life* (2 vols., 1843–47) he had unfolded secrets of personal religion and moral experience in language often of lyrical poignancy. Successive collections of hymns (1831, 1840, 1874) testified to his deep sympathy with many types of Christian devotion. Later series of *Hours of Thought on Sacred Things* (1876, 1879) carried on the application of his thought to the varied incidents of the human lot. A small book of *Home Prayers* was issued (1891) in response to the urgency of many friends, and in four volumes of *Essays, Reviews, and Addresses* (1890–91) he gathered up those of his detached writings which he wished to preserve. Even their wide range, over history, science, and philosophy, does not exhaust the whole scope of his productiveness, which included political economy and psychology. In the theological timidity and the ecclesiastical strife of the early Victorian era he stood forth (often alone) as the fearless advocate of the principle of religious freedom. Later years brought unsought appreciation. Gladstone designated him as 'the greatest of living thinkers'; and a younger philosopher (A. Seth Pringle-Pattison, *HJ* i. [1903] 444) aptly fixed the character of his service to his age by describing him as 'an ideal champion of the spiritual view of the world in a time of transition and intellectual insecurity.'

LITERATURE.—Besides the works already named, some of Martineau's earlier writings were collected by American friends in *Miscellanies*, Cambridge, Mass., 1852, *Studies of Christianity*, London, 1858, and *Essays Philosophical and Theological*, 2 vols., do. 1883. We may also name his Lectures in the Liverpool Controversy (1839), *A Study of Spinoza*, do. 1882, and *National Duties and other Sermons and Addresses*, do. 1903. See, further, A. W. Jackson, *James Martineau, a Biography and a Study*, do. 1900; J. Drummond and C. B. Upton, *The Life and Letters of James Martineau*, 2 vols., do. 1902; J. E. Carpenter, *James Martineau, Theologian and Teacher*, do. 1905.

J. ESTLIN CARPENTER.

MARTYRS.—See SAINTS AND MARTYRS.

MARY.—The following article, dealing with the cult of the Virgin Mary, starts from the Scriptural and orthodox positions (1) that our Lord Jesus Christ, being the eternal Son of God, became man, being conceived by the Holy Ghost and born of the Virgin Mary; and (2) that, inasmuch as He is thus God and man in two distinct natures and one person for ever, so is she, His mother, truly and properly described as Theotokos and Virgo Deipara—the Mother or Bringer-forth of Our Lord and God, who was God when He issued from her virgin womb, wearing the manhood which of her substance had been prepared for Him, which He had taken to Himself, which He carried with Him to the Cross, which He raised in spiritual glory from the tomb, which He wears for ever at the right hand of the Majesty on high. These things are part of the faith of the whole Catholic Church; they are treated here as historical facts.

Another matter which, though Scripture is silent upon it, unquestionably exercised a powerful influence on the development of the cult of the Virgin Mary, is assumed in this article in accordance with the view of overwhelmingly the larger part of Christendom, viz. her perpetual virginity: 'virgo concepit, virgo peperit, virgo permansit.' With the general question of the Invocation of Saints, and the merits or demerits of that practice, this article is not concerned.

The only questions, therefore, to be here discussed concern the implications of these facts. We shall inquire historically (1) what was inferred from them in the Apostolic and early ages of the Church as to the duty of Christians towards the Virgin Mother of the Lord; (2) when and how the wide-spread developments of her cult arose; and (3) the grounds on which these developments have been justified, or are rejected, by those who accept the facts.

1. In Holy Scripture.—Over and above the witness borne by the four Evangelists to our Lord's having a human mother (Mk 3^{31}, Jn 2^{1-5} 6^{42}) whose name was Mary (Mk 6^{3}), and the direct statements of two of them (Mt 1^{20}, Lk $1^{27.34}$) that she was a pure virgin when by the power of the Holy Ghost she conceived and bore our Saviour, we have in the third Evangelist several notes expressive of the high reverence and honour due to her. St.

Luke records the angelic salutation, 'Hail, thou that art highly favoured, the Lord is with thee' (1^{28}); and the angelic assurance, 'Thou hast found favour with God' (1^{30}). He makes it plain that she was the moral, and not simply the physical, instrument of the Incarnation; he brings out her wonderful faith, believing in God's power, seeking no sign, though she gets one, and asking only what course the divine call may require her to adopt (1^{34}); his narrative evinces her conscious risking 'the reproach among men with which the poor Jews still blaspheme her Son and revile herself' (Pusey, *Eirenicon*, ii. 25); and he records how 'Elizabeth, filled with the Holy Ghost,' saluted her, 'Blessed art thou among women, and blessed is the fruit of thy womb. And whence is this to me, that the mother of my Lord should come to me? . . . And blessed is she that believed' (1^{42-45}). Mary herself, in her inspired song, while acknowledging that God is her Saviour too, expects from 'all generations' a like honour to that which Elizabeth had assigned her, and speaks of 'the great things' that God had done for her ($1^{48f.}$).

Yet, while the NT thus justifies the Church's instinct of loving and reverential gratitude to the Holy Mother of the Lord, and authorizes the naming of her with lofty titles, it presents us with not one instance of her influence with Christ being invoked either in her lifetime or after her departure. At Cana, when she does interpose, she is bidden wait His time; and her advice to those whom she is sure that He will help is, 'Whatsoever *He* saith unto you, do it' (Jn $2^{4.5}$). When, on another occasion, she 'sent unto him, calling him,' He apparently did not go, but answered, 'Whosoever shall do the will of God, the same is . . . my mother' (Mk 3^{31-35}, Lk $8^{20f.}$). When a woman exclaimed, 'Blessed is the womb that bare thee,' He replied, 'Yea rather, blessed are they that hear the word of God, and keep it' (Lk $11^{27.28}$). He does not imply, of course, that Mary had not these graces—they were conspicuous in her; but He certainly puts the moral virtue higher than even her unique privilege. And when, from the Cross, He commends her to St. John saying, 'Behold, thy mother,' and him to her, 'Behold, thy son,' while to have her with him in 'his own home' (Jn $19^{26f.}$) was doubtless a precious legacy to the theologian apostle, yet the obvious meaning of our Saviour's words was rather that St. John should take care of her than that she should be his protectress (R. Stier, *The Words of the Lord Jesus*, Eng. tr., Edinburgh, 1855–58, vii. 467 ff., on Jn $19^{26.27}$). There is certainly no evidence in St. John or elsewhere in the NT that he, or any other, so much as thought of her being established as a mother to pity all Christians, and help them in their approach to Christ. On the other hand, to expound the passage, as some Protestant writers (even Stier, *loc. cit.*) have not hesitated to do, as an intimation that all Christ's earthly relationships—even Mary's to Him as His mother—ceased and determined by His death is to come perilously near the denial of His abiding manhood whereby, as our High Priest within the veil, He is still 'touched with the feeling of our infirmities' (He 4^{15}). A sufficient explanation of our Lord's neither calling her here His mother nor naming either St. John or her is supplied when we take it as an instance of His considerateness: had He betrayed the relationship, those who mocked at Him would not have been slow to insult her; and the newly re-awakened courage of the disciple might have again been shaken by the utterance of their names.

The only other notices of Mary in the NT are (1) the mention of her by St. Luke (Ac 1^{14}) in the place of honour as the first, and only one named, among the Christian women, and as still, after the Ascension, 'the mother of Jesus'; (2) the reference to her by St. Paul (Gal 4^4) as 'a woman'—an obvious allusion to the Protevangelium (Gn 3^{15}); and (3) St. John's taking from her experiences certain features for his prophetic portrait of the Church as the sun-clothed woman (Rev 12).

2. In the first three centuries.—The Christian literature of this period keeps in regard to Mary strictly to the lines of the NT. References to her are sparse; and these, though distinct as to her being the Virgin Mother of the Lord and therefore to be honoured, give no suggestion of aught that could be called a cult of her. Polycarp's short Epistle does not contain her name; but in his *Life* by Pionius there is this:

'He, according to the prophecy, . . . being born of an undefiled and spotless virgin' (xiii.).

In the *Apology* of Aristides she is simply 'a Hebrew virgin.' Ignatius, in the short recension of his seven Epistles (here regarded as genuine), is fuller.

He tells (*ad Ephes.* xix.) how the virginity of Mary deceived the Deceiver; that 'hidden from the prince of this world were the virginity of Mary and her childbearing . . . mysteries wrought in the silence of God, now to be cried aloud'; he adores our Saviour, 'Son of Mary and Son of God'; and he insists (*ad Trall.* ix. f.) that His birth of her demonstrates against the Docetists that His flesh is a reality and no semblance; but the correspondence between Ignatius and the Virgin is a Latin forgery, which never existed in the Greek, and is based on the saint's use of the word χριστοφόρος.

Justin Martyr (*Dial. cum Tryph.* c.) and Irenæus speak of her as does the Puritan Milton, as 'the second Eve.'

'The knot of Eve's disobedience was loosed by the obedience of Mary; for what the Virgin Eve had bound fast through unbelief that did the Virgin Mary set free through faith' (Irenæus, *adv. Hær.* III. xxii. 4). And again he dwells on the moral side of her part in the Incarnation: 'Mary, having a man betrothed to her and being nevertheless a virgin, by yielding obedience became the cause of salvation to herself and to the whole human race' (*ib.*).

If, however, we find Irenæus, in the barbarous Latin version of his works, calling Mary the 'advocata' of Eve, we shall do well to remember that his Greek had, apparently, συνήγορος, which implies not advocacy in our sense, but rebuke. Origen supplies one of the only two places in the Fathers where the words of our Lord from the Cross to her and to St. John have the least appearance of ascribing to her a permanent office for Christians.

'Seeing that, according to those who think soundly of her, Mary had no other son save Jesus; and that Jesus said to her, "Behold, thy son," therefore those in whom Christ lives are sons of Mary' (*in Joan.* i. 6).

But does this go further than Christ's own, 'Behold, my mother and my brethren' (Mt 12^{49}, Mk 3^{34})? Both Origen and Tertullian, like Ignatius before them, draw from her motherhood of Christ arguments against Gnostic or Docetic heresy. Yet even of the Gnostics — so strong already was the Church's faith in the Virgin-birth of the Redeemer—several were constrained to admit the fact, while others, allowing that He issued from her womb, protested that He drew nothing from her substance.

If any cult of the Virgin existed in these early centuries, it is in the records of the Church's worship at the time that we should expect to find it, rather than in the treatises of divines or the apologies of the defenders of the faith. But such accounts of the Church service of the period as have come down to us exhibit precisely the same features as do the writings of the ante-Nicene Fathers. No mention of Mary's name, no reference to her, occurs in the notices of Holy Communion in the NT; nor in the liturgical thanksgiving in the 1st Epistle of St. Clement of Rome; nor in the *Didache*; nor in Justin Martyr's or Tertullian's account of the Eucharistic service. The only place where an invocation of St. Mary could come in is at the Commemoration of Martyrs and the Commemoration of the Departed; and on this all that St. Cyprian has to say is:

'Ecclesiastical discipline teaches, as the faithful know, that at the point where the martyrs are named at the altar of God, there they are not prayed for; but for others who are commemorated prayer is offered' (*Epp.* i. [*Opera*, Oxford, 1682, p. 8]).

There is no direct evidence that among 'the martyrs' the Virgin was so much as mentioned.

The one thing in these centuries that points in the direction of any cult of her in the Church is the appearance, somewhere in the 2nd cent., of an apocryphal *Evangelium Jacobi*, which was very popular and became the basis of two later works, *Liber de Infantia Mariæ et Christi Salvatoris* and *Evangelium de Nativitate Mariæ*. It is from these that the 'traditional' names of her parents, Joachim and Anna, have been derived, and the story of Mary's nurture in the Temple from her third to her twelfth year. These books, if they were not genuine, at least met a growing and significant demand, which was not checked by their condemnation as heretical in the earliest papal *index expurgatorius* attributed to Pope Gelasius (A.D. 492–496).

3. During the period of the four great councils (A.D. 325–451).—With the conversion of Constantine Christianity became fashionable, and, as Newman puts it, the spirit of the world was poured into the Church (*The Arians of the Fourth Century*, London, 1876, p. 258). The leaders of the faithful had to raise their standard against an inrush at once of pagan sensuality and of heresies born of pagan conceptions of the Godhead. It is among the latter that we find the earliest notice in Christian history of an actual worship of St. Mary. Epiphanius reckons it a heresy (*Hær.* lxxix.) that 'certain women in Thrace, Scythia, and Arabia' were in the habit of adoring the Virgin as a goddess and offering to her a certain kind of cake (κολλυρίδα τινά), whence he calls them 'Collyridians.' Their practice (cf. Jer 44[19]) and the notion underlying it were undoubtedly relics of heathenism always familiar with female deities. Epiphanius rebukes them:

'Let Mary be had in honour, but let the Lord be worshipped' (*Hær.* lxxix. 9).

'Honour to Mary' was inevitably augmented by the Church's answer (true and necessary as that answer was) to the much more formidable heresy of Arius. Arianism, stumbling at the awful mystery of the Word made flesh (Jn 1[14]), and chiming in with the old pagan conceptions of gods older and younger, greater and less, presented to men the Eternal Son as only the first of creatures. It did not deny that Christ was born of the Virgin, but, by denying that He who issued from her womb was personally God, it lowered the greatness and the glory of her motherhood. It is not so much, however, in the interests of her dignity as for the utterance of the full truth concerning Christ that the orthodox theologians of this period are accustomed to refer to her. This holds of them all—of Cyril of Alexandria as well as of Athanasius, Basil, and the Gregorys, of Ambrose and Augustine as well as of Leo. It was in this connexion that Athanasius had spoken of her as θεοτόκος long before the Nestorian preacher shocked the congregation of St. Sophia by refusing her the title.

Athanasius gave it her because 'from the flesh of holy Mary the Son of God by essence and nature did proceed. . . . How can they wish to be called Christians who assert that the Word descended on a holy man as upon one of the prophets, and deny that He Himself became Man, taking the body from Mary?' (*Ep.* lix. 'ad Epict.' 2); and, again, because, 'when He was descending to us, He fashioned His body for Himself from a Virgin, thus to afford to all no small proof of His Godhead, in that He who formed this is also Maker of everything else as well' (*de Incarn. Verbi*, xviii.).[1]

[1] Athanasius was anxious to secure the reality of our Lord's manhood no less than His divinity; and in support of this truth also he, like Ignatius before him, appeals to Christ's birth of Mary: 'Human then, by nature, was that which was from Mary according to the holy Scriptures, and true was the body of the Lord. True it was, since it was the same with ours. For Mary was our sister, since we are all from Adam' (*Ep.* lix. 'ad Epict.' 7).

In like manner, Gregory of Nyssa, 'Have any of ourselves dared to say "Mother of Man" of that most holy Virgin the Mother of God?' (*Ep.* xix.); and Ambrose, 'Talis decet partus Deum' (*Hymn* iv. 'de Adventu Domini' [*PL* xvi. 1474]). Cyril of Jerusalem, with equal force, uses Christ's birth of Mary as demonstrating the companion truth of His real manhood.

'Believe that this Only-Begotten Son of God . . . was begotten of the holy Virgin by the Holy Ghost, and was made Man, not in seeming and mere show, but in truth; nor yet by passing through a channel, but truly of her made flesh. . . . If the Incarnation was a phantom, salvation is a phantom too' (*Cat. Lect.* iv. 9).

All the heresies, we may say, of this period were, in one form or another, denials of the Incarnation; they all fixed men's thoughts on the question propounded by our Lord Himself, 'What think ye of the Christ? whose son is he?' (Mt 22[42]). It was impossible for the Church to refute any of them without speaking, as of God His Father, so of the Virgin Mary His Mother—to reply to Macedonianism, with its denial of the Godhead of the Holy Ghost who overshadowed her (Lk 1[35]); to Apollinarianism, which, refusing to Christ a human soul, cut off from His sacred heart its thousandfold return of her love; and then to Nestorianism, which, dissolving the unity of Christ's Person, by one and the same stroke reduced the Saviour from being Himself the Word incarnate to a man in close association with the Word, and made Mary the mother only of a human infant. All these errors helped to burn in upon the mind of the Christians of that age the truth which E. B. Pusey tells us so

'startled him in his young days when first it flashed upon him that it must be true, that one of our nature, which is the last and lowest of God's rational creation was raised to a nearness to Almighty God above all the choirs of angels. . . . Yet it was self-evident, as soon as stated, that she of whom Christ deigned to take His human flesh was brought to a nearness to Himself above all created beings; that she stood single and alone in all creation or all possible creations, in that in her womb He who in His Godhead is consubstantial with the Father, deigned, as to His Human Body, to become consubstantial with her' (*Eirenicon*, ii. 24).

It is no creature-worship; it is the sense of this tremendous fact brought home to a heart inflamed with the love of the Incarnate Son that explains at once the profound solemnity of Cyril's Letter to Nestorius and the splendid eloquence of Proclus's oration on the Virgin Mother. It is not that she is the mediator (there is no hint of such a thought); it is that He is God whom she bare, whom 'she alone inexplicably housed.' Nor need we fancy (with the writer on 'Mary' in *EBr*[11]) that it was the Nicene 'solution of the Arian controversy, however correct it may have been theoretically,' that 'undoubtedly had the practical effect of relegating the God-man redeemer for ordinary minds into a far away region of "remote and awful Godhead," so that the need for a mediator to deal with the very Mediator could not fail to be felt' (*EBr*[11] xvii. 812 f.). As a matter of fact, it was the complete manhood of our Lord that the Church in the next succeeding controversies (Monophysite and Monothelete) triumphantly asserted, while at the same time carefully retaining the condemnation of Nestorianism. Indeed it has been observed that it is in the creed of Chalcedon, and not in the canons of Ephesus, that the term θεοτόκος occurs. With all the honour that they gave to her, the Fathers of this age never forgot that, if she ministered to our salvation by becoming, on and through her faith, the Mother of our Redeemer, it was through her faith in Him that she herself was saved. The great titles bestowed upon her by the Fathers relate to the fruits of the Incarnation.

'The flesh of the Virgin differs nothing from the flesh of sin; . . . but her body transmits it not to the Body of Christ, which she did not conceive through concupiscence' (Augustine, *c. Jul. Pelag.* v. 15).

And Pope Leo I. (in a passage still remaining in the Roman Breviary as one of the Lessons for Christmas Day) says that 'to [Christ's] birth alone the throes of human passion had not contributed.'

In entire consistency with this teaching of the great Fathers, we find that the worship of the Church in the conciliar period shows hardly a trace of any cult of the Virgin. There are indications that she was prayed for.

Thus in the Armenian Liturgy, 'We beseech thee that in this holy sacrifice remembrance be made of the mother of God the holy virgin Mary, and of John the baptist, of the proto-martyr Stephen, and of all the saints' (F. E. Brightman, *Liturgies Eastern and Western*, i. 440).

But she is not often mentioned. In the liturgy in the *Apostolic Constitutions* she is not even named; if she is referred to there at all, it is as included with others—'apostles, martyrs, virgins . . . whose names Thou knowest.' In other liturgical works of the period—*e.g.*, the *Statutes of the Apostles* (Ethiop. *c.* 350)—there is no mention of any commemoration of the departed, nor is there in the Arabic and Saidic versions of this book. The Eucharistic service in the *Testamentum Domini* gives thanks that the 'Word . . . was born of the Holy Ghost and the Virgin'; but its commemoration of the dead, 'Remember those who have fallen asleep in the faith, and grant us an inheritance with Thy saints,' names neither the Virgin nor any other saint. *The Pilgrimage of Silvia* also is silent concerning her, while the *Catechetical Lectures* (Lect. xxiii. on the Eucharistic service) of Cyril of Jerusalem, where we might have expected to find something, has only this:

'Then we commemorate also those who have fallen asleep before us, first Patriarchs, Prophets, Apostles, Martyrs, that at their intercessions God would receive our petition'—still no mention of Mary.

In the liturgy of the civil 'diocese' of Africa in the time of Augustine (A.D. 400) 'the only place where an invocation of the Virgin could have come in is in its commemoration of the saints and martyrs, but there is again no direct evidence that her name appeared' (*Ordo Rom. Primus*, App. iv.). Of Basil his latest editor says:

'Of any cultus of the Virgin, St. Basil's writings shew no trace.' 'Even Letter CCCLX, which bears obvious marks of spuriousness, and of proceeding from a later age, does not go beyond a recognition of the Blessed Virgin as Θεοτόκος, in which the Catholic Church is agreed, and a general invocation of the apostles, prophets, and martyrs, the Virgin not being set above these' (Blomfield Jackson, Prolegomena to 'St. Basil,' *Nicene and Post-Nicene Fathers*, viii. [1895] p. lxxiii). The passage runs: 'I invoke them to supplication to God, that through them, that is through their mediation, the merciful God may be propitious to me.'

That the departed saints, now 'with Christ' (Ph 1^{23}), do pray for us is an obvious conclusion from their perfected love; it has some sanction in the NT (Rev 6^{10}); it is argued for on this ground by Origen (*de Orat.* 31), Eusebius (*de Martyr. Palæst.* v.), and Jerome (*Ep.* lx.); and it was an easy transition to ask God that their intercessions might be heard for us; but 'Omniscience alone can hear the cry of every human heart, and Omnipotence alone can deliver everywhere,' and it was quite another thing to credit any saint, however highly exalted, with powers or prerogatives of this extent. Not so did the Fathers of the Church and the holy martyrs pray. Cardinal Newman admitted that no prayer to the blessed Virgin is to be found in the voluminous works of St. Augustine. And when, late in the 4th cent., we do find cases of direct invocation of this or that individual saint, it is in private prayer, and in regard to some more restricted matter in which that saint had been interested when on earth and might be presumed to be interested still. Of this limited sort was the prayer of Justina, mentioned with incidental approval by Gregory Nazianzen (*Orat.* xxiv. 11), 'imploring Mary the Virgin to come to the aid of a virgin in danger.' St. Mary had already been thought of as the 'virgin of virgins'—the leader of those virgin bands to whom, next to the martyrs, the Church felt that she owed a special debt. The martyrs were her witnesses to Christian truth; her virgins the conspicuous exponents of Christian purity. Virginity, be it remembered, had been praised—though not enforced—by our Saviour Himself (Mt $19^{11f.}$), and by St. Paul (1 Co $7^{37f.}$); under the pagan persecutions the virgin martyrs had won a twofold triumph; and when, on Constantine's conversion, pagan sensuality proved a menace no less formidable to morals than heresy to doctrine, virginity, organized into monasticism, became more and more alike the expression and the shield of this side of Christian virtue. Athanasius found the monks and virgins of Egypt of the greatest use to him in his contest with Arianism. He introduced monasticism at Rome; Ambrose and Martin carried it respectively to Cisalpine and Transalpine Gaul; through the latter, the trainer of missionaries, it spread over the Celtic West. Jerome carried it to Palestine; Basil was its protagonist through Asia Minor. Virginity and monasticism, no less than orthodoxy, turned the thoughts of the faithful very much towards St. Mary. If orthodoxy found, as we have seen, that Christ's birth of her was a witness at once of His Godhead and His manhood, so did monasticism boast of her as the crown of virgins. If orthodoxy called forth the panegyrics on Mary by Proclus and Cyril of Alexandria, the thought of her virginity led even more directly to her being regarded as a patroness.

It is while consoling the votaries of the virgin life that Augustine reminds them how 'the Birth from the one holy Virgin is the glory of all holy virgins: they, too, are mothers of Christ if they do the will of His Father' (*de Sanct. Virg.* v.).

Thus, too, Jerome:

'Therefore the virgin Christ and the Virgin Mary have dedicated in themselves the firstfruits of the virginity of both sexes' (*Ep.* xlviii. 'ad Pam.' 21);

and Gregory of Nyssa:

'What happened in the stainless Mary when the fulness of the Godhead which was in Christ shone out through her, that happens in every soul that leads by rule the virgin life. No longer, indeed, does the Master come with bodily presence, . . . but, spiritually, He dwells in us and brings His Father with Him' (*de Virg.* ii.).[1]

4. During the mediæval period.—For the purposes of this article, this period may be dated from the extinction of the Western Empire by Odoacer (A.D. 476) to the close of the Council of Trent (1563). Throughout this period Christianity runs in an Eastern and a Western stream; but, in spite of their divergence, there took place in both a remarkable development in the cult of the Virgin. It came to a head more early in the East. There, where the chief heresies concerning the Trinity and Incarnation had arisen, and where theological speculation was more congenial to the public taste, new forms of error on these subjects were constantly springing up, and to all these the orthodox found a complete answer in the Scripture records of our Saviour's birth of a Virgin Mother. His Virgin-birth witnessed alike the reality of both His natures and the unity of His Person; it hallowed monasticism; it rebuked the impieties first of the iconoclasts and then of the Muhammadans, while the calamities which afflicted and cut short, if they did not, till A.D. 1453, destroy, the empire in the East, were at least sufficient to impress all Christians who remained, or had been, its subjects with awestruck thoughts of Christ as the Judge of men. They remembered how, in the days of His flesh, the good centurion had, unrebuked, deemed himself not worthy to come to Christ direct (Lk 7^7), but had besought Him through the elders of the

[1] W. M. Ramsay argues that so early as the 5th cent. the honour paid to the Virgin Mary at Ephesus was the recrudescence in a baptized form of the old pagan Anatolian worship of the Virgin Mother (*Pauline and other Studies*, p. 126).

Jews. How much more, then, might they, sin-burdened, approach Him through the prayers of His spotless Mother? The 'Theologian' among the orthodox divines (Gregory Nazianzen) had, as we have seen, approved of Justina asking her help; why might not Justinian ask her advocacy for his Christian empire, and Narses look for her direction on the field of battle, and Heraclius bear her image on his banner, and Simeon Stylites, in his post-communion thanksgiving, invoke as supplicants 'all the saints . . . and with them Thy most holy Mother, . . . receive their prayers, O Christ'? (*Euchology of Orthodox Church*, tr. G. V. Shann, Kidderminster, 1891, p. 257 f.). So strong was the current of feeling that even the great liturgies, already venerable, received interpolations to express it. In some of these we can see the process going on. Thus in the Liturgy of St. Mark (Alexandrian), though originally St. Mary was simply included in the prayer that God would give rest to all the holy dead, now she is mentioned by name, 'especially the most holy, stainless, blessed, our Lady, Mother of God, and ever-Virgin,' and the sequence of thought, which still shows that she is prayed for, is interrupted by a salutation, 'Hail, thou that art full of grace . . . because thou didst bring forth the Saviour of the world.' So in St. James, the parent of all the Syrian liturgies, she had originally simply been commemorated, but now it is added 'that we may obtain mercy through their prayers and intercessions'; and in the Anaphora there is interpolated, not only the angelic salutation, but a long quotation from Proclus's glowing panegyric (Neale and Littledale, *Liturgies*[3], p. 54). The alteration is very naively made in the liturgy of the Coptic Jacobites:

'To our fathers and our brethren who are fallen asleep . . . give rest, remembering all saints . . . and most chiefly . . . the holy theotokos Mary. . . . Not that we are worthy to intercede for their blessedness . . . but . . . that standing before the tribunal of thine onlybegotten Son they may in recompense intercede for our poverty and weakness' (Brightman, i. 169).

In the Armenian Liturgy St. Mary's name remains in the Great Intercession:

'We beseech thee that in this holy sacrifice remembrance be made of the mother of God the holy virgin Mary, and of John the baptist, of the protomartyr Stephen and of all the saints' (*ib.* p. 440). But at an earlier stage the Deacon bids the worshippers 'make the holy mother of God and all the saints' their 'intercessors with the Father' (*ib.* p. 415).

The two liturgies remaining in use among the orthodox Greeks are those of Chrysostom and Basil, and are more moderate.

The latter merely mentions her in the Eucharistic Thanksgiving for Christ 'born of a woman, the holy Mother of God, ever-Virgin'; and prays that God 'would unite all of us who are partakers of the one Bread . . . that we may find mercy with all Thy saints . . . especially our all-holy, immaculate, supereminently blessed glorious Lady, the Mother of God, and Ever-Virgin Mary' (*ib.* pp. 326, 330 f.).

It is not impossible, in view of Basil's own writings, that even the last is an interpolation. The liturgy called Chrysostom's is fuller on St. Mary:

The Prayer of the Trisagion closes 'through the intercessions of the Holy Mother of God and all the Saints'; but, again, it prays for her: 'We offer to Thee this reasonable service on behalf of those who have departed in the faith . . . Apostles . . . Virgins . . . especially the most holy, undefiled, excellently laudable, glorious Lady, the Mother of God, and Ever-Virgin Mary' (*ib.* pp. 314, 331).

When, however, we turn to the less august and more popular of the authorized devotions of the Greek Church, we find her invoked in the most direct manner:

'O most holy Mother of God, light of my darkened soul, my hope, protection, refuge. I thank thee that thou hast enabled me to be a partaker of the . . . Body and . . . Blood of Thy dear Son. Enlighten the eyes of my heart . . . quicken me . . . give me tears of repentance and thanksgiving' (*Euchology*).

In the *Book of Needs*, the 'Prayerful Canon at the Departure of a Soul' teaches the dying man to cry to her:

'Known refuge of the sinful and the low, make known to me thy mercy, O thou pure one, and set me free from the hands of demons, which come about me like dogs.'

It must be admitted that such prayers are but inferences, not unnatural, from the deliberate teaching of the latest, and henceforth the most influential in the East, of the Greek Fathers, John of Damascus, that Mary is the sovereign Lady to whom the whole creation is made subject by her Son—implying, of course, that, over and above her office in the Incarnation, she is herself, through His gift, a direct giver of help to such as may seek it at her hands. It should be added that the Feast of *her* (not of Christ's) Presentation in the Temple (the story is from *Protev. Jac.*) originated in the East in the 8th cent., and was not adopted in the West till the 15th. See art. IMMACULATE CONCEPTION.

The Western Church, too, was to find through many ages the practical value of monasticism, and to carry the doctrine of celibacy to further lengths than its Eastern sister. It, too, was to have experience of errors (such as the 8th cent. Adoptianism) which, disparaging the Saviour, disparaged her also. In Spain, Hungary, and the two Sicilies, as well as through the Crusades and Algerian piracy, it was to come into painful contact with Islām. In the West too, therefore, the reaction from those errors contributed its impetus to every movement in the Virgin's honour, while manifold oppressions of the poor turned them naturally to the thought of her as the Mother of Pity, and the chivalry of the knight made her the Lady of his orisons. But the development of her cult was slow in the West. In Adamnan and Bede it is hardly perceptible; in the *Life of St. Columba* she is not mentioned.

In Bede's *HE*, St. Wilfred has a vision of St. Michael telling him, 'the Lord has granted you life, through the prayers of your disciples, and the intercession of His Blessed Mother Mary of perpetual virginity' (v. 19), and the Hymn concerning St. Ethelreda sings how 'over the Virgin Mother a shining virgin band rejoices'; and how 'her honour has made many virgin blossoms to spring forth' (iv. 20).

At Rome in the pope's (8th cent.) mass on Easter-day at the Basilica of St. Mary Major, the only mentions of her are those (1) in the Great Intercession:

'Venerating the memory first of the glorious ever-Virgin Mary, Mother of the same our God and Lord Jesus Christ; and also of Thy blessed apostles and martyrs . . . and all Thy saints; by whose merits and prayers do Thou grant that in all things we may be defended by the help of Thy protection; through the same Christ, our Lord';

and (2) in the Post-Communion:

'Deliver us, O Lord . . .; and at the intercession for us of the blessed and glorious and ever-Virgin Mary, the Theotokos, and of Thy blessed apostles . . . and of all saints, graciously give peace in our days . . . through our Lord . . .' There is no direct invocation of her, nor prayer to her (*Ordo Rom. Primus*, App. 3);

nor, indeed, is there anything more in the Canon of the Roman Mass to the present day, though in the *Proprium Missarum de tempore* this 'collect of S. Mary' is said on all Sundays in Advent:

'God, who willedst that Thy Word should take Flesh from the womb of the Blessed Virgin Mary, grant that we who believe her to be in truth the Mother of God may by her intercessions be helped before Thee.'

But neither is this, nor the *Secreta de S. Maria*, nor the *Post-Communio de S. Maria* a prayer to her; the last was indeed adopted in the English Book of Common Prayer as the collect for the Annunciation. The confession of sins in the Mass made 'to Almighty God, to the Blessed Mary, ever-Virgin . . . and to all saints,' is held to be but a recognition of the fact taught us by St. Paul, that the whole body of the Church (from which death does not separate the saints [Ro 8[38]]) suffers with the suffering of every member (1 Co 12[26]); and, inasmuch as, in like manner, the honour of Christ the Head is the honour of all His members, it cannot be wrong, it is thought, to ask, as is done in the prayer 'Suscipe sancta Trinitas,' that our memorial of Christ's Passion, Resurrection, and Ascension may redound to the honour of Mary and all saints, as well as to the salvation of all for whom they pray. These are regarded as fair inferences from the truth which we all confess, in the Apostles' Creed, of the Communion of Saints. The moderation of the Roman Missal did not suffice, however, for the popular devotions, which more and more tended to assume the forms, first, of invoking her directly to intercede for us ('ora pro nobis'), and, next, of asking her personal help for both soul and body. Two festivals really of our Lord—His Presentation in the Temple (Feb. 2), and His Conception (March 25)—became rather those of her Purification and of the Annunciation to her, while the Feasts of her Conception (Dec. 8), her Nativity (Sept. 8), and her Assumption (Aug. 15), already observed in the Eastern Churches, were introduced into the West, at first in other lands rather than in Italy or at Rome, and not always either with the same meaning or without protest.

Thus, the observance of the Assumption was appointed by the synod of Salzburg in A.D. 800, but is marked as doubtful in the capitularies of Charlemagne; literally its title imports no more than her death—the taking of her soul to God—and it is sometimes called her *dormitio*, or 'sleep.' The doctrine of her bodily assumption into heaven, derived from the apocryphal story condemned by Pope Gelasius, though widely believed, and implied in the Breviary lection from John of Damascus, is not even now *de fide* in the Roman Catholic Church, but only a 'pious opinion.' The Feast of the Visitation of the Virgin (July 2), also apocryphal in origin, was introduced from the East in the 14th cent., withdrawn from the Calendar by Pius V. (1565–72), and reintroduced by Sixtus V. (1585–90). The Nativity of Mary (Sept. 8) would be older if the sermon of Augustine, cited in its Office, be genuine, but it is commonly said that this fact is first mentioned by Andrew of Crete (*c.* 750); its observance was appointed by the synod of Salzburg in 800; two centuries later it had not become general in Italy, while (*c.* 1140) St. Bernard blames the canons of Lyons for the innovation of keeping the feast of *her* conception because it was not holy like her Nativity, St. Mary being, he held, not conceived without sin, but sanctified in the womb. Thomas Aquinas said (*Summa Theol.* III. xxix.) that the Church of Rome tolerated it but did not keep it (a not uncommon way with some in those days of treating popular devotions); and, when it did come in at Rome, in the church of St. Mary Major, it was still, so late as 1340, the festival only of the 'Sanctification of the B. V. Mary.' Underlying these different names for this festival lay the long controversy as to the sinlessness of Mary. All agreed (as all orthodox Christians must agree) that she was sanctified so as to yield a perfectly sinless manhood to the Son of God (Lk 1^{35}, He 7^{26}); but there arose in the 13th cent. a question when the process of her sanctification began, and, while divines of the date and authority of Aquinas denied her Immaculate Conception, the arguments on which Scotus based his support of it were derived wholly from abstract and *a priori* considerations. The discussion, nevertheless, tended to her exaltation above all other saints, on the ground not alone of her office, but of the grace bestowed on her. It must be confessed that some mediæval writers transgressed all bounds in the language which they employed, Peter Damian, *e.g.*, speaking of her as 'deificata' (*Serm. de Nativ. Mar.* [*PL* cxliv. 740]), while the very natural use of what Archbishop John Hamilton's *Scots Catechism* of 1552 calls the 'bonny image of the Baby Jesus and His Blessed Mother' to remind us of His gracious coming as an infant to sanctify childhood and maternity was darkened into something not far from idolatry when—as sometimes happened—one image of the Virgin (generally a black or an ugly one) was regarded and resorted to as more powerful for the help of suppliants than another.

5. From the Reformation to the present day.—The fundamental position of the Protestant Reformers, that the justification and salvation of the sinner are through faith in Christ alone, involved, on the one hand, the fullest recognition alike of His Godhead and His manhood; and the Reformers, accordingly, were at one in confessing the Catholic faith as set forth in the ancient creeds and by the great councils, which meant, of course, their acceptance of His birth of a pure virgin, and her honour as His mother. It involved, on the other hand, an insistence that the soul should come to Christ direct, and a repudiation of the idea of any creature coming between it and Him. The latter principle, it is true, could be pushed to the extreme of disparaging the helps which He has graciously provided in His Body the Church (Eph 1^{23}), for bringing men to Himself, and in the ordinances whereby 'Christ and the benefits of the covenant of grace are . . . applied to believers' (*Shorter Catechism*, 92). It brought almost everywhere the practical elimination from Protestant teaching of all thought of the departed saints having any function whatever (save that of remembered examples) towards Christians in this world. The 'Communion of Saints,' while admitted in words, was interpreted as existing simply between believers in this present world; and, contrariwise, the prayers of the living were limited to the 'Church militant here on earth.' The prominence of St. Mary in Roman Catholic devotions reacted among the Reformed in an opposite direction, till Puritanism (in certain sections) 'scrupled' even the singing of her inspired *Magnificat*, gave up the public use of the Apostles' Creed because her name occurred in it, and even so late as the publication of the *Church Hymnary* (1898) was able to secure the rejection of Bishop Richard Mant's version of the *Stabat Mater* and the deletion of the words 'Son of Mary' from H. H. Milman's hymn. It may be doubted whether such courses have helped either to a livelier faith in Jesus Christ or to a deeper love towards Him; or how far they have furthered Christian ideals of purity, chivalry, and saintliness. Puritanism, however, has not conquered either the Scottish or the Anglican Church. The former in the 18th cent. dared to speak of the Virgin in the public service in one of its 'Paraphrases' (Par. 38), and restored the use of the *Magnificat* (in metre) in another (Par. 36), and of late years 'authorized' the chanting of it in prose, as well as the recital of the Apostles' and Nicene Creeds (*Church Hymnary*, *Church of Scotland Anthem Book*, and *Mission Hymnal*). These have always kept their place in the Anglican Books of Common Prayer; and the Church of England has further secured a commemoration of St. Mary by retaining among 'the Feasts to be observed' both 'The Purification of the Blessed Virgin' (Feb. 2) and 'The Annunciation of the Blessed Virgin' (March 25). In both countries divines universally respected (*e.g.*, the Scottish Dr. W. Hanna and the English Bishops Joseph Hall and John Pearson) have spoken of her in terms of singular reverence and beauty, while W. M. Ramsay, holding, as he does, some pagan ancestry for her cultus as it exists in Asia Minor, speaks of it nevertheless as 'a purifying and elevating principle' (*Pauline and other Studies*, p. 159).

In the Roman Catholic Church there was some hope at the beginning of the Counter-Reformation that much then complained of in the extremer cult of St. Mary would be abated or put down. Something certainly was done; and the Council of Trent in its Decrees, and even in its Catechism, is fairly moderate, distinguishing, as did the older councils, between the λατρεία, due only to God, and the δουλεία or the ὑπερδουλεία, due in different degrees to His saints and servants, and insisting that the 'worship' to be paid to the Deipara must never exceed *hyperdulia*. But it is difficult to see where, in the practical system which since then has been not only permitted, but more and more encouraged, by the popes the line of difference is drawn; *e.g.*,

'Hail, O queen, Mother of Mercy! Hail, our life, our sweetness, our hope! To thee we fly, the banished sons of Eve' (Antiphon to the *Magnificat* in the Roman Breviary, reformed by order of the Council of Trent, published by order of Pope Pius V., and revised by Clement VIII. and Urban VIII.).

The Breviary, with 'the Offices since granted,' may almost be said to be now—in strange contrast to the NT—nearly as full of Mary as of Christ. On all Saturdays, and throughout the whole month of May, votive offices of the Blessed Virgin are said. The Sunday within the octave of the Nativity is 'the Feast of the Most Holy Name of Mary,' the third Sunday of Sept. that of her 'Seven Sorrows'; four Sundays in October are devoted respectively to her 'Rosary,' her 'Motherhood,' her 'Purity,' her 'Patronage,' while the old feast of her Conception (Dec. 8)—originally her 'Sanctification'—is now that of her 'Immaculate Conception,' and the bull of Pius IX. declaring this an article of faith to be received by all Christians supplies a large proportion of the lessons appointed to be read within its octave. The Breviary itself, moreover, is restrained in comparison with such books as *Le Glorie di Maria* by Alfonso de Liguori (1696–1787), the founder of the Redemptorist Order. Liguori goes far beyond the Council of Trent, for, whereas the latter says only that 'it is useful' to invoke her intercessions, he insists upon the *necessity* of doing so:

'Mary is our life, because she obtains for us the gifts of pardon . . . and of perseverance'; 'Mary is the hope of all'; 'Mary is the peace-maker of sinners with God' (ii. 1 f., iii. 1, vi. 3).

LITERATURE.—*Apostolic Fathers*, ed. J. B. Lightfoot, London, 1877–85; *Ante-Nicene Christian Library*, Edinburgh, 1867 ff.; *Select Library of Nicene and Post-Nicene Fathers*, Oxford and New York, 1886–1900; W. M. Ramsay, *Pauline and other Studies*, London, 1906; J. M. Neale and R. F. Littledale, *The Liturgies of SS. Mark, James, Clement, Chrysostom, and Basil, and the Church of Malabar*[2], do. 1869; F. E. Brightman, *Liturgies Eastern and Western*, Oxford, 1896; *The Statutes of the Apostles*, ed. G. Horner, London, 1904; *The Apostolic Constitutions in Coptic*, ed. H. Tattam, do. 1848; *The Testament of our Lord*, ed. J. Cooper and A. J. Maclean, Edinburgh, 1902; *Consecration of a Church and Altar* (Coptic), ed. G. Horner, London, 1902; *Ordo Romanus Primus*, ed. E. G. C. F. Atchley, do. 1905; *The Roman Breviary* and *Missal*; Alfonso de Liguori, *Le Glorie di Maria*, Naples, 1750; *The* [*Russian*] *Book of Needs* and *Euchology* (Russian); E. B. Pusey, *Eirenicon*, Oxford, 1865–69.

JAMES COOPER.

MĀSAI.—**I. History.**—It is advisable, first of all, to specify what we mean by the term Māsai. It is the tolerably correct designation of a widely scattered but not numerous Nilotic Negro people in E. Equatorial Africa, whose habitat, down to the beginning of the 19th cent., stretched from the Nandi plateau, the south end of Lake Baringo, and the southern slopes of Mount Kenya on the north almost to the 6th degree of S. lat. in the south. On the east they were bounded by the Bantu and Galla peoples of the region between the Tana and the Rufu rivers; on the west by the Nandi and Bantu peoples of the Sotik and Lumbwa highlands, which form the eastern limits of the Victoria Nyanza basin. The older name which this distinct race of pastoral nomads adopted for themselves—or at any rate for the pastoral and warlike section of the original tribe—was (according to A. C. Hollis) Il-maa, which in the 19th cent., if not before, became Il-māsai (spelt Maasae by some). The western and northern sections of the Māsai people, especially those sometimes known as Il-oigob, Enjámusi, or Was'ñgishu, were not only cattle-keepers and shepherds, but also industrious agriculturists. Still, the main bent of this handsome Negro race (which in bodily characteristics verges on the Hamitic negroid) was pastoral; and cattle, sheep, goats, and the domesticated ass of Ethiopia played a great part in their lives and mental considerations. All sections of the Māsai, agricultural as well as pastoral, speak a language which differs but little in its two or three dialects. The relationships of this speech lie most nearly and clearly with the Lotuka language of the Mountain Nile, with the Bari of the southern Egyptian Sūdan, with the Elgumi or Tesw, north-west of Mount Elgon, and with the Turkana of Lake Rudolf; perhaps also with other languages of the Rudolf basin. In a more remote degree Māsai is related to the other members of the great Nilotic speech-group—the Nandi languages of British E. Africa, and those of the Dinka, Shilluk, etc., of the Egyptian Sūdan. The customs and, to some extent, the beliefs of the Māsai similarly connect them with the tall Negroes of the Upper Nile basin. Clearly, the progenitors of the Māsai emigrated originally from those regions which now constitute the northern provinces of the Uganda Protectorate; but at what period there is little evidence to show, except that it was far enough back in the history of E. Equatorial Africa for the migration to have passed out of tribal recollection.[1] In all their myths and stories the Māsai think of themselves as a people indigenous to E. Africa, most of all to the regions round about Mount Kenya. This snow-crowned lofty volcano of more than 17,000 feet in altitude plays a considerable part in their traditions, and is supposed by them to be the habitation of a demigod or goddess Naiterukop,[2] who was at the same time an 'Eve' or 'Adam,' the parent, at any rate, of the higher types of humanity. The Māsai speech, like some other Nilotic languages, especially those of the south-eastern portion of the regions inhabited by Nilotic Negroes, bears evident traces of an ancient Hamitic impress, though it must be emphatically stated that neither it nor any other member of the Nilotic family can be described as Hamitic, or as other than a 'Negro' speech. But many centuries ago, perhaps as far back as the last periods of dynastic Egypt, the Kushitic section of the wide-spread Hamitic race (Caucasians tinged with Negro and perhaps Dravidian blood) profoundly impressed itself on the racial type, the speech, the culture, beliefs, and customs of the Nile Negroes. Similar action on the part of these Hamites appears to have led to the final shaping of the Bantu languages and the impulse of the Bantu conquest of the southern third of Africa. It is curious that, however 'Hamitic' the Māsai, Nandi, and other south-eastern Nilotes may be in physical and mental characteristics, their cattle, on which such a large proportion of their thoughts and beliefs is centred, are of the E. African, humped, originally Indian 'zebu' type. They do not belong to the long-horned, usually straight-backed, Galla breed, a bovine variety which seems to have originated from a wild species in W. Asia in remote Neolithic times, and to have been the earliest form of domestic cattle in ancient Egypt. These Galla oxen are nowadays found in the greater part of Abyssinia, in Darfur, Wadai, and Bornu.[3] The mysterious Ba-hima—the Galla-

[1] In the traditions of the Māsai their home-land—Kopekob or Kōpekob—lay to the north of their present habitat. They called the south 'the land of strife,' showing that their southward advance was attended by constant struggles with the preceding tribes not of Māsai race.

[2] Na-iteru-kop is a word beginning with the feminine prefix *na*, a prefix originally conveying the sense of 'mother,' but often diverging into an equivalent for 'source of,' 'place of,' 'productive of.'

[3] There are, however, traditions among the south-western Māsai that they once possessed or knew of this long-horned breed.

like aristocracy of E. Equatorial Africa — implanted this long-horned type of ancient Egyptian ox on the highlands between the Victoria Nyanza, Tanganyika, and the frontier of the Congo forest. But the long-horned Galla ox has never yet made its appearance to the east of the Victoria Nyanza or among the Māsai tribes, whose cattle are Indian in type.

2. Gods.—Though in physical characteristics the Negro element predominates in the Māsai over any other, this people is superior in mentality to the pure-blood Negro; and one is struck with a certain imaginativeness and a natural poetry in their thoughts, stories, and religious beliefs rarely found among Negro peoples, and probably due to some ancient or modern infusion of the Caucasian. The Māsai believe in a far-reaching divine power emanating from the sky high above the earth, and even above the lower regions of the atmosphere. This divinity, to which they can pray at times with real earnestness, is known usually by a female name, Eñ-ai (*Eñ-* is the feminine article, *ai*, or *gai*,[1] is the root). Eñ-ai is occasionally referred to as 'the Black God,' though in some stories or in some minds there seems to be a triad consisting of (1) Eñ-ai, the greatest and remotest of all gods, the god of the elements; (2) the benign Black God of rain, who takes a real, though far-off, interest in humanity; and (3) the surly or malign Red God, who is, on the whole, spitefully disposed towards mankind and dwells in the lower part of the atmosphere. Eñ-ai and the Black God (or both fused in one personality) would like to send the rain to the parched lands below in perpetual abundance, so that there might always be fat pastures to feed the Māsai cattle, or perpetual cultivation for the Māsai agriculturists; but the Red God frequently intervenes and intercepts the moisture so necessary to life under an equatorial sun. Distant thunder is believed to be the remonstrance of Eñ-ai at this churlishness of his subordinate deity, whom, however, he seldom bestirs himself to circumvent. Eñ-ai is known to some of the non-Māsai tribes as 'Kai' or 'Gai' without the article, and by the Māsai themselves is called by other names, such as Paasai.[2]

3. Demons.—In addition to these two gods or three gods (according as the Black and Good God is or is not identified with the Ruler of the Heavens, Eñ-ai), the Māsai believe in superhuman beings somewhat resembling the *jann* ('genii') of the Arabs—devils, it is convenient to call them. Similar beliefs reappear in the Sūdan and in many parts of the northern range of the Bantu languages, such as the Cameroons. These *jann*, or devils, trench in some of their characteristics on the werwolf conception, being in some aspects like a lion and in others like a man, or having originally taken the form of lions and then put on an appearance half human and half like an inanimate stone; or they are believed to go about looking like a lion on one side, and on the other like a monstrous human being. Their favourite home is the forest. They are mainly, if not entirely, anthropophagous in their food preferences, and do not touch wild beasts.

In one of the Māsai stories recorded by Hollis[3] it is narrated that the devil's custom is to call to human beings who pass the place of his concealment in the forest, 'Come, my brother, help me lift this load of firewood.' If they are foolish enough to proceed to his help, they are struck with a pointed stake which he carries. When any particular district was believed to be haunted by a devil and the Māsai wished to pass through it in their customary migrations in search of pasture for their cattle, they would arrange to march past the cannibals' haunt in as large a body as possible, the warriors going both in front and behind. 'Should a voice be heard issuing from the mist and calling some one, everybody remains silent, for they know that it is this devil that is calling.' In another story[1] the anthropophagous *jann* ate up all the human beings in one district except a woman, who succeeded in hiding herself with her child in a pit. As the boy grew up, he made a bow and arrows, which (presumably) he poisoned; and, when the demon, discovering their existence from the smoke of their fires, came to eat them, the boy from the branches of a tall tree shot all his arrows into the monster's body, who at first thought that it was merely the stings of gad-flies, until he succumbed to their effects. Repenting apparently in his dying moments, he gave the boy information as to how he might proceed to recover the cattle of the tribe, and most, if not all, of the people whom he had eaten. Out of gratitude these resuscitated Māsai elected the boy as their chief.

It is quite possible that this and similar stories, wide-spread over Negro Africa, refer to the lurking cannibals of some big and brutish race which lingered on in the forests of Africa long after the more open country had been populated by the modern types of man. Such grim ogres may have worn over their backs the pelts of wild beasts that they had killed, and thus have seemed on one side beast, and on the other a ghoul-like type of man.

4. Cosmology.—The Māsai believe that, when Naiterukop,[2] the demi-god of Mount Kenya, decided to start a race of true men on the earth—presumably Māsai—he found three things in E. Africa, viz. an already existing Dorobo[3] (the word is properly spelt Torobo and means 'dwarfish'), who was a kind of pre-Adamite man, an elephant, and a serpent, all of whom lived together. In course of time the Dorobo hunter killed both the serpent and the elephant mother, who, however, before her death had given birth to a calf, which escaped from the Dorobo, and in its journeying about the world met a Māsai, to whom it confided its troubles. At this juncture God Himself (Eñ-ai) intervened, and summoned both the Dorobo and the Māsai to His presence. The Māsai came, but the Dorobo seems to have delayed. The consequence was that the Māsai received God's good gifts and henceforth became rich in cattle and the master of E. Africa. Other variants of this story make Naiterukop (the divine man of Mount Kenya) the *deus ex machina* throughout, and do not invoke the intervention of the great sky-god, Eñ-ai.

5. Eschatology.—With regard to a life after death, in some of the Māsai traditions it is related that, when the man-god Naiterukop gave to their primal ancestor, Le-eyo, instructions what to say when a child died, the latter out of selfishness—because the child next to die was not his own—inverted the prayer which was to adjure the child-spirit to return. Le-eyo consequently prayed that the moon, though it died, might return again, but that the dead child might remain dead. Some time afterwards Le-eyo was likely to lose a child of his own, and therefore said the prayer rightly. But it was too late; only the first invocation of nature held good, and thus man, when he dies, never comes back, but the moon always returns.

Yet this great agony of the mind of man—this refusal to regard death as the end of all in the personalities of those whom we have loved or respected—prevails with the Māsai, athwart the repeated assertions in their folklore that 'All is over with man as with the cattle, and the soul does not come to life again.' With this people there has been a gradually growing belief (it is so also among many Bantu tribes) that a medicine-man, a great doctor, a great chief, or a very wealthy

[1] From the circumstance that this root assumes the form of *-gai* or *-kai* when borrowed by adjoining Bantu or Dorobo tribes it is possible that it was originally Eñ-gai in Māsai.

[2] A. C. Hollis, *The Masai*, Oxford, 1905, p. 346.

[3] *Ib.* p. 265 f.

[1] Hollis, p. 221 ff.

[2] J. L. Krapf, the great missionary pioneer of Equatorial E. Africa, writing in 1854 in his preface to the *Vocabulary of the Engútuk Eloikob* (the Western Māsai), thus describes the religious beliefs of the Māsai: 'At the remotest antiquity there was one man residing on "Oldoinyo eibor" (Mt. Kenya) who was superior to any human being, and whom Eñgai (heaven, supreme being, god) had placed on the mountain. This strange personage whose beginning and end is quite mysterious and whose whole appearance impresses the Wakuafi mind with the idea of a demi-god is called . . . Neiterukob. The intelligence of this strange person residing on Oldoinyo eibor reached a man named Enjemasi Enauner, who with his wife Sambu lived on Mount Sambu which is situated to the south-west of Oldoinyo eibor and is a high mountain but does not attain to the height of Oldoinyo eibor. . . . Enjemasi went to the White mountain with his wife who by the intercession of Neiterukob became fruitful and gave birth to a number of children. Neiterukob also taught Enjemasi Enauner the taming of wild cows which he saw in the forest. . . . It is to Oldoinyo eibor ("Kenia," as the Wakamba call it) that the Wakuafi resort in order to obtain the intercession of Neiterukob for getting rain, cattle, and health from the Eñgai.'

[3] The Dorobo are the nomad hunters of E. Africa, shorter in stature than the Māsai, but not very dissimilar from them in appearance, and containing many mixed strains of blood—Hamite, Negro, and possibly Bushman.

person cannot entirely cease to exist in personality even after the body is dead, buried, and decayed. It is thought by the Māsai, as by Zulus and numerous tribes of W. African Bantu, that the soul of a deceased person of importance enters one or other of the python-like snakes which frequent the vicinity of human habitations in pursuit of rats and other vermin. These (usually black) snakes are, therefore, sacred in the eyes of the Māsai, who are careful not to kill them. If a woman sees one in her hut, she pours milk on the ground for it to lick up. A variety of species of snake are even regarded as totem animals by one of the Māsai clans, who protect them against ill-treatment by the members of any other clan, and will even call on them for help if they get worsted in a fight, exclaiming, 'Avengers of my mother's house, come out!' The Māsai believed that the female snakes thus invoked would bite such as had not adopted them as a totem.

It has even been thought by some Māsai, probably not earlier than the latter years of the 19th cent., that the souls of very great chiefs are not sufficiently provided for by transmigration to a snake, but in some way go to heaven, to the abode of Eñ-ai. It is not impossible that this growing belief may have resulted from their talks with the early missionaries in E. Africa. They certainly believe that there *is* what we should define as a soul, some impalpable living essence, and that this quits a man's body when he falls asleep. Therefore a sleeper must not be too suddenly awakened lest the soul be left outside the body and the man die. In one mood the Māsai will assert that no such things as 'ghosts' exist, because they cannot be seen; in another they appear to believe that ghosts do exist and can be seen by cattle, though not by men. When a herd of cattle halts and stares fixedly at something, if it is not a lion or a leopard, it is a ghost.

6. Divination.—They also believe in omens, and, like all the Negro peoples of E. Africa, pay great attention to the cries and the actions of birds which are propitious or unpropitious. Their medicine-men practise divination of future events (1) by shaking a handful of stones out of a horn, (2) by examining the entrails of a slaughtered goat, (3) by getting drunk on mead, and then prophesying at random, and (4) by the interpretation of dreams.

7. Prayers.—The Māsai have a very real belief in God, and, if they are vague about His personality and uncertain whether they are praying to the Great God of the Firmament or to the Black God of the Upper Clouds, to one or other they occasionally make sacrifices of sheep—a rite usually conducted by the women, who, as a matter of course, pray twice a day, while men and children only occasionally utter prayers. In these prayers men and women associate the evening and morning stars, and even the snow peaks of the great mountains, Kenya and Kilimanjaro, with the Deity. They pray for children and for the health of their children, for rain, for successes in time of war, and plenty of cattle. The present writer, however, when residing many years ago at Taveita near the eastern base of Kilimanjaro, noted that the men of the Wa-Taveita (mainly Māsai in race and religion, though now speaking a Bantu language) could pray most earnestly and touchingly to Eñ-ai, the Power of the Sky, if their children were sick.

When one of their number gives birth to a child, the Māsai women gather together and take milk to the mother; they then slaughter a sheep, which is called a 'purifier of a hut,' or simply a 'purifier.' The women slaughter the animal by themselves and eat all the meat, and no man may approach the spot where the animal is slaughtered, for it is considered unlawful. When they finish their meal, they stand up and sing a song, which may be rendered approximately thus (paraphrased from Hollis):

> 'God to whom I pray,
> God who thunders and it rains,
> Give me offspring.
> To thee only every day do I pray,
> Thou morning star;
> To thee only every day do I pray,
> Thou who art of sweet savour like sage plants.
> To thee only every day do I pray,
> Who art prayed to and who hearest;
> To thee only every day do I pray.'

Women and children also pray for rain. The old men's prayer in time of drought (chanted round a bonfire of sweet-smelling wood into which is thrown a charm from the medicine-man) is:

> 'Black god, Ho!
> God water us;
> O thou of the uttermost parts of the earth,
> Black god, Ho!
> God water us.'

Young men pray that their battle raids may be successful and that they may bring back herds of cattle. All these prayers seem to be indifferently addressed both to God and to the morning and the evening star. God is not confused with the sun or the moon, but is something behind, above, beyond, and more powerful than these heavenly bodies, which are beings of either sex that alternately marry and quarrel. Of the stars other than the planets Venus and Jupiter they take little heed, with the exception of the Pleiades (the appearance of which in the heavens is indicative of seasonal changes), the Sword of Orion, and Orion's Belt. Comets are perturbing as indicative of approaching disasters.

8. Source of Māsai religion.—M. Merker, a German officer, who lived much among the Māsai of German E. Africa, published a work (first issued in 1904) in which, after discussing various Māsai beliefs and customs, he attributes these and, in part, the origin of the Māsai, to a strong wave of Semitic influence from the north, even reviving that old story, the dispersal of the Ten Tribes. It is difficult to understand how he can see anything in Māsai belief and ritual that especially suggests Jewish blood or influence and at the same time overlook the presence of similar beliefs and rites in the intervening Hamites or the Semiticized Somālis. For unnumbered centuries waves of Caucasian influence and even trickles of Caucasian blood have been passing from Western and Southern Arabia, Syria, and Egypt through Ethiopia into Nileland, the Central and Western Sūdan, and the steppes and forests and lake regions of E. Africa. The Māsai have brought their share of these beliefs, superstitions, and customs from their northernmost centre of development—somewhere, possibly, in the basin of Lake Rudolf, a region that, no doubt, was influenced from Abyssinia a score of centuries ago, as it is at the present day. At the same time, attention should be given to Merker's records of Māsai traditions and beliefs, especially as set forth in the later edition of his work (*Die Masai*, Berlin, 1910). A. C. Hollis, whose own work on the Māsai is one of importance, and Albert Steggall, a missionary long resident in the eastern part of Māsailand, both argue that Merker got his information regarding Māsai beliefs chiefly from Māsai who had long been connected with the Roman Catholic mission, and, consequently, that these informants were merely giving him versions of the Hebrew traditions in the OT. The receptivity of the Māsai mind is no doubt great; but no mission had been established in those regions a sufficient length of time for much teaching to have been imparted to Māsai boys, nor, from what the present writer knows of mission work in those regions, is it likely that either Roman Catholic or Protestant missions at that stage in their development spent much time in translating and teaching the book of Genesis to Māsai inquirers. It is more probable that the ancestors of the Māsai in their northern home were in contact with the Christian Gallas or Abyssinians, and from them imbibed those ideas of Adam and Eve and the other traditions regarding the great Patriarchs which irresistibly recall the legends enshrined in the first chapter of Genesis; or the ideas may even have percolated through N.E. Africa in pre-Christian days, when the Jews and Idumæans were influencing a good deal of W. Arabia and of Ethiopia.

The stories transcribed by Merker are not only reminiscent of the Jewish myths of Adam and Eve, Cain and Abel, Enoch, Methuselah, Lamech, and Abraham, but even extend to a personality like Moses, actually bearing the name of Musanna (or Marumi). There are even traces of a belief in a fiery serpent, of the Ten Commandments of Sinai, and of a paradise garden like Eden.

A good deal of this account of the Māsai religion must be taken in the past tense. Year by year old beliefs and traditions are fading away, and the people are becoming either absolute materialists (with the white man as their wonder-working divinity) or adherents of the various Christian missions, to which they are proving useful and influential converts.

LITERATURE.—In addition to the works of Hollis and Merker quoted throughout, see J. L. Krapf, *Vocabulary of the Engútuk Eloikob, or Language of the Wakuafi Nation*, Tübingen, 1854 (Preface is noteworthy); J. Erhardt, *Vocabulary of the Enguduk Iloigob, as spoken by the Masai Tribes in E. Africa*, Basel, 1857; J. Thomson, *Through Masăi Land*, London, 1885; H. H. Johnston, *The Kilima-njaro Expedition*, do. 1885, *The Uganda Protectorate*², do. 1904; S. L. and H. Hinde, *The Last of the Masai*, do. 1901.

H. H. JOHNSTON.

MASBOTHÆANS.—According to Eus. *HE* IV. xxii. 5 f., Hegesippus had written of the Hemerobaptists and the Masbothæans (Μασβωθαῖοι)[1] as two distinct sects 'in the circumcision among the children of Israel.' The brief characterizations of the Masbothæan sect given by the ancient heresiologists are based simply upon their etymologies of the name, which they connect either with the word 'sabbath' or with צבות, 'will,' 'purpose.' Among modern scholars A. Hilgenfeld has advanced the conjecture that the Masbothæans were the followers of the early heretic Thebuthis, also mentioned by Hegesippus, but in all likelihood the name simply means 'baptists.' In glossaries of Palestinian Aramaic the only word given for 'baptism' is *maṣbū̆'ithā*, and, as we know that among the Mandæans on the Euphrates the regular term for ceremonial immersion in running water was מצבותא (see art. MANDÆANS, p. 387ᵇ), we can hardly doubt that Μασβωθαῖοι signifies people in whose religious practice such immersions formed an outstanding element. Thus the Gr. term 'Hemerobaptists' might quite well have been applied to the same group, and the idea that the two names denoted different sects may simply have been a mistake on the part of Hegesippus. It is, no doubt, the case that in the time of Hegesippus there were among the Jews various parties which advocated the practice of immersion, each, however, after its own particular form: there were, *e.g.*, the devout, who bathed every morning and evening, and the 'bathers of the early morning,' who thought it necessary to perform an immersion before morning prayer. The term 'Hemerobaptists' would, of course, be quite appropriate for both groups.

The designation 'Masbothæans,' however, would also suit the Elkesaites, and, in fact, pointedly suggests that sect, as the Elkesaite tradition contains the name Σοβιαί, formed from the same verbal root as מצבותא (cf. art. ELKESAITES, vol. v. p. 265ᵃ). By the time of Hegesippus the Elkesaites had become so numerous in Palestine—though only, it is true, in the territory east of the Jordan—that he can hardly have remained ignorant of their existence. On these grounds, accordingly, it would seem very probable that those who had become known to him as the sect of the Masbothæans were none other than the Elkesaites.

LITERATURE.—A. Hilgenfeld, *Die Ketzergeschichte des Urchristentums*, Leipzig, 1884; W. Brandt, *Die mandäische Religion*, do. 1889, p. 180, *Elchasai*, do. 1912, p. 42 ff. On the Jewish Hemerobaptists and 'bathers of the early morning': Brandt, *Die jüdischen Baptismen*, Giessen, 1910, pp. 48–51, 92 ff.

W. BRANDT.

[1] In *Apost. Const.* vi. 6 Μασβωθέοι (ε=αι); the form *Mazbuthazi* (emend. *Mazbuthæi*) appears as a Lat. transcription of the name from the Armen. tr. of a Syr. text in one of the two MSS ed. G. Moesinger, *Evangelii concordantis expositio facta a sancto Ephræmo*, Venice, 1876, p. 288.

MASK.—A mask may be defined as a moulded surface, representing the anterior half of a head and face, and usually worn over the face of a person. Further significations are the cast taken from the face of a dead person and the parallel form in sculpture—the front half of a human head and face preserved—and the head of a fox. A division is made by W. H. Dall into 'mask' proper, 'maskette,' resembling mask but worn not upon but above or below the face, and 'maskoid,' resembling mask, but not intended to be worn.[1] This division is primarily anthropological.

The use of masks in one form or other and for various purposes has been practically universal in all stages of culture above that which the natives of Australia may be assumed to represent. The greater proportion of the Polynesian peoples are an exception. It will be most convenient to arrange the subject according to the purposes for which the mask is employed, incidentally noting details of form and manufacture and variations of general type. It may be noted at once that both in form and in use there is the usual similarity between the most widely separated races. The mask is in most cases ethnologically independent in origin.

1. Views as to the original meaning of masks.—The usual purpose of a mask is disguise by a more or less defined impersonation, impersonation alone, or, more rarely, protection, physical or moral. The figures impersonated may be real persons, imaginary persons, especially spiritual and divine, or various animals and natural objects. Robertson Smith regarded the use of animal masks in religious ceremonial as a survival of an earlier practice according to which the worshipper put on the skin of a victim, in order to 'envelop himself in its sanctity.'[2] In the form of a 'maskette' many peoples have used the heads of animals, even as a war head-dress. The ritual mask is frequently credited with the power of imparting to the wearer the qualities of what it represents. The Eskimo believe that the wearer is 'mysteriously and unconsciously imbued with the spirit' represented by the mask, and, when wearing the mask of a totem, he becomes that totem.[3] In the drama of the Pueblo Indians the actor is 'supposed to be transformed into the deity represented.'[4] The wearer of a mask in the dances of 'primitive' peoples is 'assimilated to the real nature of the being represented'—possessed by him.[5] But neither this belief nor the desire to be enveloped with sanctity can be regarded as the original factor in the invention of the mask. Dall considers the original mask

[1] W. H. Dall, 'On Masks, Labrets,' etc., in *3 RBEW* [1884], p. 93.
[2] W. R. Smith, *Rel. Sem.*², London, 1894, p. 437 f.
[3] E. W. Nelson, in *18 RBEW* [1899], pt. i. p. 394 f.
[4] J. G. Frazer, *Totemism and Exogamy*, London, 1910, iii. 227 f. *Kachina* means both 'deity' and 'masker.'
[5] H. Webster, *Primitive Secret Societies*, New York, 1908, p. 76 n.

to have been a shield held in the hand to protect the face from missiles, and later worn on the face, after which it was carved into a terrifying aspect, with the object of frightening the foe. On another line of development it became the helmet; but this view also fails to give any original psychological element. The Australians do not have the mask, but in their ceremonies they disguise the face by painting, or with down and blood. Previous to the invention of the Attic dramatic mask, the Dionysian mummers painted their faces with wine, possibly with the idea of assimilation to the deity, as in the case of the ancient Roman kings and generals, whose faces were painted with vermilion on state occasions to resemble Jupiter. But this idea is clearly secondary. Again, it cannot be argued that the mask is a development from the custom of painting the face. The two are parallel reactions to the irreducible dramatic instinct in its elemental phase of the assumption of another personality. The elaborate facial make-up of modern dramatic art is, when contrasted with the Attic masks, a fair analogy to the blackened face of the modern peasant mummer, as contrasted with the wooden masks of the N. American dancer. We may conclude that the ideas of assimilation, whether magical or religious, of terrorism, of protection, and even of disguise are secondary, and that the primary meaning of the mask is dramatic; the mask is a concrete result of the imitative instinct.

The various purposes, therefore, to which the mask is applied have no necessary development from one another, but are natural applications to particular purposes of the original mimetic instinct.

2. War masks.—These are not of frequent use. In Central and E. Africa warriors used hideous 'masks' of zebra-hide. The natives of Yucatan wore masks representing lions, tigers, and so forth, to terrify the enemy. In mediæval Europe and Japan soldiers wore helms fronted with frightful masks.[1] The frontal skull on the helmet of the German 'Death's Head Hussars' is of similar origin.

3. The mask of terror.—For other purposes than those of battle, the terrorist idea has been applied. The Chinese placed horrible paper masks on the faces of their children in order to frighten away the demon of smallpox.[2] In Africa there has been the office of 'sham devil.' In China, in order to neutralize the activity of an evil spirit, a man was masked to represent it, and placed in its sphere of operations to discourage its advance.[3] The Greek myth of the Gorgon's head was inspired by similar ideas, with which a primitive custom may be compared: in Timor-laut, in order to deceive evil spirits and prevent them from injuring the remains of a dead man, a coco-nut mask was placed near the body.[4] The further idea is here involved of protection by means of a mask which, so to say, draws the enemy's fire.

A similar use of the mask is seen in the expulsion of evils. The people of China and Celebes, when 'driving out devils,' blacken their faces or wear masks. Possibly the masked Perchten of Central Europe had originally a similar function. There may have been a mimic struggle between the Beautiful and the Ugly masks, symbolizing a struggle for the crops; masked mummers at Kayan sowing festivals represent evil spirits.[5]

4. The mask of justice.—Officers of justice or terrorism assume the personality of a supernatural inquisitor, the Vehme of mediæval Europe being a historical case. Executioners wore a mask, and possibly the black cap of the judge is an adaptation.

[1] R. Andree, *Ethnographische Parallelen und Vergleiche*, new ser., Leipzig, 1889, p. 118 ff.; Dall, p. 75.
[2] J. Doolittle, *Social Life of the Chinese*, London, 1866, ii. 316.
[3] Andree, p. 110. [4] *Ib.* p. 133.
[5] *Ib.* p. 135; J. J. M. de Groot, *Religious System of China*, Leyden, 1892 ff., vi. 977; *GB*[3], pt. v., *Spirits of the Corn and of the Wild*, London, 1912, i. 95, pt. vi., *The Scapegoat*, do. 1913, pp. 240 ff., 249.

5. The mask in secret societies.—These institutions are practically universal in the middle culture.[1] In some cases they include among their functions the administration of some form of justice. This, like all their proceedings, is carried out with mummery, and the mask is employed along with other disguise or impersonation.

The Sindungo society of Loango collects debts; the collectors wear masks.[2] The Kuhkwi, Egbo, and Egungun are other instances of these W. African societies; their masks are based on various ideas connected with the tutelary spirits of the society.[3] The Ogboni society of the Yoruba-speaking peoples is closely connected with the priesthood, and the king is obliged to submit to its decrees. The mask of Egungun represents a hideous human face; he is supposed to be a man risen from the dead, in order to spy out what is going on in the land of the living and carry off those who misbehave.[4] The Tamate of the Banks' Islands is a secret society whose name means 'ghosts.' The members possess much power, and periodically hold meetings and processions, wearing their masks.[5]

The famous Duk-duk societies[6] of New Britain, New Ireland, and the Duke of York Islands comprise practically the whole of the adult male population. In one aspect of its functions the Duk-duk is a personification of justice—judge, policeman, and executioner in one. The remarkable head-dresses worn by the operators are technically mask-like structures, representing some spiritual force in the semblance of a cassowary. The operators are two, Duk-duk representing the male and Tubuan the female cassowary. The mask worn by each is a 'huge hat-like extinguisher' of grass or palm-fibre, 6 ft. high. As far as the body-dress is concerned, it may be said to represent the cassowary, but the head is 'like nothing but the head of a Duk-duk.' A long stick is at the apex, and the 'tresses' are coloured red. The female is said to be plain, the male more gaudy. The extraordinary belief is held that the Tubuan mask gives birth to the novices when initiated into the society; and two female masks are kept from year to year for the purpose of annually breeding two Duk-duks. The persons acting seem to be lost or merged in the mask. No one is supposed to know who the actors are. The male masks appear to be burned after the ceremony.

The committees of adults who supervise the 'making of young men' are frequently dressed in disguise and wear masks. In Torres Straits on these occasions a man represents the deity Agud; he is painted all over and wears a leaf petticoat and a turtle-shell mask. Several masked *magur* (devils) frighten the novices, who are well beaten, and are told the dreadful names of the masks.[7] A 'wolf' society among the Nutkas holds initiation meetings; men wearing wolf-masks carry off the novices.[8]

[1] See Webster, *op. cit.*
[2] A. Bastian, *Die deutsche Expedition an der Loango-Küste*, Jena, 1874, i. 122.
[3] Andree, p. 135 f.
[4] A. B. Ellis, *The Yoruba-speaking Peoples of the Slave Coast of West Africa*, London, 1894, pp. 93, 107.
[5] R. H. Codrington, in *JAI* x. [1881] 287 ff.
[6] R. Parkinson, *Im Bismarck-Archipel*, Leipzig, 1887, pp. 129–134; W. Powell, *Wanderings in a Wild Country*, London, 1883, pp. 60–66; G. Brown, *Melanesians and Polynesians*, do. 1910, p. 60 ff.; Andree, p. 140; H. H. Romilly, *The Western Pacific and New Guinea*[2], London, 1887, pp. 28–34.
[7] A. C. Haddon, *Head-Hunters*, London, 1901, p. 50, also in *AE* vi. [1893] 140 f.
[8] F. Boas, in *Sixth Report on the North-Western Tribes of Canada*, London, 1890, p. 47 f.

6. The divine mask.—The shaman of N.W. America, *e.g.*, among the Makahs, has one mask for each of his familiar spirits. When giving a séance, he puts on a mask and summons the spirit with his rattle.[1] The Eskimo shamans, in making their masks, give expression to their ideas of the spirits represented. Here is a primitive source of creative plastic art. The shaman is said to be able to see through the animal-mask to the manlike face behind.[2] In the ritual of ancient Mexico the priest wore a mask representing the god.[3] On the other hand, priests in Nigeria may not wear or touch a mask.[4]

From a similar point of view the protégé of a guardian spirit wears a mask, when dancing, to represent that spirit and identify himself with it.[5] The Monumbo of New Guinea wear masks representing guardian spirits, when they appeal to them for help, fair weather, and the like, among the masks being those of kangaroos, dogs, and cassowaries. The masks, when made, are fumigated in order to 'put life into them.' They are treated with respect and addressed as if they were living persons.[6] A man wears a mask representing his totem. This practice is common in N.W. America,[7] and the belief is that the wearer becomes the totem-animal.

The image of a god may wear a mask; the Mexicans placed on the face of certain idols masks of a human face cut off from the skull and preserved. They also used elaborate masks with pyrites for the eyes, and obsidian and turquoise mosaic in bands across the face.[8] The image of the goddess 'Our Mother' wore a two-faced mask, and her priest donned a replica of this.[9]

7. The death-mask.—In connexion with the dead the mask has been exploited along interesting lines, assisting among other things the art of portrait sculpture. Besides the practice of embalming or otherwise preserving the heads of dead friends or enemies, several peoples have made masks of these. One such has been mentioned as placed upon the face of a Mexican idol, and there is a fine example in the Christy collection in the British Museum. In New Britain and elsewhere in Melanesia and New Guinea, such masks (skull masks) were worn in sacred dances.[10] The Mexicans also placed painted masks or masks of gold or turquoise mosaic on the faces of their dead kings.[11] The Aleuts covered the faces of their dead with masks.[12] The meaning of the last practice is obscure, but the Aleuts think that it is intended to protect the dead against the glances of evil spirits. Their practice of wearing masks in certain religious dances, so as not to behold the idol round which they revolve and whose glance means death, may be compared.[13] Similarly, among the Guaymis of Panama, during the initiation of young men, the women who attend upon them wear masks.[14] Basuto girls at puberty wear straw masks,[15] and Lillooet girls (British Columbia) wear goat-skin masks at the same period.[16] In Mexico, when the king was ill, the images of the gods were masked, possibly to prevent them from drawing away his soul.[1] Some idea of disguising a person dangerous or in danger may be connected with the practice, and here the mask is merely a veil. In Siam and Cambodia masks of gold were placed on the faces of dead kings. The Shans have the same custom, using masks of silver or gold.[2] These cases and the next seem to touch upon the idea of a portrait. The Egyptian mummy had an artificial face forming part of the portrait superstructure over the corpse. Death-masks proper, of gold, silver, bronze, and terra-cotta, have been found in Mesopotamia, Phœnicia, the Crimea, Italy, France, the Danube valley, and Britain.[3] The most conspicuous and complete examples are supplied by Mycenæ and Rome. In the famous shaft-graves opened at Mycenæ golden masks, 'clearly portraits,' were found, corresponding to men and children. Those at least of the latter, being of thin gold leaf, 'must have been moulded with the hand on the faces of the dead.' The masks of the men were of thicker plate, and had no eye-holes. 'The hands and feet of the children were also wrapt in gold leaf.'[4] This suggests that the informing idea was similar to that of swathing the dead, painting the face, and otherwise decorating, while protecting, the corpse. The Roman *nobiles* kept wax portrait-masks of their ancestors in the *atrium*.[5] The dead *nobilis* lay in state for seven days, during which the embalmer (*pollinctor*) took a mould of the face, which he then cast in wax, and painted with the natural colours. The mask was placed on the dead man's face, or, in case of putrefaction, on an effigy. After the burial the mask was hung in the *atrium*, possibly fixed on a bust, and under it was a *titulus* giving the name and exploits of the man represented. These *imagines* were connected by lines, giving the genealogical succession, and termed *stemmata*. The *ius imaginum* gave a man the right of having his *imago* carried in the funeral train of a descendant. The remarkable custom was that a man was followed to his tomb by all his ancestors, their masks being worn by persons as similar as possible in stature and form, riding in chariots. Marcellus was attended by six hundred of his forefathers and kin. The *imagines* were crowned with laurel on feast days. By Pliny's time the wax masks were giving way to *clipeatæ imagines*, *i.e.* medallions of metal.[6]

Since Roman times the method of securing a portrait by taking a mould of the dead man's face has been continued in the case of great personages. This is the 'death-mask' of sculpture.

8. The dramatic mask.—The secret societies of N.W. America are, in contrast with those of Melanesia and Africa, chiefly concerned with dramatic representations. Their 'masonic' privileges are important, but they exercise little authority; in fact, these societies might be described as amateur dramatic clubs, with a religious setting like that of the mediæval gilds. Frazer describes the institution as 'a religious drama' like that of ancient Greece.[7] Various purposes other than that of entertainment are fulfilled by the performances; various, too, are the characters represented, according to the constitution of the society, whether totemic or consecrated to guardian spirits or otherwise. But the essence of their

1 Dall, p. 110; Frazer, *Totemism and Exogamy*, iii. 438 f.
2 Nelson, p. 394 f. 3 Andree, p. 117.
4 N. W. Thomas, *Anthropological Report on the Ibo-speaking Peoples of Nigeria*, London, 1913, i. 58.
5 F. Boas, in *Report of U.S. Nat. Mus. for 1895* [Washington, 1897], pp. 337, 396; Frazer, *Totemism and Exogamy*, iii. 435.
6 *GB*3, pt. vi., *The Scapegoat*, p. 382.
7 Nelson, *loc. cit.*; Frazer, *Totemism and Exogamy*, iii. 275 f.
8 Dall, p. 96.
9 *GB*3, pt. vi., *The Scapegoat*, p. 287.
10 E. B. Tylor, *Anahuac*, London, 1861, p. 338; C. E. Brasseur de Bourbourg, *Monuments anciens du Mexique*, Paris, 1864–66, p. viii. pl. 43; Dall, pp. 95 f., 148.
11 Dall, p. 105. 12 *Ib.* p. 139. 13 *Ib.*
14 Frazer, *Totemism and Exogamy*, iii. 555.
15 E. Casalis, *The Basutos*, London, 1861, p. 268.
16 J. Teit, *The Lillooet Indians*, Leyden and New York, 1906, p. 263 f.

1 *GB*3, pt. ii., *Taboo and the Perils of the Soul*, London, 1911, p. 96 n.
2 J. B. Pallegoix, *Description du royaume Thai ou Siam*, Paris, 1854, i. 247; J. Moura, *Le Royaume du Cambodge*, do. 1882, i. 349; A. R. Colquhoun, *Amongst the Shans*, London, 1885, p. 279.
3 See generally O. Benndorf, 'Antike Gesichtshelme und Sepulcralmasken,' in *DWAW*, 1878.
4 Frazer, *Pausanias*, London, 1898, iii. 107.
5 Pliny, *HN* xxxv. 2 (6).
6 *Ib.*; Polyb. vi. 53; Tac. *Ann.* iii. 76, iv. 9; Serv. *ad Æn.* v. 64, vi. 802; Benndorf, p. 371; A. H. Greenidge, art. 'Imago,' in Smith's *Dictionary of Greek and Roman Antiquities*3, London, 1890–91.
7 Frazer, *Totemism and Exogamy*, iii. 550.

function is pantomime, and the mask is the means of impersonation. The masks are made of various woods—alder, maple, or cotton-wood; they are large and prominent of feature, painted red, black, and white. In some of the grotesque sort the eyes and jaws are movable, and worked by a string. Some are held by means of a mouth-bar. Some masks are two-faced, enabling the actor suddenly to change his character.[1] The masks are surrounded, as usual, with considerable mystery, and are burned or thrown away at the end of the season. For their manufacture and use there are elaborate rules. No uninitiated person may see them being made. Little masks are worn on the fingers.[2] The masks represent human persons—mythical, sometimes hideous—or animals. Ancestors, spirits, *sulia* (tutelary spirits), natural objects (*e.g.*, the sun-mask of the Kwakiutl, 'set round with seal's whiskers, and feathers, which gradually expand like a fan'[3]), animals, and birds form the subjects of a remarkably varied collection. The Tsimshians have a mask representing the thunder-bird, and at the performance mock lightning is produced and water is poured from the roof on the spectators. Salish masks represent the ancestors of the clans, viz. the wolf, owl, frog, and coyote. But, since the wearing of a mask is regarded as being unlucky, well-to-do men hire professionals to represent them. This idea may be compared with civilized prejudices against the actor's profession. The dances are pantomimic representations of the myths stored by the society, and may thus be compared with the magical pantomimes of the Australians, intended to encourage the natural processes which they represent, and, on the other hand, with the mediæval 'morality,' which was an object-lesson in good and evil. The use of the mask 'throws a sort of mysterious glamour over the performance and at the same time allows the actor to remain unknown.'[4] Apart from entertainment, the pantomimes are performed in honour of dead personages, or to bring blessings on a particular man or the community. In N.W. Brazil a very pretty pantomime is performed in honour of the dead, at which the masked actors represent the gorgeously-coloured birds and insects of the forest.[5] The drama of the Pueblo Indians is remarkable; it has features resembling those of the morality and the Greek drama. Divine beings are the characters represented by masked actors. The performances take place in the village square, and have (at least as a secondary object) the intention of procuring rain, good crops, or prosperity in general.[6]

The Lāmas of Tibet practised a regular religious drama, exactly parallel to the European morality and mystery; there were good and evil spirits, a protecting deity, men, and animals, and for all there were the appropriate masks.[7] The Burmese drama employed masks for character types such as king and minister.[8] Siamese actors wore paper masks, coloured green, red, black, or gold. A peculiarity was that the wearer did not speak; the parts were spoken by prompters.[9] In Japan the dramatic masks of paper or lacquered wood were very elaborately artistic, gods, demons, men, and animals being represented in masks by good artists.[10]

[1] J. G. Swan, 'The Indians of Cape Flattery,' in *Smithsonian Contributions*, xvi. [Washington, 1870] 69 ff.; Nelson, p. 395.
[2] Frazer, *Totemism and Exogamy*, iii. 501 f., 510; *GB*[3], pt. vi., *The Scapegoat*, p. 382; Dall, p. 123.
[3] Frazer, *Totemism and Exogamy*, iii. 344, 533; F. Boas, *Eleventh Report on the North-Western Tribes of Canada*, London, 1895, p. 52.
[4] Frazer, *Totemism and Exogamy*, iii. 312, 344, 501.
[5] Nelson, p. 394; *GB*[3], pt. vi., *The Scapegoat*, p. 381 f.
[6] Frazer, *Totemism and Exogamy*, iii. 237 f.
[7] Andree, p. 114 ff.
[8] A. Bastian, *Reisen in Birma*, Leipzig, 1866, p. 201.
[9] Bastian, *Reisen in Siam*, Leipzig, 1867, p. 503.
[10] A. Humbert, *Le Japon illustré*, Paris, 1870, i. 195.

The drama of ancient Athens, both tragic and comic, employed the mask, which had been used in the old Bacchic mummeries that seem to have produced the drama. Previously the mummers had smeared their faces with wine or covered them with fig-leaves. Similarly, the peasants of Latium wore masks of bark in the Bacchic festivals.[1] The dramatic use of masks was first established by Thespis, who previously had painted his face with white lead or purslane. Linen masks unpainted were then adopted; Chœrilus improved them; Phrynichus introduced female masks; and Æschylus added paint and generally fixed their form.[2]

The Greek mask was made of linen, or, sometimes, of cork or wood. It was large (in tragedy) to correspond to the superhuman proportions of the actors. The *onkos* (ὄγκος), a cone-shaped prolongation of the upper part of the forehead, added size and dignity to the head. The white of the eye was painted strongly, but an aperture was made for the actor to see. The mouth was permanently opened wide, and the tradition remains, unexplained, that resonance was given to the voice by means of the shape of the mask. All that the mask aimed at was the bold emphasizing of types; every feature was exaggerated, and in the huge theatres of the Greeks this fact was essential. No change of facial expression being possible and the finer shades of emotion being excluded, the mask prevented any considerable evolution of the psychological drama. 'It would be difficult to imagine the part of Hamlet played in a mask.'[3] Pollux enumerates twenty-eight styles of tragic masks. The tyrant's mask had thick black hair and beard and wore a frown. The lover's face was pale.[4] The comic mask was, in the Old Comedy, the portrait of a real person; when Aristophanes presented *The Clouds*, Socrates stood up in the auditorium to enable the audience to identify the mask of his impersonation; but, when Cleon was to be staged, the makers refused to supply a mask, such was the fear inspired by the demagogue. In the New Comedy of manners types were represented. The hot-tempered old father wore a mask with one eyebrow drawn up and the other normal; he expressed his changes of temper by turning this or that side.[5] The Roman drama dispensed with masks until the time of Roscius, who is said to have introduced them on his own account, being ugly and affected with a squint; but they had always been worn in the old-fashioned *Atellanæ*, in which an actor, when hissed, was obliged to remove his mask.[6]

In mediæval Europe and England the mask was used in the folk-drama from which the modern drama was evolved. At the Feast of Fools references are made to the wearing of masks through the period from A.D. 1200 to 1445.[7] The term 'visor' was usual for the mask. 'Mumming' and 'disguising' were terms for the various folk-plays, which were often suppressed.[8] A side-development of this drama, and a new application of the word 'mask,' were made in the 'masque' popular in Elizabethan times.[9]

The theory of Frazer as to the magical and religious origin of the drama may be tested by the special case of the mask. He writes:

[1] A. E. Haigh, *The Attic Theatre*[3], Oxford, 1907, p. 239.
[2] *Ib.* pp. 239, 242.
[3] See Aul. Gell. v. 7, and Smith's *Dict. of Gr. and Rom. Antiq.*[3], *s.v.* 'Persona'; this term refers to the resonance.
[4] Pollux, *Onomasticon*, iv. 133–141.
[5] Haigh, pp. 262, 264.
[6] Smith's *Dict. of Gr. and Rom. Antiq.*[3], *s.v.* 'Persona.'
[7] E. K. Chambers, *The Mediæval Stage*, Oxford, 1903, i. 391.
[8] *Ib.* p. 394. Skeat connects the terms 'mumming,' 'mummer,' with the Low German *Mumme* ('mask'); it is onomatopœic from *mum*, *mom*, used by nurses to frighten or amuse children, while pretending to cover the face.
[9] *Ib.* p. 400 ff.

'Actors sought to draw down blessings on the community by mimicking certain powerful superhuman beings and in their assumed character working those beneficent miracles which in the capacity of mere men they would have confessed themselves powerless to effect.'[1]

The mimetic magical ceremonies of the Central Australian natives are a strong piece of evidence in favour of this view, but it seems more probable that the native mimetic instinct expressed itself first with no particular purpose, being later applied to various magical or religious aims. It is impossible to prove that the earliest masks or even face-paints represented anything but fanciful characters of merely dramatic import.[2] The instinctive delight in personal disguise is a universal element in all the applications of the mask, and is repeated to-day in the custom of civilized peoples of wearing a mask on the upper part of the face at fancy-dress balls, which reproduce the barbaric entertainments of lower cultures. The burglar's mask is another modern reproduction of the idea of disguise, but employed for utilitarian purposes.

9. **The swinging mask.**—Cases have been cited of the mask being separated from its wearer and becoming more or less of an idol. The ancient Italian *oscilla* are an interesting parallel. These were miniature masks in wax, marble, or terra-cotta, and apparently wool, which were hung up on trees at agricultural festivals, and allowed to swing in the wind.[3] The intention may have been magical, to make the crops or vines grow, by disseminating magical force, by swinging high,[4] or by the virtue of movement.

10. **Masks in metaphor and history.**—Many obvious metaphors have been inspired by the mask, which need not be recapitulated. In history the Faux Visages, a section of the Ghibelline faction in the 13th cent., otherwise the Mascarati, are curiously repeated in name by the 'False Faces' secret society of the Iroquois.[5] 'The man in the iron-mask' is a historic mystery illustrating the permanent fascination of this element of applied psychology.

LITERATURE.—This is fully given in the article.

A. E. CRAWLEY.

MASS.—See EUCHARIST.

MAṢṢĒBHĀH.—In the OT *maṣṣēbhāh* (מַצֵּבָה) denotes a standing-stone, stele, obelisk, or pillar, sometimes conceived as being an abode of spirit or deity. The name is derived from נצב, 'to set up' (Phœn. מצבת, 'tombstone'; Arab. *nuṣb*, pl. *anṣāb*; Aram. נְצִיב; Syr. prop. name Nisibis; Palmyrene (מצב(א)). The *maṣṣēbhāh* is referred to as a heathen symbol of the Canaanites (Ex 23^{24} E, 34^{13} J, Dt 7^{5} 12^{3}), and as an adjunct to a temple of Baal (2 K 3^{2} $10^{26f.}$). It is frequently conjoined with an *ăshērāh*, which was primarily a sacred tree and later a stump or post (1 K 14^{23}, 2 K 17^{10} 18^{4} 23^{14}). *Maṣṣᵉbhôth* and *ăshērîm* were so frequent that it could be said that they might be found 'upon every high hill, and under every green tree' (2 K 17^{10}). The word *maṣṣēbhāh* is used to describe sacred stones in connexion with an altar (Ex 24^{4} E [erected by Moses], Hos 3^{4} $10^{1f.}$, Is 19^{19} [without condemnation, the article being considered usual in Hebrew worship]). The strong pillars of Tyre doomed to destruction are called *maṣṣᵉbhôth* by Ezekiel (26^{11}), and Jeremiah (43^{13}) uses the same term for the Egyptian obelisks at Heliopolis. The use of *maṣṣēbhôth* is strictly forbidden to Israelites by the Deuteronomic code and in the Law of Holiness (Lv 26^{1}), and the editor of the books of Kings estimates their character in the light of this prohibition. The earlier writers, especially E and Hosea, see no harm in these stones; but the teaching of the other prophets of the 8th cent. evoked an aversion, and Hezekiah, Josiah, and Deuteronomy insist on their destruction. Later writers, such as P, consider the altar a divinely authorized instrument of worship, and they scruple to describe the patriarchs as having anything to do with the *maṣṣēbhāh*, representing them as making altars (cf. LXX Ex 24^{4}, substituting אֲבָנִים, 'stones,' for מצבות). Hebrew monotheism, when fully developed, denuded sun and moon of their ancient divinity (Gn 1^{14-17}): 'The heaven is my throne, and the earth is my footstool: what manner of house will ye build unto me?' (Is 66^{1}). At such a period in Hebrew thought there was no longer any superstitious regard for stones, cairns, cromlechs, or menhirs.

Stones are used with no occult associations.

Samuel commemorates a victory by setting up a stone which he called Eben-ezer (1 S 7^{12}); the Temple has two pillars, Jachin and Boaz, set up in the porch (1 K 7^{21}); inscriptions are recorded on stone (Dt $27^{2f.}$, Ex 34^{1} [the Ten Words]); Rachel's grave is marked by a stone (Gn 35^{20}); Absalom in his lifetime rears a pillar, called a 'hand,' to perpetuate his memory (2 S 18^{18}); an agreement between Jacob and Laban (Gn 31^{45-48}) as to the boundary between them is marked by a stone and cairn (*galᵉʿēdh*, 'cairn of witness').

When men sought an enduring memorial, when they wished to make the deity the protector of a covenant, they often chose some form of stone as an emblem of the divine presence. Something more than this is indicated in a few instances.

Jacob set up a stone for a *maṣṣēbhāh*, poured oil upon the top of it, and called it Beth-el (Gn 28^{18-22}; Gn 35^{14} adds that Jacob poured a drink-offering thereon). As the *maṣṣēbhāh* is found associated with altars and *ăshērāh* figures in religious centres, Jacob's ceremony implies more than it states. Joshua sets up a stone saying, 'This stone shall be a witness against us; for it hath heard all the words of the Lord which he spake unto us' (Jos 24^{27} E). The use of unhewn stones for an altar (Ex 20^{25}, Dt $27^{5f.}$, Jos 8^{31}) betrays the feeling that the chisel would offend the *numen* in the stone.

Semitic and other parallels show that such instances are surviving specimens of an elaborate system of stone-worship. The *maṣṣèbhāh* is found in the cognate languages, and denotes 'lapides qui divi dicuntur' (Lampridius). Among the primitive Arabs 'the *nuṣb* serves as an altar, the victim's blood is smeared over it; hence the name *gharīy*. It is, however, more than an altar, it represents the godhead' (J. Wellhausen, *Reste arab. Heidentumes*, Berlin, 1887, p. 99). Herodotus (iii. 8) describes Arabs making a covenant.

An umpire draws blood with a sharp stone from the hand of each of the two persons making the contract, and with part of their garments he smears the blood on seven stones placed between them, invoking Orotal and Alilat. Herodotus might have added that the parties tasted each other's blood (W. R. Smith, *Kinship and Marriage*, London, 1907, p. 56 ff.).

The Canaanite high-place discovered at Gezer reveals the conspicuous place assigned to standing-stones in the cult of Palestine before the Hebrew occupation (R. A. S. Macalister, *Excavation of Gezer*, London, 1912). Phœnician coins and temples confirm the sanctity of the stone column, and the Greek name *βαίτυλος*, *βαιτύλιον*, appears to be derived from Beth-el.

'Theophrastus, in the 4th century B.C., depicts the superstitious Greek passing the anointed stones in the streets, taking out his phial and pouring oil on them, falling on his knees to adore, and going his way' (*PC*^{4} ii. 165).

Traces of like practice are recorded down to the present day. A full description of 'a shrine of pre-Islamic stone-worship' with a ritual preserving pre-historic customs in a Turkish village of Macedonia is given by A. J. Evans in his 'Mycenæan Tree and Pillar Cult' (*JHS* xxi. [1901] 99 ff.). It is due to prophetic intolerance of the irrational and immoral that so slight traces of litholatry remain in the OT.

[1] *GB*^{3}, pt. vi., *The Scapegoat*, p. 375; cf. the custom of wearing masks representing the animals about to be hunted. This may have an obviously utilitarian origin (Dall, p. 107, n.).

[2] See the collection in the Godeffroy Museum, and J. D. E. Schmelz and R. Krause, *Die ethnographisch-anthropologische Abteilung des Museum Godeffroy in Hamburg*, Hamburg, 1881.

[3] G. E. Marindin, in Smith's *Dict. of Gr. and Rom. Antiq.*^{3}, *s.v.* 'Oscilla.'

[4] *GB*^{3}, pt. iii., *The Dying God*, London, 1911, p. 283.

[5] Dall, p. 144.

'What mean ye by these stones?' asked the Hebrews; *ratio in obscuro*, answered Tacitus. To seek one principle consistently applied is as hopeless in custom as in a language. Feeling, variable and indifferent to logic, determines usage in regard to sacred stones. Mountains have inspired awe and affection—*e.g.*, Olympus, Fujiyama, Hermon, Horeb, Sinai—and it has been suggested that the sacred pillar is a little model of the Holy Hill. Meteorites have been found and treasured; and, if the host of heaven received adoration, any fragment coming on a path of light, like a falling star, or supposed to be sent amid thunder and lightning would command devotion (cf. Diana of the Ephesians and the image which fell down from Jupiter [Ac 19^{35}]; βαιτύλιον in Damascenus, quoted by Photius [A.D. 850], *Biblioth.* 342*b*, 26; 348*a*, 28; the Ka'ba at Mecca, as R. Burton thinks [*Pilgrimage to El-Medinah and Meccah*, London, 1893, ii. 300 f.], retaining its sanctity in spite of Islām). Moreover, the shadow of a pillar is a clue to the movement of the sun and the regulation of the calendar. The structures at Stonehenge 'had for the most part an astronomical use in connexion with religious ceremonials' (N. Lockyer, *Nature*, lxxiii. [1905–06] 153; see also series of Notes on Stonehenge, *ib.* lxxii. [1905] 32, 246, 270, lxxiii. 224). The same conclusion is maintained with regard to the standing-stones of Stenness in Orkney by M. Spence (*Scottish Review*, xxii. [1893] 401–417). The late Hebrew term חַמָּנִים, rendered uniformly 'sun-images' in RV (Ezk 6^{4-6}, Lv 26^{30}, Is 17^{8} 27^{9}, 2 Ch 14^{5} [cf. 14^{3}] $34^{4,7}$), probably represents the *maṣṣēbhāh* with solar associations. Palestine had a human past before the Hebrews entered it. The stone-tables (dolmens) occurring in hundreds suggested imitation; the menhirs to the east of the Jordan served as prototypes of the *maṣṣēbhāh*. Of the more obvious influences specified by the Biblical writers the commemoration of the dead has always been the strongest inspiration.

Cup-markings on the *maṣṣēbhāh* or on adjoining altars are not infrequent (cf. art. CUP- AND RING-MARKINGS). On an altar they are supposed to receive the blood of the victim; on a tombstone they would serve for food and drink offered to the dead, although a plain Turk explained the hollows on tombstones as meant to gather water for the birds. The cups are sometimes in the side, not on the upper surface of the stone; and they may be arranged in the shape of a horse-shoe. Cup-markings are held to be inconsistent with the purpose of the pillar in one case at Gezer, and the situation showed that the cups and pillar had not originated at the same period (*PEFSt* xxxvi. [1904] 112 f.). The cupped stone is cited to explain Zec 3^{9}: 'Behold the stone that I have set before Joshua; upon one stone are seven eyes: behold, I will engrave the graving thereof, saith the Lord of hosts, and I will remove the iniquity of that land in one day.'

An article by B. D. Eerdmans (in *JBL* xxx. [1911] 109–113), entitled 'The Sepulchral Monument "Maṣṣebah,"' has revived discussion on the meaning of the pillars.

'The maṣṣebah is easily explained as a house for the soul. Therefore the name of the deceased person is inscribed upon it; and the monument itself is called "soul." The male form was chosen for the graves of men, the female form for the graves of women' (p. 113).

This result has, with some reservations, been approved by E. Sellin, who adds corroborations and, in consequence, suggests striking interpretations of Is 6^{13} and $51^{1f.}$ (*OLZ* xi. [1912] 119 ff., 371 ff., 568 f.). The views of Eerdmans and Sellin are strongly contested by K. Budde (*ib.* 248 ff., 469 ff.). This indication of sex is a welcome improvement on the *suggestio concupiscentiæ* which prevailed for some time. In spite of Herodotus, ii. 106, and similar testimony in Lucian, and the phallic columns at Gezer and Petra, it appears that this was a subsidiary and occasional interpretation of the standing-stones. The feeling that the stone slab or pillar may serve as a resting-place for the soul is supported by the Jewish custom in Oriental cemeteries (בֵּית הַחַיִּים, as they are called) of giving every individual a stone. The inscribed name indicates the sex, apart from a special shape of the stone. The tombstone of a Rabbi or of a person who died of cholera has a distinctive shape.

LITERATURE.—In addition to sources cited in the art. see W. Baudissin, art. 'Malsteine,' in *PRE*³ for main works since 1685; P. Thomsen, *Kompendium der palästinischen Altertumskunde*, Tübingen, 1913, contains references to recent periodical literature.

D. M. KAY.

MASTER AND SERVANT.

—See EMPLOYERS, EMPLOYMENT.

MATERIALISM.

—Materialism is one of several types of metaphysical theory concerning the nature and number of the ultimate principles to be assumed in order to explain the universe. Dualism (*q.v.*) asserts that two independent principles must be presupposed, viz. mind and matter. Monism (*q.v.*)—in the qualitative sense—regards these two principles as simply modes or aspects of one ultimate. Monism—in the quantitative sense—is opposed to dualism in regarding one principle as sufficient. There are two kinds of such monistic theory: spiritualism, which affirms mind or spirit to be the only ultimate reality, and materialism, which makes the same assertion of matter. Thus, according to the doctrine of materialism, extended, impenetrable, eternally self-existent matter, susceptible of motion, is the one fundamental constituent of the universe; mind or consciousness is but a mode or a property of such matter, and psychical processes are reducible to physical. More precisely, there are three kinds of metaphysical materialism, thus described by Külpe (*Introd. to Philosophy*, Eng. tr., p. 117): '*attributive* materialism, which makes mind an attribute of matter; *causal* . . ., which makes it an effect of matter; and *equative* . . ., which looks upon mental processes as really material in character.'

1. History.—The atomism of Leucippus and Democritus is the earliest example of materialistic theory. According to these philosophers, the physical world is composed of invisible material particles, and mind is made up of similar atoms, smaller, rounder, smoother, and more mobile. The theory reduced all qualitative differences to quantitative (of size, form, arrangement), banished final cause or intelligent purpose from the world, denied the immortality of the soul, and interpreted the universe only in terms of mechanism and fixed law. The last element in early Greek atomism does not necessarily presuppose or involve materialistic theory, though Lange, the historian of materialism, seems to see in it the chief virtue of early materialistic speculation. The theory of Leucippus and Democritus was developed by Epicurus and Lucretius, with certain modifications.

At the beginning of the modern period the early Greek materialism was revived by P. Gassendi, who, however, deprived it of metaphysical significance by reconciling it with belief in God as Creator of the atoms. T. Hobbes, at the same time, taught a similar view, so that, though the tone of his philosophical system is materialistic, he cannot be called a thoroughgoing materialist. He strongly insisted that all that exists is body or matter, and that motion is the only kind of change in the universe. Gradually developing in England, materialism perhaps reached its climax in the writings of the French Encyclopædists (*q.v.*), after science had revealed how closely psychical states and mental development depend on the body. P. H. D. Holbach's *Système de la nature* (London, 1770), which rejects every form of spiritualism and supernaturalism, marks the culmination of this movement of thought.

Nearer to our own time materialism appeared, as a reaction from post-Kantian idealism, with renewed energy in Germany, K. C. Vogt, J. Moleschott, and L. Büchner being its leading exponents at about the middle of the 19th century. Their writings, though evincing—for the first time, perhaps, in the history of materialism—some sense of the need of an epistemological foundation for a metaphysic which resolves mental process into material, reveal great crudity of thought and knowledge in this connexion, and in spite of their popularity are of no philosophical worth to an age which is careful and critical as to epistemological presuppositions, especially such as are involved in the physical sciences. Description of physical and even mental processes, in the language of materialism, is easier to science; and this fact, together with the jubilant confidence with which science, flushed with many successes, over-hastily exaggerated its own scope and functions a generation ago, accounts for the materialistic colouring which many generalizations of natural knowledge have received—a colouring which has often been taken by students of the physical sciences, unpractised in philosophical reflexion and criticism, for an essential implication or consequence of scientific truth rightly so called. T. Huxley, who on occasion could teach materialism of the most dogmatic kind, and in another mood would capitulate to spiritualism, sought permanent refuge in agnosticism; and, since his earlier and more militant essays, materialism has found no literary champion among British scientists. In dogmatic form it is to be found to-day, perhaps, only in the literature of secularist 'free' thought. Even the monism of E. Haeckel, which is materialism in all but its name, awakens no enthusiasm among scientific students in Britain; it is rightly regarded as involving an obsolete standpoint which science, more silent and cautious—if not more critical—than formerly, has left behind.

2. The attractiveness and plausibility of materialism.—The chief outbursts of materialistic metaphysic have coincided with occasions of renewed interest in, or remarkable progress of, physical science. The emergence of this tendency to regard the world as fundamentally material, at successive epochs in the history of thought, is evidence that materialism strongly commends itself to many minds, especially to those whose studies chiefly lie in the sphere of the physical sciences.

There are many reasons for the attractiveness of materialism as a metaphysical theory or view-of-the-world to such minds, and the view possesses great plausibility when it is contemplated from the epistemological standpoint which the natural sciences, as well as the philosophy of common sense or ordinary social intercourse, take for granted. These reasons may now be specified, and the assumed theory of knowledge whence they derive their plausibility examined.

One reason why, as H. Höffding says (*Problems of Philosophy*, New York, 1905, p. 140), 'ever and again essays are made in the materialistic direction, although—since the advent of the critical philosophy—not with such dogmatic assurance as formerly,' is that our knowledge of matter, its changes and its properties, is so much greater, and so much more easy to obtain, than our knowledge of mind. Psychology is a comparatively young science. In so far as it embraces psychophysics and is pursued in its relation to physiology, even psychology deals with matter rather than with mind. And in so far as it is pursued by the analytic method—the only truly psychological one—it is a study beset with enormous difficulties. Moreover, such psychological knowledge as is forthcoming and established is rarely studied by the investigator of physical phenomena, so that he proceeds in abstraction from essential elements involved in every 'objective' fact that he examines and classifies. Psychology, again, more immediately involves metaphysics, which for the most part is as yet disputed ground. Lastly, the physical sciences owe much of their prestige to the fact that they are based on measurement, and, being thus quantitative, are capable of mathematical treatment, whereas in psychology (of the pure or analytic kind) measurement is out of the question.

The physical sciences, again, impress us with their connectedness. The connectedness of the material world exercises an overwhelming power on our minds, and especially upon the imagination. Mind, on the other hand, is discontinuous; it is known only in the form of individual minds; and these minds are not known, as yet, with anything like certainty, to communicate with each other through any other medium than that of matter. Further, we know minds only in connexion with bodies or material organisms, and, so far as observation goes, we have no knowledge of mind existing independently of body, though—again, so far as observation goes—it seems that most material 'things' exist without mind. Science teaches us also of the past history of a material world which existed for ages before organic beings, which alone experience enables us certainly to endow with minds, could exist upon it. Yet more impressive is the array of facts furnished by physiology, comparative anatomy and psychology, and pathology as to the concomitance of psychical processes with physical, their dependence on material phenomena such as the functioning of the brain, the correlation of mental development throughout the animal kingdom with organization and complexity of brain-structure, the effects upon mind of injury or disease in brain tissue, and so forth. Thus a very strong, clear, and convincing case for the priority of matter to mind, and for the dependence of the mental on the material, is presented by science; and there is much to suggest that consciousness is a property, and, indeed, a product or an effect, of matter or material process. The progress of science would seem, as Huxley put it, to have meant the extension of mechanical law and the realm of matter, and the concomitant banishment of spirit and spontaneity from the universe, and to afford as good ground for asserting mental phenomena to be effects of material as for asserting heat to be due to physical causes.

Moreover, it may be added, it is impossible to invalidate this coherent and cumulative argument for materialism from the standpoint of the physical sciences. No countercase can be made, for instance, out of the fact, if it be a fact, that to some mental events no correlated material changes within the brain have been discovered; for future research may possibly discover them, and it is precarious to stake our metaphysical theory on gaps in scientific knowledge. Nor can materialism be refuted by saying that thought, or consciousness in general, is unlike other activities or properties of matter. Heat, light, sound, and electricity are qualitatively different, yet all of them are properties of matter or of ether possessing some of the characteristics of matter. It is a baseless dogma that the effect must resemble the cause, so long as we refer to phenomenal causes and effects. Science, in its more abstract developments, does indeed reduce all diversity to quantitative difference, all causality to identity, so that heat, light, electricity, etc., are resolved into motions of matter—*i.e.* of extended and inert substance ; but at this level of analysis consciousness, looked upon as one kind of phenomenon among others, and regarded from the purely or abstractly objective point of view adopted by science, might similarly be held capable of resolution into physical antecedents. Perhaps the most that can be urged, from this epistemological standpoint, in opposition to materialism, is that the adoption of it as metaphysical truth would involve us in absolute scepticism, and therefore in doubt as to the validity of materialism. For, if thoughts and all other modes of being conscious are produced by material causes, and their co-existences and sequences are mechanically determined (so that all purposiveness is excluded), there would seem to be no reason for believing that any of our thoughts and judgments, even concerning matter, are true. This argument should suffice to dispose of the dogmatic certainty of materialism, though not necessarily of the possibility of its (indemonstrable) truth. That material change, while ever pursuing the sole path of least resistance, should throw off psychical epi-phenomena, the connexion of which is that of logical sequence, is a possibility with which the materialist must be credited, and to which, perhaps, his opponent will allow him to be welcome. A similar crux which materialism has to encounter is the order in the universe. If there be enough disorder to disturb the equanimity of the spiritualist and to put the theist in a difficulty, there is surely too much order in the world to allow the materialist to feel at home there.

3. Refutation of materialism.—But there are more telling arguments against a materialistic metaphysic than any of those hitherto mentioned. They emerge only when the question of the epistemological standpoint of physical science is raised, and the first principles and presuppositions of such knowledge are exposed to the searching light of criticism.

When science boasts of the 'objectivity' of its knowledge, it does not merely imply possession of knowledge (concerning fact) such as is universal, or capable of being common to all subjects—which is a perfectly legitimate contention; it further drops out of sight altogether, as convenient or essential to its own practical procedure, all reference to the subject of such knowledge, or to the subjective elements which are essential to the very existence of knowledge at all, and which survive in some form even when science has developed its abstractive processes to the furthest limit. Rightly recognizing that any object of universal human experience, such as the sun, is 'independent' of any individual subject's consciousness, we are often apt to speak as if such an object were similarly independent of the experience of human subjects collectively—which is a very different matter. The phenomena which science studies are not indeed the objects of individual experience, the nature of which—in complete isolation from intercourse with other individuals' experience—we can only guess or reconstruct in part ; but they are the sum of objective elements common to many individual experiences. Consciousness of an object which is not owned, a cognition which is nobody's, a phenomenon which does not appear to some subject—these things are impossible, inconceivable, and meaningless. Knowledge, moreover, as distinguished from pure passive sensation (if there be such a thing in reality), reveals the work of subjective activity and creative elaboration ; and the more generalized and abstract the principles of theoretical science become, the more, and not the less, of this teleological or subjective shaping, guided by interests, ends, and purposes, do they disclose. Thus, to consider the 'objects' of universal experience as entirely sundered from, or independent of, all subjects, to regard the phenomena of science as the phenomena *per se*, however convenient and harmless it may be for purposes of ordinary discourse and practical scientific investigation and description, is epistemologically false, or, rather, nonsensical. Yet it is precisely by the erection of this colloquial fiction into an epistemological principle that materialism and all kindred forms of thought obtain a fixed foundation. Experience—the only ultimate *datum*, the one thing which cannot be doubted or explained away without involving the assertion of its reality—is always essentially a duality in unity, subjective and objective; either aspect without the other is an impossibility. Science can ignore—so long as it confines itself to its own business—the one element in experience, the subjective, though of course its whole procedure involves subjective activity; and it ignores it so completely that its students have sometimes come to look upon what they have agreed to leave out of sight (it being none of their business) as non-existent. Objects come to be talked of as if they were really subjectless ; their independence, their priority, their exclusive reality come to be affirmed. The scientist, leaving himself out of account at the beginning, cannot discover himself at the end ; he is thus led to think that his own mind, which has largely shaped his phenomena and made them what they are for him, is but an illusion, an effect, an epi-phenomenon, a shadow cast by the machinery that he is engaged in contemplating. It is small wonder that, when science, without raising the previous question as to the nature of experience and the implications and presuppositions of knowledge, sets out in quest of a metaphysic, it should land in materialism. It is just as natural that, setting out forearmed with knowledge of the elements of the science of knowledge, it should come, when it seeks a metaphysic at all, to adopt the opposite creed of spiritualism.

Once, then, the materialist is allowed the right to talk of objects without implicated subjects, of 'purely objective' facts, of phenomena *per se*, he can proceed to lay before us an array of imposing facts and arguments which, from the standpoint conceded to him, are as irrefutable as they are impressive. But, once the epistemological assumption that objects, as known to us, can exist to be known independently of all experiencing subjects is shown to be impossible, the tables are turned. Not only do the arguments in question lose all their apparent force, but consciousness, which materialism would resolve into an epi-phenomenal effect or property of self-existent matter, is seen to be the primary reality, and matter as we know it is shown to be a conceptual construction of mind. Materialism, we conclude, misunderstands human experience, in which subjective and objective form one whole, while they are gradually differentiated only through increasingly complicated processes of conceptual distinction. The objective, moreover, is not to be identified with the material, as if these were convertible terms. Matter is a conceptual abstraction from experience, and so cannot be taken for the ground or source thereof. Atoms, again, are only figurative ideas ; and that they have to be endowed with the very attributes which, in gross matter, they were invented to explain, if not indeed with attributes that contradict all observation, is a sufficient warning against adoption of the naively realistic view that they are corporeal or material particles.

Materialism also involves the old and obsolete assumption that the so-called secondary characters of matter (colour, tone, odour, etc.) are fundamentally different from the so-called primary (extension, impenetrability, etc.). It was one of G. Berkeley's great contributions to philosophy to show that this distinction is untenable. The secondary qualities of matter have been generally admitted to be 'in our mind' and not 'in matter.' But on closer examination it is to be seen that the primary qualities are in precisely the same case. Our idea of extension, for instance, is gained only through touch or sight; and the perceived 'size' of a body depends on our distance from it. That a material object is of the same size, though at one time it may appear larger and at another smaller to a percipient, is an inference, and involves the revision of the evidence of our senses by reasoning. The extension which we attribute to a physical object, then, is inferred, and not perceived, extension; and, if we abstract from our idea of extension the sensation-elements supplied by touch or sight, nothing remains. Therefore matter possesses extension no more than it possesses colour, except as perceived by our minds. If, then, there be anything at all (which Berkeley denied) other than our minds and the direct action of God upon them which causes the sensations whence our idea of extension (or any other quality of matter) is derived, it is obvious that this something cannot be matter as it is perceived. There may be what J. S. Mill called a 'permanent possibility of sensation' independent of us, whose *esse* is not *percipi*; but, if there be, it is an entity wholly different from the 'matter' of physical science and common sense, and, for all we know, may just as aptly be described as mind or spirit. We can, therefore, without self-contradiction ascribe our sensations to God (Berkeley) or to other spiritual existences (pluralism); but we cannot ascribe them to matter as perceived. Either of the views just mentioned would explain our experience; and, unless we ascribe our sensations to the influence of other spiritual existences endowed with 'being for self,' we cannot but assume, with Berkeley, that the noumenal matter, the substratum of sensations, the substance which constitutes the permanent possibility of sensation, is but a medium or means existing solely for our sakes, and one which, from a theist's point of view, must seem superfluous. The concept of matter, then, is built on the basis of sense-impressions; and materialism uses this manifestly conceptual construction to explain the origin of sense-impressions. It thus seeks to derive the underived from the derived.

There are several other inconsistencies involved in materialistic doctrine, one or two of which may briefly be mentioned. Materialism implies that everything which happens and is accompanied by consciousness of its happening would happen equally well without consciousness; or, in other words, that consciousness makes no difference to the course of the world. But, if so, it is difficult, on the theory of evolution by survival of the fittest, which is the current scientific explanation of the origin and permanence of every organ and every function, as well as of every individual organism and every species, to account for the emergence, and still more for the development, of mind. Materialism, again, of the more thoroughgoing type, regards consciousness as the product or effect of matter, while cherishing the principle of *ex nihilo nihil fit* in its application to what physicists call 'energy.' The law of the Conservation of Energy is often held — though doubtless quite erroneously—to assert that not only is there quantitative equivalence between the energy which, in any physical change, disappears in one form and that which appears in another, but also that the sum-total of energy in the universe is constant. The latter, and illegitimate, part of the generalization has been a tenet of materialists; and it is difficult to reconcile it with their assertion that mental phenomena are caused by material. For in every such production of consciousness a disappearance of physical energy should take place, unless energy is also attributable to consciousness. The last view is so objectionable on many grounds to materialists, partly because it opens the possibility that mind can produce physical effects, that they have avoided working it out. Lastly, it is generally admitted that materialism cannot explain even the simplest type of conscious process. The difficulty of conceiving how a sensation or a feeling could be the necessary consequence or effect of motion in matter or mass-points, and of imagining how mathematical physics would cope with such a possibility, is overwhelming; and, of course, it has never been faced.

4. Recent substitutes for materialism: hylozoism.—It is not surprising, under the pressure of all these difficulties and in the light of the self-criticism to which the structure of physical science has of late been subjected, that materialism should at the present time be a practically abandoned philosophical theory. Useful as a method, it is wanting as a metaphysic; and representatives of natural science with a leaning towards metaphysical speculation and a preference for materialistic terminology adopt in its stead a monism which has much in common with the ancient doctrine of hylozoism, according to which all matter is not inert —as mathematical physics asserts for its necessary postulate—but living. Thus J. Tyndall was willing to endow primordial matter with 'the promise and potency of life'; and W. K. Clifford, in his 'mind-dust' hypothesis, and Haeckel, in his imaginative theory of atoms indwelt by rudimentary souls, go yet further, and couple hylozoism with pan-psychism.

Hylozoism is as ancient as the Ionian school of Greek philosophy, and was taught in a crude form by Thales. The Stoic doctrine of a world-soul is another form of it, revived and developed by several thinkers in the period of the Renaissance (Paracelsus, Telesio, Bruno, etc.). Hylozoism reappears again in the writings of the Cambridge Platonists (*q.v.*), as well as in the speculations of philosophers such as J. B. Robinet and G. T. Fechner; and pan-psychism—the view that all matter is psychical or has a psychical aspect—which was held by Spinoza ('omnia quamvis diversis gradibus animata' [*Ethics*, ii. prop. xiii. note]) and Leibniz, is common to the numerous advocates whom pluralism finds at the present day. It is doubtful whether hylozoism, with its assertion that all matter is organized or living, can be maintained without the further assumption of pan-psychism, that the real elements of the world, and all that we call 'things,' are psychical entities endowed with 'being for self'; and, indeed, many writers seem to use the term 'hylozoism' as if it included the latter doctrine. But, without this added implication, and taken in the etymological sense alone, hylozoism involves the repudiation of most of the consequences drawn from rigid materialism. For it denies the inertia of matter and the statement that motion is exclusively caused by external forces, crediting material bodies with capacity for self-movement, and regarding life as an inherent or essential property of all matter as such. Thus, as Kant saw, hylozoism is the death-blow to science—'science' being understood, as Kant understood it, to mean *a priori* pure or mathematical physics. The latter kind of knowledge being assumed by Kant to be necessary and universal, he could write thus:

'The possibility of living matter cannot even be thought; its concept involves a contradiction because lifelessness, *inertia*, constitutes the essential character of matter' (*Kritik of Judgment*, tr. J. H. Bernard, London, 1892, p. 304).

While Kant thus saw that hylozoism meant ruin to science in so far as it involves the calculability (by an intelligence higher than ours, though strictly finite like that imagined by Laplace) of all past and future states of the world from a sufficient knowledge of the position and motion of each of its mass-points at any given moment, modern upholders of the mind-stuff hypothesis, and of Haeckel's hylozoistic or pan-psychic theory, have not been so clear-sighted. They would retain materialism, for all intents and purposes, while changing its name. Qualitative monism is, indeed, in all its forms a position of unstable equilibrium; or, to change the metaphor, it is a half-way house (for temporary lodging) between materialism and spiritualism. And, as retreat upon materialism becomes more and more impossible, as hylozoism is seen to possess greater capacity to explain actuality than the doctrine of dead and absolutely inert matter, and as, finally, life means the power to act or change according to an internal principle, while only one such principle is known to us—*i.e.* thought, together with feeling, desire, and will, which depend upon it—it will doubtless come to be more and more plainly seen that the implications of natural science are not materialistic but spiritualistic.

LITERATURE.—F. A. Lange, *History of Materialism*, Eng. tr., London, 1877–81; R. Flint, *Anti-theistic Theories*, Edinburgh, 1879; F. Paulsen, *Einleitung in die Philosophie*, Berlin, 1893; J. Ward, *Naturalism and Agnosticism*³, London, 1907 (for epistemological questions involved); O. Külpe, *Introduction to Philosophy*, Eng. tr., do. 1897.

F. R. TENNANT.

MATERIALISM (Chinese).—Chinese religion and philosophy have been declared by many writers to be materialistic; one of them[1] went even so far as to regard materialism as a special creed taking rank with Confucianism, Taoism, and Buddhism. This view implies a misconception of materialism: a philosopher who does not believe in a personal God, or who assigns to a Supreme Being a substantial body, is not a materialist. Materialism assumes matter to be the only basis of reality. This is 'cosmological materialism,' to be distinguished from 'ethical materialism,' which sees the aim of life in egotism, pleasure, and sensuality. Both are to be found in China, but they are not at the root of her great religious systems, although materialistic tendencies may be found occasionally. Nobody will seriously think of imputing materialism to the Buddhist faith, which teaches that the visible world is nothing but a semblance, a vision without any reality. Taoism takes a similar view-point: there exists nothing except Tao, the Absolute, a supernatural, incomprehensible entity. But how about Confucianism, which has often been described as materialistic?

Confucius himself owned to a 'benevolent agnosticism,' declining all metaphysical speculations, but was not averse to popular beliefs and customs. To a disciple asking him about death he replied, 'While you do not know life, how can you know about death?' and on another occasion he made the remark, 'Show respect to the spirits, but keep aloof from them.'[2] He believed in a superior being which he called Heaven, but never used the personal name God—a fact by which he laid himself open to the charge of atheism. Probably he had no clear notion of heaven, but certainly he did not conceive it as an anthropomorphic god. Still more than Confucius himself his followers, especially the philosophers of the Sung period (12th cent. A.D.), have been denounced as materialists, but unjustly. The system of Chu Hsi, the head of this school, is a pure dualism. He recognizes two principles, matter and reason, and to the latter even concedes priority. Out of their combination the world was evolved. Matter splits into the five elements (metal, wood, water, fire, and earth); reason is the life- and mind-producing element, which also contains the virtues (benevolence, righteousness, propriety, and knowledge).

Another kind of dualism savouring much of materialism was in vogue in ancient China, and seems to have been the starting-point of Chu Hsi's philosophy. At the earlier stages of civilization religion, philosophy, and sciences are usually not yet separated. So it was in China, where we meet with the dualistic theory of *yin* and *yang* in Confucian as well as in Taoist works. It was the first germ of a natural philosophy universally accepted by the Chinese irrespective of their religious convictions or philosophic ideas. In the commentary to the *Yi King* ascribed to Tse-sse, the grandson of Confucius (5th cent. B.C.), we read that the origin of existence is due to the cosmic dual forces *yin* and *yang*; *yang* is the bright, male, generative principle, *yin* the dark, female, and receptive power; *yang* forms the heaven, *yin* the earth. Most Chinese critics look upon these principles as material substances—an interpretation open to doubt. But we have another testimony by the Taoist writer Lieh-tse of the same time, showing that he at least considered the *yin* and the *yang* to be substances. The evolution theory, though not quite scientific, reminds us of that of modern naturalists.

'The sages of old held that the Yang and the Yin govern heaven and earth. Now, form being born out of the formless, from what do heaven and earth take their origin? It is said: There was a great evolution, a great inception, a great beginning, and a great homogeneity. During the great evolution, Vapours were still imperceptible, in the great inception Vapours originate, in the great beginning Forms appear, and during the great homogeneity Substances are produced. The pure and light matter becomes the heaven above, the turbid and heavy matter forms the earth below' (Lieh-tse, i. 27).

No divine being intervenes in the creation of the world, and yet we are not justified in calling Lieh-tse a materialist, for, notwithstanding this materialistic theory, the highest principle remains Tao, a spiritual being which alone is endowed with reality; the world with all its changes is imaginary.

At an early age the Chinese had further developed this dualistic theory of *yin* and *yang* by enlarging on the working of the five elements which were conceived as physical and as metaphysical essences as well. They were believed to predominate and vanquish one another in regular turns, thus bringing about the four seasons: in spring the element wood reigns supreme, in summer fire, in autumn metal, and in winter water; to earth there is no corresponding season. The elements have their seat in different directions: wood in the east, fire in the south, earth in the centre, metal in the west, and water in the north. They are ruled by five deities, the genii of the seasons and the four quarters.

Whereas this attempt at natural philosophy is nothing but a medley of heterogeneous, more or less fanciful, thoughts, the old dualistic theory was transformed into a consistent materialistic system by the sceptic Wang Ch'ung (1st cent. A.D.). From various utterances it would appear that he thought of *yang* as a fiery and of *yin* as a watery element. The former produced the sun, the moon, and the other stars of heaven, while from water and its sediments earth, the oceans, and the atmosphere were developed. Both fluids are in constant motion, but their movement is not governed by any intelligence or subservient to the purpose of any *spiritus rector*; it is spontaneous and regulated solely by its own inherent natural laws; heaven and earth do not act on purpose, nor are they endowed with consciousness. Wang Ch'ung rejects all anthropomorphisms which have clustered

1 H. A. Giles, *Religions of Ancient China*.
2 *Anal.* xi. 11, vi. 20.

round the idea of heaven or God. The human body is formed of the two fluids, the *yin* producing the body, and the *yang* the vital spirit and the mind. At death they again disperse, the *yang*, or heavenly fluid, returning to its original state of unconsciousness. Consequently there can be no immortality, which Chu Hsi likewise disclaims.

Wang Ch'ung's materialism has not had any serious influence on the Chinese people, not because they had a horror of materialism, as many Westerners have, but owing to Wang Ch'ung's bold criticisms on the national sages, Confucius and Mencius, which they have never condoned. So far as we know, Wang Ch'ung is the only Chinese thinker who set forth a scientific system of cosmological materialism.

Already in the 4th cent. B.C. ethical materialism found an advocate in Yang Chu, the philosopher of egoism and pessimism. He maintains that in human life happiness is far exceeded by misfortune, and that this is the result of the badness of the world and of men's own doing. The practice of virtue is of no avail, because in this world the wicked thrive, and the virtuous are visited with disasters. Therefore men ought not to harass themselves in striving after unattainable or useless aims such as wealth, honour, or fame, or sacrifice themselves for others, but should enjoy their short span and be satisfied with the good that they have, for with death everything ends. In consequence of the vehement impeachments of Mencius this doctrine has never got a hold on the Chinese mind.

Both Yang Chu and Wang Ch'ung have been long buried in oblivion, until they were redeemed from it by the congenial interest of foreign admirers.

LITERATURE.—W. Grube, 'Die chinesische Philosophie,' in *Allgemeine Geschichte der Philosophie* (*Kultur der Gegenwart*, i. 5), Berlin, 1909; H. A. Giles, *Religions of Ancient China*, London, 1905; E. Faber, *Der Naturalismus bei den alten Chinesen; Werke des Philosophen Licius*, Elberfeld, 1877; L. Giles, *Taoist Teachings from the Book of Lieh Tzŭ*, London, 1912; A. Forke, 'Yang Chu, the Epicurean, in his Relation to Lieh-tse, the Pantheist,' in *Journ. Peking Oriental Society*, iii. [1893], no. 3; L. Cranmer-Byng and A. Forke, *Yang Chu's Garden of Pleasure*, London, 1912; A. David, *Les Théories individualistes dans la philosophie chinoise* (*Yang-Tchou*), Paris, 1909; A. Forke, *Lun Hêng*, Berlin, 1907-11, pt. i., 'Philosophical Essays of Wang Ch'ung'; pt. ii., 'Miscellaneous Essays of Wang Ch'ung'; S. Le Gall, *Tchou-Hi; sa doctrine, son influence*, Shanghai, 1894.

A. FORKE.

MATERIALISM (Indian).

—1. We possess several comparatively modern works which set forth the various philosophic systems of India—e.g., *Summary of all the Systems*,[1] and *Reunion of the Six Systems*.[2] The systems are arranged in the order of their increasing orthodoxy, from the author's point of view: the first, for which, as we shall see, materialism is a suitable name, is the worst of all, and the only one which is expressly in contradiction with the general conception of Indian philosophy and mysticism.

In more ancient sources—in the *Mahābhārata*, on the one side, and in the Buddhist scriptures, canonical or scholastic, on the other—we find data concerning this materialistic system which are scanty but generally in agreement.[3]

As regards the sources that would give us direct information about the materialist school only a few citations can be brought forward, and their authenticity is not certain.[1]

We are not convinced that a materialistic 'school,' a 'system,' in the exact sense of the word, existed. There have been 'materialists' who have entertained some very well-defined theories, to whom the 'spiritualists,' whether Brāhmans, Buddhists, or Jains, give different names, and whose opinions are, perhaps artificially, grouped in the works of which we have spoken.

The most characteristic name is Nāstikas, literally 'deniers,' 'misbelievers,' those who say *na asti*, οὐκ ἔστι.[2] The most famous are (*a*) Chārvākas (difficult to interpret; Chārvāka is said to be the founder of the sect; he is undoubtedly the demoniac ogre spoken of in the *Mahābhārata*);[3] (*b*) Lokāyatas,[4] 'worldly,' 'spread throughout the world' (a term which, according to T. W. Rhys Davids, denotes primarily the knowledge of nature-lore, and whose adherents are said to be the 'explainers of [the genesis of] the world'); and (*c*) Bārhaspatyas, 'disciples of Bṛhaspati' (the chaplain of the Vedic gods and the lord of wisdom).

2. In the Buddhist *Suttas* the doctrine of materialism is attributed to 'Ajita of the garment of hair,' one of the scholars and famous ascetics of the time of Buddha. He said:

> 'There is no such thing as alms or sacrifice or offering. There is neither fruit nor result of good and evil deeds. There is no such thing as this world or the next. There is neither father nor mother, nor beings springing into life without them. There are in the world no recluses or Brāhmans . . . who, having understood and realised, by themselves alone, both this world and the next, make their wisdom known to others. A human being is built up of the four elements. When he dies, the earthy in him returns and relapses to the earth, the fluid to the water, the heat to the fire, the windy to the air, and his faculties [=the five senses, and the mind as a sixth] pass into space [or ether]. The four bearers, on the bier as a fifth, take his dead body away; till they reach the burning-ground men utter forth eulogies, but there his bones are bleached, and his offerings end in ashes. It is a doctrine of fools, this talk of gifts. It is an empty lie, mere idle talk, when men say there is profit therein. Fools and wise alike, on the dissolution of the body, are cut off, annihilated, and after death they are not.'[5]

It will be seen (1) that these formulæ show a really authentic character. They are quite independent of Buddhism, for the Buddhists do not believe much more than Ajita in the use of sacrifice and offering. Perhaps they come from the Agnikas or Jaṭilas (ascetics who give burnt offerings, who have braided hair), who entered in large numbers

[1] Skr. text, ed. Calcutta, 1858, and Poona, 1906; *The Sarvadarśana-saṃgraha, or Review of the different Systems of Hindu Philosophy*, by Mādhavāchārya (A.D. 1331), tr. E. B. Cowell and A. E. Gough, London, 1882; Germ. tr. (which owes much to Cowell's work, but does not mention it) in P. Deussen, *Allgemeine Geschichte der Philosophie*, I. iii. (Leipzig, 1908).

[2] *Ṣaḍdarśanasamuchchaya*, by Haribhadra († A.D. 528), ed. L. Suali, Calcutta, 1905 (the chapter which interests us has been translated into French by L. Suali, in *Muséon*, ix. [1908] 277 ff.); among the other 'modern' sources is the *Prabodhachandrodaya*, xxvii. 18 (11th cent.).

[3] For the *Mahābhārata* see E. W. Hopkins, *The Great Epic of India*, New York, 1901, and the works on materialism cited in the bibliography; *Bhagavad-Gītā*, xvi. 6 (tr. L. D. Barnett, Temple Classics Series, London, 1905, p. 158).

[1] Citations in the 'summaries' mentioned in notes 1 and 2 on previous col.; and also in the Buddhist sources (see p. 494[a], n. 4).

[2] *Maitrī Upaniṣad*, Manu, *Mahābhārata*; the name originally extended to all kinds of sceptics, deniers of the Vedic gods, or of the Brāhmanic laws (see below).

[3] See O. Böhtlingk and R. Roth, *Sanskrit-Wörterbuch*, Petrograd, 1855-75, ii. 997.

[4] See Rhys Davids, *Dialogues of the Buddha*, i. (Oxford, 1899) 14, 110, 139, 166. C. Bendall (*Athenæum*, 30th June 1900) rightly remarks that Rhys Davids is wrong in saying: 'Of the real existence of a school of philosophy that called itself by the name [Lokāyata] there is no trace.' The traces are numerous. See also art. LOKĀYATA.

[5] *Dīgha Nikāya*, i. 55; *Saṁyutta Nikāya*, iii. 307; *Majjhima Nikāya*, i. 515, and also in the Sanskrit sources. This passage has often been translated. The version reproduced above is that of Rhys Davids, *Dialogues of the Buddha*, i. 73. Attention should be drawn to those of E. Burnouf (*Le Lotus de la bonne loi*, Paris, 1852), P. Grimblot (*Sept Suttas pâlis*, do. 1876), and R. O. Franke (*Dīghanikāya in Auswahl übersetzt*, Göttingen, 1913). The sacred writings of the Jains contain the same evidence, and confirm the Buddhist tradition (see H. Jacobi, *Jaina Sūtras*, ii. pp. xxiii, 339, 343; *SBE* xlv. [1895]).

A more complete study would describe the opinions of Pūraṇa Kassapa, another materialist contemporary with Buddha (*Dīgha*, i. 52), who denies responsibility, and teaches what is called the 'theory of non-action': 'If with a discus with an edge sharp as a razor he should make all living creatures on the earth one heap, one mass of flesh, there would be no guilt thence resulting, no increase of guilt would ensue'; and the opinions of Makkhali, who denies liberty: 'There is no such thing as power or energy, or human strength or human vigour. . . . Beings are bent this way and that by their fate, by their individual nature,' and comes very near the well-known point of view of the *Mahābhārata*, namely, the omnipotence of fate (*daiva*) and the weakness of human activity (*puruṣakāra*). It was Buddha who said that fate (*daiva*) is only the sum of our former actions.

into the primitive community, and for whom the time of novitiate was shortened 'because they believed in the retribution of actions.'

(2) Ajita does not believe in life after death or re-birth; he believes only in the four elements, earth, water, heat, wind, conceived in a materialistic sense; he therefore denies the fifth element, consciousness or cognition (*vijñāna*), which, under different names and in different manners, constitutes, in the 'orthodox' or 'spiritualistic' systems, the essential of what the West calls the 'soul.'[1] The doctrine attributed to the materialists by later sources, viz. that 'thought develops in the human body from a special mixture of the elements like the intoxicating power of the fermentation of the grain or of the juice of the sugar-cane,' arises quite naturally from this ancient theory of Ajita.

(3) Ajita denies the fruit of good and bad actions, and, consequently, morality. He is a Nāstika, a 'denier.' He certainly denies sacrifice, supernatural births, etc., but, of all these denials, the denial of the remuneration of good and bad actions is the most monstrous. The Buddhist works teach that false opinion (*mithyādṛṣṭi*) consists essentially in this denial, which destroys the 'roots of merit' and causes a man to commit all kinds of sin.[2]

Ajita seems to have led an ascetic life; but 'unbelievers,' 'deniers,' are usually 'libertines,' if we believe our sources, which attribute to them sayings like the following:

'As long as we live we ought to live happily, enjoying the pleasures of the senses. How can the body reappear after it has been reduced to ashes?'[3]

3. What leads us to believe that there was, properly speaking, a materialist school, is the double philosophical theory that our texts attribute to the deniers.

(*a*) 'The only means of knowledge (*pramāṇa*) is the immediate evidence of the senses.' All orthodox Indian schools are wrong in appealing to induction (*anumāna*) or to authority (the word of a competent person, of an omniscient being [*sarvajña*], or of the Veda).

A sentence belonging to the literature of the materialists says: 'There is nothing in man except what is visible to the senses. Look, dear friend, at what these so-called scholars call the traces of the wolf.'[4] A man who wanted to convert—let us say 'pervert'—a woman to his materialist opinions, went out of the town with her, and on the dust of the road he drew with the thumbs, index fingers, and middle fingers of his two hands, marks resembling the footprints of a wolf. In the morning the scholars said: 'Assuredly a wolf came last night from the forest; for otherwise it would be impossible that there could be a wolf's footprints on the road.' And the man said to the woman: 'See, dear friend, what clever thinkers these men are who maintain that induction proves the existence of supra-sensible objects, and who are regarded as scholars by the crowd.'

(*b*) Denying induction, these philosophers without philosophy are forced to deny causality. The name Svābhāvikas is given to the scholars who believe that things, the colour of the lotus and the sharpness of thorns, are born from the *svabhāva*, 'own nature.' Much could be said on the exact value of this word; it probably means: 'Things are not produced by causes; they are because they are.'[1]

[1] Among the questions which the Buddha refused to examine (see AGNOSTICISM [Buddhist], vol. i. p. 221b) occurs this one: 'Is the vital principle (*jīva*) the same thing as the body (*śarīra*)? Is it different from the body?' The Buddha condemns the two opposite opinions and constructs a middle way.

In order to exhaust the Pāli material on the question of materialism, one must read also the *Pāyāsi Suttanta* (see the tr. in Rhys Davids, *op. cit.* ii. 347), in which there is a discussion not only on the existence of another world, gods, etc., but also on the existence of the soul.

[2] See *Abhidharmakośabhāṣya*, ch. iv., tr. in *Muséon*, xv. [1914] 3 f.

[3] *Ṣaḍdarśanasamuchchaya*; see *Muséon*, ix. [1908] 282.

[4] *Lokatattvanirṇaya* (*Giorn. Soc. asiat. ital.* xviii. [1905] 290); *Ṣaḍdarśanasamuchchaya*, in *Muséon*, ix. 380; *Madhyamakavṛtti*, Petrograd, 1908, p. 360; *Madhyamakāvatāra*, do. 1909, p. 209.

LITERATURE.—A. M. Pizzagalli, *Nāstika, Cārvāka e Lokāyatika, contributo alla storia del materialismo nell' India antica*, Pisa, 1907, 'Sulla Setta degli Svabhāvavādinaḥ,' in *Reale Istituto lombardo di scienze e lettere*, xlvi. [1913] 104; L. Suali, 'Matériaux pour servir à l'histoire du matérialisme indien,' *Muséon*, ix. [1908] 277. Besides these special works see H. T. Colebrooke, *Essays on the Religion and Philosophy of the Hindus*², London, 1858; A. Barth, *The Religions of India*, do. 1882, Index; F. Max Müller, *The Six Systems of Indian Philosophy*², do. 1903, pp. 94–104.

L. DE LA VALLÉE POUSSIN.

MATHURĀ

MATHURĀ (Muttra).—The name Mathurā, or Muttra, is borne by both a district and a town in the United Provinces of Agra and Oudh. The District (1445 sq. m.) lies to the north of the Agra District, and includes many places sacred to the worship of Kṛṣṇa, the most notable being the small towns of Brindāban, Gobardhan, Gokul, and Mahāban (*qq.v.*). Mathurā town or city stands on the right bank of the Jumnā, on the main road from Āgra to Delhi, in 27° 30′ N., 77° 41′ E. (pop. in 1901, 60,042). The city, which is of immemorial antiquity, was placed by early Hindu writers in the country of the Śaurasenas, and was reckoned by Ptolemy (*c.* A.D. 140) to be one of the three cities of the Kaspeiraioi. He calls it Modoura (Μόδουρα), 'the city of the gods' (VII. i. 50). Arrian writes the name as Methora (Μέθορα [*Indica*, viii. 5]), and Pliny (*HN* vi. 19) uses the same spelling. An alternative Hindu literary name was Madhupura, now represented by the village Maholi, which 'is so close to the city as almost to form one of its suburbs' (Growse, *Memoir*, p. 4). Aurangzīb, who destroyed the temples, changed the name to Islāmābad or Islāmpur (*ib.* pp. 6, 35), but the new name never became current (see *Num. Chron.*, 4th ser., ii. [1902] 282). The city was plundered by Maḥmūd of Ghaznī in A.D. 1018–19 and again by Aḥmad Shāh Durrānī in 1757. The greater part of the District came under British rule in 1803.

Mathurā, one of the seven sacred cities of the Hindus, is second only to Benares (*q.v.*) in sanctity. The city and the western half of the District, known as the Braj-maṇḍal, are now associated almost exclusively with the legend and cult of the cow-herd demi-god Kṛṣṇa, but in ancient days the locality was as sacred to Jains and Buddhists as it was to Brāhmanical Hindus. The literature concerning the religious history and antiquities of Mathurā is extensive, and new objects of interest are constantly coming to light. It is impossible here to do more than indicate the importance of the locality in the history of Indian religions and the exceptional interest of the broken remains which have escaped from repeated Muslim violence.

Mathurā, being situated between the Muhammadan capitals of Agra and Delhi, was specially exposed for centuries to iconoclastic attacks. Hardly any ancient Hindu building of importance is now standing, and the valuable sculptures which make the district famous among archæologists have mostly been discovered by excavation. The sculptures and remains of buildings in an extremely fragmentary state are found in the city and for many miles round.

[1] On the Svabhāvavādins or Svābhāvikas see O. Strauss, *Ethische Probleme aus dem Mahābhārata*, Florence, 1912, p. 242; *Buddhacharita*, ix. 48 (*SBE* xlix. [1894] 99), and C. Formichi, *Açvaghoṣa poeta del Buddhismo*, Bari, 1912, p. 231; *Madhyamakāvatāra*, p. 205, tr. in *Muséon*, xii. [1911] 258 ff.; *Bodhicharyāvatāra*, Calcutta, 1911, p. 541 (ix. 117); *Gauḍapādakārikās*, Poona, 1900; *Bull. de l'École française d'Extrême-Orient*, iv. [1904] 1013; on the Svābhāvika sect in Nepāl see B. H. Hodgson, *Essays on Languages, Literature, Religion of Nepal and Tibet*, London, 1874.

The objects connected with the Jain cult have been discovered for the most part in the Kankālī or Jainī Ṭīlā (mound) to the S.W. of the city, which was the site of two Jain temples, one Digambara and the other Śvetāmbara, as well as of a remarkable *stūpa*, the only Jain monument of the kind about which details are known. In its earliest form it dated from remote antiquity, possibly from 600 or even 700 B.C. The Jain faith was vigorous in the Kushān period early in the Christian era, and the images found came down to the 11th century. At the present day Jains are few and unpopular in the Mathurā District, their principal settlement being at Kosi, where there are three temples.

The numerous Buddhist remains, which are of great interest, disclose the former existence of an important monastery founded by Huviṣka Kushān, probably early in the 2nd cent. after Christ. In Fa-Hian's time (A.D. 405) there were twenty Buddhist monasteries with some 3000 monks in the neighbourhood of Mathurā. When Hiuen Tsiang travelled, more than two centuries later, the number of monks had diminished. The Muhammadan attacks from A.D. 1018 onwards wiped out the Buddhist establishments. There are plain indications that the popular Buddhism of Mathurā included a sensual erotic element, which probably has contributed to the subsequent development of the Rādhā and Kṛṣṇa worship now specially associated with the Mathurā region. Nāga worship was much practised during the Kushān period.

Brāhmanical Hinduism appears to be the most ancient of the Mathurā religions. The Greek writers call the chief local god by the name of Herakles, and the sculpture representing the fight of Herakles with the Nemean lion is one of the most famous of Mathurā antiquities.

The temple of Kesava Deva at the Katrā on the western side of the city, rebuilt early in the 17th cent., was described by J. B. Tavernier (*c.* A.D. 1650; *Travels in India*, tr. V. Ball, London, 1889, ii. 240) as 'one of the most sumptuous buildings in all India.' Aurangzīb destroyed it in 1669, and built a mosque on the site. All the old Hindu temples in the city were destroyed by the Muhammadans at one time or another.

Archæological evidence shows that the cultus of Kṛṣṇa was well established as early as the 4th and 5th cent. after Christ (Bhitarī inscr. of Skandagupta, *c.* A.D. 456; sculptures at Maṇḍōr in Mārwār [*Arch. Surv. Ann. Rep.*, 1905–06, p. 140]), but the Vaiṣṇava cultus of Mathurā in its present form was not developed until the close of the 16th cent. under the influence of the Bengālī Gosāins of Brindāban. The history and character of the cult are well described by Growse, to whose book the reader is referred. The great temple of Viṣṇu under the name of Rang Jī, built between 1845 and 1851 by local merchant princes, is remarkable for being designed on Dravidian lines. It cost 4½ millions of rupees. The notorious erotic sect of Vaiṣṇavas founded by Vallabhāchārya (*q.v.*) (born A.D. 1479) has its headquarters in the town of Gokul.

Three Christian missions (Baptist, Church Missionary, and Methodist Episcopal) are established in the city.

LITERATURE.—*IGI*, Oxford, 1908, *s.vv.* 'Muttra,' 'Brindāban,' 'Gobardhan,' 'Mahāban'; E. Thornton, *A Gazetteer of Territories under the East India Co. and of Native States*, London, 1854, *s.vv.* 'Muttra,' 'Bindraban,' 'Gokul,' 'Goverdhun,' 'Muhabun'; J. Tieffenthaler, *Géographie de l'Indoustan*, Fr. tr. by J. Bernouilli, Berlin, 1781, pp. 201–207; F. S. Growse, *Mathurā: a District Memoir*³, with numerous illustrations, Allahabad, 1883; 'Mathurā Notes' (*JASB* xlvii. pt. i. [1878] 97–134). The antiquities are treated in detail in *Arch. Surv. of India, Reports*, ed. A. Cunningham, vols. i. iii. xi. xvii. xx., Calcutta, 1871–85, *Annual Reports*, ed. J. H. Marshall; J. P. Vogel, 'The Mathurā School of Sculpture' (*Rep.* for 1906–07, pp. 137–160), Calcutta, 1909; 'Nāga Worship in Ancient Mathurā' (*Rep.* for 1908–09, pp. 156–163), Calcutta, 1912; V. A. Smith, *The Jain Stūpa and other Antiquities of Mathurā*, Allahabad, 1901; J. H. Marshall, *JRAS*, 1911, pp. 149–153; Vogel, *ib.* 1912, pp. 118–123; J. Kennedy, 'Kṛishṇa of Mathurā,' *ib.* 1907, pp. 975–991; F. W. Thomas, 'The Inscriptions on the Mathurā Lion Capital' (*Ep. Ind.* x. [1907–08] 135–147); Vogel, *Catalogue of the Archæol. Museum at Mathurā*, Allahabad, 1910 (with detailed bibliography, pp. vi–x). See also the *Travels* of Fa-Hian and Hiuen Tsiang, the Chinese pilgrims, in any of the trr., and V. A. Smith, *A History of Fine Art in India and Ceylon*, Oxford, 1911.

VINCENT A. SMITH.

MĀTṚCHEṬA.—Mātṛcheṭa is the name of a Buddhist author, identified by the Tibetan historian of Buddhism, Tāranātha, with Aśvaghoṣa, concerning whom and the identification itself see art. AŚVAGHOṢA and the works there mentioned. It may be pointed out that the identification is made only by Tāranātha, while a much older writer, the Chinese traveller I-tsing (2nd half of 7th cent. A.D.), plainly distinguishes the two authors; further, the ascriptions of works seem not to betray either in the Chinese tradition or, with one exception (see *Kavīndravavachana-samuchchhaya*, ed. F. W. Thomas, in *Bibliotheca Indica*, new ser., no. 1309, pp. 25–29), in the Tibetan any confusion. The sole reason for the identification is the fact that both writers stood in relation to Kaniṣka. But this reason will be seen upon reflexion to have actually a contrary bearing; for nothing is more certain concerning Aśvaghoṣa than that he was a figure at the court of Kaniṣka, whereas we have an epistle from Mātṛcheṭa declining, upon grounds of old age and sickness, to visit the king. Perhaps this is the reason why Tāranātha, identifying the two poets, makes an untenable distinction between the Kaniṣka of Aśvaghoṣa and the Kanika of Mātṛcheṭa.

According to Tāranātha, Mātṛcheṭa was the son of a rich Brāhman named Saṅghaguhya, who married the youngest of ten Buddhist daughters of a merchant belonging to the city of Khorta (Gauḍa?). The time is given as during the reign of Śrīchandra, nephew and successor of Bindusāra—a statement which reflects the confusion of the Tibetan author's chronological system. The name given to the child at birth is said to have been Kāla; that he was subsequently known as Mātṛcheṭa and Pitṛcheṭa is set down to his filial devotion. We must, however, distrust the whole story; Saṅghaguhya is not a suitable name for a Brāhman, nor is a marriage with a Buddhist woman very probable. The name Mātṛcheṭa, which in later times was attached to other persons, means, no doubt, like its equivalent Mātṛdāsa, 'servant of the Mother (*i.e.* Durgā), or of the Mothers (*i.e.* the forms of Durgā)'; and this is quite in harmony with the fact that Mātṛcheṭa was at first a worshipper of Maheśvara-Śiva (Tāranātha and I-tsing) and composed hymns in his praise (I-tsing). He became an expert in *Mantra* and *Tantra* formulas and a master of dialectic. In the latter capacity he entered upon a course of controversy with the Buddhists of Oḍiviśa (Orissa), Gauḍa, Tīrahūti (Tirhut), Kāmarūpa, and elsewhere, forcing them to join the heretics, whereby he acquired the soubriquet Durdharṣa-Kāla, 'the unassailable Kāla.' At the suggestion of his mother, who hoped for his conversion by the leading doctors of her faith, he proceeded to the great Buddhist centre of Nālanda, where, in fact, he was overthrown in argument and joined the order.

According to Tāranātha, the agent of his conversion was Ārya Deva, who showed him a *sūtra* wherein he had been foretold by Buddha. If we must reject the introduction of Ārya Deva, which involves an anachronism and is due to a certain confusion (see *IA* xxxii. [1903] 346), the incident is confirmed by the statement of I-tsing that Buddha, on hearing the notes of a nightingale, had said: 'The bird, transported with joy at sight of me, unconsciously utters its melodious notes. On account of this good deed, after my Departure (Nirvâna) this bird shall be born in human form, and named Mâtriketa; and he shall praise my virtues with true appreciation' (*Record*, tr. Takakusu, p. 156 f.). We recognize here one of the prophecies (*vyākaraṇa*, *vikurvaṇa*) narrated in connexion with many Buddhist divines and others, in this case involving, perhaps, also an interpretation of the name in Prākrit form, *Mātichiṭa* = *mām atichitta*, 'transported with joy (at sight of) me.' However this may be, we have in Mātṛcheṭa's own work (*Varṇanārhavarṇana*, vv. 1–3 and 30 f.) allusions both to his previous heretical poems and to the supposed prophecy of Buddha.

The remainder of Mātṛcheṭa's career may be recorded in the words of Tāranātha (tr. Schiefner, p. 91 f.):

'At the time when Mātṛcheṭa was converted to the Buddha-doctrine, the number of heretics and Brāhmans in the Vihāras of the four quarters, who had entered the order, was very great. It was thought that, if the greatest ornament of the Brāhmans, Durdharṣa-Kāla, had shaken off his own system like the dust of his shoes and turned to the Buddha-doctrine, that Buddha-doctrine must be in truth a great marvel. Consequently there were in Nālanda alone more than a thousand Brāhman monks, and an equal number from the heretics. The Āchārya, being full of great service to religion, collected on his daily perambulations in the city for alms immense quantities of food, wherewith he entertained five hundred Bhikṣus, namely two hundred and fifty sunk in contemplation and two hundred and fifty studying, leaving them to their uninterrupted occupation. . . . The hymns composed by him are also spread abroad in all lands: as finally singers and strollers chanted them and faith in Buddha grew mightily among all the people in the land, greater service was, through the hymns, rendered to the spread of the doctrine. Towards the end of his life king Kanika sent an envoy to invite the Āchārya, who, however, as he was prevented by old age from going, composed an epistle and converted the king to the doctrine. He sent his own pupil Jñānapriya to the king as instructor. Irrespective of the *Jātaka* stories found in the *Sūtras* and other works, he desired to put into writing the ten times ten birth-stories, corresponding to the ten *Pāramitās*, which were transmitted from ear to ear by the Paṇḍits and Āchāryas: but after composing thirty-four he died. According to some biographies, it is related that, having reflected that the Bodhisattva had given his body to a tigress and so forth, he had thought he could do the same, as it was no unfeasible act. Seeing, accordingly, a hungry tigress attended by her young, he essayed to surrender his body, but at first could hardly accomplish it. But, when a still stronger faith in Buddha was kindled in him and he had with his own blood written down the prayer in seventy verses, he first gave the tigress his blood to drink, whereby he lent her weakened frame a little strength, and then surrendered his own body. Others assert that the person who thus acted was an Āchārya Parahitasvarakāntāra, who came after Mātṛcheṭa. The latter composed the abstract of the *Prajñāpāramitā* and many other *Śāstras*, and wrought many benefactions to the Bhikṣus of both the Great and the Little Vehicle: as he (Mātṛcheṭa) did not confine himself to the Mahāyāna alone, and the Śrāvakas were very devoted to him, he is greatly renowned as a general hero of the orthodox.'

The testimony of I-tsing, earlier by some 900 years, is not less emphatic (p. 157 f.):

'He composed first a hymn consisting of four hundred ślokas, and afterwards another of one hundred and fifty. . . . These charming compositions are equal in beauty to the heavenly flowers, and the high principles which they contain rival in dignity the lofty peaks of a mountain. Consequently in India all who compose hymns imitate his style, considering him the father of literature. Even men like the Bodhisattvas Asaṅga and Vasubandhu admired him greatly.

Throughout India every one who becomes a monk is taught Mâtriketa's two hymns as soon as he can recite the five and ten precepts (Sîla).

This course is adopted by both the Mahâyâna and Hînayâna schools. . . . There are many who have written commentaries on them, nor are the imitations of them few. Bodhisattva *G*ina [Dignāga] himself composed such an imitation. He added one verse before each of the one hundred and fifty verses, so that they became altogether three hundred verses, called the "Mixed" hymns. . . . A celebrated priest of the Deer Park, Sâkyadeva by name, again added one verse to each of *G*ina's, and consequently they amounted to four hundred and fifty verses (slokas), called the "Doubly Mixed" hymns.'

He proceeds to include Nāgārjuna and Aśvaghoṣa among those who imitated Mātṛcheṭa. The renown and influence echoed in these statements are further substantiated by the fact that the two hymns particularized were translated, as well as others, into Tibetan, and one of them, the 'Hymn in One Hundred and Fifty Verses' also (by I-tsing himself) into Chinese; moreover, the originals have been found in various fragments among the MS trouvailles from Chinese Turkestan, so that in due time it will be possible to form a first-hand appreciation of the poet's work. Pending the complete publication, we may base our estimate upon what has already been made public and upon the very literal Tibetan versions and the English rendering of a portion of the *Varṇanārhavarṇana* hymn, and of the whole 'Epistle to King Kaniṣka.'

The former, the 'Delineation of the Worthy to be Delineated,' is represented with obvious correctness as the earliest of the author's Buddhist compositions. Abjuring his previous heretical poems, he celebrates with great verve and abundance of poetic imagery the peerless excellences of Buddha and his doctrine. The hymn consists of four hundred verses, divided into twelve chapters with separate titles.

The 'Hymn in One Hundred and Fifty Verses' is quite similar in style and matter, as may be seen from the fragments already published, extending to about half of the poem. The amplified version (*samasyā*) with one hundred and fifty additional verses by Dignāga, constituting the 'mixed' (*miśraka*) hymn, quite corresponds to the description of I-tsing quoted above; the further amplified edition of Śākyadeva is not known. Concerning the minor hymns nothing need be said.

There are also two short tracts in verse, entitled respectively *Chaturviparyaya-kathā* and *Kaliyuga-parikathā*, the former treating of the miseries and deceptions of life, and the latter of the evils of the present Iron Age.

Undoubtedly the most interesting of Mātṛcheṭa's writings is the 'Epistle to King Kaniṣka' (*Mahārājakanika-lekha*). Beginning with excuses for not accepting the great king's invitation and for boldness in offering advice, he proceeds to counsel the young sovereign as to his moral policy, the concluding twenty out of eighty-five verses containing a pathetic appeal on behalf of dumb animals and deprecating the chase. The latter topic was familiar on Buddhist lips, as we may see from the Edicts of Aśoka. The whole epistle is full of mildness, gracious courtesy, and moral worth; that it is an old man's writing appears on the surface, and no doubt it is the latest of Mātṛcheṭa's compositions.

The statement that Mātṛcheṭa set the type for all later hymnologists is certainly so far true that all subsequent *stotras* are in the same form. This may fairly represent his quality as a poet: he displays great art in the use of language, much rhetorical skill, flow, and copiousness of matter. But the abstract nature of his conceptions, which are largely concerned with the dogmatic characteristics of the person and teaching of Buddha, and in consequence their often conventional character, place him upon a different level from his junior contemporary, the author of the *Buddhacharita*. Concerning the other writers who have been identified with him, Ārya-Śūra, Triratnadāsa, and Dhārmika-Subhūti, reference may be made to the literature given below.

LITERATURE.—i. LIST OF MĀTṚCHEṬA'S WORKS (for details of versions see the works cited below, iii.).—*Varṇanārhavarṇana-stotra*, *Śatapañchāśatika-stotra*, *Samyagbuddhalakṣaṇa-stotra*, *Triratnamaṅgala-stotra*, *Ekottarika-stotra*, *Sugatapañchatriṁśat-stotra*, *Triratna-stotra*, *Ārya-Tārādevī-stotra*, *Mātṛcheṭa-gīti*, *Chaturviparyaya-kathā*, *Kaliyuga-parikathā*.

ii. ORIENTAL AUTHORITIES.—I-tsing, *A Record of the Buddhist Religion*, tr. J. Takakusu, Oxford, 1896, pp. lv, 156 ff.; A. Schiefner, *Târanâtha's Geschichte des Buddhismus in Indien aus dem Tibetischen*, Petrograd, 1869, Index.

iii. EUROPEAN AND OTHER MODERN AUTHORS (as concerns Aśvaghoṣa see the literature at AŚVAGHOṢA).—T. Suzuki, *Açvaghosha's Discourse on the Awakening of Faith in the Mahâyâna*, Chicago, 1900, Introd.; F. W. Thomas, 'The Works of Āryaśūra, Triratnadāsa, and Dhārmika-Subhūti,' in

Album Kern, Leyden, 1903, pp. 405–408, 'Mātṛceṭa and the *Mahārājakanikalekha*,' in *IA* xxxii. [1903] 345–360, 'The *Varṇanārhavarṇana* of Mātṛceṭa,' *ib*. xxxiv. [1905] 145–163, *Kavīndravachana-samuchchhaya*, in *Bibliotheca Indica*, new ser., no. 1309 [1912], pp. 25–29; Sylvain Lévi, 'Notes sur les Indo-Scythes,' in *JA* IX. viii. [1896] 447–449, 455–456, n. 1, 'Açvaghoṣa,' *ib*. x. xii. [1908] 66–72; 'Textes sanscrits de Touen-Houang,' *ib*. x. xvi. [1910] 450–456; L. de la Vallée Poussin, 'Documents sanscrits de la collection M. A. Stein,' in *JRAS*, 1911, p. 757 ff.

F. W. THOMAS.

MATRIARCHATE.—See MOTHER-RIGHT.

MATTER.—In metaphysics matter is one of the ultimate principles or 'substances' of which phenomena are appearances or manifestations (dualism), or the sole substance in terms of which the universe is ultimately to be explained (materialistic monism, or materialism [*q.v.*]). In this sense matter is the reality, unknowable in itself, which underlies the properties of all particular things, in which those properties inhere, or by which, as impressions made on our senses, they are caused. It is the support, or substratum, of such qualities, supposed to be necessary in order to explain, in any given case, their constant co-existence as a group. The British empiricists, Locke, Berkeley, and Hume, minimized the importance of the conception of substance. Locke found the concept obscure and of little use; Berkeley dismissed matter as an abstraction and a superfluity; and Hume similarly banished spirit. Kant retained the conception in the sense of the permanent in all change. Modern phenomenalism, in so far as it preserves at all the concept of substance, and consequently of matter, regards it as denoting the unknown existent upon which physical properties somehow depend.

In the physical sciences matter is the substance—not in the sense of a metaphysical first principle, but rather in that of the 'stuff'—of which the sensible universe is composed. Its supposed action upon our sense-organs and nervous system gives rise to the totality of changing physical phenomena. Physical science dispenses with metaphysical 'matter,' as perhaps an anthropomorphism, and employs 'matter' to denote simply what is common to all material or sensible bodies, after subtraction of all their particular and diverse characteristics. In the time of Descartes, Boyle, and Locke a distinction was drawn between the primary and the secondary qualities of matter. The properties regarded as primary were extension, figure, and solidity, or impenetrability; and these were believed to inhere in matter, and to be in no way conditioned by our mind. The secondary qualities, such as colour, sound, and taste, on the other hand, were held not to subsist in matter itself; the ideas that we have of them were not supposed to be copies of anything existing independently of the mind—*i.e.*, whether perceived or not—but were regarded as due to sensations occasioned by the different size and motions of the minute particles of which matter is composed. It is doubtful whether in this respect there is any difference between the primary and the secondary qualities; and modern science retains the distinction only in so far as it tends to resolve the secondary qualities into quantitative relations, and to describe them in terms of analogies with the primary.

Absolute impenetrability, as a universal and essential property of matter, is not suggested by actual observation. Indeed, it was in all probability the observed penetrability of gross matter, especially in the gaseous form, that led to the first attempt to explain the properties of matter in terms of its atomic constitution. The happy guess of Democritus, scarcely based upon experiment or observation, was revived as a genuine scientific theory at the beginning of the 19th cent. by Dalton. The observed fact which seemed to this investigator to demand an atomic hypothesis of the constitution of matter was that chemical elements combine with one another in definite and invariable proportions by weight. This would naturally ensue if combination were the union of one or more atoms of the one element with one or more atoms of another, the atoms of each element being precisely alike in weight and in other respects, but different from those of other elements. The atomic theory has ever since Dalton's time been the foundation of the science of chemistry; and without some such hypothesis its facts and laws would be unintelligible.

But the notion of simple, impenetrable, hard atoms, such as Democritus postulated, is not free from difficulties. These atoms must be endowed with elasticity if they are to serve to explain certain physical phenomena; and this is incompatible with their simplicity. Difficulties of this kind led to the suggestion of Boscovich, that the atoms composing matter are not extended, hard bodies, but points, and centres of attractive and repulsive forces—forces whose magnitude varies with the distance between the points in such a way that no force, however great, can bring the points into coincidence. Thus extension and impenetrability were eliminated from the properties of the atom; but Boscovich's theory was never generally accepted because of the scientific prejudice against 'action at a distance,' or, in other words, because of the ingrained tendency to regard interaction between atoms to be conceivable only in terms of the kind of action with which we are familiar, viz. contact action, collision or pushing.

Another hypothesis as to the nature of the atom, and, therefore, as to the constitution of matter, is that devised by Lord Kelvin, according to which an atom is a vortex-ring of 'ether,' in an ethereal plenum capable of transmitting vibrations or waves. This hypothesis escapes at the same time the difficulties attending the notion of the impenetrable, solid, elastic atom, and those besetting the idea of action at a distance, or between isolated points. The ether had been postulated to explain the phenomena of light, and, later, those of electricity. It now also served to explain the constitution and properties of matter. It has not furnished an explanation of gravitation, and it seems to require modification if it is to supply a mechanical representation of what physicists call an electric charge. Inasmuch as the ether is non-material, it is indeed unreasonable to expect it to admit of mechanical description; for mechanical conceptions are derivable only from acquaintance with matter. On the other hand, the success which has attended such mechanical, or semi-mechanical, descriptions suggests that, if ether be not matter, it is at any rate very like it.

Lord Kelvin's kinetic theory of matter, which resolves matter into non-matter in motion, differs from that of Boscovich in that it offers a plenum instead of isolating and empty space; this plenum provides for action and reaction without resort to the notion, distasteful to physicists, of action at a distance. It differs again from Newton's in dispensing with hard atoms, while furnishing atoms which are not only extended, but also, in virtue of their rotational movement, elastic.

It has been claimed on behalf of this kinetic theory of matter that it enables the physicist to deduce material phenomena from the play of inertia involved in the motion of a structureless primordial fluid, and so achieves the ideal of ultimate simplification which scientific description or explanation seeks. This is so, though it must be borne in mind that the explanation attained is an explanation of the world only as it has been first artificially simplified by science. The further claim that physics is thus capable of reduction to a branch of pure mathematics is, however, not allowable; in going too far it refutes itself. For physics professes to deal with the real or sensible material world; it indeed passes, as it becomes more and more abstract, into 'pure' physics; but then it no longer is a science of the real, but only of the ideal or conceptual. Conceptual or pure science applies to the real world, indeed, but only partially or fragmentarily; it exhaustively describes the world in one aspect only, and leaves others out of account. Thus pure or abstract science of the material is valid, within limits, for economical description; it is not adequate to full explanation. That this is true in particular of the kinetic theory of matter can be seen at once when we grasp the fact that the primordial fluid—the non-matter to which matter is reduced, or which science substitutes for matter—is not a real thing, but an abstraction. A perfect fluid, in the first place, is a fiction, not anything known to observation. In the second place, Lord Kelvin's medium, in so far as it is describable by the negative terms incompressible, frictionless, inextensible, and structureless, differs in no respect from empty space. The one property in virtue of which it has been argued that the ether differs from space is that of inertia. But, as Ward has maintained (*Naturalism and Agnosticism*, vol. i. lect. v.), inertia, in the qualitative sense, does not suffice to supply determinateness to the primordial fluid; inertia is a property of matter, but not of modes of motion, and it is precisely the property of mass in molar bodies that, as both Clerk Maxwell and Lord Kelvin recognized, the kinetic theory of matter fails to explain. This theory of the constitution and nature of matter, therefore, belongs to the realm of symbolic description, not to that of explanation or interpretation. Science, indeed, in its higher or more abstract reaches, falls so far short of furnishing, as it was once jubilantly asserted to furnish, a complete philosophy of the world in terms of Newtonian mechanics that it professes to do no more than describe natural phenomena in so far as these are to be regarded as changes in the motion of masses. It abstracts from the qualitative properties and changes of matter, because these are not amenable to scientific method, and replaces them by hypothetically representative movements of ideal 'masses.' Matter, with its diversities of quality for perceptual experience, is not only one in kind for abstract science; as the goal and limit of abstraction is reached, or as physics passes into pure mathematics, matter becomes indistinguishable from space. It may similarly be shown that causality is eliminated by abstract science, and replaced, for descriptive purposes, by identity, change being explained and further explained until at last it is literally explained away. The development of scientific generalization in the direction of the ideal of unification and simplicity has thus not established a materialistic metaphysic or a mechanical philosophy, but has only provided a provisional symbolical description of certain aspects of the material world, valid so long as other aspects may be neglected. Such is the philosophical outcome of the scientific mode of dealing with matter.

Until recently matter was regarded as divisible only so far as to the chemical atom. There were held to be some four score fundamentally different, simple or irresolvable, kinds of matter. Matter was the primary concept of the physicist, and electricity was described more or less in terms of it. Matter was held to be strictly unchangeable in its elementary forms, the atom being supposed to be indestructible. Quite lately, however, all these beliefs have been reversed. It has been found, by a series of researches mainly conducted at, or in connexion with, the Cavendish Laboratory, Cambridge, that the atoms are not simple, but that portions of them can be split off and exist separately, and that these detached fractions, called by J. J. Thomson 'corpuscles,' are identical, from whatever different kinds of atoms they may have been broken off, and possess the same 'mass' or inertia. Thus it has become necessary to regard the atoms as complex systems, and, in spite of their differences, as built up of parts or corpuscles which are identical. Further, the corpuscle has been found to bear, or to be, a constant electrical charge (electron). Corpuscle and electron would seem to be identical, because the whole mass of the corpuscle appears to be due to its electric charge and its motion. Thus 'mass,' the most fundamental and characteristic property of matter, becomes resolvable into an electrical phenomenon; the electron is the fundamental unit alike of electricity and of matter, and matter is 'explained' in terms of electricity. An atom, in fact, is composed of a large number of units of negative electricity (electrons or corpuscles) associated with an equal number of positive units of electricity.

The full importance of the discovery and isolation of electrons cannot be indicated in an article dealing with matter, because they serve to explain the cause of the excitation of the ether-waves which produce light, and also render comprehensible other phenomena not belonging to the realm of the material. But it may be noted that the atomic (or, rather, the ultra-atomic) structure of matter, hitherto a supposition or indirect inference, has at length been experimentally demonstrated. The recent discovery and investigation of radium and other radio-active substances have led not only to the proof that the chemical elements are transmutable—helium, *e.g.*, is produced by the breaking up of radium—but also to the revelation of single atoms.

'Single atoms of Helium, shot off by Radium as α rays, have been revealed in two ways. Each atomic projectile produces a long train of electric ions as it passes through a gas before its energy is exhausted, perhaps by knocking loose corpuscles out of the molecules it encounters in its path. These ions have two effects. They make the gas a conductor of electricity, while they exist, so that, by placing the gas in a circuit with a battery and an electrometer, Rutherford has shown the effect of each α particle by the sudden throw of the needle of the instrument. Secondly, the ions act as nuclei for the condensation of mist, and, in this way, C. T. R. Wilson has made visible as a line of cloud the track of each particle' (W. C. D. and C. D. Whetham, *Science and the Human Mind*, London, 1912, p. 240).

Recent progress in science has thus furnished new light upon the question of the constitution of matter. But the ultimate question as to what matter *is* remains, as before, unsolved, and perhaps, as P. G. Tait (*Properties of Matter*, Edinburgh, 1885, p. 14) seemed to think, insoluble. To have learned that matter is electricity is not to have diminished the mysteriousness of its nature. To physical science indeed, matter, like a 'thing' or a 'fact,' is a datum. The data of science, however, are for philosophy or the theory of knowledge *constructs*. Hence it is to philosophy that we must betake ourselves if we are to hope for further elucidation of the problem contained in the question what matter is. As we have already seen, the more abstract departments of science cannot help us, because they proceed from an artificial definition of matter derived simply to make abstract science a possibility.

'The bodies we deal with in abstract dynamics are just as completely known to us as the figures in Euclid. They have no properties whatever except those which we explicitly assign to them' (J. Clerk Maxwell, in *Nature*, xx. [1879] 214).

The fundamental property thus conventionally assigned to matter with a 'let it be granted' is mass or inertia; and the science of matter is then valid of matter *if* it be wholly inert, or in so far as it is characterized by inertia. Whether any matter is wholly inert is a question; that *everything* is inert must be denied. The science of matter is no basis for a materialistic metaphysic.

For other philosophical questions connected with matter see art. MATERIALISM.

LITERATURE.—J. Ward, *Naturalism and Agnosticism*[3], London, 1907; J. J. Thomson, art. 'Matter,' in *EBr*[11]; W. C. D. Whetham, *The Recent Development of Physical Science*, London, 1904; O. Lodge, *Modern Views on Matter* (*Romanes Lecture*, 1903), Oxford, 1903; E. Rutherford, *Radio-Activity*, Cambridge, 1904; A. J. Balfour, *Reflections Suggested by the New Theory of Matter*, London, 1904.

F. R. TENNANT.

MAURICE.—The position of Frederick Denison Maurice (1805–72) in the history of English 19th cent. theology is difficult to define. He regarded himself as a simple old-fashioned Christian; but to the religious world of his time he was a most obscure and dangerous heretic. Julius Hare spoke of him as the greatest thinker since Plato, and Mill thought his intellect one of the most powerful of the age; but to most of his contemporaries Maurice seemed an obscure mystic, with a strange love for the Athanasian Creed and the Thirty-nine Articles, which much of his teaching appeared to contradict. Described as a leader of the Broad Church Party, he indignantly repudiated the epithet 'broad,' and still more the suggestion that he belonged to any 'party.' He spent much of his energy in controversy, sometimes bitter and occasionally hardly fair. Yet he was constantly on the look-out for points of agreement with his opponents, and those who knew him best were deeply impressed by his spirituality and goodness.

The paradoxes of his position may be partly accounted for by his family circumstances, and by the character of the age in which he lived. He was the son of a Unitarian minister, whose wife and daughters were converted to various forms of Evangelicalism, chiefly dissenting and Calvinistic. They were pious, clever people, much addicted to argument; and Frederick learned much from each, though he was repelled by all their theological systems. He combined his father's enthusiasm for the Fatherhood of God with his mother's conviction of the Divine Will as the root of all. His intense reverence for family relationships, together with the discordant doctrines of his loved ones, drove him to seek for some ground of unity more fundamental than doctrinal agreement. This he ultimately found in the conception of the Church as the divine family, and in the conviction that what God feels about us is far more important than what we feel about God. His view of Christ as ethically absolutely at one with the Father separated him from his Evangelical mother as well as from his Unitarian father. It precluded all idea of the Atonement as a changing of the Father's Will, as a bargain, or as a legal fiction. Similarly the popular beliefs about the Bible, the future life, and all the divine ways of working seemed to Maurice tinged with materialism. He was especially repelled by all sects, because he found in himself tendencies to fall into what he believed to be their errors. His controversial bitterness was often directed in reality against elements which he knew to be lodged in his own nature. Everywhere he discovered good, but also evil; and his position was generally a puzzle to his contemporaries.

His attitude towards politics showed the same characteristic. Growing up in the Tory reaction that followed the French Revolution and the Napoleonic wars, he was naturally disgusted by the brutalities and bigotries of this reaction. But he was almost equally opposed to a Liberalism which consisted mainly of destruction of abuses. The forces which carried Wordsworth and Coleridge into Conservatism and High Churchmanship operated strongly upon Maurice, with his reverence for the past and his attraction towards sacramentalism. For a time he hesitated. At Cambridge, after a distinguished career, he refused to take a degree, because this would have involved a profession of Churchmanship. He wrote a novel, edited the *Athenæum*, and engaged in various literary ventures. Then he decided to offer himself for ordination, and, as a preparation for this, to go through another undergraduate course, this time at Oxford. Then he published a defence of the tests by which acceptance of the Thirty-nine Articles was required from all who would obtain an Oxford degree. His arguments were, of course, fundamentally different from those used by ordinary Tories, and perhaps equally unreasonable. He afterwards admitted that his main position was untenable.

Maurice's first really important book was *The Kingdom of Christ* (1842). The book was primarily intended for Quakers. Their doctrine of 'the Inner Light' and of the supreme value of the spiritual was enthusiastically accepted by Maurice; but he set himself to proclaim the sanctity of the visible. Forms are witnesses to the invisible, and channels through which the divine spirit works. The Church is a spiritual kingdom, asserting human brotherhood, and protesting against human self-assertion and individualism, which would, if uncontrolled, destroy society. The author sometimes seems intensely Evangelical, sometimes a pronounced Catholic, sometimes a rationalist and a sort of socialist. He passes from an obscure mysticism to teaching so simple that it seems commonplace; he glances through the whole history of philosophy and theology; everywhere he discovers two tendencies, 'one belonging to the earth, one claiming fellowship with [the] Divine'; and the upward tendency is the search for that kingdom which God has provided in the Catholic Church. All this seemed orthodox enough. Its implications were not generally recognized, and in 1846 Maurice was elected to the professorship of Divinity at King's College, London.

It was characteristic that his next book dealt chiefly with the value of the non-Christian religions, the pagan philosophies, and the mediæval theologies. *The Religions of the World* appeared in 1847, and one form of the *Moral and Metaphysical Philosophy* in 1848. The latter had originally been published in 1836, but it was expanded in a series of later editions. It illustrates the wide learning of Maurice and his extraordinary capacity for discovering his points of agreement with diverse and mutually contradictory thinkers. As a history it is open to the criticism that, instead of giving a well-balanced account of systems, it presents only those aspects of them towards which the writer was attracted.

At this period Maurice was keenly interested in social movements. He invented the phrase 'Christian Socialism' as a protest against unsocial Christians and un-Christian socialists. He recognized the good in the aims of Chartists and Revolutionists. He sympathized intensely with their protests against the condition of the poor and the competitive basis of society. He set himself sternly against appeals to force, and was utterly distrustful of democratic ideals; but he started little newspapers, like *Politics for the People* and *The Christian Socialist*, with more revolutionary friends. Naturally Maurice was made responsible for the views of his less eminent associates, whom he warmly defended against the abuse of the propertied classes and their representatives. Moreover, the co-operative schemes at which he worked were regarded as an attack on capitalism, on the leading political economists, and on what was considered as the due subordination of the working classes. The 'respectable' press, secular and religious, fulminated against Maurice, and at length the Council of King's College appointed a committee to investigate the matter. But there was nothing in the Christian Socialism of Maurice inconsistent with his duties or his position as a Divinity professor.

The attack was then shifted from charges of socialism to charges of theological heresy. In 1853 Maurice published the volume called *Theological Essays.* On most points the new book was only reiterating and expanding views previously expressed; but it made clearer the author's divergence from traditional and conventional theology, especially on the subject of eternal death. He maintained, in effect, that 'eternal' means spiritual. Knowledge of God, love, truth, and the like *are* eternal life. Eternal death is not a matter of time or place, but of spiritual separation from the divine. The locality and duration of future punishment were matters outside Maurice's message, and he seems to have believed that it was also outside the message of the Bible and of the Anglican formularies. The religious world felt that much of the book was fatal to what passed as Christianity, but it was expressed in such orthodox language that it was difficult to see how Maurice could be convicted of heresy. He must, therefore, be ejected from his professorship without the formulation of any specific charges. The Council of King's College refused to adopt Gladstone's suggestion that Maurice's writings should be submitted to theological experts; and they compelled him to resign. The responsibility for their decision cannot be laid on any one party in the Church. It represented the view of the High, the Low, and the Moderate. Some High Churchmen had been at first attracted by the fervid sacramentalism of Maurice; but they soon came to suspect that his meaning was something very different from theirs. At length Pusey declared that Maurice and he were not worshipping the same God. Low Churchmen were even more disgusted with books full of intensely Evangelical sentences, which were yet fundamentally opposed to their whole scheme of salvation, their doctrine of the Fall and of the Atonement, and of the doom awaiting those who did not accept the Evangelical tenets. Broad Churchmen alone protested against the expulsion, and even they were puzzled as to how one who was so much in agreement with their hostility to the prevalent doctrines of the religious world could yet enthusiastically accept much that seemed to them superstitious and out of date. Nevertheless, the Broad Churchmen stood by Maurice, though he vigorously repudiated Broad Churchmanship. The Evangelicalism of Wilberforce and Simeon and the Anglo-Catholicism of Keble and Newman were the dominant forces in the religious world. Maurice had learned much from both. But at bottom he was opposed to both powerful parties, and few were disposed to forgive this attitude, in consideration of his enthusiastic support of some at least of their cherished principles.

Time has revolutionized the situation. At present many of the best High and Low Churchmen speak with grateful reverence of Maurice, and appear to ignore the great gulf which separates his views from their own. The fervent sincerity and piety of the *Theological Essays* are unmistakable, though to most readers much of the book seems tantalizing and obscure. More popular are *The Prophets and Kings of the Old Testament* (1853) and *The Patriarchs and Lawgivers of the Old Testament* (1855). Maurice meant by revelation a literal unveiling of truth, and especially of God's character, by a direct intercourse of the divine with the human. God literally spoke to the hearts of the old heroes, and He speaks no less directly to men's hearts in all ages. This conviction attracted Maurice especially to the Johannine books, on all five of which he wrote valuable commentaries, in which, however, he almost ignored what Higher Criticism had to say. His attitude towards the Bible was in some respects vague. Without claiming for it infallibility, he was pained by any criticism of its contents, and disposed to re-interpret rather than reject. He would not join in the outcry against Colenso and *Essays and Reviews*; but he disliked the critical spirit, and had little sympathy with plain speaking which hurt pious souls, except when it was in defence of some spiritual truth. Nevertheless, he was always ready to scandalize the religious world in cases where the traditional views seemed to him profoundly irreligious. Thus Mansel's *Bampton Lectures* (1858) practically declared that man could have no knowledge of God, except what was given him by the Bible. Such orthodox agnosticism was horrible to one who believed in a Light that lightens every man. Mansel taught, in effect, that men had no right to assume that words like 'fatherhood,' 'righteousness,' and 'justice' meant, when applied to God, all and more than what they imply in human relationships. To Maurice this seemed practically atheism; and in his book *What is Revelation?* (1859) he poured out the vials of his wrath upon the Bampton lecturer. There followed a very bitter controversy, in which Maurice for a time received little support. Gradually, however, the more spiritually-minded men of all classes rallied to his side.

Maurice's later years were spent in comparative quiet. The number of his actual disciples remained small, but his ideas spread, and the charm of his personality exercised a wide influence. It was also noticed that this mystic had proved singularly right in many of his ideas of practical reform. His Working Men's College and College for Women were imitated with more or less modification in numbers of institutions all over the country. His co-operative schemes, though unsuccessful, helped to pave the way for a great movement, conducted on less idealistic principles. Christian Socialism, under that or other names, became a great force; and meanwhile the more obnoxious features of the popular theology passed into the background, when they were not altogether dropped out of the conventional religion. Accordingly, though Maurice in books and sermons continually reiterated his old teaching, he aroused little fresh opposition. He continued to protest against popular doctrines, orthodox or liberal, but he had little to add to his old arguments. In 1866 he was appointed to the professorship of Casuistry, Moral Theology, and Moral Philosophy at Cambridge, and threw himself heartily into the duties of that position. Experts are divided as to the value of his contributions to metaphysics and to philosophy. For all departments of thought and life he claimed a theological basis, in a Father revealed in a Son through the operation of a Spirit, and witnessed to by a Catholic Church, with Bible and sacraments. Those to whom these things were either incredible or at least disconnected with philosophy and reason could regard him only as a somewhat muddle-headed mystic, however much they might reverence his character, learning, and ability.

LITERATURE.—Frederick Maurice, *The Life of Frederick Denison Maurice*, 2 vols., London, 1884, is an excellent compilation in which the editor has kept his own views and personality admirably in the background; shorter and more controversial, but adequate, biographies are given by C. F. G. Masterman (London, 1907) and W. E. Collins (do. 1902). See also T. Hughes, preface to Maurice's *Friendship of Books*, do. 1874; Leslie Stephen, art. 'Maurice,' in *DNB*, do. 1894; and the references to Maurice in J. McLeod Campbell, *Memorials*, do. 1877, and Caroline Fox, *Memories of Old Friends*, do. 1882.

J. E. SYMES.

MAY, MIDSUMMER.—Agricultural peoples throughout the world have established a ritual, more or less elaborate, about the critical periods of their common industry. This ritual, in effect, is the farmer's religion, and it may be considered the culmination of all pre-ethical animism, and its most important development prior to the great organized faiths. In the form of holiday customs its semblance survives abundantly throughout Europe, and probably not a little of its belief is latent underneath Christianity to-day.

We shall discuss its meaning below. This is perhaps less complex than has been supposed; but it is clear that the agricultural meaning is associated with the popular attitude towards the changes of the seasons, lunar and solar movements, and the growth and decay of vegetation in general. The calendar of this cult is that of the countryside, and this is even suggested by the three categories to which the terms May, midsummer, and harvest belong.

1. May.—The typical European celebration of May Day is well known. Trees, green branches, or garlands are carried round, and a King and Queen of May are appointed from among the young people. According to Mannhardt and Frazer, these objects and persons represent the tree-spirit or spirit of vegetation:

'The intention of these customs is to bring home to the village, and to each house, the blessings which the tree-spirit has in its power to bestow.'[1]

They had 'originally a serious and, so to speak, sacramental significance; people really believed that the god of growth was present unseen in the bough. . . . The idea of the spirit of vegetation is blent with a personification of the season at which his powers are most strikingly manifested.'[2]

The custom of setting up a May Tree or May Pole has been widely spread in Europe. A typical case is that of Swabia; on the first day of May a fir-tree was brought to the village, decorated with ribbons, and set up, and the people then danced round it. It remained on the village-green till the next May Day, when a new tree took its place.[3]

At a later stage, at least in England, the May Pole was permanent, while in Bavaria it was renewed at arbitrary periods of three, four, or five years.

'When the meaning of the custom had been forgotten, and the May-tree was regarded simply as a centre for holiday merry-making, people saw no reason for felling a fresh tree every year and preferred to let the same tree stand permanently, only decking it with fresh flowers on May Day.'[4]

Instead of a tree or a branch, a branch decked with flowers, or simply garlands of flowers, are frequently employed. English children use two hoops of osier or hazel, crossing at right angles, and twine flowers round them; or a pole is carried with a bunch of flowers fixed on the top.[5] In modern English folk-custom the essence of the May Pole is the long ribbons attached to the top; each of these is held by a child, and as they dance round the pole the ribbons twine round it, to be untwined when the dancers reverse.

The tree-spirit is often embodied in human form or in a living person. English children carry a doll in the garland, sometimes styled 'The Lady of the May.'[6] In Alsace a little girl is selected to be the Little May Rose, and carries a small May Tree. The Russian Lithuanians crown the prettiest girl and address her 'O May! O May!' In Brie a boy is wrapped in leaves; he is styled 'Father May.' The 'Green George' of Carinthia and Rumania is a boy covered with green branches; at the end of the procession an effigy of him is flung into the water.[7]

Here is what Frazer terms the double or bilingual representation of the tree-spirit by a tree and doll

[1] *GB*[3], pt. i., *The Magic Art*, London, 1911, ii. 59.
[2] W. Mannhardt, *Baumkultus*, Berlin, 1875, p. 315 f., quoted in *GB*[3], pt. i., *The Magic Art*, ii. 79.
[3] E. Meier, *Deutsche Sagen*, Stuttgart, 1852, p. 396.
[4] *GB*[3], pt. i., *The Magic Art*, ii. 70.
[5] *Ib.* ii. 60 ff.
[6] *Ib.* ii. 74.
[7] *Ib.* ii. 74 ff.

or a living person.[1] Instances of the single representation by a living person are numerous, such as the Little Leaf Man of Thuringia, the English Jack-in-the-Green, usually a chimney-sweep, who wore a framework covered with ivy and holly, and the innumerable May Kings and May Queens.[2] These still, in many cases, remember to announce the coming of spring, as well as to wish the people good luck.

Often the symbolism is that of a wedded pair, king and queen, lord and lady, bridegroom and bride. Trees, Frazer notes, are sometimes married to each other.[3] In some cases one party is a 'forsaken sleeper,' who is awakened by a kiss or the like. In a few cases there is an indirect representation of a marriage between the May couple.[4] The folk-drama of the marriage of Zeus and Hera in ancient Greece may be similar to the above, and certainly that of the Queen to Dionysus was identical. According to Frazer, the principle is that marriage promotes fertility.

One aspect of these customs is that the symbolic figure is supposed to ensure fertility to women and cattle as well as to vegetation and the crops. This is brought out in German and English folk-custom. The European customs are certainly to be correlated with those of other peoples, whose definite object is to promote the growth of the young crops or of the seed. In N. Morocco, for instance, during May, or at any time in spring, the women engaged to weed fields make a doll. A villager mounted on a horse runs away with it. A regular pursuit follows, and, if a man from another village succeeds in carrying it home, the village where it was made must buy it back, usually with a feast. The doll is termed *Māta*, and is dressed up as a girl.[5]

Another element besides that of the spirit of vegetation is detected here by Westermarck.

'The doll *Māta* is obviously a personification of the wheat, its vital energy; she is regarded as the bride of the field, and the ceremony itself I have heard called "the wedding of the wheats." Considering how commonly violent movements, contests, and racing are found as rites of purification, I venture to believe that the ceremony of *Māta* is originally meant to serve a similar purpose, that it is essentially a magical means of cleaning the corn, which is added to the more realistic method employed by the women on the field. At the same time, however, there may also be an idea of distributing *baraka* over the fields by racing about with the doll. Sometimes a large wooden spoon is used' for the frame of the doll.[6]

The two polar ideas of Moroccan magical belief are *l-bas*, evil magic, and *baraka*, holiness or good magic, each being a force or substance. The negative method of assisting the latter by first eliminating the former is conspicuous in Berber custom. But it would be futile to attempt to decide which method is the earlier; they are obviously complementary. A consideration to be adduced later may, however, have some significance here.

The negative aspect of agricultural ritual, viz. the imposition of tabu, has traces in European custom, especially in the prohibition of unlucky acts or times. Tabu is best exemplified, however, in lower cultures. The Dayaks of Borneo, for instance, consider the whole period of farming and all its operations to be subject to supernatural influences, while planting and harvest are especially critical times. The most elaborate tabus are imposed, and omens are constantly taken. Merriment and feasting follow the period of tabu.[7]

The Assamese proclaim a *genna* (communal tabu) at planting and harvest. The idea 'underlying the various restrictions is that men must not give time and attention to anything but the care of the crops.'[8]

[1] *GB*[3], pt. i., *The Magic Art*, ii. 73.
[2] *Ib.* ii. 80, 82, 84.
[3] *Ib.* ii. 88.
[4] *Ib.* ii. 94 f.
[5] E. Westermarck, *Ceremonies and Beliefs . . . in Morocco*, Helsingfors, 1913, p. 20.
[6] *Ib.* p. 22.
[7] W. H. Furness, *The Home-Life of Borneo Head-Hunters: its Festivals and Folk-lore*, Philadelphia, 1902, p. 160 ff.; T. B. P. Kehelpannala, in *JAI* xxv. [1895–96] 104 f.
[8] T. C. Hodson, in *FL* xxi. [1910] 300, and *JAI* xxxvi. [1906] 94.

If the Christian Lent was developed out of a period of agricultural tabu, there is complete continuity between the old and new faiths.

The question of date may here be noticed. European folk-custom has a large body of similar ritual celebrated previously to and during Lent, such as the Death of the Carnival, the Burial of Shrove Tuesday, Carrying out Death, Sawing the Old Woman, followed by a dramatic advent of Spring, Summer, or Life.[1] The former generally are dated on Shrove Tuesday, sometimes at Mid-Lent, the latter sometimes follow immediately, or at a later date—the fourth Sunday in Lent, for instance—while in Russia similar ritual in both forms is celebrated in spring and at midsummer, and also on St. Peter's Day.[2] These dates suggest that the old agricultural calendar was altered to suit the ecclesiastical.

In the majority of these Lenten customs the tree or branch or doll or person is termed Summer or Summer-tree.

'The "customs" of bringing in the May and bringing in the Summer are essentially the same. . . . The Summer-tree must likewise be an embodiment of the tree-spirit or spirit of vegetation.'[3]

With regard to the representation of Death, more prominent in the 'Summer' (Lenten) ritual than in that of May Day, Frazer's view is that it is 'an embodiment of the tree-spirit or spirit of vegetation,' the Summer-tree being often a 'revivification of the effigy of Death.' The idea is 'the death and revival of the spirit of vegetation in spring.'[4] There is also, as already noted, a natural identification of season or date with the spirit. The death is represented frequently by killing, and this may be connected with the idea of slaying the incarnate or embodied spirit while still vigorous, in order that its successor's vigour may be guaranteed.

Another feature of May ritual is the kindling of bonfires,[5] though this is most conspicuous at Midsummer-tide.

The Beltane fires of Scotland were kindled on May Day as late as the 18th century. The traces of human sacrifices at them were particularly clear and unequivocal. The most significant example is that of the north-east of Scotland. Here the Beltane fires were lit not on the first but 'on the 2nd of May, O.S. They were called *bone-fires*. The belief was that on that evening and night the witches were abroad in all their force, casting ill on cattle and stealing cows' milk. To counteract their evil power pieces of the rowan-tree and woodbine, chiefly of rowan-tree, were placed over the byre doors, and fires were kindled by every farmer and cottar. Old thatch, or straw, or furze, or broom was piled up in a heap and set on fire a little after sunset. Some of those present kept constantly tossing up the blazing mass, and others seized portions of it on pitch-forks or poles, and ran hither and thither, holding them as high as they were able, while the younger portion, that assisted, danced round the fire or ran through the smoke, shouting, "Fire! blaze an burn the witches; fire! fire! burn the witches." In some districts a large round cake of oat or barley-meal was rolled through the ashes. When the material was burned up, the ashes were scattered far and wide, and all continued till quite dark to run through them still crying, "Fire! burn the witches."'[6]

In Ireland, Sweden, and Bohemia bonfires were lighted on the first day of May; and in the last-named country the 'burning of the witches' is prominent.[7]

Bathing, washing the face with dew, and drenching effigies and mummers are common customs on May Day. The European May customs are also, among some peoples, celebrated at Whitsuntide. This date is especially marked in Russia, but also occurs in the Altmark, Bavaria, and other parts of Germany, Denmark, and Austria-Hungary. They are elsewhere celebrated at Midsummer, and on St. John's Eve or St. John's Day. One or two

1 *GB*[3], pt. iii., *The Dying God*, London, 1911, pp. 221 f., 228 f., 233 ff., 240 ff., 246 ff.
2 *Ib.* p. 262. 3 *Ib.* p. 251 f. 4 *Ib.* p. 252.
5 *GB*[3], pt. vii., *Balder the Beautiful*, London, 1913, i. 159 ff.
6 W. Gregor, *Folk-lore of the North-East of Scotland*, London, 1881, p. 167.
7 *GB*[3], pt. vii., *Balder the Beautiful*, i. 157, 159, pt. i., *The Magic Art*, ii. 65.

other dates are elsewhere found, cases apparently of arbitrary selection of a spring or summer critical day. The Swedes celebrate a minor form of the ritual on May Day, but are remarkable among European peoples for concentrating these customs upon Midsummer-tide, when May Pole, garlands, arbours, and jumping over bonfires are in great evidence.[1] It is curious that parts of Bohemia have the same date, while in Russia both Whitsun and Midsummer are celebrated similarly. The same ideas and practices are more or less equally applicable to May Day and Midsummer Day, but a Pyrenean custom suggests a special causal connexion. Here a tall tree is cut down on May Day and kept until Midsummer Eve, when it is ceremonially burned.[2]

Similarly there is a continuous connexion between the ritual and beliefs belonging to the whole trio of the critical periods, May, midsummer, and harvest. In Morocco the first day of summer (17th May) is the death of the earth, the first day of a new season, and the first day of harvest.[3] It is quite natural that green trees and green branches should be most conspicuous on May Day, and corn sheaves and the like at harvest; the preponderance of bonfires at midsummer, however, is a curiously difficult problem, whether on the theory of the tree-spirit with its corollary of sun-charms or on that of purification and *baraka*.

2. Midsummer.—Turning now to the midsummer celebrations, we find that in Sweden May Poles are set up and decorated, and the people dance round them, and bonfires are lighted to be danced round and jumped over. In Bohemia the May Pole itself is burned.[4]

In Russia on St. John's Eve a figure of the mythical personage, Kupalo, is made of straw, and 'is dressed in woman's clothes, with a necklace and a floral crown. Then a tree is felled, and, after being decked with ribbons, is set up on some chosen spot. Near this tree, to which they give the name of Marena [Winter or Death], the straw figure is placed, together with a table, on which stand spirits and viands. Afterwards a bonfire is lit, and the young men and maidens jump over it in couples, carrying the figure with them. On the next day they strip the tree and the figure of their ornaments, and throw them both into a stream.'

In some parts of Russia the ceremony is accompanied by weeping and wailing for the destroyed effigy, or by a mock combat between those who attack and those who defend it.[5] In Sardinia there is a ritual which seems to be a survival of the ancient Greek 'Gardens of Adonis.' The village swain proposes to a village girl early in spring. Then in May she sows in a pot a handful of corn, which is well grown by Midsummer Eve, when it is called *Erme* or *Nenneri*. On Midsummer Day the young couple go in a procession and break the pot against the church door. Feasting follows, and in some districts a bonfire is lighted, round which the people dance. A young couple who wish to be 'Sweethearts of St. John' clasp hands across the fire. The two 'gossips,' suggests Frazer, may correspond to the Lord and Lady of the May, and ultimately represent in flesh and blood the reproductive spirit of vegetation.[6] In Morocco smouldering fires are made on Midsummer Day or the evening before.

'Men, women and children leap over them, believing that by doing so they rid themselves of the *bas* or evil, which may be clinging to them; the sick will be cured and married persons will have offspring. Nobody is hurt by the fire since there is *baraka* in it.'[7]

In the Moroccan custom the smoke is more

1 *GB*[3], pt. vii., *Balder the Beautiful*, i. 172.
2 *GB*[3], pt. i., *The Magic Art*, ii. 141.
3 Westermarck, p. 76.
4 *GB*[3], pt. i., *The Magic Art*, ii. 65, pt. vii., *Balder the Beautiful*, i. 173.
5 W. R. S. Ralston, *Songs of the Russian People*[2], London, 1872, p. 241; *GB*[3], pt. iii., *The Dying God*, p. 262.
6 *GB*[3], pt. iv., *Adonis, Attis, Osiris*[2], London, 1914, i. 244 f., 251.
7 Westermarck, p. 79.

important than the blaze; the practical point is fumigation of men, cattle, trees, and various belongings.

It is also noteworthy that in Morocco at midsummer magic forces are supposed to be active in certain species of vegetation.[1] Fumigation by burning certain kinds of plants and the mere application of leaves and branches promote fertility, act as charms against the evil eye, and assist general well-being. There is also a custom of eating, in a quasi-sacramental manner, special foods, in which there is *baraka*.[2]

There is probably no corner of Europe in which it has not been the custom to kindle bonfires at Midsummer-tide. Besides the leaping through the fire, there are customs of throwing blazing disks through the air and of rolling burning wheels downhill.[3] A certain sanctity, as in the need-fire ceremonies, attaches to the kindling of the fire in some instances. A frequent custom is that of making gigantic figures of wicker-work, which are paraded and then burned, these midsummer giants being apparently analogous to the May Kings in their leafy garb. There are also traces of burning animals alive.[4]

Frazer derives these customs of modern Europe, especially those of N. France, from the 'sacrificial rites of the Celts of ancient Gaul,' as typified in the druidical sacrifices, and mythically in the death of Balder.[5]

Two main interpretations of these fire-rituals have been put forward. Mannhardt, originally followed by Frazer, explained them as sun-charms.[6]

At the 'great turning-point in the sun's career,' the summer solstice, primitive man 'fancied that he could help the sun in his seeming decline—could prop his failing steps and rekindle the sinking flame.'[7]

The wheel and disk are suggestive shapes. Frazer also noted the purificatory aspect of these customs.[8] Fire is a cleanser, and is frequently used for the purpose, as in the need-fire. Westermarck emphasized this aspect.

'Their primary object in many or most cases is to serve as a protection against evil forces that are active at Midsummer.'

In the Moroccan customs cleansing by fumigation is the chief idea, although there is also the ascription of positive virtue to the smoke. Westermarck finds no evidence for the sun-charm theory.[9] Later Frazer regarded the two views as being not mutually exclusive, but admitted the purificatory theory as being the more probable.[10]

Traces exist of what has been interpreted as human sacrifice by drowning on this date. Various similar customs have been interpreted as rain charms.[11] In Morocco, however, midsummer ceremonial bathing is connected with the idea of securing health by cleansing, and the same idea is attached to the European custom of rolling in dew.[12] Various kinds of divination, as is natural on special dates introductory of a new season (as midsummer is often regarded), are practised. Mock fights, tugs-of-war, games, and abuse of the ceremonial figure are common incidents. These have been interpreted as dramatic survivals of a ceremonial and magical representation of a struggle between good and evil influences, or designed to produce by homœopathic magic 'movement' in the weather or in the growth of the crops.[13] Magic plants are gathered at midsummer (see art. DEW); such are fern-bloom, fern-seed, mistletoe, and St. John's wort.[1]

For the special harvest-rites see art. HARVEST.

3. Basis of agricultural rituals.—The general theory of agricultural ritual propounded by Frazer can be connected with such primitive magical rites as the Australian *intichiuma* for developing the growth of food-plants and animals. But in many European cases it seems that the main object is to purify the sphere in which the corn grows, and many rites are concerned not with a spirit of vegetation but with vaguely-imagined evils, often in the form of witches.[2] The burning or destruction of the tree-spirit is often a doubtful proposition. It is impossible to dogmatize on the origin and first intention of these agricultural rites, but it is necessary to bear in mind the possibility that beliefs in corn-spirits and the like, and even the magical practices themselves, may be late accretions upon some simple psychological and even utilitarian facts. There is also the sense of crisis, very strong in the primitive mind. Thus, psychic reactions in sympathy with the objects concerned might lead to dramatic, but unconscious, imitations—*e.g.*, jumping to make the corn grow; in the same way imitative explanations might be made of such necessary processes as weed-burning. When established, these *ex post facto* explanations, magical, mythical, or theological, obviously tend to usurp precedence.

LITERATURE.—This is very extensive, but the main critical works are cited in the text.

A. E. CRAWLEY.

[1] Westermarck, p. 88; cf. p. 82.
[2] *Ib.* p. 90 ff. On the customs in general see Westermarck, 'Midsummer Customs in Morocco,' in *FL* xvi. [1905] 27 ff.
[3] *GB*³, pt. vii., *Balder the Beautiful*, i. 116 f., 168 f., 337 f., 340 f., 345.
[4] *Ib.* i. 269 ff., ii. 31 ff., 38.
[5] *Ib.* ii. 40 f., 87 f.
[6] *Ib.* i. 329 f.
[7] *Ib.* i. 160.
[8] *Ib.* i. 329 f.
[9] Westermarck, *Ceremonies and Beliefs in Morocco*, p. 98.
[10] *GB*³, pt. vii., *Balder the Beautiful*, i. 346.
[11] *Ib.* ii. 26 f., 30; *GB*³, pt. iv., *Adonis, Attis, Osiris*², i. 237.
[12] Westermarck, *Ceremonies and Beliefs*, p. 85 f.; *GB*³, pt. vii., *Balder the Beautiful*, i. 208, ii. 74.
[13] *GB*³, pt. v., *Spirits of the Corn and of the Wild*, London, 1912, i. 102 f.

[1] *GB*³, pt. vii., *Balder the Beautiful*, ii. 165, 287, 291.
[2] *GB*³, pt. vi., *The Scapegoat*, London, 1913, p. 158 ff.

MĀYĀ

MĀYĀ.—*Māyā*, 'illusion, appearance,' is a term in the philosophy of the Vedānta applied to the illusion of the multiplicity of the empirical universe, produced by ignorance (*avidyā*), when in reality there is only One, the *brahman-ātman*. It is not till a somewhat late period that the word assumes the technical meaning of the cosmic illusion, although this development of its sense is not an unnatural one. The word *māyā* is not uncommon even in the Rigveda, where it has the meanings 'supernatural power,' 'cunning,' 'mysterious will-power.' Sāyaṇa usually explains it by *prajñā*, 'mental power,' or *kapaṭa*, 'cunning,' 'guile,' 'deception.' Indra, *e.g.*, is said to assume many forms *māyābhiḥ*, 'by magic wiles, *or* mysterious powers'; as the possessor of this power, he is called *māyin*.

[The use of the term in the Rigveda has been thoroughly analyzed by A. Bergaigne (*Religion védique*, Paris, 1878–83, iii. 80–88; cf. A. Hillebrandt, 'Māyā,' *WZKM* xiii. [1899] 316–320). It, or such derivatives as *māyin*, *māyāvant*, is applied to the wiles of the demons conquered by Agni (v. ii. 9, etc.) and Sarasvatī (vi. lxi. 3), and especially by Indra, whether alone (i. xxxii. 4, etc.) or accompanied by Viṣṇu (vii. xcix. 4). By overcoming the *māyā* of the demons Indra won the Soma (vii. xcviii. 5). Men of evil craftiness are *māyin* (i. xxxix. 2) or *durmāyu* (iii. xxx. 15); the sorceress uses *māyā* (vii. civ. 24); but the *māyin* cannot overcome 'the primal firm ordainments of the gods' (iii. lvi. 1). The Aśvins conquer the *māyā* of the evil Dasyu (i. cxvii. 3).

On the other hand, the terms are applied to good deities. Through *māyā* Mitra and Varuṇa send rain and guard their law (v. lxiii. 3, 7); through *māyā* the sun-bird is adorned (x. clxxvii. 1). The Maruts employ it (v. lxiii. 6), and are *māyin* (v. lviii. 2), or *sumāya* (i. lxxxviii. 1, etc.). *Māyā* is known to, or used by, Tvaṣṭṛ (x. liii. 9), the Ādityas (ii. xxvii. 16), and Varuṇa and Mitra (i. cli. 9, etc.); and it is a characteristic of Varuṇa (vi. xlviii. 14, etc.); while by it the Ṛbhus attained divine dignity (iii. lx. 1). It was also employed by Agni (iii. xxvii. 7) and Soma (ix. lxxxiii. 3), and in the former deity the *māyās* of the *māyins* are united (iii. xx. 3). It was a mark of the Aśvins (v. lxxviii. 6, etc.), and even earthly sacrificers are *māyin* (ix. lxxiii. 3).

Through *māyā* Indra triumphs over the *māyin* demons (i. xi. 7, v. xxx. 6, etc.), and he 'has much *māyā*' (*purumāya*, vi. xviii. 12, etc.). Germs of the later development of the word are found in such passages as iii. liii. 8, where Indra 'assumes form after form, working *māyās* about his body,' and vi. xlvii. 18, where 'through *māyās* Indra goeth in many forms' (cf. also iii. xxxviii. 7). Sun and moon succeed each other in virtue of *māyā*

(x. lxxxv. 18), and *māyā* explains the double form of Pūṣan and Agni (vi. lviii. 1, x. lxxxviii. 6). Perhaps most significant of all is the passage x. liv. 2: 'When thou didst go, O Indra, waxing in body, speaking mighty things among folk, *māyā* was that which they called thy battles; neither now nor hitherto hast thou found a foe.'

In the Atharvaveda *māyā* was born from *māyā* (viii. ix. 5); it was milked from Virāj (on whom see Hillebrandt, *Ved. Myth.*, Breslau, 1891–1902, ii. 50–52, and Muir, *passim*), and on it the Asuras (demons) subsist (viii. x. 22). Luck in gambling is invoked by the aid of *māyā* (iv. xxxviii. 3); the black snake assumes wondrous forms (*vapus*) 'by the Asura's *māyā*' (vi. lxxii. 1); sun and moon follow one another by *māyā* (vii. lxxxi. 1; cf. xiii. ii. 11); the sorceress prevails by its means (viii. iv. 24); by *māyā* the sun makes 'the two days' (*i.e.* day and night) of diverse form (xiii. ii. 3); through Agni the *māyās* of the Asuras are repelled (iv. xxiii. 5, viii. iii. 24); yet the gods (*deva*) go about with Asura-*māyā* (iii. ix. 4).

Some idea as to the original meaning of the term *māyā* may be gained from its etymology. It has been connected with Skr. *mā*, 'to measure' (O. Böhtlingk and R. Roth, *Sanskrit-Wörterbuch*, Petrograd, 1855–75, v. 732); with Skr. *man*, 'to think' (H. Grassmann, *Wörterbuch zum Rig-Veda*, Leipzig, 1873, col. 1034; similarly P. Persson, *Studien zur Lehre von der Wurzelerweiterung und Wurzelvariation*, Upsala, 1891, p. 120; the closest cognate would be Gr. μῆτις, 'wisdom, cunning, craft'); with Gr. μῖμος, 'imitator' (G. N. Chatzidakis, Ἀκαδημ. Ἀναγνώσματα, Athens, 1902–04, i. 260); with Lat. *mīrus*, 'wonderful' (H. Ehrlich, *Zur indogerm. Sprachgesch.*, Königsberg, 1910, p. 75). The most probable connexion, however, is with a Balto-Slavic group (with which μῖμος may be connected) represented by O. Bulg. *na-mayati*, 'to nod, indicate by a sign,' Russ. *na-mayamĭ*, 'I indicate by signs, deceive,' *ob-mayakŭ*, 'deceiver,' Bulg. *za-mayvam*, 'I enchant, deceive,' Let. *mât*, 'to nod,' *ap-mât*, 'to blind, enchant.' More distant cognates are, *e.g.*, Bulg. *iz-mama*, 'deceit, swindle,' Russ. *ob-manŭ*, 'deceit,' Lith. *mõnai*, 'sorcery,' Let. *mânit*, 'to enchant,' O. H. G. *mein*, 'falsehood' (Germ. *Meineid*, 'perjury'), Little Russ. *mara*, 'phantom, dream, deception,' O. Ch. Slav. *machati*, 'to swing,' Russ. *makhŭ*, 'error,' Czech *matoha*, 'ghost,' Polish *matać*, 'to swindle, lie, deceive' (E. Berneker, *Slav. etymolog. Wörterbuch*, Heidelberg, 1908 ff., ii. 7, 15, 17 f., 4 f., 25). In Avesta we have the word *māyu*, 'skilful, clever.' The basal meaning seems to be 'to move,' hence 'to change, to deceive.' LOUIS H. GRAY.]

In Upaniṣadic literature *māyā* is first found in the *Śvetāśvatara Upaniṣad* (iv. 10) with the meaning 'cosmic illusion'; it is no longer applied simply to the juggler's art, but now connotes the illusion created by him. It is in the latter sense that the word is henceforth mainly used in philosophical literature. Śaṅkara, in his commentaries on the *Vedāntasūtras*, always used the word with the meaning 'illusion,' and the technical term employed by him became more or less stereotyped by his successors.

Although it is occasionally asserted that the idea of *māyā* is as late in origin as the use of *māyā* to describe it, there is little foundation for this view, and passages may be found in the Rigveda which show that even then it was felt that there was an underlying unity beneath apparent multiplicity; indeed, the doctrine that phenomena are unreal in relation to absolute being is common to all metaphysics.

In Rigveda, i. clxiv. 46, *ekaṁ sad viprā bahudhā vadanti*, 'that which is one the sages call by many names,' it is felt that all plurality is a matter of words only, or in x. xc. 2, where the whole universe is said to be *puruṣa* alone, it is implied that all else but *puruṣa* is illusion.

It was with the introduction of the doctrine of the *ātman* in the Upaniṣads that this denial of the existence of the empirical universe became firmly established in India as a philosophic doctrine. The conception of an all-pervading *ātman*, the 'self' of the universe, necessitates the exclusion of all that is not the self, and hence implies its unreality. The substance of the teaching of the Upaniṣads is '*Brahman* is real, the universe false, the *ātman* is *brahman* and nothing else.' Although it is not possible to quote early forms of the statement that the universe is *māyā*, or illusion, it is frequently insisted that the *ātman* is the only reality, which means the same thing—*i.e.*, all that is not the self (world, etc.) is not real; it is mere appearance or illusion. This is the teaching of Yājñavalkya in the *Bṛhadāraṇyaka Upaniṣad*:

'When the self is seen, heard, perceived, and known, the whole universe is known'; 'he who imagines there is plurality goes from death to death' (iv. iv. 19, v. 6).

With the knowledge of self phenomena become known as phases of it; they are provisionally real to a certain extent, but ignorance of the *ātman* regards them as independent of the *ātman*. We have not quite reached the stage of the later Vedānta, which regards phenomena as absolutely unreal, like a mirage. Ignorance, in the Upaniṣads, is an absence of true knowledge; in the later Vedānta it is rather an active force which conjures up the illusion of phenomena for the delusion of the self. In the Upaniṣads also we find a kind of pantheistic compromise which grants that the world does exist, but holds that the sole reality of the *ātman* is not in the least degree affected, for all is the *ātman*. This view pervades the *Chhandogya Upaniṣad*, *e.g.*:

'The *ātman* is above and below, behind and in front. The *ātman* is all the world' (vii. xxv. 2).

As time went on, *māyā* gained an ever-increasing independence as the substance *prakṛti* (nature), which was at first subordinate to the *ātman*. In post-Upaniṣadic literature the term appears frequently in a non-philosophic sense; a *mṛgamāyā* is an 'illusion gazelle' (*i.e.* not a real gazelle); a man who craftily seeks to gain money does it through *māyā*; *amāyayā*, lit. 'without *māyā*,' means 'honestly.' In these cases (for further references see Böhtlingk-Roth, *loc. cit.*) the original meaning of *māyā* persists.

In the philosophical sections of the *Mahābhārata* the term is used in its philosophical sense. Thus Viṣṇu, speaking as the supreme god, says: 'Entering into my own nature (*prakṛti*), I arise through *māyā*' (vi. xxviii. 6 f.); this explains the famous *avatāras* of the deity. 'Māyāvin' is one of the thousand names of Śiva (xiii. xvii. 1214). (On the question of *māyā* in the epic see E. W. Hopkins, *The Great Epic of India*, New York, 1901, pp. 138–142.)

The doctrine of *māyā* in the Vedānta forms the cardinal distinction from its great rival system, the Sāṅkhya (*q.v.*) philosophy. Vedānta is the system of *advaita* (non-duality); the phenomenal world does not exist; it is only *māyā*, arising from *avidyā*, that makes us erroneously think it to be real; *māyā* is overcome when he who ignorantly believed himself to be an individual realizes that in actuality he is one with the *ātman*; then only is salvation (*mokṣa*, lit. 'liberation') finally won. In the Sāṅkhya system, on the contrary, the phenomenal world is real; the Vedāntic *ātman* is ignored (Sāṅkhya is atheistic); the soul (*chit*, lit. 'thought') is involved in the woe of life because of *aviveka* (failure to distinguish between matter and soul), due to *avidyā*, etc.; salvation is gained by the complete isolation (*kaivalya*) of the soul from matter; and the soul then exists as an eternal, but unconscious, individuality. (On the distinctions between Vedānta and Sāṅkhya see especially Max Müller, *Six Systems*, p. 279 ff.)

One of the most important of the early works on Vedānta is the *Kārikā* of Gauḍapāda (8th cent. A.D.), one of whose pupils was a teacher of Śaṅkara. He is an uncompromising advocate of the doctrine of *māyā*, and strongly denies the existence of the universe. The waking world is no more real than the world of dreams. The *ātman* is both the knower and the known; his experiences exist within him through the power of *māyā*. As a rope in a dim light is mistaken for a snake, so the *ātman* is mistaken for the variety of experience (*jīva*). When the rope is recognized, the illusion of the snake at once disappears; when true knowledge of the *ātman* is attained, the illusion which makes us think of it as a multiplicity of experiences vanishes. The world has no more real existence than the snake, and, as one cannot remove or cast off what does not exist, it is wrong to speak of obtaining freedom from it. The *ātman* cannot be said to create or cause the universe any more than the rope creates the snake. Production would be either from the existent or from the non-existent; but the former is impossible, for it would be producing what already exists, and the latter is equally impossible, for the non-existent—*e.g.*, the son of a barren woman—cannot be the cause of anything; it cannot even be realized by the mind.

Gauḍapāda's monism assumed its final form in the commentaries of Śaṅkara (b. probably A.D. 788). Śaṅkara is well aware of the difficulties in the way of reconciling the various views of the Upaniṣads, and is further perplexed by the fact that as *śruti* ('revelation') they all ought to have equal weight; the latter difficulty he overcomes by his classification of knowledge as of two kinds: a higher, the knowledge of *brahman*, and a lower, including all that is not this metaphysical knowledge. He then investigates the cause of ignorance (*avidyā*), and concludes that it is to be sought in the knower. The phenomenal world is considered real so long as the unity of the *ātman* is not realized, just as the creations of a dream are thought to be real till the dreamer awakes. Just as a magician (*māyāvin*) causes a phantom, having no existence apart from him, to issue from his body, so the *ātman* creates a universe which is a mere mirage and in no way affects the self. It is through *māyā* that plurality is perceived where there is really only the *ātman*. Multiplicity is only a matter of name and form, which are the creations of ignorance, being neither the *ātman* nor different from it, through the power of illusion (*māyāśakti*). The Highest One manifests himself in various ways by *avidyā* as a magician assumes various forms by his wiles. Śaṅkara further defines two kinds of existence, empirical and metaphysical, for the first time emphasizing clearly a distinction which seems, however, to be known even in the Upaniṣads. The phenomenal universe is a fact of consciousness, and therefore has a sort of existence; all experience is true so long as the knowledge of the *ātman* is not attained, just as the experiences in a dream are real to the sleeper, until he awakes.

'. . . Therefore before the consciousness of identity with *brahman* is aroused, all worldly actions are justified' (on *Vedāntasūtras*, II. i. 121).

In spite of the discussion that has raged round it since Śaṅkara's time, the doctrine of *māyā* as enunciated by him still holds the field in India to-day and, as one of the fundamental doctrines of his Advaitist school, pervades the philosophy of the great mass of thinkers in India.

LITERATURE.—P. Deussen, *The Philosophy of the Upanishads*, Eng. tr., Edinburgh, 1906, pp. 226–239, *The System of the Vedanta*, Eng. tr., Chicago, 1912, pp. 100, 187, 228, etc., *Nachved. Philosophie der Inder*, Leipzig, 1908, pp. 24, 35, 472, 601; A. E. Gough, *The Philosophy of the Upanishads*, London, 1882, pp. 45–50, 235 ff.; Mādhavāchārya, *Sarvadarśanasaṁgraha*, tr. E. B. Cowell and A. E. Gough, do. 1882, and Deussen, *Nachved. Phil.* p. 182 ff.; Gauḍapāda, *Māṇḍūkyopaniṣatkārikā*, tr. Deussen, *Sechzig Upanishad's des Veda*, Leipzig, 1897, p. 573 ff.; Śaṅkara, *Commentary on the Vedāntasūtras*, tr. G. Thibaut, *SBE* xxxiv., xxxviii. [1890–96], and Deussen, *Sûtras des Vedânta*, Leipzig, 1887; Rāmānuja, *Commentary on the Vedāntasūtras*, tr. Thibaut, *SBE* xlviii. [1904]; Prakāśānanda, *Vedāntasiddhāntamuktāvalī*, ed. and tr. A. Venis, Benares, 1890; Sadānanda, *Vedāntasāra*, tr. G. A. Jacob², London, 1889, Deussen, *Nachved. Phil.* p. 639 ff.; F. Max Müller, *Six Systems of Indian Philosophy*, London, 1899, pp. 157, 162, 185, 367, 457; Prabhu Dutt Shāstrī, *Doctrine of Māyā*, do. 1911. For *māyā* as held by a modern Vedāntist see Max Müller, *Râmakrishna, his Life and Sayings*, London, 1898, nos. 25, 45, 64, 71, etc. Cf. also 'Literature' at artt. ADVAITA, ĀTMAN, UPANIṢADS, VEDĀNTA.

J. ALLAN.

MAYANS.—The territory of what is now the Republic of Guatemala, adjoining parts of the Republic of Honduras and of the Mexican States of Chiapas and Tabasco, and the peninsula of Yucatan, was inhabited in ancient times, as it is to the present day, by a number of different tribes, speaking allied idioms and forming a linguistic family usually designated as 'Mayan,' from the name of its most conspicuous members, the people of Yucatan. This population is to be regarded as the second of the great culture-nations of Mexico and Central America, equal to the Mexicans in material and intellectual civilization and in some ways surpassing them, but, unfortunately, much less known than the Mexicans, as regards the special traits of their civilization, their history, and the elements of their daily life. The chief ancient monuments in Central America—Palenque in Chiapas, Menche Tinamit on the Usumacinta river, Quirigua in Guatemala, Copan in Honduras, Uxmal and Chich'en Itzá in Yucatan—are the work of members of that family. They were the great astronomers and mathematicians who calculated the duration of the revolution of Venus and, perhaps, of other planets as well, and were wont to write down and handle numbers exceeding a million. They had elaborated a system of hieroglyphic writing far superior to that of the Mexicans, but only partially deciphered as yet. They were unexcelled in the apprehension and reproduction of living forms of animals and men. As a whole, their civilization and their religion were closely allied to those of the Mexicans.

In their religious practices they were not so sanguinary as the Mexicans, human sacrifices being much less numerous and in many cases being replaced by the killing of dogs. They resembled the Mexicans in their methods of prayer and offerings, fasting, and torture, and in piercing their ears and tongues and drawing threads through the holes. They also sacrificed living animals by fire to the god of fire, and in some places tortured themselves by running with naked feet over burning coals.

Like the Mexicans, the Mayans divided the year into eighteen periods of twenty days each, and they also commenced their ceremonies early in the year, in our month of January, by renewing all kinds of ceremonial utensils — incense-burners, clay-idols, and the like. This feast was called *Ocna*, and was devoted to the *chac*, the gods of labour, *i.e.* the rain-gods. When they had to make a new wooden image or, as they said, to create a god, the work began in the preceding months, and with great precautions (fasting, etc.), the artisans being confined to the house as long as the work went on. In March they had a great fire-ceremony, performed by the old men and directed to the rain-gods (*chac*) and to the old god Itzamná, who may be considered the god of life and the god of fire. This ceremony was called *tupp-kak*, 'extinguishing the fire.' They brought together every species of animal that was at hand; and, after having kindled a great fire, they killed them by cutting the breasts and tearing out the hearts, which were cast into the flame. The larger animals, such as jaguars, pumas, caimans, were not so easily captured, so they made imitations of their hearts from copal, which was their incense, and threw these into the fire. The hearts having been consumed, the priests extinguished the fire by pouring water from their jars upon it. This ceremony was intended to secure sufficient rain for the crops of the new year. Another ceremony was connected with this performance. They made a kind of terraced pyramid of stones, which seems to have been regarded as an image of the clouds. The priests anointed the lowest step with mud and the upper ones with blue colour, invoking the *chac* and Itzamná. This was, no doubt, another ceremony for bringing rain.

In April the cacao planters, who were also the great merchants, cacao being the staple merchandise of ancient Central America, celebrated a great feast to the black god Ekchuah, the god of the caravans and the merchants, to the *chac*, and to Hobnil, the god of the bee-hives. They killed a dog of the spotted colour of the cacao-pod and offered blue iguanas, feathers of wild fowl, and incense. In the month of May there was another great feast, called *Pacumchac*, celebrated to Cit chac coh, the god of war. It began with a five nights' watch in the temple of the god of war, and during this time the war-chief, called *nacom* and elected for four years by the members of the tribe, was seated on a throne in the temple of the god of war and venerated like a deity with incense-burning. The people performed a dance called *holkon-okot*, 'warrior-dance.' At the end of the five days they performed the fire-ceremony described above, after which the war-chief was taken in a solemn procession all round the temple; a dog was sacrificed, and the heart offered to the god. The heart was put into a bowl and covered by another bowl, after which the assistant priests dashed to pieces some great jars full of water—undoubtedly another ceremony intended to produce rain for the crops. A great banquet of mead and general drunkenness followed. The same banquets and drinking-bouts were repeated in the course of the next three twentieths in all the smaller villages. These feasts were called *Zabacil than*, and it is expressly stated that they were made in order that the new year might be a fertile one and bring rich crops.

The month of July was reckoned as the beginning of the new year by the Yucatecans at the time of the conquest. The twentieth (*uinal*) in question was called Pop, 'straw-mat,' meaning 'dominion,' 'reign.' They swept their houses and the village streets and renewed all objects of domestic use—plates, jars, bowls, wooden chairs, garments, and the wrappings of their idols—throwing the old ones on the dust-heaps. The priests, who had fasted for one, two, or three months, eating only once a day and abstaining from sexual intercourse, assembled in the temple and kindled new fire by friction, twirling a wooden stick in the hole of another; this new fire was put into the brazier before the idol, and all the priests and principal men burned incense with it to the idol. In the following months all the professional instruments of the different classes of the people—the books of the priests, the implements for casting lots and the fetishes of the doctors, the weapons of the hunters, and the fishing-nets of the fishermen—were consecrated by anointing them with blue colour. This feast was called *Pocam*. In the month of September the bee-keepers had a special feast at which they brought offerings of incense and honey to their god Hobnil. In the month of October, called Xul by the Yucatecans, there was a great ceremony in the village of Mani, dedicated to the god Kukulcan, the 'feathered snake,' the Yucatec translation of the Mexican god Quetzalcoatl, who was venerated as a culture-hero in Yucatan, some of the most important towns of the peninsula, Mayapan, and Chich'en Itzá, having been founded by Mexican emigrants. The last feast in the year, celebrated at the time of our months November and December, corresponded in a way to the Mexican *Izcalli*, ceremonies being performed to promote the growth of the youth and to strengthen them. Contrary to the custom of the Mexicans, the Yucatecans performed very particular and important ceremonies in the last five days of the year, which they called *xma kaba kin*, 'days without name,' *i.e.* 'unlucky' days, the names of which it is dangerous to pronounce. On these days they set up in the midst of the village the image of the deity that was to govern the coming year, this god being one of four who corresponded to the four cardinal points and followed each other in turn. These gods were: (1) for the east and the years corresponding to the east, Ah bolon tz'acab, the god of fertility; (2) for the north and the years corresponding to the north, Kinch ahau, the sun-god; (3) for the west and the years corresponding to the west, Itzamná, the old god, the moon-god and the god of fire; (4) for the south and the years corresponding to the south, Uacmitun ahau, the 'lord of the six under worlds,' the god of the dead. A number of different ceremonies and offerings were performed in honour of these gods, and the evil that was to befall the village, according to the character of the new year and of the heavenly quarter corresponding to the god thereof, was taken, represented by the figure of a demon, out of the village in the direction of the coming year.

The priests were called *ah-kin*, 'lords of days,' *i.e.* 'lords of day-signs,' 'dealers in prognostics,' 'sooth-sayers.' They were the leaders and teachers of the people—the learned men whose principal occupation was with books, pictographs, and all the traditional knowledge embodied in them. There is one marked difference between Mexican and Mayan priesthood: in Yucatan the office of sacrificer (*nacom*), who had to kill the victim, was not a highly honoured one, whereas in Mexico the highest priests and—in extraordinary celebrations, such as the inauguration of a newly-built temple—the kings themselves acted as sacrificers.

LITERATURE.—Diego de Landa, *Relacion de las cosas de Yucatan*, ed. D. Juan de Dios de la Rada y Delgado, Madrid, 1884; Diego López de Cogolludo, *Los tres Siglos de la dominacion española en Yucatan*, Campeche, 1842; E. Seler, *Gesammelte Abhandlungen zur amerik. Sprach- und Altertumskunde*, i., Berlin, 1902, iii., do. 1908; T. A. Joyce, *Mexican Archæology*, London, 1914.

EDUARD SELER.

MĀZANDARĀN.—The Persian region of Māzandarān,[1] or Ṭabaristān, is bounded on the north by the Caspian Sea and on the south by the Alburz Mountains, and extends from Astarābād in the east to the Pul-i-Rūd in the west. The winds from the Caspian bring abundant rain, and the country is heavily wooded, in contrast to the arid regions south of the Alburz. The climate is decidedly unhealthy, and the difficulty of access to the country, increased by lack of good roads, has combined with Māzandarān's insalubrity to exclude it from any generous share in the progress of Persia. It is to these disadvantages that the district owes its place in the history of religion in Irān.

Of the aboriginal inhabitants of Māzandarān we know nothing beyond the statement of Strabo (p. 515; cf. 520) that it was their custom to 'give their married women to other men after they themselves had had two or three children by them.' The *Bundahishn* (xv. 28) has a fantastic tradition of their origin, and the *Dīnkarṭ* (IX. xxi. 19) describes them as filthy and dwelling in holes.

In regard to the latter point, we may note that Firdausī (*Shāh-nāmah*, tr. A. G. and E. Warner, London, 1905 ff., ii. 58) makes the Māzandarānī White Dīv inhabit a cavern, although one thinks involuntarily of the repeated Avesta statement that demons hide under earth or dwell in caves (*Ys.* ix. 15; *Yt.* xix. 81; *Vend.* iii. 7, 10).

In the Avesta Māzandarān is the abode of the Māzainya *daēvas*, concerning whom E. W. West (*SBE* xviii. [1882] 93, n. 10) expresses the general

[1] The meaning of the name Māzandarān is not certain. The old native etymology (Ibn Isfandiyār, tr. Browne, p. 14) makes it a later form of *Mūzandarūn, 'within [a mountain named] Mūz' (so also Curzon, *Persia*, i. 354 f.; Darmesteter's etymology [*Zend-Avesta*, ii. 373, n. 321] is incorrect); but it more probably means 'Land of the Māzan Gate' (T. Nöldeke, *GIrP* ii. [1904] 178, n. 1). Ṭabaristān, the Arab. form of Pahlavi Tapurstān (on coins) or Taparīstān (*Bund.* xii. 17, xiii. 15, xx. 27), is the land of the Τάπουροι of Ptolemy (VI. ii. 6) and the Τάπυροι of Diodorus (II. ii. 3) and Athenæus (442 B; Marquart, *Ērānšahr*, p. 129). F. Windischmann's identification of Māzandarān with Media (*Zoroastr. Stud.*, Berlin, 1863, p. 229) was wrong.

view when he says that 'these demons were, no doubt, merely idolaters,' while M. N. Dhalla (*Zoroastrian Theology*, New York, 1914, pp. 8, 160) sees in them the nomads of Māzandarān and Gīlān, 'who poured down in great numbers and pillaged the possessions of the Iranians.' A number of the Avesta references to the Māzainya *daēvas* give no information as to their nature or habitat (*Ys.* lvii. 17, 32; *Vend.* ix. 13, x. 16, xvii. 9 f.). We have, however, more precise indications as to their location in the account of the threefold sacrifice by the hero Haoshyangha Paradhāta on Mt. Hara to gain the victory over 'two-thirds of the Māzainyan demons' (*Yt.* v. 22. ix. 4, xv. 8. xix. 26), for Hara (or, as it is also called in the Avesta, Hara Berezaiti, 'lofty Hara') is generally—and probably correctly—identified with Alburz, though construed in a mythological, rather than a geographical, sense (*e.g.*, Spiegel, *Erân. Alterthumskunde*, i. 191, 463, 482; Darmesteter, i. 101, n. 28; K. Geldner, *GIrP* ii. 38, and especially Geiger, *Ostīrān. Kultur*, pp. 42–45), and the 'peak' (*taēra*, *Yt.* xv. 7; cf. xii. 25; *Bund.* v. 4; *Ys.* xlii. 3) of Hara is probably Mt. Damāvand (Geiger, *loc. cit.*). The identification of Mazan (the noun from which Māzainya is derived) with Māzandarān is also made by Neriosangh (*c.* A.D. 1200), who, in his Skr. paraphrase of the Pahlavi version of the *Yasna*, renders 'Māzainya' by 'Mājandara' or 'Mājandaradeśīya' (*Ys.* lvii. 17, xxvii. 1, lvii. 32).

Closely associated with the Māzainya *daēvas* are the Varenyan *daēvas* and *dregvants*, or 'adherents of the Lie demon' (*Ys.* xxvii. 1; *Yt.* v. 22, xiii. 137, xv. 8, xix. 26; cf. Darmesteter, ii. 373, n. 33; *Yt.* x. 97, xiii. 71, and *Vend.* x. 14 are unimportant in this connexion). The land of Varena was the fourteenth best created by Ahura Mazda, but Angra Mainyu cursed it with 'untimely infirmities and non-Aryan over-lords' (*Vend.* i. 17).[1] It was 'four-eared' (*čathru-gaosha*, *i.e.* four-square or quadrangular [?]; cf. Darmesteter, ii. 14, n. 38), and was the birthplace of the hero Thraētaona or Farīdūn, who overcame Aži Dahāka (*Vend.* i. 17; *Yt.* v. 33)—a tale which was discussed at length in the lost *Sūṭkar Nask* of the Avesta (*Dīnkart*, IX. xxi. 17–24; cf. also VIII. xiii. 9, IX. xxii. 4).[2] The location of Varena is a matter of some dispute. It was certainly near Ṭabaristān (Spiegel, i. 545), but is hardly to be identified with the modern village of Verek, south of Sārī, as argued by Spiegel (i. 72, n. 2, 545) and F. Justi (*Handb. der Zendsprache*, Leipzig, 1864, p. 270 [with earlier literature], *GIrP* ii. 404). Equally uncertain is the view of C. de Harlez (*Avesta trad.*, Liège, 1875–77, i. 87, n. 2) that it was the modern Kirmān. A. V. W. Jackson (*GIrP* ii. 663) and Dhalla (*locc. citt.*) identify it with Gīlān, and Darmesteter (ii. 14, n. 38) with Ṭabaristān or Dailam. Ṭabaristān was formerly preferred by Geiger (*Ostīrān. Kultur*, pp. 127 f., 184); his later view (*GIrP* ii. 391), identifying Varena with the Caspian Gates, seems scarcely an improvement. Neriosangh was ignorant of the meaning of the term, for he renders *Varenya* by *vibhramakara*, 'confusing,' and *kāma*, 'love' (on *Yt.* i. 19; *Ys.* xxvii. 1), confounding the epithet with the later Pahlavi Varenō, the demon of lust (Jackson, ii. 660, 663; Darmesteter, ii. 373, n. 33; L. C. Casartelli, *Philosophy of the Mazdayasnian Religion under the Sassanids*, Bombay, 1889, pp. 91, 166). On the whole, Gīlān appears to be the most probable identification.

It would seem that the legend of Haoshyangha refers to an early invasion of Māzandarān and Gīlān by Iranians, and their conquest of it, at least in part. This is borne out by the local tradition of the early 13th cent., for Ibn Isfandiyār (p. 15) held that

'until the time of Jamshīd it was in the possession of the demons. He conquered them, and bade them level the mountains with the plains, fill up the lakes, drain the fens into the sea, open up the country, and distribute the rivers and streams.'

The Iranian religion found some place, at all events, in Māzandarān, for tradition sees in Spiti and Erezrāspa, who are mentioned in *Yt.* xiii. 121, two pious men who came from Māzandarān to receive the faith from Frashaoshtra, the father-in-law of Zarathushtra (*Dīnkart*, IX. xxi. 17–24).

In the Pahlavi texts the most interesting passage in the present connexion is found in the *Shikand-gūmānīg Vijār* (xvi. 28–36), which records a belief closely similar to the frequent Gnostic concept of the entanglement of light in darkness combined with a touch of the Iranian heresy of Zarvanism.

'The rain was the seed of the Māzandarāns for the reason that when the Māzandarāns are bound on the celestial sphere, whose light is swallowed by them, and, in order to pass it from them through a new regulation, discrimination, and retention of the light of Time, the twelve glorious ones show the daughters of Time[1] to the household-attending male Māzandarāns, so that while the lust of those Māzandarāns, from seeing them, is well suited to them, and seed is discharged from them, the light which is within the seed is poured on to the earth. Trees, shrubs, and grain have grown therefrom, and the light which is within the Māzandarāns is discharged in the seed.'[2]

In the *Shāh-nāmah* Māzandarān is described with little geographical accuracy (Nöldeke, ii. 178), and the Kargasārs ('Vulture-heads'), who are frequently mentioned as inhabiting the country, like the Sagsārs ('Dog-heads'), Buzgūsh ('Goat-ears'), and Narmpāi ('Strap-feet, Ἱμαντόποδες'), betray the influence of pseudo-Callisthenes upon Firdausī (Nöldeke, ii. 146, n. 3). In his proper shape the king of Māzandarān had a boar's head (Warner, ii. 75). The land itself was

'The home of warlock-dīvs and under spells
Which none hath power to loose; . . .
To go or e'en to think of going thither
Is held unlucky!' (*ib.* 36 f.).

Nevertheless, it was invaded unsuccessfully by Kai Kāūs and successfully by Rustam (*ib.* 30–41, 42–44, 57–78), one of the great achievements of the latter being the slaying of the 'White Demon,' whom Warner (ii. 27 f.) holds to be a personification of the Māzandarānīs, rendered pale by the unhealthiness of their climate. This 'White Dīv' was

'mountain-tall,
With shoulders, breast, and neck ten cords across' (*ib.* 55).

The magic exercised by the 'White Dīv' against Kai Kāūs reads like a description of a severe hailstorm (*ib.* 40); the only other point worth noting is that his blood cured failing sight (*ib.* 62).

Even in the Arab period Māzandarān remained imperfectly Islāmized. As late as the 10th cent. many of the inhabitants of Dailam and Gīlān were 'plunged in ignorance' (*i.e.* heathenism), and some were Magians, this being particularly the case with those in the mountains, valleys, fortresses, and other inaccessible places (Masʿūdī, *Prairies d'or*, ed. and tr. C. Barbier de Meynard and Pavet de Courteille, Paris, 1861–77, ix. 5). It was a

[1] With these 'non-Aryan over-lords' Geiger (p. 185, n. 2) compares the Ἀναριάκαι, a tribe dwelling along the Caspian (Strabo, pp. 507 f., 514; cf. W. Tomaschek, in Pauly-Wissowa, i. 2063; F. Andreas, *ib.* 2195).

[2] In a Turfān fragment Aži Dahāka, who was imprisoned in Damāvand, is called 'Mazan.' The adjective has thus far been found in two other passages, but in both cases the accompanying names are illegible (C. Salemann, *Manichäische Studien*, i. [Petrograd, 1908] 95). For the local Muhammadan version, according to which Solomon imprisoned in Damāvand the *jinnī* who stole his ring, see Ibn Isfandiyār, p. 36.

[1] The zodiacal signs, appointed as celestial leaders by Ahura Mazda (*Dīnā-ī-Māīnōg-ī-Xraṭ*, viii. 18).

[2] According to Darmesteter (ii. 373, n. 32) and West (*GIrP* ii. 110), the Pahlavi *Jāmāsp-nāmak* raises the question whether the Māzandarānīs were demons or men, and where their souls went after death, the reply being that they were all men, that some of them followed the religion of Ahura Mazda and others the law of Angra Mainyu, and that most of them went to heaven; but the text, as edited and translated by J. J. Modi (Bombay, 1903), contains no statement whatever on this matter.

centre of the Ḫurramite and Zaidite sects of Muhammadanism (*ib.* vi. 188, vii. 117; cf. also Ibn Isfandiyār, pp. 158, 189–193).

The Zaidites call for no special remark, but the Ḫurramites may be briefly described, as being one of the many attempts at religious syncretism in W. Asia.

The exact meaning of the name is not absolutely certain. It is usually explained as from Pers. *xurram*, 'cheerful' (*i.e.* 'Epicurean'; so T. Haarbrücker, in his note to his tr. of al-Shahrastānī's *Religionspartheien und Philosophenschulen*, Halle, 1850–51, ii. 410, and Flügel, *ZDMG* xxiii. 531, note), but it has also been derived from the town of Ḫurram near Ardābīl, which appears to have been an ancient centre of Mazdakite teaching (A. Müller, *Islam*, Berlin, 1885, i. 505, note). The present writer is inclined to trace the term to the name of Mazdak's wife, Ḫurramah, who, after her husband's execution, fled to Ray, where she carried on a successful propaganda of Mazdakite heresy, calling her teachings *Ḫurram-dīn* (cf. also C. Schefer, *Chrestomathie persane*, Paris, 1883–85, i. 170–175, where the relevant passage of Niẓām-al-Mulk's *Kitāb al-Siyāssat* [ed. and tr. in full by Schefer, Paris, 1893] is given in text and translation; for the Mazdakite heresy see art. MAZDAK).

The Ḫurramites were divided into the Bābakīyah and Māzyārīyah (the latter also called Muḥammirah, 'red-badged'). While there is abundant material regarding the rôle played for more than twenty years (815–838) in Ṭabaristān by Bābak (the Arabic spelling of the Iranian name Pāpak),[1] as well as by Māzyār,[2] for a knowledge of the special features of their sects we have only two sources—the *Fihrist* of Muḥammad ibn Isḥāq al-Nadīm (written in A.D. 987–988, ed. G. Flügel, Leipzig, 1871–72, pp. 342. 30–344. 18, tr. Browne, *Lit. Hist.* pp. 324–327) and the *Tabṣīr fī al-dīn wa-tamyīz al-firqat al-najīyat 'an al-firaq al-hālikīn* of Abū-l-Muẓaffar Ṭāhir ibn Muḥammad al-Isfarāīnī († A.D. 1078; the passage in question is ed. by Flügel, *ZDMG* xxiii. 533, note).[3]

From the *Fihrist* we learn that Bābak was the natural son of an oil-seller who migrated from Ctesiphon to the village of Bilāl-ābādh, not far from Ardābīl and Arrajān, and married, after an illicit amour with her, a one-eyed woman who later became the mother of Bābak. One day, while the boy was asleep, his mother saw a drop of blood under each hair on his breast and head, and from this she inferred that he 'was destined for some glorious mission.' Bābak later entered the service of Jāvīdān,[4] a Ḫurramī leader, and, when the latter died, in consequence of a wound received from the rival Ḫurramī chieftain, Abū 'Imrām, Jāvīdān's wife, who had engaged in an intrigue with Bābak, and who had concealed from the public the news of her husband's death, told her lover that she would tell Jāvīdān's followers that he had decided to die and cause his spirit to pass into Bābak, who was to slay the present rulers, restore the Mazdakites, and enrich his adherents. The plan was completely successful, and Bābak became the acknowledged leader of the sect, claiming to be God incarnate. After this, Bābak's mistress 'called for a cow, and commanded that it should be slain and flayed, and that its skin should be spread out, and on the skin she placed a bowl filled with wine, and into it she broke bread, which she placed round about the bowl. Then she called them, man by man, and bade each of them tread the skin with his foot, and take a piece of bread, plunge it in the wine, and eat it, saying, "I believe in thee, O Spirit of Bábak, as I believe in the spirit of Jáwídán"; and that each should then take the hand of Bábak, and do obeisance before it, and kiss it.' She then 'brought forth food and wine to them, and seated Bábak on her bed, and sat beside him publicly before them. And when they had drunk three draughts each, she took a sprig of basil and offered it to Bábak, and he took it from her hand, and this was their marriage' (Browne, p. 327).

It is thus clear that Bābak held the doctrines of *hulul* (the incarnation of God in human form), *tanāsuḫ* (passing of the soul from one body to another), and *rij'ah* (reincarnation), so that he belonged to the 'immoderate' Shī'ites as described by al-Shahrastānī (tr. Haarbrücker, i. 199 ff.; cf. Browne, p. 328). He appears to have been hostile to Islām, for Ibn Isfandiyār states (p. 153) that he 'ordered the Muhammadan mosques to be destroyed and all traces of Islām to be removed.' It is doubtful whether he was of Persian origin, for, according to the *Fihrist*, his father sang songs 'in the Nabatean tongue,' and Bābak's own tongue 'was cramped by outlandish speech' (see, further, Browne, *loc. cit.*).

To this information al-Isfarāīnī adds that the Māzyārīyah 'appealed to the religion of the Muḥammirah,' and he says:

'By night the Bābakīyah in those mountains [of Ṭabaristān] agree upon every kind of depravity with women and flute-playing, etc.; and therein [*i.e.* at night] the men and the women agree together. Then the lamps and fires are extinguished, and every one of them rises up to one of the women who chances to sit with him. And these Ḫurramīyah assert that in the Ignorance they had a king named Sharvīn,[1] whom they deem greater than the prophets; and when they mourn for the dead, in his name they pay tears and lamentations, (even) their grief for him.'[2]

It is clear that the Bābakīyah were only a later phase of the sect founded by Mazdak, but in a degenerate form, marred by the cruelty which characterized the career of Bābak, who is said to have slain at least 255,500 persons during his years of power.

LITERATURE.—F. Spiegel, *Erânische Alterthumskunde*, Leipzig, 1871–78, i. 66–70, 585–592; W. Geiger, *Ostīrān. Kultur im Altertum*, Erlangen, 1882, pp. 42–45, 124 f., 127 f., 184, 187; J. Marquart, *Ērānšahr*, Berlin, 1901, pp. 129–135; G. N. Curzon, *Persia and the Persian Question*, London, 1892, i. 354–389 (with abundant references to earlier travellers); G. Melgunoff, *O yužnomŭ berege kaspiiskago morya*, Petrograd, 1863 (Germ. tr. by J. T. Zenker, *Das südliche Ufer des kaspischen Meeres*, Leipzig, 1868); B. Dorn, *Muham. Quellen zur Gesch. der süd. Küstenländer des caspischen Meeres*, 4 vols., Petrograd, 1850–58 (edd. of the local historians Ẓāhir al-Dīn [cf. also H. Ethé, *GIrP* ii. 362], 'Alī ibn Šams al-Dīn, 'Abd al-Fattaḥ Fūmanī, and a volume of miscellaneous extracts); Muḥammad ibn al-Ḥasan ibn Isfandiyār, *Hist. of Ṭabaristān*, abridged tr. by E. G. Browne, London, 1905; G. Flügel, 'Bâbek, seine Abstammung und erstes Auftreten,' *ZDMG* xxiii. [1869] 531–542; E. G. Browne, *Literary Hist. of Persia from the Earliest Times till Firdawsī*, London, 1902, pp. 323–331. Much early literature on the history of the country has been lost—*e.g.*, 'Alī ibn Muḥammad al-Madāinī's 9th cent. *Book of the Victories of the Mountains of Ṭabaristān* and *Book of Ṭabaristān in the Days of Rašīd*, mentioned in the *Fihrist*, 103. 15. For the Māzandarānī dialect see W. Geiger, *GIrP* I. ii. [1901] 345 ff. (with copious references to earlier literature).

LOUIS H. GRAY.

MAZDA.—See ORMAZD.

MAZDAK.—**I. History.**—Mazdak, son of Bāmdādh, a Persian (probably a native of Susiana), was the leader of a communistic sect which towards the end of the 5th cent. A.D. became a formidable power in the Sasanian empire. According to some accounts, the original founder of the sect was a certain Zarādusht, son of Khurragān,[3] on whose behalf Mazdak is said to have carried on propaganda among the populace, but in any case it was under Mazdak that the sect first gained importance. His temporary success was largely due to the state of anarchy then prevailing in Persia. The emperor Kawādh, who ascended the throne in A.D. 488, finding himself opposed by the nobility and the influential Zoroastrian priesthood, entered into a close alliance with the arch-heretic and embraced his revolutionary doctrines. The governing classes were strong enough to depose Kawādh in favour of his brother Jāmāsp; but after his restoration, which took place a few years later, the power of the Mazdakites continued to increase, though Kawādh does not seem to have supported them very actively. In the concluding years of his reign a bitter struggle was waged over the succession, which the Mazdakites endeavoured to secure for one of Kawādh's sons who was devoted to their cause, while the Zoroastrian priests, in agreement with the emperor himself, regarded

[1] See the references given by Browne, *Lit. Hist.* p. 323, n. 3; C. Huart, in *EI* i. [1913] 547, and Justi, *Iran. Namenbuch*, Marburg, 1895, p. 242.

[2] Justi, p. 202.

[3] On al-Isfarāīnī see Haji Khalfa, ed. and tr. Flügel, Leipzig, 1835–58, ii. 183, no. 2390; cf. also Haarbrücker, ii. 378 ff.

[4] Cf. Justi, p. 113.

[1] See Justi, p. 290.

[2] Perhaps we may compare the nocturnal orgies against which the Gāthās polemize (*Ys.* xxxii. 10, xlviii. 10; cf. C. Bartholomae, *Gatha's des Awesta*, Strassburg, 1905, p. 33 f.; J. H. Moulton, *Early Zoroastrianism*, London, 1913, pp. 72, 129); possibly, however, it was merely a current bit of scandalous gossip without much foundation.

[3] The Mazdakites are called Zarādushtakān in the Syriac *Chronicle of Joshua the Stylite*, ed. W. Wright, Cambridge, 1882, § 20.

prince Khusrau as the presumptive heir to the throne. The course of the events which culminated in the massacre of Mazdak together with many thousands of his followers is uncertain. According to the narrative of a Persian official who was converted to Christianity and assumed the name of Timotheus (Joannes Malalas, in *PG* xcvii. 654; Theophanes, *ib.* cviii. 395), Kawādh pretended to yield to the Mazdakites, and, having appointed a day for his abdication, caused his soldiers to cut down all the Mazdakites who had assembled with their wives and children in the neighbourhood of Ctesiphon to witness the ceremony; he then gave orders that the surviving members of the sect should be seized and burned, and that their property should be confiscated. Most Muhammadan writers place this massacre in the reign of Khusrau, but the truth appears to be that, although it was carried out under Khusrau's direction and probably at his instigation, it preceded his accession (A.D. 531) by two or three years. Nöldeke assigns it to the end of 528 or the beginning of 529 (*Gesch. der Perser und Araber zur Zeit der Sasaniden*, Leyden, 1879, p. 465). The ruthless energy displayed by Khusrau on this occasion earned for him, it is said, the title of Anūshakrubān (Anūsharwān, Nūshīrwān), *i.e.* 'he of immortal spirit,' and the further measures which he took were so effectual that henceforward the Mazdakites vanish from history. That they were entirely exterminated is scarcely credible. There is some ground for the suggestion that Mazdak's ideas maintained themselves in secret and found expression in various Antinomian sects which arose in Persia during the Muhammadan period (for an account of one of these see art. MĀZANDARĀN).

2. Doctrine.—It must be remembered that the whole of our information concerning Mazdak is derived from hostile sources. The epitaph written by an intolerant sacerdotal caste over heretics who had brought it to the verge of destruction may fairly be summed up in the words 'de mortuis nil nisi malum'; and, unfortunately, we have nothing from the Mazdakite side to set against the biased narrative of our Zoroastrian and Christian authorities. On the other hand, we cannot suppose that they have altogether obscured the essential character of Mazdakism, however they may have misunderstood or misrepresented it in detail. Its socialistic basis is well described in the following passage of Ṭabarī (Leyden ed., 1879–1901, i. 893. 11 f., translated by Nöldeke, *op. cit.* p. 154):

'Among the commands which he [Mazdak] laid upon the people and earnestly enjoined was this, that they should possess their property and families in common; it was, he said, an act of piety that was agreeable to God and would bring the most excellent reward hereafter; even if he had laid no religious commandments upon them, yet the good works with which God was well pleased consisted in such copartnership.'

In another passage (Ṭabarī, i. 885. 19 f. = Nöldeke, *op. cit.* p. 141) we read:

'They [the Mazdakites] asserted that God placed the means of subsistence (*arzāq*) in the world in order that His servants might share them in common, but men had wronged one another in that respect. The Mazdakites said that they would take from the rich for the benefit of the poor, and give back to those who had little their due portion at the expense of those who had much; and they declared that he who possessed more than his share of wealth, women, and property had no better right to it than any one else. The mob eagerly seized this opportunity, . . . and the Mazdakites became so powerful that they used to enter a man's house and forcibly deprive him of his dwelling, his womenfolk, and his property, since it was impossible for him to offer resistance. . . . Soon things came to such a pass that the father did not know his son nor the son his father.'

While the principle that every man is entitled to possess an equal amount of property involves logically and practically copartnership, the removal of class distinctions, and the abolition of marriage, it may be asked from what point of view the principle itself was regarded by Mazdak, whether these results of its application formed part of his programme, and how far they were achieved by his followers. To take the last question first, Khusrau, in his speech to the priests and nobles after his coronation (Ṭabarī, i. 896. 15 f. = Nöldeke, *op. cit.* p. 160 f.), dwells upon the ruin of their religion and the heavy losses which they had incurred. The systematic regulations which he made for the purpose of compensating the sufferers, establishing the position of children of doubtful origin, etc., show that the social revolution must have developed considerably, and that the upper classes bore the brunt of it. Our authorities give great prominence to this aspect of Mazdakism, and they are justified in doing so. Mazdak was not a philosopher, like Plato, content to work out on paper a theory of the ideal communistic State. He was a militant social reformer, but he was something more. Nöldeke has remarked that what distinguishes Mazdakism from the organized socialism of modern times is its religious character, a peculiarity in which it resembles all Oriental movements of the same kind (*op. cit.* p. 459; cf. his art. 'Orientalischer Socialismus,' in *Deutsche Rundschau*, Feb. 1879, p. 284 f.). This character is preserved in the hostile Zoroastrian tradition. Mazdak's asceticism—he is said to have forbidden the slaughter of cattle for food—gave offence to the orthodox, who saw in him 'the ungodly fasting Ashemaogha' (Pahlavi commentary on *Vendīdād*, iv. 49; *SBE* iv.² [1895] 48). The passages from Ṭabarī translated above, and still more the epic narrative of Firdausī (*Shāhnāmah*, ed. Turner Macan, Calcutta, 1829, p. 1611 f.), which reflects the sentiments of the priesthood, bring out quite clearly the fact that Mazdak identified his doctrines of equality and fraternity with the religion of Zoroaster in its original uncorrupted form.

'I will establish this [communism] in order that the pure religion
May be made manifest and raised from obscurity.
Whoever follows any religion except this,
May the curse of God overtake that demon (*dēv*)!'
(*Shāh-nāmah*, p. 1613, line 11 ff.).

'Five things turn a man from righteousness;
The sage cannot add to these five:
Jealousy, anger, vengeance, need,
And the fifth one that masters him is covetousness.
If thou prevail against these five demons,
The way of the Almighty will be made manifest to thee.
Because of these five, we possess women and wealth,
Which have destroyed the good religion in the world.
Women and wealth must be in common,
If thou desirest that the good religion should not be harmed.
These two (women and wealth) produce jealousy and covetousness and need,
Which secretly unite with anger and vengeance.
The Demon (*dēv*) is always turning the heads of the wise,
Therefore these two things must be made common property'
(*ib.* p. 1614, line 7 ff.).

Without claiming that Mazdak was animated by no other motives than those which his enemies attribute to him here, we may well believe that he regarded his communistic scheme as the only sure means of enabling mankind to attain the object which Zoroaster had set before them, namely, the defeat of the powers of darkness and the triumph of the spirit of light. The astonishing success of his propaganda is to be explained by the force of his appeal to Persian idealism. He would not have gained extensive support for his social programme unless it had been, ostensibly if not in fact, the instrument by which he hoped to accomplish a great religious reformation. In the main he appears to have held fast to Zoroastrianism, and no reliance can be placed on the statements of Shahrastānī and later writers who credit him with cosmological speculations closely akin to those of Mānī.

LITERATURE.—The principal references to Mazdak which occur in Greek, Syriac, Pahlavi, Arabic, and Persian literature are collected by T. Nöldeke, *Gesch. der Perser und Araber zur Zeit der Sasaniden*, Leyden, 1879, at the beginning of the fourth excursus, 'Ueber Mazdak und die Mazdakiten,' p. 455 f., which is the best existing source of information on the whole subject, and by E. G. Browne, in his *Literary Hist. of Persia*, i., London, 1902, p. 169. See also F. Spiegel, *Erân. Alterthumskunde*, Leipzig, 1871–78, ii. 232–235; G. Rawlinson, *The Seventh Great Oriental Monarchy*, London, 1876, p. 342 f.; al-Bīrūnī, *The Chronology of Ancient Nations*, tr. C. E. Sachau, do. 1879, p. 192; Shahrastānī, tr. T. Haarbrücker, Halle, 1850–51, i. 291 ff.; *Dabistān*, tr. D. Shea and A. Troyer, Paris, 1843, i. 372 ff.; Shaikh Muhammad Iqbal, *The Development of Metaphysics in Persia*, London, 1908, p. 18 f. The collection of *rivāyats* of Dārāb Hormazdyār (ed. M. N. Unvâlâ, ii. 214–230—the edition has not yet been published) contains a long poem, written A.D. 1616, on Mazdak and Kawādh (briefly summarized by F. Rosenberg, *Notices de litt. parsie*, Petrograd, 1909, p. 51 f.).

REYNOLD A. NICHOLSON.

MEAN.—The historic varieties of significance associated with this term are all evolved from the general idea of that which comes 'between' or in the 'middle.' Hence the term has an implication of double relationship to two other terms, the primitive significance being that which is 'between' two other things in reference to space or time.[1]

As subst. and as adj. 'mean' entered Mid. Eng. from late Lat. *medianus* through O. Fr. *moien*, Mod. Fr. *moyen*. The Lat. original *medianus* (like Eng. 'middle' through its A.S. original) is connected with one of the oldest and most widely spread roots in human language. Both as subst. and as adj. 'mean,' in the sense here defined, is to be distinguished from adj. 'mean' of A.S. origin (A.S. *gemæne*, O.H.G. *gimeini*, Mod. Germ. *gemeine*, akin to *communis*), which, originally signifying 'general' or 'common' to more persons than one, acquired the sense of 'middling' or 'moderate' and then of 'low' in rank or quality, *ethically* inferior or ignoble, esp. 'avaricious' or 'penurious.'

The idea of the mean was given an ethical application by Aristotle (*Eth. Nic.* ii. 6–8), in whose doctrine of virtue it holds the central place. Virtue consists in reasonable moderation, involving the avoidance, on the one side, of excess, and, on the other, of defect; in this sense virtue holds an intermediate position, and may be said to be a mean. Here the mean is not quantitative, and the notion of 'equal distance' from the extreme is not applicable. Every habit or action may err by excess or defect; between these opposed extremes (*e.g.*, θρασύτης and δειλία) stands that degree of activity which characterizes virtuous conduct (in this instance, ἀνδρεία; cf. *Eth. Nic.* iii. 7, 1115^b–1116^a). Its 'distance' from the extremes will depend on the nature of the agent in relation to that of the moral case before him, and is therefore to be determined, not by any abstract considerations, but by the concrete rational judgment of the man of insight (φρόνιμος [*Eth. Nic.* ii. 6, 1107^a]).

This conception involves that of an adaptation or harmony of agent, act, and environment, similar to the harmony of parts displayed in a work of art; in fact, it expresses the æsthetic aspect of virtue. Aristotle is aware that, in the strictly ethical sense, virtue is always opposed to vice, and is therefore always an 'extreme' (ii. 6. 11, 1106^b 22; 17, 1107^a 6; Stewart, *Notes on the Nicomachean Ethics of Aristotle*, ii. 208). But, in laying stress on the æsthetic aspect, Aristotle is true to the Greek genius. The traditional Greek view of life made it natural that 'moderation,' 'measure,' and kindred conceptions should be appropriated to express excellence in life and action.

The typical Greek virtue is σωφροσύνη (most inadequately rendered 'temperance'), closely related to the traditional maxim μηδὲν ἄγαν. Its opposite is ὕβρις. In Homer the object of moral condemnation is of the nature of 'excess,' 'going too far'; above all, 'wickedness' is ὕβρις. In the case of the strong it is the insolence of brutality, especially in reference to the weak and the helpless; in the low and the weak it is irreverence in the presence of something higher.[2] When a man thinks of doing such things, he feels αἰδώς; if he does them, the seen and unseen witnesses feel νέμεσις, 'righteous indignation.'

There is an application of the Aristotelian principle of the mean in the general theory of knowledge, not, indeed, explicitly stated by Aristotle, but implicit in much of his thinking, as in that of Plato; it was made by Hegel into the first principle of thought and being in the applications of his Logic—his doctrine of thought as a dialectically progressive movement through the meeting of opposites—to the history of human thought and endeavour; it is this that gives to his expositions of history all their strength and value, notwithstanding the excessively rigid formalism with which the principle is applied by him in certain cases. We can seldom find clearly marked theses and antitheses (in pairs) from the opposition of which the higher truth springs; we can find only conflicting ἐνέργειαι, streams of tendency, movements of thought.

A movement involving truth mingled with error is found in conflict with another movement, involving different truths mingled with different errors. What is required is a point of view above both the conflicting principles, from which to criticize them. This is the true 'middle way,' found, not by taking what the two extreme views have in common, and disregarding all their differences, but by finding a principle which contains more truth than either of the extremes, not less truth. The value of the conflicts and oppositions of history is to suggest the need for these higher—or, to vary the metaphor, deeper—truths, and sometimes also to suggest the way to reach them.

LITERATURE.—Aristotle, *Eth. Nic.*; A. S. Grant, *Ethics of Aristotle*³, London, 1874, Essay iv.; J. A. Stewart, *Notes on the Nicomachean Ethics of Aristotle*, Oxford, 1892, i. 193–199, 202 f., 208–211, 472–475; Julia Wedgwood, *The Moral Ideal*, London, 1888, ch. iii. ('Greece and the Harmony of Opposites'); Gilbert Murray, *Rise of the Greek Epic*, Oxford, 1907, pp. 80 ff., 264 ff.; S. H. Mellone, *Leaders of Religious Thought*, London and Edinburgh, 1902, ch. i.; W. Wallace, *Logic of Hegel*², Prolegomena, Oxford, 1904, chs. xxvi.–xxxii. For the Buddhist school of the mean see art. MADHYAMAKA, MĀDHYAMIKAS.

S. H. MELLONE.

MEAN (Chinese).—Outside of Greece, the theory of the mean received formal attention only in China, which produced the classic *Chung Yung*, commonly known as 'The Doctrine of the Mean,' though more exactly rendered 'Equilibrium and Harmony' (see above, p. 90^b), the authorship of which is attributed to the grandson of Confucius, Tzŭ Ssŭ, who flourished in the 5th cent. B.C.

Heaven has conferred a spiritual nature on man, and 'an accordance with this nature is called the path [of duty],' which must never be abandoned (i. 1–2). The terms *chung* ('equilibrium') and *yung* ('harmony') are respectively absence of 'stirrings of pleasure, anger, sorrow, or joy,' and the state in which 'those feelings have been stirred, and they act in their due degree' (i. 4). Therefore, 'let the states of equilibrium and harmony exist in perfection, and a happy order will prevail throughout heaven and earth, and all things will be nourished and flourish' (i. 5). According to Confucius himself, the superior man embodies this ideal state, and 'perfect is the virtue which is according to the Mean' (ii. f.); yet some err by exceeding it, and some by falling short of it (iv. 1)—only the sage is in perfect harmony with it (xi. 3). As an example of the practical value of *chung yung*, Confucius cites the course pursued by the emperor Shun (2255–2205 B.C., according to Chinese tradition), who questioned men, 'took hold of their two extremes, [determined] the Mean, and employed it in [his government of] the people' (vi.); but yet, in spite of all, 'the course of the Mean cannot be attained to' (ix.). In a word, the superior man 'stands erect in the middle, without inclining to either side' (x. 5); if he goes beyond the mean, he checks himself; if he falls below it, he puts forth every effort to attain it (xiii. 4).

Yet 'the path is not far from man' (xiii. 1); but, even if 'common men and women, however much below the ordinary standard of character, can carry it into practice; yet in its utmost reaches, there is that which even the sage is not able to carry into practice' (xii. 2). One is not far from the path when he 'cultivates to the utmost the principles of his nature, and exercises them on

[1] From the sense of 'that which stands between two things,' the 'mean' (or plural 'means,' often used grammatically as a singular) may be used for that which produces a result, or, more generally, for any resources capable of producing a result.

[2] The case of Nebuchadrezzar (Dn $4^{27ff.}$) illustrates a form of ὕβρις, portrayed in a specifically religious setting.

the principle of reciprocity' (xiii. 3); and yet 'were the superior man to speak of his way in all its greatness, nothing in the world would be found able to embrace it; and were he to speak of it in its minuteness, nothing in the world would be found able to split it' (xii. 2). 'The superior man does what is proper to the station in which he is; he does not desire to go beyond this. . . . The superior man can find himself in no situation in which he is not himself,' and, if he fails in anything, he blames only himself (xiv. 1 f., 5). He advances in regular order from stage to stage (xv. 1), and constantly strives to advance and develop his virtuous nature that he may pursue the path of the mean (xxvii. 6). 'When occupying a high situation, he is not proud, and in a low situation, he is not insubordinate' (xxvii. 7); and it is characteristic of the superior man, though 'appearing insipid, yet never to produce satiety; while showing a simple negligence, yet to have his accomplishments recognized; while seemingly plain, yet to be discriminating' (xxxiii. 1). Among the many virtues of Confucius, special mention is made of the fact that he never swerved from the mean (xxxi. 1).

The remainder of the *Chung Yung* is devoted to laudation of filial piety, and to the duties of government, the obligation of absolute sincerity, the path of the sage, and the character of the ideal ruler—all of which depend on the cultivation of *chung yung*.

The mean is mentioned a number of times in the other Chinese Classics; *e.g.*, the *Yî King* says (xlii. 3) that the ruler should 'be sincere and pursue the path of the Mean'; but these texts add nothing to the main discussion in the *Chung Yung*.

LITERATURE.—The *Chung Yung* is most conveniently ed. and tr. by J. Legge, *Chinese Classics*, Hongkong and London, 1861–73, i. 246–298 (cf. also his Prolegomena to this vol., pp. 35–55), and again tr. by him in *SBE* xxviii. [1885] 300–329.

LOUIS H. GRAY.

MECCA.—Mecca (Arabic Makkah) is a city in Central Arabia, famous as the birthplace of Islām, and, except for a short period at the commencement of the system, at all times its chief sanctuary. A variety of the name, Bakkah, occurs once in the Qur'ān (iii. 90), and this is probably the earlier form, though the etymology is uncertain. The classical geographers, who devote considerable attention to Arabia, are apparently not acquainted with this settlement; for the Makoraba of Ptolemy (VI. vii. 32) is derived from a different root. The 'Chronicles of Mecca,' of which the earliest extant is by Azraqī († 245 A.H.), so far as they treat of the pre-Islāmic period, are collections of fables, in the main based on the Qur'ān, but to some extent influenced by the later history also. It would appear that, when Islām arose, there were no chronicles in existence dealing with the affairs of Central Arabia, and for some generations the days of paganism were regarded with a sort of horror, which prevented the preservation of precise information concerning them.

The references to the city in the Qur'ān throw little light on its early history. A *sūra* incorporated near the end of the collection (cv.) reminds the Prophet of the Owners of the Elephant, who were destroyed by birds (*abābīl*), which flung at them stones of *sijjīl*. The tradition interprets this as an expedition by Abyssinians against the Meccan sanctuary, miraculously frustrated, but it is possible that this story is an invention of exegetes, who coupled *sūra* cv. with cvi., which more decidedly deals with Mecca, and is itself a fragment, scarcely to be construed in its present form. In it the Quraish (the tribe in possession of the Meccan sanctuary) are advised to worship the Lord of this House, who has given them food after hunger and safety after fear. These two phenomena, plenty and safety, are mentioned elsewhere in connexion with the Meccan sanctuary, the former as a result, it would seem, of visits from pilgrims, whereas the latter probably means safety for refugees; but the texts are not very clear. The sanctuary itself is called in the Qur'ān either 'the house,' or 'the house of Allāh, the Sanctuary,' or the Ka'bah (a word said to mean no more than 'house,' and perhaps the Ethiopic word for 'double,' *i.e.* two-storeyed), or 'the place of prostration, the Sanctuary.' In iii. 90 f. it is called 'the first house established for mankind, blessed and a guidance to the worlds, containing manifest signs, the station of Abraham, and whoever enters it is secure.' This would by itself imply that the Ka'bah was the first house ever built, as a model for all others, and that Abraham took refuge there and made it his abode. Elsewhere (xiv. 40) Abraham states that he had settled his family by it (or in it) in spite of the sterility of the valley, in order that they might pray there regularly; and he prays that the *town* (and not the house only) might be secure. In xxii. 27 he is represented as doing in his time much the same as was afterwards done by Muhammad: he was told to purify the house for those that perform the four ceremonies called *ṭawāf*, standing, inclination, and prostration. In ii. 119 f. Ishmael is coupled with Abraham; they laid the foundations of the house, and were told to purify it as before, the ceremony called *'ukūf* being substituted for 'standing.' What may be inferred from these texts is perhaps that prior to Muhammad's time the Ka'bah was a sanctuary which enjoyed some popularity in part of Arabia, and that the right of sanctuary had to some extent been associated with the settlement of Mecca and with its inhabitants. The biography of the Prophet certainly implies that the Meccans had the very strongest objection to bloodshed, and possessed little aptitude for warfare. The association of Mecca with Abraham is unlikely to have been earlier than the Prophet, except so far as the N. Arabian tribes were known by monotheists, on the authority of Genesis, to be descended from the patriarch. It seems clear, however, that the Ka'bah was only one of many sanctuaries which were visited, and, if the word *ḥijjah*, which is used for 'pilgrimage,' be explicable from the Hebrew *ḥūg*, 'draw round,' the Arabian month which is called after it is likely to mean 'month of going-round,' *i.e.* the round of the sanctuaries, as opposed to the preceding 'month of squatting' at home. The word technically used of going round the Ka'bah, *ṭawāf*, seems also to be properly used of going a round, as, *e.g.*, is done by a sentinel, and this ceremony may be due to a confusion of thought. The pilgrimage which became stereotyped in Islām involves visits to places which are likely to have been seats of distinct sanctuaries, some at a considerable distance from Mecca.

The difficult *sūra* cvi. speaks of 'winter and summer journeying,' which is traditionally interpreted of Meccan caravans, and in the biography of the Prophet these play an important part. The Muslim archæologists suppose that the Quraish, owing to their character as 'Allāh's people,' enjoyed immunity from attack, and so had special facilities for the carrying trade. It is not easy to reconcile this with the primitive conditions which very clearly prevailed in Mecca at the rise of Islām, and the complete ignorance which the Qur'ān assumes for its inhabitants. If there be any truth in this carrying trade, it is likely to have been on a small scale.

In the Qur'ān Mecca is sometimes called 'the Mother of the villages,' *i.e.* the chief village; elsewhere the number of the villages is given as two, which the commentators suppose to mean Mecca and Ṭāif; it is more probable that only Mecca is meant. Of walls we first hear in the reign of Muqtadir (A.D. 908–932), and these did not surround the settlement, which was naturally protected by mountains, but merely blocked the passes. Snouck Hurgronje[1] is probably right in thinking that the community first gathered round the well Zamzam, which furnishes a constant supply of brackish water. The tradition gives us the names of the tribes which formed the community, but scarcely hints at any sort of municipal organization or government. Still more surprising is the absence of all mention of priests, such as we should have expected to be associated with a sanctuary. The wealth of the tribes is likely to have consisted mainly in camels, but other forms were probably known; visitors to the shrine have at all times had to pay more or less heavily for the privilege, and this source of wealth is, as we have seen, indicated in the Qur'ān. We possess only casual notices of the amounts demanded in later times, but these indicate that the piety of pilgrims often afforded a considerable revenue. The Fāṭimid khalīfs expected the governor of Mecca to make the pilgrim-tax his chief source of revenue; besides this visitors' fee, they had to pay for admission to the sanctuary, and those who brought goods had to pay import duty. Attempts were made by pious sovereigns to abolish these dues, but they had a tendency to revive, and their analogues doubtless existed in the period before the rise of Islām.

Prior to the rise of Islām it would appear that some notions of Christianity had penetrated to Mecca, and the biographies of the Prophet profess to give us the names of persons who had either adopted that system or showed some leanings towards it. There appears to be no recollection of the existence of any Christian place of worship at any time in this city. The tradition represents the pagan inhabitants as tolerant towards religious innovators and dissentients, so long as the local beliefs and practices were not assailed; but the life of such a community was so intimately bound up with the local religion that it is difficult to suppose that dissent could remain quite immune from persecution.

There is reason for thinking that the Prophet's original attitude towards the Meccan religion was uncompromising, and that his success would have involved the abolition of the ceremonies of which the Ka'bah formed the centre. His rejection by the Jews of Medīna (*q.v.*) caused him to contemplate a partial return to the system which he had abandoned, and some time before the taking of Mecca he obtained a truce enabling him to perform the pilgrimage with some ostentation. Doubtless this performance paved the way for the subjection of the place. But, when Mecca had become Islāmic, its position was modified in two important ways. On the one hand, it became the only sanctuary in Arabia; on the other hand, the presence of non-Muslims at the festival was forbidden. Since the pilgrimage was now made compulsory, Mecca lost nothing by this innovation.

It is uncertain whether the Prophet contemplated retaining Medīna permanently as his capital or at some time making his native place the seat of government. There is no doubt that there were jealousies between the two places before the Prophet's death. None of his successors (except perhaps 'Abdallāh b. Zubair, whose occupation of the khalīfate lasted some ten years) seems to have regarded Mecca as a suitable metropolis for political purposes, but its position as the central sanctuary has rarely been endangered. Certain fanatical sects, such as the Carmaṭians and Wahhābīs (*qq.v.*), have at times done damage to its monuments, and the substitution of Baghdād or Jerusalem for it is said to have been considered by Umayyad and 'Abbāsid khalīfs, although they recognized in time that such experiments would have been fatal to Islām or to their thrones.

For the history of Mecca since its adoption of Islām we possess a series of Chronicles, of which those published by F. Wüstenfeld[1] cover the first millennium from the Hijrah, and to these Snouck Hurgronje[2] has added the substance of certain unpublished records which carry the history up to our time. Regular government was then introduced, perhaps for the first time, a prefect appointed by the sovereign being responsible for the maintenance of order. This personage was leader of the ceremonies at the time of the pilgrimage, unless the sovereign either came himself or sent a special representative. The governorships of the three towns, Mecca, Ṭāif, and Medīna were at times united in the same person, at times distinct; the first was much the most important of the three. In 'Abbāsid times it was the custom, at least for a considerable period, to appoint to the governorship some member of the reigning family. It would seem that the 'Alid pretenders, who rose in a fairly constant series, usually found some support in both sanctuaries, and on several occasions they fell for a time into the hands of these persons. After the reduction of the Baghdād khalīfate to impotence—a process which began in the second half of the 3rd cent. of Islām—it would appear that the dependence of the sacred cities on the central government became lax, though historical details are wanting. About A.D. 960 an 'Alid named Ja'far made himself master of Mecca, and introduced the rule of the Sharīfs, which has lasted to our day; this word, signifying 'noble,' is applied in Muslim countries to the descendants of the Prophet. He submitted to the suzerainty of the Fāṭimids now established in Egypt, but in most respects was an independent ruler. His successors shifted their allegiance from Cairo to Baghdād and back, according to the value of the gifts received; and throughout the subsequent history of Mecca recognition has been granted without difficulty to the suzerain who offered the highest price. According to Ibn Jubair,[3] who visited Mecca in the years 1183 and 1185, the Sharīfs were of the Zaidī sect, which, while recognizing the rights of the Prophet's descendants to the succession, held that considerations of expediency might justify their being ousted; the practice of the Sharīfs was then in accordance with this doctrine. The dynasty founded by Ja'far was displaced at the beginning of the 13th cent. of our era by another, also claiming descent from 'Alī. The founder was one Qatadah, who appears to have energetically supported the rising Zaidite dynasty of San'a, but whose successors fell back into the former practice of recognizing the power which for the time was capable of displaying the greatest generosity. The 'Chronicles of Mecca' consist largely of the quarrels between Qatadah's descendants, which not infrequently had to be settled by the active interference of the Egyptian Sulṭāns, who, from the fall of Baghdād until the conquest of Egypt by the Ottomans, were ordinarily recognized as suzerains by the Sharīfs. The Sharīf 'Ajlan (1346–75), who for a time transferred his allegiance to the Mongol rulers of Persia, definitely rejected the Zaidī system and made that of Shāfi'ī dominant in Mecca, though the other orthodox systems were recognized; the dominance of the Ḥanifite school, which is the official system of the Ottoman government, dates from a much later time. A permanent garrison was first established

[1] *Mekka*, The Hague, 1888, i. 5.

[1] *Chroniken der Stadt Mekka*, Leipzig, 1858–61.
[2] *Op. cit.*
[3] ed. M. J. de Goeje, London, 1907, p. 101.

in the neighbourhood by the Egyptian Sulṭān Jaqmaq (1438–53). On the Ottoman conquest of Egypt in 1516 the allegiance of the Sharīfs was transferred without difficulty to the Sulṭān of Constantinople. The new rulers interfered with the authority of the Sharīfs to a greater extent than their predecessors, and the presence of a Turkish governor at Jeddah has constituted a permanent restriction upon it. The introduction of Turkish suzerainty also led to the adoption by the Sharīfs of an intolerant attitude towards the Shī'ites of Persia, who could only with difficulty and at some risk obtain admission to the pilgrimage. In the 17th cent., owing to the decline of the Ottoman power, the Sharīfs, who were almost always involved in family quarrels, became somewhat less dependent on Constantinople, and could even at times defy the representative of the metropolis at Jeddah. Both the sacred cities were threatened by the rise of the Wahhābite movement towards the end of the 18th cent., and indeed in 1793 and 1798 appeals for help against this new power were addressed to the Ottoman Sulṭān. This was not forthcoming, owing to the European complications in which the Porte was involved, and in 1803 Mecca was evacuated by the Sharīf, and presently occupied by the Wahhābīs, who reformed the place according to their ideas. The Sharīf was, however, after a short time re-installed on his professing to adopt the Wahhābī tenets; and for some years Turkish subjects were excluded from the pilgrimage. In 1813 an expedition sent by Muhammad 'Alī, founder of the khedivial family in Egypt, succeeded in recovering the sacred cities, and a Turkish Pasha was installed in Mecca, where, however, the rule of the Sharīf was nominally continued. After a time the Ottoman power was again represented by the governor of Jeddah.

Both the meaning and the limits of the sanctuary (*ḥaram*) were extended by Islām. The sense of this Arabic word is 'to forbid,' and a sanctuary is a place where certain acts are forbidden, of which the most important is bloodshed; it is unlikely that this prohibition before Islāmic times extended beyond the Ka'bah itself. Azraqī is very likely right in asserting that at this time the dwellings of the citizens surrounded the Ka'bah, leaving only a small area (*finā*); the growth of the Muslim community rendered the destruction of these dwellings necessary; and operations of this kind were undertaken by the second and third khalīfs. The area was further enlarged by the pretender 'Abdallāh b. Zubair, but the actual mosque surrounding the Ka'bah was first built by the Umayyad al-Walīd I. (A.D. 705–715), who erected a colonnade with marble pillars and other luxurious decorations. Further additions to the area were made by the 'Abbāsid Manṣūr (in 755), who also built a minaret, and who, in the inscription placed on his work, claims to have doubled the area. Further large additions were made by his successor, Mahdī, who at great cost had a torrent diverted with a view to bringing the site of the Ka'bah into the centre of the mosque. Yet further extensions were effected by Mutawakkil (856), who also introduced luxurious ornamentation. The frequent repairs required by the mosque were due in part to the floods by which Mecca was repeatedly visited, and to some extent to damage done during civil disorders. Under the khalīf Mu'tamid considerable extensions and restorations were again carried out in the years 894–896, and the like are recorded for the year 918 under Muqtadir. Under this khalīf serious mischief was wrought by the Carmaṭians, who massacred the pilgrims, and for a series of years practically put a stop to the institution; their atrocities culminated with the seizure in 317 A.H. of the Black Stone, which they conveyed to their headquarters in Hajar, whence it (or some substitute) was sent back twenty years later. This fetish had already been seriously injured in the time of 'Abdallāh b. Zubair, when the Ka'bah was burned down, and, in spite of great precautions, it again suffered violence at the hands of an Egyptian Shī'ite in the year 414, and not long afterwards was broken into three pieces by some Persian fanatics. The kissing of this object, which forms one of the pilgrimage rites, is not mentioned in the Qur'ān, but probably is a survival from pagan times.

In 1399 a large part of the mosque was destroyed by fire, and orders were presently given by the Egyptian Sulṭān Faraj for its restoration with increased magnificence; this was finished by 1404. In 1551 the Ka'bah itself was found to be in need of repair, but before this could be effected the question was raised whether this sacred building could lawfully be touched by the builders; and the fanatical populace were inclined to side with those holding the negative view. The precedent of Abraham and Ishmael (Qur'ān, ii. 119) finally decided the question in favour of the restoration. In 1571 orders were given for the complete rebuilding of the mosque by the Ottoman Sulṭān Salīm II., who, however, did not live to complete the work; this fell to the lot of his successor Murād III. In the colonnades the principle was followed that three marble columns should be succeeded by one of black stone from a local quarry. Details of the numbers and the location of the columns in the old and in the new mosques are given by Wüstenfeld (iv. 318, 9), together with other statistics and dates. The existing mosque appears to be substantially that erected by Salīm and his successor.

It appears, then, from this sketch of the history of the mosque that little remains in Mecca for which any considerable antiquity can be claimed. The archæological taste has rarely developed in eastern countries, and no trouble was taken either in Mecca or in Medīna to preserve historic buildings or retain ancient sites. The theoretic sanctity of Mecca has never stood in the way of leaders who wished to effect their objects by violence; and the Umayyad Yazīd, whose besieging forces were to some extent responsible for the burning of the Ka'bah in 64 A.H., did no more than would have been done by any other Muslim ruler who was engaged in suppressing a rebellion. Various buildings which figure in the early history of Islām were cleared away as the need for enlarging the temple area arose, and little regret was felt for them. On the other hand, many myths arose which have no justification in the Qur'ān; thus a stone which is called 'the station of Abraham' has acquired great sanctity, but in the Qur'ān (ii. 119, iii. 91) this phrase seems to mean only 'the dwelling-place of Abraham.' The jurist Mālik († 179 A.H.) asserts that this was restored by Omar to a place which it had occupied before the Days of Ignorance, on the faith of a chart preserved in the treasury of the Ka'bah.[1] As we have seen, the Black Stone, which is supposed to represent the 'right hand of Allāh,' is of very doubtful authenticity.

Besides the prohibition against bloodshed which theoretically covers the area occupied by the city, there are other legal peculiarities belonging to it. Closely allied to this prohibition is that against the chase, which is even extended to the cutting of trees and the plucking of herbs. This ordinance is modified in a variety of ways; it seems clear that the slaughter of noxious beasts is generally permitted, and weeding to a certain extent is also lawful. The slaughter of game has to be atoned for by compensation, on a scale fixed by the Qur'ān. There is some difference of opinion between jurists on the question whether rent may be taken for

[1] *Mudawwanat*, Cairo, 1323, ii. 212.

houses in Mecca; according to modern travellers, this question is purely academic, since the inhabitants largely earn their living by letting their houses to pilgrims.

The place of Mecca in the Muslim religion is otherwise not free from anomalies. On the one hand, it is clear that the standard of morality and piety practised by the inhabitants has at no time been particularly high, and various travellers have been shocked by their experiences; on the other hand, there is no doubt about the sanctity of the place and the spiritual benefits that accrue to those who go thither. These are not indeed free from danger; for, just as the value of good actions is higher in Mecca than elsewhere, so the debt incurred by evil deeds is there increased; and, according to the Ṣūfīs, evil thoughts and intentions are punished in Mecca, but not elsewhere. If Abū Ṭālib al-Makkī († 386 A.H.) is right, pious men in early times who went thither on pilgrimage used to pitch two tents, one within and another outside the sacred area, devoting the former exclusively to religious exercises.[1] The resulting danger was one of the reasons why continuous residence in Mecca was discouraged; two others urged by Ghazālī[2] († 505 A.H.) were the fear lest familiarity should breed contempt and the fact that absence makes the heart grow fonder. It could also be urged that, according to the Qur'ān, 'the House' is a place of returning, *i.e.* one to be visited, not made a place of residence (ii. 119).

The various sovereigns who have been protectors or 'servants' of the sanctuaries have ordinarily been lavish in marks of their favour and somewhat jealous of munificence exercised by rival potentates; among the public works executed by these benefactors the greatest amount of space appears to be devoted in the Chronicles to the aqueducts; one which conveys water from Mt. Arafat to Mecca, utilizing a channel originally constructed by order of Zubaida, wife of Hārūn al-Rashīd, occupied fourteen years (965–979 A.H.) and cost enormous sums, owing to the difficulty of piercing the rock and the primitive character of the methods in use. Numerous colleges, hospitals, and almshouses have been erected by Islāmic sovereigns and their ministers, many of them furnished with endowments. The fate of all pious foundations in Mecca, according to Snouck Hurgronje,[3] is the same: most of the houses that have any value have been at some time or other purchased in order to serve as endowment, but gradually passed from hand to hand in such a way that they retain the name *waqf* (on which see *ERE* vii. 877 f.), without serving any pious purpose. The name, however, prevents their being legally sold, yet sale is often necessary, and this is effected in fact, though new names are employed to serve instead of 'sale' and 'purchase.' An attempt was made by a Turkish resident in the middle of the 19th cent. to declare all such transactions invalid, but his removal was procured before this could be carried out.

The erection of the places of learning has not had the effect of rendering Mecca at any time a university centre, and its printing-press has contributed very little to Arabic literature; nevertheless as a gathering-place for the pious it has regularly served for the dissemination of ideas, which are worked out elsewhere. A. Le Chatelier, indeed, attributes the part played by Mecca in recent times to the influence of the Sanūsīs:

'La confrérie nouvelle rendit à la Mecque le rôle de foyer du fanatisme musulman, que lui avait fait perdre la caste sacerdotale' (*Les Confréries musulmanes du Hedjaz*, Paris, 1887, p. 19).

The author of a dialogue on Islāmic revival between Muslims of various nationalities recently placed the scene in Mecca.[1] Yet the cosmopolitan character of the pilgrimage appears from the time of the early Islāmic conquests to have rendered this sanctuary the place where it was easiest to address the Muslim world as a whole. Deeds of settlement of succession to the khalīfate were issued and deposited here by Hārūn al-Rashīd.[2] If a man wished to procure a copy of a rare work, he would have a crier advertise the want among the pilgrims.[3]

In spite of the rule which forbids access to Mecca on the part of non-Muslims, many Europeans have undertaken the pilgrimage, some indeed having adopted Islām for the purpose of carrying out this project. In *Christians at Mecca* (London, 1909) Augustus Ralli gives accounts of sixteen such visitors, beginning with Ludovico Varthema, 'a gentleman of the city of Rome,' who reached the forbidden city in 1503. Since the publication of Ralli's collection two more English travellers have been added to the list: Hadji Khan and W. Sparroy, *With the Pilgrims to Mecca, 1902*, London, 1905; and A. J. B. Wavell, *A Modern Pilgrim in Mecca*, do. 1912. Among the records of these pilgrimages that by R. F. Burton (*Pilgrimage to El-Medinah and Meccah*, London, 1855–56) is classical; it adds, however, very little topographical information to that which had been given to the world by J. L. Burckhardt (*Travels in Arabia*, London, 1829). Of the others the account of the city by Snouck Hurgronje (*op. cit.*, 1885) is the most important. In several cases the travellers were so fully occupied with the task of preserving their lives that they had no time to make observations of value; and in not a few instances the veracity of the narrators has been questioned, not without cause. Besides these accounts by Europeans there are many in existence by Muslims, some of whom have employed the French language. It is asserted that the number of the former who have succeeded in witnessing the pilgrimage and returning to tell the tale is small compared with that of those who have sacrificed their lives in the attempt; and those who have accomplished the task safely have in most cases done so by the exercise of great cunning and ingenuity. The plan of H. Maltzan (*Wallfahrt nach Mekka*, Leipzig, 1865), who, in order to pass for a Muslim, borrowed the personality of an Algerian, the latter undertaking to remain in hiding for the necessary period, may be commended both for boldness and for astuteness; it was not, however, free from danger.

LITERATURE.—The authorities are cited throughout the article.

D. S. MARGOLIOUTH.

MEDALS.—See COINS AND MEDALS.

MEDIAN RELIGION.—The religion of the ancient Medes is one of the most difficult and disputable questions in ancient Oriental history. The statements of the earlier classical authorities are not easy to reconcile with the Iranian Avesta, and fresh elements of difficulty have been introduced by the decipherment of the cuneiform inscriptions.

The actual facts are these. As far back as the 14th cent. B.C. the cuneiform documents of Boghaz Keui have shown that there was an Aryan, but not as yet Iranian, population in Mesopotamia who worshipped the gods Mithra, Varuṇa (written Uruwana and Aruna), Indra, and the two Nāsatyā, the Vedic correspondents of the Dioscuri (cf. E. Meyer, *SBAW*, 1908, pp. 14–19). In the 9th cent. B.C. this Aryan population had become Iranian,

[1] *Qūt al-qulūb*, Cairo, 1310, ii. 119.
[2] *Iḥyā 'ulūm al-dīn*, Cairo, 1306, i. 190.
[3] *Op. cit.* p. 164.

[1] *Umm al-qurā*, Port Said, 1316.
[2] Azraqī, p. 161.
[3] Yāqūt, *Dictionary of Learned Men*, ed. D. S. Margoliouth, London, 1907 ff., vi. 73.

and was settled east of the Zagros mountains, where it was known to the Assyrians as Madâ, or Medes, a name also written Amadâ, like Amardi for Mardi. From this time forward the names of the kings and chiefs of Media and the neighbouring districts mentioned on the Assyrian monuments are Iranian, and in a list of Median princes conquered by Sargon in 714–713 B.C. we find the name of Mazdaku, proving that Zoroaster's god Mazdā, 'the Wise,' was already worshipped (cf. also F. Hommel, *PSBA*, 1899, p. 132). The name of 'Mitra,' the sun-god, is also found in the tablets from Assur-bani-pal's library at Nineveh. On the other hand, Istuvegu, or Astyages, the last king of Ekbatana, is termed in the inscriptions, not 'King of Media, but 'King of the *Umman Manda*' or 'Hordes,' an archaistic title given by the Babylonians in early times to the northern barbarians, but applied in the Assyrian age to the Cimmerians and Scyths (*qq.v.*). The similarity of the names Madâ and Manda raises the question whether the Medes of the classical writers who were conquered by Cyrus were not really Scythians whose religious beliefs and practices have been transferred to their Median subjects or neighbours.

Like the Medes, the Persians also were Iranians.[1] But here again the inscriptions make it doubtful whether Cyrus and Cambyses, the founders of the Persian empire, were of pure Iranian stock, and whether the religion of Cyrus, at all events, was not the polytheism of Susa (cf. art. ACHÆMENIANS, vol. i. p. 70). Both he and his son conformed to the ancient worship of Babylonia. Gaumāta (Gomates), 'the Magian,' is expressly stated by Darius (*Bh.* [Pers. text] i. 63 f.) to have destroyed the *āyadanā*, or 'prayer-chapels,' of Persia, a word which is translated 'temples of the gods' in the Babylonian version of the Behistūn inscription. These Darius claims to have restored, along with other possessions of the Persian and Median peoples, through the help of the 'great god Auramazdā,' the creator of the earth and heavens, who in the Susian version of the Behistūn inscription (iii. 77, 79) is specially called 'the god of the Aryans.' In the eyes of Darius he occupied much the same place as that occupied by Jahweh in the OT: he was the national god of the Persians and Medes and supreme over all other gods. The existence of the latter, however, was admitted: at Behistūn Darius says that he was assisted not only by Aura-mazdā but also by 'the other gods, all that there are.' Opposed to the righteous law of Aura-mazdā was 'the Lie' (*drauga*), the Achæmenian equivalent of the Zoroastrian Angra Mainyu (Ahriman [*q.v.*]). But there is no reference to the Zoroastrianism of the Avesta in the inscriptions of either Darius or his successors; their priests, moreover, were not Magians, whose overthrow and massacre were, on the contrary, commemorated in the festival of the Magophonia;[2] and the bodies of the Persian kings seem to have been buried in the ordinary way instead of being thrown to dogs or birds of prey.[3] This, Herodotus says (i. 140), was a Magian custom.[4]

The date of Zoroaster (Zarathushtra) is uncertain, but modern scholarship is inclined to assign it to the 6th cent. B.C.; and Jackson[1] seems to be right in concluding that he arose in Media rather than in Bactria, the tradition which makes him a Bactrian being late.

Zoroaster is unknown to both Herodotus and Ctesias, the earliest mention of him occurring in a fragment questionably ascribed to Xanthus of Lydia and in Plato (*Alcib. I.*, 122). Herodotus makes the Magi a Median tribe (i. 101),[2] but he also implies that they were a class of priests (i. 140), and he describes certain of them as interpreters of dreams (i. 107). He further ascribes to them the Zoroastrian practices of reverencing the dog and destroying noxious animals (i. 140). No sacrifice could be offered without the presence of a Magus, who accompanied it with a hymn (the Avestan *Gāthā*); and there was neither altar, fire, nor libation (i. 132). The Greek historian adds (i. 131) that 'the Persians' (whose priests were the Median Magi) had 'no images of the gods and no temples or altars, considering the use of them a sign of folly.' They sacrificed to Zeus (Ahura Mazdā) on the summits of mountains, as well as 'to the sun and moon, to the earth, to fire, to water, and to the winds.' The worship of the goddess Anāhita, and presumably also of Mithra, the sun-god, referred to in two inscriptions of Artaxerxes Mnemon (*Sūsa* a, 4 f., *Ham.* 5 f.) was borrowed at a later date from 'the Arabians and Assyrians' (Herod. i. 131).[3]

On the other hand, the scourging of the Hellespont by Xerxes (Herod. vii. 35) is inconsistent with the belief that water was divine,[4] and in Herodotus's account of Magian religion Avestan dualism is conspicuous by its absence. So, too, is any reference to the doctrine of a resurrection. The simplest way of explaining these anomalies is to suppose that the religious system described by Herodotus was that of the Medes, among whom the Magi were a sort of hereditary priests, like the Levites in Israel; and that the religious system of Darius represented the religion of the Persian aristocracy, but that the origin and fundamental principles of the two were the same. The conquest of Media by Persia would have introduced the Median forms of theology among the Persian people, though their influence would have been momentarily checked by the overthrow of Gomates and his party, who perhaps would have stood in much the same relation to the Achæmenian aristocracy as the Pharisees did to the Sadducees. Meanwhile the reformer Zarathushtra had appeared in Media, where he built upon pre-existing religious beliefs and practices and attracted the Magi to his side. The result in the course of centuries was the Mazdæism of the Avesta.

LITERATURE.—A. V. W. Jackson, *Zoroaster the Prophet of Ancient Iran*, New York, 1899; C. de Harlez, *Avesta*[2], Paris, 1881; J. Darmesteter, *Le Zend-Avesta*, do. 1892–93, *Études iraniennes*, do. 1883; Eduard Meyer, *Gesch. des Altertums*, i.[2], Berlin, 1909; J. von Prášek, *Gesch. der Meder und Perser*, Gotha, 1906–10; G. Rawlinson, 'Media,' in *Five Great Monarchies of the Anc. East. World*, London, 1862–67; J. Oppert, *Le Peuple et la langue des Mèdes*, Paris, 1879; A. Delattre, *Le Peuple et l'empire des Mèdes*, Brussels, 1883 (= *Mém. couronnées . . . par l'académie royale . . . de Belgique*, xlv., pt. 1).

A. H. SAYCE.

MEDIATION.—Mediation is a word of extreme vagueness, but is here considered only in its technical or quasi-technical applications in religion. In a sense all we are and have is mediated to us somehow. Our very being comes to us through our parents. The society into which we are born and in which we are trained mediates to us most of

[1] This is the general view, but J. H. Moulton (*Early Zoroastrianism*, London, 1913, pp. 228–235) doubts whether it is correct. He hints that the Medes were the aboriginal inhabitants, and that the Magi (*q.v.*) were their priests. If this be so, the Medes were neither Iranians nor Semites. He directly states (above, p. 243b) that the Medians 'belonged to neither of the two great races which divided Nearer Asia between them.' Prášek (*Gesch.* i. 8 ff.) urges, in more detail, a similar view.

[2] For a somewhat different explanation of the Magophonia, see art. FESTIVALS AND FASTS (Iranian), vol. v. p. 874 f.

[3] See Moulton, pp. 163, 192 f., 202 f., 217; and cf. art. DEATH AND DISPOSAL OF THE DEAD (Parsi), § 15.

[4] The statement of Agathias (ii. 22), that the Medians buried the dead, whereas the Persians exposed them, is almost certainly wrong.

[1] *Zoroaster*, pp. 219–225.

[2] For the argument that Magianism was Median in origin see esp. Prášek, ii. 114 ff.

[3] W. Geiger (*Ostīrān. Kultur im Altertum*, Erlangen, 1882, pp. 488–492) derives the Zoroastrian fire-priests (*āthravans*) from Media.

[4] See, however, Moulton, p. 215 f.

what we think of as intellectual, moral, and religious convictions. The greater part of what comes under these headings is not original achievement of our own, but inheritance or education; it comes to us in some way by the mediation of others. It may be possible to make our own what is thus mediated to us, and to become possessors, as it were, in our own right of what we have inherited or been taught; but, to begin with, every creature born in time owes to mediation of some sort the whole capital with which he adventures upon independent life.

1. The NT use of the term 'Mediator.'—The technical use of the word is most easily grasped if we start from that application of it which is most definite and concrete, viz. its application to the work of Christ. There are four NT passages where this is found: 1 Ti 2^{5}, He 8^{6} 9^{15} 12^{24}. In all these passages Christ is represented as mediating between God and man. God and man have been estranged. The relation which normally subsists between them has been destroyed, and the work of the mediator is to restore it. In 1 Timothy this work is explicitly connected with the redemptive death of Christ; there is one mediator between God and men, Himself man, Christ Jesus, who gave Himself a ransom for all. The same connexion is implied in all the passages in Hebrews; there Jesus is spoken of as the mediator of a new or a better covenant. The covenant is the religious constitution under which God and men form one society, or live a common life. The old and inferior constitution, under which the ideal of religion was not realized, was the Levitical one. This was annulled because of its ineffective character, and in place of it, through the mediation of Jesus—*i.e.*, by means of, and at the cost of, His incarnation and sacrifice—comes the Christian relation of men to God. In this the ends of religion are really attained. There is real forgiveness of sins, real purification of conscience, real and abiding access to God, and all due to the mediation of Christ. This use of the term 'mediation,' which may be called the specifically Christian one, is that which has been mainly developed in later theology. Christ's work as mediator is that in which He interposes between the holy God and sinful men who are estranged from each other, and makes peace. This specifically Christian use of the term, however, is only a continuation of its use in ordinary relations. In ancient as in modern times a State or a person could offer to 'mediate' between other States or persons at war. The substantive μεσίτης is used side by side with such terms as διαλλακτής, διαιτητής, and is defined by Suidas as = εἰρηνοποιός, 'peacemaker.' The verb μεσιτεύειν, which occurs once in the NT without an object (He 6^{17}, though some here would supply τὴν ὑπόσχεσιν, 'His promise') is elsewhere usually transitive: μεσιτεῦσαι τὴν διάλυσιν εὐνοϊκῶς (Polyb. XI. xxxiv. 3) = 'to achieve the settlement by friendly mediation.' A state of hostility or estrangement, in which the making of peace is the work of a third party, and can therefore be called mediation, is the background of the primary Christian use of the term.

2. Extension of mediation in the NT from redemption to creation.—But even in the NT it is not limited to this use. It is not only that peace with God, or the forgiveness of sins, or reconciliation, or eternal life for the spiritually dead is mediated through Christ and His redemption; Christ is presented also as the mediator of creation. All that is has come into being through Him. We find this stated without explanation, as if it were self-evident, or an agreed proposition among Christians, in 1 Co 8^{6}. It is expanded in Col $1^{16f.}$ with a view to securing to Christ, who has just been referred to as the mediator of salvation (in whom we have our redemption, the forgiveness of sins [v.^{14}]), a place of dignity above all angelic powers. In Colossæ, apparently, such powers were recognized by some as mediating between God and man in a way which trenched on Christ's prerogative as the one mediator; and it was an effective method of precluding this to show that all such powers, whatever they were called, owed their very being to Christ, and could therefore in no sense become His rivals. The connexion of ideas in He 1^{2} is similar. It speaks of a Son whom God has appointed heir of all things, through whom also He made the worlds. The 'also' implies that the making of the worlds through the Son is what naturally corresponds to His being heir of all things. Probably no idea in the NT is so hard to enter into as this. When we think of Christ as mediating between God on the one hand and men alienated from God by sin on the other, we know where we are. We can speak on the basis of experience, and tell how Christ has come to us in our own estrangement, and made peace between us and God. We can speak of Him as mediator, because that is what He has been to ourselves. But creation is not a process, or an act, of which experience teaches us anything; it is not apparent that it needs to be, or that it can be, 'mediated' at all. The OT simply says that in the beginning God created the heaven and the earth. How does Paul come to say (Col 1^{16}), In Him—that is, in Christ—were all things created? How did the thought originate in his mind? What exactly did it mean to him? We cannot accept it merely on his authority, as a piece of information about the beginning of things; the content of revelation—what a man knows by the inspiration of God—never has the character of information. Unless we can enter into the origin and process of the Apostle's thought, we can never really appropriate the idea in which it rests. The idea that not redemption only but creation as well is mediated through Christ, that to Him is due and by Him must be determined not only all that we can call reconciliation but all that we can call being, is so unexpected and so astounding that we cannot but ask how it took possession of his mind.

3. Rationale of this extension in Paul.—So far as can be seen, there are only two possible explanations of Paul's attitude. One is purely formal, and reduces the idea of mediation, so far as it applies to all being, to a pure formality. It assumes that Paul had identified Christ with some supernatural being to whom this attribute or function of mediating creation already belonged, and that with the identification there went, as a matter of course, the ascription of this attribute or function to Christ. This is supposed to explain why Paul, when he introduces the idea of creation through Christ, does it *simpliciter*, without any justification or explanation: he is only doing what every one would concede who agreed with him in identifying Jesus with the Christ. But to this there are many objections. As far as can be known, there was no trace whatever in the Pharisaism in which Paul was reared of any such idea as that the Messiah was participant in the creation of the world. Further, though this may be discounted as a subjective impression, Paul writes in Colossians with passionate earnestness on this subject, and not like a man manipulating borrowed ideas which have no vital relation to his experience. And, if it be said that it is not the Jewish eschatological Messiah with whom Jesus is identified by Paul, but a supernatural being of another sort—the Logos of popular Greek philosophy, of whom such things were predicated as Paul predicates of Christ in connexion with creation—then the further question is raised, How did Paul come to make this identification? He never mentions the Logos by name. There is no indication in his writings that he knew anything about philosophy or that he had any interest in its problems. The Logos of the current philosophy, which did mediate somehow between God and the universe, was the philosophical solution of a difficulty which he had never felt: namely, how the transcendent God was to come into any relation to a material world. Paul was not troubled by this any more than the OT prophets or Jesus Himself, nor does he ever bring his doctrine of creation through Christ into any relation to it. The motive and the meaning of that doctrine must be sought elsewhere.

A real clue to his thought, as opposed to this formal one, may perhaps be found in another way. In Paul's experience as a Christian, Christ was everything. He had reconciled him to God and made him a new creature. He had put him in possession of the final truth and reality in the spiritual world, that which could never be transcended and could never fail. When he lived in Christ, he lived in the eternal world, and he felt that to that world and to the believer's interest in it everything else must be subservient. He could say, 'All things are yours' (1 Co 3^{21}); 'All things work together for good to them that love God, to them that are called according to his purpose' (Ro 8^{28}). And 'all things' here must be taken without restriction. It means not only all that happens, but all that is. Creation must in the last resort be in alliance with the God and Father of our Lord Jesus Christ, and in league with His purposes. As J. Orr put it (*The Christian View of God and the World*, Edinburgh, 1893, p. 323), it must be built on redemption lines. That is the same as to say, it must be built on Christian lines; the world in which Christians live must be essentially a Christian world. It is not a world in which anything can defeat God's purpose in Christ; it is not a world in which the final sovereignty of Christ can be frustrated; it is a world which is essentially related to Christ, to His work of reconciliation, and to His supreme place at last as heir of all things. Now, is it not legitimate to say that a world which was created for Christ was created in Him and through Him? The difficulty of apprehending what is meant by the creation of the world through Christ is only one aspect of the difficulty of apprehending Christ's pre-existence, and that again is only one aspect of the omnipresent and insuperable difficulty of defining the relations of eternity and time. If pre-existence is a legitimate way of expressing the absolute significance of Jesus—the fact that what we see in Him is the eternal truth of what God is, and that therefore He belongs to the very being of God, 'before the foundation of the world'—then the mediation of creation through Christ is a legitimate way of putting the conviction that in the last resort, and in spite of appearances, the world in which we live is a Christian world, our ally, not our adversary, or, if our adversary, one who is necessary, that in conflict with and victory over him we may prove that we have found the way of salvation. Paul does not start with the speculative idea that creation could not be immediate, and that all material and spiritual existences—things on earth and in heaven, things visible and invisible—must owe their being to the mediation of some supernatural power which is identified in his mind, we cannot tell why, with Jesus. He does not start thus, and then give this vague speculative idea a particular application when he comes to explain the Christian redemption. On the contrary, he starts with Christ and with the experience of redemption which, as a matter of fact, is mediated through Him. But the redemption thus mediated is something of absolute significance. It involves contact with ultimate realities, with the eternal truth and love of God in Christ; it kindles a light in the soul which must fall on everything in the world if we are to see it as it is; it involves no smaller a conviction than that the world is essentially a Christian world, and it is this conviction, which is still involved in Christian faith, that forms the vital content of Paul's doctrine that all things were created through Christ.

That the world has this character may, of course, be doubted. It may even be argued that no moral life, no life involving moral probation, is possible except with a background of nature which is morally indifferent; it is only in a world which is indifferent to the distinction of good and evil that man can prove his devotion to good for its own sake. But there is really no such world, though the lightning does not shun the good man's path. What the doctrine of creation mediated by Christ implies is that in the very constitution of nature it is possible to discover the same principles as are revealed in the life and work of Christ. If it were not so, no one with roots in nature would understand Christ when He appeared. The ultimate task of Christian philosophy is to discover spiritual law in the natural world. This is what Paul felt; it is what every idealistic philosophy teaches; it is the inspiration of the highest poetry; Wordsworth found in nature not an adversary or a neutral, but 'the soul of all my moral being.'

4. Mediation in the Fourth Gospel.—Without using words like *μεσίτης* and *μεσιτεύειν* the Fourth Gospel makes perhaps a more conscious and continuous use of the idea of mediation than any other book of the NT. Leaving the Prologue out of account, it is mediation in the specifically Christian sense, just as in Paul and Hebrews. The whole book might be summed up in the phrase of 14^{6}, 'No one cometh unto the Father, but by me.' It is to Jesus that men owe all the blessings which constitute salvation. They are variously described, most frequently as 'life' and 'eternal life,' but they come to men through Him and Him alone. Yet a counter or complementary truth is presented in the same Gospel. No man comes to the Father but by Jesus, yet no man comes to Jesus but him who is drawn by the Father (6^{44}). It is as though there were powers in the world antecedent to the historical Jesus which had Him in view, which prepared men to understand Him, and to welcome His mediation when He came. In the constitution of nature, in the impression which it makes as a whole on the spirit of man, in human life itself with its various experiences of success and failure, of wronging others and being wronged, of forgiving others and being forgiven by them, there is a sum or complex of forces which bears witness to Christ and constitutes a providential drawing of men by the Father to the Son.

But it is only when we receive the Son and believe in Him that we truly come to the Father. The earlier stages of religion are mediated to us through all the experiences of life; these provide for it a broad and indisputable basis here and now, and make it independent of any particular historical mediation—*i.e.*, of any mediation through persons or facts which have their place in the past. But this immediate experience of religion—a religion, as some might call it, of pure inwardness and spirituality, which has its certainty in itself, and is not at the mercy of a historical criticism for which no fact is beyond question—does not, according to the Evangelist, enable men to dispense with what is mediated through Jesus; it only enables and prepares them to appreciate it. It is consummated through Him. Only he who has seen Jesus has seen the Father. And, paradoxical as it may seem, this historical mediation does not shake the certainty of religion; the perfect religion does not become doubtful because the mediator of it lived in time. We are 'in Him that is true,' and he that believeth hath the witness in himself (1 Jn $5^{10. 20}$).

In the prologue the idea of mediation is even more explicit than in the body of the Gospel, and it is wider in its range. The first three verses are more speculative than anything in Paul, and it is difficult to think otherwise than that the author has identified Jesus with the Logos of the current philosophy, and that he is speaking of Him in terms whose antecedents are philosophical rather than evangelical. The very ambiguity of the term Logos (*ratio*, *oratio*) may have commended it to him. It suited him equally well to have Jews feel that in Christ they had God's last *word* to man, and to have Greeks feel that in Christ they were in contact with the *reason* of the world, the rational principle or truth in which all things lived, and moved, and had their being. The one knowledge and the other alike, he would have held, were mediated to men through Jesus. It is by no means clear, however, that the prologue makes the Logos, as distinct from the historical Jesus, the mediator either of a universal revelation of God to man or of a special revelation of God to Israel. The interest of the Evangelist in such speculative ideas is perhaps less than has been assumed. The traditional and somewhat grandiose interpretation of the prologue, according to which the Incarnation does not appear until $v.^{14}$—an interpretation which has so commended the passage to those who delight in the idea of a general revelation in nature and history culminating in a final and adequate revelation in Christ—is almost certainly wrong. The movement of thought in the prologue is spiral. The Incarnation appears already in $v.^{4}$, and the history of Christianity up to the time of the writer is summarized in $v.^{5}$. Revelation in its full and specifically Christian sense, the mediation to men of that knowledge of God which is eternal life, is accomplished only through Jesus, the Word made flesh. The difference from Paul may be said to lie in this: in Paul Jesus mediates revelation through redemption (we know God as Father because He saves us by His Son), whereas in John He mediates redemption through revelation (we are saved from sin and death because through Jesus we have the knowledge of the Father). But the distinction is true only when it is not pressed. In both writers it is the specifically Christian sense of mediation that is vital: Jesus is the mediator between God and men. The wider sense of mediation, according to which Jesus mediates creation as well as redemption, while it is found in both, has not the same emphasis. The apostles seem to feel that their religion ultimately implies this, but it is not this that directly inspires or sustains it.

5. Mediation and Jesus' consciousness of Himself.—The most important of questions to the Christian religion is whether this specific sense of mediation, which is not only recognized by but pervades all the apostolic writings, is confirmed when we turn to the mind of Christ Himself. He never speaks of having anything to do with the creation of the world, but was He conscious of being in any sense a mediator between God and men? Did He stand between them to any intent? Did men in any sense owe to Him either the knowledge of God or reconciliation to God, or were these supreme spiritual blessings immediately open to them, in independence of Him? The questions have been answered in both ways. Harnack's famous *dictum* (*Das Wesen des Christentums*, Berlin, 1900, p. 91), that in the gospel as preached by Jesus the Son has no place, but only the Father, is so qualified by other statements that its author can hardly be cited for the negative. Much more uncompromising representatives of this side are J. Weiss and W. Heitmüller. The former, in *Das Urchristentum* (Göttingen, 1914, p. 364), in discussing the relations of faith in Christ and faith in God (in Paul), explicitly renounces the idea of a necessary mediator of salvation. Christ was there, as a matter of fact, and therefore Paul had to give Him a place in his religion somehow; but Weiss, with a sense of his own daring,[1] declares that there was no necessity for His mission and work in the nature of God, and that God's eternal love, though Paul knew it only through Christ, must have had its way even if Christ had failed the redeeming work of the Father, or if God in the fullness of His love had been able to dispense with the sacrifice of Christ. There is not, indeed, any appeal here to the mind of Christ, with regard to mediation, but there is the expression of a conviction which forecloses any such appeal. In Heitmüller's *Jesus* (Tübingen, 1913) the denial is even vehement:

> 'It is quite beyond doubt that according to the preaching of Jesus we have to do in religion only with an immediate relation of man to God: between God and man nothing and no one has place, not even Jesus. Religious significance in the proper sense Jesus in any case does not claim' (p. 73).

But Heitmüller feels a certain embarrassment when he deals explicitly with some words of Jesus. He admits that they disclose not merely a prophetic but a superprophetic consciousness—*e.g.*, the well-known passage Mt 11^{27}. To be the bearer of a unique revelation, the Son *simpliciter*—it almost terrifies us to think of it. It is not a divine self-consciousness, but it is almost more than human. It might impel us to ask whether it was compatible with soundness and clearness of mind. 'Here is the point at which the form of Jesus becomes mysterious to us, almost uncanny' (p. 71). Further on, he speaks of the riddle as insoluble (p. 89), but apparently he thinks that he has reduced it to less disquieting proportions when he writes (p. 126) that Jesus seems to have claimed for Himself *only* that He is the way to the Father. It is difficult to see how He could have claimed more. The opposite view, that the place which the NT generally assigns to Jesus, as the indispensable mediator between God and men, is in harmony with Jesus' consciousness of Himself, is argued in the present writer's *Jesus and the Gospel* (London, 1908, p. 159 ff. on the self-revelation of Jesus). The argument covers both the Johannine idea of the mediation of the knowledge of God (as in Mt 11^{27}) and the Pauline idea of the mediation of redemption (as in Mk 10^{45}). What it does not expressly extend to is the speculative idea that creation as well as revelation and redemption is mediated through Christ.

6. Other mediators than Jesus.—Emphasis is laid in the NT on the exclusive character of Christ's mediation: there is one God, and one mediator between God and men. This is the idea of such passages as Ac 4^{12} ('none other name'), Col $2^{9f.}$ ('in him dwelleth all the fulness of the Godhead bodily, and in him ye are made full'), and He 7^{24} (the priesthood which does not pass to, or cannot be trenched upon by, another), as well as of Jn 14^{6}. What is in view in these passages is the idea that Christ in His work of reconciliation may have rivals or competitors, powers which in independence of Him prepare for His work, or supplement it, or enable men to dispense with it. This is unambiguously and exhaustively denied. The idea of mediation in the Christian sense has no application but to Him. Spiritual beings, whatever their name or degree—principalities, powers, dominions—owe their own being to Him, and have their functions,

[1] 'Wir müssen es aussprechen . . . ehrlicherweise muss man sagen' (*ib.*).

whatever they are, in a world which He has reconciled to God.

The exclusiveness of His mediation with regard to nature (being) as well as redemption is strongly asserted both in Col 1[16] and in Jn 1[3]. Probably in both these passages, as well as in 1 Ti 2[5], there is reference to forms of Gnosticism which it is difficult for us to define. For ancient thought generally, and therefore for ancient religion, the world was full of invisible powers of a personal or quasi-personal sort, and these easily asserted a place for themselves in the religious life. They came between God and the soul in ways that we cannot appreciate, and the interest of the apostles is to expel from the relations of God and the soul every power but that of Jesus. Their argument is that of experience against uncontrolled imagination. The controversies of later theologians, Catholic and Protestant, on the mediation (intercession) of saints are like this, but not identical. Those who admit that we can pray for one another have no ground for denying that the saints can pray for us. All that is to be said is that we do not know anything about it; but whatever the saints may do for us they can do only in dependence on Jesus, not as mediators who might bring us to God apart from Him. For statements on opposite sides of this question see Calvin's *Institutio*, III. xx. 20–27; *Westminster Confession*, ch. xxi. 2; Thomas Aquinas, *Summa Theol.*, III. qu. xxvi. art. 1 f.; S. J. Hunter, *Outlines of Dogmatic Theology*, London, 1895–96, §§ 574, 607; K. von Hase, *Handbuch der protestant. Polemik*[7], Leipzig, 1900, p. 294.

7. Mediation in the OT.—If we look back from the NT to the OT, we find much everywhere which can be described in terms of mediation, though *μεσίτης* occurs only once in LXX (Job 9[33]), where, according to T. K. Cheyne (*EBi*, col. 3003), it answers to בֵּינֵינוּ, and means a person who could interpose with authority between Job and his imperfect or arbitrary God—an arbitrator who would see justice done. This is akin to the *διαιτητής*, defined by Aristotle as *ὁ μέσος*, and often found in Greek as a synonym of *μεσίτης*; but it is hardly the equivalent of the NT *μεσίτης*, whether we regard revelation or reconciliation as that which comes to men through Him. If we confine our attention to the relations of God and man, in which the term mediation is properly applied, both aspects of it pervade the OT. Revelation, or the knowledge of God, is mediated to men through the prophet. It is not necessary to ask here how it is mediated to the prophet himself; for the purposes of religion he obtains it immediately. He stands in God's council and hears His voice; it is the voice of God Himself, or such an echo of it as the prophet's voice can utter, that is heard when He speaks. There is no external criterion for distinguishing the true voice of God from a voice which speaks lies in His name. The secret of the Lord is with them that fear Him (Ps 25[14]); they have, without knowing it, what the NT calls (1 Co 12[10]) the gift of 'discernment of spirits.' As revelation is mediated through the prophet, so in the largest sense is reconciliation through the priest. The Levitical system may have been very imperfect—it was destined, indeed, to perish by its inadequacy; but the idea of it was to enable men to approach God, to give them peace with Him, to put it in their power, in spite of all that they had done, to have communion with God, living as members of a society of which He was the head. The Levitical system does not, of course, exhaust what the OT exhibits of the mediation of reconciliation. Much importance is attached to prayer: the hour of irremediable ruin is come—the final breach between God and His people—when Jeremiah hears that, though intercessors like Moses and Samuel stood before Jahweh, they could not turn His heart toward Israel (Jer 15[1]). The ministry of intercession mediates for man to God, as well as the ministry of sacrifice—unless we reduce the latter to the former, and regard sacrifice as in essence 'embodied prayer.' It is another form, possibly a form inferior to intercession because less spiritual, of showing the cost at which reconciliation is mediated to sinful men.

8. Later developments of mediation.—Though the main content of mediation in the OT may be condensed under prophecy and priesthood, it is not quite exhausted there. Especially in post-Exilic literature, where the transcendence of God is emphasized till it depresses the soul, we find intermediate beings appear whose functions are wider and less defined. Sometimes they have to do with the creation of the world, sometimes with its government in nature or in history; sometimes they are specially concerned with Israel's fortunes, or with the giving of the law; sometimes they are interested in individual men, attaching themselves to pure souls and making them prophets or sages. Foreign influences as well as philosophical necessities determined the form of such thoughts, and they grew to have a larger and larger space in many minds. In A. Bertholet's *Bibl. Theol. des alten Test.*, Tübingen, 1911, § 32, there is a sufficient account of this faith in intermediate beings (*Hypostasenlehre*), so far as it can be derived from the Greek Bible. The most important of them was Wisdom, though Wisdom, curiously enough, in spite of Mt 11[19], Lk 11[49], seems to have fallen out of favour in the NT, and is not once mentioned where we might most have expected it, in the Johannine writings. Perhaps this was due, as J. Grill has suggested (*Untersuchungen über die Entstehung des vierten Evangeliums*, Tübingen, 1902, p. 199 f.), to the frequency with which in Gnosticism *σοφία* represented a lost æon which had to be redeemed (cf. *ERE* vi. 236 f.). Next in importance to Wisdom came the Word or Logos. On this see W. Bousset, *Die Religion des Judentums*[2], Berlin, 1906, p. 399, and cf. art. LOGOS, § 2. The doctrine of the Logos as 'mediating' is developed at great length and with infinite inconsistency in Philo. It can be best studied in E. Bréhier, *Les Idées philosophiques et religieuses de Philon d'Alexandrie*, Paris, 1908, ii. ch. ii. f. It is perhaps not unfair to say that in Philo the Logos mediates between God and the *κόσμος*; that it mediates, further, between God and man as made in the image of God and participant in reason, but that it is not a mediator in the specifically NT sense of the term, *i.e.*, a mediator of redemption betweer God and sinners. The verbal coincidences between Philo and the NT often, perhaps always, conceal a wide divergence of meaning. A full discussion of what Jewish belief in mediating powers eventually came to may be found in F. Weber, *Die Lehren des Talmud*, Leipzig, 1886, ch. xiii. He enumerates five: (1) the angel Meṭaṭrôn, (2) the Word, or *Mēmrā* (*q.v.*), of Jahweh, (3) the *Shᵉkhînāh*, (4) the Spirit of God, and (5) the *Bath Qôl*, or heavenly voice through which revelation is given. Where the mind starts with these generalities, whether in a more speculative or in a more religious interest, it does not seem able or impelled to bring them to any convergence upon a single mediator; but the NT writers, starting from their experience of Christ as the only and the real revealer of God and reconciler of sinners to Him, are able to regard all these doctrines of mediating hypostases as hints or suggestions of what they possess in Jesus, and are not afraid in a manner to identify Him with them all. Whatever they promised or were intended to secure has been finally made good and secured through Him. He is the Wisdom of God —the Key to the world of nature, of history, and of all human life; He is the Word made flesh; Paul can even say (2 Co 3^{17}) that in His exaltation He is the Spirit. All mediation between God and sinful men is summed up and exhausted in Him. He is Himself our Peace. But all mediation, if the name is legitimately extended in this sense, between God and creation is also transacted through Him. The last, however, is not the starting-point; the mind rises to it only inferentially through an overpowering impression of the absolute significance of Jesus as the mediator of reconciliation; it is one way of expressing the conviction that He is the Beginning and the End, the First and the Last.

9. Subordinate sense of mediation (means of grace).—Mediation in a subordinate sense is the subject of the whole doctrine of the means (*media*) of grace; that is, of the divinely appointed ordinances through which the salvation of Christ is brought home to man. Grace is mediated through these ordinances, especially, according to Protestant theology, through the Word, sacraments, and prayer. The conditions under which the use of them becomes effectual for salvation—*i.e.*, the terms on which grace really is mediated through them—are stated in all the confessions in more or less experimental and argumentative forms.

Comparative religion offers examples of mediation more or less analogous to those here considered. Wherever there are religious institutions and customs, they are mediatorial. It is through them that the spirit of a religion is conveyed to those who are brought up within its pale. Sometimes there are what A. M. Fairbairn used to call 'developmental coincidences' between other religions and Christianity where there is no real interdependence. Thus Mithra was called μεσίτης in the first instance as dwelling in the air which is midway between heaven and hell. But the local meaning deepened into a moral one. Mithra became mediator between the inaccessible and unknowable God who reigns in the ethereal spheres and the human race which lives its restless life here below. He is addressed as great Mithra, messenger of the gods, mediator of the religion of the elect (F. Cumont, *Les Mystères de Mithra*^{3}, Brussels, 1913, pp. 129, 139, 146). Similar phenomena are abundant in the religions of India. But we nowhere find a religion of which we can say, as has been said of Christianity, that it is what it is because of the presence in it of the mediator.

LITERATURE.—As the idea of mediation involves that of the nature of Christianity, and especially raises the question whether Christ has a necessary place in the Christian religion, and, if so, what precisely that place is, and what it implies as to Christ Himself (Christology), the literature is really co-extensive with that of Christian theology. Older discussions of main aspects of the subject are to be found in J. Butler, *Analogy of Religion*, ed. J. H. Bernard, London, 1900, pt. ii. ch. v., and J. Martineau, *Studies of Christianity*, do. 1875, 147 ff. Besides the works mentioned in the article, all modern writings on NT theology are more or less relevant, but the formal treatment of it, even in the Jesus-Paul literature, is not frequent.

JAMES DENNEY.

MEDICINE.—See DISEASE AND MEDICINE.

MEDICINE-MEN.—See SHAMANISM.

MEDĪNA.—Medīna, in Arabic with the article, means 'the Town,' as opposed to the desert (Qur'ān ix. 102, 121), and is the name usually given to the city whither Muhammad fled from Mecca, sometimes interpreted as 'the Prophet's City.' Its proper name was Yathrib (*ib.* xxxiii. 13), evidently the Ἰάθριππα of Stephanus Byzantinus (*s.v.*) and the Λαθρίππα of Ptolemy (VI. vii. 31), apparently identical in origin with the Egyptian Ἄθριβις (indeed a form Athrib is mentioned). Another name which is sometimes cited is Ṭaibah or Ṭābah, to be compared with the Hebrew Ṭôb (Jg 11^3, etc.), and perhaps with the Greek Θήβη, meaning 'fragrant' or 'good.' Many more names are collected by Samhūdī (893 A.H.) in his monograph on Medīna (*Khulāṣat al-wafā*, Cairo, 1285), but these are mostly honorific epithets; one, however, which he quotes from the OT is Salqah, which should rather be Salkah (Jos 12^5, etc.); but this identification is certainly erroneous.

Since Stephanus Byzantinus gives the relative adjective of Yathrib as Ἰαθριππηνός, it must have been the home of some persons known to the Græco-Roman world not later than the 6th cent. A.D.; and to the end of the 7th cent. there probably belonged one 'John of Yathrib' mentioned in a letter of James of Edessa 'to John Stylites'; this Yathrib is identified with Medīna by some writers (*ZDMG* xxiv. [1870] 263), but it is difficult to suppose that there can have been a 'presbyter of Yathrib = Medīna' at that time. For the early history of the place, then, as well as the later we have to rely exclusively on Muslim authorities, who naturally have much to say about a town which played so important a part in the history of their system. It is unfortunate that their notices of its pre-Islāmic history are mainly fabulous, though they must contain a little fact as well.

The settlement, which is often called 'Between the two lābas,' *i.e.* volcanic formations, was at the commencement of Islām a joint one of Arabs and Jews. The former were grouped in two tribes, the Aus and the Khazraj, whereas of the latter three tribal names are handed down—Qainuqā', Quraish, and Naḍīr. The native Jewish tradition appears to know nothing of these colonies, whose names surprise us; for the last two are clearly Arabic, and the first apparently so. They are supposed to have had a dialect (or jargon?) of their own, some fragments of which are preserved in the Qur'ān (iv. 48), but are exceedingly puzzling. This fact would seem to militate against the supposition that they were Arabs who had adopted Judaism. If we are justified in attributing to them some of the Jewish matter that is found in the Qur'ān, they must have been acquainted with portions of the Oral Tradition, to which there are occasional references; and it is practically certain that the early Islāmic lawyers were indebted to proselytes from these communities for certain technicalities and even whole maxims. The personal names which are preserved are partly Hebrew, partly Arabic.

The Muslim tradition represents the Jews as further advanced in civilization than the Arabs of Medīna, and engaged both in trade, including lending money on security, and in cultivation of the soil; the date was the most important product. Further, they are said to have had schools, and to have written Arabic in Hebrew script, as was done at a later time and is done even now. They were under the protection of their Arab neighbours, and were occasionally compelled to fight in the tribal wars, much against their inclination.

Between the Aus and the Khazraj there was a long-standing feud, which led to the parties summoning the Prophet in the manner recorded in his biography.[1] Hellenic antiquity, which furnishes many analogies to that of the Arabs, provides illustrations of this expedient for putting an end to civil strife. He called his new adherents Anṣār, 'Helpers,' a name which, according to the Qur'ān (iii. 45, lxi. 14), originally belonged to the apostles, and doubtless is a popular etymology of Nazarene.

Like many other statesmen, the Prophet found in external warfare the best remedy for civil strife; and, since at least for some years all new adherents were required to migrate to Medīna, the

[1] Ibn Hisham, ed. F. Wüstenfeld, Göttingen, 1860, p. 286 ff.

town grew vastly in magnitude and importance during his despotism. Neither he nor his immediate successors had any taste for architecture or other forms of art, and, though building must have gone on for the housing of the increasing population, it was, like the Prophet's mosque and domestic quarters, of a primitive kind. There are traditions, probably deserving credit, that the former had to be repeatedly enlarged and repaired during this period; but reconstruction on a considerable scale appears to have taken place first in the time of the Umayyad Walīd b. 'Abd al-Malik, who gave orders in the year 88 for the destruction of the older building and the houses of the Prophet's wives, and the inclusion of the whole area in a new mosque covering 200 × 200 cubits. According to Ṭabarī (*Chronicle*, Leyden, 1879–1901, ii. 1194), the khalīf demanded and obtained assistance from the Byzantine emperor, both in materials and in workmen. The new mosque was elaborately decorated, and rewards were offered to the artists, who, however, according to Samhūdī's authorities, were at times guilty of profanity. The whole was under the direction of Omar b. 'Abd al-'Azīz (afterwards khalīf), who introduced a *miḥrāb* and four minarets.

In 160 A.H. further additions were made by order of the khalīf Mahdī, and his successors repeatedly repaired and decorated it. The whole building was burned down in the year 654 A.H., and restored chiefly by the Egyptian Sulṭāns, whose successors continued to adorn and enlarge it. It was again burned down in 886 A.H., and rebuilt by order of Qāïtbāï with great magnificence. This was in the time of the local historian Samhūdī, who was absent at the time of the fire, but lost much of his property owing to it. Qāïtbāï's is the existing mosque. Architectural details connected with the various buildings are given by R. F. Burton (*Pilgrimage to El-Medinah and Meccah*, London, 1855–56, vol. i. ch. xvii.), who also adds some details for the period since Samhūdī. Apparently a certain amount of destruction was effected by the Wahhābīs, who also plundered the treasures; but, when they had been forced to evacuate the place in 1815, the damage was made good.

Visitation of Medīna is not incumbent on Muslims, but it is regarded as a dutiful act, the Prophet having said: 'Whoso performs the pilgrimage and fails to visit me deals undutifully by me' (quoted by Ḥarīrī, *Maqāma* xxxii.). The visit is, of course, to the Prophet's grave, which is the chief object of interest in the sanctuary; for the Sunnīs those of his first two successors and his daughter, who lie beside him, are also of importance. For a description of the tomb itself, which is screened off, Burton goes to the traveller Ibn Jubair (ed. M. J. de Goeje, London, 1907, p. 121), neither having seen it himself nor having met any one who had. According to Ibn Jubair, a place is supposed to be left vacant beside the others for Isā b. Maryam (*i.e.* the Christian Saviour). The European fable of Muhammad's coffin being suspended by a magnet between heaven and earth seems to be unknown to Islāmic writers, though it bears some resemblance to a story told about that of Timur-Lenk, which, according to Ibn Iyās (*History of Egypt*, Cairo, 1311, i. 347), had to be so suspended because the earth was unwilling to receive it. Various superstitions connected with this tomb are to be found in the works of European travellers, especially that of J. F. Keane (*Six Months in the Hejaz*, London, 1887, p. 225). By some puritan sects the visitation of the tomb is regarded as idolatrous, but this view is unusual.

Medīna remained the political capital of Islām during the reigns of the Prophet's first three successors, but lost that position in the civil wars which followed the death of the third. In normal times it counted as an annex of Mecca (*q.v.*), whose governor was responsible for it; hence there is a dearth of native chronicles, and Samhūdī makes use of the casual notice in the travels of Ibn Jubair, somewhat as modern European writers use the passage. On the other hand, owing to the continued residence of the Prophet's widows and such of his companions as were students or devotees, it became the first university of Islām, where what are called 'the Islāmic Sciences' were founded. Numerous jurists arose in Medīna, and presently a canon of seven was formed. The people of the place claimed that the governors should consult them about all cases which came before them for trial. As late as 200 A.H. its jurists or traditionalists were regarded as more scrupulous than others (D. S. Margoliouth, *The Early Development of Mohammedanism*, London, 1914, p. 73). On the whole, the school of Medīna, associated with the name of Mālik ibn Anas (*q.v.*), was supposed to attach more importance to tradition and less to inference than the school of 'Irāq, which had been founded by Abū Ḥanīfa. The differences which resulted were not of primary importance, though discussion at times raged fiercely (see LAW [Muhammadan]).

For at least the Umayyad period Medīna was supposed to be the seat of literary criticism as well. When a question arose in Damascus at the court of one of these khalīfs concerning the source of a certain line of poetry and the relative merits of certain poets, the khalīf sent to the governor of Medīna, ordering him after his sermon in the mosque to refer these matters to the congregation, which proved able to decide them (*Aghānī*, Cairo, 1285, viii. 180). It would seem that the beginning of Islāmic libraries is to be sought in Medīna; the poems of the Prophet's court-poet, Ḥassān b. Thābit, were kept there, and the copy was renewed when it showed signs of evanescence.

LITERATURE.—Of the work of Samhūdī cited above the abridgment was published 1285 A.H.; the original, of about thrice the bulk, exists in the Bodleian Library. The portion of it which deals with places of interest in the neighbourhood is summarized by F. Wüstenfeld, *Das Gebiet von Medina*, Göttingen, 1873. Accounts of the modern condition of the place are to be found in many of the records of pilgrimages, most recently in those of Hadji Khan and Wilfred Sparroy, *With the Pilgrims to Mecca, 1902*, London, 1905, and A. J. B. Wavell, *A Modern Pilgrim in Mecca*, do. 1912.

D. S. MARGOLIOUTH.

MEDITATION.—See DEVOTION AND DEVOTIONAL LITERATURE.

MEDITATION (Buddhist).—See BODHISATTVA, vol. ii. p. 752 f., DHYĀNA.

MEEKNESS.—**1. OT conception.**—The Hebrew word for meekness (עֲנָוָה) is closely connected with the ideas of humility, poverty, and affliction. A great feature of OT literature is the attempt which it constantly reveals to reconcile with the facts of experience the principle that righteousness brings prosperity, while wickedness is inevitably followed by disaster. In view of the apparent contradiction of this principle by the facts of life, some OT writers (Ps 37, Job) attempt to vindicate the ways of God to man, and to establish the ultimate reality of this principle by insisting that the suffering of the righteous and the success of the wicked are only temporary. In the end divine justice will compensate the 'meek' (who are thus identified with the righteous), while the transient prosperity of evil-doers will end in calamity and downfall.

2. NT conception.—Christian teaching derives the conception of meekness from the OT, but enlarges and spiritualizes its meaning and application. The deep significance attached to this conception in the NT lies in its identification of the loftiest ideal with the profoundest reality. The meek man is thus defined as one who not only 'counts it better to suffer than to do wrong' (Plato), but as one who 'resists not evil' (Mt 5[39]). He is the one who surrenders the *immediate* interests of life, but in so doing he is not emptying his life but rather filling it with larger interests. 'In ceasing to contend for his own rights against others he makes the rights of all others his own.' Accordingly, Jesus calls upon His disciples to surrender even the most obvious rights of property (Mt 5[40]). But the ground of such surrender is not the denial of individual rights on the part of Christ. On the contrary, He assigns the highest importance to individual work, and He confers upon the meek a title not only to the Kingdom of Heaven, but also to the inheritance of the earth (Mt 5[5]). Such possession, however, is to be realized only through spiritual development; that is to say, such possession is not to be won by self-assertion or by insistence upon individual interest, but only as the individual identifies the common welfare of men with his own. Hence Christ's refusal to take part in a selfish struggle for private gain, and His ultimate conquest of all opposition by depriving others of the very power of setting up interests in opposition to His own.

3. Philosophical conception.—(1) *Its place in the history of ethics.*—While other ethical systems have in many cases been characterized by lofty ideals of conduct, the profound conception of meekness indicated in the preceding paragraph is distinctive of Christian ethics. The ethical ideal has generally been conceived as pleasure in some form or other. Hedonism (*q.v.*) conceives it as the pleasure of the moment, but the objection to this view is that such transient pleasure cannot satisfy a consciousness that is not momentary. Eudæmonism (*q.v.*) seeks to repair this defect by setting up the happiness of the life as a whole as the *summum bonum*, but a fatal limitation of this view is that the happiness of life as a whole is incalculable. The balance of pleasures and of pains cannot be adjusted, and the values of competing pleasures cannot be quantitatively determined though they may be qualitatively distinguished. The same criticism applies to Utilitarianism (*q.v.*), for the greatest happiness of the greatest number is still less calculable than the happiness of the individual life as a whole. A further criticism applies to all three forms of Hedonistic ethics—the criticism that pleasure, if sought for itself, is not found. This radical defect can be met only by a radical change of ethical ideal. What the nature of the new standard is to be will depend upon the point of view taken. If this be the standpoint of Christian ethics, then the ultimate moral standard cannot be lower than the attainment of perfection; and an essential factor in the rule of conduct by which this ideal is to be realized is the quality of meekness (πρᾳότης, πραότης, later form πραΰτης). True humblemindedness, gentleness, consideration for others, self-respect without vanity, reverence, and perfect humility—for all these qualities are connoted by the term 'meekness'—alone lead, according to Christian ethics, to the realization of moral perfection, and at the same time to the attainment of real temporal prosperity. In NT phraseology the meek are most truly happy (or blessed), because theirs is not only the Kingdom of Heaven, but also the inheritance of the earth.

But how is such a quality of character, which has for its distinctive feature an utter absence of self-assertion, actually to achieve the conquests and acquire the possessions which are thus ascribed to it?

(2) *Its relation to the doctrine of evolution.*—According to the principle of natural selection, it has been argued that in the evolutionary process the unworthy or 'unfit' must be set aside in order to make way for the survival of the fittest. There are some, therefore, who maintain that by supporting such institutions as hospitals, almshouses, and sanatoria we are retarding the process of evolution. It is argued that we are thus breeding degenerates and criminals, consumptives and lunatics, and, worst of all, taxing the sane, healthy, and law-abiding citizens for their support.

But this view fails to recognize all that the doctrine of evolution implies. It confuses this principle with that of letting the weakest go to the wall. It is hardly necessary to point out that by adopting such a principle we should blunt our finer feelings and should therefore sink in the moral scale. And the cost in time, money, and efficiency for other pursuits that is entailed in our care for the aged and diseased is negligible when compared with the moral gain. Thus we find that the preservation of the infirm and consideration for the weak are strictly compatible with, and, indeed, an essential factor in, the law of evolution, inasmuch as they tend to develop a quality of human character which has the highest survival value. The growth of the spiritual Kingdom and the dominance of the world by meekness and humility are thus progressively realized.

LITERATURE.—*HDB*, art. 'Meekness'; cf. art. 'Sermon on the Mount,' vol. v. p. 19; W. S. Bruce, *The Ethics of the Old Testament*, Edinburgh, 1895, *The Formation of Christian Character*[2], do. 1908; H. Sidgwick, *Outlines of Hist. of Ethics*, London, 1886, esp. ch. iii.; J. S. Mackenzie, *Manual of Ethics*[4], do. 1904.

A. J. HORROCKS.

MEGARICS (Μεγαρικοί).—Euclides of Megara is generally regarded as the founder of the Megaric school, though it would be more correct to keep the name for his successors a generation or two later. Euclides himself was an Eleatic and also an 'associate' (ἑταῖρος) of Socrates. The account of his philosophy given by E. Zeller (*Philosophie der Griechen*, II. i.[4], Leipzig, 1889, p. 244 f.) is vitiated by his adoption of Schleiermacher's identification of the Megarics with the 'friends of the forms' (εἰδῶν φίλοι) of Plato's *Sophist*. It is quite impossible to reconcile the few facts we know about the teaching of Euclides with the theory of plurality of forms, and Proclus, in his commentary on Plato's *Parmenides* (p. 149, ed. V. Cousin, Paris, 1820–27), states quite distinctly that the 'friends of the forms' were the 'wise men of Italy,' that is to say, the Pythagoreans. On such a point Proclus's testimony is conclusive, for he had access to and was familiar with the works of Plato's immediate successors.

The most trustworthy account that we have of the Megaric doctrine is that of Aristocles, the teacher of Alexander of Aphrodisias (2nd cent. A.D.), some extracts from whose *History of Philosophy* are preserved in the *Præparatio Evangelica* of Eusebius (xiv. 17). Its Eleatic origin is at once apparent from these, and Aristocles expressly says that it was first the doctrine of Xenophanes, Parmenides, Zeno, and Melissus, and later of Stilpo and the Megarics. In the first place, they made it their business to 'throw' (καταβάλλειν, a metaphor from wrestling) all sensation and appearance, and to trust in reasoning alone. The method which they adopted was that elaborated by Zeno, a method which was known as 'dialectic' by its admirers and as 'eristic' by its critics. It consisted in showing that two contradictory but equally cogent conclusions could be established with regard to everything without exception, and that there was therefore no truth at all in any of the appearances presented to our senses. That is what Plato calls ἀντιλογία, and we still possess a curious fragment of a work in the Doric dialect, generally known as the *Dialexeis* (the name is without authority), which applies the method to certain ethical antinomies. It is most natural to regard this work as a product of Megara, and we know that the Megarians clung with special tenacity to their native dialect.

The effect of this criticism is to leave us with nothing but the One or the Whole (τὸ ἕν, τὸ ὅλον) and to deprive the Many and the Parts of all claim to reality. That was the doctrine of Parmenides, but there is evidence that Euclides understood it in a rather different sense than the founder of his school, and it is here that we can trace the influence of Socrates. The One of the Eleatics had been a continuous, corporeal *plenum*, whether finite (Parmenides) or infinite (Melissus), but Euclides took the step of identifying it with the Good, which was 'called by many names, such as God, Wisdom (φρόνησις), and Mind (νοῦς).' It was in this way that 'the Absolute' made its first appearance in the history of philosophy, and its claim to be the sole reality was based on the inherent contradictoriness of all appearance.

The philosophy of Euclides had a very great influence on Plato, who had taken refuge with him at Megara after the death of Socrates, and it is to this influence that we may most probably ascribe the unique position assigned to the Good in the *Republic*. It was impossible, however, for Plato to acquiesce permanently in an Absolutist doctrine of any kind; for that excluded from Reality what he was most interested in, the Soul, and especially the best Soul of all, namely God. The *Parmenides* and the *Sophist* are chiefly occupied with this problem, and it is plain that Plato believed himself to have disposed finally of the Absolute. That led, of course, to a breach between the Academy and their fellow-Socratics of Megara, and from this time forward we may discern the beginnings of a distinct Megaric school. As was natural, the negative dialectic was more zealously cultivated than the central doctrine of Euclides. When an abstract Absolute has been set up, there is not much more to be said about it, but the dialectical method is always available for the criticism of rival philosophies. Aristotle was naturally the chief object of the Megaric attack, which was led by Eubulides. Aristotle's own logical theory was to a large extent moulded by this situation, and the title given to his course on fallacies, the *Sophistici Elenchi*, bears witness to it; for, since the time of Plato's *Sophist*, the old term had been revived as a name for thinkers of the class known later as Megarics. The fallacies exposed by Aristotle are, in fact, for the most part, Megaric arguments, and that is the explanation of the sense in which the words 'sophism' and 'sophistry' have been used from that time to the present day. Many of these sophisms are well known, such as the Liar (ψευδόμενος), the Veiled Man (ἐγκεκαλυμμένος), the Heap (σωρείτης), and the Bald Man (φαλακρός). As an extreme specimen, we may take the argument of the Horns: 'What you have not lost, you have. You have not lost horns. Therefore you have horns.' Some of the arguments are more serious, however, and raise the problem of continuity. The influence of Zeno is still felt in the *ratio ruentis acervi* (σωρείτης λόγος), referred to by Horace (*Epist.* II. i. 45). The most important of all from a historical point of view, however, was the κυριεύων of Diodorus Cronus († *c.* 307 B.C.), which continued to be discussed in the schools for centuries. Aristotle's favourite doctrine of potentiality and actuality (δύναμις and ἐνέργεια) was specially objectionable to the Megarics, and Diodorus set himself to destroy the conception of possibility altogether. The argument may be stated thus: 'Nothing impossible can proceed from anything possible. But it is impossible that anything in the past should be other than it is. If it had ever been possible still further in the past for it to be other than it is, then an impossibility must have proceeded from a possibility. Therefore it was never possible that it should be other than it is. Therefore it is impossible that anything should happen which does not actually happen.' Chrysippus confessed that he could not solve this, and Epictetus still busied himself with it.

The definite constitution of the Megaric school as a philosophical sect was the work of Stilpo of Megara, who for some time after the death of Aristotle (322 B.C.) was the most important philosophical personality in Greece. When Ptolemy I. took Megara in 307 B.C. he tried to induce Stilpo to return with him to Alexandria, but the invitation was declined. From the few facts that are told of him it is plain that he revived the positive side of the doctrine of Euclides and insisted on the sole reality of the One. He argued that to speak of man is to speak of nobody; for it is not to speak of A any more than of B. In the same way, he refused to admit that a cabbage shown to him was cabbage. There was a cabbage in just the same sense ten thousand years ago. As he further denied the real existence of forms or species (εἴδη), whether in the Aristotelian or in the Platonic sense, it followed that everything was mere appearance. But what distinguished Stilpo from all his predecessors, so far as we know, and what made Megaricism a reality for the first time, was the ethical principle which he deduced from this apparently barren Absolutism. It was the only ethical principle that such a doctrine can yield, that of quietism and insensibility. Plato's nephew Speusippos had already maintained that pleasure and pain were both evils, and that good men aim at imperturbability (ἀοχλησία), and the word 'apathy' (ἀπάθεια) occurs in the Platonic *Definitions* (413 A), which belong to the early Academy. In his *Ethics* (1104ᵇ, 24) Aristotle alludes to those who define the various forms of goodness as ἀπάθειαι and ἠρεμίαι. But it was Stilpo who made the doctrine live. Teles, who was his fellow-citizen and a little later in date, holds him up as the great example of indifference to the vicissitudes of fortune. It is unnecessary to suppose that he was influenced in this direction by the Cynics; for the doctrine follows quite naturally from his denial of reality to the world of sense, which he certainly derived from a very different source. As Zeno of Citium was a disciple of Stilpo, we may certainly regard him as a spiritual ancestor of Stoicism. The same tendency was represented by the school of Eretria, whose chief representative was Menedemus (*c.* 352–278 B.C.), and which regarded itself as an offshoot of the school of Elis, which looked upon Phædo as its founder. We know little about it, but its existence bears witness to the growth of the quietist ideal and its intimate connexion with a metaphysical theory which rejects the appearances of the world and holds fast to the One conceived as absolute.

LITERATURE.—There is little literature dealing with the Megarics outside the general histories of Philosophy, and what there is may be regarded as antiquated. It will be sufficient to mention C. Mallet, *Histoire de l'école de Mégare et des écoles d'Elis et d'Erétrie*, Paris, 1845.

JOHN BURNET.

MEIR. — Rabbi Meir, a Jewish sage who flourished in Palestine in the 2nd cent., belonged to the fourth generation of the Tannāîm (Rabbis of the age of the Mishnā); he was one of the foremost disciples of Rabbi Aqiba, and helped, with them, to give a new impulse to 'the study of the Law' (*i.e.* the consolidation and development of Jewish religious thought and practice) after the troubles attending the persecution under Hadrian. So great was the estimation in which he was held that, by one authority, those disciples are styled 'Meir and his associates' (*Midr. Rab.* to Lv 1[11]). Learning, mental acuteness, and a ready wit combined with a lofty character to make him the remarkable man he was. His parentage and birthplace are either uncertain or unknown. Contrary to the Talmudic practice, he is cited without a patronymic, and his doubtful descent gave rise to the legend which made him a son of Nero, a fabled convert to Judaism (*Giṭṭîn*, 56*a*). Even his real name, Meashah (Moses), was half-forgotten. When Aqiba, flouting the edict of the Roman authorities, continued to teach, Meir stood by him (*Tôs. Beᵉrākhôth*, ii. 6). His other masters were Rabbi Ishmael, to whom he went because he deemed himself intellectually unequal to the task of following Aqiba's discourses, and—a still more interesting fact—Elisha ben Abuyah, who was later to become an apostate and a declared friend of the Romans. From the latter, recreant though he was, Meir did not altogether dissociate himself in after years. He listened to his doctrine, and made discreet use of it.

'Like one who eats dates, he devoured the fruit, but threw away the stones' (*Ḥăgîgāh*, 15*b*).

His motive was not exclusively love of learning; there united with it grateful regard for one who had once been a cherished teacher, and likewise the hope of winning back the renegade; but his relations with Elisha were viewed with suspicion, and were partly the reason why his reputation with his contemporaries fell short of his posthumous fame.

Returning to Aqiba later on, Meir was ordained by that master, and began to teach in the Rabbinical schools. In his discourses he availed himself largely of the Haggādā (the homiletical method of Scriptural interpretation) and also of fables and parables. Thus it was said of him in later times that 'when Rabbi Meir died the parable-makers died with him' (*Sôṭāh*, 49*a*). He is credited with being the author of three hundred fables, of which only a few have been preserved in the Talmudic writings (*Sanhedrin*, 38*b*). His knowledge of Latin and Greek also helped him in his Biblical lectures. His acquaintance with the sacred text was so extensive and precise that, when once, on his travels in Asia Minor, he entered a synagogue on the eve of the Feast of Purim and found that there was no copy of Esther forthcoming for public recital, he wrote out the entire book from memory (*Tôs. Meᵉgillāh*, 2). For this intimate knowledge of the sacred text he was doubtless largely indebted to his profession as a scribe. Compared with the exegetical methods of his immediate teachers, his own mode of interpretation may be said to have been rationalistic. Keen and bold dialectic played a large part in his expositions, so that it was said of him (*Sanh.* 24*a*) that, in his lectures, he was like one who uprooted mountains and ground them together. He amazed and perplexed his colleagues by his daring decisions.

'He would declare the unclean permitted and the forbidden clean, and give his reasons' (*'Erûbhîn*, 13*b*).

It was usual to regard consecutive passages in the Bible as necessarily having a common subject-matter; Meir, however, held a different opinion. There are many such passages, he declared (*Siphrē* to Nu 25[1]), which have no organic connexion. This originality of his was viewed differently by different minds. Some admired his rationalism and courage; 'Meir's very staff,' they cried, 'teaches knowledge' (Jerus. *Neᵉdhārîm*, ix. 1). Others disapproved. 'Enough, Meir,' protested his colleagues when once he was more than usually daring (*Midr. Rab.* to Ca 1[12]). Nevertheless, as Hamburger remarks (ii. 707; as to the protest see I. H. Weiss, *Gesch.* ii. 15), in virtue of his qualities of mind and heart, he breathed into Judaism the breath of a new life. As to the Hălākhā (the body of decisions on ritual practice), his orderly and logical arrangement of the material contributed greatly to make the compilation of the Mishnā possible. He was a stringent upholder of the ritual Law; but he was even more strict with himself than with others.

'Never have I presumed to set aside, in my own personal practice, the decisions of my colleagues when those decisions have been more stringent than mine' (*Shabbāth*, 134*a*).

His strength of character is further illustrated by his opposition to Simeon ben Gamaliel II., then presiding over the Sanhedrin at Usha. To Meir had been assigned the office of *ḥākhām* of that body (as to the duties of that functionary see *JE*, art. 'Ḥakam'). Holding Simeon's knowledge of the Law inadequate, and resenting the President's excessive regard for his own dignity, he conspired with Rabbi Nāthān, one of his associates, to secure the Patriarch's deposition. Simeon, however, defeated the plot, and it was the conspirators who were ejected. Later on Nāthān was re-admitted, but Meir sturdily refused to make the necessary submission, and he narrowly escaped excommunication in consequence.

His domestic life was at once happier and sadder. His wife Beruria (Valeria) is one of the great women of the Talmud. The daughter of the martyr Rabbi Hananiah ben Teradion, who suffered under Hadrian, she was noted for both learning and moral worth. The touching story which records her wonderful fortitude in the hour of crushing calamity has been told again and again.

During Meir's absence at the academy one Sabbath eve, their two sons suddenly died. Beruria withheld the sad tidings from her husband until the day of peace was ended. Then she told him of it in a parable. 'A friend,' she said, 'left me some jewels to keep for him years ago—so long ago that I had come to look upon them as my own. Now, of a sudden, he has claimed them; but I find it hard to part with them. Must I really give them up?' 'Why ask such a question?' answered Meir, 'you should have restored them already.' 'I have done so,' she replied, as she led him to the death-chamber (*Midr. Mishlē* to Pr 31[10]).

This is not the only instance in which the Talmud is just enough to admit that one of its greatest sages was taught by a woman; Beruria instructs her husband in the higher knowledge on another notable occasion.

Annoyed by the pin-pricks of uncouth neighbours, Meir angrily calls down imprecations upon his tormentors. His wife rebukes him. 'Rather,' she protests, 'let us pray that they may live to repent; for the Psalmist's supplication is not "Let sinners be consumed out of the earth," but "Let sin be consumed"' (the allusion is to Ps 104[35], where the Hebrew is susceptible of Beruria's interpretation; for the story see *Beᵉr.* 10*a*).

The Rabbi, despite a certain severity and intolerance, was worthy of his wife. His defects were the defects of his qualities. If sometimes he set his face like a flint towards other men's weaknesses, he was strong and brave when life's sorrows touched himself. He, too, could preach and practise the great duty of submission.

Echoing Ec 5[2], he says, 'Let thy words before God be few; school thyself to say, "Whatever God doeth He doeth well"' (*ib.* 60*b*). And, again, 'As we should thank God for the good, so should we praise Him for evil' (*ib.* 48*b*). God Himself suffers with His sorrowing children (*Mish. Sanh.* vi. 5).

Expounding in novel fashion the verse, 'A good name is better than precious ointment; and the day of death than the day of one's birth' (Ec 7[1]), he said that death, the common lot of men, is good for those who pass hence with a good name (*Beᵉr.* 17*a*). Again, he said that what, according to Gn 1[31], God saw and proclaimed 'very good' at the Creation was death (*Midr. Rab.* to the verse). The section of the Mishnā known as *Ābhôth*

(Ethics of 'the Fathers') assigns a typical maxim to each of the great Talmudic Rabbis. The maxim associated with Meir reads as follows:

'Limit thy toil for worldly goods and give thyself to the Torah; but be lowly of spirit towards all men' (*Ābhôth*, iv. 10).

Meir was clearly no Pharisee of the baser sort; to be a sage was, for him, to have an incentive not to pride, but to humility. To study the Law, too, was not an end in itself; it must be made an impulse and inspiration to the noble life. Thus in another utterance of the sage he pictures God as saying:

'Devote thyself with all thy heart and soul to know my ways and to watch at the gates of my Law. Keep my Law in thy heart and my fear before thine eyes; guard thy mouth from sin, and purify thyself from all transgression. Then will I be with thee always' (*Ber.* 17*a*).

Equally notable are his teachings concerning social duty. Men are not to be judged by outward appearances.

'Look not at the flask, but at what it contains; there is many a new flask that contains old wine, many an old flask which has not even new wine in it' (*Ābhôth*, iv. 20).

Nor are men to be judged by the honey of their words. If we have two friends, one of whom admonishes us and the other flatters, we should love the former, for he is leading us heavenwards (*Ābhôth de R. Nāthān*, 29). He preaches sincerity even in the small things of social intercourse; he warns us against inviting a friend to dinner when we know that he will not accept the invitation, and against offering him a present which we believe he will not take (*Bŏraithā Ḥûllîn*, 94*a*; *Tôs. Bābhā Bathrā*, vi. 14). It is a man's duty to adapt himself to the ideas and customs of the community in which he lives; in Rome he should do as Rome does. The angels, the sage points out, when they came down to earth and appeared to Abraham, ate like mortals; when Moses went up to heaven, he neither ate nor drank (*Midr. Rab.* to Gn 18^{8}). Applying to Aaron the words (Mal 2^{6}), 'he did turn many away from iniquity,' Meir thus characterized the great high priest:

'If Aaron chanced to meet a bad man, he was careful to salute him; so that, when the latter next time meditated an evil deed, he said to himself, "Woe is me! how shall I then look Aaron in the face?" In like manner, if two men quarrelled, Aaron would go to one of them and say, "See, my son, what thy friend is doing; he is beating his breast, rending his clothes, and crying: 'Woe is me! how can I look my friend in the face, seeing that I have sinned against him?'" Then he would go and say the same to the other; so that at length they embraced and were reconciled' (*Ābhôth de R. Nāthān*, 12).

Meir has left many maxims on the self-regarding duties also. He exhorts us to contentment with our worldly lot. 'Who is rich?' he asks, and he answers, 'He that hath peace of mind with his riches' (*Shab.* 25*b*). 'He that feels shame,' he says elsewhere, 'will not quickly be led into sin' (*Nedhārîm*, 20*a*). The sin of Samuel's sons (1 S 8^{3}), he declared, lay in their demanding what was due to them (*Shab.* 56*a*). The Law (Ex 22^{1}) ordains that a man who steals an ox must make fivefold restitution; but, if he steals a sheep, the restitution is only fourfold. The difference is to be explained by the fact that, unlike sheep, the ox is a toiling animal. 'Here,' cries Meir, 'is a proof of the worth of labour in the sight of God!' (*Mekhîltā* to the verse). In common with the Rabbis who lived under Roman rule, and with the early Christians (see E. Gibbon, *Hist. of the Decline and Fall of the Roman Empire*, London, 1901-06, ii. 17), he condemns the theatre and the arena. The one is 'the seat of the scornful' (Ps 1^{1}), the other a place of execution (a reference to the cruelties of the gladiatorial contests) (*Ābhôth de R. Nāthān*, 37; *'Ābhôdhāh Zārāh*, 18*b*). He emphasizes the futility of human ambitions by an apt remark: man, he says, is born with his hands clenched as though he would grasp the whole world; he dies with his hands wide open, for he takes nothing with him (*Midr. Rab.* to Ec 5^{14}).

Unbending to the ignorant (*'am ha-areṣ* [*q.v.*]) and the schismatic among his own people, Meir shows himself tolerant and liberal towards men of alien creed.

The Gentile who gives himself to the study of the Law is as worthy as the Jewish High Priest; for Holy Writ (Lv 18^{5}), speaking of God's statutes, says that if a *man* do them, he shall live by them—a man, not a priest or a Levite (*Bābhā Qammā*, 38*a*; *Sanh.* 59*a*).

He had many conversations with Gentiles, chiefly polemical.

One of these opponents designates Israel a people contemned of God, driven by the Master from His house, and put in subjection to other lords. 'God,' argues the controversialist, 'has made you exiles in our midst; why, then, do you not assimilate with us?' Meir protests against the theory. 'Rather,' he affirms, 'we are to be likened to a son whom his father has discarded because of his evil life, but whom the paternal heart is ready to take back if he return penitently' (A. Jellinek, *Bêth ham-Midrash*, Leipzig, 1853-78, i. 21). 'If,' asks another disputant, 'your God loves the poor, why does He not sustain them?' 'In order,' Meir replies, 'to give us an opportunity of escaping Gehenna by the practice of loving-kindness' (*Bābhā Bathrā*, 10*a*).

Like Aqiba, his master, Meir is pictured by the Talmud (*Qiddûshîn*, 81*a*) as undergoing the temptation of St. Anthony. Satan, so runs the legend, appears to the sage in the form of a beautiful woman, who would entice him with her wiles. But he escapes them. The legend puts in concrete shape the traditions concerning the Rabbi's unyielding rectitude which gathered about his name. Another story tells of a journey which he once made to Rome in order to rescue from a house of ill-fame his wife's sister, who had been taken captive after her father's martyrdom. It is said that his mission was successful (*'Ābhôdhāh Zārāh*, 18*a*).

Born, it is believed, in Asia Minor, Meir died in that country. He enjoined his disciples to bury him on the seashore, so that the waters which laved the land of his fathers might touch his bones (Jerus. *Kilayîm*, 32*c*). 'He had no equal in his generation' is one Talmudic appreciation of him (*'Ērûbhîn*, 13*b*); and, in a public eulogy pronounced on him at Sepphoris, Rabbi José declared him to be 'a great man and a saint, but humble withal' (Jerus. *Ber.* ii. 7).

Of all the Tannaim, Meir's name is most widely known among the people. In the house of every pious Jew there is a money-box hung on the wall, in which the inmates deposit their alms for the poor of Palestine. This box bears the inscription 'Mêîr, Ba'al han-Nēs' ('Meir, the wonder-worker'), an allusion to the miraculous power attributed to him in Talmudic and popular lore (see *JE* viii. 435).

LITERATURE.—W. Bacher, *Die Agada der Tannaiten*, Strassburg, 1890-1903; Hamburger, artt. 'Beruria,' 'Mair R.,' 'Religionsgespräche'; H. Graetz, *Geschichte der Juden*, Leipzig, 1866-78, iv. (Eng. tr., London, 1891-92, ii.); *JE*, art. 'Meir'; I. H. Weiss, *Geschichte der jüd. Tradition*, Wilna, 1904, ii. 90 ff.

MORRIS JOSEPH.

MELANCHOLY.—In Greek physiology the bodily constitution of an individual, his appearance, his liability to disease, and also his mental character were explained by the proportions in which the four humours were distributed in his framework. These were blood, yellow bile, black bile, and phlegm, the predominance or excess of which gave respectively the sanguine, the choleric, the melancholic, and the phlegmatic 'temperament.' Melancholy (μέλας and χολή) was thus the mental disposition of the melancholic temperament. The terms passed into literary and popular use, although the doctrine of the four humours, on which the distinctions were based, was forgotten or discarded. The names seemed, in fact, to correspond to certain broad differences, bodily and mental, among men, and writers on insanity are still careful, in their description of cases, to indicate the 'temperament' of each patient. The differences are now made to depend either upon the blood or upon the nervous system, or both. If the blood is decisive, the difference may be sought either in its substance—the number of red corpuscles, etc.—or in its circulation; if the nervous system, in the strength or the rate of reaction, or both. Henle made use of the conception of nerve-tone, which has since been retained and developed (*Anthropologische Vorträge*). No part of the nervous system, he showed, is ever wholly at rest during life; every stimulus finds a certain degree of excitation already present in the nerve-endings and nerve-fibres on which it acts; what we call rest is, therefore, a moderate degree of activity, which may rise or fall, and which is maintained by internal stimuli, acting through the blood. This is the 'tonus' of the nerves, their preparedness for action; the higher the tonus, the stronger the re-action. On the nerve-tone will, therefore, depend the sensitiveness of the individual, his prevailing emotional attitude, and his quickness and firmness of response. A low tone shows itself in the dull, heavy expression of face (in the phlegmatic, *e.g.*), the relaxed muscles, the deliberate movements, the tendency to 'run to fat'; a high tone in the vivid complexion, alert expression, and quick movements of the sanguine or choleric. The melancholic, according to Henle, has also a high nerve-tone, but reacts through the emotional or affective system, rather than the voluntary; whereas the choleric relieves feeling by prompt and strenuous action, the melancholic is denied this advantage; his melancholy is the brooding upon and nursing of emotions, a habit from which genius, or, it may be, merely hypochondria and hysteria, spring. Wundt's simple formula has been widely accepted: that temperament is primarily a question of emotion, that emotion undergoes two forms of change, one in intensity, or strength, the other in rate; hence the fourfold division: strong and quick—choleric; strong and slow—melancholic; weak and quick—sanguine; weak and slow—phlegmatic. Strong emotions under modern conditions mean a predominance of pain; slowness of change means that the mind takes time to follow out its own thoughts, is not wholly absorbed by the present but looks to the evil ahead. These tendencies characterize the melancholic (*Grundzüge der physiol. Psychologie*[5], iii. 637). The scheme is too simple to fit the complexities and subtilties of human character, however, and there is no general agreement even as to the number of distinct temperaments, as many as nine having been suggested.

1. Melancholy and pain.—Melancholy differs from the other dispositions in being a well-recognized temporary emotion or mood, as well as a prolonged or permanent trait, and also in being in an extreme form the most prominent symptom of a definite form of insanity—melancholia or mental depression. It has formed the theme of one of the most wonderful books in our language—*The Anatomy of Melancholy*, by Robert Burton, first published in 1621.

The melancholy with which he deals, and of which the 'causes, symptoms, prognostics, and cures' are set forth with such fertility of illustration, is 'an habit,—a chronick or continute disease, a settled humour,' but it is built up, as he recognizes, out of 'melancholy in disposition,' which is 'that transitory *Melancholy* which comes and goes upon the smallest occasion of sorrow, need, sickness, trouble, fear, grief, passion, or perturbation of the mind, any manner of care, discontent, or thought, which causeth anguish, dullness, heaviness and vexation of spirit, any ways opposite to pleasure, mirth, joy, delight, causing frowardness in us, or a dislike. In which equivocal and improper sense, we call him melancholy that is dull, sad, sour, lumpish, ill-disposed, solitary, any way moved, or displeased. . . . Melancholy in this sense is the character of Mortality' (i. 164 [ed. London, 1896]).

It might be said that this temporary melancholy is merely mental pain, however caused, and that the permanent disposition or habit is a state of mind in which mental pain is the dominant tone. The expression of melancholy is that of pain, the pale face, the drawn look, lips and eyebrows turned slightly downwards at the corners; the respiration slow and sighing, the pulse-beat slow, the temperature lowered, the nutrition-processes, including the appetite, impaired, so that the body seems insufficiently fed. One of the immediate consequences is also a loss of sensitiveness to outer impressions; they lose in clearness and distinctness; the judgment follows suit, and the whole mental character is, even though only for the moment, changed for the worse. In particular, egoism develops:

'The patient thinks only of himself and his sufferings; altruistic passions, family affection yield to an egoism of the most exacting and extreme type' (H. Beaunis, *Les Sensations internes*, Paris, 1889, p. 193 ff.).

Mental pain may be less acute, but it is more persistent than physical pain, and it has the same reverberation throughout the organism. The distinction between the two is probably artificial; mental pain accompanies all physical pain, while in its turn physical pain—discomfort, loss of nervous tone—is a constant accompaniment of mental pain. The most common cause of the former, physical pain, is the over-excitation or exhaustion of some sensory or motor nerve; so the most common cause of the latter, mental pain, is the over-strain or exhaustion of the brain centres and tracts concerned in ideation, emotion, memory, and will. Love and over-study were two of Burton's causes of melancholy. So melancholy may be regarded as a pain of fatigue, as due to excessive functioning on the emotional or intellectual side, especially when the strain has not been rewarded with success.

The extraordinary persistence of melancholy, the difficulty of distracting the mind from it, is due, as Beaunis urges, not merely to the fact that its causes—the desires, the memories—are persistent, but also to 'the sentiment of the irreparable, which is at the root of almost all mental pains, the idea that all is lost and without hope. The mother who knows that she will never see again the child that has died in her arms, the artist who sees that he will never be able to realise the ideal of his dreams, the inventor whose discovery is held up to ridicule, the poet whose verses, that he believes to be inspired, are laughed at, the thinker who seeks for truth and finds only doubt, the Christian who sees the foundering of his belief and of his faith, all have this sentiment of the irreparable, of the lost beyond return, which leaves behind only nothingness and despair' (*ib.* p. 234).

2. Melancholy and the sense of values.—Melancholy is the mood of an imaginative mind; it is true that an animal is sometimes described as 'melancholy'; a dog that has lost his master, a wild animal in captivity in a narrow space, a bird deprived of her mate: death, even self-inflicted death, is known to have followed such misfortunes. So a child may be 'melancholy' after the loss of a mother or a playmate. But in the strict sense melancholy is an adult and a human infirmity. Probably the time of its greatest frequency is the period of adolescence; in middle and old age it tends to disappear, to be replaced in senility, occasionally, by a state outwardly similar, but inwardly different. Byron's lameness and Heine's and Leopardi's delicate constitutions have suggested that physical disease may be the predisposing cause to melancholy; but, as Metchnikoff points out, Schopenhauer preserved his melancholy and pessimism to a vigorous old age, while there are innumerable cases of patients suffering from serious and even deadly diseases, yet retaining their native lightness of heart. If anything, melancholy is more common among the young, healthy, and vigorous. It does not really depend upon the health at all, but upon the sense or 'sentiment' of life. The typical case is Goethe, who in his own youth passed through the torment which he describes in *The Sorrows of Werther*, and had thoughts of suicide, but in his old age is described as casting off the sickly and morbid side of his character, replacing it by a serene and even joyous love of life (E. Metchnikoff, *Essais optimistes*, pt. viii.). The intensity of feeling is greater in the young than in the old, both for pleasure and for pain; hence they are more impressionable; but this is not due to the greater vitality or sensitiveness of their nervous system, but rather to the fact that the older man is better able, through his experience, to interpret the impressions, to see them in their true perspective, and in relation to life as a whole, whereas for the young each impression is taken in isolation, is weighed only in its relation to the immediate needs or desires of the self. Hence the vivid colouring of their life, the higher happiness, and the deeper pain. In the same way melancholy is more frequent in men than in women, in the northern races than in the southern races of Europe. A northern race, perhaps because its civilization is a more recent growth, is more conscious of itself, and less conscious of the wider group in which the loss of one individual is compensated by the gain of another. It was mainly from Russia, Germany, and Scandinavia that the melancholy school of writers of last century—the Fin de Siècle—came. Suicides are said to increase in number northwards, and one of the most common causes of suicide is melancholy (see Burton's disquisition on suicide [i. 495]; and Metchnikoff, p. 306). At the back of all melancholy is fear—fear of pain in the first instance, then fear of loss, of failure, of death, of society's judgment upon oneself. The greater the value, or, rather, the greater the appreciation of a good, the greater the pain at its loss, and the greater the pain at the prospect of its loss. Hence melancholy is, paradoxically, more common in the idealist than in the materialist. Paul Bourget, writing of Baudelaire, finds the key to the profound melancholy of this rather repulsive figure in the mysticism and idealism of his early faith. When such a faith, the faith in the eternal, has been strongly held, its object deeply adored, the loss of faith in it, and of love, is irreparable. The individual may no longer have the intellectual need to believe, but he still has the need to feel as when he believed. The desires remain, strengthened by habit, and in the sensitive soul their influence is irresistible; yet their satisfaction is impossible. Melancholy then is the effect of failure of adaptation to the environment, in matters of faith and belief. The stronger the resistance of facts to the realization of the thinker's dream, the deeper his melancholy. To the mystic soul faith is not the mere acceptance of a formula or of a dogma; God is not for it a word, a symbol, an abstraction, but a real being in whose company the soul walks as a child in its father's, who loves it, knows it, understands it.

Once an illusion so strong and so sweet has gone, says Bourget, no substitute of less intensity will suffice; after the intoxication of opium, that of wine seems mean and paltry. Driven away at the touch of the world, faith leaves in such souls a gap through which all pleasure slips away. The more the sufferer tries to escape, the more securely is he held, until at last there remains as his only satisfaction 'the redoubtable but consoling figure of that which frees from all slaveries, and delivers from all doubts,—Death' (Paul Bourget, *Essais de psychologie contemporaine*, Paris, 1892, p. 21).

Still deeper is the melancholy of unsatisfied desire, when the failure of satisfaction lies, not in the resistance of external circumstance, but in the inability of the subject to enjoy, an inability which is itself a mark of exhaustion; it is the soul that has lived most, felt most strongly, indulged its passions to the full, till its power to feel is almost destroyed, that finds life most unbearable.

'Le mensonge du désir qui nous fait osciller entre la brutalité meurtrière des circonstances et les impuissances plus irréparables encore de notre sensibilité' (*ib.* p. 142).

It is the melancholy of nature after the storm, of evening, of the grey light that comes after the sunset, of the brown tints of autumn trees—exhaustion or decay after stress and life.

Less tragic is the melancholy that is associated with pensiveness, deliberation, thought, as in Milton's *Il Penseroso*—the melancholy of the poet and of the philosopher. Beaunis connects this also with pain, however. When man reflects, he is forced to recognize, according to Beaunis, that he is born to pain, and that pleasure is only an accessary in his life.

'There is no physical pleasure which can compensate for an hour of *angina pectoris*, no mental enjoyment which does not disappear before the pain caused by the death of one we love, no intellectual pleasure which is not annulled when we think of how much is unknown in our fate. Pessimism, an irrefutable pessimism, is at the root of every reasoning, of every meditation' (p. 222).

Happily, he adds, most men do not reflect or meditate upon the fate either of themselves or of others; their interest faces outwards, not inwards; they have no time to worry over problems that great minds have found insoluble; or, if they do worry over them, they are able to set their worries at rest by the acceptance of a solution ready-made, on the authority of the Church or the pastor.

3. Melancholy and exhaustion.—The essential nature of melancholy has been probed more deeply from the point of view of pathology, and in various ways the idea of exhausted or decreased energy has been brought into connexion with the known laws of mental activity.

To Bevan Lewis melancholy means nervous enfeeblement; the subject is no longer able to do easily and smoothly even the most familiar and habitual acts; it is only with effort that he can think, or attend to what he hears or reads.

'It appears to us that the true explanation is due to mental operations being reduced in level so far as to establish conscious effort in lieu of the usual unconscious operations, or lapsed states of consciousness which accompany all intellectual processes. The restless movements of the intellectual eye (in the artist, poet, etc.), as well as those of the state of maniacal excitement, bespeak in the former case the exalted muscular element of thought, and in the latter a highly reflex excitability, but in the melancholic these muscles of relational life are usually at rest, the eye is fixed, dull, heavy, sluggish in its movements and painful in effort, the eyelids are drooped, the limbs motionless. The only muscles in a state of tension are those which subserve emotional life, viz. the small muscles of expression' (*Textbook on Mental Diseases*, p. 121). 'Failure in the muscular element of thought has as its results on the subjective side, enfeebled ideation and the sense of objective resistance' (*ib.* p. 122).

The eye sees less clearly, the mind interprets less accurately; the will acts less vigorously, and less effectively; it may be that the motor ideas, which are the cues, if not the excitants, of action, cannot be formed or recalled accurately in the mind; hence apathy and inaction. The environment, the non-ego, appears as antagonistic or foreign to the self; it is no longer the world in which we moved freely and easily, therefore pleasantly, but one which is new and strange, which resists our efforts and counters our desires. The result is a rise in the subject-consciousness; the mind is thrown back upon itself. The man broods upon his sufferings, which become his wrongs, and, in interpreting or explaining them, suspicion of others is the simplest and therefore the most frequent way out.

According to Pierre Janet's interpretation, melancholy represents a stage on the way to *misère psychologique*, or psychic misery, with its accompanying disaggregation of the personality, and subjugation of the conscious by the subconscious or unconscious self. There are innumerable degrees of attachment and detachment of acts and ideas to the self. In thought-reading and in table-turning we have simple instances of how acts are carried out which correspond to ideas or thoughts in the mind of the subject, yet the acts are neither voluntary nor conscious on his part; he is aware of the result, not of his own agency in it. In spiritualism—the possession of the medium by the supposed spirit of the dead, who gives through the medium information which the latter, in his normal state, is wholly unaware of enjoying—we have a more systematized form of the same thing.

Finally, in hypnotism, in hysteria, morbid impulses, fixed ideas, and obsessions, there are vivid examples of how thoughts, or, rather, systems of thought, though formed by the individual, may yet by the conditions of their occurrence appear entirely foreign to him; he is their slave, they take possession of him, he is carried away by them. Passions, of the source of which the patient is wholly unaware, dating back perhaps to a forgotten childhood, may yet lead to actions for which he cannot recognize his responsibility, which he may indeed forget immediately afterwards and, therefore, wholly fail to connect with his 'real' self. He is unaware even that he was the physical agent; any proof of this that can be brought forward must have a shattering effect upon the self-consciousness; the patient feels that he no longer has a grip of himself, that he may do some incredible act of violence, cruelty, immodesty, or crime. He becomes estranged from himself—and this doubleness is itself an added source of depression; it is the same in effect whether the two personalities succeed each other in time, as alternating personalities, or exist simultaneously, although acting separately; the disaggregation means an impairment of the self, often revealed by an actual loss of intellectual power, weakened concentration of attention and will. The subject becomes morbidly curious about his own feelings, his strength of will, his health, his prospects in life, etc. This subjectivity is the essence of the melancholy disposition. It remains to ask what is the cause of the disaggregation of consciousness, the psychological misery, of which melancholy is so prominent a symptom. According to Janet, the cause may be either physical or mental; physical, as the exhaustion of a prolonged illness, or of a sudden shock, or continued over-exertion, as in heavy physical strain; or mental, as in the shock of terror, excessive grief, prolonged mental worry, strong emotional excitement (*e.g.*, religious). The great vital crises, at puberty, adolescence, and the change of life, with the feeling of strangeness which the loss of old and the gain of new sensations and impulses bring, are common causes of at least a temporary disaggregation and depression. The theory is not widely different in effect from that of Bevan Lewis; in both it is the co-ordinating power that fails, through nervous exhaustion; the elementary impressions and impulses fall apart, as it were, into their primitive independence; the subject seems out of touch with his environment, is unable to face the tasks of his social or occupational life. According to the degree of disaggregation or rise of subject-consciousness, there may be simple melancholy, hysteria, or actual insanity (P. Janet, *L'Automatisme psychologique*, pt. ii. chs. iii. and iv.).

4. Melancholy and personality.—The sense of mystery, of strangeness, of possession, that occurs in melancholy deserves to be considered in detail. In melancholy, as has been shown above (§ 3), the sensations are less clear, their threshold is higher, the perceptions based upon them are blurred, partly from the relaxation of the muscles of attention, partly from the absorption of the mind by the pain, real or imaginary. The individual neither sees nor hears so clearly as before; the commonest objects may look strange, the most familiar voice sound different; but these things are interpreted not as a change in the experiencing subject, but as a change in the objects experienced. One's friends, one's country, one's world have changed, and the subject is unable to face the great activity required to adapt himself to the new sphere. Still greater is the loss of clearness in the memories. The most vivid experiences, when they can no longer be clearly and definitely recalled, tend to lose the warmth and intimacy which memories of 'my own experiences' should possess, as compared with those of others of which I have merely heard or read. Thus in mental exhaustion and depression the memories of my own life lose their emotional tone; they seem to belong to another than myself. It is true that this state lends itself to analysis, and that the habit of analysis, once formed, may continue when normal life has returned.

Amiel is said to have written: 'The desire to know, when it is turned upon the self, is punished like the curiosity of Psyche, by the flight of the beloved object; the outward-facing look makes for health; too prolonged a looking inwards brings us to nothingness. By analysis I am annihilated.' And again, 'All personal happenings, all special experiences are for me pretexts to meditation. Such is the life of the thinker. He depersonalises himself every day; if he consents to experiment and to act, it is the better to understand; if he wills, it is to know what will is. Although it is sweet to him to be loved, and he knows nothing sweeter, there again he seems to himself to be the occasion of the phenomenon rather than its end. He contemplates the spectacle of love, and love remains for him but a spectacle. He is nothing but a thinking subject, he retains nothing but the form of things' (see L. Dugas and F. Moutier, *La Dépersonnalisation*, Paris, 1911, p. 138 ff.).

This is an exact description of the frame of mind in the milder forms of melancholy, as that of the poet or artist, like Byron, Edgar Allan Poe, Heine, the young Goethe, etc. Shakespeare's Hamlet is a classical instance; they are not real experiencers, real agents, or lovers, but mere play-actors so far as emotion is concerned. Probably, however, their descriptions are the more accurate in that they are not blinded by passion, as is the cheerful ordinary mortal.

A somewhat different way of putting the case of melancholy might be drawn from the writings of S. Freud and others of his or allied schools—viz. that depression springs from the influence of a morbid complex on the personality. The complex may be any strong emotional experience, shock, terror, social disaster, etc. Wishes, desires, more or less closely connected with the shock-complex, are repressed, at first consciously, while suggestive ideas and associations, which arise from the same root, are expelled from the mind when they enter it. But a train of thought, when expelled, and a wish, when repressed, do not on that account cease to exist. They continue to live in the subconscious or in the unconscious, and may, so long as they are incomplete or unrealized, influence the conscious life indirectly. They may do this in two ways: (*a*) the complex draws off to itself, for its repression, a considerable degree of the available psychic energy; the individual is mentally weakened. As we have seen above, the greater effort required for the simplest, most habitual acts is felt as strain, as exhaustion, as pain; the self, with its distresses and difficulties, becomes more and more the centre of attention. (*b*) But, further, the complex, though itself driven below the level of consciousness, and shut off from direct connexion by the 'censor' of consciousness, is still enabled during moments of relaxation, half-sleep, reverie, distracted attention, etc., to send disguised messengers through. These take the form of dreams, phobias or terrors, obsessions, sudden impulses, etc. For the most part these dreams and impulsive acts are protective; they are a means of realizing, in however imperfect a way, the wish inspired by the complex; but the subject himself may be wholly unaware of this origin and of their meaning; they seem like an invasion of his personality by a foreign one. Painful experiences and memories have a far greater tenacity of life than pleasant; they have a high degree of 'perseveration,' as it has been called, *i.e.* the tendency to force their way into consciousness, of their own accord, and without any apparent stimulus or associative link. And, again, even the slightest of associations is enough to drag up the painful complex or its substitutes. On the other hand, such memories are not 'sociable'; they do not bring other thoughts in their train; especially they lack 'determination'-value, the tendency to direct the mind systematically from one thought to a train of others; they tend to clog thought. The subject becomes more and more conscious of inefficiency in his profession or in his social life; and the consciousness of failure has the usual consequence of making the actual failure all the greater.

5. Melancholy and pessimism.—Melancholy and pessimism are two sides of the same state of mind, the one expressing the subjective attitude and disposition, the other the theoretical interpretation. Happiness becomes a dream which is never realized, and which it seems hopeless to pursue. Subjectively, indifference, apathy, want of feeling; objectively, death, seem the only desirable things. The ideas, imaginations, and suggestions that arise in the mind of the melancholic, according to a well-recognized law (see Störring, *Mental Pathology*, p. 222 ff.), tend to be of the same emotional tone as that of the disposition in which they are called up, *i.e.* painful, depressing; the melancholic sees only the sad, the tragic, the bitter side of things, the pain that is suffered, the sins and crimes and follies that are committed, not the pleasures, the kindness, the goodness, that are in things. Hence melancholy, whatever its source, has played a powerful part in religious movements. It is not only that religion and its history furnish the melancholy mind with a cohort of images of the most terrifying type, but also that the consciousness of the suffering self sends it to religion, to the idea of sin and its punishment, as the most obvious and nearest interpretation; and, finally, that religion offers the only adequate relief and hope of escape. Religious melancholy is the subject of one of Burton's most curious dissertations (pt. iii. sect. iv. membrum i.), and James's *Varieties of Religious Experience*, lects. vi. and vii., on 'The sick Soul,' give a modern presentation. It is there shown how, as in Tolstoi's case, melancholy may be accompanied by a total change in the estimate of the values of things: things that seemed of the utmost value before now seem worthless; they excite no emotion or interest whatever; and a consequence of this is that the world, and people, look different and are thought of differently—as strange and unreal. It is also shown that in a rational being the strangeness and change of feeling incite to a search for a reason, for an explanation, either directly in oneself or in the action of other beings upon oneself. Either of these ways may lead to religious conversion and relief.

6. Moroseness.—The pathologist Pinel, in his treatise on *Mental Alienation*, depicted melancholics as of two distinct types—the one filled with enthusiasm for art, for literature, for all that is great and noble, or, among ordinary people, merely pleasant, lively, and affectionate, yet apt to torment himself and his neighbours by bursts of anger and chimerical suspicions; the other is the type to which the Emperor Tiberius and Louis XI. of France belonged—men who are gloomy and taciturn, deeply suspicious of others, fond of solitude. Suspicion of others is the dominant mark, with cunning and duplicity of the most dishonourable and cruel kind, which, if power is added, become fiercer and less restrained as age increases (P. Pinel, *L'Aliénation mentale*[2], Paris, 1809, p. 161). This represents with some accuracy the morose type of melancholy. Moroseness springs from the disposition to regard others as having secret designs upon one's property or life or place, and to avoid them in consequence. It involves extreme self-centring and misanthropy. Melancholy is a disease of the imaginative, moroseness of the unimaginative mind—the man who does not aspire beyond that which he has already attained, the man of narrow range of ideas, unable to appreciate the values that others place upon things, especially the ideal values. Probably the pivot of the morose character is, like that of melancholy, fear or anxiety.

As de Fursac has said of the miser, 'It is undoubtedly true that from insecurity springs anxiety, and that anxiety becomes a torture and a source of trouble for the mind. It has for effects the diminution of activity, the development of defensive tendencies to the detriment of the expansive tendencies, the cult of absolute security, and the horror of risk. It is intimately bound up with insociability' (*L'Avarice*, p. 23).

This is true also of the insecurity of power or of position, in narrow and selfish characters; there is no sense of the solidarity of the race, even of the family; the morose man sees only the bad side, the weaknesses of his neighbours; he has no sympathy with or any kind of feeling for others; he is vindictive, and, if opportunity allows, savage, brutal, cruel.

LITERATURE.—R. Burton, *The Anatomy of Melancholy*, Oxford, 1621 (by 'Democritus Junior'; the author's name was subscribed to an 'Apologetical Index' at the end of the volume). For the history of the theory of the 'temperaments' see W. Volkmann, *Lehrbuch der Psychologie*, Cöthen, 1894 f., i. 205 ff.; J. Henle, *Anthropologische Vorträge*, Brunswick, 1876, p. 101 ff.; and W. Wundt, *Grundzüge der physiologischen Psychologie*[5], Leipzig, 1902–03, iii. 637 ff.; J. Sully, *Pessimism: a History and Criticism*[3], London and New York, 1891; W. James, *The Will to Believe*, do. 1897 ('Is life worth living?' p. 32 ff.); Élie Metchnikoff, *Essais optimistes*, Paris, 1907 (pt. vii. 'Pessimisme et optimisme'; pt. viii. 'Goethe et Faust'); P. Janet, *L'Automatisme psychologique*, Paris, 1889, and *Les Obsessions et la psychasthénie*, do. 1903; T. S. Clouston, *Clinical Lectures on Mental Diseases*[5], London, 1898; W. James, *The Varieties of Religious Experience*, New York and Bombay, 1902; J. Rogues de Fursac, *L'Avarice, Essai de psychologie morbide*, Paris, 1911; G. Störring, *Mental Pathology in its Relation to Normal Psychology*, tr. T. Loveday, London, 1907; W. Bevan Lewis, *A Text-book on Mental Diseases*, do. 1889.

J. L. McINTYRE.

MELANESIANS.—1. Extent and limits of the subject.—The region of the South Pacific, which is called Melanesia, is well defined, except on the western side. The boundary on the east lies between Fiji, which is Melanesian, and Samoa, which is Polynesian. To the south the Melanesian island of New Caledonia is separated by a considerable space of ocean from New Zealand, which is Polynesian, as are the small islands of Micronesia on the north from the Melanesian Solomon group, but to the west the islands of Melanesia overlap New Guinea. Some of the inhabitants of that vast island are Melanesian, at any rate in language; but, though Melanesians have been called Papuans, there can be no doubt that Papua, or New Guinea, cannot be placed as a whole in Melanesia. Five distinct groups of islands are without question Melanesian: (1) the Solomon Islands, with the groups which connect them with New Guinea; (2) the Santa Cruz group; (3) the Banks' Islands and New Hebrides; (4) New Caledonia, with the Loyalty Islands; and (5) Fiji.

The first discovery in Melanesia was that of the Solomon Islands by Spaniards, under Mendaña, in 1567. In 1595 the same voyager discovered Santa Cruz; and in 1606 Quiros and Torres discovered the New Hebrides and Banks' Islands. The Dutch discovered Fiji in 1643. French voyagers in the latter part of the 18th cent., and finally Captain Cook in his second great voyage, completed the general survey of all the groups. In the records of these passing visits it is vain to seek for information concerning the religion of the natives. The discoverers saw what they believed to be temples, idols, worship and invocations of devils; they interpreted what they saw, as succeeding voyagers have done, according to their own conceptions of savage beliefs. It was not till missionaries, about the middle of the 19th cent., began to live in closer intercourse with the native people and to learn their languages that any certain knowledge of Melanesian religion could be gained. The following account represents in the main the knowledge which has been gained by the Melanesian Mission of the Church of England. The religion of the Fijians is considered in another article (see FIJI). The account here given has been drawn from the Solomon Islands, the Santa Cruz group, the Banks' Islands, and the Northern New Hebrides. It has been gathered from natives of those groups in native language, and much of it has been gained from what educated natives have written in a native language. Very little, however, has come from the Western Solomon Islands or the Southern New Hebrides; but there is every reason to believe that religious beliefs and practices in these islands do not differ considerably from those of the central parts of Melanesia.

2. Basis of Melanesian religion.—From whatever source they may have derived it, the Melanesians generally have held the belief that their life and actions were carried on in the presence and under the influence of a power superior to that of living man. This power, they thought, was all about them, attached to outward objects, such as stones, and exercised by persons, *i.e.*, either by men, alive or dead, or by spirits who never were men. This 'sense of the Infinite,' as Max Müller (*Lectures on the Origin and Growth of Religion* [*HL*], London, 1878, lect. i.) calls it, was the foundation of the religious beliefs of the Melanesians; the general object of their religious practices was to obtain the advantage of this power for themselves. This power is impersonal, and not physical in itself, although it is always put in motion by a person; and all remarkable effects in nature were thought to be produced by it. It is not fixed in anything, but can abide and be conveyed in almost anything. All spirits, beings superior to men, have it; ghosts of dead men generally have it, and so do some living men. The most common name for it is *mana* (*q.v.*). The methods by which living men use and direct this power may well be called magical; the controlling force lies generally in words contained in chanted or muttered charms. If worship is addressed to beings who are not living men, and if the use of their power is sought from them to do good or to do harm, it is because such beings have this *mana*; the forms of words have efficacy because they derive it from the beings which have *mana*; a common object, such as a stone, becomes efficacious for certain purposes because such a being gives it *mana* power. In this way the influence of the unseen power pervades all life. All success and all advantage proceed from the favourable exercise of this *mana*; whatever evil happens has been caused by the direction of this power to harmful ends, whether by spirits, or ghosts, or men. In no case, however, does this power operate, except under the direction and control of a person—a living man, a ghost, or a spirit.

3. Objects of worship.—The objects of religious worship, therefore, were always persons to whom prayer or sacrifice was offered, or in whose names charms were recited, with the view of gaining supernatural power, or turning it, either directly or indirectly, to the advantage of the worshipper. These personal objects of worship are either spirits or ghosts. By spirits are meant personal beings in whom the spiritual power already mentioned naturally abides, and who never were men; by ghosts are meant the disembodied spirits or souls of dead men. To keep these distinct is essential to the understanding of Melanesian religion. Natives themselves are found to confuse them at times, while Europeans are usually content to call all alike deities, gods, or devils.

(1) *Spirits.*—A native of the Banks' Islands, where spirits are called *vui*, wrote the following definition:

'What is a *vui*? It lives, thinks, has more intelligence than a man; knows things which are out of sight without seeing; is powerful with *mana*; has no form to be seen; and has no soul, because it is itself like a soul' (see Codrington, *Melanesians*, p. 123).

The *wui* of the Northern New Hebrides is of the same nature. Yet such spirits are seen, in a shadowy, unsubstantial form; and there are many spirits called by the same name to whom the definition does not accurately apply, while the stories concerning them treat them as if they were men with superhuman and quasi-magical powers. Still the natives steadily maintain that these are not, and never were, men. In the Solomon Islands beings were believed to exist who were personal, yet who had never been men, and who lacked the bodily nature of men, but they were very few and enjoyed little religious consideration. The term which is applied to such beings is also applied to some who had undoubtedly existed at some time as men. The question arises whether those beings, concerning whom stories were told and believed in the Banks' Islands and New Hebrides which showed them to be like men of more than human power and intelligence, should not be called gods. Such were Qat in the Banks' Islands, Tagaro, Suqe (in various forms of the names) in the New Hebrides, and Lata in Santa Cruz. To such as these it would certainly not be improper to apply the word 'god.' But the native word by which they are known, such as *vui*, is applicable also to other beings for whom 'god' is too great a name, this category including elves, fairies, nameless beings of limited influence whose nature is still spiritual, so to speak, not corporeal. To describe all these, to distinguish them from dead men, the best general term seems 'spirit'; and it is to these beings that the religion of the New Hebrides and Banks' Islands looks, as possessing and wielding *mana*, the power which must be called spiritual, which men have not in themselves, and which they seek to obtain for their advantage by sacrifices, prayers, and charms.

(2) *Ghosts.*—It makes the matter clear if this term be used when the beings spoken of are simply men who are dead in the body while that part of them that is not bodily retains activity and intelligence. In the Banks' Islands and New Hebrides the word used is merely 'dead man,' such as *tamate* or *natmas*. In the Solomon Islands a very common word in various forms is *tindalo*. The question again occurs whether these should not rather be called gods. There are certainly some to whom prayers and sacrifices are offered, whose place and time in human life are forgotten or unknown, and whose existence as persons possessed of powers far superior to those of living men is alone present to the belief of the existing generation. Such may not unreasonably be called gods. But, whereas in the Eastern groups such beings are plainly called 'dead men,' it seems more correct, and serves better for clearness, to use an English word which shows them once to have been living men, and separates them from any such beings as are believed never to have belonged to human kind. The word 'god' cannot be a translation of 'dead man.' Where, as in the Solomon Islands, a distinct name, such as *tindalo*, is in use, this objection to the use of the word 'god' does not so plainly apply. Yet the natives emphatically declare that every *tindalo* was once a man, that the *tindalo* is the spirit (*tarunga*) which once was the seat and source of life, intelligence, and power in a man who was then in the body. The living men who worship the *tindalo* regard themselves as possessed of that non-corporeal nature which alone remains in the dead, and is the seat of the dead

man's superhuman power. They believe that some of them have a measure of that power, derived by them from the dead. They believe that, when they are dead, they will also, it may be, receive a great access of this power. The difference which they recognize between themselves and the *tindalo* is that they are alive and have but a comparatively small measure of spiritual power. But it should be understood that every living man does not become a *tindalo* after death. The large majority of men are of no great importance, and show no remarkable powers in their lifetime; alive they are nobodies, and such they remain when dead. But there are always some living men who show qualities which give them success and influence. Such success and influence are not ascribed by the natives to natural qualities, but to the possession of that spiritual power which they have obtained from the *tindalo* with whom they live in communication. When a great man dies, it is expected that he should prove to be a *tindalo*, a ghost worthy of worship, an effective helper, one whose relics will put the living in communication with him. Thus, after the death of Ganindo, a chief, a famous fighting man of Florida, his name was invoked and a sign of his power sought from him. On proof of this power a shrine was built for him, his head, his tools, and his weapons were preserved in it, and sacrifices with invocation were offered to him there. Such a one might, indeed, appear to European visitors to be a god; but to the natives of the place, who now worshipped him, and among whom he had lived as one of themselves, it was his ghost, in the common English sense of the term, who was among them.

Again, the question may arise whether this is not the worship of ancestors. The ghost of a dead man, however, who was well remembered in the flesh, and who was often, no doubt, younger in years than some of his worshippers, is not an ancestor. The natural tendency is, as new objects of worship of this character arise, and as one great man after another dies, to neglect and desert the ghosts and their shrines of the past generation, while the newer wonders and powers attract faith and veneration to new ghosts and shrines. As the object of worship thus became more of an ancestor, he was less an object of worship. But certainly there are some concerning whose time and place of life the natives profess themselves to be ignorant, but whose names, such as Daula and Hauri in Florida, are known to all, and who are now universally believed to be very powerful *tindalo*, though in ancient times they lived in human form on the island. These may be called ancestors, and they are worshipped, but not as ancestors.

The personal beings towards whom the religion of the Melanesians turns, with the view of obtaining their *mana* for aid in the pursuits, dangers, and difficulties of life, are thus spirits and ghosts; and it is remarkable that the Melanesians are thus divided by their religious practices into two groups. In the Western group, as in the Solomon Islands, there is a belief in spirits who never were men, but worship is directed to the ghosts of the dead; in the Eastern group, as in the Northern New Hebrides, the ghosts of the dead have indeed an important place, but worship is in the main addressed to spirits who have never been men. And in the arts of life and in the advance from savagery towards civilization, the Solomon Islander who worships ghosts certainly ranks before the New Hebrides man who worships spirits.

4. Prayers.—The Melanesian native, believing himself surrounded with unseen persons who can help him, naturally calls upon them in distress, just as he called upon his father as a child. Such appeals are not prayers according to the meaning of the various native words which would be translated 'prayer' in English. Prayers in the native sense are forms of words; and, strictly speaking, they are formulas which are known only to some, and which have in themselves a certain efficacy and even compelling force. It may be said that exclamatory appeals in case of danger at sea and in the extremity of sickness are prayers in a true sense of the term, which yet to the native are not strictly prayers, because they have public utterance and an elastic form. A man in danger by the sea may call on his father, grandfather, or some ancestor to still the storm, lighten the canoe, and bring it to the shore; when fishing he may beg for success, and when successful may thank his helper. But in such cases a formula, if one were known, would always be preferred, and that would be a prayer in the native sense of the word. Charms, muttered or sung under the breath for magical purposes and in the treatment of sickness, are easily distinguished; but it must be said that in Florida, an important centre of Christian teaching in the Solomon Islands, the word used for Christian prayer is taken from these charms.

It is remarkable that in the Banks' Islands and the Northern New Hebrides, where spirits have a more important place in native religion than ghosts, all prayer must be addressed to the ghost of a dead person. Indeed, every proper form begins with the word *tataro*, which is, no doubt, a word meaning 'ghost.' It is true that in danger at sea a man will call on dead friends to help him, but this is not a true prayer (*tataro*) because no formula is employed. It is also true that men in danger call on spirits, either with or without a formula; but neither is a true *tataro*, since it is not addressed to ghosts. Many forms of words, moreover, which are true *tataro* prayers, are formulas for cursing as well as for petition. Such are used when a man throws a bit of his food aside before eating, and pours a libation before drinking *kava*, or when he pours water into an oven, since in them he asks for benefits to himself and mischief to his enemies. A *tataro* prayer is a spell; a call for help in danger is a cry.

5. Sacrifices.—There can be little doubt that sacrifices properly so called have a place in Melanesian religion. One simple form is probably universal. A fragment of food ready to be eaten, a bit of betel-nut, and a few drops of *kava* poured as a libation are offered at a common meal as the share of departed friends, who are often called by name, or as a memorial of them with which they will be gratified. This is accompanied with a prayer. With the same feeling of regard for the dead, food is laid on a grave or before a memorial image, and is then left to decay, or, as at Santa Cruz, is taken away and eaten by those who have made the offering. In a certain sense, no doubt, the dead are thought to eat the food. Yet the natives do not apply to these offerings the words which connote sacrifices in the strict sense of the term. In the Western Islands the offerings in sacrifices are made to ghosts and consumed by fire as well as eaten; in the Eastern groups they are made to spirits, and there is no sacrificial fire or meal. In the former nothing is offered but food; in the latter native money has a conspicuous place.

(1) *In the Solomon Islands.*—A sacrifice in San Cristoval, one of the Solomon Islands, has been thus described in writing by a native of the place:

'In my country they think ghosts are many, very many indeed, some very powerful, some not. There is one who is principal in war; this one is truly mighty and strong. When our people wish to fight with any other place, the chief men of the village and the sacrificers, and the old men, and the men elder and younger, assemble in the place sacred to this ghost;

and his name is Harumae. When they are thus assembled to sacrifice, the chief sacrificer goes and takes a pig. . . . The pig is killed (strangled), not by the chief sacrificer, but by those whom he chooses to assist him, near the sacred place. Then they cut it up; they take great care of the blood lest it should fall upon the ground; they bring a bowl and set the pig in it, and when the pig is cut up the blood runs down into this. When the cutting up is finished, the chief sacrificer takes a bit of flesh from the pig, and he takes a cocoa-nut shell and dips up some of the blood. Then he takes the blood and the bit of flesh and enters into the shrine, and calls that ghost and says, "Harumae! Chief in war! we sacrifice to you with this pig, that you may help us to smite that place; and whatsoever we shall carry away shall be yours, and we also will be yours." Then he burns the bit of flesh in a fire upon a stone, and pours down the blood upon the fire. Then the fire blazes up greatly to the roof, and the house is full of the smell of pig, a sign that the ghost has heard. But when the sacrificer went in he did not go boldly, but with awe; and this is the sign of it: as he goes into the holy house he puts away his bag, and washes his hands thoroughly, to show that the ghost shall not reject him with disgust' (Codrington, p. 129 f.).

The pig thus sacrificed was eaten by the worshippers. When this account was written, the older people well remembered Harumae as a living chief.

In the neighbouring island of Mala a native gives the names of seven kinds of sacrifice. (1) A man returning from a voyage puts food before the case which contains the relics of his father. (2) In sickness, or where failure of a crop shows that some ghost has been offended, a pig is offered as a substitute for the man whom the offended ghost is plaguing, and is strangled and burned whole on the stones of a sacred place, together with mixed food. The sacrificer calls aloud upon the offended ghost and upon many others, and sets a bit of the food which he has left unburned before the relic case of the dead man to whose ghost the pig was offered. (3) To 'clear the soul,' a pig or dog is killed and cooked; the sacrificer calls upon the ghost by name to clear away the mischief, and throws the sacrifice into the sea or sets it in the place sacred to the ghost invoked. (4) This is performed in the house of the sick person who is to benefit by it. A pig or dog is cooked and cut up; the names of the dead members of the family to which the ghost to be propitiated belonged are called out, with a petition to each on behalf of the sick man; the sacrificed animal is eaten by the males who are present. (5) (6) (7) are sacrifices of firstfruits—yams, flying-fish, and canarium nuts—which are presented as food to the ghost concerned, with the invocation of his name, and set in a sacred place.

In Florida and Ysabel, both belonging to the Solomon group, sacrifice is of the same character. There are those who know, having been taught by their fathers or mother's brothers, how to approach the powerful ghosts of the dead, some of whom were the objects of a more public and some of a more particular worship. Such a ghost of worship, called a *tindalo*, had his shrine in which his relics were preserved. The officiating sacrificer is said to 'throw the sacrifice.' A certain *tindalo*, whose worship and influence are not local, is called Manoga. A native writes:

'He who throws the sacrifice when he invokes this *tindalo* heaves the offering round about, and calls him, first to the East where rises the sun, saying, "If thou dwellest in the East. where rises the sun, Manoga! come hither and eat thy mashed food." Then turning he lifts it towards where sets the sun, and says, "If thou dwellest in the West, where sets the sun, Manoga! come hither and eat thy food." There is not a quarter towards which he does not lift it up. And when he has finished lifting it he says, "If thou dwellest in heaven above, Manoga! come hither and eat thy food. If thou dwellest in the Pleiades or in Orion's belt; if below in Turivatu; if in the distant sea; if on high in the sun or in the moon; if thou dwellest inland or by the shore, Manoga! come hither and eat thy food"' (Codrington, p. 131 f.).

Whether, as in this case, the offering be vegetable food or whether it be a pig, a piece is consumed in the fire within the shrine, and the people without partake of the sacrificial food. In these islands, moreover, the sacrifice of the firstfruits must precede the general use of the products of each season.

Human sacrifices were occasionally made, and such were thought most effectual for the propitiation of an offended ghost. In this case the victim was not eaten by the assistants as when a pig was offered; but a piece of flesh was burned for the ghost's portion, and bits were eaten by young men to get fighting power, and by the sacrificer who had made the offering.

In the island of Santa Cruz the flesh of pigs or vegetable food is placed before the stock of wood that represents a person recently deceased for him to eat; feather-money and betel-nuts are laid out for ghosts, and food is thrown to them at sea. These are distinctly offered for the ghost to eat or use, but they are soon taken up and disposed of by the offerers as common things. Such offerings resemble those of food laid on graves or at the foot of an image in the Solomon Islands, which would not there have the name of sacrifices; but the full sacrifices of the Solomon Islands, as has been shown, have the sacrificial characteristics of intercession, propitiation, substitution, and a common meal.

(2) *In Banks' Islands and New Hebrides.*—To offerings here, no doubt, the name of sacrifice is far less properly applied, and yet it is almost necessary to employ it. The offerings are made in almost all cases to spirits, but in some cases to the ghosts of dead men. The offering is generally native money; nothing is killed or burned, nothing eaten; and the offering is laid upon a stone, cast into water, or scattered upon a snake or some other creature, the stone, the creature, or the sacred spot being chosen because of its connexion with the spirit who is to be conciliated or from whom benefits are sought. Access to the spirit is to be obtained through the sacred object; but the common worshipper or suppliant cannot obtain this access by himself, and is consequently obliged to use the services of a go-between who knows the stone or whatever it may be and through it is able to know and to approach the spirit. The worshipper generally gives native money to the 'owner,' as he is called, of the sacred object, who then gives a little money to the spirit, and perhaps pours the juice of a young coco-nut on the stone, while he makes his request on behalf of his client. There is thus an intercession, a propitiation, an offering of what the suppliant values and the spirit has pleasure in receiving. So far it is a religious action of a sacrificial character, and is distinct from prayer. In the New Hebrides, besides similar sacrifices to spirits, offerings are made to the ghosts of powerful men lately deceased, either at their graves or in the places which they haunt. Men who know these and have access to them take mats, food, and pigs (living or cooked) to the sacred place, and leave, or profess to leave, them there. Nowhere in these islands is there an order of men who can be called priests. The knowledge of the spirits and of the objects through which access to them can be obtained is open to all, and is possessed by many. Most of those who possess it have received it secretly from their fathers or elder relatives, but many have found it by happy accident for themselves, and have proved their connexion with the spirit by the success of their ministrations.

6. Sacred places and objects.—The sanctity which belongs to such stones or sacred spots as have been mentioned in connexion with sacrifice has, of course, a religious character. Native life in Melanesia is, for the most part, in continual contact with the prohibitions and restrictions which belong to this religious feeling. The sacred character of the object, whatever it may be, is derived from one of two causes: it may lie in the nature and associations of the thing itself, or it may be conferred by men who have the *mana*, the spiritual power, to confer it. It may be said, generally speaking, that among these sacred objects there are no idols, in the strict sense of the term. It is true that images are made more or less in all quarters to represent the dead, being set up as memorials at funeral feasts, in burial-places, in canoe houses, and in places of general assembly. They are treated with respect; offerings of food are made, and other valuable things are occasionally laid before them; but the images are memorials of men deceased, likenesses to some extent, and representations; they are not worshipped, and are sacred only because of what they represent.

(1) *Stones.*—Sacred places almost always have stones in them. The presence of certain stones gives sanctity to the place in which they naturally lie; and, when a place has for other reasons become sacred, stones which have that character are brought and placed there. Here again recurs the important distinction between spirits and ghosts. The stones of the burial-place of a powerful man receive *mana* from him, or a man who had *mana* is buried near sacred stones, thus connecting the ghost and the stone. In other cases, the stone is believed to have such a relation to a spirit, who never was a living man, that it acquires a mysterious quality, and becomes the means by which the man who has the knowledge of the stone can have access to the spirit. Many sacred stones then are sepulchral, and this is usually the case in the Solomon Islands. The sacrifices already described are offered upon stones. A stone is also frequently sacred in the Eastern Islands because a *vui* (spirit) belongs to it. In this group stones may be divided into those that naturally lie where they are reverenced and those which have *mana* derived for various reasons from a spirit, and which are carried about and used for various purposes, and as amulets. The natives emphatically deny that the connexion between stones and spirits is like that which exists between the soul and body of man. Certain stones are kept in houses to protect them from thieves; and, if the shadow of a man falls on one of these, the ghost belonging to it is said to draw out his life and eat it. It has been supposed that the ghost which consumes the man's life must correspond in the stone to the soul in a living man; but the natives do not believe that the ghost dwells in the stone, but by it or, as they say, at it; they regard the stone as the instrument used by the spirit, which is able to lay hold on the man by the medium of his shadow.

(2) *Trees, streams, and living creatures.*—Trees are sacred because they grow in a sacred place, or because they have a sacred snake, *e.g.*, that haunts them. Some have a certain inherent awe attaching to their kind. The natives deny that they ever regarded a tree as having anything like a spirit of its own corresponding to the soul or *animus* of man. Streams, or rather pools, are sacred as the haunts of ghosts in the Western, and of spirits in the Eastern groups. The reflexion of a man's face upon such water gives the ghost or spirit the hold upon the man's soul by which it can be drawn out and its life destroyed. Among living creatures which are sacred, sharks have a conspicuous place. If one of remarkable size or colour haunts a shore or rock in the Solomon Islands, it is taken to be some one's ghost, and the name of the deceased is given to it. Before his death a man will give out that he will enter into a shark. In both cases it is well understood that the shark to which the ghost has betaken himself was, before it was thus occupied, a common shark; but, now that he is in it, the place where the man lived is visited by the fish, and the neighbours and relatives of the deceased respect and feed it. A spirit, known to some one who sacrifices for it, can, in like manner, be introduced in the Banks' Islands into a shark, which thus becomes familiar. In the Solomon Islands a crocodile may be a *tindalo*, since the ghost of a recent ancestor may possibly have entered it, or may be known to have entered it. Almost any living creature that haunts a house, garden, or village may well be regarded as conveying a ghost. Among birds the frigate-bird is conspicuous for its sacred character in the Solomon Islands; the ghosts of deceased men of importance find their abode in them, and indeed ancient and widely venerated *tindalos* dwell in them. In all the groups there is something sacred about kingfishers. Snakes receive a certain veneration wherever they are found in a sacred place. The original female spirit, that never was a human being, believed in San Cristoval to have had the form of a snake, has given a sacred character to all snakes as her representatives. In the Banks' Islands, and still more in the New Hebrides, snakes with which certain *vui* associate themselves, and which therefore have much *mana*, are worshipped and receive offerings of money in sacred places. One amphibious snake is firmly believed to appear in human form to tempt a young man or woman.

Is, then, the religion of the Melanesians altogether an animistic religion? Nowhere does there appear to be a belief in a spirit which animates any natural object, tree, waterfall, storm, stone, bird, or fish, so as to be to it what the soul of a man, as they conceive it, is to his body, or, in other words, so as to be the spirit of the object. The natives certainly deny that they hold any such belief; but they believe that the spirit of a man deceased, or a spirit never a man at all, abides near and with the object, which by this association receives supernatural power, and becomes the vehicle of such power for the purposes of those who know how to obtain it.

7. Magic and charms.—The belief in magic and the use of magic and charms do not perhaps properly belong to religion; but among Melanesians it is hardly possible to omit this subject. The foundation of religion is the belief in the surrounding presence of a power greater than that of man; and in great part the practice of religion comes to be the method by which this power can be turned by men to their own purposes. The natives recognize, on the whole, a regular course of nature in the greater movements of things which affect their lives, but at every point they come in touch with what they take to be the exercise by men of the power which they derive from either ghosts or spirits. By means of this power, men who know the proper formula and rite can make rain or sunshine, wind or calm, cause sickness or remove it, know what is beyond the reach of common knowledge, bring good luck and prosperity, or blast and curse. No man has this power of himself, but derives it from a personal being, the ghost of a man deceased, or a spirit of a nature which is not human. By charms (certain forms of words muttered or chanted, which contain the names of the beings from whom the power is derived) this power becomes associated with the objects through which the power is to pass. These things are personal relics, such as hair or teeth, remains of food, herbs and leaves, bones of dead men, and stones of unusual shape. Through these objects wizards, doctors, weather-mongers, prophets, diviners, and dreamers do their work. There is no distinct order of magicians or medicine-men, just as there is no separate order of priests; the knowledge of one or more branches of the craft is handed down from father to son, from uncle to sister's son, or, it may be, is bought and sold. Many men may be said to make a profession of magic, and to get property and influence thereby. A man cannot, it may be said, be a chief without a belief that he possesses this supernatural power. There is no doubt that those who exercise these arts really believe that a power resides in them, though, indeed, they are conscious of a good deal of deceit.

A great part of this is sympathetic magic, and seems to the people to have reason in it. The failure of some charm or of some magician does not discredit charms or magic, since the failure is due to the counteraction of another and stronger charm; and one doctor who has failed has been, secretly or openly, opposed by another who has on his side a more powerful ghost or spirit. Thus the people were at every turn in contact with the unseen world and its powers, and in this religion was certainly at work. It is not necessary to go into this subject in any detail. With regard to sickness, it is often said that savages do not believe that any one is naturally sick. That is not the case in Melanesia, in the case of such troubles as fever and ague; but any serious illness is believed to be caused by ghosts or spirits; and the more important the patient is the more reasonable it seems to ascribe his sickness to some ghost or spirit whom he has offended, or to the witchcraft of some enemy. It is not common to ascribe sickness to a spirit in those groups where spirits have so great a place in the religious regard of the people. There it is the ghosts of the dead who inflict sickness, and can be induced to remove it; for there is a certain malignity belonging to the dead, who dislike to see men well and living; a man who was powerful and malevolent when alive is more dangerous than ever when dead, because all human powers which are not merely bodily are believed to be enhanced by death. So, whether to cause sickness or to remove it, the doctor by his charms brings in the power of the dead. A wizard is paid by a man's enemy to bring the malignant influence of the dead upon him; he or his friends pay another to bring the power of other dead men to counteract the first and to save the endangered life; the wizard who is the more powerful—who has on his side the more or the stronger ghosts—will prevail, and the sick man will live or die accordingly. Two parties of such hostile ghosts are believed in San Cristoval to fight the battle out with ghostly spears. All success and prosperity in life, as well as health and strength, are held to depend on the spiritual power obtained by charms or resident in objects which are used with charms; the Melanesian in all his employments and enterprises depends upon unseen assistance, and a religious character is thus given to all his life.

8. Tabu.—This word, commonly *tapu* or *tambu* in the islands of Melanesia now under consideration, and established as an English term, was taken from the islands of Polynesia. In Melanesia the belief prevails, clearly marked by the use of distinct words in some islands, that an awful and, so to speak, religious character can be imposed on places, things, and actions by men who have the *mana* to do it. A place, *e.g.*, in which a powerful man has been buried, where a ghost has been seen, which a spirit haunts, is holy and awful of itself, never to be lightly invaded or used for common purposes. But a man who has the proper power can tabu a place as he chooses, and can forbid approach to it and common use of it. Behind the man who exercises this power is the ghost of the dead or the spirit whose power the man has. Tabu implies a curse. A chief will forbid something under a penalty. To all appearance it is as a chief that he forbids, and as of a chief that his prohibition is respected; but in fact the sanction comes from the ghost or spirit behind him. If a common man assumes the power to tabu, as he may and sometimes does, he runs a serious risk; but if, on the other hand, he forbids the gathering of certain fruit, and sets his mark upon it, and then, as often naturally happens, some one who has disregarded his prohibition and taken the fruit falls ill or dies, this is at once a clear proof that the tabu is real, and any future prohibition made by him will be respected. Thus to a considerable degree, in the Banks' Islands at least, men of no great consequence, as well as the societies which are there so numerous, set marks of prohibition which meet with respect. Every such prohibition rests upon an unseen power; there is in it no moral sanction, but there is the consciousness of the presence of the unseen which certainly works much for morality. What is wrong in itself is by no means always tabu; but what is tabu is very often what the natives recognize as wrong in itself. For it must not be supposed that Melanesians know no moral distinction of right and wrong. Disobedience to parents, unkindness to the weak and sick, are no doubt common, but there is a general feeling, both strong and marked, that it is right to respect and love parents, and wrong to be unkind. Neighbours will carry food to the sick whose friends neglect them, and very plainly express their blame. Those who lie freely upon occasion respect truthfulness, and say that it is bad to tell lies.

9. Totemism.—If totems, properly so called, exist among Melanesians, they must be considered in treating their religion. A totem is defined by J. G. Frazer (*Totemism and Exogamy*, London, 1910, i. 3 f., 8) as being 'a class of material objects which a savage regards with superstitious respect, believing that there exists between him and every member of the class an intimate and altogether special relation.' The relation between a man and his totem has partly a religious and partly a social character. It is held that 'the members of a totem clan call themselves by the name of their totem, and commonly believe that they are actually descended from it.' Each one, moreover, 'believing himself to be descended from, and therefore akin to, his totem, the savage naturally treats it with respect. If it is an animal he will not, as a rule, kill or eat it.'

(1) Florida, in the Solomon Islands, where the native system as it is understood by themselves has been carefully explained by natives of some education, affords probably the best field for consideration of the subject. The people are divided into six exogamous kindreds, called *kema*, each with its distinguishing name, descent following the mother. Two of these kindreds are named from living creatures, a sea-eagle and a crab. Each of the six has some object which its members must avoid, and which they must abstain from eating, touching, approaching, or beholding. This is the *mbuto* of the *kema*. In one case, and one case only, this *mbuto* is the living creature from which the kin takes its name. The Kakau kin may not eat the *kakau* crab, and that crab might accordingly be regarded as the totem of that Crab kindred. But the other kin which takes its name from a living creature, the Eagle kindred, is quite at liberty to kill or eat that bird; it, therefore, cannot be the totem of that kin. Again, a member of the Eagle kindred may not eat the common fruit pigeon, which is his *mbuto*, and would say that the pigeon was his ancestor. Here, then, the pigeon appears as the totem of the Eagle kin; they cannot eat it; it is their ancestor. But was a pigeon their ancestor

in the sense that they are descended from it? Decidedly not. It was a human ancestor who associated himself with the pigeon; the pigeon represents the dead man, the pigeon is a *tindalo*, a dead man of power. A native writes:

'We believe these *tindalo* to have been once living men; and something that was with them, or with which they had to do, has become a thing forbidden, *tambu*, and a thing abominable, *mbuto*, to those to whom the *tindalo* (once a living man) belongs' (Codrington, p. 31 f.).

That is to say, the pigeon represents the human ancestor; the man begat the generations of his kindred before he died and entered into a pigeon. The pigeon is not truly an ancestor, nor is it truly a totem. The native writer goes on to give the example of another kindred which avoids the giant clam, the traditional ancestor of which haunted a certain beach. That ghostly ancestor is represented by the clam on that beach, and a native will say that the clam is his ancestor, but without meaning more than he means when he says that an ancient weapon in a shrine is a dead chief, a *tindalo*, that is, belongs to him.

(2) In another of the Solomon Islands, Ulawa, not long ago the people would not eat the fruit of the banana, and had ceased to plant the tree. The elder natives would give to the fruit the name of a powerful man whom they remembered living, and say that they could not eat him, thus accounting for their avoidance of the banana as food. The explanation was that this man, before his death, announced that after death he would be in banana fruit, and that they were not to eat it. Soon he would have been an ancestor, the banana would be an ancestor, while clearly there was no descent from a banana in the belief of the people. This, then, is no totem, though it may illustrate the origin of totems.

(3) In the New Hebrides, in Aurora Island, there is a family named after the octopus. They do not call the octopus their ancestor, and they freely eat it; but their connexion with it is so intimate that a member of the family would go to the reef with a fisherman, call out his own name, and say that he wanted octopus, and then plenty would be taken. This, again, seems to approach totemism.

(4) In the Banks' Islands and New Hebrides, however, there is what comes very near to the 'individual totem.' Some men, not all, in Mota conceived that they had a peculiar connexion with a living creature, or it might be a stone, which had been found, either after search or unexpectedly, in some singular manner. If this was a living thing, the life of the man was bound up with its life; if an inanimate object, the man's health depended on its being unbroken and secure. A man would say that he had his origin in something that had presented itself to him. In Aurora also, in the New Hebrides, a woman dreams or fancies that there is something—*e.g.*, a coco-nut—which has a particular relation to her unborn child, and this the child hereafter must never eat.

10. Societies, mysteries, and dances. — (1) *Societies.*—A very conspicuous feature of native life in the Torres Islands, Banks' Islands, and New Hebrides is the universal presence in those groups of a society, called by some form of the name *supwe*. There are, or were, certain objects commonly in view which, at first sight, could not fail to connect this with the religion of the people. The visitor to a village would see platforms built up with stones, with high, pointed, shrine-like little edifices upon them, within which were the embers of a fire below and images in human form above. If he hit upon a festival, he would see such images carried in the dance. But such appearances show, as a matter of fact, nothing else than the presence of this society, since they are merely the hearth and the emblems of the men of high rank in the *supwe*, an institution which is entirely social, and has no religious character. To gain advance and distinction in it requires, no doubt, the spiritual power of *mana*, as does every other form of success, and so sacrifices, prayers, and charms are used; and doubtless the *supwe* is under the sanction of tabu. It is also true that a man's position after death is believed to depend in some measure on his rank and his liberality in this society. But the account of it cannot come under the head of religion.

(2) *Mysteries.*—A religious character attaches much more truly to the mysteries, the mysterious secret societies which hold an important place in native life in the Solomon Islands and in the Eastern groups. The lodges of these societies appear to visitors to be temples and seats of religious worship; the images within them seem to be idols. The mysteries are closely fenced by a strict initiation, and a rigid tabu guards them; to those outside the secret and unapproachable retreats the mysterious sounds and the appearance of the members in strange disguise convey a truly religious awe. In fact, the mysteries are professedly methods of communion with the dead, the ghosts which are everywhere, more or less, objects of religious worship. In the Banks' Islands the name of the mysteries was simply 'the Ghosts.' Yet, although within the mysterious precincts the ordinary forms of sacrifices and prayers were carried on to gain the assistance of the dead and communion with them, there was no esoteric article of belief made known and no secret form of worship practised. There were no forms of worship peculiar to the society, no objects of worship of a kind unknown to those without. There was no 'making of young men,' no initiation without which the native could not take his place among his people. The women and the children, perhaps, really believed that what they saw and heard was ghostly, but many an accident betrayed the neighbour in disguise; and the neophyte, when introduced into the sacred place, found himself in the company of his fellows of daily life. Still, since the presence of the dead was professed and believed, and since so much of the religion of the Melanesians, particularly in the Solomon Islands, was concerned with the ghosts of the dead, it is true that these secret societies and mysteries belong to the religion of the people.

(3) *Dances.*—This is by no means the case with dances. All the societies have their dances, which are part of the mysteries, and which it is the first task of the neophyte to learn. But there are dances everywhere in the public life of the people which, however difficult, all boys and young men desire to learn, and have to learn in secret before they can perform them at the feasts. The ghosts in Hades, in their shadowy life, dance as living men do. Visitors are too apt to speak of 'devil dances' and 'devil grounds'; but it may be said to be certain that dances, as such, have no religious or superstitious character in Melanesia.

11. Creation, cosmogony. — The consciousness of the relation of men to a creator is commonly accepted as a chief ground of natural religion. Consequently, when natives are asked (perhaps very imperfectly) who made them and the things around them, and they give the name of the maker to whom their origin is ascribed, they are thought to name their creator; and it is assumed that this creator is the chief object of their worship. Thus Qat, under the name Ikbat, was thought at first to be the chief deity at Mota; and the name of the supposed creator has elsewhere been taken as the name of God. But creation, the making of men and things, is by no means a proof of very great power, or a ground for great reverence, among Melanesian people. It may almost be said that relation to a creator has no religious influence at all, though reference to Qat as the maker of men is made in correcting children in the Banks' Island. The existence of the world, as the natives conceived of it, and the course of all the great movements of nature, are quite independent of that creative power which was ascribed to certain spirits. The makers were spirits. In the Solomon Islands the belief in Kahausibware is characteristic. She was a female spirit in the shape of a snake; she made men, pigs, coco-nuts, fruit-trees, and food in San Cristoval; death had not yet appeared. There was a woman who had a child. The snake strangled the child; the mother chopped the snake in pieces; thenceforward all good things changed to worse, and death began. Respect is shown to snakes as the progeny or representatives of this female spirit, but she cannot be said to be worshipped.

In the Banks' Islands and the New Hebrides, as has been stated before, spirits are the principal objects of worship, and they are also believed to have had much to do with the fashioning of the world of man. Yet it must be borne in mind that they are by no means held to be originators; they came themselves into a world existing under circumstances such as those in which men now live, where there were houses and canoes, weapons and ornaments, fruits and gardens. In the Banks' Islands Qat held the highest place. He was born the eldest of twelve brothers, who dwelt in a village in Vanua Lava. There Qat began to make men, pigs, trees, rocks, as the fancy took him, in a land which already existed. His chief assistant in his work was another spirit (*vui*) named Marawa ('spider'); his brothers envied and thwarted him; when he made a wife for himself, they tried to kill him; he instructed them and played tricks on them. There were other spirits in the world when he was born, some enemies whom he had to overcome. From one of these spirits, dwelling in another group, named Night, he bought the night to relieve the tedium of perpetual daylight. Finally, when the world was settled and furnished, he made a canoe in the middle of the island of Santa Maria, where now is the great lake, collected his wife and brothers and living creatures into it, and in a flood caused by a deluge of rain was carried out into the sea and disappeared. The people believed that the best of everything was taken away by Qat, and looked for his return. Though no longer visible, he still controlled to a great extent the forces of nature, and he heard and answered the cries of men. In a way the natives looked upon him as an ancestor as well as their creator, but they were emphatic in their assertion that he was never a man himself; he was a spirit, a *vui*, of a nature different from that of man; and, because a spirit, he was master of all magic power, and full of that *mana* which was at work in all around. It is, however, scarcely possible to take him very seriously or allow him divine rank, even though he is the central figure in the origin of things and his influence is present and effective. In the New Hebrides nearest to the Banks' Islands Tagaro takes the place of Qat. He is no doubt the Tangaroa of Polynesia. He made things as Qat did; he had his brothers, ten of them, and there was another, Supwe, who thwarted Tagaro and made things wrong. Tagaro also went back to heaven. In other islands Supwe appears as the chief of this band of great spirits. In Santa Cruz, Lata corresponds, but not very closely, to Qat and Tagaro, since he also made men and animals.

These greater spirits are named and known as individual persons. Besides these, in all the islands are spirits innumerable and unnamed. These are they whose representative form is very often a stone, who haunt the places which their presence makes sacred, who associate themselves with snakes, sharks, birds, and the various things through which men can communicate with them and draw from them the spiritual power from which comes all manner of success in life, and which can be turned to injury as well as succour. It may safely be said that these spirits were not malignant beings, though they were spiteful at times and were willing to do mischief to the enemies of their worshippers. The multitude of beings who in the Solomon Islands have power in storms, rain, drought, calms, and especially in the growth of food—the *vigona*, *hi'ona*, and others—seem to belong rather to the order of spirits than to that of the ghosts of the dead, and such they are acknowledged to be, though the natives speak of them as ghosts.

Thus the world of the Melanesians was populous with living beings, visible and invisible, with men, with the ghosts of the dead, with spirits great and small; and pervading and surrounding all was a power which belonged to all spirits, to the dead as such, and to many men; all these could direct it and employ it, and it was everywhere at hand. The world so inhabited was bounded to the Melanesians by the circle of the sea which surrounded the islands which were known to them, a circle which varied in place and size according to the position of the centre. The old world of the Banks' Islanders did not include the Solomon Islands; that of the Solomon Islanders was a much wider world. Wherever the circumference of the circle fell the sky was supposed to shut down fast upon it. Under this firmament the sun and moon made their journeys; and the stars hung in it. The heavenly bodies were not thought to be living beings, but rather rocks or islands. In the sun and moon were inhabitants with wives and families, in whom the sun and moon were personified and about whom many stories were told; but these have no religious character.

12. Death and after death.—Without some belief in a life after death, as well as in a power superior to that of living man, it is plain that the Melanesian religion could not be such as has been described. This implies a belief in a soul of man, though what that is they find it difficult to explain. They naturally use different words in their different languages, and these words convey various metaphors, when they are properly understood, the use of which probably involves a certain inconsistency. It may safely be said, however, that, whatever word they use, the Melanesians mean that there is something essentially belonging to man's nature which carries life to the body, which is the seat of thought and intelligence, which exercises a power which is not of the body, which is invisible, and which, after it has become separate from the body in death, still has an individual existence. It is in a sense a spirit, and in some islands is so called; but it is quite distinct from those spiritual beings that never were the souls of men and therefore never disembodied. The soul can go out of a man in a dream or a faint; it can be drawn out of the body or injured in the body by magic or spiteful ghosts or spirits; when finally separated from the body in death it becomes a ghost. Such a soul is peculiar to man. It is true that, as will be seen in the account of Hades, there is something which is like the ghost of a pig, of a weapon or ornament, something that remains and has a shadowy form; but the natives will not allow that even a pig, an intelligent and important personage with a name, has a soul as a man has.

(1) *Death.*—It was not part of the original nature

of men that they should die. In stories the first men are represented as changing their skins, as snakes cast their slough, and returning to youth and strength, until by some accident or folly life could no longer be so renewed, and death came in. When it came, the way to the abode of the dead was opened and men departed to their own place, Hades. The funeral rites do not require description. The disembodied spirit is not thought generally willing to depart far from the body which it has left or the place in which it has lived; but, the body being buried, or otherwise disposed of, the ghost proceeds to its appointed place.

(2) *Hades.*—There is a great difference between the conception of the Solomon Islanders and that of the Banks' Islanders and New Hebrides people with regard to the place where the dead take up their abode. In the Eastern Islands Hades is in the under world; in the Solomon Islands the dead, though there is an under world, depart to islands and parts of islands belonging to their own group, and from Florida they were conveyed in a ghostly canoe, a 'ship of the dead.' In all parts of Melanesia alike the condition of the dead in these abodes is an empty continuation of the worldly life; in all parts the ghostly life is not believed to be eternal, except in so far as the native imagination has failed to follow their existence with any measure of time. But, though the dead congregate in Hades, they still haunt and frequent the homes of their lifetime, are active among the living, and, as has been shown, in the Solomon Islands the religion of the living is mainly concerned with the worship of the dead. In these islands the weapons, ornaments, and money of a man of consequence are buried with him or placed on his grave. Whether these decorate the dead or serve his use in Hades is uncertain. It is as when a dead man's fruit-trees are cut down, as they say, as a mark of respect; he ate of them, it is said, while he was alive, he will never eat again, and no one else shall have them.

The notion is general that the ghost does not at first realize its position, or move with strength in its new abode; and this condition depends to some extent on the period of the decay of the body; when that is gone, the ghost is active. It is to expedite this activity that in some parts the corpse is burned.

While in a general way the ghosts of the dead pass to their Hades above ground, there are some which have their principal abode in the sea. Before his death a man may declare his purpose of taking up his abode in a sea-bird or a shark, or the dead body may be sunk into the sea and not buried. These sea-ghosts have a great hold on the imagination of the natives of San Cristoval and the adjacent islands, and were frequently represented in their carvings and paintings. They appear as if made up of fishes, and fish are the spears and arrows with which they shoot disease into the living.

In Santa Cruz the dead, though they haunt the villages, go into the great volcano Tamami and pass below. In the Banks' Islands the common Hades has many entrances; in this they have villages in which they dwell as on earth, but in an empty life. The ghosts hang about their graves for a time, and it is not desired that they should remain, though at the death-feasts they have a portion thrown for them. The great man goes down to Panoi with his ornaments, that is, with an unsubstantial appearance of them. In the Northern New Hebrides there are passages to Hades at the ends of the islands, the northern or southern points, by which ghosts go down, and also return. In Lepers' Island the descent is by a lake which fills an ancient crater. Living persons in all these islands have gone down to see their dead friends; they have seen the houses, the trees with red leaves, and the flowers, have heard the songs and dances, and have been warned not to eat the food of the ghosts.

(3) *Rewards and punishments.*—There remains the important question whether the condition of the dead is affected by the character of the living man; whether the dead are happier or less happy, in better or in worse condition, according as they have been, in native estimation, good men or bad on earth.

(*a*) *Solomon Islands.*—It cannot be said that in these islands the moral quality of men's lives affects their condition after death. When the canoe of the dead took the ghosts of Florida across to the neighbouring island of Guadalcanar, they found a ghost of worship, a *tindalo*, with a rod which he thrust into the cartilage of their noses to prove whether they were duly pierced. Those who passed this test had a good path which they could follow to the abodes of the dead; those who failed had to make their way as best they could with pain and difficulty. In Ysabel they present themselves to the master of their Hades at a pool, across which lies the narrow trunk of a tree. They show their hands; those who have the mark of the frigate-bird cut in them are allowed to pass; those who have not the mark are thrown from the trunk into the gulf beneath and perish.

(*b*) *Banks' Islands and New Hebrides.*—In these islands there is something which approximates to a judgment of a moral kind. It is true that, as a man's rank in the world has depended very much upon the number of the pigs he has slain for feasts, so the ghost fares badly who has not so done his duty by society. So in Pentecost Island, when the ghosts leap into the sea to go below, there is a shark waiting which will bite off the nose of a man who has not killed pigs; and in Aurora a fierce pig is ready to devour the ghost of a man who has not planted the tree that supplies material for the mats which are so highly valued. But there is a kind of judgment, a discrimination between good and bad, which has a moral character, and is, perhaps, well worthy of remark. Thus in the Banks' Islands it was believed that there was a good Hades and a bad. If one man had killed another by treachery or witchcraft, he would find himself opposed at the place of descent by the ghost of the man whom he had wronged; he dreaded the path which led to the bad place, and wandered on the earth. If a man had been slain in fair battle, his ghost would not withstand the ghost of the man who slew him. The bad, they said, were not admitted to the true Panoi, the Hades where there were flowers, though but shadows, and the empty semblance of social life. But who was the evil man? It was answered, 'One who killed another without cause or by charms, a thief, a liar, an adulterer.' Such in their Hades quarrel and are miserable; they haunt the living and do them what harm they can. The others, who lived as they ought to live, abide at least in harmony in Panoi after death.

It is very likely that these notions of something like retribution in the under world have not entered very deeply into the native mind, and are not generally entertained. But that such beliefs should have been received at all is enough to show that their sense of right and wrong has been carried by Melanesians into their prospect of a future state, a view which can hardly have failed to have something of a religious tendency, even if it cannot be said to prove in itself the existence of a religion which these islanders undoubtedly possess.

LITERATURE. — J. Lubbock, *The Origin of Civilisation*, London, 1870; E. B. Tylor, *PC*[4], do. 1903; A. W. Murray,

Missions in Western Polynesia, do. 1862; R. Steel, *The New Hebrides and Christian Missions*, do. 1880; J. Inglis, *In the New Hebrides*, do. 1886; G. Turner, *Samoa*, do. 1884; C. M. Woodford, *A Naturalist among the Head-Hunters, Solomon Islands, 1886–88*, do. 1890; H. H. Romilly, *The Western Pacific and New Guinea*, do. 1886; H. B. Guppy, *The Solomon Islands and their Natives*, do. 1887; R. H. Codrington, *The Melanesians: their Anthropology and Folklore*, Oxford, 1891.

R. H. CODRINGTON.

MELETIANISM.—There were two Meletian schisms, each having considerable influence on the fortunes of the Arian controversy. The earlier took its name from the Meletius who was bishop of Lycopolis in Egypt; the later from the Meletius who was consecrated bishop of Antioch in A.D. 360.

1. The Meletian schism in Egypt.—Μελήτιος (Epiphanius) or Μελίτιος (Athanasius) was bishop of Lycopolis in Egypt, and his dispute with Peter, bishop of Alexandria, led to a schism which received attention at the Council of Nicæa. According to Athanasius (*Apol. c. Arianos*, 59), Meletius was condemned about A.D. 305 or 306, so that the quarrel was already of long standing when the Council assembled. The origin of it is extremely obscure. As Hefele points out (*Councils*, Eng. tr., i. 343 ff.), there are three separate accounts: (1) in documents discovered by Maffæi and published in M. J. Routh, *Reliquiæ Sacræ*, Oxford, 1814–18, iv.; (2) in the writings of Athanasius; (3) in Epiphanius. All these differ in their details as to the origin of the schism. The first of the three documents preserved in Routh is a letter of certain Christians in prison who were afterwards martyred by Diocletian (Eus. *HE* viii. 10). It is supposed that the actual writer of the letter was Phileas, bishop of Thmuis. Meletius is addressed as a fellow-minister (*comminister*, the document being preserved in Latin), so that the schism has evidently not yet begun, and he is blamed for ordaining clergy in strange dioceses, without the consent of his fellow-bishops or even of Peter of Alexandria. The second document is a note, added by an anonymous hand, to say that after the martyrdom of the bishop Meletius had gone to Alexandria and found two discontented men, Arius and Isidore, and proceeded to excommunicate the visitors (περιοδευταί) appointed by Peter, who thereupon wrote the letter which makes the third of our documents, to the people of Alexandria, bidding them to avoid all communion with Meletius. From this very early and contemporary evidence we learn that Meletius's offence was that of trespassing on the rights of Peter and the other bishops by conferring orders out of his own diocese. It is to be noticed that these irregularities took place before the deposition of Meletius. Athanasius says nothing about the irregular ordinations. In his *Apology against the Arians* (ch. 59) he gives as the cause of the deposition of Meletius that he had been guilty of many offences, particularly of having sacrificed to idols and of having calumniated the bishops of Alexandria, Peter, Achillas, and Alexander (ch. 11). In his *Letter to the Bishops of Egypt and Libya* he asserts (ch. 22) that the Meletians were declared schismatics fifty-six years before, and that the Arians thirty-six years ago were convicted of heresy. Socrates (*HE* i. 6) gives practically the same account as Athanasius, and may, as Hefele suggests, have copied from him. The third version of the origin of the schism, however, differs materially from those which we have hitherto considered. It is given by Epiphanius (*Hær.* lxviii.), and printed in Routh (iv. 105). Meletius, says this writer, was a perfectly orthodox bishop. Indeed, he credits him with having accused Arius to Alexander, with whom Meletius, though a schismatical bishop, was on good terms. The real cause of the dispute was, according to Epiphanius, the question of the treatment of the lapsed. But Epiphanius's account, as Hefele shows, is full of inaccuracies, and contradicts the earliest evidence, as when, *e.g.*, he makes Meletius a fellow-prisoner with Peter. But he may have been correct as to the underlying cause of the schism, Meletius being, like Novatian at Rome and the Donatists in Africa, the representative of the severe disciplinarians. Epiphanius had, moreover, special knowledge of the Meletians from their schism having spread to his native place, Eleutheropolis. Perhaps because of his doctrinal orthodoxy, Meletius and his party were treated very leniently by the Council of Nicæa. It may be that canon 6, affirming the authority of the bishop of Alexandria, was directed against them; but in the synodal letter (Soc. *HE* i. 9) Meletius was not permitted to ordain or appoint clerics any more, and those whom he had ordained were to be admitted to the Church (μυστικωτέρᾳ χειροτονίᾳ) and to rank below the clergy ordained by Peter and his successors. Athanasius was much troubled by those schismatics who joined his opponents; and from their ranks came his bitter enemies, the priest Ischyras, Arsenius, and many others. Athanasius bitterly regretted the decision of Nicæa in this matter (*Apol. c. Arianos*, 71 f., where a list of the followers of Meletius is given). The schism lasted down to the middle of the 5th century (Soc. *HE* i. 8).

LITERATURE.—Besides the historians and Athanasius, C. J. Hefele, *A History of the Christian Councils*, Eng. tr., i.[2], Edinburgh, 1894, p. 341 ff.; A. P. Stanley, *Lectures on the History of the Eastern Church*, London, 1884; H. M. Gwatkin, *Studies of Arianism*[2], Cambridge, 1900; H. Achelis, art. 'Meletius von Lykopolis,' in *PRE*[3].

2. The Meletian schism at Antioch.—The importance of the disputed episcopal succession at Antioch is due to the fact that it hindered the good understanding between the Roman and Alexandrian Churches and those Asiatic Christians who, though at heart orthodox, were less uncompromisingly Nicene than many of the Athanasian party. The dispute, which lasted for more than fifty years, ranged the great saints and Fathers of the later years of the 4th cent. in opposite camps. Against St. Basil, St. Gregory of Nazianzus, St. Flavian of Antioch, and St. John Chrysostom were opposed St. Damasus of Rome, St. Ambrose of Milan, St. Peter of Alexandria, and, much against his will, St. Athanasius himself. The merits of the controversy are perhaps as evenly distributed as the names on either side. To understand it aright it is necessary to trace the divisions of the patriarchal Church of Antioch from the days of the Nicene Council. Eustathius, the bishop, who had been one of the foremost champions of the accepted creed, was the first to suffer in its cause, being deprived of his see in A.D. 330, though not without a serious tumult in the city, owing to the machinations of Eusebius of Cæsarea and the 'conservative' faction. The see of Antioch was now filled by prelates who were hostile to the Nicene formula—Eulalius, Euphronius, Flacillus, Stephen, and Leontius, the last of whom, by prudently concealing his real opinions on vexed questions, preserved peace till his death in 357. He was succeeded by Eudoxius, 'the worst of all the Arians,' who was installed as bishop of Constantinople in A.D. 360. It now became necessary to provide a successor at Antioch, and Meletius was chosen, being supposed to be a man of peace in accord with the party in power (F. Cavallera, *Le Schisme d'Antioche*, p. 72, note). In his sermon, however, on Pr 8^{22} he declared himself on the side of the Nicenes (Epiph. *Hær.* lxxiii.), and was at once deposed and exiled, and Euzoïus put in his place. Thus Meletius, once the Arian nominee, had become a Catholic confessor. Since the deposition of Eustathius, the faithful Nicene remnant had remained apart under the care of the priest Paulinus, and did not enjoy the prospect of communicating with the followers of Meletius, who, unlike them, had not borne the burden of the contest. The party of Paulinus, however, was not considerable—perhaps its insignificance induced Euzoïus, who is said to have had a regard for its leader, to allow it the use of a small church. Meletius's party, on the other hand, was numerous and increasing owing to the popularity of the bishop, and it seemed probable that under him the Catholics would ultimately be united. In 362 Athanasius held the small but important Council of Alexandria (see ARIANISM, vol. i. p. 780). A synodal letter, the *Tomus ad Antiochenos*, was sent to Antioch by the hands of the bishop Eusebius of Vercelli, who had attended the Council; but on his arrival he found that his companion in exile, Lucifer, bishop of Caliaris in Sardinia, had taken upon himself to consecrate Paulinus bishop of the old Nicene party at Antioch. As far as Antioch was concerned, the schism was unimportant. Meletius was universally beloved, and his moderation in regard to the points at issue in the controversy was more in consonance with Asiatic and Syrian Christianity than the uncompromising attitude of Alexandria and the West. Nor was Athanasius averse to a settlement, which let bygones be bygones, and allowed the good work done by Hilary of Poictiers in reconciling the bishops of Asia Minor to the Nicene Creed to bear fruit. But, not wishing to disavow Lucifer, the bishop of Alexandria recognized Paulinus, as did also the Roman see. The dispute had now reached a stage at which principles were involved not unlike those which made the unhappy Donatist schism so incurable in Africa—the difference being that the Donatists (*q.v.*) rejected bishops who had been unfaithful in regard to heathenism, and the Eustathians of Antioch those who had once been infected with heresy. The Roman see under Damasus declared unhesitatingly for Paulinus; but throughout the East Meletius was regarded as the champion of orthodoxy; and he was a sufferer under Valens for his adherence to the Nicene Creed. The Cappadocian fathers, Basil and the two Gregorys, were devoted to Meletius, and John Chrysostom belonged to his church and was first ordained reader and afterwards deacon by him. The schism at Antioch embittered the life of St. Basil, who in vain appealed to Athanasius to recognize Meletius, and was seriously troubled by the uncompromising support which Damasus gave to Paulinus. Things were further complicated by Apollinaris, the famous bishop of Laodicea, who, though condemned for his erroneous opinions, is recognized not only as a defender of Nicene theology, but also as one of the profoundest thinkers of his time (see APOLLINARISM). Among his friends was the presbyter Vitalius, who had been made priest by Meletius, but was ultimately consecrated by Apollinaris as rival bishop to Paulinus (*c.* 375). Thus, including the Arians, the Church of Antioch was now divided into four parties, the three Nicene bishops being Meletius, Paulinus, and Vitalius. Strangely enough, not a shadow of suspicion rested on any one of these three rivals in regard to character. Meletius and Paulinus were both recognized as saints, while, despite the suspicious orthodoxy of his consecrator, Vitalius was highly respected by the most honoured churchmen of the day. Some hope of ending the schism was given when the six leading presbyters of the Church agreed to recognize either Meletius or Paulinus, if one survived the other. In 381 Meletius was at Constantinople, taking a leading part in the Second General Council. This Council was destined to affirm the creed of Nicæa and reunite the Church, though it proved unable to bring peace to the distracted community at Antioch. Meletius died during the Council; and, for some unexplained reason, Flavian, one of the six presbyters who had agreed to recognize Paulinus if he survived, consented to be consecrated successor to Meletius. His action appears on the face of it indefensible; but, as he proved a remarkably saintly bishop, there may be some extenuating circumstances for his conduct of which we are not aware. The appointment of Flavian was one of the reasons for the Roman see's regarding the Council of Constantinople with disfavour. Paulinus was supported by the bishops of Egypt, Cyprus, and Arabia, whilst Palestine, Syria, and Phœnicia adhered to Flavian. Theodosius recognized Flavian, and, when the serious affair of the statues was causing anxiety in the city, it was he as its bishop who pleaded the cause of the people at Constantinople (A.D. 387). Paulinus died in 388; and before his death he consecrated Evagrius in his place—a most uncanonical proceeding. The Westerners seem to have supported the claims of Evagrius, and Ambrose urged Theodosius to compel Flavian to come to Italy and submit his claims to the decision of the Church there; Theophilus of Alexandria was naturally opposed to him, as were Epiphanius and Jerome. When, however, Evagrius died, no rival bishop was consecrated. On Chrysostom's appointment to Constantinople (398) he managed to heal the schism so far as Alexandria and Rome were concerned; and Flavian placed the names of his two rivals—Paulinus and Evagrius—on the diptychs of the Church. The Eustathians continued to hold separate meetings till the time of Alexander (414–415), who healed the schism by an act of Christian courtesy, visiting the Eustathian church on Easter day and being accorded a hearty welcome by the congregation. The schism was finally ended when Kalandion, patriarch of Antioch (481–485), brought back the relics of Eustathius. The schism of Antioch would be no more than a somewhat dull chapter in ecclesiastical history were it not for the underlying causes, indispensable for the right understanding of the intricate questions which make the religious divisions of the East so complicated. As has been indicated, there was a singular absence of bad feeling and, we may add, of bad motives. We hear nothing of the disorder and even crimes which mark the course of the Donatist schism. But throughout we can see how incompatible were the ideals of the great patriarchates of Rome and Egypt with those of the East. Meletius, Flavian, John Chrysostom, and Nestorius, the great Antiochenes, all felt the encroachments of the bishop of Alexandria supported—except in the case of Chrysostom—by Rome. What has been called the Meletian schism was a foreshadowing of troubles to come which rent the Church asunder, and it is a phase in the long struggle between the rival theologies of Alexandria and Antioch, which dates from the days of Origen.

LITERATURE.—Eusebius, *Vita Const.* iii. 59–62; Rufinus, *HE* i.; Philostorgius, *HE* v.; Socrates, *HE* ii.–vi.; Sozomen, *HE* iv.–vi.; Theodoret, *HE* ii.–v.; Epiphanius, *Hær.* lxxiii.; Basil, *Epp.* 66, 120, 214, 258; Ambrose, *Epp.* 12–14, 56; Jerome, *Epp.* 15, 16; Greg. Naz., *Ep.* 240, *Carm.* II. ii. 1514–1624; Chrysostom, *Panegyrics* on Meletius and Eustathius; C. J. Hefele, *Hist. of the Councils of the Church*, Eng. tr., ii.², Edinburgh, 1896, pp. 275, 278, 346, 378, etc.; H. M. Gwatkin, *Studies of Arianism*², Cambridge, 1900, p. 211 ff.; A. Harnack, *Lehrbuch der Dogmengeschichte*³, Leipzig, 1894, Eng. tr., *Hist. of Dogma*, London, 1894–99, iv. (esp. p. 89 ff.); F. Cavallera, *Le Schisme d'Antioche, ive siècle*, Paris, 1905.

F. J. FOAKES-JACKSON.

MEMORY. — I. **Use of the term.** — (*a*) The term 'memory' can be used in a wide biological sense to signify retention of the effects of stimulation. In this sense it is regarded by some writers as a fundamental attribute of living matter—a view which was put forward by Ewald Hering in 1870, in a paper read before the Imperial Academy of Science at Vienna, 'On Memory as the Universal Function of Organized Matter.' Wherever there is life with growth and development, there memory must be predicated, since each new process is the outcome of the old and implies its retention.

Memory is a faculty not only of our conscious states, but also, and much more so, of our unconscious ones. . . . Our ideas do not exist continuously as ideas; what is continuous is the special disposition of nerve substance in virtue of which this substance gives out to-day the same sound which it gave yesterday, if it is properly struck. . . . The reproductions of organic processes, brought about by means of the memory of the nervous system, enter but partly within the domain of consciousness, remaining unperceived in other and not less important respects. . . . The memory of the so-called sympathetic ganglionic system is no less rich than that of the brain and spinal marrow. . . . A muscle becomes stronger the more we use it. . . . After each individual action it becomes more capable, more disposed towards the same kind of work, and has a greater aptitude for repetition of the same organic processes. It gains also in weight, for it assimilates more matter than when constantly at rest. We have here . . . the same power of reproduction which we encountered when we were dealing with nerve substance. . . . This growth and multiplication of cells is only a special phase of those manifold functions which characterize organized matter. . . . Reproduction of performance, therefore, manifests itself to us as reproduction of the cells themselves, as may be seen most plainly in the case of plants, whose chief work consists in growth, whereas with animal organism other faculties greatly preponderate.'[1]

Hering states the doctrine of the heredity of acquired characteristics with great simplicity.

'We have ample evidence of the fact that characteristics of an organism may descend to offspring which the organism did not inherit, but which it acquired owing to the special circumstances under which it lived. . . . What is the descent of special peculiarities but a reproduction on the part of organized matter of processes in which it once took part as a germ in the germ-containing organs of its parent, and of which it seems still to retain a recollection that reappears when time and occasion serve?'[2]

For Hering the marvels of instinct are but the marvels of habit handed on from generation to generation.

'He who marvels at the skill with which the spider weaves her web should bear in mind that she did not learn her art all on a sudden, but that innumerable generations of spiders acquired it toilsomely and step by step.'[3]

Samuel Butler, in *Life and Habit* (1877), set forth the same doctrine, although he was at that time ignorant of Hering's paper. Into a later book, entitled *Unconscious Memory*, he incorporated a translation of the German lecture.

At the present day a similar view of memory is presented by such biologists as Francis Darwin, R. Semon, and H. S. Jennings. It should be noticed that in such a biological doctrine of memory there is no necessary reference to consciousness. The structural development and behaviour of plants and animals may testify to memory in this wide sense without thereby giving evidence of consciousness.

(*b*) In a psychological use of the term such a reference is essential. As generally understood in psychology, memory denotes the retention of experience, and its subsequent reproduction with the consciousness that it belongs to the past. To remember is to refer back. The distinction between memory as a conscious experience and memory as a biological fact has been emphasized by H. Bergson in his distinction between the memory which imagines and the memory which repeats. All our bodily habits are memory in the latter sense, but not necessarily in the former. Acquired skill implies practice with the retention of past progress, but in the exercise of skill there need not be any conscious reference to those past exercises whereby this skill was acquired. Both forms of memory may be combined when performed habit or acquired skill is guided on any occasion by a conscious reference back to past efforts, successes, and failures. For Bergson the relation of the two forms of memory portrays the relation of body to soul; each may enter into the service of the other.

'The bodily memory, made up of the sum of the sensori-motor systems organized by habit, is then a quasi-instantaneous memory to which the true memory of the past serves as base . . . the memory of the past offers to the sensori-motor mechanisms all the recollections capable of guiding them in their task and of giving to the motor reaction the direction suggested by the lessons of experience. . . . But, on the other hand, the sensori-motor apparatus furnish to ineffective, that is unconscious, memories, the means of taking on a body, of materializing themselves, in short, of becoming present. For, that a recollection should reappear in consciousness, it is necessary that it should descend from the heights of pure memory down to the precise point where *action* is taking place.'[1]

James Ward would subscribe to the biological doctrine of memory, but finds it meaningless save as interpreted in terms of the psychological.

'Nay, the bare term "retention" itself, and all cognate terms, such as "trace" or "residuum," are meaningless unless some present circumstance can be related to the past; thus they presuppose memory. The analogy of inscribed records is a favourite resort of those who strive to elucidate the nature of memory by physical imagery; we find it again and again in Locke, for example. Such an analogy is about on a par with that between the eye and a telescope—the one is a natural, the other an artificial, organ or instrument of vision; but neither will explain seeing as a psychological fact.'[2] 'Records or memoranda alone are not memory, for they presuppose it. *They* may consist of physical traces; but memory, even when called "unconscious," suggests mind; . . . the mnemic theory then, if it is to be worth anything, seems to me clearly to require not merely physical records or "engrams," but living experience or tradition.'[3]

(*c*) 'Memory' may be used to denote the retention of past experience without reference to the explicit reproduction of such experience. The essential difference of this use of the term from the biological use lies in the word 'experience' with its implication of mental processes. Writers on psychiatry, such as Morton Prince, S. Freud, and C. G. Jung, use the term 'memory' for the influence of past on present experience, whether the subject is conscious of such influence or not.

'When we conceive of memory as a process we have in mind the whole mechanism through the working of which this past experience is registered, conserved and reproduced, whether such reproduction be in consciousness or below the surface of consciousness.'[4]

In this sense all perception and all behaviour involve memory. Not only so, but these writers would include in their reference past experience of which the individual took no conscious note. Sensations received, and actions performed, with no consciousness of their occurrence, are said to be remembered and to be of great importance in determining future experience.

(*d*) As usually interpreted, memory belongs to cognition, but, inasmuch as all experience cannot be reduced to processes of cognition, so, it may be urged, neither can the retention and reproduction of experience. Such a theory requires that the emotional aspect of experience, feeling-tone, and conation be reproduced in memory as emotion, as feeling-tone, and as conation. Just as these aspects of consciousness are never experienced alone 'in abstracto' but always in a concrete whole of experience, so they will never be reproduced 'in abstracto,' but in a concrete whole with an idea or with an object of sense-perception in this or that action. In this article memory will be treated as implying the retention of past experience and the explicit reproduction of such experience in the form of ideas.

2. Reproduction of ideas.—It is a disputed point whether ideas of past experience ever arise spontaneously in consciousness or are always suggested by the datum of present consciousness. Evidence in favour of the former view is found in the experimental work of G. E. Müller and F. Schumann, A. Binet, and other experimental psychologists.

[1] *Ap.* S. Butler, *Unconscious Memory*, pp. 109, 116, 117 f.
[2] *Ib.* pp. 118, 122.
[3] *Ib.* p. 129.

[1] Bergson, *Matter and Memory*, p. 197.
[2] Ward, *Naturalism and Agnosticism*[2], London, 1903, ii. 157.
[3] Ward, *Heredity and Memory*, p. 55 f.
[4] Morton Prince, *The Unconscious*, p. 2.

The latter view certainly represents the commoner form of memory. The attempt to classify the relation in which the suggested idea stood to the present consciousness gave rise to the 'laws of association.' The types of relationship, contiguity in time and place, similarity and contrast, were erected into principles of explanation. The present datum x was said to suggest the past experience y because previously x and y had been contiguous in time or place, or because they were similar, or, again, because they contrasted—three very different lines of explanation (see art. ASSOCIATION). Modern writers seek to find an explanation for this association of past and present in the direct and indirect connexions of experience brought about through our purposeful activities. Association is but a special form of the bonds existing between different moments of experience in virtue of the organization of experience into systems. Direct or indirect participation in some common system or whole constitutes the bond of union which enables a present datum to suggest past experience. The laws for the organization of experience, for the formation of spatial wholes, temporal wholes, trains of perception, trains of ideas, systems of conduct, are the ultimate principles of association. The conditions which determine the actual line of association followed on any given occasion are of two kinds—those which relate to the whole in which the present datum and a particular past experience participate, and those which relate to the special circumstances of the present moment of suggestion.

A whole which is closely organized will form a stronger basis for association than one which is loosely organized or which lacks a definite principle. A whole which has occurred repeatedly or recently is more influential than one which is of rare or long past occurrence. Experimental investigations have served to demonstrate the efficacy of close organization, intrinsic interest, repetition, and recency in determining suggestion. As illustrative of the influence of close organization one may cite H. Ebbinghaus's work with nonsense syllables. The only principle for organization was the spatial arrangement and time sequence of a string of syllables—*e.g.*, duk, lil, bap, pom, etc.—memorized by reading aloud. Any interference with the spatial and temporal organization of the series rendered rememorizing of the same syllables slower, and the difficulty of rememorizing the syllables was in proportion to the degree to which the original spatial and temporal organization was disturbed. As compared with a whole which has meaning—*e.g.*, a passage of prose or verse—these strings of nonsense syllables are more difficult to memorize, a fact which illustrates the influence of an intrinsic interest as a basis of organization. The work of L. Steffens and P. Ephrussi has emphasized the importance of attention with respect to the basis of organization. It has proved more economical to memorize material by repeating it as a whole than to memorize it piecemeal, provided the material is such as can be attended to without undue difficulty. Continuity of interest is preserved by this so-called 'global' method, whereas it is destroyed by the artificial sections of the 'partial' or piecemeal learning. The value of rhythm in organizing a sequence of experiences has been shown by Müller and Schumann, and is a commonplace of school practice. The influence of repetition in rendering suggestion certain and swift is illustrated by Müller and Schumann's researches. Experimental work by Müller and A. Pilzecker demonstrated the effect of recency in determining which of two possible lines of association suggestion should follow.

Of the conditions relating to the moment of suggestion, two seem to be predominant — the emotional attitude of the individual, and the trend of his ideas. The influence of the first on the line of association is demonstrated by the emotional congruity between the attitude of the present and that of the experience recalled; in a Micawber-like mood we forget failures and recall only ambitions and achievements. The importance of the trend of present consciousness has been shown in much recent work. An investigation by H. J. Watt brought out the control over association exercised by the *Aufgabe*, or task, before the mind at the moment. On the relevance or irrelevance of the reproduced idea depends very largely the serviceableness of our memory in any given difficulty. Appositeness for the purpose of the present moment, for what W. James termed 'the topic' of the stream of thought, will give one line of association the advantage over another.

A question which has become important for psychology is dissociation. Some writers hold that, just as experience becomes organized into wholes and these wholes are interrelated one with another in still larger organizations, so also there takes place the opposite process, viz. dissociation. Through dissociation certain episodes of past experience or certain aspects of that experience drop out of a given organization; such episodes cannot then be reproduced; no suggestion of normal consciousness can connect itself with the dissociated contents of past experience. The theory is of great importance to psychopathology in its bearing on the amnesia of hypnosis and hysteria and on multiple personality. The process whereby the insulation of non-suggestible memories is brought about is described differently by different writers. Dissociation is the line of description followed by Morton Prince; repression (without the implication of dissociation) in virtue of some pain value is the line of description followed by the Freudian school.

3. Obliviscence and reminiscence.—The failure of reproduction, whatever may be the view taken as to disintegration, is by no means the same psychical fact as failure of retention; inability to recall does not in itself prove obliviscence or the decay of past experience. Whether there can be total obliviscence, whether any experience can cease to be influential in mental life, may be open to dispute. Certainly it would seem that many experiences cease to be retained as explicit ideas. In the absence of any interest to organize items of experience obliviscence would be the natural fading out of processes which had fulfilled their function. Ebbinghaus's experiments with nonsense syllables, already referred to, furnished a typical curve of the rate of forgetting such items. The principle of organization was mere spatial and temporal contiguity; no interest gave value to the series of syllables or rendered one syllable of greater worth than another. Ebbinghaus's curve shows that after an interval of twenty minutes 41·8 per cent of any series learnt was forgotten, after an interval of an hour 55·8 per cent was forgotten, after twenty-four hours 66·3 per cent, after six days 74·6 per cent, after thirty-one days 78·9 per cent. The fading away of the processes is rapid at first and very gradual afterwards. Experimental work, however, would also seem to indicate that experience does not necessarily begin to fade from the moment when it ceases to be 'present' experience. On the contrary, there is a certain amount of evidence that processes ripen or mature, the reproduction of past experience being clearer or fuller after some short lapse of time than immediately after the original occurrence. Some of the experimental work of A. Jost suggested this, and recent work with school-children has brought out the same feature. Thus, if the amount of ballad poetry which children aged 12 can reproduce correctly immediately after learning be represented by 100, the amount which they can reproduce forty-eight hours later without any further learning will be 110. A similar increase in content reproduced is found in other kinds of school material. In the case of nonsense syllables, although forty-eight hours later some syllables can be reproduced which have not been remembered immediately after learning, the total amount reproduced is less. This tendency for 'reminiscence,' as it has been termed, is more marked in children than in adults. The greater organization of adult consciousness would enable any experience to attain its full value and association speedily, and, when reproduced, it is already developed, and henceforward decay rather than growth will be its life-history. In the case of the less organized experience of the child it may well be otherwise. The meaning and association of an experience would develop more slowly, and might be incomplete when the demand for reproduction followed at once upon its first reception.

4. Function of imagery.—Past experience reproduced as ideas depends very largely upon imagery. Imagery is of the same character as sense experience—visual, auditory, tactual, motor, etc. Francis Galton proposed grouping individuals into classes according to the kind of imagery used in reproduction—*e.g.*, an audile, one who reproduced past experience in terms of auditory imagery, heard words descriptive of the facts recalled. Most people were said to belong to a mixed type, *i.e.* to use all varieties of imagery. It would seem, however, that the kind of imagery used, even by a so-called audile or a visualizer, depends very largely upon the idea reproduced and the purpose for which it is reproduced. The fragmentary character of images, their instability and lack of localization as compared with sense presentations, has always been recognized. The schematic and symbolic character of imagery with respect to the idea for which it stands has received more attention in recent research. The function of imagery would seem to be to provide a focus for attention, and thereby to give clearness and definiteness to ideas. It has been noticed that, where the process of reproduction takes place with difficulty or where a train of ideas develops slowly, there the presence of imagery is marked, and the imagery seems indispensable to the realization of the ideas in question. Where, on the other hand, ideas are reproduced easily or a train of ideas develops rapidly or is familiar in its character, there imagery is sketchy and in some cases scarcely recognizable. The question has been raised whether reproduction is possible without imagery, without even the symbolic imagery of words standing for the ideas reproduced. Here, as in so many other psychological problems, no dogmatic answer is possible in the present state of knowledge. There is much patient research in connexion with the question, and from it there should arise a clearer conception of the problem and of its solution.

On the development of memory and memory training see art. DEVELOPMENT (Mental).

LITERATURE.—S. Butler, *Unconscious Memory*, London, 1880; J. Ward, *Heredity and Memory*, Cambridge, 1913; H. Bergson, *Matter and Memory*, Eng. tr., London, 1911; H. Piéron, *Evolution de la mémoire*, Paris, 1910; Morton Prince, *The Unconscious*, New York, 1914; S. Freud, *The Pathology of Everyday Life*, Eng. tr., London, 1914; H. Ebbinghaus, *Über das Gedächtnis*, Leipzig, 1885: E. Meumann, *Ökonomie und Technik des Gedächtnisses*, do. 1908; G. F. Stout, *Manual of Psychology*³, London, 1913, bk. iv. ch. iii.; H. J. Watt, *The Economy and Training of Memory*, do. 1909.

BEATRICE EDGELL.

MĒMRĀ.—The tendency of Hebrew imagery to personify abstract powers, such as sin, sheol, wisdom, is evident also in the manner in which the divine word or speech is represented in poetry and elevated language. God's fiat by which creation came into being and continues to exist is spoken of as emanating from Him to execute His will. By the word of Jahweh 'were the heavens made' (Ps 33^{6}). 'He sendeth his word, and healeth them' (107^{20}). In Is 55 the word proceeding from God's mouth assumes form and accomplishes His will as His plenipotentiary. In the Apocrypha also we meet with a few instances where the word stands for God:

It was the word that descended on the offspring of the fallen angels to pierce them with the sword (*Jub.* 5^{11}); it entered Abraham's heart (12^{17}); it slew the first-born in Egypt; 'thine all-powerful word leaped from heaven out of the royal throne' (Wis 18^{15}).

But, while these instances are of rare occurrence in the Targumim—though nowhere else in Jewish post-Biblical literature—the word is already hypostatized under the form of *Mēmrā*. The Aram. *mēmar*, emph. state *mēmrā*, from *emar*, 'to speak,' signifies, like λόγος, from λέγειν, 'a word,' without the additional meaning of 'reason' connoted by λόγος. It occurs about 180 times in the Onḳelos Targum, 100 times in the so-called Jerusalem Targum, and 320 times in the pseudo-Jonathan (in the last two also דִּבּוּרָא) for God.

It stands either in the const. state—*e.g.*, Gn 15^{6} 'He believed in Jahweh' (Onḳ. renders 'in the Mēmrā of Jahweh'), Ex 19^{17} 'Moses brought forth the people before the Mēmrā of Jahweh' (in Jonathan 'before the Shᵉkhînāh'), Nu 23^{21} 'The Mēmrā of Jahweh their God is their support, and the Shᵉkhînāh of their king is among them'—or with suffixes: 'It is a sign between my Mēmrā and you' (Ex 31^{13}); 'This Mēmrā is a consuming fire' (Dt 9^{3}); 'I will shield thee with my Mēmrā until I have passed by' (Ex 33^{22}). It was employed by the Targumists in the place of God wherever anthropomorphisms, anthropopathisms, or any act inconsistent with the nature of a transcendent God, are predicated. Thus, 'By my Mēmrā I have founded the earth, and by my strength I have hung up the heavens' (Is 48^{13}). The mouth of Jahweh becomes the Mēmrā of Jahweh (Gn $3^{8.\,10}$). The Israelites said: 'Behold, Jahweh our God has shown us his glory (îḳārā), and his greatness, and we have heard the voice of his Mēmrā' (Dt 5^{24}). It is His Mēmrā that repents (Gn 6^{6} etc.); God swears by His Mēmrā (Nu 14^{35}); 'for my sake' is rendered 'for the sake of my Mēmrā' (Is 48^{11}). The Mēmrā gave the Law (Ex 20). 'These are the statutes . . . which Jahweh made between his Mēmrā and the children of Israel' (Lv 26^{46}). The Mēmrā accomplished the exodus from Egypt (Ex 3^{12}, etc.). 'Jahweh thy God, his Mēmrā, is thy help who brought thee out of the land of Egypt' (Dt 20^{1}). Isaiah saw 'the glory of the Shᵉkhînāh of the King of the worlds Jahweh Sᵉbhāôth' (Is 6^{5}), and then heard 'the voice of the Mēmrā' (6^{8}).

The above are only a few typical passages of the use of the Mēmrā (for an exhaustive list see F. Weber, *Jüdische Theologie*, Leipzig, 1897, p. 180; A. Edersheim, *Life and Times of Jesus*⁴, London, 1887, ii. 659 ff.; he was followed by W. Fairweather in *HDB* v. 284). What, then, did the Targumists understand by the Mēmrā? A cursory glance at the Aramaic version will be necessary before we answer this question. The demand for a version in the Aramaic vernacular by the returned exiles must have been supplied very early; it is difficult to say how far back we are to place the institution of the office of the Mᵉthûrgᵉmān ('Dragoman,' 'Interpreter'), who rendered into the vernacular each verse of the Law and each three verses of the Prophets, as they were read publicly in the synagogue (cf. the office of the Ἑρμηνευτής in the early Christian communities). The frequent repetition must have produced a stereotyped version. The exclamation of Christ on the Cross in the Aramaic of Ps 22^{1} indicates that the Bible was familiar to Him in that language; and St. Paul's quotation of Ps 68^{18} in Eph 4^{8} is more in accordance with the Targum than with our Mas. Text or the LXX. A written Targum on Job existed at the time of Gamaliel (*Shab.* 115*a*). Although neither Origen nor Jerome mentions the existence of a Targum, that of Onḳelos had already at that time the position of a kind of authorized version.

'R. Jehudah says, whosoever transplants a verse (of the Bible) as it stands misrepresents the text, and whosoever adds to it is a blasphemer. Let him render it in accordance with *our Targum*' (*Ḳid.* 49*a*).

Jewish scholars agree that this refers to Onkelos (*e.g.*, Maimonides, in *Yad*, Îshūth viii. 4; see also L. Zunz, *Gottesdienstliche Vorträge*[2], Frankfort, 1892, ch. v.). The aim of the version was to give a correct rendering of the text. Where he differs from the original he does so in favour of the Hălākhā and popular usages:

Ex 23^{19} 34^{24}, Dt 14^{21} are rendered 'Ye shall not eat flesh with milk'; 'the fruit of the goodly tree' (Lv 23^{40}) is already called *ethrôg*. 'The Passover shall be eaten in *one assembly*' (Heb. 'one house') (Ex 12^{46}) in accordance with *Pesaḥ*. 86*a*.

It is obvious that the version was intended to embody Palestinian theology for popular use, and deviation from the original in the case of the names and acts of God was to guard against misconception of the nature and irreverent usage of the name of God. We find, accordingly, the divine unity insisted on:

Elōhîm with a plural predicate is rendered in the singular (Gn 35^{7}); Dt 4^{35} is translated 'to know that Jahweh is God, there is none beside him'; 'Who is like unto thee among the gods?' (Ex 15^{11}) becomes 'There is none beside thee. Thou art God'; so 18^{11} 'Jahweh is great, and there is no other God.'

Jahweh may not even be contrasted with other gods. Not even may the term 'god' be applied to other divinities.

They are either 'errors,' 'abominations' (Gn 35^{2}), or 'terrors' (31^{32}); 'he brought him up to the high place of his terror' (Heb. 'Ba'al') (Nu 22^{41}).

To avoid contrasting God with man or ascribing the same action to both, Onḳelos would introduce a paraphrase: 'They believed in the Mēmrā of Jahweh and in the prophecy of Moses' (Ex 14^{31}), 'the people murmured against the Mēmrā of Jahweh and strove with Moses' (Nu $21^{5.7}$); or the construction would be changed into the passive: 'Let it not be spoken to us from before Jahweh' (Ex 20^{19}). The same construction is employed when human actions and passions are ascribed to God:

'The voice of the lad was heard before God' (Gn 21^{17}); 'the labour of my hands is revealed before God' (31^{42}); 'it is revealed before me' (Heb. 'I know') (Ex 3^{19}); a Mēmar from before Jahweh came to Abimelech (Gn 20^{3}); 'Balaam met with a Mēmar from before Jahweh' (Nu $23^{3.4}$). This construction explains Onḳelos's rendering of Dt 33^{27}, which accidentally resembles Jn 1^{10} 'By his word the world was created.' In the place of זרעת עולם, 'the everlasting arms,' he reads, like the Peshiṭta version, זרע העולם 'he (the Mēmrā) sowed (=created) the world,' which in the passive assumed the above rendering.

It is evident that a version made under the influence of rigid uncompromising monotheism and accepted as embodying Rabbinic theology would avoid the assumption of an intermediate being distinct from God. To compare the Mēmrā with Philo's Logos would credit the Targumists with more theosophy than they otherwise claim, and it would be also unaccountable why only this term and nothing more of Philonic exegesis and mysticism should have found its way into the Targums. Its use in all the Targums rather warrants the assumption that its adoption is older than the Alexandrian Logos. We are inclined to think that it was introduced by the M^{e}thūrg^{e}mānîm when the name IHVH ceased to be pronounced and before Adonai was substituted, some time during the Persian period. The Mēmrā, therefore, is the deity revealed in its activity, just as the Sh^{e}khînāh and Îḳārā represent the divine majesty and glory. The term is based on Gn 1^{2}, emphasizing the fact that the world came into being by divine command.

Onḳelos uses Mēmrā when speaking of human authority:

'The Mēmar of Pharaoh' (Heb. 'the mouth of Pharaoh') (Gn 45^{21}); 'he does not receive our Mēmrā' (Heb. 'will not obey our voice') (Dt 21^{20}).

LITERATURE.—Besides the works referred to in the art. see *JE*, art. 'Memra'; S. D. Luzzatto, *Philoxenus*, Vienna, 1830; W. Bousset, *Die Religion des Judentums im neutestamentl. Zeitalter*[2], Berlin, 1906, p. 399.

A. E. SUFFRIN.

MEN, THE.—In the Gaelic-speaking portion of Scotland 'the Men' were for about two centuries the recognized leaders of religious thought, and the popular representatives of spiritual and evangelical worship. They were called 'the Men' because they were laymen, and not ministers. The circumstances in which they arose varied in different districts; the causes to which they owed their origin admit of little doubt.

In the reign of James VI., Robert Bruce, the eminent Edinburgh preacher, was banished to Inverness. In a letter, written in Feb. 1613, to Sir James Semple, the laird of Belvise, the exiled minister says:

'If his Hieness wold command me to the scaffold, I have a good conscience to obey him, and it wold be more welcome to me nor this lingering death that I am in' (D. Calderwood, *Hist. of the Kirk of Scotland*, Edinburgh, 1842–49, vii. 183).

The 'lingering death' which Bruce deplored resulted in the establishment in Inverness of meetings for prayer and fellowship, and in the gathering together of bands of godly men whose influence continued to mould the religious life of the Highlands for many generations.

After the restitution and re-establishment of Episcopacy in Scotland in 1662, nearly 300 ministers relinquished their livings, and their places were filled in the greater number of parishes by ministers who did not possess the confidence of the people. In the more populous districts of the South, the unity of the people, and their devotion to Presbyterianism, enabled them to maintain their religious zeal by means of 'conventicles,' meetings for purposes of worship held in despite of the law. In the North a number of the ministers readily turned Episcopalian, and retained their livings. The people were less devoted to Presbyterianism, but, even so, the more devout among them were roused to opposition by the manner in which the vacant livings were filled. The parishes were large, the population was sparse, and combined action for the holding of religious meetings was almost impossible. Religious instruction was for a time neglected. The 'curates,' as the new incumbents were called, exercised little or no influence. When ministers were no longer regarded as leaders of the people in sacred things, there rose to take their place men of devout lives, of integrity of character, familiar with the Scriptures, and recognized as possessing spiritual gifts, who, going from parish to parish to hold meetings, were accepted as religious guides.

At a later period, the arbitrary manner in which patronage was exercised in the Presbyterian Church, and acquiesced in by Church courts, revived the influence and importance of an institution which had already obtained a foothold in many districts. Bands of earnest Christians boldly denounced legal arrangements which ignored religious needs and aspirations, and the people honoured them for doing so. Interest in a common object drew them together. They deplored the low state of religion in the land, they yearned for spirituality of worship and a greater knowledge of Holy Scripture among their countrymen. They held monthly or quarterly meetings for prayer and fellowship. These were occasions of high spiritual enjoyment. Sometimes the company sat up during the whole night, and passed the time in prayer and praise and spiritual conversation.

In order to prevent any misconstruction of their aims they provided themselves in some cases with carefully drafted constitutions. A document, dated 17th September 1788, setting forth the objects and rules of the society of the Men in Ross-shire shows that, while they deplored the low state of religion throughout the land, they did so not in a spirit of self-righteousness; they were at the same time faithful in dealing with one another. Among various evils they note, 'thrusting in ministers on reclaiming congregations with the force of the law of patronage—pastors who have nothing in view but the fleece.' The same document gives as one of the rules of the society: 'Thirdly, as the Word of God requireth, that we should consider one another, to provoke unto love and good works; therefore, if one or more of us see or hear anything unbecoming in the walk, conduct, or expressions of one another, that we be free with one another according to the Scripture rule: "Go tell thy brother his fault," etc. (Mt 18^{15}); "Thou shalt not hate thy brother in thine heart: thou shalt in any wise rebuke thy neighbour, and not suffer sin upon him"' (Lv 19^{17}). It adds: 'We are aware that this our meeting together, out of different parishes, will be misconstructed; but, so far as we know ourselves, we have no divisive views in it; nor do we make a faction, and we desire to give none offence.'

Soundness of judgment characterized their utterances and their conduct. Their activity was far removed from that fanatical enthusiasm into which religious zeal frequently degenerates. One exception, still referred to with bated breath, when referred to at all, indicates their general abhorrence of fanatical excess. They organized meetings for prayer and the reading of Scripture among the people. The first Sabbath school in Ross-shire was opened by one of them—Findlater, known as the 'Quaker merchant.' Before the Bible was translated into Gaelic, many of them were experts in making a running translation from the English version into the language of the people. The more gifted among them expounded the Word, and not a few became eloquent and powerful preachers, though lacking the training of the schools. The deep respect of the people for an ordained ministry was reflected in the fact that these spiritual guides, even when their influence was most powerful, were called not ministers or preachers, but 'the Men' (*na Daoine*).

By 'the Men' the evangelical spirit was kept alive in large districts, and the comforts of religion were administered in many a stricken home and in many a remote hamlet. They generally set apart one night of each week for prayer, and another for fellowship or conference. On the latter a portion of Scripture was selected to be the subject of discussion. This passage was referred to as the *Bonn Ceist*, or the 'Question.' The Men, each in turn, gave an exposition, generally bearing on experimental religion, and thus their gifts of speech and of scriptural interpretation were developed. Fitness to expound Scripture in public assemblies, combined with blamelessness of life, secured recognition as one of the Men. This exercise became so popular that, whenever the Sacrament of the Lord's Supper was administered, a day was set apart for the Men. Generally it was the Friday between the Fast-day and the day of Preparation. It was known as *là na Ceist* ('the day of the Question'). Great gatherings were expected when popular Men came to 'the Communion.' Worshippers often travelled long distances, and from far and near; multitudes, who never became church members, attended faithfully on the Men's day.

The presiding minister opened the service with praise, prayer, and the reading of Scripture, and afterwards called for the passage which was to become the 'Question.' One of the more highly honoured of the Men announced a passage, indicating its bearing on Christian experience, and requesting speakers to deal with some such topic as 'marks by which God's children are distinguished from the world,' 'marks of true conversion,' 'marks of saving faith,' etc. Then the presiding minister called upon the most aged and experienced Christians present to give the 'marks' to their fellow-Christians. This service was generally held in the open air. Its popularity was such that the largest church could seldom contain the congregation gathered that day. 'To rise to the question' on a Communion Friday stamped the speaker with the hall-mark of public recognition. Henceforward his position was assured. He was one of 'the Men.'

The popularity of the Men was a menace to the Church wherever its services were not characterized by evangelical faithfulness. Many of them would not partake of the Sacraments at the hands of ministers of whom they did not approve, and approved ministers were prevented by ecclesiastical discipline from receiving those who held aloof from the worship of their own parishes. Resolutions against the Men were passed in Presbyteries and Synods, but all efforts to crush them only increased their popularity. The people believed in them, honouring them for the strictness of their lives, and frequently asserting that they were possessed of the gift of prophecy.

In earlier times, wherever the doctrines of grace were faithfully proclaimed, the Men were faithful to the Church, and they undoubtedly created a taste for the more spiritual and evangelical preaching which began early in the 19th century. With the revival of evangelicalism the special circumstances in which they proved a religious force passed away. But power and influence once acquired are not readily abandoned. In many districts the Men heartily welcomed and warmly supported an evangelical ministry; in others they persistently and fiercely opposed all ecclesiastical influence. The estrangement continued too long. In parts of Sutherland, Inverness, and Ross-shire they continued to stand aloof, and in the more northern districts they formed bodies known as 'Separatists.' The more they diverged from the Church the more they developed contempt for all learning except a literal knowledge of the Authorized Version of Scripture. They became narrow and intolerant. Utterly disregarding all outward culture, they attempted to force upon the people a religion of loveless gloom. From one extreme it was easy to pass to others. Antinomianism was openly professed in some districts, and exorcism was practised in others. These fitful throes were the spurious imitations of a life that had gone. In later times opposition to instrumental music and church choirs, a severe observance of the Sabbath, a blind devotion to the recognized translation of Scripture, a general condemnation of scholarship, and a zeal for the doctrine of election which merged into fatalism characterized generally the scattered fragments of a body whose sway was at one time both powerful and beneficent.

But the old spirit has not altogether disappeared. A different type is occasionally met with. 'Men,' tender-hearted and spiritually-minded, still preserve the best traditions of a past age. In the absence of the minister one of these may be found here and there to conduct the Sunday service in church or meeting-house. Standing at the precentor's desk, equally ready to give an extempore address or to read a portion of some 18th cent. divine, he follows devoutly the usual order of service, except that he does not pronounce the benediction. These Men live saintly lives, they are honoured by the people, and they help to preserve the simplicity and spirituality of religion.

LITERATURE.—A. Auld, *Ministers and Men in the Far North*², Edinburgh, 1891; D. Sage, *Memorabilia Domestica*, Wick, 1889; J. Kennedy, *The Days of the Fathers in Ross-shire*, Edinburgh, 1867.

G. R. MACPHAIL.

MEN OF GOD.—*Lyudi bozhii*, or 'Men of God,' is the self-assumed name of a Russian sect who regard themselves as the only true worshippers of God; they believe that God is to be found only among themselves, ordinary Christian church-goers being, in their view, worldlings. By the outside world they are usually known as 'Khlysti,' *i.e.* 'Flagellants,' though they themselves repudiate this title. As a matter of fact, they are essentially not flagellants but dancers, flagellation being a mere accompaniment of the dance, and not even a universal practice. The name is probably a corruption from 'Christŭ,' the oldest traceable title by which they designate themselves as those who have Christ in their midst, in their leaders.

Although the Men of God have many 'Christs,' they are not a Christological sect in the proper sense of the word, for their Christology is only one side of their doctrine of spiritual ecstasy; that is to say, they are a secret sect who practise asceticism and fall into trances. Their principal means for drawing down the Spirit is dancing (*radeniye*); other devices are the singing of songs, of which they have a great number, couched in highly poetical language, and fasts. A member of this sect who succeeds in receiving the Spirit in full measure becomes a Christ or even a God Zebaoth (a Christ of the highest rank) or a Mother of God; those who receive the Spirit in a less degree are invested with the title of one of the apostles, or of the ecclesiastical saints, and honoured as prophets or prophetesses. In their belief, even Jesus of Nazareth first became a Christ only through receiving the Spirit at His baptism. While these persons have received the Spirit as a permanent possession, ordinary members of the community may obtain Him temporarily through the same means.

Besides severe and often protracted fasts, complete sexual abstinence is a feature of their asceticism. Those who enter the sect as married people must henceforth live as brothers and sisters. Others are, as a rule, not permitted to marry at all, but may take a young woman into their house as 'spiritual sister' in 'spiritual marriage,' exclusive of sexual intercourse. The latter constituted the trespass of Adam and Eve, and is condemned as the sin κατ' ἐξοχήν; in accordance with this view, childbirth is regarded as extremely sinful, while children are despised as 'little sins.' Generally speaking, the Men of God aim at a monastic style of living, their houses being arranged as convents and the women wearing a kind of nun's dress. Like all Russian sectaries, they enforce complete abstinence from intoxicating liquors; even coffee, and in many communities tea also, is forbidden. On the whole the Khlystic system of morals lays so much stress on the mortification of the flesh (the resurrection of which they deny) that it has not been able to set up a practical ideal of life. Altruism appears among them essentially as sympathy, which has to display itself in the bestowal of alms. Besides practising asceticism, they lay great stress on the voluntary endurance of persecution from the State and from the Church, and the sect is persecuted even to the present day as 'extremely pernicious.' In earlier centuries the persecution was excessively brutal; attempts were made to crush them by the rack and the scaffold, but in vain, and they furnished many martyrs. Since the beginning of the 19th cent. those methods have been replaced by imprisonment and transportation to the Caucasus and Siberia.

The Men of God, however, seek to show the courage of their opinions not by open confession of their faith, but by concealment of it, and it is precisely their obstinacy in this matter that has often brought upon them increased severity of punishment. This concealment of their belief is due to their view of the Holy Spirit, whom they regard as a power which shuns observation, revealing Himself in secret and averse from publicity. If a man talks about the Spirit, he loses Him. Consequently not only are their ecstatic religious services secret, but they generally conceal the fact of their adherence to the sect. They outwardly conform to the State Church, and attend Confession and Holy Communion, although they spit out the wine afterwards. They themselves celebrate communion with *kvas* (a sour drink from rye meal and malt) or with water.

Any one who desires admission into the sect must, at an initiatory rite, conducted with an extremely elaborate ceremonial, swear a solemn oath that under no circumstances whatever, not even under the severest persecution, will he disclose his belief either to his nearest relatives or to the ecclesiastical confessor. In reality this sect thoroughly despise the State Church as 'the world,' the kingdom of Satan, and regard the 'popes' (clergy) as Jewish priests and Pharisees. In opposition to the Orthodox Church, they are sure that they are the only true Church, the Kingdom of God on earth, because they alone possess the Spirit of God. The services of the Orthodox Church are useless, since they dispense with dancing, the proper means for bringing down the Spirit from heaven.

The Men of God have also services in which there is no dancing; these are the 'usual conferences,' and consist in singing, and the reading and exposition of Holy Scripture; but they are only assemblies for attracting adherents, and they hint darkly at the 'better services.' In reality the source of revelation for this sect is not Holy Scripture, but the Spirit which descends on them during the dance. Any one who feels the desire for the 'better services' must undergo long preparation before he is received into the sect by one of the leaders and admitted to them. In the 'better services' a kind of frenzied dance takes place, consisting of a series of variously arranged movements performed singly and collectively, while songs are sung without any instrumental accompaniment. The object of the dance is to induce at least some of the performers to fall into an ecstasy (named the 'bath of regeneration,' since the *radeniye* is regarded as the real spiritual baptism in opposition to the mere water-baptism of the Church). The 'Christs,' 'Mothers of God,' prophets and prophetesses especially, but sometimes also the ordinary members of the community, when in the ecstatic state, break into improvised doggerel, and prophesy the 'common fate' of their sect and the 'private fate' of individual members. This secret service closes with a common meal—the 'love-feast'—which is regarded as the true communion. The services generally begin in the evening, and continue far into the night.

The sectaries have also provided a substitute for the other sacraments of the State Church. But the ritual varies in the different congregations and even in the same congregation, according to circumstances. The Men of God do not believe, with the Orthodox Church, that a sacrament must have the prescribed form in order to be efficacious; in their view, the Spirit operates unfettered and creates for Himself whatever form He chooses. They seem to have special rites of their own, such as dancing round a tub filled with water at the summer solstice. Here, doubtless, we have to do with a relic of Slavic heathenism, and vestiges of heathen ideas are also found in their songs and liturgical formulæ. This rite, however, has received a Christian colouring in the vision of the 'golden Christ,' who appears out of the steam above the vessel.

The attribution of sexual excesses and sacrificial rites to the Men of God appears, according to the Russian official reports themselves, to be utterly slanderous and merely a device of the State Church to combat the sect, and brand as hypocritical an asceticism which is more strenuous than her own.

Our earliest sources of information regarding the sect, which they call 'Christovshtchina,' are Yevrosin (who wrote in 1691), Dimitri, bishop of Rostov (who wrote between 1702 and 1709), and Theophylact Lopatinski (1745), and further information is found in the reports of two trials of Khlysti held at Moscow between 1733–39 and 1745–57. The first shows the sect reckoning its adherents for the most part in the Moscow monasteries, among monks and nuns and peasants connected with the monasteries; it also comprised some tradespeople. In the monasteries it seems to have marked a reaction against deeply-rooted immorality. It also spread beyond Moscow, to the district of Moscow itself, to Yaroslav and Uglitch, and to the town of Venyov, south of Moscow. In the first trial Prokofi Lupkin, a soldier of the bodyguard (*streletz*), appears as 'Christ,' his wife, Akulina Ivanovna, and the nuns Nastasya and Marfa (who were both finally beheaded in Petrograd) as 'Mothers of God.' Altogether more than 300 persons were condemned.

According to the reports of the second trial, the sect had considerably diminished in the Moscow monasteries, but, on the other hand, had spread much more widely among the peasant population as far as Petrograd and in the government districts of Vladimir and Nijni-Novgorod, while, at the same time, Moscow maintained its central position as the head-quarters of the sect.

Moscow was the scene of operations of the 'Christs' Serge Osipov, Vasili Stepanov, and, more famous than these, Andreyan Petrov, who, known as the 'Happy Idiot,' had the entrée to the houses of the aristocracy, and carried on his propaganda there for the sect not entirely without success. The communities of Khlysti in other places also possessed 'Christs' and 'Mothers of God.'

Lupkin and Petrov belong to the seven 'Christs' named by the legend which describes the origin of the Men of God (as the seventh they reckon Selivanov, the founder of the Skoptzy sect, which split off from the Khlystovshtchina in 1772). Since the reports of the trials prove the correctness of the assertions of their tradition regarding the seven 'Christs' and the 'Mothers of God' Akulina and Nastasya, the tradition may be trusted as to what it relates concerning the earlier 'Christs' Danila Philipov and Ivan Suslov. Of these the first is said to have also ranked as 'God Zebaoth' and to have founded the sect about the middle of the 17th cent. in the government district of Kostroma, while the second, as his disciple, spread it in the Oka and Volga districts and introduced it into Moscow. The evidence of Dimitri and Theophylact as to the founder of the Khlystovshtchina applies to Suslov; but ancient songs of the Khlysti speak of one 'Christ,' Averyan, who lived in the 14th cent., and of another, Yemelyan, who laboured in Moscow in the time of Ivan the Terrible. The majority of Russian scholars consider the sect much older than historical information reaches. Although the attempt to derive it from the heathenism of the Slavs and Finns must be pronounced unfortunate, owing to the decidedly Christian character of the sect, the suggestion which derives it from the Bogomils (*q.v.*) seems extremely credible; but, on the other hand, the Khlysti are entirely devoid of a trace of the Bogomilian cosmology, and they suggest rather the Messalians or Euchites (*q.v.*).

In the 19th cent. Kostroma and Moscow maintained their central importance in an ideal sense as places hallowed by tradition, especially in consequence of the intense activity of the 'Mother of God,' Ulyana Vasilyevna. The actual centre, however, was shifted in the middle of the century south-eastward into the government districts of Nijni-Novgorod, Samara, and Tambov, through the activity of Radayev and the 'Christs' Vasili Shtsheglov and Avvakum Kopylov. The former, with his peculiar mystical teaching, and like some later 'Christs,' takes a special place among the Khlystovshtchina inasmuch as, by appealing to the trance-producing spirit, he caused asceticism to fall into abeyance, and shamefully abused the devotion of his female followers. On the other hand, Vasili Shtsheglov and the 'Christs' resembling him have no immoral rites ascribed to them, but merely unchastity.

In the further course of the century the centre of the sect was pushed still further southward into the Caucasus territory, especially through the conspicuous energy of Kopylov's pupil, Perphil Katasonov. He and his followers again took the title 'God Zebaoth,' and ruled not only all the communities of the Caucasus, where the Khlysti, under their new name 'Shaloputy' ('eccentrics'), lead a considerably harassed existence, but also those of Southern Russia upwards to Smolensk, each of which has its own 'Christ.' Many Khlysti communities honour as a Christ the orthodox 'Father John of Kronstadt,' famous through Russia for his faith-healing.

The Khlysti communities are not large, since they depend for their increase, as they must, on account of their sexual abstinence, almost entirely on proselytism. Although they are now generally to be found everywhere in the Russian Empire where there are Russian peasantry, their total number, which can be only approximately reckoned, cannot exceed 200,000. Their significance for the national life, however, is, on account of their sober, industrious mode of life, far greater than this number would lead one to suppose. This article, the attitude of which is very different from that of Russian scholars, is based upon the writer's book, *Die russischen Sekten*, i. (Leipzig, 1907), which, besides the Khlysti, deals with such sects as the Skakuny, Malyovantzy, and Paniyashkovtzy, all of which are dependents of the different bodies of the Khlystovshtchina. The latter have assumed special forms as they passed from the sphere of influence of the Greek Orthodox Church to that of the Lutherans, the Stundists, and the Molokani ('Milk-drinkers'). Among the Lutheran Finns of Ingermannland the sectaries are called Skakuny ('Hoppers'). Kondrati Malyovanny founded a sect intermediate between the Khlystovshtchina and Stundism in Tarashtcha in the government district of Kieff about 1890, and his teaching caused an epidemic of trance-phenomena. The Molokani-Khlysti are called Pryguny ('Jumpers'). There were, and still are, numerous other bodies which, on account of some peculiarity, split off from the sect. Although the 'Worshippers of Napoleon,' who used to revere him as a 'Christ,' seem to have died out, the Adamites, who seek to get rid of modesty as a relic of the Fall, and, therefore, go naked at divine service and in their houses, still exist to-day. The sect of the Paniyashka regard the body as not only sinful but directly possessed by the devil, and intensify their asceticism accordingly.

LITERATURE.—The most important Russian works on the sect are: I. Dobrotvorski, *Lyudi bozhii: Russkaya sekta tak nazyvayemych duchovnych christian* ('The Men of God: the Russian Sect of the so-called spiritual Christians'), Kasan, 1869; fragments of this have been translated into German by A. Pfizmaier in *SWAW* civ. [1883] and *DWAW* xxxiv. [1884] and xxxv. [1885]; N. Reutski, *Lyudi Bozhii i Skoptzy* ('The Men of God and Skoptzis'), Moscow, 1872; K. Kutečov, *Sekty Khlystov i Skoptzov* ('The Sects of the Khlysti and Skoptzis'), Kasan, 1882, [2]Stavropol, 1900; A. Rozhdestvenski, *Khlystovshtchina i Skoptzshestvo v Rossii* ('Khlystovshtchina and Skoptzism in Russia'), Moscow, 1883. There are also numerous articles in newspapers.

K. GRASS.

MENCIUS.—**1. Life.**—Mencius, or Meng-tse (371–288 B.C.), second only to Confucius in the annals of orthodox Chinese philosophy, was born in Tsou of a family whose ancestral home was in Lu, the native State of Confucius. While still very young, he lost his father; he was educated by his mother, who is famous among the women of China for the care with which she brought up her son. Nothing is known of his other preceptors, except that they were of the school of Confucius, whom Mencius regarded as supreme among men, and proposed to himself as example (*Mencius*, II. i. 2, IV. ii. 22). When we get certain knowledge of him, he is a person already well known and accompanied by disciples, moving from one State to another according as the reception of himself and his doctrines was favourable or otherwise, accepting such gifts as he deemed consistent with his self-respect, and devoting himself to the exposition of his views on ethics and politics. This he did with acumen and considerable liveliness, frequently using illustrations, some of which are famous.

From the man of Sung, who assisted his corn to grow long by pulling it up, we are to learn the need of patience in the development of character (II. i. 2). The moral absurdity of not putting an immediate end to unrighteous practices is illustrated by the man who stole his neighbour's fowls, and who replied to one who remonstrated with him, 'I will diminish my appropriations, taking only one fowl a month till next year, and then I will make an end of the practice' (III. ii. 8). The Niu mountain, whose natural vegetation is destroyed by axes and bills and the browsing of cattle, is a figure of human nature, which, through the occurrences of daily life, loses its native goodness and cannot regain it during the brief respite of the night or the calm of dawn (VI. i. 8).

In addressing himself to the princes and governors of his time, Mencius may sometimes have been guilty of undue compliance with the faulty dispositions of those with whom he dealt (I. ii. 5); if so, it was from no unworthy motive, but only to secure the more ready acceptance of his teaching. For the most part he spoke his mind with an admirable freedom, not overawed by 'the pomp and display' of the great (VII. ii. 34), but acting according to his own teaching that respect is best shown by giving righteous counsel (II. ii. 2). Mencius is quite conscious of his own worth. He alone in his age could bring tranquillity and good order to the empire (II. ii. 13). His words will not be altered by any future sage (III. ii. 9). He has, accordingly, a keen sense of the respect due to him (II. ii. 11, IV. i. 24), though he occasionally employs unworthy shifts to maintain his dignity (II. ii. 2). Looking on himself as the continuer of the Confucian teaching (VII. ii. 38), he regarded it as an urgent duty to oppose the teachings of Yang and Mo (III. ii. 9). This he did with vigour and acuteness, while always willing to receive repentant heretics without reproaches, not tying up the leg of a pig which had already been got back into the pen (VII. ii. 26). The last twenty years of his life Mencius spent in Lu, where, with the assistance of his disciples, he prepared that sole record of his teaching which is called by his name and now forms one of those standard writings known as *The Four Books*.

2. Ethics.—Mencius's view of human nature is fundamental. Man's nature is good in the sense that 'from the feelings proper to it it is constituted for the practice of what is good' (VI. i. 6). The four cardinal virtues—benevolence, righteousness, propriety, knowledge—are not infused into man from without, but have their rise from the feelings of commiseration, of shame and dislike, of modesty and compliance (reverence and respect [VI. i. 6]), of approving and disapproving (II. i. 6). These four principles are accepted as psychological facts not reducible, *e.g.*, to any form of self-interest (II. i. 6). All that is needed for perfect virtue, in which a man becomes possessor of himself (III. i. 4), is that these innate principles be developed (II. i. 6, VII. i. 15; cf. also 'All things are already complete in us' [VII. i. 4]); and for this human nature is self-sufficient; failure arises not from lack of ability, but simply from not making the necessary effort (I. i. 7, IV. i. 10). From another point of view Mencius analyses human nature into *chih* ('mind,' 'will,' νοῦς) and *ch'i* ('passion-nature,' ψυχή). The former is supreme, but the latter is not to be violently suppressed, but developed in accordance with righteousness. Otherwise one's nature suffers defeat—as it also suffers defeat through action in which the mind feels no complacency. The mating of the passion-nature with righteousness is to be accomplished only by persistent practice of righteousness; but, given a mind set on righteousness, this result necessarily follows (II. i. 2). The violent suppression of the passion-nature, by which the integrity of a man's being is impaired, must be distinguished from the abscission of desires in an ethical interest (VII. ii. 35). Mencius, in basing his ethics on human nature, appears to have been not unaware of the ambiguity of the term 'nature.' Such seems to be the drift of a Socratic argument in which he maintains that 'the nature is not to be confounded with the phenomena of life' (VI. i. 3 [Legge's tr.]). Elsewhere he points out that there are desires which are natural, but in connexion with them there is the appointment of heaven, and the superior man does not say of them, 'It is my nature.' There are also moral propensities which are the appointment of heaven, but which the superior man recognizes rather as natural (VII. ii. 24). In things equally natural there is a gradation of worth, which can be recognized by thinking (VI. i. 14 f.). Moreover, the sense of shame, which a man may not lack (VII. i. 6 f.), is indicative of his having a moral constitution, which alone is properly his nature. In the possession of this nature, good in its composition, all men are alike, evidence of this being found in the fact that, as in matters of physical taste, music, and beauty there are common standards, so also is it in morals (VI. i. 7). This originally good nature is the child heart (IV. ii. 12), which differentiates man from the lower animals (IV. ii. 19); and in possessing it the ordinary man is of one kind with the sages (II. i. 2, III. i. 1), who simply have apprehended before me what my mind also approves (VI. i. 7). The sages, however, are spontaneously what other men attain to by effort (IV. ii. 19, VII. ii. 33), though they, too, learned from other men (II. i. 8). The great man is he who does not lose his child heart (IV. ii. 12); but for most men it is lost, and the grand aim of education is its recovery (VI. i. 11). Morality is the supreme task laid on each man (IV. i. 19), which requires unremitting diligence (VI. i. 9, VII. ii. 21). Nothing can be done with self-satisfied conformists to current standards, those 'thieves of virtue' (VII. ii. 37); for it is necessary that morality should criticize itself (VII. i. 5). The way to sage-like virtue begins in ordinary duties (VI. ii. 2), and the carrying out of principles already possessed by all (VII. ii. 31). Vigorous action according to the law of 'reciprocity' is the closest approximation to perfect virtue (VII. i. 4). It is also perhaps hinted that virtue is the mean between extremes (II. i. 9, IV. ii. 6 f., 10). For self-direction it is of the greatest importance 'to estimate the mind,' *i.e.*, to become acquainted with the real nature of one's motives (I. i. 7), and second thoughts are often best (IV. ii. 23). Life presents a series of alternatives of which the higher is, by reflexion, to be chosen in spite of the seductions and obscurations of sense (VI. i. 15). Righteousness is to be preferred before life itself (VI. i. 10). The righteous man is beyond the reach of calamity (IV. ii. 28, VII. i. 21). The only inevitable calamity is self-incurred (IV. i. 8). True greatness is to practise virtue for the sake of oneself and of others, superior to the seductions or threats of riches, honours, poverty, and force (III. ii. 2). To rejoice in virtue breeds unconscious grace of deportment, which is the perfection of music (IV. i. 27; cf. VII. i. 21). 'Benevolence, righteousness, self-consecration, fidelity, with unwearied joy in these virtues—these constitute the nobility of Heaven' (VI. i. 16). Realized virtue is sure of a transforming influence on others (IV. i. 12); failure to evoke a response should lead to self-examination (IV. i. 4). Virtue cannot be selfish; to find purity by withdrawing from all contact with evil one must become an earthworm (III. ii. 10). Each man is responsible to the extent of his moral attainment for the instruction of others (V. i. 7), and to instruct others is the greatest fidelity (II. i. 8, III. i. 4), while neglect of this duty degrades the virtuous to the level of those whom they should teach (IV. ii. 7). Of the special virtues, filial piety is the only one that is referred to in any detail. Mencius quotes the definition of it as serving one's parents with propriety, burying them with propriety, and sacrificing to them with propriety (III. i. 2). The service of parents is the greatest of all services and the root of all others; it has regard not only to physical sustenance, but to the wishes of the parents (IV. i. 19); and it takes unquestioned precedence of duties to wife or children (IV. ii. 30). Filial piety completes itself in the funeral rites (IV. ii. 13); and, in view of the importance of sacrifice to ancestors, lack of posterity is the gravest instance of unfilial conduct (IV. i. 26).

3. **Politics.**—Mencius has no scheme of social reconstruction. Existing social usages (*e.g.*, concubinage) and the existing political arrangement—an empire consisting of small States, each with its own king, but owning the supremacy of one State whose ruler is emperor—all this Mencius simply accepts. What he is concerned with is the rectification of moral relations within this existent social framework. He follows the current analysis into the five relations of father and son, sovereign and minister, husband and wife, old and young, friend and friend; and desires the cultivation of the corresponding virtues, affection, righteousness, harmony in difference, order, fidelity (III. i. 4). Of these relations that male and female should dwell together is the greatest (V. i. 2); and within the family we have in service of parents and obedience to elder brothers the fundamental exemplifications of benevolence and righteousness (IV. i. 27, VII. i. 15). Mencius opposes any such obliteration of natural relations as he finds in Mo's doctrine of universal love. Men have 'a root,' *i.e.*, they have a special relation to their parents and therefore a special duty corresponding thereto (III. i. 5). So, too, Mencius opposes all pantisocratic schemes, and teaches that society implies a differentiation of function in which those who labour with the mind govern, and those who labour with their strength are governed (III. i. 4), and in which the teacher of righteousness has his due place (III. ii. 4). In Mencius's doctrine of the State two points are to be noted especially: the emphasis on morality and the democratic bias. Rule is based not on force, but on willing submission accorded to virtue (II. i. 3, IV. ii. 16). If the ruler be virtuous, his influence will extend to all his subjects (IV. i. 20, ii. 5). There is no secret of statecraft—it needs only that the ruler give scope to the innate goodness of his nature (I. i. 7, II. i. 6). Let him dismiss all talk of 'profit,' and think only of benevolence and righteousness (I. i. 1). In the disordered times of Mencius such a benevolent government, having regard for the people's welfare (IV. i. 3, 9), would be immediately successful (II. i. 1). The truly benevolent ruler has no enemy within the empire (VII. ii. 4). Rulers are the shepherds and parents of their people (I. i. 4, 6), and must make it their first business to see that they (the people) have a certain livelihood, for without that they will abandon themselves to crime (I. i. 7). Mencius is very emphatic on the necessary precedence of a sound economic condition.

> 'When pulse and grain are as abundant as fire and water, how shall the people be other than virtuous?' (VII. i. 23).

Agriculture, therefore, and then education are prime interests of State (III. i. 3). The strength of a kingdom is in its morale (I. i. 5, IV. i. 1). Destruction is only self-incurred (IV. i. 8). A wise prince will be guided by his ministers (I. ii. 9), but he is himself ultimately responsible for the government of his State (I. ii. 6); he must treat his ministers with respect (II. ii. 2), regarding them as his hands and feet, and they will then regard him as their belly and heart (IV. ii. 3). In the appointment of ministers members of old established families are to be preferred, an ancient kingdom being one in which there are families with this tradition of service (I. ii. 7). Indeed, the art of governing lies in securing the approbation of these great families (IV. i. 6). New men, however, are not to be excluded (I. ii. 7); only the ruler must seek those by whom he may be taught (II. ii. 2). The love of what is good is the main qualification for being a minister, since those who have good thoughts will gladly lay them before him (VI. ii. 13). Let the ruler be guided in the appointment and dismissal of ministers by the voice of the people (I. ii. 7). In a State the people are the most important element; the spirits of the land and grain are the next; and the sovereign is the lightest. Therefore to gain the peasantry is the way to become emperor (VII. ii. 14). The voice of the people is determinative of the sovereignty in a kingdom (I. ii. 10), and in accordance with it a prince may rebel even against the emperor (I. ii. 3). For a sovereign forfeits his rights by wickedness and becomes a 'mere fellow' (I. ii. 8), and, if not removed by the members of the royal house (V. ii. 9) or other ministers (VII. i. 31), he may be removed by the leader of a righteous rebellion. He who takes on him this duty of removing his sovereign must be sure that he is 'the minister of heaven' (II. i. 5, ii. 8). He who is such is marked out by the appointment of heaven showing its will by his personal action and his conduct of affairs, which are such as to win universal submission.

> 'Heaven sees according as my people see; heaven hears according as my people hear' (V. i. 5).

All wars of ambition are condemned (IV. i. 14, VII. ii. 2), and ministers who encourage the ambitions of their prince are 'robbers of the people' (VI. ii. 9). If right government prevails in the empire, the princes of the feudatory States will be submissive one to another in proportion to their virtue, and not in proportion to their strength (IV. i. 7). As for the details of a truly benevolent government, 'never has any one fallen into error who followed the laws of the ancient kings' (IV. i. 1), whence sovereigns should imitate Yao, and ministers Shun (IV. i. 2, VI. ii. 10).

4. **Religion.**—References in the writings of Mencius to religious worship are merely incidental, and show that he accepted without criticism such worship of spirits and of ancestors as was then current. Of more interest are his references to heaven. He quotes, with approval, from the *Shu King*, or *Book*

of History, the saying that heaven, having produced the inferior people, appointed for them rulers and teachers to be assisting to God (I. ii. 3). As heaven protects all, so, in glad imitation, should the ruler of a great State protect a small State, while the ruler of a small State should recognize the decree of heaven and be willing to serve the great State (I. ii. 3). Such obedience to heaven ensures preservation, while disobedience entails destruction (IV. i. 7). So, generally, 'calamity and happiness are men's own seeking' (II. i. 4), although heaven's decree and man's causality are both recognized:

'That which happens without a man's causing it is from the ordinance of heaven' (V. i. 6).

There is a decree for everything, and a man should receive submissively what can be correctly ascribed thereto; but he who understands what is meant will not stand under a precipitous wall, nor can death under fetters be justly ascribed to heaven's decree, though death in the discharge of duty may be so attributed (VII. i. 2). Man's duty, therefore, is to do the right and leave the issues to heaven (I. ii. 14, VII. i. 1), which in its painful discipline of individuals has moral ends in view (VI. ii. 15, VII. i. 18). From man's nature we can know heaven; and to preserve one's mental constitution and nourish one's nature is the way to serve heaven (VII. i. 1). To have no shame before heaven is one of the things in which the superior man delights (VII. i. 20). Heaven is the realized ideal after which man aspires (IV. i. 12). Specially suggestive is this saying:

'Though a man may be wicked, yet if he adjust his thoughts, fast, and bathe, he may sacrifice to Shang-ti' (IV. ii. 25; for the full connotation of Shang-ti see art. GOD [Chinese]).

5. In conclusion a few miscellaneous points may be noted. Mencius indicates the correct method for understanding Nature by obedience and not by violence in the investigation of her phenomena (IV. ii. 26). He gives us a good canon of interpretation:

'Those who explain the Odes [*i.e.* the classical *Shi King*] may not insist on one term so as to do violence to a sentence, nor on a sentence so as to do violence to the general scope' (V. i. 4).

To this may be added his comment on the *Book of History*, which may perhaps be generalized:

'It would be better to be without the Book of History than to give entire credit to it' (VII. ii. 3).

LITERATURE.—J. Legge, *The Chinese Classics*, Hongkong and London, 1861-73, ii. The prolegomena and translation, without the Chinese text, are published separately, *The Life and Works of Mencius*, London, 1875. See also E. Faber, *The Mind of Mencius*, tr. A. B. Hutchinson, London, 1882.

P. J. MACLAGAN.

MENDELSSOHN.—Moses Mendelssohn, otherwise Rabbi Moses of Dessau, philosopher, writer, and Bible translator, was born 6th Sept. 1729 at Dessau, where his father, Mendel, was a poor scribe and teacher in a family descended from Rabbi Moses Isserles, a distinguished Talmudist and philosopher of the 16th cent., known as 'Rema.' Moses Mendelssohn was taught Rabbinics by the local Rabbi, David Fränkel, who published a commentary on the Palestinian Talmud in 1742. Fränkel was called to the Rabbinate of Berlin in that year, and the young student followed him there in 1743.

At Berlin Mendelssohn was taught French and English by A. S. Gumperz, and taught himself Latin and Greek. His taste for philosophy was inspired by the study of Maimonides' 'Guide of the Perplexed.' He earned a precarious livelihood as tutor in the home of a well-to-do Jewish silk merchant, Isaac Bernhard, in whose warehouse he afterwards, and throughout his life, was employed as book-keeper. His evenings and all his leisure he devoted to philosophy. He was a follower of Wolf and Leibniz, but was much influenced by the English School of empirics, especially Locke and Shaftesbury. His acquaintance with Lessing, who was also born in 1729, began in 1754, when he defended Lessing's drama *Die Juden* against adverse criticism. Lessing became his lifelong friend, and dubbed him the second Spinoza. It was Lessing who had Mendelssohn's first work printed —the *Philosophische Gespräche* (1755). In 1755 they collaborated in an anonymous and piquant attack on the Berlin Academy—*Pope ein Metaphysiker!*, and the next year Mendelssohn translated Rousseau's *Discours sur l'origine . . . de l'inégalité parmi les hommes*, though he ridiculed the author's partiality for man in a state of nature. Though M. Steinschneider (*Cat. libr. Hebr. in Bibl. Bodleiana*, Berlin, 1852-60) enumerates 39 separate Hebrew works of his, and though he wrote Hebrew poetry when a child of ten, it is as a writer of classical German that Mendelssohn became famous. His essay on æsthetics, *Vom Erhabenen* (1757), was studied by Schiller and Herder. In admiration, rather than in Lessing's pity and terror, he found the moral object of Tragedy. The stories about his friendship with Frederick the Great are legendary. On the contrary, he criticized the king's *Poésies diverses* in 1760, and found fault with him for writing in French. The royal displeasure was so great that he was threatened with expulsion from Berlin, but the Marquis d'Argens intervened, and as a 'philosophe mauvais catholique' pleaded with his Majesty as a 'philosophe mauvais protestant' to grant to the 'philosophe mauvais juif' the privilege of residence.

In 1763 Mendelssohn was awarded by the Berlin Academy a prize of 50 ducats for his essay *Ueber die Evidenz der metaphysischen Wissenschaften.* In 1771 the Academy elected him a member, but Frederick the Great refused to confirm the appointment, and no protest, not even that of Queen Ulrica of Sweden, was of any avail to get the king to alter his decision with regard to the 'berühmter Jude.' Among his own brethren, and especially in Berlin, Mendelssohn enjoyed the highest esteem. In 1764 he was freed from Jewish communal dues, and in 1772 further honour was shown to him by his co-religionists.

His Socratic Dialogue called *Phaedon, oder über die Unsterblichkeit der Seele* was published in 1767, and created an immense sensation. It was translated into nearly all European languages. A Hebrew translation by I. B. Bing, with a preface by N. H. Wessely, appeared in 1787, and an English translation by C. Cullen in 1792. That work showed a notable reaction against the free thought of Voltaire, and was welcomed by the learned as well as by those in high places, from Winckelmann to Prince Carl of Brunswick. It was the first book of philosophy read and discussed by Goethe and later by Schiller, and dissuaded from suicide many disappointed or degenerates. Mendelssohn rapidly acquired a unique position among the intellectuals of Berlin. His chief friends, besides Lessing, were Hamann, Gleim, Wieland, and Herder, and the Swiss writers Zimmermann, Iselin, Gessner, and Lavater.

The last was the famous physiognomist, immortalized by Darwin; but it was in his capacity as a very zealous pastor that he caused the Jewish philosopher much trouble and annoyance. He publicly dedicated his translation of C. Bonnet's *Palingénésie philosophique* (1769) to Mendelssohn, and urged him to abandon Judaism and become a Christian. The Jew, having obtained the sanction of the 'Consistorium zur Censur,' replied in his *Schreiben an den Herrn Diakonus Lavater zu Zürich* (1770), manfully defending his position. It was not only yesterday that he had examined the evidences of his own religion. What but conviction would induce him to remain a persecuted Jew? He would never change his religion.

This reply produced a storm of protest. J. B. Kolbele in his *Antiphädon* (1770) was among those who heaped invective upon him in various pamphlets, of which his best biographer, M. Kayserling, gives a full list. Next year an anonymous *Pro-memoria* appeared in his defence.

The attack, though it injured his health, turned his thoughts to Judaism and the Jews. As early as 1761 he had prepared a Hebrew Commentary on the Logic of Maimonides, and had presented the MS to one Samson Kalin, who published it as his own.

Perhaps his most important work, so far as his influence on his co-religionists was concerned, was his translation of the Pentateuch into classical German with a *bîûr*, or commentary, in Hebrew. His first assistant was Solomon Dubno († 1813), who quarrelled with Mendelssohn in 1780. Mendelssohn's brother Saul took Dubno's place in the translation of Exodus, but Hartwig Wessely, a scholar born rich, but afterwards impoverished, later became his chief collaborator. This translation of the Pentateuch met with much opposition from the orthodox Rabbis Landau, Jacob Lissa, Elijah Wilna, and Hirschel Levin (formerly chief Rabbi of London and then of Berlin) because of what they thought a heretical mistranslation in Lv 19^{17}, where 'thou shalt rebuke thy neighbour' was toned down to 'canst'; but the storm of opposition ceased, largely through the aid of Italian Rabbis, who, though orthodox, were also enlightened.

Mendelssohn's translation of the Psalms, which had been begun before 1770, was not completed for thirteen years. During this period the translator took up the work only spasmodically and just when some particular Psalm suited his mood of the moment. It was intended for Christian rather than for Jewish readers, and it was first printed in German characters, not Hebrew. The publisher Maurer bought the MS for 500 thalers and published it in 1783, but lost money by the publication; next year it was published in Hebrew characters with a *bîûr* by one Joel Löwe. The Song of Deborah and the Song of Songs were the other Bible translations completed by Mendelssohn. His commentary on Ecclesiastes he had published anonymously in 1769. It was clear and sympathetic, but, though greatly admired by Herder, is notable chiefly for a novel division into sections, differing from the traditional chapters. Mendelssohn was a keen opponent of the higher criticism of those days, and scouted Bishop Benjamin Kennicott's textual alterations of the Bible. One immediate result of the translation was a change in the course of education of Jewish boys, and the inculcation of German rather than Jewish ideas. Part of the Jewish Liturgy was also translated by him, viz. the Haggādā, a Passover service—a fact which seems to have escaped the notice of bibliographers.

In 1776 Mendelssohn collected money—and students—for the unsectarian college 'Philanthropin' of Dessau. In 1781 he and his rich disciple, Isaac Daniel Itzig, founded the Jewish Free school in Berlin, the first institution of the kind, where not only Bible and Talmud, but also German, French, and sciences were taught by Jewish and Christian teachers. Similar institutions were afterwards founded on the same plan in Breslau and other cities.

After his wife's death, Lessing had to battle for tolerance in his *Anti-Goeze*, and conceived the idea of meeting the theologians with a comedy. This was the orgin of his famous drama *Nathan der Weise*, which appeared in 1779, and which was in some respects a development of his youthful production *Die Juden*. Lessing himself founds the play on the story of the Jew Melchizedek in Boccaccio's *Decameron*. About no German work except Goethe's *Faust* has so much been written. Nathan is Mendelssohn, Recha his daughter Dorothea, the templar Lessing, the Swiss widow Daja is intended for Lavater, the dervish is Mendelssohn's mathematical friend Abraham Wolf Rechenburg, and so on. The play itself is not a plea for Jews and Judaism, but for toleration and humanity, and an attack upon religious persecution of all kinds. In Vienna it was confiscated. The controversy engendered by *Nathan der Weise* led to a plea for the civil emancipation of the Jews by C. W. von Dohm (*Über die bürgerliche Verbesserung der Juden*, Berlin, 1781), translated into French by Mirabeau (London, 1787). Six hundred copies of this translation were forwarded to Paris for the use of the French States General, but lost in that troublous time, and eventually burnt in the Bastille. In 1782 Mendelssohn published a translation of Manasseh ben Israel's *Esperança de Israel* (Amsterdam, 1650), with an introduction pleading for emancipation. He was again reproached for remaining a Jew, or for being a 'wobbler' between Judaism and Christianity, and this induced him to write his *Jerusalem* (1783), a work on religious power and Judaism. In this book, translated into English in 1783, he vindicated his Judaism and explained why he was not a Christian. It is a plea for the separation of State and Church, and urges that 'Kirchenrecht' is incompatible with true religion. Judaism, he urged, has no dogmas or chains upon belief; Joseph Albo († 1444), who had reduced the thirteen creeds formulated by Maimonides to three (cf. *ERE* iv. 246[a]), was no heretic. Judaism required conformity with ceremonial law, but tolerated complete liberty of opinion.

In a Reader for his children, Mendelssohn substitutes in the creeds the words 'I recognize as true and certain' for the words 'I believe.' Ceremonial laws he regarded as a sort of living scripture and the great bond between Jew and Jew, urging that, even if their utility were no longer clear, they were still binding. Actions are our duty, but creeds, symbols, and formulas are the fetters of reason. In this way he reconciled the deism of Leibniz and the English deists with revealed law. His *Jerusalem* and his unfinished *Betrachtungen über Bonnet's Palingenesie* are both pleas for toleration, but not for uniformity of belief. In both he warns his disciples against prejudice, superstition, and even enthusiasm. *Jerusalem* excited an enormous sensation. Kant said that it was incontrovertible, and wrote a highly appreciative letter about it; Mirabeau said that it ought to be translated into every European language; Michaelis found fault with its condemnation of Anglican bishops for consenting to sign the Thirty-nine Articles, and Mendelssohn had to explain his position in the *Berliner Monatsschrift*, of which he was one of the founders in 1783. By some contemporaries he was attacked as an atheist and by others as a 'Talmud Rabbi,' but he saw no inconsistency between his philosophical belief and his faith. His Hebrew works are written entirely from the Rabbinical standpoint, and he was a good Talmudist, as is proved by his correspondence with Jacob Emden.

Mendelssohn's *Morgenstunden*, like his Bible translation, was in the first instance intended to lead his son Joseph to a true belief in God. Its publication, in 1785, was designed as a refutation of Spinozism itself as well as of the charge that Lessing was a Spinozist. In 1853 Alexander von Humboldt, in a letter to M. Mortara, described how, in his youth, he and Mendelssohn's sons had heard these very *Morgenstunden* given forth by the philosopher in his study. In the first part Mendelssohn proves the existence of God; the nature of the Divine Being and His characteristics were to be treated in the second part. Its philosophy is an attempt to advance upon the sensualism of Wolf by the help of English empiricism. He claimed that human common sense, when working hand in hand with reason, was infallible.

Though self-taught, Mendelssohn was neither a dilettante nor a popular philosopher. Hegel depreciates him as a philosopher, but, as a writer of German, his style furnishes the best example of German prose after Goethe and perhaps Lessing. Its characteristic was its Socratic irony. A predecessor of Kant, his writings are far easier to understand. Kant himself was proud that the Jewish scholar had attended one of his lectures, and was always polite to him, though he expressed disappointment that Mendelssohn had not reviewed his *Kritik der reinen Vernunft*, when it appeared in 1784. Simultaneously with the publication of the *Morgenstunden* appeared F. H. Jacobi's treatise *Ueber die Lehre des Spinoza an den Herrn Moses Mendelssohn*. Lavater had rebuked him for not being a Christian; Jacobi now charged him with atheism. He was profoundly disturbed by what he considered a cruel attack, and retaliated with his address *An die Freunde Lessings*. He brought the manuscript to his publisher Voss on 31st Dec. 1785, and died two days later of a paralytic stroke. There is little doubt that Jacobi's attack, in which Lavater, Herder, and Goethe had all sided against the Jewish philosopher, brought about his end.

He left three sons and three daughters. His sons Joseph and Abraham founded the famous banking house of Mendelssohn and Co., which still exists. The former in 1840 reviewed Rossetti's *Dante*. The great musician Felix Mendelssohn was Abraham's son; another grandson, G. B. Mendelssohn, edited the philosopher's complete works in 1843–45.

Mendelssohn's first biographer, his pupil I. A. Euchel, described him as short and broad-shouldered, but feeble and pigeon-breasted, with thick black hair, dark complexion, bright eyes, and high forehead, a voice soft and gentle, and in conversation crisp and persuasive, but never long-winded (*Tôlᵉdhôth Rambamân*, Berlin, 1786).

There is much difference of opinion among Jews as to whether his influence has been beneficial to them or not. The general view seems to be that it has proved better for Jews than for Judaism. His chief opponents were the 19th cent. Russian intellectuals known as the Maskhîlîm, especially Perez Smolenskin, who denounced him for denying Jewish nationalism, belittled his knowledge of the wisdom of Israel, and characterized him as a merchant rather than a Rabbi. Yet without doubt he was the first and most typical of modern Jews, the first to identify himself with another nation and yet remain a Jew.

'Judaism, which hitherto had impressed the whole mental activity of the Jew,' says Segal in *Aspects of Hebrew Genius* (p. 183), 'was narrowed down by Mendelssohn into a mere religion. . . . He separated the man from the Jew. . . . To Mendelssohn's followers such a dual life became difficult. . . . Traditional Judaism did not easily lend itself to be compressed and squeezed. . . . Mendelssohn's followers experienced the conflict between Judaism and Germanism at every step. . . . They threw off the burden of Judaism. . . . But . . . the period of the great apostasy . . . was followed by a period of religious reform and the readjustment of Judaism to the new conditions of Jewish existence.'

Jewish nationalists of the present time, not quite fairly, regard Mendelssohn as the chief cause of the desire for assimilation felt by a small section of their co-religionists. Mendelssohn was an apologist for religion in general rather than for Judaism in particular. That was his chief merit in a Voltairean age and in sceptical Berlin. The finest epigram about him, and one which he himself would have appreciated, is the distich,

'Es ist ein Gott, das sagte Moses schon,
Doch den Beweis gab Moses Mendelssohn.'

LITERATURE.—M. Kayserling, *Moses Mendelssohn*, Leipzig, 1862, ²1888, is the standard biography; H. G. R. Mirabeau, *Sur Moses Mendelssohn, sur la réforme politique des Juifs et en particulier sur la révolution tentée en leur faveur en 1753 dans la Grande Bretagne*, London, 1787; M. Samuels, *Memoirs of Moses Mendelssohn*², do. 1827; M. Schwab, *Moses Mendelsohn: sa vie et ses œuvres*, Paris, 1868; M. Kayserling, *Moses Mendelssohn; Ungedrucktes und Unbekanntes*, Leipzig, 1883; E. Schreiber, *Moses Mendelssohn und seine Verdienste um das Judenthum*, Bonn, 1879; *REJ*, *passim*; M. Tuzber, *Ṣidqath Môsheh*, Hebrew Manuscript (MS Adler no. 162); A. S. Isaacs, *Step by Step*, Philadelphia, 1910.
E. N. ADLER.

MENNONITES.—'Mennonites' is the name applied to those Protestant Christians who, on such subjects as the management of the congregation, baptism, oath-taking, ecclesiastical discipline, civil office, and the bearing of arms, agree wholly or partly with Menno Simons, from whom they derive their name.

1. Distribution.—The Mennonites have congregations in Switzerland (1500 souls), Germany (18,000), France (1200), Russia (70,000), the United States (about 120,000), and Canada (about 90,000); those in the Netherlands, though not the greatest in number (65,000), are the most important section.

(*a*) *Switzerland.*—Their true fatherland is Switzerland; they originated there in 1524, when Konrad Grebel and Felix Manz, members of the congregation of Zwingli, dissatisfied with their leader, condemned the baptism of infants as 'the greatest abomination of the devil and the Roman pope.' They founded a separate congregation in 1525 and baptized their members on confession of faith; a year afterwards they rejected the oath. It is possible, though not probable, that their opinions are connected with those of sects of the Middle Ages, especially the Waldenses. They wished to re-establish the Christianity of apostolic times and preserve only the two 'ceremonies' ordained by Christ; therefore they denied the Christian character of the civil authority, rejected paid ministry and the use of the sword, and demanded the exercise of the apostolic excommunication.

In the persecutions of the 16th cent. many of them died as martyrs or fled to South Germany, where they propagated their tenets. In the 17th cent. also the Mennonites in Switzerland were oppressed by the government; imprisonment and deportation to the Italian galleys greatly diminished their number. Again, at the beginning of the 18th cent., the persecution recommenced, and even in 1811 the Mennonites were molested. In the midst of these sufferings there arose differences between them: the more rigid—called 'Ammansche' or 'Amische' after their leader Jacob Amman—disapproved of every luxury, and demanded that in case of excommunication all intercourse, even between husband and wife, should be, during the period of excommunication, broken off; the less rigid followed Hans Reist; the names of these parties (also 'Obere Mennoniten' and 'Untere Mennoniten') are still preserved among the Mennonites of America.

At the present day the Mennonites in Switzerland are enjoying a new prosperity. They are now free citizens of the State, which allows them exemption from oath-taking and from military service. They have their own organ, *Der Zionspilger* ('The Pilgrim to Zion').

(*b*) *Germany.*—The Mennonites in Germany have continued to survive in spite of great difficulties and oppressions. In the year 1867 they were obliged to give up one of their characteristics, viz. their defencelessness. Many of them, however, agreed with the resolution of the government, and obtained permission from it to serve in the baggage-train of the army. Interest in their history has been aroused recently by the writings of L. Keller and Mrs. A. Brons; and, in 1884, in order to prevent the decline of their little number, the Mennonites founded the *Vereinigung der Mennonitengemeinden im deutschen Reiche* ('Union of the Congregations of Mennonites in the German Empire'). Their periodical, *Mennonitische Blätter*, has been issued since 1854.

They have congregations in Alsace, the Bavarian Palatinate, Baden, Würtemberg, Hesse, Nassau, at the lower part of the Rhine, in Westphalia, East Friesland, at Hamburg, Friedrichstadt, and in West and East Prussia.

(*c*) *France*.—In France the Mennonites held their first conference at Toul in 1901; their paper, *Christ seul*, appeared in 1908.

(*d*) *Russia*.—An emigration of Mennonites to Russia took place when the celebrated empress Catharine had promised them great territories in her empire, where they would be permitted to live according to their own religion and customs. About 2000 left Prussia in 1788; and many others followed them until 1824. At first they suffered many trials, not the least of which were due to discord among themselves. As they persisted in their belief in apostolic succession, their congregation needed an elder who had received the imposition of hands. They prospered, however, in their new fatherland, which gave a shelter also to the fugitive Mennonites from Hungary. At present they have congregations in the districts of Jekaterinoslaw and Tauria, Warsaw, the Crimea, Saratow, Samara, Caucasus, and Chiwa. In their colonies the school management is excellently ordered, the church affairs are managed by the elders of the congregation, and the preachers, selected from among the brethren, fulfil not only the duties of their ministry, but also those of their civil calling.

In 1874 a great danger threatened the Mennonites: exemption from military service was abrogated, and thus the privilege conceded to them by the empress Catharine and the emperor Paul was annihilated. Large numbers of Mennonites prepared to quit Russia; in the years 1874–80 more than 15,000 left for America. This made an impression upon the Russian government; the emperor sent the minister, F. E. I. von Todtleben, to them; after mutual deliberation the resolution was made that the Mennonites could perform their military duties in the forestry of the State. This favourable arrangement has been maintained ever since; the Mennonites, however, according to their old traditions, have always sought to relieve the sufferings of war.

(*e*) *America*.—The Mennonites are far more numerous in America than in any other country. The first colonists were Dutchmen who, about 1650, settled in New Amsterdam (now New York). Under the pressure of the heavy persecutions in the Rhine-land, thirteen families at Crefeld resolved to emigrate to the New World. They landed on 6th October 1683, three pioneers having already bought 8000 acres of land in Pennsylvania from William Penn, and they founded Germantown (now part of Philadelphia). Seven other families followed in 1688; and from that time the emigration continued during the whole of the 18th cent. and still more during the 19th. In 1820 Swiss Mennonites came to America, followed in 1836 by many South Germans, and afterwards, as we have said, by whole congregations from Russia, besides one from Galicia and one from West Prussia.

The emigrants formed many friendly connexions with the Quakers and other sects, but they preserved their independence. They came with the hope of remaining free from all hindrances in following their own customs and institutions; some of them even entertained the desire to establish in the New World the true Kingdom of God according to His Ordinance. It was only after long deliberation that they dared to entrust the ministry of baptism and of the Lord's Supper to an elder who had not received the imposition of hands in Europe; and even now the most rigid of them will not permit their fellow-members to enter a 'church.'

The Mennonites have a great regard for their past history—and not unjustly. Their forefathers were the first to protest against slavery; they committed their scruples to writing on 18th April 1688, and delivered the document to the magistrate. In a manly and Christianlike spirit they declared: 'Freedom of conscience reigns here, which is right and rational, and personal freedom ought to reign here for every one, criminals of course excepted.' In the War of Independence their defencelessness was respected; nevertheless many emigrated in 1786 to Canada, as they could not approve of insurrection against the British government. Conservative in all things, they have not even yet, after two centuries, given up their old language, 'Pennsylvania Dutch.'

The Mennonites in America are divided into: (1) Old Mennonites, who form the great majority; their periodicals are the *Mennonitische Rundschau* and *The Herald of Truth* (the Germ. ed., *Herold der Wahrheit*, has ceased to appear since 1901—an evidence of the decline of the German language among them); (2) 'Amish' Mennonites; and (3) the 'General Conference.' Since 1860 the last-mentioned party has endeavoured to form an organization between all the Mennonites of America, respecting the autonomy and the peculiarities of each congregation. The foundation of Bethel College at Newton, Kans., was favoured by them.[1]

2. Characteristics.—Wherever Mennonites are found—in Switzerland or in Germany, in Russia or in France, in the United States or in Canada—they are known as excellent husbandmen, simple in their manners, blameless in their behaviour, honest, conscientious, and diligent, so that most of them are in easy circumstances. In consequence of their seclusion the civilization of later times has had little influence on them; they are very conservative and often suspicious of opinions which differ from their own. (An exception must be made in the case of the German Mennonites who live close to the frontiers of the Netherlands—East Friesland, Westphalia, and on the Rhine; they have been influenced by the Dutch Mennonites [see below].) They have remained where their forefathers stood three centuries ago; in order to understand their opinions, it is, therefore, necessary to consult the writings composed by their fellow-believers in the 16th and 17th centuries.

3. Religious beliefs.—The oldest defenders of baptism after confession of faith entertained a strong aversion to the papal hierarchy. They would not reform the Roman Catholic Church; they would destroy it by the foundation of separate and wholly autonomous congregations. The preachers were elected by the majority; there was no tie between the congregations except that of community of faith and of love. According to the example of the segregation of Israel, the people of the Lord, from the Gentiles, the congregation of Christ ought to be separated from the world; this was done by the external bond of laws and commandments that formed a sort of fence round the true believers. As the congregation of the Lord consists only of believing and regenerate children of the Lord, only those who are sufficiently advanced in years and experience, and, therefore,

[1] One of the most renowned professors of this college was C. H. Wedel, author of the *Abriss der Geschichte der Mennoniten*, Newton, 1900–04, who died in 1910.

able to believe, can be admitted into the congregation by baptism. Hence they highly valued baptism as a token of the confession of faith, but they did not acknowledge the baptism of children as a baptism; he who was baptized as an infant was not baptized at all. The name of Anabaptists (*q.v.*), therefore, was an undeserved nickname, given them by their enemies.

They sought to maintain the purity of the congregation by excommunication, and taught that true believers must avoid all intercourse with an excommunicated member. The charge has often been brought against them that, since they regard themselves as the perfect or holy congregation of the Lord, they do not admit that they are poor lost sinners. Their lives and their writings, however, contradict this accusation most positively. It is true that they separated themselves from all those who were of a different opinion, but it was from fear of seduction. By the simplicity of their manners and their dress they showed their rejection of the world. A wedding outside of the congregation was a 'worldly,' a sinful, wedding. They were strangers on the earth; therefore no interference with the powers of the world, no using of the sword, was permitted. The oath is forbidden, not only by the gospel (Mt 5^{34} and Ja 5^{12}), but also for conscience' sake, since in the spiritual Kingdom of God on earth the truth is the highest and the only law. By their sharp contrast between the world and the congregation—the natural and the spiritual—they insisted on the necessity of regeneration; but their doctrine on this subject is legal rather than evangelical in character. They teach that regeneration is an OT contrition, awakened in the soul by the threats and the promises of God, who moves us through these to avoid sin and to live according to His will. These threats and promises are written in His word; therefore it is the seed of regeneration. They meant in good faith to be orthodox, but their dislike of all scholastic terms and their desire to use only the phrases of the NT caused them, sometimes, to disagree with the faith of the Church; hence they refused to acknowledge the Holy Ghost as a person—they called Him a power of God—and yet they believed that they professed purely the doctrine of the Trinity. They rejected every dogma from which they feared damage to the practice of their piety, for the tenor of their religious life was above all things practical; hence they repudiated most positively the Calvinistic tenets of predestination, irresistible grace, and the perseverance of the saints. In the doctrine of the Lord's Supper they followed Zwingli; but, for them, it was more a token of mutual love and unity. They combined with it the rite of feet-washing.

Such were the tenets of the community with which Menno Simons (1496–1561) became connected in 1536. He had been a priest at Witmarsum in Friesland, but after a long inward struggle he left the Roman Catholic Church. From that time he defended in sermons, writings, and disputations the opinions of his fellow-believers so eagerly that they were called after him—Mennonites. They had already suffered heavy losses by persecutions; but they struggled bravely on; no torture—not even death at the stake—could terrify them. The congregation in Amsterdam was founded in 1530 by Jan Volkerts Trijpmaker, who died a martyr in 1531. In his preaching he always exhorted his followers to be peaceful and obedient to the magistrate, but Jan Matthijs, by his fanatical impetuosity, prepared the way for the notorious Jan Beukels of Leyden (John of Leyden), whose fatal doctrine was that the time of enduring oppression had passed away, that the sword must be drawn, and that the true believers were summoned to subjugate the kingdoms of the world, and especially Münster. The majority, however, disapproved of such violence; every day during the winter of 1534 the congregation of Amsterdam enrolled about one hundred additional members; and a party of forty insurgents, who on 10th May 1535 conquered the town-hall of that city, found no support. When the terrible tragedy of Münster had terminated, a separation took place throughout the Netherlands between the rebellious and the moderates—the latter party being called at first Obbenites and then Mennonites.

These increased greatly in spite of all obstacles, but their unity was soon broken by disagreement about the practice of excommunication. The more lenient Mennonites lived chiefly in Waterland (a part of North Holland); hence they were called Waterlanders. The more rigid were the Flemish and the Frisian Mennonites; but among those parties so many schisms have occurred that it is impossible to enumerate them all. Let it suffice to say that the Waterlanders formed the most tolerant and liberal party. They would not apply the epithet 'believing' or 'unbelieving' to any one on account of his particular opinions on articles of faith with which God in His word has not clearly connected salvation or condemnation. They even took an interest in the things of this world; *e.g.*, they supported with their money the great William of Orange in his efforts to liberate the Netherlands from the Spanish yoke. Afterwards many of them held magistracies, but the influence of the State Church has put an end to that.

The Mennonites exercised a remarkably attractive influence upon the Brownists who, from 1593, had settled in Amsterdam to evade the persecution in England (see art. BROWNISM). One of them, John Smyth, came to Holland in 1606; with his friend, Thomas Helwys, he forsook Brownism in 1608, administered baptism on confession of faith, and founded a separate congregation. A year afterwards he tried to amalgamate it with the Mennonites; in this his followers were successful (1615). Helwys, on the contrary, though he entertained friendly relations with the Mennonites, maintained his independence; he returned to England in 1611. His followers, influenced by Edward Barber (1641), came to the conclusion that only baptism by immersion was legal. Henceforth they called themselves Baptists, and broke off community of faith with the Mennonites.

In the 17th cent. Socinianism exercised such a great influence on the Mennonites that the Reformed theologian, J. Hoornbeek, could write: 'Anabaptista indoctus Socinianus, Socinianus autem doctus Anabaptista.' The more conservative desired to defend themselves against the intrusion of this dreaded heresy by maintaining the old confessions of faith—a dangerous measure, for these confessions had never had any binding authority. At last a great schism took place in 1664 between the liberal and the orthodox members ('Lamisten' and 'Zonisten'). With regard to the practice of Christian charity, however, the unity was not severed; the two parties worked together to relieve their suffering brethren in the Palatinate and elsewhere.

In the golden age of the Dutch Republic many of its poets and painters—among them probably the celebrated Rembrandt—were Mennonites. They formed more than one-tenth of the whole population, but as a rule neither the nobility nor the lower classes joined their ranks.

In the 18th cent. their number declined for many reasons. The lay-preachers, elected from among the brethren, no longer satisfied the congregations; consequently, a great number of families passed into the State Church. The foundation of a theological seminary in Amsterdam (1735) did not produce any lasting improvement. At many places, fortunately, the piety of the forefathers continued, and the spiritual well-being of the people and the spreading of a higher civilization were objects of great care. The *Teyler's Genootschap* ('Society of Teyler') and the *Maatschappij tot Nut van 't Algemeen* ('Society for the Promotion of the General Good')—two institutions that to this day do a large amount of useful work—were founded in 1778 and 1784 by Mennonites.

They fully agreed with the Revolution of 1795, for their old ideals appeared to them to be realized by it; they gladly supported it by many sacrifices, but their prosperity greatly declined in the hard times of Napoleon. To improve this state of things the *Algemeene Doopsgezinde Sociëteit* ('General Society of Mennonites') was founded at Amsterdam in 1811 by some wealthy congregations, and at present all the Mennonite congregations are members of it. This Society took upon itself the care of the theological seminary and the support of the indigent congregations. By its influence the desirable end was obtained that all the congregations, in the course of time, possessed only ministers who had received a university education. From that time their seclusion from the other Protestants ceased. In the theological sciences the Mennonites are diligent and able co-operators (*e.g.*, S. Hoekstra, J. G. de Hoop Scheffer, A. W. Wybrands, C. Sepp, S. Cramer). Often their ministers preach to congregations of another confession—in other words, they exchange pulpits. The professors of their seminary are also professors of theology at the university of Amsterdam.

Still the Mennonites have remained congregationalists; they are zealous for the entire independence of each congregation. Consequently, in the respective congregations there is some difference in the form of public worship—*e.g.*, in the use of psalters and hymn-books—and there is also a difference in the manuals used for religious teaching. Nevertheless, they are strongly attached to each other and to their community, and promote their common interests in fraternal unanimity. Their ministers are elected by the majority of the brethren (and often also of the sisters) or, in many congregations, by the church-committee. They are not ordained and wear no official dress, for they form no class and have no authority.

In regard to baptism and oath-taking the opinions of the Mennonites are unchanged. Self-reliance, evident in the voluntary act of becoming a member of the congregation, is still the condition of membership, so that they would rather abolish the whole rite of baptism than permit the baptism of infants. They have no confessions of faith and would not tolerate them. They dislike dogmatic speculations, and hold that the characteristic of a true believer is not his creed but his life. Hence, their toleration allows persons of very different opinions to live peacefully together in the same congregation. The majority of them are liberal; the more conservative profess a Biblical orthodoxy.

Their original tenets concerning ecclesiastical discipline, bearing of arms, and civil office are at present abolished. Considering that the Mennonites form little more than one-hundredth part of the population, it is a significant fact that an important number of ministers, representatives of the nation, burgomasters, etc., have for many years belonged to them. The connexion with the Mennonites of other countries is maintained chiefly by the means of the missionary society, which propagates the gospel in Java and Sumatra. The missionaries and the contributions come principally from their foreign brethren.

LITERATURE.—The literature concerning the Mennonites is very extensive, but there is no good history of them, based on the advanced science of our days. The most important works on the subject are the following:

i. *GENERAL WORKS.*—J. H. Ottius, *Annales Anabaptistici*, Basel, 1672; C. H. A. van der Smissen, *Kurzgefasste Gesch. der Mennoniten*, Summerfield, Illinois, 1895; A. Brons, *Ursprung, Entwickelung und Schicksale der Mennoniten*[3], Amsterdam, 1912; C. H. Wedel, *Abriss der Gesch. der Mennoniten*, Newton, Kans., 1900–04.

ii. *SPECIAL WORKS.*—C. A. Cornelius, *Gesch. des Münsterischen Aufruhrs*, Leipzig, 1855–60; L. Keller, *Gesch. der Wiedertäufer und ihres Reichs zu Münster*, Münster, 1880; M. Schoen, *Mennonitenthum in Westpreussen*, Berlin, 1886; J. P. Müller, *Mennoniten in Ostfriesland*, Emden, 1887; D. Musser, *The Reformed Mennonite Church*, Lancaster, Pa., 1878; S. W. Pennypacker, *Hist. and Biographical Sketches*, Philadelphia, 1883; H. P. Krehbiel, *The Hist. of General Conference of the Mennonites of N. America*, Canton, O., 1898; C. H. Smith, *The Mennonites of America*, Goshen, Ind., 1909; S. Blaupot ten Cate, *Geschiedenis der Doopsgezinden in Nederland*, 5 vols., Leeuwarden and Amsterdam, 1839–47; S. Hoekstra, *Beginselen en leer der oude Doopsgezinden*, Amsterdam, 1863; a great number of essays in the annual periodical *Doopsgezinde Bijdragen*, 50 vols., Amsterdam, Leeuwarden, and Leyden, 1861–1912; *Bureau of the Census, Special Reports*, 'Religious Bodies, 1906,' ii. [Washington, 1910] 402–428; Schaff-Herzog, vii. [1910] 299–310. An almost complete bibliography of the writings concerning the Mennonites of all times and all countries will be found in the new catalogue of the library of the congregation of the Mennonites at Amsterdam (at present in the press).

W. J. KÜHLER.

MENTAL RESERVATION.—It seems to be universally admitted that there are cases in which we should do a grave wrong by supplying a questioner with the information which he demands, and that we are, therefore, justified in misleading him. Yet there is considerable difficulty as to the ethical grounds on which such deception can be defended. Does it not necessarily involve either implicit or explicit falsehood? And can a lie ever be right? The problem is an old one, and moralists have answered it in different ways. The doctrine of mental reservation is the solution offered by many theologians both mediæval and modern. This doctrine depends so closely on the traditional Roman Catholic teaching as to the intrinsic malice of lying that in order to explain it it will be necessary first to state briefly what that teaching is.

Roman Catholic theologians are unanimous in holding that a lie is always and necessarily sinful: there can be no such thing as a permissible lie. This is the teaching of St. Augustine (*de Mendacio, contra Mendacium ad Consentium, Enchiridion*, xvii. ff.); and every Roman Catholic theologian of weight is in agreement with him. The utterances of Scripture on the subject are, they believe, quite decisive, and leave no room for dispute. Moreover, the Scholastic theologians reach the same conclusion on rational grounds. A lie, they teach, does not necessarily presuppose the wish to deceive; it consists in the intentional assertion of what is contrary to a man's inward thought ('sermo prolatus cum intentione dicendi falsum'). The liar may know that his lie will not deceive; yet, so long as he intends to assert what is false (and is not manifestly joking), his words are a lie. Nature has provided us with the power to express our thoughts by external signs. He who employs this faculty to convey to others the very opposite of his thought is violating moral order; he is using his power for an illegitimate purpose; and his act contains an intrinsic turpitude. The wish to deceive is an aggravation of the offence; but it is not requisite to make the words a lie (Thomas Aquinas, *Summa Theol.* II. ii. qu. 110, artt. 1, 3). Falsehood is, further, an offence against justice; we owe the truth to our fellow-men. But, even apart from this aspect of it, the act is intrinsically evil.

It is plain that, where so strict a view is taken as to the obligation of truth, the cases which we are considering constitute a grave difficulty. Whatever be the circumstances, a lie can never be justified. Augustine seems to have thought that the only choice lay between silence and a frank declaration of the truth irrespective of consequences (*de Mend.* xiii.). But it is clear that this does not solve the problem; for in many cases silence is equivalent to an admission; and it may well be that to answer the question proposed, whether by words or by silent assent, would constitute a flagrant breach of justice. A violation of the elementary principles of justice is not a whit less wrong than a sin against veracity.

Here, then, arises the question as to the permissibility of 'mental reservations.' A speaker is said to employ a mental reservation when his statement is true only if qualified by a restrictive clause, and when he does not openly express this clause but 'reserves' it within his own mind. Thus, *e.g.*, should a member of the Government reply to some impertinent inquiry regarding matters of State, 'I do not know,' his answer is in all likelihood qualified by such a reservation, and is to be understood as signifying, 'I do not know in my capacity of a private citizen.'

The general verdict of theologians is that a man may lawfully use mental reservations under certain given conditions, viz. if there be a real need of preserving a secret, and if the external circumstances are such as to indicate that the words may have to be understood in a restricted sense. Where these conditions are present, he may use reservation, even with the full prevision that, for one reason or another, his questioner will not advert to the restriction. Thus, to take a classical example, if murderers inquire of a man whether their intended victim is lying concealed in his house, it is allowable for him to reply that no one is concealed there; for the circumstances are such that even the murderers themselves should be aware that the words may have to be understood with a restrictive clause: 'No one is concealed there, of whom I can justly speak to men like yourselves.' Mental reservations of this kind are termed *restrictiones late mentales.* It is only in a loose sense (*late*) that they can be called 'mental'; for their presence is externally recognizable through the circumstances of the case.

It is contended that these statements are not in any sense falsehoods. For it is a principle universally admitted that, in judging of the meaning of words, we must take into consideration the circumstances in which they are used. No one regards the prisoner's plea of 'Not guilty' as a lie. The concrete surroundings show that his words signify only that he is not guilty juridically, in the eye of the law. A priest is not looked on as guilty of falsehood when he professes never yet to have heard of some matter which was long since revealed to him in confession; all are aware that what is spoken in confession is to him as if it were unknown. In each case the circumstances indicate that the words may be employed in a restricted sense. Taken in that sense, they are true: they correspond with the speaker's real judgment. The same holds good in the cases where we are justified in using mental reservation; the circumstances show that there may be a qualifying clause.

It may be urged that in a mental reservation we use language with the deliberate purpose of deceiving another, and that this is, to all intents, falsehood. But the objection is not, in fact, justified. In the first place, our true purpose is not to deceive but to protect our secret—a thing that we have every right to do. We may not, indeed, in order to do so, tell a lie; but we are not bound to supply the questioner with the information which he unjustly seeks to extort. And, secondly, in such cases it is more correct to say that the questioner deceives himself than that we deceive him. He is well aware that to such a question we may be unable to give a full answer without the betrayal of a secret, and he must expect an evasion. If he chooses to take it as an unqualified statement of the whole truth, let him attribute the error to his own folly. We may be the occasion of his mistake; we are not, properly speaking, its cause.

It stands to reason that mental reservation may be employed only where there is real necessity of preserving a secret, and where there is no other way of so doing; to employ such a method in matters of little moment would not be mental reservation, but plain falsehood. In the ordinary intercourse of daily life men assume that no exception will be taken to their inquiries, and that the replies which they receive will be frank; there is nothing in these matters to suggest to them the possibility of a restricted reply. This, however, is not the case if the restriction is such as to be manifest to all except the extremely unobservant. Under such circumstances a comparatively slight cause—*e.g.*, to set aside an inconvenient question—will be justification enough. Again, if the person who asks has a right to demand the information from us, then, unwelcome as the question may be, we must answer fully. It would not, *e.g.*, be justifiable to practise mental reservation to the income-tax commissioners.

In the 16th cent. a prolonged controversy arose as to the permissibility of the *restrictio pure mentalis*, viz. a mental reservation the presence of which is not indicated by any external circumstances whatever. The first to put forward this opinion appears to have been the famous canonist Martin de Aspilcueta ('Doctor Navarrus'; 1491–1586). His authority was so great that he was followed by not a few authors of note, including L. Lessius, A. Diana, etc. On the other hand, theologians no less eminent maintained what is clearly the case, that such reservations differ in no way from falsehoods. This was the view emphatically taught by P. Laymann, J. Azor, G. de Coninck, and many others. In 1679 Innocent XI. condemned three propositions drawn from the works of those who defended the use of the *restrictio pure mentalis* (H. Denzinger and C. Bannwart, *Enchiridion Symbolorum*[11], Freiburg, 1911, nos. 1176–1178). Since that time the opinion has been acknowledged to be theologically indefensible.

Protestant moralists reject the doctrine of mental reservation, and those of them who deal with the cases at issue solve the problem by adopting a less rigorous view as to falsehood than is taken by the Roman Catholic theologians. They teach that the malice of lying consists in its being an offence against justice, truth being a debt which we owe our fellow-men; and that, where that debt ceases, falsehood is legitimate—thus, *e.g.*, Grotius (*de Jure Belli et Pacis*, III. i. 11), J. Milton (*Treatise of Christian Doctrine*, in *Prose Works*, London, 1848–53, v. 115–119), Jeremy Taylor (*Ductor Dubitantium*, in *Works*, London, 1828, xiii. 351), W. Paley (*Principles of Moral and Political Philosophy*, bk. iii. ch. 15, in *Works*, London, 1821, i. 135). For reasons given above this view is regarded as erroneous by the Roman Catholic theologians.

LITERATURE.—P. Laymann, *Theologia Moralis*, Munich, 1630, III. iv. 13; T. Raynaud, *Opusc. de Æquivocatione et Mentali Restrictione*, in *Opera*, Lyons, 1665, xiv. 71; D. Viva, *Theses Damnatæ ab Alex. VII., Innoc. XI., Alex. VIII.*, Padua, 1708; G. J. Waffelaert, *Dissertation sur la malice du mensonge*, Bruges, 1884; J. H. Newman, *Apologia pro Vita Sua*, London, 1864, Appendix 8; T. Slater, artt. 'Lying,' 'Mental Reservation,' in *CE*; A. Ballerini, *Opus Theologicum Morale*, Prato, 1890, VI. ii. 4; and the moral theologians generally.

Protestant criticism: R. Sanderson, *De juramenti promissorii Obligatione*, London, 1647, præl. vi. n. 6; E. Stillingfleet, sermon xvii. (1679), in *Works*, London, 1710, i. 253; O. Zöckler, art. 'Reservatio Mentalis,' in *PRE*[3].

G. H. JOYCE.

MERCY.—Mercy, as an ethical quality predicable of both God and man, may be usefully distinguished from love or kindness as connoting in its object a certain inferiority, whether natural or spiritual. It excludes the idea of equality, in this or that relation, as between giver and receiver. In the Bible the divine mercy signifies active pity for the guilty or the miserable; it is manifested in countless ways, but pre-eminently in the bestowal of salvation in Christ, and may therefore be described as the form assumed by divine love in the presence of the sinful or the frail. Either moral failure or creaturely weakness is sufficient to evoke it, and both things are always found in all men. Hence mercy in God is rather a permanent disposition than merely an intermittent source of specific acts. As exhibited at its noblest in Jesus' personal demeanour, mercy has in it nothing of condescension, which is an attitude bordering on scorn; it was because He sought to establish with them such communion of spirit as might produce inward renewal that Jesus showed compassion to the needy, and under these circumstances mercy became the instrument of His trust in the divine capacities of man. Ere long Jesus was able to call the recipients of His mercy by the closer name of 'friends.'

The ascription of mercy to God implies a positive estimate of religious cognition, or at least the rejection of some negative estimates which have figured prominently in 19th cent. philosophy. To say of mercy, with Shakespeare, that 'it is an attribute to God Himself,' is the equivalent of holding that anthropomorphic judgments do not necessarily or substantially falsify our apprehension of the divine reality, and that moral qualities which faith sees in God are not essentially different from qualities in men called by the same names.

Apart from special tenets of the schools, Christian minds have usually held that the divine mercy is characterized, or even constituted, by two qualities. (1) It is free; it is not forced by any outward constraint, nor does it come to manifestation as the automatic response of reason to the facts of the world. God is love, love which has its measure in the Cross; and His mercy, as everlasting as Himself, is greater than we could either ask or think. It is misleading to speak of Him as constrained to mercy, if we mean simply that His action is the free expression of a perfectly loving Will; His pity is evoked, not by merit, or by tears of repentance, but by the need or ruin of His creatures. (2) It is absolute, and covers the whole of human life; it accepts no limit from human prejudice, but puts all men in debt for every good gift. For St. Paul the mercy of God has the aspect of miracle or paradox as being vouchsafed to the unworthy and even to the actively hostile, whose worth it creates but does not presuppose. Our part is not to measure or explain it, but rather to enjoy it with wonder and adoration.

Yet the best religious thought has never held the divine mercy to be incompatible with hostility to sin. Ethically pure compassion is a real capacity for holy anger; there is no mercy in allowing a bad man to go on in badness. Doubtless to an evil conscience mercy and judgment appear to be in conflict, but for Jesus both were living expressions of the Father's love.

Mercy in God asks for mercifulness in man. In the parable of the Unmerciful Servant (Mt 18[23-35]) Jesus made this plain for good and all. Mercy for Him is an element in the righteousness of the Kingdom, and it has been pointed out that 'it needed much to be inculcated in Christ's time, when sympathy was killed by the theory that all suffering was penalty of special sin, a theory which fostered a pitiless type of righteousness' (A. B. Bruce, in *Expositor's Greek Testament*, i. [1897] 99). To seek at God's hands a pity which we refuse to others is insincere; not only so, but in the absence of a merciful spirit we are morally incapable of appreciating the free, unbought mercy of God. Hence the promise to the merciful that they shall receive mercy (Mt 5[7]) expresses one aspect of the moral nature of things.

Human mercy must take the mercy of God as its model and inspiration. Like its exemplar, it is not to be accurately doled out in proportion to the receiver's deserts; in its perfectness it will rather exhibit a certain abandonment and overflowing munificence, and will ask no questions about the offender save as to his penitence. But feeble and complaisant mercy is as demoralizing as indiscriminate charity. 'Be ye merciful, even as your Father is merciful' (Lk 6[36]) is a call for discipline no less than lenity.

The supreme motive of mercifulness, whether to the guilty or to the necessitous, is not the natural desire to be treated mercifully in our own time of need; it is the thankful memory of pity bestowed on us by God. And the living sense that from the mercy of God all our hopes begin, the sight of its glorious freedom and absoluteness in Christ, is far more than a mood of comfortable security; it is charged with moral inspiration enabling Christian men to do and bear all things for the sake of the unmeasured divine love that for them has made all things new.

LITERATURE.—R. C. Trench, *New Testament Synonyms*, ed. London, 1901; H. Jacoby, *Neutestamentliche Ethik*, Königsberg, 1899; T. C. Hall, *History of Ethics within organised Christianity*, London, 1910; W. Herrmann, *Communion of the Christian with God*, Eng. tr.², do. 1906.

H. R. MACKINTOSH.

MERCY (Indian).—Adequately to discuss the significance and operation of the quality of mercy within the range of the Indian peoples would demand a book or treatise of no inconsiderable length. All that is practicable within the limits of an article is to attempt to exhibit the natural qualities and general tendencies that have been at work, to estimate the efficacy and worth of the influences that have been brought to bear, and to indicate the broad results in the character and disposition of the inhabitants of the country, as they are found in evidence at the present day. It is manifest that environment and ethnological origin and development, no less than religious prejudice and ethical culture, have contributed to a resultant quality or characteristic which can be defined only in the most general terms.

It is clear, moreover, that, from early historical times at least, the expression of this quality in the races of India has been obstructed and almost stifled in two directions, the one more or less a consequence of the other. The barriers raised by caste, which became only more formidable with the lapse of time, while permitting or even enjoining the exhibition of kindliness, generosity, and pity within the narrow caste limits, formed insuperable obstacles to the exercise of these qualities without, and therefore tended inevitably to isolation and degradation. And religious pride and prejudice, allying themselves with caste distinctions, promoted the growth of a narrow partisanship and class organization, within which the development of a spirit of fraternity and human kindliness was as little practicable as that of community of interest. The earlier periods of Indian history and social life also show clearly the presence of those feelings of mutual hostility and dislike which exist universally among groups of primitive peoples dwelling in a wide land, among whom isolation and the difficulties of communication are an effective ground of suspicion and of perpetual fear of that which presents itself as of unknown character and intentions. Thus the suspicion engendered by mere strangeness leads not seldom to acts of cruelty, which ultimately obtain the sanction of custom and are fortified by religious precept and rule. An unreasoning dread of that which is exceptional, rather than any other natural impulse, is probably at the basis of all such ruthless practices. The angry and hostile feelings thus aroused check the growth of the spirit of sympathy and mercifulness; and the latter must wait for the rise of a wider and more intelligent and generous outlook upon life and human relationships.

The claims, moreover, of a religious ritual which not only sanctioned, but enjoined, animal sacrifices were hostile to the development of the kindlier qualities of pity and regard for the weaker or less fortunate members of the tribe or community. Familiarity with the taking of life has always tended, not only in India, but elsewhere, to deaden sensibility and to bring into play the harsher and more cruel passions. When the sacrificial act claims the sanction of religion, and is transformed into a sacred rite and duty, the performance of which in all its rigid details is obligatory and of the highest merit, the debasing effect of custom and habit is reinforced by an appeal to the strongest human motives and prejudices. That which in many instances it would revolt a man to do for himself he will do determinedly and with a clear conscience under what he conceives to be divine authority. The elaborate Vedic sacrifices, with their large demands and imposing ritual, could have had in this respect only one consequence—to familiarize men's minds with thoughts of savagery, and to close their hearts and ears to the cry for compassion. With facilities for mutual intercourse and the advance of civilization, and with a higher estimate of the value of life in all its forms, these practices changed their character, or tended altogether to disappear. Offerings of fruit or flowers, or models in paste of animal form, took the place of the living sacrifice at the altar, and bear witness to an alteration of feeling on the part of the worshipper, and a desire to free his ritual from acts and observances which had become repugnant to a more cultivated and sensitive nature.

It is probable also that a distinction should be made—a distinction due to racial characteristic as well as to natural environment—between the primitive peoples of India and the later Aryan tribes, who entered the country in successive bands of invasion from the north-west and north. The latter were swayed by the gentler, more peaceable, and kindly temperament incident always to the pastoral habit of life. Eventually this tendency, though with many a set-back and cross-current, triumphed, and gave its general tone to the character and disposition of the entire Indian people. The primitive tribes, for the most part isolated from one another in gloomy and treacherous forest homes, received a training which developed the suspicious and harsher elements of human nature, brought into prominence the rugged aspects of nature as a whole, and was calculated to present few attractive features of generosity or humanity. Thus they were taught lessons of stern pitilessness and disregard of the life or well-being of others, and more or less unconsciously cultivated a disposition akin to that of the wild beasts against which they had continually to be on their guard. These two currents of thought and feeling may be traced all through the course of Indian history, and are observable at the present time among the racial and caste divisions of the country. It is to the credit of the innate courtesy and sympathetic kindliness of the native Indian that a merciful and generous spirit has, on the whole, maintained itself against religious and social prejudices, and, in the face of influences from within and from without, has to a large extent prevailed against isolating class-feeling and sectarian pride.

In the Indian sacred books the duty of pitifulness and compassion to all is a constantly recurring theme. Mercy (*dayā*) and abstinence from injury to life (*ahiṁsā*) are primary obligations. Especially in the *Bhagavad-Gītā* (*q.v.*), and in the type of religious thought and experience which it represents, the enforcement of this duty occupies a prominent place. The true Brāhman may be known by his friendliness to all; and not only the Brāhman, but other castes also, are bound by the same rule. The best sacrifice is that which refrains from doing hurt to any creature; respect should be shown for the life and happiness of even the lowliest of creatures, and no animate being should ever be subjected to injury or wrong. In a similar manner the religious teaching of the schools that are in sympathy with the *Bhagavad-Gītā* repeats and enforces the same responsibility. Two comments upon these injunctions are perhaps natural and inevitable. They seem, in the first place, to show more regard for animal than for human life; it is probable that the original authors assumed the latter, or regarded it as inclusively stated in the larger precept. And, further, the interpretation placed upon the rule has been, at least to the Western mind, in practice so one-sided and exaggerated as to destroy in large part its operative worth. The general tendency, however, it can hardly be doubted, has been in the direction of the cultivation of the qualities of mercy and mutual consideration. These qualities naturally find little or no statement or emphasis in the books on law or ritual, or among the regulations for the detailed observance of the sacrifices. The Vedic hymns, while they extol the forbearance and mercy together with the justice of the gods, leave it a matter of inference rather than of command that men should follow in their steps. In general it may be said that the decisive influence upon Indian character and belief has been exercised not by the ritual precepts, but by the humanitarian teaching of the *Bhagavad-Gītā*, by the popular epic poetry, and by the tradition of the lives of the heroes of olden time.

The first organized protest against the sacrificial rule in the interests of a kindlier and more humane spirit was made by Buddhism. The character of Gautama Buddha, as depicted in the extant literature and stereotyped in painting and sculpture, is singularly gentle and attractive. In practice as well as by precept he would seem to have urged the duty of forbearance and brotherliness to all; to do no harm to any living thing was a rule enjoined upon all who desired to unite themselves to his company and be enrolled among his disciples; and the purpose of the law which forbade the Buddhist monk to move from place to place during *Vassa*, the season of the rains, was at least as much to avoid the otherwise inevitable destruction of animal and insect life which would ensue, at a time when the multiplicity and activity of all such life are most apparent, as in recognition of the difficulties of travel incident to the season. Hindu monks and ascetics appear also to have observed *Vassa*, although not so universally or to the same extent. The merciful spirit, of which the rule of *ahiṁsā* was the outcome and logical conclusion, pervaded Indian Buddhism as long as it remained in its native land, found expression in the acts and edicts of its greatest emperor, Aśoka, and emphasized and extolled a generous tolerance towards the feelings and opinions of others, which, with rare exceptions, has characterized its attitude and life in all countries to which it has been carried. In India the influence which it exerted in this respect was strong, and remained as a permanent force in the life of the people after the Buddhist faith itself had become decadent and had perished from the land. In the wider aspect also, and as illustrating this spirit, Buddhism alone of the great religions of the world has never been guilty of persecution.

Jainism, the ancient sect contemporary with Buddhism and possessed of similar views and doctrines, inherited also from Hinduism the principles of mercifulness and regard for life in all its manifestations, but carried these principles to an extravagant and abnormal length. Even noxious creatures, however irritating or insignificant, may not be destroyed; and the literal interpretation of the injunction to do no hurt to living beings has led with them to practical inconveniences of a serious nature, which are not counterbalanced by an equivalent development of the qualities of a real compassion. Buddhism, moreover, in the days of its strength in India, made provision for sick, infirm, or worn-out animals in special hospitals; and similar institutions, established and maintained by adherents of the Hindu and Jain faiths, for many centuries past and even at the present time, bear witness to a compassionate spirit worthy of all commendation. To Western thought, however, these institutions appear not seldom to defeat their own object, and to be accompanied by contradictions in feeling and practice which it is difficult to reconcile with the spirit of the implied religious teaching. The form has been preserved and the letter of the law obeyed; but the meaning and motive of the whole have, in many instances at least, lost their force and been disregarded in the external fulfilment of an obligation which satisfied the conscience, but did little to effect a change in the character or disposition of the individual.

With the coming of the Muhammadans a new spirit invaded India, antagonistic to the old, the consequences of which were great and permanent. Born of religious fanaticism, and nurtured in the camp and on the field of battle, the warlike spirit of Islām bore down all religious opposition and refused to accept the symbol and confession of faith of the vanquished creed. From the minds of the conquerors religious fanaticism, in alliance with a temper naturally stern and self-contained, had banished all feelings of compassion towards aliens or foes. Thus a spirit of inhumanity, based ultimately upon religious precept and belief, not only inculcated indifference to life where the honour or extension of the faith was concerned, but urged the entire elimination of the infidel by force of arms. In a further respect also, and that wholly new to India, the example set has been followed with results calamitous for the whole peninsula, the untoward effects of which have only begun to be repaired within comparatively recent years. There is no evidence that before Islām led the way religious prejudice or rivalry ever found expression to any considerable extent in overt acts of persecution. The warfare between the sects was waged by word and argument in the schools and royal courts, but not by violence. The followers of Muhammad taught men to throw the sword into the scale; and the spirit of division and hatred has never since that time been other than latent on both sides, ready to spring to arms and perpetrate cruelties on any violation of religious comity or outrage upon religious conviction.

Two further external influences deserve consideration, but are of very unequal weight and importance. Of non-Christian ethical systems that of the Parsis is unrivalled for its merciful spirit and regard for the poor and necessitous of its own religious community; and the large-hearted generosity of wealthy members of the Parsi faith has always been beyond praise. In general, however, the obligations of kindliness and mutual helpfulness are valid towards those of their own faith alone; and, except by way of example, it cannot be said that their principles or practice have made any deep impression on the nation as a whole. Their numbers, moreover, are too few, and their social severance from Hindu and Muhammadan alike too complete, to enable them to exercise a wide-spread influence for good in this respect. They are and remain strangers in the land, whose character and life have been for the most part for themselves alone, neither shared in nor sought as a pattern by those among whom their lot was cast.

With Christianity it has been entirely otherwise. From the beginning it threw itself into the national and social life of the country, and, as far as the religious sentiment and pride of its opponents would permit, endeavoured to permeate society with its principles and to uplift the people as a whole to the level of its own ethical ideal. The influence of its temper and teaching has always been wider than the limits of its acknowledged churches or professed disciples. Its example has been pervasive and powerful, and mainly through its preaching and its schools it has exercised a far-reaching ethical influence on the doctrines and practice of the Indian peoples. Whether or how far early Buddhism was indebted to Christianity for moral precept and belief remains an open question, to which it is improbable that any definite or certain answer can ever be given. The later centuries, however, afford abundant evidence of the extent of Christian influence and the attractiveness of Christian ideals in modifying the hold of cruel rites upon the popular mind and in securing, although not always permanently, the acceptance of higher standards of right and mutual regard.

The influence described was never stronger than during the last and present centuries, and it was especially marked in the reform movements of the 19th cent., whose leaders never hesitated to acknowledge their indebtedness to Christian teaching and to the Christian Scriptures. Ram Mohan Roy, Keshab Chandra Sen, and others, to a large extent accepted the principles of the Christian faith, while repudiating its more distinctive doctrines (see art. BRĀHMA SAMĀJ). Moreover, it was on the ethical side that most would seem to have been learnt and adopted. The broad and kindly tolerance of all sects, which is a marked feature of the religious life of the Reformed churches, the gentle habit of mind and speech, and the regard for the rights and consideration for the needs and sufferings of others, if not altogether due to the leaders' knowledge and appreciation of Christian principles, were thereby greatly strengthened. With the exception of the Arya Samāj (*q.v.*), however, which exercises a growing ascendancy in many directions, the contribution of these sects to the spirit and thought of India has not been so effective or lasting as at one time was anticipated. The leaven of their influence has been restricted in its range, although within these limits a genuine effect has been produced.

At the basis of Indian religious and moral

thought, therefore, at least in its earlier stages and as regards the conception of the nature of the gods, lay a belief in the generally beneficent and merciful character of the divine powers. The Vedic deities are, for the most part, kindly disposed towards mankind. It is reasonable to suppose that in those remote ages also the quality of mercy found a place among the attributes of the gods because it was appreciated and practised by their worshippers. On the other hand, the awesome and threatening character which a nature-religion often and quite naturally assumes must not be overlooked. The two elementary characteristics or tendencies met, and, being incapable of complete reconciliation, existed side by side throughout the entire development of Indian spiritual and ethical history. Like most Orientals the Indian is by nature gentle and disposed to kindliness and generosity; and this aspect of his disposition found expression in the *Bhagavad-Gītā* and kindred works, and was put into practice by those sects which more or less sincerely acknowledged its authority and were permeated by its spirit. Lower and darker forms of religious faith maintained a cruel and blood-stained ritual, the effect of which on those who followed it could not fail to promote hardness and insensibility to suffering or need. And the more influential systems of philosophy, if not actively hostile to considerations of humanity and brotherly love, at least stood aside, and found their interest and life in a region where the kindly mutual relations upon which mercy is dependent have no part.

It may be said, therefore, that the Indian faith that heaven is merciful has, on the whole, found expression in the Indian creed, and been translated into Indian practice. To generalize, however, with regard to races so diverse in origin, history, and character, on any but the broadest and most general basis, is impracticable. The cross-currents in the case of India are exceptionally numerous owing to the many elements that have entered into the life of the inhabitants of the country. An appreciation can take account of little more than the general characteristics of the majority, their habit of mind, and mode of action. These considerations, however, justify to the fullest extent the description of the native peoples of India as by nature indulgent and merciful.

LITERATURE.—The subject is discussed more or less incidentally in all works on the religions and philosophy of India. See artt. HINDUISM, JAINISM, PARSIS, BHAKTI-MĀRGA, BRĀHMA-SAMĀJ.

A. S. GEDEN.

MERCY (Muslim).—To despair of God's mercy is one of the great sins, for mercy is one of the attributes of God, and to doubt whether He will show it implies disbelief in this divine attribute.

'O my servants who have transgressed to your own hurt, despair not of God's mercy, for all sins doth God forgive' (Qur'ān, xxxix. 54). 'Who despaireth of the mercy of his Lord, but they who err?' (xv. 56).

The words 'In the name of God, the Merciful One,' form the heading of all chapters of the Qur'ān except the ninth. *Al-Raḥmān*, the Merciful One, is one of the names of God; it is used in some *sūras* for Allāh. The Qur'ān refers in various ways to the mercy of God. The angels who celebrate His praises cry out: 'Our Lord! thou dost embrace all things in mercy and knowledge' (xl. 7). Satan is said to have claimed mercy on the ground that he was a thing and, therefore, part of the 'all things.' The reply is that the mercy refers only to the obedient and 'adds to the ruin of the wicked' (xvii. 84). The 'treasuries of the mercies of the Lord' is a Qur'ānic expression, and the word 'mercy' is used as a description of divine books. The book of Moses is spoken of as a guide and a 'mercy' (xi. 20). The Qur'ān is frequently called a 'mercy.'

'O men, now hath a warning come to you from your Lord, and a medicine for what is in your breasts, and a guidance and a mercy to believers' (x. 58). 'And we send down of the Qur'ān that which is a healing and a mercy to the faithful, but it shall add to the ruin of the wicked' (xvii. 84).

It is said of those who follow Jesus that God put into their hearts 'mercy and compassion' (lvii. 27); but this is not consistent with the denunciation of them (ix. 29–35) and the prohibition of friendship with them (v. 56). The words probably apply to Christians who become Muslims, for the passage goes on to address those who believe:

'Fear God and believe in His apostle; two portions of His mercy will He give to you; He will bestow upon you a light to walk in' (lvii. 28).

The two portions are: one for believing in Muhammad, and one for belief in the former prophets (Baiḍāwī). The light is either the Qur'ān to enable the convert to walk in the right path, or, if the walking refers to the bridge (*al-Ṣirāṭ*) finer than a hair, over which all must pass at the Last Day, then the 'light' is true faith which will preserve its possessor in his perilous walk over that bridge. One chapter of the Qur'ān (lv.) is called *Sūrat-al-Raḥmān*, the 'chapter of the Merciful One,' and begins: 'The Merciful One hath taught the Qur'ān, hath created man, hath taught him articulate speech.' The phrase 'God is merciful' is in constant use, and in practical daily life has overshadowed the idea of His righteousness and justice. It too often leads to complacency and self-satisfaction. A man commits sin and says, 'God is merciful': so, instead of leading to repentance and amendment of life, his idea of the mercy of God too often tends to make disobedience easy and safe.

LITERATURE.—There is no special literature on the subject; see literature under SALVATION (Muslim).

EDWARD SELL.

MERIT (Introductory and non-Christian).—In the earlier stages of religious development, as is attested by abundant examples in artt. BLEST, ABODE OF THE (Primitive and Savage), ESCHATOLOGY, and STATE AFTER DEATH, the moral character of life in this world is not a factor either for securing immortality at all or for determining rank and status in the future world, whether immortality be attained by an individual or be vouchsafed to all. In these early stages earthly position, notably chieftainship, or a particular manner of death—*e.g.*, in battle—is a requisite qualification for life in the future world; character, whether good, bad, or indifferent, has no weight in deciding the question. When, however, religion advances, when immortality is not conferred automatically (if the religion in question believes it to be conferred at all), but is a boon which must be achieved by long and toilsome endeavour, then three conditions—sometimes separated, but usually combined in greater or less degree—are imposed: works, faith, and love.

The ideal combination of these three requisites is found in but one religion—Christianity; and within Christianity only Roman Catholicism gives full recognition in its official statements to all three. The doctrine of the merit of good works has fared poorly. Some religions practically ignore it, notably the Bhakti-mārga (*q.v.*) of India and the Ṣūfīism (*q.v.*) of Persia. In both of these the attitude may be due to what they regard as undue stress on good works in Hinduism and Muhammadanism respectively; but, on the other hand, over-emphasis on faith and love to the exclusion of good works is dangerously apt to degenerate into an antinomianism which is a pitiful parody of religion at its best. Love alone is practically the sole condition of salvation to the Ṣūfī and to the follower of the Bhakti-mārga; faith is scarcely concerned except in so far as one naturally believes with firmness what one loves with fervour. Faith and works are the essential bases of Mandæanism (W. Brandt, *Mandäische Religion*, Leipzig, 1889, pp. 171–174). Mere intellectual faith, without love or works, has never been held, so far as the writer knows, to avail for salvation, except possibly in extreme Lutheranism.

The stress laid by St. Paul on justification 'by faith apart from the deeds of the law' (Ro 3^{28}; cf. 5^{1}, Gal 2^{16}) must not be wrested from its context in the Apostle's teaching, for he himself tells us that love is greater even than faith (1 Co 13), and that 'faith worketh by love' (Gal 5^{6}; cf. 1 Th 1^{3}, 1 Ti 1^{5} etc.). There was reason for him to speak disparagingly of works—it was necessary for him to combat the excessive nomism of Judaism. But St. Paul was a man of balanced judgment, and to say that he condemned all works because he deprecated reliance on them alone would be a misrepresentation of his true attitude. He recognized the value and the merit of good works (2 Co 8 f.), enjoining the church at Philippi to 'work out your own salvation with fear and trembling' (Ph 2^{12}), and at Thessalonica to establish their hearts 'in every good work and word' (2 Th 2^{17}). There is no doubt that he would have subscribed heartily to the famous passage of St. James (Ja 2^{17}; cf. v.^{20}) that 'faith, if it have not works, is dead in itself.'

The doctrine of the merit accruing from good works may be viewed from two sides—from the side of man and from the side of the deity. From the human side, the more good a man does, or even tries to do, the greater is the merit which he deserves; from the divine side, it is recognized, practically by Christianity alone, that no man can be so rich in good works as to merit salvation; 'all have sinned, and fall short of the glory of God' (Ro 3^{23}); all human righteousness is, as Isaiah said (Is 64^{6}), but as 'pannus menstruatæ.'

Only a shallow thinker would stress the apparent antinomy here set forth; the two partial truths blend harmoniously in the perfect truth of the Christian faith. Indeed, the Christian is saved solely by merit, though not by his own. Our Lord Himself could say, as His earthly life drew to its close, that He had accomplished the work which His Father gave Him to do (Jn 17^{4}), and He emphasized the necessity of work (5^{17} 9^{4}). Only through the work consummated on Calvary did salvation come to man; only through the merit of the Sacrifice of the Atonement can we hope at last to attain to heaven (cf. Council of Trent, sess. v. ch. 3, sess. vi. chs. 3, 16, can. 10).

In the primitive stages of religion its essence may be regarded as works. Beliefs are fluid; ritual is stable; every rite must be performed with minute scrupulosity. If the proper rites are thus exactly observed, the result is certain (provided, of course, that no stronger counter-force opposes); and, if a happy hereafter is the object of such rites, that blessedness is thereby assured (cf. *PC*^{3} ii. 90 f.). Not all, however, are content with the discharge of minimum requirements and, consequently, with minimum results. If one wishes for more, he must do more; perhaps, also, it will be well for him to provide a store against unforeseen contingencies. In that case also he must be more energetic in the doing of such works as will effect such a result; it is even possible that merits may be deliberately amassed for the purpose of achieving results unattainable for those who are content with the requirements imposed on every one; and in some cases the merits thus stored up are available for others as well as for him who originally accumulates them. The doctrine of the merits of our Lord's Passion and, in Roman Catholic theology, of the merits of the saints at once come to mind in the latter connexion; and the Roman Catholic dogma of the merit of works of supererogation also falls within this general category.

The doctrine of merit is, on the whole, a characteristic of the higher types of religion. We find it, it is true, among the lower races, as when the Brazilian Içanna 'say that the souls of the brave will become beautiful birds feeding on pleasant fruits, but cowards will be turned into reptiles' (*PC*^{3} ii. 7); and a similar belief is recorded of the African Maravi and of the Santal of India (*ib.* pp. 8, 10). Elsewhere, as among the Nicaraguans and the Negroes of Guinea, the good alone enjoy immortality, the wicked being annihilated (*ib.* p. 22 f.). Among the Greenlanders the condition of happy immortality is to have been a hard worker in this life (*ib.* p. 86; the manner of death—*e.g.*, by drowning or in child-birth—is also a factor). In all these cases, which might be much multiplied —*e.g.*, from African and American Indian tribes (*ib.* p. 94 f.)—the distinction between 'good' and 'bad' must invariably be interpreted by the standards of the particular peoples concerned. If this is done, there is undoubtedly a very real ethical basis and a true morality—even though quite rudimentary—as the foundation of the belief in the future destiny of the soul.

The doctrine of merit is much developed in the higher religions, as in Egyptian (cf. art. ETHICS AND MORALITY [Egyptian], § 7 f.) and Vedic (cf. Muir, v. [1872] 284 ff.), and reaches its non-Christian culmination in the Zoroastrian triad of 'good thoughts, good words, and good deeds' as antithetic to 'bad thoughts, bad words, and bad deeds.' The course of the evolution is well summarized by E. B. Tylor (*PC*^{3} ii. 84 f.):

'The idea of the next life being similar to this seems to have developed into the idea that what gives prosperity and renown here will give it there also, so that earthly conditions carry on their contrasts into the changed world after death. Thus a man's condition will be a result of, rather than a compensation or retribution for, his condition during life. . . . Through such an intermediate stage the doctrine of simple future existence was actually developed into the doctrine of future reward and punishment.'

Turning to the higher religions, we observe, first, that the teaching of Muhammadanism on the subject of merit is practically to the effect that good works are requisite, but that the true believer, being guided by Allāh to perform them, is, in reality, saved only by divine grace, while the wicked are punished eternally for the sins which they have committed, and for their refusal to submit to divine guidance. The problem is complicated here by the fatalism of Muhammadanism (see art. FATE [Muslim]).

At the Last Day 'every soul shall be recompensed as it hath deserved: no injustice on that day' (Qur'ān, xl. 17). It is equally true that whosoever of the 'People of the Book' 'believeth in God and the last day, and doeth that which is right, shall have their reward with their Lord' (ii. 59; cf. ii. 76, 106, 215, iii. 194, iv. 60, 121–123, 172, v. 73, vii. 40, xi. 14, xxv. 64–76; the idea is closely paralleled by Ac 10^{35}); and elsewhere faith is conjoined with observance of almsgiving and the appointed times of prayer (ii. 2–4), while throughout faith and works go together (*e.g.*, iii. 190–199). The whole attitude of Islām on this matter may thus be summarized from the earliest *sūra* (xxxvii. 22–55) which deals extensively with it:

'Gather together those who have acted unjustly, . . . and guide them to the road for hell. . . .
But on this day they shall submit themselves to God. . . .
"Just, therefore, is the doom which our Lord hath passed upon us." . . .
Ye shall surely taste the painful punishment,
And ye shall not be rewarded but as ye have wrought,
Save the sincere servants of God! . . . .
"But for the favour of my Lord, I had surely been of those who have been brought (unto damnation)."'

In a word, the saved declare (vii. 41): 'Praise be to God who hath guided us hither! We had not been guided had not God guided us!' (cf. also E. M. Wherry, *Comprehensive Commentary on the Qurân*, London, 1882-86, ii. 12, note 31, and index, *s.v.* 'Salvation').

The most complete development of the theory of merit among the ethnic religions is undoubtedly found in India. The main aspects have already been considered at length in the art. KARMA, where it will be seen that the Indian concept of merit is closely connected—as it is in several other religious systems—with belief in transmigration (*q.v.*) and in asceticism (*q.v.*). One aspect, however, calls for mention here—the accumulation of merit for the attainment of supernatural results in this life.

On the theory of sacrifice as set forth by the *Brāhmaṇas—i.e.*, that it is a rite which *ipso facto* compels the result at which it aims—it follows that the accumulation of merit not only by sacrifice but also in other ways will constrain the gods themselves to bow before the might of the ascetic. This power may be used for good or for evil, according to the purpose of him who possesses the merit in question. The records of India are full of stories of sages who have won enormous powers by the accumulation of merit, almost wholly by asceticism.

Thus, Bali conquered Indra and all the other gods except Viṣṇu, and ruled the world until Viṣṇu outwitted him; Chyavana constrained Indra to do his will (*Mahābhārata*, iii. 122-125); the particularly ill-tempered Durvāsas by his curse brought the gods so completely under the power of the demons that only the famous churning of the Ocean of Milk, which produced the *amṛta* ('ambrosia'), restored the divine sway (*Viṣṇu Purāṇa*, i. 9); Hariśchandra's patience under trial deservedly raised him to heaven, though he unhappily boasted of his merit and fell, but, repenting in mid-air, still remains in his aerial city half-way between heaven and earth (*Mārkaṇḍeya Purāṇa*, i. 7 ff.): Kaṇḍu's austerities, like those of many other sages, were so perilous to the gods that Indra sent the Apsaras Pramlochā to seduce him (*Viṣṇu Purāṇa*, i. 15); Kārtavīrya thus obtained great boons, which he used wisely (*ib.* iv. 11); the demon Rāvaṇa, the evil figure of the *Rāmāyaṇa*, won supernatural power by the merit of his austerities; Viśvāmitra, whose conflicts with the almost equally merit-endowed Vasiṣṭha form an important theme in the earlier Sanskrit literature, rose to be a Brāhman instead of being merely a Kṣatriya (Muir, i.[2] [1872] 317 ff.). Indeed, the idea recurs constantly throughout Sanskrit literature, the implication being always that the sage owes his power solely to the merit which he has accumulated; and in modern folk-belief the same supernatural might is accredited to the Yogī and Faqīr.

In later Zoroastrianism merit conditions very strictly one's position in the future world. Through full renunciation of sin and complete confession of it 'the duty and good works which were before performed' come back to a man (*Šāyast lā-Šāyast*, viii. 5-9). Those whose good and evil exactly balance go neither to heaven nor to hell, but to Hamēstagān, the 'Ever-stationary' (cf. L. H. Gray, *Muséon*, new ser., iii. [1902] 178), which in one text (*Dātistān-ī-Dīnīk*, xxiv. 6, xxxiii. 2) is divided into two parts, one for those whose goodness slightly preponderates, and the other for those whose evil minutely overbalances the scale. Not only is punishment in keeping with one's sin (cf. M. N. Dhalla, *Zoroastrian Theology*, New York, 1914, pp. 56 f., 273-275, 280 f.), but in the future world justice is so strictly observed that even the good deeds of a wicked man receive reward.

'For instance, a man whose whole body was either cooked in the caldron or was undergoing some other torment had one of his legs stretched out unmolested, because he had either shoved a wisp of hay before a hungry animal that was tied and could not reach it or killed some noxious creatures with it. He had not done any other good deed his whole life long' (Dhalla, p. 281, with reff.; cf. also L. C. Casartelli, *Philosophy of the Mazdayasnian Religion under the Sassanids*, Bombay, 1889, p. 167 f.).

Merits avail, as the doctrine of the merits of the saints teaches, not only for one's self, but also for others. This has been recognized by other religions as well as by the older form of Christianity. In the Buddhist *Upasampadā-kammavāchā*, or ritual

for admission to the Buddhist priesthood, the candidate prays: 'Let the merit that I have gained be shared by my lord. It is fitting to give me to share in the merit gained by my lord' (J. F. Dickson, *JRAS*, 1875, pp. 7, 9). Buddhism, however, stands almost alone in thus transferring merit during this life. The transfer of merit from the living to the dead is less common, although the Marcionite practice of 'baptizing for the dead' may possibly belong here (cf. J. Bingham, *Antiquities of the Chr. Church*, London, 1843-45, iii. 451-456). It is, however, taught by the Roman Catholic Church that, in virtue of the article of the Communion of Saints, the faithful living may transfer their merits for the benefit of souls in purgatory. More frequently the transfer is made in the future world, particularly at the examination of a recently arrived soul. Thus, in Muhammadanism, according to al-Ghazālī (*Perle précieuse*, ed. and tr. L. Gautier, Geneva, 1878, p. 79 f.), the man whose good and evil exactly counterbalance is bidden by Allāh to borrow some small merit from a more fortunate soul that the balance may be turned in his favour (for other solutions of this problem cf. the discussions connected with the al-A'rāf of Qur'ān, vii. 44-46, and see J. B. Rüling, *Beiträge zur Eschatologie des Islam*, Leipzig, 1895, p. 37 f.; M. Wolff, *Muh. Eschatologie*, do. 1872, p. 85). In late Zoroastrianism sacrificial merit (*kirfak*) of which the officiating priest is unaware goes to the treasury (*ganj*) of the angels, who give the ensuing enjoyment 'to the soul of that person who has at once become righteous in mind' (*Šāyast lā-Šāyast*, viii. 4).

LITERATURE.—*PC*[3] ii. 83-107; *MI* i. 86, 96-99, 299-302, ii. 360 f., 550-552.

LOUIS H. GRAY.

MERIT (Christian).—Merit is, properly speaking, an ethical idea. It implies the existence of at least three things: (1) a moral law under which man is placed, (2) a free will which enables him to obey it, and (3) a system of rewards and punishments by which obedience or disobedience to the law is sanctioned. Meritorious conduct is such as is agreeable to the law, and is at the same time voluntary; as meritorious, it claims honour or reward. Demerit, on the other hand, is the mark of such voluntary conduct as is not correspondent to the law; conduct to which this mark attaches demands punishment (for this general conception of merit see J. Martineau, *Types of Ethical Theory*[3], Oxford, 1889, ii. 80 ff.).

In Christian theology the idea of merit is closely connected with that of good works; and there is an important inter-confessional controversy between Roman Catholicism and Protestantism concerning the relation between the two. Both confessions recognize the ethical character of Christianity by declaring good works necessary to salvation, but, while Catholicism views good works, with certain limitations, as meritorious of eternal salvation, Protestantism denies that the standpoint of merit is at all valid in the Christian life.

1. The Jewish and Hellenistic doctrine of merit.—The conception of the merit of good works and the demerit of disobedience was inherited by Christianity and Judaism. It does not belong, strictly speaking, to the prophetic religion of Israel. While the prophetic religion is, above all things, ethical, and its demand is for righteousness, the point of view under which right conduct is regarded is, in the first place, rather that of loyalty to Jahweh than that of the accumulation of merit and demerit, and the consequent hope of reward and fear of punishment. Typical of the prophetic attitude to the subject is such a sentence as Mic 6[8] 'He hath shewed thee, O man, what is good; and what doth the Lord require of thee, but to do justly, and to love mercy, and to walk humbly with thy God?' Nevertheless, there is always the idea in reserve of a judgment by which evil-doers are to be cut off; and in such a passage as Is $1^{19f.}$ the alternative of reward for obedience and punishment for disobedience is very clearly propounded (cf. also $3^{10f.}$).

With the codification of the prophetic morality in the Law, however, the standpoint of merit became much more clearly defined. In Dt 27–29, *e.g.*, the whole duty of religion is brought under the heads of the blessing which rewards obedience to the divine commandments and of the curse which follows disobedience. In Dt 6^{25} 24^{13} also is found the important idea of a 'righteousness before God' established by the performance of the precepts. Prophecy after the establishment of the Law tends more and more to be conformed to the legal standpoint. The general idea of reward and punishment is applied in a very atomistic way to the individual by Ezekiel (cf. 3^{16-21} 18^{1-32}; other notable passages of a similar general tendency in later prophecy are Is 65^{11-15} 66^{14-18}, Mal 3^{1}–4^{3}).

The practical way in which the motives of the hope of reward and fear of punishment operated in the post-Exilic legalism can be studied in Proverbs and Ecclesiasticus (cf. Pr 19^{17}, Sir $12^{1ff.}$ $29^{14f.}$). It should be noted, however, that so far there is no idea of rewards or punishments in a future life. The life after death is conceived in all the earlier stages of the Jewish religion as without moral distinction. In the further development of religion during the Greek period, however, moral distinctions are extended into the next life, while in the Palestinian Judaism antagonistic to Greek influence the scribes further developed the preceding legalism into a complete formalism.

In this formalism the different moral duties are regarded in great detail and in separation from one another. The moral task is not viewed as a whole, but as the sum of single observances. The duties of fasting, prayer, and almsgiving are especially prominent. Reward varies precisely as performance:

'He who performs one precept has gotten to himself one advocate; and he who commits one transgression has gotten to himself one accuser' (*Pirḳê Ābhôth*, iv. 15, ed. C. Taylor², Cambridge, 1897, p. 69).

The reward is partly present, partly future; where this world fails fully to reward or punish, the next world redresses the balance.

The result of this atomistic conception of moral duties is to give great prominence to the external and ceremonial duties. It leads naturally to that idea of righteousness by works which was so prevalent in Pharisaic circles in NT times.

Life under the Law was certainly not wholly formalism and externalism. Examples of real heart religion were still to be found among the Jews of this time. C. G. Montefiore rightly insists that the tendency to formalism represents only one aspect of the later Judaism, and that it is not fair to judge it by this aspect alone (see *Origin and Growth of Religion as illustrated by the Religion of the Ancient Hebrews* [*HL*], London, 1897, lect. ix.). The same truth is emphasized by G. Dalman in his *Worte Jesu* (Eng. tr., *The Words of Jesus*, Edinburgh, 1902).

Nevertheless, the formalistic aspect of the religion of the scribes must here be emphasized, for the following reasons: (1) it distinguishes it from the earlier prophetic stages of the prophetic religion of Israel; (2) it explains the protest of the NT against the religion of the scribes; (3) it still influences the Roman Catholic conception of merit.

'Just because the catechisms for the elementary schools adduce passages like Dn 4^{24} [*sic*], To 12^{8} for the Roman Catholic doctrine of good works, we must go back to the religion of Judaism' (K. Thieme, in *PRE*³ xxi. 110).

A brief glance at Hellenistic Judaism of the same period will conclude this part of our survey. The morality of the book of Wisdom and of Philo combines with the Jewish idea of obedience to the Law Plato's philosophical doctrine of virtue. On the subject of moral retribution Wisdom remains practically one with the earlier Ecclesiasticus. Philo, however, further distinguishes himself both from the Wisdom literature and from the teaching of the scribes by avoiding the principle of 'atomism' and carrying back all virtues to one root, love or faith. The punishment of sin, moreover, he regards as a living death, the reward of virtue as communion with God (see J. Drummond, art. 'Philo,' in *HDB* v. 207).

As regards the views of educated paganism, when Christianity came into being, the doctrine of Plato was a formative influence.

Plato 'in several dialogues expresses the thought that a judgment upon all souls takes place at death, at which they receive, κατὰ τὴν ἀξίαν (*Phædo*, 113 E), both the reward for their good and the punishment for their evil deeds (*Rep.* x. 614 ff., *Gorg.* 523 ff., *Phædo*, 113 f.). Here, however, the mere conception of merit is overlaid by the other, that he who strives after righteousness and virtue seeks ὁμοιοῦσθαι θεῷ, and therefore will not be overlooked by God (*Rep.* x. 613 A B)' (J. Kunze, in *PRE*³ xx. 501).

The last thoughts carry us beyond the sphere of the doctrine of merit. Nevertheless, there can be no doubt that in paganism, as well as in Judaism, the view that regards God above all things as a rewarder of good and evil, and tends to review His relation to men under legal analogies, was the dominant and most usual religious theory. The total position of things is well summed up by Schultz in *SK* lxvii. 9:

'When Christianity entered the world and found its first expression in the dominant Jewish circles, as well as among the spokesmen of the idealistic Hellenic popular culture, the thought of a divine repayment deciding according to legal standards, and therefore of a merit or demerit of men according to which their fate was to be settled, was a self-evident axiom. A different relation of man to God, now that the prophetic type of religion had ceased to be influential, was not in general imaginable. With faith in God as the representative of the moral order of the world, there appeared to be evidently given the faith that He rewards and punishes according to the rule of human law.'

2. The doctrine of the NT.—The teaching of Jesus links itself on to that of the OT prophets, and also to that better side of the later Judaism upon which Montefiore and Dalman insist. It is, in the first place, essentially ethico-religious; religion and morality are completely blended in it. Jesus demands of His disciples an absolute conformity with the will of God (Mt 5^{48}), a righteousness better than that of the scribes (5^{20}). Without this none can enter into the kingdom of heaven (7^{20}). This better righteousness is, however, not to be attained by a closer conformity to the Law. Jesus further teaches that the only true righteousness is heart righteousness; that, apart from a right motive, outward conformity to the Law is worthless. Again, the idea of God as the Father, so central in His teaching, is the very antithesis of and makes impossible a legal conception of the relation of man to God. The righteousness which Jesus demands is, therefore, in the end just the spirit of sonship, energizing in the imitation of the Father (5^{48}).

While thus rejecting the legalism of the scribes, Jesus employs in His ethical teaching the current ideas of reward and punishment. That righteousness shall be rewarded and wrong-doing punished He reiterates again and again (Mt $5^{1ff.}$ 6^{19} 19^{21} etc.). He speaks once (unless it be the Evangelist) of 'good works' (ὑμῶν τὰ καλὰ ἔργα, Mt 5^{16}); he did not reprove the question: 'What shall I do that I may inherit eternal life?' (Mk 10^{17}); in His answer, moreover, He points the asker to the keeping of the commandments. Cf., further, the teaching of the parables of the faithful and unfaithful servants

(Mt 24$^{45ff.}$), and of the talents (25$^{14ff.}$), and observe again the principle expressed in Mk 4^{24}.

The principle of merit, therefore, occupies a somewhat ambiguous position in the teaching of Jesus. On the one hand, there are fundamental doctrines which appear to leave no room for it; on the other, we find in places a general recognition of it. The position of things in the NT as a whole is much the same.

The rest of the NT corresponds exactly in its ethical demands with the teaching of Jesus Himself. The *necessity* of righteousness is absolute, alike for the Jewish Christianity of the Epistle of James and the anti-Jewish Christianity of Paul, as well as for the other NT writers (cf. Ja 1$^{21f.}$, Gal 5$^{19-21}$, Eph 5^{5}, 1 Jn 3$^{7-12}$ esp. v.^{9}). Throughout the NT also the doctrine of the Fatherhood of God is fundamental, though not so dominant as it is in the teaching of Jesus. The idea of retribution according to works is also generally prevalent. Paul, indeed, in the most important cycle of his teaching—that upon justification—appears to exclude the principle of merit altogether. Justification is by faith alone: by the works of the Law no man can be justified (Ro 3^{20} 4^{5}, Gal 2^{16} 3^{11}; observe especially the direct exclusion, in so many words, of the principle of merit in Ro 4$^{4f.}$). Yet the Apostle teaches also that reward and punishment are according to men's works; and he regards this doctrine as axiomatic, feeling himself here on common ground not only with the Jews, but also with the Græco-Roman world (Ro 2$^{6ff.}$; cf., further, 2 Co 5^{10} 9^{6}, Gal 6^{9}, 2 Th 1^{9}, and also Col 3^{24}, Eph 6^{8}, 1 Ti 4^{8}, 2 Ti 4^{8}).

Even more prominent is the doctrine of retribution according to works in the Apocalypse, and the Epistles of James, 1 Peter, and to the Hebrews (cf. Rev 2$^{10-20}$ 3$^{5. 12. 21}$ etc., Ja 3^{18} 4^{10}, 1 P 1$^{9. 17}$ etc., He 10^{35} 11$^{26. 35}$ 12^{2}). The current idea of retribution is therefore almost universal in the NT, though, as Schultz says (*op. cit.* p. 13), 'without systematic development.' Only in the Gospel and Epistles of John is it almost wanting. The reason for this is assigned by Schultz as follows:

'At bottom there is no room for it. The true life work, which the community elect of God performs, is belief in the Son of God, and in this belief eternal life is already given, as possession and as hope' (p. 13).

Here, then, enters a problem which the NT writers do not themselves seem to have felt much. What is the relation of the doctrine of retribution, which the NT has in common with the current thought of its age, to the specifically Christian ideas, such as those of the Divine Fatherhood, or of justification by faith? This is a problem whose full significance was later to be brought to light. We may, however, refer here to the passages in the NT which suggest the limitations with which the doctrine of retribution is to be taken.

To begin with Jesus Himself, when He describes, as He often does, the relation of God to men by comparing it to that of a master and his household servants (cf. Mt 24$^{45ff.}$ 25$^{14ff.}$, Lk 17^{9}), He thereby does away with the idea of merit and reward in the strict sense.

'The servant in the sense of antiquity can acquire no merit. He is δοῦλος ἀχρεῖος, even when he has done all he should (Lk 17^{9}). His master can reward him, but that remains at bottom an act of good pleasure' (Schultz, p. 15).

In the one instance where Jesus actually does speak of paid labourers, and so leaves the way open for the strict idea of reward according to merit, He emphasizes by contrast the truth that God will not be bound by this rule, but reserves to Himself the right of graciously transcending it (Mt 20$^{1f.}$).

Finally, Jesus opens out the view of a reward which belongs rather to the personality revealed in the work than to the performance as such.

'Only where the tree is good, can the fruit be good (Mt 12^{33} 13^{33}). It is the conduct of life, the πρᾶξις, which is recognized and rewarded in the individual deeds' (Schultz, p. 14).

Paul, again, suggests a reconciliation between the idea of justification by faith and judgment according to works in the conception of good works as the fruit of the Spirit (Gal 5$^{22f.}$).

'Where justification is, there is also the gift of the Spirit, and therefore also good works. Thus the verdict of present justification and of the future judgment must coincide' (R. S. Franks, *Man, Sin, and Salvation*, London and Edinburgh, 1908, p. 128 f.).

Again, in Eph 2$^{8-10}$ good works appear not as a condition, but as a result, of salvation. 'Sometimes, however, the ethical interest so predominates that Paul even comes to represent future salvation as conditional on perseverance in faith and obedience' (*ib.* p. 129). Cf. Ro 8^{17}, 1 Co 9$^{24-27}$, Ph 3$^{8-14}$ with exposition given by Franks (*ib.*).

Finally, we may take into account the recession of the idea of retribution in the Johannine writings, which has already been noticed. The tendency in the NT, at any rate in the most important parts of it, is in general to limit the principle of merit and retribution in favour of the doctrines of grace. But it must be admitted that such limitation is by no means universal or absolute (it is least observable in the minor NT writers); and there remains, therefore, a fundamental antinomy in the Christian religion, as originally stated, which theology is called upon to solve. How difficult the task is, the history of doctrine reveals.

3. The doctrine of merit in the Christian Church.—We begin with primitive Gentile Christianity, and note that the whole cycle of Christian ideas by no means passed over equally to the Gentile Christians — what they received was naturally conditioned by their previous preparation. As to the necessity of good works, we find an intense moral earnestness in primitive Gentile Christianity. But, further, the idea of the twofold retribution according to works (reward or punishment) was familiar to the whole Græco-Roman world; hence this element of NT doctrine was easily assimilated, and, indeed, emphasized in more than its proper proportion, so much so that we have to recognize in the early Christian Church a return to a great extent to the Jewish doctrine of works. The doctrines, on the other hand, which should have prevented this return, such as, above all, the Pauline doctrine of justification by faith, found but little receptivity awaiting them. Hence the doctrine of good works in the Apostolic Fathers is very similar to that of the Jewish Rabbis. Christianity appears as a new law, and eternal life as the reward of keeping it. Just as in later Judaism, stress is especially laid on the merit of fasting and almsgiving. Cf. *2 Clem.* xvi. 4 (almsgiving becomes a mitigation of sin); *Barn.* xix.; *2 Clem.* iii. 3 f., viii. 4–6, ix. 5; Hermas, *Sim.* IX. xxviii. 5, X. ii. 4. We actually find already the idea of a work of supererogation (Hermas, *Sim.* V. iii. 3: 'If thou doest a good work beyond the commandment of God, thou shalt win for thyself more abundant glory').

In the Greek Fathers this line of thought continues, side by side, indeed, with the idea of grace, with which, however, it is never properly correlated. A more important and characteristic development belongs to Western theology, and begins with Tertullian. Himself a jurist, he gave to the doctrine of good works an essentially juristic stamp, which it has never lost in Latin Catholicism. A typical sentence is:

'A good deed has God as its debtor, just as also an evil one, because a judge is a rewarder of every cause' (*de Pœn.* 2).

Tertullian, in fact, looks upon the whole life of the Christian after baptism as strictly a life under the Law, its motives hope of reward and fear of punishment, and the result determined purely according to legal standards. All good works are in general meritorious; merit, however, in a peculiar sense attaches to such as go beyond the strict demands of God—*e.g.*, fasting and the maintenance of virginity. Retribution is strictly according to merit (*Scorp.* vi., *de Pat.* x., *ad Scap.* iv.).

These ideas are continued by the later Latin Fathers. Ambrose, however, begins to correlate them with the idea of divine grace—a work completed by Augustine. The latter still maintains that eternal life must be won by merit, and that good works establish merit, but the divine grace alone can enable men to perform good works, so that all our merits are God's gifts, and, when God crowns our merits, He crowns in reality simply His own gifts (*Ench.* cvii., *Ep.* cxciv. 19).

The teaching of Augustine is systematized and modified by the mediæval schoolmen. The idea that eternal salvation must be merited by good works is common to them all. Baptismal grace simply puts men into a condition to win merit. Works are not properly meritorious unless done from an inner principle of love (*caritas*), which is infused in the heart by the Spirit of God. Alexander of Hales, however, modified this doctrine by distinguishing between two degrees of merit, 'meritum de congruo' and 'meritum de condigno,' and two degrees of grace, 'gratia gratis data,' general grace, and 'gratia gratum faciens,' saving grace. He further taught that, while 'meritum de condigno,' or merit to which God owes a reward in strict justice, is possible only by the help of saving grace, 'meritum de congruo,' which God rewards because His mercy goes beyond strict justice, is possible by the help of general grace. In this way even the first grace can be merited (F. Loofs, *Dogmengeschichte*[4], Halle, 1906, p. 544 f.). Thomas Aquinas was more cautious. He denied the possibility of merit before baptism. All merit, however, so far as it proceeds from the free will is 'de congruo'; so far as it proceeds from grace, it is 'de condigno' (*ib.* p. 549 f.). Duns Scotus taught that 'meritum de congruo' was possible to a man 'in puris naturalibus' according to God's 'potentia absoluta,' not, however, according to his 'potentia ordinata' (*ib.* p. 596 f.). Finally, the Nominalist, Gabriel Biel, the disciple of William of Occam, taught without hesitation that he who does what is in him can merit 'de congruo' the grace which enables him 'de condigno' to merit salvation (*ib.* p. 615). It is from this point that the Reformation antithesis to the Roman Catholic doctrine of good works takes its start. Luther, returning to Paul's principle of justification by faith, declares that the doctrine that salvation can be merited by good works, however modified by a reference to the co-operation of divine grace, is absolutely opposed to the pure gospel.

We ought to notice that Luther's point of view is not altogether without parallel in the Middle Ages. Above all others Bernard of Clairvaux presents similar thoughts.

'He is foolish and mad, whoever he be that trusts in any merits of his life, who trusts in any religion or wisdom but only humility' (*de Diversis*, sermo xxvi. 1; other passages are given in A. Ritschl, *Rechtfertigung und Versöhnung*, i., Eng. tr., p. 99).

Luther, however, elevated what was thus occasionally expressed in the Middle Ages as a devotional point of view into the central doctrine of the faith. This teaching, in its ultimate form—there were many stages of development—is that salvation is by faith alone. Works are not the condition of righteousness, but righteousness received as a divine gift by faith is the condition of good works. Faith works by love, and its natural fruits are good works.

In opposition to Luther's view the Roman Catholic Church at the Council of Trent stamped with its approval the mediæval doctrines of good works (see sess. vi. can. 32). R. Bellarmine briefly sums up the Roman Catholic point of view when he says: 'The common opinion of all Catholics is that good works are truly and properly meritorious, and that not merely of some particular reward, but of eternal life itself' (*de Justificatione*, v. 1 [*Disputationes*, Ingolstadt, 1588–93, vol. iii.]).

Protestantism as a whole, both Lutheran and Reformed, completely agrees with the position of Luther, as expressed above. In the early Lutheran Church there was, however, a controversy as to the necessity of good works. If they were not to be regarded as the meritorious cause of salvation, the question was in what relation they stood to it. Melanchthon used phrases which were thought to imply that good works, though not the ground of justification, were nevertheless a *causa sine qua non* of our acceptance with God. To this mode of expression Luther objected, as good works are the consequence, and in no sense the condition, of justification. Agricola, a pupil of his, went further, and taught that good works are not necessary to salvation, the believer being not under the Law but under grace, and accepted for Christ's sake apart from any works of his own. Luther denounced this view also, maintaining that the Law remained under the gospel, not indeed as a means of justification, but as a revelation of the will of God as to what men ought to do (C. Hodge, *Systematic Theology*, London and Edinburgh, 1872–73, iii. 238).

The controversy was renewed not long afterwards in consequence of the doctrine of George Major, professor at Wittenberg, who had also been a pupil of Luther and Melanchthon. Major was accused of teaching that good works were necessary to justification, but denied this. He maintained that good works were not necessary as meritorious of salvation, but were necessary as fruits of faith. He admitted that the sinner was in a state of salvation as soon as he believed, but taught that, if his faith did not produce good works, it was not saving faith. N. von Amsdorf, his chief opponent, taught, on the other hand, that, though the statement that good works were necessary to salvation might be true in a general way, it was misleading. Good works are necessary to sanctification, but not to salvation in the proper sense, which is identical with justification. Amsdorf went so far as even to say that good works were harmful to salvation (*op. cit.* p. 239 f.).

These controversies were closed by the Formula of Concord (1580), which, on the one hand, condemns the statement that good works are necessary to salvation, but, on the other, equally rejects the doctrine that they are harmful to salvation. Men are to be shown how necessary it is to exercise themselves towards God in good works, but also how necessary it is to avoid all thought of good works in the matter of justification. Finally, the Formula condemns the idea that faith in Christ can consist with intentional or wilful sin (cf. *F. C. Epitome*, ed. Leipzig, 1857, ix., 'de Bonis Operibus').

The Formula of Concord closes the history of the doctrine of good works in orthodox dogmatics. It remains now only to notice that, since the Formula was composed, the whole question of the place of good works in Christianity has passed into a new phase. The essentially ethical character of modern Protestant theology, with its emphasis on the teaching of the OT prophets, and still more on that of Christ, makes the question whether good works are necessary to salvation seem almost absurd. At the same time, in the sense in which the Formula of Concord denies that good works are necessary to salvation, modern Protestant theology is absolutely at one with it. It repudiates the Roman Catholic conception of salvation by merit, and views good works, in essential agreement with the prophets, with Christ, and with Luther, as the expression of the filial attitude towards God.

There is, however, a powerful tendency not simply to deny the applicability of the category of merit to the matter of justification, but to regard it as a complete intruder in the domain of Christian theology. Justification by faith is regarded by Ritschl not as an alternative to justification by works, coming in in view of the failure of the latter, but as from the first the only method of salvation. The consequence of this view is an attempt to remove from theology the conception of the reward of good works in any other sense than that of their immanent fruition. The Pauline doctrine of twofold retribution is regarded simply as a remnant of Pharisaism or as a dialectic concession to his Jewish opponents (cf. Ritschl, *Rechtfertigung und Versöhnung*, ii. 319; also W. Beyschlag, *NT Theol.*, Eng. tr., Edinburgh, 1895, ii. 179; H. J. Holtzmann, *Lehrbuch der neutestamentl. Theol.*, Freiburg i. B., 1896–97, ii. 129). Our Lord's use of the category of reward is regarded as merely popular and not fitted to be the basis of a theological statement (cf. Holtzmann, i. 192 f.).

The question is really that of the rights of 'natural theology' within the Christian religion. The doctrine of twofold retribution has always been regarded as one of the pillars of a natural theology. Ritschl, however, regards the whole of the traditional natural theology, and in particular the doctrine of a twofold retribution, as due to the Hellenization of Christianity, and as being no proper part of Christian theology (cf. *Rechtfertigung und Versöhnung*, iii. 24 f., Eng. tr., p. 260 f., also ii. 318 f.), maintaining that the doctrine of twofold retribution, in a word, is Jewish or Greek but not Christian. The Ritschlian doctrine on this point has been by no means generally accepted. Many would still agree with C. Gore when, commenting on Ro 2[13], he speaks of natural religion as the necessary and essential basis of all evangelical teaching (*The Epistle to the Romans*, London, 1899, i. 108 f.). It must, however, be admitted that the co-existence in the NT of the doctrine of justification by faith and of reward according to works remains one of the antinomies of the Christian religion, of which, if the Ritschlian position be refused, no satisfactory synthesis has yet been attained. And, further, Ritschl is surely right when he says that 'the rubric of good works is unsuitable as a comprehensive designation of the ethical side of Christianity' (iii. 627, Eng. tr., p. 663). The phrase 'good works' suggests just that Pharisaic atomism which is the very opposite of the teaching of Christ, and, while employed in the NT like many other phrases derived from Jewish thought, it is not one in which the specific genius of Christianity comes out, but rather one in connexion with which there is a perpetual danger of a reversion to a lower stage of religion.

LITERATURE.—The usual Biblical Theologies and Histories of Dogma; also the great systematic theological works, among which A. Ritschl's *Rechtfertigung und Versöhnung*[3], Bonn, 1889, is specially important (Eng. tr., *Justification and Reconciliation*, vol. i., Edinburgh, 1872, vol. iii.[2], do. 1902, vol. ii. still untranslated). The great monograph on merit is H. Schultz, 'Der sittliche Begriff des Verdienstes und seine Aufwendung auf das Verständniss des Werkes Christi,' in *SK* lxvii. [1894] 7–50, 245–313, 445–553. See also artt. 'Verdienst' and 'Werke, gute,' in *PRE*[3].

ROBERT S. FRANKS.

MERLIN.—The name Merlin is a modification, first found in its Latinized form Merlinus, of the Welsh Myrddin or Merddin. That the latter form in Welsh is not a mere orthographical variant of the former is shown by a line of the poet Dafydd ab Gwilym (middle 14th cent.), which attests the pronunciation with *e* in the first syllable. In mediæval romance Merlin played a prominent part, in close conjunction with the Arthurian legend, as a prophet and as a magician. In the earliest references which we have to him in Welsh literature he appears as a bard, while, later, he is represented in Welsh and other prophetic literature as a seer, until finally, in the Merlin romances, his character as a magician predominates. The origin of the name Myrddin or Merddin is uncertain, and it is only by accident that it has become identical with the second element of Caer Fyrddin, the Welsh name for Carmarthen, since, in that name, Myrddin (in its mutated form Fyrddin) is the later phonetic equivalent of the Celtic Mori-dūnon ('the fortress near the sea'). The reason for the substitution of *l* for *dd* (=soft *th*) in the Latin and other forms of the name is uncertain. Probably it was due to the absence of the soft sound of *th* from these languages, and the consequent necessity for substituting for it some other sound, but it is not clear why that sound should have been *l*. As for the derivation of the name, it may be stated that there is one obstacle, and that a doubtful one, to its derivation from the Latin Martinus. This should give Merthin (with hard *th*), but there is a bare possibility that this form might change to Merddin, in accordance with a Welsh sound-change of *th* to *dd* which operated in certain words, but which was arrested before it affected all instances of *rth*. There is probably an instance of this sound-change in the place-name Gogerddan, in Cardiganshire, which doubtless stands for 'Gogerthan,' another form of 'Gogarthan,' a diminutive of Gogarth ('an eminence'). This derivation of Merddin is only a possibility; but, if it is sound, it is just conceivable that some of the early legends of Merlin contain distorted accounts of St. Martin, to whom St. Ninian is said to have dedicated the church called *Candida Casa* or Whithorn. A magician called Melinus is mentioned in the *Vita Patricii* of Jocelyn (x. 79, ed. *AS*, II Mar. [1865] 556), written in the 12th cent., but whether or not the name stands for Merlinus is uncertain; in the *Vita Patricii* which is ascribed to Bede, though more probably by Mellanius Probus (ed. J. Colgan, *Acta Sanctorum . . . Hiberniæ*, Louvain, 1645–47, ii. 51–63), he is called Locrus. It is interesting to note that Adamnan in his *Life of St. Columba* makes no mention of Merlin.

1. Merlin in Welsh legend.—So far as the earliest allusions to Merlin in purely Welsh literature are concerned, it is clear that his name belonged to the same legendary zone as the majority of the heroes and saints commemorated in early Welsh literature and included in early Welsh genealogies, namely to that of the 'Men of the North,' who are represented as having come into Wales from Northern Britain, more especially from the region of the Clyde and the Forth. This is the zone, *e.g.*, of Cunedda Wledig, Urien Rheged and his son Owain, of St. Kentigern (the patron saint of Glasgow and of St. Asaph), Caw, Rhydderch Hael, Gwenddolen, Cynon ab Clydno Eiddin, and of Arthur himself. The débris of the ancient British legendary cycle is to be found in Nennius, as well as in poems of the *Black Book of Carmarthen*, the *Book of Aneirin*, the *Book of Taliessin*, and the *Red Book of Hergest*, while fragments of the same cycle may be detected in the *Mabinogion*, the *Triads*, and the *Bruts*. It is in the *Book of Aneirin*, a MS of the 13th cent., but containing much older material, that the first reference to Merlin by name occurs in Welsh literature, in the phrase 'he defended the fair song of Mirdyn,' the form 'Mirdyn' in this passage being undoubtedly a variant for 'Myrdin,' the mediæval Welsh equivalent of the Myrddin of later Welsh.

Since it is clear that the legend of Myrddin (Merlin), in its earlier developments, must have arisen on British soil and have been circulated in the ancient British tongue, it will be of interest, before considering its later evolution in Latin and other non-Welsh sources, to review the forms in which we find it in the literature of Wales. Unfortunately, the Welsh materials of the Merlin legend do not go further back than the 12th cent., but they doubtless embody more primitive features, though it is no longer easy to determine these elements with certainty. The Myrddin legend owed its popularity in Wales, in the 12th cent. and later, to its convenience as a vehicle for the enunciation of prophecies as to the ultimate success of the Welsh in their struggle against the English. In this form of the legend Myrddin is represented as having, in the battle of Arderydd (often wrongly written Ardderyd), caused the death of the son of his sister Gwenddydd, who apparently was the wife of Rhydderch Hael, a prince of Strathclyde, who, in the battle in question, was the opponent of another Northern prince, Gwenddolen, with whose court Myrddin as a poet appears to have been connected. According to this Welsh legend, smitten with remorse, he flees in his frenzy, under the pursuit of Rhydderch Hael and his hounds, to the Forest of Caledonia (Coed Celyddon), to which, in Welsh mediæval legend, allusion was sometimes made as the home of sprites and departed spirits. In his flight the bard's sole companion is a little pig, and with his companion he reaches the shelter of an apple-tree in the heart of the forest. Under this apple-tree he is represented as uttering prophecies concerning future events in the history of Wales. It would appear from some of Myrddin's utterances that, in the course of his wanderings, communications were sometimes made to him by a female friend, who bears in Welsh the name Chwimbian or Chwiplein, who is probably the original of the Viviane of the later Merlin romances. It is possible that, in earlier forms of the legend than those known to us from Welsh literature, this nymph or Egeria may have originally played a less shadowy part than that which comes to view in Welsh 12th cent. legend, when the chief use of the Myrddin story was as a vehicle for encouraging vaticinations. It is noteworthy that in no part of early Welsh literature, not even in the *Black Book of Carmarthen*, which was written in the Priory of Carmarthen in the latter half of the 12th cent., is there any attempt to connect Myrddin with Carmarthen (in Welsh, Caer Fyrddin), as was done by Geoffrey of Monmouth. Hence we may conclude that the story of the connexion of Merlin with the North and with the battle of Arderydd—fought, according to the *Annales Cambriæ* (ed. *Monumenta hist. Britannica*, i., London, 1848, pp. 830–840), in A.D. 573—was traditional and well-established. The Northern associations of the story are further confirmed by the fact that Nennius mentions a Riderch Hen (*Hist. Brit. ad ann.* 597, ed. *Mon. hist. Brit.* i. 75), who is probably to be identified with Rhydderch Hael, while the life of St. Kentigern (xlv., ed. and tr. A. P. Forbes, *Historians of Scotland*, v., Edinburgh, 1874) names a Rederech, who is doubtless also to be identified with the same person, and a Laloiken, or Laloicen, whose name is clearly the same as that of Llallogan, identified with Myrddin in a poem purporting to be a conversation between Myrddin and his sister Gwenddydd, found in the *Red Book of Hergest* and generally known as the *Kyvoessi Myrdin* ('The Conversation of Myrddin'). H. L. D. Ward (in *Romania*, xxii. [1893] 504 ff.) has published another version of the Laloiken story, from two fragments in the Brit. Mus., and has adduced conclusive evidence to show that Llallogan (Laloiken) is a proper name, found, *e.g.*, in a Breton document called the *Redon Cartulary* as Lalocant and Lalocan (see *Romania*, xxii. 504). The simpler form of Llallogan, Llallawc (=Llallog), is probably a purely Welsh variant. It may be stated that the precise site of Arderydd (given in an older form in the *Annales Cambriæ* as Armterid) has not been fixed with certainty, the usual identification with Arthurel being based on a false pronunciation, but it is probable that the name Gwenddolen survives in the place-name Carwhinelow (Caer Wenddolen) near Carlisle. In the fragments given above, Laloiken is said to have been driven mad by the events of the great battle 'in campo inter Lidel et Carwanolow situato.'

The attribution of prophecies in Welsh literature to a bard Myrddin is not an isolated phenomenon, but is also found in the case of the Welsh poet Taliessin, in whose case, as in that of Myrddin, a legendary nucleus has survived, the chief feature of which is an account of his transformations. It is probable that the connexion of the name Taliessin with prophecy was earlier than that of Myrddin, as is suggested by a statement put into the mouth of the latter in the first poem of the *Black Book of Carmarthen*, in a dialogue between him and Taliessin about the battle of Arderydd, to the effect that Myrddin's prophecy would be widely known *after* that of Taliessin. The conception of a poet that is implied in the utterance of such vaticinations resembles the mediæval idea of Vergil, who was then viewed more as a prophet and magician than as a poet (see D. Comparetti, *Vergil in the Middle Ages*, Eng. tr., E. F. M. Benecke, London, 1895). As for the genesis of such prophecies as those of Myrddin, the original models were probably the so-called *Sibylline Oracles*, and such imitations of them as bridged over the time between the period of their composition and the Middle Ages. In the Middle Ages and even later there was a congenial mental atmosphere for the composition of prophecies and the practice of magic, nor was an interest in vaticinations confined to Wales, as may be seen, *e.g.*, in the popularity of such writers of prophecies as Atterbury, Bannister, John of Bridlington, Thomas of Erceldoune, and others in England, not to speak of Merlin himself.

In the *Black Book of Carmarthen* (12th cent.) the two chief forms of prophecy that are associated with the Myrddin legend are those known as the *Afallenau* ('The Apple-trees') and the *Hoianau* ('The Hails'). Both poems contain prophetic allusions, mainly to events of the 12th cent. in Wales. The former poem mentions Coed Celyddon ('the forest of Caledonia'), which was represented as the scene of the Myrddin legend, as well as Prydyn (Pictland) in the North, Mon (Anglesey), Ardudwy (N.W. Merioneth), Dinwythwy (near Carnarvon) in N. Wales, Cors Fochno and Pumlumon (Plynlimmon) in Cardiganshire, and the rivers Tawe, Taf, Teifi, Towy, Machafwy, and Edrywy in S. Wales. The *Hoianau* poem refers to the disagreement between Henry II. and Henry III., and also to the Welsh prince, Llewelyn ab Iorwerth, lord of Gwynnedd or N.W. Wales. There are allusions in this poem to Gwynedd (N. W. Wales), and to Tir Ethlin, the Land of the Heir-Apparent, which was the district situated in N. Wales between the rivers Conway and Clwyd. The student of the prophetic allusions of these poems would do well to consult the Introduction and notes of J. Gwenogvryn Evans's edition of the *Black Book of Carmarthen*. Here, again, most of the topographical allusions are to places in S. Wales, such as Dyfed (S.W. Wales), St. Davids, Milford Haven, Mynwy (Monmouth), y Sarffren and Castell Collwyn in Radnorshire, together with the rivers Taradyr, Mynwy (the Monnow), Machafwy, and Teifi, while there are also allusions to certain famous battles of early Welsh history, which are probably taken from some current bardic list of such battles.

In the *Book of Taliessin* (14th cent.) there is a similar prophetic poem (but without any account of the Myrddin legend itself), put into the mouth of Myrddin under the title *Arymes Prydein Fawr* ('The Prophecy of Great Britain'). The events which are foretold are similar in character to those of the *Afallenau* and *Hoianau*. There are other poems in the MS which, without expressly mentioning Myrddin, are clearly cognate with the Myrddin poems already mentioned.

In the *Red Book of Hergest* (14th cent.) there are two poems which have clear links of affinity with the *Afallenau* and *Hoianau*, but which may have been composed later. They undoubtedly belong, like the latter, to the Welsh Myrddin tradition. These two poems are (1) *Kyvoessi Myrdin a Gwendyd y chwaer*, 'The Conversation of Myrddin with his sister Gwenddydd,' and (2) *Gwasgargerd Vyrdin yn y bed*, 'The Diffused Song of Myrddin in the grave.' Though there are allusions which make it clear that their writers were familiar with the legend of the Northern Myrddin, Myrddin in these poems is little else than the instrument of prophecy. It may be of interest to note that a common feature of the Myrddin and other prophecies of the Middle Ages was an expectation of the return of the princes Cynan and Cadwaladr to life, in order to lead jointly the Welsh forces to victory over the English.

It is in the *Kyvoessi* poem that the term Llallogan, already mentioned, occurs. Though this word is doubtless in origin a proper name, yet W. O. Pughe (*Nat. Dict. of the Welsh Lang.*[3], Denbigh, 1832, *s.v.*) interpreted both it and *llallawg* as meaning 'twin brother.' It is not improbable that the term was misunderstood in this sense, even by the author of the *Kyvoessi*, since he makes Gwenddydd speak of 'my *llallogan* Myrddin,' while the term *llallawg*, as a synonym for *llallogan*, is doubtless invented from it by analogy. In the original narrative on which the *Kyvoessi* poem was based, Llallogan was doubtless a proper name, as it is in the Life of St. Kentigern, in the passage 'in curia eius (Rodarci) (erat) homo fatuus vocabulo Laloicen,' and it is this Laloicen that is identified in the *Scotichronicon* (iii. 31; ed. W. Goodall, Edinburgh, 1759), as in the *Kyvoessi* poem, with Merlin. Poems xix., xx., and xxi. of the *Red Book of Hergest* (in Skene, *Four Ancient Books of Wales*) clearly belong to the same cycle as the preceding.

Occasional references to Myrddin are found in the Welsh poets of the Gododin period (A.D. 1100–1300), as, *e.g.*, in Cynddelw's *Elegy to Owain Gwynedd* (*Myvyrian Archaiology of Wales*[2], Denbigh, 1870, p. 152[a]), where the poet says that Owain was 'fairer than Myrddin.' Gwynfardd Brycheiniog, too (*ib.* p. 193[b]), speaks of the Lord Rhys of Deheubarth (S. Wales) as having been prophesied by Myrddin. Elidr Sais (*ib.* pp. 243[a], 244[b]) refers to Myrddin's brilliancy in song, and likewise Gwilym Ddu o Arfon (*ib.* p. 277[a]) speaks of 'the excellent Myrddin of the stock of Meirchion.' The poet Sefny-n, also, in an elegy on Iorwerth Gyrriog, compares the dead bard to Myrddin (*ib.* p. 334[b]). Further, a cynical and sarcastic poet, Madog Dwygraig, satirizes the *Afallenau* in one of his poems called *Dychan i Ferch* ('A Satire on a Woman'). In Dafydd ab Gwilym (poem xxviii.) there is an echo of the fame of Myrddin as a poetic lover, while in poem xlvii. he is said 'to have made with the craftsmanship of love a house of glass about a mistress.' The few other allusions to Myrddin in Dafydd ab Gwilym are unimportant. Later legend (see MS 162 in the Peniarth Collection, now in the National Library of Wales, Aberystwyth, written about 1600) associated Myrddin with the Island of Bardsey, off the coast of Carnarvonshire, and located his grave there (cf. R. Higden, in *Polychronicon* [ed. T. Gale, Oxford, 1691, i. 187]), and Giraldus Cambrensis may have had this legend in view when he spoke of Merlinus Celidonius' grave (see below) as being shown near Nevyn in Carnarvonshire.

That Wales was not without an interest in the prophecies of the Sibyl, which are probably the prototypes of the Merlin and similar vaticinations, is shown by the fact that MS 5 of the Peniarth Collection, belonging to the second quarter of the 14th cent., contains a Welsh translation of the Sibylline prophecies, called *Llyma Prophuydolyaeth Sibli doeth* ('Here is the prophecy of the wise Sibyl'), based on the *De Sibillis* of Isidore of Seville. This translation is also found in the *Red Book of Hergest* (cols. 571[a]–577), and in Peniarth MS 14, pp. 45–57. The latter bears the title 'The Sibyl's Dream,' and belongs to the middle of the 13th century. It differs both from the versions of Peniarth 5 and from the *Red Book* text. The popularity of prophecies in this and the subsequent century in Wales is further shown by the inclusion in Peniarth MS 3, written about 1300, of the *Kyvoessi* poem, together with the *Afallenau* and *Hoianau*, while MS 20 of the same collection (15th cent.), by its inclusion of the same poem and the addition to it of a further prophetic extension, shows that this popularity continued. This is further proved by the fact that we find in the *Cwtta Cyfarwydd*, a MS written at varying dates from 1415 to 1456, copies of the *Afallenau* and *Hoianau* with the *Gwasgargerd Vyrdin* poem together with English prophecies by Bridlington, Bannister, Thomas of Erceldoune, and others. We find the *Afallenau* and *Hoianau* in Peniarth MS 59, a MS of the first half of the 16th cent., while, in the latter half of that century and in the 17th, the Welsh Myrddin poems still continued to be copied, as we see from Llanstephan MS 41 (1610–30), now in the National Library of Wales.

In the foregoing account the fortune of the Arderydd or Northern legend of Merlin, with the associated prophecies, has been traced. The Merlin thus depicted is sometimes called in Latin 'Merlinus Silvestris,' and in Welsh 'Myrddin Wyllt' ('Merlin the Wild'); while another Latin name by which he is known is that of 'Merlinus Celidonius' or 'Caledonius,' being so called in order to distinguish him from Merlinus Ambrosius, who is a creation of Geoffrey of Monmouth, through the substitution of Merlinus for the Ambrosius of a narrative which Geoffrey found in Nennius. A later MS of the *Annales Cambriæ*, in its account of the battle of Arderydd, reflects the Merlinus Silvestris tradition, in its addition to the original entry of the words 'inter filios Elifer et Guendoleu filium Keidiau: in quo bello Guendoleu cecidit: Merlinus insanus effectus est.' In keeping with the Northern conception of Merlin already mentioned, but also influenced by Geoffrey's account in connexion with the name Laloicen, the Life of St. Kentigern (*Scotichronicon, loc. cit.*) refers to Merlin's suffering in the words that are put into his mouth: 'Ego sum Christianus, licet tanti nominis reus, olim Guortigirni vates, Merlinus vocitatus in hac solitudine dira patiens fata,' though the influence of Geoffrey is here unmistakable in the reference to Vortigern.

2. The Vita Merlini.—This is a Latin hexameter poem, giving, in verses of considerable ease and fluency, an account of Merlin's life and adventures. Nearly all writers upon it have taken it, owing to its dedication, to be the work of Geoffrey of Monmouth, but the legend which it embodies is so entirely different from that given in Geoffrey's *Historia* that it is in the highest degree improbable that he is its author. The legend which it incorporates and expands is essentially that of the Welsh *Afallenau* and *Hoianau* and of the 'Laloicen' tradition that is contained in the Life of St. Kentigern. Ferdinand Lot has published an analysis of the *Vita Merlini* (*Annales de Bretagne*, xv.), and has shown it to be later than the Laloicen fragments already mentioned; but he too readily assumes that Geoffrey was its author, and goes too far in seeking to trace the influence of the *Vita Merlini* on the Welsh Myrddin poems of the *Black Book of Carmarthen* and of the *Red Book of Hergest*, with the exception of the first poem of the former, which purports to be a dialogue between Myrddin and Taliessin. The Latinized proper names of the *Vita Merlini* show quite clearly that they were formed by some one who was familiar with the Welsh names of the Myrddin legend, such as Ganieda for Gwenddydd, Telgesinus for Taliessin, and the like. At the same time, there are important departures from the Welsh form of the legend, as, for instance, the opposition of Guennolous to Merlin; but in the *Vita Merlini*, as in the *Afallenau*, there are prominent allusions to apples, and the whole setting of the Latin poem and of the Welsh poems, in spite of certain discrepancies, is for the most part the same. The *Vita Merlini*, however, contains one name, Mældinus, which, as Lot has pointed out, is probably derived from an Irish rather than from a Welsh source, being, in all likelihood, that of the hero of the voyage of Mælduin. Though the *Vita Merlini* appears to be the work of some one other than Geoffrey, it appeared during his lifetime, having been written about 1148, while he died in 1154. It was dedicated to Bishop Alexander's successor, Robert, who was a man of considerable influence at the court of Stephen. The poem is of great interest as showing the popularity of the Northern and Welsh type of the Merlin legend in cultured circles in Britain in the 12th cent., but familiarity with Geoffrey's history is already shown by the reference to Vortigern (l. 681).

3. **Merlin in Geoffrey and in the Chronicles.**—The introduction of the figure of Merlin into the mediæval Chronicles is due to Geoffrey of Monmouth, who deliberately transformed the Ambrosius of one of his sources, Nennius, into Merlinus. This is clear from the fact that, in the Prophecy and in the last part of the preceding book, Geoffrey calls Merlin Ambrosius Merlinus. The innovation in question was first made by Geoffrey, when he published 'The Prophecy of Merlin' as a separate work, before the appearance of his *Historia Regum Britanniæ*. This Prophecy must have been published early enough for Ordericus Vitalis to quote from it, as he does in bk. xii. of his *History*, written about 1136 or 1137. Later it was incorporated in Geoffrey's *Historia*, and forms bk. vii. of that work. The Ambrosius with whom Geoffrey identified Merlin first comes to view in Gildas (*de Excidio Britanniæ*, xxv., ed. *Mon. hist. Brit.* i. 15), as Ambrosius Aurelianus, but the first to make him into a legendary person was Nennius, who describes him (xli.-xlv.) as a child without a father, for whom Vortigern searched, by the advice of his sorcerers, in order to render stable the foundations of a tower that he was building. He was found, according to Nennius, in the field or plain of Elleti, in the region of Gleguissing (=Glywyssing in Monmouthshire), and in Nennius's narrative he is also associated with the ancient Carnarvonshire fort of Dinas Emrys (Emrys being the Welsh derivative of Ambrosius), near Beddgelert, and is represented as a sorcerer (*magus*), who prophesies the final overthrow of the English by the Welsh. Ambrosius in Geoffrey appears as a separate character (*Hist. Brit.* viii. 1), but the rôle which he plays in that author was filled in Nennius by Guorthemir (Vortimer). It is Geoffrey, too, that first connects Merlin with Carmarthen (*Hist. Brit.* vi. 17).

Another new element which Geoffrey introduced into the story, and which became a notable feature of the Merlin romance, was the suggestion that the boy's father was a supernatural being of the type known by the name of *incubus*. The suggestion made by Nennius, that the boy was the son of a Roman consul, is omitted by Geoffrey. The idea of introducing an *incubus* into the story probably came from a reminiscence of the pseudo-Bede (*de Elem. Phil.*, bk. i. [*PL* xc. 1131]), who doubtless reflects a view put forward by St. Augustine. The germ of the conception of Merlin as a sorcerer was already in Nennius, and the idea of putting prophecies into his mouth was ready to Geoffrey's hand, and even then a practice of the times, as is seen by Geoffrey's own references (ii. 9, xii. 18) to the prophesying of the eagle at Shaftesbury. Giraldus Cambrensis, too, quotes prophecies of Merlin that are not found among those given by Geoffrey (see R. H. Fletcher, *Arthurian Material in the Chronicles*, Boston, 1909, p. 93, note 1). He makes a distinction between Merlinus Ambrosius and Merlinus Silvestris (or Celidonius), and attributes to the former only prophecies taken from Geoffrey, and he likewise states (*Itin. Camb.* ii. 6, 8) that he discovered, in an out-of-the-way locality, a copy of the prophecies of Merlinus Celidonius in the British tongue. Geoffrey gives prominence to Merlin's powers, not only as a prophet, but as a magician, and represents him as one whose magic power conveyed Stonehenge from Ireland to Salisbury Plain and changed the forms of Uther and his companions. In Geoffrey, however, Merlin is not mentioned later than Uther's reign, but subsequent legend and romance could not resist the temptation to associate him with Uther's son, Arthur. In romance, Merlin, as a magician, tended to come more and more into prominence, until at last he became a figure second only to that of Arthur himself.

In the case of subsequent chronicles the following points may be noted. The Welsh *Brut Tysilio*, an adaptation of Geoffrey's *History*, shows a development on the lines of the later Romances, and probably under their influence. For example, Merlin is represented as owing his birth to the machinations of Lucifer and other evil spirits, and the increased prominence of the magical conception of his character is seen by the statement that he, by his magic art alone, is able to draw the stones that are to be carried from Ireland to Salisbury Plain as far as the ships, after the complete failure of the warriors. The same tendencies may be noted in Wace, who omits Merlin's prophecies, with the exception of those about Vortigern, on the ground that they are unintelligible to him, while he invests Merlin throughout with superhuman powers, and does not even mention any mechanical assistance in the transmission of the blocks of Stonehenge. Traces of romantic influence come to view also in the Chronicle called *Draco Normannicus* (*c.* 1170; ed. R. Howlett, *Chron. of the Reigns of Stephen*, etc., London, 1884–89, ii. 589–757), which, it may be stated, contains many allusions to the section of Merlin's prophecies that relate to the first half of the 12th century.

In Layamon's *Brut* there are a few additional touches to the story of Merlin, such as Merlin's explanation that the immediate cause of the fall of the tower which Vortigern was trying to build was the fighting of two dragons with one another at midnight. In this narrative, again, there is a marked emphasis on the supernatural conception of Merlin, which shows itself on the side both of supernatural knowledge and of supernatural power. There are some points of contact in the narrative with the *Vita Merlini*, as in the account of the discovery of Merlin in a forest, at Uther's instance, when he wished for his aid to obtain Igerne as his mistress.

In the Latin hexameter poem called *Gesta Regum Britanniæ* (ed. F. Michel, London, 1862), Merlin is entirely supernatural, as, *e.g.*, where he transmits the stones to Stonehenge by means of magical songs, or where he magically changes Uther's form. Merlin, too, gives Arthur new strength in his contest with Frollo. Here, again, there is a link with the *Vita Merlini*, where it is said that Arthur was conveyed to an ever-to-be-remembered island, on which a royal maiden dwelt. In the case of other chronicles, some omit the prophecies or certain of them, as, for instance, Alfred of Beverley (*c.* 1150; ed. T. Hearne, Oxford, 1716), who omits most of them, and Richardus Cluniacensis (in 1162), who omitted the prophecies in the first edition of his *Universal Chronicle* (ed. L. A. Muratori, *Antiquitates Italicæ medii ævi*, Milan, 1738–42, iv. 1079–1104), but who found it advisable to include them in his second and third editions. Again, it is clear that all chronicles did not share equally in the tendency to exaggerate the powers of Merlin; *e.g.*, Ralph Niger in his *Chronicon* (ed. R. Anstruther, London, 1851) has a mere allusion to Merlin's transportation of the stones of Stonehenge.

There are, as already stated, traces in Giraldus Cambrensis of an attempt at the fusion and reconciliation of the Caledonian tradition and that of Geoffrey, in his theory of the existence of two Merlins. He follows Geoffrey in his connexion of Merlinus Ambrosius with Carmarthen, while he knows of the madness of Merlinus Caledonius, but attributes it not to remorse at having killed his sister's son, but to fright at the sight of an apparition in the air. Giraldus, like many of the chroniclers who succeeded Geoffrey, succumbed to the temptation of bringing Merlin down to the time of King Arthur. One story, which Giraldus records (*Itin. Camb.* ii. 6), to the effect that Merlinus Caledonius had been found near Nevyn in Carnarvonshire, is probably connected with the legend that associated him with the island of Bardsey. Merlin's burial appears to have been located in some traditions at Carmarthen, where a 'Merlin's Grave' was pointed out, while in Scotland it was located at Drummelzier, anciently Dunmeller, in Tweed-dale.

The wide-spread popularity of the prophecies of Merlin may be gauged by the fact that two Latin poems appear to be extant embodying a number of them from the pen of a Scandinavian monk called Gunlangus Leifi of Thingeyra, while a similar MS in the Copenhagen Library was translated into English, with the History of Hulfdan Einar, and published in London in 1718 (see San-Marte, *Die Sagen von Merlin*, Halle, 1853, p. 18).

In 1185–89 there appeared a commentary on the prophecies of Merlin by Alanus de Insulis, and in 1603 it was published at Frankfort. In this commentary Alanus testifies to the existence, in the Brittany of his day, of a strong belief in the prophecies in question. Further, John of Cornwall, a disciple of Peter Lombard, commented on these prophecies publicly in the University of Paris (see *Prophetiæ Merlini cum expositione Johannis Cornubiensis*, *ap.* K. J. Greith, *Spicileg. Vatican.*, Frauenfeld, 1838, p. 98). The credence given to the Merlin prophecies continued, in Britain and in France, well into the 17th cent., if not later, and the Council of Trent sought to counteract the considerable effects of this popularity by putting the prophecies on the Index. A similar attitude of mind to that of the Council of Trent is reflected in the work called *Vincentii Bellovacensis Speculum Historiale* (xx. 20). For English editions of the Life and Prophecies of Merlin, see Literature.

4. Merlin in romance.—Merlin first comes to view as a character of romance proper in a poem of which only a fragment has come down to us, probably dating from the 12th cent., and usually attributed to Robert de Borron (ed. Paris and Ulrich, in their ed. of the *Huth Merlin*; see Lit.). This poem was the basis of a French prose work which forms the Romance of Merlin, and this, again, is thought to be partly the work of the same author. It has come down to us in two forms, the first being generally called the 'ordinary' or 'vulgate' Merlin, while the second is known as the *Suite de Merlin*. Of the latter work Malory's first four books are an abridgment, and from it is derived one of the minor Arthurian stories, namely that of Balin and Balan. In the Merlin romances, as in the later developments of the Arthurian story (see ARTHUR, ARTHURIAN CYCLE), there is an ecclesiastical or theological development, the leading motive which led to the birth of Merlin being the conspiracy of the world of demons to produce an Antichrist, who would be the means of rendering the work of the Incarnation ineffective. Thus the birth of Merlin is represented as a kind of counter-incarnation, and, through the machinations of the demons, he is brought into the world as the child of a woman whose family has been ruined by the evil spirits, and who is herself seduced by a demon. Providentially, however, Blaise, the confessor of Merlin's mother, baptizes the child as soon as it is born, and thereby brings it into the Christian fold. The child, nevertheless, retains, though a Christian, the demonic gifts of magic and prophecy, and these powers he puts to beneficial use even in his infancy, by saving his mother's life and startling her accusers by revealing their family secrets. The narrative then proceeds on the lines of Geoffrey's *History* in the account of his relations with Vortigern, Ambrosius, and Uther. After this, Arthur is represented as having been committed as an infant to Merlin's care, and Merlin hands him over to Antor, who brings him up as his own son. It is Merlin who reveals to Arthur the fact that he is the son of Uther Pendragon and Igerne, and it is to Merlin that Arthur looks for guidance and counsel during the earlier period of his rule. At the termination of this period Merlin vanishes from Arthur's court. The stories accounting for his disappearance vary in different forms of the romance. One story states that he was betrayed by a maiden called Niniane or Viviane, probably the Chwimbian of Welsh legend; but in some versions of this narrative she is represented as a water-fairy, in others as a king's daughter. With this lady Merlin is in love, and she, in the spirit of Delilah, obtains from him the secret of his magic power, and uses this knowledge to cast him into a profound sleep and to imprison him alive in a rocky grave. According to this account, Merlin uttered a loud cry, called the 'Brait,' before he died. Apparently this form of the story was the most popular. In another version his prison is not of stone but of air; and, though Merlin in this prison can see and hear everything, he can be seen by none. He can also hold converse with wayfarers who pass his prison, and one of these happens to be Gawain. The prose *Perceval* contains another form of the story, according to which Merlin is not imprisoned by his mistress, but retires of his own accord to an edifice called an 'Esplumeor,' which he himself builds, after which retirement he is never more seen. The Romance of Merlin eventually became a long introduction to the prose Lancelot and to the Arthurian cycle generally.

The Romance of Merlin, as already indicated, is to be found first in the fragmentary poem, attributed to Robert de Borron, giving, however, only the introductory part of the story, in a single MS of the Bibliothèque Nationale, and, secondly, in the prose version based on this poem in combination with the early history of the Grail, which bears the name *Joseph of Arimathea*. In two cases the Merlin story forms a small Arthurian cycle through the addition of a *Perceval* and a *Mort Artus*. Of the 'ordinary' or 'vulgate' Merlin, which is a long and elaborate romance, several copies are extant. This story is continued in two forms, each of which has survived in a single MS. One of these is called the *Huth Merlin*, after the distinguished patron of learning, Alfred Huth, who bore the expense of its publication. It is a version of which Malory made use in his rendering of the story, and the Spanish and Portuguese translators also based their versions upon it. The other sequel is MS 337, also in the Bibliothèque Nationale, and is called by Paulin Paris the *Livre Artus*.

In English the earliest form of the Merlin Romance is a metrical translation called *Arthour and Merlin*, which was made from French at the beginning of the 14th cent.; and a later translation, generally known as the great prose Merlin, was made about the middle of the 15th century. Spenser (*Faery Queen*, canto iii.) alludes to Merlin, and there is reference to his deception by the Lady of the Lake in Ariosto (*Orlando furioso*, canto iii. st. 10). The romantic development of the Merlin story is doubtless mainly due to the desire of the French *trouvères* to bring the legend of Merlin, like those of Arthur and Tristan, into harmony with the general civilization and culture of their time. In the 19th cent. Tennyson utilized the Merlin legend in his *Idylls of the King*, and gave a version of his own of the character of Viviane.

5. Merlin in satire.—Like the other mediæval romances, that of Merlin tended, in the eyes of a more critical age, to provoke satire, and so it is not strange that Cervantes ridicules and parodies it in his *Don Quixote*, while Rabelais also parodies the prophecies in his *Pantagruéline prognostication certaine, véritable et infaillible*, composed about 1533, while in his *Gargantua* he exposes the life and prophecies of Merlin to further ridicule. The contrast between the spirit of Cervantes or Rabelais and that which delighted in the prophecies and romance of Merlin illustrates the change from the characteristic mental attitude of the Middle Ages to that of later times.

LITERATURE.—H. L. D. Ward, *Catalogue of Romances in the British Museum*, i., London, 1883; W. F. Skene, *The Four Ancient Books of Wales*, 2 vols., Edinburgh, 1868; J. Gwenogvryn Evans, *The Black Book of Carmarthen*, Pwllheli, to subscribers only, 1906; Geoffrey of Monmouth, *Prophetia Merlini*, ed. San-Marte (A. Schulz), Halle, 1853; J. Rhŷs and J. G. Evans, *The Text of the Bruts from the Red Book of Hergest*, Oxford, for subscribers only, 1890; *Gaufridi Arthurii . . . de vita et vaticiniis Merlini Caledonii carmen heroicum*, London, 1830; San-Marte, *Sagen von Merlin*, Halle, 1853; F. Michel and T. Wright, *Vita Merlini*, Paris and London, 1837; H. O. Sommer, *Le Roman de Merlin, or the Early History of King Arthur* (from French MS Add. 10292 in Brit. Mus. [c. A.D. 1316]), London, to subscribers only, 1894, *The Vulgate Version of the Arthurian Romances*, ed. from MSS in Brit. Mus., vol. ii., 'Lestoire de Merlin,' Washington, 1908; G. Paris and J. Ulrich, *Merlin, Roman en prose du xiiie siècle d'après le manuscrit appartenant à A. H. Huth*, Paris, 1886; *Arthur: Arthour and Merlin*, ed. W. B. D. D. Turnbull, Edinburgh, 1838; E. Kölbing, *Arthour and Merlin*, Leipzig, 1890; H. B. Wheatley, *Merlin or the Early History of King Arthur*, with valuable introductions and bibliography, 2 vols., London, 1899; J. Rhŷs, *Hibbert Lectures*, London and Edinburgh, 1888; F. Lot, in *Annales de Bretagne*, xv. [1899–1900]; H. L. D. Ward, in *Romania*, xxii. [1893]; A. C. L. Brown, in *RCel* xxii. [1901]; R. H. Fletcher, *Arthurian Material in the Chronicles*, Boston, 1906; L. A. Paton, 'Merlin and Ganieda,' in *Modern Language Notes*, Baltimore, June 1903; J. G. Evans, *Catalogues of Welsh MSS* (for Hist. MSS Comm.), London, 1898–1910; Wynkyn de Worde, *Lytel Treatys of the Byrth and Prophecy of Merlin*, do. 1510 (known only through the last leaf of its reprint, pub. 1529, said by the late Bernard Quaritch to be extant); T. Heywood, *The Life of Merlin, surnamed Ambrosius, his Prophecies and Predictions*, London, 1641, *Merlin's Prophecies and Predictions Interpreted*, do. 1651; *Merlin's Life and Prophecies*, do. 1658; *The Life of Merlin, surnamed Ambrosius*, Carmarthen, 1812, London, 1813; *Les Prophécies de Merlin*, 3 vols., Paris, 1526; *La Vita de Merlino*, etc., Venice, 1507; *Prophetia Anglicana et Romana, hoc est, Merlini Ambrosii Britanni . . . vaticinia, una cum septem libris explanationum in eandem Prophetiam . . . Alani de Insulis*, Frankfort, 1603, [2]1608; art. 'Merlin,' in *Dublin Univ. Magazine*, June 1865; 'Merlinus-spá,' in G. Vigfússon and F. Y. Powell, *Corpus poet. boreale*, Oxford, 1883; T. Malory, *Morte d'Arthur*, 1st ed., London, c. 1485; *Historia di Merlino*, Venice, 1480; *El baladeo del sabio Merlin*, Burgos, 1498; Hersart de la Villemarqué, *Myrdhin ou l'enchanteur Merlin*, Paris, 1862; T. Stephens, *The Literature of the Kymry*, Llandovery and London, 1849; San-Marte, *Die Arthursage*, etc., Leipzig, 1842; F. G. Freytag, *Dissertatio de Merlino Britannico*, Naumburg, 1737; F. E. de Mézeray, *Hist. de France*, Paris, 1685; Giraldus Cambrensis, *Itin. Camb.*, London, 1801, Rolls Series, do. 1861–91; Tennyson, *Idylls of the King*, 1st ed., do. 1859; Sharon Turner, *A Vindication of the Genuineness of the Ancient British Poems*, do. 1803; *Catastrophe Mundi or Merlin Reviv'd* (anon.), do. 1683; A. Nutt, *Studies on the Legend of the Holy Grail*, do. 1888; J. Rhŷs, *Arthurian Legend*, Oxford, 1891; C. Chabaneau, *Fragments d'une traduction provençale du roman de Merlin*, Paris, 1883. Further literature is given by V. Chevalier, *Répertoire des sources hist. du moyen âge bio-bibliog.*, new ed., Paris, 1905–07, col. 3202 f.

E. ANWYL.

MESMERISM.—See HYPNOTISM.

MESSALIANS.—See EUCHITES.

MESSIAH.—I. *SCOPE OF THE ARTICLE.*—Much confusion is caused by the fact that the term 'Messianic' is used in a much wider range of meaning than 'Messiah.' It has come to be applied by Christian writers to everything in the OT which is thought to refer, however vaguely, to the coming and work of Christ or to the Church, while, even where this implication is wanting, it is given very generally to all passages which speak of the hope of a better and glorious future. 'Messiah,' on the other hand, refers definitely to a person, and it would seem, therefore, that the term 'Messianic' should be confined to passages which imply the coming of an extraordinary person, normally regarded as a king, who is to be in a special sense sent and endowed by God, and whose advent is to mark the end of a world-age. It would, indeed, be an advantage if the looser use of 'Messianic' could be dropped; it suggests that, in the hope of a Golden Age, the principal and original element was the expectation of a Saviour-King, which might here and there be ignored, or which might be assumed to be implied even where it was not actually mentioned. In fact, however, the reverse is the case; the oldest and the most general expectation is that of the era of happiness, and with this the hope of the Messiah was sometimes combined in later times. For it is quite clear that a majority of the OT passages which deal with the hopes of a glorious future do not speak of the King of the future at all; Jahweh Himself is the agent of deliverance and of judgment; He alone is Saviour and Redeemer in the OT; the nation as a whole, or the dynasty of its kings, is the object of His favour. In such cases the Christian interpreter may have good ground for maintaining that, from the religious point of view, such hopes were realized in the coming of Christ, but historically they are not the same as the expectation of a Messiah, and can be called Messianic only in the lax sense. All this wider expectation belongs to the subject of eschatology (*q.v.*), and this article will, therefore, be confined to the consideration of the Messiah in the strict sense, and the term 'Messianic' will be used only in connexion with him. It may be added that, while eschatology does not always imply a Messiah, neither does the

Messiah himself always appear in a strictly eschatological setting.

II. *MEANING OF THE WORD.*—The term 'Messiah' represents the Heb. Māshîaḥ, the Aram. Meshîḥā, 'anointed one.' It is used quite generally in the OT as an epithet, both of priests (Lv 4⁵ 6²² etc., and perhaps Dn 9²⁵) and of kings, esp. of Saul (1 S 12³ etc.), while in Is 45¹ it is applied to Cyrus. Nowhere in the OT does it occur in its later technical sense, which is first found in *Enoch* and *Psalms of Solomon* (see below, IV. 1). In the OT language any Jewish king is 'the Lord's anointed,' and the phrase is in no way confined to a single pre-eminent king. In Ps 105¹⁵ and 1 Ch 16²² 'anointed ones' occurs in the plural, of the patriarchs. Dalman[1] suggests that Messiah in its later sense is a shortened form of 'Jhvh's Anointed,' and that no single passage of the OT was responsible for its adoption.

'Christ' is, of course, Χριστός, the Gr. equivalent, which translates the Heb. Māshîaḥ in the Septuagint. In view of discussions connected with its use in the NT, it is well to note that it is sometimes used without the article even when it is an epithet standing in apposition to a proper name —*e.g.*, 1 S 26⁹· ¹¹.

The general significance of anointing is discussed in the art. under that heading. In view of the fact that 'Messiah' did not become a technical term till late, the primitive meaning of anointing is quite irrelevant in considering the ideas associated with the figure; *e.g.*, even if it be true that anointing was originally transferred from the image of the god to the king, we cannot argue that the Messiah was regarded as a divine being. Anointing had come to denote the two ideas of consecration and endowment.

III. *TEACHING OF THE OT.*—In order to discover the general trend of the OT teaching it is essential first to discuss, however briefly, the exegesis of the separate passages which speak, or may be reasonably thought to speak, of the coming of a Messiah; in no other way is it possible to realize the precise extent and nature of the hope. The examination is complicated not merely by difficulties of interpretation, but also by questions as to authenticity and date. Here it should be noted that, if critics reject as late certain passages which refer to the Messiah, it is by no means always from any *a priori* unwillingness to allow the Messianic hope to be of early date or to find it in a particular prophet, but because on external evidence such passages seem to be inconsistent with the context. In many cases they presuppose the Exile in a way which seems to be impossible in a pre-Exilic writer; in others the note of hope and promise seems to nullify the message of judgment and punishment which occupies the central place. Here the criterion to be applied is a very delicate one. How far did threats and promises actually exist side by side in the message of the same prophet? At what point do the promises become so contradictory of the threats that they can be regarded only as later insertions? However these questions may be answered in any particular case, it may not be superfluous to point out that, when a passage is regarded as 'unauthentic' and late, it does not lose its value, either historical or religious; and it still remains evidence of the Messianic hope, only in a different age and circle from that to which it is commonly assigned. The principle being admitted that the prophetic books are composite works, comprising elements of various periods, each case must be judged solely on its merits.

1. **The data.**—It will be well to begin with 2 S 7 as the passage which is most clearly typical of the OT belief, at any rate on one side. It seems to be Deuteronomic in tone, and can hardly be earlier than the reign of Josiah. Its main purport is to insist on the permanence of the Davidic dynasty (vv.¹¹· ¹⁶). In its context this is contrasted with the fall of Saul's house (v.¹⁵), but we may also assume an implied contrast with the various short-lived dynasties of the Northern Kingdom (cf. Hos 8⁴). The passage itself does not speak of any single pre-eminent or final successor of David and is in no way eschatological, but precisely in proportion as the actual occupants of the throne proved themselves unworthy would it be natural to look for some one king who could realize the ideal. And, if at the same time there were other expectations of a wonderful Saviour, the two lines of hope would easily coalesce. At any rate, the personal Messiah in the OT is nearly always associated with the Davidic dynasty, and the references in the early prophets which have any claim to be regarded as Messianic are all connected with it. They may, indeed, be older than 2 S 7, and in any case this passage will hardly be the origin of the hope; it rather embodies and gives literary form to something which already existed.

In Am 9¹¹⁻¹⁵ there is a promise of the restoration of the Davidic dynasty, with no reference to a personal Messiah, but the passage is almost certainly an Exilic addition (so J. Wellhausen, K. Marti, G. A. Smith, etc., though S. R. Driver* defends it with some hesitation).

In Hosea it may not be necessary, with Marti and Volz, to reject all passages which speak of future happiness, but the only verse which is in any way Messianic in the strict sense is 3⁵, 'Afterward shall the children of Israel return, and seek the Lord their God, and David their king.' Here, again, the stress is laid on the Davidic dynasty; but either the whole verse or at least the words 'David their king' are of doubtful authenticity.

The crux of the question with regard to early Messianic prophecy is reached when we come to Isaiah.

(*a*) Is 7¹⁴ᶠᶠ·.†—Until a new factor was introduced by considerations derived from comparative religion, it was becoming generally agreed that the passage had no reference to the birth, miraculous or otherwise, of a Saviour-child or king at all. As Gray points out, the promised sign is not necessarily a marvel or miracle (cf. Ex 3¹², 1 S 2²⁷ᶠᶠ·), but is to be found 'in the chain of events predicted.' By the time a child shortly to be born reaches a certain age the promised deliverance will have come. His name Immanuel does not imply the divinity of the child, or even that he will play a rôle as God's agent in the deliverance (as a matter of fact, there is not the least hint that he does anything of the sort), but, after the common Hebrew usage, expresses the point of view of the parents; it is the reverse of Ichabod (1 S 4²¹). H. Gressmann,‡ however, and others argue that the passage is intelligible only if we suppose an already existing belief in the advent of a divine Saviour-child, who is to be born mysteriously. On this view the virgin is 'the virgin of prophecy,' the mother spoken of in the tradition; 'butter and honey' are the food of the gods, as in Iranian and Greek myth; and the whole passage

[1] *The Words of Jesus*, p. 291; see p. 292 for later Jewish use of the term.

* *Cambridge Bible*, 'Joel and Amos,' Cambridge, 1897, p. 119 ff.

† Reference should be made to the very full and excellent discussion of this and the other Isaianic passages in G. B. Gray, *ICC*, 'Isaiah,' Edinburgh, 1912.

‡ *Der Ursprung der israelitisch-jüdischen Eschatologie*, Göttingen, 1905, p. 272 ff.; A. Jeremias, *Babylonisches im Neuen Testament*, Leipzig, 1905, p. 64 ff.; C. F. Burney, *JThSt* x. [1908–09] 580 ff. For criticism see C. Clemen, *Primitive Christianity and its Non-Jewish Sources*, Eng. tr., Edinburgh, 1912, p. 143.

has a mythological background. The theory has an undeniable fascination, but its main hypothesis cannot yet be regarded as proved (see below, 2 (*d*)). In this case it rests on the probably false assumption that the sign must be of a miraculous nature. Further, neither the article nor the noun in *hā'almāh* requires the meaning put upon it. If we reject the reference to the wife of Isaiah or Ahaz or to some other particular mother, the definite article may be generic as in Am 3^{12}, while it is now generally agreed that *'almāh* does not necessarily denote virginity, and is certainly not the word which would have been chosen if the supernatural character of the birth without a human father had been the point to be emphasized. 'Butter and honey' may be merely a symbol of plenty, a variant of the common 'milk and honey.'[1] But perhaps the chief objection to the mythological view is to be found in the fact, to which attention has already been called, that Immanuel does not play any part in the deliverance, nor does he afterwards appear as a factor in this or any other prophet's hopes for the future. The apparent reference to Immanuel in 8^{8} is quite meaningless; there has been nothing to suggest that the child is the king to whom the land belongs, and we should probably read with LXX 'for God is with us' (cf. v.^{10}).[2]

(*b*) Is $9^{6ff.}$ is a passage of a very different character. We have here a true Davidic Messiah, but it is important to note that the restoration is the work of Jahweh Himself; the child is not himself a conqueror, but is born to be Prince of Peace. The fourfold name is remarkable, and, as Gray points out, 'mighty God' must not be toned down to 'mighty hero'; it is unique in the OT. Clemen[3] admits that all four titles are 'perhaps mythological,' and the passage suggests the influence of the *Hofstil* (see below). The child apparently ascends the throne at once—a suggestion that it is empty at the time of his birth; this may perhaps imply an Exilic date, though there is nothing else in the passage itself which necessitates its being placed later than Isaiah.[4] It is, in fact, the clearest and best passage to establish an early expectation of a Messiah. It is, however, very remarkable that the passage seems to have had no influence on later literature, being never referred to either in the OT or in the Apocalypses or the NT.[5]

(*c*) Is $11^{1ff.}$ had, on the contrary, a great influence on later thought, and lies behind the picture of the Messiah as drawn in many apocalyptic passages; in particular, the term 'Branch' became technical. Here, again, the Messiah is Davidic, with a special endowment of the Spirit. We note, too, the stress laid on the return of the Golden Age—a feature which may be derived from foreign mythology. At any rate, we have the Davidic Messiah in a clearly eschatological setting; v.^{1} seems to imply a date after 586 B.C.;[6] the metaphor is that of a tree cut down to the stump and sending out fresh shoots, which would describe exactly the revival of the kingdom after its ruin at the fall of Jerusalem.

Mic $5^{2ff.}$ is peculiarly difficult.* Omitting minor questions of reading and exegesis, the main points are as follows. (*a*) The passage follows, though it may not be originally connected with, an eschatological passage in ch. 4 (cf. Is 2) where there is no mention of a Messiah. (*b*) It speaks of a Messianic king born at Bethlehem Ephrathah, and, therefore, Davidic; in spite of his humble origin (so G. A. Smith, *The Twelve Prophets*, London, 1896, i. 413 ff.), he is to be a great and apparently a peaceful ruler. Is more than this hinted at? In particular, does v.^{2b} imply pre-existence or merely the antiquity of the family from which he springs? And what is the meaning of 'she which travaileth'? Gressmann and others explain it of the divine mother, and J. M. P. Smith admits this, but regards the verse as a late gloss, implying a Messianic interpretation of Is 7^{14}; the change of person from both v.^{2b} and v.^{4} is very awkward, and so is the contradiction between Jahweh's abandonment of His people and the previous verse. But, even if a mysterious birth is hinted at, there is no suggestion that the mother is a virgin or that the child is in any way connected with Immanuel. Whatever the date of the verse, it is far better to follow some of the older commentators (Calvin, Orelli, etc.) and see in the phrase a reference to the birth-pangs of Zion in $4^{9f.}$, where exactly the same word is used for 'travaileth,' while in both passages the return of the remnant is referred to (cf. Hos 13^{13}, Is 26^{17}, where the same figure of travail is used). 'She which travaileth' is, therefore, Zion personified. (*c*) Verse ^{2} certainly implies that there is no reigning king and, therefore, suggests an Exilic date. (*d*) Verse $^{5ff.}$ seem to belong to a different prophecy (tr. 'This'—not 'This man'—'shall be our protection'). The Messiah drops out, and the confidence of the passage rests on a different basis.†

In Jeremiah the main stress is laid on the continuance of the Davidic line, and this figures prominently in the book as we have it—a feature which is significant in view of the Deuteronomic origin of the fundamental passage 1 S 7. In $23^{5ff.}$‡ we have the righteous Branch or Shoot (*ṣemaḥ*, not *nēṣer*, as in Is 11), with the name Jahweh Ṣidqēnū, 'The Lord our Righteousness,' perhaps with an ironic reference to Zedekiah, the reigning king. But the application of the same term to Jerusalem in the parallel passage (33^{16}) shows that the main stress is on the dynasty rather than on any single or final representative, and this feature appears clearly in 17^{25} 22^{4} ('kings sitting upon the throne of David'),§ while in $33^{14ff.}$ a very special emphasis is laid on the covenant with David, interpreted as meaning that he should never want a successor. In 30^{9} ('they shall serve the Lord their God, and David their king, whom I will raise up unto them') the reference seems to be to each successive representative rather than to any single descendant, or to a belief in the actual return of David himself. Finally, we note that Jahweh Himself is consistently the agent of deliverance, the Davidic king appearing only after the salvation is completed.

The general presentation in Ezekiel agrees with that of Jeremiah. We have references to 'David my servant,' as the ruler of the future (34^{23} 37^{24}), with pictures of the Golden Age and a strong

[1] It is not necessary for our present purpose to enter on the vexed question whether the passage is a threat or a promise; in either case we must suppose a certain amount of later insertions or of combination of passages written at different periods. Those who regard the passage as a threat take 'butter and honey' as a symbol of scarcity and nomadic fare—a view which Gray criticizes severely.

[2] The fact that the LXX has this rendering here suggests that its rendering παρθένος in 7^{14} does not, as is often argued, imply that it interpreted the passage Messianically. For, if it had done so, it would surely not have dropped the only other possible reference to the divine child.

[3] P. 145.

[4] See Gray, *ad loc.* (p. 168), for a criticism of R. H. Kennett's argument (*The Composition of the Book of Isaiah*, London, 1910, p. 71) that the word used for 'boot' means a military boot worn by Syro-Greek soldiers, this implying a Maccabean date. Gray himself leaves the date open.

[5] Dalman, p. 317, n. 1.

[6] So Gray, etc.; Driver, B. Duhm, and G. A. Smith, however, keep the Isaianic date; see *HDB* ii. 488, for Smith's arguments.

* See J. M. P. Smith, *ICC*, 'Micah, Zephaniah and Nahum,' Edinburgh, 1912, *ad loc.*; Gressmann, pp. 278, 284.

† P. Haupt, in *Trans. of the Congress for the History of Religions*, Oxford, 1908, i. 268, argues for a Maccabean date; so Marti.

‡ C. H. Cornill and Marti accept the passage as genuine.

§ So in 3^{15} 23^{4} the rulers in the happy future are shepherds, in the plural (cf. the 'saviours on mount Zion,' Ob ^{21}).

stress on the presence of Jahweh Himself. In $17^{22ff.}$ the cedar twig planted on the mountain of the height of Israel may be a reference to the prophecies of Isaiah (?) and Jeremiah, while 'until he come whose right it is' (21^{27}) suggests the Shiloh prophecy of Gn 49^{10}.* On the other hand, in the ideal State of chs. 40 ff. the 'Prince' is only one of a series of kings, and plays a very subordinate part in the reformed Jerusalem. The general impression given by Ezekiel is that he was acquainted with popular hopes of an individual Messiah and, in particular, with the promises attached to the Davidic dynasty; these were too strong to be entirely ignored, but the priest-prophet himself had little real interest in them.

In Hag 2^{23} Zerubbabel is to be the ruler in the Messianic Age. So in Zec 3^8 6^{12} † he is the 'Branch' and the servant of Jahweh. The importance of the passages is twofold: (*a*) we have the first undoubted example of the identification of a historical person with the Messiah; (*b*) the reference to the Branch shows, even more decisively than in Ezekiel, that earlier prophecies were being studied and interpreted in accordance with contemporary conditions.

Zec 9^9 belongs to another and a later prophecy. Though the ass may originally have been the symbol of royalty (cf. Gn 49^{11}), it here stands for humility. The king is victorious over his enemies ('saved' rather than 'having salvation'), but the stress is on the peaceful character of his rule. He is not explicitly Davidic.

In the Psalms we are concerned with a group of royal Psalms, especially 2, 45, 72, 89, 110, 132. Here we are met with almost insoluble problems as to date, since there is not even the *a priori* presumption which we have in the case of passages which stand in the writings of a particular prophet. Further, we must allow for the possibility of glosses in the course of the many editings through which the various Psalters passed; such glosses may have emphasized a supposed Messianic reference—*e.g.*, Ps 72^{8-12}.‡ In all these Psalms we find startling language used of kings, the extent of their dominion, and their power, usually with stress on the Davidic covenant. It is common ground that such language was never strictly true of any Israelite king in either kingdom. Are these Psalms, then, addressed to the expected Deliverer of the future, *i.e.* to the Messiah? The objection to this view is the strong impression made in most cases that a definite living king is addressed; *e.g.*, Ps 45 is clearly an actual marriage song and is accepted as such, *e.g.*, by Kirkpatrick and Briggs. And, if some of these Psalms are to be understood historically, the general similarity of language suggests that the same principle is to be applied to all. A. F. Kirkpatrick,§ in fact, argues that all have a primary historical reference, of course without prejudice to their spiritual application. In interpreting the language we are helped by the existence of the *Hofstil*, or 'Court style,' to which Gressmann ‖ and others call attention. Exaggerated language of this kind was a regular feature of the court addresses and poems in honour of Oriental monarchs; cf. the language of Ps 21^{4-8}, which is certainly addressed to an actual king. It is possible that this *Hofstil* in Israel, and perhaps elsewhere (see below, **2** (*d*)), included elements derived from the Messianic expectation. If it was believed that some one member of the Davidic dynasty should be the greatest of all, it was natural for the admirers of any king to suggest on his accession that he and no other was the long-desired. In this case the Psalms may be called quasi-Messianic, and at least illustrate the nature of the Messianic hope.

A warning against too strict an interpretation of this *Hofstil* is to be found in the phenomena presented by the Babylonian hymns. We find Nannar addressed as 'begetter of gods and men,' 'King of kings who has no judge superior to him'; but then precisely the same flattery is offered to Asshur, Ishtar, or Nebo.

As H. F. Hamilton points out (*The People of God*, London, 1912, p. 8), 'the ascription of universal dominion to so many of them [*sc.* the gods] was merely a piece of inexpensive flattery which no one mistook for serious truth. . . . It was a sound policy to avoid too much partiality.'

In the same way we must beware of laying too much stress on the uniqueness, majesty, or finality ascribed to the king addressed in any particular Psalm. Its language, taken literally, may seem to be applicable only to a unique Messiah, but in the mouth of an Oriental its application is less strict or exclusive.

The following points are further to be noted. (i.) As in the Prophets, the stress is on the Davidic covenant; 2 S 7 seems to be continually before the poets' eyes. This is especially marked in Ps 89, which refers to the nation and the dynasty, the nation itself being personified in v.$^{40ff.}$ (cf. Is 5, Ps 80^{12}). So 'firstborn' in v.^{27} seems to refer to the description of Israel in Ex 4^{22}, while 'servant' in v.^{39} suggests a parallel with 2 Isaiah. The Psalm as a whole is a prayer for the restoration of the dynasty and the nation, rather than for the coming of any particular king who is to mark a new epoch. The same applies to Ps 132, though 'horn of David to bud' (v.^{17}) may refer to 'the Branch.' Ps 45, however, is not Davidic (Briggs and Sellin ascribe it to N. Israel), nor is Ps 110 except in the title.

(ii.) The language of the Psalter had great influence on later Messianic ideas, terms being used which afterwards became titles of the Messiah. As they occur in the Psalter they are, however, hardly technical; they are not used of one definite figure or king to the exclusion of all others. We have 'anointed' (Ps 2^2 $89^{38.51}$ $132^{10.17}$) used in its general sense (see above, § II.), 'son' (2^7, probably not in 2^{12}), 'firstborn' (89^{27}), while 'thy throne, O God' (45^6), *may* imply deification.*

(iii.) Ps 110 stands alone in speaking of a priest-king, who is not, however, Levitical; it is very generally regarded as Maccabean, referring to Simon (see, however, Briggs, *ad loc.*).

There remain a few other OT passages, mainly fragments of poetry embedded in the historical books, which require brief notice.

Gn 49^{10}.†—It may be taken for granted that Shiloh is not a personal title of the Messiah. The first hint of such a view is found in the Talmud (*Sanh.* 98*b*), and it was not so used till the versions of the 16th century (Driver). The reading and interpretation are both doubtful, but it is possible that the passage is Messianic—'until he come whose right it is' (Ezk 21^{27}; see above) may be a reference.‡ The question then arises whether the

* As showing that earlier prophecies were by this time definitely studied, see 38^{17}, where there is a re-editing of Jer 3–6, Zeph 1^7.

† The text is in disorder; Zerubbabel must have been originally mentioned in 6^{11}; cf. 'crowns' in the plural and 'them both' in v.^{13}. Possibly when the power was centred in the high priest the text was deliberately altered, giving us perhaps the first example of the Levitical Messiah (see Driver, *Cambridge Bible*, *ad loc.*).

‡ See C. A. and E. G. Briggs, *ICC*, 'Psalms,' Edinburgh, 1906–07, *ad loc.*

§ See *Cambridge Bible*, 'Psalms,' Cambridge, 1892–1912, vol. i. p. lxxvi ff.

‖ P. 250 ff.; E. Sellin, *Der alttestamentliche Prophetismus*, Leipzig, 1912, p. 169 ff.

* So Gressmann, p. 256. This interpretation, however, which is that of LXX and He $1^{8f.}$, is open to grave objections; note esp. that in v.^{7} we have 'Jahweh thy God.' Briggs supposes an interpolated address to God; Kirkpatrick favours, out of the many suggestions, 'thy throne is the throne of God,' or else 'thy Throne shall be for ever and ever,' *Elohim* having been substituted for an original *jhjh* or *jhvh*, misread as Jahveh.

† See Commentaries by Driver and Skinner, *ICC*, *ad loc.*

‡ O. C. Whitehouse, however (*DCG* ii. 172), thinks that the Genesis passage is moulded on Ezekiel.

verse is a late addition on the basis of the Isaianic prophecies (Driver), or whether, with Gunkel, Gressmann, and Sellin, we are to regard it as a fragment of pre-prophetic eschatology, not specifically Davidic. But it is a strange eulogy to say that Judah shall rule only till the great one from elsewhere comes. Skinner holds that the reference is simply to the Davidic dynasty; Judah is to be independent till it is merged in the kingdom of its hero.

Of Gn 3[15] the most that can be urged in the way of Messianic interpretation is that the passage is a prediction of the ultimate victory of man, the seed of the woman, in the conflict with evil, typified by the serpent. The 'seed' cannot be understood as referring to any definite descendant of Adam in the singular. The same applies to the other predictions in Genesis with regard to the seed of Abraham, where the thought is of the nation; the exegesis of St. Paul in Gal 3[16] is admittedly untenable.

Nu 24[17] is usually understood as referring to David's conquest of Moab. But, on the ground that 'star' suggests a semi-mythological figure, Sellin* and others find in the passage a trace of a primitive Messianic hope; others regard it as Messianic but late. Note that the passage is certainly corrupt at the close.

Dt 33[17] may refer only to the dominion of Ephraim (the Song belongs to the N. Kingdom), but Sellin† again urges that the hyperbole is too strong and that we have an echo of an early Messianic hope, transferred to Ephraim. In later times the passage influenced the idea of the Messiah ben Joseph.‡

Dt 18[15] (applied Messianically in Ac 3[22] 7[37]) is clearly a promise of a succession of prophets, not of a single and final prophet.

A word must be said with regard to the Servant passages of 2 Isaiah. Very few critics now consider these to be Messianic in the strict sense, the reference being either to the actual nation or to the ideal Israel. This is so clear in the early songs that it must also hold good of Is 53; this is best understood of the sufferings of the Exile, which are seen to have a redemptive value not only for the nation, but for the world as a whole.§ Gressmann,‖ however, on the ground of the obscure and oracular character of the language, argues that the writer is using already existing material which would be understood by his readers. Is 53 is a mystery hymn, addressed to a dying and rising God; He is treated as an eschatological figure, parallel to that of the Messiah, who is here neither Davidic nor specifically a king. It cannot be said that there is any real evidence for this view (for a criticism see Clemen, p. 149). Nor, again, is it possible to find a suffering God or Messiah in Zec 12[10], which clearly refers to some historical martyr.

In Dn 7[13ff.] ¶ there can be little doubt that the figure of 'a son of [a] man' appearing 'on' or 'with the clouds of heaven'** is, in the context, a symbol of Israel itself, a human being in contrast to the 'beasts,' the hostile world empires. But it is equally clear that the expression came to be understood of a personal Messiah (see below, IV. 2 (*d*) (2)), and it is urged with some reason that it did not originate with Daniel, but had a history behind it. The figure is introduced as familiar, and no explanation is given in the ch. of the coming with clouds, which may, therefore, be assumed to be a recognized element in the conception. Gressmann[1] believes that we have a figure of foreign origin, parallel with the Messiah and afterwards identified with him. To Sellin[2] he is the Messiah transformed, the *Urmensch*, or 'primal man,' of Paradise, who is to return once more; Clemen[3] is inclined to agree with this explanation of the origin.

In 9[25f.] the references in the AV to the Messiah are certainly misleading.[4] In v.[25] 'the anointed one, the prince,' is either Cyrus or Jeshua; in v.[26] he is Onias the high priest.

2. Survey of OT teaching.—(*a*) From our review of the OT passages it becomes clear that the expectation of the Messiah in the strict sense occupied a comparatively subordinate place.[5] The fact that in a large number of books and passages which deal with the future he is not mentioned at all is of the greatest significance as showing that his coming was not an essential or invariable element in the national hopes; *e.g.*, he is never mentioned in Zephaniah, which is entirely eschatological, nor in Joel. It cannot be assumed, as the Christian interpreter often unconsciously assumes, that the Messiah is in such cases taken for granted. There is, in fact, no hint of him, and often no room for him. Further, even in books or groups of writing where we have found possible references to him, there are many passages where he is completely ignored (*e.g.*, in Isaiah). The idea is introduced suddenly and sporadically and as suddenly dropped. Jahweh Himself is always the Redeemer and Saviour, and this is the essential and unvarying element in the OT teaching; the stress is on His coming and manifestation and not on that of any representative.[6]

(*b*) There are constant references to hopes connected with the dynasty of David, and these sometimes take the form of the expectation of another David, a specially endowed ruler. During the degradation and after the fall of the monarchy the earlier period was naturally idealized and became to the nation its Golden Age, while it became more and more necessary that he who was to revive its glories should be regarded as no ordinary man, but as the special representative of Jahweh.

(*c*) The way in which the references to the Messiah are introduced and the fact that they are so frequently enigmatic in form suggest that the Messianic belief was, above all, an element in the popular religion. It is wanting in the Priestly writings, and, as we saw, Ezekiel seems to have been somewhat suspicious of it; the prophets do not use it consistently, and it appears and disappears in an extraordinary way. Its connexion with the kingdom would commend it to the mind of the people, while religious teachers could avail themselves of it only with caution and reserve, though it could not always be entirely ignored. It is obvious that these were, in fact, the features which determined Christ's attitude to the hope in later times.

(*d*) In recent years the whole subject has been reconsidered in the light of comparative religion.[7] Gunkel and, especially for our present subject, Gressmann have urged that Jewish eschatology, including the Messianic hope, is not a new development in the prophetic or Exilic periods, but that it goes back to a far earlier age and is really not specifically Jewish at all. They argue that the hope of a semi-divine Deliverer, or *Heilbringer*,

* P. 171. † *Ib.*

‡ Bousset, *Religion des Judentums*, p. 265.

§ See art. JUDAISM, vol. vii. p. 583b. ‖ P. 301 ff.

¶ The literature is very extensive; reference may be made to Driver, *Cambridge Bible*, 'Daniel,' Cambridge, 1900, Dalman, p. 241 ff., and to artt. in the Dictionaries, *s.v.* 'Son of Man.' For the linguistic problem see art. JESUS CHRIST, vol. vii. pp. 516–519.

** It is pointed out that '*on* the clouds,' which is read by LXX, is used only of God; Dalman regards this as the original reading; Bousset, p. 301, n. 1, the reverse.

1 P. 340 ff. 2 P. 177. 3 P. 82.

4 See, for a full discussion of the traditional and other interpretations, Driver, 'Daniel,' *ad loc.*

5 See E. Kautzsch, *HDB* v. 694, 713.

6 Dalman, p. 295 f.; Sellin, p. 193.

7 H. Gunkel, *Schöpfung und Chaos*, Göttingen, 1895; Gressmann, *Der Ursprung der israelitisch-jüdischen Eschatologie*; Sellin, *Der alttestamentliche Prophetismus*; T. K. Cheyne, *Bible Problems*, London and New York, 1904; W. O. E. Oesterley, *Evolution of the Messianic Idea*, London, 1908; criticisms in Gray, 'Isaiah,' and Clemen.

was a common possession of the ancient world, especially in Egypt and Babylonia, and that the OT language is intelligible only when understood as one expression of that hope. Sellin essentially agrees as to the antiquity of the belief, which he regards as not merely pre-prophetic but as pre-Davidic, while he rejects the hypothesis of its foreign origin, being ready to admit foreign influence only in colouring and details.[1]

We have already had examples of the principles of this school as applied to such passages as Is 7, Mic 5, etc. It is further suggested[2] that the Messiah is the *Urmensch*, or primal man, the hero-king of Paradise, who is to return with the Golden Age at the end. Gressmann rightly points out that the Messiah is the prince of peace rather than a conqueror; *i.e.*, he is the king of the Golden Age restored by Jahweh. Sellin[3] develops this idea. Job 15^7 suggests a tradition of the first man as pre-existent with God and sharing His wisdom; he finds a trace of this in Gn 3^6, 'to make one wise,'[4] while the same word is used in Jer 23^5, Is 52^{13}; cf. the stress on wisdom in Is 11^2. He is, further, the 'son of man' of Ps 8 and of Daniel, while his pre-existence is hinted at in Is 49^1 51^{16}. Gressmann further argues that the idea of world dominion cannot be Hebrew in origin; cf. Ps 72^8, where the river Euphrates is the centre of empire (it cannot be a boundary parallel to the 'ends of the earth'). Again, it is suggested that the descriptions of Jahweh ascending the throne and becoming king must have originally referred to a divine Messiah; the latter, Gunkel and Zimmern believe, is Babylonian in origin, while the same may be the case with the *Hofstil* in general.

The point of view is fascinating and has been argued with great ingenuity, but it has been generally felt that it lacks definite proof when we come to the details, whether of the OT passages or of the supposed parallels. As we have seen, the interpretation of the crucial passages is very doubtful. The Immanuel passage does not seem to refer to the Messiah hope at all, while, if 'she which travaileth' in Micah is understood of Zion, the idea of a mysterious origin disappears; the Shiloh passage is open to so many interpretations that it is very unsafe to build on it. It is quite true that with regard to eschatology in general (and it must be remembered that the view which we are considering starts from eschatology and not from the Messianic hope in particular) the prophets from Amos onwards give the impression of dealing with ideas already to some extent familiar, and it is equally true that the same is sometimes the case with the Messianic passages, but this does not justify us in finding the solution of every obscure passage in hypothetical popular traditions. We have already argued that the way in which the allusions to the Messiah are introduced does suggest that the idea was general and popular, used only occasionally and with some reserve by the prophets, so that it cannot be regarded as the discovery of any one of them. But of its great antiquity there is no real evidence. The passages in which it occurs are in many cases placed late on quite definite grounds, and we could hardly prove that it existed before the Exile except in the form of expectations connected with the permanence and glory of the house of David. We must, in fact, admit that data are wanting whereby we might fix with any certainty the period in which the hope arose. We can only say that the way in which the allusions are introduced does militate against its origin being placed in the Exilic period, in spite of the lack of definite evidence to the contrary, though

[1] Pp. 176, 191, 228 ff. [2] Gressmann, p. 286 ff. [3] P. 179 ff.
[4] Skinner and *Oxford Heb. Lexicon*, however, translate הִשְׂכִּיל, 'to look at.'

they do not in any way carry it back to a dim antiquity.

A similar verdict of 'not proven' must be passed on the hypothesis of a foreign origin (with regard to foreign influence on details, such as in the *Hofstil* and partial parallels, especially at a later period, the case is somewhat different). The preceding discussions have already dealt with many of the points. Sellin[1] discusses the supposed parallels in some detail, and concludes that there is no real parallel to the expectation of a divine deliverer to come at the *end* of history or to usher in a new era. The most that we find is a yearning for the return of the Golden Age of Paradise, together with the courtier's flattery applied to some particular king that he will be the one to bring this about—*e.g.*, the famous Letter to Assurbanipal. A. H. Gardiner[2] has shown that the Leyden Papyrus has been misinterpreted and contains no reference to a 'Messiah,' while the Golenischeff Papyrus refers to a contemporary king Amen-em-het I. In all these cases we have examples of *Hofstil*, with the natural hope that each new king will bring in an era of peace and happiness, but no real evidence of a genuine expectation of a Messiah, which, Sellin concludes, is peculiar to Israel: 'The ancient East knows no eschatological king.'[3]

To return to the OT, the hypothesis of the wide-spread expectation of a Redeemer-King is not necessary to explain its language. We have in the earliest Messianic passages expectations connected with the revival and increased glory of the dynasty of David. There are also the eschatological hopes of the return of the Golden Age, which probably go back to a comparatively early period; this is to be brought about by Jahweh Himself; but, since all critical periods of progress are in actual experience connected with the appearance of some specially great individual (Israel was familiar with the work of an Abraham, a Moses, a David, or an Elijah), it was natural to believe that this salvation of Jahweh might be mediated by His earthly representative, who would then be looked for among the descendants of David; in this way the national and the eschatological hopes would easily be combined as we find them combined in the late passage Is 11. So far from the Davidic Messiah being the precipitation of widely diffused ideas of a world Saviour, the latter seems to have developed later as the offspring of the union of national and eschatological hopes.

IV. *DEVELOPMENT SUBSEQUENT TO THE OT.*—**I. The data.**—In passing to the period covered by the Apocrypha and the apocalyptic literature, it will be well again to begin by some examination of the actual data.[4]

(*a*) *Books where the Messianic hope is ignored.*—In the eschatology of the Apocrypha, with the exception of 2 Esdras, the Messianic hope is practically ignored. It is just possible that there may be a hint of it in the reference to the coming of the 'faithful prophet' in 1 Mac 14^{41} (cf. 4^{46}), but, if so, the hope appears in a very attenuated form. In 2^{57} the permanence, or, in the context, the restoration, of the Davidic kingdom is mentioned with no reference to the Messiah. In the rest of the books, though there may be hints of the Messianic kingdom in the wider sense (*e.g.*, 2 Mac 2^{18}, Bar 4^{21}, Sir 44–50), nothing is said about a personal Messiah. Wis 2 ff. deals with the sufferings of the righteous in a way that recalls Is 53, and with the future life, but is clearly not Messianic.

[1] P. 231 ff.; see also Clemen.
[2] *Admonitions of an Egyptian Sage*, Leipzig, 1909.
[3] P. 177.
[4] The references are generally to the *Apocrypha and Pseudepigrapha of the Old Testament*, ed. R. H. Charles, Oxford, 1913, as well as to Charles's editions of the separate books; the dates given are generally those adopted by him; see also his *Eschatology*[2].

A similar silence is found in some of the apocalyptic literature, and here this silence is all the more significant since the writers are dealing directly with the hopes for the future. The Messiah does not figure in *Enoch* i.–xxxvi., lxxii.–lxxxii., xcii.–cviii., except in cv., where 'my Son' is suddenly introduced; Charles regards the chapter as an independent fragment. In the pictures of the Golden Age in *Jub.* i. 29, xxiii. 26 there is no Messiah; in xxxi. 18 he figures, though not prominently, as the descendant of Judah and as ruler in the temporary Messianic kingdom; Charles, however, considers the clause to be an interpolation. In the *Assumption of Moses*, which comes from a 'Pharisaic Quietist,' there is again no reference; Taxo (ix. 1) cannot be the Messiah;[1] Jahweh Himself is the avenger, and Moses the only mediator. The Messiah is in the same way ignored in 3 and 4 Mac., the *Secrets of Enoch*, the *Letter of Aristeas*, and the later parts of the *Apocalypse of Baruch*.

(*b*) *Books where the Messiah is mentioned.*—In *Enoch* lxxxiii.–xc. (166–161 B.C.) the Messiah appears after the judgment as the 'white bull,' a human figure, with no very active or definite rôle. In the 'parables,' however (xxxvii.–lxxi.; 94–64 B.C.), we have rich material. Especially in xlv.–lvii. he is the central figure, the pre-existent Son of man, judge, ruler, champion, and revealer. Besides Son of man, he is called 'the Elect One' and 'the Righteous,' titles which appear in the NT. 'Messiah' or 'His Anointed' also occurs in xlviii. 10, lii. 4, and Charles regards these as the first example of the use of the word as a technical title, though Dalman[2] strikes out the passages as interpolations.

In the *Testaments of the Twelve Patriarchs* the salient point is that the Messiah is descended from Levi, and is a priest (cf. Ps 110); see *Test. Reub.* vi. 7–12, *Test. Levi*, viii. 14, xviii., *Test. Jud.* xxiv. 1 ff., etc. In *Test. Jud.* xxiv. 5 f., however, we find the usual Messiah ben Judah; so perhaps *Test. Naph.* iv. 5. According to Charles, the former conception is the original, and the book dates from 109–106 B.C., the palmy days of Hyrcanus, the Maccabean dynasty, which came of a priestly family, being then regarded as Messianic. But, after the breach between it and the Pharisees, and the infamies of Hyrcanus' successors, additions were made to the book, reverting to the ordinary view. The conception of the Messiah is that he is a priest and a warrior, sinless, with power over evil spirits, and bringing sin to an end; the ethical note is strongly marked.

In the *Psalms of Solomon* (70–40 B.C.) there is no reference to the Messiah in i.–xvi., though the future deliverance is dealt with. In xvii. and xviii., however, there is a very important description. He is Davidic in contrast to the non-Davidic dynasty of the Hasmonæans; though himself human, he comes with the power and special endowments of God; he is to conquer the nations and purge Jerusalem of sin. The whole picture is full of enthusiastic and vigorous touches, but there are no transcendent traits in the conception. The end and the duration of the Messiah's kingdom are not clear, but 'throughout his days' in xvii. 42 suggests that he is regarded as mortal. He is called 'His' or 'the Lord's anointed,' the title being here certainly a technical one, its first occurrence, if the passages in Enoch are rejected.[3]

In the *Sibylline Oracles*, iii. 49 (168–51 B.C.), we read of 'a holy prince' who is to reign over the whole earth for all ages, though, somewhat inconsistently, judgment follows; iii. 652 (*c.* 140 B.C.) speaks of a king from the sunrise sent by God who is to bring peace to every land. In the later fifth book (before A.D. 130) we have (in 108) again a king sent from God who apparently destroys Nero *redivivus* (Antichrist), while 414 ff. speak of a 'blessed man' from the plains of heaven, who destroys evil-doers and sets up the new temple.

The *Fragment of a Zadokite Work*,[1] first published by S. Schechter in 1910, is placed by Charles in 18–8 B.C. and by most scholars before A.D. 70, and seems to have come from a reforming party among the priests. 'A Teacher of righteousness' has already appeared (i. 7, etc.), and a Messiah is expected (ii. 10, viii. 2 [?], ix. 10, 29, xv. 4, xviii. 8) who is to arise 'from Aaron and Israel.' Charles interprets this phrase as pointing to the sons of Mariamne and Herod. This is not quite certain, but the Messiah is clearly Levitic, as in the *Testaments*, the book being marked by hostility towards Judah. The 'Teacher of righteousness' or the 'Lawgiver' (viii. 5) is a forerunner of the Messiah, though at a considerable interval, and is identified with the 'star' of Nu 24^{17}, the 'sceptre' of the same passage being applied to the Messiah.

In the composite (*Syriac*) *Apoc. of Baruch* the Messiah appears in the three earlier Fragments, A^1, A^2, A^3, written before A.D. 70. In xxix. f. (A^1) he is revealed mysteriously, apparently from heaven, whither he returns in glory; his rôle is a passive one, and the whole conception is materialistic. In xxxix. f. (A^2) and lxxii. ff. (A^3) he is the warrior slaying enemies and ruling over the Gentiles; the influence of Is 11 is marked. In lxx. 9 the phrase 'my servant Messiah' occurs, but the whole verse is regarded as an interpolation. In the three later Fragments, B^1, B^2, B^3, there is the so-called Messianic Kingdom without a Messiah.

4 (2) Esdras is again composite. In $7^{27ff.}$ (*Ezra Apocalypse*) we have the remarkable conception of 'My Son the Messiah' revealed with his companions and dying after a reign of 400 years (cf. 14^9). In 12^{32} (the 'Eagle Vision') he is the Lion of the seed of David who destroys sinners; the text has been interpolated to represent him as pre-existent and dying at the end, in order to agree with 7^{27}. Of chief importance is the 'Son of man' vision (ch. 13), where the Messiah is 'the man,' as in Daniel, 'My Son,' pre-existent, destroying the ungodly by the fire of his mouth and the breath of his lips, and restoring the ten tribes to the heavenly Zion.

Philo makes only very slight references to the Messiah, who is really foreign to his system. That he is mentioned at all must be regarded as a concession to the popular standpoint. *De Execrat.* 8 f. speaks of the restoration of Israel on one day; the dispersed are to return led 'by a divine superhuman appearance, which, though unseen by all others, is visible only to the delivered.' So in *de Præm. et Pœn.* 15–20 the Messiah is a man of war, reference being made to Nu 24^7.

In the same way the Messiah is recognized by Josephus only very occasionally, and that in a way which shows that he did not take the subject very seriously. In *BJ* VI. v. 4 he practically treats Vespasian as the Messiah in the sense that he is to be the destined 'governor of the habitable earth'; cf. the account of his interview with the same emperor in III. viii. 9, and see Suet. *Vesp.* ch. 4, and Tac. *Hist.* v. 13,[2] passages which are good evidence that the existence of the Messianic hope was a

[1] See Charles, *ad loc.*; F. C. Burkitt, *Jewish and Christian Apocalypses*, London, 1914, p. 39.
[2] P. 269.
[3] In xvii. 36 'Anointed Lord' (χριστὸς κύριος) is generally recognized as a mistranslation or misreading of 'the Lord's Anointed.'

[1] Besides the works already quoted see also a survey of recent literature on the book by J. W. Lightley, in the *London Quarterly Review*, Jan. 1915, p. 15.
[2] See *JE*, *s.v.* 'Messiah,' for similar ideas connected with Alexander, on the basis of the interview recorded in Jos. *Ant.* XI. viii. 5.

recognized feature of Judaism. In *Ant.* X. x. 4 he refuses to explain the 'stone' of Dn 2^{45} on the ground that his history is not concerned with the future.

As evidence of popular views, though not of the belief of Josephus himself, we have the various quasi-Messianic risings which he records: Theudas (*Ant.* XX. v. 1), the Egyptian (*Ant.* XX. viii. 6, *BJ* II. xiii. 5), and the unnamed impostor (*Ant.* XX. viii. 10).

A *Samaritan Hymn for the Day of Atonement*,[1] dated A.D. 1376, but certainly embodying earlier material, speaks of the Messiah under the title *Taeb*, which probably means 'the Restorer,' though A. Merx explains it as *rediens, i.e.* probably Moses, whose return was expected. This *Taeb* is not supernatural, but restores the lost dominion of the people, and is a prophet, the conception being based on the figure of Moses in opposition to the beliefs of the Jerusalem Jews. He dies after 110 years, and his death is followed by the Judgment and the end. Jn $4^{25ff.}$ shows the antiquity of some Messianic belief among the Samaritans (cf. Jos. *Ant.* XVIII. iv. 1).

2. Survey of the teaching.—(*a*) We note the sporadic character of the Messianic hope, as in the OT. Certainly the Messiah is mentioned somewhat more frequently, and when he appears we have in some cases a few more details, but it is still true that until the fall of Jerusalem he is not an essential element in Jewish religious thought or even in its eschatology.[2] If it were not for the NT, we should never have imagined that there was a period when the expectation of his coming could be taken for granted as accepted in almost all circles and as the centre of the hope for the future. This aspect is sometimes discussed (*e.g.*, W. Baldensperger, *Die messianisch-apokalyptischen Hoffnungen des Judentums*, Strassburg, 1903, p. 92 ff.) as though the problem were the disappearance of the Messianic hope during the Maccabean period. If our interpretation of the evidence is correct, this misrepresents the facts, since there is nothing to show that the hope was at any previous period either universal or essential. It may be true[3] that the figure of the Davidic king came to seem too small for the larger stage on which Israel now found itself, and that the rule of the Maccabees left the pious Jew for a time well content, but it is best to recognize that the data are insufficient for anything like a chart of the rise and fall of the Messianic hope. The one thing we can say is that in the 1st cent. A.D. the Messianic hope had become more universal than ever before. We recognize that even then it is absent in the *Ass. of Moses*, and is not taken very seriously by Philo or Josephus; but the NT evidence is indisputable, and is confirmed by the fact that the Messiah is an integral part of the creed of later Judaism. The explanation is probably to be sought in the political circumstances of the day and in the dislike of the rule of the Herods and the Romans.

(*b*) There is some evidence which suggests that, as before, the hope was mainly an element in the popular religion. The Apocalypses in which it figures were largely popular products, and the NT proves that its chief strength lay among the people;[4] the popular risings recorded in Josephus show the same thing.

(*c*) We may see two influences at work which tended to throw into higher relief the person and function of the Messiah. From the religious side there was the growing tendency to remove God from active interference with the affairs of the world and to fill His place with a series of intermediate beings.[1] Hence the rôle of the Messiah becomes more important, and functions which in the OT are ascribed to Jahweh Himself are now transferred to him. He becomes the Deliverer and Saviour, as in the *Sib. Or.*, Baruch, and Esdras, and the new conception thus meets a real religious need. Again, as outward conditions became more hopeless, it was inevitable that he who was to restore the nation should be increasingly conceived of as endowed with supernatural powers, or as himself more than man. His coming is to affect the whole world, though it is still always regarded from a strictly Jewish and national standpoint. As a keener interest is taken in the fate of the individual, so the conception is linked with beliefs in judgment and resurrection, and receives altogether a more decided and more varied eschatological colouring, though we remind ourselves once more that it is not an *essential* element in the eschatology of the time.[2]

(*d*) Attempts to distinguish varying types of the hope at different periods and in different classes of writings are not always very convincing. We can, however, trace a double development,[3] though the two lines overlap, and each includes contradictory elements derived from the other—*e.g.*, in the combination of the conceptions of a Warrior-Conqueror and of a supernatural Avenger and Judge, or of earthly and heavenly bliss.[4] (1) We have the conception, which is essentially that of the OT, of the Messiah as a human figure, however miraculously endowed, a warrior and a conqueror, and the Son of David. This is seen best in the *Psalms of Solomon* (where the title 'Son of David' occurs for the first time), and is implied in many passages of the Gospels dealing with the popular hope, especially in the attempts to make Christ king, and in the charges brought at His trial, as well as in the Messianic movements mentioned by Josephus. This Messiah is to conquer the nations (*Sib. Or.* iii. 653, v. 108 f., 416 ff.; Bar 39^7 70^9) and sometimes to convert them (*Test. Jud.* xxiv. 6; *En.* xlviii. 5), though their conversion is also often disconnected from the Messiah (To 13^{11} 14^6, *En.* xc. 30, etc.).

Parallel to this conception is that of the Messiah ben Levi,[5] found in the *Testaments* and the *Zadokite Fragment* (cf. Ps 110), and represented in the NT by the heavenly priesthood of Christ in Hebrews.[6]

(2) We find a belief in a transcendent Messiah, connected chiefly with the title 'Son of man,' in the parables of *Enoch* and 4 Esdras (cf. also *Sib. Or.* v. 414). The phrase is derived from Daniel, and, whatever its meaning and origin there, there can be no doubt that in *Enoch* and Esdras it has a definite Messianic significance;[7] it is possibly even a recognized technical title.[8] The fact is, as Baldensperger[9] points out, that Daniel, though not

1 See A. Cowley, 'Samaritan Doctrine of the Messiah,' in *Exp*, 5th ser., i. [1895] 161 ff.; Bousset, pp 258, 265.

2 It is possible that the place of the Messiah was sometimes taken by Michael, as a parallel figure; in Dn 12^1 he, and not the Messiah, is the champion of Israel; so in *Ass. Moses*, x. he is the angel who avenges Israel; note his prominence in Rev 12. Bousset (*Die Offenbarung Johannes*, Göttingen, 1896, *ad loc.*) suggests that the Christology of Hermas can be understood only by seeing that Christ takes the place formerly filled in Jewish thought by Michael; cf. also Rev 14^{14}, where the Son of man on the cloud seems to be an angel; note the language of v.[15].

3 Bousset, *Rel. des Judentums*, p. 255 ff.

4 *Ib.* p. 257.

1 See Baldensperger, ch. ii.

2 This eschatological colouring, the signs of the coming of the Messiah ('the Messianic woes,' etc.), the duration and nature of the Messianic kingdom, and its relation to the Judgment and Resurrection, together with the varying ideas as to the fate of the Gentiles therein, are dealt with in art. ESCHATOLOGY, to which reference should be made. See also Schürer, *HJP* II. ii. 137 ff.; W. V. Hague, *JThSt* xii. [1910] 57.

3 See Hague, p. 72 ff.

4 Baldensperger, p. 111 ff.

5 We have not sufficient material to justify us in regarding this as a specifically Sadducean conception as opposed to a Pharisaic Messiah ben David.

6 For connexion with the *Testaments*, etc., see H. Windisch, *Hebräerbrief*, Tübingen, 1913, p. 67.

7 Dalman, p. 243.

8 So Charles, *Eschatology*², p. 261.

9 P. 97 ff.

in itself directly Messianic, revived hopes for the future and prepared the way for the apocalyptic Messiah.[1] This transcendent Messiah plays an active rôle as champion of the righteous in *Enoch* lxii. 2, and still more decidedly in 4 Es $13^{9ff.\ 37ff.}$. The most significant feature, however, is his appearance as judge, not only of men and the nations, but of evil spirits (*Enoch* lv. 4, etc.); this function is not ascribed to the human king. Except in 4 Es 12^{32}, a Christian interpolation, the transcendent Messiah is never represented as a descendant of David—a fact which may throw light on our Lord's question (Mk $12^{35ff.}$); He may have been following a recognized line of thought which found the Davidic descent too narrow for the great conception. As is well known, He never speaks of Himself as 'Son of David.' We may note that, though the Apocalypses apparently reject the Davidic descent, they yet use Davidic passages, such as Is 11, Ps 72, 89, in their picture of the Messiah.[2]

(*e*) *Pre-existence and mysterious origin.* — The Son of man is clearly in some sense pre-existent in *Enoch* (*e.g.*, xlviii. 3, 6, xlvi. 1) and in 4 Es 13 and perhaps in 7^{27} 12^{32}, though the former passage is doubtful, and G. H. Box regards the latter as interpolated.[3] The question arises how far a personal pre-existence is really implied. In Jewish thought everything of supreme value was regarded as pre-existing in the mind of God, perhaps to some extent under the influence of the Platonic doctrine of ideas. This applied to such things as the Law and the Temple, while even Moses is pre-existent in *Ass. Moses*, i. 14, iii. 12; it is this sort of pre-existence that is ascribed to the Messiah or his 'Name' in the Targums.[4] But it must be allowed that in *Enoch* and Esdras the Messiah seems to be regarded as pre-existent in a personal sense and revealed from heaven, and this was certainly the view of St. Paul. It should, however, be noted that in 4 Es 7^{28} 'my Son, the Messiah' who is thus revealed dies after 400 years; *i.e.*, he is not a divine being.

This point of view should be distinguished from the hints which we have of the mysterious origin and birth of the human Messiah, since the Son of man of *Enoch* and Esdras is, of course, not born as a man at all. We have doubted the existence of such ideas in Isaiah and Micah, but they are clearly found at a later period—*e.g.*, in the mysterious star of *Test. Levi*, xviii. and in the king ἀπ' ἠελίοιο of *Sib. Or.* iii. 652 (cf. Bar 29^{3}). We have definite evidence of the belief in Jn 7^{27}, Justin Martyr (*Dial.* 8, 110), and the Talmud, the general idea being that the Messiah was to be born in secret (at Bethlehem) and hidden on earth, or even in Paradise, until the time of his revelation.[5] Some such tradition seems to underlie Rev 12; on the question of foreign influence see below, (*g*).

At the same time the passages cited as evidence of a belief in his birth of a virgin or divine mother are unreliable.[6] *Test. Jos.* xix., which seems to speak of a virgin-birth, is with good reason regarded by Charles as corrupt; so in *Enoch* lxii. 5, lxix. 29 he reads for 'son of a woman' 'Son of man,' while the *Midrash Ekhāh* on La 5^{3} is obscure and of very doubtful date. Nor, again, can 'the travail pangs of the Messiah' imply anything of the kind; the expression is figurative, and applies to the Messiah, not to his mother. According to Justin, *Dial.* 49, the Jewish belief is that the Messiah is to be born ἄνθρωπος ἐξ ἀνθρώπου.

To the circle of ideas connected with pre-existence belongs the identification of the Messiah with the first or the spiritual man.[1] Something has been said of the theory that this underlies the figure of the Son of man (see above, III. 2 (*d*)). Philo (*Leg. Alleg.* i. 31, p. 49, *de Op. Mundi*, 134, p. 32) knows of an earthly and a spiritual man, the latter, whose creation is recorded in Gn 1, coming first, while the former is the man of Gn 2. St. Paul (1 Co $15^{45ff.}$) represents the spiritual man as coming *after* the psychic or earthly, evidently opposing the other view, and identifies him with the Messiah. So in *Test. Levi* the Messiah brings back Paradise, while the Samaritan title *Taeb* seems to mean 'Restorer' (cf. χρόνοι ἀποκαταστάσεως in Ac 3^{21}). The general idea in St. Paul, however, is the identification of Christ with the ideal archetypal man,[2] as opposed to the historical Adam, and not with any first king of Paradise.

(*f*) *Forerunners of the Messiah.*—The starting-point is Mal 3 f., where Elijah is to return before the Day of Jahweh (cf. Sir 48^{10}); the Messiah is not mentioned, and possibly Elijah is a kind of substitute for him.[3] In the Gospels, however, he has become a forerunner of the Messiah (Mk 1^{2} 6^{15} 8^{28} 9^{11}, Jn 1^{21}). There are again traces of a belief in the return of Moses, based on Dt 18^{15}, and the two are combined in the Transfiguration; these are probably the 'two witnesses' of Rev 11^{3}. In the later Antichrist legend the two witnesses are Enoch and Elijah,[4] who were translated without death. There are also hints of other 'companions' of the Messiah in 4 Es 6^{26} 7^{28} 13^{52}; Ezra appears as such in 14^{9}, Baruch in Bar 76^{2}, Jeremiah in 2 Mac 2^{1} 15^{13}; cf. Mt 16^{13}. We may compare the two predecessors of Saoshyant (see below, (*g*)).

(*g*) *Foreign influence.* — We were doubtful of theories which traced the origin of the Messianic idea to foreign sources, but this does not exclude the possibility of foreign influences at a later time on the details of the conception. Such influence is undoubtedly found in the development of Jewish Apocalyptic. We cannot discuss the wider question of the syncretistic character of its eschatology in general, but must confine ourselves to points which directly affect the conception of the Messiah. Naturally it is in the transcendent Messiah that foreign and mythological traits appear most clearly. Hague,[5] following Gressmann, argues that such ideas lie behind 4 Es 13, and even goes further in holding that a star myth is implied in the appearance of the man 'from the sea.' He also traces[6] the whole idea of a mysterious revelation of the Messiah to Is 45^{15}, 'Verily thou art a God that hidest thyself, O God of Israel, the Saviour,' which, he agrees with Gressmann,[7] cannot be of Jewish origin. He traces it to language such as that used by Assurbanipal: 'I was born in the midst of mountains which no man knoweth . . . thou (Ishtar) . . . hast brought me forth from the mountains, hast called me to shepherd thy people.' Many critics[8] argue in the same way with regard to the conception of a miraculous birth, comparing the language used by Sargon I. ('My mother was poor, my father I knew not'), the beliefs connected with Saoshyant, and the legends of the birth of Cyrus, Alexander, and others; there is, in fact, a general tendency to regard extraordinary men as

[1] Dn 7^{13} is interpreted Messianically by Aqiba (*c.* A.D. 120), and gave rise to the later name for the Messiah, *Ănānî*, 'Cloud Man' (Dalman, p. 245).

[2] Dalman, p. 318.

[3] The LXX of Ps 109 [110]^{3}, ἐκ γαστρὸς πρὸ ἑωσφόρου ἐξεγέννησά σε, suggests some kind of pre-existence.

[4] In *JE*, *s.v.* 'Messiah,' it is, however, argued that there are traces in Rabbinic literature of a real pre-existence of the Messiah.

[5] Dalman, p. 301; Hague, p. 83.

[6] Jeremias, p. 30; see Clemen, p. 292.

[1] See H. Lietzmann, *Handbuch zum NT*, Tübingen, 1910, on 1 Co $15^{45ff.}$; Clemen, p. 152 ff.

[2] This conception seems to occur in *Barnabas* v. 5, vi. 12. For later developments see Bousset, *Hauptprobleme der Gnosis*, Göttingen, 1911, p. 172 ff., *Kyrios Christos*, do. 1913, p. 25 f.

[3] Baldensperger, p. 96.

[4] Bousset, *The Antichrist Legend*, Eng. tr., London, 1896, p. 203 ff.

[5] P. 90 ff. [6] P. 83. [7] P. 311.

[8] Jeremias, pp. 28 ff., 38, 46 ff.; Cheyne, *passim*.

wonderfully born, and this was particularly marked with regard to Egyptian and Babylonian kings. Without pronouncing on the question of direct influence, we may admit that we find the same general tendency at work with regard to beliefs as to the origin of the Messiah, but always with the important proviso that we have found no real evidence, except in Christian circles, of the idea of his birth from a virgin or divine mother, nor have we yet found any complete parallel to the expectation of a final eschatological king.[1]

Something must be said of the possible influence of Zoroastrianism.[2] Here, again, we would at once admit a general influence in the sphere of eschatology. Moulton allows this, though to a less extent even than Clemen. He draws attention to Bousset's[3] admission that Parsi influence must have come to Israel by way of Babylon 'when strongly tainted with Babylonian elements,' and argues, further, that Zarathushtra himself had very little influence in the West. Hence, all that the Jews can have known was Parsiism in a comparatively debased form, as represented by the Magi (*q.v.*), and this compels us to regard most of the parallels between the higher doctrines of the two religions as pure coincidences. We are concerned here mainly with two points.

(1) A great deal has been said of the connexion between Yima, the first man, and the Messiah. It is held[4] that this lies behind the idea of the 'Son of man' (see above, III. 1 and 2 (*d*)), which, Clemen agrees, 'comes ultimately from Parsiism.' There is, no doubt, some connexion between Yima and the fall story, though Moulton[5] holds that Parsiism is the borrower. Further, as Bousset allows, there is the important difference that, while Yima is king of Paradise, *der Urzeit*, the Messiah is king *der Endzeit*, and there is no trace of this transformation in Iranian legend. We may add that there is also no trace in Hebrew legend of the Messiah as originally king of the first Paradise (see above, (*c*)).

(2) There is undoubtedly a remarkable similarity between the Messiah and Saoshyant, which is originally an epithet rather than a title. The renovation of the world 'is accomplished by the present labours of "those that will deliver," the *saošyantō*. In the Gathas these are simply Zarathushtra himself and his fellow-workers, whom the Prophet's faith pictures as assuredly leading on an immediate regeneration.'[6] The hope failed, and Zarathushtra himself was to return as Saoshyant. This is certainly the one real parallel with the Messiah proper, but it seems impossible to suppose any direct influence. Moulton[7] dismisses it among 'the certainly fortuitous coincidences,' while Bousset[8] holds that the connexion is between Saoshyant and the forerunner Elijah, rather than with the Messiah himself. At the same time there may have been some reaction between the two, affecting details of the conceptions, especially in the idea of the Messiah coming from the sunrise; cf. the ἀπ' ἠελίοιο of *Sib. Or.* iii. 652, and the LXX ἀνατολή for 'branch' in Jer 33^{15}, Zec 6^{12} (cf. Lk 1^{78}).[9]

We must also allow for the influence of Græco-Roman ideas[1] affecting at any rate the periphery of the Messianic hope and its development under Christianity. After Alexander the title σωτήρ ('Saviour') became common, with deification of kings and emperors, accompanied by hints of their wonderful origin. We may instance the well-known Priene inscription, with the legends connected with Augustus. But here, again, it is doubtful whether we really have proof of the existence of a belief in a final world-Saviour who is to usher in a new era, or only the inevitable court flattery which regards each king as greater than any of his predecessors. The single exception is Vergil's famous Messianic *Eclogue*.[2] Here, whether the child who is to be born be the son of Octavian and Scribonia or not, we have a remarkable and almost unique agreement with OT conceptions—the era of Paradise and its king, the Golden Age following on his conquests, plenty without toil, animals sharing in the regeneration, together with the ethical note. Whether through the Sibylline Books or directly through the LXX, Jewish teaching may have penetrated to Roman literary circles, or we may have an echo of Zoroastrianism.[3] On the other hand, the parallel may point to an independent spread of something like a Messianic hope in pagan circles.

(*h*) *Interpretation of prophecies.*—A feature of this period is the habit of working on earlier prophecies—a tendency which we have found as early as Ezekiel and Zechariah; for a later example see To 14^{5}.[4] In the apocalyptic books there are certain prophetic passages and ideas which became part of the stock-in-trade and are constantly referred to in dealing with the Messianic hope. The chief are Dn 7, Is 11,[5] used continually (*e.g.*, *Ps. Sol.*, Bar.), Ps 2[6] (*e.g.*, *Ps. Sol.*), Ps 45 (*e.g.*, *Test. Jud.* xxiv. 1), Nu 24^{17}, the star of which is applied Messianically in *Test. Levi* xviii. 3, *Jud.* xxiv. 1, but understood of the Teacher of Righteousness in *Zad. Frag.* ix. 8.

We have in this use of prophecy many examples of the scribal methods[7] working mechanically on the data and fusing the old and new into a single picture, of course not without contradictions. The application of a passage does not decide its historical meaning, but only the interpretation which had come to be put upon it. The vagaries of later Rabbinism had already begun—*e.g.*, the interpretation of Am $5^{26f.}$ in *Zad. Frag.* ix. 5 ff. We have an interesting example of independence in 4 Es $12^{12f.}$, where the interpretation of the fourth kingdom as given in Dn 7^{23} is definitely rejected.

It is important to ask in this connexion whether by the first cent. A.D. the OT was in any circles interpreted as pointing to a Suffering Messiah. It is almost certain that it was not. The conception in 4 Es 7 is the quite different one of a human Messiah who is to die after a reign of 400 years (cf. the Samaritan *Taeb*). There is no evidence that Is 53 was interpreted Messianically until a later period, and, when it is, the verses which speak of suffering are applied not to him but to the nation.[8]

[1] For foreign influences in Rev 12 see Bousset, *Offenbarung*, *ad loc.*, and Cheyne, p. 77 ff., with criticism in Clemen, p. 303 ff.

[2] See art. ESCHATOLOGY, vol. v. p. 381, with literature there cited, and add J. H. Moulton, *Early Zoroastrianism*, London, 1913, esp. Lect. ix., 'Zarathushtra and Israel,' with discussions in Clemen (summary on p. 368). W. Fairweather (*HDB* v. 297, 307) accepts influence in details without supposing direct borrowing.

[3] *Rel. des Judentums*, p. 550.

[4] Gressmann, p. 290 ff.; Bousset, *Rel. des Judentums*, p. 257 ff.; Clemen, p. 154 ff.

[5] P. 308.

[6] Moulton, p. 158.

[7] P. 309.

[8] *Rel. des Judentums*, p. 584, n. 2.

[9] See A. Smythe Palmer, *HJ* v. [1906–07] 156.

[1] Bousset, *Rel. des Judentums*, p. 258; Jeremias, p. 58 ff.; A. Deissmann, *Light from the Ancient East*, Eng. tr., London, 1911, p. 368 ff.

[2] See J. B. Mayor, W. W. Fowler, and R. S. Conway, *Virgil's Messianic Eclogue*, London, 1907.

[3] So Moulton, p. 91, interpreting the simile of the closing lines as a reference to the story that Zoroaster laughed when he was born.

[4] It may be remarked that there are hardly any traces in the LXX of an attempt on the part of the translators to introduce a Messianic meaning; χριστός is never introduced where the Heb. has not Messiah. Is 7 is no exception (see above, III. 1), but the title of Ps 45, 'Song of the Beloved,' for 'Song of Loves,' may be intended to suggest a Messianic interpretation. For ἀνατολή for 'Branch' see above, (*g*).

[5] But not Is 9 (see above, III. 1) or 7.

[6] This, however, is comparatively rare (Dalman, p. 268 ff.).

[7] Baldensperger, p. 104.

[8] V. H. Stanton, *HDB*, art. 'Messiah'; see, further, Driver and A. D. Neubauer, *Jewish Interpreters of Is. liii.*, London, 1877;

The most decisive proof of this position comes from the NT. It is clear that the death of the Messiah was not expected in any quarter, and that the crucifixion of Jesus was the great stumbling-block, while it was not easy to find proof of its necessity from the OT. The story of the Ethiopian eunuch (Ac $8^{27ff.}$) seems to be intended to call attention to an interpretation of Is 53 which is evidently not that generally accepted. The admissions of Trypho (Justin, *Dial.* 68, 89 f.) do not express the Jewish belief, but are put into his mouth under the stress of the argument, while the 'pangs of the Messiah' do not refer to his personal sufferings, but to the woes which are to precede his coming.

The Messiah ben Joseph, who does, in fact, die, in contrast to the Messiah ben Judah, appears clearly only after A.D. 135. According to Bousset,[1] he is the Messiah of the ten tribes, slain in the battle by Gog and Magog; the conception seems to be derived from Dt 33^{17}, Zec 12^{10}, and certainly has no connexion with Is 53. It is possible that this figure is connected with the failure and death of Bar Kokhba, explaining them on the lines of the expectation of a preliminary Messiah who was to fall in battle against the enemies of Israel (Rome).

V. *DEVELOPMENT UNDER CHRISTIANITY.*—The starting-point of the evidence of the NT, and especially of the Gospels, is the way in which the Messianic hope is represented as universal. As we have seen, it is taken for granted in the Apocalypses where it occurs, but it is still sporadic in its appearances, and the future can be painted without reference to it. But in the Gospels the expectation of the Messiah is common to all. It appears, indeed, to be taken more seriously by the common people than by their leaders; but Pharisees, priests, and Sadducees all accept the hope without questioning its validity. The point at issue is only whether Jesus is really the Messiah. As regards the nature of the hope, it would appear, as against A. Schweitzer, that it was at least as much political and national as transcendent, corresponding closely to what we find in *Ps. Sol.* The Messiah is to be a king descended from David, and his rule will be opposed to that of the Romans.

A full discussion of our Lord's own attitude to His Messianic claims will be found in art. JESUS CHRIST. We may here emphasize the salient points. (*a*) As against W. Wrede, it is certain that He did regard Himself as in some sense the Messiah. He did not, indeed, proclaim Himself as such in His public teaching; it was His 'secret,' discovered by St. Peter at Cæsarea Philippi, and first avowed to the world at His trial. (*b*) His favourite designation of Himself in this connexion was 'Son of man,' the title being chosen as containing in it elements of transcendence and mystery, and as free from the political implications of Messiah, and still more of Son of David, a title which He avoids. The difficulty is to reconcile His use of this phrase with the absence of any public proclamation of His claim, since from its use in *Enoch* we should infer that it would at once be recognized as a synonym for 'Messiah' itself. The difficulty is eased by eliminating, on literary grounds, a certain number of the passages in which it occurs (cf., *e.g.*, Mt 5^{10} with Lk 6^{32}, or Mt 16^{3} with Mk 8^{27}), while in others its use is ambiguous, since it might be supposed to refer to some other unnamed person (Mk 8^{38}). It is not, however, possible, except by somewhat drastic criticism, to eliminate all passages where it is used publicly of Himself or privately to the disciples before St. Peter's confession.[1] We must, therefore, suppose, in spite of *Enoch*, that it was regarded as Messianic only in certain circles, and that it could still be used, as in Ps 8 and Ezekiel, in a wider sense.

(*c*) He did not regard Himself as the Messiah merely in the strict sense in which we have used the term, but as gathering up in Himself the various lines of OT hopes and promises. It does not, however, appear that direct argument on the basis of the OT played any considerable part in His teaching, except as recorded in the Fourth Gospel. The proofs from the OT in the NT seem rather to reflect a later stage of controversy between Jew and Christian, in which each adopted the same scribal methods of interpretation.

(*d*) Christ added considerably to the content of the Messianic hope, especially in His teaching as to the necessity of the death of the Messiah. It is not possible to decide with any certainty as to the lines by which He was led to this conviction, though it was, no doubt, helped by a growing recognition of the hostility of the ruling powers to His claims and of the inevitable results of their attitude. Further, He must have meditated on the deeper teaching of the OT as implying, especially in Ps 22 and Is 53, that the means of redemption and the condition of glorification were to be found only in suffering, and this quite independently of whether such passages technically applied to the Messiah or not. Though in Acts and 1 Peter the Servant passages are directly quoted, they are used but little in the Gospels, and hardly at all in Christ's own teaching (see Lk 22^{37}, Mk 10^{45} $12^{6ff.}$). It would seem, then, that as the ultimate source of His conviction we are forced to fall back on an intuition which the Christian will regard as a revelation from the Father.

In the light of the expectation of the Parousia, the idea of a twofold advent of the Messiah was introduced, assuming that Jesus was not merely 'the Messiah of the future' during His lifetime. There is no trace in earlier literature of any belief in two comings of the Messiah.

(*e*) It follows, finally, that the title 'Messiah' or 'Christ,'[2] as used in the NT and in Christian literature generally, has a far richer meaning and content than any that we have felt justified in ascribing to it in earlier periods. It gathered into itself the ideas associated with the Wisdom and Logos,[3] and came to include the whole work of redemption from sin and spiritual regeneration accomplished by Jesus. He has become the centre of history and the inaugurator of a new age in a way which both differs from and transcends anything that we find in the OT or Apocalypses as associated with the future Deliverer. He is the mediator of a new covenant and the bearer of a new revelation to a world of which the outward conditions remain unaltered, while with the passing of the Jewish State the nationalist element dropped away once for all. At the same time, the title 'Christ,' with its historical associations, is a reminder, even to those to whom the promises of the OT may mean little in themselves, that the coming of Jesus of Nazareth was not something new and unexpected, but was the true climax of the long preparation of the chosen people. In particular, the fact that functions which in the OT are reserved for Jahweh and not for the Messiah

Dalman, *Der leidende und der sterbende Messias*, Berlin, 1888; Schürer, II. ii. 184. Bousset, *Kyrios Christos*, p. 27 ff., agrees, though he leaves open the bare possibility that the wide-spread myths of the dying and rising god may have influenced Jewish Messianic ideas.

[1] *Rel. des Judentums*, p. 264, *Antichrist Legend*, p. 103. But in *JE*, *s.v.* 'Messiah,' the connexion with the ten tribes is denied.

[1] But see Dalman, *Words of Jesus*, p. 260 ff.

[2] It must be remembered that 'Christ' tends to become a proper name and to lose its technical Messianic implications; the distinctive title of Jesus in Hellenistic Christianity is κύριος ('Lord'). See Bousset, *Kyrios Christos*, esp. p. 94 ff.

[3] Note that in Philo the Logos largely takes the place of Messiah; in *de Conf.* 14, p. 414, the 'branch' of Zec 6^{12} is applied to the Logos. Cf. also art. LOGOS.

are in the NT transferred to Christ is of the deepest significance. The real desire of the highest spirits of Israel was not so much for a representative of Jahweh, however exalted, as for a revelation of God Himself. Christian belief finds this satisfied in the Incarnation, and we shall not be disturbed when we find that the OT says comparatively little about the Messiah. The vital question is whether the hopes which it entertained with regard to the coming of God did find their fulfilment in the Christ.

VI. *THE MESSIAH IN LATER JUDAISM.*[1]—From the end of the 1st cent. A.D. a belief in the Messiah was an integral part of the Jewish creed—a proof that the representation of the universality of the hope which we find in the NT is substantially correct. The Messiah is indeed strangely absent from the Mishna, possibly owing to fear of Rome, but he figures both in the Palestinian and in the Babylonian recensions of the *Shᵉmôneh 'Esrêh*—a fact which indicates that his presence therein must date from the 1st cent. A.D.—and appears constantly in the Talmud. The failure of the Bar Kokhba rising in A.D. 135 marks an important stage. Attempts to anticipate the Messiah's coming were then abandoned, the principle being 'a plague on those who calculate the end,' and the political side was almost dropped. What remained of it was transferred to a temporary Messianic Kingdom, in which Israel was to be restored to Palestine, this national kingdom being, generally speaking, only preparatory to the *'ôlām hab-bā*, the world to come, where universalistic features are found. The Messiah is Son of David[2] and an earthly deliverer, though in some sense pre-existent and appearing mysteriously (see above, IV. 2 (*e*))—features which need not imply divinity. With the fall of Jerusalem apocalyptic fell into disfavour,[3] and with it the belief in a transcendent Messiah. Polemic with Christians also worked in the same direction, and to this we may attribute the disuse of the title 'Son of man'; the form of the Beatitude in Lk 6[22] may be a hint of such controversies.[4] The spiritual side is strongly emphasized in the Rabbinic teaching by its insistence on the need for repentance as the condition of the coming of the Messiah, while we also find considerable detail as to the features of the Messianic era, the Messianic woes, etc.

The twelfth article of the present Jewish creed, as drawn up by Maimonides, is as follows: 'I believe with perfect faith in the coming of the Messiah, and though he tarry I will wait daily for his coming.' Liberal Judaism, however, would seem to have abandoned the hope of a personal Messiah, though it still retains the Messianic hope in a wider and spiritualized sense[5]—a sense in which it may fairly claim to have the general trend of the OT on its side.

LITERATURE.—The literature bearing on special points has been indicated in the course of the article. The following may be mentioned in relation to the whole subject: J. Drummond, *The Jewish Messiah*, London, 1877; V. H. Stanton, *The Jewish and the Christian Messiah*, Edinburgh, 1886; E. C. A. Riehm, *Die messian. Weissagung*, Gotha, 1885, Eng. tr., *Messianic Prophecy*², Edinburgh, 1900; C. A. Briggs, *Messianic Prophecy*, Edinburgh, 1886, and *The Messiah of the Gospels*, do. 1894; P. Volz, *Die vorexilische Jahweprophetie und der Messias*, Göttingen, 1897; E. Schürer, *GJV*³, Leipzig, 1898, Eng. tr., Edinburgh, 1890; W. Bousset, *Die Religion des Judentums im neutestamentlichen Zeitalter*², Berlin, 1906; G. H. Dalman, *Die Worte Jesu*, Leipzig, 1898, 1902, Eng. tr., Edinburgh, 1909; R. H. Charles, *Eschatology, Hebrew, Jewish, and Christian*², London, 1913; together with relevant sections in works on OT and NT Theology, and articles in the Bible Dictionaries.

C. W. EMMET.

[1] See Dalman, *Words of Jesus*, p. 291 f., etc.; *JE*, *s.v.* 'Messiah'; Oesterley and Box, *Religion and Worship of the Synagogue*, London, 1907, p. 205 ff.

[2] Yet Aqiba, who spoke of the thrones of Dn 7 as prepared for God and David, supported Bar Kokhba, who was not Davidic!

[3] Burkitt, ch. i.; see *JE*, *s.v.* 'Messiah,' for traces of belief in a transcendent Messiah in later Judaism.

[4] Baldensperger, pp. 140, 168.

[5] See C. G. Montefiore, *Outlines of Liberal Judaism*, London, 1903, pp. 280, 314; also art. JUDAISM, vol. vii. p. 608, etc.

MESSIAHS (PSEUDO-).—From the final loss of the independence of the Jewish State until within a few generations ago, Jewish history has known the frequent advent and passing of self-styled Messiahs, prophets of hope in the darkest periods of the Diaspora, self-appointed leaders of the Jewish race in the Return to the land from which their ancestors were exiled. The appearance of a Messiah was often, especially in the case of the earlier ones, accompanied by revolts and uprisings, and these almost invariably occurred at times when, and in localities where, anti-Jewish persecution was prevalent. Moreover, these Messianic movements were frequently, especially in the latter cases, of a political nature. The religious aspect of the rising was, however, seldom absent, and in many instances the new teacher, anxious to signalize his activity and to secure his influence by religious innovations, endeavoured to subvert the basic teachings of Judaism, to which, in consequence, considerable harm sometimes occurred. New sects were created on some occasions; on others wholesale adoption of Muhammadanism or Christianity took place.

Although it is to some extent customary to include a number of Jewish reformers and revolutionists in the category of pseudo-Messiahs, only a proportion of these agitators in reality attributed to themselves the Messianic semi-divinity. Others, often against their own wish, were hailed by their enraptured followers as the divine leader, promised in Jewish tradition to bring the scattered and troubled people back to their inheritance. Just as there existed a belief in an Ephraimitic Messiah who was to be the forerunner of the Davidic Messiah, so, among the pseudo-Messiahs, many pretended to be not the Messiah Himself but His forerunner. The opening of the Christian era saw in the Holy Land a number of these local minor Messiahs. Thus we learn from Josephus (*Ant.* XX. v. 1; also Ac 5[36]) that about A.D. 44 one **Theudas**, claiming to be a prophet, told his followers that he would divide the Jordan and enable them to cross dry-shod. They collected on the bank of the river for the miracle to be performed, but before the prophet could take steps to carry out his prophecy the whole party was massacred by a detachment of Roman soldiery. A similar fate overtook the followers of another Messiah, an Egyptian. They collected, it is said to the number of 30,000, on the Mount of Olives to watch the fall of the walls of Jerusalem at the command of their leader, but the proceedings were interrupted by Felix and his soldiery (Jos. *Ant.* XX. viii. 6, *BJ* II. xiii. 5; and Ac 21[38]). A third pretender preparing to lead the people into the wilderness was destroyed together with his followers by Festus the Procurator (Jos. *Ant.* XX. viii. 10).

A Messiah of a different description was **Menaḥem**, the son of Judah the Galilæan and the grandson of Hezekiah the leader of the Zealots. He seized the city of Masada together with a large store of arms, with which he supplied his followers, and then attacked Jerusalem. In battle with the soldiers of Agrippa II. Menaḥem was successful, and as a result captured Antonia, one of the defences of the capital. Emboldened by his success, Menaḥem claimed the leadership of all, and thus aroused the jealousy of his colleagues and was assassinated. Menaḥem was the last Judæan Messiah before the destruction of the Temple. Contemporary with these Messiahs of the 1st cent., similar personages arose among the Samaritans, all of whom, after an existence more or less brief, passed away. Prominent among them were Simon **Magus**, who endeavoured to induce the early Christians to join his movement, but who is said ultimately to have become converted to Christianity, together with many of his followers, and **Dositheus**, who, instead of restoring the Hebrew State, founded a Samaritan sect that survived until the 6th century.

The destruction of the Temple led for a time to a cessation of pseudo-Messianic activity. For sixty years no new Messiah arose until at length, on the accession of Hadrian, the milder government of Trajan gave way to sterner rule. The repressive policy of the Romans aroused once more the spirit of the Jewish people still unsubdued. A rebellion broke out and a leader was immediately to hand in the person of **Bar Kokhba** or Bar Kozibah (probably from the name of his birthplace). Of the personality of this leader little is known. His original name is even doubtful. It is conjectured that he was one Simeon of Cozeba (1 Ch 4[22]) or Chezib (Gn 38[5]). The name Bar Kokhba, or 'son of a star,' was given to him by the famous R. Aḳiba, who believed that in him was fulfilled the prophecy: 'There shall come forth a star out of Jacob . . . and shall smite through the corners of Moab, and break down all the sons of Sheth' (Nu 24[17]). Bar Kokhba does not appear to have adopted the designation of Messiah himself. This dignity was attributed to him by R. Aḳiba and other sages. On the outbreak of the rebellion, the whole province, composed of Judæa, Samaria, and Galilee, was evacuated by the Romans. The army of the Jews at this time has been estimated at as many as from 400,000 to 580,000 fighting men. Unfortunately, little is known of the campaign, but it is certain that the Roman garrison and the generals in command at the time of the outbreak proved respectively inadequate and incapable. The services of Julius Severus, the greatest soldier of the age, were requisitioned from Britain, where he had been waging an arduous war with the martial natives, to recover the prestige of the Roman arms. But even he, with unlimited resources, was at first compelled to remain on the defensive, and trusted to his tactics of cutting off detached parties and supplies to wear out his formidable enemy. In the course of the operations 50 general engagements were fought, and with every victory the numbers of Bar Kokhba's followers increased. From the most remote of the Jewish colonies men came to fight under his banner. Recruits were not drawn solely from Israel; Bar Kokhba's army included non-Jews in its ranks. Those who could not fight helped to fill the rebel coffers. At first the campaign proved a series of successes for the pretender. Jerusalem was soon captured, and served as a capital for Bar Kokhba, who was proclaimed king, and duly carried out the duties of sovereignty. For three years the Holy City remained in his possession, and during that time his armies succeeded in taking 50 walled towns and 985 villages. At length the tide turned. After a desperate struggle, Jerusalem was captured by the Romans, and no two stones of its buildings were left standing on one another. Other towns fell into the same hands until, of all the territories of Bar Kokhba, the town of Bither alone remained. Here the hero made his last stand, but not with the undivided support of the inmates of the fortress. Dissensions broke out among the garrison, and on the 9th of Ab, already the blackest anniversary in the Jewish calendar, Bither was stormed, Bar Kokhba killed, and his body brought in triumph to the Roman camp.

During the pacification that followed the males were slain by the thousand, and the women and children sold into slavery. Unheard of and unspeakable tragedies were enacted. In Bither alone more are said to have been slain than those who took part in the Exodus from Egypt. The number of dead was counted by hundreds of thousands. All those who were able escaped from a country which offered them the only alternatives of slavery and death with torture. Many fled to Arabia, and the considerable Jewish population of that country, even to this day, may be reckoned one of the results of Bar Kokhba's abortive insurrection. R. Aḳiba, who had been thrown into prison at the outbreak of the rebellion, died under torture at its conclusion. The war led to the final breach between the Jews and Judæo-Christians. The latter suffered severities at the hands of Bar Kokhba and his followers, in consequence of their refusal to join in the national uprising.

The fatal results of the Bar Kokhba movement discouraged for some centuries personation of the Messiah. In fact, an attractive opportunity did not occur again until the 5th cent., when, in accordance with a Talmudic computation, the day of the Messiah was supposed to be at hand. It was at this juncture that such a one, self-styled **Moses**, appeared in the island of Crete. Of his origin or his subsequent fate nothing is known. He induced the Jewish population of the island to support his pretensions, and on a specified date promised to lead them dry-shod to the mainland. On the appointed day the Jews gathered round him on a promontory and at his direction some threw themselves into the sea, expecting a path to be opened for them through the waters. The miracle did not occur. Many of the enthusiasts were drowned; others were rescued. The Messiah himself disappeared.

The pretender next to come under notice was **Isaac ben Ya'ḳūb Obadiah Abū 'Īsā al-Iṣfahānī**, who flourished at Iṣfahān at the end of the 7th century. There are two estimates of his claims. The one was that he was merely the forerunner of the Messiah, the other that he was the Messiah Himself. His call came to him through a sudden and miraculous cure from leprosy, and in support of his divinity his disciples pointed out that, although an illiterate before his call, he was able after that event not only to read and write, but even to compose books. The affairs of the khalīfate were at that period in a chaotic condition, and a military movement, such as Isaac's soon became, had good chances of success. The pretender and his followers met the army of the khalīf in battle at Rai (Rhagæ), but Abū 'Īsā was defeated and slain, and with his death the rising came to an end. The movement, however, did not die with its founder. It survived among the 'Īsāvites, the earliest of the Jewish sects of the Diaspora, who did not disappear until a couple of centuries later. Abū 'Īsā's influence on 'Anān, the founder of the Ḳaraites (*q.v.*), and on his ritual was, however, more enduring.

Abū Īsā left at least one disciple of influence. **Yudghān of Hamadān**, called al-Rā'ī ('the shepherd'), did not himself claim to be more than a prophet, although his admirers, in accordance with precedent, insisted on his Messiahship. His teachings showed undoubted traces of Ṣūfīism, then at the opening of its career; they were opposed to anthropomorphism, and to a great extent resembled those of his master Abū 'Īsā. After Yudghān's death his disciples adopted an additional doctrine —that of the immortality of their master, who, they contended, was not dead, but would appear again.

Contemporary with Yudghān al-Rā'ī was **Serenus**, a Syrian, who was both a political and a religious reformer. He promised to restore the Jews to the Holy Land, and, perhaps in consequence, his influence spread as far as Spain. His career commenced in A.D. 720, but was very short-lived. He was speedily captured and brought before the khalif Yazīd II., to whom he excused himself by stating that he had never been serious in his claims; he had merely been amusing himself at the expense of his co-religionists. Serenus was accordingly handed over to the latter for punishment, while his followers, repenting of their heresies, were re-admitted to the fold.

For the next three centuries and a half no Messiah arose in Israel. Then there was in the West a small group of unimportant pretenders: in France (*c.* 1087), at Cordoba (*c.* 1117), and at Fez (*c.* 1127). Of these there are practically no records beyond the mere mention by Maimonides. About 1160, however, one of far greater importance arose in Kurdistān. **David Alroy** (or Alrui) came from the north of Persia, probably Ādharbaijān, being a member of one of the free Jewish tribes which claimed descent from the Ten Tribes, and to which the Afghāns, the Afrīdīs, and Paṭhāns of to-day trace their ancestry. The period was again one of political disorganization. One great element of disturbance was the efforts of the Crusaders to recover and to keep possession of the Holy Land. Moreover, intertribal warfare was incessant, and the weakness of the Sultan led almost to a paralysis of the Government. It was in these circumstances that Alroy visited Baghdād, and on his return to his own people he raised the standard of revolt. A large following immediately collected, and Alroy, who had meanwhile proclaimed himself the Messiah, determined to break the yoke of the Muhammadans and to lead the Jews back to Palestine. From this point truth and legend have so intermingled in the story of Alroy that it is impossible to disentangle them. His command of the magic arts led to the acceptance of his mission far and wide. Only the Jews of Baghdād were sceptical, but his hold on the others was so strong that those in Baghdād were quite incapable of suppressing the movement. Alroy is said to have been summoned by the Sultan, to have appeared in answer to the summons and proclaimed his divine mission, to have been cast into prison, and to have miraculously escaped. Despite his magic powers, Alroy's movement was undoubtedly a failure. In all probability he was killed in an unsuccessful attack on the stronghold of Amadia. According to a less reliable version, the governing powers, unable to overthrow the Messiah by fair means, bribed his father or father-in-law to put him to death. On the death of Alroy his followers, in order to appease the Sultan, had to pay a considerable fine. In Alroy's instance also the pretender's death did not mean the end of his cult. The sect of Menaḥemites, named after Menaḥem, the traditional designation of the Messiah, adopted by Alroy, continued for many years.

A century passed before the next prominent pseudo-Messiah appeared upon the scene, but before that period, in 1172, a minor prophet arose in Yemen. His course lasted but a year, at the end of which term he was beheaded, it is said at his own request, in order to show by his return to life that he was indeed the Messiah.

Abraham ben Samuel Abulafia was born at Saragossa in 1240. While still a youth he was attracted to kabbalistic studies, and it was as a kabbalist rather than as a pseudo-Messiah that his career was of most influence. His life was spent in wandering from town to town and from country to country. In 1281 he was in Rome attempting to convert the pope to Judaism—of course without success. His boldness involved him in imprisonment, from which he is said to have escaped miraculously. Four years later, when in Sicily, Abulafia proclaimed himself the Messiah, and announced the millennium for the year 1290. The year denoted came and went, but the millennium still tarried. Abulafia continued his picturesque career for one more year and then disappeared from history. He also, however, left his spiritual descendants, for his teachings were continued by two of his disciples, **Joseph Jikatilla** and **Samuel**, both of Medinaceli. Where Abulafia had failed, they were little likely to succeed, and it was but for a moment that these two meteors flashed in the firmament.

Immediately following them came **Nissim ben Abraham of Avila**, who pointed to 1295 as the year of the millennium. There were sufficient believers to fill the Synagogue on the appointed day, there eagerly to await the divine manifestation; but again disappointment was the prevailing emotion, and, when the watchers found mystic little crosses on their garments, many, accepting them as heavenly manifestations, embraced Christianity. The fate of the prophet, as of many of his predecessors, is unknown.

A century later **Moses Botarel of Cisneros** appeared. As a prophet he was of little consequence. In 1502 **Asher Lämmlein** suddenly arose in Istria and announced that, if the people would prepare themselves, the Messiah would appear that very year. At his suggestion fasting, prayer, and almsgiving became general throughout the empire. Jews and Christians alike accepted his teachings and prepared for the advent of the Messiah and the return to the Holy Land. Here again the precedent was followed: no Messiah appeared; the prophet disappeared.

At the close of the 14th cent. **Jacob Carson** (or **Carcasoni**), a minor prophet, appeared in the north of Spain, and **David Reubeni**, the picturesque emissary of his brother the mysterious king of Khaibar, or the East, also came upon the scene. Khaibar, according to the generally accepted locality of the kingdom, was a district in S. Arabia inhabited by nomad tribes of Israelites, although the view has been put forward that Reubeni came from India (see E. N. Adler, in *Aspects of the Hebrew Genius*, p. xxii, and *Auto de Fé and Jew*, p. xxx).

Reubeni arrived at Venice in 1524 after having visited Palestine and Egypt. He immediately proceeded to Rome, where he procured an audience of the pope, Clement VII., to whom he announced that he had been sent by his brother to obtain allies and assistance in his war with the Sultan. In support of his claims Reubeni brought letters of introduction from Portuguese officers in the East. The Jews of Italy found the means for him to proceed to Lisbon, and he arrived in Portugal in 1525, with the view of inducing the king, John III., to ally himself with the king of Khaibar. For a time the Portuguese policy seemed to favour such an alliance, and King John definitely promised a fleet of 8 ships and 4000 cannon for the assistance of his new ally. At the same time the pressure that was being put upon the Marranos of Portugal was relaxed, doubtless out of deference to the susceptibilities of Reubeni.

The embassy, the ambassador, and the circumstances that surrounded them, as well as the accompanying legends that immediately began to be woven, endowed Reubeni with almost superhuman powers in the eyes of the Jews, for whom the only hope lay in the future to which all their faculties were ever strained. The interest and excitement aroused by his advent were no less intense among the Marranos than among the Jews themselves. Miraculous powers, a semi-divinity, were attributed to him. If any proof of these claims were needed, his existence as a Jew unmolested at the court of one of the most relentless of the persecutors of Jews and Judaizers was considered sufficient. The people looked eagerly towards him and expected, not a momentary palliation of their tortures, but a final release.

By no means the least of those who were dazzled by the appearance and favour of Reubeni was **Solomon Molkho** (previously Diogo Pires) (*c.* 1501–32), an official of the Government, of Jewish descent. Pires, who was a young man of great promise, aroused by the stir caused by Reubeni's mission, abandoned Christianity, adopting his ancestral Judaism in place of it, and endeavoured to attach himself as a disciple to the newcomer. The latter, however, severely discouraged all conversions to Judaism, fearing probably lest in consequence of them trouble might react on him and his mission, and Molkho found little or no favour with him. Molkho's conversion to Judaism had placed his life in great jeopardy; and, deprived of the protection of Reubeni for which he had hoped, he left Portugal for Turkey. In the East Molkho, although hitherto supposed to be quite unlearned in Jewish lore, is said to have displayed a remarkable acquaintance with that subject, and by his eloquence and learning, and the mysterious manner in which he had acquired the latter, he soon collected around him a school of disciples who considered him almost divine. His teachings went without disguise far into the domain of mysticism. By him the advent of the Messiah was foretold for 1540, and the sack of Rome in 1527, an oft-foretold precursor of the millennium, seemed to confirm Molkho's prophecies. The one ambition of the prophet was to earn a martyr's crown, and in pursuance of this aim after a brief sojourn in Turkey he returned to Christendom.

As was expected by Reubeni, the conversion and flight of Molkho, added to other incidents, shook the position which Reubeni had acquired at the Portuguese court. The royal promises, although made apparently in good faith, lacked fulfilment, and the undoubted excitement of which he was the cause among the Neo-Christians of the kingdom rendered his continued presence among them most undesirable; and, after having spent a year at the Portuguese court, Reubeni was asked to withdraw. The ship in which he sailed was wrecked on the coast of Spain, and for a time he was in the hands of the Inquisition. His release was, however, ordered by the emperor, Charles V., and he settled at Avignon, then under the sovereignty of the pope. From Avignon Reubeni removed to Italy, preceded everywhere by the mysterious reputation which he had acquired, and followed by a host of believers, who hailed him as the precursor of the Messiah and even as the Messiah Himself.

Meanwhile Molkho had also come to Italy with the reputation which he had acquired in Turkey, enhanced, if possible, and a following that grew in numbers from day to day. In Rome Molkho, imbued with Messianic tendencies, had visions and foretold floods and earthquakes, which, it must be added, subsequently occurred. More valuable to him, however, were the favour and protection which he had obtained from the pope, Clement VII., and from some of the cardinals. With their assistance he was able to defy his enemies, who were drawn not only from among the emissaries of the Inquisition, but also from the Jews, some of whom shrewdly considered his influence and pseudo-Messiahship harmful rather than beneficial to Jewry. His critics among his own community were, however, numerically insignificant, and his influence among the Jews increased until he became indeed their accepted prophet. By Graetz Molkho has been described at this period of his career as 'the Jewish Savonarola' (*Hist.* ix. 274). In order to avoid the flood which he had foretold would overtake Rome, Molkho repaired to Venice, and here he met once again the first inspirer of his enthusiasm, David Reubeni. His position in regard to Reubeni had, however, undergone a change since their previous meeting; his fellow-prophet, Molkho, met him now, not as a disciple, but as an equal.

Reubeni was still endeavouring to obtain assistance for his brother, the king of Khaibar, and from the authorities in Venice he received some encouragement in his mission. After the flood Molkho returned to Rome, where he was received with enthusiasm as a successful prophet. The pope, the cardinals, and the ambassadors of the Powers vied with one another in their flattering attentions to him. His influence was so great at this period that he was able to secure the indefinite postponement of the introduction of the Inquisition into Portugal; but his Jewish enemies, especially Jacob Mantin of Venice, were untiring, and they ultimately succeeded in securing his arrest by the Inquisition as a renegade Christian, and Molkho was condemned to be burned. All the preparations for the *auto da fé* were made and the victim was in due course consumed by the flames. It was then discovered, however, that the pope, in order to protect his favourite, had gone to the length of substituting another victim, and that Molkho himself was safely hidden within the papal apartments. In the circumstances it is not surprising that Molkho was smuggled out of Rome at the first opportunity.

Molkho thereupon rejoined Reubeni, and the two decided to journey to Ratisbon to plead with the Emperor the cause of the Jews of Khaibar. There is a tradition that advantage was taken of the interview with Charles to endeavour to convert him to Judaism, and it was possibly this attempt that led to the arrest of both the ambassadors. They were put into chains and carried to Mantua, where at the Emperor's request Molkho was again tried by the Inquisition and sentenced to be burned. At the last moment pardon was offered him on condition that he returned to the Christian fold, but he rejected the offer with scorn. He had only one cause for repentance, was his reply, and that was that he had been a Christian in his youth. Molkho's ambition was thereupon gratified and he earned a martyr's crown. Some of his addresses were published by him in 1529 under the title of *The Book of Wonder*. Reubeni was taken to Spain and there handed over to the Inquisition. His ultimate fate is surrounded by mystery, but he appears to have died while in the hands of the Holy Office. The evidence that he was burned is insufficient. A copy of Reubeni's diary is in MS at the Bodleian. Graetz published a portion in his *History*[3], ix., and Neubauer published the whole of it in *Mediæval Jewish Chronicles*, ii.

Concerning the existence of Reubeni there can be no legitimate doubt. His mission, however, is not so well authenticated, and there are those, no mean authorities, who consider him to have been merely a charlatan and impostor. Graetz (ix. ch. 8), for instance, judging from the language of Reubeni's *Journal*, expressed the belief that it had been written by a German Jew, and Neubauer held the same view, only more positively. Rieger and Vogelstein (*Gesch. der Juden in Rom*, ii. 41–46, 53–58) are also very sceptical about his *bona fides*, but they express the opinion that he did come from Arabia. Adler (*Auto de Fé and Jew*, p. 30 ff.) seems to have more confidence in Reubeni's credentials, but locates the source of his embassy at Cranganore in India.

Strictly speaking, neither Molkho nor Reubeni should perhaps be included in the list of pseudo-Messiahs, for neither ever claimed divinity. They were Messiahs for the most part against their own inclinations. The same may be said of **Isaac ben Solomon Ashkenazi Luria** (Ari) (1534–72), the founder of the modern kabbala. An ascetic and a mystic, he never pretended to be more than the forerunner of the Messiah, not the Messiah Himself. His principal disciple, **Hayyim Vital Calabrese** (1543–1620), was acclaimed by his master as possessing a soul unsoiled by sin. Around him also a group of mystical legends have collected. On Luria's death Vital succeeded to his position and also claimed to be Messiah ben Joseph, the precursor of Messiah ben David. Both Luria and Vital made Safed the scene of their principal activities. In the time of Vital a rival Messiah arose in the person of **Abraham Shalom**, who in 1574 sent a message to Vital pointing out that the latter was only Messiah ben Joseph, but he, Shalom, was Messiah ben David. He offered, moreover, to shield Vital from the death that would otherwise have been his fate.

The most remarkable and influential of all the pseudo-Messiahs was **Shabbathai Ṣebi**, born, the son of a Sephardi agent of an English mercantile firm, at Smyrna, on the 9th of Ab (the anniversary of the destruction of Jerusalem and a fast day in the Jewish calendar), 1621 or 1626. He is generally believed to have died on the Day of Atonement in 1676. Even as a boy Shabbathai was noteworthy for his physical beauty and his strange introspective habits. For the ordinary learning of the Jew, that of the Talmud, he had no liking, and the time spent by him at the school of R. Joseph Escapa was for the most part wasted. On the other hand, the kabbalistic mysteries of the *Zôhăr* had a great attraction for his mind. He threw himself ardently into the study of them, and endeavoured, by carefully following out the ordinances laid down therein, and especially by the practice of asceticism, himself to solve the mysteries that the *Zôhăr* professes to offer its students. On attaining manhood, Shabbathai had already acquired a considerable reputation as a kabbalist, which was enhanced by his mode of life, his obvious belief in his magical powers, and his determined aversion to marriage, probably without precedent in the society in which he lived. Meanwhile Shabbathai's father had learnt, through his correspondents in England, something of the hopes and beliefs of the English millenarian sects, then prominent in English thought, and had in particular been apprised of the identification of the year 1666 with the opening of the millennium. By a coincidence, according to the computations of the *Zôhăr*, the year 1648 was to mark the appearance of the Jewish Messiah. Shabbathai, encouraged by these signs and by the almost worshipful attitude of his father, who attributed the whole of his material good fortune to his son's saintliness, by nature and education already prepared for the rôle that he was about to adopt, revealed himself in the latter year to a select circle of his followers as the Messiah. In support of his claim he uttered the Tetragrammaton—an act permitted only to the high priest in the Temple on the Day of Atonement. Shabbathai remained at Smyrna for some years after this event, surrounded by a circle of fervent believers, but with little if any influence outside of the district in which he lived. He and his teachings were closely watched by the Rabbinical authorities, who ultimately, considering that he had overstepped the permissible limits, excommunicated him and his disciples on account of their heresy, and banished him from Smyrna. This occurred about 1654 (according to Graetz, 1651).

From Smyrna Shabbathai is believed to have gone to Constantinople, supported in every sense by his disciples and strengthened in particular by two of them — Moses Pinheiro, a man of some scientific knowledge and of mature years, and Abraham Yachini, a distinguished preacher, who, by means of an alleged ancient MS of very doubtful authenticity, rendered Shabbathai still more steadfast in the belief in his own divine mission. It is doubtful whether Shabbathai, if he ever intended to visit Constantinople, did so on this occasion, but it is certain that he arrived at Salonica, where mysticism was likely to find a sympathetic atmosphere, shortly after his banishment from Smyrna. In Salonica Shabbathai showed himself even more intoxicated with the consciousness of his new rôle than he had been at Smyrna, and his acts led here also to his practical expulsion by the Rabbis. After leaving Salonica the new Messiah spent some time wandering about the Orient, promulgating his views and his claims in every city that he visited and gaining adherents in all parts. In 1660 he was in Cairo, where he remained for about two years. There he gained a valuable supporter in the person of Raphael Joseph Chalebi of Aleppo, a mystic who had long awaited almost with impatience the coming of the Messiah, and whose wealth and influence were both extensive.

The approach of the apocalyptic year, 1666, attracted Shabbathai to Jerusalem, where, suppressing temporarily his extravagances, he built up an influence over the people on less theatrical bases. As the representative of the people of the city, he was sent abroad to obtain funds for their relief from an impending calamity, and the success of his mission rendered him all the more popular among the grateful people in whose midst he was sojourning. While in Cairo, Shabbathai succeeded in yet another mission. A Polish Jewess, who at the age of six had been left an orphan and whose subsequent career was almost as romantic as that of Shabbathai, was at the time in Leghorn, where she was reputed to be living an immoral life. Of great beauty and, moreover, of an eccentric disposition, she was already famous beyond the limits of the town, and her announcement that she was intended as the bride of the Messiah made her known to even a wider circle. In fact, her renown spread as far as Cairo, where it came to the ears of Shabbathai; he sent for and married her, declaring that she was his divinely appointed spouse.

Shabbathai thereupon returned to Palestine. Passing through Gaza, he met there Nathan Benjamin Levi, otherwise known as Nathan Gazati, who immediately became the leading advocate of the new Messiah and took unto himself the rôle of Elijah, the forerunner of the Anointed. One of his first steps was to announce the opening of the Messianic Age for the following year, 1666. This prophecy, together with many subsidiary ones, was promulgated far and wide, spreading even to the shores of the North Sea. These claims were, however, not by any means encouraged by the authorities at Jerusalem, and Shabbathai thought it well to find a more congenial centre for his activities. He returned to Smyrna, his journey thither taking the form of a triumphal progress which culminated in a reception at his destination, remarkable for its enthusiasm. At Smyrna, overwhelmed by his reception, he put the final touch to all the rumours that were current regarding his divinity, and formally announced his Messiahship. He was forthwith entrusted with absolute power as the sole ruler of the local Jewish community. Wherever Jews were to be found, the rise of the new Messiah attracted attention. The business of the exchanges of Europe was neglected in order that the latest of miracles might be discussed. The merchants of the North Sea ports wrote to their agents in the Levant for information. Tribute poured in upon the 'King of Kings.' Embassies were sent to him from the four corners of the earth. In the synagogues he was publicly hailed as the Messiah, and those who doubted went in danger of their lives. Even among the Christians believers in his mission were to be found. In Hamburg Protestants went to their pastor and said: 'We have almost certain accounts not only from Jews, but also from our Christian correspondents at Smyrna, Aleppo, Constantinople, and elsewhere in the East that the new Messiah of the Jews does many miracles, and the Jews of the whole world flock to him. What will then become of the Christian doctrine and the belief in our Messiah?' Prophets, male and female, in accordance with Joel's prediction (Jl 2^{28}), arose and exclaimed in Hebrew, a language with which they were supposed to have no acquaintance: 'Shabbathai Ṣebi is the true Messiah of the Race of David; to him the crown and the kingdom are given!' The daughters of R. Peḥina, Shabbathai's bitterest enemy, blessed the name of the pretender, as had been foretold. In Persia the Jewish agriculturists refrained from work on account of the advent of their deliverer who would lead them back to the Promised Land.

At the beginning of the year 1666 Shabbathai left Smyrna for Constantinople, but before doing so he distributed the kingdoms of the earth among his principal followers. As soon as he had landed on European soil, he was arrested by an officer of the Sultan, who placed him in chains, and it was in this condition that Shabbathai approached the capital. Despite his undignified landing, Shabbathai's popularity in no wise languished, and he was received by hosts of believers in his divinity, who, by the gifts which they brought, enabled the 'Messiah' to secure a considerable alleviation of the lot that would otherwise have fallen to him. Shabbathai's courage did not, however, equal his popularity; and, when questioned by the authorities regarding his claims and intentions, he replied that he was merely a Rabbi sent from Jerusalem to collect funds for charitable purposes. Despite this falling away, the influence of the pretender, instead of waning, grew stronger, and in his prison in Constantinople Shabbathai held a court which was attended by Muhammadans and Jews who alike proclaimed his divinity. After two months the prisoner was removed to Abydos, and there his court was continued with, if possible, even greater success than in the capital. His renown and exaggerated reports of the royal manner in which he was treated spread throughout the civilized world. The castle of Abydos became a place of pilgrimage to Jewries far and near. In parts of Europe the Jews made preparations for the return to Palestine under Messianic guidance. In innumerable synagogues prayers for the pretender's welfare were regularly offered; and with every day the excitement both within Abydos and throughout the world increased. Meanwhile Shabbathai, in order apparently to justify his existence, abrogated certain of the Jewish fast days.

Shabbathai's fall was due to the appearance of a rival, one **Nehemiah Ha-Kohen**, who posed as a forerunner of the Messiah. Shabbathai, learning of Nehemiah's prophecies, summoned him to Abydos. After a long journey Nehemiah arrived. An interview with Shabbathai was followed by dissatisfaction on both sides. Nehemiah, fearful of assassination by the Shabbathaians, fled to Constantinople, where he embraced Muhammadanism and denounced to the authorities the treasonable intentions of his rival. Removed to Adrianople, Shabbathai at length realized the critical position in which he was placed. Hoping thereby to save his life, he also embraced Muhammadanism, and was followed in this course by his wife and some of his adherents. The Sultan was much pleased at this act and appointed the pretender one of his doorkeepers. Shabbathai, in order to retain his hold upon the Jews, announced: 'God has made me an Ishmaelite; He commanded, and it was done. The ninth day of my regeneration.' His apostasy, despite the loyalty to him of many of his adherents, shattered his influence in Jewry, and hosts of Jews, their eyes at length opened by the last act of their prophet, repented bitterly of their support of the movement. For a time, in consequence of the schism caused by Shabbathai's apostasy, Turkish Jewry was in great danger of extermination, the fear of wholesale conversions to Muhammadanism being accompanied by that of the massacre of those who refused to follow Shabbathai's example. Powerful influences, however, warded off the latter danger.

Shabbathai seems never to have abandoned his Messianic claims. He managed to found a Judæo-Muhammadan sect of believers, the Dönmeh, who have survived, especially in Salonica, to the present day. After a time he fell into disgrace, was deprived of his office, and banished to Dulcigno, where he died, it is believed in 1676, leaving behind him a controversy which long continued in Israel. The Dönmeh are in a sense crypto-Jews, inasmuch as, while outwardly conforming to Muhammadanism, they practise certain Jewish or debased Jewish rites in secret. There is, however, in practice little secrecy concerning their difference from the Muhammadans, from whom, although they mix in commerce, socially they keep carefully aloof.

Shabbathai was succeeded by quite a shoal of petty Messiahs. The first of the line was **Jacob Querido**, or Jacob Ṣebi, who was the real founder of the sect of Dönmeh. He was in reality the brother of Shabbathai's fourth wife, who for her own purposes pretended that he was her son by the Messiah. Querido's principal doctrine was that the redemption could not come about until the world was either entirely good or entirely wicked, and, as the latter state was by far the easier of attainment, he preached and practised licentiousness in order that the day of the millennium might dawn. Querido died at the end of the 17th cent., and was succeeded in due course by his son **Bereḥiah** (*c.* 1695–1740). Other Shabbathaian Messiahs who flourished at this period were **Miguel** (Abraham) **Cardoso** (1630–1706), a Marrano, **Mordecai Mokiaḥ** (*c.* 1650–1729) of Eisenstadt, **Löbele Prossnitz** († *c.* 1750), and **Judah Ḥasid**. These were all, more or less, prophets of Shabbathai so long as he survived, and they endeavoured to step into his place when he died. Mokiaḥ flourished and preached in Italy and Poland. Prossnitz was of the class of clumsy conjurers; nevertheless he attracted many adherents in Austria and Germany. Ḥasid, who was a leader of the sect of Ḥăsîdhîm, 'the Ultra-holy,' traversed Europe at the head of a considerable following whom he led to Jerusalem. He died, however, immediately after his arrival in that city, and with his disappearance his followers were left leaderless and destitute.

The last of the most prominent of the successors of Shabbathai was **Jacob Frank** (1726–91). He was born in Podolia, where his first occupation was that of distiller. His original name was Jankiev Lejbovicz, but he obtained the new surname of Frank from the subjects of the Sultan in whose midst he sojourned for a long time. An undisguised charlatan and an apostate from more than one faith, he pursued a career of unceasing warfare against Rabbinical Judaism, and in the peculiar views to which he gave expression he described himself as the re-incarnation of all the prophets and Messiahs who had preceded him. In Turkey he obtained considerable renown on account of his kabbalistic learning, and on the return to his birthplace the remnants of the Shabbathaian party, who were known as Zoharites, appointed him their prophet. The Talmudists, however, disapproved most vehemently and forcibly of his teachings, which were leading directly to the destruction of Judaism and of morality in Poland. Frank and the Frankists were excommunicated, but they found a powerful friend in the bishop of Kamenetz, whom they ingratiated by pretended points of strong resemblance between their faith—which was bitterly opposed to Rabbinic Judaism—and Christianity. With his assistance the tables were turned, and for a time the upper hand was gained over the orthodox element in Jewry. With the death of the bishop, however, another change came over the fortunes of the parties. The position of the Frankists became precarious, and in order to secure the safety of his followers Frank instructed them to accept baptism, he himself setting the example. Conversions to Christianity followed on a considerable scale; but, when the converts were discovered to be leading double lives, and, while outwardly Christians, to be following Jewish practices in secret, the attention of the ecclesiastical authorities was directed towards them. Frank was himself arrested in 1760 on a charge of heresy and imprisoned in the castle of Czentschow, where he remained for thirteen years. This imprisonment did not by any means put an end to his movement or his teachings, and his prison became a centre for the promulgation of his doctrines. The invasion of the Russians in 1772 led to his liberation, and he was then free to make a triumphal progress through Poland, Bohemia, and Moravia. He lived in state until his death in 1791, latterly as the Baron of Offenbach, in various continental capitals, always with an immense retinue and a vast treasure, derived from his infatuated adherents, at his command. His later history, however, hardly belongs to the annals of Jewry, for his influence on Judaism had ceased long before his death. His followers, the Frankists, although for a time they kept themselves apart as pseudo-Jews of a peculiar description, were ultimately absorbed into the population in whose midst they lived.

Frank was the last of the series of pseudo-Messiahs to be accepted seriously by any considerable section of Jewry, but there is one other who deserves mention, before the catalogue of these actors on the world's stage is brought to a close. **Moses Hayyim Luzzatto** (1707–47) differed considerably from most of his predecessors in the rôle in which he also essayed to live. With most, if not all, of them there was a spirit of charlatanry manifest. Not even Luzzatto's most determined enemy could sincerely suggest any such charge against him. One might almost say that he was merely a victim of his own delusions; his predecessors for the most part found the victims of their delusions outside of themselves. Luzzatto, the cultured son of wealthy Italian Jewish parents, was a poet by nature as well as by profession. Early in life, however, he fell under the influence of the kabbalists and the *Zôhār*, and soon the mysteries of this literature took complete possession of him and he firmly believed himself to be divinely inspired. He even went so far as to create unaided a second *Zôhār*, and by the work of his own hands and mind he was convinced of his divine mission. A circle of young devotees soon settled round him, and his fame began to spread to the confines of Jewry. The leaders of orthodox Judaism in Germany were scandalized and, after some difficulty, brought pressure to bear upon the newly arisen prophet to undertake to refrain from teaching, by means of either the spoken or the written word, the new doctrines. Luzzatto gave the desired promise, but was unable to observe it for very long, and, when he once more reverted to the forbidden studies, he was excommunicated by the board of Rabbis of Venice. Ultimately Luzzatto wandered to Palestine, where he died of plague shortly after his arrival.

LITERATURE.—On the general subject of pseudo-Messiahs relatively little has been written. The principal references to the subject are to be found scattered in works on post-Biblical Jewish history. *JE* x. contains a general résumé of the subject with supplementary articles in other volumes dealing with individual pretenders to the Messiahship. Pseudo-Messiahs in general are also dealt with by **Joannes à Lent**, in *Schediasma historico-philologicum de Judæorum Pseudo-Messiis*, Herborn, 1697; **M. Gaster**, in *Jewish Chronicle*, Feb. 11 and March 11, 1898; and **A. M. Hyamson**, *Gentleman's Magazine*, ccxc. [1901] 79–89. For the individual pseudo-Messiahs, **H. Graetz**, *Geschichte der Juden*, Leipzig, 1868–78, Eng. tr., London, 1891–92, should be consulted. In addition, for Theudas see **Josephus**, *Ant.* xx. v. 1; **Eusebius**, *HE* ii. 2, and **E. Schürer**, *HJP* I. ii. 168. For Dositheus see **S. Krauss**, in *REJ* xlii. [1901] 27–42; **A. Büchler**, *ib.* 220–231, and xliii. [1901] 50–71; **D. Oppenheim**, in *Magazin für die Wissenschaft des Judenthums*, i. [1874] 68; **S. Krauss**, *Griech. und latein. Lehnwörter in Talmud*, etc., ii. [Berlin, 1898] 192; **J. W. Nutt**, *Fragments of a Samaritan Targum*, London, 1874, pp. 47–52; **E. Renan**, *Histoire des origines du christianisme*, v. [Paris, 1877] 452; **L. Herzfeld**, *Geschichte des Volkes Israel*², ii. [Leipzig, 1863] 606; **S. Schechter**, *Documents of Jewish Sectaries*, Cambridge, 1910; **K. Kohler**, in *AJTh* xv. [1911] 404–435. For Bar Kokhba see **Eusebius**, *HE* iv. 6; **Dio Cassius**, *Hist. Rom.* lxix. 12–14; **Schürer**, *HJP* I. ii. 257 ff.; **Arsène Darmesteter**, in *REJ* i. [1880] 42 ff.; and **J. Derenbourg**, 'Quelques Notes sur la guerre de Bar Kozeba,' in *Mélanges de l'École des hautes études*, Paris, 1878. For Isaac ben Ya'ḳūb of Iṣfahān see **A. I. Silvestre de Sacy**, *Chrestomathie arabe*, Paris, 1826, i. 307. For David Alroy see *The Itinerary of Benjamin of Tudela*, ed. **M. N. Adler**, London, 1907, pp. 77–81; **A. Neubauer**, *Mediæval Jewish Chronicles*, Oxford, 1887–95; **D. Kaufmann**, in *REJ* xvii. [1888] 304; **A. Neubauer**, *ib.* iv. [1882] 188–191. For Abraham ben Samuel Abulafia see **M. H. Landauer**, in *Literaturblatt des Orients*, 1845, p. 381 ff.; **A. Jellinek**, *Beiträge zur Geschichte der Kabbala*, Leipzig, 1852, pt. ii., and *Philosophie und Kabbala*, do. 1854; **Philip Bloch**, *Geschichte der Entwickelung der Kabbala*, Trèves, 1894, p. 46 ff.; **H. Vogelstein** and **P. Rieger**, *Geschichte der Juden in Rom*, Berlin, 1896, i. 247 ff. For Moses Botarel see **A. Jellinek**, 'Biographische Skizzen,' in *Literaturblatt des Orients*, 1846, p. 187 f.; **M. Steinschneider**, *Jüdische Literatur*, Frankfort a. M., 1893, pp. 110–128. For David Reubeni and Solomon Molkho see **E. N. Adler**, *Auto de Fé and Jew*, London, 1908, chs. v. and vi., and *Aspects of the Hebrew Genius*, ed. L. Simon, do. 1910, p. xxii ff.; **A. Neubauer**, *Mediæval Jewish Chronicles*, ii.; **D. Kaufmann**, in *REJ* xxx. [1895] 304–307, xxxiv. [1897] 121–127, x. [1885] 288; **Vogelstein** and **Rieger**, *Gesch. der Juden in Rom*; and **S. Schechter**, *Studies in Judaism*, ii., London, 1908, p. 222 ff. For Isaac Luria see **Steinschneider**, *Jüd. Lit.* p. 456; **C. D. Ginsburg**, *The Kabbalah*, London, 1865, p. 134; **Schechter**, *Studies in Judaism*, ii.; and **E. J. Worman**, in *REJ* lviii. [1909] 281 f. For Hayyim Vital Calabrese see **Schechter**, *Studies in Judaism*, ii. For Shabbathai Ṣebi and Samuel Primo see **Abraham Danon**, in *REJ* xxxvii. [1898] 103–110 and lviii. [1909] 270–291; **N. Brüll**, 'Sabbathai Zebi und seine Anhänger,' in *Populärwissenschaftliche Monatshefte*, xii. [1892] 6, 25, 80; **E. Finkel**, in *Ost und West*, v. [1905] 51 ff.; **Ludwig Geiger**, 'Deutsche Schriften über Sabbatai Zebi,' in *Zeitschrift der Geschichte der Juden in Deutschland*, v. [1892] 100–105; **M. Horschetzky**, 'Sabbathy Zwy, eine biographische Skizze,' in *Allgemeine Zeitung des Judenthums*, ii. [1838] 520 ff.; *The Restauration of the Jewes*, London, 1665; *Several New Letters concerning the Jews*, do. 1666; *A New Letter concerning the Jews*, do. 1666, *The History of the three late famous Impostors*, do. 1666; **D. Kaufmann**, in *REJ* xxxiv. [1897] 305–308, and in *Allgemeine Zeitung des Judenthums*, lxii. [1898] 364; **A. Epstein**, in *REJ* xxvi. [1893] 209–219; **David de Gunzbourg**, *ib.* xxvii. [1893] 144 f.; **A. Freimann**, *Sammelband kleiner Schriften über Sabbathai Zebi und seine Anhänger*, Berlin, 1912. For the Dönmeh see also **A. Danon**, *REJ* xxxv. [1897] 264–281, in *Allgemeine Zeitung des Judenthums*, li. [1887] 538 ff., and in *Actes du onzième congrès des orientalistes*, Paris, 1898, iii. 57; **H. Graetz**, 'Ueberbleibsel der Sabbat. Sekte in Salonichi,' in *Monatsschrift*, xxxiii. [1883] 49 ff.; **Paul Rycaut**, *The History of the Turkish Empire from the Year 1623 to the Year 1677 containing the Reigns of the three last Emperours* . . ., London, 1687; **J. T. Bendt**, 'Die Dönmes oder Mamin in Salonichi,' in *Ausland*, lxi. [1888] 186–190 and 206–209, and *Revue des Écoles de l'Alliance israélite*, v. [1905] 289–323. For Miguel Cardoso see **M. Gaster**, *History of the Ancient Syna-*

gogue, London, 1901, p. 109 ff.; and M. Mortara, in *REJ* xii. [1886] 301 ff. For Jacob Frank see H. Graetz, *Frank und die Frankisten*, Breslau, 1868; A. Theiner, *Vetera Monumenta Poloniæ . . . ex Tabulariis Vaticanis Collecta*, iv. [Leipzig, 1864] 158–165. For Luzzatto see Franz Delitzsch, *Zur Gesch. der jüdischen Poesie*, Leipzig, 1836, p. 89 ff.; I. M. Jost, *Gesch. des Judenthums und seiner Sekten*, iii. [do. 1859] 179 ff.; L. Zunz, *Literaturgeschichte*, Berlin, 1865–67, p. 449; *Autobiografia di S. D. Luzzatto*, Padua, 1882; D. Kaufmann, 'Poésie de Moise Hayyim Luzzatto,' in *REJ* xxxix. [1899] 133 ff., xxiii. [1891] 256 ff.

ALBERT M. HYAMSON.

METALS AND MINERALS.—I. Metals.—Fire and metallurgy may be regarded as the two main bases of material culture. The results of the modern applications of steam and electricity have been described as 'puny and insignificant when compared with those which followed the discovery of metals by the men of the stone age';[1] and with the finding of the art of extracting metal from ore 'human culture was revolutionised.'[2] Possibly the first attempts at utilizing metals were made by applying a modification of hammer-work on stone to fragments of surface-ore. Copper and its alloys, especially a native bronze, would naturally be observed first; but the usual order of discovery—copper, bronze, iron—is not absolute; the order varied in different regions. For instance, it is unlikely that the West and Central Africans found any metal earlier than iron, which is so abundant in their country.

Observing the importance to humanity of the discovery of metals and the invention of metallurgy, philosophers have inclined to attribute them to some remarkable cause. Lucretius, *e.g.*, imagined a mighty conflagration; this, in consuming forests covering metalliferous ground, would reduce the outcropping ore to a metallic state.[3] But, with the discovery of fire-making, there are many possibilities, and various lines of discovery may have converged. Gowland suggests that the origin of metallurgy is to be found in the camp-fires of the Neolithic age.[4] When these were made on metalliferous soil, the lumps of metal melted out would at once attract the attention of a stone-working people, and the blows of the stone hammer on the hot and malleable mass would indicate its possibilities. The camp-fire may thus be regarded as the prototype of the most elaborate modern furnaces.[5]

Naturally, a feeling of the importance of metals, and a primitive appreciation of the 'marvels of science' in connexion with the working of them and of their mechanical capability, reacted upon early man with the results usually found when superstition meditates on critical things. The body of beliefs about metals and, in a less degree, minerals is enormous, but reducible to a few simple types which are found everywhere and survive in peasant psychology to this day. Special properties of this or that metal or mineral are taken into account, and cultural reactions of all kinds modify the various beliefs and usages. These may be typically exemplified without unnecessary multiplication.

In common with all skilled crafts in early culture, the miner and the worker in metal are regarded with wonder, and often with its entailed superstitious feelings.

Among the Bangala of the Upper Congo no one is allowed to step over a smith's fire or blow it with his mouth; such acts would pollute the fire and cause bad workmanship. The smith is supposed to use witchcraft in order to perform his smithing well. Neighbouring peoples simply regard the smith with respect.[6] Some African smiths form sacred gilds; the mythical Wayland Smith of Scandinavian lore is a natural deification, as is part at least of the figure of the Greek Hephaistos.

[1] W. Gowland, 'Copper and its Alloys in Prehistoric Times,' *JAI* xxxvi. [1906] 15.

[2] *Ib.* Probably the first iron used was not meteoric or telluric, in spite of cases among the Eskimos.

[3] v. 1250 ff.

[4] *Op. cit.* p. 17.

[5] Gowland, *op. cit.*, and 'The Metals in Antiquity,' *JRAI* xlii. [1912] 235–287.

[6] J. H. Weeks, in *JRAI* xxxix. [1909] 456.

The usual tabus and animistic beliefs are attached to the working of metals, to mining, and to the ore and metal themselves.

The tin-miners of Malaysia have a remarkable code of tabus and body of superstitious ideas, but they are outnumbered by the Chinese workers, who, however, as will be seen, have a similar faith. The ore is supposed not only to be alive but to grow, to be able to move from place to place, to reproduce itself, and to have special likes or affinities for certain people and things, and *vice versa*. 'Hence it is advisable to treat tin-ore with a certain amount of respect, to consult its convenience, and what is, perhaps, more curious, to conduct the business of mining in such a way that the tin-ore may, as it were, be obtained without its own knowledge.'[1] Of the tabued acts observed by the miners, the chief are that no living creature may be killed in the mine; that the *sarong* may not be put on; that shoes may not be worn, or an umbrella used. Numerous charms are employed by the 'mining wizards' for the purpose of clearing away evil spirits and to induce the ore to show itself.[2] The Malay *pawangs* ('medicine-men'), or mining wizards, used to enjoy 'an extraordinary reputation, some of them being credited with the power of bringing ore to a place where it was known that no ore existed, . . . to possess the power of sterilising such ore as existed, and of turning it into mere grains of sand.' No one but him was allowed to wear a black coat at the mine. He used a special language (*bahāsa pantang*, 'tabu language') for his professional duties, and he had 'a wonderful "nose" for tin.'[3] Sometimes each separate grain of ore was credited with personality.[4] It was believed that tin could 'announce its presence by a peculiar noise heard in the stillness of night.'[5] Sometimes the personality of the tin is described as a buffalo, in which shape it makes its way underground,[6] this being perhaps a sophistication of the lode.

'In Sumatra the spirits of the gold mines are treated with as much deference as the spirits of the tin-mines in the Malay Peninsula. Tin, ivory, and the like, may not be brought by the miners to the scene of their operations, for at the scent of such things the spirits of the mine would cause the gold to vanish. . . . In some cases, for example in removing the grains of the gold, a deep silence must be observed; no commands may be given or questions asked, probably because the removal of the precious metal is regarded as a theft which the spirits would punish if they caught the thieves in the act. Certainly the Dyaks believe that gold has a soul which seeks to avenge itself on men who dig the precious metal.'[7]

In Manipur the iron-ore deposits are under the protection of an *ūmang lai* ('forest god'), who is propitiated before the iron is worked.[8] He capriciously moves the iron about. His symbol is a piece of iron a few inches square. The *lai-harauba* ('pleasing the god') is an annual festival. 'The first thing to be done is to bring the lai into a state of activity. Ordinarily speaking he is supposed to remain inert, unless offended in any way.' He 'particularly affects two plants called Leisang Leirel and Langthei, and when he is about to be pleased the Leirangba, a specially selected official, has to fetch them.' The plants are placed in the house of the *lai*, and then taken in a brass vessel by an old lady to the river. She wades about, suddenly stumbles, and then emerges with a vessel full of water. The god has now come.[9] A procession with music is made to the *lai-pham* ('god's place'), where his images (the pieces of iron) are set out. By them is placed the vessel, and a service of prayer and praise is celebrated, after the lighting of a sacred fire for the sacrifice. The god's servants or priestesses are two old women, termed *maibis*, who are often inspired by him and babble incoherently. If a man is similarly possessed by the god, he is known as *maiba* and during the ceremonies wears the dress of a *maibi*. Dramatic performances end the list of events.[10]

The last example is a perfect one for showing the development of an organized cult around a metal and the processes of its acquisition. There is some vagueness, which is worth noting, as to whether the metal itself is personified. As for its being deified, this is hardly to be inferred here or elsewhere.

The god appears to be rather the owner of the site, resembling the Hebrew Baals.

The Malays regarded gold in a similar way. The gold 'spirit' is 'believed to be under the care and in the gift of a *dewa*, or god.' It has the form of a golden roe-deer.[11] The theriomorphism is analogous to that of tin.

The same ideas are found at the other side of the world.

Gold was regarded by the Central Americans as possessed of 'divine qualities,' and it was gathered in fasting and penance.[12]

[1] W. W. Skeat, *Malay Magic*, London, 1900, pp. 250, 259 f., quoting A. Hale, in *JRAS* xvi. [1885] 303–320.

[2] Skeat, pp. 269, 267.

[3] *Ib.* pp. 250, 256, 253.

[4] *Ib.* p. 265 f.

[5] *Ib.* p. 263.

[6] *Ib.* p. 250.

[7] *GB*³, pt. ii., *Taboo and the Perils of the Soul*, London, 1911, p. 409 f., quoting J. L. van der Toorn, in *Bijdragen tot de Taal-, Land- en Volkenkunde van Nederlandsch Indië*, xxxix. [1890] 100; M. T. H. Perelaer, *Ethnographische Beschrijving der Dajaks*, Zalt-Bommel, 1870, p. 215.

[8] J. Shakespear, in *JRAI* xl. [1910] 349.

[9] *Ib.* p. 351.

[10] *Ib.* p. 352 ff.

[11] Skeat, pp. 271, 251.

[12] Bancroft, *NR* iii. 500.

An interesting detail with regard to the personality of metals is supplied by Malay superstition. The Malays believe that so long as gold is in the earth it has a soul. When the gold is taken by man, the soul flies away.[1] The idea is parallel to those found in agricultural lore; presumably the corn-spirit leaves John Barleycorn when he is ground, if not when he is reaped. The idea is elaborated in Celebes, on the principle that the soul may be retained and will assist the usefulness of the implements when made.

Among the Alfoers of Celebes iron-working is a prominent industry. Iron is credited with a soul, which is apt to desert the metal under the hammer. Every smithy, therefore, includes a bundle of *lamoa* ('gods'), consisting of wooden imitations of iron implements, and in this the soul of the iron resides. '"If we did not hang the *lamoa* over the anvil, the iron would flow away and be unworkable" on account of the absence of the soul.'[2]

This is an interesting application of the principle of the external soul.

The Chinese in their elaborate animism have not neglected metals. They consider metals and ores when in the ground to possess a *shen* ('soul') of animal or human shape, and this figure is either the mineral or a spirit guarding it. 'Gold, jade, and pearls . . . are the *tsing* of Heaven and Earth.'[3]

A particular development is towards the Scandinavian idea of gnomes. The Chinese have tales of silver men and of 'women in white'; when they were attacked and knocked down, they disappeared, and silver mines were found on the spot.[4]

The same kind of analogy connects various metals with various things, according to colour or other properties. The Greeks of to-day call jaundice 'the golden disease,' and heal it on the homœopathic principle with a decoction from an English sovereign, English gold being the best.[5]

One or two examples of the miscellaneous wonder-lore which has gathered round metals may be cited.

Fern-seed, itself a mythical vegetable gold-dust, guides to hidden treasures.[6] A Malay recipe for turning brass into gold is to kill a wild pig, and sew up in it a quantity of 'scrap' brass; then pile timber over it, and burn it; when grass has grown over the remains, 'dig up the gold.'[7] Paracelsus made a magic ring of a mixture of all metals joined under certain constellations,[8] and Van Helmont concocted a ring of magic metal which cured disease.[9] An obvious connexion is practically universal between gold and the sun, silver and the moon. Silver is the lunar metal; hence peasants like to have silver in their pockets when they see the new moon, and to turn it for luck, *i.e.* doubling.[10] Throughout the world magnetic iron and ore have excited wonder.

The relative value of the familiar metals is the same in superstition and ordinary usage. It is interesting to note that the Hindus regarded alloys as impure, and never used them for religious purposes.[11] Here may be detected the notion of mixture, adulteration, as a component of the idea of impurity. Another popular division of metals is into 'precious' and 'base.' The Chinese consider gold 'the most genuine matter.'[12] In all the analogous estimates found in every age it would seem that æsthetic ideas supersede economic. Clearly the æsthetic value of gold and silver rather than their importance as currency is to the fore, and either view preponderates over the mechanical importance of iron.

A similar predilection is shown in the genealogies of the metals.

Manu said that gold and silver arose from the union of water and fire.[13] In Chinese philosophy tin 'is produced by the influence of the feminine principle in nature, being classed between silver and lead. The metal arsenic generates itself in two hundred years and after another two hundred years is converted into tin. Tin, being a product of the feminine principle, has tender qualities. When it is submitted to the influence of the masculine principle, it is converted into silver. It is sometimes found that wine kept in tin vessels has a poisonous action on man, which proves that the arsenic had not been completely transformed into tin.'[1]

1 A. C. Kruijt, *Het Animisme in den indischen Archipel*, The Hague, 1906, p. 164.
2 *GB*³, pt. vii., *Balder the Beautiful*, London, 1913, ii. 154, quoting Kruijt, in *Mededeelingen van wege het Nederlandsche Zendelinggenootschap*, xxxix. [1895] 23 f., xl. [1896] 10 f.
3 J. J. M. de Groot, *The Religious System of China*, Leyden, 1892 ff., iv. 332, 328.
4 *Ib.* iv. 332 f.
5 *GB*³, pt. i., *The Magic Art*, London, 1911, i. 80.
6 *GB*³, pt. vii., *Balder the Beautiful*, ii. 287 ff.
7 Skeat, p. 188.
8 W. G. Black, *Folk-Medicine*, London, 1883, p. 174.
9 *Ib.* p. 176.
10 Tylor, *PC*⁴, London, 1903, ii. 302 f.; cf. H. Oldenberg, *Rel. des Veda*, Berlin, 1894, pp. 81, 88 f.
11 Râjendralâla Mitra, *Indo-Aryans*, Calcutta, 1881, i. 241.
12 De Groot, iv. 331 f.
13 *SBE* xxv. [1886] 189.

This notion of transmutation of metals is a curious parallel to modern discoveries of the degeneration of radium into a series of filial metals. The search of the alchemists for the philosopher's stone included a similar hypothesis.

According to the Pahlavi *Bundahišn*, gold, silver, iron, brass, tin, lead, quicksilver, and adamant arose from the various members of the dead Gāyōmart; and 'on account of the perfection of gold it is produced from the life and seed.'[2] The Pahlavi *Šāyast lā-Šāyast* speaks (xv. 15) of the duty of 'propitiating' melted metal, *i.e.* practising 'habits of the heart so unsullied and pure that, when they shall drop melted metal upon it, it does not burn.' But the ordeal slays a sinner. Metal, especially gold and silver, is a 'counterpart of Shatvairō himself in the world.'[3] From the divided body of Indra, according to the *Śatapatha Brāhmaṇa*, metals arose, as well as all kinds of substances and living creatures; *e.g.* from his navel came lead.[4] The five elements in Chinese natural philosophy are water, fire, wood, metal, and earth. Wood produces fire, fire earth, earth metals, metals water, and water wood.[5] The idea of animal souls for metals already referred to has probably no cosmological intention.

In the multitudinous superstitions relative to the protective, curative, or dangerous properties of metals or metallic implements, the analogy of their relative value and efficiency—*e.g.*, between gold and steel—seems to predominate. The *Śatapatha Brāhmaṇa* lays down that the slaughtering-knife for the horse should be of gold, that for the *paryaṅgyas* of copper, and that for the other sacrifices to Prajāpati of iron. Gold is a symbol of the nobility, copper of heralds, messengers, and the like, iron of the peasantry.[6] The intrinsic value of gold, its brilliance, analogous to fire and the sun, connect it with vitality. Hence its extraordinary popularity as a panacea to this day among the Chinese, in the form of leaf, dust, decoction, or grease. It is placed in the mouth of the dead to assist revivification and to delay decomposition.[7] The Chinese also put mercury in coffins in order to preserve the body.[8] With no knowledge of embalming they endeavour to insulate, as it were, the coffin against decay. The use of quicksilver may be referred to the analogy between a moving and apparently living metal of worth and organic life. British folklore advises rubbing ringworm with silver.[9]

Metals, in virtue of their various properties, are used both as medicines and as amulets, in either case dependent on magical notions. The Burmese believe that the wearing of silver and gold is itself protective, and base metals may be used in default of precious.[10] Lumps of gold are worn under the skin to secure invulnerability. There is a common practice of covering amulets with gold-leaf to add to their efficacy.[11] For a person to wear something, as if a part of himself, which has a value of its own, adds to his own value and resisting power. On the same line of reasoning, metals of worth are the more useful in warding off ghostly enemies. In European as in Semitic folklore, the most efficacious bullet against a witch is one of silver, or a crooked sixpence;[12] but all metals have efficacy in this direction.

The property of resistance is common to most metals; the precious metals possess the further properties of beauty and value. The strength and hardness of iron make it a favourite charm.

1 Gowland, *JRAI* xlii. 247 f.
2 *SBE* v. [1880] 183.
3 *Ib.* p. 375 f.; M. N. Dhalla, *Zoroastrian Theology*, New York, 1914, pp. 37, 94, 232 f.
4 *SBE* xliv. [1900] 215.
5 De Groot, iii. 955, 957.
6 *SBE* xliv. 303 f.
7 De Groot, iv. 331, 330.
8 *Ib.* i. 281.
9 Black, p. 182.
10 W. L. Hildburgh, in *JRAI* xxxix. 402 f.
11 *Ib.* p. 406.
12 *GB*³, pt. vii., *Balder the Beautiful*, i. 316.

To keep off evil spirits, mourners in India carry a piece of iron—a key or a knife or any iron object. In Scotland after a death a piece of iron was placed in all the provisions in the house 'to prevent death from entering them,' and similar customs obtain in Ceylon and Morocco.[1] 'When Scotch fishermen were at sea, and one of them happened to take the name of God in vain, the first man who heard him called out "Cauld airn," at which every man of the crew grasped the nearest bit of iron and held it between his hands.'[2] To this day in parts of Scotland there survives a queer superstition about 'pigs' and 'iron.' It is unlucky to utter the words 'sow,' 'swine,' or 'pig' when fishing;[3] if you hear a man do so, you must shout 'Cold iron.'

It is a mere coincidence that in modern medicine iron is used as a tonic and that in early culture its 'strength' was absorbed by men.

The people of Nias wear iron arm-rings to keep off evil spirits or witchcraft; and they place iron by the side of sleeping infants for the same purpose. In Sarawak biting a piece of iron is a similar protection. The Torajas believe that iron strengthens one's soul, and hold ceremonies at smithies for this purpose. The people of Halmahera drink water in which iron has been dipped.[4] In Surinam iron arm-rings are supposed to strengthen the wearer.[5]

Several Malay sultans have in their regalia a sacred lump of iron, 'a piece of old scrap-iron with supernatural powers.'[6] Long iron nails are used by the Malays to protect new-born infants, betel-nut scissors to drive away evil spirits from the dead, and a sword is put in a strange river before a man will drink of it. When eating alone in the forest a man will sit on his sword, not only to drive away evil but to 'confirm' himself. Such iron implements are called 'representatives of iron.'[7] Scraps of iron are used in ointments for curing the sick.[8]

The supernatural power of a sharp instrument is, of course, to be added in many cases to the intrinsic power of iron and steel as such.

Lead appears but rarely in superstition. The Atharvaveda speaks[9] of a charm against demons and sorcerers by means of lead. Here, as in mediæval Europe and classical antiquity, the softness and malleability of the metal, and perhaps its weight, were possibly connected with ideas of image-making, for which it is as convenient as wax. The practice of injuring a person by damaging his image or effigy is world-wide. Curses inscribed on leaden tablets were common objects of Greek and Roman superstition; a leaden arrow, in classical belief, destroyed love.[10]

The virtues of metal may be enhanced, as is seen in the last-cited cases, by the form and purpose of the manufactured article. The ring has the additional advantage of enclosing and keeping safe; the coin has the further values of currency and of the personality whose head is stamped on the obverse. British folklore adapted the royal 'touch' for King's Evil by using crown-pieces bearing the head of King Charles I. Sufferers from paralysis or rheumatism collected coppers from the charitable at the church-door, and these were commuted into silver rings which were worn to cure the infirmity.[11]

The acoustic properties of metals have also been important in popular religion.

'The idea that the sound of brass or iron has power to put spirits to flight prevailed also in classical antiquity, from which it may have been inherited by mediæval Christianity.'[12]

In the Far East the virtues of the gong as a repeller of evil are well known. Brass is considered by the Chinese the most effective metal for repelling demons;[13] the sound of a brass instrument is the most terrifying.

A remarkable set of beliefs and practices has a strong tabu against the use of iron and the substitution of other metals or substances, previously used o. not. These rules usually apply to critical circumstances and persons.

Iron was not allowed to touch the body of the king of Korea. The Archon of Platæa was forbidden to touch iron. Tools of iron might not be introduced into Greek temples, and the Arval Brothers offered an expiatory sacrifice when an iron graving-tool was used. Roman priests were not allowed iron razors. The hair of the Flamen Dialis might be cut only with a bronze knife. It appears that the Greeks ascribed purificatory powers to bronze. The Pawnees, Hopis, Hottentots, and Gold Coast Negroes retain stone implements for sacred purposes. Circumcision is performed with a quartz knife by the Hottentots and the Ovambo.[1] Among the Damaras blood was ceremonially drawn from the slayer of a man or a lion, but with a flint knife.[2] The druids cut the sacred mistletoe with a golden sickle. When making need-fire, the Scots removed all iron from their persons. In making the Yule-tide fire-wheel (*clavie*), the hammering must be done with a stone. Similar tabus were observed in ancient Palestine and Italy. No iron tool was employed in making Hebrew altars or in the building of the Temple at Jerusalem. The Roman Pons Sublicius, a sacred bridge, was made and repaired without any use of iron or even bronze. Hindus have believed the use of iron for buildings to be productive of epidemics.[3]

Frazer considers that the tabu against iron in ceremonial 'perhaps dates from that early time in the history of society when iron was still a novelty, and as such was viewed by many with suspicion and dislike.'[4] Thus, when iron ploughs were introduced in Poland, some bad harvests followed, and the farmers reverted to the wooden implements.[5] The hypothesis is inconclusive. Iron and steel are used in virtue of their death-dealing qualities to ward off supernatural (no less than physical) evil, and weapons made from them are essentially dangerous weapons. Now, ceremonies practised at critical seasons or with reference to persons or things in a critical and sensitive condition call for special treatment with special apparatus, or at least for peculiar delicacy and care. This attitude is quite a sufficient reason for the employment of less dangerous tools, such as flint, quartz, or the human hand in critical operations, and it also sufficiently explains the ceremonial use of flint or bronze instead of iron, and particularly the use of gold or silver in connexion with very sacred persons or things. In Morocco the last sheaf of harvest is regarded as an incarnation of the *baraka* of the crop. It may not be cut with a sickle of steel or iron, but is plucked with the hand. Compare with this the Moroccan custom of placing steel and salt underneath the stack of wheat in order to keep off the attacks of *znūn*.[6] In the first case, steel is evidently too dangerous a substance for dealing with the delicate sanctity of the Bride of the Fields; in the second, its very dangerousness makes it an ideal defence. It is quite possible that in certain sacred operations—*e.g.*, circumcision and cutting the mistletoe—the phenomenon of rust, indicating decay, may also have been a deterrent from the use of iron. This, or the general notion of the dangerousness of hard metals, may have inspired the Chinese rule that metal buttons may not be used on grave-clothes. They would 'give trouble to the dead by injuring his body while it is decaying in the grave.'[7] On the other hand, the Chinese use gold, jade, and mercury to retard the decay and facilitate the future revival of the dead.

1 *PNQ* iii. [1886] 60; W. Gregor, *Folk-lore of the North-East of Scotland*, London, 1881, p. 206; *PC*[4] i. 140; F. Liebrecht, *Gervase von Tilbury*, Hanover, 1856, p. 99 ff.; R. C. Thompson, *Semitic Magic*, London, 1908, p. xxix.

2 *GB*[3], pt. ii., *Taboo and the Perils of the Soul*, p. 233.

3 *Ib.* note.

4 Kruijt, *Het Animisme*, pp. 161, 163.

5 K. Martin, in *Bijdragen tot de Taal-, Land- en Volkenkunde von Nederlandsch Indië*, xxxv. [1886] 24.

6 Skeat, p. 273, note. 7 *Ib.* p. 274. 8 *Ib.* p. 429.

9 i. 16. 10 *Myth. Vat.* III. xi. 18.

11 Black, pp. 142 f., 174.

12 J. G. Frazer, in *JAI* xv. [1886] 88.

13 De Groot, vi. 944 f.

1 *GB*[3], pt. ii., *Taboo*, p. 227; W. E. Griffis, *Corea*, London, 1882, p. 219; Plut. *Aristides*, xxi., *Præcepta ger. reipub.*, xxvi. f.; G. Henzen, *Acta Fratrum Arvalium*, Berlin, 1874, p. 128 ff.; Macrobius, *Sat.* v. xix. 13; schol. on Theocritus, ii. 36; G. B. Grinnell, *Pawnee Hero Stories*, New York, 1889, p. 253; J. G. Bourke, *The Snake Dance of the Moquis of Arizona*, London, 1884, p. 178 f.; T. Hahn, *Tsuni-Goam*, do. 1881, p. 22; *GB*[3], pt. ii., *Taboo*, p. 227.

2 *GB*[3], pt. ii., *Taboo*, p. 176.

3 E. S. Hartland, *Science of Fairy Tales*, London, 1891, p. 306; C. F. G. Cumming, *In the Hebrides*[2], do. 1883, p. 226; 1 K 6[7], Ex 20[25]; Dion. Hal. *Ant. Rom.* iii. 45, v. 24; Pliny, *HN* xxxvi. 100; *IA* x. [1881] 364.

4 *GB*[3], pt. ii., *Taboo*, p. 230. 5 *Ib.* p. 232.

6 E. Westermarck, *Ceremonies and Beliefs, etc., in Morocco*, Helsingfors, 1913, p. 25 ff.

7 De Groot, i. 64.

2. Minerals. — The religious associations of minerals in general are fewer and less marked than those of metals, except in the case of salt. The use, however, of stones of various sorts and shapes as fetishes and vehicles of magic is very widely spread; but, as it demands a special study (see art. STONES), it is touched upon here only to illustrate the general attitude towards the mineral world.

Australian medicine-men possess sacred stones full of strength, more or less regarded as 'living spirits.' They swallow them or rub their heads with them to acquire their virtue.[1] In Melanesia magic and worship are closely connected with sacred stones. The stone is not the *vui* (the spirit) nor is the *vui* in the stone, but there is a 'connexion.' The stone is, as it were, the 'outward part' or 'organ' of the *vui*, and the owner of such a stone is its priest.[2] These stones are kept in houses in order to bring *mana* to the inmates. There are special stones for promoting the growth of the crops and for bringing rain or sunshine. The stone is rubbed with food—*e.g.*, coco-nut—to induce it to act. Food placed on a stone and then eaten gives *mana* to the eater.[3]

Both shape and material are concerned in the prestige of sacred stones.

The Australians are partial to a small round black stone, which is easily manipulated; the medicine-man cures a disease by pretending to extract such a stone from the patient's body.[4] In some tribes every man carried a round black pebble of magic power, *bulk*; placing this in contact with anything coming from an enemy sent the magic force into his body, procuring his death or sickness.[5] Rock-crystal, or quartz, is a favourite material for these purposes.[6] Australian medicine-men used bits of rock-crystal for making rain, curing or causing disease, and poisoning water. To cure disease they would extract a piece of rock-crystal, alleging that a hostile sorcerer had placed it in the patient's body.[7] To make rain the sorcerer breaks off a piece of rock-crystal and spits it towards the sky.[8] White quartz is used for this purpose in Queensland. The stones are fixed to a stick and placed at the bottom of a pool, while in some parts a quartz crystal is ground to powder, which is scattered over the women, who pretend that it is rain,[9] the liquid appearance of the crystal possibly suggesting its connexion with rain. The Wa-wamba of Central Africa anoint a rain-stone and place it in water; Mongolians use a bezoar stone.[10] In the Banks' Islands a round stone, called 'sunstone' (*vat loa*), is decorated with radiating feathers and hung in a tree to produce sunshine.[11] In New Guinea a 'wind-stone' is tapped with a stick to produce wind. If it were struck heavily, a hurricane would result. The people of Vancouver have a number of stones, each representing a particular wind, and the required wind is obtained by slightly moving the corresponding stone.[12] Pebbles, being obviously suitable for counting (cf. *calculus*), are naturally used as representatives of persons; in Scottish folk-ritual at Hallowe'en each member of a family is represented by a stone.[13] In Greece a black stone is placed on the head to produce strength, and people carry stones on their heads while jumping over the bonfire.[14]

The use of crystals of quartz or other mineral for 'seeing' is world-wide, and needs no special illustration here (see art. CRYSTAL-GAZING). Again there is to be noted the analogy between the crystal and the liquid stage.

In the Middle Ages the term 'bezoar' covered mineral as well as animal concretions.[15] One variety was the 'madstone,' curative of madness and poisoning.[16] The adder-stone was worn to cure whooping-cough, amber to ward off croup, the snake-stone to remove serpent's poison, the load-stone to cure rheumatism, in recent Scottish custom.[17] Precious stones particularly have in all ages commanded interest by their unique beauty of colour, sparkle, or phosphorescence. The Greeks wore 'amethysts' to prevent intoxication; agate was a panacea of disease; the bloodstone checked bleeding.[1]

The lore of jewels is a subject in itself, but mainly built up of fanciful analogy rather than of genuine superstition. But the Dayaks, among others, suggest the same elements of animism as have prevailed in the case of metals, when they regard a special form of diamond as 'the soul of diamonds.'[2] At the other end of the scale there is the modern English burglar who carries a lump of coal in his pocket as a charm, possibly a charm for invisibility.[3]

The ceremonial use of flint implements for extraordinary purposes, while steel is used for ordinary, has been alluded to above.

The fine jade of China has attracted to itself almost a special cult; it is identified with the heavens, since all precious substances are from the sky. Like gold, it possesses intense vital force, or *yang*. Some jade is of a beautiful azure colour—a fact with which its heavenly origin may be connected. Chinese folklore has stories of jade-wine flowing from mythical rocks of jade. Jade prolongs life, and even produces immortality.[4] In folk-medicine it was used as a sovereign panacea, and administered as a decoction or ointment. Jade-water was procurable from streams flowing by jade rocks, or was made with powdered jade.[5] In accordance with the idea that death is a protracted sleep, the Chinese place in the mouth of the dead objects possessing vital energy (*yang*) to facilitate revival and retard decomposition, such being jade, jasper, nephrite, and agate. Jade, the most precious mineral, being identified with the heavens, intensifies the souls, or *shen*, of those in contact with it; and the same was the case with gold, sometimes identified with jade.[6]

'When the Sovereign fasts, the jade which he swallows is procured by the Manager of the Jade Stores.'

This would accelerate his intercourse with disembodied *shen*, the object of his fast.[7] There were many stories of a luminous variety of jade.[8]

The discovery of salt[9] and its employment in food-preparation constitute an epoch as socially important as the discovery of metals. Neither has been achieved by the Australian natives; and many metal-using savages are still ignorant of salt. But its discovery generally comes early in culture, though long subsequent, in most cases, to the discovery of metal. Owing, perhaps, to its quasi-medicinal properties, as much as to its effect on food stuffs, salt has attracted an extraordinary amount of superstitious and religious attention. The bond, *e.g.*, created in Arabic and other customs by eating salt together is in the highest degree sacred, and may deserve the name of 'salt-communion.' Very holy obligations were 'covenants of salt.'[10] Salt has analogies with blood and all 'strong foods'; on another side it has analogies with 'strong' metals like iron. Primitive peoples ignorant of salt are supposed to correct its absence from their food by drinking fresh blood.

Harmless superstitions about salt have lasted into modern civilization, owing to its having been a sort of symbol of food-communion and of the common meal.

In mediævalism the salt separated the family from the retainers in hall.[11] In Leonardo's fresco of the Last Supper, Judas was to be recognized by the salt-cellar which he had overturned; the detail is visible in the copy by his pupil, Marco d' Oggiono, in the Brera Gallery.

1 K. L. Parker, *The Euahlayi Tribe*, London, 1905, p. 35.
2 R. H. Codrington, in *JAI* x. [1881] 275.
3 *Ib.* pp. 276, 278.
4 J. Dawson, *Australian Aborigines*, Melbourne, 1881, p. 59.
5 L. Fison and A. W. Howitt, *Kamilaroi and Kurnai*, Melbourne, 1880, p. 251 f.
6 It is shown as a mystery to boys at initiation (Fison and Howitt, p. 283).
7 E. J. Eyre, *Expeditions into Central Australia*, London, 1845, ii. 316, 359.
8 A. L. P. Cameron, in *JAI* xiv. [1885] 362.
9 W. E. Roth, *North-West-Central Queensland Aborigines*, Brisbane and London, 1897, p. 167 ff.
10 *GB*[3], pt. i., *The Magic Art*, i. 305.
11 Codrington, *JAI* x. 278.
12 *GB*[3], pt. i., *The Magic Art*, i. 322.
13 *Ib.* pt. vii., *Balder the Beautiful*, i. 230.
14 *Ib.* p. 211 f.
15 Black, p. 145 ff. 16 *Ib.* pp. 144, 146. 17 *Ib.* p. 182.

1 Black, p. 176. 2 Kruijt, *Het Animisme*, p. 160.
3 Black, p. 219. 4 De Groot, i. 275, 272 f.
5 *Ib.* iv. 330. 6 *Ib.* i. 269, iv. 328.
7 *Ib.* i. 271. 8 *Ib.* i. 277 f.
9 First found in the form of rock-salt and marsh-salt.
10 Nu 18[19], 2 Ch 13[5]; J. Wellhausen, *Reste arab. Heidentums*[2], Berlin, 1897, pp. 124, 189; I. Benzinger, *JE*, *s.v.* 'Salt.'
11 The Latin *salinum* was placed in the centre of the table, and rendered it sacred.

Salt has been much used in sacrifice, indicating the analogy between sacred and ordinary meals. *Mola salsa* was offered by the Latins to the *lares*, and salt was sprinkled by Greeks and Latins on the head of the sacrificial animal. On the other hand, the Rabbi Chia, in the 3rd cent., stated that in all salt there is some portion of the salt and sulphur of Sodom, which blinds the person whose eyes it touches.[1] We thus get the two poles usually found belonging to sacred substances, positive and negative, *optimum* and *pessimum*.

Salt has been widely used in protective and curative magic, and the association of ideas may be the same as is seen in the word 'preserve.'

Lao and Siamese women after childbirth washed themselves daily with salt and water, salt being a protection against witchcraft.[2] Moors carry salt in the dark to keep off ghosts,[3] and in Teutonic countries it is placed near infants to protect them.[4] In Morocco it is put in the wheat stack to guard it from *znūn*, and is sprinkled on the hand-mill before grinding the corn.[5] British folk-custom has the charm of carrying salt withershins round a baby before taking it to be baptized.

Salt is a cure for many sicknesses, and procures disenchantment.[6] Like blood and iron, it is a favourite medium for the oath; in early Teutonic custom the swearer dipped his finger in salt, and then took the oath.[7]

As with other trades, sacredness has attached to salt-mining.

In Laos salt-miners observe continence and other tabus.[8] In ancient Germany salt-working was a sacred business.[9] The peoples of Central America worshipped a 'goddess,' Huixtocihuatl, of salt, who was believed to have invented the pan-process.[10]

Prohibitions against the use of salt are instructive for the theory of tabu. Certain professions, and persons in certain states, are forbidden to use salt, as they are forbidden other critical substances.

Mourners may eat no salt among Hindus, Africans, and other peoples. Priests and medicine-men (as among the Egyptians, the Dards, and Central and S. Americans) may eat no salt throughout their lives.[11] The salt-tabu of the Egyptian priesthood is especially emphasized.[12] When travelling, the Central African might not use salt. If he did, and his wives were not behaving well, the salt would act as 'a corrosive poison.'[13] During the ceremonies of firstfruits among the Yuchi Indians of California continence and abstinence from salt are ordered,[14] as is also the case after a solemn communion with a god by the Huichol Indians.[15] No salt may be used in cooking the flesh of the beast or any food at the Gilyak Bear Festival.[16] Some Dayaks after taking heads may not eat salt, or touch iron, or have intercourse with women. Baganda fishermen have the same combined tabu.[17] In Indian ritual the young student, after being brought to his teacher, and the newly-married pair must abstain from salted food for three days.[18]

The following is a luminous instance of the ætiology of the associations of salt.

Among the Nyanja-speaking tribes of British Central Africa the girl at puberty is secluded and may eat no salt. After the seclusion she is married. On the wedding-night she puts salt in the relish which she cooks, and this is set out next morning for relatives to rub on themselves, though not if the husband is impotent.[19]

On this and similar customs, viz. that women at their periods may not put salt in food, lest husband and children contract a disease, Frazer says:

[1] J. Basnage, *Hist. des Juifs depuis Jésus-Christ*, The Hague, 1716-26, iv. 1224.
[2] C. Bock, *Temples and Elephants*, London, 1884, p. 260.
[3] A. Leared, *Morocco and the Moors*, London, 1876, p. 275; Black, p. 131.
[4] Grimm, *Teutonic Mythology*, tr. J. Stallybrass, London, 1882-88, iii. 1049.
[5] Westermarck, pp. 27, 31, 47.
[6] Black, p. 131.
[7] Grimm, iii. 1049.
[8] *GB*[3], pt. ii., *Taboo*, p. 200.
[9] Grimm, iii. 1047.
[10] *NR* iii. 369 f.; *GB*[3], pt. vi., *The Scapegoat*, London, 1913, p. 283, pt. vii., *Balder the Beautiful*, i. 244.
[11] Frazer, *Totemism and Exogamy*, London, 1910, iv. 223-227.
[12] Plut. *de Is. et Osir.* xxxii.
[13] J. Macdonald, in *JAI* xxii. [1893] 104.
[14] F. G. Speck, *The Yuchi Indians*, Philadelphia, 1909, p. 86 f.
[15] *GB*[3], pt. v., *Spirits of the Corn and of the Wild*, London, 1912, ii. 93, quoting C. Lumholtz.
[16] *Ib.* p. 195, quoting L. von Schrenck.
[17] *GB*[3], pt. ii., *Taboo*, pp. 167, 194.
[18] Oldenberg, pp. 411, 413 f.
[19] *GB*[3], pt. vii., *Balder the Beautiful*, i. 26 f., quoting R S. Rattray.

Abstinence from salt is somehow associated with the idea of chastity. 'Primitive man connects salt with the intercourse of the sexes and therefore forbids the use of that condiment in a variety of circumstances.'[1]

A psychological analysis is assisted by the Rabbinical theory of *kilayim*, the mixture of things differing in species or substance, and by the principle underlying the contrast between Apollo and Dionysus in Greek thought. Persons in a crisis must be chaste; the keynote of chastity is avoidance of alien influence, of mixture. The Apolline ideal is static, that of Dionysus dynamic. The votaries of the latter god celebrated orgies with consumption of flesh, wine, and blood. The principle of the orgy, whether alcoholic, cannibal, flesh-eating, or sexual, is distinctly dynamic—a stimulation of human energy to the utmost degree. Movement and change are among its characteristics; and, in a humble way, salt, as producing chemical change, is in the list of dynamic vehicles. In connexion with sexual intercourse it is analogous to leaven; there is some idea of the process of fermentation, so to say, about the sexual act, as well as the expenditure of vital energy in an ultra-dynamic process.

Alum and sulphur[2] are used, but in a far less degree, as magical substances. Alum is an Egyptian charm against the evil eye,[3] and both are employed in Morocco to protect ploughing oxen from the evil eye.[4] Cinnabar was used in Greek charms for producing invisibility.[5]

The use of coloured ochres, chalk, pipeclay, gypsum, kaolin, and other earths for decorating the body on ceremonial occasions is very widely spread in the lower culture. Magical ideas naturally attach to bituminous deposits and such sources of rock-oil as are found in Western Asia. Chinese folklore includes magical use of oil.[6]

3. In metaphor.—The metallic and mineral world has naturally developed a large literature of metaphor. Gold is in the OT a symbol of purity, of nobility, and of value, and 'brass' (=bronze or copper) is used in the OT as a symbol of hardness.[7] Iron connotes strength and severity—'a rod of iron,' 'a yoke of iron,' 'walls of iron,' 'an iron sinew.'[8] A teacher of the law, said the Rabbis, must be as hard as iron. Being also breakable into pieces, it is a symbol of the Tôrāh with its numerous parts.[9]

The symbolism of Dn 2 and 7 comparing the kingdoms of the world to metals was popular in mediæval literature.

'Gold is Babylon; silver is Media; copper is Greece; iron is not mentioned either at the time of the First or of the Second Temple, since it symbolises Edom (Rome), which had destroyed the Temple.'[10] The Iranians had a longer series of ages—gold, silver, brass, copper, tin, steel, iron.[11]

Philo elaborated a metallic symbolism: gold is wisdom; copper perception.[12] The Sabians associated each planet with a metal, of which the statues of the planetary god were made;[13] and in Mithraism the soul passed through seven gates, each of a different metal — lead, tin, bronze, iron, alloy, silver, and gold—and each corresponding to a planet as well as to a psychic quality.[14] Hesiod's famous metallic series of the ages of the world inspired a considerable literature. The first age, which was the best, was golden; that in which

[1] *GB*[3], pt. vii., *Balder the Beautiful*, i. 28.
[2] O. Gruppe, *Griech. Mythol. und Religionsgesch.*, Munich, 1906, p. 889.
[3] E. W. Lane, *Modern Egyptians*, London, 1836, i. 323.
[4] Westermarck, p. 16.
[5] Thompson, p. lxvii.
[6] De Groot, i. 23.
[7] Job 23[10], La 4[1], Is 13[12], Dt 28[23], Lv 26[19], Job 6[12] 40[18], Is 48[4].
[8] Dt 28[48], Ps 2[9], 2 Mac 11[9], Is 48[4].
[9] *Ta'an.* 4*a*; *Suk.* 52*b*; S. Krauss, art. 'Metals,' in *JE*.
[10] Krauss, *loc. cit.*
[11] *SBE* v. 199 ff.
[12] *De Leg. Alleg.* (Mangey, i. 25) iii. 4.
[13] Krauss, *loc. cit.*; J. H. Gladstone, in *Nature*, April 1898, pp. 594-598.
[14] Origen, *c. Cels.* vi. 22; cf. Gruppe, p. 1037.

we live is iron.[1] The principle behind this is æsthetic.

In Italy Saturn and in Greece Cronus 'was believed to have been a king who reigned in heaven or on earth during the blissful Golden Age, when men passed their days like gods without toil or sorrow, when life was a long round of festivity, and death came like sleep, sudden but gentle, announced by none of his sad forerunners, the ailments and infirmities of age.'[2]

LITERATURE.—To the authorities cited add R. Andree, *Die Metalle bei den Naturvölkern*, Leipzig, 1884; O. Schrader, *Sprachvergleichung und Urgesch.*[3], Jena, 1907, ii. 3-99; K. B. Hofmann, *Das Blei bei den Völkern des Altertums*, Berlin, 1885; V. Hehn, *Das Salz*[2], do. 1901; R. Garbe, *Die ind. Mineralien*, Leipzig, 1882. A. E. CRAWLEY.

METAMORPHOSIS.—1. Evidence for the belief.—Metamorphosis, transformation, or shape-shifting is a power universally believed in at low levels of culture. It survives at higher levels, especially among the masses, though it is also found in myths which are current among the educated or where popular belief tends to take the form of dogma, as when 17th cent. theologians accepted the werwolf superstition as a fact. The evidence for this universal belief is copious, and is found in myths, legends, and sagas, as well as in poetry from all lands; in folk-tales, of which it is one of the commonest themes or the most important incident, as, *e.g.*, in the 'Transformation Combat' or the 'True Bride' cycle;[3] in existing folk-belief, whether among savages or the peasantry; in the writings of modern travellers, explorers, and missionaries, as well as in older literature—Egyptian, Babylonian, Hindu, Greek, and Celtic.

2. Varieties of metamorphosis.—Metamorphosis is asserted of every order of beings and even of inanimate things. (*a*) As far as men are concerned, where the belief is current all men do not necessarily claim the power of transformation, but any man will readily admit that others have this power. Hence we have beliefs in the existence of distant tribes or groups possessing the power of transformation. Generally those who are credited with this power are medicine-men, shamans, sorcerers, wizards, and witches. To multiply instances is unnecessary; suffice it to say that, wherever such a class of people is found, shape-shifting is always one of their magical powers. No European peasant believes that he can change his form, though his savage ancestors did so; with him the belief survives in his firmly-rooted opinion that every witch can do so (see LYCANTHROPY). Among certain peoples, however, every one is believed to have some connexion with an animal form. Thus among the nations of W. Africa the bush-soul, one of the souls which each man possesses, exists in an animal; in Indo-China one of the souls of a man has the power of appearing as a man or as a wer-animal. This aspect of the subject is fully discussed under LYCANTHROPY.

While metamorphosis into animal form is more general, that into tree, plant, or flower is also found here and there. Besides this, numerous myths and tales from all parts of the world explain the origin of some tree or plant by saying that it sprang from the body—the arm, leg, head, or blood of some human being. Similarly, men are sometimes held to have sprung from plants. Where a tree springs from a dead human being the identity of the two is obvious, and here the stories may be based on the fact that trees often do grow from the barrows of the dead. They are supposed to be tenanted by the dead man's spirit or are identified with the man himself.[4]

The medicine-man or wizard has also the power of transforming others. He may supply them with magical means to change their form, but more usually he himself casts a spell upon them and transforms them. This is usually done through malice—and no incident is commoner in folk-tales than this—but it is sometimes meted out as a punishment, though transformation for this reason is generally the act of the gods. In such cases the transformation may be for a longer or shorter period, but it is often of a permanent character.

Instances are found at all levels of culture. Classical mythology knew many such punishments for impiety. The incident enters also into Christian tradition, though it is derived from earlier sources. Thus Christ is represented as a tired traveller who is refused food or on whom a trick is played by a peasant or a Jew, and the result for them is the punishment of transformation to animal form. In many cases groups of megaliths are said to be human beings changed to stone for some act of impiety—the idea perhaps originating in the belief that the stones embody ghosts of the dead buried beneath them.[1] Other instances of petrifaction, in some cases also for a punishment, are found in all mythologies—Australian, American Indian, Greek, Hebrew, etc. The idea of petrifaction may be connected with the fact that many rocks bear some resemblance to human form.[2] In folk-tales the power of petrifying is usually in the hands of witch or wizard, and a touch with a wand, binding the victim with the witch's hair, or the repeating of a spell suffices. Cf. Medusa's head.

(*b*) The power of transformation on the part of men was reflected back upon the gods in all mythologies, from the lowest to the highest—Bushman, Australian, Polynesian, Peruvian, Celtic, Greek, Hindu, Egyptian, etc. There was no limit to the forms which they could take, animal or human, in order to serve their purposes—to escape danger, to benefit men, to carry on amours, and the like. As in Egypt, men looked forward to being able to assume any form in a future life, like the gods.[3] The gods, too, as has been seen, had the power of causing metamorphosis as a punishment to men.

(*c*) Demons and supernatural beings of all kinds were also believed to have similar powers. The *jinn* of Arabia, the *bhūts* of India, the devils of early and mediæval Christianity,[4] the water-horses and other monstrous beings of popular belief, can assume any shape to carry out their ends. Often the form is that of an attractive girl or youth who lures away a human victim to destruction. Ghosts of the dead may appear as animals, or project themselves into animals temporarily, but there is a wide-spread belief in their more permanent assumption of animal forms (see ANIMALS, vol. i. p. 493[b]).

(*d*) Animals themselves are sometimes believed to be capable of self-transformation. This is true of the fox in Japan and China and of the tiger in Malaysia (see LYCANTHROPY), and the seal and similar animals are well known in folk-belief to have the power of changing into human shape.

(*e*) Inanimate objects may also be changed into other forms by magical power. The best instance of this occurs in the Transformation Flight group of *Märchen*, in which, *e.g.*, a girl escaping with her lover throws down small objects which become a forest, a mountain, or a lake, and impede the progress of the pursuer (see MacCulloch, *CF*, p. 171 ff.). Examples of this are found not only in European and Asiatic folk-tales, but in Samoan, American Indian, and Basuto stories.

3. Origin of the belief in metamorphosis.—An examination of the enormous mass of evidence for the belief in metamorphosis suggests that man's idea of personality, or perhaps rather of the forms in which personality may lurk, is an exceedingly fluid one. There has everywhere been a stage of human thought when no clear distinction was drawn between man and the rest of the universe, between human and animal, between animate and

1 Hesiod, *Works and Days*, 109-201.
2 *GB*[3], pt. vi., *The Scapegoat*, p. 353.
3 J. A. MacCulloch, *CF*, pp. 159, 164 f.
4 *Ib.* p. 115; G. Allen, *Evolution of the Idea of God*, London, 1897, p. 147 f.; A. Lang, *Myth, Ritual, and Religion*[2], i. 154 f.

1 A. J. Evans, 'The Rollright Stones and their Folk-lore,' *FL* vi. [1895] 5 ff.
2 L. J. B. Bérenger-Féraud, *Superstitions et survivances*, Paris, 1896, ii. 371 ff.; MacCulloch, *CF*, p. 156; A. Lang, *op. cit.* i. 151 ff.
3 E. A. W. Budge, *Egyptian Magic*[2], London, 1901, p. 230 f.
4 L. F. A. Maury, *La Magie*, Paris, 1860, p. 103; cf. 2 Co 11[14] and the *Apocryphal Acts*, *passim*.

inanimate. In this stage of thought animate and inanimate are equally believed to be alive; men, animals, and things have the same feelings and passions, or act and speak in the same manner. Or, when the idea of soul or spirit is attained, all are equally alive by virtue of the possession of such a soul or spirit. Such beliefs in the underlying similarity of all things hindered men from having a clear notion of personality. It was not fixed and unalterable; it might assume various forms. There was thus obtained a practical, working belief that men, animals, and spirits or gods, as well as inanimate things, might assume some other form than their own from time to time. Hence it is not surprising to the savage if what he now sees as a man he sees immediately after as an animal or a bush. Where the idea of spirit or soul exists, and where it is thought that the spirit can leave its containing body, nothing is easier than to believe further that it can enter for a time into an animal or a tree. Other lines of thought also served to support the belief in the solidarity of men, animals, and things, and in metamorphosis. Totemism, with its assertion of the kinship of a human clan and an animal or plant species, has given rise to various myths which are rooted in this primitive stratum of thought, and in turn have served to deepen it. Thus it is sometimes thought that at first 'all animals were as men,' as the Algonquins say,[1] and only later took animal form. As the Hareskin Indians think, in the beginning men were animals and animals were men, but afterwards changed their rôles; or, according to the Zuñis, all things were originally animals, but now men, trees, etc., are degenerate animals with souls which can leave their bodies.[2] Again, men were once animals who became men—a common Polynesian belief.[3] Where a clan of one totem dislike the animal which is the totem of another distant clan, they may come to regard the men of that clan as possessed of its nature and liable to assume its form. In all such cases, whether totemistic in origin or not, it is easy to see that men and animals might be supposed to revert temporarily to the other forms which once were theirs.

It is also possible that an analogy between the habits of certain animals and those of human beings, in life or after death, may have aided the belief in metamorphosis. Thus, where ghosts of men are believed to return to the house in which they lived and which is also the haunt of such animals as snakes or rats, it is easy to imagine that these are forms of the dead man. This is the case in Zululand with the snake. Night-roaming animals like the cat, tiger, or wolf might be identified, as they were, with witches, who also roamed in darkness.

Hallucination might be a potent factor in aiding the belief. Savages have often declared that they have witnessed such a change of shape. The preconceived idea suggested the hallucination, and it in turn gave support to the belief. Or persons to whom drugs had been administered might have hallucinations of themselves as animals, as in classical and mediæval instances (see LYCANTHROPY, § 2). Madness, again, has also had its part to play. Its victims, especially where the belief in metamorphosis prevails, often imitate the cries, motions, and actions of animals, and this could only serve to establish the belief more securely. The wer-wolf superstition was largely moulded out of such cases of mania (see LYCANTHROPY, § 3).

[1] C. G. Leland, *Algonquin Legends of New England*, London, 1884, p. 109.
[2] E. Petitot, *Traditions indiennes du Canada nord-ouest*, Paris, 1886, p. 275 f.; F. H. Cushing, *Zuñi Folk-Tales*, New York, 1901, Introd. p. ix.
[3] G. Turner, *Samoa a Hundred Years Ago*, London, 1884, pp. 296, 330.

The custom of dressing in an animal skin at sacred dances, or before a bear-hunt, or of wearing animal-masks in war, would also aid the belief in metamorphosis. The frenzy of the dance would suggest self-transformation to the dancer, while the onlookers or the enemy would imagine that they saw human animals. There is no doubt also that medicine-men have often strengthened the belief by exploiting it—*e.g.*, dressing as an animal, imitating its howls and its actions.[1]

In practice the belief in the power of metamorphosis of men is generally limited to the medicine-man, sorcerer, etc., who transforms his victims usually by a spell, talisman, or potion. Self-transformation is caused in many ways, most of them magical. Sometimes, however, it is the result of a divine, supernatural, or demoniac gift.

See, for a further discussion and examples, the art. LYCANTHROPY; cf. also TRANSMIGRATION.

LITERATURE.—A. Lang, *Myth, Ritual, and Religion*², London, 1899, i. 118 f., 150 f.; J. A. MacCulloch, *CF*, do. 1905, ch. vi., 'Transformation'; E. B. Tylor, *PC*⁴, do. 1903, *passim*.

J. A. MACCULLOCH.

METAPHYSICS.—It is not easy to give a quite satisfactory definition of metaphysics. The name throws no real light upon its nature, having referred originally merely to the order of some Aristotelian treatises; but it suggests that the subject is concerned with topics that can be properly dealt with only after the more special sciences (which may be taken to include the vital sciences as well as the more purely physical ones) have been discussed. For the purpose of this sketch, it may suffice to state that the subject of metaphysics is the most fundamental problems of knowledge and reality. It will be convenient to divide the treatment of it into three parts: (1) the general nature of knowledge, (2) the conception of reality and its chief applications, and (3) the bearings of metaphysics on other subjects, especially ethics and religion.

1. Knowledge.—The first thing that has to be noticed about knowledge is the ambiguity of the term. It is here employed in a very wide sense; but it is very commonly understood in a narrower one. Thus, knowledge is frequently distinguished from those modes of apprehension which are called sensation, perception, and imagination. It is thus confined to those modes of apprehension which involve definite thought or conception. Again, it is common, especially since the time of Kant, to contrast knowledge with belief. It is now customary to use the term 'cognition' to include all these modes of apprehension; and it is in this extended sense that the term is here employed. But even cognition is generally distinguished by recent psychologists from other modes of consciousness, which are called feeling, or affection, and willing, or conation. There are valid grounds for these distinctions, but it is important to remember that, so far as we are directly aware of these distinguishable aspects of our consciousness, they are, in the widest sense of the word, known or cognized. We apprehend pleasantness and unpleasantness and the fact of striving just as truly as we apprehend sounds or colours, trees or stars, triangles or systems of philosophy. There are, however, some differences in our ways of knowing which it is very necessary to bear in mind. The most fundamental are those that have been expressed by the terms 'simple apprehension and judgment,' 'immediacy and mediacy,' 'acquaintance and description,' 'enjoyment and contemplation,' 'experiencing and experienced.'[2] It may be well to take the last of these first. Whenever there is knowledge of any kind, there is some one who knows

[1] See M. Dobrizhoffer, *Account of the Abipones*, London, 1822, ii. 77; R. M. Dorman, *The Origin of Primitive Superstitions*, Philadelphia, 1881, p. 248; cf. LYCANTHROPY, § 3.
[2] These are the antitheses that are specially emphasized by G. F. Stout, W. Hamilton, B. Russell, S. Alexander, and C. Lloyd Morgan respectively.

and something that is known. Knowledge does not exist *in vacuo*, but at some particular centre; and that centre is not primarily aware of itself, but of some particular object. Whenever any one reflects upon his knowledge, however, he at once becomes aware of this double aspect: he realizes not only that something is apprehended, but that he apprehends it. What exactly *he* is, and what the *something* is that he apprehends, are matters for further consideration; but the general fact can hardly be disputed. Now, when any one reflects further upon his knowledge, and especially when by intercourse with his fellowmen he is able to compare his own knowledge with that of others, he very soon comes to realize that some of the things that he apprehends are more closely connected with his particular way of apprehending them than others are. He finds that some things are cognized by others in substantially the same way in which they are cognized by him. To this class belong especially facts relating to number, to spatial and temporal order, to the forms of objects in space and time, and to the general conditions under which such objects occur. Such things come to be regarded as being in a special sense objective, *i.e.* as being independent of the particular nature of the being by whom they are apprehended. Some other things are more open to doubt in this respect. There is not the same amount of agreement about colours as there is about forms; and there is still more difference of opinion with regard to the extent to which beauty and ugliness, agreeableness and disagreeableness, are to be ascribed to particular objects that we apprehend. Thus we are led to distinguish some of the things that we know as not specially belonging to ourselves, but being simply objects that we contemplate; and others as being more peculiarly our own, things that we have or enjoy, things that are not merely experienced, but that are bound up with our attitude as experiencing. The things that appear to be most emphatically in the latter class are such characteristics as pleasantness and unpleasantness, beauty and ugliness, emotional experiences, values; but the division between these and such experiences as those of taste, smell, colour, etc., is not a very sharp one. Hence, instead of placing objects in one or other of these divisions, we may be led rather to recognize a subjective and an objective aspect in *all* modes of apprehension.[1]

Once this important distinction has been duly recognized, the next that claims our attention is that between immediate and mediate apprehension. Some things are known to us in a quite direct way, and cannot be doubted. When any one has an experience of pain, he may be very uncertain with regard to its source and even with regard to the part of his organism to which it is to be referred; and he may even have some difficulty in distinguishing clearly between the pain that he is experiencing and some other fact that he is experiencing or that he has experienced; but he cannot really doubt that he is having this experience, whatever he may be, and however the object of his experience is to be described or interpreted. Every man is in some degree 'a man of sorrows and acquainted with grief,' and he cannot have any doubt about the grief with which he is acquainted, though he may be quite unable to analyze or describe it, or to explain how it has arisen. As soon as we begin to analyze, to describe, or to explain, we enter into the region within which doubt is possible. Even the naming of an experience may involve some error;[1] for to name it implies that we class it along with some other experiences, and we may be wrong in supposing that it is essentially the same or similar. It may be that what I call my grief should be more properly characterized as simple unpleasantness or as resentment or remorse; and, when I think that I am grieving over my neighbour's misfortunes, I may in reality be considering rather the way in which they affect myself. Knowledge ceases to be immediate as soon as it ceases to be the simple apprehension of something and becomes, implicitly or explicitly, a judgment about something. Here also, however, we have to recognize differences of degree. Though we may conceivably be in error in thinking that grief is the right name for what we are experiencing, yet, if we are really 'acquainted with grief,' we can hardly be mistaken in thinking that what we are experiencing is of the same general kind as what we have experienced before. But we may easily pass to something that we cannot so immediately know. When Lady Constance says, 'Grief fills the place up of my absent child,' we are not likely to be ignorant of what she means by grief, and we can partly apprehend what the rest of her statement means; but, if we have never had any similar experience, our apprehension has very little immediacy. We may even be inclined to doubt whether it has any real meaning at all. It is a description of something that might be apprehended, but with which we do not happen to be acquainted.

Now, the various theories of knowledge turn largely on the distinction between what is immediate and what is mediate, and between what is subjective and what is objective. One theory of knowledge which, in different forms, has played a very conspicuous part in the history of philosophy is to the effect that we have no immediate knowledge of anything but what is essentially subjective. One of the most extreme forms of this theory is found in the doctrine of Descartes, that the only thing of which we are immediately certain is the existence of the self as a conscious or thinking being. What he really brings out, however, is rather that everything of which we are immediately conscious certainly exists as something apprehended. What thus certainly exists is a complex, including certain objects that are apprehended and the fact of their apprehension. But Descartes considered that the objects thus apprehended might be properly described as being 'in the mind,' and that the individual mind should be regarded as a persistent thing within which such objects are contained; and he called the objects 'ideas.' He was thus led to think that the individual mind exists both as something known, *i.e.* as an 'idea,' and as something that persists in a way that is independent of its being immediately known, whereas the other objects that are known are known only as having what he calls 'objective reality,' *i.e.* the kind of reality which consists simply in their being immediately known. But he recognized that *some* of these other objects carry with them the suggestion of a more complete reality than that which belongs to them in the simple fact of their immediate apprehension; and he sought, by various arguments, to give grounds

[1] The lack of words to distinguish properly between the subjective and the objective aspects of cognition has been a great source of confusion. Sensation, *e.g.*, has had to do duty both for sensing and for what is sensed; and it is only very recently that it has been common to distinguish between perception and percept, conception and concept. Even now we do not readily grasp what Goethe meant when he said that all the thinking in the world (subjective activity) may not bring us to thought (the apprehension of an objective concept). It is largely the failure to realize this distinction that makes it so difficult for most people to understand such an 'Idealism' as that of Plato or Hegel, in which 'ideas,' or 'thoughts,' mean certain objective forms, orders, or universals. The 'New Realism' has greatly helped to make this distinction clearer.

[1] The difficult subject of error, its nature and conditions, cannot be here discussed. But see the references given at the end of this article.

to justify the belief in this more complete kind of reality. In doing this, he founded the doctrine which has been referred to as that of 'representative ideas,' which had a great influence on subsequent speculation. According to this doctrine, the individual mind may be compared to a picture-gallery, the pictures being 'ideas.' One of the pictures is the picture of itself, and that must be supposed to have been always in it. Some others, such as that of God, must also be supposed to have been always there. Some may be supposed to have been painted by itself. Some are daubs of no particular significance. But there are some that appear to be portraits; and these may be supposed to be the portraits of other beings outside the mind, and to have been, as it were, handed in by them. This is, no doubt, a somewhat crude way of stating it; but it appears to be substantially what Descartes sought to maintain; and, with some modifications, it reappears in the writings of several other philosophers. Berkeley dealt it a severe blow by contending that, if we see pictures only in a gallery, we have no ground for supposing that they ever exist in any other way than in a gallery; and Hume improved on this by arguing that, if we see only the pictures, the gallery is an unwarranted supposition. The metaphor that he uses is that of actors on a stage. We see the actors only, and have no reason to suppose that there is a stage. This reduced the whole doctrine almost to an absurdity; and the conception of 'representative ideas' was denounced with considerable force by Thomas Reid. What he had to put in its place, however, was not very clear. Kant took a more fruitful line by urging that we cannot without absurdity regard our knowledge as being confined to what is immediately apprehended by us at any time. We have to recognize certain fundamental orders, such as those of space, time, and causation, which carry us beyond our immediate data and inevitably suggest a coherent system of connexions. In his 'Refutation of Idealism' he urges, against Descartes and Berkeley, that the recognition of such a coherent order is more directly involved in the apprehension of objects distinct from the self than in the apprehension of the subject; and that our knowledge of the persistent reality of the self must, consequently, be regarded as derivative. He contends, however, that the order that we are bound to recognize in the objects which we apprehend is an order that can never be completely systematized, and must, consequently, be treated as 'phenomenal' and distinguished from the real order, which may be supposed to belong to 'things in themselves,' and which we are led to postulate chiefly on moral grounds. But Kant's doctrine carried conviction at least with regard to the necessity of recognizing that some kind of reality belongs to the more mediate forms of apprehension as well as to those that are more immediate. When the significance of this is fully realized, it leads to the doctrine that may be characterized as that of 'epistemological realism,' *i.e.* the doctrine that everything that we in any way cognize has a kind of reality which is not simply to be identified with the fact that it is immediately apprehended at a particular moment.

The acceptance of a doctrine of this kind gives a new interest to the study of the objects of cognition. So long as these objects are regarded merely as a flow of presentations, the interest in them tends to be almost purely psychological—*i.e.* it is directed simply to the way in which they come to be apprehended by the individual consciousness. When they are regarded as things possessing permanent characteristics and permanent orders of their own, they become the subject-matter of an independent study, and may almost be said to have given rise to a new science. This is the science that has been called by Meinong *Gegenstandstheorie*. It is the attempt to distinguish and arrange the different kinds of objects that we apprehend. It is obvious that there is a very great variety of such objects, when this term is understood in its most comprehensive sense. We apprehend, *e.g.*, a great variety of sense-data—sounds, colours, pains, strains, and so forth; we apprehend a great variety of percepts—stones, plants, animals, etc.; we apprehend orders, such as those of time and space, intensive and qualitative differences, causal dependence, etc.; we apprehend hypotheses, valuations, distinctions of beauty and ugliness, good and evil, etc. The study of these corresponds to some extent to the doctrine of categories; but, when it is approached from this point of view, it becomes very much more comprehensive than any of the lists of categories that are commonly set forth; and, in fact, it has a rather different aim from that implied in any of these lists. The problems raised by any such attempt to distinguish and arrange the various types of objects are evidently of a fundamental character, and seem, therefore, to belong properly to the subject-matter of metaphysics. It is possible, however, to discuss some of them to a considerable extent without any definite attempt at a systematic metaphysical construction. This brief indication of the general nature of these problems must suffice here.

2. Reality.—The study of the theory of knowledge and *Gegenstandstheorie* leads to the recognition that, in one sense at least, there is no meaning in the antithesis between the real and the unreal. As Parmenides and Plato urged, pure non-being is not to be thought or spoken of. But there is still a sense in which the things that we apprehend may be said to be more or less real. Sometimes our apprehension of things is very incomplete; and, when we gain a fuller apprehension of them, we may be said to know them more truly. Again, the things that we know are in many cases parts of larger wholes; and, so long as we do not apprehend the wholes of which they are parts, we cannot be said to have a full apprehension even of the parts. This is at least the case when they are parts of an organic unity. We could not be said to know much about the brain if we did not understand the function which it fulfils in the life of the organism. Our apprehension of the part, in such a case, is not the apprehension of what is unreal; but it may be said to be less real when it is thus apprehended than it is when its relations to the whole are understood. And, if the universe is an organic whole, this distinction will apply to the apprehension of all the objects in it. Hence there may still be a sense in which it is legitimate to speak of an antithesis between appearance and reality, or of different degrees of reality, though both these expressions are open to some objection. Now, in apprehending and arranging the various objects of our cognition, we are at least trying to regard them as forming a complete cosmos, such that every object has a definite place in the total order; and constructive metaphysics, as distinguished from *Gegenstandstheorie*, tries to find the way in which the objects of our experience can be so regarded. Here we are met at the outset by various forms of scepticism. Such a scepticism as that of Hume, no doubt, is effectively removed by a more thorough doctrine of knowledge, such as that of Kant. But even Kant ends with the view that our knowledge is only of appearance, and that we can never hope to apprehend things as they are in themselves; and such an agnosticism is defended, in different ways, by a considerable number of philosophical writers. If it is strictly pressed, it means that we have to be content with the theory of knowledge, supplemented by *Gegenstandstheorie.* The doctrine of the newer Realists, of whom Meinong is one of the ablest representatives, tends in this direction, though the supporters of it vary considerably in their applications. In the case of Kant himself, the attitude is modified by the two circumstances that, on the one hand, he had not fully reached the point of view of *Gegenstandstheorie,* not having completely freed himself from the subjectivism of Hume, while, on the other hand, he recognized that, though we cannot know anything about things as forming a real cosmos, we are justified in entertaining certain beliefs with regard to such reality, chiefly on moral grounds. This view of belief, as contrasted with knowledge, has been developed by the Pragmatists, who maintain that the ultimate ground of belief is not knowledge, but rather practical need. In general, the Pragmatists hold, further, that there is no real need to think of the world as a complete cosmos; but this is not an essential part of the Pragmatists' point of view. Bergson, again, while agreeing with the Pragmatists that our purely intellectual beliefs are based on practical needs, thinks that it is possible to reach a more perfect knowledge by means of intuition—a view which to some extent connects him with such earlier philosophers as Plotinus and Schelling. All these ways of thinking, and perhaps some others as well, tend to discredit the attempt to form a constructive doctrine of the objects of knowledge as constituting a cosmos. Yet the attempt continues to be made; and Kant at least recognized that, however futile it may be,[1] it is hardly possible for the human intelligence to refrain from trying it, when the scientific interest has been fully developed in it. All that can be done here, however, is to indicate some of the chief ways in which this attempt has been made.

The earliest attempt at a constructive theory of the cosmos, and certainly one of the most interesting and remarkable, is that which is set forth in the *Upaniṣads.* The difficulties of the subject, especially at so early a stage of human thought, prevent it from being dealt with in a perfectly lucid way; and it relies, in consequence, partly on poetic metaphor and partly on vague paradox; but the doctrine that the cosmos is to be conceived as an unchanging spiritual unity, manifesting itself, especially in human life, in a process of slow development, appears to be definitely indicated; and this view, showing itself most clearly in the conception of a long series of successive embodiments,[2] gained a firm hold on Eastern thought. It is a view to which Western thought also has recurred from time to time; but in general Western thought starts rather from the multiplicity of existing things, and makes only very tentative efforts to apprehend the central unity. Among the Greeks the earliest attempts to frame a theory of the unity of the cosmos took the form of a somewhat crude hylozoism, such as that of Thales. Pythagoras is supposed to have introduced conceptions more akin to those of the East; but, if so, they became gradually modified among his followers through the influence of the more materialistic ways of thinking that were current around them, and eventually through the growing interest in mathematical conceptions. In the end their speculative doctrines seem to have been largely lost in a barren formalism and a rather fantastic play with numerical analogies. The early representatives of the Eleatic school were perhaps more faithful to the conception of the unity of the cosmos; but in the poem of Parmenides it is difficult to distinguish what is to be taken literally from what is only metaphor. He sometimes seems to deny altogether the reality of multiplicity and change; but perhaps he meant only that the cosmos as a whole has to be thought of as one and unchanging, though change and multiplicity are contained within it. In any case, a view of this kind would have been very difficult to set forth clearly with such technical language as he had at his disposal; and it is probable that his views were not well understood by his followers. Anaxagoras recognized very definitely the essential unity of the cosmos and connected it with mind or reason; but he does not draw any clear distinction between mind and matter, and, in attempting to contrast the order that is brought about by mind with a pre-existing disorder, he makes use of an antithesis which is as difficult to justify as that between the real and the unreal.[1] It is with the philosophy of Plato that we first come upon a really coherent attempt to set forth a conception of the cosmos; and, in many respects, it may be doubted whether that attempt has ever been surpassed. His main conception is that of the Good as the principle of order; and he combines this with the recognition of a number of subordinate principles, all regarded as universal types in accordance with which the particular objects of our experience are formed. This view was made in some respects clearer by the Aristotelian conception of a hierarchy of forms leading up to the perfect intelligence; but, on the whole, Aristotle's main interest lay rather in the establishment of special sciences on the basis of this conception of fundamental forms. Plotinus, at a considerably later time, working largely under the influence of Oriental sources, but helped by the Platonic doctrines, succeeded more fully than any one else in ancient times in arriving at a conception of a cosmic system unfolding itself by a process from unity to multiplicity and returning into unity again; but his views are difficult to disentangle, and he tends at times to appeal to a mystical intuition rather than to a clearly reasoned doctrine.

In more modern times the system of Spinoza is the first attempt at a thorough constructive theory of the cosmos. In his emphasis on the unity of the whole he recalls Parmenides. The fact that Parmenides described it as finite, while Spinoza insisted on its infinity, is perhaps a somewhat superficial difference; for they probably understood the term 'infinity' in different senses. More significant is Spinoza's antithesis, derived from the Cartesian philosophy, between the unity of the spatial world and that of the world of thought, and his attempt to represent these two forms of unity as essentially identical. This results in a quasi-mathematical conception of the universe, and makes it appear as what James describes as a 'block universe.' Leibniz endeavoured to remove this defect by his conception of monads, which has served as the basis for subsequent theories of spiritualistic Pluralism. Yet he combines the conception of the complete independence of the monads with the recognition that they are parts of a world-order, the nature of which is definitely

1 Kant's view of its futility is mainly based on the difficulties which he brings out in his 'antinomies.' The solution of these is one of the main problems of constructive metaphysics; but this subject is too large and difficult to be discussed here. Hegel's dialectic is the most elaborate attempt to deal with such difficulties. Attempts have also been made by H. Bergson, B. Russell, and others.

2 The philosophical conception of the continuity of spiritual life ought, no doubt, to be distinguished from the cruder forms of the doctrine of reincarnation; but this is a subject that can only be hinted at here. The bearings of modern philosophy on this subject are best brought out by J. M. E. McTaggart, *Some Dogmas of Religion,* London, 1906, and B. Bosanquet, *The Value and Destiny of the Individual.*

1 The meaninglessness of any conception of pure chaos or disorder, such as that with which Anaxagoras appears to start, is well brought out in Bergson's *Creative Evolution,* Eng. tr., London, 1911.

determined, and which is selected as the best from an infinite number of possible world-orders. How possibility is to be distinguished from actuality is one of the most difficult problems that are raised by his philosophy;[1] but, on the whole, it must be confessed that his philosophy in general, notwithstanding its great ingenuity, is much more remarkable for the number of problems that it suggests than for the convincing character of the solutions that are proposed. His attempt was followed by a great deal of critical work, especially that done by Hume and Kant; and the constructions that followed upon this critical work are deserving of more careful attention.

The most important is that of Hegel, and it is also one of the most difficult to interpret. What can be said with confidence is that, by means of a more definite interpretation of the Platonic dialectic, he made a very thoroughgoing attempt to arrange all the fundamental concepts involved in thinking about the world in a definite order from the simplest to the most complex. By this means he sought to show that a certain conception of spiritual unity is the most comprehensive of all conceptions, and the only one by means of which a coherent view of the universe can be obtained. He then proceeds to interpret the non-human world ('nature') and the world of human life ('spirit') as an order of growth through which the spiritual significance of the whole is gradually unfolded. It is generally recognized that a considerable part of the working out of his dialectic carries conviction, but that there are several places in which the movement is difficult to follow. The treatment of human life is generally recognized as being highly instructive, while the interpretation of 'nature' is much more open to criticism. No subsequent writer, however, has succeeded in making substantial improvement on the general view of the cosmos that Hegel has presented. Most of those who have made attempts at definitely constructive work are chiefly distinguished from Hegel by the more tentative character of their doctrine. They seem to provide, at most, only the *disjecta membra* of a more complete system. Some of them may also be criticized on the ground that they rest on a subjective conception of knowledge, in a few cases approximating even to the point of view of Berkeley. But into the details of their work we cannot here enter.

It may seem disappointing, after so many centuries of more or less continuous philosophic endeavour, that it should not be possible to refer more definitely to results that are generally accepted as conclusive. But it is hardly surprising that the interpretation of the whole should present more difficulty than that of some special parts. It is probably necessary that we should have a fairly thorough appreciation of the kinds of order that are contained in the parts before we can have any definite conception of the order that is involved in the whole. By the help of mathematics we are getting a more and more thorough insight into the relations that are involved in the orders of number and space. The Platonic conception of Good has been made more definite by modern discussions of orders of valuation. Physical science is helping us to interpret the causal order with more and more definiteness. Such dialectical discussions as those of Bradley, and such attempts to determine the various kinds of objects as those that are made by Meinong, may be expected to throw fresh light on the most fundamental concepts, and thus supply new instruments for the reinterpretation of the whole. But probably our interpretation must always remain, to some extent, tentative.

[1] No sharp distinction can be drawn between the possible and the actual. To say that anything is possible is to say that it would be if—; and what would be depends entirely on the structure of the actual. In general, things are said to be possible in philosophy when they are not inconsistent with the structure of some special order (*e.g.*, time or space), though they may be inconsistent with the structure of the cosmos. An action, *e.g.*, is possible when it would happen if some one chose to do it. This is well brought out in G. E. Moore's *Ethics*.

3. Bearings of metaphysics on other subjects.—It would be a great mistake to suppose that the value of metaphysical speculation is to be measured exclusively by its success in providing us with a coherent doctrine of the cosmos. Any one who thinks seriously about the ultimate problems of knowledge and reality is almost bound to make some attempt to think about the universe as a whole; but the discussion of the special problems may be treated as an end in itself, and the value of such discussion is to be found largely in the light that it throws on other subjects that are commonly and conveniently regarded as distinct. The debt of the special sciences to metaphysical discussion could not easily be over-estimated. Almost all the special sciences, especially those that are concerned with human affairs, were first established on a firm foundation by Aristotle, who used in their establishment his fundamental conceptions of form and matter, potentiality and actuality, together with his general doctrine of categories and causes. The atomic theory was mainly due to Leucippus and Democritus, working on the foundations that had been laid by the Eleatics. Mathematics, physics, and astronomy owed much to the Pythagoreans and, in later times, to the metaphysical analyses of Descartes, Leibniz, and Kant. Some of the most important ideas of modern biology were anticipated by the early hylozoists; and, in many other ways, the foundations of almost every department of knowledge and action can be traced to metaphysical analysis. This tends to be forgotten owing to the fact that, once the results of such analysis have been well established, they are incorporated in the body of the special sciences and arts and habits of life, and the work of clearing up the fundamental principles is largely ignored; just as, in our more ordinary life, we are sometimes apt to forget the labours of those by whom the means of living are provided. Hence it may be worth while to make some reference here to the fundamental conceptions that seem to be involved in several of the most important subjects.

(*a*) *Psychology.*—The fundamental aim of psychology appears to be that of studying the growth of cognition in the individual mind. It may seem strange to say this in view of some recent attempts to produce a 'psychology without cognition,' which does not appear to differ very markedly from other forms of psychology. But in general the roots of any subject, like those of a plant, may often with advantage be kept out of view. We may have 'psychology without a soul,' because we can take the soul for granted; and it is certainly not the business of psychology to consider the soul except as cognizing or cognized. We may even have 'psychology without cognition,' just because it is entirely concerned with that, and consequently need not single it out as one of the special things with which it has to deal. So we may study wealth without welfare, though apart from welfare wealth would have no meaning. Naturally, in studying psychology, it is the modes of apprehension, rather than the fact of apprehension, that chiefly call for attention. But, whether we are considering sense-data or objects of perception or feeling or desire or emotion or attention or thought or will, the primary question for psychology is, What is it that we apprehend? That there are very many modes of apprehension seems clear, but they are all forms of cognition. The recognition of this ought to guard us against any attempt to divide up our conscious life into separate faculties, though it leaves us free to recognize many distinctions and many stages of growth. Hence psychology is best studied genetically;[1] but it is important to guard against the misconception that, in studying the order of growth in our cognition, we are either explaining cognition itself or accounting for its special modes[2] or giving an account of the genesis of the objects that are cognized. The order of the growth of cognition is one thing; other things have orders of their own. These are perhaps the chief ways in which the consideration of the fundamental problem of psychology may help to guard us against misconceptions in its study.

(*b*) *Logic.*—The fundamental conception of logic appears to be that of implication. It sets itself to consider the conditions under which one bit of knowledge may be taken to imply another. In order to discover this, it is necessary to determine the precise significance of the knowledge from which we start. Hence the importance of definition and of what are called the 'laws of thought,' the aim of which is to ensure fixity of meaning. Obviously, if A fluctuated in meaning, its implications could not be determined. Formal logic is concerned simply with the attempt to tie down meanings and to discover what they imply. In more concrete forms of logic the doctrine of causation is the chief instrument for the discovery of implications. Hume did much to clear up the general signification of causation by doing away with the obscure conception of efficiency and substituting that of a definite order of sequence. Kant urged that the sequence is essentially logical rather than temporal, and that the general principle of implication—if A, then B—has to be accepted as expressing a necessary order among phenomena. More recent discussions have given still more definiteness to the conception.[3] The dialectic of Hegel is another way in which implications can be brought out. According to this, every conception implies its opposite. The value of these methods cannot be discussed here; but it seems clear that the general significance of implication is one of those ultimate problems that concern metaphysics.

(*c*) *Mathematics.*—The mathematical sciences are closely connected with formal logic. As soon as the general characters of the orders of number and space have been made apparent, the working out of their implications requires no extrinsic considerations. The relations contained in these orders are, however, more complex than the relation of a predicate to a subject or of an individual to a class. But there are many orders from which implications can be directly drawn—*e.g.*, the order of time and that of value. Hence it seems possible to regard mathematics as one of several ways in which the general principle of direct or formal implication can be developed.

It may be well to notice one caution that is suggested by metaphysical reflexion with regard to the application of mathematics. The conclusions reached by the study of the two orders of number and space are so precise and convincing, and some of them can be so readily applied to spatial and temporal objects, that there is a considerable temptation to regard all of them as being directly applicable to such objects. Such an assumption does not appear to be legitimate. It may be doubted, *e.g.*, whether some of the speculations with regard to possible dimensions of space, in excess of three, have any direct application to existing objects. A similar caution is necessary with regard to the conception of infinity. On this point reference may be made to the art. INFINITY.

[1] This method was, to all intents, inaugurated by Aristotle, who showed in this, as in many other respects, a sounder grasp of the essentials of the subject than many of its later exponents have had.

[2] It is here that the 'associationist' psychology and such a genetic psychology as that of H. Spencer are at fault.

[3] See esp. B. A. W. Russell, 'On the Notion of Cause,' in *Aristotelian Society's Proceedings*, xiii. [1912–13].

(*d*) *The natural sciences.*—The natural sciences have nearly always presented a stumbling-block in the way of metaphysical construction. This is due chiefly to the apparent lack of definite order in what are sometimes called the 'brute facts' of the natural world. Hegel compared nature to a bacchantic dance. For Plato also, and for many others,[1] it has tended to appear as a falling off from the unity and intelligibility that are postulated by the conception of a complete cosmos. The objects of nature seem to differ in kind, and no continuity in the ordering of kinds is readily discoverable. This applies to the objects of sense as well as to the objects of perception. There seems to be a gulf fixed between colours, sounds, smells, pains, etc., as well as between mechanical systems, chemical combinations, and organic bodies. Hence it has been sought to bridge these gulfs by teleological conceptions—*i.e.* by the view that differences of kind are to be interpreted by reference to the conception of value, as in some way required for the constitution of the 'best possible world.' But this is at most a postulate; and it is generally recognized that we are not entitled to apply this interpretation in any direct way in the scientific study of natural objects. Apart from this, the chief forms of order that are available are those of time and space, extensive and intensive magnitude, causation, and the general law of continuity in the quantity of what is called energy (a conception that is perhaps still in need of more precise determination). No doubt the doctrine of evolution supplies, to some extent, another principle of order; but it is erroneous to suppose that the earlier stages in this order can be regarded as, in any direct way, implying the later. Epigenesis, or, as Bergson has called it, 'creative evolution,' has to be, in some form, recognized—*i.e.* the doctrine that what comes later is distinct in kind from what comes earlier. It does not follow from this, however, that there is not a definite and intelligible order. But there are still fundamental problems in the study of nature for which metaphysics can as yet offer no very satisfying solution. Still, there is at least the suggestion that a solution might be found in the conception of value. Evolution, in particular, is very naturally thought of as a progress, though a somewhat discontinuous one, towards what is intrinsically better.

(*e*) *Æsthetics.*—In æsthetics at least the conception of value becomes prominent; and its legitimacy within this sphere, where it is applied very largely to objects that can be perceived or imagined, is hardly open to dispute. It is true that sometimes what is described as beautiful may have little claim to be regarded as more than pleasant, and even pleasant only to certain individuals. In this case the valuation is highly subjective, and may hardly deserve to be described as a definite valuation at all. But in the higher forms of art at least an effort is being made to produce something that has intrinsic value; and in some cases it is difficult to resist the conviction that something that is intrinsically valuable—something that may properly be described as 'a joy for ever'—has actually been secured. But the science of æsthetics is still largely in the making.

[1] Cf., *e.g.*, what is said by Aristotle in *Met.* xii. 10, where the lack of order in nature is likened to the life of a slave to whom, on account of his low estate, a certain licence is permitted. The religious conception of a 'Fall' appears to be closely connected with this. See H. S. Chamberlain, *The Foundations of the Nineteenth Century*, London, 1909, ii. 34.

(*f*) *Ethics.*—It is in ethics rather than in æsthetics that the conception of intrinsic value comes definitely into prominence. Ethical writers may differ in their views of what is intrinsically valuable—whether it is the good will or pleasure or some form of perfection or completeness of self-conscious life—but almost all recognize that in the moral life men are engaged in the effort to realize something that is intrinsically good, and in the end what is intrinsically best. Yet it is difficult to make the conception of such an ultimate good perfectly clear; and some are inclined to doubt its validity. It must be confessed that we seem to begin with valuations that have little conscious ground. Our primitive likings appear to be based on organic needs; and it is only gradually that we are led to regard them as means to ends that have a truer and more lasting value. We begin with organic impulses, and advance through the pleasant to the beautiful and good. Hence the moral life is still, on the whole, as it was in the time of Socrates, a struggle towards a good that is very imperfectly apprehended, and sometimes even not very consciously pursued. It tends to be guided by custom, convention, positive laws, and generally recognized opinions rather than by any clear apprehension of a good that can be either defined or attained. But in ethical science some attempt is made to define it; and this involves a discussion that may properly be called metaphysical. The discussion of its attainability seems even to involve a general theory of the cosmos.

Apart from the fundamental conception of intrinsic value, the most important problem that concerns ethics is that of freedom. This is closely connected with the conception of value and also with that of causation. It is doubtful whether any definite meaning can be given to moral freedom except that which may be expressed by saying that choice has a real place in the chain of causes; and choice can be interpreted only as a mode of valuation. It is essentially preference, *i.e.* the regarding of one thing as essentially more valuable than another. Thus the problems of value and causation are those that chiefly connect ethics with metaphysics.

Ethical valuations have important bearings on economics and politics; but these cannot be considered here. Nor can we attempt to appraise the significance of what is described by Nietzsche as the 'transvaluation of all values' (*Umwertung aller Werte*).

(*g*) *Religion.*—A chief element in the higher forms of religion consists in a certain intensification of the moral consciousness by its more definite concentration on the conception of intrinsic value—as in such sayings as 'What shall it profit a man, if he shall gain the whole world, and lose his own soul? Or what shall a man give in exchange for his soul?' (Mk 8[36]). This intensification is generally combined with the conviction that the object of ultimate valuation is real and attainable. A conviction of this kind is sometimes based on a definite metaphysical doctrine. At other times it is based rather on some form of intuition or of revelation, or on the authority of some great teacher, or simply on the intrinsic force of the moral principle itself. The founders of religions and their most influential prophets have generally connected their teaching with some doctrines of a more or less explicitly metaphysical character. Buddhism, which is perhaps the most purely ethical form of religion that has ever had an extensive influence, seems to be rather intimately connected with those Indian forms of metaphysical construction that had their origin in the *Upaniṣads*. It conceives of what has ultimate value as the realization of the higher self, to be achieved by the control of the lower, and especially by the suppression of the lower forms of desire—a process which is supposed to be, in general, attainable only through a cycle of reincarnations. The doctrine of the Pythagoreans, which was largely religious, had a somewhat similar character; and the influence of Plato, so far as it can be described as religious, tends, on the whole, in the same direction; as that of Plotinus even more definitely does. Christianity was perhaps in its origin less definitely metaphysical; but it has been to a large extent interpreted, in the course of its historical development, by means of Platonic and more or less kindred conceptions, and in some of its more recent phases is hardly distinguishable from the more esoteric forms of Buddhism. The relations have been thus expressed by Holmes:

> 'Plato reasoned about God. Buddha kept silence about him. Christ made him the theme of his poetry. . . . As a speculative thinker he does not compete with Plato. As a systematic teacher he does not compete with Buddha. But as a source of spiritual inspiration he has no rival' (*Creed of Buddha, ad fin.*).

The gospel of love is the most inspiring, because it implies, when its meaning is fully developed, that everything has value—a more thorough optimism than anything that is involved in the Platonic Good or the Buddhist Nirvāṇa (whatever the exact interpretation of that may be).[1] It is sometimes urged that metaphysical and religious views of the cosmos, by representing the attainment of the moral ideal as involved in the nature of things, have a certain tendency to weaken the moral motive, by making it appear that individual effort is unnecessary. No doubt some metaphysical systems have claimed to advance 'beyond good and evil'; and the same may be said of some forms of religion. But, on the whole, none of the deeper forms either of metaphysical construction or of religious insight has represented the ideal as attainable in any other way than through the individual choice of what is best.

LITERATURE.—The literature of the subject is so vast that only a selection can be made. A. E. Taylor, *Elements of Metaphysics*, London, 1903, gives a good general survey. F. H. Bradley, *Appearance and Reality*[2], do. 1908, supplies the most remarkable of recent attempts at metaphysical construction. L. J. Walker, *Theories of Knowledge*, do. 1910, should be consulted. On the special subject of error, the essay by G. F. Stout, in *Personal Idealism*, do. 1902, is very valuable; and it should be supplemented by reference to B. A. W. Russell, *Philosophical Essays*, do. 1910, and F. H. Bradley, *Essays on Truth and Reality*, Oxford, 1914. A. Meinong's views about *Gegenstandstheorie* will be found in his *Untersuchungen zur Gegenstandstheorie und Psychologie*, Leipzig, 1904, and his *Gesammelte Abhandlungen*, do. 1913. His important book *Ueber Annahmen*, do. 1902, [2]1910, throws much light upon the subject. On the various attempts at metaphysical construction the Histories of Philosophy must be referred to; E. Caird, *The Evolution of Theology in the Greek Philosophers*, Glasgow, 1904, and R. Adamson, *The Development of Modern Philosophy*, Edinburgh, 1903, may be specially commended. On some of the earlier phases of speculation E. Schuré, *Les grands Initiés*[4], Paris, 1899, Eng. tr., London, 1912, is extremely interesting, though perhaps some of his statements are too conjectural and lack evidence. A. Drews, *Plotin*, Jena, 1907, is instructive on a philosopher who is too little known. G. F. Stout, *Analytical Psychology*, London, 1909, indicates the most fundamental problems in that subject. On formal logic J. N. Keynes, *Studies and Exercises in Formal Logic*,[4] do. 1906, and F. C. S. Schiller, *Formal Logic*, do. 1912, may be consulted—the former is constructive, the latter critical. On the foundations of the more concrete type of logic A. Ruge and W. Windelband, *Encyclopædia of the Philosophical Sciences*, do. 1913, furnish all that is needed. J. M. E. McTaggart, *Studies in Hegelian Dialectic*, Cambridge, 1896, and *A Commentary on Hegel's Logic*, do. 1910, supplies interesting material, both for interpretation and for criticism. B. Croce, *What is living and what is dead in the Philosophy of Hegel*, Eng. tr., London, 1915, gives perhaps the most searching examination of the Hegelian method. On mathematics, B. A. W. Russell, *Principles of Mathematics*, Cambridge, 1903, should certainly be consulted. The *Principia Mathematica*, London, 1910–13, by the same writer, in conjunction with A. N. Whitehead, may be referred to as showing the way in which the logical foundations of the subject can be worked out. J. Ward, *Naturalism and Agnosticism*[2], do. 1903, discusses the foundations of the natural sciences. W. Ostwald, *Vorlesungen über Naturphilosophie*, Leipzig, 1902,

[1] The contrast, in this respect, is well, though perhaps too emphatically, brought out by H. S. Chamberlain, i. 187–200.

may also be specially referred to. B. Croce, *Æsthetic as Science of Expression and General Linguistic*, Eng. tr., do. 1909, is probably the most instructive of recent works on the basis of that subject. On ethics reference should be made to the art. ETHICS (by J. H. Muirhead). The conceptions of value and freedom are well discussed by G. E. Moore, in his *Ethics*, do. 1912. The philosophical significance of the conception of value is brought out with great wealth of illustration by B. Bosanquet in *The Principle of Individuality and Value*, do. 1912, and *The Value and Destiny of the Individual* (*Gifford Lectures*, 1912), do. 1913. A. Meinong, *Psychologisch-ethische Untersuchungen zur Werth-Theorie*, Graz, 1894, and C. Ehrenfels, *System der Werththeorie*, Leipzig, 1897–98, are also important on this subject. The *Gifford Lectures* have done much to show the metaphysical foundations of religion. Perhaps E. Caird, *The Evolution of Religion*, Glasgow, 1893, J. Royce, *The World and the Individual*, New York and London, 1900–01, and J. Ward, *The Realm of Ends*, Cambridge, 1911, are the most noteworthy, in addition to those already mentioned. *The Creed of Christ*[3], London, 1906, and *The Creed of Buddha*, New York, 1908, by E. G. A. Holmes, are interesting as bringing out the relations between the two highest forms of religion, and emphasizing the metaphysical conceptions that underlie them. H. Höffding's emphasis on 'the conservation of values' as the fundamental aspect of religion in his *Philosophy of Religion*, London, 1906, has also a very special interest; and so has the characterization of 'the free man's worship' in B. Russell's *Philosophical Essays*. The general views expressed in this art. are further developed in the artt. ETERNITY and INFINITY, in the writer's articles in *Mind*, new ser., xxii. [1913], 'A Sketch of a Philosophy of Order,' and xxiii. [1914], 'The Meaning of Reality,' and *A Manual of Ethics*[5], London, 1915, esp. bk. ii. ch. vi. Reference may also be made to artt. EPISTEMOLOGY and ERROR AND TRUTH.

J. S. MACKENZIE.

METEMPSYCHOSIS.—See TRANSMIGRATION.

METEORS, METEORIC STONES.—See PRODIGIES AND PORTENTS.

METHOD (Logical).—Besides the ideals proper to the concept, the judgment, and inference, there are certain secondary ideals for thought in general. These supplement the primary ideals in a way comparable with that in which, according to the ethics of Butler, the 'adaptations of human nature to virtue' supplement the 'eternal fitnesses of behaviour' which had been described by Clarke. The secondary ideals should be stated with definite reference to the order and process of thinking, whereas the primary ideals are descriptions of truth when thought.

A wide licence has been taken by logical writers in articulating method, methodology, and applied logic; and it is here proposed tentatively to name as secondary ideals systematization, reform, and development. The course of thought must be such as to approach reality in the subtlety of its constituents and the complexity of their interconnexion; to reconstitute concepts, judgments, and inferences, in correspondence with it; and to realize the mutual support that these give to each other, as dealing with the same cosmos.

Method emerged from an outworn analytic and dialectic of Aristotelian origin, and won a place in modern logical theory, chiefly through the use of the topic made by Descartes in introducing his reformation of philosophy, and through the canonic of empirical science introduced by Bacon; and Kant's subsequent definition of it was in fair accordance with the Cartesian tradition:

'Just as the doctrine of elements in logic has for its aim the conditions of perfectness in a knowledge related to an object . . . so, general methodology, as the second part of logic, ought to treat, in contrast with it, the form of science in general, or the way to evolve science from a diversity of knowledge' (*Logic*, § 96).

An even more explicit reference to the course of our thinking is desirable, because only in some relation to ordered sequence can the ideals of concept, judgment, and inference become a personal discipline, and give not a mere consciousness of 'validity' or of 'fallacy,' but a development of our natural 'sense of method' (cf. J. Brough, *The Study of Mental Science*, London, 1903, p. 5 ff.). The sense of method is an estimate of the extent to which the several faculties proper to a conviction have actually played their part in it.

1. Systematization.—The most general impulse of thinking is to make a double approach to reality, by analysis and by synthesis. The impulse has been recognized in various logical contexts; in Aristotle's distinction between problems of reason or of essence and problems of fact or of existence; in Descartes's rule of method to divide the difficulties of an investigation, and his rule to conduct our thoughts in the order of simple to complex; in Newton's requirement that natural philosophy should proceed from compounds to ingredients, from motions to forces, and, in general, from effects to causes, before explaining phenomena by causes as principles. The impulse follows, as it were, an indefinitely receding horizon. There is neither simplicity nor complexity that is final, whether in the world of possible perceptions or in the extensions which scientific imagination may make into the imperceptible.

'Scientists have tried to find it [the 'simple fact'] in the two extremes, in the infinitely great and in the infinitely small'—the astronomer in distances so great as to reduce a star to a point, the physicist in the atom, the biologist in the cell (H. Poincaré, *Science and Method*, Eng. tr., London, 1914, p. 19).

Even simplicities so laboured as these are provisional, if only because the structure of systematic science based on them is provisional.

'In the . . . advance of science an uninterrupted, but progressive series of mental constructions . . . gives us an approximate [but only approximate] idea of the inter-connected system of Reality' (F. Enriques, in *Encyclopædia of Phil. Sciences*, i. 234).

Under this impulse the course of thinking will lead to the actualization of the primary ideals of concept, judgment, and inference, but does not in itself commit our whole nature, as they do, to expectation, submission, and reaction. Its more immediate end is reform within the ideational content.

2. Reform.—Analysis and synthesis provide for continuous revision and reconstitution of such ideational contents as have previously been available for actualizing the primary ideals.

'Only inasmuch as we are set free from the accidental associations of ideas formed through single perceptions, by a happy variety of observations and a steady attention to their distinctions and resemblances do we gradually become cognizant of the more general and essential connections, and our conception of things ever more and more adequately' shows the necessary presuppositions of the understanding 'to hold good in the heterogeneous materials of the actual world' (H. Lotze, *Microcosmus*, Eng. tr., London, 1885, bk. ii. ch. iv. § 4 [i. 236]).

The 'perceptions' here spoken of are 'already permeated with the results of sifting critical energy of mind,' but the spirit of reform, more expressly than that of systematization, claims to pass by any warnings from ancient realism as to the sanctity of universals, and equally by those of our modern pure logic as to identities, necessities, and systematic coherencies. Its claim is among the inevitable paradoxes of permanence and change.

(*a*) *Individuation.*—Even the unity of the individual, of 'that which is neither said of any subject nor contained in any subject' (Aristotle), 'the "It" without anything added' (Occam), 'the point in the tissue of reality where it accepts the predicate' (Bosanquet), may be newly isolated and identified. This unity is more directly imposed in perception and is more firmly sustained by social reference and consent than the conceptual, yet there still continues scientific controversy on the more optional identities, such as independent organs or organisms in botanical or zoological growth, concrete standards of measurement in calculation; and even as to whether units are possible at all within the flow of psychical life, or whether a distinction of persons should be made when consciousness has become pathologically discontinuous.

(*b*) *Classification.*—The special store of concepts embodied in the language of a people or in technical terminology may be seen in course of reform, as needs and circumstances without methodical analysis modify the meanings of words. A more methodical initiative in reform proceeds through classification by 'natural kinds,' persistent 'species,' 'types,' or evolutionary 'series'—*e.g.*, metals, grasses, temperament, organisms. But classification can follow only where individuation leads; and also our ultimate interests lie in actual events, open to our influence, rather than in the stereotyped possibilities in a thing, a class, a group, or a series.

(*c*) *Tabulation.*—With the purpose of practical control of nature, Bacon urged the tabulation of instances of event.

'Natural and experimental history is so various and diffuse, that it confounds and distracts the understanding, unless it be ranged and presented to view in a suitable order. We must therefore form Tables and Arrangements of Instances, in such a method and order that the understanding may be able to deal with them' (*Novum Organum*, ii. 10).

If our dealing with them is not by way of further analysis into the elements of natural 'form' as Bacon intended, but is numerical, the tables become 'statistics'; and statistics may be summarized through 'graphs'; and the duplication of tables into affirmative and negative may be avoided by 'averages'; and inevitable lapses from accuracy may be regularized as 'probable error.'

(*d*) *Hypothesis.*—Method can pursue the synthesis of simple elements required in judgment, while still suspending the assent or final submission of our nature to its necessity. The course of thought freely varies its subjects and predicates, expands each tentative 'form,' 'causal connexion,' or 'law' into exemplifications, or each imagined 'fact' into natural consequences, and verifies these as independently true or real, or as not so. Many recent writers, including Jevons, Sigwart, and Bosanquet, teach that such a development and trial of ideas is essential for all inductive inference. Thus, if a pencil of light is a composite of vari-coloured rays, and is passed through a prism, we shall see the spectrum band; if the process is reversed, we shall reconstitute the untinted whiteness. If eoliths are of human origin, they should serve some purpose, and our ingenuity may discover one.

(*e*) *Colligation.*—A hypothesis may command an indefinite number of such exemplifications or consequences, both already known and waiting for verification. Thus the theory of elliptical orbits for planetary motion covered many planetary positions already registered, and the possibilities of further registrations. This is the 'colligation of facts by means of appropriate conceptions' (Whewell, *Novum Organum Renovatum*, bk. ii. iv.), or the discovery of 'types of order' (Royce, in *Encyc. of Phil. Sciences*, i. 90)—an achievement of intelligence which Whewell considers to be all that is serious in scientific investigation, but which Mill considers as an operation 'subsidiary to induction,' that is to say, to induction as inference (*Logic*, bk. iii. ch. ix. § 3, bk. iv. ch. ii.).

Lotze in his 'pure logic,' and independently of 'methods of investigation,' undertook to exhibit a serial order of schemata for judgment and inference, in which was shown an increasing complexity of conceptual distinctness.

'The various forms of thought will be arranged in an ascending series, in which each higher member attempts to make good a defect in the preceding one, due to its failure to satisfy, in regard to its own particular problem, the general impulse of thought to reduce coincidence to coherence' (*Logic*, Introd. § 11).

Thus the categorical form 'S is P,' is followed by the hypothetical, 'if S is X, it is P.' The syllogism, if not a mere *petitio principii*, involves the further conceptions which constitute the induction and analogy supporting its premisses, and these, again, send their roots into larger systems of classification and explanation. Thus the reform of a single concept—*e.g.*, the atom in chemistry, the cell in biology, the vibration in acoustics—may call for readjustments throughout increasing complexities of science.

3. **Development.**—But in method, as in organic life, the whole may decide the part. Nature is more than a 'tissue of uniformities,' as Mill described it. It is a unity. And the ideal of development means that the system of our thinking reacts upon its diversity of content. In perceptual observation, historical narrative, and explanatory conceptions of fact objects and instances are made possible by the growth of knowledge as a whole.

(*a*) *Perceptual extensions.*—Fields of perception beyond those of the natural senses may be opened through science—*e.g.*, in space by the telescope and microscope, in time by the chronoscope and bioscope, in composition of substances by the spectroscope and radioscope. And extensions of sensitivity may be supplemented by artificial mechanisms of record, the chronograph, logograph, and automatograph.

(*b*) *Historical interpretation.*—Records of past events may be given new values by cumulative means of interpretation. Even mere relics may, through a convergence of interpretative hypotheses, as with the relics of pre-historic man, newly disclose remoter ages for methodical retrospect. That our foresight of events yet to come is not similarly from time to time newly lengthened is connected with the fact that here the way of hypothesis cannot be confirmed by verification. Methodical procedure can only assume a number of alternatively possible events, and assign to each a probability.

(*c*) *Explanatory theory.*—A given fact newly known, or more fully observed, may present many varied facets for hypothetical explanation. A chipped flint may be conceived as a geological product, an elastic molecular substance, a surface chemically stained, a contrivance of manufacture, a tool of purpose. And on each facet may centre a separate stress of hypothesis. We may collect contributory explanations of fact in a science predominantly concrete, such as archæology, geology, geography. On the other hand, in sciences comparatively or purely abstract, we may systematize hypotheses among themselves, as empirical, derivative, or ultimate, making exemplification or consequence incidental only—*e.g.*, in physiology, chemistry, mathematics, ethics. But the deepest difference within the 'form of science' is that between *a priori* science, where exemplification or consequence flashes into inference under the magic of intuitive construction, described by Descartes, and empirical science, where the ordered sequence aims and waits to fulfil the primary ideals of inference in '*a posteriori* synthetic judgments' (see artt. INFERENCE and LOGIC).

LITERATURE.—See works mentioned under art. LOGIC. The historical progress may be followed in the works of Aristotle (*Posterior Analytics* and *Topics*), Descartes (*Regulæ*, and *Method*), Arnauld, Bacon, and Whewell (*Philosophy of Discovery*, London, 1860) as mentioned; and in J. Herschel, *Preliminary Discourse on the Study of Natural Philosophy*[2], London, 1851; W. Whewell, *History of Scientific Ideas*[3], do. 1858, and *Novum Organum Renovatum*[3], do. 1858. Of recent logical systems, those of J. S. Mill, R. H. Lotze, C. W. von Sigwart, W. Wundt, and J. Venn (*Empirical Logic*[2], London, 1907) give prominence to method. Besides the definitely methodological books of Davidson, Venn, Jevons, Pearson, and Poincaré, also mentioned, the following may be referred to on special topics: G. C. Lewis, *Methods of Observation and Reasoning in Politics*, London, 1852; G. Gore, *Art of Scientific Discovery*, do. 1878; E. Naville, *La Logique de l'hypothèse*, Paris, 1880; H. Hughes, *Theory of Inference*, London, 1894; T. B. Strong, and others, *Lectures on the Method of Science*, Oxford, 1906; H. Poincaré, *Science and Hypothesis*, Eng. tr.[2], London, 1914; F. Enriques, *Problems of Science*, Eng. tr., do. 1914; J. Royce, 'The Principles of Logic,' in *Encyclopædia of Philosophical Sciences*, vol. i., Eng. tr., do. 1913.

J. BROUGH.

METHODISM.—I. *HISTORY AND POLITY.*—In this article we shall confine ourselves to a description of the origin, growth, and leading features of the Methodism which is connected with the name of John Wesley. The Methodism within the Church of England which resulted in the rise of the Evangelical party is not within our province (see EVANGELICALISM).

1. The rise of Methodism.—According to Wesley, the 'first rise' of Methodism was in Oxford, in November 1729; the second, in Savannah, Georgia, in April 1736; and the third, in London, on 1st May 1738. We pass over the Methodism that found expression in the 'Holy Club' at Oxford, and in the 'Society' formed by Wesley in Savannah, and strike the path which leads to the origin of Methodism as an existing organization. The date, 1st May 1738, is significant. Wesley had returned to England, having learned many bitter lessons in Georgia. By his contact with the Moravians he had been enlightened and disheartened concerning his religious experience. He had learned that, although he had 'followed after the law of righteousness,' he had not attained to it. His disappointment at discovering that he had been pursuing a wrong path was intense. The Moravians explained his failure by showing him that he had not sought righteousness 'by faith, but as it were by works.' His conversations with them left in his mind the unanswered question, What is the faith that leads to salvation? Waiting in London for a solution of the problem that baffled him, he assisted in forming one of the Religious Societies so numerous at the time. His instinct for 'fellowship' was one of the dominant forces of his life, and explains much that happened in his career. The Religious Society which he joined met in the house of James Hutton. It owed much of its character to the advice of Peter Böhler, a Moravian to whom Wesley was unspeakably indebted for spiritual guidance. The Society was founded on 1st May 1738. Rules were drawn up for its management, and, as was the case in Savannah, the members of the Society who were intent on cultivating a deeper religious life were divided into little companies called 'bands.' The Society grew, and its meeting-place was changed to a room in Fetter Lane. At first the Society, like the other Religious Societies, was in connexion with the Church of England; subsequently it was dominated by Moravian influences, and this connexion was broken.

2. Wesley's spiritual crisis.—Methodism, as it now exists, can be understood only by realizing the facts concerning the progress of Wesley's religious experience. By much conversation, by close study of the NT, by prayer 'without ceasing,' he advanced from an intellectual understanding of the meaning of 'saving faith' to the understanding that comes through experience. While he was in the stage of an ever-brightening intellectual apprehension, he preached the doctrine of 'salvation by faith' in many of the London churches. He taught it as it stands in the *Homilies*; but it was resented by clergymen and their congregations, and the churches were closed against him. In this way a policy of exclusion from the churches was commenced, which, after a time, profoundly affected Wesley's relation to the Church of England.

During this preliminary stage, Wesley was oppressed with a 'burden' which was to him 'intolerable'—the burden of unpardoned sin. That load was lifted on 24th May 1738, in a 'room' in Aldersgate Street, the meeting-place of one of the Religious Societies.

'I felt I did trust in Christ, Christ alone for salvation; and an assurance was given me that He had taken away *my* sins, even *mine*, and saved *me* from the law of sin and death' (*Journal*, i. 476).

In that decisive hour he entered into an experience, new so far as he was concerned, but an old experience not only among Moravians but also among many Churchmen and Dissenters. It is an extraordinary fact, however, that it had become unintelligible to the mass of English Christians. Wesley's 'conversion' filled him with the spirit of the evangelist. He would gladly have borne his testimony in the churches, but he was compelled to wait until a wider sphere opened before him.

3. Beginning of field-preaching.—In April 1739 Wesley found his opportunity, and began his evangelistic work. George Whitefield, a member of the Oxford 'Holy Club,' had entered into the experience of 'conscious salvation' before Wesley, and had made a deep impression in Bristol by the preaching of the 'new doctrines.' Being excluded from the churches, he went into the open air, and addressed great crowds of people in Bristol and at Kingswood. Having to leave England for America, he wrote to Wesley asking him to take his place; Wesley consented, and on 2nd April 1739 he commenced his famous campaign of 'field-preaching.' In addition to preaching in Bristol and to the Kingswood colliers, he got into close touch with the Religious Societies in the city. His genius for administrative reform found scope in them. He divided them into 'bands.' The Societies in Baldwin Street and Nicholas Street so increased that it became necessary to build a 'Room' for their accommodation. A site was secured near the Horsefair, and the 'Room' was opened on 3rd June 1739. Afterwards Wesley went to London to assist in composing disputes which had arisen in the Fetter Lane Society. He again met Whitefield, who, being detained in England, had spent his time in preaching to multitudes in Moorfields, on Kennington Common, and elsewhere. Wesley joined him in his field-preaching. On 11th November 1739 he held a service amid the ruins of 'the King's Foundery of cannon,' a building near Moorfields, which had been shattered by an explosion. Wesley acquired the site and built a 'Room' upon it, which became famous in Methodist history. Some who indulge in regrets concerning the separation of the Methodists from the Church of England point to the building of these 'Rooms' as 'the parting of the ways'; Methodists maintain that it was the closing of the churches that led to the opening of the 'Rooms.'

4. First Wesleyan Societies.—While he was still a member of the Fetter Lane Religious Society, Wesley formed a Society of a different type at the Foundery. It was started, probably, in the latter end of the year 1739, and is looked upon as the Mother Society of Methodism. In July 1740 Wesley was practically excluded from the Fetter Lane Society. Those who left with him joined the Society at the Foundery. By that time Societies, under the special direction of John and Charles Wesley, existed in London, Bristol, and Kingswood. In 1742 Newcastle-upon-Tyne was visited by Charles Wesley, who formed a Society there on the new pattern. These Societies are called by John Wesley, in the 'Rules' which he drew up for them and published in 1743, 'The United Societies,' and they were the nucleus of the Methodist Church. In the 'Rules' a Society is described as 'a company of men, having the form and seeking the power of godliness; united in order to pray together, to receive the word of exhortation, and to watch over one another in love, that they may help each other to work out their salvation.' In these new organizations the 'band' system was a prominent feature; but, in addition, the Societies were divided into 'classes,' each containing about 12 persons who were placed under the care of a 'leader,' not only for their own spiritual edification, but also that Wesley might be assisted in his pastoral supervision. At first the leaders visited the members at their houses; but, that method proving inconvenient, the members were expected to meet their leader at some fixed place, week by week. The 'Rules' mentioned above are still, with slight alterations, the 'general rules' for Methodists, the 'particular rules,' passed in after years, being contained in the disciplinary 'codes' of the different Methodist churches. In the classes contributions, usually a penny a week, were made for the poor. At a later date these contributions were given for the support of the ministry, a special poor-fund being raised from other sources. Stewards were appointed to manage matters of finance, and the leaders met the ministers and stewards of each Society once a week to pay in the moneys that they had received, and to give information concerning any member who was sick or might need special pastoral attention. Out of these arrangements the Leaders' Meeting arose, which became an integral part of the Methodist organization. The oversight of his Societies weighed heavily on Wesley's mind. He never worshipped numerical success; he was not content to gather together a miscellaneous crowd of people of whom he knew nothing. He supplemented the work of the leaders by visiting the members himself in their homes, and met them once a quarter in the classes for personal conversation on their religious experience. If satisfied, he gave them tickets in recognition of the fact that they were members of the Methodist Society.

5. Attitude of the clergy.—Those who have studied the constitution of the Religious Societies will note the affinities and divergences between them and the United Societies. One line of divergence was caused by circumstances which Wesley deeply regretted. The Religious Societies were in close connexion with the Church of England, and many of their members were frequent communicants at the churches. Wesley would have gladly preserved this connexion and practice; but such a course was made impracticable by the conduct of the clergy. In some places they arranged among themselves to repel the Methodists from the Lord's Table. In Bristol, on 27th July 1740, Charles Wesley and a company of Kingswood Methodists were sent away from the sacrament in Temple Church. Charles Wesley, therefore, administered the Lord's Supper to the Methodists in the school at Kingswood which had been built for the training of the colliers' children. In Newcastle-upon-Tyne a similar crisis arose. It is significant that in Newcastle the difficulty was aggravated by the fact that three of the dissenting ministers of the town agreed to exclude from the communion all who would not refrain from hearing the Wesleys. The effect of these exclusions, and of Charles Wesley's action, was speedily seen. The Methodists were diverted into a path which gradually but decisively diverged from the Church of England.

6. Enlisting of lay-preachers.—Another line of divergence from the practices of the Religious Societies must also be noted. John Wesley's conversion made him an evangelist. He longed to proclaim the gospel not only to select companies but to the world. His heart responded to the counsel of Lady Huntingdon: 'Attempt nothing less than all mankind' (*Journal*, iii. 48, note 1). But how could that advice be followed by a man in his circumstances? His work taxed all his strength. Charles Wesley helped him, especially in the opening years of his mission, and a few friendly clergymen gave him occasional assistance; but such help was inadequate. The double task of the pastoral care of his Societies and the evangelization of the country was too great for a single man. But the way opened. He had great skill in discovering and using the working-powers of laymen, and he soon found himself at the head of an order of lay-preachers who shared with him the hardships and the successes of his work. In 1738 and 1739 laymen had preached with his consent, but the order of lay-preachers is usually considered to date from 1740. The importance of this step cannot be exaggerated. The lay-preachers were divided into 'itinerants,' 'half-itinerants,' and 'local preachers.' They first abandoned their business and gave themselves entirely to the wandering life of the evangelist, under Wesley's personal supervision. For that work, at the beginning, they got no pay; later on a small sum was given them; but many years elapsed before they were rescued from the pinch of poverty. Assisted by them, Wesley went out 'to reform the nation, particularly the Church, and to spread Scriptural holiness over the land' (*Minutes of Conference*, i. 446). Wesley's work as an evangelist, an educationalist, a philanthropist, a social reformer, and a pioneer in enterprises that have deeply affected the condition of the nation must be passed over here. Some idea of the toils of himself, his preachers, and those who were associated with them in his Societies may be gathered from the fact that, when he died in 1791, there were 136,622 members in the Methodist Societies in Great Britain and Ireland, in other parts of the British Dominions, and in the United States of America.

7. Institution of the Conference.—It is now necessary to indicate certain facts which have determined the character of modern Methodism. While Wesley was 'the head of his order,' and spoke the last word in matters of administration, he thoroughly believed that there is safety in 'a multitude of counsellors.' He consulted the bands, the leaders, and persons of experience in his Societies, but the chief evidence of his reliance on the counsel of others is to be seen in the conferences which he held with the clergy who helped him, and with his lay-preachers. He also assembled the stewards at intervals in different parts of the country and conversed with them on financial and spiritual subjects. Out of his annual conferences with the clergy and lay-preachers, with whom lay-officers of the Society were sometimes associated, arose 'the Yearly Conference of the People called Methodists.' Towards the end of his life the vagueness of this description of the Conference was seen to be a danger. The power to appoint preachers to the numerous chapels that had been built would revert after Wesley's death to the Conference so inadequately described. To meet this contingency, on 28th Feb. 1784 Wesley signed a Deed Poll explaining the words 'the Yearly Conference of the People called Methodists,' and declaring 'what persons are members of the said Conference, and how the succession and identity thereof is to be continued.' One hundred 'preachers and expounders of God's Holy Word' then 'under the care of and in connexion with' Wesley were declared to be the Conference, and they and their successors, to be chosen in the manner laid down in the Deed, were 'for ever' to be 'the Conference of the People called Methodists.' This Deed Poll received decisive confirmation in 1835, when the Lord High Chancellor, Lord Lyndhurst, and the Vice-Chancellor, Sir Lancelot Shadwell, upheld its validity in trials which took place in their courts. In his judgment the Vice-Chancellor affirmed that the Conference had been 'the supreme legislative and executive body' in Methodism since the death of Wesley.

The Conference in Wesley's day was more than

a consultative assembly. It took complete oversight of preachers and people. It kept an eye on the moral character and doctrinal beliefs of the preachers, and stationed them in their Circuits. We shall accentuate only one part of its functions. In the form of 'Model Deed' for the settlement of chapels then called 'Preaching Houses,' published first in 1763, a clause appears which constitutes Wesley's *Notes upon the New Testament* and his four volumes of *Sermons* as the standard by which trustees were to judge the orthodoxy of the preachers appointed by the Conference. We may also add that the rights of trustees were strengthened by the clause in Wesley's Deed Poll which provided that, with the exception of clergy of the Church of England, the Conference might not appoint a preacher to the same chapel for more than three years successively.

8. Provision for the sacraments.—One other point remains to be considered at this stage. The question of the administration ot the sacraments to the Societies had to be settled. The bulk of the Methodist people would not go to the parish churches for the sacrament of the Lord's Supper, and provision for its administration in their own chapels was urgently desired. In November 1778 Wesley opened his new chapel in City Road, London. In that chapel the sacraments were administered as they had been in some of the other Methodist chapels in London and the country. Wesley was pressed to extend similar privileges to the rest of his Societies. He saw, however, that, if he yielded, he would have to qualify and appoint some of his lay-preachers to administer the sacraments; and, in his opinion, such appointment necessitated ordination. Time and circumstances led him to a solution of the problem. In 1769 he had sent two of his lay-preachers to New York to direct the work which had been begun there by certain Methodist local preachers. The work in America proved very successful, but the War of Independence gave it a new complexion. The Anglican clergy were scattered, and many of the Methodists had been without the sacraments for years. The Americans would have solved the difficulty by ordaining a sufficient number of their lay-preachers, but Francis Asbury, who had been sent out as a preacher from England by Wesley, checked this movement and advised that Wesley should be consulted. Wesley had satisfied himself that he, as a presbyter, had the power to ordain other presbyters; but he hesitated to do so. In 1784 the American crisis became acute; so, after much thought, he appointed Dr. Thomas Coke, a clergyman who acted with him, and Francis Asbury as 'superintendents' in N. America, and two other preachers as 'elders.' With the exception of Asbury, who was in America, these preachers were set apart by Wesley, assisted by other presbyters of the Church of England, by the imposition of hands. In this way the American difficulty was met, and the Methodist Episcopal Churches, which now number their membership by millions, entered on their remarkable career. Wesley afterwards ordained preachers for Scotland and for Foreign Mission stations. At last he took a still more decisive step in this direction. In 1788 he ordained Alexander Mather 'deacon,' 'elder,' and 'superintendent,' and in 1789 he ordained Henry Moore and Thomas Rankin 'presbyters,' empowering them to administer the sacraments in England. He exhorted them to maintain as close an association as possible with the Established Church; but, when that association was no longer practicable, they were to proceed to confer on other preachers the 'orders' which they had received (see *Proc. Wesleyan Hist. Society*, ix. 145–154).

9. Influence of Charles Wesley.—John Wesley is justly considered as the founder of the Methodist Church, and we have, in the main, dwelt on his actions in describing the origin and development of the United Societies. It would be unpardonable, however, if we failed to emphasize the services of his brother, Charles Wesley. During the early days of the 'Revival' he was a daring and successful evangelist, facing the violence of mobs and rivalling his brother in the activities of the wandering preacher's life. Later he settled down in Bristol, and then in London, and his itinerant work was restricted. But his influence as a hymn-writer was strong, and it is still felt not only in Methodism but throughout the Protestant Churches. He died on 29th March 1788.

10. Events following Wesley's death.—John Wesley died on 2nd March 1791. His death produced a dangerous crisis. Many thought that the time had come when the Methodist Societies would fall in pieces. Their stability had been secured, in great part, by his firm and reasonable autocracy. Was that autocracy to be exercised by a successor? The answer was in the negative. Then how was the supervision to be maintained which he had exercised over preachers and people during the intervals between the annual meetings of the Conference? The Conference gave the answer by dividing the kingdom into Districts, each containing a small number of Circuits, the preachers in which, being formed into committees, were answerable to the Conference for the maintenance of Methodist discipline. The functions of these Committees were enlarged from time to time, and chairmen, appointed by the Conference, were placed over them. This arrangement has been greatly developed in more modern times. The Committees have grown into District Synods, which exercise great influence in the administration of Methodism.

After Wesley's death the demand for the sacraments became urgent. The party most favourable to the Church of England was first in the field and issued manifestos against administration by the preachers. These provoked replies, and a controversy on the subject was continued until 1795, when an arrangement was made between the Conference and the representatives of the trustees of chapels. This arrangement, contained in the 'Plan of Pacification,' led to the administration of the sacraments in all Methodist chapels. As to ordination, it was decided that the reception of a preacher into 'full connexion with the Conference' should carry with it the right of administration without ordination by imposition of hands. In the case of Foreign Missionaries an exception was made, and they were ordained as in the time of Wesley. In 1836 the Conference determined that all its ministers should be ordained by the imposition of hands.

11. 'Plan of Pacification.'—Another subject of cardinal importance pressed for settlement. The question had to be answered, Who shall possess the predominant ruling power of Methodism? The country, at the time of Wesley's death, was agitated by the discussions which had accompanied the American War of Independence and the French Revolution. The doctrine of 'the sovereignty of the people' fascinated many minds, and led to a strong wish on the part of some to introduce into Methodism a democratic form of government. But the most serious contest was between the claims of the Conference and of the trustees of chapels. That contest was settled, for the time being, by the 'Plan of Pacification' and by certain regulations that were passed at the Leeds Conference of 1797. In these documents we find the fundamental principles which still govern the Mother Church of

Methodism. The pastoral power of the preachers was safeguarded; but its exercise was limited by giving to the Leaders' Meeting additional rights, as representing the Societies, while matters of finance were placed more completely under the control of the Circuit Quarterly Meetings in which laymen predominated. Thus, in 1795 and 1797, was instituted that remarkable 'balance of power' which is a peculiarity of the system of Methodism. The settlement was almost universally approved. Out of a membership of nearly 100,000, about 5000 persons who were desirous of a democratic form of government united themselves into a Society under the leadership of William Thom and Alexander Kilham, and became the Methodist New Connexion.

12. Connexional system of Wesleyan Methodism.—Speaking of Methodism in the present time, we may say that the Wesleyan Methodist Church, the mother church of the Methodists, has pursued its course along the lines laid down by John Wesley. The Connexional system is intact. The Circuits consist of the several Societies within their boundaries, the Districts are composed of the Circuits in their areas, and 'the Connexion' is the aggregate of all the Societies, Circuits, and Districts in those countries in which Methodism is established in association with the Conference. This great organization is kept together by the unifying power of the Conference. Every attempt to introduce the principle of 'Circuit independency' has been successfully resisted. It is impossible here to describe minutely the organization of Wesleyan Methodism. It is the result not only of the work of Wesley, but of the continuance of his work, done in his spirit, for more than a hundred years since his death. We may briefly note some of the changes which have taken place in the Conference since the Deed Poll was signed in 1784. The specific naming of the 100 preachers who composed the Conference produced excitement and ill-feeling, especially among preachers who were not nominated in the Deed. In 1791 the Conference, in accordance with Wesley's request conveyed in a letter, resolved that all preachers who were 'in full connexion' should enjoy every privilege that the members of the Conference enjoyed. That resolution almost completely allayed the ill-feeling that had been excited.

13. Lay-representation and the constitution of Conference.—The action of the Conference in 1876, however, is of still greater interest. Although no alteration can be made in the composition of the Conference created by Wesley's Deed Poll, save by process of civil law, it has been found possible to associate laymen, as well as ministers, with 'the Hundred.' The Conference, which assembles annually towards the end of July, now meets in two Sessions. Its representative Session is held first, and consists of 300 ministers and 300 laymen. The resolutions they pass are made valid by the confirming vote of the 'Legal Conference.' Some of the lay-representatives are chosen by the ministers and laymen present at the preceding Conference; but the greater number are elected by the separate vote of the laymen assembled in the representative Sessions of the District Synods held in May. Those Sessions have been much enlarged, not only by the inclusion of many laymen who are members of District sub-Committees, but also by the addition of the representatives of the Circuit Quarterly Meetings, which, in their turn, have been greatly enlarged through alterations made in the composition of the Leaders' Meetings. The most striking of the alterations in the Leaders' Meetings is the addition to them of persons elected by the Society Meeting in each place to represent the members of the Society. The votes for the laymen and the duly qualified women chosen to attend the Conference represent a wide constituency. As there is a permanent ministerial element in the Representative Session of the Conference consisting, for instance, of members of 'the Hundred,' there is also a permanent lay element. It is composed of the lay-treasurers of certain funds, along with 48 laymen elected by the votes of ministers and laymen present at the Conference. One-third of this number retire annually, and are not eligible for immediate re-election. In the Representative Session it is estimated that nearly 60 members of the Hundred will be present, a quorum of 40 being necessary for the transaction of business, according to the Deed Poll. To these are added several ministerial officials, such as chairmen of Districts who are not members of the Hundred, 8 representatives of foreign missionaries, and others. The rest of the 300 ministers are chosen by the votes of the ministers in the Pastoral Session of each Synod in Great Britain, the number of ministerial and lay-representatives being governed by the principle of proportion of members of Society in the several Districts. The Representative Session of the Conference deals with all questions in which the expenditure of money is involved, and reviews the work done by the committees of ministers and laymen that have managed the affairs of the several Church 'Departments' during the year. New legislation may also be proposed on subjects within the province of the Session, but such new legislation is not confirmed until it has been submitted to the Representative Sessions of the Districts for consideration and report.

At the close of the Representative Session the Pastoral Session is held. This consists of the 'Legal Hundred,' the ministers who have been members of the Representative Session that year, and other ministers who have received the permission of their Synods to attend. When the scheme of lay-representation was adopted, it was agreed that all questions of doctrine, discipline, and the stationing of ministers should be reserved to the Pastoral Session, as also the management of the Book Room, the great publishing department of Methodism. The Pastoral Session exercises strict discipline over the ministers of the Connexion, and also considers all appeals in cases of discipline affecting members. The Circuit Quarterly Meetings have a right to memorialize the Conference, in both its sessions, on Connexional subjects, and to propose alterations in Methodist rules and regulations. When 'provisional legislation' is passed by the Conference in its Pastoral Session, that legislation has to be submitted for the consideration of the ministers of the Districts when assembled in the Pastoral Session of the Synods.

14. Home and Foreign Missions.—The work of Methodism has always been deemed of greater importance than its machinery. The wide-spread character of that work may be judged from the *Minutes of Conference* annually published. The work of the Home and the Foreign Missionary departments is worthy of special consideration. In recent years the evangelistic campaign has been quickened by the erection of large Mission Halls in some of the principal towns of England. The example of renewed evangelistic enterprise in Wesleyan Methodism has made a deep impression on the Churches of Great Britain and other countries. The Foreign Missionary work of Methodism dates from 1769. The work gradually increased. In 1785 appointments in the United States, Nova Scotia, Newfoundland, and Antigua appear in the *Minutes of Conference.* Working in connexion with the Conference, Coke was the leading spirit of Methodist Foreign Missionary enterprise until his death in 1813. In that year the work became more completely organized, and the present Wesleyan Methodist Missionary Society was formed. In estimating the importance of the work done by that Society, it must be remembered that its present operations are carried on in a field that is only a fragment of the area once occupied. Independent and affiliated Conferences formed in the United States, Canada, France, S. Africa, and Australia have taken over almost all the work which was begun by the British Conference in the several countries mentioned.

the Eastern Section, 6,794,471, and, in the Western Section, 25,934,076, making a total of 32,728,547.

The statistical tables show that there are many separate Methodist Churches in the world. It must, however, be understood that the divisions that have occurred have not been caused by doctrinal differences; in almost all cases they have arisen from varying opinions concerning ecclesiastical constitution and administration. In the Western Section the 'colour question' has had an influence on the number of churches.

I. CHURCHES OF THE EASTERN SECTION.

	Churches.	Ministers.	Local preachers.	Members and probationers.	Churches.	Sunday Schools.	Sunday School officers.	Sunday School scholars.
1.	Wesleyan Methodist . . .	3,066	24,836	664,958	12,542	9,428	139,099	1,094,950
2.	Primitive Methodist . . .	1,192	16,241	211,691	5,136	4,176	59,338	463,821
3.	United Methodist . . .	895	6,239	165,722	3,021	2,374	42,556	317,657
4.	Irish Methodist	244	628	29,648	398	353	2,582	25,834
5.	Wesleyan Reform Union . .	21	520	8,366	195	179	2,746	21,754
6.	Independent Methodist . .	414	..	8,769	159	157	3,051	27,703
7.	French Methodist . . .	40	84	1,690	124	70	225	2,456
8.	S. African Methodist . . .	253	5,797	117,146	3,930	788	2,893	39,329
9.	Australasian Methodist . .	1,069	4,701	150,890	6,554	4,021	23,086	218,170
	Total for Eastern Section, 1910	7,194	59,046	1,358,880	32,059	21,546	275,576	2,211,674

II. CHURCHES OF THE WESTERN SECTION.

	Churches.	Ministers.	Local preachers.	Members.	Churches.	Sunday Schools.	Sunday School officers.	Sunday School scholars.
1.	Methodist Episcopal . . .	20,755	14,718	3,489,696	30,305	35,590	374,118	3,579,999
2.	Methodist Episcopal Church (South)	7,877	4,584	1,883,043	16,457	15,980	127,761	1,337,108
3.	Methodist Church, Canada .	2,655	2,589	340,091	3,672	3,678	36,503	340,897
4.	African Methodist Episcopal .	6,774	6,302	606,106	5,630	5,695	39,310	316,000
5.	African Methodist Episcopal (Zion)	3,488	3,024	547,216	3,298	..	..	..
6.	Methodist Protestant . . .	1,362	490	188,437	2,390	2,123	17,812	141,899
7.	Coloured Methodist Episcopal .	2,901	6,194	234,721	2,857	3,011	12,044	219,999
8.	Free Methodist	1,122	802	32,112	1,163	1,154	7,662	44,275
9.	Wesleyan Methodist . . .	598	192	19,178	571	491	2,523	21,211
10.	Primitive Methodist . . .	72	93	7,407	98	95	1,511	12,900
11.	Union American Methodist Episcopal	138	..	18,500	255	78	481	3,372
12.	African Union Methodist Protestant	200	..	4,000	125	66	441	5,266
13.	Congregational Methodist . .	337	..	15,529	333	182	1,146	8,785
14.	Congregational Methodist (Coloured)	5	..	319	5	..	..	..
15.	New Congregational Methodist .	59	..	1,782	35	27	143	1,298
16.	Zion Union Apostolic (Coloured)	53	..	3,059	45	36	212	1,508
17.	Independent Methodist . .	2	..	1,161	2	..	..	..
18.	Reformed Methodist . . .	18	..	357	11	..	..	..
19.	Reformed Methodist Union Episcopal (Coloured)	40	..	4,000	58	54	204	1,792
20.	British Methodist Episcopal (Coloured)	20	6	700	21	18	125	..
21.	Japan Methodist . . .	138	81	12,322	107	300	1,150	25,826
	Total for Western Section, 1910	48,614	39,075	7,409,736	67,438	68,578	623,146	6,062,135

NOTE.—The returns for local preachers and for Sunday Schools are in some instances incomplete.

III. SUMMARY OF EASTERN AND WESTERN SECTIONS.

Eastern Section	7,194	59,046	1,358,880	32,059	21,546	275,576	2,211,674
Western Section	48,614	39,075	7,409,736	67,438	68,578	623,146	6,062,135
Total	55,808	98,121	8,768,616	99,497	90,124	898,722	8,273,809

15. Statistics of world Methodism.—It is only at the decennial meetings of the Ecumenical Conference, when representatives of the Methodist Churches in both hemispheres meet, that an idea of the wide-spread influence of Methodism can be gained. Those Conferences were instituted in 1881, the latest being held in Toronto in 1911. The carefully compiled statistics presented to that Conference speak for themselves.

It was estimated that the members and adherents of the Methodist Churches, in 1910, numbered, in

There is one Church, bearing the Methodist name, which is not represented in the Ecumenical Conference — the Welsh Calvinistic Methodist Church. Its history and organization should be studied in Williams's valuable book (*Welsh Calvinistic Methodism*). The Church is closely connected in origin with Whitefield's work in Wales. The doctrinal difference, indicated in its title, suggests a reason for its unique position among Methodist Churches.

16. Methodist Episcopal Churches.—The success

of Methodism in the United States of America has been remarkable. We have mentioned some facts concerning its origin in 1769, and the action of Wesley in ordaining Coke as a Superintendent, and two other preachers as presbyters, in 1784. When Coke arrived in America, he ordained Francis Asbury as a Superintendent. Asbury's work and influence have left a deep mark on Methodism in the United States. Like Wesley, he was a man of high spiritual tone. He rivalled Wesley in evangelistic enterprise, and gathered around him men who possessed the courage and devotion of the pioneer preacher. The War of Independence had made the whole country the sphere of the most enterprising Evangelism. In settled towns, in clusters of huts, in lonely backwoods, the Methodist preacher became a familiar figure, as he preached and formed and visited his little Societies. The growth of the churches in the immense areas in which the pioneers worked necessitated the helpful supervision not only of the Superintendents but also of 'Presiding Elders,' who rode hither and thither, constantly giving inspiration and guidance to the scattered evangelists and churches. For a considerable time the work was carried on in close connexion with the British Conference, and on lines similar to those followed in England. A Conference was held in the States in 1773, at which time there were 6 Circuits, 10 preachers, and 160 members. From these small beginnings American Methodism has advanced to its present position.

The Methodist Episcopal Church and the Methodist Episcopal Church (South) occupy the chief positions among the Methodist Churches of the United States. They separated in 1844, in consequence of discussions which involved the question of slavery. We may refer to some of the constitutional arrangements of the Methodist Episcopal Church. The members of the Church are divided into local Societies, one or more of which constitute a 'pastoral charge.' A quarterly conference is organized in each 'pastoral charge.' The 'travelling preachers' throughout the States are members of their several Annual Conferences, the sessions of which they are obliged to attend. In addition to the ministerial Annual Conferences, a General Conference is held every four years composed of delegates from all the Annual Conferences in the States. It consists of pastors and lay-delegates, the admission of the latter into the General Conference dating from 1872. The ministerial delegates are elected by the Annual Conferences, each of which is entitled to one delegate at least. The General Conference fixes the ratio of representation and the manner of election. Every four years a Lay Electoral Conference is constituted within the bounds of each Annual Conference for the purpose of voting on constitutional changes to be submitted to the General Conference, which is the supreme legislative assembly. The Lay Electoral Conference is composed of lay-members, one from each pastoral charge, chosen by the lay-members of each charge over twenty-one years of age, in such manner as the General Conference has determined. Each Lay Electoral Conference is entitled to elect as many lay-delegates to the General Conference as there are ministerial delegates from the Annual Conference. In the General Conference the 'General Superintendents,' as the bishops are called in the *Discipline of the Methodist Episcopal Church*, preside in such order as they determine; but, if no General Superintendent is present, the Conference elects one of its other members to preside *pro tempore*. The presence of two-thirds of the whole number of delegates constitutes a quorum for the transaction of business. The General Conference elects by ballot as many General Superintendents as it may deem necessary from among the 'Travelling Elders,' as the former Presiding Elders are now called. The Conference has full power to make rules and regulations for the Church, under the limitations and restrictions laid down in the *Discipline*. The principal restrictions are that it cannot revoke, alter, or change the *Articles of Religion*, which were prepared by John Wesley, and which first appeared in *The Sunday Service of the Methodists in the United States of America*, published in 1784. Nor can the General Conference establish any new standards, or rules of doctrine, contrary to the present existing and established standards. In addition, it cannot change or alter any part or rule of government so as to do away with episcopacy or destroy the plan of General Superintendency. It is also unable to revoke or change the 'General Rules' of the Church. Those 'Rules' are, with slight variations, the 'Rules of the Society of the People called Methodists,' as drawn up by John Wesley in 1743. As to the procedure of the General Conference, the *Discipline* shows that, in voting, the ministers and laymen vote together; but it is provided that a separate vote 'by orders' may be taken on any question when it is requested by one-third of either order of delegates present and voting. In all cases of separate voting the concurrence of the two orders is required for the adoption of the proposed measure. If the proposal concerns a change of the constitution, a vote of two-thirds of the General Conference is required. Such, in bare outline, is a sketch of some of the outstanding features of the organization of the Methodist Episcopal Church, but it should be supplemented by a study of the book of *Doctrines and Discipline* (1912). In J. H. Rigg's *Comparative View of Church Organisations* there is a chapter on American Episcopal Methodism which contains important information enabling the student to compare the constitution of the Mother Church of Great Britain with that of the Methodist Churches in the United States. For many years the visits of fraternal delegates, representing the Conferences of Great Britain and Ireland and America, have served to strengthen the bond of union between the Methodists of the two countries. The American Methodists hold a conspicuous position among the Churches devoted to the work of Foreign Missions.

17. Early secessions.—We have mentioned the first important Methodist secession in England, taking place in 1797. As the Methodist New Connexion is now part of the United Methodist Church, it is not necessary to describe its original constitution. In 1810 a small Society, numbering 10 members, was formed by Hugh Bourne in Staffordshire, and became the germ of the Primitive Methodist Church. In 1815 a Society, consisting of 22 persons, was formed by William O'Bryan in Devonshire out of which arose the Bible Christian Church. The reasons for the institution of these two Societies were similar. In the former case Hugh Bourne and William Clowes, two earnest evangelists, were indisposed to submit to the restrictions of Methodist discipline and manner of work. They sought and found a sphere in which they could have a larger freedom. They made no attempt to agitate the Church from which they were separated. They gathered their members out of the neglected classes, and displayed in their work much of the spirit of ancient Methodism. The same may be said of William O'Bryan, the founder of the Bible Christian Church.

18. Primitive Methodist Church.—Next to the Wesleyan Methodists, the Primitive Methodists hold the strongest position in Great Britain. The constitution bears, in several points, a strong resemblance to that of the Wesleyan Methodist Church, but there is a marked difference in the composition of the Conference. H. B. Kendall, in his *Handbook of Primitive Methodist Church Principles and Polity* (London, 1913), says:

'The Deed Poll provides that members shall be formed into Classes, Societies, Circuits, and Districts, and that Societies shall have their Leaders' Meetings, and Circuits their Committees and Quarterly Meetings' (p. 61).

Dealing with the functions of the Annual Conference, he sets forth the provisions of the Primitive Methodist Deed Poll. First of all, the Conference is to be composed of 12 Permanent Members, irremovable from office except for incompetency or incapacity. Next, it is to be composed of other persons not exceeding 4, whose appointment is to be made by a by-law of the Conference. These may be ministers or laymen, official or unofficial members. Lastly, the Conference is also composed of delegates, who have been elected thereto by their District Meetings, one-third of whom must be travelling preachers and two-thirds laymen, and no layman is to be appointed who is not a local preacher, or a class leader, or a Circuit steward. After long consideration and much discussion it was decided by the Conference of 1876 that the number of delegates to be sent by each to the highest court should be determined by the number of members in the District, 3000 being made the unit for one minister and two laymen (p. 61 f.). Kendall is of opinion that the Primitive Methodist polity is a 'modified Presbyterianism,' one evidence of the fact being that the Churches are jointly governed by ministers and lay-officials, and that all ministers are in theory equal, the Superintendent differing from his colleagues only in function and responsibility (p. 62). Up to the present the Primitive Methodists have not shown any strong desire for corporate union with other Methodist Churches. Their Foreign Missionary work is confined to Africa.

19. United Methodist Church.—In 1827, 1835, and 1849 there were secessions from the Wesleyan Methodist Church resulting from serious controversies concerning questions of government and administration. The first was occasioned by the introduction of an organ into one of the chapels in Leeds. In its course constitutional questions were raised touching the power of the Conference, which re-emerged at a later stage. In 1835 the creation of the Theological Institution for the training of candidates for the ministry roused strong opposition. The first occasion of the disturbance was soon nearly forgotten, and the controversy turned into an attack on the constitution of the Wesleyan Methodist Church. The agitation was elaborately organized and vigorously conducted in all parts of the country, and brought about the secession of several thousands of members, who formed themselves into the Wesleyan Association. The Association held its first Annual Assembly in Manchester in 1836. The Leeds reformers of 1827 joined the new Church.

The largest of all the secessions from the Wesleyan Methodist Church took place in 1849. Its immediate cause was the action taken by the Conference in dealing with certain anonymous publications in which the personal character of ministers holding high official responsibility was attacked. But, as before, the controversy soon involved the question of the constitution and, especially, of the power of the Conference. It is difficult to state the number of persons lost to the Wesleyan Methodist Church through this agitation. The aggressive work of Methodism was paralyzed for several years. When the strife subsided, it was found that the number of members in the Wesleyan Methodist Church was nearly 100,000 less than when the agitation began. The 'Reformers' of 1849–52 formed themselves into a distinct community, which, by union with the Methodist Association, became 'the United Methodist Free Churches.'

In 1907 an Act was passed by Parliament authorizing the union of the Methodist New Connexion, the Bible Christians, and the United Methodist Free Churches, under the name of 'The United Methodist Church.' The constitution of the new Church shows the usual indications of compromise; but it retains the strong marks of original Methodism. The Conference, which is composed of ministers and laymen in equal numbers, meets once a year. It includes the President and Secretary, the President-designate, 12 ministers and 12 laymen, who form, in a sense, a permanent nucleus, the Connexional officers, the representatives of District Meetings, and such representatives of Connexional Funds and Institutions as the last preceding Conference has determined. The whole number of the Conference, exclusive of the Guardian Representatives and Connexional officers, is about 300. The Conference appoints a General Connexional Committee which exercises a 'general oversight over the affairs of the United Methodist Church during the intervals between the Conferences.' The authority of the Church Meeting, the Leaders' Meeting, and the Circuit Quarterly Meeting is great. These meetings are, to a considerable extent, independent of the Conference, but the Conference has certain rights which it can exercise in cases calling for its interference. The constitution of the United Methodist Church may be studied in the *General Rules*, approved by the Conference in September 1907, a new edition of which was published in 1911. Foreign Missionary work is being done by this Church in China, Africa, Central America, and the W. Indies.

20. Smaller Methodist Churches.—The Wesleyan Reform Union consists of those Churches and Circuits which held aloof from the amalgamation producing the United Methodist Free Churches. In 1859 a constitution was formed which is fully described in a pamphlet published by the Wesleyan Reform Union Conference, the latest edition being issued in 1896.

In 1805 several small Churches formed a union which held its first Annual Meeting in Manchester. The distinctive characteristics of the churches so united are an unpaid ministry, conjoined with the free church-life of the Quakers and the doctrines and methods of Wesleyan Methodism (J. Vickers, *Independent Methodism* [Wigan], 1910, p. 3). In 1898 this union assumed the name of the Independent Methodist Church. Its churches are situated chiefly in Lancashire, Yorkshire, and the northern counties, with some outlying churches in Nottinghamshire and Leicestershire, and a few besides in Bristol and the south-west. The Independent Methodists excel in Sunday School work.

Although sharply divided by constitutional distinctions, the Methodists of England have so much in common, especially in their practical work, that they are being drawn nearer together. The Ecumenical and other Conferences have done much to promote the spirit of fraternity among them. In Canada and other countries the Methodist Churches have united, and Methodist reunion in England is often sympathetically discussed.

LITERATURE.—i. POLITY, ETC.—*Minutes of the Yearly Conference of the People called Methodists*, published annually, 1744–1914; *Reports of Proceedings of Ecumenical Methodist Conferences*, 1881, 1891, 1901, 1911; *Rules of the Society, etc., with Statements concerning Church Membership*, published by direction of Conference (1913); C. Wansborough, *Handbook and Index to the Minutes of the Conference*, London, 1890; *The Sunday Service of the Methodists*[4], do. 1784; *The Book of Public Prayers and Services for the Use of the People called Methodists*, do. 1883; *Doctrine and Discipline of the Methodist*

Episcopal Church, New York, 1912; **J. S. Simon**, *A Summary of Methodist Law and Discipline*^{4}, London, 1914; **D. J. Waller**, *The Constitution and Polity of the Wesleyan Methodist Church*^{3}, do. 1905; **J. H. Rigg**, *The Connexional Economy of Wesleyan Methodism*^{2}, do. 1879; **G. Turner**, *The Constitution and Discipline of Wesleyan Methodism*, do. 1841; **J. Benson**, *An Apology for the People called Methodists*, do. 1801; **J. Beecham**, *An Essay on the Constitution of Wesleyan Methodism*^{3}, do. 1851; **J. Crowther**, *A Portraiture of Methodism*, do. 1811, ^{2}1815; **E. Grindrod**, *A Compendium of the Laws and Regulations of Wesleyan Methodism*, do. 1842; **S. Warren**, *A Digest of the Laws and Regulations of Wesleyan Methodists*^{2}, do. 1835; **W. Peirce**, *The Ecclesiastical Principles and Polity of the Wesleyan Methodists*^{3}, do. 1873; **W. Redfern**, *Modern Developments in Methodism*, do. 1906; **C. Welch**, *The Wesleyan Polity illustrated and defended*, do. 1829; **J. H. Rigg**, *A Comparative View of Church Organisations*^{3}, do. 1897; **J. S. Simon**, *A Manual for Class Leaders*, do. 1892; **J. G. Rogers**, *Church Systems in the 19th Century*, do. 1881.

ii. HISTORY.—**C. J. Abbey** and **J. H. Overton**, *The Eng. Church in the 18th Century*^{3}, 2 vols., London, 1896; **J. Stoughton**, *Hist. of Religion in England*^{4}, 8 vols., do. 1901; **W. E. H. Lecky**, *Hist. of England in the 18th Century*^{5}, 7 vols., do. 1899–1901, ch. viii.; **H. S. Skeats** and **C. S. Miall**, *Hist. of the Free Churches of England, 1688–1891*, do. 1891; **J. Hunt**, *Religious Thought in England*, 3 vols., do. 1870–73, iii.; **W. Myles**, *A Chronological Hist. of the People called Methodists*^{4}, do. 1813; **G. Smith**, *Hist. of Wesleyan Methodism*, 3 vols., do. 1859; *A New Hist. of Methodism*, ed. W. J. Townsend, H. B. Workman, and G. Eayrs, 2 vols., do. 1909; **C. H. Crookshank**, *Hist. of Methodism in Ireland*, 3 vols., do. 1885–88; **J. S. Simon**, *The Revival of Religion in England in the Eighteenth Century*, do. 1907; **W. Williams**, *Welsh Calvinistic Methodism*^{2}, do. 1884; *A Jubilee Memorial of the Bible Christian Connexion*^{2}, do. 1866; *Proceedings of the Wesleyan Historical Society*, 9 vols., Burnley, 1898–1914; *Centenary of Methodist New Connexion*, London, 1897; **H. B. Kendall**, *Origin and Hist. of the Prim. Methodist Church*, 2 vols., do. 1905; **J. Petty**, *Hist. of the Prim. Methodist Connexion*, do. 1870; **B. Gregory**, *A Handbook of Scriptural Church Principles and of Wesleyan Methodist Polity and History*, do. 1888, *Side Lights on the Conflicts of Methodism*, do. 1898; **J. R. Gregory**, *A Hist. of Methodism*, 2 vols., do. 1911; **G. Alexander**, *Hist. of the Methodist Episcopal Church South*, New York, 1894; **N. Bangs**, *Hist. of the Methodist Episcopal Church*, 4 vols., do. 1839–41; **J. M. Buckley**, *History of Methodism in the United States*, 2 vols., do. 1896; **J. F. Hurst**, *Hist. of Methodism*, do. 1902–04, vols. i.–iii., 'British Methodism' (by **T. E. Brigden**), vols. iv.–vi., 'World-Wide Methodism,' vol. vii., 'American Methodism'; **H. N. McTyeire**, *Hist. of Methodism*, Nashville, 1884; **A. Stevens**, *Hist. of Methodist Episcopal Church*, 4 vols., New York, 1864–67; **A. Sutherland**, *Methodism in Canada*, London, 1903; *Centennial Volume of Canadian Methodism*, Toronto, 1891; **J. Dixon**, *Methodism in America*, London, 1849; **D. Young**, *Origin and Hist. of Methodism in Wales and the Borders*, do. 1893; **D. Butler**, *John Wesley and George Whitefield in Scotland*, do. 1899; **G. G.** and **M. G. Findlay**, *Wesley's World Parish*, do. 1913; **W. Moister**, *Hist. of Wesleyan Missions in all Parts of the World*, do. 1871; *Report of Wesleyan Methodist Missionary Society*, 1913 (contains brief sketches of each Mission); **J. M. Buckley**, *Constitutional Hist. of Amer. Methodism*, New York, 1909; **D. Sherman**, *Hist. of the Revisions of the Discipline of the Methodist Episcopal Church*, Cincinnati, 1874; **J. J. Tigert**, *Constitutional Hist. of Amer. Episcopal Methodism*, Nashville, 1894. There are numerous Colonial and local Histories: **G. Osborn**, *Outlines of Wesleyan Bibliography*, London, 1869; **R. Green**, *The Works of John and Charles Wesley: A Bibliography*, do. 1896; **W. J. E. Bennett**, *The Church's Broken Unity—Methodism*, do., n.d.; **W. J. Townsend**, *The Story of Methodist Union*, do., n.d.; **J. Telford**, *The Methodist Hymn-Book Illustrated*, do. 1906.

iii. BIOGRAPHY.—**J. Hampson**, *Memoirs of John Wesley*, 3 vols., Sunderland, 1791; **T. Coke** and **H. Moore**, *Life of John Wesley*, London, 1792; **J. Whitehead**, *The Life of the Rev. John Wesley and of the Rev. Charles Wesley*, 2 vols., forming a *Hist. of Methodism*, do. 1793–96; **H. Moore**, *The Life of the Rev. John Wesley*, 2 vols., do. 1824–25; **R. Southey**, *The Life of Wesley and the Rise and Progress of Methodism*, 2 vols., do. 1820; **R. Watson**, *Life of the Rev. John Wesley*, do. 1831; **L. Tyerman**, *Life and Times of John Wesley*^{6}, 3 vols., do. 1890, *Life of the Rev. George Whitefield*, 2 vols., do. 1876, *The Oxford Methodists*, London and New York, 1873, *Wesley's Designated Successor, John Fletcher*, London, 1882; **J. Telford**, *Life of John Wesley*, do. 1886, *Life of Rev. Charles Wesley*, do. 1886; **T. Jackson**, *Life of Charles Wesley*, 2 vols., do. 1841; *The Works of John Wesley*, 14 vols., do 1829–31; **J. H. Rigg**, *The Living Wesley*^{3}, do. 1891; **E. Clarke**, *Susanna Wesley*, do. 1886; **J. Kirk**, *The Mother of the Wesleys*^{3}, do. 1866; **W. H. Fitchett**, *Wesley and his Century*, do. 1906; **J. H. Overton**, *John Wesley*, do. 1891; **C. T. Winchester**, *Life of John Wesley*, do. 1906; **R. Green**, *John Wesley, Evangelist*, do. 1908; *The Lives of Early Methodist Preachers*, ed. T. Jackson, 6 vols., do. 1871; **F. W. Briggs**, *Bishop Asbury: A Biographical Study for Christian Workers*, do. 1874; **W. Arthur**, *Life of Gideon Ouseley*, do. 1876; **J. W. Etheridge**, *Life of the Rev. Thomas Coke, D.C.L.*, do. 1860, *Life of the Rev. Adam Clarke, LL.D.*, do. 1858; **T. P. Bunting** and **G. S. Rowe**, *Life of Jabez Bunting*, do. 1887; **D. Benham**, *Memoirs of James Hutton*, do. 1856; **Mrs. R. Smith**, *Life of Henry Moore*, do. 1844; **R. Chew**, *Life of James Everett*, do. 1875; **J. Grundell** and **R. Hall**, *Life of Alexander Kilham*, Nottingham, 1799; *Life of Alexander Kilham*, London, 1838; *Life and Times of Selina, Countess of Huntingdon*, 2 vols., do. 1840; **Julia Wedgwood**, *John Wesley and the Evangelical Reaction of the Eighteenth Century*, do. 1870; **W. W. Stamp**, *The Orphan House of Wesley*, do. 1863; *The Journal of the Rev. John Wesley, A.M.*, ed. Nehemiah Curnock, standard ed., 8 vols., do. 1909–15; *The Journal of Charles Wesley*, 2 vols., do. 1849; **T. Jackson**, *The Centenary of Wesleyan Methodism*, do. 1839; **A. D. Godley**, *Oxford in the Eighteenth Century*, do. 1908; **J. H. Rigg**, *The Churchmanship of John Wesley*^{2}, do. 1886; **R. D. Urlin**, *The Churchman's Life of Wesley*, do. 1880; **H. W. Holden**, *John Wesley in Company with High Churchmen*, do. 1874; **I. Taylor**, *Wesley and Methodism*, do. 1851.

JOHN S. SIMON.

II. *DOCTRINE.*—Let us look into the soul animating the body which has been described. Methodism was the offspring of the Evangelical Revival that took place in England during the 18th cent.; its doctrine was moulded under the religious conditions of that age.

1. Methodism and deism.—A rationalistic deism then largely prevailed amongst educated men—a system of thought which fenced God off from mankind behind the laws of nature and bounded human knowledge by the limits of sense-perception and logical reason. The Deity was treated as an absentee from His world; and men consequently became godless in practice as in thought. The Revival swept down these artificial barriers. God was realized in living contact with His children. The sense of the divine was recovered; the transcendent became again immanent to consciousness. Accordingly, 'the life of God in the souls of men' was Wesley's definition of religion; 'the work of God' was the habitual Methodist designation for the Revival, because in its phenomena God's immediate action upon human nature was discerned. Hence the emphasis laid in the teaching of the Wesleys on 'the witness of the Spirit' (Ro 8). The doctrine of assurance—the personal certainty of the forgiveness of sins and of restored sonship toward God — was the outstanding feature of original Methodism. To most Churchmen of the time professions of this kind appeared a strange 'enthusiasm' (see G. Lavington, *The Enthusiasm of Methodists and Papists considered*^{3}, London, 1833); that a man might know his sins forgiven was deemed a dangerous presumption. Along with the Fatherhood of God, the Deity of the atoning Saviour and of the witnessing and sanctifying Spirit came to be freshly recognized; an arrest was made of the Socinianism which by the middle of the 18th cent. was rife among both Anglicans and Dissenters.

2. Methodism and Calvinism.—The Methodist forces were soon divided on the question of predestination. Predestinarianism, like deism, magnifies the transcendence of God at the expense of His immanence, reducing finite will to an illusion and making man, even in his acceptance of divine grace, the passive creature instead of the consenting child of God. The Puritan theology, in its prevailing strain, was intensely Calvinistic; and to it Whitefield, with the Welsh Methodist leaders and the Evangelical clergy generally, adhered, while the Wesleys espoused Arminian views upon election and grace, in this respect inheriting the High Anglican tradition. But the spring of their universalism lay in the sense of God's mercy to mankind revealed within their own breast and interpreted in the broad light of the NT; they sang:

> 'The boundless grace that found out me
> For every soul of man is free!'

They could not preach that God 'willeth all men to be saved' under the reservation that He has doomed some, of His mere pleasure, to perdition; as Christ's ambassadors, they cried, without any misgiving, 'Ye all may come, *whoever will*!' The

Wesleyan teaching lifted a cloud from the character of God; it brought salvation to thousands who had deemed themselves predestined reprobates. Wesley vehemently contended against another tenet of Calvinism, maintained by contemporary Evangelicals—that of the necessary inherence of sin in the redeemed. The current orthodoxy limited the salvation of Christ in the degree of its attainability as well as in the persons by whom it is attainable. John Wesley arrived at the conviction that the man who is 'in Christ' may become even on earth a thoroughly 'new creature,' that it is possible to be actually 'cleansed from all sin' through 'the blood of Jesus' (1 Jn 1^7)—'freed' (as he would say) 'from the last remains of sin'; on the strength of God's promises and the warrant of experience, he taught his people to seek and expect the power to keep continually the Two Commandments of Jesus and so to become altogether holy and happy. To this effect he used to quote the Communion Prayer, 'that we may perfectly love thee, and worthily magnify thy holy Name,' insisting that this is to ask from God no boon beyond His giving. From the moment of conversion the Methodist was set at war with 'inbred sin,' inspired by the prospect of its extirpation. The Class Meeting, with this ideal before it, became a school of holiness. The 'glorious hope of perfect love' proved an abiding spring of spiritual ardour and a powerful spur to moral endeavour. Sometimes the extravagances and self-delusions of unbalanced minds discredited the doctrine of Perfect Love; to such abuse all earnest religious teaching is liable. But the sight of the goal of faith given to Methodism quickened and sustained the race for multitudes. The endurance of the Wesleyan Revival is due to the spiritual breadth and sanity of its programme. In this sense Wesley defined the object of Methodism as being 'to spread Scriptural Holiness throughout the land.' The hymns of Charles Wesley are the best exposition of Methodism in the fundamental respects which we have stated; they served as its keenest weapon in the arduous conflict which it waged with Calvinism. Along with the hymns, the doctrine which inspired them has leavened the whole Methodist Church.

3. Methodism and Moravianism.—Methodism owes a peculiar debt to the Moravian Brethren; their hand led the two Wesleys out of 'the legal wilderness' into the liberty of the sons of God. From this simple people, as well as from William Law and the mystics, John Wesley learned deep lessons respecting faith and inward religion. But there came here also a parting of the ways. Leading members of the Unitas Fratrum in England, and others of Wesley's early associates, were infected with the mystical tendency to despise the external duties of religion. Regarding the inner light and the Holy Spirit's witness as the sum of Christianity, men of this persuasion treated fellowship and Church order as superfluities; some of them verged in theory, if not in practice, upon Antinomianism. Among the latter the maxim was current, which Wesley denounces as an 'enthusiastic doctrine of devils,' that 'we are not to do good unless our hearts are free to it'—in other words, that we should leave disagreeable duties undone (this was a temporary, but widely operative, aberration in Moravianism). In this outbreak Wesley saw the peril of the Revival; he raised a barrier against it in the 'Rules of Society' (dated 1st May 1743), which bear strongly upon private and social duty, and by the mutual oversight secured through the Class Meeting. Thus the experimental in religion was balanced by the practical; inward holiness found in outward holiness its complement and safeguard. Methodism recognized that, while salvation is 'through faith' alone, a true faith 'works by love'; it enforced the teaching of St. James side by side with that of St. Paul, and found the two entirely consistent. Their home-training and Anglican schooling stood the Wesleys in good stead at this crisis.

4. Methodism and the Church of England.—John and Charles Wesley were sons and ministers of the Church of England, and taught (as they supposed) her true doctrine. John Wesley quoted the *Articles* and *Homilies* in vindication of his most oppugned tenets. For the guidance of his people he revised the Thirty-nine Articles, reducing their number by omission and abbreviation to 25 (so printed in the Wesleyan Methodist Service Book): the changes are in many instances significant. There disappear, with others, artt. viii. ('Of the Three Creeds'), xiii. ('Of Works before Justification'), xv. ('Of Christ alone without Sin'), xvii. ('Of Predestination and Election'), xx. and xxi. ('Of the Authority of the Church' and 'Of the Authority of General Councils'), xxiii. ('Of Ministering in the Congregation'), and xxxiii. ('Of Excommunicate Persons'). The title of art. xvi. becomes 'Sin after Justification' instead of 'Sin after Baptism,' and 'Ministers' is substituted for 'Priests' in xxxii.; 'Traditions' is paraphrased by 'Rites and Ceremonies' in xxxiv., the substance of the art. being preserved with notable alterations in detail. 'The Civil Magistrates' (xxxvii.) Wesley turns into 'the Rulers of the British Dominions,' adding 'his Parliament' to 'the King's Majesty,' merging 'Ecclesiastical and Civil' in 'all Estates,' and concluding with the first paragraph of the art.; he ignores the Royal Supremacy over the Church. The artt. on 'the Sacraments' and 'the Lord's Supper' are reproduced almost *verbatim*; but that 'Of Baptism' is curtailed, the definition ending with the words 'sign of . . . new Birth'; the statement that by baptism persons are 'grafted into the Church' is avoided, while the clause commending 'the Baptism of young Children' is retained. Art. ix., 'Of Original or Birth-Sin,' is also cut down materially: the Wesleyan teaching on Sanctification appeared to conflict with the assertion that 'this infection of nature doth remain, yea in them that are regenerated.' The reference to 'flesh' and 'bones' is dropped from the art. 'Of the Resurrection of Christ.' The general effect of the recasting is to emphasize the Protestant and Evangelical character of the formulary, to set aside the principle of State-establishment, and to eliminate Calvinism.

5. Doctrinal standards.—Neither the Articles of Religion nor any other Anglican document or dogmatic creed was laid down by Wesley as the ground of Christian fellowship. The revised Articles of Religion were, however, from the first incorporated, with certain necessary local adaptations, in the constitution of the Methodist Episcopal Church of America (see *Doctrine and Discipline*, etc., of this Church, pp. 21–26). 'There is only one condition previously required,' the Rules state, 'in those who desire to enter these [the Methodist] Societies, viz. a desire to flee from the wrath to come, to be saved from their sins.' This 'narrow gate' leads into the true way; the earnest seeker of salvation approves Christ and the gospel as the sick man his remedy; a deep repentance affords the best guarantee for orthodoxy. To his preachers, however, Wesley prescribed his *Notes on the NT* and the first four volumes of *Sermons* (ed. 1787–88, containing 44 Discourses) for the basis of a common understanding. These standards are introduced into the Model Deed regulating the trusts upon which Wesleyan Methodist church-fabrics are secured, and into the ordination vows of the ministers. Every Local Preacher also declares his assent to 'the general doctrine' contained in the above writings as being 'in accordance with the holy Scriptures.' While they present no formal confession or dogmatic scheme, the *Notes* and *Sermons* contain the full evangelical creed in solution; they are a working standard framed for a preaching ministry, and have proved a sufficient regulative canon for a Church that retains its Evangelical consciousness and is concerned above all things to preserve the life-conveying spirit of these authoritative documents. A Conference Resolution of 1807 forbade the tenure of office in the Societies to any person 'holding opinions contrary to the total depravity of human nature, the Divinity and Atonement of Christ, the influence and witness of the Holy Spirit, and Christian Holiness, as believed by the Methodists.'

6. Four salient points. — The characteristic features of Methodist teaching may be summed up as follows.

(1) *Universal redemption.* — Wesley and his preachers proffered in the name of Jesus Christ 'a free, full, and present salvation' to every sinner —a salvation based on the Sacrifice of the Cross, bestowed on condition of 'repentance toward God and faith toward our Lord Jesus Christ,' and certified inwardly by the witness of the Spirit of God bringing peace of heart and the sense of God's fatherly love, and outwardly by a life of holy obedience.

(2) *Entire sanctification.*—Methodism holds the gospel to be as large in its intension as in its extension, to be designed for the 'rooting out' from human nature of 'every plant which the Heavenly Father planted not'; it encourages the Christian man to look for the perfect cure, in himself and in his race, of sin's disease. The Rules of Society, illustrated by Wesley's social work, virtually include the community with the individual man in the scope of Christ's redemption.

(3) *The fellowship of believers.*—Methodism stands for Christian brotherhood. It honours the ministry and cherishes the two sacraments; but, in its view, the proof of Church-membership lies essentially not in observance of sacraments, nor in obedience to priests, nor in subscription to creeds, but in the fulfilling on the part of Christ's brethren of His law of love by their seeking one another's company and bearing one another's burdens.

(4) *Ordered Christian service.*—'This is the love of God, that we keep His commandments': the Wesleyan Rules of Society were conceived as an application of the commandments of Christ to the situation of the Methodist people in early days. Interpreted with good sense and according to the spirit in which they were framed, those rules are found applicable to later times and to the circumstances of Methodists all over the world. They signify that the Christian man is Christ's in body as in spirit, and is called in concert with his fellows to bend everything in life to the furtherance of God's kingdom upon earth.

The above sketch is a narrative, not a criticism —a narrative of the genesis of Methodism as a product of and a factor in the life of Christendom. The changes which the system has undergone in thought and spiritual character, due to its wide expansion and the reaction upon it of later religious movements, cannot here be traced. Suffice it to say that through its manifold divisions and diversities of government a striking identity of doctrine prevails. Ecumenical Methodism retains the stamp of its origin.

LITERATURE.[1]—John Wesley, *Works*[3], 14 vols., London, 1829–31 (chiefly important for doctrine are *Sermons*, *Doctrine of Original Sin*, *Appeals to Men of Reason and Religion*, *Plain Account of Christian Perfection*, and *Plain Account of the People called Methodists*); *The Methodist Hymn Book*, do. 1904, *A Collection of Hymns for the Use of the People called Methodists*[4], do. 1792; *Poetical Works of John and Charles Wesley*, ed. G. Osborn, 13 vols., do. 1868–72; John Fletcher, *Works*, 8 vols., do. 1844 (esp. *Checks to Antinomianism*, *A Rational Vindication of the Catholic Faith*, and *Socinianism Unscriptural*); J. Benson, *An Apology for the People called Methodists*, do. 1801; R. Watson, *Theological Institutes*[8], 4 vols., do. 1850; E. Hare, *Treatise on the Scriptural Doctrine of Justification*[2], do. 1839; R. Treffry, *Inquiry into the Doctrine of the Eternal Sonship of the Lord Jesus Christ*[3], do. 1849; T. Jackson, *Wesleyan Methodism a Revival of Apostolical Christianity*[4], do. 1839; W. Cooke (M.N.C.), *Christian Theology*, do. 1846; J. Stacey (M.N.C.), *The Christian Sacraments Explained and Defended*, do. 1856; D. D. Whedon (A.M.), *The Freedom of the Will*, New York, 1874; W. B. Pope, *Compendium of Christian Theology*[2], 3 vols., London, 1879, *Person of Christ*, do. 1871, [2]1875, *A Higher Catechism of Theology*, do. 1885; J. H. Rigg, *Modern Anglican Theology*[3], do. 1880, *Oxford High Anglicanism*[2], do. 1899; M. Randles, *First Principles of Faith*, do. 1884; W. F. Slater, *Methodism in the Light of the Early Church*, do. 1885; A. Sulzberger (G.M.), *Christliche Glaubenslehre*[2], Bremen, 1889; J. A. Beet, *Through Christ to God*, London, 1892, *The New Life in Christ*, do. 1895, *The Last Things*[2], do. 1905, *A Manual of Theology*, do. 1906; T. G. Selby, *The Holy Spirit and Christian Privilege*, do. 1894; J. Chapman, *Jesus Christ and the Present Age*, do. 1895; J. S. Lidgett, *The Spiritual Principle of the Atonement*, do. 1897, *The Fatherhood of God*, Edinburgh, 1902; R. W. Moss, *The Range of Christian Experience*, do. 1898; H. C. Sheldon (A.M.), *System of Christian Doctrine*[2], New York, 1912, *Hist. of Christian Doctrine*, 2 vols., revised, do. 1905; F. Ballard, *The Miracles of Unbelief*[7], Edinburgh, 1911, *Theomonism True*, London, 1906; W. J. Townsend (U.M.), *Handbook of Christian Doctrine*, do. 1905; O. A. Curtis (A.M.), *The Christian Faith*, do. 1905; Milton S. Terry (A.M.), *Biblical Dogmatics*, New York, 1907; A. S. Peake (P.M.), *Christianity, its Nature and its Truth*, London, 1908; G. G. Findlay, *Fellowship in the Life Eternal*, do. 1909; A. L. Humphries (P.M.), *The Holy Spirit in Faith and Experience*, do. 1910; W. A. Grist (U.M.), *The Historic Christ in the Faith of To-Day*, do. 1910; W. T. Davison, *The Indwelling Spirit*, do. 1911; J. Mudge (A.M.), *The Perfect Life in Expression and Doctrine*, New York, 1911; H. B. Workman, *Methodism*, Cambridge, 1912; *The Chief Corner-Stone, Essays towards an Exposition of the Christian Faith for To-day* (by various Wesleyan writers), ed. W. T. Davison, do. 1914.

GEORGE G. FINDLAY.

MEXICANS (Ancient).—The territory of what is now the Republic of Mexico was inhabited in ancient times—as in part it still is—by a great diversity of nations and tribes. The plains of Northern Mexico were the domain of tribes of a low culture stage, living mostly without fixed abode, relying chiefly on the produce of the chase, and to some extent on agriculture. These tribes, of whom we know very little, received from the Mexicans the general name of Chichimecs. The more cultivated nations were concentrated in the central highlands, and in the ravines, valleys, and coast-plains of Southern Mexico. Though belonging to different linguistic stocks, and differentiated as to their advancement in culture, art, science, and political power, they were, nevertheless, identical in the special traits of their civilization, forming, so to speak, one great geographical culture province.

The name Mexicans belongs properly to the inhabitants of the city of Mexico or Tenochtitlan, who were otherwise called Aztecs, but the designation was extended to all tribes and tribal fractions who spoke the same idiom, and were known to the citizens of Mexico by the name Naua or Nauatlaca, *i.e.*, 'speaking intelligibly.' Their abodes in historical times were the central highlands, the Federal District, the States of Mexico, Puebla, and Morelos, and the territory of Tlaxcala, where they lived intermingled with fractions of the Otomi nation, with Mazauas, Matlatzincas, Popolocas, and other primitive nations. From that central home parts of the Mexican nation emigrated, in pre-historic times, to the Atlantic coast, reaching as far as Guatemala, San Salvador, and the coasts and islands of the great lake of Nicaragua. Those were the tribes particularly connected with the mythical name of Toltecs. To the Maya-speaking people of Guatemala these emigrants were known

[1] The letters A.M. attached to the name of authors signify American Methodist; G.M., German Methodist; M.N.C., Methodist of the New Connexion; P.M., Primitive Methodist; U.M., of the United Methodist Church; the undistinguished names are Wesleyan Methodist.

by the name of Yaqui, which seems to be but another name of the Toltecs, who were commonly designated by the Mexicans as the Tonatiuh iixco Yaque, 'those who went to the rising sun.' For all these tribes, undoubtedly, a long succession of ages of cultural development must be taken into account, since their civilization, at the time of the Conquest, might have equalled, at least in many respects, that of the ancient nations of the other side of the globe. Their religion had reached a correspondingly advanced stage of development, and was very elaborate, while their pantheon was unusually rich.

1. Religious ideas. — As with all the other nations of the world, the religious faith and the metaphysical ideas of the Mexicans had in part developed from attempts to grasp the connexion between the things of this world according to the principle of causality; in part they were the outcome of religious practice, and the crystallization of magic ceremonies, intended to produce certain effects by way of imitation. The great problems that presented themselves to the human mind because of the movement of the sun, the changes in the shape of the moon, and the varying location of the 'great star'—the morning star—have been treated by the Mexicans in a great number of mythical tales and mythical personifications.

The most prominent and the most widely worshipped Mexican god, of whom the largest number of tales and myths were reported, Quetzalcoatl, the 'feathered snake,' the creator of men, the wind-god of the later priestly school, was, in fact, nothing else than a mythical personification of the moon, who in her decrease travels to the east, *i.e.*, draws every day nearer to the sun, and finally dies away in the rays of the rising sun. It was believed that, when dying, this god, or his heart, was transformed into the morning star. The counterpart of this deity, Tezcatlipoca, the young warrior, who was regarded as the watching eye, the god who sees and punishes all kinds of sin, and the sorcerer who roams about in the night, is, in reality, the new, waxing moon who makes her appearance in the evening sky, and will travel on in the night, as the eye of the night. On the other hand, deities like Centeotl, the 'maize-god,' have developed from certain religious practices—*e.g.*, the placing of maize-stalks or young maize-ears in the houses, in order to get rich crops. Xipe Totec, the 'flayed,' the god who wears a human skin, the hide of a sacrificed man, has probably originated from well-known ceremonies celebrated in the beginning of the year in the time of sowing, in order to bring about the re-birth of vegetation. The two classes of deified beings met in the one great idea that the celestial powers, the sun, the moon, and the god of thunder and lightning, were at the same time the promoters of the growth and ripening of the fruit, and in the conviction that the new-born god (the rising sun) and the increasing agency (the waxing moon) were the causes of all birth and growth and of all that maintains and keeps up human life, and that they were the source of human life itself.

The spirits of the dead are to be added to these two classes — the ancestors, the founders of the tribe who had died in ancient times, and who had lived when the sun had not yet made its appearance in the sky. These deified ancestors were believed to awaken and to live in the night and, consequently, were identified with the stars. Xiuhtecutli, the god of fire, who had likewise existed in the 'time of darkness and night,' before the birth of the sun, and was, accordingly, named Ueueteotl, the 'old god,' became in some way the prototype of these ancestral gods.

2. Origin of the world.—The Mexicans believed that heaven, earth, and the sun had not been created at once, but that four ages of a somewhat imperfect creation had preceded the formation of the present world. The first of these pre-cosmic creations was named Ocelotonatiuh, 'jaguar-sun.' This was the sun of darkness, or sun of the earth, for the jaguar was considered to be the animal that swallowed the sun in time of eclipse, and, as the earth was the realm of darkness, the jaguar was identified with the earth. This first period came to an end by darkness, when the jaguars were eating men. The second period was called Ecatonatiuh, 'wind-sun.' This period came to an end by great revolving storms, and men were transformed into apes. The third period had the name Quiauhtonatiuh, 'rain-sun,' meaning 'fire-rain.' In this period fire rained from the sky, volcanic ashes and lapilli were strewn over the earth, and reddish lava-cliffs arose. Men were transformed into birds. The fourth period was called Atonatiuh, 'water-sun.' In this period a great deluge took place, men were transformed into fishes, and the sky fell down upon the earth. The fallen sky was raised by the joint action of the gods Quetzalcoatl and Tezcatlipoca, and the earth was revived. It was only then, in the year called *ce tochtli*, 'one rabbit,' that the present world was created. Its name is Olintonatiuh, or 'earthquake-sun,' because this present world is to be destroyed by earthquakes. One year after this creation, in the year *ome acatl*, 'two reed,' the god Mixcoatl, 'cloud-snake,' the god of the North—or Tezcatlipoca in the form of Mixcoatl—'drew fire out of the wooden sticks,' kindled fire by means of the fire-drill. Then men were created, and war was begun, in order that there might be human hearts at hand for nourishing the sun. The first who was killed in war, *i.e.*, was captured in war and offered on the sacrificial stone, was Xochiquetzal, the goddess of the moon, for it is the moon who dies every month in conjunction with the sun, and by her death gives life and strength to the rising sun.

Men being created, and war being commenced, there was opportunity for the creation of the sun. At the end of the first half of the first Mexican cycle of 52 years, in the year 'thirteen reed,' the sun was created.

The gods assembled in Teotiuacan, the ancient city of the sun, and took counsel, asking each other who should take charge of lighting the world. The first who offered himself was Tecciztecatl, the moon-god. Again the gods asked which other deity would take charge of lighting the world. As no one replied, the gods requested Nanauatzin, the 'bubonic,' the luetic god, to undertake it, and he consented. The gods kindled a great fire in the *teotexcalli*, the 'divine stove,' and Tecciztecatl tried first to throw himself into the fire, but he was afraid and drew back. Then Nanauatzin shut his eyes and threw himself at once into the fire, and after him Tecciztecatl did the same. This took place at midnight. Then the gods conjectured in what direction the sun was to rise. It was in the east, where the sun rose at day-break, followed by the moon. The chroniclers relate that originally the moon possessed the same splendour as the sun, but the gods struck her in the face with a rabbit, so that her splendour darkened, and now the figure of the rabbit is seen on the face of the moon. After having risen, the sun and the moon stood still for four days and four nights, whereupon the gods resolved to sacrifice themselves in order to give life to the sun. After the gods had killed themselves, the sun commenced to move, and ever since has made his regular courses, alternating with the moon.

3. Origin of men.—When heaven and earth were created, the gods took counsel and asked where to get beings to dwell on the earth. Then Xolotl, the dog who jumps down from the sky—the god who carries the setting sun to the under world—went to the kingdom of the dead to fetch a bone of the dead. When he had given his message to Mictlantecutli, the king of the dead, the latter asked him to move four times round the sepulchre in the stone-circle, blowing the conch. The god called upon the worms to make a hole in the shell, and thus he blew the conch. The king of the dead gave the bone to him, but ordered his vassals to follow him and to dig a pit in his way. There the god stumbled and fell, the bone slipped out of his hand, fell to the ground, and was broken in pieces. The god was much grieved, but he arose, picked up the fragments, and brought them to Tamoanchan, a region situated far in the west.

There the goddess Ciuacoatl or Quilaztli ground down the fragments on the grinding-stone, and put the pulverized material into the *chalchiuhapaztli*, the bowl hollowed out of a precious stone, and set with gems. On this pulverized material Quetzalcoatl sprinkled blood drawn by piercing his penis with a knife. In this way men were generated, and food was found for them in the same region of the west. It was the maize, whose place the black ant and the red ant showed to the god.

4. Heaven, earth and under world, and the abode of the dead.—The Mexicans were of opinion that from the earth (*tlalticpac*) upwards there were thirteen regions or heavenly spheres (*ilhuicatl*), and from the earth downwards there were nine regions or under worlds (*mictlan*). The second, third, and fourth of the heavenly spheres were the regions where the moon and the clouds, the stars and the sun moved, while the uppermost or thirteenth region was the abode of Ometecutli, Omeciuatl, or Tonacatecutli, Tonacaciuatl, the gods of generation. The second of the under-world regions was the Chicunauhapan, the 'nine streams,' the water that encircled the realm of the dead and was in a way identified with the ocean of the western region. The third under-world region was the *tepetl imonamiquian*, the gateway by which the sun entered the under-world region. The undermost region was the abode of Mictlantecutli and Mictecaciuatl, the lords of the dead. To this under-world region there went, however, only the men and the women who had died in their homes from sickness, injury, or the infirmities of age. Men who were drowned, struck by lightning, or carried away by malignant fever or contagious disease were believed to be taken by Tlaloc, the rain-god. Their corpses were not burned, but buried, blue colour—the colour of water and rain—having been put on their foreheads. They went to Tlalocan, the home of the rain-god, situated on a great mountain in the east, a paradise of vegetation, in order to serve him there. Men killed in war or sacrificed on the sacrificial stone and women who had died in childbed belonged to a third order, and went to heaven, to the house of the sun. The warriors went to the east, to receive the rising sun and to accompany him up to the zenith. The women had their dwelling in the west, in the region of the setting sun. In the morning they climbed up to the zenith, where, at noon, they received the sun from the hands of the warriors, and accompanied him on his downward course. At sunset they delivered the sun to the dwellers in the under-world region, for at night the sun illumines the under world, and the dead awaken and live.

5. Principal deities.—A detailed study of Mexican mythology and the character of the Mexican gods leads to the conclusion that the forefathers of the Mexicans worshipped the sun, the moon, the morning star, the hearth-fire, the maize-god, and the other deities of vegetation, the god who pours down the beneficial rain, and a host of *numina* and spirits who were believed to dwell in particular places, as mountains, caves, water-holes, etc. In the course of time those cosmic potencies assumed very different shapes in the mythopoetic imagination of the people, coalescing in part with a deified ancestor, or being merged in certain regional festivals, thus giving rise to certain well-defined divine personages, who in the different tribes, towns, and villages were acknowledged as the *altepeyollotli*, the 'heart (or living principle) of the town.'

Thus Uitzilopochtli, the war-god, the particular protector of the citizens of Mexico (Tenochtitlan), must originally have been the rising sun, or the morning star. His mother conceived him from a feather-ball coming down from the sky. Her other children, the Centzon Uitznaua, the 'four hundred Southerns' (the stars), and their elder sister Coyolxauhqui (the moon), seeing their mother pregnant, wished to kill her, but just at this moment Uitzilopochtli was born. Armed with shield and spear, he came forth from his mother, decapitated his elder sister Coyolxauhqui, and drove the 'four hundred Southerns' from the 'Snake-mountain' (the sky). The other war-god Camaxtli, or Mixcoatl, the god of the Tlaxcaltecs, the 'shooting god,' was probably a mythic conception of the morning star. Tlaloc was the rain- and thunder-god and the god of the mountains. He had his residence on the top of a mountain in the east, where he owned four chambers and four barrels, from which his servants, dwarf-gods, bailed out the water and poured it down on the earth. Stone images of this deity are to be found all over the country. Tezcatlipoca was the god of the Tezcocans and of the tribes dwelling on the slopes of the volcano. He was the sorcerer who roams about in the night, the god who sees and punishes sin, and the patron of the *telpochcalli*, the club-house of the young warriors; and certainly developed from the conception of the new, waxing moon. Xiuhtecutli, the 'lord of the turquoise,' or Ixcoçauhqui, the 'god with the yellow face,' the god of fire, was the tutelary deity of the citizens of Tlatelolco and their brethren on the western mountain slope, the Tepanecs of Tacuba and Coyouacan. Tonatiuh, the sun, and Metztli, or Tecciztecatl, the moon, had in ancient times been worshipped at Teotiuacan, north of the valley of Mexico, and two great pyramids dedicated to them are still to be seen in that place. The moon alone was the principal deity of the inhabitants of Xaltocan and of the province of Meztitlan, on the borders of the Huaxteca. Quetzalcoatl, the 'feathered snake,' the creator of human life, the wind-god, was another conception of the waning and resuscitating moon. He was the great god of the merchants of Cholula and all the Mexican commercial colonists, down to the provinces of Guatemala and San Salvador. Xipe Totec, 'our lord, the flayed,' the god of the sowing time, the god of vegetation, was generally worshipped in the whole country; but it seems that the Nauatl tribes on the borders of the State of Oaxaca, the inhabitants of Tehuacan, Cozcatlan, and Teotitlan del Camino were particularly addicted to his cult. He is also called god of the goldsmiths, because the goldsmiths, located in the town-quarter, or clan Yopico, regarded him as their tutelary deity. Xochipilli, the 'flower-prince,' the lord of the green maize, the god of food, had his worshippers all along the Atlantic slope. He was believed to be incorporated in the Quetzalcoxcoxtli, the wild fowl that chants in the morning. He had a brother called Macuilxochitl, 'Five flowers,' or Auiateotl, 'the god of voluptuousness,' who was the deity of pleasure, of music, dancing, gaming, and debauchery. Ome tochtli, 'two rabbits,' the pulque-god, the Mexican Bacchus, was the town-god of Tepoztlan, in the State of Morelos.

Female deities were Couatlicue, the mother of Uitzilopochtli, worshipped in Mexico City; Ciuacouatl, the female warrior, the goddess of Colhuacan; Itzpapalotl and Quilaztli, the earth-goddess and the fire-goddess of the towns of Quauhtitlan and Xochimilco; Teteo innan, the 'mother of the gods,' or Toci, 'our grandmother,' also called Tlazolteotl, the 'goddess of ordure,' or Tlaelquani, 'mire-eater' (*i.e.* sinner); she was generally worshipped as a harvest-goddess; Xochiquetzal, the goddess of flowers and of love, had her worshippers throughout the country, and a magnificent pyramid dedicated to her is still to be seen in Xochicalco, south of Cuernavaca. All these goddesses, without any doubt, were originally moon-goddesses, but developed into goddesses of fertility and generation, into earth-goddesses and patronesses of women's art. Chalchiuhtlicue, the 'goddess whose garments are precious stones,' was the impersonation of running water, brooks, and lakes; Uixtociuatl that of the salt water, and accordingly the patroness of the salt-makers. Centeotl, the maize-god, was represented either as a female or as a male deity, and was particularly related to the gods of generation, the authors of life.

6. Religious practices.—The Mexicans were penetrated by a feeling of absolute dependence on their gods. They regarded them as the givers of all things and as those who inflicted punishments upon them, and they were convinced that most of these punishments were brought down on them by their own sins. In order to obtain the favour of their gods or to appease their wrath, they used to address them with prayers, to present offerings to them, to humiliate themselves in their presence, and to torture themselves in their honour. In the work compiled by Bernardino de Sahagun, the original of which was written in Aztec, he has preserved many prayers directed to several gods, distinguished by a high and noble feeling, and by a wonderfully refined and poetic language, while another chapter of the same work contains twenty ancient and very curious songs, which they used to sing in honour of their gods at the different anniversary festivals (text, Germ. tr., and commentary in E. Seler, *Gesammelte Abhandlungen zur amerikan. Sprach- und Altertumskunde*, Berlin, 1902–08, ii. 959–1107).

The offerings which the Mexicans were accustomed to bring to their gods consisted of food and garments, flowers and green twigs (*acxoyatl*) to adorn their altars, copal, rubber, and different kinds of aromatic herbs to burn, and piles of wood to heap up and kindle on the top of their temple-pyramids. They humiliated themselves in the presence of their gods by eating earth (*tlalqualiztli*), *i.e.*, by touching the earth with the finger and putting it to the mouth. When they requested something from their gods, and before every festival dedicated to them, they fasted, eating only once in the day, avoided red pepper sauce and every kind of spices, abstained from sexual intercourse, and did not wash their heads. When the request which they had to make was a very earnest one, they tortured themselves by piercing their tongues, or the margin of their ears, sometimes drawing stalks or threads through the hole made in the tongue, and offering the blood issuing from their wounds, collecting it on agave leaves. If they had committed a sin such as intercourse with the wife of another man, and wished to atone for it, they went to the priests of the goddess Tlaçolteotl and made confession, and the priests, after having heard the confession, imposed some penance—*e.g.*, to go naked in the night to some shrines of the 'women-goddesses' (*ciuateteó*), there to deposit garments made of the common bark-paper. By performing this penance they were believed not only to have got rid of the sin committed, but also of the punishment for it enjoined by the law. A Mexican religious practice that excited the curiosity and even the amazement of the Christian priests was the so-called 'eating of the god' (*teoqualiztli*). At a certain festival a number of devotees assembled, and, after having made an image of the god from the paste obtained by grinding certain seeds, the high priest sacrificed the image and cut it into pieces. The assembled persons ate the pieces, and those who had partaken were obliged to pay for a year all expenses for the cult of the god in question.

Finally, the Mexicans felt compelled to bring living beings as an offering to their gods. They sacrificed to the fire-god by casting into the fire all kinds of animals that could be found in the fields, and they also offered human prisoners in the same way. The warriors who had captured them brought them, their limbs tied together, and hanging on a pole, like captured game, for the fire-god was the god of war and of the chase. The Mexicans killed quails by decapitating them, as an offering to the sun and other deities such as Uitzilopochtli, for the quail was the spotted bird, the image of the starry sky.

They fastened prisoners with extended arms and legs to a wooden frame, and shot them with arrows. This was a sacrifice for the earth-goddess, and was intended to fertilize the earth. There is no doubt that it was originally meant as an imitation of the sexual act. They decapitated a woman as an image of the 'mother of the gods'—the moon-goddess, the harvest-god—and flayed her, for the old moon, the waning moon, is cut into pieces, and her splendour is stripped off. Yet she would revive, and therefore the flayed skin of the victim was donned by a man who, in the following ceremonies of the feast, represented the goddess.

The Mexicans practised to a terrible extent the offering of human hearts, torn out of the bodies of living men. They used for that purpose a sacrificial stone of a rounded pyramidal shape. The victim was thrown backwards on the top of it, his extended arms and legs were held by four men, and the sacrificer, armed with a big stone knife, made a broad cut across the breast, under the ribs, and, putting in his hand, tore out the heart. The heart itself was presented to the sun, and with the blood they moistened the mouth of the idols, while the heads of the sacrificed were put in rows on poles. The body was delivered to the man who had captured the prisoner and had presented it as a sacrifice. He cooked the flesh with maize, and made a feast of it with his relatives and friends. With the thigh-bone of the dead man he made a bundle that was hung up on a high pole in the middle of the house-courtyard. This was a token of the valour of the owner, and probably, at the same time, a fetish for luck and protection.

7. Annual festivities.—The Mexicans divided the year into eighteen sections of twenty days each and five remaining days. On each of these twentieths they had a feast with many elaborate ceremonies, dedicated successively to various special deities, all these feasts being intimately connected with the exigencies of the different sections of the year with regard to the culture of the soil, sowing, and harvesting, and with the changing aspects that in the different years those important affairs presented to the anxious eye of the labourer. They commenced with the ceremonies early in the year—in the time of our February. At that time, in the houses and on sacred spots—mountains, caves, water-holes, and localities considered as the abodes of the rain-gods—they set up poles to which papers painted with the emblems of the *numina* of these localities were attached; and they carried children, who were bought from their parents, to the same localities and sacrificed them to the rain-gods, in order that these divinities might grant rain in sufficient quantity for the crops of the new year.

In the second twentieth they celebrated a great feast to Xipe Totec, the god of vegetation, a form of the ancient moon-god. This was just before sowing, and it seemed to those ancient philosophers to be necessary to fertilize the earth, that she might receive the germ and bring forth the crops. For this important business a sacrifice of value and a vigorous man were required.

They took a prisoner of war, the most gallant whom they had at hand, and with him performed a ceremony that was in a way a testing. He was fastened by a rope to the central hole of a stone of flat cylindrical shape, the so-called *temalacatl* (spinning wheel of stone). There he had to fight with four other men until he was exhausted, after which they bound him, with extended arms and legs (*mamaçouhticac*), to a wooden frame, where he was shot with arrows, so that the blood might drop on the earth and fertilize it. This was the original form of the ceremony, as it is seen in the pictographs, and as it was performed in certain ancient towns up to the time of the conquest. In Mexico City, however, when the prisoner was exhausted and no longer able to defend himself, he was sacrificed in the regular way, by cutting the breast and tearing out the heart; and many prisoners were sacrificed in the same way after him. The bodies of the sacrificed were skinned, and the skins donned by certain men who represented the god in the following ceremonies, to show by this garb that the earth-god had put on a new cloak. From this custom this second annual feast was called Tlacaxipeualiztli, 'flaying men.' The feast concluded with a great ceremonial dance, where priests disguised as maize-ears, maize-stalks, and other vegetables, or as beings connected with the fields, exhibited to the people the abundance of food which the new year was expected to bring.

In the third and fourth twentieths, called Toçoztli, 'awakening,' the temples and shrines were adorned with green stalks, and the ears destined for sowing were brought to the temple of the maize-goddess to be consecrated. The fifth feast, called Toxcatl, fell at the time when the sun, shifting to the north, came to the zenith. This was regarded as the real feast of the new year, and the present writer has shown, in his explanation of the Humboldt Codices, that the day-names by which the Mexicans designated the different years correspond to the days with which the feast Toxcatl began. In this feast a living image of the god Tezcatlipoca, *i.e.*, a prisoner of war who in the disguise of this god had represented him all the year round, was sacrificed, and immediately replaced by another prisoner, who, invested with the paraphernalia of the god, had to represent him in the new year. The sixth twentieth, the time when the rainy season set in, was celebrated by a general and severe fasting of all the priests of all the temples, including the little boys in the priestly schools. The Mexicans ate at this feast a certain meal prepared with maize in grain and beans, called *etzalli*, whence it bears the name Etzalqualiztli, the 'eating of the meal of maize and beans.' In the seventh and eighth twentieths the sprouting of the young maize-ears was celebrated by a ceremonial dance of the kings and rulers of the town, and a general feeding of the people, the feast being called Tecuilhuitl, the 'feast of the kings.' The ninth and tenth twentieths were called Tlaxochimaco and Xocotl uetzi, 'when the Xocotl comes down (or is born),' or Miccailhuitl, the 'feast of the dead.' At these festivals living prisoners were thrown into the fire as a sacrifice to the god of fire, and the image of Xocotl or Otontecutli, the 'god of the Otomi,' the 'soul of the dead warrior,' having the shape of a bird, a butterfly, or of a mummy packet, was placed on the top of a high pole, and brought down by the male youth, vying with each other in climbing to the top.

The eleventh twentieth, called Ochpaniztli, 'sweeping the roads,' was the harvest feast, and at the same time a great expiation ceremony, by which evil was taken out of the town.

A woman representing Teteo innan, the 'mother of the gods,' having been decapitated at midnight and flayed, a priest put on the skin and represented the goddess in the following ceremonies. From a portion of the skin of the thigh, a mask was made and worn by the son of the 'mother of the gods,' Centeotl-itztlacoliuhqui, the maize-god, the 'curved obsidian knife,' who is described as the god of cold and punishment, and is, in fact, only another form of the morning star, the son of the moon-goddess. The principal ceremony consisted in a ceremonial impregnation of the goddess by Uitzilopochtli, and, on the way to meet the god, Teteo innan was accompanied by warriors and by phallic deities called Cuexteca (men of the province of the Huaxteca). Ceremonial dances followed, where Teteo innan was replaced by the maize-goddess. At the end of the feast warriors, racing with each other, took the mask out of the town, and buried it somewhere in the territory of their enemies. The goddess herself, *i.e.*, the priest wearing the skin of the victim, was likewise driven out of the town, and the skin was hung up, beyond the boundaries of the town, on a frame-work dedicated to Teteo innan, being her sanctuary.

In the twelfth twentieth, called Teotleco, the Mexicans celebrated the return of their gods, *i.e.*, of the fire-gods, who were reputed to have gone out of the country during the rainy season. The feast may also be called the 'birthday of Uitzilopochtli.' It concluded with another fire-ceremony, in which living prisoners were thrown into the flames. The thirteenth feast, called Tepeilhuitl, the 'feast of the mountains,' was another harvest feast, when the pulque-gods—the gods of fecundity—were honoured by sacrifices, and offerings were brought to the rain-gods, *i.e.*, to the gods of the mountains. The fourteenth feast, called Quecholli, was dedicated to Mixcoatl, the god of hunting and war, and was celebrated by a great ceremonial hunting. Arrows and other weapons were made.

The fifteenth feast, called Panquetzaliztli, 'raising the banners,' was the great feast of the god Uitzilopochtli, when the myth of the birth of this god and the victory which he obtained over his brethren, the Centzon Uitznaua (the stars), were dramatically represented by a combat between the warriors and the prisoners designated for sacrifice. The fire-snake, the weapon with which Uitzilopochtli had killed his sister Coyolxauhqui, came down from the upper platform of the temple to burn the offerings heaped up on the great cylindrical stone at the foot of the staircase leading up to the platform. The sixteenth feast, Atemoztli, was dedicated to the rain-gods. The seventeenth, Tititl, was a commemoration feast of the dead, at which the *ciuateteô*, the 'women-goddesses,' *i.e.*, the deified women, the spirits of the women who died in child-bed, and their patroness Ilamatecutli, the old goddess, the goddess of fire, played an important part. The eighteenth and last feast was called Izcalli, 'increasing,' and was dedicated to Xiuhtecutli, the god of fire, who was honoured by offerings of all kinds of animals thrown into the flames. The god was represented in this feast by two different figures—at one time as a god of vegetation, clothed in green quetzal-feathers and wearing a mask of turquoises and green stones, and at another time as the god of the burning fire, clothed in feathers of the red macaw and wearing a mask of red and black stones. The five last days of the year, called *nemontemi*, were deemed unlucky. No feast was celebrated on them, nor any business of importance taken in hand.

Other ceremonies were performed to the deities who were believed to rule certain days, according to the name of the day in question, these names being composed of one of the numbers one to thirteen and of one of the twenty day-signs. As these names, in the different years, were not assigned to a fixed date—the initial days of the years bearing different names—the feasts of the rulers of the days were denominated 'movable feasts.'

8. Priests.—For the performance of all these ceremonies, filling out, in the true sense of the word, nearly the whole year, and for the regular service of the different gods, many priests were employed, called *tlamacazquê*, 'servants.' They were divided into different classes, such as the *tlenamacaque*, 'incense-burners,' the *teouaquê*, 'guardians of the idols,' the *quaquacuiltin*, 'old priests,' and the *ometochtzin*, 'pulque priests,' who were at the same time the musicians and the singers. At the head of all these priests there were in Mexico City two high priests, called Quetzalcoatl Totec tlamacazqui and Quetzalcoatl Tlaloc tlamacazqui, *i.e.*, the special priests of the two great gods, Uitzilopochtli and the rain-god

Tlaloc, whose sanctuaries were situated close to one another on the top of the principal pyramid.

9. **General characteristics.**—In spite of their adherence to bloody sacrificial rites, the Mexicans were sober, honest people, of tender susceptibility, governed by laws of a high moral standard, respecting the rights of property, detesting lying and falsehood, cheerful with their friends, brave in war, and unflinchingly obedient to their native kings. Their governors and princes exercised arbitrary power, but were restrained by unwritten laws, handed down from their forefathers, and by public opinion. Their punishments were severe, but never cruel. Vices such as drunkenness and untruthfulness arose with the misery and slavery of the Spanish times. In material culture, too, the Mexicans were nearly equal to their conquerors. Spanish government did not add very much to their cultural standard, and to-day the Indians are, if not the most refined, certainly the most honest, component of the population of the Mexican territory.

LITERATURE.—B. de Sahagun, *Hist. general de las cosas de Nueva España*, Mexico, 1829; T. de Benavente Motolinia, *Memoriales* (= L. G. Pimentel, *Documentos históricos de Méjico*, i.), do. 1903; D. Duran, *Hist. de las Indias de Nueva España*, do. 1867; E. Seler, *Altmexikan. Studien* (*Veröffentlichungen aus dem königl. Museum für Völkerkunde*, i. [1888], vi. [1899]), *Codex Borgia*, 2 vols., Berlin, 1904–06, *Gesammelte Abhandlungen zur amerikan. Sprach- und Altertumskunde*, 3 vols., do. 1902–08; T. A. Joyce, *Mexican Archæology*, London, 1914; W. Lehmann, 'Traditions des anciens Mexicains,' *Journ. de la Soc. des Américanistes de Paris*, new ser., iii. [1906].

EDUARD SELER.

MEXICANS (Modern). —An intimate knowledge of the religion of the ancient peoples of Mexico is necessary in order to understand the religious life of the present native population of the country. On first acquaintance with the people an impression is given that the Roman Catholic religion is everywhere present, yet many of the pre-Columbian religious ideas remain. Too much cannot be said of the energies and the fervour of the Roman Catholic priesthood in their attempts to Christianize the natives. The originality of their methods and their enthusiasm for the work resulted in a marked success. They learned the native languages, and collected much data upon the customs and religion of the people, and to these early accounts we owe practically all our knowledge of the pre-Columbian life.

The clergy soon noted the ability of the people to read in pictures, and this was turned to account in their teaching of the Roman Catholic Catechism. Figures were drawn on large pieces of cloth representing most ingeniously, in a series of pictures, the various teachings of the Church. These pictures were also made in books, some of which, according to N. Leon (*Am. Anth.*, new ser., ii. [1900] 726), are still used among the Mazahuas of Michoacan. A more ambitious attempt was made by the priests to teach the natives the Latin words of the Lord's Prayer and other Articles of the Church. A native monosyllabic word was selected, the sound of which was similar to a syllable of the Latin word, and this word was represented by a picture. The first syllable, *pa*, of *pater*, was shown by a picture of a flag, which in Nahuatl was *pantli*, and the second syllable, *ter*, was represented by a drawing of a stone, *tetl* in Nahuatl. In this way, picture by picture, the native word was known, and each word recalled a similar word or syllable in the Latin.

J. de Torquemada tells us (*Monarquia Indiana*, Madrid, 1723, xv.) that the Christian priests illustrated the vicissitudes and the instability of life by pictures representing a great expanse of water on which were vessels manned by sailors. On one ship Indian men and women were praying, with garlands of roses in their hands, and they went to heaven accompanied by angels, while on another vessel the Indians were shown fighting with one another, ogling women, becoming intoxicated, and receiving glasses of wine from devils. According to J. de Acosta's statement (*The Natural and Moral Hist. of the Indies*, ed. C. R. Markham, London, 1880, bk. vi. ch. vii.), in illustrating the doctrine of the Trinity, God was pictured with three carved heads, and St. Peter and St. Paul were drawn as two carved heads with keys and sword. As Sapper remarks:

> 'It is easy to suppose that this sort of picture must have been absolutely incomprehensible to an Indian, but there is little doubt that the effect of these pictures was extremely favourable to the spread of Christianity' (*Globus*, lxxx. 126).

The Spanish *padres* were not content with these mnemonic and symbolic methods of teaching the Christian religion, but soon learned the languages of the country, translated the Catechism into the various dialects, and preached in the native tongues. Priests taught the Indians how to record their languages phonetically by the use of the Spanish characters, and from the early days of the Conquest there was a constantly increasing amount of printed and MS material in the languages of the different peoples of Spanish America.

With a knowledge of the native languages, together with the names and attributes of the various gods, the Spanish priests had a wonderful asset in their teaching, and they used their knowledge to good effect. Their explanation of the native pantheon was an earnest attempt to incorporate it, as much as possible, into their own religion, and, accordingly, we find many of the ancient myths turned into a new setting, with the saints now figuring as the actors in the ancient tales. It is difficult to determine how much of this transformation was due to the initiative of the priests of the new faith, and how much may be attributed to the Indians' own attempts to reconcile their old religion with the new. Knowing the tendency of primitive man to explain everything in terms of his own mental fabric, we may suppose that many of the strange metamorphoses which came about were the natural result of implanting ideas upon an older foundation, but a result not recognized or authorized by the Church. In many cases the gods of the ancient religion were incorporated into the new, as when the three most important gods were sometimes turned into the Trinity, while the lesser gods became the saints of the Church. The evil one already had a counterpart in the Mexican religion; among the Mayas he was Kisin, the earthquake.

The present population of Mexico may be divided, for the purposes of this article, into four classes as regards their religion: (1) those of Spanish descent who are true Roman Catholics; (2) those of mixed descent who are nominally Roman Catholics, but still retain some of the ancient pre-Columbian religious ideas; (3) those of mixed blood who are fundamentally pagans from the Christian point of view, with religious rites coloured by Roman Catholic teaching; and (4) those who show no trace of the Roman Catholic teaching, and still continue to practise the ancient religion. It is, of course, impossible to draw a hard and fast line between any two of these classes; the two middle divisions are differentiated only by the degree in which the Christian or the native religion predominates.

Class I.—In the large cities and towns there is a numerous population of Spanish-speaking people who have little or no Indian blood, and these carry out the rites and ceremonies of the Roman Catholic Church as practised in Spain. The festivals of the Church are celebrated with great pomp and ceremony. An interesting survival of the teaching of the early Franciscans is seen in the *Nacimientos*, the *Pastorales*, and the Mystery Plays performed at Corpus Christi and at other times. Soon after the Conquest the sacred dramas, so popular in Spain at that time, were introduced into Mexico, and were regarded as an important means of propaganda.

Class 2.—The casual observer seldom sees any of the native element among the peoples who have been placed in this division, and he considers the population good Roman Catholics. It is only after close intimacy extended over a considerable period of time, together with a knowledge of the nature of the native practices, that one gradually finds that the underlying principles of the religion are based on the native ideas rather than upon the Christian faith. The veneer of Roman Catholicism is removed, and the native religion stands out clearly. The greater part of the population of Mexico are of mixed blood, with a strong preponderance of the Indian over the Spanish strain. This type of native is present even in the large cities and towns, where a great proportion of the people fall into Class 2, whose religion is Roman Catholic, with an undercurrent of the old ideas. The *gente* of Mexico City, *e.g.*, are of this class.

Holy Week throughout Mexico is a time of great religious enthusiasm. In addition to the Passion Plays which have already been mentioned, there is a constant round of festivals, many of which are strongly flavoured by the native elements. The season of prayer and fasting appeals to the natives, some of whom wear the crown of thorns and flagellate themselves. From Holy Thursday until the Gloria of Saturday the bells of the churches are silent, and the *matracas*, or rattles, take their place. Each child and adult has a rattle, and the streets are full of vendors, each selling some sort of noisy toys. On the *Sabado de Gloria* new fire is struck from the blessed flint. The burning of Judas is a common sight in every Mexican town; figures of Judas, representing him as a man or woman, a negro, a soldier or a knave, a devil or a gentleman, are burned in every village plaza. Many of these figures contain jars filled with various objects, and, when the container is broken, the contents fall into the struggling crowd. Firecrackers and rockets often form the hands and feet of these Judas figures. It is a time of much merriment.

In Mexico City on *Viérnes de Dolores*, the eve of Palm Sunday, there is a long procession of decorated boats in the Viga Canal; and flowers, small shrines, and altars are displayed everywhere, the native love of flowers and their varied use of them as decoration being seen at this time at its best. These religious festivals play a very important part in the life of the people.

The custom of erecting wooden crosses along the roads and trails is very common in Mexico. The traveller, in passing one of these crosses for the first time, usually deposits a stone or a flower before it.

It is on the magical side of the religion that we find the greatest number of survivals at the present time. Symbolic and contagious magic abounds among all strata of the population. Some of their ideas are, of course, derived from the Spanish element, but the greater number are purely native. Hypnotic suggestion is the important feature in all the ceremonies which deal with healing the sick. The air is full of evil spirits, which linger round the entrances of the villages, and precautions must be taken to placate or outwit them.

Class 3.—This class is represented in the small *pueblos* in the country districts, where the headman of the village performs the offices of the Church, except at infrequent intervals when the priest of the district makes his visit to celebrate Mass and to perform marriages and baptisms. The native religious ideas are much in evidence, for the visits of a priest of the Church are often too infrequent to make much headway against the presence of the strong native religious element. This cannot be stamped out among the people, and it remains a sturdy growth unless persistent and energetic efforts are made to counteract its influence by Christian teaching. It is among people of this class that the blending of pre-Columbian and Christian ideas may best be studied.

The native elements come to the front especially in connexion with agriculture and the burial of the dead. Incense is burned and offerings are made to the gods of fertility at the time of sowing; other gifts are presented to the gods of rain; in some cases offerings are given to the wind-gods when the burning of the brush of the maize-field is undertaken; and abstention from sexual intercourse before the planting is another of the survivals. Among the Otomi an idol is buried in the maize-field, another is kept in the domestic house, and a third in the granary. The hunter may burn incense for a successful hunt, the traveller for a prosperous journey. Every house has its *santo*, or saint, often the crudest kind of picture or image, and the firstfruits of the harvest are usually placed before this shrine; in time of sickness and death many offerings are made and incense is burned. It is the nature of the gifts and the spirit in which they are made, rather than the act itself, that show the pre-Christian ideas.

In many of the prayers the native element is seen. Sapper tells (*Das nördl. Mittel-Amerika*, p. 270) of the Kekchi praying, 'Thou art my mother, thou art my father,' a form common in the *Popol Vuh* (*q.v.*). The Indian origin of many of the prayers is seen in the poetical form, the parallelisms, the antitheses, and the repetitions of single words and phrases. Seler tells of a stone idol discovered in a cave in the State of Puebla before which offerings of flowers, eggs, and wax candles were found. In another case the visiting *padre* saw, to his indignation, a stone idol occupying the place of honour beside the crucifix, on the altar of the village church. In a cave in Oaxaca a pottery incense pan and two turkey feathers were discovered, the feathers having undoubtedly been used in connexion with the sacrifice of human blood, so common a part of the religious ritual of the ancient Mexicans. These definite examples will show the hold which the older ideas have upon the people, who are nominally good Roman Catholics.

Class 4.—The number of individuals who have been placed in this division is comparatively small, and, as might be expected, they are found only in the most unsettled and inaccessible portions of the country. They show practically no influence from the outside world in their customs, their languages, or their religion. Spanish is seldom understood, and the native languages show little change from those portions which were recorded by the early Spanish conquerors. It is among these people that one can obtain a clear picture of the pre-Columbian aborigines. The polytheistic ideas are still maintained, and many of the gods now worshipped may be identified with the ancient deities of the people —Sakaimoka of the Huichols, *e.g.*, is recognized as the old rain-god, Tlaloc. It is seldom that the ancient gods of the sun, the moon, the morning star, and other planets can be noted in the present pantheon, although among the Seri of Lower California the sun and moon find a place among the gods, and among the Tarahumare there is a 'father-sun' and 'mother-moon.' Among the present-day Mayas the sun and moon are servants of the gods.

Worship by means of prayer, divination, and sacrifice takes many different forms. Human sacrifice has been abolished, although there are a few sporadic cases where it has been reported within the last century. Blood sacrifice is not uncommon among people of this class, the ear and other parts of the body being cut with a stone knife, and the blood allowed to drop upon the idols. Offerings of food and drink now form the main portion of the religious practices of the population, although burning of copal or other incense to the gods is also very common. Compulsory intoxication —a common feature of the ancient religion—is still carried out by means of the *pulque* of the Mexicans, the *hikuli* of the Huichols, the *tesvino* of the Tarahumare, and the *balche* of the Lacandones. Divination is practised in many forms, and among many peoples there is a class of soothsayers who look into the future by means of the movements of sacrificed animals, the smoke of the incense, the crystal, the image on the surface of a basin of water, and many other ways. The prayers of the Cora, collected and translated by Preuss (*Die Nayarit-Expedition*), furnish an excellent criterion of the native point of view towards the gods and religion in general. The dances of the people are often held for magical purposes. Among the Tarahumare, *e.g.*, the dance is a prayer, a petition for prosperity for the harvest, or for health and freedom from ill-fortune.

The idea of renovation, the renewal of the incense-burners and the cleansing of the houses and of the places of worship at certain times of the year, is an ancient practice. Among the Lacandones, at the main ceremony of the year, when the firstfruits are offered, the entire collection of incense-burners is renewed. The old ones are 'dead,' and new ones are made to take their place. Priests no longer form a distinct class by themselves in Mexico, but the head-man of the village or the head of the family now performs the priestly functions, and among some of the tribes the class of *shamans* still remains. It is claimed that one-fourth of the Huichols (*q.v.*) of Northern Mexico are *shamans*; the name of the tribe signifies 'the doctors or healers.' It is they who have the power to look into the future and who understand and interpret the will of the gods. Religious temples, so common a feature of the pre-Columbian culture, no longer play a part in the religious life, though the Lacandones still make pilgrimages to the ruined structures where they believe their gods reside, carrying with them incense-burners and other offerings. The religious practices are usually carried on either in the domestic habitations or in a house set apart for the purpose, this house being called *topina*, 'the house of all,' among the Huichols. Women are usually excluded from these religious places, except at the termination of the worship, when general feasting takes place, and the offerings, previously made to the gods, are consumed by the worshippers. Perhaps the best example of a people who have had no contact with Spanish ideas are the Lacandones, who live in the State of Chiapas on a tributary of the Usumacinta River, which forms a portion of the boundary between Mexico and Guatemala. The early efforts of the Spanish to Christianize these people met with failure, and they have remained undisturbed for three hundred years. The customs, and especially the religion, of this people are important as an aid in understanding much of the life of the early Maya tribes, and many of the ceremonies are counterparts of those represented in the pre-Columbian MSS.

A geographical survey of the principal religions of the native Mexicans shows an interesting change from north to south. From the religious point of view, the ideas of the tribes of Sonora and Chihuahua are directly associated with those of the natives of the south-western portion of the United States: the religion of the Puebloan peoples and of the Navahos and Apaches shows a striking similarity to the religious ideas of the Huichols, the Cora, and other peoples of Northern Mexico. The rain and the importance of rain are the prime factors in the religion of all these peoples. The symbolism of the Huichols centres in the phenomena of nature. In Central and Southern Mexico the religious ideas of the present native population show a great number of survivals of the ancient religion of the formerly highly cultured peoples belonging to the Nahua, the Maya, and kindred civilizations.

LITERATURE.—D. G. Brinton, 'Das Heidentum im christlichen Yukatan,' *Globus*, lix. [1891] 97–100; M. R. Cole, 'Los Pastores, a Mexican Play of the Nativity,' *Memoirs of the Amer. Folk-lore Soc.* ix. [1907] 1–234; C. Lumholtz, 'Symbolism of the Huichol Indians,' *Memoirs of the Amer. Mus. of Nat. Hist.* iii. [1900] 1–128, *Unknown Mexico*, New York, 1903, *New Trails in Mexico*, do. 1912; K. T. Preuss, 'Parallelen zwischen den alten Mexikanern und den heutigen Huicholindianern,' *Globus*, lxxx. [1901] 314 f., *Die Nayarit-Expedition*, Leipzig, 1912; K. Sapper, *Das nördliche Mittel-Amerika*, Brunswick, 1897, 'Ein Bilderkatechismus der Mazahua in Mexico,' *Globus*, lxxx. 125 f.; E. Seler, 'Götzendienerei unter den heutigen Indianern Mexicos,' *Globus*, lxix. [1896] 367–370 (=*Gesammelte Abhandlungen zur amer. Sprach- und Alterthumskunde*, Berlin, 1902–08, ii. 87–93); O. Stoll, *Suggestion und Hypnotismus in der Völkerpsychologie*, Leipzig, 1894; A. M. Tozzer, *A Comparative Study of the Mayas and the Lacandones*, New York, 1907.

A. M. TOZZER.

MICHAELMAS.—I. The origin of the festival and the Michael churches in Italy.—The *Martiloge in Englysshe*, translated by Richard Whytford of Syon monastery and printed by Wynkyn de Worde in 1526, records the Roman and Sarum tradition of the origin of the festival:

'The xxix day of September. In the moũt of gargane the reuerend memory of saynt Mychaell the archaũgell where a chirche of hym is cōsecrate that is but of poore buyldyng yet notw^t^standyng it is adourned w^t^ many grete vertues' (Henry Bradshaw Society, iii. [1891] 153).

The Sarum Missal in the calendar has: '3 kl. Oct. Michaelis archangeli,' and in the text: 'Michaelis archangeli' (*Miss. ad usum . . . Sarum*, Burntisland, 1861–83, pp. 25^{xx}, 918). The calendar of the Westminster Missal of 1362–86 has: 'iii kl. Oct. Sancti Michaelis archangeli' (H. Bradshaw Soc. i. [1891] p. xiii). The Missal of Robert of Jumièges, an English Service-Book written, probably at Winchester, between the years 1008 and 1023, has in the *Kalendarium*: 'iii. Kl. Oct. Sci. Michahelis archangeli.' The rubric in the text reads: 'iii Kal. Oct. Dedicatio Basilicae Sancti Michahelis Archangeli' (H. Bradshaw Soc. xi. [1896] 17, 215). This agrees with the title in the Leofric Missal (A), a French MS of the first half of the 10th cent.: 'iii. Kal. Oct. Dedicatio basilicae sancti Michahelis archangeli' (*Leofric Missal*, ed. F. E. Warren, Oxford, 1883, p. 162). The *Kalendarium* of the Leofric Missal (B), a Glastonbury MS of the latter part of the 10th cent., has: 'iii. Kl. Oct. Sci. Michahelis archangeli' (*ib.* p. 31). The Leofric Missal (A) is a Gregorian Sacramentary, and the title is based upon that in the Codex Vaticanus (ii.) published by Muratori: 'iii Kalendas Octobris id est xxix Die mensis Septembris. Dedicatio Basilicae Sancti Angeli' (L. A. Muratori, *Liturgia Romana Vetus*, Venice, 1748, vol. ii. col. 125). This is evidence of the 9th century.

The earlier Gelasian Sacramentaries carry the evidence back to the 7th century. The Vatican MS of the 7th or early 8th cent. has 'Orationes in Sancti Archangeli Michaelis.' The Rheinau MS and the S. Gall MS, of the 8th or early 9th cent., have the title: 'Dedicatio Basilicae Angeli Michaelis' (H. A. Wilson, *The Gelasian Sacramentary*, Oxford, 1894, p. 200).

The rubric in the Leonian Sacramentary throws still further light on the origin of the festival. It stands alone in assigning it to 30th Sept. and not 29th Sept., but it adds a note of locality which differs from that of the later Roman tradition: 'Prīd. Kāl. Oct. N̄ Basilicae Angeli in Salaria' (C. L. Feltoe, *Sacramentarium Leonianum*, Cambridge, 1896, p. 106). Feltoe refers to a 9th cent. MS at Padua, which reads: '29 Sept. Dedic. basil. S. angeli Michahelis via Salaria' (*ib.* p. 203). Martin Rule, in his 'Analytical Study of the Leonian Sacramentary' (*JThSt* ix. [1908] 515 ff., x. [1908] 54 ff.), traces the materials of this Verona MS of the 7th cent. to three collections made during the pontificates of Leo I. (440–461), Hilarus (461–468), and Simplicius (468–483). This carries the evidence of the rubric to the 5th century.

The festival is, therefore, in its origin the dedication festival of a church. The evidence is not confined to the liturgical books of the Roman rite. The early Mozarabic rite is represented in a MS of the 11th cent. at Paris (Bibl. Nat. nov. acq. lat. 2171). In a short treatise, *Adnuntiationes Festivitatum*, the festival is announced thus: 'Adveniente diae il. festivitas erit dedicatio sancti Micahelis archangeli vel sociorum eius' (MS 2171, p. 25). And in the *Martirum Legium*, a calendar in the same MS under Sept. 29, is: 'iii. (Kal. Oct.) dedicatio sancti Micahelis arcangeli' (G. Morin, 'Liber Comicus,' *Anecdota Maredsolana*, i. [1893] 392, 402). A contemporary MS from the same Spanish monastery of Silos in Old Castile (Brit. Mus. Add. MS 30851) has two hymns: 'in diem Sancti Micaeli Arcangeli,' where reference is made to the 'socii.' The first hymn has the line: 'ut glorietur in deo cum consortes socios'; and the second: 'Urielo Gabrielo Rafaelo socius' (*Mozarabic Psalter*, H. Bradshaw Soc. xxx. [1905] 254, 256). The Ambrosian rite in the 12th cent. refers to the 'dedicatio in monte Gargano.' The *Kalendarium* has: 'iii. k. Oct. s. Michaelis in monte Gargano,' and the *ordo pro denariorum divisione*: 'dedicatio s. Michaelis in monte Gargano' (Beroldus, ed. M. Magistretti, Milan, 1894, pp. 11, 17).

i. *The Castello S Angelo at Rome.*—Quentin has sifted the further evidence of the Martyrologies. The earliest entry is that of the Martyrology of Bede: 'iii. Kl. Oct. Dedicatio ecclesiae sancti angeli Michaelis.' This is modified by the Mâcon MSS: 'Romae, dedicatio basilicae sancti angeli'; by the Clermont MS: 'Romae, dedicatio basilicae sancti Mikaelis archangeli'; and by the Bologna MS with the insertion of the words 'miliario sexto' between 'Romae' and 'dedicatio.' The earliest evidence supports that of the Leonian Sacramentary, and points to the dedication of a church at the sixth mile-stone on the Via Salaria. The MSS of Toul and Remiremont read: 'In Monte Gargano, dedicatio basilicae sancti Michaelis archangeli.' This is the source of the entry in the Martyrology of Ado, archbishop of Vienne, *c.* 870; but he adds:

> 'Sed non multo post, Romae, venerabilis etiam Bonifatius pontifex ecclesiam sancti Michaelis nomine constructam dedicavit, in summitate circi, criptatim miro opere altissime porrectam. Unde et isdem locus, in summitate sui continens ecclesiam, inter nubes situs vocatur' (Quentin, *Les Martyrologes historiques*, p. 561).

The entry in the Martyrology of Ado is the most ancient testimony to the consecration of the tomb of Hadrian to St. Michael. A century later Liutprand of Cremona witnesses to this church on the top of the Castel S. Angelo:

> 'Munitio vero ipsa . . . tantae altitudinis est, ut ecclesia quae in eius vertice videtur, in honore summi et caelestis miliciae principis archangeli Michaelis fabricata, dicatur sancti Angeli ecclesia usque ad caelos' (*ib.* p. 561).

Baronius also identified the Church of St. Michael 'inter nubes' with the Castle of S. Angelo, assigning its dedication to Boniface III. (606) or Boniface IV. (607–614), in memory of the staying of the plague under Gregory the Great (C. Baronius, *Martyrologium Romanum*, Venice, 1602, p. 544).

ii. *The church on the Via Salaria.*—The dedication festival of Sept. 29 would seem to have three steps in historical progress. The earliest has reference to the church on the Via Salaria, the second to the Apulian church on Monte Gargano, the third to the church on the Castel S. Angelo. The sixth mile-stone on the Via Salaria is north of the site of Fidenæ, somewhere between Castel Giubileo and Casale Marcigliano. The Casali Sette Bagni, which lies on the hill-side north of the little stream of the Allia, cannot be far from the old Basilica of St. Michael. The evidence from the Michael shrine near Spoleto, which was known for its healing springs, may explain the origin of the dedication.

iii. *The church on Monte Gargano.* — Monte Gargano juts out from the north end of Apulia into the Adriatic. The Michael shrine is on the Monte S. Angelo, about ten miles from Manfredonia, the ancient Sipuntum. The dedication is assigned to the last years of the 5th century. Baronius refers to it under the year 493 (*Annales Ecclesiastici*, ed. Mainz, 1601–05, sub anno xliii.; cf. his *Martyr. Rom.*, p. 261). The 'Apparitio S. Mich. Ang.' is kept on May 8. The *Liber Pontificalis* of Anastasius Bibliothecarius reads: 'Huius temporibus inventa est Ecclesia sancti Angeli in Monte Gargano' (*Liber Pont.* ch. 50, S. Gelasius). It was a great centre of pilgrimage in the 10th century. Otto III. visited the sanctuary in 998. The fact rests on the credible witness of the *Vita S. Romualdi* of Petrus Damianus (F. Gregorovius, *Storia della città di Roma*, Ital. ed., Venice, 1872–76, iii. 559). In the church was a spring of water which was held to be a cure for fever:

> 'Ex ipso autem saxo quo sacra contunditur aedes: ad aquilonem altaris dulcis et nimium lucida guttatim aqua dilabitur: quam incolae stillam vocant. Ad hoc et vitreum vas . . . argentea pendet catena suspensum . . . denique nonnulli post longas febrium flammas hac austa stilla celebri confestim refrigerio potiuntur salutis' (B. Mombritius, *Sanctuarium*, ed. duo Monachi Solesmenses, Paris, 1910, i. 391).

iv. *The Michael sanctuary in Umbria.* — The Antonine *Itinerary* thus notes two stations on the way from Rome to Milan by the Via Flaminia: 'civitas spolitio . . . mil. vii: mutatio Sacraria . . . mil. viii.' This 'mutatio' is placed at Le Vene, near Spoleto (*Itin. Ant. Aug.*, ed. G. Parthey and M. Pinder, Berlin, 1848, pp. 288, 378). Wesseling rejects the theory of P. Cluver that this referred to a sanctuary of Jupiter Clitumnus, and accepts that of L. Holstein that there was a Christian sanctuary on this site when the *Itinerary* was written (P. Wesseling, *Vet. Rom. Itineraria*, Amsterdam, 1735, p. 613). H. Leclercq states definitely that the sanctuary cannot have been dedicated to the 'God of Angels' before the epoch of Theodosius, or at the latest before the beginning of the 5th century. The inscriptions of the *Tempio di Clitunno* belong to this date. The inscription over the central door reads: 'S̄C̄S̄ DEUS ANGELORUM QUI FECIT RESURRECTIONEM.' Leclercq says:

> 'Cet édifice, dont la première destination n'était pas chrétienne, et qui portait primitivement le nom de sacrarium, n'a pu être transformé et dédié au Dieu des anges qu'à l'époque de Théodose' (*DACL*, art. 'Anges,' p. 2147).

And again, after examining the theory of H. Grisar that these buildings (*i.e.* the Tempio di Clitunno and the Church of S. Salvatore at Spoleto) are works of a school of the 12th cent., he concludes:

> 'Nous pensons donc, jusqu'à nouvelle démonstration, que contrairement à l'opinion de Luc Holstein, le *tempietto di Clitunno* a eu une destination primitivement païenne, il fut un de ces *sacraria* qui bordaient en assez grand nombre la rive du Clitunne pour avoir fait donner le nom de *Sacraria* au gîte d'étape situé entre Spolète et Trevi' (*ib.* p. 2149).

The consecration of the healing water of the Clitumnus to the God of Angels suggests a similar origin for the basilica on the Via Salaria, and may perhaps lie behind the dedication on Monte Gargano. The early Christian association of angelic agency with healing springs is recognized in Jn 5[4]. Leclercq states that there is evidence of the prevalence of the cult of angels in Umbria from the first half of the 5th century. The Church of S. Salvatore outside the walls of Spoleto is on the site of a small church originally dedicated to St. Michael in 429. There is another in the parish of Mandorleto near Perugia, of the same epoch, called in the inscription: 'basilicam sanctorum angelorum' (*ib.* p. 2148).

2. The Michael churches in the East.—i. *St. Michael of Khonai.*—The Church of St. Michael the Archistrategos was the centre of the angel cult of Asia. When the hill-station of Khonai took the place of Colossæ in the 7th cent., the Church of Colossæ became known as the Church of St. Michael of Khonai. The legend tells that St. Michael had saved the people of the Lycus valley from inundation by clearing the gorge outside Colossæ. The miracle of Khonai in its present forms is of the 9th cent., but it represents the foundation legend of the great Church of Colossæ. W. M. Ramsay has no doubt of the identity of the Church of St. Michael of Khonai with the Church of Colossæ. The raid of the Turks in 1189 swept along the Lycus valley. Khonai on the hill-side escaped them, but the threshing-floors along the valley were destroyed, and the great church was burnt (Nicetas Choniates, *Annales de Isaaco Angelo*, bk. ii. ch. 2 [*Hist. Byzant.*, Venice, 1729, xii. 210]). The legend also explains the origin of a spring of sweet water on the north of the city (Ramsay, *Cities and Bishoprics of Phrygia*, i. 214 ff.). St. Michael of Khonai in the later Christian legend takes the place of the Zeus of Colossæ of pagan tradition. The power associated with Zeus was in the Christian period attributed to St. Michael. Ramsay sums up the importance of the legend in its bearing on early Christian history:

'The worship of angels was strong in Phrygia. Paul warned the Colossians against it in the first century (Col. ii. 18). The Council held at Laodiceia on the Lycus, about A.D. 363, stigmatised it as idolatrous (Conc. Laod. Can. 35). Theodoret, about 420-50 A.D., mentions that this disease long continued to infect Phrygia and Pisidia (Interpr. Ep. Col. ii. 16). But that which was once counted idolatry, was afterwards reckoned as piety' (*Church in the Roman Empire*, London, 1893, p. 477).

ii. *Asia.*—Michael the Archangel was honoured throughout Asia. His name is preserved in Mikhayil near Prymnessos, in Mikhalitch on the Sangarios, and in other city names (Ramsay, *Phrygia*, i. 31 f.). He is connected with the introduction of Christianity into Isaura, and is associated with the cities of Akroinos-Nicopolis and Gordium-Eudokias. Sozomen speaks of the cures wrought at the Michaeleion, a shrine built by Constantine on the north shore of the Bosphorus (*HE* ii. 3). Its ancient name was Hestiæ, and was traditionally associated with a temple built by the Argonauts (Cedrenus, *Hist. Comp.* [*Hist. Byzant.* vii. 96]; Ramsay, *Church in Rom. Emp.*, p. 477, n.). It was 35 stadia from Constantinople, and is now represented by Arnautköi.

Procopius describes the rebuilding of this basilica by Constantine, and the building of another under the dedication of St. Michael at Proochthous on the Asiatic shore (Procopius, *de Ædificiis*, i. 8). He built another on the Asiatic coast at Mokadion (*ib.* i. 9). Procopius also mentions the Michael churches erected by Justinian at Antioch (*ib.* ii. 111) and at the healing springs of Pythia in Bithynia, with a house of rest for the sick (*ib.* iv. 3), while at Perga in Pamphylia stood a ptocheion of St. Michael (*ib.* v. 9).

iii. *Constantinople.*—There are important references to the Michael churches of Constantinople and the neighbourhood in the *Imperium Orientale* of Anselmo Banduri (*Hist. Byzant.*, xxiii. and xxiv.) and in the *Constantinopolis Christiana* of C. D. du Cange (*Hist. Byzant.* xxii.). The latter gives a list of fifteen churches (*Const. Christ.* iv. 3) in the city and five monasteries in the suburbs (*ib.* iv. 15). The chief festival of St. Michael in the Eastern Church is kept on Nov. 8.

iv. *Alexandria.*—The *Annals* of Eutychius of Alexandria († 940) have a legend connected with a Michael church in Alexandria. It was on the site of a temple of Saturn, in which had been an image of brass named Michael. The image was broken up, and the pagan festival was transferred to St. Michael (R. Sinker, *DCA*, p. 1179).

3. The Michael churches in the West.—In Italy and the East, headland, hill-top, and spring sanctuaries now dedicated to St. Michael were formerly sacred sites of earlier religions. The associations rest frequently on folk-lore; the testimony is that of legend and tradition or place-name. The same associations are to be expected in the West. In some cases the legend may be traced; in others it may linger in folk-lore, and can be looked for only in local tradition. But, given an ancient dedication to St. Michael and a site associated with a headland, hill-top, or spring, on a road or track of early origin, it is reasonable to look for a pre-Christian sanctuary.

i. *Headland and coast churches.*—On the French coast are St. Michel near the mouth of the Loire, St. Michel on the Pointe du Raz in Brittany, St. Michel en Grève to the south of Lannion, the Île St. Michel near the Cap de Frehel, and, best-known of all, Mont St. Michel. The legend associated with Mont St. Michel suggests the tradition of an ancient sanctuary of Celtic heathendom. The giant slain by Arthur on the site is said to have come from Spain, the Hades of Celtic mythology (Rhŷs, *Celtic Heathendom*, p. 90 f.). He is said to have ravished Elen, who is equated with a goddess of Welsh mythology (*ib.* p. 161). Thus, by the overthrow of a giant by the champion of Christendom, the Celtic sanctuary becomes the sanctuary of St. Michael.

Among the coast and headland churches in England are St. Michael's Mount, the church of Lyme Regis, and that of Bere near Seaton, all of ancient origin. There are also St. Michael near the mouth of the Camel opposite Padstow, St. Michael, Mawnan, overlooking Falmouth Bay, and St. Michael-Caer-hayes. On the west coast there is a Michael church at Workington in Cumberland; on the east coast, Garton in the East Riding, Sidestrand and Ormesby St. Michael, in Norfolk; on the south coast, Newhaven in Sussex and East Teignmouth, Devon. With a few exceptions the majority are in Dorset, Devon, and Cornwall, where the old lore lingered longest.

ii. *Hill-top churches.*—These are to be found throughout the West, sometimes as hermitage chapels, sometimes as town and village churches. St. Michel is the central church of Limoges, the Augustoritum or metropolis of the Lemovices. St. Michel is also the central church of Castelnaudary on the old road between Carcassonne and Toulouse. These sites are frequently the high-places consecrated to early religious rites. The church of Penkridge in Staffordshire is dedicated to St. Michael. Penkridge is the Celtic site of the ancient city of Pennocrucium, 'a place-name which bears evidence to the worship of the heathen god in the centre of ancient Britain' (Rhŷs, *Celtic Heathendom*, p. 202 f.). It is the Brythonic equivalent of the Irish *Cenn Cruach*, 'the Chief of the Mound,' who bowed before the staff of St. Patrick.

Penkridge was formerly the sanctuary of the Celtic Zeus.

A Michael church may often witness to some pre-historic centre of religious worship.

The story of a bull is associated with the foundation-legend of the Church of St. Michael 'in Monte Gargano.' The legend rests on a 'libellus' which was kept in the church. Garganus, a rich citizen of Sipuntum, missed his bull from the herd:

'Quem dominus collecta servorum multitudine per devia queque requirens, invenit tandem in vertice montis foribus cuiusdam asistere speluncae. Itaque promotus cur solivagus incederet: statim corripit ira motus arcum, et appetit illum sagita tossicata que venti flamine retorta: eum a quo iacta est mox versa percussit' (Mombritius, *Sanctuarium*, i. 390; cf. Hereford Breviary in Chapter Library, Worcester, 15th cent., *ap.* H. Bradshaw Soc. xl. [1911] 339).

The sanctity of the bull-shrine is here vindicated. The terror is averted by the dedication of the site to St. Michael.

The life of St. Francis of Assisi alludes to the forty days' fast in honour of St. Michael. It was kept 'ad heremum Alvernae.' It was on the occasion of one of these fasts that the birds gathered round his cell. They are called his 'sorores aviculae' (Mombritius, *Sanct.* i. 512). The vision of the stigmata is assigned to the same sanctuary.

'Biennio itaque antequam spiritum rederet caelo . . . perductus est in montem excelsum seorsum: cui nomen Alvernae. Cum igitur iuxta solitum morem quadragessimam ibidem ad honorem archangeli Michaelis ieiunare coepisset . . . coepit immissionum cumulatius dona sentire' (*ib.* i. 524).

iii. *The spring churches.*—The dedication of wells and springs to St. Michael may be noted in the Michael churches of Askerswell, at the head of the Asker Valley in Dorset, at Barwell in Lincolnshire, and at Houghton-le-Spring in Durham. In Portugal near Leiria on the Monte de São Miguel a warm and a cold spring issue close together from the Olhos de São Pedro.

There is a remarkable example of a Michael church in association with a spring at Llanmihangel near Llantwit Major in Glamorganshire. The church is in a dell, and just outside the N.W. corner of its churchyard is a spring. The spring-head is ornamented with the bust of a woman, and the water used to issue from the breasts. It is now (April 1915) nearly filled up with mud.

iv. *The Llanfihangel churches in Wales.*—It has been noted by W. L. Bevan (*Dioc. Hist. of St. David's*, London, 1888, p. 36, *ap.* Willis Bund, *The Celtic Church of Wales*, p. 336) that the Michael churches in the diocese of St. David's, to the number of forty-five, with one exception, are in the country districts. It has been suggested by Willis Bund (p. 336) that they mark a second stage in the spread of Christianity in Wales:

'The group of Michael churches would therefore represent the villages of the lay tribe that had become Christian, but which still belonged to the lay tribe, and so could not be called by the name of the Saint, or the tribe of the Saint, or of his family. They thus form a group which marks the spread of Christianity. . . . The term selected was one that would celebrate the victory of the cross over the Pagan' (*ib.* p. 336).

The Michael churches of Anglesey bear out this suggestion. There are four of them; and they are all in the near neighbourhood of sites of great antiquity, associated with the legend and myth of Wales. Llanfihangel-ty'n Sylwg, on the coast north-west of Beaumaris, is within the pre-historic site of Bwrdd Arthur. Llanfihangel Tre'r Beirdd derives its name from the ancient Carneddau Tre'r Beirdd. It lies to the east of Llanerchymedd. Llanfihangel-yn-Nhowyn, south-east of Valley, is near the site of Cær-Ellen. Llanfihangel Esceifiog is parochially connected with the old site of Plas Berw. This association of the Michael churches of Anglesey, taken together with the evidence of the churches in Italy and the East, can hardly be accidental. It would seem to support the evidence that the Michael churches occupy the shrines and sites of Celtic heathendom.

v. *The Michael churchyards.*—The churchyard of St. Michael's at Lichfield is referred to in the MS *Historia Ecclesiæ Lichfeldensis* in the Cathedral Library at Lichfield. It was a venerated site even in the time of St. Augustine:

'Corporibus occisorum sepelliendis insolitae magnitudinis coemeterium quod fano Divi Michaelis adiacet, fertur inserviisse; quod ferunt Augustino, qui Anglorum Apostolus dicitur, cum illas insulae partes inviserat, religione venerabile fuisse' (MS *Hist. Eccl. Lichf.*, *ap.* H. E. Savage, *The Church Heritage of Lichfield*, Lichfield, 1914, p. 14).

A note 'de Cemeteriis' in the same MS speaks of certain national burial-places in the early ages of the Church:

'In primordiis nascentis Ecclesiae Anglicanae cemeteria erant rara, pauca sed amplissima et spaciosa: ut cemeterium Avelloniae sanctum in quo Rex Arthurius sepultus est; cemeterium Doroverni Cantiorum; Eboraci Brigantium; Lindisferne; atque adeo cemeterium Divo Michaeli sacrum Lichefeldiae ab Augustino Anglorum Apostolo, ut fama est, consecratum' (*ib.* p. 14).

There is a passage in Bede which probably refers to a similar burial-place in the neighbourhood of Hexham:

'Est mansio quaedam secretior, nemore raro et vallo circumdata, non longe ab Hagustaldensi ecclesia . . . habens clymeterium sancti Michahelis archangeli, in qua vir Dei saepius, . . . manere cum paucis, atque orationibus ac lectioni quietus operam dare consueverat' (*HE* v. 2).

The Church of St. Michel at Bordeaux is on the site of an ancient cemetery, the soil of which has the property of preserving the bodies.

vi. *The Angel Victor in Ireland.*—The *Genair Patraicc*, the hymn of St. Fiacc in honour of St. Patrick, has two references to St. Michael under the name of Victor. In v. 4 it is by his command that Patrick went across the seas:

'Asbert Victor fri gniad
Mil con tessed for tonna,'

'Said Victor to Milchu's bondsman, that he should go over the waves' (*Irish Liber Hymnorum*, H. Bradshaw Soc. xiii. [1898] 98, xiv. [1898] 32).

In l. 47, an angel sends Patrick to Victor, who stopped him from going to Armagh at his death:

'Dofaith fa-des co Victor,
ba he ar·id·ra·lastar,'

'He sent him south to Victor: it was he [Victor] that stopped him' (*ib.* xiii. 102, xiv. 34).

The gloss on v. 4 reads:

'Victor. i. angel communis Scotticae gentis sein: quia Michael angelus Ebreicae gentis, ita Victor Scottorum' (*ib.* xiii. 98).

The translation of the Irish gloss on v. 46 reads:

'i.e. to meet him, to summon him to go to Victor. He was his soul-friend, and he is the common angel of the Gaels [aingel coitcend na ńGoedel]; sicut est Michel Iudeorum ita Victor Scotorum' (*ib.* xiii. 102, xiv. 184).

The hymn seems based on notes written by Muirchu Maccu Mactheni in the 7th cent. and preserved in the Book of Armagh. The hymn itself belongs to the 8th century (*ib.* xiv. 176). The name Victor may be traceable to the *inlatio* of the Mozarabic Missal for Michaelmas:

'E celo missus: iniquum hostem perimens submittet in inferno: et ipse victor exultans victori plaudet: a quo victor manebit' (*Missale Mixtum dictum Mozarabes*, ed. A. Lesley, Rome, 1755, p. 392).

It is a point of affinity between the liturgical uses of Ireland and Spain.

But the name Michael is not sunk in the title Victor. J. H. Bernard, in his note on the Hymn of St. Colman Mac Murchon in honour of St. Michael, says:

'St. Michael was very popular in Ireland. In the Second Vision of Adamnan we read in section 19: "the three hostages that were taken on behalf of the Lord for warding off every disease from the Irish—are Peter the Apostle, and Mary the Virgin, and Michael the Archangel." There are a large number of fragmentary Irish poems in praise of St. Michael in the manuscript collection of the Royal Irish Academy. There were churches dedicated to him in many localities; the place-name *Temple-Michael* still exists in 6 or 7 counties' (H. Bradshaw Soc. xiv. 133).

4. The Michaelmas goose.—There is an old saying: 'If you eat goose on Michaelmas-day you will never want money all the year round' (Hone, *Every-Day Book*, i. 1339). In Herefordshire in 1470, 'one goose fit for the lord's dinner on the feast of St. Michael the archangel' was due as part of service or rent for land (*ib.*). G. Gascoigne, in his poems published in 1575, alludes to a similar custom:

'At Christmasse a capon,
At Michaelmasse a goose,
And somewhat else at New-yeres tide,
For feare their lease flie loose' (*ib.*).

Such customs lie deep in the folk-lore and religious ideas of a people. Geese have sacred associations. They saved Rome ('anseres non fefellere: quibus sacris Junoni' [Livy, v. 47]). The goose-pond, or 'fuente de las ocas,' is still preserved in the cloister court of the cathedral of Barcelona. The cathedral is built on the site of a Roman temple—a temple ascribed to Hercules. Some columns in an adjoining street still witness to the antiquity of the site. There were sacred geese in the Greek temples (*ERE* i. 518). Geese were tabu to the ancient Britons ('leporem et gallinam et anserem gustare fas non putant' [Cæs. *de Bell. Gall.* v. 12]). They also have a place in the story of St. Werburga ('in Wedune mansione, quod est iuxta Hamptoniam . . . infinita aucarum silvestrium . . . multitudo' [*Nova Legenda Anglie*, ed. C. Horstmann, Oxford, 1901, ii. 423]). The witness of East and West, the folk-lore and legend of Britain, alike point to the sacred associations of the Michaelmas goose. This established Michaelmas custom rests, together with the sites of so many of our Michael churches, on a foundation of primitive religion, and in Britain they are no less sacred to Christianity for thus keeping alive the deep-rooted religious convictions of Celtic heathendom.

5. The liturgical meaning of the festival: St. Michael and All Angels.—The festival of Michaelmas is specially in honour of St. Michael, but the words of the *officium* or *introit* to the mass in all Western uses are: 'Benedicite Dominum omnes angeli.' The festival thus includes All Angels. The English Prayer-Book entitles the festival 'St. Michael and All Angels.' The Colbertine Breviary of *c.* 1675 (H. Bradshaw Soc. xliii. [1912] p. xxxvi) agrees in this title: 'S. Michaelis et omnium Angelorum.' The Dedication of the Great Hall of the Baths of Diocletian in 1564 under the title *S. Maria degli Angeli* shows the same intention.

The Collect 'Deus, qui miro ordine'—'the services of Angels and men in a wonderful order'—is common to all the uses. Its subject is the ministry of angels. The gospel, offertorium, and postcommunio are also common to all. The Gospel—'Quis putas maior'—refers to the guardianship of the angels, the Offertory—'Stetit Angelus'—to the incense of prayer, the Postcommunio—'Beati Archangeli tui Michaelis'—to the intercession of St. Michael. The Epistle common to the Roman and Sarum and most of the Western uses—'significavit Deus quae oportet fieri cito'—commemorates the Angel of the Apocalypse (H. Bradshaw Soc. xii. [1897] 1595).

The Epistle in the English Prayer-Book, 'There was war in heaven,' represents a different strain of liturgical tradition, and celebrates the victory of St. Michael over the dragon, 'that old serpent, called the devil and Satan, which deceiveth the whole world.' The Westminster Missal of *c.* 1375 has this Epistle as a First Lection, followed by the usual Epistle, 'Significavit Deus.' It is a rare instance of two prophetical lessons before the gospel, which of itself shows the influence of Gallican use. This inference is strengthened by its use as the First Lection in the Mozarabic *Missale Mixtum* (ed. Lesley, p. 389). It also appears as a Matins lesson in the Milan Breviary (*Breviarium Ambrosianum*, Milan, 1896, Pars Aestiva, ii. Prop. de Tempore, p. 403). Wickham Legg traces it in the Missals of Durham, Abingdon, and Sherborne among old English uses; and in that of Rouen of 1499 and the Cistercian Missal of 1627 (H. Bradshaw Soc. xii. 1595).

The English Epistle is inspired by the thought of the triumph of Christianity over heathenism, and belongs to the same cycle of ideas as the Angel Victor in Ireland.

LITERATURE.—*DACL*; Henry Bradshaw Society; *DCA*; F. Arnold-Forster, *Studies in Church Dedications*, London, 1899; W. Hone, *Every-Day Book*, do. 1830; H. Quentin, *Les Martyrologes historiques*, Paris, 1908; W. M. Ramsay, *Cities and Bishoprics of Phrygia*, Oxford, 1895-97; J. Rhŷs, *Celtic Heathendom*3, London, 1898; J. W. Willis Bund, *The Celtic Church in Wales*, do. 1897.

THOMAS BARNS.

MICIUS.—'Micius' is the latinized form of the words otherwise transliterated Mih Tsze, or Mo Tsze, meaning 'the philosopher Mih.' His personal name was Teih (or Ti). He was a native of the State of Sung, and is regarded by some as a younger contemporary of Confucius (E. Faber, E. H. Parker), and by others as 'very little anterior to Mencius' (J. Legge). His opinions are preserved in 71 chapters arranged in 15 books; but 18 of the chapters, in some cases along with their very titles, have been lost. Faber speaks of him as an ancient Chinese socialist, and Parker calls him 'a Quixotic Diogenes,' head of 'the school of simplicity, socialism, and universal love' (*China and Religion*, London, 1905, p. 67). It is this doctrine of universal love by which he is best known, largely because of the criticism of it by Mencius (*q.v.*). All social disorders in the empire, and between persons, families, or States, spring from selfishness, and would be impossible if men loved the persons, families, and States of others as they love what belongs to themselves. Such universal love may be difficult; but, if men can be induced to sacrifice their lives for the sake of pleasing their sovereign, how much less difficult should they find it to practise universal love, which, moreover, would be responded to by love. Others would follow if only rulers would lead the way by administering their government on this principle, taking pleasure in it, stimulating men to it by rewards and praise, and aweing them from opposition to it by punishment and fines. Micius adduces the ancient kings as examples, for equally with Confucius he builds on the ancient books. What gives rise to hate and all its evils is the principle of making distinctions. In spite of the brevity of life and the selfish desire to make the most of it for oneself, each man should be for the other as for himself. There is no one who would not prefer as his friend or his sovereign one who practises universal love rather than one who acts on the opposite principle. To the objection that universal love is injurious to filial piety Micius replies that the filial son is one who wishes to secure the happiness of his parents by inducing men to love and benefit them, and that to love and benefit the parents of others is precisely to secure for one's own the same treatment in return (bk. iv.). It is here that Mencius joins issue with the Mihist I Tsze. Taking Micius's doctrine as inculcating *equal* love to all, he argues from the actual facts of human nature, pointing out that a man's affection for his brother's child is not merely the same as his affection for the child of his neighbour, and that man is related in a special way to his own parents, heaven having made man to have this one root (Mencius, bk. iii. pt. i. ch. 5, pt. ii. ch. 9). Legge admits that Micius appears to lose sight of the other sentiments of the human mind in his exclusive contemplation of the power of love, but denies that Micius taught equal love to all. It is true that we do not find in Micius the phrase 'without difference of degree,' used by I Tsze, though it may be held that I Tsze represents the logic of his master's doctrine. I Tsze also exposed himself to Mencius's criticism by his exaggeration of his master's teaching on simplicity in funeral rites (Mencius, bk. iii. pt. i. ch. 5). Micius did no more than discourage extravagance on utilitarian grounds, as being of no profit to men or gods, while he allowed all that was necessary for a decent interment (Micius, bk. v. ch. 25). Among other points worthy of notice are these. In bk. iii., on the value of uniformity, Micius holds that men originally were hopelessly at sixes and sevens, each having his own view of right, and that order is based on submissive acceptance of the judgment of the supreme ruler, whose judgment, however, must conform to heaven if heaven-sent punishments are to be avoided. Hence the piety of the ancient kings. Micius is firmly convinced of the existence of spiritual beings, the instruments of heaven's righteous administration, and so far affirms the necessity of religious belief for social stability (bk. viii.). Of two chapters criticizing the Confucian school one survives, though Chinese editors are inclined to deny this reference of his remarks. On the whole Micius deserves Legge's praise of him as 'an original thinker,' who exercised a bolder judgment on things than Confucius or any of his followers.

LITERATURE.—J. Legge, *Chinese Classics*, London, 1867–76, ii. Prolegomena; E. Faber, *Die Grundgedanken des alten chinesischen Socialismus*, Elberfeld, 1877.

P. J. MACLAGAN.

MICMACS.—See ALGONQUINS (Eastern).

MIDRASH AND MIDRASHIC LITERATURE.—The term *midrāsh* (from the root *dārash*, 'to seek,' 'inquire') signifies 'research,' 'inquiry,' 'study.' Applied by the Chronicler to historical writings of didactic import,[1] as the Midrash of the Prophet Iddo (2 Ch 13^{22}) and the Midrash of the book of Kings (2 Ch 24^{27}), it assumed later, with the advent of the *sôfᵉrîm*, or scribes, upon the stage of Jewish history, the connotation of free exposition or exegesis of Scripture, eventually becoming a general term for pure theoretic study as opposed to a practical pursuit of knowledge.[2] From the latter usage the Jewish academy received its name *bēth ham-midrāsh*, 'house of study.' In a narrower sense, *midrāsh* is employed to mean any specific exposition of a Scriptural passage differing essentially from the *pᵉshāṭ*, the literal meaning (the plural form in such case being *midrāshôth*), and the name is then transferred to a collection of such free expositions, known collectively as *midrāshîm*, Midrashic works.[3]

The intellectual activity of the Rabbis with regard to this free exposition of the Bible was developed along two distinct lines, the Hălākhāh and the Haggādāh, and a few brief remarks on the basic differences between these two currents of Rabbinic thought, flowing in parallel streams, are of paramount importance. Reduced to their bare etymology, the terms signify: *hălākhāh*, 'way of acting,' 'habit,' 'rule of conduct'; *haggādāh* (also known in its Aramaic form *'aggādāh* or *'agādā*), 'narrative,' 'explanation.'[4] The Hălākhāh confines itself to the legalistic aspect of the Scriptures; the Haggādāh to their moralizing and edifying aspect. From the Rabbinic standpoint, the Bible is a microcosm in which is reflected every move and event of the great universe. One teacher comments: 'Turn it, and again turn it; for the all is therein, and thy all is therein' (*Sayings of the Jewish Fathers*, p. 96). It requires only the light of a great thinker to extract from its compact pages all this esoteric wisdom; like a hammer which strikes the inherent sparks from the rock, it is possible to unravel all the secrets which lie beneath the surface of the cold letter of the text (*Sanh.* 34*a*). The Hălākhāh takes up this work of rekindling the mystic spark of knowledge in the legal field; in all other fields of human activity that task is undertaken by the Haggādāh. The Hălākhāh relies, for its powers, mainly on the intellectual and logical faculties of man; the Haggādāh on the imaginative and emotional faculties. The Hălākhāh strives to preserve the letter of the law by insisting on the observance of all the details in the ritual; the Haggādāh, by a well-defined analysis of the relation of man to his environment, seeks to preserve its spirit.[1]

Midrashic study, therefore, assumes a twofold aspect. On the one hand, it is concerned with the evolution of legalism—the Hălākhāh; on the other, it centres about the problems of God, man, and the universe—the Haggādāh. The origin of Midrashic study is shrouded in the gloom of antiquity. The Rabbis themselves often assign Midrashic interpretations of Scripture to Biblical personages, but such statements are not to be taken literally. A noteworthy instance of this occurs in the Mishna (*Shᵉḳālîm*, vi. 6): 'This is the midrash which Jehoiada, the high-priest, taught,' etc. By such assertions the Rabbis probably meant to emphasize the continuity and binding force of the traditional law. There can be no doubt, however, that this free method of inquiry into Scripture was well established during the period of the early scribes, the men of the Great Synagogue, who took up the reconstructive work initiated by Ezra.[2] The author of Daniel uses Midrashic exegesis quite liberally in interpreting the words of Jeremiah ($25^{11f.}$ 29^{10}) in his famous prophecy of the weeks (ch. 9). With the advent of the scribes Midrashic study becomes a permanent institution in the Jewish intellectual world and passes through its process of evolution during the succeeding ages. Three historical periods are generally distinguished: (*a*) the period of the *sôfᵉrîm*, or scribes, 400 B.C.–A.D. 10; (*b*) the period of the *Tannāîm*, the early Rabbinical authorities, A.D. 10–220; (*c*) the period of the *Ămôrāîm*, later Rabbinic authorities, A.D. 220–500. The historical side of the development of Midrashic study has been ably dealt with in the works of L. Zunz, *Die gottesdienstlichen Vorträge der Juden*, Frankfort, 1892; Z. Fränkel, *Hodegetica in Mischnam*, Leipzig, 1859, and *Introductio in Talmud Hierosolymitanum*, Breslau, 1870; D. Hoffmann, 'Zur Einleitung in die halachischen Midraschim' (*Beilage des Rabbiner-Seminars zu Berlin*), 1887; and especially in the works of W. Bacher, *Die Agada der Tannaiten*, Strassburg, 1903, *Die Agada der babylonischen Amoräer*, do. 1878, and *Die Agada der palästinischen Amoräer*, do. 1892–99. Only few traces remain of the Midrashic exegesis of the early scribes (cf. *Mishnāh Sôṭāh*, viii.; *Ma'ăsēr Shēnî*, v. 10 f.). During the second period, the Tannāitic, Midrashic study must have developed to grand proportions, as is evident from the fact that the various schools of Rabbis, begin-

1 Cf. S. R. Driver, *Introduction to the Literature of the OT*[9], Edinburgh, 1913, p. 529.

2 *e.g.*, Rabban Simeon, the son of Gamaliel, adds: 'Not the *midrāsh* (pure theoretic study) is the groundwork, but the deed' (*Sayings of the Jewish Fathers*, ed. C. Taylor[2], Cambridge, 1897, p. 5, Heb. text).

3 Cf. W. Bacher, *Die exegetische Terminologie der jüdischen Traditionsliteratur*, Leipzig, 1899–1905, i. 103.

4 Bacher (*JQR* iv. [1892] 406–429) derives this word from the formula *maggîd shᵉ*, 'the text explains that,' in use in the earliest Midrashic works.

1 Cf. I. H. Weiss, *Zur Geschichte der jüdischen Tradition*[2], Wilna, 1904, iii. 220.

2 The following passage is of interest as confirming this position. Rabbi Levi says: 'We have received this midrash from the men of the Great Synagogue. Wherever Scripture uses the expression "and it came to pass," the phrase generally implies calamity' (*Mᵉgillāh*, 10*b*). Parallel passages on the authority of a number of different teachers are found in *Bᵉrēshîth Rabbā*, xlii. 3; *Wayiḳrā Rabbā*, xi. 7; *Rûth Rabbā*, i. 7 proœm.; *Estēr Rabbā*, i. 1 proœm.; *Pᵉsiḳtā Rabbāthî*, 5. In these the period of the Babylonian Exile is assigned as the date for this midrash (cf. N. Krochmal, *Môreh Nebûkhê haz-Zᵉmān*[2], Warsaw, 1894, p. 224).

ning with Hillel, laid down specific rules for exegesis to keep the study within definite bounds.[1] The period of the Âmôrâîm was most prolific in the field of Midrashic research, most of the collections, in fact, having their beginnings during that period.

1. Halakhic Midrāshîm.—The legalistic exegesis of Scripture did not proceed in an unsystematic manner. Each school of Rabbis would hand over the results of its work to the next in the form of rules of legal hermeneutics which were derived from a collation of similarly worded passages in the Pentateuch. Accordingly, the school of Hillel, at the beginning of the first century of our era, left seven such rules, which, in the school of Rabbi Ishmael, were later amplified into thirteen.[2] These are either based on some logical syllogism or of purely exegetical character. Thus the seven original rules laid down by the school of Hillel embrace the following: (1) the inference from minor and major (at the bottom of which is *a fortiori* reasoning); (2) the analogy of expressions; (3) the generalization of one special provision; (4) the generalization of two special provisions; (5) the effect of general and particular terms; (6) the analogy made from another passage; (7) the explanation derived from the context.[3]

From the school of Rabbi Ishmael a complete commentary on the legal portion of the Pentateuch was issued, the following parts of which have been preserved.

(*a*) The *Mᵉkhîltā* (Aramaic for 'rule' or 'measure'), which is the earliest Rabbinic work extant, is a running commentary to the legal portions of Exodus. It begins with the injunction concerning the Paschal lamb in $12^{1ff.}$, and ends with the injunction concerning the kindling of fires on the Sabbath (35^3). A large portion of Haggadic material has also been added. In the *Mᵉkhîltā*, as well as in all the other Halakhic Midrāshîm, the activity of the Rabbis in the legal field is analyzed; in the Mishna it is synthesized. The *Mᵉkhîltā* went through the hands of later redactors, whose work is still traceable. The *editio princeps* was Constantinople, 1515, and the two critical editions are *Mechilta . . . von I. H. Weiss* (Vienna, 1865) and *Mechilta de Rabbi Ismaël . . . von M. Friedmann* (do. 1870).[4]

(*b*) The existence of a commentary to Leviticus from the same school is posited by Hoffmann ('Einleitung,' pp. 72–76) from fragments preserved in various places in Rabbinic literature.

(*c*) The Halakhic Midrash to Numbers from the same school is the *Sifrē* to Numbers, forming a running commentary to $5\text{–}35^{34}$ with omissions. The work is generally bound together with the *Sifrē* to Deuteronomy, and both were, for a long time, considered of similar origin. The latter work, however, originated in the school of Rabbi Aḳiba. The name *Sifrē* probably means 'books.' The first edition was printed in Venice, 1545, and a critical edition was issued by M. Friedmann, *Sifre debé Rab* (Vienna, 1864).

(*d*) Fragments, from the same school, of a commentary to Deuteronomy were published by D. Hoffmann, in *Jubelschrift zum siebzigsten Geburtstag des Dr. Israel Hildesheimer*, Berlin, 1890, pp. 1–32.

Opposed to the methods pursued by the school of Rabbi Ishmael was the more rigoristic school of Rabbi Aḳiba. The latter, in expounding the law, followed a method known as 'extension and limitation' (*ribbûî û-mi'ûṭ*), introduced by his teacher, Nahum of Gimzo. According to this system, it was necessary to consider the amplifying or limiting value of certain particles used in the Pentateuch when considering the legal question involved in the passage, in order to include the additions of tradition or to exclude what it no longer sanctions. Thus the particles 'even,' 'every,' 'also,' 'with' were considered as amplifying, the particles 'but,' 'only,' 'from' as limiting, the original law. Rabbi Aḳiba's disciples included the most distinguished teachers of the Law, such as Rabbi Me'îr, Judah ben 'Ilāi, Simeon ben Yôḥāi, and Yôsê bar Ḥălaftā. His disciple, Aquila, followed his methods of exegesis in his Greek version of the OT. From the school of Rabbi Aḳiba the following Halakhic Midrāshîm have been preserved: (i.) the *Mᵉkhîltā* of Rabbi Simeon ben Yôḥāi on Exodus, contained in the *Midrāsh hag-Gādhôl*, and published by D. Hoffmann (*Mechilta de Rabbi Simon b. Jochai*, Frankfort a. M., 1905);[1] (ii.) the *Sifrā* or *Tôrath Kôhănîm*, 'the Law of the Priesthood,' which is a most complete running Halakhic commentary to Leviticus, and was edited by Rabbi Ḥiyya (middle of 2nd cent.; cf. Hoffmann, 'Einleitung,' p. 22); the *editio princeps* was Venice, 1545, and the standard edition is *Sifra, Commentar zu Leviticus . . . nebst Erläuterung des R. Abraham ben David und I. H. Weiss . . . herausgegeben von Jakob Schlossberg*, Vienna, 1862; (iii.) the *Sifrē Zūṭā*, the Halakhic commentary to Numbers from the school of Rabbi Aḳiba, existing only in fragmentary form in various collections, foremost among which is the *Yalḳūṭ Shimᵉ'ônî*, the *editio princeps* of which uses the expression *Zūṭā*, 'smaller,' to distinguish this Midrash from the *Sifrē* to Numbers mentioned above (cf. Hoffmann, 'Einleitung,' pp. 59–66); and (iv.) the *Sifrē* to Deuteronomy, which is the legal commentary to this book issuing from the same school. It is usually bound with the *Sifrē* to Numbers emanating from the school of Rabbi Ishmael (cf. above).

These Midrashic collections are but small remnants of the great number of such works which the ravages of time have destroyed. They were compiled, for the most part, during the first two centuries of our era. While their scope is primarily Halakhic, the Haggadic content in each instance forms no mean proportion, for the Rabbis felt themselves bound by no rigorous division-line in arranging their material. The later Mishna and Talmud are similar extensive collections which comprise the greatest efforts of the Rabbis in the realm of Hălākhāh and Haggādāh.

To illustrate the methods of the Halakhic Midrash the following passage, in which the legal aspect of tort is discussed, will be of interest:

'"Eye for eye" [Ex 21^{24}] means a money-compensation. This, however, is a mere assertion; perhaps we are actually to understand the passage in its literal sense. Says Rabbi Eleazar: "Scripture unites in one passage [Lv 24^{21}] the two injunctions, 'He that killeth a beast shall make it good: and he that killeth a man shall be put to death.' For what purpose is this collation?—in order to establish a like precedent for the laws of tort in the case of man and beast. Just as the damage inflicted on a beast is punishable by a fine, so the damage inflicted on a human being is punishable by a fine." Rabbi Isaac adds: "In the case where one's beast had repeatedly inflicted death on several human beings, Scripture specifically imposes a fine on the owner to escape a deserved death-penalty [Ex $21^{29f.}$]; in this case, where the Scriptural penalty is only the loss of an eye, there is all the more reason to believe that the text meant to allow a money compensation"' (cf. *Mᵉkhîltā of Rabbi Ishmael, Mishpāṭîm*, 8).

The binding force of the decisions of the Rabbis with regard to their interpretations of the Mosaic law is clearly expressed in the following:

'Concerning the authority of the words of the scribes, Scripture says [Dt 17^{11}]: "According to the tenor of the law which they shall teach thee." It does not say which the Torah

1 Cf. S. Horovitz, in *JE* viii. 549.
2 For these see *JE* x. 511 f.
3 Cf. *Tôseftā, Sanhedrîn*, ch. 7; *Ābhôth of Rabbi Nathan*, ch. 37; and *Sifrā*, introductory ch.
4 Cf. J. Winter and A. Wünsche, *Die jüdische Litteratur*, Trèves, 1894, i. 371–410; and *JE* viii. 554 f.

1 Cf. S. Schechter, *Midrash Haggadol*, Heb. preface, Cambridge, 1902; I. Lewy, 'Ein Wort über die Mechilta des R. Simon,' *Jahresbericht des jüdisch-theologischen Seminars 'Franckelscher Stiftung,'* Breslau, 1889; and L. Ginzberg, in *Festschrift zu I. Lewy's 70ten Geburtstag*, do. 1911, pp. 403–436.

shall teach thee, but rather which *they* shall teach thee. . . . Furthermore, it enjoins, "Thou shalt not turn aside from the sentence which they shall shew thee, to the right hand, nor to the left," which means that thou shalt listen to their opinions in reference to what is right, if they tell thee that it is right, and in reference to what is left, if they tell thee that it is left; and even if they were to tell thee concerning the right that it is left, and concerning the left that it is right, thou must yield to their opinion' (*Shîr hash-Shîrîm Rabbā*, i. 2).

2. Haggadic Midrāshîm.—The Haggādāh is the expression of the philosophy of Jewish life, and, as a result, had a wider appeal than the more abstruse Hălākhāh. With a keen appreciation of the consoling powers of the Haggādāh, Rabbi Isaac informs us:

'Generations before, when the penny had a freer circulation, there was a desire to listen to lectures on Mishnah and Talmud: but to-day, however, when the penny is scarce, there is only a desire for Scripture and Haggādāh' (*Pᵉsîḳtā of Rav Kahana, Baḥôdesh hash-Shelîshî*).

The Haggadic Midrāshîm are of two kinds: (1) exegetical, and (2) homiletic. The first form running commentaries to the text of the various books of the OT, and in this respect follow the method of the Halakhic Midrāshîm. They are, however, frequently introduced by several proems —opening remarks generally based on some text in the Hagiographa—which is rather a characteristic of the homiletic Midrāshîm. The latter are collections of homilies or sermons which were delivered during the Sabbath and festival services in the synagogues, and which were based on the portion of the law read during such service. The homiletic Midrāshîm, therefore, differ essentially, in structure as well as in the treatment of their subject-matter, from all the other Midrashic works. They are regularly introduced by proems in which a passage from the Hagiographa or Prophets is explained and introduced into the context. Several homiletic works (notably the *Tanḥûmā*) also resort to a Halakhic exordium. The lesson of the day is then attached to the opening verses of the portion of the law read during the service, the text being often used merely as a basis for a lesson on morals quite fully developed. The homilies close, for the most part, with verses of encouragement, prophesying the redemption of Israel and the advent of the Messianic era. Two cycles of homiletic Midrāshîm are in existence: (*a*) those originating in the three-year-cycle of Scriptural Sabbath readings then in vogue in Palestine—the *Sᵉdhārîm* cycle [1]—and (*b*) those based on the readings during the special Sabbaths in the Jewish calendar (occurring before Purim and Passover) and on the festivals and fast-days —the *Pᵉsîḳtā* cycle.

3. Exegetical Midrāshîm.—Of these the oldest and most important is *Bᵉrēshîth Rabbā*, a Haggadic commentary to Genesis.[2] It is the first in the collection known as *Midrāsh Rabbā*, or *Midrāsh Rabbôth*, which comprises ten Midrashic works, one for each book of the Pentateuch, and one for each of the Five Scrolls (the books of Esther, Canticles, Ruth, Lamentations, and Ecclesiastes). The works included in this collection are of a miscellaneous character, and their time of composition extends from the 6th to the 12th cent.—the period in which the different Haggadic Midrāshîm were redacted. Of the Haggadic Midrāshîm *Bᵉrēshîth Rabbā* is, no doubt, the oldest as well as the richest from the point of view of subject-matter. Like most of the Midrāshîm, it had its origin in Palestine, and was put into its final form no later than the 6th century. Older authorities assign the work to Rabbi Hoshaiah, a Palestinian teacher of the 3rd cent. (with whose remarks the book opens), but he cannot be responsible for the work in its present form. The historical and legendary content of Genesis furnishes ample material for Haggadic exposition. The ten Midrashic works forming the collection *Midrāsh Rabbā* were printed for the first time in Venice, 1545. The standard edition is that of Wilna, 1878–87. The collection was translated into German by August Wünsche in *Bibliotheca Rabbinica, eine Sammlung alter Midraschim*, Leipzig, 1880–85, and L. Shapiro translated a part of *Bᵉrēshîth Rabbā* into English (*Midrash Rabba*, New York, 1906).

Ēkhā Rabbāthî, a Haggadic commentary to Lamentations, is also a very early exegetical Midrash, and is included in the *Midrāsh Rabbā*. This work (as well as *Bᵉrēshîth Rabbā*) is introduced by many elaborate proems followed by commentary to the text of Lamentations. The book is especially rich in anecdotes and legends of the pathetic events that transpired during the destruction of Jerusalem. A critical edition has been issued by S. Buber, *Echa Rabbati*, Wilna, 1899.

Shîr hash-Shîrîm Rabbā is an exegetical Midrash to Canticles, included in the *Midrāsh Rabbā*. The entire work is an elaborate allegorical rendition of the relation between God and Israel implied in the dialogues between the shepherd and his bride.

Rûth Rabbā (also included in the *Midrāsh Rabbā*) is an exegetical Midrash to Ruth. The book is introduced by a series of proems, and the conversion of Ruth furnishes many a beautiful lesson to the Rabbinical commentators.

Ḳôheleth Rabbā (also included in the above collection) is an almost complete exegetical commentary on Ecclesiastes. The author utilized much of the material found in the Talmud and in various earlier Midrashic works, and mentions several sources by name—a sign of the late origin of the Midrash.

Finally, *Estēr Rabbā* is an exegetical commentary on Esther included in the *Midrāsh Rabbā*. This is one of a number of extant Haggadic Midrāshîm to the book of Esther, very popular because of its use during the Purim festival. The others were published by S. Buber, *Sammlung agadischer Commentare zum Buche Esther*, Wilna, 1886, and *Agadische Abhandlungen zum Buche Esther*, Cracow, 1897.

Besides the above-mentioned Midrāshîm to the Five Scrolls, Buber published several other extant Midrāshîm to the books of Canticles, Ruth, Lamentations, and Ecclesiastes, in *Midrasch Suta*, Berlin, 1894.

There are still extant several Haggadic Midrāshîm dealing with the remaining books of Scripture. There can be no doubt that originally such exegetical works existed on all the books, but they have been lost. Foremost among them is *Midrāsh Tᵉhillîm*, a Haggadic commentary to the book of Psalms. It is also known as *Shôḥēr Ṭôbh*, 'He that seeketh good' (Pr 11[27]), which are also the opening words of the book. This Midrash is especially rich in the rhetorical devices employed by the Haggadists—analogies, legends, fables, maxims, etc. A critical edition was issued by Buber (*Midrasch Tehillim*, Wilna, 1891). A Midrash to the book of Samuel has, likewise, been preserved, known as *Midrāsh Shᵉmû'ēl*. It is a collection of Haggadic comments on the book, gleaned from various parts of Rabbinic literature. The first edition of the work was Constantinople, 1517. A critical edition was issued by S. Buber (*Midrasch Samuel*, Cracow, 1893). *Midrāsh Mishlē* is an incomplete Haggadic Midrash to Proverbs. The comments in this Midrash are exceptionally brief, so that the work approaches the character of a Biblical commentary. A critical edition was

[1] Cf. J. Theodor, in *Monatsschrift für Geschichte und Wissenschaft des Judenthums*, xxxiv. [1885–87] 356.

[2] For introductions to the various Midrashic works cf. *JE*, under each title; Winter and Wünsche, i. 411–601; and the introductions to the separate works.

issued by S. Buber (*Midrasch Mischle*, Wilna, 1893). The Midrāshîm to the books of Isaiah and Job are mentioned by older authorities, and, of the latter, extracts are found in the collection, *Yalḳūt Mākhîrî* (to Is 61[11]), and in a few other old works. Several fragments of a Midrash to the book of Jonah have been published by A. Jellinek (*Beth ham-Midrasch*, Leipzig, 1853–77, i. 96–105); and by C. M. Horowitz (*Sammlung kleiner Midraschim*, Berlin, 1881).

Finally, there are in existence a number of works known as *Yalḳūṭîm*, 'collections,' which are in the nature of thesauri to all the books of Scripture, and which give (with their proper sources) a wealth of Haggadic material for each of the books. Three of these works are very important: the *Yalḳūṭ Shimᵉʿônî*, frequently known merely as *Yalḳūṭ*, ascribed to Rabbi Simeon, the preacher (last edition, Wilna, 1898), the *Yalḳūṭ ham-Mākhîrî*, ascribed to Rabbi Machir ben Abba Mari, only portions of which have appeared (Buber, *Yalkut Machiri . . . zu den 150 Psalmen*, Berdyczew, 1899), and the *Midrāsh hag-Gādhôl*, of which the part to Genesis has been published by Schechter (*op. cit.*), and the part to Exodus by D. Hoffmann (Berlin, 1913–15).[1]

4. Homiletic Midrāshîm.—The purely homiletic Midrāshîm belonging to the *Sᵉdhārîm* cycle (based on the triennial readings of the Pentateuch in the synagogues of Palestine) are: (1) the *Tanḥūmā*, (2) *Aggādath Bᵉrēshîth*, and (3) the four remaining works in the *Midrāsh Rabbā* on the four last books of the Pentateuch. The *Tanḥūmā* (also known as *Yᵉlammᵉdēnû*, 'Let him teach us,' because of the frequent use of this formula to introduce the Halakhic exordiums in the Midrash) is a complete homiletic commentary to the Pentateuch, extant in two versions, containing also special homilies for the days of the *Pᵉsîḳtā* cycle. A third version is known to have existed. A critical edition was issued by Buber (*Midrasch Tanchuma*, Wilna, 1885). *Shᵉmôth Rabbā* on Exodus, *Wayiḳrā Rabbā* on Leviticus, *Bᵉmidhbar Rabbā* on Numbers, and *Dᵉbhārîm Rabbā* on Deuteronomy are four homiletic works of different origin belonging to the same cycle. Of these the homilies to Leviticus are, no doubt, among the oldest, and are characterized by a frequent use of popular sayings and proverbs to illustrate the lesson of the day. The other three works include many homilies that are already found in the *Tanḥūmā* collection. *Aggādath Bᵉrēshîth* is a collection of homilies to portions of Genesis and to portions of the Prophets and Psalms, and was edited by Buber (*Agadath Bereshith*, Cracow, 1902).

Two collections of homilies of the *Pᵉsîḳtā* cycle have been preserved: (1) *Pᵉsîḳtā of Rav Kahana*, and (2) *Pᵉsîḳtā Rabbāthî*. The first consists of thirty-four homilies on the lessons for the special Sabbaths and the feast days. It was edited by Buber (*Pesiḳta . . . von Rav Kahana*, Lyck, 1868). The *Pᵉsîḳtā Rabbāthî* is a later work, and also contains homilies for the special days of the *Pᵉsîḳtā* cycle. It was edited critically by M. Friedmann (*Pesîḳta Rabbathi*, Vienna, 1880).

5. Style and content of the Haggadic Midrash.—In order to make their teachings most effective, the Rabbis resort to well-known rhetorical devices.[1] Foremost among these is the use of the *māshāl*, 'analogy.' The analogy, or extended metaphor, is a well-known figure in literary composition; in the hands of the Rabbis it reached the zenith of its didactic powers. The analogies were drawn from two sources—first, from the events of every-day life, and, secondly, from the institutions of the Roman empire, during which period the Rabbis lived. On the subject of the political institutions of Rome as depicted in the *māshāl* an interesting volume of no mean size has been written (I. Ziegler, *Die Königsgleichnisse des Midrasch beleuchtet durch die römische Kaiserzeit*, Breslau, 1903). On the comparative side, Paul Fiebig has contributed an interesting volume on the differences between the Rabbinic and the NT use of the *māshāl* (*Altjüdische Gleichnisse und die Gleichnisse Jesu*, Tübingen and Leipzig, 1904). The analogy was most helpful in explaining difficulties in the textual narrative, and often in accounting for extraneous matter in Scripture not quite adaptable to preaching purposes. A few examples will suffice to illustrate the use of the *māshāl*.

A *matrona* once asked Rabbi Yôsê bar Ḥălaftā, 'Why does Scripture say: "He giveth wisdom unto the wise, and knowledge to them that know understanding" [Dn 2[21]]? It were meet that the passage should read, "He giveth wisdom unto the unwise, and knowledge to them that have no understanding."' This Rabbi Yôsê met with the following: 'Let me give you an analogy. If two men, one poor and one wealthy, were to approach thee to borrow a sum of money, to whom wouldst thou lend the money, to the poor man or to the rich?' 'Of course to the rich man,' she replied, 'for, in the event of its loss, he still has assets from which I might recover, whereas from the poor man I could not get a penny.' Thereupon Rabbi Yôsê replied: 'Would that thy ears would hear what thy mouth doth utter! If the Holy One, Blessed be He, were to grant wisdom to simpletons and fools, they would decant this wisdom from the public baths, the theatres, and at other unseemly moments; He therefore granted wisdom to the wise, who confine it to its proper place in the synagogue and the academy' (*Ḳôheleth Rabbā*, i. 7).

In commenting upon the fact that the Pentateuch does not enumerate by name the participants in the sedition of Korah, the Rabbis use the following *māshāl*:

Rabbi Judah, the son of Simon, explained, on the authority of Rabbi Levi ben Parta—'This may be compared to the son of a decurion who once committed a theft in the public bath, and the keeper of the bath does not desire, for tactful reasons, to reveal his name; but describes him as "a handsome youth dressed in white." Similarly the Pentateuch does not mention the names of all the participants in the sedition of Korah, but merely describes them in the following terms: "princes of the congregation, called to the assembly, men of renown"' (Nu 16[2]; cf. *Bᵉmidhbar Rabbā*, xiii. 5).

Another form of the *māshāl* was the fable or parable. Collections of parables are already associated in the Jewish world with the name of the wise king, Solomon, who is said to have spoken 'of beasts, and of fowl, and of creeping things, and of fishes' (1 K 4[33]). In the Talmud two collections are mentioned on several occasions—a collection of fox-fables and a collection of date-tree parables (cf. *Sukkāh*, 28*a*; *Bābhā Bathrā*, 134*a*). The OT uses the parable in the speech of Jotham (Jg 9[8-15]) and in that of Jehoash (2 K 14[9]). A casual example will illustrate its use in the Midrash. In the following, the fable of the fox and the fishes is effectively employed by Rabbi Aḳiba:

During one of the persecutions, when the study of the Torah was forbidden under penalty of death, Pappus discovered Rabbi Aḳiba busily engaged in its study. Pappus asked him, 'Rabbi, art thou not endangering thy life in transgressing the royal mandate?' Whereupon Rabbi Aḳiba replied, 'Let me give thee an analogy in the following story: Once the fox rambled alongside the bank of a river and, beholding the fishes, exclaimed, "Come out to me, and I shall hide you from all harm in the crevices of the rock, where you will never fear capture." To which the fishes replied, "Thou, who art the most clever of beasts, art nothing more than a simpleton. Our whole life depends on the element of water, and thou wouldst have us leave it for the dry land." Similarly, the life of Israel is wrapped up

[1] Besides the collections already mentioned, there are special Haggadic works of didactic import based upon a large amount of material in previous works, but not arranged in the form of commentaries to the Scriptures. Such are the *Pirḳê dᵉ Rabbi Ĕlîʿezer*, Warsaw, 1879; *Tannā dᵉbhê Ĕliyāhû*, crit. ed., M. Friedmann, Vienna, 1907; and the whole collection known as *Smaller Midrāshîm*, dealing with Haggādāhs on special subjects, such as the Decalogue, the death of Moses and Aaron, etc., scattered in various collections, and especially in the works of Jellinek (*op. cit.*); C. M. Horowitz (*op. cit.*, and *Bêth ʿEḳedh Hāʿagādôth*, Frankfort, 1881); S. A. Wertheimer (*Battê Midrāshôth*, Jerusalem, 1893); L. Grünhut (*Sammlung älterer Midraschim*, do. 1858–94); and J. D. Eisenstein (*Ôṣar Midrāshîm*, New York, 1915). The Midrash known as *Leḳaḥ Ṭôbh* (ed. Buber, Wilna, 1880), of Tobiah ben Eliezer, is not a true Midrash, but rather a commentary on the Pentateuch.

[1] For the following, cf. Zunz, pp. 102–179; and Krochmal, pp. 222–230.

in one element—the study of the Torah, as it is written, "For he is thy life, and the length of thy days" [Dt 30^{20}], and thou wouldst have me leave it because of personal danger' (*Tanḥûmâ Tābhô*, 4; *B^{e}rākhôth*, 61*b*).

Another means of impressing a lesson is the aphorism, maxim, or proverb. The OT already contains extensive gnomologies in proverbial form. The wisdom of the great Ben Sira later added to this original store, and the *Sayings of the Jewish Fathers* is a historically arranged gnomology written in the Tannāitic period, and comprising the most important maxims of the learned teachers from the time of Simon the Just to the period of the Âmôrāîm. A later author, Rabbi Nathan, is said to have made a large collection of such maxims; and in the *Âbhôth of Rabbi Nathan* (ed. Schechter, Vienna, 1887) a substratum of his original work remains. This work is characterized by the frequent use of the numerical proverb, in which a number of sayings are associated by means of a numerical key.[1] The material in these collections, as well as the sayings current among the masses (generally introduced by the formula 'as the people say'), was employed by the Rabbis in teaching their lessons. Many of these proverbs are also found in the Gospels.[2] For example, the well-known saying in the Sermon on the Mount, 'With what measure ye mete, it shall be measured unto you' (Mt 7^2), is very frequent in Haggadic literature (cf. *Tanḥûmâ*, *B^{e}rēshîth*, 33; *T^{e}hillîm*, xxii. 2; and *Mishnāh Sôṭāh*, i. 17). Similarly, 'Enough for the servant that he be as his lord' (Mt 10^{25}) is found in *Tanḥûmâ*, *L^{e}kh L^{e}khā*, 23; *T^{e}hillîm*, xxvii. 5; and in the Talmud (*B^{e}rākhôth*, 58*b*). Only a few of these gems can be quoted here:

'A single coin in an empty jar makes a loud noise' (*T^{e}hillîm*, i. 21, and, in the Talmud, *Bābhā M^{e}ṣî'ā*, 85*b*). 'Say to the bee, I want not thy honey and I crave not thy sting' (*T^{e}hillîm*, i. 21; *B^{e}midhbar Rabbā*, xx. 10). 'Woe to the dough which the baker condemns as unfit' (*T^{e}hillîm*, ciii. 14). 'Woe to the living who implores aid of the dead, woe to the hero who intercedes with the weakling, woe to the seeing who ask help from the blind, and woe to the generation whose leaders are women' (*ib.* xxii. 20).[3]

Another rhetorical device for impressing a lesson is the pun. This leads into the field of Rabbinic humour. Scripture has set the precedent for its usage in carefully executed word-plays and puns especially on the names of individuals.

'And she bare Cain, and said, I have gotten' (Heb. *ḳānîthî*) (Gn 4^1). 'God shall enlarge (*yaft*) Japheth' (*yefeth*) (Gn 9^{27}). The prophet Isaiah (5^7) very eloquently says, 'He looked for judgment (*mishpāṭ*), but behold oppression (*miśpāḥ*); for righteousness (*ṣ^{e}dhāḳāh*), but behold a cry' (*ṣ^e'āḳāh*).

Similarly, the Rabbis take great liberties in punning on proper names.

'Wherefore was the prophet called Jeremiah? Because, during his life, Jerusalem was left in a state of ἐρημία' ('desolation') (*Ḳôheleth Rabbā*, i. 2). 'The name of the daughter-in-law of Naomi was Orpah because she turned her back (*'ōref*) to her mother-in-law. The name of the other was Ruth, because she apprehended (*rā'athāh*) the words of her mother-in-law' (*Rûth Rabbā*, ii. 9).

The Rabbis decide from a pun that the language of the creation was Hebrew.

'"She shall be called Woman ['*ishshāh*], because she was taken out of Man ['*îsh*]" [Gn 2^{23}], from this it is evident that the Torah was given in the holy tongue.' Rabbi Phinehas and Rabbi Ḥilkiah claim the following on the authority of Rabbi Simon: 'Just as the Torah was given in the holy tongue, so was the world created with the holy tongue. For, hast thou ever heard anyone derive a form *gynia* from the word *gyne* (Gr. γυνή, 'woman')? Or does one derive *anthropia* from the word *anthropos* (Gr. ἄνθρωπος, 'man'), or *g^{e}bhartā* from *gabhra* (Syr. for 'man')? But one does say '*ishshāh* [Heb. for 'woman'] from *'îsh* [Heb. for 'man']"' (*B^{e}rēshîth Rabbā*, xviii. 4).

The Massoretic variations of the Heb. text of the Bible open up new channels for Haggadic exegesis. The Midrash often assigns explanations for the defective writing in the text or for the marginal variations (*ḳ^{e}rî* and *k^{e}thîb*). The following is an example:

'"When it giveth its colour (lit 'eye') in the cup" (Pr. 23^{31}) is rendered "the script reads 'in the purse' (Heb. *bakkîs*), not 'in the cup' (Heb. *bakkôs*), referring, on the one hand, to the drunkard, who giveth his eye in the cup; and, on the other hand, to the merchant who fixeth his eye on his purse"' (*Tanḥûmâ Sh^{e}mînî*, 7).

The Midrash also employs the well-known kabbalistic method of exposition, *g^{e}maṭriā*, which consists in deducing hidden meanings from the numerical value of the letters in the Heb. words.[1]

Finally, the Midrash employs the anecdote to advantage. The value of the anecdote as a didactic force is generally recognized. But, more than this, we are to seek in the anecdote for historical events witnessed by contemporaries, for folk-lore, for primitive conceptions of natural science, etc. Only a few examples can be given here. The following pathetic tale is one of a series of anecdotes depicting the events that transpired during the destruction of the Holy City:

'The story is told of Miriam, the daughter of Naḳdimôn [Nicodemus], whom the sages had granted an allowance of 500 (*sic*) gold denarii for her daily ointment expenditures, and who maligned them for it in the words "Thus mistreat your own daughters!" . . . Says Rabbi Eleazar: "So sure may I be of seeing [Zion's] consolation as I am that I saw her [some time after the destruction] in Acco, picking barley-grains from beneath the stalls of horses, and I applied the Biblical verse to her case, 'If thou know not, O thou fairest among women, go thy way forth by the footsteps of the flock, and feed thy kids beside the shepherds' tent'" (Ca 1^8)' (*Êkhā Rabbāthî*, 1, 48).

The superstitions of the day were shared alike by Rabbi and priest. Many are the stories told of demons infesting wells and desert places (cf. *Tanḥûmâ*, *B^{e}rēshîth*, 27; *ib.* *Ḳ^{e}dhôshîm*, 9), often driven out through the opportune intervention of the Rabbi who called magical formulæ to his aid. Very often the heathen practices of antiquity are recorded. Thus, in *Êkhā Rabbāthî* (proem 23), it is said, 'The Arab slays a lamb and inspects the liver for the purpose of auguring future events.' This practice is well known to students of *Kulturgeschichte*. Philosophy, primitive conceptions of science, natural history—all cater to the one end of teaching a lesson in ethics or morals, which is ever the ultimate aim of the Haggadic Midrash.

LITERATURE.—This is given throughout the article.

SOLOMON T. H. HURWITZ.

MIGRATION.—See RACE.

MIKIRS.—I. Name and history.—The people known to the Assamese by the name Mikir are one of the numerous Tibeto-Burman races of Assam. Their own name for themselves is Ārlèng, which (like many other tribal names in this region and elsewhere) means 'man' in general. Their numbers, according to the Census of 1911, were 106,259—a large total for a homogeneous Tibeto-Burman group in Assam; of these 736 were classed in the returns as Hindus, 1182 as converts to Christianity, and the remainder as animists. The race occupies the central portion of the Assam range, looking north to the Brahmaputra, and the isolated mountainous block south of that river between Nowgong and Sibsāgar called the Mikir Hills; a few have settled in the plains of Nowgong and Kāmrūp, and north of the river in the Darrang district, and follow plough cultivation, but the main strength of the tribe is found in the hilly region of the Kāmrūp (about 11,000), Khāsi and Jaintia Hills (15,600), Nowgong (45,000) and Sibsāgar (25,000) districts. They are essentially a hill race, practising the form of cultivation by axe, fire, and hoe known as *jhūm*. Their remembered history, like that of most tribes of the kind, goes back a very short distance in time. There is reason to believe, from the local names of places and streams, that they once occupied the

[1] A. Wünsche has collected all the numerical proverbs in the Talmud and the Midrash in *Die Zahlensprüche im Talmud und Midrasch*, Leipzig, 1912 (reprinted from *ZDMG* lxv.–lxvi.).

[2] For the Haggādāh, as used by the Church Fathers, the work of L. Ginzberg is important (*Die Haggada bei den Kirchenvätern*, i., Amsterdam, 1899, ii., Berlin, 1900).

[3] Among the great number of collections of Rabbinic proverbs the work of M. Schul (*Sentences et proverbes du Thalmud et du Midrasch*, Paris, 1878) deserves mention.

[1] In Heb. the letters have numerical values.

southern portion of the hill tract north of the Kachar valley, where they are not found at the present day; it is certain that they afterwards resided in mass in the eastern portion of the Jaintia Hills, as subjects of the Jaintia Raja; and a still clearer tradition relates that, being harassed by warfare between Khāsi (or Jaintia) chiefs, they resolved to move into territory governed by the Āhoms, and thereupon migrated into the tracts which they now hold in the Nowgong and Sibsāgar districts. This migration probably took place, as can be gathered from the Āhom annals, about A.D. 1765. As the figures just given show, large numbers continued to live in the Khāsi and Jaintia Hills and along the Kāmrūp border, which tract they call Nihàng, the territory into which they migrated in the east being called Nilīp. They are a peaceful and unwarlike race, and are said to have given up the use of arms when they placed themselves under the protection of the Āhom kings. Their traditions tell of fights with the Hill Kachāris, or Dīmāsā, but these were anterior to the migration into Jaintia territory, or at any rate to that into the Āhom dominions.

2. Physical characteristics. — Physically they present the ordinary features of the Tibeto-Burman hill races of Assam: a light yellowish-brown complexion, an average height of about 5 feet 3 inches, cephalic index 77·9. The nose is broad at the base, and often (but not always) flat, with a nasal index of 85·1 and an orbito-nasal of 107·7. The facial hair is scanty, and only a thin moustache is worn. The front of the head is sometimes shorn; the hair is gathered into a knot behind, which hangs over the nape of the neck. The body is muscular, and the men are capable of prolonged exertion. They have been largely employed (like the Khāsis) as porters in frontier expeditions in Assam, and carry heavy loads, the burden being borne upon the back and secured by a plaited bamboo or cane strap passing round the forehead; this, however, is the general method of carriage from Nepāl eastwards along the whole sub-Himālayan region, and not peculiar to the Mikirs. The staple food is rice, fish, and the flesh of pigs, goats, and fowls, but meat is chiefly eaten at sacrifices. The flesh of cows is not eaten, nor is milk drunk. Large quantities of rice-beer are made and consumed, being prepared by each household, and spirit is also distilled. Opium is used to a large extent, as by other races in Assam. Tobacco and betel-nut are also commonly used.

3. Marriage and inheritance.—The Mikir people are divided into three sections, called Chintòng, Rònghàng, and Āmrī. These, however, are only local names, the first representing that portion of the tribe inhabiting the Mikir Hills, the second the central portion, in the hilly parts of Nowgong and N. Kachar, and the third those in the Khāsi and Jaintia and Kāmrūp Hills. The whole tribe, wherever settled, is divided into five large exogamous groups, and these into sub-groups. The five main groups are called Ingtī, Teràng, Lèkthē or Inghī, Teròn, and Timung. Within each of these groups intermarriage cannot take place. The scheme of society is patriarchal, the children being counted to the father's group. The most usual marriage, however, is between first cousins on the mother's side, and the maternal uncle occupies a privileged position at the funeral ceremonies; this may be a custom adopted from the Khāsis, among whom the strictly matriarchal system prevails. Ordinarily the son on marriage brings his wife home to his parents' house; but, if he has to make a payment to his father-in-law, he may stay a year, two years, or even for life, according to agreement, giving his work to the family in return for his bride. There are traces of a former condition of things analogous to that which obtains among the Nāga tribes, in which the boys of a village lived together in the *teràng*, or bachelors' house, and the unmarried girls are said also either to have had their own *teràng* or to have lived in that of the boys, when promiscuous intercourse and illegitimate births were common. This practice, however, no longer obtains anywhere. The marriage-tie is said to be ordinarily observed with strictness, but divorce is permissible. Polygamy has been adopted sporadically from the Assamese, but generally monogamy prevails. The sons inherit; if there are none, the brothers; after them the deceased's nearest agnate of his own exogamous group. The wife and daughters get nothing, but retain their personal property, ornaments, clothes, etc.

4. Gods.—The religion of the Mikirs has been to some extent affected by ideas borrowed from the Khāsis, and in a larger degree by Hinduism. One of their gods, Pirthàt Rēchō (the god of thunder), bears a Khāsi name; but borrowings here are chiefly noticeable in the funeral ceremonies and the methods of divination. Hinduism has contributed the name of Jòm, or Yama, as the god of the dead, and the abode of spirits is called Jòm-āròng, or 'Yama's town.' Possibly Mahādeva may be the original of Ārnàm-kethē (='the great god'), who is a house-god worshipped by a triennial sacrifice; and one of the gods, called Ārnàm-pārō (='the hundred-god'), includes under this name Kāmākhyā, the Hindu goddess of Nīlāchal above Gauhāti. The original Mikir conception of deity is, like that of the rural population of India generally, open to the adoption into the pantheon of any divine agency venerated or propitiated by their neighbours. The word *ārnàm* ('god') may be generally defined as 'anything felt to be mighty or terrible.' All natural objects of a striking or imposing character have their divinity. The sun and moon are regarded as divine, but are not specially propitiated. Localities of an impressive kind, such as mountains, waterfalls, deep pools in rivers, great boulders, places where a river disappears underground, have each their *ārnàm*, who is concerned in the affairs of men and has to be placated by sacrifice. Such local divinities of the jungle are propitiated chiefly to avert mischief from tigers, which are a terrible plague in some parts of the Mikir country.

Besides these divinities of flood or forest, there are other deities of a more specific character. These may be classified into house-gods, concerned in the welfare of the household, and gods concerned in the prosperity of the village generally, while a third class preside over various kinds of disease or trouble. The most important of the house-gods is Hèmphū ('head of the house,' or 'householder'), who owns all the Mikir people. With him is associated Mukràng, who is slightly lower in dignity. These two gods, the preservers of men, are approached by the sacrifice of a fowl or goat. Everybody can sacrifice to them at any time, and Hèmphū must be invoked first in every sacrifice, being the peculiar owner of men. Pèng, another house-god, lives in the house, and gets the offering of a goat, sacrificed once a year in the space before the house; maize, rice, and a gourd of rice-beer are placed for him above the verandah of the house, and the first-fruits of the harvest are offered to him. Ārnàm-kethē, already mentioned, is another house-god, but lives in heaven, not, like Pèng, in the house itself. He is propitiated by the sacrifice of a castrated pig once in three years. Both Pèng and Ārnàm-kethē have to be specially invoked to take up their abode in the house, and their introduction to it is generally due to the action of a diviner (*uchē*), called in on the occurrence of a case of sickness, who declares (after the appropriate incantations) that Ārnàm-kethē or Pèng wishes to join the household. If it were not for this, Mikir families would generally be satisfied with Hèmphū and Mukràng.

The village or communal gods are called Rèk-ànglòng (='mountain of the community') or Inglòng-pī (='great mountain'), and Ārnàm-pārō, already mentioned. The Mikir villages are nomadic, moving from place to place as the soil in the neighbourhood becomes exhausted. Rèk-ànglòng is the god of the hill on which the village stands, the *deus loci*, with whom they have to be at peace. He is worshipped in the field, and only men eat the sacrifice, which is a fowl or goat per house once a year. Ārnàm-pārō is the name of a god who takes a hundred shares of rice, rice-flour, betel-nut, and the red spathe of the plantain-tree cut up; the name seems to be a collective, and to indicate all the divine powers in the neighbourhood. He is worshipped with a white goat and a white fowl. These two gods figure particularly at the *Ròng-kēr*, or great annual festival, celebrated for the most part in June at the beginning of the year's rainy-season cultivation, or in some villages during the cold weather. The sacrifice is eaten in common by the men only of the village, and they keep apart from their wives on the night of the festival. The observances correspond with the custom of *genna* (village tabu), which is common among the neighbouring Nāga tribes.

The gods named above are all invoked and propitiated to grant prosperity and avert misfortune, both generally and specially. There are, besides, numerous gods who take their titles from the special diseases over which they preside or which they are asked to avert; such gods are called after rheumatism, cholera, barrenness among women, goitre, phthisis, stone, diarrhœa, dysentery, smallpox, black and white leprosy, elephantiasis, etc. Each worship has its appropriate ritual, often of a complicated character. Among these deities perhaps a trace of Hinduism may be discovered in the name for smallpox, *pī-āmīr*, 'the mother's flowers': in Assamese and Hindī the goddess of smallpox is known as 'the mother' (Mātā, or Sītalā Māī). It is difficult to draw the line which divides the gods, *ārnàm-ātum*, who preside over these plagues from the demons or devils, *hī-ī*, who are also said to cause continued sickness. They too are propitiated with sacrificial offerings in the same manner as the gods.

An interesting name in the list of gods is Lām-āphū, 'the head or master of words,' a power probably of modern origin. He is the deity sacrificed to by a man who has a case in court; the sacrifice is a young cock, which should be offered at night, secretly, by the sacrificer alone, in a secret place.

There is no worship of trees or animals, and the gods have no visible shape, temples, or shrines. Idols are not in use. At the time of the sacrifice the gods to whom it is offered are addressed in set forms of words by the worshipper, but there does not appear to be any separate class of priests charged with the sacrificial ritual. The animal sacrificed is beheaded, as in Hindu sacrifices, by a stroke delivered from above with a heavy knife.

5. Diviners.—The most important person with reference to the worship is the diviner (*uchē*, fem. *uchē-pī*), who decides on the deity to be invoked. Here, again, there does not appear to be any caste or hereditary function: any one may be an *uchē*. The diviners are of two kinds—the inferior, generally a man, called *sàng-kelàng-ābàng*, 'he who inspects grains of rice,' whose art is acquired by instruction and practice; and the superior, called *lodèt* or *lodètpi*, invariably a woman, who works under the inspiration or *afflatus* of divine powers. The services of these persons are generally sought in cases of sickness, the *lodèt* being inquired of in the more serious cases.

The humbler practitioner proceeds by arranging grains of rice, taken at random from those left in the pot, in particular fashion in small heaps; the grains in the heaps are then counted, and, if the odd numbers predominate, the omen is good. Cowries are sometimes used instead of grains of rice. Another way, apparently borrowed from the Khāsis, is to arrange in a circle, equidistant from a point marked on a board, as many little heaps of clay as there are gods suspected in the case, each heap being called by the name of a god. An egg is then sharply thrown at the point marked in the middle of the board; when it breaks and the yolk is scattered, that heap which receives the largest splash of yolk, or towards which the largest and longest splash points, indicates the god responsible for the affliction. Another mode is to hold upright in the hand a long iron knife of special form, called the *nòkjīr*, which is invoked by a spell to become inspired and to speak the truth. The holder then asks questions of the *nòkjīr* as to the probability of the sufferer's recovery and the god responsible for his sickness, and the *nòkjīr* shakes at the correct answer and name.

The *lodèt* is an ordinary woman (not belonging to any particular family or group) who feels the divine *afflatus*, and, when it is upon her, yawns continually and calls out the names and will of the gods. Her assistance is invoked when witchcraft (*mājā*) is suspected.

She bathes her hands, feet, and face in water in which the sacred basil (*ocymum sanctum*, the *tulsī* of Indian languages) has been steeped, and begins to shake and yawn. A gourd of rice-beer is brought, of which she drinks some, and begins to call out the names of gods, and they descend upon her. She is now inspired, and, when questioned, indicates, by indirect and riddling answers, the enemy who has bewitched the sufferer, or the gods to whom sacrifices must be offered.

Charms are much used for the treatment of disease, as they are everywhere else in India, and do not present any special features. Oaths and imprecations take the place of ordeals, the speaker inviting evil on himself if he swears falsely or fails to perform a promise.

6. Funeral ceremony.—The most elaborate celebration is the funeral ceremony, of which a long account, full of detail, is given in Stack and Lyall's monograph on *The Mikirs* cited at the end of this article. Much money is spent upon it, and it is spread over several days. It is the only occasion on which dances are performed by the young men of the village or music used, except (to a much less extent) at the harvest-home. The ceremony is considered obligatory in all cases except that of a child who has been born dead, or who has died before the after-birth has left the mother; in such cases the body is buried without any ceremony. Victims of smallpox or cholera are buried shortly after death; but the funeral service is performed for them later on, the bones being dug up and duly cremated. When a person is killed by a tiger, if the body or clothes are found, they are buried at a distance from the village, because the tiger is supposed to visit the burial-place. Such persons cannot gain admittance to Jòm-āròng unless elaborate funeral and expiatory ceremonies are performed for them. Being killed by a tiger is generally imputed to the victim's sin; his spirit is believed to dwell in the most dreary of the places where dead men's spirits go. Except in such cases, the dead are disposed of by cremation, the burnt bones being afterwards buried.

What is chiefly noticeable about the ceremony, as described in the work referred to, is the confident assumption of the continued existence of the dead person's spirit, for whom food, specially prepared by the *uchē-pī*, or divining woman, is set apart; the insistence upon the due performance of the rites in order to get admission to Jòm-āròng; and the use of dancing, which is marked by its name (*chomàng-kàn*) as adopted from the Khāsis, in the ceremony. If the deceased is a person of unusual importance, a still more elaborate ceremony is required, and monumental stones, upon the model of those erected by the Khāsis, are set up.

7. Ideas of future life.—Apart from the ritual of

the funeral, the Mikirs seem to have a strong conviction of the survival of the dead. They speak of having seen the 'shade' or 'image' (*ārjàn*) of a dead man; a sickly or neurotic person catches such glimpses in the house, on the road, etc. *Phārlō*, 'spirit,' is used both of living persons and dead. They say of one deceased, 'Last night in my spirit I saw him,' where *phārlō* is the spirit of the sleeping man. When such glimpses are experienced, betel and food are set aside in the house, and after a time thrown away. After a death a chant is composed, setting forth the parentage and life of the dead, and ending: 'You will now meet your grandparents, father, deceased brother, etc., and will stay with them and eat with them.' As already mentioned, food is regularly provided for the spirit until the completion of the funeral; after that there are no regular offerings, but occasionally a man or woman puts aside from his or her own share of food a portion for the dead, as, *e.g.*, when another funeral reminds them of those who have died before. There is said to be no fear of the dead coming back to trouble the living. The Mikirs' conception of 'Jòm's town' is that everything there is different from the earth-life. An idea, perhaps borrowed from Hinduism, is said to prevail that the spirits of the dead do not stay for ever in Jòm-āròng, but are born again as children, and this goes on indefinitely. On the other hand, Stack records, in the words of his informant, the following:

'The Mikirs give the names of their dead relations to children born afterwards, and say that the dead have come back; but they believe that the spirit is with Jòm all the same' (*Mikirs*, p. 29).

8. Conclusion.—The unwarlike character of the Mikirs has prevented them from becoming, like their neighbours, the Nāgas and Kukis, split up into different units, with hostile feelings towards all outside the community, and with languages gradually diverging more and more from the common standard. Their speech is very uniform wherever they are found, and a large amount of co-operation and friendly intercourse exists among them. On the other hand, the group differs very much, in habits, institutions, and particularly in language, from the other tribes by whom they are surrounded. A study of their speech and social institutions has led to the conclusion that they should be classed with those tribes which form the connecting link between the Nāgas and the Kuki-Chins, and that the preponderance of their affinities lies with the latter race, especially with those dwelling in the south of the Arakan Roma range, where the Chin tends to merge into the Burman of the Irawadi valley.

LITERATURE.—All that has as yet been put on record about the Mikirs is summarized in the volume in the series of Assam Ethnographical Monographs entitled *The Mikirs*, from the papers of E. Stack, edited, arranged, and supplemented by C. J. Lyall, London, 1908.

C. J. LYALL.

MILINDA.—Milinda is the Indian name for the Greek king of Bactria called in Greek Menander. When Alexander's empire broke up on his death, Greek soldiers on the east of India founded separate States, and the names of about thirty of them and their successors are known by their coins. Of these the most powerful and successful was Menander, who must have reigned for at least thirty years at the end of the 2nd and the beginning of the 1st cent. B.C. He died probably about 95 B.C., but we know neither the boundaries of his kingdom nor how far he was merely over-lord, rather than the actual administrative sovereign over the various portions of his vast domain. He is the only one of those Greek or half-Greek potentates whose memory has survived in India; and he is there remembered, characteristically enough, not as a political ruler, nor as a victor in war, but as an intelligent and sympathetic inquirer into the religious beliefs of his subjects.[1]

This has found expression in a very remarkable book, the *Milinda Pañha* ('Questions of Milinda'). Just as in one of the most popular of the Dialogues of the Buddha Sakka, the king of the gods, is represented as coming to the Buddha to have his doubts resolved, so in this work the Greek king is represented as putting puzzles in religion to Nāgasena, a wise teacher among the Buddhists of his time. In all probability it was with the *Sakka Pañha Suttanta* in his mind that the author of the *Milinda Pañha*, whoever he was, framed his work.

The *Milinda Pañha* is divided into seven books. The first is introductory, and is very cleverly so drawn up as gradually to raise the expectations of the reader regarding the great interest of the encounter of wit and wisdom which he will find in the following books. Bk. ii., 'On ethical Qualities,' and bk. iii., 'On the Removal of Difficulties,' contain a number of questions, put by the king and answered by Nāgasena, on the elementary doctrines of Buddhism. On the conclusion of this book the king is converted, and devotes himself to a long and careful study of the text of the Pāli canon. In bk. iv., the *Meṇḍaka-pañha*, or 'Dilemmas,' the king submits to Nāgasena the difficulties which he has met in the course of his studies. The discussion of these difficulties leads up to and culminates in the meaning of *nirvāṇa*, and closes with an eloquent peroration on that subject.

Having thus brought his reader up to the bracing plateau of emancipation, the author proceeds in the next book, the *Anumāna Pañha*, 'Problem of Inference,' to describe what is to be found there. In an elaborate allegory of the City of Righteousness he sets out the various mental and moral treasures enjoyed by the *arahant* who has reached in this life the ideal state. The next book, the *Dhutaṅgas*, 'Extra Vows,' is devoted to an exaltation of those who have adopted the ascetic practices so called. The last book, incomplete in our existing MSS, consists of a long list of types of the *arahant*, showing how he has, *e.g.*, five qualities in common with the ocean, five with the earth, five with water, and five with fire. The details of sixty-seven such similes are given. Of the remaining thirty-eight only the list is given, the detailed explanations being lost.

There are peculiarities both of merit and of defect in this book. The author, or authors, have an unusual command of language, both in the number of words used and in the fitness of the words chosen in each case. There is great charm in the style, which rises occasionally throughout the book to real eloquence; and there is considerable grasp of the difficult and important questions involved. On the other hand, there is a great weakness in logic. The favourite method is to invent an analogy to explain some position, and then to take for granted that the analogy proves the position taken to be true; and quite often, when the right answer to a dilemma would be a simple matter of historical criticism, the answer given savours of casuistry, or is a mere play on the ambiguity of words. Then the author, though he naturally avoids the blunders so often repeated in European books against Buddhism—that *nirvāṇa*, *e.g.*, is a state to be reached by a 'soul' after it has left the body, or a state not attainable except by a 'priest' or a 'monk'—does not stand on the ancient Path. His description of the *arahant*, whom he calls a *yogī* (a term not found in the older books), lays more stress on those qualities afterwards ascribed to the *bodhisattva* (*q.v.*) than on those belonging to the Path, or mentioned (of the

[1] See the authorities quoted in Rhys Davids, *Questions of King Milinda*, i. (*SBE* xxxv.) pp. xviii-xxiii.

arahant) in the *Nikāyas*. His Buddhology has advanced beyond that of the *Nikāyas*. The ethics of the Aryan Path are barely referred to; the doctrine of causation, the necessity of seeing things as they really are (*yathābhūtaṁ pi jānanaṁ*), is not even mentioned, notwithstanding its cardinal importance in the earlier teaching. The author devotes a whole book to the *dhutaṅgas*, a term not occurring in the *Nikāyas*, and in that book manifests a spirit entirely opposed to the early teaching.[1] All these peculiarities of style and mental attitude are uniform throughout the work. It would seem, therefore, most probable that it was the work either of one author or of one school within a limited period of the history of that school. Probably the latter will eventually be found to be the right explanation.

The work is four times quoted as an authority by the great Buddhist commentator, Buddhaghoṣa.[2] It is the only work outside the Pāli canon which he thus quotes. It is also quoted as an authority in the *Dhammapada* commentary (i. 127).[3] All these references may be dated in the 5th cent. A.D. They are taken from the second, third, and fourth books, which at least must be considerably older than the works in which the *Milinda* is quoted as an authority. None of the quotations is exactly word for word the same as the corresponding passage in Trenckner's edition of the text,[4] and the present writer has pointed out elsewhere the various interpretations possible of these interesting, though slight, discrepancies.[5] In one passage (p. 102 of the text) Buddhaghoṣa seems to have the better reading. Nāgasena is also quoted in the *Abhidharma-kośavyākhyā*, a Sanskrit Buddhist work which may be dated in the 6th cent. A.D.[6] There are also several incidental references in Chinese 'translations' of Indian books. When we know the dates of the latter, and can be sure that the references really occur in them, those references may have importance.

At the beginning of the work (p. 2 of the text) there is a table of contents giving the titles of the subdivisions of the book. The editor, V. Trenckner, also gives us titles, which differ, however, from those in the table of contents given in the text. Hīnaṭikumburē's translation into Siṁhalese[7] likewise gives titles, presumably from the much older Pāli MSS which he used. These titles differ from both the other lists. Trenckner, who has certainly made one glaring mistake (p. 362), gives no *apparatus criticus* for his titles; and, as he used only three of the seven MSS of the work known to exist in Europe,[8] one would like to be informed also as to what readings are given by the other four. Even for the canonical books the discrepancies in the subsidiary titles are very frequent, and it is often probable that such titles are later than the text to which they refer. It is clear that, pending further information, Trenckner's titles to the divisions of the *Milinda* cannot be relied on as original.

B. Nanjio, in his most useful catalogue of Chinese Buddhist books,[9] gives under no. 1358 the title of one called *Nāsien Bikhiu King*, 'Nāgasena the Bhikkhu's Book.' The attempt to reproduce the sound of the words of this title suggests that the words before the translator must have

[1] See above, *ERE* ii. 71[b].
[2] See the references given in Rhys Davids, *op. cit.* pp. xiv-xvi.
[3] *Dhammapada A.* i. 380 might, at first sight, be taken for another, but it is from *Majjhima*, ii. 51.
[4] The *Milinda-pañho*, ed. V. Trenckner, London, 1880.
[5] *Op. cit.* p. xv ff.
[6] See Rhys Davids' note in *JRAS*, 1891, pp. 476–478, and Max Müller, *India, What can it teach us?*, London, 1883, p. 209.
[7] See on this translation Rhys Davids, *Questions of King Milinda*, i. p. xii ff.
[8] *Ib.* p. xvii.
[9] *Catalogue of the Chinese Translation of the Buddhist Tripiṭaka*, Oxford, 1883.

been, not Sanskrit (*bhikṣu*), but Pāli (*bhikkhu*) or some other Indian dialect akin to Pāli. J. Takakusu has discussed the date of this work, which purports to be a translation of some Indian book with the same title.[1] It is first mentioned in a catalogue dated A.D. 785–804, and subsequently in others. But, though the compilers of all these catalogues are usually careful to give the name or names and the date of the translators or authors of the books which they mention, they do not do so in this case. They add, however, a remark:

'The translator's name is lost, and we register it as belonging to the Eastern Tsin dynasty (A.D. 317–429).'

So we have a book known to have existed at the end of the 8th cent., and then believed, on grounds not recorded, to have existed in the 4th cent. A.D. There is no evidence that the original was in Sanskrit.

There are two recensions of this book in Chinese, the longer one about half as long again as the shorter one. The difference arises mainly from the omission in the shorter of two long passages found in the longer. In other matters the two are much the same. These omissions are probably due to a mere mistake, perhaps of the translator, perhaps of the printer, and the two recensions may be considered as really one. This bears to the Pāli text the following relation.

The translation into English by the present writer consists of 580 pages. The Chinese corresponds more or less to 90 of these pages (one recension omitting about 34 of those 90). The paragraphs corresponding in Chinese and Pāli are those on pp. 40–135 of the English version. But there are seven or eight omissions, and three additions of whole paragraphs, and quite a number of smaller variations or discrepancies.[2] It is clear that there is some connexion between the Chinese and Pāli books. It is possible that the Indian original (for there was only one) of the Chinese book may be the original out of which the Pāli was developed, mainly by the addition of the last three books. It is equally possible that the Indian work translated into Chinese was itself derived from an older work in seven books, and that its author or authors omitted the last three books as dealing with *arahant*-ship, in which he (or they) took no interest. This would be precisely in accord with the general feeling in the north-west of India at the period in question—the end of the 3rd cent. B.C. The doctrine of an emancipation to be reached in this life by strenuous mental exertion was, not unnaturally, yielding place to a doctrine of salvation in the next life through *bhākti*, personal devotion to a deity. The psychological details of the old system of self-control rather bored people. So the *Milinda* may, quite possibly, have been reduced to a short and easy book, with the sting of *arahant*-ship taken out of it.

A solution of this *Milinda* problem would be of the utmost importance for the elucidation of the darkest period in the history of Indian literature. Unfortunately, each of the alternatives suggested above involves great difficulties, and none of the scholars who have written on the subject has so far been able to persuade any other to accept his conclusions. The evidence at present available is insufficient. When the Tibetan translation has been properly examined, when all the quotations from the *Milinda* in the Pāli commentaries are edited, when all the references elsewhere (and especially those in the numerous Buddhist Sanskrit works still buried in MSS) have been collected, we shall be better able to estimate the value of the external evidence as to the history of the *Milinda* literature in India. When an adequate compari-

[1] *JRAS*, 1896, p. 12 ff.
[2] See the comparative table given by F. O. Schrader, *Die Fragen des Königs Menandros*, p. 120 f.

son has been made between the words used and the ideas expressed in the Pāli *Milinda* and those found in the canon on the one hand and the commentaries on the other, we shall have more valuable internal evidence than is yet available. The lists of about a hundred words peculiar to the *Milinda* published by the present writer in 1890[1] was necessarily inadequate, and has not since then been improved upon.

LITERATURE.—*Milindapañho*, ed. V. Trenckner, London, 1880; T. W. Rhys Davids, *Questions of King Milinda*, *SBE* xxxv. [1890], xxxvi. [1894]; F. Otto Schrader, *Die Fragen des Königs Menandros*, Berlin, n.d., but probably 1906; R. Garbe, *Deutsche Rundschau*, cxii. [1902] 268 ff. (reprinted in *Beiträge zur indischen Kulturgeschichte*, Berlin, 1903, p. 95 ff.); A. Pfungst, *Aus der indischen Kulturwelt*, Stuttgart, 1891; J. Takakusu, 'Chinese Translations of the Milinda Panho,' *JRAS*, 1896, pp. 1–21; Rhys Davids, 'Nāgasēna,' *ib.*, 1891, pp. 476–478; E. Specht, 'Deux Traductions chinoises du Milindapañho,' *Trans. of the 9th Oriental Congress*, London, 1893, i. 518–529; M. Winternitz, *Gesch. der ind. Literatur*, ii., Leipzig, 1913, pp. 139–146; L. A. Waddell, 'A Historical Basis for the Questions of King "Menander,"' *JRAS*, 1897, pp. 227–237; Hinatikumburē Sumaṅgala, *Milinda Praśnaya* (Siṁhalese), Colombo, 1877. For the historic Milinda see V. Smith, *Early Hist. of India*³, Oxford, 1914.

T. W. RHYS DAVIDS.

MILITARISM.—See WAR.

MILK (Primitive Religions).—That milk should have become an object of sacred importance in the mind of early man was inevitable. All food was sacred, and milk, so beneficial in every way, has been accorded a special place among the objects of religious veneration by mankind at nearly all stages of his development. Anthropologists have not specifically dealt with the first stages in the domestication of animals, except as a part of the larger question of totemism. There are people who have practically no tamable animals, and these are in the lowest stages of savage culture. An observation of O. T. Mason is clearly indicative of where these first stages must be looked for.

> 'Women were always associated especially with the milk- and fleece-yielding species. Before the domestication of milk-yielding animals and in the two continents where they were not known in aboriginal times, the human mother had to suckle her young two or three years until they were able to walk at her side and partially take care of themselves. The effect of this upon her nature and all social life was on one side in her favour, but on the other dreadfully increased her burdens and retarded the growth of population' (*Women's Share in Primitive Culture*, London, 1895, p. 151).

The two continents here referred to are America and Australia, and E. J. Payne has succinctly summarized the economical and social results of the absence of milk-producing animals (*Hist. of America*, Oxford, 1892, i. 287–292).

These results may be contrasted with the corresponding condition of the people inhabiting the European, Asiatic, and African continents, who have, as far as observation goes, always possessed milk-producing animals. Milk takes an important part in their religious belief and ceremonial. It is not clear, however, whether the diverse practices obtaining among the varied races of these continents have any relationship as stages in the evolution of man's religious attitude towards milk. Consideration of the subject from this point of view can be conducted only by the widest survey of the evidence, and it will be well to approach it from the highest form to which religious belief concerning milk has attained and proceed thence to some of the lower forms of the cult.

The use of milk in religion has reached its climax among the Toda tribes of India. The sanctity of the dairy among these people is the chief element in their religion. The gods take part in the churning, and the dairy organization marks off two great clan divisions: 'The most important dairy institutions of the Todas belong to the Tartharol, but their dairymen are Teivaliol' (W. H. R. Rivers, *The Todas*, London, 1906, p. 680). The milk of the buffaloes is sacred. The ritual connected with the buffalo and with the dairy is 'certainly of a religious character,' and there can be little doubt that the dairy formulæ 'are intercessory and that they bring the dairy operations into definite relations with the Toda deities' (*ib.* p. 231). The dying are given milk to drink when on the point of death (W. E. Marshall, *A Phrenologist amongst the Todas*, London, 1873, p. 171), and the dead body is taken into the dairy (Rivers, 339 ff.). From these facts, carefully marshalled by Rivers, it is clear that these people have developed the sanctity of milk to its highest point. With them it is an essential feature of organized worship.

There is nothing like this in any other part of the world. It is the highest specialized use of milk in religious observance. The sacred character of milk in other parts of the primitive world is shown by its use in various ceremonies of a religious character, but not in connexion with an organized religious cult, as among the Todas. Both in Africa and in India these ceremonies reach a high grade in places, but do not attain the Toda level. Perhaps the royal milk-drinking observances of the king of the Unyoro, a section of the Bantu people in Africa, affords the nearest parallel (J. G. Frazer, *Totemism*, London, 1910, ii. 526–528) to the Toda practice. An interesting Kaffir folktale, 'The Story of the Bird that made Milk' (G. M. Theal, *Kaffir Folk-lore*, London, 1882, pp. 1–46), appears to be founded on the first use of milk and refers to events which preceded the use of milk, but it contains details which bring it within the general condition of the African beliefs. 'They used to get milk from a tree. This was got by squeezing, and the people who drank it were always thin.' The Kaffirs now drink a kind of fermented milk, and it is noticeable that, 'when poured out for use by the master of the household, who is the only one permitted to touch the milk sack, a portion is always left behind to act as leaven' (*ib.* p. 195). These are clearly religious practices which require further investigation, but in the meantime it is permissible to classify them as less developed in form than the Toda example.

Every one knows the reverence paid to the cow in India; but, in spite of the attempt of the early mythologists to identify the cow with the higher forms of Hindu religion (A. de Gubernatis, *Zoological Mythology*, London, 1872, i. 1–41), the fact remains that the cow is not a god. The reverence for the cow is quite human in its character, and the 4th book of the *Laws of Manu* contains the clearest evidence of this.

Crooke points out that respect for the cow in India is of comparatively modern date, and gives some interesting data to show the lines along which it has developed (*PR* ii. 226–236). This view is confirmed by the uses to which the products of the cow were put. According to Viṣṇu, a house is purified by plastering the ground with cow-dung, and land is cleansed by the same process; cows alone make sacrificial oblations possible by producing sacrificial butter, and among six excellent productions of a cow which are always propitious milk and sour milk are included (*Institutes of Vishnu* [*SBE* vii. (1900)], xxiii. [1883] 56–61).

On the other hand, the evidence from the Panjāb is that, when a cow or buffalo first gives milk after calving, the first five streams of milk drawn from her are allowed to fall on the ground in honour of the goddess (D. C. J. Ibbetson, *Panjāb Ethnology*, Calcutta, 1883, p. 114). It is also a protective from the evil eye, and has various uses in magic and divination. This suggests that in the Panjāb milk is on its way towards a definitely religious position.

In Europe the once sacred character of milk is indicated by the evidence of folk-lore, which records

[1] *Questions of King Milinda*, i. p. xlii ff.

the protective measures which have to be taken to secure it against harm from witches and other malevolent powers (*GB*[3], pt. i., *The Magic Art*, London, 1911, ii. 52 f.).

The best examples are found in Russia, where the people on Midsummer eve drive the cattle through the fire to protect the animals against 'wizards and witches, who are then ravenous after milk' (W. R. S. Ralston, *Songs of the Russian People*[2], London, 1872, p. 391). This rite affords the explanation of a curious story told of an Irish prince, Bress, son of the Fomorian Elatha. It is related of him 'that he arrogated to himself the milk of all the hairless dun cows in the land,' and he 'caused a great fire of ferns to be made, and all the cows in Munster to pass through it, so that they might fulfil the necessary conditions, and their milk become the royal property' (H. d'Arbois de Jubainville, *Irish Mythological Cycle*, Eng. tr., Dublin, 1903, p. 95). Included in this tradition are the following ritual observances—the restriction to cows of a single colour, the passing through fire to secure protection, and the right of the king to a royal supply of milk. The restriction as to colour also appears elsewhere in Irish folklore (C. Plummer, *Vitæ Sanctorum Hiberniæ*, Oxford, 1910, vol. i. p. cxlvi, and K. Meyer and A. Nutt, *Voyage of Bran*, London, 1895–97, ii. 186). The legend of the Dun Cow of Whittingham near Preston is of the same order, the attacking witch being successful in this case (J. Harland and T. T. Wilkinson, *Lancashire Legends*, London, 1882, pp. 16–19).

Ritual in custom and ritual in myth are parallels, and it would be well to inquire whether in folklore there is more than this suspicion of sanctity in the attitude of popular belief as to milk. The milkmaid is almost everywhere an important personage in the social fabric of the village, and her utensils share her importance. The present writer differs from Lady Gomme in her explanation of the famous game of 'Milking Pails' as a mere teasing of the mother (*Dict. of Traditional Games*, London, 1894–98, *s.v.*) in that it appears to be a cumulative estimate of the superior value of the milking-pail as an article of domestic use, and it is pertinent to note in this connexion that the Irish chieftain had 'in his house constantly a cask of milk' (*Anc. Laws of Ireland*, Dublin, 1865–1901, iv. 311). That milk was poured on the ground is attested by J. G. Dalyell (*Darker Superstitions of Scotland*, Glasgow, 1835, p. 193), and W. Gregor states that at death all the milk in the house was poured out on the ground (*Folklore of N.E. of Scotland*, London, 1881, p. 206). This must have originally been an offering to the earth-god as in the Panjāb. In Ireland it is called an oblation to the fairies (W. G. Wood-Martin, *Traces of the Elder Faiths of Ireland*, London, 1902, ii. 7), and the fairies are the successors of the gods. It was offered every Sunday on Brownie's stone in the island of Valay and other islands (M. Martin, *Western Islands*, London, 1716, pp. 67, 110).

This brings us very close to the stage when milk was a sacred object in the cult of the gods. In the Christian Church it was substituted for wine in the elements of the communion. This was afterwards prohibited by canon law (Dalyell, p. 193, quoting Gratian, *Decretalia*, p. 111), but it may be surmised that it originated as one of the surviving rites of ancient pagan religion. St. Bridget was in some degree regarded as the special patron of milking, as appears in the beautiful milking-songs of Scotland (A. Carmichael, *Carmina Gadelica*, Edinburgh, 1900, i. 261–275), and she was at her birth bathed in milk (*Lives of Saints from the Book of Lismore*, ed. Whitley Stokes, Oxford, 1890, pp. 184, 318). St. Bridget is in many of her attributes a pre-Christian goddess, and her association with milk in the surviving forms once more takes us back to ancient pagan religion.

That bathing in milk was also a death rite is shown both in traditional ballad lore and in traditional games. In the beautiful ballad of 'Burd Ellen,' preserved by R. Jamieson (*Popular Ballads and Songs from Tradition*, etc., Edinburgh, 1806, p. 125), is the verse:

> 'Tak up, tak up my bonny young son,
> Gar wash him wi' the milk.
> Tak up, tak up my fair lady,
> Gar row her in the silk.'

Lady Gomme has analyzed the different versions of the children's game of 'Green Gravel,' and has shown from the general movements of the game that it is derived from a funeral rite. This view is confirmed by the fact that the most constant formulæ in the game rhymes include the line,

> 'Wash them in milk and clothe them in silk'
> (i. 172).

There seems little doubt that these words are survivals of an ancient burial rite.

In the religions of antiquity there is more definite evidence. J. E. Harrison, in her discussion of primitive baptism (*Prolegomena to the Study of Greek Religion*, Cambridge, 1903, p. 596 f.), asks 'what was the exact ritual of the falling into milk? . . . Did the neophyte actually fall into a bath of milk, or . . . is the ritual act of drinking milk from the beginning metaphorically described?' and, in spite of a useful parallel from Egyptian ritual, comes to the conclusion that 'of a rite of immersion in milk we have no evidence.' This, however, cannot be quite true if St. Bridget represents, as there is strong evidence to prove, an early Celtic goddess who has brought into her Christian attributes traditions and rites of pre-Christian origin. There is the further example of the Picts in Ireland saving themselves from the poisoned arrows of their Fir-Fidga enemies by taking a bath filled with the milk of one hundred and twenty white hornless cows, where the single colour condition is again repeated. The rite of bathing in milk attributed to St. Bridget was certainly not of Christian origin any more than the offering of milk and honey in early baptismal rites was Christian (*ib.* p. 597 f.), and we must take it that these rites come from early Celtic religion. The offerings of milk and honey were made to the nymphs and to Pan (Theocr. *Id.* v. 53 f. and 58 f.), and to this day in modern Greece they are made to the Nereids (J. C. Lawson, *Modern Greek Folklore*, Cambridge, 1910, p. 150 f.).

To sum up the evidence—it would appear that in primitive religions there are three stages in the sacred characteristics attributed to milk: (1) where it is a definite part of the dominant religious cult; (2) where it is extensively used in religious ceremonial, but is not an exclusive or predominant element in the ceremonial; (3) where it is looked upon as a religious object, and is, consequently, subject to danger from outside forces, from which it demands various forms of protection. The survey seems to make it clear that the unique example of the Todas is a highly specialized development of the religious conception of milk, and not a normal condition, while the evidence of folklore and of the religion of antiquity leads us to conclude that the endowment of milk with sacred properties arose from its enormous social influences, which led to specialization of its use on solemn and important occasions. This would be the normal position of milk in religious thought. A last stage is represented by the necessity of protecting it from malignant influences. This is survival from the normal stage, and arises only when it was no longer a protective force itself.

LITERATURE.—This is given fully in the article.

L. GOMME.

MILK (Civilized Religions).—**1. As food and sacrifice.**—Since man is a mammal, milk is universally known; and, as man early learned to use the milk of goats, cows, and camels, milk became a natural symbol of nourishment. The ancient Egyptians sometimes pictured the heavens as a woman with hanging breasts, and sometimes as a cow with full udder,[1] thus suggesting that the heavens nourished men. The Babylonians suggested, similarly, that milk is the divinely given nourishment of man by picturing the mother-goddess with breasts so full that she must support them with her hands.[2] Since milk is so universal an element of human diet, it is but natural that it should have been offered at times in sacrifice to deities, as meat, meal, and firstfruits were. Thus in *Yašt* xv. of the Avesta there is frequent mention of a sacrificial gift of boiled milk, and it was mingled with *haoma* (*q.v.*) in sacrifice.[3] Among the Arabs flesh seethed in milk is still a common dish,[4] yet the Hebrews were prohibited from boiling a kid in its mother's milk. W. R. Smith thought that this was because milk for boiling is usually sour, so that such boiling would involve the offering of a fermented sacrifice, or that possibly milk was here regarded as a substitute for blood.[5]

2. In a supposed Semitic myth.—In the OT 'flowing with milk and honey' is a phrase frequently used to designate the fertility of Palestine. It occurs in Ex $3^{8.\,17}$ 13^{5} 33^{3}, Lv 20^{24}, Jer 11^{5} 33^{22}, and Ezk $20^{6.15}$. Curdled milk (the modern *laban*) and honey are also mentioned in Is 7^{15} as the food of the child that is to be named 'Immanuel.' It occurs again in the same chapter (7^{22}), where it is more difficult to interpret, and where its occurrence may be due to editorial redaction. The phrase 'flowing with milk and honey' occurs in the J document (*c.* 850 B.C.), and continued to be used till the time of Ezekiel. T. K. Cheyne[6] in 1901 noted that the phrase is more poetical than the context seems to justify, and suggested that it might be a survival of a description of Israel's idealized past. Since ancient poetry is always tinged with mythology, he thought it not improbable that this phrase was of mythological origin. Usener[7] in 1902 held that the phrase was of mythological origin, and that it was borrowed by the Hebrews from Iranian mythology, where, according to him, we hear of heavenly honey and holy cows. The phrase had, he thought, descended by one line to the Hebrews and by another to the Greeks, who described the food of the infant Zeus on Crete as curds and honey. Stade,[8] in commenting on Usener's article, claimed that the phrase 'flowing with milk and honey' was not used earlier than the time of Ezekiel, that in the J document and Jeremiah it was a later addition, and that Usener was right in claiming that in Jl 3^{18} the use of the figure was due to Greek influence. Whether 'curd and honey' could have been a mythological phrase introduced from Assyria, he thought, was a problem for Assyriologists. H. Zimmern[9] in the next year, 1903, claimed from the Assyriological side that honey and curd played a great rôle in the Babylonian cult, and that it was of mythological origin, though he offered little proof for the statement. Finally, Gressmann[10] in 1905 endeavoured to work this view into an elaborate scheme of Hebrew mythology, which formed, he believed, the basis of the prophetic eschatology.

Before accepting this view, it should be noted just what part milk and curdled milk, or *laban*, played in the life of the Hebrews. Milk, like wine, was in early Israel a symbol of prosperity and plenty. An old poet sang of Judah:

'His eyes shall be red with wine,
And his teeth white with milk' (Gn 49^{12}).

Laban was a dish so relished as an article of diet that Abraham is said to have offered it to his guests (Gn 18^{8}), and Jael to the tired Sisera (Jg 5^{25}); honey and *laban* along with wheat, barley-meal, beans, and lentils were furnished as food to David and his men (2 S 17^{27-29}). It is natural, therefore, that *laban* and honey, the two most delicious viands known to them, should enter into poetical descriptions of abundance, fertility, or prosperity (see Dt $32^{13f.}$, Job 20^{17} 29^{6}, Sir 39^{26}). The natural uses of these articles of food are sufficient to account for these poetic allusions.

The strongest arguments of the mythological school rest, however, on the highly-coloured language of Joel and later apocalyptic writers, and upon supposed Assyrian parallels. In Jl 4^{18} (EV 3^{18}) we read:

'And it shall come to pass in that day that
The mountains shall drop sweet wine,
And the hills shall flow with milk
And all the water-courses of Judah
Shall flow with water.
And a spring shall come forth from the house of Yahweh
And water the valley of Shiṭṭim';[1]

in the *Sibylline Oracles*, iii. 744 ff.:

'For Earth the universal mother shall give to mortals her best
Fruit in countless store of corn, wine and oil.
Yea, from heaven shall come a sweet draught of luscious honey,
The trees shall yield their proper fruits, and rich flocks,
And kine and lambs of sheep and kids of goats.
He will cause sweet fountains of white milk to burst forth';

and again, *ib.* v. 281 f.:

'But the holy land of the godly alone shall bear all these things.
An ambrosial stream distilling honey and milk shall flow from rock and fountain for all the righteous.'[2]

In view of the aridity of the desert, it would seem to need no mythology, but only a little poetic exaggeration, to lead to the designation of Palestine by the nomads as a 'land flowing with milk and honey.' The use of these viands in the life of the Hebrew nation easily accounts for the poetic use in Deut. and Job, and these in turn furnish the point of departure for the later more hyperbolic language in Joel and the *Sib. Or.* Unless we can find some outside parallels, there is, then, no need for the mythological hypothesis.

Most of the Assyrian parallels hitherto cited turn out to be unreal. Thus a passage cited by Zimmern simply enumerates honey and *laban* along with oil, wool, gold, and silver as desirable things.[3] Another passage deserves more attention. It is part of an incantation for driving the demon of sickness from a man's body. It runs:

'*Laban* from a pure stable they shall bring,
Milk from a pure corral they shall bring,
Over the pure *laban* from the pure stable utter an incantation:
May the man, son of his god, become pure!
May that man become pure as *laban*!
Like that milk may he become pure!'[4]

It is clear that no mythological meaning can be involved in this passage. It is the purity of the *laban* and the milk that is emphasized. A mythological quality is as much out of place as it would be in the Avesta, when milk is enumerated among the foods which may be given to a woman who has

[1] See J. H. Breasted, *History of Egypt*, New York, 1909, p. 55.
[2] See, *e.g.*, M. Jastrow, *Bildermappe zur Religion Babyloniens und Assyriens*, Giessen, 1912, Tafel 7, No. 23.
[3] *Yasna*, x. 13; *Nyāyišn*, i. 16; *Nirangistān*, 76; it is also an offering by itself in *Yasna*, iii. 1, 3, iv. 1; *Visparad*, xi. 3; *Nir.* 57, 60, 108.
[4] See *PEFSt*, 1888, p. 188, and W. R. Smith, *Rel. of Semites*², London, 1894, p. 221 n.
[5] W. R. Smith, *loc. cit.*
[6] *EBi* ii. 2104 f.
[7] *Rhein. Museum für Phil.* lvii. 177–195.
[8] *ZATW* xxii. 321–324.
[9] *KAT*³, p. 526.
[10] *Ursprung der israel.-jüd. Eschatologie*, pp. 209–221.

[1] So J. A. Bewer, in *ICC*, 'Obadiah and Joel,' Edinburgh, 1912, p. 140 f.
[2] H. C. O. Lanchester, in R. H. Charles, *Apocrypha and Pseudepigrapha*, Oxford, 1913, ii. 391, 402.
[3] H. Zimmern, *Ritualtafeln für den Wahrsager, Beschwörer und Sänger*, Leipzig, 1901, p. 239.
[4] *Cuneiform Texts from Bab. Tab. etc. in Br. Museum*, xvii., London, 1903, pl. 23, ll. 170–181; cf. Jastrow, *Rel. Bab. und Assyr.* i. (Giessen, 1905) 347.

brought forth a still-born child, in order to effect her purification (see *Vendīdād*, v. 52, vii. 67). Milk is here only one of several ingredients—meat, bread, wine, water. As she had first to drink ox-urine, the milk can hardly have been chosen for mythological reasons. Another fragmentary text which has been frequently cited on the basis of an indefinite reference by Friedrich Delitzsch[1] runs as follows:[2]

> 'Crown of . . .
> For the shepherd of the black-headed [people] . . .
> I pray a prayer . . .
> A sceptre of lapis lazuli may his hand [grasp] . . .
> For the shepherd of the black-headed [people] . . .
> Honey and *laban* abundantly . . .
> The mountain bearing produce . . .
> The steppe, the field bearing fruit . . .
> The orchards bearing fruit . . .
> On his left hand may the god Sin . . .
> To the king in person may they do homage!'

This is clearly a prayer for a Babylonian ruler. The petitioner asks that great fertility and prosperity may come in his time. The language resembles that of Joel and the Sibyl, but the imagery is capable of as natural an explanation as is that of the Hebrew seers.

The other passage which has been thought to show that the Babylonians and Assyrians held mythological views of milk and honey occurs in an incantation. The part in question reads:

> 'Pure water bring into its midst.
> The exalted lord, the great serpent of heaven,
> By his pure hands shall establish thee;
> Ea to a place of purity shall bring thee,
> To a place of purity shall bring thee,
> With his pure hands shall bring thee,
> Into honey and *laban* shall bring thee.
> Water of an incantation he shall put to thy lips,
> Thy mouth with an incantation he shall open.'[3]

Here at last we have a passage that moves in such a realm of heavenly unreality that it may fairly be regarded as based on a myth, but the mythical part does not centre at all in the honey and *laban*, but in the action of the god. Honey and *laban* are used to denote a place of fertility and plenty, and it may fairly be claimed that they were introduced here from such usage as that of the preceding passage, and are no necessary part of the myth.

The Semites probably had their origin as a separate people in Arabia,[4] which was a land of deserts and oases. It was thus that the oasis and its palm-tree became one of the symbols of paradise and an emblem of the Golden Age, and finally entered as one of the elements into the Christian symbolism of the New Jerusalem.[5] It seems probable that in the primitive language of the desert an oasis or a fertile land like Babylonia and Palestine may have been designated as a 'land flowing with milk and honey.' The occurrence of the phrase among both Babylonians and Hebrews points in this direction; it probably had an origin in their common ancestry. As the phrase is lacking, however, in the description of paradise both in Gn 2, 3 and in Ezk 28, it can hardly have formed an integral part of the traditions of the Golden Age, or have entered as an important element into the mythology of the Semites.

Indeed, in the paradise story of Gn 3 the food which makes man like God is not milk and honey, but the fruit of a tree. So in the corresponding Babylonian story, the Adapa myth, it was not milk and honey, but 'food and water,' that might have gained immortality for Adapa.[6] As these accounts are doubtless both variants of the same primitive paradise myth, it is impossible to resist the conviction that milk and honey formed no part of that myth among the Semites, but was simply a descriptive phrase employed by the dwellers in the desert to describe fertile lands—a phrase which survived both in Babylonia and in Palestine, and which came only in post-Exilic times among the Hebrews to designate a Golden Age that was still future.

3. In the Avesta.—Among the Persians these ideas apparently did not in the early time play a prominent rôle. Milk was offered in sacrifice and was used in certain incantations, as noted above. Homage was rendered to it,[1] and it was regarded as a divinely purified provision in the breasts of females, as was the seed in males;[2] a prosperous woman was 'rich in children and rich in milk.'[3] The cow was regarded as a beneficent animal guarded by Ahura Mazda as he guarded all other things on which the prosperity of people depends,[4] but in no sense a heavenly animal. So far from Jews having borrowed a myth from Persians, as Usener thought, the elements of the supposed myth appear only in the later syncretistic Mithra cult, and would seem to have been borrowed from the Semites.

4. In the Vedas.—In India milk was viewed as a symbol of nourishment. The Atharvaveda regards a house full of nurture as one full of milk,[5] and the earth is a mother who can pour forth milk for her suppliants.[6] Nevertheless in the Rigveda both milk and honey were employed in the ritual, though they were both subordinate to the all-prevailing *soma*. When milk was used as an offering, it was sometimes sweet and sometimes sour, both kinds of offerings being recognized.[7] As in Iranian ritual, the milk was often mixed with *soma*, the lacteal element sometimes being sour.[8] Honey was in the same way used as an offering; sometimes it was mixed with *soma*,[9] but sometimes with milk. Thus Rigveda, VIII. iv. 8, addresses Indra:[10]

> 'With honey of the bees is the milk mixed;
> Come quick, run and drink!'

Milk was created in kine by Varuṇa, even as he gave cool breezes to the forests, swiftness to horses, wisdom to the heart of man, lightning to the clouds, the sun to the sky, and *soma* to the mountains (Rigveda, V. lxxxv. 2). This reveals a high estimate placed upon milk and honey as foods, but lacks any mythical element,[11] as does the passage (X. lxiii. 3) in which the sky (*dyau*) gives milk to the All-Gods.

The Sanskrit poets often allude to the ability of the swan to separate milk from water; but this, as C. R. Lanman has shown, has no mythological significance. It is a reference rather to the fact that these birds fed on the milk-like juice of the lotus stalks, which grew beneath the water.[12] Similarly the religious teachers of India often use as an illustration of a changing existence the relationship between sweet milk, sour cream, and butter, not because they saw anything mythological in them, but because they illustrated change in forms of existence.[13]

In India, then, it can only be said that milk and honey were so highly valued as food that they

[1] In George Smith, *Chaldäische Genesis*, Leipzig, 1876, p. 285 n.; cf. Kennedy, 'Honey,' in *EBi*, col. 2104, and G. B. Gray, in *ICC*, 'Isaiah,' Edinburgh, 1912, i. 129 f.
[2] H. C. Rawlinson, *Cuneiform Inscriptions of Western Asia*, iv., London, 1891, no. 3, 1–27.
[3] *Ib.* 25, 39–55*a*.
[4] See G. A. Barton, *Sem. Origins*, New York, 1902, ch. i.
[5] *Ib.* p. 96, n. 1, and Barton, *The Roots of Christian Teaching as found in the OT*, Philadelphia, 1902, pp. 262–266.
[6] Cf. *KB* vi. 97–99.

[1] *Yasna*, vi. 17, vii. 26, viii. 1, xvi. 8.
[2] *Ib.* lxv. 5.
[3] *Vend.* xxi. 6, 7; *Yašt* xxiv. 13, 49.
[4] *Vend.* v. 20.
[5] Atharvaveda, IX. iii. 16.
[6] *Ib.* XII. i. 9 f., 59.
[7] Cf. Hillebrandt, *Ved. Myth.* i. 219–222.
[8] *Ib.* p. 222.
[9] *Ib.* p. 243 f.
[10] *Ib.* p. 238.
[11] For the various sacrifices into which milk entered as an element (sacrifices to the dead, new and full-moon sacrifices, etc.) see A. Hillebrandt, *Rituallitteratur: Vedische Opfer und Zauber* (=*GIAP* iii. 2), Strassburg, 1897, pp. 95, 110, 111, 117, 131, 135, 160, 172, 186.
[12] *JAOS* xix. [1898] 151–158.
[13] Cf. H. C. Warren, *Buddhism in Translations*, Cambridge, Mass., 1900, pp. 114, 134, 149.

naturally formed a part of the most valued offerings to the gods. Perhaps the proper mixture of these viands was supposed to have some magic significance, for one passage (Rigveda, IX. xi. 2) says that they were mixed by the *atharvans*;[1] but there is no trace of such a myth as some have supposed for the Semites.

5. In Egypt.—In Egypt, as already noted, the sky-goddess was pictured as either a woman or a cow with full breasts; but this was only to symbolize her nurture of her earthly children. If milk had in early Egyptian thought any mythological significance, we should expect to find it prominent among the foods promised to the deified kings to whom the pyramid-texts of the Old Kingdom promised a place among the gods. True, the departed king is frequently represented as suckled by the sky-goddess or some other divinity connected with Re. The goddess is once thus addressed: 'O mother of this king Pepi . . . give thy breast to this king Pepi, suckle this king Pepi therewith.' The goddess replies: 'O my son Pepi, my king, my breast is extended to thee, that thou mayest suck it, my king, and live, my king, as long as thou art little.'[2] Milk was, then, the food of the celestials only during their heavenly childhood. When Pepi was grown, he was promised 'bread which cannot dry up' and 'beer which cannot grow stale.'[3] Later he is given a 'snared fowl.'[4] Bread is called 'the bread of the god.' Pepi is invited to 'sit down to thy thousand of bread, thy thousand of beer, thy thousand of oxen, thy thousand of geese, thy thousand of everything whereon the god liveth.'[5] Another source of food for the deified king is the tree of life situated in a mysterious isle at a distance, and this king Pepi sought and attained.[6] This tree of life is probably a survival from a desert and oasis life similar to that of the Semites.[7] Milk plays very little part in these Egyptian myths.[8] It is only the food of the deified kings during that part of their celestial life which corresponds to childhood on earth.

6. In Græco-Roman literature.—Among the Greeks and Romans, as among the Semites and people of India, milk and honey were delicacies that were much appreciated, and their use goes back to an early time. Libations of milk and honey were, according to the *Iliad*,[9] poured out for the dead, and such libations appear to have continued down to the Christian era.[10] In case of pestilence milk and honey were among the offerings presented at the sacred mountains of Pelion and Ida;[11] and, before eating, milk, honey, and bread were offered to Hestia.[12] Milk and honey were also symbols of plenty and prosperity. Thus Pindar († 442 B.C.) says:

> 'Rejoice, my friend! Lo, I send you, though at late hour, this honey mixed with white milk, fringed with the froth of blending, a draught of song conveyed in the breathings of Aeolian flutes.'[13]

Though here metaphorical for sweet poetry, the metaphor attests the use of milk and honey as delicacies. In course of time both milk and honey became symbols of plenty. Thus Tibullus († 18 B.C.) says:

> 'The oaks themselves give honey, and beyond the sheep
> Bring udders of milk ready to the hand of the care-free.'[14]

Similarly Ovid:

> 'Now rivers of milk, now rivers of nectar run,
> And yellow honey distils from the green ilex.'[1]

With these poets milk and honey have become emblems of the Golden Age, but with many others they are simply symbols of plenty.[2]

Latin writers are, of course, dependent on Greek models for their imagery, and it is possible that Tibullus and Ovid were influenced directly or indirectly by Semitic ideas. A usage of milk and honey, however, which goes back to Homeric times cannot have been borrowed from the Persians. Possibly it may have come from Semitic Mesopotamia through the Hittites, since Hittites appear to be mentioned in the *Odyssey*,[3] but we know as yet too little of Hittite ritual to regard this as more than a remote possibility. Possibly, too, it may have been carried to the Ægean lands by Phœnicians, but it is quite as probable that the uses of milk and honey developed in the Ægean lands independently of Semitic ideas.

7. Among Christians.—The many references to milk and honey in Patristic literature collected by Usener[4] are clearly echoes of Joel and the Sibyl. Some curious Christian myths connected with the milk of the Virgin Mary are, however, still current in Bethlehem and its vicinity. There is at Bethlehem a cave called the 'Milk Grotto.'[5] A legend has it that the Holy Family once took refuge there, and that, as the Virgin nursed the Child, a drop of her milk fell on the floor. Because of this it is still believed that a sojourn in the grotto not only increases the milk of women and animals, but cures them of barrenness. In reality this legend arose to Christianize a grotto that was originally a shrine of Ashtoreth.[6]

All about Bethlehem the limestone crumbles and forms little white pebbles about the size of peas. These are accounted for by the story that a drop of the Virgin's milk fell on the rock, and that these pebbles are the miraculous result. Similarly it is said that, as the Virgin nursed the Child by the wayside, a drop of her milk fell on a thistle, which on this account became flecked with white and is called 'Mary's thistle.'[7] These myths are the outgrowth of the transfer to the Virgin of the old grotto of the mother-goddess, and are really much more exotic to Christianity than the quotation in the Patristic writers about the Golden Age.

In the early Church the newly baptized were given milk and honey to taste (or, in some Western churches, milk and wine) as symbolizing their regeneration through baptism (cf. 1 Co 3^2, He 5^{12}, 1 P 2^2). By the twenty-fourth canon of the Third Council of Carthage (397) this milk and honey was to be consecrated at the altar on Easter Even, the most solemn day for baptism; but the use has been forbidden since the Trullan Council of 692.[8]

LITERATURE.—A. Hillebrandt, *Vedische Mythologie*, Breslau, 1891–1902, i. 219–222, 238–244; A. A. Macdonell and A. B. Keith, *Vedic Index*, London, 1912, i. 67, 208 f., 234, 338, 490 f.; T. K. Cheyne, *EBi*, 2104; H. Usener, in *Rheinisches Museum für Philologie*, lvii. [1902] 177–195; B. Stade, in *ZATW* xxii. [1902] 321–327; H. Gressmann, *Ursprung der israelitisch-jüdischen Eschatologie*, Göttingen, 1905, pp. 209–221; C. Clemen, *Primitive Christianity and its Non-Jewish Sources*, Edinburgh and New York, 1912, p. 143 ff.; O. Dähnhardt, *Sagen zum Neuen Testament*, Leipzig, 1909, ch. xviii.

GEORGE A. BARTON.

1 See Hillebrandt, *Ved. Myth.* i. 238.
2 See K. Sethe, *Die altägyptischen Pyramidentexte*, ii. (Leipzig, 1910) §§ 910–913, and J. H. Breasted, *Development of Religion and Thought in Ancient Egypt*, London and New York, 1912, p. 130.
3 Sethe, i. [1908] § 859.
4 *Ib.* ii. § 1394.
5 *Ib.* § 2026 f.; Breasted, p. 132.
6 *Ib.* i. § 484; Breasted, p. 134.
7 Barton, *Sem. Or.* p. 117 f.
8 So W. Max Müller in a private letter to the writer.
9 xxiii. 170 f.
10 Cf. Eur. *Orestes*, 114 f., and Vergil, *Æn.* iii. 66.
11 O. Gruppe, *Griech. Mythol. und Religionsgesch.*, Munich, 1906, p. 248.
12 Silius Ital. vii. 184.
13 *Nem.* iii. 76 ff.
14 I. iii. 45 f.

1 *Metam.* i. 111 f.
2 Cf. Aristoph. *Birds*, 749; Horace, *Odes*, II. xix. 9 f. IV. ii. 27, *Epod.* xvi. 47–50; and Vergil, *Ecl.* iv. 30.
3 xi. 520 f.
4 *Op. cit.*
5 See K. Baedeker, *Palestine and Syria*[5] (Eng. tr.), Leipzig, 1912, p. 106 f.
6 Cf. Barton, in *BW* xxiv. [1904] 178, n. 21.
7 Cf. O. Dähnhardt, *Sagen zum NT*, ch. xviii.
8 J. Bingham, *Antiquities of the Chr. Church*, London, 1843-45, iv. 50–52, v. 35.

MILL, JAMES AND JOHN STUART.—The two Mills, father and son, occupy a unique position in the history of British thought. They were, after Bentham, the greatest figures in the utilitarian school and the leaders of the philosophical radicals in politics.

1. James Mill.—Next to Bentham, James Mill was the force that moulded the early expression of utilitarian doctrine. He was a Scotsman by birth, the son of humble parents (his father a country shoemaker and his mother a farmer's daughter), born at North Water Bridge, on the North Esk, in the parish of Logie-Pert, Forfarshire, on 6th April 1773. By his intellectual ability and his indomitable power of work, he raised himself to the commanding position that he ultimately attained. His early education was received at the parish school of his native place, and afterwards at Montrose Academy, where he had as schoolfellow Joseph Hume. From Montrose Academy he went to Edinburgh University (in the palmy days of Dugald Stewart), where he graduated M.A. in 1794, and forthwith proceeded to the study of Divinity, and was licensed as a preacher of the gospel in the Church of Scotland in 1798. The ministry, however, was not destined to keep him long. Being appointed tutor to the only daughter of Sir John Stuart of Fettercairn (Member of Parliament for Kincardineshire), he came under the special notice of Sir John, and went with him to settle in London in 1802. He was not long in London before he made his presence felt. In 1803 we find him active in originating *The Literary Journal* and making many contributions to it. In 1804 he produced his pamphlet on the *Corn Trade*. Thenceforth he contributed articles, in an unceasing flow, to innumerable periodicals and magazines—*The Philanthropist*, *The Annual Review*, *The Westminster Review*, *The London Review*, *The Edinburgh Review*. But his most outstanding essays were written for the Supplement to the fifth edition of the *Encyclopædia Britannica*, the chief of them being on 'Government,' 'Education,' 'Jurisprudence,' and 'Laws of Nations.' A reprint of the *Encyclopædia* articles was made in book form and had a wide influence. For about eleven years (from 1806 to the end of 1817) he worked strenuously at his *History of British India*, which, on its publication, produced a great impression. The immediate result was his appointment to a post in the India House, in the department of Examiner of India Correspondence, where he became head of the office in 1830. Besides a little book on the *Elements of Political Economy* (1821), largely reproducing Adam Smith, but embodying also the distinctive principles of Ricardo, he produced his great psychological work, the *Analysis of the Phenomena of the Human Mind*, which was brought out in 1829. This at once raised him to the position of psychologist in chief of the utilitarian school, filling the gap that had been left in the elaborate and multifarious teaching of Bentham. With Bentham himself Mill was on terms of the most intimate friendship, and the master regarded him as his most stalwart disciple. So staunch a Benthamite, indeed, was Mill that it has been doubted whether he was anything more than a brilliant reproducer of Bentham's opinions. That, however, does Mill an injustice. He was no mere echo, but a voice. His psychology alone proves it; and he was potent as a political force to an extent that even Bentham hardly equalled. When he died (his death took place in London, on 23rd June 1836), he was generally admitted to be the great inspiring spirit of radicalism and the one man who could have made the radical propaganda the success that it had become. In the year before his death (1835) appeared his *Fragment on Mackintosh*. This is really a vigorous defence of empiricism against intuitionism, though it assumes the form of a vehement criticism of Mackintosh, and is chiefly valuable as presenting Mill's philosophical positions in a clear and condensed light, rendered all the more effective by the polemic setting.

Mill's fame as a psychologist rests on his consistent experientialism, his thoroughgoing application of association to the phenomena of the mind, and his uncompromising insistence on the power of associationism to explain the mind and all its processes. But this has already been brought out in the art. ASSOCIATION, and need not be further dwelt on. A word, however, may be said on his psychological ethics. Mill's ethics is essentially hedonistic: the human will is moved by pleasure (or the avoidance of pain) and by this alone; and with a view to the attainment of pleasure (or to the getting rid of pain) men habitually act. But there is such a thing as disinterested conduct; and by the utilitarian himself benevolence is regarded as the supreme virtue. How, then, explain this? In the first place, Mill has recourse to the distinction (of which Bentham had made so much) between motive and intention, and maintains that, while our intention in benevolence is disinterested, our motive is interested; in other words, a benevolent action pleases the individual, gives him satisfaction, else he would not do it, but it also promotes the happiness of others. Now, this being pleased with acting benevolently towards another—what else is it than the individual identifying another's happiness with his own? And what more could be demanded of him? 'Can any greater degree of social love be required,' asks Mill, 'than that the good of others should cause us pleasure; in other words, that their good should be ours?' (*Frag. on Mackintosh*, p. 294). Then, again, there is the ethical principle of transformation (the phrase is not Mill's) to be considered—the principle that we see at work in the miser, whose nature is so changed by his traffic with money that the original desire of money for the pleasure that it can procure him becomes ultimately the desire of money for its own sake. What happens in the case of the miser happens in the case of disinterestedness and benevolence. Although individual pleasure lies at the root of a man's benevolent action, he has come, through continued intercourse with men and the experience of mutual help, to submerge the thought of his own pleasure and make benevolence itself his end.

What, then, of conscience, with its intuitions and its vaticinations? Conscience to Mill is not a simple and elementary faculty in human nature, but the product of association. That gives to it its power, and explains its peculiarities, and indeed constitutes its value. The ultimate test of morality is utility: right and wrong are qualities of conduct and are to be gauged by the tendency of actions to produce pleasure or pain.

Education occupied a large share of Mill's attention. As a utilitarian radical, he was eager that the people should be educated—educated so as to develop and improve their intelligence, and render them fit to be worthy citizens. Hence, he took a practical interest in the educational movement of the time, and entered as a keen polemic into the controversy between the Lancasterian and the Bell systems of education; he tried to establish a school (but failed) on the principles of Bentham laid down in his *Chrestomathia* ('Study of useful things'): and he was one of the small band of ardent educationists who originated the University of London. But his claim to honour as an educationist rests on his broad-minded theory of education, as developed in his *Encyclopædia* article, where education is shown to be the work of a man's life-time, where the roots of it are laid in associationist psychology, and where the principles of Helvetius regarding the almost unlimited power of education in transforming the individual are vigorously enforced.

In the realm of jurisprudence Mill made for himself a great name in the sphere of international law. His *Encyclopædia* article on that subject is, within its limits, almost perfect. It might be elaborated at points and more fully illustrated, but it is everywhere wise and suggestive. Particularly striking are its handling of the rights of nations in the time of war, and its treatment of the possibility of an effective court of arbitration in international quarrels.

As a philosophical politician Mill achieved fame by his theory of government. It is not a theory that is invulnerable. It lays itself open to objection as to the adequacy of its analysis of human nature; it was attacked by Macaulay on the ground of its deductive method and disregard of the inductive mode of procedure; and Sir James Mackintosh attacked it on the side of its extreme advocacy of popular representation, which seemed to ignore the danger of democratic tyranny, or the abuse of power on the part of the 'masses' in defiance of the interests of the 'classes.' The foundation of the theory is that the individual man is by nature self-centred, that he aims at pleasure for self and as much of it as he can obtain, and that, in his pursuit of personal interest, he is ready to lay hold of everything that ministers to his gratification, regardless of the pleasures and desires of others. Hence the need of government, and its meaning: government just signifies keeping one man from grasping at and mercilessly pursuing what belongs to another. But the members of a government are themselves men, with men's selfish passions and readiness to tyrannize over others, and, consequently, need themselves to be restrained. The restraint comes and only can come from the people; and the only tolerable form of government is a representative government — a government where the people's representatives act as a check on legislative abuse. It is only when the people are governed by men elected by themselves and representing them that the interests of governors and governed can be identified. Yet this identification of interest is liable to be broken through, if the representatives are not themselves watched. A body of representative men, if left entirely to their own actions, will have 'sinister' interests and may become as selfish and oppressive as an individual may be. The safeguard lies in frequent parliamentary elections: thus only (so it appeared to Mill) could the people retain a proper hold on their own representatives.

Into social reform Mill threw himself with much energy. Reforming zeal was the great characteristic of the utilitarians. This was but the practical side of their all-controlling principle, the general welfare, or the greatest happiness of the greatest number. Prisons and prison discipline, mendicancy, the Poor Laws, and such like engaged his pen; and it was through the influence of his views, to no small extent, that subsequent reforms were effected.

2. **John Stuart Mill.**—The eldest child of James Mill was John Stuart Mill (born in London on 20th May 1806; died at Avignon, in France, on 8th May 1873). His early education was conducted solely by his father, who, although constantly occupied in literary and exacting work, did not grudge to act as schoolmaster to his son. His method of teaching was altogether of an exceptional kind; and, although the result of it was also exceptional, the method has not been imitated by others or regarded as generally practicable. At three years of age the boy was set to learn Greek, which was his chief study for the next five years, English and arithmetic being added as secondary subjects. This created in the youthful learner a love for Greek—not only for the language, but for the literature and the thought of Greece—that lasted throughout his life. There is nothing more noticeable in his writings than his genuine appreciation of the dialectic method of Plato and his constant use of the Socratic mode of inductive defining, in order to secure clear concepts and exact verbal expression of them, with a view to truth. At the age of eight, the boy had Latin added to his Greek; and, by the time that he was fourteen years of age, he was indoctrinated into the principles of logic, psychology, and political economy. These were stiff subjects for a boy of that age; but they were the subjects in which he afterwards excelled.

All the time that these subjects were being set as tasks, the father was making the boy his constant companion, sharer in his daily walks, and, through his conversation and judicious cross-questioning, was gradually developing the boy's mind and imparting to him clearness and exactness of thought and confidence in thinking. This Socratic procedure was supplemented at the earliest moment by making the boy himself a teacher. He was set to superintend the education of the younger members of the family, thereby enabling him to gain further clearness of ideas and to strengthen his intellectual faculty. No wonder that the precocity of young Mill became proverbial.

A further stage in his education was a year's sojourn in France, as the guest of Sir Samuel Bentham, at the age of fourteen. This introduced him to the French language and to French literature and politics; and, through excursions in the Pyrenees and elsewhere, aroused in him an enthusiasm for natural scenery and a love for botany and zoology. These things all influenced him in later life.

On his return from France, he was further taken in hand by his father. He was now directly introduced to Bentham's teaching, in the French translation and exposition of it in P. E. L. Dumont's *Traités de législation* (London, 1802). 'The reading of this book,' he says (*Autobiography*, p. 64), 'was an epoch in my life; one of the turning points in my mental history.' At this time also he studied Roman law under John Austin, the jurist.

At the age of sixteen, the youth was beginning to feel his intellectual independence. Burning with enthusiasm for Bentham, he started a Bentham Club of young men, which he designated 'The Utilitarian Society.' Somewhat later he became a member of 'The Speculative Society,' and was also a prominent figure among the youths who met, at stated times, in George Grote's house for discussion of philosophical and economic questions. Later he took an active share in 'The Political Economy Club.' Thus was the development of young Mill's thought and mind further aided by a variety of powerful intellectual agencies.

In 1823, at the age of seventeen, came his appointment, by the East India Company, to the post of Assistant Examiner, under his father, in the Office of the Examiner of India Correspondence. This continued till he reached the position of Chief of the office in 1856—two years before the abolition of the East India Company.

A turning-point in his life was his break-down in health in 1826. There is little doubt that hard work, long-continued and unintermitted, and the over-strain of early education under his father's tuition were largely the cause of this. But there was something more. There was the emotional nature of the young man, which had been cramped but not destroyed by his father's one-sided training, craving for satisfaction. The end of the crisis was what he himself regards as analogous to a 'conversion.' It came in large measure through study of the poetry of Wordsworth and the philosophy of Coleridge, and showed itself in a revolution both in his intellectual opinions and in his character. He was no longer the undiscriminating follower of Bentham that he had been; he was no longer neglectful of the emotional side of human nature. He emerged from the ordeal a new man, with wider mental outlook and deeper and intenser sympathies. The extent of the change may be seen by reference to his two remarkable essays on Bentham and Coleridge, republished in vol. i. of his *Dissertations and Discussions* (London, 1859-67).

Another important factor in his life was the influence over him of Mrs. Taylor, who became his wife in 1851.

His work in connexion with literary journals was enormous. He wrote articles almost without number and on an exhaustless variety of subjects (philosophical, political, economic, social). They began with *The Westminster Review* and extended to other magazines—especially *The London Review* and, afterwards, *The London and Westminster Review*. They are valuable as enabling us to trace the development of his opinions, the growth of his views in philosophy, and the gradual modification of his radicalism in politics.

His first great intellectual work was his *System of Logic, Ratiocinative and Inductive*, which appeared in 1843. This was followed, in due course, by his *Essays on some Unsettled Questions of Political Economy* (1844), and *Principles of Political Economy* (1848). In 1859 appeared his little treatise on *Liberty*, and his *Thoughts on Parliamentary Reform*. His *Considerations on Representative Government* belongs to the year 1860; and in 1863 (after first appearing in magazine form) came his *Utilitarianism*. In 1865 came his *Examination of Sir William Hamilton's Philosophy*; in 1867 his Rectorial *Inaugural Address* at St. Andrews University, on the value of culture; in 1868 his pamphlet on *England and Ireland*; and in 1869 his treatise on *The Subjection of Women*. In 1869 also was published his edition of his father's *Analysis of the Phenomena of the Human Mind*, with many valuable notes illustrative and critical by J. S. Mill himself, by Bain and Grote, and by Andrew Findlater. His two posthumous works are his *Autobiography* (1873) and his *Three Essays on Religion* (1874). To these have to be added the two large volumes of *Letters* (ed. Hugh S. R. Elliot) published in 1910.

A phase of Mill's life has still to be noted—his parliamentary career. In the Parliament of 1865-68 he sat as Radical member for Westminster. Three things in chief did he advocate in the House of Commons—women suffrage, the interests of the labouring classes, and land reform in Ireland.

In philosophy J. S. Mill's fame rests chiefly on his *Logic*, his *Political Economy*, and his *Examination of Sir William Hamilton*, to be taken in connexion with his notes in his edition of his father's *Analysis*.

As a logician he stands out as the great empiricist who formulated and elaborated inductive logic, who re-stated and in part revolutionized deductive logic, who made systematic application of logical principles to the moral sciences (including politics), and who enforced, in polemic form, the power of experience to be the criterion or ultimate test of truth. The brilliancy of his thought and the clearness of his style (including an unwonted aptitude for felicitous illustration, ranging over a wide field of knowledge) cannot be too highly praised. The stimulus to the student derivable from a study of his *Logic* is undoubted. The epoch-making character of his great work must be acknowledged without reserve. But how far he has succeeded in bridging the gulf between inductive and syllogistic logic may be disputed—even Bain, his intimate friend and associate, has his doubts (see his *Dissertations on Leading Philosophical Topics*, London, 1903, pp. 21-26); and empirical logic has made great advances since his day. On the other hand, it must be allowed that these advances were rendered possible only through Mill's work.

In psychology Mill upheld the associationism of his father, but gave a more attractive expression of it as 'mental chemistry.' He carried forward his psychology into theory of knowledge and formulated his doctrine of psychological idealism (founding on Berkeley), which, resting on the empirical genesis of knowledge through the various senses operated by association, issues in the conception of matter or objective reality as 'the permanent possibility of sensations' and of mind as 'the permanent possibility of feeling.' In the case of mind, however, there is a peculiarity: it is *conscious* of its states. This we must accept, as it is given in our experience, but we must accept it as inexplicable—no further account of it is possible. He was unbending in his opposition to those who base truth on intuition. Not that he denied the fact of intuition, but he demanded that it should be tested by experience, so that it may not become (as it had become to a school of philosophers at the time) the bulwark of prejudice and irrationality and the hindrance to intellectual, political, and social progress.

Mill's great work on *Political Economy* (equal in originality of thought and in importance to his *Logic*) is a clear exposition of the various branches of the science—wealth, distribution, consumption, and exchange, and all the various topics that arise out of these. It shows him also as a keen, but fair, critic. But his chief merit lies in his widening the scope of political economy and removing from it the reproach of being 'the dismal science.' This he did (partly under the influence of Auguste Comte) by infusing into it human feeling and associating it with the philosophy of society. Economic principles were now conjoined with their practical applications, and a transformation took place. Not only do we have a minute and scientific handling of such things as labour, capital, rate of interest, money, international trade, and all the other points that the ordinary political economy dealt with, but also a stimulating discussion and wise treatment of such deeply interesting problems as the future of the labouring classes, the land question, socialism, etc. In explanation of the exceptional popularity of the treatise he himself says:

> 'It was, from the first, continually cited and referred to as an authority, because it was not a book merely of abstract science, but also of application, and treated Political Economy not as a thing by itself, but as a fragment of a greater whole; a branch of Social Philosophy, so interlinked with all the other branches, that its conclusions, even in its own peculiar province, are only true conditionally, subject to interference and counter-action from causes not directly within its scope: while to the character of a practical guide it has no pretension, apart from other classes of considerations' (*Autobiog.*, p. 236).

That is, doubtless, absolutely correct.

Mill's utilitarian ethics, as expounded in his *Utilitarianism*, is extraordinarily significant; both the matter and the style fascinate, not less than the glow of conviction that permeates the whole. Justice has rarely been done to it by opponents, because they have failed to see (*a*) that it is not a treatise of pure abstract reasoning, but one written out of the living conviction of a man who loved his fellow-men; (*b*) that it is practical in its object, and not merely theoretical; and (*c*) that, although it sets forth pleasure or happiness as the standard and test of human conduct, it makes supreme the conception of man as a social being and conditions all by the conception of the general welfare. His view of the human will as determined by character, and of character as formed *by* a man, and not *for* him, is his contribution to the solution of the free will problem, and his defence of the position that there can be such a thing as a *science* of ethics—and, if of ethics, then also of economics.

Mill as a political thinker is a great subject. As a radical democrat, he loved the people and worked hard for them in parliament and out of it. But he would not submit in any degree or for a moment to their irrational desires and expectations. They had to be led and not followed. He was acutely conscious of their tendency to tyrannize and their selfish disregard of justice. He was exceptionally alive to their readiness to domineer over minorities; hence, he powerfully advocated the principle of parliamentary proportional representation. Thus alone, he thought, could minorities of electors get their rights. He saw the people's jealousy and suspicion of the educated and refined classes of society; hence, he stood fast by the principle of plurality of votes, as determined by culture and social position. He was very sensitive to the tendency in the masses to act unscrupulously and in an underhand fashion; therefore he opposed vote by ballot.

On the other hand, he was a strong upholder of the liberty of the individual; and he gave a powerful defence of individualism in his treatise *Liberty*—a defence of the right of the individual to hold his own opinions and to give free expression to them, and his right to live in such a way as seemed fit to himself, so long as his mode of living did not interfere with the rights and liberties of others. In the same spirit, though he was quite alive to the necessity of the government dictating and controlling within limits, and, therefore, restricting the liberty of the individual to that extent, he thought that the less government interfered the better: his legislative principle, with necessary qualifications, was *laissez-faire*.

Another object that lay near to Mill's heart was that of women suffrage. His book on the subject has exhausted the handling of the theme from that point of view. But he added active support to theory by consistently advocating universal franchise in parliament, and by pushing on and personally guiding the Women Movement in London and the provinces.

The problems of the universe were constantly in Mill's thoughts. He puzzled himself long and anxiously over the question of the freedom of the will, and ultimately reached the deterministic solution that has just been referred to. The nature of the external world and of the human ego also exercised his mind; and his doctrine of 'psychological idealism' was the result. But there still remained the problem of God. With the conception of the Deity as 'the Absolute,' unknown and unknowable, to whom no attributes (such as knowledge, mercy, and love) could be applied, he had no sympathy. His criticism of H. L. Mansel's view, as set forth in his Bampton Lectures on *The Limits of Religious Thought* ([5] London, 1870), is scathing and effective. But Mill's thought on the great theme is best given in his supremely interesting posthumous *Essays*. His honesty of character and his 'indifferency to truth' (as Locke would express it) here come out in a very striking fashion. Discouraged from theistic thinking by his father in his early training, and not encouraged to it by his utilitarian friends and fellow-thinkers in after life, he yet had that openness of mind that would willingly receive truth to whatever extent it might reveal itself. He fain would have been optimistic in his view of the universe, but he could not; and the most that he could do was to allow a conception of God that conserved His goodness but limited His power. In face of our harrowing experience of Nature 'red in tooth and claw with ravin' and of the unutterably hard and harsh experiences of life in general, he could not rise to the idea of a Great Power who was All-loving, Omniscient, and Omnipotent. But he was willing, or, at any rate, not unwilling, to believe in a Power of Goodness or of Love who would, if He could, subdue evil and put an end to suffering and misery and was only hindered by the recalcitrant circumstances of the world. This admission, combined with his admiration of Jesus of Nazareth as the highest of ethical teachers, shows his power of detachment from early upbringing and from immediate social environment, and his readiness to respond to the light whenever it came. This was the noblest trait of his character.

Mill's nature was, in many ways, an attractive one, characterized by high and sterling qualities. He was generous in his outlook and sympathetic with men in their struggles, aspirations, and doubts. He was eager to be fair in his estimate of others and of their opinions, and always ready to admit that there is likely to be some truth in every doctrine and belief that has been sincerely held; there was nothing of the persecutor in him. His disinterested regard for truth was unbounded; and he took little care to cloak or hide unpalatable opinions, but expressed himself freely without regard to personal consequences. He delighted in championing persons and causes that he conceived to be unjustly treated by society or by the law of the land. His public spirit was intense; and he never feared to attack legislative or other injustices, and to uphold unpopular views, in the interest of the working classes or of the downtrodden. His life was consistently devoted to one end—furtherance of the good and welfare of his fellow-men.

LITERATURE.—J. Grote, *Exploratio Philosophica*, Cambridge, 1865, *An Examination of the Utilitarian Philosophy*, do. 1870, *A Treatise on the Moral Ideals*, do. 1876; T. Ribot, *La Psychologie anglaise contemporaine*, Paris, 1870, Eng. tr., London, 1873; H. Sidgwick, *The Methods of Ethics*, London, 1874, [7]1907, *Outlines of the History of Ethics*, London and New York, 1886; A. Bain, *James Mill: a Biography*, London, 1882, *John Stuart Mill: a Criticism*, do. 1882; C. Douglas, *The Ethics of John Stuart Mill*, Edinburgh and London, 1897, *John Stuart Mill: a Study of his Philosophy*, do. 1895; Leslie Stephen, *The English Utilitarians*, London, 1900; H. Höffding, *A History of Modern Philosophy*, Eng. tr., do. 1900; P. Janet and G. Séailles, *A History of the Problems of Philosophy*, Eng. tr., do. 1902; E. Albee, *A History of English Utilitarianism*, London and New York, 1902; A. Seth Pringle-Pattison, *The Philosophical Radicals*, Edinburgh and London, 1907; J. MacCunn, *Six Radical Thinkers*[2], London, 1910; J. Seth, *English Philosophers and Schools of Philosophy*, London and New York, 1912.

WILLIAM L. DAVIDSON.

MILLENNIUM.—See ESCHATOLOGY.

MILTON.—1. Life.—John Milton was born in London at the Spread Eagle in Bread Street, Cheapside, on 9th Dec. 1608. He was the eldest son of John Milton, a London scrivener, whose conversion to the faith of the Anglican Church had led to his being disinherited by his father, a yeoman of Shotover Forest and a staunch Roman Catholic. The poet inherited the stubborn self-will of his grandfather and the more sensitive and cultured spirit of his father, from whom he also derived his taste for music. From the first the boy was studious, and his father supplied him with the best teachers. When in 1625 (Feb. 12) he entered Christ's College, Cambridge, at the age of sixteen, he had already acquired, under his first tutor, Thomas Young (a graduate of

St. Andrews), and at St. Paul's School, under the older and the younger Alexander Gill, a mastery of Latin, a competent knowledge of Greek, and even some acquaintance with Hebrew. 'From the twelfth year of my age I scarce ever forsook my nightly studies for bed before midnight' (*Defensio Secunda*, 1654). In English poetry he was familiar with Joshua Sylvester's translation of Du Bartas (1605), Fairfax's *Tasso* (1600), and probably Spenser, Drummond, and others. The older Gill was a reader of English literature, but probably Shakespeare and play-books were not welcomed in a religious family like that of the scrivener's, where 'last of all, not in time, but as perfection is last, that care was ever had of me, with my earliest capacity, not to be negligently trained in the precepts of Christian religion' (*Apology for Smectymnuus*, 1642). Milton was not attracted by the dialectical and theological studies of Cambridge. The lines *At a Vacation Exercise* and some Latin pieces show that he took his part in the prescribed work, but his favourite studies were literary and classical, 'grave orators and historians,' the 'smooth elegiac poets,' from whom he passed in 'riper years' to 'the shady spaces of philosophy; but chiefly to the divine volumes of Plato and his equal [*i.e.* contemporary] Xenophon.' To a knowledge of the classical poets he added now the Italians, 'the two famous renowners of Beatrice and Laura,' the 'lofty fables and romances' of Boiardo and Ariosto (*Apology for Smectymnuus*, Introd.). On the world of mediæval romance Milton looked out through Italian windows, but he was familiar (later, at any rate) with Geoffrey of Monmouth and probably with Malory. The poems of this period, both English and Latin, bear witness to the double source of Milton's poetic inspiration—classical literature and the Biblical Christianity of Puritan England. The finest expression of these, not always entirely compatible, tastes is the tender (an epithet so rarely applicable to Milton's poetry) and beautiful ode, *On the Morning of Christ's Nativity* (1629); while some lines of the *At a Vacation Exercise* and the short odes, *On Time* and *At a Solemn Music*, show the poet of *Paradise Lost* 'mewing his mighty youth' and meditating the sublimest flights of religious song:

'Yet I had rather, if I were to choose,
Thy service in some graver subject use,
Such as may make thee search thy coffers round,
Before thou clothe my fancy in fit sound:
Such where the deep transported mind may soar
Above the wheeling poles, and at Heaven's door
Look in, and see each blissful deity,' etc.
(*At a Vacation Exercise*, 29 ff.).

Milton left the University in 1632 without taking orders, and the next six years of his life were spent at Horton in the quiet prosecution of his studies in classical literature, history, mathematics, and music, with occasional visits to London to purchase books, to visit the theatre, to be an onlooker perhaps at Court ceremonials,

'Where throngs of knights and barons bold
In weeds of peace high triumphs hold' (*L'Allegro*, 119 f.),

and to enjoy the company of friends, among whom the first place was held by Charles Diodati. A young Italian girl, too, of whom we know only that her first name was Emilia, seems to have touched his fancy and occasioned the writing of his earliest Italian verses. The experience is perhaps referred to in the seventh of his Latin elegies. During these years he also extended his knowledge of English poetry from Chaucer and *Piers Plowman* to Shakespeare (at Cambridge he had already written his famous lines for the second folio), Jonson, and the later Elizabethans. All the poems written at this period bear witness to this native and Elizabethan influence, and some of them, as *L'Allegro* and *Il Penseroso*, are composed in a lighter, more secular and Epicurean vein than any English pieces (some of the Latin elegies are very much in this vein) had been or were ever again to be written by Milton. But in *Comus, or A Maske Presented at Ludlow Castle* (1634), which he composed at the invitation of Henry Lawes, all the resources of Milton's learning and art were employed to set forth his deepest ethical and religious convictions, his passionate love of purity, his sense of the dependence of all human virtue on the protecting grace of God. The theme of the second book of the *Faerie Queene* is rehandled by a poet of a higher moral temper and a no less, though more controlled and classically educated, sense of beauty.

Milton had gone to Cambridge with a view to taking orders, and, though he left without doing so, there is no evidence that he had ceased to be, when he settled at Horton, an orthodox Anglican. He was a communicant; he had signed the Articles; nothing had yet betrayed that he was by conviction a Presbyterian in his views on Church government; while on the doctrine of predestination in its relation to the human will his position was always closer to that of the Arminians than to that of the Calvinists. What alienated Milton from the Church of England was less its dogma than its practice, the rigour of Laud and the identification of Episcopacy with the Court and its arbitrary policy. His intense and ideal love of liberty was awakened, and the first notes of the coming storm were heard in *Lycidas* (1638), the most passionate, plangent, and musical poem which Milton had yet written. In the same year he went abroad, still intent rather on self-culture and the preparation for the task of writing a great poem than on controversy and theology. In Paris he met the Dutch *savant* Hugo Grotius, whose *Adamus Exul* was one of the sources of *Paradise Lost*. He spent two months in Florence, conversing and interchanging Latin and Italian verses with young Academicians. He proceeded to Rome, where he visited the Vatican Library and the English College, and heard Leonora Baroni sing at the palace of Cardinal Barberini. The elevated strain of compliment in the Latin verses addressed to her betrays the influence of Italian preciosity. At Naples he met Manso, Marquis of Villa, Tasso's patron and Marino's, and in a Latin poem addressed to him prays that he may find a like patron when he undertakes to sing of

'reges,
Arturumque etiam sub terris bella moventem,
Aut dicam invictae sociali foedere mensae
Magnanimos Heroas, et (O modo spiritus adsit!)
Frangam Saxonicas Britonum sub Marte phalanges!'
(*Sylvæ*, 'Mansus,' 80 ff.).

But Milton was not destined to sing of kings or the knights of the Round Table. The meeting of the Long Parliament determined him to return home, and he made his way back to England by Venice and Geneva to plunge soon into that long course of controversy, ecclesiastical and political, which determined the choice of themes, the doctrinal framework, and the temper and spirit of *Paradise Lost*, *Paradise Regained*, and *Samson Agonistes*.

The first of the controversies into which Milton plunged with ardour and vehemence was that concerning Church government, and the rival claims of a Presbyterian and Prelatical organization. In the first pamphlet, *Of Reformation in England* (May–June 1641), he raises the question why the English Reformation had lagged behind that on the Continent and attacks Episcopacy and English bishops and their 'policy' from Cranmer and Ridley to the promoters of the war with Scotland, closing with an amazing denunciatory prayer. *Of Prelatical Episcopacy* (June–July 1641) is an examination of the origin of Episcopacy in reply to a tract by Archbishop Ussher. Of the other pamphlets two, *Animadversions upon the Remonstrant's Defence against Smectymnuus* (July 1641) and *An Apology against a Pamphlet called a Modest Confutation of the Animadversions of the Remonstrant against Smectymnuus* (March–April 1642), were contributions to a controversy on Episcopacy between Hall and certain now little-known Puritan divines, of whom Thomas Young was one. The most fully reasoned and interesting statement of Milton's ideal Presbyterianism is contained in *The Reason of Church Government urged against Prelaty* (Jan.–March 1641–42). Two undercurrents of thought run through the main stream of controversy, rising to the surface from time to time, the one with unmistakable and eloquent distinctness, the other with less obtrusive yet sufficient clearness. The first of these concerns the great poem which he was meditating; the other shows him full of high thoughts concerning the mysteries of love and marriage. The Puritan movement had heightened men's ideals both of purity and of marriage, and Milton was as impassioned a champion of chastity as he was an enemy of asceticism. Love had touched his fancy in youth, but, when in May 1643 he married, it was clearly the act of one whose choice of the individual was too hastily determined by an ideal regard for the wedded estate; and the result was, what, as Milton himself complains, is more often the fate of the chaste and unworldly student than of the libertine, the discovery that in the wife whom he had chosen was to be found none of the qualities that he had so fondly anticipated, no intellectual help-meet, but an 'unconversing inability of mind,' 'a mute and spiritless mate,' begetting 'that melancholy despair which we see in many wedded persons' (*Doctrine and Discipline of Divorce*, i. 4). Others have experienced the same misfortune and in the end have managed to work along; but Milton was no average man, and he turned passionately round to discover an escape, and that one which should enjoy the approval of his own conscience and the Christian Church. *The Doctrine and Discipline of Divorce Restored* (Aug. 1643) was written and published (anonymously and without licence) before his wife had given any definite ground for separation. An enlarged and improved edition appeared in February 1644 with a signed introductory letter to 'the Parliament of England with the Assembly.' A second tract, *The Judgment of Martin Bucer concerning Divorce*, followed in July of the same year, vindicating Milton's position against critics; and to the same end he issued in March 1645 *Tetrachordon*, a discussion of four passages in Scripture, and *Colasterion*, a savage onslaught upon a certain Joseph Caryl, one of the licencers. Incidentally the divorce controversy called forth the most famous of Milton's pamphlets, *Areopagitica, A Speech . . . for the Liberty of Unlicens'd Printing* (Nov. 1644).

The outcry which the divorce pamphlets evoked opened Milton's eyes to the interval that separated his ideal Church from the Presbyterian Church which its votaries were seeking to invest with all the divine right and intolerant authority of the overthrown Episcopal Church of England, and helped him to formulate his own conception of Christianity as independent of any visible and authoritative Church. He never, therefore, identified himself with the Independents, but from this time to the close of the Commonwealth his sympathies were with that party in politics; and, when the death of the king completed the rupture between them and the Presbyterians, Milton came forward as the champion of regicide and the impugner of all connexion, whether of authority or endowment, between Church and State.

On 13th February 1649—a fortnight after the execution of Charles—appeared *The Tenure of Kings and Magistrates*, 'proving that it is lawfull, and hath been held so through all Ages, for any who have the Power, to call to account a Tyrant or wicked King, and after due conviction to depose and put him to death, if the ordinary Magistrate have neglected, or deny'd to do it. And that they who, of late, so much blame deposing are Men that did it themselves.' The sting in the tail of this bold title is intended for the Presbyterians, who are roughly handled throughout as hypocrites and revolters from their own principles. The *Eikonoklastes*, of the same year, follows chapter by chapter the *Eikon Basilike* in Milton's most scornful style. To Salmasius and other impugners of the King's execution Milton replied in his first and second *Defensio pro populo Anglicano* (1651, 1654). The *Defensio contra Morum* (1655) was a savage onslaught on one who, he believed, had slandered himself. His last purely political pamphlet, the *Ready and Easy Way to Establish a Free Commonwealth* (March 1660), was published on the eve of the Restoration.

That conception of the Church's influence and authority as purely spiritual which is evident in Milton's first sketch of an ideal Presbyterianism, and had been intensified by his rupture with the Presbyterians, led him to disapprove of Cromwell's attempt to combine religious endowment with a wide though still limited toleration; and his own position was expounded in the *Defensio Secunda* (in the middle of a eulogy of the Protector and his associates) and, after Cromwell's death, in *A Treatise of Civil Power in Ecclesiastical Cases* (Feb.–March 1659). When the Rump superseded Richard Cromwell and the question of tithes was raised, Milton published his *Considerations touching the likeliest Means to remove Hirelings out of the Church* (Aug. 1659), a bitter onslaught on the clergy, Presbyterian or Independent, who claimed tithes or fees instead of trusting to the 'benevolence and free gratitude' of their flocks. Milton's last religious works were the short pamphlet *Of True Religion, Heresy, Schism, and what best Means may be used against the Growth of Popery* (1673) and the body of divinity *De Doctrina Christiana*, on which he had been busy for many years, but which was not printed till 1825.

Throughout the rule of the Commonwealth Milton's life had been the twofold one of a private student and tutor (to children living in or coming to his house) and of a servant of the State as Latin secretary to the Council of State (1649–59). The incidents of his private life are few. In 1653 his wife died, and in 1656 he married Catharine Woodcock, whose early death in 1658 is referred to in the most touching of his sonnets. His marriage with Elizabeth Minshull in 1663 was a convenient arrangement.

During all these years Milton had written very little poetry. From 1640 to 1642 his mind had been full of his great projected work, and the commonplace-book preserved at Trinity College, Cambridge, shows the steady trend of his thoughts towards a drama on the subject of the Fall. Two sketches of the drama are set down, and his nephew, Edward Phillips, reports that the speech of Satan at the opening of the fourth book of *Paradise Lost* is part of the original scheme. The interest of controversy and the shock of his unhappy marriage interrupted the work and it was not resumed till 1658. In the interval the only English poems which Milton wrote were some sonnets on public events or persons and private incidents in the dignified manner of his Italian predecessors in similar poems, and in Italian form, for even the device of running the sense on from octave to sestet (which has been thought a device peculiar to himself) had been practised by Italian poets known to Milton. In 1658 *Paradise Lost* was resumed in epic, not dramatic, form; was composed to dictation, corrected, and completed by 1665; and published in 1667. It was followed in 1670 by *Paradise Regained*, an epic on 'the brief model' of the book of Job, and *Samson Agonistes*, Milton's sole experiment in those 'dramatic constitutions wherein Sophocles and Euripides reign.'

2. Thought and works.—Of Milton's early poems no more need be said here. Apart from their rare poetic beauty they bear delightful witness to the delicate purity and profound piety of the poet's childhood and youth, combining in an effect of unique and too transitory loveliness literary and classical culture with the finer spirit of a Puritanism which was not yet heated and hardened by the fires of religious and political controversy. The purpose of the present article is to outline the creed of Milton as it took shape in the years of storm and stress which followed his return to England and to consider the reflexion of this creed, and the temper which it at once expressed and intensified, in his longer poems.

In his earliest pamphlets Milton ranges himself on the side of the Presbyterian reformers of the Anglican Church. The Scriptures are the sole authority for the right government of the Church, which is not a matter that has been left to human discretion and experience to devise. God, who shaped to its minutest detail the government and worship of the Jewish temple, 'should he not rather now by his own prescribed discipline have cast his line and level upon the soul of man which is his rational temple, and, by the divine square and compass thereof, form and regenerate in us the lovely shapes of virtues and graces, the sooner to edify and accomplish that immortal stature of Christ's body which is his church, in all her glorious lineaments and proportions?' (*Reason of Church Government*, i. 2). But the NT recognizes only two orders, bishops or presbyters (they are the same thing) and deacons—so Paul writes to Timothy ('not once naming any other order in the Church'). Prelacy is an addition of man's devising and ambition ('Lucifer . . . was the first prelate angel') opposed to 'the reason and end of the gospel' (*ib.* i. 3 ff.).

But, when Milton came to state the respect in which Episcopal jurisdiction opposes the reason and end of the gospel, he parted company at once (how far consciously it is hard to say) with his Scottish and English sympathizers, and with the actual practice of dominant Presbyterianism. For his objection to Episcopal jurisdiction is the, for Milton, fundamental principle 'that jurisdictive power in the Church there ought to be none at all.' His objection is to the archidiaconal courts with their penalties and fines, and the Star Chamber. Over the outward man, person, and property, authority belongs to the State, which is not concerned with inner motives but with 'the outward peace and welfare of the commonwealth, and civil happiness in life' (*ib.* ii. 3). The authority of the Church is over the inward and spiritual man, and her sole weapons are instruction, admonition, reproof, and, finally, excommunication, the last to be so used as always to keep open the door of reconciliation to repentance. The motive to which the Church appeals is not terror, but shame, 'the reverence and due esteem' in which a man holds himself 'both for the dignity of God's image upon him and for the price of his redemption which, he thinks, is visibly marked upon his forehead,' making him account 'himself a fit person to do the noblest and godliest deeds, and much better worth than to deject and defile, with such a debasement, and such a pollution as sin is, himself so highly ransomed and ennobled to a new friendship and filial relation with God' (*ib.*). Such a conception of Christian conduct as springing from a man's sense of his own worth, a worth conferred by God from the beginning and renewed by redemption, is as characteristic of Milton, nurtured on the Bible but nurtured also upon the classics, as it is alien to the general trend of Protestant thought in Milton's England, which laid more stress on man's worthlessness than on his worth, and appealed less to shame as a motive than to fear of death and the judgment to come. Bunyan and Milton are separated by a wide gulf; and the noble temper of Milton's early lines *On Time* shows as little of Ronsard's or Shakespeare's regretful sense of the ravages of 'Time's fell hand' as of such a preacher as Donne's awed apprehension of the terror and the ecstasy of the Christian's death. And the idea of a Church whose authority is purely spiritual is even more remote from the thought and practice of Presbyterianism in power whether in Geneva, Holland, or Scotland. It was not to promote general toleration that the Scottish Presbyterians signed the Solemn League and Covenant.

Milton was quickly made aware of the interval that separated him from the Presbyterians by the publication of his pamphlets on divorce. The opposition which they excited seems to have taken him by surprise, but the anger which followed was intense and coloured all his subsequent thought. Repelled by Protestant orthodoxy—though he maintained strenuously that some of the greatest Protestant divines were on his side—he was driven to reconsider the whole question of orthodoxy; and he set out, with all the confidence of Satan voyaging across the 'wild abyss' of chaos, to articulate a creed for himself in the dogmatic manner of Trent and Westminster. The record of this progress is to be found in the controversial pamphlets, the elaborate *De Doctrina Christiana*, and, finally, in *Paradise Lost* and *Paradise Regained.*

Two principles control all Milton's findings. The first is that the ultimate arbiter of every question is the individual reason and conscience 'than which God only is greater.' The mind of each man is absolutely free to try all things and hold fast by his own conclusions uncontrolled by State or Church. This liberty is 'the fundamental privilege of the Gospel, the new birthright of every true believer, Christian liberty' (*A Treatise of Civil Power*, etc., also *De Doctrina Christiana*, Dedicatory Epistle). No one could assert more absolutely the fundamental principle of the Renaissance—the emancipation of the individual; and Milton approaches the solution of each question in the spirit of the later age of reason, with this difference that he accepts as a fundamental experience not to be reasoned upon—more than one can reason upon the fact of an external world—the Christian consciousness of sin and of redemption and regeneration through Christ as set forth in the Scriptures. This directs us to the second of the principles on which Milton's conclusions rest. The final source of all saving religious knowledge is the Bible. It is on this that the emancipated mind must exercise itself, from this its conclusions must be drawn. Milton's method, therefore, in discussing every question which he takes up, from the divinity of Christ to the liberty of the press, is twofold when the subject admits of both lines of argument: firstly, what does reason declare?—and Milton is as confident of the competence of *a priori* reasoning on political and social questions as any later theorist of revolution; secondly, what has Scripture declared, to what conclusion does it lead us when different passages are duly compared and when all are interpreted in the light of the Christian law of charity, in the spirit of the words 'the sabbath was made for man, and not man for the sabbath'? The one consideration to which Milton never condescends is expedience, the difficulties and the practical means of obviating these revealed by experience; he has none of Burke's reverence for 'prudence constituted as the god of this lower world.'

Milton's polemical pamphlets are, accordingly, a bewildering blend of ideal reasonings, high *a priori* principles set forth in glowing and harmonious but elaborately Latinized periods; a pedantic, at times captious and wrong-headed, citation and cross-examination of Biblical texts; truculent polemic, condescending not infrequently to coarse personal abuse; and withal a general absence of the mellower wisdom that proceeds from experience and charity. There is much to inspire and delight in these pages burning with fires that are perhaps not yet altogether extinct but in general have died down; there is little to interest the statesman. If Milton's pamphlets yet live, it is as eloquent statements of high and abstract ideals, to ignore which altogether is to reduce political expedience to sheer opportunism.

The divorce pamphlets have nothing to say upon the difficult problems of children and the mutual relations of the family and the State. They combine elevated reflexions on the ideal significance of marriage as a spiritual rather than a carnal union (regarded solely from the point of view of the man) with a tedious, passionate, wrong-headed attempt to reconcile Christ's prohibition of divorce 'but for adultery' with Moses' permission. God cannot have at any time permitted sin. The later command cannot have been intended, therefore, to annul the earlier, but merely to check certain prevalent abuses. Milton was not without apprehension of the fact of moral and religious progress. He went beyond the English Protestantism of his day in asserting that under the new dispensation the Mosaic moral as well as ceremonial law had been abolished. But the new law was, he maintained, a law of liberty, of greater responsibility because of greater freedom. Such a rigid law of marriage as the Churches asserted was a curtailment of the liberty which even the Law had granted, a fresh enslavement of the spirit to the letter. Looking at the question exclusively from the man's point of view, he advanced to an assertion of divorce as the private concern of the individual and to a defence of polygamy (*De Doctr. Christ.* i. 10).

The *Areopagitica* was an overflow from the divorce controversy, and is a magnificent *a priori* vindication of freedom of thought and speech as the fundamental condition of the successful quest of truth. The practical difficulties which have beset the attempt to find a solution, other than a compromise varying in different countries, lay outside Milton's ken; nor could he foresee all the evils that have attended the freedom allowed to a Chauvinist or a commercial press to deceive and to pervert.

The same lofty but *a priori* idealism combined with exposition of texts and interchange of personalities characterizes the pamphlets, Latin and English, written to vindicate the execution of Charles I., and those on, what became his favourite themes, an unendowed clergy and a universal toleration of all religious bodies, the Roman Catholic Church alone excluded. Of the original and inalienable rights of subjects and the duties and responsibilities of kings Milton writes with all the passion of a mind nurtured upon classical republicanism and OT history, and heated by the fires of civil war:

> 'There can be slain
> No sacrifice to God more acceptable
> Than an unjust and wicked king'
> (Seneca, *Herc. Fur.* 992, tr. in *The Tenure of Kings and Magistrates*).

The doctrine of the civil contract is buttressed by precedents from the turbulent annals of Israel, the early history of the Britons, the rebellions in Scotland and Holland. Of the real difficulties of the problem, as Hobbes saw them, of the fact that somewhere in every society there is and must be an authority against which no rights can be pleaded, Milton shows no suspicion. He was at work recasting with the utmost confidence the government of England at the moment of the Restoration. His sympathies were aristocratic: the best should rule. Of the difficulty of securing this he knows nothing. Hooker's claim for a divine sanction attaching to usage and expedience is spurned by Milton's contempt for tradition, confidence in *a priori* reasoning, and conception of the Bible as the sole oracle of God, of authority in *all* fields of thought and experience. His Latin orations and English pamphlets on the issue between parliament and king made no enduring contribution to the political thought of the 17th century.

Milton's denunciation of an endowed clergy—a subject on which he found himself at variance with his hero Cromwell—and his claim for complete tolerance of all religious differences of opinion were the natural outcome of that conception of the purely spiritual character of ecclesiastical authority with which he set out, of his growing dislike of the Presbyterian clergy and their claim to usurp the privileges and intolerance of their Anglican predecessors, and of the purely individualistic character of his philosophical Christianity. From rejecting ecclesiastical discipline and authority Milton was driven onward by a ruthless logic to the denial that any regard is due, in religion or ethics, to the collective consciousness of Church or society. Yet without such collective consciousness, however imperfectly developed, is either religion or morality possible? For Milton every man is his own Church; his creed the product of his own study of the inspired text. The true heretics are those who follow a Church against their conscience and their convictions based on Scripture. Congregations of like-minded men, meeting to worship together, Milton seems to assume there will always be; but for the service of a clergy, except to teach the young and to exhort the careless, there is no need.

> 'If men be not all their life-time under a teacher to learn logic, natural philosophy, ethics or mathematics, which are more difficult—certainly it is not necessary to the attainment of Christian knowledge that men should sit all their life long at the feet of a pulpited divine' (*The likeliest Means to remove Hirelings*).

Let there be a voluntary, simple, itinerant clergy living by the labour of their hands and the free-will offerings of the richer congregations.

This conception of Christian doctrine as something as definable and demonstrable as mathematics (but easier of comprehension) is crucial for a right apprehension of what Milton was in quest of throughout these years of theological and political polemic—that justification of God's ways to men which was to be the theme of his great poem. For a study of that thought as finally articulated we must go to the *De Doctrina Christiana*. 'Joannes Milton Anglus Universis Christi Ecclesiis Necnon Omnibus Fidem Christianam Ubicunque Gentium Profitentibus' are the dedicatory words of the MS in which was set down the creed of the Church of John Milton, the final result of his resolve to have done with traditions and definitions, councils and assemblies, and to formulate for himself, from a study of the text of Scripture, a complete and articulate body of divinity and morality.

The creed so formulated is, as might have been anticipated, at variance in essential respects with the creed both of orthodox Protestantism and of historical Christianity. Milton's faith might be described as Protestant Christianity accommodated to the spirit of the classical Renaissance, for the points on which Milton stands most resolutely aloof from orthodox Calvinist Protestantism are just those in which the latter seemed to compromise the dignity and liberty of the human mind which the Renaissance had re-asserted.

In this respect Milton's Arianism, though the most startling, is not the most important of the dogmas which he formulates. Yet it reflects the poet's temperament, and is in harmony with the religious tone of the two epics. The doctrine of the divinity of Christ regarded on its psychological side is the expression of the transcendent worth ascribed by the Christian consciousness to the personality and life of Jesus; it is the intellectual expression of a passionate devotion. Milton's reverence for the 'author and finisher' of the Christian faith is sincere and profound, but it is not animated with the ardent flame of love which throbs in Dante's *Divina Commedia* or Bunyan's *Pilgrim's Progress* or Thomas à Kempis' *Musica Ecclesiastica*, or many others of the great distinctively Christian works of feeling and imagination. A high and austere monotheism is of the innermost texture of Milton's soul.

The same high, not to say proud, soul is revealed in Milton's refusal to accept the Calvinist doctrine of predestination and the complete corruption of man's soul after the Fall—his refusal to sacrifice the reality of human freedom, the intrinsic worth of human nature. Predestination, he declares, extends to election only, not to reprobation. It did not determine man's fall, but the means of his redemption, since God foresaw that of his own free will man would fall:

'For man will hearken to his glozing lies,
And easily transgress the sole command,
Sole pledge of his obedience: so will fall
He and his faithless progeny. Whose fault?
Whose but his own? Ingrate, he had of me
All he could have; I made him just and right,
Sufficient to have stood, though free to fall'
(*Paradise Lost*, iii. 93 ff.).

The redemption purchased by Christ is in the same way freely offered to all, not to an elect, predestined number. To all, God gives grace, 'though not in equal measure yet sufficient for attaining knowledge of the truth and final salvation':

'for I will clear their senses dark
What may suffice, and soften stony hearts
To pray, repent, and bring obedience due.
To prayer, repentance, and obedience due,
Though but endeavoured with sincere intent,
Mine ear shall not be slow, mine eye not shut' (*ib.* 188 ff.).

Nor — and here again Milton diverged from orthodox Protestantism—is all apprehension of and aspiration after good extinguished in man as a result of the Fall. The result, indeed, of Adam's sin is not only guilt but spiritual death, which is 'the obscuration to a great extent of that right reason which enabled man to discern the chief good,' 'that slavish subjection to sin and the devil which constitutes, as it were, the death of the will.' Yet the divine image in man's soul is not wholly extinguished.

'This is evident, not only from the wisdom and holiness of many of the heathen, manifested both in words and deeds, but also from what is said Gen. ix. 2 *the dread of you shall be upon every beast of the earth*, v. 6. *whoso sheddeth man's blood by man shall his blood be shed; for in the image of God made He man.* These vestiges of original excellence are visible, first, in the understanding. Ps. xix. 1 *the heavens declare the glory of God*; which could not be if man were incapable of hearing their voice. . . . Nor, secondly, is the liberty of the will entirely destroyed' (*De Doctr. Christ.* i. 12 [Sumner's tr.]).

Man retains sufficient liberty at least to endeavour after righteousness, at least to make him responsible for his sins, though its power is so small as to afford him no subject for boasting.

In accordance with the same high regard for the will, for conduct as the test of a living religion, Milton refuses to accept the orthodox distinction of faith and works and the ascription of justification to the former alone. In the text 'A man is justified by faith without the deeds of the law' (Ro 3^{28}), he insists that stress must be laid on the words 'of the law.'

'For Paul does not say simply that a man is justified without works, but without the works of the law; nor yet by faith alone, but "by faith which worketh by love," Gal. v. 6. Faith has its own works which may be different from the works of the law. We are justified therefore by faith, but by a living not a dead faith; and that faith alone which acts is accounted living. James ii. 17. 20. 26' (*ib.* i. 22).

The same spirit makes Milton assert more completely than the Westminster Confession the liberty of the Christian under the new dispensation. It is not the ceremonial law alone that is abolished, but the entire Mosaic law, including the Decalogue (*ib.* i. 26 f.), the place of which is taken by a higher law 'written not in tables of stone, but in fleshy tables of the heart,' the law of love given in our Lord's words, 'Thou shalt love the Lord thy God with all thy heart, and with all thy soul, and with all thy strength, and with all thy mind; and thy neighbour as thyself' (Lk 10^{27}). In the Decalogue is included the Fourth Commandment (*ib.* i. 10, ii. 7), on which English Puritanism laid so much stress. In his first pamphlet Milton had joined in the general condemnation of the Book of Sports and its instigation to 'gaming, jigging, wassailing and mixed dancing' on 'that day which God's law, and even our reason, hath consecrated.' But in *The likeliest Means to remove Hirelings*, 'the seventh day is not moral, but a convenient recourse of worship in fit season, whether seventh or other number.' Our rigid observance is an unnecessary cause of separation from the Reformed Churches of the Continent. The argument (*e.g.*, of the Westminster Confession) that the Jewish law of the Sabbath had been transferred intact to the first day of the week is invalid (*De Doctr. Christ.* ii. 7).

'Under the gospel no one day is appointed for divine worship in preference to another, except such as the church may set apart of its own authority for the *voluntary* assembling of its members, wherein, relinquishing all worldly affairs, we may dedicate ourselves wholly to religious services as far as is consistent with the duties of charity' (*ib.*).

Such are some of the most important divergences of Milton's creed from the creed of the Protestant Churches around him. Of this creed *Paradise Lost* and *Paradise Regained* are the poetical setting forth. Like the *Divina Commedia*, the *Paradise Lost* is not primarily an epic, but a didactic exposition of a theological creed; and, as all the details of Dante's creed may be discovered in the *Summa* of Thomas Aquinas, so Milton's conception of God, of Christ, and of the angels and devils is that which he has set down more drily in the *De Doctrina*; and the purpose which Milton declares he has in view—

'To justify the ways of God to men'—

is theologically conceived. His poem is not an attempt to reconcile the heart and the imagination to truths already accepted. It is a restatement in poetic form of these doctrines in such a way as will finally justify God and indict man. 'Therefore thou art inexcusable, O man, whosoever thou art that judgest' (Ro 2^{1}).

Looked at steadily from this point of view, it cannot justly be said that *Paradise Lost* will bear comparison with the *Divina Commedia* or the *De Natura* of Lucretius. Take away from either of these poems the high purpose that shines through them, and half their beauty is gone. It is its symbolic, mystic character that gives sublimity to every detail of Dante's heaven and hell. Few to-day read *Paradise Lost* with any desire to discover Milton's creed, or, if they do, will accept with any conviction, any such willing suspension of criticism as it is the function of poetry to beget, his justification of God's way to men, this stern and harsh rendering of Paul's 'as in Adam all died.' The time is past in which Milton's poem was read almost as if it were the Bible itself, the poetic presentation of those momentous events as if they actually occurred, to judge of the justice or injustice of which was forbidden. Now we can see that the epic form and the spiritual intention of the poem are not capable of being harmonized. The poem is held together from the first line to the last by the miracle of Milton's style—a veritable 'cloth of gold' encrusted with all the barbaric spoil of his multifarious learning—and by the miracle of his verse harmonies. But, when we look beneath this dazzling surface, we see that the unity is not so complete as we imagined, that a magnificent epic story is troubled and rendered abortive by the cramping theological purpose. All that is greatest in *Paradise Lost* is the product of Milton's creative, mythopœic faculty working as freely on the scanty material of Biblical record and ecclesiastical tradition as did Homer or any primitive poet when shaping and embroidering popular myths. But the result has nothing in it that is essentially Christian. The splendid scenes of the opening books—Satan and his companions debating in hell, Satan voyaging through chaos or descending through the heavenly bodies in the first freshness of their creation, the scenes in Eden, the wars in heaven—these might be fragments from the primitive myths of some forgotten religion, and perhaps nowadays we should read them with greater and less troubled interest if we might do so without the necessity of a reference to our own religious traditions and feelings, without having to ask ourselves 'Is this our God? Is this the Second Person of the Trinity?' For, as Milton approaches his proper theme, in the theological disquisition in heaven, in the story of the Temptation and what follows, we cannot but feel, despite frequent beauties, a steady subsidence of the creative power of the opening; the didactic displaces the epic poem. The magnificent promise of the opening books seems to be unfulfilled. The great characters there brought upon the stage achieve nothing. Even the Satan of the Temptation strikes us as not quite the Satan of the first and second books, of whose dauntless, passionate soul we should have expected some action larger, more magnificent, than this rather over-elaborately treated temptation of a not too wise woman. The simple Bible story will not adapt itself to the classical epic treatment. The large, creative movement of the earlier episodes is lost as the poet feels himself confined by the original story and the didactic purpose.

The harmonizing of story and didactic is better achieved in *Paradise Regained*, Milton's epic on the 'brief model' of the book of Job; but it is so because the didactic and argumentative strain is, as in Job, dominant throughout. The poem is a finely wrought presentation of Milton's ideal Christian virtues, obedience, temperance, and the scorn of worldly glory. But, beautiful poem as it is, austere in spirit and chaste yet rich in texture, there is none of the wonderful creative power of the great episodes and characters in the longer poem; and its austerity of tone marks its limits as a religious poem, for obedieuce, temperance, and unworldliness are Christian virtues only as they flow from or lead to charity, and but little of the radiance of Christian love illumines and warms this severe and stately poem.

The passion which sleeps under Milton's austerest lines flowed forth like a flood of lava in the work which closed his career. *Samson Agonistes* has the rare interest and beauty of the personal passages in *Lycidas* and *Paradise Lost*. Unfettered by Scriptural details or didactic purpose, Milton pours into the artificial mould of classical tragedy all the passionate feeling with which he reviewed the course of his own life and the history of the cause with which he had identified himself so wholeheartedly. The never-closed wound of his first marriage, the loss of his sight, the defeat of the high hopes which he had conceived for his country as a chosen people, a Kingdom of God on earth, the triumph of the hated prelates and the despised

> 'sons
> Of Belial flown with insolence and wine'—

all found utterance in the severely moulded lines and choruses of this tragedy, not a lament, as Treitschke called it, but the last utterance of Milton's indomitable will, that unshakable self-confidence which he called faith in God—a fitting close to the career of the loftiest soul among English poets:

> 'Samson hath quit himself
> Like Samson, and heroicly hath finish'd
> A life heroic' (*Samson Agonistes*, 1709 ff.).

Of Milton's supreme greatness as a poet there is no question. In sustained loftiness of soul, elaborate magnificence of language, and mastery of varied cadences he has no superior. His works have become the touchstone of poetic taste, for, unless a reader has an ear and taste for the technique and music of poetry, he may not find much to attract him in Milton; if he does, he will find endless delight. To the question whether he is also to be considered a great Christian poet a more modified answer must be given. A study of his articulated creed bears out the impression communicated by his poetry that Milton's was not an *anima naturaliter Christiana*. His was rather the soul of an ancient Stoic, blended with that of a Jewish prophet, which had accepted with conviction the Christian doctrine of sin and redemption. The spirit of his poetry wants two of the most distinctively Christian notes—humility and love. Milton's soul was as proud as Dante's; he was less conscious of the failing (*Purg.* xiii. 186 ff.). It is the absence in all his poetry of the note of passionate self-surrender to the love of Christ that separates him, not only from Dante, but from a Puritan like Bunyan, an Anglican like Herbert, a Roman like Crashaw and Vondel, among his contemporaries. It was on another side that Christianity claimed Milton. His work begins and ends in the idea of liberty and its correlative duty, human freedom and the responsibility that it carries with it of living

> 'As ever in the great Taskmaster's eye.'

God is, for Milton, indeed the great Taskmaster, but he rejoices in the tasks; 'the victories of the conscience are gained by the commanding charm which all the severe and restrictive virtues have for him' (Emerson, in *North Amer. Review*, xlvii. [1838] 65); for Milton freedom is obedience in the highest and hardest tasks. To restore this freedom is the great service of Christianity, the fruit of Christ's perfect obedience and the regenerating work of the Holy Spirit. Christianity alone is perfect liberty, a liberty that no human authority, Church or State, may limit. Milton, with all his defects, is an ethical and religious poet because of the conviction which his poetry imparts that, in the words of a recent French writer,

> 'God is for Milton the all in all of life. There is no more terrible evil than sin which separates us from God; there is no more sublime mystery than the Redemption which reconciles us to God' (P. Chauvet, *La Religion de Milton*, Paris, 1909, p. 241).

All his acts and writings were inspired by his desire that the Kingdom of God might come on earth, be it that his conception of that Kingdom was in some way maimed and incomplete, that it was not always given him to distinguish between his own will and God's:

> 'O, may we soon again renew that song,
> And keep in tune with Heaven, till God ere long
> To His celestial consort us unite,
> To live with Him, and sing in endless morn of light!'
> (*At a Solemn Music*, 25 ff.).

LITERATURE.—i. *EDITIONS.*—Edd. of Milton's poems are numerous, but a really good annotated ed. has yet to be made. T. Newton's ed. (London, 1749–52) is still valuable because of its collection of classical sources. Of later edd. mention may be made of D. Masson's (London, 1874) and W. Aldis Wright's (Cambridge, 1903). Collected edd. of the prose works are J. Toland's (Amsterdam, 1698), T. Birch's (London, 1738, 1753), and J. A. St. John's (Bohn's Libraries, 1836). Some of the pamphlets—*e.g.*, *Areopagitica*—have been edited separately.

ii. *CRITICISM.*—The criticism of Milton begins with Dryden's epigram and includes J. Addison, *The Spectator*, Dec. 1711–May 1712; S. Johnson, *Lives of the Poets*, London, 1778–81; S. T. Coleridge, *Literary Remains*, do. 1836–39, *Seven Lectures*, do. 1856; T. B. Macaulay, *Critical and Historical Essays*, do. 1854 (the essays on 'Milton' appeared in the *Edinburgh Review*, 1825, on the occasion of the publication by C. R. Sumner of the newly-discovered *De Doctrina Christiana*, Cambridge, 1825); R. W. Emerson, 'Milton,' *North Amer. Rev* xlvii. [183$] 56 ff.; W. S. Landor, *Imaginary Conversations*, London, 1846; T. De Quincey, *Collected Works*, do. 1853, vols. vi., x.; E. H. A. Scherer, *Études critiques de littérature*, Paris, 1876; H. von Treitschke, *Historische und politische Aufsätze*[2], Leipzig, 1865; J. R. Lowell, *Among my Books*, Boston, 1876; Matthew Arnold, *Mixed Essays*, do. 1879, *Essays in Criticism*, 2nd ser., do. 1888; Mark Pattison, *Milton* (*English Men of Letters*), London, 1879; T. H. Ward, *English Poets*, do. 1880; E. Dowden, *Transcripts and Studies*, do. 1888; R. Garnett, *Life of John Milton*, do. 1890; W. Raleigh, *Milton*, do. 1900.

H. J. C. GRIERSON.

MĪMĀṀSĀ.—*Mīmāṁsā* in Sanskrit signifies 'investigation,' 'explanation.' The word is usually employed as the title of one of the six systems of philosophy recognized as orthodox by the Brāhmans. The Mīmāṁsā system is most closely related to the Vedānta (see art. VEDĀNTA); for in them both the subjects of ancient Indian speculation which meet us in the Brāhmaṇas and Upaniṣads are methodically developed.

The two systems form a connected whole in the sense that the Mīmāṁsā comprises the ritualistic doctrine of works, the Vedānta the doctrine of salvation by knowledge. Each, while limited to its own sphere, makes reference also to the other, so that it is impossible to doubt that they received a literary form at the same time. It is due chiefly to this close connexion with the Vedānta doctrine, and in the second place probably to the form into which it has been cast, that the Mīmāṁsā has found a place in India among the philosophical systems; for with philosophy its particular subject-matter has nothing to do.

Mīmāṁsā as a name of the ritualistic system is an abbreviation of *Pūrva-* or *Karma-mīmāṁsā*, 'first explanation,' or 'explanation of the function of work.' These names are explained by the connexion of the system with the Vedānta, which on its side is termed *Uttara-* or *Brahma-mīmāṁsā*, 'second explanation' or 'explanation of the All-Soul,' also *Śārīraka-mīmāṁsā*, 'explanation of the incarnation' (of Brahma). The oldest and most important text-book of the Mīmāṁsā is the *Mīmāṁsādarśana* of Jaimini. H. Jacobi places the composition of this work (and the contemporary completion of the Vedānta- or Brahma-sūtras) between *c.* A.D. 200 and 450 (*JAOS* xxxi. [1911] 1 ff.).

The aim of the Mīmāṁsā is to give rules for the correct interpretation of those Vedic texts whose subject is the Brāhmanical ritual. Since these texts contain in great parts an imperfect and obscure description of the ceremonies, and, besides, are interspersed at every step with speculations on the mystical meaning of the separate acts and implements, the assistance of rules was, in fact, absolutely necessary for the sacrificer, who believed that he had to dread the most serious consequences from the least mistake in ceremonial observance. The Mīmāṁsā offers a solution of all doubts which might present themselves with regard to the details of the sacrifice, and also professes to remove the discrepancies which are actually found in the Vedic texts. These last, however, according to the view of the Mīmāṁsā, are in every instance only apparent. The system, moreover, discusses at the same time the rewards which are offered for the correct performance of the sacrifice; so that the Mīmāṁsā is a compendium of the special theology of the Brāhmans.

The Mīmāṁsā does not recognize the existence of God. Nevertheless this fact interferes as little here as in the Sāṅkhya and the other systems with belief in the supernatural beings of the popular Indian faith. If we ask on what authority the instruction given with regard to the sacrifice and its consequences rests, the Mīmāṁsā answers that the Veda needs no authority, but is eternal and uncreated; and that its revelation concerns only things existing from eternity, and self-evident. This conviction is in India maintained with remarkable tenacity, and is strangely opposed to the entirely personal wishes, for the most part quite worldly, which were continually presented to the gods by the authors of the ancient Vedic hymns. In reality the teachers of the Mīmāṁsā associate the word *Veda* less with these ancient hymns than with the ritualistic texts of the second period of Vedic literature, in which the individuality of the authors is not so prominent.

It has been already remarked that the form in which the Mīmāṁsā is presented may have contributed towards its being regarded, in spite of its essentially unphilosophical character, as a system on a level with the other five systems of Indian philosophy. For the contents of the Veda are here classified under definite categories, and every subject of investigation is explained according to a method which represents already a high degree of logical skill in arrangement. This methodical and established scheme, which the other schools also adopt as their standard, contains the following five divisions: (1) the proposition, (2) the doubt as to its correctness, (3) the erroneous method of treating the question, (4) the refutation of the erroneous method by the true argument, (5) the result of the investigation. Occasionally also, for the purpose of establishing the special doctrines of the Mīmāṁsā, questions of philosophical import are discussed. This is true especially of the proposition that sounds and therefore words are eternal, and likewise the connexion of words with their meaning. On the basis of this theory the Mīmāṁsā teaches that the relation of word and meaning is not dependent on general agreement, but that the meaning is naturally inherent in the word. The Mīmāṁsā was compelled to propound this theory in order to protect the Veda from the suspicion of fallibility which attaches to all human works. If the Veda were to be regarded not as a collection of books composed or inspired, but as something uncreated, existing independently from eternity, then the connexion of the words of which the Veda is composed, with their meaning, could not be the result of human activity; but the words, and in the last resort the sounds that form the words, must have existed from all eternity—a view which could have held sway only within the narrow horizon of a school to which one language alone was known.

LITERATURE.—*Mīmāṁsādarśaṇa*, ed. Maheśachandra Nyāyaratna, Calcutta, 1873–89; *Arthasaṅgraha*, ed. G. Thibaut, Benares, 1882, Introductory Remarks; A. Barth, *Religions of India*[3], London, 1891; F. Max Müller, *Six Systems of Indian Philosophy*, do. 1899, ch. v.; *Sarva-darśana-saṅgraha*, tr. E. B. Cowell and A. E. Gough, 2nd ed., do. 1894, ch. xii.

R. GARBE.

MINÆANS. — See ARABS (ANCIENT), SABÆANS.

MIND.—Questions of empirical psychology and of the relations between body and mind are discussed in other articles (see BODY, BODY AND MIND, BRAIN AND MIND). The present article must be limited to a discussion of the metaphysical theories of mind. Owing to the peculiar position which these problems occupy in philosophy, as well as in the study of ethical and religious problems, it is advisable, first of all, to make explicit some of the epistemological problems which especially confront the student of the nature of mind; and, in order to do this, we must, in view of numerous traditional complications which beset the theory of the knowledge of mind, open our discussion with some general statements concerning the nature of problems of knowledge.

The history of epistemology has been dominated by a well-known contrast between two kinds of knowledge, namely, perceptual knowledge and conceptual knowledge. This dual contrast seems insufficient to supply us with a basis for a really adequate classification of the fundamental types of knowledge. It is proposed in the present article to base the whole discussion upon a threefold classification of knowledge. Having begun with this threefold classification and briefly illustrated it, we shall go on to apply it to the special problems which we have to face in dealing with mind. We shall then consider in some detail what kinds of mental facts correspond to the three different kinds of knowledge thus defined. In conclusion, we shall deal with some problems of the philosophy of mind in the light of the previous discussion.

1. Perception and conception as fundamental cognitive processes.—A careful study of the processes of knowledge, whether these occur in the work of science or in the efforts of common sense to obtain knowledge, shows us three, and only three, fundamental processes which are present in every developed cognitive activity and interwoven in more or less complicated fashion. Of these two have been recognized throughout the history of science and philosophy, and their familiar contrast has dominated epistemology. The third, although familiar and often more or less explicitly mentioned, was first distinguished with sharpness, for epistemological purposes, by the American logician, Charles Peirce. We shall speak first of the two well-known types of cognitive process, perception and conception.

The name 'perception' is used in psychology with special reference to the perceptions of the various senses. We are here interested only in the most general characteristics of perception. William James has used, for what is here called perception, the term 'knowledge of acquaintance.' He distinguishes 'knowledge of acquaintance' from 'knowledge about.' In the simplest possible case one who listens to music has 'knowledge of acquaintance' with the music; the musician who listens in the light of his professional knowledge has not only 'knowledge of acquaintance,' but also 'knowledge about'; he recognizes what changes of key take place and what rules of harmony are illustrated. A deaf man who has learned about the nature of music through other people, in so far as they can tell him about it, but who has never heard music, has no 'knowledge of acquaintance,' but is limited to 'knowledge about.' 'Knowledge of acquaintance' is also sometimes called 'immediate knowledge.' In the actual cognitive process of the individual human being it never occurs quite alone, since, when we know something perceptually or by acquaintance, we also always have more or less 'mediate' knowledge, *i.e.*, one who listens to music, but who also considers the person of the artist, the relation of the music to the programme, the name of the composer, or the place of this experience in his own life, has in his knowledge that which is more than the immediate hearing of the music.

'Knowledge about' includes, on occasion, mental processes which may vary very widely and which may be mingled with 'knowledge of acquaintance' in ways which are far too complex to analyze here. But 'knowledge about' is especially opposed to 'knowledge of acquaintance' in one class of cases which need to be emphasized through the use of a special name. We may name that class by calling the kind of knowledge involved in it by the name already used, 'conceptual knowledge.' Conceptual knowledge is knowledge of universals, of relations, or of other such 'abstract' objects. The Socratic-Platonic theory of knowledge called attention from its very beginning to universals and relations, and consequently made this type of knowledge specially prominent.

No doubt, even if one is disposed to cling to this merely dual classification of knowledge, one may well question whether all knowledge which is not merely 'knowledge of acquaintance' is of the grade of conceptual knowledge. For there is much 'knowledge about' concerning which we should all hesitate to say that it is knowledge of universals. Socrates himself, in his effort to define the knowledge of universals, met at the start with the fact that much of our knowledge of universals is confused and inarticulate. But if, for the moment, we neglect the intermediate cognitive states in which we more or less mingle 'knowledge of acquaintance' and conceptual knowledge, or possess conceptual knowledge in imperfect degrees of development, we may readily admit that this traditional dual classification of cognitive states is sufficient to call attention to a distinction which is of the utmost importance, both for empirical science and for metaphysics.

While the distinction between perceptual and conceptual knowledge is of great importance in determining the distinction between the deductive and the inductive methods in the sciences, the classification of these two modes of cognition does not of itself suffice to determine what constitutes the difference between inductive and deductive science. When we have clear and accurate conceptual knowledge, we are in general prepared to undertake scientific processes that in the case of further development will involve deductive methods. Thus, in particular, a conceptual knowledge of universals leads, in the mathematical sciences, to the assertion of propositions. Some of these propositions may appear at the outset of a science as axioms (*q.v.*). Whether accepted as necessarily true or used merely as hypotheses, these propositions, either alone or in combination, may, and in the mathematical sciences do, form the starting-point for a system of rational deductions. The type of knowledge involved in this deductive process will be, in the main, the conceptual type. In what sense and to what degree a 'knowledge of acquaintance' enters into a process of mathematical reasoning we have not here to consider. All will admit that the sort of knowledge which dominates such a deductive process is 'abstract,' is concerned in reaching results which are true about the propositions that themselves form the premisses of the deduction. And so our knowledge concerning numbers, the operations of a mathematical science, and similar cases form exceptionally good instances of what characterizes conceptual knowledge in its exact and developed form.

In the inductive use of scientific methods we find a more complicated union of the perceptual and the conceptual types of knowledge. When a hypothesis, such as Newton's formula for gravitation, or Galileo's hypothesis concerning the laws of falling bodies, is stated, the type of knowledge involved in formulating and in understanding the hypothesis is prevailingly conceptual. When the hypothesis is tested by comparing the predictions based upon it with experience, the test involves appealing at some point to perceptual knowledge, or 'knowledge of acquaintance.' The processes of experiment used in an inductive science might seem to be typical cases of processes involving perceptual knowledge. And experiments unquestionably do involve such knowledge. But an experiment reveals a truth, because it brings concepts and percepts into some sort of active synthesis. Upon such active synthesis depends the process of validation which is used as the basis for the definition of truth used by recent pragmatists (see ERROR AND TRUTH).

In so far as we insist upon this dual classification of fundamental processes of cognition, the questions which most come to our notice, regarding both knowledge and its objects, concern (1) the relative value of these two cognitive processes, and (2) the degree to which, in our actual cognitive processes, or in ideal cognitive processes (such as we may ascribe to beings of some higher order than ours), the two can ever be separated. These two questions have proved especially momentous for the theory both of knowledge and of reality.

(1) Regarding the relative value of the two fundamental types of cognition, Plato, as is well known, held that conceptual knowledge is the ideal type, the right result an expression of reason. Conceptual knowledge gives truth; perceptual knowledge gives illusion or appearance—such is, on the whole, the Platonic doctrine. In recent discussion the pragmatists—and still more emphatically Bergson—have insisted upon the relative superiority of the perceptual type of knowledge. The familiar expression of this view is the thesis of recent pragmatism that conceptual knowledge has only a sort of 'credit value'; perceptual knowledge furnishes the 'cash of experience'; conceptions are 'bank notes'; perceptions, and perceptions only, are 'cash.' The statement of Bergson goes further, and declares that, if we had unlimited perceptual knowledge, *i.e.* 'knowledge of acquaintance' whose limits and imperfections we had no occasion to feel, because it had no limits and no imperfections, then conceptions could have no possible interest for us as cognitive beings. In other words, we use concepts, *i.e.*, we seek for a knowledge of universals, only when our perceptions in some way fail us. Conceptual knowledge is in its very essence a substitute for failing perceptual knowledge. The opposition between Plato and Bergson regarding this estimate of the relative significance and truthfulness of the two kinds of cognitive processes is thus characteristic of the contrast which is here in question. Of course all the philosophers admit that, in practice, our knowledge makes use of, and from moment to moment consists in, a union which involves both conceptual and perceptual processes.

(2) On the question whether the two foregoing types of knowledge, however closely linked in our normal human experience, can, at least in ideal, be separated—*i.e.*, whether a knowledge by 'pure reason' is possible on the one hand, or a knowledge of 'pure experience' is ever attainable on the other hand—the historical differences of opinion are closely related to well-known metaphysical controversies. For Plato, as (in another age, and in a largely different metaphysical context) for Spinoza, it is at least in ideal possible for philosophy, or for the individual philosopher, to attain a purely intellectual insight into the realm of 'ideas' or into the nature of the 'substance.' For various forms of mysticism, as well as for theories such as the one set forth in the *Kritik der reinen Erfahrung* (Leipzig, 1888-90) of R. H. L. Avenarius, a mental transformation may be brought about through a process which involves either a practical or a scientific correction and gradual suppression of erroneous intellectual illusion; and, at the limit of this process, reality becomes immediately and perceptually known, without confusion through abstractions.

The 'radical empiricism' of James's later essays makes use of a theory of knowledge which attempts, as far as possible, to report, apart from conceptual constructions, the data of pure experience.

2. Interpretation through comparison of ideas as a third fundamental cognitive process.—It is an extraordinary example of a failure to reflect in a thoroughgoing way upon the process of knowledge that until recently the third type of cognitive process to which we must next refer has been neglected, although every one is constantly engaged in using and in exemplifying it.

When a man understands a spoken or written word or sentence, what he perceives is some sign, or expression of an idea or meaning, which in general belongs to the mind of some fellow-man. When this sign or expression is understood by the one who hears or who reads, what is made present to the consciousness of the reader or hearer may be any combination of perceptual or conceptual knowledge that chances to be in question. But, if any one cries 'Fire!', the sort of knowledge which takes place in my mind when I hear and understand this cry essentially depends upon this fact: I regard my fellow's cry as a sign or expression of the fact either that he himself sees a fire or that he believes that there is a fire, or that, at the very least, he intends me to understand him as asserting that there is a fire, or as taking an interest of his own in what he calls a fire. Thus, while I cannot understand my fellow's cry unless I hear it, unless I have at least some perceptual knowledge, and while I equally shall not have a 'knowledge about' the nature of fire, and so a 'knowledge about' the object to which the cry refers, unless I am possessed of something which tends to be conceptual knowledge of his object, my knowledge of my fellow's meaning, my 'grasping of his idea,' consists neither in the percept of the sign nor in a concept of its object which the sign arouses, but in my *interpretation* of the sign as an indication of an idea which is distinct from any idea of mine, and which I refer to a mind not my own, or in some wise distinct from mine.

It is to be noted that, however we reach the belief in the existence of minds distinct from our own, we do not regard these minds, at least in ordinary conditions, as objects of our own perceptual knowledge. For the very motives, whatever they are, which lead me to regard my perceptions as my own even thereby lead me to regard my fellows' perceptions as never present within my own field of awareness. My knowledge of my own physical pains, of the colours that I see, or of the sounds that I hear is knowledge that may be called, in general terms, perceptual. That is, these are objects with which I am, or upon occasion could be, acquainted. But with my fellow's pains I am not acquainted. To say this is merely to say that, whatever I mean by 'myself' and by 'the Alter,' the very distinction between the two is so bound up with the type of cognition that is in question that whatever I am acquainted with through my own perception is *ipso facto* my own object of acquaintance. Thus, then, in general, perceptual knowledge has not as its object what is at the same time regarded as the state of another mind than my own.

But, if the mind of my fellow, in particular his ideas, his feelings, his intentions, are never objects of perceptual knowledge for me, so that I am not directly acquainted with any of these states, must we regard our knowledge of the mind, of the ideas, of the intents, purposes, feelings, interests of our fellow-man as a conceptual knowledge? Is our fellow-man's mind the object of a concept of our own? Is the fellow-man a universal, or a relation, or a Platonic idea? Wherein does he differ from a mathematical entity or a law of nature? Unquestionably we regard him as possessing conceptual knowledge of his own, and also as engaged in processes of knowledge which may be conceptual, or which may involve any union of percept and concept. But the fact remains that neither by our own perceptions can we become acquainted with his states of mind, nor yet by our own conceptions can we become able to know the objects which constitute his mental process. In fact, we come to know that there are in the world minds not our own by interpreting the signs that these minds give us of their presence. This interpretation is a third type of knowledge which is closely interwoven with perceptual and conceptual knowledge, very much as they in turn are bound up with it, but which is not reducible to any complex or combination consisting of elements which are merely perceptual or merely conceptual.

Every case of social intercourse between man and man, or (what is still more important) every process of inner self-comprehension carried on when a man endeavours to 'make up his own mind' or 'to understand what he is about,' involves this third type of cognition, which cannot be reduced to perception or to conception. It is to this third cognitive process that, following the terminology which Peirce proposed, we here apply the name 'interpretation.'

In order to distinguish more clearly the three types of cognition, we may say that the natural object of perception is some inner or outer datum of sense or of feeling, such as a musical tone, a colour, an emotional state, or the continual flow of the inner life upon which Bergson so much insists. For these are typical objects of perceptual knowledge, *i.e.* of 'knowledge of acquaintance.' The typical objects of conceptual knowledge are such objects as numbers, and relations such as identity and difference, equality, and so on. But typical objects of interpretation are signs which express the meaning of some mind. These signs may be expressions of the meaning of the very mind which also interprets them. This is actually the case whenever in memory we review our own past, when we reflect upon our own meaning, when we form a plan, or when we ask ourselves what we mean or engage in any of the inner conversation which forms the commonest expression of the activity whereby an individual man attains some sort of explicit knowledge of himself.

The form of cognitive process involved in the social relations between man and man is essentially the same as that involved in the cognitive process by which a man makes clear to himself his own intent and meaning. For, despite well-known assertions to the contrary on the part of Bergson, nobody has any adequate intuitive 'knowledge of acquaintance' with himself. If such perceptual or intuitive knowledge of the self by the self were possible, we should not be obliged to acknowledge that the world of human beings is dominated by such colossal and often disastrous ignorance of every man regarding himself, his true interests, his real happiness, his moral and personal value, his intents, and his powers, as we actually find characterizing our human world. In brief, man's knowledge, both of himself and of his neighbour, is a knowledge which involves an interpretation of signs. This thesis, very ably maintained by Peirce in some of his early essays, involves consequences which are at once familiar and momentous for the theory of knowledge.

That the type of knowledge involved whenever signs are interpreted is a fundamental type of knowledge which cannot be represented either to perception or to conception can be exemplified in most manifold ways, and will appear somewhat more clearly through the illustrations given below. It may be useful to point out here that, while all our interpretations, like all our perceptual and conceptual knowledge, are subject to the most manifold illusions in detail, it still remains the case that, whenever one is led to attempt, propose, or believe an interpretation of a sign, he has actually become aware, at the moment of his interpretation, that there is present in his world some meaning, some significant idea, plan, purpose, undertaking, or intent, which, at the moment when he discovers its presence, is from his point of view not identical with whatever idea or meaning is then his own.

If somebody speaking to me uses words which I had not intended to use, I may misunderstand the words, or I may not understand them at all. But, in so far as I take these words to be the expression of a meaning, this meaning is one that just then I cannot find to be my own—*i.e.*, these words do not express my ideas, in so far as these ideas are by me interpreted as my own. The cognitive process here in question divides, or at least distinguishes, that part of the objects, ideas, or meanings in question into two distinct regions, provinces, or modes of mental activity. One of these regions is interpreted at the moment as 'my own present idea,' 'my own purpose,' 'my own meaning'; the other is interpreted as 'some meaning not just now my own,' or as 'some idea or meaning that was once my own'—*i.e.*, as 'my own past idea,' or as 'my neighbour's meaning,' or perhaps as 'a meaning that belongs to my social order,' or 'to the world,' or, if I am religiously minded, 'to God.' In each case the interpretation that is asserted may prove to be a wrong one. Interpretation is fallible. So, too, is conception, when viewed as a cognitive process, and so is perception, whose character as 'acquaintance with' is no guarantee of its accuracy, whether mystical apprehension or ordinary observation is in question. The fact for our present purpose is not that our human knowledge is at any point infallible, but that there is the mode or type of cognition here defined as interpretation. Interpretation is the knowledge of the meaning of a sign. Such a knowledge is not a merely immediate apprehension, nor yet a merely conceptual process; it is the essentially social process whereby the knower at once distinguishes himself, with his own meanings, ideas, and expressions, from some other self, and at the same time knows that these selves have their contrasted meanings, while one of them at the moment is expressing its meaning to the other. Knowledge by interpretation is, therefore, in its essence neither mere 'acquaintance' nor yet 'knowledge about.'

There is another way of expressing the distinction of these three kinds of knowledge which proves useful for many purposes. Knowledge of the first kind, 'knowledge of acquaintance,' may for certain purposes be characterized as 'appreciation.' Conceptual knowledge, owing to the means often employed in making a concept explicit, may be for many purposes called 'description.' In each case, as will be noted, the main character of the type of knowledge in question can be designated by a single term, namely, appreciation or description, just as in the foregoing these two types of knowledge have been designated each by a single term, acquaintance in one case and conception in the other.

In designating the instances of interpretation it is well to note that every interpretation has three aspects. For the one who interprets it is an expression of his own meaning. With reference to the object, *i.e.* to the sign, or to the mind whose sign this is, the interpretation is the reading or rendering of the meaning of this mind by another mind. In other words, every interpretation has so far a dual aspect: it at once brings two minds into quasi-social contact and distinguishes between them or contrasts them. In the light of this contrast and with reference to the direction in which it is read, the two minds are known each in the light of the other. As has already been said, the two minds in question may be related as a man's own past self is related to his present or future self. And in fact, as Peirce has pointed out, every act of interpretation has also a triadic character. For the cognitive process in question has not only a social character, but what one may call a directed 'sense.' In general, when an interpretation takes place, there is an act B wherein a mental process A is interpreted, read, or rendered *to* a third mind. That the whole process can take place within what, from some larger point of view, is also a single mind with a threefold process going on within it has already been pointed out. Thus, when a man reflects on his plans, purposes, intents, and meanings, his present self, using the signs which memory offers as guides, interprets his past self to his future self, the cognitive process being well exemplified when a man reminds himself of his own intents and purposes by consulting a memorandum made yesterday for the sake of guiding his acts to-day. Every explicit process involving self-consciousness, involving a definite sequence of plans of action, and dealing with long stretches of time, has this threefold character. The present self interprets the past self to the future self; or some generally still more explicit social process takes place whereby one self or quasi-self has its meanings stated by an interpreter for the sake of some third self.

Thus, in brief, knowledge by interpretation is (1) an expression (by an 'interpreter') of (2) the idea or meaning whereof some other mind gives a sign, and (3) such an expression as is addressed to some third mind, to which the interpreter thus reads or construes the sign.

3. Self-interpretation, comparison of one's own ideas, and knowledge of time.—When such interpretation goes on within the mind of an individual man, it constitutes the very process whereby, as is sometimes said, he 'finds himself,' 'comes to himself,' 'directs himself,' or 'gets his bearings,' especially with reference to time, present, past, and future. In the inner life of an individual man this third mode of cognition, therefore, appears at once in its most fundamental and simplest form as the cognitive process whose being consists in a *comparison of ideas*. The ideas compared here belong in one sense to the 'same self'; but they differ as the ideas of 'past self' and 'future self'; or, in various other ways, they belong to different 'quasi-minds.'

That such a process is, indeed, irreducible to pure perception, to pure conception, or to that active synthesis of the two which James has in mind when he uses the term 'idea,' readily becomes manifest if we consider what takes place when two 'ideas' are 'compared,' whether these two belong to men who are 'different individuals' or to the past, present, or future selves of one who is, from another point of view, the same man.

An 'idea,' when the term is used in the sense which recent pragmatism[1] has made familiar and prominent, is not a mere perception, nor a mere collection or synthesis of various perceptions, images, and other immediate data; nor yet is it a mere conception, whether simple or complex. It is, for James and his allies, a 'leading,' an 'active tendency,' a 'fulfilment of purpose,' or an effort towards such fulfilment, an 'adjustment to a situation,' a seeking for the 'cash,' in the form of sense-data, such as may, when found, meet the requirements, or 'calls,' made by the conceptual aspect of the very idea which is in question. This concept has, in Bergson's phrase, its 'credit value.' Eventual sense-data may furnish the corresponding 'cash.' The idea is the seeking for this 'cash.' When the wanderer in the woods decides to adopt the idea that 'yonder path leads me home,' he makes an active synthesis of his concept of home and of his present sense-data. This active synthesis, expressed in his idea, 'I am homeward bound,' is a 'leading,' which, if he is successful, will result in furnishing to him, when his wanderings cease, the perceptions of home which constitute the goal of his quest. This, then, is what is meant by the term 'idea' in that one of its senses which pragmatism has recently most emphasized.

In this way we may also illustrate how the cognitive process possesses the two forms or aspects which have usually been regarded as the only fundamentally distinct aspects of knowledge: perception and conception. We meanwhile illustrate that active *union* of these two which constitutes the 'idea' as defined by recent pragmatism. But we do not thus illustrate an aspect of cognition which is equally pervasive and significant, and which consists in the *comparison of ideas*. It is just this aspect of cognition upon which our present theory most insists. For by what process does the wanderer, when he reaches home, recognize that this home which he finds is the very home that he had sought? Not by the mere presence of a 'home-feeling,' not by a perception which, merely at the moment of home-coming, pays the 'cash' then required by some then present conception of home, but by a process involving a comparison of his ideas about his home, at the moment when he reaches home, with his memories of what his ideas were while he was lost in the woods and while he still inquired or sought the way home.

In order to consider what such a comparison essentially involves, it is not necessary to suppose that the act of comparison must take place in a form involving any high grade of self-consciousness, or depending upon a previous formation of an elaborate system of ideas about the self, the past, and similar objects. The essentially important fact is that whoever begins, even in the most rudimentary way, to take account of what seems to him as if it were his own past, whoever is even vaguely aware that what he has been seeking is the very object which now he finds, is not merely perceiving the present, and is not conceiving the past, and is not simply becoming aware of his present successes and disappointments as present facts—he is comparing his ideas of present success or failure with his ideas of his past efforts. This comparison is essentially an interpretation of some portion of his own past life, as he remembers that life, in the light of his present successes or disappointments, as he now experiences them. A third cognitive process is then involved. This interpretation compares at least two ideas: (1) the past idea or 'leading' (*e.g.*, the past search for home by the path through the woods); (2) the present success

[1] See W. James, *Pragmatism*, London, 1907.

or failure (*e.g.*, the reaching home itself, or getting to the close of some stage of the wandering); and, in making this comparison, this interpretation estimates the result, perhaps in the light of one's idea of one's own future ('and henceforth I need search no more'), or perhaps in the light of one's idea of one's entire self ('I have succeeded,' or 'I am a knower of the truth,' or 'So much of the world of reality is mine'). In any case two comments may be made upon every such act of comparing two ideas and interpreting one in the light of the other.

(1) Unless such processes of comparing ideas were possible, and unless, in at least some rudimentary form, it took place, we could never make even a beginning in forming a coherent view of our own past and future, of our own selves as individuals, or of selves not our own. Our ideas both of the Ego and of the Alter depend upon an explicit process of comparing ideas. The simplest comparison of ideas—such as the case upon which recent pragmatism lays so much stress—the comparison upon which the very idea 'my success' also depends, the comparison, namely, which is expressed by saying, 'What I sought at a past moment is the very same as what, at the present moment, I now find,' is an instance of an act of interpretation, and is not reducible to the two other types of knowledge.

(2) All such processes of comparison are equally characteristic of the cognitive activity which goes on during our explicitly and literally social life and of the cognitive activity which is needed when we think about our relations to our own individual past and future. In brief, neither the individual Ego nor the Alter of the literal social life, neither past nor future time can be known to us through a cognitive process which may be defined exclusively in terms of perception, of conception, and of the ideal 'leadings' of the pragmatists. The self, the neighbour, the past, the future, and the temporal order in general become known to us through a third type of cognition which consists of a comparison of ideas—a process wherein some self, or quasi-self, or idea interprets another idea, by means of a comparison which, in general, has reference to, and is more or less explicitly addressed to, some third self or idea.

4. The relation of the three cognitive processes to our knowledge that various minds exist and to our views about what sorts of beings minds are.—The use of the foregoing classification of the types of cognitive processes appears of special importance as soon as we turn to a brief outline of some of the principal theories about the nature of mind which have played a part in the history of philosophy. Nowhere does the theory of knowledge show itself of more importance in preparing the way for an understanding of metaphysical problems than in the case of the metaphysics of mind. No attentive student of the problem of mind can easily fail at least to feel, even if he does not very explicitly define his feeling, that in dealing with the philosophy of mind both common sense and the philosophers are accustomed to combine, sometimes in a very confused way, a reference to different more or less hypothetical beings, while the ideas that are proposed with regard to the nature of these beings are of profoundly different types.

Thus it may be a question for common sense or for a given metaphysical doctrine as to whether or not there exists a so-called soul. Now it makes a great difference for the theory of the soul whether the kind of soul which is in question is viewed as in its essence an object of a possible immediate acquaintance or perception, as an object of a possible adequate conception, or as an object whose being consists in the fact that it is to be interpreted thus or so. Unless the three kinds of cognition are clearly distinguished, the one who advances or tests a given theory of the soul does so without observing whether he himself is speaking of the soul as a possible perception, or is treating it as if it were, in its inmost nature, an object which can be known only through some adequate conception. If one has called to his attention the fact that he is speaking now in perceptual and now in conceptual terms of the mind or soul which his theory asserts to be real, he may then attempt to solve his difficulties in the way which recent pragmatism has emphasized, *i.e.*, he may declare that his doctrine is of necessity a 'working hypothesis' about the nature of the soul, that it is, of course, in part stated in conceptual terms, but that the concepts are true only in so far as they prove to be somewhere directly verifiable in terms of immediate percepts.

Yet nowhere does recent pragmatism, in the form in which William James left it, more display its inadequacy as a theory of knowledge than in the case where it is applied to an effort to define the truth of hypotheses concerning mind, or to test such truth. For, as a fact, nobody who clearly distinguishes his neighbour's individual mind from his own expects, or can consistently anticipate, that his neighbour's mental states, or that anything which essentially belongs to the inner life or to the distinct mind of his neighbour, can ever become, under any circumstances, a direct perception of his own. For, if my neighbour's physical pains ever became mine, I should know them by immediate acquaintance only in so far as they were mine and not my neighbour's. And the same holds true of anything else which is supposed to be a fact essentially belonging to the individual mind of my neighbour. At best I can hope, with greater or less probability, to *interpret* correctly the meaning, the plan, or some other inner idea of the mind of my neighbour; but I cannot hope to go beyond such correct interpretation so far as to perceive my neighbour's mental states. For, if my neighbour's states became the immediate objects of my own acquaintance, my neighbour and I would so far simply melt together, like drops in the ocean or small pools in a greater pool. The immediate acquaintance with my neighbour's states of mind would be a knowledge neither of himself as he is in distinction from me nor of myself as I am in distinction from him. For this general reason 'working hypotheses' about the interior reality which belongs to the mind of my neighbour can never be 'converted into the cash of experience.' My neighbour's mind is never a verifiable object of immediate acquaintance, precisely as it is never an abstract and universal idea. The one sort of knowledge for which recent pragmatism has no kind of place whatever is a knowledge, statable in pragmatistic terms, concerning my neighbour's mind.

James himself follows a well-known and ancient philosophical tradition by declaring that our assertion of the existence of our neighbour's mind depends upon the argument from analogy. Because of similar behaviours of our organism we regard it as by analogy probable that both our neighbour's organism and our own are vivified by more or less similar mental lives, so that we have similar experiences. But to regard or to believe in the mind of our neighbour as an object whose existence is to be proved through an argument from analogy raises a question whose answer is simply fatal to the whole pragmatistic theory of knowledge. Surely an argument from analogy is not its own verification. For pragmatism the truth of a hypothesis depends upon the fact that its conceptual constructions are capable of immediate verification in terms of certain facts of immediate experience. But my neighbour's inner states of mind can never become for me objects of immediate acquaintance, unless they become my states of mind and not his, precisely in so far as he and I are distinct selves.

The hypothesis that our mental lives are similar may thus be suggested by analogy or may be stated in terms of analogy; but the analogy in question is essentially unverifiable in the required terms, *i.e.*, in terms of immediate perceptions. For my neighbour can immediately perceive only his own states, while I, in so far as I am not my neighbour, can verify only my own states. From the point of view, then, of the argument from analogy, my neighbour, in observing his own states, does *not* verify my hypothesis in the sense in which my hypothesis about him demands verification, namely, in terms of the experience of the self who makes the hypothesis. From this point of view, the problem of the mind of my neighbour remains hopeless.

It is possible, of course, to say of the foregoing argument from analogy what is also said both by common sense and by science, on the basis of a theory of truth which is in its essence conceptual and realistic. One can, of course, assert that in actual fact the mental states of my neighbour really exist and are in a certain relation which makes it true to say that they are analogous to mine. This real relation may be asserted to be as much a fact as any other fact in the universe. If this fact of the real analogy is granted, then it may be declared that my hypothesis to the effect that my neighbour's mind is a reality is actually true. This, however, is precisely the type of truth which William James's pragmatism undertakes to reject.

A very different appearance is assumed by the whole matter if we recognize that there is a third kind of knowledge, which is neither conceptual nor perceptual, and which is also not the sort of union of conception and perception which is completely expressible in terms of the favourite metaphor of Bergson and the pragmatists, namely, the metaphor of the conversion of conceptual credits or bank-notes into perceptual cash, *i.e.*, into immediate data of experience. For interpretations are never verified merely through immediate data, nor through the analysis of conceptions. This is true whether I myself am the object of my own interpretation or my neighbour is in question. If we seek for metaphors, the metaphor of the conversation, already used, furnishes the best means of indicating wherein consists the relative, but never immediate, verifiability of the truth of an interpretation.

When I interpret (whether my own purposes or intents or the ideas of another man are the objects which I seek to interpret), what I first meet in experience is neither a matter of acquaintance nor a mere 'knowledge about.' What I meet is the fact that, in so far as I now understand or interpret what I call myself, I have also become aware, not immediately but in the temporal process of my mental life, that ideas have come to me which are not now my own, and which need further expression and interpretation, but which are already partially expressed through signs. Under these circumstances, what happens is that, as interpreter of these signs, I offer a further expression of what to me they seem to mean, and I make the further hypothesis that this expression makes more manifest to me both the meaning of this sign and the idea of the mind or self whereof this sign gave partial expression. It is of the essence of an expression which undertakes to interpret a sign that it occurs because the sign already expresses a meaning which is not just at the present moment our own, and which, therefore, needs for us some interpretation, while the interpretation which at the moment we offer is itself not complete, but requires further interpretation.

In literal conversation our neighbour utters words which already express to us ideas. These ideas so contrast with our own present ideas that, while we find the new ideas intelligible, and, therefore, view them as expressions of a mind, we do not fully know what they mean. Hence, in general, our neighbour having addressed us, we in reply ask him, more or less incidentally or persistently, whether or not this is what he means—*i.e.*, we give him back our interpretation of his meaning, in order to see whether this interpretation elicits a new expression which is in substantial agreement with the expression which we expected from him. Our method in a conversation is, therefore, unquestionably the method of a 'working hypothesis.' But since this 'working hypothesis' refers to our neighbour's state of mind, it is never conceivably capable of direct verification.

Nor does what the pragmatists are accustomed to call the successful 'working' of this hypothesis consist in the discovery of any perceptible fact with which we get into merely immediate relation. Our interpretation of our neighbour satisfies our demands, precisely in so far as our interpretations, which are never complete, and which always call for new expressions and for further interpretations, lead to a conversation which remains, as a whole, essentially 'coherent,' despite its endless novelties and unexpected incidents.

Our whole knowledge of mind, in so far as by this term we mean intelligent mind, not only depends upon, but consists in, this experience of a consistent series of interpretations, which we obtain, not merely by turning conceptual 'credits' into the 'cash of immediate acquaintance,' but by seeking and finding endlessly new series of ideas, endlessly new experiences and interpretations. This never-ended series of ideas, in so far as we can hold them before our minds, tends to constitute a connected, a reasonable, a comprehensible system of ideal activities and meanings. The essence of mental intercourse—we may at once say the essence of intelligent mental life and of all spiritual relations—not only depends upon, but consists in, this coherent process of interpretation.

Or, again, an interpretation is not a conceptual hypothesis which can be converted into 'perceptual knowledge'; it is a hypothesis which leads us to anticipate further interpretations, further expressions of ideas, novel bits of information, further ideas not our own, which shall simply stand in a coherent connexion with one another and with what the original interpretation, as a hypothesis, had led us to expect. When I deal with inanimate nature, I may anticipate facts of perception, and then my hypotheses about these facts 'work,' in so far as the expected perceptions come to pass. But, when I deal with another mind, I do not merely expect to get definable perceptions from that mind; I expect that mind to give me new ideas, new meanings, new plans, which by contrast are known at each new stage of social experience to be not my own, and which may be opposed to my own and in many respects repellent to me.

But it is essential to the social intercourse between minds that these endlessly novel ideas and meanings should, through all conflicts and novelties and surprises, retain genuine coherence. Thus, in dealing with other minds, I am constantly enlarging my own mind by getting new interpretations, both of myself and of my neighbour's life. The contrasts, surprises, conflicts, and puzzles which these new ideas present to me show me that in dealing with them I am dealing with what in some respects is not my own mind. The coherence of the whole system of interpretations, ideas, plans, and purposes shows me just as positively that I am dealing with a mind, *i.e.*, with something which through these expressions constantly interprets itself, while, as I deal with it, I in turn constantly interpret it, and even in and through this very process interpret myself. It will and must be observed that this Alter, with which I have to deal, both in reflecting on my own mind and in seeking for new light from my neighbour, is never a merely single or separable or merely detached or isolated individual, but is always a being which is of the nature of a community, a 'many in one' and a 'one in many.' A mind knowable through interpretation is never merely a 'monad,' a single detached self; its unity, in so far as it possesses genuine and coherent unity, tends, in the most significant cases, to become essentially such as the unity which the apostle Paul attributes to the ideal Church: many members, but one body; many gifts, but one spirit (Ro 12[4ff.])—an essentially social unity, never to be adequately conceived or felt, but properly the object of what the Apostle viewed, in its practical and religious aspect, as the spiritual gift of charity, in its cognitive aspect as interpretation: pray rather that ye may interpret (1 Co 14[13]).

5. Metaphysical theories of the nature of mind.—(*a*) *Predominantly perceptual theories.*—The nature of mind may be defined by a given metaphysical theory mainly in terms which regard mind as best or most known through possible 'perceptions' or through possible 'acquaintance' with its nature. Such theories have been prominent throughout the whole history of human thought. They depend, first, upon ignoring the fact that what is most essential to the mind is known through the cognitive process of interpretation. They depend, further, upon making comparatively light of the effort to give any abstract conceptual description of what constitutes the essence of mind. They depend upon turning to what is sometimes called 'introspection,' or, again, 'intuition,' to bring about an immediate acquaintance with mind.

Since, in general, any one who forms a predominantly perceptual idea of what mind is very naturally is not depending solely upon his own personal experience, but upon the experiences which he supposes other minds to possess, these perceptual theories of the nature of mind actually make a wide use of the reports of other people and so, more or less consciously, of arguments from analogy.

The simplest and vaguest, but in some respects the most persistent, of all theories of mental life appears, upon a largely perceptual basis, and also upon a basis of an argument from analogy, in countless forms of so-called 'animism.' Leaving aside all the historical complications, we may sum up the animistic theory of mind thus. We perceive, within ourselves, certain interesting processes which include many of our feelings, embody many of our interests, and characterize many of our activities. These activities, which in ourselves we more or less directly observe, are closely connected with the whole process of the life of the organism, *i.e.*, of the body in whose fortunes each one of us is so interested. That which produces all these feelings, awakens in us all these interests, vitalizes our own body, and forms for each of us a centre of his own apparent world—this is the mind. The mind, then, strives and longs. It feels pain and pleasure. It prospers as the body prospers, and suffers as the body suffers.

Analogy shows that other people have such minds. These minds are as numerous as the organisms in question. They resemble one another and differ from one another, much as the organisms resemble and differ from each other. An extension of this analogy, on the basis of many motives, leads us to regard the world about us as containing many minds which are not connected with human bodies—at least in precisely the same way in which our minds are connected with our bodies. When the vast mass of superstitious beliefs which have made use of such analogies and such experiences can be more effectively controlled through the advances of the human intelligence, this primitive animism tends to pass over into theories of which we find some well-known examples in early Greek philosophies. These early Greek theories of mind appear, on a somewhat primitive and already philosophical level, as 'hylozoistic.' The world, or, at all events, the organic world, has life principles in it which vary as the organisms vary, and which are also of a nature that feeling and desire reveal to ourrelatively immediate 'knowledge of acquaintance' with our own minds.

The theories of mind of this type have played a great part in the life both of philosophy and of religion. As a general theory, animism has proved very persistent, and that for obvious reasons.

One of the Hindu *Upaniṣads*[1] well suggests both the origin and the logical basis—such as it is—of these theories when, in an allegory, it represents the question arising within the body as to where and what the soul most is. The question is disputed amongst the various bodily organs, each asserting itself to be the principal seat of life and also of mind. To discover which view is true, the members of the body take turns in leaving the organism. When the eyes go, blindness ensues, but life and mind continue, and so on with various other members. But, when the breath starts to leave the body, all the other members together cry, 'Stay with us! You are the life, you are the soul, you are the self or Ātman.'

This allegory sufficiently indicates how primitive, how vague, and how stubborn is such a perceptual theory of mind when defined in terms of immediate intuition, and of a more or less pragmatic testing of various views about the physical organism.

Later in its origin, but continuing in its influence to the present day, is another perceptual theory of mind, which the later *Upaniṣads* present at length, and which, in another form, is exemplified by a notable assertion of H. Bergson in his *Introduction to Metaphysics*[2]—namely, that of one object at least we all have intuitive knowledge, this object being the self. The entire history of mysticism, the history also of the efforts to discover the nature of mind through introspection, can be summarized by means of these instances in the Hindu *Upaniṣads* that discover the true self through the experiment with breathing, and of the latest vision of Bergson, who defines the nature of mind, and also its contrast with body, in terms of the *élan vital*; for all these views emphasize, in various more or less primitive, or in more or less modern, forms, essentially the same theory of mind: the essence of the mind is to be known through immediate acquaintance. That which Schopenhauer calls the will to live, that which Bergson characterizes in the terms just mentioned, that which the shamans and medicine-men of all the more intelligent tribes have sought to know, is, in every case, mind viewed as an object of possible perception.

In the history of thought such perceptual theories of mind have become more highly developed and diversified, and have assumed other and very widely influential forms, by virtue of an insistence that we have an immediate perception of what is variously called 'mental activity,' 'the active soul,' or 'the principle of individual selfhood.'

[1] *Bṛhadāraṇyaka Upaniṣad*, VI. i. 7–14, tr. in P. Deussen, *Sechzig Upanishad's des Veda*, Leipzig, 1897, p. 503.

[2] Eng. tr., London, 1913.

Motives which as a fact are not statable in purely perceptual terms have joined with this fondness for defining mind in perceptual terms to make emphatic the assertion that this theory of mind ought to be stated in expressly 'pluralistic' terms. It has, consequently, been freely asserted that we 'immediately know' our own self to be independent, to be distinct from all other selves, and thus to be unique. Since it is also sometimes asserted that we know, or that we 'know intuitively,' upon occasion, the fact that we can never be directly acquainted with the conditions of our neighbour's mind, such perceptual theories have given rise to the so-called problem of 'Solipsism.' For, if we know mind by perception only, and if we are sure of it only when we perceive it, and if each of us can perceive only his own mind, then what proves for any one of us that there is any mind but his own? The analogy which primitive animism so freely and so vaguely used becomes, for the critical consciousness, questionable. In consequence, the problem of Solipsism has remained in modern times a sort of scandal of the philosophy of mind.

The solution of the problem of Solipsism lies in the fact, upon which Peirce so well insisted,[1] that no one of us has any purely perceptual knowledge of his own mind. The knowledge of mind is not statable, in the case either of the self or of the neighbour, in terms of merely immediate acquaintance. If the truth of this proposition is once understood, the entire theory of mind, whether for metaphysics or for empirical psychology, is profoundly altered. Until this inadequacy of knowledge through acquaintance to meet the real end of human knowledge is fully grasped, it is impossible to define with success either the mind or the world, either the individual self or the neighbour.

(*b*) *Predominantly conceptual theories.*—As is the case with every highly developed doctrine, the conceptual form is very naturally assumed by any philosophical theory of mind which seeks for theoretical completeness. The conceptual theories of mind have been in history of two general types: (1) the purely conceptual, *i.e.* 'the abstractly rational' metaphysical theories; and (2) the more inductive conceptual theories based upon the more or less highly developed 'empirical psychologies' of the period in which these theories have flourished. We need not enumerate these theories or give their history.

Of principal importance in their history have been (1) that type of vitalism whose most classical representative is the Aristotelian theory of mind; (2) the monistic theory of mind, which often depends not so much upon the general metaphysical tendency to define the whole universe as One, but rather upon the effort to conceive mind and matter by regarding them both as the same in substance; and (3) the various types of monadology, which are characterized by the assertion of the existence of many real and more or less completely independent minds or selves, whose nature it is either to be themselves persons or to be beings which under certain conditions can assume the form of persons.

Of those various important theories which are expressed in the predominantly conceptual form that of Aristotle is very deeply and interestingly related to primitive animism on the one hand, while, on the other hand, it looks towards that development of the idea of the distinct individual self upon which more modern forms of monadology have depended.

Whatever special forms the conceptual theories of mind may assume, the well-known problem remains: How are these conceptions of the various mental substances, or principles, or monads, which are each time in question related to the sorts of experience which the psychologists, the students of the natural history of mind, have at any stage of knowledge discovered or may yet hope to discover? From the point of view of modern pragmatism, conceptual theories of mind might be entertained as 'working hypotheses' if they led to verification in perceptual terms.

In fact, the modern physical sciences, in conceiving the nature of matter, deal with manifold problems, but use conceptual hypotheses regarding the nature of matter which are, in a large measure, subject to pragmatic tests. Molecules and atoms and, of late, various other types of conceptual physical entities, which were formerly supposed to be incapable of becoming objects of physical experience, now appear to come within the range of the experimenter's verifications. Therefore the processes of the experimental verification of physical hypotheses have, on the whole, a direct relation to the sort of knowledge upon which the pragmatists so much insist. The 'conceptual credits' of physical hypotheses are, on the whole, verifiable in terms of the 'perceptual cash' of laboratory experience. When this is not the case, there is a tendency towards such direct verification. Hence physical hypotheses, at least regarding what is generally called the phenomenal nature of matter, have generally proved to be topics for an inquiry within the strict realm of inductive science.

But it has been, in the past, the reproach of the conceptual theories about the nature of mind that no pragmatic test can be discovered by which one might learn what difference it would make to an observer of mental processes and, in particular, of his own mental processes whether minds are 'soul substances,' or Leibnizean monads, or not, or whether the introspective observer of his own sensations or feelings is or is not himself a Leibnizean monad or Aristotelian 'entelechy'; or, again, whether he is essentially persistent and indestructible. Thus, from the pragmatic point of view, the majority of these conceptual hypotheses regarding the nature of mind show little sign of promising to prove more verifiable than they thus far have been. In consequence, the outcome of conceptual views regarding the real nature of mind has been, for many reasons, on the whole sceptical. In fact, the whole nature of mind cannot be adequately conceived, and could not be so conceived even if one's power to perceive mental processes were increased indefinitely, unless another type of cognitive processes were concerned in such an enlargement. For a mind is essentially a being that manifests itself through signs. The very being of signs consists in their demanding interpretation. The relations of minds are essentially social; so that a world without at least three minds in it—one to be interpreted, one the interpreter, and the third the one for whom or to whom the first is interpreted—would be a world without any real mind in it at all. This being the case, it might well be expected that a conceptual theory of mind would fail precisely as a perceptual theory fails. Such theories would fail because they do not view the cognitive process as it is and do not take account of that which is most of all needed in order even in the most rudimentary fashion to grasp the nature of an intelligent mind.

(*c*) *Theories making use of the cognitive process of the interpretation.*—Despite the inadequate development of the doctrine of interpretation thus far in the history of epistemology, there have not been lacking theories regarding the nature of mind according to which mind is an object to be

[1] See Royce, *Problem of Christianity*, ii.

known through interpretation, while its manifestations lie not merely in the fact that it possesses or controls an organism, but in the fact that, whether through or apart from an organism, it expresses its purposes to other minds, so that it not merely has or is a will, but manifests or makes comprehensible its will, and not merely lives in and through itself, as a monad or a substance, but is in essence a mode of self-expression which progressively makes itself known either to its fellows or to minds above or below its own grade.

That theories of mind which are based upon such a view have existed, even from very primitive times, is manifest wherever in the history of religion a consultation of oracles, discovery of the future or of the will of the gods through divination, or, in fact, any such more or less superstitious appeals to other minds, and readings or interpretations of these appeals, have taken place. Primitive belief in magic arts has apparently, on the whole, a conceptual type of formulation. Therefore magic has been called the physics of primitive man. It depends upon the view that man is subject to laws which, if he could discover them, he could use for his purposes, just as we now make use of the known laws of physics for industrial purposes. The supposed realm of magic arts is thus analogous to our present realm of industrial arts. The view of pragmatism—that primitive magic is not true merely because its hypotheses regarding how to cause rain or how to cure diseases do not 'work'—is in this case fairly adequate to express the situation both epistemologically and metaphysically.

Moreover, as we have seen, animism, in its more primitive forms, expresses a predominantly perceptual theory of mind, and whether such a theory, either of mind or of the relations between mind and the physical world, is held in some simple form by the medicine-man of an obscure tribe or is impressively reiterated in a Hindu *Upaniṣad*, or is fascinatingly placed in the setting of a modern evolutionary theory by Bergson, makes comparatively little difference to the essential views of the philosophy of mind which are in question. But that view of the nature of mind which gained, apparently, its earliest type of expression when men first consulted, and hereupon more or less cautiously interpreted, the oracles of their gods has (as befits a theory of mind which is founded upon a fundamental cognitive process) persisted throughout the history of human thought. This way of viewing mind has, in fact, persisted in a fashion which enables us to distinguish its expressions with sufficient clearness from those which have had their origin either in the conceptions of primitive magic or in the perceptions which guided primitive animism.

From the point of view of the cognitive process of interpretation mind is, in all cases where it reaches a relatively full and explicit expression, equally definable in terms of two ideas—the idea of the self, and the idea of a community of selves. To an explicit recognition of what these two ideas involve a great part of the history of the philosophy of mind has been devoted. Both ideas have been subject to the misfortune of being too often viewed as reducible either to purely conceptual terms or to purely perceptual terms. If the self was defined in predominantly conceptual terms, it tended to degenerate into a substance, a monad, or a mere thing of some sort. Under the influence of a too abstract epistemology (such as the Kantian) the self also appeared as the 'logical ego,' or else as the 'pure subject.'

The fortunes of the idea of the community have been analogous. In religion this idea has proved one of the most inspiring of the ideas which have gradually transformed tribal cults into the two greatest religions which humanity possesses—Buddhism and Christianity. In ancient philosophy the community, viewed as the soul 'writ large,' inspired some of the most fruitful philosophical interpretations of Plato, Aristotle, and the Stoics. In the general history of civilization loyalty, which is identical with the practically effective love of communities as persons that represent mind on a level higher than that of the individual, is, like the Pauline charity (which is explicitly a love for the Church universal and for its spirit), the chief and the soul of the humanizing virtues—that virtue without which all the others are but 'sounding brass or a tinkling cymbal.' Yet, in the history of thought the idea of the community has greatly suffered, less frequently from the attempt to view it as the proper object of a direct mystical perception than from the tendency to reduce it to a purely conceptual form. As a conceptual object the 'mind of the community,' the 'corporate mind,' has tended to be thought of as an entity possibly significant in a legal or in a sociological sense, but difficult, and perhaps unreal, in a metaphysical sense.

Experience shows, however, that the two ideas —the idea of the individual self and that of the community—are peculiarly adapted to interpret each the other, both to itself and to the other, when such interpretation is carried on in the spirit which the religion of Israel first made central in what undertook to be a world religion, and which the apostle Paul laid at the basis both of his philosophy of human history and of his Christology.

Modern idealism, both in the more vital and less formal expressions of Hegel's doctrine and in its recent efforts at a social interpretation of the self, of the course of human evolution, and of the problems of metaphysics, has already given a partial expression to a theory of which we tend to become clearly aware in proportion as we recognize what the cognitive process of interpretation is, and how it contrasts with, and is auxiliary to, the processes of conception and perception. Only in terms of a theory of the threefold process of knowledge can we hope fully to express what is meant by that form of idealism which views the world as the 'process of the spirit' and as containing its own interpretation and its own interpreter.

LITERATURE.—The epistemology of Charles Peirce is discussed at length by the present writer in *The Problem of Christianity*, London, 1913, ii. (in Index, *s.v.* 'Peirce,' references will be found which will serve as a guide to the understanding of Peirce's theory of knowledge, and its relation to the metaphysical theories of the nature of mind).

JOSIAH ROYCE.

MIND AND BODY.—See BODY AND MIND.

MIND AND BRAIN.—See BRAIN AND MIND.

MINERALS.—See METALS AND MINERALS.

MÎNÎM.—Certain persons of Jewish origin mentioned in the Talmud and contemporary Rabbinical literature, usually with severe disapproval, are called Mînîm. Considerable difference of opinion has existed upon the question who the Mînîm were; but the view is now generally, though not universally, held that they were mainly Jewish-Christians. This theory has the support of Graetz, Jost, Weiss, Bacher, and Lévi; the chief opponent is Moritz Friedländer. The writer of this article, from an independent study of the evidence, decides for the Jewish-Christian interpretation, while admitting a wider denotation in a few passages. The evidence, consisting of the whole of the passages (so far as they are known to him) where mention is made of the Mînîm, is presented in full in the writer's work

Christianity in Talmud and Midrash, to which the reader is referred for details which cannot be given in the short space of this article.

The book *Siphrê*, § 115, p. 35ᵃ, quoting Nu 15[39] 'And ye shall not walk after your heart,' says, 'This is Mînûth'—meaning that this is the state of mind, or principle of conduct, characteristic of the Mînîm. This is the earliest attempt at a definition of the term, though the word itself was in use earlier. It amounts to saying that a 'Mîn' (singular of Mînîm) was one who followed the dictates of his own selfish nature as against those of the lawful authority. The result of doing so is, indirectly, the rejection of beliefs and practices enjoined on those who hold the true religion. A Mîn, accordingly, disregards the authority of the Rabbis, as teachers of religion and expounders of the Torah both written and unwritten, and also maintains doctrines and practices which are not those of the true religion. Tos. *Sanh.* xiii. 4 f. has the following censure on the Mînîm:

'The sinners of Israel, and the sinners of the nations of the world, descend into Gehenna, and are judged there twelve months. . . But the Mînîm, and the Apostates, and the betrayers, and the Apîqôrôsîn. . . . Gehenna is shut in their faces, and they are judged there for generations of generations.'

If the term Mînîm denoted all unfaithful Jews, there would be no need of four descriptive names. The distinction between the four is as follows. The betrayers (Mᵉsôrôth) are political informers, 'delators.' Apostates are those who wilfully and openly transgress some part of the ceremonial law, thereby proclaiming their disloyalty. Apîqôrôsîn are 'Epicureans,' free-thinkers, whether Jewish or Gentile. The Mînîm are those who are false at heart, but who do not necessarily proclaim their apostasy. They are the more dangerous because more secret; they are not an open enemy, but the foe within the camp; and it is in accordance with this that the Talmud refers to the Mînîm more frequently and with more hostility than to the other classes of unfaithful Jews. The Mîn might be an apostate or a delator, and could hardly fail to be a free-thinker; but the real nature of his offence was moral rather than intellectual.

Why was the name Mîn given to such persons? Various derivations of the word have been given, some of them mere fanciful guesses. The best explanation seems to be that proposed by Bacher (in *REJ* xxxviii. 45) and accepted by I. Lévi (*ib.* p. 205), according to which *mîn* (מין) is at first the ordinary word for 'sort,' 'kind,' and is translated in the LXX, Gn 1[12], by γένος. Figuratively the word is used to denote a 'sect' (αἵρεσις), and more particularly the sect of the Sadducees (τὸ Σαδδουκαίων γένος, Jos. *Ant.* XIII. x. 6, where ἡ Σαδδουκαίων αἵρεσις is also used). Gradually the term lost the meaning of 'sect' and took on that of 'sectary,' the Jew who separated himself from the community and adopted false doctrines. If this explanation is correct, it throws light on the fact that in the Rabbinical texts the reading sometimes varies between Mîn and Ṣaddûkî (Sadducee). It is usually said that the latter word is due to the Christian censor, who objected to the word Mîn, but in some cases the reference is certainly to the Sadducees, while yet the word Mîn, or possibly both words, may have been read. The writer of this article proposed another derivation of the word Mîn (*op. cit.* p. 362), but now surrenders it in favour of the one just set forth.

The Mînîm, then, were Jewish heretics of some kind. The question is, Of what kind? The answer resolves itself into a choice between Jewish-Christians and Jewish-Gnostics. That they were Jews is beyond dispute, for a Gentile is never called a Mîn, unless in one or two instances through ignorance or inadvertence. The only conspicuous advocate of the Gnostic interpretation is Friedländer (*Der vorchristliche jüdische Gnosticismus*; cf. also a defence in reply to criticism in *REJ* xxxviii. 194 ff.), but it is a serious defect of Friedländer's book that the argument is based on Rabbinical texts from which he strikes out, as interpolations, passages of crucial importance, without mentioning the fact. By this method any hypothesis could be proved. Bacher and Lévi, in articles in *REJ* (xxxviii. 38, 204) have severely handled Friedländer's hypothesis as well as his peculiar method of proof, and Lévi elsewhere refers to it as 'cet échafaudage de propositions puériles' (*RHR* li. [1905] 412). The evidence for the view that the Mînîm were Jewish-Christians may be briefly summed up as follows. In many of the passages where they are mentioned there is nothing distinctive, certainly nothing definitely Christian; but in a few passages a connexion between Mînûth and Christianity is so definitely stated that it cannot be excluded from neutral passages except on the ground of equally definite statements to the contrary. Such contrary evidence is not to be found, and even Friedländer does not produce any. (1) In a famous passage, Bab. '*Ăbhôdhāh Zārāh*, 16*b* (and in three other places), it is told how a certain Rabbi Eliezer (end of 1st cent.) was arrested for Mînûth. He accounted for this afterwards by saying that he had once met 'one of the disciples of Jesus the Nazarene, by name Jacob of Kᵉphar Sᵉkhanyā,' who told him the exposition of a text and added, 'Thus hath Jesus the Nazarene taught me.' Also, in the same treatise, p. 27*a*, the same Jacob is called 'Jacob the Mîn,' and it is said that he offered to cure a sick man, while in Tos. *Ḥull.* ii. 22 f. the same Jacob proposed to work his cure 'in the name of Yeshûa' ben Pandîrā,' *i.e.* Jesus. (2) In Bab. *Shabb.* 116*a* there are mentioned, in close connexion, the books of the Mînîm and the Evangelion, *i.e.* the Gospels. (3) The characteristic doctrine of the Mînîm—that of Two Powers in Heaven—is closely allied to, if not identical with, the teaching of the Ep. to the Hebrews, and is not the Gnostic doctrine of the Demiurgus. The connexion of this doctrine with Christianity is shown by a passage in Pᵉsîqtā *Rab.* xxi. 100*b*: 'If the son of the harlot saith to thee, "There are two Gods,"' etc., where 'the son of the harlot' denotes Jesus.

The combined force of these arguments, which could be supported in great detail if space allowed, seems conclusive in favour of the Jewish-Christian interpretation; and this view is strongly confirmed by a passage in Jerome:

'Usque hodie per totas Orientis synagogas inter Iudaeos haeresis est, quae dicitur *Minaeorum*, et a Pharisaeis nunc usque damnatur; quos vulgo Nazaraeos nuncupant, qui credunt in Christum, filium Dei, natum de virgine Maria, et eum dicunt esse qui sub Pontio Pilato passus est et resurrexit, in quem et nos credimus; sed dum volunt et Iudaei esse et Christiani, nec Judaei sunt nec Christiani' (*Ep.* cxii. [lxxxix.] 13 [*PL* xxii. 924]).

The general conclusion to be drawn from the evidence, of which the foregoing is the most important, is that, wherever in the Talmud and Midrash mention is made of the Mînîm, the author of the statement intended to refer to Jewish-Christians. At the same time it is possible that the Rabbis attributed to Mînîm actions or opinions which, in fact, were not those of Christians; and, further, that the Rabbis occasionally applied the term Mîn to Gentiles as being enemies of Judaism.

The references to the Mînîm in the Rabbinical literature are few and fragmentary. The passages where they are mentioned amount to about 120, most of which contain either polemical dialogues between a Mîn and a Rabbi or allusions to heretical interpretations of texts, although a few are anecdotes of events in connexion with the Mînîm. It is not possible to construct a history of the Mînîm; the material is sufficient only to give a few glimpses of them, and to throw some little light upon their relations with orthodox Jews.

The Mînîm, as stated above, were apostates who concealed their apostasy, and it was necessary, therefore, to have some means of detecting them. This was the object with which the Formula against the Mînîm was introduced. It is stated (Bab. *Ber.* 28*b*, 29*a*) that R. Gamaliel II. (president of the Sanhedrin at Jabneh) said to the Rabbis: 'Is there any one who knows how to compose a Benediction of the Mînîm?' Samuel the Little stood up and composed it. The following year he forgot it, and sought to recall it for two and even three hours, and they did not call him up (from the lectern). The 'Benediction' of the Mînîm was an addition made to the Eighteen Benedictions (*Sh*e*môneh 'Esrēh B*e*rākhōth*), which are short prayers, some of them very ancient, forming the nucleus of the Jewish liturgy. The twelfth in order, as composed or adapted by Samuel the Little, runs: 'May there be no hope for the Mînîm.' Those who were Mînîm could not, of course, join in this prayer, and would be detected. The introduction of this formula marks the official condemnation of the Mînîm by the Rabbis; and the date may be placed at A.D. 80, or thereabout. This does not imply the separation of the Mînîm from the strict Jews at and after that time; they were still to be found, as Jerome says, in all the synagogues of the East in his time; but it is true, nevertheless, that the Mînîm did to some extent possess a separate organization, with synagogues of their own.

The reason why a formula of detection against the Mînîm became necessary about A.D. 80, was, in part, that the Temple had been destroyed ten years before. As long as the Temple stood, Jewish-Christians in Jerusalem appear to have taken part in the ritual observances equally with non-Christian Jews. After the destruction of the Temple, however, it was possible to argue that the ceremonial law was not merely *de facto* suspended (as the Jews admitted), but *de jure* abrogated; and this is the link which connects the original Jewish-Christians with the Mînîm. The latter appear, from the notices of their doctrines, to have held a theology closely akin to that set forth in the Ep. to the Hebrews; and, if so, the inference is ready to hand that it was the symbolic interpretation of the ceremonial law that opened the way for a Christology more highly developed than that of the original Jewish-Christians.

The hostility towards, and dread of, the Mînîm were at their height in the 2nd cent.; afterwards they declined, till in the 4th cent. we find comparatively friendly relations with them. The Mînîm of Cæsarea applied to R. Abahu to find them a teacher, and he sent them R. Saphra, a Babylonian Jew of unquestioned orthodoxy (Bab. *Ăbhôdhāh Zārāh*, 4*a*). The meaning of this gradual change is that at first it was not evident to the Rabbis that the Christian Church would not develop on Jewish-Christian lines. When, in course of time, it appeared that the Mînîm did not represent the strength of the Christian movement, there was the less reason to dread it; there was less danger to Judaism from a Gentile Christianity than from a Jewish form of it. Of Gentile Christianity the Rabbinical literature takes scarcely any notice. Space does not allow of illustrations of the polemics between Mînîm and Jews, or of the anecdotes which represent the former as being not only apostates but licentious. It must suffice to say that they appear to have been a dwindling sect, in Judaism but not of it, spurned alike by Jews and by Christians. In their theology they departed from the strict monotheism of Judaism, and held a doctrine—called the Doctrine of the Two Powers in Heaven—which corresponds with the relation between God and Christ set forth in the Ep. to the Hebrews. No mention is made in any of their polemical discussions of the Messiahship of Jesus, nor is there more than one very slight trace of the doctrine of the Trinity (Jerus. *Ber.* 12*d*, 13*a*). Jerome identifies them with the Nazarenes, and the corresponding name, *Nôṣrîm*, is found in two passages (Bab. *Ăbhôdhāh Zārāh*, 6*a*; Bab. *Ta'an.* 27*b*). The name Ebionite does not occur in the Rabbinical literature.

LITERATURE.—See the Histories of H. Graetz, London, 1891-92, I. M. Jost, Leipzig, 1857-59, and I. H. Weiss, Vienna, 1887; W. Bacher and I. Lévi, artt. in *REJ* xxxviii. [1898] 45 ff., 205 ff.; M. Friedländer, *Der vorchristliche jüdische Gnosticismus*, Göttingen, 1898, *Die religiösen Bewegungen . . . im Zeitalter Jesu*, Berlin, 1905, and *REJ* xxxviii. 194 ff.; R. T. Herford, *Christianity in Talmud and Midrash*, London, 1904; *JE*, art. 'Min.'

R. T. HERFORD.

MINISTRY (Early Christian).—An attempt will be made in this article to collect the more important facts in connexion with the ministry as far as the first five or six centuries of our era are concerned. About the facts themselves there is general agreement; but the interpretation of the facts has been disputed. A summary will be made, as briefly as possible, of the theories that have been deduced from the facts as to the institution of a ministry by our Lord, and its development in subsequent ages. But a discussion of these theories is not part of the design of the article.

1. The Apostolic Age.—In Acts and in the Epistles of the NT we find in active operation a ministry of two kinds, itinerant and local.

i. THE ITINERANT MINISTRY.—We read of apostles, prophets, and evangelists, all of whom come under this heading. The first of these terms includes at least a few (even in the early ages) who were not of the Twelve (see below, § 2). The qualification of an apostle seems originally to have been that he should have seen our Lord, and have been His 'witness' (Lk 24^48, Ac 1^8). Thus, when the vacancy in the number of the Twelve has to be filled up, the qualification mentioned by St. Peter is that the person chosen should have 'companied with [the Eleven] all the time that the Lord Jesus went in and went out among' (or 'over,' ἐπί) them, 'beginning from the baptism of John, unto the day that he was received up from' them; so that he might become a witness with them of Jesus' resurrection (Ac 1^21f.). St. Paul received his qualification, though in a different way, at his conversion (cf. Gal 1^1, 'An apostle, not from men, neither through man, but through Jesus Christ, and God the Father'). That St. Barnabas and the others mentioned below (§ 2) had seen Christ is not stated, but is quite probable. Hegesippus says (Eus. *HE* ii. 1) that Barnabas was one of the Seventy. This qualification may have been waived in the sub-apostolic period.

Hort (*Christian Ecclesia*, p. 28) thinks that the word 'apostle,' which is of comparatively rare occurrence in the Gospels, referred originally only to the mission to the villages, though such passages as that about judging the twelve tribes (Mt 19^28, Lk 22^30) were indications of the extended signification of the name which we find in Acts.[1] It is clear, however, from Lk 6^13 (the reading in ‖ Mk 3^14 is doubtful) that our Lord gave them the title; and that He intended more than a mere mission to the villages by the designation appears almost certain from such passages as Lk 12^41-43, where He speaks of a commission for future ages (see below, § 9). St. Luke certainly uses the name without reference to the mission to the villages.

Christian prophets are frequently mentioned in the NT—Agabus and others (Ac 11^27f. 21^10); those at Antioch, 'prophets and teachers,' including

[1] The name 'apostles' for the Twelve is found, according to Westcott and Hort's text, only in Mt 10^2, Mk 3^14 6^30, Lk 6^13 9^10 17^5 22^14 24^10, and not at all in Jn, though 13^16 seems to be an allusion to the title.

Barnabas and Saul, also Symeon Niger, Lucius of Cyrene, and Manaen (Ac 13^{1}); Judas and Silas (15^{32}); and an unstated number in 1 Co 12$^{28f.}$ (see § 2) 14$^{29-33}$. Prophets are mentioned as a class in Eph 2^{20} 3^{5} 4^{11} (see § 2), possibly in 1 Th 2^{15}; also in Rev 18^{20} 22^{9}. They are coupled in Eph. and Rev. with apostles.[1] They are described as receiving revelations (1 Co 14$^{29ff.}$). Christian prophetesses are also mentioned (Ac 21^{9}, Philip's daughters). But it may be doubted if 'prophets' ought to be described as a class of the ordinary Christian ministry. Their office was purely charismatic (see below, § 3).

It is otherwise with 'evangelists.' These are mentioned in Ac 21^{8} (Philip), Eph 4^{11} (see below, § 2), 2 Ti 4^{5} (Timothy). This name would seem to be that given to those who, though not apostles, because they had not the qualification stated above, yet were itinerant officials and not of the local ministry. Eusebius (*HE* iii. 37) gives the name to those who 'occupied the first place among the successors (διαδοχῆς) of the apostles' and were itinerant preachers of the gospel. He says that, when they had only laid the foundations of the faith in foreign places, they appointed others as pastors (ποιμένας) and then went on to other countries and nations. A few lines later he talks of 'pastors or evangelists,' and seems to mean by the former the local, by the latter the itinerant, ministry.

Apostles and prophets are also mentioned in the *Didache* (§§ 10-13), a manual probably of the beginning of the 2nd century. These were normally itinerant officials, and were perhaps identical (see *Did.* § 11). The value of this evidence is discounted by J. A. Robinson (*JThSt* xiii. [1912] 339), who thinks that the writer does not describe the conditions of his own day, but those which he thought had been in force at an earlier time. This theory, however, is very doubtful (for Robinson's earlier view see his *Com. on Ephesians*^{2}, London, 1904, p. 98, n.).

The function of the itinerant ministry was evangelistic (cf. 1 Th 2$^{8f.}$, 1 Ti 2^{7}). The itinerants might settle for a time at a place, as Timothy settled at Ephesus, Titus in Crete, and St. Paul himself at various places where he founded churches; but this was not their normal work. In the *Didache* it is recognized that a prophet may settle in a place (§ 12 f.).

ii. THE LOCAL MINISTRY.—Under this heading are included in the NT 'bishops,' 'presbyters,' and 'deacons.' For other names of these officials see § 2. The functions of the local ministry were administrative and pastoral. Thus baptism seems to have been specially entrusted to it (cf. 1 Co 1^{14}, and perhaps Ac 19^{5}; ct. v.^{6}). In the beautiful story of St. John and the young robber related by Clement of Alexandria (*Quis dives*, 42), the apostle does not himself baptize the young man, but gives him over to the local bishop-presbyter to baptize (see below).

(*a*) *Bishops.*—During the period covered by the NT, we read of this name being given to Christian ministers only in Gentile churches—at Philippi (Ph 1^{1}), at Ephesus (Ac 20^{28}, 1 Ti 3$^{1ff.}$), in Crete (Tit 1$^{7ff.}$). So St. Peter, writing to the churches in most of the provinces of Asia Minor, uses the participle ἐπισκοποῦντες, 'exercising the bishop's office' (1 P 5^{2}). That the 'bishops' are the same as 'presbyters' in the Apostolic Age seems to follow from a comparison of Ac 20^{17} with 20^{28}, where the same individuals are called by both titles; and of 1 Ti 3$^{1-7}$ with 5$^{17-19}$, the first of which passages describes the qualifications of 'bishops,' the second of which gives regulations for 'presbyters' as for those who have already been mentioned in the Epistle; and of Tit 1^{5} with v.^{7} ('appoint presbyters in every city . . . for the bishop must be blameless'); also from the use by St. Peter of ἐπισκοποῦντες when speaking of presbyters (see above, and 1 P 5^{1}). The same thing is apparently found in Clement of Rome (*Cor.* 42, 44), where the local ministers are called 'bishops and deacons,' and yet 'presbyters' are spoken of, and their 'episcopate' (ἐπισκοπή). He says that the apostles knew through our Lord Jesus Christ that there would be strife over the name of the episcopate. In the *Didache* also (§ 15) the local ministry consists of 'bishops and deacons.' Perhaps 'presbyter' expressed the rank, and 'bishop' the function.

Hort (pp. 98 f., 189-212) takes a different view. He holds that the words 'bishops' and 'deacons' are used in a non-technical sense in the NT as meaning 'those who have oversight' and 'those who minister.' He thus interprets the words in Ac 20^{28}, 1 Ti 3$^{1ff.}$, and deduces the conclusion that the same holds good in Ph 1^{1}, where ἐπισκόποις and διακόνοις have no article. He does not deny that 'deacons' may have become the name of the officials before the Pastoral Epistles were written, but he thinks that St. Paul uses the word in a non-technical sense.

(*b*) *Presbyters.*—The name was perhaps taken over by the Christians from the Jews, who gave it to the members of the Sanhedrin and others. But inscriptions show that the heathen Greeks used it for members of a corporation, and the same thing appears from the papyri. A. Deissmann thinks (*Bible Studies*, Eng. tr., Edinburgh, 1901, p. 154 ff.) that the Christians of Asia Minor may have adopted the term, not from the Jews, but from the Greeks. In Egypt, as Deissmann shows (p. 233), pagan priests were called 'presbyters.' [It may be added that inscriptions also prove that the title ἐπίσκοπος was used for certain officials in Greek-speaking countries in pre-Christian times (Deissmann, p. 230 f.).] In the early Church the name 'presbyter' was specially used, as it would seem, at Jerusalem (Ac 11^{30} 15^{2} etc. 16^{4} 21^{18}), but it was also used by the Christian Jews of the Dispersion (Ja 5^{14}), and in the Gentile communities, for Paul and Barnabas appointed 'elders in every church' on a journey in Asia Minor (Ac 14^{23}).

The identity in the NT of 'bishops' and 'presbyters' was completely forgotten before the end of the 2nd century. Thus Irenæus (*Hær.* III. xiv. 2), referring to Ac 20$^{17ff.}$, speaks of St. Paul meeting at Miletus bishops and presbyters from Ephesus *and the other cities*; the last four words are no doubt due to the plural 'bishops,' as to Irenæus the idea of more than one bishop (in the sense in which the word was used in his day) in any city would be quite foreign. Clement of Alexandria, at the end of the century, was also ignorant of the identity; he speaks (*Pæd.* III. xii. 97) of commands in Holy Scripture given to presbyters, bishops, deacons, widows (in that order), as to distinct persons. In *Quis dives*, 42, he speaks of a single 'bishop' in one of the cities of Asia in St. John's time; this is doubtless historically correct, yet we may notice that a few lines later he calls the bishop 'the presbyter.' This is an instance of that fluidity of phraseology which we shall have occasion to notice below (§ 2). In the 4th cent. Jerome and other Fathers had learnt that the bishops and presbyters of the NT were the same persons (see references in Lightfoot, *Philippians*, p. 98 f.).

(*c*) *Deacons.*—These ministers are mentioned in the NT in Ph 1^{1}, 1 Ti 3$^{8. 10. 12f.}$ only. They are not found in the Epistle to Titus. They are also mentioned, together with 'bishops,' in Clement of Rome and the *Didache* (as above). The usual view has been that they represent the Seven whose appointment is recorded in Ac 6. Others think

[1] In Eph 2^{20} the Church is said to be built upon the foundation of the apostles and prophets (no article before 'prophets'). Both here and in 3^{5} prophets come after apostles, and Christian prophets must therefore be meant. Hort (p. 165) gives good reasons for thinking that here (not in 4^{11}) the same persons are meant by both designations. All the apostles were probably prophets, though all the Christian prophets were not apostles.

that the Seven were the prototypes both of the diaconate and of the presbyterate, and that at some time after St. Stephen's death the office was divided into those two branches. Another view is that the appointment of the Seventy (or Seventy-two) in Lk 10^{1} was the foundation of the presbyterate. The Seven of Ac 6 were appointed in the first instance for the administration of relief (v.^{3}), but that they were also preachers of the gospel is seen from the history of Stephen and Philip, and might be inferred from their solemn ordination with prayer and laying on of hands.

iii. THE POSITION OF JAMES THE LORD'S BROTHER AT JERUSALEM.—Christian antiquity agrees in giving St. James a local ministry at Jerusalem, and yet in making him, in a real sense, equal to the Twelve, and in ascribing to him rule or presidency over the presbyters, though nothing is said of any autocratic powers possessed by him. This account of his position is borne out by the NT writers. In Ac 12^{17} Peter bids those who are assembled in Mary's house tell of his escape 'unto James and to the brethren.' In $15^{13ff.}$ James presides over, or at least takes a leading part in, the apostolic council, and gives the decision, *i.e.* interprets the evident sense of the assembly. In 21^{18} Paul and his companions visit him assembled with the presbyters in a formal meeting. In Gal 1^{19} he is, perhaps, called an apostle (see § 2); he and Cephas are visited by Paul at Jerusalem. In 2^{9} he is named before Cephas and John, and the three are 'reputed to be pillars.' In 2^{12} the Jewish Christians who come from Jerusalem to Antioch are said to come 'from James.' Of the Fathers the earliest to bear witness to St. James's position in Jerusalem is Hegesippus, known as the father of Church history (*c.* A.D. 160). He says that 'James, the brother of the Lord, succeeded to the government of the Church in conjunction with the apostles' (Eus. *HE* ii. 23); he describes the appointment of Symeon, a cousin of the Lord, as 'the next bishop' (iv. 22). So Eusebius, who depends on Hegesippus, says (iii. 11) that they pronounced Symeon to be worthy of the throne of that diocese (παροικία), and (iii. 32) that Symeon was the second bishop of the Church of Jerusalem; in the former passage he says that there was a second Apostolic Council on the occasion of Symeon's election. The last statement is very doubtful; but the tradition probably gave rise to the detailed pseudepigraphy of the Church Orders, which assign all sorts of directions to the apostles. The same supposed council has been thought by some to have decreed the establishment of diocesan episcopacy; but the latter was probably of gradual growth rather than the result of an enactment of a formal council (see below, § 4). The position of James is also spoken of by Clement of Alexandria (*Hypotyposes*, bk. vi., quoted by Eus. *HE* ii. 1):

> 'Peter, James, and John, after the ascension of our Saviour, as if also preferred by our Lord, strove not after honour, but chose James the Just bishop of Jerusalem. . . . The Lord after His resurrection imparted knowledge to James the Just and to John and Peter, and they imparted it to the rest of the apostles, and the rest of the apostles to the Seventy, of whom Barnabas was one.'

The phrase about imparting knowledge to James may probably be a reference to 1 Co 15^{7}. The description of him as 'bishop of Jerusalem' is an anachronism of nomenclature, but it roughly describes his position. His office at Jerusalem is a favourite theme in the 'Clementine' literature, but the date of these works is uncertain.

iv. ANGELS IN THE APOCALYPSE.—The 'angels' in Rev 1^{20}–3^{22} have been taken by some to be the chief ministers of the Church in the province of Asia. But this interpretation is so doubtful that no argument can be built upon it.

v. There is no certain trace of any local officials in the NT inferior to the 'bishops and deacons.' Interpreters are mentioned in 1 Co 14^{28}, for those who speak with tongues (cf. 12^{10}). But there is no indication that an ecclesiastical office is intended.

2. Fluidity of phraseology.—It is important to remember that the names of Christian ministerial offices were not stereotyped in the Apostolic Age. Many theories have been erroneously built on the supposed identity of offices in different centuries, because of the identity of names. In the earliest age the names of the orders of the ministry were in a fluid condition, even if the functions and duties of the offices were fixed, which is doubtful.

(*a*) *The name 'apostle.'*—This is used in the NT of the Twelve (see above, § 1). It is also used of certain other persons who had equal authority with the Twelve in the early Church—Paul, Barnabas, probably James the Lord's brother (see Lightfoot, *Galatians*^{5}, pp. 84, 95; cf. 1 Co 15^{7}), probably also Andronicus and Junias, who were 'of note among the apostles' (Ro 16^{7}; but some think that the latter was the name of a woman), perhaps Silvanus, who was associated with St. Paul in writing to the Thessalonians (1 Th 2^{6}; cf. 1^{1}). Timothy might have been included under the same designation but that he is excluded from it by 2 Co 1^{1}, Col 1^{1}, doubtless because he had not seen Christ (see § 1). The name is also used in the NT of messengers simply (2 Co 8^{23}, Ph 2^{25}), and of our Lord Himself (He 3^{1}; cf. Jn 20^{21}). In the Syriac-speaking churches it was given to any missionary; and so the Greek-speaking Irenæus says (*Hær.* II. xxi. 1): 'After the twelve apostles, our Lord is found to have sent forth seventy others.' Tertullian (*adv. Marc.* iv. 24) gives the name to the Seventy as well as to the Twelve ('he chose also seventy other apostles besides the twelve'). Note that St. Luke (10^{1}), in describing the appointment of the Seventy, says that Jesus 'sent them forth' (ἀπέστειλεν), whence the name ἀπόστολος comes at once. It means 'one commissioned.' Certain persons, called 'false apostles,' arrogated the name to themselves (2 Co 11^{13}, Rev 2^{2}).

(*b*) *The names 'bishop' and 'presbyter.'*—We have already seen that the name 'bishop' was used in the 1st cent. in a sense different from that which it afterwards acquired. And we may notice how fluid was the phraseology with regard to both 'bishop' and 'presbyter.' Our Lord is called a 'bishop' in 1 P 2^{25}; St. Peter a 'presbyter' in 1 P 5^{1} (συμπρεσβύτερος), St. John in 2 Jn ^{1}, 3 Jn ^{1}. In the 2nd cent. the term 'presbyters' came to be used somewhat as we use the term 'the Fathers.' We may also notice how easy was the change from 'presbyter' to 'old man'; so much so that it is not always easy to determine in any given passage which translation ought to be taken. In 1 P 5^{5} St. Peter, who has been addressing the presbyters, suddenly says: 'Likewise, ye younger [men], be subject to the elder' (πρεσβυτέροις). Clement of Rome (*Cor.* 1) says: 'Submitting yourselves to your rulers (ἡγουμένοις), and rendering to the presbyters [Lightfoot: 'older men'] among you honour,' etc.; and so in § 21. A little later Polycarp, after saying that 'the young men must be blameless,' goes on to exhort the Philippians to submit themselves 'to the presbyters and deacons' (*Phil.* 5). The association of the presbyterate and old age survived for a long time. It is found in the *Apostolic Church Order* (Bohairic version), where it is said that presbyters should live 'after the manner of old men' (§ 18; H. Tattam, *Apost. Const. in Coptic*, London, 1848, p. 20). The ordination prayer of a presbyter in the *Testament of our Lord* (*c.* A.D. 350?) speaks by a paranomasia of 'the Spirit [masc.] of the presbyterate who doth not grow old' (i. 30). Pseudo-Pionius (4th cent.) in the *Life of Polycarp* (§ 17; Lightfoot, *Apost.*

Fathers, pt. ii., 'Ignatius and Polycarp,' iii. 447 f.) unhistorically makes Polycarp to be an old man before he is ordained presbyter. So perhaps Hermas, *Vis.* ii. 4 (2nd cent.), where the presbyters are the officials of the πρεσβυτέρα ('aged woman'), who is interpreted as the Church. Gregory of Nazianzus (*Orat.* xlii. 11, 4th cent.) speaks of the presbyters being 'honoured for years and wisdom.'

(*c*) *The name 'deacon.'*—In addition to the use of the word διάκονος in the non-ecclesiastical sense of a 'servant,' as in Mt 22^{13}, Jn $2^{5.9}$, and elsewhere in the Gospels, and (metaphorically of a ruler as God's servant) in Ro 13^4, or of a 'follower' (of Christ) in Jn 12^{26}, we have it used frequently of others than the ordinary 'deacons.' Our Lord is called a 'deacon' in Ro 15^8 ('deacon of the circumcision'); St. Paul in Col $1^{23.25}$, 2 Co 3^6 6^4 (pl.), Eph 3^7, 1 Co 3^5 (also Apollos); Timothy in 1 Th 3^2 (Westcott-Hort's text), 1 Ti 4^6 (cf. the technical use of διάκονος in $3^{8ff.}$); Epaphras in Col 1^7; Jewish Christians in 2 Co 11^{23}. Satan's 'deacons' are mentioned in 2 Co 11^{15}. This fluidity of expression would be realized by the English reader if the translation 'deacon' (instead of 'minister') were adopted throughout, and if it were borne in mind how often διακονία and διακονέω are used in the NT, always in the non-technical sense of 'service' and 'to do service.'

(*d*) *St. Paul's lists of the ministry* show a great fluidity of nomenclature. But they do not give technical names to the various classes of the ministry. In 1 Co 12^{28} we have: apostles, prophets, teachers, powers, charismata of healings, helps, governments, kinds of tongues. These cannot all be offices; some are (as we see from v.^{29}) purely charismatic, namely powers (working of miracles), healings, tongues. Probably no orders of the ministry are here explicitly enumerated, but only the different kinds of work done in the Christian Church. On the other hand, officials of the ministry are enumerated in Eph 4^{11}, where we have apostles, prophets, evangelists, pastors[1] and teachers (the last two are one class). These offices are said to be 'for the perfecting of the saints unto the work of ministering,' *i.e.*, to equip the members of the body for the function of service to the whole (Robinson, *Ephesians*^{2}, p. 98 f.; the RV inserts a comma after 'saints,' but the two clauses probably go together). In this list we have no 'bishops,' 'presbyters,' or 'deacons,' and yet these officials existed at Ephesus (Ac $20^{17.28}$, 1 Ti $5^{17ff.}$). Hence in this Pauline list we cannot look for technical designations, but rather for a description of the work done by different officials. The 'pastors and teachers' appear to be the local ministry. In Ro $12^{6f.}$ we have the abstract charismata or gifts: prophecy, ministering (διακονία), teaching, exhortation, giving [alms], ruling, showing mercy. In 1 Th 5^{12} we have leaders (προιστάμενοι); cf. 1 Ti $3^{4f.12}$ 5^{17}, where this word is used of 'bishops' and 'deacons.'

(*e*) *Fluidity of 'hieratic' language.*—In the NT and the sub-apostolic writers the word ἱερεύς is not used of a Christian minister, though Christians as a body are called 'priests' and 'a priesthood' (ἱεράτευμα) in 1 P $2^{5.9}$, Rev 1^6 (cf. Rev 5^{10} 20^6), just as all Israel had been 'priests' (Ex 19^6). Our Lord Himself is called a 'priest' or 'high priest' (ἀρχιερεύς) in He 3^1 $5^{5f.}$ $7^{17.26}$ 10^{21}, etc. Clement of Rome, Ignatius, and Irenæus do not use 'hieratic' language of the Christian ministry, but the *Didache* says of the Christian prophets: 'they are your high priests' (§ 13). Polycrates, bishop of Ephesus, *c.* A.D. 190, says (quoted by Eus. *HE* v. 24) that St. John was a priest, wearing the mitre (or 'golden plate,' πέταλον); but the meaning is not clear.[1] Justin Martyr (*c.* A.D. 150) calls the Christian body 'the true high-priestly race of God' (*Dial.* 116). Tertullian at the end of the century speaks of the bishop as 'high-priest' ('summus sacerdos,' *de Bapt.* 17), and, in reference to the Christian ministry, speaks of 'functions of priesthood' ('sacerdotalia munera,' *de Præscr.* 41). Hippolytus, early in the 3rd cent., uses similar language (*Hær.* i. pref.): 'We being their [the apostles'] successors and participators in this grace of high-priesthood,' etc. In Cyprian the bishop is frequently called 'sacerdos,' and his office 'sacerdotium.' The *Older Didascalia* (3rd cent.) calls the bishops 'high-priests' (Funk, *Didasc. et Const. Apost.*, Paderborn, 1905, i. 102), and says that the Jewish priests and levites now correspond to the deacons, presbyters, widows, and orphans. The names 'high-priest' for the bishop, and 'priests' and 'levites' for the presbyters and deacons respectively, were frequently used in the 4th cent. and onwards, and are often found in the Church Orders (for references see Maclean, *Ancient Church Orders*, p. 67, n.). In the ordination prayer for a presbyter in the *Apost. Const.* viii. 16 (*c.* A.D. 375) and in the Epitome known as *Constitutions through Hippolytus*, § 6 (Funk, ii. 80), his functions are called ἱερουργίαι, 'priestly duties.' Of other 4th cent. writers we may take as an example Epiphanius, who uses ἱερεύς for a Christian priest (*Exp. Fid.* 21), and whose 'priesthood' (ἱερωσύνη) includes subdeacons, but not readers (*ib.*). Jerome calls his famous treatise on the ministry 'Concerning priesthood' (Περὶ ἱερωσύνης). At the Council of Laodicea (*c.* A.D. 380, can. 27, 30), 'hieratics' (ἱερατικοί) are the bishops, priests, and deacons, as opposed to the 'clerics' (κληρικοί), who include the minor orders. In *Apost. Const.* iii. 15, and in the *Apost. Canons*, 63 (*c.* A.D. 400), the minor orders are included among the 'hieratics.' In the Syriac-speaking Churches the word *kāhnūthā* (which is the translation of ἱερωσύνη) is used for all orders of the ministry.

The use of this language does not mean that a new conception of the ministry was entertained by those in whose writings it is first found. It was not likely to be used as long as any Jewish priests or levites were in the ranks of the Christian ministry. For example, Barnabas was a levite (Ac 4^{36}), and could not well have been called a 'priest' without considerable confusion. When 'hieratic' language was first used in the Christian Church, it was a new nomenclature, but did not imply any new functions. It is a fallacy to describe some 2nd cent. Christian writers as unsacerdotal, and some as sacerdotal. The use of 'hieratic' language meant that the writers who employed it ascribed to Christian officials the ministry delivered by the Great, and in the strictest sense the Only, High Priest, our Lord Himself. The writers like Ignatius who do not use 'hieratic' language are even more emphatic about the authority of the ministry than those who do.

3. Charismatic ministry.—This term properly indicates those who are endowed with any spiritual gifts, called χαρίσματα ('gifts') in 1 Co 12^4 or simply πνευματικά ('spiritual [things']) in 12^1 14^1; but it is conveniently used for those who had 'extraordinary' charismata. We must distinguish between the 'charismatic' and the official ministry. As long as extraordinary charismata continued, the two went on side by side. Yet the same person might be of

[1] The word 'pastor' or 'shepherd' (ποιμήν) is used of our Lord in He 13^{20}, 1 P 2^{25} (cf. 1 P 5^4, Jn $10^{11.14}$). It was often applied to bishops by later writers (e.g., *Apost. Const.* ii. 1). The verb ποιμαίνειν is used of the Christian ministry in Jn 21^{16}, Ac 20^{28}, 1 P 5^2 (cf. Jude ^{12}). In Ac 13^1 'prophets' and 'teachers' are joined together (cf. 1 Co 12^{28}).

[1] H. Delff's theory is that the 'beloved disciple' (whom he distinguishes from the apostle John) was a native of Jerusalem and belonged to one of the high-priestly families (W. Sanday, *Criticism of the Fourth Gospel*, Oxford, 1905, p. 99 f.).

both ministries; thus St. Paul was an apostle, and yet spoke with tongues more than all (1 Co 14[18]). The charismata enumerated in 1 Co 12[8-10] include wisdom, knowledge, faith, healings, miracles, prophecy, discerning of spirits, tongues, interpretation of tongues. Of these probably the most prominent was prophecy. For the passages in which Christian prophets are mentioned see § 1, above; these, however, do not imply that Agabus, Judas, Silas, and others held office in the Church as prophets, though they may have done so in another capacity. It is recognized that any one might receive a revelation, and so be a 'prophet' (cf. 1 Co 14[30]). Thus those whom we should call 'laymen,' as not being of the official ministry, spoke in the Christian assemblies (*ib.*). But women were not allowed to do so (v.[34]), though they might be prophetesses (Ac 21[9]). In 1 Co 14 the charisma of tongues is somewhat disparaged as compared with prophecy.

Prophecy long continued. For the prophets in the *Didache* see above, § 1. Quadratus, early in the 2nd cent., was renowned for his prophetical gifts (Eus. *HE* iii. 37). Polycarp is called in the letter written by the Smyrnæans 'an apostolic and prophetic teacher' (*Mart. Pol.* 16; A.D. 155 or 156). Hermas received revelations, and his *Shepherd* (*c.* A.D. 150?) was widely received as a prophetic writing. Even in the 4th cent. the Church Orders speak of charismata, and in particular of revelations, being expected; *e.g.*, the *Test. of our Lord* speaks of those expected by the bishops, presbyters, widows, and by any Christians (i. 21, 23, 29, 31 f., 40); gifts of healing or of knowledge or of tongues are referred to as being a possible endowment of any Christian (i. 47). Such a one was not to be ordained ('a hand is not laid on him'), but to be had in honour (*ib.*). See also below, §§ 6–8.

The term 'charismatic ministry' is capable of being misunderstood, as if the official ministry was considered a purely mechanical one, and only of human appointment. But St. Paul clearly recognizes the official ministry as charismatic in another sense. Timothy had the charisma in virtue of his ordination (1 Ti 4[14]). The official ministry had the 'spiritual gift,' though it was not of the same nature as that of those who had extraordinary endowments; and the two ministries, as we have seen, might overlap.

4. Bishops, presbyters, and deacons from the 2nd cent. onwards.—(*a*) *Bishops.*—In the Epistles of Ignatius (*c.* A.D. 110) we find bishops in the later sense of the word fully established. We may here make an endeavour to collect the facts with regard to the diocesan episcopate, postponing a statement of the theories that have been advanced as to its origin. The phrase 'diocesan episcopate' is perhaps the best that we can use, as it begs no question as to the relation of the bishop to the presbyter; the phrase 'monarchical episcopate,' which is used by many writers, is open to this objection.

The establishment of bishops in the later sense in the Churches of the province of Asia and elsewhere is ascribed by a steady tradition to John the Apostle. Clement of Alexandria (*Quis dives*, 42) says that 'after the tyrant's death' John 'returned to Ephesus from the isle of Patmos,' and 'went away, being invited, to the contiguous territories of the nations, here to appoint bishops, there to set in order whole Churches, there to ordain such as were marked out by the Spirit.' Tertullian similarly says (*adv. Marc.* iv. 5) that 'the order of the bishops' [of the Seven Churches of Asia, or of all the Churches of the province] 'when traced up to their origin' rests 'on John as their author.' And the *Muratorian Fragment* (*c.* A.D. 180?) says that John was exhorted by 'his fellow disciples and bishops' to write his Gospel. Ignatius speaks of bishops being established all over the world (*Eph.* 3). But we do not find the diocesan episcopate established in all places at an equally early date. Thus Ignatius writes to the Philippians, but makes no mention of their bishop. Clement of Rome (*c.* A.D. 95) likewise omits all reference to a bishop at Corinth when writing to the Corinthians. It is, of course, possible that the office at Philippi and Corinth was vacant at the dates of these letters; but this hypothesis cannot be proved, and the deduction has usually been made that the diocesan episcopate was not established in these two places so soon as elsewhere. The position at Rome at the end of the 1st cent. has been considered doubtful. Clement writes in the name of his Church (not of the presbyters), but he does not call himself its bishop, nor does he name himself at all; we have to gather information about the authorship of this Epistle from subsequent writers. Clement obviously held a prominent position in the Roman Church; and, though nomenclature and organization matured themselves more slowly at Rome than elsewhere, the testimony of all antiquity must be taken as showing that he held the first place in it. Thus Irenæus makes Clement the third bishop of Rome in the list which he gives of bishops of that city up to his own time (*Hær.* III. iii. 3). He says that Linus, the first bishop, received the office from the apostles Peter and Paul, and that Anacletus succeeded him, and was in turn succeeded by Clement. Before Irenæus, Hegesippus had already made a list of the bishops of Rome, as all the Greek MSS and the Syriac versions of Eus. *HE* iv. 22 assert (see Lightfoot, *Apost. Fathers*, pt. i., 'Clement,' i. 154). The alternative (rejected by Lightfoot but accepted by Harnack) of διατριβήν for διαδοχήν is a conjecture based on the loose paraphrase of Rufinus. But, as Hegesippus's list is not extant, we cannot tell where it began. We notice that Ignatius, in writing to Rome, mentions no bishop there, and that, as G. Salmon remarks (*Introd. to the NT*[6], London, 1892, p. 519, n.), all through the first two centuries the importance of the bishop of Rome is merged in the importance of his Church. Dionysius of Corinth (*c.* A.D. 170) writes to the Church of Rome, not to Soter its bishop, though he mentions him in the third person.

Long before the end of the 2nd cent. the diocesan episcopate was universal, so much so that writers like Clement of Alexandria, as we have seen, did not know that the 'bishops' of the NT were the same as the presbyters. It is therefore unnecessary to carry further an investigation into the spread of the system in the 2nd century (for detailed information reference may be made to Lightfoot, 'Dissertation,' in his *Philippians*). But it is desirable to refer to the conception of the episcopate which we find in the works of Cyprian, bishop of Carthage in the middle of the 3rd century. Ignatius and Irenæus had described the bishop as a centre of unity, and Cyprian emphasizes this still more in his treatise *de Unitate Ecclesiæ* and in his *Epistles*. In this connexion he dwells strongly on the sin of schism from the visible unity symbolized and guarded by the bishop. It has been said that he 'magnified his office,' and extended its claims to autocracy; yet no one emphasizes more than he the necessity of constitutional action on the part of the bishop, and his obligation to carry his clergy and laity with him (see below (*b*)). He also dwells on the election of the bishops by the people (see art. LAITY, § 4). There is no real foundation for Hatch's view, from which his German translator Harnack dissents, that the rule that there should be only one bishop in each community was not fully established before Cyprian's time, and was due to his dispute with Novatian (*Organization of the Early Christian Church*, p. 103; for an account of Cyprian's view of the ministry reference may be made to Gore, *The Church and the Ministry*[5], pp. 151–156, with his quotations in the footnotes).

It would seem that at the first the primary object of a local ministry was liturgical. Thus the *Didache*, immediately after mentioning the Sunday worship (§ 14), continues: 'Appoint (χειροτονήσατε) for yourselves *therefore* bishops and deacons' (§ 15). And so in the succeeding ages one of the principal functions of the diocesan bishop was to celebrate the Eucharist. In the Church Orders of the 4th and 5th centuries the newly-consecrated bishop himself begins to exercise his functions by doing so, rather than the principal consecrator, as in modern times. The same idea underlies the ancient practice, still preserved in some parts of Christendom, of 'concelebration,' that is, of the newly-ordained presbyters joining aloud with the bishop who has just ordained them, in consecrating the Eucharist. (In the early ages concelebration was not confined to ordinations.) We may compare the custom, which also survives, of a newly-ordained deacon reading the liturgical gospel, that being one of his functions which he immediately begins to discharge. In this connexion we may notice that the bishop and the presbyter were the only persons allowed to celebrate the Eucharist (see art. LAITY, § 5 (*a*)).

The Council of Nicæa enacted that bishops were not to be translated from one see to another (can. 15; A.D. 325). But this rule was almost immediately disregarded (see Athanasius, *Apol. c. Arian.* 25). The Nicene Council applied it also to presbyters and deacons.

(*b*) *Presbyters*.—In early Christian literature the presbyters are frequently recognized as the councillors of the bishop. Ignatius, who says that the presbytery is attuned to the bishop as strings to a lyre (*Eph.* 4), bids the people submit to the bishop and presbyters (*Eph.* 2, 20, *Trall.* 13), and do nothing without them (*Magn.* 7, *Trall.* 2 f., 7); he speaks of 'the bishop presiding (προκαθημένου) after the likeness of God, and the presbyters after the likeness of the council (συνεδρίου) of the apostles' (*Magn.* 6); in *Smyrn.* 8, the bishop is compared to our Lord, and the presbyters to the apostles (cf. *Magn.* 13: 'with your revered bishop and with the fitly-wreathed spiritual circlet of your presbytery, and with the deacons who walk after God'). In the same way, more than a century later, Cyprian says (*Ep.* xiv. [v.] 4, 'To the presbyters and deacons') that he had determined from the beginning of his episcopate to do nothing without the advice (*consilium*) of the presbyters, and the concurring feeling (*consensus*; see art. LAITY, § 8) of the people. The presbyters are here recognized as councillors of the bishop in a higher sense than the laity. This is not quite the same position as in *Ep.* xxxviii. (xxxii.) 1 ('To the presbyters, deacons, and people'), where Cyprian speaks of consulting them all before he ordained clergy. This is the equivalent of the more modern *Si quis* or public intimation of a proposed ordination. Origen likewise compares the 'councillors' and 'rulers' of the Church with those of the city, clearly meaning the presbyters and the bishop (*c. Cels.* iii. 30). A similar state of things is seen in the *Older Didasc.* (ii. 28, 3rd cent.; Funk, i. 108), where it is said that the presbyters are 'honoured as apostles and councillors of the bishop, and the crown of the Church, for they are the council and curia of the Church.' The derived *Apost. Const.* (ii. 28) use nearly the same language.

It is for this reason that the bishop had his throne in the church with the presbyters sitting round him on either side. Thus in the *Apost. Ch. Ord.* (*c.* A.D. 300; for the Syriac text and tr. see *JThSt* iii. [1901] 59) the presbyters are appointed by the bishop, and sit on either side of him, those on the right being the regulators of the service of the altar, those on the left the regulators of the people; and the presbyters are 'sharers in the mysteries' with the 'shepherd' (the bishop; see above, § 2). In the *Older Didasc.* (ii. 57; Funk, i. 158), the *Apost. Const.* (ii. 57), and the *Test. of our Lord* (i. 19) the same arrangement is found. In the last-mentioned manual the more exalted and honoured presbyters, who 'labour in the word,' sit on the right, and 'those of middle age' (*i.e.* the younger ones; see above, § 2 (*b*) for the association of the presbyterate and old age) sit on the left. For an ambiguity as to the position of the bishop and presbyters when ministering at the altar, see Maclean, *Ancient Church Orders*, p. 37.

The presbyters were charged with celebrating the Eucharist, at least when the bishop was absent (see above), and with pastoral duties to the flock. In the 4th cent. the *Apost. Const.* thus sum up the functions of bishops and presbyters (viii. 28):

'The bishop blesses, but does not receive the blessing; he lays on hands (χειροθετεῖ), ordains (χειροτονεῖ),[1] offers (the Eucharist), receives a blessing from bishops, but not at all from presbyters; the bishop exercises discipline (καθαιρεῖ) over every cleric who deserves discipline, except over a bishop, for alone he cannot (do this). The presbyter blesses, but does not receive the blessing except from a bishop or fellow-presbyter, and so he gives it to a fellow-presbyter; he lays on hands but does not ordain; he does not exercise discipline, but he separates those inferior to him,' etc.

An interesting feature is that the presbyter is allowed to confirm, for this seems here to be the meaning of χειροθετεῖν,[2] blessing and ordaining being mentioned as different actions. Ordinarily the presbyter baptized, and brought the neophyte to the bishop for confirmation; this is the regular practice in the Church Orders and was the earlier custom in both East and West. In the East the presbyter has for many centuries confirmed, both in the Orthodox and in the Separated communions, but he uses chrism consecrated by the bishop. The same thing is also found in the West, but only in exceptional cases. Innocent I. in his *Epistle to Decentius* (§ 3; A.D. 416) shows that Western presbyters had the power by custom, though he did not approve of their exercising it. The Council of Orange (A.D. 441) says (can. 1, 2) that in the absence of a bishop a presbyter may receive penitent heretics, marking them with the chrism and benediction, *i.e.* (apparently) confirming them. Still earlier the first Council of Toledo (A.D. 400) shows the same thing by implication. It forbids (can. 20) a presbyter to consecrate the chrism, and allows only a bishop to do so, but says that deacons or subdeacons shall fetch the chrism from the bishop before Easter. The Council of Carthage, A.D. 390 (can. 3), also forbids presbyters to consecrate the chrism. This implies a regular practice of confirming by presbyters (for further references see Duchesne, *Christian Worship*, p. 338, n.). For Egypt we have the evidence of the writer known as Ambrosiaster (*in Eph.* iv. 12), who says that in that country the presbyter 'signs' (*consignat*) if the bishop be not present; and we read the same in *Quæst. Vet. et Nov. Test.* § 101, printed as an appendix to vol. iii. of the Benedictine ed. of Augustine (another reading there has 'consecrate,' *i.e.* consecrate the Eucharist). Lightfoot ('Disserta-

[1] One good MS reads: 'ordains, does not lay on hands.'

[2] It has, however, been interpreted of the absolution of penitents. C. H. Turner (*JThSt* xvi. [1915] 61), who adopts the alternative reading, interprets this 'laying on of hands' of the custom of the presbyters laying on hands at the ordination of a presbyter. Against this, however, is the fact that in the *Apost. Const.* that custom is not mentioned, and is perhaps negatived (see below, § 8 (*a*)).

tion,' p. 231) makes the surely strange error of supposing that this 'consignatio' means 'ordination.'[1]

There are traces in our period of a very close connexion between presbyter and bishop. Thus in the *Canons of Hippolytus*, which in their present form are perhaps of the 4th cent., but which adhere very closely to their 3rd cent. source, we read that a bishop and a presbyter are ordained with the same prayer except for the name of the office, and except that in the case of the presbyter enthronization is omitted. 'The bishop is in all things put on an equality with the presbyter, except the name of the throne and ordination, for the power of ordination is not given to him,' *i.e.* to the presbyter (can. iv.; ed. H. Achelis, Leipzig, 1891, §§ 30–32). So in the *Egyptian Church Order* (§ 32) there is only one ordination prayer for bishop and presbyter. The later Church Orders have separate prayers.

A bishop is still called a 'presbyter' in the 2nd and later centuries (see, *e.g.*, Iren. *Hær.* III. ii. 2, 'successions of presbyters,' which in iii. 2 he explains as 'successions of bishops'). In his letter to Victor Irenæus speaks of 'the presbyters before Soter who presided over the Church which thou rulest' (Eus. *HE* v. 24). Dionysius, bishop of Alexandria (*c.* A.D. 258), speaks of 'my fellow-presbyter Maximus' (Eus. vii. 11). For Clement of Alexandria see above, § 1 (*b*), and for Firmilian see below, § 8 (*a*).

(*c*) *Deacons.*—This was a numerous and important order in all the early ages. The deacon's functions are summarized by the author of the *Apost. Const.* (viii. 28), by saying that he does not bless or baptize or offer [the Eucharist], but that, when a bishop or presbyter has offered, he gives [the sacrament] to the people, not as a priest (ἱερεύς) but as one who ministers to the priests. He is described in the oldest as well as in the later liturgies as assisting at the Eucharist, and especially as saying the short exhortations and the ectene, or litany (see, *e.g.*, the liturgies in the *Test. of our Lord* and in the *Apost. Const.* viii.); he keeps order in service time (*Test.* i. 34; *Older Didasc.* ii. 57, etc.); he assists at baptism in all the Church Orders which describe the rite; in some authorities he is allowed to baptize in the absence of bishop and presbyter (see art. LAITY, § 5); he often reads the liturgical gospel at the Eucharist (Sozomen, *HE* vii. 19; *Test.* i. 27), as at this day in the West; he administers the eucharistic gifts in Justin Martyr (*Apol.* i. 65), and often in the Church Orders (for details see J. Cooper and A. J. Maclean, *Test. of our Lord*, Edinburgh, 1902, p. 223; for *Apost. Const.* see above); he has many pastoral duties, such as visiting the sick (*Test.* i. 34, *Apost. Const.* ii. 32, 44, iii. 19, *Egyp. Ch. Ord.* 33), entertaining strangers (*Test.* i. 34), arranging for burials[2] (*ib.* and Eus. *HE* vii. 11). The deacon also attends to the eucharistic offerings and is often the almoner of the Church (*Older Didasc.* ii. 57; *Apost. Const.* iii. 19). In some authorities the bishop and presbyters exercise the discipline of the laity through the deacons (*Test.* i. 36 f.; *Apost. Const.* ii. 16; *Ethiopic Didasc.* § 4). As time went on, deacons pressed their claims and relegated several of their lesser functions to the minor orders. We find several writers repressing deacons for this reason—*e.g.*, Cyprian (*Ep.* iii. [lxiv.] 13, 'ad Rogatianum'), the Council of Arles (can. 15; A.D. 314), which says that many deacons attempted to celebrate the Eucharist, that of Nicæa (can. 18; A.D. 325), and almost all the Church Orders, the *Test. of our Lord* being a solitary exception, for in that manual the position both of deacons and of 'widows who preside' is greatly extolled.

(*d*) *Number of the clergy.*—Cornelius, bishop of Rome, writing to Fabian or Fabius, bishop of Antioch, A.D. 251 (the letter is given by Eus. *HE* vi. 43), enumerates the various orders and classes at Rome as follows: one bishop (about this he is emphatic), 46 (*var. lect.* 36) presbyters, 7 deacons, 7 subdeacons, 42 acolytes, 52 exorcists, readers, and doorkeepers, and more than 1500 widows and persons in distress (for the minor orders see below, § 6). But in unimportant places the clergy were much fewer. In the *Apost. Ch. Ord.* (*c.* A.D. 300) there were: one bishop, 3 presbyters, 3 deacons (so the Syriac), one (?) reader, 3 widows. In the *Test. of our Lord* (*c.* A.D. 350?) we have (i. 34), besides the bishop, 12 presbyters, 7 deacons, 14 subdeacons, 13 'widows who preside' (the Greek original no doubt had προκαθήμεναι). Seven was a very ordinary number for the deacons, because of the Seven in Ac 6. Sozomen says (*HE* vii. 19) that even in his day (5th cent.) there were only 7 deacons in Rome, though 'in other Churches the number of deacons is a matter of indifference.' The Council of Neo-Cæsarea, appealing to Acts, says that even in the largest towns there are not to be more than 7 deacons (can. 15; *c.* A.D. 314, or perhaps a little later). The number twelve for the presbyters in the *Test. of our Lord* may be due to the comparison of their order to the apostles. Eutychius (10th cent.) describes Alexandria in old days as having had twelve presbyters; but his evidence is quite untrustworthy (see below, § 8 (*d*)).

(*e*) *Age of ordination.*—At Neo-Cæsarea it was enacted (can. 11) that no one was to be ordained presbyter before he was thirty years of age, because our Lord then began to teach. This became the general rule for many centuries. There was no similar rule about bishops, but the 2nd can. of Nicæa says that no novice in the faith is to be ordained presbyter or bishop. The minimum age for deacons seems to have been twenty-five. The Council of Hippo (A.D. 393) says that no one is to be ordained at all under that age (can. 1); but this rule can hardly have applied to the minor orders, for the same Council (can. 18) speaks of readers who are appointed as quite young boys. So Cyprian (*Ep.* xxxviii. [xxxii.] 1) and Socrates (*HE* vii. 41) speak of very young readers. The *Gallican Statutes* (*c.* A.D. 500; see below, § 6 (*c*)) say that a bishop must be of the 'prescribed age,' but does not say what that is (§ 1).

It may be convenient to note here some later rules as to age of ordination. The Maronite rule is that a presbyter must be over 30, for the reason stated above (H. Denzinger, *Ritus Orientalium*, Würzburg, 1863–64, ii. 148), and a deacon must be over 21 (*ib.* p. 128). The East Syrian or Nestorian *Sunhādhūs*, or 'Book of Canon Law' (VI. iv. 2; Maclean and W. H. Browne, *Catholicos of the East*, London, 1892, p. 201), says that readers must not be ordained till past boyhood, subdeacons when nearly grown up, deacons a little later, presbyters about 18, though (it adds) the ancient age was 30. The Anglican minimum age for deacons is 23, for presbyters 24, for bishops 30, and this is the usual Western custom; some relaxation of the rule has rarely been made in the case of deacons.

5. Development of the supervisory offices.—(*a*)

[1] The present writer can find no good instance of 'consignare' or its Greek equivalent σφραγίζειν, or their substantives, being applied to ordination. The Greek σφραγίς and its Oriental equivalents usually refer to baptism or confirmation, or both, or to the sign of the cross; by analogy Tertullian (*adv. Valent.* 1) uses 'consignare' of admission to the Eleusinian mysteries (see also Lightfoot, *Apost. Fathers*, pt. i., 'Clement,' ii. 226, n.; Maclean, *Ancient Church Orders*, p. 109). In the *Verona Latin Fragments* (ed. Hauler, p. 110) 'consignare' is used in contradistinction to ordination, for the part played by the presbyters at a presbyter's ordination (see below, § 8 (*a*)): 'The presbyter at the ordination (*ordinatione*) of a presbyter signs (*consignat*) when the bishop ordains (*episcopo ordinante*).' Ducange (*Glossarium Mediæ et Infimæ Latinitatis*, Paris, 1840–50, Niort, 1883–87) gives no instance of *consignatio* meaning 'ordination,' though he gives instances of its meaning 'confirmation.' Suicer (*Thesaurus*, 3199) gives one instance from pseudo-Dionysius Areopagita (*Eccl. Hier.* v. p. 312 [*PG* iii. 509]) of σφραγίς meaning 'ordination,' but this instance is very doubtful.

[2] It has been suggested that 'the young men' of Ac 5[6. 10] (note the definite article) who buried Ananias and Sapphira were prototypes of the deacons in this respect. For the *copiatæ*, or 'grave-diggers' (mentioned by Epiphanius, *Exp. Fid.* 21), and the *parabolani* (visitors of the sick) see J. Wordsworth, *Ministry of Grace*, p. 195 f.

Metropolitans.—The name is first found in the 4th cent., before which there is no certain trace of provincial organization, the 'eparchy' in the *Apost. Ch. Ord.* being apparently the civil province. At Nicæa metropolitans are mentioned by that name (can. 4, 6), and the word 'eparchy' is apparently used of an ecclesiastical province, though, as the civil and ecclesiastical provinces normally coincided, this is not quite certain. At the Council of Antioch *in Encæniis* (A.D. 341) metropolitans are recognized in effect, though the name is not given to them (can. 9, 19); 'the bishop presiding in the metropolis' (*i.e.* in the civil capital) is the phrase used, and the corresponding verb is employed in can. 19. The word 'metropolitan' is used at Laodicea (can. 12; *c.* A.D. 380). On the other hand, there is no mention of a metropolitan in the Church Orders, and this is a cogent argument against their being dated later than the 4th cent., and for their not being assigned to any of the great centres like Alexandria or Antioch. In these manuals the neighbouring bishops come together for the election of a bishop, and the whole assembly of bishops, clergy, and laity elect, just as they do in Cyprian (*Ep.* lxvii. 5, 'To the clergy and people in Spain'); but there is no metropolitan. There is perhaps just a faint trace of a primacy in *Apost. Const.* viii. 4, which speaks of 'one of the first bishops' saying the ordination prayer of a bishop; and so in the *Arabic Didasc.* (*c.* A.D. 400?; § 36, 'the first bishop among them'). But this is all. A rather stronger trace is to be seen in the *Apost. Canons* (can. 35 [also numbered 34 or 33]; *c.* A.D. 400). After the 4th cent. metropolitans became practically universal.

Although there was no regular organization of provinces before the 4th cent., yet bishops of certain important cities, like Rome, Carthage, Alexandria, Antioch, wielded great influence over the neighbouring bishops. We see this in the case of Cyprian. At Nicæa the authority of the bishops of Alexandria and Rome is spoken of as an ancient custom, and no one is made bishop without the metropolitan (can. 6). Alexandria is to have, as before, authority over Egypt, Libya, and Pentapolis, *i.e.* over more than one civil province (*ib.*). The growth of this influence was promoted by the holding of synods, when external circumstances permitted. Synods would ordinarily be held in the 'metropolis' (chief town) of the civil province or eparchy, and the bishop of that city would naturally preside. So the civil metropolis tended to become the ecclesiastical metropolis. But this was not always the case with synods. At that of the bishops of Pontus held to consider the Paschal question, Palmas as the oldest [bishop] presided (Eus. *HE* v. 23). Palmas was bishop of Amastris (iv. 23). At the end of the 4th cent. the Council of Hippo decreed that a bishop of a principal see (*prima sedes*) was not to be called 'princeps sacerdotum' or 'summus sacerdos,' but simply 'primæ sedis episcopus' (can. 25). Thus the name 'metropolitan' was apparently not in use in the province 'Africa'; and Hefele thinks that, except at Carthage, the metropolitan rights went to the oldest bishop of the province, and that the same thing held good in Spain before Constantine's time (*Hist. of the Councils*², Eng. tr., Edinburgh, 1872, i. 162).

In spite of his position at Carthage, Cyprian affirms that all bishops are equal. Thus in *de Unitate*, 5, he says that the episcopate is one and that all bishops are full partners in it with joint and several responsibility; for this is the meaning of his phrase 'cuius a singulis in solidum pars tenetur.' So in *Ep.* lv. (li.) 21, 'ad Antonianum,' he says that every bishop disposes and directs his own acts, and will have to give an account of his purposes to the Lord. Cf. also *Epp.* lvii. (liii.) 5, lix. (liv.) 14, both to Cornelius; Cyprian says that appeals are not to be carried outside the province in which the cause began.

The custom of giving the pallium to metropolitans hardly falls within the limits of this article (see *DCA* ii. 1174).

(*b*) *Patriarchs.*—The name 'patriarch' was probably borrowed from the Jews. In the LXX of 1 Ch 27^{22} it is used for the head of a tribe, and in 24^{31} and some MSS of 9^{9} 23^{20} for the head of a πατριά, or subdivision of a tribe. In the NT it is used of David (Ac 2^{29}), the sons of Jacob ($7^{8f.}$), and Abraham (He 7^{4}). In 4 Mac 7^{17} 16^{22} (ed. W. R. Churton, *Uncanonical and Apocryphal Scriptures*, London, 1884) it is used of Abraham, Isaac, Jacob, and others. In the early centuries of our era a Jewish 'patriarch,' or representative of the nation, is several times mentioned—*e.g.*, by Cyril of Jerusalem (*Cat.* xii. 17; A.D. 348), who speaks of the Jews' 'recent measures relative to their patriarchs as they now call them.' The Emperor Hadrian (A.D. 134?) refers to the Jewish patriarch in his letter to the consul Servianus about religion in Alexandria (see Lightfoot, 'Dissertation,' p. 225). Hadrian visited Egypt A.D. 130. In Christian literature we find the term first applied to Christians non-officially. Basil seems to use it as equivalent to 'bishop' when he says (*Ep.* clxix. 'ad Greg.') that the deacon Glycerius assumed the style and title of patriarch. An example in Gregory of Nyssa's *Funeral Oration on Meletius, bishop of Antioch* († A.D. 381), when he exclaims 'Behold these your patriarchs,' is perhaps purely oratorical; he is referring to the bishops who attended the second Ecumenical Council at Constantinople. Gregory of Nazianzus explicitly uses the term of senior bishops (*Orat.* xlii. 23): 'aged bishops or, to speak more accurately, patriarchs.' But it came to be used of the bishops of Rome, Constantinople, Alexandria, Antioch, and Jerusalem, though not by canons of councils till long after our period—not before the 9th cent.; the whole subject is treated in detail by Hatch in *DCA* ii. 1573 (art. 'Patriarch'). The growth of the authority of these sees is shown by the 6th can. of Nicæa, and the 28th of Chalcedon; the latter was rejected by the bishop of Rome. The ultimate result was the joining together of several provinces or eparchies, each of which was governed by its own metropolitan, under a single patriarch, whose jurisdiction was somewhat loosely defined, just in the same way as in civil affairs several 'eparchies' were grouped together into one *diœcesis*, which was a very different thing from our 'diocese.'

(*c*) *Archbishops.*—This term, which in the West became the customary title of metropolitans, was not so used in the East. It was a title of honour conferred on bishops of some of the greatest sees, though its application was not always uniform. In the 4th cent. Epiphanius uses the term (*Hær.* lxix. 3) of Meletius, bishop of the Thebais, and (lxviii. 1) of the bishop of Alexandria. At Chalcedon (A.D. 451) it is applied to the bishops of Constantinople, Alexandria, and Rome (can. 28, 30; the last is not considered to be a canon proper; see Hefele, iii. 422).

(*d*) *Chorepiscopi.*—These 'country-bishops' were assistants to the diocesan bishops for the work of the rural districts. In the Greek-speaking Churches and in the West they were, at least normally, bishops—such is the trend of the evidence, though Morinus denies it—but in the Syriac-speaking Churches, at a later date, they were often confused with the περιοδευταί, or 'visitors,' and were presbyters. They somewhat resembled the assistant ('suffragan') and coadjutor bishops of the present day, in that they worked under the direction of the diocesan bishop, though their functions were not entirely the same. They are first mentioned at Ancyra (can. 13 [see below, § 8 (*b*)]; A.D. 314), Neo-Cæsarea (can. 14; A.D. 314 or a little later), Nicæa (can. 8; A.D. 325). From the 10th can. of the Council of Antioch *in Encæniis* (A.D. 341) we may perhaps gather that not all chorepiscopi were bishops, for it uses the expression 'even if they have received consecration as bishops.' They are also mentioned by Athanasius (*Apol. c. Arian.* 85), Basil (*Ep.* xxiv. etc.), and other 4th cent. writers. But they are not referred to in the Church Orders, and it is probable that they were to be found only in the busy centres, from which, as we have seen above (*a*), these manuals did not come. In the *Edessene Canons*, *i.e.* the Syriac *Teaching of the Apostles* (see *Ante-Nic. Chr. Lib.*, 'Syriac Documents,' p. 42 f.), a 'ruler' is to be appointed as head over the village presbyters; and these 'rulers' must have been itinerant visitors, for a reference is made to Samuel also making visits from place to place and ruling (can. 24; *c.* A.D. 350). The Council of Sardica in Illyricum (*c.* A.D. 347, or earlier) does not appear to recognize the existence of chorepiscopi. The 6th can. says that a bishop is not to be ordained in a village or small town for which one presbyter suffices, for it is not necessary there that a bishop should be made, lest the name of a bishop and his authority become cheap (the authenticity of these canons is disputed).

Among the functions of the chorepiscopus were the appointment and ordination of minor orders, but not as a rule of deacons and presbyters. To ordain these he must have the explicit consent of the diocesan bishop who had appointed him (Antioch *in Encæniis*, can. 10). He could also confirm; see the 3rd can. of the Council of Riez or Regium in Provence (Hefele, iii. 157; A.D. 439). Schismatic bishops when reconciled were sometimes made chorepiscopi, as there could not be more than one diocesan bishop in each see (Nicæa, can. 8; Socrates, *HE* i. 9; Riez, can. 3). Lightfoot ('Dissertation,' p. 233, n.) looks upon chorepiscopi as a survival of the 'presbyter-bishops' which his theory of the origin of the diocesan episcopate postulates (see below, § 10); but there is absolutely no evidence for this survival, and indeed it is very unlikely that chorepiscopi existed before the 4th century.

An attempt was made towards the end of that century to abolish the office. The Council of Laodicea (can. 57; *c.* A.D. 380) forbids their appointment for the future, and says that there are to be only periodeutæ (apparently presbyters), while chorepiscopi who had already been appointed were to act only with the consent of the diocesan bishop (this points to a certain self-assertiveness on the part of the chorepiscopi). But this canon did not put an end to the office. Chorepiscopi are found frequently in the Far East (see below), and were revived in the West for a time (Hefele, i. 18). There were some of this order present at the Council of Ephesus, A.D. 431, but not at that of Chalcedon, A.D. 451.

In the East Syrian *Sunhādhūs* (vi. 1) there are three orders of the ministry, each with three subdivisions. In the second order (the presbyterate), chorepiscopi or periodeutæ (both these names are transliterated into Syriac) form the first subdivision, and seem to be identical. Their duties were to visit the villages and monasteries as representatives of the bishop (Maclean-Browne, *Catholicos of the East*, p. 182). They were not specially ordained, for the *Sunhādhūs* says that bishops 'ordain all readers, subdeacons, deacons, and presbyters, give a blessing to periodeutæ, and say a prayer over archdeacons' (*ib.*).

(*e*) *Archdeacons.*—Neither the name nor the office of an archdeacon is found before the end of the 4th century. The name is found in the *Pilgrimage of 'Silvia'* ('*Etheria*'), which has usually been assigned to that date, though some place it later; but even there it is not the name of a distinct office. Neither the name nor the distinct office is found in the Church Orders, though in the *Test. of our Lord* the principal deacon has certain duties assigned to him. Some writers at the end of, or later than, the 4th cent. give to certain famous deacons the name 'archdeacon,' as when Augustine calls Laurence by that title (*Serm. de diversis*, cxi. [ed. Ben. ccci.] 8); so Theodoret (*HE* i. 25) calls Athanasius the 'leader of the chorus of deacons, though a young man.' There is no archdeacon in Cornelius's list of Roman officials (above, § 4 (*d*)). Jerome (*Ep.* cxlvi., 'ad Evangelum') mentions archdeacons as an order, and after his time they were common in both East and West. In the *Ordo Romanus Primus* the archdeacon plays a very important part in the eucharistic liturgy at Rome (*e.g.*, §§ 18, 20, ed. E. G. C. F. Atchley, London, 1905). But this work is probably of the 8th cent., though founded on a similar document of the 6th (Atchley, p. 7). The archdeacon was at first a deacon, and in some cases the senior deacon succeeded automatically to the office; but Sozomen (*HE* viii. 9) speaks of Chrysostom appointing Sarapion as archdeacon, and therefore he could not have succeeded automatically. There was only one in each diocese in the time of Jerome (*loc. cit.*). For the later development of this office see *DCA* i. 136.

In the East Syrian Church the archidiaconate is the middle subdivision of the second order, *i.e.* of the presbyterate (see above). The office is still used in that Church as an honorary one, and an influential presbyter is appointed 'arkān,' or archdeacon. In the West the office is in frequent use, and in most Western countries each bishop has at least one archdeacon, called the 'eye of the bishop.' The archdeacon is a senior presbyter, deputed to relieve the bishop of some of his minor functions.

6. Development of the lesser offices.—At an early date we find the existence of some orders of the ministry lower than those of bishops, presbyters, and deacons. We read at various times of subdeacons, readers, singers, interpreters, doorkeepers, acolytes, exorcists. There was also a ministry of women — widows, presbyteresses, deaconesses. It must be noted, however, that some of these offices were not always and in all places reckoned as orders; *e.g.*, exorcists were long considered to exercise a charismatic ministry, and were reckoned as being outside the ordinary roll of the clergy.

(*a*) *Readers* (ἀναγνῶσται, *lectores*).—This is probably the oldest of the minor orders. In Justin Martyr's description of the Eucharist (*Apol.* i. 67; *c.* A.D. 150) the reader of the lections plays an important part, though Justin may not mean that he was of a separate order in the ministry. In the *Apost. Ch. Ord.* (§ 19; *c.* A.D. 300) he comes before the deacon, and Harnack thinks (*Sources of the Apost. Canons*, Eng. tr., London, 1895, p. 71 f.) that his office was at first a charismatic one, and that he was not originally included among the clergy. Stress is laid in the manual just named on the necessity of the reader being learned. He must be 'able to instruct' or 'narrate' (διηγητικός), and he 'fills the place of an evangelist.' This qualification is not always insisted on in the case of a bishop; this Church Order says (§ 16) that, if a bishop does not know letters, at least he is to be meek. The *Test. of our Lord* also insists that the reader must be learned, and have had much experience (i. 45). Probably he had, at first, the duty of expounding what he read; but, when he was limited to the mere reading of the lections, his position fell, as it did at Rome in the middle of the 3rd century (see above, § 4 (*d*), where the readers are classed with the exorcists and door-keepers, below the acolytes). In the other Church Orders the reader comes, sometimes before, and sometimes after, the subdeacon. In *Sarapion's Sacramentary* (§ 25; *c.* A.D. 350) the minor orders are 'subdeacons, readers, and interpreters.' There are indications in some of the authorities that readers were not numerous. The *Older Didasc.* and the *Apost. Const.* (ii. 28; Funk, i. 108 f.) suggest that it is probable that a church may not have a reader at all; and in several Church Orders there is an indirect indication that there was only one in each place (Maclean, *Ancient Church Orders*, pp. 14 f., 87). Readers come below deacons in Tertullian (*de Præscr.* 41). They are frequently mentioned in Cyprian; and they often had the important duty of reading the liturgical gospel at the Eucharist: this they did from a desk, or *ambo* (*Ep.* xxxix. [xxxiii.] 4, 'About Celerinus'). In the Diocletian persecution they had the custody of the Scriptures (J. Wordsworth, *Ministry of Grace*, p. 189).

(*b*) *Subdeacons* (ὑποδιάκονοι, ὑπηρέται, *subdiaconi, ministri*).—These officials, whose chief duty was to assist the deacons at the Eucharist and in their other functions, are mentioned in the 3rd cent. by Cornelius at Rome (above, § 4; he speaks of seven) and Cyprian in Africa (*Ep.* xxxiv. [xxvii.] 3, 'To the presbyters and deacons': he speaks of two subdeacons by name and a certain acolyte), and in the *Older Didasc.* (E. Hauler, *Verona Latin Fragments*, Leipzig, 1900, p. 40; Funk, i. 116; see below). In the 4th cent. we find them in Spain at Elvira (can. 30; *c.* A.D. 305; no other minor order is mentioned in these canons), in Egypt in *Sarapion's Sacramentary* (§ 25), in the Church Orders (but not in the *Apost. Ch. Ord.*), at Neo-Cæsarea in Cappadocia (can. 10; A.D. 314 or later), at Antioch *in Encœniis* (can. 10; A.D. 341), at Laodicea (can. 20–22, 25; *c.* A.D. 380), and in Athanasius (*Hist. Arian. ad Monachos*, 60; A.D. 358). At Neo-Cæsarea and Laodicea, and in *Apost. Const.* iii. 11, and elsewhere the subdeacon is called ὑπηρέτης, or 'minister.' The existence of subdeacons in the East before the 4th cent. has been disputed, and it has been thought that the passage in the *Didascalia* where they are mentioned is an interpolation; yet it occurs both in the Latin and in the Syriac versions. Eusebius (*HE* viii. 6) makes their existence in most parts of the East during the Diocletian persecution uncertain. He says that a royal edict directed that the presidents (προεστῶτες) of the Church everywhere should be imprisoned, and that the prisons were filled with bishops, presbyters, deacons, readers, and exorcists; he omits any mention of subdeacons here. In the *Canons of Hippolytus* (can. xxi. [ed. Achelis, § 217]) they are mentioned together with presbyters and readers, in a passage where deacons are omitted; but this may be due to the present (4th cent. ?) form of the *Canons*; the omission of deacons may be a mere clerical error.

(*c*) *Acolytes, or collets* (ἀκόλουθοι, *acolythi, acoliti*).—These are first mentioned by Cornelius (above, § 4), and by Cyprian (*loc. cit.*). They are also mentioned in the *Gallican Statutes* (as J. Wordsworth has conveniently named them [*Ministry of Grace*, p. 58]) or *Statuta Ecclesiæ antiqua*, a collection of canons which used to be ascribed to the so-called 'Fourth Council of Carthage' (can. 6; Hefele, ii. 410; their real date is *c.* A.D. 500). Acolytes assisted at the Eucharist, and performed various minor functions in the services. They are found only in the West, where they became very numerous. Cornelius says that there were 42 at Rome in the 3rd century. As there were 14 regions in that city, there would be one deacon or subdeacon and three acolytes for each region (Harnack, *Sources of the Apost. Can.*, p. 95). An acolyte was sent by Cornelius as a messenger (Cyprian, *Ep.* xlix. [xlv.] 3).

(*d*) *Singers* (ψάλται, ᾠδοί, ψαλτῳδοί, *cantores, psaltæ*, etc.).—In the earlier Church Orders singers are mentioned, but not as a separate order. They had, however, already become such in the *Apost. Const.* (iii. 11, vi. 17; *c.* A.D. 375), at Laodicea (can. 23), in the *Apost. Canons* (can. 43 [42], 69 [68]; *c.* A.D. 400), and in the Arabic translation of the *Test. of our Lord* (i. 45), which adds a chapter to that manual about their appointment, and reduces the lesser orders in the *Test.* (see above, § 4) to 'four subdeacons and readers, three widows and singers'; the date of this Arabic translation is unknown. Singers are a separate order also in the *Gallican Statutes* (can. 10).

(*e*) *Interpreters* (ἑρμηνεῖς, ἑρμηνευταί, *interpretes*).—These are not mentioned in the Church Orders. They naturally are found only in bilingual countries. Eusebius mentions them in Palestine (*Mart. Palest.*, longer version, § 1, tr. A. C. McGiffert, p. 342 [*Nic. and Post-Nic. Fathers*]); he says that Procopius was a reader, interpreter, and exorcist. Sarapion (§ 25) mentions them in Egypt, Epiphanius (*Exp. Fid.* 21) in Syria and Palestine. In the *Pilgrimage of 'Silvia'* ('*Etheria*') we read (vii. 5) that at Jerusalem some spoke Greek only, and some Syriac only, and that, as the bishop, though he knew Syriac, yet spoke only in Greek, a presbyter stood by to translate the bishop's Greek into Syriac. For 1 Co 14^{28} see above, § 1 (*e*).

(*f*) *Doorkeepers* (πυλωροί, *ostiarii*).—These are mentioned in Cornelius's list, and in the *Apost. Const.* (ii. 57, iii. 11), and the *Ethiopic Didasc.* (§ 10), but not in the other Church Orders, which retain (as indeed do also the *Apost. Const.*, rather inconsistently) the old direction that deacons are to guard the doors. For the devolution of the deacon's functions see above, § 4 (*c*).

(*g*) *Exorcists* (ἐξορκισταί in the NT, Josephus, and elsewhere, but ἐπορκισταί in *Apost. Const.* viii. 26, and Epiphanius, *Exp. Fid.* 21, *exorcistæ*).—Jewish exorcists are mentioned in Lk 11^{19} (where 'your sons' can hardly mean the disciples, but must be the Jews), Ac 19^{13}, and Jos. *Ant.* VIII. ii. 5 (he is speaking of the time of Solomon). Christian exorcists are mentioned by Cornelius, as above, and by Firmilian, who in his letter to Cyprian speaks of exorcists in Cappadocia twenty-two years before his time (Cyprian, *Ep.* lxxv. [lxxiv.] 10). But the Christian exorcizing of demons is mentioned by Justin (*Dial.* 85, *Apol.* ii. 6), Tertullian (*de Idol.* 11, *de Præscr.* 41), Origen (*c. Cels.* vii. 4). On the other hand, candidates for baptism were exorcized by the bishop before Easter (Maclean, *Ancient Church Orders*, p. 97; T. Thompson, *Offices of Baptism and Confirmation*, Cambridge, 1914, p. 28). The Council of Laodicea (can. 26) says that no one may exorcize in churches or houses unless authorized by the bishop. The office of an exorcist was at first entirely charismatic, and he was not originally one of the clergy (see below, § 8 (*g*)). We can well understand that unrestrained exorcism became an abuse, and that exorcists needed stringent regulations.

(*h*) *Ministry of women.*—It is not very easy to distinguish between the 'widows' who were on the Church roll for relief and those who were, in some sort, in the ministry. The widows in Ac 6^1 come under the former category; those of 1 Ti 5^{3-16} perhaps under both, for v.$^{11ff.}$ seem to imply ministering. A deaconess, Phœbe, is mentioned in Ro 16^1, though Hort (*Christian Ecclesia*, p. 208) thinks that διάκονος (fem.) is here used in a non-technical sense, and merely means that Phœbe ministered to the needs of the Church. Many think that 'women' in 1 Ti 3^{11} (γυναῖκας without article) means deaconesses; note the qualifications for deacons which precede and follow.[1] We also read of Prisca (Priscilla) joining with Aquila in his evangelistic work (Ac 18^{26}); this was no doubt in private teaching, as St. Paul forbids a woman to speak in church (1 Co $14^{34f.}$, 1 Ti $2^{11f.}$). In the Christian literature after the NT we find frequent mention of a ministry by women. In the *Apost. Ch. Ord.* one of the 'widows' is to visit the sick, while the other two are to pray and receive spiritual revelations (see above, § 3). In the *Test. of our Lord* the 'widows who preside' (προκαθήμεναι) are an important order; they are also called 'presbyteresses,' as corresponding to presbyters, while deaconesses are mentioned as corresponding to deacons; deaconesses carry the Eucharist to a sick woman (ii. 20), just as a deacon does to a sick man (cf. Justin Martyr, *Apol.* i. 65). At Laodicea presbyteresses (πρεσβύτιδες) are identified with 'those who preside' (can. 11); and their appointment for the future seems to be forbidden, though the interpretation is not quite clear. In early times widows or deaconesses were employed especially in the baptism of women. The deaconess is sometimes called ἡ διάκονος (Ro 16^{1}), but usually ἡ διακόνισσα (Nicæa, can. 19; *Apost. Const.* viii. 19; Epiphanius, *Exp. Fid.* 21). For further details see Maclean, *Ancient Church Orders*, p. 83 f.; J. Wordsworth, *Ministry of Grace*, ch. v.

It may be interesting to give here Epiphanius's list of clergy and other classes of Christians in *Exp. Fid.* 21. He mentions bishops, presbyters, deacons, subdeacons, readers, virgins, monks, ascetics, widows, 'those who marry honestly,' deaconesses (especially for baptism), exorcists, interpreters, grave-diggers (or *copiatæ*, see above, § 4 (*c*)), doorkeepers; and he adds: καὶ ἡ πᾶσα εὐταξία.

(*i*) *Promotion.*—It is a common, and in the West the usual, thing for a deacon and the lower officials to be in due course promoted; but it is doubtful if this was often the case in the first three centuries. The 'good step' (βαθμὸν καλόν; see § 8 (*g*)) of 1 Ti 3^{13} has been interpreted by Ambrose, Jerome, and some moderns, of promotion, though this is not very probable, and does not well suit the rest of the verse. The only instance of such a course in the 1st cent. is perhaps Philip, who in Ac 8 is one of the Seven, without authority to lay on hands, but in Ac 21^{8} is called 'the Evangelist,' that is (probably) one of the 'apostolic men' like Timothy and Titus who, though not apostles, yet shared the apostolic office (above, § 1 (*a*)). But, at any rate from the 4th cent., perhaps earlier, promotion from the lower to the higher offices became common. Those of readers and subdeacons are referred to in the *Test. of our Lord* (i. 44 f.), *Apost. Const.* (viii. 22, readers), and are implied by Basil (*Ep. canon. tert.* ccxvii. 69). Cyprian (*Ep.* xxxix. [xxxiii.] 5, 'To the clergy and people') speaks of promoting readers to the presbyterate—this was because they had been confessors (cf. § 7 below). The promotion of deacons is mentioned in the *Apost. Ch. Ord.* 22 (to the episcopate), *Apost. Const.* viii. 17 f., *Ethiop. Ch. Ord.* 24, and probably in the *Test.* i. 38; explicitly also in the *Codex Canonum Ecclesiæ Africanæ* (can. 31; Hefele, ii. 470). Polycarp is said by the 4th cent. pseudo-Pionius (see above, § 2 (*b*)) to have been successively deacon, presbyter, and bishop (§§ 11, 17, 23); and the Council of Sardica (can. 10, if genuine) says that a bishop must have been a reader, deacon, and presbyter, some time before becoming bishop.

7. Honorary offices. — It appears from the Church Orders that confessors, *i.e.* those who had been apprehended in the persecutions and had confessed their religion, but had escaped martyrdom, enjoyed an honorary presbyterate. A confessor (ὁμολογητής) had 'the honour of the presbyterate by his confession' (*Egyp. Ch. Ord.* 34; *Ethiop. Ch. Ord.* 25; *Canons of Hippolytus*, vi. [ed. Achelis, 43–47], *Test. of our Lord*, i. 39). It is, however, enacted in these manuals that, if a confessor is wanted for a bishop, he must receive the laying on of hands, or ordination. There is no evidence that confessors were ever allowed to minister, or to celebrate the Eucharist, without ordination. Indeed the *Canons of Hippolytus* (*loc. cit.*) say that a confessor has not got the form of the presbyterate, but he has obtained its spirit. An honorary presbyterate was possible, as there were many presbyters in each place; but an honorary episcopate was not possible, both because there was only one bishop in each see and because the bishop had the duty of ordaining others, which an unordained person could not do. It is noteworthy, and a sign of the earlier date of the Church Orders above mentioned, that the *Apost. Const.* (viii. 23; *c.* A.D. 375), while giving honour to confessors, yet repress their undue claims. This work says that a self-asserting confessor is to be cast out; confessors are not to be ordained unless wanted as bishops, priests, or deacons, in which case they are to be ordained. It says nothing about the honorary presbyterate.

That confessors were in some cases entitled to an honorary office is not the same thing as saying that confessors were preferred to others for the higher offices of the Church when they became vacant. Tertullian (*adv. Valent.* 4) tells us that Valentinus was indignant, when he expected to become a bishop, because another was preferred before him by reason of a claim which confessorship (*martyrium*) had given him. It is not said that the confessor who was preferred was made bishop without being ordained. Eusebius (*HE* v. 28), quoting an unnamed writer about the heresy of Artemon, mentions a confessor Natalius who was chosen by the heretics as their bishop, apparently because of his confessorship (early 3rd cent.). Hippolytus (*Hær.* ix. 7) relates how Callistus, having been imprisoned in Sardinia, succeeded Zephyrinus at Rome as bishop. Asclepiades, a confessor, became bishop of Antioch (Eus. *HE* vi. 11). But these and other instances prove nothing as to confessors becoming bishops without ordination.

8. Transmission of the ministry.—In this section we enter on the consideration of a series of facts whose significance is much disputed. An endeavour will be made to state the whole of the facts as far as they are relevant to the early period with which this article deals. For a description of rites used in transmitting the ministry see art. ORDINATION.

(*a*) In the NT we find, in the case of the Seven (Ac 6^{1-6}), that the people 'elect' (v.^{5} ἐξελέξαντο), while the apostles 'appoint' (v.^{3} καταστήσομεν) and set apart by prayer and imposition of hands (v.^{6}). In 14^{23} Paul and Barnabas 'ordain' (χειροτονήσαντες) presbyters 'for' the people of Pisidian Antioch, Iconium, etc. The word used is a general one, and does not necessarily imply laying on of hands. It is used for election by a show of hands, or (as here) simply for appointing. In the case of the elders (presbyters) at Ephesus, Hort (*Christian Ecclesia*, p. 99) remarks that there is no indication that St. Paul appointed them. Yet the phrase 'the Holy Ghost hath made you bishops' (Ac 20^{28}) cannot be pressed to mean a direct authority of the presbyters received from God without human intervention, such as St. Paul himself had (Gal 1^{1}). God works through human means; and the analogy of $6^{3f.}$ 14^{23} will lead us to suppose that, though

[1] Another interpretation makes these 'women' the wives of the deacons; but then we should have expected the article.

the people probably elected their presbyters, St. Paul appointed them. St. Luke is not accustomed to repeat details of this nature. In 1 Ti 4[14] the presbytery are said to have laid hands on Timothy, and in 2 Ti 1[6] St. Paul is said to have done so; probably here we have the counterpart of the custom which is found in later ages of the presbyters and bishop joining in the ordination of a presbyter (see below). In 1 Ti 5[22] Timothy lays on hands, though it is doubtful if ordination is here referred to. In Tit 1[5] Titus 'appoints' (καταστήσῃς) presbyters in every city in Crete. We may notice, by way of analogy, another laying on of hands in Ac 8[17] 19[6], which is not ordination; this is reserved for the apostles in those passages, though ordinarily they did not baptize (8[13] 10[48] 19[5], 1 Co 1[14-17]).

For the sub-apostolic period we have very little evidence on the point which we are now considering. But Clement of Rome describes in general terms how the ministry was appointed.

'[The apostles] preaching everywhere in country and town, appointed their first-fruits, when they had proved them by the Spirit, to be bishops and deacons. . . . They appointed (κατέστησαν) the aforesaid persons [the bishops and deacons], and afterwards they provided a continuance,[1] that if these should fall asleep, other approved men should succeed to their ministration. Those therefore who were appointed by them (the apostles), or afterward by other distinguished (ἐλλογίμων) men with the consent of the whole Church . . . these men we consider to be unjustly thrust out from their ministration' (*Cor.* 42, 44).

Here we have popular election, and 'appointment' (κατάστασις; for this word see art. ORDINATION) by 'distinguished men,' *i.e.*, not by the 'bishops and deacons,' but by such *viri apostolici* as Timothy and Titus.

For the 3rd cent. we have evidence that only bishops (in the later sense) could then ordain; for Novatian had to get, by a disreputable trick, three bishops to ordain him (see below (*e*) and (*f*)). Firmilian of Cappadocia, writing to Cyprian about the re-baptism of heretics (Cyprian, *Ep.* lxxv. [lxxiv.] 7 f.), denies that heretics can baptize, and says that 'all powers and graces are established in the Church where the presbyters preside who possess the powers both of baptizing and of imposition of hands and of ordaining.' Then, referring to St. Paul's having baptized (*sic*) John Baptist's disciples again, and having laid hands on them that they might receive the Holy Ghost, Firmilian goes on to say that the 'bishops of these times' can by imposition of hands alone give the Holy Spirit (*i.e.* by confirmation). His argument is against admitting heretics without re-baptism, because of St. Paul's action in Ac 19; but his words necessarily mean that none in his day but bishops could receive heretics by confirmation. With regard to the words which he uses in the earlier part of the paragraph, we may remark that by 'presiding presbyters' he must, being himself a bishop in the later sense of the word, mean bishops, even if he alludes to the custom of the presbyters joining in the ordination of a presbyter (see below); and it is significant that Cyprian translates Firmilian's πρεσβύτεροι by 'maiores natu' and 'seniores,' not by 'presbyteri'; cf. also § 4 in the same Epistle: 'we the presbyters and prelates.' We notice here another instance, besides those mentioned above in § 4 (*b*), of bishops being still called πρεσβύτεροι.

At least from the 4th cent. onwards we find explicitly stated the rule that only a bishop can ordain; possible exceptions will be noted below. As the *Canons of Hippolytus*, though not in their present form of the 3rd cent., reproduce very faithfully the language of their source, which probably goes back to Hippolytus's time, and may even have been written by him, it seems likely that this explicit rule also goes back to Hippolytus's time at least (see iv. [ed. Achelis, § 32]: 'the power of ordaining is not given to [a presbyter]').

In and after the 4th cent. (we have no earlier evidence on the point) we find a custom which is still prevalent in the West, that at the ordination of a presbyter the presbyters should lay on hands together with the bishop, though he alone says the prayer of ordination. This is found in the *Egyp. Ch. Ord.* (§ 32), the *Ethiop. Ch. Ord.* (§ 22), the *Test. of our Lord* (i. 30), the *Gallican Statutes* (§ 3; Hefele, ii. 411), and the *Verona Latin Fragments* (Hauler, pp. 108–110). These manuals emphasize the fact that the bishop acts alone in ordaining a deacon. This (as the last manual says) is because the deacon is ordained for the service of the bishop, and does not take part in council with the clergy, while 'on a presbyter the presbyters also lay (their) hands, because of the common and like spirit of the clergy (*cleri*); for a presbyter can only receive, he cannot give [this spirit], and therefore he does not ordain the clergy, but at the ordination of a presbyter he signs when the bishop ordains' (see above, § 4 (*b*)).

The custom of presbyters joining in the laying on of hands when a presbyter is ordained was apparently not known to the writer of the *Apost. Const.* He says (viii. 16): 'When thou ordainest a presbyter, O bishop, lay thy hand upon his head in the presence of the presbyters and deacons, and pray,' etc. He uses almost exactly the same words about the ordination of a deacon, while he does not, as the other Church Orders do, emphasize the fact that a bishop acts alone in ordaining a deacon. So in iii. 20 we read, according to the best MSS: 'A presbyter and a deacon [are to be ordained] by one bishop and [so are] the other clerks.' Three MSS here read 'by one bishop and the other clerks'; but this cannot in any case be the right reading, for deacons were never ordained by the bishop and presbyters jointly, and moreover 'clerks' must here mean the minor orders. See also above, § 4 (*b*).

The limitation of the power of ordaining to bishops is found in a large number of writers. For the *Canons of Hippolytus* see above. The *Apost. Const.* say that a presbyter cannot ordain even the minor orders (iii. 11, 20, viii. 28). So also the *Ethiopic Didasc.* (§ 14) limits ordination to bishops. Jerome, who energetically enunciates the closeness of relation between bishop and presbyter, yet denies that the latter can ordain: 'What does a bishop,' he writes, 'that a presbyter does not *except ordination?*' (*Ep.* cxlvi. 1, 'ad Evangelum'). The case of Ischyras, which happened early in the 4th cent., is important in this connexion, and is related by Athanasius (*Apol. c. Arian.* 11 f., 76). Ischyras had been ordained presbyter by Colluthus, who was, Athanasius tells us, never other than a presbyter. When after the Meletian schism in Egypt at the beginning of the 4th cent. Alexander (bishop of Alexandria, A.D. 313–326) admitted the presbyters who had been ordained by Meletius (bishop of Lycopolis), Ischyras was not even numbered among them, and therefore he did not receive ordination in that quarter (§ 11); but he was ordained presbyter by Colluthus, and all ordained by that man were, after the schism, reduced to the rank of laymen; and, Athanasius adds, no one doubts it (§ 12). The same writer quotes (§ 76) a letter of the clergy of Mareotis (in Egypt) saying that Ischyras was no presbyter; that he had been ordained by Colluthus who *pretended to the episcopate* [this is significant for the point of view of the clergy of Mareotis]; and that all ordained by Colluthus resumed (at the end of the schism) the same rank that they had before, and so Ischyras proved to be a layman. Alexander himself, in a letter quoted by Theodoret (*HE* i. 3), accused Colluthus of 'making a trade of Christ for lucre,' and says that he set up his sect before Arius's separation. Colluthus was declared by the Council of Alexandria (A.D. 324) to be only a presbyter. We must notice that the refusal to

[1] ἐπιμονήν. This is a conjecture; the MSS have ἐπινομήν, ἐπιδομήν, and the Syriac versions apparently read ἐπὶ δοκιμήν or ἐπὶ δοκιμῇ (see Lightfoot, *Apost. Fathers*, pt. i., 'Clement,' ii. 132). Gore (*Church and the Ministry*, p. 288, n.) renders 'gave an additional injunction,' retaining ἐπινομήν on the strength of a recently discovered Latin version, which has 'legem dederunt.'

recognize Ischyras' ordination was not due to the fact that Colluthus was in schism (as also Meletius was), but to the fact that he was only a presbyter, and therefore could not ordain (on Colluthus see also Epiphanius, *Hær.* lxix. 2).

We may now consider certain possible exceptions to the above-named rule.

(*b*) *The 13th canon of Ancyra* (A.D. 314).—This canon, according to one reading, seems to say that under certain circumstances a presbyter was allowed in Galatia to ordain. It runs thus:

'It is not permitted to chorepiscopi to ordain presbyters and deacons, ἀλλὰ [μὴν] μηδὲ πρεσβυτέρους (*var. lect.* πρεσβυτέροις) πόλεως, unless permission be given by the bishops in writing in every (*var. lect.* another) parish' [*i.e.* diocese].

The words left untranslated are uncertain both as to the reading and as to their signification. The dative πρεσβυτέροις is adopted by Lightfoot, who translates 'nor even to city presbyters, except permission be given in each parish by the bishop in writing.' This would recognize that city presbyters might, if allowed by the bishop, ordain. On the other hand, Routh, Gore, and Rackham read the accusative, and the last writer has gone into the readings with great care (in *Studia Bibl. et Eccles.*, iii. [Oxford, 1891] 139, 194). This would forbid chorepiscopi to ordain city-presbyters without leave. If so, there is still a doubt as to the meaning of ἀλλὰ μὴν μηδέ. Routh renders 'much less'; Gore 'no, nor'; while Rackham follows Lightfoot here and translates 'not even'—he takes the middle clause as a parenthesis, and understands the canon to say that chorepiscopi may not ordain presbyters and deacons in another parish, not even may they ordain town-presbyters (in their own parish) without the bishop's permission. On the whole, the readings of this canon are so uncertain that no argument can safely be built upon it. It is a decided objection to Lightfoot's general interpretation that, if it were the true one, this canon would stand absolutely alone in 4th cent. literature; the Alexandrian case (see below) is quite different. Another objection is that it would place the city-presbyters on a higher level as to powers of ordination (cf. 'not *even*') than the chorepiscopi, who at any rate were normally bishops. For detailed discussions on this canon see Lightfoot, 'Dissertation,' p. 232 f.; Gore, *Church and Ministry*[5], note D, p. 338.

(*c*) *The Canons of Hippolytus* say (ii. [ed. Achelis, § 10]) with regard to the ordination of a new bishop that 'one of the bishops and presbyters, who lays his hand on his head,' is to say the ordination prayer. This canon has sometimes been quoted as if it said that 'one of the bishops *or* presbyters' is to do so. As we have seen, the *Canons* say that a presbyter cannot ordain, and therefore this is clearly not a permissible interpretation. But what does the canon mean? Gore (p. 132, n. 5) supposes that in the original (we have the *Canons* only in a translation of a translation) the direction was that one bishop and one presbyter were to lay on hands and to say the prayer. This would be in accordance with the close relation between these orders elsewhere hinted at in the *Canons* (see above, § 4 (*b*)). Yet this explanation does violence to the grammar of the text as we have it; for all the verbs are in the singular. Another explanation may therefore be preferred, that 'unus ex episcopis et presbyteris' means 'one who has both the episcopate and the presbyterate,' for we have already seen (in § 4 (*b*)) that a bishop was not considered to cease to be a presbyter when he became bishop. The facts of the transmission of the *Canons* make it precarious to fix certainly on any one translation of the words; but they cannot be adduced as an exception to the rule which we are considering.

(*d*) *The succession at Alexandria.*—Much more important than the above is a peculiarity said to have existed at Alexandria in the earliest ages. (The matter is full of difficulties and may be studied in detail in Lightfoot, 'Dissertation,' p. 230 f., and in *JThSt* ii. [1901] 612 f. [E. W. Brooks, Turner], iii. [1902] 278 [Gore].) Jerome says (*Ep.* cxlvi., 'ad Evangelum') that at Alexandria till the middle of the 3rd cent. the presbyters nominated (*nominabant*) as bishop one of their own number, and placed him in a higher grade, as if an army were to appoint (*faciat*) a general, or deacons were to choose from their own body one whom they knew to be diligent, and to call him archdeacon. He then goes on to deny that a presbyter can ordain, in the words cited above (*a*). Somewhat similarly, Severus, Monophysite patriarch of Antioch in the 6th cent. (we have his letter only in a Syriac translation), says that the bishop of Alexandria used in former days to be appointed (the Greek verb was doubtless καθίστασθαι) by presbyters, but 'afterwards the solemn (or mystical?) institution of their bishops has come to be performed by bishops.' The word rendered 'institution,' *mettasrhānūthā*, may mean either 'election' or 'ordination' (R. Payne-Smith, *Thesaurus Syriacus*, Oxford, 1879–1901, ii. 2737). Jerome may mean, as some later writers understood him to mean, that the Alexandrian presbyters elected their bishop from their own number, and that no further ordination was necessary; we should thus have, as an exceptional custom, a body of what we may call presbyter-bishops, who had been entrusted when they were ordained with the full powers of the ministry, including the ordination of others, though they delegated the function of ruling to one of their number. Or the meaning may be that, unlike other presbyters, the presbyters of Alexandria had the right of electing their own bishop without the intervention of the neighbouring bishops.

Confirmation of Jerome's statement has been found in three writers besides Severus. Ambrosiaster's testimony, however, as we have already seen in § 4 (*b*), is irrelevant. In the apophthegms of the Egyptian monk Poemen (*JThSt* ii. [1901] 613) it is said that certain heretics accused the archbishop of Alexandria [probably Athanasius or his successor] of having his ordination (χειροτονία) from presbyters. This was in the latter half of the 4th cent., and Jerome distinctly states that the custom which he mentions had ceased a hundred years before. Certainly Athanasius was elected by the people and the bishops, and ordained by the latter (cf. art. LAITY, § 4). Poemen, in his meekness, made no reply; but, though the accusation was doubtless a pure calumny, it may probably be an echo of some former peculiarity at Alexandria. The third writer is Eutychius, an Arab patriarch of Alexandria in the 10th cent., who says that the twelve presbyters of Alexandria, when the patriarchate was vacant, chose one of their number, and the remaining eleven laid their hands on him, and blessed him, and created him patriarch, and that this lasted till the time of Bishop Alexander (A.D. 313–326). Those who are familiar with the late ecclesiastical histories of the Eastern Churches, which are full of fables and of impossible statements, will hesitate to accept Eutychius's testimony as an independent confirmation of Jerome. He probably depends on Jerome at third or fourth hand, and it is not surprising that he flatly contradicts him.

We are, then, met with a perplexing series of contradictory statements. But they can hardly be all dismissed as entirely devoid of truth. Probably there was at Alexandria in very early times some peculiarity in the appointment or in the ordination of bishops, whether it took the form of the presbyters electing him or of their ordaining him. A great difficulty in the way of the latter supposition is the fact that Jerome makes the change to have taken place in the time of Origen. Yet Origen, who suffered much from the autocratic authority of the bishops of Egypt, and especially of the bishop of Alexandria, and who was prompt to castigate bishops for going beyond their powers, gives no hint that in his own day a great change was taking place by which the Alexandrian presbyters were being deprived of their rights (on this point see, further, Gore, *Church and Ministry*[5], p. 127 f.). On the whole, the remark of C. H. Turner (*JThSt* ii. 613) seems just, that 'it becomes harder than ever to discover the history and character of this exceptional system in detail.'

(*e*) *Some other exceptions* which have been alleged are due to a misapprehension. Thus Paphnutius, a presbyter and hermit in the Scetic desert in Egypt in the 4th cent., is said by his younger contemporary Cassian, the historian of Oriental hermits (*Conferences*, iv. 1), to have 'promoted' a certain Daniel to the diaconate and presbyterate. The meaning here must certainly be 'to nominate,' as is often the case even with the words 'constituere,' 'ordinare,' and the like. We read, *e.g.*, of kings 'ordaining' bishops and popes (see Gore, p. 341). To suppose that at the end of the 4th cent. a presbyter in Egypt laid on hands to ordain, and that Cassian, writing at Marseilles in the 5th cent., mentioned it without surprise, would indeed be an anachronism. Another instance is the statement by Cyprian that Novatus, a schismatical presbyter in Africa in the 3rd cent., appointed (*constituit*) Felicissimus deacon (*Ep.* lii. [xlviii.] 2, 'ad Cornel.'). The meaning here is capable of being tested. A few lines later on Cyprian says that Novatus, who had 'made' (*fecerat*) a deacon, 'made' [Novatian] a bishop. But Cornelius tells us (Eus. *HE* vi. 43) that Novatian got three rustic bishops from a remote part of Italy to come to Rome, and when they were drunk to ordain him 'through a counterfeit and vain imposition of hands.' Thus 'making' a deacon or bishop here means 'getting him ordained.' [Eusebius calls Novatian 'Novatus'; on this see *DCB* iv. 58.] The story of Aidan lies outside our period, but it may be here briefly referred to. Bede says (*HE* iii. 5) that the seniors of Iona, A.D. 634 or 635, 'ordaining' (*ordinantes*) [Aidan] bishop, sent him to their friend King Oswald to preach the gospel. Here 'ordaining' can only mean 'procuring the ordination of.' We know that the Irish and Columban monks had a bishop with them for episcopal acts, though they had no system of diocesan episcopacy. But in any case it is impossible to believe that Bede, the ardent upholder of the customs of Rome, would have accepted (as in fact he did accept) Aidan as a true bishop if he had been ordained by presbyters only.

(*f*) *Bishops ordained by not fewer than three bishops.*—The earliest example of this rule, as a definite enactment, is at the Council of Arles in Gaul (A.D. 314), which says that ordinarily seven, but at any rate not fewer than three, bishops are to take part in the ordination of a bishop (can. 20). The 4th canon of Nicæa says that a bishop is to be appointed (καθίστασθαι) by all the bishops of the eparchy (province); at any rate at least three shall meet and ordain, the other bishops giving their assent in writing. The *Apost. Const.* (iii. 20) say that a bishop is to be ordained (χειροτονεῖσθαι) by three bishops, or at least by two, and is not to be appointed (καθίστασθαι) by one; so *Apost. Canons*, 1, *Ethiopic Didasc.* § 16. But this rule must have been in force long before the 4th century. Cornelius was ordained by 16 bishops (Cyprian, *Ep.* lv. [li.] 8, 24, 'ad Antonianum'). Novatian was ordained, as we have seen (*e*), by three; had the rule not been then in force, he would have been content with getting a single bishop to ordain him. Much stress is laid by Athanasius on the number of bishops who took part in his own election (see art. LAITY, § 4). At the third Council of Carthage (A.D. 397) it was proposed that twelve bishops should be the minimum; but this proposal was not carried (Hefele, ii. 408).

An exception to the rule is found at Rome, where, at least from the 6th cent. onwards, the pope acted alone in consecrating bishops (Duchesne, p. 361). And in the Celtic Church it was common for a bishop to be consecrated by a single bishop.

The object of the rule seems to have been to secure the assent of the comprovincial bishops to the election. But in the ordination itself there is a variety of usage as to what part the bishops took (see art. ORDINATION).

(*g*) *Appointment of the minor orders.*—In the 4th cent., when minor orders were developed, there was a certain discrepancy of usage as to whether certain classes of persons were 'ordained' at all, *i.e.* set apart by some solemn ceremony; and also a distinction was frequently made between ordination with, and ordination without, laying on of hands. Basil distinguishes the ministers who were ordained without it from those 'in orders' (ἐν βαθμῷ, *Ep. can. tert.* ccxvii. 51). So the *Apost. Canons* (82 [81]) speak of the χειροτονία βαθμοῦ, meaning 'ordination to the higher ministry.'[1]

In the *Test. of our Lord* (i. 44 f.), *Canons of Hippolytus* (vii. [ed. Achelis, § 48 f.]), *Egyp. Ch. Ord.* (35 f.), *Ethiop. Ch. Ord.* (27), subdeacons and readers are ordained without imposition of hands; so the reader in the *Const. through Hippolytus* (13); and the subdeacon in the *Gallican Statutes* (§ 5), which take the same thing for granted in the case of the ordination of an acolyte, exorcist, reader, doorkeeper (§§ 6–9). On the other hand, the *Apost. Const.* (viii. 21 f.) press the laying on of hands, and appoint it for the ordination of both subdeacon and reader. The *Const. through Hippolytus* appoint it for a subdeacon (11), but not for a reader.

In many of these manuals persons holding charismatic offices are not ordained at all. Such are confessors, virgins and ascetics, widows, exorcists. But there are exceptions, in which some of these classes receive an ordination of some sort, though without imposition of hands. In the *Test.* widows 'who preside' are ordained (i. 41); in the *Canons of Hippolytus* (viii. [ed. Achelis, § 53 f.]) one who wishes to be ordained because he has the gift of healing is not to be ordained until it is made clear that the gift is of God (other manuals say that one who has a charisma is not to be ordained, *i.e.* merely for that reason); in the *Gallican Statutes* (§ 7) an exorcist is ordained, and a book is given him in which the exorcisms are written. Virgins (ascetics) receive a blessing on their profession, not from presbyters, but only from the bishop, in *Gallican Statutes* (§ 11) and the 3rd canon of the Council of Carthage, A.D. 390 (Hefele, ii. 390).

9. The institution of a ministry by our Lord.—We now enter upon the consideration of theories as to the origin and development of the ministry. There are two main trends of opinion, and an attempt will be made to summarize them, without going into questions of detail, and without going beyond general principles.

(*a*) It is held that our Lord founded a ministry to be a means of bestowing grace on the Church and for its government. For this purpose He founded an apostolate, and gave to it a commission apart from the Church at large. It is clear from Acts, and to a certain extent from the Epistles, that the apostles exercised an authority over the Church, and it is difficult to conceive that that authority was due to delegation from the people themselves. Of such a delegation there is no trace in the NT, and the position of the apostles after Pentecost appears to presuppose a distinct commission from our Lord Himself. The ministerial commission, whether given to the apostles or to the Church as a whole, was not bestowed till after the Resurrection; but our Lord foretells the gift in more than one passage. Whatever be the true exegesis of the promise to St. Peter after his confession of the Christ (Mt $16^{18f.}$), and of the phrase, 'Upon this rock I will build my Church,' the

[1] For βαθμός in 1 Ti 3^{13} see above, § 6 (*i*). The word is used in Eus. *HE* iii. 21 and at the Council of Ephesus (can. 1, A.D. 431) in the sense of the 'position' or 'order' of bishops.

passage about giving the keys of the kingdom of heaven carries a commission of binding and loosing, *i.e.* of government. It is not a commission then given, but a promise that it will be given; and the promise was fulfilled after the Resurrection. The commission is, however, not here promised to the Church as a whole. On the other hand, in Mt 18[17f.] the Church (ἐκκλησία) is spoken of as exercising discipline, and our Lord then gives (apparently to the Twelve, but this is disputed) that promise of binding and loosing which had already been given to St. Peter. 'The supernatural authority does inhere in the Church as a body, but the Church has (not by her own but by Christ's authority) executive officers, and it is through them that her judicial power is put into effect' (Gore, *Church and Ministry*[5], p. 207). A distinct stewardship, however, apart from the powers promised to the whole flock, is foretold in the parable of Lk 12[41-48]. This parable, as F. Godet remarks (*Com.*[4], Eng. tr., Edinburgh, 1887, ii. 108), assumes that the apostolate will be perpetuated till Christ returns, a ministry of the word established by Christ. The same writer adds that the theory which makes the pastorate emanate from the Church as its representative is not Biblical; this office is rather an emanation from the apostolate, and therefore mediately an institution of Jesus Himself. It may be added that in the parable the stewardship is appointed by the Lord (note the future: 'shall set over his household'), in order that the household may be fed, and that it will last until the Lord comes.

The ministerial commission was given after the Resurrection, but it is disputed whether it was given to the apostles or to the Church at large. The commission in Jn 20[21-23], with the gift of the Holy Ghost (*i.e.* πνεῦμα ἅγιον without the article) and the power of binding and loosing, was given on the evening of Easter Day, when only ten of the apostles were present, Thomas being absent (v.[24]). It was distinctly a 'mission': 'As the Father hath commissioned (ἀπέσταλκε) me, I also send (πέμπω[1]) you.' But it is uncertain whether others were present on this occasion besides the Ten. 'The disciples' are mentioned (v.[19]), but this often means the apostles. In the description in Lk 24[33ff.], which seems to refer to the same appearance of our Lord, we read of 'the Eleven and them that were with them.' The number 'eleven' is only a general way of speaking, for Thomas was not present; in this passage there is no word of any commission. Putting the passages together, we may conclude that it is probable that others besides the Ten were present, but the indications point to the commission having been given only to the apostles. That Thomas had the commission given to him at another time can only be conjectured. In the First Gospel the commission is given when the 'eleven disciples' are assembled on the mountain in Galilee: 'All authority hath been given unto me in heaven and on earth. Go ye therefore,' etc. It has been suggested by H. Alford (*Com. in loc.*) that others besides the Eleven were then present, because 'some doubted.' But this is against the grammar. The 'some' must have been certain of the Eleven; nor is it at all improbable that the apostles, or some of them, though they believed on Easter Day, yet allowed doubts to assail them afterwards. This hesitating faith was characteristic; it was finally confirmed only by the Pentecostal gift. We do not know what account St. Mark gave of the ministerial commission; but the author of the Appendix certainly conceived the commission as having been given to the Eleven ('Mk' 16[14ff.]).

[1] This word 'marks nothing more than the immediate relation of the sender to the sent,' while the other verb denotes a delegated authority (see B. F. Westcott, *Com. in loc.*).

The more probable conclusion seems to be that the special ministerial commission was given to the apostles to hand on in perpetuity to succeeding generations, although the Church at large was given a supernatural authority to be exercised by divinely appointed ministers. For a fuller exposition of this view see Gore, *op. cit.*, ch. iv. and (in the later editions) note M.

(*b*) A very different view is taken by Hatch (*Organization of the Early Christian Church*) and Hort (*The Christian Ecclesia*). Hort holds that the commission was given to the Church as a whole, and that the Church as a whole appointed the apostles, whose authority was due to the spontaneous homage of the Christians in Judæa. He thinks that the apostles were not commissioned by our Lord to govern the Church, but only to be witnesses of His resurrection; that they were not, strictly speaking, officers of the Church as the Seven were (p. 231). He doubts if they had any authority outside Judæa. An indefinite authority grew up round them because they were personal witnesses. 'The Ecclesia itself, *i.e.* apparently the sum of all its male adult members, is the primary body, and, it would seem, even the primary authority' (p. 229). With regard to the commission in Jn 20, Hort thinks that others besides the apostles were probably present, and that, though perhaps the charge was 'directly and principally' spoken to the apostles, yet it was spoken to them as representing the whole community (p. 32 f.). [There is no scriptural authority for Hort's addition of 'adult male' to the narrative.]

On these various views it may be remarked that it is common ground that the apostles were given the commission as representing the Church. The point in dispute is whether they received a commission from our Lord direct, distinct from the Church, *i.e.*, whether they derived their authority from Him immediately or from the people to whom they were to minister.

10. The origin of the diocesan episcopate.—We may in conclusion state very briefly the main theories which have been advanced to account for the universal existence of the diocesan episcopate from the 2nd cent. onwards.

(*a*) The first view is that the diocesan episcopate is the successor to the apostolate, but localized. The old local ministry was represented by the presbyters and deacons of the later period; and the supervisory ministry of the apostles, which was formerly itinerant, by the bishops who were now settled in one place. In this view the complete commission, which was held at first by the apostles, was given to certain *viri apostolici* and then to bishops (in the later sense) only, and presbyters and deacons never from the first possessed the commission to hand on the ministry to others. This was the more usual patristic view. For an able statement of it reference may be made to Gore, *The Church and the Ministry*.

(*b*) The second view is that the diocesan episcopate was evolved, by apostolic direction, from the presbyterate; or, to speak more accurately, from the body of presbyter-bishops. This evolution was effected by one of the members of this body being given certain sole powers, notably that of ordaining. In this view the old presbyter-bishops had the complete ministerial commission, even as the apostles had it, but the complete commission was restricted at an early date to one of their number. This is the view of Jerome, Ambrosiaster, and some other Fathers. It may be studied in J. B. Lightfoot's 'Dissertation,' which upholds it.

It is clear that either of these views is compatible with either of those described in § 9. On the one hand, the second view is compatible with the highest doctrine of apostolic succession, such as Jerome himself held. And, on the other hand, the first view is compatible with the belief that the apostles derived all their authority from the people.

Whatever view be taken of the matters touched on in this and the preceding section, it is important to notice a point on which all are agreed. The Christian ministry is not vicarious, but representative. The members of it do not form a class having a closer relationship to God than the laity, for every Christian holds personal communion with the divine Head of the Church (Lightfoot, pp. 181, 268; Gore, p. 76). All have direct access to God, and the minister does not perform the people's religion instead of them. He represents the people to God by acting as their mouthpiece, but the worship which he offers is the people's and not merely his own. The sacrifice of prayer and praise is offered by all, though the minister may be the only one who gives audible utterance to it. He represents God to the people, as the human instrument by whom the word is preached and the sacraments are administered. But he is not a barrier between God and the people.

LITERATURE.—The following works represent very various opinions, Anglican, Presbyterian, Roman Catholic, and others: J. Morinus, *de Sacris Ordinationibus*, Paris, 1665, 2nd ed., Antwerp, 1695; C. Gore, *The Church and the Ministry*[5], London, 1902 (1st ed., 1889); J. B. Lightfoot, 'Dissertation on the Christian Ministry' (in his Commentary on *Philippians*), 1st ed., 1868 (quotations from edition of 1903); see also his appended note on 'bishop' and 'presbyter,' p. 95 ff.; T. M. Lindsay, *The Church and the Ministry in the Early Centuries*, London, 1902; E. Hatch, in *DCA*, artt. 'Archdeacon,' 'Orders, Holy,' 'Ordinal,' 'Ordination,' 'Priest,' 'Patriarch' (a large fund of antiquarian information will be found in these articles), also *Organization of the Early Christian Church*, London, 1881; A. W. Haddan, in *DCA*, art. 'Bishop'; B. Shaw, in *DCA*, art. 'Metropolitan'; A. J. Maclean, *The Ancient Church Orders*, Cambridge, 1910; L. Pullan, *The Christian Tradition*, London, 1902, chs. 3, 4; R. C. Moberley, *Ministerial Priesthood*, do. 1897; F. J. A. Hort, *The Christian Ecclesia*, do. 1897 (posthumous); J. Wordsworth, *The Ministry of Grace*, do. 1901; L. Duchesne, *Christian Worship: its Origin and Evolution*[4], Eng. tr., do. 1912.

A. J. MACLEAN.

MINOTAUR.—1. The myth.—Minotaur (ὁ Μινώταυρος, ὁ Ταῦρος ὁ Μίνω καλούμενος,[1] 'the Minos-bull' or 'bull of Minos') is in Greek myth the offspring of Queen Pasiphae's union with a bull, and is represented as a man with a bull's head and tail. As Apollodorus tells the story,[2] her husband, Minos, had become king of Crete through the good-will of Poseidon; after telling the people that the gods had chosen him and would grant whatever he asked, he prayed Poseidon to send a bull from the sea that he might sacrifice it. But he broke his vow, for, when the splendid creature came forth from the deep, he added it to his herd and offered a substitute on Poseidon's altar. To punish him the god inspired Pasiphae with an unnatural passion, gratified through the artifice of Daidalos, who concealed her in a wooden cow. She bore a child, Asterios, surnamed 'the bull of Minos,' who had a bull's head, but was otherwise like a man. Warned by an oracle, Minos imprisoned the monster in the labyrinth built by Daidalos. Moreover, the bull from the sea was made savage by Poseidon, and it was one of the labours of Herakles to capture it and carry it to the Peloponnese; thence it wandered to Marathon in Attica, and ravaged the country. Androgeos, son of Minos, having come to Athens and beaten all opponents at the games, King Ægeus challenged him to go forth against the bull, which killed him.[3] Minos, to avenge his son, made war on Athens, and exacted as a condition of peace that every year (every ninth year, according to Plutarch, *Theseus*, 14) the Athenians should send seven youths and seven maidens to be devoured by the Minotaur. On the third occasion Theseus, who had overcome many robbers and, last of all, had captured the Marathonian bull, was chosen or offered himself as one of the victims. When he landed in Crete, Ariadne, daughter of Minos, fell in love with him, and, on his promising to take her to Athens as his wife, contrived with Daidalos that he should escape from the labyrinth, giving him a clew of thread which he was to make fast at the entrance. Holding the thread, he penetrated to the Minotaur's lair and slew him with his fists. Then he made his way out and escaped by night with Ariadne and his companions.

[1] Paus. I. xxiv. 1.

[2] Apollod. II. v. 7, III. i. 3, xv. 7, Epit. i. 7 ff.

[3] Schol. Plato, *Minos*, 321 A.

Apollodorus omits the incident of Minos' ring and Poseidon's recognition of Theseus as his son.[1] The story is further rounded off by Pherekydes;[2] Theseus sacrifices the Minotaur to Poseidon, and the injured god at last gets his due.

In this form the story owes much to Attic dramatists, who depicted Minos as a cruel tyrant, while the general tradition saw in him a wise law-giver and founder of Hellenic civilization.[3] The Attic version became an intricate romance in which Daidalos was almost as much the hero as Theseus. It credits Athens through him with the miracles of Minoan craftsmanship. It emphasizes Minos' fraud on Poseidon, because the god's son, the Attic prince Theseus, is to be the instrument of his vengeance. When, outwitted by Theseus, Minos imprisons the other Athenian hero, Daidalos makes himself wings, and his escape is the motive for Minos' futile campaign and ignominious death in Sicily.

The genuine Cretan elements in the rambling composite tale are the sea-born bull, so closely resembling the divine lover of Europa, the Minotaur and the labyrinth, both figured on coins of Knossos, and the fall of the Minoan Empire in a Sicilian expedition (cf. Herod. vii. 170). The break between pre-historic and Hellenic Crete was in many respects complete, but the coins make it probable that the legend of a bull-monster clung to the pre-historic palace at Knossos, and was adopted by the Dorian settlers. A. J. Evans, the excavator of the site, has shown how the complex of ruined walls, adorned with frescoes of bull-fights, in which boys and girls took part, and processions of tribute-bearers, must have helped to shape the story.[4] The name of the labyrinth is explained with the help of λάβρυς, the Lydian word for 'double-axe,'[5] as meaning 'house (or place) of the axe,' a sacred emblem which stood in shrines within the palace and was often engraved on its walls and pillars. This may have been the ancient name of the palace, placed under the protection of a deity with whom both axe and bull were closely associated (hence the frequent juxtaposition of double-axe and horns; see art. ÆGEAN RELIGION, vol. i. p. 145, fig. 5). The remarkable preservation of the ruins proves that they were respected by the Greek and Roman inhabitants, perhaps as the remains of the labyrinth, which the ancients located at Knossos. Diodorus mentions 'the foundations of Rhea's house and a cypress-grove

[1] Paus. I. xvii. 3, describing a painting of the 5th cent. B.C. by Mikon; cf. Bacchylides, xvii.

[2] Frag. 106 (*FHG* i. 97)=schol. to *Od.* xi. 320 (Theseus is told how to surprise the Minotaur as he sleeps in the μυχός, evidently the central point of a conventional maze; cf. § 3 below).

[3] This conflict of views is discussed in the Platonic dialogue *Minos*, 318D and 320E, and in Plut. *Thes.* 15. Both writers remark that Minos made a mistake when he quarrelled with a city like Athens, whose tragic poets could make or mar a reputation.

[4] *JHS* xxi. [1901] 109 ff., *BSA* viii. [1901–02] 103.

[5] Plut. *Quæst. Græc.* 302A. A cognate form would be the name of Labraunda, the Carian town where an axe-wielding Zeus was worshipped.

which has been hallowed since ancient times'[1] as existing there in his day; the tabus attached to such a precinct go far to account for the survival of the pre-historic walls in the midst of a classical city. He denies that any trace of the labyrinth remained,[2] but seems to be combating an accepted belief; Philostratus,[3] writing early in the 3rd cent. after Christ, mentions the labyrinth as the chief 'sight' of Knossos. Late writers[4] transfer the tradition to the subterranean passages of a quarry above Gortyna, described by P. Belon[5] and other travellers.

2. The Minotaur in ancient art.—In the Cretan art of the bronze age we meet with a series of hybrid monsters, combining a human body with various animal-heads, which seem to represent demons (cf. ÆGEAN RELIGION, vol. i. p. 145); the types may have been influenced by the animal-headed deities of Egypt or have been generated locally by ritual dances in which animal-masks were worn. Among them is a Minotaur-like figure, the most significant instance being a clay seal-impression from Knossos which shows a seated monster with calf's head and forelegs and a bearded man standing before it.[6] Bull-headed men appear in the archaic art of Greece and Etruria, and until the reforms of Marius a figure of this kind was one of the standards of the Roman army.[7] The earliest representation of Theseus and the Minotaur is a small gold plaque from Corinth (Berlin Museum,[8] a work of *c.* 600 B.C.). In the second half of the 6th cent. the slaying of the Minotaur appears on black-figure vases, and, according to Pausanias, the Minotaur was twice figured among the mythological groups on the Amyclæan throne: (*a*) bound and led captive by Theseus (cf. the sacrifice to Poseidon mentioned by Pherekydes), (*b*) being slain by him.[9] At first isolated, the killing of the Minotaur is associated on later black-figure and red-figure vases with other deeds of Theseus, a cycle which took shape at the beginning of the 5th cent., when the Attic hero was exalted into a second Herakles. The Minotaur is drawn as a man with a bull's head and tail; his body is often spotted or brindled, and once sprinkled with stars (in allusion to his name Asterios), once with eyes, like that of Argos.[10] He is naked and unarmed, but sometimes clutches one or more stones. Theseus usually attacks him with a sword, but an interesting group of vase-paintings shows him dragging the dead monster out from a building with columns; here we may suspect the influence of stage-representations. Athene, Ariadne, and even Minos are sometimes present as spectators. Later designs treat the combat as a wrestling-match, the finest example being a bronze relief from Pergamon now in the Berlin Museum.[11] In sculpture we have a metope of the Theseion at Athens, fragments of a group found on the Acropolis (where Pausanias saw and described it), and fragments of two other groups in Rome, all representing the combat.[12] Campanian wall-paintings show Theseus standing over the dead Minotaur, while the rescued boys and girls press round, and some mutilated marble groups seem to have represented the same scene.[1]

Evans traces the origin of the Cretan type to certain Egyptian cylinders found in the Delta, which influenced Cretan sealstones from about the VIth dynasty onwards. These in their turn borrowed types from early Babylonian cylinders.[2]

3. The labyrinth in art.—On coins of Knossos the labyrinth is represented by a pattern of increasing complexity, advancing from a simple fret-pattern, through a more or less elaborate swastika, to a developed maze.[3] On several vases of the 5th cent. the scene of Theseus's combat with the Minotaur is indicated by a panel of mæanders and similar patterns, evidently a conventional representation of the supposed ground-plan.[4] The labyrinth, in fact, became assimilated to the mazes which have been familiar in most parts of Europe from antiquity to the present day—a large subject which cannot be fully discussed here.[5] In Italy, where the maze had been known as the Game of Troy (*Truia* inscribed upon a maze on an early Etruscan vase), the name 'labyrinth' took its place, and the Minotaur is figured in the centre of several Roman mosaic mazes. Similar pavements were constructed in Christian churches; they are especially common in the cathedrals of N. France—Chartres, Amiens, and others; they were known as *Domus Dedali* or *Chemin de Jerusalem*, and to tread their windings was a recognized form of penance. It seems that the original use of the maze, wherever found, was to serve as the track of a ritual dance. Plutarch tells a story which was evidently intended to establish a connexion between Greek dances of this type and the Minotaur legend; Theseus had landed at Delos on his voyage home, and with his companions danced a dance 'which is still kept up by the Delians' in imitation of the windings of the labyrinth.[6]

4. Explanations of the myth.—(*a*) *Rationalistic.*—According to Philochorus,[7] the Cretans said that the Minotaur was a general named Taurus whom Theseus defeated at an athletic meeting; the tribute-children were kept prisoners in the labyrinth and given as prizes to the victors; or else he was a captain whom the Athenians beat in a sea-fight. A modern writer, E. Fabricius,[8] who assumed that the quarry near Gortyna was the labyrinth, explained its narrow entrances as a device for the guarding of prisoners made to work in its galleries, and supposed that this gave rise to the story of the tribute-children.

(*b*) *The Minotaur as an old bull-god.*—W. H. Roscher[9] equated Minotaur = Cretan bull = Minos. E. Bethe[10] has argued that Minos, son of the bull-Zeus and husband of Pasiphae, who bears a bull-son, was originally the bull-god himself. The story of Theseus and the Minotaur is a doublet of the stories of Herakles vanquishing the Cretan bull and Theseus capturing the bull of Marathon; in each case the story is allegorical and represents

1 Diod. v. 66; cf. Evans, in *BSA* x. [1903–04] 51, *Scripta Minoa*, Oxford, 1909, p. 103.
2 Diod. i. 61.
3 Philost. *Vita Apollon.* iv. 34.
4 The first is Claudian, *de Sexto Consul. Hon. Aug.* 634, written in A.D. 404.
5 *Les Observations de plusieurs singularitez*, Paris, 1553, bk. i. ch. vi.; plan in T. A. B. Spratt, *Travels and Researches in Crete*, London, 1865, ii. 49.
6 *BSA* vii. [1900–01] 18, fig. 7*a* (cf. 7*b* and 7*c*), 133, fig. 45.
7 Pliny, *HN* x. 16.
8 *Archäol. Zeitung*, xlii. [1884] pl. 8, fig. 3.
9 Paus. III. xviii. 11, 16.
10 Probably a mistake on the part of the vase-painter, who copied a stage-dress, the edges of which are seen at wrists and ankles. The vase is in the British Museum (E 48), and is signed by Douris (see A. B. Cook, *Zeus*, i., Cambridge, 1914, p. 494).
11 A. Baumeister, *Denkmäler des klass. Altertums*, Munich, 1884–88, fig. 1875.
12 S. Reinach, *Répertoire de la statuaire grecque et romaine*, Paris, 1897–1904, ii. 693.

1 Baumeister, fig. 1876; Reinach, ii. 510.
2 *Scripta Minoa*, i. 122 ff., *Nine Minoan Periods* (in the press).
3 *Brit. Mus. Coin Catalogue, Crete*, London, 1886, pl. iv. ff.; Cook, i. 476 ff.
4 Illustrated by P. Wolters, in *SMA*, 1907, p. 113 ff., plates I.–III.
5 For the literature see J. G. Frazer, *GB*3, pt. iii., *The Dying God*, London, 1911, p. 76 ff.; and Cook, i. 484–490. Evans found maze-patterns painted on wall-plaster at Knossos; in his forthcoming *Nine Minoan Periods* he derives the labyrinth-pattern in Crete, through the simple key-pattern, from the Egyptian sign for 'the palace in its court' which was taken over into the Minoan system of hieroglyphs.
6 Plut. *Thes.* 21. Lucian, *de Salt.* 49, mentions the 'labyrinth' in a list of Cretan dances.
7 Quoted by Plut. *Thes.* 16.
8 Roscher, *s.v.* 'Labyrinthos.'
9 *Über Selene und Verwandtes*, Leipzig, 1890, p. 136 ff.
10 *Rhein. Mus.* lxv. [1910] 214 ff.

the overthrow of Cretan rule. Herakles, who goes to Crete to capture the bull, stands for the Dorian colonists; Theseus, who overcomes the same bull in Attica, delivers the country from a Cretan conqueror.[1] On somewhat different lines J. E. Harrison argued in a paper read before the Hellenic Society in 1914 that the slaying of the Minotaur, son of the sea-born bull, expresses the downfall of Cretan sea-power; 'the Minotaur was the primitive "point de repère" round which ultimately crystallised the complex figure of Poseidon.'

(*c*) *The solar interpretation.*—Pasiphae's name connects her with the moon;[2] her bull is often held to be the sun. Two recent writers have seen in the Minotaur a human actor impersonating the sun-god. J. G. Frazer maintains 'that Cnossus was the seat of a great worship of the sun, and that the Minotaur was a representation or embodiment of the sun-god,' and suggests that Ariadne's dance, the track of which was the labyrinth, may have been an imitation of the sun's course in the sky.[3] A. B. Cook, after showing that in Cretan myth the sun was conceived as a bull and that the labyrinth was 'an *orchestra* of solar pattern presumably made for a mimetic dance,' goes on to suggest that the dancer who imitated the sun masqueraded in the labyrinth as a bull—the Minotaur, in fact, was the Knossian Crown Prince wearing a bull-mask, a piece of ritual borrowed perhaps from Egypt.[4]

(*d*) *The suspicion of human sacrifice.*—The Minotaur, like the horses of Diomede, is a man-eater; the myth implies that it was necessary for Minos to gratify this appetite. W. Helbig[5] saw in the story another version of Kronos devouring his children; Kronos was banished by Zeus to the under world, the Minotaur by Minos to the labyrinth. There was a tradition that in old days in Crete the Kouretes had offered human sacrifices to Kronos,[6] and the 'feast of raw flesh'[7] which Euripides mentions in the famous chorus from his tragedy *The Cretans*, as part of the initiation to the service of Idaian Zeus, was open to a similar suspicion; in a recently discovered fragment of this play Pasiphae taunts her husband in terms which leave no doubt as to the charge.[8] Euripides probably had in mind the Cretan mysteries in which the votaries tore with their teeth a living bull in commemoration of the eating of the boy Zagreus by the Titans.[9] But these mysteries stand in no direct relation, so far as can be seen, to the substratum of Minoan religion; they explain the cannibal element in the Euripidean story, but not the bull-form of the man-eating demon. Frazer has conjectured that in Crete, as in other parts of the Mediterranean, children were sacrificed to a Moloch-like image with the head of a bull.[10]

Phœnicians and Carthaginians sacrificed children to a bronze image of Kronos (=El?), so contrived that victims laid on its outstretched hands fell into a furnace beneath.[11] Rabbinic writers describe Moloch's image in similar terms, and add that it had the head of a calf.[12] Now Talos, the brazen coast-guard of Crete, who killed strangers by hugging them to his red-hot breast, was by some called Tauros (Apollod. I. ix. 26), and a gloss of Hesychius makes him a by-form of the sun-god. A tradition

[1] *Rhein. Mus.* lxv. 218, 225.

[2] Paus. III. xxvi. 1.

[3] *Op. cit.* p. 77.

[4] *Op. cit.* i. 490 ff.; cf. Diod. i. 61.

[5] Roscher, ii. 3011.

[6] Porphyry, *de Abst.* ii. 56, and Eusebius, *Præp. Evang.* IV. xvi. (p. 156), both quoting from a lost work by Istros on Cretan sacrifices.

[7] Eur. *Cretes*, frag. 472 (Nauck).

[8] *Berliner Klassikertexte*, Berlin, 1907, v. ii. 75.

[9] Firmicus Maternus, *de Errore prof. rel.* vi. 1 ff.

[10] *Op. cit.* p. 74 f.

[11] Diod. xx. 14; schol. Plat. *Rep.* 337 A, and other passages collected by M. Mayer, in Roscher, ii. 1501 ff.

[12] See references in Cook, i. 723, note 1.

as old as Simonides connects him with Sardinia and with human sacrifices there;[1] recent excavations have shown that the Sardinians of the bronze age worshipped a bull-god in subterranean temples.[2] Suggestive as these combinations are, however, we have no real evidence of any cult of the Minotaur, nor of human sacrifice to a Cretan bull-god;[3] at most they prove that the Greeks were familiar with the rites of adjoining countries and used them to add a touch of horror to the local legends of Knossos.

LITERATURE.—This is sufficiently cited throughout the article.

R. C. BOSANQUET.

MIRACLES.—1. Introductory.—Miracles have often been studied *in vacuo*—a method which does not tend to belief in them. It is better to have a standard of comparison, to study them in the light of those alleged of their chief worker, who, if any one can work miracles, is most likely to have done so. This is the point of view that will be taken in this article. Christ's miracles suggest unusual and striking power, presumably divine, used for beneficent ends, not to cause wonder, and this points to the essence of miracle. We therefore define miracle as an occasional evidence of direct divine power in an action striking and unusual, yet by its beneficence pointing to the goodness of God. Mere wonders, by whomsoever wrought, would have a thaumaturgic aspect and would not reveal character—*e.g.*, spiritualistic marvels. Christ calls His miracles *ἔργα*, 'works,' or *σημεῖα*, 'signs.' *Σημεῖα* may be combined with *τέρατα*, 'wonders,' in describing what the Jews seek or the work of false Christs. His own miracles are not called by Him *τέρατα*, though He calls them *δυνάμεις*, 'powers.' But the stress is on that of which they are signs—the love of God.

All three words—'works,' 'signs,' 'powers'—are used by Christ in describing His disciples' miracles, by the Evangelists, and by friends and critics. The first two are favoured in the Fourth Gospel.[4] In Acts and Epp. *τέρατα* and *δυνάμεις* are combined with *σημεῖα* in speaking of Christ's and the apostles' miracles. In Rev 13^{14} the beast, in 16^{14} devils, in 19^{20} the false prophet, work *σημεῖα*; cf. 2 Th 2^{9} and Mt $7^{22f.}$.[5] Rev $12^{1.3}$, *σημεῖον ἐν τῷ οὐρανῷ*, throws light on the sign expected by the Pharisees (Mk 8^{11}, Lk 11^{16}).

2. Miracles in the lower culture.—Whether the savage does or does not believe in a cosmic order is uncertain. Some savage mythologies certainly seem to suggest that he does. But he believes that the medicine-man, or shaman, has power to alter certain concrete events—*e.g.*, to produce rain in time of drought, to allay storms, etc. In so far as he recognizes any order in nature, this action is really supposed to be *contra naturam* and thus corresponds to the popular view of miracles. Hence it is not only a religious view of the universe which suggests to the savage mind an elasticity in the order of nature, as Frazer insists.[6] It is elastic to the magician, as it is elastic to the divinity. This power of altering events is the power of magic in which every savage believes. He himself may practise it to some extent by means of fetishes obtained in various ways, but in that case the power is in the fetish. But more usually he attributes magical power to the

[1] Hesych. *s.v.* Ταλῶς· ὁ ἥλιος; Zenobius, *s.v.* Σαρδόνιος γέλως; Suidas, *s.v.* Σαρδάνιος γέλως.

[2] *Bull. Paletnol. Ital.*, 1909, pp. 159–177; *Mon. Ant. dei Lincei*, xxiii. [1915] 313–436. These *θόλοι* may be the very buildings which Greek writers attributed to Daidalos; see pseudo-Arist. *de Mirab.* 100 (2); Diod. iv. 29, v. 15.

[3] G. Murray, *Rise of the Greek Epic*[2], Oxford, 1911, p. 156 ff., thinks that Minos' periodic visits to the cave of Zeus imply a ceremony of sacrifice and rejuvenation, and asks whether the tribute-children may not have died with, or for, the king in the cave of the bull-god.

[4] Cf. also *τὰ θαυμάσια* (Mt 21^{15}), *τὰ ἔνδοξα* (Lk 13^{17}), *παράδοξα* (Lk 5^{26}).

[5] It is a fact that psychic gifts are often possessed by unattractive and bad people.

[6] *GB*[3], pt. i., *The Magic Art*, London, 1911, i. 224, pt. vii., *Balder the Beautiful*, do. 1913, ii. 305.

medicine-man, to traditional culture-heroes,[1] to the gods ('white' or beneficent magic), or to sorcerers (those who practise 'black' or anti-social magic). Magic is a sort of thaumaturgic miracle, and is looked upon as something abnormal. If it were a normal thing, it would have no aspect of mystery, as it has, and the magician would not be regarded as he is by his fellows. For the savage magic is mysterious, and everything mysterious is more or less abnormal, magical, miraculous. Magic or thaumaturgic miracle, as believed in by the savage, includes power over nature—producing or stopping rain, sunshine, and wind; curing sickness, exorcizing spirits and demons, and removing barrenness; producing fertility or increasing the food-supply; causing success at hunting or fishing; causing sickness, injury, or death. Other powers are shape-shifting, invisibility, and raising the dead. Generally the power by which these things are supposed to be done comes from an exterior entity of which some persons possess a large share —the Melanesian *mana*, the Annamese *tinh*, the Siouan *wakan*, etc.[2] It is that which 'works to effect everything beyond the ordinary powers of man, outside the common processes of nature.' It is a miraculous power, a theoretical force by which the savage accounts for magic in all its forms. Why magic should have come to be believed in, why some men should have been thought to possess magical power, is not clear, though various causes might be suggested. One of these is the unexplained phenomena of the *x* region—telepathy, hypnotism, cure by suggestion, clairvoyance, inspirational possession.[3] These exist among savages, and would be regarded as magical, as to us they are supernormal. They would suggest other powers still more fantastic. Magic or thaumaturgic miracle belongs to a quite primitive stage of thought, but many of the actions attributed to the shaman are reproduced in the miracles ascribed to Lao-tse, Buddha, Muhammad, or to ethnic and Christian saints.

3. The miraculous in the ethnic religions.—Miracles occur plentifully in religions at a higher level than those of savagery, and are freely ascribed to the great ethnic teachers and to saintly persons or ascetics in those religions. Asceticism and austerity are, in fact, sometimes a necessity as well as a guarantee of miracle, as they are also in the case of Christian saints.

As for the great religious founders, it should be clearly noted that they themselves made no claim to work miracles. This statement is supported by their own sayings in most cases, or it may be proved from the early writings describing the origins of these religions. In the *Gāthās*, the earliest part of the Avesta, there are no miracles, and no very high place is ascribed to Zoroaster.[4] Confucius was largely indifferent to spiritual matters and avoided anything dealing with the supernatural. He is most unlikely to have made any claim to miracles, and in fact he said:

'To search for what is mysterious, and practise marvellous [arts], in order to be mentioned with honour in future ages:—this is what I do not do.'[5]

Lao-tse was opposed to all magic, and was a man of humble mind. Buddha himself protested against miracles, and, though he knew of miraculous acts, he was indifferent to them. When a disciple gained an almsbowl by a display of miracles, he caused it to be broken and forbade these.[1] Some sayings of his point to his dislike of miracles:

'There is no path through the air, a man is not a Samaṇa by outward acts'—perhaps a reference to the supposed gift of walking on air. When an *arhat* flew through the air, Buddha is represented as rebuking him: 'This will not conduce either to the conversion of the unconverted, or to the increase of the converted, but rather to those who have not been converted remaining unconverted, and to the turning back of those who have been converted.' He also said: 'I command my disciples not to work miracles.'[2]

Muhammad also knew of miracles, but he disliked them and wrought none himself. The people demanded signs, but he disclaimed these, usually on the ground that they are powerless to convince. In earlier ages they had been regarded as lies or sorcery, not as divine acts. God's revelation to the Prophet was the true miracle, and the Qur'ān contained it.[3]

Nor did any one of the great ethnic teachers lay claim to divinity. Yet, in spite of this and of their own utterances about miracles, miracles are freely ascribed to them, sometimes even in the actual works which contain such disclaimers. How soon this process began it is difficult to say, yet probably no very long time was necessary for the growth of miraculous legend. In many cases, however, as in similar instances in Christian hagiography, it is possible to trace the growth of a miraculous story in successive versions of the same incident.[4] The miracles and supernatural events associated with the lives of these men are either connected with their conception and birth or acts alleged to have been performed by themselves. The miracles of the former class are invariably lacking in lives contemporary, or nearly so, where these exist. There is sometimes a semi-miraculous origin (Lao-tse, Zoroaster, Buddha), but not a virgin-birth, for both parents are concerned in the act of conception.[5] The moment of birth is hailed by a great variety of portents on earth, in the sky, or in the lower regions. Unearthly lights are seen, mysterious music is heard. Prophecies of future greatness are made. The child himself speaks, laughs, stands, walks, or announces his intention of saving the world. Or, again, the child is miraculously saved from persecution and danger of death. There are also wonderful signs at the death of some ethnic teachers, especially at Buddha's death.[6]

For wonders associated with the birth of a *bodhisattva* or with the Dalai Lāma in Tibet, see *SBE* xi. 46; L. A. Waddell, *The Buddhism of Tibet*, London, 1895, pp. 247, 249; and for those connected with future beings in Zoroastrian belief, *SBE* xlvii. 105 f., 111 f., 115 f.

In the case of miracles of the second group beneficent actions are extremely rare, *i.e.* miracles performed to benefit others. As a rule, the miracles merely exalt their worker, and sometimes they are of a kind to force belief in him. Lao-tse is said to have raised the dead, and Buddha to have healed wounds; but these are occasional, and are in a minority compared with the great number of thaumaturgic acts.[7] These largely consist of power over nature and complete control over its processes, and are often of a most

1 See HEROES AND HERO-GODS; G. Grey, *Polynesian Mythology*, London, n.d. [1855], p. 11 f.; R. H. Codrington, *The Melanesians*, Oxford, 1891, pp. 156, 163, 168.

2 Codrington, pp. 118 f., 191; P. Giran, *Magie et religion annamites*, Paris, 1912, pp. 21, 22, 157; E. S. Hartland, *Ritual and Belief*, London, 1914, p. 26 ff.

3 O. Stoll, *Suggestion und Hypnotismus in der Völkerpsychologie*², Leipzig, 1904; A. Bastian, *Ueber psychische Beobachtungen bei Naturvölkern*, Leipzig, 1890; A. Lang, *The Making of Religion*², London, 1900.

4 Cf. J. H. Moulton, *Early Zoroastrianism*, London, 1913, p. 80.

5 *Lī Kī*, xxviii. 1. 20 (*SBE* xxviii. [1885] 303 f.); cf. G. G. Alexander, *Confucius the Great Teacher*, London, 1890, p. 290.

1 T. W. Rhys Davids, *Buddhism*, London, 1880, p. 71.

2 *Dhammapada*, xviii. 254 (*SBE* x. [1881] pt. 1, p. 63 f.); *Chullavagga* (*SBE* xx. [1885] 81); E. Burnouf, *Introd. à l'histoire du bouddhisme indien*, Paris, 1844, p. 170.

3 See Qur'ān, v. 110, vi. 34, x. 21 f., xvii. 60, xxvii. 10 f. (*SBE* vi. [1900] 113, 119, 195, 233, ix. [1900] 7, 35 f., 46, 92, 100, 106, 111).

4 Cf. Rhys Davids, p. 13 f.; W. Muir, *Life of Mahomet*, London, 1878, pp. 369, 590, 599.

5 *SBE* xl. [1891] 313, xlvii. [1897] 18 ff., 138 ff., xix. [1883] 2 ff.; *Lalitavistara*, tr. P. E. Foucaux, Paris, 1884–92, *passim*. Cf. J. A. MacCulloch, 'Comp. Religion and the Historic Christ,' in *Religion and the Modern World*, London, 1909, p. 130 ff.

6 *SBE* xi. [1900] 44, etc.; Rhys Davids, p. 14.

7 R. K. Douglas, *Confucianism and Taoism*, London, 1877, p. 179 ff.; *SBE* xvii. [1882] 83.

grotesque and obviously improbable kind. Buddha made floods recede, or passed miraculously from one side of the river to another. Levitation, flying through the air, and ascent to heaven are frequent miracles, or, as in the case of Buddha, treading on water, entering earth as if it were water, and passing through a wall.[1] Understanding or influencing the thoughts of others *à distance*, change of form, and invisibility occur. Frequently the miracle-worker saves himself from accident or death.

Some of these miracles are simply repetitions of the magical acts attributed to medicine-men. They are traditional stock incidents easily fitted on to the life of any person. Others are sheer inventions. Others may be exaggerations of actual events, perhaps in some cases of real supernormal powers possessed by this or that teacher, or of great shrewdness or spiritual insight. But they are generally of a most unlikely character, and have seldom a beneficent purpose, nor is there any historic evidence for them, even if they were of such a kind as would require it.

In most of these religions miracles are commonly attributed to saints, sages, and ascetics. They bear a similar character in widely distant regions and under different creeds, and often run on parallel lines. Here again these miracles bear a curious likeness to many which are ascribed to Christian saints. Taoist, Zoroastrian, Buddhist, Hindu, and Muhammadan all believe in the possibility of the miraculous in the case of gifted persons. In Taoism those who through asceticism and saintliness 'rise to the Tao' become like gods and are superior to the laws of nature.[2] In Buddhism the cause is profound meditation. By this the *arhat* gains transcendent faculties—the five *abhijñās* ('magical powers') and *iddhi*, saintship, but also the power of working miracles.[3] Holy men in Islām possess similar powers as a result of their faith, piety, and self-denial. They are also helped to them by the *jinn* and by knowledge of the divine name.[4] The range of these wonders in the different religions is very wide. It includes a great variety of powers over nature—the production or cessation of storms or sunshine, causing the sun to stand still, drinking up rivers, superiority to fire or water (*e.g.*, not being wet in heavy showers, or walking or passing through water); superiority to the limitations of matter and space (a common Buddhist attribute), the power of invisibility, change of form or of sex, invulnerability, levitation and swift passage through space, penetrating walls, mountains, earth, lengthening beams of wood, opening doors without keys, swift transference from one place to another. Again, light is made to stream from the fingers or hands, or miraculous supplies of food are provided. Inanimate objects are made to act as if alive. Supernormal knowledge of distant events or of men's thoughts is asserted. The power of exorcizing and dispelling demons commonly occurs. Less rarely the cure of disease and the removal of barrenness and even the raising of the dead are found.[5] One method of curing disease used by Muhammadan wonder-workers is to pass the hand over the part affected — perhaps a species of mesmerism.[1] As to these miracles as a whole, there is no evidence that they ever occurred, and, as Burton says of the incredible miracles of Islām, collateral or contemporary evidence is never sought for.[2] The question of supernormal powers will be discussed later.

Occasionally, especially in Buddhism, Hinduism, and Islām, miracles are wrought by relics or at the graves of saints. As far as Buddhism is concerned, these are of a very dazzling kind. In Islām they are mainly, though not wholly, works of healing or the removal of barrenness.[3] In the case of the latter the spirit of the dead saint begets the child —a form of primitive belief (see FAIRY, § 9, vol. v. p. 687).

Such miracles are occasionally said to cause belief. Those to be wrought in future ages on behalf of Zoroastrianism will make all mankind believe in the good religion (*e.g.*, causing the sun to stand still). Those wrought by Buddhists also cause conversion, especially incredible marvels in the world of nature.[4]

4. Classical miracles.—This group, as it includes so largely miracles of healing, may be considered by itself. These were mainly the result of divine rather than human agency and they cluster around the practice of incubation (*q.v.*), or 'temple-sleep.' The patient, after ritual and sacrifice, slept in the temple; in the course of his sleep he dreamed that the god touched and healed, or opened his body and cured him (? an operation under hypnotic influences), or indicated a remedy either directly or by symbolic means. The actual healing was speedy or more gradual, and in some instances—*e.g.*, that of Aristides in his *Sacred Orations*—it was prolonged over many years, yet the god was always supposed to intervene. The *stelæ* recording miraculous cures found at Epidauros are obviously fictitious—a kind of advertisement of the shrine.[5] There is no reason, however, to doubt that cures of a more or less miraculous aspect did take place—the result of faith-healing or of a strong mental suggestion, aided by all the adjuncts of the place (the ritual, the dream, the medicaments).[6] It is not impossible that in sleep the subconscious self may cause dreams about diseases, of the early indications of which it has become aware, or might even suggest a cure. The dream-cures may have been based on phenomena of this kind. The hero-god mainly concerned was Asklepios, who was thought once to have been a human healer and to have raised the dead, while wonderful events—*e.g.*, brilliant light—were associated with his birth.[7]

Healing miracles were also wrought by images of gods, heroes, or famous persons. Other miracles were wrought by such images—they moved, wept, spoke, and gave advice—and there are numerous parallels to this in all religions, even in Christianity.[8] Mythology and popular belief also ascribed

[1] *SBE* xi. 21, xvii. 104, xix. 222, 240, 251; P. Bigandet, *The Life or Legend of Gaudama*, Rangoon, 1866, i. 218.

[2] J. J. M. de Groot, *Religion in China*, New York, 1912, p. 182 f.

[3] *SBE* xxi. [1884] 1 ff., xi. 40, 207 f., 214; Rhys Davids, p. 174 f.; art. MAGIC (Buddhist), § 1. These powers sometimes result from religious exaltation in a previous life.

[4] E. W. Lane, *The Modern Egyptians*, London, 1836, ii. 45, *Arabian Society in the Middle Ages*, do. 1883, p. 49; *PR* i. 218.

[5] For these miracles see Douglas, p. 225 and *passim*; de Groot, pp. 84 f., 152, 186, 271; *SBE* xlvii. 72, 105 f., 111 f., 115 f., xxi. 421 f., 426, 428 f., xvii. 3, 76, 270, xiv. [1882] 309, xix. 260, xx. 8, 394, 396, xxi. 268; *PR* i. 7, 36, 191; R. C. Temple, 'The Folklore in the Legends of the Panjab,' *FL* x. [1899] 396 ff.; M. Monier-Williams, *Brāhmanism and Hindūism*[4], London, 1891, pp. 247, 266.

[1] R. Burton, *History of Sindh*, London, 1851, p. 229.

[2] *Ib.* p. 229.

[3] S. Beal, *Romantic Legend of Sâkya-Buddha*, London, 1875, pp. 92, 94; *SBE* xxxvi. [1894] 174 f.; S. I. Curtiss, *Primitive Semitic Religion To-day*, London, 1902, pp. 75 ff., 115 ff., 157 f.; Lane, ii. 54; Temple, *loc. cit.*; *PR* i. 184 f.

[4] *SBE* v. [1880] 231 f., xxi. 421, 426, 428.

[5] *CIG* iv. 951 f.

[6] For incubation see E. Thrämer, in Pauly-Wissowa, ii. 1686 f.; P. Kavvadias, Τὸ ἱερὸν τοῦ Ἀσκληπίου, Athens, 1900; M. Hamilton, *Incubation*, London, 1906; artt. HEALTH AND GODS OF HEALING (Greek), INCUBATION.

[7] Pliny, *HN* xxvi. 3; Julian, *c. Christianos*, p. 300, ed. K. J. Neumann, Leipzig, 1880.

[8] Clem. Alex. *Cohort. ad Gentes*, xi. (32); Plutarch, *Aratus*, 32; Lucian, *Deorum Conc.* 12, *Philops.* 18 f.; L. J. B. Bérenger-Féraud, *Superstitions et survivances*, Paris, 1895–96, ii. 10 f.; O. Weinreich, *Antike Heilungswunder*, p. 137 ff.; J. Grimm, *Teutonic Mythology*, tr. J. S. Stallybrass, London, 1882–88, i. 114 f., iv. 1320 f.; cf. *ERE* vi. 553b.

great wonders to relics of gods or heroes. Some of these were multiplied exactly as mediæval relics. They were miraculously found, and various places disputed their possession.[1] Healing also took place at tombs of heroes. Less common are miracles by human wonder-workers. Tacitus speaks of Vespasian curing blindness and lameness,[2] and the fictitious life of Apollonius of Tyana by Philostratus contains miracles at his birth and death, healings, and exorcizing of demons. He may have had supernormal healing gifts, but some of the stories are modelled on the NT miracles. Others are told by none but Philostratus.[3] The emissaries of the impostor Alexander of Abonoteichos (*q.v.*), according to Lucian's life of him, credited him with healing and with raising the dead.

5. On the whole the miracles of ethnic religions do not possess an air of truth. They are incidents ascribed to this or that person, some of whose doings, on account of his greater insight or skill, may have seemed miraculous. Some, however, may be supernormal phenomena. As to the cases of healing, they are seldom asserted of individual teachers, but rather in connexion with shrines and relics. Suggestion or hypnotism may explain such as are genuine. Whether any influx of life or healing power from another sphere was also present is a question which must always be an open one (see § 12).

6. **Miracles in the OT.**—Roughly speaking, the miracles of the OT fall into two groups, those connected with Moses and Joshua, and those connected with Elijah and Elisha. The documents describing these are of a date far removed from the events described, and their evidential value is thus small. Some of the miraculous events are doublets of each other, and in those of Elijah and Elisha a kind of artificial parallelism is to be observed. The narratives are in some cases composite, and a more or less non-miraculous substratum may be traced. Many of the miracles have a strong thaumaturgic aspect, and they suggest that, as in the case of ethnic religious teachers and the Christian saints, it was not enough that the outstanding character, insight, and leadership of Moses or Elijah should be recorded, but miracles should also be ascribed to them. While, in the case of Elijah and Elisha, it is not impossible that they had some gift of healing—which might then be the *point d'appui* of the miraculous legend attached to their history—it is remarkable that in the case of the greater prophets, save once with Isaiah (2 K $20^{9f.}$), there is no thaumaturgic element. The idea of God which the miracle stories reflect is not of the loftiest kind, but rather that of men at a lower spiritual level. The spirit animating some of the miracles resembles that which animates barbarous men. There is aggressiveness, ruthlessness in dealing with human life where men do not know or worship God, and intolerance. Few of the miracles have that beneficent aspect which we find in the majority of the NT miracles. Again, there is a certain materialism in the method of describing the miracles—*e.g.*, in the idea of speaking face to face with God. Some of the miracles are magical, and are alleged to have been copied by pagan magicians (Ex $7^{11f. 22}$ 8^7). Others seem to reflect the traditional beliefs of the Semites—*e.g.*, that of God's manifestation in fire—or are traditional stories rather than true histories. Some, no doubt, have a symbolic value, as when a record of spiritual revelation is told in material terms (the burning bush, the revelation to Elijah—the latter a reminder that miracles as outward phenomena parallel to thunder, fire, etc., are a lower kind of testimony to God). Some of the miracles—*e.g.*, the ten plagues—are regarded as direct divine interpositions. It is possible, doubtless, to suppose that God made use of existing phenomena to effect His purposes. It is equally possible that phenomena coincidental with a crisis in the nation's history may have been regarded as direct Providential interpositions. Especially would this be the case if prayer for deliverance had preceded them. Such answers to prayer must not be ruled out, and all such answers have a miraculous aspect. They show the superiority of spirit to matter (see below, § 16). This is also true of the event on Carmel, when Jahweh's superiority to Baal was clearly seen in answer to Elijah's prayer. There was some divine intervention, even if that is explained thaumaturgically or associated with rather ruthless methods. Again, we need not doubt that God led His people 'with a mighty hand, and with an outstretched arm, . . . and with signs, and with wonders' (Dt 26^8). We need not doubt that in the movements of history He does 'make a way to His indignation' (Ps 78^{51}) against the unrighteous. But whether the leading and interpositions were in the manner depicted is open to question. A strong belief in divine deliverance might easily lead to the formation of legendary accounts of it. The real miracle in the OT is the growth of the idea of God, the strong sense of the divine presence in the world, divine guidance in the affairs of the universe and of men. The real religion of the OT lies elsewhere than in the accounts of separate miracles. It is found in the growth of a spiritual religion, in such documents as that which tells of creation, in the records of spiritual experience and aspiration, in the phenomenon of prophetism.

7. **The miracles of Christ.**—(*a*) When the documents composing the Gospels are examined, it is found that even in the earliest there is no non-miraculous substratum; all alike contain miracles. By every one Christ's teaching is admitted to be marvellous, yet authentic. This raises a presumption that the marvellous deeds are also authentic. The date of the documents is sufficiently near to the events recorded to admit of authenticity, and the evidence is as good as anything short of signed scientific evidence is likely to be. The writers were men who knew themselves to be witnesses, and had regard for truth.

(*b*) Christ ascribes His miraculous power to God, as He does His teaching (Jn 14^{10}). There is a real divine work being done (Lk 11^{20}, Mk 5^{19}, Lk 8^{39}; cf. Jn 9^3 $11^{4. 40. 42}$ 14^{10}). So also the witnesses of the miracles regard them (Mk 2^{12}, Mt 9^8 15^{31}, Lk 7^{16} 9^{43} 18^{43}). Yet power is inherent in Christ, as the method of the miracles shows, or the definite 'I will' (Mk 1^{41}). Here also the people recognize this inherent power (Mk 7^{37}). All power is delegated from God, as Christ taught. Hence the power to work miracles is not necessarily confined to Christ (Mt 12^{27}), though He has that power in a supreme degree.

(*c*) Christ as sinless is a moral miracle without *a priori* likelihood, therefore there need be no *a priori* objection to His miracles, which generally tend to rectify an unnatural, disordered state in the world. Unlike Buddha, Christ had not to grope His way to perfection—an instructive contrast. The sinless Christ was in unison with the forces of the divine will. Hence power to cure disease flowed from Him who was untouched by disease.[1] So, also, in whatever way He was divine

[1] Paus. v. 13. 7; *HN* xxviii. 4; Herod. i. 67 f.; Plutarch, *de Genio Socr.* 4 f., *Theseus*, 36; P. Decharme, *Mythologie de la Grèce antique*, Paris, 1879, p. 302 f.; L. F. A. Maury, *Hist. des religions de la Grèce antique*, do. 1857–59, ii. 52.

[2] Tac. *Hist.* iv. 81; Suet. *Vesp.* 7.

[3] *In Honour of Apoll. of Tyana*, ed. J. S. Phillimore, Oxford, 1912, pp. lxxvi, lxxx, text iii. 38, 39, iv. 45, viii. 5.

[1] Cf. D. W. Forrest, *The Christ of History and of Experience*, Edinburgh, 1897, pp. 117 f., 157; A. Morris Stewart, *The Crown of Science*, London, 1902, pp. 74, 80.

He was certainly more than man. His powers would thus be greater than those of ordinary men, and might therefore be miraculous.

(*d*) Christ's miracles are in harmony with His personality and teaching. There is an air of naturalness and ease about the miracles not found elsewhere. He never doubts His own power to work them, never falters in exercising it. His method, unlike that of other healers or exorcists, causes amazement, showing that it was not similar to theirs. He casts out demons with a word, or *à distance*, and no mere faith-healing or magical exorcism accounts for these cures. Yet there is an economy in the use of miracles which we do not find in ethnic narratives, while, again, Christ never works miracles for Himself.

(*e*) But, if miracles are so easily ascribed to great ethnic teachers, why should they not have been ascribed to Christ? This is certainly a possibility, nor need we deny that there was time enough for a miraculous legend to grow. But all the facts must be faced. The greater part of the Gospels is from eye-witnesses who had no wish to deceive. No miracles are recorded of John the Baptist. The basis of the narrative is true, and it contains miracles as well as the wonderful teaching. In several cases the teaching is intimately connected with the miracles, indeed springs out of them.[1] If Christ wrought miracles at all, it is not impossible that there would be a tendency in a biographer to exaggerate the miraculous. But, again, the miracles as a whole are very different from those ascribed to ethnic teachers, as may be seen by comparison. We have every reason to believe that Christ wrought miracles, even if the truth of any given miracle cannot be asserted or demands investigation. The miracles are in keeping with Christ's personality, and *vice versa*, and the impression made by them on the people, on inquirers (Jn 3^{2}), and on hostile critics who admitted their truth is of great importance.

(*f*) Comparing Christ with ethnic teachers or Christian saints, we find that they never claimed to work miracles, and disliked them, while Christ made such a claim. If He refused to work a sign from heaven (Mk 8^{11}), this is really a proof of His power to work signs of a kind,[2] but not of the kind so liberally allowed to ethnic teachers. Christ's miracles are beneficent, never egotistical like Buddha's or even those of Christian saints; their setting is different from those of the ethnic religions; they are harmonious with the character of the worker; they have invariably a moral and spiritual quality not found elsewhere.

(*g*) Miracles, properly regarded, assist faith. But was this the primary purpose of Christ's miracles? Were they mere credentials of His mission? This is doubtful. Beneficence was primary, and often forestalled the faith of the person concerned (Mk 3^{1}, Lk 7^{11}, Jn $5^{2\text{ff.}}$), as it did in the case of demoniacs. Crowds of people were doubtless influenced by the miracles, especially by their unique character, for they produced fear or amazement even if that was followed by praise to God (Lk 7^{16}, Mt 15^{31}). The result was that crowds of people flocked to Christ and forced on Him a popularity which He disliked and from which He sometimes withdrew (Mk 1^{45}, Lk $5^{15\text{f.}}$). One whose credentials were miracles would have acted otherwise. The multitude connected the miracles with Christ's Messiahship (Mt 12^{23}, Jn $16^{14\text{f.}}$)—a belief which He did not at first encourage (cf. Lk 4^{41}, Mk 1^{25} $3^{11\text{f.}}$). When John sends to know if He is Messiah, He points to His works of mercy (Mt $11^{2\text{ff.}}$); the stress is on these, rather than on Messiahship. Miracles are not wrought to cause belief in it; miracles are works of mercy, and their merciful rather than their miraculous character is important. They are part of a spiritual mission rather than proofs of it. Disbelief in the worker's power shows hardness of heart, for the mercy and love displayed, rather than the miraculous power, are spurned (cf. Mk $3^{21\text{f.}}$ 5^{17} 6^{43}, Mt $11^{21\text{-}23}$, Lk $10^{13\text{-}15}$). Mere popularity was distasteful, and silence about a cure is often enjoined.

The exception in Mk 5^{19} is explainable because Christ was unknown in Gadara and was leaving it. What the man was to tell of was the divine mercy.

True, Christ's compassion often overcame His dislike of mere popularity, while this popularity might sometimes indicate a genuine faith and love. But, if Christ works miracles at all to evince faith, it is not the faith of a fickle crowd, but the faith of the individual. Such an individual or those who intervened for him would already have faith, and that faith would be augmented (Jn 4^{53}, Lk $17^{15\text{f.}}$). Yet even here it is an existing confidence that is rewarded rather than a divine mission that is proved.

Christ does not appear to rank His 'works' very high, as the phrasing of Jn 5^{36} shows. Works are of less importance than the personal appeal of Christ (Jn $10^{37\text{ff.}}$; cf. $14^{10\text{f.}}$). Christ's personality and His words are witnesses far more than His works (Jn $5^{40\text{f.}}$ $6^{33\text{f.}}$; cf. 8^{51}). This lower position corresponds to the refusal to work a sign to sceptics; cf. also Jn 20^{29}.

The disciples followed Christ first as a result of the impression which His personality had made on them. Later the effect of His miracles—those only of the non-healing group—on them is sometimes noted. In spite of the comment in Jn 2^{11}, the disciples must already have believed. In other cases new thoughts are suggested to them, or a confession of belief is made (Mk 4^{41} 6^{51}; cf. Mt 14^{33}). The miracles, however, were not wrought primarily for these purposes, but to quell fears or to confirm existing confidence. Even the lesson of the withered fig-tree is not that of the power of Christ, but of faith in God and of what faith can do (Mt 21^{20}). The true attitude is seen in Jn 21^{7}, when recognition follows the miracle. The act is consonant with a personality already known and loved. The cumulative effect of miracles was no doubt to quicken understanding of Christ, and we remember that the great miracle of the Resurrection was what finally convinced the disciples of Christ's true nature.[1] Still, on the whole, the miracles were not meant to force belief or to act as credentials. They were part of a divine mission, and had their value, but it was rather that of contributing to a better understanding of a personality, not as a proof of it, and that because they were signs (σημεῖα) of a divine compassion. As for the people, their amazement was at the authority, ease, and naturalness of Christ's method, seen also in His teaching (Mk $1^{22.\,27}$; cf. Mt $7^{28\text{f.}}$). Signs are part of a revelation which confirms itself, for, when as thaumaturgic displays they are sought,[2] refusal follows, or a symbolic answer, or some piece of spiritual teaching.[3]

There is no real contradiction in Jn 15^{24}, for elsewhere the works are a witness to divine love (3^{2} 7^{31} 9^{33} $10^{32\text{-}37}$), not as a mere proof of it, but because they are done out of love. Men who do not see such love are spiritually blind, and to that degree in sin (cf. Mt 11^{20}, Mk 10^{20}). In the miracle on the paralytic, which is said to witness to divine authority, Christ's authority had been derided, and proof was necessary (Mk $2^{10\text{f.}}$). In the case of the raising of Lazarus, this is done that 'they [disciples and bystanders] may believe' (Jn $11^{15.\,42}$). Many bystanders did believe; others did not. Yet Martha's existing faith is the condition of this miracle (cf. v.$^{25\text{ff.}}$ with v.^{40}).

[1] Cf. F. Godet, *Lectures in Defence of the Christian Faith*^{3}, Edinburgh, 1895, p. 114 f.; A. B. Bruce, *The Miraculous Element in the Gospels*, do. 1886, p. 104.

[2] *Pace* P. W. Schmiedel, *EBi*, col. 1881; cf. J. R. Seeley, *Ecce Homo*^{5}, London, 1866, Preface, p. viii.

[1] Even by the apostles miracles are seldom referred to as having an evidential character. Cf. A. T. Lyttleton, *The Place of Miracles in Religion*, London, 1899, p. 53 f.

[2] Lk 11^{16} 16^{31}, Mk 8^{11}. Such a sign from heaven is seen in Rev $12^{1.\,3}$.

[3] Mk $8^{11\text{f.}}$, Mt 12^{38} $16^{1\text{f.}}$; cf. Jn 2^{18} 4^{48} 6^{30}. Lk $11^{6.\,29}$.

Here and elsewhere in this Gospel a theory of its author that miracles cause belief is at work (2^{11} 9^{3} 11^{4}). In this miracle belief of a specific kind—in Christ's power over death—is to be taught to those who believed in Him already.

Generally healing is the reward of faith, Christ's power working with the person's faith. There is thus more than subjective faith-healing, for with Christ there is 'power to heal,' obvious enough where the faith of the person healed is not in question. Where there was no faith, but *conscious* opposition, miracle was naturally impossible (Mk 6^{5}). Christ could have forced a miracle, but this was against His method, though even here He did heal 'a few' who believed. A writer who recorded this was not one who was likely to invent or imagine miracles. Christ also Himself had faith in God, as His words show (Mk $9^{23.\,29}$ $11^{22f.}$; cf. Mt 14^{21}).

The miracle in Mk $5^{28ff.}$ shows in a crude way that power to heal was in Christ, and was made effective by the patient's faith. In Mt $9^{20f.}$ the woman thought that by merely touching His garment healing would follow (cf. Mk 3^{10} 6^{56}, Mt 14^{36}, Lk 6^{19}). Christ was somehow aware of this, and, rewarding her faith, healed her. Mark and Luke suggest that He was aware of the woman's touch by power going out of Him. This would seem to reduce the miracle to magic.

(*h*) *Possession.*—Not all but only certain kinds of sickness were regarded by the Jews scientifically or colloquially as possession. Only once does Mark connect bodily disease with possession ($9^{17f.}$); Matthew and Luke do so on three occasions. In Mk 9^{17} a dumb spirit is mentioned; Luke (8^{36}) makes it a case of possession, Matthew (17^{15}) of epilepsy (σεληνιάζεται, 'epileptic'), though later the demon is said to be cast out. Epilepsy was a kind of intermittent possession (cf. Mt 4^{24}), as also was lunacy (Mk $5^{1f.}$; cf. Jn 10^{20}), or any apparent eccentricity.[1] The recorded cases are eight in number, with a few general instances. Whatever be the explanation of possession, the fact of the cure is not in question. Christ's healing of it was thorough, masterly, immediate, probably permanent,[2] and sometimes *à distance*. His method was not that of mere exorcism, as has been insisted.[3] Both the manner of the cure and its result show that it differed in degree, if not in kind, from that of the exorcist. Yet Christ taught that others might or did use it, if they had faith (Mt $17^{17f.}$, Mk 11^{23}). Serious cases are healed by a word, and the superlative nature of the cure is recognized even by hostile witnesses (Mk 3^{22}; cf. 6^{16}).[4] It had thus a miraculous quality: here was the 'finger' or the 'spirit' of God (Lk 11^{20}, Mt 12^{28}).

Possession by a demon is a world-wide savage explanation of sickness, and, as a survival at higher levels, of certain diseases, where the symptoms seemed to suggest the demon's movements or his speech in a voice different from that of the patient. But was the disease more than epilepsy, lunacy, hysteria, *clounisme*, or such a psycho-pathological state as that of alternating personality, 'temporary control of the organism by a widely divergent fragment of the personality, self-suggested in some dream-like manner into hostility to the main mass of the personality'?[5] In such cases the person may believe himself possessed by the devil, or he may speak in another voice, simulate another personality, or develop automatic writing.[6] As to epilepsy,

'No demon could by possibility produce more fearful results by entering into a man than I have often seen resulting from epilepsy.'[1]

Supernormal knowledge is often a characteristic of those believed to be possessed, knowledge of which the ordinary self could not be aware. This is ascribed to the demon; rightly it should be ascribed to the subconscious self or the fragmentary personality. In the NT the demoniacs show knowledge of Christ which He wishes to be kept secret, or they assume that He has power over them.[2] The fragmentary or subconscious self, identifying itself with a demon, speaks in accordance with the belief that Messiah would destroy demoniac power and asserts that Jesus is Messiah. Yet these men, in lucid intervals, may have heard that He was so regarded. Thus their knowledge would not be supernormal. Lunatics often dread one particular person.

A man's belief in his possession by a demon is paralleled by the belief that he is a wolf. Both are pathological states, and where the belief in transformation disappears lycanthropy is apt also to disappear. This is more or less true of the belief in demons and the supposition of possession (see LYCANTHROPY).[3]

Demon-possession as a belief continued long after, as it had existed long before, Christ's time. It is not explained, therefore, by saying that demons were allowed to torment men while He lived, so that His power might be seen. If Christ then accommodated Himself to an existing belief, yet He did not accept it in all its current forms, and some at least of what is ascribed to Him may be the thoughts of His reporters.[4] Christ could hardly have cured the patients save by sympathetically accepting their point of view. So also for the sake of refuting an argument He accepts the point of view of the Pharisees, without categorically saying that He actually casts out demons (Mt $12^{27f.}$, Lk 11^{19}; cf. Mt 12^{43}, Lk $10^{17ff.}$). An accurate explanation would not have been understood, and might even have gone beyond present-day science. Or, with power to heal, was Christ's knowledge here limited? Did He believe in possession? In any case there is no doubt about His healing this strange disease instantly and permanently, and differently from exorcists, or from modern physicians in the cases of apparent possession. Of course it is a large assumption to say that there are no existences which might not take possession of a human personality and act through it.[5] Psychical research tends to admit that there are such existences in the case of discarnate human spirits, but has no evidence of diabolical or hostile possession.[6] This, of course, does not exclude such possession—*e.g.*, by some alien power at the centre of man's being where consciousness and will reside. Yet an unexplained mental disease is not necessarily possession. In a sense, it is true, there was possession if disease was caused by sin or vice, disease being objectively regarded as evil. But there is no clear proof that the cases cured were directly the result of sin.

For alleged demon-possession in modern China and elsewhere see J. L. Nevius, *Demon Possession and Allied Themes* (London, 1897), though it is doubtful whether the cases are not explainable on other grounds. Much of the evidence comes from Christian natives, whose earlier belief in demons was still strong. Healthful and life-giving influences of Christianity may explain the cures where pagan methods failed, as Justin long before asserted (*Apol.* ii. 6) and also H. A. Junod, of Thonga cases (*The Life of a South African Tribe*, Neuchâtel, 1912–13, ii. 460). On Nevius's theory see W. R. Newbold, *Proc. of Soc. for Psychical Research*, xiii. [1897] 602.

(*i*) *Healing.*—Christ's miracles of healing are not explainable by M. Arnold's 'moral therapeutics,' *i.e.* the cure of neurotic diseases by mental influ-

[1] Mt 11^{18}, Jn $7^{19f.}$ 10^{20}; cf. Mk $3^{21f.}$

[2] This is implied in Mk 5^{15}; cf. 9^{26} and 16^{9}. Cf. Bruce, p. 191. W. Bousset, *Jesus*, Eng. tr., London, 1906, p. 50, regards the cures as temporary, appealing curiously to Mt $12^{43ff.}$.

[3] As by J. M. Thompson, *Miracles in the NT*, London, 1911, p. 37. For the Jewish method see Josephus, *Ant.* VIII. ii. 5.

[4] Cf. Mk $1^{27f.}$, Mt 8^{13} 9^{33}, Lk 4^{36}, Jn 11^{37}.

[5] F. W. H. Myers, *Human Personality*, London, 1903, i. 200; cf. B. Sidis, *The Psychology of Suggestion*, New York, 1910, p. 283 f.; B. Sidis and S. P. Goodhart, *Multiple Personality*, New York, 1905.

[6] Cf. Lang, *Making of Religion*², p. 139 f.; O. Lodge, *The Survival of Man*, London, 1909, p. 111, and *passim*; Myers, *passim*.

[1] T. S. Clouston, *Unsoundness of Mind*, London, 1911, p. 237.

[2] Cf. Ac 16^{16}.

[3] Cf. Bruce, p. 187.

[4] John does not appear to accept the theory of demon-possession, though he refers to the Jewish belief.

[5] The demons, if they existed, were not necessarily like the horrible figures of later imagination.

[6] Myers, ii. 198.

ences. Many of these diseases were not neurotic, and were such as do not yield to mental treatment, while the evidence for their cure is as good as that for neurotic cases.[1] Occasional miracles at Lourdes are also wrought on more than neurotic diseases, and they suggest an influx of healing power from without. But Christ's miracles of this kind are more than occasional. Here surely some healing power—'the power of the Lord' (Lk 5^{17})—wrought through Him. It was neither variable nor uncertain, and it enabled the patient to throw off disease immediately. It was communicated to the sick by an act of will, a word, a touch, or sometimes *à distance*, perhaps by telepathy. To this use of such a power there is no authentic parallel. If it be said that Christ had merely superior access to an *x* region, to which others might have access, yet His access was so superior as to be miraculous. His faith in the power awakened faith in the patient, so that in a sense there was suggestion both from without and from within. There was more than mere 'faith-healing,' a word which is apt to be used loosely. If it is used as mere auto-suggestion, there was obviously more than that. Diseases which apart from scientific diagnosis were plainly most serious were cured without difficulty. If Christ merely did what one day may be more generally possible,[2] at least He did act perfectly in a way as yet undiscovered.

(*j*) *Raising the dead.*—The instances of this are so few in number as to raise a presumption of their truth, for here is exactly where miracles would probably be exaggerated in a fictitious narrative.[3] The possibility of catalepsy or trance cannot be excluded, yet we may assume that Christ would know the truth. To Him, indeed, death was no more than a sleep (Mk 5^{39}, Jn $11^{11\text{-}14}$), from which the sleeper might be roused in the presence of the Lord of life, who could command the return of the principle of life to the lifeless body, whenever He was beside the dead.[4]

(*k*) *The nature group.*—The evidence for these miracles is as good as for those of healing. Here again their small number—six (or, admitting duplicates, five)—suggests genuineness, as do also generally the narratives which relate them, as well as the manner of the relation. The attempts to interpret them as symbolic teaching related as miraculous action do not command respect any more than the various rationalistic methods of explaining them away. The real questions are concerned with their adequacy to the occasion, with the power involved—was it one accessible to others?—with the method of its use—to excite wonder or to minister beneficence. Was there again a real breach of the order of nature?—a statement which no one is competent to assert (§ 15). For, though it is easy to assume a 'reversal of the natural physical order,'[5] some of the miracles of healing are just as contrary to our experience. If Christ's was a unique personality, we must take account of what may be proper to Him either in or out of nature. Such a one on occasion may as easily walk on the sea as on dry land. These miracles suggest the superiority of the spiritual and moral order to the material. They, with one possible exception, are in keeping with the personality and character of the worker. The question of adequacy[6] to the occasion may be safely answered

[1] See R. J. Ryle, 'The Neurotic Theory of the Miracles of Healing,' *HJ* v. [1907] 572 ff.

[2] See a suggestive passage in Stewart, p. 182 ff.

[3] Contrast the large number of raisings from death by the relics of St. Stephen alleged by St. Augustine, *de Civ. Dei*, xxii. 8.

[4] Little touches of exaggeration in the story of Lazarus need not detract from the essential fact.

[5] W. Sanday, *Bishop Gore's Challenge to Criticism*, pp. 19, 23 f.

[6] There is no question of working these miracles in answer to any demand for a sign.

in the affirmative as regards stilling the tempest, walking on the sea, and feeding the multitudes. In the first two, lessons of faith were immediately taught, but they also have a permanent value in this direction as well as in showing the supremacy of spirit to matter. In the third the adequacy is seen in the beneficence of the action involved. It is more difficult to prove adequacy in the case of the change of water to wine. Was it probable that such a great miracle would be wrought to enhance the joy of a wedding-feast? Yet the narrative has an air of genuineness, though, if it were performed for symbolic reasons also, these are not hinted at. As to the power involved, it is certainly beyond that of men in the cases of stilling the tempest, changing water to wine, and multiplying food. Yet, in a universe ruled by divine will, was it impossible for one in whom that will was supreme to use it to still a storm, or to perform such probably creative acts as the other miracles involve? No breach of the order of nature is involved, for in the first two there is but a quickening of natural processes—the storm would sooner or later have ceased; a change is slowly effected in the moisture taken up by the growing vine. In the third, though the act is incomprehensible to us, can it be said that there was any breach of nature involved? While it is not impossible that a miraculous aspect has been here given to a non-miraculous action, the narratives have a genuine air, and the numerous different rationalistic explanations suggest that there is an inexplicable fact. In the case of walking on the sea a supernormal power which might be open to others might be suggested, if the story of D. D. Home's[1] floating in the air be accepted, or if there is genuine fact behind the numerous stories of levitation. The difference, however, is that Christ used such a power consciously and purposively; this is not observable in the other cases.[2]

The withering of the fig-tree presents difficulties as to adequacy, and because it is contrary to the principle that Christ never wrought miracles for Himself. The tree was destroyed because it had no fruit for Him. Is He likely to have acted thus? There is no hint in the story or its context that it is an acted parable. While we need not question Christ's power, it is open to us to seek explanations of the origin of such a story, and these are much easier to find, and have much more verisimilitude, than those offered for the other nature miracles.

(*l*) The story of the stater and those of the draught of fishes need not be interpreted miraculously. The first appears to involve supernormal knowledge and directive purpose in bringing the fish to the spot, and this is again contrary to the principle of economy in the miraculous observed elsewhere, for the money might easily have been obtained otherwise. Probably an ordinary incident has been given a miraculous aspect. As to the others, there is no note pointing to the miraculous (as, *e.g.*, in Mk 4^{41} $6^{51f.}$, Jn 2^{11}), and it is perhaps not necessary to assert it here.

(*m*) *Incarnation and virgin-birth.*—The idea of incarnation involves no breach of an order of nature, for we have no evidence that such an event was necessarily contrary to any existing order. It begins a new order, and it is a superlative instance of what all are familiar with already—the influence of spirit on matter. To such an event virgin-birth may have been necessary and consonant, since no ordinary child was concerned. Sinlessness is as much a miracle in the moral as virgin-birth in the physical sphere, but it need not be said that the latter was necessary to the former. This is a theological speculation, not found in early writers who speak of the Virgin-birth,[3] nor in the NT itself.

[1] H. H. L. Carrington, *The Physical Basis of Spiritualism*, London, n.d., p. 378.

[2] Evidential value is also found in the fact that this is the sole instance of such a miracle in Christ's life, unlike those of miraculously crossing a river so often told of Buddha.

[3] *E.g.*, Ignatius, *ad Ephes.* 19; cf. *Asc. of Isaiah* x. 8–xi. 19.

Parallels to incarnation and virgin-birth have been alleged from pagan sources, but there is no real analogy. The idea of divinity becoming really incarnate in human flesh was alien to Jewish thought, and probably also to pagan. Hence it is really impossible to assert that the story was invented in Jewish-Christian circles at the early date involved. That it is an early story is undoubted, and the evidence for the two versions of it in Matthew and Luke must go back to Joseph and Mary.[1] There is some evidence that it was known even in Christ's lifetime that He was not Joseph's son—a knowledge apt to be perverted by hostile critics. As to the story itself, it has only to be compared with the versions of it in the Apocryphal Gospels to see how an existing story could be exaggerated without being recast. The lack of such exaggeration in Matthew and Luke points to genuineness. Comparative mythology is often relied on to show that virgin-birth is a universal myth, but examination of the instances shows no real parallel. A human or divine father regarded in a material sense, or some material means, is always involved. This is true even of the late miraculous stories of the birth of Buddha, whose human father appears all through, and also of the birth of the future saviour Saoshyant in Zoroastrianism.[2] Yet, even if such stories were more nearly parallel, the question should be faced—Do myths never come true?

(*n*) *The Resurrection.*—Arguments against the Resurrection usually make much of the discrepancies in the narratives. Are these more than may be looked for regarding such an event? Or do they really discredit the central fact to which all bear witness? Without discussing them in detail, it may be said that they offer evidence as good as that for the Crucifixion, and, if they do not prove a real resurrection, do they prove anything at all about Christ? Certain facts are important: the empty tomb, the definite date never varied from, as well as the personality involved—no ordinary man whose resuscitation to a normal human life might be rejected, as Huxley would have rejected that of the hypothetical ordinary man[3]—and the vast change effected in the apostles' characters and methods of action. We may here consider the main modern explanations.

(1) Visions, subjective or objective, or telepathic impressions are really inadequate to account for the story. No such experiences have ever produced such a result, and they could not have given rise to the story of the Resurrection or of the empty tomb, or have so changed the disciples. A phantom would only have made them afraid (Lk $24^{37f.}$). The disciples already knew of the existence of Christ's spirit, for this was the common Jewish belief, and as Jews they also looked forward to a future resurrection. How then could such alleged communications from such a spirit have so altered them or originated such a belief in the Resurrection with the definite meaning which the word had to any Jew? If it be said that it was precisely this Jewish belief in a future resurrection that made the disciples imagine that their experience of a phantasm was really that of a Risen Christ, this is in effect to make them the most credulous and untrustworthy of men—which no one really believes of them.

(2) Equally inadequate is the theory which would derive the story from myths and cults of slain and risen gods. It is claiming too much to assert that the apostles were influenced by these, supposing they knew of them, which is unlikely. Was there anywhere a myth of a god who had died and risen again on earth? The revival even of Osiris took place in the Other-world. No such myth had ever been applied to the history of any man, as the theory supposes it to have been to that of Jesus. Such myths were sensuous, and had sprung out of nature-cults. How could they originate a whole new world of ethical and spiritual ideas? The theory produces the greater out of the less with a vengeance, and sets aside every shred of historical evidence, while it has never explained why Christianity supplanted such myths and cults as it is alleged to have sprung from.[1]

On neither theory is the Resurrection or its vast results explainable, and each postulates a miracle as great as the miracle of the Resurrection itself. The change involved in the Resurrection is beyond our ken; yet there was a change, not merely the resuscitation of a dead body. We know too little of the laws of the universe to assert that such a change is impossible, or that there is no law of resurrection of whose working Christ's resurrection is the first instance. The new theories of matter seem to make the change conceivable, if the 'basis' of matter is to be found in a strain in the ether giving rise to the electrons of which the atom is composed. Ether is described as sub-material, while electrons might conceivably be resolved into ether again. Matter would thus be destroyed.[2] Others regard matter as a complex of energies.[3] If these theories be true, might not Christ's body be resolvable without corruption into the ultimate constituents of matter and then re-formed as a new etherial body, since ether is sub-material, the indwelling spirit moulding it as if it were a material body, yet not subject to the limitations of such a body? At all events these new theories lessen the difficulties in the way of accepting the Resurrection.

(*o*) *The Ascension* was probably a final vanishing (Lk 24^{31}) from the sight of the apostles, interpreted conventionally and symbolically as ascension, and, as far as the vision of angels is concerned, objectively. Heaven being regarded as a place above, this was inevitable, and was in keeping with the symbolism of up and down, high and low. Christ vanished out of space conditions into a higher state, and this is the essential truth behind the descriptions, while it is the natural corollary of the Resurrection.

8. Miracle in the Apostolic Age.—The miraculous powers included in the apostolic commission may have received additions—*e.g.*, raising the dead (Mt 10^{8})—while some are allegorical (Lk 10^{19}). Mk $16^{17f.}$ probably is an addition mingling the authority with the record in Acts and this passage in Luke. Certain it is that some miraculous power was transmitted to the apostles or made accessible by their faith. In Acts we see it at work. Faith on the part of the recipients of cure is also clearly in evidence, sometimes of a superstitious kind (5^{15} 9^{11}) perhaps resulting in cures by auto-suggestion. St. Paul both appeals to these powers of healing and refers to them (Ro 15^{19}, 1 Co $12^{9f. 28f.}$, Gal 3^{5}). They are regarded as credentials of the apostolic mission—perhaps not a sound theory. Those who believed because they saw signs and wonders had not the highest faith,

[1] For arguments *a silentio* see A. C. Headlam, *The Miracles of the NT*, p. 277 f.; and, regarding the genealogies, J. Moffatt, *Introd. to the Literature of the NT*, Edinburgh, 1911, p. 250 f.

[2] See J. A. MacCulloch, in *Religion and Modern Thought*, p. 130 ff.; C. Clemen, *Primitive Christianity*, Eng. tr., Edinburgh, 1912, p. 288 ff.

[3] T. H. Huxley, *Hume*, London, 1879, p. 137.

[1] Pagan sceptics never tried to derive the Resurrection story from their own mythology. See, further, J. A. MacCulloch, in *Religion and the Modern World*, p. 137 ff.

[2] O. Lodge, *The Ether of Space*, London, 1909, pp. 83, 87, *Life and Matter*, do. 1905, pp. 28, 32 f., *Man and the Universe*[2], p. 172, *Modern Views on Matter*, Oxford, 1903, p. 13; W. C. D. Whetham, *The Recent Development of Physical Science*[4], London, 1909, pp. 36, 244 f., 256 f., 280 ff.; T. G. Bonney, *The Present Relations of Science and Religion*, do. 1913, p. 25 f.

[3] Whetham, p. 265 f.

unless the signs were accepted as tokens of divine love. It is obvious that St. Paul meant more than mere faith-healing, some actual miraculous gift, by his χαρίσματα ἰαμάτων or ἐνεργήματα δυνάμεων (1 Co 12[9f.]). There was, in some cases at least, the influx of divine power into the diseased. In the case of Eutychus it is doubtful if a miraculous return to life is intended. In that of Dorcas it is so, though some unusual recovery from apparent death may have been locally exaggerated into a miracle.

The account of Pentecost and its marvels describes an incursion of the spiritual audibly and visibly into the material world. Such an incursion would be difficult to describe, but it is no more than what might be expected on such an occasion. A distant analogy may be found in the phenomenon of light or of a cold breeze accompanying phantasmal appearances.[1] As to speaking with tongues, the phenomenon is perhaps no more than ecstatic utterance, and it is one which is apt to be degraded. The kindred phenomena of trance-utterance and inspirational address studied in our day have little value. Whatever might be the value of the tongues at Pentecost or at other times, St. Paul came to have a low opinion of the gift. The effect of a spiritual invasion would vary with the nature of the person invaded. The real miracle of Pentecost was the power shown by St. Peter and his fellows, and the spiritual results following.

The stories of release by means of an angel have been regarded as symbolic accounts of connivance or friendly interposition interpreted as divine aid. Yet, if other orders of beings exist, they might so intervene, and might have power over matter. The real question is one of adequacy to the occasion, and we find no such intervention in the case of James (Ac 12[2]).

St. Paul's experience on the way to Damascus is really similar to that of the Resurrection appearances, though there is more splendour, so that he is blind for a season. If these appearances are accepted, St. Paul's 'vision' at once falls into place, even if the accounts vary. That he himself should cause blindness is perhaps no more wonderful than that he should heal. Did his words cause a temporary auto-suggestion of blindness to Elymas? The incident of the viper (28[3ff.]), though viewed as miraculous, is not necessarily so. This is also true of the death of Ananias and Sapphira. Emotional shock might account for the deaths, and this would lend itself to a miraculous interpretation.

9. Ecclesiastical miracles.—The question as to the time when miracles ceased, if at all, used to be much debated. Some supposed that they continued down to the 3rd, 4th, or 5th cent.; others, like Middleton, made them end with the age of the apostles and characterized all later records of them as stupid and untrue.[2] The evidence alleged for miracles is continuous to the present time; how far it is based on fact is an open question if miracles are possible at all. The miracles of some individuals in the early Church are far more amazing and numerous than those of Christ. They were wrought not only on the sick or the dead, but on nature. Miracles of the last class are of a most stupendous character, incredible on the face of them and quite beyond all adequacy to the occasion. The age was doubtless one of considerable credulity, when miracles had to be forthcoming to rival those of paganism, in which the ecclesiastical writers believed, though attributing them to demons. Many accounts of miracles are too rhetorical to be taken seriously—*e.g.*, the Benedictine editors of Chrysostom's account of the miracles of St. Babylas say that it is rhetorical and for the most part destitute of truth.[3] In some cases, again, natural

[1] Cf. Myers, ii. 128, 323, 515, 538; E. Gurney, F. W. H. Myers, F. Podmore, *Phantasms of the Living*, London, 1886, i. 550, and *passim*; Carrington, p. 366.

[2] C. Middleton, 'Free Enquiry into the Miraculous Powers which are supposed to have subsisted in the Christian Church,' *Miscellaneous Works*[2], London, 1755.

[3] *Opera*, Paris, 1718–38, ii. 530 (= *PG* l. 527 f.).

or perhaps supernormal events have been interpreted miraculously. Many are wrought to support some doctrine or practice not always of the essence of Christianity—*e.g.*, the use of relics, *at bottom* a species of fetishism. Some concern the Eucharist, but many of these are magical rather than miraculous.

Some miracles copy those of the Bible. Others are such as are found in ethnic sources—*e.g.*, changing the course of a river, drying up a lake, causing a staff to become a tree.[1]

The healing of the sick and the possessed is referred to from the time of Justin[2] onwards. The evidence for many of these miracles is of a very slender kind; credulity accepted them, sometimes pious fraud suggested them; but their possibility need not be denied. Gifts of healing may have existed with certain persons who had faith to use spiritual power or to aid the faith of others. In 'an age of spiritual exaltation and spaciousness, of enlarged consciousness and deepened faith and more buoyant hope'[3] such miracles might be expected. On the other hand, there are few instances of such cures as our Lord performed. Most are wrought in connexion with relics or the Eucharist. That cures should thus occur need not be doubted. Where the power of these was believed in or the patient's faith was strong, suggestion might heal, even if there was no power to heal in these media themselves.[4] There may also have been an influx of power from another sphere, as a reward of faith or an answer to prayer, and this would be a miraculous cure (§ 12). So in the case of exorcism, while, here again, the use of relics or the Eucharist is found quite as much as prayer, it need not be doubted that the patient might respond to the treatment, which was really a form of suggestion. Indeed, where the resources of a spiritual religion were called upon, why should not these have brought calm and order to the disturbed mind? (see § 7 (*h*)). There is, however, no such evidence for cures as exists for Christ's healing method. Patients continued to be afflicted at intervals in many cases. Exorcism tended to become a business, and the 'cure' was often of a very drastic kind.[5]

The most circumstantial accounts of raising the dead come from St. Augustine.[6] These are all connected with the shrine or relics of St. Stephen. The evidence is perhaps no more than hearsay, and there is no real proof that the persons were really dead. Elsewhere Augustine describes what was really a case of trance as the return from death.

10. Mediæval miracles. — During the Middle Ages nothing seemed too incredible to be related or believed. Every saint was expected to work miracles, and miracles freely adorned the popular Lives of the saints. It was said of St. Vincent Ferrer that it was a miracle when he performed no miracle. Any saint in whom a particular district, monastery, or church was interested was apt to have many miracles attributed to him. The people seemed incapable of being content with his spiritual victories; these had to take material form, to be symbolized as miracles. As in the earlier period, many miracles were alleged in support of particular doctrines or practices—the cult of the Virgin and saints, of relics, the Eucharist, the use of images. Protests were made from time to time by theologians, but in vain.[7]

[1] Some of these are accepted by J. H. Newman, *Two Essays on Biblical and on Eccles. Miracles*[2], London, 1870.

[2] *Apol.* ii. 6, *Dial.* 39, 85.

[3] W. F. Cobb, *Spiritual Healing*, p. 45.

[4] The right reception of the Eucharist might have effect in ill-health. Cf. the words, 'preserve *thy body* and soul.'

[5] J. Bingham, *Origines Ecclesiasticæ*, London, 1821–29, i. 284, iii. 182, v. 335.

[6] *De Civ. Dei*, xxii. 8. Prayer was also used, but the relics are mainly in evidence.

[7] See passages in J. A. W. Neander, *General History of the Christian Religion and Church*, Eng. tr., London, 1851–58, vii. 433 f.

The folk expected miracles, and miracles were freely provided for them. Many of the miracle stories are repeated in countless Lives of saints; one biographer plagiarized freely from another, and later Lives are often more full of miracles than the earlier Lives of the same saint. Biblical miracles were freely imitated; only in any given case they were multiplied a hundredfold. Other miracles belong to a floating tradition, and repeat those already found in ethnic sources or in classical writings. Some are versions of folk-tale incidents. Frequently the quite ordinary or the particular gifts of a saint were exaggerated into miracles. Others can be traced to a misunderstanding of Christian artistic *motifs*—*e.g.*, the stories of saints carrying their heads in their hands can be traced to pictures where they were thus represented to symbolize their death by decapitation—or to the visions or hallucinations of hysterical devotees, though these were supposed to belong to the highest state of ecstasy, in which reason played no part. All these miracles may be divided into four classes: (*a*) miracles wrought on nature, often of a most extravagant type—arresting the sun's course, hanging a cloak on a sunbeam; (*b*) miracles wrought by or upon inanimate objects—the numerous moving, talking, smiling images, already met with in paganism, or the opening of locked doors at the touch of a saint's finger; (*c*) miracles occurring to a saint—*e.g.*, light streaming from his fingers, talking at birth, carrying fire, bilocation, levitation; and (*d*) miracles of healing, exorcism, and raising the dead.

The practice of incubation passed over to the Christian Church and was mainly associated with St. Cosmas and St. Damian, but the cures were often of a prolonged character. The methods were much the same as in pagan temples, *mutatis mutandis.*[1] As to healing miracles in general, what has already been said of these applies here also (cf. also § 12).[2]

Possibly some miracles were actual instances of supernormal phenomena of the *x* region, so long scoffed at, but now more or less investigated by science. There are incidents corresponding to cases of hypnotism, telepathy, clairvoyance and clairaudience, telekinesis—the movement of objects without being touched—appearances of phantasms of the living or dying (perhaps that which underlies cases of bilocation), and the occasional superiority of the senses to outward effects (carrying fire). Of these as well as of levitation there has been a constant tradition through the ages, and in the mass of alleged occurrences there may have been some genuine instances. Such phenomena are not necessarily miraculous or even evidence of saintliness. On the other hand, if mind can communicate with mind, communications from another sphere may be made to minds on this earth, and these would have a miraculous quality—*e.g.*, the voices and visions of Jeanne d'Arc or those which prefaced the healing of Dorothy Kerin.[3] The communication may be coloured by the preconceptions of the percipient—a divine message may appear as a voice or vision of Virgin or saint, or a case of real spiritual healing may be associated with belief in a relic. Divine power might also be manifested from time to time through the supernormal phenomena referred to, making them miraculous. There should, in fact, be no cleavage between normal and supernormal and supernatural in our appreciation of the divine working.

11. Modern miracles.—These are mainly connected with healing, though supernormal phenomena in connexion with spiritualism have been claimed as miraculous.[1] Typical cases are associated with shrines and relics—*e.g.*, the cures at the tomb of the Abbé Paris or by the Holy Thorn related by Pascal[2]—or are accomplished by various personages representing every form of Christianity, or by mind-cures, faith-healing (*q.v.*), and Christian Science (*q.v.*).

The cures at Lourdes (*q.v.*) are associated with the vision of the Virgin seen by Bernadette Soubirous in 1858, though nothing was said to her about these. The number of pilgrims amounts to some 600,000 yearly, but no more than 2 per cent of the cures are regarded as 'miraculous.' Some vouched for are of an almost instantaneous nature.[3] Christian Science is associated with a theory of the unreality of matter and of pain. Disease is the result of false thinking. The Divine Spirit heals by casting out 'mortal-mind.'[4]

All these various methods of healing are traced to the spiritual value and truth of the creed or theory or practice with which they are associated. Yet some of them flatly contradict each other. They are rather means by which a cure is mediated, quite apart from their truth or value. A key to the problem is perhaps found in 'spontaneous cures' occurring in medical practice, which may be traced to suggestion. This is probably the main factor behind the cures effected by these various methods. It is the power of the unconscious as well as of the conscious self over the body, when once an idea has been accepted.[5] Existing beliefs are strengthened; new hopes are initiated; fears and inhibitions are removed; and the physical processes by which pathological conditions are removed begin to be affected. Thus in all the various methods 'the differences are subjective rather than objective, differences in the mind of the sufferers, rather than in any scientific evidence as to the nature of the healing agency.'[6] Susceptibility to suggestion may vary, and it should not be forgotten that there may be evil as well as healthful suggestions. But that it is a real psychic process is undoubted.[7] The suggestion may come from belief in a relic, a saint, or from the 'mystic theism' of Christian Science. The main fact is that it often works, even if the cures are seldom instantaneous, though they may occur in a quicker manner than in ordinary physical therapeutics. We are still left to inquire, however, whether any other exterior force works in connexion with the vital healing force inherent in the organism, and set in motion by suggestion. If so, we should be in presence of the miraculous. This possibility must now be considered.

12. Mental and spiritual healing in relation to Christ's miracles of healing.—Psychic forces affect the body in normal life, and of these suggestion is one. But is there also at times, with the healing suggestion or as an answer to prayer, an influx of exterior, divine, spiritual power to heal? This would correspond to the exaltation of mind by spiritual influences in inspiration. It would be a particular and outstanding instance of what we find everywhere, if all life is dependent for its energy on some all-environing Life. It might not be regarded as miraculous or supernatural, for, if miracle is part of the process of the universe, in a sense it is natural. But in so far as the result testifies clearly to processes outside our ken, to the power of a divine person thus making Himself

[1] L. Deubner, *Kosmas und Damian*, Leipzig, 1907; M. Hamilton, p. 109 f.

[2] For these groups of miracles see *AS*; J. J. von Görres, *Die christliche Mystik*, Regensburg, 1836–42; Gregory of Tours, *de Miraculis*; A. Butler, *Lives of the Fathers, Martyrs, and other Principal Saints*, Dublin, 1833–36; S. Baring-Gould, *Lives of the Saints*², London, 1897–98; cf. W. R. Inge, *Christian Mysticism*², do., 1912, pp. 143 f., 264; J. A. MacCulloch, 'Saintly Miracles,' *ExpT* xix. [1908] 403 ff.

[3] On this see E. L. Ash, *Faith and Suggestion*, London, 1912.

[1] A. R. Wallace, *Miracles and Modern Spiritualism*; see § 14.

[2] D. Hume, 'Of Miracles,' *Essays and Treatises on Several Subjects*, ii. 131, ed. Green and Grose, ii. 88; B. Pascal, *Œuvres complètes*, Paris, 1858, ii. 143.

[3] J. Jörgensen, *Lourdes*, London, 1914, p. 161 f.; A. T. Myers and F. W. H. Myers, 'Mind Cure, Faith Cure, and the Miracles of Lourdes,' *Proc. of Soc. for Psych. Research*, ix. [1893] 160–210.

[4] M. B. G. Eddy, *Science and Health*, Boston, 1902, *passim.*

[5] B. Sidis, *The Psychology of Suggestion*, pp. 15, 180.

[6] Myers, i. 213.

[7] It is accepted by medical science; see *British Medical Journal*, Supplement, July 15, 1911, p. 211.

known, the current of whose energy is entering our life for a particular purpose, this is a sign, or miracle. The spirit has let loose 'life-giving forces which sweep before them the evils of sickness and disease.'[1] There is more than mind-cure; faith has tapped a divine source, and it has aided the unconscious mind. That this has never taken place cannot be affirmed, though a leader of the movement for applying the spiritual powers of the Church to disease[2] in conjunction with medical treatment is still seeking for an authentic instance. The appeal to spirit in one form or another has been made in all religions where healing was practised, and doubtless the divine spirit has not confined His work to any one of them, if thus He works at all. But, while uncertainty attaches to all mental therapeutics, our Lord's healing methods were never uncertain. He always set free the healing power, the divine life which healed, whether His own or acting through Him as a perfect channel, unsusceptible to disease. This is seen by His words, 'I will, be thou clean.' The result was swift and certain cure. Thus Christ as healer differs in degree and kind from all media of occasional cures. That He cannot effect such cures where perfect faith exists is not credible.[3]

13. **Hostile criticism of miracles.**—Though the Schoolmen were probably refuting current objections to miracles, no serious criticism appeared until the 17th cent. with *Spinoza's* attack. The laws of nature are the decrees of God. Miracles cannot happen because they violate the order of nature, and thus God would be contradicting Himself, for nature is fixed and changeless. Miracles could tell us nothing of God, since they surpass our powers of comprehension.[4]

Spinoza's view is mechanical and takes no account of the interaction of existing 'laws,' their interference with each other without violating the order of nature. This may also be true of miraculous action. The material universe may be subject to the spiritual order. God may bring in new forces from time to time, or combine existing forces for a definite end, and His guidance exists through all. Moreover, even if miracles are incomprehensible, they do tell us certain definite things about God, as Christ's miracles did. Spinoza's pantheistic doctrine of God deprived God of all real freedom.

The *Deists* opposed miracles on the ground of a fixed order of nature. God, having made the world, never interfered with it, and to assert miracle was a kind of treason to Him. Hence the Gospel miracles were explained away or allegorized. Miracle was a possibility, but it never occurred. This also was the position of *David Hume*, whose argument, aimed at Roman Catholic miracles primarily, was regarded by him as invulnerable. Miracle was a violation of the laws of nature by a particular volition of deity, of whose attributes or actions, however, we could know nothing otherwise than from our experience of them in the ordinary course of nature. No testimony could establish a miracle, unless its falsehood would be more miraculous than the alleged miracle itself. The belief in miracles arises from the pleasing sensations which they arouse, and they are common adjuncts of religious enthusiasm. A miracle could never be proved so as to be the foundation of a system of religion.[5]

Huxley criticizes Hume's argument on the ground that every event is a part of nature and proof to the contrary is impossible. 'Calling our often verified experience a law of nature adds nothing to its value,' since we cannot affirm that the experience will be verified again. Any seeming violation of the laws of nature would be investigated by science, and its existence would simply extend our view of nature. Miracle is conceivable, and involves no contradiction, yet evidence for it must be complete.[1] It may be added that Hume's 'experience' is such as he only would admit. His own criterion of evidence, even when fulfilled, is at once rejected by him,[2] and some of his admissions—*e.g.*, as to the hypothetical eight days' darkness—tell against his own argument. A particular volition of deity may reveal a world transcending ours without violating laws of nature, which are also volitions of deity. Christ's signs are part of our experience of the working of God. As to miracles establishing a doctrine, the argument has little force now. Miracles of healing, *e.g.*, need not prove the truth of the system in which they are found (§ 11), and it is questionable whether any ethnic system was founded on a miraculous basis. Christ, not His miracles, established Christianity, but His miracles are inherent in His religion in a way that those alleged of ethnic teachers are not.

German rationalism, represented by *H. S. Reimarus*, opposed miracles as impostures effected by Christ. *H. E. G. Paulus*, however, regarded them as ordinary or perhaps unusual events interpreted by readers as miracles—a thing which the authors of the Gospels never intended, though they sometimes had mistaken ordinary action for miracle. *D. F. Strauss* started, like Paulus, from the Spinozan principle, and regarded miracles as legendary accretions—a halo of wonder placed round Christ's head by the early Church, because the Messiah had been expected to work miracles. Yet, mythical as they are, the miracles are symbols of metaphysical ideas.

Literary criticism in the persons of *E. Renan*, *M. Arnold*, and *W. E. H. Lecky* set aside miracle altogether. 'Miracles do not happen,' was Arnold's catchword. Renan maintained that Jesus had to either renounce His mission or become a thaumaturgist. Miracles were a violence done to Him by His age—a statement incompatible with Lk 13^{32}—and yet He believed in miracles, and had no idea of an order of nature. Arnold, while opposed to explaining miracles in detail, thought it a mistake to rest Christianity on miracle, for, when that was discredited, as he believed it had been, Christianity was apt to go with it. Both Renan and he admitted some truth in the miracles of healing, but Renan's description of these comes short of what is said of their thoroughness and ease, and is, in fact, grotesque.[3] Arnold's idea of 'moral therapeutics' assumes that illness was due to sin, while Christ, as bringer of happiness and calm, addressed the moral cause of disease. Such a method might be used extensively in the healing art.[4]

The assumption that illness was due to sin is not proved, and some healing miracles are not explainable by moral therapeutics. In any case Christ had a power which has not been imitated, and the other miracles are quite as well attested as those of healing.

The literary pantheism favoured by *R. W. Emerson* (*q.v.*) saw miracle everywhere, therefore definite miracles nowhere. Miracle as taught by the churches was a monster.[5] Christ's miracles are explained by saying that He felt man's life and doings to be a miracle—an insufficient account of σημεῖα.[6] There is some truth, however, in the saying that 'to aim to convert a man by miracles, is a profanation of the soul.'[7] Not dissimilar is *Carlyle's* 'natural supernaturalism,' though he admitted that such an event as the raising of one from the dead would violate no law, but prove the entrance of some deeper law.[8]

Materialism rejects miracle altogether and refuses to investigate individual miracles — too often the attitude of science. Agnosticism, as represented by *Huxley*, admitted the possibility of miracle, but, in the event of such 'wonderful

[1] Cobb, p. 224.
[2] McComb, Worcester, and Coriat, *Religion and Medicine*, p. 4.
[3] Cf. the remarks of P. Dearmer, *Body and Soul*, p. 315; J. M. Hickson, *The Healing of Christ in His Church*, n.d., and *The Healer*, *passim*.
[4] *Tractatus Theologico-Politicus*, Eng. tr., London, 1862, ch. 6.
[5] *Op. cit.* ii. 115 ff. For the sources of Hume's argument see J. H. Burton, *Life and Correspondence of D. Hume*, Edinburgh, 1846, i. 57.

[1] Huxley, *Hume*, p. 129 ff.; cf., for further criticism, T. De Quincey, 'On Miracles as Subjects of Testimony,' *Works*, Edinburgh, 1862, vii. 224 f.
[2] Cf. ii. 122, 131 with p. 483.
[3] *Vie de Jésus*, Paris, 1863, ch. xvi.
[4] *Literature and Dogma*, p. 126 ff. (*Works*, London, 1903, vii.).
[5] *Works*, Riverside ed., London, 1898, i. 128; cf. ii. 66.
[6] *Ib.* i. 128.
[7] *Ib.* i. 131.
[8] *Sartor Resartus*, bk. iii. ch. 8, *Essays*, iv. 37.

events' happening, would widen its view of nature. All that would thus be shown would be that all experience, however long or uniform, is apt to be incomplete. There would be no necessary divine power behind such a wonderful event.

But, while science might investigate any 'wonderful event,' has it yet explained even an ordinary event? Christianity regards all events as expressions of divine will, direct or indirect, and such as are miraculous are more striking evidence of that, not just because they arouse wonder, but because of their appeal to what is ethical or spiritual in us. They witness to the supremacy of spirit over matter (§ 15).

On the whole, the scientific attitude to miracle is less hostile now than it once was. Many scientific men are also religious men, and the new vistas open to science have made a spiritual interpretation of the universe more possible.

14. The defence of miracles.—The *Apologists* generally connected miracles with prophecy, and showed that they fulfilled predictions of such deeds made long ago. They are by no means the sole evidence for Christianity, though, as the Greek Fathers maintained, they might help those who through sin could not see God in His works. Origen pointed out that Christ's miracles were not done for show, like a juggler's wonders, and that, unlike a juggler, He demanded a new way of life.[1] The Fathers commonly appealed to the miracles done in their day, and *Arnobius* devotes much attention to miracles as proving Christ's divinity. *Augustine* first gives a philosophy of the miraculous. God's will is the ultimate source of all things, and nothing can be *contra naturam* which happens by God's will. Everything is natural, not to us, but to God. Miracles are part of an established order. They are not *contra naturam*, but may be contrary to what is known to us of nature.[2] The *Schoolmen* start from this idea of uniformity, forestalling the ideas of science, but not on experimental grounds. There is a higher and a lower order of nature, the former at once natural and supernatural, God's ideal plan. In it are *causales rationes et primordiales* of miracles. In the actual order, known to us, with its chain of causes and effects, miracles could not originate, but these have the capacity for higher powers being inserted in them—all parts of God's original plan. Miracles are not such to God, who can interfere with the *ordo secundarum causarum* which is subject to Him. Miracles are *prœter hanc ordinem*—the order known to us—but not *contra naturam*.[3] Again, as the course of things can be changed by creaturely power, so God's power may bring an event to pass otherwise than in the usual course, so that men may know His power. This is equivalent to the view that there may be guidance of forces in nature to a particular result which may appear miraculous to us (§ 15). Later the idea came generally to be held that miracles were a real suspension or violation of the laws of nature, the view attacked by Spinoza and Hume, both sides arguing as if all nature's 'laws' were known to them. *Bishop Butler* wisely points out that, while we see nature carried on by general laws, God's miraculous interpositions may have also been by general laws of wisdom. Nature is plastic to Him, and these laws are unknown to us. There may be beings to whom the miraculous is as natural as ordinary nature is to us. Butler was arguing against the Deists, but he sometimes forestalls Hume's objections, as when he says that miracles should be compared not with ordinary but with extraordinary events in nature. With the Schoolmen he tends to regard miracles as part of the original plan of things. He again forestalls Hume when he argues that fraudulent miracles do not

1 *c. Cels.* i. 68; cf. iii. 22.

2 *c. Faustum*, 26, *de Civ. Dei*, xxi. 7 f., *de Gen. ad Lit.* vi. 13.

3 Cf. Aquinas, *Summa Theol.* I. cv., cvi., *Summa c. Gentiles*, III. xcix. f.

disprove those of Christianity, but he is on less sure ground when he says that Christianity was offered and received on the ground of miracles publicly wrought to attest its truth. *J. B. Mozley* continued Butler's position that miracles are necessary to a revelation,[1] but argued, with him, that no miracle could make us accept anything contrary to moral or true religion. There is order, cosmos, in nature, but the mechanical expectation of recurrence which would keep out miracle cannot be proved true. Anything contradictory to experience might be either some event in accordance with an order of nature or a direct divine interposition, spirit prevailing over matter. Such a miraculous event, as the act of a Personal Being, would show moral will and intention and be evidence of a higher world. The order of nature might be suspended, if there was use in suspending it. But the laws of nature would be suspended, not the laws of the universe, which would be a contradiction. Suspension of the laws of nature is possible, and it happens—*e.g.*, where the laws of matter are suspended by the laws of life. If spirit be regarded as above matter and capable of moving it, miracle becomes possible.

In opposition to German rationalism *Schleiermacher*, in his *Der christliche Glaube* (Amsterdam, 1830–31), maintained that nature admitted of new elements, consonant as it was to God's will and work, even if conditioned by it. Nature may contain the cause of the miracle, but it appears only when God calls it forth. Christ had a supernatural origin and, as sinless, was a moral miracle. Yet the Virgin-birth, Resurrection, and Ascension were set aside along with many of the miracles, though miracle was admitted, since God has complete power over nature. Our belief in Christ, according to him, does not depend on miracles. Thus, though Schleiermacher still opposes certain miracles, he offers a constructive theory of miracle. Later *A. Ritschl* refused to regard miracles as contrary to natural law, and held that they were akin to Providential action. *J. Kaftan* argues from the same side that 'laws of nature' are unreal, a mere formula allowing us to grasp the course of nature. Miracle is such an unusual event as will awaken us in a special manner to God's living government of the world. He works in all things, but can use special means to enable faith to trace His presence.[2] *Hermann Lotze* also refuses to regard miracle as setting aside laws of nature. The miracle-working power, by virtue of its internal connexion with the inner states of things, can alter these and so modify the result of the laws. Law is thus turned to account. Even if there be mechanical necessity, this change in the internal state of things subject to it causes it to produce an external miraculous phenomenon. The elements of the universe are not 'selfless and void points of attachment for unalterable forces,' but living parts of the living One. No law is altered when miracle occurs, but the bearers of the forces obedient to these laws are altered. The conditioning cause of miracles is in God and nature both, hence there is no arbitrariness in miracles. Yet Lotze sets aside Christ's miracles, partly because the change in man's conceptions of nature has made them dubious.[3]

On the whole, modern theology tends to regard the universe as plastic to God and miracles as the evidence of will. Even man can produce effects in nature not producible by nature itself. Such a view is elaborated by *H. Bushnell*.[4] Again, as by

1 *Eight Lectures on Miracles.* Miracles, far from being a decisive proof of revelation, have now themselves to be proved!

2 *Truth of the Christian Religion*, Eng. tr., Edinburgh, 1894, ii. 393 ff.

3 *Microcosmus*, Eng. tr., Edinburgh, 1885, i. 450 f., ii. 478 f.

4 *Nature and the Supernatural*, London, 1863. See *ERE* iii. 45b.

J. R. Illingworth, divine immanence is made the ground of miracle. There is unity rather than uniformity in nature; it is due to spirit which uses matter for its purposes. The moral aspect of miracles is also emphasized by him and by other writers. Christ's miracles do not interfere with law, but restore laws which were broken. Disease is here regarded as due to sin. As to the Resurrection, there is no reason why a sinless soul should not resume at will a sinless body.[1] The supremacy to an extraordinary degree of spiritual force over the mere material is also emphasized by *A. C. Headlam* in his recent book on miracles.[2]

From a spiritualistic point of view *A. R. Wallace* argues for miracles on the ground that intelligent beings, unperceived by us, have power over matter, producing supernormal phenomena, the occurrence of which has been noted in all ages. By this view he claims that Christ's miracles as well as answer to prayer find new support.[3]

15. The question of the miraculous.—Miracles are not fortuitous events, breaking in upon a fixed order of nature. Both they and that order are evidences of divine will. The more the nature of the universe is revealed to us, the more impossible is it to believe that it all merely happened, that there was no guidance or control to produce such a vast and complex result. This impossibility is only the more increased by recent discoveries in science. If there is an infinite number of ultimate elements all of precisely the same form, it is most unlikely that all these should have happened upon the same form. Neither matter nor energy possesses the power of automatic guidance and control. Hence some form of guidance is essential, some directing mind and will. Life is outside the categories of matter and energy, yet it can use both, guiding and controlling them in accordance with the laws which govern them. Such guidance should not be denied to a supreme will and source of all life. But, if such guidance is granted, then miracles—particular instances of that guidance—become possible. A fixed order of nature does not necessarily mean that nature is self-contained and self-sufficing or subject to unalterable mechanical necessity. We do not know all of that order, nor is it likely that it is the only possible order. We cannot assert that a limit has been set to every combination of matter and energy, to every method of guiding these, to every possible result. If so, a miracle is not a breach of the order of nature, which, modifying St. Augustine's formula of known and unknown, may be regarded as one of which we do not know everything. As to the 'laws of the universe,' all that this means is governance of the universe according to law. If things always happen in an unvarying sequence, this does not exclude guidance, nor does it mean that the ultimate cause of the sequence has been discovered. Nor, if some phenomenon happened but once, would it be outside law or happen apart from guidance. Man can interfere with nature, utilizing its forces to produce new results, without breaking any single law of nature. What man can do is possible for the mind and will behind the universe. Law, again, if it exist in the material, must also exist in the super-material universe which interacts with the former. By its laws those of the material universe may be suspended, and in so far as any such action is purposive and beneficent it reveals a law of love, a universe governed all through according to law by a competent and good will. A miracle would thus be a beneficent and intelligent control and guidance of existing forces in accordance with law by a supreme spiritual power, and this is precisely what we find in the miracles of Christ. They were natural actions to Him, either because of what He was or because He was in perfect harmony with that supreme spiritual power.

It is easy to hold a wrong idea of the uniformity of nature or, rather, its unity, to adopt Illingworth's *dictum*. Theology has been apt to insist upon miracle as a sort of catastrophic gap in an existing uniformity. Science has tended to forget the possibility or, rather, the fact of endless variety in that uniformity. Such variety is only the more in evidence with the new discoveries of science, which now postulates either an energy as the only physical reality or a sub-material basis of matter with a psychical significance. But, apart from that, how endless is the diversity even in a uniform nature, not even two blades of grass precisely the same! Nor is life explainable in terms of mechanical uniformity. It uses and controls matter and energy, and may exist apart from them.[1] Unity, with endless variety, is a better description of the universe than mere mechanical uniformity. In the interaction of the forces of the universe a slight increase of one force will produce a different result. And, if the forces, the interaction, the result, are guided and controlled, this would not detract from, but only augment, the theory of science that this is an orderly universe. Such guidance and control are not occasional but continuous, for a true theology can never postulate a God outside the universe, interfering with it on occasion. He always does what is best for it, and all that the universe contains—not merely its physical contents—is utilized for definite ends. Thus, if a slight increase of one force in any combination of forces—a re-arrangement of forces—will produce a different result from what is generally produced, miracle becomes possible. The result would show more definitely will and beneficence in the guiding process. Science might investigate this result, might even conceivably reproduce it. Could it explain the process? Could it tell how Christ could do such things in a pre-scientific age? There must have been some influence working with Him or in Him to produce such purposive, intelligent results. Science might create life, say, out of certain chemical combinations of dead matter. But could it explain why precisely that combination, that arrangement of forces or conditions, produced life? There would not be an act of creation, but the setting in motion of certain forces already possessing the potency of life. Why or how they possessed this would remain unexplained.

As there are physical so there are moral and spiritual facts, not explainable in terms of the former, though they interpenetrate. Miracles, as such, are not isolated physical phenomena or prodigies. They are not unrelated to any moral or spiritual sequence. They have a moral and spiritual purpose, a clear relation to surrounding circumstances. Unlike the vast majority of ethnic miracles, Christ's miracles have that moral and spiritual quality which differentiates them from physical prodigies. They are distinct revelations of God or of God's nature in relation to the universe and man. As in a less degree in all His miracles, so in a higher degree in the Resurrection, there is a union of physical and spiritual, such as is seen also wherever mind and life control matter and energy. Matter is here completely controlled, spiritualized, and such an event could scarcely have been imagined or invented. All miracles imagined or invented would have been little else than wonders. But Christ's miracles, with their spiritual and moral quality, are continuous with the

[1] *Divine Immanence*, chs. iv. and v., *The Gospel Miracles*.
[2] *The Miracles of the NT*.
[3] *Miracles and Modern Spiritualism*.

[1] O. Lodge, *Life and Matter*, p. 133 ff.; J. S. Haldane, *Mechanism, Life, and Personality* London, 1913, p. 60; cf. H. Bergson, *Creative Evolution*, Eng. tr., do., 1911, p. 13.

system of the universe as a whole. So again many alleged supernormal phenomena are not miracles; they do not show a direct moral, purposive action on the part of a divine power, but reveal unsuspected and unexplained human powers. If God directs the whole universe, miracles are in no sense a rectifying of His own mistakes. They are instances of the overcoming of evil and disorder in a universe where these exist and where evil may have been necessary to the world-process, a stage on the way to perfection. Yet that perfection is being brought about, and miracles are an instance of this, since they clearly show God's purpose, more clearly perhaps than the more quietly-working process. They show, as Lotze says, that God is so related to matter that it cannot resist Him at all. So Christ's healing miracles show that spirit and will are superior to the causes which produce disease. Thus in no sense is miracle *contra naturam*; rather is it an expression of divine action in ways which may contradict our ordinary experience, *i.e.* our real ignorance of the universe.

The unchanging nature of radium might have been regarded as an unalterable law; yet the lapse of time (it takes 2500 years for an atom of radium to change) would show that this was a mistaken view, a parable of our knowledge of the laws of the universe.

The divine will, acting normally in certain ways, may act in different ways, perhaps in our limited view contrary to these. One set of laws is put aside for the moment, just as man can transcend the physical order by his will. Yet order is not interrupted, for the whole order of nature—all that happens—is just the divine will to which, *e.g.*, a swift 'miraculous' process of healing may be as natural as a slower process, or the turning of water to wine as natural as the slower growth of the vine. In either case there is a quickening of a natural process, and yet to God that quickening may be perfectly normal. Does this take away the miraculous from what we call 'miracle'? In a sense it does, for we tend to draw too straight a line between natural and supernatural. All events, inasmuch as they express the divine will, are natural, yet they are supernatural in so far as they all end for us in mystery. What constitutes a miracle is its quality, its instant suggestion of divine power and goodness. Man's spiritual vision is clouded, and he does not always see these in the ordinary event, nor is that always the fullest revelation of God. All things speak of God, but some speak more clearly. Yet these are by no means abnormal; they do not occur on inadequate occasions, nor do they contradict the fundamental laws of experience. The reign of law is not set aside, for the ways in which miracle is brought about are still in accordance with law, even if the miracle happen but once.

Certain persons, for no very obvious reason, seem to possess supernormal powers, or these are manifested through them; others have genius; others, men of God, have spiritual gifts. What powers may not be open to one like Christ, in whom divine power existed and whose sinless will was in perfect harmony with God's? He claimed to possess divine power, and He said that He came to do the Father's will. Things were therefore natural to Him which might have been unnatural to another. Yet His miracles were in subordination to the moral miracle of His sinless personality, and therefore in harmony with it. Divine power and goodness overflowed, as it were, from Him upon nature and man. His miracles are perfect examples of the control of the material by the spiritual, and they prove that all force, all guidance, are in the last resort spiritual. Yet the real reason for following Him was Himself, not His signs. The power by which He wrought these was in Him because of what He was. It might be open to all who live upon the same plane, as He pointed out.

As has already been said, there is no evidence in Christ's miracles of the lawless breaking of a 'law of nature.' Rather is it as if existing forces were being directly influenced, whether neutralized or quickened, or as if a new force was working with a natural force to produce a result different from what the latter could produce. In the case of healing disease a slow process gives place to a swifter process. So in the calming of the sea a natural process is heightened. In either case there is the power of will. When walking on the sea, Christ must have exerted a power which witnessed to some law quite as much as the law which for the moment it displaced. When water was changed into wine, was this more marvellous *for Christ* than the transmutation of one element into another as proved possible by science?

In the case of feeding the multitudes analogy is more difficult to find. Were bodily needs forgotten through a miraculous mental exaltation, so that a sacramental partaking of a small portion of food sufficed? This does not account for the fragments that remained. We cannot trace the method, but our limited vision need not detract from its miraculous aspect. Those most concerned believed that a miracle had occurred, unless the texts are wholly fictitious.

In Christ it is not a question of divinity breaking through a humanity in acts which are superhuman, but of a constant superiority to humanity in one who is its perfect type. It is therefore no stranger that His actions should be more wonderful than those of other men than that His teaching or His sinless life should surpass theirs.

Apart from the general control or guidance of the universe, divine will may work through normal or supernormal actions, or may act directly in specific cases, for what are to us miraculous purposes. Speaking is a normal action, but where a man speaks under the influence of the Spirit there is inspiration. Healing by suggestion is supernormal, but, if the suggestion is aided by spiritual influences, there is a miraculous cure. Again, as in some of Christ's miracles, we trace more direct action upon material things. Such action may be regarded as supernatural because mysterious; yet to God it is natural. All action, human or divine, is part of an ascending series; we cannot say where the natural ends and the supernatural begins; what we can assert is that Christ's confidence in His power or in God's power working through Him never faltered. He intimates that, if men had faith enough, they could do even greater works. Have we yet sounded 'the abysmal depths of personality,' or used to the full the power of the divine spirit working with us?

16. Prayer.—The relation of miracle to prayer may be briefly touched on. If miracle is a special instance of divine control, then answer to prayer has a miraculous aspect. Human mind and will can control existing physical forces or overcome the laws which govern them. There is readjustment without catastrophe. To every single fact there are countless antecedents, and a little of less or more will produce a new result, as is seen, *e.g.*, by the different chemical products obtainable by even the slightest increase in the number of similar atoms combining with others to produce these. Man himself can produce new effects in the physical world. Must we deny this power to God? He can surely guide, deflect, or neutralize one force by another, or act directly upon matter and energy so that a new result will follow, subject, of course, to every limitation of reason and order. How little exercise of power on God's part would be necessary to cause rain in answer to prayer! Since man and man's actions and thoughts, hence also his prayers, are a part of the forces of the universe, when we do not pray, the result, even in the physical world, may be different from what it would have been had we prayed. Prayer is energy, and earnest prayer cannot be useless, even if its result is not just what man wants. If God's plan for the universe is so far conditioned by man's misuse of free will, how speedily will that plan be accomplished when man's will is at one with God's! It is His will that we pray, and every answer to prayer, as a direct manifestation of His will, is so far miraculous, and yet, like all miracle, quite natural. God foresees all that will happen in the universe; therefore He foresees whether we shall pray, and whether any particular prayer will be answered in one way or another. If the occurrence of certain things in God's plan depends on prayer, then we must pray. Are we then not free? Still we have the feeling of acting as free agents, and feeling is perhaps here truer than reason.

LITERATURE.—The following works for the most part deal exclusively with miracles. For others, patristic, scholastic, and modern, see references in the article. J. Bois, *Le Miracle moderne*, Paris, 1907; T. G. Bonney, *The Present Relations of Science and Religion*, London, 1913; A. B. Bruce, *The Miraculous Element in the Gospels*, do. 1886; G. Campbell, *A Dissertation on Miracles*, Edinburgh, 1823; C. G. Clarke, art. 'Wonders,' in *DCA* ii. 2041 ff.; W. F. Cobb, *Spiritual Healing*, London, 1914; E. O. Davies, *The Miracles of Jesus*, do. 1913; P. Dearmer, *Body and Soul*, do. 1909; H. Farmer, *Dissertation on Miracles*, do. 1771; P. Fiebig, *Antike Wundergeschichten zum Studium der Wunder des Neuen Testamentes*, Bonn, 1911; A. C. Headlam, *The Miracles of the NT*, London, 1914; D. Hume, 'Of Miracles,' in *Essays and Treatises on Several Subjects*, Edinburgh, 1804, *Essays*, ed. T. H. Green and T. H. Grose, London, 1907; J. R. Illingworth, *Divine Immanence*, do. 1898, *The Gospel Miracles*, do. 1915; H. Latham, *Pastor Pastorum*, Cambridge, 1891; Abbé Lecanu, *Dictionnaire des prophéties et des miracles*, in J. P. Migne, *Encyclopédie théologique*, ser. ii., vols. xxiv., xxv., Paris, 1844–66; W. E. H. Lecky, *History of Rationalism*, London, 1865; J. J. Lias, *Are Miracles Credible*[2]? do. 1890; Oliver Lodge, *Man and the Universe*, do. 1908; S. McComb, E. Worcester, and I. H. Coriat, *Religion and Medicine*, do. 1908; Conyers Middleton, 'Free Enquiry into the Miraculous Powers which are supposed to have subsisted in the Christian Church,' *Miscellaneous Works*[2], do. 1755; J. B. Mozley, *Eight Lectures on Miracles*, do. 1865; J. H. Newman, *Two Essays on Biblical and on Ecclesiastical Miracles*[3], do. 1873; H. Langhorne Orchard, *The Attitude of Science towards Miracles*, do. 1910; Blaise Pascal, *Pensées, Questions sur les Miracles, Œuvres*, Paris, 1758; O. Pfleiderer, *The Early Christian Conception of Christ*, Eng. tr., London, 1905; R. Reitzenstein, *Hellenistische Wundererzählungen*, Leipzig, 1906; C. A. Row, *The Supernatural in the NT*, London, 1875; P. Saintyves, *Le Discernement du miracle*, Paris, 1909; W. Sanday, *Bishop Gore's Challenge to Criticism*, London, 1914; T. B. Strong, *The Miraculous in Gospels and Creeds*, do. 1914; M. Carta Sturge, *The Truth and Error of Christian Science*, do. 1903; F. Temple, *The Relations between Religion and Science*, do. 1884; J. M. Thompson, *Miracles in the NT*, do. 1911; T. Trede, *Der Wunderglaube im Heidentum und in der alten Kirche*, Gotha, 1901; R. C. Trench, *Notes on the Miracles of our Lord*[2], London, 1847; A. R. Wallace, *Miracles and Modern Spiritualism*, do. 1896; O. Weinreich, *Antike Heilungswunder*, Giessen, 1909; J. Wendland, *Miracles and Christianity*, tr. H. R. Mackintosh, London, 1911.

J. A. MACCULLOCH.

MIRACLE-PLAYS, MYSTERIES, MORALITIES.

—**1. Introduction.**—As was indicated in the introduction to the art. DRAMA, the origin of the mediæval drama, like that of the Greek, is to be found in religious observances. It is true that from the earliest reigns of Norman kings in England secular pageants were common features of any day of special rejoicing; but these were not strictly dramatic in their nature, nor did they contribute to the essential development of the form. The true beginning of the long course which leads up to Shakespeare and Racine is found in the Churches; the most striking fact in the history of the mediæval drama is its evolution from the simplest germs in the responses of the liturgy into an elaborate new form without the influence of either antecedent or contemporary dramatic material. Though many steps and many dates in the history of the Miracles and Moralities are still to be discovered, and their due place to be assigned to many influences, it is possible to write a clear history of the drama in the Middle Ages from its origin in the antiphonal tropes of the liturgy to its final expression in the great Passion-plays, 'Mystères,' and 'Miracle-cycles.'

The probability of some survival of classical influence in the mediæval drama has led some writers to trace all possible ancient dramatic and mimetic traditions in the period between the closing of the theatres and circuses in the 6th cent. to the establishment of a developed liturgical drama in the 10th and 11th; but, notwithstanding the efforts of the modern Greek scholar K. N. Sathas (Ἱστορικὸν δοκίμιον περὶ τοῦ θεάτρου καὶ τῆς μουσικῆς τῶν Βυζαντινῶν, Venice, 1878) and his followers to found the mediæval religious drama on the ruins of the ancient Greek, preserved in Byzantium and carried to the west by the returning crusaders, it is the opinion of most scholars that no more can be said than that there was possibly a continuance of the mimetic tradition, kept alive by wandering, outlawed entertainers—a tradition that may have helped the development of the drama by aiding the survival of some feeling for dramatic form, and may later have had a part in the secularization of the religious drama. (For the Byzantine stage see K. Krumbacher, *Geschichte der byzantinischen Litteratur*[2], Munich, 1897, pp. 644–648, 746–749; for the views of Sathas, J. S. Tunison, *Dramatic Traditions of the Dark Ages*, Chicago, 1907; for the subject in general, Chambers, *The Mediæval Stage*, i. ch. i.)

2. The liturgical drama.—The antiphon, of Eastern origin, introduced into Italy by St. Ambrose, was the germ from which the mediæval drama developed. Certain antiphonal services had many dramatic possibilities, which more or less unconsciously began to take form in the tropes, or interpolations in the liturgical text for certain feast-days. The most important from the standpoint of dramatic history were the tropes of the Easter mass, the earliest dramatized form of which is the 'Quem quæritis.' This, assigned to about the year 900 and ascribed to the trope-writer Tutilo of St. Gall (Karl Young, 'The Origin of the Easter-Play,' in *Publications of the Modern Language Assoc. of America*, March 1914), seems to have developed into a considerable play as a trope of the introit for the day, and to have sent out branches which, combining with other ceremonies, such as the 'Visitatio sepulchri,' and other dramatic forms, such as the 'Prophetæ,' grew into the great Passion-plays and Miracle-cycles.

This earliest form is:

'Interrogatio.
Quem quaeritis in sepulchro, Christicolae?
Responsio.
Jesum Nazarenum crucifixum, o caelicolae.
Non est hic, surrexit sicut praedixerat;
ite, nuntiate quia surrexit de sepulchro.
Resurrexi.'

The last word, 'Resurrexi,' is the first word of the Easter introit. By textual accretions, partly by additions from the Vulgate, but more often by 'free composition,' and by the development of a dramatic setting (the 'sepulchrum') and truly dramatic personalities (the three Marys, the angel at the tomb, etc.), this trope grew into a well-developed though brief liturgical play (MS Brescia, 15th cent., quoted by Young), and attained a much larger development as a 'Visitatio sepulchri' at the end of Easter matins.

The altar served as the setting for the 'Quem quæritis' plays, as was natural, for it symbolized the tomb of Christ (Young, p. 45). This made easy the transition to the use of the 'Quem quæritis' as part of the 'Sepulchrum' ceremony at Easter matins (the 'Elevatio crucis' following the 'Adoratio crucis' and 'Depositio crucis' on Good Friday; the ceremonies were symbolical of the burial and resurrection of Christ). This second and dramatically more fruitful use of the 'Quem quæritis' grew by textual additions, such as the sequence 'Victimæ paschali,' and by additions of incident—first, details of the Biblical story (*e.g.*, the visit of the three Marys to the tomb, and of Peter and John); secondly, secular imaginative details (*e.g.*, the visit of the Marys to the 'unguentarius,' or dealer from whom they bought the necessary spices, a character who later became popular in the vernacular Passion-plays).

Though there was a considerable dramatic development of the 'Quem quæritis,' it remained strictly a liturgical drama; it was chanted, the parts were taken by churchmen, there was little real dialogue, and the setting was of the simplest. In certain late forms there are introduced motives that do not belong to the events of Easter morning, such as the kiss of peace accompanying the greeting 'Surrexit Christus,' or the 'Tollite portas' ceremony prescribed by the ritual for the dedication of a church. These point to the possibility of a development of the Easter play which, however, was not to take place in the 'Quem quæritis' proper. This matter will be considered in speaking of the Passion-play.

But the 'Quem quæritis' was not the only drama of Easter-week. The 'Peregrini,' attached to the vespers of Easter Monday, established in the 12th cent., was known in England, France, and Germany. The simplest form tells of the journey to Emmaus and the supper there (Petit de Julleville, *Les Mystères*, i. 67; Chambers, ii. 37). In others Mary Magdalene appears, or the Virgin and the other Marys greet the risen Christ; or a new scene is added of the incredulity of Thomas; or there is even a merging of a developed form of the 'Quem quæritis,' the 'Peregrini,' and the Easter morning ceremony of the 'Elevatio crucis.'

Parallel with the plays of the Resurrection, other liturgical plays developed as parts of the office of other feasts. The Christmas season was the most productive; but there were plays for Epiphany and certain saints' days, particularly that of St. Nicholas. Though evidence of their existence has been found, the plays for many occasions have entirely disappeared. A Christmas drama, the 'Pastores,' commemorating the visit of the shepherds, grew out of a Christmas introit-trope, modelled on the Easter 'Quem quæritis.' It begins 'Quem quaeritis in praesepe, pastores, dicite.' It is purely liturgical, very simple in form, and of infrequent occurrence in the MSS, but is of interest for its connexion with the ancient and still popular representations of the crib, or *crèche*, of the infant Christ (see BAMBINO), and for its influence on the more fruitful dramatic forms into which it was absorbed. The essence of the play is the visit of the shepherds, a crib with images of the Virgin and Child, the announcement of the birth of Christ by a boy 'in similitudine angeli,' the singing of the 'Gloria in excelsis' by the angels and a hymn by the shepherds, a dialogue between the shepherds and two priests 'quasi obstetrices,' the adoration of the shepherds, and a final hymn.

A more common form of Christmas drama was the 'Stella,' a play of the visit of the Magi, originally consisting of antiphons and simple prose dialogue, representing the following of the star, the visit to the Infant, the offering of gifts, and the warning to the Magi (Creizenach, *Geschichte des neueren Dramas*, i. 60; Chambers, ii. 45; Petit de Julleville, i. 51; texts in du Méril, *Origines latines*, and in Coussemaker, *Drames liturgiques*). The simplest and probably the earliest examples are from Rouen and Limoges. This form of liturgical play developed early. Dates are uncertain, but MSS of the late 11th cent. have the play in a well-developed form. As the Easter 'Quem quæritis' centred about the 'Sepulchrum' and that of Christmas about the 'Præsepe,' the 'Stella' had as its starting-point the star. A gilt star, the points sometimes holding candles, was lowered from a hole in the ceiling or held up by an assistant. Like the Nativity plays, the 'Stella' developed partly from dumb show, and the simpler forms continued parallel with the expanded forms and outlived them.

The dozen or so complete extant versions of the play vary considerably. The drama developed by the representation, in action instead of narrative, of the visit to Jerusalem, by the addition of various scenes in which Herod plays a part, as, *e.g.*, his anger at the escape of the Magi and his order for the massacre of the innocents, and even the actual representation of the massacre, and finally the lament of Rachel, which had received independent dramatic treatment. As Chambers puts it, 'the absorption of the motives proper to other feasts of the Twelve Nights into the Epiphany play has clearly begun' (ii. 48). This absorption was to result in certain larger and more complex plays made up by the joining of the 'Pastores,' the 'Stella,' and the 'Rachel.' It is only in view of the result from this fusion and of the expansion of certain parts that the 'Stella' is of great importance for the later history of the drama. The part of Herod grew by expansion and emphasis even to take the first place in the English Corpus Christi cycles.

More important for the future of the mediæval drama than any of the forms thus far considered was the 'Prophetæ,' which had a curious origin, first studied by Sepet (*Les Prophètes du Christ*). It was based on the apocryphal *Sermo contra Judæos* attributed in the Middle Ages to St. Augustine, but really of later origin, and used in many churches as a lesson in the Christmas offices. In the passage so employed, the author invokes thirteen witnesses to the divine mission of Christ and calls upon them to predict His coming. The prophets invoked are Isaiah, Jeremiah, Daniel, Moses, David, Habakkuk, Simeon, Zacharias, Elisabeth, John the Baptist, Vergil, Nebuchadrezzar, and the Sibyl. The dramatic growth of this sermon had certainly begun by the 11th century. In the earliest forms the play follows the sermon closely, but is written in verse. Classical language and even direct quotations from the *Eclogues* appear in the prophecies of Vergil and the Sibyl. In later examples from Laon and Rouen the dialogue is expanded, the 'precentor' is replaced by two 'appellatores' or 'vocatores,' and Balaam is added to the prophets. More remarkable is the little added drama of Balaam and his ass, which has been considered by many writers the origin of the notorious Feast of the Ass, but which is perhaps more probably a reaction from the disturbing festival. In the Rouen text the part of Nebuchadrezzar is also expanded into a miniature play: Shadrach, Meshach, and Abed-nego refuse to worship the image, are cast into the fiery furnace, and escape all harm, whereupon the king testifies to the might of the coming Saviour.

It will be seen that at this stage of development the 'Prophetæ' necessitated a much more complex setting than was usual with liturgical drama—the throne of the precentor, the fiery furnace, distinct costumes (described in the rubrics), Balaam's ass. This was a beginning of the complexity that was to characterize the great Miracles.

This complexity and the fusion alluded to above may be seen in a Latin play preserved in a 13th cent. MS (Royal Library, Munich; text in du Méril). It is a combination of most of the Christmas dramatic forms. St. Augustine sits with the prophets at his right, the chief of the synagogue and the Jews at his left. The prophets foretell the Messiah; the head of the synagogue is angered at their blasphemies. A new character, the 'bishop of the children,' interposes the suggestion that St. Augustine shall be questioned. The Rabbi in anachronistic and pedantic words argues the impossibility of the Virgin-birth, and St. Augustine answers. The argument is taken up by the choirs of prophets and Jews, the one singing 'Res miranda,' the other 'Res neganda.' So far the play is an expanded 'Prophetæ,' still mostly liturgical in feeling and form. The prophets take their places in the church, and a play of the Annunciation begins abruptly. This part is brief. The Scriptural dialogue between the Virgin and the angel is followed by the visit of Elisabeth. The next direction is that Mary 'vadat in lectum suum . . . et pariat filium.' The choir hails His coming, and immediately the 'Stella' begins. A star shines forth, the three kings follow it, and appear before Herod; an angel announces the coming of Christ to the shepherds (the 'Pastores' element). The devil hints that the angel has deceived them, but they are convinced by the chanting of the 'Gloria in excelsis' by a heavenly choir; they seek the cradle and worship Christ; they meet the Magi bearing gifts. The Magi are warned not to return to Herod, who orders the killing of the innocents. The mothers lament their lost children (the 'Rachel' element); Herod falls dead, and is seized by demons. An angel sends Joseph into Egypt. The king of Egypt advances, accompanied by a choir singing 'choses fort profanes.' The Holy Family arrives in Egypt; the idols fall, and the priests, unable to restore them, are converted. Finally the choir chants a malediction against Herod and the Jews. The last part is free and individual in composition. Petit de Julleville thinks it unlikely that it was played in church (because of the 'episcopus puerorum'), and that more likely it was given in a monastery school.

As this play well represents the form attained by the liturgical drama through the combination of types and free composition, certain plays founded on the stories of Daniel and Lazarus represent another development—the expansion of single scenes in the older plays into independent dramas. Most interesting, because the first liturgical play attributed to a definite author, is the 'Daniel' of Hilarius, a cosmopolitan Goliardic scholar, disciple of Abelard, who flourished in the first half of the 12th cent. (text in J. J. Champollion-Figeac, *Hilarii versus et ludi*, Paris, 1838, and in du Méril). The 'Historia de Daniel representanda' opens with the feast of Belshazzar; the mystic words appear, and Daniel interprets them; Darius enters Babylon with his army and kills Belshazzar; Daniel appears at court, refuses to worship the king, and is thrown to the lions; the angel brings Habakkuk to him; Daniel is again in favour. The play is expanded by choruses in honour of the various personages, 'conductus Danielis,' 'conductus regine,' etc. The chant to Daniel (as also in the similar play from Beauvais) is a hymn in honour of the birth of Christ. This, as well as the rubrics, indicates the connexion of the play with the liturgy; but the note at the end, 'This done, if the play has been given at matins, let Daniel sing the Te Deum, if at vespers the Magnificat,' indicates that it was not a regular part of the office. In this partial detachment from the liturgy we see the beginnings of that development which was to take the drama entirely out of the hands of the clergy.

3. The secularization of the drama.—The indications of a tendency to make the liturgical drama more popular that we have seen in the expansion of certain themes in the 'Prophetæ,' in the freer and more poetical composition of many of the later liturgical plays, in their comparatively independent position in relation to the Church offices, are emphasized by the gradual change in the language, spirit, and setting of the plays, as they progressed towards that final and almost complete secularization which should take them out of the Church and out of the control of the clergy, and make them great popular spectacles rather than expositions of Christian faith. The degrees of popularization were innumerable. In the 15th cent., even when the purpose was edification, whole scenes were often frankly amusing and vulgar, with no religious significance whatever—*e.g.*, in the scene or playlet of Mak and the shepherds in the Towneley cycle, and in the comic scenes of the German Passion-plays.

The vernacular came by slow degrees to replace Latin. At first the two languages appear side by side; in the earliest examples the local speech appears only in refrains or in the lines of a few minor characters, or in the less impressive passages. But there is no discoverable rule; the same character may speak Latin in one passage, French in another. One of the earliest cases of the two languages used together is the 'Sponsus,' a 12th cent. play of the wise and foolish virgins from Limoges (text in *Romania*, xxii. [1893]; du Méril). Here a considerable part is in the 'langue d'oc'; the angel who announces the coming of the bridegroom speaks only French, the virgins both languages. The refrains are in French. The final words in which Christ condemns the foolish virgins are first Latin and then French, ending thus, perhaps to make the lesson clear and impressive to the congregation:

'Amen dico
Vos ignosco,
Nam caretis lumine;
Quod qui perdunt [MS pergunt]
Procul pergunt
Hujus aulae limine.
Alet, chaitivas! alet, malaureas!
A tot jors mais vos penas livreas;
En efern ora seret meneias.'

Occasionally, as in the 'St. Nicholas' of Hilarius, the vernacular is found only in the refrains. In other plays it is a translation of the preceding Latin lines—an indication of the reason for the use of the common tongue—as in the 12th cent. 'Adam' (text from Tours, first ed. by V. Luzarche, Tours, 1854; K. Bartsch, *Chrestomathie de l'ancien français*[4], Leipzig, 1880), and in many German plays. Latin and the vernacular were even mingled in the lines, as in the Beauvais 'Daniel' (text in Coussemaker, no. iv.):

'Vir propheta Dei, Daniel, vien al Roi,
Veni, desiderat parler à toi,' etc.

Some late dramas are wholly in the vernacular, except for refrains or certain impressive passages.

In France particularly the development of the drama was marked by the adoption of a more varied versification. The earliest liturgical plays were entirely in prose, the later ones mostly in verse.

In these later forms 'the versification is rather complicated, very varied; almost all are written in stanzas. But these stanzas differ in the number of lines and in metre; the lines are syllabic, but vary in length from four syllables to ten' (Petit de Julleville, i. 23).

Dactylic hexameters also are used, sometimes leonine, as in the lament of Rachel in the Fleury 'Interfectio puerorum' (cf. Petit de Julleville, i. 49; text in du Méril; MS in Orléans Library):

'O dolor! O patrum mutataque gaudia matrum!'

Occasionally lines are quoted or imitated from the classics; *e.g.*,

'Quae rerum novitas aut quae vos causa subegit
Ignotas temptare vias? Quo tenditis ergo?
Quod genus? Unde domo? Pacemne huc fertis, an arma?'
(cf. *Æn.* viii. 112-114).

As important as this change in language is the

gradual secularization of the spirit of the plays. The last part of the composite Munich play referred to above will illustrate this point. Though written in Latin, one part is an original secular poem in praise of spring, filled with pagan allusions and with no liturgical or Biblical connotation. The introduction of the comic element and of the melodramatic in the passages relating to Balaam's ass and Herod points to an equally strong secular influence, one that was to lead to some of the most striking and unfortunate developments of the great Miracles and even of the Passion-plays of the 15th century. We must not make the mistake of ascribing all the crude humour and vulgarity of Miracles to a naive and simple taste for such things; as Petit de Julleville points out, even in plays as early as those of Hilarius a conscious vulgarization has begun, a conscious appeal to an audience rather than a congregation, and the author's intention is even satirical.

The secular tendency which perhaps had most to do with the final almost complete secularization of the mediæval drama was the elaboration of the setting required by the constantly increasing length and complexity of the plays; for this development brought about the transference of the plays to the open (first the churchyard or square in front of the church, then the main square of the town, or several places at once), and, still more important, gradually brought the plays under the control of the laity. It is a long way from the simple 'sepulchrum' or 'præsepe,' the two chanted parts, the lack of appropriate costume, of the 'Quem quæritis' to the varied setting, the many characters, the costumes of the 'Conversio Pauli' (Petit de Julleville, i. 69; text from Fleury MS, mentioned above, in du Méril, and in Coussemaker, no. xiii.) with its several 'sedes' for Saul, Judas, etc., its two scenes, Jerusalem and Damascus, its armed men, and its 'lectus' for Ananias, or the Munich 'Prophetæ' described above, with its 'sedes' for the prophets, its 'lectus' for the Virgin, its shining star, its mouth of hell, its many characters. Henceforth the change in setting was one of degree rather than of kind; the elaboration merely followed the increasing complexity of the plays as they added one incident after another. Within the church, the crucifix, the altar, the 'sepulchrum,' the rood-loft (representing heaven), and the crypt furnished the chief accessaries of the play. To these, which were in the sanctuary and choir, were probably added in the more elaborate plays 'sedes,' 'domus,' and 'loca' extending down the nave. This natural arrangement was apparently followed when the drama left the church, as in the 12th cent. Norman 'Resurrectio.' Chambers (ii. 83) suggests such an arrangement of the 'lius,' 'mansions,' and 'estals' required by the prologue, following the analogy of a Donaueschingen Passion-play of the 16th cent., the plan of which is extant (given in Froning, *Das Drama des Mittelalters*, p. 277). The prologue gives the order of the required sets: the crucifix, the monument ('sepulchrum'), the gaol, heaven, hell, Emmaus, Galilee, and six 'estals' or 'sedes.' The only other extant French religious play of the same period, the 'Adam,' shows even better how far the drama had outgrown the simplicity of the 'Quem quæritis.' The Latin rubrics indicate not only a complex setting, but great care in stage management, even extending to the gestures and voice of the actors.

For instance: 'Let there be built a paradise in a higher place; around it let there be draperies of silk. . . . There shall be sweet flowers and foliage; various trees from which shall hang fruits. . . . Then the Saviour shall arrive, clothed in a dalmatic; before him shall be placed Adam and Eve, Adam in a red tunic, Eve in a woman's white robe and a veil of white silk' (Chambers, ii. 80).

The rubrics mention not only the costumes for all the characters, and the localities—paradise, hell, a cultivated field—but also 'properties'—a spade, a rake, chains for the devils to use, cauldrons for them to beat upon, flames.

The development of the liturgical drama was practically complete by the 13th century. Thereafter the growth was mainly outside the church, secular and more vernacular, much more rapid and national. The liturgical drama was much the same in different countries, but the vernacular religious plays took on national characteristics in the 14th cent.; so that thenceforth, to be understood with any clearness, the special literary types that developed must be studied by countries. Furthermore, the influence of particular authors and of particular methods of representation makes itself felt.

4. England.—The early dramatic history of England is difficult to trace, for much the larger number of plays have been destroyed. The development of the liturgical drama in England must be partly guessed at from that of France. Only the slightest indications of what it originally was are extant. The earliest dramatic piece is the 'Quem quæritis' from the Winchester troper dating probably from about 979 (text in W. H. Frere, *The Winchester Troper*, London, 1894). This is not nearly so simple as the St. Gall 'Quem quæritis' mentioned above. More interesting is the very full account of the 'Quem quæritis' ceremony in Bishop Ethelwold of Winchester's *Concordia regularis*, which probably dates from 965 to 975 (Chambers, ii. 14, 306; text in *Anglia*, xiii. [1891] 365). This includes a simple trope not much more elaborate than the St. Gall one. Of it, however, Chambers (ii. 15) says:

'The liberal scenario of the *Concordia regularis* makes plain the change which has come about in the "Quem quæritis" since it was first sung by alternating half-choirs as an introit-trope. Dialogued chant and mimetic action have come together, and the first liturgical drama is, in all its essentials, complete.'

The only other extant English text of the liturgical period is a 14th cent. 'Quem quæritis' from Dublin. But church inventories, account-books, and statutes indicate the existence of the 'Pastores,' 'Peregrini,' 'Resurrectio,' 'Stella,' 'Prophetæ,' etc., at a number of places, including York, Lichfield, Salisbury, and Lincoln; and William Fitzstephen, writing of the late 12th cent. in London, records

'repraesentationes miraculorum quae sancti confessores operati sunt, seu repraesentationes passionum quibus claruit constantia martyrum' (*Vita S. Thomæ*, quoted by J. P. Collier, *History of English Dramatic Poetry*², London, 1879, i. 11).

Of a Beverley 'Resurrectio' (*c.* 1220) the (bilingual) text of only one actor's part remains. So little do we know of this early period that it cannot be decided whether the liturgical drama passed directly from Latin to English, or whether there intervened a Norman-French period.

The full development of the English Miracle-play came in the 14th cent., and during the next two centuries and more it can be studied more clearly from extant texts. Whether or not the English drama received a special impulse from the establishment of the Corpus Christi festival in 1311, the most characteristic English dramatic form, the Corpus Christi processional cycles, were founded soon after that date. The Chester plays were probably given first in 1328. The dates of the establishment of the other cycles are not known, but references to them are found as follows: Beverley, 1377; York, 1378; Coventry, 1392. In 1350 there is a reference to a 'ludus filiorum Israelis' at Cambridge. From this time on there was the greatest activity throughout the country.

It will be impossible to analyze at all adequately even the chief monuments of the period under consideration; the four great Corpus Christi cycles and the minor instances of dramatic activity can hardly be mentioned. Generally the English Miracle-plays were represented in separate scenes, each by a different trade-gild, on its own 'pageant'—

'a high scafolde with two rowmes, a higher and a lower, upon four wheeles. In the lower they apparelled them selves, and in the higher rowme they played. . . . They begane first at the abay gates, and when the firste pagiante was played it was wheeled to the highe crosse before the mayor, and so to every streete . . . to se which playes was greate resorte, and also scafoldes and stages made in the streetes in those places where they determined to playe theire pagiantes' (Archdeacon Rogers' description of a play at Chester, 1594, quoted by Pollard, *English Miracle Plays*, p. xxv).

Though the plays were given by the gilds, they were under the direction of the town council, which made the strictest rules concerning the manner, thoroughness, and promptness of the performance—*e.g.*, at York (1415):

'And all maner of craftsmen yat bringeth furthe ther pageantez in order and course by good players, well arrayed and openly spekyng, upon payn of lesyng of C.*s*, to be paide to the chambre without any pardon' (*York Plays*, ed. Lucy Toulmin Smith, p. xxxiv).

The plays of the cycle were not the work of one author, but an 'organic growth.' The number of gilds acting varied; hence there was also a variety in the number of plays or scenes. The play for each gild was often slight in subject—*e.g.*, 'Adam and Eve, an angel with a spade and a distaff assigning them to work,' played by the armourers at York. An outline of the subjects of the York cycle (probably composed towards the middle of the 14th cent.) will give an idea of the wide range of the plays:

the Creation, the Temptation, the Fall, Noah and the Ark, the Sacrifice of Isaac, Moses in the Wilderness, the Prophecies of Christ, the Annunciation, the Birth of Christ, the Shepherds, the Magi, the Slaughter of the Innocents, Christ in the Temple, the Temptation, the Woman taken in Adultery, the Raising of Lazarus, Judas, the Last Supper, the Crucifixion, the Harrowing of Hell, the Resurrection.

Although this list is incomplete, we can see in it all the elements that we have found in the Continental liturgical plays, and may be permitted to suppose that the Miracle-cycles developed by the extension and amalgamation of liturgical forms such as the 'Prophetæ,' the 'Stella,' the 'Pastores.' Though, like their French and German contemporaries, the authors allowed themselves considerable freedom in expanding the Biblical text (as, *e.g.*, in the part of Herod), yet the characters most freely drawn are almost exclusively those of persons to whom neither Scripture nor legend ascribes either name or individuality. Such personages as Cain's 'garcio,' or servant, Noah's wife, the shepherds, are introduced for the sake of relief—often inappropriately, it seems to us, as in the Crucifixion scene.

'It is to this desire for dramatic relief that we owe the story of Mak and his sheep-stealing in the Coventry cycle—our first English comedy' (Pollard, p. xli).

In the Coventry cycle there are various characters that link the Miracle with the Morality, the dramatic form more characteristic of the later years of the pre-Elizabethan drama. Such characters appear as Death, Veritas, Misericordia, Pax. The earliest known English Morality is lost. It was a 14th cent. play,

'setting forth the goodness of the Lord's Prayer . . . in which play all manner of vices and sins were held up to scorn, and the virtues were held up to praise' (J. Toulmin Smith, *English Gilds*, London, 1870, p. 137).

The earliest Morality that has survived is 'The Castle of Perseverance.'

Its purpose was 'to trace the spiritual history of *Humanum Genus* . . . from the day of his birth to his appearance at the Judgment Seat of God, to personify the foes by whom his pathway is beset, the Guardian Angel by whose help he resists them, and the ordinances of Confession and Penance by which he is strengthened in his conflict' (Pollard, p. xlvi).

The play is wordy but impressive; it has logical development and unity of purpose. The stage directions show that it was elaborately presented. The most famous morality is 'Everyman,' composed in the 15th cent.; it is thoroughly dramatic in language and treatment.

The great Moralities were followed by shorter ones dealing with narrower subjects—'didactic interludes,' Pollard calls them. From these are derived most of the common notions regarding Moralities. One of the earliest is 'Hycke Scorner.' Some are written in praise of religion, others in praise of learning (*e.g.*, the 'Interlude of the Four Elements'). Some of the later interludes are real plays, in the modern sense—*e.g.*, 'A New and Pleasant Enterlude; intituled the Marriage of Witte and Science,' licensed 1569–70. The amusing lines, the act-division, and the characterization make the play modern rather than mediæval. John Heywood's plays illustrate still better the change that was taking place in dramatic art—a change which was to lead rapidly to the splendid Elizabethan drama.

5. **France.**—The development of the liturgical drama outlined above carried us into the 12th century. In France there are few plays known of the 12th and 13th centuries, the period when the drama became thoroughly secularized. Of the 12th cent. two plays are known, Jean Bodel's 'Jeu de Saint Nicolas' and Rutebeuf's 'Miracle de Théophile.' In the 14th cent. the French drama first acquired its national character. Petit de Julleville says that forty-three plays of the period are extant, all except one being 'Miracles de Notre Dame.' Here we have a form not found generally in other countries. That there must have been other forms of plays in this century is certain; the derivation of the dramas of the 15th cent. from those of the 12th and 13th makes this clear. Forty of the plays of the Virgin are in one MS in the Bibliothèque Nationale. These plays, however they vary in story and in source, all have as a central theme a miraculous event brought about by the intervention of the Virgin—always a mechanical and unexpected intervention. In other respects—in style, stage-management, songs—the plays are so similar as to make them seem, if not the work of one author, at least the répertoire of one company; and this is the more likely as such plays were performed by societies, called 'Puys,' formed for the purpose.

In the 15th cent. for the first time the word 'Mystère' appears as a dramatic term, and in this century it meant a representation of either Biblical story or the lives of saints. The NT was more used than the OT, for, as we have seen, the interest of the Middle Ages in the OT was chiefly in the foreshadowing of the redemption of mankind. This view accounts for the inequality and lack of dramatic feeling in the use of OT story. Furthermore, the mediæval drama was not original; it did not build up a play from a situation as did Corneille or Racine, but transcribed Scriptural narrative regardless of dramatic effect.

Though the French 'Mystères' seldom approach the completeness of the English cycles, they are often cyclical in form and extremely long. The famous 'Passion' of Arnoud Gretan is about 65,000 lines, a length attained not merely by prolixity but by following the career of each of the apostles after the Crucifixion. The French Passion-plays, the most notable of the 'Mystères,' centred, of course, around the Passion, which they developed in a painfully realistic manner; but they were extended at the pleasure of the author by the addition of any scenes preceding or following the main event. The Mysteries based on the legends of the saints, also popular in this period, had often a local interest.

'Many were composed for a certain province, city, or brotherhood, in order to celebrate a patron saint, to commend a relic, or to give sanction to a pilgrimage' (Petit de Julleville, i. 230).

6. Germany.—The early texts are scarce in Germany, but from those that are extant it appears that the liturgical play had much the same history as in other countries, and that the transition from the Latin to the vernacular took place in the same manner. As early as the 12th cent. the Tegernsee 'Anti-christus' (text in Froning, p. 206), though written in Latin, has several secular characteristics: an ambitious plan, allegorical figures, and particularly a political motive, for it is 'a subtle vindication, on the one hand, of the Empire against the Papacy, on the other of the "rex Teutonicorum" against the "rex Francorum"' (Chambers, ii. 64). In the 14th and 15th centuries the religious drama flourished in Germany, its most characteristic form being the Passion-play, of which numerous texts survive. There were also some cycles, such as those for Corpus Christi from Swabia (15th cent.). The Passion, which came in the 14th and 15th centuries to be the chief theme of the religious drama in France and Germany, had seldom been represented in the liturgical drama. The nearest approach to a Passion-play was found in the dialogued versions of the 'Planctus Mariæ.' The earliest Passions seem to have been in Italy (Siena, *c.* 1200; Padua, 1244). The earliest text is German from Benediktbeuern. Like other mediæval dramatic forms, the Passion-play grew by additions and by amalgamation with other forms, either 'prefigurations' of Christ or events following His Passion. By the 14th cent. the form was well developed, but its main period in Germany was from 1400 to 1515. Great 'Passions' were played at Frankfort, Alsfeld, Friedberg, and other towns. Some, as at Eger and Donaueschingen, were cyclical in extent.

7. Modern survivals.—Traces of mediæval dramatic custom can be found here and there in Europe to the present day. In general the survivals are no more than dumb show like the popular *crèche*, or representation of the infant Christ at Christmas, which is, however, rather a reversion to the ceremony from which the Christmas play was derived than a survival of the play. Most notable in this way are the representations of the Passion-play that have been either kept alive in out-of-the-way places or revived, most famous among them being that of Oberammergau. The first mention of it is in 1633, and the oldest text, dating from about 1600, contains traces of two earlier texts (K. Trautmann, *Oberammergau und sein Passionsspiel*, Bamberg, 1890). In 1662 the text was altered by the weaving into it of the version of Sebastian Wild, the Augsburg Meistersinger, and parts of that of Johann Aelbel. In the middle of the 18th cent. it was further remodelled by the Benedictine Rosner after the model of the Jesuit drama, and in 1780 Rosner's bombastic version was simplified by Knipfelberger. Its present simple and dignified form is the work of two authors, P. O. Weiss and M. Daisenberger. The play is given every ten years, in pursuance of the original vow on deliverance from pestilence. Other versions of the Passion-play have been performed in recent times at Brixlegg and Vorderthiersee in the Tyrol and at Höritz in southern Bohemia (A. Hauffen, *Ueber das Höritzer Passionsspiel*, Prague, 1894). Representations of this kind occur to this day in southern Italy (T. Trede, *Das geistliche Schauspiel in Süditalien*, Berlin, 1885).

LITERATURE.—i. GENERAL.—W. Creizenach, *Geschichte des neueren Dramas*, Halle, 1893 ff.; E. K. Chambers, *The Mediæval Stage*, 2 vols., Oxford, 1903; bibliography in Chambers, ii. p. xiii ff., and in F. H. Stoddard, *References for Students of Miracle Plays and Mysteries*, New York, 1887; lists of texts in Chambers, ii. 407-461, and Petit de Julleville, *op. cit. infra*, ii.

ii. LITURGICAL PLAYS.—Léon Gautier, *Histoire de la poésie liturgique au moyen âge*, vol. i., 'Les Tropes,' Paris, 1886; C. E. H. de Coussemaker, *Drames liturgiques du moyen âge*, Rennes, 1860; Carl Lange, *Die lateinischen Osterfeiern*, Munich, 1887; E. du Méril, *Origines latines du théâtre moderne*², Paris, 1896; M. Sepet, *Les Prophètes du Christ*, do. 1878, *Origines catholiques du théâtre moderne*, do. 1901.

iii. ENGLAND.—A. W. Pollard, *English Miracle Plays*, Oxford, 1890; K. L. Bates, *The English Religious Drama*, New York, 1893; C. Davidson, *English Mystery Plays*, New Haven, 1892; texts, *The Chester Plays*, re-ed. H. Deimling, London, 1893; *The Digby Plays*², ed. F. J. Furnivall, do. 1896; *Ludus Coventriæ*, ed. J. O. Halliwell, do. 1841; *Towneley Plays*, re-ed. G. England and A. W. Pollard, do. 1897; *York Plays*, ed. Lucy Toulmin Smith, Oxford, 1885.

iv. FRANCE.—G. Paris and U. Robert, *Miracles de Nostre-Dame*, 8 vols., Paris, 1876–93; L. Petit de Julleville, *Histoire du théâtre en France: les Mystères*, 2 vols., do. 1880.

v. GERMANY.—R. Froning, *Das Drama des Mittelalters*, Stuttgart, 1891; L. Wirth, *Oster- und Passionsspiele bis zum 16ten Jahrhundert*, Halle, 1889; J. E. Wackernell, *Altdeutsche Passionsspiele aus Tirol*, Graz, 1897; E. Wilken, *Geschichte der geistlichen Spiele in Deutschland*, Göttingen, 1872; G. Milchsack, *Die Oster- und Passionsspiele*, Wolfenbüttel, 1880.

vi. ITALY.—F. Torraca, *Il Teatro italiano dei secoli XIII, XIV, e XV*, Florence, 1885; A. d'Ancona, *Origini del teatro italiano*², Turin, 1891, *Sacre Rappresentazioni dei secoli XIV, XV, e XVI*, Florence, 1872; A. Lumini, *Le Sacre Rappresentazioni italiane*, Palermo, 1877.

A. I. DU P. COLEMAN and A. D. COMPTON.

MIRROR.—The invention of the mirror[1] seems to coincide with the beginnings of the higher civilization, following upon the institution of metallurgy. It is clearly an instance of adaptation of the polished reflecting surface of metals. The Egyptian mirror apparently set the mode for all subsequent developments of the instrument, at least in the Western world.

1. Mirrors of the ancients.—These were almost invariably hand-mirrors for ladies' toilette purposes. The Egyptian were made of bronze (not brass, as often stated), or similar mixed metal. From six to eight inches in diameter, they were elliptical in shape, with the long axis at right angles to the handle, which also served as a stand. The polish was extraordinarily fine, and in some cases still remains.[2]

Mirrors are not mentioned in Homer, but were used in classical Greek times, and borrowed by Rome. Few Greek mirrors are extant, but their shape suggests derivation from Egypt, as does that of the Roman mirror from Greece. Both Greek and Roman artificers preferred the absolutely circular form, with the handle as in the Egyptian original. They were usually made of bronze, with 20 to 30 per cent of tin; some specimens are silver or silver-plated. The Romans developed the box-mirror, consisting of two circular disks joined by a hinge. At the back of Greek and Roman mirrors embossed work was usual.[3] The most numerous collections are from Etruria. The Etruscans were sedulous imitators of Greek art, and much of their work on mirror-backs is interesting and intelligent, though lacking the fineness of Greek technique. Pliny notes the manufacture of glass mirrors backed with tinfoil at Sidon,[4] but the invention did not succeed, and had to be repeated in the Middle Ages. The Romans made large mirrors also, similar to the modern cheval-glasses, but fixed in the walls of rooms, and working up and down like a window-sash.[5] The mirror-case was especially developed

[1] The word is derived from Lat. *miratorium* (*mirari*) (*OED*, *s.v.*). Similar formations are found in Skr. *darpaṇa*, 'mirror'; Gr. δρωπάζω, δρώπτω, 'see'; Pers. *āyīnah*, Baluchi *ādēnk*, 'mirror'; Av. *dī*, 'see'; O.H. Germ. *spiagal*, Germ. *Spiegel*, 'mirror'; Lat. *speculum*; O. Ch. Slav. *zrŭcalo*, 'mirror,' *pozrŭcati*, 'see.' The mirror is also connected with the shadow—O.H. Germ. *scûkar*, 'mirror,' *scû*, 'shadow'; O. Ir. *scathán*, 'mirror,' *scáth*, 'shadow'; O. Ir. *scaterc*, 'mirror,' for **scáth-derc*, 'shadow-seeing' (C. C. Uhlenbeck, *Kurzgefasstes etymol. Wörterb. der altind. Sprache*, Amsterdam, 1899, p. 122; W. Geiger, *ABAW*, 1 Cl. xix. i. [1890] 113; O. Schrader, *Reallex. der indogerm. Altertumskunde*, Strassburg, 1901, p. 784). Here also belong Heb. מַרְאָה, 'mirror,' רָאָה, 'see.'

[2] J. G. Wilkinson, *Manners and Customs of the Ancient Egyptians*², London, 1878, ii. 350.

[3] W. Wroth, in Smith's *Dict. of Gr. and Rom. Antiquities*³, *s.v.* 'Speculum' (κάτοπτρον [class.], ἔσοπτρον, ἔνοπτρον).

[4] *HN* xxxvi. 26 (193); one was found at San Remo.

[5] J. H. Freese, in *EBr*¹¹, *s.v.*

by artists. Metal mirrors were known in northern India by the Christian era,[1] and they were used to some extent by the Central American peoples,[2] while the Hebrews were familiar with them at an early period for women's use.[3] In Greek art Aphrodite is sometimes represented as holding a mirror; and in the Indian marriage ritual a mirror is placed in the left hand of the bride to enable her to dress her hair.[4] A mirror and a comb are not infrequently found on Scottish sepulchral monuments of the early mediæval period, but their precise signification is still uncertain.[5]

2. Mediæval mirrors.—The mirror-case continued to be popular among the rich, but the mirror itself became smaller, and was usually carried on the person.

'Probably the largest mirror known in the Middle Ages did not exceed the size of a plate.'[6]

The circular shape was retained.

'The reflecting surface was usually of polished steel or other metal, and steel mirrors were still in use in the sixteenth century.' There is a reference to a 'round "looking-glass" of Catherine of Aragon, which was probably a polished metal surface with a sheet of glass over it. An arrangement of this sort had been employed since the thirteenth century, and in the inventories of the Dukes of Burgundy, dating from the fifteenth century, we hear of the *Verre à mirer*, evidently a looking-glass.'[7]

This method is a noteworthy, but futile, attempt at a combination of metal and glass.

'Considering the great quantity of glass manufactured for windows from the thirteenth century onward, it would have been curious if the idea of employing a substance admitting of so high a polish had not suggested itself to the mirror-makers of the day. But until a really satisfactory metallic backing was discovered, the advantage of a looking-glass over a steel mirror would be slight, and this fact may account for the persistence of the latter for domestic use down to so late a period. The amalgam of mercury and tin which gives the modern looking-glass its efficiency was not known before the sixteenth century.'[8]

A final improvement was effected in the middle of the 19th cent. by the French invention of plate-glass. Backing for glass was known in the 13th cent., and in the 14th there was a gild of glass-mirror-makers in Nüremberg, but it was first in Venice that mirror-making acquired commercial importance.[9]

The mirror naturally has lent itself to the production of curiosities, mostly the result of experimentation. The effects of concave and convex surfaces seem to have been known at an early time in both the East and the West. The 'magic mirror' of China and Japan reflects on a screen an image of its back.[10] In mediæval Europe small spherical glass mirrors were known as *Ochsenaugen*. The use of reflectors to produce light and heat was early discovered, as by the Greeks and Central Americans.[11] Mirror-writing is often practised by ambidextrous persons, as by Leonardo, and it also occurs pathologically in forms of aphasia.

3. Superstitions connected with the mirror.—The property of reflecting images naturally inspires wonder, and thus tends to produce superstitious beliefs and practices. Most of these are connected with the common idea that the reflexion of a person is his soul.

'A savage who had been made to look into a mirror exclaimed, "I gaze into the world of spirits!" One of Darwin's children, at nine months old, turned to the looking-glass on hearing his name called.'[12]

These two cases illustrate the connexion between soul, self, and consciousness. The philosophy of Hinduism was fond of mirror-analogies when discussing this connexion.

'The person . . . that is seen in the eye, that is the Self. . . . This is *Brahman*.'[1] 'The person that is in the mirror, on him I meditate.' 'I meditate on him as the likeness. Whoso meditates on him thus, to him a son is born in his family who is his likeness, not one who is not his likeness.'[2]

In the simpler thought of uncultured peoples, however, the reflexion is a spiritually real soul.

The Andamanese 'do not regard their shadows, but their *reflections* (in any mirror) as their souls,'[3] and in one account of the Fijians a man's likeness 'in water or a looking-glass' was regarded as his soul.[4] Savages of New Guinea when first looking into a mirror thought their reflexions were their souls,[5] while the New Caledonians believed that their reflexions in mirrors or water were their souls,[6] and the Macusis of Guiana held the same belief about the reflexion in the eye of another.[7] Many terms for the soul point to the same notion. The Melanesian *atai* ('soul') means 'reflexion,'[8] and the same meaning belongs to many terms among the Indonesians.[9]

Hence the frequent notion that there is something uncanny about a mirror, a belief which culminates in the idea that the reflecting surface has abstracted and retains the soul.

There is a pool in a Saddle Island river (Melanesia) into which any one who looks dies; the malignant spirit takes hold of his life by means of his reflexion in the water.[10] The Zulus have a similar terror of looking into any dark pool; a beast therein will take away their reflexions.[11] The Aztecs supposed that to see one's reflexion in water wherein a knife had been placed meant a stab to the soul,[12] and the Galelarese forbid their children to look in mirrors, which will take away their beauty.[13] Manu said (in rules for a *snātaka*): 'Let him not look at his own image in water.'[14] The old Greeks had the same maxim; to dream of seeing one's self reflected foreboded death, and Frazer explains the story of Narcissus on these lines.[15] The Rabbis laid it down that one must not look into a mirror on the Sabbath, unless it were fixed on a wall. Later they forbade men generally to use mirrors, as being effeminate, reserving, however, the privilege to their own relatives, as being 'close to the government.'[16] The Rabbinical idea was doubtless merely puritanical.

With these notions is connected the custom of covering mirrors or turning them to the wall after a death.

'It is feared that the soul, projected out of the person in the shape of his reflection in the mirror, may be carried off by the ghost of the departed, which is commonly supposed to linger about the house till the burial.'[17]

This practice is widely spread over Europe, and occurs in Islām.[18] Similarly, sick persons should avoid looking into a mirror, and it is advisable for a bride to refrain from using a mirror in modern Greece.[19] Since the mirror holds the soul, it is said to be extremely unlucky to break a looking-glass.[20]

'A mirror,' say the sectarian Russian Raskolniks generally, 'is an accursed thing.'[21]

1 *Milinda-pañha*, IV. i. 60 (*SBE* xxxv. [1890] 189).
2 *GB*³, pt. i., *The Magic Art*, London, 1911, ii. 243.
3 J. Jacobs, in *JE*, *s.v.*'; Ex 38⁸, Is 3²³, Job 37¹⁸, 1 Co 13¹². AV 'glass' refers to the metal mirror.
4 A. Hillebrandt, *Rituallitteratur* (=*GIAP* iii. 2), Strassburg, 1897, p. 65.
5 J. Anderson, *Scotland in Early Chr. Times*, 2nd ser., Edinburgh, 1881, pp. 51, 62, 68, 178, 181 f.
6 *Guide to the Mediæval Room, British Museum*, 1907, p. 213.
7 *Ib.*
8 *Ib.* p. 213 f.
9 *EBr*¹¹, *s.v.*
10 *Ib.*
11 Archimedes was said to have set fire to enemy ships by means of gigantic mirrors or burning glasses.
12 H. Höffding, *Outlines of Psychology*, Eng tr., London, 1891, p. 7.

1 *Chhāndogya Upaniṣad*, VIII. vii. 3 (*SBE* i. [1900] 135).
2 *Kauṣītaki Upaniṣad* iv. 11 (*SBE* i. 304).
3 E. H. Man, 'On the Aboriginal Inhabitants of the Andaman Islands,' *JAI* xii. [1882] 162.
4 T. Williams and J. Calvert, *Fiji and the Fijians*, London, 1858, i. 241.
5 J. Chalmers, *Pioneering in New Guinea*, London, 1887, p. 170.
6 *GB*³, pt. ii., *Taboo and the Perils of the Soul*, London, 1911, p. 92.
7 E. F. im Thurn, in *JAI* xi. [1882] 363.
8 R. H. Codrington, *The Melanesians*, Oxford, 1891, p. 250 f.
9 A. C. Kruijt, *Het Animisme in den Indischen Archipel*, The Hague, 1906, p. 13. See generally *GB*³, pt. ii., *Taboo*, p. 92 ff.; A. E. Crawley, *The Idea of the Soul*, London, 1909, p. 196 ff.
10 Codrington, in *JAI* x. [1881] 313.
11 H. Callaway, *Nursery Tales, etc., of the Zulus*, Natal and London, 1868, p. 342 f.
12 *GB*³, pt. ii., *Taboo*, p. 93, quoting B. de Sahagun.
13 *Ib.*, quoting M. J. van Baarda. For further instances cf. J. von Negelein, *ARW* v. [1902] 24–26.
14 iv. 38 (*SBE* xxv. [1886] 135).
15 *Loc. cit.*
16 Jacobs, in *JE*, *s.v.*, quoting *Shab.* 149*a*.
17 *GB*³, pt. ii., *Taboo*, p. 94 f.; cf. *PR*² i. 233.
18 Jacobs, *loc. cit.*; *GB*³, pt. ii., *Taboo*, p. 95.
19 J. C. Lawson, *Modern Greek Folklore and Ancient Greek Religion*, Cambridge, 1910, p. 10.
20 F. T. Elworthy, *Evil Eye*, London, 1895, p. 83, and esp. von Negelein, p. 23 f.
21 *GB*³, pt. ii., *Taboo*, p. 96.

On the other hand, a mirror, as when set in a ring, may be used to repel demons.[1]

Divination by means of a reflecting surface is an ancient and world-wide practice, its principle being that figures representing the souls of persons at the moment or in future actions may be seen. A pool of ink is a common substitute for the mirror (cf. art. CRYSTAL-GAZING), and a combination of mirror and pool of water was used at Demeter's sanctuary at Patræ, where was a sacred spring, but its use was permitted only in cases of sickness.

'They tie a mirror to a fine cord, and let it down so far that it shall not plunge into the spring, but merely graze the surface of the water with its rim . . . they look into the mirror, and it shows them the sick person either living or dead.'[2]

It is also used, especially in German and Slavic lands, to discover one's future husband or wife.[3]

Divination by mirrors is a variety of a wide-spread method of 'seeing,' the most frequent instrument being the crystal ball.[4] A magic mirror possessed of the power of speech is not uncommon in folk-tales;[5] and in Shintoism actual worship is rendered to mirrors which, originally presented to deities, have come to stand for the divine beings themselves.[6]

The supernatural associations of mirrors are chiefly the foregoing, but one or two of a miscellaneous order may be noted, as illustrating the general subject.

Pausanias describes a temple near Megalopolis, within which was a mirror fixed on the wall. 'Any one who looks into this mirror will see himself either very dimly or not at all, but the images of the gods and the throne are clearly visible.'[7] The Greeks kindled sacred fires by means of the mirror or crystal, and the same was the case in China and Siam, while in the Inca kingdom the new fire was kindled at the summer solstice by means of a concave mirror turned to the sun.[8]

4. The mirror in metaphor.—The optical properties of the mirror are so important and impressive that all civilized thought is permeated by ideas derived thence. One or two only can be cited. The Hebrew parœmiographer says: 'As in water face answereth to face, so the heart of man to man,'[9] while the Buddhist *suttas* speak of 'a way of truth, called the Mirror of Truth.'[10] Mirror was a favourite component of titles of books in Elizabethan literature, in its meaning of 'true description,' and its meaning of 'pattern, exemplar, model' is similar. Shakespeare writes 'the mirror of all Christian kings.' 'To hold as 'twere the mirror up to Nature' uses the simplest connotation of the term. An interesting metaphor is used of psychic processes; 'the mirror of the mind' occurs both in Chaucer and in Shakespeare. Among new sources of metaphor are the two remarkable biological and chemico-physical analogies to the optical fact of mirror-image (in which right becomes left and *vice versa*). All vertebrate animals, many invertebrate, and the leaf and other systems of plants are bilateral, one side being the mirror-image of the other, while the formation of right-handed and left-handed crystals is connected with the division of acids into right and left according to the effect produced in relation to polarized light.

LITERATURE.—With the exception of the well-known archæological works on antique mirrors and popular folklore collections, the relevant literature is included in the article.

A. E. CRAWLEY.

MISHMIS

MISHMIS.—The Mishmis are a tribe who inhabit the Mishmi hills, a section of the mountain ranges on the northern frontier of Assam, which shut in the eastern end of the Brahmāputra valley, between that river and the Dihāng, a region practically unexplored, consisting of steep ridges, covered as a rule with tree forest, and including some peaks 15,000 ft. in height (*IGI* xvii. [1908] 377 f.). They are divided into four tribes, speaking three distinct but probably connected languages. The most western tribe is known as Midu, Midhi, Nedu, or Chūlīkaṭā, 'hair-cropped'; they inhabit the Dihāng valley with the adjoining hills. To their east are the Mithun, or Bebijiyā, 'outcasts,' who speak practically the same language. East of the Bebijiyās are the Taying or Digāru Mishmis, beyond the Digāru river. The Mijus are still further east, towards the Lama valley of Dzayul, a sub-prefecture of Lhāsa. Most of these live beyond the British frontier. The numbers counted at the last three Censuses in Assam were 217, 98, and 271 (*Census Rep. Assam*, 1891, i. 203; 1901, i. 139; 1911, i. 134).

1. Ethnology.—The Mishmis have been identified by some authorities with the Miaotzu or Hmeng, the aborigines of Yunnan, whose name has been interpreted to mean 'children of the soil,' 'roots,' or as a contemptuous reference to their 'simple dirt' (J. G. Scott and J. P. Hardiman, *Gaz. Upper Burma*, pt. i. vol. i. [Rangoon, 1900] p. 597 ff.).

'So far as the means at our disposal permit us to draw conclusions, it seems most probable that these four tribes belong neither to the Tibeto-Himalayan nor to the Assam-Burmese branch of the Tibeto-Burman languages. They seem to be descendants of clans which, when the parting of the ways between the two branches took place, accompanied neither, but made their own way at different periods into the hills overlooking the Assam valley from the north' (G. A. Grierson, *Census Rep. India*, 1901, i. 263).

2. Relations with the British Government.—The British first came in contact with the Mishmis in 1825, when Lieut. Burlton reported that the 'Mishmah' were inhabited by tribes 'who were very averse to receive strangers.' Other officers visited them between that time and 1851, when M. Krick, a French missionary, was murdered by them. Then followed a succession of outrages. In 1885 one of their headmen was taken to visit the Calcutta Exhibition. Soon after his return he died, and the tribe, holding the British Government responsible for his loss, decided that the head of a British subject should be buried with him, in order to propitiate his spirit. So they slew a British subject and carried off his head. An expedition in 1899–1900 reduced them to submission, and since that time they have given little trouble. But they are keen tappers of rubber, and it has been found expedient to prevent them from crossing the Brahmāputra into British territory for that purpose (B. C. Allen, *Gaz. Lakhimpur*, 1905, p. 55 ff.).

3. Religious beliefs.—The best account of their religious beliefs is that by E. T. Dalton, *Descriptive Ethnology of Bengal*, Calcutta, 1872, p. 16 f.:

'The religion of the Mishmis is confined to the propitiation of demons whenever illness or misfortune visits them. On these occasions the sprig of a plant is placed at the door to intimate to strangers that the house is for the time under *tabu*. They appear to have no notion of a supreme or benevolent deity. They worship Mujidagrah as a god of destruction, Damipaon as god of the chase and knowledge, and Tabla as a god of wealth and disease, and a great many others without name. It appears both from Lieutenant Rowlatt and the Abbé Krick's notes that the Mishmis have priests, but they are few in number and have to be brought from a distance when required. M. Krick describes one that he saw at a funeral ceremony. . . . For several days previous to the arrival of a priest, an attendant was employed in singing a devotional chant to the accompaniment of a small bell. There was also a preliminary sacrifice of a red cock and hen, the blood of which was received in a vessel containing some other fluid, and the mixture carefully examined, as it is supposed to indicate if the result will be fortunate or otherwise. At last the priest arrived, dressed like an ordinary chief, but he wore a rosary of shells, and, attached

1 *PR*[2] ii. 35 f.
2 Paus. VII. xxi. 12 (tr. J. G. Frazer, London, 1898).
3 Von Negelein, p. 28.
4 Eng. 'mirror' has the meanings of 'a magic glass' or 'crystal' (*OED*, *s.v.*).
5 *CF*, p. 34 f.
6 W. G. Aston, *Shinto*, London, 1905, pp. 218, 72, 134 f.; cf. L. A. Waddell, *Buddhism of Tibet*, do. 1895, pp. 393, 445.
7 Paus. VIII. xxxvii. 7.
8 *GB*[3], pt. i., *The Magic Art*, ii. 243 ff.
9 Pr 27[19].
10 *Mahāparinibbāna-sutta* ii. 8 (*SBE* xi. [1900] 26).

to the front of his headdress, two appendages like horns. For two days, at intervals, the priest and his son employed themselves in singing chants, marking the time by waving a fan and ringing a bell; on the third day he put on his chief's Tibetan robe, and assumed what may be regarded as his pontifical dress—a tight-fitting coat of colored cotton, a small apron, a deer skin as a mantle; from his right shoulder descended a fringe of long goats' hair dyed bright red, and over his left shoulder he wore a broad belt embossed with four rows of tigers' teeth, and having attached to it fourteen small bells. On his head he placed a bandeau ornamented with shells, and round the knot of hair at the top of his head a movable plume which turned like a weathercock. This was followed by a wild demoniacal dance; but whether a *pas seul* by the priest, or one in which the people generally joined, we are not informed. The object was, however, to make as much noise as possible to frighten the devils. After this, lights were all extinguished, till a man suspended from the roof obtained a fresh light from a flint. He was to be careful not to touch the ground as he produced it, as the light thus obtained was supposed to be fresh from heaven [cf. *GB*[3], pt. i., *The Magic Art*, London, 1911, ii. 234 ff.; pt. vii., *Balder the Beautiful*, do. 1913, i. 2 ff.]. When the burial is of a person of note, animals are slain, and the skulls arranged round the tomb [cf. *ERE* i. 499; *PR* ii. 225; L. A. Waddell, *The Buddhism of Tibet*, London, 1895, p. 484 n. 1], and under the shed built over the grave, raw and cooked flesh with grain and spirits are placed (the share of the dead), and all the arms, clothes, and implements he was in the habit of using when living. The poor, it is said, bury the dead without much ceremony, or throw the bodies into the river.'

About 1872—the writer gives no clear dates—T. T. Cooper (*The Mishmee Hills*, London, 1873) visited the tribe, and gives some account of their appearance, dress, manners, and customs (p. 180 ff.).

An earthquake occurred, and they told the chief, Chowsam, 'that the devil residing in a neighbouring mountain had been angry, and rent the side of the mountain' (p. 193).

'The Mishmees being polytheists, though of the lowest order, it was not difficult to make Poso [another chief] understand the existence of one Great Spirit above all' (p. 197). 'The Mishmees,' he said, 'are very unfortunate. We are everywhere surrounded by demons; they live in the rivers, mountains, and trees; they walk about in the dark and live in the winds; we are constantly suffering from them. . . . In answer to a question as to which demon he thought the strongest, after some hesitation he said that the demon of fire was the strongest and most dangerous, as he dried up the water and burnt the mountains; he was also good-natured, as he warmed them and cooked their food' (p. 198).

'As to religion, their notions are very vague. Polytheism, encumbered with all the rites and ceremonies of fetishism, is their true creed. The yearly sacrifice and feast in honour of their deceased parents shows that they have some idea of a future state, but I could not find out their particular ideas, as death is a disagreeable subject of conversation among them, and Chowsam always declined to interpret questions relating to it' (p. 238). 'The two most important ceremonies of the Mishmees are undoubtedly those attending deaths and marriages. In the case of sickness a soothsayer is called in, and he generally prescribes the sacrifice of fowls or pigs, according to the state of the patient. These sacrifices he orders as a propitiation of the demon who is supposed to be instrumental in causing sickness. When death ensues, particularly in the case of a chief, mhittons [*mithan*, also called *gayāl*, *bos frontalis* (W. T. Blanford, *Fauna of British India, Mammalia*, London, 1890–91, p. 487 ff.)], pigs and fowls are killed without stint, and all the old men and women feast to their heart's content, hospitality being considered a great virtue. They eat in honour of the departed, talking the while of his great and good qualities. The body is burnt after two days, and the ashes are collected and placed in a miniature house, erected close to the family residence. This unique tomb is then surrounded by some of the skulls collected by the chief during his lifetime, which serve as a monument of his past hospitality, while the rest of his treasures are divided amongst his sons, the son-and-heir taking the lion's share. When there are no sons the skulls go to the nearest male relations. The eldest son takes the title of gam, or chief, and holds a yearly feast in honour of his deceased father, which is considered one of the most sacred observances among them' (p. 237).

When Cooper suffered from an abscess in his ankle, a soothsayer or exorcist was called in. He was dressed like the other Mishmis, but allowed his hair to fall in long, unkempt masses over his shoulders. After inspecting the patient's foot, he stripped himself naked except for a small loincloth, and produced a handful of rushes from his waistbelt. These he began to plait and unplait, accompanying the operation with a buzzing noise, as though he were counting. Occasionally he would place his hand on the painful spot, and then shake the rushes over it, keeping his eyes shut the whole time. After nearly an hour he announced that two fowls must be killed, which would ensure recovery. He declined to answer what devil had been at work, and what effect the rushes had on him (p. 252).

LITERATURE.—The chief authorities are quoted in the article.

W. CROOKE.

MISHNA.—See TALMUD.

MISSALS.—See RITUAL.

MISSION (Inner).—*Die innere Mission* is the name used in Germany to describe the sum-total of those efforts which are made by the Protestant Churches to ameliorate the conditions of the suffering of the poor and to bring the institutions and usages of society into harmony with the will of God. It is to be distinguished from *Die äussere Mission* ('foreign missions') in that it confines its activities to Germany and Germans resident or sojourning in foreign lands. It is an endeavour to overcome the heathenism found within the borders of a country professedly Christian. It is to be distinguished from mere humanitarian effort in that it definitely makes temporal and material aid a means to spiritual redemption, and from the official activity of the pastors and paid officers of the Church in that it works through the voluntary agency of individual Christians or groups of Christians, the pastor's office being to arouse the spirit of willingness and marshal its powers for the purpose of redeeming love. It aims at realizing in sacrificial service the universal priesthood of believers.

The movement originated after the close of the Napoleonic Wars when orphan homes were established for children whose parents had lost their lives in the war (Johannes Falk, Graf Adalbert von der Ricke, C. Heinrich Zeller). A number of societies and institutions arose organized on a large scale for the care of the poor, the nursing of the sick, and the saving of destitute children. This grew out of the pietistic movement (see PIETISM), and was largely inspired by the efforts of Great Britain in the foreign missionary field, the foundation of the Bible Society, the work of Mrs. Elizabeth Fry, and the City Missions. Conspicuous among the leaders were Johann Hinrich Wichern (1808–81), who in 1833 founded at Hamburg the *Rauhe Haus* (a reformatory institution built upon the household system with a training home for lay-workers), and Theodor Fliedner (1800–64), who in 1826 founded at Kaiserwerth the first society for prison-visiting in Germany, in 1833 the first refuge for discharged female prisoners, and in 1836 the famous *Diakonisseninstitut* for the training of nurses and infant teachers.

The name 'Innere Mission' was first employed in a narrower sense by Friedrich Lücke, of Göttingen, in *Die zweifache, innere und äussere Mission der evangelischen Kirche* (Hamburg, 1843), to mean work among the lapsed members of the different Christian communities and the fortifying of a weak church with the help of a strong, while Wichern broadened out the meaning of the term to include all practical Christian work in the homeland and among Germans in foreign lands (*Diaspora*).

It was Wichern who first organized the movement on a comprehensive scale in 1848. The revolution of that year roused the Church from its apathy, and opened its eyes to the glaring evils of heathendom which had grown up in the midst of the nation. A Church Diet was summoned at Wittenberg, where 500 representatives of Protestant German Churches assembled. Standing on Luther's grave, Wichern delivered a memorable address, picturing the wide-spread power of the paganism which had arisen in their midst and the fruits which it had produced, and calling upon the

Churches to join hands in remedying these evils. He sketched on large and statesmanlike lines the programme of the remedial activities needed, and proposed the formation of a central committee (*Centralausschuss*), consisting of ministers and laymen, to make a survey of the fields of work, place the various societies already at work in touch with one another so as to save overlapping, point out the need of new effort and help such effort to succeed, guide the movement as a whole, and, above all, make it clear that all the several ministries, of whatever kind, were animated by the one divine spirit of redeeming love in Christ. Thus was established a free confederation of all the activities of the Protestant Churches, so far as these were extra-official. The object of the Innere Mission, as defined in the first report of the *Centralausschuss*, is 'that the Christian Church with all its resources, and through all its agencies, may fill and quicken the whole life of the people in all ranks of society, inspire all social arrangements and institutions with the might of a love energizing heart and life—and through all its living members labour to save the neglected and the poor.' The Innere Mission was to be 'the practising doctor in the great hospital of the people.' Its programme and policy are set forth in full in *Die innere Mission der deutschen evangelischen Kirche, eine Denkschrift an die deutsche Nation*, written by Wichern at the instance of the Central Committee and published in April 1849. This book sets out the scope of the work and the relations of that work to the activities of the State on the one hand, and of the Church on the other. For twenty years Wichern remained practically the directing spirit. Pamphlets (*Fliegende Blätter*) were published annually at the *Rauhe Haus* giving reports of the various agencies carried on.

The most comprehensive survey of the work is given in two Jubilee publications of the *Centralausschuss* in 1899 (*Statistik, Fünfzig Jahre*). These contain reports by different authoritative writers on the work done in each of the following departments:

(1) The care of children, crèches, infant schools, care of cripples, Sunday schools and children's services, refuges and orphanages, country holidays for city children.
(2) The care of adolescents, associations and homes for apprentices and journeymen, schools of domestic economy, Rescue homes, *Jugendbund für entschiedenes Christentum* (analogous to Christian Endeavour Societies).
(3) The care of tramps and the homeless, colonies for unemployed, homes for girls, railway-station missions, Girls' Friendly Societies and Lodges, missions to soldiers and sailors, river and canal boat population, railwaymen, navvies, brickyard-workers, waiters.
(4) The quickening of the Christian spirit, city missions, men's brotherhoods, support of weaker Churches, Christian art associations, lectures.
(5) Work among emigrants and Germans in foreign lands (*Diaspora*), pastorates at holiday resorts.
(6) Care of the poor, sick, and infirm, district nursing associations, Red-cross work in war, homes for imbeciles, epileptics, inebriates, blind, deaf and dumb.
(7) Combating of social evils, Sunday observance, housing reform, prison missions, temperance work, savings banks, anti-gambling work, friendly societies, building societies, Christian education.
(8) Christian literature, dissemination of Bibles, tracts, and sermons, periodicals, libraries, colportage.
(9) Organization of Inner Mission according to province and district, conferences.
(10) Training of workers for prisons, asylums, unemployed colonies, nursing, etc., courses of instruction for social workers.

As the result of the Innere Mission the whole of Germany has been covered with a network of philanthropic agencies, imbued with the Christian spirit; the social conscience has been quickened and enlightened, and the efforts of the Churches have been co-ordinated and wisely directed. The State has co-operated. In 1852 the brothers of the *Rauhe Haus* were allowed to act as warders in Prussian prisons, and Wichern was commissioned to visit the prisons, investigate their conditions, and suggest reforms. Later, Wichern was appointed Councillor of the Ministry of the Interior and made a member of the *Evangelischer Oberkirchenrat.* The work of the Innere Mission paved the way for the social legislation which followed the Franco-German War. The most notable results of the Innere Mission are the mobilization of women for Christian work, especially in sick-nursing, the Elberfeld system of poor-relief and its extension to other German towns, and the work of Pastor F. v. Bodelschwingh (b. 1831), who founded at Bielefeld a colony for epileptics and unemployed, and organized, with the help of the Government, the national scheme of relief-stations for tramps.

In the Church the Innere Mission has given the laity, and especially women, their sphere of service; it led to the official institution of the diaconate in the Evangelical Church in 1856, and gives material expression to the universal priesthood of believers. It has filled a place in the educational system by caring for orphans and infants, and counteracting the movement for the secularization of schools.

The movement has affected other countries, especially Switzerland (J. A. Bost), Denmark (Wilhelm Beck), Norway (P. Harem), and Holland (O. G. Heldring). Florence Nightingale received her first training at Kaiserwerth. The work of Thomas Guthrie (Ragged Schools), William Pennefather (Mildmay Conference), and John Brown Paton (Lingfield Homes for epileptics, training colony for unemployed at Wallingford, National Home Reading Union, Social Institutes, Boys' Life Brigade, Girls' Life Brigade, Civic Leagues of Help) was consciously influenced by the Innere Mission. In 1873 J. B. Paton and Francis Morse summoned a conference at Nottingham 'to consider the practical relations of Christianity to the social wants and evils of our time,' at which Paton expounded the Innere Mission of Germany, and a union of all existing Christian charities and societies working for social ends was formed at Nottingham. W. T. Stead took up the same idea in his agitation for a Civic Church. The nearest approach in England has been the organization of Civic Leagues (or Gilds) of Help (beginning 1906), which represent an attempt to adapt the Elberfeld system to the conditions of English city life and bring all the social activities of the civic community into touch with each other.

LITERATURE.—J. H. Wichern, *Die innere Mission der deutschen Kirche*, Hamburg, 1849, *Kongressvorträge*, do. 1891 (see esp. 12 theses at Second Stuttgart Congress, 1850), *Prinzipielles zur inneren Mission* (*Collected Works*, vol. iii.), do. 1902; T. Fliedner, *Kurze Geschichte der Entstehung der ersten evang. Liebesanstalten zu Kaiserwerth*, Kaiserwerth, 1856, *Nachrichten über das Diakonissenwerk in der christlichen Welt alter und neuer Zeit und über die Diakonissenanstalt zu Kaiserwerth*[5], do. 1867; T. Schäfer, *Die weibliche Diakonie in ihrem ganzen Umfange dargestellt*, Hamburg, 1879–80, *Leitfaden der inneren Mission*, do. 1903; *Monatsschrift für die innere Mission*, Gütersloh, 1876 ff. (ed. T. Schäfer); I. Nitzsch, *Praktische Theologie*, Bonn, 1867–68, vol. iii.; F. Oldenberg, *J. H. Wichern: sein Leben und Wirken*, 2 vols., Hamburg, 1884–87; G. Uhlhorn, *Die christliche Liebestätigkeit*, Stuttgart, 1882–90, vol. iii.; P. Wurster, *Die Lehre von der inneren Mission*, Berlin, 1895; P. Wurster and M. Hennig, *Was jederman heute von der inneren Mission wissen muss*, Stuttgart and Berlin, 1902; W. Martius, *Die innere Mission, ihre Bedeutung und ihr Wesen, ihr Verhältnis zu Kirche und Staat* (*ein Wort zur Orientirung und zur Mahnung*), Gütersloh, 1882; J. B. Paton, *The Inner Mission of Germany and its Lessons for us*, London, 1888; W. Fleming Stevenson, *Praying and Working*, do. 1887; J. S. Howson, *Deaconesses*, do. 1862; Florence Nightingale, *Account of the Institution for Deaconesses*, do. 1851; R. Volf, *Indre Mission, dens Historie og Grundtanker i kort Udtog*, Copenhagen, 1870.

Adverse critics have not been wanting: F. v. Holtzendorff, *Die Brüderschaft des rauhen Hauses, ein protestantischer Orden im Staatsdienst*, Berlin, 1861; F. A. W. Diesterweg, *Die innere Mission in ihrer Gefährlichheit*, Berlin, 1852; G. Rasch, *Ein protestantisches Mönchkloster in Moabit*, 1870.

J. L. PATON.

MISSIONS.

Buddhist (M. Anesaki), p. 700.
Christian—
Early and Mediæval (C. R. Beazley), p. 705.
Roman Catholic (M. Spitz), p. 713.
Christian—
Protestant (H. U. Weitbrecht), p. 727.
Muhammadan (T. W. Arnold), p. 745.
Zoroastrian (L. H. Gray), p. 749.

MISSIONS (Buddhist).—I. **In China.**—Buddhist missionary enterprises outside of India were started by King Aśoka in the latter half of the 3rd cent. B.C. On the other hand, a later Chinese record informs us that in 217 B.C. (in the reign of Shih-Huangti of the Tsin dynasty) eighteen Buddhist monks were brought to the capital of the empire. The authenticity of the information may be questioned, but, when we take into account the facts that Chinese Buddhists used to ascribe the 7th cent. B.C. to Aśoka's reign, and that, in spite of that, the date of the story almost agrees with the historical date of Aśoka, the tradition seems not to be a mere forgery. About one hundred years after that event, as stated in an official record, another contact of Buddhism with the Chinese took place. An expedition sent to the Western regions by the Emperor Wu, the most ambitious sovereign of the former Hān dynasty, in 121 B.C. brought a golden statue and prisoners; and in 2 B.C. the Yuechi ambassadors are said to have brought some Buddhist scriptures. These stories point to the spread of the Buddhist missions in Central Asia in the centuries immediately after Aśoka's missionary enterprises.

Historical records agree in assigning to A.D. 67 the first official introduction of Buddhism into China. The Emperor Ming, stimulated by a dream, sent an expedition in search of the golden man of whom he had dreamt (A.D. 64), and, when the expedition returned in 67, it brought not only Buddhist statues and scriptures, but also two monks, both Indians, Kāśyapa Mātaṅga and Dharmarakṣa by name. The first Chinese Buddhist book, containing the forty-two sayings of Buddha, was written by Kāśyapa, and translations of several texts are said to have followed it. The Pai-ma, or White Horse Temple, was built in Loyāng, the capital, and soon after the emperor's brother built another temple. Conversions *en masse* are said to have taken place in 71, many nobles and Taoist priests being among the converts. The new religion was received with open arms and heart; the way must have long been prepared for it.

There is a gap of about eighty years between the mention of the first missionaries and the advent of two other monks, one of whom was Shih-kāo of Parthia, who came to China in 148 and worked till 170. He is said to have been of royal blood and to have left his country because of the fall or decline of his own royal family. This is one of the evidences that Buddhism had a strong foothold in Parthia and Central Asia. It is quite conceivable that Chinese Buddhism had its source close to China's western borders at that time. Shih-kāo's works are mostly texts from *Āgamas*,[1] the counterparts of the Pāli *Nikāyas*, and some of them treat of hygienic matters, connected with the practice of counting the respirations, or *ānāpāna*. Perhaps we may see here the first of the medical works of the missionaries.

For a century after the great Parthian translator we have only scanty records of missionaries, yet we have reason to suppose that missions were going on slowly. The Buddhist propaganda in this period consisted chiefly in translations of the scriptures and in miracle-working. Certainly the works of art and architecture in a new style, aided by elaborate rituals and music, were great attractions; the Pai-ma temple is said to have been decorated with mural paintings representing Buddha and his saints; but the worship of Buddha's relics and the miracles worked by them are mentioned oftener than the works of art. The relics (*śarīra*, Chin. *shöli*) were represented by pearls of mysterious origin, and the miracles ascribed to them were mostly the rising of variegated mists from them. Little is heard of works of charity, though they are sometimes mentioned later than the 4th century. That the translations played a great part in the Buddhist missions is proved by the work done during the five centuries after the first undertaking. This was quite natural, because the Chinese already had rich literatures, both Confucianist and Taoist, when Buddhism came to China, and the new religion found it urgent to confront them with scriptures of its own.

Besides the translations, the first apologetic writing is ascribed to A.D. 195, and a series of apologetics and polemics followed.[1] This literature continued throughout the whole history of Chinese Buddhism. Its most flourishing period was in the 4th and the 5th centuries, during which Taoism was a powerful rival of Buddhism. These polemics were mostly carried on by native teachers, while foreign missionaries were occupied with translations.

Though polemics do not belong properly to missionary works, we may here consider one instance, in order to throw a side-light on our subject. In 195 Mou-tzu, a Confucianist convert, wrote 37 sets of questions and answers in defence of his new faith. These questions may be divided into two groups: (1) those from the Confucianist side, asserting that Buddha's ascetic religion was against humanity, and (2) those from the Taoist side, asserting that immortality (or, rather, physical longevity) was attainable only by Taoist practices, not by Buddhist teaching. Mou-tzu defended his religion with abundant quotations from Confucius and Lao-tse, but the doctrines with which he confronted the attacks were really Buddhist. The transcendental idealism of supreme enlightenment was the position which he assumed against Confucianist positivism, and the teaching of impermanency of physical life was his standing-ground against Taoist mysticism.[2] This may be taken as a typical example of the apologetic writings of the period.

The fall of the Hān dynasty in 220 and the subsequent division of the country into the Three Kingdoms were of great significance for the history of the nation, both politically and religiously. From this time down to the close of the 6th cent. the country was divided into many contending dynasties and kingdoms, and in a country like China, where the ruler's will determines everything, the fate of the Buddhist mission was always influenced by the vicissitudes of the ruling dynasties. Centres of missions were identical with the residences of dynasties, and the missionaries worked under their patronage, or were expelled by rulers who preferred Taoism to Buddhism. Under these circumstances three important centres of the mission grew up:

[1] Cf. B. Nanjio, *Catalogue*, p. 382; Anesaki, 'The Four Buddhist Agamas in Chinese,' in *TASJ* xxxv. 3 [1908], pp. 17 f., 28–34.

[1] There are collections of these writings; see Nanjio, nos. 1471, 1472, 1479, 1480, 1481.

[2] The question begins with 'Who is Buddha?' The answer to it shows that the author was acquainted with Buddha's life through information which is very similar to the *Lalitavistara*. Some critics doubt even the existence of this person, on the ground that the polemic literature flourished not earlier than the 4th cent., but we omit discussion of the question and follow the legend.

(1) Chāng-ān (the modern Sing-ān), (2) Lo-yāng (on the Hoang-ho) in the north, and (3) Chien-yeh (the modern Nanking) in the south. During the first half of the 3rd cent. the last two were the respective capitals of two of the Three Kingdoms, while the third was situated far in the west, beyond the reach of Buddhist influence. After a short interval of unity (280–302) these three places remained as the three centres of China in all the vicissitudes of rulers and States. Thus the missionaries who came to China by land routes worked mostly in the north, deriving their sources from Central Asia or the north-west of India, though some went further to the south.

The 4th cent. was a period of confusion in China, caused by a hopeless division of the country and by intrusion of invaders from the north. Yet Buddhist missions proceeded to cover the greater part of the land, and many of the contending rulers welcomed missionaries from Central Asia. One of these men, Fo-t'u-cheng, who came in 310 to Lo-yāng from a 'western country,' laboured not as a translator but as a social worker. It is said that he was 'well versed in magic formulæ and saved many people from diseases and sufferings by his supernatural attainment.' No fewer than 893 monasteries and sanctuaries were established by him, and his 'disciples' numbered 10,000. But his significance in Chinese Buddhism lay perhaps more in his having educated one of the most powerful thinkers, Tao-ān, than in his actual works; though he laboured mostly in the north, his influence was later propagated to the south by his disciples.

The demarcation between north and south became more conspicuous when, at the beginning of the 5th cent., two comparatively powerful dynasties divided the country into two. While the northern, the Wei dynasty, patronized those who came from or through Central Asia, the southern, the Sung dynasty, invited missionaries from S. India, who came by the sea route. Moreover, the repeated persecutions of Buddhists by Taoist rulers of the northern dynasties drove many missionaries and Chinese monks to the south, and it was through them that a start was made in establishing groups of men of similar tendencies, which became the origin of sectarian division in Chinese Buddhism.

Among those who worked in the north the most prominent was Kumārajīva, a native of Karachar. He came to Chāng-ān in 401, having been invited by the prince of the Tsin dynasty, and, being highly patronized by the latter, he worked there with great success for more than ten years. His lectures were attended by crowds from various classes of people, and his work of translation was assisted by the best scholars and men of letters. It is no wonder that the translations ascribed to him are ranked as classical Chinese, and that his translation of the *Lotus of the True Law* ([*q.v.*] *Saddharmapuṇḍarīka*) remains the most valued and revered of the Chinese Buddhist scriptures.[1] Kumārajīva was apparently a monk, but his conduct was very irregular, for he lived with many concubines; yet his talent was so appreciated and his fame so high that his patron and the people honoured him, despite his neglect of Buddhist discipline and in spite of attacks heaped upon him.

A powerful rival, however, appeared in the person of Buddhabhadra, who was invited to Chāng-ān in 398. He is believed to have arrived at the coast of Shantung by the sea route, having once failed to come by land. In contrast to Kumārajīva, he observed austere rules of monastic life, and instructed his followers in discipline and in meditation. At last a critical rupture between the two great men broke out, and Buddhabhadra took refuge in the south, where Tao-ān's disciples were living secluded in a monastery on Mount Lu-shan, in the modern province of Chiang-hsi. The leader of the group was Hui-yüan († 416), and its members were monks, poets, and philosophers who were disgusted with the troubles of the world and devoted themselves to meditation and conversation with one another. Here Buddhabhadra found men more congenial than the Buddhists of the north, and instructed them further in the secrets of Buddhist mental training. In this group of thinkers we see Chinese Buddhism quite acclimatized to the native soil, especially to the poetic and transcendental mood of the southern Chinese, and preparing for further union of Buddhist meditation with Chinese quietism. It was on this ground that a definite school of meditation, known as Shan-no (Skr. *dhyāna*), later established itself and further impressed Buddhism with the poetry of the valley of the Yang-tzu. Although the followers of the Shan-no school trace their origin to Bodhidharma, who is believed to have come to China by sea in 520, the further source is to be found in the group of recluses at Lu-shan who welcomed Buddhabhadra. After all, we can assign the foundation of Chinese Buddhism, relatively apart from foreign missionaries, to Tao-ān and Hui-yüan. Yet, parallel with this native movement, missionary work was proceeding, both in the north and in the south.

As we have mentioned, the south welcomed Indian missionaries, many of whom came by sea, and we find a sudden growth of sea-communication with India from the dawn of the 5th century. The pioneer of the sea-voyage from Ceylon to China was the famous pilgrim Fa-hian, who arrived at Shantung in 414, and who was followed by a series of Buddhists who sailed to China and worked mostly under the patronage of the southern dynasties. The most eminent of these was Guṇavarman, who came to Canton from Ceylon, *via* Java, in 424. He laid the foundations of two monasteries called Chao-t'i (Chetiya) and Ch'i-yuan (Jetavana) in Nanking. Here he instructed his followers in the strict discipline of the Vinaya and instituted the system of ordination, as an initiation into Buddhist mysteries, by establishing a special centre for the purpose, after the model of the Sīmā of Nālandā (*q.v.*). The arrival of a number of Siṁhalese nuns in 434 under the leadership of a certain Tissara (?) was probably connected with his institutions and intended for starting nunneries after the model of Sinhalese Buddhism. Another group of nuns came from Ceylon in 438. Among those who followed the footsteps of Guṇavarman are to be mentioned Kālayasas and Dharmamitra, both translators of Mahāyāna texts; Guṇabhadra, the translator of the *Saṁyukta-āgama*; and Saṅghabhadra, the translator of the Pāli *Samanta-pāsādikā*, a commentary on the Vinaya written by the famous Buddhaghoṣa. The last of these is said to have come together with his master, a Tripiṭaka-āchārya.[1]

In the 6th cent. we have two notable instances of sea-journeys. One was the journey of Bodhidharma, mentioned above, who is said to have remained silent for nine years after his arrival in China, but who yet succeeded in impressing his spiritual influence and in opening a powerful stream of meditative naturalism in China and Japan.

[1] Later in the 6th cent., the Indians Bodhiruchi and Jñānagupta, the famous translators of many Mahāyāna texts, worked in the north.

[1] See J. Takakusu, *Pali Chrestomathy*, Tokyo, 1900, pp. lxxiv–lxxvi, and *JRAS*, 1896, pp. 416–439. Takakusu's conjecture that this 'master of the Three Baskets' might have been Buddhaghoṣa himself is plausible, but requires further confirmation. The translation of the *Samanta-pāsādikā* is dated 489.

The next instance was the voyage of Paramārtha, who arrived in China in 546 and was invited to Nanking in 548. To him we owe the translations of many of Asaṅga's and Vasubandhu's works and some other books. He was the first propagator of the Yogāchāra Buddhism in China, even before Yuan-chwang, the great translator of the 7th century.

Thus the Buddhist missionaries came to the Middle Kingdom from two sides by two routes, one *via* Central Asia and the other *via* Ceylon.[1] Their works of translation laid the foundation for the further development of their religion in the East, and have given us a rich store of information. On the other hand, we must not forget the pious zeal of the Chinese pilgrims who went to the West in search of truth and scriptures, the most prominent of whom was Fa-hian. It is related that the missionaries coming eastward and the pilgrims going westward met one another everywhere in the 5th and 6th centuries. By the conjoint labour of these men were completed the translations of the four *Āgamas*, together with several of their single parts; the Vinaya texts in various versions, belonging to different schools;[2] and the important Mahāyāna texts, such as the *Lotus*, the *Flower-garland* (*Avataṁsaka*), etc. From these works we can see how Buddhist ideas and expressions were naturalized in the Chinese language, which is totally of different structure from the originals. These books and expressions now form an integral part of the Chinese language and literature.

Up to the 5th cent. Buddhist missions in China consisted chiefly in the work of translation, though we may suppose that popular propaganda was not neglected. Besides these, the monastic institutions were an integral part of the Buddhist religion. The first translation of the *Pratimokṣa* (Pāli *Pātimokkha*) and the regular monastic discipline based on it were carried out by Dharmakāla, an Indian, who came to Lo-yāng in 250. In the 5th cent. we see a further establishment of the regular method of ordination under the government's patronage and supervision, carried out by Guṇavarman in the south, as mentioned above. The sustenance of these ordained monks and nuns was eagerly patronized as a deed of great merit by rulers as well as private persons. We hear that, when, in 446, Emperor Tā-wu of the northern Wei dynasty persecuted Buddhists, there were 3,000,000 of these monks and nuns in his territory alone. This may be an exaggeration; but it is quite conceivable that there were 83,000 ordained patronized by the Emperor Wu (reigned 502–549) of the Liāng (southern) dynasty, the great protector of Buddhism, and himself an ordained monk. Besides these regular monks many ascetics were revered as saints by the people, and they contributed much to the propagation of the religion, but as much to the dissemination of superstitions. They formed an eclectic element in Buddhism by adopting Taoistic and Indian ways of living and practices, but there were some who were really saintly, or at least beyond the world. Their lives are described in the *Book of Saints and Miracles* (Nanjio, no. 1484), and many of them are hardly to be distinguished from the Taoist 'men of mountains.' The people accustomed to look upon the Taoist miracle-workers as holy men were also attracted to these Buddhist 'saints.'

We can mention only one instance of a definite record of charitable work. That was a method of famine relief, called *Seng-chi-su*, or 'Church grain' (*Seng-chi* = Pāli *Saṅghika*), which was inaugurated by Thān-yao, a man of unknown origin, in the southern kingdom in 469; a certain percentage of the crops was stored in monasteries and distributed in cases of famine.

While missionary work was advancing, the foundations of doctrinal division, based on the schools prevalent in India, began to arise. The man who stood foremost in systematic treatises on doctrines was Tao-ān, mentioned above, who wrote commentaries and essays and emphasized the vacuity of the phenomenal world. In his time a translation of an *Abhidharma* text (Nanjio, no. 1273) was produced, and prepared for the promulgation of Vasubandhu's philosophy by Paramārtha sixty years later. The group of Lu-shan, already mentioned, was another sign of sectarian division, and these men opened the way for the later growth of the meditative Shan-no school and of the pietistic religion of the Buddha Amitābha. These were, however, only precursory movements for real sectarian division and dogmatic systematization; a really independent growth of Chinese Buddhism and formation of branches date from the latter half of the 6th cent., and then we pass from the missionary stage.

The unity of China achieved by 580 and the rise of the glorious T'āng dynasty in the beginning of the 7th cent. mark a new era of Chinese history, political as well as religious; and we may close our survey of the Buddhist missions with this time. It remains to be added that, in the 8th cent., the mystic Buddhism, known as the Mantra sect, was introduced by two foreign missionaries, Śubhakarasiṁha and Amoghavajra. This form of Buddhism became influential in Japan after the 9th century. Towards the close of the 10th cent. there was again an influx of Indian missionaries, but they are of no great significance.

2. In Tibet.—As in the case of China, the early history of Buddhism in Tibet is shrouded in nebulous legends. The missionaries dispatched by King Aśoka touched the Tibetan borders, probably along the western parts of the Himālayas; but it is more than a hundred years after his time that legend tells us of the establishment of a Buddhist temple on the Tibetan side of the mountain range. This legend and the story of the miraculous descent of four caskets containing Buddhist treasures, in the 4th cent. A.D., may be taken as indications of Tibet's contact with Buddhist missions. Dismissing these legends, the first date that can be assigned with certainty for Buddhism in Tibet is the 7th century. The reigning king was Srong-btsan Gam-po († 698), and Buddhism was introduced into Tibet by his marriage with a Chinese princess and also with a Nepālese princess. The former marriage is confirmed by Chinese history; the name of the princess was Wen-ch'eng, and the marriage took place in A.D. 641. She brought with her Buddhist statues and books, and probably some priests, and established a firm footing for Buddhism in that country, which had gradually been coming into contact with the religion through its eastern and southern borders. The Nepālese princess was the agent in introducing the occult worship of the Buddhico-Hindu goddess Tārā, the event which determined to a great degree the nature of Buddhism destined to prevail in Tibet.

The legends concerning this introduction of Buddhism into Tibet and the succeeding events throw little light on the nature of the missionary labours undertaken by the Buddhists; we are

[1] According to Nanjio, App. ii., among 72 translators who worked between 67 and 420, there were 15 Indians, 7 Yuechis, 5 Parthians, 7 Kubhans, 21 from the western countries and 17 Chinese; among them 22 worked in the south, of whom 5 were Chinese. Among 43 workers who worked between 420 and 550, 14 were Indians, 10 from Kubha and other western countries, 4 Siṁhalese and Indo-Chinese, and 4 uncertain. Among them 27 worked in the south.

[2] For the whole extent of the work done up to 520 see Nanjio, pp. xiii–xvii; for the *Āgama* texts see Anesaki, *op. cit.*

told only of the actions taken by the rulers and their ministers. Certainly the propaganda proceeded among the people by supplying them with new objects of worship and new methods of cult, but the most important factor in determining the fate of the new religion was in the hands of the rulers. The stimuli given by the Buddhist consorts of Srong-btsan Gam-po caused him to send his able minister Thummi Sambhota to India, where he performed a great service for Buddhism and for Tibet by inaugurating a Tibetan alphabet after the model of the Skr. Devanāgarī. Translation of Buddhist books, partly from Chinese, but much more from Sanskrit, was made possible by this system of Tibetan letters. A decisive step in the work of translating Buddhist books into Tibetan was taken more than a century later, in the reign of Khri-Srong De-btsan (reigned 740–786), who was a successful conqueror of borderlands. It was he who invited learned Buddhists from India and gave a decided turn to the nature of Tibetan Buddhism, because those Indians mostly advocated occult mysticism based on the belief in the efficacy of *dhāraṇī*, or mystic formulæ, and magic practices. Among these agents of mystic Buddhism we mention two names: Padmasambhava (or 'Lotus Growth,' with an allusion to the lotus as the womb of the cosmos), who introduced many writings, and his disciple, Pagur Vairochana, the 'Great Translator.'

The 9th cent. was a period of confusion in Tibet, and the fate of Buddhism passed through various vicissitudes in association with the inclination of the rulers and with their rise and fall. From the latter part of the 10th cent. we see fresh streams of N. Indian Buddhists and a firmer establishment of mystic Buddhism. Besides the translations, many original writings, historical and doctrinal, were composed in Tibetan; and the missionary stage may thus be closed in this period. After all, accessible material concerning Buddhist missions in Tibet is scarce, and what is known relates only to political support by the government, and to translations produced by foreigners and Tibetans.

The 13th cent. was an epoch-making period in the history of Tibetan Buddhism, in connexion with the conquest of Asia by the Mongol Kublai Khān. Buddhist missions seem to have been active before this time in Mongolia, and the Mongol conquerors were partly converted to Tibetan Buddhism, though all of them were eclectics of promiscuous nature. Tibetan Buddhism was definitely established as a theocracy by the energy and ability of Phagspa, the ally of Kublai Khān, and its influence was extended to the northern countries and even to China. The definitely independent, and totally isolated, growth of Tibetan Buddhism is to be dated from the latter part of the 14th cent., when the Mongol dynasty in China fell and the Tibetan reformer Tsong-Kha-pa arose.

3. In Korea.—When, in the 4th cent., Buddhism was being naturalized in Chinese culture, its propagation further eastwards began. At that time Korea was divided into three kingdoms and several minor States. Of these three Koryö (or Kokuryö) was situated in the north, and first came into contact with Buddhism. In 374 two monks, Atao and Shuntao, both of whom are said to have been foreigners, were invited from N. China to the capital of Koryö (the modern Pien-yang), and in the next year two temples [1] were built for them, while in 384 a certain Mālānanda was welcomed by the court of Păikchyöi, which was situated in the middle of the country. Historical records tell of the construction of temples and of the arrival of missionaries, both Indian and Chinese, from China, but little information is given of how they worked in their propaganda, this fact being partly due to the circumstance that these records were compiled by the Confucianists of the anti-Buddhist dynasty of the 15th century.

The Buddhist propaganda advanced to the southern extremity of the peninsula in the middle of the 5th century. An ascetic, nicknamed the 'Black Foreigner,' preached the Three Jewels in the south and is said to have cured a princess of the Silla kingdom by means of incense and spells. He was followed by some missionaries who came to the south and gained hold of the people's minds. The worship of Buddha was received officially by the king of Silla in 528, and this monarch and his successors were not less zealous in the Buddhist cause than the rulers of the north. The construction of temples and organization of Buddhist rites came into vogue. A king who ruled in 540–576 became a monk, and his consort became a nun; and the propaganda advanced so far in his reign that a Korean priest was appointed archbishop of the realm of Silla.

4. In Japan.—In nearly a century and a half Buddhism had converted the whole of Korea, and it was quite natural that the tide of the mission should also reach Japan, which had a close communication with the peninsular States and had introduced Chinese learning in the beginning of the 5th century. The religion was first advocated by the Korean immigrants, and then by some natives. After these preparations, it was presented officially by the king of Păikchyöi to the Japanese court as a sign of homage and friendship in 538 (the date is usually, but erroneously, given as 552). The presents consisted of a gilt statue of Buddha, scriptures, banners, and other ritual instruments,[1] and the message which accompanied these presents said:

> 'This teaching (*dharma*) is the most excellent of all teachings. It brings infinite and immeasurable fruits to its believers, even to the final enlightenment (*bodhi*). Just as the *Chintāmaṇi*[2] jewel is said to give inexhaustible wealth to its possessor, so the jewel of this glorious Law never ceases to give response to those who seek for it. Moreover, it has come to Korea from India, far distant, and the peoples of the countries lying between these two are now all adherents of it,' etc.

These words, accompanied with a fine image and works of art, were a marvellous revelation to a people who knew only how to invoke spirits supposed to be little superior to men. The court, on the other hand, was divided into two parties, one favourable to the new worship, and the other hostile, the point of their dispute being whether the newly-offered deity was more powerful than the national deities or not. The hidden motive of the difference, however, was the political clan strife, intermingled with the difference of progressive and conservative policies. During fifty years of strife the fate of the new religion seemed always wavering. But the presents were followed by an incessant influx of priests, monks, artisans, and physicians, as the rearguards of the religion. It was natural that elaborate rites and the practice of medicine should be most effectual means in the conversion of a rather primitive people like the Japanese at that time. Though the religion was not yet accepted officially by the court, some sovereigns cherished it as their faith, and the Soga family, the head of the progressionists, became its zealous advocates. They built topes and temples, and we hear of a nunnery founded by the family in 584. The fall of the conservative party in 587 marked a decisive step in the progress of Buddhism, and to commemorate this event a temple was built,

[1] The names of these temples, Syo-mun and I-pul-lan, sound neither Chinese nor Korean.

[1] Cf. W. G. Aston, *Nihongi*, ii. 65 f.

[2] The *chintāmaṇi* is a mythical jewel; Aston's translation, 'to his heart's content,' is not accurate.

for the first time at State expense. The erection of these and other Buddhist buildings caused constant importations of Buddhist statues, utensils, etc., accompanied by missionaries and artisans, and these displays of art were associated with works of charity. Three institutions—an asylum, a hospital, and a dispensary—were attached to a temple built in 593, and similar institutions were founded here and there in the subsequent centuries.

In the regency of Prince Shōtoku, the Constantine of Japan (reigned 593-622), the new religion became the State Church. Not only were missionaries and learned monks invited from Korea, but direct communication with Chinese Buddhism was opened (605), and Japanese monks were sent to China for study. The number of the Korean missionaries who worked in this period was considerable, and their achievements in preaching religion, in teaching science, especially astronomy, and in other matters, were a great credit to them; but the new religion found native teachers in less than a hundred years after its introduction. The prince himself gave lectures on Buddhist scriptures and organized various institutions. In short, the Buddhist propaganda in this century consisted first in the display of forms, then in works of charity, chiefly medical practices, and lastly in teaching. The mission, however, did not extend very far from the capital in Yamato. The acceptance of Buddhism was closely connected with the diplomatic relations with the Korean States and China, on the one side, and with the efforts to centralize the government and to unite the divided clans by religion, on the other. The development of religious institutions and the management of State affairs assisted each other.

After the decisive step of the adoption of the Buddhist faith had been once taken, the progress of the religion was sure and steady. Its influence was propagated gradually from the capital to the provinces. Many Korean immigrants, some of whom were usually monks and nuns, were offered homes in various provinces, and the number of native workers increased, some of whom studied in China or Korea. The donations given not only to large monasteries and to clergy of higher ranks, but also to the poor and aged monks and nuns, show how numerous were the ordained natives and immigrants. Besides these Korean and Japanese priests, a certain number of Chinese, Indians, and other foreigners carried on the Buddhist propaganda, the most famous of whom were Kanjin, a Chinese, and Bodhisena, an Indian. The former founded the central institution for ordination and monastic discipline, and was appointed archbishop (754–763 in Japan).[1] He was also an organizer of medical practice and founded a botanical garden. The Indian was of the Brāhman family Bhāradvāja. He came to Japan in 736 with his Annamese and Chinese followers, some of whom were musicians, and worked as a bishop till his death in 760, being known as the 'Brāhman bishop.' These missionaries brought many useful arts and things Indian, which contributed to the influence of the religion, such as musical instruments, Indian harps, and the bas-relief in the Græco-Bactrian style, preserved in the Imperial treasury, dating from the 8th century. Among the native workers there were some learned men, who laboured mostly in the capital as teachers and bishops; others were practical men who worked in the provinces in bridging rivers, constructing roads, canals, harbours, and ponds, opening mountain passages, planting avenues, etc. We do not know how or where these men learned their arts and crafts, but their works were so wonderful to the people that many miraculous stories are told of them even to this day. The mention of some Ainu monks, whom the court favoured with gifts in 689, shows the advance of the propaganda to the far north-east.

The elaborate system of ritual, medical work, etc., which had been the chief means of the propaganda, remained in vogue for a long time. The distribution of medical stores and the dispatch of combined bands of monks and physicians into the provinces are constantly mentioned in the 8th century. In addition to these methods, religious ceremonies for the welfare of the ruling families and for the tranquillity of the country became the order of the day in the court as well as in the temples, and were patronized by the government and by the nobles. These pious deeds were extended to the provinces, and scriptures were distributed wherever there were any priests. The founding of provincial cathedrals (*kokubun-ji*) was followed by the founding, near the capital, of the central cathedral, which was dedicated to the great statue of Lochana Buddha, now known as the Daibutsu in Nara, and was completed in 754. These works and dedications converted the whole of Japan into a Buddhadom before the close of the 8th century. There are many remains of these works to this day, and Japan owes the sculptures, which have never been excelled by later works, to the same period.

It is obvious that the methods of the religious mission contributed to the unification of the country. Charitable works were regarded in the provinces as the boons not only of the Church but also of the State; splendid religious buildings were held to be signs of the power of the court. It was not merely by the mysterious efficacy of the worship and ceremonies that the security of the throne and the tranquillity of the country were maintained and increased; the Buddhist mission in the provinces during these two centuries was at the same time a political mission.

By the 9th cent. the unity and centralization of the national government were complete. From that time Japanese Buddhism began to stand on its own feet, even though the Japanese Buddhists were still indebted to their co-religionists on the continent. The two brightest stars of the Buddhist history of Japan, Dengyō († 822) and Kōbō († 835), were once students in China, but these two men opened the way for the development of Japan's own Buddhism. Thus the beginning of the 9th cent. may be taken as the end of the Buddhist mission in Japan.

One thing remains to be added, viz. a new influx of Chinese influence in the latter half of the 13th century. The introduction of the Zen (*dhyāna*) Buddhism, which was produced by Bodhidharma in China, as mentioned above, necessitated a fresh influx of monks and artists, whose great influence upon Japanese art, literature, and social life in the 14th and 15th centuries must be recognized. Tea, fans, kakemono, and similar things, now known in the West as 'things Japanese,' Japan owes to these communications with Chinese Buddhism.

Taking a general survey, we see a remarkable contrast between the Buddhist missions in China and those in Japan. In China works of charity seem to have played rather an insignificant part and translations of scriptures an important part; the opposite was the case in Japan; no Japanese translation of the Buddhist scriptures was made till quite recent times. Chinese has remained the sacred language of Japanese Buddhism almost throughout, though there have been some original writings in Japanese. This antithesis is due to the different levels of civilization on which China and Japan stood at the time of the introduction of Buddhism.

[1] *Travels of Kanjin*, tr. J. Takakusu (in preparation).

LITERATURE.—B. Nanjio, *A Catalogue of the Buddhist Tripiṭaka*, Oxford, 1883, Introd. and App. ii.; *Nihongi*, tr. W. G. Aston, London, 1896, ii.; W. E. Griffis, *The Religions of Japan*, do. 1895, ch. x.; L. Hearn, *Japan, an Attempt at Interpretation*, New York, 1904, ch. x.; A. Lloyd, *The Creed of Half Japan*, London, 1911, first part; E. Schlagintweit, *Buddhism in Tibet*, Leipzig, 1863.
M. ANESAKI.

MISSIONS (Christian, Early and Mediæval).—**1. From the close of the Apostolic Age to the conversion of the Empire (c. A.D. 100–323).**—Missions were the main external activity of the Christian community in the earliest time. Before the middle of the 2nd cent. (*c.* 140) Justin Martyr claims for them a very wide field of operations—not merely over the Helleno-Roman world, but beyond.

'There exists not a people, whether Greek or barbarian, or any other race, by whatsoever title or manners they may be marked out, however ignorant of arts or of agriculture, whether they dwell under tents or wander in covered waggons, among whom prayers are not offered in the name of a crucified Jesus to the Father of all things' (*Dial. c. Tryph.* 117).

Much to the same effect, but more guardedly, Irenæus tells us (*c.* 180) that even then many barbarous nations held the Christian faith, written not with pen and ink, in books or papers, but by the Holy Spirit in their hearts (*adv. Hær.* III. iv. 2). Tertullian likewise (*c.* 200) boasts of the rapid spread of the Church:

'We are a people of yesterday, and yet we have filled every place belonging to you . . . your very camp, palace, . . . forum . . . we leave you your temples only. We can count your armies; our number in a single province will be greater' (*Apol.* 37).

Britons beyond the Roman pale, Sarmatians, Germans, and Scythians are among the more distant races that he reckons as already touched by Christianity (*adv. Judæos*, 7). Origen (*c.* 230–240) declares the gospel not merely to have won myriads of converts among 'all nations,' but, more precisely, to have penetrated into many parts of the barbarian world (*c. Cels.* i. 27, ii. 13); while Arnobius (*c.* 304) denies that any nation of the barbarians was then without some Christian influence (*adv. Gentes*, i. 16, ii. 5). From Eusebius (*c.* 320–330) we hear of the ex-Stoic Pantænus of Alexandria undertaking a missionary journey to India about 180 (*HE* v. 10); here Pantænus is said to have found a Gospel of St. Matthew in Hebrew which had been left there by the apostle Bartholomew. Even if by this 'India' is understood the 'Lesser' or 'Third India' of some early geographers, including parts of the S. Arabian shore-lands and of Abyssinia, this is a noteworthy journey. Origen again, about 215, was invited to teach the Gospel in Arabia, and accepted the invitation (Eus. *HE* vi. 19). From Edessa in N. Mesopotamia, where the Church was firmly settled by 150, Christianity was propagated in the Persian kingdom, even to Bactria. Bishop John, 'of Persia and Great India,' attended the Nicene Council in 325. Armenia, which may, however, be reckoned as usually within the Roman Empire, or at least within its sphere of influence, till the disasters of the later 4th cent., was won by the Church, shortly before the winning of the Empire, at the end of the 3rd century. Gregory the Illuminator was the leading person of this mission (*c.* 302), and Armenia was the first country in which Christianity was adopted as the national religion. In the early days of Constantine (*c.* 311) Bishop Hermon of Jerusalem sent missionaries (Ephraim and Basil) to 'Scythia' and to the Crimea, part of which at least may be considered Roman. About A.D. 100 St. Clement, the fourth bishop of Rome, had been martyred at Kherson, representing the modern Sevastopol.

2. From the conversion of the Empire to the rise of Islām (c. 323–632).—Important extensions of Christianity followed the conversion of Constantine.

(*a*) *Africa.*—Among these one is African. The Abyssinian Church was founded, or at least Christianity became the religion of the nation, from about 330, through the work of missionaries from Alexandria. Frumentius, a follower of Athanasius, who consecrated him as bishop of Ethiopia, or Nearer India, was the leader of this mission. From 356, again, the Arian emperor Constantius entered on a far-reaching scheme of Arian proselytism in Abyssinia, Southern and South-Western Arabia, and the coast lands of Persia and India, as far as the Indus, and perhaps beyond. Even before 250, perhaps by 200, Christianity had begun to spread among the native African tribes, on the fringe of the Roman Empire, in modern Tunis and Tripoli. In the 6th cent., in the reign of Justinian, and largely through the influence of the empress Theodora, Christianity was planted among the Nubians (from *c.* 548). Till the 14th cent. a Nubian Church maintained itself, though cut short by Muhammadan conquest, when, less fortunate, if not less heroic, than the Abyssinian (protected by its highlands, and saved, at a critical moment, by Portuguese aid), it succumbed to Islām.

(*b*) *Asia.*—In Asia, beyond the limits of the Empire, Christianity, Orthodox or Nestorian, went far afield, before the outbreak of Muhammadan conquest in the 7th century. Bishop John, 'of Persia and Great India,' as we saw, attended the Nicene Council in 325; in 334 we hear of a bishop of Merv; the line of the metropolitans of 'Babylon' (*i.e.* Ktesiphon and Seleukeia [Σελεύκεια ἡ ἐν Βαβυλῶνι]) likewise began in the 4th cent.; and in the same period the Persian Christians suffered fierce persecutions from the government, largely at Magian instigation. In the 4th cent. a Syrian mission went to Malabar. Arnobius even speaks vaguely of Christianity having been preached among the 'Seres,' or Chinese of the interior—'China as approached by land'—before the conversion of Constantine, but this is unsupported and in itself doubtful.

In the 5th cent. Nestorius and his followers were cast out of the Church (431); a Nestorian communion was rapidly organized; and a wonderful missionary energy was shown by this 'Protestantism of the East.' In 498 the Nestorian patriarchate of Babylon or Ktesiphon was set up; this in 762 followed the 'Abbāsid khalīfs to their new capital of Baghdād. About 505 Christianity reached China in Nestorian form. In 551 Nestorian monks brought the eggs of the mulberry silkworm from China to Constantinople. Before 540 Nestorian bishops appeared at Samarqand and Herat, and from the same time we have sepulchral evidences of Nestorian Christianity as far as the Semiryechensk, or 'Seven Rivers,' district of the Balkhash basin, close to the Russo-Chinese frontier of to-day. These funeral monuments extend from A.D. 547 to 1027, but are mostly of the 10th and early 11th centuries; they commemorate clergy, laymen, and women. One refers to a priest 'sent round to visit the churches,' perhaps something of a missionary. Gregory of Tours in the 6th cent. collected some information about Indian Christianity, partly from an Indian Christian who had come to Western Europe from the 'Thomas Country' near Madras. Nestorian missions had now penetrated to India, and were transforming the native Christianity.

Cosmas Indicopleustes of Alexandria, the author of the *Christian Topography*, who in his earlier life was probably a Nestorian himself, describes the vast extent of an Eastern Christianity, beyond the Imperial limits, which must have been largely Nestorian, about 550. Churches were then to be found, he declares, in Ceylon, Malabar, and Socotra, with 'a bishop and clergy ordained and sent from Persia'; in Bactria and among the Huns; in Mesopotamia, Scythia, Hyrcania, and other lands east of the Euxine (see bks. iii. and xi., esp. p. 178 f. of B. de Montfaucon's ed. [*Coll. nova Patr. et Script. Græc.*, Paris, 1706, ii. 113 ff.]=*PG* lxxxviii. 168 f.). At no time, perhaps, till the Russian colonization of North Asia was Christianity more strongly supported in Eastern lands than at this time.

(*c*) *Europe.*—St. Patrick's conversion of Ireland (from *c.* 430) opened to Christendom a land that had never been Roman, and was practically unknown to Continental Europe, after Honorius withdrew the legions from Britain. The full discovery of Ireland was the work of Christian missionaries. Within a century of St. Patrick's death the Irish took up a great mission-work of their own. From about 550 to 800 the Irish Church showed its greatest energy abroad, and perhaps reached its highest prosperity at home. Its followers preached with remarkable success among the English who had overrun Eastern Britain. They carried the gospel further into Caledonia than Agricola had ever carried Roman conquest. Some of their pioneers reached the Orkneys, the Faroes, the outermost Hebrides, and even Iceland (of the last Irish monks were the first discoverers, in 795).

Despite the fictions with which the early history of Scotland is overlaid, it need not be questioned that some progress was made by Christian missions beyond the Firth of Forth even in the 5th century. St. Ninian, the founder of 'Candida Casa' in Galloway, who was apparently working in the south-west and centre of modern Scotland about 390–430, is specially associated with these enterprises.

The Roman mission dispatched by Pope Gregory I. to England in 597 was concerned with a country lying within the Old Empire, and so outside the proper field of this article. It was, however, the commencement of a movement which in course of time penetrated to non-Roman lands—Scotland, Ireland, Central Germany, the Scandinavian kingdoms—and played a great part in winning them to Christianity, or in turning them from their native Church to Roman allegiance.

3. From the rise of Islām to the Crusades (632–1096).—The vigour, or at least the extent, of Nestorian missions in South Asia in the first age of Islām is evident from a letter of bitter complaint from the Nestorian patriarch to the bishop of Fārs (or 'Persia' proper) about 650. It was owing to his neglect, the patriarch declares, that the people of Khorāsān had lapsed from the faith, and that India, 'from Fārs to Colon' (Kulam, or Quilon, near Cape Comorin), was now being deprived of a regular ministry. We find the same patriarch writing to the Christians of Socotra and of Balkh, and undertaking to provide a fresh supply of bishops for his spiritual subjects of the Upper Oxus. His successor, in order to appease an old quarrel between the Christians of Bactria and the metropolitan of Persia, visited Balkh about 661.

But the crowning achievements of early Nestorian enterprises were in China, and of these we have an account in the famous monument of Si-gan Fu. In 635–636 a missionary, who appears in the Chinese Record as 'Olopan' (Rabban), entered the 'Flowery Land,' and reached Si-gan Fu, the capital of the Tang dynasty. He had come, we are told, from 'Great China' (the Roman Empire); he was received with favour; his teaching was examined and approved; his Scriptures were translated for the Imperial library; and within three years an Imperial edict declared Christianity a tolerated religion. With the speculative fairness of his race (and of one of the greatest of Chinese rulers) T'ait-sung welcomed any religion whose spirit was 'virtuous, mysterious, and pacific.'

The radical principle of the new faith, he thought, 'gave birth to perfection and fixed the will.' It 'was exempt from verbosity, and considered only good results.' Therefore it was 'useful to man, and should be published under the whole extent of the Heavens. . . . And I command the magistrates to erect a temple of this religion in the Imperial city, and twenty-one religious men shall be installed therein.'

T'ait-sung's successor was no less friendly.

'He fertilized the truth, and raised luminous temples [Christian Churches] in all the provinces,' till they 'filled a hundred cities. . . . The households were enriched with marvellous joy.'

'Olopan' himself became a 'Guardian of the Empire,' and 'lord of the Great Law.'

Then followed, from about A.D. 683, a time of disfavour and oppression. Chinese conservatism rallied against the new worship.

'The children of Che [Buddhists] resorted to violence, and spread their calumnies; low-class men of letters put forth jests. . . .'

But after a time the Nestorian Church in China, as in India (and about the same time), revived. Fresh missionary enterprise was one cause of this, in both fields.

In A.D. 744 'there was a religious man of Great China named Kiho, who travelled for the conversion of men'; on his arrival in the Middle Kingdom, illustrious persons united 'to restore the fallen Law.' In 747 the emperor brought back 'the venerable images' to the Temple of Felicity, and firmly raised its altars; with his own hand he 'wrote a tablet' (probably for the great church of the capital). His three successors all 'honoured the luminous multitude.' One observed Christmas by burning incense; another 'instituted nine rules for the propagation of the doctrine'; various high officials of the court, a member of the council of war, and several governors of provinces 'rendered perpetual service to the luminous gate.' The inscription closes with words of thankfulness; never had the mission been more prosperous than when 'in the year of the Greeks 1092 (A.D. 781), in the days of the Father of Fathers, the Patriarch Hanan-Yeshuah, this marble tablet was set up with the history of the . . . preaching of our fathers before the kings of the Chinese.' Hanan-Yeshuah died in 778, but news of his death would naturally take a considerable time to travel from Baghdād to Si-gan Fu.

The general truthfulness of this record (the most remarkable witness that we possess of Christian activity in the Further East before the 13th cent.) is supported by what we know of the Chinese mission from other sources.

Between 714 and 728 the Nestorian patriarch appointed the first metropolitan for China; in 745 the Chinese emperor decreed the name of 'Roman temples' to the Christian churches of his empire; about 790 the patriarch of Baghdād sent a new metropolitan to Si-gan Fu, and after his murder at the hands of robbers a successor was dispatched, with six other bishops and a party of monks.

Like the Chinese mission, the Indian was revived in the middle of the 8th century. About 745 a party from Baghdād, Nineveh, and Jerusalem, under orders from the arch-priest at Edessa, arrived in India, with the merchant Thomas — the 'Armenian merchant' of Gibbon (*Decline and Fall of the Roman Empire*, ed. J. B. Bury, London, 1896–1900, v. 150).

In 774 the Hindu ruler of the Malabar coast granted a charter, graven on copper, to the Christians of his dominions. A famous inscription discovered in 1547, on St. Thomas Mount near Madras, probably of the 8th cent., but perhaps even earlier, another charter of 824, to the Malabar Christians, the journey of Bishop Abraham about 800 from Basra to China, and the Arab references to the strength of Christianity at this time and down to the Far Eastern revolution of 878, may also be cited. Finally, the continuance of the lines of metropolitans in China, India, and the Merv region, and the permission granted them, about 850, to be absent from the central councils of the Nestorian Church (at or near Baghdād, every four years), are other fragments of evidence to the vigour of Nestorian missions at a time (*c.* 750–850) which perhaps marked the close of their greatest development.

From the end of the 9th cent., however, this Nestorian expansion began to be seriously checked. The Nestorians had been in high favour, not only with the Chinese emperors, but also with the Muhammadan khalifs, as guides to the Greek treasures of letters, science, and medicine. But, as Arabic learning progressed, the Nestorian position became less important and privileged; the spread of Islām tended more and more to contract the area still left open for Nestorian activity in many regions; and in China the old conservatism revived. The disorders of 878 and the years following produced another Chinese reaction against alien importations. The baleful effects of civil war were attributed to foreign devilry, and in the next century Chinese Christianity much declined. Thus a Muslim writer of the later 10th cent. (*c.* A.D. 987) reports a conversation in Baghdād with a monk who had been sent to China seven years before, and had returned in despair on finding but one person of his faith still extant there. This was probably pessimism. Nestorianism, even to the 14th cent., maintained a certain position in the Far East; it was the only form of Christianity that the Polos found (and in many a city they found it) scattered, however thinly, throughout the Chinese Orient; in the 11th cent. it had won fresh triumphs in Central Asia. About 1007–08 the Khān of the Keraits (one of the four main branches of the Mongol Tatars, living in the basin of Lake Baikal) was converted to Nestorian Christianity. With him doubtless went many, perhaps the bulk, of his tribe; and in this event is apparently the ultimate source of the tradition of 'Prester,' Presbyter, or Priest, 'John.' In all its earliest forms this tradition is not African, but Asiatic; it refers to a Christian potentate in the 'extremity of the East' or the heart of Asia, supposed to unite in himself royal and sacerdotal power and office, to have great military and political importance, to rule extensive dominions, and to uphold the faith of the Cross, though surrounded by unbelievers, and cut off by vast distance from the main body of the Church. This is the story, as it takes shape in the 12th cent., and as it is referred to by the great European travellers of the 13th; not till the 14th (from *c.* 1330) do we find it transferred to Africa and associated with the 'Emperor of the Ethiopians' or Negush of Abyssinia.

In Northern Europe, beyond the limits of the Old Empire, the Roman missions advanced rapidly in the 8th cent., after success in England had once been achieved, and largely as a result of the reflex action of that English mission. The movement that Gregory had started flowed back upon the Continent with new force from the converted island. In Frisia, Thuringia, and Bavaria the tribes beyond the Rhine were gradually converted by Frankish, Irish, and English missionaries in the obedience of Rome; chief among these was the church-statesman and martyr St. Boniface or Winfrith of Crediton (680–755), who became the 'apostle of the Germans,' the first bishop of Mainz and primate of Germany, the reformer of the Frankish Church.

Charles the Great's very forcible conversion of the Old Saxons, between the Ems and the Elbe, again advanced the borders of Christendom on the North (772–804). The same emperor compelled the prince of the Slav Czechs of Moravia to receive baptism (801); but the real conversion of this people, as well as of the neighbouring sister-race of Bohemia, was begun by the Byzantines Cyril and Methodius of Thessalonica, the 'apostles of the Slavs,' from about 863. Cyril had already worked with great success among the (Turkish?) Khazars of S. Russia. Like Ulfilas with the Gothic script, Cyril and his brother formed a Slav alphabet still prevailing in Russia, Serbia, and Bulgaria, and in Moravia down to the 16th century. Greek formed the basis of the 'Cyrillic' letters in most cases; but some were entirely new—either invented by the missionaries or adapted from various Oriental writings. By the diplomacy of Pope Nicholas I. Cyril and Methodius were brought into close relations with, and obedience to, Rome, and all their Central European work was turned to the profit of the Roman Church. By the end of the 9th cent. the victory of Latin Christianity among most branches of the Czechs may be accepted as complete.

The conquests of Charles the Great brought Frankish Christendom into close proximity to the Scandinavian peoples and the Slavs of the North European plains, and soon after the death of Charles the conversion of these races was seriously commenced. Ansgar or Anskar, the 'apostle of the North,' was born about 801, and about 826 left the monastery of Corbie for the 'Northern mission.' First he worked (with his helpers) in Nordalbingia (or Holstein) on the Danish border, and in Schleswig; obliged to quit this field by a pagan reaction, he made his way even to Sweden in 829, preached before the king, won a great measure of success, and in 831 was consecrated the first archbishop of Hamburg. He was driven hence by a Scandinavian invasion about 845; but in 848 he was appointed to the vacant see of Bremen, with which the missionary diocese of Hamburg was now united. He resumed his work in Denmark (848–853), won the favour of the Danish king, converted a large part of the people, and again opened his campaign in Sweden (*c.* 853). At his death in 865 Danish, Swedish, and perhaps even Norse Christianity had been securely founded, though complete triumph was not reached for more than a century.

The Bulgarians of the Balkans, settled within the limits of the Old Empire, received Christianity from Constantinople about 845–865, largely by means of the patriarch Photius. This gain was fiercely disputed between Rome and the East, for the Bulgarian Czar, instructed and probably baptized by Photius, also turned his inquiring mind to Pope Nicholas I., and received from him a further supply of Christian teaching and practical advice. The struggle over Bulgaria was one of the chief surface-causes for that schism of Eastern and Western Christianity which now became decisive, and was never really healed again. But the Orthodox Church remained in possession of her Bulgarian gains—in spite of the appeal of Nicholas to listen first to Rome amidst the claims of conflicting teachers, and to cleave to that Church 'which had always been without spot, or wrinkle, or any such thing.'

In the 9th cent., after the sack of Iona by the Northmen (806), the relics of St. Columba seem to have been translated to Dunkeld, which became for a time the centre of Scottish Christianity—till St. Andrews, from about 905, took its place.

Poland perhaps received its first knowledge of Christianity from Bohemia and Moravia. From about 967 the court and ruling classes accepted the new faith in its Roman form, and before 1000 the establishment of Latin Christianity was completed, under the great conqueror Boleslav, who first raised Poland to the position of an important European State.

The earliest mission among the heathen Prussians was probably undertaken by Adalbert (or Voytyech), second bishop of Prague, who travelled into Prussia in 996, and was martyred on the shores of the Frische Haff in April 997. Boleslav 'the Great' of Poland, who had encouraged this mission, placed the martyr's relics at the court-town of Gnesen, which now became an Archbishopric.

The Hungarians, whose attacks on Germanic and Italian Europe were finally ended by the defeat on the Lechfeld in 955, at the hands of Otto the Great, were rapidly won to the Western Church by mission enterprise. By about 975 considerable progress had been made; the reigning Hungarian prince Geisa (972–997) was a nominal, if semi-pagan, Christian; but the complete victory of Christianity was gained by the first king, Stephen 'the Saint,' baptized by Adalbert of Prague about 983. Stephen was called to succeed his father Geisa in 997; he took the royal title in 1000; he put down the pagan opposition; and before his death in 1038 he had completed the establishment of the Latin Church in his kingdom, had organized that kingdom with remarkable success, and had given it a first impression of civilization. He founded colleges, hospitals, and monasteries for Hungarians in Rome, Ravenna, Constantinople, and Jerusalem, and his hospitality to pilgrims was so generous that the overland route through the Hungarian plain came to be generally preferred by the mass of those travelling from Western Europe to Constantinople and Syria.

Roman Christianity, as introduced by Ansgar, won the allegiance of the king, court, and ruling classes of Denmark in the days of Harold Blaatand, or 'Blue Tooth,' a century after Ansgar, from about 966. Yet even after this there was a pagan reaction, accompanied by some persecution (1000–04), under Svend, or Swegen, 'Forkbeard,' the conqueror of England, who vacillated between the old heathendom and the new faith, but finally embraced the latter, after his triumph in the West. Cnut the Great, Svend's son and successor (1014–35), was almost a Danish Clovis, and identified his policy with the work of the Christian Church in all ways.

Christianity in Sweden, likewise founded by Ansgar, did not become the faith of the court and the governing classes till the end of the first millennium, under Olaf the 'Lap-King' (955–1022). Pagan reactions still occurred till far on in the 11th cent., a final one on the eve of the First Crusade—but the battle was really won by 1020.

The first faint beginnings of (Latin) Christianity in Norway may also be traced back to Ansgar's time. Under Haakon I. (935–961) it began to struggle for predominance; the king for a long time endeavoured to promote it, but in his later years, for political and other reasons, he yielded much to the wishes of the pagan party. Heathen and Christian struggled for ascendancy till the short and brilliant reign of Olaf Tryggvason (995–1000), who forced the gospel on the bulk of his subjects with every kind of violence and every art of persuasion. The work was completed by Olaf the Saint, the godchild and third successor of Tryggvason (1015–30).

From Norway Christianity was carried to the Norse colonies of Iceland and Greenland. The German priest Thangbrand, a truly militant missionary, who killed opponents in single combat, was sent to Iceland by Olaf Tryggvason in 997; in 1000 the new faith was accepted (with some important concessions to heathenism) in a National Assembly; and at the same time the gospel reached Greenland, where it soon won the allegiance of the colonists.

Leif Ericson, probably the first discoverer of America, was commissioned by Olaf Tryggvason in 1000 to proselytize his countrymen, on his return from the court of Norway to his home in Eric's Fiord, but the missionary journey was interrupted by storms, which drove Leif to Vinland (Nova Scotia ?).

Russia was not really won till the time of Vladimir the Great ('St. Vladimir,' 986–1015). The patriarch Photius, it is true, claims (*c.* 867) that the fierce and barbarous Russians had already been converted by the missions of the Eastern Church, but even a century later the mass of the people were thoroughly heathen. Decisive Christian success began with the conversion of Olga, the princess-regent of Kieff, and widow of the grand-prince Igor, who visited Constantinople in 955, and was there baptized into the Greek Church. The full triumph of the faith was delayed for a generation by the refusal of Olga's son Svyatoslav to abandon his heathenism. The work was finished by Vladimir, son and successor of Svyatoslav, and the most effective and powerful head of the Russian people that had yet appeared, under whom Russia gave premature and deceptive promise of playing a first-class part in the world, in the 10th and 11th centuries. After his capture of the Imperial (Byzantine) dependency of Kherson in the Crimea (on the site of the later Sevastopol), and his marriage with an Imperial princess in 988, he accepted the Christianity of the Eastern Church; and his court and the mass of his people followed the example of the grand-prince of Kieff. The progress of the faith was both rapid and deep; no part of Europe became more intensely attached to its Christianity, and no nation perhaps has done more to spread the Christian faith, as it has understood the same. Vladimir died in 1015, but under Yaroslav the Lawgiver (1019–54), who with his father must rank as the chief Russian statesman of the earlier and freer age—before the Tatars—the establishment of the Church was completed.

4. From the First Crusade to the end of the mediæval time (1096–1453).—Thus, before the close of the 11th cent., nearly all Europe had been won to Christianity of the Roman or the Greek allegiance, and the borders of Christendom had been extended, to North and East, far beyond the limits of the Old Empire—to Greenland and Iceland, to Norway, Sweden, and Denmark, to the shores of the Baltic, the plains of Poland, the Carpathian highlands, and the western regions of Modern Russia—Kieff, Smolensk, Novgorod. Novgorod enterprise, it is probable, had by 1096 carried the religion as well as the trade of that great Republic into some of the regions and among some of the tribes of the furthest North and North-East—in the White Sea basin and in the valleys of the Dvina and Pechora.

A little later, in 1121, the bishop of Greenland undertook what was probably a missionary journey to America—he 'seeks Vinland'—but we hear no more of him.

Christendom, as thus constituted, included some pagan *enclaves*, mainly along the South and East of the Baltic, such as the countries of the Lithuanians, the Finns of Finland (and N. Russia), the Old Prussians, and the Wends and other Slavs of Pomerania and other lands afterwards included in Eastern Germany. In the 12th cent. much of this land began to be won. The Finns of Finland were conquered by the Swedes in a war which had something of a crusading character (*c.* 1157–58), and the profession of the Roman Catholic faith was gradually enforced. Russian Christianity meanwhile appears expanding in the far North and East by its foundation of the St. Michael's monastery, on the site of Archangel (in the 12th cent.), and of the important Novgorod colony of Vyatka, north of Kazan (1174). Latin Christianity accompanied the early victories of Germanism beyond the Elbe in the 10th century. The pagan and anti-German reaction which set in about 983 was equally injurious to Teutonic Christendom and Empire, and much of the new mission ground was lost. Polish and German attempts to convert the Pomeranians led to small result till well on in the

12th cent., when Otto of Bamberg (in 1124–28) became the 'apostle' of this country. From the time when the main German advance beyond the Elbe was permanently resumed, about 1130, the progress of Christianity was rapid between the Elbe and the Oder; and the extension of the bishoprics of Magdeburg, Oldenburg, and Ratzeburg witnessed to this. German colonization followed German conquest, and, as the colonists were at least nominal Christians, the Church grew steadily stronger.

German Christianity (accompanying German colonization) was planted as far east as the Düna or Western Dvina (the river of Riga) in the later 12th cent.; some Bremen merchants formed a settlement on or near the site of Riga about 1158, and about 1168 Meinhard, an Augustinian canon of Holstein, headed a mission to Livonia. The work was difficult, for the Livonians were a faithless race who professed the proper sentiments when advantage was to be gained from them, but turned upon the mission with mockery and insult when they no longer needed its help (Meinhard built them not only churches, but fortifications). An eclipse brought the missionaries into peril—they were accused of swallowing the sun. Their danger was hardly less when they were justly suspected of a more successful cultivation of the land than was then usual in Livonia. Baptisms were constantly 'washed off' in the Dvina by lapsed converts. Meinhard, consecrated bishop of Livonia in 1170, died in 1196, without having achieved much success. His second successor, Albert of Apeldern and Riga, had superior fortune, tact, and abilities. He organized a Livonian Crusade (permitted by Innocent III. to rank as a fulfilment of the vow for the Holy War in Syria); he enlisted considerable forces of warriors and missionaries; in 1200 he founded, or re-founded, the city of Riga as a new base for conquest and proselytism, and as the seat of the bishopric; and in 1202 he started the *Fratres Militiæ Christi*, the 'Knights' or 'Brethren of Christ,' or 'of the Sword,' the *Schwertträger* or *Port-glaives* of German and French historians, an important element in the Teutonic Order and a main source of its dominion on the Baltic. Pope Innocent gave the 'Sword-Brethren' the statutes of the Templars. Albert's mission-crusade had rapid success, and most of Livonia was baptized before the close of 1206.

A mission in Esthonia was commenced a little earlier than this by Bishop Fulk, formerly a monk of La Celle; and Dietrich, Meinhard's chief lieutenant in Livonia, became bishop of Esthonia in 1213. He was killed in 1218, and the next bishop transferred the headquarters of the mission (now thoroughly German) to Yuryev, Derpt, or Dorpat, in 1224. A Danish mission in Esthonia, at this time largely in Danish hands, was organized from Reval, which became a bishopric in 1218. Even in Lithuania a Roman mission appears to have started in the first half of the 13th cent., but its progress was slow, and general or definite success was not attained till the first Union of Poland and 'Litva' in 1386.

In 1236–37 the 'Sword-Brethren' united with the Teutonic Knights, founded at Acre in 1190, and summoned to help in the conquest and conversion of Old Prussia in 1226. They had much in common—an origin from Bremen, a constitution on the model of the Templars, the patronage of the Virgin, the protection of the emperors, the 'duty of fighting for the Cross,' the championship of the German race and German interests against all other.

This brings us to the Prussian crusade and mission. The early unsuccessful attempts at proselytism in Old Prussia, mainly under Polish patronage, have been noticed. In 1207 the Poles began again, with better appearance of success. In 1215 a Prussian bishop was consecrated. But a violent heathen reaction soon followed, accompanied by massacre, and by the destruction, it is said, of 250 churches. The supporters of the mission now fell back on the idea of a holy war, and in 1218 Pope Honorius III. allowed a Prussian Crusade as a substitute for the Syrian. In 1226 the Teutonic Order, already despairing of much permanent effect in the Levant, though its nominal headquarters remained at Acre till 1291, was invited to help, and terms were made between the grandmaster, Hermann of Salza, and the Poles, mainly represented by duke Conrad of Mazovia. The emperor Frederic II., the intimate friend and patron of Hermann, gave the fullest support in his power, bestowing on the Order the sovereignty of all such territories as they had acquired by gift or should win by conquest. A long, bloody, and desperate struggle of over fifty years brought about (by 1283) the complete submission of the Prussians, the partial extermination of the race, the enforced conversion of the remainder, and the German colonization of a great province which was to become one of the most Teutonic of lands, and to give name, by union with Brandenburg, to the chief German State of modern times, the creator and core of the present German Empire.

The opening of intercourse in 1245 between Western Europe and the new Mongol masters of Asia, through the embassies sent by Pope Innocent IV. to the Tatar courts, proved to be the beginning of an important and romantic chapter of mission history. Among the distant enterprises of the Christian Church, or the forgotten incidents of past intercourse between remote civilizations, there are few more interesting than the early Roman missions in Further and Central Asia, and in the border-lands of Eastern Europe. We have seen how, in the earlier Middle Ages, Nestorian missionaries carried the gospel to China, Turkestan, and the Indies. Almost to the close of the crusading period, their creed was practically the sole representative of the Nazarene faith in Asia, outside the narrow limits of the shrunken Byzantine Empire and the crusading principalities. But in the 13th cent. the Church of Rome began to be heard of in the depths of 'Tartary,' and between 1245 and 1255 the great overland travellers of the first generation, the Friars John de Plano Carpini, William de Rubruquis or Rubrouck, and Andrew of Longumeau, appeared in the Mongol courts, on the Volga, or in the Baikal or Balkhash basins. Yet their work was primarily that of diplomatists, of envoys from the pope or the king of France, in their capacity as Christian leaders; the missionary was not prominent in their work; Rubruquis alone, of this famous group, seems to have spent time or energy in doctrinal discussions or proselytizing efforts, and even he does not claim in any way to have founded a mission church in Asia or in Russia.

The Polos, again, who represented Roman Christendom among the Mongols from 1260 to 1295, and gave us our first good account of the Chinese and Indian worlds and of so much of Central Asia, cannot be considered active propagandists. Kublai Khān expressed a desire for official Christian instructors; but his wish remained unfulfilled. Marco Polo and his relatives were primarily merchants, adventurers, men of the world. No mission work can be credited to them.

But, while the Polos were still in China, the founder of the Latin churches both in Cathay and in India started on his way. Friar John de Monte Corvino, a Franciscan like Carpini and Rubruquis, and a man of untiring energy, courage, and patience, began his life-work in Asia about 1275, and in 1289 was sent by Pope Nicolas IV. with letters to the great men of the Tatar empire and of neighbouring lands—the supreme Khān in Cathay, the Īlkhān in Persia, the 'emperor of Ethiopia,' and others. Corvino reached Cathay in 1292 or 1293, apparently by the South Asiatic sea-route from Ormuz, making a long halt upon the way in the Madras region (or 'St. Thomas's country'). He achieved conspicuous success in the Far East; he was repeatedly reinforced from home; and his work led to the creation of a regular Roman hierarchy, with at least two bishoprics, in the 'Middle Kingdom.' He was even credited, by one tradition, with the conversion of a Mongol-Chinese emperor. To him is due not only the first planting of Western Christianity in China and in the Indies, but the earliest noteworthy Christian account of South Indian climate, people, manners, and customs, and some valuable evidence upon the overland and oversea routes which connected the Levant and the Far East, as well as upon the association of Western traders and Western missionaries in the European penetration of Asia.

Corvino seems to have made his way into Persia by much the same route—through Sivās, Erzerum, and Kars—as merchants then took between the Gulf of Scanderoon and Tabrīz. At Tabrīz, however, he was joined by a 'great merchant and faithful Christian,' Peter of Lucolongo, and with this companion he turned aside from the continental main track and made his way south into India, with the view of there taking ship for Cathay (1291). Some time, however, was yet to elapse before the friar committed himself to the frail barks of the Indian seas—'flimsy and uncouth, without nails or iron of any sort, sewn together with twine like clothes, without caulking, having but one mast, one sail of matting, and some ropes of husk' (cf. *Münchner gelehrte Anzeigen*, xxii. [1855] 175).

In the sacred region of St. Thomas's shrine, near Madras, he remained eighteen months, and here died his comrade, Nicolas of Pistoia, 'on his way to the Court of the Lord of all India.' He was buried in the Church of St. Thomas, while Corvino transmitted to Europe (22nd Dec. 1292) a quaint and memorable sketch of the Deccan and its people from his own observation—one of the earliest pictures of Indian life drawn by a Roman Christian or Western European — which seems to have awakened the papacy to the possibilities of Hindu conversion. Meantime, while Friar John was writing, the Polos were off the Coromandel coast —on their return to Europe—and here Messer Marco Millione may have met the man who was to represent Christendom in the 'Middle Kingdom' during the next thirty years, as the Venetian merchants had done for the past thirty.

We next meet with Corvino in China itself—at the Imperial city. His second letter (of 8th Jan. 1305) is dated from Peking, or 'Cambalec,' and tells how for eleven years, from 1293, he had laboured in Cathay; how he had struggled against prejudice and calumny; how brilliant successes had followed dismal failures; and how, in 1304, he had at last been joined by a colleague, Friar Arnold of Cologne. Probably he landed at the great port of 'Zayton,' or Amoy, in Fo-kien; apparently he made his way immediately to Peking. In any case, he failed to convert the emperor, Tīmūr Oljāitū, son and successor of Kublai, and a great favourer of the Buddhist lamas—'nimis inveteratus in idolatria,' as Corvino puts it. But he was not long without a triumph. In his first year at Cambalec he won the Nestorian Prince George, 'of the family of the great King Prester John of India' (Wadding, *Annales Minorum*, vi. 69). George died in 1299, but before his death he found time to build a fine church for his new allegiance, 'called the Roman Church,' at a place twenty days' journey from Peking—perhaps at Tatung in Shan-si, just east of the great Ho-ang-ho elbow, where Friar Odoric seems also to fix 'the capital of Prester John' (*ib.* vi. 70). The 'Prester John' and Prince George here referred to are probably of the royal house of the Kerait Tatars, of the Baikal basin, apparently converted to Nestorian Christianity in the 11th century (cf. above, p. 707ᵃ). Nor was this all. Prince George's heir was named after the missionary; a translation of all the Roman service-books was ordered and begun; many Nestorians embraced Corvino's faith.

With the death of King George, however, the sky was again overcast; apostasy succeeded conversion; there was no more translation of the Latin ritual; and Corvino was left alone to endure the slanders of the Nestorians—a community 'professing the Christian name, but deviating from the Christian faith,' and now so powerful in Cathay that they would tolerate no Christian rivals (*ib.* vi. 69).

At last the prospect brightened; a leading enemy confessed; in 1303 the friar was at last permitted to live at court; in 1304 Brother Arnold joined him; with a little more aid the emperor himself, 'Imperator Cham,' might be gained. The writer was now old and grey, more with toil than with years, for he was but fifty-eight; yet he was now building a second church in Peking; New Testament and Psalms he had just done into the 'language most used among the Tatars.' For one thing he still yearned—news of Europe, of the Church, of his Order. Twelve years had passed in silence; and now a farrago of incredible blasphemies about the court of Rome, the Order of St. Francis, and other matters of the Western world had been spread abroad by a Lombard surgeon newly come to Cathay—'ante duos annos,' otherwise in 1302 or 1303. Brother John, therefore, on every account was anxious for fresh help; but, warned by his own troublous sea-voyage, he laid down the best route for subsequent travellers—by the Crimea, the Volga, and the Steppes. By this overland path, travelling along with the Imperial messengers, a man might get through to Peking in six months.

Corvino's third letter is also from Peking, and was written on Quinquagesima Sunday, 13th Feb. 1306. Its tone is hopeful; its record is one of steady progress. In 1305 a new church and adjoining mission buildings had been commenced in 'Cambalec'; the emperor honoured the friar above all other 'prelates' at his court; and, like Kublai, his great ancestor, he desired earnestly to see envoys from the see of Rome and the nations of Western Christendom. With such a soil to work upon, the writer joyfully anticipated the harvest that might reward the friars who had lately arrived in Persia and the Crimea.

In a postscript Corvino tells of yet another triumph. Some time previously, either during his stay in India or after his arrival in the Flowery Land, an embassy from Ethiopia had waited on him with entreaties to come over and help them, to visit their country himself, or to send good preachers there. Since the days of St. Matthew and his disciples, they declared, they had never seen a Christian teacher. It is with Nubian Christianity that tradition especially associated St. Matthew; the local Church, though long doomed, was not everywhere extinct; and the earlier 14th cent. saw more than one effort of the Roman see to win this difficult and dangerous country.

Corvino addressed these letters to the Brethren of the Franciscan and Dominican missions in Persia and the Steppe lands of Southern Russia. His appeal was not unheeded; and the authorities of the Church, fired with his own enthusiasm, took up the mission that he had begun with something of the spirit that he desired.

New conquests seemed now to open before the Church of Rome. Friar John was created archbishop of Cambalec (with exceptional powers) in the spring of 1307, and seven bishops (of whom three only persevered) were dispatched to consecrate and help the new primate of Cathay. In 1308 these three suffragans—Gerard, Peregrine, and Andrew—reached China, and carried out the consecration of Corvino. Each of them appears successively in the history of the mission as bishop of 'Zayton' in Fo-kien, where a powerful Latin mission was gradually established, and where some Genoese traders appear to have settled in the early years of the 14th century. A Franciscan tradition maintained that the emperor Khaishan Kuluk (1307–11), third of the Yuen, or Mongol, dynasty in China, and grandson of the great Kublai, was converted by Monte Corvino; and it may have been the news or legend of this success that led Clement V. in 1312 to send three more suffragans to the aid of Archbishop John; in any case, we find one of these later bishops, Peter of Florence, becoming head of a monastery in this harbour-town of 'Zayton.'

The remaining fragments of our knowledge of Corvino are soon told. In 1322 he appoints Andrew of Perugia, one of his first group of suffragans, to the see of 'Zayton'; in 1326 Andrew, writing home, refers to the Archbishop, without naming him; and about 1350 the Franciscan chronicler, John of Winterthur, makes a confused allusion to what is evidently Corvino's first Peking letter, supposed by the annalist to be the work of a nameless Franciscan of Lower Germany, possibly the very Arnold of Cologne who joined the mission in 1304. Lastly, in 1328, we hear of the death of that aged missionary who first carried Roman Christianity as an active faith to India and China, who perhaps converted the 'Emperor of Emperors,' and who was the first and last effective European bishop in the Peking of the Middle Ages.

The best days and brightest hopes of the Chinese mission really closed with the life of its founder; but the Church at home showed no consciousness of failing energy. A certain Brother Nicolas, apparently a Franciscan like Corvino, was nominated to succeed him, and, with twenty friars and six laymen, set out for Cathay. We are not sure, however, that he ever reached the Middle Kingdom. All that we do know of his journey is that he arrived at Almalig, the modern Kulja, now on the Central Asian frontier of China and Russia, that he received good treatment there, and that in 1338 Pope Benedict XII. wrote to the Chagatai Khān (June 13), thanking him for his kindness to Nicolas.

Meanwhile, a little earlier (in 1338), an embassy from the Great Khān then reigning—Tīmūr Ukhagatu—had appeared before Benedict XII.; and with this embassy letters had arrived from certain Christian princes of the Alan nation in the Khān's service, begging for a bishop and legate worthy to replace Corvino. In reply to these communications, four Franciscan envoys and a large company of less important representatives carried the papal briefs from Avignon, by way of Naples, Constantinople, Kaffa in the Crimea, and Almalig-Kulja, to Peking, which they reached in 1342. After four years in China they returned, like the Polos, by the southern waterway from Amoy to Ormuz, making a lengthy stay in Southern India, and finally re-appearing at Avignon in 1353. The historian of this embassy, John de Marignolli, draws a glowing picture of the prosperity of the Roman Catholic mission in the Far East; but of the mission history after this time we know almost nothing. Of one thing we may be certain: the Chinese national reaction which broke out in 1368 set the Ming dynasty upon the throne, and expelled the Mongol Yuen, put an end for centuries to Western Christianity and to European trade within the Middle Kingdom. When this calamity befell, it is said that the friars, flying across Asia from Peking to Sarai and the Volga, carried with them the relics of the Grand Khān converted by Corvino.

In Persian, Mesopotamian, Armenian, and Caucasian lands the religious explorations of the Western Church began about the middle of the 13th century. The Dominicans penetrated to Tiflis about 1240; in 1255 Rubruquis found several friar-preachers in Armenian towns, and tells us of their travels to Tabrīz as well as to Tiflis. Yet it was only with the Tatar conquest of Baghdād, and with the overthrow of the khalīfate, in 1258, that Roman Catholic influence assumed real importance in Persia. From this time to the early years of the 14th cent., Latin missions and Latin trade played an important part in the empire of the Īlkhāns; several of Hulagu's successors seem to have been 'almost persuaded' to accept some form of Nazarene faith; not till about 1304 did they definitely end their religious hesitation by embracing Islām. Even then, for more than half a century, Rome struggled bravely against the current; though her cause might be declining, she continued to maintain the airs of a conqueror—founding bishoprics, creating provinces, vaunting the submission of heretical patriarchs. In 1318 we hear of the inauguration of a complete Persian hierarchy, with a metropolitan at the Īlkhāns' capital of Sulṭāniyah (a little south of the Caspian), whose jurisdiction included not merely Persia, but also Central Asia, India, and 'Ethiopia.'

Yet after the death of Abū Sa'īd, the last true Īlkhān, in 1336, Roman proselytism seems to have completely lost touch of the governing classes among the Mongols of South-West Asia; in the age of Tīmūr (1380–1405) the Islāmizing of the latter was fairly complete. The Middle, like the Farther East, though less completely, shut its door on Christian enterprise before the age of Henry the Navigator.

The first trace of a Roman Catholic mission in India is the visit of Monte Corvino to the Madras region in 1291–92, an incident of deep significance in the history of mankind, not only as evidencing a fresh opening of intercourse between India and Europe, but also as bearing upon the Persian and Chinese enterprises of the Roman Church, and as representing the first joint effort of the Franciscan and Dominican Orders, under papal direction, upon the remoter heathendom of Southern and Eastern Asia. The chief incident in this chapter of European enterprise is the foundation of a Roman mission in the Bombay region and in Malabar, and the establishment of a Roman bishopric near Cape Comorin a generation later (1321–30). In the *Letters* and *Marvels* of Bishop Jordanus, the first and apparently the only occupant of this see in the Middle Ages, in the *Recollections* of John de Marignolli, in the Travel Record of Friar Odoric, and in the official *Annals* of the Franciscan Order and of the Roman Church, we learn a little about this remarkable undertaking. Its history cannot be traced below the middle of the 14th cent. (*c.* 1349–50); but its leader's references to Latin intercourse with Nubia and Abyssinia, and plans for a European fleet upon the Indian Ocean—like his repetition of Indian prophecies of a coming European domination, and his personal conviction of the ease with which such domination could be established—are among the curious things of mediæval literature.

We have seen something of the vigour with which the Latin missions and Western commerce of this time fought to win and maintain a position in China, in India, and in Persia. During the same period (*c.* 1245–1370) the fates of Christianity and of Islām were decided in Higher Asia, and Latin missionaries and traders fought no less keenly, no less vainly, than in Cathay and Persia for the victory of their creed and commerce in Turkestan, in the Volga basin, and in the Crimea. But of the latter enterprises we have a slenderer record, and what we know of them is frequently incidental to the larger story of Roman Catholic proselytism in the Celestial empire or in Irān.

Before the great Tatar invasion of Eastern Europe, in 1237–43, Dominican missionaries had penetrated into the countries lying east of the Middle Volga, even if the expeditions of Carpini and Rubruquis in 1245–55 had not to any large extent the character of proselytizing ventures. It was apparently in the early part of the 14th cent., and especially under Uzbeg Khān (1321–40), that Rome exerted herself most strenuously for the winning of the North-Western Mongols, and that the mission stations at Astrakhan on the Lower, and at Kazan on the Upper, Volga, at Torki, and other places on the west shore of the Caspian, at Khiva, near the Lower Oxus, at Samarqand, and at Kulja in the Balkhash basin, by the Russo-Chinese frontier of to-day, came into being. Even more, perhaps, than in China or India, these Latin outposts, from the Caspian to the Kama, from the Caucasus to the Altai, represent the exploring spirit of the European at this time in its most daring form. For where could the enmity of nature and men be defied more recklessly? Where in all the known world could distance, barbarism, sterility, and fanaticism present a more formidable combination of obstacles?

Even as late as 1362 we find traces of Roman Catholic effort in Northern Tartary. But about this year the Latin missions in Central Asia may be supposed to have ended in a final storm of persecution; and before Tīmūr's death, in 1405, European missionary activity had really withered away in other Western Mongol lands.

In Europe the later 14th cent. witnessed the conversion of the last considerable people which still professed heathenism. The 'Litva,' or Lithuanians, whose central region is the Vilna country, had become an important power by conquest from the Russian nation, now lying, for the most part, helpless and crushed beneath the heel of the Mongol Tatars. Most of Western Russia had fallen into their hands (some valuable districts had become Polish), and the Lithuanian dukes aspired to a great position in the world. In 1382 the Polish throne was left to a woman, the daughter of Lewis 'the Great'; and Yagielo (or 'Jagellon'), the 'Litva' prince, hoped that by marriage with this heiress (in spite of her strong distaste for his person) he might become one of the chief European sovereigns. His hopes were realized; and a Roman Catholic Polish-Lithuanian State was thus founded by the marriage- and conversion-treaties of 1386. This State gradually became a Polish empire under one faith and one sovereign, with one (terribly defective) constitution and administration (1501; 1569). With Vitovt, or Vitold, the last great 'Litva' conqueror, ended the brief hope that Lithuanian conversion might after all turn to the profit of the Eastern Church.

For 'Prince Vitovt,' the Russian annalist laments, 'had previously been a Christian . . . but he renounced the Orthodox faith, and adopted the Polish, and perverted the holy churches to service hateful to God' (*Chronicle of Novgorod*, A.D. 1399).

In the 14th cent. we also hear of the progress of Russian missions, the pioneer or attendant of Russian colonization, in the most distant regions of North-Eastern Europe. About 1376 the monk Stephen, afterwards canonized as the apostle of Perm ('Stephan Permsky'), founded the earliest Christian church on the Upper Kama. It was a venture of some risk, for a former missionary in this country had been flayed by the natives, 'while they were yet but infants in the faith.' Before his death (in 1396), however, Stephen had confounded the heathen priests and sorcerers of the Kama, overthrown the idols of the *Voipel* and the 'Golden Old Woman,' stopped the sacrifice of reindeer, secured the triumph of Christianity, and founded Moscovite influence in a region from which, two centuries later, Moscow overthrew the Siberian Khānate. Under Stephen's successors, Andrew, Isaac, and Pitirim (1397–1445), the Russian Church took root in the Pechora country, just as it did on the White Sea during the same period, through the foundation of the most famous monastery of the Far North in the island of Solovki, or Solovetsky (1429). The Solovetsky monastery began with the hermitage of the monk Savvaty, or Savvatii, in 1429; after this, Zosima, with the sanction of Archbishop Jonas of Novgorod, joined in founding the community which became so celebrated. On the neighbouring mainland Christian enterprise appears much earlier: the St. Michael monastery, the germ of Archangel city, was established in the 12th cent. by Archbishop Ivan of Novgorod. In Lapland, again, religious enterprise accompanied political and commercial. Like Stephen in the Kama, and Isaac in the Pechora, Iliya of Novgorod and Theodorite of Solovetsky appear as apostles of faith and culture to Kola and the Lapps.

The Portuguese, in their great oversea expansion of the 15th cent., especially from 1445, undertook mission-work with enthusiasm, perseverance, and at least considerable temporary success. Even from the beginning of his enterprise (*c.* 1415) Prince Henry 'the Navigator' did not entirely forget the duty of proselytism, though at first more absorbed by the idea of Crusade. His biographers, even in his earlier years, emphasize his purpose of 'extending the Catholic religion,' of 'showing the natives the way of the holy faith,' of 'making increase in the faith of Christ.' The new slave-trade was used to help to create a native African Church. From 1445 a policy of friendly intercourse with the Negroes of the Sūdan and the Moors of the Sahara was adopted, as leading to conversion, as well as trade, in place of the raiding and kidnapping of earlier time. For the prince's purpose was 'to make Christians of them.' Professed missionaries were soon (before 1453) sent out to Negroland. But the history of this development, and most of the Portuguese success in the mission-field, belong to times after the close of the mediæval period.

LITERATURE.—Jerome, *de Viris Illustribus* (*e.g.*, ch. 36); Eusebius, *HE* (*e.g.*, v. 10); Socrates, *HE* (*e.g.*, i. 19); Sozomen, *HE* (*e.g.*, ii. 24); John of Ephesus; John Malalas; Cosmas, *Topographia Christiana* (*e.g.*, bks. iii., xi.); Dicuil, *de Mensura Orbis Terræ* (*e.g.*, vii. 11–14); C. Baronius and O. Raynaldus, *Annales Ecclesiastici*, Rome, 1646–77 (*e.g.*, 356, 1260, 1267, 1274, 1278, 1285, 1338, 1370); Gregory Abulfaragius, *Historia Compendiosa Dynastiarum*, ed. E. Pocock, Oxford, 1663 (*e.g.*, 427); J. S. Assemani, *Bibl. Orientalis*, Rome, 1719–28 (*e.g.*, III. i. 130 f., 155–157; ii. 77–175, 413–617); Carpini and Rubruquis, ed. M. A. P. d'Avezac, in *Recueil de Voyages*, iv. [1839] (*Mém. de la Soc. géographique de Paris*), ed. C. R. Beazley in Hakluyt Soc. Publications, London, 1903; Corvino and Jordanus, in L. Wadding, *Annales Minorum*², Rome, 1731–45, vi.; Andrew of Perugia, Pascal of Vittoria, etc., *ib.* vii.; J. de Marignolli, in *Fontes Rerum Bohemicarum*, Prague, 1873–82, iii.; *Chronicle of 'Nestor'* [Kieff Chronicle]; *Chronicle of Novgorod*; *Chronicon Livonicum Vetus*; J. L. von Mosheim, *Historia Tartarorum ecclesiastica*, Helmstadt, 1741; I. Halberg, *Extreme Orient*, Gothenburg, 1906; A. Harnack, *Expansion of Christianity*, London, 1904–05; H. Zimmer, *Celtic Church*, Eng. tr., do. 1902; A. Hauck,

Kirchengesch. Deutschlands, Leipzig, 1886–1905; J. Labourt, *Christianisme dans l'empire perse sous la dynastie sassanide*, Paris, 1904; A. Fortescue, *The Lesser Eastern Churches*, London, 1913; Beazley, *The Dawn of Modern Geography*, do. 1897–1906, i. 205–242, ii. 275–381, iii. 160–309; J. C. Robertson, *Hist. of the Christian Church*, do. 1876, esp. i. 214–216, 411–418, ii. 204 f., 254 ff., iii. 30–37, 62–80, 457–480, iv. 73–116, v. 278–288, vi. 356–377, vii. 416 ff., viii. 333 ff.; G. Milne Rae, *The Syrian Church in Malabar*, Edinburgh, 1892; A. E. Medlycott, *India and the Apostle Thomas*, London, 1905; J. A. Letronne, *Matériaux pour l'hist. du Christianisme*, Paris, 1833; T. Wright, *Early Christianity in Arabia*, London, 1855; *Trans. of Russian Archæological Society* (Oriental section); G. Pauthier, *De l'Authenticité de l'inscription nestorienne de Si-ngan-fou*, Paris, 1857; G. T. Stokes, *Ireland and the Celtic Church*[3], London, 1892; N. M. Karamzin, *Hist. of Russia*, Petrograd, 1842, vol. v.; V. O. Klyuchevsky, *Lives of the Saints as Historical Material*, Moscow, 1871.

C. RAYMOND BEAZLEY.

MISSIONS (Christian, Roman Catholic).—When Jesus Christ, the Son of God and the Redeemer of mankind, had fulfilled His divine mission in the world, had sealed it with His death, and endorsed it by His resurrection, He empowered His apostles, and through them His Church, to continue the same in His name and by His authority. That apostolate of salvation was to be catholic, or universal in space, doctrine, and time, to teach all nations all things at all times (Mt 28^{18-20}). Mindful of the Last Will and Testament of Christ, the Church has always looked upon missionary work as an essential and solemn obligation, and upon its progress as an unfailing gauge of her vitality. Since the day of Pentecost, when she received her baptism by the Holy Spirit, the Church has carried on the apostolate with more or less success in the midst of constant persecutions from within and from without, and in spite of unfavourable political conditions and anti-Christian legislation. The missionary character which she displayed in apostolic and sub-apostolic times equally manifested itself in the Celtic, Germanic, and Frankish missionaries, till the Benedictine missionaries SS. Gregory, Augustine, Wilfrid, Boniface, Ansgar, and Adalbert gave to the missionary movement its definite shape. When in subsequent ages new countries were discovered or opened up, the Orders of St. Francis and St. Dominic became important factors in the missions among the followers of Islām and the Mongols, in Morocco and Egypt, in Syria and Palestine, India and China. In 1252 a special missionary congregation was formed out of members of the two orders known as *Societas peregrinantium propter Christum*. A new impetus to the Roman Catholic apostolate was given when, in the 14th, 15th, and 16th centuries, Spain and Portugal took the lead in exploration, conquest, and commerce in the East and the West. They gave freely of the wealth that they had won in their respective colonies to found missions, schools, and colleges for the propagation of the faith, and their fleets never set forth without having on board missionaries—Augustinians, Dominicans, Franciscans, or Jesuits—destined for the peaceful conquest of souls. To avoid political troubles and to further the cause of Christianity, Pope Alexander VI. in 1496, by the famous line of demarcation, assigned the East to the Portuguese and the West to the Spaniards, and with a remarkable zeal they devoted their protection for nearly three centuries to the spread of the gospel, though this Protectorate had its serious disadvantages for a healthy development. Franciscan missionaries accompanied Columbus in 1493, and they were followed by others to the Antilles (1500), Mexico or New Spain (1519), Yucatan, Guatemala, and Honduras, Nicaragua and Costa Rica. In S. America the Franciscans had missions in Colombia and Venezuela, in Peru and Ecuador. At the request of the king of Spain Franciscans went to Chile and Bolivia, to the Indians in the Pampas of Argentine and in Gran Chaco, and in 1538 they landed in Southern Brazil. When in 1664 Narváez undertook an expedition into Florida, five Franciscans went with him, and from there they extended their work to New Biscaya, New Mexico, Arizona, Texas, and California. French Franciscans were the first missionaries in Canada (1615) and Nova Scotia, while in Africa they continued their work in Morocco, Tunis, Tripoli, Egypt, and Abyssinia.

The Society of Jesus, founded by St. Ignatius Loyola (†1556) in 1534, placed itself from the very beginning at the disposal of the Church for missionary work. St. Francis Xavier inaugurated in 1542 the Roman Catholic apostolate in India, Ceylon, Malacca, and Japan. Under Francis Borgia (1565–72) Jesuit missionaries were sent to Florida, Mexico, Peru; under Acquaviva (1581–1615) to Canada, Chile, Paraguay, the Philippines, and China; under Vitelleschi (1615–40) to Tibet, Tongking, Maranhão, etc. What the suppression of the Society of Jesus (1773) meant for the Roman Catholic apostolate may be best realized by the fact that by one stroke of the pen the Church was deprived of 3300 Jesuit missionaries alone in that year.

Besides the Franciscans and Jesuits, other missionaries belonging to various religious orders were engaged in the mission field of the Roman Catholic Church, although not to so large an extent. Among these may be mentioned the Theatines (1524), Capuchins (1528), Barnabites (1533), Oratorians (1575), Carmelites (1565), Augustinians (1588), Lazarists (1624), the missionary seminaries of Rome (1608) and of St. Sulpice (1642), and, lastly, La Société des Missions Étrangères of Paris (1663). For the sake of unity and conformity all these various missionary organizations were finally centralized from Pope Gregory XIII. (1572–85) to Gregory XV. (1621–23). By the brief of 22nd June 1622 (*Inscrutabili*) the latter, with the help of the Carmelite Thomas a Jesu and the Capuchin Girolamo da Narni, instituted the Congregatio de propaganda fide, or Propaganda, whose sphere of jurisdiction has recently been circumscribed by Pius X. (29th June 1908). The Congregation consists of 25 cardinals with a cardinal-prefect, 4 secretaries, 10 minutanti, and some 50 consultors. Their chief work is to establish and circumscribe the boundaries of the missionary jurisdictions or districts, *i.e.* mission, prefecture, vicariate, diocese, etc., to entrust the particular field to the various missionary societies, to appoint the missionary superiors, etc.

Thus from the beginning of the 16th cent. the Roman Catholic Church carried on her apostolate throughout the world in N. and S. America, in Africa and the adjacent islands, in Asia, China, India, etc. On the other hand, the struggles and the storms which she had to endure in the 18th cent. from the tyrannical absolutism of European rulers, from the crippling tutelage of the State, from a false philosophy, the Encyclopædists (*q.v.*), and finally from the French Revolution and the subsequent suppression of almost all the religious orders and missionary societies, brought her apostolate to a temporary standstill, till it was revived between 1820 and 1830.

The 19th and so far the 20th centuries are witnesses of the unswerving fidelity of the Church to the command of Christ and a pledge of her vitality and energy in the mission field. Unsupported by emperors and kings as her protectors and promoters, nay, hampered in her efforts by Roman Catholic governments and anti-Christian legislation, she has carried on the work of reconstruction and reorganization, has recovered her ground, and, finally, has carried her propaganda into every corner of heathen lands. The ancient orders have taken up their work in the field, new missionary societies have been founded during the course of the century, training colleges have been established, and religious orders of women, formerly almost excluded from the missions, are now to be found everywhere, about 20,000 taking their share in the educational, charitable, and industrial work. To support the missionaries and the missions materially, the Association for the Propagation of the Faith (1822) and the Society of the Holy Childhood have done good work, while Popes Gregory XVI., Pius IX., Leo XIII., and Pius X., as well as the Roman Catholic hierarchy throughout the world, have given their support to promote the revival of missionary work among the heathen.

According to H. A. Krose (*Katholische Missionsstatistik*, Freiburg, 1908), the total result of missionary work on the part of the Roman Catholic Church in the 19th cent. amounted to 8,321,963 converts from paganism. This flock is attended by 12,305 missionary priests, of whom 5369 are natives, 4863 brothers, and 17,284 sisters, with 30,414 stations, 22,736 churches, 17,834 schools with 791,878 pupils. When we add the results of the Roman Catholic missions since the time of the Reformation, we have in the Roman Catholic mission field 30,000,000 native converts.

According to Karl Streit (*Katholischer Missionsatlas*, Leipzig, 1906) there were: 7933 European and 5837 native priests, 5270 brothers, 21,320 sisters, 24,524 catechists, 42,968 stations, 28,470 churches, 7,441,215 native members, 1,517,000 catechumens, 24,033 schools with 840,974 pupils, etc. The *Atlas Hierarchicus*, by the same author, published at Paderborn in 1913, does not give a summary of the apostolate.

The review of missionary societies and their respective missions given on the opposite page will help the reader to understand the position of the Roman Catholic missions in our own days.

I. *ASIA*.—As far as missionary work in its strictest sense is concerned, Asia may be divided into: (1) India Proper, or the British Empire of India with Ceylon, Burma, and Malay Peninsula, (2) the Chinese Empire, including Mongolia, Manchuria, and Tibet, (3) Indo-China, with Siam and Laos, and (4) the Japanese Empire, with Korea. The early history of missions in this continent has been outlined in the 'Early and Mediæval' section, above.

1. **British India.**—British India and Ceylon, with an area of 1,800,000 sq. miles and a population of some 300,000,000 souls, is one of the most important and probably one of the most difficult mission fields of the Roman Catholic Church owing to the babel-tongued tribes (120), the many non-Christian religions (Hindu, Brāhman, Buddhist, Muhammadan, pagan) and Christian denominations (40), and the prejudices of the highly developed caste system.

In 1498 Vasco de Gama landed in Calicut, the capital of Malabar, accompanied by the Trinitarian Pedro de Covilham, who in 1500 became the protomartyr of the missions in India. In the same year eight secular priests and eight Franciscans arrived with Pedro Alvarez Cabral, three of whom were put to death by the Muhammadans. Yet, in spite of persecution and death, the Franciscans, and after 1503 the Dominicans, went forth to India as the pioneer missionaries, to sow the seed of Christianity in Cochin (1503) and Goa (1510), and gradually extended their work to Bombay, Madras, Damão, Bengal, Agra, Ceylon, Mailapur, etc., under Fathers Antonio do Lazal (1530), do Porto, and Padrão. To establish the Church on a firm footing Pope Paul III. erected the bishopric of Goa (1534) with Bishop John of Albuquerque as its first occupant; the see was raised to an archbishopric by Paul IV. (1557) with three suffragans at Cochin (1557), Cranganore (1600; archbishopric 1605), and Mailapur (1606). Two Franciscans, James of Borbas and Vincent of Lagos, founded the college of St. Paul at Goa for the purpose of training a native clergy.

In 1541 the Jesuits entered the mission field of India and, at the request of John III. of Portugal, St. Francis Xavier, accompanied by Paul of Camerino and Francis Mansilhaes, set out to inaugurate a new period of missionary labours. From Goa he extended the faith to the Fishery Coast, Travancore (1544), Cochin, Quilon, and Ceylon. His Jesuit successors took up and carried on his work: de Nobili among the Brāhmans of Madura (1605–48), Tanjore, and Mysore (30–100,000 converts), Criminalis on the Fishery Coast (90–130,000 converts) (1602), de Britto among the Maravas (1693), Acquaviva at the court of Akbar the Great; Father Goes penetrated from India into China, and Andrada crossed the Himalayas and went to Tibet. They were followed by other members of the Society such as da Costa, Martinez, Laynez, Bouchet, Martin, Calmette, Cœurdoux, and Constantine Breschi (1700–40). Franciscans in Agra and Delhi, Capuchins in Madras (1642), Barnabites and Augustinians (Archbishop Menezes of Goa [1594–1610]) in Hyderabad and Bengal, Theatines and Oratorians (Father Vaz, apostle of Ceylon [† 1711]) shared with them in this new harvest of souls in India, whilst, after 1656, the Carmelites worked for the return of the Syrian Christians of Malabar to Roman Catholic unity.

With so many missionary labourers in the Indian mission field, hopes of a speedy conversion of India were entertained, and, no doubt, would have been realized to some extent, had Portugal remained faithful to the duties and sacred obligations that she had promised in connexion with the Padroado—the right of patronage—which the Holy See from Leo X. to Paul V. (1514–1616) had granted to her kings. When, however, the power and the influence of Portugal began to decline and the Dutch and the English took her field in the East, the supply of missionaries became limited, the missionaries themselves were put to death or expelled, the churches were destroyed, and the native Christians were cruelly persecuted. The Sultan Tippu Sahib of Mysore between 1782 and 1799 put 100,000 Christians to death, forced 40,000 into apostasy, and sold 30,000 as slaves to Muhammadan dealers. The dispute regarding concessions to Hindu usages or Malabar rites, commencing with de' Nobili in 1606 and ending in 1744 with the bull of Benedict XIV., *Omnium sollicitudinum*, greatly divided the missionaries to the disadvantage of their work, which suffered a heavy blow by the suppression of the Society of Jesus in the Portuguese dominions in 1755, in the French possessions in 1762, and throughout the world in 1773. There were at this time 150 Jesuits in Goa, 47 in Malabar, and 22 in Pondicherry. True, their places were partly filled by Capuchins, by the Missionary Seminary of Paris (1776), and by some native priests, who were ordained without a vocation or an adequate education. Thus the missions in India, which in 1700 numbered some 1,500,000 or even 2,500,000 Roman Catholics, were only ruins and wreckage (500,000 or even less) in 1800. The archbishopric of Goa, with its three suffragans of Cranganore, Cochin, and Mailapur, numbered 340,000 members with 400 priests, and outside the Goanese jurisdiction there were four missions—Agra, with 5000 converts under the care of 10 Capuchins, Pondicherry, with 42,000 and 6 priests, the Carmelite missions of Malabar, with 88,000 converts and 5 priests, and Ceylon, with 1 missionary and 20 native priests for 50,000 members. All this was due to the anti-Christian policy of Pombal and the neglected obligations of Portugal's right of the Padroado. The Holy See,

ROMAN CATHOLIC RELIGIOUS ORDERS AND MISSIONARY SOCIETIES, AND THEIR FIELDS OF WORK.

Name.	Abbreviation.	Founded.	Mission-fields (A.D. = Archdiocese, D. = Diocese, Prel. = Prelature, V. = Vicariate, P. = Prefecture, M. = Mission).
Augustinians (Hermits) . .	E.S. Aug.	1526	V. North Hu-nan, Cooktown; P. Amazonas.
,, (Recollects) . .	,, ,,	1588	V. Casanare; P. Palawan; M. in Brazil.
Benedictines	O.S.B.	1529	Prel. Rio Branco; Abbeys of New Nurcia; Seoul; V. Dar-es-Salam; P. Katanga and North Transvaal; M. Drisdale River; Indians in U.S.A.
Capuchins	O.F.M. Cap.	1528	D. Candia, Agra, Allahabad, Lahore; A.D. Simla; V. Arabia, Caroline-Marianne, Erythrea, Gallas, Somali, Goajira, Guam, Seychelles, Sophia; P. Araucania, Bettiah, Southern Borneo, Caqueta, Upper Solimões, Miso Calanga, Belgian-Ubanghi, Rajputana, Sumatra; M. Mardin, Syria, Trebizond, Kephalonia, etc.
Carmelites (Discalced) . . .	O. Carm.	1562	D. Quilon, Verapoly, Mesopotamia, Kurdistan, Armenia; M. Baghdād.
Dominicans	O. Pr.	1216	V. Amoy, Canelos y Macas, Curaçao, Fo-kien, Central-East and Northern Tongking; P. Shikoku, Urubamba; M. Mossul, Trinidad, E. Uuelle.
Franciscans	O.F.M.	1209	Palestine; V. Aleppo, S. and N. Shan-si, E. and N. Shantung, N. and Central Shen-si, S. Hu-nan, S.-W., N.-W., and E. Hu-peh, Egypt, Morocco, Zamora; P. Rhodes, Tripoli, Ucayali; Prel. Santarem; M. Mozambique.
Jesuits	S.J.	1534	D. Calcutta, Bombay, Galle, Madura, Mangalore, Poona, Trichinopoly, Trincomalee; V. Batavia, Kiang-nan, S.-E. Chih-li, Central Madagascar, British Guiana, British Honduras, Jamaica; P. Alaska, Kwango, Zambesi; M. Albania, Syra, Tinos, Armenia, Adana, Syria, Philippines, Australia, U.S.A., Mexico, Cuba, Colombia, Ecuador, Peru, Chile, Argentine, Brazil, Japan.
Lazarists	C.M.	1625	D. Ispahan; V. Abyssinia, S., E., and N. Kiang-si, S. Madagascar, C., S.-W., N., E., and Maritime Chih-li, E. and W. Che-kiang; M. Macedonia, Constantinople, Syria, Palestine, Egypt.
Marists	S.M.	1816	V. Fiji, New Caledonia, New Hebrides, Central Oceania, Samoa, Solomon Islands.
Missionary Seminaries—			
Lyons	M.A.	1856	V. Benin, Dahomey, Gold Coast, Nile Delta, Ivory Coast, Liberia; P. E. and W. Nigeria, Korhoga; M. Negro Missions U.S.A.
Milan	S.M.	1850	D. Krishnagar, Hyderabad; V. E. Burma, S. and N. Ho-nan, Hongkong.
Mill Hill	S.M.H.	1866	A.D. Madras; V. Upper Nile; P. N. Borneo, Kashmir; M. Auckland, Congo, Philippines, Maori, Panjāb.
Paris	M.E.P.	1658	A.D. Tokio; D. Nagasaki, Osaka, Hakodate, Pondicherry, Mysore, Coimbatore, Kumbakonam, Malacca; V. Seoul, Taiku, N. and S. Manchuria, S., E., and W. Sze-ch'uen, Tibet, Kientchang, S., W., Upper, and Maritime Tongking, E., W., and N. Cochin China, Cambodia, Siam, Malacca, Laos, S. and N. Burma; P. Kwang-tung, Kwangsi, Kwei-chow, Yun-nan.
Parma	S.P.	—	W. Ho-nan.
Rome	S.S. Apostl. Petri et Pauli	1867	S. Shen-si, Lower California.
Scheutveld	C.i.c.M.	1865	V. E., C., and S.-W. Mongolia, N. Kansuh, Upper Congo; P. S. Kansuh, Upper Kassai; M. Kulja, Philippines.
Steyl	S.V.D.	1875	V. S. Shantung, Togo; P. Kaiser Wilhelmsland, Niigata; M. Philippines, Mozambique, Dutch India, Negro Missions U.S.A., and among Indians in S. America.
Turin (la Consolata) . . .	M. Cŏnsol.	1901	V. Kenia; P. S. Kaffa.
Verona	F.Ss.C.	1867	V. Sūdān.
Missionary Societies—			
Congregation of the Holy Ghost	C.Sp.S.	1703 and 1842 United in 1848.	V. Bagamoyo, Kilimanjaro, Zanzibar, N. Madagascar, French Upper Congo, Gabun, Loango, Senegambia, Ubanghi, Sierra Leone; P. Lower Katanga, Upper Cimbebasia, Portuguese Congo, French Guinea, North Katanga, Nossi Be, Lower Niger, Senegal, Teffe; M. Bata, Lunda, Cunene, Réunion, Mauritius, Hayti, Guadeloupe, Martinique, Trinidad, Ubanghi-Chari, Landana.
Algerian Miss. or White Fathers	P.B.	1868	V. N. and S. Nyanza, Kivu, Unyamyembe, Tanganyika, Upper Congo, Nyassa, Bangweolo, Sahara; P. Ghardaia; M. Sūdān, Algiers, Jerusalem, Kabylia.
Picpus	C.Ss.CC.	1800	V. Hawaii, Tahiti, Marquesas; P. Kaiser Wilhelmsland.
Pallotinians	P.S.M.	1835	V. Cameroons; M. Kimberley, Australia, Brazil.
Oblates of Mary Immac . .	O.M.I.	1816	D. Jaffna; A.D. Colombo; V. Athabasca, Basuto, Keewatin, Mackenzie, Natal, Oranje, S. Transvaal, Kimberley; P. Lower Cimbebasia, Yukon.
Missionaries of the S. Heart .	M.S.C.	1854	D. Port Victoria; V. New Pomerania, British New Guinea, Gilbert Islands, Marshall Islands; P. Dutch New Guinea; M. Philippines, Brazil.
Salesians of Don Bosco . .	C. Sal.	1846	V. Mendez-Gualaquiza, N. Patagonia; P. S. Patagonia.
Missionaries of Immac. Heart of Mary	C.M.F.	1849	V. Fernando Po; P. Choco.
Company of Mary a Montfort .	S.M.M.	1705	V. Llanos de S. Martin, Shire; M. Hayti.
Priests of S. Heart of Jesus .	S.Ss.C.	1877	V. Stanley Falls; M. Belgian Congo.

Salvatorians (S.D.S. 1881), P. Assam; **Premonstratensians** (O. Praem. 1120), P. W. Uuelle; **Silvestrines** (O. Silv. 1231), D. Kandy; **Trappist Missionaries** (R.M.M. 1909), Natal; **Trinitarians** (O.Ss.Tr. 1198), P. Benadir; **Redemptorists** (C.Ss. Redempt. 1732), V. Surinam (Dutch Guiana), Matadi; **Passionists** (C.P. 1735), Bulgaria; **Assumptionists** (A.A. 1845), Missions in the Orient; **Salesians of Annecy**, D. Nagpur; **Oblates of St. Francis of Sales**, Great Namaqualand, Orange River.

recognizing the inadequacy and the unwillingness of Portugal, began to provide for the neglected field of India. Hitherto only missionaries of Portuguese origin had been admitted, and this by way of Lisbon and Goa. For years Portugal left the bishoprics vacant and in 1827 withdrew all material subvention. The misery was too evident, and Gregory XVI. took matters into his own hands without consulting the interests of Portugal. India was opened to all Roman Catholic missionaries irrespective of nationality or religious orders. In 1837 the French Jesuits entered Madura, and they were followed by the Germans (Bombay and Poona 1854, 1857), the Belgians (Calcutta 1859, Galle 1895), and the Italians (Mangalore 1878). The Missionaries of Paris took up their work in Malacca (1840) and Burma (1857), those of Milan in Krishnagar (1855), Hyderabad (1863), and E. Burma (1866), the Oblates in Jaffna (1847) and Colombo (1883), etc. In 1832 the Propaganda asked Portugal either to fill the vacant sees or to renounce the Padroado. As no answer arrived for two years, Gregory XVI. began to institute vicars-apostolic in Bengal and Madras (1834), in Ceylon and Pondicherry (1836), etc. But new trials and difficulties commenced. The Portuguese Government protested against sending missionaries into India and against the establishment of new vicariates without the consent and the co-operation of the kings of Portugal, and the patriarch of Goa placed himself at the head of a schism in India—the Goanese schism—which was maintained under the patriarchs of Goa, Joseph de Silva y Torres and Joseph de Matta. Pius IX. tried in 1857 to come to a settlement, but this was accomplished only by Leo XIII. on 23rd June 1886. A million and a half of native Christians were again under the allegiance of the Holy See when on 1st Sept. 1886 Leo XIII. established the hierarchy in India—8 archbishoprics: Goa, Verapoly, Colombo, Pondicherry, Madras, Calcutta, Agra, and Bombay, to which Simla was added in 1910, the patriarch of Goa holding the dignity of primate, and twenty-five dioceses, etc. For the furthering of the mission work Leo XIII. also established a papal delegation for India in 1884, which since then has been administered by the titular archbishops Agliardi (1884–87), Ajuti (1887–92), and Zaleski.

The first thirty years of the Indian missions after the reorganization under Gregory XVI. was a period of reconstruction in gathering together and strengthening in the faith the remnants of the old Roman Catholic congregations. With the decline of the Goanese schism and establishment of the hierarchy a steady flow of conversions began, and since then remarkable progress has been made, more conspicuously among the Tamil races in S. India and Ceylon, less so in the Aryan lands of the north. In 1887 the numbers of Roman Catholics in India were:

India	989,381	1,224,427
Ceylon	207,692	
Three vicariates of Burma .	27,354	

According to the Census of 1911 (including Burma):

Native Roman Catholics of the Latin Rite .	1,394,000
Native Roman Catholics of the Syrian Rite	413,142
Eurasian and European Roman Catholics .	97,144
Total . .	1,904,286
Ceylon (native Roman Catholics) . .	322,163
Total for India and Ceylon .	2,226,449

To complete the survey of the Roman Catholic missions in British India, we subjoin the general statistics taken from the *Atlas Hierarchicus* (1913): the hierarchy consists of 9 archbishoprics, 22 dioceses, 3 vicariates, and 4 prefectures, with 1268 foreign and 1230 native priests, 638 brothers, 3592 sisters, 2776 catechists, 4920 native teachers, 2,215,682 Catholics, 1108 principal and 7208 secondary stations, 5891 churches, 27 theological seminaries with 1121 students of theology, 2843 elementary schools with 163,696 pupils, 519 higher schools with 32,616 boys and 15,273 girls, 290 orphanages with 14,706 orphans, 48 hospitals, 175 dispensaries, 18 printing presses, etc.

2. China.—The revival of Roman Catholic missionary activity in China after the close of the mediæval period dates from the time when the Jesuit Father Ricci was allowed to settle there (1583). Science was to pave the way for religion and missionary work. In 1600 Ricci went to Peking and with the help of his Jesuit brethren started missions at Canton, Nanking, and Kian-si, receiving converts from the highest to the lowest classes of the population, till his death in 1610. The persecution which broke out in 1617 was brought to a speedy end by the invasion of the Manchu Tatars. In 1628 the Jesuit Adam Schall arrived in Peking, gained great influence by his learning, and turned it to the advantage of religion. In the meantime the Dominicans, who in 1625 had established themselves on the island of Formosa, had also opened missions in Fu-kien. One of these Dominican missionaries, the native priest Gregory Lopez, or A-Lo, known as the Chinese Bishop, the first and the only Chinaman who has been raised to the episcopate, rendered the greatest services to the Roman Catholic Church in his native land (1654).

At the request of Bishop Pallu, Clement X. divided China, which had hitherto been under the jurisdiction of the bishop of Macao, into two vicariates and entrusted the northern part to Gregory Lopez, consecrated bishop at Canton in 1685.

About this time the emperor K'ang-hi, a pupil of Father Schall, repealed all the edicts against the Christians, and the missionaries who had been imprisoned were released and resumed their work. Like Fathers Ricci and Schall, Father Verbiest, another learned Jesuit, who arrived in China in 1660, became the favourite of the Mandarins, and K'ang-hi appointed him president of the faculty of mathematics and gave the missionaries permission to preach the gospel throughout China.

Through the influence of Verbiest and his learned successors Christianity made great progress within a century, and when he died the Roman Catholic Church was in a flourishing condition, honoured at Court, professed by the highest mandarins, and numbering about 300,000 members. Since, however, the Roman Catholic religion was not officially recognized, and the natives were forbidden by law to embrace the faith, the local mandarins put many obstacles in the way and caused many a local persecution, till Father Gerbillon, in 1692, obtained an edict from the emperor giving full liberty to all his subjects to embrace and practise the Roman Catholic religion.

But, whilst the Church was enjoying peace from without, she was sadly disturbed from within by a controversy about the Chinese rites, *i.e.* the lawfulness of taking part in the Chinese ceremonies in honour of Confucius and of using the word *Tien* ('heaven') to express the idea of God, and whether the prostrations and sacrifices in honour of Confucius and of the ancestors were merely civil ceremonies or connected with idolatry and superstition. Instead of preaching the gospel, converting the infidels, and applying their abilities to other clamant duties, missionaries of the first class wasted their talents, time, and work in useless and fruitless discussions, for Jesuits and Dominicans were divided in their opinions. Father Ricci, as well as the Chinese bishop, Gregory Lopez, and most of the Jesuit missionaries, considered the Chinese rites as merely civil ceremonies, while the Dominicans strongly objected to this view. In 1693, however, the controversy became acute by the action of Bishop Maigrot, vicar-apostolic of Fu-kien, who condemned the rites and threatened with interdict all the missionaries who refused to conform to his command. To settle the dispute, a papal legate was sent to China in 1705, who, owing to lack of tact, only offended the emperor.

In 1706 K'ang-hi made all the priests in China promise that they would teach nothing contrary to the received usages in China, and in the following year issued an edict threatening death to all who should preach against the rites. Alarmed lest the Government should be provoked to harsher measures, the Jesuits appealed to Rome, asking for instructions. A new papal legate arrived in China in 1721 with letters to K'ang-hi, assuring him that the Holy See would ask nothing more than that the Christians should be allowed to pay their respects to the dead in a manner not prejudicial to their religion. In spite of this decision the controversy continued till 1742, when Benedict XIV. condemned the rites and forbade the Christians to take part in them. After peace was restored, Jesuits and Dominicans, Franciscans and Augustinians, priests of the Society for Foreign Missions of Paris and Lazarists worked hand in hand for the evangelization of China. Some shed their blood, while others, such as Gerbillon, Bouvet, and Parenin, became the scientific advisers to the Court or wrote learned books and treatises or published works of piety for their converts. The emperor K'ang-hi, during his long reign of sixty years, treated the Christians with justice, revoked all the edicts against them, raised them to the highest offices in the empire, and made the ministers of the Christian religion his companions, friends, and advisers. He died in 1721 without embracing Christianity, although he desired to be baptized in his last illness.

After the death of K'ang-hi, a reaction took place. His son and successor, Yung-chin (1722–35), drove the missionaries from the Court, and ordered them to leave the country, with the exception of Father Parenin and three of his colleagues. A general edict of persecution was issued in 1724, the missionaries were seized and banished, and 300 churches were destroyed or turned into pagan temples, while 37 Manchu princes who had become Christians, with 300 of their servants, were sent into exile (1724). The accession of K'ien-lung (1735) to the throne of China mitigated for a time the severity of the anti-Christian laws, but in 1745 a new persecution broke out in Fu-kien, where, in the following year, Bishop Sanz and four Dominicans were tortured and beheaded, and soon the flame spread to other provinces. All the hatred was turned against the priests, who were obliged to seek refuge in flight.

Scarcely had the Church recovered from her trials when a new misfortune overtook her. The Jesuits, who from 1583 to 1773 had worked in China as elsewhere, were suppressed. At the request of the Propaganda, the Lazarists took charge of the Jesuit missions in China—*i.e.* four large churches in Peking and the missions in 13 out of 18 provinces—in 1783. For many years, however, the Lazarists were unable to send a sufficient number of missionaries to continue the work of the Jesuits; seven missionaries seem to be all that were sent from 1773 to 1793. Finally the French Revolution cut off the supply of missionaries from France, and for over thirty years the Lazarists were unable to send a single priest to China. The Roman Catholic Church in China, which in the reign of the emperor K'ang-hi is said to have numbered 800,000 members, was reduced at the beginning of the 19th cent. to 220,000, divided among the Lazarists at Peking and Nanking, the Franciscans in Shan-si, the Dominicans in Fu-kien, the Missionaries of Paris in Sze-ch'uen, and the Portuguese secular priests at Macao and Canton.

Yet, in spite of bloodshed and persecution, of cruel edicts issued by the emperors, and the anti-Christian hatred of provincial and local mandarins, and notwithstanding anti-foreign policy fostered by the literati and carried into effect by members of secret societies, the Taiping and Boxers, the Roman Catholic Church has made good progress during the course of the 19th and specially since the beginning of the 20th century. The Franciscans and Dominicans, the Jesuits and Augustinians, the Lazarists and the Missionaries of Paris who had been in the Chinese missions for the last two centuries, have strengthened their ranks and extended their work, while new missionary societies founded in the 19th cent., such as the Scheutveld and the Steyl missionaries, and the missionary seminaries of Milan, Rome, and Parma, have opened up new fields, and all the European missionaries engaged in China have strengthened their ranks with a large number of native priests.

True, the opening of the 19th cent. did not promise a bright future, for Kia-k'ing (1795–1820) proved to be one of the greatest persecutors, having revived the old anti-Christian laws. Bishop Dufresse was beheaded in 1825, Father Clet in 1820, and Father Perboyre in 1840. But China was shaken to her very foundations when in 1842 Britain declared war on her and compelled her to open certain ports, while France demanded religious liberty for the Roman Catholic missionaries in 1844. The Chinese Government acceded, and in 1844–45 two edicts were issued by which Christianity received legal recognition in the empire, and in 1846 a third ordered the restoration to Roman Catholics of all the churches which they had lost since the reign of the emperor K'ang-hi. The eighty missionaries who at this period were at work in China were strengthened in 1841 by the arrival of the first missionaries of the Society of Jesus, who were once more entrusted with one of their former fields of labour, the vicariate of Kiang-nan.

Though religious liberty was granted by the edicts of 1844, 1845, and 1846, they remained a dead letter in many of the provinces in the interior. In 1851 the emperor Hien-fêng revoked them, and renewed those against the Christians. The murder of Father Chapdelaine (1856) brought matters to a crisis. France joined Britain in a war against China, and the result was the Treaty of Tientsin (1858) and the Convention of Peking (1860); the churches were restored as well as the religious and charitable institutions, the missionaries obtained free passports throughout the empire, the faithful were guaranteed unrestricted exercise of their religion, and all the edicts against the Christians were abrogated. Yet the Christians were not safeguarded from local persecutions, which broke out in Kiang-si, Kwang-tung, Sze-ch'uan, Hu-nan, and finally in Tientsin in 1870. After the accession of Kwang-su in 1875 the Roman Catholic Church enjoyed a long period of peace, and, though the empress Tsz'e Hsi was not favourable to Christianity, yet she did nothing against its progress and development. In 1895 and 1899 the French minister in Peking obtained new concessions for the Christians, among them the privilege that the Roman Catholic missionaries were put on an equality with the Chinese local authorities—a privilege which was cancelled a few years later.

The political plunders of Europe in China, by taking Kiaochow (Germany, 1897), Talienwan (Russia, 1898), Wei-hai-wei (Britain, 1898), and Kwang-chou-wan (France, 1898), resulted in the Boxer riots, which brought sad days for the missions. Bishops, priests, and sisters lost their lives; churches, schools, and hospitals were levelled to the ground; and native Christians were slaughtered. Peace was restored only when a strong international army entered Peking on 14th Aug. 1900 and ten foreign Powers dictated their terms in the Chinese Capital on 7th Sept. 1901. A movement towards the Roman Catholic Church then began, a great number of Chinese entering the list of the catechumens, and it has steadily advanced since the Boxer rising. The overthrow of the Manchu dynasty in China and the proclamation of a Chinese republic have not interfered with missionary work. Yuan-Shi-Kai, the first president of the new republic, promised absolute religious liberty, mandarins and governors eulogized the tact of the Roman Catholic missionaries, and Christian and non-Christian sects look up with admiration to the spiritual power of the Church whose missionaries are living examples of the poverty, zeal, and heroism of apostolic times.

During the flourishing period of the Roman Catholic Church in China, from 1583 to 1773, the hierarchy was not developed, though the Propaganda had resolved in 1651 to appoint a patriarch, two or three archbishops, and twelve bishops. In 1577 Gregory XIII. created the diocese of Macao for China and Japan, which was divided into two, viz. Macao and Funay (Japan) in 1587. In 1659 Alexander VII. erected within the diocese of Macao two vicariates for China, and to satisfy Portugal Alexander VIII. created the dioceses of Peking and Nanking under the jurisdiction of Goa, to which were added three vicariates, viz. Shan-si, Fu-kien, and Sze-ch'uan. In 1800 there were in China five missionary districts divided between the Franciscans (Shan-si), the Dominicans (Fu-kien), the Missionary Society of Paris (Sze-ch'uan), the Lazarists (Peking, Nanking, Hu-nan, Hu-peh, Kiang-si), and the secular priests (Macao) with 200,000 members. Fifty years later the number had increased to 18 districts with 330,000 members, in 1890 to 40 ecclesiastical jurisdictions with 601,000 members; in 1905 we find 43 vicariates with 931,000 members, and in 1911–12, 48 vicariates and prefectures with 1,345,376 members (1913 = 1,431,000; 1914 = 1,605,107) and 496,912 catechumens.

According to the *Atlas Hierarchicus*, we find for China and her dependencies, Mongolia and Manchuria, the following statistics: 49 missionary dioceses or vicariates and prefectures, 1365 European and 721 native priests, 247 European and 86 native brothers, 743 European and 1429 native sisters, 4327 male and 2752 female catechists, 7191 native teachers, 1,406,659 native Christians and 613,002 catechumens, 1442 principal and 13,806 secondary stations, 9214 churches and chapels, 54 theological seminaries with 1638 students, 6974 elementary schools with 129,320 (?) pupils, 157 higher schools with 4439 (?) boys and 906 (?) girls, 392 orphanages with 29,198 inmates, 97 hospitals, 427 dispensaries, and 21 printing presses.

3. **Indo-China.**—Indo-China, the bridge between India and China, the most easterly of the three peninsulas of S. Asia, is politically divided into Upper and Lower Burma (British), the Malay Peninsula (British and Siamese), Siam (independent), French Indo-China, which consists of Cochin China, Annam and Tongking, Cambodia and Laos, covering a total area of some 735,000 sq. miles with a population of 35,000,000 or 40,000,000 souls. As Burma and the Malay Peninsula are—ecclesiastically—included in British India, we have to deal here only with French Indo-China, Cambodia, Laos, and Siam.

The area of French Indo-China has been estimated at 262,000 or 309,000 sq. miles with a population of 16,000,000 or 21,000,000 inhabitants. The first attempts to preach the gospel in French Indo-China were made in the 16th cent. by a French Franciscan, Bonfer (1554), and two Portuguese Dominicans, Gaspard of the Cross, who penetrated into Cambodia, and Sebastian de Cantu; both were put to death in Siam in 1569. These were followed by Lopez Cordoso, Sylvester Azevedo, and John Madeira, who preached in Siam and Cambodia, while Louis Fonseca and Diego Advarte (martyred in 1600) went to Cochin China in 1596. These early missionaries, however, had little success. When the Jesuits engaged in the missions of Japan were expelled in 1614, they made their way to Indo-China; such were Francis Buzoni, Diego Carvalho, and Francis del Pina, who in 1615 entered Cochin-China and Cambodia in 1617, and they were followed by Alexander of Rhodes, the pioneer missionary of Indo-China, in 1624. From Cochin-China Father Julian Baldinoti extended the work to Tongking in 1626. In a short period of time the Church made such rapid progress that, in spite of repeated persecutions, the number of Christians amounted to 108,000 in 1641, while Father Tissanier on his arrival in 1658 found 300,000 converts under the charge of only 6 Jesuit priests and 30 lay catechists. To plead the cause of the Church in Indo-China and the insufficient number of workers, Father Rhodes returned to Europe to appeal for help. In the meantime persecutions raged against the native Christians in 1644, 1645, and 1647; but, on the other hand, a new missionary society was founded in Paris (Les Missions Étrangères), whose members were to become the instruments for a rich harvest in the East. Among the first missionaries of the Society of Paris we find Fathers Chevreuil, Haingues, Brindeau, Mahot, and Vachet. To strengthen the work Pope Alexander VII. appointed in 1659 two members—the actual founders of Les Missions Étrangères—viz. Francis Pallu and Pierre de la Motte Lambert, as vicars-apostolic of Tongking and Cochin China. Under their administration parishes were established, schools and seminaries were opened for the training of a native clergy, and de la Motte founded a congregation of native sisters called 'Les Amantes de la Croix.' A persecution which broke out in 1664, during which the Jesuits were temporarily expelled till 1669, greatly reduced the number of native Christians, partly by martyrdom, partly by apostasy, so that on the arrival of the Missionaries of Paris there were only 100,000 Christians left, but this number was increased to 200,000 in 1681. To strengthen the position of the missionaries Pallu in 1672 urged Colbert, the French minister, to establish commercial relations between France and Indo-China, and persuaded Louis XIV. to use his influence on King Le-hi-tong to allow the freedom of Christian worship. In 1678 the vicariate of Tongking was divided into Eastern and Western Tongking; the former, since then divided into Northern and Central, was entrusted to Spanish Dominicans, and the latter to the 'Missions Étrangères' of Paris.

The rapidly growing religious influence exercised by both bishops and priests led to renewed persecutions, which have scarcely been interrupted till our own day. Yet in 1737 we find there 250,000 Christians, *i.e.* 120,000 under the care of the Jesuits, 80,000 under the Missionaries of Paris, 30,000 under the Augustinians, who in 1676 had entered the field, and 20,000 under the Dominicans. This number was not only maintained but increased in spite of civil wars and uninterrupted persecutions during the 18th cent., and notwithstanding the suppression of the Society of Jesus and the consequent decrease of European missionaries. In 1800 we find the following table of statistics:

Cochin China: 1 vicar-apostolic, 5 missionary and 15 native priests, 50,000 native Christians (Missionaries of Paris).
Tongking W.: 1 vicar-apostolic, 6 missionary and 63 native priests, 120,000 native Christians (Missionaries of Paris).
Tongking E.: 1 vicar-apostolic, 4 missionary and 41 native priests, 140,000 native Christians (Dominicans).

3 bishops, 15 missionary and 119 native priests, 310,000 Christians.

In the meantime a political movement had taken place in Indo-China which at first seemed very favourable to the spread of Christianity, but which in reality became the cause of serious hindrances, obstacles, and persecutions. During the civil war which commenced in 1777, Nguyen-anh, the ruler of Cochin China, implored the help of the European

Powers against the rebellious Tai-Shans. Britain, Holland, and Portugal willingly offered their help, but Pierre-Joseph Pigneaux de Béhaine, since 1771 vicar-apostolic of Cochin China, offered to enlist the help of France, and Nguyen-anh accepted the proposal. Accompanied by Prince Canh, the king's son, Pigneaux set out for France, and, as plenipotentiary of the Annamese king, signed a convention on 28th Nov. 1787, according to which France was to assist Nguyen-anh to recover his throne. But to his dismay the bishop, on his return to the East, found that France had abandoned the project, and, therefore, he persuaded 20 officers and 500 men of Pondicherry to come to the rescue of the king, who defeated his enemies and in 1802 proclaimed himself as emperor of Indo-China and Annam under the name of Gialong.

Owing to this success Gialong was favourable to Christianity, which made splendid progress throughout the Annamese empire. This period of peace (1802–20), however, was only a preparation for future trials. In 1819 the Christian community included 4 bishops, 25 European and 180 native priests, 1000 catechists, and 1500 sisters. Gialong was succeeded by his son, Minh-mang (1821–41), a cruel and profligate tyrant and a bitter enemy of Christianity and foreigners. He dismissed his father's trusted friends, summoned all the missionaries to appear at court, and resolved to obliterate the very name of Christianity within his realm. Though his object was defeated for a time, he issued a new edict in Jan. 1833, ordering all Christians to renounce their faith, to trample the crucifix under foot, to raze all churches and religious houses to the ground, and to punish all the missionaries with the utmost rigour. Hundreds of Christians, 20 native and 9 European priests, and 4 bishops fell as victims to this tyrant—Fathers Gagalin (1833), Marchand (1835), Cornay (1837), de la Motte (1840), Mgr. Borie (1838), and Mgr. Delgado (1838), 84 years old. The persecution abated under Minh-mang's successor, Thieu-tri (1841–47), who did not possess the energy of his predecessor, and was afraid of Britain's successes in China and of a threatened interference of France. Instead of being annihilated, the Church's missionaries and converts increased year after year in spite of all the edicts and tortures of Minh-mang. In 1840 we find:

Cochin China: 1 vicar-apostolic, 1 coadjutor, 10 missionary and 27 native priests, 80,000 Roman Catholics.
Tongking W.: 1 vicar-apostolic, 8 missionary and 76 native priests, 180,000 Roman Catholics.
Tongking E.: 1 vicar-apostolic, 1 coadjutor, 6 missionary and 41 native priests, 160,000 Roman Catholics.

3 bishops, 2 coadjutors, 24 missionary and 144 native priests, 420,000 Roman Catholics.

To facilitate the work of the missions in the Annamese empire, Gregory XVI. in 1844 divided Cochin China into two vicariates, Eastern and Western, and W. Tongking into Western and Southern in 1848, while in 1850 Cambodia and N. Cochin China were also raised to vicariates.

Though King Thieu-tri did not shed the blood of the priests, yet they did not escape imprisonment; such were Fathers Gali, Berneux, Charrier, Miche, and Duclos, who were set free by Captain Levêque of the *Héroine* in 1843. This and similar interferences by the French in 1847 and 1856 provoked the resentment of King Tu-duc (1847–83), whose reign of 36 years is one uninterrupted period of persecution of the bishops, priests, and Christians. In 1848 he issued an edict setting a price on the heads of the missionaries, and in 1851 he ordered the European priests to be cast into the sea and the native priests to be cut in two; Fathers Schäffler (1851), Bonnard, and Minh (1852) were martyred. In 1855 a universal proscription of Christians followed, and in 1857 Bishop Pellerin, vicar-apostolic of N. Cochin China, appealed to Napoleon III. to intervene. In August 1858 France and Spain, roused by the slaughter of their countrymen, took joint action, and seized Touran (1858) and Saigon (1859). The persecution meanwhile raged with unabated vigour. Bishops Diaz, Hermosilla, Garcia, Cuenot, etc.—altogether 5 bishops, 28 Dominicans, 3 Missionaries of Paris, 116 native priests, over 100 native sisters, and 5000 Christians—were put to death, 100 towns, all centres of Christian communities, were razed to the ground, 40,000 Christians died of ill-treatment, and all the possessions of the remainder were confiscated. Peace was restored in 1862, when Annam ceded to France the southern provinces of Cochin China and guaranteed freedom of religious worship. That peace, however, did not last long; it was broken by the interference of the French freebooters Dupuis, Dupré-Garnier, and Philastre, and Mgr. Puginier, vicar-apostolic of W. Tongking, became involved to the detriment of the missions. A new treaty was signed between France and Annam on 15th March 1874, which again guaranteed religious freedom and the safety of the missionaries, and from 1874 to 1882 the Christians enjoyed a period of relative peace, till the Annamese mandarins disregarded the treaty and compelled France to interfere. Hue was captured on 25th Aug. 1883, the Annamese were defeated, and on the same day the new treaty was signed, and on its ratification, 23rd Feb. 1886, Annam became a French protectorate. Yet, before this was accomplished, the Christians, who were considered as friends of France and enemies of Annam, had to suffer severely. At the close of the year 1886 Tongking, Cochin China, and Laos had to mourn the loss of 20 European and 30 native priests, and 50,000 Christians; E. Cochin-China alone lost 8 European and 7 native priests, 60 catechists, 270 sisters, 24,000 Christians, 17 orphanages, 10 convents, and 225 chapels, etc. Yet the blood of the martyrs has been here as elsewhere the seed of Christianity, and surely during the 28 years of peace the Roman Catholic Church has made marvellous progress in Indo-China, and has never been in so flourishing a condition as she is to-day. Of this the statistics given below are ample proof.

Siam.—The first Roman Catholic missionary who entered Siam was the French Franciscan, Bonfer, who preached the gospel there from 1550 to 1554, but without result. He was succeeded by two Dominicans, Jerome of the Cross and Sebastian de Cantu, who converted some 1500 Siamese from 1554 to 1569, when they were put to death. The Dominicans were replaced by Jesuits in 1606 and 1624, and in consequence of a persecution the field was abandoned till 1662, when Alexander VII. made it a vicariate and in 1669 entrusted it to the Missionary Society of Paris with Mgr. Laneau as its first bishop. The Siamese king, Phra Narai, in 1687 signed the treaty of Louvo with Louis XIV. of France, by which the Roman Catholic missionaries obtained permission to preach the gospel throughout Siam. This was done till 1727, when a serious persecution broke out which lasted without interruption for the rest of the century. After the Burmese inroads and wars were over, the 12,000 Siamese Christians were reduced to 1000 with Bishop Florent and 7 native priests in charge. In 1826 and 1830 fresh European missionaries arrived, among them Fathers Bouchot, Barbe, Pallegoix, and Courvezy. In 1834 Courvezy was appointed bishop, and under his administration Siam had 6590 Roman Catholics with 11 European and 7 native priests. His successor, Bishop Pallegoix (1840–62), the best Siamese scholar and the most successful missionary among the Laos, induced Napoleon III. to renew the French alliance with

STATISTICS OF THE ROMAN CATHOLIC MISSIONS IN INDO-CHINA AND SIAM.

Missionary Districts.	Missionary Societies.	Priests. Foreign.	Priests. Native.	Brothers.	Sisters. Foreign.	Sisters. Native.	Catechists.	Seminarists.	Native Roman Catholics.	Catechumens.	Principal Stations.	Out-stations.	Churches.	Elementary Schools.	Pupils.	High Schools.	Pupils.	Orphanages.	Orphans.	Hospitals.
N. Tongking, 1883	Dominicans	19	25	—	10	45	80	53	33,474	126	25	218	190	—	—	—	—	16	356	2
E. Tongking, 1848	,,	14	45	5	10	96	137	115	63,398	435	25	330	296	—	—	2	150	6	400	4
Central Tongking, 1848	,,	19	100	—	7	431	310	181	240,947	430	45	593	638	—	—	—	—	5	400	4
Upper Tongking, 1895	Sem. of Paris	27	20	—	6	42	103	58	25,239	449	32	138	137	169	2,526	—	—	4	127	8
W. Tongking, 1678	,,	45	102	16	52	349	422	275	141,216	946	47	809	523	663	19,837	2	650	10	2016	7
Maritime Tongking, 1901	,,	38	67	—	12	140	198	164	98,000	1,012	31	369	364	626	16,008	—	—	13	2008	—
S. Tongking, 1846	,,	35	88	—	—	162	290	277	142,404	677	78	486	408	182	4,892	—	—	6	205	12
N. Cochin China, 1850	,,	43	62	14	11	573	47	113	58,895	1,930	60	261	235	68	2,318	3	300	3	185	2
E. Cochin China, 1659	,,	65	42	—	4	271	89	166	61,047	2,000	32	503	490	57	735	—	—	25	581	1
W Cochin China, 1844	,,	57	79	31	70	648	80	125	70,467	1,457	85	170	235	168	9,514	2	575	12	713	13
Cambodia, 1850	,,	48	41	4	42	202	74	157	45,920	1,500	38	117	170	129	6,634	1	90	8	701	9
Laos, 1899	,,	32	4	—	8	14	62	4	12,509	149	23	56	64	53	1,414	—	—	19	195	7
Total		442	675	70	232	2,973	1,892	1,688	993,516	11,105	521	4,050	3,750	2,115	63,878	10	1,765	127	7,887	69
Siam, 1662	Sem. of Paris	45	21	18	35	87	21	44	24,025	296	23	33	56	76	3,740	4	858	17	523	7

King Mongkut of Siam (1856). Thanks to the broadmindedness of Mongkut (1851–68) and Chulalongkorn (1868–1910), the Roman Catholic missions in Siam enjoyed peace under Pallegoix's successors, Bishops Dupont (1862–72) and Vey (1875–1909). In 1875 there were in Siam 11,000 Roman Catholics, 17 European and 7 native priests, with 30 churches; in 1913 we find 24,000 Roman Catholics, 45 European and 21 native priests, 35 European and 87 native sisters, 23 principal and 33 secondary stations, 56 churches, 76 elementary schools with 3740 pupils, and 4 high schools with 858 students under Bishop M. J. Perros.

The missions in Laos, which were commenced in 1876 and formally opened in 1883, were separated from Siam as a vicariate in 1899. In 1913 we find there 32 European and 4 native priests, 8 European and 14 native sisters, 12,500 Roman Catholics with 23 principal and 56 secondary stations, and 64 churches and chapels with 53 elementary schools.

4. Japan.—The existence of the island empire of Nippon, or Ji-pen, 'the Land of the Rising Sun,' was first revealed to the Western world by the Venetian traveller Marco Polo (1295–98), under the name of Cimpangu, but was not visited by Europeans until three centuries later. Famous among these was the Portuguese Mendez Pinto, who, on 23rd Sept. 1543, landed on Tanegashima and became instrumental in the conversion of three shipwrecked Japanese, Anjiro and his servants. In 1549 St. Francis Xavier, accompanied by the Jesuit Cosmo de Torres and by Brother Fernandez, set out for Japan and landed at Kagoshima, whence he extended his work to Hirado, Hakata, Yamaguchi, Meako, and Bungo, forming everywhere nuclei of promising Christian centres. Before his departure to China in 1551, St. Francis had obtained new helpers from Goa, such as Fathers Balthasar Gago, Gaspar Berse, Edward da Silva, and Peter de Alcavera, who were later on joined by Gaspar Coelho, Vilela, Louis Froes, Melchior, and Antonio Diaz. For forty years the Jesuits remained in sole charge of the missions in Japan, and their work progressed under the protection of Nobunaga, then actual ruler of Japan (1573–82). Torres is said to have baptized 30,000 converts and built 50 churches from 1549 to 1570. Thirty years after the death of St. Francis, we learn from Coelho's annual report for 1582 that at that time 'the number of all Christians in Japan amounts to 150,000 with churches great and small 200 in number.' Down to the year 1563 there had never been more than 9, down to 1577 only 18, and to 1582, 72 members of the Society engaged in the Japanese mission-field. In 1582 a Japanese embassy, consisting of four Japanese princes and a Japanese Jesuit, went to Rome and were received in audience by Gregory XIII. In the meantime Nobunaga had died that same year, and his successor, Hideyoshi Taikosama, became a fierce persecutor of the Christians, ordering the destruction of all the churches and the immediate expulsion of all the Roman Catholic priests (1587). The return of the Japanese embassy from Rome in 1590 and the arrival of Father Valignani with new European Jesuits effected a change, however, and the Japanese Christians began to breathe more freely. In 1593 the Japanese missions numbered 56 European Jesuit priests, 11 European scholastics, 87 Japanese Jesuit brothers, 5 Japanese and 3 Portuguese novices with 23 residences, and about 300,000 or even 600,000 members. Pius V. had appointed the Jesuit Antonio Oviedo bishop of Japan with Melchior Carnero as his coadjutor, but the latter died at Macao, and his successor, Sebastian Morales, who was appointed by Sixtus V., came only as far as Mozambique. Bishop

Pedro Martinez, also a Jesuit, appointed in 1591 and consecrated at Goa in 1595, arrived in Japan in the following year. In 1593 four Spanish Franciscans—Peter Baptist of San Estevan, Bartholomew Ruiz, Francis de Parilla, and Gonsalvus—arrived in Japan and started work at Meako, Nagasaki, and Osaka, thus trespassing upon the privilege granted by Gregory XIII. in 1585 to the Jesuits. The progress of Christianity roused the Bonzes, who accused the Roman Catholic missionaries of being only political agents of Spain and Portugal, and Hideyoshi gave the signal for a cruel persecution, during which 6 Franciscans, 15 Japanese Tertiaries, 3 Japanese Jesuits, and 2 servants, known as the '26 martyrs of Nagasaki,' were put to death on 5th Feb. 1597. Instead of destroying Christianity, however, the persecution only helped to make it known. Hideyoshi died in 1598, and his successor, Jeyasu Daifusama (1605–15), left the Church in peace, which was then governed by the Jesuit Bishop Luiz Serqueyra. In 1602 the Jesuits were reinforced by Franciscans, Dominicans, and Augustinians, and by the year 1613 we find in Japan 130 Jesuits and some 30 priests belonging to the other missionary societies. The actual number of native Christians, however, is doubtful. Between 1549 and 1598, 500,000, between 1598 and 1614, 152,000, and between 1614 and 1630, 25,000 adults were baptized, and we are told that the actual number of native Christians in 1614 amounted to 1,800,000. But the peace and prosperity were the prelude to one of the most terrible persecutions begun by Jeyasu for some unknown reason. In 1614 Bishop Serqueyra died and was succeeded by the Franciscan martyr, Bishop Louis Sotelo, who was burned alive in 1624. In order to weaken the Christians the Shogun arrested 117 Jesuits and 27 other missionaries, together with the Roman Catholic leaders, and transported them to the Philippines (1614); but many of them returned.

Jeyasu died in 1615 and was succeeded by Hidetada, who renewed the edicts of his father, and from 1617 to 1640 the persecution went on without interruption. The 'Great Martyrdom' took place at Nagasaki on 2nd Sept. 1622, when 10 Jesuits, 6 Dominicans, 4 Franciscans, and 32 Japanese nobles were put to death. Jemitsu, the following Shogun, is said to have killed about 20,000 every year from 1623. Over 200 of the missionaries, some 800 native catechists, and 200,000 Christians suffered actual martyrdom. From the year 1638 Christianity appeared to be extinct in Japan; though sporadic efforts were made by Jesuits in 1642 and later, all these failed. Father John Sidotti was the last Roman Catholic priest who entered Japan (1708), and he was put to death on 15th Dec. 1715.

The blood of so many martyrs, however, was not destined to be shed in vain. When in 1832 Gregory XVI. erected the vicariate of Korea, Japan was included. In 1844 Father Forcade and Ko, a catechist, landed on Liu-Kiu Island, and they were joined by Father Leturdu in 1846. In the same year the vicariate of Japan was erected with Father Forcade as vicar-apostolic. But Japan was still a forbidden land till, in 1853, the United States broke down the barriers by a treaty, which was followed by others with Great Britain, Russia, etc., and Father Petitjean was able to build a Roman Catholic church at Nagasaki, which, on 17th March 1865, became instrumental in finding that there were in Japan still 25 Christian villages with several thousand Christians who for 200 years had kept the faith. In 1866 Petitjean was appointed vicar-apostolic. Though some minor persecutions broke out, the Church made progress, and in 1873 the laws and edicts against Christianity were abolished. In 1876 Japan was divided into two vicariates, and under Leo XIII. two more were added in 1888 and 1891, till on 15th June 1891 Leo XIII. re-established the Roman Catholic hierarchy, *i.e.* the archdiocese of Tokyo with three suffragan sees of Nagasaki, Osaka, and Hakodate, which were placed under the care of the Missionaries of Paris, to which have since been added the prefectures of Shikoku (1904) and of Niigata (1912) under the care of the Dominicans and the Missionaries of Steyl. The number of Roman Catholics, which in 1870 amounted to 10,000 with 13 priests, reached 23,000 in 1880, 44,000 in 1891 with 82 European and 15 native priests, 63,000 in 1910 with 150 European and 33 native priests, and 69,755 in 1913.

Korea.—From 1636 to 1876 Chosen, 'the Land of the Morning Calm,' was known only under the name of the 'Hermit Kingdom of the Far East' on account of the rigorous enforcement of her policy of isolation against all foreigners. Yet Roman Catholic missionaries made their way and found their faithful children in Korea, whose very name became known in Europe as the symbol of persecution and martyrdom. When, in 1592–94, Taiko Sama of Japan sent his soldiers to Korea, the Jesuit Gregorio de Cespedez accompanied the troops as chaplain to the numerous Roman Catholics in the army, and in his spare time instructed the Koreans also, baptizing, on his return to Japan in 1593, some 300 Korean prisoners of war. Nothing, however, is known of the fate of his converts in Korea, as in the beginning of the 17th cent. all traces of Christianity had disappeared from the land. In 1783 Seng-hun-i, one of the Korean *literati*, joined the annual embassy to Peking and interviewed there Alexander de Govea, the Franciscan bishop, who baptized him by the name of Peter. On his return he was joined by two friends, Pieki and Il-sini, who became the pioneers of Christianity in Korea. From 1784 to 1794 they received some 4000 neophytes into the Church, who were persecuted by the Bonzes from 1785 to 1791. An attempt made by de Remedios in 1791 to penetrate into Korea failed. In 1794 Father Jacob Tsiu (*alias* Padre Jayme Vellozo), a Chinese priest, succeeded in entering, and for six years continued the apostolate, during which time he baptized 6000 converts and thus increased the flock from 4000 to 10,000 souls. In 1801 new edicts were published against the 'new religion'; among the martyrs were Peter Seng-hun-i, Father Tsiu, and 300 of his flock. For thirty years the Christians in Korea remained without a pastor in spite of repeated requests both to Peking and to Rome, owing to persecutions in China. In 1827 the mission field of Korea was entrusted to the Société des Missions Étrangères of Paris, and on 9th Sept. 1831 Korea was made a vicariate with Bruguière as its first bishop, Fathers Chastan and Maubant being his only assistants. The bishop died in the sight of Korea, while Fathers Maubant and Chastan reached Seoul in 1836 and 1837 respectively. At the end of the year the newly-appointed bishop, Imbert, arrived and found the flock reduced from 10,000 to 6000, which was increased to 9000 two years later, when the bishop and the two priests were put to death (1839). In 1845 Bishop Ferréol, accompanied by Fathers Daveluy and Kim, the first native Korean priest, took over the field, but the latter died the death of a martyr in the following year. From 1846 to 1866 the Church in Korea enjoyed comparative peace, during which numerous converts were made both under Ferréol and under his successor, Bishop Berneux—from 11,000 to 25,000. This was the most flourishing period in the annals of the Church in Korea, which then possessed 2 bishops (Berneux and Daveluy) and 10 priests. In 1866 the persecution raged again, and during it the 2 bishops with 7 priests were put to death and 3 priests had to leave the country. In 1867 attempts were made to reopen the mission, but failed. In 1869 Ridel was appointed bishop, but was not able to enter Korea until 1874, was expelled in 1877, and died in 1884. The treaties of Korea with Japan, the United States, Britain, France, and Austria again opened the gates of the Hermit Kingdom. Bishop Blanc found on his arrival in 1883 only 13,000 Roman Catholics out of 25,000 in 1866, but the flock numbered 16,590 at his death in 1890. During the long reign of Bishop Mutel (since 1890) the missions in Korea, which was declared an independent kingdom in 1895, a Japanese protectorate in 1905, and a Japanese general residency in 1910, have enjoyed freedom. In 1897 we find 32 European and 3 native priests with 32,217 members in 497 stations, in 1909, 46 European and 10 native priests with 68,016 members. At the request of Bishop Mutel, Korea was divided in 1910 into the two vicariates of Seoul and Taiku, and numbered, in 1913, 58 European and 17 native priests with 59 principal and 978 out-stations, and 150 churches with 80,500 members.

II. *AFRICA*.—There is hardly a more glorious chapter to be found in the annals of the Roman Catholic Church than that of Africa. After the decay of early Christianity there, except for a few sadly corrupted remnants surviving in Kabylia, and among the Copts and the Abyssinians, Africa remained for many centuries a closed continent to Christianity, though the Franciscans and Dominicans, the Trinitarians and the Order of Our Lady of Mercy tried their best in the 13th, 14th, and 15th centuries to alleviate the lot of Christian captives and to instil the lessons of Christianity into the hearts of the Muhammadans of Morocco, Tunis, and the Barbary States. When in the 15th cent. the Portuguese, under the leadership of Henry the Navigator, son of King John I. of Portugal, began their discoveries and expeditions along the west coast of Africa, passed Cape Bojador (1433), reached the Rio de Ouro (1442), and doubled Cape Verde (1444), they unfurled the banner of the Cross. In 1471 they crossed the equator, Diego Cam discovered the Congo (1484), Bartholomew Diaz doubled the Cape of Good Hope (1487), while Vasco da Gama came as far as Mozambique, Malindi, and Mombasa (1497). Pope Alexander VI. in 1494 assigned to Spain all the lands discovered and still to be discovered 370 miles west of Cape Verde Islands, and to Portugal all the land to the east, with the one obligation to further the propagation of Christianity and to support mission work in the east and west. Dominicans and Franciscans, Augustinians and Jesuits, Capuchins and Carmelites, supported by secular priests, vied with one another in carrying into effect the command of Christ 'to teach all nations.' Bishoprics were founded on the adjacent islands of the Dark Continent, viz. Las Palmas in the Canary Islands, Funchal in Madeira (1514), São Thiago do Cabo Verde (1532), São Thomé (1534), etc. King Emmanuel of Portugal took a special interest in the evangelization of the Congo, and from 1505 to 1512 sent annually some missionaries of different religious orders (Dominicans, Franciscans, and Augustinians), who, supported by the native King Alphonsus, made good progress. The bishop of St. Thomas (Gulf of Guinea), to whose jurisdiction the Congo belonged, adopted the title of bishop of the Congo, transferred his see to San Salvador, and erected a chapter consisting of 28 canons. As the missionaries already engaged in the Congo did not suffice for the growing demands, St. Ignatius, at the request of the king of Portugal, sent some Jesuits—among them Fathers Vaz, Ribera, Diaz, Soveral, Noguera, Gomez, etc.—who founded a college at San Salvador. From 1554 to 1592, 8 bishops occupied the see of San Salvador, and, when in 1592 the bishopric of Angola was united with that of the Congo, the see of San Salvador was transferred to St. Paul de Loanda. With the growth and expansion of Portuguese power in the E. and W. Indies, however, Portugal neglected to supply the Congo with a sufficient number of missionaries, so that in 1587 we find only 12 priests for thousands of Christian villages. King Alvaro II. therefore applied to Rome for help in 1608; but it was only in 1640 that 6 Italian Capuchins under Francis of Pamplona were sent, and these were strengthened between 1648 and 1683 by Italians and Portuguese, such as Dionysius Mareschi, Bonaventure Carriglio, Joseph of Antiquera, Jerome of Puebla, Francis of Monteleone, and Anthony Zuchelli, as well as by Carmelites who arrived in the Congo in 1659. It seems that these earlier missionaries extended their work as far as Stanley Pool and to the valley of the Kassai. Carmelites, Franciscans, Jesuits, and secular priests also started missionary work in Senegambia, Sierra Leone, the Gold Coast, Benin, Angola, and Upper and Lower Guinea. Among these pioneers we may mention the Jesuits Barreiva († 1612), Fernandez, Barros, Almeida, Netto, and Alvarez, and the Capuchins Bernardine Renard and Angelus of Valencia. On the east coast missionary work was commenced soon after its discovery—in Mozambique by the Jesuits Sylveira (martyred 11th Aug. 1561), Acosta, and Fernandez; at Sofala by the Dominicans (1586) John dos Santos, John de Pietate, and Nicholas de Rosario; in Madagascar by the Lazarists (1648) Nacquart de Champmartin, Gondren, and Bourdaise (1657). In Egypt the Franciscans continued their work among the Copts, and the Jesuits among the Ethiopians (Bermudez, John Nuñez, Andrew Oviedo, Melchior Carneiro, etc.).

The various wars waged between the Dutch and the Portuguese, the slave-trade which was encouraged by the Christian European Powers, the civil feuds among the natives, the more promising colonies in the east and in the west, and the decrease of Portuguese power in Africa soon made the Portuguese forget their solemn obligation, and, instead of furthering the welfare of Christian civilization, they only became a standing obstacle to the work of evangelization, since they would not allow any missionaries but Portuguese in their colonies. Unable—or, rather, unwilling—to support the missionary work, the flourishing churches on the west and east coasts of Africa became weaker and weaker, and social, political, and religious disturbances, such as the sectarian policy of Pombal, the anti-Roman Catholic attitude of Holland and England, and, finally, the French Revolution, brought every missionary enterprise in Africa to a standstill. According to Louvet (*Les Missions catholiques au XIXième siècle*), the total number of Roman Catholics of continental Africa at the beginning of the 19th cent., including Uniate Copts and Abyssinians, amounted to 47,000.

With the formation of the Society for the Propagation of the Faith in 1822 we perceive the first signs of a change for the better. The conquest of Algiers by France in 1830, which broke down the ramparts of Muhammadan fanaticism, and the reopening of the missions among the Copts in Egypt and their kindred in Abyssinia by de Jacobis in 1839 were the preludes to the Christian awakening of the Dark Continent. The son of a Jewish Rabbi was destined to take up anew the Roman Catholic missions in Africa and to inaugurate the magnificent apostolic movement, for Libermann became the founder of the Missionary Society of the Holy

Heart of Mary and the Holy Ghost, usually called the Congregation of the Holy Ghost, whose members (since 1843) have devoted themselves to the evangelization of the Negroes in Senegambia and Gabun (1844), Sierra Leone (1864), the Portuguese Congo (1873), French Guinea (1878), Cimbebasia (1879), Kunene (1882), Loango (1883), Lower Nigeria (1885), Ubanghi (1887), Zanzibar (1863), Bagamoyo (1891), N. Madagascar, etc. When Mgr. Marion de Bresillac returned from the depth of India to France in 1858, his feelings were drawn to the Dark Continent, and he founded the African Missionary Society of Lyons, whose fields principally lie in the districts known as the 'White Man's Grave'—Dahomey (1861), Benin (1868), Gold Coast (1881), Ivory Coast (1895), Liberia (1906), E. and W. Nigeria, Korhogo (1912), and the Nile Delta. Ten years later another missionary society came into existence, viz. the Missionaries of Our Lady of Africa, or the White Fathers, whose field of action extended rapidly from Algeria to Kabylia, from Tunis to the Sahara and the Sūdān, till the bold hand of its founder, Cardinal Lavigerie, came to drive it, in spite of all obstacles, right to the heart of the African continent. To-day they have charge of 11 missionary districts—Kabylia, Gardaia, W. Sūdān, Nyasa, Bangweolo, Upper Congo, Tanganyika, Unjanjembe, S. and N. Nyanza, and Kivu, with 187,129 members, 196,000 catechumens, 138 principal stations, 502 priests, 52 brothers, 244 sisters, 2289 catechists, 85 native sisters, 2 native priests, 30 students in minor orders, 378 aspirants, 1974 schools with 79,521 pupils, and 341 charitable institutions.

Besides these three African Missionary Societies *par excellence*, work is also carried on by the orders which in days gone by laboured as pioneers in Africa, such as the Franciscans (Egypt, Tripoli, Morocco), the Capuchins (Erythrea, Galla, Somaliland, Seychelles), the Trinitarians (Benadir), the Lazarists (Abyssinia, S. Madagascar), the Jesuits (C. Madagascar, Kwango, Zambesi), and the Missionary Seminary of Verona (C. Africa), the Benedictines of St. Ottilien (Dar-es-Salam, Lindi), the Trappists (Natal, Congo), the Belgian, English, and German missionary societies of Scheut (Congo Free State), of Mill Hill (Upper Nile), of Steyl (Togo), the Oblates of Mary Immaculate (Natal, Transvaal, Orange, Kimberley, Lower Cimbebasia, Basuto), etc.

The missionaries, if they do not precede the explorers or conquerors, accompany them; nowhere are they wanting. From the valleys of the Atlas to the highland plains of Abyssinia, from the Sūdān to the Cape, on the great rivers and lakes, in the desert plains and in the equatorial forests, in the heart of the continent and in the islands, the Cross of Calvary is found to-day set up as the sign of redemption. Where the missionaries have been able to labour they have laboured, and where they could only die they have died. According to the *Katholische Missionen*, Oct. 1912, Africa, as far as it is a missionary country, consists of 6 dioceses, 44 vicariates, and 28 prefectures apostolic, 1 prelature nullius, and 7 independent missions, with 1,100,000 native members and some 600,000 catechumens. When we add the dioceses of Africa and her islands which are not under the jurisdiction of the Propaganda, and, therefore, do not fall under the heading of the African mission field strictly speaking, we find the total number of Roman Catholics amounting to 3,742,000—insignificant when compared with the number of inhabitants, which is said to amount to 165,000,000 or 180,000,000 or even 200,000,000 souls.

III. *N. AND S. AMERICA.*—When, in 1492, Columbus landed on the island of San Salvador, he found a brown-skinned people whose physical appearance confirmed him in his opinion that he had at last reached India, and he called the inhabitants, therefore, 'Indios,' or 'Indians.' Subsequent navigators and explorers found that the same race was spread over the whole continent from the Arctic shores to Cape Horn, and that the people were more or less everywhere alike in their main physical characteristics, whence they extended the name 'Indians' to these aborigines in both S. and N. America with the exception of the Eskimos in the extreme north. Much has been written about the atrocities and cruelties of the white invaders—Spanish, French, Portuguese, Dutch, and English—committed against the Red Men, the original inhabitants and owners of the soil. The Roman Catholic Church, from the very outset of the political conquest of S., C., and N. America, has acted as the protectress of the downtrodden Indians, and her missionaries—Franciscans, Dominicans, Jesuits, and Hieronymites such as Las Casas, Montesino, Nobrega, and Anchieta—have taken up their cause of liberty and religion. Lopez de Vega, one of the greatest Spanish poets, unfolds the whole aim and purpose of the Spanish conquerors in S. America in two lines:

'Al rey infinitas tierras
Y a Dios infinitas almas,'

i.e. 'to extend the boundaries of the Spanish empire over the vast territories of the new world and thereby to gain an infinite number of souls to God.' Religion was her great end and aim, her all-pervading motive. The soothing influence of the Roman Catholic missionaries in S. America is still to be seen in the splendid churches and colleges and the thousands and millions of devoted converts; and, as long as Spain remained faithful to her solemn obligations, she was successful and prosperous. The destruction of the Indian missions, in which the Roman Catholic missionaries had worked for two hundred years, was due to the anti-Roman Catholic policy and legislation of Spain and Portugal; the revival is to be ascribed to the efforts of Pius IX., Leo XIII., and Pius X., who worked in harmony with the rulers of the different States and republics through their apostolic delegates. To describe the Roman Catholic missionary work among the Indians in S. and C. America would mean to write the history of the Roman Catholic Church in the colonial period of these countries from 1520 to 1820. It may suffice to note the work of the Franciscans and the Jesuits during this period.

Franciscan missionaries accompanied Columbus in 1493, and they were followed by others to the Antilles in 1500, to Mexico or Nova Hispania (Peter of Ghent, Martin of Valencia, Molina, Ribeira, the famous Zummaraga [1548], the first archbishop of Mexico, and Martin of Coruña), to Yucatan (Didacus of Landa [1579]), Guatemala and Honduras (Peter of Betancour and Maldonado), Nicaragua and Costa Rica. In S. America the Franciscans had missions in Colombia and Venezuela (John a S. Philiberto [1527], Louis Zapata, and Ferdinand Larrea) with some 200,000 baptized Indians, in Peru (Mark of Nizza and Jodokus Ryke), in Ecuador and Ucayali (Philip Luyando, Dominic Garcia, and Francis Alvarez [1686]). At the request of the king of Spain, Franciscans went to Chile (1553) (Martin of Robleda and Angelus of Espineira (1778]), to Bolivia (Andrea Herrero [1838] and Antonio Comajuncosa [1814]), and into the Pampas of Argentine and to Tucuman (Francis Solanus [1610]). In 1538 they landed in S. Brazil (Bernard Armenta, John de los Barrios [1547], Bernardine of Cardenas, and Louis Bolaños [1629]).

Between 1565 and 1572 Jesuit missionaries went to Florida, Mexico, and Peru, and, under Claudius Acquaviva (1581–1615), the second successor of St.

Ignatius, to Chile and Paraguay, and later on to Maranhão. Names such as Nuñez, Correa, Nobrega, and Anchieta have become household words among the Indians in S. America, while the name of Azevedo, who, with 39 of his fellow-missionaries, suffered martyrdom in Brazil (1570), stands for loyalty to duty. At the time of the suppression of the Society of Jesus the Jesuits were represented in Brazil by 445, in Maranhão by 146, in Paraguay by 564, in Mexico and California by 572, and in New Grenada, Chile, Peru, and Ecuador by 192, 242, 526, and 209 members respectively.

Equally famous among the defenders of the Indians are the Dominicans Las Casas, Louis Bertrand, Antonio Montesino, Dominicus de Betanzos, Dominicus Ortiz, the Augustinian Francis John de Medina, etc. With the suppression of the religious orders and the downfall of the Spanish supremacy in S. and C. America came also the destruction of the flourishing missions. The Christian Indians and Negroes were allowed to drift, nay, were often driven back into paganism, were slaughtered by their cruel white taskmasters, their plantations were destroyed or ruined, their schools and churches were reduced to ashes, and the missionary work which had been accomplished among them by the self-sacrificing heroes of Christian charity during two hundred years with the greatest outlay of money and valuable lives was destroyed. The political upheaval and the masonic influence in the beginning of the 19th cent., with the subsequent scarcity of priests in the S. American Republics, scarcely allowed the missionaries to resume their work among the remaining Indians and Negroes. In recent years the Propaganda has once more appealed to willing workers among the various religious orders and missionary societies for help to establish missionary work among the Indians; yet it remains a difficult task to obtain a precise record of their work, since most of them are at the same time engaged among the numerous European colonists in the S. American Republics. In the following we give only the names of the vicariates, prefectures, and missions in the various States, the dates of their erection, and the missionaries engaged.

Colombia: V. Goajira (Capuchins), 1905; V. Casanare (Augustinians), 1893; V. Llanos de S. Martin (Society of Mary), 1903; P. Caquetá (Capuchins), 1904; P. Choco (Immaculate Heart of Mary), 1908.

Guiana: V. Demerara (Brit. Guiana) (Jesuits), 1837; V. Surinam (Dutch Guiana) (Redemptorists), 1825 (1852); Cayenne (French Guiana) (Congregation of the Holy Ghost), 1643 (?).

Ecuador: V. Canélos y Mácas (Dominicans), 1893; V. Mendez y Gualaquiza (Salesians), 1893; V. Napo (Jesuits), 1893; V. Zamora (Franciscans), 1893.

Peru: P. Amazonas (S. Leon) (Augustinians), 1900; P. Ucayali (Franciscans), 1900; P. Urubamba (Dominicans), 1900; M. Putumayo (Franciscans), 1912.

Brazil: Prel. Santarem (Franciscans), 1903; M. Rio Branco (Benedictines), 1907; Prel. Araguaya, 1911; P. Rio Negro, 1910; P. Solimões (Capuchins), 1910; P. Teffé (Congregation of the Holy Ghost), 1910.

Argentine-Paraguay: V. Patagonia N. (Salesians), 1884; P. Patagonia S. (Salesians), 1883; Gran Chaco and Pampas (Franciscans).

Chile: V. Autofagasta (secular priests), 1895; V. Tarapaca (secular priests), 1894; P. Araucania (Capuchins), 1901.

Mexico: V. California, 1874.

Central America: V. British Honduras (Jesuits), 1888 (1893).

Antilles: V. Curaçao, 1842; V. Jamaica (Jesuits), 1837.

Krose (*op. cit.*) reckons the number of the uncivilized Indians in America at 1,500,000 or 1,750,000, *i.e.*, Brazil, 600,000; Paraguay, 100,000; Argentine, 30,000; Chile, 50,000; Peru, 350,000; Bolivia, 250,000; Ecuador, 200,000; Colombia, 150,000; Venezuela, 60,000. To these must be added some 200,000 or 250,000 Coolies, Negroes, and Chinese. In these missions European colonists live side by side with the Indians, etc. According to Krose, some 401,000 are Roman Catholics, and, allowing some 150,000 as being Europeans, there remains a Roman Catholic Indian and Negro population of 250,000 souls. In the whole mission field there were 476 priests, 230 brothers, 435 sisters, 418 stations, and 340 churches. In C. America and the W. Indies there are still 500,000 or 600,000 pagans, among whom Jesuits, Dominicans, Redemptorists, and Lazarists are at work, some 180 missionaries among 330,000 native Roman Catholics.

The United States of America are composed of former British, Spanish, and French colonies, and their population—91,972,266 (Census of 1910)—consists of a small remnant of the original American Indians (270,000, according to some, 330,000 or 444,000, according to other writers), of imported Negro slaves and their descendants (9,827,763), of yellow or Asiatic immigrants (146,863), and of white or European settlers and their descendants. In the former Spanish (Florida, Texas, New Mexico) and French (Louisiana) colonies the Roman Catholic missionaries have worked for the conversion and Christian civilization of the Indians from the beginning of the colonial epoch. Dominicans entered Florida in 1560, and they were supported in 1568 by the arrival of 12 Franciscans, 5 secular priests, and 8 Jesuits, among whom we may mention Fathers Martinez, Segura, de Quiros, and de Solis. In Texas and New Mexico Spanish Franciscans—Marcos of Nizza, John of Padilla, and Louis of Escalon—had commenced in 1539, but made little progress. In Arizona Francis of Porras (1683) and in California Juniper Serra (1784) commenced missionary work among the Indians, and along the Mississippi we find Father Marquette. The conquest of N. America by the white immigrants drove the Indians further and further, and 'spoliation, outrage, and murder' were the orders for almost one hundred years. According to H. G. Ganss ('The Indian Mission Problem, Past and Present,' in *The Catholic Mind*, no. 13 [New York, 1904]), there remain in the United States some 270,000 Indians, of whom 100,000 are Roman Catholics, 40,000 Protestants (74,000?), 110,000 'follow the old ways,' and 20,000 have no Church affiliation. According to Streit (*Atlas Hierarchicus*, 1914), there are in the United States 440,931 Indians, of whom 64,741 (67,255) are Roman Catholics. These are scattered in 33 dioceses, possess 306 churches, and are attended by 163 priests (Benedictines, Franciscans, Jesuits, etc.) and 391 sisters; 100 schools are attended by 7359 children. Famous among the Indian missionaries in the 19th cent. are Father de Smet and Bishop Marty.

The Negro population in the United States (one-ninth of the whole population), descendants of the slaves who for two hundred and fifty years had been imported into America, have for the last fifty years been emancipated, but are still treated as outcasts. Owing to hostile legislation, the Roman Catholic Church had for many decades a poor chance of alleviating the miserable conditions of the Negroes, since baptism was considered inconsistent with the state of slavery. After the emancipation of the Negroes (1863) and the second Plenary Council of Baltimore (1866), Archbishop Spalding raised his voice for their conversion. The same course was pursued at the third council (1884) by Archbishop (Cardinal) Gibbons, who established a commission for Roman Catholic missionary work among the Negroes and the 'Catholic Board for Mission Work among the Colored People.' It is difficult to obtain the exact number of Negroes professing the Roman Catholic religion in the United States, since some live in coloured parishes while others are mingled with the white population, and of the latter a report is hardly ever made. The *Catholic Encyclopædia* (xii. [1911] 629) gives the number as amounting to 200,000 or 225,000, while, according to the *Atlas Hierarchicus*, there are only 103,436 scattered in 33 dioceses, with 109 churches, 162 priests (Josephites, Missionary Society of Lyons, Congregation of the Holy Ghost, and Mission of Steyl), and 173 schools with 14,181 pupils.

The 'Catholic Board for Mission Work among the Colored People,' in its semi-annual publication, *Our Colored Missions*, 1912, gives the following statistics: churches, 72; priests working exclusively for Negroes, 99; schools, 126 with 11,270 pupils; charitable institutions, 27 with 2520 inmates; Roman Catholics, 260,000. Two religious orders of priests devote themselves exclusively to coloured missions, namely the Josephite Fathers and the Fathers of the African Missions (Lyons). Besides these two there are eight other orders of men in the field: the Jesuits, Franciscans, Dominicans, Marists, Lazarists, Fathers of the Holy Ghost, Fathers of the Divine Word, and the Capuchins (see also *Our Negro Missions*, by the Fathers of the Divine Word, Techny, Ill., U.S.A., 1914).

In Canada the descendants of the aborigines are divided into four families: (1) the Huron Iroquois, (2) the Innuits or Eskimos, (3) the Dénés, (4) the Algonquins. In 1905 their total number amounted to 107,637, of whom 85,553 lived inside, the others outside the reservations. In the earliest days of the French colonial period Franciscans in 1615, Jesuits in 1625, and Sulpicians in 1657 devoted themselves to the conversion of the Algonquins and the Huron Iroquois—some 100,000 souls. Famous among these missionaries are d'Olbeau, Le Caron, Viel, Sagard (Franciscans), Brébeuf, Lallemant, Lejeune, Garnier, Chabanel, Daniel, Jogues, Jolliet, and Marquette (Jesuits). In 1659 the ecclesiastical hierarchy was established in Canada, and the Church entered from the missionary to the colonial period among the immigrants.

Of the 107,637 Indians to-day 35,060 are Roman Catholics; the remainder, with the exception of 10,906 who are still pagans, belong to various Protestant denominations, who are scattered in 33 dioceses. The Roman Catholics are attended by some 160 priests in over 110 stations, with 104 schools, and 200 sisters.

IV. *OCEANIA.*—The southern realm of islands which stud the Pacific Ocean has been named Oceania, and for convenience of reference has been divided into four districts, viz.

Australia with Tasmania.
Melanesia (New Guinea, New Pomerania, Bismarck Archipelago, Solomon Islands, New Hebrides, Loyalty Islands, New Zealand).
Micronesia (Marianne, Caroline, Marshall, and Gilbert Islands).
Polynesia, comprising all the smaller islands between Hawaii in the north and Easter Island in the east.

Discovered in the 16th and 17th centuries by Spanish and Portuguese admirals, such as Balboa, Magellan, Mendana, Quiros, and de Torres, who were followed by Dutch, French, English, and German explorers—Roggewein and Tasman, La Pérouse and d'Urville, Cook and von Humbold—they remained more or less in obscurity till the beginning of the 18th and even the 19th century. That Roman Catholic missionaries set their foot on the islands soon after their discovery, although only occasionally, is certain. Padre Pigafetta accompanied Magellan to the Ladrone Islands in 1521, another priest landed on the Marquesas in 1595, two Spanish missionaries visited Tahiti in 1774, and Abbé de Quelen converted a few natives in the Hawaiian group in 1819. As Spanish and Portuguese supremacy declined, the discoveries were of little consequence to Christianity, and, owing to the political and religious revolution in Europe, the suppression of religious orders, and the scarcity of missionary vocations and pecuniary support, the Roman Catholic missions were to a large extent neglected in the Pacific. The Marianne and Caroline groups were the only ones where progress was made. The former was visited by the Jesuit Diego de San Vittore, who landed with four other Jesuits on Guam in 1668, and these were followed by five more in 1670; but nearly all the Spanish missionaries were killed in 1670, 1672, and 1684. From 1700 to 1766 the Marianne missions were entrusted to German Jesuits, who in 1731 extended their work to the Carolines. After the suppression of the Jesuits the Marianne Archipelago was handed over to Spanish Augustinians in 1786, and the latter were replaced by German Capuchins in 1907.

Several attempts were made by the Jesuits on the Philippines to open a mission in the Caroline Islands in 1700, 1708, 1709, and 1721, but all of them failed, till Father Cantova succeeded in 1731. Owing to the serious loss of lives, however, the Jesuits abandoned the field, and it was only in 1886 that twelve Spanish Capuchins were able to resume missionary work once more in the Carolines; they remained in charge till 1904. In 1911 the German Marianne and the Carolines were united into one vicariate-apostolic with Walleser as its first bishop, while the United States possession of Guam was made an independent vicariate in charge of Spanish Capuchins. The vicariate of Guam numbered, in 1913, 12,000 Roman Catholics, and that of Marianne-Caroline had 5395 in 1914. With the exception of these two island groups, the beginning and development of Roman Catholic missionary enterprise in the Pacific belong to the 19th and 20th centuries. It was on 7th July 1827 that Alexis Bachelot, accompanied by Abraham Armand, Patrick Short, and Robert Walsh of the Picpus Society, landed in Honolulu (Hawaii) to resume the apostolate in Oceania, the whole of which was placed under the ecclesiastical jurisdiction of Solages, then prefect-apostolic of Mauritius (1830). Three years later the vicariate of Oceania was established, and in quick succession the Roman Catholic missions were extended to the various island groups and entrusted to the two pioneer missionary societies in the Pacific, viz. the Missionaries of the Sacred Heart (Picpus) and the Society of Mary (Marists). From 1827 to 1845, under Cardinal Prefect Capellari of the Propaganda and under his pontificate as Gregory XVI., the Society of Picpus sent its missionaries to Hawaii (1827), the Gambier Islands (1834), the Marquesas (1838), and Tahiti (1841), while the Marists went to Wallis, Tonga, New Zealand (1837), New Caledonia (1843), Fiji (1844), and Samoa (1845). Gregory XVI. divided Oceania into two distinct vicariates: Eastern (1833–44) and Western Oceania (1836–48), from which Central Oceania was separated in 1842. These three vicariates form, so to speak, the roots of the ecclesiastical jurisdictions in the Pacific. From the Eastern vicariate were separated those of Hawaii, Marquesas, and Tahiti (1844 and 1848), and from the Central those of New Caledonia (1847), Samoa (1851), and Fiji (1863 [1887]), while W. Oceania was divided into the vicariates of Melanesia (1844–89) and Micronesia (1844–97). From Melanesia were separated New Guinea and New Pomerania (1889), and from Micronesia the Gilbert (1897) and the Carolines (1886). Some of the groups were again divided and subdivided, such as New Guinea and New Pomerania, from which were separated the Solomon (1897–98) and the Marshall Islands (1905). The Marianne group depended upon the diocese of Cebu (Philippines) till it was made an independent vicariate. The divisions demanded new helpers in the ever-expanding field, and during the colonial period of Oceania (1882–1903) three other missionary societies were asked to help: to the Capuchins were entrusted the Caroline (1886 and 1904) and the Marianne Islands (1907), to the Picpus Society the Cook or Hervey Archipelago and Kaiser Wilhelmsland W. (1913), to the Society of the Divine Word (Steyl) Kaiser Wilhelmsland E. (1896), to the Marists the New Hebrides (1887) and the Solomon Islands (1898), and, finally, to the Congregation of the Sacred Heart (Issoudun) New Pomerania (1882), New Guinea, British and Dutch (1884 and 1903), the Gilbert (1888) and the Ellice

STATISTICS OF ROMAN CATHOLIC MISSIONS IN THE PACIFIC OCEAN, 1913.

Mission districts. V. = Vicariate. P. = Prefecture. M. = Mission.	Year of Foundation.	Missionary Society.	European priests.	Native priests.	European brothers.	Native brothers.	European sisters.	Native sisters.	Catechists, male.	Catechists, female.	European Roman Catholics or descendants.	Native Roman Catholics.	Catechumens.	Non-Roman Catholics.	Principal stations.	Secondary stations.	Churches and chapels.	Catechetical seminaries.	Pupils (Catechists).	Elementary schools.	Pupils.	Higher schools.	Boys.	Girls.	Orphanages.	Orphans.	Dispensaries.	Printing presses.
Marianne and Carolines, V.	1886 1911	Capuchins.	16	—	16	—	10	—	1	2	50	4,730*	300	27,856	13	9	17	—	—	22	894	—	—	—	—	—	3	1
Guam, V.	1911	„	6	—	2	—	12	—	?	?	?	12,000	?	2,000	6	—	10	—	—	?	?	—	—	—	?	—	—	—
New Pomerania, V.	1889	Congr. of Sacred Heart.	37	—	43	—	34	—	83	49	140	20,417	1,934	300,000	31	102	90	3	89	131	4,698	2	34	23	18	633	28	1
Kaiser Wilhelmsland E., P.	1896 1911	Society of Divine Word.	29	—	23	—	40	—	6	—	—	2,410	1,200	150,000	17	—	19	1	12	26	1,500	—	—	—	—	—	17	1
Kaiser Wilhelmsland W., P.	1911	Picpus Congr.	—	—	—	—	—	—	—	—	—	—	—	—	—	—	—	—	—	—	—	—	—	—	—	—	—	—
New Guinea, V.	1889	Congr. of Sacred Heart.	26	—	21	—	38	—	8	—	180	4,767	2,300	300,000	12	22	28	—	—	39	1,258	—	—	—	2	?	19	1
N. Solomon Islands, P.	1898	Society of Mary.	12	—	4	—	11	—	4	—	?	480	649	100,000	5	?	14	—	—	12	350	—	—	—	—	—	—	—
S. Solomon Islands, V.	1897 1912	„	16	—	2	—	8	—	41	11	67	3,000	1,500	150,000	10	54	51	1	32	50	416	—	—	—	1	4	—	1
New Hebrides, V.	1901 1904	„	26	—	6	1	17	3	40	—	400	1,500	2,500	68,000	17	6	21	1	35	28	443	—	—	—	1	?	—	—
New Caledonia, V.	1847	„	57	—	7	10	22	29	18	—	29,234	10,783	?	16,000	31	26	82	1	?	43	4,744	5	244	285	1	65	—	—
Marshall Islands, M.	1905	Congr. of Sacred Heart.	6	—	6	—	15	—	6	—	6	730	140	10,000	5	3	7	—	—	5	182	4	25	40	—	—	5	—
Gilbert Islands, V.	1897	„	23	—	12	—	19	—	95	—	50	14,037	385	12,000	18	125	117	1	20	100	2,266	9	60	143	6	216	27	1
Fiji Islands, V.	1863 1887	Society of Mary.	33	—	12	18	47	50	247	—	350	12,000	?	128,000	18	273	85	2	92	44	2,915	4	100	170	—	—	—	—
Central Oceania, V.	1842	„	24	4	—	—	19	28	52	—	—	9,940	?	16,862	16	?	34	1	60	31	2,446	4	—	347	—	—	—	—
Samoa (Navigator Island), V.	1851	„	20	4	13	—	15	10	96	96	250	7,854	180	40,000	14	106	83	1	40	106	2,016	4	85	79	—	—	—	1
Sandwich (Hawaiian Isl.), V.	1848	Picpus Congr.	37	—	35	—	68	—	—	—	30,000	15,000	?	102,000	22	—	106	—	—	14	2,335	3	710	510	1	30	—	—
Marquesas, V.	1848	„	9	—	2	—	8	—	21	—	130	2,488	?	800	9	28	37	—	—	—	—	—	—	—	—	—	—	1
Tahiti, V.	1833 1848	„	30	—	8	—	25	—	80	—	2,000	5,800	150	30,500	56 (?)	8	80	—	—	20	1,950	—	—	—	—	—	—	1
Dutch New Guinea, P.	1902	Congr. of Sacred Heart.	20	—	15	—	10	—	35	—	?	3,500	360	650,000	9	?	19	—	—	40	1,325	—	—	—	—	—	—	—
			427	8	227	29	418	120	833	158	62,857	131,436	11,598	2,104,018	309	690	900	12	380	711	29,738	35	2855		30	948	99	9

* According to *Katholische Missionen*, July 1914, the Roman Catholic population of the Marianne-Carolines is 5395, that of Guam, 12,400.

Islands (1897), and, lastly, the Marshall Islands (1899).

Where eighty years ago there were—with the exception of the Marianne group—scarcely any Roman Catholics, and no priest or bishop, we find to-day an established hierarchy, with 14 bishoprics, 4 prefectures-apostolic, and 1 mission with 131,000 native and 63,000 European members, 427 priests (8 native priests), 227 brothers, 418 sisters, 1000 stations, 990 churches and chapels, and 700 schools with 30,000 pupils. The population of Oceania proper (without Australia and Tasmania) amounts to 2,650,000 or (without New Zealand, no longer a missionary country) 2,000,000, or, according to others, 1,340,000 souls. The Roman Catholic population is, therefore, comparatively small, and the work, especially in New Guinea, the Solomon group, and other islands, is little advanced. But, bearing in mind the social, moral, religious, political, ethnological, and linguistic problems of the various groups and their natives, the unhealthy climate, in many cases absolutely unsuitable for Europeans, the variety of dialects even among the inhabitants of the same islands, and, lastly, the hostile attitude of some of the European Powers that have divided the islands among themselves towards every Christian enterprise, and the fierce opposition displayed against the Roman Catholic missionaries from 1830 to 1880, the Roman Catholic Church has made slow but sure progress. She has become a Christianizing and civilizing factor in the Pacific, and as such she is now acknowledged by the various European governments and their representatives, by explorers and tourists, and by missionaries of every denomination, whatever their attitude towards the tenets of the Roman Catholic Church may be.

Famous among the Roman Catholic missionaries in the Pacific are the two pioneer missionaries (later bishops), Bataillon (1843–77) of C. Oceania, the founder of the missions in New Caledonia, Fiji, Samoa, and Rotuma, and his fellow-worker, Pompallier of W. Oceania, Bishop Epalle, who was murdered in 1845, Bishop Rouchouze of E. Oceania, etc. Nor must we forget Father Chanel, the proto-martyr of the Pacific and the apostle of Futuna (1841), Father Damian Deveuster, the leper apostle of Molokai, or Fathers Bontemps of the Gilbert and Castanié of the Cook Islands, and, lastly, Brother Eugene Eyraud, the lay apostle of Easter Island.

As space does not allow of a detailed history of the interesting work of Roman Catholic missionary enterprise in the Pacific, we give on p. 726 a table of statistics which will tell the story of the heroic work which the missionaries have achieved within the years 1830–1913 under very trying circumstances of persecution, hunger, poverty, and death.

In the following table of statistics we give the summary of missionary work during the 19th cent. and the results of previous centuries since the Reformation. These statistics we borrow from Krose (*op. cit.* p. 123).

A.—SUMMARY OF R.C. MISSIONS IN THE 19TH CENT. (STATISTICS, 1908).

Mission field.	Roman Catholics.		Priests.		Mission helpers.		Stations.	Churches.	Schools.	Pupils.
	Total.	Of European origin.	Total.	Native.	Brothers.	Sisters.				
Asia	6,299,886	138,000	9,086	5,237	2,930	11,996	25,157	17,837	13,083	504,074
Australia and Oceania	170,054	—	392	9	291	531	547	553	497	20,634
Africa	853,931	130,000	1,842	123	1,357	3,668	3,702	3,418	3,392	193,813
America	998,092	170,000	985	?	285	1,089	1,008	928	862	72,357
Total *A*	8,321,963	438,000	12,305	5,369	4,863	17,284	30,414	22,736	17,834	790,878

B.—RESULTS OF FORMER CENTURIES.

Asia	6,700,000	10,000
Africa	1,038,000	15,000
America	14,250,000	—
Total *B*	21,988,000	25,000
Totals *A* and *B*	30,309,963	463,000

LITERATURE.—H. Hahn, *Gesch. der kathol. Missionen seit Jesus Christus bis auf die neueste Zeit*, 5 vols., Cologne, 1857–65; F. Schwager, *Die kathol. Heidenmission der Gegenwart*, Steyl, 1907–09; L. E. Louvet, *Les Missions catholiques au xixme siècle*[2], Paris, 1898; J. B. Piolet, *Les Missions catholiques françaises au xixme siècle, ou La France au dehors*, 6 vols., do. 1901–02; P. M. Baumgarten, *Das Wirken der kathol. Kirche auf dem Erdenrund*, 3 vols., Munich, 1901–03; A. Huonder, *Die Mission auf der Kanzel und im Verein*, 3 vols., Freiburg, 1912–14; R. Streit, *Missionspredigten*, do. 1913–14; H. Fischer, *Jesu letzter Wille*, Steyl, 1906, Eng. tr., *Our Lord's Last Will and Testament*, London, 1910; P. Manna, *Operarii autem pauci*, Milan, 1909, Eng. tr., J. Glinchey, *The Workers are Few*, Boston, 1911; K. Streit, *Atlas Hierarchicus*, Paderborn, 1913; H. A. Krose, *Kathol. Missionsstatistik*, Freiburg, 1908, *Kirchl. Handbuch*, vols. i.–iv., do. 1907–13; J. Schmidlin, *Die kathol. Missionen in den deutsch. Schutzgebieten*, Münster, 1913, *Zeitschr. für Missionswissenschaft*, vols. i.–iv., do. 1911–14; F. Schwager, *Die brennendste Missionsfrage der Gegenwart: Die Lage der kathol. Missionen in Asien*, Steyl, 1914; A. Huonder, *Der einheimische Klerus in den Heidenländern*, Freiburg, 1909; M. Spitz, 'The Native Clergy in Heathen Lands,' in *Illustrated Catholic Missions*, 1909–10; A. Launay, *Hist. générale de la société des missions étrangères*, 3 vols., Paris, 1894; A. Brou, *Les Jésuites missionnaires au xixme siècle*, Brussels, 1908; M. Spitz, 'Franciscans and Foreign Missions,' in *Illustr. Cath. Miss.*, 1911; *Les Missions catholiques*, 47 vols., Lyons, 1868–1915; *Die kathol. Missionen*, Freiburg, 1873 ff.; *The Illustrated Catholic Missions*, London, 1886 ff.; *The Missions Overseas* (Annual Review), do., 1907 ff.; R. Streit, *Führer durch die deutsche kathol. Missionsliteratur*, Freiburg, 1911; art. 'Missions,' in *CE*.

M. SPITZ.

MISSIONS (Christian, Protestant).—I. *INTRODUCTION.*—The missions of the Reformed Churches of Christendom seem at first sight to be discontinuous from those of the mediæval Church and from the post-Reformation missions of the Roman Church. While the Roman Church carried on extensive missions from the 16th to the 18th cent., the Reformed Churches during the same period were doing practically nothing. Indeed, their divines, when they touched the subject of the Christian obligation to evangelize the world, were mainly occupied in elaborating arguments to show that the command of Christ to do this had lapsed in their day. The causes of this inaction are complex.

After the great crisis of the Reformation the Protestant countries of Europe had not only to adapt their religious life to new conditions, but also to maintain their political existence against powerful hostile combinations. Meanwhile it was to Spain and Portugal, the great representatives of the old creed, that the discovery of America and of the Cape route to India had fallen. To them, accordingly, the pope had committed authority over the newly-found regions of America and Africa as well as the E. Indies, and this dominion they were able, to a considerable extent, to make effective. The revival of the Roman Church which followed the Reformation naturally threw much of its best force into these national undertakings, sanctioned by 'holy Church.' With the armies and administrators of Spain and Portugal went the priests and friars, whose task it was to bring these new territories into the Roman obedience.

With the 17th cent. began the colonial expansion of England, which resulted in the Christianization of N. America, not by the labour of missionaries, but by the migration of Christian peoples. A little later the Netherlands, freed from the rule of Spain, began to take over the dominions of Portugal in the East, and eventually founded a great empire in the Malay Archipelago; they also colonized the extremity of S. Africa and thereby founded a white nation in yet another temperate clime. To the Dutch also largely belongs the credit of opening commercial relations with China and Japan. Meanwhile, in the course of the 18th cent., the great Indian empire of Britain came into existence, and, following on this, relations with the Further East developed during the 19th century. The same period saw the penetration of Africa from south, east, and west, and its partition between Western Powers, among whom Britain and, latterly, Germany represented the Reformed faiths. It was through these political developments that the missionary sphere of the Protestant nations was opened up, so that, when their religious life was effectually revived towards the close of the 18th cent., the missionary call of an open world for which they were specially responsible came to Reformed Christendom with irresistible force.

When we have indicated the main features of the expansion of Protestant nations, we have indicated also the main lines of their missionary development as compared with that of the primitive and the mediæval Church. At first Christianity was conscious in principle of its universal destiny, but was practically confined by a limited world-outlook and the lack of communication between East and West. In the Middle Ages the Church on the one side was straitened by Islām, and on the other was grappling with the unfinished task of absorbing and training the barbarian nations of Europe. In both these periods the evangelist and the evangelized were, on the whole, of similar races and of cultures not radically different. In the modern period the world-outlook has become complete and practical, while, with the facility of intercourse, the immensely greater progress in arts and sciences since the 15th cent. by the Christianized nations has made the intellectual and social difference between the Christian and the non-Christian far greater than at any earlier time. This is at once the advantage and the impediment of modern missions as compared with ancient.

Modern missions generally are continuous with the primitive expansion of Christianity, and in the case of Protestant missions in particular we must go back to the primitive records of the faith and to its early history in order to estimate their work. But in so doing we are at once struck by certain outstanding contrasts connected with the historical situation. Since in primitive times the missionary and his hearers belonged broadly to the same level of culture and to the same sphere of thought and language, and were members of the same or similar communities, the whole range of problems connoted by the terms 'home base' and 'foreign field' was for them non-existent, and the economic problem of modern missions was present only in germ, or even in an inverted form, financial help being sent by the daughter Churches to the mother. Not unconnected with this feature of early conditions is another fact. The propagation of the faith was the work of the Church in each place, whether through its officers or through its ordinary members, for the Church itself was the evangelizing body. Hence in the early records of expansion the professional missionary, as distinguished from the ordinary minister or layman, is conspicuous by his absence. There were great leaders in the work of evangelization among the bishops and others, but for associations distinct from the Church, set apart for evangelism, there was no place. Finally, the political relation of the missionary to his hearers was either simply that of a fellow-subject of the same great empire or that of a stranger from a land of no very different conditions.

Following on the adoption of Christianity as the religion of the Roman State, the irruption of the barbarians, and the rise of monasticism, these conditions were modified. The missionary trained and set apart for the work appears on the scene, more often as a member of an order than as an isolated evangelist. The conversion and control of virile and turbulent barbarians seemed to demand a sterner discipline than the Church alone could exercise; repeatedly the arm of the State was vigorously used, and orders came into existence that were half-monk, half-warrior, such as the Knights of St. John and the Order of Teutonic Knights. The Christianization of the West was largely accomplished through monastic and military agencies, though the individual missionary was not absent. In Asia the wide-spread missionary work of the Nestorians had little of the political element, but it went down before the great onrush of Asiatic migrations—either under the military impact of Islām or under the unified forces of Buddhism. On both sides of the world the faith spread or receded amid the reciprocal contact and strife of nations whose land-frontiers were contiguous. The more stringent organization of missionary work and the training of the worker had made progress, but the political factor had deteriorated its texture.

The doctrine of the Reformation insisted on the liberty of the individual conscience and the freedom of individual access to God, together with the absolute sovereignty of His grace in the work of salvation. The result of this in principle, although slowly realized in practice, was the elimination of the political factor from the spiritual activity of the Church, more especially in missionary work. The missions of the counter-Reformation were still closely linked with political conquest and administration, but so also were the earlier Dutch Protestant missions in the East. Both were in reality survivals of the mediæval method. The modern missionary method, both in the Roman and in the Reformed communions, is substantially that of free associations, working on a basis of voluntary co-operation. The missionary orders of the Roman Church have indeed retained continuously their historical organization, adding new orders, as needed, on a similar basis; but the missionary societies of Protestant Christendom are, in effect, an expression of the same principle, only that in them the exercise of individual freedom has been combined with obedience to superimposed organization and discipline for a common purpose. It would not be correct to say that Protestant missions are differentiated from Roman by a lack of direct subordination to Church authority, for many of them are directly administered by the governing bodies of their Churches. There is, however, this obvious difference, that the missions of the Roman Church are all co-ordinated and guided by a single central authority which is conspicuously lacking in Protestant Christendom. On the other hand, the Protestant organizations are now systematically endeavouring to gain the benefits of unity, together with those of freedom, by voluntary co-operation and co-ordination in missionary work, not only as between Churches but also as between nations.

II. *HISTORY.*—**1. Formation and development of societies.**—Up to the 18th cent. the missionary societies in Britain and on the Continent were closely connected. The Dutch East India Company, founded in 1602, was enjoined by its charter to care for the conversion of the heathen in the newly-won possessions of the Republic, and it appointed preachers for the purpose; but the work was carried on mechanically under government pressure. After a century the number of registered Christians in Ceylon was 350,000, in Java 100,000, and in Amboyna 40,000, but few were left of these myriads in Ceylon after English rule came in, and only a small minority in Java under Dutch rule. In New England the Pilgrim Fathers at first had to defend life and property against the Indian tribes who surrounded them, but in 1646 John Eliot, pastor of Roxbury, gave himself to work among the aborigines, learning their language, carefully teaching them, and gathering them into organized churches—the first real Protestant missionary enterprise. In 1649 the Corporation for the Propagation of the Gospel in New England was formed, and it is still extant, but its activities have consisted chiefly in the collection of funds. In 1698 the efforts of Thomas Bray, Rector of Sheldon, Warwickshire, resulted in the formation of the Society for the Promotion of Christian Knowledge. During the 18th cent. this aided the Danish-Halle Mission and other missions in India, but its principal work since 1813 has been the publication and circulation of Christian literature, both at home and abroad. In 1701 the Society for the Propagation of the Gospel was founded to provide clergy for the colonies and dependencies of Great Britain and also to take steps for 'the conversion of the natives'; but little was done for the latter object till after 1817. These three societies are connected with the Church of England.

The revival of spiritual religion in Germany known as Pietism (*q.v.*) resulted in two missionary movements during the 18th century. Frederic William IV., king of Denmark, feeling responsibility for his colonial dominions, found the men whom he needed in Bartholomæus Ziegenbalg and Heinrich Plütschau, followers of the great Pietist leader, Hermann August Francke. They were sent out in 1705 to the Danish settlement of Tranquebar in S. India, and there founded a work which was developed by many successors of note, especially Christian Friedrich Schwartz (1749–98). Their work was partly maintained by the S.P.C.K. The other far-reaching missionary movement of German origin was the Moravian. Members of the Unitas Fratrum of Moravia, driven from their homes for their faith, were settled by the Pietist Nikolaus Ludwig, Count von Zinzendorf, on his estate at Herrnhut in Saxony in 1722. Very soon their zeal led them to send missionaries to the Negroes of the W. Indies and to the Greenlanders who had been evangelized by the Norwegian, Hans Egede, but were left after his return uncared for. This was the beginning of a world-wide work, carried on by a community never numbering more than 40,000 souls in Europe, but with 100,000 converts abroad, and a roll of more than 2000 missionaries, sent out since its foundation. See, further, art. MORAVIANS.

The Presbyterian Society for the Promotion of Christian Knowledge, founded in Scotland in 1709, deserves mention, because among a few missionaries whom it sent to the Indians of N. America was David Brainerd, the evangelist of the Delaware Indians. He died after only three years' work, but his biography powerfully influenced William Marsden of New Zealand, William Carey and Henry Martyn of Bengal, and many others.

By the middle of the 18th cent. these early movements of Protestant missions had greatly slackened owing to the religious deadness which had overtaken the various Churches. But the antidote to this was already working in the evangelical revival connected on the Continent with the names of Francke and Zinzendorf, and in England with those of John Wesley (1703–91) and George Whitefield (1714–70). The inevitable result in the revival of zeal for the evangelization of the outside world became manifest towards the end of the century. The two great leaders and their immediate followers were ministers of the Church of England, but, owing to the deadness of her leaders and people, the movement, while powerfully influencing the Church, resulted in the formation of the strongest of the Protestant bodies, the Methodists of England and America. But it was to another dissenting body that the missionary call first came effectively. The great pioneer William Carey and his fellows founded the Baptist Missionary Society in 1792. In 1795 followed the second society, at first called simply the Missionary Society. It was founded by Church of England, Independent, and Presbyterian ministers. In 1796 two Scottish associations were established, known as the Edinburgh and Glasgow Societies. In 1799 Evangelical members of the Church of England decided to establish the Church Missionary Society, and the undenominational society already mentioned became known as the London Missionary Society. Though others are not excluded, it has since then practically remained the organ of the English Congregationalists. The British and Foreign Bible Society was set on foot in 1804 by the joint action of churchmen and dissenters. The Wesleyan Methodists had already been carrying on missionary work in East and West since 1786 under the personal guidance of Thomas Coke, but after his death in 1814 they established their own society. The societies named, together with the revived operations of the S.P.G., represent the formative beginnings of Protestant missionary work in Great Britain. The American Board of Commissioners for Foreign Missions, formed mainly by Congregationalists in 1810, and the American Baptist Missionary Union (1814) were the earliest societies in America. Before sketching the development of these and indicating the minor societies, it is desirable to mention two outside movements which greatly influenced the history of missions in Africa and the East.

It is reckoned that the African slave-trade during the hundred years preceding 1786 conveyed no fewer than 2,000,000 Negroes into British colonies, chiefly the W. Indies and British N. America; but even in England Negroes were sold and bought till the judgment pronounced by Lord Chief Justice Mansfield in 1772: 'As soon as any slave sets his foot on English ground, he becomes free.' This formed the starting-point for the campaign against the slave-trade in the entire British possessions, carried on within and without Parliament by William Wilberforce from 1789 till its victorious climax amid the throes of the Peninsular War in 1807. The abolition of the slave-trade did not as yet do away with slavery in British possessions outside the United Kingdom, nor with the slave-trade carried on by foreign nations. But it gave a powerful impulse to missionary work among Negroes, and arrangements were made at Sierra Leone for the reception of liberated slaves, of whom many thousands were settled there under the care of C.M.S. missionaries, the same thing being done later on the E. African coast near Mombasa. Meanwhile, the agitation against slavery in the British dominions was continued by Wilberforce and his successors till it was crowned with success in the Emancipation Act of 1833, which liberated 1,000,000 slaves in the W. Indies at a cost to the State of £20,000,000 paid to the owners as compensation. Slavery in the United States, and the trade that fed it, continued till Emancipation Proclamation in 1863. Since then what remained of slavery under Christian rule has been abolished, and slavery in Muslim and pagan lands has been greatly limited. As a result of the shifting of populations, there are now some 12,000,000 Christianized Negroes in the United States and W. Indies, apart from those who have been brought in through missionary effort in Africa.

In the East the greatest of all colonial empires was built up by English merchant adventurers. The East India Company dates its charter from the year 1600, but for 150 years little was done for the spiritual benefit of its European servants, and nothing for the evangelization of the natives of the land. After the battle of Plassey in 1757 things improved somewhat among Europeans, but, when Parliament, on the motion of Wilberforce, in 1793 was ready to afford facilities for missionary work in India, the opposition of the E.I.C. threw out the clauses, and for the next twenty years Christian missionaries were rigorously excluded from its territories. At length in 1813, when the E.I.C. charter was once more revised, not only was the entry of missionaries conceded, but an ecclesiastical establishment was provided for Europeans, the representatives of which have done not a little to forward the cause of missions.

i. BRITAIN.—The later development of British societies, especially Anglican, was strongly influenced by several religious movements. The Irish Revival of 1859 affected England in 1860 and gave an impetus to the formation of undenominational societies, such as the China Inland Mission. In 1875 Dwight L. Moody's first revival in London and the first Keswick Convention marked the beginning of a movement which resulted in an immense growth of missionary zeal, both in offerings and in service on the part of university men, especially in connexion with the C.M.S. The Tractarian Movement had influenced one side of the Church of England for a generation before it began to appear extensively on the mission-field during the last quarter of the century.

(*a*) *Anglican.*—The *Society for the Propagation of the Gospel* in 1817 was supporting a few clergy and schoolmasters in the N. American colonies and elsewhere. From that time it began its missions to non-Christians (1823) by sending men to Bengal and to S. India, where Robert Caldwell was distinguished as linguist and bishop. It has carried on all its missions under the direct superintendence of the diocesan bishops in the mission-field, and it has included in its activities the provision of ministration to white men in the colonies and on the continent of Europe. Its work among non-Christians has steadily increased and now absorbs £165,000 out of an income of £250,000. In India it has occupied Calcutta, Lucknow, Delhi, Bombay, Madras, Assam, and Burma. In 1821 it advanced to S. Africa, in 1848 to Borneo, in 1862 to the Pacific, in 1863 to N. China, in 1873 to Japan, in 1889 to Korea, in 1892 to Manchuria, and in 1903 to Siam. By constitution the S.P.G. is as broad as the Church of England, but as a matter of fact it has represented mainly the High Church side. It has developed in varying degrees the community type of missions. The Oxford Mission to Calcutta (1881) is now independent; the Cambridge Mission to Delhi and the Cawnpore Christ Church Brotherhood are still connected with the S.P.G. Its most flourishing missions are those to the Tamils of Tinnevelly and to the Kols of Chotā Nāgpur, both in India.

The principal other societies of this type are: (1) the *Melanesian Mission*, founded in 1846 by George A. Selwyn, afterwards bishop of Lichfield, and carried on by the martyr John C. Patteson; (2) the *Universities Mission to Central Africa*, a response made in 1859 to the call of David Livingstone, who appealed to the youth of Oxford and Cambridge to carry on his work. Bishop Edward Steere was its most distinguished scholar and statesman.

The earliest missionaries of the *Church Missionary Society*, like those of the S.P.G. and S.P.C.K., were Germans, and the Basel Missionary Institution, established in 1815, supplied no fewer than 88 C.M.S. missionaries, including the Arabic scholar and writer, K. G. Pfander, and the E. African explorers, J. Rebmann and L. Krapf. Its first mission was in W. Africa (1804). India was entered in 1813, when 'Abd-al-Masīḥ, the disciple of Henry Martyn, opened work at Agra. In 1814 Madras and New Zealand were occupied; Travancore in 1816; Ceylon in 1818; N.W. Canada in 1822; in 1820 C. T. E. Rhenius began work in Tinnevelly. In 1837 L. Krapf first went to E. Africa, and in 1841 H. W. Fox and L. L. Noble began the Telugu Mission in S. India. In 1847 China was entered by W. A. Russell and R. H. Cobbold. In 1850 the Sindh Mission was begun, and in 1852 the Panjāb Mission was started at Amritsar. The N.W. Frontier was first touched at Peshāwar in 1854, British Columbia in 1856, and Kashmīr in 1864. Uganda was opened up in 1876, Persia and Japan in 1869, Egypt (the revival of a previous mission) in 1882.

The C.M.S. represents the Evangelical school of the Church of England, in touch with the more pronounced Anglicanism on the one side and with nonconformist and interdenominational effort on the other. Its missionaries, after the first supply of German recruits, were drawn largely from its college at Islington, but of late years they have been furnished in increasing numbers by the universities. It is the largest of the Protestant missionary societies, with a missionary roll of 1340, an annual income of £400,000, and 450,000 adherents in the mission-field.

The *Church of England Zenana Missionary Society*, founded in 1880, works side by side with the C.M.S. in India and China. In 1913–14 it had 224 women missionaries, 27,239 pupils in zenanas and schools, and an income of £60,000. The *South American Missionary Society* (1851) carries on the Patagonian work begun by Allen Gardiner, and also works in Paraguay and S. Chile.

Most of these societies have associations in Ireland and Scotland, but the contributions and missionaries from those countries are not separately given.

(*b*) *English Free Churches.* — Only the chief societies can be dealt with here. The earliest is the *London Missionary Society* (1795). The discoveries of Captain John Cook moved the founders to send their first mission to the South Sea Islands, where John Williams, after years of work, was martyred on the island of Erromanga (1839). In 1798 S. Africa was occupied, and the labours of Robert Moffat, followed by those of his yet more distinguished son-in-law, David Livingstone, became classical. The most remarkable of L.M.S. missions was that in Madagascar, founded in 1820, and resumed, after long expulsion of the missionaries, with extraordinary fruitfulness. In N. and S. India L.M.S. work has been going on since 1804, extending to Bengal, the United Provinces, Madras, and Travancore. Robert Morrison of this society was the first missionary to enter China (1807), and missions are now planted in S., C., and N. China. C. Africa was taken up as a memorial to Livingstone in 1877. In 1913–14 this mission had 294 missionaries, an income of £214,000, and 316,000 adherents.

The *Baptist Missionary Society*, founded in 1792 on the impulse of William Carey, cobbler, preacher, missionary, and linguist, sent him out as its first messenger. Moved by the narrative of Cook's voyages in the South Seas, his first desire was to go there, but his destination was changed to India, and, being debarred by the E.I.C.'s regulations from settling in British territory, he started the first mission in Bengal at the Danish settlement of Serampore. This became the centre of a unique literary and linguistic work, carried on by Carey with the help of his colleagues, Joshua Marshman and William Ward. From Bengal the English Baptists extended their work eastwards to Assam, north-westwards to Agra, Delhi, and Simla, and southwards to Orissa; also to Ceylon, where a considerable work is done, to three provinces of China, and in Africa to the Lower and Upper Congo; they also did work in Kamerun, which was eventually made over to German missionaries when their government occupied the country. In 1913–14 they had 463 missionaries, an income of £99,000, and 25,170 Church members.

The Wesleyan Methodists had already begun work in the British W. Indies under Thomas Coke in 1786, and in W. Africa from 1811. After his death the *Wesleyan Methodist Missionary Society* was founded as a separate organization, and the work advanced in 1814 to Ceylon, in 1815 to S. Africa, in 1817 to India, in 1822 to Australasia, and in 1851 to China. In the last region, and in S. Africa and the W. Indies, many of the churches are no longer under the management of the society. Like the Baptists in the north of India, the Wesleyans in the south have done much for the cause of vernacular literature. In 1913–14 their missionaries numbered 392, their income was £130,000, and their adherents 307,000.

Of societies connected with the minor sects of Methodism it must suffice to mention the Methodist New Connexion (1824), working in China; the United Methodists (1837), in China, E. and W. Africa, and Jamaica; and the Primitive Methodists (1869), in Africa. The Methodist missions generally are an integral part of the Church organizations. The Welsh Calvinistic Methodists (1840) are, properly speaking, Presbyterian. They have an exceptionally successful work among the Khāsis of the Assam hills.

For convenience we may add here the *Friends' Foreign Mission Association* (1865), working in Madagascar, India, Ceylon, China, and Syria. Like the Moravians, though very much later in time, the Friends prosecute their missionary operations to an extent that is in striking contrast to the smallness of their community, reckoned, as it is, at some 30,000 members.

(*c*) *Presbyterian.* — The Presbyterian societies, like the Methodist, are part and parcel of the Church organization.

Scottish Churches. — The *Glasgow* and *Scottish Missionary Societies*, founded in 1796, carried on their work in the face of considerable indifference and even opposition. In 1824, at the instance of John Inglis, the General Assembly undertook a mission to India, and the sending out in 1829 of Alexander Duff, followed by Murray Mitchell and John Wilson, marked an epoch in the history of educational missions in India, which these men opened up with marvellous ability and zeal. The work at Lovedale in Kaffraria (1841) became famous among industrial missions. At the Disruption in 1843 the missionaries in India and Kaffraria cast in their lot with the Free Church, and this new body soon greatly increased its operations, adding Natal, Nyasaland, the New Hebrides, Syria, and S. Arabia. Since the union of the Free Church with the United Presbyterians the United Free Church field has included operations in W. Africa, the W. Indies, China, and Japan. The work of the Established Church was also revived and extended in India, C. Africa, and China.

The *English Presbyterian Church* (1847) is working in China, Formosa, the Straits Settlements, and India; the *Irish Presbyterian Church* (1840) in Manchuria and India.

All these societies have their organizations for women's missionary work, in some cases distinct from the main body, but mostly as a department of it. Generally speaking, the women's societies or auxiliaries are later developments, for it was hardly practicable to send out unmarried women as missionaries till after the middle of the last century; before this, work among women was carried on by the wives of missionaries, to whom some of the most important organizations owe their foundation and development. In the figures given the women's work is included in that of the main society.

(*d*) *Undenominational.* — Among undenominational societies we notice the two most prominent. The *Indian Female Normal School and Instruction Society* was founded in 1852 for the educational purposes indicated in its name. In 1880 the majority of the Church of England members seceded, and started the *Church of England Zenana Missionary Society.* Under the new name of the *Zenana, Bible, and Medical Mission* the original body has continued to co-operate with Church of England and Presbyterian missions in India, and has developed medical work. The *China Inland Mission* was founded in 1865 by J. Hudson Taylor, who had already worked in China as an evangelist from 1853. Vocation and spiritual preparation are insisted on, but not high educational attainments; careful training, however, is given in language-schools on the field. No direct appeals for funds are made at the home base, and no fixed salary is guaranteed to the missionary. The plan of advance has been to 'occupy' province after province by stationing missionaries in the inland provincial capitals, instead of remaining in or near the treaty ports on the coast. The sending out of seven Cambridge athletes in 1885 created great enthusiasm. The work of the C.I.M. has spread rapidly and given an impetus to advance by other societies into Inland China. In the Boxer Rebellion of 1900 the martyr roll of missionaries of this society far exceeded that of any other. The

Salvation Army has been doing missionary work, principally in India, since 1883; its operations have been mostly of a social kind, such as industrial undertakings and reclamation of certain criminal tribes. The *North Africa General Mission* works mainly in Algeria and Morocco; the *Egypt General Mission* as indicated by its name; the *Regions Beyond* and the *Sudan United Missions* in W. and C. Africa.

(*e*) *Missionary publishing societies.*—In all Protestant missionary work the rule has been to give converts and others access to the Christian Scriptures as soon as possible. Occasionally this may have resulted in premature productions which have afterwards been the cause of misunderstanding or hindrance, but, taken as a whole, the translation of the Scriptures into the languages of the non-Christian world has been one of the most signal and fruitful achievements of modern missions. The Bible, as a whole or in part, is now printed in about 500 languages and dialects. The great bulk of this work has been and is being done by the *British and Foreign Bible Society* (1804), which has issued 487 of these versions up to 1914. The number of these is being increased year by year, and the work of revision of older versions in the light of the best scholarship is constantly proceeding. Many scores of these languages possessed neither book nor script before they were reduced to writing by the missionaries, who soon followed up the spelling-book and the school-reader with the Gospels, and gradually added the whole NT and in many cases the OT also. The B. and F.B.S. circulated, in 1914, 10,162,413 copies of the Scriptures. It received a charitable income (exclusive of sales) of £90,000. The *National Bible Society of Scotland* and the *Trinitarian Bible Society* in the same year circulated respectively 2,762,616 and 154,952 copies in 13 and 2 languages (besides those dealt with by the larger society).

For the production of Christian literature of a more general kind the *Society for the Promotion of Christian Knowledge*, already noticed, is the oldest society. It helps Church of England missions in all parts of the world, principally with books of devotion and theology, but also with works of a more general nature. It has published in 99 languages. The *Religious Tract Society* (1799), with an income (apart from sales) of £17,196, does a similar work on an interdenominational basis, and it has been the means of founding several daughter societies in India and China. It publishes in 200 languages. The *Christian Literature Society for India* was founded in 1858 as a Christian reply to the mutiny. Under John Murdoch (1859–1904) it developed a wide-spread activity in production, both of educational works and of religious and general literature. A similar *Christian Literature Society for China* has done much in producing high-class literature under the leadership of Timothy Richards and others. The *Nile Mission Press* at Cairo (1902) produces Arabic literature for missions to Muslims in the Near East. But the mission presses at work in the four quarters of the globe run into many hundreds.

ii. AMERICA.[1]—The *American Board of Commissioners for Foreign Missions*, founded in 1810, sent out its first missionaries to India in 1812; but, owing to the hostile attitude of the E.I.C., they did not secure a footing in W. India till 1814, and in the same year they entered Ceylon. The other principal steps forward were to Oceania (1819), W. Africa (1830), S.E. Africa (1835), China (1847), and Japan (1869). Since the separation from this Board of the Dutch Reformed and the Presbyterian missions the A.B.C.F.M. represents the Congregationalists of the U.S.A. Income, £200,978; missionaries, 615; adherents, 193,742.

The *American Baptist Missionary Union* came into existence in 1814, when Adoniram Judson entered Burma. In 1827 he began a remarkably successful work among the Karen tribe, which has come over in masses to Christianity. Another Indian mission of the A.B.M.U. in the Telugu country (from 1840) has been the sphere of a large movement. The Union entered China in 1843, the Congo Territory in 1866, and Japan in 1872. The Southern Baptist Convention, an off-shoot from the main body, carries on missions in China, W. Africa, and Japan. Income, £222,885; missionaries, 701; adherents, 505,600.

The *Methodist Episcopal Church* represents the Wesleyan movement in the U.S.A. The larger, or Northern, branch carries on its missions to non-Christians in S. India (1833), China (1847), N. India (1856), Japan (1872), Korea (1885), and Malaya (1889). The Southern branch began missionary work in 1846, and carries it on in India, China, and Japan. The foreign work of this denomination has spread rapidly and widely. Income, £296,506; missionaries, 1396; adherents, 687,368.

The *Presbyterian Church in the U.S.A.* is also a leading missionary force. It separated its work from that of the A.B.C.F.M. in 1837, and has missions in Syria, Persia, India, Siam, W. Africa, China, and Japan. Its educational work in India especially is of a high order. The Presbyterians of the Southern States (*Presbyterian Church in the U.S.A.*; 1861) work in China, Japan, Congo Territory, and Korea. The *United Presbyterian Church* (1859) maintains a vigorous work in China, India, and Egypt (the last named chiefly among Copts); in their Panjāb Mission accessions have been very large. The *Dutch Reformed Church* (1832) works in China, Japan, India, and on the Persian Gulf. The *Disciples of Christ* have missions in China, Japan, India, and Turkey. The first of these denominations in 1914 had an income of £561,142, 1537 missionaries, and 370,238 adherents.

The *Lutheran Churches of the U.S.A.*, numbering over 2,000,000 communicants (and, say, 10,000,000 adherents), are divided into six chief sects, whose first mission was undertaken in 1841. They work mainly in India, where their most important mission is in the Telugu country. Income, £68,907; missionaries, 81; adherents, 70,426.

The total figures for Protestant Missions in N. America amount to 6627 missionaries and 1,396,631 adherents.[1]

Canada has eight leading Protestant missionary societies. The principal of these are the *Baptist*, the *Methodist*, the *Presbyterian*, and the *Anglican*.

In addition to the Boards connected with the various Churches, one organization, connected with no Church in particular, has powerfully influenced the missionary life of all, not only in America, but in the United Kingdom, and on the continent of Europe. The going out of the 'Cambridge Seven' to China in 1884 excited great interest among the students of America as well as among those of Great Britain, and at a conference of students summoned in 1886 by Moody at Mount Hermon, Mass., the *Student Volunteer Missionary Union* was formed on the basis of a declaration by each member of his or her intention to become a foreign missionary. The same movement continued in a less organized form in Britain till it was formally established there also, in Edinburgh, in 1892. It soon became evident that the appeal for missionary

[1] The figures given are exclusive of work among Indians or others in home territories. Unless otherwise specified, they are for the year ending Dec. 1914. Generally speaking, these American Boards are part of the official organization of their respective Churches. The principal ones only are mentioned.

[1] It is impossible to estimate accurately the distribution of income between home and foreign missions.

service could not be effective without a strengthening of the general Christian life of the student world at large, and in 1893 the *Student Christian Movement for Great Britain and Ireland* was started. This has now a membership of over 9000 students, including those in theological colleges, and it is affiliated to the *World's Student Christian Federation*, with a membership of over 180,000 students in some 40 countries. The S.V.M.U. has become a department of the more general work. Since 1896 it has systematized the study of missions among its members and outside by the formation of study circles and the provision of suitable textbooks for them. The Liverpool Conference of 1912 co-ordinated the foreign missionary and home social problems of the movement more closely than before, and the S.C.M. works at the solution of both as inseparable the one from the other. From the British branch of the S.V.M.U. over 2000 students have left in thirteen years for the mission-field; 700 are still in college, and 600 are undergoing post-collegiate training for missionary work. The Union sends out no missionaries itself, but only through the societies.

iii. GERMANY.—In the latter part of the 18th cent. the Danish-Halle Mission died out, its missionaries being taken over by other societies. The *Moravians* quietly continued their work and celebrated their first centenary in 1832 with much cause for rejoicing; their influence was felt, too, in new undertakings elsewhere. During their second century the work has increased till it embraces 21 mission-fields, mostly in America, but also in Africa, Australia, and India. The income from home contributions is little more than one-third of the total expenditure, the balance being met from free-will offerings in the mission-field, government grants, and trade profits. The fields of work are largely the most remote and inhospitable lands, such as Greenland, Labrador, Alaska, the Mosquito Coast, N. Australia, and Lesser Tibet.

Other German Protestant missionary efforts began with the training of missionaries for societies outside of Germany. Johann Jaenicke from 1800 to 1827 carried on a missionary seminary in Berlin whose *alumni* were sent out from Holland and England. They included pioneers in Tinnevelly (C. T. E. Rhenius) and China (C. Guetzlaff). In S. Germany Christian life was strongest in Würtemberg, Baden, and German Switzerland, and here missionary interest resulted in the foundation of the *Basel Missionary Institute* in 1815, from which 88 candidates were passed on to the C.M.S., many of whose early missions were founded or conducted by them. In 1822 the *Basel Evangelical Missionary Society* was founded, largely through the efforts of Christian Gottlieb Barth. Their first permanent mission was started on the Gold Coast in 1828. In 1843 work was begun on the south-west coast of India, in 1846 in China (Kwantung), and in 1886 Kamerun, becoming a German colony, was taken over from the Baptist Missionary Society. The Industrial Association connected with the Basel Mission has taken a lead in industrial work in S. India, where it carries on weaving, tile-making, etc., at Mangalur and other centres.

The *Berlin Missionary Society* sent out its first missionaries to Africa in 1834, and in 1872 it took over work in S. China, and in 1891 in E. Africa. The valley of the Wupper in Rhenish Prussia was a strong centre of active Christian life, and here, after much preliminary work, the *Rhenish Missionary Society* was founded in 1828. This, too, began work first in S. Africa, extending in 1834 to Borneo, in 1862 to Sumatra, in 1865 to Nias, in 1846 to China, and in 1887 to Kaiser Wilhelmsland. The missions in S. Africa have attained a large measure of self-support, and in Sumatra many Muhammadans have been brought in, together with masses of pagans.

The year 1836 saw the foundation of three German societies. The *Bremen Missionary Society* has had a chequered career, its principal mission being in W. Africa, where the deadly climate has carried off many missionaries. The *Leipzig Missionary Society* was first established in Dresden, and transferred to Leipzig by its director, K. Graul, in 1848. It makes more use of university graduates as missionaries than do the other German missions, which generally employ seminarists. It also more than others represents the pronounced Lutheran element. The Leipzig M.S. in 1840 took over what remained of the old Danish-Halle Mission, and in 1892 it opened work in German E. Africa. The *Gossner Missionary Society* was founded by a Berlin pastor of that name. He began on his own responsibility to train missionaries in Scripture and the devotional life, and within 22 years he had sent out 178 to Australia, British and Dutch India, N. America, and W. Africa. Not a few of them proved able and successful evangelists. After Gossner's death in 1858 many of them joined other societies, but the work among the Kols of Chotā Nāgpur, which had been specially fruitful, was put under a board, since then known as the Gossner M.S. Notwithstanding the secession of several missionaries with their flocks to the S.P.G. in 1868, the Gossner Mission (113,000 adherents) represents the largest group of Christians in the Province of Bengal.

Another mission which belongs to the extreme Lutheran section of German Protestantism, and which also owes its origin to the enterprise of a single man, is the *Hermannsburg Missionary Society*, begun by Ludwig Harms in 1849. After parting with certain fields to others, this mission has work now in S. Africa and India.

Besides the eight societies mentioned above, the following have been founded later: *Schleswig Holstein* (1877), *Neukirchen* (1882), *General Evangelical Protestant* (1884), *Berlin Missionary Society for E. Africa* (1886), together with a number of minor bodies, including several small societies for women's work. The G.E.P. Society is the only body representing a modernist standpoint approximating to Unitarianism. It has a few missionaries in Japan.

iv. HOLLAND.—Owing, perhaps, to the State propagation of the faith in former years, independent missionary societies have not multiplied here so rapidly as elsewhere. The *Dutch Missionary Society*, founded in 1797, has worked in the Malay Archipelago, and the results of its work have largely—especially in Minahassa in Celebes—been taken over by the Established Church, which maintains 36 pastors and 26 assistants, who minister both to converts and to colonists. A number of minor societies have been formed from time to time. The Dutch missions have had considerable success among the Muslims of their colonies.

v. FRANCE.—In France the cause of Protestant missions is represented by the *Société des Missions Evangéliques*, founded in Paris in 1824. Its chief mission is the very successful one among the Basutos in S. Africa with which the name of François Coillard is connected. It has also taken over work from English and American societies in territories such as Madagascar, Gabun, and the Society Islands, which had come under French domination. In French Switzerland the *Mission Romande* was founded in 1879; it works in N. Transvaal and Delagoa Bay.

vi. SCANDINAVIA.—In Scandinavia the *Danish Missionary Society* was founded in 1862, and works in S. India and China. The *Norwegian Missionary*

Society (1842) has missions among the Zulus and in Madagascar. There are minor missions connected with the China Inland, the Alliance, and other societies. Sweden also has had its own *Swedish Missionary Society* since 1835, working in S. India and S. Africa, and a *Swedish Missionary Union*, since 1878, with missionaries in Algeria, the Congo, Ural, Persia, China, and Chinese Turkestan, besides minor associations. Finland has a *Lutheran Missionary Society* with work in S. Africa and *Free Church* missions in China and India.

vii. BRITISH COLONIES.—The British colonial Churches of various denominations maintain a considerable and increasing amount of missionary work. This is done partly through societies locally formed, partly by assisting the older societies in home lands. Australia and New Zealand, in addition to work among their own aborigines, send men and women principally to Asiatic countries, the S. African churches to the pagans of their own territories, the now independent W. Indian Churches to their own neighbours and to their race-fellows in Africa. In India and China, though very few churches are as yet self-supporting, various indigenous missionary societies have been formed, such as the *Tinnevelly Missionary Society* and the *National Missionary Society*, for work in various parts of India. These two had 2416 adherents, 5 missionaries, and an income of about £4000 in 1912.

2. Preparation of missionaries.—In the beginnings of societies the first step taken was frequently the establishment of a missionary seminary. As a rule, the candidates required some school training before entering on their theological course. The fact that many of them had been engaged in trades or handicrafts rendered them all the better suited to the pioneer work which largely fell to their lot, but not a few distinguished scholars developed among them. The Free Churches in England and America have drawn their missionaries mainly from the theological colleges of their denominations, but the Scottish Churches have usually sent out graduates of the universities. In the Anglican Church, missionary seminaries have a more important position, the most prominent being the C.M.S. College at Islington (797 missionaries up to 1913, of whom 13 are bishops) and St. Augustine's College at Canterbury (307 and 5 respectively). On the Continent the great majority of missionaries are seminarists, but their training is generally most thorough, and they seem to have produced as many scholars in proportion as the university-trained men. In American missions it is difficult to distinguish accurately between university and non-university men. In any case, both there and in Europe the S.V.M.U. has greatly tended to bring men and women of good university attainments into the missionary ranks—a tendency emphasized by the rapidly increasing demands of higher education in the mission-field.

Till recently good theological training with a university degree was considered the *ne plus ultra* of missionary preparation from the intellectual side. But since the beginning of this century the conviction has been gaining ground that the task of the missionary demands, besides these, a technical training proper to it. This opinion was voiced by Commission VI. of the Edinburgh Conference, which recommended the establishment of Boards of Study for the special preparation of missionaries both in Britain and in America. This was carried into effect. The American Board of Missionary Studies is working on a somewhat wider basis, taking in theological subjects as well as others, whereas the British Board of Study, by mutual agreement, as an interdenominational body, deals only with general subjects (history and methods of missions, phonetics, linguistics, comparative and special study of religions, ethnography, anthropology, sociology, hygiene, business methods, educational methods). Some colleges already give themselves more or less to the teaching of these subjects: in America the Kennedy School of Missions at Hartford, Conn., the Missions Department of Yale University, the Bible Teachers' Training School, New York, the College of Missions, Indianapolis, the Cincinnati Missionary Training School, in Britain the U.F.C. Women's Missionary College, Edinburgh, and the Kingsmead Training Institution, Birmingham, take up many of these subjects, and it is in contemplation to merge the British Board of Study in a Central College of Missionary Study.

3. Missionary conferences.—The lack of unity and co-ordination in Protestant missions has long exercised the minds of their promoters, and the effort has been made to overcome this difficulty by gatherings for common counsel. The general missionary conferences thus far were held in Liverpool in 1860 (126 members); London, Mildmay Park, 1878 (158 delegates); London, Exeter Hall, 1888 (1494 delegates); New York, 1900 (2300 members); and Edinburgh, 1910 (1206 delegates). The bulk of the membership in these has consisted of delegates of missionary societies and boards, supplemented by missionaries from the field and experts of eminence. The composition of these conferences has become increasingly interdenominational and international; and in Edinburgh not only did High Anglicans attend as members, but messages of greeting were received from Greek and Roman prelates, while Asiatics, Africans, Australasians, Americans, and Europeans of many nationalities took part. The conferences have no legislative or executive authority, but the 'findings' which are formulated as the result of their debates exercise great practical influence on missionary work and methods. The reports of these conferences form a valuable record of the progress of missionary life and policy and a storehouse of missionary thought and argument. The report of the Edinburgh Conference especially (in 9 vols., London and New York, 1910) is indispensable to the student of missions. Its investigations and discussions are carried on by a Continuation Committee which publishes the quarterly *International Review of Missions*. The same kind of work has been carried on in the mission-field by periodical conferences of representatives from different missions at such centres as Madras and Shanghai, and in 1912–13 J. R. Mott convened a series of Continuation Committee Conferences in India, China, and Japan, the findings of which are published in a bulky volume (New York, 1913). By these and other means a large amount of practical union in work has been attained, and the tendency in the mission-field and at the home base towards closer unity has been promoted.

4. The field.—i. AMERICA.—The spread of Christianity in this continent has been mainly through immigration. Paganism is now only a fringe of the total population of 170,000,000. The work of Protestant missions has been chiefly in N. America, among Eskimos, Indians, and Negroes. For our purposes the W. Indian Islands and Guiana go together with N. America. S. America has been touched in Patagonia and Paraguay.

(*a*) *Eskimos.*—The Norsemen who immigrated to Greenland in the Middle Ages had a bishopric of their own, but both they and their faith died out before the 18th century. In 1721 a Norwegian pastor, Hans Egede, having heard of them, repaired to the west coast of Greenland and began work among the Eskimos under great difficulties owing to their utter indifference. It was continued, however, by his son, and eventually taken up by the Danish M.S. The west coast population in this region is Christianized, and missionary work is going on among the pagans of the east coast. Further south on the west coast the Moravians, beginning in 1733, founded the settlement of New Herrnhut, and from that centre Christianized the tribes, so that in 1899 they were able to hand over this territory to the care of the Danish Church. In Labrador since 1771 the scattered Eskimos have been mainly brought in by the Moravians, and they are cared for with the help of trade carried on by the mission ship 'Harmony.' On the other side of the continent the U.S. territory of Alaska contains a relatively considerable population of Eskimos, besides Aleutians, Indians, immigrant Chinese, and white men. Here in 1877 a Presbyterian mission was founded, followed by Moravians, American Anglicans, and others, totalling about 6000 Christians. The race, about 40,000 in number, is intellectually apathetic and feebly organized; hence its contact with white traders has been unfavourable to the development of independent Church life, but missionary work has meant their salvation from extinction through strong drink, disease, and exploitation.

(*b*) *Indians.*—These number now in the U.S. and Canada under 400,000. Over one-half live on reservations; the rest are scattered among their white fellow-citizens. From the 17th cent. onwards the relations of the colonists, whether French, English, or Dutch, with the Indians were those of perennial warfare and commercial exploitation, till the peace of the country was fully established and a more sensible and humane policy was gradually introduced. Missionary efforts were never entirely wanting. John Eliot (from 1646), David Brainerd (from 1743), and David Zeisberger (from 1745) gathered many thousands of Indians into Christian congregations of peaceful citizens, but again and again their work was destroyed by civil war. The later and more gradual settlement of Canada was advantageous to the Indian population, as the missions of all Churches were able to gain a hold, before land-grabbing and commercial greed came strongly to the fore. The first Protestant mission was begun in the Hudson's Bay Territory in 1820; it has been developed largely by the C.M.S., and much heroic work was done by its pioneers among the sparse native population before the colonists came in. Now the whole dominion is parcelled out in dioceses of the Anglican Church, and work among the Indians is carried on by other denominations also, Presbyterians and Methodists being specially active. Since the separation from England the evangelizing of Indians in the U.S. has been more and more taken over by the various Churches, and the still pagan Indians are a small remnant. Their assimilation as citizens of the Republic is still an incomplete process.

(*c*) *Negroes.*—These number (including coloured or mixed population), in the U.S. 9,827,763 (1910), and in the W. Indies 1,280,000. Their introduction into the latter dates from the Spanish conquest, into the U.S. from 1640. Organized missions among the U.S. Negroes practically began about 1860, but during their time of slavery large numbers had been Christianized, especially by the Methodists and Baptists. The bulk of these Negroes are now connected with the various Protestant Churches. In 1913 they contributed about £20,000 for home missions and £10,000 for foreign missions, besides maintenance of churches, ministry, and education. The Negroes of Cuba and Haiti are but little touched by Protestant work, but in the remaining islands they are incorporated into self-supporting churches, the result of previous missionary effort, and their economic condition is less complicated by an overweight of white population than in the U.S. They number about 1,000,000.

(*d*) *S. America.* — The territory of Guiana is closely connected with the W. Indies. Anglicans, Moravians, and Methodists have gathered converts amounting to 90,000. These are partly from among the E. Indian indentured coolies working on the sugar-plantations (who are also to be found on the islands). Catechists and clergy of Indian nationality work among them, and coolies returning home help to spread the faith in India.

Of the 38,000,000 in S. America the aborigines number about 5,000,000, mostly belonging to the Roman Catholic Church. Protestant missions have touched them in Patagonia, where the work set on foot by the heroic pioneer, Allen Gardiner, changed the opinion of Charles Darwin as to the susceptibility of a savage race to higher culture. The Indians of the Chaco in Paraguay have also begun to come in, and the mission among them has been recognized by the government of the Republic as the best mediator between white and coloured peoples.

ii. AFRICA.—(*a*) *W. Africa.*—It is this part of the continent that, owing to the slave-trade, has had the earliest and most intimate connexion with Protestant lands, especially with N. America. The endeavour to influence Africa directly by means of the liberated slave is chiefly represented by the little republic of Liberia, founded in 1824 by the American Colonisation Society. The Christian Negroes who settled there were hardly ripe for administering the Free State proclaimed in 1847, but from this centre work is being carried on by sundry societies among the neighbouring non-Christians. A certain number of American Negroes have been sent as missionaries to Africa by their Churches in the U.S.A., but the effective shaping of their work is a problem that awaits solution.

The north-west coast of Africa as far as the Senegal borders on sparsely-inhabited Muhammadan territory which has scarcely been entered as yet. From this to the mouth of the Congo is the region of Protestant mission-work.

At Sierra Leone the settling of liberated slaves began in 1808, after the abolition of the slave-trade, and its capital received the name Freetown. Up to 1846, 50,000 African slaves had been brought there, chiefly by British cruisers. For years great loss of life was experienced among the C.M.S. and other missionaries who worked there, and among the welter of tribes represented the only common language available was English. To some extent the varying elements were sifted out, and Christianity spread by means of those who rejoined their kindred elsewhere. In 1852 an Anglican bishopric was constituted, and in 1861 the Church, in which meanwhile education had spread rapidly, was made self-governing. It carries on missions among its pagan neighbours. Here and elsewhere in W. Africa the missionary comes into contact increasingly with Muslims from the north. Among a population of 75,000 in the colony 57,000 are Protestant Christians.

The Gold Coast Colony has a population of 1,500,000. The western part is worked by Wesleyan missionaries, the eastern by the Basel Society. The latter, since 1828, has penetrated effectively into the back country formerly under Ashanti rule; the Wesleyans, too, have moved into the northern territory. The country is being opened up by railways, and the rapid increase of commerce is enriching the Christian community here as elsewhere in W. Africa, to the advantage of self-support, but not always to that of spiritual life and morals. The Christian community now numbers upwards of 30,000.

The German colony of Togoland, next on the

east, has considerably developed missionary work from that country, during the last few years, among the Ewe nation. Good linguistic work has been done. The community numbers some thousands.

The work in the lower basin and delta of the Niger has assumed increased importance since the constitution of Nigeria, the richest of Britain's African possessions, as a Crown Colony, with a population of 18,000,000. The first mission stations (from 1846 onwards) were started to look after natives of the Yoruba country who had returned from Sierra Leone to their own people. Lagos, the great port of the palm-oil trade, and the large interior towns of Abeokuta and Ibadan were occupied, and considerable Christian communities were gathered, amounting (1913) in the Yoruba province to 50,000. Economic development is going on rapidly, and the demand for education, especially in English, is increasing year by year.

After the Niger had been opened up by three voyages of exploration (1841, 1854, 1857), an African priest of the C.M.S., Samuel Crowther, was sent to this region. He planted several stations, and in 1864 was consecrated bishop. The work was carried on by Africans, with some vicissitudes but with substantial progress, till Crowther's death in 1891, when W. Equatorial Africa was placed under an English bishop, assisted by two Africans, the wealthy churches of the Delta being granted self-government. In N. Nigeria the town of Lokoja had been occupied in 1865, but it was not till the end of the century that an effective advance was made into this territory, where a predominantly Muhammadan population alternates with large patches of paganism, while the spread of Islām continues in a southerly direction. The work here is still in its beginnings. In Calabar at the south-east corner of Nigeria a Christian community of 11,000 has been gathered in by the U.F.C. mission.

Kamerun, a German colony since 1884, was originally evangelized by English Baptists, but their work was taken over mainly by the Basel Society, who were pushing into the back country before the outbreak of the great European war. The Christians number about 15,000 out of an estimated population of 3,000,000.

The Congo River was first opened up completely by Stanley in 1876–77, and the Congo Free State, under the protection of Belgium, has been the scene of rapid missionary advance along the river. Yakuso, the furthest point, near Stanleyville, is 1200 miles from the mouth. Among the first explorers in detail were the English Baptists G. Grenfell and W. H. Bentley from 1879 onwards. Other missionaries of various nationalities followed. Owing to the difficulties of climate and the great multitude of tribes and languages, progress has been limited, but some dozen societies are now at work in this area. Indigenous churches are being formed, and elementary education is being pushed.

The characteristic problems of the W. African missions generally are presented by the constant advance of Islām from the north, the demoralization of commercial intercourse caused by the liquor-trade, and the unsettling effects of a rapid acquisition of wealth formerly undreamt of. On the other hand, the removal of the evils connected with the slave-trade, the increase in prosperity and intelligence, and the creation of a Christian standard of conscience and morals, with the opportunity given to the natives of rising to a higher life, are elements in appreciable progress towards the regeneration of the Negro peoples.

(*b*) *S. Africa.*—In this we include the regions south of the river Kunene on the east and the Zambesi on the west. It contains three African races: the Bantu (including Zulus and Kafirs), the Nama or Hottentot, and the Bushman, the last two scarcely remaining pure, the first virile and prolific. The climate being temperate, Christianity has spread by immigration from western nations, and the white population is reckoned at 1,300,000. Hence the racial problem is at its acutest in S. Africa, and it specially affects the work of missions, which aim at raising the native populations to a higher level, religious, moral, and social, and at giving them the best education which they are capable of assimilating. The earliest Dutch colonists regarded the natives as an inferior class of beings whom it was both lawful and expedient to keep in subjection, and this attitude has not been confined to one section of the white races. Thus there has been a persistent prejudice against, and often actual antagonism to, the work of missions, sometimes aggravated by lack of prudence on the part of the missionary and by unbalanced policy on the part of the government. The conviction is gaining ground, however, that without the moral influence of Christianity the problems resulting from the contact and blending of two cultures cannot be thoroughly solved. Among some 4,000,000 natives there are now about 750,000 Christians, the result of the work of 30 missionary societies belonging to 8 nationalities. The racial factor is especially in evidence in the 'Ethiopian Movement,' composed of groups of congregations who in 1892 formally seceded from their missionary connexions. Some of them in 1899 joined the Anglican Church as 'the Ethiopian Order'; the remainder do not appear to be progressive either in internal life or in external expansion.

In what became in 1886 German S.W. Africa the principal work has been done by German missionaries of the Rhenish Society since the forties. The fruits of their persevering and systematic efforts have suffered greatly through colonial wars. Protestant Christians in the colony number, by last figures, 13,000.

The largest indigenous Christian population is in Cape Colony, numbering 1,145,000 out of a total of 2,500,000; it comprises westwards, broadly speaking, bastardized Hottentots, and, eastwards, Kafirs of relatively pure race. The Moravians, who began work in 1737, were followed in 1799 by the L.M.S., whose missions in Bechuanaland are remarkable for their great pioneers, R. Moffat and, above all, Livingstone. Through the persistence of John Mackenzie and the intervention of the British Government, all attempts to block the northward way of the missionary were frustrated, and the path of the gospel was opened up to the C. African lakes and eventually from the Cape to Cairo. The converts of the L.M.S. in Cape Colony now form a Congregational Union with some 35,000 adherents. Efforts of later dates are represented by the adherents of the Wesleyans (over 90,000, now independently organized), Rhenish M.S. (16,000), Berlin M.S. (50,000), and Scottish Presbyterians (25,000). The majority of the white colonists belong to the Dutch Reformed Church, which for a long time held aloof from missionary work. Since the middle of the 19th cent. its attitude has changed, and it carries on missions within and beyond Cape Colony. In the latter it counts over 80,000 native Christians, the majority of whom are under the charge of its parochial clergy. The Anglican Church in the three dioceses of the Colony claims over 70,000 adherents.

Among the Zulus and Swazis of Natal the work of many denominations has been greatly hindered by frequent and destructive wars, but Christian congregations have grown, and some converts have been gained from among the Indian coolies. Basutoland, blessed with a more quiet development since it became a Crown Colony in 1884, has been worked principally by the Paris M.S., which now counts about 70,000 adherents. Among the Bechuanas of the Transvaal and Orange River Colony Dutch, Anglican, Wesleyan, and Lutheran missions have gathered a Christian community of considerable importance. The problems of moral and social development are greatly complicated by the congestion of labourers, both Christian and non-Christian, in the mine compounds of Johannesburg and the Rand. The thinly-populated Bechuanaland Protectorate includes Khama's Country, where a Christian African prince rules his people well.

Madagascar has been a land of great vicissitudes in missionary work. The first missionaries of the L.M.S. began work with considerable success among the Hovas, the ruling race of the central province, in 1820. In 1836 the accession of a hostile queen brought about the expulsion of the missionaries, and for twenty-five years the Christians were severely persecuted, yet they increased considerably. In 1861 a new ruler recalled the missionaries, and, when another queen was baptized in 1869, conversions began in masses. To cope with the situation other societies, Friends, S.P.G., and Norwegians, entered the island. In 1895 Madagascar was annexed by France, and Protestant mission work was so severely hampered that the L.M.S. was fain to give over a large part of its work to the Paris M.S. The total number of Protestant Christians in Madagascar is estimated now at 287,000, while the scholars number 44,577.

(c) *E. and C. Africa.*—Missionaries helped to open up these lands both from the east coast and from the interior southwards. In 1844 Ludwig Krapf, a German in C.M.S. service, landed on the island of Mombasa and began work on the mainland opposite. He planned (1) to carry a chain of mission stations across Africa from Mombasa to Gabun; (2) to establish on the east coast a colony for liberated slaves like that in Sierra Leone on the west; and (3) to work for an African ministry under an African bishop. The second of these objects was accomplished at Freetown in 1874; the first and third are in process of realization now. In 1846 Krapf was joined by Johann Rebmann. After nine years Krapf was invalided; Rebmann held on for twenty-nine years. By their discovery of the snow-peaks of Kilimanjaro and Kenia on the equator, and of the great inland-sea of Nyanza, they revolutionized the geography of C. Africa, and their linguistic labours prepared the way for later workers in a fruitful field.

The yet greater work of David Livingstone is part of history. From his first station of Kolobeng in S. Africa he constantly pressed northwards, crossed Africa from east to west, and opened up the lake regions of Nyasa and Tanganyika, exploring ceaselessly till he died at Ilala in 1873. In his opinion the end of the geographical feat was the beginning of the missionary enterprise. He desired to uproot the slave-trade, and to open up Africa to legitimate commerce and to Christian culture with faith as its root. The Universities Mission to Central Africa undertaken by members of the Church of England, the L.M.S. mission on Lake Tanganyika, and the Scottish Presbyterian missions in Nyasaland are the direct results of his lifework; but it affected the whole missionary enterprise of inland Africa. To Stanley it was given to complete the work of Livingstone by his exploration of the Congo valley, and in the course of it he gave the impulse which has resulted in the formation of a virile Christian State in the centre of Africa, now the kingdom of Uganda. Stanley found the king, Mutesa, hesitating between the claims of Christianity and Islām. Through a Swahili Christian interpreter he put the Christian case before the monarch and straightway appealed to English Christendom to enter this open door. The result was the sending of the well-known C.M.S. mission in 1875. The murder of James Hannington and the barbarous persecution of the early converts only served to increase zeal and enthusiasm. After sundry conflicts and imminent risk of abandonment by the Colonial Office, Uganda became a British Protectorate, under which mission work has gone forward peacefully. The country now contains 96,000 Protestant Christians, with a somewhat larger number of Roman Catholics and a smaller number of Muhammadans. The schools contain scholars up to a secondary standard. The growing Church now forms an effectual breakwater against the rising tide of Islām.

The two protectorates of E. Africa, the English and the German, have each brought the country under civilized administration, and the British Government has opened up its territory by a railway, preceded or accompanied by missionaries. The English work in German territory has been partly made over to German missions since the establishment of the colony in 1884, but a group of C.M.S. missions remains round Mpwapwa, and another of the U.M.C.A. opposite Zanzibar. The German work is chiefly on the northern frontier and on the north shore of Lake Nyasa and its vicinity. The principal missions of the Nyasaland Protectorate are those of the Scottish churches, with the two industrial centres of Livingstonia in the north and Blantyre in the south—fit memorials of the great Scottish missionary pioneer. His successors have seen the slave-trade entirely wiped out and fierce animist tribes subdued by the influence of Christian love, exemplified in medical missions, and brought under training in civilized industry and commerce. The Anglo-Egyptian Sūdān in its Muhammadan parts is closed to missionary effort by government ruling; among the pagan Dinkas, Azandi, and other tribes missionary work is in its first stages.

iii. OCEANIA.—Missions in Oceania date from 1769, and owe their first impulse to the interest excited by the story of Cook's voyages in the South Seas. The major part of this area is suitable for European colonization, and the aborigines belong to more or less primitive states of culture, in which their physical as well as mental stamina has remained weakly. Owing partly to this and partly to unscrupulous exploitation by white settlers and traders, the result of contact with the white races has been the rapid diminution, and in some cases, as in Tasmania, the entire extinction, of the native races. The work of missions has therefore largely consisted in the rescue of weaker races from extermination through contact with exponents of higher civilizations not imbued with the Christian spirit. In no part of the world have the results of missions been more rapid and wide-spread, but stability is sometimes lacking. The effects of kidnapping, strong drink, and disease have been appreciably counteracted.

Work in *New Zealand* was started by Samuel Marsden in 1814, and after a time made rapid progress. In 1840 the islands became a British colony; unfortunately wars broke out, and in 1864 the strong Hau Hau apostasy, a recrudescence of pagan cults mixed with Christian heresies, drew away great numbers. In spite of this the leading missions of the C.M.S. and Wesleyans were able, before the end of the century, to make over their converts to the local Church organizations. The New Zealand Parliament also has its Maori members. The Maori population of New Zealand is about 50,000, of whom some 30,000 belong to Reformed communions. There appears to be some hope that, in place of declining, the native population is beginning to increase.

In *Australia* the aborigines have dwindled to 74,000, living mostly in the northern parts of the continent. After several abortive attempts missions, with a strong industrial element, have been continuously carried on since 1851 by English bodies of various denominations, as well as by Moravians and Lutherans. Despite pessimism, the aborigines have proved susceptible to the elevating influence of the gospel, and decadence has been to some extent arrested, though independence is not yet in sight. The number of Protestant Christians is computed at 6000.

The *Islands of the Pacific* may be roughly grouped into Polynesia (south of Hawaii), Melanesia (west of Polynesia), and Micronesia (north of Melanesia). Among the larger islands of Polynesia, Hawaii, now a United States territory with Honolulu for its capital, was first evangelized by the American Board from 1820 onwards and Christianized within fifty years. It has sent out and supported missionaries to several other islands. Tahiti, occupied by missionaries of the L.M.S., had a similar history, but after the annexation of the group by France it became necessary to transfer the work to the Paris M.S. Raiatea, the sphere of the famous John Williams, has remained in British connexion. In the Tonga and Viti, or Fiji, Islands the Wesleyans have been the principal workers. Practically the entire population is Christian, and is efficiently ruled by princes of the same faith. Education is wide-spread, and evangelists from Fiji have carried the faith to many other islands.

Melanesia has a population of 475,000, of whom 111,000 are Protestant Christians. The gathering in of these numbers has cost not a few missionary lives, owing to resentment on the part of islanders who had been oppressed by traders. The missionaries are British, German, Dutch, and Norwegian. The martyrdom of Bishop Patteson in 1871 called forth much enthusiasm and service, and during his long life John G. Paton of the United Presbyterian Mission saw 20,000 natives converted in the New Hebrides and contributing £1300 in one year for Church purposes.

On the Micronesian Islands, now under British, German, and American protection, developments since 1852 have been similar. Missionaries from Australia have taken part. Roman Catholic work is stronger here than in the other islands; out of 30,000 Christians the Roman Catholics claim 12,000.

New Guinea, or Papua, was first entered in 1871, when Christians from L.M.S. missions in Polynesia volunteered for the work, in which many of them laid down their lives. They had a great leader in James Chalmers (1876–1901). The Christians now number 35,000. Anglican, Wesleyan, German, and Dutch missionaries have taken part.

In various parts of Oceania, especially Australia, Hawaii, and Fiji, missionary work is carried on among the Asiatic immigrants from India, Japan, and China with the help of native preachers from those countries, not without some result. The barriers of caste and social opposition are less rigid than at home, but the restraints of conventional morality are also loosened.

The total population of Oceania, excluding Australia and New Zealand, is reckoned at some 2,000,000, of whom 320,000 are Christians.

iv. INDIA.—The impact of Christianity on India has been conditioned by certain outstanding features of the land and people. The peninsula is isolated by land and sea. The culture of the people ranges from the most primitive to a highly developed, though stationary, form. Its religion contains a similar variety of cults, ranging from spiritual adoration to cruel and obscene orgies, all bound together intellectually by a subtle pantheistic philosophy, socially by the unique system of caste (*q.v.*). Its contact with the outer world during recent centuries has been mainly through the immigration of foreign invaders, who have brought with them the monotheistic religion and polity of Islām, so that Indian Musalmāns now constitute by far the largest Muslim nation of the world. Most recently, however, India has come into connexion with a seafaring nation of the West more intimately than any other Asiatic land. Here, as elsewhere, the missionary has employed in the first instance the agencies of preaching and persuasion, but the form which the results of his work have assumed has mainly been determined by the conditions of the classes to whom he has addressed his message. To bring out the chief features of it, we may deal with 'mass movements,' education, and philanthropy as main channels of evangelization.

The earliest form of Christianity in India is that of the Syrian Churches of Travancore and Cochin, which probably owe their origin to the Nestorian community of Persia, whose members traded with the Malabar Coast in their early days. From about the 4th cent. a trading and landholding community accepted the Christian faith, and has continued as a local caste to the present day. Early in the last century they were aroused from lethargy by contact with Anglican Christianity, and the work of the C.M.S., first in combination, and afterwards side by side, with the Syrians, has stimulated reform and progress, both in education and in evangelizing zeal. The work of St. Francis Xavier, Roberto de' Nobili, and other great Roman Catholic missionaries of the Portuguese period is principally in evidence now in the masses of fisher folk and other labouring castes in the west and south of India; and in the earliest Protestant missions the same factor of community-movements appears. In the Danish-Halle Mission of the 18th cent. the greatest name is that of C. F. Schwartz (landed 1750, died 1798). The 20,000 Christians whom he gathered in Tanjore and elsewhere were mainly from the village labourers. After his death the work dwindled, till it was taken over by the Anglican Church, and during the first half of the 19th cent. the work of the C.M.S. and S.P.G. in Tinnevelly (principally among the palm-tree climbers), together with that of the L.M.S. in S. Travancore, yielded much more than half the entire number of Protestant converts in India, and naturally also the best organized churches. In 1851 these missions had 51,355 adherents, the remainder of the Madras Presidency 23,821, and all the rest of India 16,916. In the succeeding sixty years these missions and others in S. India have greatly developed, largely through the agency of American societies. The Protestant Christians now number 870,425 (besides over a million and a half Roman Catholics and Syrians), and they contribute £33,721 to the support of worship and schools. The Indian ministry includes 492 ordained men as against 487 foreign missionaries, and the self-administration of the churches is on the increase. Self-extension, too, is shown by the activity of more than one mission of the Indian Churches. The largest is the Tinnevelly Missionary Society, with an income of 12,000 rupees, 4 ordained men, and 2000 converts in a mission which they carry on in the Nizam's territory. Part of their work was made over to the diocese of the first Indian bishop, V. Azariah of Dornakal, when he was consecrated in 1913.

In Travancore a similar movement has made headway in the L.M.S. and C.M.S. missions, which now number 73,000 and 57,000 Christians respectively. Still more wide-spread is the movement in the Telugu country north of Madras. Here, especially since the great famine of 1877–78, the out-caste village labourers have pressed into the churches in myriads. The Christians belonging to Anglicans, American Baptists, Lutherans, and others are estimated at some 150,000.

In Bengal an older movement in the forties of the last century left a considerable church in the Nadiyā district; more recently the Nāmaśūdras of E. Bengal are turning their hopes towards Christianity, and the B.M.S. has admitted some hundreds from among them. In the United Provinces of Agra and Oudh the Chamārs (leather-workers) and sweepers have been principally gathered in by the American Methodist Episcopalians, who record congregations numbering 102,000 adherents, while other Protestant missions have 22,000. The most rapid movement during the last decade was in the Panjāb, where the Christians entered in the government Census returns had increased from 37,000 in 1901 to 163,000 in 1911 chiefly in the American Presbyterian missions.

The movements among the Indian village proletariat which have resulted in these large and growing accessions to Christianity all form part of one upward tendency of populations representing pre-Aryan inhabitants, enslaved by the Aryan conquerors and kept for millenniums in servitude, but now afforded the opportunity of emancipation by rulers whose political and social ideals are bound up with Christianity and whose rule has been accompanied by active Christian efforts of teaching and philanthropy. The effect of these efforts in raising the masses who have responded to them is expressed thus by the Hindu Census superintendent of the Mysore State:

'The enlightening influence of Christianity is patent in the higher standard of comfort of the converts, and their sober, disciplined and busy lives' (*Census of India, 1911*, Calcutta, 1913, vol. i. pt. i. p. 138).

To this we may add that evidences of spiritual regeneration and devotional life are also to be found.

The populations so far referred to are the 'untouchables' who live among the Hindus and Musalmāns of the plains. They may number (accuracy is very difficult to secure) some 30,000,000. But there are some 10,000,000 more of non-Hindu aborigines, living mainly in hilly regions, among whom the Christian faith has found ready entry. Such are the Karens of Burma, the Khāsis of Assam, the Kols and Santāls in Bengal. The Christian communities among these amount to some 200,000 persons. Both among these and among the out-castes the expansion of the movement appears to be limited only by the capacity of the Christian Church adequately to shepherd and educate the candidates for discipleship. The effect of education and Christian influence in raising the status of the Christian community as compared with its Hindu and Muhammadan neighbours has been very marked. Some progress has been made in improving their position as agriculturists; in the Panjāb the Christians have been recognized by Government as an agricultural tribe, and in the irrigation colonies there are several flourishing villages of Christian cultivators, holding land direct from the State.

Education of a simple kind, including that of girls, was from the first a regular part of missionary activity, but it was brought into prominence by the Scottish missionary, Alexander Duff (1830–57). He set out to evangelize the upper classes of Bengal by means of higher education, given through the medium of the English language, which, through the efforts of Macaulay and others, had already been adopted by Government as the vehicle of learning for India. Duff was assisted in his plans by Rājā Rām Mohan Ray, the founder of the Brāhma Samāj (*q.v.*). Duff's converts were counted rather by the score than by the hundred, but they included men who made their mark on the Christian Church as leaders throughout N. India. His school also had a powerful effect on the development of the Brahmā Samāj and other liberal movements in Hinduism, and not less did he influence the educational policy of the Government of India, which in 1854 founded departments of public instruction, and in 1857 established universities in Calcutta, Madras, and Bombay, followed later by others in Lahore and Allāhābād, and recently by a Hindu university at Benares and a Muslim one at Aligarh. Duff's school soon developed into a college, and no fewer than 8 other colleges were founded in different parts of India during Duff's lifetime. The most noteworthy contemporary of Duff as an educator was John Wilson of Bombay, who founded the college which bears his name, and added to his English work a profound acquaintance with Hinduism. There are now 38 Protestant missionary colleges in India, containing, in 1912, 5447 students, including 61 women, the latter practically all Christians. Of the total, 4481 students were Hindus, 530 Muhammadans, and 436 Christians. There is a fully-organized missionary college for women in Lucknow; and a college department works in connexion with a girls' high school in Lahore.

The work of elementary and secondary education was powerfully forwarded by the system of grants-in-aid which the Government instituted in 1854. The grants are made in proportion to the educational efficiency of schools, regardless of the religion of the managers. Educational efficiency being greatest among the missionaries, they have earned the chief portion of the grants, though their lead in this respect is no longer so marked as it was. Their secondary schools number 283, with 62,602 boys and 8400 girls; 880 boarding-schools contain 22,193 boys and 17,566 girls, all Christian. In 87 theological schools 1852 students are in training, and 127 training-schools have 1904 male and 1173 female students. The boarding-schools are partly secondary and partly primary. The result of secondary education in conversions has been small, but the influence on social ideals and practice and on religious thought has been very great. The care bestowed on the education of the Christian community, especially the women, has made it, with the exception of the Parsis, the most literate in India, far above the average of the Hindus generally, and little, if any, behind the Brāhmans. The number of Christian officials and teachers is large in proportion to the size of the community, and it is not easy to keep pace with their need for a highly educated ministry, while satisfying the wants of the large rural populations. The provision of elementary education for these is the most urgent missionary problem of the day. True, the elementary pupils in mission schools throughout India number about 450,000, but the great majority of these are non-Christian. In missionary colleges and schools of every kind 576,371 persons were being educated in 1912—about one in ten of all pupils.

Christian literature took its first effective start with the work of the great pioneer, William Carey (1793–1834). Together with Marshman and Ward, he worked chiefly at Bible translations into a multitude of different languages, and also founded a missionary college in Serampore. Most of these versions were mere *ballons d'essai*, but the Bengali became the foundation of all further work in that tongue. Henry Martyn at the same time produced his remarkable Urdu version of the NT, and a long line of translators and authors followed, supported by the publishing societies mentioned above. Krishna Mohan Banerjea among Hindu converts, 'Imād-al-Dīn among Muslims, and John Murdoch among English writers and publishers of Christian literature are outstanding names. Besides Bible versions there is also an incipient Christian literature in all the principal Indian languages, amounting in some of them to several hundred works. These are directed both to the training of the Christian Church and to convincing and persuading outsiders.

Among the philanthropic auxiliaries to the gospel message, medical work takes a foremost place. The effective prosecution of this in India dates from the middle of last century, when W. Lockhart of the L.M.S. was sent to Travancore, and Henry M. Scudder of the American Board to Ceylon. The chain of medical missions on the N.W. Frontier was begun in Kashmīr in 1864, and has since then extended to Peshāwar, Bannu, Derā Ismāīl Khān, and Quetta. The attitude of a turbulent, fanatical, and treacherous Muhammadan population has been greatly modified by the work of medical missions, and, while converts have shown their faithfulness in martyrdom, Christian Scriptures and literature, illustrated by the example of disinterested Christian love, have penetrated far into regions otherwise inaccessible to the missionary. Similar effects have been produced on the intolerance of the caste-proud Hindu, and, while suffering is impartially relieved, regardless of creed or condition, the ministry of healing has brought many to the discipleship of the Healer. The first qualified woman-doctor came to India in 1880, though medical work by women had been carried on long before. Medical missionary women have led the way in relieving the once hopeless suffering of secluded Indian womanhood, given over to treatment by ignorant and clumsy midwives and barber-women. Of the Indian women-doctors now serving under the Dufferin Fund and other public bodies the great majority are Christians, with a sprinkling from the Brāhma Samāj.

Closely allied with general medical work is that of the leper missions. Of the unfortunate leper community, hitherto uncared for, several thousands are under care in Christian institutions, and many of them have accepted Christianity. Christian institutions for the blind and the deaf and dumb are the only ones for these classes in India. Famine orphanages are common, and have furnished an appreciable fraction of the Christian community, especially in N. India; these have in recent years found imitators among non-Christians, and, owing to the influence and example of mission schools and colleges, the conception and practice of social service are spreading among Indian students, as shown by the society of the 'Servants of India,' promoted by G. K. Gokhale.

India affords the largest and most influential sphere of work among the Muslims of the world. Its Musalmān community numbers 65,000,000, and it is both specifically Indian in type and cosmopolitan by ties of religion—a fact which gives this community a greater political importance than its numerical proportion to the Hindu population would warrant. The largest Muhammadan community of India, that of Bengal, now numbering 24,000,000, came under British rule after the battle of Plassey in 1757, but the first effective Christian work among them was done by the chaplain-missionary Henry Martyn when he translated the NT and much of the OT into the Muhammadan *lingua franca* of India—the Urdu, or camp dialect of Hindōstānī. His one convert, 'Abd-al-Masīḥ, was the forerunner of many ex-Muslims who have joined the Christian ministry. It is impossible to estimate accurately the number of converts among the laity, but with their descendants they must run into several myriads. The circulation of the Scriptures, which the Muslim professedly recognizes as divine, is especially effective as a means of evangelism.

Among the Buddhists of Burma and S. Ceylon the results of work have been similar to those among the middle classes in India; *i.e.*, conversions have been sporadic, occasionally in families, with here and there outstanding personalities. The Census of 1911 gave the number of Protestant Christians in India as 1,452,759, compared with 970,385 in 1901. The largest proportion is in S. India (626,000), where the work has been established longest and is most systematic. The distribution elsewhere varies chiefly according to the incidence of mass movements. Protestant Christians in other parts number: Bengal, 178,000; United Provinces, 135,000; Panjāb, 155,000; Bombay, 51,000; Central Provinces and C. India, 24,000. In the native States they are generally fewer — *e.g.*, Haidarābād, 29,000; Mysore, 9,000; Panjāb States, 500; Kashmīr, 700.

Syncretism, in the shape of reform movements, both religious and social, is much in evidence. The earliest organized body of this kind is the theistic Brāhma Samāj, founded in 1828 by Rājā Rām Mohan Ray—a small sect, but influential owing to the social standing, literary ability, and philanthropic zeal of its members. The teaching of its sections ranges from a modified Hinduism to a kind of Unitarian Christianity with Indian atmosphere. The Ārya Samāj (*q.v.*), founded in 1875 by Dayānand Sarasvatī, represents a cruder modification of original Hinduism, professing to hold to the Vedas as absolutely inspired, and accordingly forcing their interpretation to fit modern standards. It has a strong political and nationalist vein, and is bitterly hostile to Christianity; but it has done good work in the cause of education and social reform. It prevails chiefly in the Panjāb and United Provinces. In Bombay the Prārthanā Samāj (*q.v.*) does a similar work. These bodies, following missionary example, are beginning to interest themselves in the amelioration of the depressed classes by education, and the Ārya Samāj actually admits them and also Muhammadans into the 'Vedic religion' by a ceremony of purification (*śuddhī*).

Modernist movement among the Muhammadans dates from the efforts of Sir Sayyīd Aḥmad, who began in 1858 to arouse his fellow-religionists to the imperative need for English education, which resulted in the establishment of the Anglo-Muhammadan College at Alīgarh and the All-Indian Muslim Conference. It has also produced something of a school of liberal theology. A more wide-spread movement was inaugurated by Ghulam Aḥmad of Qādiān in the Panjāb in the year 1879. He, like Dayānand, harked back to his sacred Scriptures, and treated the Qur'ān as verbally inspired, interpreting it in a new fashion with an eye to modern thought. This sect, too, is strongly opposed to Christianity, and some members of it have started a mission to England at Woking. Despite their attitude of opposition, these new sects all owe more or less of their originating impulse and of their specific doctrine to the message of Christian missions. The Indian national movement has a tendency to bring the reformed sects nearer together, and its influence is being felt in the Christian community also in a certain touchiness and impatience of foreign influence. At the same time there are signs of an increased feeling of responsibility for the evangelization of

India, marked by the establishment of the National Missionary Society and other efforts.

The Dutch possessions known as Indonesia were previously under Hindu rule, but since the 12th cent. they have gradually been overrun by Muslim chieftains, and out of the total population of 38,000,000 all but 2,000,000 are now Muhammadan. The Dutch East India Company, while building up its Eastern empire, also Christianized the natives after a fashion, but their condition at the beginning of the 19th cent. was very low. Since then it has improved, and the so-called permanent congregations (*gevestigte gemeenten*) are under the care of clergy appointed and maintained by the State; churches of later converts are from time to time placed under this organization. Modern missionary work began in the second decade of last century, and has been carried on mainly by Dutch and German missionaries on the four principal islands of Sumatra, Java, Celebes, and Borneo, as well as on some of the smaller ones. Large numbers of converts have been gathered in Java, in the Batak country on the north coast of Sumatra, and in the Minahassa district of Celebes. In the second of these an effective barrier has been erected to the inland advance of Islām. The total number of converts from Islām in these islands is estimated at 40,000.

v. CHINA.—In contrast with India, China has but one standard language and literature, and may therefore be regarded as a unity, despite its size and diversity. Modern missionary work was begun by Robert Morrison of the L.M.S. in 1807. He baptized the first convert in 1814, and before his death (1834) he had translated the Bible into Chinese, besides writing many pamphlets. But neither he nor his colleague, Robert Milne, was able to enter the jealously-guarded empire of China; they could only reside in the Portuguese settlement of Macao or in British territory at Malacca. The opening of China to foreign intercourse, including missionary effort, was the result of a series of wars, internal and external, the first of which, while it helped to admit the missionary, did much to discredit his message. The three 'opium wars' of 1842, 1858, and 1860 resulted in the opening of twenty-four 'treaty ports' to foreign intercourse, and it was in these, especially Shanghai, Hangchow, Tientsin, and Canton, that Protestant missions first gained a footing. Up to 1850, 3 English societies, 1 German, and 7 American had begun work, and the converts may have amounted to 100. The preponderance of American workers in China became more marked as time went on, and the same is true of Japan.

The next great convulsion was an internal one, the Taiping rebellion, which lasted from 1850 to 1864, and was eventually suppressed by the 'ever victorious army' of a Western leader, General Charles George Gordon, himself in deep sympathy with Christian missions. The leader of the rebellion had once come under the influence of a Christian missionary, and he claimed to have received a divine revelation to destroy idolatry and to put an end to the Manchu dynasty. The second of these aims was accomplished half a century later by another great convulsion, and we may believe that the Taipings did much towards preparing the way for the first, which is yet to come; but we may also be thankful that their iconoclasm did not prematurely succeed before the constructive forces of Christian faith and practice were ready to step into the breach. Meanwhile, missions on the coast were increasing their work, and the year after interior China had been quieted (1865) Hudson Taylor formed the China Inland Mission, which led the way to the formation of a network of stations during the last half century, now extending to the remotest interior of the Republic. This mission alone now numbers 1076 foreign missionaries, as against 473 of all societies and nationalities in 1877. In that year the number of converts was reckoned at 13,000.

The final break-up of the Manchu dynasty was first marked by the Boxer outbreak of 1900, directed, with the connivance of the Empress, against both foreigners and Chinese Christians; 135 missionaries, with 53 of their children, were killed, and some 16,000 Chinese Christians were massacred, many of them accepting death willingly rather than deny the faith. A strong impression was created by the refusal of missionary societies to accept a money indemnity from the Chinese Government for the missionary lives laid down freely for the gospel. During the succeeding decade the number of foreign missionaries in China increased almost 50 per cent (2785 to 4175, including wives of missionaries), and the number of converts more than doubled (204,672 to 469,896 in 1910). In 1913 the number of 'full members' was given as 235,303. Counting children and other adherents who are not included in their statistics by many bodies, the total may be estimated at about 500,000. Foreign missionaries, including wives, are 5186, and Chinese workers 17,879.

The revolution of 1911–12 was the final stage in the opening up of China to Western culture and Christianity. There has, it is true, been a slight reaction from the abolition of Confucianism as the religion of the State, but a stronger power than the iconoclasm of the Taipings is shaking the foundations of the old cults, namely the re-casting of the world-old system of Chinese education in Western and 20th cent. moulds. Moreover, the official request made by the Chinese Government on 27th April 1913 for the prayers of its Christian subjects, whatever motives of policy may have inspired it, was a recognition of Christianity as a power affecting deeply the interests of the nation; and Sun Yat Sen, the leader of the Cantonese revolutionary section and almost of the Republic, is a Christian who seeks to model his political policy on the principles of the Bible. Happily, too, the establishment of the Chinese Republic has coincided with the final abolition of the Indian opium traffic once forced on China by Britain.

The situation thus created has offered to the Christian Churches unexampled opportunities of access to the educated classes of China. These had hitherto looked with contempt on teachers who in very few cases could master the intricacies of their literature, but now they are ready to welcome Western language, literature, and science. Great efforts have been made, especially by the American missions, to grapple with the task of providing centres of higher education on a Christian basis throughout China, and in this, as well as in general work, the tendency towards co-operation between allied bodies is strong and helpful. No fewer than 9 university colleges are in effective operation, 7 in coast provinces, 1 in the centre, and 1 in the west. In several the medical faculty is strong, and Christian missions at present lead in the training of qualified doctors for China. There are some 264 mission hospitals (1913) with 126,788 in-patients and 2,129,774 out-patients for the year. Among the agencies which have been particularly active in taking advantage of the present opportunities the Y.M.C.A. has been specially in evidence. The evangelistic meetings conducted by J. R. Mott, and still more by George Sherwood Eddy (1912–14), were attended by large audiences of educated Chinese, sometimes up to 4000, in many of the principal towns of China. Among the hearers were officials of high rank, of whom one was baptized, while thousands of men promised to study the Bible, and hundreds have actually joined the Christian Church.

The creation of a Christian literature for China has been carried on mainly by co-operation between the missions represented in the Christian Literature Society for China, under the guidance of Timothy Richards and others. The rapid opening of the mind of China to appreciation and reception of Western thought has given missionary scholars both the opportunity and the task of providing not only religious but general and scientific literature for readers, whether Christian or non-Christian. Both this and the work of Bible translation in China have been greatly facilitated by the existence of a common standard of written language, though versions of the Bible are being produced in several local vernaculars, as also in a popular form of the Mandarin. The circulation of the Bible is increasing by leaps and bounds; in 1910 a million and a half copies of Bibles, New Testaments, or single books were circulated; in 1914 two million and a quarter.

The first L.M.S. woman missionary to China was appointed in 1868. The work among women has been greatly hampered by the custom of footbinding and by social prejudice, but these have been in great measure overcome, largely as the result of missionary effort, and the desire for the education of women is greatly on the increase; some are using their education not only to qualify for the medical and teaching professions, but also for social service. Over 600 members have been enrolled in a Student Volunteer Movement for the Christian ministry, putting aside prospects of lucrative careers. The tendency in this class is to work for the formation of an indigenous Chinese Church free from Western control, and some progress is being made in the self-support of native churches. Meanwhile the various cognate bodies which have hitherto been carrying on separate missions, such as Anglicans, Presbyterians, and Methodists, are amalgamating their organizations as a first step towards larger union.

In the outlying provinces of China work is still in its beginnings. It is furthest advanced in Manchuria, where Presbyterians and Lutherans have a community of some 33,000. The devoted work of James Gilmour (1870–91) in Mongolia left little visible result, and the societies which are following it up are gathering a few converts amid great difficulties. In Chinese Tibet these are insuperable, and the only quarter from which the gospel has entered that land is Little (or Western) Tibet, belonging to India, where Moravian missionaries have some small congregations, and have done much for the investigation of Tibetan language, literature, and history. Among the Muslims of Chinese Turkestan Swedish and China Inland missionaries are in the early stage of work.

vi. Japan, Korea, and Formosa.—Here, as in China, we have countries in which, after periods of notable success on the part of Roman Catholic missions, the native rulers have turned upon them as politically dangerous, and have violently persecuted the Christian Church, almost to extinction, till, through political changes, intercourse with the West has been resumed, but on a different footing, and with this the way has been opened for missions of the Reformed communions also. In the case of Japan this re-opening dates from the year 1859, when American missionaries were the first to settle in the country. The first Protestant Christian was baptized in 1864, but meanwhile persecution of Christians continued, sometimes with severity, till the Revolution of 1868, which once more brought the Mikado to power, and inaugurated the modern government of Japan. G. Ensor (C.M.S), who arrived in 1869, was the first English missionary, but full religious toleration was not granted till 1873, to be speedily followed by the serious suggestion that Christianity should be made the State religion. This was, however, negatived, and subsequently there was a distinct reaction against foreign influences, among which Christianity was included, especially during the first decade of this century. But a swing back of the pendulum was indicated by the action of the Minister of Education in 1912, when he announced that the Government had resolved to recognize Christianity, alongside of Shinto and Buddhism, as a religion deserving of encouragement, expressing, at the same time, the hope that Christianity would conform itself to national aspirations. In this connexion it is noteworthy that the Christian message in Japan has appealed specially to men of culture. A quite disproportionate number of Christians are found among members of Parliament, high military and naval officers, doctors and professors, and Count Okuma has recorded that 'the indirect influence of Christianity has poured into every realm of Japanese life' (*Intern. Review of Missions*, Oct. 1912, i. 654). The number of Protestant Christian adherents in Japan may be reckoned at about 100,000. Forty per cent of the mission stations are said to be self-supporting. Three-fourths of the converts are attached to one or another of four amalgamated Churches representing the Anglican, Congregational, Presbyterian, and Methodist missions respectively. The great majority of the Protestant missions have established an organization for the promotion of common work, called the 'Federated Missions of Japan.' This has formed a general Christian Literature Society, and promoted joint efforts for evangelization, both in the towns and in the hitherto neglected rural districts.

The work of missionary education bulks less largely at present in Japan than in China, owing to the fact that from the first opening of the country education has been steadily taken in hand by the State, which now provides a completely organized system of education from the primary schools (at which attendance is compulsory) up to the universities and technical schools. There are 14 Protestant middle schools, with about 5500 scholars, and two colleges of university grade, of which the Doshsisha College at Kyoto, founded by Joseph Niishima, has 700 students. Elementary missionary education is backward, as Christian children have access to well-worked Government schools. The educational work of the Y.M.C.A. has been much appreciated in Japan, and has strongly influenced the student world; and the Y.W.C.A. is reaching women increasingly. Christian missionary efforts among the aboriginal Ainus of Yezo have been appreciated by the Japanese Government, who bestowed a decoration on John Batchelor of the C.M.S. in recognition of his work for this dying race.

Among the dependencies of Japan, Formosa, first entered in 1865, now has some 30,000 Christians. Korea, after three and a half centuries of absolute seclusion, was not effectively entered till 1882, first by American missionaries, and, in 1890, by Anglicans. The growth of the work has been phenomenal, especially in the years following the Russo-Japanese war of 1905–06. Adherents in 1913 numbered 185,000, over 19,000 children were under education in mission schools, and 20 hospitals and 23 dispensaries were in operation. This progress has been accompanied by remarkable zeal in the study of Scripture and by reformation of life.

vii. The Near East.—Under this term we include the lands, stretching from Morocco to Persia, in which Islām first arose and spread. Owing to the long dominance of Islām the work of Christian missions to Muslims in this region is either non-existent or in its infancy. For our present purpose, we are not dealing with missions to the surviving Abyssinian, Coptic, Armenian, Syrian, Nestorian, or Jacobite Churches. We may, however, note that the educational work carried on among Oriental Christians, principally by American missionaries, in the Turkish empire and Egypt has resulted in the formation of considerable Protestant communities, whose progress in intelligence, morality, and zeal has raised the Christian name in the eyes of the Muslims and reacted favourably on the ancient churches by stimulating a desire for reform and progress. There is among the Protestant Orientals also the dawn of a desire to evangelize the Muslim—a feeling that had been eradicated from the Oriental Christian by a thousand years of oppression and misrule, which prevented him from seeing in the Muslim anything but an irreconcilable tyrant. The most effective missionary work done by men of these nationalities is that of Bible colporteurs. The Muslim verbally acknowledges the Scriptures of the OT and NT to be inspired, and, if once induced to study them, he is in many cases led to see that the theory of their corruption subsequently to Muhammad is a figment of his divines. Thus their witness to Christ, as well as their incompatibility with the Qur'ān, is a powerful influence in the conversion of the Muslim. The British and Foreign Bible Society employs in the countries referred to 71 colporteurs, and has 27 depots, through which 128,926 copies of Bibles, Testaments, and portions are circulated. Individual conversions through these means are fairly frequent, but the building up of Christian communities is a slower process, hampered by special obstacles.

In Morocco, Algeria, Tunis, and Tripoli, among a total population of about 14,000,000, work is carried on mainly by the N. Africa Mission and other undenominational agencies. There are converts here and there. The principal agency, besides that of colportage, is schools, which are elementary. In Egypt work was begun in 1854 by the American United Presbyterians, principally among the Copts, and resuscitated by the C.M.S. in 1882. Considerable access has been gained among the Effendi class, and a number have been baptized, while medical work has to some extent reached the masses, in both town and country. Schools, primary and secondary, contain 17,094 pupils (largely of Coptic faith or origin), and a scheme for the establishment in Cairo of a Christian university is being actively promoted by American missionaries. German and English missionaries are pushing out into the Anglo-Egyptian Sūdān, and, though Christian propaganda is barred among the Muslims of that region, yet in Omdurman some educational work is being done. Cairo is the chief literary centre of the Muhammadan world, and from the Christian side vigorous efforts are being made by the Nile Mission Press, an Anglo-American undertaking, to produce and circulate evangelistic literature in Arabic.

In Asia Minor and Syria Protestant work has been done chiefly by American missions working among the ancient churches. The system of education which they have developed, from primary schools to colleges, especially the Roberts College in Constantinople, has notably affected the Muslim community in thought and attitude towards Christianity. Medical missions, in Palestine especially, have tended in the same direction. Arabia is touched on its outskirts at Baghdād, Bahrain, and Aden by schools, medical work, and colportage. Persia was first entered by Henry Martyn, when he completed his translation of the NT at Shīrāz in 1811. In 1829 K. G. Pfander visited Persia, and wrote his celebrated *Balance of Truth*, laying the foundation of a Persian Christian literature, built upon later by W. St. Clair Tisdall and others. In 1871 American Presbyterians organized work among the tribes of N. Persia, and in 1875 S. Persia was occupied by R. Bruce of the C.M.S. Medical and educational work has developed largely, and the demand for schools on a Western model far exceeds the power of the missionaries to supply it. The modernist sect of Bahaism, sprung from the Bābī reform movement, has borrowed freely from Christianity but does not so far make much return (see art. BĀB, BĀBĪS). Throughout these missions work among women, visiting, teaching, and medical, has initiated or helped on the movement perceptible in Muslim lands for the elevation of the female sex.

viii. MISSIONS TO JEWS.—The Jewish population of the world is approximately 12,000,000. Protestant missionary work among them is carried on by 95 societies, maintaining 500 men and 350 women missionaries. The *London Society for Promoting Christianity among the Jews* (253 missionaries; income in 1914, £51,000) is the principal one. Statistics are quite imperfect. Some 250 of the Anglican clergy are converts or sons of converts from Judaism. J. F. de le Roi estimates baptisms during the 19th cent. in Protestant churches at 72,740; Roman Catholic, 57,300; Greek, 74,500. The theologians Neander and Edersheim, the missionary bishops Schereschewsky, Hellmuth, Alexander, and Gobat, were Christian Jews.

III. *GENERAL ASPECTS.*—1. **Principles.**—As a result of the work of missions by the Reformed Churches since the end of the 18th cent. there is now a growing community of some 6,000,000 native Christians belonging to the most varied races and cultures, from the primitive aborigines of Australia to the progressive people of Japan. Yet in the age which has seen this unexampled expansion of Christianity in every direction the question has been raised whether Jesus of Nazareth ever intended that His disciples should carry the message of His redemption into all the world, though it is fully allowed that the world mission of His faith was the legitimate and necessary consequence of the principles which He enunciated and exemplified. To suppose that the Originator of this life and teaching, which have persisted in spreading their vitalizing influences among the nations for nineteen centuries, was Himself without desire for or intention of producing such an effect would be to face the most insoluble enigma of history. The development which we have sketched makes it abundantly clear that the mainspring of this world-wide enterprise of missions has been the conviction that its promoters and messengers were carrying out the conscious purpose and explicit command of the Saviour of the world. At the same time it would be unnatural that the reconstruction of thought which our age is experiencing in every sphere of life should leave the conception of foreign missions entirely unaffected. Among the Reformed Churches more especially Zinzendorf's motto of 'souls for the Lamb' as the one goal of missionary effort has expanded, under the influence of teachers like G. Warneck in Germany and B. F. Westcott in England, into the wider and deeper conception of a call to regenerate the nations spiritually, morally, intellectually, and socially, and to build up the universal Church of Christ. Moreover, the results of research into Christian origins have helped us, with a truer historical perspective, to test our contemporary missionary work by the example and spirit of the Apostolic Age. From subsequent early and mediæval history, too, the Churches have been learning lessons of the manifold adaptation of the form of missionary work to the conditions and needs of different ages and peoples, and of these lessons the whole modern development is an amplification. But this larger sweep of outlook and effort has by no means made the first aim of individual conversion superfluous. On the contrary, this remains the vital centre of the whole, and it is as this is expanded and co-ordinated in the larger aim that the true end of missionary work is attained.

2. **Methods, apostolic and contemporary.**—The radical question is raised again and again whether the close following of the methods of St. Paul is not the true solvent of our most fundamental difficulties, particularly of the lack of spiritual and economic independence in our mission churches. Were the evangelist to make brief sojourns instead of settling down, to devolve authority straightway on native helpers instead of keeping them in long tutelage, to demand instead of giving pecuniary assistance, Christian congregations might, it is urged, be smaller, but they would be stronger and self-reproducing. Each of these paths has been tried in modern missions, generally with scant success, for the same end under different conditions may demand different means. Where there was a Jewish diaspora standing at the threshold of Christianity, teaching and discipline had been assimilated which may now require a generation; where habitat and civilization of evangelist and evangelized were practically identical, the problems now arising from disparity of civilizations and distance of abode were non-existent. Recognizing these and other special difficulties and defects of modern missionary work, we have to seek their solution not in the forms of apostolic, or any other, evangelism, but in the principles embodied in those forms. Thus in the adventure of faith undertaken by the C.I.M., which has so remarkably opened up China to the gospel, we have a contemporary adaptation of the Pauline method, rapidly following the main lines of communication and occupying the chief cities of an empire which in culture and administration offers much analogy to that of Rome. Or, again, in the revival of community life in the brotherhoods and sisterhoods of Anglican missions we have a useful adaptation of early and mediæval monasticism to the conditions of the mission-field of to-day. But both of these have the defects of their qualities.

The effect of modern thought on the adaptation of NT principles to contemporaneous missionary work may be traced in the development of the chief missionary methods. The mission school and college have no precedent in apostolic times, and they differ greatly from the cloister school of monastic missionaries, their original purpose being to serve as a means of conveying the message to the children of the literate, or would-be literate, classes who are otherwise not easily reached, and of bringing them into the Christian Church when they have arrived at years of discretion. The most notable effect of earlier educational work was the conversion of men of mark, who exercised great influence on the development of the Church. Within the last generation this aspect of the work has receded into the background; the conception of educating the mind of a nation and creating an atmosphere permeated by Christian ideals has exercised increasing influence on missionary educators, especially in high schools and colleges, and it is certain that their successes have lain mainly in this direction. The value of such preparation of the community for the eventual reception of Christ as Lord and Master is immense, and it may be hoped that much of the work which commonly falls to be done after conversion is thus being accomplished beforehand. But there is need of balanced judgment and steadfast will, lest elaboration of the scaffolding delay or even prevent the erection of the building. Similarly, in the now indispensable work of medical missions the physical benefits conferred were at first entirely subsidiary to the spiritual aim; but the conception of a Kingdom of God to be realized in things temporal as well as spiritual has led to emphasis upon the fact that the work of healing, even apart from any spiritual effects, is a worthy aim of the missionary. This involves the risk that the medical missionary may be merged in the philanthropist. The modern medical missionary would not, if he could, ignore the demand for the greatest possible scientific efficiency, for he will not allow Christian zeal to be the bosom friend of second-rate professional skill; yet he will lay the decisive emphasis of his calling on the specific aim of the missionary to carry home his message. Again, in the delivery of that message by the general missionary a comparative study of religion and sociology has modified the method of approach by the Christian messenger to non-Christians. He is less inclined to attack their observances and rites than to elicit the need latent in each human heart of something higher, less prone to controvert their doctrines and deities than to set forth Christ in life and teaching. The conviction is gaining ground among his hearers that he is no ruthless iconoclast of their national religion, but a sympathetic guide who would lead them to satisfactions which it fails to supply. But, if he is to do this, his aim must still be that they may be 'redeemed from the vain manner of life handed down from their fathers' (1 P 1[18]) and come to know the only true God. Without attacking concrete sin and error this cannot be done. The manner of controversy has been rightly modified, and it is well to use points of agreement as a basis for approach; but the reason for adopting one faith in place of another cannot lie in their points of resemblance, but only in those of difference. Hence controversy or polemic, in the right form, can never become obsolete as a missionary weapon. Once more, in the case of missionary work for women its first, and most worthy, aim was simply to deliver sisters whom the Christian woman found in degradation, ignorance, and suffering from these evils into the liberty of Christian womanhood. As, in the course of generations, they laboured for this end, the great task of training new types of Christian motherhood suited to each nation gradually dawned upon them, and they became aware that they had stimulated a greater awakening than they had dreamed of among the women of China, India, and Africa. But Christian personality remains the key of the position, and the feminist movement, which is growing in East and West alike, finds its true regulative everywhere in the principles of the gospel.

3. **Cognate activities.**—A bare mention must suffice of the achievements of missionaries in works ancillary to their main calling. The names of Livingstone, Krapf, and Rebmann among explorers, of James Legge, R. Caldwell, H. A. Jaeschke, and Carl Meinhof among philologists, and of R. Codrington and John Roscoe among anthropologists are but a few among many. In civil life, too, missionaries have sometimes held a prominent place—*e.g.*, C. F. Schwartz in Tanjore and John Mackenzie in Bechuanaland; and in India municipal offices have occasionally been held by them. To outsiders these public services have been a vindication of the missionary's usefulness; to some among the missionary public it has seemed that they might be a hindrance to it. In the nature of things such services must remain exceptional, rendered by isolated individuals who possess the ability and energy. As by-work they have been of service; were they more than this, they would prove a hindrance.

4. Results and problems.—The present condition of the world mission-field shows off-shoots of the Reformed Churches in every stage of growth. Their members, as always, vary in genuineness and strength, but everywhere they include whole-hearted followers of Christ, and, as a body, they have advanced greatly in tone and conduct from their former non-Christian manner of life. The animist, the pantheist, the agnostic, and the deist have come to believe in one almighty Father, one sinless Saviour, one indwelling sanctifying Spirit. From this faith grow the fruits, both of higher morality and of social amelioration, enhanced culture, and intellectual progress. In many directions the desire is shown to hand on the benefits of the gospel to others, and readiness to make sacrifices in so doing is evident. It has been remarked that the churches of the mission-field have produced no first-class heresy, implying thereby a lack of serious intellectual striving. But other causes may more reasonably be assigned for this. The intellectual training and status of the foreign teacher is so far superior, in the great majority of cases, to that of his converts that it would be difficult for them to maintain positions contrary to those which he has laid down—all the more so as the possible variations of intellectual formulation have been fairly fully worked out by previous heresies, the weaknesses of which have been pointed out to them. Moreover, no inconsiderable part of the effect produced by Christian missions is to be found in the change of attitude, the new beliefs and ideals of conduct, individual and social, taken over from them by the still non-Christian world. In this process the analogues of early Christian heresies are to be found in the teachings of bodies outside the Christian Church. Thus the Brāhma Samāj reform of Hinduism represents a kind of Arianism; the Bahai offshoot of Islām would stand for one variety of Gnosticism, and theosophy (*q.v.*) for another. Generally speaking, syncretism is largely practised, and in many cases by men of noble character who are striving for a reconciliation of the old and the new, but the religion of the amateur collector is not more likely to stand now than in the early centuries, though it is a pitfall of which the abler intellects of the young churches need to beware.

Analogous to this is the problem of unity in the Reformed Churches. The majority of the divisions which have sprung up in the West from local and temporary causes have naturally no meaning to the Eastern convert; and the same holds good of many dividing lines in doctrine. The resulting tendency to unity in faith and practice, in face of powerful opposing forces, is healthy and hopeful. There is, however, a danger that members of the young churches should regard all distinctions in doctrine and discipline indiscriminately as mere Western peculiarities which may be swept aside in order to construct an edifice of truly indigenous Christianity. A sound attitude of the missionary teacher towards questions of race and nationality will do much to meet this danger.

Next to the essential spiritual element no factor in missionary work is more weighty than the social progress which it has initiated or stimulated. From these successes a difficulty often springs. In the contact of two deeply-separated civilizations the convert naturally assimilates that of his Western teacher, but without the exercise of wisdom and restraint he may evolve a mere caricature of Western culture without its balance and restraint, thereby repelling alike his own countrymen and his Western fellow-Christians; and among higher races he may acquire needs and habits which will involve him in economic difficulties. Meanwhile, Western culture and commerce are ceaselessly flooding into mission lands, and the change of life connected with them is affecting non-Christians scarcely less than Christians. As a result of this the efforts of the missionary to promote a simple indigenous style of living may be resented as intended to repress the progress of the native Christian. One of the missionary's most difficult and delicate tasks is to decide and to convince his charges what is justly due to the decencies and progress of Christian life and what is illegitimate as ministering to extravagance and parasitic growth.

Thus social progress is intimately connected with the great difficulty presented by the economic dependence of the mission churches on their parents at the home base. The amount annually expended by home churches on the maintenance of ministers, preachers, and teachers of indigenous races is estimated at £7,000,000. The amount recorded as raised by the native churches in the same connexion is £1,500,000. Allowing for a liberal margin of error, the disparity is still immense, even when we consider that a large number of the converts are drawn from impoverished strata of society whose financial weakness must be great for some time to come. Almost every advance is dependent on fresh exertions made by the mother churches, who also contribute largely to the maintenance of worship, pastoral care, and teaching. In the last resort the economic dependence of mission churches is part of the larger problem of the economic dependence of the coloured races on the white, and in all probability the one will not be solved without the other.

Everywhere we are brought up against the racial problem. It was there from the first, and the success of missions has been in proportion to that of the messenger in understanding and treating with wise sympathy people of a foreign race. As the races have become conscious of their common ideals, traditions, and interests, the racial question in the mission-field has developed into the national. Everywhere the missionary is met, actively or passively, by insistence on the rights of the race in its own sphere and a demand for equal opportunity, as against the old idea of the inherent superiority of the white man. The opposition thus engendered reacts against the white man's religion, and there is on each continent a restiveness and impatience of control on the part of converts and churches such as did not exist a generation ago. To deal with this firmly and sympathetically as a sign of healthy growth, and as a pathway to new and fruitful relations, is the part of wisdom. Premature independence and unduly delayed emancipation both have their dangers. Smartness and efficiency may be made an idol; but it is also a temptation to take the easy path of lowering the ideals of the gospel, and this leads to deterioration. The problem is to be solved only by patient, tenacious charity on the part of the missionary who understands the national and racial feeling, and whose watchword is the responsibility of the stronger.

LITERATURE.—H. U. Weitbrecht, *Bibliography for Missionary Students*, Edinburgh, 1913. Special mention may be made of: G. Warneck, *Outline of a Hist. of Protestant Missions*, do. 1906 (new Germ. ed., Berlin, 1913), *Evangelische Missionslehre*, 5 vols., Gotha, 1897–1903; J. S. Dennis, *Christian Missions and Social Progress*, 3 vols., Edinburgh, 1899–1906; *Report of the World Missionary Conference*, do. 1910; J. R. Mott, *The Continuation Committee Conferences in Asia, 1912–13*, do. 1913; J. Warneck, *Paulus im Lichte der heutigen Heidenmission*, Berlin, 1913; J. N. Farquhar, *Modern Religious Movements in India*, New York, 1915; C. H. Robinson, *Hist. of Christian Missions*, Edinburgh, 1915.

H. U. WEITBRECHT.

MISSIONS (Muhammadan).—The materials for the history of Muhammadan missionary activity are much less abundant than those for the history of the propagation of Christianity. Muhammadan historians appear to have been singularly incurious as to the spread of their own faith, and only scanty references to conversions are found at rare intervals in the vast historical literature of the Muhammadan world. The absence of a priesthood in Islām, implying the setting apart of a separate body of men as exponents of the doctrines of the faith, has had its counterpart in a lack of ecclesiastical annals; there have been no Muslim missionary societies (except towards the end of the 19th cent.), no specially trained propagandists, and very little continuity of missionary effort; even the religious orders of Islām, which have at times done much for the spread of the faith, have not cared to set on record the story of the success that has attended their preaching. There is, therefore, nothing in Muhammadan literature to correspond to the abundant materials for the history of Christian missions provided in the biographies of Christian saints, the annals of the Christian religious orders, and the innumerable journals and other publications of the various Roman Catholic and Protestant missionary societies. In fact, the fullest details as to Muslim missionary activity are generally to be found in the writings of the Christian clergy who have watched with apprehension the rapid extension of Islām. Yet to this poverty of information from Muhammadan sources there is one notable exception, namely, the biography of Muhammad himself. The missionary activity of Islām begins with the life of the founder, and the numerous biographies of the Prophet are full of stories of his efforts to win over unbelievers to the faith.

In the Qur'ān itself, the duty of missionary work is clearly laid down in the following passages (here quoted in chronological order according to the date of their revelation):

'Summon thou to the way of thy Lord with wisdom and with kindly warning: dispute with them in the kindest manner' (xvi. 126). 'They who have inherited the Book after them [*i.e.* the Jews and Christians] are in perplexity of doubt concerning it. For this cause summon thou (them to the faith), and walk uprightly therein as thou hast been bidden . . . and say, In whatsoever Book God hath sent down do I believe: I am commanded to decide justly between you: God is our Lord and your Lord: we have our works and you have your works: between us and you let there be no strife: God will make us all one: and to Him shall we return' (xlii. 14). 'Say to those who have been given the Book and to the ignorant, Do you accept Islām? Then, if they accept Islām, they are guided aright: but if they turn away, then thy duty is only preaching' (iii. 19). 'Thus God clearly showeth you His signs that perchance ye may be guided, and that there may be from among you a people who invite to the Good, and enjoin the Just, and forbid the Wrong; and these are they with whom it shall be well' (iii. 99 f.). 'To every people have we appointed observances which they observe. Therefore let them not dispute the matter with thee, but summon them to thy Lord: Verily thou art guided aright: but if they debate with thee, then say: God best knoweth what ye do' (xxii. 66 f.). 'If any one of those who join gods with God ask an asylum of thee, grant him an asylum in order that he may hear the word of God; then let him reach his place of safety' (ix. 6).

Further, the faith of Islām was to be preached to all nations, and all mankind were to be summoned to belief in the One God.

'Of a truth it [*i.e.* the Qur'ān] is no other than an admonition to all created beings, and after a time shall ye surely know its message' (xxxviii. 87 f.). 'This (book) is no other than an admonition and a clear Qur'ān, to warn whoever liveth' (xxxvi. 69 f.). 'We have not sent thee save as mercy to all created beings' (xxi. 107; cf. also xxv. 1 and xxxiv. 27). 'He it is who hath sent His apostle with guidance and the religion of truth, that He may make it victorious over every other religion, though the polytheists are averse to it' (lxi. 9).

In the hour of Muhammad's deepest despair, when the people of Mecca turned a deaf ear to his preaching, when the converts that he had made were tortured until they recanted and others had to flee from the country to escape the rage of their persecutors, the promise was revealed:

'One day we will raise up a witness out of every nation' (xvi. 86).

The life of the Prophet himself presented, for succeeding generations, an ensample of Muslim missionary activity. When he began his prophetic career, his first efforts were directed towards persuading his own family; his earliest converts were his wife, Khadījah, his adopted children, Zaid and 'Alī, and some members of his immediate circle. He did not begin to preach in public until the third year of his mission, but he met only with the scoffing and contempt of the Quraish. In the fourth year of his mission he took up his residence in the house of al-Arqam, one of the early converts, and many Muslims dated their conversion from the days when the Prophet preached in this house, which was in a central position, much frequented by pilgrims and strangers. The conversion of 'Umar b. al-Khaṭṭāb about two years later was a source of great strength to the little band of Muslims, who now began publicly to perform their devotions together round the Ka'bah. Though Muhammad continued to teach for ten years, the number of converts remained very small, and an attempt to win adherents outside Mecca, in the town of Ṭā'if, ended in complete failure; but some pilgrims from Yathrib (or, as it was afterwards called, Medīna) showed themselves to be more receptive, and Muhammad sent one of his early converts, Muṣ'ab b. 'Umair, to Yathrib to spread the faith in that city. Muṣ'ab's mission was so successful that in the following year he was accompanied by more than seventy converts in the pilgrimage to Mecca; they invited Muhammad to take refuge in Yathrib, and he accordingly migrated thither in September 622—a date which was afterwards adopted as the beginning of the Muhammadan era. In Medīna the little Muslim community gradually developed into a political organism that spread over the greater part of Arabia before the death of Muhammad in 633, and political expediency tended to thrust purely religious considerations into the background; but the proselytizing character of the new faith was not lost sight of, and the Arab tribes that submitted to the political leadership of Muhammad accepted at the same time the faith that he taught. But of distinctively missionary activity there are only scattered notices, and for some time after the death of Muhammad there is a similar lack of evidence of distinctively proselytizing effort on the part of the Muslims during the expansion of Arab rule over Syria, Persia, N. Africa, and Spain, though in all these countries large numbers of persons from among the conquered populations passed over to the dominant faith. There is one notable exception in the case of the pious 'Umayyad khalīfah, 'Umar b. 'Abd al-'Azīz (717–720), who was a zealous propagandist and endeavoured to win converts in all parts of his vast dominions from N. Africa to Transoxania and Sind.

With the decline of the Arab empire the Muslim world was faced with the task of converting its new rulers. The conversion of the Turks proceeded very slowly; the earliest converts appear to have been the Turkish soldiers who took service under the khalīfah in Baghdād; there are a few legends of proselytizing efforts in Turkestan, but the history of the conversion of the Turkish tribes is obscure, and Islām seems to have made little way among them before the 10th cent., when the Seljūq Turks migrated into the province of Bukhārā, and there adopted Islām. The conversion of the main body of the Afghāns probably belongs to the same period or a little earlier, though national tradition would carry it back to the days of the Prophet himself.

A more formidable task was the conversion of the Mongols, and here Islām had to enter into competition with two other missionary faiths, Buddhism and Christianity, both of which at the outset met with greater success. The devastations of the Mongols had brought ruin to the centres of learning and culture in the Muhammadan countries which they overran, and it was only by slow degrees that Islām began to emerge out of the ruins of its former ascendancy and take its place again as a dominant faith. From the latter part of the 13th cent. converts began to be made from among the Mongols, and a new epoch in Muslim missionary history then commenced, in which the religious orders, and the Naqshbandī in particular, played a prominent part. In the profound discouragement which filled the Muslims after the flood of the Mongol conquest had poured over them their first refuge had been in mysticism, and the *pīr*, or spiritual guide, who during this period began to exercise an increasing influence, became of special importance among the proselytizing agencies at work. The first Mongol ruling prince to profess Islām was Baraka Khān, who was chief of the Golden Horde from 1256 to 1267; according to one account, he owed his conversion to two merchants whom he met coming with a caravan from Bukhārā; but the conversion of their prince gave great offence to many of his followers, and half a century later, when Uzbeg Khān (who was chief of the Golden Horde from 1313 to 1340) attempted to convert the Mongols who still stood aloof from Islām, they objected, 'Why should we abandon the religion of Jenghīz Khān for that of the Arabs?' In other parts of the Mongol empire the progress of Islām was still slower and more fluctuating, and it did not become the paramount religion in the kingdom of the Īlkhāns of Persia until 1295, or among the Chaghatāy Mongols until three decades later. The first Muhammadan king of Kāshgar (which the break-up of the Chaghatāy dynasty had erected into a separate kingdom) was Tūqluq Tīmūr Khān (1347-63), who is said to have owed his conversion to a holy man from Bukhārā, by name Shaikh Jamāl al-Dīn; but so late as the end of the 16th cent. a dervish named Isḥāq Walī found scope for his proselytizing activities in Kāshgar and the neighbouring country, where he spent twelve years in spreading the faith.

The extension of Mongol rule over China gave an impulse to the spread of Islām in that country; though Muslim merchants had been found in the coast towns from a much earlier period, the firm establishment of their faith in China dates from the 13th cent., and the settlements of immigrants from the west, which were founded from that period, developed into the great communities of Chinese Muslims of the present day—through various causes, of which proselytism has been one. The rise of the Mongols was also incidentally the cause of renewed missionary activity in India; Islām had gained a footing in Sind and on the Malabar coast as early as the 8th cent., and in the north after the establishment of Muhammadan rule at the close of the 12th cent., but the terror of the Mongol arms caused a number of learned men and members of religious orders to take refuge in India, where they succeeded in making many converts.

To the period of the Mongol conquests—though in no way connected therewith—is traditionally ascribed the first establishment of Islām in the Malay Archipelago. Sumatra appears to have been the first island into which it was introduced —probably by traders from India and, later, Arabia; but the extension of the new faith was very slow, and even to the present day large sections of the population of this island remain unconverted. The conversion of Java, according to the native annals, began in the 15th cent. and spread from this island into the Moluccas and Borneo. The arrival of the Portuguese and, later, of the Spaniards, in the 16th cent. checked for a time the growing influence of Islām in the Malay Archipelago, and the rival faiths of Christianity and Islām entered into conflict for the adherence of its peoples; but the oppressive behaviour of the Spaniards and their attempts to enforce the acceptance of their religion ultimately contributed to the success of the Muslim propagandists, who adopted more conciliatory methods for the spread of their faith, intermarried with the natives, and conformed to their manners and customs. The missionary activity of Islām has been carried on spasmodically in these islands up to the present day—for the most part by traders. From the very nature of the case, there has been little historical record of their labours, and this little is chiefly found in the reports of Christian missionaries. Legendary accounts of the arrival of the earliest apostles of Islām in several of the islands have been handed down, but they are uncritical and of doubtful historical value.

The history of the spread of Islām in India by missionary effort is not quite so scanty, but it has largely been overshadowed by the absorbing interest of political events; for, though the Indian Muhammadans have produced a large body of historical literature, their references to the propaganda of their faith in these histories are few. The biographies of saints, however, and local traditions contain many references to a successful propaganda, and, among much that is legendary and fantastic, there is evidence of the activity of a number of missionaries from the beginning of the Muhammadan period. Among these may be mentioned Shaikh Ismā'īl, a Bukhārī Sayyid who preached in Lahore in 1005, Sayyid Nādir Shāh, the patron saint of Trichinopoly (where he died in 1039), and 'Abd Allāh, who landed in Cambay in 1067, and is said to have been the first missionary of the Musta'lī Ismā'īlī sect (known in India as 'Bohorahs'). Towards the close of the same century another Ismā'īlī missionary, but of the Khojah sect, Nūr al-Dīn (generally known as Nūr Satāgar), carried on a successful propaganda in the Hindu kingdom of Gujarāt. In 1236 there died in Ajmer one of the greatest of the saints of India, Khwājah Mu'īn al-Dīn Chishtī, who settled in that city while it was still under Hindu rule and made a large number of converts; ten years later died one of the apostles of Islām in Bengal, Shaikh Jalāl al-Dīn Tabrīzī, the forerunner of a long series of missionaries in that province. Of importance in the history of Islām in the Panjāb is the settlement in that part of India of saints of the Suhrawardī order; *e.g.*, to the preaching of Bahā' al-Dīn Zakarīyā, and of Sayyid Jalāl al-Dīn and his descendants, many of the tribes of the Panjāb owe their conversion. These are but a few out of the long series of preachers of Islām who carried on a distinctively missionary work, side by side with the various influences, social and political, that contributed to the spread of Islām in that country.

Of the vast history of the spread of Islām in Africa it is not possible here to give more than a brief sketch. For the early period of the Arab conquest of Egypt and N. Africa, though conversions took place on a large scale, there is little evidence of active missionary effort. The opposition of the Berbers in the west and the Nubians in the Nile valley checked for a time the southward movement of Muslim influences. By slow degrees, however, Islām penetrated among the Berbers, but acquired an ascendancy over them only when it assumed the form of a national movement with the rise of the native dynasties of the Almoravids in the 11th, and the Almohads in the 12th, century. The Berbers introduced Islām into the lands watered by the Senegal and the Niger, and Arabs from Egypt spread their faith in the eastern Sūdān during the 12th cent., to which period the conversion of Kordofan and Kanem appears to belong. In the 13th cent. the Mandingos come forward as zealous missionaries of Islām, to be followed by the Hausas, whom they had converted, and the Hausas have carried their faith with them from one end of the Sūdān to the other. Their propagandist efforts were intermittent, however, and many parts of the Sūdān remained untouched by Muslim influences until the 19th century.

Except in India and the Malay Archipelago, there are few records of Muslim missionary activity from the 15th to the 18th century. Nevertheless many conversions occurred during this period; *e.g.*, the Turkish conquests in Europe in the 14th and 15th centuries were followed by conversions to Islām on a large scale, and in the 17th cent. thousands of Christians in Turkey in Europe went over to the religion of their rulers; similarly the conquests of Aḥmad Grāñ in Abyssinia (1528–43) were signalized by numerous conversions to Islām; but there is little evidence of any direct propagandist efforts on the part of the Muslims.

A great revival of the missionary spirit of Islām followed the Wahhābī reformation; this movement stirred the whole of the Muslim world—either to sympathy or to opposition—and thus directly or indirectly gave the impulse to the great missionary movements of the 19th century. In India the Wahhābī preachers aimed primarily at purging out the many Hindu practices that caused the Muslims to deviate from the ways of strict orthodoxy, but incidentally they carried on a propaganda among unbelievers, and their example was followed by other Muhammadan missionaries, whose preaching attracted to Islām large numbers of converts throughout the country. In Sumatra Wahhābī reformers stirred up a revival and made proselytes. But a more momentous awakening was felt in Africa. 'Uthmān Danfodio returned from the pilgrimage to Mecca full of zeal for the Wahhābī reformation, and under his leadership his people, the Fulbe, who had hitherto consisted of small scattered clans living as shepherds, rose to be the dominant power in Hausaland; the methods of the Fulbe were violent and political, and they endeavoured to force the acceptance of Islām upon the pagan tribes which they conquered. On the other hand, a peaceful propaganda was carried on in the Sūdān by members of the Amīrghaniyyah and Qādiriyyah orders; the former takes its name from Muhammad 'Uthmān al-Amīr Ghanī, whose preaching won a large number of converts from among the pagan tribes about Kordofan and Sennaar; after his death in 1853 the order that he founded carried on his missionary work. The Qādiriyyah order had been introduced into Western Africa in the 15th cent., but awoke to renewed life and energy in the 19th. Up to the middle of that century most of the schools in the Sūdān were established and conducted by teachers trained under the auspices of the Qādiriyyah, and their organization provided for a regular and continuous system of propaganda among the heathen tribes. Another order, the Sanūsiyyah (founded in 1837), has also been very active and successful in proselytizing.

A fresh outburst of Muslim missionary zeal in Africa exhibited itself when the greater part of that continent was partitioned among the Powers of Christian Europe—Britain, France, and Germany; by establishing ordered methods of government and administration, and by facilitating communication by means of roads and railways, they have given a great stimulus to trade and have enabled that active propagandist, the Muslim trader, to extend his influence in districts previously closed to him and to traverse familiar ground with greater security.

Throughout the course of Muhammadan history Islām has at times received large accessions of converts for various reasons—political and social—wholly unconnected with missionary enterprise, at the same time it has always retained its primitive character as a missionary religion, without, however, having any permanent organization to serve as a medium for its expression. Societies for carrying on a continuous propaganda were unknown in the Muslim world before the last decades of the 19th cent., and such Muslim missionary societies as are now found in Egypt and India appear to have owed their origin to a conscious imitation of similar organizations in the Christian world. The most characteristic expression of the missionary spirit of Islām is, however, found in the proselytizing zeal of the individual believer, who is prompted by his personal devotion to his faith to endeavour to win the allegiance to it of others. Though there have been religious teachers who may be looked upon as professional missionaries of Islām, especially the members of the religious orders, it is the trader who fills the largest place in the annals of Muslim propaganda; but no profession or occupation unfits the believer for the office of preacher of the faith, nor is any priestly ministrant needed to receive the convert into the body of the faithful. Some observers, entitled to respect for their knowledge of the Muhammadan world, have gone so far as to say that every Muslim is a missionary:

'À tout musulman, quelque mondain qu'il soit, le prosélytisme semble être en quelque sorte inné' (Snouck Hurgronje, *RHR* lvii. [1908] 66). 'The Muslim is by nature a missionary . . . and carries on a propaganda on his own responsibility and at his own cost' (W. Munzinger, *Petermann's Mittheilungen*, 1867, p. 411).

However exaggerated such an opinion may be, stated thus as a universal, it is certainly true that there is no section of Muslim society that stands aloof from active missionary work, and few truly devout Muslims, living in daily contact with unbelievers, neglect the precept of their Prophet:

'Summon thou to the way of thy Lord with wisdom and with kindly warning' (Qur'ān, xvi. 126).

Even the prisoner will on occasion take the opportunity of preaching his faith to his captors or to his fellow-prisoners. The first introduction of Islām into Eastern Europe was the work of a Muslim jurisconsult who was taken prisoner, probably in one of the wars between the Byzantine empire and its Muhammadan neighbours, and was brought to the country of the Pechenegs (between the lower Danube and the Don) in the beginning of the 11th cent.; before the end of the century the whole nation had become Muhammadan. In India, in the 17th cent., a theologian, named Shaikh Aḥmad Mujaddid, who had been unjustly imprisoned, is said to have converted several hundred idolaters whom he found in the prison. Women as well as men are found working for the spread of their faith; the influence of Muhammadan wives made itself felt in the slow work of converting the pagan Mongols, and in Abyssinia in the first half of the 19th cent. the Muhammadan women, especially the wives of Christian princes, who had to pretend a conversion to Christianity on the occasion of their marriage, brought up their children in the tenets of Islām and used every means to spread their faith. In the present day the Tatar women of Kazan are said to be zealous propagandists of Islām.

The individualistic character of Muhammadan missionary effort partly explains the absence of detailed records of conversion; there is a similar lack of the common apparatus of modern Christian missions—*e.g.*, tracts and other missionary literature for general distribution; but in learned circles a vast controversial literature has been produced, to which some of the ablest of Muslim thinkers have contributed—*e.g.*, al-Kindī († 873), al-Mas'ūdī († 958), Ibn Ḥazm († 1064), al-Ghazālī († 1111), etc., as well as a number of converts who have written apologies for their change of faith and in defence of their new religion.[1] Several documents making a direct appeal to unbelievers have been preserved; the earliest of these are the letters[2] which Muhammad addressed to the great potentates of his time, the emperor Heraclius, the king of Persia, the governor of Yaman, the governor of Egypt, and the king of Abyssinia. To the reign of al-Ma'mūn (813–833), who himself is said to have been zealous in his efforts to spread the faith of Islām, belongs the interesting treatise of 'Abd Allāh b. Ismā'īl al-Hāshimī, in which he makes an impassioned and affectionate appeal to his Christian correspondent to accept Islām.[3] Of a much more formal character are the two letters, one in Arabic and the other in Persian, which the Tīmūrid prince, Shāh Rukh Bahādur, addressed in 1412 to the emperor of China, inviting him to 'observe the law of Muhammad, the Apostle of God, and strengthen the religion of Islām, so that he might exchange the transitory sovereignty of this world for the sovereignty of the world to come.'[4] A similar royal missive was sent by Mawlā'ī Ismā'īl, Sharīf of Morocco, to King James II. in 1698.[5] Coming from such an exalted source, these documents have been preserved, while the efforts of humbler folk have remained unrecorded. The publication of tracts and periodical reports of missionary societies makes its appearance only in the latter part of the 19th century.

LITERATURE.—Some attempt to give a bibliography of the scattered notices of Muslim missionary activity is made in *The Preaching of Islam*², London, 1913, by the present writer. For the early period the most valuable source is *Annali dell' Islām*, by Leone Caetani, Milan, 1905 ff., with exhaustive references to authorities, both Christian and Muhammadan. China is the only country to which any detailed monograph on the spread of Islām has been devoted, in Marshall Broomhall, *Islam in China*, London, 1910; see also *Mission d'Ollone, Recherches sur les Musulmans chinois par le commandant d'Ollone*, etc., Paris, 1911 f. For different parts of Africa separate monographs have appeared, *e.g.*, C. H. Becker, 'Zur Geschichte des östlichen Sūdān' and 'Materialien zur Kenntnis des Islam in Deutsch-Ostafrika,' *Der Islam*, i. and ii., Strassburg, 1910, 1911; G. Bonet-Maury, *L'Islamisme et le Christianisme en Afrique*, Paris, 1906; A. Le Chatelier, *L'Islam dans l'Afrique occidentale*, do. 1899; M. Klamroth, *Der Islam in Deutschost-afrika*, Berlin, 1912. For the Malay Archipelago see the article 'Mohammedanisme' and the various place-names in *Encyclopaedie van Nederlandsch-Indië*, ed. P. A. van der Lith and J. F. Snelleman, Leyden, 1899–1905; C. Snouck Hurgronje, *Nederland en de Islâm*², do. 1915; G. Simon, *Islam und Christentum im Kampf um die Eroberung der animistischen Heidenwelt: Beobachtungen aus der Mohammedanermission im Niederländisch-Indien*, Berlin, 1910. Much material may be gathered from the works of travellers in Muhammadan countries, from the journals and other periodical literature published by the various Roman Catholic and Protestant missionary societies, and from the periodicals specially devoted to the study of Islām, viz. *Revue du monde musulman*, Paris, 1906 ff., *Der Islam, Zeitschrift für Geschichte und Kultur des islamischen Orients*, Strassburg, 1910 ff., *The Moslem World, a Quarterly Review of current Events, Literature, and Thought among Mohammedans*, London, 1911 ff., *Mir Islama*, Petrograd, 1912 ff., and *Die Welt des Islams, Zeitschrift der deutschen Gesellschaft für Islamkunde*, Berlin, 1913 ff.

T. W. ARNOLD.

MISSIONS (Zoroastrian).

— Zoroastrianism began as a distinctly missionary religion. According to tradition, Yima (on whom see art. BLEST, ABODE OF THE [Persian]) was the first mortal asked by Ahura Mazda 'to remember and to cherish' the faith (*Vend.* ii. 3), but he professed himself unequal to the task and—unless the tradition is devoid of all meaning—contented himself with extending the domain of Iranian temporal power. Previous to the rise of Zoroaster there is no record of any conscious endeavour to propagate Iranism, which, like all religions which have no personal founder, was non-missionary.[1] With Zoroaster's advent, however, the attitude changed, and he himself, convinced that his religion was 'the best for existent beings, to further my creatures when followed in accord with righteousness' (*Ys.* xliv. 10), and that it would confer blessing for all eternity (*Ys.* liii. 1), besought Ahura Mazda and Aša to reveal to him their divine plan that he could rightly know how to proclaim (*srāvayaēmā*) the religion (*Ys.* xlix. 6), to the end that he might 'convert all men living' (*yā jvantō vīspēng vāurayā*, *Ys.* xxxi. 3). The potency of the faith would convert many hearers (*Ys.* xlvii. 6), and the promise of Paradise would turn the wicked (*Ys.* xxviii. 5). Indeed, a later text (*Yt.* xiii. 87–94) celebrates the greatness of Zoroaster, destined to spread the Mazdayasnian faith over all the world. Such was the merit of the religion that, if a non-believer accepted it and did not sin in future, all his past transgressions, even the most heinous, were forgiven (*Vend.* iii. 40 f.).

Zoroaster was successful in winning to his doctrine King Vīštāspa of Bālkh, who spread the faith with his conquests (cf. *Yt.* xiii. 99 f.; *Šāh-nāmah*, tr. A. G. and E. Warner, London, 1905 ff., v. 76 f., 85; A. V. W. Jackson, *Zoroaster*, New York, 1899, pp. 80–92); and among the converts were Turanians,[2] such as Fryāna and his descendant Yōišta (*Ys.* xlvi. 12; *Yt.* v. 81, xiii. 120), Arejahvant (*Yt.* xiii. 113), Frārāzi (*Yt.* xiii. 123), Saēna (*Yt.* xiii. 97; cf. *Dīnkarṭ*, IX. xxxiii. 5), and Isvant (*Yt.* xiii. 96; *Dīnkarṭ*, *loc. cit.*). Zoroaster is represented as praying that he may be able to cause heads of houses, villages, districts, and lands to think, speak, and act in accordance with the religion (*Ys.* viii. 7), and missionaries went afar 'to them who in [other] lands seek for righteousness' (*Ys.* xlii. 6), while, according to a Persian *rivāyat*, some account of the Zoroastrian propaganda was contained in the lost Vīštāsp Nask of the Avesta (*SBE* xxxvii. [1892] 424). Itinerant (*pairi-jaθan*) priests are mentioned side by side with those who laboured at home (*dainhāurvaēsa* [*Vīsp.* iii. 3, ix. 2; *Yt.* xxiv. 17]), and in some cases such priests were evidently invited abroad, since they are

---

1 For an account of such writings see Moritz Steinschneider, *Polemische und apologetische Litteratur in arabischer Sprache, zwischen Muslimen, Christen und Juden*, Leipzig, 1877; Ignaz Goldziher, 'Ueber muhammedanische Polemik gegen Ahl al-kitâb,' *ZDMG* xxxii. [1878] 341 ff.

2 On the doubtful authenticity of these letters see Caetani, *Annali dell' Islām*, i. 725 ff.

3 *Risālah 'Abd Allāh b. Ismā'īl al-Hāshimī ilā 'Abd al-Masīḥ b. Isḥāq al-Kindī*, London, 1885, pp. 1–37.

4 E. Blochet, *Introduction à l'histoire des Mongols de Fadl Allah Rashid ed-Din*, London, 1910, p. 249 f.

5 *RHR* xlvii. [1903] 174 ff.

1 In one of the Aramaic papyri from Elephantine a Persian is mentioned as head of a city (perhaps Syene; cf. E. Sachau, *Aram. Papyri und Ostraka aus . . . Elephantine*, Leipzig, 1911, pp. 51–54) in the reign of Darius II., and is described as a 'Mazdayasnian' (מזדיזן). Since this word (Av. *mazdayasna*) is frequently used in the Younger Avesta to denote a Zoroastrian (cf. C. Bartholomae, *Altiran. Wörterbuch*, Strassburg, 1904, col. 1160 f.; the borrowed Armenian *mazdezn* is employed in the same sense [H. Hübschmann, *Armen. Gramm.*, Leipzig, 1895–97, i. 190]), it may possibly support the theory (opposed by the present writer in art. ACHÆMENIANS, but advocated by J. H. Moulton, *Early Zoroastrianism*, London, 1913, p. 39 ff.) that the Achæmenians were Zoroastrians. On the other hand, the writer has always maintained that the Achæmenian Persians were Mazdayasnians in the rigid sense of the word, so that the Av. term would prove little in this connexion.

2 The ethnology of the Turanians is uncertain. They have commonly been supposed, since the days of F. Max Müller, to be non-Iranian, but this seems to be true only in part. Their names, as recorded in the Avesta, are Iranian, and the *Šāh-nāmah* (i. 189) records that they were descended from Tūr, son of Farīdūn, while the name Tūra appears to be Iranian (Bartholomae, col. 656). It is possible that they were Scyths (J. Marquart, *Ērānšahr*, Berlin, 1901, pp. 155–157; S. Feist, *Kultur . . . der Indogermanen*, do. 1913, pp. 405 f., 425, 471; cf. art. SCYTHS). While they may well have been a congeries of races, like the Scyths, they appear to have been regarded, by the Avesta, as nomad Iranians as opposed to the pastoral folk who evolved the Avesta. See, further, art. TURANIANS.

described as 'desired afar' (*dūraē-frakāta* [*Yt.* xvi. 17]). On the other hand, the missionaries sometimes encountered opposition, as when Keresāni sought to suppress them, but was driven from his kingdom by Haoma (*Ys.* ix. 24), though the present writer is inclined to regard this account as an Iranian reflex of a Vedic myth, the rôle of the hero being reversed, as is the case also in certain other figures surviving from the period of Indo-Iranian unity.[1] When, in like manner, the Pahlavi *Šikand-gūmānīk-Vijār* states (x. 67 f.) that the sons of Vištāspa 'even wandered to Arūm [the Byzantine empire] and the Hindūs, outside the realm, in propagating the religion,' the tradition of missionary activities in these countries (on which see Jackson, pp. 85–90) deserves no credence, and equally apocryphal is the statement of the *Dīnkarṭ* (*SBE* xxxvii. p. xxxi) that the Avesta was translated into Greek.[2]

From the close of the Avestan period to the dynasty of the Sasanids (224–651), there is almost a blank in the history of Zoroastrianism, for neither Seleucids nor Parthians seem to have taken much interest in the religion.[3] Nevertheless, there was considerable diffusion, if not of orthodox Zoroastrianism, at least of Iranism during this time. We have already had occasion to note the spread of Iranian concepts in Cappadocia as shown in the month-names of that country (art. CALENDAR [Persian], vol. iii. p. 130ᵃ); and a curious amalgamation of Semitic and Iranian religious ideas is revealed by a Cappadocian Aramaic inscription of the 2nd cent. B.C. (M. Lidzbarski, *Ephemeris für sem. Epigraphik*, i. [1902] 67–69), which runs as follows:

'This (?) Dēn-Mazdayasniš (רינמזריסנש־א), the queen (?), the sister and wife (אחתא ואנתתא) of Bēl, spake thus: "I am the wife of King Bēl." Thereupon Bēl spake thus to Dēn-Mazdayasniš: "Thou, my sister, art very wise, and fairer than the goddesses; and therefore have I made thee wife of Bēl (?)." The reference to *xvaētvadatha* (on which see MARRIAGE [Iranian], § 2) is also of interest.[4]

An inscription of Antiochus I. of Commagene (1st cent. B.C.) at Nīmrūd Dāgh is of much value as the expression of the religious fervour of a prince who traced his lineage, on the paternal side, to the Achæmenians themselves, and also as showing the character of a late Zoroastrian cult in a foreign land. The relevant portions of this text (ed. most conveniently by W. Dittenberger, *Orientis Græci inscript. selectæ*, Leipzig, 1903–05, no. 383 [i. 593–603]) may be summarized as follows (cf. also F. Cumont, *Textes et monuments figurés relatifs au culte de Mithra*, Brussels, 1896–99, i. 11, 233, 238, ii. 89–91, and below, p. 754ᵇ):

'I considered piety (εὐσέβειαν) not only the strongest foundation of all things good, but also the sweetest joy to men, and held it to be the criterion both of fortunate power and of blessed usefulness (κρίσιν καὶ δυνάμεως εὐτυχοῦς καὶ χρήσεως μακαριστῆς); throughout my life I was seen by all to deem holiness (ὁσιότητα) both the most faithful guardian and the inimitable delight of my kingdom' (11–19); and to this all his success during a long and hazardous career was due. When he ascended his ancestral throne, he appointed a common abode for all the gods (κοινὴν θεῶν ἁπάντων . . . δίαιταν), adorned their images with every device according to ancient Persian[1] and Greek regulation, and honoured them with sacrifices and laudations (μορφῆς μὲν (ε)ἰκόνας παντοίαι τέχνηι καθ' ἃ παλαιὸς λόγος Περσῶν τε καὶ Ἑλλήνων—ἐμοῦ γένους εὐτυχεστάτη ῥίζα—παρέδωκε κοσμήσας θυσίαις δὲ καὶ πανηγύρεσιν [20–34]). He was not, however, content with this. Having determined to found a mighty monument (ἱεροθεσίου) most nigh the heavenly thrones (οὐρανίων ἄγχιστα θρόνων), where, after he had sent his soul 'to the heavenly thrones of Zeus Oromasdes,' his body might slumber 'till boundless time,'[2] he declared that holy spot to be the common enthronement of all the gods, who were imaged in token of his piety (34–53). Accordingly, he set up statues of Zeus-Oromasdes, Apollo-Mithra-Helios-Hermes, Artagnes [Verethraghna]-Herakles-Ares, Commagene, and himself[3] in gratitude for the 'immortal care' (ἀθανάτου φροντίδος) which had aided him in all his times of trial (54–66). He made every provision for the upkeep of the shrine, the priests of which were to wear Persian vestments (71 ff.). Besides the sacrifices enjoined by old and new custom alike, he directed that the anniversary of his birth and of his coronation be observed annually by all, and that in each month the priests should commemorate the days—the 16th and the 10th—on which the gods had caused these two events to take place. All this is safeguarded by a law which 'my voice spake, but the mind of the gods ratified' (121 f.).

At the festivals the images of the gods should be clad in Persian fashion and be crowned with golden diadems (132–139); incense and perfumes were to be offered (142 f.), and an abundant feast was to be provided for all comers (146–161). The service at these banquets was performed by *hierodouloi* (*q.v.*), who, with their children, were inalienable (161–191), as were also the villages, etc., dedicated for the maintenance of the shrine (191–205); and the inscription closes with the hope that the dedicator's children will follow his example, and with blessings on those who observe his will and curses on those who seek impiously to undo his work (205–237). For a fragmentary inscription which begins in closely similar fashion see Dittenberger, no. 404 (i. 621 f.).

As regards India, we note that on the coinage of the Kuṣān kings Kaniṣka (*q.v.*) and Huviṣka (1st–2nd cent. B.C.) a number of Zoroastrian deities appear along with Greek and Hindu gods and effigies of the Buddha (M. A. Stein, 'Zoroastr. Deities on Indo-Scythic Coins,' in *BOR*, 1887, pp. 155–166; and especially A. von Sallet, *Zeitschr. für Numismatik*, vi. [1879] 386–409; A. Cunningham, 'Coins of the Kushâns, or Great Yue-ti,' in *Numismatic Chron.* III. xii. [1892] 40–82, 98–159 and plates xiv.–xxiv.; P. Gardner, *Coins of the Greek and Scythic Kings of Bactria and India in the Brit. Mus.*, London, 1886, pp. 129–161 and plates xxvi.–xxix.; *Cat. of Coins of the Ind. Museum* [Calcutta], Calcutta, 1893–96, iv. 39–50; further literature in E. J. Rapson, *Indian Coins*, Strassburg, 1898, p. 18).

According to a section (ch. cxxxvi. [cxxxix.]) of the *Bhaviṣya Purāṇa* written after the middle of the 6th cent. A.D., priests called Magas were brought from Šākadvīpa ('Scyth-[is] land') to serve sun-temples. This is scarcely to be construed as Iranian propaganda; for the function of these foreign priests see art. SAURAS AND MAGAS, and cf. D. B. Spooner, *JRAS*, 1915, pp. 63–89, 405–455.

With the rise of the house of Sāsan Zoroastrianism not merely revived, but again developed a markedly missionary spirit. According to the *Dīnkarṭ* (ed. and tr. P. B. and D. P. Sanjana, Bombay, 1874 ff., vol. x. p. 12), Ahura Mazda commands that the faith be spread through the world; and in elucidating the meaning of Av. *fravarāne*, 'I profess,' the Pahlavi commentators add that every Zoroastrian endeavours to propagate the religion among all mankind, while the highest praise attaches to the quondam non-believer who renounces his former tenets in favour of Zoroastrianism (*SBE* xviii. [1882] 415). Sapor II. (309–379), aided by his great priest Ādarbād (on whom see Justi, *Namenbuch*, p. 49), worked zealously in the cause of proselytism (*Dīnkarṭ*, vol. ix. p. 579), and the *Dīnkarṭ* (vol. viii. p. 26) directly sanctions propaganda by force. That this was by no means a

[1] Keresāni is apparently to be identified with the Vedic Kṛśānu, an archer who shot at the eagle which was carrying off Soma (Rigveda, IV. xxvii. 3 f.; cf. A. Bergaigne, *Religion védique*, Paris, 1878–83, iii. 30 f.; A. Hillebrandt, *Ved. Myth.*, Breslau, 1891–1902, i. 448 f.; A. A. Macdonell, *Ved. Myth.*, Strassburg, 1897, p. 137). For Keresāni see F. Justi, *Iran. Namenbuch*, Marburg, 1895, p. 161 (J. Darmesteter's identification of him with Alexander the Great [*Zend-Avesta*, Paris, 1892–93, i. 80–82] is quite improbable).

[2] Contrariwise, much of a very second-rate character was current in Greek under the names of Zoroaster, Ostanes, Hystaspes, etc. (J. A. Fabricius, *Bibliotheca Græca*, Hamburg, 1705–28, i. 245–252, 92–95); cf. also the folk-medicine and magic ascribed to Zoroaster in *Geoponica*, I. vii. f., x., xii., II. xv., V. xlvi., VII. v. f., xi., X. lxxxiii., XI. xviii. 11, XIII. ix. 10, XV. i.

[3] On the Parthian religion see G. Rawlinson, *Sixth Great Orient. Monarchy*, London, 1873, pp. 398–402; F. Justi, *GIrP* ii. [1904] 486 f.; A. V. W. Jackson, *ib.* p. 694; J. M. Unvala, 'The Religion of the Parthians,' in *Sir Jamsetjee Jejeebhoy Madressa Jubilee Vol.*, Bombay, 1914, pp. 1–10. Cf. also art. PARTHIANS. For the Seleucids see E. R. Bevan, *House of Seleucus*, London, 1902, i. 290 f.

[4] It is implied in *Yt.* xvii. 16 that Daēna (Religion personified) is the *daughter* of Ahura Mazda and Ārmaiti, but she is neither his sister nor his wife.

[1] Cf. art. IMAGES AND IDOLS (Persian). The term 'laudations' (πανηγύρεσιν) looks very like a literal translation of Av. *yašta*, 'Yašt,' panegyric of an individual deity.

[2] τὸν ἄπειρον αἰῶνα may possibly translate Av. *zrvan akarana*.

[3] For the brief individual inscriptions to all these see Dittenberger, nos. 384–388 (i. 604–606).

merely academic attitude is amply proved by the records of persecution of the Christians by the Sasanid rulers in Persia.[1] The Pahlavi portion of the *Nīrangistān* (ed. D. P. Sanjana, Bombay, 1894, fol. 16a, 17a) bears witness to the admission of proselytes, and the Pahlavi *Māṭīgān-ī-Hazār Dāṭistān* (ed. J. J. Modi, Poona, 1901, p. 1; tr. Bartholomae, *WZKM* xxvii. [1914] 347 ff.) states that a slave belonging to a Christian should be ransomed by Zoroastrians from his master if such a slave embraces Parsiism, though he is not to be set free if he becomes a Zoroastrian together with or after his master.

During the period under consideration there was some extension of Zoroastrianism in China (cf. Jackson, pp. 278–280), though no details are thus far known. It would appear, however, from the discoveries made by M. A. Stein, A. Grünwedel, A. von Le Coq, and P. Pelliot in Turkestan, where Buddhist, Persian, Turki, Greek, and Chinese relics lie intermingled, that Zoroastrianism passed along the great trade-routes. It may be doubted whether there was any active propaganda.[2]

We have just seen that the Sasanids proceeded by force against non-Zoroastrians in Persia; they pursued a similar course in Armenia. Ample proof of this is given in the Armenian historians,[3] and much further information is doubtless to be gleaned from the hitherto untranslated Acts of the Armenian Martyrs.[4] As an example it will be sufficient to summarize the data of the 5th cent. writer Elisæus (*Hist. of Vartan*, tr. C. F. Neumann, London, 1830):

All non-Zoroastrians were oppressed in Armenia from the reign of Aršak III. (341–367) till that of Artašēs IV. (422–429). The Persian Yazdagird II. (438–457) followed this example, urged by the Zoroastrian priests to 'exterminate the sect of the Christians,' and he deprived them of their property and martyred those who remained steadfast. Some he induced to become apostates by money and high rank, saying, 'Oh that you would but receive the doctrine of the Magi into your souls! Oh that you would but exchange the heresy of your souls for the true and excellent laws of our gods!' The Magi exhorted him, if he would prove his gratitude for his power and his victories, to make Zoroastrianism dominant everywhere. In the course of his endeavours the Zoroastrians promulgated an interesting Zarvanite statement of theology, to which the Christians replied (pp. 11–20). The persecution provoked a revolt, which was not suppressed until the Christian leader, Vardan, fell in battle in 451. The whole account of Elisæus shows the clash of two religions, each of uncompromising character. Cruelty and craft were only too evident, but the spirit of sincere conviction must be recognized.

With the overthrow of the Sasanian dynasty by the Arabs the missionary enterprise of Zoroastrianism practically came to a close. The plight of those who remained in Persia was—and is—too wretched to allow more than a reluctant and hostile toleration at best from the dominant Muhammadanism.[1] Those who, in the 7th cent., migrated to India and thus gave rise to the communities of Parsis (*q.v.*) were received with none too warm a welcome. As Dhalla observes (p. 323), with regard to their abstention from propaganda in India,

'The precarious condition in which they lived for a considerable period made it impracticable for them to keep up their former proselytizing zeal. The instinctive fear of disintegration and absorption in the vast multitudes among whom they lived created in them a spirit of exclusiveness and a strong feeling for the preservation of the racial characteristics and distinctive features of their community. Living in an atmosphere surcharged with the Hindu caste system, they felt that their own safety lay in encircling their fold by rigid caste barriers.'

Nevertheless, a certain amount of proselytizing continued as late as the 18th cent., especially in the case of slaves purchased from low-caste Hindus. Such procedure, however, instead of being welcomed as extending the faith, aroused hostility on social grounds, some Parsis being unwilling to permit such converts to prepare sacred cakes (*drons*) for the festivals or to allow the proselytes to be exposed after death on the Parsi 'Towers of Silence.' The question was referred more than once to the Zoroastrians in Persia, whose replies were in favour of admitting converts. From the point of view of orthodox Zoroastrianism, there cannot be the slightest question that the ruling of the Irānī (Persian) Zoroastrians was right. On the other hand, it was felt by the Parsis of India that an influx of low-caste Hindus would be prejudicial to the purity of their Iranian community.

The only cases in which proselytism has been urged in recent years have been instances in which a Parsi has married a non-Zoroastrian wife, or has desired to have children born by such a wife, or by a non-Zoroastrian mistress, received into the Parsi community. In all these cases admission has been granted only in the face of intense opposition.

The motives of the converts have been, in practically every instance, worldly, not religious, and the conversions have been purely nominal. Parsis hold that such proselytes are harmful to the faith, and that, if converts are admitted at all, it must be under conditions which put the sincerity of the neophytes' religious convictions beyond suspicion. The Zoroastrian community has no organization for training new converts; the matrimonial opportunities of Parsi girls are lessened by the possibility of converting prospective wives of other religions; and the admission of illegitimate children of Parsis is felt to be virtually a condoning of immorality.

This attitude—so different from that of Zoroaster and of Zoroastrianism until the migration to India —is fraught with grave possibilities to Parsiism. The age of marriage is rising, and the birth-rate is falling. There is a steady leakage towards agnosticism (not towards conversion to Christianity, Muhammadanism, or any form of Hinduism). Even among those who regard themselves as Zoroastrians there is much laxity. Theosophy (*q.v.*) is making a form of 'esoteric' Zoroastrianism which can scarcely be reconciled with the Avesta. Some of the radical wing of the 'reforming' party, at the other extreme, rationalize the religion until it becomes a travesty of its real content. Against all this must be reckoned many wisely conservative Parsis, both priests and laymen,[2] but whether, so long as all accessions from without are forbidden, they can advance and extend the 'good religion' is a question for the future.

LITERATURE.—M. N. Dhalla, *Zoroastrian Theology*, New York, 1914, pp. 11–13, 72–75, 198 f., 323–325, 367 f.; letter of Rustamji Edulji Dastur Peshotan Sanjana to the writer (5th July 1915).

LOUIS H. GRAY.

MISTLETOE.—See CELTS, vol. iii. p. 295 f.

[1] S. E. Assemani, *Acta martyrum orientalium*, Rome, 1748; P. Bedjan, *Acta martyrum et sanctorum*, Paris, 1890–97; G. Hoffmann, *Auszüge aus syr. Akten pers. Märtyrer*, Leipzig, 1880; J. Labourt, *Christianisme dans l'empire perse sous la dynastie sassanide*, Paris, 1904; L. H. Gray, 'Zoroastrian . . . Material in the Acta Sanctorum,' in *Journ. of the Manchester Egyp. and Orient. Soc.*, 1913–14, pp. 37–55; further material is given in the Bollandists' *Bibliotheca hagiographica orientalis*, Brussels, 1910. For Zoroastrian hostility towards Christianity and Judaism see artt. JESUS CHRIST IN ZOROASTRIANISM, JEWS IN ZOROASTRIANISM. Justi (*GIrP* ii. 521, 529 f.), followed by A. J. H. W. Brandt (*Mandäische Religion*, Leipzig, 1889, p. 162, note 1), holds that the persecutions were political rather than religious in motive, the Nestorians enjoying State protection and even favour, whereas the Catholics, owning allegiance to a non-Persian power, were objects of hostility.

[2] As illustrating the extent to which Iranian ideas were current in China it is interesting to note that a long Manichæan treatise exists in Chinese (ed. and tr. E. Chavannes and P. Pelliot, 'Un Traité manichéen retrouvé en Chine,' in *JA* x. xviii. [1911] 499–617, XI. i. [1913] 99–199, 261–394).

[3] M. Brosset, *Collection d'historiens arméniens*, Petrograd, 1874–76, *Deux historiens arméniens*, do. 1870; V. Langlois, *Collection des historiens anciens et modernes de l'Arménie*, Paris, 1867–69.

[4] *e.g.*, J. B. Aucher, *Sanctorum acta pleniora*, 12 vols., Venice, 1810–14; L. Alishan, *Bibliotheca Armeniaca*, 22 vols., do. 1853–61; *Vitæ et passiones sanctorum*, 2 vols., do. 1874; *Vitæ patrum*, 2 vols., do. 1855 (all in Armenian only). The 'Passion of SS. Abdas, Hormisdas, Šahin, and Benjamin' is tr. by P. Peeters, *Analecta Bollandiana*, xxviii. [1909] 399–415. For further details see the *Bibl. hag. orient.* cited above.

[1] See art. GABARS and the literature there cited, to which may now be added five papers by Khudayar Sheriyar in the *Jejeebhoy Jubilee Vol.*, pp. 299–318, 432–438.

[2] On all these movements see esp. J. N. Farquhar, *Modern Religious Movements in India*, New York, 1915, pp. 84–91, 343–346.

MITHRAISM.—The religion generally known by this name, which enjoyed a wide-spread popularity in the centuries immediately preceding and following the Christian era, centred in the worship of Mithra, a divinity worshipped in the Indo-Iranian period by the two most easterly branches of the Aryan race, as is shown by the fact that his name appears in the form Mitra among the gods of the Vedic pantheon and in that of Mithra in the early religious poetry of Persia. The name coincides in form with a common noun which in Sanskrit means 'friend' or 'friendship' and in Avestan 'compact,'[1] and it would seem to follow that from the earliest times the conception of Mithra was an ethical one.

1. Mitra in Vedic religion.—In the only hymn addressed exclusively to him in the Rigveda (iii. 59) Mitra is said to 'bring men together, uttering his voice' and to watch the tillers of the soil 'with unwinking eye'—phrases which suggest a solar divinity; and from the numerous hymns in which Mitra and Varuṇa are conjointly addressed it is abundantly clear that both divinities are manifested in the celestial light. In the *Brāhmaṇas*, indeed, the view prevails that Mitra represents the light of day, especially that of the sun, while to Varuṇa belong the 'thousand eyes' of night. This seems, however, to be a later refinement, the beginnings of which may be traced in the Atharvaveda, especially IX. iii. 18, where Mitra uncovers in the morning what Varuṇa has concealed. The theory of Oldenberg,[2] that the group of divinities known as Ādityas, who are said in Rigveda IX. cxiv. 3 to have been seven in number,[3] originally represented sun (Mitra), moon (Varuṇa), and five planets, and was borrowed from a Semitic race, has little to commend it. It is more probable that Varuṇa was by origin the all-encompassing vault of heaven (√*var*, 'cover'), Mitra the light which proceeds therefrom. Ethically the two gods were probably differentiated in the Indo-Iranian period, Varuṇa being the supreme upholder of physical and moral order, Mitra the all-seeing witness who guarantees good faith between man and man. This is not so clear in the Vedas as in the early religious poetry of Persia, where the place of Varuṇa is taken by Ahura Mazda (='Wise Lord,' the word Ahura corresponding to Skr. *asura*—a term which in later Vedic literature means 'demon,' but in the Rigveda is applied to gods, more especially to Varuṇa and Mitra, and is plausibly suggested to have connoted the possession of occult power).

2. Mithra in Iran.—Among the Iranian peoples the worship of Mithra attained an importance which it never possessed in India. The early history of this worship is very obscure, owing to the uncertainties which beset the interpretation of the Avestan texts. From the inscriptions found by H. Winckler at Boghaz-keui in 1907,[4] especially the treaty between the Hittite king Subbiluliuma and Mattiuaza, the son of Tushratta, king of Mitanni, it appears that Mitra, Varuṇa, Indra, and the Nāsatya, or 'Twins,' were worshipped in the district of Mitanni in the 14th cent. B.C. Eduard Meyer ('Das erste Auftreten der Arier in die Geschichte,' *SBAW*, 1908, p. 14 ff.) regards this fact as a proof that an Aryan community existed in Mitanni; in *EBr*[11] xxi. 203 he suggests that the Aryans in question were a caste ruling over a non-Aryan people. It is, however, uncertain whether we should regard them as the ancestors of the Iranians, and even possible (as J. H. Moulton has suggested, *Early Zoroastrianism*, London, 1913, pp. 7, 26) that we have here the relic of a prehistoric migration backward from India to the North-West. It is to be observed that the name Varuṇa is otherwise unknown in Iranian texts, whilst Ahura Mazda, who takes his place, appears under the form Assara Mazāsh in an Assyrian list of divinities of about 650 B.C. (published by F. Hommel, *PSBA*, 1899, pp. 127, 138), and had, no doubt, been borrowed from an Iranian people at a considerably earlier date. To the same period belongs a tablet from the library of Assurbanipal in which Mithra is identified with Shamash (R. iii. 69, 5, l. 72). Our next evidence dates from the Achæmenian dynasty. The inscriptions of Cyrus, it is true, throw no light on his worship of Iranian divinities, and Darius I. mentions Ahura Mazda only; but the evidence of theophoric names (Μιτραδάτης [Herod. i. 110, 121], Μιτροβάτης [*ib.* iii. 120, 126, 127], and, earlier still, Μιτραγαθής, if this is the correct reading, in Æsch. *Pers.* 42) makes it plain that Mithra was prominent in the Persian pantheon,[1] while Artaxerxes Mnemon (403–358 B.C.) names as his divine protectors Ahura Mazda, Anāhita, and Mithra (*Art. Sus.* a, 4 f., *Ham.* 5 f. [O. Pers. text]). The coupling of Mithra with the goddess Anāhita reminds us of the confusion between the two of which Herodotus is guilty in the passage (i. 131) in which he describes the Persian religion, and identifies Μίτρα with the 'Assyrian' Mylitta (an appellative of Ishtar).

3. Mithra in early Zoroastrianism.—We have next to consider the position of Mithra in the religion of Zarathushtra. Adopting the position (1) that the *Gāthās* go back to the time of the Prophet himself, and that this was not later (and very possibly earlier) than the traditional date (7th cent. B.C.), and (2) that the *Yashts*, at any rate as regards the metrical portions, are not many centuries later,[2] we observe that Mithra is never mentioned in the former, and was ignored by Zarathushtra in his reform. It may even be possible to go further, and to hold that the Prophet regarded him as a *daēva*, or demon, whose worship was to be banished from the pure faith. In *Ys.* xxxii. 10 we hear of the teacher of evil who 'declares that the Ox and the Sun are the worst thing to behold with the eyes,' which may perhaps refer to the nocturnal sacrifice of the bull by Mithraists; and it is also possible that the Ox-Creator (*Gēush-tashan*) named in *Ys.* xxix. 2 was a substitute for Mithra devised by Zarathushtra. These are only conjectures;[3] but we shall find in later Mithraic ritual abundant proofs of the survival of primitive conceptions such as Zarathushtra endeavoured to eradicate. It is not necessary here to discuss the difficult questions regarding the measure of success attained by the Prophet's reform and the origin of the counter-movement (perhaps Magian) which restored the more primitive worships. It may be worth mentioning, however, that in the Persian calendar, which there is reason to think (on astronomical grounds) was introduced into Cappadocia by Darius I.,[4] the names of the months are derived from divine names, which include those of Mithra

[1] These words are connected by etymology with the base **mei*, 'exchange,' seen in Lat. *com-munis*, Goth. *ga-mains*, M.H.G. *ge-mein*, etc.; see K. Brugmann and B. Delbrück, *Grundriss*[2], Strassburg, 1897 ff., II. i. 346, and especially A. Meillet, *JA* x. x. [1907] 143–159.

[2] *Religion des Veda*, p. 185 ff.

[3] Six Ādityas are enumerated in Rigveda II. xxvii. 1, and eight in X. lxxii. 8 f.

[4] Cf. H. Winckler, 'Die Arier in den Urkunden von Boghazköi,' *OLZ*, 1910, pp. 289–301.

[1] Cf. also the names Μιθροβαρζάνης (Corn. Nepos, *Datam.* vi. 3, Diod. Sic. xv. xci. 5), Μιθροβουζάνης (Diod. XVII. xxi. 3; Arrian, *Anab.* I. xvi. 3), Μιτραφέρνης (Nicolaus Damasc. *FHG* iii. 363), Μιθροπαύστης (Plut. *Themist.* 29), Μιθραύστης (Arrian, *Anab.* III. viii. 5), etc. (F. Justi, *Iran. Namenb.*, Marburg, 1895, pp. 208 f., 213, 216 f., and esp. Cumont, *Textes*, ii. 76–85, 464–466).

[2] A popular account of the present state of the question will be found in J. H. Moulton's *Early Religious Poetry of Persia*, Cambridge, 1911, and further details in the same author's *Early Zoroastrianism*.

[3] Moulton, *Early Zoroastrianism*, pp. 129, 357.

[4] See excursus, *ib.* p. 430 ff.

(but not Anāhita) and the six Amesha Spentas (or Amshaspands), which are among the most characteristic features of Zoroastrianism properly so called. For our knowledge of Mithra-worship among the Persians we naturally turn to the *Mihir Yasht* (*Yt.* x., Eng. tr. in *SBE* xxiii. [1883], by J. Darmesteter, more accurately in German by F. Wolff, *Avesta . . . übersetzt*, Strassburg, 1910, pp. 198–221). The opening lines of the poem show clearly the high position enjoyed by Mithra, although, as a *yazata* ('adored one') he stood technically on a lower level than the six Amshaspands of Zarathushtra's creed.

'Thus spake Ahura Mazda to the holy Zarathushtra : When I created Mithra, lord of wide pastures, then, O Spitama, I created him as worthy of sacrifice, as worthy of prayer as myself, Ahura Mazda' (*Yt.* x. 1).

The *Yasht* speaks with no uncertain voice either of the physical or of the ethical character of the god :

'The first of the spiritual *Yazatas*, who rises over the Mountain [1] before the immortal sun, driver of swift horses ; who foremost attains the gold-decked, fair summits, whence he surveys the whole dwelling-place of the Aryans, he, the most mighty' (*Yt.* x. 13).

This is clearly neither the sun himself nor any individual object, but the heavenly light in general, and it suits well with the recurring formula of the hymn :

'To Mithra, the lord of wide pastures, we sacrifice, the truth-speaking, eloquent in assembly, the thousand-eared, the shapely, the myriad-eyed, the exalted, (lord of) the broad look-out, the strong, the sleepless, the vigilant' (*Yt.* x. 7, etc.).

Here the ethical and the physical are already combined ; and in the second stanza of the hymn the god and the 'promise' or 'compact' over whose fulfilment he watches are almost identified ; for Zarathushtra is thus addressed by Ahura Mazda :

'Break not the compact [*mithrem*], whether thou make it with the faithless or with the righteous fellow-believer, for Mithra stands for both, for the faithless as for the righteous.'

Throughout the *Yasht* the invincible might of Mithra is invoked against the *mithradruj*, which may be translated either 'deceiver of Mithra' or 'promise-breaker.' It is this guardianship of truth and good faith that gives Mithra his special character ; but he is also invoked, like other divinities, as the protector of the needy,

'whom the poor man, who follows the teaching of righteousness, when wronged and deprived of his rights, with uplifted hands invokes for help' (*Yt.* x. 84), and his aid is sought 'in both worlds, in this world of the body, and in the world of the spirit' (*ib.* 93).

The last trait may remind us that among the functions of Mithra was that of assisting the souls of those departed in the faith on their journey to Paradise.

He is implored to 'be present at our sacrifice, come to our libations . . . bear them for atonement, lay them down in the House of Praise' (*Yt.* x. 32).

It is natural, therefore, to find as his companions Sraosha ('obedience') and Rashnu ('justice'), who, in later Zoroastrianism,[2] are found beside Ahura Mazda in the Final Judgment. In the *Yasht*, however, they figure as his henchmen in the great struggle between the powers of light and darkness.

'Mithra strikes terror into them, Rashnu strikes a counter-fear into them, Sraosha drives them together from every side toward the protecting angels' (*Yt.* x. 41).

Throughout the poem Mithra appears as pre-eminently a god of battles ; he was, therefore, especially fitted to become, as he did in later times, the favourite deity of the Roman soldier. Of the ritual of Mithra-worship the *Yasht* tells us little ; *haoma* (*q.v.*) and milk were offered to him in libation ; and the Mazdayasnian is bidden to sacrifice 'beasts small and great, and birds that fly,' and to prepare himself for the sacrifice by ablutions and penance (*Yt.* x. 119–122).[1]

4. External influences on Mithraism.—(*a*) *In Babylonia.* — The picture thus sketched — and nothing essential would be added by drawing on the later portions of the Avesta or the Pahlavi texts—is in many ways very different from that of Mithraism as known to us from the inscriptions and monuments of the Roman period, and the problem of accounting for the difference is one which the evidence at present available does not enable us to solve. It is, however, clear that the transformation was due partly to Babylonian influence, partly to contamination with beliefs current in Asia Minor. The former influence, no doubt, began to exert itself at an early date, since the confusion of which Herodotus was guilty, in identifying Mithra (as a supposed female divinity) with Ishtar, and the coupling of Mithra with Anāhita (*q.v.*), who, in spite of her associations with the Oxus, was a goddess of an easily recognized Semitic type, point to a close *rapprochement* between Persian and Babylonian cults. The most important feature of later Mithraism, due to Chaldæan influence, was the prominence of astrolatry. There is nothing to show that this was a feature of early Iranian religion, whereas we know that the observation of the heavenly bodies and the belief in their influence on the affairs of men were of great antiquity in Babylonia. When, therefore, we find the busts of sun and moon and the circle of the zodiac standing features in Mithraic monuments, we can have no doubt as to the ultimate source of this element; nor can it be questioned that the elaboration of a body of doctrine, expressed in and through myth and symbols, also took place in the Farther East, although the details of the process escape us. We can say no more than that the dualism of Iranian religion furnished a clue both to the cosmic process and to the destiny of the individual soul, and that the results which flowed from the doctrine were worked out in detail on the banks of the Euphrates. The brief account of Zoroastrianism given by Plutarch in the *de Iside et Osiride*[2] shows us how far the Magians had already carried the transformation of the simple Persian faith into that which meets us in the *Bundahishn* and other Pahlavi texts of the Sasanian era, and enables us to rely on these to some extent for the interpretation of doubtful details in the evidence. Essential features are: (1) the separation in the material universe of the province of Ahura Mazda, 'withdrawn beyond the sun as far as the sun is from the earth,' from that of Angra Mainyu, the prince of darkness, and the intermediate position of Mithra, the μεσίτης ; and (2) the doctrine that the soul is a divine spark of light descending from the highest heaven and acquiring a gross and earthly envelope which taints it with corruption and makes its existence on earth a continual struggle with the power of evil. The moral consequences of this doctrine, particularly the inspiring conception of Mithra, the Mediator, as at once the commander under whom the individual shares in the fight against the prince of darkness and the Redeemer[3] who grants to his faithful servants final deliverance from the body of death, followed by the return of

[1] *Hara berezaiti* is the name elsewhere applied to the peak upon which 'Ahura Mazda the Creator fashioned for Mithra a dwelling where is neither night nor darkness, nor chill wind, nor hot, nor death-dealing sickness, nor pollution wrought by demons, nor do mists rise thereon' (*Yt.* x. 50). To the Iranian this meant Mt. Alburz.

[2] See L. C. Casartelli, *Philosophy of the Mazdayasnian Religion under the Sassanids*, Bombay, 1889, pp. 79–81 ; Dhalla, *Zoroastrian Theology*, p. 239 f. ; Cumont, *Textes*, i. 37.

[1] At the close of the *Yasht* (x. 145 ; cf. 113) Mithra and Ahura are jointly invoked, just as Mitra and Varuṇa are in the Vedic hymns.

[2] Ch. xlvi. f.

[3] In a Manichæan Turfān fragment Mithra is designated as 'redeemer and benefactor' (*bōxtār ūd xvābar*, C. Salemann, *Manichaeische Studien*, i. [Petrograd, 1908] 4 d, 2 [p. 6]).

the purified spirit to the sphere from which it came, we may believe to be characteristically Iranian; to Chaldæa we shall attribute the elaboration of the astrological dogmas connected with the influence exercised by the planets upon the soul in its passage through their spheres, and the prominence given to the conception of Destiny as revealed in the unchanging order of the heavenly process, carried on throughout unending time (*zrvan akarana* in later Zoroastrianism). Fatalism was the necessary corollary of these doctrines; but its acceptance in theory did not prevent Mithraism from becoming an intensely practical creed, full of stimulus for the activity of the individual.[1]

(*b*) *In Asia Minor.*—It is much more difficult to say what was the effect upon Mithraism of its diffusion throughout Asia Minor.[2] We have no contemporary evidence for the stages by which this took place, but it is at least probable that the later Achæmenian kings, who were, as we have seen, ardent votaries of Mithra and Anāhita—Artaxerxes Ochus is said[3] to have erected statues of the goddess in many places—established the worship of these divinities in the outlying portions of their dominions. It was not long before they became assimilated to those which were indigenous to the land; Anāhita was readily identified with the Great Mother whose worship was so deeply rooted in Anatolia (see art. MOTHER OF THE GODS), and thus the way was paved for an alliance between Mithra and Cybele (*q.v.*). Mithra himself took the shape of Men in Pontus (see below), and was assimilated in art with Attis (*q.v.*), in spite of the profound differences of nature and function between the two. More than this we can hardly say, for the primitive features of Mithraic ritual, to be considered later, were not necessarily borrowed, but may go back to Iranian antiquity. The *taurobolium*, however, is believed by Cumont (i. 334 f.) to have been taken over by Mithraism from the cult of the Great Mother. The propagation of Mithraism in the West had its political as well as its religious side. One of the earliest conceptions of Iranian religion was that of the 'glory,' or *hvarenō*.[4] This was conceived as a kind of mystical effulgence or aureole derived from the heavenly light, and possibly borrowed some of its features from the widely diffused conception of the external soul. In the story of the Fall, embodied for the Iranians in the myth of Yima, sin entailed the loss of this precious talisman; and in the *Mihir Yasht* the *dush-hvarenō*, 'he of evil glory,' is the man who 'thinks that Mithra sees not all his evil deeds and lying' (*Yt.* x. 105). But the *hvarenō* was more especially the talisman of the royal house of Irān, and as such is the main subject of an entire *Yasht* (*Yt.* xix.), which deals with those who have or will possess it, beginning with Ahura Mazda himself and ending with Saoshyant, the future deliverer of the world from evil, but giving in the main, as Darmesteter points out (*SBE* xxiii. 286), 'a short history of the Iranian monarchy, an abridged Shāh Nāmah.' Historically, therefore, the *hvarenō* is the token of Iranian kingship and the talisman which gives victory over the Turanian. Naturally enough, the Near Eastern dynasties which sprang from the wreck of Alexander's empire were anxious to secure this token of legitimacy, and were therefore fervent worshippers of Mithra, 'the spiritual *Yazata* who rides through all the Karshvars, bestowing the *hvarenō*' (*Yt.* x. 16). The prevalence of this conception is but thinly veiled by the disguise which the *hvarenō* attained among half-Hellenized Asiatics as the Τύχη βασιλέως. It was doubtless at the courts of these mushroom monarchs that the Hellenization of Mithraism, which was the indispensable condition of its further diffusion, was brought about. In this respect our most instructive monument is the enormous cairn set up by Antiochus I. of Commagene (69–38 B.C.) on the tumulus of Nimrūd Dāgh, on either side of which was a terrace with identical series of five statues.[1] These, as the king tells us in his inscription, represented (1) Zeus-Oromasdes (=Ahura Mazda), (2) Apollo-Mithras-Helios-Hermes, (3) Artagnes-Herakles-Ares (= Verethraghna, 'victory'), (4) Commagene, (5) Antiochus himself; of the last the king says that by setting up the fashion of his own form he has 'caused the honour of ancient deities to become coeval with a new Τύχη.' The identification of Mithras with three Greek divinities illustrates the elastic methods of syncretism; Hermes is probably chosen as the guide of souls in the world beyond the grave,[2] and, at the same time, it may be, with allusion to the planet assigned to him (in common with Apollo) by the Greeks, since Antiochus was a convinced astrologer and has left us his horoscope in relief on the retaining-wall of the terrace; yet Mithras is also, as so often later, identified with the sun himself. Antiochus's father, it may be added, was one of the numerous bearers of the name Mithradates; and another of the reliefs shows Antiochus clasping the right hand of Mithras, represented in Persian costume with the radiate nimbus. This grouping of the god with the ruler whom he protects is a motive which recurs in various quarters, especially, as M. I. Rostowzew[3] has shown, in Scythia. On the coinage of Trapezus (Cumont, ii. 189–191) Mithras, in Persian costume, appears on horseback —in one instance flanked by the figures of Cautes and Cautopates (see below); hence we are able to recognize him in the mounted divinity (generally trampling on a prostrate foe) represented on various works of art found in the tumuli of the Scythian princes in the Caucasus and Southern Russia. A notable example is the silver *rhyton* from Karagodeuashkh,[4] where Mithra, holding sceptre and drinking-horn, is faced by a Scythian prince, also mounted, who uplifts his right hand in the gesture of adoration.

5. Contact with Greece and Rome.—It was in Asia Minor that Greek art was enlisted in the service of Mithraism and created the sculptural types which were diffused throughout the West and form the chief source of our knowledge of the cult. The group of Mithras the bull-slayer, to be described presently, though ultimately inspired by the bull-slaying Nike of the Athenian acropolis, is manifestly the creation of a Pergamene artist, and adorned every sanctuary of Mithras. In spite of this fact, however, it is to be noted that Mithraism never became popular in Greek lands; it is not found, *e.g.*, at Delos, where so many foreign cults flourished in the later Hellenistic age, and its

[1] 'Astral theology' as a system is foreign to the Avesta; the worship of Tishtrya (=Sirius), to whom *Yt.* viii. is addressed, forms no real exception to this rule. Of the constellations only the Great Bear is mentioned in this hymn (*Yt.* viii. 12).

[2] That Mithraism came to Asia Minor from Semitic sources is proved by the Græco-Aramaic bilingual inscriptions of Cappadocia, in one of which (from Rhodandos) a Persian records how he ἐμάγευσε μίθρῃ (*Comptes rendus de l'acad. des inscriptions*, 1908, p. 434), and also (as Cumont points out) by the fact that the form Μαγουσαῖοι is a transliteration from the Aramaic.

[3] Clem. Alex. *Protrept.* 5.

[4] The word appears in the compound names which the Greeks wrote Τισσα-φέρνης, Φαρνά-βαζος, etc. Cf. for other names Justi, pp. 90–98, 178, 181 f., 493. On the 'glory' itself see especially E. Wilhelm, 'Hvarenō,' in *Sir Jamsetjee Jejeebhoy Madressa Jubilee Vol.*, Bombay, 1914, pp. 159–166.

[1] For this inscription see K. Humann and O. Puchstein, *Reisen in Klein-Asien und Nord-Syrien*, Berlin, 1890, p. 262 ff., and cf. Cumont, ii. 89–91, 187–189.

[2] Cf. the dedication 'Deo invicto Mithræ Mercurio' found at Stockstadt together with a statuette (F. Drexel, *Das Kastell Stockstadt*, Heidelberg, 1910, p. 86; Cumont, *Mystères*[3], p. 146).

[3] *Predstavlenie o monarchitcheskoi vlasti v Skithii i na Bospore*, Petrograd, 1913, p. 4 ff.

[4] *Ib.* pl. i. 1.

traces are rare (and generally of Imperial date) throughout the Hellenized East, in Syria, Egypt, etc. Even in the 2nd cent. A.D. Lucian writes of Mithras as a barbarian god, οὐδὲ ἑλληνίζων τῇ φωνῇ (*Deorum Conc.* 9).

The cult of Mithras is said by Plutarch (*Pomp.* 24) to have been brought to Rome by Cilician pirates taken captive in 67 B.C., and there is no reason to doubt the statement; but it certainly failed to achieve the popularity already attained by some other Oriental religions until almost the close of the 1st cent. after Christ, for the earliest Mithraic inscription as yet found in Rome was set up by a freedman of the Flavian dynasty (*CIL* vi. 732 = Cumont, ii. 105 f.), and, although the British Museum contains a statuary group of Mithras and the bull dedicated by a slave of Ti. Claudius Livianus, *præfectus prætorio* in A.D. 102 (Cumont, ii. 228; cf. 106), Mithraic monuments and inscriptions do not become common in the West until the Antonine period.

6. Diffusion in the Roman world.—(*a*) *By the army.*—The diffusion of Mithraism was largely the work of the army. Pontus, Cappadocia, Commagene, and Lesser Armenia—precisely those regions in which the specialized form of the cult had been developed—were recruiting-grounds largely drawn upon by the Romans, even while as yet only client-kingdoms of the empire, and still more when they were annexed and became provinces. During the Parthian wars under Claudius and Nero a considerable Oriental element thus entered the service of Rome, largely as auxiliaries, but also in the legions. Whether or no the soldiers of the Third Legion who saluted the rising sun at the second battle of Betriacum (A.D. 69) were Mithraists, it is at least certain that the Fifteenth, which served in the Parthian wars of Nero and was transferred by Vespasian to the Danube, brought the cult of Mithras to its camp at Carnuntum in A.D. 71. Another important centre of the cult in the same region was Aquincum, the headquarters of Legio II. Adjutrix, founded by Vespasian from the sailors of the Ravenna fleet, who, as freedmen, were doubtless in many instances of Oriental birth. But the wide spread of Mithraism on the frontiers was largely due to the auxiliary corps—*alæ* and *cohortes*—raised in the East under the Flavian and succeeding dynasties and used to garrison the line of the Danube and the Rhine or the Vallum in Northern Britain. Except for a relief found in London (Cumont, ii. 389 f.), all the Mithraic monuments and inscriptions found in Britain belong either to the legionary camps at Isca (Caerleon-on-Usk [*CIL* vii. 99 = Cumont, ii. 160]) and Eboracum (York [Cumont, ii. 391 f.]) or to the forts on or near the wall, such as Borcovicum (Housesteads [*CIL* vii. 645–650 = Cumont, ii. 161, 393–396]), Amboglanna (Birdoswald [*CIL* vii. 831 = Cumont, ii. 162]), Bremenium (High Rochester [*CIL* vii. 103 = Cumont, ii. 162]), Vindobala (Rutchester [Cumont, ii. 392 f.]), and others. So, too, in the Two Germanys the sanctuaries of Mithras (with some few exceptions[1]) are found either in legionary camps, such as Vetera Castra, Bonna, and Moguntiacum (Cumont, ii. 389, 385 f., 381–383), or in the forts along the *limes Germanicus*, where they are lacking in none of the principal posts—Butzbach, Friedberg, Saalburg, Heddernheim, Grosskrotzenburg, Osterburken, Böckingen, Murrhardt (*ib.* ii. 354–360, 472 f., 362–381, 351–354, 348–351, 154), and others. We have already mentioned the military settlements of Carnuntum and Aquincum, on the Upper Danube, as centres of Mithraism; the same might be said of practically every important post on that river down to its mouth—*e.g.*, Vindobona, Brigetio, Viminacium, Oescus, Durostorum, and Troesmis (*ib.* i. 363, ii. 329, 275, 130, 489 f., 272), to name the principal centres. In Africa also the camp of the Third Legion at Lambæsis, and several military posts, such as Mascula and Sitifis (*ib.* ii. 168, 170, 405 f.), have furnished Mithraic monuments; and in the countries where traces of Mithraism are relatively rare they are often found in the colonies of veterans—*e.g.*, Emerita (Merida) in Spain[1] (*ib.* ii. 166) and Patræ in Greece.

(*b*) *By slaves.*—Next in importance to the army, in the diffusion of Mithraism, came the slave population employed by the State, the municipalities, or private individuals. The first class comprises more especially the employés of the custom-houses and the State-properties, such as mines and quarries. Thus in the Danubian provinces, especially Dalmatia and the Pannonias, the *stationes* of the customs-barrier at which the *vectigal Illyrici* was levied have furnished a number of Mithraic dedications, due to slaves and freedmen in the public service, several of whom bear Greek names and were, therefore, doubtless natives of the Eastern provinces. Again, the presence of numerous Mithraic monuments in Noricum (*ib.* ii. 150–152, 335–339, 472) is accounted for, not so much by the military occupation—though the station of Commagene, which clearly takes its name from an auxiliary regiment, forms a natural exception—as by the mines owned by the State in that province. In Italy the *servi publici* of the municipalities contributed largely to the spread of the religion. At Sentinum, which has yielded an inscription (*CIL* xi. 5737 = Cumont, ii. 121) giving a list of thirty-five *patroni* of a Mithraic congregation, the slaves and freedmen of the municipality figure side by side with *ingenui*; at Nersæ a slave employed as *arcarius* restored a Mithræum (*CIL* ix. 4109 f. = Cumont, ii. 120). It goes without saying that private slaves—especially in the households of the wealthy in Rome itself—played a large part in the spreading of Mithraism.

(*c*) *By trade-routes.*—We may in part trace to imported slaves the spread of Mithraism along the trade-routes which were in communication by sea with the Eastern Mediterranean, though doubtless the merchants themselves were often worshippers of Mithras. Thus in the African provinces, apart from the military stations mentioned above, the only traces of Mithraism are to be found in such coast towns as Cæsarea, Cirta, or Rusicade (Cumont, ii. 171, 168, 170, 406 f.); in Southern Gaul we can trace by the presence of Mithraic monuments the spread of the cult on the trade-route which followed the valley of the Rhone and in the towns of Narbonensis, which were always open to transmarine influence from their nearness to Massilia; and Aquileia, whence the trade of the Mediterranean found its way into Central Europe, was itself both a centre of Mithraic worship and a stage in its further diffusion. It is thus, *e.g.*, that we must explain the remarkable prevalence of Mithraic monuments in the upper valley of the Adige and on the Brenner route to the Upper Danube, as well as on the North-Eastern route *via* Emona and Poetovio. No province of the empire is richer in remains of Mithraism than Dacia, where all the principal sites—Sarmizegetusa, Apulum, Napoca, Potaissa, etc. (Cumont, ii. 131–139, 280–306, 308–319)—have furnished material of this kind. We can hardly explain this entirely by the influence of the army which occupied Dacia and the neighbouring Danube provinces, and are forced to conclude that among the settlers planted by Trajan in the

[1] Four out of twenty-six, according to Toutain (see below, p. 756a).

[1] It may be noted that an officer of the Seventh Legion dedicated an altar in this sanctuary (*L'Année épigraphique*, 1905, no. 25). The finds have recently been published fully by Pierre Paris (*RA* ii. [1914] 1 ff.).

province and drawn 'ex toto orbe Romano' (Eutrop. viii. 6) were many Orientals who brought with them their native faiths, among which the worship of Mithras soon assumed a commanding position.

7. Geographical and social distribution.—The geographical distribution of the monuments of Mithraism may most easily be grasped by an examination of the map which accompanies Cumont's volumes, upon which the sites, when they have been found, are marked in red. It will be seen at a glance that, except in the places and districts of which mention has already been made, traces of the cult are few and far between. In Greek lands, in Western Gaul, and in Spain, taken together, the sites where its monuments have been found may almost be counted on the fingers. Hence Toutain[1] has argued that the cult of Mithras never became widely diffused in the West, outside the army and certain regions in direct communication with the East, and that the notion that it was at one time not far from achieving the triumph which was reserved for Christianity is much exaggerated. Toutain leaves out of account Rome and Italy—which makes his presentation of the evidence one-sided. But he endeavours to reinforce his argument by a consideration of the social condition of the adherents of Mithraism. He points out with justice that the dedicators of votive sculptures and the builders or restorers of Mithraic sanctuaries are very largely drawn from the official classes and provincial governors, military commanders, or *procuratores*, etc., employed in the civil administration. As early as the age of the Antonines we find *legati* and *tribuni militares* among the votaries of Mithras; in the reign of Commodus, M. Valerius Maximianus, governor of Dacia, dedicates an offering to 'Sol invictus Mithras' (*CIL* iii. 1122=Cumont, ii. 133); under Septimius Severus, C. Julius Castinus, governor of Pannonia, consecrates an altar to Mithras (*CIL* iii. 3480=Cumont, ii. 141), and the number of similar instances is multiplied in the 3rd cent. after Christ, while imperial *procuratores* in Noricum and Dacia follow their example. It would be natural to infer that Mithraism was at least favourably regarded by the government; and, in fact, we learn from the *Historia Augusta* (cap. 9) that Commodus was initiated into the mysteries, while an inscription of the age of the Severi (*CIL* vi. 2271=Cumont, ii. 100) mentions a 'sacerdos invicti Mithrae domus Augustanae,' and the largest Mithræum at present known was discovered in 1912 in the Thermæ of Caracalla; in this was found an inscription in honour of Zeus-Helios-Sarapis-Mithras,[2] and this unusual identification is explained by Caracalla's special devotion to the Egyptian divinity. This imperial patronage goes far to explain the popularity of Mithras-worship in the 3rd cent.; it also accounts for the fact that, though by no means confined to the public services, military and civil, it was mainly found among their members and took no general hold on the population of the western provinces, so that the withdrawal of imperial favour was a fatal blow.

8. Grades of initiation.—Our knowledge of the doctrines and ritual of Mithraism is largely drawn from the inscriptions and monuments discovered in the Mithræa, to the interpretation of which something is contributed by ancient texts, especially those of Christian apologists. The most important of these is a passage of St. Jerome (*Ep.* cvii.), who describes the destruction of a 'cave of Mithras' and the 'monstrous images' used in the initiation of the votaries, who are enumerated as follows: *Corax*, *Gryphus* (MSS *nunphus* or *nymphus*), *miles*, *leo*, *Perses*, *heliodromus*, *pater*. These names are naturally taken to indicate seven grades through which the neophyte passed in succession; and this is confirmed by other texts. The inscriptions found in a Mithræum in Rome (*CIL* vi. 749 ff.=Cumont, ii. 93 f.) mention ceremonies described by the words 'tradiderunt hierocoracica, leontica, persica, heliaca, patrica'; the adjectives clearly correspond with five of the grades mentioned by St. Jerome. We find also 'ostenderunt (*or* tradiderunt) cryfios (chryfios).'[1] The last word seems to be equivalent to *κρύφιος*, and has been substituted for the corrupt *nymphus* in the text of St. Jerome. The title *pater* (or *pater patrum*) for the highest grade is common in inscriptions; and a passage of Porphyry refers as follows to the others:

> τοὺς μὲν μετέχοντας τῶν αὐτῶν ὀργίων μύστας λέοντας καλεῖν, τὰς δὲ γυναῖκας ὑαίνας, τοὺς δὲ ὑπηρετοῦντας κόρακας· ἐπί τε τῶν πατέρων . . . ἀετοὶ γὰρ καὶ ἱέρακες οὗτοι προσαγορεύονται· ὅ τε τὰ λεοντικὰ παραλαμβάνων περιτίθεται παντοδαπὰς ζῴων μορφάς (*de Abstin.* iv. 16).

We infer that the *κόραξ* was a low grade, and that initiation into the mysteries proper began with that of *leo* (cf. τοῖς τὰ λεοντικὰ μυουμένοις [Porph. *de Antro Nymph.* 15]). The mention of women called ὕαιναι stands alone; it has been proposed to read λεαίνας, and some confirmation may be found in the discovery of a tomb at Œa in Tripoli in which a husband and wife were buried and described as *leo* and *lea* (*Comptes rendus de l'acad. des inscriptions*, 1903, p. 357 ff.). For the 'eagles' and 'hawks' independent evidence is not forthcoming, unless two inscriptions from Lycaonia which mention ἀετοί are Mithraic (cf. *Bonner Jahrbücher*, 1902, p. 12). Porphyry, it will be noticed, speaks of the animal disguises worn by the *leones*. In the *Quæstiones veteris et novi testamenti* falsely attributed to St. Augustine (*PL* xxxv. 2348) we read how 'some flap their wings like birds and imitate the voice of the crow; others roar after the manner of lions'; and the passages quoted are strikingly illustrated by a relief found at Konjica, in Bosnia, carved on the reverse of a slab which shows the usual subject of Mithra the bull-slayer (see below).

In the centre of the scene are two figures reclining on a couch, in front of which is a table with four loaves marked with a cross; beside the table are seen a lion and a bucranium. On either side are two figures; on the left a *κόραξ*, *i.e.* a man wearing the mask of a crow, and a 'Persian,' distinguished by his dress; to the right a *leo*, wearing a lion's mask, and a figure the upper portion of which is unfortunately lost. It will be noticed that the *miles* of St. Jerome does not appear in the other sources—though the use of the term in Mithraism is confirmed by a passage of Tertullian (*de Præscr. Hær.* 40) and by the title *miles pius* in two inscriptions from Wiesbaden (*CIL* xiii. 7570, 7571), in Greek στρατιώτης εὐσεβής (inscription of Amasia, *Recueil des inscr. du Pont*, Brussels, 1910, 108). It is possible, therefore, that the mutilated figure of the Konjica relief represents the *cryfius*, and that the *miles*, though he belonged to the rank and file of Mithras's soldiery, was not admitted to partake in the mysteries. He was, however, initiated by a ceremony described by Tertullian (*de Corona*, 15); a crown was set before him, *interposito gladio*, and then placed on his head, but removed by the neophyte, who exclaimed 'Mithras is my crown.'

In the passage previously quoted Tertullian speaks of a soldier of Mithras as 'branded in the forehead'; and the καύσεις μυστικαί of which Gregory of Nazianzus speaks (*Orat.* iv. 70 [*PG* xxxv. 592]) may refer to this. Tertullian (*de Bapt.* 5) also mentions a Mithraic purification 'per lavacrum' resembling the rite of baptism; and it is to be noted that the Mithræa which have been excavated either contain natural springs or have water specially laid on. Of the ceremonies which accompanied the higher degrees of initiation we know little; Porphyry (*loc. cit.*) tells us that the *leo* had both hands and tongue purified with honey, which was also used in the initiation of the *Persa*. In the passage quoted above Gregory of Nazianzus mentions the βάσανοι to which the initiates were sub-

[1] *Les Cultes païens dans l'empire romain*, ii. 144 ff.
[2] *Notizie degli Scavi*, 1912, p. 323.

[1] A relief from Arčer, now at Sofia (*ARW* xv. [1912] pl. i. 4), shows a kneeling figure wearing the 'Phrygian' cap, partly hidden by a veil held by two other figures. Rostowzew (p. 53) explains this with reference to the phrase quoted in the text.

jected; and his commentator Nonnus (*PG* xxxvi. 989, 1009, 1012) enlarges on this topic and speaks of 'eighty punishments' by water and fire, frost, hunger, thirst, and journeyings, in an ascending scale of severity. These may to some extent be imaginary; but it must be remembered that the *Mihir Yasht* (§ 122) speaks of ablutions and stripes. Tertullian (*de Præscr. Hær.* 40) uses the phrase 'imago resurrectionis,' which suggests a simulated death; and the biographer of Commodus tells us that the emperor 'sacra Mithriaca vero homicidio polluit.'[1] Thus the little that we know of the Mithraic rites of initiation shows that they were of a type well known in primitive religion, and carry us back to a stage far earlier than the developed theology of later Iranian times. Nor can we say more of the rites in which the initiates partook; Christian writers found an analogy to the eucharist in the Mithraic communion of bread and water (ἄρτος καὶ ποτήριον ὕδατος [Justin, *Apol.* i. 66], *panis oblatio* [Tert. *loc. cit.*]), which seems to be represented on the Konjica relief.

9. Sanctuaries, ritual, and monuments. — The central act of worship in Mithraism, however, appears to have been the sacrifice of the bull, the prototype of which was the slaying of the bull by Mithra himself, represented in relief in every Mithraic sanctuary. These places of worship were described by the term *spelæum* (*CIL* iii. 4420 = Cumont, ii. 146), for which we also find *crypta* (*CIL* iii. 1096 = Cumont, ii. 132) and *antrum* (*CIL* vi. 754 = Cumont, ii. 94), and were often established in natural caves or grottoes, as, *e.g.*, on the north slope of the Capitol at Rome, beneath the church of Araceli. As a rule, however, the place of the grotto was taken by a subterranean crypt, approached by a stairway; the chapels attached to private houses were naturally placed in cellars—*e.g.*, the Mithræum below the church of San Clemente in Rome. It should be noted that the Mithræa are never of great size, and, where the adherents of the worship were numerous, the number of *spelæa* was multiplied. Thus Ostia possessed five, Aquincum at least four, and Carnuntum three sanctuaries. The more elaborate examples show a fore-court, or *pronaos* (the term is used in *CIL* xiv. 61), leading to a small chamber, whence the staircase descended to the crypt in which the mysteries were celebrated. This was traversed by a central passage, on either side of which were *podia* about six feet broad with inclined surfaces. Whether, as Cumont supposes, the worshippers knelt upon these, or reclined upon them while partaking of the ceremonial banquet, it is hard to say. At the extremity of the crypt, which often took the form of an apse (called *exedra* in *CIL* iii. 1096), was placed the relief of Mithras and the bull, often accompanied by other sculptures, such as figures of Cautes and Cautopates or the lion-headed Kronos.

The symbolism of these monuments is not easy of interpretation, and ancient texts help us little. In the central scene, the type of which (as was mentioned above) was certainly fixed by a Pergamene artist, probably in the 2nd cent. B.C., Mithras, clothed in the conventional costume which in Greek art signified the Oriental, places his left knee on the back of a bull, and, seizing its horn (or muzzle) with the left hand, plunges a knife into its throat.[2] The scene of the action is a cave, the prototype of the *spelæum*, which sometimes contains plants or even trees. A scorpion fastens on the testicles of the dying bull, while a dog, and usually a serpent also, drink the blood which flows from the death-wound. A crow is almost always present, perched either on Mithras's mantle or on the edge of the cave. Finally, we have a significant detail in the ears of corn in which the tail of the bull terminates (or which, in some instances, spring from the wound). In interpreting the scene we must also take into account a second representation with which the reverse of the slab is decorated at Heddernheim (Cumont, ii. pl. viii.). Here Mithras stands beside the body of the slain bull, holding a drinking-horn in his left hand and receiving from the hands of the sun-god a bunch of grapes. On either side are the figures of children holding baskets of fruit; in the background a radiate cap is planted on a pole; and in an upper register we have a scene in which a central figure, unfortunately defaced, is surrounded by animals (dogs, wild boar, sheep, ox, possibly horse). The explanation of these scenes can hardly be doubtful. We read in the *Bundahishn* (esp. xiv. 1) of the bull which was the first creation of Ahura Mazda, and was slain by Ahriman, but through its death gave birth to vegetable life on the earth; from its spinal marrow 'grain grew of fifty-five species, and twelve species of medicinal herbs.' Moreover, its seed was 'carried up to the moon, where it was purified and produced the manifold species of animals' (*ib.* 3). From its blood, again, sprang 'the grape-vine from which they make the wine' (*ib.* 2). Though we cannot definitely trace this cosmogony to earlier Avestan sources, it is indubitably of great antiquity; and the Mithraic monuments offer a remarkable modification of it. Here the central doctrine that the death of the bull was the source of life, both animal and vegetable, remains the same; but the killing of the animal is not the act of the evil spirit, but a sacrifice performed by Mithras himself, probably acting as the minister of Ahura Mazda, whose messenger we may see in the crow.[1] The function of the creatures of Ahriman (scorpion and serpent) is limited to that of endeavouring to nullify the miracle in process. But the significance of the scene was not only cosmological; it was also eschatological, for the new creation to which the Zoroastrian looked forward at the end of time was to be heralded by the sacrifice of a second bull, this time by the 'redeemer' (Saoshyant) (*Bundahishn*, xxx. 25). Nor can we doubt that these myths, like so many others, were interpretations of a rite older than mythology, and that the sacrifice of the bull was in origin intended to promote fertility and ensure the annual renewal of life on the earth, the bull being chosen as the victim on account of his great generative power.

10. Myth.—The myth of which Mithras was the hero and the slaying of the bull the culminating episode can no longer be reconstructed in its details, but many of its episodes are represented on the monuments. The reliefs of the bull-sacrifice are often enclosed in a framework broken up into small panels, on each of which an episode of the myth is shown. The chief of these are the following.

(1) *Birth of Mithras from the rock.*—On several monuments the figure of the god is seen emerging from a rock, the 'petra genetrix' of several inscriptions (*CIL* iii. 8679 = Cumont, ii. 139, etc.); cf. the expressions θεὸς ἐκ πέτρας (Firmicus, *de Err. prof. relig.* 20), πετρογενὴς Μίθρας (Lyd. *de Mens.* iii. 26), etc. The scene is sometimes completed by the addition of a shepherd or shepherds who witness the miraculous birth.

(2) *Mithras and the tree.*—On some monuments the figure of Mithras is seen half-concealed by a tree from which he seems to be emerging, or, again, which he is stripping of its foliage. The first might be considered as a variant of the birth-scheme, if it did not occur on the same monuments; in any case, it seems to show that Mithras was on one side a vegetation-spirit.

(3) *The archer and the rock.*—Mithras, in Oriental costume,

[1] *Vita Commodi*, ix. 6. The statement of Socrates (*HE* iii. 2) that human sacrifices were offered in Mithraism is unworthy of credence.

[2] In the best examples Mithras wears an expression of pathos, as though he were the unwilling instrument of heaven; A. Loisy (*RHR* lxvi. [1913] 538) suggests that this is because god and victim are, in a sense, one; but this seems fanciful. The 'Alexandroid' type used by the artist was a 'romantic' creation.

[1] For the crow in Zoroastrian literature cf. *Bundahishn*, xix. 22.

discharges an arrow at a rock, from which a stream gushes out; a kneeling figure receives the water in his hands or refreshes his throat. Sometimes a suppliant kneels before Mithras and implores him to perform the miracle.

(4) *Mithras and the sun.*—Here there is a series of scenes, of which the following are the most important: (*a*) investiture of the sun by Mithras; the sun-god kneels before Mithras, who places the radiate crown on his head with the left hand, while in the right hand he holds an indistinct object, probably a drinking-horn; (*b*) alliance of Mithras and the sun; the two figures are represented clasping the right hand in token of friendship; (*c*) Mithras conveyed in the sun's chariot across the ocean, represented as a reclining figure in the style of Greek art; (*d*) banquet of Mithras and the sun (sometimes with other guests); they recline on a couch, generally holding drinking-horns, and before them is a small table with viands.

(5) *Mithras and the bull.*—Though the slaying of the bull is never found except as the principal scene, other episodes of the legend are often used in the decoration of the side-panels. The following are the chief: (*a*) and (*b*) the bull in a boat, the bull issuing from a gabled building; these two scenes, when found on the same monument, are always in juxtaposition; in one case (a relief found at Saarburg in Lorraine) two figures in Oriental costume are setting fire to the building; (*c*) the capture of the bull; this is represented in a series of scenes, which display, first the bull at pasture, then Mithras seizing it by the horns, vaulting on its back and riding on it, and eventually either carrying it on his shoulders or, more often, dragging it by the hind-legs, while its fore-feet hang on the ground; the last scene seems to be described by the word *transitus* (*CIL* iii. 14354, 27 and 28).

(6) *Scenes in which Mithras takes no part.*—These are either simple representations of other divinities in the form given to them by Greek art, such as the unexplained head of the Osterburken relief (perhaps = Kronos), the figures of the Earth-goddess, of Atlas, of Oceanus, and the three Fates, or scenes in which Zeus is shown, either receiving the thunderbolt as the symbol of power at the hands of Kronos or in combat with the giants.

No successful attempt has been made to explain the series of representations just described; the last class, no doubt, clothe in Greek form conceptions derived from Persian sources, the identification of which can at best be a matter of guess-work.[1] We can, however, be certain that, whatever the original content of the Mithraic legends, it had been profoundly modified by the astral religion of Babylonia. Mithras, as we saw, was by origin a god of the heavenly light; and it is possible that his birth from the rock may symbolize either the appearance of the dawn on the mountain-tops or the effulgence of light from the vault of heaven conceived as a solid dome. At any rate, there can be no doubt as to the meaning of the two torch-bearers, dressed in the same Oriental costume as Mithras himself, who regularly appear on either side of the scene of the bull-slaying, and are also found at the birth of Mithra. One holds his torch aloft, the other lowers it, and these actions clearly symbolize the rising and setting of the sun,[2] so that Mithras and the torch-bearers form a triad hinted at in the phrase Μίθρας τριπλάσιος (pseudo-Dionys. Areop. *Ep.* vii. 2).[3] But the monuments show that the heavenly phenomena played a still more important part in Mithraism. Mention has been made of the lion-headed figure of human form, wrapped in the coils of a serpent, of which a large number have been found in Mithræa. The figure often has four wings and holds in its hands a pair of keys, or a sceptre and thunderbolt. The symbolism of the figure would be easy of comprehension even apart from the fact that we find the signs of the zodiac engraved on its body in some instances. It represents eternal time, the *zrvan akarana* which became the chief divinity in one of the theological systems that sprang up in the bosom of later Zoroastrianism, and seems to have been described in Greek as Κρόνος, though we have no direct proof of this.[4]

[1] Explanations differing in some respects from those of Cumont are given by Toutain, *RHR* xlv. [1902] 145 ff.

[2] But see also § 9 *sub fin.*

[3] No explanation can be given of the names Cautes and Cautopates applied, as the inscriptions show, to these figures; that they were by-forms of Mithras himself is proved by the full expression 'Deo M(ithræ) C(auto)p(ati) S(oli) I(nvicto),' *e.g. CIL* vii. 650 = Cumont, ii. 161.

[4] F. Legg (*PSBA* xxxiv. [1912] 138 ff.) prefers to see in this figure a representation of Ahriman, whose worship by Mithraists is attested by dedications 'deo Arimanio' (Cumont, ii. 98, 141). A mutilated relief at York (Cumont, ii. 393) seems to represent this figure with some variation from the usual type, and the inscription (also mutilated) contains the name ARIMANIV(S).

The zodiac is also commonly found either as a framework enclosing the scene of the bull-slaying or, as in most of the reliefs from the *limes Germanicus*, as a border to the upper edge of the *spelæum* in which this takes place. In addition to this, the more elaborate reliefs are almost always decorated with busts of sun and moon, while many also exhibit the planets, or symbols which represent them.[1] We also find the seasons and the winds; and it is beyond doubt that the lion,[2] the *crater*,[3] and the serpent must be combined with these last as emblems of the elements. It may be added that the sea (*oceanus*) and heaven (*cælus*) are both mentioned on a stele from Heddernheim (Cumont, ii. 156). It is clear, therefore, that in the Mithraic mysteries a complete system of cosmography was taught; nor can there be any doubt of its application to the soul and its destiny. The doctrine of the microcosm, which pervades all the speculations of later antiquity, was popularized by the Stoics, especially by Posidonius, and, together with the astrological doctrines which accompanied it, was derived from Oriental sources. It formed part of the common stock of teaching imparted to the votaries of the various 'other-worldly' religions (of which Mithraism was one) which became diffused throughout the West from the beginning of the Christian era onwards. We should be able to give a more definite account of Mithraic eschatology if we could assume that the 'Mithrasliturgie' published by Dieterich from the Paris magical papyrus (*Bibl. Nat. Suppl. Grec.* 574) deserved that name. This document, committed to writing about A.D. 300, is in its present form part of the stock-in-trade of an Egyptian magician, and is interspersed with *voces magicæ* and supplemented by directions for its use in the *séances* of this practitioner. The question is whether the compiler made use of a genuine Mithraic document; this is suggested by the opening words, which may be translated as follows:

> 'Be gracious unto me, Providence and Fortune, to me, who am writing down these, the first of all traditional mysteries, and grant immortality to my only child, an initiate worthy of this mighty power, which the Great God, the Sun, Mithras, bade his archangel transmit to me, that I alone, an eagle, might soar through the heavens and behold all things.'

It is to be noted that this private revelation made by the initiator to his 'only child' resembles those of the *Corpus Hermeticum* (the product of an Egyptian school of theosophy) rather than the ritual of a community; also that the 'eagle' is introduced into the text by a conjectural emendation of Dieterich. In the revelation itself we find nothing that distinguishes Mithraism from other theosophies, and a good deal which is definitely Egyptian; Dieterich lays stress on the 'golden shoulder of the ox, which is the Great Bear,' which he would recognize in the object held by Mithras in the investiture of the sun as represented on a relief from Virunum (Cumont, ii. 336, fig. 213); but the identification is extremely doubtful; other examples of the same subject show nothing at all resembling an ox's shoulder, and in any case the conception is specifically Egyptian. On the whole, therefore, it is safer to regard the papyrus as

[1] On a relief from Apulum (Cumont, ii. 311) we find a series of the following four objects: (*a*) sacrificial knife, (*b*) altar, (*c*) *pileus*, (*d*) tree, repeated seven times. These symbols represent the elements, and their repetition indicates that each planet contained all four.

[2] 'Ardentis naturæ sacramenta leones Mithræ philosophantur' (Tert. *adv. Marc.* i. 13).

[3] παρὰ τῷ Μίθρᾳ ὁ κρατὴρ ἀντὶ τῆς πηγῆς τέτακται (Porph. *de Antro Nymph.* 18).

nothing more than a syncretistic product.[1] It is likely enough, however, that the ascent of the soul through the seven spheres was taught in the Mithraic mysteries; Celsus (*ap.* Origen, *c. Cels.* vi. 22) explicitly tells us of a 'ladder with seven gates' made of the seven metals assigned to the planets which was shown to the initiates; Porphyry, quoting a certain Eubulus, who attributes to Zoroaster the doctrine that the 'cave' was a symbol of the universe, of which Mithras was the creator, speaks of it as containing *κατὰ συμμέτρους ἀποστάσεις σύμβολα τῶν κοσμικῶν στοιχείων καὶ κλιμάτων*;[2] and it can be no accident that in one of the Mithræa at Ostia six semi-circles are traced on the floor of the central passage, while six planets are represented on the walls of the *podia* and the signs of the zodiac on their upper surface (Cumont, ii. 243–245). Beyond this all is speculation; and Porphyry himself probably knew little more than we do, for he mentions (*de Abstin.* iv. 16) as his chief authority on the mysteries a certain Pallas, who explained the animal disguises worn by the initiates either as symbols of the zodiacal constellations or as shadowing forth the doctrine of metempsychosis (which Eubulus also stated to be Mithraic). It is not necessary to repeat the astrological speculations, confused in themselves, by means of which Porphyry endeavours to interpret the symbols of Mithraism; but there can be no doubt that the all-pervading influence of astrolatry affected Mithraic doctrines. Thus we sometimes find that the figures of Cautes and Cautopates hold the symbols of the bull and the scorpion, the signs which mark the beginning of spring and winter.

11. Final phase.—In its final phase Mithraism was absorbed into the 'solar pantheism' which supplied Roman society in the 3rd and 4th centuries with a theology reconciled with contemporary philosophy and science, and became, under Aurelian, the official religion of the Roman State.[3] 'Sol invictus,' as the ruler of the universe was called in a phrase of Oriental associations, was represented on earth by the emperor, and his identification with Mithras was far easier than many others which syncretism was able to effect. Thus 'invictus Mithras,' 'deus invictus Mithras,' or (in full) 'deus Sol invictus Mithras' became the commonest title of the god. It was with this modification that Mithraism bade fair during the last quarter of the 3rd cent. A.D. to become a world-religion. The State-cult of Sol was no more fitted than the worship of the emperor to satisfy the religious instinct; but Mithraism could supply the defect through its mystical teaching and its ties of brotherhood; and it was, besides, *par excellence* the religion of the army and the official classes. In A.D. 307 Diocletian, Galerius, and Licinius, meeting in conference at Carnuntum, dedicated an altar to Mithras, 'fautori imperii sui,' in one of the oldest centres of his worship in the empire; but the victory of Constantine dispossessed him in favour of a rival creed, which had struck its roots more deeply in those populations of the empire which were less immediately in touch with the legions and the official hierarchy. It became clear that the vogue of Mithraism was in large measure an artificial one, created by the powerful machinery of the imperial government. When Mithraism sank from a position of privilege to one of toleration, and before long became an object of persecution, its days were numbered. It lingered on, on the one hand, in certain less civilized outposts of empire and in the Alpine valleys, while, on the other, it became the symbol of a lost cause to the group of cultured pagans which maintained the defence of paganism in the senate-house. The emperor Julian, whose oration, *εἰς βασιλέα Ἥλιον*, is a characteristic exposition of 'solar theology,' was a votary of Mithras; but his attempt to revive the defunct creed of the pagan emperors and to give it an organization resembling that of Christianity was still-born. After his death persecution began in earnest, and, as far as the evidence enables us to judge, the destruction of Mithræa was wide-spread during the reign of Gratian. The letter of St. Jerome quoted above, which enumerates the seven Mithraic grades, describes such an act performed in Rome by Gracchus, *præfectus urbi* in A.D. 377. The latest inscriptions in which Mithras is named are those of the group of senators belonging to the society of which Macrobius's *Saturnalia* gives us a picture. Vettius Agorius Prætextatus († A.D. 385) is called 'pater sacrorum' (*CIL* vi. 1779=Cumont, ii. 95) and 'pater patrum' (*CIL* vi. 1778=Cumont, ii. 95), and these inscriptions are the latest datable evidences of the cult. The measures of Theodosius gave the death-blow to the practice of pagan worship; and the Mithræum at Saarburg in Lorraine was destroyed in his reign.

12. Relations with other cults.—Mithraism lent itself readily to alliances with other worships, especially those of female divinities, which supplied what it was unable to offer to women; and it seems to have been specially associated with the cult of the Magna Mater. We find their sanctuaries adjoining each other at Ostia and on the Saalburg; dedications are commonly made simultaneously to both divinities; and the *taurobolium*, which (whatever its origin) was certainly attached to the worship of Magna Mater in the West, received an added significance when interpreted in terms of Mithraism, in which the life-giving blood of the bull became the pledge of immortality. In the Danube region a curious by-form of Mithraism is revealed to us by a series of reliefs and leaden plaques which have been interpreted by Rostowzew in the article (in Russian) quoted above. Here a female goddess, whose attribute is a fish, no doubt a local derivative of Anāhita, is accompanied by two mounted figures, in whom we must recognize a duplication of the horseman Mithras found on the coasts of the Black Sea.

LITERATURE.—The great work of **Franz Cumont**, *Textes et monuments figurés relatifs aux mystères de Mithra*, 2 vols., Brussels, 1896–99, supersedes all previous treatises, a list of which he gives in vol. i. p. xxi ff.; he has also published an abridgment of his larger work under the title *Les Mystères de Mithra*3, Paris, 1913, in which the bibliography of the subject is brought up to date; the earlier editions of this work have been translated into English and German. Among recent works the most important are **A. Dieterich**, *Eine Mithrasliturgie*2 (ed. R. Wünsch), Paris and Berlin, 1910, and **J. Toutain**, *Les Cultes païens dans l'empire romain*, Paris, 1908–11, vol. ii. ch. iv., 'Le Culte de Mithra.' Other works and articles dealing with special points are referred to in the course of the article. For the Vedic Mitra see **A. A. Macdonell**, *Vedic Mythology*, Strassburg, 1897, §§ 13, 44, and authorities there cited, especially **A. Hillebrandt**, *Varuṇa und Mitra*, Breslau, 1877; **H. Oldenberg**, *Die Religion des Veda*, Berlin, 1894; **A. Eggers**, *Der arische Gott Mitra*, Dorpat, 1894. For the Avesta Mithra see especially **M. N. Dhalla**, *Zoroastrian Theology*, New York, 1914, pp. 103–111.

H. STUART JONES.

MOAB.—The name 'Moab,' like that of the neighbouring peoples, Israel, Edom, Ammon, Aram, etc., appears to have been the name of a race rather than of a district, for, as G. A. Smith has pointed out (*EBi*, art. 'Moab,' § 1), in Nu

[1] We do not even knew what was the language officially used in the Mithraic communities. The inscriptions are naturally for the most part in Latin. Some Persian words occur—*e.g.*, *nabarze* (usually connected with Pers. *nabard*, *nabardah*, 'courageous'; this etymology, proposed by G. Kuun, *Arch. epigr. Mitteilungen*, vi. [1882] 107, is uncertain because of the Pahlavi form, *n(i)parṭ*, 'battle'; Persian was scarcely spoken as early as the Mithraic period), as an epithet of Mithras, and *nama sebesio*, where *nama* probably='praise' (cf. Cumont, i. 314, note 2).

[2] *de Antro Nymph.* 6.

[3] For this see esp. Cumont, 'La Théologie solaire,' *Mémoires présentés à l'acad. des inscriptions*, xii. [1909].

21$^{11-15}$ (cited by F. Brown, S. R. Driver, and C. A. Briggs, *A Heb. and Eng. Lexicon of the Old Testament*, Oxford, 1906, p. 555, as evidence that the name Moab=' territory of Moab'), 'in v.^{13} Moab is parallel to the Gentilic Amorite ; in v.^{15} also it is the people.' The derivation and meaning of the name are unknown. The etymology מֵאָבִי, 'from my father,' given in Gn 19^{37} (LXX), which doubtless gave rise to the malicious story of Moab's origin, is merely popular. Since Moab and Ammon are represented as related to Israel through Lot, Abraham's nephew, whereas Esau is Jacob's twin brother, we may conclude that at the time when these stories took shape the Israelites considered that the Moabites and Ammonites, though of kindred stock, were by no means so closely related to them as Edom. Moab is said to be descended from Lot's elder daughter (Gn 19^{37}); therefore it was probably supposed that the settlement of Moab preceded that of Ammon. Whether the Moabites themselves possessed any tradition of a migration from Mesopotamia may well be doubted, the statements of Gn 11^{31} 12$^{4f.}$ being perhaps mere inferences from the belief that the Israelites were connected with Mesopotamia. Since, however, the expression 'children of Lot' (Dt 2$^{9.19}$, Ps 83^{8}) scarcely rests directly upon Gn 19$^{37f.}$, Lot was probably more prominent in early times than the OT as a whole would imply ; but whether the Moabites and Ammonites regarded themselves as 'children of Lot,' or succeeded them in the districts which they occupied, cannot be determined. The late antiquarian note in Dt 2^{10} implies that the population of Moab was not altogether homogeneous, while the place-names clearly show Canaanite influence.

The constant boundary of Moab on the west was the Dead Sea and the Jordan ; the north, east, and south frontiers varied from time to time. Probably the Wādy el-Ḥasy represents the farthest extent of Moabite territory to the south and the Ḥajj road that to the east. The Wādy Nimrīn, some 8 miles north of the Dead Sea, may be taken as the extreme northern limit (see G. A. Smith, *op. cit.* § 2).

Beyond the mere mention of Moab as included in the conquests of Ramses II. nothing is known of its history before the period of the Israelite invasion of Palestine. According to Nu 21$^{21-31}$, shortly before the arrival of Israel, an Amorite king, Sihon, seized the Moabite territory north of the Arnon. What circumstances determined the Israelite invasion of Palestine from the east is not certainly known, but it is not unlikely that the Israelites attacked Sihon in response to an appeal from the Moabites (as Wellhausen, *EBr*^{9}, art. 'Israel,' has suggested), and that it was only after the defeat of Sihon that the Moabites discovered that their allies had no intention of giving up the fruits of their victory. There is certainly no valid reason for disputing the general historicity of the tradition. The statement that Reuben was the first-born son of Israel naturally implies that Reuben was the first tribe to obtain a settlement, while the assignment of Moabite territory to Reuben, and the belief that Moses died and was buried there, as well as the tradition that the Israelites crossed the Jordan near Jericho, all point to a belief that N. Moab was occupied at least for a time by Israel. After the invasion of W. Palestine, however, the Israelites were disintegrated and engaged in a perpetual conflict with the Canaanites, Philistines, etc. (see art. ISRAEL), with the result that the Moabites were able to recover their own. The tribe of Reuben, in spite of its reputation for bravery, was nearly exterminated (Gn 49$^{3f.}$, Dt 33^{6}), and Moabite rule was extended even over the Jordan valley west of the river. For a time, indeed, Moabite aggression was checked by Ehud, but we find Israel and Moab again at war during the reign of David, and perhaps also during that of Saul.[1] But, although David's treatment of Moab is said to have been drastic enough, Moab was not incorporated in Israel. The Moabites merely 'became servants to David, and brought presents' (2 S 8^{2}). It may be inferred that Reuben had already been nearly exterminated or practically absorbed in Moab. Whether Moabite influence was strong in Jerusalem in the days of Solomon, notwithstanding 1 K 11$^{1-8.33}$, is very doubtful ; Solomon's idolatry is described in terms of a later age. It was probably during his reign or that of Rehoboam that Moab recovered independence.

Under the vigorous rule of Omri the Moabites again felt the hand of Israel. According to the inscription of Mesha (found at Dîbān [Heb. Dîbhôn] in 1868, commonly called the Moabite Stone), the period of Israelite domination occupied forty years.[2] It is not necessary to suppose that Mesha's inscription is earlier than the events recorded in 2 K 3, for it is clear from that account that the campaign of the allied kings was unsuccessful. Moreover, an ancient king in recording his achievements was naturally silent about his reverses.

The independence which Moab recovered under Mesha was perhaps lost again in the reign of Jeroboam II. It is, however, impossible to speak with certainty on this point, for the south limit of Jeroboam's kingdom is given as 'the sea of the Arabah' (2 K 14^{25}), and may refer only to the north of the Dead Sea. For 'the sea of the Arabah' Amos (6^{14}) speaks of 'the brook of the Arabah,' which has been identified with 'the brook of the '*Ărābhîm*' or 'willows' (Is 15^{7}), which by some has been identified with the Wādy el-Ḥasy. These identifications are, however, by no means certain, and the order of names in the preceding verses of Is 15 suggests that 'the brook of the willows' is to be sought in the north of Moab. Amos (2^{3}) mentions a judge of Moab in lieu of a king, and it has accordingly been argued that at the time Moab possessed no king of its own ; but this cannot be decided with certainty.

During the Assyrian period Moab appears to have shown more prudence than the Israelite kingdom in bowing to the storm. Tiglath Pileser exacted tribute, and, although in 711 B.C. Sargon mentions Moab in conjunction with Philistia, Judah, and Edom as having formed an alliance with Egypt, Moab probably avoided an invasion by a timely submission. It continued subject to Sennacherib, Esar-haddon, and Assurbanipal, and, according to 2 K 24^{2}, furnished troops to Nebuchadrezzar against Jerusalem. Doubtless in Moab as in Judah there was throughout a party bent on regaining the national independence, and at the beginning of the reign of Zedekiah of Judah (Jer 27) this party appears to have been in power. Yet no actual revolt from Nebuchadrezzar seems to have taken place, and Moab afforded an asylum to fugitive Jews (Jer 40^{11}). It is not improbable that after the destruction of Jerusalem the policy

1 The summary of Saul's wars (1 S 14^{47}) bears such a strong resemblance to that of David's (2 S 8) that it may be doubted whether there was any definite tradition of a campaign of Saul against Moab. Hostilities between Saul and Moab would not indeed be inconsistent with 1 S 22$^{3f.}$, and David, when he succeeded to the throne, would at once stand in a different relation to the king of Moab from that which he had occupied as a rebel against Saul.

2 A discussion of the way in which this statement is to be harmonized with the Biblical chronology lies outside the scope of this article. It is to be noted that, although by 'the son of Omri' Mesha probably means Ahab, the expression would not preclude a later successor (see W. H. Bennett, *The Moabite Stone*, pp. 20–22).

of Moab coincided with that of the king of Ammon, who apparently intended by the murder of Gedaliah to compel Judah to join a confederacy against the Chaldæans.

Moab was menaced, however, by a danger even more formidable than that from Assyria or Babylonia: east and south the country was exposed to invaders from the desert, and Ezekiel ($25^{8f.}$) already perceived the coming disaster. The criticism of Jeremiah (48), which describes the devastation of Moab, is extremely difficult; the chapter, however, appears to be to a great extent a cento of various earlier passages, and this in itself implies a late date. Is $15–16^{12}$, which is used by the author of Jer 48, notwithstanding the corrupt condition of the text and later modifications, gives a clearer picture of Moab's disaster. Here it is evident, if we argue from the names of places which may be identified with tolerable certainty, that the invader advances from south or south-east to north or north-west, and therefore cannot be the Assyrian, Chaldæan, or Persian, but must be a foe from the desert.[1] With this invasion the national existence of Moab came to an end, though Jewish writers long continued to mention the country by the old name (Is 25^{10}, Ps 60^8 83^6 108^9). It is remarkable that the name Moab does not occur in 1 Maccabees. It is found, however, in Dn 11^{41}, and Josephus (*Ant.* I. xi. 5, XIII. xiii. 5, xv. 4) uses the term 'Moabites' to denote the Nabatæan Arabs.

The language of Moab, as we know from Mesha's inscription, was Hebrew, differing only dialectically from the language of the OT. It is, indeed, not impossible that what we regard as peculiarities of Moabite speech once belonged also to the spoken Hebrew of W. Palestine. Although portions of the OT are earlier than the 9th cent. B.C., they were probably long preserved in an oral form, in which case peculiarities of dialect may well have been modified.

The land of Moab affords many proofs even in these days of its former fertility and prosperity. The OT has several references to the cities of Moab, many of which are named, and mentions its vineyards as well as its sheep. Being situated off the direct line of communication between Egypt and the great Asiatic empires, it was less liable than W. Palestine to be made a battlefield, though doubtless there was constant need of warding off the attacks of dwellers in the wilderness. On the whole, however, Moab seems to have had a far more peaceful history than Israel. In the words of Jer 48^{11}, 'Moab had been at ease from his youth, and had settled on his lees, and had not been emptied from vessel to vessel, neither had he gone into captivity.'

The religion of Moab presents many parallels to the popular religion of Israel in pre-Exilic times. There is no evidence, however, that any great Moabite prophets, if such existed, could point, as did the Israelite prophets, to a tradition of purer religion in the past. Like Israel, Moab had taken possession of a land containing stone circles (in OT language, *gilgāls*) and other primitive monuments, and it is probable that in the land of Moab, as in W. Palestine, some of these were adapted to the worship of the later strata of population. From the occurrence of such names as Baal-Meon and Baal-Peor it may be inferred that the pre-Moabite religion of the land resembled the pre-Israelite religion of W. Palestine, and was in fact Canaanite. This inference is confirmed by the occurrence of the curious compound 'Ashtar-Chemosh' (Moabite Stone, line 17); for Ashtar is probably a masculine form of the name familiar to us as Ashtoreth, and

[1] See R. H. Kennett, *The Composition of the Book of Isaiah*, London, 1910, p. 34 f.

the combination of it with Chemosh suggests that some ancient sanctuary of Ashtar or Ashtoreth had been appropriated by Chemosh, just as the ancient sanctuaries of Canaan in W. Palestine came to be considered sanctuaries of Jahweh. We know both from the OT and from the Moabite Stone that Chemosh was the national god of Moab exactly as Jahweh was the national God of Israel. Indeed, the Moabite conception of Chemosh appears to have coincided with the ordinary Israelite conception of Jahweh. The name Chemosh appears compounded in proper names precisely as the name Jahweh. Thus Mesha's father's name was Chemosh in combination with some word which has been variously read as *melekh* and *gad*; a Chemosh-nadab (cf. the Israelite name Jonadab) paid tribute to Sennacherib; and the name Chemosh-yaḥī (cf. the Israelite Jehiah) is inscribed on a gem found near Beirūt (*EBi*, art. 'Chemosh'). Mesha speaks of Chemosh in precisely the same terms as an Israelite of his day might have used in speaking of Jahweh, and in Nu 21^{29} the Moabites are called 'the people of Chemosh' and also his 'sons' and 'daughters.' Evidence of the existence of other cults in pre-Moabite times may be found in the occurrence of such a name as Nebo, but there is no reason for supposing that such worship continued among the Moabites. The name Dawdah, or Dawdoh, occurs on the Moabite Stone (line 12) apparently as a divine name; but, since Ataroth, where the altar-hearth of Dawdoh was seized, was Gadite, the name throws no light on Moabite religion. Whatever the worship of Chemosh may have been before the permanent settlement of Moab, it is extremely probable that it was thenceforth largely intermingled with Canaanite elements. The OT makes it abundantly clear that the worship of Jahweh was tainted in precisely the same way, and Nu 25 affords no evidence that Moab was worse than Israel in this respect; only, whereas, by the 6th cent. B.C., Israelite religion had to a considerable extent been purged of the grosser Canaanite elements, that of Moab remained unreformed. Besides religious prostitution, indications of the prevalence of drunkenness in Moab have been found in Gn $19^{32ff.}$, Jer 48^{26}; and, having regard to the references to vine-culture, this is not improbable, though the Israelites were scarcely in a position to throw stones. It is related (2 K 3^{27}) that Mesha, when hard pressed by Israel, sacrificed his son, and we may therefore assume that human sacrifice was a definite feature of Moabite religion. Human sacrifice, not only of the infant first-born, but on occasion of other victims also, was common in Israel down to the 7th cent. B.C. Mesha's sacrifice of his son should probably be compared, not with 2 K 16^3, Mic 6^7, for in the case of Ahaz probably only the ordinary offering of the infant first-born is meant, but rather with Jg $11^{30f.}$ Cf. also Gn 22, 2 S 21^9, 1 K 16^{34}. Further evidence of the general agreement of Moabite religion with that of Israel is to be found in Mesha's boast (Moabite Stone, line 17) that he has banned or made tabu the population of Nebo.

The danger to Israel of intimate intercourse with a people closely akin in race, speaking the same language, and holding religious ideas similar to those of which the prophets had so earnestly laboured to rid Israel, was clearly perceived by the Israelite reformers, and will partly account for the stringent law in Dt 23^3, though political considerations may also have dictated this.

LITERATURE.—See the excellent articles on 'Moab' in *HDB* and *EBi*; also W. H. Bennett, *The Moabite Stone*, Edinburgh, 1911, with the bibliography there given (p. 64).

R. H. KENNETT.

MOCHI.—See CHAMĀRS.

MODERATION. — Cicero in an interesting passage expresses some hesitation as to the proper Lat. equivalent of the Gr. word σώφρων:

'Veri etiam simile illud est, qui sit temperans, quem Graeci σώφρονα appellant, eamque virtutem σωφροσύνην vocant, quam soleo equidem tum temperantiam, tum moderationem appellare, nonnunquam etiam modestiam; sed haud scio an recte ea virtus frugalitas appellari possit' (*Tusc. Quæst.* iii. 8).[1]

He proceeds to describe the virtue in question as follows:

'Eius videtur proprium, motus animi appetentis regere et sedare, semperque adversantem libidini, moderatam in omni re servare constantiam.'

Moderation, according to this view, is a part of temperance. If temperance consists in self-control in regard to the pleasures of sense, moderation is self-control exercised in less difficult spheres. Limitation (*modus, moderatio*) is, of course, a feature in all virtue; this idea has a long history in the philosophy of Greece, and takes formal shape in Aristotle's doctrine of 'the mean' which gives expression to the peculiarly Greek notion that virtue in its essence means 'harmony, grace, and beauty in action' (see A. Grant, *The Ethics of Aristotle*², London, 1866, vol. i. essay iv.).[2] The word 'moderation,' however, is in Christian ethics specially assigned to the virtue which 'in least things sets the limit.' If temperance is concerned with strong passions, moderation controls those which are less vehement. Such, at any rate, is the view of Aquinas in his discussion of *modestia* (*Summa*, II. ii. 160).

Following the guidance of Aquinas, we find that 'moderation' is chiefly concerned with four matters: (1) the desire of excellence or superiority; (2) the desire of knowledge; (3) the outward actions concerned with the conduct of life, business, and recreation, work and rest, etc.; (4) apparel, furniture, and the external apparatus of life.

Each of these points is fully discussed by Aquinas in II. ii. 161–169.

(1) As regards the desire of superiority, the virtue which moderates it and regulates it is humility (*q.v.*).

(2) The virtuous control of the desire of knowledge is called by Aquinas *studiositas* as opposed to a form of excess which he calls *curiositas* (cf. Aug. *Conf.* X. xxxv. 54). Little needs to be added to the discussion in the *Summa* (II. ii. 166, 167). We may, however, call attention to a fine passage in Bernard (*in Cant.* xxxvi. 3), who points out that in 1 Co 8² St. Paul 'non probat multa scientem, si sciendi modum nescierit.' Christian moderation, he says in effect, will prescribe the limitations under which knowledge should be pursued, in respect of the choice of subjects, the degree of zeal, and the purpose of the student. He lays great stress on the question of motive. Those who wish to know merely for the sake of knowing give way to 'turpis curiositas.'[3] Those who pursue knowledge 'ut aedificent' are guided by charity; those who seek it 'ut aedificentur,' by prudence (cf. T. Wilson, 'Maxims of Piety and Morality,' no. 429 [*Works*, Oxford, 1847–63, v. 423]).

(3) Moderation in the matter of work and recreation and other corporal actions and movements is discussed in *Summa*, II. ii. 168. What Aquinas says practically amounts to this—that man's external behaviour is to be consistent with his dignity as a reasonable being and with the claims made upon him as a member of a community. What St. Paul means to imply in the words σεμνός and κόσμιος is here in point (1 Ti 3²·⁴), as to which Trench (*Synonyms of the NT*, Cambridge, 1854, § xcii.) draws the following distinction:

'Whatever there may be implied in κόσμιος,[1] . . . something more is involved in σεμνός. If the κόσμιος orders himself well in that earthly πολιτεία, of which he is a support and an ornament, the σεμνός has a grace and dignity not lent him from earth; but which he owes to that higher citizenship which is also his,' etc.

Aquinas deals at length with the question of recreation, but says little as to the duty of moderation in work. This point is one which has its importance for us owing to the conditions of modern industrial life. It has been said of the Anglo-Saxon race that 'an excess of industry,' 'intemperate labour,' is one of its most prominent characteristics (A. Wylie, *Labour, Leisure, and Luxury*, new ed., London, 1887, p. 19). Christian moderation implies such self-restraint in the matter of labour as will give fair play to the faculties, spiritual and mental, which are not absorbed in the business of life (on this point W. Law writes suggestively in his *Serious Call*¹⁰, London, 1772, ch. iv.). On the other hand, pleasure-worship is a more obvious peril of our time. In every class there are multitudes who are 'lovers of pleasures more than lovers of God' (2 Ti 3⁴), and the result is seen in a wide-spread enfeeblement of will and conscience. Recreation is, of course, a duty which we owe to our nature—a duty distinctly implied in the Fourth Commandment, and there is a virtue concerned with the due regulation of the natural desire for relief from labour.

'Ludendi etiam est quidam modus retinendus' (Cic. *de Off.* i. 29; cf. 34).

We can scarcely on this point improve upon the maxim of Aristotle that in determining the right mean in such matters tact alone (ἐπιδεξιότης) can decide, *i.e.* a sense of fitness trained by exercise and reflexion.[2] Aquinas points out that, as there can be sinful excess in the matter of amusement, so there may be a wrong defect, for a man in social intercourse must 'show himself friendly' (Pr 18²⁴).

'It is contrary to reason for a man to make himself irksome to others, taking no pains to please them and even hindering their pleasures' (*Summa*, II. ii. 168. 4 resp.).

Still, since amusement is to be sought with a view to labour (Arist. *Eth. Nic.* x. 6. 6: παίζειν ὅπως σπουδάζῃ), happiness does not consist in amusement, and to make a serious business of it is 'foolish and very childish' (*ib.*). Christian *tact* in these matters was what the Puritans of the 17th cent. lacked. They were credited with the opinion that 'no honest mirth or recreation is lawful or tolerable in our religion' (see the *Declaration* of Charles I. of 18th Oct. 1633, which may be found in H. Gee and W. J. Hardy, *Documents illustrative of Eng. Church Hist.*, London, 1896, p. 528 ff.). The Puritan, says J. R. Green, lacked 'all sense of measure and proportion in common matters.'[3] John Bunyan's sin which 'he could not let go' was 'a love of hockey and of dancing on the village green.' It was in the midst of 'a game of cat' that the converting voice 'did suddenly dart' into his soul (Green, v. 103 f.).

(4) The virtue of moderation finally finds scope in the *minutiæ* of external apparel, furniture, and other conveniences of life (cf. Cic. *de Off.* i. 39: 'eadem mediocritas ad omnem usum cultumque vitae transferenda est'; see also i. 35, and cf. Basil, *Hom. de Humilitate*, vii., and Ambrose, *de*

[1] Cf. *Orat. pro Deiot.* ix. 26: 'Ego frugalitatem, id est, modestiam et temperantiam, virtutem esse maximam iudico' (quoted by Aug. *de Beata Vita*, 31). Ambrose, in *de Off. Min.* i. 43, treats moderation and temperance as synonymous.

[2] Cf. Aug. *de Nat. Boni*, 3; Aquinas, *Summa*, II. ii. 141. 7.

[3] Cf. Seneca, *Ep.* lxxxviii. 36: 'Plus scire quam sit satis, intemperantiae genus est.'

[1] Theodoret (on 1 Ti 3²) remarks that the word κόσμιος implies good behaviour in voice, appearance, and gait, ὥστε καὶ διὰ τοῦ σώματος φαίνεσθαι τὴν τῆς ψυχῆς σωφροσύνην.

[2] The virtue concerned with recreation, according to Aristotle, is εὐτραπελία, for which *urbanitas* or *comitas* might be a fair Latin equivalent. As to the peculiarly Greek grace of εὐτραπελία see *Eth. Nic.* iv. 8; cf. Thuc. ii. 38, 41.

[3] *Hist. of the English People*, London, 1895–96, v. 102; cf. Ambrose, *de Off. Min.* i. 18 [78], who derives *modestia* 'a modo scientiae quid deceret.'

Off. Min. i. 18). We may note that the word κόσμιος is applied to the dress of women (1 Ti 2[9]), and a similar expression, ἐν καταστήματι ἱεροπρεπεῖς, is found in Tit 2[3]. The principle implied seems to be that a person's dress is to be proportioned to his station or office in life, or to the occupation in which he may chance to be engaged (work, or recreation, or worship).[1] Law goes to the root of the matter when he represents 'Paternus' as advising his son on these points:

'Let your dress be sober, clean, and modest, not to set out the beauty of your person, but to declare the sobriety of your mind, that your outward garb may resemble the inward plainness and simplicity of your heart. For it is highly reasonable, that you should be *one man*, all of a piece, and appear outwardly such as you are inwardly' (*Serious Call*, ch. xviii.).[2] As to the dress of women see what is said of 'Miranda' (ch. ix.).

It may be objected that this entire account of 'moderation' is somewhat arbitrary. The fact is that moralists have evidently found difficulty in distinguishing between the different spheres of action in behaviour which are regulated by moderation, sobriety, and temperance respectively. There is, however, practical convenience in following the line suggested by Aquinas. He may be criticized as over-systematic, but we need not suppose that his classification is intended to be exhaustive. The virtue which 'in minimis modum ponit' will be differently estimated according to the various circumstances in which men find themselves placed:

'Quaerendum etiam in omni actu quid personis, quid temporibus conveniat atque aetatibus, quid etiam singulorum ingeniis sit accommodum. Saepe enim quod alterum decet, alterum non decet' (Ambrose, *de Off. Min.* i. 43 [212], speaking of moderation).

It remains to add that the word 'moderation' occurs in AV only in Ph 4[5] (τὸ ἐπιεικές). In RV the word is translated 'forbearance.' The grace which St. Paul has in mind—'considerateness' or 'reasonableness'—is, of course, a form of that beautiful 'moderation' which Wilson describes in 'Sacra Privata' (ed. Oxford, 1849, p. 41 [*Works*, v. 31]) as 'the way of an happy life':

'Lay nothing too much to heart; desire nothing too eagerly; rejoice not excessively, nor grieve too much for disasters; be not violently bent on any design; nor let any worldly cares hinder you from taking care of your soul; and remember, that it is necessary to be a Christian (that is, to govern one's self by motives of Christianity) in the most common actions of civil life.'

This is essentially the spirit enjoined by St. Paul (1 Co 7[29-31]). Cf. Ambrose, *de. Off. Min.* i. 18 [70]:

'Magna igitur modestia, quae cum sit etiam sui juris remissior, nihil sibi usurpans, nihil vindicans, et quodammodo intra vires suas contractior, dives est apud Deum.'

LITERATURE.—Ambrose, *de Officiis Ministr.* i.; Thomas Aquinas, *Summa Theologiæ*, II. ii. 161-169; J. Taylor, *Holy Living*, ch. ii. § 5; H. Martensen, *Christian Ethics (Individual)*, Eng. tr., Edinburgh, 1881, § 170; J. Ruskin, *Modern Painters*, pt. 3, sect. i. ch. 10 (on the relation of moderation to art).

R. L. OTTLEY.

MODERATISM.—See EVANGELICALISM.

MODERNISM.

—Modernism is the name given by the papal encyclical which condemned it to a complex of movements within the Roman Communion, all alike inspired by a desire to bring the tradition of Christian belief and practice into closer relation with the intellectual habits and social aspirations of our own time. These movements arose spontaneously and, for the most part, in entire independence of one another during the last decade of the 19th century. Since they had thus a common inspiration and a common purpose, it was neither unnatural nor unfair that the authority which condemned them should unite them under a common designation in a common censure. Yet it is necessary to insist that, in the earlier stages of their development, the various movements grouped together and logically correlated by the author of the encyclical *Pascendi* had little or no conscious connexion, and that it was only the external pressure of adversity that gradually forced them at a later period into mutual relations of a more intimate kind.

It may be well in the first place to sketch briefly the history of this complex movement as a whole, and then to give some account of the various forms which it has assumed. These may perhaps be treated most conveniently under the heads of (*a*) apologetic, (*b*) historical criticism, and (*c*) ecclesiastical and social reform.

1. History.—It must not be forgotten that the Vatican Decrees were the result of a liberal movement in the Church. For its founders, or at any rate for most of them, Ultramontanism was the vision of a Roman Catholicism freed from the entanglements of ancient dynastic contentions and in its new independence pledged to the spiritual leadership of the rising democracies. It was natural that the movement should find its fruitful seed-bed in the countries which had yielded most readily to the spell of the Revolution. Lamennais, Lacordaire, and Montalembert were its chief names in France; in Italy, Gioberti and Rosmini. But the hopes of the earlier Ultramontanism, open to all the winds of the century, perished in 1848. The consolidation of the spiritual empire of the papacy was to be achieved by other instruments and in another spirit. The Council of the Vatican seemed, both to the victors and to the vanquished, to be the definite reproof of the generous dreams which had made it possible. Its reactionary character was accentuated by contemporary happenings—the consolidation of the Italian kingdom at the expense of the temporal power, and the establishment of the Third Republic in France. Yet, in fact, a new era had dawned. Both in the intellectual and in the political spheres new and strange problems urgently demanded the attention of Roman Catholic scholars and thinkers. Many among them felt that the Church was in danger of being paralyzed by the Syllabus and the Vatican decrees, and were resolved that this danger must at all costs be averted. The accession of Leo XIII. in 1878 seemed to give them their opportunity. His numerous encyclicals, while conservative and traditional in tone and perhaps still more so in intention, were nevertheless so framed as to be capable of being turned to account by the progressives. Of these encyclicals, three may be specially recalled: *Æterni Patris* (4th Aug. 1879), which enjoined a return to the traditional metaphysics of St. Thomas Aquinas as the necessary foundation for the demonstration of the chief points of Christian belief; *Rerum Novarum* (15th May 1891), which dealt with the condition of the working classes; and *Providentissimus Deus* (18th Nov. 1893), which expressly condemned 'disquieting tendencies' in Biblical interpretation 'which, if they prevailed, could not fail to destroy the inspired and supernatural character of the Bible.' The warnings and counsels contained in these documents were resumed and reinforced in a further encyclical, dated 8th September 1899, and addressed to the archbishops, bishops, and clergy of France. It may be said that the whole history of Leo XIII.'s pontificate, its success and its failure, is to be found in a comparison of the last of these documents with its three predecessors. Such a comparison reveals a growing alarm on the part of authority at the development both of those new tendencies in apologetic or exegesis which it had attempted to repress and of the social action of the clergy which it had encouraged.

[1] In classical writers sentiments of this kind occasionally occur: *e.g.* Hor. *Carm.* I. v. 5; Ter. *Heaut.* II. iii. 47; Cic. *de Off.* i. 36: 'a forma removeatur omnis viro non dignus ornatus; et huic simile vitium in gestu motuque caveatur.'

[2] We are reminded of the advice of Polonius to Laertes in *Hamlet*, act i. sc. 3. Ambrose says strikingly (*de Off. Min.* i. 18 [71]): 'Vox quaedam est animi, corporis motus.'

That alarm was not without justification. It is in France, intellectually and politically the most highly developed country of the Roman Communion, that the reason for it can be most clearly traced. In 1875 the French episcopate secured from the government of the Third Republic the right to establish what were practically Roman Catholic universities free from all State control. Of the foundations thus authorized the most important was the Catholic Institute of Paris, which came into existence in 1878. Among its first professors was Louis Duchesne, a scholar who, though then only thirty-five years of age, had already achieved considerable reputation as an ecclesiastical historian of wide knowledge and independent judgment. Three years afterwards one of Duchesne's pupils, Alfred Loisy, a young priest belonging to the diocese of Châlons, was appointed to the chair of Hebrew at the Institute. Both scholars claimed the right to apply a rigorously scientific method to their respective spheres of research, the one to ecclesiastical history, the other to Biblical exegesis. Their contention was that it was not only possible, but necessary, to distinguish between the requirements of history and of faith. Duchesne's critical boldness in the treatment of ecclesiastical legend speedily aroused the hostility of the traditionalists, and in 1885 he was compelled to suspend for a year his course at the Institute. It was not till 1893 that Loisy was forced to resign his chair—a resignation which was followed by the condemnation, in the encyclical *Providentissimus*, of the principles of Biblical interpretation which he had upheld. During the decade of his connexion with the Institute, however, a group of scholars had been formed who, having become teachers in their turn, carried an enthusiasm for the critical method into the other Catholic Institutes and many of the diocesan seminaries.

The new movement towards a positive theology, as it was called, had its effect also upon the lay world. The beginning of the nineties was marked in intellectual France by what Brunetière described as 'the bankruptcy of science.' This meant that science had proved unequal to the needs of life, that man could not live by science alone, and that religion was coming into its own again. But, if it meant a revolt against scientific dogmatism, it meant equally a revolt against philosophic dogmatism. New tendencies in philosophy were beginning to appear which assigned to the will or to the total activity of the human spirit the principal rôle in determining truth. A young Roman Catholic philosopher, Maurice Blondel, turned these new tendencies to account in the interests of Christian apologetic in a thesis entitled *L'Action*, sustained before the Sorbonne for his doctor's degree on 7th June 1893. A year or two earlier, a group of young members of the university, attracted by the new spirit among the teaching clergy and prepared to find in it a promise of reconciliation between religion and contemporary knowledge and ways of thought, had founded a society which was to embrace those who desired to retain or regain religious belief without sacrifice of intellectual honesty. The society (its title, *L'Union pour l'action morale*, sufficiently indicated its object) had among its members religious freethinkers, Roman Catholics, Protestants, and Jews. On the occasion of a congress of Roman Catholic youth, held at Grenoble in May 1892, Leo XIII. had written a letter to the bishop of Grenoble in which he declared that it was the part of Christian wisdom to promote the co-operation of all men of goodwill, whether believers or those who, while not believers, were yet *naturaliter Christiani*, in the pursuit of individual and social good. This declaration was received with enthusiasm by the members of the new Union, and its president, Paul Desjardins, sought an interview with the pope and obtained from him the assurance of his entire sympathy with its aims. Meanwhile many of the younger clergy had found in the encyclical *Rerum Novarum* and in Leo XIII.'s advice to French Roman Catholics to rally to the Republic the long-awaited opportunity of religious action upon the democracy. Numerous Roman Catholic democratic journals were started, the democratic clergy were invited by many bishops to explain their views to the students of the diocesan seminaries, and public conferences were organized at which men of all shades of democratic opinion were welcomed.

Thus throughout the French Church a new era of intellectual and social activity seemed suddenly to have dawned under the immediate sanction of authority. Leo XIII.'s later pronouncement, it is true, aimed at keeping in check the various phases of the complex movement which his earlier encyclicals had been interpreted as in some degree encouraging. Yet up to the end of his pontificate no individual condemnation had taken place, and that though it was believed that determined efforts had been made to procure the condemnation of Loisy's first attempt to utilize the results of his critical studies for popular apologetic purposes in his little book *L'Évangile et l'église*. This book, published towards the end of 1902, was afterwards described by its author as '(1) a historical sketch and explanatory account of the development of Christianity, and (2) a general philosophy of religion and an essay in the interpretation of dogmatic formulas, official Symbols, and conciliar definitions, with a view to bringing them into agreement, by the sacrifice of the letter to the spirit, with the data of history and contemporary ways of thinking' (*RHLR* xi. [1906] 570). It precipitated a ferment which had been slowly and silently working throughout the Roman Church during twenty years. In Italy, Germany, England, America, and even in Spain, Loisy was suddenly hailed as an interpreter of ideas which had long been more or less clearly present to many minds. His treatment of religion on its side of human growth had welded together the philosophical and the more strictly theological elements of the new apologetic method. His treatment of the nature of ecclesiastical authority in the *Autour d'un petit livre* (a sequel to *L'Évangile et l'église*) served to demonstrate to the social reformers within the Church a close kinship between their own aims and methods and those of the theological reformers. Loisy had all unconsciously become the nucleating centre of a movement which knit together all the various elements of reform and extended its ramifications throughout large sections of the Roman Catholic world.

The election of Pius X. to the papal chair was an opportunity for stern dealing with this new threat to the fixity of Roman Catholic tradition. For some years before the death of his predecessor the peril of the new doctrines had been vehemently proclaimed by the traditional theologians, notably by C. F. Turinaz, the bishop of Nancy, and J. Fontaine of the Society of Jesus. Leo XIII. had probably no sympathy whatever with the attempted reconciliation between the Church and modern life, but he had himself aimed at some reconciliation, and he therefore shrank from direct condemnation. Pius X. had no such difficulty. Reconciliation implied that tradition was perfectible, which he could not admit. He hastened, within a few months of his election, to strike at both the theological and the social activities of the reformers. On 16th December 1903 five of Loisy's books were placed on the Index, and two days afterwards a *motu proprio* was issued which aimed at regulating 'popular Christian action.' The war, which was to be waged during the next four years, had been declared. A varied and continued literary activity, on the one side, was met by repeated condemnations, on the other. Loisy indeed made a formal submission, and devoted himself in silence to the preparation of his great work on the Synoptic Gospels. But Blondel's 'philosophy of action' was popularized by Lucien Laberthonnière, a priest of the Oratory, in a series of articles published for the most part in the *Annales de philosophie chrétienne*, and afterwards issued in two small volumes—*Essais de philosophie religieuse* and *Le Réalisme chrétien et l'idéalisme grec*. In the *Quinzaine*, a review edited by Georges Fonsegrive, a professor of the university, another university professor, Edouard Le Roy, inaugurated a discussion of the nature of religious dogma which provoked a considerable controversy. Le Roy afterwards published, in the form of a volume entitled *Dogme et critique*, a collection of replies to his critics, together with the original articles. In Italy Antonio Fogazzaro, the novelist, launched a programme of ecclesiastical reform, having for its object a general renewal of Christian life, in his novel *Il Santo* (Milan, 1906). In the same country Giovanni Semeria, a Barnabite, did much by his lectures on both the historical and the philosophical aspects of apologetics to disseminate the new ideas, while Romolo Murri, a secular priest of the diocese of Fermo, continued his crusade on behalf of Christian democratic action, undismayed by numerous manifestations of hostility on the part of authority. Among his chief supporters in this crusade was Salvatore Minocchi, a professor of Hebrew at Florence, who had also become known as a Biblical critic through his studies of the Psalms and of Isaiah. In England the movement was represented principally by the writings of George Tyrrell, a member of the Society of Jesus, and Friedrich von Hügel. The latter had read a paper on the progress of OT criticism as it concerned the Hexateuch at a Roman Catholic Congress held at Fribourg-in-Switzerland in 1897, which afforded ample evidence of his accurate scholarship and of the freedom of his critical method and conclusions. Since then he had been engaged on an important work on *The Mystical Element of Religion* (it was not published till 1908), which revealed his originality and depth as a thinker on all the problems connected with religion, while it gave further proof of his competence as a critical historian. Meanwhile he had contributed articles to the *Quinzaine*, *Il Rinnovamento*, and other Modernist reviews, notably a reply to an article by Blondel which had impugned the right of criticism to a complete autonomy in the religious domain, and a defence of critical conclusions with regard to the Pentateuch against a judgment of the papal Biblical Commission affirming its Mosaic authorship (27th June 1906). Tyrrell was already widely known for his frank and bold handling of religious difficulties, but it was his acknowledgment of the authorship of *A Letter to a University Professor*, which had been privately circulated, and his consequent expulsion from the Society of Jesus (Feb. 1906), that brought him to the forefront of the Modernist movement and made him its universally acknowledged leader till his death in July 1909. In Germany the movement was for the most part confined to an agitation for ecclesiastical reform. Franz Xavier Kraus, a professor at Freiburg-im-Breisgau, was the determined opponent of Ultramontanism. An Ultramontane he defined as 'one who places the Church before religion, who identifies the pope with the Church, who is ready to sacrifice a clear decision of his own conscience to the sentence of an external authority' ('Kirchenpolitische Briefe,' ii., in *Allgemeine Zeitung*, Supplement, 1895, no. 211; the letters were signed 'Spektator,' one of the pseudonyms adopted by Kraus; see Schnitzer, *Der katholische Modernismus*, in the series *Die Klassiker der Religion*, p. 39, where the letter is given in full as the work of Kraus). Kraus, however, died in 1902, too early to be involved in the distinctively Modernist controversies. Hermann Schell, a professor in the Theological Faculty at Würzburg, had as early as 1896 published a book entitled *Katholizismus als Prinzip des Fortschritts*, which provoked long and bitter controversy. As a result certain bishops of Northern Germany forbade their priests to attend his lectures. Two years afterwards controversy was renewed over Schell's views on eternal punishment, and four of his books were placed on the Index. Schell made a formal submission after receiving an assurance from the bishop and the Theological Faculty of Würzburg that such submission did not imply any sacrifice of conviction on his part. But he withdrew none of the condemned books from circulation, and continued till his death in 1906 to be the leader of a strong liberal movement in German Roman Catholicism. Among his most influential disciples were Albert Ehrhard of Strassburg, Joseph Schnitzer of Munich, and Hugo Koch of Braunsberg.

Pius X. did not fail to reply to the growing menace of this movement. During the years 1905–06 he issued a series of encyclicals in condemnation of the Christian Democratic movement in Italy. Another series of decisions by the Biblical Commission which Leo XIII. had appointed in 1902 reproved the audacities of criticism in questioning accepted beliefs as to the authorship and authenticity of certain books of Scripture. In April 1906 the works of Laberthonnière and Fogazzaro's *Il Santo* were condemned by the Congregation of the Index. But it was not till the beginning of 1907 that the storm burst in its full fury. Murri was suspended 'a divinis' on 15th April. Two days later the pope delivered an allocution in which he denounced the new movement as 'the compendium and poisonous essence of all heresies,' and called upon the cardinals to aid him in eradicating these evils from the Church. At the end of the same month the Cardinal Prefect of the Index wrote to Cardinal Ferrari, archbishop of Milan, enjoining him to procure the suppression of *Il Rinnovamento*, a Modernist review which had been launched at the beginning of the year. The Cardinal Prefect's letter was remarkable not only for the strong terms in which it denounced the review as 'notoriously opposed to Catholic spirit and teaching,' but also because it took the unusual course of expressly naming certain writers—Fogazzaro, Tyrrell, von Hügel, and Murri. In May the archbishop of Paris, inspired, no doubt, by similar action on the part of the Cardinal Vicar, prohibited the reading of Le Roy's *Dogme et critique*, and at the same time forbade any priest in his diocese to collaborate in Loisy's *Revue d'histoire et de littérature religieuses*. The professors of the Catholic Institute of Paris were at the same time forbidden by the bishops who controlled that seat of learning to contribute to *Demain*, a small Modernist weekly which had been founded at Lyons in 1905. In June Pius X., in a letter of felicitation to Ernst Commer, a professor at Vienna, who had written an attack upon the theology of Hermann Schell, described those who had projected a monument to Schell's memory as 'either ignorant of Catholicism or rebels against the authority of the Holy See,' though among them were the archbishop of Bamberg and the bishop of Passau.

By this long series of censures the way was

prepared for a more stringent and inclusive condemnation of all the various heresies, exegetic, apologetic, philosophical, and social, that were troubling the Roman Catholic world. That condemnation was pronounced in the decree of the Inquisition, *Lamentabili sane exitu*, dated 3rd July 1907, and the encyclical *Paecendi Dominici gregis*, of 8th September in the same year. The decree *Lamentabili* was a mere collection of sixty-five propositions which were to be condemned. No indication was given of the sources from which they had been derived, and no writer was condemned by name, but thirty-eight of the propositions were directly concerned with Biblical criticism, and Loisy, in some notes on the decree which he published at the beginning of the following year, accepted its condemnation as directed in large measure against himself. The encyclical *Pascendi* was a document of much greater importance, and was recognized as such by the leading Modernists. Tyrrell met it with vigorous criticism and open defiance in two articles which appeared in the *Times* on 30th September and 1st October, in the full knowledge that he was exposing himself to the severest censures of the Church. On 28th October a more detailed reply was published in Rome under the title *Il Programma dei modernisti*. The encyclical had deduced from an unsound philosophical principle all the various errors which it grouped together under the name of Modernism, and it maintained that the false conclusions of the Modernists with regard to history, dogma, and the Bible were all the necessary result of an erroneous philosophy. To this the *Programma* replied that it was, on the contrary, the undeniable results of historical criticism that had made necessary a new apologetic of some kind.

The attitude of Tyrrell and of the authors of the *Programma* revealed a determination to resist the action of authority. The watchword of this resistance was to be 'No schism.' Even if excommunicated, the Modernist leaders were resolved to claim their inalienable right of spiritual domicile within the Church. Authority might cut them off from its outward communion, but could not affect their inward communion with it. Tyrrell expounded the new policy in an article contributed to the *Grande Revue*, and remained till his death its most consistent adherent. But the difficulty of giving effect to the policy soon became apparent. The chief difficulty lay in the economic dependence of the Modernist clergy, which prevented their action in the open. On the morrow of the publication of the *Programma*, *e.g.*, the reading of the book was forbidden to the faithful and its authors were excommunicated. But, as they still remained anonymous, the effect of their protest upon the outer world was largely discounted. Yet it was in Italy that resistance to the encyclical was most obstinate and prolonged. In spite of the assiduous suppression of Modernist journals, both scientific and social, new ones continually appeared in that country. Among these the most influential was *Nova et Vetera*, founded in January 1908, in which for the first time theological views of a decidedly negative character, such as found expression in the *Lettere di un prete modernista*, published at Rome in the same year, began to appear. Meanwhile condemnations were launched against the leaders who had appeared in the open. Loisy was formally excommunicated on 7th March 1908. The same sentence was pronounced against Murri, who had been elected as a deputy to the Italian Chamber, on 22nd March 1909. Tyrrell had been deprived of the sacraments on 22nd October 1907. The same fate befell Schnitzer at the beginning of February 1908. Minocchi was suspended 'a divinis' in January of the same year, and in the following October voluntarily withdrew into secular life. This series of personal condemnations was followed up and completed by a blow aimed at the Christian Social movement in France. The *Sillon*, the organ of the movement, was formally condemned on 25th August 1910, and its promoters ordered to work henceforward for social reform under the direction of their respective bishops. Marc Sangnier, the lay leader of the movement, made his submission, but Pierre Dabry, its most prominent clerical representative, withdrew into secular life.

The various measures of repression set forth in the encyclical *Pascendi* having failed, after a lengthened trial, to produce the desired effect, Pius X. issued, on 1st September 1910, the *motu proprio Sacrorum Antistitum*, in which he enjoined the imposition of a special oath of adhesion 'to all the condemnations, declarations, and prescriptions contained in the encyclical *Pascendi* and the decree *Lamentabili* upon all professors of seminaries and Roman Catholic universities and institutes on admission to their office and upon all ordinands. It fell, however, not to a priest or even to a layman, but to a woman, to make a protest against what she conceived to be a violation of Christian liberty. Maude Petre, the biographer of Tyrrell, having been called upon by the bishop of the diocese in which she resided to subscribe to the condemnations contained in the encyclical *Pascendi* and the decree *Lamentabili* as a condition of her admission to the sacraments, refused to do so on the ground that such subscription would imply a readiness to defend, if necessary with her life, every word of those documents as being equally important for faith with the Apostles' Creed itself. About the same time an anonymous document, purporting to represent the views of a numerous group of ecclesiastics belonging to all the French dioceses, appeared in a Parisian newspaper, the *Siècle*. It contained a declaration that its authors desired, before taking the oath under constraint, to protest before God and the Church that they did not regard their act of submission as in any way binding upon their consciences or as implying any modification of their opinions. Whether with this reservation or not, the anti-Modernist oath was generally taken by most of those suspected of being Modernists, and the history of Modernism as an open movement in the Roman Catholic Church had come to an end.

2. Forms.—(*a*) *Apologetic of immanence.*—It was the aim of the philosophic Modernists, notably of Laberthonnière, to establish the cardinal points of Christian belief by the aid of the modern evolutionary or dynamic view of the universe. That involved a departure from the traditional scholastic method of apologetic. But they did not abandon scholasticism arbitrarily, simply because it was old. On the contrary, it was their sincere belief that the Aristotelian metaphysic and logic utilized by the scholastic theologians provided a less perfect instrument for the illustration and defence of specifically Christian belief than the more modern conceptions of life. It is, *e.g.*, an essential part of Christian belief that God is personal and that He is Creator. But it is only in the light of a dynamic conception of the universe that the full significance of these affirmations is disclosed. The God of Aristotle was a logical abstraction, the ultimate Idea. Creation was but the logical derivation of the divine Idea in specific forms towards a passively receptive matter. It was in no sense a productive effort realizing new life. But that is just what the Christian belief demands. For it God is the sovereign source of power, and that power goes forth, must by its very nature go forth, in a real creative effort issuing in new life independent of and yet closely united with its source. And the very essence of that new life is again real creative action. For action is always creative, an extension of life beyond itself, its prolongation into another life, not itself, of which it remains the constitutive principle. Thus creation is God's transcendent reality introducing itself into the world and becoming immanent in it. And this act of creation is the act of the divine love by which God is eternally pledged to His world, by which His world, becoming self-conscious in man, needs and can receive His grace. Again, as Laberthonnière points out, it is just because God is not the 'pure act' of Aristotle, but the power which by His own nature acts continually, that we can conceive of a plurality, a society engendered within the unity of His own Being. The doctrine of the Trinity assumes a vital and not a merely formal character.

Thus the reality which we assign to life, because we already feel it there, is itself the motive of our belief in the personality of God. That personality is not a mere idea to which we attain by logical inference. It is a vital inference from our total experience of life as free creative action. That experience implies a more or less conscious communion of each separate creative unit with an original infinite source of creative life, and of all the units with one another in and through that life. All the terms which this essentially religious experience has formulated to express itself—communion, inspiration, revelation, faith, judgment—imply a concretely personal character in God. On the other hand, these terms, when interpreted to us and by us through the logical abstractions of the Aristotelian metaphysic, lose much of their distinctively religious significance. The conception of faith, *e.g.*, as an assent of the intelligence to the truth acquired extrinsically, by the teaching of a divinely deputed authority, fails to do justice to its concrete reality. That concrete reality of faith is an immediate response of the whole personal nature to the personal divine action upon it, a response in virtue of which it recognizes authority and the measure in which authority mediates the divine action to it. The intellectual element in faith exists, but it exists as a derivative from some profounder and more vital action of faith. So, again, revelation, when conceived as the final and imperfectible deposit of truth-statements to be imposed upon the intellect from without, is shorn of much of its religious character. Assent to such a revelation need not be religious at all. The real concrete revelation of God is to the whole personal nature apprehending His action upon it. And the perfect instruments of that revelation are Christ, the Incarnate Word, and the life of His Church in so far as it is a real extension of His life. The thought of the Church, its dogmas, its truth-statements, are but the partial and ever-perfectible translation in terms of one aspect of man's activity, his power of intellectually apprehending reality, of its living apprehension of God in Christ. Thus even the Gospels themselves are not a completed revelation. They indeed enshrine the perfect revelation of the Christ-life. But that revelation can be apprehended only in proportion as it is lived, and by those by whom it is lived. The Gospels were but the earliest attempt of those who had lived it to read and interpret its mysteries. Thus history is not of merely accidental importance to Christianity, but is, on the contrary, of its essence. As Laberthonnière frequently puts it, Christianity has dared to conceive of God *sub specie temporis*. God condescends to weave the texture of His vast designs with human hands. The divine inspiration of each individual life is a free product of the total inspiration of past humanity and a contribution towards all future inspiration. So tradition acquires a vital, and not a merely formal, value.

(*b*) *Historical criticism.*—It was the aim of the philosophical Modernist to vindicate the Church as the supreme organ of the vital religious tradition of mankind. The historical Modernist sought to do the same thing in his own special field of study. The orthodox apologist, grounding himself on the closed character of revelation as imperfectible truth-statement, had to prove the practically formal identity of the dogmatic statements of the Church to-day with the Scriptural revelation. For the historian, however, the admission of such formal identity was impossible. The development of dogma from the most general to the most exact forms of statement, from the simplest to the most complex and detailed forms, was a fact of history. As a historian, the Modernist had merely to trace the development and expose its character. But, as a Christian apologist (the rôle which alone constituted him a Modernist), he had to undertake the much more difficult task of reconciling this development of dogma with its permanent truth-value. This he attempted to do by distinguishing between the spirit and the form of each dogmatic statement, ascribing to the former an absolute and permanent, to the latter a merely relative, instrumental, and mutable value. By the spirit of a dogma such apologists meant its witness to some aspect of religious experience which was necessary to the reality of the religious life, and therefore universal or capable of becoming universal. But that witness could pass current between mind and mind only by the aid of some intellectual symbol capable of suggesting the actually experienced reality. Such symbols, necessarily shaped by the intellectual methods and habits of their period of growth, were clearly perfectible. But the growth of dogma was something more, and more truly organic, than the adaptation, as it were consciously and from without, of more perfect thought-forms to a constant experience. For thought reacts upon life, the clear perception of an experience upon the experience itself, enlarging and deepening its import. And so many of the Modernist apologists were ready to find in the more developed forms of dogma a fuller expression of its spirit, the experienced reality actually deepened by the more adequate form of the witness to it. A similar method of treatment was applied by the Modernist historian to the growth of ecclesiastical government and institutions and all the formal aspects of the Church's life. As a historian, he had to deny the orthodox contention that the actual fabric of Church order had been instituted by Christ Himself. But he claimed that the Church as a society had grown out of the spirit of Christ, and that each stage in the evolution of its order could be shown to have been the necessary means, under the circumstances of its particular historical moment, of preserving or extending the operation of that spirit.

(*c*) *Ecclesiastical and social reform.*—Yet the movement did not propose simply to divinize the existing Church. Her actual institutions came into existence in a distant past in response to the needs of the spirit then operating within her. But to-day those institutions may be suffocating her true life. They may even, as Fogazzaro's saint suggests, be introducing false and destructive spirits into her system—'the spirit of falsehood, the spirit of clerical domination, the spirit of avarice, the spirit of immobility' (*Il Santo*, pp. 336–342). Yet none of the chief Modernist writers can be said to have put forward any definite programme of ecclesiastical reform. They urge rather that Church authority should remember of what spirit it is, what spirit it exists to serve and extend.

'The Church is the hierarchy with its traditional concepts, and it is the world with its continuous hold upon reality, with its continuous reaction upon tradition; the Church is official theology, and the inexhaustible treasure of Divine truth which reacts upon official theology; the Church does not die, the Church does not grow old, the Church has in its heart more than on its lips the Living Christ, the Church is a laboratory of truth in continuous action' (*ib.* p. 293).

Only when possessed by such a conception of her character and mission will the Church discover what reforms she needs to make her equal to both in the profoundly changed circumstances of contemporary life. It is the conception which has inspired the Modernist social reformer also. He has aimed at making Christianity the leaven of national, political, social, and economic life, and therefore the principle of a larger and humaner life which may embrace and harmonize all these. He has conceived of the Church as an instrument of world-civilization rather than of world-renunciation, and of world-renunciation only in so far as it is involved in and necessary to a genuine world-civilization. And so he has tried to understand sympathetically and to co-operate with all the generous hopes and endeavours of the modern democratic movement, whether among Churchmen or among those who are outside the Church's pale. It has been perhaps the chief burden of his offence in the eyes of authority. The Modernist social reformer has been at one with the Modernist ecclesiastical reformer in thinking that the Church needs especially to be saved from the danger of becoming increasingly a clerical autocracy, exacting from the laity as the sum of their duty a passive submission to its decrees. It may be said in conclusion that the one purpose which was common to all the allied but independent movements grouped together under the name of Modernism was the self-reform of the Church, a reform inspired by belief in life, in the totality of human action, as itself most likely to provoke man's need of God and to ensure a genuine satisfaction of that need—a reform, therefore, which was to be sought along the lines of contemporary thought and action. It was a generous purpose, arising out of a genuine revival of intelligent religious faith. Though authority, taking a different view of the religious needs of the time and of the method of their due satisfaction, has succeeded in suppressing the open activity of the movement, it is as yet impossible to predict its ultimate success or failure. One thing, however, may with some confidence be asserted, viz. that its apparent failure for the moment has been due less to the action of authority than to the prevailing lack of interest among the Latin peoples in thought about or discussion of religious questions. If that interest should ever be revived, it is certain that it will demand and procure throughout the Latin churches reforms similar in inspiration, in range, and in effect to those for which the Modernist leaders contended during the last decade of the 19th cent. and the first decade of the 20th.

LITERATURE.—For the history of Modernism the following books are the most important: A. Houtin, *Histoire du modernisme catholique*, Paris, 1912, *La Question biblique chez les catholiques de France au xixe siècle*, do. 1902, and *La Question biblique au xxe siècle*, do. 1906; J. Schnitzer, 'Der katholische Modernismus,' in *Zeitschrift für Politik*, v. 1 [1911]; J. Kübel, *Geschichte der katholischen Modernismus*, Tübingen, 1909; M. Petre, *Autobiography and Life of George Tyrrell*, London, 1912; A. Loisy, *Choses passées*, Paris, 1913. Among the chief Modernist documents are: A. Loisy, *L'Évangile et l'église*, Paris, 1902, *Autour d'un petit livre*, do. 1903, *Simples réflexions*, do. 1908, and *Quelques Lettres*, do. 1908; G. Tyrrell, *A Much-Abused Letter*, London, 1906, *Lex Orandi*, do. 1904, *Lex Credendi*, do. 1907, *Through Scylla and Charybdis*, do. 1907, *Medievalism*, do. 1908, *Christianity at the Cross-Roads*, do. 1909; L. Laberthonnière, *Essais de philosophie religieuse*, Paris, 1903, *Le Réalisme chrétien et l'idéalisme grec*, do. 1904; E. Le Roy, *Dogme et critique*, do. 1907; F. von Hügel, *The Mystical Element of Religion*, London, 1908; G. Semeria, *Scienza e fede*, Rome, 1903, *Dogma, gerarchia, e culto*, do. 1902; R. Murri, *La Vita religiosa nel Cristianesimo*, do. 1907, *Della Religione, della chiesa, e dello stato*, Milan, 1910; U. Fracassini, *Che cos'è la Bibbia*, Rome, 1910; *Il Programma dei modernisti*, do. 1907, Eng. tr., London, 1908. To these may be added an excellent anthology, representative of the chief Modernist writers of Germany, France, Italy, and England, selected by J. Schnitzer, and published under the title *Der katholische Modernismus* in the series *Die Klassiker der Religion*, Berlin, 1912. Unfortunately this anthology bears the same title as the same author's critical study of Modernism mentioned above. The chief pontifical condemnations are conveniently given in Denzinger[11], nos. 1701–80 ('Syllabus errorum'), 2001–65 ('Lamentabili'), 2071–2109 ('Pascendi'), 2145–47 (anti-Modernist oath); and all the documents are collected by A. Vermeersch, *De Modernismo tractatus*, Bruges, 1910 (cf. also his art. 'Modernism,' in *CE* x. [1911] 415–421).

A. L. LILLEY.

MOGGALLĀNA.—Moggallāna was one of the two chief disciples of the Buddha. He was a Brāhman by birth, and his mother's name is given in the *Divyāvadāna* (p. 52) as Bhadra-kanyā. Nothing is known of his youth, but in a very early document[1] we are told the story of his conversion.

There was a Wanderer (or Sophist) at Rājagaha named Sañjaya.[2] Moggallāna and a friend of his, another young Brāhman from a neighbouring village, had become 'Wanderers' (*paribbājakā*) under Sañjaya. Each had given his word to the other that the first to find 'ambrosia' should tell the other. One day his friend, Sāriputta, saw Assaji, another Wanderer, passing through Rājagaha on his round for alms. Struck by Assaji's dignified demeanour, Sāriputta followed him to his hermitage and, after compliments had been exchanged, asked him who was his teacher and what was the doctrine he professed, seeing that his mien was so serene, his countenance so bright and clear. 'There is a great man of religion, one of the sons of the Sākiyas, who has gone forth from the Sākiya clan. He is my teacher; it is his doctrine I profess,' was the reply. 'Well, what is the doctrine?' asked Sāriputta. 'I am but a novice, only lately gone forth. In detail I can not explain, but I can tell you the meaning of it in brief.' Sāriputta told him that that was just what he wanted—the spirit, not the letter, of the doctrine. Then Assaji quoted a verse:

'Of all phenomena sprung from a cause
The Teacher the cause hath told;
And he tells, too, how each shall come to its end,
For such is the word of the Sage.'

On hearing this verse Sāriputta obtained 'the pure eye for the truth'; that is, the knowledge that whatsoever is subject to the condition of having an origin is subject also to the condition of passing away. (This is the stock phrase in the early Buddhist books for conversion.) He at once acknowledged that this was the doctrine that he had sought for so long a time in vain. He went immediately to Moggallāna, and told him that he had found the ambrosia, and, when he explained how this was, Moggallāna agreed with him in the view that he had taken, and they both went to the Buddha and were admitted into his order.

The story here summarized is repeated, in almost identical terms, in various commentaries.[3] It is curious in two ways. In the first place, who, on being asked to give the spirit of the Buddhist doctrine in a few words, would choose the words of Assaji's verse? One may search in vain most manuals of Buddhism to find any mention of the point raised in the verse;[4] and yet the verse has been so frequently found on tablets and monuments in India that Anglo-Indians are wont to call it, somewhat extravagantly, 'the Buddhist creed.' The Buddhists, of course, have no creed in the European sense of that word, but any one who should draw up one for them ought to include in it a clause on this matter of causation. The quotation may very well have made a special impression upon Sāriputta and Moggallāna. They had already renounced the sacrifice as a satisfactory solution of the problems of life, and were seeking for something more satisfactory than the vague hints now to be found only in later passages, such as *Īśā* 14, where the ambrosia is brought into a mystic connexion with cause and with passing

1 *Vinaya*, ed. H. Oldenberg, i. 39–44; translated in Rhys Davids and H. Oldenberg, *Vinaya Texts*, i. 144–151.

2 It is not stated that he was the same as the Sañjaya of *Dīgha*, i. 58, the famous 'eel-wriggler.'

3 *Dhammapada Com.* i. 85–95: *Theragāthā Com.* on verse 1017; *Aṅguttara Com.* on i. 83, etc.

4 But see the chapter on causation in C. A. F. Rhys Davids, *Buddhism*, London, 1912, pp. 78–106.

away. Here, in this new theory of causation, was a quite different view of things, which seemed to these inquirers to meet the case.

It is also, at first sight, curious that they should have called this particular doctrine 'ambrosia' (*amata*). Though this expression was no doubt first used of the drink that preserved the gods from death, it must before the rise of Buddhism have acquired, among the Wanderers, the secondary meaning of salvation as being the ineffably sweet.[1] It is true that the other idea of salvation, as being a deliverance (from evil, or from the eternal round of rebirths and redeaths), is also found in pre-Buddhistic works (see MOKṢA). But it was natural, in the beginnings of speculation, to have varying attempts at the expression in words of so complicated a conception; and it is improbable that the early Buddhists invented such a phrase as ambrosia, connoting, as it does, so much of the earlier polytheism.

Moggallāna is frequently mentioned in the canon, and usually with the epithet Mahā ('the Great'). A number of verses ascribed to him, including one long poem and several shorter ones, are preserved in the anthology called *Theragāthā* ('Psalms of the Brethren').[2] The *Dīgha* is curiously silent about him; but a whole book is assigned to him in the *Saṁyutta*;[3] and about two score of passages in the *Majjhima* and the *Aṅguttara*, and elsewhere in the *Saṁyutta*, record acts done or words spoken by him.[4] We need not give the details of these passages. The general result of them is that he was considered by the men who composed them to have been a master of the philosophy and of the psychological ethics, and especially of the deeper and more mystical sides, of the teaching. There is, *e.g.*, an interesting passage where the Buddha compares Sāriputta with Moggallāna:

'Like a woman who gives birth to a son, brethren, is Sāriputta to a young disciple, like a master who trains a boy so is Moggallāna. Sāriputta leads him on to conversion, Moggallāna to the highest truth. But Sāriputta can set forth the four Aryan Truths and teach them, and make others understand them and stand firm in them, he can expound and elucidate them.'[5]

In one characteristic Moggallāna is stated to have been supreme over all the other disciples. This is in the power of *iddhi* ('potency').[6] Both word and idea are older than the rise of Buddhism; and the meaning is vague.[7] The early Buddhists, trying, as they often did, to pour new wine into the old bottles, distinguished two kinds of *iddhi* —the one lower, intoxicating, ignoble; the other higher, temperate, religious.[8] The former has preserved for us the belief common among the people, the latter the modification which the Buddhists sought to make in it. The former reminds us of the *mana* of the South Seas, or the *orenda* of some American tribes, or sometimes of the strange accomplishments of a spiritualistic medium. Birds have *iddhi*, with especial reference to their mysterious power of flight.[9] Kings have *iddhi*[10] of four kinds (differently explained at *Dīgha*, ii. 177 and *Jātaka*, iii. 454). It is by the *iddhi* of a hunter that he succeeds in the chase.[11] *Iddhi* is the explanation of the luxury and prosperity of a young chief.[12] By *iddhi* one may have the faculty of levitation, or of projecting an image of oneself to a distant spot, or of becoming invisible, or of walking on water, or of passing through walls, or of visiting the gods in their various heavens.[1] All these are worldly *iddhi*, the *iddhi* of an unconverted man. That of the converted, awakened man is self-mastery, equanimity.[2] Both these kinds of potency were regarded as natural, that is, neither of them was, according to Indian thought, what we should call supernatural. And neither of them, in Buddhist thought, was animistic, that is, either dependent upon or involving the belief in a soul as existing within the human body.

In both these respects of *iddhi*, the worldly and the spiritual, Moggallāna, in the oldest records, is regarded as pre-eminent. An amusing and edifying story is preserved of the way in which, like an ancient St. Dunstan, he outwits the Evil One.[3] We are also told how, in order to attract the attention of the gods to the very elementary exposition of ethics that he thought suitable to their intelligence, he shook with his great toe the pinnacles of the palaces of heaven.[4] Other instances of Moggallāna's instructing the gods are given in the *Moggallāna Saṁyutta* referred to above, and in the *Aṅguttara* (iii. 331, iv. 85), while two anthologies, probably the latest and certainly the most dreary books in the canon, the *Vimāna Vatthu* and the *Peta Vatthu*, consist entirely of short poems describing interviews which Moggallāna is supposed to have had with spirits in the various heavens and purgatories.

Most of the episodes in which Moggallāna figures are localized, that is, the place where the incident or conversation took place is mentioned by name. The names are very varied, and it is clear that no one place could be regarded as his permanent residence.

Tradition has preserved no further account of his life, but the manner of his death is explained in two commentaries, the two accounts being nearly identical.[5] Both Sāriputta and Moggallāna died in the November of the year before the Buddha's death, just before the Buddha started on his last journey.[6] Sāriputta died a natural death; Moggallāna, it is said, was murdered, at the instigation of certain jealous Jain monks, by a bandit named Samana-guttaka, at the Black Rock cave on the Isigili Hill near Rājagaha.

When Cunningham opened the topes (memorial mounds) at Sānchī, he found in one of them two boxes containing fragments of bone and inscribed respectively 'Of Sāriputta' and 'Of Moggallāna the Great' in Pāli letters of Aśoka's time.[7] A similar discovery was made in the neighbouring group of topes at Satdhāra.[8] It is evident that more than two centuries after their death the memory of the two chief disciples had not yet died out in the community, and that the Buddhist laity who erected these monuments considered it suitable that their supposed relics should be enshrined in the same tomb.

The name Moggallāna was occasionally adopted as their name in religion by candidates for the order until the 12th cent. of our era. The belief that the power of *iddhi* had been actually exercised by Moggallāna the Great and others in the ancient days is still held by those of the orthodox who adhere to the ancient tradition, though, except as practised long ago, the belief in it soon died out. There is no evidence, later than the canon, of any

1 Cf. the use of the phrase by a non-Buddhist, and before the first sermon had been uttered, at *Vinaya*, i. 7, 8.
2 *Theragāthā*, 1146–1208, tr. C. A. F. Rhys Davids, in *Psalms of the Early Buddhists*, ii. 387 f.
3 *Moggallāna Saṁyutta*, iv. 262–281.
4 See the index volumes to these works.
5 *Majjhima*, iii. 248.
6 *Aṅguttara*, i. 23; cf. *Milinda*, 188, and *Divyāvadāna*, 395.
7 See art. MAGIC (Buddhist), § I.
8 *Dīgha*, iii. 112, 113.
9 *Dhammapada*, 175; but the commentary, iii. 177, interprets the passage otherwise.
10 *Udāna*, p. 11.
11 *Majjhima*, i. 152.
12 *Dīgha*, ii. 21; *Aṅguttara*, i. 145.

1 The stock passages are at *Dīgha*, ii. 83; *Majjhima*, i. 34, 494; *Aṅguttara*, i. 255, iii. 17, 28.
2 *Dīgha*, iii. 113.
3 *Majjhima*, i. 332 ff.
4 *Ib.* i. 252 ff.
5 *Jātaka Com.* v. 126; *Dhammapada Com.* iii. 65 ff.
6 *Jātaka Com.* i. 391.
7 A. Cunningham, *The Bhilsa Topes*, London, 1854, p. 297.
8 *Ib.* p. 324.

contemporary cases of the lower, worldly *iddhi* of the unconverted man.

LITERATURE.—*Vinaya Piṭaka*, ed. H. Oldenberg, London, 5 vols., 1879–83; T. W. Rhys Davids and H. Oldenberg, *Vinaya Texts* (*SBE* xiii. [1881], xvii. [1882], xx. [1885]); C. A. F. Rhys Davids, *Buddhism*, London, 1912; *Dhammapada Commentary*, ed. H. C. Norman, Oxford, 1906–14 (*PTS*); *Therīgāthā Commentary*, ed. E. Müller, do. 1893 (*PTS*); *Saṁyutta*, ed. L. Feer and C. A. F. Rhys Davids, do. 1884–1904 (*PTS*); C. A. F. Rhys Davids, *Psalms of the Early Buddhists*, do. 1909–13 (*PTS*); *Aṅguttara*, ed. R. Morris and E. Hardy, do. 1885–1910 (*PTS*); *Milinda-pañha*, ed. V. Trenckner, London, 1880; *Divyāvadāna*, ed. E. B. Cowell and R. A. Neil, Cambridge, 1886; *Majjhima*, ed. V. Trenckner and R. Chalmers, Oxford, 1888–99 (*PTS*); *Udāna*, ed. P. Steinthal, do. 1883 (*PTS*); *Dhammapada*, ed. S. Sumangala, do. 1914 (*PTS*); *Dīgha*, ed. Rhys Davids and J. E. Carpenter, do. 1890–1911 (*PTS*).

T. W. RHYS DAVIDS.

MOKṢA (Skr., also *mukti*) **and VIMUTTI** (Pāli, also (*vi*)*mo*(*k*)*kha*).—These terms, other prefixes being sometimes substituted, are all derivatives from *much*, 'to let go,' 'discharge,' 'release,' and, with varying import, are identical in primary meaning with our 'deliverance,' 'emancipation,' 'freedom,' 'liberty,' 'release.' Whichever equivalent be selected, the inquirer may start with two general way-marks. In the first place, the concept in question has a negative side, viz. a having got loose from, or rid of, and a positive side, viz. the cœnæsthesis, or general sense of expanded outlook, calm, security, attainment, power to be and do, without which the 'getting freed from' were in some cases too costly a gain. If these two aspects be held together in the mind, then the common terms for them, stated above, may—and this is the second way-mark—be considered as, more perhaps than any other idea, the pith and kernel of the religious faiths of India, and as coming nearer to the Christian 'salvation' than any other. It should, however, be added that the concept grew within those faiths, and that it was by no means always and everywhere given this paramount emphasis and importance. Awareness of emancipation as such, or of its absence and desirability, is not patent in the earliest recorded expressions of the Indian mind. The vital importance of solidarity, either with tribal custom and convention or with the decrees and the very life of his gods, is far more pressing on the man of primitive culture than is any revolt or self-exclusion from, or independence of, any order or destiny, socially or divinely imposed on all. Moreover, the particular deliverances or riddances that came in time to be generalized under a common notion varied in kind.

Before making good these general considerations by analysis, it may be well to guard the reader of translations from Indian literature against gaining an inaccurate idea of the frequency of allusions to 'freedom,' etc. Perhaps no language is as rich in privative or negative inflexions as is that of the Indian classics, whether it be Vedic, Prākrit, Pāli, or Sanskrit. We have ourselves a few terms where the negative form exceeds, in inspiring emphasis, the positive form—*e.g.*, independence, infinite, immortality, etc. Such terms are very numerous in Indian literature, and it often happens, notably in translations by Max Müller and Fausböll, that, to give the force or elegance of the originals, words with a negative prefix—*a*, *ni*, *vi*—are rendered by 'free from,' and even 'freedom from.'

Thus we find such renderings as 'free from evil,' *a-pāpa*; 'free from fear,' *a-bhaya*; 'free from grief,' *vi-śoka*; 'free from desire,' *niṣkāma*; 'free from the body,' *a-śarīra*; 'free from decay, death,' *vi-jara*, *vi-mṛtya*, *a-mṛta*; and many others, notably, 'being freed from good and freed from evil,' *vi-sukṛta*, *vi-duṣkṛta*, *i.e.* 'sundered from (*vi*) the well-done and the ill-done,' in other words, rid of the effects of his actions or *karma* (*Kauṣītaki Upaniṣad*, i. 4).

Many other 'liberties' taken by the lavish use of 'free from' go to swell this misconception. The phrase just quoted occurs in an archaic account of *saṁsāra*, or transmigration. Now, it is true that the *mukti*, or *mokṣa*, concept centres in the release of the soul or self, not only from this body, but also from all future bodies. But the only term expressive of release here is in the translation. 'All who depart from this world go to the moon . . . if a man make reply [on arriving] to the moon, it *passes him on*' (*atisṛjate*), *i.e.* he does not return to be reborn on earth. This is translated, in *SBE*, 'sets him free.' Further on, in ii. 7, in an ancient sun-hymn occurs the unique appellation *varga*, 'twister' or 'turner': 'Thou art the twister! twist thou the sinning of me' (*vargo 'si pāpmānaṁ me vṛṅdhi*). This is translated (*ib.*): 'Thou art the deliverer, deliver me from sin.' In the *Taittirīya Upaniṣad*, ii. 9: 'he frees himself' is, literally, *spṛṇute*, 'he saves himself.' In the *Bṛhadāraṇyaka Upaniṣad*, IV. iv. 23, Regnaud renders *uparatas* (M. Müller: 'satisfied,' Deussen: 'entsagend') by 'libre de tout désir.' In the *Chhāndogya Upaniṣad*, VIII. i. 6, the words rendered 'freedom in all the worlds' are, literally rendered, 'faring as they list' (*kāmachāra*); and in *Maitrāyaṇa Upaniṣad*, i. 2, 'had obtained freedom from all desires' (M. Müller) is, in the original, 'had turned to renunciation' (Deussen).

It is very possible that the translators were encouraged in this habit by consulting the mediæval commentaries of Śaṅkara, in whose philosophy *mokṣa* was a well-evolved concept, and who uses it liberally in his paraphrases.

For instance, in *Kaṭha Upaniṣad*, II. vi. 18—'Nachiketa became free from passion (*vi-raja*) and obtained Brahman'—the last clause is explained as 'became freed' (*mukto 'bhavad*).

In being thus advised to discount much factitious emphasis laid in these ancient works on a notion that was evolving in them, the reader may contend that most at least of the translations criticized render only what is really implicit in the various riddances referred to, namely, a liberty emerging through the abandonment of this or that. It is true that the Indian mind did indeed work its way to a positive concept of *mokṣa* or *vimutti* chiefly through an austere elimination viewed as the getting relieved of discarded burdens. Even a Buddhist commentator of probably the 5th cent. A.D. chose to define *vimokha* as so-called 'because of the being set free (*vimuchchanato*) from opposing things' (*Puggala-Paññatti Com.*). But the state of emancipation, as a conscious assurance, belongs none the less to that more evolved and positive side of its psychology which, in the West, is usually associated with political autonomy and social or personal self-congratulation. The freedom in which the Indian gloried was spiritual:

'O free indeed! O gloriously free am I
In freedom from three crooked things . . .
Ay, but I'm free from rebirth and from death,
And all that dragged me back is hurled away'
(*Psalms of the Sisters*, 11).

'Henceforth in the real (or true) Brahman he becomes perfected and another. His fruit is the *untying of bonds*; without desires he attains to bliss imperishable, immeasurable, and therein abides' (*Maitrāyaṇa Upaniṣad*, vi. 30).

And *Kathā-vatthu*, ix. 1, is intended to bring out the fact that, whereas one enters on 'the Path' to salvation, full of a sense of dangers to be got rid of, the gradual putting off of 'fetters' converts this consciousness into expectation of the bliss of perfected deliverance, *i.e.* of Nibbāna.

For *vimutti* is 'comparable to' Nibbāna, and 'the holy life is planted on, and leads to and culminates in Nibbāna' (*Majjhima*, i. 304; *Saṁyutta*, v. 218).

There is but the faintest anticipation of this in the Vedas. The only 'setting free' in those pages is the resting-place (*vimochana*) where horses are eased for a while from harness. Gods are called upon to deliver from sin—but it is such 'as clings to our bodies' (*Rigveda*, VI. lxxiv. 3; cf. I. xxiv. 9, VIII. xviii. 12, *muñchatam*)—and to let the enemy catch snares and be slain (VII. lix. 8). But such a prayer as 'May I be *detached from death* like a gourd from its stem, but *not from the immortal* [*amṛta*]' (*ib.* 12) is the precursor of the later thought. Beyond such expressions the vocabulary of freedom was, it would appear, unborn.[1] The Brāhmanas give, in the elaborate ritual of the altar-building, a rite to be chanted while laying the 'bricks of saving' (*spṛtah*), that is, from evil

[1] *Mukti* is said in O. Böhtlingk and R. Roth (*Sanskrit-Wörterbuch*, Petrograd, 1855–75, v. 801) to occur once in the *Śatapatha Brāhmaṇa*, but it is a faulty reference, and the present writer cannot trace it.

and from death (*Śatapatha Brāhmaṇa*, VIII. iv. 2), but elsewhere (XI. iii. 3) it is said that none but a *brahmachārin* or *religieux* is exempted by Brahman from death, and only on the condition that he daily tends the sacred fire. Not here any more than in the Vedas does the grasp and realization of an emancipated consciousness appear. It is still apparently only inchoate in the Upaniṣads ranked as the oldest. Of these the *Kena Upaniṣad* is silent on the matter. In the *Aitareya Āraṇyaka*, an ancient mystic nature-monologue, there are hymns prescribed for rites proficiency in which brings the compassing of 'all desires.' These desires are enunciated—long life, luck, wealth, fame, etc.—but 'liberty' is not among them. Progress in spirituality is revealed in the *Taittirīya* and *Chhāndogya Upaniṣads*, but the emancipation-spirit is still immature. The former shows the growth of it at the end of the second part:

'He who knows the bliss of that Brahman whence speech, whence mind turn back, not finding it, . . . tortures not himself with: "What good have I left undone? What evil have I done?" He, knowing this, saves himself.'

The latter (*Chhāndogya*, VI. xiv. 2) shows a parallel growth in the parable of the man brought blindfold from his Gandhāra home into the desert, and thence, with sight restored, directed how to get home again; even so does one who has gained true knowledge through his teacher know that

'I shall only so long belong to this [system of rebirth] till I am emancipated (*vimokṣye*); then I shall go home' (so Deussen).

And in the closing section occurs the favourite simile for deliverance:

'Freeing myself from the body, as the moon frees himself from Rāhu's jaws, I go into the world of Brahman.'

The same simile is hinted at in the *Kaṭha Upaniṣad*:

'He who has perceived the soundless, the intangible . . . the eternal . . . the unchangeable, is freed from the jaws of death' (I. iii. 15).

But in the following passage (*ib.* II. v. 1) we see how the idea is finding expanded expression:

'There is a town with eleven gates of the Unborn, of thought influctuate. Whoso approaches (Deussen: 'honours') it, he grieves no more and, emancipated, is set free (*vimuktaś cha vimuchyate*). Verily this is that.'

From what 'set free' is not unambiguous (M. Müller: bonds of ignorance; Deussen: the body), but 'liberty' is becoming realized as an ideal.

Turning now to the long *Bṛhadāraṇyaka Upaniṣad*, we come at length to an emphatic designation of certain attainments as constituting 'liberty' (III. i. 3 ff.). The priest asks the Veda-teacher how he who institutes a sacrifice may be freed from the influence and thraldom of death, of day and night, and of the waxing and waning moon, and how the bright worlds shall be reached up a stairless sky. By this or that celebrant priest are given the several replies, and to each reply is added: '*That* is liberty, *that* is utter liberty (*sā muktiḥ sā atimuktiḥ*).' These are then termed the *atimokṣas*.

It is noteworthy that, while these four 'liberations' are alone so emphasized, aspiration does not (in the adjacent section) stop at heaven. Urged by another interlocutor, a Kṣatriya, again and again, with proffered largess, to 'speak of that higher thing which avails for emancipation,' Yājñavalkya, the Veda-teacher, finally discourses of the soul and of beholding the soul as God.

'Scarce visible and old there lies a path
That reaches into me, was found by me.
Thereon the wise whose is the Brahma-lore
Fare onward to the world of light, and thence
O'erpassing that are utterly released'
(*utkramya svargaṁ lokam ito vimuktāḥ*).

'As the slough of a snake lies on an anthill dead and cast away, there lies this body, but that disembodied, that immortal, that life, is Brahman only, only light' (IV. iv. 8, 7).

This with its context is not designated as *atimokṣa*, or as *mukti*. When we find again the snake-skin simile, in the *Praśna Upaniṣad*, V. 5, where the emancipation described is that of spiritual ecstasy rather than of a disembodied spiritual unity, or full realization of the same, the freedness, on the one hand, is made more explicit, and, on the other, the liberation is described as 'from evil.' But, whether emancipation be from the power of the body during life or from the body itself and from all subsequent bodies at final death, the main positive consciousness, realized in this early stage of Vedāntist *mokṣa*, is, intellectually, discernment of the identity between the Absolute, Brahman or Ātman, and the soul located in man, and, emotionally, the sense of security and assurance resulting therefrom. For the individual becomes invested with the powers, negatively expressed, of the Absolute Being: undecaying, imperishable, unattached, unbound, unlimited, unsuffering, etc. (*Bṛhadāraṇyaka Upaniṣad*, IV. ii. 4).

'If a man clearly beholds this self as lord of all that is and will be, . . . who has entered into this patched-together hiding-place, he is creator, maker of all, his is the world, he is the world . . . then is he no more afraid' (*ib.* IV. iv. 13, 15).

Proceeding to the less ancient Upaniṣads, such as may have been influenced by Buddhist and other developments, we find in the 'Upaniṣad of the Shavelings' (*Muṇḍaka*) the compound *parimuchyanti* (III. ii. 6), 'completely freed':

'They who have grasped the sense of Veda-lore,
All anchorites, their inmost being purged
In earnest resignation, at the final death
In Brahma-heaven become immortal, wholly freed.'

But in the *Śvetāśvatara Upaniṣad*, and the allied but perhaps still later *Maitrāyaṇa Upaniṣad*, the reader finds himself among new ideas jostling against the older ones. These are yet present—soul and Brahman, release from life and death, and knowledge as giving release—but the current has widened, if not deepened. The theism of Yoga, the theory of separate souls and their self-emancipation from conditioned, mutable concomitants of the Sāṅkhya system, the critical, scientific attitude of Buddhism, and the tragic earnestness of the two former and of Jainism—all these have caused a revolution in outlook that strikes a new note at the very first words:

'Om! The Brahman teachers say: What is the primal cause, what Brahman? Whence are we?' (*Śvetāśvatara Upaniṣad*, i. 1).

Through it all the *mokṣa*-idea appears as the work of a creator:

'The Deva' or Īśvara ('Lord'), 'himself self-caused, is the condition (the cause) of the maintenance and the movement (*sthiti, saṁsāra*), the bondage and the liberation (*bandha, mokṣa*) of the world' (*ib.* vi. 16). To know him, to 'see, making his own being a lamp, the being of the Lord,' is to have 'all fetters fall away, all sufferings destroyed, and the ceasing of birth and death come to pass' (*ib.* i. 11, ii. 15). 'I, seeking for freedom, take in him my refuge, supreme Causeway to that-which-is-not-dead (*amṛtasya paraṁ setuṁ*), Fire that burneth where no fuel is' (*ib.* vi. 18 f.).

'As soon a man might wrap the atmosphere
About himself like any cloak, as reach
The end of suffering, not knowing God' (*ib.* vi. 20).

Yet both here and in the *Maitrāyaṇa Upaniṣad* the Ātmanistic monism is none the less maintained, and all personal deities are recognized as names of the self (IV. v. f., VI. v. 8).

Much, it is true, is made of a disparate 'element-soul' or self, bound by the fetters of the fruits of good and evil, crippled, and as one in prison, till 'by knowledge, by *tapas* (austerities), by meditation he is freed from those things by which he was filled and overcome, and obtains union with the Ātman' (IV. ii. 4).

Yet this concept no longer satisfies:

'Having seen his own self as the Self (or soul), he becomes selfless (*nirātman*); and, in virtue of selflessness he is to be conceived as immeasurable, unconditioned. This is the highest mystery, betokening emancipation . . . through selflessness he has no part in pleasure or pain, but attains absoluteness (*kevalatva*)' (VI. xx. f.)—

a wondrous blend of Buddhist and Sāṅkhya concepts.

Yet another new term reveals a fresh and notable development of the *mokṣa*-consciousness, that of 'autonomous,' or independent—*svatantra* (V. xxviii. 38):

'Independent, standing on his own greatness, he contemplates the cycle of rebirth as it were a rolling chariot-wheel' (that has ceased to convey him). Cf. the 'autonomy' prescribed in and vital for Buddhism (*Dīgha Nikāya*, ii. 100, and elsewhere).

The psychology also of the *process* of self-liberation has attained an interesting development (*Maitrāyaṇa Upaniṣad*, VI. xxxiv.). *Manas* (*i.e.* the mental mechanism of sense-cognition, a narrower concept than 'mind') is, like Īśvara himself, called 'the cause of bondage and of liberty.' And to bring it to its right anchorage, to bring it, in fact, 'to an end in the heart' (the seat of the soul) —'that is knowledge, that is *mokṣa* . . . that man is wholly freed (*parimuchyate*).' Nor does this austere discipline, nor does the evolving power of introspection dull the rapture associated in the earlier books with this setting free. With a poet's licence, or through theistic influence, the poet pictures the Absolute soul (Brahman) as reciprocally 'longing for a true (or real) man' (*ib.* VI. xxx.).

That the yet later Upaniṣads could use *mokṣa* as practically synonymous with religion appears in the *Mukti Upaniṣad*, which recommends him who seeks for *mokṣa* to study the *Māṇḍūkya Upaniṣad*, and, if that suffice not, certain others, and so on till all are included. The one named consists in a concise effort to define the essence (*sāra*) of the soul or Brahman. More pertinent is the definition of *mokṣa* in another of the aforesaid Upaniṣads, the *Sarva-sāra*, as the destruction of the illusion that the material body, or any other factor of the phenomenal self, is the Ātman ('soul'), who is God. The illusion is the bond, ignorance its cause. (This illusion is the first of the 'Ten Fetters' of Buddhism.)

Mokṣa as the supreme aspiration runs through that best known portion of the *Mahābhārata* epic called the *Bhagavad-Gītā*. The allusions occur almost entirely in the parts judged by R. Garbe to be older (see BHAGAVAD-GĪTĀ). We find *mokṣa* applied to liberation from evil (iv. 16), from the body (v. 23), from lusts and anger (v. 26), from decay and death (vii. 29), from works (ix. 28), from the illusion of opposites (xv. 5). But, however the bondage be conceived, release is effected, here also, by a spiritual union with Brahman, conceived as, or as behind, Īśvara, lover of the human soul, who invites his utter self-surrender, and bestows on him, in virtue of that surrender, release from this or that form of limitation (cf. ix. 26 f., xii., xiii. 9 f.). Another section of the epic is called 'the *mokṣa*-doctrine'; yet it is in the *Anugītā* section that the complete picture of the emancipated individual occurs (*Adhyāya*, 19). In this we see him contemplating Ātman, attaining Brahman, sunken in this one goal, oblivious as to the past, freed from results, heedless of 'this' or 'that.' Yet he is a friend to all, suffering all, master of sense and self, fearless, wrathless, meek, upright, treating all creatures as if they were he, indifferent to opposites, lost to social and domestic ties, wanting naught, cleaving to naught, detached. 'He is in every sense free.' All classes, the trader and the labourer, too, may enter on this upward way, and even women, but much more the Brāhman and the Kṣatriya who study, joy in their duty, and hold the Brahma world as highest; for the fruit of achievement is liberty, and the utter abatement of ill. Beyond that lies no greater bliss.

This notable climax is in complete harmony with Buddhist thought. It is more than probable that, before the epic attained its final form, the influence of Buddhist culture had made itself deeply felt, and that to it is largely due the breaking down of class and sex disability to attain the highest, the humaneness of the lonely saint, and the crucial emphasis on the ending of suffering. *Dukkha* ('ill') is not, of course, absent from the earlier Vedāntic literature, but it attains emphasis only in that which must have felt the impress of Buddhism, to say nothing of Jainist and Sāṅkhyan influence. Now, in the doctrine of Arahantship, or the release from continued deaths and rebirths by the perfected character, *vimutti* is not only dominant to the same extent as is *mukti* (*mokṣa*) in Vedānta, but the treatment of it is more consistent and therefore, perhaps, simpler. In it *vimutti*, *vimutta*, 'freedom,' 'freed,' express the actual and consciously realized achievements; *vimok(k)ha* nearly always refers to certain prescribed courses of rapt mentality, whereby such a state might be sooner acquired, or, if acquired independently, quickened —a sort of morning sacrament (*Dīgha Nikāya*, ii. 112; *Puggala-Paññatti Com.* [*JPTS*, 1914, p. 177]):

'He who before he breaks his fast can touch
Mental emancipation's eight degrees,
In grade ascending and so back again'
(*Psalms of the Brethren*, 1172).

Hence the terms 'freed by understanding,' 'freed-both-ways,' meaning emancipated by the work of understanding only, or emancipated both thus and by the eight *vimokhas* or similar exercise in *samādhi* (cf. *Majjhima Nikāya*, i. 477).

Moreover, *vimutti*, as expressing final achievement, with the rapturous assurance of it, was at the heart of the Buddhist Dhamma from the first. In that which is recorded as his second sermon—the *Anatta-lakkhaṇa Sutta* (*Vinaya Texts*, i. 101; cf. 107)—Gotama Buddha stated how emancipation grew out of the rejection of the cosmic soul as immanent in and identical with the sense of individual personality ('self' being only an abstract idea inseparable from bodily and mental factors). Perception of the absence of Ātman-qualities (permanence, omniscience, bliss) in these denuded them of factitious attraction. Craving to renew them in future lives fell away. The freed individual knew that he was free, and thenceforth needed only to await the final hour in quieted but blissful well-being and righteous living. Again, in sending forth his first missionaries, the Buddha named as his and their supremely adequate qualification:

'I am freed from all snares human and divine; ye are freed from all snares human and divine . . . Go ye now . . . for the welfare of the many . . .' (*Vinaya Texts*, i. 112 f.).

The subjective awareness of the freed state, held to be also valid objectively, is further enhanced by the use of such terms as 'realizing,' 'touching,' 'tasting' (*Dīgha Nikāya*, iii. 230; *Majjhima Nikāya*, i. 477; *Aṅguttara Nikāya*, ii. 244, i. 36, iv. 203, etc.).

'Wherefore thus must ye study: "more and ever more striving our very best shall we realize supreme emancipation"' (*Aṅguttara Nikāya*, iii. 218).

'Having liberated his mind with respect to things that should be let go he touches perfect liberty' (*ib.* ii. 196; cf. 244).

'The eight deliverances (*vimokhā*) are to be realized by personal contact' (*Dīgha Nikāya*, iii. 230).

'Few are they who obtain the taste of liberty' (*Aṅguttara Nikāya*, i. 36).

'As the ocean has but one taste, that of salt, so has Nibbāna but one taste, that of emancipation' (*ib.* iv. 203; *Vinaya Texts*, iii. 304).

Awareness of full attainment was realized as a timeless moment of ecstatic consciousness (*Kathāvatthu*, iii. 4), but the reverberations formed an abiding joy:

'Gladness springs up within him, and rapture thereto; the thoughts of his enraptured consciousness become tranquillized; thus tranquillized he knows bliss; and in that bliss his consciousness is stayed' (*Dīgha Nikāya*, iii. 241, 'The five occasions of emancipation'; cf. i. 73).

Imagination plays about the term:

'He with fair flowers of Liberty enwreathed,
Sane and immune, shall reach the perfect peace'
(*Psalms of the Brethren*, 100).

'Above the rolling chariot of this earthly life spreads the silken canopy of emancipation' (*Saṃyutta Nikāya*, iv. 293).

And in the later *Questions of King Milinda*:

'As the ocean is all in blossom with the innumerable . . . ripple of its waves, so is Nibbāna all in blossom, as it were, with the innumerable, diverse, delicate flowers of purity, knowledge, emancipation' (IV. viii. 69).

Arahantship, again (*ib.* v. 17), is called

'the Exalted One's jewel of emancipation (*vimutti-ratana*), chief diadem of all.'

The three terms here brought together—Nibbāna, Arahantship, emancipation—are largely, though not wholly, coincident in range, presenting different aspects of the ideal, Nibbāna: the having eliminated 'the fires' of evil and of craving for continued life human or divine; the contemplation of an Ātman-less Absolute; Arahantship: supreme positive attainment in life on earth; Vimutti: the subjective aspect of both, the negative force in it never far off:

'Let go (*muñcha*) that which has been, let go what will be,
Let go what thou art midst of, thou that dost
Transcend Becoming! On every side freed-minded
Thou'lt not again come toward birth and dying'
(*Dhammapada*, 348).

But the self-knowledge that he *is* free is a clause in the formula confessing Arahantship:

'Emancipated by right (or perfect) gnosis (*sammadaññā-vimutta*)'; 'in him thus set free there arises the knowledge "freed"!' . . . (Nikāyas, *passim*; *Dialogues*, i. 93).

And the unity connecting the negative and positive aspects may be discerned in the *Sutta Nipāta* verses:

'In whom no sense-desires do dwell,
For whom no craving doth exist,
Who hath crossed o'er [the sea of] doubt:—
What sort of freedom [waits] for him?
No other freedom [waits] for him' (1089 f.).

In the Nikāyas *vimutti* and Nibbāna are declared to be 'comparable' one with another (in the same thought-category, *Majjhima*, i. 304). But in the *Dhamma-saṅgaṇi vimutti* is distinguished into higher mental freedom and Nibbāna (p. 234; cf. *Dīgha Nikāya*, i. 174).

As the subject of a distinct group (*khandha*) of religious experience, *vimutti* is ranked in the *Suttas* fourth with the groups 'ethics' (*sīla*), concentrative studies (*samādhi*), and insight (*paññā*, *Majjhima*, i. 214; *Aṅguttara Nikāya*, i. 125, *passim*), while for the Arahant a fifth was reckoned: knowledge and intuition of *vimutti* (*vimutti-ñāna-darsana*, *ib.* i. 162, etc.). Closely associated with the fourfold path to Arahantship, and called, later, modes of progress, avenues, or channels to *vimutti*, are the studies in 'Emptiness,' 'the Signless,' 'the Not-hankered-after' (*Dīgha Nikāya*, iii. 219; *Saṁyutta*, iv. 295–297; *Dhamma-saṅgaṇi*, 344 f., and *Compendium of Philosophy*, London, 1910, p. 216).

A very frequent allusion to emancipation in the Nikāyas is that of *chetovimutti paññāvimutti*, corresponding fairly well to emancipation of heart and head. The systematic expansion of ethical emotion was not peculiar to Buddhism (see LOVE [Buddhist]). But the founder of Buddhism is represented (*Saṁyutta*, v. 118) as claiming that he alone inculcated in such exercises emancipation of the heart.

In this way, in suffusing the idea of more and more beings with (1) love—'let all beings be void of enmity and malevolence,' (2) pity—'let all be set free from suffering,' (3) sympathy—'let all be happy and fortunate,' (4) equanimity—'all are the owners, the heirs of their deeds,' these mental exercises, if fully practised, result in a thorough self-mastery through complete emancipation from the respectively opposed moods of (1) enmity, (2) harmfulness, (3) antipathy, (4) passion (Ledi Sadaw, Mahāthera, in a letter to the writer).

Taken alone, apart from that supreme enfranchisement from all the conditions for rebirth, they constituted the best way to Brahma-heavens.

'*Sāriputta*: This, I told Dhānañjani, is the way to share existence with the Brahma gods.

The Buddha: Why did you establish Dhānañjani in that inferior Brahma-world, when there was more to be done?

Sāriputta: I judged, lord, that these Brāhmans preferred that heaven' (*Majjhima*, ii. 195).

'All other bases of meritorious acts which are stuff for rebirth (*opādhika*) are not to be compared to the emancipation of the heart by love. That takes all those up into itself, as the moon outshines the stars, the sun the mirk, the morning star the night, shining in radiance and in splendour' (*Iti-vuttaka*, 19–21).

But to be emancipated by intuition or insight is to have broken all the ten 'fetters' by the four successive stages of the Ariyan Path—Stream-winning, Once-Returning, Never-Returning, Arahantship—and to have reached the going-out of all fevered desires as to lives on earth or in the heavens (*Dīgha Nikāya*, iii. 108).

'For not by the slothful nor the fool, the undiscerning, is that Nibbāna to be reached which is the *untying of all knots*' (*Iti-vuttaka*, 102).

The mountain ranges of *vimutti* were the haunts of those who, 'with the world well lost,' had developed the symptoms of life's culminating in its final end. Hence it is in the two works containing the legacies of such matured creatures—the *Sutta-Nipāta* and the anthologies of *Theras* and *Therīs*—that the theme of emancipation is maintained most steadily:

'Come now, let us see Gotama, who lion-like
Doth roam alone . . .
. . . and let us ask of him
How can we be set free from snare of death?
Declare to us who ask as to the way
How may a man from sorrow be set free'
(*Sutta-Nipāta*, 164 f.).

'Passed he away fraught with the seed of rebirth,
Or as one wholly free? That would we know'
(*Psalms of the Brethren*, 1274).

'And as the sun rose up out of the dawn
Lo! then my heart was set at liberty' (*ib.* 477).

'Whose range is in the Void and the Unmarked
And Liberty:—as flight of birds in air
So hard is it to track the trail of him' (*ib.* 92).

'And see, O Master! Sundarī who comes
To tell thee of Emancipation won
And of the night no more to be reborn;
Who hath herself from passion freed (*vītarāgā*),
Unyoked from bondage' (*Psalms of the Sisters*, 334).

'Tho' I be suffering and weak and all
My youthful spring be gone, yet have I come,
Leaning upon my staff, and clomb aloft
The mountain peak. My cloak thrown off,
My little bowl o'erturned: so sit I here
Upon the rock. And o'er my spirit sweeps
The breath of Liberty!' (*ib.* 29, 30).

'Passion abandoned, hatred and illusion,
Shattered the bonds, nor is there any trembling
In that the springs of life are wholly withered:—
Like the rhinoceros let him wander lonely'
(*Sutta-Nipāta*, 74).

'E'en as a fish that breaks its net in ocean,
E'en as a fire that turns not back to burnt stuff:—
Like the rhinoceros let him wander lonely' (*ib.* 62).

'Dwelling in love, in pity, and in freedom,
In friendly joy, in balance, each in season,
Nought in the world disturbing his composure:—
Like the rhinoceros let him wander lonely' (*ib.* 73).

The evolution of *mukti*, or *mokṣa*, in Jainism cannot be adequately dealt with till its early literature is more fully accessible. As evolved, the idea is clearly presented above (art. JAINISM, vol. vii. pp. 468, 470).

Similarly the (*vi*)*mokṣa*, or *apavarga*, concept of Sāṅkhyan thought, which survives in mediæval commentaries, and which, even in the aphorisms on which these are based, shows a later and a more habile metaphysic than such as the foregoing discussions reveal, will be dealt with in art. SĀṄKHYA. In those aphorisms (*Sūtras*) the individual soul, called *puruṣa*, is conceived as 'neither bound, nor liberated, nor migrating' (lxii.), as is the rest of man's nature, physical and mental. Emancipation consists in having discerned the 'subtle difference between this [dual] nature (*pradhāna*) and the soul' (xxxvii.). 'By knowledge is liberation (*jñānena chā'pavargo*), by the opposite is bondage' (xliv.). With this knowledge the work of good and evil is done; the union of soul and organism may 'go on like the potter's wheel revolving from the effect [of his impact]' (lxvii.) after the finished pot is removed, but, when nature thereupon ceases to act, the soul obtains absoluteness (*kaivalyam āpnoti*) (lxviii.).

LITERATURE.—Works quoted from: *The Upanishads*, tr. Max Müller, *SBE* i. [1879], xv. [1884]; P. Deussen, *Sechzig Upanishad's des Veda*, Leipzig, 1897; P. Regnaud, *Matériaux pour servir à l'histoire de la philosophie de l'Inde*, Paris, 1876–79 (translates many selections, giving the original as well); P. Deussen, *Vier philosophische Texte des Mahâbhâratam*, Leipzig, 1906, *Allgemeine Geschichte der Philosophie*, i. pt. 3, iv. 6, do. 1908; *Vinaya Texts*, tr. T. W. Rhys Davids and H. Oldenberg, 3 vols., *SBE* xiii., xvii., xx. [1881–85]; *Questions of King Milinda*, tr. T. W. Rhys Davids, *SBE* xxxv.–xxxvi. [1890–94]; the four *Nikāyas*, *Dhammapada*, *Sutta-Nipāta*, and other Pāli works: publications of the PTS, London, 1882 f. (the two last tr. Max Müller and V. Fausböll, *SBE* x.[3] [1898]); *Psalms of the Early Buddhists*, 2 vols., and *Points of Controversy* (*Kathāvatthu*), *PTS*; *Dialogues of the Buddha*, tr. of *Dīgha Nikāya*, i. (in *SBB*, ii., iii.). The blend of theism and 'ātmanism' handed down from the stage of Vedāntist thought indicated in the *Maitrāyaṇa* and *Śvetāśvatara Upaniṣads*, and developed in the *Bhagavad-Gītā*, may be studied in P. Narasimha's description of *mukti* in 'The Vedântic Good,' *Mind*, Jan. 1915. Another interesting account of *mokṣa*, with a criticism on P. Deussen's treatment of the place of moral considerations in the doctrine, is by Dvijadas Datta, 'Moksha, or the Vedântic Release,' *JRAS* xx. pt. 4 [1887–88], p. 513.

C. A. F. RHYS DAVIDS.

MOLINISM.—There is no problem in theology more difficult than that which has reference to the knowledge and causality of God, on the one hand, and the liberty and eternal destiny of human beings, on the other. The problem includes three difficulties: (1) How is it possible to reconcile God's foreknowledge with the freedom of the human will? (2) If the entire physical reality of our free acts proceeds from God as the First Cause, how is it possible for our will to be a free cause, or for evil actions to be imputed to us? (3) Given the sincere will of God to save all men, how account for the terrible fact that many die without the light of faith and never attain to eternal salvation?

The endeavours of theologians to throw light on these difficulties have brought forth two systems: Thomism and Molinism. The doctrine of the Thomists, which is the old traditional doctrine of St. Augustine and St. Thomas Aquinas (*qq.v.*), was attacked by Molina at the close of the 16th cent.; since then an unending controversy has raged in Roman Catholic schools of theology.

I. *HISTORY OF THE CONTROVERSY.*—In the 13th cent. St. Thomas Aquinas, a Dominican, synthesized the sum of human knowledge with regard to God as the First Cause and Final End of all things in a work called the *Summa Theologica*. Herein is contained all that the human mind, aided by revelation, can know concerning God's providence, universal causality, grace, etc. So great became the renown of St. Thomas for the solidity and sublimity of his doctrine that at the Council of Trent the *Summa Theologica*, alone of all theological treatises, was thought fit to be used in consultation with the sacred Scriptures. The Order of St. Dominic is sworn to love and defend the doctrines of St. Thomas as by hereditary right; and it is their loyalty to these doctrines that has earned them the well-merited name of Thomists.

At the close of the 16th cent. the Jesuit Luis de Molina (1535–1600) published a new doctrine on predestination, grace, free will, etc. The basis of the whole system is the so-called *scientia media*, a theory borrowed by Molina from his master, Pedro da Fonseca, who, knowing it to be entirely new and against the traditional doctrine, had not dared to publish it. Molina's book was published at Lisbon in 1588 and is entitled: *Concordia liberi arbitrii cum gratiæ donis, divina præscientia, providentia, prædestinatione et reprobatione.* Had this theory been known, says Molina, Pelagianism would never have existed, Luther would not have denied free will, and Semi-Pelagianism would easily have been stamped out. Molina further adds that St. Augustine and the other Fathers would have unanimously approved of this theory of predestination and this manner of conciliating free will with the foreknowledge and providence of God, if it had been propounded to them (*Concordia*, ed. Paris, 1876, p. 548). This new doctrine, however, did not arrest the teachings of Michael Baius, nor did it prevent the rise of Jansenism (*q.v.*), but was itself the cause of an unending and bitter controversy which has lasted for centuries between Thomists and Molinists. The above assertions of Molina aroused the indignation of the followers of St. Augustine and St. Thomas. Dominic Bañes vigorously attacked the new theory, and so great was the dissension caused by the ensuing controversy that in 1594 the matter came before Pope Clement VIII., who, in 1598, instituted a special board of inquiry, known as the 'Congregatio de Auxiliis.' There were, in all, 181 assemblies of this congregation, which debated the doctrines under discussion. Three condemnations in succession were drawn up by the consultors against Molina. On 13th March 1598 they declared that the *Concordia* and the doctrine of Molina must be unreservedly condemned. On 19th Dec. 1601 they condemned 20 propositions taken from the *Concordia*. At the assembly of the Cardinals (8th March 1606) it was decided to give orders to the consultors to draw up a bull for the condemnation of 42 propositions taken from the *Concordia*. The bull was actually prepared for publication, but on 28th Aug. 1607 Paul V. held a congregation of cardinals in which it was decided to postpone the condemnation. The result of the 'Congregatio de Auxiliis' was, then, a moral defeat for Molinism. So forcibly was this brought home to Acquaviva (the General of the Jesuits) and his counsellors that the Congruism of F. Suarez was substituted for Molinism and imposed upon the Society by Acquaviva by his decree of 14th Dec. 1613. For more than 200 years Congruism (see below, p. 776[b]) was taught by the Jesuits in obedience to the decree of Acquaviva, but pure Molinism has now been revived by some Jesuit theologians.

In this matter an important point to be noted is the declaration of Paul V. that both Molinism and Thomism agree in *substance* with Catholic truth, but differ only as regards the *mode* of explaining the efficacy of grace, *both of which opinions may be held.* Innocent XII., in reply to the University of Louvain (7th Feb. 1694), and Benedict XIII., in a brief (*Demissas preces*, 6th Nov. 1724), vindicated the Thomistic doctrine of the efficacy of grace *ab intrinseco* and the gratuity of predestination. Lest, however, the words uttered by Benedict XIII. should be understood to minimize the doctrines of Molinism, Clement XII. said (2nd Oct. 1733):

> 'We do not wish the eulogies (which we iterate, approve, and confirm) of our predecessors (Clement XI. and Benedict XIII.) in praise of the Thomistic school to detract in any way from the authority of other Catholic schools' (*Bullarium Ord. Præd.* viii. 291).

Since the encyclical *Æterni Patris* of Leo XIII. (4th Aug. 1879), Roman Catholic schools of theology have done their utmost to claim as their own not only the doctrine, but the very name of St. Thomas Aquinas. In spite of the remonstrances of Thomists, Molinists have endeavoured to drag St. Thomas to their side, and even to impose on St. Thomas the theory of *scientia media*, which, before Molina, was not even dreamed of ('ne per somnium quidem'), as C. Tiphanus, himself a Jesuit, declares.[1] The first crossing of swords took place between R. P. Beaudoin and C. Mazzella. Not long after, G. Schneemann published a work in 1881, in refutation of which A. M. Dummermuth published a work at Paris in 1886, which contains a complete demonstration of the mind of St. Thomas. In 1893 V. Frins essayed a reply, and in refutation of this Dummermuth published another work in

[1] *De ordine deque priori et posteriori*, 24.

1895. Since then there have been many minor publications, chiefly in theological and philosophical *Reviews*.

II. *ESSENCE OF MOLINISM*.—1. **Natural order.** —(1) *God's foreknowledge and free will*.—The knowledge of God, considered in itself, is one and indivisible; considered with reference to objects which are the term of His knowledge, it is divided according to the diversity of objects into speculative and practical, into necessary and free, etc. The division which concerns us now is that into the knowledge of vision (*scientia visionis*) and the knowledge of simple understanding (*scientia simplicis intelligentiæ*). The former has reference to things which have existed, exist, or will exist; the latter has reference to the purely possible, *i.e.* to objects which have not existed, do not, and will not exist (cf. *Summa Theol.* I. qu. 14, art. 9). Now, if this division is adequate, God must know a future free act by the 'knowledge of vision.' But, according to St. Thomas (I. qu. 14, art. 8, and art. 9 ad tertium), this knowledge necessarily implies an act of God's will or a divine decree. Hence a future free act is known by God by virtue of, in fact *in*, His decree, and therefore no future free act can exist unless God decrees its existence. This is the doctrine of the Thomists.

For Molina this is subversive of the freedom of the human will. Hence, he says, a means must be found whereby God knows a future free act before, and independently of, the divine decree. Now there is a third kind of object, continues Molina, which neither is purely possible nor yet belongs to the category of those objects which, in some difference of time, have actual existence. There is the future event which would exist if certain conditions were realized, which, however, will *not* be realized. Under this head are to be classed all those free acts which, though never destined actually to exist, would exist if certain conditions were fulfilled. These are called conditioned future events (*futura conditionata*, or *futurabilia*); and God knows these by the *scientia media*, a knowledge which is midway, as it were, between that of vision and that of simple understanding. Although a future conditioned event is that which will never come to existence, because the condition on which it depends will never be fulfilled, the *scientia media*, as such, abstracts from the realization or non-realization of such a condition; hence, by the *scientia media*, God explores and knows, with infallible certainty, what the human free will will infallibly do by its own innate liberty (consent or dissent, do this act or that, etc.) if it be placed in such or such circumstances. God, if He wishes, *e.g.*, Peter to consent, to do this act, etc., decrees to put Peter in these or those circumstances, and decrees conditionally to grant His help or concurrence for the particular action determined upon by Peter's free will (see below, 'simultaneous concourse'). In this decree, which follows the foreknowledge of the future free act, Molinists say God knows the absolute future consent without prejudice to the free will; but the certitude of His knowledge is due, not to the intrinsic efficacy of the decree, but to the *scientia media*, which sees the consent before the decree.

The unanimity among Molinists is mainly negative, namely, that God does not know future free acts in any absolute, actual decree of His will; but, as regards the medium in which God sees a future free act, *quot homines, tot sententiæ*.

(*a*) Molina and, after him, R. Bellarmine, M. Becanus, etc., teach that God knows the future free act in the super-comprehension of the free will; *i.e.*, God's knowledge penetrates into the innermost recesses of the will and sees there what it will infallibly do in such and such circumstances. This is the direct denial of free will, for the certain knowledge of an effect in its cause is the knowledge of a necessary effect. (*b*) Therefore Suarez taught that God knows the future free act in His decree foreseen as future. But it is impossible even to conceive of a future decree in God: the divine decrees are eternal, and are therefore neither past nor future. Unable to answer this, Suarez had recourse to another medium: (*c*) God knows future acts in their truth, which is either formal or objective. The reality of the future free act is the objective truth; the proposition expressing that reality is the formal truth. Some Molinists (G. Vasquez, M. Liberatori, H. Kilber, D. Palmieri, etc.) hold to the formal truth, asserting that of two contradictory propositions expressing a future contingent event one is determinately true, the other determinately false from all eternity, and this independently of God's will; but God knows all truth; therefore . . . This medium is rejected, not only by all Thomists, but by many Molinists, by Billot, G. Lahousse, etc. Others (F. Suarez, J. B. Franzelin, Mazzella, etc.) hold to the objective truth, since the truth of a proposition expressing the future depends on the objective truth of a future event. This medium is rejected by other Molinists—by Lahousse, who says that God sees future free acts, not in their truth, as such, but in their reality (*in ipsismet*). Billot, among others, refutes this. Others—J. Kleutgen, P. Carnoldi, T. de Régnon—failing to find a medium which does not involve absurdities, admit the *scientia media*, but acknowledge their ignorance as to its process of operation. Hence, the *scientia media*, invented to explain a difficulty, is the greatest difficulty of all.

(2) *God's causality and free will*.—God is the First Cause; therefore no being or mode of being can escape His causality. Thomists teach that in virtue of the divine decree the human will is physically, *i.e.* efficiently, predetermined by God to produce a free act. This divine influx precedes the action of the will by a priority of nature and causality, and applies the will to act (*i.e.*, makes the will pass from the state of not acting to the state of acting), thus rendering the will *in actu primo* capable of freely determining itself *in actu secundo*. The free will infallibly consents to that to which it is premoved; *i.e.*, the premotion is efficacious; yet the power to dissent remains with the will, for the premotion, divinely efficacious, effects that, although the will has the power to dissent, it infallibly consents and does not dissent. According to pure Molinism, the divine influx does not precede the action of the free will, but simultaneously co-operates with it, helping, as a partial cause, to produce the same action and the same effect. This divine action, called 'simultaneous concourse,' is, therefore, not received into the will, but is rather alongside of it, and is received immediately into the action and effect of the will. In order to safeguard the universal causality of God, it is said that, although God and the free will are partial causes of the free act, nevertheless the effect is wholly produced by God as the First Cause, and wholly by the will as the secondary cause. The simultaneous concourse is not efficacious, but is, of its very nature, indifferent, and is modified or determined by the free will, and hence can be used for volition or nolition, for this act or that act, indiscriminately, according to the determination of the free will. Other Molinists reject this simultaneous concourse, and admit a kind of premotion, *i.e.* a physical influx received into the faculty of the will previous to the determination (action) of the will. By this influx the will is moved and determined to general or universal good,

but of itself the influx is indifferent and inefficacious for this or that particular good: without any further influx from God, the will determines itself to act, not to act, to do this, or to do that.

Thomists are accused of making God the cause of sin by the physical premotion which is efficacious, but the difficulty of sin has to be solved by Molinists also. Physical premotion effects, it is true, that the will cannot but infallibly do that to which it is premoved, but no Thomist allows that God predetermines to sin *qua* sin (see THOMISM): the simultaneous concourse of the Molinists is a co-operation of God with the will, not indeed to produce the sinful action as sinful, but to produce the physical reality of the action. It is a lesser evil to co-operate than to make another commit a sin; Molinists have chosen a lesser evil, but have not solved the difficulty.

Against the two theories of Molinism with regard to the divine influx Thomists object that neither safeguards the universal causality of God. The self-determination of the will is not nothing; it is a reality, which, therefore, cannot escape God's causality. To argue, as does a recent Molinist (Lahousse, *Theol. Nat.*, Louvain, 1888, cap. 9, art. 3, no. 502), that there seems no reason why this quality (*i.e.* the determination of the will whereby it makes itself pass from the state of not willing to the state of willing) cannot be efficiently produced by a created being is not only to beg the question, but manifestly to deny, in very words, God's universal causality.

2. Supernatural order.—(1) *Grace and free will.*—Against Pelagians both Thomists and Molinists defend the necessity of grace for the production of a salutary act. Against Semi-Pelagianism both defend the necessity for the very beginnings of faith, and for the desire to do a salutary work. Both teach the absolute gratuity of actual grace, even for the very beginnings (*prima gratia vocans*) of justification. Against Calvin, Luther, and Jansen both teach that sufficient grace is given to all without exception, and that, under the influence of efficacious grace, the freedom of the will remains intact. The first point of difference between Thomism and Molinism concerns the nature of sufficient and efficacious grace, which both agree to be a division of actual grace. For the Thomist efficacious grace is entitatively, *i.e.* intrinsically (*ab intrinseco*), different from sufficient grace. Sufficient grace gives the proximate power of producing a salutary act; it raises the will to a supernatural level, and constitutes it *in actu primo* capable of performing a salutary act; but in order to produce that act *de facto* an efficacious grace (which is a physical premotion in the supernatural order) is necessary. Hence sufficient grace in Thomism gives the *posse*, efficacious grace the *agere* (see THOMISM). For the Molinist the same grace can be sufficient or efficacious; it remains sufficient if the will resists; it becomes efficacious if the will consents. Grace, therefore, is efficacious, not intrinsically or of its very nature, but extrinsically, by the consent of the will (*gratia efficax ab extrinseco*). In the natural order, as said above, the divine indifferent concourse is not received into the will, nor does it precede the action of the will, but in the supernatural order it precedes (owing to which it is called *gratia prœveniens*) the action of the will, and is received into it, thus elevating and making the will the principle *in actu primo* of the salutary act (this saves Molinism from Semi-Pelagianism). Prevenient grace is a physical reality produced by God in the soul moving it (owing to which it is called *gratia excitans*) morally (not physically, *i.e.* efficiently) to consent; it co-operates (owing to which it is called *gratia co-operans*) with the will to elicit a salutary act; but the consent does not follow infallibly, because this grace is not of its very nature, or intrinsically, efficacious (cf. Molina, *Concordia*, qu. 14, art. 13, disp. 41). According to this doctrine, one and the same grace can be merely sufficient for one individual and efficacious for another; further, a lesser grace can be efficacious for one person, while a greater grace can remain merely sufficient for another. Nevertheless, an efficacious grace is a greater boon than a grace merely sufficient. Thus, God from all eternity foresaw (by the *scientia media*) that, if He gave grace A to Peter, he would consent, but, if He gave grace B, Peter would not consent. When, therefore, God gives to Peter grace A, which He foresees will be efficacious, that grace is a greater gift than grace B, which He foresees would be merely sufficient (Molina, L. Lessius, Mazzella, H. Hurter, Palmieri, P. Tepe, etc.).

Bellarmine, Suarez, Vasquez, etc., modified this doctrine, and held what is called Congruism. In this form of Molinism sufficient grace is not indeed intrinsically different from efficacious grace, but differs only as regards the manner in which it affects the will. Efficacious grace (called *gratia congrua*) is that which is so accommodated to man's temperament and to the circumstances of time and place that the will infallibly, but freely, consents; sufficient grace (*gratia incongrua*) is that which is not so perfectly adapted to a man's character and to the circumstances of time and place, etc., and hence the will *de facto* resists. If, therefore, God wishes Peter to consent to grace, He decrees to give him congruous grace—*i.e.* a grace perfectly adapted to Peter's character—to put him in the most fitting circumstances, etc.

(2) *Predestination.* — According to the two theories of grace in the Molinist system, there are two theories of predestination: predestination due to foreseen merits (*post prœvisa merita*) and gratuitous predestination (*ante prœvisa merita*).

(*a*) *Predestination due to foreseen merits.*—God truly and sincerely wishes all to be saved (the salvific will of God); to all he gives sufficient grace. Foreseeing, by the *scientia media*, who will consent to grace and persevere in it, God predestines them to glory. In this opinion predestination to glory presupposes the good use of grace and is therefore not gratuitous (Lessius, Vasquez, Becanus, Franzelin, H. Tournely, etc.). As is evident, this theory entails all the insoluble difficulties of the *scientia media*. Moreover, all that man has he receives from God, according to St. Paul (Ro 11[35f.] 'Who hath first given to him, and it shall be recompensed unto him again? For of him, and through him, and unto him, are all things'; cf. 1 Co 4[7] 'What hast thou that thou didst not receive? but if thou didst receive it, why dost thou glory, as if thou hadst not received it?'). Now Pelagians, Semi-Pelagians, and Molinists deny the gratuity of predestination, for no other reason than because they presuppose something on man's part which is the reason why God predestines some to glory and not others. The Pelagians presuppose good works, the Semi-Pelagians the beginning of good works, and Molinists the good use of grace. But, if all these things are from God, He cannot look for or await them in order to predestine some and not others; on the contrary, He gives even the good use of grace to some because he pre-elected them to glory. In accordance, then, with the teaching of St. Paul, with the doctrine of St. Augustine and St. Thomas, Thomists, and some Molinists of high repute, teach the absolute gratuity of predestination, *i.e.* irrespective of foreseen merits.

(*b*) *Gratuitous predestination.*—God wishes all to be saved; to all He gives sufficient grace. By a special act of love and mercy He elects some to glory in preference to others, without any other reason than that of His own divine will. To the chosen He gives graces by which they will infallibly reach heaven (Suarez, Bellarmine, J. de Lugo, Billot, etc., and all Thomists, after St. Augustine and St. Thomas). On this point there is practically no difference between Thomists and this group of Molinists; the difference between them has reference to another question treated above, namely, the origin of the efficacy of grace. Some Congruists teach that God gratuitously elects certain ones, not to glory, but to congruous grace, to which they will infallibly consent, and in which they will persevere. Foreseeing this consent by the *scientia media*, God predestines them to glory. Against the latter opinion Thomists object, in particular, that God is made to act in a manner that implies the denial of an axiom received as true not only by all schools of philosophy but by common sense. In the order of actual realization the means must necessarily precede the end; but in the order of intention the end must precede the means, for it is impossible to choose and adapt means to an end without a preconception of the end. Now, since God must act as an intellectual being, He must (according to this axiom) first of all conceive the end, then choose the means for obtaining that end. But grace, good use of grace, merit, are the means, and glory is the end. Therefore He must first predestine to glory before He predestines to congruous grace. In the Congruist theory He does exactly the opposite. To this simple and irrefragable argument no Congruist has ever essayed a reply that is not suicidal. Molina also teaches the gratuity of predestination (*Concordia*, qu. 22, art. 4, 5, disp. 1, membr. xi.), but his explanation is very different from that of the majority of those who follow him. In eternity God knows all possible universes, infinite in number; in each universe or order there is a series of free acts, all of which God knows by the *scientia media* independently of any act of His will. In each of these possible orders certain people are predestined, not, indeed, through the efficacy of a divine decree (which as yet has not intervened), but through grace made efficacious by the consent of the human will, in which the will perseveres unto the end. The omniscient God knows all this by the *scientia media*. By His own free will, without any regard whatsoever to foreseen merits, He gratuitously decrees to bring one of these orders to existence. The difference between Molina and Suarez on this point comes to this, that the former teaches predestination to glory before a prevision of absolute future merits, but after the prevision of conditioned future merits, whereas the latter teaches predestination to glory before prevision of future merits, whether absolute or conditioned. Molina explains his own theory in a manner more subtle and more profound than any of his followers. But, apart from the insuperable difficulty of the *scientia media*, there are difficulties in this explanation which absolutely destroy free will. We deny absolutely that a free act can be connected with any one order; it is the denial in very words of the freedom of the act. It is absolutely false that a free act is connected with any circumstances whatever, in the sense that, given the circumstances, a particular free act must follow. All those possible universes are contradictions, and have therefore no reality or conceivability; God, therefore, could not conceive them.

(3) *Reprobation.*—It is a defined doctrine of Catholic faith that no one is destined by God to eternal damnation except after a prevision of demerits; this is called 'positive reprobation.' In the theory of gratuitous predestination, by the very fact that God gratuitously elects some and not others, those not chosen will infallibly not be saved; hence a reprobation of some sort is concomitant with the predestination of some to glory; this is called 'negative reprobation.' The difficulty is to conciliate negative reprobation with the universal salvific will of God. Suarez and his followers say it is a 'positive act of nolition to elect'; some Thomists (as J. B. Gonet, V. Contenson, etc.) that it is a 'direct exclusion from glory'; others (as A. Goudin, C. R. Billuart, etc.) that it is the 'omission of an effectual election' to heaven. It is, however, very difficult to safeguard the salvific will of God if negative reprobation be a positive act on God's part. Why not say, therefore, that it is the entire absence of any act of the divine will, whether of volition or nolition? It is the mere absence of the act of assumption.

LITERATURE.—I. *HISTORY.*—Theodorus Eleutherius (Livinus de Meyer), *Historia Controversiarum de divinæ gratiæ auxiliis sub Summis Pontificibus Clemente VIII. et Paulo V.*, Antwerp, 1705; A. Leblanc (Hyacinthe Serry), *Historia Congregationis de auxiliis gratiæ sub Summis*, etc., Louvain, 1700, *Prælectiones*, ii., 'Opusc. Schola Thomistica Vindicata,' Venice, 1742; J. Platel, *Auctoritas contra prædeterminationem physicam pro scientia media historice propugnata*, Lyons, 1665; C. H. Amat de Graveson, *Epistolæ Theologico-Historico-Polemicæ*, Bassano, 1785, lib. ii. cap. 1; C. R. Billuart, *Le Thomisme triomphant*, Liège, 1731, *Apologie du Thomisme triomphant*, do. 1731; G. Schneemann, *Controversiarum de divinæ gratiæ liberique arbitrii concordia initia et progressus*, Freiburg, 1881; A. M. Dummermuth, *S. Thomas et doctrina præmotionis physicæ*, Paris, 1886, *Defensio doctrinæ S. Thomæ Aq. de præmotione physica*, Louvain, 1895; V. Frins, *S. Thomæ Aq. doctrina de cooperatione Dei*, Paris, 1893; T. de Régnon, *Bañes et Molina*, do. 1883; H. Gayraud, *Thomisme et Molinisme*, Toulouse, 1889–92; P. Mandonnet, 'Notes d'histoire thomiste,' *Revue Thomiste*, 1914, pp. 667–675.

II. *THE DOCTRINE.*—L. de Molina, *Concordia liberi arbitrii cum gratiæ donis*, etc., Paris, 1876, qu. 14; M. Becanus, *Summa Theologiæ Scholasticæ*, Lyons, 1621, 'De Deo,' cap. 18; L. Lessius, *De Perfectionibus moribusque divinis*, Paris, 1875, lib. iv., *De gratia efficaci et decretis divinis*, do. 1878; D. Ruiz de Montoyo, *De Scientia Dei*, do. 1629, disp. 20; C. Tiphanus, *De ordine deque priori et posteriori*, Rheims, 1640; F. Suarez, *Metaphysica*, Paris, 1866, disp. 19, 22, *Opuscula* (in *Opera Omnia*, do. 1858, xi.), i. 'De concursu, motione, et auxilio Dei,' ii., 'De scientia Dei futurorum contingentium,' iii., 'De auxilio efficaci,' *De Gratia*, Paris, 1867, Prolegom. 2; J. B. Franzelin, *De Deo uno*, Rome, 1883, sect. 4; A. Goudin, *Tractatus Theologici*, Louvain, 1874; C. R. Billuart, *Summa S. Thomæ*², Arras, 1867–72, tom. i. diss. 5–9, tom. iii. diss. 5; N. del Prado, *De gratia et libero arbitrio*, Fribourg, 1907.

ÆLRED WHITACRE.

MOMENTARY GODS.—'Momentary gods' (*Augenblicksgötter*) is an expression coined by H. Usener (*Götternamen*, Bonn, 1896, p. 279), and one whose credentials are open to question. It must certainly be admitted that the phenomena which Usener brings under the term are of very diverse kinds. It is true, of course, that human beings whose minds are dominated by fetishistic and animistic ideas may, under the influence of a momentary impression, ascribe to objects or occurrences a divine or dæmonic character; but the question is whether it is worth while to differentiate such procedure from the general mass of fetishistic and animistic phenomena by the use of a special term. Thus we frequently meet with the practice of worshipping the lance or other weapon (L. Deubner, *ARW* viii. [1905], Beiheft, p. 71), such being often invoked to witness an oath (Æsch. *Sept.* 529; schol. Apoll. Rhod. i. 57); but these facts in reality furnish reasons for doubting whether the weapon was only then deified, and suggest rather that it was thought of as permanently possessed of divine qualities. Thus, too, while Vergil makes Mezentius say: 'dextra mihi deus et telum quod missile libro,'[1] and is imitated in this artifice by later epic authors (Silius Ital. v. 118, vi. 137; Statius, *Theb.* iii. 615, ix. 548), such poetic fancies throw no light whatever upon primitive religious feeling. The lightning-flash smiting down upon

[1] *Æn.* x. 773.

the earth is regarded everywhere with a religious dread, and Greeks and Romans alike avoided all contact with the spot where it had struck, this being for the former a consecrated place (ἠλύσιον, ἐνηλύσιον), and for the latter a *bidental*, which is explained by the phrase 'fulgur conditum.'[1] Thus the lightning-flash actually came to be regarded as a divine being: some of the Diadochi adopted the name Keraunos; in Seleucia Seleucus Nicator instituted a cult of the κεραυνός (Appian, *de Rebus Syr.* 58), the existence of which is attested by numerous coins; and there is an Orphic hymn dedicated to this deity. Keraunos is often represented as subordinate to Zeus, who in this capacity is called Keraunios, Kataibates, and Kappotas, just as Juppiter Fulgur is designated Fulgurator and Fulminator (Usener, *Kleine Schriften*, iv. Leipzig, 1913, p. 471). The natural phenomenon here involved is, of course, one of relatively rare occurrence, and but seldom arrests special attention by leaving visible traces of its action, but the worship of lightning, in its essential features, cannot be separated from that of winds and meteoric stones. Quite a different case, again, is presented by the worship of the last sheaf, or of the harvest-wreath (Gr. εἰρεσιώνη), and by other practices which have been explained by W. Mannhardt;[2] the harvest-wreath, which was wound round with white and red woollen threads, and for the year remained hanging at the door as an amulet for the house, is unmistakably a fetish, *i.e.* a sacred object fashioned and consecrated by human beings (R. M. Meyer, *ARW* xi. [1908] 320); in the last sheaf, however, and things of similar formation, is concealed the corn-spirit which, according to animistic ideas, renews the life of the corn, but, while it is only at harvest-time that the spirit becomes in a manner manifest to sight, it is in reality always present, and is therefore not a 'momentary god' in the proper sense. Usener likewise adduces the conceptions of the δαίμων and the *genius* of the individual. It is very difficult to come to a definite conclusion regarding the ultimate origin of these conceptions; they have undoubtedly been influenced in part by ideas of the soul, and, in the case of the δαίμων, by the notion of 'possession' (J. Tambornino, *De antiquorum dæmonismo*, Giessen, 1909), while the snake-form of the *genius* seems to point in quite a different direction (W. F. Otto, in Pauly-Wissowa, vii. 1155 ff.). In any case, the present writer can see no rational grounds for bringing δαίμων and *genius* under the category of 'momentary gods.'

While, however, the conception of 'momentary gods' is thus in part a rather indeterminate one, and in part of limited significance, the introduction of the term 'special gods' (Germ. *Sondergötter*) has proved to be of real advantage. This term, too, we owe to Usener, who framed it on the suggestion of E. Lehmann in connexion with Varro's *di certi*; like the latter, the special gods are deities with a clearly defined sphere of action, and thus closely allied to the momentary gods. Usener has shown that in the development of religion—so far, at least, as Greece was concerned—they are anterior to the great deities, and this result might, no doubt, be very widely generalized. Unmistakable examples are found in Greek heroes like Euodos (G. Kaibel, *Epigrammata Græca*, Berlin, 1873, no. 825), Myiagros (Paus. VIII. xxvi. 7), Teichophylax (Hesych. *s.v.*), or Horophylax (*JHS* viii. [1887] 236), who never had more than a local significance and a narrow sphere of action. Other beings of this type were absorbed by the great Olympian (*i.e.* Homeric) deities; thus Kourotrophos (also in plur., *Ephem. Arch.*, 1899, p. 143) was originally an independent deity who at length became a mere epithet of Ge, Artemis, Demeter, etc., and Zeus Erechtheus, Athene Hygieia, etc., are to be interpreted in the same way. We may even venture to say that the displacement of these special deities by the Olympians was one of the most important processes in the development of Greek religion within historical times.[1] Among the Romans such special deities are found more especially in the Indigitamenta (*q.v.*), in which every particular operation—*e.g.*, in agriculture—was assigned a distinct tutelary spirit—Vervactor, Redarator, Imporcitor, Insitor, Obarator, Occator, Sarritor, Subruncinator, Messor, Convector, Conditor, Promitor. It is said, indeed, that even the *lupanaria*, *culinæ*, and *carceres* had each their special deity (Tertull. *ad. Nat.* ii. 15).[2] From this, however, we derive but scanty information as to the earlier state of things which had been disturbed by the incursion of the Greek religion; even in Varro's lists of these gods we already find many names of extraneous origin, and we are quite unable to say what degree of importance attached to the individual deities.

Very valuable data are furnished by the accounts of the Lithuanian special gods, as critically discussed by Usener (*Götternamen*, p. 79; cf. Deubner, *ARW* ix. [1906] 281; O. Schrader, *ERE* ii. 31 f.); here we find Austheia, the goddess of bees, Babilos, the honey-god, Budintaia, the goddess who arouses from sleep, Kiauliukruke and Kremata, the swine-gods, Meletele, the goddess of the colour blue, Raugupatis, who causes the fermentation of beer, and Wejopatis, the lord of the wind. Kindred figures are found among the Letts.

As regards the existence of such special deities in other religions—with the exception, however, of the heathenism that was not wholly submerged by the Roman Catholic Church (see below)—our knowledge is at fault, partly from lack of materials and partly from lack of research. We may unhesitatingly take for granted, however, that, *e.g.*, the pantheons of the Vedas and the Avesta[3] correspond with that of Homer in presenting various types of deities, and that the place of the great gods who hold sway in these literary monuments was, among the people, *i.e.* in the living religion, taken by a multitude of less imposing beings, of whom, it is true, our knowledge is most imperfect. The Phœnician religion provides an instructive example; here it was not, strictly speaking, a single self-identical Baal to whom divine honours were paid; on the contrary, each several tribe and city had its own special Baal, and worshipped him as a tribal or tutelary deity. The data which lie most readily to hand are found in countries where residual elements of heathen views still co-exist with or underlie the Roman Catholic religion in the practice of saint-worship, and have to some extent been countenanced by the Church (D. H. Kerler, *Die Patronate der Heiligen*, Ulm, 1905). Thus, *e.g.*, among the Zamaites of Prussia, St. Agatha took care of the household fire and St. Nicholas was the guardian of boatmen, St. Apollonia cured toothache and St. Laurentius rheumatic pains, St. Crispin was the patron of shoemakers and St. Goar of potters.[4] In the Vosges St. Abdon is believed to drive away fleas, St. Catherine to secure husbands for maidens, St. Sabina to

1 Amm. Marcell. xxiii. 5.13: 'hoc modo [*i.e.* fulmine] contacta loca nec intueri nec calcari debere fulgurales pronuntiant libri.'

2 *Antike Wald- und Feldkulte*, Berlin, 1877.

1 Cf., however, the criticism by L. R. Farnell, 'The Place of the "Sonder-Götter" in Greek Polytheism,' in *Anthropological Essays presented to . . . Tylor*, Oxford, 1907, pp. 81–100.

2 The necessary corrections of Usener's statements in this connexion will be found in G. Wissowa, *Gesammelte Abhandlungen zur röm. Rel.- und Stadtgesch.*, Munich, 1904, p. 304, and W. F. Otto, *Rhein. Mus.* lxiv. [1909] 449, 468.

3 On Iranian 'special gods' cf. the remarks of J. H. Moulton, *Early Zoroastrianism*, London, 1913, pp. 69–71, 105, 150. A notable instance is Verethraghna, 'Victory.'

4 On the saints who exercised an official function Deubner, *De Incubatione*, Leipzig, 1900, is well worth consulting.

allay the pangs of love, and so on. A number of these tutelary offices of saints are universally recognized by the Roman Catholic Church, and are entered in the *Diario Romano*, in which we are told, for instance, that St. Blasius cures sore throat and St. Liberius pains due to calculus, and that St. Martha protects from epidemics. Almost every district has its own particular patron saint, and in many cases clings to him with marked tenacity.

LITERATURE.—This has been sufficiently indicated in the article.

W. KROLL.

MONADISM.—See LEIBNIZ.

MONARCHIANISM. — Monarchianism is a term generally used to designate the views of those heretics who, to safeguard the Divine unity (*monarchia*), so refined away the distinction of the Divine Persons as to destroy the Trinity. Hippolytus has left us a summary account of their origin. A certain Noetus, so he tells us, was the protagonist of these ideas; they were upheld by his disciple, Epigonus, and further propagated by the latter's disciple, Cleomenes.[1] From Epiphanius we gather that Noetus must have died shortly before A.D. 250.[2] But Hippolytus, who appears to have been martyred about A.D. 240, and who composed his *Philosophumena* between the years 230 and 235,[3] says in his *Tractate against Noetus*, i., that he 'died not very long since.'[4] And this seems more probable; for Cleomenes, the disciple of Noetus's disciple Epigonus, according to the *Philosophumena*,[5] caused much trouble during the pontificates of Zephyrinus and Callistus, viz. 198–222.[6]

Hippolytus endeavours to show that Noetus's views were in reality only those of the philosopher Heraclitus the Obscure, who held that 'the Father is an unbegotten creature who is creator.'[7]

Noetus and his disciples hold, says Hippolytus, these Heraclitean tenets, for they say 'that one and the same God is the Creator and Father of all things; and that when it pleased Him, He appeared.'[8] And again: 'When the Father had not been born, He [yet] was justly styled Father; and when it pleased Him to undergo generation, having been begotten, He Himself became His own Son, not another's.' 'In this manner,' adds Hippolytus, 'he thinks to establish the sovereignty [of God], alleging that Father and Son, [so] called, are one and the same [substance], not one individual produced from a different one, but Himself from Himself; and that He is styled by name Father and Son, according to vicissitude of times.'[9]

Hippolytus, as we have seen, says that Noetus set forth his views as a means of upholding the Divine sovereignty, but, as a fact, the term *monarchia* (μοναρχία) was ambiguous and could be used as the watchword of both parties. Thus Eusebius tells us[10] that St. Irenæus wrote a work, *de Monarchia*, against those who held that God was the author of evil. Similarly Justin Martyr has left a treatise, *de Monarchia*, to prove that God is the sole governor against paganism;[11] see also Athenagoras, *Legatio* viii.[12] But, as was only natural, the Apologists previous to the Council of Nicæa were faced with the grave difficulty that, while combating polytheism, they had to maintain the divinity of Christ without impairing the Divine unity. And it must be acknowledged that, in insisting upon the divinity of Christ, they often, through lack of precision in their choice of terms, laid themselves open to the charge of ditheism. Thus Hippolytus says that Callistus reproached the opponents of Noetianism with being ditheists;[1] and Pope Dionysius felt himself compelled to point out that in opposing Sabellius many 'divide and cut to pieces and destroy that most sacred doctrine of the Church of God, the Divine monarchy, making it as it were three powers and partitive subsistences and godheads three.'[2] An example of this unintentional vagueness may be found in Justin, *Dial.* cxxix., and, what is even more remarkable, in those who most strenuously resisted the Noetians and their successors, the Sabellians. Thus Novatian, while insisting on the divinity of Christ and urging the precision with which Christ Himself says 'I and the Father are one' (ἕν, 'one,' that is, in the neuter, and consequently not in person, but in substance or nature), yet offers no explanation of how this can be. The retort was obvious: Then you hold that there are *two* Gods![3] Even Tertullian, in spite of his lawyer-like precision of terms and his undoubted orthodoxy on this point—even in his Montanist days—has some most misleading expressions which the post-Nicene writers would have avoided at all costs.[4] Yet these things are inevitable, and it is by such discussions, with occasional lapses from exactitude on either side, that the Church can come to a full knowledge of the deposit of truth.[5]

A remarkable exception to this prevailing vagueness is furnished by Athenagoras, who, in his *Legatio*, says:

'The Son of God is the Logos of the Father, in idea and in operation; for after the pattern of Him and by Him were all things made, the Father and the Son being one. And, the Son being in the Father and the Father in the Son, in oneness and power of spirit, the understanding and reason (νοῦς καὶ λόγος) of the Father is the Son of God. But if, in your surpassing intelligence, it occurs to you to inquire what is meant by the Son, I will state briefly that He is the first product of the Father, not as having been brought into existence (for from the beginning, God, who is the eternal mind [νοῦς], had the Logos in Himself, being from eternity instinct with Logos [λογικός]); but inasmuch as He came forth to be the idea and energizing power of all material things.'[6]

Nor is it surprising that these so-called Monarchians should have had a strong following. God is One. For this monotheism the prophets had fought and prevailed. But, if God is One, then, though there may be diversity of actions *ad extra*,

1 *Phil.* ix. 2. 2 *Hær.* lvii. 1 (*PG* xli. 994 f.).

3 See A. C. McGiffert's 'Eusebius' (*Nicene and Post-Nicene Fathers*, i. [1890]), note on *HE* VI. xxii. 1.

4 Hippolytus, *Fragments* (from A. Gallandus), in *Ante-Nicene Fathers*, ix. [1883] pt. ii., p. 51.

5 IX. ii., vi. f.

6 Zephyrinus was pope, A.D. 198–217; Callistus reigned only five years, 217–222; cf. *HE* V. xxviii. 3 and VI. xxi. 1, with McGiffert's notes.

7 *Phil.* ix. 4. 8 *Ib.* ix. 5. 9 *Ib.*

10 *HE* V. xx. 1.

11 Περὶ Θεοῦ Μοναρχίας, tr. in *Ante-Nicene Fathers*, ii. [1892] 329 ff. (*PG* vi. 311), but probably not the work referred to by Eusebius, *HE* IV. xviii. 4; and note Origen, *Com. in Ep. ad Titum* (*PG* xiv. 1304): 'philarchiae morbo languentes dogmata statuerint.'

12 Athenagoras, Πρεσβεία (*PG* vi. 903; *Ante-Nicene Fathers*, ii. 375 ff.).

1 *Phil.* ix. 7. Much capital has been made out of Hippolytus's violent attacks on the orthodoxy, and, indeed, on the personal character, of Popes Zephyrinus and Callistus. But Hippolytus himself says (*Phil.* ix. 7) that Callistus excommunicated Sabellius, though he maintains that Callistus did so out of fear of himself, Hippolytus. Perhaps the best commentary on Hippolytus's diatribes is furnished by the absolute silence of all other writers of the period.

2 Quoted by Athanasius, *Epistle in Defence of the Nicene Definition*, 26 (*PG* xxv. 462); J. H. Newman, *Athanasius*, Oxford Library of the Fathers, 1842–44, i. 45; also *Ante-Nicene Fathers*, xviii. [1895], 'Tertullian,' iii. 385–387, a fragment of an epistle or treatise of Dionysius, bishop of Rome, against the Sabellians; cf. also Dionysius of Alexandria, *adv. Sabellium*, given in Eusebius, *Præp. Evang.* viii. 19 (*PG* x. 1270); Mansi, *Concilia*, i. col. 1011.

3 Novatian, *de Trin.* xi.–xviii., xxvii.

4 Thus in *adv. Prax.* iii. (*PL* ii. 158) he speaks of the angels as being 'members of the Father's own substance,' and in iv. (*ib.* 159) of the *monarchia* as 'committed' by the Father to the Son.

5 Cf. St. Augustine's remark apropos of the re-baptism controversy: 'Quomodo enim potuit ista res tantis altercationum nebulis involuta ad plenarii concilii luculentam illustrationem confirmationemque perduci, nisi primo diutius per orbis terrarum regiones multis hinc atque hinc disputationibus et collationibus episcoporum pertractata constaret? Hoc autem facit sanitas pacis, ut, cum diutius aliqua obscuriora quæruntur et, propter inveniendi difficultatem, diversas pariunt in fraterna disceptatione sententias, donec ad verum liquidum perveniatur, vinculum permaneat unitatis, ne in parte præcisa remaneat insanabile vulnus erroris' (*de Baptismo c. Donatistas*, II. iv. (5) [*PL* xliii. 129]; the whole passage is worth reading in this connexion).

6 Athenagoras, Πρεσβεία, x. (*PG* vii. 907; *Ante-Nicene Fathers*, ii. 385); cf. xxiv. (*PG* vii. 946).

there can be no such diversity of action *ad intra* as shall imply distinction of Persons. But Christ is God, and Christ suffered upon the Cross. Therefore the Father suffered![1] The conclusion seemed compelling; but the Noetians and Sabellians shrank from it and endeavoured to explain that this suffering of the Father was in some sense not really His.[2] Theirs was a strong position. They seemed to be the advocates of orthodoxy against the orthodox themselves. It was in vain that the latter rejoined: Then, according to your argument, it is the Father who sits at His own right hand! For, while the NT as a whole clearly taught the divinity of the Son and the distinction of Persons, yet there were certain texts which, while maintaining the former, seemed expressly to deny the latter. Thus Praxeas insisted on 'I and the Father are one' (Jn 10^{30}); this it was easy to explain in a monotheistic sense, as Tertullian does.[3] But it was not so easy to explain 'He that hath seen me hath seen the Father; and I am in the Father, and the Father in me' (Jn $14^{9f.}$). Tertullian treats this passage at considerable length,[4] but it can hardly be said that his answer precludes the retort: Then there are *two* Gods!

It is only when we turn to such an analysis of these passages as is furnished by Athanasius (*e.g.*, on Jn 14^{10}, in *Orat.* iii. 23) and Augustine (*Tract.* xix. 13, xxi. 4, xxii. 14) that we realize the distinction between ante- and post-Nicene clearness of expression when handling the questions ventilated by the Noetians and their successors. St. Phœbadius († *c.* A.D. 393) puts the dilemma clearly:

> 'If we speak of one God in the singular, excluding the word "Second Person," we thereby approve that mad heresy which says that the Father Himself suffered. If, on the other hand, we admit of number combined with division, then we join hands with the Arians who hold that God was made from God, and who say that He fashioned a new substance out of nothing. We must, then, hold to the rule which confesses that the Father is in the Son and the Son in the Father, to the rule which while preserving the oneness of substance acknowledges an economy (*dispositionem*) in the Divinity.'[5]

Both sides, then, claimed to be the sole upholders of a true conception of the Divine monarchy:

> 'Marcellus and Photinus,' says Athanasius, 'negative Christ's existence before ages, and His Godhead and unending Kingdom, upon pretence of supporting the divine monarchy.'[6]

Tertullian states the case in his usual pithy manner:

> 'We, say they, maintain the monarchy. . . . Yes, but while the Latins take pains to pronounce *monarchia*, the Greeks refuse to understand *œconomia* . . . for, extolling the *monarchia* at the expense of the *œconomia*, they contend for the identity of Father, Son, and Spirit.'[7]

And then he puts his finger on the real difficulty which the Noetians had to face:

> 'Praxeas put to flight the Paraclete, and he crucified the Father!'[8]

Hence the opprobrious nickname for the so-called Monarchians—Patripassians,[9] *i.e.* 'those who made the Father suffer' in the person of the Son. Methodius († *c.* 312), commenting on Rev 12^{1-6}, likens those who have gone astray with regard to one of the Three Persons in the Trinity to the third part of the stars that fell:

> 'As when they say, like Sabellius, that the Almighty Person of the Father Himself suffered.'[1]

It is of interest to note how these heresies shaded off into one another. Thus Sabellius apparently denied that he was a Patripassian; but, in order to do so, he seems to have held that our Lord came into being only on His human birth.[2] The Arians, on the contrary, said 'before the ages,' thus agreeing, so it would seem, with the Patripassians. Again we note that, whereas Sabellius claimed to rank as a Monarchian, yet the Arian bishops, writing to Alexander, say:

> 'We do not do as did Sabellius who, *dividing the One*, speaks of a Son-Father.'[3]

Thus their ground of complaint against Sabellius was precisely that on which he plumed himself on not doing, viz. separating the Divine *monarchia.* Similarly Athanasius says:

> 'Sabellius supposed the Son to have no real subsistence, and the Holy Spirit to be non-existent; he charged his opponents with dividing the Godhead.'[4] And once more: 'Sabellius, dreading the division invented by Arius, fell into the error which destroys the Personal distinctions.'[5]

It must, however, be remembered that no one can at this date say what precisely were Sabellius's opinions, partly because of the inevitable fluctuations through which he passed, partly, and chiefly, because history is apt to confuse him with his disciples, as in the passage last quoted from Athanasius.[6]

How grievous were the ravages worked by these Monarchian views can be seen by the frequent condemnations of them in the shape of Sabellianism. Thus Pope Damasus condemned them in the Council held at Rome in 380 (or [?] 382):

> 'We anathematize those also who follow the error of Sabellius in saying that the Father is the same as the Son.'[7]

Similarly, in the ecumenical Council of Constantinople (A.D. 381) the first canon is directed against various shades of Arianism, and finally against the Sabellians, Marcellians, Photinians, and Apollinarists.[8] By the time of the provincial Council of Braga (561) we see how these Monarchian principles have verged into Priscillianism and are tainted with Manichæism.[9] The same comprehensive condemnation was repeated in the Lateran Council of 649 (can. xviii.).[10] Lastly, Eugenius IV. found it necessary to remind the Jacobites, in his decree dated 4th Feb. 1441, that the Church 'condemns Sabellius for confusing the Persons and for thus altogether doing away with the real distinction between them.'[11]

The subsequent ramifications of the Monarchian tenets do not concern us here. Suffice it to say that they spread very widely, though in forms which varied considerably from those originally set forth. Thus Eusebius mentions that Beryllus, bishop of Bostra, 'deserted the ecclesiastical standard,' *i.e.* the Rule of Faith, and asserted that Christ did not pre-exist in a distinct form of His own, neither did He possess a divinity of His own, but only that of the Father dwelling in Him.[12] This is clearly a derived form of Monarchianism. The most prominent, perhaps, among the later

[1] Tert. *adv. Prax.* xxix. (*PL* ii. 194).
[2] *Philos.* ix. 5; cf. x. 23.
[3] *Adv. Prax.* xxii. (*PL* ii. 183).
[4] *Ib.* xxiv.; cf. Novat. *de Trin.* xxviii. (*PL* iii. 940–942).
[5] *Liber c. Arianos*, xxii. (*PL* xx. 29 f.); cf. also Zacchæus, *Consultationes*, ii. 15 (*ib.* 1135).
[6] Athanasius, *De Synodis*, 26 (vi.) (*PG* xxvi. 731); Newman, *Athanasius*, i. 114.
[7] *Adv. Prax.* iii. (*PL* ii. 158), and ix. (*ib.* 164). Tertullian's use of the term *œconomia* is unusual. In the NT it generally refers to the ministry of the Word of God (*e.g.*, 1 Co 9^{17}); also to the divine counsel as fulfilled in the Incarnation (Eph 1^{10}). And thus it is used by the Greek Fathers of the mystery of the Incarnation (cf. J. C. Suicer, *Thes. eccles.*, Amsterdam, 1728, *s.v.*). But here Tertullian uses it of the relationship of the Three Persons of the Trinity, a usage of which Suicer takes no notice.
[8] *Ib.* i. (*PL* ii. 156). Of Praxeas himself very little is known. Hippolytus apparently knows nothing of him, though, if we are to argue from his silence, we could equally well argue from Tertullian's silence regarding Noetus, Cleomenes, and Sabellius. For some of the views which have been held regarding his identity see *DCB*, *s.v.* 'Praxeas.'
[9] Cf. Augustine, *Tract.* xxxvi. 8, *in Joan.*; cf. xxxvii. 6, lxx. 2, lxxi. 2 (*PL* xxxv. 1667, 1672, 1819, 1820); and Origen, *Com. in Ep. ad Titum* (*PG* xiv. 1304).

[1] *The Banquet of the Ten Virgins*, discourse ix. ch. 10 (*Ante-Nicene Fathers*, xiv. [1906] 77).
[2] Athanasius, *Orat.* iv. 3 (*PG* xxvi. 471); cf. Newman, i. 114, ii. 529, n.
[3] Newman, i. 97.
[4] Athanasius, *adv. Apoll.* i. 21 (*PG* xxvi. 1130); W. Bright, *Historical Writings of Athanasius*, Oxford, 1881, p. 114.
[5] *Ib.* ii. 3 (*PG* xxvi. 11380); Bright, p. 120.
[6] *Orat.* iv. 3 (*PG* xxvi. 471); Newman, ii. 529.
[7] Mansi, iii. 481, 486.
[8] *Ib.* iii. 557.
[9] *Ib.* ix. 774, canons 1–14.
[10] *Ib.* x. 1151.
[11] *Ib.* xxxi. 1735.
[12] *HE* VI. xxxiii. 1, with McGiffert's notes.

Monarchians were the Priscillianists. They are of interest by reason of the strange influence which they had on the Latin text of the Gospels[1]—*e.g.*, indirectly on 1 Jn 5^7. To them are due the Monarchian *Prologues* which have attracted so much attention in later years.[2]

It is usual to embrace under the heading Monarchianism the so-called Adoptianist heresies. But, while it is true that the Adoptianists may be regarded as the legitimate outcome of the Monarchians, yet they approach the question from an entirely different standpoint. For Adoptianism is a Christological heresy, whereas Monarchianism, at least in its original form as Patripassianism, concerns the Father rather than the Son. To embrace the two heresies under one heading is to obscure the issue. See art. ADOPTIANISM.

LITERATURE.—In addition to the works referred to throughout the article, see A. Harnack, *History of Dogma*, Eng. tr., London, 1894–99, ii., iii., *s.v.* 'Modalism'; J. A. W. Neander, *History of the Planting and Training of the Church by the Apostles*, ed. Bohn, do. 1851, ii.; Harnack, art. 'Monarchianismus,' in *PRE*[3]; J. H. Newman, *The Arians of the Fourth Century*[3] (written previous to the discovery of Hippolytus's *Philosophumena*), London, 1871; J. Chapman, art. 'Monarchians,' in *CE*; *DCB*, *s.vv.*; L. J. Tixeront, *Histoire des dogmes*[2], i. Paris, 1905, ch. viii.

HUGH POPE.

MONASTICISM.—I. *ETYMOLOGY; DEFINITION.*—The word 'monasticism' is derived from the Gr. word μόνος, 'alone,' 'solitary,' from which a whole family of words has been formed: μονή and μοναστήριον, 'monastery'; μοναχός, 'monk' or 'solitary'; μονάζειν, 'to lead the solitary life'; μονάζοντες, 'solitaries'; μονάστρια, 'nun'; μοναδικός, μοναχικός, μοναστικός, μονήρης, 'monastic'; μονάζουσα, μοναχοῦσα, μοναχή, 'nun'; τὸ μοναχικόν, 'monasticism'; μοναστικῶς, 'monastically'; μοναχισμός, 'monachism.'[3]

In Latin this word has given *monachus* and its derivatives, *monacha*, *monachatus*, *monachare*, *monachizare*, *monachismum*, *monachatio*, *monasterium*, and a few other words.[4]

'Interpretare vocabulum monachi, hoc est nomen tuum: quid facis in turba qui solus es?' (Jerome, *Ep.* xiv. [*PL* xxii. 350]). 'Sin autem cupis esse quod diceris, monachus, id est solus, quid facis in urbibus, quae utique non sunt solorum habitacula sed multorum?' (*Ep.* lix. [*PL* xxii. 583]).

All these words, derived as they are from the same root, indicate the idea of solitude, of isolation. This solitude must not, however, be interpreted as implying absolute isolation—such as that of the hermit in the desert. As we shall see, the term 'monk' has come to be applied to men living the same life in common—a life in which they are indeed separated from the world, but not from one another.

In common usage the word 'monasticism' is often incorrectly extended to embrace the idea of the religious state in general, comprising even those religious orders which cannot be regarded as belonging to this category — such, *e.g.*, as the Dominicans and Franciscans, the Jesuits and other clerks regular. Strictly speaking, the term should be reserved for the form of religious life led by those who, having separated themselves entirely from the world, live in solitude—as, in fact, the etymology of the words 'monk,' 'monastery,' etc., clearly indicates. We shall see below (§ III.) in what the special characteristics of the monk properly so called consist, the special conditions of the monastic life, and its various types. The monks, in fact, form a class apart among what are known as the 'religious orders'; they must be distinguished from those that are commonly termed the 'mendicant orders' or 'friars'—*e.g.*, Dominicans, Franciscans, or Carmelites—from the clerks regular, such as the Jesuits, and from other forms of the religious life and religious congregations—*e.g.*, the Redemptorists, Oratorians, Sulpicians, etc. (see art. RELIGIOUS ORDERS).

At the present day monks are represented in the Catholic Church by the Basilians and other monks of the East; by the Benedictines, Cistercians, Camaldolese, Olivetans, Carthusians, and other religious families of less importance. They must be distinguished from the ascetics who existed in the early ages of the Church, and who were simply Christians living a more austere life in the world. Nevertheless, after the monastic life properly so called had been instituted, many of these ascetics of both sexes entered the monasteries; hence we find the name 'ascetic' applied sometimes to the monks also (see, *e.g.*, the *Peregrinatio Etheriæ*; cf. art. ASCETICISM, vol. ii. p. 63 f.). The canons regular and the military orders should also be distinguished from the monks, although there were many points of contact between them. We are not, however, concerned with them here.

II. *MONASTICISM OUTSIDE OF CHRISTIANITY.*—Monasticism cannot be regarded as an institution belonging exclusively to Christianity, although it is chiefly in that religion that its full development is to be sought. Examples occur in the non-Christian religions as well, and we shall see in what relation these stand to Christian monasticism.

1. Worship of Sarapis.—In recent years it has become the fashion to see in the κάτοχοι—pagan recluses who lived in the temples of Sarapis and their dependencies—the authentic ancestors of the Christian monks. Weingarten, to whom this theory owes its origin, has even maintained that St. Pachomius, the founder of Christian cenobitism, not only drew a large part of his Rule from the usages of these κάτοχοι, but had been himself a κάτοχος of Sarapis, before his conversion to Christianity, at the Sarapeum of Chenoboscium. This theory, however, rests on a series of unverified hypotheses. Pachomius was never a κάτοχος. All that can be gathered from the most ancient life of this saint is that he withdrew to an abandoned temple of Sarapis, and that, while there, he had a vision of God—not, however, of the pagan divinity, but of the God of the Christians. Moreover, the analogies that have been drawn between these *hierodouloi* and the cenobites of Christianity are only apparent.[1]

2. Neo-Platonism.—The Alexandrian school of philosophy in the 2nd and 3rd centuries taught a kind of mysticism, more philosophical than religious, in which moral ideas and ascetic practices occupied an important place. The attempt has been made to find in this mystic philosophy the source of Christian asceticism. The latter, however, was in existence before this date, and under a very different form. Moreover, it seems difficult to avoid the conclusion that the Alexandrian philo-

[1] Thus note canon xvii. of the Council of Braga (A.D. 561): 'If any one reads the Scriptures which Priscillian corrupted in accordance with his own erroneous views . . . let him be anathema' (Mansi, ix. 774).

[2] John Chapman, *Notes on the Early History of the Vulgate Gospels*, Oxford, 1908, chs. xii.–xv.

[3] J. C. Suicer, *Thesaurus ecclesiasticus*, Amsterdam, 1728, *s.vv.*; E. A. Sophocles, *Greek Lexicon of the Roman and Byzantine Periods*, Boston, 1870, *s.vv.*

[4] C. du F. du Cange, *Glossarium*, ed. L. Favre, 10 vols., Niort, 1885–87, *s.vv.*

[1] With regard to this question of κάτοχοι and cenobites cf. H. Weingarten, 'Der Ursprung des Mönchtums im nachkonstantinischen Zeitalter,' in *ZKG* i. [1877] 1 ff.; E. Preuschen, *Mönchtum und Sarapiskult: eine religionsgeschichtliche Abhandlung*, Giessen, 1903; E. Revillout, 'Le Reclus du Sérapéum, sa bibliothèque et ses occupations mystiques,' in *REg* i. [1880] 160, also *Rapport sur une mission en Italie*, Paris, 1878, p. 38; P. Ladeuze, *Étude sur le cénobitisme pakhomien*, Louvain, 1898, p. 37; J. Mayer, *Die christliche Ascese*, Freiburg, 1894, p. 37; Brunet de Presle [C. M. Wladimir], 'Mémoire sur le Sérapéum,' in *Mémoires présentés par divers savants*, I. ii. [1852] 575; A. Bouché-Leclercq, 'Les Reclus du Sérapéum de Memphis,' in *Mélanges Perrot: Recueil de mémoires concernant l'archéologie classique, la littérature et l'histoire anciennes*, Paris, 1903, p. 21 f.; A. Rusch, *De Serapide et Iside in Græcia cultis*, Berlin, 1907; Leclercq, art. 'Cénobitisme,' *DACL* ii.[2] 3053–3056.

sophy, far from influencing Christianity, was itself deeply imbued with Christian ideas (cf. ASCETICISM, vol. ii. p. 65b).[1]

3. Druidical communities.—It will be enough to mention the theory of Alexandre Bertrand, who saw in the druids the ancestors of the Christian cenobites. This theory, which regards the monks not only as the imitators, but as even the legitimate descendants of the communities and brotherhoods of the old Celtic religion, has no solid foundation, and has been unanimously rejected by specialists; hence we need not discuss it in detail.[2]

4. Orphic communities.—Orphism, which had so much in common with Pythagoreanism, had, like it, a certain resemblance to Platonism and Neo-Platonism; it counselled practices of asceticism, some of which resemble those of Christianity. It imposed on the 'pure' and the 'holy' a rigorous system of penances and privations, among which were the practice of vegetarianism and numerous purifications. Although our information regarding these *thiasoi*, or Orphic societies, is not very extensive, we know that they were not only spread throughout Greece, but were also found in Italy, Africa, Gaul, and the whole of the Western world. Lactantius alludes to these confraternities (*de Div. Instit.* i. 22 [*PL* vi. 242 f.]). There were rites of initiation, mysteries, prayers, hymns, and unbloody sacrifices, which were celebrated during the night. But the doctrines and mysteries of Orphism have a very special character of their own and very little in common with those of the Christian religion.[3]

5. Buddhist asceticism.—Both Buddhism and Brāhmanism possess institutions that have certain characteristics analogous to those of Christian monasticism. In the sacred books of the Hindus mention is made of hermits forming colonies and dedicating their lives to the study of the Vedas and to the contemplation of Brahman. They are vegetarians, and practise mortification in all its forms. While in Brāhmanism the monastic life has preserved its eremitic character, in Buddhism we find it, on the contrary, in the cenobitic form. The monks live together in monasteries, in the practice of poverty—as mendicants, in fact—and celibacy. Such monasteries are still to be found in Japan, Korea, China, India, and Ceylon.

The lamaseries of Tibet are the most curious examples of this form of monasticism. The monastic capital of Tibet (*q.v.*) is Lhāsa, and of the 30,000 inhabitants of this city 10,000 are monks, who are divided among 2500 monasteries. In the provinces of China there are also monasteries of this kind, some of which contain from 300 to 400 bonzes. They have the head shaven, and spend their time reciting prayers and performing ceremonies before the statue of Buddha. Many of them condemn themselves to a life of absolute silence, others to complete immobility.

The *faqīrs* of India offer another variety of the life of mortification and renunciation. A. Hilgenfeld and other writers have tried to establish the influence of these institutions on Christian monasticism. But it is easy to show, with the advance of scholarship, that it is the contrary that is true, and that certain practices of Buddhist monasticism owe their inspiration to Christian influence.[1]

6. Monasticism among Jews and Muhammadans.—(*a*) *Essenes.*—The Essenes (*q.v.*) may be regarded as one of the most striking examples of the monastic life outside of Christianity. Whether they be looked on as a sect, as a tribe, or as a religious community, the Essenes (150 B.C.) offer all the principal characteristics of the cenobitic life—community of goods, practice of poverty and mortification, prayer, and work, meals and religious exercises in common, silence, celibacy, etc. Although there is no direct relationship between them, it is nevertheless true that both Essenian and Christian asceticism derived much of their practice from the same source, viz. the Jewish religion.

(*b*) *Therapeutæ.*—The Therapeutæ (*q.v.*), whose very existence has been disputed, are described by Philo (*de Vita Contemplativa*) as cenobites, leading a life almost identical with that of the Christian cenobites. This description bears so striking a resemblance to the life led by Christian monks that more than one writer has been led to deny its authenticity as a work of Philo and to uphold the opinion that it is a Christian compilation undertaken with the view of providing a venerable ancestry for the Christian cenobites. Renunciation of the world, prayer, life in common in real monasteries, vigils, chants carried out by alternate choirs, the practice of fasting and other mortification—such are the chief characteristics of the life of the Therapeutæ. Nevertheless, they do not seem to have exercised any direct influence on Christian monasticism.[2]

(*c*) *Nazirites.*—The Nazirites (*q.v.*) were men who lived an austere life, abstained from wine and all fermented liquors, never cut their hair, avoided scrupulously all legal impurities, and took a vow to consecrate their lives to God. They had certain practices in common with the monks, although their ideal was not the same. Regarding such resemblances we may point out that, as in the case of the Essenes, since Christianity itself had its ancestor in Judaism, it is not astonishing that there should be certain resemblances between their respective institutions on many points.[3]

(*d*) *Rechabites.*—Some (cf. T. K. Cheyne, *EBi* iv. [1903] 4019) regard the Rechabites as forming 'a sort of religious order, analogous to the Nazarites,' and St. Jerome himself saw in them the precursors of the monks (*Ep.* lviii., 'ad Paulin.,' 5 [*PL* xxii. 583]). But such analogies should not be pressed too far. The Rechabites were distinguished by certain special observances, such as abstinence from wine, the prohibition against building houses, and the obligation to live in tents, but it is difficult to see in them anything more than a tribe of Bedawī such as still exist in these days and observe the customs of their ancestors with such zeal.[4]

(*e*) *Muhammadans.*—Muhammadanism has given birth to several 'religious orders,' the chief of which are the Qādirī, the Maulavī, the Baqtāshī, the Rufā'ī, etc. The monks are called Dervishes ('poor'); they live together, 20, 30, or 40 at a time,

[1] T. Keim derives Christian asceticism from this source (*Aus dem Urchristenthum*, Zürich, 1878, p. 204 f.). Against this theory cf. D. Völter, *Der Ursprung des Mönchtums*, Freiburg, 1900, p. 39, and G. Grützmacher, 'Mönchtum,' in *PRE*³ xiii. 217.

[2] A. Bertrand, *Nos Origines*, iv. *La Religion des Gaulois: Les Druides et le druidisme*, Paris, 1897, pp. 417–424, appendix J, 'Les grandes Abbayes chrétiennes d'Irlande, d'Écosse, et du Pays de Galles, heritières des communautés druidiques de ces contrées'; cf. G. Boissier, in *Journal des Savants*, 1898, pp. 578–580; G. Dottin, 'La Religion des Gaulois,' in *RHR* xxxviii. [1898] 151 f.

[3] Cf. E. Zeller, *Die Philosophie der Griechen*, Tübingen, 1844–52, i. 88; L. F. A. Maury, *Hist. des religions de la Grèce antique*, Paris, 1857–59, iii. 300; O. Gruppe, *Die griech. Culte und Mythen*, Leipzig, 1887; E. W. T. Maass, *Orpheus*, Munich, 1895.

[1] Cf. Grützmacher, in *PRE*³ xiii. 217; Heimbucher, *Die Orden und Kongregationen der katholischen Kirche*, i. 54 f.; J. J. Bochinger, *La Vie contemplative ascétique et monastique chez les Indiens et chez les peuples bouddhistes*, 1831.

[2] On the Therapeutæ and the question of the authenticity of the famous treatise of Philo, cf. Leclercq, in *DACL* ii.² 3063. Since the works of H. Massebieau and F. C. Conybeare on the subject, the authenticity of the treatise would seem to be solidly established.

[3] Cf. G. Less, *De Nazireatu*, Göttingen, 1789; J. B. Wirthmüller, *Die Nazoräer*, Ratisbon, 1864; B. Duhm, *Die Gottgeweihten in der alttestamentl. Religion*, Tübingen, 1905.

[4] Cf. A. Calmet, 'Dissertations sur des Réchabites,' in *Commentaire littéral* (*Jérémie*), Paris, 1724–26, pp. xliii–liii; *HDB* iv. 203.

in a monastery under a head (*shaikh*). The Dervishes wear a long robe of coarse stuff. Reception into their order is preceded by a time of probation, which lasts sometimes 1001 days. As regards their religious practices, these Muhammadan monks have prayers, sacred dances, and sometimes penances, such as the privation of sleep, immobility (ensured by fetters on the feet), fasting, and solitude (see art. DERVISH). Many of them are also mendicants. Some of the orders claim to go back to the time of the Prophet himself, although he had said 'In Islām there are no monks,' and although no mention of the monastic life is to be found in the Qur'ān. Even during the lifetime of Muhammad, however, the Ṣūfīs gave themselves up to certain practices of monasticism and lived together in community (see art. ṢŪFIISM). Abū Bakr and 'Alī, contemporaries of the Prophet, formed, with his approval, communities of the same kind. Other orders were founded on the same model in Egypt, Arabia, Persia, and Turkey. There were no fewer than 27 monasteries in the island of Crete alone. One of the most celebrated of Muhammadan monasteries, that of Konia in Asia Minor, possessed 500 cells.[1]

III. *CHRISTIAN MONASTICISM.*—Is Christian monasticism derived from one or other of these sources, or is it an original institution? This is a question that has often been discussed. On account of certain undeniable resemblances between Christian monasticism and the various forms just described, some writers have not hesitated to regard the one as the child of the other. But in this case, as in that of the history of all institutions, however striking such resemblances may appear at first sight, they are not sufficient of themselves to establish a relationship. This is a principle now accepted by all serious students of history. To prove relationship between the institutions of Christianity and those of other religions, it is necessary to produce facts clearly demonstrating that one institution has been derived from the other. This, however, still remains to be done. We shall therefore regard Christian monasticism as a plant that has grown up on Christian soil, nourished exclusively on the principles of Christianity. This seems, for the moment at least, to be the only theory that can safely be maintained.[2]

i. PRINCIPAL CHARACTERISTICS. — Christian monasticism possesses certain characteristics all of which are not equally essential, but which, nevertheless, when taken together, are necessary to constitute a monk.

1. Poverty, chastity, humility, and obedience.—The first monks, after the example of the Christian ascetics, practised poverty, chastity, and humility —virtues which, along with obedience, soon came to be regarded as essential to the monastic life. In order to carry out the evangelical counsels and to imitate the life led by Christ Himself and, after Him, by the apostles and first disciples, it was necessary to give oneself up to these virtues:

'Beati pauperes spiritu' (Mt 5³); 'si vis perfectus esse, vade, vende quae habes, et da pauperibus' (Mt 19²¹); 'non potestis Deo servire et Mammonae . . . ne solliciti sitis animae vestrae quid manducetis, neque corpori vestro quid induamini,' etc. (Mt 6²⁴ᶠ·). 'Sunt eunuchi qui seipsos castraverunt propter regnum coelorum. Qui potest capere, capiat' (Mt 19¹²). Cf. St. Paul (1 Co 7⁷ᶠ· ³²⁻³⁵). 'Si quis vult post me venire, abneget semetipsum, et tollat crucem suam, et sequatur me' (Mt 16²⁴; cf. 10³⁸).

The first monks, like the ascetics before them, took these words of the gospel literally and abandoned all that they had in order to live in poverty and by the labour of their hands. They practised chastity under the form of complete celibacy and perfect continence. The practice of obedience consisted in following in the footsteps of Jesus Christ, recognizing Him as their Master, and in submission to those who represent Him here below. In the case of the cenobites this obedience was the result of their very life itself. The moment that many monks united to live together, they were obliged to adopt a rule of life which would be the same for all, and to submit to the authority of a head. This, again, was but to obey Christ, by showing obedience to the Rule or to him who was its guardian. Schenoudi of Atripe obliged his monks to make a profession of obedience to the Rule of the monastery. This profession was a written and signed engagement, and was preserved in the archives of the monastery.[1] The greater number of monasteries had the same custom under one form or another. These virtues were taught and practised by all the early monks, and, as soon as monastic customs began to be drawn up and codified, we find severe laws laid down to ensure their practice.

2. Mortification (fasting, etc.).—Along with these virtues we find others which in reality flow from them or complete them, and which were always practised by the monks and prescribed by the different Rules. Mortification is essential to the practice of asceticism; it takes the form of the renunciation of the pleasures of sense (chastity, celibacy, fasting, etc.); work, silence, prayer even, may all be considered forms of mortification. As in all schools of asceticism (Neo-Platonist, Buddhist, etc.), fasting is considered one of the essential exercises of the Christian 'athlete'; Jesus taught it to His disciples and practised it Himself; and it was regarded by the monks as one of the most efficacious of all exercises of mortification. The history of the early solitaries tells of intrepid fasters who passed two, three, and even five days without touching food. The custom of taking food only once during the week from Monday to Saturday which was observed by those known as 'Hebdomadarii' was common.[2] There is, in fact, no monastic Rule in which restraint in matters of food and drink is not arranged for.

It is chiefly in the monasteries of the East (Syria, Palestine, Asia Minor) that one comes across extraordinary forms of mortification; though these must be regarded as exceptional cases, they cannot be passed over in silence. There were, first of all, the Stylites and the Dendrites, who condemned themselves to perpetual immobility, the former on their columns, the latter on the branch of a tree. Then there were the βοσκοί, or 'Browsers,' mentioned by Sozomen. These were solitaries of Mesopotamia, and were so called because they lived on grass like cattle. Others, again, chained themselves to a rock, or bore on their shoulders a species of cangue, or yoke. Sozomen also speaks of a Syrian monk who abstained from eating bread during eighty years.[3] All these are exceptional cases, and are even regarded by some as mere eccentricities, recalling the practices of the *faqīrs* of India. It should be noted carefully that the monastic Rules not only never prescribe such feats of strength, but even condemn them.[4]

[1] Heimbucher, i. 51 f.; art. 'Dervich,' in *Kath. Lexicon*, iii. 1527 f.

[2] It should be remarked that this is the conclusion now reached by writers of very different opinions, such as Berlière, *L'Ordre monastique*, Leclercq, *loc. cit.*, Grützmacher, *loc. cit.*, and Workman, *The Evolution of the Monastic Ideal*, p. 86 f. An exception must be made, as we have already pointed out, for certain Jewish institutions, since between Jews and Christians many principles and religious ideas are held in common.

[1] E. Amélineau, *Mémoires publiés par les membres de la mission archéologique française au Caire*, IV. i. [1888] 234–236.

[2] Cf. F. Cabrol, *Étude sur la Peregrinatio Silviæ; les églises de Jérusalem; la discipline et la liturgie au IVᵉ siècle*, Paris, 1895, p. 135 f.

[3] Soz. *HE* vi. 33 f. (*PG* lxvii. 1391 f.); cf. C. Clermont-Ganneau, 'L'Abstinence de pain dans les rites syrien, païen et chrétien,' in *Recueil d'archéologie orientale*, ii. [1898] 134, n. 45.

[4] Cf. Leclercq, in *DACL* ii.² 3143 f.

3. Work.—Certain fanatics, such as the Messalians or Euchites (*q.v.*), maintained that the life of a monk should be entirely given up to prayer; hence they condemned all work or other forms of activity. This tendency was early reprobated by the Church; all monastic founders or legislators realized the danger of such exaggerations; and one and all signalized the vice of idleness as the one most to be dreaded in the monastic life. St. Augustine, in his treatise *de Labore Monachorum*, condemns this error, and shows the real necessity of work for those who follow the monastic vocation. Already in the East, during the 4th cent., it was an established principle that the monk should live by the labour of his hands. The work of the monk was of two kinds: (*a*) manual, and (*b*) intellectual.

(*a*) *Manual.*—The manual labour of the early monks consisted chiefly in the weaving of mats or the cultivation of the soil. These occupations had as their principal motive not so much interest or gain as mortification in addition to all the mortifications already forming part of their existence, and especially the avoidance of idleness. The proceeds of their work were usually handed over by the monks to the poor or to the prisoners, or else they served to sustain the community itself (Cassian, *de Cœnobiorum institutis*, x. 22 [*PL* xlix. 388 f.]). In the case of the monks of the West this manual work was carried out in so orderly and methodical a manner that it resulted in the clearing of a large part of the waste-land of Europe.[1]

The various arts and crafts had also their place in monastic activity, but in the West rather than in the East. A monastery came, in course of time, to form a little city in itself. Founded, as most monasteries then were, far from the towns and centres of worldly activity, they were obliged to provide for themselves, and, besides cultivating the soil, the monks had to give themselves to the exercise of the various trades necessary for their wants—*e.g.*, baking, carpentry, weaving, etc. In addition to the arts of drawing and miniature painting, architecture, sculpture, and the fine arts were cultivated with great success.

(*b*) *Intellectual.*—The intellectual work of the monks consisted chiefly in the *lectio divina*, *i.e.* the reading and study of the sacred Scripture and other holy writings. In the West this part of the monastic curriculum underwent a great development. More and more time was given to intellectual work. The copying of ancient MSS in the scriptorium of the monastery became one of the principal occupations of the monk, and it is to this fact that we owe the preservation of the greater part of the works of classical antiquity. The arts of calligraphy, drawing, painting, and the illumination of MSS soon followed as a natural consequence, and some monasteries had attached to them studies, from which came forth works of art that are now among the most precious possessions of the libraries of Europe.[2]

(*c*) *External work; the sacred ministry.*—The monks, especially in the East, retired from the world into solitude, there to lead lives of prayer and labour apart from all intercourse with it. They took part in the external ministry of the Church only on rare occasions and by force of special circumstances. A number of monasteries, however, received 'oblates,' *i.e.* children consecrated from an early age by their parents to the monastic state. These it was necessary to instruct; hence schools were established in the monasteries, some of which became famous and were attended by secular students as well.[1]

In the West the monks were led in time to take up in certain countries—*e.g.*, England and Germany—the work of evangelizing the people. They thus became missionaries, and had, in fact, a large part in bringing about the conversion of Europe.

4. Prayer.—But it was always clearly understood that neither work nor any other occupation should absorb the whole of the monk's activity. A considerable part of his time was always devoted to prayer. In substance this prayer consisted in meditation on, or recitation of, the Psalter, which was distributed according to the days of the week or the hours of each day. It was organized more methodically when regular monasteries began to be established in greater numbers; and from it has evolved the divine office as we now have it, with its different 'Hours' for the night and the day—Matins, Lauds, Prime, Tierce, Sext, None, Vespers, and Compline.[2]

5. Silence.—Silence, recommended by philosophers as a necessary condition for meditation or intellectual research, was one of the practices most rigorously enforced in the monastic life. In the case of the hermits, living in complete isolation, silence was practically absolute, and rare were the occasions on which they could indulge in conversation. They did, however, occasionally visit one another, and sometimes returned to their monasteries for a certain length of time. For the cenobites talking was naturally of more frequent occurrence, but severe regulations were established on this point in the greater number of monasteries.

6. Solitude.—Solitude, as in the case of silence, was interpreted in a more or less wide sense. For the anchorites, hermits, and Stylites, living in their caves, in their tombs, or on their pillars, solitude was absolute and complete. For the cenobites it consisted rather in their separation from the world, in the practice of silence, and in certain restraints. It is this need of solitude that may be said to have given to monastic architecture its principal characteristics and the disposition of its various parts. The monastery was enclosed by walls; one gate alone gave access to it. Communication with the outside world was subject to strict control, and, to render the necessity less frequent, the monastery, like a little city, was to be self-contained. There were exercised all the different trades and crafts demanded by the needs of the community.

7. Stability.—Stability, *i.e.* the engagement undertaken by a monk to remain all his life in the same monastery, was only an accidental condition of the monastic state, and was not established everywhere. In certain regions a monk could, without any breach of his vows, pass from one monastery to another. The abuse of this custom, as seen in the wandering monks, or 'Gyrovagi' (see below, iii. 6), and other considerations as well, led to the establishment of stability as a law of the monastic state, which little by little became general. St. Cæsarius of Arles imposes it in his Rule, and also St. Benedict.[3]

[1] H. Hallam, *Middle Ages*[4], London, 1826, iii. 436; M. Guizot, *Hist. de la civilisation en France*[6], Paris, 1851, i. 378; M. P. E. Littré, *Études sur les barbares et le moyen âge*, Paris, 1867; Berlière, ch. iii., 'L'Œuvre civilisatrice'; E. Levasseur, 'Le Travail des moines dans les monastères,' *Séances et travaux de l'acad. des sciences morales et polit.*, Nov. 1900, pp. 449–470; C. Duvivier, 'Hospites: Défrichements en Europe, et spécialement dans nos contrées aux XIe, XIIe et XIIIe siècles,' *Revue d'hist. et d'archéol.* i. [1859] 74–80, 131–175.

[2] Cf. art. 'Bibliothèque,' in *DACL*.

[1] For the monastic schools cf. L. Maitre, *Les Ecoles épiscopales et monastiques de l'occident*, Paris, 1866; A. T. Drane, *Christian Schools and Scholars*, London, 1867; G. von Detten, *Ueber die Dom- und Klosterschulen des Mittelalters*, Paderborn, 1893; Berlière, 'Les Ecoles abbatiales au moyen âge,' in *Messager des fidèles*, vi. [1884] 499–511, also *L'Ordre monastique*, iii. 116 f.

[2] L. Duchesne, *Christian Worship*, Eng. tr.[4], London, 1912, p. 446, 'The Divine Office'; S. Bäumer, *Gesch. des Breviers*, Freiburg, 1895; P. Batiffol, *Hist. du bréviaire romain*, Paris, 1893, Eng. tr., London, 1898.

[3] A. Malnory, *Saint Césaire, évêque d'Arles*, Paris, 1894, pp 10–12; *Regula Sancti Benedicti*, cap. lviii.

ii. CUSTOMS, ORGANIZATION, HIERARCHY, CONSTITUTIONS OF THE MONASTERY, RULES, COSTUME.—The hermits and anchorites lived separate and alone in the desert; hence they were their own masters. It often happened, however, that the hermit, sensible of the dangers resulting from this independence, would submit himself to the direction of another, whom he regarded as his spiritual father. Sometimes colonies of hermits were formed under the direction of a head, to whom the others rendered obedience. Again, we find hermits living near a monastery of cenobites, to which they were obliged to return at certain times, generally on Saturday and Sunday and on feast-days. With regard to the monastic hierarchy and the organization of authority among the cenobites, great variation is to be observed in primitive ages. It was generally, however, fairly simple in character. At the head of the monastery was a superior, at once spiritual father and temporal administrator, who was known by the various titles of archimandrite (ἀρχιμανδρίτης), hegumenos (ἡγεμών, ἡγεμονεύς, ἡγούμενος), abbot (ἀββᾶς and ἄμμα),[1] προεστώς, præpositus, or provost, etc. This superior governed the community, sometimes with the help of an assistant and other officials who fulfilled various charges, such as cellarer, porter, etc. He was generally assisted also by a council composed of the older members of the community (*seniores*). The office of the seniors, who were nominated by the superior himself, expired at the end of the year. The government of these monastic societies was a monarchy rather than an oligarchy; often it was even an absolute monarchy.[2] The cellarer (κελλαρίτης, whence *cellerarius*, 'cellarer'), the official who had charge of the stores of the monastery, had, as a rule, very wide powers over the temporal affairs of the monastery. Sometimes the abbot, as already mentioned, was assisted in his office by an official who ranked second after himself in the monastery; sometimes there was a third as well (prior and subprior).

The monasteries thus constituted usually enjoyed complete autonomy. There was nothing resembling the modern order or congregation, in which the different religious houses are united under a superior-in-chief or 'general,' and depend upon one house, which is the mother-house of the whole congregation. In the West it was not till the time of St. Benedict of Aniane that the idea of grouping monasteries together under a central authority was actually realized. For example, St. Basil in his Rule, which was the law everywhere in the East, contents himself with giving a few general principles as to the choice of the superior and the exercise of authority. In certain monastic colonies, too, the organization was very rudimentary in character. St. Anthony and St. Hilarion, *e.g.*, were the spiritual and temporal heads of the communities founded by them, and unity and order were maintained by visiting the various houses subject to them (*Vita S. Hilarionis*, ch. iii.).

Nevertheless, even in the early age of monasticism, we have instances of the attempt to group certain monasteries together under a central authority. Pachomius, *e.g.*, formed his monasteries into a real 'congregation.' He visited each house in turn; he assembled the superiors together four times a year in what closely resembled the general chapters of later days. In these assemblies the interests and affairs of the various communities were discussed and settled. Pachomius himself nominated the superiors of the different houses, and a 'procurator-general' for the whole confederation. Tabenna, the head-house of this congregation, was an almost military organization. The monks were divided into companies, often under an official called the dean; ten companies formed a further division, at the head of which was another official. At an early period the Rules, or constitutions, of the various monasteries came to be written down. A great number of these exist, some of which can be safely attributed to the most ancient masters of the monastic life. We shall speak only of the principal ones.

[1] The word 'abbot' did not originally designate the superior (cf. J. M. Besse, *Les Moines d'Orient*, Paris, 1901, p. 168; also art. 'Ama,' *DACL* i.[2] 1306–1323).

[2] Monastic government has even been presented as a kind of 'spiritual democracy' (Workman, p. 132). This is true, in a sense, but the monastic form of government cannot in reality be ranged under any very definite category. It possesses the characteristics alike of monarchy, oligarchy, and democracy.

The *Regula Antonii* cannot be regarded as the work of St. Anthony himself, but it is extremely ancient.[1] This collection of maxims on the monastic life was brought together in Egypt, in the course of the 6th cent., but there is nothing against the belief that many of them are authentic and of much earlier date than the collection itself.[2] The same may be said of the authenticity and age of the *Regula ad Monachos Macarii Alex.* (*PG* xxxiv. 967–970), and the *Regula ad Monachos Serapionis, Macarii, Paphnutii et alterius Macarii* (*PG* xxxiv. 971–978).

The Rule of St. Basil (Ὅροι κατὰ πλάτος, *Regulæ fusius tractatæ*; Ὅροι κατ' ἐπιτομήν, *Regulæ brevius tractatæ* [*PG* xxxi. 889–1052, 1080–1305], tr. Rufinus, in L. Holste, *Codex Regularum*, Paris, 1661, i. 67 f.; cf. C. T. G. Schoenemann, *Bibl. Patr. Latina*, Leipzig, 1792–94, i. 619 ff.) has had a wide influence on Oriental monasticism, and is at the present day practically the only Rule existing. Even in the West its influence was considerable, as may be seen—to cite but one example—from the reference made to it in the Rule of St. Benedict. A long letter, written by St. Basil to St. Gregory of Nazianzus before the drawing up of his Rule, may be regarded as an outline or rough draft of the latter.[3]

The Rules attributed to St. Pachomius and to Schenoudi, although not authentic in the same sense as the Rule of St. Basil, are, nevertheless, substantially their work in spite of later retouching and additions.[4] The Rule of Pachomius, written originally in Coptic, was translated into Greek and Latin (Ladeuze, p. 272). There are three texts of the Rule of Schenoudi (cf. *Monuments de la mission archéologique française au Caire*, iv. 235 f., and Leclercq, in *DACL* ii.[2] 3111).[5]

The Book of the Governors of Thomas of Marga, of the 6th cent., describes the life led by the cenobites and anchorites of the Nestorian monastery of Beth-Abhe in Mesopotamia.[6]

In the West, besides Cassian, whose two works exercised the widest influence on monasticism in that part of the world,[7] we must mention the Rule of St. Benedict, *Regula S. Patris Benedicti*.[8]

Other Rules are: the *Regula incerti auctoris*, later than the works of Cassian, but earlier than the Rule of St. Benedict (Holste, *Codex Regularum*, ed. M. Brockie, Augsburg, 1759, i. 137 f.), the *Regula Sanctorum Pauli et Stephani*, almost contemporary with that of St. Benedict (*ib.* i. 138 f.), the Rule for nuns attributed to St. Augustine, *Ep.* ccxi. (*ib.* i. 141). For this Rule and those of SS. Fructuosus and Isidore, see, further, V. iii. 1 (*d*) below.

Several Rules written for the Celtic monks are in existence. The Rule written in verse, and attributed to St. Ailbe, is not, strictly speaking, a Rule. That attributed to St. Columba is a short collection of prescriptions and maxims of asceticism, and was written for the use of solitaries. There are also other documents of the same character, attributed with more or less likelihood to St. Comgall of Bangor and others. The Rule of

[1] Cf. B. Contzen, *Die Regel des heil. Antonius*, Metten-gymnasialprogramm, 1895–96; *Apophthegmata Patrum* (*PG* lxv. 71–440); *Verba Seniorum* (*PL* lxxiii. 739–810); and J. B. Cotelier, *Ecclesiæ Græcæ Monumenta*, Paris, 1677–86, i. 524.

[2] Regarding the edd. of these maxims, cf. K. Krumbacher, *Gesch. der byzantinischen Litteratur*[2], Munich, 1897, p. 188; C. Butler, *The Lausiac History of Palladius*, 2 vols. [*TS* vi.], Cambridge, 1898–1904, pp. 208–215; S. Vailhé, 'Les Apophthegmata Patrum,' in *Echos d'Orient*, 1902, pp. 39–46; Leclercq, *loc. cit.*

[3] St. Basil, *Ep.* ii. (*PG* xxxii. 223–233; cf. Paul Allard, 'St. Basile avant son épiscopat,' *Revue des questions historiques*, lxiv. [1898] 29 f.); Zöckler, *Askese und Mönchtum*, p. 287; A. Kranich, *Die Ascetik in ihrer dogmatischen Grundlage bei Basilius dem Grossen*, Paderborn, 1896; K. Holl, *Enthusiasmus und Bussgewalt beim griechischen Mönchtum: Studie zu Symeon dem neuen Theologen*, Leipzig, 1898, p. 140 f. On the authenticity of the Rule of St. Basil cf. Leclercq, in *DACL* ii.[2] 3147 f.

[4] For the discussions to which these Rules have given rise cf. Ladeuze, p. 259 f.

[5] P. E. Lucius, 'Die Quellen der ältesten Gesch. des ägyp. Mönchtums,' *Zeitschrift für Kirchengeschichte*, vii. [1885] 163 f.

[6] E. A. W. Budge, *The Book of the Governors: Historia Monastica of Thomas, Bishop of Marga, A.D. 840*, ed. from Syriac MSS, 2 vols., London, 1893.

[7] See below, V. iii. 1 (*b*).

[8] On the Rule of St. Benedict, the authenticity of which is incontestable, and its various edd. see below, p. 792[b], note 1.

St. Columban, his Penitentiary, and that of St. Cummian, are the only ones the authentic character of which is really established.[1] At an early date collections were made of all these monastic Rules.[2]

The question of monastic costume is one with regard to which the different Rules show a bewildering variety. It is also, from the archæological point of view, one of the least clear. It seems that there was originally no special dress for monks. The only rule on this point seems to have been that the monk in his character of ascetic should, like certain ancient philosophers, show in his costume the outward sign of the poverty and humility of his state of life and of his detachment from the things of this world. Even St. Benedict, at a time when monasticism already had customs and traditions both numerous and of long-established date, does not seem to have given much importance to the form, colour, or quality of the habit worn by his monks (*Regula*, ch. lv.). Nevertheless, at an early date certain garments worn by the monks, and borrowed in all probability from the peasant population among whom they lived, came to be regarded as traditional, and in time even had a mystic meaning attached to them, as in the case of the liturgical vestments. In spite of this the monastic habit must always be carefully distinguished from the latter category.

We may now enter into greater detail regarding the various garments worn by the ancient monks both in the East and in the West. Many of these garments are still in use among their descendants.

The ancients did not know the use of linen. The tunic of wool was their only under-garment (*λεβιτίον, κολοβή, colobium*). The monks adopted this. It had short sleeves or was sleeveless. The anchorites often wore the tunic made of goatskin or camel's hair, which acted as a veritable hair-shirt (Cassian, *Instit.* i. 8 [*PL* xlix. 74]). The tunic was girded by a cincture, which recalled that worn by John the Baptist ('zona pellicea circa lumbos suos,' Mt 3[4]), and which soon became an essential part of the monk's habit. It was usually made of leather (*cinctura, zona, ζώνη, balteus, cingulum*, etc.).[3] The hood and the scapular are also characteristic of the monastic habit. The first (*cucullus, cucullio*) was originally merely a covering for the head. It was, in fact, the ordinary head-covering of peasants, and is found in both East and West. It protected the head against the heat or the cold, and could be thrown back at will on the shoulders.[4] The hood came in time to be attached to a garment covering the shoulders and breast to protect them against the weather, and finally developed, after various transformations, into the cowl—an ample vestment falling in wide folds to the feet and with large sleeves. The cowl is the distinctive choir-habit of the monk. The scapular (*scapulare*) seems to be peculiar to Benedictine monks, since there is no mention of it before the time of St. Benedict. Still it is evident, from the text of his Rule, that it was not his own invention. By some it has been compared to an analogous garment worn by Eastern monks; but it is more probable that it was originally a kind of blouse or smock-frock with hood attached, such as was worn by peasants in the neighbourhood of Monte Cassino. St. Benedict prescribes it as a working dress—'scapulare propter opera.' It was worn to protect the rest of the habit, and replaced the cowl. Its etymology indicates that it covered the shoulders.[5]

The Eastern monks usually went barefooted. St. Pachomius, however, gave his monks sandals, and St. Benedict speaks of 'pedules et caligae,' which seem to have been a kind of stocking, or sock, and sandals. Archæologists have disputed at length as to the exact meaning of these terms and also regarding the other parts of the monastic habit.[1]

iii. DIFFERENT TYPES OF MONKS.—The monks may be divided into various classes.

1. **Hermits.**—The hermits (ἐρημῖται, from ἔρημος, 'desert') lived in solitude in the desert; St. John the Baptist, and later St. Paul the Hermit and St. Anthony, were the first of these.

2. **Anachorites or anchorites** (ἀναχωρηταί, from ἀναχώρημα, 'retreat').—This title is synonymous with the first, and indicates those monks who practised the solitary life. This form of the monastic life is the most ancient; it spread, first of all, in Egypt, then in Palestine and Syria, through the whole of the Eastern world, and, finally, in the West.[2] In course of time the Camaldolese, Carthusians, Hermits of St. Augustine, and certain other institutions of like character arose. These may be grouped under the class of anchorites or hermits, since they have preserved, along with the cenobitic element in their lives, many of the characteristics of the eremitic state.

3. **Recluses and Stylites.** — With the hermits and anchorites must be classed the recluses and Stylites, who, on account of their relatively small number, may be regarded as exceptional cases. The former lived enclosed in cells, sometimes completely walled up and communicating with the exterior only by means of a small window. The latter, who are found almost exclusively in the East, lived on the top of a pillar, more or less elevated from the ground.[3]

4. **Dendrites.** — The Dendrites (from δένδρον, 'tree') lived in trees.

5. **Cenobites** (from κοινόβιος, 'one who lives in common with others').—This was the general term for all monks living together in community. During the primitive period the comparative advantages and excellence of the solitary and cenobitic forms of monastic life formed the subject of frequent discussions. St. Basil stoutly maintains his preference for the cenobitic life over the eremitic life, and his preference is shared by St. Benedict. It is undeniable that in early days the eremitic life had the greater number of adherents; but in course of time it declined, even in the East, while, in the West, it cannot be said ever to have existed except as an exceptional state of things. After the 16th cent. it almost completely disappeared.[4]

6. **Sarabaites and Gyrovagi, or Circumcelliones.**—Among the other monastic types, ancient authors draw attention to the Sarabaites and the Gyrovagi, who were regarded as an evil kind of monks. The first, mentioned by St. Jerome under their Syriac name of 'Remoboth' (*Ep.* xxii. 34 [*PL* xxii. 419]), lived together in twos and threes in a monastery, in order to live a life without

[1] Holste gives two other Rules attributed to SS. Comgall and Columba. For this question see L. Gougaud, 'Inventaire des règles monastiques irlandaises,' in *Revue Bénédictine*, xxv. [1908] 167–184, 321–333; O. Seebass, *Ueber Columba von Luxeuils Klosterregel*, Dresden, 1883; Leclercq, in *DACL* ii.[2] 3212 f.

[2] The earliest and most celebrated of these collections is that made by St. Benedict of Aniane († 821), entitled *Concordia Regularum* (*Concordia Regularum nunc primum edita ex Bibliotheca Floriacencis Monasterii, notisque et observationibus illustrata ab H. Menard O.S.B.*, Paris, 1638 [=*PL* ciii. 701–1380]); cf. L. Traube, 'Bibliotheca Goerresiana,' in *Neues Archiv für ältere deutsche Geschichtskunde*, xxvii. [1902] 737 f. For other attempts of this kind see J. Trithemius, Aubert Le Mire, etc.; cf. also Heimbucher, i. 76. Of more recent date: L. Holste, *Codex Regularum Monasticarum et Canonicarum*, 3 vols., Rome, 1661, completed by Brockie, *Holstenii Cod. regular. etc. nunc auctus, amplificatus et observ. criticis historicis illustratus*, Augsburg, 1759 (*PL* ciii. 393–700).

[3] Cf. art. 'Ceinture,' in *DACL* ii.[2] 2779 f.

[4] Daremberg-Saglio[3], i. fig. 2094; artt. 'Birrus,' *DACL* ii.[1] 907 f., and 'Capuchon,' *DACL* ii.[2] 2127 f.

[5] Cf. *RA*, May–June 1892, pp. 331 and 333, for representation of peasants wearing the scapular; cf. also J. Mabillon and L. d'Achéry, *Acta Sanctorum O.S.B. sæc.*, Venice, 1733–38, v. præf. p. xxxi, *Annales O.S.B.*, Paris, 1703–39, i. 505.

[1] See especially A. Calmet, *Commentario litterale, istorico, e morale sopra la Regola di S. Benedetto*, Arezzo, 1753, ii. 179 ff., and the *Commentaire sur la règle de S. Benoît* by (D. Delatte) the abbot of Solesmes, Paris, 1913, p. 394 f. On the question of monastic costume in general cf. P. Bonanni, *Ordinum religiosorum in ecclesia militante catalogus eorumque indumenta*, 5 vols., Rome, 1722; Hélyot, *Hist. des ordres monastiques, religieux et militaires*, etc.; R. A. S. Macalister, *Ecclesiastical Vestments*, London, 1896, App. I., 'Costumes of the Religious Orders'; J. Braun, *Die liturgische Gewandung im Occident und Orient*, Freiburg i. Br., 1907.

[2] Cf. Heimbucher, i. 41.

[3] For the recluses cf. *Hist. Laus.* 43; Theodoret, *Hist. rel.* 29, 30, etc. (*PG* lxxxii. 1490–1494); R. M. Clay, 'The Hermits and Anchorites of England,' in *The Antiquary's Book*, London, 1914; Heimbucher, i. 145, note; for the Stylites, all quotations in H. Delehaye, *Les Stylites*, Brussels, 1895; Vailhé, 'Les Stylites de Constantinople,' in *Echos d'Orient*, 1898; for the different classes of monks cf. Besse, p. 19 f.

[4] Cf. Synod of Vannes, 465, canon 7; Synod of Agde, 506, canon 38; G. D. Mansi, *Concilia*, Paris reprint, 1901–13, vii. 954, viii. 331.

either rule or law, following no other rule than that of their own will or caprice. The Gyrovagi or Circumcelliones ('vagabonds') went from monastery to monastery, demanding a lodging for a few days, and scandalizing all true Christians by their excesses.[1]

7. Catenati.—As the name indicates, these monks loaded themselves with chains. They took no care of their bodies, allowed their hair and beards to grow neglected and untrimmed, went barefooted, and wore a black cloak (Leclercq, in *DACL* ii.[2] 3218).

8. Apotactites (from ἀποτάσσεσθαι, 'to renounce'; cf. Lk 14[33]).—These formed a class intermediary between the earlier ascetics and the monks properly so called. They are found in Jerusalem, in the East, and in Asia Minor. Some of them followed the example of the Gyrovagi, and spent their life wandering about, and some fell into the heresy of the Encratites.[2]

IV. *HISTORY OF MONASTICISM*.—i. ORIGIN OF THE MONASTIC LIFE; THE ASCETICS. — The ascetics of early Christianity may be regarded as the ancestors of the monks. The greater number of the characteristics of which we have already spoken as belonging to the essence of the monastic life are found among the ascetics—poverty, celibacy, the practice of mortification, fasting, silence, prayer, etc. The ascetics were, in fact, simply monks living in the world.

'Asceticism and cenobitism are inseparable. Asceticism is an individual phenomenon, cenobitism is a social institution.'[3]

It was but natural that, as Christians gradually became more worldly, the ascetics should retire from their midst and betake themselves to the desert; and here we have the origin of true monasticism—the first monks were ascetics living retired from the world in the desert.

This is not the place to enter upon a detailed history of these Christian ascetics (see art. ASCETICISM). But it may be remarked, in passing, that Christian asceticism, while recognizing among some of the prophets and just men of the Old Law (such as Isaiah, Jeremiah, and John the Baptist) its ancestors or forerunners, claims, above all, as its source and foundation the doctrine of Jesus Christ, who taught renunciation under all its forms. Not to mention certain texts occurring in the writings of the Apostolic Fathers—in those, *e.g.*, of Tertullian, Origen, and Clement of Alexandria, whose 'true Gnosticism' offers many characteristics of asceticism — one may consult certain documents that will give assistance in arriving at a knowledge of this movement precursory of monasticism, especially the *Epistles* of pseudo-Clement 'To Virgins' and the work of pseudo-Cyprian, *de Singularitate Clericorum*.[4]

ii. MONASTICISM IN THE EAST.—**1. Sources.**—The question of the authenticity and truthfulness of the documents on which the history of the early years of Eastern monasticism is founded has given rise, in recent years, to lengthy and impassioned disputes.

(*a*) *Vita Pauli*.—The *Vita Pauli*, written by St. Jerome, is sometimes considered to have no serious historical basis. The first of the hermits withdrew to the desert not before the middle of the 3rd cent., and, towards the end of his life, would have made the acquaintance of St. Anthony.[1]

(*b*) *Vita Antonii*.—If the authentic character of St. Jerome's life of Paul the first hermit be denied, it is St. Anthony who must be regarded as the father of the eremitic life. The *Vita Antonii*, attributed to St. Athanasius, has serious historical foundation, despite the discussions of which it also has been the subject.[2] In it St. Athanasius describes the life of a man whom he has himself known, and who died between 356 and 362. According to this life, Anthony was born at Coma, or Comon, in the middle of Egypt. At the age of 20, on hearing the passage in the Gospel of St. Matthew regarding the rich young man (19[17ff.]), he sold his belongings and put himself under the direction of an ascetic in order to learn the practice of Christian renunciation. Then he retired to the desert and led the life of a hermit for twenty years, a number of disciples gathering round him. During the persecution of Maximian, he went to Alexandria to fortify his brethren in the faith, returning there again, later on, to refute Arius. Living retired in his desert, he visited from time to time the colonies of hermits who had been his disciples and who peopled the desert. He died in 356 (or 362), at the age of 105. We have already seen what is to be thought of his Rule. The letters and sermons attributed to him are not more authentic in character (*PG* xl. 963–1066).

(*c*) *Lausiac History of Palladius*.—Another document which has been much disputed is the *Lausiac History of Palladius* (*PRE*[3] xiii. 219); it recounts the origins of monasticism. Weingarten and Lucius see in it nothing more than a romance, and Amélineau has further complicated the question by the unjustifiable use of the Coptic sources. Butler, in his excellent work on the subject, *The Lausiac History of Palladius* (Cambridge, 1898–1904, i. 257–277), has re-established the real text and demonstrated its importance from the historical point of view.[3]

(*d*) *Rufinus*.—Rufinus of Aquileia († 410) travelled through Egypt in order to visit the most celebrated solitaries, and his *Historia Monachorum* furnishes interesting details on the monastic life in that country.[4]

(*e*) *Cassian*.—Far more important for the history of monastic institutions, customs, and teaching are the two works of Cassian—*de Institutione Cœnobiorum* (12 books), and *Collationes Patrum* (24 Conferences). Cassian, like Rufinus, travelled about from one monastic colony to another in Egypt and Palestine in order to be initiated into the manner of life there observed.[5]

(*f*) *Peregrinatio Etheriæ*.—The *Peregrinatio ad loca sancta*, of which the date has been so much disputed, but which can, in all probability, be assigned to the latter half of the 4th cent., is the account of a pilgrimage to the monasteries of Egypt, the peninsula of Sinai, Palestine, and Syria, and gives many interesting details regarding the hermits and the monasteries of the period.[6] There are many other sources of Eastern monastic history, but the historians and writers of the 4th, 5th, and 6th centuries, such as Eusebius, Theodoret, Sozomen, Socrates, etc., afford less room for discussions as to authenticity and credibility, and their testimony serves to control the truth of the accounts furnished by Palladius, Rufinus, and the others.

2. History.—Apart from the life of St. Anthony, summarized above, the general lines of monastic history in the East may be presented as follows.

(*a*) *Egypt*.—Amun (Ammonius), a contemporary of St. Anthony, founded colonies of hermits in

[1] For these different kinds of monks cf. Cassian, *Collationes*, xviii. ch. iv. f. (*PL* xlix. 1093 f.), and *Institutiones*, v. 36, with the notes by A. Gazée (*PL* xlix. 255); *Regula S. Benedicti*, i.; *Regula Magistri*, i.; St. Jerome, *Ep.* xxii. 'ad Eustochium' (*PL* xxii. 419 f.); St. Augustine, *de Opere Monachorum*, 28 (*PL* xl. 575 f.).

[2] Cf. art. 'Apotactiques, Apotaxamènes,' in *DACL* i.[2] 2604 f.; Cabrol, *Étude sur la Peregrinatio Silviæ*, p. 135 f.

[3] Leclercq, in *DACL* ii.[2] 3048 f.; cf. Zöckler, *Askese und Mönchtum*.

[4] Cf. Leclercq, in *DACL* ii.[2] 3078–3090; Heimbucher, i. 86 f.; N. M. Antonelli, 'Dissertatio de Ascetis,' in *Sancti Patris Jacobi Episcopi Nisibeni sermones, cum præfatione, notis*, etc., Rome, 1756; S. Schiwietz, 'Vorgeschichte des Mönchtums oder das Ascetentum der drei ersten christl. Jahrh.,' in *Archiv für kath. Kirchenrecht*, i. [1898] 3 f., ii. 305 f.; and especially F. Martinez, 'L'Ascétisme chrétien pendant les trois premiers siècles de l'église,' in *Les Etudes de théologie historique de l'Institut Catholique de Paris*, Paris, 1914.

[1] Weingarten, *PRE*[2] x. 760; Grützmacher, *PRE*[3] xiii. 217, and *Hieronymus*, Leipzig, 1901, i. 160; see, however, in favour of the reality of his existence, Butler, *Laus. Hist.* i. 231; Workman, p. 96.

[2] On the *Vita Antonii* cf. Weingarten, 'Ursprung,' p. 21 f.; H. Gwatkin, *Studies of Arianism*, Cambridge, 1882, pp. 102–107, *Arian Controversy*[4], London, 1898, p. 48; F. W. Farrar, *Lives of the Fathers*, Edinburgh, 1889, i. 451; in favour of the historicity, A. Robertson, 'Athanasius,' in *Post-Nicene Fathers*, iv., Oxford, 1892, p. 189; Butler, i. 178 ff.; Workman, p. 354.

[3] Cf. Ladeuze, *op. cit.*; E. Preuschen, *Palladius und Rufinus: ein Beitrag zur Quellenkunde des ältesten Mönchtums* (*TU*), Giessen, 1897.

[4] The authenticity and veracity of the *Historia Monachorum* have also been the subject of much discussion, but it has a certain historical value. For discussions regarding the text see the works of Butler, Ladeuze, and Preuschen, already cited in reference to Palladius; see also Leclercq, in *DACL* ii.[2] 3098 ff.

[5] Cabrol, art. 'Cassian,' in *DACL* ii.[2] 2348–2357; O. Bardenhewer, *Patrology*, Eng. tr., Freiburg i. Br., 1908, p. 515 ff. The text of the Rule of Cassian, which was believed to be lost, has recently been discovered in Munich and at the Escurial (cf. H. Plenkers, *Untersuchungen zur Überlieferungsgesch. der ältesten lateinischen Mönchsregeln*, Munich, 1906, pp. 70–84).

[6] *Sanctæ Silviæ Aquitanæ Peregrinatio ad loca sancta*, ed. G. F. Gamurrini, Rome, 1887; other edd.: P. Geyer, Vienna, 1898, E. A. Bechtel, Chicago, 1902; cf. M. Férotin, 'Le véritable Auteur de la Peregrinatio Silviæ, la vierge espagnole Etheria,' in *Revue des questions historiques*, lxxiv. [1903] 367–397; and *PRE*[3] xviii. 345–347.

Lower Egypt, and was the father of monasticism in Nitria.[1] His disciples lived in huts and met together in the monastic church on Saturdays and Sundays. There were 8 priests in the colony to carry out the liturgical functions for the community. According to the *Lausiac History*, there were 600 hermits in the desert of Nitria. Idleness was carefully excluded, each monk being obliged to provide for himself by his own labour. In the evening psalms and hymns were chanted. The discipline of the life was very strict. Ammonius died before 356. His disciples continued his traditions in Nitria. The theological works of Origen were studied there, and the 'tall brothers,' Ammonius, Dioscorus, Eusebius, and Euthymius, who made such a disturbance in the theological world later on, belonged to this monastic family.[2]

About six miles to the south of the mountain of Nitria was the Desert of Scete, where another colony of hermits was established. The brethren observed perpetual silence; as at Nitria, they assembled in church for the offices only on Saturdays and Sundays. Their cells were either mere caverns in the rocks or else wattled cabins. Macarius the Greater († 383 or 387) was the first of these hermits. He has left behind him among the *Apophthegmata* a series of remarkable maxims and homilies that show him to have been one of the founders of Christian mysticism.[3] Macarius the Younger, Evagrius Ponticus, and Mark the Hermit are also figures that stand out among these solitaries.[4] The Desert of Scete still preserves the ruins of their ancient monasteries, one of which, known as the monastery of St. Macarius, is inhabited by a few Coptic monks.[5]

Besides Nitria and Scete, the whole of Egypt was strewn with hermitages—the Thebaid, Lycopolis, Kopres, Oxyrhynchus (where there were to be found, it is said, 10,000 monks and 20,000 nuns), and Arsinoë, where there were also 10,000 monks (*Hist. Laus.* 5, 18).

In Upper Egypt the name of Pachomius attracted special attention. He was instructed in the monastic life by a venerable hermit named Palamon, and established himself at Tabenna (Tabennîsi)—a name that was to remain famous in monastic history. Pachomius is the real founder of the cenobitic life. His disciples lived together under the same roof and were subject to the same discipline. Other monasteries were founded which followed the same observance, and thus cenobitism was established. Regarding the organization of the Pachomian monasteries see above (p. 785; cf. also W. E. Crum, *Theological Texts from Coptic Papyri, edited with an Appendix upon the Arabic and Coptic Versions of the Life of Pachomius, Anecdota Oxoniensia*, Semitic ser., pt. ii., 1913).

While speaking of Pachomius, we must not omit to mention one of his disciples named Schenoudi of Atripe, whose history has been revealed recently through Coptic MSS, and who, although he did not exercise so marked an influence as Pachomius, played an important part in the history of the cenobitic life. The profession of obedience which he imposed on his monks is the oldest document of this kind that we possess, and it marks a stage in the history of monastic Rules. Schenoudi made the attempt to combine the eremitic with the cenobitic life, and he succeeded to a certain extent.[1]

1 *Hist. Monast.* 30; *Hist. Laus.* 8; Sozomen, i. 14 (*PG* lxvii. 900 f.); Socrates, iv. 23 (*PG* lxvii. 509 f.); L. Bulteau, *Essai de l'hist. monast. d'Orient*, Paris, 1678; Besse, *op. cit.*; S. Schiwietz, *Das morgenländische Mönchtum*, Mainz, 1904; R. N. C. Curzon, *Visits to Monasteries in the Levant*, London, 1849.

2 P. van Couenbergh, *Etude sur les moines d'Egypte depuis Chalcédonie jusqu'à l'invasion arabe*, Louvain, 1914.

3 *Apophthegmata Patrum*, in Cotelier, *Ecclesiæ Græcæ Monumenta*, i. 24 (*PG* lxv. 257 f.); *Homilies*, in A. Gallandi, 'Prolegomena in Vitas et Scripta SS. Macariorum,' *Bibl. Vet. Patr. Ant. Script. Eccles.*, Venice, 1765–81, vii. 3 f. (*PG* xxxiv. 449 f.).

4 *Hist. Laus.* 20, 86.

5 G. Steindorff, 'Durch die libysche Wüste nach der Oase des Grysiter Ammon,' *Berliner Lokalanzeiger*, 18th March 1900.

(*b*) *Sinai.*—From Egypt the monastic life soon spread as far as the Sinaitic peninsula, on which there were later several flourishing monasteries. St. Nilus the Sinaitic († *c.* 430) and St. John Climacus were its shining lights, and may be regarded as the great doctors of the ascetic life. The *Peregrinatio Etheriæ* gives interesting details regarding the monasteries of Sinai (see below iii. I (*d*)).

(*c*) *Palestine.* — The monastic foundations of Palestine were no less illustrious. It will suffice to quote the names of Hilarion of Gaza, a disciple of St. Anthony of Egypt, and especially those of Melania the Elder at the Mount of Olives, Paula, and St. Jerome.[2] In this region monasticism made considerable headway. The number of monasteries and lauras rose to 100, and the influence of these religious houses in the quarrels between Origenism, Eutychianism, Monotheletism, and iconoclasm was very important. It would be impossible to give here even a résumé of this history; we must be content to refer the reader to the authors cited in note 2 below, and also to the attempt at a classification of some of the Palestinian monasteries in Leclercq, *DACL* ii.[2] 3165–3175. It was only with the Arab invasion of Palestine that the progress of these monasteries was arrested.

(*d*) *Syria.*—Syria became at an early period a land of monasteries. It has even been questioned whether the monastic life there was not indigenous, *i.e.*, whether it did not, as in Egypt, spring directly from the native practice of asceticism—which must be regarded as an early phase of monasticism—or whether, on the other hand, it was an importation from without. The latter opinion seems to be the more likely. The Syriac life of Mark-Arogin, beneath its legendary surface, contains a residue of history that can be extracted with little difficulty. According to this history, he came from a Pachomian monastery, established himself among the mountains near Nisibis, and died there in 363, leaving behind him a flourishing monastic house.[3] The recently edited works of Aphraates give some curious information about other solitaries (μονάζοντες), who seem to have been ascetics living in the world rather than real monks.[4]

At Edessa and in Osrhoene we have Julian regarded as the founder of monastic life in that country, and especially Ephraim the Syrian, a contemporary of St. Basil. He lived many years as a hermit, then went to study monastic tradi-

1 With regard to Schenoudi see Amélineau, *Mémoires publiés par la mission archéol. au Caire*, iv. [1885 f.], i.; J. Leipoldt, *Schenute von Atripe und die Entstehung des national-ägyptischen Christentums* (*TU*), Leipzig, 1903; Ladeuze, *Revue d'histoire eccl.* vii. [1906] 76–83; Revillout, 'Les Origines du schisme égyptien; le précurseur et inspirateur Senuti le prophète,' in *RHR* viii. [1883] 401–467, 545–581; Amélineau, *Vie de Schnoudi*, Paris, 1889; Leclercq, in *DACL* ii.[2] 3104 f.

2 *Hist. Laus.* 117–129; 'Vita Melaniæ Junioris,' *Analect. Boll.* viii. [1884] 11 ff.; Zöckler, 'Hilarion von Gaza,' in *Neue Jahrbücher für deutsche Theologie*, iii. [1894] 146–178; Vailhé, 'Les premiers Monastères de la Palestine,' in *Bessarione*, iii. [1897] 39–59, 209–225, 334–356, iv. [1898] 193–210; A. Couret, *La Palestine sous les empereurs grecs*, Paris, 1869, pp. 326–636.

3 P. Bedjan, *Acta Martyrum et Sanctorum*, Paris, 1890–97, iii. 376 f.; J. Labourt, *Le Christianisme dans l'empire perse sous la dynastie sassanide*, do. 1904, p. 302 f.

4 Cf. a discussion on this point in R. H. Connolly, 'Aphraates and Monasticism,' in *JThSt* vi. [1904–05] 522–539; F. C. Burkitt, 'Aphraates and Monasticism,' *ib.* vii. [1905–06] 10–15, *Early Christianity outside the Roman Empire*, Cambridge, 1899, and *Early Eastern Christianity*, London, 1904. See, further, Connolly, 'Some early Rules for Syrian Monks,' in *Downside Review*, xxv. [1906] 152–162; G. Bert, *Aphrahat's, des persischen Weisen, Homilien: aus dem Syrischen* (*TU*), Leipzig, 1888, ed. J. Parisot, Paris, 1894 (cf. esp. 6th hom. to the ascetics); P. Schwen, *Afrahat, seine Person und sein Verständnis des Christentums*, Leipzig, 1907.

tions under the guidance of St. Basil, and perhaps visited Egypt also. He is one of the principal scholars of the Syrian Church, and his numerous works contain much information regarding the monastic life.[1]

There were colonies of hermits in Cilicia, round about Antioch, and in the Desert of Chalcis in the 4th century. The Desert of Chalcis was known as the Thebaid of Syria, and there St. Jerome lived as a hermit from 373 to 380.[2] In the 5th cent. the first of the Stylites, St. Simeon, makes his appearance in the north of Syria (Theod. *Hist. Rel.* 26 [*PG* lxxxii. 1464 ff.]). This strange form of monastic life survived as late as the 15th century.[3]

(*e*) *Asia Minor.*—In Asia Minor in the 2nd cent. Montanism (*q.v.*) had appeared—a movement in the direction of an excessive ultra-asceticism. In Pamphylia in the 4th and 5th centuries the Euchite or Messalian monks allowed themselves to be carried away by the same excessive views, and appear also to have undergone Manichæan influences. They were always resisted by the Church and were finally condemned, but revived during the Middle Ages in the sects of the Paulicians and Bogomils.

Eustathius of Sebaste, who introduced monasticism into Armenia, Paphlagonia, and Pontus, was of Egyptian origin and a disciple of Arius. He exercised a wide influence on monasticism in that part of the world and also spread his errors abroad. His disciples, the Eustathians, were condemned by the Church.[4] The Council of Gangra, in 340, gives valuable information concerning the history of the ascetics and monks and the excesses of some of those whom it condemns.[5]

(*f*) *Cappadocia.*—It was chiefly in Cappadocia and under the inspiration of St. Gregory of Nazianzus, St. Gregory of Nyssa, and St. Basil, the real legislator of the monks of the East, that monasticism started its true development. Basil had become acquainted with the monastic life in Syria and in Palestine. He declared himself distinctly in favour of the cenobitic type, and it was for cenobites that he wrote his Rule, or rather his Rules (see above, p. 785b). The Rule of St. Basil has remained in use in the East to the present day. It does not enter into details, but lays down in general the virtues and duties of the monastic state. The monk is the perfect Christian; the ascetic life does not consist merely in carrying out certain practices, but in the sanctification of one's whole being and in the love of one's neighbour. One must raise up and perfect nature and not destroy it. Christian perfection completes, elevates, and purifies the wisdom of the ancients. In his monasteries the education of children was undertaken, and work was recommended and encouraged. The public prayer of the community was already organized, and we find the various Hours of Matins, Tierce, Sext, None, Vespers, and the Night Office (μεσονύκτιον).[6]

(*g*) *Cyprus.*—According to St. Jerome, monasticism was brought to the island of Cyprus by Hilarion. St. Epiphanius, who had himself been a monk in Palestine, defended the monks with ardour.

(*h*) *Constantinople.*—When Palestine and Egypt had ceased to be the chief centres of monastic life in the East, it was Constantinople, and, later, Mt. Athos, that succeeded to that position. The foundations attributed to Constantine or to the time of his immediate successors can, however, be admitted only with reserve.[1] It was not till towards the end of the 4th and especially during the course of the 5th cent. that monasticism began its development at Constantinople. In the reign of Justinian there were no fewer than 80 monasteries at Constantinople,[2] and the emperor legislated for the monastic life as for all other institutions of the empire. The Acœmetæ and the Studites deserve a long study to themselves; they have already formed the subject of monographs, to which we can here only draw attention in passing. The names of St. John Damascene and Theodore the Studite recall the long strife maintained by the monks on the question of the iconoclasts.[3]

(*i*) *Mount Athos.*—From the 9th, but especially during the 10th, cent. the peninsula of Mt. Athos, in the Ægean Sea, became a monastic centre of the highest importance, and formed a kind of monastic republic. Safe in their monasteries, built for the most part on steep cliffs, defended by the sea and by the thickness of their walls, the monks of this peninsula, which is connected with the mainland only by a narrow isthmus, were able to defy all attacks, and the cenobitic life has been maintained there up to the present day. The history of this monastic colony may be given in a few words. The origin of monasticism on Mt. Athos is obscure. The first testimony on which we can depend is found in the 9th cent., but it is probable that long before that there were hermits living among the rocks and in the forests of this peninsula, so well fitted for the solitary life. The year 963 is the date of the foundation of the first great monastery by St. Athanasius, one of the most celebrated of the Athos monks. From this date onwards foundations followed one another in rapid succession. The great monasteries of Iviron, Vatopedi, Xeropotamos, Esphigmenon, Dochiaru, Agios Paulos, etc., rose up in different parts of the holy mountain from the 10th to the 14th century. The latest in date is the monastery of Stavronikita, founded in 1542. A number of smaller houses and simple hermitages depend upon these greater monasteries. The Rule followed is that of St. Basil. The monasteries form a kind of confederation or little republic, which is represented by 20 members, constituting at once a parliament and a tribunal under the direction of 4 presidents, one of whom has the title of πρῶτος. In each monastery the ἡγούμενος enjoys supreme authority. In the 14th cent. the idiorrhythmic form of life (ἰδιορ-ῥυθμία) was introduced, in accordance with which, in certain of the monasteries, the monks possess money of their own and enjoy a number of dispensations. Autonomous during a certain period, the governing council of Mt. Athos was finally subjected to the jurisdiction of the patriarch of Constantinople. Under the various governments and dynasties that succeeded one another in the East—the Comneni, the Palæologi, even the Turks themselves, and the hospodars of Wallachia—the liberty of the monks of Mt. Athos was always respected. Painting, architecture, and calligraphy were cultivated with success, and their libraries contain MSS of the highest value.[4]

[1] Ephraim, *Opera omnia*, Rome, 1734–46; for the other edd. cf. *PRE*³ v. 406; R. Duval, *Hist. politique, religieuse et littéraire d'Edesse jusqu'à la première croisade*, Paris, 1891, pp. 150–161; Bardenhewer, pp. 387–393.

[2] Cf. Grützmacher, *Hieronymus*, i. 155 f.

[3] Delehaye, *op. cit.*; see also above, p. 786b.

[4] F. Loofs, 'Eustathius von Sebaste,' in *PRE*³ v. 627–630.

[5] Mansi, ii. 1095–1106; C. J. Hefele and H. Leclercq, *Hist. des conciles*, Paris, 1907 ff., i. 1029.

[6] E. F. Morison, *St. Basil and his Rule*, Oxford, 1915.

[1] Cf. E. Marin, *Les Moines de Constantinople depuis la fondation de la ville jusqu'à la mort de Photius* (330–898), Paris, 1897; J. Pargoire, 'Les Débuts du monachisme à Constantinople,' in *Revue des questions hist.* lxv. [1899] 68–72; art. 'Constantinople,' in *DACL* ii.² 1445–1448.

[2] Cf. Marin and Pargoire, *locc. citt.*

[3] See 'Acémètes,' in *DACL* i.² 307–321; A. Tougard, 'La Persécution iconoclaste d'après la correspondance de St. Théodore Studite,' in *Revue des questions hist.* vi. [1890] 80–118.

[4] V. Langlois, *Le Mont Athos et ses monastères*, Paris, 1867; W. Gass, *Zur Gesch. der Athos-Klöster*, Giessen, 1865; A. Riley, *Athos; the Mountain of the Monks*, London, 1887; E. Miller, *Le Mont Athos*, Paris, 1889; Porphyrius Uspensky, *Hist. of*

iii. MONASTICISM IN THE WEST.—1. **Before St. Benedict.**—(*a*) *Rome and Italy.*—It has been remarked, and with justice, that while, in the inscriptions of the catacombs, careful mention is made of all the various degrees of the ecclesiastical hierarchy—even down to that of *fossor*—no allusion has ever been found to ascetic, anchorite, cenobite, monk, or nun.[1] The existence at Rome of monks, of consecrated virgins, and of monasteries at that period cannot, however, be denied. We leave on one side the legend of Boniface and Aglæ, which is, moreover, of Eastern origin.[2] Constantia, daughter of Constantine, gathered together around the tomb of St. Agnes a community of virgins. It was in a Roman monastery also that St. Marcellina, sister of St. Ambrose, consecrated herself to God (352–366.)[3] Pammachius, another Roman patrician, along with Fabiola, lived the ascetic life, and founded near the mouth of the Tiber a hospice which was served by monks.[4] St. Athanasius arrived in Rome after 339, accompanied by two Egyptian monks. He remained there three years and inspired this community, so deeply Christian in spirit, with admiration of and sympathy with the monastic ideal of the Thebaid. He made proselytes even from among the highest society of Rome, and Marcella, daughter of the widow Albina, along with Melania the Elder, devoted herself to the life. A community of ascetics and cenobites was founded on the Aventine, from which stand out names such as those of Sophronia, Asella, Paula, and Fabiola. The favour shown towards such institutions by Pope Damasus and, in particular, the arrival in Rome of St. Jerome, who became the spiritual father of the community on the Aventine, greatly accentuated the movement.[5] The attempt made by Vigilantius to oppose it in favour of monasticism had no other result than that of starting a controversy with St. Jerome, from which Vigilantius came forth utterly crushed and humiliated (*c.* 385).[6]

In the rest of Italy the progress of monasticism was scarcely less rapid than in Rome itself. In the middle of the 4th cent. Eusebius of Vercelli, till then exiled in Egypt, returned to his church (in 363) and obliged the clergy of his cathedral to submit to the monastic rule of life. His example was soon followed in Milan, under St. Ambrose, and at Aquileia,[7] while Cremona, under the bishop Vincent (407–422), Novara, under the bishop Gaudentius (397–417), Bologna, Ravenna, under St. Peter Chrysologus, Pavia, under the bishop Ennodius, and Turin, under the bishop Victor, all favoured the monastic movement.

In S. Italy, besides Nola with its illustrious bishop, St. Paulinus, we find monasteries at Naples, at Capua, and in Etruria, Sabina, Umbria, Picenum, at Tusculum, Monte Calvo, Fundi, on the banks of Lake Fucino, on the islands off the Mediterranean coast of Italy, Gorgona, Capraja, Sardinia, and the Isle of Cabis (near Torrentum).[1] It would be difficult to draw up even a simple catalogue of these monasteries, so numerous were they.

Cassiodorus (*c.* 570) was contemporary with St. Benedict. It has even been conjectured that his Rule was borrowed from the latter, but this is no more than a conjecture. What is certain is that the minister of Theodoric, on his property of Vivarium, gave the example of a monastery where the ascetic practices of the monastic life were allied with a high degree of intellectual culture. While, on the summit of Mt. Morius, the hermits gave themselves up to their solitary vocation, in the monastery built at the foot of the mountain the cenobites spent their time in the diligent copying of MSS.[2]

(*b*) *Gaul.*—Monasticism, which was to play so considerable a part in Gaul, was established there at an early date (2nd half of the 4th cent.) and with great éclat by St. Martin of Tours. At first it took the eremitic form. The disciples of St. Martin lived as hermits, meeting for exercises in common only on certain occasions. The first monastery founded in Gaul was that of Ligugé, in 360. There were, besides, Marmoutier (Martini Monasterium) and, no doubt, a great number of other houses, for we read that 2000 monks were present at the obsequies of St. Martin.[3] St. Martin wrote no Rule for his monks, and the latter seem simply to have followed the general traditions of the ascetic life. Several of his disciples applied themselves in company with their master to the work of the apostolate. This would explain why this first attempt at monasticism in Gaul did not leave any lasting traces behind it.

We find, about the same date, that there were monks at Rouen, in the Morinie (Boulonnais, Artois, W. Flanders), in the forests, along the seacoast, and even in the islands of the coasts.[4]

St. Sulpicius Severus, the historian of St. Martin, established a community of ascetics in his villa of Primuliacum.[5] Gregory of Tours († 594) gives in his works most valuable information regarding the monastic movement in Gaul in the 5th and 6th centuries. The greater number of the monks whose lives he wrote, while possessing their own characteristic spirit, are still largely under the influence of the teaching of St. Martin.

The most interesting of all these experiments in the monastic life at this period is the foundation of the celebrated monastery of Lérins on an island of that name off the coast of the Mediterranean near Cannes. Monastic life, inaugurated there towards the year 410 by St. Honoratus, was to continue through many long centuries, almost without interruption, to our own day. It was at the beginning a mingling of the eremitic and cenobitic elements. Both manual and intellectual work were held in honour, and great was the influence exercised by the monks of Lérins throughout the Middle Ages.[6] It will be sufficient, for this earlier

Athos and its Monasteries, 3 vols., Kieff and Moscow, 1845–92 (Russ.); Curzon, *op. cit.*; E. M. de Vogüé, *Syrie, Palestine, Mont Athos, Voyage au pays du passé*, Paris, 1876; Krumbacher, pp. 511–515, 1058 f.; D. Placide de Meester, *Voyage de deux bénédictins aux monastères de Mont Athos*, Paris, 1908; V. Vannutelli, *Monte Athos e le meteore*, Rome, 1888; K. Lake, *Early Days of Monasticism on Mt. Athos*, Oxford, 1909.

1 Leclercq, in *DACL* ii.[2] 3175.

2 *AS*, May, iii. 279–283; Duchesne, 'Notes sur la topographie de Rome,' in *Mélanges d'archéol. et d'histoire*, x. [1890]; Franchi de Cavalieri, 'Dove fu scritta la legenda di S. Bonifacio?' in *Nuovo bollettino di archeol. cristiana*, vi. [1900] 205–234; A. Dufourcq, *Études sur les Gesta Martyrum romains*, 4 vols., Paris, 1900–10, i.; cf. *Anal. Boll.* xx. [1901] 337 f.

3 E. Spreitzenhofer, *Die Entwicklung des alten Mönchtums in Italien von seinen ersten Anfängen bis zum Auftreten des heil. Benedikt*, Vienna, 1894, p. 29; Leclercq, *DACL* ii.[2] 3176.

4 Cf. G. B. de Rossi, *Bollettino di archeol. cristiana*, 1866, p. 103.

5 C. Daux, 'Amédée Thierry et les premiers monastères d'Italie aux IVe et Ve siècles,' in *Revue des questions hist.* xxi. [1877] 404–473.

6 On Vigilantius cf. below, p. 791b.

7 Spreitzenhofer, p. 13 f.; F. Ughelli, *Italia sacra*, 9 vols., Rome, 1644–62, iv. 747, 580, vi. 44, etc.; Albers, 'El Monachismo prima di S. Benedetto,' *Rivista Storica Benedettina*, x. [1915].

1 Cf. Spreitzenhofer and Leclercq, *locc. citt.*

2 *Works of Cassiodorus*, ed. J. Garet, Rouen, 1679 (*PL* lxix. and lxx.); A. Franz, *M. Aurelius Cassiodorus Senator*, Breslau, 1872; Chevalier, *Répertoire: Bio-Bibliographie*, *s.v.* 'Cassiodore.' For his library cf. A. Olleris, *Cassiodore conservateur des livres de l'antiquité latine*, Paris, 1841.

3 Sulpicius Severus, *Vita S. Martini*; F. Chamard, *Saint Martin et son monastère de Ligugé*, Paris, 1873; E. Martène, 'Hist. de Marmoutiers,' in *Mémoires de la société archéol. de Touraine*, Tours, 1874–75; Lecoy de la Marche, *Saint Martin*, do. 1881; A. Hauck, *Kirchengesch. Deutschlands*, Leipzig, 1898, p. 52 f.

4 Malnory, *op. cit.*

5 A. Curie-Seimbres, *Recherches sur les lieux habités par Sulpice Sévère, premiers monastères institués en Aquitaine*, Tarbes, 1875; F. Mouret, *Sulpice Sévère à Primuliac*, Paris, 1907.

6 Malnory, *op. cit.*; L. Alliez, *Hist. du monastère de Lérins*, 2 vols., Draguignan, 1862; P. Lahargou, *De schola Lerinensi, ætate merovingiaca*, Paris, 1892; *DACL* ii.[2] 3196–3198.

period, to cite the names of Vincent of Lérins and Salvianus.

Another important influence exercised over the development of monasticism in Gaul during this period was that of Cassian. His works were in reality the first monastic code in Gaul (see above, p. 787b), and, it may be said, in the whole of the West. He founded the monastery of St. Victor at Marseilles, which became renowned, and other monasteries also.[1]

St. Cæsarius, bishop of Arles, must also be regarded as one of the principal monastic legislators at this date.[2] We can only mention the monasteries founded by Leonian in the diocese of Vienne, by St. Theudaire in Isère, in the Isle Barbe, at Condat (St. Claude), and at St. Maurice of Agaune, and by SS. Romanus and Lupicinus in the Jura.[3]

(c) *Britain, Ireland, the Celts.*—The monastic life was established fairly early among the Celts and Anglo-Saxons, and underwent an extraordinary development among them. Its introduction into Great Britain was due to St. Germanus, bishop of Auxerre, who came to the island in 430 to restore ecclesiastical discipline. In Wales Llan Lltud, Llancarvon, Ti-Gwen, and Bangor soon became renowned. Some of the monks from these monasteries—St. Gildas, St. Lunain, St. Paul Aurelian, and St. Samson—established the monastic life in Brittany (Armorica), where it also made great advance.[4] Monasticism in Ireland has much in common with that of Brittany, to which it seems, in fact, to owe its origin. The name of St. Columba and that of his foundation at Iona stand out conspicuous in its history.[5] Another saint whose name we must not forget to mention among the Celtic monks, although his chief foundation, Luxeuil, belonged to Gaul, is St. Columban, the rival and namesake of Columba. His Rule, inspired entirely by the principles and traditions of Irish monasticism, spread rapidly in Gaul and disputed for a time the predominance of that of St. Benedict.[6]

(d) *Spain.*—In Spain the beginnings of the monastic life are somewhat obscure. The Council of Elvira (*c.* 300) makes no allusion whatever to either ascetics or virgins. The *Peregrinatio Etheriæ* belongs to the last quarter of the 4th century. It is the account of her journeying in the East and her pilgrimages to the holy places, sent to her nuns in Spain by a Spanish virgin named Etheria, or Egeria, who was, in all probability, abbess of the community to which she writes.[7] We find further traces of the ascetic and monastic life among the Priscillianists of Spain, in this century. Priscillian gave himself out as an example of asceticism (see art. PRISCILLIANISM). It has

[1] *Cartulaire de l'abbaye de St. Victor de Marseille*, 2 vols., Paris, 1857.

[2] Malnory, *op. cit.*

[3] L. Niepce, *L'Île Barbe: son ancienne abbaye*, Lyons, 1890; P. Benoit, *Hist. de l'abbaye et de la terre de Saint-Claude*, 2 vols., Paris, 1890–92; B. Krusch, 'Vitæ Patrum Jurensium,' *Mon. Germ., Script. Merov.*, iii. [1896–97] 125–166; Duchesne, 'La Vie des Pères du Jura,' *Mélanges d'archéol.*, xviii. [1898] 1–18; Leclercq, in *DACL* ii.[2] 3197–3198; Besse, *Les Moines de l'ancienne France: Période gallo-romaine et mérovingienne*, Paris, 1906.

[4] A. de la Broderie, 'Les Monastères celtiques aux VIe et VIIe siècle,' in *Annales de Bretagne*, ix. [1893] 183–209, 379–394, *Hist. de Bretagne*, Rennes, 1896, i.; J. W. Willis-Bund, *The Celtic Church of Wales*, London, 1897; *DACL* ii.[2] 3207.

[5] C. F. R. de Montalembert has devoted to the history of the Celtic and Anglo-Saxon monasteries a large portion of his book, *Les Moines d'Occident*, Paris, 1860–77; see esp. bks. x.–xiii.; see also L. Gougaud, *loc. cit.*

[6] Seebass, *op. cit.*; Malnory, *op. cit.*; L. Gougaud, 'L'Œuvre des Scotti dans l'Europe continentale,' in *Revue d'hist. ecclés.* ix. [1908] 21–37, 255–277; G. Bonet-Maury, 'St. Colomban et la fondation des monastères irlandais,' *Rev. Hist.* lxxxiii. [1903] 277–299.

[7] Cf. above, p. 787b.

recently been shown that the *Regula Consensoria Monachorum*, attributed at first to St. Augustine, then to a contemporary of St. Fructuosus, probably comes from a Priscillianist source, in the 5th century. It is a Rule for cenobites, original in character.[1]

The Rule of St. Isidore († 636) and that of St. Fructuosus of Braga (*c.* 660) also deserve mention. They enjoyed considerable success until the advent of the Rule of St. Benedict in Spain, which became there, as in almost the whole of the Western world, the only Rule for monks.[2]

Vigilantius, who represents the element hostile to the monks and ascetics, was a priest at Barcelona in 396. During the year 409 the invasions in Spain, as everywhere else, resulted in the destruction of the monasteries. Mention of this is to be found in the chronicles of the period.[3]

The Council of Tarragona, in 516, turned its attention to the monks.[4] St. Martin, abbot of Dumio near Braga, who is known as St. Martin of Braga, and who had been a monk in Palestine and played so important a part in the history of the conversion of the Suevi, laboured at the restoration of the monastic life in Spain.[5]

Two other bishops, SS. Leander and Isidore, also worked for the same end. The first wrote a Rule for the use of virgins, and the second drew up a Rule for monks.[6] The latter was already known to St. Leander, the friend of St. Gregory the Great, and to Tajo, bishop of Saragossa (*c.* 650), the great admirer of the works of St. Gregory and of his *Dialogues*, in which the praises of St. Benedict are set forth. This bishop did much to spread the knowledge of these works in Spain.[7] Besides these names, we find, between the date of the conversion of Visigothic Spain (587) and that of the Arab invasion (711), those of certain monks and hermits—the African Donatus, who, along with 70 monks, also from Africa, took refuge in the monastery of Servitanum, in the province of Valencia; St. Emilian, who enjoyed a wide-spread cultus in Spain; the hermit, Valerius, in the neighbourhood of Astorga, etc.[8]

(e) *Africa.*—In Africa the first monastic centre seems to have been formed around the person of St. Augustine. This saint had studied the monastic life both in Rome and in Milan, and, on his return to Tagaste, he installed himself with some of his friends in a house, where they gave themselves to the practices of asceticism. Ordained priest, he founded a second monastery at Hippo, where he lived himself till he was made bishop in 396. He then transformed his episcopal dwelling into a monastery like those of the bishops of Milan, Vercelli, and others at this time, and so founded what we may call a 'cathedral monastery,' or, as he himself called it, *monasterium clericorum.* Others of the African episcopate soon followed this

[1] Ed. in Holste-Brockie, *Codex Regularum*, i. 136 f., and in *PL* lxvi. 993–996; cf. D. de Bruyne, 'La *Regula consensoria*: Une règle des moines priscillianistes,' in *Revue Bénédictine*, xxv. 83–88.

[2] On the *Regula Communis* of St. Fructuosus see T. Herwegen, 'Das Pactum des heil. Fructuosus von Braga,' in *Kirchenrechtl. Untersuchungen*, xl. [1907] 71–79; and Leclercq, in *DACL* ii.[2] 3223. With regard to the *Pactum* of St. Fructuosus and the *Pacta*—a curious form of religious profession—besides Herwegen, see R. Klee, *Die Regula Monachorum Isidors von Sevilla und ihr Verhältnis zu den übrigen abendländischen Mönchsregeln jener Zeit*, Marburg, 1909.

[3] Cf. Leclercq, *L'Espagne chrétienne*, Paris, 1906, p. 213 f.

[4] *Ib.* p. 241.

[5] Leclercq, in *DACL* ii.[2] 3222; Albers, 'El Monachismo prima di S. Benedetto; il monachismo nella Spagna,' *Rivista stórica Benedettina*, ix. [1914].

[6] Leander, *Libellus ad Florentinam*, in *PL* lxxii. 874–894; Isidore, *Regula Monachorum*, in *PL* lxxxiii. 867–894.

[7] Tajo of Saragossa, *PL* lxxx. 720 ff.

[8] Cf. Montalembert, ii. 186 f.; Leclercq, *L'Espagne chrétienne*, p. 325 f.

example, and Hadrumetum, Uzala, Calame, Cirta, Mileve, and Carthage became real centres of monastic life. The *Regula pro Monachis* attributed to St. Augustine is not his under this form, as we have already said, but it is drawn from his letter (ccxi.) to religious bodies of both sexes living in poverty and chastity, passing their time in prayer and ascetic practices, and in certain works of charity. The counsels of the great bishop are characterized by the charity, discretion, breadth of mind, and high spirituality to which all his works bear witness.[1] We have already spoken of his famous treatise, *de Opere Monachorum*, composed in the year 400.

The Vandal persecution was unable to destroy all these monasteries, but it arrested for the time the progress of monasticism in Africa. Byzantine rule (533–709) restored peace and liberty, and a true renaissance of religion took place, in which monasticism naturally benefited. Several new monasteries were founded, notably at Ruspe and at Tebessa. The ruins of the latter still exist.[2] But the Muhammadan invasion was to destroy monastic life in Roman Africa as well as Christian life in general.

(*f*) On the Danube, in the region of Noricum, we have to mention the wonderful work among those people of St. Severinus († 482), called 'the apostle of Noricum.'[3]

2. From St. Benedict to the 13th century.—St. Benedict, born at Nursia (*c.* 480), died at Monte Cassino (*c.* 540), deserves a place apart in the history of Western monasticism. The influence exercised by his Rule in the West may be compared to that of St. Basil in the East. Having dwelt, at first, as a hermit among the Sabine mountains, he later gathered disciples round him, founded monasteries at Subiaco and Monte Cassino, and wrote a Rule which, after the lapse of two centuries, was to become the one monastic Rule of the West. It may, in fact, be said that the history of Western monasticism is practically identical, for the greater part of the Middle Ages, with that of the Benedictines.[4] The Rule of St. Benedict, which is divided into 73 chapters, is written for cenobites, and addresses itself exclusively to those who follow that form of monastic life. It teaches the virtues of humility, obedience, and poverty, and enjoins the practice of silence, hospitality, and manual work. It regulates the hours for prayer and lays down the order of the psalmody. The monastery forms, as it were, a little city or, better, a complete society provided with all its necessary organs. At the head of all is the abbot, assisted by his provost, or prior, and his seniors, while at the head of every 10 monks is the dean. Then there are the cellarer, who is charged with the temporal affairs of the monastery, and the various other officials that divide between them the different functions necessary to the well-being of the house. The monastery should, as far as possible, provide for itself and possess a garden, a mill, and all the necessary offices and work-shops. The sick, too, are to be specially taken care of, and the monks and the *oblati* receive necessary instruction. Guests are to be received with honour. Those who offend against the Rule must receive punishment according to their deserts.[1] Such is, in summary, the Rule of St. Benedict—a Rule characterized by great simplicity, but in which is clearly reflected that spirit of wise discretion and justice which was the genius of the Roman character, while at the same time it is penetrated through and through by the purest spirit of Christian asceticism, and rivals in its discretion and its sublimity of view the Rule of St. Basil itself.

St. Gregory († 604), the greatest of all the popes of the early Middle Ages, in giving to this Rule the support of his authority and in recounting, in his *Dialogues*, the life and miracles of its author, assured its predominance over all other monastic Rules. He himself founded a monastery in his own house (the Monastery of St. Andrew, on the Cœlian), in which the Rule of St. Benedict was observed, and sent to England one of its monks, his disciple St. Augustine, who, while commencing the work of converting the Anglo-Saxons, at the same time implanted in their midst that Rule which was destined to take such firm root there and to spread far and wide over the land.

(*a*) *England.*—The Christianity established by St. Augustine among the Anglo-Saxons was thoroughly monastic in character. In the greater number of towns—*e.g.*, at Canterbury, York, London, Ripon, Peterborough, etc.—the monastery was the centre of the new Christianity. The church of the monastery became the cathedral, and the abbot the bishop of the diocese that was thus gradually formed. The kingdoms of the Saxon heptarchy were one after another converted by the disciples or successors of St. Augustine, and the history of the four centuries extending from the death of St. Augustine in 605 to the Norman Conquest in 1066 is one of the finest parts of the history of Western monasticism.[2] It would be impossible to give even a summary of it here. We cannot do more than cite some of the principal characters and the names of the chief monasteries that stand out in its pages. Among the former we have the abbots and monks Aidan, Oswald, Wilfrid, Theodore, Cuthbert, Benedict Biscop, Aldhelm, Boniface, Bede, Alcuin, Odo, Dunstan; among the latter are Canterbury, Westminster, Malmesbury, York, Lindisfarne, Ripon, Peterborough, Jarrow, Wearmouth, Croyland, Whitby, Coldingham, Tynemouth, and Hartlepool. Even after the Norman Conquest in 1066 the history of monasticism in England does not come to an end. It was still flourishing in the 11th cent., and the Normans, far from destroying the English monasteries, founded new ones. Lanfranc and Anselm, archbishops of Canterbury, re-peopled the Saxon monasteries with colonies of monks brought over from the famous abbey of Bec and from other Norman monasteries. Cluny, too, made several foundations in the country, and the Cistercians, in their turn, established themselves at Waverley, Rievaulx, Fountains, and many other places. St. Stephen Harding, who exercised so great an influence on the order of Cîteaux and gave it its organization, was an Englishman. The order

[1] Cf. Leclercq, *L'Afrique chrétienne*, Paris, 1904, ii. 73–77, and *DACL* ii.[2] 3225 f.; Besse, *Le Monachisme africain*, Paris, 1900; Albers, 'Il Monachismo prima di S. Benedetto; il monachismo in Africa,' *Rivista stórica Benedettina*, ix.

[2] H. Saladin, 'Rapport sur une mission en Tunisie,' in *Archives des missions scientifiques*, 3rd ser., xiii. [1887] 179–181; cf. C. Diehl, *Nouvelles archives des missions scientifiques*, iv. [1893] 331–335, also *L'Afrique byzantine*, Paris, 1896, p. 429 f. For a list of the monasteries cf. Leclercq, in *DACL* ii.[2] 3231, and *L'Afrique chrétienne*, ii. 73–77.

[3] *AS*, Jan. i. 483, 497; L. S. le Nain de Tillemont, *Mémoires pour servir à l'hist. ecclés. des 6 prem. siècles*[2], Paris, 1701–12, xvi.

[4] On St. Benedict and the Benedictines see Mabillon, *opp. citt.*; G. Krätzinger, *Der Benediktinerorden und die Kultur*, Heidelberg, 1876; Berlière, *Mélanges d'hist. bénédictine*, Maredsous, 1897–1902; Bulteau, *Abrégé de l'hist. de l'ordre de saint Benoist jusqu'à la fin du IXe siècle*, 2 vols., Paris, 1684; see esp. Chevalier, *Répertoire: Topo-bibliographie*, *s.v.* 'Bénédictins.'

[1] On the Rule of St. Benedict see the edd. and works of E. Schmidt (Ratisbon, 1891), E. Woelfflin (Leipzig, 1895), L. Traube (Munich, 1898), C. Butler, Morin, etc., as cited in art. 'Bénédictins,' in *DACL* ii.[2] 664; Plenkers, *op. cit.*

[2] It is to this history of the Anglo-Saxon and Celtic monks that Montalembert has consecrated the greater part of his history of the monks of the West; see also W. Dugdale, *Monasticon Anglicanum*, new ed., London, 1817–30; E. L. Taunton, *The English Black Monks of St. Benedict*, 2 vols., do. 1897; F. A. Gasquet, *English Monastic Life*, do. 1904.

of Savigny, which also had numerous foundations in England, was absorbed by that of Cîteaux. But with the 14th and 15th centuries English monasticism began to decline.[1]

(*b*) *France.*—However great the success of the Benedictine life in England, it may be said with truth, if its history be regarded as a whole, that France was the land of its predilection. The story of the Rule of St. Benedict being brought to Merovingian Gaul by his disciple, St. Maurus, and of the latter's foundation of the abbey of Glanfeuil on the banks of the Loire as the first Benedictine monastery in that country, has been contested.[2] Whatever the truth of this question may be, it is certain that the Rule was introduced into France at an early date—from the beginning of the 7th cent.—and it spread there with such rapidity that it soon succeeded in supplanting the Rule of St. Columban and in imposing its authority on all the monasteries. A synod held at Autun, in 670, speaks of it as though it were the only monastic Rule in existence, and that of Châlons, in 813, declares formally that it is followed in almost all the monasteries of the country.[3] The movement attained its apogee under Charlemagne, the great protector of the Benedictine monks, and under his son, Louis le Débonnaire. The reform of St. Benedict of Aniane witnesses at once to the unity and to the vitality of Benedictine life.

It is again in France that we must seek the origin of the important monastic reform of which Cluny was the cradle, and which, little by little, spread beyond the limits of France into Italy, Spain, England, Germany, and Poland. The abbey of Cluny, near Macon, was founded by William, Duke of Aquitaine, in 910; the monks were brought from the abbey of Baume, where the Constitutions of St. Benedict of Aniane were followed; hence the Cluniac reform sprang from that of the 9th century. Its first abbots, Bernon, Odo, Mayeul, Hugh, Odilo, and Peter the Venerable, raised Cluny to the highest degree of prosperity and extended its influence to every country in Christian Europe. The work of Cluny, in the religious, social, and political order, was considerable; during the 10th, 11th, and a part of the 12th centuries it exercised an unrivalled influence on Christian morals and institutions. From the political and religious points of view, it offered to the popes valuable and indispensable assistance in their struggle against the emperors of Germany, and the latter, as well as the kings of France, were obliged, more than once, to reckon with the powerful abbey.

Among the monasteries that accepted the Cluniac reform and flourished under it must be cited especially the great abbeys of Moissac, St. Martial, Uzerches, St. Jean d'Angély, St. Bertin, St. Germain d'Auxerre, and Vézelay in France, and Cava, Farfa, and S. Paolo fuori le mura in Italy.[4]

At the very moment when the influence of Cluny began to decline, a new star arose on the monastic horizon. On 21st March 1098, Robert, abbot of Molesmes, founded in the diocese of Dijon the abbey of Cîteaux, which was to become the centre of a new reform of Benedictine life. While Cluny, although careful to remain faithful to the spirit of St. Benedict, had become the seat of culture, of the liberal arts, and of letters, and had exercised considerable influence on the external world, Cîteaux, under the inspiration especially of St. Bernard, returned to an austerer conception of the monastic life. All sumptuousness and solemnity, even in the liturgical offices, were proscribed, monastic architecture was reduced to its simplest expression, and intellectual and artistic culture was set on one side, manual labour and the exercise of every kind of hard work taking its place.[1]

The Cistercian reform, whose influence, while not to be compared with that of Cluny, was nevertheless of considerable importance, especially during the 12th cent., spread beyond France and took in a large number of monasteries in other countries. It continued to exercise its influence till the end of the Middle Ages, and was revived on a new basis in the 17th cent. in the celebrated reform of La Trappe under the Abbé de Rancé.[2]

(*c*) *Germany.*—Before the introduction of the Benedictine Rule into Germany, monastic life was but feebly represented in that country. The Anglo-Saxon monks, SS. Pirmin and Boniface, with their disciples, brought to Germany, along with their missionary zeal, the traditions of Benedictine life, which scarcely existed there at that period, the only known trace during the 6th cent. being found in the life of St. Eugendus.[3]

During the 7th and 8th centuries the Celtic monks of St. Columban came into Germany and founded a number of monasteries. Among these we may mention St. Gall, Ebersmünster, Moyen-Moutier, St. Odile, Honau (Onogia), and Aschaffenburg, not to speak of those at Strassburg, Mainz, Cologne, Ratisbon, Würzburg, Erfurt, and Heggbach.[4]

In 1185 all the Scottish monasteries of Germany were united to form a congregation, under the jurisdiction of the abbot of St. James of Ratisbon, by Innocent III. Gradually the numbers of Scoto-Irish monks that were at first continually coming into Germany began to diminish, and by the 15th cent. they were replaced, in most of the monasteries, by Germans. This congregation ended by entering that of Bursfeld and becoming one with it. Mention, however, is made in the 17th cent. of a Scottish abbot, Ogilvie by name († 1646).

Reichenau on Lake Constance began, in 724, a history glorious in monastic annals, and Murbach, Fritzlar, Hersfeld, Heidenheim, and Bischofsheim are scarcely less famous. Fulda, in the days of its prosperity, counted 100 monks among its inmates and became a nursing-ground for missionaries, of whom the chief were to play an important part in the history of Christian Germany. Such were Sturmius, Willibald, Wunibald, and also SS. Walburga, Lioba, and Thekla. Synods held in Germany in 744 and 745 discussed monastic affairs and prescribed that all monks were to live according to the Rule of St. Benedict. Worthy of special

1 Dugdale, *op. cit.*; *Annales Monastici*, ed. H. R. Luard, Rolls series, 5 vols., London, 1864–69, and several other vols. of the series; *A Hist. of the English Church*, ed. W. R. W. Stephens and W. Hunt, London, 1899–1910, ii. 273, iii. 306; L. Janauschek, *Origines Cistercienses*, Vienna, 1877, i. 22 f.

2 C. de la Croix, *Fouilles archéol. de l'abbaye de Glanfeuil*, Paris, 1899; C. Port, *Dict. histor. de Maine-et-Loire*, do. 1879, iii. 428–431.

3 Hefele-Leclercq, *Conciles*, iii. 1144; Besse, *Les Moines de l'ancienne France*, Paris, 1906.

4 P. Lorain, *Essai historique sur l'abbaye de Cluny*, Dijon, 1839; J. H. Pignot, *Hist. de l'ordre de Cluny*, 3 vols., Paris, 1868; E. Sackur, *Die Cluniacenser in ihrer kirchlichen und allgemeingeschichtlichen Wirksamkeit bis zur Mitte des elften Jahrh.*, 2 vols., Halle, 1892–94; Berlière, *L'Ordre monastique*, p. 188 f.; cf. Chevalier, *Répertoire: Topo-bibliographie*, *s.v.* 'Cluny'; and esp. A. Molinier, *Les Sources de l'hist. de France*, Paris, 1901–04, I. ii. 234–244.

1 P. Guignard, *Les Monuments primitifs de la règle cistercienne*, Dijon, 1878; Janauschek, *op. cit.*; H. d'Arbois de Jubainville, *Etude sur l'état intérieur des abbayes cisterciennes*, Paris, 1858; Berlière, *op. cit.* pp. 271–274; Chevalier, *Répertoire: Topo-bibliographie*, *s.v.* 'Cisterciens.'

2 La Trappe (in the diocese of Séez, Orne). On La Trappe and its history see Chevalier, *Répertoire: Topo-bibliographie*, *s.v.* 'Trappe.'

3 Achéry and Mabillon, *Acta Sanctorum O.S.B.*, i. 558; cf. Hauck, ii. 732 f.; Heimbucher, i. 226.

4 A. Bellesheim, *Gesch. der kathol. Kirche in Irland*, 3 vols., Mainz, 1890–91, i. 338 f., 585 f., 'Die Benediktinerstiftungen in dem Rheinland,' in *Studien und Mittheilungen*, ix. [1888] 445 f.

mention in this connexion is the Synod of Aix-la-Chapelle in 802, famous for the legislation which it laid down for the monks. Under Dukes Ottilo and Tassilo, no fewer than 29 cloisters were founded, some of which have left a name behind them in history—*e.g.*, Tegernsee, Benediktbeuern, Polling, Wessobrunn, Kremsmünster, Scharnitz, and Metten.

Charlemagne and Louis the Pious were the great protectors of the Benedictine monks. At their courts were to be seen Alcuin, Adalhard, Wala, Angibran, Arn, Ansegise, Paul the Deacon, and, above all, Benedict of Aniane, the great monastic reformer. The Cluniac reform found its way also to Germany, where it commenced a new era of activity and prosperity for the monastic life. The monasteries of Reichenau, St. Maximin of Trèves, Echternach, St. Emmeran of Ratisbon, Tegernsee, St. Maurice of Magdeburg, and Weissenburg flourished anew under its protection. Einsiedeln, whose patron was St. Meinrad, a hermit who died in 861, became likewise the centre of an important monastic reform,[1] which extended to the abbeys of Petershausen, Disentis, Pfäffers, St. Blaise and Muri, Hohentwiel, Kempten, Ebersberg, and Rheinau (near Schaffhausen). The monastery of St. Emmeran of Ratisbon in its turn introduced its own customs into the monasteries of St. Peter of Salzburg, Tegernsee, Prüll, Weltenburg, and several others. Ulrich of Ratisbon (or of Cluny, † 1093) was one of the most active agents in the Cluniac movement in Germany and Switzerland.

Hirsau, or Hirschau, founded about 830, was also of great importance from the monastic point of view. The constitutions of this monastery were adopted by 150 other monasteries. Hirschau, as well as Cluny, offered valuable assistance to St. Gregory VII. in his struggle against investitures and against the abuses among the clergy. Like the great Burgundian abbey, it also had much influence on art, architecture, and culture in general. The reform of Hirschau, while keeping its own spirit intact, was, to a large extent, inspired by that of Cluny. The annals of the abbey were written by Trithemius and Baselius.[2]

Another reform, which, like that of Hirschau, drew much of its inspiration from Cluny, while keeping certain special characteristics of its own, made itself felt not only in Italy, the land of its birth, but in Germany also. This was the reform inaugurated by the monastery of Fructuaria (Früdelle), near Turin, founded in 1003. Its constitutions were adopted by many Italian monasteries and in Germany, notably by the monasteries of Gorze, St. Maximin of Trèves, St. Blaise, in the Black Forest, and by Muri, Garsten, Gottweig, Lambach, etc.[3]

Besides these reforms issuing from within the monastic order itself, mention must be made of the efforts made by ecclesiastical councils to bring back the monasteries to the practice and observance of the Rule. In particular may be cited the Synod of Rouen (1074), and those of Poitiers (1078), Rome (1083), London (1112), and Paris (1212-13). The decrees of the last council, which received the approbation of Innocent III., exercised a great influence on the monastic order as a whole. The 4th Council of the Lateran (1215) established rules that are still in force at the present day, especially as regards the convoking of general chapters—a kind of monastic council, composed of abbots and delegates from the various monasteries, wherein are discussed matters relating to the discipline and general interests of the monastic life.[1]

[1] On Einsiedeln see *Annales Einsidlenses*, in Pertz, *Mon. Germ. Hist. Script.* iii. [1839] 145 ff.; Chevalier, *Répertoire: Topo-bibliographie, s.v.* 'Einsiedeln.'

[2] J. Trithemius, *Chronicon Monasterii Hirsaugiensis*, Basel, 1560; P. Giseke, *Ausbreitung der Hirschauer Regel durch die Klöster Deutschlands*, Halle, 1877; cf. Heimbucher, i. 253, note 2.

[3] Albers, *Untersuchungen zu den ältesten Mönchsgewohnheiten*, Munich, 1905; cf. Heimbucher, i. 256; Berlière, *L'Ordre monastique*, p. 189.

3. From the 13th to the 20th century.—In the 13th cent., whilst monasticism, in spite of all these attempts at reform, continued to decline, new forms of the religious life arose which answered better perhaps to the spirit of the age, but which none the less drew numerous souls athirst for perfection and formed a current which, although not actually inimical to the ancient monastic institutions, was nevertheless very distinct from it. Such were the great Dominican and Franciscan orders and a few other religious families inspired with the same principles. No other attempt at monasticism that was really original and powerful remains to be considered, with the possible exception of the congregation of St. Maur. Hence it will be sufficient to give a brief outline of the principal characteristics of monastic history during the last centuries of the Middle Ages.

The great schism of the West and the Hundred Years' War dealt another terrible blow to the monastic orders, but the attempts at reformation were not less numerous than in the preceding centuries. The Council of Constance (1414-18) consecrated some of its decrees to the reformation of the Benedictine order, and was the factor that inspired a great meeting, comprising 131 abbots of various monasteries, which was held at Petershausen in 1417. In 1418 Pope Martin V. sent the abbot of Subiaco, Nicholas Seyringer, to Melk, the great Austrian abbey, to lay the foundation of that restoration of monastic life. The enterprise was successful, and a great number of the monasteries of Austria, Bavaria, and Swabia rallied to the movement—*inter alia*, Mariazell, Seittenstetten, St. Peter of Salzburg, Kremsmünster, St. Emmeran of Ratisbon, Braunau, Tegernsee. The great Italian abbeys of Subiaco and Farfa also accepted this reformation. In other respects all these monasteries remained independent and did not form a real congregation.[2]

The Council of Trent dealt with the question of monasteries as it did with all other Christian institutions. The 25th Session (3rd Dec. 1563) treats *de regularibus et monialibus*, renews the decree of Innocent III. and of the 4th Lateran Council, unites the exempt monasteries to form congregations, institutes, general chapters, and cloisters, and legislates concerning visitors, presidents of congregations, novices, and the election of superiors and nuns; in a word, it establishes a collection of rules and laws concerning the monastic life.[3] Congregations were immediately after founded on those principles.[4]

Even more important than the Melk reformation, so far at least as Germany is concerned, was that of Bursfeld. Founded in 1003 on the banks of the Weser and colonized by Corby, this abbey was destined to play an important part in monastic history from the 15th century. John

[1] We have already seen that, even as far back as the time of St. Pachomius, the endeavour was made to unite monasteries in a species of federation; another example of this occurs in the 9th cent., under the authority of St. Benedict of Aniane. But it is not, in reality, till the 11th cent. that we find among the Cistercians the usage of general chapters properly so called. From the Cistercians the practice passed to the Benedictines, and from them to other orders (cf. Berlière, 'Les Chapitres généraux,' in *Mélanges d'hist. bénédictine*, 4th ser., Maredsous, 1902, p. 52 ff., and Heimbucher, i. 274 f.).

[2] A. Schram, *Chronicon Mellicense*, Vienna, 1702; M. Kropff, *Bibliotheca Mellicensis*, do. 1745; F. Keiblinger, *Gesch. des Benedictinerstiftes Melk*, 2 vols., do. 1851, 1869; Berlière, 'La Réforme de Melk au XVe siècle,' in *Revue Bénédictine*, xii. [1895] 204 ff.

[3] Petrus ab Audomaro (Walloncapello), *Institutionum monasticarum secundum Concilium Tridentinum Decreta*, Cologne, 1584.

[4] See the list in Heimbucher, i, 300 f.

Dederoth († 1439), who had already reformed the abbey of Clus, took Bursfeld in hand in 1433 and also Rheinhausen. The three monasteries remained closely united. In 1446 the abbot of Bursfeld became the president of the congregation. The constitutions show a solid organization, with general chapters, visitors, and every means of safeguarding the observance of piety and regularity. The success of this reformation grew from day to day. The cardinal of Cusa,[1] Nicholas V., and Pius II. became its ardent promoters. At the death of Abbot Johann von Hagen (1469) the congregation numbered 36 monasteries, which later increased to 230. In 1579 the abbey of Bursfeld, which up to this time had been the head-house of the congregation, went over to Protestantism under the influence of Julius of Brunswick, and the congregation was itself secularized in 1803.[2]

We have already spoken of the monastic origins in Spain. For a long time the Rule of St. Isidore was observed in that country, side by side with that of St. Benedict. The Synod of Coyaca (1050) prescribed that either the Rule of St. Isidore or that of St. Benedict should be observed in all monasteries in Spain. Not many years later, however, the influence of Cluny began to be felt and to spread throughout Spain; gradually it predominated, until it finally eliminated the observance instituted by St. Isidore. In the 14th and 15th centuries two important congregations rose up, those of Valladolid (1390) and Monserrat (1492). The latter made foundations in Portugal, Peru, and Mexico.[3] The movement of the claustrales at Saragossa and at Tarragona were less important.[4]

The Low Countries were a monastic land for centuries. Wilfrid of York, on the occasion of a journey to Rome in 678, having been thrown on the shores of Friesland, was there welcomed with great warmth. After his return to his monastery at Ripon, he sent over Willibrod, one of his monks, who established himself at Utrecht, and became the great apostle of Friesland, having St. Boniface as a fellow-labourer for some time. Other missionaries soon came from Iona, and, like England, the country became Christian and monastic at the same time. The most celebrated of these foundations was the monastery of Echternach.[5]

The Reformation in Germany in the 16th cent. led to the expulsion of the monks from their monasteries, the closing of monastic buildings, and the handing over of their revenues to laymen, and especially to Protestant princes. A great number were sacked. It has been calculated that in the Peasant War more than 1000 monasteries and castles were destroyed. A few monasteries were, however, saved from the general ruin (cf. Heimbucher, i. 295).

In England the effects of the Protestant Reformation were still more terrible for the monasteries. In 1524 the Holy See had caused Cardinal Wolsey to make a visitation of the monasteries, and one of the consequences of this general visit was their confiscation and almost complete secularization by Henry VIII. and his minister Thomas Cromwell (1534). Elizabeth finished the work of destruction in 1560. Scotland's turn came later on (1559–1560). In all it has been estimated that 578 monasteries, of which 63 were Benedictine, were confiscated. Besides the falls and lamentable defections there were not wanting monks who became martyrs, and who paid with their lives their fidelity to their vows.[1] Benedictine life was maintained throughout all these centuries of persecution, and the Anglo-Benedictine congregation has preserved the inheritance of its ancestors to the present day.

The Reformation which destroyed the monasteries in England and Germany did not succeed in establishing itself in France. There the monasteries held out. The 17th cent. was marked by an important monastic restoration, the Benedictine congregation of SS. Vannes and Hydulphus in Lorraine and that of St. Maur in France. These two congregations, with an end and a constitution that were similar, had for their common object to re-establish a stricter mode of observance in Benedictine monasteries and to bring back the monks to the rigorous practices of the Benedictine Rule. The very large part played by the congregation of St. Maur in intellectual work bore splendid fruits and helped to found a school of erudition that has given to France a Mabillon and a Montfaucon, a Denys de Sainte-Marthe, a d'Achéry, a Coustant, a Ruinart, etc.—a school that has never been equalled.[2]

A certain number of new orders which practised the monastic life and accepted the Rule of St. Benedict as their fundamental guide may be regarded as branches of the Benedictine order. We can give only a very brief outline of their history here.

(*a*) *Sylvestrines.*—The first of these orders sprung from the Benedictine trunk is the Sylvestrines, so called from the name of its founder, Sylvester Gonzelin, of the family of Gozzolini († 1267). In 1227 he retired to Osimo and followed the Rule of St. Benedict, adding new austerities, until in a short time a few ancient monasteries took their place under the new discipline. At the time of its greatest prosperity it comprised 56 monasteries, the greater part of which were in Italy and a few in Portugal and Brazil. At the present day this number is greatly diminished. The church of St. Stephen del Cacco in Rome now belongs to them.

(*b*) *Celestines.*—The Celestines are a more important branch than the Sylvestrines. They owe their foundation to the pope of that name, St. Celestine V., who at first was a hermit on Monte Morone in the Abruzzi, and then at Mt. Majella. He endeavoured to combine under one manner of life the cenobitic principle of the Benedictines and the practices of the anchoretic life. When he became pope, he protected and favoured the order which he had founded, approved of its constitutions, and accorded it many privileges. His congregation, having made numerous foundations in Italy, spread into France, Saxony, Bohemia, and the Low Countries. It possessed 150 monasteries, of which 96 were in Italy and 21 in France.[3]

(*c*) *Olivetans.*—The Olivetans were founded by Bernard Tolomei († 1348), a professor of Law at Siena, who, in company with a few companions, retired to Mount Oliveto, some leagues from Siena,

1 For this great man's influence in the reformation of the monasteries of Germany, Switzerland, and Spain, cf. Heimbucher, i. 292, note.

2 On Bursfeld see J. G. Leuckfeld, *Antiquitates Bursfeldenses*, Leipzig and Wolfenbüttel, 1713; Berlière, 'La Congrégation de Bursfeld,' in *Revue Bénédictine*, xvi. [1899] 360 f., 385 f., 481 f., 550 f.

3 Hélyot, vi. 236 f.; Curiel, *Congregatio Hispano-benedictina*; cf. *Studien und Mittheilungen*, xxv., xxvi., xxvii.

4 Besse, *Revue Bénédictine*, xvii. [1900] 275 f.

5 O. Reiners, *Die St. Willibrod-Stiftung in Echternach*, Echternach, 1895; Heimbucher, i. 233; Chevalier, *Répertoire: Topo-bibliographie*, *s.v.* 'Echternach.'

1 A. Savine, *English Monasteries on the Eve of the Dissolution*, Oxford, 1909; Gasquet, *Henry VIII. and the English Monasteries*, London, 1888; Taunton, *op. cit.*

2 On St. Vannes and St. Hydulphus congregation see Hélyot, vi. 272 f.; on St. Maur, *ib.* p. 286; Heimbucher, i. 305 f.; B. Pez, *Bibliotheca Benedictino-Mauriana, seu de ortu, vitis et scriptis patrum Benedictinorum e congr. S. Mauri in Francia*, Augsburg, 1716; P. Le Cerf de la Viéville, *Bibliothèque historique et critique des auteurs de la congr. de St. Maur*, The Hague, 1726, etc.; cf. Heimbucher, i. 305; Chevalier, *Répertoire: Topo-bibliographie*, *s.v.* 'Bénédictins.'

3 Cœl. Telera di Manfredonia, *Historie degli uomini illustri per santità del ordine dei Celestini*, Bologna, 1648; on Celestine V. cf. *AS*, May, iv. 418–537, and Heimbucher, i. 279.

whence his congregation takes its name. They lived as hermits, while following the Rule of St. Benedict in so far as its main principles are concerned. Pope John XXII. gave his approbation to their constitutions. Fourteen years after its foundation more than 100 monasteries, including Monte Cassino, had rallied to this mode of life. Their principal monasteries were those of San Miniato in Florence, and Settignano and S. Francesco Romana at Rome. Among their members are counted 4 cardinals, 5 archbishops, 30 bishops, and a few savants, such as Lancelotti, Bianchieri, etc.[1]

(*d*) *Humiliati, Pulsano, and Monte Vergine.*—Three other orders or congregations—the Humiliati, Pulsano, and Monte Vergine—are also offshoots in Italy of the Benedictine tree. The first was founded in the 12th cent., with the aid of St. Bernard, by St. John Oldrado († 1159) near Cosmo, but later they joined the partisan demagogues of Arnold of Brescia and then the Waldenses. St. Charles Borromeo made a futile attempt to reform them; the rebel monks tried to get rid of the saint by endeavouring to bring about his death, and were consequently suppressed by St. Pius V. in 1571.[2] The order of Pulsano, which never made any great progress, was founded in Apulia by St. John de Matera († 1139).[3] That of the Guilhelmites, or hermit Benedictines of Monte Vergine, was founded by a friend of St. John de Matera—St. William (Lat. Guilielmus) of Vercelli († 1142), who had at first lived as a hermit on Monte Vergine, in the neighbourhood of Naples. He had a certain number of followers, and built several other monasteries in Italy and even as far off as Sicily. The monastery of Monte Vergine became and has remained the centre of a very flourishing pilgrimage.[4]

(*e*) *Fontavellane.*—Among the reforms in the Benedictine order we must not omit to mention that of Fontavellane under the inspiration of Dominic of Foligno († 1031) at Faenza in Umbria. St. Peter Damian († 1072) was its most powerful and most fervent promoter, and St. Dominic le Cuirassé ('the armoured') is also one of its glories. Its Rule added new austerities to those of St. Benedict's. In 1570 it was united to the Camaldolese.[5]

(*f*) *Camaldolese.*—This was one of the most numerous and most powerful of the congregations of the Benedictine order. They essayed to combine the cenobitic with the anchoretic mode of life. At one time they numbered 2000 monks, and their history is intermingled with the most important events of the Church in Italy in the 11th century. Their founder was St. Romuald († 1027), who was at first abbot of San Apollinare in Classe at Ravenna, and withdrew thence to Campo Maldoli (whence the name 'Camaldoli' or 'Camaldolese') in the Apennines with a colony of hermits.[6]

(*g*) *Vallombrosa.*—The order of Vallombrosa was founded by St. John Gualbert († 1073) at Vallombrosa in Tuscany. The founder, who was not ignorant of the attempt of the Camaldolese, also took up the idea of uniting the anchoretic life with the cenobitic mode, basing his plan on the Rule of

[1] S. Lancelotti, *Historiæ Olivetanæ*, Venice, 1623; Hélyot, vi. 192 f.

[2] For the Humiliati cf. P. Sabatier, *S. François d'Assise*, Paris, 1894, p. 158 (Eng. tr., London, 1901); H. Tiraboschi, *Memorie degli Humiliati*, Modena, 1766; *Vetera Humiliatorum Monumenta*, 3 vols., Milan, 1766–69; Hélyot, vi. 152 f.

[3] Hélyot, vi. 135 f.

[4] T. Costo, *Storia dell' origine del S. luogo di Monte Vergine*, Venice, 1691; G. Giordano, *Croniche di Monte Vergine*, Naples, 1648; Hélyot, vi. 122 f.

[5] R. Biron, *Vie de Saint Pierre Damien*, Paris, 1908.

[6] A. Florentinus, *Historiarum Camaldulensium*, etc., Florence, 1575; G. Grandi, *Dissertationes Camaldulenses*, Lucca, 1707; cf. Chevalier, *Répertoire: Topo-bibliographie*, *s.v.* 'Camaldules.'

St. Benedict. This congregation, like that of the Camaldolese, also played an important part under Leo IX. and St. Gregory VII. in the reformation of the Church in its fight against simony.[1]

(*h*) *Grammont and Fontevrault.*—France, which, in Cluny and Citeaux, had given birth to the two most illustrious reformations of the Benedictine order, has still two more interesting attempts to its credit, although of much less importance—the order of Grammont and that of Fontevrault. The first resembles the Camaldolese order. Its founder, St. Stephen of Muret, near Limoges († 1142), where he lived a very mortified life, withdrew to Grandmond, or Grammont, a place which was at that time a desert in the same country. His order was more or less of a success in France, and at one time numbered about 60 monasteries.[2] Fontevrault (*Fons Ebraldi*), in the Department of Maine-et-Loire, gave its name to the order founded by Robert d'Arbrissel, who renewed an ancient institution, namely, that of double monasteries.[3] The founder's influence as a missionary and preacher was enormous, and at his death 3000 monks and nuns were united under his guidance. His Rule spread to England and Spain, but Fontevrault remained the principal house. The most rigorous discipline maintained the spirit of St. Robert in the monasteries thus brought together.[4]

There were also a few partial reformations that arose in certain great abbeys which we might call monastic capitals, Chaise-Dieu, L'Abbaye de Cluse, Sasso-Bigno, Sauve Majour, Le Bec, Thiron, Savigny, Saint-Sulpice, and Cadouin.[5]

(*i*) *Mechitarists.*—The Mechitarists represented one of the most curious attempts at reform in the Benedictine order. Mechitar (Mechithar or Mekhitar, † 1749) was an Armenian who, with the object of enlightening his fellow-countrymen concerning the Roman Catholic Church, resolved to found an order consecrated to the work of the mission and the education of youth and the composition or the translation of Catholic works. In Armenia he was subjected to long persecutions on the part of the schismatics, but, far from being discouraged, he succeeded in founding his congregation in Armenia. His most celebrated foundation, however, was in the island of St. Lazarus, near Venice; it became a very active centre for Armenian studies. The monastery of Vienna, founded in 1810, is also celebrated for its printing-press and its seminary.

(*j*) *Carthusians.*—The Carthusians, like the Camaldolese, represent a mixture of the anchoretic and the eremitic modes of life in Western monasticism. St. Bruno, their founder, withdrew to the desert of the Chartreuse (whence the name 'Carthusian') in the diocese of Grenoble, France, where he established a little colony of hermits, whose successors have succeeded in keeping together and maintaining their traditions down to the present day. A great number of foundations were made throughout all the nations of Europe. In a Carthusian monastery each monk lives in his own cell and cultivates his little garden. They come together only for divine office in choir, for conference, or for chapter, and on certain days they meet in the common refectory and for the weekly walk. They have always been noted for their fervour,

[1] V. Simius, *Catalogus virorum illustrium congregationis Vallis Umbrosæ*, Rome, 1693; Hélyot, v. 298 f.

[2] J. Levêque, *Annales ordinis Grandi-Montensis*, Troyes, 1662.

[3] On the double monasteries cf. Mary Bateson, 'Origin and early History of double Monasteries,' *Trans. of the Royal Hist. Society*, xiii. [1899] 137–198; J. Varin, 'Mémoire sur les causes de dissidences entre l'église bretonne et l'église romaine,' *MAIBL* v. [1858] 165 f.

[4] H. Nicquet, *Hist. de l'ordre de Fontevraud*, Angers, 1586, Paris, 1642; M. Cosnier, *Fontis Ebraldi exordium*, Masserano, 1641.

[5] For the details cf. Heimbucher, i. 265.

and among them there have been a few ascetic writers of high merit. Some of their chapter-houses are celebrated for their architectural beauty and for the art treasures which they contain.[1]

The 19th cent. was one of restoration for monasticism. While in England, Germany, Austria, and Italy the ancient monastic congregations and the great abbeys were maintained in spite of all difficulties, some attempts at monastic restoration were made in France, Italy, Switzerland, Germany, and America. It will suffice to refer the reader to the article 'Benedictine Order,' in *CE* ii. 443–465, for a fuller account of these attempts (cf. Heimbucher, i. 600).

V. *CONCLUSION*. — In an article that must necessarily be brief, we have been able to give only a very short summary or historical outline. To give it any degree of completeness one should study in detail the influence exercised by the monks on the Church and on society in general; consider what has been their work of sanctification, of charity, of apostleship; enumerate the services which they have rendered to civilization as savants, litterateurs, artists, agriculturists, and, at times, as politicians. It would then be seen that, although vowed by their monastic profession to a life of retreat and renunciation, which is the kernel of their vocation, the monks have accomplished a work that has been equalled by no other society down to the present day.

If this résumé of monastic history had any pretensions to completeness, some mention should here be made of the nuns, in whose ranks are found characters as remarkable as those of Lioba, Mechtild, Gertrude, Hildegarde, Roswitha, and others. From the historical point of view, however, this is unnecessary. The nuns brought no new element into the monastic life, but were content to follow in the footsteps of the monks under the influence of the great reformers of the monastic order.

LITERATURE.—U. Berlière, *L'Ordre monastique des origines au XIIe siècle*, Maredsous, 1912; E. C. Butler, 'Monasticism,' in *Cambridge Medieval History*, i., Cambridge, 1911, pp. 521–542, 683–687; U. Chevalier, *Répertoire des sources historiques du moyen-âge: Topo-bibliographie*, Paris, 1894–1903, *s.vv.* 'Ascètes, Ascétisme,' 'Moines'; H. J. Feasey, *Monasticism: What is it?* London, 1898; J. O. Hannay, *The Spirit and Origin of Christian Monasticism*, do. 1903; A. Harnack, *Das Mönchtum, seine Ideale und seine Geschichte*, Giessen, 1895 (cf. *Reden und Aufsätze*, i. [Giessen, 1904]), Eng. tr., London, 1901; M. Heimbucher, *Die Orden und Kongregationen der katholischen Kirche*, Paderborn, 1896 f.; P. Hélyot and M. Bullot, *Histoire des ordres religieux*, 8 vols., Paris, 1860 (orig. ed. 1714–19); H. Leclercq, art. 'Cénobitisme,' in *DACL* ii.[2] [1910] 3047–3248; C. Montalembert, *Monks of the West*, Eng. tr., London, 1896; H. B. Workman, *The Evolution of the Monastic Ideal from the Earliest Times down to the Coming of the Friars*, do. 1913; O. Zöckler, *Askese und Mönchtum*, 2 vols., Frankfort, 1897.

For a complete bibliography see Heimbucher, i. 46 f.; art. 'Monasticism,' in *CE* x. 463, 464, 467, 472; art. 'Mönchtum,' in *PRE*[3] xiii. 214 ff.; Berlière, *op. cit.* (bibliography at the end of each chapter), and *Bulletin d'hist. bénédictine*, 1907–12, Suppl. to *Revue Bénédictine*, Maredsous, 1912; Butler, *op. cit.* pp. 683–687; Leclercq, *loc. cit.*, and Chevalier, *Répertoire: Topo-bibliographie, locc. citt.*

F. CABROL.

MONASTICISM (Buddhist).—**I. The monastic order.**—The monastic order in Buddhism, as instituted by Gautama Buddha himself, was not essentially a new creation in India, but was derived from ancient Hindu usage and practice. Separation from the world, in the solitary existence of a hermit or ascetic or in regulated communities, had been almost from time immemorial a characteristic feature of Indian life. In adopting the principle of monastic rule and self-discipline as the basis of his religious system, and defining this as the sole way of religious attainment, the Buddha presented to his hearers no new doctrine or ideal, but urged and enforced a duty familiar to them from the teaching of their own sacred books. The distinctive feature of the Buddhist order, in which it was differentiated from its predecessors, and to which, in large part at least, it owed its wide extension and success, was the removal of all restrictions of caste. Membership of the order was open to all from the highest to the lowest, without distinction of race or birth. All alike were bound by the vow of poverty, relinquished all personal or individual possession of worldly goods, and sought in meditation and spiritual endeavour that deliverance from the bonds of existence and misery which, the Buddha taught, could never be achieved in the turmoil and distraction of a life in the world. To indicate, therefore, the life of renunciation and strenuous pursuit of the highest aim to which they pledged themselves the monks were known as *bhikṣus*, 'beggars,' *śramaṇas* or *śrāmaṇeras*, 'endeavourers,' the latter term being given to the novices or junior monks, and *sthaviras*, 'elders,' to those who were the senior or ruling members in the monasteries. The community of monks as a whole was known as the *Saṅgha*, or order, and with the Buddha himself and the *Dharma*, the sacred rule or law, formed a Buddhist triad, each member of which was idealized and invested with a sacred character, and ultimately became the object of a definite worship.[1] On the sculptures the Saṅgha is represented as a man holding a lotus in his hand, the symbol of stainless purity.

In inception and intention the monasteries were not the established homes of the monks. To the latter no permanent abodes were assigned, but they were to follow the wandering life of an ascetic or beggar, dependent for their livelihood upon the gifts of the laity, their only shelter the trees of the forest, or booths constructed of leaves and branches (*parṇaśālā, pannasālā*). Only during *Vassa* (*Varṣa*), the season of the rains, when travelling became impracticable or could be prosecuted only at the grave risk of injury to living beings, was it incumbent upon them to remain in a definite place or a permanent building. Caves, either natural or artificially excavated in the rock, seem to have been among the favourite dwelling-places of the early Buddhist monks. Gautama is represented as giving permission for five different kinds of abodes (*pañcha lenāni*): 'I allow you, O Bhikkhus, dwellings of five kinds, vihāras, aḍḍhayogas, storied dwellings, attics, caves.'[2] The more elaborate and permanent dwellings were, in the first instance, apparently always the gifts of wealthy laymen, who desired in this way to do honour to Gautama himself or to the order which he had founded. A usual name for the larger monasteries was *saṅghārāma*, the abode or delight of the Saṅgha; and the term *vihāra* was employed also to denote the temple where the images were enshrined, in a building which, in the great monasteries at least, was usually distinct from the main hall.

It became necessary, moreover, at an early date to place restrictions upon the absolute freedom of entrance into the order. Such restrictions took the form of the prohibition of admission to those suffering from any mental or bodily defect, as the blind or lame, and to the vicious in habit or life,

[1] A. Miræus, *Origines monasteriorum Carthusianorum per orbem universum*, Cologne, 1609; G. Corbin, *Hist. sacrée de l'ordre des Chartreux*, Paris, 1653; C. Le Couteulx, *Annales Ordinis Cartusiensis*, new ed., 8 vols., Neuville-sous-Montreuil, 1888–91; on the bibliography of the Carthusians cf. Chevalier, *Répertoire: Topo-bibliographie*, *s.v.* 'Chartreux.'

[1] Thus in the 'three-refuge formula' which every candidate for admission into the order was required to repeat the Saṁgha is personified, and to each in succession the suppliant applies for protection and aid: *Buddhaṁ śaraṇaṁ gachchhāmi, Dharmaṁ śaraṇaṁ gachchhāmi, Saṅghaṁ śaraṇaṁ gachchhāmi*, 'I seek refuge in the Buddha, the Religion, and the Order' (*Mahāv.* i. 12. 4).

[2] *Chullav.* vi. 1. 2; *SBE* xx. 158; cf. *Mahāv.* i. 30. 4, where these are termed 'extra allowances'; *aḍḍhayoga* is explained by the commentator to mean a gold-coloured Bengali house.

gamblers and those involved in debt.[1] The consent of parents also was required in the case of a minor. No distinction or priority of caste, however, was ever recognized in Buddhism, although it seems to have been true that the earliest converts were for the most part Brāhmans. Inasmuch as in and through the order alone was final deliverance to be attained, it was an essential feature of the Buddha's gospel that no accident of birth should hinder a man from entering upon and prosecuting the path that led to salvation, to *nirvāṇa*. It was impossible for the layman to work out his own salvation while in the world, fettered by its ordinances and under the spell of its attractions. He must renounce the world and become a monk, that, undistracted and at leisure, he might pursue the highest ends and win for himself final deliverance.

The earliest ceremony of admission to the monastic order appears to have been as simple as possible, and confined to a recital of the 'three-refuge formula,' together with a declaration on the part of the applicant of his desire to become a monk. At first Gautama himself received and admitted all candidates. Later he entrusted this right to the monks themselves, each monk being permitted to ordain one novice. This rule again was found to be too strict, and ultimately the only limit to the number that a monk might himself receive was the condition of efficient oversight.[2]

On admission the candidate provided himself with the usual almsbowl and the appropriate three vestments (*trichīvara*) which constituted almost his sole possessions.[3] The colour of the robes seems to have been originally dull red or reddish-yellow, as worn by most of the Hindu ascetics, but varies at the present time in different countries; in the south it is usually yellow. They were to be made in patches or torn pieces, like the rice-fields of Magadha.[4] Besides the almsbowl the ordained monk carried also with him a staff, a razor and tooth-pick, and a water-strainer, the last in order to ensure that no living creature should inadvertently be destroyed by him when drinking. The use of the rosary in addition was a practice of later origin. Frequently the robes were the gift to the Buddha or his disciples of wealthy laymen, who sought to secure merit for themselves by generosity to the order.

Upon converts from other sects who came desiring to receive *upasampadā* a probation (*parivāsa*, 'sojourn,' 'delay') of four months was imposed. Fire-worshippers and Jaṭilas (wearing the *jaṭā*, *i.e.* with matted hair), however, were to be accepted forthwith, on the ground of their orthodox belief; Śākyas also, because of their kinship with the Buddha.[5]

The daily routine of monastic life admitted of little variation. The day began early with recitation and prayers, followed by the regular round for alms. Silently and with downcast eyes the monks moved in procession and presented themselves before the householders' doors, to receive whatever food might be placed in their bowls. For this they were not allowed to make request, as the Brāhman students and ascetics were accustomed to do. Whatever was bestowed they were to accept with gratitude; if no gift were offered, they were to pass on to another house without showing resentment. On their return a simple noon-day meal was followed by rest and meditation, the day closing with service and recitations in the temple or hall of the monastery. In most of the monasteries regular instruction was given to the *śrāmaṇeras*, or junior monks, and an elementary education was thus available for the entire male population. There were no public services, however, within the monasteries, nor any worship in the usual sense of the term. Only in *Vassa* did the monks ordinarily engage in preaching, or place themselves at the service of the laity for the reading of the Scriptures or prayer. Twice a month at the new and full moons on the *uposatha* days, the days of abstinence and fasting, the *pratimokṣa*,[1] or confession of sin, was to be formally recited at a full chapter of the monks. Later a weekly recitation was instituted, which included the intermediary days, on the seventh and twenty-first of the lunar month.[2]

In intention and practice, therefore, the Saṅgha formed a brotherhood, within which no distinction was made of rank or birth; age, learning, and seniority formed the only title to authority and respect. The control of the monasteries was in the hands of the *sthaviras*, the elders or senior monks. The *upādhyāyas* or *āchāryas* were ordained members of the fraternity, of some years' standing, qualified by character and learning to give instruction and to conduct the recitations and prayers. The novices or junior monks were required to devote themselves to study, to perform the necessary services of the monastery buildings, to wait upon the senior monks, and sometimes to attend them when they moved abroad. All alike pledged themselves to obey the rules and discipline of the order. There were, however, no irrevocable vows. The monk was free at any time without blame to discard his robes and return to the world. In this way in some Buddhist countries the entire male population passed through the monastery schools, and for a longer or shorter period wore the yellow vestments. By his return to the world the monk definitely desisted from his endeavour to secure for himself deliverance from suffering and misery; for only within the order, according to the teaching of the Buddha, was salvation to be attained. Lay brethren also (*upāsaka*, 'worshipper,' 'servant') were admitted to the monastery as labourers and servants, and upon them a less strict discipline and obligation were imposed. Nothing further probably was required of them than to recite the 'three-refuge formula.' They took no part in the regular life of the monastery, did not join in the daily itinerancy for alms, and were in all matters under the direction of the monks. The outside laity also were accustomed to visit the monasteries to make offerings at the shrines.

The rules of extreme poverty incumbent upon the monks individually did not extend to the monasteries in their corporate capacity. These might be and often were powerful and wealthy corporations, possessed of great resources, and wielding a corresponding influence in the neighbouring districts. Their property consisted for the most part of land and the revenues of estates or villages which had been granted to them in perpetuity by wealthy patrons, whose piety and liberality earned its recompense in the merit which thereby accrued to the donor. Gifts in money as well as in kind were frequently bestowed. Sometimes also these donations took the form of the building and furnishing of monasteries for the use of the brethren. Such benefactions are recorded within the lifetime of Gautama himself. He gave his permission for the dedication of the estate and buildings, expressed his pleasure at the meritorious service of his followers, and prophesied of the future good which

[1] *Mahāv.* i. 39–76.

[2] *Ib.* 52, 55. See art. INITIATION (Buddhist).

[3] The regulations with regard to clothing appear to have been in part polemical and directed against the Jain ascetics, who went about unclothed.

[4] *Mahāv.* viii. 12.

[5] *Ib.* i. 38.

[1] Pāli *pātimokkha*, 'release,' 'liberation.' That the term ordinarily conveyed this meaning there can be no doubt. Its original significance is in dispute (see Kern, pp. 74 and note, 85 ff.).

[2] Kern, p. 99 f.

would be theirs as a certain reward. In respect, however, of their wealth and resources the monasteries of Buddhist countries differ to a considerable extent. In Ceylon, with the exception of a few that are more influential and renowned, the buildings are small, and shelter few inmates. In Mongolia and Tibet they are large and elaborately furnished and decorated, and frequently occupy imposing positions of great natural beauty. Burma and Siam possess buildings of much architectural merit; and the monasteries and temples of Japan are not excelled for stateliness and charm by any in the whole Buddhist world. The Chinese monasteries have suffered much from neglect and decay, and in many instances have within recent years been altogether abandoned, or diverted to secular purposes.

2. Nuns.—Apparently only with much reluctance did the Buddha consent to the establishment of an order of nuns (*bhikṣuṇīs*, Pāli *bhikkhunīs*). The traditional account relates that at the thrice-repeated request of Mahāpajāpatī, Gautama's aunt and nurse, strongly supported by Ānanda, the Buddha gave his permission for women to 'go out from the household life and enter the homeless state under the doctrine and discipline proclaimed by the Tathāgata.' The concession, however, would prove disastrous, so Gautama prophesied, to the prosperity and duration of the faith which he taught; the pure religion and the good law would endure only for five hundred years instead of a thousand. On the same occasion he prescribed the obligations and duties of the *bhikkhunīs* contained in 'Eight Chief Rules,' to which they were bound in strict obedience. The regulations involved subservience to and dependence upon the order of monks in all respects. A nun even of a hundred years' standing was to rise and respectfully salute even the youngest monk, nor was a nun to venture to admonish a monk, though she must submit to receive admonition from him. Further a nun may not keep *Vassa* in a district in which no monk is resident.[1] It is probable that the ordination of women as *bhikkhunīs* and the establishment of nunneries are in reality due to a later age than that of the founder of Buddhism. The institution has never become popular or gained a strong hold in any Buddhist country; and the number of the nuns has always been small relatively to the number of monks.

3. India.—The Chinese pilgrims, Fā-Hian, Hiuen-Tsiang, and others, in the 5th and following centuries of the Christian era, found monasticism flourishing in N. India, and the great monasteries with their thousands of learned and studious monks exercised a powerful and attractive influence. They belonged in almost equal proportion to the two great schools of Buddhist doctrine, the Hīnayāna and the Mahāyāna (*qq.v.*). In the time, however, of the visit of Hiuen-Tsiang, the most renowned of the Chinese monks (A.D. 629–645), they seem to have been losing ground everywhere to the rival sects of the Brāhmans. The most famous Buddhist monastery was that at Nālanda, the modern Barāgāon near Gayā (*q.v.*), a description of which is given by the latter pilgrim.[2] See, further, art. NĀLANDA.

4. Ceylon.—In Ceylon the power and influence of the community during the early centuries of the Christian era, under the rule of the native Ceylonese kings, who were enthusiastic Buddhists, attained a high level, and were exercised not only ecclesiastically but also in political affairs. The rulers themselves received *abhiṣeka* (*q.v.*) at the hands of the monks, who not only offered advice and exercised authority in matters of State, but as judges decreed penalties for breaches of the law. On the other

[1] *Chullav.* x. 1; *SBE* xx. 320 ff.
[2] S. Beal, *Si-yu-ki*, London, 1906, ii. 167 f., 170 ff.

hand, the kings interfered in the maintenance of ecclesiastical discipline, and are themselves said to have taught publicly and expounded the principles of the religion. The most flourishing period of monastic life, when the communities of the monks were most numerous and wealthy, appears to have been from the 2nd cent. B.C. to the 10th cent. after Christ, when the Tamil invaders from S. India began to overrun the northern half of the island, which was then the chief home of religious faith and prosperity, destroying the monasteries and introducing the beliefs and practices of Hinduism. Towards the close of the 12th cent. a brief revival of national religion took place with the re-establishment of national independence under Parākrama the Great († *c.* A.D. 1197). After the death of the king, however, a decline of national and religious life again set in, during which the monasteries and schools of Buddhism manifested little vigour or initiative, and, although the religious life of the community maintained itself outwardly, it gradually fell to a low level of intelligence and spirituality. Only within the last few years have there been signs of a renewed vitality and interest in the purer doctrines and principles of the faith, and of energy or zeal on behalf of its preservation and extension.

The chief authority for the history of the order in Ceylon is the *Mahāvaṁsa*, or 'Great Chronicle,' a native record of religious and political events in the island from the introduction of Buddhism by Mahinda (Mahendra), the son, or, according to Hiuen-Tsiang, the younger brother, of Aśoka, at the close of the 3rd or the beginning of the 2nd cent. B.C., to the reign of King Mahāsena in the earlier part of the 4th cent. A.D.[1] There is also a collection of devotional 'songs' or 'psalms' of the monks (*Theragāthā*) contained in the *Sutta-Piṭaka* of the Pāli Scriptures, which throws much light on the thoughts and aspirations of the inmates of the monasteries, and gives on the whole a high conception of their piety and self-denying spirit. A similar collection of *Therīgāthā*, 'Songs of the Nuns,' forms part of the same *Piṭaka*.[2] The defect of the *Mahāvaṁsa* regarded as an authority, over and above its obvious exaggeration of details and naive acceptance of miraculous traditions intended to glorify the course of Buddhist history, is its partisan character. Written in the interest and from the point of view of the monks of the Mahāvihāra at Anurādhapura, the capital city of N. Ceylon and for many centuries the centre of Buddhist monastic life and enterprise, it takes no account of the development of doctrine or teaching in the two great rival communities of the Abhayagiri and the Jetāvana monasteries, each with an independent life of its own. For a period of more than ten or twelve centuries, to the close of the 12th cent. A.D., when the leading sects were reunited, no record is available of the activities or influence of these two important monastic institutions. Apparently they were protestant in their beliefs and practices as regarded the leading and established church of the Mahāvihāra. To what extent, however, their teaching diverged from the orthodox standard, or their manner of life was nonconformist, we have no means of ascertaining.[3]

[1] See *Mahāvaṁsa*, tr. into Eng. by W. Geiger and M. H. Bode, Oxford, 1914, with Introduction and references to other literature. The text of the *Mahāvaṁsa* was edited and published by Geiger for the *PTS* in 1908, and an earlier tr. by G. Turnour and L. C. Wijesiṁha was reprinted at Colombo in 1889.
[2] The Pāli text of both collections was edited by H. Oldenberg and R. Pischel, London, 1893. Translations of the *Therīgāthā* and *Theragāthā* by C. A. Rhys Davids under the titles of *Psalms of the Early Buddhists, the Sisters*, and *Psalms of the Early Buddhists, the Brethren*, were published at Oxford in 1909 and 1913.
[3] See Cave, *Ruined Cities of Ceylon*; Copleston, *Buddhism in Magadha and Ceylon*[2], ch. xxiv.

More recently there has been a recrudescence of sectarian differences in the island. These, however, concern monastic usage and habit rather than belief; and in the latter respect there is little if any variation throughout Ceylon. There are three chief sects, the origin of which appears to have been due in all instances to external initiative and influence; and one of these at least seems to owe its existence to a distinct protest against laxity of demeanour and rule. The earliest and most numerous sect is known as the Siamese, established about the middle of the 18th cent. by a number of monks from Siam, who came to Ceylon to restore, it is said, the true succession which had been lost. About fifty years later a separation took place, apparently on disciplinary, not doctrinal grounds, and the Amarapura sect was founded, its leaders being monks who owed their rank and ordination to the Burmese city. The third and protestant sect, the most recent and numerically the least important, is the Rāmanya or Rangoon. The Siamese is the most wealthy and numerous, including among its followers about half of the monks of the island. Most of the important and popular temples and shrines are in their hands. From ten to fifteen per cent belong to the Rāmanya. These last pledge themselves to a stricter observance of the vow of poverty, and neither individually nor collectively do they own, as do the others, landed property. They follow also a simpler mode of life, and avoid with the greatest scrupulousness all contact with the worship or customs of Hinduism. Outwardly the sects differ in the manner in which the yellow robe is worn; the Siamese leave the right shoulder uncovered, but the Rāmanya and the Amarapura draw the robe over both shoulders. The Rāmanya is most influential in the southern part of the island, the Siamese in the central provinces; but the latter is said to be losing ground to its younger rival.[1]

The monasteries of Ceylon are for the most part small, rarely containing more than from ten to twenty monks. The few larger and more important institutions alone, as at Kandy, will accommodate up to forty inmates. In the country districts frequently only two or three monks live together. Recitation, confession, and preaching by the monks take place especially at new and full moon, and on the mid-days intervening; thus four times in the lunar month. More formal services last for ten days or a fortnight without intermission, and are carried out at the expense of wealthy laymen, who by charity to the monks secure merit for themselves. During the three months of *Vassa* (*Was*) the monks leave the monasteries and live in the villages, either in specially constructed sheds or booths or by invitation in the houses of rich laymen, who entertain them generously at their own expense. The rule that in the season of the rains, corresponding in Ceylon to our late summer and autumn, no journeying may be undertaken is interpreted in the sense that no monk may be absent from his village or temporary home for more than six or seven days.[2]

5. **Siam.**—Perhaps the most distinctive feature of Siamese monastic rule is the control exercised by the monarch. Otherwise the habit and discipline of the monks are similar to the practice of Ceylon. The king is visitor and patron of the monasteries, and himself nominates the *sangkharat*, or archbishop, the supreme ecclesiastical dignitary of the country. He selects for the office one of the four chief abbots, who are entrusted severally with the control of the northern and southern provinces of the kingdom, the general oversight of morals and ritual, and the management of the interests of the wandering monks or ascetics who are unconnected with any of the *wats*, or monasteries. These hermits, who make their home in the jungle, are now few in number, but are said to have been very numerous in former times. The inmates of the monasteries themselves frequently spend a considerable part of the year in journeying from one shrine or sacred place to another. Parties of these pilgrims are known as *phra todông*, and as they file in procession along the roads they form a picturesque element in the country side. Each monk is accompanied by a *sisya*, or attendant, who carries his almsbowl and other utensils, and a portable shelter or tent consisting of a large Chinese umbrella, which is set up in the ground at halting-places and a white cloth thrown over it. There are also a few nuns, known as *chi-sông*, who live for the most part in huts in the neighbourhood of the monasteries. They are usually women advanced in years who are without relatives to provide for their well-being or maintenance. There are no regular nunneries.

The four chief abbots, together with four coadjutors or assessors, form a sort of Court of Final Appeal in all matters of religious or ecclesiastical administration or discipline. The general control is in the hands of provincial ministers of the Church, who exercise jurisdiction within districts that correspond usually with the civil divisions of the country. The ecclesiastical organization, therefore, is parallel to the civil; and the ruler of the State is supreme over all.

In Siam, as in Burma, the rule obtained that every male member of the nation should at some time in his life take upon himself the monastic vows, and become resident in a monastery. The accepted minimum period of residence was three months; after this the monk was free to return to the life of a layman. Most of the boys also passed through the monastery schools, receiving an elementary education in reading and writing and the fundamental doctrines of Buddhism. The layman retained an attachment to the monastery of which he had been an inmate, and once at least in the twelve months, at the religious celebrations in the autumn at the close of *Was*, brought gifts and new robes for the use of the monks during the coming year. At the more important monasteries in Bangkok the king himself, as head of the Church, goes in procession with much ceremony, bearing rich presents and costly robes for the monks. In all the festivals and numerous public holidays the monks take a considerable if unofficial part, and are the recipients of much attention and many generous gifts. In Siam the obligation of individual and personal poverty is less strictly observed than in most Buddhist countries. In some instances the monastic cells are adorned with books and pictures and furnished with ornaments and other objects of luxury, and the monks may be seen driving about the streets in carriages. The majority, however, live a simple life, and are regular in their duties and apparently sincere in their devotion. The monasteries also frequently derive considerable revenues from land or other endowments granted to them by Government, or from the gifts of private donors.

The routine of life within the monasteries is practically the same as in Burma and elsewhere in the south. The day begins and ends at an early hour. Morning prayers in the *bôt*, the principal hall or temple of the monastery, before the great gilded image of the Buddha, are followed by the usual early begging round. The food placed in the bowl is received in silence, and eaten

[1] See Copleston, ch. xxvii., 'Modern Monastic Life,' where other and minor differences between the sects will be found recorded; A. S. Geden, *Studies in the Religions of the East*, London, 1913, p. 556 ff.

[2] *Mahāv.* iii. 1 ff.; Copleston, pp. 129 f., 261 f.

immediately on the return to the monastery. No solid food is taken after mid-day. The intervals in the morning and afternoon are occupied with study and meditation and in giving instruction, in recitation from the sacred books, or in preaching. The usual title of the monk is *phra*, 'saint,' or *telepoin*. The latter name is said to be of Môn origin, signifying 'our Master.' The Japanese term *bonze* is also in use among Europeans.

6. Burma.—The monastic life of Burma is in its essential features similar to that of Ceylon. The monastic buildings themselves, however, are on a far more elaborate and costly scale, and the lives of the monks are more strictly ordered and devotional. The monasteries also have been more closely in touch with the laity, both because the monks have mingled freely with the people in their festivals and religious ceremonies and, more especially, on account of the influential position which they have occupied as centres of learning and education. Previous to the establishment of European missionary and Government institutions, which to an increasing extent have supplanted them, every Burmese lad passed through the monastery schools, owed whatever book knowledge he possessed to the teaching of the senior monks, and for a longer or shorter period himself participated as a recognized member of the community in the orderly life of the monastery.[1] Thus, although the majority returned to a secular life and to the pursuit of agriculture or trade, the entire male population of Burma had practical acquaintance with the life of a monk, and knew from within his requirements and aspirations. The system contributed effectively to national unity and strength, and for many centuries made of the Burmese a literate people, even if the standard of attainment was not very high. The boys learnt also respect for their elders and habits of regularity and obedience which served them well in their after careers. See art. BURMA AND ASSAM (Buddhism in).

7. Tibet.—The distinctive feature of the monasticism of Tibet is its elaborate and gorgeous ritual, recalling in many respects the ceremonial of the Roman Catholic Church. The similarity is due for the most part to the influence of the early Nestorian missionaries, who, while leaving little trace of their doctrinal teaching, succeeded in impressing upon the religious life of the country much of the outward form and observance which had been developed in Western lands and on Christian foundations. But, further, the Lāmaist ritual includes ceremonies of exorcism and magic, accompanied by music, dancing, and dramatic performances, the whole most widely divergent from the spirit and simplicity of primitive Buddhism, the source of which is to be found in the ancient native superstitions and practices of the people, which the Buddhist missionaries from India tolerated either from necessity or of choice, if they did not actually foster them. The monastic communities of Tibet are wealthy and powerful, with large revenues and possessions. The buildings themselves are often of great size, sheltering as many as ten thousand inmates, and are imposing rather from their unrivalled position on the sides or summits of lofty rugged hills than from any architectural excellence. At the other extreme, among the anchorites and hermits has been developed a rigorous and cruel asceticism, which is no less opposed to the true Buddhist spirit, but which is closely allied to and probably derived from the Śaivite mysticism and practices of N. India. See art. LĀMAISM.

8. Central Asia.—That for a considerable period Central Asia was the home of a broad and vigorous Buddhist life has long been known. That life naturally centred in the monastic communities established in the several cities on the important roads of pilgrimage and traffic that skirted the central desert of sand on the north and south. In the countries, however, that were subjected to Muhammadan invasion and conquest little trace of the faith remains. The Chinese pilgrims repeatedly make mention of monasteries with large numbers of inmates whose zeal and piety excited their admiration;[1] these for the most part if not entirely were adherents of the Mahāyāna school. Their narrative, nevertheless, conveys the impression that the real influence of the faith upon the character or habits of the people beyond the monastery walls was but slight. Recent exploration and excavations have entirely confirmed the record of the Chinese, and suggest a fairly strong and prolonged Buddhist hold upon the country. Ruined *stūpas* are numerous, and bear witness to Buddhist traditions and the presence of Buddhist monks. The monastic buildings themselves would be of less solid construction, and either have perished or are unrecognizable.[2]

9. China.—Of the monastic life of other Buddhist lands which follow the Mahāyāna with more or less concession to native modes of thought and superstitions there is little further that requires notice in a general survey. It will be sufficient to refer to the articles on the several countries. The main character and type have been everywhere preserved, but the details of mode of life and profession have varied greatly with environment and the genius of the people. In China the monks have occupied generally a degraded position, with a few honourable exceptions, holding a creed and practising a ritual in which there was more of sorcery and magic than of Buddhist faith. The exceptions were the highland monasteries, and those remote from the centres of population, where the monks, though ignorant, were simple, kindly, and pious, seeking salvation through self-denial and right living. The nuns were no less degraded and for the most part despised. Recent events in China, however, with the diversion of numerous temples and monasteries to educational purposes, the desertion or destruction of others, and the spread of Western influence and science, have entirely changed the situation as far as the religious life and thought of the people are concerned. It is not easy to forecast what the ultimate effect upon Buddhism will be, or how far it will modify or even destroy so essential and characteristic a feature of the Buddhist faith as monasticism has ever been. That the effect will be profound and far-reaching there can be no doubt.[3]

10. Korea.—The monastic institutions of Korea resemble those of China, whence both doctrine and practice have been derived. Religiously as in other respects the country has always been dependent on its greater neighbour to the south, and neither in belief nor in rule of life does Korean Buddhism present much that is novel or of interest. Overshadowed by Confucianism and ancestor-worship, it has developed few distinctive features, and has for some centuries exercised a decreasing influence on the thought and habits of the people.

[1] See art. EDUCATION (Buddhist), vol. v. p. 177 ff.

[1] *e.g.* Kashgar, Beal, ii. 306 f.; Khotan, *ib.* 309 ff., Fa-Hian, ch. iii. (Legge, p. 16 ff.); Yarkand, Beal, ii. 307 f.; Sarikol, *ib.* 298 ff.

[2] Cf. M. A. Stein, *Ancient Khotan*, 2 vols., Oxford, 1907, *passim*, and *Ruins of Desert Cathay*, 2 vols., London, 1912; artt. by L. Giles, J. Pelliot, and others, in *JRAS*, 1914, etc. Stein found that the memory of the Chinese Buddhist pilgrim, Hiuen Tsiang, is still retained at the 'Halls of the Thousand Buddhas,' in the west of the province of Kansu, and elsewhere in Central Asia to the present day. The tradition of his learning and devotion, and of the miraculous powers with which he was credited, proved to be a real power in the minds of the priesthood.

[3] Hackmann, *Buddhism as a Religion*, bk. iii. ch. vi.; Edkins, *Chinese Buddhism*²; Wieger, *Bouddhisme chinois*, i., 'Monachisme,' p. 133 ff.

The monasteries are usually small, the number of inmates rarely exceeding twenty-five or thirty, and sometimes, as in Ceylon, no more than three or four monks are found living together. The more important institutions are grouped around the capital, but none are allowed within its walls. Their numbers also are decreasing. The monks themselves command little respect, and are drawn, for the most part, as in China, from the lower classes. The example and influence of Japan also may perhaps be traced in the character of some of the buildings, which are fortified and built on high ground to dominate the country at their base. In the neighbourhood of Seoul a few nunneries exist.

The most distinctive feature of Korean monasteries is the presence of pictures on the walls. These are drawn and coloured on paper and mounted on silk, and usually represent scenes from the lives of the Buddha. Often the entire surface of the interior walls is thus hung with pictures, presenting a remarkable contrast to the monasteries of other lands. Externally the walls are covered with paintings in bright colours of *bodhisattvas* or other supernatural beings. The sanctuaries often contain only a single image, rarely more than two or three; and these are small, and for the most part of clay or wood. Metal images are almost if not entirely unknown.

In their dress the monks have preserved the national costume in the form of a long cloak with sleeves, worn over all, and generally white. The head is shaved, in conformity with Buddhist practice, but not the beard. The shaven head, however, is not branded after the Chinese custom, although branding may be effected on other parts of the body, as the breast or arms. The order is recruited mainly from boys received by dedication or adoption in early childhood. Endowments are not numerous. Most of the monasteries are dependent for their maintenance upon the gifts of the laity, or, where opportunity serves, upon the personal labour of the monks in the cultivation of the temple lands.

11. **Japan.**—The temples and monasteries of Japan are large and well-appointed, and give the impression of a reality of creed and life which is almost altogether wanting to those on the continent. The numerous Buddhist sects of Japan have their home and distinctive life in the monastic communities, and the monasteries themselves in the details of their architecture present varieties of construction according to the sect to which they belong. In creed and belief the sects differ greatly among themselves, and have few features in common with the Buddhism of the south. In the past the activity and strenuousness of the national life found their almost complete counterpart in the monasteries, which formed associations of fighting monks at war with one another, oppressing and plundering the common people. In more settled times speculative thought, mystical, devotional, and idealistic, has been highly developed, perhaps most conspicuously in the 'Sect of the Pure Land,' who hold a theistic creed, and expound and practise a moral code which has much in common with that of the NT. Accompanying a revived religious life also, at different periods of the nation's history, missionary effort and preaching have been prosecuted with zeal and success. Both at home and in China a similar work of propagandism is being carried on at the present time with much devotion and energy.[1]

12. **Conclusion.**—It is natural to compare and contrast the monastic principles and life of Buddhism with those of the Christian orders of the Early and Middle Ages in Europe. In the general features of discipline and government there is much obvious similarity. All communities vowed to poverty and a celibate life, whether Hindu, Muhammadan, Buddhist, or Christian, almost of necessity organize themselves on somewhat similar lines. The essentially distinctive features of Buddhist monasticism would seem to be two: (1) the practice of literal mendicancy, which takes the form of a daily round, equipped with staff and begging-bowl, to receive whatever portions of food the charity of the householders may bestow. In the countries where the Mahāyāna type of Buddhism has prevailed this custom is not and probably never has been obligatory or usual. It forms a distinct and characteristic element, however, of early Buddhist rule and observance. (2) According to Buddhist teaching, salvation is to be found only within the limits of the order. The layman can achieve his own deliverance only if and when he dons the robe of the monk, and takes upon himself the monastic vows. He must seek refuge from the world in a life of retirement, meditation, and self-denial, for not otherwise can the fetters of *karma* be broken and *nirvāṇa* gained. In Buddhist polity and doctrine, therefore, the order holds a pre-eminent place distinct from and above that which it occupies in any other great religious system.

LITERATURE.—A selection only from a great and ever-growing literature can here be given. Many important works have been referred to in the course of the article. The original sources are available in the translations of *SBE* and elsewhere: *SBE* xiii. [1881], xvii. [1882], xx. [1885], 'Vinaya Texts,' xi. [1900] 'Buddhist Suttas,' xlix. [1894] 'Buddhist Mahāyāna Sūtras'; H. C. Warren, *Buddhism in Translations*, Cambridge, Mass., 1896; T. W. Rhys Davids, *Dialogues of the Buddha*, pts. i. and ii., London and Oxford, 1899 and 1910; cf. H. Hackmann, *Buddhism as a Religion*, Eng. tr., London, 1910; P. D. Chantepie de la Saussaye, *Lehrbuch der Religionsgeschichte*[3], 2 vols., Tübingen, 1905, i. 104–114, ii. 74–122; H. Kern, *Manual of Indian Buddhism*, Strassburg, 1896, pp. 73–101; T. W. Rhys Davids, *Buddhism*, new ed., London, 1910; R. Spence Hardy, *Manual of Budhism*[2], do. 1880; R. S. Copleston, *Buddhism in Magadha and Ceylon*[2], do. 1908, chs. xii.–xiv., xxiv., xxvii.; H. W. Cave, *Ruined Cities of Ceylon*, new ed., do. 1900; Shway Yoe, *The Burman, his Life and Notions*[3], do. 1910, chs. iii. f., xii. f., xv., xx. f.; V. C. Scott O'Connor, *Mandalay and other Cities of Burma*, do. 1907; W. A. Graham, *Siam*[2], do. 1912; L. A. Waddell, *Buddhism of Tibet or Lamaism*, do. 1895, pp. 169 ff., 255 ff., and *Lhasa and its Mysteries*, do. 1905; P. Landon, *Lhasa*, 2 vols., do. 1905; J. Edkins, *Chinese Buddhism*[2], do. 1893; E. H. Parker, *China and Religion*, do. 1905, ch. iv.; L. Wieger, *Bouddhisme chinois*, i., 'Monachisme,' Paris, 1910, p. 133 ff.; R. F. Johnston, *Buddhist China*, London, 1913; A. J. Little, *Mount Omi and Beyond*, do. 1901, chs. iv.–vi.; B. H. Chamberlain, *Hand-book for Travellers in Japan*[7], do. 1903; artt. ASCETICISM (Buddhist), EDUCATION (Buddhist), HĪNAYĀNA, IMAGES AND IDOLS (Buddhist), and on the several Buddhist countries.

A. S. GEDEN.

MONASTICISM (Hindu). — The habit of monasticism owes its origin, it has been said, to the natural tendencies of mankind towards mysticism and asceticism. These are developed, set in order, and satisfied, in the rule and restraint of the monastic life. In India, more perhaps than elsewhere, the practice is of very great antiquity; and the motives and instincts suggested, although true in general of the rise and history of Indian monasticism, in two respects at least render an insufficient account of the causes at work. In the routine existence of the monasteries, as far as this is distinct from the solitary or wandering life of the hermits and ascetics, mystical devotion has played but a small part. Mysticism in India has shunned companionship. The mystic aim has been the chosen and cherished pursuit of the lonely ascetic. And the latter, the ascetic motive or ideal, has been overwhelmingly predominant among the causes that have urged such great numbers of Indian men and women at all times to adopt the monastic robes and manner of life. A third motive, however, exercised a powerful influence in determining the choice of the monastic profession. This was

[1] Hackmann, bk. iii. ch. viii.; Geden, *Studies in the Religions of the East*, p. 368 ff.

the Indian view of life as a whole. By the Indian life has ever been regarded as essentially evil, and relief from the burden and sorrow of existence as the chief and final goal. In many forms of Indian doctrine, especially the Buddhist, but also in that of Hindu leaders and teachers before Gautama, this end was to be achieved only in and through a monastic dedication and life. It was impossible for the layman, distracted by the cares and encumbered by the possessions of the world, to secure salvation. Emancipated from these, he was free to devote himself to the highest aim, and to win his way to deliverance (*mokṣa* [*q.v.*]).

A second respect in which historically Indian monasticism in general has been distinguished from Buddhist or Christian is the deficiency of co-ordination or of a central control. The various orders have been for the most part loosely organized, and that from want not of organizing power but of inclination and will. The ideal of the Indian monk or ascetic is not and never has been a fixed residence and occupation, but rather freedom to wander at pleasure, to visit the various sacred places and shrines, and to dispose his manner of life and his time independently in all respects as seemed best to himself. Apparently the habits and methods of the monastic life have undergone little change or development since the earliest ages. The mendicant, or wandering ascetic, rather than the resident community of monks, has been the characteristic feature of Indian religious life; and the monasteries have served in a greater degree as lodging- or rest-houses than for fixed and permanent habitation. The earliest delineations of Indian social and religious life present the same features as are seen in modern times—a large drifting population of mendicants and ascetics, who find only a temporary home in the monasteries, and after a longer or shorter stay move on entirely as their own inclination prompts.

The habitual practice of a life thus ordered and determined is of extreme antiquity in India. It would seem to be based ultimately upon the Hindu regulation of the four *āśramas* (*q.v.*), according to which every Brāhman towards the close of his life must renounce the world and adopt the homeless life and the ascetic garb. In intention, therefore, no low-caste or out-caste man could become a monk, but only the 'twice-born.' In practice, of course, the wandering population is recruited from all castes; and many follow the life as an easy and convenient mode of gaining a subsistence without trouble to themselves.[1] The ancient Indian custom, familiar to Indian thought and in closest harmony with Indian ideals, formed the model for the great Buddhist and Jain communities of monks, and gave to them precept and habit and rule. Only in organization did the daughter communities go far beyond anything that was developed in Hinduism. Here the preference for an independent and self-regulated life proved itself the stronger, and broke away from all attempts at a settled and established order or government.

The Hindu monasteries, or 'maths' (Skr. *maṭha*), are invariably of small size, providing accommodation for only a few inmates. Except at the important pilgrim centres, as Hardwār or Benares (*qq.v.*), where durable buildings of brick are found, they are often little more than a collection of huts or cells ranged around a central court-yard. Permanent quarters are provided for the *mahant*, or presiding abbot, of the monastery and his resident students. The remaining buildings are occupied at the periodical festivals by the members of the order to which the monastery belongs. Attached are a temple or shrine for the service of the deity, and in the larger monasteries at least a separate *dharmaśālā*, or rest-house, for the accommodation of travellers. The term *maṭha* appears to have been originally applied to the solitary hut of the religious recluse, and then to similar dwellings of the communities of hermits living together in the forest in the practice of austerities. Of such a woodland hermitage an attractive description is given in Kālidāsa's *Śakuntalā*. The name was ultimately extended to include all more or less permanent homes or residences for the monks. The maths exist in considerable numbers all over India, but the inmates for the most part live a retired life, keeping to themselves, and both they and their homes are little known to outsiders or Europeans. Each sect or monastic order has its own maths, that of the founder of the order being regarded as the chief. There is, however, no central control, nor any interference in the management or affairs of another monastery. The older monastic buildings are of the simplest character and architecture. Later more elaborate buildings were erected, sometimes of more than one storey; but they never compete in size or architectural pretensions with the great Buddhist *vihāras*. When the latter faith died out in Bengal, some of its monasteries passed into Hindu keeping and were appropriated for the use of Hindu monks.

To erect a monastery for the service of the monks and wandering ascetics has always been regarded as an act of religious merit. The math is the gift of a generous and pious layman; and of such donors there has never been any lack in India. In most instances an endowment for the upkeep of the monastery is provided either at the time of erection or by subsequent grant, and this is increased from time to time by the gifts of patrons who endeavour thus to secure merit for themselves. The individual monk is bound by a vow of poverty, but the monasteries often become exceedingly wealthy in revenue and lands. Since the monks themselves do no manual labour, nor indeed work of any kind, the lands are usually farmed out to Hindu lay-proprietors. The management, however, by the temple authorities of their large revenues has sometimes been so defective that the British Government has been compelled to interfere, and take over temporarily the control of the monastic estate.

The Hindu monk is known as *yatin*, one who curbs his passions and has renounced the world, or *vratin*, the devotee who has taken upon himself the vows of renunciation and consecration. The former term is technical among the Jains also, but is said to be regarded with disfavour. The *naiṣṭhika* is the religious student, who engages himself to remain with the *guru* as pupil and disciple after the close of the regular period of service as a *brahmachārin*. The titles *yogin* and *sannyāsin* are more appropriate and more usually applied to the wandering ascetic, without home or stated means of livelihood. The former denotes the Hindu mystic and saint, who endeavours to attain to union with God by the way of self-control and asceticism. The *sannyāsin* has 'cast off' all worldly fetters and attachments, and is separated from all earthly wants or ties. *Bhikṣu*, 'beggar,' describes rather the common characteristic of the class. In the Pāli form of *bhikkhu* it has become the usual term for the Buddhist monk; Hindu usage ordinarily gives the preference to other names. All monks depend for their livelihood solely upon the charitable gifts of the laity. The daily round with the begging-bowl for doles of food at the door of the Hindu householder is never made in vain, and the flow of Indian charity and

[1] The abbot of a monastery in the Panjāb made complaint to J. C. Oman of the crowd of idle and worthless *sādhus* who charged themselves upon him and took advantage of his hospitality (*Mystics, Ascetics, and Saints of India*, p. 262 f.).

hospitality to ascetics is unstinted. The red- or yellow-coloured robe of the monk is an unfailing passport to generosity and benevolence all over India. Such generosity accrues to the merit of the giver, and has no regard to the character or motive of those who receive the alms. Among the latter there are not a few whose robes cover avarice and greed, or perhaps more often mere indolence and a desire to save themselves the trouble of providing for their own wants. But there are also among them sincere men, often of considerable learning, earnest and devoted in their pursuit of the truth.

The Sanskrit law-books contain rules and regulations for the guidance of the ascetic life. The sixth book of Manu is entirely devoted to this subject. Hermits and ascetics are to beg for their food once a day, to be indifferent to their reception, neither vexed at a refusal nor exultant when their bowl is well filled, to restrain their senses and appetites, eating little, and always to be on their guard lest they accidentally destroy life, watching the ground before them as they move, that their feet may not crush any living thing.[1] The same purpose is in view in the rule that a monk must not change his residence during *Vassa*, the season of the rains.[2] Elsewhere it is provided that students, ascetics, and others shall be free from tolls and taxes.[3] They are not to be allowed to bear witness in the law-courts,[4] probably because, being separated from the world, their testimony with regard to its doings would necessarily be unreliable; nor do they inherit property.[5] Penances also are prescribed for those who for successive days omit to go on the begging round or neglect their other duties.[6] The oversight of the monastery and the responsibility for entertaining itinerant monks or strangers are in the hands of a presiding elder or abbot (*maṭhādhipati*). Around him usually is gathered a band of young disciples, who are instructed by him in the Hindu scriptures and render him personal service in accordance with ancient immemorial custom. There is, however, no definite or fixed hierarchy or gradation of office. The inmates of the monastery are free to come or go at their own will, and neither their movements nor their actions are in any way controlled. They must wear the monastic garb, observe the vow of poverty, and depend entirely upon the bounty of others for their daily sustenance. Beyond these simple conditions they do as they please. The actual possessions which the monk or *sannyāsin* carries with him vary to a slight degree with the sect to which he belongs. The essentials are the robes and a begging-bowl; to which are usually added a staff, water-pot, and rosary, a strainer, a pair of sandals, the materials for smoking and betel-chewing, and perhaps one or more vessels for carrying or cooking food.

The vows (*vrata*) which the ascetic or monk undertakes to observe are five in number: avoiding hurt to any living creature, truthfulness, abstinence from theft, self-restraint, and liberality (Skr. *ahiṁsā*, *satya*, *asteya*, *brahmāchārya*, *tyāga*). These have been adopted, with the exception of the last, in the Jain and Buddhist systems. There are also five lesser vows: equanimity of mind, obedience to the *guru*, gentleness, cleanliness, and purity in eating.[7] The third is explained as having reference to the danger to living beings involved in rough or hasty conduct. There is considerable difference between the sects in respect of the degree of ascetic self-denial or actual discomfort and pain which they voluntarily endure. Śaivite monks are, as a rule, more extreme in their manner of life and austerities. The Vaiṣṇavites allow themselves greater liberty and seldom, if ever, inflict upon themselves the prolonged bodily tortures by which the others seek to gain notoriety or accumulate merit. In all the monasteries the chief Hindu festivals are observed with religious rites and free entertainment for visitors, and the introduction or appointment of a new abbot is attended with much ceremony. Of the routine details of the ordinary monastic life, however, little is known.

The Sikhs also have monasteries of their own and religious orders. The three principal are those of the Akālins, Nirmālins, and Udāsins (*qq.v.*).[1] They vary in both their dress and manner of wearing the hair, some being shaven and others displaying the loose dishevelled locks of the typical *sādhu*. In one instance at least in a monastery visited by J. C. Oman the *mahant* wore robes differing from those of the ordinary monk—a white long-sleeved coat or tunic and a turban of bright colours. The chief and largest monastery is at Amritsar (*q.v.*) near the Golden Temple, built of brick in two storeys and with two open courts, belonging to the Udāsin sect. The other sects also possess monasteries and temples of considerable size. In all a large part of the religious worship consists in the reading of the *Granth* (*q.v.*), and sometimes of other Hindu sacred books. Except at the seasons of the great festivals the monasteries are usually almost deserted, but on these occasions they are thronged with monks and others who have come to join in the feasting and religious ceremonies.

The monastic institutions of the Jains in some respects hold an intermediate position between those of the Hindus and the Buddhists. Their rule and order are more definitely framed than the former, but are less exacting than the Buddhist and allow more freedom to the individual. As in Buddhism also, the existing system or practice of the Brāhman monks or ascetics formed the model on which the founder of the Jain faith ordered his own community. Mahāvīra himself is said to have had a following of fourteen or fifteen thousand monks, and more than twice that number of nuns. Over the monastic schools into which the community was divided were placed eleven chief disciples, or *gaṇadharas*, or twelve if Gośāla be reckoned, who proved himself the unworthy rival and opponent of his master. Jain writers are said to compare the twelve disciples of their founder with the twelve apostles of Christ, and to assign to Gośāla the part of Judas the traitor.

The prevision and independence of the founder of Jainism are shown in the recognition which he accorded to the laity. It has been urged with much probability that this was one of the chief facts that enabled Jainism to withstand the stress of persecution and the steady pressure of the dominant Hinduism, when Buddhism, based solely upon a priesthood, decayed and fell away. Mahāvīra established four orders of society within his system, each with its respective functions and rights: monks (*bhikṣus* or *yatins*) and nuns (*bhikṣuṇīs*), laymen (*śrāvakas*) and laywomen (*śrāvikās*). The Jain laity thus hold a definite place in the Church by the side of the ecclesiastical order. The Digambaras, however, refuse to women the right to enter the order, and assert that they cannot attain salvation (*mokṣa*).

The five vows of the Jain monk are the same as those of the Brāhman ascetic with the ex-

[1] Manu, vi. 55 f.; cf. Baudh. II. x. 18. 4 ff.; Vas. x. 7 f.; *Khād. Gṛhyasūtra*, II. v. 16.

[2] Gaut. iii. 13; Baudh. II. vi. 11. 20.

[3] Manu, viii. 407; cf. vii. 133; Vas. xix. 23; Āpast. ii. 13 ff.; Viṣṇu, v. 132.

[4] Manu, viii. 65; Baudh. i. 13; Nārada, i. 158, 182.

[5] Vas. xvii. 52.

[6] Viṣṇu, xxviii. 52; cf. *Sāṅkh. Gṛhyasūtra*, II. xii. 6 ff.

[7] Baudh. II. x. 18. 1 ff.; cf. Gaut. iii. 11 ff.; A. S. Geden, *Studies in the Religions of the East*, London, 1913, p. 610 ff.

[1] Cf. art. ASCETICISM (Hindu), vol. ii. p. 94.

ception of the last, for which is substituted *aparigraha*, the renunciation of all desire, *i.e.* entire indifferentism.[1] This was the aim also of the Hindu monk; and it is probable that this was the original meaning of the fifth vow in Hinduism, although it is now differently explained. A sixth vow is said to be undertaken by some of the Śvetāmbaras, never to eat after dark lest they should inadvertently destroy life; others declare that this rule is implicit in the first, *ahiṁsā*. To this duty of avoiding in every way injury to life Jains of every sect attach greater importance than either Hindu or Buddhist monks. The Jain layman is hardly less rigorous and careful than the monk. All Jain ascetics carry a piece of cloth to place over their mouths lest they should cause injury when inhaling.[2] The stricter sect of the Sthānakavāsins (Dhuṇḍhīas) wear the mouth-cloth always, by night as well as by day; the other sects are less scrupulous. These precautions against the taking of life do not under all circumstances apply to the monk's own life. When the twelve necessary years of asceticism have been passed, which every monk observes in imitation of the founder of his faith, religious suicide is not only innocent but an act of merit and may be even a duty. Most of the *gaṇadharas* are said to have thus ended their lives by voluntary starvation, and the practice is reported to have been not infrequent in former times.

In addition to the mouth-cloth the Jain monk bears the usual begging-bowl, and a strainer for his drinking-water. The members of all sects carry also an instrument for sweeping the path before them, which in the case of the Digambaras is usually a peacock's feather; the Śvetāmbaras and Sthānakavāsins use a broom, of greater or less size. The head is shaved, and the two last-named sects wear the monastic robes of five pieces, of a white or yellow colour. The Digambaras ('sky-clad') go about unclothed. These last are for the most part found in the south of India. All monks are subject to the vow of personal poverty, but it is said that in many instances this is evaded, even to the extent of carrying coin or bank-notes on their person.

The monastic life both of the monks and of the nuns is ordered on similar lines to the Buddhist. In the ordinary course the inmates of the monastery rise early, and each then makes confession of the known or unknown sins of the past night, and proceeds to the temple for morning worship. This consists in meditation, bowing down before the idol with recitation of a sacred *mantram*, and in *pradakṣiṇa*, or circumambulation, which is performed four or seven times. About ten in the morning the round is made to beg for food. One monk, however, goes on behalf of all the inmates of the monastery; and in this respect Jain practice differs from Hindu or Buddhist. The food may not be eaten in the houses of the laity, but is brought back to the monastery and divided among all. According to rule the begging round should be made only once a day, but it is often repeated in the afternoon. After returning confession is made to the *guru* before partaking of the morning meal. The hours from one to three are devoted to study; and, if an afternoon circuit is undertaken for alms, it is succeeded, as in the morning, by confession. The second and last meal of the day is taken about sunset, and no monk is allowed to leave the monastery after dark.[3]

[1] For a full statement and discussion of the Jain vows see Stevenson, *Heart of Jainism*, p. 234 ff.

[2] It is usually supposed that the purpose of this is to avoid killing insects or minute animalcules in the air by drawing them into the mouth. Mrs. Stevenson, however, maintains, on the authority of some of the Jains themselves, that it is done lest the air itself should suffer harm (*Heart of Jainism*, pp. 100, 227).

[3] Stevenson, p. 228 ff.

Initiation (*dīkṣā*) into the monastic order takes place at the hands of a priest after a year's probation. The novice lays aside his lay garments and ornaments, and adopts the robes of a monk. Within the monastery itself three grades or orders are recognized, based upon seniority or the choice of the community. The ordinary *sādhu*, monk or ascetic, of not less than a year's standing, may be elected *upādhyāya*, and it then becomes part of his duty to give instruction to the younger monks. Further powers of administration and discipline, including the right of excommunication, are in the hands of the *āchārya*, who is appointed on the ground of seniority, or for recognized knowledge and ability. Confession is usually made to the *āchārya*. For the greater part of the year most of the monks itinerate from place to place. It is only during the rainy season and at the principal festival seasons that the monasteries are fully occupied.

LITERATURE. — M. Monier-Williams, *Brāhmanism and Hindūism*[4], London, 1891; J. C. Oman, *Mystics, Ascetics, and Saints of India*, do. 1903 (cf. his *Cults, Customs, and Superstitions of India*[2], do. 1908, pt. ii. ch. iv.); Mrs. Sinclair Stevenson, *Notes on Modern Jainism*, Oxford, 1910, *Heart of Jainism*, Oxford and London, 1915. The last-named work is the most complete and reliable account of Jainism yet published. Cf. also artt. ASCETICISM (Hindu), FESTIVALS AND FASTS (Jain), HINDUISM, vol. vi. p. 701.

A. S. GEDEN.

MONEY.—Money is the name applied to the instrument devised by man which enables him conveniently to effect exchanges of goods and services. It was a great advance upon barter when an intermediary was adopted by the trafficking parties that provided at the same time a measure of values and a generally acceptable medium of exchange. As man advanced from simple barbarism, he acquired some elementary forms of personal wealth, and the practice of exchanging with others to satisfy his growing diversity of wants would naturally arise; in course of time the advantage of possessing an intermediary which formed a unit of comparison of worth and represented a standard of values would come to be recognized. For this purpose objects of common utility or ornament were early adopted—oxen, cattle, sheep, furs, slaves, shells, nuts, precious stones, and bits of metal are examples of the various substances used as money in different circumstances and stages of civilization. These selected substances illustrate the kinds of wealth that were accumulated as stores of value and used as means of paying tribute and debt. They thus became also a form of what is called 'capital' in modern economics.

Gradually the defects of some of the various substances employed to satisfy the money-function became apparent in their inconvenient bulk and lack of divisibility for small payments, their perishableness and absence of equality and stability. Thus by degrees the essential attributes of good money emerged; it was found that the superior metals (gold and silver) possessed in an exceptional degree the qualities desirable in a good medium and a measure of value. Money should have stability in value; it should be durable, portable, divisible; it should be easily recognizable and capable of being coined. No substances possess and retain all these attributes absolutely, but gold and silver display them in the highest degree; consequently they have been generally adopted for money by civilized nations. Since they are natural products, variations in their supply create some fluctuations in value, as do also changes in demand which follow on the growth of population and the irregularities of trade. But, on the whole, gold has responded best to the needs of society as a basis for its complex and ever increasing trade and commerce. Standard money has the attribute of universal acceptability; it commands confidence that it will be promptly received by others without loss of value. It measures the value of the services of labour; and wages as well as goods are estimated in terms of money. The value of goods, when expressed in money, is called their price.

The business of money-changing, of banking and finance, consists largely in the manipulation of money in its various forms and of obligations—debts, credits, loans, etc.—expressed in terms of money. These claims are discharged either by gold and silver or by documents (notes, cheques, bills, etc.), *i.e.* by paper money, representative of sums of metallic money and ultimately redeemable in standard coin.

The introduction of credit-instruments, as the paper substitutes for gold are called, is an extension of the money-function and a refinement upon the employment of metallic money. It is virtually a kind of return to barter; for, while it diminishes the use of coin, it simplifies exchanges and substitutes for payment in metal a promise on paper; this representative money becomes a valuable commodity and multiplies business by its convenience. Debts are set off against debts by means of credit-instruments, substitutes for money that circulate quickly; they become a peculiar currency of promises or claims that do temporary duty, and they are easily transmitted by post; thus they vastly facilitate the business of exchange. The term 'credit' implies that these instruments are promises, and they rest in the long run upon the recognized metallic basis—gold; therefore an adequate amount of gold must be accumulated and safely stored in order to give stability and confidence to the system.

In OT times money was always weighed (Gn 23[16]). This was a necessary precaution in earlier periods, but in modern times the process of coining, exercised as an exclusive function of the Government, confers absolute certainty, accuracy, and uniformity, and inspires confidence; the stamped coin carries with it evidence of the amount and value of the gold that it represents, where gold is the accepted standard of value. The subsidiary coins of silver and bronze are legal tender only within moderate limits, viz. two pounds in silver, and twelve pence in bronze in Great Britain; they are only token coinage, and do not correspond to their intrinsic value in metal, which is small. The value of gold, like that of other commodities, depends ultimately upon the law of supply and demand; the value varies with the amount available for money purposes, for large quantities of the precious metals are absorbed in the arts and as personal ornaments.

The quantity theory of money—*i.e.* that the value varies inversely as the quantity—assumes that all exchanges are made in the standard coin, but the use of paper substitutes, while it does not nullify the abstract theory, introduces modifications too technical for detailed explanation in an article which is mainly descriptive. The system of substituting paper currency for the standard coin requires for security that such paper shall be convertible into gold on demand. To provide this most essential requisite an adequate cash reserve of gold must be maintained. This is one of the responsible functions of the Bank of England. The management and control of the reserve are matters too intricate for present discussion. The excessive issue of inconvertible paper—*i.e.* of notes which cannot be met by gold on demand—has led many countries into great difficulties, and has frequently caused much loss and suffering. Paper currency debased by over-issue drives out gold, destroys confidence, raises prices, and produces financial disaster; business is checked, and the injury falls with peculiar severity upon the wage-receiving classes, who find that their wages paid in paper at such times fall greatly in buying power. There is no remedy but the re-instatement of the currency on a sound basis. A large number of interesting economic problems arise in connexion with the use of money; they are, however, too technical for present consideration, which is restricted to a general account of the nature and services of this useful instrument of civilization. Money is a powerful factor in the spread of civilization, in advancing progress, in distributing the varied products of nature throughout the world. Money, in fact, may rank with roads, vehicles, beasts of burden, railways, steamships, posts, and telegraphs in the advancement of human material well-being. The oft-quoted passage, 'The love of money is the root of all evil,' is frequently misapplied as casting a slur upon money itself and upon those engaged in occupations concerned with its employment. The dictum was, however, intended as a condemnation of greed, selfishness, worldliness, and absorption in gain; its profound truth and seriousness render it in no sense condemnatory of the use of money, which is of as great service to society in the distribution of products as a ship, a railway, or any other instrument subservient to the material needs of man. In many of the remarks of Jesus in the parables and in the gospel narratives reference is made to money in its ordinary uses; in all these cases its practical utility is taken for granted and its economic service is unquestioned.

LITERATURE.—W. S. Jevons, *Money and the Mechanism of Exchange*, London, 1875; J. S. Nicholson, *Treatise on Money, and Essays on Monetary Problems*[3], Edinburgh, 1895; F. A. Walker, *Money in its Relations to Trade and Industry*, London, 1880; H. Withers, *The Meaning of Money*, do. 1909; J. W. Gilbart, *Hist. and Principles of Banking*[3], do. 1837; W. Bagehot, *Lombard Street*, do. 1873, new ed., do. 1910; G. J. G. Goschen, *Theory of the Foreign Exchanges*, ed. do. 1896; G. Clare, *The ABC of Foreign Exchanges*[4], do. 1905.

G. ARMITAGE-SMITH.

MONGOLS.—1. Ethnology and habitat.—Like the Ainus and the Dravidians (*qq.v.*), the Mongols are a race distinctively Asiatic. They fall into three great divisions—Buriats (*q.v.*), Western Mongols (Kalmuks), and Eastern Mongols. The habitat of the Kalmuks extends from the Hoang-ho to the Manich (a tributary of the Don), their special centres being Astrakhan and the Caucasus, Zungaria, N.W. Mongolia, Alashan, N. Tibet, and the Chinese province of Kokonor. The Eastern Mongolians inhabit chiefly Mongolia, the southern portion being divided into a number of tribes, such as the Tumets and Chakhars, while the northern section consists of the more homogeneous Khalkas.

The Mongolian type is best represented by the Kalmuks and the Khalkhas:

> 'Nearly average stature (1m. 63–64); head, sub-brachycephalic (ceph. ind. on the liv. sub. 83); black straight hair, pilous system little developed; the skin of a pale-yellow or brownish hue, prominent cheek-bones, thin straight flattened nose, Mongoloid eyes,' etc. (J. Deniker, *Races of Man*, London, 1901, p. 379).

Another peculiar characteristic of this race is the 'Mongolian spot,' small dark patches of pigmentation, especially in the sacrolumbar region, frequently observable in infants, but disappearing in early childhood. The 'Mongolian spot' is not, however, restricted to the Mongols; it occurs sporadically elsewhere, instances having been noted, *e.g.*, among the modern Indians of Mexico (cf. also Deniker, p. 51).

As a result of migrations, the Mongolian race has spread far beyond its original habitat. It has profoundly affected the Chinese (particularly in the south) and Japanese; in Bengal and Orissa the crossing of Mongolian with Dravidian has given rise to the Mongolo-Dravidian type, and other 'Mongoloid' types appear in the Himālaya region and in the Far East.

The chief Asiatic area occupied by non-Buriat

Mongols (Kalmuks, Khalkas, etc.) is bounded on the north by Siberia, on the south by China, on the west by Russian Turkestan and Chinese Turkestan, and on the east by Manchuria. It forms a high but depressed undulating plateau, roughly 2500 feet in altitude, hemmed in by an immense double or triple chain of forest-covered mountains, known together as the Hingan and Yinshan, on the one side, and by the Altai range and its offshoots on the other. Although the greater portion is Gobi (a Turki word), or 'Great (Desert) Expanse,' and is destitute of rivers sufficiently broad and deep to impede seriously the swooping movements of horsemen, there are plenty of salt lakes (only one of which escapes into Russia by a river), innumerable oases and pasture lands, suitably located sweet-water wells, and even cultivable or forest lands dotted about and available in turn at different seasons of the year to the nomads who know the peculiarities of the country so well. This fact explains how armies of millions can easily move on the simple condition that they possess sufficient cattle, horses, sheep, and camels to drive before or with themselves as food and clothing; nothing else matters, for wood and iron can be picked up by the way at various well-known places, and women with babies can be carried with the tents in huge carts. This vast rim of mountain range nearly all round constitutes a huge watershed, and on the outer side rivers run into Manchuria, Russia, and Turkestan; but the gravelly expanse of Gobi with its parched atmosphere soon causes the sources flowing into the depressed desert portions of Mongolia to dry up or disappear into the sands, so that in many places recourse must be had to rude cisterns or reservoirs, automatically collecting fresh water after each summer storm. The Onon and Kerulon rivers, the valleys of which have during the past 2000 years witnessed the successive rise to political prominence of several obscure tribes, bring the north centre of Mongolia proper into direct water communication with Siberia (*i.e.* Russia) and N. Manchuria (*i.e.* China).

2. Civilization and religion.—Mongol family life has been admirably described in a series of articles written (anonymously) by a Protestant missionary for the *Chinese Recorder* (a Shanghai publication) in 1875. Immovable property is scarcely conceived of, and the idea of personal property and individual rights is almost equally lacking, except in reference to one's horse and saddle, clothing, and weapons. Even one's wife—who, so far as nature allows it, seems to be the absolute equal of her husband—is only a life interest, for all wives (except one's own actual mother) pass over on the death of their temporary possessor, with the felt tent and the stock-pot, to the eldest son, or, failing sons, to brothers, cousins, or uncles. In case of great warlike expeditions, of course, there are temporary aggregations of men, and the modern Mongols, like the Turks and Huns, always have an annual tryst; but as a rule tribes scatter, families scatter, and individuals scatter, so that the *yurtā*, or the felt tent (or *mêng-gu bo*, as the Chinese call it in E. Mongolia), is the sole economical unit. In 1760 the entire Kalmuk nation, four subdivisions, consisted of only 200,000 tents all told, *i.e.* before they were conquered. In the distance, on the prairie or grassy plain north of the Great Wall, one sees one or more black spots like dung-heaps. These turn out on closer inspection to be felt *bo*, firmly attached by long ropes to pegs or other firmer anchorages fixed in the ground. It is the correct thing to make some sound on approaching; otherwise one or more powerful dogs, often of Tibetan breed, may attack the intruder. The tents are composed of thick felts, arranged to withstand the wind and snow. According to wealth or poverty the interior is hung with handsome or shabby stuffs, and the exterior is sometimes additionally protected with Chinese oil-paper or other such impervious material; but severe simplicity is the general rule; all luxury is makeshift. If a man has horses and dogs, or even only one horse and one dog, and maybe works for someone else as a herd, he is a poor man; a rich man may have as many as 1000 or more horses and 100 or more camels (all of the two-humped or Bactrian kind), not to mention sheep and goats (never pigs); but, rich or poor, the mode of life is always the same—rough, strong, home-made clothes, harness, and equipment; one or two trunks to contain treasures and best clothes; a hospitable reception for any traveller, poor or rich; no tables or chairs; and a fixed etiquette as to privacy, precedence, or the right to squat in certain honoured or tabued places. No one who carefully reads all that has been recently written about the eastern and western nomads from the Shilka to the Volga can doubt that in physique, mode of life, and even in basic language, they are and always in historical times have been practically the same people, *i.e.* a congeries of tribes whose national designations have no deeper significance than that from time to time an eponymous hero or a brilliant family, clan, or tribe has succeeded in bringing most other tribes under his or its own name or banner.

With regard to the modern Mongols—especially the Khalkas—who had (sometime before the Manchus seized their opportunity of taming them through Lāmaism and saintly influences) already succumbed to drink and earlier strong religious influences, they may be said to have now entirely lost the ferocity, warlike initiative, and passion for plunder that characterized the conquering hordes of Jenghiz Khan in the early 13th century. Even Jenghiz himself, though a mere shamanist, or casual 'idolater,' and, so far as is known, destitute of any religious training, seems to have been by natural rectitude of character susceptible to ethical influences when not injudiciously thrust upon him; and this quite spontaneously, for he sent for and respectfully consulted a humble Chinese Taoist philosopher who travelled all the way from Shan Tung to Samarqand to advise him as to the humanity of his own warlike proceedings.[1]

The religion of the Kalmuks and of the Eastern Mongols is Lāmaism (*q.v.*); the older Mongol religion, however, was shamanism, which is retained by the Buriats (*q.v.*).

3. Present-day distribution.—When the Chinese Ming dynasty in 1368 sent the Mongol tyrants in Peking back to their steppes, the old division into the Western or right 'wing' and the Eastern or left 'wing'—practically Kalmuk and Khalka—was reverted to by the ejected Mongols, and these two wings were subdivided into the *Djirgughan Tumen*, or 'Six Myriads.' When the Manchus conquered or conciliated the Chakhars and other inner (Eastern) Mongols in 1628–33 (*i.e.* before they became emperors of China in 1644 as well as Manchu emperors), they organized all of them except the Chakhars into six *chogolgan*,[2] or 'leagues' (translated by the Chinese word *mêng*, 'sworn alliance'). These six leagues, four east (Chih Li) and two west (Shan Si), are again subdivided into 24 *aimak*, or 'tribes' (translated by the Chinese word *pu*; this word *aimak* occasionally appears in Chinese Jenghizide history as *aima*, and in Chinese Manchu history occasionally as *aiman*).

[1] See E. Bretschneider, 'Travels of the Taoist Ch'ang Ch'un,' *Chinese Recorder*, v. [1874] 173–199, vi. [1875] 1–22; also 'Traces of Christianity in Mongolia in the XIII century,' by the archimandrite Palladius, *ib.* vi. [1875] 104–114.

[2] W. F. Mayers, *The Chinese Government*, Shanghai, 1878, suggests that, in so doing, the Manchus were continuing the principle of the Six Myriads, and (pending the conquest at a later date of the Khalkas and Kalmuks) were applying it to the Inner Mongols along the Great Wall.

This is not the place to introduce a discussion on language or a long list of native Mongol tribal names; but it may be mentioned as specially significant that the Khartsin tribe of the Chosotu league are the absolutely direct descendants of Jenghiz and Kublai; they now occupy the steppes north of Jêhol (thrice visited in 1869–71 by the present writer).

Besides the 24 tribes of Inner Mongols under their own native *jassaks*, and irregularly subdivided into 49 flags, or banners, there is still a more intimate class of Inner Mongols known as the 'herdsmen,' who are not ruled by their own princes at all, but by the military governors at Tenduc, Kalgan, and Jêhol. The extramural area of which Kalgan (='the gate' in Mongol) is the governing centre is popularly known as Chakhar, a word derived from the leading tribe, called during the Ming dynasty Chakhar, or Chakhan-r. There are also the Mongols of Kokonor, descendants of a collateral branch of Jenghiz's family, with whom have been associated a number of Kalmuk tribes from the west; they also intermarry with the Manchus, but were not entitled, like the Inner Mongols, to style themselves 'cousin.' Besides these main divisions, there are the Tumet tribes of N. Shan Si, the Bargu, the Urianghai, the Mingad, the Jakchin, and other odd remnants mostly of Kalmuk type, which for convenience are ranked among the herdsmen, and are under the administration of one or the other of the Manchu (now Chinese) *tutungs*, or military governors, from Uliassutai in the west to Jêhol in the east.[1]

The Outer Mongols mainly consist of two races—the Khalkas and Kalmuks—between whom there were prolonged and bloody wars until the Manchus (after having subdued the Inner Mongols and China itself) reduced both to complete subjection. Even after the ejection of the Jenghizide dynasty from China, when both classes of Mongols were thrust back upon their deserts, they frequently crossed the desert and fought incessantly between themselves, besides, separately or in unison, making raids upon the Ming empire. The Khalka area is easily recognizable on any map because the four (originally three) tribes or khanates into which they are divided are usually plainly marked as the Tushêtu, Tsetsen, Jassaktu, and Saïnnoïn khanates; the last-named was carved out of the first, during the Ming dynasty, by the Dalai Lāma of Tibet as a reward for services rendered to the Yellow-hats at the expense of the Red. These four Khalka tribes, or khanates, were again subdivided into over 80 flags, or banners, but this arrangement was complicated by two of their banners having been incorporated with the Inner Mongols, whilst, on the other hand, three Kalmuk banners were incorporated with the Khalkas. The other two of the four Khalka khanates used to fall under the high political influence of the Mongol *hutuktu*, or saint, at Urga, who had a Manchu resident to keep things right. A certain proportion of the Kalmuk race was moved to the neighbourhood of Lake Kokonor after the Manchu conquest of 1753–54, and it there falls under the control of the Chinese military governor at Si-ning. These Mongol tribes are divided among themselves; the Kalmuks have their own local saints both in the west and at Kokonor, but the Khalkas, though kinsmen, are almost hereditary enemies. Nor can the Khalkas easily coalesce with the 49 flags or 24 tribes of Inner Mongols. The latter represent the true historical Tata, as the immediate descendants of the Jenghizides were officially styled by the Ming dynasty; after nearly 200 years of warfare with China they joined the Manchus honourably and nearly as equals, for they were never conquered, as the Khalkas and Kalmuks were some generations later. They have always been kindly treated by and have intermarried with the Manchus, some of whose emperors have married pure Mongol women, recognizing them as legitimate empresses of China. When the Republic was first declared in 1912, there was some talk of the Inner Mongols from a racial point of view joining their countrymen, the Khalkas, under the united rule of the rebellious *hutuktu* at Urga, but this uprising was averted by the moral delinquencies of the *hutuktu*, the political acumen of President Yüan, and the lack of sympathy between the pure outer nomads and their inner brethren, who are now by long habit more or less impregnated with Chinese civilization, political privilege, and economic luxury.

LITERATURE.—P. J. Strahlenberg, *Deseription . . . particularly of Russia, Siberia, and Great Tartary*, London, 1738; J. Bell, *Travels from St. Petersburg . . . to divers Parts of Asia*, Glasgow, 1763; P. S. Pallas, *Sammlungen hist. Nachrichten über die mongol. Völkerschaften*, Petrograd, 1776–1801; B. Bergmann, *Nomadische Streifereien unter den Kalmücken*, Riga, 1804–05; I. J. Schmidt, *Forschungen im Gebiete der älteren . . . Bildungsgesch. der Völker Mittelasiens*, Petrograd, 1824; E. R. Huc, *Souvenirs d'un voyage dans la Tartarie, le Thibet et la Chine*, Paris, 1850 (Eng. tr., London, 1852); J. Gilmour, *Among the Mongols*, London, 1883; A. A. Ivanovski, *Mongolen-Torguten*, Moscow, 1893; P. S. Popov, *Report on the Nomads of Mongolia*, Petrograd, 1895 [Russ.]; P. K. Kozlov, *Mongoliya i Kamŭ*, do. 1905–08; G. N. Potanin, *Očerki sěvero-zapadnoi Mongolii*, do. 1881–83 (esp. vol. iv.; cf. also *FLJ* iii. [1885] 312–328); J. Curtin, *Mongols in Russia*, London, 1908, and *Journey in S. Siberia*, do. 1910; A. Pozdněev, *Mongoliya i Mongoly*, i., Petrograd, 1896; J. A. Šiteckij, *Skizzen des Lebens der astrachan. Kalmyken*, Moscow, 1893; J. de Guignes, *Hist. gén. des Huns, des Turcs, des Mongols et des autres Tartares*, Paris, 1756–58; C. d'Ohsson, *Hist. des Mongols*, Amsterdam, 1852; H. H. Howorth, *Hist. of the Mongols*, London, 1876–88; D. Pokotilov, *Ist. vostočnych Mongolov v period dinastii Min*, Petrograd, 1893; L. Cahun, *Introd. à l'hist. de l'Asie*, Paris, 1896; E. Blochet, *Introd. à l'hist. des Mongols de Fadl Allah Rashid ed-Din*, Leyden, 1910; W. Schott, 'Älteste Nachrichten von Mongolen und Tataren,' *ABAW*, 1845; P. Bureau, 'Les Tartares-Khalkas,' *Science Soc.* v. [1888] 392–417, vi. [1889] 67–84, 345–372, vii. [1889] 472–496; A. A. Ivanovski, 'Zur Anthropologie der Mongolen,' *AA* xxiv. [1896] 65–90; F. Birkner, 'Zur Anthropologie der Mongolen,' *Archiv für Rassen- und Gesellschaftsbiologie*, i. [1906] 809–821; D. Banzarov, *Černaya věra ili šamanstvo i Mongolov*, Petrograd, 1891; E. M. Köhler, 'Ein Religionsfest der Mongolen,' *Deut. Rundschau für Geog. und Statistik*, xxii. [1900] 539–551; C. Braig, 'Eine mongol. Kosmologie,' *Philosoph. Jahrb.* ii. [1890] 135–152, 291–306; C. Koehne, 'Recht der Kalmücken,' *ZVRW* ix. [1891] 445–475; A. Pozdněev, 'Kalmykckiya skazki,' *Zapisski vostoč. otděleniya Imp. Russ. Archeolog. Obščestva*, iii. [1889] 307–364, iv. [1890] 321–374, vi. [1892] 1–68, vii. [1893] 1–38, ix. [1895] 1–58, x. [1897] 139–185, and *Mongolskaya chrestomatiya*, Petrograd, 1900; B. Laufer, 'Skizze der mongol. Lit.,' *Keleti Szemle*, viii. [1907] 165–261.

E. H. PARKER.

MONISM.—1. The term.—The term 'monism' was coined by Christian Wolff (1679–1754), and was used by him to denote the philosophical theories which recognized only a single kind of reality, whether physical or psychical, so that he could apply the name 'monists' equally well to the materialists and to the so-called idealists of his age. It is easy to understand why the word in this artificial sense should never come into general use, and in fact it was so employed only sporadically by individual thinkers of the 18th century. In the 19th cent. the term 'monism' came to be used by the disciples of Hegel as designating their own peculiar mode of thought; thus, *e.g.*, K. F. Goeschel, in 1832, published a work entitled, *Der Monismus des Gedankens* ('The Monism of Thought'). In this sense too, however, the term had but a limited usage. In point of fact, it first found a place in current speech as the designation of a philosophical movement closely related to the modern theory of biological evolution, and it was, in particular, the biologist Haeckel and the philo-

[1] See Parker, 'Manchu Relations with Mongolia,' 'Campaigns against the Khalkas and Oelots,' and other papers on this subject in *China Rev.* xv. [1886–87], xvi. [1888–89]; also a paper on 'Kalmuck Organization,' *ib.* xxiii. [1898–99].

logist Schleicher who brought the word into general currency. In Germany the philosophical movement referred to has found concrete expression in a 'monistic society' (*Monistenbund*), which has drawn to itself a considerable body of adherents. Nevertheless, certain other applications of the term still maintain their ground. In especial, the name 'monism' is given to the philosophical theory which, instead of subordinating the soul to the body, or the body to the soul, interprets them as equivalent aspects of a single fundamental process, and on this ground constantly refers each to the other. Of monism in this sense Spinoza is generally regarded as the leading exponent. Finally, taking the term in its widest sense, we might apply it to every mode of thought which seeks to transcend the distinction between the physical and the psychical, and to reach an ultimate unity. The fact that these various significations are often mingled together in common usage has led to great confusion and much unprofitable controversy.

2. Monism as expressing an inherent need of the mind.—In its widest sense monism is the expression of a demand which no philosophy and no religion can in the last resort evade. The human mind at length refuses to allow the real to fall apart into the irreconcilable opposites of body and soul, of nature and spirit; and every system of thought must ultimately arrive at some kind of unity. In this sense Christianity itself is a monism—a spiritual monism—since it traces all reality to the divine Spirit. In the philosophical realm, however, monism usually stands for the Spinozistic view, which recognizes an exact correspondence between extension and thought, the visible and the invisible, finds the same laws and forces to work in each, and interprets the order and connexion of thought as identical with the order and connexion of things (Spinoza, *Eth.* ii. prop. 7: 'ordo et connexio idearum idem est ac ordo et connexio rerum'). This view has the advantage of providing a solution of the simplest kind for a problem which cost Spinoza's predecessors much trouble—the problem, namely, of the interaction of soul and body; for, on this theory, according to which the two series of facts proceed side by side quite independently, and yet remain ever in mutual harmony, there is no interaction at all, the specific data of either series being explained by the relations of that series alone. Modern psychology, in following up this theory, has propounded the doctrine of 'psychophysical parallelism,' and strives to apply the doctrine to mental and bodily processes in detail. As this whole mode of thought apparently permits each aspect to develop its own distinctive character, without severing it or keeping it apart from the other, it has proved remarkably attractive to the human mind.

3. Its tendency to one-sidedness.—Its power of attraction, however, lasts only as long as we keep to the general outlines of the problem, and every attempt to give the idea a more precise application encounters great difficulties, and results in giving the preponderance to one or other of the two sides: either the physical becomes predominant, and the psychical a mere reflexion or concomitant of it, or else the psychical is assigned the superior position and the physical becomes simply its outward expression or a means to its ends. Thus monism inevitably breaks up into two forms—an idealistic and a naturalistic—and there never has been, nor can there ever be, a pure monism, *i.e.* a monism maintaining a perfect equipoise between body and spirit. The clearest exemplification of this is found in Spinoza himself; a closer scrutiny of his thought shows that he is never purely monistic, but always leans more either to naturalism or to idealism—the former in the groundwork, the latter in the consummation, of his system, as appears more especially in his *Ethics*. In the beginning of that work the supreme factor, the core of the real, is nature, while psychical life is a mere representation of the natural process, and simply follows its order; at the close, however, this naturalism is transmuted into an idealism, for Spinoza's doctrine that all reality is supported and integrated by a divine life, and that nature only moulds that life into visible form, as well as the doctrine that man is capable of assimilating the whole universe, and of attaining infinity and eternity by the intellectual love of God ('amor dei intellectualis'), cannot be called anything but idealism. Whatever Spinoza may have meant, he certainly did not reach a pure monism; and the subsequent development of philosophical thought shows that the monistic movement always inclines either to the one side or to the other.

(*a*) *Idealistic monism.*—The classical period of German literature was dominated by an idealistic monism, and, in particular, Goethe gave his full adherence to the view. In the philosophy of the period, this type of idealism found powerful support in Schelling's philosophy of identity. Yet, while in art and philosophical thought the outer and inner worlds were made closely dependent upon each other and were firmly interlinked, they were not regarded as of co-ordinate authority; on the contrary, the universe of reality seems here to be pervaded by an inner life, and the union of the visible and the invisible world is brought about upon the basis of the spirit. It was, however, strongly insisted upon that the inward life cannot come to its own, or realize itself perfectly, without in some way embodying itself and taking perceptible form in the external. Here we have the genesis of an æsthetic and philosophical monism of the idealistic type.

(*b*) *Naturalistic monism.*—On the other hand, the monism frequently associated with the modern theory of evolution exhibits a naturalistic tendency. It regards the physical world as the essential substance of the real, and differs from materialism only in the circumstance that it conceives the psychical, not as derived from physical processes, but as present from the first even in the most minute elements of the material world, and as forming an essential constituent therein. Even so, however, the psychical is not thought of as attaining to independence and spontaneity; it has no powers or laws peculiarly its own, but is in every respect subordinate to, and wholly interwoven with, external nature; nor again, on this theory, is human life endowed with any special significance or accorded any distinctive vocation. It is true that this naturalistic monism, in its theory of practical life, recognizes the ideal ends of the Good, the True, and the Beautiful, and undertakes the task of furthering them. But it can do so only by contravening its own naturalistic principles, and thus it comes to exhibit the fatal inconsequence of theoretically recognizing unity as its supreme aim while in practice falling into an absolute contradiction between thought and action.

The progress that this theory of naturalistic monism, in spite of its inherent flaws, is making in contemporary life, in Germany at least, is due to the concurrence of various causes. Nature, formerly so often sadly ignored, has come to mean more and more for the modern mind. Not only does she reveal ever more fully the delicate texture of her being, but in yielding herself to the practical arts she has added vastly to our command of the environment. The importance of the material factor for human well-being is much more widely recognized in modern civilization than was once the case. The result of these various developments is that

Nature now exercises a much more profound influence even upon our thoughts and convictions than she formerly did. This does not, of course, lead necessarily to a naturalistic philosophy, nor was there any great danger of such an issue as long as high spiritual ends held sway among human beings and dominated their common efforts. But such spiritual ends have been, if not entirely lost sight of, yet largely obscured, in the development of modern life; with regard to the ultimate questions of human existence mankind is now in a state of grave disunion, and common effort has given place to widely divergent tendencies. Amid so much diversity regarding the content of the spiritual life, the longing for a single all-embracing theory of existence readily attracts men to the path of naturalism, which proffers what seems to be the simplest and most intelligible solution of the great problem. In reality, therefore, it is the defects of the opposite view that here lend strength to monism.

Another factor which—in Germany at least—operates in favour of naturalistic monism is found in the perplexities that have emerged in the province of religion and the Church. That religion at the present day bristles with problems, and that the minds of men differ widely in the treatment of them, are facts that cannot be denied even by those for whom religion is a supreme interest. In Germany, however, the situation is greatly aggravated by the intimate relations between Church and State, since in such circumstances the doctrines of religion readily come to be felt as a restraint imposed by the State upon thought; and, where large numbers are already alienated from religion, or in dubiety regarding it, there is a natural tendency to look with sympathy upon movements that set forth with perfect candour the conflict of ideals, especially the conflict between natural science and the teaching of the Church, and seek to bring it to a decisive settlement. From this position the monist may regard himself as a champion of freedom and truth.

4. Its function and limitations.—When we have in this way explained the spread of naturalistic monism, we have at the same time shown its limitations. It possesses a certain power and has also a degree of rightful authority as long as it maintains a critical attitude and provides incentives to special tendencies of thought; and this condition is fulfilled when it insists upon a higher recognition of the natural factor in human life, and demands that the assured results of modern science shall not be ignored by those who speak in the name of religion. Its weakness, again, shows itself in the positive aspect of its work, and in its claim to serve as a guide to human life and to satisfy the human soul. For such ends it has, in truth, nothing to offer but an intellectual interpretation of things—an interpretation which purports, by improving our conceptions of nature and by showing that man forms part of nature, to be able to supply the human heart with powerful impulses and endow it with happiness. But between ends and means, between claim and achievement, there is a wide disparity. The scientific procedure of monism, moreover, suffers from the defect of confusing natural science with the philosophy of nature, and of too rashly transforming the results of natural science into principles of the cosmos, while giving no recognition at all to the peculiar character of spiritual life or the process of universal history. But, whatever judgment we may pass upon this modern monism, it is certainly a notable feature in the life of the present day.

LITERATURE.—A. Bain, *Mind and Body*[2], London, 1873; R. Eisler, *Geschichte des Monismus*, Leipzig, 1910; R. Eucken, *Main Currents of Modern Thought*, Eng. tr., London, 1912; A. Forel, *Gehirn und Seele*[11], Leipzig, 1910; C. Lloyd Morgan, 'Three Aspects of Monism,' in *Monist*, iv. [1894] 321; G. J. Romanes, *Mind and Motion and Monism*, London, 1895; W. Ostwald, *Vorlesungen über Naturphilosophie*[3], Leipzig, 1905, *Monistische Sonntagspredigten*, Berlin, 1911 ff.; J. Wendland, *Monismus in alter und neuer Zeit*, Basel, 1908; and esp. E. Haeckel, *Natürliche Schöpfungsgeschichte*, Berlin, 1868, [10]1902, Eng. tr.[4], London, 1892, *Anthropogenie*, Leipzig, 1874, [5]1903, Eng. tr., *The Evolution of Man*, London, 1905, *Der Monismus als Band zwischen Religion und Wissenschaft*, Bonn, 1893, Eng. tr., London, 1894, *Die Welträthsel*, Bonn, 1899, Eng. tr., *The Riddle of the Universe*, London, 1900.

R. EUCKEN.

MONKEY.—See ANIMALS.

MONOLATRY AND HENOTHEISM.

MONOLATRY AND HENOTHEISM.—A whole group of words, some of them classical, are compounded with μόνος as a prefix. Ecclesiastical usage added not a few others—*e.g.*, 'monogamy,' marriage only once, re-marriage after the death of one's wife being forbidden, 'Monophysites,' 'Monotheletes.' To these was added, in modern times, 'monotheism' (*q.v.*); this term was touched with ambiguity, since it was sometimes a synonym for unitarianism. Last of all, apparently by Julius Wellhausen,[1] 'monolatry' was coined to express not belief in the sole existence of one god, but restriction of worship to one object of trust and loyalty, although other races might admittedly have other supernatural helpers.

If the first half of the word shows it to be akin to monotheism, its affinities on the other side are with idolatry (see IMAGES AND IDOLS). Christian usage, from the Bible downwards, vacillates between interpreting idolatry as image-worship and as worship of 'false' gods in the sense of non-existent beings. In the Roman Catholic Church the distinction is made between *latria*, worship paid only to the Persons of the Trinity, and *dulia*, veneration of the saints (even the Blessed Virgin receives not *latria*, but *hyperdulia*). Both in the Roman and in the Greek Churches *adoratio* (προσκύνησις) or *dulia* is rendered to images or icons of the Divine Persons and saints, as well as to the Gospels, relics, etc. (cf. Denzinger[11], nos. 302, 337, 342, 985 f.).

Unhappily, there is another term which habitually presents itself as a synonym for monolatry and as a rival—henotheism. This word was coined by F. Max Müller while under the influence of Schelling. In a review of Renan, entitled 'Semitic Monotheism,' and contributed to the *Times* in 1860 (reprinted in *Chips from a German Workshop*, i. [1867], and again in *Selected Essays*, ii. [1881]), Müller, while repudiating Renan's theory of a monotheistic instinct peculiar to the Semites, finds at the basis of all religion a crude or vague faith in the divine, not yet articulated either into polytheism or into monotheism, and calls this 'henotheism.' As thus defined on its first emergence, henotheism is a hypothetical construction, belonging to a period earlier than recorded history. E. von Hartmann[2] is fairly in line with this when he speaks of henotheism as 'the original nature-religion'; as the 'indifference of mono-, poly-, and pan-theism'; as the 'identity of essence of all the gods.'

Much greater importance, however, attaches to Müller's later usage, introduced in a 'Lecture on the Vedas' of 1865 (also reprinted in *Chips*, i. and *Essays*, ii.). Here we have a pair of synonymous terms—'henotheism' and 'kathenotheism'—which refer to a well-marked historical phenomenon. Study of the Vedas had impressed Max Müller with the way in which each deity, out of a large recognized pantheon, is treated in turn as if the supreme or even the sole god. While Indian religion offers the classical illustration of

[1] T. H. Huxley (*Nineteenth Cent.*, xix. [1886] 495) is quoted by *OED* in this sense; Robertson Smith is also quoted (*OTJC*, Edinburgh, 1881, p. 273; 'natural . . . Semitic monolatry').

[2] As summarized in O. Pfleiderer, *Phil. of Religion*, Eng. tr., London and Edinburgh, 1886–88, iii. 19.

this attitude, it recurs elsewhere. Max Müller recognizes it in Greece, Italy, and Germany (*HL*, 1878, London, 1879, p. 286), as well as in Finland (*Contributions to Science of Mythology*, London, 1897, p. 264). Both these books speak of 'henotheism or kathenotheism' (*HL*, p. 271), 'kathenotheism or by a shortened name henotheism' (*Contributions to Science of Mythology*, p. 140). When P. Asmus describes the whole of 'Indo-germanic' religion as henotheistic,[1] because of the alleged tendency of all its divinities to pass into each other, he is inspired by Max Müller's second usage, though he distorts it.

It may seem to us that Müller has himself been guilty of a certain confusion. But the worst confusion of all is introduced by Pfleiderer (*loc. cit.*), without regard to either of Müller's definitions, and in conscious opposition to Hartmann and Asmus. He recognizes—distinctively among the Semites—not, of course, a monotheistic instinct, but a 'national or relative monotheism which in the case of Israel was the porch to pure monotheism' (iii. 34 n.); and this he calls henotheism. We cannot wonder if high authorities have proposed to suppress the term 'henotheism' because of its ambiguity (*e.g.*, J. Estlin Carpenter, in *EBr*[11] xxiii. 72[a]; H. Oldenberg, *Rel. des Veda*, Berlin, 1894, p. 101, note 1; E. W. Hopkins, 'Henotheism in the Rig Veda,' in *Class. Studies in Honour of H. Drisler*, New York, 1894, pp. 75–83, *Religions of India*, Boston, 1895, p. 139 f.; A. A. Macdonell, *Vedic Mythology*, Strassburg, 1897, p. 16 f., with references to earlier literature).

'Kathenotheism' is regarded by Carpenter as already extinct. The word is cited by E. B. Tylor (*PC* ii. 354), but has certainly found little favour.

One might have wished to see 'kathenotheism' and 'monolatry' spared, as names for two very different approaches towards monotheism, while the word 'henotheism' might either be wholly suppressed or else generalized to include both kathenotheism and monolatry, together with any other workings of monotheistic tendency that fall short of monotheism properly so called. There is much significance for theists in irrepressible movements towards recognition of one great help, one supreme power, one sovereign goodness.

Allan Menzies's distinction (*Hist. of Religion*[4], London, 1911, ch. iv. p. 55; he has been good enough to confirm or explain his meaning in a private letter) between henotheism and kathenotheism follows Pfleiderer (and makes henotheism cover exactly the phenomena of monolatry). But any suggestion that this distinction is Max Müller's own must be repelled. Cf., further, Müller's *Physical Religion*, 1891 (Glasgow Gifford Lecture of 1890), p. 181 n.: 'It is to be regretted that other scholars should have used the name henotheistic in a different sense from that which I assigned to it. Nothing causes so much confusion as the equivocal use of a technical term [but is Müller himself quite clear of blame?], and the framer of a new term has generally had the right of defining it.'

The classical region of monolatry is the religion of Israel, whose phenomena, as we saw, probably suggested the name. The First Commandment (of the greater Decalogue, Ex 20 or Dt 5) crystallizes the requirement and carries it into the moral region. Kindred Western Semitic races—possibly other races too—may have known something similar, upon its lower side. Moab or Ammon or Edom may have been loyal to the tribal god in mere patriotic prejudice. Loyalty to the God of righteousness, in Israel or in all lands under heaven, means vastly more. The only real justification for monolatrous behaviour is the monotheistic fact. It is indeed true that 'the distinction between monolatry and monotheism' is often a narrow one (art. GOD [Biblical and Christian], vol. vi. p. 253). It is also true that there will be an element of monolatry in religion as long as earthly conditions endure. Human faith—theistic, or fully Christian—is no bare recognition of facts which exist independently of our attitude. Faith is choice of God and a pouring out of our humble all in His service.

[1] Pfleiderer, iii. 20.

LITERATURE.—Besides the references given above, see art. GOD (Biblical and Christian), noting both 'monolatry' (vol. vi. pp. 251[b], 252[a], and 253[b]) and 'henotheism' (pp. 252[ab], 275[b], 276[a], 277[a], 283[b], 289[b]). The student must carefully observe in what sense either word is employed by the different writers. 'Kathenotheism' is not employed at all in the articles.

ROBERT MACKINTOSH.

MONOPHYSITISM.—I. Before the Monophysites.—The name 'Monophysites,' as denoting a party in the Christian Church, ought in strict usage to be applied only to those who regarded as erroneous the doctrine formulated as a standard by the Synod of Chalcedon (A.D. 451), *i.e.* the doctrine of the two natures (δύο φύσεις), divine and human, in the one person (ὑπόστασις or πρόσωπον) of Jesus Christ, and who took as the watchword of their faith 'the one nature of the incarnate Word of God' (μία φύσις τοῦ θεοῦ λόγου σεσαρκωμένου). The doctrine of the single nature of Christ, however, did not then emerge for the first time, and we begin by narrating the history of Monophysitism prior to the rise of the Monophysites proper.

The formula μία φύσις is first found among the Arians (see art. ARIANISM, vol. i. p. 775 ff.). **Lucian of Antioch** and his followers had spoken of the one divine or, more properly, semi-divine nature (φύσις or ὑπόστασις, the two terms not being as yet distinguished) of the Logos, in which inhered liability to suffering (πάθη) and limited knowledge (ἀγνοεῖν). **Eudoxius of Constantinople** († A.D. 370) acknowledged the Word made flesh but not become man (σαρκωθέντα, οὐκ ἐνανθρωπήσαντα), who had not assumed a human soul, but became flesh in order to manifest Himself to us as God through the flesh as through a curtain; it was therefore quite wrong to speak of two natures (δύο φύσεις), since the Word was not man in the full sense (τέλειος ἄνθρωπος), but God in the flesh (θεὸς ἐν σαρκί), *i.e.* viewed as a whole, one composite nature (μία τὸ ὅλον κατὰ σύνθεσιν φύσις). **Apollinaris of Laodicea** (see art. APOLLINARISM, vol. i. p. 606 ff.) expressed himself in similar terms, though in a line of thought directly contrary to that of Arianism. It was his firm conviction that the perfect God (θεὸς τέλειος) had descended upon the earth, and in this belief he felt that he was at one with the Nicæans as opposed to the Arians; but no less decisively he maintained also that two complete entities cannot become a unity (δύο τέλεια ἓν γενέσθαι οὐ δύναται), and thus that the union of perfect deity with complete manhood is impossible (εἰ ἀνθρώπῳ τελείῳ συνήφθη θεὸς τέλειος, δύο ἂν ἦσαν). Hence Apollinaris, in writing to the emperor Jovian, expressed himself as follows:

'We acknowledge, not two natures in the one Son, one worshipped and the other not worshipped (μίαν προσκυνητὴν καὶ μίαν ἀπροσκύνητον), but one nature of the Divine Word (μίαν φύσιν τοῦ θεοῦ λόγου), incarnate, and worshipped together with His flesh in one worship (σεσαρκωμένην καὶ προσκυνουμένην μετὰ τῆς σαρκὸς αὐτοῦ μιᾷ προσκυνήσει)' ('Επιστολὴ πρὸς 'Ιοβιανὸν τὸν βασιλέα [J. Dräseke, 'Apollinarios von Laodicea,' *TU* vii. [1892] 3, 4, p. 341; H. Lietzmann, 'Apollinaris von Laodicea und seine Schule,' *TU* i. [1904] 1, p. 250]).

This, however, involves a deification of the flesh, and it is but a short step to the inference that all the conditions which rendered the Logos liable to suffering during His earthly course are in the flesh brought into connexion with the divine nature (παθητὴν εἶναι τὴν τοῦ θεοῦ θεότητα).

For a time Christian theology was in danger of surrendering to this illusory logic, as was the case, *e.g.*, when it undertook the task of coming to terms with the Antiochene school (see art. ANTIOCHENE THEOLOGY, vol. i. p. 584 ff.). The Christological interest of the Antiochenes, in contradistinction to that of the Apollinarians, culminated in the view that a perfect humanity was retained along with perfect deity in Christ. These theologians, accordingly, spoke of two natures (δύο φύσεις or δύο ὑποστάσεις) in the one Christ—since for their conceptions, too, φύσις and ὑπόστασις were equivalent terms—and thus seemed to endanger the unity of His person. Their leading opponent, **Cyril of Alexandria,** was supremely concerned to maintain this unity, but he did it only by leaving out of account every element of human personality in the Saviour. According to Cyril, we must assume that two natures, the divine and the human, existed in Christ before He became man, and that at His becoming man these two natures were fused together in an indissoluble unity (συνέλευσις δύο φύσεων καθ' ἕνωσιν ἀδιάσπαστον ἀσυγχύτως καὶ ἀτρέπτως), and could thus be distinguished only in theory (θεωρίᾳ μόνῃ). To denote this divine-human nature Cyril likewise availed himself of the formula μία φύσις τοῦ θεοῦ λόγου σεσαρκωμένη; he borrowed it from a confessional work of Apollinaris — the Περὶ τῆς σαρκώσεως τοῦ θεοῦ λόγου (cf. *ERE* i. 608), of which, it is true, he believed that Athanasius was the author. We can see how closely he approaches Apollinaris at this point. The Alexandrian, nevertheless, did not proceed to the conclusions drawn by the Laodicean, who rejected the view that the Saviour had assumed a complete humanity and a ψυχὴ λογική. To Cyril the formula remained a religious postulate, and he used all the resources of an artificial logic to give it also a theological validity. Here he takes φύσις simply as a κοινόν; the divine-human nature, however, is something new in relation both to the divine nature and to human nature, and the properties of these, viz. sovereign majesty and passibility respectively, may be in mutual communication in Christ without forcing us to assume that there is any blending of them. In this way, accordingly, two natures go to form one (ἐκ δύο φύσεων μία φύσις [or ὑπόστασις]).

To follow such intricate theories was a task beyond the power of simple and unlearned minds. It is true that, of the subtleties of Cyril's discriminative logic, **Eutyches,** the aged archimandrite of a monastery near Constantinople, had come to a knowledge of the idea expressed in the phrase μετὰ τὴν ἕνωσιν μία φύσις, but precisely on that ground he would not grant that Christ's bodily form was identical in character with the human (ὁμοούσιος ἡμῖν); at the local Synod of Constantinople in 448, addressing the tribunal of bishops, he declared, οὐκ εἶπον σῶμα ἀνθρώπου τὸ τοῦ θεοῦ σῶμα; and, although in the course of the proceedings he further modified his statements, he was condemned on the ground of the Docetic tendencies which he could not conceal (see art. DOCETISM, vol. iv. p. 832 ff.). Thenceforward, in the memory of the Church the name of Eutyches was one of reproach, and Eutychianism was stigmatized as heresy. Another group who would not renounce the idea of δύο φύσεις μετὰ τὴν σάρκωσιν were those who in their deepest hearts assented to the formula μία φύσις τοῦ θεοῦ λόγου σεσαρκωμένη defended by Cyril. For them it served to ease the situation that a distinction was now being made between the terms φύσις and ὑπόστασις. This distinction, in fact, soon came to be quite as important as that between οὐσία and ὑπόστασις in the doctrine of the Trinity. In the development of that doctrine the latter distinction had served to make intelligible how three divine persons (ὑποστάσεις) could participate equally in the divine being (οὐσία); and in like manner it was now thought possible to explain how two natures (φύσεις), the divine and the human, could equally inhere in one person (ὑπόστασις), viz. Jesus Christ.

The theologians of the West, from the days of Tertullian, had been accustomed to speak of the 'duplex status, non confusus, sed coniunctus, in una persona, deus et homo Jesus.' What they called *natura* (*substantia*) found an equivalent expression in φύσις, and *persona* could be rendered by ὑπόστασις. In reality, therefore, the best solution of the problem seemed to be that formulated by Pope **Leo** in his letter to Flavian of Constantinople (dated 449; the so-called Τόμος Λέοντος, *Ep.* xxviii., 'ad Flavianum') as follows:

'Salva proprietate utriusque naturae et substantiae et in unam coeunte personam suscepta est a maiestate humilitas, a virtute infirmitas . . . agit utraque forma (μορφή) cum alterius communione, quod proprium est . . . propter hanc unitatem personae in utraque natura intelligendam et Filius hominis dicitur descendisse de coelo . . . et rursus Filius Dei crucifixus dicitur et sepultus' (*PL* liv. 755 ff.).

What was subsequently termed the *communicatio idiomatum* (ἀντίδοσις τῶν ἰδιωμάτων) thus already finds clear expression in Leo's words. Nevertheless Gibbon is quite right in saying:

'An invisible line was drawn between the heresy of Apollinaris and the faith of St. Cyril; and the road to paradise, a bridge as sharp as a razor, was suspended over the abyss by the master-hand of the theological artist' (*Decline and Fall of the Roman Empire*, v. 126).

In point of fact, while Western theology thus avoided the extreme of Apollinarism, it was menaced by the spectre of the Antiochene peril. Here too it could be said: 'incidit in Scyllam qui vult vitare Charybdin,' and at all events the doctrine of the two natures in one person (Dyophysitism, or, grammatically more correct, Diphysitism) not only failed to compose perturbed minds, but actually fanned the latent elements of controversy into flame. In this controversy the disputants, moving on the lines of Cyril (and Apollinaris), went back to the watch-word μία φύσις; now, however, they spoke, not of the one incarnate nature of the divine word, but of the one nature of the incarnate word (σεσαρκωμένου, not σεσαρκωμένη), the intention being to indicate decisively that the point involved was not μία φύσις merely μετὰ τὴν σάρκωσιν. We now proceed to trace the history of this Monophysitism properly so called.

2. The Council of Chalcedon and its results.—After Cyril's death in 444 the episcopal throne of Alexandria was occupied by **Dioscurus,** a man destitute of theological learning and possessed with a more daring ambition than even his predecessor. His great aim was to secure the supremacy of Alexandria, and the Alexandrian theology, in the Eastern Church, and, as long as he had the ear of the emperor, and Rome did not contest his claims, he seemed to be on the fair way to attain his end. At his instigation Theodosius II. summoned a general Synod to meet in Ephesus in 449 (shortly afterwards stigmatized by Leo I. as *latrocinium*, σύνοδος λῃστρική, 'the Robber Synod'). Here, with the assistance of the civil power, and the physical violence of fanatical Egyptian monks, he succeeded in giving full effect to his claims; and, while Eutyches, who enjoyed the protection of Dioscurus, was restored to the communion of the Church, Flavian of Constantinople, Domnus of Antioch, and Theodoret of Cyrus were deposed. The triumph of Dioscurus, however, was but short-lived, for not only did he damage his case by his ruthless dealings, but he committed the blunder of irritating Leo by refusing, in spite of the protest of the Roman legate, to have the *Epistula ad Flavianum* read at the Council. The result was a swift revulsion. The emperor died on 28th July 450, and his sister Pulcheria, the moving spirit of the administration, had even before his death come to recognize that the transference of the ecclesiastical centre of gravity from the capital to Alexandria, and the consequent liberation of the Church from political control, might be attended with the gravest consequences. As empress, with the acquiescence of her husband, the military commander Marcian, who was little interested in ecclesiastical or doctrinal affairs, she actively promoted a plan of co-operating with Leo to put an end to the theological dispute at a great assembly of the Church and thus to restore the ecclesiastical balance in the East.

To achieve this desirable end was the task of the fifth Ecumenical Council, held in 451 at **Chalcedon** in the vicinity of Byzantium. The deposition of Dioscurus, as it could quite well be justified on grounds of ecclesiastical polity, was effected without difficulty. The demand that Leo's doctrinal letter should be accorded the authority of a symbol, however, was resisted with the utmost tenacity by a majority of the members. After protracted discussions the Council at length agreed—not, indeed, without menaces from the throne—upon a formulary designed to make for reconciliation, although, as a matter of fact, it involved, in its most decisive passage, a rejection of the Cyrillian tradition. The formulary, which was carried on 22nd Oct. 451, starts from a recognition of the Councils of Nicæa (325), Constantinople (381), and Ephesus (431), and reproduces the Nicene and the so-called Nicæno-Constantinopolitan creed; it then affirms that Cyril's letters to Nestorius and the Orientals, as well as Leo's *Epistle to Flavian*, have been adopted as attestations of the true faith. It next proceeds to the confession of belief in Jesus Christ as perfect God and perfect man, consubstantial with the Father according to His deity, consubstantial with us according to His humanity, in two natures (*ἐν δύο φύσεσιν*, not *ἐκ δύο φύσεων* as in portions of the literary tradition), without confusion or change, without division or separation (*ἀσυγχύτως, ἀτρέπτως, ἀδιαιρέτως, ἀχωρίστως*). The confession ends with a statement already quoted from Leo's letter, now rendered as follows:

> *τῆς τῶν φύσεων διαφορᾶς ἀνῃρημένης διὰ τὴν ἕνωσιν, σωζομένης δὲ μᾶλλον τῆς ἰδιότητος ἑκατέρας φύσεως καὶ εἰς ἓν πρόσωπον καὶ μίαν ὑπόστασιν συντρεχούσης.*

A decree, promulgated (7th Feb. 452) by the two emperors Marcian and Valentinus III., imposed severe penalties upon all who should henceforth dispute in public regarding the faith; offending clergy and army officers should be deprived respectively of their priestly and military status, and others proceeded against by law. Dioscurus was exiled to Gangra in Paphlagonia, where he died in 454.

The results of the Council were not long in manifesting themselves. In *Palestine* an active revolt broke out among the monks. Juvenal, bishop of Jerusalem, who had become prominent at Ephesus (449) as an energetic partisan of Dioscurus, had at Chalcedon, in fear of a diminution of his ecclesiastical power, deserted the Alexandrian and his protégé Eutyches, and had also accepted the formula, taking part, indeed, in its final revision. By this defection he lost the confidence of a large and influential body of monks in Palestine, who elected the monk Theodosius as bishop in opposition to him. The spiritual leader of the insurgents was Peter the Iberian, monk and bishop of Mayuma, the port of Gaza. The rebellious monks found a patroness of high rank in the empress-dowager Eudocia, then resident in Jerusalem. It is told of one of these fanatics that, when Leo's *Epistle* was brought to him, he took it to the tombs of the Fathers and asked whether he should accept it or not, and that a voice cried from the tomb:

> 'Cursed be the ungodly Leo, robber of souls, as his name signifies; cursed be his profane *Tomus*; cursed also be Marcian and the ungodly Pulcheria; cursed be Chalcedon and its Symbol and all who yield acceptance to it; cursed be he who acknowledges two natures in Christ, the Son of God, after the union' (E. Renaudot, *Hist. patriarcharum Alexandrinorum Jacobitarum*, Paris, 1713, p. 120).

This wild outburst of hate expresses most appositely the state of feeling then prevalent in Palestine. By A.D. 453, however, the movement was suppressed for the time by military measures.

In *Egypt* the situation was still more troublesome. A certain Proterius was forcibly thrust by the government upon the Alexandrians as bishop in place of Dioscurus. On the accession of the emperor Leo I. (457–474), the presbyter Timotheus Aelurus (*i.e.* 'the Weasel'), who had been on friendly terms with Cyril and was known as a rigid Monophysite, was raised to the episcopal throne by methods of sheer violence. At Easter, 457, Proterius was murdered by the populace in the baptistry of the cathedral church, while Timotheus purged the Egyptian sees of Diphysites, and pronounced the anathema upon Chalcedon ('the Synod,' as it now comes to be called in the sources). Timotheus held his position until 460, when, after fierce conflicts, he was driven from Alexandria and banished to Gangra; he was subsequently sent to Cherson, and there devoted himself to the composition of a 'Refutation of the doctrine laid down at the Synod of Chalcedon,' a work which only recently (1908) came to light in an Armenian translation.

The patriarchate of *Antioch* was likewise kept in a state of unrest by long protracted dissensions. Here the presbyter Petrus Fullo (*Γναφεύς*, 'the Fuller'), who in no long time supplanted Bishop Martyrius, zealously opposed the teaching of the Council, and contended for the doctrine that God had been crucified (*ὅτι θεὸς ἐσταυρώθη*). To the liturgy he added the singing of the Trisagion (Is 6^3) supplemented by the phrase *ὁ σταυρωθεὶς δι' ἡμᾶς*; and he also introduced the 'Credo' (the Nicene) into the Mass, probably with a view to emphasizing his opposition to the Chalcedonian formula, as also, however, to Eutychianism. But his tenure of the see did not last long, for in 471 the emperor Leo ordered him to be deposed. The imperial government thus found itself confronted by a serious task. On the one hand, it was a matter of urgency to preserve unity between East and West, between Byzantium and Rome, and this could be done only if there was no deflexion from the lines marked out at Chalcedon; on the other, those in the East whose dissatisfaction and resentment were due to the Council had to be restrained, pacified, and, if possible, reconciled to what had been done. The emperors Zeno (474–491) and Anastasius (491–498) exerted all their energies to establish ecclesiastical equilibrium in the East, but they failed altogether in the task of maintaining peace with Rome at the same time. A proceeding of signal importance was the attempt of Zeno (482) to gain acceptance for a new formulary, the so-called *Henotikon*, in place of the Chalcedonian symbol. The Henotikon was designed to give emphatic expression to what was common to all parties, and accordingly it recognized the Councils of Nicæa, Constantinople, and Ephesus as witnesses to the faith, disclaimed Nestorius and Eutyches, and condemned every one who 'now or ever, at Chalcedon or elsewhere, thought or thinks otherwise.' The formulæ expressing the doctrine of the natures of Christ were adroitly kept in the background, so that every cause of offence might be removed. In spite of all, however, the project of the emperor failed of complete success. It is true that Acacius, the court-patriarch of Constantinople, and Petrus Mongus (*i.e.* 'the Stammerer'), who now occupied the episcopal chair of Alexandria instead of Timotheus Aelurus, worked straightforwardly for the union of the warring factions, but the policy of reconciliation was repudiated by the uncompromising Monophysites, especially in Egypt, where the extremists (*ἀκέφαλοι*) actually severed themselves from the rest of their party. On the other hand, the convinced Diphysites, including the Acœmete monks of Constantinople, bitterly resented the virtual repudiation of Chalcedon. The most serious result was the rupture of good relations with Rome. This was due in part, no doubt, to the dogmatic problem, but certainly not less to jealousy of the ever-growing ascendancy of the Constantinopolitan bishop as 'ecumenical patriarch'—a title that now begins to gain currency. Thus the rupture of communion between East and West which was brought about in 484 by Felix III. of Rome presents itself as the outcome of an inner necessity. That ecclesiastic excommunicated Acacius, and demanded that in the *causæ Dei* the emperor should subordinate his own will to that of Christ's priests. The two communions remained apart for thirty-five years. The first overtures for peace were made by the emperor Anastasius in negotiations with Pope Hormisdas, the proposal of calling another general synod being taken as a basis; but the demands of the Roman pontiff, who insisted upon the recognition of Chalcedon and the condemnation of the now long deceased Acacius, brought the negotiations to an end. It was not till the accession of Justin I. (518–527), who left the administration of affairs to his nephew Justinian, that the hour of re-union struck. To win Rome seemed well worth a sacrifice; and all Rome's conditions were accepted, the name of Acacius, as well as those of the emperors Zeno and Anastasius, being removed from the diptychs of the Church.

This renewal of amity with Rome, purchased at so great a cost, carried with it, of course, a complete rupture with the Monophysites. During the reign of Anastasius the latter had gradually won a position of greater influence in Church politics. Anastasius too, no doubt, tried to steer a course in line with the Henotikon, but his own Monophysite convictions tempted him, especially towards the close of his reign, to show an imprudent complaisance to the more fiery and impetuous spirits in the Monophysite camp, and it is not without good cause that his name stands in the Monophysite calendar of saints. The aggressive movement of the malcontents began in Syria, where the Monophysites, under the leadership of Severus of Antioch and Philoxenus of Hierapolis (cf. § 3), gained an ascendancy over the Henoticists. At the Synod of Tyre (513, or, more probably, 515) they renounced the Council of Chalcedon, and thus publicly proclaimed their repudiation of the policy directed from Constantinople. Palestine, too, was the scene of a Monophysite reaction, while in Egypt they completely gained the upper hand. The change of policy begun in Justin's reign was dictated mainly by a desire to put an arrest upon these successes. A fierce persecution was the result, especially in the diocese of Antioch, many bishops, including Severus and Philoxenus, being banished from their sees.

3. The Monophysite theology.—The views of the Monophysites regarding the theological problem were by no means homogeneous. The one point in which the sect were unanimous was their opposition to Leo's *Tomus* and the symbol of Chalcedon —that idol with the two faces, as Zacharias Rhetor called it. Only a few of them drew from the doctrine of the one nature the Docetic inferences of Apollinaris or even of Eutyches. The majority tried to keep to the lines marked out in the theology of Cyril. This was the case, *e.g.*, with Timotheus Aelurus, and, above all, with Severus of Antioch, ecclesiastically the most influential, and theologically the most outstanding, champion of moderate Monophysitism, while Julian of Halicarnassus and Philoxenus of Hierapolis were more extreme in their views.

Severus, born *c.* 465 at Sozopolis in Pisidia, was the grandson of a bishop and the son of a town-councillor. He studied grammar and rhetoric at Alexandria and law in Beirût. While in Alexandria he had been in touch with pietistic circles (φιλόπονοι), but was converted through the influence of Zacharias Scholasticus, subsequently his biographer, in Beirût. He was baptized, and gave himself devotedly to fasting and prayer. In a short while he joined the monks of Peter the Iberian's monastery at Mayuma; for a time he lived as a hermit in the Desert of Eleutheropolis, and afterwards built a monastery of his own, soon winning great renown as a director of souls. In 508–511 we find him in Rome, acting as the representative of the monks who were being persecuted for their Monophysite principles. At the court of Anastasius he laboured for the principle of the Henotikon. At the expulsion of Flavian he was raised, despite the opposition of the suffragan bishops, to the patriarchal chair of Antioch (6th Nov. 512). The Synod of Tyre (515; cf. § 2) marks the summit of his work as an ecclesiastic. He was very active in the visitation of his diocese, and was most willing to preach either within or beyond the confines of his episcopal city. At the accession of Justin (Sept. 518), however, he was driven from his see, and fled to Alexandria. Considerably later, the administration of Justinian seemed to open a prospect of further ecclesiastical activity for Severus, who expected that the conferences in Constantinople (533) would set the seal of success upon his efforts. But the fall of Anthimus (cf. § 4) brought disaster to him too; he was excommunicated in 536, and withdrew to the desert country southwards from Alexandria. He died at Xois, on the Sebennitic arm of the Nile, probably on 8th February 538 (not 543).

Of his numerous writings all that has come down to us in Greek is fragments in Catenæ and anthologies. There are, however, Syriac translations of his works by Paul of Callinicus, Jacob of Edessa, and others. Of his exegetical and doctrinal writings may be mentioned ἀποκρίσεις πρὸς Εὐπράξιον κουβικουλάριον, and κατὰ Ἰωάννου γραμματικοῦ τοῦ Καισαρείας. Other writings worthy of note are his λόγοι ἐπιθρόνιοι or ἐνθρονιστικοί (125 homilies dating from the years he spent in Antioch, ed. R. Duval and others in the *Patrologia Orientalis*, Paris, 1906 ff.), his letters, extant in 23 books (bk. vi. ed. E. W. Brooks, London, 1902–04), and his hymns (the so-called Octoëchus, ed. E. W. Brooks, *Patrologia Orientalis*, 1910; cf. also art. HYMNS [Greek Christian], vol. vii. p. 8b).

Philoxenus, whose native name was Xenaya, was a student in Edessa while Ibas was bishop of that city, and we may thus infer that he was born *c.* 450. From Edessa he went to Antioch, where his ardent championship of the Henotikon brought him into conflict with the patriarch Kalandion, who had him expelled from the city. In 485 he was ordained by Peter the Fuller as Metropolitan of Hierapolis (Mabug). From the time when Flavian of Antioch, who was an adherent of Chalcedonian views, held office, Philoxenus appears as the spokesman of the Monophysite party in the patriarchate; subsequently, however, he was thrown into the background by Severus. Like the latter, he was eventually exiled (518 or 519), being sent first to Thrace, and then to Gangra in Paphlagonia, where, perhaps in 523, he died a violent death. He ranks as one of the most eminent of Syrian writers, though most of his works still lie dormant in the British Museum and other libraries; of those that have been published the most important is the *Discourses on Christian Doctrine* (tr. E. A. W. Budge, London, 1894–95).

Our knowledge of **Julian** rests upon very meagre data. The date of his birth is unknown. While bishop of Halicarnassus in Caria, he was concerned in the intrigues which led to the downfall of Macedonius, patriarch of Constantinople, in 511. He was himself expelled from his bishopric in 518, and took up his abode in the monastery of Enaton, outside the gates of Alexandria. Here he was embroiled in a doctrinal controversy with Severus (see below), who was then resident in that city, and this resulted in a temporary rupture within the party. At the death of the Monophysite patriarch Timotheus IV. the followers of Julian were able to secure the chair for their candidate, Gaianus, in place of the regularly elected Theodosius, and Theodosians and Gaianites were soon involved in a bitter strife. Of Julian's later fortunes we have no knowledge, nor, indeed, can we say definitely whether he was alive when, for the second time, the ban was pronounced upon him at Constantinople in 536. Of his writings we still possess a number of letters from his correspondence with Severus, and a Commentary on Job, transmitted in a Latin translation, and wrongly ascribed to Origen.

It was far from the minds of Severus and those who shared his views to argue for a fusion of the divine and the human in the person of Christ. Their insistence upon the singleness of Christ's nature after the Incarnation rested upon their conviction that the hypothesis of two natures necessarily implied two subjects or individual entities. What they found specially objectionable was the inference drawn in Leo's letter from the permanently distinct character of each nature—the inference, namely, that in the unity of Christ's person each nature, while no doubt in communication with the other, maintains its own distinctive function. According to the Monophysites, the theory that ascribed to each of the two natures a distinct mode of action (ἐνέργεια) divided the one Christ into two πρόσωπα, since no nature could possibly assert itself (ἐνεργεῖν) that did not remain self-subsistent (ὑφίστασθαι); the hypothesis of two φύσεις led to that of two ὑποστάσεις, and so to the abhorred heresy of Nestorius. In conformity with the position of Cyril, and with a mode of expression first met with in the writings of pseudo-Dionysius the Areopagite, viz. ἀνδρωθεὶς θεός and His καινὴ θεανδρικὴ ἐνέργεια (cf. art. MONOTHELETISM, § 1, p. 822[a]), Severus took as the basis of his speculations the inherently complete divine nature and person of the Logos. The Logos, in His act of assuming flesh—flesh animated by rationality—becomes flesh and man, and, as man, is born of woman, but still remains, even as He had been, One, since, in virtue of such an indissoluble union, and without detriment to His inherent character, He transmutes and transfigures the flesh with His own glory and power. The united elements thus form a composite nature and a divine-human hypostasis, and it is to this that all His activities are to be traced.

The thesis that the body of Christ was subject to the laws of nature was deemed of the utmost importance by the Severians and Theodosians, who saw in it an expression of the identity of essence between that body and our own, and were thus able to avoid the heresy of Eutyches. It was precisely this thesis, however, that gave offence to the extremists of the party. To Julian and his followers it was simply inconceivable that Christ's body had been subject to corruption (φθορά), which has been a characteristic of human nature since the Fall. In order to understand the precise usage of this term in the present connexion, we must note that it did not refer to the φθορά which denotes the complete dissolution of the body into its elements at death; all parties were at one in asserting that Christ's body was not subject to φθορά in that sense, *i.e.* as decomposition. The question at issue here had to do with the natural infirmities of the human body (ἀνθρώπινα πάθη)—its liability to hunger, thirst, weariness, sweating, weeping, bleeding, and the like. The view of Julian, Philoxenus, and the Gaianites was that, while Christ certainly hungered and thirsted, it was because He desired, not because He required (οὐκ ἀνάγκῃ φύσεως), to do so—because, in short, according to the divine counsel (κατ' οἰκονομίαν), He had voluntarily taken upon Himself human pains and needs. He was the Son of man, as man was before the Fall, while all other men, though sons of Adam too, were possessed of a body and a soul of a nature that was due to Adam's fall.

We are thus able to understand the heretical designations applied by the warring Monophysite parties to one another. The Julianists or Gaianites charged their opponents with phthartolatry, the worship of the corruptible. These 'phthartolaters,' however, retorted upon their accusers with the epithet 'aphthartodocetists' or 'phantasiasts,' *i.e.* those who would change the reality of Christ's human experience into a mere appearance. As a matter of fact, the latter view was quite a natural inference, and many of the extremists were led astray by it. The most extravagant view seems to have been reached by those Gaianites who asserted that the body of Christ, from the moment of its union with the Logos, should be regarded not only as uncorrupted (ἄφθαρτον) but also as uncreated (ἄκτιστον). These were stigmatized as 'aktistetes' by their opponents, whom in return they called 'ktistolaters,' *i.e.* 'worshippers of that which was created.' Divisions arose even among the Severians themselves. Themistius, a deacon, taking his stand upon such Scripture passages as Mk 13^{32} and Jn 11^{34}, maintained that, as the body of Christ was subject to natural conditions, so its animating spirit could not be regarded as omniscient. To the adherents of this doctrine their opponents applied the name 'agnoetes.'

4. Justinian and the new orthodoxy.—On 1st August 527 Justinian became sole emperor of Rome. It does not fall to us here to set forth fully his far-reaching ecclesiastical policy in its transforming effect upon all things. The decisive factor in his attitude towards the West was his recognition of the Roman chair as the supreme tribunal of the Church, though this did not prevent him, after his victory over the Goths, from giving the popes an experience of his autocratic power. The defection of the Eastern Church gave the imperial ecclesiastic many an anxious hour. He soon came to recognize that his persecution of the Monophysites (see § 2 at end) had been a grave error. Little as he might wish to displace once more the orthodoxy now officially recognized, he could hardly help desiring to reconcile the Monophysites, especially as the empress Theodora was working with growing fervour for the rehabilitation of the party with which she sympathized in her devout moods. A few years after Justinian's accession to the throne, accordingly, negotiations were opened with the insurgents, and the most eminent of the bishops deposed in 518—not, however, including Severus—were summoned to Constantinople, where, it was hoped, they would be won over at a religious conference. In this conference, on the orthodox side, only such theologians were to take part as unequivocally accepted the thesis that one of the Trinity had suffered in the flesh (ἕνα τῆς τριάδος πεπονθέναι σαρκί). This Theopaschite formula was manifestly a friendly overture to the Monophysites. But the 'Collatio cum Severianis' (533 [or 531]), after two days of verbal controversy, came to nothing. On 15th May 533 Justinian issued an enactment in which he once more declared Chalcedon to be a standard of faith co-ordinate with the three earlier councils. The negotiations with the Monophysites were, nevertheless, still proceeding, and communications were now opened with Severus as well. Severus, yielding to reiterated pressure, went at length to the capital, where in 535 Anthimus, a protégé of the empress Theodora and a theological partisan of Severus himself, had been raised to the episcopate. But the interlude was not of long duration. In the following year (536) Pope Agapetus was able so to influence the emperor that the doctrinally suspect patriarch was superseded by the orthodox Menas. It is nevertheless the case that, during the entire reign of Justinian, the Monophysites firmly maintained their position at the court, while in Syria and Egypt their ecclesiastical power was supreme (cf. § 5).

Justinian himself made zealous efforts to comprehend the points of the doctrinal controversy. His great aim was to reconcile the teaching of Cyril and the Symbol of Chalcedon. In this he found effective support in that most eminent of his theologians, **Leontius of Byzantium** († 543 as a monk in Palestine), who, in his Ἐπίλυσις τῶν ὑπὸ Σευήρου προβεβλημένων συλλογισμῶν, κατὰ Νεστοριανῶν καὶ Εὐτυχιανιστῶν and other writings, won renown as a prolific author and an able assailant of the Severian Christology. The theology of Leontius is based wholly upon the Aristotelian logic. A novel feature of it, however, was his ingenious application of the idea that the ὑποστῆναι of Christ's human nature was ἐν τῷ λόγῳ, so that that nature is not ἀνυπόστατος, but ἐνυπόστατος. The term 'enhypostasis' operated like a spell. It seemed to obviate in the happiest way all the difficulties that beset the doctrine of the God-man. By its means the Chalcedonian Symbol could, without violation of its actual words, be interpreted in the sense of

Cyril's doctrine. It was nevertheless the use of this expression that led to the introduction of scholasticism into the Byzantine theology.

Justinian died in 565. Under his successors the Monophysites of the city and diocese of Constantinople had much to bear, and their harsh experiences have been graphically described by John of Ephesus, himself a Monophysite, in his Church History. Negotiations for a union of the warring factions, it is true, were once more resumed, but were foredoomed to failure by the circumstance that the ecclesiastics of the imperial court would not surrender the understanding with Rome, while the Monophysites regarded that understanding as the root of all evil. The consequence was that in the course of the 6th cent. the Monophysite communities in the Byzantine patriarchate were destroyed one after another. The Churches of Egypt and the Eastern provinces, on the other hand, remained quite impervious to the ecclesiastical influence of the capital, and the severance of the purely Monophysite communion from the Catholic Church became ever the more complete.

5. The independent Monophysite churches.—The Monophysites of *Syria* never ceased to regard the banished Severus as the rightful patriarch of Antioch, and declined to recognize the standing of those who were successively appointed to the office by the emperor. The organizer of their church life was **Jacob Barâdai** (*i.e.* 'he with the horse-cloth'; † 578), who, originally a monk in Constantinople, had been ordained, *c.* 541, bishop of Edessa by Theodosius of Alexandria (cf. § 3), then also resident there; and in consequence the Syrian Monophysites came to be called Jacobites. Barâdai, in his long journeys in W. Asia and Egypt, instituted communities, and consecrated patriarchs, bishops, presbyters, and deacons. The chief representatives of literature in Syria were nearly all Monophysites.

In addition to Severus, Philoxenus, and Julian (cf. § 3), the following writers of the earlier period deserve mention: Jacob of Sarug († 521), the author of widely read metrical homilies, which earned for him the title of 'Flute of the Holy Spirit'; Sergius of Resaïna († 536), physician and priest, who translated into Syriac several works of Aristotle and Galen, as also of the pseudo-Dionysius Areopagitica; Jacob of Edessa († 708), equally renowned as theologian, liturgical writer, philosopher, historian, exegete, and grammarian; George, bishop of the nomadizing Arabs, a writer whose letters have come down to us in large numbers. Of the mediæval authors one of the most prominent was Bar Hebræus (Abulfaraj; † 1286), whose *Chronicle* forms one of the most important sources of information regarding Monophysitism.

From the time when Islām became the dominant power in Syria, the Jacobites decreased in numbers more and more. At the present day there are some 200,000 of them in the Turkish empire, and about 1,000,000 in India—on the Malabar coast and in Ceylon. Their ecclesiastical superior (formerly entitled 'maphrian,' now 'katholikos') resides in the monastery of Deir-Safaran, near Mardin. Efforts made by the Jacobites, from the close of the 18th cent., to effect a union with Rome had a very meagre result. At the present day the Roman Catholic Syrians number about 30,000, and are subject to a patriarch, who takes his title from Antioch, but lives in Mardin.

In *Egypt* the conflicts between the Severians and the Julianists or Gaianites (cf. § 3) at length ruptured the unity of Monophysitism, which, nevertheless, became the faith of nearly the whole Coptic population. The patriarch of the orthodox, the Melchites (*i.e.* 'Imperials'), who was also procurator of the province, could count upon the homage of very few outside the higher official ranks in Alexandria and some of the larger towns. The Monophysite propaganda was carried also to the Nubians and the Alodians. From 616 marauding bands of Persians ravaged the religious stations on the Upper Nile, and it was only after the Arabs, with the hearty good-will of the Copts, took possession of the country that the Monophysite patriarch ventured to leave his place of refuge in the Upper Egyptian desert. During the Middle Ages the condition of the Coptic Church was a fairly prosperous one, but subsequently it was sorely harassed and ravaged by Muslim fanaticism, and it is only within recent times that it has been able to make a fresh advance. The Christian Copts of the present day still maintain their Monophysite creed (see, further, art. COPTIC CHURCH).

Finally, Monophysitism penetrated also to *Armenia*. The Armenians, while still engaged in battling for their own faith with Parsi Mazdæism, were quite unaffected by the dogmatic controversies of the Imperial Church. The expanding propaganda of the Persian Nestorians, however, induced them to adopt the Henotikon of Zeno (cf. § 2). Thereafter they maintained close relations with the Syrian Monophysites, and at the Council of Dvin, in 554, they overtly accepted the more radical position represented by Julian of Halicarnassus. From that time they have remained faithful to Monophysitism, though they subsequently gave their adherence to the more moderate Severian school.

LITERATURE.—i. *SOURCES.*—(*a*) Decrees of the Councils, Declarations of Synods, papal briefs.

(*b*) *Historical works and Chronicles.*—Zacharias Rhetor (Scholasticus), shortly after the accession of Anastasius, wrote, from the Henotic standpoint, a record of ecclesiastical events from the Council of Chalcedon to the death of Zeno (extant only in a Syriac version; see below, under *Historia Miscellanea*); Theodorus Lector, Anagnostes in the Church of St. Sophia in Constantinople at the beginning of the 6th cent., wrote, from the orthodox standpoint, a history of the Church from Nestorius to Justin I., which now exists only in fragments; Johannes Malalas, *Chronography*, composed in Justinian's reign; Evagrius, *Ecclesiastical History*, written after 546 (ed. J. Bidez and L. Parmentier, London, 1899); Theophanes Confessor, *Chronography*, composed between 810 and 815 (ed. C. de Boor, Leipzig, 1883–85). Of the Latin chroniclers Liberatus, *Breviarium causæ Nestorianorum et Eutychianorum*, is worthy of note. The most important of the Syrian authorities are: *Chronicon Edessenum* (ed. I. Guidi, in *Corpus Scriptorum Christianorum Orientalium*, 'Chronica Minora,' I. i., Paris, 1903), dating from the middle of the 6th cent.; *Historia Miscellanea*, a compilation of the same period by an unknown Monophysite writer, and including the history of Zacharias Rhetor mentioned above (ed. K. Ahrens and G. Krüger, Leipzig, 1899; also F. J. Hamilton and E. W. Brooks, London, 1899); John of Ephesus († *c.* 585), *Ecclesiastical History* (3rd part ed. W. Cureton, Oxford, 1853).

(*c*) *Various.*—The *Plerophories* of Johannes Rufus of Mayuma, a collection (*c.* 515) of the sayings, prophecies, visions, and revelations of various distinguished Monophysites, and especially of Peter the Iberian (ed. F. Nau, in *Patrologia Orientalis*, Paris, 1911); the biography of Peter the Iberian, probably by the Johannes Rufus just named (ed. R. Raabe, Leipzig, 1895); *Vitæ virorum apud Monophysitas celeberrimorum* (ed. E. W. Brooks, in *Corpus Script. Christ. Orient.*, 'Scriptores Syri,' III. xxv., Paris, 1908); the biographies of the Syrian monks Euthymius and Sabas, by Cyril of Scythopolis († after 557), etc.

ii. *MODERN WORKS.*—L. S. Le Nain de Tillemont, *Mémoires pour servir à l'hist. ecclésiastique des six premiers siècles*[2], Paris, 1701–12, xv. f., E. Gibbon, *The Hist. of the Decline and Fall of the Roman Empire*, ed. J. B. Bury, 7 vols., London, 1901–06, and C. W. F. Walch, *Hist. der Kezereien . . . bis auf die Zeiten der Reformation*, Leipzig, 1762–85, vi.–viii., are still indispensable. Of more recent works on the general history of the period the following deserve special mention: J. B. Bury, *A Hist. of the Later Roman Empire*, London, 1889; H. Gelzer, 'Abriss der byzantinischen Kaisergeschichte,' in K. Krumbacher's *Gesch. der byzantinischen Literatur*[2], Munich, 1897; C. Diehl, *Justinien et la civilisation byzantine au vi*[e] *siècle*, Paris, 1901; and W. G. Holmes, *The Age of Justinian and Theodora*, London, 1905–07. On the questions of literary history the reader should consult (in addition to Krumbacher) W. Wright, *A Short Hist. of Syriac Literature*, London, 1894, and R. Duval, *La Littérature syriaque*[3], Paris, 1907. Of Histories of the Church and of Dogma, the most important are the following: I. A. Dorner, *Entwicklungsgesch. der Lehre von der Person Christi*, ii.[2], Berlin, 1853 (Eng. tr., Edinburgh, 1861–63); C. J. von Hefele, *Conciliengeschichte*[2], Freiburg, 1873–90, ii. (1875) (best form now in the Fr. revised ed. of H. Leclercq, Paris, 1907–13); A. Harnack, *Lehrbuch der Dogmengeschichte*[4], Tübingen, 1909–10, ii. (Eng. tr., London, 1894–99); L. J. Tixeront, *Hist. des dogmes dans l'antiquité chrétienne*, 3 vols., Paris, 1906–12, iii.; L. Duchesne, *Hist. ancienne de l'église*, Paris, 1906–10 (only to the close of the 5th cent. A.D.), iii.; the best monograph on the subject is J. Lebon, *Le Monophysisme sévérien*, Louvain, 1909. In writing the present article the author has drawn upon his contributions to *PRE*[3] ('Julian von Halikarnass,' 'Justinian I.,' 'Monophysiten,' 'Philoxenus,' 'Severus,' 'Zacharias Scholastikus,' etc.), and upon his *Handbuch der Kirchengeschichte*, i. (Tübingen, 1911); additional literature will be found both in the articles and in the book.

G. Krüger.

MONOTHEISM.—In the history of religion monotheism, the doctrine that 'there is one God,' or that 'God is One,' is somewhat sharply opposed to a very wide range of beliefs and teachings. The contrast, when it appears in the religion of a people, or in the general evolution of religion, tends to have an important bearing both upon religious practices and upon religious experience, since to believe in 'One God' means, in general, to abandon, often with contempt or aversion, many older beliefs, hopes, fears, and customs relating to the 'many gods,' or to the other powers, whose place or dignity the 'One God' tends henceforth to take and to retain. If these 'many,' as the older beliefs, which some form of monotheism replaces, had dealt with them, were themselves for the older faiths 'gods,' then the monotheism which is each time in question opposes, and replaces, some form of 'polytheism.' This is what happened when Judaism and Muhammadanism replaced older local faiths. If one were satisfied to view the contrast in the light of cases closely resembling these, and these only, then the natural opponent of monotheism as a belief in 'One God' would appear to be, in the history of religion, polytheism as a belief in 'many gods.'

Since, however, there are various religions and many superstitions which recognize the existence of powers such as, despite their more or less divine character, lack some or all of the features which naturally belong either to God or to gods, and since demons, the spirits of the dead, or magic powers may be in question in such religions, the name 'polytheism' can hardly be quite accurately applied to the whole class of beliefs which are in any important way opposed to monotheism. So, in the history of religion, monotheism has two opponents: (1) polytheism proper, and (2) beliefs that recognize other more or less divine beings besides those that are properly to be called gods.

In the history of philosophy, however, monotheism has a much narrower range of contrasting or opposing beliefs. Polytheism, as an explicit doctrine, has played but a small part in the history of philosophy. To the doctrine 'God is One' or 'There is one God,' where this doctrine forms part of a philosophy, there are opposed forms of opinion which are often classified under three heads: (1) philosophical pantheism, (2) philosophical atheism, (3) philosophical scepticism regarding the divine beings. The modern name 'agnosticism' has been freely used for a philosophical scepticism which especially relates either to God or to other matters of central interest in religion.

Frequently, in summaries of the varieties of philosophical doctrine, the term 'pantheism' has been used as a name for such philosophical doctrines as 'identify the world with God.' Pantheism is often summed up as the doctrine that 'All is God,' 'Everything is God,' or, finally, 'God is everything.' But a more careful study of the philosophical doctrines which have gone under the name of pantheism, or which have been so named by their opponents, would show that the name 'pantheism' is too abstract, too vague in its meaning to make any clear insight easily obtainable regarding what ought to constitute the essence of a philosophical pantheism as opposed to a philosophic monotheism. The two propositions (1) 'God is One,' and (2) 'God is identical with all reality,' or 'with the principle upon which all reality depends,' are not, on the face of the matter, mutually contrary propositions. How far, in reference to a given creed, or theology, or religious tradition, the first proposition appears to be contrary to the second depends upon the special interpretation, and sometimes upon the special prejudices of critics, sects, or philosophers of a given school.

One who asserts the 'unity of God' may or may not be laying stress upon the fact that he also makes a sharp distinction between the reality called God and other realities—*e.g.*, the world. That such sharp distinctions are often in question is an important fact in the history of philosophy. Nevertheless the doctrine that 'God is One' has been philosophically maintained at the same time with the doctrine that 'God is all reality.' For such a view, the two doctrines would simply be two ways of expressing the same centrally important fact. One who wishes to understand the numerous controversies, subtle distinctions, and religious interests which at one time or another have been bound up with the name 'pantheism' must be ready to recognize that the term 'pantheism,' when used without special explanation, is a poor instrument for making clear precisely where the problem lies. In brief, one may say that, while the term 'pantheism' has been freely employed by philosophers, as well as by those who are devoted to practical religious interests, it is, as a historical name, rather a cause of confusion than an aid to clearness. The proposition, 'God is One,' has, despite the complications of doctrine and of history, a comparatively definite meaning for any one who advances a philosophical opinion concerning the nature of God. But the proposition, 'God is all,' or 'God is all reality,' has, in the history of thought, no one meaning which can be made clear unless one first grasps all the essential principles of the metaphysical doctrine of the philosopher who asserts this proposition, or who at least is accused by his critics of asserting it.

If we endeavour, then, to make clearer the essential meaning of the term 'monotheism' by contrasting the historical forms of monotheism with philosophical doctrines which have been opposed to it, we may attempt to solve the problem of defining what is essential to philosophical monotheism by dwelling upon a contrast which, especially in recent discussion, has been freely emphasized. One may assert, *e.g.*, that in speaking of the nature of the 'One God' who is the essential being of monotheistic belief, either (1) one holds that God is 'immanent' in the world, thus asserting the doctrine of the 'divine immanence,' or (2) one holds to the doctrine of the 'transcendence' of God, thus asserting that the divine being in some fashion 'transcends' the world which He has created or with which He is contrasted. But here, again, one deals with two doctrines which, in certain philosophical contexts, do not appear to stand in contrary opposition to each other. For, as is well known, there are philosophies which insist that God is in a certain sense 'immanent' in the world, and also in a certain sense 'transcendent' in His relation to the world. Aristotle, in a well-known passage (*Met.* xii. 10), gave a classic expression of the relations of the doctrines which are here in question, when he stated the question as to whether the divine being is related to the world as the 'order' is to the army, or as the 'general' is to the army. Aristotle replied by saying that 'in a certain sense' God is *both* the 'order' of the world and the 'general,' 'although rather the general.' Thus the opposition between divine immanence and divine transcendence does not precisely state the issue and class of issues which one finds playing the most important part in the history of philosophical monotheism (see art. IMMANENCE).

Another attempt to get the issue between monotheism and the contrasting or opposed philosophical doctrines clearly before the mind may take the well-known form of declaring that monotheism, properly so called, lays stress upon the 'personality of God,' while the opposed or contrasting doctrines, which so often are regarded as constituting or as tending towards pantheism, have as their essential feature the tendency to view God as 'impersonal.' From this point of view, it would be of the essence of monotheism to declare that the One God is a person, while it would be of the essence of those doctrines which are opposed to monotheism to declare, in a fashion which might remain simply negative, that the divine being is not personal. It would then remain for further definition to consider whether the divine being is 'superpersonal' or is 'merely material,' or, again, is 'unconscious,' or is otherwise not of a personal character.

But the difficulty in this way of defining the contrasts which have actually appeared in the history of thought lies in the fact that the very conception of personality is itself, in the history of philosophy, a comparatively late as well as a decidedly unstable conception. It is fair to ask how far the most widely current modern ideas of personality were present to the minds of such Greek philosophers as Plato and Aristotle. All the ideas of personality which philosophers may now possess have recently been vastly influenced by the whole course of modern European civilization. The problem of how far the Occidental and Oriental minds agree regarding what a 'person' is is one about which those will be least likely to dogmatize who have most carefully considered the accessible facts. In fact, the whole experience of the civilized consciousness of any nation or philosopher is likely to be epitomized in the idea of personality which a given philosophy expresses. It seems, therefore, inconvenient to make one's classification of the philosophical doctrine about the nature of God depend upon presupposing that one knows what a philosopher means by the term 'person.' It is true that whoever makes clear what he means by 'person' will thereby define his attitude towards nearly all fundamental philosophical problems. But the idea of personality is, if possible, more difficult to define than any other fundamental philosophical idea. Therefore, to define monotheism as a 'belief in a personal God' will give little aid to the understanding of what sort of belief is in question, so long as the idea of what constitutes a person remains as obscure as it usually does.

A still further effort has been made to define monotheism by making explicit reference to philosophical doctrines concerning the question whether the world was created or is self-existent. As a matter of fact, that set of Christian theological doctrines and of scholastic interpretations of Aristotle which goes by the name of 'creationism' has played an important part in the history of the more technical forms of monotheism. Yet the issues regarding creation are, after all, special issues. How they bear upon the problem of monotheism can hardly be understood by one who has not already defined monotheism in other terms. Creationism is the familiar doctrine that 'the world was created by God.' This doctrine can become clear only if one first knows what one means by God.

The effort to make some further advance towards unravelling the great variety of interwoven motives which appear in the history of monotheism, and which have been suggested by the foregoing considerations, will be aided by attempting, at this point, once more to review the issues with regard to the nature of God, but now from a somewhat different point of view. The problems, both about 'God' and about 'the gods,' have everywhere been inherited by the philosophers from religions whose origins antedated their philosophy. In a few cases, notably in the case of Greece on the one hand and India on the other, the origin of the philosophical traditions regarding the divine being can be traced back to ancient religious tendencies, while the transition from religion to philosophy is fairly well known, and passes through definite stages. In one other instance, the transition from a tribal religion to a form of monotheism which was not due to philosophers but which has deeply influenced the subsequent life of philosophy is also decidedly well known, and can be traced in its essential details. This is the case of the religion of Israel. Now in the three cases in question —that of India, that of Greece, that of Israel—the rise of a doctrine which is certainly in each case a monotheism can be fairly well understood. The three forms of monotheism which resulted led in the sequel to contrasts of doctrine which, in the case of the history of philosophical thought, have been momentous. Ignoring, then, the complications of early religious history, ignoring also the effort further to define and to classify those doctrines which have been summarized in the various definitions of monotheism and its opponents which we have just reviewed, it seems well to reconsider the important varieties of philosophical belief regarding the divine being in the light of the great historical contrast of the three forms of monotheism which India, Greece, and Israel put before us. We shall discard the name 'pantheism,' and make no attempt to define the contrast between divine immanence and divine transcendence, or to speak of the problem in what sense God is personal and in what sense impersonal. Nor can we here exhaust the varieties of philosophical opinion. But the threefold contrast just given will help us to make clearer the philosophical issues of monotheism by naming certain varieties of philosophical thought which have both a definite historical origin and a great influence upon the character of opinion about the divine being. Simplifying the whole matter in this somewhat artificial but still well-founded way, we may say that, from the historical point of view, three different ways of viewing the divine being have been of great importance both for religious life and for philosophical doctrine. No one of these three ways has been exclusively confined to the nation of which the form of opinion in question is most characteristic, and in the history of philosophical thought the three motives are interwoven. But a comparatively clear distinction can be made if we emphasize the three contrasting doctrines, and then point out that these doctrines, while not exclusively due each to one of the three nations or to philosophies which have grown out of the religious traditions of the nation in question, are still, on the whole, fairly to be associated, one with the tradition of Israel, the second with the influence of Greece, and the third with the influence either of India or of nations and civilizations which, in this respect, are closely analogous in spirit to the civilization of India.

(1) The monotheism due to the historical influence of the religion of Israel defines God as 'the righteous Ruler of the world,' as 'the Doer of justice,' or as the one 'whose law is holy,' or 'who secures the triumph of the right.' The best phrase to characterize this form of doctrine, to leave room for the wide variety of special forms which it has assumed, to indicate its historical origin, and also to imply that it has undergone in the course of history a long process of development, is this: 'the

ethical monotheism of the Prophets of Israel.' We include under this phrase that form, or type, or aspect of monotheism, which characterizes philosophies that have been most strongly influenced, directly or indirectly, by the religion of Israel.

(2) The monotheism which has its historical origin very largely in the Greek philosophers defines God as the source, or the explanation, or the correlate, or the order, or the reasonableness of the world. It seems fair to call this form 'Hellenic monotheism.' In the history of philosophy, and especially of that philosophy which has grown up under the influence of Christianity, this idea of God has, of course, become interwoven—sometimes consciously, sometimes unconsciously—with the ethical monotheism of Israel. But, when a philosophy of Christian origin is in question, while in some respects this philosophy, if positively monotheistic, is almost sure to be strongly influenced by ethical monotheism, the most important and essential features of the philosophy in question will be due to the way in which it deals with the relation between the order of the world and the nature of the 'One God.' Aristotle's statement of his own problem regarding whether God is identical with the 'order' or is related to the world as the 'general' is related to the army is a good example of the form which the problem of monotheism takes from this point of view.

(3) The third form of monotheism is very widespread, and has actually had many different historical origins. In the history both of religion and of philosophy this form of monotheism, somewhat like the Ancient Mariner, 'passes, like night, from land to land' and 'has strange power of speech.' Often unorthodox at the time or in the place where it is influential, it has indirectly played a large part in the creeds of various times and places. Usually fond of esoteric statements of doctrine, and often condemned by common sense as fantastic and intolerable, it has had many times of great popular influence. The official Christian Church has had great difficulty in defining the relation of orthodox doctrine to this form of opinion. In the history of philosophy the more technical statements of it have formed part of extremely important systems.

This form of monotheism is especially well marked in the early history of Hindu speculation. It is often called 'Hindu pantheism'; and it is indeed fair to say that it is in many respects most purely represented by some systems of belief and doctrine which have grown up on Indian soil. On the other hand, it has a less exclusive relation to Indian philosophy than the Hellenic form of monotheism, in its later history, has to Greek philosophy, so that the connexion here insisted upon between this kind of monotheism and the early history of Hindu philosophy must be interpreted somewhat liberally. In fact, at the close of the history of Greek philosophy this third form of monotheism appeared as a part of the Neo-Platonic philosophy. Yet in this case an Oriental origin or direct influence is extremely improbable. Examples of the tendency of this form of monotheism to take on new forms, and to be influenced by other motives than those derived from the religion or philosophy of India, are to be found in the recent revival of such types of doctrine in various forms of 'intuitionalism' and 'anti-intellectualism' in European thought.

The essence of this third type of monotheism is that it tends to insist not only upon the 'sole reality of God,' but upon the 'unreality of the world.' The name 'acosmism' therefore is more suggestive for it than the name 'pantheism.' It might be summed up in the proposition 'God is real,' but all else besides God that appears to be real is but an 'appearance' or, if better estimated, is a 'dream.' If we attempt to make more precise the vague word 'pantheism' merely by saying, 'God and the world are, according to pantheism, but one,' the natural question arises, 'If they are but one, then which one?' But what we may now call, in a general way and upon the general historical basis just indicated, 'Indic monotheism,' whether it appears in Hindu philosophy, in Spinoza, or in Meister Eckhart, tends to assert, 'The One is God and God only, and is so precisely because the world is but appearance.' This definition of the third form of monotheism relieves us of some of the ambiguities of the term 'pantheism.'

The threefold distinction now made enables us similarly to review some of the great features of the history of philosophical monotheism in a way which cannot here be stated at length, but which, even when summarily indicated, tends to elucidate many points that have usually been unduly left obscure.

The ethical monotheism of the Prophets of Israel was not the product of any philosophical thinking. The intense earnestness of the nation into whose religious experience it entered kept it alive in the world. The beginnings of Christianity soon required philosophical interpretation, and in any such interpretation the doctrine of the righteous God must inevitably play a leading part. In the course of the development of the Church this doctrine sought aid from Greek philosophy. Consequently, the whole history of Christian monotheism depends upon an explicit effort to make a synthesis of the ethical monotheism of Israel and the Hellenic form of monotheism. This synthesis was as attractive as, in the course of its development, it has proved problematic and difficult. The reason for the problem of such a synthesis, as the philosophers have had to face that problem, lies mainly in the following fact. Whether taken in its original form or modified by philosophical reflexion, ethical monotheism, the doctrine that 'God is righteous,' very sharply contrasts God, 'the righteous Ruler,' or, in Christian forms, 'God the Redeemer of the world,' with the world to which God stands in such ethical relations. On the other hand, for the Hellenic form of monotheism, the problem which Aristotle emphasized about the 'order' and the 'general' indeed exists. But in its essentials Hellenic monotheism is, on the whole, neutral as to the kind of unity which binds God and the world together. Our later philosophies, in so far as they are founded upon Hellenic monotheism, must therefore attempt explicitly to solve the problem which Aristotle stated. And, on the whole, such philosophies tend towards answering the question as Aristotle did: God is both 'order' and the 'general' of the army which constitutes the world. Hellenic monotheism, moreover, is influenced by strongly intellectual tendencies. On the other hand, the monotheism of Israel was, even in its ante-philosophical form, a kind of voluntarism. God's law, viewed as one term of the antithesis, the world which He rules, or which He saves, viewed as the other, are much more sharply contrasted than Aristotle's 'order' and 'general' tend to be. When, in the development of the philosophies which grew out of the Greek tradition, the Hellenic concept of the Logos (*q.v.*) assumed its most characteristic forms, its intellectual interests were, on the whole, in favour of defining the unity of the divine being and the world as the most essential feature of monotheism. But, at each stage of this development, this intellectual or rational unity of the Logos and the world gradually came into sharper and sharper conflict with that ethical interest which naturally dwelt upon the contrast between the righteous

Ruler and the sinful world, and between divine grace and fallen man.

Therefore, behind many of the conflicts between so-called pantheism in Christian tradition and the doctrines of 'divine transcendence' and 'divine personality,' there has lain the conflict between intellectualism and voluntarism, between an interpretation of the world in terms of order and an interpretation of the world in terms of the conflict between good and evil, righteousness and unrighteousness.

Meanwhile, in terms of this antithesis of our first and second types of philosophical monotheism, we can state only half of the problem. Had the monotheism of Israel and the Hellenic doctrine of God as the principle of order been the only powers concerned in these conflicts, the history both of philosophy and of religion would have been, for the Christian world, far simpler than it is. The motives which determine the third idea of God have tended both to enrich and to complicate the situation.

It is true that a direct connexion between ancient Hinduism and early Christian doctrine cannot be traced. But what we have called, for very general reasons, the Indic type of idea of God became, in the course of time, a part of Christian civilization for very various reasons. As we have seen, the doctrine that God alone is real while the world is illusory depends upon motives which are not confined to India. In the form of what has technically been called 'mysticism,' this view of the divine nature in due time became a factor both in Christian experience and in philosophical interpretation. The Neo-Platonic school furnished some of the principal technical formulations of such a view of the divine nature. The religious experience of the Græco-Roman world, in the times immediately before and immediately after the Christian era, also in various ways emphasized the motives upon which this third type of Christian monotheism depends. The Church thus found room within the limits of orthodoxy for the recognition, with certain restrictions, of the tendency to view the world as mere appearance, ordinary life as a bad dream, and salvation as attainable only through a direct acquaintance with the divine being itself.

The very complications which for philosophy have grown out of the efforts to synthesize Hellenic monotheism and the religion of the Prophets of Israel have repeatedly stimulated the Christian mystics to insist that what the intellect cannot attain, namely, an understanding of the nature of God and His relation to the world, the mystic experience can furnish to those who have a right to receive its revelations. Philosophy—intellectual philosophy—fails (so such mystics assert) to solve the problems raised by the contrasts between good and evil, between God and the world, as these contrasts are recognized either by those who study the order of the universe or by those who thirst after righteousness. What way remains, then, for man, beset by his moral problems, on the one hand, and his intellectual difficulties, on the other, to come into real touch with the divine? The mystics, *i.e.* those who have insisted upon the third idea of God, and who have tested this idea in their own experience, have always held that the results of the intellect are negative, and lead to no definite idea of God which can be defended against the sceptics, while, as the mystics always insist, to follow the law of righteousness, whether with or without the aid of divine grace, does not lead, at least in the present life, to the highest type of the knowledge of God. We approach the highest type of knowledge, so far as the present life permits, if we recognize, in the form of some sort of 'negative' theology, the barrenness of intellectualism, and if, meanwhile, we recognize that the contemplative life is higher than the practical life, and that an immediate vision of God leads to an insight which no practical activity, however righteous, attains. To teach such doctrines as matters of personal experience is characteristic of the mystics. To make more articulate the idea of God thus defined has formed an important part of the office of theology.

Without this third type of monotheism, and without this negative criticism of the work of the intellect and this direct appeal to immediate experience, Christian doctrine, in fact, would not have reached some of its most characteristic forms and expressions, and the philosophy of Christendom would have failed to put on record some of its most fascinating speculations.

It is obvious that, on the face of the matter, the immediate intuitions upon which mystical monotheism lays stress are opposed to the sort of insight which the intellect obtains. Even here, however, the opposing tendencies in question are not always in any very direct contrary opposition in the thought or expression of an individual thinker or philosopher. Thus, in an individual case, an exposition of mysticism may devote a large part of its philosophical work to a return to the Hellenic type of theism. That this was possible the Neo-Platonic school had already shown (see art. NEO-PLATONISM). Wherever Christian monotheism is strongly under the Neo-Platonic influence, it tends to become a synthesis of our second and third types of monotheism. In such cases the monotheism is Hellenic in its fondness for order, for categories, and for an intellectual system of the universe, and at the same time devoted to immediate intuitions, to a recognition that the finite world is an appearance, and to a definition of God in terms of an ineffable experience, rather than in terms of a rational system of ideas. Such a synthesis may, in an individual system, ignore the conflicts here in question. Nevertheless, on the whole, the opposition is bound to become, for great numbers of thinkers and, on occasion, for the authorities of the Church, a conscious opposition. And the opposition between the ethical and the mystic types of monotheism is in general still sharper, and is more fully conscious. Despite all these oppositions, however, it remains the case that one of the principal problems of Christian theology has been the discovery of some way to bring the third of the ideas of God, the third of the tendencies to define God as One, into some tolerable and true synthesis either with the first or with the second of the three types of monotheism, or with both.

In the technical discussions of the idea of God which have made up the introductory portions of many systems of so-called 'nature theology,' it has been very general for the philosophers of Christendom to emphasize the Hellenic type of theism. The so-called philosophical 'proofs of the divine existence' make explicit some aspect of the Hellenic interest in the order and reason of the world. The 'design argument,' first stated in an elementary form by Socrates, and persistently present in popular theology of the monotheistic type ever since, is an interpretation of the world in terms of various special analogies between the particular sorts of adaptation which the physical world shows us and the plans of which a designing intelligence, in the case of art, makes use. The so-called 'cosmological argument' reasons more in general terms from the very existence of this 'contingent' world to the Logos whose rational nature explains the world. The highly technical 'ontological argument' insists upon motives which arise in the course of the effort to define the very nature of an orderly system. In its briefest statement the ontological argument is epitomized by Augustine when he defines God as 'Veritas' and declares that Veritas must be real, since, if there were no Veritas, the proposition that there is no Veritas would itself be true. The more highly developed forms of the ontological argument reason in similar fashion from our own ideas of the nature of the Logos, or of the rationally necessary order system of the universe—in other words, from the realm of Platonic ideas, in so far as it is manifested through and to our intellect, to the reality of such a system beyond our intellect.

It has been insisted, and not without very genuine basis, both in religion and in the controversies of the philosophers, that all such efforts, through the intellect, to grasp the divine nature lead to results remote from the vital experience upon which religious monotheism and, in particular, Christian monotheism must rest, if such monotheism is permanently to retain the confidence of a man who is at once critical and religious. Into the merits of the issues thus indicated, this is no place to enter. In any case, however, both the warfare of the philosophical schools and the contrast between intellectual theology and the religious life have often led to philosophical efforts to escape from the very problems now emphasized to some more immediate intuition of the divine, or else to assert that there is no philosophical solution to the religious problem of theism. Thus intellectualism in theology, in the forms in which it has historically appeared, has repeatedly tended to bring about its own elimination. The more highly rational it has become, and the more its apparent barrenness, or its inability to combine the various motives which enter into the three different monotheistic tendencies has become manifest, the more the result of a careful analysis of the intellectual motives has led either to the revival of mysticism or to a sceptical indifference to philosophical theism. To say this is merely to report historical facts.

Some negative results of the more purely Hellenic type of monotheism became especially manifest through the results of the Kantian criticism of reason and of its work. It is extremely interesting, however, to see what, in Kant's case, was the result of this criticism of the traditional arguments for the existence of God. By temperament Kant was indisposed to take interest in experiences of mystic type. For him, therefore, the failure of the intellect meant a return to the motives which, in no philosophical formulation, but in the form of an intensely earnest practical faith, had long ago given rise to the religion of Israel. Therefore the God of Kant is, once more, simply the righteous Ruler. Or, as Fichte in a famous early essay defined the idea, 'God is the moral order of the world.' This Kantian-Fichtean order is, however, not the Hellenic order, either of the realm of Platonic ideas or of the natural world. It is the order of 'the kingdom of ends,' of a universe of free moral agents, whose existence stands in endless contrast to an ideal realm of holiness or moral perfection, after which they must endlessly strive, but of whose real presence they can never become aware through a mystical vision or by a sure logical demonstration. The righteous man, according to Kant, says: 'I will that God exists.' Kant defines God in terms of this will. Monotheism, according to this view, cannot be proved, but rationally must be acknowledged as true.

Yet, in his *Critique of Judgment*, Kant recognized that the requirement to bring into synthesis the intellect and the will, and to interpret our æsthetic experience, *i.e.* our acquaintance with the kind of perfection which beauty reveals—this ideal, a synthesis of the ethical, the intuitional, and the rational—remains with us. And, despite all failures, this ideal is one from which philosophy cannot escape.

The revived interest in intuition and in religious experience which has characterized the transition from the 19th to the 20th cent. has once more made the mystical motives familiar to our present interest. The permanent significance of the ethical motives also renders them certain to become prominent in the attention of serious-minded men, even though the Kantian formulation of the ethical ideals seems for the moment, in our mobile contemporary philosophical and religious thought, too abstract and rigid. And so we are not likely, in future, to accept any merely one-sided Hellenism.

While no attention can here be given to the solutions of the problem of philosophical monotheism which have been proposed during the last century, the problem of monotheism still remains central for recent philosophy. It may be said that dogmatic formulations are at the present time often treated with the same indifference which is also characteristically shown towards the faith of the fathers, viewed simply as a heritage. Nevertheless, the problems of philosophical monotheism remain as necessarily impressive as they have been ever since the early stages of Christian theology. They are as certain to survive as is philosophy itself. What the whole history of the monotheistic problem in philosophy shows becomes to-day, in view of our explicit knowledge of the philosophy of India, and in view of our wide comparative study of religions, more explicit than ever. Philosophy is a necessary effort of the civilized consciousness, at least on its higher level. Monotheism is a central problem of philosophy. This problem is not to be sufficiently dealt with by merely drawing artificial or technical distinctions between Platonic or Neo-Platonic theories; nor can the problem be solved by calling it the problem of the immanence of God as against His transcendence. The question 'Is God personal?' becomes and will become more explicit in its modern formulation the more we become aware of what constitutes a person. Meanwhile, as was remarked above, the problem of monotheism has other aspects besides the problem of personality.

The essentials of the great issue remain for us, as for our fathers, capable of formulation in the terms which have here been emphasized. To repeat, the philosophical problem of monotheism is (1) In what sense is the world real? (2) In what sense is the world a rational order? (3) In what sense is the world ethical? The effort to answer these questions cannot be made by exclusive emphasis on one of them. For, as we have seen, the problem of monotheism requires a synthesis of all the three ideas of God, and an answer that shall be just to all the three problems. Whether monotheism is true or not can be discovered, in a philosophical sense, only through a clear recognition of the contrast of the three ideas of God, and the synthesis which shall bring them into some sort of harmony. The further discussion of the nature of this harmony does not come within the scope of this article (see art. God [Biblical and Christian]).

LITERATURE.—I. Kant, *Kritik der reinen Vernunft*, Riga, 1781, 'Dialektik,' iii., 'Das Ideal der reinen Vernunft,' tr. J. M. D. Meiklejohn, London, 1860, p. 350 ff.; G. W. F. Hegel, *Vorlesungen über die Beweise für das Dasein Gottes*, printed as a supplement to *Vorlesungen über die Philosophie der Religion*, in *Werke*, Berlin, 1832–87; J. Martineau, *A Study of Religion*, Oxford, 1888; Evelyn Underhill, *Mysticism*[3], London, 1912; W. R. Inge, *Christian Mysticism*, do. 1899; J. Royce, *The World and the Individual*, New York, 1900–01.

JOSIAH ROYCE.

MONOTHELETISM.—I. **The problem.**—The Monenergistic or Monothelete controversy seems at first glance to be a mere sequel to the Monophysite conflict, a knowledge of which is assumed in the present article. On a closer examination, however, we see that the later controversy has a character of its own, since it shows how the adoption of the orthodox Diphysite point of view was not regarded as leading necessarily and directly to Dithelete conclusions. In the art. MONOPHYSITISM (p. 811 ff.) it was indicated how the new orthodoxy came to terms with the problem of the two natures in the one person of Jesus Christ—the problem raised by the Symbol of Chalcedon. The person of the God-man was conceived as arising from the person (ὑπόστασις) of the Logos, which assimilated the human attributes, and upon which, as the core of personality, human nature was, so to speak, engrafted by the process of ἐνυπόστασις. On this hypothesis it might seem entirely justifiable to ascribe everything that Christ said or did to the one volitional activity (ἐνέργεια) of the God-man, and actually, indeed, to regard all as emanating from His undivided will (θέλημα). Such a view, moreover, could be supported by the evidence of earlier Fathers. Cyril, with reference to Lk 8^{54}, had said of Christ: μίαν τε καὶ συγγενῆ δ' ἀμφοῖν [*i.e.* word and hand] ἐπιδεικνὺς τὴν ἐνέργειαν; and it was possible, above all, to adduce the witness of a passage in the fourth Epistle of the pseudo-Dionysius—a passage containing the phrase μία θεανδρικὴ ἐνέργεια, which was destined to play so important a part in the coming days. The Monenergists were possessed with the idea that the redemptive activity of the God-man emanated wholly and solely from His divine nature, that nature providing the stimulus which was mediated by His rational soul and brought to realization in His body. Nor had even the natural operations of Christ as a rational being their source in His human nature purely by itself, as that nature subsisted, not by itself alone, but in the divine nature conceived as inherently personal. Hence that which in Christ corresponds to human nature was itself the work of God: it was one energy, whose source is God, and whose instrument was His humanity; it was one will, and that will was divine. To Sergius of Constantinople (cf. § 2) it seemed perfectly obvious that the rationally endowed body of Christ effected its natural movements only in accordance with the measure assigned by His divine will, and that, just as our bodies are governed by our rational souls, so the whole complex of Christ's human nature was constantly directed by His deity.

The objections urged by the opposite party against this theory of the oneness of Christ's ἐνέργεια were based upon the feeling that it surrendered the distinctively human element in Christ's activity, since it implied that His human nature was a mere passive instrument, and must therefore be conceived as inanimate or, at least, as nonrational. Such a view, however, was in reality a reversion to Apollinarism (*q.v.*); and, even if the Monenergists did not go so far, yet their idea of the one composite energy really presupposed that of the one composite nature as held by the Severians. In point of fact, the theses of the Monenergists approximate very closely to those of the Severians—the more moderate party of the Monophysites. As the Monenergists themselves came to recognize this, they surrendered the phrase μία ἐνέργεια and rallied around the ἓν θέλημα. This position they regarded as unassailable, since two wills (as distinguished from mere impulses or natural tendencies to action) seemed inevitably to involve two subjects endowed with volition (δύο ὑποστάσεις). They rightly recognized that, if there was in the God-man a will which diverged from His divine will, that divergent will could spring from nothing else than an ungodly tendency in the nature which He had assumed. Such a view, however, would have been in conflict with the doctrine of the sinlessness of Christ's human nature, in which all parties were at one, and would therefore have been accounted blasphemy. Gregory of Nyssa, writing long before, had said: τὸ ἐκείνου θέλειν οὐδὲν ὑπεναντίον τῷ θεῷ, θεώθεν ὅλον. The adverse party was wont to appeal to passages like Mt 26^{39}, where the human will and the divine will seem to stand in opposition; but the Monotheletes sought to show from the Fathers that, on a strict interpretation of this text, Christ had a human will κατ' οἰκείωσιν only. They did not mean to deny the presence of a human activity in the one will of Christ, but they held that this activity was entirely due to His divine will. In relation to His divine ἐνέργεια, they maintained, the human ἐνέργεια becomes a πάθος, and, when Gregory said of Christ that His soul wills, he meant that the volition of Christ's soul was due to the will of the Deity who was personally united with His soul, and that, accordingly, it was divine volition in a human form.

The Monenergists and Monotheletes sought to support their contention also on the ground that the phrase δύο ἐνέργειαι had never yet been heard in the doctrinal controversy; and, while this claim was not absolutely valid, yet Sergius could say with some show of reason that none of the θεόπνευστοι τῆς ἐκκλησίας μυσταγωγοί, *i.e.* none of the recognized Fathers of the Church, had made use of the phrase. As regards the formula of the δύο θελήματα, again, the Monothelete case was a still stronger one. In earlier writers the phrase δυὰς θελημάτων is used only as expressing a final consequence foisted upon those who held the doctrine of the two natures. The use of the phrase in a positive sense can be traced only in a single work, written—if genuine—before the Monothelete controversy, viz. the treatise περὶ τῆς ἁγίας τριάδος καὶ περὶ τῆς θείας οἰκονομίας ascribed to Eulogius of Alexandria († 607). But, while the Ditheletes were thus unable to call tradition to their aid, they operated all the more zealously with the inherent logic of their case. In point of fact, no logical objection could be urged from the standpoint of the new orthodoxy, as, *e.g.*, from that of Leontius of Byzantium, against the procedure of ascribing δύο φυσικαὶ ἐνέργειαι to the δύο φύσεις. Indeed, it was, more than all else, this logical inference, *i.e.* the consistent development of the position affirmed in the formulæ of Chalcedon, that helped the doctrine of the two wills to gain the day. It is true that the contradiction involved in the doctrine of the two natures was rendered still more palpable in that of the two wills. But those who had come to terms with the former doctrine had no difficulty in accepting the latter, and it is the aim of the following historical sketch to show how this point was reached.

2. The beginnings of the controversy.—The secession of the Monophysites did serious damage to Byzantium and its Church. It smoothed the way for the advance of the Arabs and of Islām. Far-seeing and energetic politicians sought to arrest the mischief by working for the ecclesiastical reconciliation of the eastern and southern provinces of the empire. The most outstanding figures in this movement were the emperor **Heraclius** (610–641) and the patriarch **Sergius** (610–638). Sergius, a Syrian born of Jacobite parents, was already giving his mind to the thought of union in the early years of his tenure of office. He caught at the watchwords μία ἐνέργεια and μία θέλησις ἤγουν ἓν θέλημα, which had apparently been introduced into the controversy by the Alexandrian Monophysites, and he succeeded at the outset, on the basis of the doctrine implied by these expressions, in winning the emperor's approval of his designs. Soon afterwards (622) Heraclius issued an edict proscribing the doctrine of the *δύο ἐνέργειαι*. But, although Sergius brought all the weapons of patristic learning to bear upon the Armenian and Syrian Monophysites, the negotiations made little headway. It was not until 633 that indications of real progress began to show themselves. **Cyrus,** patriarch of Alexandria, whom Heraclius had translated to that city from Phasis in Lazica, succeeded in bringing about a union with the Theodosians, *i.e.* the Monophysites (see art. MONOPHYSITISM, § 3). The doctrinal programme drawn up by Cyrus, while setting the doctrine of the two natures in the forefront, guarded it carefully by special clauses; it distinctly recognized the Cyrillian terminology of the one incarnate nature, and it adopted the Areopagite formula of the one theanthropic energy. The Monophysites had some grounds for thinking that, as one of our sources puts it, it was not they who made alliance with Chalcedon, but rather Chalcedon with them. About this time, too, the metropolitan church succeeded in effecting an understanding with the Armenian, though this did not last long. The greatest triumph, however, was the winning of **Athanasius,** the Jacobite patriarch of Antioch; for now the occupants of the three great Oriental sees were all on the same side. But at this juncture the union that had been brought about with such difficulty was gravely imperilled by the action of a Palestinian monk.

This was **Sophronius,** who had at an early date maintained relations with the Alexandrian patriarchs Eulogius and John the Merciful. He now made his way from Palestine to Egypt in order to lodge a protest with Cyrus against the articles of union, in which he thought he discerned Apollinarism. As Cyrus hesitated to withdraw the articles at the request of Sophronius, the latter proceeded to Constantinople and tried to induce Sergius to delete the expression *μία ἐνέργεια* from the document. The patriarch was not prepared to take that step, but for the sake of peace he agreed to send his Alexandrian colleague a letter recommending him to have done with the dispute as to one *ἐνέργεια* or two, but forbidding him to sanction the thesis of the two wills, which he stigmatized as blasphemous (*δυσσεβές*). With this Sophronius was satisfied. Sergius, moreover, secured another triumph in gaining the support of Pope Honorius for his pacific policy (cf. § 3). Shortly afterwards (634) Sophronius was appointed to the see of Jerusalem. He broke away at once from the accepted understanding by referring in his inaugural encyclical to the two natures, though he certainly avoided any overt acceptance of the doctrine of the two wills. His action was deeply resented by Sergius, and Honorius tried, though without success, to persuade him to drop the objectionable expression. Eventually the emperor issued a decree, framed by Sergius—the so-called Ecthesis of 638—forbidding all mention either of one energy or of two energies: of one, because the mention of it might lead to a denial of the two natures, and of two, because two energies seemed logically to involve two mutually antagonistic wills.

3. **The case of Honorius.**—Honorius of Rome, by reason of his attitude in the Monothelete controversy, was, as will be explained below (§ 5), put under the ban by an Ecumenical Council. This proceeding has had such important consequences in the war of the confessions that the historian cannot afford to ignore it. Here we must first of all ask what Honorius had really said. The missive in which he explained his theological position to his colleague in Constantinople is extant only in a Greek translation, but the agreement of this translation with the Latin autograph was definitely confirmed at the Council. In this letter Honorius had set in the foreground his desire that the controversy as to one or two energies should be allowed to rest or relegated to the grammarians. The introduction of the new phrases into the doctrinal terminology might bring those who used them under suspicion either of Eutychianism or of Nestorianism. He nevertheless adhered impartially to the view that, whatever decision might be made between the hypothesis of the one and that of the two energies, it was at all events necessary to accept the doctrine of a single will (*ὅθεν ἓν θέλημα ὁμολογοῦμεν τοῦ κυρίου Ἰησοῦ Χριστοῦ*); for, as the Son of God had assumed a pure and supernaturally begotten human nature, the idea of a second will, disparate or antagonistic (*διάφορον ἢ ἐναντίον θέλημα*), was simply out of the question. Passages like Mt 26^{39} or Jn 5^{30}, in which Christ seems to mark a contrast between His own will and the will of God, did not in any real sense indicate a different will, but simply referred to the economy of His assumed humanity (*οὐκ εἰσὶ ταῦτα διαφόρου θελήματος, ἀλλὰ τῆς οἰκονομίας τῆς ἀνθρωπότητος τῆς προσληφθείσης*). Christ, as our example, adopted this manner of speaking for our sake, *i.e.* in order that we should follow His footsteps, not seeking our own will but the will of God.

The letter of Honorius reveals throughout an intelligent and accurate grasp of the situation. To reproach its writer with having adopted the doctrine of the one will is simply an anachronism, for that doctrine had not yet become ecclesiastically suspect. Even Sophronius himself, in fact, as has already been said, had not put the doctrine of the two wills upon his programme, and the question as to the Monotheletism of Honorius is of a piece with that regarding the Monophysitism of Cyril of Alexandria. We might venture to say, indeed, that, if Honorius had, a generation later, occupied the Roman chair in place of Agatho, he would have given the same judgment as the latter did, and thus, to speak paradoxically, would have pronounced his own condemnation. Agatho and the Council of 681 stood face to face with a situation of a totally different kind. As Monotheletism had then become a thing of evil repute, they were simply bound to condemn it, and, in doing so, they could not avoid reprobating the missive of Honorius as well. Above all, however, we must not forget that Agatho not only refrained from protesting against the anathematization of his predecessor, but by the voice of his legate actually gave it his sanction. In the following year Pope Leo II. expressly ratified the condemnation in a communication to the emperor, in which he spoke of Honorius as one 'qui hanc apostolicam sedem non apostolicae traditionis doctrina illustravit, sed profana proditione immaculatam fidem subvertere conatus est.' This judgment is, no doubt, unduly severe, and, measured by the standard of historical truth, positively false. Still, it certainly shows the remarkable freedom from prejudice with which the authority of a pope in matters of doctrine could then be viewed even in Rome itself. It is quite incompetent, on the other hand, to bring the case of Honorius into the question of papal infallibility. If we keep in mind the provisions of the Vatican dogma regarding the import and scope of the pope's infallibility, we shall see at once that they do not apply at all to the missive of Honorius. If the latter is declared to be without error, the same attribute might with equal justification be applied to any other utterance of a pope.

4. **Byzantium and Rome in conflict.**—After the

death of the emperor Heraclius, and the brief reigns of his two sons, his grandson, **Constans II.** (641–668, son of Constantine III.), was raised to the throne in consequence of a court revolt. Constans, too, adhered to the Ecthesis, which, however, had meanwhile encountered a keen resistance, especially among the clergy of the West. In Rome Pope John IV. officially condemned Monotheletism; the N. African bishops raised a vigorous agitation against it; and soon the whole western province was ringing with passionate debate. Constantinople, on the other hand, remained loyal to the Ecthesis. The patriarch Pyrrhus, who had succeeded Sergius, was deposed by Constans on political grounds, being superseded by Paul, a man of like doctrinal views with himself. Pyrrhus went to Africa, and there intervened vigorously in the conflict. With Maximus, an abbot of Constantinople, who had likewise removed to Africa, he conducted a discussion the records of which are among the most notable documents of the whole controversy. Here Maximus proved the victor.

This **Maximus** was the most eminent and effective champion of Ditheletism, and his constancy to his creed won him the title of 'Confessor.' He was born *c.* 580 at Constantinople. His career was that of a high State functionary, and he acted as imperial secretary in the reign of Heraclius. From 630 he lived in the monastery at Chrysopolis (now Scutari), where he soon attained to the dignity of an abbot. He worked energetically on behalf of Ditheletism both in Africa and at Rome, and it was at his instigation that the Lateran Council of 649 (see below) was summoned. As the part which he thus played ran counter to the policy of the emperor, he was at length put upon his trial. In 653 he was arrested and taken to Constantinople, and two years later he was banished. In 662 the unfortunate man was once more subjected to a legal process, as a result of which his tongue was cut out and his right hand struck off, and he died within the year in Lazica on the east coast of the Euxine. The best known of his extant works is his *Scholia* to the pseudo-Dionysian writings, and it was, in fact, the comments of Maximus that secured the Church's recognition of these texts.

The vehement opposition of the Ditheletes, however, did not wholly fail to influence the ecclesiastical policy of the emperor. Already in 648 Constans, acting on the advice of the patriarch Paul, had issued a decree, the so-called Typus, declaring that the dispute regarding the doctrine of the wills must come to an end at once. The Typus, unlike the Ecthesis, avoids all argumentation on matters of detail; disobedience to its provisions was to be visited with severe ecclesiastical and civil penalties. Bnt the Ditheletes would not be silenced. They had now their centre in Rome, and a Council conducted in 649 by Pope **Martin** in the Constantinian basilica of the Lateran Palace, and attended also by the Greek monks who had fled to Rome, affirmed, in explicit conformity with the declaration of Chalcedon, its adherence to the doctrine of two wills and two energies corresponding to the two natures of Christ. The action of Martin raised an agitation in both East and West, and the emperor, bitterly resenting this, as well as the pope's friendly relations with the exarch Olympius, then lying under suspicion of high treason, had him sent to Constantinople (653), and, after a criminal trial, banished to the Chersonese, where in 655 death released him from his sufferings.

5. The 6th Ecumenical Council and the end of the controversy.—For a time it appeared as if the new policy of peace would be attended with success. Pope Vitalian entered into friendly alliance with the emperor; ecclesiastical communion between East and West was tacitly restored; and, when Constans visited Rome in 663, he was received with due imperial honours. At the murder of the emperor, however, the antagonism broke out more fiercely than ever, and the dissension led to a fresh rupture of ecclesiastical relations. Such a state of matters was felt by the politicians, as formerly in Justinian's time, to be intolerable; and to deal with it the emperor **Constantine IV.** Pogonatus (668–685) resorted to the plan of holding an imperial Synod. In November 680, accordingly, the Eastern prelates, together with the legates of Pope **Agatho,** assembled in the Hall (τροῦλλος, hence 'Trullan' Council) of the imperial palace at Constantinople. This Council, which sat, with considerable interruptions, until September 681, is recognized officially by both Churches as the 6th Ecumenical Council. The members, with abundant excerpts from the Fathers in their hands, carried the debate from one point to another, until at last the Roman representatives won acceptance for the doctrine of the two wills, and procured the condemnation of its opponents, living and dead alike, including, as we saw above (§ 3), Pope Honorius. The Roman point of view is set forth in the comprehensive statement laid by Agatho before the emperor—a document that came to be regarded as a counterpart to the Tomus of Leo I. (cf. art. MONOPHYSITISM, § 1). In the Symbol of the Council the terms in which the Chalcedonian formula defines the relation of the two natures are applied to the two inherent wills (*δύο φυσικαὶ θελήσεις ἤτοι θελήματα*). Thus the two wills corresponding respectively to the two natures are not opposed to each other (*οὐχ ὑπεναντία*); on the contrary, the human will is obedient to the divine and omnipotent will to which it is subject (*ἑπόμενον τὸ ἀνθρώπινον αὐτοῦ [i.e. τοῦ λόγου] θέλημα καὶ μὴ ἀντιπίπτον ἢ ἀντιπαλαῖον, μᾶλλον μὲν οὖν καὶ ὑποτασσόμενον τῷ θείῳ αὐτοῦ καὶ πανσθενεῖ θελήματι*), for it was necessary that, while the will of the flesh must indeed act, it should be subordinate to the divine will. Just as the flesh of the God-Logos (*τοῦ θεοῦ λόγου*) is called flesh, and is flesh, so the natural will of this flesh is called, and rightly called, the will of the God-Logos. And, as His holy and stainless animate flesh was not taken away in being made divine (*θεωθεῖσα οὐκ ἀνῃρέθη*), but remained within its own limitations and relations (*ἐν τῷ ἰδίῳ αὐτῆς ὅρῳ καὶ λόγῳ διέμεινεν*), so the human will likewise was not abolished in the act of deification, but was still preserved.

Agatho did not live to see the triumph of his cause, and it was left to his successor, Leo II., to secure the acceptance of the Council's decrees in the West. The most zealous antagonist of Ditheletism in the East, Macarius, patriarch of Antioch, was prevented from doing further mischief by confinement in a monastery. The second Trullan Council, the so-called Concilium Quinisextum (692), homologated the condemnation of Monotheletism. This does not mean, of course, that the conflict was wholly at an end, and, in fact, it was intermittently fanned to fresh outbursts by the wranglings of the Byzantine court. Eventually the emperor Philippicus Bardanes (711–713) undertook to deal with it, while his successor, Anastasius II. (713–715), restored the authority of the Council of 680–681. But Monotheletism was still faithfully adhered to by the Maronites of Mt. Lebanon.

LITERATURE.—i. *SOURCES.*—(1) Letters and other written communications of those who took part in the controversy, as found in the documents of the Lateran Synod and the 6th Ecumenical Council; (2) contemporary works, esp. the writings of **Maximus Confessor** (*Opuscula theologica et polemica ad Marinum, Disputatio cum Pyrrho*) and statements in **Anastasius Sinaita**, Περὶ τοῦ κατ' εἰκόνα καὶ καθ' ὁμοίωσιν, bk. iv. (A. Mai, *Script. Vet. Nova Coll.*, Rome, 1821, vi. 193 ff.); (3) later chronicles and historical works, as, *e.g.*, the Ἱστορία σύντομος of the patriarch Nicephorus, and the Χρονογραφία of Theophanes.

ii. *MODERN WORKS.*—The reader should consult the works cited at the art. MONOPHYSITISM; those of **Gibbon, Walch, Dorner, Hefele, Harnack,** and **Krumbacher** are well worth attention also as regards Monotheletism. The disputes in Armenia touched upon in § 2 of the present article are discussed with special care in **G. Owsepian**, *Die Entstehungsgeschichte des Monotheletismus nach ihren Quellen geprüft*, Leipzig, 1897. The best recent discussion of the case of Honorius—though from the standpoint of papal infallibility—is given in J. Chapman, *The Condemnation of Pope Honorius*, London, 1907 (= *Dublin Review*, cxxxix. [1906] 129 ff., cxl. [1907] 42 ff.). For the relation of the present art. to the writer's artt. in *PRE*[3], cf. the closing note in the literature of art. MONOPHYSITISM.

G. KRÜGER.

MONSTERS (Biological).—'Monstra vocantur quia monstrant.' This ancient platitude may seem ridiculous to-day, but it has not yet lost its meaning entirely. Doubtless in a modern civilized society the birth of a two-headed lamb, of a 'bull-dog calf,' or of a cyclopian child no longer excites attention as a portent of disaster or proof positive of witchcraft. Yet to a certain section of the community the objects present opportunities of enlarging the common store of biological knowledge. The specimens themselves demonstrate eloquently the possibilities of aberration in the processes of normal development and growth. They testify to the existence of numerous independent forces or influences, balanced delicately under normal circumstances. They point to a disturbance of the balance. They reveal the nature of individual influences, as manifested when one has been exerted in excess, to the exclusion or suppression of the countervailing factors.

In biology monsters are regarded as extreme instances of developmental varieties. Variations of lesser degrees constitute the class of 'abnormalities,' although, as explained in art. ABNORMALITIES (Biological), no hard and fast line separates the two groups. Many monstrous formations are determined by disturbances affecting the embryo or the fœtus, though the post-natal period of growth is by no means free from disorders productive of a comparable result. And instances of the latter kind, such as retarded adolescence, or precocious senility, may be included fairly with others showing the extreme tenuity of the neutral zone between health and disease.

The study of monsters falls naturally into two divisions: (*a*) the investigation of their actual structure, and (*b*) research into the mode of their production.

(*a*) On the anatomical side a classification has been attempted, and it is based upon consideration of the part or parts actually affected. In view of the vast number of categories thus recognized, only the most cursory survey is possible here; and, instead of rehearsing the long list of classes and their subdivisions, it must suffice to note that, while the whole body has suffered in some cases, in others certain parts only will be found to be distorted.

The developmental history of monsters shows us that, as a general rule, the departure from what is normal will be greater and more complete in proportion as the disturbance was early in its occurrence. For in the first phases of development, when the total mass of the embryo is almost infinitesimally small, even a slight error will affect the rudiments of every organ and structure that is to be perfected subsequently. At this point again two distinct groups of monsters must be contrasted. In some cases the uterus may void its contents prematurely as a shapeless mass; to this, in human pathology, the antiquated term 'mole' is still applied. Or, again, the disturbance may lead to partial 'gemination,' *i.e.* to some distorted kind of twin-formation. Thus twins of equal size may continue to grow though connected with each other, and at the birth may produce such a phenomenon as the 'Siamese twins.' In other instances of this class the twins are quite unequal in point of size and, it may be, of development. As a result, an almost normal child may be born with an imperfect twin attached to it. The two are then distinguished as the 'autosite' and 'parasite' respectively. The parasite is most commonly attached to the autosite in or about the middle line of the body. It may present almost any appearance, from that of a mere wart-like excrescence to that of a headless trunk with arms and legs. In rare instances the parasite has been found to be entirely enclosed within the body of its host, so that it is not visible externally at all.

Lastly, in yet another class of monsters, the process of gemination may have been complete but unequal, and one twin is born in a normal state, while the other is represented by a spherical mass, consisting of various tissues and rudiments of organs in the most complete confusion. Even the latter may be maintained alive throughout the intra-uterine period of existence.

Apart from these instances of 'twinning,' we may notice that certain particular structures such as the heart or the brain may be defective to the point of obliteration, while a large class bears witness to interference with such normal processes as the formation of the face or the closure of the walls of the body to protect the viscera.

(*b*) The study of the normal processes of development throws a flood of light on the problem of explaining the particular aberration responsible for the occurrence of a monster. Physiological investigations have dealt with the nature of the disturbing causes, and to these we shall now turn.

The artificial production of monsters first claims attention. In fish-hatcheries the occurrence is accidental and unwelcome, yet the frequency with which grotesquely-formed individuals appear among the fry is so well known as to be almost a matter of common knowledge. The eggs of the domestic fowl have been used for experimental purposes for at least fifty years past. In this department of biology the name of the French observer, C. Dareste, deserves special mention. The more usual modes of procedure are to subject the eggs during artificial incubation to selected abnormal influences. These may be of the nature of magnetic force, variations of temperature, or, again, the disturbances caused by partially varnishing the eggs, or by subjecting them to incessant rotation. In these ways various physical agencies have been shown to be influential in producing monstrous forms. Eggs of other animals (often those of Invertebrates) have been employed to test the effects of chemical agents or of altering the chemical constitution of the media in which the developing eggs normally rest. Such ova have also been the subjects of experiments in which the fertilizing element has been varied.

Physiological research of this kind has established clearly the susceptibility of the egg-cell to a variety of influences, whether these be physical, mechanical, or chemical. At this point another possibility seems to demand notice. The influence of so-called maternal impressions has long been discussed by those who are not prejudiced on this subject. Only the highest forms of life are suitable for observation or research in this respect, and it cannot be said that the potency of such impressions has been established.

Turning more particularly to human beings, it may be mentioned that medical research has shown that certain monstrous developments, viz. Acromegaly and Achondroplasia, are due to the excess or deficiency of certain fluids which normally pass with the blood to bathe the tissues of the body. In this department of research only the first steps have been taken as yet.

In such ways the anatomical study of monsters shows the investigator what parts have suffered, while the physiologist is able to point to the disturbing element. Thus we are left with the impression that, where the balance of reacting forces is so delicate, no absolute standard of what is a normal form is possible. A normal individual is connected with others which we call abnormal by an infinite number of intermediate forms. And the abnormal examples in turn lead on to monsters.

That which is born is the outcome of a host of interacting forces. Its capacity to maintain existence and to reproduce its kind depends first upon its conformation, and then upon the environment in which it finds itself. Two remarks may be made in conclusion. Though the attribute of vast size is commonly associated with our ideas of monsters, yet from the biological point of view this is not necessary, and huge monsters are but representative of one out of many possibilities.

And lastly, while in this article the occurrence of monstrous forms among animals has been reviewed, it is to be remembered that most of the considerations here set forth are applicable equally to the vegetable kingdom.

LITERATURE.—Special mention may be made of C. Dareste, *Recherches sur la production artificielle des monstruosités*, Paris, 1877; other contributions to the literature are so numerous as to preclude even a partial enumeration here. Reference is made specially to the exhaustive bibliography provided by E. Schwalbe, *Morphologie der Missbildungen*, Jena, 1906.

W. L. H. DUCKWORTH.

MONSTERS (Ethnic). — **1. Various kinds of monsters.**—The existence of monstrous beings, human, animal, or diabolic, is believed in at all levels of culture. They are referred to or described in stories, traditions, or myths, or they are depicted or represented in some artistic form. Among savages monstrous animals are often supposed to exist, like the Bun-yip of Australian tribes—a mythic water-monster who carries off women—or the monsters or dragons said to swallow youths at initiation in New Guinea.[1] Frequently more or less distant tribes are believed to have some monstrous or abnormal feature—one eye, more than two eyes, eyes under the arms, vast ears, two or more heads —to be headless or featureless or of great size, or to possess tails. Ghosts, especially ghosts of those who have died a violent death, are often visualized as monsters of a more or less horrible kind, usually with a fondness for human blood. Among barbaric peoples similar beliefs are found, especially in Oriental mythology and folk-lore. Here whole classes or tribes of monstrous beings exist, like the *rākṣasas* of Hindu myth—hideous fiends with shape-shifting powers—or the evil *jinn* or the ghouls of Arabic belief, or the satyrs, centaurs, and cyclopes of Greek mythology. Here also human tribes of monstrous form are a subject of popular belief. The people of Jābah (Java?) were supposed by the Arabs to have their heads in their breasts.[2] Herodotus describes some of the tribes supposed to live beyond the region of the Scythians —men with goats' feet, men with one eye (the Arimaspi)—and other tribes believed in by the Libyans —monsters with dogs' heads or headless with eyes in their breasts.[3] Pliny also writes copiously about such tribes.[4] Irish mythology speaks of tribes of men with dog, or cat, or goat heads.[5] Tribes or individuals covered with an abnormal growth of hair are often mentioned by ancient or mediæval travellers from the Carthaginian Hanno onwards.[6] In Egypt monstrous creatures were often figured on tombs, and the god Bes is depicted as a dwarfish but monstrous and repulsive figure.

1 R. Neuhauss, *Deutsch-Neu-Guinea*, Berlin, 1911, iii. 296, 402 f., 489, 493 f.

2 S. Lane-Poole, *Arabian Society in the Middle Ages*, London, 1883, p. 45.

3 iv. 25, 27, 191.

4 *HN* vii. 1 ff.

5 J. A. MacCulloch, *The Religion of the Ancient Celts*, Edinburgh, 1911, p. 217.

6 A. F. Le Double and F. Houssay, *Les Velus*, Paris, 1912, p. 136 ff.

The monstrous creatures of Babylonian and Assyrian art are well-known—winged bulls or lions with human heads, and other abnormal forms. These were set in front of entrances as a means of frightening away evil spirits, and a similar use of hideous figures is known elsewhere (see DOOR, vol. iv. p. 848 f.), at both lower and higher levels.[1]

Among the folk everywhere monstrous beings have a real existence to the imagination, and are doubtless survivals of similar beings believed in by their forefathers. But the influence of Christianity was often to give a sinister aspect to the supernatural beings of the older paganism. The water-horse and water-bull of Celtic lore are typical examples of monsters which have still a real existence to the folk in remote districts. Demoniac beings are also often envisaged as monsters, and everywhere more or less repulsive giants and dragons have been subjects of popular belief (see DEMONS AND SPIRITS, GIANTS).

The mythologies of most races tend to give a demoniac, gigantic, or monstrous form to the supernatural enemies of culture-heroes[2] or the gods—Tiāmat and her brood in Babylonia, the opposing hosts of beings whom Rā daily conquered in Egyptian belief, the demons, giants, or monsters who strive with gods in Hindu, Greek, Teutonic, or Celtic myth. They typify chaotic powers as opposed to and conquered by the powers of order, and hence they constantly tend to be regarded as evil, while their opponents embody righteousness and goodness.

As early as the days of primitive man monstrous forms have been depicted in various ways. Thus in caves at Marsoulas and Altamira grotesque faces may represent demons, while other curious hybrid figures, half-human, half-animal, have been variously interpreted, but may represent monsters of the imagination of the Stone Age.[3] Savage art tends to give all its human or supernatural subjects a grotesque, if not monstrous, form, often, no doubt, from lack of skill, but there is sometimes a deliberate exaggeration, in a horrible or grotesque direction, of features or of one or more members of the body. This monstrosity of feature is also seen in masks worn on ceremonial occasions by savages, and often meant to represent the faces of particular spirits.[4] Indian art delighted to represent its divinities as many-headed or many-armed—a method which has spread into adjacent countries.[5] Tibetan representations of demons or gods are often repulsive in their monstrosity. Reference has already been made to the monstrous Babylonian figures. In mediæval and later Christian art demons and the devil were depicted in the most sinister and horrible form possible—half-human, half-animal, or with exaggerated features, tusks, horns, tails, or with faces on chest, stomach, or knees.[6]

2. Origin of the belief in monsters.—Probably no single origin is to be looked for. There may have been different origins for the belief as a whole, or particular monstrous forms may have had an origin different from that of some other forms.

(*a*) Imagination is doubtless responsible for much of the monstrosity that is attributed to men, mythical animals, or demons in mythology or primitive art. As man's imagination peopled the world around him with spirits, so these appeared to his imagination as 'gorgons, hydras,

1 Cf. a monstrous figure for scaring evil spirits from the Nicobar Islands (*Handbook to the Ethnographical Collections, Brit. Museum*, London, 1910, p. 77; cf. *ERE* iii. 435a).

2 Cf. *ERE* vi. 638 f.

3 W. J. Sollas, *Ancient Hunters and their Modern Representatives*, London, 1911, p. 247.

4 R. Andree, *Ethnographische Parallelen und Vergleiche*, new ser., Leipzig, 1889, p. 107 ff.; W. H. Dall, 'On Masks, Labrets,' etc., 3 *RBEW* [1884], p. 67; *Handbook to the Ethnographical Collections, Brit. Museum, passim.* See also art. MASK.

5 Cf. HAND, HEAD, for other instances.

6 This is particularly noticeable in illuminated MSS or in pictures of the Temptation of St. Anthony type. Cf. Le Double and Houssay, *passim.*

and chimæras dire.' There was a constant tendency to visualize the creatures of belief as human and yet as more than human, as animal and yet as more than animal. As man drew little distinction between himself and animals, as he thought that transformation from one to another was possible, so he easily ran human and animal together. This in part accounts for animal-headed gods or animal-gods with human heads. Or, where gigantic superhuman strength, wisdom, or productiveness was concerned, man represented these to himself by forming images of the beings who possessed them with numerous or enormous heads or arms or phallus.[1] There is little doubt also that the lack of skill in depicting the human form tended to fill with suggestions of monstrosity the minds of those who gazed on such images.

(*b*) This last fact may have in turn influenced the dreams of men, and, as dream figures were realities, such forms were believed to have a real existence. But, apart from that, and especially when we consider the way in which dreams are deliberately cultivated by the medicine-man (see AUSTERITIES), they have, no doubt, had strong influence in the creation of monsters, of which the mind in waking hours could no more rid itself than could Frankenstein escape his monstrous creation. The combination of existing but diverse forms would easily occur in sleep, and such monstrous forms would play a part in the drama enacted during the hours of sleep. Such forms, seen in sleep by men to whom dreams had an intense reality, became a real part of the contents of the actual world in which they lived.[2] Primitive and savage men are like children, and they no doubt had their night terrors, caused by fantastic or horrible figures seen in dreams and still appearing to haunt them when sleep was rudely broken by the effect of fear. Again, hallucinations seen in waking hours by those whose mental balance was deranged might also aid in the creation of monsters, as they form part of the world inhabited by persons with certain kinds of mental affliction.

'Long rows of horrible characters may pass in endless procession before the strained and wearied eyes; pictures of a vividness scarcely ever realised in normal life are presented, in which the most horrible acts are being committed by personages of frightful mien.'[3]

Such hallucinatory appearances, described to the sane, would by them be accepted as real, and it is probable that the medicine-man, living an abnormal life and given to seeing visions, is never quite sane. But, again, the savage in his waking life is probably the subject of hallucinatory impressions to a far greater extent than the civilized man. His psychic state when awake bears a close resemblance to his psychic state when asleep. What he thinks he sees is actual to him, and every illusion, however incredible or monstrous, is a fact.[4] Even in cultured Egypt there were figured on the tombs the monstrous forms which the deceased thought he had seen in his lifetime.[5]

(*c*) Monsters, again, may owe their origin to a basis of fact. Any large predatory animal whose coming and going was obscure would tend to be envisaged in still more awful guise. Some, indeed, have argued that belated survivals of now extinct animals may have suggested the dragons and other monsters of folk-tale and tradition, and, if this were true, it is certain that the impression made by them would easily become legendary.[1] Most savages have traditions of monstrous animals, which are really exaggerated forms of actual animals seen by their ancestors, but unknown to their descendants in their new habitat—*e.g.*, the monstrous lizards of Maori tradition are the crocodiles of the land whence the Maoris migrated.[2]

Perhaps actual abnormal or monstrous births may have assisted in the formation of mythical monsters, or would tend to be regarded in popular belief as matters of common occurrence. Thus in China the standard histories are full of such prodigies.[3] It is certain also, apart altogether from the possibility of abnormal births as a result of bestiality, that men have often speculated upon this or imagined the effects of such unnatural unions between different species of animals or between beasts and human beings. This is seen in universal folk-lore and in ancient myth, as well as in the half-gossiping histories and chronicles of bygone days and in the pseudo-scientific works on natural history from the time of Pliny onwards.[4] Mediæval theology also believed that the union of demons and human beings resulted in the birth of monsters.

The brutality or merely the hostility of other tribes, nearer or more distant, would inevitably cause them to be regarded in a still more sinister or monstrous aspect. Horrible deformities were attributed to them, or this or that feature was exaggerated, or habits of a peculiar vileness were ascribed to them—*e.g.*, forms of loathsome cannibalism. Even remoteness or ignorance of such tribes would invest them with distorted forms. Here, probably, is to be seen the origin of the belief in those monstrous tribes already alluded to. Invading peoples, behaving with brutality, are sure to be regarded as monsters. In the same way the monstrous cannibalistic ogres of folk-tale are exaggerated forms of actual cannibals (see CANNIBALISM). Again, where certain deformities are assumed by warriors to strike terror into their opponents, where faces are painted or tatued, masks or animal head-dresses worn, these are apt to become a real part of the men themselves.[5] They are regarded as monsters rather than as men.

(*d*) Lastly, the misinterpretation of fact may easily give birth to monsters. This is especially seen where the bones of fossil animals of large size have been regarded as those of monsters or giants, or their tusks as the claws of monstrous birds—the griffin or the rukh. Hence the rise of many myths about these beings—*e.g.*, of how they were slain by gods or spirits beneficent to men.[6]

There is no doubt that the belief in the existence of monstrous forms has had a profound influence on the mind of man, probably for the reason that, as has been proved experimentally, any abnormal shape has a strong power of suggestion.[7]

LITERATURE.—U. Aldrovandi, *Monstrorum Historia*, Bonn, 1642; E. P. Evans, *Animal Symbolism in Ecclesiastical Architecture*, London, 1896; C. Gould, *Mythical Monsters*, do.

1 Cf. HAND, HEAD; cf. the images of Hermes and similar images among the Bushmen, Admiralty Islanders, tribes of the Niger Coast, Yorubans, Fijians, etc. See A. Lang, *Myth, Ritual, and Religion*², London, 1899, ii. 275; *JAI* xxviii. [1899] 110; A. B. Ellis, *The Yoruba-speaking Peoples*, London, 1894, p. 78; T. Williams, *Fiji and the Fijians*, i., do. 1858, p. 177.

2 Cf. L. Laistner, *Das Rätsel der Sphinx*, Berlin, 1889, for the creation of myths and mythical beings from dreams.

3 B. Hollander, *The First Signs of Insanity*, London, 1912, p. 237.

4 S. Freud and his school have argued that the mythopœic faculty is one akin to dream fancy. Myth is a kind of waking dream. See his 'Der Dichter und das Phantasieren,' in his *Sammlung kleiner Schriften zur Neurosenlehre*, Leipzig, 1911 f. Cf. K. Abraham, *Traum und Mythus*, Vienna, 1909.

5 A. Wiedemann, *Religion of the Ancient Egyptians*, Eng. tr., London, 1897, p. 179. The sphinxes, griffins, etc., were thought to be real creatures of the desert.

1 J. A. MacCulloch, *CF*, p. 395.

2 K. M. Clark, *Maori Tales and Legends*, London, 1896, pp. 79, 184; E. Shortland, *Traditions and Superstitions of the New Zealanders*², do. 1856, p. 73.

3 J. J. M. de Groot, *Religion in China*, New York, 1912, p. 271.

4 Le Double and Houssay, pp. 228 ff., 239; MacCulloch, *CF*, pp. 253 ff., 277; de Groot, p. 277.

5 Cf. B. Thomson, *Savage Island*, London, 1902, p. 127 f.; C. I. Elton, *Origins of English History*², do. 1890, p. 241; MacCulloch, *Rel. of Ancient Celts*, p. 217; Y. Hirn, *Origins of Art*, London, 1900, p. 272.

6 E. B. Tylor, *Early Hist. of Mankind*², London, 1870, p. 306 ff.

7 Cf. Boris Sidis, *The Psychology of Suggestion*, New York, 1910, p. 42 f.

1886; F. Hedelin, *Des Satyres brutes, monstres, et démons*, Paris, 1888; Joannes Damascenus, *De Draconibus*, in Migne, *PG* xciv. 1599 ff.; Pliny, *HN*; P. Sébillot, *Le Folk-lore de France*, Paris, 1904–07, vol. iii.

J. A. MacCulloch.

MONTANISM.—**1.** The movement now generally known, from the name of its founder, as Montanism had its birth at a village called Ardabau in the part of Mysia adjoining Phrygia, probably not far from Philadelphia (Ramsay, *Cities and Bishoprics of Phrygia*, p. 573). There, as it seems, about A.D. 156, Montanus, a recent convert, who had been a pagan priest, began to prophesy. His prophesyings were accompanied by strange phenomena resembling those associated with demoniacal possession. In what way his exercise of the prophetic charisma was regarded by his opponents as differing from that of the genuine prophets we have various hints from nearly contemporary documents: he spoke while he was actually in a state of ecstasy; the true prophets received their message in ecstasy, but did not deliver it till their faculties returned to a normal condition. Moreover, the 'ecstasy' of Montanus was a kind of madness, deliberately induced, whereas prophets, acknowledged as such by the Church, even when in a state of ecstasy, were of sound mind; the so-called ecstasy of Montanus was, in fact, not ἔκστασις, but rather, as a contemporary writer (*ap.* Eus. *HE* v. xvi. 7, 14) calls it, παρέκστασις. In agreement with these statements an oracle of Montanus declares that the prophet is as a lyre played upon by the divine plectrum; and the form in which most of his extant utterances are cast implies that he was a mere passive instrument, and that the phrases which fell from his lips were actually the *ipsissima verba* of the Deity. His opponents reminded him of the style of the ancient prophets, who as human agents proclaimed the will of God—'Thus saith the Lord.'

2. After a time—as seems to be implied, a considerable time—Montanus was joined by two women, Maximilla and Priscilla, or Prisca, who with his sanction deserted their husbands, and who also claimed to possess the prophetic charisma. Their utterances were similar in matter and in manner to those of their leader.

3. There can be no doubt that Montanus maintained that this 'new prophesying' differed essentially from all preceding prophecy. Thus the novelty of its form was to be explained. It was the fulfilment—so it was alleged—of the Lord's promise of the coming of the Paraclete (Jn 14^{12-18}). The apostles had not the perfection of the Holy Spirit (1 Co 13^{8-10}); this was reserved for the new prophets, of whom Christ spoke in Mt 23^{34}. This is stated to be the Montanist doctrine by many writers, and it is the basis of the exaggerated assertion of Eusebius (*HE* v. xiv.) that Montanus claimed that he himself was the Paraclete.

4. It is not clear whether in the earliest period the prophetesses were regarded as mouth-pieces of the Paraclete in the same sense as Montanus. Eusebius suggests the contrary when he reports that, while Montanus was held to be the Paraclete, the women were 'as it were prophetesses of Montanus' (cf. Did. Alex. *de Trin.* iii. 41. 2; pseudo-Tert. *Hær.* 7). It is possible that at first they were put in a lower position, Mt 23^{34}, but not Jn 14^{12-18}, being taken as referring to them; and that it was only at a later time, perhaps after the death of Montanus, that they were regarded as on a par with him.

5. It is evident that the acceptance of the 'new prophecy' as embodying the final teaching of the Paraclete, and as in some sense superseding earlier revelation, was the cardinal principle of Montanism. This is made manifest by the very phrase 'new prophecy' constantly used by its adherents; by the title πνευματικοί which they arrogated to themselves, as distinguishing them from other Christians (ψυχικοί) (Tert. *passim*; Clem. Alex. *Strom.* iv. 13 [*PG* viii. 1300 C]); and by the polemics of anti-Montanist writers, whose argument was mainly directed to proving that this 'so-called prophecy' was in truth a false prophecy proceeding from the spirit of evil.

The charisma was not regarded as confined to Montanus and 'the women.' Theodotus, *e.g.*, was an ecstatic, and was reported to have died while in an ecstasy.

6. We are not surprised to learn that this sudden outburst of prophecy, and the claims that were made for its leaders, provoked much opposition. Many of those who heard Montanus and his companions would have silenced them. Two Phrygian bishops made an ineffectual attempt to 'prove and refute' the spirit that spoke in Maximilla; another, who had come from Anchiale in Thrace, attempted to exorcize Priscilla. At first, we are told, the movement advanced slowly: 'but few of the Phrygians were deceived.' But after a time, it seems, the majority of the Phrygian Christians became adherents of Montanus. Thus only can we account for the fact that at an early period his followers were commonly spoken of as 'the Phrygians,' and their teaching as 'the heresy of the Phrygians' (οἱ Φρύγες, ἡ κατὰ Φρύγας αἵρεσις, whence the Latin *cataphryges, cataphrygiani*). In due course formal protests were issued by the bishops. While the movement was still in its infancy, Claudius Apollinarius, bishop of Hierapolis, wrote a treatise against it, to which were appended the signatures of many bishops, at least one of whom came from Thrace. Other confutations of the new teaching followed it (Eus. *HE* v. xvii. 1). Many synods met in Asia and excommunicated its adherents. On the other hand, the Montanists used scathing words about the ecclesiastical rulers, and stigmatized them as slayers of the prophets. They put forth treatises in which the arguments of their opponents were answered. It is impossible to determine with accuracy the date of the inevitable crisis; but it is certain that in Phrygia before the year 177 the Montanists were excluded from the Catholic Church (Eus. *HE* v. iii. 4; cf. xvi. 22, which clearly refers to the persecution under Marcus Aurelius).

7. It is difficult to fix the date of the beginning of the prophesying of Montanus. The choice is usually held to lie between A.D. 172, under which year Eusebius records the origin of the movement in his *Chronicon*, and A.D. 156–157, which is supported by Epiphanius (*Hær.* xlviii. 1). It is not clear, indeed, that these two dates are inconsistent, for Eusebius may be giving the year, not of the earliest prophesying of Montanus, but of some prominent event which he regarded as the starting-point of the 'heresy'—*e.g.*, the migration to Pepuza (see below, § 9), or the promulgation of one of Montanus's more startling innovations. In any case it is probable that Eusebius's date is a mere inference from the fact that Claudius Apollinarius wrote his anti-Montanistic treatise—which Eusebius appears to have dated on insufficient grounds after 174 (Lawlor, *Eusebiana*, p. 150 f.)—'when Montanus with his false prophetesses was in the act of introducing his error' (*HE* iv. xxvii.). It must therefore be regarded with caution. It is to be observed that Apollinarius wrote some time after Montanus had been joined by 'his false prophetesses' (*ib.* v. xix. 3)—an event which was itself probably a good deal later than the beginning of the prophesying. Further, (1) the history of which a short account has been given in the preceding section requires a period of a good many years; and (2) Maximilla, the last of the three leaders, died in 179–180. The movement must have enjoyed the advantage of their supervision for a sufficiently long time to give it the strength and stability which it undoubtedly possessed. These considerations point to an origin much before 172. The earlier date is therefore to be preferred, though with the misgiving which necessarily attaches itself, in such matters, to the statements of Epiphanius. He has certainly fallen into error in one passage (perhaps two) in which he gives dates connected with the Montanist movement (*Hær.* xlviii. 2, li. 33).

8. That the Paraclete was manifested in Montanus, and in him and his companions revealed the fullness of Christian teaching, was, as we have seen, the original and essential doctrine of Montanism. But, since it was the office of the Paraclete to supplement the teaching of Christ, it was to be expected that this doctrine would be made the basis of a system differing at many points from the teaching of the Church as usually understood. Montanus, it is true, did not consciously deviate from ecclesiastical dogma. His opponents bear witness that he accepted the canonical Scriptures and was orthodox with regard to the resurrection of the dead and the doctrine of the Trinity. But in another sphere his 'innovations' were considerable.

9. Not long after the beginning of the prophesying Montanus crossed the Phrygian border and established himself with his followers at a city called Pepuza, which Ramsay (pp. 213, 573) places west of Eumenia, and not far from the Phrygian Pentapolis. Pepuza, with the neighbouring village of Tymion, he named Jerusalem. To this settlement, which was thenceforward the centre and holy city of Eastern Montanism, he endeavoured to gather adherents from all quarters. These facts, coupled with the lavish promises made by the prophets to their adherents and certain predictions of Maximilla (Eus. *HE* v. xvi. 9, xvii. 4; Epiph. *Hær.* xlviii. 2), apart from a more explicit oracle attributed to another prophetess (Epiph. *Hær.* xlix. 2), would lead us to the conclusion that the 'new prophecy' taught men to expect in the near future, at Pepuza, the final Parousia of the Lord (*ib.* xlviii. 14). The primitive Montanists, in fact, held the doctrine of chiliasm, but chiliasm of a new kind. It was this hope of the Parousia at their Jerusalem that gained for them the name of Pepuzians.

10. Connected in some measure with their chiliastic teaching was their view of the prophetic office in the Church. The prophetic charisma was not an occasional gift, bestowed as the need for its exercise arose; according to the dictum of 'the Apostle' (1 Co 13[8f. ?]), it was perpetual, one of the notes of the Church. Consequently Montanus, Maximilla, and Priscilla received their office in a line of succession. Quadratus and Ammia of Philadelphia were the links which connected them with Agabus, Judas, Silas, and the daughters of Philip (Eus. *HE* v. xvii. 3, 4; Epiph. *Hær.* xlviii. 2). But, since Montanus and his companions were the channels of the ultimate revelation, they were the last of the prophetic succession. After them would come the end.

11. Again, the exalted position given to the 'new prophets' led naturally to the assignment to them of prerogatives generally regarded as belonging to the bishops, and thus to a conflict between the prophets and the regular hierarchy. The prophets had the power of absolution (orac. *ap.* Tert. *de Pud.* 21). This power they shared with the 'martyrs' or confessors (Eus. *HE* v. xviii. 7).

12. Once more, the association with Montanus of two prophetesses involved the recognition that women might hold high office in the Church. Maximilla and Priscilla seem to have made independent contributions to Montanist teaching (Hipp. *Phil.* viii. 19; cf. Did. Alex. *de Trin.* III. xli. 3; *ZKG* xxvi. 486); and they were probably in the habit of prophesying in the congregation (Eus. *HE* v. xvi. 9: ἀκαίρως). There is evidence that, at any rate in later times, other women followed their example (Orig. *ap.* Cramer, *Cat.* v. 279), or even outdid it; for we read of a prophetess in Cappadocia in the 3rd cent., perhaps a Montanist, who baptized and celebrated the Eucharist (Firmilian, *ap.* Cypr. *Ep.* lxxv. 10), of female bishops and priests, and of virgins who regularly officiated in the congregation at Pepuza (Epiph. *Hær.* xlix. 2 f.; Did. Alex. *de Trin.* III. xli. 3).

13. Montanus made laws regarding fasts (Eus. *HE* v. xviii. 2: ὁ νηστείας νομοθετήσας; cf. Hipp. *Phil.* x. 25; Tert. *de Iei.* 13). This does not mean, apparently, that he increased the number or the rigour of fasts, but rather that he reduced them to rule, eliminating thereby the element of free will in such matters, making them a duty to be observed by all Christians alike, and not only by those who used them as a means for attaining higher perfection. Among these ordinances (perhaps a later development, due to 'the women' [Hipp. *Phil.* viii. 19]) were some which enjoined abstinence from particular kinds of food (ξηροφαγίαι, ῥαφανοφαγίαι). There is some evidence that in Phrygia the Montanist rule as regards the number of fasts fell below Catholic custom (Soz. *HE* vii. 19, where the two weeks of Lent seem to correspond to the 'duae hebdomadae xerophagiorum' of Tert. *de Iei.* 15), while in the West it did not greatly exceed it (see de Labriolle, *La Crise*, p. 399 f.). The regulations about fasting are therefore to be regarded as instances of the Galaticizing or legal tendency which was descried in Montanism by its adversaries (Tert. *de Iei.* 14). This was the natural outcome of a system which invested the exhortations of the prophets with a divine sanction, giving them the character of unalterable laws, to be observed as ends rather than as means for the attainment of holiness.

14. Under the same category may be brought the Montanist repudiation of second marriages. For on this point their divergence from the Church must not be exaggerated. The Church discouraged second marriage; the Montanists held it to be fornication. That which the Church permitted in special cases the Montanists excluded by a law which admitted no exception.

15. We learn (Eus. *HE* v. xvi. 20, xviii. 5) that the Montanists held martyrs (including confessors) in high honour, and even set special store by their opinion on questions of doctrine and practice. But this was no peculiar feature of their system; it reflected the general feeling of the age. And, when they went a step further and allowed them the power to forgive sins, they were in agreement with the orthodox of the West (Tert. *de Pud.* 22), if not also with those of Phrygia. It must be added that there is no proof of the statement, often made, that Phrygian Montanism inculcated a severe asceticism, or that its adherents were more antagonistic to heathenism than other Christians in the same district, or displayed special eagerness for martyrdom. Such evidence as exists points in the opposite direction (Lawlor, *Eusebiana*, pp. 127–135).

16. Montanism, after its severance from the Church, though it retained the hierarchy of bishops, priests, and deacons, developed in its organization some peculiar features. Montanus was responsible for the innovation (as it was esteemed) of salaried preachers, and for the institution, doubtless connected therewith, of collectors of money, headed, as it seems, by a steward (ἐπίτροπος [Eus. *HE* v. xvi. 14]). St. Jerome (*Ep.* xli. 3) reports, in agreement with an ordinance of Justinian (*Cod. Just.* I. v. 20. 3), that the hierarchy consisted of the patriarch of Pepuza, κοινωνοί (apparently the successors of the stewards), bishops, and inferior ministers.

17. Of the peculiarities of Montanism here enumerated some were a revival—perhaps rather a survival—of the belief and practice of an earlier period; such, *e.g.*, are the recognition of prophets as a permanent order (1 Co 12[28], Eph 4[11]; *Didache*, 11 ff.), the prohibition of second marriage (Athenag. *Leg.* 33; Theoph. *ad Autol.* iii. 15; Iren. III. xvii. 2), chiliasm (Just. *Dial. c. Tryph.* 80; Eus. *HE* III. xxxix. 12 f.). Others are in harmony with what is known of the Oriental religious temperament, especially that of the Phrygians, and may be accounted for by the influence of environment. Among these are the 'enthusiasm' of the prophets (Bonwetsch, *Gesch. des Montanismus*, p. 62 ff.), the ministry of women, and the expectation of an immediate Parousia (Hipp. *in Dan.* 18 f.; Orig. *c. Cels.* vii. 8–10). The substitution of Pepuza for the literal Jerusalem may be due to the same influence. It had, at any rate, the practical advantage of providing a holy city in the district from which Montanus drew the greater number of his adherents.

18. It is not necessary to pursue the history of

Eastern Montanism in detail. For some years after the death of Maximilla, the last of the original trio, in 179–180, there were no prophets, and the Church and the world enjoyed peace—facts which, as anti-Montanistic writers pointed out, disproved the claims of the first prophets. But the spread of the sect was not permanently checked thereby. A revival of prophecy seems to have taken place shortly before A.D. 200 (Eus. *HE* v. xviii. 3–12), and ultimately adherents of the movement were found in every part of Asia Minor, in Egypt (Clem. Alex. *Strom.* iv. 13 [*PG* viii. 1300 C]; Did. Alex. *de Trin.* etc.), and even in Constantinople, though they were always most numerous in Phrygia. The sect survived the stringent edicts of various emperors, and was perhaps not wholly extinguished till the period of the Turkish invasion (Ramsay, p. 574).

19. Before we turn to its history in the West, some important facts may be mentioned. The early Montanists were prolific writers. Their controversial tracts have been referred to above (§ 6). Here it is to be noted that Caius (*c.* A.D. 200) accuses them of composing new Scriptures (Eus. *HE* VI. xx. 3), while other authorities attribute numerous writings to Montanus, Maximilla, and Priscilla. A certain Asterius Urbanus compiled a collection of oracles of the prophets (*ib.* V. xvi. 17); and Themiso 'wrote a Catholic Epistle in imitation of the Apostle' (*ib.* xviii. 5). An anonymous author quoted by Eusebius alludes to literature of this class when he states that he hesitated to write against the Montanists for fear of being charged with adding to the Canon (*ib.* xvi. 3). It is clear that the 'new prophecy' was propagated by writing as well as by oral teaching.

A necessary result of this was a tendency to division. The Montanists must have regarded the writings of their own prophets as of at least equal value with the Scriptures: they constituted in fact, if not in intention, an enlargement of the Canon. It was inevitable that they should be used, like the canonical Scriptures, as authoritative expositions of dogmatic Christianity, and that, like them, they should be variously interpreted. By the end of the 2nd cent. there were two parties of Montanists, who took different sides in the Monarchian controversy, and both of them appealed to the oracles of the prophets as well as to the Scriptures (Hipp. *Phil.* viii. 19; pseudo-Tert. *Hær.* 7; Did. Alex. *de Trin.* ii. 15, iii. 18, 23, 38, 41; *ZKG* xxvi. 452 ff.; Tert. *adv. Prax.* 2, 8, 13). Thus the authority ascribed to the writings of the prophets produced a tendency to the formation of parties differing from one another in matters of faith, and probably also in matters of discipline. This tendency would be greater if, as seems likely, such writings were not collected into a *Corpus*. Each community would follow the teaching of such books as they happened to possess, without the obligation of harmonizing it with that of the books possessed by other communities.

20. A similar tendency is revealed in the fact that in the earliest times, apart from the title of Phrygians, which merely indicated the place of its origin (Clem. Alex. *Strom.* vii. 17), there was no generally accepted name for the sect. The various communities seem to have been commonly designated by the names of local leaders. Thus we hear of the followers of Proclus or of Æschines (pseudo-Tert. *Hær.* 7), the adherents of Montanus, Alcibiades, and Theodotus (Eus. *HE* v. iii. 4), the followers of Miltiades (*ib.* xvi. 3: probably the Montanists of the Pentapolis), the Priscillians, and the Quintillians (Epiph. *Hær.* xlix. 2; on the latter name see Voigt, *Eine verschollene Urkunde des antimontanistischen Kampfes*, pp. 107, 129 f.). Apparently the last name of this class to emerge was that with which we are most familiar, 'Montanists' (first found in Cyril, *Cat.* xvi. 8). There are also nicknames, which we may suppose to have been merely local, and to have witnessed to local customs (cf. Jerome, *in Gal.* ii. 2). Such are the Artotyritæ of Galatia (from the use of bread and cheese in the mysteries), the Tascodrugitæ (from a peculiar way of holding the hands in prayer; of this Passalorynchitæ is a variant form; cf. Ramsay, p. 576), and the Ascodrugitæ or Ascitæ of Galatia (from orgies connected with a wine-skin [Epiph. *Hær.* xlviii. tit. 14; Filast. 49, 76; Aug. *Hær.* 76]). It is perhaps scarcely correct to speak of Montanism as a sect. In its later stages it was rather a congeries of sects somewhat loosely held together by an acknowledgment of the manifestation of the Paraclete in Montanus (cf. Voigt, p. 131).

21. The earliest notice which we possess of any knowledge of the Montanist movement in the West appears in the year 177. In that year the Christians of Gaul, acting as ambassadors for the peace of the churches, wrote letters to Pope Eleutherus and to the brethren in Asia and Phrygia expressing their opinion of the movement. Since Eusebius (*HE* v. iii. 4) pronounces their judgment 'pious and most orthodox,' it may be inferred to have been, on the whole, anti-Montanist. And this conclusion is confirmed by an examination of the account of the persecution at Vienne and Lyons, written at the same time (de Labriolle, *La Crise*, p. 225 ff.). If we may judge from two passages of Irenæus (*Hær.* III. xi. 9, IV. xxxiii. 6 f.), who was their emissary to Rome, though they avoided the extreme position of the Alogi (see art. LOGOS, above, p. 137[a]), who in their zeal against Montanism rejected the Johannine writings, and though they refused to deny the existence of prophetic gifts or the right of women to prophesy in the church, they yet condemned the followers of Montanus as schismatics. It would seem that Eleutherus confirmed their judgment.

It is difficult to explain this incident without supposing that there was at the time a Montanist propaganda in Rome. No doubt the Montanist missionaries there were quickly followed (perhaps preceded) by representatives of the orthodox party in Phrygia; and it may be conjectured that among these was Avircius Marcellus of Hierapolis in the Pentapolis, 'the chief figure in the resistance to Montanism in the latter part of the second century' (Ramsay, p. 709). He certainly visited Rome with a purpose in some way connected with the welfare of the Church; and in one of the passages from Irenæus just referred to there are phrases which recall both the labours of the Gallican Christians for the peace of the churches (cf. Iren. *Hær.* IV. xxxiii. 7 with Eus. *HE* v. iii. 4) and a treatise dedicated to Avircius almost at the time when his famous epitaph recording the visit to Rome was written (cf. Iren. *Hær.* IV. xxxiii. 6 with Eus. *HE* v. xvi. 7 f., and see Ramsay, pp. 709 ff., 722 ff.).

22. Twenty-five years later, under Pope Zephyrinus, a fresh attempt was made to introduce Montanism into Rome. The Montanist leader Proclus held a disputation there with Caius, which was afterwards published, and some fragments of which remain (Eus. *HE* II. xxv. 6 f., VI. xx. 3). The pope favoured the 'new prophecy,' and had actually put forth 'letters of peace to the churches of Asia and Phrygia'; but in the end, under the influence of Praxeas, these letters were withdrawn (Tert. *adv. Prax.* 1). There were doubtless later attempts of the same kind; one is referred to by St. Jerome (*Ep.* xli.). But Montanism was never strong in Rome, and it is not heard of there after the beginning of the 5th century.

23. It secured some foothold in Spain. But of its history in that region we know nothing except that it had some adherents there at the end of the 4th century (Pacianus, *Ep.* i. 1 ff.).

24. In Africa the propaganda had more success. By the end of the 2nd cent. knowledge of the 'new prophecy' had reached Carthage—perhaps from Rome, less probably direct from Phrygia—and it gained there its most illustrious convert in the person of Tertullian. St. Augustine seems to have gone beyond his evidence when he stated that Tertullian at first opposed the movement; he was certainly in later life a sincere and ardent champion of the teaching of Montanus, as he understood it.

25. The qualifying words are necessary; for Montanism, as it appears in the pages of Tertullian, differs so much, and withal is so little conscious of difference, from the Montanism of Phrygia that we are compelled to suppose that his acquaintance with the teaching of the prophets was imperfect. He can hardly have received direct instruction from Eastern Montanists; his knowledge of their tenets must have been, in the main, derived from books, including a collection (*de Fuga*, 9; note the words 'et alibi') of the oracles of Montanus and Priscilla (he never quotes Maximilla by name), which was apparently incomplete.

Tertullian accepted, without reserve, the claim of the prophets to inspiration by the Paraclete. But, though he speaks of prophetic speech in a state of ecstasy (*de Iei.* 3), we find no hint in his writings of the strange phenomena which were the normal concomitants of Montanist prophecy in the East. He tells us (*de An.* 9) of a sister who fell into an ecstasy during a church service; but she was not permitted to communicate the revelation which she had received till the congregation had departed. None of the usual anti-Montanist arguments (see Epiph. *Hær.* xlviii. 3–8) would have had any force against ecstasy so well controlled as this. Tertullian, indeed, identifies ecstasy with *amentia* (*adv. Marc.* iv. 22, v. 8), but with such qualifications of the meaning of *amentia* (*de An.* 45) as to bring him very near to the standpoint of Eastern orthodox writers. Moreover, with habitual inconsistency, he affirmed, in direct opposition to the Phrygians, that the apostles had the fullness of the Spirit.

Further, Tertullian seems to betray no consciousness of the doctrine that there was a succession of prophets from the days of the apostles to Montanus. In his view prophecy ceased with the Baptist (*de An.* 9, *de Iei.* 12), till it was restored in the prophets of the Paraclete.

Again, Tertullian never mentions Pepuza. He was a chiliast, and he expected the Parousia in the near future; but he believed that it would take place in Jerusalem (*adv. Marc.* iii. 24). He cannot have read the oracle (Epiph. *Hær.* xlix. 1) which declared that the New Jerusalem would descend at Pepuza.

Tertullian agreed with the Phrygians in allowing to the prophets authority to absolve from sin, though he has some difficulty in reconciling this view with his own opinion that certain sins are unpardonable (*de Pud.* 19, 21). But he is indignant with those who hold that martyrs have a like prerogative (*ib.* 22).

On another subject he is in conflict with the Phrygians. He will not permit a woman 'to speak in the church, nor to teach, nor to baptize, nor to offer, nor to assume any function which belongs to a man' (*de Virg. Vel.* 9). If the sentence had been less trenchant, one might have supposed that it came from an anti-Montanist polemic.

26. Thus Tertullian rejected much that in Asia Minor was counted Montanist. And he added much, especially in the direction of rigorism, of acute opposition to paganism, and of avidity for martyrdom. For it is not to be assumed that, when his later views differ from his earlier, and when he proclaims them as taught by the Paraclete, they were really derived from primitive Montanism. Thus in his *de Fuga* he denounces flight in persecution as sinful, though in his *ad Uxorem* (i. 3) he counts it lawful; and in his *de Pudicitia*, forsaking the milder teaching of the *de Pœnitentia*, he denies the power of the Church to forgive grosser sins. But in the former case he quotes oracles which make no reference to flight, and in the latter one which flatly contradicts his thesis (*de Fuga*, 9, *de Pud.* 21). In both, the oracles are more in harmony with his earlier than with his later opinions. Visions also enabled him to add, now a new doctrine (*de An.* 9), now a fresh rule of discipline (*de Virg. Vel.* 17), to the official teaching of the 'new prophecy.'

27. Even on subjects in which he was in entire accord with Eastern Montanism we find no essential difference between his earlier and later teaching; *e.g.*, he expressed disapproval of second marriage in his pre-Montanist treatise *ad Uxorem*; the arguments used are identical with those of his *de Exhortatione castitatis* and *de Monogamia*, including that founded on the nearness of the end, which is more strongly stated in the earlier work. His description of marriage as a form of fornication occurs in all three. The result of his adoption of Montanist principles is seen merely in the fact that an absolute prohibition takes the place of a strong expression of disapproval; or, in other words, that he draws the logical conclusion from his argument. Here, as elsewhere, he found in oracles or visions only a new sanction for opinions already formed.

28. Thus we see that, if the form of Asiatic Montanism was largely determined by environment, and possibly by the influence of individual leaders, the form of African Montanism, or, as it was afterwards rightly called, 'Tertullianism,' was determined by the personal force of Tertullian himself, and doubtless in some degree by the environment which moulded his character. We cannot forget that the home of Tertullianism was later to become the home of Novatianism and Donatism.

29. If it be asked, What was there in Montanism to attract such a man as Tertullian? it must be remarked that he was unaware of, or ignored, many of those features of the movement which to Eastern opponents caused most scandal. There remained the proclamation of the inspiration of the living Church, burdened with a few corollaries, most of which had been anticipated by his own thinking. Premising this, we may accept the answer of Swete (*Holy Spirit*, p. 79): 'For Tertullian the interest of Montanism lay chiefly in the assurance which the New Prophecy seemed to give that the Holy Spirit was still teaching in the Church.' It need only be added that the acceptance of the Montanist oracles as embodying the teaching of the Paraclete was made easier for him by the support which they seemed to give to opinions which he maintained in opposition to other Christians.

30. The Tertullianists seem to have become an insignificant body after the death of their founder. They are never referred to by St. Cyprian, in spite of his veneration for Tertullian. The last adherents of the sect returned to the Church when St. Augustine was at Carthage, and he reports that, when he wrote his work on heresies, their basilica was in Catholic hands (*Hær.* 86).

LITERATURE.—i. *PRINCIPAL SOURCES.*—The oracles of the prophets (ed. with commentary in de Labriolle, *La Crise*, pp. 34–105); the anonymous writer of A.D. 192 (quoted Eus. *HE* v. xvi. f.); Apollonius (*c.* A.D. 200, quoted *ib.* xviii.); the early document worked up in Epiphanius, *Hær.* xlviii. 2–13 (A.D. 180–200); **Hippolytus**, *Syntagma*, represented by pseudo-

Tertullian, *adv. Omnes Hæreses*, Epiph. *Hær.* xlviii. 1; Filastrius. *Liber de Hæresibus*; Hippolytus, *Philosophumena*, viii. 19, x. 25 f., *in Dan.* iii. 20; the early document underlying Didymus Alex. *de Trinitate*, iii. 41, and the Μοντανιστοῦ καὶ ὀρθοδόξου διάλεξις (ed. G. Ficker, in *ZKG* xxvi. [1905] 446 ff.); Montanist treatises of Tertullian.

ii. *MODERN LITERATURE.*—J. de Soyres, *Montanism and the Primitive Church*, Cambridge, 1878; G. N. Bonwetsch, *Die Geschichte des Montanismus*, Erlangen, 1881, art. 'Montanismus' in *PRE*[3]; G. Salmon, art. 'Montanus' in *DCB*; H. G. Voigt, *Eine verschollene Urkunde des antimontanistischen Kampfes*, Leipzig, 1891; W. M. Ramsay, *Cities and Bishoprics of Phrygia*, Oxford, 1895-97, pp. 573-576, chs. xvi., xvii.; A. Harnack, *History of Dogma*, Eng. tr., vol. ii.[2] London, 1897, ch. iii., art. 'Montanism' in *EBr*[11]; H. B. Swete, *The Holy Spirit in the Ancient Church*, do. 1912, ch. iv.; H. J. Lawlor, *Eusebiana*, Oxford, 1912, essay ii.; P. de Labriolle, *La Crise montaniste*, Paris, 1913, *Les Sources de l'histoire de Montanisme*, do. 1913 (text of all passages relating to Montanism in early writers, with introduction).

H. J. LAWLOR.

MOON.—See SUN, MOON, AND STARS.

MORAL ARGUMENT.—'Moral argument' is distinguished from logical either in the nature of the facts to which appeal is made or in the assurance which the conclusion expresses. It is possible that both implications are associated with its meaning. But in general it is often used to denote some probability in the nature of it as distinguished from the certitude of logical argument.

It is probable that the term derived its specific import from the implications of the 'moral argument' for the existence of God and immortality in the Kantian philosophy. In this method of 'proving' them Kant remarked the impossibility of meeting the demands of the moral law in this life, and, as this law required the adjustment of duty and happiness, he sought this realization in a life to come. To effect this adjustment the existence of God was supposed to be required. This argument was assumed to be valid when all the logical arguments for the same conclusion were null and void. The want of absolute assurance implied in the conclusion was transferred to all arguments which gave what is called 'moral certainty.'

It also derives part of its meaning from the implication that the moral order of things favours or expresses the ultimate significance of what lies behind it. That is, the assumed rationality of things is taken to imply the nature of the causal agency behind it, and the 'moral argument' is an expression of what is supposed to be implied by the admission of an actual moral order in the world, while the logical argument is supposed to be limited to a physical order and its implications.

A fuller exposition of Kant's moral argument for the existence of God and immortality is the following:

> Happiness is the natural condition of a rational being in the world, and is the natural accompaniment of virtue. In fact, the moral law itself requires a union or synthetic connexion between virtue and happiness. But in the present natural order this ideal union is not effected, and we cannot treat the world as rational unless it provides for this connexion between them. The connexion requires an infinite time for its realization, and hence we have to postulate immortality as the condition of realizing the demands of the moral law which holds valid for the present. Immortality thus becomes a necessity of a rational order. But this union of virtue and happiness, not being a necessary one, requires the causal interposition of something to bring it about. Since we postulate immortality as the condition of rationality, we postulate the existence of God to effect the realization of happiness in connexion with virtue The argument, thus, is that morality, if valid and binding at all, requires God and immortality to make its imperatives rational and its rewards possible.

LITERATURE.—I. Kant, *Kritik der reinen Vernunft*, ed. G. Hartenstein, Leipzig, 1867, iii. 531-540, and *Kritik der praktischen Vernunft*, ed. Hartenstein, do. 1867, v. 137-140; B. P. Bowne, *Theory of Thought and Knowledge*, London, 1897, pt. ii. ch. v.; Kuno Fischer, *Immanuel Kant und seine Lehre*, Munich, 1882, ii. 113-126.

JAMES H. HYSLOP.

MORAL EDUCATION LEAGUE.—Following on the rise of the Ethical Movement (*q.v.*) in England, a number of persons interested in the training of the young began to study methods of imparting moral instruction on an ethical basis pure and simple, and in such a manner as to meet the needs of children drawn from all denominations. The Union of Ethical Societies seized the opportunity of an approaching election of the London School Board to invite a wide variety of societies to send delegates to a conference. In July 1897 the delegates met under the presidency of Frederic Harrison, and adopted a policy of which the two leading statements were as follows:

> (1) 'That there is urgent need of introducing systematic moral instruction without theological colouring into the Board schools in place of the present religious teaching.'
>
> (2) 'That this moral instruction should be made the central, culminating and converging point of the whole system of elementary education, giving unity and organic connection to all the other lines of teaching, and to all the general discipline of the school life.'

A direct result of this conference was the establishment of the Moral Instruction League at a well-attended meeting in St. Martin's Town Hall on 7th December 1897, and annual meetings have been regularly held and reports issued since January 1898. The original object, 'to substitute systematic non-theological moral instruction for the present religious teaching in all State schools,' was changed, in 1901, to the purely constructive policy 'to introduce systematic non-theological moral instruction into all schools.' On the same principle, the object was, in 1909, relieved of the phrase 'non-theological,' and made to run thus: 'To urge the introduction of systematic moral and civic instruction into all schools, and to make the formation of character the chief aim in education.'

At the same time the title of the society was altered to the Moral Education League. The League, however, definitely affirms that it 'works on a non-theological basis,' and both its considerable output of literature and its practice during the seventeen years of its history (1898–1915) have obviously exhibited its detachment from all forms of sectarian and denominational principles. Its supporters in the earlier stages made attempts, with some success, to induce parents to take advantage of the Conscience Clause of the Education Act of 1870, withdraw their children from religious instruction, and apply for special moral lessons. These efforts ceased as the League became more absorbed in its scheme for building up a sound method of civic teaching, and for illustrating that method by lessons publicly given under the direction of a Moral Instruction Circle. The Circle was nominally conducted by the Union of Ethical Societies, but naturally proved very useful to the League as a means of propaganda, and it was maintained for several years. Active dissemination of the League's views by meetings, in the press, and among Education Committees and Members of Parliament gradually leavened public opinion. In 1904 the Government Education Code appeared with a preface in which character-training was emphasized; in 1905 the official volume of *Suggestions for the Consideration of Teachers and Others concerned in the Work of Public Elementary Schools* contained a section on the formation of character; and in 1906 the Code, issued by Augustine Birrell, directed local authorities to devote 'greater and more systematic attention' to the subject, though the choice of 'direct' or 'incidental' methods was left open. In 1909 a debate on moral instruction, led by G. P. Gooch and William Collins, took place in the House of Commons, and a deputation, largely composed of League representatives, waited upon the Minister of Education (W. Runciman) in May of the same year. Since that date the League has been quiescent in the political field, and has mainly devoted its energies to influencing the opinion of educationists and the general public. A return issued by the League in 1908 showed that, of the 327 local education authorities in England and Wales over 100 had taken definite action in emphasizing moral instruction in their schools, in some cases by setting apart a lesson in the secular time-table, but usually by incorporating special moral elements in the religious course; and twenty authorities had adopted the syllabus drawn up by the League. Besides this syllabus, which supplies a detailed series of notes for the seven standards, the literature of the League includes a number of text-books by A. M. Chesterton, Baldwin, Waldegrave, Robson, Reid, Wicksteed, and F. J. Gould, numerous pamphlets, a Quarterly (beginning April 1905), and a volume designed for use in India (*Youth's Noble Path*, 1911). The education authorities in Bombay, Ceylon, and Mysore have evinced practical interest in the methods of the League; and significant sympathy has been shown by H.H. the Gaekwar of Baroda, and many other Indians as well as Anglo-Indians. Each annual report testifies to a spirit of inquiry aroused in various colonies and foreign countries. A remarkable testimony to this spirit was afforded in 1907, when a committee of inquiry into moral instruction and training in schools examined witnesses and collected papers, its report being published in two volumes in 1908 (vol. i. 'United Kingdom,' vol. ii. 'Foreign and Colonial'). The inquiry was carried on independently; but several members of the League sat on the Committee and contributed to the volumes just named. A still more striking reinforcement of the League's endeavours appeared in 1908 in the shape of the first International Moral Education Congress, held in London under the secretaryship of G. Spiller. A similar congress was held at The Hague in 1912.

F. J. GOULD.

MORAL LAW.—The concept of law is one of the two concepts which may be taken as fundamental in an ethical system. According as we start from the idea of a good to be attained or of a law to be obeyed, we have a teleological or a jural theory of ethics. The former of these was the characteristic type of Greek theories; the latter became predominant in Christian times. Under the teleological conception morality is looked upon as fundamentally a matter of self-expression or self-realization, and its laws are regarded as rules for the attainment of a good which every man naturally seeks. It is in this sense that Socrates was able to maintain his paradoxical position that no man is willingly vicious and that all vice is ignorance. Such a position is essentially a naturalistic one, implying a native goodness in human nature which needs only enlightenment to realize its natural good. Moral conduct is the rational pursuit of happiness.

In a jural system of ethics, on the other hand, human nature is conceived as divided against itself and therefore in natural opposition to the good. Morality is not a harmonious development of natural powers guided by the idea of happiness, but a life of discipline and subordination to an authoritative law. It is not the natural value or the pleasure of an act that renders it moral, but its value as commanded by the law. It is not commanded because it is good, but it is good because commanded.

It is evident, therefore, from this distinction of starting-points and attitudes that the term 'moral law,' in its strict meaning, denotes an imperative, regarded as having practical efficacy in conduct. The idea is of an order which is to be imposed upon human nature and, accordingly, to be accepted by the rational will. One must, therefore, distinguish between such an imperative, which does not rest upon any natural desire for happiness, and a moral rule or law in the teleological sense of the term. The moral laws, in the teleological view, are not imperative, but counsels of prudence, pointing out the best ways for the attainment of happiness. Their practical efficacy rests upon a natural desire for satisfaction, and hence, in their hypothetical character, they have more the nature of uniformities in the scientific sense of the term 'law.' They are rules of applied psychology. Although such rules are often spoken of as laws, yet, lacking the element of imperativeness, they are perhaps better not designated by that term.

Historically, the conception of morality as law is an early one, primitive morality consisting in obedience to tribal custom regarded as ultimately imperative for the individual. When ethical reflexion awakes, however, with its scepticism and questioning of authority, the natural view of morality is the teleological one, and the concept of moral law gives way to that of good. Experience and a deepening of the moral and religious consciousness, such as occurred in the Hellenistic age and in early Christian times, revived the dualistic idea of morality, and we have the Christian theories with their central doctrine of moral law and obligation. While these were at first theological in character, in modern philosophy we find the idea of law maintained also upon a natural basis.

Considered with reference to the nature of moral law and its authority, three types of system may be distinguished: (1) theological, (2) natural, and (3) rational.

1. Theological. — In the theological systems moral law is regarded as a rule of conduct which has its ground in the nature or will of God and not in the nature of man or in the consequences involved in obedience or disobedience to the law. The rule may be for the good of man, but it is for his good because it is the divine will, and not the divine will because it is for his good. 'Man's chief end is to glorify God and to enjoy him for ever.' God is the beginning and the end of the moral world, man but an incident in the creation. Sometimes it is the will, sometimes it is the intellect, that sets the standard, but in all cases systems of this type are theocentric in nature. To this type belong the various forms of scholastic theory, so far as they succeed in really breaking away from their classical originals, as well as the chief systems of Protestant moral philosophy.

The serious difficulty in theological systems has always been the question of the authority of the divine law and its hold over the individual. Emphasis upon the divine has tended by contrast to raise new centres of interest in the human, and men have always refused to remain satisfied with the idea of a law whose basis is outside themselves. The significant element has therefore been found either in the consequences of the law for man, in which case we have a utilitarian principle, or in the human nature itself, under which hypothesis we have a natural basis for morals.

2. Natural.—Natural law as a basis for morals may therefore be described as an order of human nature, known to be such by the unaided reason of man, and recognized as binding without reference to the desires or pleasures and pains of the sentient life. Man knows himself as properly of a certain nature, and cannot reasonably depart from the rules involved in its realization. These rules are not imposed from without, but are the expression of his own nature and binding only as such. To be moral is to be truly a man, and to be truly a man is to be truly a rational animal. The norms of reason are the moral laws. This type of theory was prevalent in the earliest period of modern ethics, and represented the attempt to place morals upon a rational basis. The general idea takes various forms as it is expressed in the Stoic formulæ of Grotius and the Neo-Platonic doctrines of the Cambridge Platonists and their like. While theistic in their philosophical implications and foundations, these systems agree in their desire to free morals from theological authority and to found them upon an immanent rather than a transcendent basis. Yet in so doing they tend to lose their jural character and revert to the teleological type of their Greek originals. The dictates of reason which reveal these moral or natural laws are indeed authoritative, but their authority really rests upon the value of the good end or ideal which they express. Moral law, when rationalized, ceases to be supreme, whence it was very easy for the transition to be made from these Platonizing systems to the early forms of English utilitarianism. Indeed, in spite of their legal terminology, it is hardly accurate to include them at all under the jural type; they are the natural compromises of the transitional period.

3. Rational. — The rational interpretation of moral law finds its clearest expositor in Kant. It is true that Butler formulated the traditional English theory of conscience half a century earlier, but even in his conception the supremacy of conscience does not involve independence of consequences; its function is to decide between the rival interests of self-love and benevolence, not to dictate a law irrespective of either. It was Kant's merit, as he conceived it, to separate out the pure principle of a moral law and present it free from any admixture of motions drawn from a consideration of consequences. To be moral is not to seek to satisfy a desire for anything, however good, but to obey a dictate of reason determined by nothing outside its own rationality. A moral law is thus a categorical imperative addressed by the reason to a being not naturally inclined to obedience. The motive to obedience is respect for the law itself whose authority we feel in our sense of moral obligation. The law, as grounded neither in the nature of God nor in its consequences for man, is thus absolute and the expression of a free reason which commands of itself alone, or is autonomous—to use Kant's term. That there is such a categorical imperative is the only fact given us by pure reason, and that, if there are free beings, they must govern themselves by such laws is evident; but how there can be free beings at all, and how we as sentient beings can be subject to such absolute dictates of reason—these are matters involved in the mysteries of personality. The form of such a law, as independent of consequences, must be abstract. Be rational, or 'act from a maxim fit for universal law,' is the formula. It is thus essentially negative—a critical test rather than an informing principle. No act is to be done whose maxim is not capable of universalization, but no principle is given us, apart from experience, by which to determine any positive control for the will.

In its illustration of this rational concept of moral law, Kant's theory also illustrates most adequately the jural concept of morality in general, the essence of which, as in Kant's system, is the primacy and absoluteness of law. In the theological forms the law tends to become heteronomous and foreign, and hence immoral, while in the natural systems it tends to subordinate itself to the concept of good and thus lose its jural character. In Kant's system alone is it at once a law and absolute.

LITERATURE.—F. C. French, 'Concept of Law in Ethics,' in *Philos. Rev.* ii. [1893] 35–53, also published separately, 1892; E. Zeller, *Vorträge und Abhandlungen*, Leipzig, 1865–84; H. J. S. Maine, *Ancient Law*10, London, 1906; Thomas Aquinas, *Summa Theologica*; H. Grotius, *De Jure Belli et Pacis*, Amsterdam, 1720; R. Cudworth, *Treatise concerning Eternal and Immutable Morality*, London, 1731; J. Butler, 'Sermons on Human Nature,' *Works*, ed. J. H. Bernard, do. 1900; I. Kant, *Fundamental Principles of the Metaphysic of Ethics*, tr. T. K. Abbott, do. 1895.

NORMAN WILDE.

MORAL OBLIGATION.—The word 'obligation' comes from Lat. *obligare*, and implies that we are bound to some rule or norm. While legal obligation involves, in any last analysis, some external coercion, moral obligation assumes an inner compulsion, a sense of the personality being bound by that which may have no external authority to enforce it, and which, indeed, may be but very imperfectly formulated. Language bears witness to a universal human experience of a sense of this obligation or 'oughtness.' Even the most primitive speech reveals the sense of an inner compulsion, an inner voice that says 'I must.' In its actual history, however, this inner compulsion has rarely been quite separated from the sense of some external coercion. We find it first expressed in a series of more or less definite inhibitions. Its earlier chapters are written in a series of commandments, saying, 'Thou shalt not,' and this primitive morality is based upon customary and largely external usage. It is, moreover, shaped and sustained in an increasingly elaborate system of 'tabus,' which form a link between the external and internal authorities. The realization of an internal authority as compelling as any external coercion is a relatively recent conception. Indeed, only quite recent discussions have clearly distinguished in theory what practical purpose early made definite, namely, that to the extent that coercion becomes foreign to the agent's will, to that extent it ceases to be the agent's action. Moreover, older moral reflexion failed to draw any sharp line between the sense of moral obligation, as a category of the practical understanding, and that empiric content of the rule or norm to which the moral agent feels himself bound.

1. Uncritical religious intuitionalism ascribed both the sense of moral obligation and the content of the ethical code to an innate sense, and regarded both as a divine implanting in the human soul. Thus to both was ascribed a certain absolute and fixed character that often ended in an unreal and static morality. Religious and philosophical history and reflexion have revealed the fact that all codes are, in part at least, subject to change according as social and economic conditions change. And, as it became clear that empiric morality was thus conditioned, the question naturally arose whether the whole sense of moral obligation was not equally empiric and destitute of any normative or permanent character. Men began to seek its origin in the ebb and flow of human tradition. Thus arose the question of the seat of this inner voice and the historic genesis of conscience.

2. Greek intellectualism was prone to seek the origin of this sense of obligation in the rational process. Plato represents Socrates as identifying all moral obligation with rational insight, and he himself taught that morality recognized the given heavenly types or norms of conduct in the eternal ideas of the good. And, though Aristotle parted company at this point with Plato, and saw the social and empiric character of the ethical norms, yet on the whole Greek intellectualism never succeeded in keeping clearly apart these two elements in every ethical situation—the code of morals to which a moral agent is bound and the inner compulsion by which he is bound. Hellenistic ethics thus swung between an uncritical intuitionalism and an equally uncritical empiric rationalism. It may now be taken for granted that, though the discursive reason is and always must be concerned in every ethical situation, and is more particularly interested in the critical analysis of every given code of ethics, nevertheless it is vain to seek the origin of the sense of moral obligation in the rational process alone. Nor can we successfully resolve moral obligation into clear rational insight into consequences of any kind.

3. **Critical rationalism** began with the work of Hobbes, Locke, and Hume. Locke had little difficulty in showing how untenable was the uncritical intuitionalism that sought for innate codes of morals. But both Hume and Hutcheson leave unanalyzed a 'moral sense' as something ultimate. This moral sense Adam Smith, in his brilliant ethical treatise, sought to resolve into sympathy, or at least to trace its origin to sympathy as a natural attribute of man. It was distinctly on the basis of this critical rationalism that Bentham and the two Mills made their famous analysis of the sense of moral obligation in terms of utility, and more especially of social utility. So far as this empiric rationalism dealt with the codes of morals found in human history, it was fruitful and stimulating in a high degree. At the same time, it became increasingly evident that empiric utilitarianism could build no bridge from the socially useful to the sense of personal responsibility to be socially useful. And, when John Stuart Mill conceded an intuitive capacity for estimating values as higher and lower, and thus also a capacity for the intuitive recognition of moral values as higher over against other types of value, clear-eyed critics of rational utilitarianism realized that Bentham's system had gone into bankruptcy.

4. **Biological evolution**, however, infused new life into the discussion as to whether the origin of the sense of moral obligation might not be found in the socially useful. It was suggested by Darwin himself that the conflict of instincts, and the survival of groups obeying the instincts that made for group-preservations, would in a long process of development link the socially useful with the morally right, and this line of inquiry has been followed up by Leslie Stephen, Alexander Sutherland, E. Westermarck, L. T. Hobhouse, and others. The exceedingly useful light that this line of research has thrown upon the gradual development of empiric codes of conduct has led to confusion of the two issues involved. It may be readily conceded that the socially useful has determined in a measure, perhaps we may say in large measure, what men consider morally right, but the origin of the category 'moral obligation' remains unexplained. Evolutionary analysis has not as yet succeeded in building a bridge between the socially useful and the sense of moral obligation to the group. Somewhere at some time such a sense must appear in unmoral life as a variation, and, this variation having been once assumed, law and morals link themselves with group purpose, as von Ihering abundantly shows (*Der Zweck im Recht*[3], esp. vol. i. ch. vi.), but the biological analogy has been distinctly overworked, and it is becoming increasingly evident that evolutionary philosophy must assume variations and does not explain them. Thus on the ethical field origins are no more explained than on the biological, and the sense of a moral obligation cannot so far be successfully analyzed into unmoral elements. Moreover, even in detail the sense of individual moral obligation presents many difficulties in connexion with the socially useful, for historically it is easy to show that the sense of moral obligation has time and again protected courses of conduct patently socially detrimental.

5. **Critical intuitionalism** is therefore in many different phases reasserting itself, and, especially on the ethical field, there are many attempts to re-state more satisfactorily the position of Kant and Lotze. There is some return to Jacobi and Fries, and the philosophies of Wundt, Eucken, Eisler, James, and Bergson are suggesting new formulations for the sense of moral obligation as a category of the practical reason incapable of further analysis —an empty concept, it is true, in this form, whose content is given in empiric experience and is subject to the laws of evolutionary process and progress, among which laws the socially useful is one of the most important factors. Thus from the psychological point of view Wundt and James, as well as Eisler and others, assume the capacity for moral distinction and the sense of moral obligation, without attempting to analyze the category further, while realizing that the content of moral appreciation is a subject for scientific examination, and has its own evolutionary history. From this point of view the feeling of moral obligation arises as a variation, and maintains itself by its social usefulness. Bergson has as yet given no development of his philosophy along ethical lines, but the revival of a critical intuitionalism has found support in his main contention, and followers of Fries and Jacobi see in the sense of moral obligation the evidence of a capacity for reaching beyond the phenomenal, and link this with a re-statement of the Kantian argument for God's existence. According to this school, the fundamental significance of the sense of moral obligation is the compelling power of the purposeful character of life. The unity of our mental and spiritual life demands that moral judgments be not irrational, even though complete rationalization may be beyond our power. However divergent the empiric codes of social behaviour may be, the existence of a moral obligation is an element everywhere; hence the very rational process itself is involved in a defence of the inherent validity of moral obligation.

6. **Conclusion.**—Moral obligation may then be said to so far defy any further ultimate analysis, and its origin is as mysterious as are all other origins and variations. It is a category of the practical reason, and is in so far super-rational, but the contents of the moral judgment are subject to the rational process, as in the sphere of the phenomenal. Thus the total ethical complex reveals rational, sympathetic, eudæmonistic, and hedonistic elements. But into no one of these can the fundamental sense of personal obligation be quite successfully resolved. Moreover, this sense of inner compulsion, covering as it does fields of action which no external coercion could regulate, is everywhere becoming the regulative principle of human society, displacing in the moral man outward law, and giving the sense of new freedom, because our obligation is the categorical imperative of the informed conscience, and has its seat within, and is not based upon, outward law with its concomitant of external coercion.

LITERATURE. — Aristotle, *Nicomachean Ethics*, tr. F. H. Peters[10], London, 1906; Cicero, *de Officiis*; James MacCosh, *The Intuitions of the Mind*, London, 1860, esp. pt. ii. bk. iv.; J. Locke, *Essay on the Human Understanding*, do. 1828; D. Hume, *A Treatise of Human Nature*, Edinburgh, 1739–40; F. Hutcheson, *A System of Moral Philosophy*, Glasgow, 1755 (cf. W. R. Scott, *Francis Hutcheson: His Life, Teachings, and Position in the History of Philosophy*, Cambridge, 1900); Adam Smith, *Theory of Moral Sentiments*[8], London, 1797; J. Bentham, *Introduction to the Principles of Morals and Legislation*, new ed., do. 1823; James Mill, *Analysis of the Phenomena of the Human Mind*, do. 1829; John Stuart Mill, *System of Logic*, do. 1843, esp. pt. i. ch. iii.; Leslie Stephen, *The Science of Ethics*, do. 1882; Alexander Sutherland, *The Origin and Growth of the Moral Instinct*, do. 1898; James Martineau, *Types of Ethical Theory*, Oxford, 1885, esp. vol. ii. bk. ii.; I. Kant, *Theory of Ethics*, tr. T. K. Abbott, London, 1895–98; W. Wundt, *Ethik*, Stuttgart, 1886, Eng. tr., London, 1897–1901; J. F. Fries, *Wissen, Glaube und Ahndung*, ed. L. Nelson, Göttingen, 1905; R. von Ihering, *Der Zweck im Recht*[3], Leipzig, 1893–98; H. Spencer, *Principles of Ethics*, London, 1910; James Seth, *A Study of Ethical Principles*[12], New York, 1911; F. Paulsen, *System der Ethik*[3], 2 vols., Berlin, 1894, Eng. tr., London, 1899.

THOMAS C. HALL.

MORAL SENSE.—The term 'moral sense' is practically equivalent to 'conscience,' and shares the field of ethics with such principles as rectitude and duty, happiness and social health. In the form of συνείδησις, the term 'conscience' appears as early as Periander and Bios (Stobæus, p. 192. 21); as an approving and fortifying moral sense, Epictetus uses the synonym συνειδός (bk. iii. ch. xxii.), while the disapproval of *conscientia* is referred to by Cicero (*Laws*, i. 14). Upon the basis of a natural moral sense, St. Paul speaks of the Gentiles as those who performed by nature (φύσει) the works of the law, being guided by conscience (συνείδησις, Ro 2[15]). The appreciation of an inner moral sense distinct from external commandment seems to have been indicated by Sophocles in the *Antigone*, where the heroine appeals to a higher principle of action, while she repudiates the established law; the Sophists' distinction between φύσις and θέσις further marks off the internal sanction of conduct from all forms of external statutes. However important the principle of a moral sense may appear to be, it cannot be denied that the most profound moral systems have been elaborated in independence of it. Socrates based Greek ethics upon the general principle of knowledge, whence Plato and Aristotle, Stoic and Epicurean, perfected the ancient ethical ideal, leaving the ethics of conscience to the minor moralists. The meagre development of ethical theory in mediæval times failed to develop the notion of a natural moral sense; it is in modern systems of ethics that the analysis of the moral sense is to be found; even here such ethical philosophies as those of Kant and Spinoza were perfected without appealing to a special sense of morality.

When modern ethics began with Hobbes, it was the opposition to relativism and egoism that led R. Cumberland (*de Legibus Naturæ*, London, 1672) to postulate conscience and benevolence as the true foci of conduct, although it was the latter principle that received chief emphasis. As a deist, Shaftesbury insisted upon a 'natural sense of right and wrong' (*Inquiry concerning Virtue*, London, 1699, bk. i. pt. iii. 2), which he identified with conscience, and thus spoke of 'religious conscience' and a 'displeasing consciousness' (bk. ii. pt. ii. 1). With F. Hutcheson the moral sense was discussed more æsthetically than ethically in the form of a disinterested regard for universal humanity, whence he inquires,

'If there is no moral sense . . . if all approbation be from the interest of the approver, What's Hecuba to *us* or *we* to Hecuba?' (*Inquiry concerning Moral Good and Evil*, London, 1725, sect. i. 2).

J. Butler was the first to subject the moral sense to exact psychological analysis, whence he regards conscience as the 'principle in man by which he approves or disapproves his heart, temper, and actions' (*Sermons upon Human Nature*, London, 1726, serm. i. [*Works*, ed. J. H. Bernard, London, 1900, i. 31]). This inward sense of approval and disapproval is further regarded as a principle of 'reflexion' whose essence is that of 'authority' (serm. ii.). Butler tends to complicate the problem when he asserts that the dictate of conscience is ever in accordance with the impulses of reasonable self-love, while the supreme sanction of the moral sense is found in the principle of harmony with nature.

Among the ethical idealists of the 18th cent., Richard Price and Kant opposed the notion of a moral sense as such, and sought in reason the ultimate moral authority. In his *Review of the Principal Questions and Difficulties in Morals* (London, 1758), Price denies the validity of Hutcheson's 'moral sense,' and appeals to the 'understanding' as the ground of ethical distinctions, although Price's treatment of the understanding makes it possible for him to depart from mere rationalism, and repose in a Platonistic 'intuition' (ch. i. sects. i., ii.). Kant, who derived moral distinctions autonomously from reason, whence also springs the categorical imperative, treats the moral sense with contempt when he says:

'As to moral feeling, this supposed special sense, the appeal to it is indeed superficial when those who cannot *think* believe that feeling will help them out, even in what concerns general laws' (*Metaphysic of Morals*, tr. T. K. Abbott, London, 1889, p. 61).

In its treatment of the moral sense, then, the Enlightenment (*q.v.*) insisted upon something even more rationalistic than conscience.

If the tendency of the 17th and 18th centuries was to regard the moral sense as something rational, the tendency of the 19th and 20th centuries has been to reduce the principle in question to the social. In the middle of the 18th cent. Adam Smith inaugurated the career of social ethics when he sought the source of moral sentiment in 'sympathy.' The first to raise the question concerning the *origin* of moral sense, Smith had no hesitation in founding the ideas of propriety, merit, and duty upon the instinct of natural sympathy (*Theory of Moral Sentiments*, London, 1759). A century later Darwin connected the moral with the biological, and thus made the moral sense dependent upon the predominance of the social tendency in man. To 'sociability' Darwin adds the principle of 'reflexion,' without which the social could not have become ethical, so that the ideals of Butler, to whom Darwin pays due tribute, have not been wholly lost to view (*Descent of Man*, London, 1871, ch. iii.). Equally significant with the departure from the rational is the change from the individualistic to the social; for, where Butler identified conscience and reasonable self-love, Darwin united conscience with the non-egoistic in human nature.

When biological ethics transferred the seat of the moral sense from the self to society, much of the phenomenology of conscience, shame, approval, obligation, etc., seemed intelligible; at any rate, 'scientific' ethics has assumed that the social is conclusive, as appears from such a work as L. Stephen's *Science of Ethics* (London, 1882), where biological, social, and ethical are firmly linked (ch. viii.). In opposition to Stephen, and in the general style of Butler, J. Martineau has insisted upon the rational and individualistic conception of the moral sense (*Types of Ethical Theory*, Oxford, 1885, vol. ii. bk. ii. ch. ii.).

Where the moral individualism of the 18th cent. has practically succumbed before the advance of social ethics, there has arisen an æsthetic individualism which, while not allying itself with the moral-sense theory, has not failed to make vigorous warfare upon the social conception of life. Beginning with the romanticism of Friedrich Schlegel and the realism of H. B. Stendhal, and advancing with the *Décadence* of C. P. Baudelaire, this anti-social view has come to a climax in Nietzsche, who stigmatizes the compunctions of the social moral sense as so much 'bad conscience' from whose terrors he would emancipate mankind (*A Genealogy of Morals*, tr. W. A. Haussmann and J. Gray, London, 1899, pt. ii.). In the same manner Ibsen speaks of the modern man as one who, suffering from 'sickly conscience,' stands in need of a 'robust conscience' (*The Master Builder*, tr. E. Gosse and W. Archer, London, 1893, act ii.), while H. Sudermann, with more direct reference to social ethics as such, speaks derisively of the 'conscience of the race' (*The Joy of Living*, tr. E. Wharton, London, 1903, act iv.). Similar expressions of anti-social immoralism may be found in Anatole France, August Strindberg, and Bernard

Shaw. Thus, the status of the moral sense in contemporary thought seems to consist of a dogmatic assertion of the social on the part of science and a violent repudiation of the principle by culture.

LITERATURE.—M. J. Guyau, *Esquisse d'une morale sans obligation ni sanction*[2], Paris, 1881; P. Rée, *Die Entstehung des Gewissens*, Berlin, 1885; J. G. Schurman, *The Ethical Import of Darwinism*, New York, 1887; W. Wundt, *Ethik*, Stuttgart, 1886; F. Brentano, *Vom Ursprung sittlicher Erkenntniss*, Leipzig, 1889; T. Elsenhaus, *Wesen und Entstehung des Gewissens*, do. 1894; J. Dewey and J. H. Tufts, *Ethics*, London, 1909; C. G. Shaw, *The Value and Dignity of Human Life*, Boston, 1911. CHARLES GRAY SHAW.

MORAL THEOLOGY.—See CASUISTRY.

MORALITIES.—See MIRACLE-PLAYS, MYSTERIES, MORALITIES.

MORALITY.—See ETHICS AND MORALITY.

MORAVIANS.—**1. History.**—The Moravian Church, or the Unitas Fratrum, belongs to the historic Churches of Christendom. For more than four and a half centuries it has never wavered in its claim to be a part of the Catholic Church, possessing the historic episcopate and the three orders of the ministry, administering the sacraments and preaching the Word according to apostolic precept, laying special emphasis on the importance of Christian unity, the cultivation of personal religion, and the necessity of personal service.

Whatever obscurity surrounds certain points in its history, there is nothing doubtful as to its origin. It dates from the year 1457; Bohemia was the land of its birth; and the more spiritually-minded followers of John Hus were its first members. Hus, the gifted rector of the University of Prague, an earnest reformer and eloquent preacher, owed much of his religious enlightenment to the writings of Wyclif, introduced into Bohemia by the wife of Richard II., a princess of that country. After his martyrdom at Constance in 1415 the greater part of his followers took up the sword in defence of their religious liberties. Some were pacified by concessions, such as their partaking of the cup as well as of the bread at the Holy Supper; but others, whose convictions went deeper, the Puritans of their day, withdrew from political life, retired to a remote corner of the country, and settled down in the Barony of Lititz. Here they formed themselves into a religious community on NT lines, in which many of the institutions of the early Christian Church were revived, under the leadership of duly elected elders. At the Synod of Lhota in 1467 they further proceeded to elect their own ministers, and for these they obtained ordination from the Waldenses (*q.v.*), whose bishop, Stephen, consecrated Michael Bradacius as the first bishop of the Unitas. The episcopate was given and received in the conviction of its apostolic origin, coming from the Eastern, not the Western, Church, transmitted possibly through the so-called sects, such as the Euchites, the Paulicians, the Cathari, etc. The validity of these orders was recognized even by the enemies of the Unitas; and, as the step thus taken involved complete ecclesiastical separation from Rome, it resulted in fierce persecution, despite which, however, the membership increased, the congregations multiplied, and the Church's influence spread far and wide, not merely in Bohemia, but beyond its borders also. The name adopted was *Jednota Bratrská*, the Latin rendering of which, 'Unitas Fratrum,' fails to give the exact meaning; 'Ecclesia Fratrum,' 'the Church of the Brotherhood,' would be more correct. The leaders in those early days were Peter of Cheltcic, Gregory the patriarch, and Lucas of Prague—men of very different temperaments, but of equal devotion. The Church's doctrines soon became distinctly evangelical; thus, at the Synod of Reichenau in 1495, the Brethren decided the great question, 'How shall a man be justified before God?' by the answer, 'Through the faith of our Lord Jesus Christ and the righteousness which is of God.' They laid special stress on Christian character and conduct; hence their strict discipline, which later excited the admiration of the Reformers. By the year 1500 they had over 200 congregations with more than 100,000 members; and in 1535 these figures had doubled themselves. It was the Brethren who issued the first hymn-book in the vernacular, in 1501; they set up some of the finest printing-presses in Europe, and used them largely for the production of their own translation of the Bible, which is still the standard Bohemian version of to-day. Their schools had a well-deserved reputation; Bohemia's best literature was the product of their scholars. Their church music became famous, especially for the congregational part-singing. Family worship was a feature of their homes; the children were early grounded in the Scriptures; the catechisms were clear, concise, and practical. The Church government was Presbyterian, with the Synod as the supreme court. Under its authority the bishops controlled their own dioceses, and they alone ordained; the presbyters preached and administered the sacraments; the deacons acted as assistants. Infant-baptism was practised, followed by confirmation.

As the Church expanded, it came to include three separate branches, in Bohemia, Moravia, and Poland; yet the three remained organically one, and thus the Unitas became the earliest International Protestant Church. Its history during the greater part of the 16th and 17th centuries is one long record of persecution, broken by intervals of rest and of official favour. It suffered terribly during the period of the Counter-Reformation, especially after the disastrous battle of the White Mountain in 1620. A veritable 'Book of Martyrs' might be compiled dealing with the days when Rome set itself to exterminate the Unitas. Its foremost leaders among the nobility were executed, its clergy imprisoned, its members sent to the mines or kept in dungeons; its churches were closed, its schools destroyed, its Bibles and hymn-books, catechisms and histories were burned. More than 36,000 families fled from Bohemia, and with them their sole surviving bishop, John Amos Comenius, the herald of humanistic and religious training for the young. He was at that time the leading educationist in Europe, and his writings still rank among the standard authorities. His wanderings took him to Poland and Holland; and he was also invited to England to re-organize the very defective system of education which prevailed in that country. Much sympathy for the Bohemian martyrs had already been aroused during the Commonwealth, when Cromwell offered the Unitas a home in Ireland; and this continued afterwards also, when collections on its behalf were made in many of the Anglican churches. In the belief that the days of the Unitas were numbered Comenius drew up a remarkable document in which he says:

'As in such cases it is customary to make a Will, we hereby bequeath to our enemies the things of which they can dispossess us; but to you our friends (of the Church of England) we bequeath our dear Mother, the Church of the Brethren. It may be God's will to revive her in our country or elsewhere. You ought to love her even in her death, because in her life she has given you an example of Faith and Patience for more than two centuries' (*Ratio Disciplinæ*, Amsterdam, 1660, Dedication).

He also secured the episcopal succession, apart from the Polish branch in which it still continued, by having his son-in-law, Peter Jablonsky, consecrated as bishop by Bishop Bythner at Milenezyn in Poland.

With the death of Comenius in 1672 the first part of the history of the Unitas ends. The second part opens at Herrnhut, in Saxony, where in 1722 a company of fugitives from the Moravian border valleys, in which isolated families of the ancient Church had still preserved the faith of their fathers, found a refuge on the estate of a young nobleman, Count Nicolas Ludwig von Zinzendorf. They were soon joined by others from Bohemia; and in association with a number of German Pietists they formed themselves into a society similar to those which then existed within the Lutheran Church. But this did not satisfy the descendants of the Unitas; they insisted that they were not Lutherans, they belonged to a much older Church; and, being now in the possession of a certain amount of religious liberty, they desired its re-establishment. To this Zinzendorf was at first opposed, till from a chance copy of the writings of Comenius he learned what the history of the Unitas had been, how glorious its past, how evangelical its doctrine, how strict its discipline, how firm its faith and steadfastness under suffering. Almost unconsciously he found himself being led on to devote his life, his means, and his talents to the re-organization of this venerable Church, and its equipment for further service. But the Renewed Church was not of Zinzendorf's creation. Its points of contact with the Unitas lie in the personal descent of many of its members, in the church regulations which were again introduced, and, above all, in the orders of the ministry, which in 1735 were restored, when David Nitschman was consecrated bishop by Bishop Daniel Ernst Jablonsky, whose father had received the succession from Bythner with the written commission of Comenius.

The little community at Herrnhut rapidly increased and developed in spite of the banishment of Zinzendorf by order of the Saxon Government, on the ground of his having introduced unauthorized religious novelties and of teaching false doctrine. Its fame spread far and wide, since in it a striking union of spiritual life with good works and industrial activity was to be seen. The danger of a narrow type of Pietism (*q.v.*) was averted by a wonderful experience of revival and a wave of evangelizing zeal, which visited the Church in 1727, under the impulse of which it embarked on that particular work in the doing of which lay the pledge of its continued existence. At the beginning of the 18th cent. foreign missions were almost entirely unknown among the Reformed Churches; it was left to the Moravians to inaugurate the modern missionary movement. This dates from the year 1732, when two of the Brethren set out to evangelize the enslaved Negroes in St. Thomas, willing to become slaves themselves if that should be the only way of winning them for Christ. In the same spirit others went to the Eskimos in Greenland; others settled in S. America, and carried the gospel for the first time to the natives in the Dutch Colony of Surinam. Work was also begun among the N. American Indians, to whom David Zeisberger devoted sixty-three strenuous years of life. In S. Africa these early missionaries were to be found teaching Hottentots and Kaffirs the faith of Jesus. They penetrated to Persia and Ceylon, they preached in Egypt and Algiers, they established their stations on the Gold Coast and in eight of the W. India Islands, they started a mission to the Jews—and all this as pioneers, and within a few years after the founding of that little Saxon village whose inhabitants numbered only some 600. They formed the first Protestant Church that recognized and attempted to fulfil the duty of world evangelization; and in this effort they stood alone for sixty years. This early characteristic of the Renewed Church still remains its outstanding distinction; and that is why, alone among all others, it possesses no separate missionary society, since the whole Church is the society, and within it the principle prevails that 'to be a Moravian and to further missions are identical.'

From Herrnhut strong religious influences began to spread at home as well as abroad among the students in the German universities, the landowners in the Baltic provinces, the merchants of Amsterdam, and the military in Berlin. Zinzendorf and his Brethren were invited everywhere, and, as the result of their evangelistic work, societies or congregations, known as 'settlements,' sprang up in Denmark, Holland, Russia, and Switzerland, and in several of the German principalities. Each became, like Herrnhut, an industrial as well as a religious centre, for the apostolic rule of being 'diligent in business' as well as 'fervent in spirit' was insisted on. It was largely by means of these industrial undertakings, supplemented by the unstinted generosity of Zinzendorf, that the cost of the mission work was met—not to mention the fact that most of the missionaries provided for their own necessities.

The first official visit was paid to England in 1735; and here it was that Peter Böhler three years later met with John Wesley and became the means of his spiritual enlightenment. Here also the name 'Moravian' came into use; given originally as a convenient nickname (like 'Methodist'), it has now gained a kind of permanence, though it cannot be regarded as satisfactory, since it emphasizes only one point, and that a comparatively unimportant one, in the long history of the Unitas.

The Moravian influence was unquestionably one of the main factors in the early days of the Evangelical Revival; for a time it equalled that of the Methodists. Moravian evangelists preached throughout the length and breadth of the United Kingdom, leaving their mark especially in Yorkshire and the Midlands; and, through the preaching of John Cennick, to a yet greater degree in Ireland and the west of England.

In America also the Church took root in the middle of the 18th cent., around two centres, Bethlehem in Pennsylvania, and Salem in N. Carolina; and from each of these two places it spread rapidly. Thus the Church came to consist again of three distinct provinces, according to the different nationalities—German, English, and American. These form the home base, and, though widely separated, they are organically one. Each province is independent as regards the conduct of its own affairs, elects its own bishops, appoints its own administrative boards, and legislates for itself through its own synods. The main outward bond of union between the parts (and the seat of final authority) is the so-called General Synod, made up of delegates from all the provinces. This bond may seem a very slight one, yet through these many years the spirit of brotherhood in Christ has been strong enough to prevent any kind of schism in the body.

The death of Zinzendorf in 1760 had important results. It involved a severe financial strain which at one time threatened disaster and dissolution, but it also led to the framing of a distinctive system of church government, the settlement of its constitution, the definition of its doctrine, and the reorganization of its undertakings. The administrative centre still lay in Germany, where during the latter part of the 18th cent. the Moravians found themselves in the forefront of the controversy with rationalism; they became the recognized champions of orthodox Evangelicalism. Here also their influence was as far-reaching as in England, though in a different way. In this case it was due largely to the writings and the personality of Bishop August Gottlieb Spangenberg, originally a professor at Halle. It made itself felt in the universities; Schleiermacher learned his religion and gained his conception of the historic Christ at a Moravian college; and Kant, the philosopher of Königsberg, referred his students, when searching for peace, to 'the little Moravian church over the way; that,' he said, 'is the place in which to find peace.'

2. **Characteristics.**—(*a*) *Diaspora.*—A unique feature of the Church's work on the Continent was, and still is, the so-called Diaspora, an extensive agency for promoting spiritual life and fellowship within the National (Protestant) Churches. It is carried on in many parts of Germany, in Denmark, Norway, Sweden, Switzerland, and Russia; and, according to synodal resolution, no worker in it is allowed to seek converts for the Moravian Church from among the members of other communions. The effort is in the interests of the Kingdom of God as a whole, supplementary to the existing religious agencies, and is designed to strengthen and promote the unity of believers. This accounts to a great extent for the good-will shown to the Moravians by those who know the disinterested nature of their labours, and the catholicity of their spirit. Had there been more denominationalism, no doubt a larger numerical increase would have resulted, but it would have meant the loss of that kindliness of mutual feeling which has marked the Church's relationship to other Christian communities.

(*b*) *Education.*—Another Moravian characteristic is the educational system, officially recognized and regarded as belonging to the Church's work and responsibility. Love of education, and enthusiasm for it, formed a part of the inheritance which had come down from the days of the Unitas. It was held that, just as the Church had its mission to the heathen, who had never heard the gospel, so had it also a mission to the young to ground and train them in its divine precepts. To carry this out was a priceless privilege ordained of God, to be undertaken with prayer, and to be done for Him. In this spirit numerous boarding-schools were opened in Germany, Holland, England, Switzerland, and America; many of them have become famous, not only on account of the education given, but also by reason of the pupils who have gone forth from them, men distinguished in almost every calling and rank of life. The standard was high; and, if in many cases the discipline was strict, it was always blended with the kindly influences of a distinctly Christian atmosphere.

(*c*) *Missionary zeal.*—The third, and the most characteristic, feature of Moravianism is its missionary zeal. Never since the beginning of the work in 1732 has this waned; the Church has sent forth its sons and daughters in an unbroken stream, in some cases through five generations of the same family. Most of its congregations have their representatives in the missions, and through these living links the bond of sympathy with the foreign field is maintained. The Church's energies flow largely along this channel, in support of what represents, and is felt to be, its God-appointed work in the present as much as in the past, a glory that has not faded. Hence the surprisingly large number of Moravian missionaries in proportion to the membership; and also the relatively high standard of financial support. Whilst in the Protestant Churches at large the proportion of missionaries to members is about 1 to 5000, among the Moravians it is 1 to 60. These are the words of J. R. Mott on the subject:

'If members of the Churches in Great Britain and America gave in like proportion [as the Moravians], then the Missionary contributions would aggregate over £12,000,000 per annum instead of some £3,000,000. And if they went out as Missionaries in corresponding numbers, we should have a force of nearly 400,000 foreign workers, which is vastly more than the number of Missionaries estimated as necessary to achieve the evangelisation of the World' (*Report of New York Ecumenical Missionary Conference*, New York, 1900, i. 97).

The work abroad has to a great extent been among primitive races, some of them now approaching extinction, in out-of-the-way parts, in lands that are peculiarly unpromising and uninviting, and that have been neglected by every one else. These have been taken up by the Moravians in accordance with Zinzendorf's early desire and determination, when, as a school-boy, he established among his companions the so-called 'Order of the Mustard Seed,' for the purpose of seeking the conversion of the heathen, having in mind 'especially such as others would not trouble themselves about.' Thus the Moravian Brethren were the pioneers in work among the lepers, first in the Cape Colony, where as early as 1818 a missionary and his wife cut themselves off from their fellow-Europeans, and settled down in a lonely valley among the poor outcasts, in order to care for their bodies as well as their souls. The result was remarkable, for within six years over 90 of the lepers were converted and baptized. Afterwards the work was continued on Robben Island, a sandy stretch lying off Cape Town; and still later a spacious hospital has been built outside the walls of Jerusalem, where the aim is to gather all the lepers of Palestine, and to alleviate the sufferings caused by this dread disease.

Continuous expansion has marked the missionary enterprise of the Church, till now it is to be found in every continent. The fields are as follows: Labrador, Alaska, California, the W. Indies (Jamaica, St. Thomas, St. John, St. Croix, Antigua, St. Kitts, Barbadoes, Tobago, Trinidad, San Domingo), the Mosquito Coast, Nicaragua, Demerara (British Guiana), Surinam (Dutch Guiana), S. Africa, East and West, Nyasa and Unyamwezi (in German E. Africa), W. Himalaya, and N. Queensland—14 different countries, 343 stations, with 1503 preaching places. The workers include 367 European and American missionaries, among them doctors, educationists, deaconesses, etc., 48 ordained native ministers, 459 native evangelists, 1663 native helpers; with a total of 107,379 souls in their care. The annual expense amounts to £114,000, exclusive of the Leper Home, which costs an additional £1500 per annum. Mission colleges exist in England, Germany, America, the W. Indies, and S. Africa; hospitals in Labrador, Jerusalem, Surinam, and Kashmīr, where Zenana work is also carried on.

The above figures, if not large in themselves, are strikingly so when compared to the size of the home Church. This consists of the continental congregations, in Germany, Austria, Switzerland, France, Denmark, Russia, Sweden, and Norway; the British province (England, Scotland, Ireland, and Wales); and the American provinces, North and South. The last-named have 134 congregations; in Great Britain there are 45, and on the Continent 30—or 74, if the Diaspora centres are included. A joint undertaking of the whole Church, apart from the foreign enterprise, is the evangelization of the lands of its birth and early history, viz. Bohemia and Moravia. Work among the young is carried on in both day and boarding-schools; the home Sunday schools number 179, and have 23,000 scholars; abroad there are 189 schools, with 1430 teachers, and over 25,000 scholars. In England an agency known as the Rural Mission works on lines somewhat similar to the Diaspora on the Continent.

3. **Worship.**—The worship of the Church com-

bines the liturgical element with a large measure of freedom in extempore prayer—a blending of order and liberty. The British Book of Worship includes two liturgies for public service, an alternate form of prayer, a confession of faith, and formularies for the baptism of infants and of adults, for confirmation, ordination, marriage, and burial—and combined with these is a newly-revised collection of hymns of all ages. It is the latest successor of the first Protestant hymn-book ever issued. The Church's ritual is marked by simplicity and directness of purpose, due largely to a wise caution in the use of symbolism, and also to a dislike of whatever would serve to quench the spiritual impulse of the moment. A stately dignity marks the special services and the doxologies in use at the consecration of bishops and the ordination of ministers. The same applies in a measure to the confirmation service, which, as in the Greek Church, is not considered an exclusively episcopal function, but may be performed by a presbyter. At all these services the surplice is worn, as well as at the administration of the sacraments. The Apostles' Creed is in use as representing the oldest, simplest, and most generally accepted expression of the faith of Christendom; and in addition a special confession, based on that compiled by Luther and made up mainly of a connected sequence of Scripture passages, is recited on the great Church festivals, such as Easter, Whitsunday, etc. In it the Trinitarian belief of the Church finds marked emphasis—the Fatherhood of God, the Creator of all things and the Author of salvation; the redemptive and mediatorial work of the Son in His perfect humanity, the 'Lamb of God' once slain, now risen and glorified; the presence and power of the Holy Spirit, 'Who proceedeth from the Father, and Whom our Lord Jesus Christ sent after that He went away . . . that He should abide with us for ever.'

4. Doctrine.—The main points of doctrine as held and taught are defined in the Church Book under the following heads: the doctrine of the total depravity of human nature; the doctrine of the love of God the Father; the doctrine of the real Godhead and the real humanity of Jesus Christ; the doctrine of our reconciliation unto God and our justification through the sacrifice of the Cross; the doctrine of good works as the evidence of faith; the doctrine of the fellowship of believers; the doctrine of the Second Coming of the Lord; and the doctrine of the Headship of Christ over the Church, which is His Body. Thus in essence the theological position is that of the Nicene Creed, the XXXIX Articles, the Augsburg and the Westminster Confessions; but, since no one Creed can be said to be a complete statement of the whole range of Christian dogma, liberty is allowed for difference of view in non-essentials. The Holy Scriptures are regarded as the only rule of faith and conduct, the basis of all teaching, and the final court of appeal. More stress is laid on Christian life and character than on perfect agreement of opinion. Devotion to Christ, and personal union with Him, form the foundation of the Brotherhood. The Church has kept itself free from anything approaching sectarian peculiarities of doctrine, and this because it came out from Rome on the broad ground of gospel truth and liberty, and did not separate itself from any other Evangelical Church.

5. Constitution and government.—The constitution and government of the Church, which at one time was something of an oligarchy, is now essentially democratic, as may be seen from the fact that in the General Synod, which meets every six years and controls the funds and the work of the entire body, the elected members outnumber those who have a seat in virtue of their office. The same applies to the provincial synods, and also to the authorities of the individual congregations. The principle at work in Church affairs is that of 'the government of the people, by the people, and for the people,' under the sole headship of Christ. The bishops have no administrative powers on account of their position, though, as a matter of fact, a bishop is almost invariably the president of the board of elders which directs the work of each province. These boards are elected by synod, the members holding office only during the inter-synodal period; they are responsible to the synod for their administrative doings. The foreign missions, as the concern of the whole Church, stand under the management of an international mission board, on which each of the home provinces, as well as the foreign field, is represented. This has at present its seat in Herrnhut, though it might just as well be located anywhere else. In addition there is a general directing board of the Unity, which has to see to the carrying out of the principles laid down by the General Synod in regard to constitution, doctrine, worship, orders, congregation rules, and discipline. It exercises also the functions of a court of appeal; it summons the General Synod, and acts as the standing representative of the Church in its entirety.

All appointments in the ministry are made by the directing boards of the respective provinces; each congregation is entitled to suggest names for the filling of a vacancy, and each minister has the right to accept or decline a call sent to him. The different provinces make their own arrangements for the training of their students, whilst in all the various colleges the standard is equally high. The normal course includes the work necessary for a University Degree in Arts, which each student is expected to gain; then follows a three years' study of theology. As a rule, some period is devoted to teaching in the boarding-schools. Later on comes ordination, in the first instance as a deacon when acting as assistant minister; and, on being appointed to a separate charge, a second ordination admits to the presbyterate. Thus the Church possesses and combines within itself many of the features which in other cases separate some of the larger religious bodies. Its orders are strictly episcopal, for only bishops can ordain, but its government is presbyterian. Its teaching is distinctly evangelical, though no formal subscription to any specific Creed is demanded, or expected, from ministers or members. The individual conscience is bound by no formularies; the bond of union lies not so much in a common Confession as in the exercise of mutual love as the supreme mark of discipleship. Infant-baptism and confirmation are practised; at the Holy Supper the wafer is generally used; the Church seasons are observed with very special stress on the services of Holy Week and Easter. In some of these observances there is a marked element of ritual, hallowed by the usage and tradition of past centuries; but at the same time the Church is as free from the bondage of form and ceremony as it is from all sacramentarianism.

The whole body, scattered over the world's surface, on the Continent, in Great Britain, in America, and in the 14 mission-fields, is still an organic Unity, each portion maintaining its own national characteristics, the Germans attached to their German ways, the English and Americans equally loyal to their own country's interests and customs. Jointly they form an international brotherhood, composed of men of many races and differing opinions, all banded together, not to propagate any special system of church government, or any kind of ritual, or any particular point of doctrine, but to evidence and promote the oneness of believers in Christ, and to prove the possibility of a union, organic as well as spiritual, which rises above all barriers of nationality and opinion. The Moravian Church does not work in opposition to any other evangelical Church, nor does it seek to increase its membership by any system of proselytizing. Its aim is to gather into the fold of Christ those who are still outside, and then to further that growth in grace and that fruitfulness of service which are the divinely appointed means for the spread of the Kingdom of God among the children of men. It is above all else a missionary and a union Church.

LITERATURE.—i. *ANCIENT CHURCH.*—Anton Gindely, *Gesch. der böhmischen Brüder*, Prague, 1857–58; Jaroslav Goll, *Quellen zur Gesch. der böhmischen Brüder*, do. 1878–82; E. de Schweinitz, *Hist. of the Unitas Fratrum*, Bethlehem, Pa., 1885; J. T. Müller, *Die deutschen Katechismen der böhmischen Brüder*, Berlin, 1887.

ii. *RENEWED CHURCH.*—David Cranz, *Ancient and Modern Hist. of the Brethren*, Eng. tr., London, 1780; A. G. Spangenberg, *Life of Count Zinzendorf*, Eng. tr., do. 1836; J. E. Hutton, *Hist. of the Moravian Church*², do. 1909; G. Wauer, *Beginnings of the Brethren's Church in England*, do. 1901; E. R. Hassé, *The Moravians* ('Leaders of Revival' Series), do. 1912, and *Count Zinzendorf* (in preparation); J. E. Hutton, *Hist. of Moravian Missions* (in preparation); J. T. Hamilton, *Hist. of the Moravian Church*, Bethlehem, Pa., 1900, and *Hist. of the Missions of the Moravian Church*, London, 1901; cf. also *Bureau of the Census, Special Reports*, 'Religious Bodies: 1906,' Washington, 1910, ii. 494–499; and see art. HUSSITES.

E. R. HASSÉ.

MORBIDNESS.—The term 'morbidness' as applied to moral and religious states of mind is popular rather than scientific. It designates particularly any unduly depressed state connected with one's moral or religious status. Little effort has been made thus far to discover a scientific differentia for religious and moral disease or morbidness. One author,[1] essaying a moral pathology, treats largely of ordinary moral faults and classes as pathological even such habits as result from mistaken conceptions of the moral life. Here 'pathological' loses all definite meaning; as well might we class as morbid the misspelling of a word. On the other hand, neurologists and medical writers tend, on the whole, to limit moral and religious morbidness to certain phenomena of the insanities, such as the delusion that one is God or Jesus Christ, or that one has committed the unpardonable sin. While it is difficult to differentiate between sanity and insanity, a useful mark of the insane is that they are incapable, for the time being at least, of fulfilling their social functions. Thus, all the insanities are cases of moral inability and, in this sense, of moral morbidness.

There is, however, a broad expanse of moral morbidness that is neither insanity, on the one hand, nor, on the other, mere deflexion from a moral ideal through erroneous thinking or through the common instinctive impulsions. The best example is the moral distortions frequently found among adolescents. Under the stress of the neural and intellectual re-organization that is going on at this period of life, the following types of morbidness are not uncommon.

(1) Excessive or minute introspection of one's desires, motives, or choices, often with the application of excessively severe standards to one's self. In religious communions that emphasize such experiences as conversion, regeneration, and the witness of the Spirit, this introspection often consists in a search for signs of the divine presence or of divine operations within one's soul.

(2) Hypersensitiveness to moral and religious situations and distinctions. To be wrong at all is to be heinous; only perfection is really good—this is the attitude of mind. This is what is often called 'morbid conscience.' The victim of it is likely to put absurd emphasis upon the exact performance of trifles that seem to be duties. Habitual self-condemnation or censoriousness towards others may also appear.

(3) A passion for certitude, and refusal to live by the ordinary, commonsense assumptions, probabilities, and 'rule o' thumb' devices of mature practicality. Sometimes a sense of uncertainty becomes almost an obsession. The victim feels uncertain, for instance, whether he has locked the door, although he knows, in the ordinary sense of 'knowledge,' that he has done so. So, also, he may feel that he ought or ought not to do a certain thing, although he understands, in a way, that his feeling is unreasonable.

(4) Feverish or self-annihilating devotion to a person, a cause, or an ideal. Here morbidness consists partly in emotional excess, partly in the egregious self-assertion upon which the supposed sublimity of self-obliteration depends.

(5) In the four types thus far named we behold a sort of psychical congestion and soreness. A fifth type displays the opposite—insensibility and failure to function in the presence of normal stimuli. Callousness towards the pains and pleasures of others and lack of a sense of obligation are its marks. In less extreme cases the callousness appears only in spots, as towards some one person, human interest, or kind of duty.

These adolescent twists illuminate the whole subject of moral and religious morbidness. For, if the five types be broadly interpreted, they will be found to cover all cases of such morbidness at whatever stage of life. Here we have over- and under-sensitiveness, excess of action and defect of it, excess and defect of introspection, over- and under-caution, and disproportion in thinking. This is not normal or healthy, yet it includes no insane delusions and no such failure of practical adjustment as puts one outside the pale of social toleration.

The causation of morbidness in the sense that now grows towards definiteness includes two factors: neural depression (or at least lack of vitality), and some incidental experience that starts an unfortunate mental habit. The fundamental facts with which we have to deal are excess, defect, and distortion of emotion. Not infrequently morbid persons cherish a conviction that their mental processes are rational rather than emotional even though observers easily discover the lack of emotional balance. Conduct, and what passes as reason, are alike determined by some congestion or soreness, or by abnormal callousness. These emotional tendencies are primary psychical signs of neural conditions. The depression may be a hereditary or temperamental trait, an incident of a disease, or the product of an internal irritant, of a drug, or of fatigue. The reason why morbidness occurs so frequently in adolescence is that the pubertal change and the consequent re-organization of habits put extraordinary demands upon the nervous system. To this cause must be added the peculiar loads in school life, economic life, and social life that our occidental customs impose upon youth. Finally, in many cases sexual perversions and difficulties connected with the firm establishment of a healthy sexual life increase the tendencies to depression. In mature life the same general principles apply. Morbidness may safely be assumed, in practically all cases, to spring partly out of nerve depression, which, in turn, may have many causes.

The last of the five adolescent types enumerated does not readily reveal its neural basis. Moral insensibility, indeed, may not seem to require any special neural basis. May it not be a matter of

[1] A. E. Giles, *Moral Pathology*, London, 1895.

mere habit? Habit might, perhaps, account for it in older persons, but, whenever a child or youth exhibits it, the presumption is that strength for a full social reaction is lacking. Let it be remembered that socialized conduct is an achievement that implies power to feel in particular ways, and to resist and organize impulses. In the games of children and youth 'foul play' is often simply the resort of individuals who have not sufficient muscular strength or mental power to hold their own while playing the game according to the rules. In social situations that present stimuli of normal strength a child of normal powers will react socially unless some positive counter training has preceded. Persistent unresponsiveness to social stimuli is strongly suggestive of constitutional weakness or of incidentally depressed vitality.

But the neural basis of morbid moral and religious states is not nearly the whole explanation of them. Neural depression is generic rather than specific; it puts consciousness into a minor key, but it does not of itself construct the melody. The particular reaction depends upon particular stimuli and upon incidental as well as permanent subjective conditions. The same neural background may be present in a person who worries about his soul's salvation and in one who worries about his health. Further, habit plays a leading rôle in the whole matter. A morbid reaction, once induced in a period of weakness, may become fixed as a habit, and so persist even after the original neural depression has been partly or wholly removed. The relation beween moral and religious morbidness and neurasthenia is often close. In both we find a general background of neural depression and a foreground of habitual ideas and practices, often highly systematized and therefore regarded as rational.

A gloomy theology or moral theory rarely, if ever, produces settled morbidness in the absence of predisposing nervous weakness or depression. Healthy and nervously strong persons, if they accept such doctrines at all, usually hold them in a theoretical way for the most part, or yield to their terrors only now and then when attention is specially directed to them. There is truth in the popular observation that, if men really believed in the grim theology that some of them profess, they would 'go wild.' The fact that, even in circles in which such theologies are accepted, men pursue and enjoy the common values of life, such as family, home, property, and social recognition, is direct evidence that any settled emotional realization of the prevailing belief depends upon something more than a set of ideas. If, however, any individual in such a circle has a tendency to nervous weakness, religious instruction may easily become the decisive factor in producing morbidness of a serious kind. In the aggregate the spiritual havoc thus wrought is undoubtedly large, although the cases of it are scattered. It is most unfortunate that among those who are susceptible to such injury are many persons whose sensitiveness and fineness of organization adapt them for high tasks. It is sometimes, no doubt, the possible prophet, poet, reformer, or thinker whose energies are fruitlessly introverted by depressing instruction.

LITERATURE.—G. Vorbrodt, 'Zur Religionspsychologie, Prinzipien und Pathologie,' *Theologische Studien*, Jena, 1906, pp. 237–303, argues against the view that religion as such is a morbid phenomenon. Josiah Moses, *Pathological Aspects of Religions*, Worcester, Mass., 1906, gives an extended analysis of religious extremes of various sorts. E. D. Starbuck, *The Psychology of Religion*, London, 1899, shows that conversion is, in general, a normal rather than abnormal phenomenon, chiefly of adolescence (ch. xiii.), but he presents numerous cases of adolescent doubt, brooding, depression, and introspection (ch. xvii.). G. A. Coe, *The Spiritual Life*, New York, 1900, also discusses adolescent difficulties, particularly doubts and morbid conscience. As already indicated, A. E. Giles, *Moral Pathology*, London, 1895, is not significant for our topic. A popular discussion of depressive states of the neurasthenic type will be found in E. Worcester and others, *Religion and Medicine*, New York, 1908. See also J. Bresler, *Religionshygiene* (pamphlet), Halle, 1907.

GEORGE A. COE.

MORDVINS.—I. Introduction and sources.—The Mordvins form a branch of the Finno-Ugrian race (cf. vol. vi. p. 22[b]), and consist of two tribes called respectively the Erzä and the Moksha. Our knowledge of their ancient religion, coming, as it does, almost exclusively from a time when, in name at least, they had been converted to Christianity by the Russians, and when they could practise the rites of their earlier faith only in secret, is very scanty and defective. After the Mordvin people, as a whole, in consequence of the victory by which the Russians finally overthrew the Tatar khanate of Kazan (1552), had come under the sway of the conquerors, measures of a more or less violent nature were taken here and there to convert them, and were continued in the 17th century. It was not, however, till about 1740–50 that they came to submit *en masse* to the rite of Christian baptism, and the following decades witnessed the disappearance of the last vestiges of their heathenism. Yet for a long time their conversion was, in the main, a merely nominal change, and, accordingly, even in quite recent times the exploration of remote districts has yielded much valuable material for the elucidation of their ancient religion.

Our earliest information on the subject comes from an Italian traveller, G. Barbaro, who visited the district now called Eastern Russia in 1446, and who gives a short account of how the victim was dealt with in the horse-sacrifice of the Moksha tribe. The notes on the religion and sacrificial practices of the Mordvins made by N. Witsen, a Dutchman, at the close of the 17th cent. are altogether negligible; nor can we gather much of value from the accounts of P. J. Strahlenberg, K. Müller, I. Lepechin, J. G. Georgi, and P. S. Pallas, in the 18th century. A more useful source (in spite of errors due to misapprehension) is the Russian MS written by a land-surveyor named Miljkovič in 1783, and several times printed (most recently in *Tambovskija Eparchialjnyja Vědomosti*, no. 18, Petrograd, 1905, p. 815 ff.). From the middle of the 19th cent. we find in Russian newspapers and periodicals (especially those of the provinces), as in other publications, sporadic notices and descriptions of local conditions. Accounts of a more general character have been given by Meljnikov, Mainov, and Smirnov (cf. Literature at end). Meljnikov (writing *c.* 1850) draws his material mainly from MS sources; but, as regards the ideas of the gods, deals with his data too freely, and adds imaginative embellishments. The same may be said of Mainov, who, some thirty years later, devoted himself to the investigation of Mordvin ethnography, and even travelled over the Mordvin district; in many points he merely follows Meljnikov. A much more valuable production is that of Smirnov, who carefully utilizes the available literature as well as a number of MS sources, and also draws upon his own observations. The following account is based not only on the published sources, but also upon collections made by the present writer among the Mordvins themselves, and the fairly abundant MS material subsequently forwarded by native Mordvins to the Finno-Ugric Society in Helsingfors; it likewise draws upon some (in part very valuable) MSS dating from the middle of the 19th cent. and now in the keeping of the Imperial Geographical Society, or else deposited in the Asiatic Museum of the Imperial Academy of Sciences, Petrograd. The latter group of MSS had been already used in part, though very unscientifically, by Meljnikov and Mainov.

2. The dead.—Life after death was regarded as a direct continuation of earthly life. The departed in their graves live and occupy themselves in much the same way as they did upon earth—hence the articles required by them were placed beside their bodies in the grave. In death as in life kith and kin are still together, so that the graveyard is the counterpart of the village; there is no realm of the dead in a universal sense. From the graveyard the human-like shades come forth to visit the living. Each family worships its own dead, the foremost and mightiest of whom is the first who was buried in the particular graveyard, *i.e.* the progenitor of the family (together with his wife), who was often still spoken of by his own name and was honoured with the title of 'ruler of the graveyard' (*kalmon' kirdi*). The prevailing idea seems to be that this progenitor should not belong to too remote a past; thus among certain Erzä Mordvins in the government of Saratov, who migrated thither some 200 or 250 years ago, the earliest ancestors to whom worship is accorded are positively stated to have been the first settlers—the memory, and thus also the worship, of the earlier generations having faded away. Festivals in honour of departed individuals are celebrated during the first year after death—one immediately after burial, and others at specified times, as, *e.g.*, six weeks, or the fortieth day, after death, from which time onwards the shade of the dead becomes more closely attached to the corpse in the grave, while prior to that time it lingers chiefly in its former home or, it may be, in places which the living person had been accustomed to visit. At this festival the previously deceased members of the family are believed to be in attendance, and are implored to take the newly departed into their midst.

General festivals for all departed ancestors (*pokštšat babat*, or *at'at babat*, 'grandfathers and grandmothers' [=ancestors]), again, are celebrated at least twice a year, in spring and autumn (latterly the dates of both the individual and the general festivals were for the most part brought into accordance with those of the commemorative celebrations appointed by the Russian Church). The ancestors are invited in due form to a feast in the village, the several houses of the family-group being taken in rotation for this banquet of the living with the dead. According to a tradition from the beginning of the 17th cent., joint festivals for the dead were in an earlier period held by larger family-groups or clans also at intervals of some fifty years. Formerly, animal-sacrifices were offered at the celebrations, and the ceremonies connected with them contain features that seem to point to a still earlier practice of human sacrifice. The living approach the ancestors with prayers and gifts in all circumstances in which, as they think, they require the help of these ancestors either for their own benefit (particularly in cases of illness, which may be sent by the ancestors themselves, if angered) or in order to injure others. Moreover, at the sacrificial feasts which are held by the community in honour of the (nature-) gods, the ancestors are in some districts conjoined with these as objects of worship, being invoked in the prayers immediately after the deities, and besought for the same earthly blessings—success in tillage and cattle-rearing, good fortune, and health. The dead, when thus present by invitation, are welcome guests, from whose benignity all good things may be expected—though at the close of the festival, it is true, they are driven away, sometimes with threats—but, when they appear on their own initiative, they are greatly feared, especially as causing disease. Peculiar terrors are excited by the dead who perish by accident—*e.g.*, by drowning—or who for other reasons have not received proper burial, as also by those who die without surviving kindred; such unfortunates are, accordingly, attended to only in the festivals for their own ancestors.

In connexion with the ceremonial of this ancestor-worship, special mention must be made of the fact that at the festivals for deceased individuals, according to some older accounts, a wooden image or a doll representing the dead was set on the bench by the festal table; subsequently this was replaced by articles of clothing belonging to him. At these festivals, however, the departed has also a living representative, a person of the same sex and of about the same age, who acts his part, and is treated by those present as if he were the deceased. He presents himself in the clothes of the dead, and frequently is conducted from the graveyard, and then, at the end of the feast, taken back to it. According to some accounts, he never speaks at all, but partakes heartily of the banquet, and receives the tokens of respect accorded by those present. Other accounts inform us, however, that he carries on an active conversation with them: he tells them of the life of the under world, and of those who have gone there before him; he gives them good counsel, admonishing them to live in unity, to abstain from theft and excessive drinking, to look well after their cattle, and the like; he blesses man and beast, settles disputes regarding inheritance, etc.

According to some authorities, the dead, during their existence in the grave, undergo a second experience of death, passing thereby 'into a higher state,' in which they no longer maintain direct relations with those living upon the earth, but have intercourse only with those who have died once, and through the latter alone influence the fortunes of the living.

Although the ancestors are worshipped and invoked like the gods, and to some extent conjointly with them, the two classes are, nevertheless, rigidly distinguished from each other. Still, there seem to be cases where the people have quite forgotten the human origin of a dead person whom they worship, and he is invoked as a 'god' (*pas*). Among the Erzä in the governments of Kazan and Samara we find a deity called Staka pas, 'the heavy god,' who is honoured with special sacrificial festivals, and is entreated not to launch 'his heaviness' (*i.e.* evil generally) upon the people. In some parts a divine pair bearing various proper names—*e.g.*, Onto and Bonto (who are popularly supposed to be husband and wife)—are invoked by the epithet of Staka pas, while elsewhere the 'heavy god' is addressed in the sacrificial prayers also as Kan pas, Kuvan pas, and regarded as living 'in the black earth.' The word *kan*, the signification of which is now unknown to the people at large, is simply the Tatar *kan*, 'prince,' so that *kan pas* means 'the god-prince'; *kuvan*, again, is in all likelihood traceable to the Turkish princely title *kagan* in its Chuvash or Bulgar phonetic form *kogan* or *kugan* (with *o* or *u* instead of the common-Turk. *a*), which, though it has not come down to us, would correspond perfectly to the Mordvin *kuvan*. As the Mordvins, in part at least, were at one time among the subject peoples of the Volga Bulgars, the ancestors of the Chuvashes of to-day, we may be permitted to conjecture that the 'heavy god' was originally the spirit of a high Turkish ruler; similarly, the other heavy gods, such as Onto, etc., perhaps represent native princes of a bygone age.

With the Mordvin cult of the dead is probably connected in some way also the worship of the deity or spirit called Keremet (Erzä) or Kerämät, Kerämäd (Moksha), a name of Chuvash origin (in the Chuvash tongue of to-day, *Kirämät*, originally an Arab. word). Among the Mordvins this deity bears the title *soltan*, *salhta*, which is obviously the same as the Arabo-Turkish *sulṭān*. What is told of him among the Mordvins is meagre and inconsistent. Among the Moksha, according to an early account, he was a deity of great prestige and power, and superior to all others in his influence upon everyday life—in no sense a malign spirit, like Keremet among the Cheremisses. Although he bears a name of foreign origin, and was regarded by the Moksha as 'born and bred with the earth'—a fact which shows that the people had no idea of his human origin—it would seem, nevertheless, that his worship contains certain elements of a former native hero-cult. In the legal proceedings of the community oaths are taken in the name of Kerämät, and it is believed that he punishes those who are guilty of crime.

3. **Nature.**—(*a*) *Air and sky.*—In the Erzä tribe the deity of the sky is called Vere-pas, *i.e.* 'the god who is above.' We also find mention of Ski-pas and Niške-pas or Niške, the latter of whom, while now identified by some of the Erzä with Vere-pas, was originally in all likelihood a distinct god (probably of foreign origin). In a number of ancient MSS the name Niške occurs in the form Ineške, whence it appears that the name is really a synthesis of *ine*, 'great,' and the first element in the divine name Ski-pas just mentioned. *Ski*, again, is a participle of an obsolete verb *ška-*, meaning 'bear,' 'procreate,' so that Ski-pas signifies literally 'the generative god,' 'procreator-god,' and Niške, 'the great procreator.' The sky-god of the Moksha is called Škaj—a name corresponding exactly to the Erzä Ski—or, with the addition of the term for 'god,' which among the Moksha is still found in the more primitive dissyllabic form *pavas*, Škabavas (also Škabas and Škajbas), which accordingly corresponds in form with the Erzä Ski-pas. In the prayers he receives the designation Värdä, 'he who is above,' or Ot's'u, 'the great one' (see above, the explanation of the Erzä name Niške). The Erzä Niške or Niške-pas has a consort named Niške-ava, 'Mother Niške,' who is worshipped at any rate by women in their homes (she is now often identified with the Virgin Mary, the Theotokos); he has also two daughters, Kastargo and Vezorgo, while in the songs we likewise hear of a son. Among the Moksha the wife of the sky-god is, so far as is known, mentioned, along with a daughter, only in a single song, where she is called Škabas-ava, 'Mother Škabas.' Strahlenberg states that the highest deity of the 'Mordvins' (by which term he obviously means the Erzä tribe) is Jumishipas; in the first portion of his name, *jumi*, we have perhaps a cognate form of the Cheremiss term Jumo, applied to both the sky-god and the sky, and of the stem in the Finnish *jumala*, 'god,' while the second element is either equivalent to Si-pas, 'sun-god,' or, more probably, an incorrect form of Ski-pas (see above).

Among the Mordvins generally the sky-god ranks as supreme among the gods, and to him must frequently be offered the first sacrifice and prayer. It may be noted, however, that, according to a report from the middle of the 19th cent., the Moksha, or at least part of them, did not offer sacrifice to Skaj at all, but simply, at the beginning of every sacrificial festival, addressed him with a brief prayer for protection.

A special deity of thunder, who is worshipped in the communal sacrificial feasts, is found among the Erzä. He is named Pur'gine (lit. 'thunder'), or Pur'gine-pas ('the god Thunder,' 'thunder-god'), and the worshippers beseech him to send a beneficial rain, but not the noisome hail; his figure has been strongly influenced by that of the prophet Elijah in popular Russian belief. Among the Moksha thunder is called *at'am*, a derivative of *at'a*, 'grandfather,' 'old man,' and this, together with the fact that the rainbow is termed *at'am-jonks* (*jonks* = 'bow,' 'cross-bow'), seems to indicate that the Moksha also personified thunder, though the imperfect sources certainly say nothing of a thunder-cult among them.

In the prayers and elsewhere the sun as well as the moon is designated a god (*pas*, *pavas*), viz. Tši-pas (Erzä), Si-bavas (Moksha), 'the god sun,' 'sun-god,' and Kov-bas, Kov-bavas, 'the god moon,' 'moon-god.' Special oblations are accorded to the sun at the sacrificial feasts. The worship of the moon seems to involve no more than that, when a person first descries the new moon, he bows before it with a prayer for good health, and promises it a whole (*i.e.* uncut) loaf. The morning and the evening glow are invoked, with Russian proper names attached to the terms, almost exclusively in magic formulæ—*e.g.* as 'morning-glow Mariya,' 'evening-glow Dariya'—and were probably derived, along with the formulæ themselves, from the Russians, resembling in this the spirits of midday and midnight, and others of similar character, which are likewise designated by Russian proper names in the magic formulæ.

Among the deities of the sky should perhaps be included a goddess styled Azĕr-ava, 'mistress,' who, in addition to Kerämät, was once highly revered among the Moksha, at least in some districts. She was said to dwell 'in the high place, in the upper parts of the atmosphere,' and bore the epithets 'rain-bringer' and 'corn-begetter'; she seems, however, to have been rather closely related in some way to Kerämät, as in the local law-courts oaths were taken in her name and in his (see above). Here, too, may be mentioned an obscure goddess named Ange-pate or Ange-pate pas (*pate*, more correctly *pat'a*, means 'elder sister'), who is said in one MS to have been worshipped among the so-called Teryuchans (Russianized Erzä in the government of Nijni Novgorod), but is otherwise unknown.

The name Ujsud or Ujvĕs'id—a word of obscure origin—is used among the Moksha to denote a host of spirits who move about in the upper atmosphere amid harmonious sounds (mingled, indeed, with inharmonious) and to whom girls make offerings of their hair. Should one who catches a glimpse of these spirits at once implore them to send him good fortune, he obtains his wish, though at times their gift may be death. With this host may be compared the celestial spirit known among the Chuvashes as Kĕvak Xuppi, 'the gate of heaven'—the personification of some luminous appearance: 'when the gate of heaven opens, one obtains what one asks for.'

In some districts the Mordvins worshipped the wind, mostly under the name of Varma-ava, 'mother wind,' 'wind-mother,' both privately and at the communal sacrifices; and in her divine capacity she was specially implored not to damage the corn and hay crops. Worship, with offerings of food, was accorded also to frost, usually as Moroz-at'a or Kelme-at'a, 'old man frost,' but only within the house; the ceremonial of this cult is manifestly of Russian origin, as is probably also the spirit itself.

(*b*) *Earth, field, and grain.* — Mastor-ava, 'mother earth,' 'earth-mother,' especially among the Erzä, appears as one of the most revered of deities, being often named, indeed, immediately after the sky-god; thus in the songs we often find the set phrase, 'First he bowed before the sky-god, and then before mother earth.' At the communal sacrifices the Erzä besought her to give them a good harvest and to bestow good health upon the tillers of the field. She seems sometimes to have borne the epithet Mastor-pas, 'god earth,' 'earth-god,' although elsewhere Mastor-pas appears as a distinct (male) deity, whom people invoked in their imprecations to bring their enemies to destruction. The Moksha, too, had their Mastĕr-ava, 'mother earth,' but in their official worship her place is taken by Paks′-ava, 'mother field,' 'field-mother,' or Paks′-azĕrava, 'field-mistress,' 'field-hostess,' or, again, Noru-paks′ä, 'corn-field.' Among the Erzä there is little mention of the spirit of the tilled field; here, along with 'mother earth,' we find the place of that spirit usually taken by Norov-ava, 'mother corn,' 'corn-mother,' also designated Norov-pas, 'the god (goddess) corn,' to whom, among the Moksha, corresponds S′or-ava (or sometimes Noru-ava), 'mother corn'; S′or-ava, however, is found mainly in the magic formulæ and the songs. Each tilled field had its own particular spirits. For the meadow likewise there was a special presiding spirit, called Nar-azĕrava, 'mead-mistress,' or the like; but, as far as we know, she was not the object of a distinct cult, or, at most, she was presented before the hay harvest with a few pieces of bread, accompanied by a prayer for her protection.

(c) *Forest and tree.* — The forest-spirit — each forest has one of its own—is usually designated Vir-ava, 'mother forest,' 'forest-mother,' and is now generally an evil-disposed being, whose characteristics (with the exception of her sex and her large breasts) have been borrowed in detail from Lješyj, the evil forest-spirit of the Russians (on the Lješyj see *ERE* iv. 628); she is not worshipped. According to our older records, however, the forest-mother, who among the Moksha is also known as Vir-azĕrava, 'forest-hostess,' 'forest-mistress,' was a friendly deity, to whom hunters and those who gathered fruits, berries, or mushrooms prayed for protection against wild beasts, serpents, and ill-luck of all kinds, and for success in their efforts, presenting her at the same time with small oblations of food, drink, and money. Among the Moksha similar petitions are addressed also to Virĕ-pavas, 'the god forest.' While, according to the extant sources, the forest-spirits were not worshipped at the communal sacrifices, it seems likely from certain reports that such worship was paid to particular trees—oak, lime, birch, pine —which were entreated to grant prosperity to crops and cattle; we read, *e.g.*, of Tumo-pas, 'the god oak,' 'oak-god,' to whom were addressed prayers for rain. In the spells there is frequent mention of Čuvto-ava, 'tree-mother,' who, as in the case of many other spirits, was asked to pardon some supposed injury unwittingly done to her—*e.g.*, by a push—and who punished the offender by afflicting him with disease.

(d) *Water.*—The water-deity common to all the Mordvins is Ved-ava, Vedmastor-ava, 'mother water,' 'water-mother,' known among the Moksha also as Ved-azĕrava, 'water-hostess,' 'water-mistress.' She holds an important position in the cultus, principally as the spirit who presides over the fecundity of the earth, of women, and of cattle —though, at least latterly, less as the sender of fish, probably on account of the small importance of fishing as an industry. Each distinct body of water—river, brook, lake, fountain, well—has its special presiding spirit, who may bear a more definite name — *e.g.*, Rav-ava, 'mother Volga,' 'Volga-mother,' Ăs-ava, 'mother fountain,' etc. In the songs we find mention also of a 'sea-mother' (Mor′ava), probably of Russian origin; with her should perhaps be identified the Ot′s′uved-azĕrava, 'sea-mistress' (*ot′s′u-ved*, lit. 'great water,' also 'sea'), of an older Moksha account, although our informant interprets her name as Ot′s′u ved′-azĕrava, 'the great water-mistress,' *i.e.* as denoting a universal supreme water-goddess, 'the ruler of all local waters.' In an Erzä sacrificial prayer we find Veden′-kan, 'khan or prince of water,' or Ved-kan, 'water-prince' (the sense of the word *kan*, which is of Tatar origin, is not known to the people generally); mention is made also of Lis′man′ girde pas, 'the god who presides over the well.' A special water-spirit is Ved-eräj, 'water-dweller,' or Vetsa-eräj, 'he who inhabits the water'; there are, in fact, many such spirits; they are malignant beings, who, like vampire spirits, lie in wait for newly-born children, devour the grain that has been cursed by an enemy, etc. So far as we know, they are not worshipped. It is probable that these water-spirits, our information regarding whom is very meagre, were originally the souls of persons who had been drowned.

(e) *Fire.*—Among the nature-spirits should also be included Tol-ava, 'fire-mother,' 'mother fire,' who is often named in magic formulæ and in songs, but of whose public worship we know virtually nothing.

4. House, court-yard, etc.; the village.—The spirit of the dwelling-house bears various names. Among the Moksha it appears as Kud-azĕrava or Kudži-azĕrava, 'house-mistress,' 'house-hostess,' and also as Kud-ava, 'house-mother,' and Kudži-pavas, 'house-god,' 'the god house'; while among the Erzä we find Kudon′-tšin′ pas, 'god of the house' (*tši*, *ši* or *ži* being the analogue of *kudo*, *kud*, 'house'), or Keren′ šotskon′ pas, 'god of the lime-bark and the beams,' 'lime-bark and beam-god,' sometimes (perhaps through a misunderstanding and corruption of the original name) Ker′an′ šotškon′ pas, 'the god of the hewn beam, *or* beams,' and in some districts also Kudo-jurtava, 'house-mother' (lit. 'dwelling-place-mother of the house').[1]

The dwelling-place as a whole, *i.e.* the court-yard, the dwelling-house, and its adjoining buildings, which the Mordvins designate by the name *jurt*, a word borrowed from the Tatar language, has a special spirit of its own, the Jurt-ava, 'dwelling-place-mother,' known among the Moksha also as Jurt-azĕrava, 'dwelling-place-mistress.' This spirit, especially among the Erzä, has in many cases dispossessed the above-mentioned household-spirit in the proper sense, and taken its place; in this capacity it is also called Kudo-jurtava (see above) by way of distinguishing it from Kardas-jurtava, 'dwelling-place-mother of the yard,' and is represented as a dwarfish female being, or as a cat-like creature, which lives under the stove, being thus obviously connected with the Russian domestic spirit Domovoj (on which see *ERE* iv. 626 f.), which likewise lives near the stove, and has the form of a dwarf or a cat. Common to all the Erzä is a special spirit of the court-yard named Kardas-s′arko, 'court-*s′arko*' (a word of obscure meaning in this connexion), who

[1] More particularly in the magic formulæ we find a vast number of domestic spirits, *quasi*-personifications of various parts of and articles in the living-room, and generally described as 'mothers,' 'mistresses' or 'rulers'—*e.g.*, Pätnakud-azĕrava (Moksha), 'stove-mistress,' Uštuman′ kirdi (Erzä), 'ruler of the stove,' Kenkš-ava, 'door-mother,' etc. Among the Moksha Kujgĕrĕš, and among the Erzä T′r′amo, is a benevolent domestic sprite of dwarfish human form, who, however, is not worshipped. He brings to his master whatever of other people's property the latter may desire, but a task must be set for him every night, else he will begin to carry his master's goods to others. Those who wish to obtain such a spirit must keep an egg of a hen or a cock (!) from seven to twelve weeks in the armpit, remaining meanwhile under the floor; it is then hatched out. It is also possible to kill this spirit. The name T′r′amo seems to be derived from the verb *t′r′a*, 'to nourish,' while Kujgĕrĕš is probably a compound formed of *kuj*, 'serpent,' and *korĕš*, 'owl,' and thus originally meant 'serpent-owl'—though the Mordvins no longer think of it as having such a form. With this we may compare the fact that, *e.g.*, among the Lithuanians the analogous spirit, the Kaukas (on which cf. *ERE* iii. 696), is represented now as an owl and now as a fiery dragon; cf. also the myth of the basilisk.

lives beneath a stone situated in the court,[1] and is generally represented as a male, though sometimes as a female. Among some of the Moksha we hear of a court-spirit named Koram-ot′s′unä, 'the chief of the court,' while others speak of a special spirit called Kaldas-ava, 'cattleyard-mother.'

To these house- and court-spirits sacrifices are offered by the individual family at stated seasons, and also on special occasions—the birth of a child, the birth of a cow's first calf, etc. At the legal tribunals held by the head of the household with his family, according to an early Moksha account, it was the practice to swear by the house- and the dwelling-place-spirits as well as by deceased ancestors. As protectors of the cattle we also find, sometimes even at the communal sacrifices, certain saints of the Russian Church—*e.g.*, Frollavrol (a distortion of two saints' names, Flor and Lavr), surnamed Alašan′-pas, 'horse-god,' Nastasija (Russ. Anastasia), with the epithet Reven′-pas, 'sleep-god(dess)'; Miljkovič mentions also a 'swine-god' (Tuon′-pas), etc. Moreover, the store-pit, the bathroom, the threshing-place, etc., had each its special presiding spirit, usually designated 'mother,' or (among the Moksha) 'mistress,' 'hostess,' as, *e.g.*, Ban′-ava, 'bathroom-mother,' or Ban′-azĕrava, 'bathroom-mistress,' and on certain definite occasions offerings of food and drink were presented to these spirits. Likewise the bee-garden, sometimes forming part of the house-garden, sometimes situated in the forest, had its particular spirit: Neškĕper-ava (Moksha), 'bee-garden-mother,' Neške-pas (Erzä), 'beehive-god,' etc. Mention is made even of an alley- or lane-god (Ul′t′s′a-pas). The village, too, had its spirit, named Vel-ava, 'village-mother,' or Vel-azĕrava, 'village-mistress,' or Velen′-pas, 'god *or* goddess of the village'; this spirit was worshipped at the communal sacrifices.

5. Evil spirits.—To this class belong the spirits called *šajt′an* ('Satan'; pl. *šajt′at*), who dwell in marshes and waters (especially in deep parts), but also on dry land, in caverns. They beget children; they appear in various forms, including that of a fish. In the Mordvin spells they are found also as servants of the wicked earth-god Mastor-pas (see above, p. 845ᵃ). The Erzä believe in a distinct spirit of curses, 'the ruler of the curse,' called Ert, 'curse,' Ert-pas, 'curse-god,' 'the god curse' (also Erks), and is anthropomorphically figured as having a wife and a large family. Another evil spirit is Ävĕs′, or Jävĕs′ (Moksha), Eves′, Evs′ (Erzä), called also Idem-eves′ (*idem*, 'fierce'), etc. According to a Moksha account, this spirit and his wife produce seventy-seven children every year; every year, however, the whole family is killed by thunder except two, who in the following year beget other seventy-seven, and so on. The Erzä seem to regard this spirit as a wicked sorcerer, who flies in the air as a meteor. Numerous diseases are personified, and addressed as 'mother'; some of these disease-spirits, too, are thought of as married people, while others take the form of chickens, etc.

6. General observations on Mordvin mythology.—Among the Mordvins the personification of the deities (nature-spirits) is of a very feeble character, especially in the cultus—a fact signally attested by linguistic usage, and more particularly by that of the sacrificial prayers. Thus the 'rising and setting sun-god (god sun)' and 'the moon-god (god moon) who moves in a circle' are simply the sun and the moon in their visible form, but regarded as animate; in the sacrificial prayers there is nothing that would point to their personification, and, while in the mythology the sun is depicted as a maiden and the moon as a man, this is probably due to foreign influence. Nor can the designation 'mother' (*ava*), which—with the epithet *kirdi*, 'ruler' (fem.), *e.g.*, Mastoron′ Kirdi Mastor-ava, 'earth-mother, the ruler of the earth'—is the general term of most frequent occurrence in the names of the deities, be regarded as implying the attribution of personality to any particular deity;[1] these 'mothers,' in fact, are, especially in the sacrificial prayers, only the amorphous and indistinct 'souls' of natural objects, etc. Thus men 'dig' the earth-mother, and 'sow corn in her'; the field-mother—in place of whom the 'tilled field' is sometimes invoked—may 'be crushed by the horse's foot,' and 'carried away to another person's field'; the corn-mother, it is true, appears in a popular lyric as singing songs in the festive attire of a Mordvin woman, but this personification is not long maintained, for in her song the corn-mother speaks of herself thus: 'I was sown in the morning twilight, reaped in the evening twilight, thrown into the granary in order to be brewed into small beer at Easter, and baked into pastries at Christmas'; the water-mother 'streams,' or 'wells forth like silver'; the fire-mother 'blazes,' and so on. So, too, with the household-spirit, we can still to some extent distinctly trace the original idea that it is the animate dwelling-house itself, or, in other words, the amorphous soul of the house. Thus we find it said in a Moksha magic prayer, 'Kud-azĕrava ('house-mistress'), pardon him who built you and heats you'; in an Erzä petition of similar character we read, 'Kudo-jurtava ('house-mother'), above is thy lime-bark [the roof is thatched with this], beneath are thy beams'; while a parting utterance of a girl who has just been married runs, 'Dear house [=soul of the house], I have sojourned much in thy warm house.'

In conjunction with the spirits designated 'mothers' (*avat*) and 'mistresses' or 'hostesses' (*azĕr-avat*) are found the correlative (male) 'old ones' (*at′at*) and 'lords' or 'hosts' (*azĕrht*)—*e.g.*, Ved-at′a, 'water old one,' Ved-azĕr, 'water-lord,' Kud-at′a, 'house old one,' Kud-azĕr, 'house-lord.' They are for the most part absent from the sacrificial prayers, belonging rather to the sphere of the magic formulæ and of folklore, where such married couples are even represented as having children. Here we have obviously a later development, perhaps not unconnected with ancestor-worship, in which male and female progenitors are generally named together as married pairs. It is only in the case of the god of the sky and the god of thunder that personification has reached a more advanced stage. These two deities are always represented as human-like figures, and it is mainly with them that the few myths current among the Mordvins have to do. Thus, the thunder-god appears in the songs as the son-in-law of the sky-god Niške, while the latter, again, finds a wife for his son (of whom otherwise nothing has come down to us) in a Mordvin maiden whom he bears up to the sky in a silver cradle upon a chain. This myth-making process, which perhaps was to some extent due to foreign influence, does not, however, appear in the worship—the sacrificial prayers—at all, while among the Moksha the name of the sky-god, the form of which certainly suggests personification (*škaj*, 'procreator'; see above, p. 844ᵃ), is also used as the designation of the natural sky—*e.g.*, in the phrase *škajs′ mazems′*, 'the sky reddens.' The older conception of nature as animate merely, but not personal, still tends to maintain its ground, and to impede the process of personification.

Virtually no limits were set to the practice of ascribing life to inanimate things. In the magic formulæ we find that, *e.g.*, plants, the claw of an otter, the handle of a pan, a distaff, a laundry beetle (the last three are invoked by the magician

[1] The blood of sacrificial animals is allowed to run into the cavity under this stone.

[1] Cf. the Mordvin name for the pupil of the eye: *s′elme-ava*, lit. 'eye-mother.'

as his 'elder sisters'), are all endowed with life, and their aid is sought to expel disease.

It is manifest that, in the course of centuries, the religion and worship of the Mordvins have been affected by foreign (Aryan, Lithuanian, Turkish) influence, as is shown, for one thing, by a number of mythological terms—*e.g.*, *pavas*, *pas*, 'god' (cf. O. Ind. *bhagas*, O. Pers. *baga*), Pur′gine, the thunder[-god] (cf. Lith. *perkúnas*), Kerämät (=Chuvash Kirämät), Šajt′an, an evil spirit (cf. Tatar Šajtan, Chuvash Sujttan); in later times they have also been greatly influenced by Russian popular beliefs, especially in ancestor-worship.

7. Worship.—Besides the oblations performed at home by the individual family, usually under the direction of the head of the household or his wife, and accorded mainly to the domestic spirits and to ancestors, every village community held its own sacrificial feasts, in which the participants frequently arranged themselves in groups corresponding to their families or clans. From certain reports and indications, however, it would seem that at an earlier time there were joint sacrificial festivals for larger districts. The places at which sacrifices were paid to Kerämät appear to have been fenced in. On at least some of the sacrificial sites stood a simple building without windows, which, like the ordinary dwelling-house, was called *kudo*, and was used for religious purposes. The deities were not represented in material forms—the obscure indications of such likenesses found in Russian sources probably refer to representations of the dead. The offerings comprised all kinds of edible animals, from horses to fowls, while, as has already been said, allusions to an earlier practice of human sacrifice are not wholly absent from the tradition. Parts of the sacrificial animal—especially, but not exclusively, the inner parts—were presented to the deities, and in the sacrifices in honour of the dead the idea that the soul of the victim is to serve the dead person in his under-world life is brought out quite distinctly. There are indications that the colour of the animal sacrificed corresponded with that of the natural phenomenon or the object worshipped, so that the earth-spirit received a black animal, and so on. The ceremonial of the sacrifices to the nature-deities sometimes included magical actions (analogous magic), while the form of the prayer used occasionally recalls that of a magic formula—*e.g.*, 'Sky-god, may the corn prosper!' The ceremonies have, on the other hand, been noticeably influenced by the cult of the dead; thus, in the sacrificial feast, the sky-god, like the dead in the mortuary feast, had a human representative, who in his stead responded to the person praying.

The notices regarding the sacrificial priests show great divergences. According to some accounts, there were priests and priestesses—designated respectively *in-at′a*, 'great old man,' and *im-baba*, 'great old woman,' among the Moksha—who held a life appointment, and who did duty also at marriages and in the legal proceedings of the community, while other reports indicate that they were selected for definite periods of longer or shorter duration. In addition to the designations just given, we find the following: *at′a*, 'old man,' *voz-at′a*, meaning something like 'sacrificing old man,' *oznit′s′a*, 'he who sacrifices *or* prays,' *ozni-baba*, 'the old woman who sacrifices *or* prays,' and *pokš-baba*, 'great old woman.' In some of the sacrificial feasts both sexes took part, but there were also distinct festivals for males and females respectively. The public worship of the deities was connected in the closest way with agriculture, the principal employment of the people, and also with the related industry of cattle-rearing, and the deities were specially besought to grant success in these. In the cult of the nature-deities there is no trace whatever of an ethical element, prayers being addressed to them for earthly boons alone; but that element, as already indicated, does not seem to have been wholly absent from the cult of the dead, or from the worship of Kerämät (and the obscure Azěr-ava), and the spirits of the house and the homestead.

8. Magic.—From the sacrificial priest should be distinguished the sorcerer and sorceress, although there is certainly a suggestion that the priests were selected from the family or caste of the sorcerers. The latter are now usually designated by a term borrowed from the Russian, viz. *orožija*, *voražjä* (Russ. *vorožeja*), but we find also a genuine native term, *sodit′s′a*, *sodaj*, 'he (she) who knows.' These sorcerers prophesy; they discover lost things; they find out the causes of disease and all misfortune with the aid of forty-one (or forty) beans or other objects like beans, or by gazing into water freshly drawn from a well in the early morning, or by looking into the face of the person afflicted; they cure diseases by magic spells and magic prayers conjoined with the appropriate offerings, and among these prayers there is a specially large number in which a spirit (*e.g.*, the earth-mother) is solicited to pardon a presumptive injury unwittingly done to him by a fall, a push, etc., and punished by a visitation of disease or other calamity. Other kinds of disease (disease-spirits) are driven out by threats and by magic practices, special magic formulæ serve to protect against the evil eye, and so on. Magic might, of course, be employed also to cause injury.

The magic formulæ and associated practices of the Mordvins show, on the whole, strong evidence of Russian influence, or, to speak more accurately, have for the most part been borrowed from the Russian people.

LITERATURE.—Besides the writings cited in § 1, cf. **P. Meljnikov**, 'Očerki Mordvy,' in *Russkij Věstnik*, v. xxi. [1867]; **W. Mainov**, 'Les Restes de la mythologie mordvine' (=*Journal de la société finno-ougrienne*, v.), Helsingfors, 1889; **I. N. Smirnov**, 'Mordva. Istoriko-etnografičeskij očerk,' in *Izvěstija Obščestva Archeologii, Istorii i Etnografii pri Imper. Kazanskom Universitetě*, x.–xii. (also separately, Kazan, 1895; contains abundant references to further literature; Fr. tr. P. Boyer, *Les Populations finnoises des bassins de la Volga et de la Kama*, Paris, 1898, pt. ii.); **H. Paasonen**, 'Über die ursprünglichen Seelenvorstellungen bei den finnisch-ugrischen Völkern und die Benennungen der Seele in ihren Sprachen,' in *Journal de la société finno-ougrienne*, xxvi. [1909] (also separately); **V. J. Mansikka**, 'Über russische Zauberformeln,' etc. (with Finno-Ugric supplement), in *Annales Academiæ Scientiarum Fennicæ*, i. [1909]; **U. Holmberg**, 'Die Wassergottheiten der finnisch-ugrischen Völker,' in *Mémoires de la société finno-ougrienne*, xxxii. [1913] 132–159; **H. Paasonen**, 'Mythologisches, Etymologisches,' *ib.* xxxv. [1914]; **M. E. Evsevjev**, 'Bratčiny i drugie religioznye obrädy mordvy Penzenskoj gubernii,' in *Živaja Starina*, xxiii. [1914].

H. PAASONEN.

MORMONISM.—See SAINTS, LATTER-DAY.

MOSQUE.—See ARCHITECTURE (Muhammadan in Syria and Egypt).

MOTHER.—See CHILDREN, FAMILY, MOTHER-RIGHT.

MOTHER OF THE GODS (Greek and Roman).—The Mother of the Gods was identified by Homer (*Il.* xv. 187) and Hesiod (*Theog.* 634) with Rhea, the wife of Cronos. She was famous in legend for having prevented Cronos from swallowing Zeus by providing him instead with a large stone which she had wrapped in swaddling-clothes (Hes. *Theog.* 485 ff.; Apollod. i. 5). The story was localized in Crete, which thus became the fabulous birth-place of Zeus. There is some evidence of an old-established cult of the Mother of the Gods at various places on the mainland, although the name Rhea scarcely appears in this connexion. Thus, there was an altar of the Mother of the Gods in the agora at Athens (Æschin. i. 60), and a sanctuary (μητρῷον [Paus. I. iii. 5]), which was used as a record office (Lycurg. 66). An ancient festival, known as Galaxia, on the occasion of which a barley cake was boiled in milk, was celebrated in her honour (I. Bekker, *Anecd. Græca*, Berlin, 1814–21, p. 229. 5). The ætiological legend which ascribes the foundation of the sanctuary to the expiation required for the murder of a Phrygian μητραγύρτης (schol. Aristoph. *Plut.* 431; Phot. *Lex.* p. 268. 7) shows clear traces of the later conviction that the worship of the Great Mother had been imported from Asia Minor. The same influence[1] may be present when Pindar speaks of a sanctuary of the Mother close to his own gate, where she was worshipped in conjunction with Pan (*Pyth.* iii. 77 ff. [137 ff.]), and the scholiast, who does not hesitate to identify her with Rhea, relates that Pindar himself set up her statue near his house in consequence of a stone image of the Mother of the Gods having fallen from the sky at his feet. Pausanias (VIII. xxx. 4) records the existence of a ruined temple of the Mother of the Gods at Megalopolis in Arcadia, and of another, which was roofless, close to the sources of the Eurotas and the Alpheus, and of two lions made of stone in its immediate neighbourhood (*ib.* xliv. 3). But the oldest of her temples in the Peloponnese, containing a stone image of the goddess herself, was at Acriæ in Laconia (*ib.* III. xxii. 4).[2] Yet another temple was at Corinth (*ib.* II. iv. 7) with a stone throne, and a stone image of the goddess.

From the 5th cent. at least Rhea came to be identified with the Phrygian Great Mother (Eur. *Bacch.* 58 ff., 127 ff.), whose influence in Greek religion was henceforth increasingly important. Already in the Homeric prelude (*Hymn* xiv.) the Mother of the Gods is addressed as rejoicing in the clash of cymbals, the beating of drums, the blare of pipes, and the roar of wolves and lions. In another passage (Soph. *Phil.* 391 ff.), where the name of Rhea is not mentioned, she is clearly referred to as the mother of Zeus, and is identified with the Phrygian Mountain-Mother, the mistress of the swift-slaughtering lions. She is there also addressed as 'all-fostering Earth,' and there are other passages in which the earth-goddess is described as Mother of the Gods (*Hym. Hom.* xxx. 17; Solon, frag. 36. 2; Soph. frag. 268)—a title which she might well have claimed as mother and wife of Uranus according to the Hesiodic theogony (117 ff.). But it is impossible to explain the worship of the Mother of the Gods as merely a development from the vague conception of a motherly earth. The identification of the Mother of the Gods by certain 5th cent. poets (Eur. *Hel.* 1301 ff.; Melanippides, frag. 10 [T. Bergk, *Poetæ Lyrici Græci*[4], Leipzig, 1878–82, iii. 592]; Pind. *Isthm.* vii. 4) with Demeter, who, according to the received genealogy, was a daughter of Rhea (Hes. *Theog.* 454), is a further cause of perplexity. The existence of a Metroum at Agræ (*FHG* i. 359; J. G. Frazer, *Pausanias*, London, 1898, ii. 204), where the lesser mysteries were celebrated in honour of Demeter, may assist those who maintain that the Athenian Mother was another form of Demeter Θεσμοφόρος (L. Preller and C. Robert, *Griech. Mythologie*, i.[4], Berlin, 1887, p. 651). Lastly, we must take into account the antiquity of the cult of the Mountain-Mother in Crete, which has been abundantly established by the archæological discoveries of recent years. Most significant in this connexion is the impression of a signet-ring found at Cnossos, which represents the goddess standing on the apex of a mountain and guarded on either side by a lion (see art. MOUNTAIN-MOTHER).

To disentangle the actual course of development from these extremely complicated facts is one of the most puzzling tasks within the sphere of Greek mythology. The leading consideration is that, though the name of Rhea was often associated with Cybele, the identity of the two goddesses was never so completely merged that the Rhea of the Greek theogonies did not remain distinct from the partner of Attis (Gruppe, *Griech. Mythologie*, p. 1521). Some modern investigators hold the opinion that the fusion did not take place until the period subsequent to the Persian Wars (J. Beloch, *Griech. Geschichte*, Strassburg, 1893–1904, ii. 5_3). Others, while maintaining that the cult of the Mother belonged to the oldest stratum of Greek religious thought, believe that her legend and ritual passed from Crete to the Greek settlements in Asia Minor, where she was completely assimilated to Cybele in the 7th cent. or earlier (Gruppe, p. 1526 f.). Beyond this lies the question whether the goddesses subsequently identified were in origin entirely distinct (Wilamowitz, in *Hermes*, xiv. [1879] 195), or whether the Phrygian Cybele and the Cretan Rhea both developed in their separate manifestations from an identical substratum of belief belonging to the pre-Hellenic and pre-Phrygian inhabitants of Crete and Asia Minor (P. Kretschmer, *Einleitung in die Gesch. der griech. Sprache*, Göttingen, 1896, p. 194 f.). Modern theory inclines to go further (A. Rapp, in Roscher, ii. 1660), and to distinguish from Rhea a Greek Mother of the Gods, whose relation to the Phrygian Mother is to be explained by the fact that she belonged to a period anterior to the separation of Greeks and Phrygians. It is argued that, though the evidence of the cult of Rhea is scanty, its existence as distinct from that of the Mother of the Gods is well attested in Arcadia (Paus. VIII. xxxvi. 2), at Olympia (schol. Pind. *Ol.* v. 10), and at Athens (Paus. I. xviii. 7). To this it has been replied (*CGS* iii. 296) that the double title justified the establishment of distinct sanctuaries, and that it was quite possible for Greek travellers who found in Crete the worship of a great maternal goddess of fertility, bearing the name of Rhea, to transfer her cult to the mainland, using sometimes her original name, and sometimes the title μήτηρ θεῶν, in reference to their own god Zeus, whom they affiliated to her. From this point of view it becomes significant that the cult of the Mother prevailed especially in districts which are known to have been affected by Cretan influences. Instances of such coincidence are the appearance of the Idæan Dactyls at Olympia (Paus. V. vii. 6) and the legendary connexion of Athens with Crete. Moreover, the result of recent Cretan discoveries enables us to gauge better the extent of the influence which Cretan civilization must have exercised in pre-historic times. On the other hand, although Cybele did not appear in myth as the Mother of the Gods, the supposition that she was originally distinct from Rhea, and that some accidental resemblance led to their coalescence, seems to be refuted by the remarkable agreement of the traditions relating to the two goddesses. Thus, the birth of Zeus in a cave on Mt. Ida in Crete corresponds to the worship of Cybele in the hollows of Trojan Ida (Eur. *Or.* 1449; Lucr. ii. 611 ff.); the stone which Rhea offered to Cronos to the sacred stone of Cybele at Pessinus (Livy, xxix. 11); the noisy rites of the Cretan Curetes to those of the Phrygian Corybantes (Lucian, *de Salt.* 8); and the Idæan Dactyls, the attendants of Rhea,

1 Pindar (frag. 80) is the earliest writer who is known to have given the name Cybele to the Mother of the Gods (cf. Aristoph. *Av.* 875 f.).

2 The reference of Pausanias to Mt. Sipylus indicates the permanence of the belief that the μήτηρ θεῶν was identical with the goddess worshipped in Asia Minor. There is a curious reference to the cult of an anonymous Mother-goddess in Alexis, frag. 267, ii. 395 K.

were located both in Phrygia and in Crete (Soph. frag. 337).

Since it appears to be established that there was a primitive cult in Crete and Asia Minor, and to a lesser degree in Greece proper, devoted to the celebration of the Mother of the Gods, or Great Mother, but, on the other hand, the specifically Oriental features attending the ritual of Cybele were regarded as essentially foreign to Greek sentiment and were introduced to the mainland at a comparatively late period, it must be inferred that the character of the Asiatic cult had been largely modified by barbarian, especially Semitic, influences. The native Hellenic conception of the Mother is best illustrated by an Attic relief (now at Berlin) dated about 400 B.C. and in the form of a ναΐσκος, where the beautiful and benign figure of the goddess is represented enthroned and holding the tympanum, with lions couching at her feet (reproduced by Rapp, p. 1663, and by Farnell [*CGS* iii. pl. xxxiv.]).

The general characteristics of Cybele-worship have been described elsewhere (see artt. ATTIS, CYBELE), and consequently we may limit ourselves to the impression which it made upon Greek civilization at various epochs. Attis was a youth beloved by Cybele, and the story of their relations is parallel to that of Aphrodite and Adonis. According to the various narratives, none of which is earlier than the Hellenistic age, Attis was either a hunter who, like Adonis, was killed by a boar (Hermesianax, *ap.* Paus. VII. xvii. 9), or a hind (Theocr. xx. 40) that mutilated himself under a pine-tree and died from loss of blood (Ov. *Fast.* iv. 223 ff.). At the festival held in his honour a mimic representation of his death, burial, and resurrection took place, in which a pine-log was substituted for the corpse (*GB*² ii. 130 ff.).

The story, which attests the identification of Cybele with her Semitic counterpart Ishtar or Astarte (Lucian, *de Dea Syria*, 15), must have been current in Asia Minor from a very early date; for clear traces of Attis are recognizable in Herodotus's narrative of the death of Atys, the son of Crœsus, at a boar-hunt (Herod. i. 34 ff.), and the herdsman Anchises, the favourite of Aphrodite, is obviously a double of the herdsman Attis. Theopompus, the comic poet, whose plays belong to the end of the 5th and the beginning of the 4th cent., refers to the association of Attis with Cybele (frag. 27, i. 740 K.), and it is probable that the name is to be recognized in the cry ὕης ἄττης mentioned by Demosthenes (xviii. 260) in his famous account of the vulgar initiation-rites—doubtless of Asiatic origin—in which Æschines took part as an acolyte. In classical times these barbaric cults became familiar to the common people as a congeries of superstitious practices (C. A. Lobeck, *Aglaophamus*, Königsberg, 1829, i. 116; Lucian, *Icarom.* 27, etc.), so that the worship of Attis and the Mother was apt to become confused with the observances proper to Dionysus (Strabo, p. 470), Sabazius (Aristoph. *Av.* 875), and Artemis (Diog. frag. 1 [A. Nauck, *Tragicorum Græcorum Fragmenta*², Leipzig, 1889, p. 776]). With Artemis in particular Cybele was associated as the protectress of lions, bears, panthers, and other wild beasts; and with Hecate, who was identified with Artemis at an early date, she shared the title Antæa (schol. Apoll. Rhod. i. 1141; Hesych. *s.v.*) as the sender of nocturnal apparitions (Gruppe, p. 1539).

The worship of the Mother was distinguished from the indigenous Greek cults chiefly by its emotional, ecstatic, and mystical character. Indeed Phintys the Pythagorean pronounced that participation in the rites of the Mother was inconsistent with the requirements of womanly modesty (Stob. *Floril.* lxxiv. 61). In the Corybantic initiation-rites the novice was placed on a chair (θρόνωσις), while the celebrants danced round him, accompanied by the wild notes of soul-stirring music (Plat. *Euthyd.* 277 D, *Legg.* 790 D). Although, in consequence of the syncretism already explained, the mysteries of Cybele are sometimes associated with the Eleusinian mysteries of Demeter, the symbolic words of initiation, as recorded by two of our authorities (Clem. Alex. *Protrept.* I. ii. 13, p. 14 P.; schol. Plat. *Gorg.* 497 C), are undoubtedly derived from the Phrygian worship of the Great Mother: 'I have eaten from the timbrel, I have drunk from the cymbal, I have borne the sacred vessel, I have entered into the bridal chamber' (J. E. Harrison, *Prolegomena to the Study of Greek Religion*, Cambridge, 1903, p. 158). The last phrase relates to the mystical communion between the goddess and her lover, which was ritually enacted all over the East, whether in connexion with the names of Cybele and Attis, of Aphrodite and Adonis, or of Isis and Osiris (*GB*² iii. 159 ff.).[1] It was common to each of these legends that the lover was put to death and afterwards restored to life, if not always in the same incarnation. The mystical marriage may have been in its origin a magical process intended to stimulate the reproductive forces of nature, while the subsequent death and resurrection of the priest-king represented the annual decay and revival of vegetation.[2] The self-mutilation of Attis, which is, of course, the transference into myth of a primeval custom of priestly emasculation, though at first sight not easy to reconcile with the other data, probably belonged to the same circle of ideas. Whether we should regard the act in its primary intention as the final oblation by means of which the votary seeks to assimilate himself to the essential nature of the goddess (E. Meyer, *Gesch. des Altertums*², Stuttgart, 1907-09, I. ii. 649), or whether it was intended to secure the continued fruitfulness of the Earth-mother and the renewal of her crops (*GB*³, pt. iv., *Adonis, Attis, Osiris*, London, 1907, p. 224 ff.; Cumont, in Pauly-Wissowa, vii. 681), is not altogether certain, and the two ideas are not necessarily inconsistent with each other. Considerations bearing on the question may be deduced from the fact that the severed genitals were dedicated in the sanctuary of Rhea-Cybele (schol. Nicand. *Alex.* 8), and from the statement of Lucian that they were thrown into some particular house from which the Gallus received female raiment and ornaments (*de Dea Syria*, 51). Anyhow, it is unnecessary to suppose that the custom was introduced into the cult owing to a fresh impulse of mysticism which, moving from East to West, perhaps in the 6th cent., aimed at the liberation of the worshipper from the indulgence of sensual desires (Gruppe, p. 1542). Certainly asceticism was by no means characteristic of the begging priests of the Mother (μητραγύρται),[3] who earned their living by vulgar quackeries imposed upon the superstitious masses, and who, although they are first known to us from the fragments of the poets of the New Comedy (Μητραγύρτης, a play of Antiphanes, ii. 74 K.; cf. Menand. frag. 202, iii. 58 K.), were probably familiar figures in Athens at a much earlier date (R. C. Jebb, on Soph. *Œd. Tyr.* 388 [*Tragedies*, Cambridge, 1904]; cf. Plat. *Rep.* 364 C). It may be conjectured with some probability that the influence of this traffic was considerable, although

[1] Gruppe, p. 1541, points out that the names θαλάμαι, καλύβαι, and παστάδες given to sanctuaries of Cybele (schol. Nicand. *Alex.* 8; Hesych. *s.v.* Κύβελα; *Anth. Pal.* ix. 340. 4) are to be interpreted in the same way.

[2] The notion that Cybele and Attis stand for the generative principle and its terrestrial process survives in the Neo-Platonic treatise of Sallustius περὶ θεῶν (iv.; tr. G. Murray, *Four Stages of Greek Religion*, New York, 1912, p. 191 ff.).

[3] Some of these may have been eunuchs (Babrius, cxxxvii. 1).

the conception of the frenzied Galli who scourged themselves with whips (Plut. *adv. Colot.* 33, p. 1127 C), and lacerated their flesh with knives (*Anth. Pal.* vi. 94. 5), cannot be traced to an earlier source than the Alexandrian writers (Cumont, *op. cit.*, col. 675), and has become known to us chiefly through Latin literature (*e.g.*, Sen. *Agam.* 723; Lucr. ii. 614 ff.).

In the year 205 B.C. a Sibylline oracle was discovered by the Decemviri, directing them, as a condition of success in the war, to introduce into Rome the worship of the Great Mother of Pessinus (Livy, xxix. 10). Accordingly, the sacred stone, which was then in the custody of Attalus, king of Pergamus, having been removed by him from its original home at Pessinus (L. Bloch, in *Philol.* lii. [1895] 580 ff.), was brought to Italy in circumstances of great ceremony, and reached its destination in the year 204. Strange happenings marked its arrival. The ship conveying the sacred object grounded on a sandbank in the Tiber. Then Claudia Quinta, a noble matron whose freedom of speech had provoked censorious tongues to slander, prayed to the goddess that her character might be cleared by the ordeal, if she succeeded in drawing off the ship after strong arms had failed. The ship at once began to follow her direction, and Claudia's innocence was triumphantly vindicated (Ov. *Fast.* iv. 291 ff.; Suet. *Tib.* 2; Tac. *Ann.* iv. 64). On the 4th of April the goddess was received as a temporary guest, until a permanent home could be provided for her, in the temple of Victory on the Palatine, and the day was set apart for a festival to be known as the Megalesia, on which gifts were presented to the shrine, and a *lectisternium* and public games were held (Livy, xxix. 14). Ten years later scenic performances were for the first time exhibited at the Megalesia (*ib.* xxxiv. 54). Subsequently, thirteen years after the contract had been placed, a temple on the Palatine for her sole and separate occupation was dedicated to the Magna Mater Idæa on the 10th of April 191, when the *Ludi Megalenses* were included for the first time in the State calendar (*ib.* xxxvi. 36). Somewhat later, if not immediately, they were extended so as to occupy the entire interval between the 4th and 10th of April (*CIL* i.^{2} 314). On the first day of the festival the *prætor urbanus* made a solemn offering to the goddess in her temple (Dion. Hal. *Ant. Rom.* ii. 19). The third day was reserved for the performance of stage-plays (Ov. *Fast.* iv. 377), and we know that four of the extant works of Terence were presented on this occasion. Races (*circenses*) were held on the last day (Marquardt, *Röm. Staatsverwaltung*^{2}, iii. 501), and in the age of Nero and Domitian these had become by far the most popular feature of the whole celebration (Juv. xi. 193). The recurrence of the festival was marked by general merrymaking and licence; clubs were formed to promote social enjoyment (Cic. *de Senect.* 45); and so lavish was the expenditure of the upper classes on reciprocal hospitalities that in 161 a sumptuary law was found necessary to restrain it (Aul. Gell. ii. 24).

In the last two centuries of the Republic the participation of State officials in the cult was limited to the extent already described; but, dating from the time of Augustus, who restored the temple of the Magna Mater after it had been burned down in A.D. 3, there is evidence of a further ceremony of a primitive character which took place on the 27th of March. This was known as the *lavatio*, when the symbolic stone and possibly also the knife of the Gallus (Mart. III. xlvii. 2) were conveyed, by the direction of the Quindecimviri, through the Porta Capena, and washed in the waters of the Almo, which debouches into the Tiber just outside the city (Ov. *Fast.* iv. 337; Lucan, i. 599). In all other respects the administration of the cult was left in the hands of its foreign ministers, particularly the Galli with their Archigallus (*CIL* vi. 2183), and no Roman citizen was allowed to acquire any official status in relation to it. The Phrygian priests, however, were permitted on stated occasions to march in procession through the city in their sacerdotal dress, singing their wild songs to the accompaniment of flutes and tympana (Dion. Hal. *loc. cit.*), and collecting alms from the bystanders (Cic. *de Leg.* ii. 22).

In the latter part of the 2nd cent. a complete re-organization of the cult seems to have taken place. Henceforth, as the evidence of numerous inscriptions shows, Roman citizens were permitted to assume priestly offices subject to the approval of the Quindecimviri, but the privilege was exercised chiefly by the freedman class. To the ceremony of the *lavatio* on March 27th there was now added a further festival of five days, the opening ceremony of which on March 15th was denoted *Canna intrat* on the Calendar of Philocalus (*CIL* i.^{2} 264), while the remaining four days, the 22nd, 24th, 25th, and 26th of March, were designated respectively *Arbor intrat*, *Sanguen*, *Hilaria*, and *Requietio*. The ceremonial represented in detail the various incidents of the story of Attis with which we are already familiar. On the 22nd the procession of reed-bearers (Cannophori) which entered the city was intended to recall the fact that Attis as a child was exposed among the bulrushes of the river Gallus (Julian, *Or.* v. 165 B). Similarly on March 22nd the Dendrophori carried to the temple on the Palatine a pine-tree, encircled with fillets of wool and adorned with violets, as a representation of the tree under which Attis mutilated himself. The day of blood (24th) was given up to lamentation for the death of the god, and, whereas originally the act of self-mutilation was then performed by the priest, subsequently it was sufficient for the Archigallus to make an incision in his arm and symbolically to sprinkle his blood (Tert. *Apol.* 25). The climax of the festival was reached in the rejoicings over the resurrection of the god which occupied the day of the *Hilaria*. It was recognized in antiquity that the renewal of the sun's power after the vernal equinox was hereby symbolized (Macrob. *Sat.* I. xxi. 10), and that the whole festival was devised to celebrate the decay and re-birth of vegetation (cf. Plut. *de Is. et Osir.* 69 [378 F]). Modern scholars have noticed the parallel presented by our Lenten and Easter services, which occupy a corresponding position in the calendar (*CGS* iii. 301).

It remains to mention the rite known as *taurobolium*, performed on 28th March, the existence of which is attested by a series of inscriptions extending from the 2nd to the end of the 4th century. Although during this period it was invariably linked to the service of the Great Mother, there is no doubt that it belonged originally to the cult of some other deity, and it has been conjectured that this was the Persian goddess Anāhita, who had been identified with Ἄρτεμις Ταυροπόλος (F. Cumont, *Rev. archéol.* xii. [1888] 132 ff.). There is also much obscurity in the details of the rite. In the earlier period the chief incident of the *taurobolium* and of the certainly similar *criobolium* was the sacrifice of a bull or a ram; but at a later date, according to both the epigraphic (*e.g.*, *CIL* vi. 511) and the literary (Prudent. *Peristeph.* x. 1011 ff.) records, the recipient of the *taurobolium* stood in a cavity having a perforated roof through which the blood of the bull was poured over him so that he might suffer a 're-birth.' The whole ceremony was under the control of the Quindecimviri.

In the Roman Imperial period the cult of the

Great Mother, by passing under State control, lost many of its original characteristics; but the power of the Roman organization was such that, by the adoption of suitable accretions from outside, and by its association with the cults of Isis and Mithra, it exercised during the last days of paganism a wider and more potent influence than at any earlier time.

LITERATURE.—E. Gerhard, *Ueber das Metroon zu Athen und über die Göttermutter der griech. Mythologie*, Berlin, 1851; A. Rapp, in Roscher, ii. 1638 ff.; W. Drexler, *ib.* ii. 2910 ff.; L. R. Farnell, *CGS*, Oxford, 1896–1909, iii. 289–306; O. Gruppe, *Griechische Mythologie und Religionsgeschichte*, Munich, 1906, pp. 1521–1555; Grant Showerman, *The Great Mother of the Gods* (= *Bulletin of the University of Wisconsin*, no. 43, phil. and lit. series, i. 3 [1901]); F. Cumont, in Pauly-Wissowa, ii. 2247 ff., vii. 674 ff.; H. R. Goehler, *De Matris Magnæ apud Romanos cultu*, Meissen, 1886; J. Marquardt, *Röm. Staatsverwaltung*, iii.[2], Leipzig, 1885, p. 367 ff.; G. Wissowa, *Religion und Kultus der Römer*, Munich, 1902, pp. 263–271; G. E. Marindin, in *Dict. Gr. and Rom. Antiq.*,[3] London, 1891, ii. 155, *s.v.* 'Megalesia.'

A. C. PEARSON.

MOTHER-RIGHT.—1. Introduction.—Mother-right is a form of social organization in which the rights of a person in relation to other members of his community and to the community as a whole are determined by relationship traced through the mother. In this condition the duties which a person owes to society, the privileges which he enjoys, and the restrictions to which he is subject are regulated, and their scope is determined, by the relations in which the person stands to his mother's relatives and his mother's social group.

Mother-right is a highly complex condition in which a large number of social processes are involved. The following are the chief elements that can be distinguished.

(1) *Descent.*—This term should be limited to the process which regulates membership of the social group, such as clan, caste, family, etc. In mother-right descent is matrilineal; a person belongs to the social group of his mother. The use of the term is most appropriate when the community is divided into distinct social groups, and this distinctness is most pronounced in the clan-organization in which the practice of exogamy separates the social groups called clans clearly from one another. The social organizations based on the family or kindred are made up of social groups less clearly distinguishable from one another, and, though we may speak of descent in the family whether in the limited or extended sense, the term is here less appropriate.

(2) *Kinship.*—In a community based purely on mother-right kinship would be traced solely through the mother and would not be recognized with the relatives of the father. Everywhere in the world, but especially among peoples who possess the clan-organization, kinship carries with it a large mass of social duties, privileges, and restrictions (*ERE* vii. 705), and in a typical condition of mother-right these social functions would exist only in connexion with the mother's relatives. We have no evidence, however, of the existence of any society in which kinship is not recognized with the relatives of the father, although in many cases the functions are very restricted as compared with those of relationship traced through the mother, good examples being those in which marriage is allowed with any of the father's relatives, but is strictly forbidden with equally near relatives on the mother's side.

(3) *Inheritance.*—In a condition of typical mother-right children would inherit nothing from the father; their rights to property would be determined solely by relationships through the mother. Mother-right does not imply that rights in property should be vested either mainly or exclusively in women. On the contrary, in many cases in which children inherit nothing from the father, women are debarred from holding property, though they form the channel by which it is transmitted from one member of the community to another. The usual rule of inheritance in mother-right is that the property of a man passes to his brother or his sister's son. Often it passes from brother to brother, and, on the death of the last surviving brother, to a sister's son.

(4) *Succession.*—This term is most conveniently used for the process whereby rank, office, or other social distinction is transmitted. In mother-right succession usually follows the same rules as inheritance, a chief, priest, or other holder of rank or office being succeeded either by his brother or by his sister's child.

(5) *Authority.*—Mother-right has often been supposed to imply mother-rule, but in the great majority of the societies which furnish us with examples of mother-right authority is definitely vested in the male—in the father or oldest male as the head of the household, and in the chief as the head of the tribe or corresponding social group. In some societies, however, authority in the household is vested in the mother's brother, giving rise to a form of social organization which has been called the 'avunculate,' and the authority of the mother's brother in one form or another is very common, not only associated with other features of mother-right, but in societies in which descent, inheritance, and succession are patrilineal. Only very rarely is authority in the household vested in the mother or oldest female. The term 'matriarchate,' which is often used loosely as the equivalent of mother-right, should be limited in its scope to this condition of mother-rule. Many societies exist in which women are chiefs or monarchs, but, as a rule, this condition is not associated with mother-right. Among peoples over whom women rule the father is usually the head of the household.

(6) *Marriage.*—Mother-right in its typical form is associated with a mode of marriage, most suitably called 'matrilocal,' in which the husband lives with his wife's people. In its extreme form the husband may be only an occasional visitor to his wife's home, so that the children grow up with little or no social obligation towards their father, and live under the authority of the mother and the mother's brother.

In a state of typical mother-right a person would belong to his mother's social group. He would not recognize the existence of any kind of social duty except towards his mother's relatives, and would ignore the relatives of his father; property, rank, and office would pass solely through women. It is not a necessary feature of mother-right, however, that authority should be vested in the woman. It might be so vested, but, if the woman is not the ruler, it would be vested in her brothers. In mother-right in its most typical form the father should have no authority in the household.

The condition thus described as typical mother-right occurs very rarely, being found most purely among such people as the Iroquois and Seri Indians of N. America and the Khasis of Assam. In many cases which have been regarded as examples of mother-right some of the social processes included under this head depend on the tie with the mother, while others are determined by relationship traced through the father, producing social conditions of the most varied kinds. Thus, while descent is matrilineal, succession may be patrilineal. Kinship is everywhere, so far as we know, recognized through the father as well as through the mother, and authority in the household is often paternal where descent, inheritance, and succession are all matrilineal. Moreover, a mixture of social groupings may be present, one of which may be patrilineal while the other is matrilineal, this being especially the case when local organizations accompany different forms of exogamous grouping.

There are cases in which matrilineal processes show themselves only in certain departments of social life. Thus, a people who possess patrilineal institutions in general may yet show the presence of matrilineal practices in connexion with slavery. The children of a free father and a slave mother may be slaves even if the father is of high rank, while the children of a free mother and a slave father may be free, and even noble, if the mother belongs to the nobility.

Another condition in accordance with mother-right is that in which marriage between half-brother and sister is allowed when they are the offspring of one father and different mothers, while it is forbidden when they are of the same mother by different fathers. The form of marriage which is forbidden would be impossible with mother-right, while that which is allowed would be natural, provided that the mothers belonged to different exogamous groups.

Another large group of matrilineal practices is characterized by the authority of the mother's brother. Among a people who practise patrilineal descent, inheritance, and succession the mother's brother has sometimes more authority than the father, and this authority may be accompanied by a number of other social functions which show that the tie with the mother's brother is closer than that with the father. Thus, mother's brother and sister's son may hold their property in common, or the sister's son may take the goods of his uncle without restraint. The mother's brother may act as the special guardian and instructor of his nephew, he may initiate him into the mysteries of secret societies, or may take the leading part in such rites as circumcision and its variants, ear-boring, knocking out teeth, and other operations.

2. Distribution and varieties.—Owing to ignorance or neglect of the complexity of mother-right on the part of ethnographers, the available evidence often leaves us uncertain how far the social processes of a people correspond with those of mother-right.

(1) *America.*—Mother-right[1] exists in America in an especially pure form. Not only are descent, inheritance, and succession purely matrilineal among many of its peoples, but the woman takes a place in social life which would justify the use of the term 'matriarchy.' A striking example of this condition is found among the Iroquois and Hurons,[2] where women are the heads of the households, elect the chiefs, and form the majority of the tribal council. Almost as striking an example occurs among the Pueblo Indians, where, with the exception of the Tewa,[3] descent is matrilineal, the house is the property of the woman, marriage is matrilocal, and the children are regarded as belonging to the mother. Other purely or predominantly matrilineal stocks are the Caddoan (Pawnee, Arikara), the Muskhogean (Creek, Choctaw, Seminole), the Yuchi, and the Timucua.

In other cases matrilineal and patrilineal tribes are found among one stock. Thus, though the Siouan tribes are mainly patrilineal, the Biloxi, Tutelo, Crow, Hidatsa, Oto, and Mandan are matrilineal; while among the Winnebago the sister's son formerly succeeded, a woman could be chief, and the mother's brother exercised much authority.[4] Again, though the majority of Algonquians are patrilineal, the Mohegans are matrilineal, succession formerly passed to the sister's son among the Ojibwa,[1] and there is evidence of matrilineal inheritance and of the authority of the mother's brother among the Menomini.[2] Another stock with both modes of descent is the Athapascan. While the outlying Navaho and Apache in the south are matrilineal, the main body of the people in the north vary. The western tribes, such as the Loucheux, Takulli, Tahltan, and Knaiakhotana, have matrilineal moieties or clans with inheritance and succession in the female line. The eastern tribes, on the other hand, are made up of bands within which social rights pass patrilineally.[3] The tribes of California, broken up into a large number of linguistic stocks, are organized in villages. Marriage is often matrilocal, but inheritance and succession are patrilineal. A totemic clan-organization has been recorded among the Miwok, and the totemic organization of the Yokut is said to be associated with matrilineal descent.[4] The Yuman stock practise patrilineal descent, but have also another form of social grouping which may stand in some relation to mother-right.[5] The local form of organization seems to prevail in the Shoshonean stock, except among the Hopi, who are, however, Pueblo Indians in general culture though they speak a Shoshonean language. This form of organization also extends northwards as far as the Salish, beyond whom the Kwakiutl form an intermediate link with the matrilineal Heiltsuk, Haida, Tsimshian, and Tlingit. The Tsimshian show traces of a mixture of matrilineal and patrilineal modes; for, though a man belongs to his mother's clan, he takes the name of his father's totemic crest as part of his personal name.[6] This mixture is still more evident among the Kwakiutl, where a man belongs to his father's clan, but takes the totemic crest of his wife's father when he marries, and transmits it to his son, who bears it till his marriage, when, in his turn, he takes the crest of his father-in-law.[7]

It is very doubtful whether the Eskimos possess any form of clan-organization. The chief social unit seems to be the family, the social rights of which pass from a father to his children.

Southward of the United States, the Seri Indians possess mother-right in a most complete form.[8] Women take the chief place in government, sometimes putting their decisions into execution themselves, while in other cases their brothers execute their wishes and are consulted by them in cases of difficulty. The husband only visits his wife and takes a very unimportant place in her household, though he may occupy a leading place in another household in his capacity of mother's brother.

We have little knowledge of the social organization of the peoples of Central America, but the Aztecs appear to have been matrilineal, at any rate so far as succession was concerned, the ruler being followed by his brother or by his sister's son.

Our knowledge of the social organization of S. America is more fragmentary than in any other part of the world, but there are definite records of the presence of mother-right in several regions and facts which suggest its presence elsewhere. One centre of the practice is the Santa Marta peninsula in Colombia,[9] where the Goajiro are

1 For general information regarding America see Morgan, *Ancient Society*, pp. 62–185; *HAI* i. [1907], ii. [1910]; J. R. Swanton, *Amer. Anthropologist*, vii. [1905] 663.

2 See Morgan, *League of the Iroquois*, Rochester, N.Y., 1851, pp. 84 f., 325 f.; J. W. Powell, *1 RBEW* [1881], p. 19 ff.

3 *Amer. Anth.* xiv. [1912] 472.

4 J. Carver, *Travels through the interior Parts of N. America*, London, 1778, p. 259; Radin, *Amer. Anth.* xii. [1910] 214.

1 Morgan, *Ancient Society*, p. 166.

2 W. J. Hoffman, *14 RBEW*, pt. i. [1896] p. 11 ff.; A. Skinner, *Anth. Papers, Amer. Mus. Nat. Hist.* xiii. [1913] 20.

3 C. Hill-Tout, *British North America*, London, 1907, p. 143 ff.

4 C. H. Merriam, *Amer. Anth.* x. [1908] 562.

5 A. L. Kroeber, *ib.* iv. [1902] 276; J. P. Harrington, *JAFL* xxi. [1908] 344 n.

6 F. Boas, *Rep. Brit. Assoc.*, 1889, p. 819.

7 Boas, *Rep. U.S. Nat. Mus.*, 1895.

8 W J McGee, *17 RBEW*, pt. i. [1898] p. 9 ff.

9 F. A. A. Simons, *Proc. Roy. Geogr. Soc.* vii. [1885] 789; F. L. Nicholas, *Amer. Anth.* iii. [1901] 606.

organized in totemic clans with matrilineal descent. Property passes to the sister's sons, and compensation for injury goes chiefly to relatives on the mother's side. Among the Aruacs, who are said to have been the original inhabitants of the peninsula, we have no record of the nature of the social organization; but the people trace their descent to an ancestress, and women take an important place in social life.[1] Another centre of mother-right is in British Guiana,[2] where the Arawaks practise matrilineal descent and matrilocal marriage. The neighbouring Warau and Makusi are also said to be matrilineal. If a Makusi woman marries a man of another tribe, the children will belong to the Makusi; but, as it is said that these people may marry the daughter of the sister, it is improbable that they have a matrilineal clan-organization. Apparently this region is in an intermediate condition, and the presence of patrilineal succession among the Siusi,[3] a branch of the Arawaks, also points in this direction. The Arawaks who have wandered into Brazil are matrilineal,[4] and there is another centre of mother-right in this country on the Kulisehu branch of the Xingu River.[5] The Bakaïri of this region are matrilineal in that the children of the Bakaïri woman who marries a man of another tribe belong to the Bakaïri, and this is true of other tribes; but, as in British Guiana, we do not know of any definite matrilineal clan-organization. Succession appears to be in an intermediate condition, a chief being succeeded by his son, his sister's son, or his daughter's husband. The mother's brother shares the exercise of authority with the father.

Among other peoples of S. America, such as the Caingang[6] and the Tsoroti,[7] there is matrilocal marriage; but we do not know whether this custom is associated with other features of mother-right.

(2) *Oceania.*—Since the great majority of Polynesians do not possess any form of clan-system, and we know little of their local organization, the nature of descent is doubtful; but where the clan-organization exists, as in Tikopia, it is definitely patrilineal.[8] The communism of the people also makes the nature of inheritance doubtful, but there is certainly no evidence of any of the modes of transmission which accompany mother-right. Chiefs are usually succeeded by their children, and this mode of succession also holds of hereditary occupations. In Tonga, however, succession may pass to the sister's son, and a woman may be chief in several parts of Polynesia. As a rule, the father has authority in the household; in some islands, such as Tonga and Tikopia, the mother's brother has certain social functions, but not of a kind that shows any special exercise of authority. In New Zealand,[9] and perhaps elsewhere, matrilocal marriage is frequent.

Micronesia, on the other hand, is the seat of definite mother-right. In the Marshall and Mortlock Islands and in the Carolines, with the exception of the island of Yap, the matrilineal mode of transmission is general.[10] In Ponape there are exogamous clans with matrilineal descent, and property passes to the sister's sons.[1] Only in Yap does the son follow his father, who elsewhere is said to be a stranger to his children. Marriage appears to be largely matrilocal. In the Marianne Islands all that we are told is that the woman commands absolutely in the house.[2] In the Pelew Islands there are exogamous totemic clans with matrilineal descent.[3]

Melanesia has usually been regarded as one of the most definite examples of mother-right; but, even where descent is matrilineal, its social organization departs so widely from the typical condition as to make it doubtful whether the term should properly be used.[4] Descent is often matrilineal, but follows the father in New Caledonia, and in many islands of the New Hebrides as well as in one part of Santa Cruz. In other places, such as most parts of Fiji and one region of the Solomons, the absence of a clan-organization makes the nature of descent doubtful. Chieftainship is always patrilineal where it is hereditary at all, and inheritance is in an intermediate condition. Property passes to the children in some places and to the sisters' children in others, while elsewhere different kinds of property follow different rules of inheritance. In Santo in the New Hebrides, people take the totem of the father as part of the personal name, but belong to the mother's clan, and in Vanua Levu in Fiji, where there is matrilineal descent, a man pays special respect to the totem of his father, though he belongs to his mother's clan and inherits her sacred land.[5] Matrilocal marriage is not frequent even where descent is matrilineal, and there are often definite social relations between a man and his mother's brother, though not always of a kind to show any special exercise of authority on the part of the uncle.

(3) *Australia.*—There are at least four forms of social grouping in this continent: the moiety, the matrimonial class, the local group, and the totemic group; since two or more of these may co-exist, there may be more than one rule of descent.

Wherever there is a simple dual organization, as among the Dieri and Ngarabana (Urabunna) of Central Australia, descent is matrilineal so far as the moiety is concerned.

The peculiarity of descent in the case of the matrimonial class is that it is neither patrilineal nor matrilineal, but the child belongs to a class different from that of either father or mother. Where marriages follow the orthodox rule, it is not possible to tell definitely the nature either of descent of the class or of the moieties of which the classes may be regarded as subdivisions. Marriages do not always follow the ordinary rules, however, and A. R. Brown has used the exceptional marriages of certain eight-class tribes as the means of detecting the true nature of descent.[6] By means of evidence provided by R. H. Mathews he shows that among the Arunta the children of the chief form of irregular marriage belong to the class to which they would have belonged if they had been the children of the man by a regular marriage, thus showing that descent among this people is determined by the father. Among the Tjingilli, on the other hand, the children of an irregular marriage belong to the group to which they would have belonged if they had been the offspring of the union of their mother with a husband married according to rule, showing that here descent is properly matrilineal so far as the class is concerned.

1 W. Sievers, *Reise in der Sierra Nevada de Santa Marta*, Leipzig, 1887, p. 91 f.
2 R. Schomburgh, *Reise in Britisch-Guiana*, Leipzig, 1847, i. 169, ii. 314; E. F. im Thurn, *Among the Indians of Guiana*, London, 1883, p. 185 f.
3 T. Koch-Grünberg, *Zwei Jahre unter den Indianern*, Berlin, 1909, pp. 68, 109.
4 C. F. P. von Martius, *Zur Ethnographie . . . Amerika's*, Leipzig, 1867, p. 690 f.
5 K. von den Steinen, *Unter den Naturvölkern Zentral-Brasiliens*2, Berlin, 1897, p. 285 f.
6 Borba (Barbo ?), *Globus*, l. [1886] 235; Ambrosetti, *ib.* lxxiv. [1898] 245.
7 E. Nordenskiöld, *Indianerleben*, Leipzig, 1912, p. 92.
8 W. H. R. Rivers, *Hist. of Melanesian Society*, Cambridge, 1914, ii. 239.
9 R. Taylor, *Te Ika a Maui*, London, 1855, p. 164.
10 J. Kubary, *Mitt. der geogr. Gesellsch. in Hamburg*, 1878–79, p. 224.

1 F. W. Christian, *The Caroline Islands*, London, 1899, p. 74.
2 C. Le Gobien, *Hist. des îles Mariannes*, Paris, 1700, p. 59.
3 J. Kubary, *Die socialen Einrichtungen der Pelauer*, Berlin, 1885.
4 Rivers, ii. 90.
5 A. M. Hocart, *Man*, xiv. [1914] 2.
6 *Man*, x. [1910] 55, xii. [1912] 123.

The local group is probably always patrilineal, but this form of social grouping has been largely neglected by ethnographers, and we must await further information to show whether this mode of descent is universal.

The totemic grouping shows great variety of descent. Sometimes the totemic group corresponds with the local group, and where this is so descent is necessarily patrilineal. In other cases, where the totemic groups form subdivisions of the matrilineal moieties, they are of equal necessity matrilineal. Among the Dieri there are two forms of totemic organization: one kind of totem, called *pintara*, is transmitted from father to son together with special knowledge of legends and rites, while a man takes another kind of totem called *madu* (the *murdu* of Howitt) from his mother. The intermediate condition of the people between matrilineal and patrilineal transmission of the totem is shown by the fact that the father often transmits his *madu* as well as his *pintara* to his son. Each man also obtains from his mother or her relatives special knowledge of legends, etc., relating to his maternal ancestors.[1]

The communistic habits and the poor development of personal property in Australia make the subject of inheritance of little importance, but in so far as it exists it seems to follow the same lines as descent of the moiety or class. Thus, among the Arunta, whose irregular marriages point to patrilineal descent, certain objects, and especially *churinga*, or ancestral bull-roarers, pass from a man to his son, or, if he has no son, to his brother and his brother's son. Among the Tjingilli and other tribes whose irregular marriages show them to have matrilineal descent, property passes into the possession of the mother's brothers or the daughter's husbands, the inheritors being men of the moiety of the mother of the dead man. The latter mode of inheritance also occurs among some of the tribes of the northern territory.[2]

Since the Australians have neither chiefs nor priests, the subject of succession is also quite unimportant. The special powers of a wizard or leech are acquired by special processes of initiation. Perhaps the topic which comes most definitely under this head is the knowledge of native legends and rites, the double character of which among the Dieri has already been considered. Elsewhere this kind of knowledge is closely connected with totemism, and probably follows the laws of transmission of the totem.

(4) *New Guinea.*—The most definite example of mother-right in this region occurs among the Massim of the south-eastern islands.[3] This people, who speak a Melanesian language, practise mother-right in a purer form than is found anywhere in Melanesia proper. Not only does a man belong to the totemic clan of his mother, but property passes to his sister's children in some localities, and everywhere a chief is succeeded by his brother or his sister's son. In parts of the Papuan Gulf descent is probably matrilineal, but succession to the rank of chief is patrilineal. Another locality where mother-right apparently prevails is on the Mamberamo River, in the Dutch portion of New Guinea,[4] where a boy belongs to his mother's tribe, and wears its distinctive dress, even when he lives with his father's people.

Elsewhere in New Guinea patrilineal customs are found, though here and there indications of mother-right occur. Thus in the Mekeo district, which has a form of the dual organization, descent sometimes passes in the female line, and among the neighbouring Pokao descent is sometimes matrilineal, and a woman may be chief and be succeeded by her child. Among the Koita, Motu, Roro, and Mekeo peoples the mother's brother has certain social functions, and these functions are highly developed in the western islands of Torres Straits, where, side by side with patrilineal descent, inheritance, and succession, the mother's brother has more authority than the father.[1]

[1] O. Siebert, *Globus*, xcvii. [1910] 48.
[2] B. Spencer, *Native Tribes of the Northern Territory of Australia*, London, 1914, p. 250.
[3] C. G. Seligmann, *The Melanesians of British New Guinea*, Cambridge, 1910, p. 435 f.
[4] M. Moszkowski, *ZE* xliii. [1911] 323.

(5) *Indonesia.*—Father-right prevails throughout the greater part of the Malay Archipelago. There is a peculiar form of matrilocal marriage in one part of the Timor,[2] in which the husband returns to his own home after a time, leaving behind him his children, who inherit their mother's property.

In several parts of Sumatra mother-right is present in its most definite form.[3] Among the Malays of Minangkabau, of Upper Padang, and certain other districts there are matrilineal clans and the extreme form of matrilocal marriage in which the husband continues to dwell in his mother's house and only visits his wife. The people live in long houses, which accommodate a family in the extended sense, consisting of persons descended from one woman, the head of the household being the eldest brother of the leading woman. He takes the place of a father to his sister's children, who inherit his property after it has been enjoyed by his brothers and sisters. A form of organization intermediate between the condition of Minangkabau and father-right occurs in Tiga Loereng, where husband and wife live together, but the father has little power over his children, authority being exercised by their mother's eldest brother. Property belonging to husband or wife at the time of marriage passes to their respective clans, but that acquired by them after marriage is divided between their children and their sisters' children.

(6) *Asia.*—There are no examples of mother-right in E. Asia, with the possible exception of the Ainus in the north and Cambodia in the south. Among the Ainus relationship through the mother is said to be more important than that through the father, and the mother's brother is the most important member of the family group, but we have no definite information about descent or inheritance. The peoples of Siberia are usually organized in patrilineal clans, but matrilocal marriage is frequently present.[4]

In India there are two centres of mother-right. One of these, represented by the Khasis and Synteng of Assam, affords a most definite example of the condition.[5] Descent is matrilineal in the clan, which is traced back to an ancestress and embraces kindred groups consisting of the female descendants of a great-grandmother. The house and other property belong to the women, and the husband or father has no authority except in those cases in which, at some time after marriage, he removes his wife and children to another house. Property is inherited by daughters, the house and its contents go to the youngest daughter, and, in default of daughters, the inheritance passes to a daughter of a mother's sister. The *siem*, or chief, is a man, except in Khyrim, but is succeeded by his brother or the son of his eldest sister. The neighbouring Wár people show an intermediate

[1] *Rep. Cambridge Exp. to Torres Straits*, v. [1904] 144.
[2] H. O. Forbes, *A Naturalist's Wanderings in the Eastern Archipelago*, London, 1885, p. 457.
[3] For a more complete account of the distribution of mother-right in this island, see J. G. Frazer, *Totemism and Exogamy*, ii. 185 ff.
[4] M. A. Czaplicka, *Aboriginal Siberia*, Oxford, 1914, p. 23 f.
[5] P. R. T. Gurdon, *The Khasis*, London, 1907, p. 63 f.

form in that both men and women inherit, but the youngest daughter obtains an additional share. The Gāros, who live to the west of the Khasis, and the Megam, or Lynngam, who are a fusion of Khasi and Gāro, practise a form of mother-right closely resembling that of the Khasis. Though a man cannot inherit property and can possess only that acquired by his own exertions, he nevertheless exercises some control over the property of his wife, and can even appoint a member of his clan, usually his sister's son, to exercise this control in the event of his death.[1] Among the Kochs of N. Bengal, who are in contact with the Gāros, marriage is matrilocal, and a man is said to obey his wife and her mother.[2]

The other Indian centre of mother-right is on the Malabar coast, where matrilineal descent, inheritance, and succession are practised by the Nāyars, northern Tīyans, and other peoples, including even the Muhammadan Māppilas, or Moplahs, of N. Malabar. This system of law, known as *marumakkatāyam*, is closely connected with the so-called polyandry of this part of India. In the unions of Nāyar women with Nambutiri (Nambūri) men, which are habitual in this region, the father has so little to do with his own children that he cannot touch them without pollution.

Elsewhere in S. India where descent, inheritance, and succession are patrilineal, matrilocal marriage occasionally occurs in the form known as *illatam*. This custom is especially followed in families where there is no son, male heirs being obtained by the daughter staying at her own home after marriage. Matrilocal marriage also occurs in Ceylon.

Several peoples of the Caucasus show traces of mother-right. Thus, in marriages between slaves and free persons the child follows the station of the mother, and a woman may habitually go to her father's house for the birth of her children.[3] The maternal uncle has much authority, and in Georgia takes the leading part in all that concerns blood-revenge.[4]

The earliest record of mother-right comes from Lycia, where, according to Herodotus, the people took the mother's name, and the status of children in marriage between free and slave was determined by the condition of the mother.

Among the Arabs of Yemen succession passes to the sister's son, and many records of the Semites of Arabia and Palestine have been regarded as evidence of an early condition of mother-right.[5] The marriage between half-brother and sister, of which the story of Abraham affords an example, accompanies mother-right elsewhere, and several passages in the OT, such as Gn 31^{43} and Jg 8^{19}, suggest this form of social organization.

At the present time the mother's brother has some degree of authority in Palestine, and a formula used in the Bedu (Bedawī) marriage ceremony shows that great importance is attached to motherhood.[6]

(7) *Africa.*—The Semites of N. Africa are definitely patrilineal, but in some Arab tribes of the Anglo-Egyptian Sūdān the wife returns to her own home for the birth of every child—a custom probably connected with matrilocal marriage. Though the Hamitic Beja are now patrilineal, there are records which show that five centuries ago they counted genealogies in the female line and practised succession to the sons of sister and daughter.[1] Among the Bogo, Barea, and other allied Hamitic or partially Hamitic peoples the mother's brother takes an important place in social life, though the patrilineal character of their institutions is otherwise very definite.[2]

The Nubas of S. Kordofan form a striking exception to the patrilineal institutions of most of the mixed Hamitic and Negro Nilotic peoples, such as the Shilluks and Dinkas; as boys grow up, they spend more and more time with their mothers' brothers, who are held to be more closely related to them than their fathers. Property is transmitted to the sister's sons, and a man lives for some time with his wife's people.[3] The Māsai, Nandi, Suk, and other partially Hamitic peoples of the northern part of tropical E. Africa are purely patrilineal.

The Bantu peoples show much variety in the mode of transmission of social rights. About Lake Nyasa and the Rovuma River[4] there are a number of definitely matrilineal tribes, such as the Wa-Yao, Achewa, Wa-Makonde, and Wa-Makua. The children take the totem of the mother, a chief is succeeded by his sister's son, and the mother's brother is regarded as the nearest relative and the natural guardian of his sister's children. The Anyanja practise both modes of descent, but the patrilineal sections are said to have derived this form of transmission from the Angoni, a branch of the Ama-Zulu. This people, together with the Ama-Xosa,[5] Ba-Suto,[6] Ba-Thonga,[7] and other Bantu peoples of S.E. Africa, are definitely patrilineal, though the mother's brother exercises much authority.

Passing northwards from Lake Nyasa, we find a more or less gradual change from matrilineal to patrilineal descent.[8] The Wa-Sagara and Wa-Digo are definitely matrilineal, while among the tribes about Lindi inheritance and succession pass to the sister's children. In other tribes, such as the Wa-Niamwesi and Wa-Jagga, the mode of descent varies according as the bride-price has or has not been paid, the children belonging to the mother's people in the latter case and to that of the father in the former. In general in this region the social institutions tend to become more patrilineal on passing from the coast to the interior.

The Ba-Ganda, Ba-Hima, Ba-Nyoro, and other Bantu peoples of Uganda are definitely patrilineal.[9] The only exceptional feature is that, while the mode of succession is purely patrilineal, the king of Uganda belongs to the totemic clan of his mother, though he also takes certain other totems connected with royalty.

The Bantu of the northern part of the Belgian Congo are mainly patrilineal.[10] Among the Ba-Ngala children inherit, but the mode of descent is determined by a family council, which usually ordains that a child shall take the totem of its

1 A. Playfair, *The Garos*, London, 1909, p. 62 f.
2 B. H. Hodgson, *Proc. Asiat. Soc. Bengal*, xviii. [1849] 707.
3 W. Sobolsky, *Russ. Rev.* xii. 2 [1883] 176.
4 M. Kovalevsky, *Tableau des origines et de l'évolution de la famille et de la propriété*, Stockholm, 1890, p. 21.
5 See W. Robertson Smith, *Kinship and Marriage in Early Arabia*, new ed., London, 1903; G. A. Wilken, *Het matriarchaat bij de oude Arabieren*, Amsterdam, 1884, Germ. ed., Leipzig, 1884; and J. R. Wetzstein, *ZE* xii. [1880].
6 Mrs. H. H. Spoer, *FL* xxi. [1910] 270 ff.

1 See Seligmann, *JRAS* xliii. 649.
2 W. Munzinger, *Ost-afrikanische Studien*, Schaffhausen, 1864, pp. 207, 477 f., 527 f., *Ueber die Sitten und das Recht der Bogos*, Winterthur, 1859, p. 75.
3 The writer is indebted to Professor and Mrs. Seligman for this information.
4 H. H. Johnston, *British Central Africa*, London, 1897, p. 471; A. Werner, *British Central Africa*, do. 1906, p. 252 ff.; K. Weule, *Native Life in East Africa*, Eng. tr., do. 1909, p. 309.
5 G. Fritsch, *Die Eingeborenen Süd-Afrika's*, Breslau, 1873, p. 117.
6 E. Casalis, *Les Bassoutos*, Paris, 1859, p. 190.
7 H. A. Junod, *Life of a South African Tribe*, Neuchâtel, 1912, i. 221 f.
8 J. Kohler, *ZVRW* xv. [1902] 27; H. Cole, *JAI* xxxii. [1902] 305 ff.
9 J. Roscoe, *The Baganda*, London, 1911, p. 128 ff., *The Northern Bantu* (in press).
10 J. H. Weeks, *Among Congo Cannibals*, London, 1913, p. 111 f.

father. Here the same rule holds as in E. Africa; social institutions become more matrilineal on passing from the interior towards the coast. Mother-right also occurs in Loango and Angola.[1]

Among a group of Bantu peoples in the S.W. Free Congo[2] property and rank are transmitted to the brother or the sister's son, and among one of these peoples, the Ba-Mbala, kinship is said to be counted farther in the female than in the male line. Not only is succession matrilineal, but the mother of the chief enjoys great esteem, if not authority. We are not told of any definite social groups with either line of descent, but respect is shown to animals by not eating their flesh, and this *ikina bari* is transmitted from father to son. This institution is almost certainly a kind of totemic grouping, so that these people show a condition almost exactly the reverse of that found in Melanesia, descent being patrilineal, while inheritance and succession are mainly matrilineal. If, as seems almost certain, the *ikina bari* is a form of totem, we have here an example of the connexion of totemism with patrilineal descent, and this association comes out still more strongly among the Ova-Herero of S.W. Africa. This people possess two distinct forms of social grouping, one matrilineal and the other patrilineal, and the most recent and trustworthy account[3] shows that, while there is no definite association of animals or plants with the matrilineal *eanda*, the patrilineal *oruzo* is definitely totemic.

In Nigeria and the countries west of it, we find an interesting series of transitions between mother- and father-right. The westernmost people of whom we have knowledge are the Tshi-speaking peoples of the Gold Coast.[4] They have totemic groups with matrilineal descent, property passes to the eldest brother born of the same mother, and, in default of brothers, to the eldest sister's son. Only if there are no nephews does the son inherit; and, if there is no son, the chief slave inherits. Succession passes to the brother and the sister's son. In addition to the totemic clans, called *abusua*, there are also groups, called *ntoro*, which appear to have a totemic character.[5] In these groups descent is in the male line, or, as the people themselves put it, 'a person takes the fetish of his father and the family of his mother,' the condition thus having a remarkable resemblance to the two totemic groupings of the Dieri of Australia. Among the neighbouring Fanti-speaking peoples the son inherits only the property of the mother, a slave inheriting the property of a man if he has no sister's son.

Among the Ewe-speaking peoples of Dahomey[6] kinship is counted through females in the lower, and through males in the upper, classes. Among the former property passes to the brother and to the sister's son, while a chief is succeeded by his son. The Ewe of Togoland are said to count relationship through the father rather than through the mother, but the mother's brother is the proper heir. It is noteworthy that the knowledge of the art of circumcision is transmitted from father to son.[7] Among the next people, passing eastwards, the Yoruba,[8] we do not know of any definite rule of descent, but the people are said to trace kinship

1 O'Hier de Grandpré, *Voyage à la côte occidentale d'Afrique*, Paris, 1801, i. 109.

2 E. Torday and T. A. Joyce, *Les Bushongo*, Brussels, 1910, *JAI* xxxv. [1905] 398 ff., xxxvi. [1906] 39 ff., 272 ff., *JRAS* xxxvii. [1907] 139.

3 E. Dannert, *Zum Rechte der Herero*, Berlin, 1906.

4 A. B. Ellis, *The Tshi-speaking Peoples*, London, 1887, pp. 234, 297.

5 C. H. Harper, *JAI* xxxvi. 178 ff.

6 A. B. Ellis, *The Ewe-speaking Peoples*, London, 1890, p. 177 f.

7 J. Spieth, *Die Ewe-Stämme*, Berlin, 1906, p. 120.

8 A. B. Ellis, *The Yoruba-speaking Peoples*, London, 1894, p. 174.

in both lines, and a chief is succeeded by his son. That kinship through the mother is regarded as of great importance is shown by the fact that children of one father by different mothers are scarcely considered as blood-relatives. The property of a man passes to his sons, and that of a woman to her daughters. Next to the Yoruba come the Edo,[1] who practise two forms of marriage. In one, the *amoiya* marriage, apparently the more regular, the children belong to the clan of the father, while in the other, called *isomi*, they belong to the mother's clan, unless they are bought by the father, or unless in later life they elect to stay in their father's country. In the Sobo country, whence the Edo are said to have come, there is matrilocal marriage. The Ibo,[2] still farther eastward, practise male descent, and property passes to the sons, except in the *idebwe* form of marriage, corresponding with the *isomi* marriage of the Edo, in which the children belong to their mother's clan and are the heirs of their mother's father. As a rule, a man allows his daughter to contract this form of marriage only when he has no son, the custom thus resembling the *illatam* of S. India.

(8) *Europe*.—There is hardly a European people of antiquity to whom some form of mother-right has not been ascribed.[3] Perhaps the clearest evidence comes from the Basques, among many of whom the father has little authority, whereas women hold property, and transmit rights to their children, even when they cannot exercise them themselves.[4] According to Strabo,[5] women were the heads of families in Spain, and the Picts are said to have been matrilineal,[6] the chief line of evidence being that where the fathers of kings are mentioned they are neither kings nor Picts, but belong to neighbouring tribes. Among the Celts the king and magician are said to have been succeeded by the sister's son.[7] In Ireland the sister's son was important,[8] and the frequent mention of this relative in English ballads has led F. B. Gummere[9] to infer the close relation between a man and his mother's brother which is one of the features of mother-right. The account by Tacitus[10] of the authority of the mother's brother affords the chief evidence in favour of mother-right among the Teutons, but the position of a woman at the head of the genealogical tree of the Lombards and passages in the *Nibelungenlied* and *Edda* point in the same direction.[11] The inscriptions on tombs and other facts point to the prevalence of some form of mother-right among the Etruscans,[12] and this form of organization has also been claimed for the early inhabitants of Latium.[13] The evidence for matrilineal institutions among different elements of the population of Greece has been much discussed.[14] Perhaps the

1 N. W. Thomas, *Edo-speaking Peoples of Nigeria*, London, 1910, i. 47 f.

2 Thomas, *Ibo-speaking Peoples of Nigeria*, London, 1913, i. 31, 86, ii. 60.

3 O. Schrader, *Reallex. der indogerm. Altertumskunde*, Strassburg, 1901, pp. 564–566, 576; H. Hirt, *Die Indogermanen*, do. 1905–07, p. 706 f.; B. Delbrück, 'Das Mutterrecht bei den Indogermanen,' *Preuss. Jahrbücher*, lxxix. [1895] 14–27.

4 E. Cordier, *De l'Organisation de la famille chez les Basques*, Paris, 1869, p. 42 f.

5 P. 165.

6 McLennan, *Studies in Ancient History*, p. 102; H. Zimmer, *Zeitschr. der Savigny-Stiftung für Rechtsgeschichte*, xv. [1894] 209.

7 J. Rhŷs, *Celtic Folk-lore*, Oxford, 1901, p. 637.

8 H. d'Arbois de Jubainville, *Cours de littérature celtique*, Paris, 1883–1902, vii. 187.

9 *An English Miscellany presented to Dr. Furnivall*, Oxford, 1901, p. 133.

10 *Germ.* 20, *Ann.* xii. 29.

11 L. von Dargun, *Mutterrecht und Raubehe*.

12 Bachofen, *Die Sage von Tanaquil*, p. 281 f.

13 W. Ridgeway, *Proc. Brit. Acad.* iii. [1907–08] 32.

14 See, among many other works, McLennan, *Studies in Ancient History*, p. 235; H. J. Rose, *FL* xxii. [1911] 277 ff.

strongest evidence is that in Athens half-brother and sister were allowed to marry when by the same father. Lastly, though in, rather than of, Europe, may be mentioned the Gypsies of Transylvania,[1] among whom a father shows little interest in his children, who remain with their mother's people if their mother dies and their father, as usual, marries a woman of another 'clan.'

3. Mixture-forms.—The preceding survey has shown not only that descent may follow one mode of transmission, while other social processes, such as inheritance and succession, may follow another, but that there may also be two kinds of descent. This is especially frequent where a local grouping is combined with exogamous clans or moieties, the usual rule being that the local grouping is patrilineal, while the grouping in clan or moiety is matrilineal. Another kind of mixture is that found among the Dieri of Australia and the Tshi of W. Africa, in which there are two forms of totemism with different modes of descent. The condition of the Ova-Herero of S. Africa, where a patrilineal totemic grouping is combined with matrilineal clans which are probably non-totemic, affords another example of the combination of two modes of descent. A less definite condition is that in which, combined with one or other definite mode of descent, there are customs which bring a person into definite social relations with relatives on the side from which descent is not counted. An interesting example occurs among the widely separated Tsimshian of N. America and the people of Santo in the New Hebrides. In both of these localities a person belongs to the totemic clan of his mother, but takes the totem of his father as part of his personal name. Another form of totemism which shows mixture of the two modes of transmission is found among the Massim of New Guinea and the people of Vanua Levu in Fiji, where persons belonging to the social group of the mother pay special respect to the totem of the father. A still more eccentric example is that of the Kwakiutl of the N.W. Pacific coast, who belong to the clan of the father, but are indirectly brought into relation with the clan of the mother by receiving from the father the totemic crest which he had adopted from the father of his wife when he married.

4. Associated conditions.—It is not at present possible to connect mother-right with race. It occurs side by side with father-right and with intermediate forms among many peoples, including the Australian, Melanesian, Indonesian, Bantu, W. African Negro, and N. American Indian. At the present time it is absent among Caucasian and Mongolian peoples, but it is doubtful if this has always been so. There is more reason to connect mother-right with scale of culture. Most of the peoples who practise it rank low in the scale, but there are definite exceptions to this generalization in the Khasis of Assam, the people of the west coast of India, the Minangkabau Malays of Sumatra, and many tribes of N. America.

As already pointed out, mother-right in its purest form can occur only in conjunction with the clan-organization, but it is not connected with any special form of this organization. The dual system, in which the whole community forms two exogamous moieties, is always matrilineal in Melanesia and, where not complicated with a class-system, in Australia, but the dual systems of N. America are sometimes patrilineal.

Totemism is still less habitually associated with either form of descent. As was said above, one people may even possess two forms of totemism, one associated with matrilineal and the other with patrilineal descent. The special regard for the father's totem which accompanies some cases of matrilineal transmission suggests a peculiar connexion of totemism with father-right, and other considerations also imply that the totemic organization tends to be patrilineal.[1] Social organizations founded on a local basis, especially those with local exogamy, are usually patrilineal, and in societies devoid of the clan-organization, in which kinship is equally important on the two sides, it is exceptional for inheritance and succession to be matrilineal.

If mother-right is especially connected with the clan-organization, we should expect to find it associated with the classificatory, or 'clan,' system of relationship, and so it is. We do not know of any people with definite mother-right who do not use the classificatory system. The correlation is especially striking in Africa, in more than one part of which classificatory and kindred systems exist side by side. Thus, in the Anglo-Egyptian Sūdān the only people who use the classificatory system are the Nubas, and they are also the only people to practise mother-right. Again, in the series of peoples of W. Africa who show so definite a transition from matrilineal to patrilineal institutions (see above, p. 856[a]) it is the Tshi, with their classificatory system, whose social institutions are most clearly matrilineal.

There is some reason to suppose that mother-right may be peculiarly associated with agriculture. In N. America typical clan-systems are found especially in the maize country,[2] and in Africa mother-right seems to be present especially among peoples who live chiefly by agriculture, while father-right is associated with pastoral life. The association is, however, by no means universal.

5. Survivals of mother-right.—By this expression is meant social customs found in societies organized on a patrilineal basis which are the natural concomitants of mother-right and are, therefore, assumed to be vestiges of the earlier presence of this form of society. The most prominent of the customs which have been so regarded is the relation between a man and his mother's brother. Many peoples among whom descent, inheritance, and succession are patrilineal show the existence of just such relations between a man and his sister's child as are prominent among the social practices of mother-right. That they are such survivals is especially probable where they show the authority of the mother's brother, while the power of the nephew to take any of the property of his uncle is also a natural survival of a social condition in which the sister's son is heir to his uncle's goods. Advocates of the view that these relations between a man and his mother's brother are survivals of mother-right regard it as psychologically natural that such rights to authority or property would not easily be relinquished, but would persist in one form or another long after the formal laws of the community had ordained a different disposition of authority or property.

The marriage of half-brother and sister when of the same father but different mothers has also been regarded as a survival of mother-right. In a society which attached any great importance to kinship through the father such a marriage would be impossible, while it is natural among people who pay special regard to kinship through the mother. When, therefore, this form of marriage is found among a patrilineal people, it has been held to point to an antecedent condition of mother-right.

Other survivals of mother-right have been seen

[1] H. von Wlislocki, *Vom wandernden Zigeunervolke*, Hamburg, 1890, p. 66.

[1] For Melanesia see Rivers, ii. 337.
[2] Swanton, *Amer. Anth.* vii. 671.

in tradition and myth. It is frequently the case among matrilineal peoples that the descent of the clan or tribe is ascribed to a female ancestor, and the belief in a female ancestor among a patrilineal people has been regarded as a survival of mother-right. A similar supposed survival is the widespread mythological theme of unwitting patricide.[1] This absence of knowledge of the father would be natural in the more pronounced forms of matrilocal marriage, and, in consequence, the occurrence of the theme in the mythology of a people has been regarded as evidence that the people were once in a stage of mother-right. Amazon-legends have also been interpreted as relics of mother-right.

Less direct is the relation of certain social customs, such as the *couvade* and the cross-cousin marriage. According to one theory, the *couvade* is associated with the desire on the part of the father to assert his rights over his child, and those who adopt this explanation of the custom will regard it as a survival of mother-right when it is found in a patrilineal society. Again, there is reason to believe that in some parts of the world the cross-cousin marriage (see above, p. 425 f.) has come into existence through the desire of a father that his son shall acquire his property by marrying a woman who would be one of his heirs under a condition of mother-right. Another custom which may be a survival of mother-right is the rule found in several parts of Africa that the daughter or sister of a king shall not bear children. Such a prohibition would put an end to succession by the sister's son.

Etymology has also been called upon for evidence of former mother-right. Thus, the fact that the Chinese word for clan-name means 'born of a woman' has been held to point to matrilineal descent in China,[2] and the derivation of the Arabic word for 'clan' has been adduced to support a similar conclusion in the case of early Semitic society.[3]

6. History.—In several parts of the world we have definite evidence that a condition of mother-right has changed either into one of father-right or into a form of social organization in which social rights are recognized with the relatives of both father and mother. Thus there is evidence that some form of mother-right once existed in Europe, while in the Sūdān there is historical proof that five hundred years ago the Beja, who are now definitely patrilineal, kept their genealogies in the female line and transmitted property to the sons of sister or daughter. In Melanesia, again, and in some parts of America, there is positive evidence of a change from matrilineal to patrilineal institutions, the transition being still in progress in some parts of Melanesia. On the other hand, there is no unequivocal evidence from any part of the world of a change having taken place in the opposite direction. Consequently, it has been held by many students that the change from matrilineal to patrilineal institutions has been a universal feature of the history of human society, and this proposition has become a dogma among many anthropologists.

This dogma has recently been attacked from two quarters. The idea of the priority of mother-right is supported in many parts of the world by the low state of culture of the peoples who possess this form of social organization, but, as already pointed out, this is not universally true, and students of the ethnology of N. America have been led to question the dogma, largely because the matrilineal Iroquois and Pueblo Indians are among the most advanced peoples of the continent. The other line of attack is closely connected with a change which has recently taken place in the attitude of many students towards the history of social institutions. The idea that any product of human society, such as mother-right, has been universal is closely connected with the belief that human society as a whole has been the product of a relatively simple process of evolution which has proceeded everywhere on similar lines and passed through similar stages. To those inspired by this belief it was only necessary to show that mother-right has often changed into father-right, and it followed that this order must have been universal. Among many students, however, the conviction has been growing that human society is not the product of a simple process of evolution, but has been built up by a highly complex process in which a vast variety of forms have been produced by blending of cultures. If the transitions between mother-right and father-right have arisen as the result of the mixture of peoples, we should not expect to find that one form has always preceded the other, but it is probable that in the vast complexity of human progress matrilineal should sometimes have been superposed on patrilineal institutions, and that sometimes father-right would have changed into mother-right. One school of students who have adopted this point of view, viz. that of which F. Graebner and W. Schmidt are the most distinguished adherents, believe that in most parts of the world matrilineal migrants have settled among earlier patrilineal peoples, so that the main change has been from father-right to mother-right, and not in the reverse direction. According to them, people possessing the dual organization with matrilineal descent have settled among patrilineal totemic peoples, and have thus produced the various forms intermediate between the two kinds of society which are found in so many parts of the world. According to this school, the undoubted changes from matrilineal to patrilineal institutions which are found in certain regions are the result of later movements, the change in Melanesia, *e.g.*, being due to relatively late Polynesian settlements, and that in N. America to European influence.

There is much reason to suppose that Graebner and Schmidt have gone too far in their reaction against the prevailing view, and that the evidence on which they base their opinions is fallacious. But, while it is almost certain that by far the most frequent process throughout the world has been a transition from mother- to father-right, the reverse change may have occurred. The region which presents the strongest evidence of a change in this direction is N. America. Not only do some of its matrilineal peoples, such as the Iroquois and Pueblo Indians, possess the most advanced cultures of the continent, but, where one people, such as the Déné or northern Athapascans, practise both lines of descent, it is the less cultured who use the patrilineal mode. Moreover, it is said that there is definite evidence that matrilineal institutions have been taken over from others by people who were previously patrilineal or were devoid of any form of clan-organization. Several peoples of N. America possess a custom which provides a mechanism for changing one mode of descent into another. Personal names are often definitely connected with a moiety or clan, each social group having names especially reserved for its members. Among some matrilineal people of N. America, such as the Shawnees, a father gives his own clan-name to his child, thus taking a definite step towards the transference of the child to his own social group. This or some similar mechanism might well have come into play to assist a change in the opposite direction.

One of the cases most often put forward by

[1] M. A. Potter, *Sohrab and Rustem.*
[2] H. A. Giles, *China and the Chinese*, New York, 1902, p. 27.
[3] Wilken, Germ. ed. p. 38.

American ethnologists as an example of change from father- to mother-right is that of the Kwakiutl.[1] This people practise patrilineal descent, but the peculiar system by which a man takes the crest of his wife's father has been ascribed to the influence of their northern matrilineal neighbours, the Tsimshian and Haida. Other examples are the Athapascan tribes bordering on the Tlingit, who are said to have adopted the matrilineal dual organization of the people, and the Babine branch of the Takulli, another Athapascan tribe who are said to have taken their matrilineal four-clan system from the Tsimshian.

In other parts of the world there is definite evidence that the change has been from the matrilineal to the patrilineal mode. There is a large body of evidence pointing to the change having been in this direction in Melanesia;[2] but even here it is possible that certain conditions, such as the highly developed mother-right of the Massim of New Guinea, may have been assisted by some later matrilineal influence. In Africa, again, there is much reason to believe that the change has been in the patrilineal direction. The transition from matrilineal to patrilineal institutions which occurs among the peoples of W. Africa from the Tshi to the Ibo points to the gradual infiltration of immigrants coming from the north-east, who became the chiefs of those among whom they settled. While introducing their patrilineal institutions completely in the east, they did not succeed in altering descent among the general body of the people as they progressed westwards. The transitions found among the Bantu and the association of patrilineal transmission with high development of culture among such people as the Ba-Ganda and Ama-Zulu would seem to be the result of the settlement of a patrilineal pastoral people among a matrilineal population who, till then, had thriven upon agriculture.

7. Origin.—Until we know the history of this form of social organization, it is hardly profitable to discuss its origin at length, but some of the leading views which have been put forward may be mentioned.

In the first place, mother-right has been widely held to be the natural consequence of sexual promiscuity and group-marriage. The less important is fatherhood in a society, the more will that society be driven to base its social rights upon the mother. Another view is that matrilineal descent is a secondary consequence of matrilocal marriage. Where a husband merely visits his wife and is only an outsider in her household, descent and other social processes must be expected to rest on the relation between mother and child. A third view regards mother-right as a social state which has resulted from the dominance of woman, and especially from her importance in agriculture. As already seen, there is reason to connect mother-right with a high development of the art of agriculture, especially in N. America, and it is noteworthy that it is in this continent that we have our clearest evidence of the dominance of the woman.

LITERATURE.—J. J. Bachofen, *Das Mutterrecht*, Stuttgart, 1861, 2Basel, 1897, *Die Sage von Tanaquil*, Heidelberg, 1870, *Antiquarische Briefe*, Strassburg, 1881; J. F. McLennan, *Studies in Ancient History*, 1st ser., London, 1876; L. H. Morgan, *Ancient Society*, do. 1877; L. von Dargun, *Mutterrecht und Raubehe und ihre Reste im germanischen Recht und Leben*, Breslau, 1883, *Mutterrecht und Vaterrecht*, Leipzig, 1892; A. Giraud-Teulon, *Les Origines du mariage et de la famille*, Paris, 1884; C. N. Starcke, *The Primitive Family*, London, 1889; E. B. Tylor, *Nineteenth Century*, xl. [1896] 81 ff.; E. Grosse, *Die Formen der Familie und die Formen der Wirthschaft*, Freiburg and Leipzig, 1896; M. A. Potter, *Sohrab and Rustem*, London, 1902; E. S. Hartland, *Primitive Paternity*, do. 1909; J. G. Frazer, *Totemism and Exogamy*, do. 1910. Cf. also A. H. Post, *Grundriss der ethnolog. Jurisprudenz*, Oldenburg and Leipzig, 1894-95, i. 71-79, 83-90, 212-216.

W. H. R. RIVERS.

[1] F. Boas, *Rep. U.S. Nat. Mus.*, 1895, p. 334.
[2] Rivers, ii. 90, 319.

MOTIVE.—**1. Different senses.**—The term 'motive' is used in philosophy and psychology in four different senses.

(1) In the first and most general sense it means any force, of an internal or mental character, which impels to action or prevents some kind of action, be the force conscious or unconscious, and the action voluntary or non-voluntary. Thus Bentham defines motive as 'any thing that can contribute to give birth to, or even to prevent, any kind of action' (*Principles of Morals and Legislation*, p. 46). In this sense motive includes what Reid calls mechanical principles of action, such as instinct and habit, and also what Bentham calls 'speculative' motives, which influence acts that rest purely in the understanding.

(2) In a second sense 'motive' is taken with a more restricted signification, as limited to some end which we present to ourselves and of which we are conscious. Bentham has this meaning in view when he defines motive as 'any thing whatsoever, which, by influencing the will of a sensitive being, is supposed to serve as a means of determining him to act, or voluntarily to forbear to act, upon any occasion' (*ib.*). Such motives are termed by Bentham 'practical,' and are, he holds, ultimately reducible to pleasure and pain, though whether it be the expectation of the pain or the pain which accompanies that expectation that is the motive he leaves undetermined (p. 47, note). This contains the germ of an important distinction. In motives in this sense we may distinguish two things: a subjective and affective element, sometimes called affect, a spring of action, *Triebfeder*; and an objective, presented or intellectual element. Whether this subjective element is reducible to pleasure or pain, or includes more, and in what relation it stands to the objective, intellectual element and to the conative factor in mind, are among the most difficult questions in the psychology of the feelings. Here it is taken as standing in relation to certain volitions as a spring of action (see Morell, *Outlines of Mental Philosophy*, pt. vii. chs. i. and ii.; Baldwin, *Handbook of Psychology*, ii. 313-315, 332 f., 354; Stout, *Manual of Psychology*3, bk. i. ch. i.; Mellone and Drummond, *Elements of Psychology*, Edinburgh and London, 1907, ch. iv.). Cf. Bentham's figurative and unfigurative motives (*infra*).

(3) A third sense of the word 'motive' occurs in the writings of Green and his followers. According to the teaching of Green, something more is required to constitute a motive than the conscious presentation of an end. In the analysis of one of Green's followers, the voluntary satisfaction of a want involves five things:

'(1) The want. (2) The feeling of the want. (3) An idea of an object by which the want can be satisfied. (4) An idea of the satisfaction actually taking place, the work of the imagination. (5) The presentation of this satisfaction as, under the circumstances, the greatest good. The self identifying itself with the attainment of the object; finding in the realisation of the idea. not the satisfaction of a want merely, but the satisfaction of self' (D'Arcy, *Short Study of Ethics*2, p. 32).

It is only to this last stage (5) that Green and D'Arcy apply the term 'motive.' Hence the doctrines that a conflict of motives is impossible and a strongest motive an absurdity (Green, *Prolegomena to Ethics*, bk. ii. ch. i.).

(4) A fourth sense of the word 'motive' belongs to Kant. Kant reserves the term *Bewegungsgrund* for the objective ground of the volition, which he opposes to the subjective ground of the desire, or the spring (*Triebfeder*). The objective ground of the self-determination of the will is the end which is assigned by reason alone, and is free from all

mixture of passion and sensuous affection (*Werke*, ed. Rosenkranz and Schubert, viii. 55; Abbott, *Kant's Theory of Ethics*[6], London, 1909, p. 45). Such objective ends are common to us with all rational beings, and are to be distinguished from subjective ends, to which we are impelled by natural disposition. Unlike all inclination and fear, respect or reverence for the moral law is an effect, not a cause (Kant, *Werke*, viii. 21, note). Regarded as a spring, this feeling acts negatively only.

In these four senses of the word 'motive' we see a progressive change of meaning from that of a mere impelling force, not even necessarily accompanied by consciousness, to that of an internal impulsion to the existence of which consciousness is essential; passing thence to the idea of an object which gives satisfaction; finally ending in Kant in the conception of motive as an object which is free from, and even opposed to, all subjective ground of desire. Green's view, though later in point of time, seems not so developed as that of Kant, since in Green the object is still made to be a motive by relation to a want or internal principle of desire, though such want or desire is again conceived as dependent on the object with which the self identifies itself. Kant's distinction of motive and spring and relegation of these terms to different classes of action get rid of the wavering between contradictory points of view implicit in Green's doctrine.

Whether we shall give to the term 'motive' the extensive signification contained under (1) may appear a mere question of the use of language; but, as is the case in most questions of terminology, important issues lie concealed beneath the purely verbal discussion. This extensive use of the word early aroused dissent. Reid in 1793, criticizing Crombie's 'Essay on Philosophical Necessity,' said:

'I understood a motive, when applied to a human being, to be that for the sake of which he acts, and, therefore, that what he never was conscious of, can no more be a motive to determine his will, than it can be an argument to convince his judgment.

Now, I learn that any circumstance arising from habit, or some mechanical instinctive cause, may be a motive, though it never entered into the thought of the agent.

From this reinforcement of motives, of which we are unconscious, every volition may be supplied with a motive, and even a predominant one, when it is wanted' (Reid, *Works*, ed. Hamilton, p. 87).

Reid then acutely remarks that 'this addition to his [Crombie's] defensive force takes just as much from his offensive,' since it undermines the evidence for the necessary action of motives known or felt. In other words, necessitation by efficient is fatal to necessitation by final causes. At this stage the distinction seems to turn upon the presence or absence of consciousness. But, even if we regard consciousness as the condition of the existence of motive in sense (2), this does not prevent the motivation or impelling force being essentially mechanical as when non-voluntary in sense (1). Green's doctrine tries to evade this by assigning to self-consciousness the power of determining the predominance of the motive which actually does succeed, while still admitting that the end to which we thus determine ourselves is assigned by the pathological or affective element. Kant, on the other hand, assigns to reason a power of determining action to an end, which is quite independent of, and even opposed to, the pathological feeling. 'Motive' in this sense has passed over entirely from the meaning of an impelling force to that of an object determined and decided upon by reason.

These distinctions are closely bound up with the inquiry regarding the freedom of the will. If our will is possessed of an original power by which it can control the direction in which it utters itself, then the causal action of motives must be distinct from mechanical impulsion; they may induce, or incline, but do not determine, according to inevitable law. If, on the other hand, our will has no such power, what we call inducing and inclining must be merely the subjective side of the collision of predestined forces, of which we are the theatre or rather the play itself. If this be the case, the appearance of a causation, which may yield to conscious motives, but is not controlled by them, must be an illusion. The illusion demands explanation. This Münsterberg undertook to furnish in his *Willenshandlung* (1879). In *Man's Place in the Cosmos* ([2] Edinburgh and London, 1902), J. Seth Pringle-Pattison gives an acute analysis of Münsterberg's views. According to Münsterberg, the will is only a complex of sensations. Our activity, whether the inner activity of attention or the outer activity of muscular contraction, appears to us to be free, just because the result of the activity is already present in idea, and is, in all cases, accompanied by the sensations flowing from previous motor innervation. The feeling of innervation itself is 'just the memory-idea of the movement, anticipating the movement itself.' In the *Grundzüge der Psychologie* (1900) Münsterberg's position is modified by a Fichtean point of view. The 'action theory of mind' here put forward makes the consciousness of sensation dependent on motor discharge. It, therefore, precludes any theory of action other than that of mechanical causation. Nor is this conclusion altered by the theory of taking an attitude (*Stellungnahme*) towards the world, which Münsterberg puts forward. Such activity as lying outside consciousness could not even give rise to the illusion of voluntary activity.

It was maintained by Hartley (*Observations on Man*, London, 1810, i. 522) that 'to prove that a man has free will in the sense opposite to mechanism, he ought to feel that he can do different things while the motives remain precisely the same,' and that here 'the internal feelings are entirely against free will where the motives are of a sufficient magnitude to be evident,' while he admits a power of resisting motives. Such a power, on Hartley's view, can come only from some other and stronger motive; that is, there is no intrinsic power of resisting motives. The attribution to the self of an intrinsic power of strengthening indefinitely certain desires, which then become motives (in Green's sense), seems the essence of the third theory of motives. There is an illusory atmosphere of determinism about Green's theory. The will is determined by motives. That desire only is a motive which is successful. There is no conflict of motives, nor any strongest motive. But then the strongest desire is made to be the strongest, *i.e.* to be a motive by the action of the eternal consciousness which is perpetually reproducing itself in us, and which helps to constitute, in cognition and action, all the objects of knowing and will. Is now this action of the eternal consciousness something from all eternity, unalterably the same? The result is practically identical with Hartley's—the only freedom in it is that the ego, since it determines the motive, is consequently, in being determined by the motive, determined by itself. This is only Spinozistic necessity. But, if the action of the eternal ego on the finite ego is not so predetermined, is something which, at the moment of decision, may fall out differently on different occasions, notwithstanding identity of desire and circumstances, then such action is not different from free will in the ordinary sense, and implies a surplus of undetermined or self-determined free activity of the ego, as in the Kantian doctrine.

Green's theory of motives must be carefully distinguished from a modern psychological doctrine, to which it bears a strong verbal resemblance. Green says (*Proleg. to Ethics*, p. 93) that an appetite or want 'only becomes a motive, so far as upon the want there supervenes the presentation of the want by a self-conscious subject to himself and with it the idea of a self-satisfaction to be attained in the filling of the want.' Stout, too, says (*Manual of Psychology*[3], p. 709):

'Motives are not mere impulses. They come before consciousness as reasons why *I* should act in this or that way. They are not independent forces fighting out a battle among themselves, while the Ego remains a mere spectator. On the contrary, the motives are motives only in so far as they arise from the nature of the Self, and pre-suppose the conception of the Self as a determining factor. From this it follows that the recognised reasons for a decision can never constitute the entire cause of decision. Behind them there always lies the Self as a whole, and what this involves can never be completely analysed or stated in the form of definite reasons or special motives.'

The great verbal similarity of this to what Green says is evident. But to Green the self-conscious subject, through determination by which a want becomes a motive, is 'a principle of other than natural origin,' is, in fact, an entity of a sort. To Stout the self as a whole, even if what it involves can never be completely analyzed or stated, is not an entitative principle eternal or otherwise, but, rather, the 'thought of the self.' In deliberation, he says, 'the concept of the Self as a whole will not directly tend to reinforce or suppress a desire' (p. 708).

'A certain line of action being suggested as possible, I contemplate myself as I shall be if I put it in execution, so as to make it part of my actual life-history, and on the other hand I contemplate myself as I shall be if I leave it undone. I follow out this representation of a hypothetical Self in more or less detail until that turning-point in the process which is called Voluntary Decision emerges' (*ib.* p. 709).

This theory, that motives arise and are constituted by relation to the conception of self, whether we take it in Green's metaphysical or in Stout's psychological form, as a *general* theory of motives, seems not to be true. That very many motives are determined by conscious relating of the end in view to the self is true—notably the self-regarding ones. But it is difficult to regard altruistic motives as necessarily related to the concept of self. They may sometimes be so, but not necessarily or universally. The highest moral ends are disinterested. The disinterested character of æsthetic emotion has been emphasized by Burke and Kant, Hegel and Schopenhauer. Molinos, Fénelon, and Madame Guyon have maintained the possibility of a disinterested love of God. It must, therefore, be admitted that, while the analysis of the term 'motive' given under (2) and (3) is in many cases a correct and complete analysis, there are other cases where, even if impelled towards the end by some subjective affective element, the self-conscious satisfaction of this impulse need form no part of the objective end in view nor even of the subjective impelling force.

It is when we come to the fourth sense of the term 'motive'—the strict sense given to it by Kant—that we find the most striking detachment of the term from all association with the subjective self. It may still bear relation to something universal, common to the individual selves, but the ends are then ends in which the individual self loses its individuality. They are objective. This is the essential of morality to Kant, and the point which separates the ethics of Kant from the ethics of Green. It was to retain in the moral motive the reference to self that Green was compelled to characterize the good as the 'perfection of human character' or 'self-devotion to the perfecting of man.' D'Arcy (*Short Study of Ethics*[2], p. 277) has seen this defect in the ethics of Green. The defect is, however, a necessary outcome of Green's initial position. To Kant, on the other hand, reason, not the mere self, is able to give itself an end, which, though realized in the matter of desire, is independent of the relation of that matter to the particular self. Kant is often criticized as if the categorical imperative set up ends, detached from all the material of desire and inclination, as if purely formal ends existed by themselves. It is the impenetration of particular desires and inclinations by the categorical law of duty that gives to the individual the absolute value expressed in that form of the categorical imperative which is expressed: 'so treat humanity whether in thine own person or that of another always as an end and never as a means.'

We have, therefore, in our highest ends, moral, æsthetic, and religious, the singular paradox that in them an element, which comes into existence only through particular feelings and inclinations, becomes, as regards its essential character, independent of these and a motive of selfless and disinterested action.

In the above discussion we have considered the several distinct senses in which the term 'motive' may be used. There are, however, some ambiguities connected with its use which, while not really adding to the multiplicity of senses, might nevertheless appear to do so. Bentham says:

'Owing to the poverty and unsettled state of language, the word *motive* is employed indiscriminately to denote two kinds of objects, which, for the better understanding of the subject, it is necessary should be distinguished. On some occasions it is employed to denote any of those really existing incidents from whence the act in question is supposed to take its rise. The sense it bears on these occasions may be styled its literal or *unfigurative* sense. On other occasions it is employed to denote a certain fictitious entity, a passion, an affection of the mind, an ideal being, which upon the happening of any such incident is considered as operating upon the mind, and prompting it to take that course, towards which it is impelled by the influence of such incident. Motives of this class are Avarice, Indolence, Benevolence, and so forth. . . . This latter may be styled the *figurative* sense of the term *motive*' (p. 46 f.).

The real incidents—motives in the unfigurative sense—are:

'1. The *internal* perception of any individual lot of pleasure or pain, the expectation of which is looked upon as calculated to determine you to act in such or such a manner; 2, any *external* event, the happening whereof is regarded as having a tendency to bring about the perception of such pleasure or such pain.'

Each of these is further distinguished according as it is in *prospect* or in *esse*, meaning by the former the posterior possible object which is looked forward to as the consequence of his action [or inaction], by the latter, the present existing object or event which takes place upon a man's looking forward to the other.

These distinctions partly depend on Bentham's doctrine that the only motives are pleasure and pain, which has been ably criticized by Sidgwick (*Methods of Ethics*, bk. i. ch. iv.). They may be reduced to those drawn by Fleming (*Manual of Moral Philosophy*, ed. London, 1870, p. 176) between 'the external object, the internal principle, and the state or affection of mind resulting from the one being addressed to the other.' The internal principle may be dismissed as, at any rate for the purposes of this article, a 'fictitious entity.' The distinction, however, between the external object and the resulting state or affection of mind has an important bearing on the foregoing discussion. It might seem plausible to say, as Fleming says, that 'speaking strictly it [the term 'motive'] should be applied to the terminating state or affection of mind which arises from a principle of human nature having been addressed by an object adapted to it; because it is this state or affection of mind which prompts to action.' This is true in all cases where an affection is the spring of action. But there are cases in which the affection does not exist, or the action takes place without, or contrary to, its prompting. In the 'beautiful soul' in Schiller's *Anmuth und Würde*, affection produces moral results, but, to Kant, true moral action is independent of such affection. In art, however much feeling may guide, it cannot be considered as the motive. In true art it cannot even be said that there is a conscious image or ideal which impels the artist to produce. In art, as Schelling says, the ego is unconscious in regard to its product (*System des transcendentalen Idealismus*, vi., Tübingen, 1800 [*Sämmtl. Werke*, Stuttgart, 1856-61, iii.]).

An important distinction is that between motive and intention. The nature of intentionality is thus stated by Bentham:

'Let us observe the connexion there is between intentionality and consciousness. When the act itself is intentional, and with respect to the existence of all the circumstances *advised*, as also with respect to the materiality of those circumstances, in relation to a given consequence, and there is no mis-supposal with regard to any preventive circumstance, that consequence must also be intentional. In other words, advisedness, with respect to the circumstances, if clear from the mis-supposal of any preventive circumstance, extends the intentionality from the act to the consequences' (p. 44).

The distinction itself is most clearly expressed by Martineau (*Types of Ethical Theory*², ii. 272):

'The *Intention* comprises the whole contemplated operations of the act, both those for the sake of which, and those in spite of which, we do it. The *Motive* comprises only the former.'

Dividing the intention as Martineau does into persuasives, dissuasives, and neutral consequences, it is only the first that fall under the heading of 'motive' (cf. Mill, *Utilitarianism*, London, 1879, ch. ii. p. 27; Muirhead, *Elements of Ethics*², p. 61; Mackenzie, *Manual of Ethics*, p. 64 ff.).

This excludes from intention all motives in sense (1) which are unconscious or involuntary. It includes motives in senses (2) and (3). It is more difficult to say whether it includes motives in sense (4). The particular object or end is certainly included in the intention, but the law which the will gives to itself, while controlling and determining the intention, seems not necessarily to form part of it. The act, even if done for the sake of the law, has not the law in its universality as its end. To make Martineau's statement true we must understand 'persuasives' in an affective sense.

2. Classification of motives.—The various classifications reflect the difficulties which have attended the foregoing discussions. Our impulses or active principles are classified by Reid into mechanical, animal, and rational; but only to the last two does he apply the term 'motives.' Stewart has criticized this classification on the grounds that 'mechanical' cannot be applied to instincts and habits (which is done by Reid), nor to any of our active principles. It is capricious to call our appetites animal principles, because common to man and brutes, and to distinguish our instincts as mechanical, in regard to which our nature bears so strong an analogy to the lower animals. Mechanical principles of action produce their effect without any will or intention on our part. Animal principles of action require intention and will, but not judgment. Rational principles of action require not only intention or will, but judgment or reason. Stewart censures Reid for including under animal principles of action the desire of knowledge, of esteem, pity, patriotism, etc.

Stewart's own classification falls under five heads: (1) appetites, (2) desires, (3) affections, (4) self-love, (5) moral faculty. This classification has been ably criticized by Martineau (ii. 134).

McCosh gives the following classification of the orective or motive powers, or, as he prefers to say, of the motive and moral powers:

i. The native appetencies of the mind leading to emotions. These include: (1) the inclination to exercise every native power voluntarily or involuntarily; (2) the desire to receive pleasure and avoid pain; (3) the appetites: tendencies to seek for knowledge, esteem, society, power, property; (4) an inward principle that impels to seek for the beautiful; (5) the moral power as a prompting energy; (6) unselfish motives prompting to action in relation to other beings, *e.g.* sympathy.

ii. The will not as furnishing incitements, inducements, or motives, but as seated above these, sanctioning, restraining, and deciding among them.

iii. The conscience—a cognitive power involving certain beliefs and judgments (*Intuitions of the Mind*, p. 242 ff.).

More important than any of these classifications is that of Martineau (ii. 129-175). He begins by distinguishing between two sets of impelling principles in man: (1) 'those which urge him, in the way of unreflecting instinct, to appropriate objects or natural expression,' and (2) 'those which supervene upon self-knowledge and experience, and in which the preconception is present of an end gratifying to some recognized feeling' (p. 135). The former he calls primary springs of action, the latter secondary. Under the primary come—(1) propensions: including organic appetites and animal spontaneity; (2) passions: antipathy, fear, anger; these do not arise as forces from the needs of our own nature, but are rather what we suffer at the hands of objects; (3) affections: parental, social, compassionate; these operate as attractions towards other persons; (4) sentiments: wonder, admiration, reverence; these direct themselves upon *ideal relations*, objects of apprehension or thought that are above us, yet potentially ours.

Under the secondary principles which are characterized by their *interested* nature or invariable aim to produce certain states of ourselves come—(1) secondary propensions: love of pleasure, money, power; (2) secondary passions: malice, vindictiveness, suspiciousness; (3) secondary affections: sentimentality; (4) secondary sentiments: self-culture, æstheticism, interest in religion.

The secondary series is the self-conscious counterpart of the primary series. These principles give rise to ulterior combinations, such as love of praise, emulation, fellow-feeling. In addition to these are prudence and conscience, but neither is, according to Martineau, a positive principle, so as to range in the series of impulses. Each exercises a judicial function—prudence among the secondary principles, conscience over the whole.

If we examine these various classifications, we shall find much to confirm the wide view of motives which we have taken. Martineau's distinction of primary and secondary springs of action directly contradicts the narrow view of motives taken by Green, which would limit motives to those associated with the notion of self. Such association gives rise to secondary springs of action. Again, some of these classifications rightly regard conscience and the moral faculty as motive powers prompting to action and yet *per se* incapable of being identified with an affective element. In Martineau's theory the moral element consists in relative position in a scale of excellence intuitively discerned. Other moralists might seek to analyze further in what this excellence consists, and this analysis might be dangerous to the intuitive scale, might show that the position of a spring varies with circumstances; but the insight that the moral element is not an affective spring of action, in either the primary or secondary form, remains; and with it remains the necessity of recognizing a fourth form of motive, the motivity of which, whether proceeding from an autonomy of the will itself or from a recognition of an intrinsic authority in certain imperatives of action, or from a recognition of superiority or authority in inward springs or outward courses of conduct, demands a unique position for itself in the classification of those forces which impel the human will to action.

LITERATURE.—J. M. Baldwin, *Handbook of Psychology*, New York, 1889-91, ii. 'Feeling and Will'; J. Bentham, *Principles of Morals and Legislation* (*Works*, ed. J. Bowring, Edinburgh, 1859, i.); T. H. Green, *Prolegomena to Ethics*, Oxford, 1883; I. Kant, *Grundlegung zur Metaphysik der Sitten*, and *Kritik der praktischen Vernunft* (*Sämmtl. Werke*, ed. K. Rosenkranz and F. W. Schubert, Leipzig, 1838-40, viii.); C. F. D'Arcy, *Short*

*Study of Ethics*², London, 1912; T. Reid, 'Letters,' *Works*², ed. W. Hamilton, Edinburgh, 1849; J. Martineau, *Types of Ethical Theory*², Oxford, 1886, ii.; D. Stewart, *Philosophy of the Active and Moral Powers*, Edinburgh, 1828; H. Münsterberg, *Grundzüge der Psychologie*, Leipzig, 1900, i.; J. McCosh, *Intuitions of the Mind*³, London, 1893; J. D. Morell, *Introd. to Mental Philosophy*, do. 1862; J. S. Mackenzie, *Manual of Ethics*⁴, do. 1900; J. H. Muirhead, *Elements of Ethics*², do. 1906; H. Sidgwick, *Methods of Ethics*⁷, do. 1907; G. F. Stout, *Manual of Psychology*³, do. 1913.

G. J. STOKES.

MOUNTAINS, MOUNTAIN-GODS.—

There are few peoples who have not looked upon mountains with awe and reverence, or who have not paid worship to them or to gods or spirits associated with them in various ways. Their height, their vastness, the mystery of their recesses, the veil of mist or cloud now shrouding them, now dispersed from them, the strange noises which the wind makes in their gorges, the crash of a fall of rock, or the effect of the echo, their suggestion of power, their appearance of watching the intruder upon their solitude—all give to them an air of personality, and easily inspire an attitude of reverence and eventually of worship. They are next thought to have a spirit akin to, yet greater than, man's, and such a spirit may become separate from the mountain and exist as a god of the mountain. The natural dangers encountered by the traveller or mountain-dweller, as well as the mystery of gorge, precipice, or cavern, suggest the presence of spirits, dangerous or at times beneficent, and in many cases also ghosts of the dead are thought to haunt the mountains. Their summits, being near the sky and often surrounded by cloud, suggest their connexion with gods of sky or rain; or the remoteness and mystery of their peaks cause them to be regarded as dwellings of gods or of ghosts.

Sporadically we find no cult of mountains or mountain-spirits, but that is generally where no cult of nature exists, or, of course, where no mountains exist. Where they are feared, it is generally as much because of the demons supposed to infest them as because of their own suggestion of terror. The horror of mountains found in writers from Waller to the time of Scott, Byron, and Wordsworth was perhaps a literary affectation as much as genuine lack of appreciation. Wordsworth's 'voice of the mountains' has generally made a strong appeal to men and has given a great impulse to the imagination.

1. The personification of mountains.—The various impressions which mountains made upon men's minds led to their being regarded as alive, or possessed of a power lurking behind their massive forms, and, finally, to their personification in a greater or less degree. The next stage was that the mountain-god—the personified mountain which received worship—became a god of the mountain, separate from it, yet connected with it. It is difficult in particular cases to say which of these stages is intended, or to disentangle them, since the human mind so easily adopts either attitude; and, even where a god of the mountain is worshipped, the mountain itself still looms vast and, as it were, personal. In this section we shall examine instances where the mountain seems to be worshipped for itself alone or to be regarded as sacred and to some extent personal.

The Choles of Itza regarded one particular hill as god of all the mountains, and on it burned a perpetual fire.[1] To the Huichol Indians every hill and rock of peculiar shape is a deity,[2] and hills as well as lakes, rain, etc., are tribal gods of the Thompson Indians.[3] The Mexicans had gods of mountains (§ 2), but they regarded all mountains as divine and personified them. Iztaccihuatl was the wife of Popocatepetl. Molina describes the hill Huanacauri as the chief *huaca* of the Incas.[4] In Korea mountains are personified, and the idea of guardianship, *e.g.*, of towns, is associated with them (cf. § 5). Yet there are also spirits of mountains.[5] In Japan the term *kami*, applied to deities, is likewise applied to mountains, which are supposed to possess great power.[6] Similarly in China, where spirits of mountains have always been worshipped, mountains themselves are included among the *shen*, or beneficent gods. There are ten principal mountains included among the *t'i-ki*, or earth-gods—the five *yoh*, of which the greatest is T'ai Shan in Shantung, and the five *chen*.[1] Of each of these there is one in each chief cardinal point (the four mountains), and one in the centre. The chief minister of Yâo was called 'president of the mountains.'[2] To these, or to their spirits, sacrifices are made on the great altar of the earth at the summer solstice. Other mountains are also included in the category of gods and in the official worship (see also § 7).[3] In Tibet Mt. Kanchinjunga was once an object of worship, but is now regarded as the dwelling of a god of the same name. There are four great deified mountains in Tibet.[4] In Media and in Phrygia gods were identified with mountains, and a cult was paid to them on their summits.[5] Among the Celts a cult of mountains, as well as of gods of mountains, is to be traced. One inscription was 'To the Mountains'; the mountains are often invoked in spell or prayer or invocation in Irish texts; and Gildas speaks of the 'blind people' who adored mountains and other parts of nature.[6] While the Greeks adored divinities associated with mountains, some mountains still retained a degree of personification—*e.g.*, Mt. Ida as a nymph.[7] In India as early as the Rigveda (VII. xxxv. 8) there is a direct appeal to the mountains: 'May the mountains be propitious to us.' The Himālaya is king of mountains, the great divine range *par excellence*, pre-eminently sacred. It 'cannot be shaken,' and it is the abode of the dead, of mighty creatures, and of living saints and ascetics, as well as the haunt of demons of all kinds. But its own virtues are supreme. To think of it is to gain vast merit; to see it is to have one's sins removed. It was personified as Himavat or Harivaṁśa, father of Gaṅgā and Umā Devī, or Pārvatī, the mountain-goddess, identified with one of the peaks.[8]

An ancient story tells how Pārvatī covered up the eyes of Mahādeva when he was performing *tapas* on Himavat. Flame burst from his forehead and scorched the mountain; but, when she assumed a submissive attitude, her father was restored to his former condition.[9]

Among the aboriginal tribes of India mountains are personified. The Santāls sacrifice to Marang Burū, at once a mountain and a god. Other tribes have no other gods but mountains, rivers, and the dead.[10] Among the Semites mountains and hills had been personified, and many of them were regarded as peculiarly sacred—the dwelling-place or seat of a god (§ 5). But the evidence is mainly that of cults upon hills or high places to a god associated with these (§ 7). The pagan Slavs are described as worshipping mountains.[11]

Where a god associated with a hill or mountain bears a name similar to it, it is probable that the mountain personified gave this name to the subsequent god of the mountain. A Celtic god Poeninus was god of the Pennine Alps, Vosegus was god of the Vosges mountains. Cf. other examples above.

Evidence of the personification of mountains is also to be found in the sporadic cases of alleged descent from mountains, possibly because these mark the region whence some tribe took its origin or migrated.

The Navahos thought that they came from the bowels of a great mountain near the San Juan.[12] Some Mexicans regarded the mountain Cacalepei as their mother.[13] The Iranian kings were supposed to have descended from the mountain Ushidarena.[14]

2. Gods and mountains.—Besides being personified, mountains are associated with clearly defined gods, either as their occasional or as their more permanent seats or abodes, or there are gods of the mountains distinct from these as personified.

The house of the Māsai god Ngai (Eñ-ai) is in the snows of Kilimanjaro.[15] Among the Yoruba there is a god of the mountains called Oke. In Hawaii several distinct deities of the volcano Kilauea were recognized, each of these being connected with some part of it.[16] Among the Todas most deities are associated with hills, each occupying a separate peak, on the summit of which is a stone circle, barrow, or cairn.[17] The

---

1 *NR* iii. 122.
2 *FL* xii. [1901] 108.
3 *Ib.* xi. [1900] 398.
4 W. H. Prescott, *Hist. of the Conquest of Mexico*, London, 1843. ii. 41; C. R. Markham, *Narratives of the Rites and Laws of the Yncas*, do. 1873, p. 13.
5 *FL* xi. 328 f.
6 W. G. Aston, in *FL* x. [1899] 317.

1 J. J. M. de Groot, *Religion in China*, New York, 1912, pp. 16, 201 ff.
2 *SBE* iii. [1879] 35.
3 *Ib.* xxxix. [1891] 244; de Groot, *loc. cit.*
4 L. A. Waddell, *Buddhism of Tibet*, London, 1895, p. 370 f.
5 Diod. Sic. ii. 13; L. F. A. Maury, *Hist. des religions de la Grèce antique*, Paris, 1857–59, iii. 185.
6 J. A. MacCulloch, *Religion of the Ancient Celts*, Edinburgh, 1911, pp. 39, 172; Gildas, *de Excidio Britanniæ*, ii. 4.
7 Apollodorus, I. i. 6.
8 Crooke, *PR* i. 60 f., 62; Muir, *Orig. Skr. Texts*, i.² [1872] 130; *Milinda-pañha*, IV. viii. 16.
9 Muir, iv.² [1873] 269 f., quoting *Mahābhārata*, xiii. 6355 ff.
10 *PR* i. 61; E. W. Hopkins, *Religions of India*, Boston, 1895, p. 537; cf. *ERE* ii. 482ᵇ.
11 L. Leger, *La Mythologie slave*, Paris, 1901, p. 190.
12 *NR* iii. 121.
13 Prescott, ii. 41.
14 *SBE* xxxi. [1887] 200, note 2.
15 J. Thomson, *Through Masai Land*, London, 1885, p. 445.
16 W. Ellis, *Polynesian Researches*, London, 1832–36, iv. 248 f.
17 *FL* xviii. [1907] 103.

Khonds worship a god of hills, and among the Kols the great deity Marang Burū, or 'Great Mountain,' is the rain-god, Marang Burū being a conspicuous peak in Chotā Nāgpur which is either the god himself or his dwelling-place. Before the time of rain elaborate ceremonies take place on the mountain for rain and a fruitful season.[1] Mt. Shasta is thought by American Indian tribes to have been made of snow and ice by the Great Spirit from the sky, after which he stepped down upon it and hollowed it out as a wigwam where he might live on his visits to earth.[2] Among the Thompson Indians the 'Old Man' is a being living on high mountains, and there making rain or snow by scratching himself.[3] The Master of Life is thought by other tribes to dwell in the Rocky Mountains.[4] The Mexicans thought that Tlaloc, god of rain, dwelt on the highest mountain-tops where the clouds gather. Other gods, his lieutenants, bearing his name, dwelt in hills and were worshipped as gods of water and of mountains. The cult of Tlaloc was of great importance, and was connected with festivals of the first rank.[5] In Central India the sun-god is supposed to dwell on hills, and isolated rounded hills are hence called 'sun-rays.' Several outstanding peaks of the Himālaya are the seat of gods—Kailāsa of Śiva and Kubera—and a title of Śiva is the 'mountain-god.' Other mountain chains or peaks are associated with divinities—*e.g.*, the Vindhya ranges with Mahārāṇī Vindhyeśwarī, the goddess of the range. In earlier times Rudra was believed to dwell among the mountains, or on their tops, and Durgā was called 'the dweller in Mandara.'[6] Manu is said to have descended on a slope of the Himālaya called 'Manu's Descent,' and to have tied his ship to a peak after the flood.[7] As has been seen, there is a constant confusion between the mountains personified and the personal gods of mountains in India. In Greece certain gods were closely associated with mountains. The habitual cult of Zeus on mountain-tops, like that of the Mexican Tlaloc, shows his earlier connexion with rain, cloud, and lightning sent down from the heights, and he probably had been identified with and had absorbed similar earlier gods there worshipped—*e.g.*, at Mt. Lykaion in Arcadia (Zeus Lykaios). In several other instances the mountain where the cult took place gave a title to the god—*e.g.*, Zeus Olympios (here the cult no longer was observed), Zeus Laphystos (Bœotia); on Mt. Pelion he was worshipped as Zeus Akraios.[8] Clouds resting on peaks where Zeus as rain-god was worshipped were a sign of rain.[9] Hermes had a temple on the summit of Mt. Cyllene, and Apollo on the hill of Phigaleia. Artemis was also worshipped on high places in Arcadia. The Cretan Mother-goddess, like the Phrygian Cybele (*q.v.*), was represented standing on a hill (cf. art. MOUNTAIN-MOTHER). Cybele was the Mountain-mother (*μήτηρ ὀρεία*),[10] and she loved the mountain and its recesses, called by her name *Κύβελα*.[11] Another divinity associated with mountains was Pan, who was born on Mt. Lykaios and had one of his sanctuaries there. Several mountains—*e.g.*, Mt. Mænalus, Mt. Lampea—were sacred to him. There he loved to hunt, and there he might be heard piping.[12] The personalized nymphs were also of the mountains, and were worshipped there. They had caves on Mt. Cithæron, and gave oracles from them. Certain nymphs, called *Ὀρεστιάδες* or *Ὀρειάδες*, presided over mountains, and were companions of Artemis.[13] Mt. Olympus was supposed to be the seat of the gods, with the palace of Zeus on its summit. In Cappadocia, according to Strabo,[14] a mountain was called after a god Omanos. Some Babylonian gods were called 'ruler of the mountains,' and Enlil is described as 'the great Earth-Mountain'—a reference to Babylonian cosmogony and to the belief that he was god of all the forces of life. For his worship, and later that of all the gods, an artificial mountain was erected in the plain.[15] The world-mountain was the seat of the gods. Among the Celts gods were associated with hills, where some cult was offered to them, or with mounds. Within these they were believed to have retired on the coming of Christianity, and there they live as fairies.[16]

For Berbers see *ERE* ii. 506.

3. Ghosts dwelling on mountains.—To some extent the belief that ghosts haunt mountains or that the Other-world of the dead is situated on a mountain-top may have arisen from the custom of burying the dead on hills, but the belief often exists where this custom is not found. It was doubtless connected with the fact that mountains are lofty and touch the clouds or are swathed at times in mists. They are near the sky-land which is so often associated with the dead. They are lofty and mysterious; and, as they are the dwelling-place of gods and spirits other than human, it was natural enough to regard them as also the habitation of ghosts.

Burial on hills is only one of many methods of disposing of the dead, and is by no means universal. It is found among the Comanches, Arapahos, and other N. American tribes, the Caribs and Patagonians, in Arabia and Tibet, and among the Parsis where no *dakhma* exists (the body is surrounded by stones, not buried). Hill-burial was also favoured by the Norsemen.[1]

In Melanesia the idea that ghosts dwell on mountains is frequently found—*e.g.*, in British New Guinea (life like that of earth [Koita]; a blissful Elysium [Aroma]; ghosts as a light or a fungus [Roro-speaking tribes]), and among the Kai of German New Guinea (ghosts as animals haunting wild glens). In the D'Entrecasteaux group is the spirit-mountain Bwebweso, the happy spirit-land which the ghosts reach by a snake-bridge over a chasm. No mortal dare climb it or speak above a whisper when passing it.[2] In Tahiti the heaven of the dead, Tamahani, is on a mountain on the north-west side of Raiatua, and frequently in Polynesia a mountain-top or rocky defile or the surrounding mists are the abode or resort of ghosts.[3] In the Shortland Islands the dead go to certain mountains, and, after remaining there for some time, depart to a volcano.[4] Among the Dayaks of Borneo hill-tops are associated with ghosts. The heaven of the Idaans and other tribes is on the top of Kina Balu, and the ghosts feed on the moss on its sides. Among the Sea Dayaks a hero who becomes the object of a cult is buried in a lonely spot on the crest of a hill.[5] Various African tribes have similar beliefs.

The Akamba think that ghosts dwell on hills, and that volcanic veins are their paths. Sacrifice is made to them there, and they fear to approach the hill among the woods of which the ghosts dwell.[6] Among the Kagoro ghosts dwell in groves or on mountains.[7] The Bondei god, Mlinga, is a mountain, and souls go thither, storms come from it, and in war drums are heard upon it. Death is the penalty for trespassing on it.[8] The Anyanja hear the ghosts talking on their spirit-hill, or drums beating. To hear these is dangerous.[9] Malagasy ghosts and animal spirits reside in a great mountain in the north.[10]

In N. America the Sonora Indians thought that ghosts dwelt in caves and rocks, the echo being their voices.[11] Of other tribes it is said that souls of the dead go to Wakondah, who dwells in the Rocky Mountains, and there live in bliss.[12] Tlalocan, a Mexican Elysium in the mountains, was the place of souls of those sacrificed to Tlaloc and of those who died of leprosy or by drowning or lightning.[13] The Hindus regarded the Himālaya as the home of the sainted dead.[14] One Chinese paradise is in the Kuen-lun mountains, and is for those who attain holiness or divinity; many tales are told of its wonders.[15] Similar beliefs lingered on in the W. Highlands. Certain clans had hills 'to which the spirits of their departed friends had a peculiar attachment,' and which were supernaturally lit when a member of the clan died.[16]

In pagan Slavic belief the dead must climb a steep glass mountain, on whose top is paradise, and in *Märchen*, Scandinavian and Slavic, this idea reappears as the rescue of a princess or a fair being from the top of a glass mountain by a hero.[17]

The road which the soul has to traverse to the region of the dead is often a difficult one, and in some savage instances it passes over mountains, or the entrance to the Other-world is from a cave in a volcanic vent (see DESCENT TO HADES [Ethnic], § 1).

1 Hopkins, p. 528; E. T. Dalton, *TES* vi. [1867] 34.
2 *NR* iii. 90 f.
3 *FL* xi. 398.
4 W. Irving, *Astoria*, London, 1839, p. 142.
5 *Ib.* pp. 324, 343 ff.
6 *PR* i. 61, 63; Hopkins, pp. 461, 416.
7 *Satapatha Brāhmaṇa*, I. viii. 1. 5 f.
8 Paus. I. xxxi. 4, xxxii. 2, IV. iii. 9. xxxiii. 2, VIII. ii., xxxviii. 3, IX. xxxiv. 5; *CGS* i. 50 f.
9 Theoph. *de Signis Tempestatum*, i. 20, 24.
10 *CGS* iii. 296.
11 L. R. Farnell, *Greece and Babylon*, Edinburgh, 1911, p. 109.
12 Paus. VIII. xxiv. 4, xlii. 3, xxxvi. 8; *CGS* v. 382, 432.
13 *CGS* v. 424; Homer, *Il.* vi. 420; Paus. IX. iii. 9.
14 xi. p. 521.
15 Farnell, *Greece and Babylon*, p. 104; G. F. Moore, *Hist. of Religions*, Edinburgh, 1914, i. 202.
16 MacCulloch, p. 66.

1 H. R. Schoolcraft, *Indian Tribes of the U.S.*, Philadelphia, 1853–57, ii. 133; W. H. Brett, *Indian Tribes of Guiana*, London, 1868, p. 125; R. Fitzroy, *Narrative of Voyages of the Adventure and Beagle*, do. 1826–39, ii. 158; J. L. Burckhardt, *Notes on the Bedouins and Wahabys*, do. 1831, i. 280; A. V. W. Jackson, *Persia Past and Present*, New York, 1906, p. 394; cf. *ERE* iv. 422[b], 510[b].
2 C. G. Seligmann, *The Melanesians of British New Guinea*, Cambridge, 1910, p. 189; J. Chalmers and W. W. Gill, *Work and Adventure in New Guinea*, London, 1885, p. 86; R. W. Williamson, *The Mafulu Mountain People of British New Guinea*, do. 1912, p. 267 f.; R. Neuhauss, *Deutsch-Neu-Guinea*, Berlin, 1911, iii. 112, 150 f.; G. Brown, *Melanesians and Polynesians*, London, 1910, p. 399 f.
3 Ellis, i. 331, 516.
4 *FL* xvi. [1905] 115.
5 S. B. St. John, *Life in the Forests of the Far East*, London, 1862, i. 172, 278; H. Low, *Sarawak*, do. 1848, p. 245; I. H. N. Evans, *JRAI* xlii. [1912] 380; C. Hose and W. McDougall, *The Pagan Tribes of Borneo*, London, 1912, ii. 10; cf. *ERE* ii. 683[a].
6 C. Dundas, *JRAI* xliii. [1913] 535, 548.
7 A. J. N. Tremearne, *JRAI* xlii. 159.
8 G. Dale, *JAI* xxv. [1896] 232 f.
9 *FL* xxii. [1911] 257.
10 Ellis, *Hist. of Madagascar*, London, 1838, i. 429 f.
11 *NR* iii. 529.
12 Irving, p. 142.
13 *PC* ii. 61.
14 *PR* i. 60.
15 De Groot, *Religion in China*, p. 175.
16 R. G. MacLagan, *FL* viii. [1897] 208.
17 W. R. S. Ralston, *Songs of the Russian People*[2], London, 1872, p. 109 f.; *CF*, p. 368 f.

In Mexican belief the soul of one dying a peaceful death had to pass between two mountains which threatened to meet and crush him, if he were not armed with a passport.[1] Mt. Demavend in Persia was the resting-place of the blessed on their way to paradise,[2] and Mt. Albūrz was one of the supports of the Chinvat bridge. In ancient Egyptian belief the 'Mountain of the West,' through which lay the road to the region of the dead, was guarded by Taûrt or Hathor, who is represented emerging from the mountain,[3] where Rā also sits. At the tomb the coffin was set on a small sandhill, representing the mountain.[4]

Many folk-tales and myths tell of a deliverer, some *rex quondam, rex futurus*, like Arthur, who is one day to return as the saviour of his people.[5] In some of these he is in fairyland or heaven, but 'the cruder and more archaic belief is that he sleeps within the hills.'[6] Sometimes he is seen there by one who has been able to penetrate into the hill. Such tales are told of Arthur, Merlin, Fionn, Bruce, and many another hero, and there are innumerable Celtic, Teutonic, and Slavic instances.[7] The story is also found in Korea.[8] Hartland suggests that these heroes are gods of the earlier faiths, vanquished by Christianity but not destroyed.[9] So in Irish myth the Tuatha Dé Danann had retired within the hills.[10] But, while this is not impossible, the idea seems to be linked more directly with that of the dead being alive in grave or barrow or in hills (as in Scandinavian belief), whence they might come in the hour of their people's need.

4. Mountains as the abode of spirits.—Besides being the seat of gods, mountains are also peopled, like other parts of nature, by spirits, or are haunted by fierce demons.

In Australia Twanjirika is the mountain-spirit of the S. Arunta, and in the Lake Macquarie district Yaho lived on the tops of high mountains and was hostile to the blacks. The Arunta also fear spirits called *oruntja*, dwelling on a hill.[11] In British New Guinea the Koita dread a spirit living on a hill which they will not approach, but a spear made from a tree growing near it is peculiarly effective.[12] In Polynesia spirits people the mountains and are generally dangerous.[13] The *yaku* of the Veddas people rocks and hill-tops, among other places, and are named from them. They send disease, and are much feared. Some of these *yaku* are spirits of the dead—of headmen or their wives. They also have a dangerous aspect—sending sickness or stealing children—and are placated by offerings.[14] The Kayans and other tribes of Borneo believe in spirits manifesting themselves in parts of nature—*e.g.*, mountains. Spirits of this kind are called *toh*, and are malevolent; hence people are careful not to offend them. The most dangerous are found on the most rugged summits, which the natives will hardly approach.[15] Among the Lushei Kuki clans *lashi* are beings dwelling in precipices and controlling animals, but demons people hills, streams, etc., and cause much trouble.[16] In Chitral bad spirits with feet turned backwards dwell on Tirich Mir.[17] Among the Oraons every rock and natural feature is haunted by demons, and this is true of every part of India.[18] The Himālaya is the dwelling of innumerable beings, its recesses the haunt of demons, its caves of witches and fairies. Other hills are equally infested and consequently feared. As early as Vedic times such beliefs are found, and in the *Mahābhārata* witches are said to live in mountains.[19] In Korea the spirits of mountains are duly worshipped by sacrifices, and on every pass is a shrine where prayer is made to them or an offering laid. They control tigers and give the hunter power to catch them.[1] In China mountain spectres are much feared, and evil spirits haunt mountains, their power being proportionate to the size of these. Only on certain days should mountains be crossed, and only after fasting and purification. The genii of mountains are more friendly and have a regular cult (§ 7).[2] In Indo-China the Thai believe in the *phi* dwelling on steep mountains, who have the power of imitating storms by night.[3] In Annam female spirits or fairies called *chu vi* dwell in forests and mountains, and for each hill there are genii good and bad.[4] Among the Bantu of S.E. Africa demons haunting mountains are much feared.[5] On the other hand, the Awemba believe in guardian spirits attached to hills, etc., who send rain and fertility.[6] For similar Berber beliefs see *ERE* ii. 506[b]. The Babylonians thought that evil spirits dwelt on mountain-tops.[7] In Persia Demavend is the home of genii and demons,[8] and wizards assemble there. It is a general Muhammadan belief that the mountains of Qāf, supposed to be the circular boundary of the earth, are the chief abode of *jinn* and *ifrits*.[9] European folk-lore makes hills and mountains one of the dwelling-places of elves, fairies, dwarfs, and similar beings,[10] and the *devs* (demons) of Armenian folk-belief live in mountains,[11] while fairyland is often within a hollow hill (see art. FAIRY, § 11). So the Serbian *vilas*[12] and the Nereids of modern Greece haunt hills and mountains. Certain mountains were trysting-places of spirits, demons, and witches—*e.g.*, the Horselberg, the Brocken, the Puy de Dôme, and innumerable others in every part of Europe, these gatherings probably being reminiscent of sacrificial rites in pagan times on the same spots.[13]

5. Sacred mountains.—Wherever mountains are personified or associated with gods or are the seat of a cult, their sacredness is obvious. But some mountains have a peculiar sanctity. Legend clusters thickly round them, and they are places of pilgrimage or sources of merit.

Among the Western Nandi there is a sacred hill called Chepel-oi, the hill to which the spirits set fire. Ghosts are supposed to fire the grass there annually, and no Nandi will go near it.[14] In Japan Fuji-yama is the sacred mountain, regarded as a goddess or connected with a goddess of the same name.[15] Pilgrims ascend its summit in vast numbers annually, and it is a frequent object of Japanese art. The Kwan-lun mountains are the sacred mountains of Taoism, and have given rise to numerous fanciful legends.[16] In early Hinduism Mt. Mandara in Bihār was a kind of Olympus. It formed the stick with which the gods churned the ocean for ambrosia. But more usually Himavat (Himālaya) is the sacred mountain-chain, 'the divine mountain, beloved of the gods.' As has been seen, it is extolled as a god. There are many temples on it, and it is the object of innumerable pilgrimages. It is inhabited by beings whose mere presence adds value to the merit of the penances of ascetics (see also § 1). Other mountains are sacred —*e.g.*, the Vindhya range—an object of devotion and prayer, and have their temples or shrines.[17] In ancient Persia Albūrz or Hara Berezaiti was peculiarly sacred, the first of mountains. The sun and stars revolved round it; light came from it and returned there; on it was no night or darkness, no cold, no wind, no sickness; on it the Amesha Spentas built a dwelling for Mithra, and he looks upon all the material world from it; below it was the Chinvat bridge. All mountains are said to have grown from its roots.[18] In the Qur'ān Ṣafa and Marwah are said to be 'beacons of God,' and pilgrims are advised to compass them about. Idols formerly stood upon them and were worshipped, but Muhammad ordered their destruction, though the visitation of the mountains is an important part of the Hajj rites.[19] Mt. Sinai was also regarded as sacred, and oaths were taken by it.[20] Among the Semites several mountains were sacred as the dwelling- or resting-place of gods or the

1 *NR* iii. 537.
2 *FL* xii. 274.
3 A. Wiedemann, *Rel. of the Ancient Egyptians*, London, 1897, p. 169 f.
4 *Ib.* p. 236.
5 E. S. Hartland, *Science of Fairy Tales*, London, 1891, pp. 205, 228 f.
6 *Ib.* p. 207.
7 MacCulloch, p. 344; J. Grimm, *Teutonic Mythology*, tr. J. S. Stallybrass, London, 1882–88, p. 953 ff.
8 *FL* xi. 327 f.
9 Hartland, p. 229.
10 MacCulloch, p. 66.
11 N. W. Thomas, *Natives of Australia*, London, 1906, p. 213; Spencer-Gillen[b], p. 496.
12 Seligmann, p. 183.
13 Ellis, *Polyn. Res.* i. 331; A. Bastian, *Allerlei aus Volks- und Menschenkunde*, Berlin, 1888, i. 46; T. Waitz and G. Gerland, *Anthropologie der Naturvölker*, Leipzig, 1859–72, vi. 295 f.
14 C. G. and B. Z. Seligmann, *The Veddas*, Cambridge, 1911, pp. 140, 153 f.
15 Hose-McDougall, ii. 1, 23, 25.
16 J. Shakespear, *JRAI* xxxix. [1909] 375, *The Lushei Kuki Clans*, London, 1912, p. 65.
17 *FL* xiii. [1902] 183 f.
18 E. T. Dalton, *Descriptive Ethnology of Bengal*, Calcutta, 1872, p. 258; *PR* i. 62.
19 *Milinda-pañha*, IV. viii. 16; *PR* i. 60 ff., 261; H. Oldenberg, *Die Religion des Veda*, Berlin, 1894, p. 39 f.; Hopkins, p. 415 f.

1 *FL* xi. 328 f.
2 De Groot, *Rel. System of China*, Leyden, 1892 ff., iv. 109; R. K. Douglas, *Confucianism and Taoism*, London, 1877, p. 244.
3 A. Bourlet, *Anthropos*, ii. [1907] 619.
4 P. Giran, *Magie et religion annamites*, Paris, 1912, pp. 134, 222.
5 G. M. Theal, *Records of S.E. Africa*, vii. [1901] 405.
6 J. H. West Sheane, *JRAI* xxxvi. [1906] 151.
7 M. Jastrow, *Religion of Babylonia and Assyria*, Boston, 1898, p. 260 f.
8 E. C. Sykes, *FL* xii. 262, 274; S. Lane-Poole, *Arabian Society in the Middle Ages*, London, 1883, pp. 37, 104.
9 *SBE* vi. [1900] p. lxix f.; cf. W. W. Skeat, *Malay Magic*, London, 1900, pp. 14, 81.
10 Grimm, pp. 448, 452, 455, 474. Cf. the stories of the Venusberg, *ib.* p. 935. See also E. H. Meyer, *Germ. Mythologie*, Berlin, 1891, pp. 126–128, 158 f.
11 M. Abeghian, *Armen. Volksglaube*, Leipzig, 1899, p. 111 f.
12 M. E. Durham, *JRAI* xxxix. 86.
13 Grimm, pp. 1051 ff., 1619 f.
14 A. C. Hollis, *The Nandi*, Oxford, 1909, p. 100.
15 *FL* xx. [1909] 251.
16 *SBE* xxxix. 244, xl. [1891] 70.
17 Hopkins, p. 358 f.; M. Monier-Williams, *Brāhmanism and Hindūism*[4], London, 1891, p. 349; *Buddha-charita*, vii. 39 ff.
18 *Yt.* x. 50 f., xii. 23; *Bund.* v. 3–8, viii. 2–5; *Dāṭistān-i-Dīnīk*, xcii. 5; *Dīnkarṭ*, IX. xx. 3, xxii. 4.
19 Qur'ān, ii. 153.
20 *Ib.* xcv. 2.

scene of a cult (§ 7). Sinai was sacred before Israel received the Law from it, and it is specifically called the mount of God in OT (Ex 3^{1} 4^{27} 24^{13}, 1 K 19^{8}). Several other sacred mountains are also mentioned there—Moriah, Nebo (perhaps originally the seat of the god Nebo), Hor, and Zion (Gn 22^{14}, Dt 32^{49}, Nu $20^{22ff.}$, Is $2^{2f.}$ 25^{6}). The last remained sacred in much later times as the central seat of worship, and was regarded as God's holy mountain, the 'mountain of the Lord's house.'[1] In ancient times Mt. Atlas in Morocco was held in great reverence. Religious fear seized those who approached it, and the Libyans are said to have regarded it as a temple and a god, the object by which they swore, and a statue.[2]

In China mountains have a curious importance, especially the two groups of five already referred to and other sacred mountains. According to the doctrine of *feng-shui* (*q.v.*), every house, temple, field, etc., should be so situated that the beneficent influences of the universe may be freely exercised upon it. These influences are modified by the configuration of the earth. Hence hills intercept noxious influences—*e.g.*, bad winds—or they send far and wide the beneficent influences of water, the chief element in nature; or they are bearers of heavenly influences to man; or, standing around a town, they symbolize the animals of the four quarters, and bring it prosperity. The shape of hills or of any part of them may also influence a village or its inhabitants for good or evil. Hence it is important to select a site near a favourable contour, or a hill or rock in which there is a beneficial combination of elements, as given in the books of geomancy.[3] Similar ideas are found in Korea. Towns, houses, and graves must have their guardian peaks, and care must be taken to avoid or to counteract hostile influences from a hill. People are born according to the nature of the hill on which graves of ancestors are—*e.g.*, a craggy hill denotes a warrior. There are currents or veins of influence in mountains, and prosperity depends on the proper circulation of these.[4] In India it is held that mountains as well as rivers or temples are places which destroy sin, this being especially true of Himavat.[5] In the *Laws of Manu*, however, it is said that a student who has completed his term is not to reside long on a mountain.[6] In Zoroastrianism mountains are said to have been created by outgrowth from the root of Albūrz, the first mountain, in 18 years, after their substance was formed in the earth during 1000 years. High mountains, being near heaven, are apt to become seats of heavenly beings. On the top of one Ahura revealed the law,[7] and mountains are said by the Spirit of Wisdom to be moderators of wind, warders-off, rest-places, and supports of rain-clouds, smiters of Ahriman and the demons, and maintainers and vivifiers of the creation of Ahura Mazda.[8] Of 'him who goes to the lofty mountains' their glory is said to 'bless him and be friendly' (cf. Himavat, § 1).[9] Some are said to have been made by Ahura Mazda.[10] Yet their creation is connected in the *Bundahišn* with the rushing in of the spirit of evil,[11] and at the restoration of all things earth is to receive its original perfect state of a level plain, because mountains are the work of the evil spirit.[12] Even Albūrz, whose summit supports the Chinvat bridge, will no longer exist.[13] Perhaps also this conception accounts for the tabu in the *Sad-dar* against women after child-birth looking at a hill.[14] J. H. Moulton regards this idea, so contrary to Parsi and Aryan notions of the sacredness of mountains, as one of the beliefs brought in by Magian influences, neither Aryan nor Semitic, and superimposed upon Zoroastrianism.[15] A similar idea is seen in the description of the Buddhist paradise, Sukhāvatī, which will be level and contain 'no black mountains nor jewel mountains, nor Sumerus, king of mountains, nor Chakravāṭas, great kings of mountains.'[16] The friendly influence of the hills is especially marked in the OT, as is natural where so many of them were sacred, and Zion was in particular the seat of God's house.[17] They are symbols of God's might, yet are subject to Him. They melt like wax before Him or smoke at His touch. They rejoice with the worshipper, or are bidden to do so, or they break forth into singing before the return of the exiles. They are symbols of God's righteousness; they bring peace and righteousness to the people.

[1] For many others see **Baal**, vol. ii. p. 287a, and references there: cf. Ps $48^{1.\,2}$ 87^{1}.

[2] *HN* v. 1; Max. Tyr. *Dissert.* viii. 57; see **Berbers**, vol. ii. p. 506.

[3] De Groot, *Religious System of China*, iii. 947 ff., *Religion in China*, pp. 285, 294 ff., 301, 314; cf. *Shih King*, iii. 5.

[4] *FL* xi. 329 ff.

[5] *Vasiṣṭha Dharmaśāstra*, xxii. 12; *Baudhāyana Dharmaśāstra*, III. x. 12.

[6] iv. 69.

[7] So the Mosaic Law was revealed from Sinai. In Gnostic books Christ's esoteric revelations are given on a mountain—perhaps a combination of Mt 5^{1} 24^{3} and 28^{16}. Cf. also the *Apocalypse of Peter*.

[8] *Dīnā-ī-Maīnōg-ī-Xrat*, lvi. 2–6; cf. also *Yt.* i. 31; *Bund.* viii. 2–5; *Selections of Zaṭ-sparam*, vii. 1–7.

[9] *Šayast lā-Šayast*, xix. 12.

[10] *Nyāyišn*, v. 5 f.

[11] *Bund.* viii. 1 ff.

[12] *Bund.* xxx. 33; cf. Plutarch, *de Is. et Osir.* 47: 'the earth having become flat and level.'

[13] *Bund.*, *loc. cit.*

[14] *Sad-dar*, xvi. 4.

[15] *Early Zoroastrianism*, London, 1913, pp. 214, 403.

[16] *Sukhāvatī-vyūha*, 17. Is 40^{4} is probably not analogous, but cf. Rev 16^{20}.

[17] Ps 121^{1} 125^{2}; cf. J. Ruskin, *Modern Painters*, 'The Mountain Glory.'

6. Fabulous mountains. — As the preceding section has shown, actual mountains are often regarded in a mythical light — *e.g.*, Albūrz in Zoroastrian belief, Himavat in Hindu, Kwan-lun in Taoist. Some mythologies, however, have invented mythical mountains, mainly in connexion with cosmogony.

Among such is the Bab. 'mountain of the world' (§ 9 (*b*)). In Hindu and, more particularly, Buddhist mythology Meru or Sumeru, the abode of the gods, occupies a prominent place. It is the primeval and the chief of mountains, the 'golden mountain.' It holds fast the earth, yet it swayed at the coming of Buddha.[1] It is 84,000 miles high, and is surmounted by the heavens. Seven concentric rings of vast mountains surround it, with intervening seas. Between these and an eighth outmost ring are the four continents.[2] Round Meru the sun, moon, and planets revolve. In Tibet the Lāmas offer to the Buddhas daily the universe in effigy; Meru is represented by a dole of rice in the middle.[3] In Muhammadan belief the mountains of Qāf are believed to encompass the earth and its surrounding ocean like a ring, as Albūrz was held to do in Zoroastrian belief.[4] They are of green chrysolite, and are the chief abode of the *jinn*. Our earth is one of seven successive earths, rising above each other, and supported by a rock communicating with Qāf by veins or roots, the origin of earthly mountains. In Malay belief Qāf (which may = the Caucasus) is being bored through by people called Yājūj and Mājūj, and, when they succeed, the world will come to an end. The Malays believe in the existence of a central mountain Mahameru—a borrowing from Hindu belief.[5]

7. Cult of mountains.—A cult offered to mountains or to divinities connected with them cannot be sharply divided from a cult on mountains, whether that is to such gods or to others. In some cases, no doubt, mountain-tops were selected for altars, shrines, or temples because of their supposed nearness to heaven—one seat of the gods.[6] Here and there, however, the difference can be seen even in the same religion.

Among the Nandi, after harvest the people of each geographical division hold a feast on the top of a hill, and in drought people look to Tindiret or Chepusio hill every morning and say, 'Rain, Tindiret!'[7] The savage Malays of Malacca sacrifice to the mountain-spirits on the summits, make a wish, addressing the spirit, and then partake of the sacrifice. This may be done three times, if not successful; should a third visit fail, another mountain is visited.[8] Among the American Indian tribes Bancroft says that a direct worship of hills was unusual, but there was a liking for hills and mounds as places of worship.[9] The Thompson Indians, however, offered the first berries of the year to the mountains, an old man dancing and holding the offering up to them.[10] The Mexicans worshipped mountains and mountain-gods, and, when no hills were available for temples, made artificial mounds, or *teocalli*, for worship. Effigies of the mountains were made of dough and eaten in connexion with human sacrifices to the Tlalocs and mountains.[11] Infants and hairless dogs were also sacrificed on high mountains.[12] In China from ancient times mountains and rivers share with heaven the reverence of the State. There are many historical notices in the sacred books of this or that emperor or king worshipping towards the hills or going to famous hills and sacrificing the appropriate sacrifices to them, usually to the five mountains (§ 1), or to the spirits of the hills.[13] This was done on festivals, at the successful conclusion of war,[14] or on the occasion of a progress through the kingdom. In this way rest was given to the spirits of the hills.[15] Omission to sacrifice to any of these spirits was an act of irreverence, and the ruler was deprived of part of his territory.[16] At Peking is the great altar of 'Empress Earth,' and here at the summer solstice, when sacrifices to heaven are made, the emperor sacrifices to earth's chief components—mountains, rivers, and seas. Similar sacrifices are offered to the ten mountains on other State occasions, as well as to the ranges dominating the site of the imperial mausoleums.[17]

[1] *Fo-sho-hing-tsan-king*, I. i. 25 (*SBE* xix. [1883] 5); *Mahābhārata*, III. clxiii. 14; cf. I. xvii. 5, I. xviii. 1.

[2] Waddell, p. 78; S. Beal, *Buddhism in China*, London, 1886, p. 172 f.

[3] Waddell, p. 397 f.

[4] *Yt.* v. 21, xix. 1.

[5] Lane-Poole, pp. 37, 100, 104 f.; Skeat, p. 1 f.

[6] In the *Lî Kî* (VIII. ii. 12) ancient kings appointed wise men who ascended famous hills and there announced to heaven the good government of the princes.

[7] Hollis, p. 47 f.

[8] W. W. Skeat and C. O. Blagden, *Pagan Races of the Malay Peninsula*, London, 1906, ii. 326 f.

[9] *NR* iii. 122.

[10] J. Teit, *Thompson Indians of British Columbia*, p. 345 (*Jesup N. Pacific Expedition, Memoirs of Amer. Museum of Nat. Hist.*, 1900).

[11] *NR* iii. 123, 343 ff.

[12] *Ib.* p. 330 f.; *FL* xviii. 276.

[13] *Lî Kî* III. ii. 14–16, iii. 6, VIII. ii. 7, ii. 12.

[14] *Shû King*, II. i., III. i. 9 f., V. iii. 1.

[15] *Shih King*. i. 8.

[16] Cf. Douglas, pp. 12, 80 f.

[17] De Groot, *Rel. in China*, pp. 194 f., 201 f.

In India from early times a cult has been paid to or on mountains (§ 1). The *Institutes of Viṣṇu* say that mountains are excellent places for performing *śrāddhas*,[1] and the *Gṛhyasūtras* speak of an oblation of butter made on a mountain to east or north.[2] The cult of sacred mountains, on which shrines or temples are commonly built, has already been referred to. Aboriginal tribes attach a high importance to this cult, and many sacrifices and rites take place upon hills and mountains (Santāls, Korwas, Kols, etc.).[3] In Korea people go once a year to worship the popular god of hills. Pilgrims ascend mountains for merit, and carry a pebble, which is placed on the heap at the top dedicated to this god.[4] In ancient Persia there are frequent references in the sacred books to worship and sacrifice being offered to mountains 'glorious with sanctity,' or 'brilliant with holiness.'[5] The mountains which give understanding are worshipped with libations, as part of the liturgical service.[6] The *Yasna* mentions worship of Sraosha by Haoma on 'the highest height of high Haraiti,'[7] and Herodotus speaks of the custom of ascending the highest peaks and offering sacrifices to Zeus, calling the whole vault of the sky Zeus, probably some Zoroastrian sky-god representing the primitive Indo-European god of the sky.[8] In Greece numerous mountains were crowned by temples dedicated to some particular god, but no deity was so much worshipped on mountain-tops as Zeus, who from his heights was supposed to rule the world. The Greek cults on high places were of ancient date, and perhaps concerned gods supposed to dwell in heaven, rather than gods of the heights. In modern Greece monasteries often stand on the site of these ancient mountain-shrines.[9]

Pausanias describes the cult of Zeus on Mt. Lycaon. There was a mound of heaped-up earth for an altar with two pillars facing the rising sun. Here also and on Mt. Tmolus the priest performed certain rites for the production of rain.[10] In ancient Anatolia festivals in honour of Cybele were celebrated on the tops of Ida and Berecyntus, where she was supposed to reside, and where the trees were sacred to her and never cut down.[11]

Among the Samogitæ on a certain mountain-top there was a perpetual fire in honour of the god Pargn, who controlled thunder and tempest.[12] Among the Semites hills or high places were favourite places of worship, and are frequently referred to in OT in connexion both with pagan tribes or peoples and with Israel. Jahweh was commonly worshipped on high places, and was supposed to dwell there, according to an older stratum of thought, while Israel also offered sacrifice and incense on them to the local gods—the Beālîm of hills—or other gods from time to time (cf. Hos 4^{13}, Jer 2^{20} 3^{6} 17^{2}, Ezk 20^{28}, 1 K 11^{7} 14^{23} 2 K 16^{4} 17^{10}). For the Canaanite cults see Dt 12^{2}, Nu 33^{52}; Moab, Is 15^{2} 16^{12}; cf. Nu 22^{41}–23. The references to the worship of Jahweh on high places, whether natural or artificial, are frequent—*e.g.*, 1 S $7^{1.17}$ $9^{12f.}$, 2 S 15^{32}, 1 K 3^{4} $18^{20f.}$, Jg 6^{26}, Dt 27^{4}.

Archæological research has discovered remains of many 'high places,' often on hills, and even now remains of temples and sacred groves are to be seen on Hermon and other mountains. On some mountains worship and sacrifice still take place, and circular enclosures of stone crown the summits.

Aaron has a shrine on Mt. Hor, and is supposed to visit it twice a week. Muhammadan saints have also shrines on hill-tops.[13] In European folk-survivals from earlier paganism, ritual acts—*e.g.*, 'hill-wakes' or bonfires at May-day or midsummer—often take place on hills.[14]

Many high places are probably artificial constructions.

The Bab. temple-tower (*ziqqurat*) was an earthly copy of the world-mountain, and served the purpose of the worshippers, whose ancestors had been accustomed to worship on heights, gaining nearer access to heaven (cf. *ERE* i. 690b). The Mexicans and other American peoples built mounds, pyramids, or *teocalli*, where no hills were available for worship. Some of these mounds were of great size. On them sacred buildings were erected, and the higher these could be placed the more sacred they seemed. *Teocalli* were also erected on high mountains. The mounds are found in the bottom lands, though occasionally on higher ground.[1]

Heaps of stones, often dedicated to the local genius on the highest point of mountain-passes, to which every traveller adds a stone, are found in all parts of the world and at all stages of culture. The added stone may be an offering (in Ladakh the mountain-spirit is said to be offended if no stone is given[2]), or may carry off weariness (it is often alleged that weariness leaves the traveller when he offers it), or the contagion of evil, or it may drive away evil spirits, or it may be a materialization of the prayer made at the moment. See LANDMARKS, vol. vii. p. 794 f.; *GB*³, pt. vi., *The Scapegoat*, London, 1913, p. 11 ff.

In all religions which have encouraged asceticism men have chosen to live a solitary life among mountains, partly because of their loneliness, partly because of their sacred associations. Their living there tended to increase the sacred aspect of some mountains.

In India Himavat has always been the resort of saints and ascetics.[3] Buddhist monasteries in Tibet are often on almost inaccessible heights, like many in Eastern Christian regions. Taoist hermits have been fond of mountains,[4] as also have Christian ascetics.

8. Symbolism.—Mountains are everywhere symbolic of strength and everlastingness (cf. the frequent phrase in OT 'the everlasting hills,' though compared with Jahweh they are as nothing). To the Hebrews they were symbols of Jahweh's righteousness, His kindness, His guardianship.[5] In the *Yî King* a mountain is a symbol of resoluteness.[6] The Bab. Bel is called 'the great mountain,' or 'the great Earth-Mountain.'[7] The Zulus speak of their king as being 'high as the mountain,' or address him as 'Yon mountain,'[8] and elsewhere 'mountain' is a title of honour.[9] Buddha is said to be composed and firm as Sumeru, or he is called 'the golden mountain,' and he is illustrious among men as Sumeru among mountains.[10] The name *montagne* was given to the extreme French Revolutionists, who occupied the higher part of the hall where the Assembly met.

9. Mountains in cosmogony.—(*a*) The creation of mountains is referred to in some cosmogonies.

In an American-Indian myth they were made by the crow and the hawk from mud brought up by a duck.[11] In W. Australia one myth tells how they were made from a heap of roots which a man kicked in all directions.[12] A Maori myth describes how the mountains and valleys of New Zealand were carved out by the knives of Maui's brothers, and an Australian myth of the god Bunjil and his knife is like this.[13] Scandinavian, Cochin-Chinese, and Orphic myths recount how the mountains were made from the bones of a giant or of Zeus.[14] An Indian myth regards certain mountains as offshoots from the Himālaya, brought for Rāma when he was building a bridge[15] (see also §§ 5, 6).

(*b*) As to the ordinary observer the sky seems near the tops of mountains, so many myths regard it as so near as to be easily reached from them;[16] or, again, the mountains, real or mythical, support the sky or the heavens.

---

1 lxxxv. 58.
2 *Gobhila-Gṛhyasūtra*, IV. viii. 14.
3 Monier-Williams, p. 349 f.; Hopkins, p. 358 f.; cf. *ERE* ii. 482b.
4 *FL* xv. [1904] 449.
5 *Yasna*, i. 14, ii. 14, iii. 16, xxii. 26, xlii. 2, etc.; *Visparad*, i. 6, ii. 8.
6 *Yt*. i. 31.
7 lvii. 19.
8 Herod. i. 131; cf. Moulton, pp. 60 f., 391 ff.
9 *FL* xii. 501; *CGS* i. 50 ff.
10 Paus. VIII. ii.; W. R. Paton and E. L. Hicks, *Inscriptions of Cos*, Oxford, 1891, no. 382.
11 F. Cumont, *The Oriental Religions in Roman Paganism*, Chicago, 1911, p. 47 f.; Virgil, *Æn.* ix. 85.
12 *FL* xii. 298.
13 See W. W. Baudissin, *Studien zur semitischen Religionsgeschichte*, Leipzig, 1876–78, ii. 231 f.; S. I. Curtiss, *Primitive Semitic Religion To-day*, London, 1902, pp. 79 ff., 139, 142 f.; P. S. P. Handcock, *Latest Light on Bible Lands*, do. 1913, p. 244. Cf. BAAL, vol. ii. p. 287, HIGH PLACE, vol. vi. p. 678 f.
14 *FL* xxii. 36; *GB*³, pt. vii., *Balder the Beautiful*, London, 1913, i. 149.

1 *NR* iii. 123, iv. 765 ff.; F. S. Dellenbaugh, *North Americans of Yesterday*, New York, 1901, pp. 195, 206, 391.
2 *FL* xv. 448; cf. *Royal Commentaries of the Yncas*, tr. C. R. Markham, London, 1869–71, bk. ii. ch. 4.
3 *PR* i. 60.
4 De Groot, *Rel. in China*, pp. 84, 139.
5 Ps 36^{6} 72^{3} 125^{2}; cf. Is 54^{10}.
6 App. ii. sect. i. hex. iv. (*SBE* xvi. [1882] 271).
7 Farnell, *Greece and Babylon*, p. 104.
8 A. F. Gardiner, *Narrative of a Journey to the Zoolu Country*, London, 1836, p. 91; J. Shooter, *Kafirs of Natal*, do. 1857, p. 290.
9 H. Spencer, *Principles of Sociology*, London, 1893, i. 367.
10 *Fo-sho-hing-tsan-king*, I. i. 49, IV. xix. 1549; cf. V. xxiv. 1890.
11 *NR* iii. 124.
12 *FL* xx. 341.
13 A. Lang, *Myth, Ritual, and Religion*², London, 1899, i. 186; R. Brough-Smyth, *Aborigines of Victoria*, do. 1878, i. 423.
14 Grimm, pp. 559, 570.
15 *PR* i. 63.
16 K. L. Parker, *More Australian Legendary Tales*, London, 1898, p. 84; G. Turner, *Samoa a Hundred Years Ago*, do. 1884, p. 13; *JAI* xvi. [1886] 233 [Borneo]; E. A. W. Budge, *Egyptian Magic*², London, 1901, p. 51 f.; *ERE* ii. 682b.

Mt. Atlas was formerly known as 'the Pillar of Heaven.'[1] In Bab. cosmogony the sky rested on the 'mountain of the world,' *i.e.* the world itself conceived as a hemispherical mountain with gently sloping sides.[2] In Hindu and Buddhist cosmogony the various heavens are arranged on and above the mythical Mt. Meru in an ascending series (see COSMOGONY [Buddhist], [Hindu]). Fragments of Celtic myth suggest that with the Celts also a mountain supported the sky—*e.g.*, a mountain near the sources of the Rhone was called 'the column of the sun,' perhaps bearing up the sky while the sun revolved round it.[3] We may note the Greek myth of the Titans piling Mt. Ossa on Olympus, and Pelion on Ossa, in order to scale heaven.[4]

(*c*) In Hebrew story the ark rested on Mt. Ararat after the Flood (Gn 8[4]). So in Bab. myth the 'mountain of the land of Nitsir' held the ship fast and did not let it slip, and on its top Utnapishtim offered sacrifice and incense to the gods.[5] The Hindu flood-myth tells how the fish bade the seven *ṛṣis* bind the ship to the highest peak of Himavat. Manu descended from it on Himavat; hence the northern mountain is called 'Manu's descent'[6] (cf. DELUGE).

LITERATURE.—C. Albers, *De Diis in Locis Editis Cultis apud Græcos*, Zutphen, 1901; F. F. von Andrian, *Der Höhencultus asiatischer und europäischer Völker*, Vienna, 1891; T. C. Banfield, *De Montium Cultu*, do. 1834; R. Beer, *Heilige Höhen der alten Griechen und Römer*, do. 1891; J. Ruskin, *Modern Painters*, London, 1843–60, pt. 5, esp. ch. 19 f.; E. B. Tylor, *Primitive Culture*[4], do. 1903, ii.

J. A. MACCULLOCH.

MOUNTAIN-MOTHER.—The Mountain-Mother is the only Greek divinity certainly known to be of pre-historic origin. In the accompanying figure we have a seal-impression of late Minoan style (*c.* 1500 B.C.) found at Knossos.[7] It is of cardinal importance and embodies, indeed, nearly all that we certainly know of the Mother. She wears the typical flounced Minoan skirt, and,

Impression of signet-ring showing Mountain-Mother and pillar-shrine.

holding either sceptre or lance, stands flanked by guardian lions on the peak of her own mountain. To the left is a Minoan shrine with pillars and 'horns of consecration'—the symbols that connect her with plant and animal life, the pillar being only a shaped and stylized tree. The mountain stood for earth, and the earth is Mother because she gives life to plants, animals, and man. 'Earth sends up fruits, so praise we Earth the Mother' (Γâ καρποὺς ἀνίει, διὸ κλῄζετε ματέρα γαῖαν) was the litany chanted by the priestesses of Dodona.[8]

On the seal figured here the Mother rules alone, with an ecstatic male worshipper before her, but on other gems a male divinity appears, sometimes descending from the sky. It is noticeable, however, that he is always young and manifestly subordinate. In Cretan religion the male divinity is sometimes a child, the necessary attribute of motherhood, sometimes a young man, and sometimes a sky-power fertilizing Mother Earth; but always the Mother is dominant. This dominance of the Mother divinity is of prime importance, and is in marked contrast to the Olympian system of Homer, where Zeus the Father reigns supreme. The Mother- and the Father-cults are, in fact, characteristic of the two strata that go to the making of Greek religion—the southern (Ægean or Anatolian) stratum has the dominant Mother-god, the northern (Indo-European) the dominant Father-god, the head of a patriarchal family, who is, ostensibly at least, the monogamous husband of a subordinate wife. The northern religion obviously reflects patrilinear, the southern matrilinear, social conditions. A further distinction is of importance—the Homeric patriarchal Olympus is the outcome of a 'heroic' condition of society; it emphasizes the individual; it is the result of warlike and migratory conditions; the worship of the Mother focuses on the facts of fertility, and emphasizes the race and its continuance rather than the individual and his prowess. Mother-worship is of the group rather than of the single worshipper. We find the Mother and her subordinate son or lover attended always by groups of dæmonic personages—Kouretes, Korybantes, Telchines, Dactyls, Satyrs, and the like.

A further characteristic of this southern matrilinear group-worship of the Mother is that it is mystical and orgiastic. The mysteries all centre not on Zeus the Father, but on the Mother and the subordinate son—Demeter in Greece, whose daughter, Kore, is but her younger form, and Rhea or some other form of the great Mother; the Dionysos of the mysteries is son of the Earth-Mother. The reason is simple; mysteries are now known to be simply magical ceremonies, dramatic representations of birth, marriage, and death, enacted with a view to promoting fertility. Mysteries, in fact, spell magic, and the mysteries of the Mother stand again in marked contrast to the rational worship of the Olympian Father. In the Olympian system the worshipper approaches his god as he would his fellow-man, with prayer, praise, and presents; his action is rational and anthropomorphic, not magical, not mysterious, not orgiastic.

The mysteries of the Mother are based, like all other mysteries, on initiation-ceremonies, which have for their object to prepare the boy for adult life and especially for marriage (see INITIATION [Greek] and KOURETES AND KORYBANTES). Each young man, each member of the band of Kouretes, or grown youths, became by initiation not only the son but the prince-consort of the Mother; he went through a mystical and magical ἱερὸς γάμος.[1] This explains at once the expression used by Euripides (*Bacchæ*, 120), ὦ θαλάμευμα Κουρήτων. It also elucidates the confession made by the Orphic initiate, Δεσποίνας δὲ ὑπὸ κόλπου ἔδυν χθονίας βασιλείας.[2] Marriage is the mystery *par excellence.* In the matrilinear worship of the Mother the series of consorts was perennial. In Crete the fructifying of the Mother was mimetic and dramatic; in some Asia Minor cults it was attended by the horrors of castration.[3] In the *Cretans* of Euripides (frag. 472, Nauck) the mystic 'held aloft the torches of the Mountain-Mother' (μητρί τ' ὀρείῳ δᾷδας ἀνασχών), the blazing torch being a familiar fertilizer and purifier of fields and crops.

To the Olympos of Homer—a product of the Achæan heroic age—the Mother was never admitted; even Demeter had there only a precarious footing. But in post-Homeric days, when north and south were fused, a place was found for her in a more elastic pantheon as Mother of the Gods.

[1] Herod. iv. 184.
[2] L. W. King, *Babylonian Religion and Mythology*, London, 1899, p. 29 f.
[3] MacCulloch, p. 228.
[4] Homer, *Od.* xi. 315 f.
[5] King, p. 135.
[6] *Śātapatha Brāhmaṇa*, I. viii. 1. 1 ff.; *Mahābhārata*, iii. 12,790 f.
[7] A. Evans, *BSA* vii. [1900–01] 29, fig. 9.
[8] Paus. x. xii. 10.

[1] A. B. Cook, *Zeus*, i., Cambridge, 1913, p. 650.
[2] J. E. Harrison, *Prolegomena*, p. 668.
[3] For an explanation of the practice see J. G. Frazer, *Adonis, Attis, Osiris*[2], London, 1907, p. 224.

She lent many of her sacred animals, attributes, and traits to the women-goddesses of Greece—to Hera her ἱερὸς γάμος, and sometimes her lion, to Artemis her function as πότνια θηρῶν, to Aphrodite her dove, to Athene and the Erinyes her snakes, to Demeter her mysteries. How far these several goddesses were indigenous forms of the Mother, how far they were directly immigrant from Crete, cannot certainly be stated, but undoubtedly the dominant Mother with the male attendant—*e.g.*, Attis and Adonis—half son, half lover, is echoed in Hellenic mythology in the figures of the great patroness-goddesses with the heroes whom they protect, in Hera and Jason, in Athene and Perseus. The Mother has many names—Rhea, Cybele, Dindymene, Ma—but her functions remain the same; her characteristic attributes and sacred animals—lion, bull, and goat—vary with the culture and local surroundings of her worshippers. Cf., further, art. MOTHER OF THE GODS (Greek and Roman).

LITERATURE.—Roscher, *s.vv.* 'Meter,' 'Gaia'; Daremberg-Saglio, *s.v.* 'Cybele'; L. R. Farnell, *Cults of the Greek States*, Oxford, 1896–1909, iii. 289–306; J. E. Harrison, *Prolegomena to the Study of Greek Religion*, Cambridge, 1903, pp. 260–286 and 497–501, and *Themis*, do. 1912, p. 492; A. Dieterich, *Mutter Erde*, Leipzig, 1905: see also art. ÆGEAN RELIGION, vol. i. p. 142. For the Hittite form of the Mother see H. A. Strong and J. Garstang, *The Syrian Goddess*, London, 1913.

J. E. HARRISON.

MOURNING.—See DEATH AND DISPOSAL OF THE DEAD.

MOUSE.—See ANIMALS.

MOUTH.—In many ways the mouth is of importance from a religious point of view. It is that by which man speaks to the gods in prayer, or utters or sings their praises; many wind instruments used in sacred rites are blown by its means (see MUSIC); sacred things and persons are kissed with the lips, and the kiss has an important part to play not only in sexual but in social and religious life, while it has also a large folklore of its own.[1] Silence is sometimes even more important than speech with the lips in religion and magic as well as in social affairs.[2] Laughter is also a function of the mouth, and plays a large part in life, while it has likewise a ritual and folklore aspect.[3] The *Bhagavad-Gītā* regards the body as 'the city of nine portals,' of which the mouth is one.[4] Voice and breath are two of the immortal parts of the body, according to the *Śatapatha Brāhmaṇa*, and it calls Indra the breath and Sarasvatī the tongue.[5] On the lips sit the seven *ṛṣis* (the senses), and the tongue is an eighth which communicates with Brahman.[6] In the account of the creation of the different classes in the Rigveda, priests are said to be from the mouth of the primeval man.[7] In the Egyptian *Book of the Dead* the god Anubis has charge of the lips, as other gods have of other parts of the body.[8]

Hell is often conceived in Christian literature and art as a monster with a vast mouth into which souls fall and are swallowed, as already Sheol in Hebrew thought (Pr 1[12]; cf. Nu 16[32f.]). In Scandinavian mythology Hel has also a gaping mouth. Mythology often makes night a monster which devours the light or the sun. Cf. Skr. *rajanīmukha*, 'the mouth of night,' evening.

1. The mouth and the soul.—Whether the soul is regarded as a breath, a mannikin, or a tiny animal, the mouth is one of the orifices by which it may leave the body either during life or at death.[1] Popular sayings like 'to have one's heart in one's mouth' or 'the soul on the lips' illustrate this.[2] It is also seen in the precaution taken by the Hindus of snapping the thumbs to keep the soul back[3] when any one yawns. The soul may escape from the mouth during sleep, as is illustrated by many tales where, in the form of a small animal, it has been seen doing so. By preventing its re-entering one can cause the death of its owner.[4] At death, in the belief of many peoples, the soul finally makes its exit by the mouth. In the *Mahābhārata* (iii. 297) Yama opens the mouth of Satyavīn while he sleeps and draws out his soul, which is afterwards given to his wife, who replaces it in his mouth. Ovid tells how Hylonome applied her lips to those of the dying Cyllarus to prevent his breath leaving him.[5] Homer says that life cannot return once it has passed the lips.[6] On the frescoes of the Campo Santo, Pisa, the soul is depicted as a sexless child leaving the body by the mouth. Similar beliefs are common among savages and with the folk everywhere. Hence, where the soul as a ghost is feared, precautions are sometimes taken to prevent its egress from the mouth. The mouth and other orifices are forcibly closed or stopped up, as among the S. Australians, Itonamas and Cayuvavas (S. America), Malays, New Caledonians, and Marquesas Islanders.[7] In some cases the jaws are bound for the same purpose, and it is possible that, where this is done merely to keep the mouth closed, its real origin may be traced here.[8] The Ainus bind the mouth of a fox when killed first at a hunt, lest its ghost come forth and warn other animals of the hunter's coming.[9]

On the other hand, the desire of recalling the soul to the body gives rise to certain practices connected with the mouth. In China it is stuffed with things endued with vital energy, so that, if the soul returns, revival of the body may be aided and decomposition prevented. Among these are certain minerals, cowries, pearls, grain, and coins, and a ritual is prescribed for the purpose.[10] Similar practices are found in Bali (gold ring on tongue), in Tongking (gold and silver in mouth), and elsewhere.[11] De Groot holds that the placing of a coin in the mouth of the dead had the same purpose. This practice is best known from its use among the Greeks and Romans, but it is also recorded in India (small pieces of gold in mouth, etc., or melted butter allowed to trickle down [Hindus]; coin, etc., placed with dead [non-Aryan tribes]), and among the Litu-Slavs and Teutons.[12] This has been generally regarded either as a fee for the ghostly ferryman, as held by Greeks and Romans themselves, or as part of a gift to the dead, or a commutation of such a gift.[13] The Chinese practice, however,

[1] See KISSING; cf. J. Grimm, *Teutonic Mythology*, tr. J. S. Stallybrass, London, 1882–88, pp. 1101, 1632.
[2] *Ib.* pp. 1102, 1633; cf. Ps 141[3], Ja 3[5ff. 9f.], and Carlyle's frequent praise of silence.
[3] See LAUGHTER; S. Reinach, 'Le Rire rituel,' *Cultes, mythes, et religions*, Paris, 1905–12; Grimm, pp. 1100 f., 1632.
[4] v. 13.
[5] x. i. 3. 4, XII. ix. 1. 14 (cf. IX. i. 1. 13, v. 2. 4).
[6] *Bṛhadāraṇyaka Upaniṣad*, II. ii. 3.
[7] Rigveda, x. xc. 12; cf. also J. Muir, *Orig. Skr. Texts*, i.[2] [1872] 10.
[8] A. Wiedemann, *Religion of the Ancient Egyptians*, London, 1897, p. 272.

[1] Grimm, p. 828 ff.
[2] Seneca, *Nat. Quæst.* iii. præf. 16; Herodias, *Mim.* iii. 3 f.
[3] *PNQ* ii. [1887] 114, § 665.
[4] Grimm, pp. 1082 f., 1548, 1625 f.; R. Chambers, *The Book of Days*, Edinburgh, 1863, i. 276.
[5] *Metam.* xii. 424 f.
[6] *Il.* ix. 409.
[7] J. G. Frazer, *JAI* xv. [1886] 82, and references there; *JAI* viii. [1879] 393; A. d'Orbigny, 'L'Homme américain,' in *Voyage dans l'Amér. méridionale*, Strassburg and Paris, 1839, iv. pt. ii. pp. 241, 257; W. W. Skeat, *Malay Magic*, London, 1900, p. 401; *Annales de la propagation de la foi*, xxxii. [1860] 439; M. Radiguet, *Les derniers Sauvages*[2], Paris, 1882, p. 245.
[8] See DEATH, vol. iv. pp. 473[b], 498[b], 501[a]; cf. 485[a] for Japanese ceremonies for keeping the mouth shut.
[9] J. Batchelor, *The Ainu and their Folk-lore*, London, 1901, p. 504.
[10] J. J. M. de Groot, *Rel. System of China*, Leyden, 1892 ff., i. 269 ff., 278.
[11] *Ib.* i. 279 note.
[12] Lucian, *de Luctu*, 10; cf. *ERE* iv. 474[a], 505[b], 477[a], 480[b], ii. 22[a]; Grimm, pp. 831, 1550, 1785.
[13] A gold coin was put in the dead man's coffin in the W. Isles to pay the ferryman, but the reason is perhaps a classical borrowing (A. Carmichael, *Carmina Gadelica*, Edinburgh, 1900, ii. 238).

throws new light on the subject, and points to a possible origin for the same practice elsewhere, though it came to be regarded otherwise.

To the same origin may be ascribed the practice of filling the mouth of the corpse with food before burial. This, often regarded as a sacrificial feeding of the dead, may have been intended as a means of recalling the soul, though each instance must be examined in its own context, and it must be admitted that quite different reasons are often given by those who practise this rite. Yet, if the dead used earthly food, this would keep them from eating the food of the Other-world, which binds the eater to that world. Thus they might be able to return.[1]

It is found among the Thô of Tongking (*ERE* iv. 418a), some Papuan and Polynesian tribes, and the Badayas (de Groot, i. 357 f.). In the Panjāb leaves of the *tulasi* plant and Ganges water are placed in the mouth as offerings to Yama, that he may be merciful to the dead (*PR* ii. 69). In S.E. India the Kumi fill the corpse's mouth with rice and rice-beer (T. H. Lewin, *Wild Races of S.E. India*, London, 1870, p. 230). At the funeral feast of the father among the Kukis food is placed beside him and his pipe is put in his mouth, and he is bidden to eat because he is going on a long journey (*ib.* p. 273). The ancient Persians dropped *haoma* juice, which produces immortality, or some pomegranate seeds into the mouth of the dying (*ERE* iv. 502b). With this may be compared the practice of putting the Host in the mouth of the dead, which was condemned at the 3rd Council of Carthage and at other councils and synods (J. Bingham, *Origines Ecclesiasticæ*, London, 1829, v. 338, vii. 344).

Of course, if the dead are to be fed at all, it is most natural to place food in the mouth, and in some instances a tube connected with the mouth is made to protrude from the grave so that nourishment may be poured down through it.[2] Where head-hunting is practised, the heads or, rather, the spirits connected with them are often fed by having food placed in the mouth.[3] The Egyptian ceremony of 'opening the mouth and eyes' was performed that the deceased might see and eat the food offerings and utter the right words in the right manner.

As a preparatory rite the mouth and eyes of the mummy or statue representing the deceased were rubbed with part of the food to excite the appetite. Then the *sem* priest addressed the deceased: 'I have set in order for thee thy mouth and thy teeth. I open for thee thy mouth, I open for thee thy two eyes. I have opened thy mouth with the instrument of Anubis, the iron instrument with which the mouths of the gods were opened.' Mouth and eyes were touched with this instrument, and Horus was asked to open the mouth of the deceased as he had opened that of Osiris. With another instrument the lips were touched so that right words might be spoken. Then the mouth was touched with other articles to give life and colour to the lips, and touched again so that the jaw-bones might be established; and, finally, food was then placed in the mouth.[4]

The establishing of the jaw-bones probably refers to an old custom of dismemberment. Various texts speak of restoring the jaw-bones and the mouth in the reconstituted body. The lists of the members of Osiris include lips, mouth, and jaw-bones,[5] and there may have been an ancient rite of cutting out the jaw-bone and preserving it separately. This is done by some African and Melanesian tribes.

In Uganda the king's jaw-bone is cut out and preserved in a special house, where it is consulted as an oracle, as the spirit is supposed to attach itself to it.[6] Widows among the tribes of the Hood peninsula carry the husband's jaw-bone.[1] The Tamos of German New Guinea exhume the corpse after some months and with great ceremony remove and preserve the lower jaw. Similar customs are observed by other tribes of this region.[2] Again, the Saa (Solomon Islands) preserve it with the skull in a hollow wooden image of a fish or in the public canoe-house.[3] In New Britain the jaw-bone is worn by a relative as a means of obtaining its owner's help.[4]

These customs are perhaps akin to that of making trophies of the jaw-bone or lips of enemies, as in Ashanti, Dahomey, Tahiti, etc. (see HEAD, vol. vi. p. 534b), if the purpose is to secure power over the ghost of the dead man.

The Egyptian custom should be compared with the 'way of purifying the three deeds'—body, mouth, and heart—as practised on the deceased by the Shingon sect in Japan.[5] Among the Basoga the lips of the dead are smeared with oil.[6]

2. Hostile spirits and the mouth.—The mouth as a spirit-opening is naturally one which is exposed to the entry of hostile spirits which take possession of a man. In India *bhūts* are thought to enter by the mouth, and in Egypt in common opinion all kinds of evil spirits try to do the same. Various customs are more or less clearly connected with this belief, and have for their object the warding off of such noxious influences. Eating in private is one of these; uttering a charm or performing some ritual act after yawning is another; scrupulous teeth-cleaning, as with the Hindus, is a third; veiling the face is a fourth.[7] Probably the wide-spread custom of knocking out or filing the teeth, usually at puberty, is also connected with these dangers at initiation to man's food.[8] Though, from the savage point of view, tatuing the lips or boring one or both lips and inserting feathers or a wooden or metal plug, which is often increased to large dimensions, is regarded as ornamental, the origin of the practice is perhaps magical. The lip-ornament is a protective charm against spirits entering by the mouth door, or perhaps also against the escape of the soul. This custom is found among the Eskimos, Haidas, and other N. American tribes, and very commonly in S. America (the most extravagant use of it being among the Botocudoes), as well as among many African tribes.[9]

3. The mouth and the breath.—As the soul or life is so often connected with the breath—whether breath in general, or, as has been suggested, the last breath—which may be expelled by a sneeze or yawn, and which leaves the body finally at death,[10] certain rites in connexion with the mouth have arisen. In some instances a relative receives the last breath into his own mouth, by application of his lips to the dying man's, or by a kiss.[11] The Alfoors, on the other hand, close the mouths of animals at a birth lest they swallow the infant's soul, and the mother and others in the house must keep the mouth shut.[12] The breath, again, may have life-giving properties. Hence the Eskimo *angekok* will breathe on a sick man to cure him or give him a new soul;[13] or, as among the Bribri Indians, the medicine-man purifies a woman after

1 Cf. *ERE* iii. 561 f., iv. 653b, v. 682a.
2 A. B. Ellis, *Land of Fetish*, London, 1883, p. 134 (Old Calabar).
3 C. Hose and W. McDougall, *Pagan Tribes of Borneo*, London, 1912, ii. 21, 118; H. Ling Roth, *Natives of Sarawak*, do. 1896, ii. 170.
4 H. M. Tirard, *The Book of the Dead*, London, 1910, p. 23 ff.; E. A. Wallis Budge, *Egyptian Magic*, do. 1899, p. 195 ff., *Osiris and the Egyptian Resurrection*, do. 1911, ii. 49, 92. *The Book of the Making the Spirit of Osiris* says, 'O Form, thou hast thy mouth, thou speakest therewith. Horus has preserved for thee thy mouth. O Form, thy jaw-bones are on thee firmly fixed.' Cf. *The Book of Opening the Mouth*, ed. and tr. Budge, London, 1909, ii. 162.
5 Budge, *Osiris and the Egyptian Resurrection*, i. 387, ii. 49.
6 J. Roscoe, *The Baganda*, London, 1911, p. 109 ff., *JAI* xxxi. [1901] 130; J. F. Cunningham, *Uganda and its Peoples*, do. 1905, p. 226; J. H. Speke, *Journal of the Discovery of the Source of the Nile*, do. 1908, p. 207.

1 R. E. Guise, *JAI* xxviii. [1899] 211.
2 B. Hagen, *Unter den Papua's*, Wiesbaden, 1899, p. 260; R. Neuhauss, *Deutsch-Neu-Guinea*, Berlin, 1911, p. 82.
3 R. H. Codrington, *The Melanesians*, Oxford, 1891, p. 262.
4 G. Brown, *Melanesians and Polynesians*, London, 1910, p. 183.
5 *ERE* iv. 490b.
6 H. H. Johnston, *The Uganda Protectorate*, London, 1902, ii. 718.
7 See *PR* i. 240, ii. 22, 47, and references.
8 A. E. Crawley, *The Mystic Rose*, London, 1902, p. 135 f.
9 A. P. Maximilian von Wied-Neuwied, *Reise nach Brasilien*, Frankfort, 1820, ii. 5 ff.; *Handbook to Ethnographical Collections, Brit. Mus.*, London, 1910, *s.v.* 'Lip-piercing'; O. Stoll, *Das Geschlechtsleben in der Völkerpsychologie*, Leipzig, 1908, p. 98 ff.; W. H. Dall, 'On Masks, Labrets,' etc., *3 RBEW* [1884], p. 73; H. S. Stannus, *JRAI* xl. [1910] 316.
10 So E. Monseur, 'L'Ame poucet,' *RHR* li. [1905] 374.
11 See instances in *ERE* iv. 415a (Nias), 505b.
12 W. F. A. Zimmermann, *Die Inseln des indischen und stillen Meeres*, Berlin, 1860–65, ii. 386.
13 F. Nansen, *Eskimo Life*, London, 1893, p. 227.

child-birth by breathing on her.[1] Healing by breathing or blowing upon a patient is also found among American Indian medicine-men and in Oriental countries. On the other hand, the breath as connected with the life may contaminate sacred objects. Hence these must not be breathed upon, or the mouth must be covered when one is near them.

In Timor the common people, in addressing the Raja, place the hand before the mouth, lest they profane him by their breath.[2] Among the Parsis the priest must cover his mouth and nose with a thick veil—the *paitidāna*—on approaching the sacred fire and other sacred objects.[3] Giraldus Cambrensis relates of the sacred fire in the shrine of St. Brigit at Kildare that it must not be breathed on by those who tended it—probably an earlier pagan Celtic tabu.[4] Similarly the *Laws of Manu* forbid the Brāhman to blow the sacred fire with his mouth.[5] A tabu of this kind is found among the Balkan Slavs in connexion with the sacred house-fire on the hearth.[6] Shinto priests have also to veil their mouths when cooking the sacrificial food, and so have the cooks in the Mikado's kitchen.[7] Saxo Grammaticus tells of a shrine at Rügen so sacred that the priest might not breathe in it, but had to go to the door for that purpose.[8] On the other hand, a Maori chief would not blow upon a fire lest his sacred power should pass to it and so to the food cooked on it, and then to the eater of the food, causing his death.[9]

The old custom of 'scoring above the breath,' *i.e.* making an incision on a witch's forehead to neutralize her evil power, may have been connected with the idea that her evil life-influence came forth with the breath.[10] Saliva, as connected with the mouth, is at once a tabued thing and a source of danger and magic influences and also a safeguard—*e.g.*, against witchcraft—as well as of use in healing rites (see SALIVA).[11]

See also BREATH.

LITERATURE.—This is given throughout the article.

J. A. MACCULLOCH.

MOZOOMDAR.—See BRĀHMA SAMĀJ.

MUGGLETONIANS.—The followers of the London prophets, John Reeve (1608–58) and his cousin Lodowicke Muggleton (1609–98), were designated 'Muggletonians.' Both Reeve and Muggleton were originally Puritans, but Reeve became a Ranter and Muggleton dropped all public worship, being attracted by Boehme's writings and by the prophecies of John Robins and Thomas Tany. In 1651 Muggleton had inward revelations interpreting the Scriptures; Reeve had the same experience next year, and on 3rd–5th Feb. 1652 Reeve announced an audible commission urging him to rebuke Robins and Tany and constituting him the last messenger of the third and final dispensation, Muggleton being his 'mouth.' They were the two witnesses of Rev 11, to announce a new body of doctrine and to declare the eternal destiny of individuals. By 27th July 1652 their *Transcendent Spirituall Treatise* was complete for publication. They declared that all succession had ceased for 1300 years, and, when challenged to prove their new commission, their last resort was to curse their opponents; a few accidents or deaths from fear established their credit. Being imprisoned for blasphemy in 1653, they issued two more pamphlets. Demands for new truth were met by Reeve laying down six principles, published 15th Aug. 1656, as to the person of God, person of angels, person of devils, condition of Adam at his creation and how he lost his estate, heaven and glory, hell and death. The same year a full exposition appeared in *The Divine Looking Glass, or the Third and Last Testament*, printed in the style of the AV.

The leading doctrines run thus. Matter is eternal and independent of God; this earth is the centre of the universe, sun and moon being fixed in the firmament about as big as we see them. God is one and eternal, with a material body rather larger than human, clear as crystal. The One God came to earth as Jesus, entrusting the temporary charge of the universe to Elijah. Angels have spiritual bodies and rational natures; Adam's body was natural, and his soul spiritual. Eve, however, is the important person; one angel and one only fell; he tempted her, entered bodily into her, and there dissolved, whence was born Cain. Eve tempted Adam to carnal intercourse, and thence arose Abel and Seth. Thus in the world are two distinct races, cursed and blessed. The soul is mortal, generated with the body, and returning to dust, whence it shall rise with the body. At the resurrection each person shall be re-created where he died, the wicked lying immovable in eternal lonely misery.

Reeve died in 1658, and Lawrence Clarkson aspired to fill his place, publishing three works. At the Restoration Muggleton was abandoned by many, but he regained his influence, even over Clarkson. He added the new doctrine that God has ceased intervening in the world, so that prayer is useless. For the next few years he was at war with the Friends, till William Penn, in 1672, published his *New Witnesses Proved Old Heretics*. A second secession took place in 1670 in consequence of his Nine Assertions, but Alexander Delamaine and John Saddington vigorously supported him. In 1676 G. Sheldon found some followers near Ashford. Next year he was again indicted for blasphemy, pilloried, imprisoned, and fined. He then wrote his autobiography, and, though no new revelation came, he was highly respected during the rest of his life for practical counsel. An anonymous attack by Bishop J. Williams in 1694 was promptly repelled by Thomas Tomkinson, who, in 1699, published his correspondence and autobiography, under the title *Acts of the Witnesses*.

Though one early revelation was quite explicit, that the end of the world was imminent, belief persisted. Many works were reprinted in 1756, after Swedenborg announced a kindred system, and others were written. Then James Birch led a reformation back to the views of Reeve; but, in 1778, he claimed direct inspiration, so that a secession took place, known especially in Pembroke and Bristol, as well as in London till 1871. A revival occurred about 1829–31, resulting in a fine edition of the primary works in three quarto volumes; and *The Looking Glass* was reprinted even in 1846. Prayer and preaching not being practised, public worship was confined to reading the standard books aloud, and singing the *Divine Songs*; the chief reading-room was in New Street, off Bishopsgate Street. Since 1870 worship seems to have ceased, though annual meetings were held at Denby in Derbyshire within living memory.

LITERATURE.—Sources are cited in the article; for bibliography see Joseph Smith, *Bibliotheca Anti-Quakeriana*, London, 1873. Modern studies are: Alexander Gordon, *The Origin of the Muggletonians*, Liverpool, 1869, *Ancient and Modern Muggletonians*, do. 1870; A. Jessopp, *Coming of the Friars*, London, 1888.

W. T. WHITLEY.

MUHAMMAD.—I. **Historical sources.**—Muhammad († 7th June A.D. 632; called also Aḥmad, and by poets Maḥmūd) Abu'l-Qāsim, sometimes

1 H. Pittier de Fábrega, *SWAW*, phil.-hist. Classe, cxxxviii. [1898] 20.

2 A. Featherman, *Social History of the Races of Mankind*, London, 1881–91, ii. 465.

3 J. Darmesteter, *Le Zend-Avesta*, Paris, 1892–93, i. p. lxi, ii. pp. xv, 214, note 31, 241, note 1; M. Haug, *Essays on the Sacred Language, Writings, and Religion of the Parsis*³, London, 1884, p. 243; cf. Strabo, xv. 3. 14.

4 Gir. Cambr. *Top. Hib.* ii. 34 f.

5 iv. 53.

6 *AE* xiii. [1900] 1.

7 G. F. Moore, *History of Religions*, Edinburgh, 1914, i. 104.

8 Saxo Grammaticus, *Danish History*, tr. and ed. O. Elton, London, 1894, p. 393.

9 R. Taylor, *Te Ika a Maui*², London, 1870, p. 164.

10 See M. M. Banks, 'Scoring a Witch above the Breath,' *FL* xxiii. [1912] 490 f.

11 See *GB*³, pt. ii. *Taboo*, London, 1911, p. 287 ff.; J. G. Bourke, *Scatologic Rites of all Nations*, Washington, 1891, p. 348 f.; *JAFL* iii. [1890] 53 f.; *Proc. Soc. Ant. Scotland*, iv. [1855] 212; *CF*, p. 193.

localized as Al-Tihāmī ('of the Tihāmah' [Mutanabbī, ed. F. Dieterici, Berlin, 1861, p. 331]), known by his followers as 'the Apostle *or* the Prophet of Allāh,' and also by numerous other names, variously estimated at 30, 300, or even 1000 (see the collection in Qasṭallānī's *Mawāhib Laduniyyah*, Cairo, 1278, iii. 133–179), was the founder of the religious and political system called in Europe after him, but named by him Islām or Ḥanīfism. The event in his life which furnishes his followers with an era, viz. his migration (*hijrah*) from Mecca to Medīna, is fixed by synchronism with the Jewish Day of Atonement for 20th September, A.D. 622. That era was introduced several years after his death, and, indeed, for the purpose of arranging the events in his career, by his second successor 'Omar I. (Mubarrad [† 285 A.H.], *Kāmil*, Cairo, 1308, i. 325), whereas the calendar on which it is based uses a lunar year of 354 days, introduced by the Prophet near the end of his life. Since both the calendars and the eras previously employed in Central Arabia are only vaguely known, and the story of 'Omar implies that he had not before heard of an era (which perhaps is confirmed by the fact that the word used for 'era' signifies 'month-making'), accurate dating of events in the Prophet's life is impossible. There is, however, an allusion in the Qur'ān (xxx. 1) to the victory of Chosroes in the Nearer East, which took place A.D. 616, and this agrees with the tradition that Muhammad preached for some ten years in Mecca before his migration. Probably the earliest written account of him is that in the Armenian *Chronicle of Sebeos* (Armen. text, Petrograd, 1879, pp. 104–106; Russ. tr. by K. Patkanian, do. 1862, pp. 116–118), of the 7th cent.; it is very scanty, giving little more than the statement that he was an Ishmaelite who taught his countrymen to return to the religion of Abraham and claim the promises made to the descendants of Ishmael. His career may, therefore, be said to be known entirely from Islāmic sources, which contain no biography that is quite contemporary. The earliest work that was intended to be a chronicle of his life is that by Muḥammad b. Isḥāq (*c.* 150 A.H.), who composed his *Sīrah* ('Biography') for the 'Abbāsid Khalīfah Manṣūr (136–158 A.H. = A.D. 754–775) at least a century and a quarter after the death of his subject. This work does not appear to exist in its entirety, though probably the bulk is preserved in the *Compendium* of Ibn Ḥishām († 218 A.H.) and the *Chronicle* of Ṭabarī († 310 A.H.). Its author was in communication with eminent members of the Prophet's family, but is said to have been a man of indifferent morals, besides being a Shī'ite and a Qadarī (believer in the freedom of the will); he employed versifiers to compose poems to be put into the mouths of the personages who figure in his narrative; and his credibility was otherwise impugned.[1] Contemporary with Ibn Isḥāq was Mūsā b. 'Uqbah († 141), whose collection of *Campaigns* was studied in Cairo as late as the 15th cent., but of which hitherto only some fragments have been discovered (ed. E. Sachau, *SBAW*, 1904), and those of little value. Shāfi'ī († 204) quotes this author once for what is clearly an edifying fable (*Umm*, Cairo, 1321, iii. 100). Later by some fifty years is the work of Wāqidī († 204), which to some extent embodies the same materials as the work of Ibn Isḥāq; and somewhat later still the encyclopædic work of Ibn Sa'd († 230), secretary of Wāqidī, on the Prophet, his family, and his followers. The memoirs or table-talk of the Prophet's associates were collected and tabulated (with infinite repetitions) by the jurist Aḥmad b. Ḥanbal († 241), and the recollections of these persons, after being critically sifted, were arranged in the order of subjects for the use of lawyers by numerous authors shortly after this date, and by some considerably earlier. Very little of this material has historical value. In the main, then, our knowledge of the Prophet's career comes from the work of Ibn Isḥāq.

There is reason for thinking that shortly after Muhammad's death some sketch of his life, comparable to the Christian *paradosis*, was communicated orally to those who embraced Islām, enabling them to understand allusions in the Qur'ān; but this is likely to have been brief, and statements in early law-books indicate that considerable uncertainty prevailed with regard to events of primary importance in the Prophet's biography. It is of interest that the Khalīfah 'Abd al-Malik (65–86 A.H.) wrote to 'Urwah b. Zubair (born 22) for an account of the battle of Badr, and his letter in reply is preserved by Ṭabarī (i. 1284)—as usual, not from a copy but from oral tradition. This personage was born twenty years after the event, and appears in treating the subject to have consulted the Qur'ān. Another letter of this jurist in reply to a question about the sense of the Qur'ān has the appearance of a conjecture as to its meaning rather than of a historical tradition (Ṭabarī, *Commentary*, xxviii. 24). The general suspicion of and objection to written matter other than the Sacred Book which prevailed prior to the foundation of Baghdād, and indeed for some time after, prevented the perpetuation of memoranda or memoirs which would have formed a secure basis for the biography. Although the work of Ibn Isḥāq contains a certain number of ostensibly contemporary documents—*e.g.*, letters and State-papers—their authenticity seems in every case liable to question, not only on internal grounds, but because different authorities are in disagreement about them. It is, indeed, clear that no official collection was ever made of Muhammad's correspondence, treaties, and rescripts; Shāfi'ī († 204), who appears to have made accurate search in Arabia, could find nothing in writing referable to the Prophet except the Qur'ān and one apocryphal document, of which he knew only by hearsay. Contemporary treaties, produced in ancient and modern times, have been shown to be fabrications by the anachronisms which they contain (see Yāqūt, i. 248).

The Qur'ān appears to be for the most part authentic, but those who collected it avoided chronological arrangement as much as possible, combining in the same *sūrahs*, or chapters, matter belonging to widely different periods. In order to use it for historical purposes the reader has to interpret it by Ibn Isḥāq's biography; but there are many cases in which that biography appears to be conjectural interpretation of the Qur'ān. It is true that the commentaries on the latter, of which one on an enormous scale was compiled by the historian Ṭabarī in the middle of the 3rd Islāmic cent., profess to locate most or all of the texts; but, unfortunately, they give a variety of locations, and leave on the mind the impression that nothing was certainly known or remembered about the 'occasions of revelation' beyond what the texts themselves imply.

If, in spite of these considerations, the general trustworthiness of Ibn Isḥāq's narrative is probably to be maintained, there are three reasons for this. (1) The practice ascribed to the second Khalīfah of assigning pensions to the Muslims, which varied with the length of time during which they had been members of the community, accounts for the existence of lists of fighters in various battles, and for the preservation of the chronological order of

[1] See Yāqūt, *Dictionary of Learned Men*, ed. D. S. Margoliouth, London, 1907 ff., vi. 399–401.

those battles, since each was followed by some accessions. (2) The biography rarely has recourse to the supernatural, and, when this element is introduced, it does not appear to affect the causation; where, *e.g.*, angels or the devil take part in battles, they do not really contribute to the result. (3) The character which the narrator ascribes to his prophet is, on the whole, exceedingly repulsive. To this may be added the fact that, although Ibn Isḥāq wrote for an 'Abbāsid patron, he takes very little trouble to glorify his ancestor 'Abbās, whereas he paints a pleasing picture of Abū Ṭālib, the uncle of the Prophet, whose son 'Alī was the head of a family which also claimed to succeed the Prophet. Hence it is clear that this biographer has not as a rule yielded to the temptations which lead astray men in his position.

2. Life.—For the present purpose the briefest sketch of the Prophet's career, as Ibn Isḥāq narrates it, will suffice.

It is not possible to throw any serious doubt on the location of Muhammad as a member of a numerous Meccan family, though the name of his father excites suspicion, since 'Abdallāh' (the equivalent of 'some one') is used at a later period as a substitute for an unknown name; perhaps it is in this case a substitute for a name of which the second element was that of a pagan deity. Few have accepted the suggestion of Sprenger[1] that the name 'Muḥammad' itself was adopted by the Prophet when he entered on his prophetic career; for the name is found in pre-Islāmic inscriptions, and its connexion with the prophecy Hag 27, 'and the desire (*ḥemdath*) of all nations shall come,' seems to be an afterthought; there is therefore no reason for supposing that this name or its variants had Messianic associations. According to the biography, the life of Muhammad falls into four periods. (1) For forty years he lived as a pagan at Mecca (which comes into history with his enterprise, not having been mentioned previously). At the age of twenty-five he married a woman much older than himself, who bore him one or more sons (who died in infancy) and four daughters. In his fortieth year he became the recipient of revelations, wherein the office of prophet was conferred upon him. (2) For three years he carried on private propaganda, winning some adherents in his own family, among his private friends, and among the humbler classes in the town. (3) For ten years he carried on his mission publicly in Mecca, for the greater part of the time under the protection of his uncle Abū Ṭālib, who was not a believer; after his death the mission had for a time to be transferred to Ṭā'if, until another protector could be found among the Meccan magnates. Meanwhile a temporary refuge had been obtained for the Prophet's persecuted followers in Christian Abyssinia. Towards the end of this period the continuance of civil war at Yathrib (Medīna) suggested to some of the inhabitants the desirability of securing a prophet to settle their disputes. Muhammad was invited to undertake this task, and accepted; but he wisely sent his followers before him to Yathrib to serve as a bodyguard when he arrived; he himself escaped with difficulty from Mecca, where danger was anticipated from this move. (4) Once in Medīna, he proceeded to organize his followers as an army, ruthlessly suppressed internal opposition, secured the alliance of various Arabian tribes, and started raiding the Meccan caravans. Involved in war with his former fellow-citizens, he inflicted on them a series of defeats, culminating in the capture of the city in the eighth year of his migration. By the end of his life he had imposed his doctrine on the whole of Arabia, exterminating the Jewish communities, with few exceptions, rendering the Christian communities tributary, and abolishing paganism.

So far as this career is that of a military and political adventurer, countless parallels could be adduced. A man who can organize an armed force and lead it to victory may rise from obscurity to autocracy anywhere. Probably every century of Islām has its tale of such personages. The 'Abbāsid, Fāṭimid, Buwaihid, Seljūq, and Ottoman dynasties all arose in this way; and in most of these the religious appeal played an important part. The success of the founders was clearly due not to the objective truth of the doctrines with which they were associated, but to their skill as organizers and military leaders. In Muhammad's case, owing to the amount of information which we possess about him, it is easier to analyze the qualities which produced success than where the records are scantier. In the first place, his ability to gauge the capacities of others was abnormal; hence in the choice of subordinates he seems to have made no mistakes. In the second place, he was thoroughly familiar with the foibles of the Arabs, and utilized them to the utmost advantage. The stories of his successes as told by Ibn Isḥāq indicate a complete absence of moral scruple; but they also show a combination of patience, courage, and caution, ability to seize opportunities, and distrust of loyalty when not backed by interest, which fully explain the certainty with which results were won. If his age is correctly recorded, and no events of great importance in his early life concealed, his military career began when he was over fifty; this seems astonishingly late, yet analogies, if not parallels, can be found. Surprise is also excited by the ease with which the Arabs abandoned their gods and goddesses, readily accepting the logic of the stricken field; for, though new prophets arose after Muhammad's death, there appears to have been no recrudescence of paganism. Yet to this, too, some analogies can be discovered. The fact of primary importance in the rise of Islām is that the movement became considerable only when its originator was able to draw the sword and handle it successfully. That he was summoned to Yathrib was doubtless due in part to the presence of a Jewish element in that community, intellectually further advanced than the Arab tribes, which at first evidently favoured this advocate of monotheism; that he was able to make the fullest use of that opportunity was due to his own ability. The only difficulties which are to be found in his career are, therefore, those which render all history difficult. It is impossible to say why one man should be more gifted than his fellows, or why opportunities should occur for the development of special talents.

According to the Qur'ān (xliii. 30), he was not a 'great man' in his city, and, if the words of xciii. are to be taken literally, he lost his parents at an early age, and at some period was poor and burdened with a family. The question whether he could read and write has been much discussed, and it is unfortunate that we do not know certainly whether those accomplishments formed the basis of education in Mecca when he was a lad; there is, however, some slight reason for supposing that they did. The evidence indicates that he could do both of them, but not well. Thus, when he records the charge made against him of copying the ancient history which he reproduced in the Qur'ān from dictation (xxv. 5 f.), he does not rebut it by the assertion that he could not write. The tradition makes him a tradesman, and can even name his partner and the goods in which he dealt. Some have tried to find evidence of this in the language of the Qur'ān, which undoubtedly takes metaphors from sale and barter, profit and loss; but whether it does so to a greater extent than other books may be doubted. Some stories say that he was employed by his first wife Khadījah in the conduct of a caravan; and others tell of him following this occupation early in life.

It is, on the whole, probable that he travelled in his youth, for, though the geography of the Qur'ān is vague, the descriptions of travel which it contains seem to be based on personal experiences. Moreover, the charge of ignorance which is repeatedly made against the people of Mecca is more likely to have been brought by one who had some acquaintance with a higher civilization.

3. Origins and development of system.—The tradition does, indeed, name precursors of Muhammad at Mecca, among them a relative of his wife who had either copied or translated a portion of a gospel. Since Christianity had made progress in both N. and S. Arabia, it is not unlikely either that missionaries had found their way to Central Arabia, or that travellers thence had had their curiosity aroused and made inquiries into the system. The phenomena of the Qur'ān on the

[1] *Das Leben und die Lehre des Mohammad*, i. 158.

whole render it improbable that any part of it is based on book-learning; for, though in one place the Psalms are quoted with fair accuracy (xxi. 105 = Ps 37^{29}), the nature of the references is ordinarily explicable only as the reproduction of hearsay. Thus it cites (liii. 37 f., lxxxvii. 19) 'the Scrolls of Moses and Abraham' for maxims that are analogous to those occurring in the Prophets or the NT, though not quite identical with them; and the mode of quotation implies that the writer had a vague notion of the book cited, such as actual perusal would have corrected. Further, the form assumed by the proper names and the religious technicalities indicates a great variety of linguistic sources; for in these Ethiopic, Greek, Syriac, Hebrew, and perhaps other languages are represented. Some of the proper names are not at present traceable to any version of the Scriptures—*e.g.*, Ṭālūt for Saul, 'Īsā for Jesus. Moreover, from the manner in which the Biblical narratives are told it is difficult to imagine that the writer was acquainted with the continuous history of the Bible; he knows only stories out of it. All this points to the probability that Muhammad heard the stories from narrators of different nationalities, who translated them orally into Arabic, leaving on their hearer a decidedly vague impression, in spite of the fact that they interested him keenly. Besides the canonical books, various uncanonical works contribute to the matter of the Qur'ān, which, in addition, refers to prophets not mentioned elsewhere. The Prophet was charged with employing as mentor a resident in Mecca, and after the migration to Medīna, where there were Jews, he may have been able to utilize the Biblical learning of one or other among his converts. But it seems probable that what was reproduced during the Meccan period had been heard from travelling companions or from Jews and Christians whom he had met in foreign parts.

Prior to his call Muhammad is said to have practised ascetic retirement on Mt. Ḥirā, and for this an old technicality, *taḥannuth*, is preserved, which is said to mean 'to acquire merit,' and certainly has nothing to do with the Heb. *tᵉḥinnôth*, 'supplications.' The call itself evidently took the form of a command to read, which the Prophet reluctantly obeyed. The communications embodied in the Qur'ān were, according to the tradition, made to the Prophet and uttered by him in trance; he would wrap himself in a blanket and perspire copiously at the time. A certain number of these stories may be inference from *sūrahs* lxxiii. and lxxiv., where the Prophet is addressed as 'Thou that art wrapped up,' combined with *sūrah* xcvi. (supposed to be the first revelation), where he is bidden 'read.'

The form of the utterances at times approaches verse, *i.e.* a series of sentences in which the same quantity and quality of syllables are reproduced, the termination of each unit being marked by rhyme, whereas more usually rhyme only, and this of a somewhat loose character, is observed. The relation of this Qur'ānic style to the verse and rhymed prose of classical Arabic is an enigma which cannot at present be solved. An artifice based on the recurrence of letters is obviously literary; *i.e.*, it depends for its existence on the practice of writing, since only those who are accustomed to read and write think of their words as agglomerations of letters; to the illiterate the word, if not the sentence, is the unit. Indeed, in what is supposed to be the earliest revelation the deity is said to have taught with the *calamus*, or reed-pen. The existence of poets before the Qur'ān is attested by a *sūrah* which is directed against them (xxvi.) and a text in which the deity states that He had not taught Muhammad poetry (xxxvi. 69). If the poetry which existed before the Qur'ān was analogous to the classical poetry, the people of Mecca cannot have been in the state of naive ignorance with which the Qur'ān credits them; yet the poetry which is ascribed to the Umayyad period—*i.e.* the second half of the 1st Islāmic cent.—is to a great extent clearly authentic, while its authors represent the continuance of a pagan tradition. With regard to rhymed prose, probably we have nothing in this style that is certainly genuine and older than the 2nd cent. of Islām. It is, however, a much easier performance than verse, though no less dependent on writing. Oracles are supposed to have been delivered in it by pre-Muhammadan wizards.

Now the respect of ignorance for knowledge is a well-attested phenomenon, displayed in the desire of the Prophet that Jews and Christians should not be molested in the exercise of their creeds. It is therefore unlikely that the poets and wizards who preceded Muhammad presented a higher stage of education; hence, according to natural sequence, the style of the Qur'ān would seem to come between such naive jingles as may have counted for versification in Arabia and the highly artificial products with which we meet in the Umayyad period. It would follow that all the pre-Islāmic poetry as well as all that ostensibly belongs to the time of the Prophet and his immediate successors is spurious; but, as has been seen, the spuriousness of that which is incorporated in the Prophet's biography is otherwise attested; and the most distinguished philologists of the early 'Abbāsid period, to whose labours we owe our collections of early poetry, were unscrupulous fabricators.

The Prophet, then, claimed to introduce literature into his native language, and the form was probably modelled on the quasi-poetic experiments which had preceded the Qur'ān. It is, however, very noticeable that in his lifetime his book resembled a newspaper in having a fluid rather than a stationary existence; it was as a whole continuous, but each number had ephemeral importance. The theory was gradually evolved that it was a reproduction of a divine archetype, first as a series of copies, then as a single copy. The complete development of this theory was not possible before the collection of the Qur'ān; and the Prophet himself never thought of attempting such an undertaking.

The difference between his first conception of a prophet and that current in ancient Israel, before the literary prophet had arisen, was perhaps not very great. The oracles were partly spontaneous, partly required for emergencies; their form differed from that of ordinary speech by the presence of an artifice; and the prophet delivered them in what spiritualists call 'the superior condition.' At times the oracles were supplemented by dreams. Further, the Hebrew prophet was a 'warner,' which is one of the epithets applied by Muhammad to himself; he foretold misfortunes, which, however, were ordinarily contingent, since it was his business to indicate the line of conduct whereby they could be averted. Muhammad's notions of prophecy seem to have been chiefly influenced by those cases in which the prophet also claimed to be the head of the community, its priest and its king.

Attempts have been made by Sprenger and others to specify the epileptic fits which in Muhammad's case ostensibly accompanied the revelations; but it is doubtful how far these are to be regarded as real occurrences. It is clear that he was a man of great physical strength, since his life as tyrant of Medīna was spent in constant military expeditions, added to the cares of a rapidly increasing community, of which he was at once priest, legislator, ruler, and judge. Yet we never hear of his health breaking down under the strain. The 'fits' seem to have been experienced only when they were required for the delivery of the revelations, and in no case to have interfered with his activities.

A message must have matter as well as form, and, when Muhammad became head of a State, his Qur'ān served as government organ, containing rescripts and something like an official chronicle of important events, with comments upon them. But before the migration the matter was not so easily supplied. To a certain extent it reproduces narratives from the Christian Bible, which *ex hypothesi* could not have been known to Muhammad from books, and therefore must have been communicated to him by direct inspiration, and so are a proof of the miraculous character of the whole work. The chief purpose of these and of the other messages is to insist on the importance of obeying God's messengers implicitly.

It is not easy to say whether Muhammad had any desire to inculcate any particular doctrine, for there appears to be none which he was not prepared to abandon under political pressure, and the tradition represents his followers as far more attached than himself to the dogmas. The main doctrines of the early teaching are the future life, the unity of God, and the folly of idolatry. Since he ultimately retained in his system the kissing of the Black Stone (cf. *ERE* vii. 743[a]), it is difficult to treat the campaign against idolatry as quite serious. The doctrine of the future life was preached in the early days as a warning of the approaching end of the world and the Day of Judgment; yet he had afterwards to make the martyrs in his cause enter paradise at once, and his enemies enter hell immediately after death—a belief not easily reconciled with the former. According to Ṭabarī, during the Meccan period he at one time, under stress, issued a revelation admitting the Meccan goddesses to his pantheon; and, though this text was expunged from the Qur'ān, the apology for it, viz. that it was the devil's interpolation, remains (liii. 19–23, xxii. 51; see *ERE* vii. 150). He even consented at one time to erase his title 'Apostle of God' from a document, when it stood in the way of the ratification of a treaty. Even the formula with which the *sūrahs* and other documents commence shows clear signs of compromise: 'In the name of Allah the Raḥmān the Merciful.' Since the last adjective is an Arabic rendering of the second, which is Aramaic, used as a divine name by Jews and pagans, and in Arabic not an epithet, but a name, some mystery must lie behind the employment of this name with a translation following it. The tradition suggests that the name 'Allāh' was familiar to the Meccans, but not the name 'Raḥmān,' which, indeed, had been adopted by one or more false Messiahs. In certain parts of the Qur'ān, however, it may be said to be dominant. This formula, then, was doubly accommodated to Meccan prejudices.

The tradition does not conceal the fact that the 'canons of Islām' were of slow growth; it is probable that the part of the programme which never varied was the restoration of the religion of Abraham. One of Muhammad's precursors, Zaid b. 'Amr, is represented as travelling with the view of discovering the religion of this patriarch, from whom the tribes of N. Arabia, according to Genesis, are descended. It is not probable that his name was known in Mecca before Muhammad introduced it; but in doing so he was treading on safe ground, since the 'people of learning,' *i.e.* Jews and Christians, were agreed about the relationship. If the tradition is to be trusted, the new system was called by the Meccans 'Ṣābism,' a name connected historically with Ḥarrān, where a cult of Abraham is likely to have existed; the Ḥarrānians appear to have been called Ḥənpē, 'heathens,' by their Christian neighbours, and possibly this is the solution of the puzzling name 'Ḥanīf' applied in the Qur'ān to the religion of Abraham, and synonymous with 'Muslim,' which, according to the same book (vi. 163), was a title invented by the patriarch. The Qur'ānic tales about Abraham are traceable to the Jewish Midrash; what is chiefly known about his religion is that he was an iconoclast, and was not one of the *mushrikūn*, *i.e.* polytheists. When the Prophet decided to make the Meccan pilgrimage part of his system, he ascribed the building of the Ka'bah to Abraham and Ishmael (ii. 119 ff.), and brought the prayer-ceremonial into connexion with the former. It is probable, though not certain, that both that ceremonial and the fasting month are Ḥarrānian.

There is reason for thinking that, besides the prohibition of idolatry, the earliest form of Islām enjoined certain daily ceremonies which were afterwards developed and regulated until they became stereotyped as the five *ṣalawāt*; and it is not easy to dissociate from these the theory of legal purity, which, however, seems to have existed in parts of pagan Arabia, since some of the technicalities are found in Sabæan inscriptions. Of the actual growth of the ritual or liturgy nothing certain is known; the prayer which corresponds with the *Paternoster*, and is called the *Fātiḥah* ('Opener') because it is prefixed to the Qur'ān, contains polemical references to Jews and Christians ('those who have incurred anger and those who go astray'), which point to a late period in the Prophet's career; for his hostilities with the Jews did not commence until after the migration, and those with Christians were some years later. Moreover, the prayer-ceremonies were connected with military drill, which is unlikely to have been required before the raising of an army was contemplated.

The other canons or main institutions of Islām—the pilgrimage, the fasting month, and the tax called 'alms' (*zakāt* or *ṣadaqah*)—belong to the Medīna period, though they cannot be precisely dated. The establishment of the first indicates the Prophet's resolve to conciliate so far as possible the pagans of Mecca, and to abandon Judaism, which on his arrival at Medīna he was inclined to adopt; it belongs to the same policy as that which dictated his making the Meccan temple the direction of prayer instead of Jerusalem (ii. 139 f.). The fasting month, whatever its origin, is evidently a military exercise; on the one hand, it accustoms the fighting men to endure privation, and, on the other, it trains them to turn night into day. The alms or income-tax of 2½ per cent is organized poor relief. An innovation which is at least as important as the canons, though it is not termed one, is the tabu on intoxicants (ii. 218, v. 92), which is said to have been introduced in the third year of the migration, and appears to belong to military discipline. There may, however, be some truth in the idea of W. G. Palgrave[1] that this tabu is definitely anti-Christian in intent.

It is probable, then, that the positive parts of Islāmic teaching belong to the period after the migration, and that these were largely suggested by the Judaism which the Prophet got to know there. His usual plan when he adopted institutions was to disguise the borrowing; but he also introduced serious modifications. Thus, in the case of the Sabbath he not only shifted the day from Saturday to Friday, but reduced the time when business might not be transacted to the period occupied by the mid-day religious service (lxii. 9 f.). Instead of the elaborate system of

[1] *Central and Eastern Arabia*, London, 1865, i. 428.

food-tabus which occupies so prominent a place in the Mosaic code, he adopted the minimum retained by the Council of Jerusalem, recorded in Ac 15, with the tabu on swine's flesh which some think was originally to be found in those regulations (ii. 168, v. 4, xvi. 116). He held that each of the communities (Jewish and Muslim) might eat the food of the other, and, indeed, went out of his way to record in the Qur'ān what he supposed to be the Jewish rules on the subject (vi. 147).

From Christianity he appears to have taken very little in the way of either doctrine or practice. His first relations with Christians seem to have been friendly, and, as has been seen, during the Meccan period he is said to have found a refuge for persecuted followers at Christian Axum; at a later period he used eulogistic language of Christian monks whom the Qur'ān had affected to tears (v. 85 ff.). He supposed (v. 116) the Christians to worship three deities, Allāh, the Virgin Mariam, and 'Īsā, whom he identified with the spirit of God, but also called 'a Word' (iv. 169). When he became acquainted with the division of Christendom on the subject of the nature of Christ, he conceived that it was his mission to settle the dispute; it is noticeable that he fully accepted the Virgin-birth and the Ascension, though not the Resurrection, as he denied that Christ had been crucified; but he rejected with vehemence the doctrine of the divinity of Christ (xix. 17 ff., iii. 40 ff., iv. 156). Sprenger fancies that he horrified his Christian visitors by his *ḥarīm* as much as he shocked his Jewish subjects by his ignorance of the OT;[1] what is certain is that the embassy from Christian Najrān which waited on him in Medīna, when his power was making progress in Arabia, ultimately eschewed religious discussion and resigned themselves to the payment of tribute.

4. Relation of system to paganism.—Comparison between Muhammad's system and that of those which it displaced in non-Christian Arabia is difficult owing to the fragmentary nature of our information about the latter. The name applied to the heathen Arabs in the Qur'ān, *mushrikūn*, if it really means 'those who assign associates to Allāh,' would imply that these pagans were to some extent monotheists, *i.e.* recognized one Supreme Power; but it is curious that the subordinate deities are called 'their' partners, *i.e.* of their worshippers (vi. 138). It is likely that the communities had their tribal and local cults, the abolition of which was regarded as a preliminary for the political union of Arabia. In order to employ monotheism for a political and, indeed, imperialistic object the deity had to be treated as a tribal god, favouring one community and hostile to all others. The men whose accession to Islām after the migration led to its great military successes, especially Khālid b. al-Walīd and 'Amr b. al-'Āṣ, appear to have had little or no religious conviction, but to have been moved by admiration for the Prophet's military and diplomatic skill, and anxious to serve under so able a chief. So far as religion entered into their consideration, they probably thought of the god of the community as leading it in war, and found the deity of the Muslim society able to defeat the others. More devout members of that society regarded the Prophet as able to call in the divine aid whenever he was in need of it. As the political programme increased, doctrine diminished in importance; and the institution of practices seems to have been based on the desire to give the new system the equivalent of what other systems possessed, in order that those others might have no rival attractions.

5. The Prophet's sincerity.—The question of Muhammad's sincerity in his claim to be the spokesman or προφήτης of the deity has often been discussed, and various views have been held on the subject; as examples we may quote that of Sprenger, who regards Muhammad's assertions on this subject as a case of epileptic mendacity,[1] while L. Caetani finds no contradiction between his supposed elaborate preparation of revelations and his ascription of them to direct communication from the deity.[2] The former view, as has already been seen, is scarcely tenable; nor does the latter correspond with the facts, for the revelations furnish little indication of elaborate preparation, and, when once delivered, they appear to have been neglected; there are, indeed, traditions of collections of revelations having been made by some of his followers, but it seems certain that Muhammad himself kept no such collection. Caetani's theory, however, is probably sound to this extent, that in Muhammad's case, as in those of many other men of vast energy and ability, there was a belief or consciousness of being directed by the deity, which, however, by no means led to his trusting anything to chance; and, while the angels whom he declared to have won his battles were partly pious, partly poetical personifications of the heroism of his followers, he was fully conscious of the value of attributing his victories to these supernatural auxiliaries; to be defeated by angelic cavalry was no discredit to any foe. He was also quite conscious of the value attaching to the right to dictate the moral law.

6. Moral reforms.—As a moral reformer Muhammad has to his credit the abolition of infanticide, which, if we may trust the Qur'ān (xvi. 61 f., lxxxi. 8 f.), was commonly practised in Arabia in the case of female infants. On the other hand, serious evil was caused by his institution (v. 91) of compensation for oaths, *i.e.* the principle that an oath might be violated at the pleasure of the person who had sworn it, if he performed some sort of penance. While the Qur'ān scarcely formulates any general principles of morals, it on the whole insists on *moderation*, and probably aimed at no considerable departure from current notions on these matters. Hence it tolerates polygamy and unlimited concubinage, and assumes the institution of slavery. In the matter of the blood-feud Muhammad did not contemplate complete abolition, but he endeavoured to mitigate its consequences and favoured mild reprisals (ii. 173–175). With the institution of private property and the acquisition of wealth he found no fault, and he deprecated extravagance in almsgiving as in other matters. The quality of personal courage he rated very high, and, though he often inspired it by the promise of paradise, it is clear that his followers were largely persons who required no such stimulus to make them brave. The ascetic morality afterwards taught by Ṣūfī preachers and, if the tradition is to be believed, approved by some of Muhammad's early adherents finds little support in any interpretation of the Qur'ān that is reasonably literal, and clearly receives no countenance from the Prophet's own career, if any credibility attaches to his biography. Like other sovereigns, he claimed a large share of the booty won in his raids as his perquisite, and appropriated territory as his domain.

It is not clear, then, that Muhammad can be credited with any considerable reform except in the matter of infanticide, whereas in the subordination of the family tie to the religious brotherhood he appears to have weakened one social sanction without introducing any other equally strong by way of compensation. The history of this sub-

[1] ii. 371.

[1] i. 207 ff.

[2] *Annali dell' Islamo*, Milan, 1905 ff., i. 204 ff.

ordination can be traced in the Qur'ān rather more continuously than most institutions.

Where moral codes are drawn up, as is the case in several *sūrahs*, honour to parents is given a high place in the list of commandments. When Abraham is first introduced, he prays for his parents; then he becomes involved in a dispute with his father on the subject of idolatry, but promises to pray for him; and this, when Abraham next comes on the scene, he actually does. But after the migration, when the younger generation were joining Muhammad against the wishes of their parents, such filial duty towards their unbelieving parents was thought undesirable; hence they are forbidden to pray for the latter, and Abraham's conduct is excused on the ground that he had made the promise; finally, Abraham himself is represented as repudiating all parental claims, and his conduct is declared exemplary except for his undertaking to pray for his father (xiv. 42, xix. 42–49, xxvi. 70 ff., xliii. 25, lx. 115, lx. 4).

This is only one example of the movement in the direction of intolerance which the Qur'ān exhibits as it proceeds. The Prophet undoubtedly wished to make Muslim life as sacrosanct within the Muslim world as in the old tribal system the tribesman's life had been within the tribe; but in this he failed, since his first followers eventually waged civil war with each other, and in the history of Islām the victims of massacres by Muslim Sulṭāns have frequently been Muslim communities, and, indeed, families claiming descent from the Prophet himself.

7. Toleration.—On the question of religious toleration the Qur'ān contains a series of utterances belonging to different periods, and varying from large-minded tolerance to extreme fanaticism. In one text (v. 73) future happiness is promised to four communities—believers, Jews, Ṣābians, and Christians—on condition of their believing in Allāh and the last day, and doing good works; in another the last three communities are mentioned with the pagans and the Mazdæans in a context which implies that the prospect before them is less satisfactory (xxii. 17). At times no form even of controversy is permitted except rivalry in kindness; elsewhere the Muslims are told to fight with other communities relentlessly until they accept Islām or pay tribute, which they are to bring in humiliation. Friendship with members of other communities is forbidden. The most intolerant utterances are the latest ones, but the progress in this direction does not seem to have been regular. The permission granted the Muslims to conceal their faith if confession is dangerous (iii. 27, as ordinarily explained) is characteristic of a system which is more political than religious. The ultimate system adopted was to permit the existence of communities which professed to follow a revealed book, but to disarm them and make them tributary; this condition is identified by some jurists with that of slaves. The existence of communities to which this description did not apply was forbidden. Since the chief Christian doctrine is said in the Qur'ān (xix. 92) to be so blasphemous as to be calculated to produce a general convulsion of nature, this toleration, though praiseworthy, is clearly illogical; for we can scarcely conceive a convulsion of nature being averted by the payment of a moderate poll-tax.

8. Legislation. — As a legislator Muhammad probably perpetuated current practice rather than introduced a fresh system, and the Qur'ān is on many grounds ill-suited for a basis of jurisprudence. It is imperfect, self-contradictory, and destitute of order. So far as any principle can be traced in its arrangement, the collector seems to have been anxious to avoid any semblance of chronological order, whence, in the case of conflicting enactments, it has to be supplemented by tradition. Where there is anything like systematic treatment of any topic—*e.g.*, the laws of inheritance in *sūrah* iv.—the signs of improvisation are very apparent; and even a little consideration should have shown the barbarity and folly of the punishment of hand-cutting for theft (v. 42). There is a curious tradition that on his death-bed Muhammad desired to frame a code for the guidance of the community; but to those who supposed that they had in the Qur'ān the actual word of God this utterance not unnaturally seemed delirious. The State, however, suffered very seriously for the want of guidance in the matter of appointing successors to the sovereign; and until the introduction of European codes it was never able to get rid of the doctrine that all law was to be got from the Qur'ān or the Prophet's equally inspired conduct, and so lacked the power to legislate on a sound basis.

9. Philosophy.—Though it is not probable that Muhammad had any liking for metaphysical speculation, the rôle which he had assumed rendered it necessary for him to formulate views on various matters which any form of religious propaganda brings to the front. The reduction of these questions and their answers to precise and philosophical form probably belongs to a later age, and, indeed, in the tradition Muhammad names sects which came into existence a century or more after his death; but in a vaguer form the Qur'ān deals with them, and so furnishes a basis for theology, though one of doubtful firmness. His theory of the deity is, on the whole, naively anthropomorphic; the Allāh of the Qur'ān has been compared to a magnified Oriental despot. A royal court is formed by the angels; Jibrīl conveys messages to the Prophet (ii. 91), whereas others are sent, mounted on horses, to fight the Prophet's battles (iii. 125, viii. 9, ix. 26, 40). Other intelligent beings are the *jinn*, or *shaiṭāns*, whose prince is Iblīs; the second word is taken from the Ethiopic, the third from the Syriac transliteration of the Greek; the δ of διάβολος was mistaken for the Syriac sign of the genitive, somewhat as Ὀδύσσεια gets transformed into *Liber essentiæ*. To these the Prophet preaches (perhaps through a vague reminiscence of 1 P 3[19]), and some are converted (xlvi. 28–30, lxxii. 1 ff.). Satan himself is the power that makes for evil, causes men to forget, and even interpolates the oracles of prophets. He has the divine permission to mislead mankind for a season (xv. 37–39). The Qur'ān, on the whole, seems to favour the theory of predestination, but there are passages which contradict it, and to those who impugn it an evasive answer rather than a rejoinder is given (see art. FATE [Muslim]). The resurrection of the body is taught in a crude form, and the future life is thought of as one of bodily pains and pleasures; hence metaphysical questions concerning the soul are scarcely touched. The creation is narrated mainly as in Gn 1, but with the addition of some apocryphal matter. The teleological argument for the existence of God is often emphasized.

10. The Prophet's apologists.—The distinction drawn in the case of the founder of Christianity by D. F. Strauss[1] between the historical and the mythical can be accommodated to that of the founder of Islām, though as regards Muhammad we have not so much to sift canonical documents as to contrast the impressions left by the biography of Ibn Isḥāq with the character of the Prophet as it appears at later periods of Islām. That biography, as will be seen, left room for some important supplements and called for modification in certain respects.

The character attributed to Muhammad in the biography of Ibn Isḥāq is, as has been seen, exceedingly unfavourable. In order to gain his ends he recoils from no expedient, and he approves of similar unscrupulousness on the part of his adherents, when exercised in his interest. He profits

[1] *Das Leben Jesu für das deutsche Volk bearbeitet*, Leipzig, 1864, p. xxiv.

to the utmost from the chivalry of the Meccans, but rarely requites it with the like. He organizes assassinations and wholesale massacres. His career as tyrant of Medīna is that of a robber-chief, whose political economy consists in securing and dividing plunder, the distribution of the latter being at times carried out on principles which fail to satisfy his followers' ideas of justice. He is himself an unbridled libertine and encourages the same passion in his followers. For whatever he does he is prepared to plead the express authorization of the deity. It is, however, impossible to find any doctrine which he is not prepared to abandon in order to secure a political end. At different points in his career he abandons the unity of God and his claim to the title Prophet.

This is a disagreeable picture for the founder of a religion, and it cannot be pleaded that it is a picture drawn by an enemy; and, though Ibn Isḥāq's name was for some reason held in low esteem by the classical traditionalists of the 3rd Islāmic cent., they make no attempt to discredit those portions of the biography which bear hardest on the character of their Prophet. The theory that this person's conduct was a model for his followers has in consequence done serious mischief.

Apologies for Muhammad were started in the 18th cent. by H. de Boulainvilliers,[1] who was favoured by Gibbon because this apology provided some instruments against Christianity. More importance was attached to the lecture of Carlyle on 'The Hero as Prophet,' incorporated in the collection called *On Heroes and Hero-Worship* (London, 1841), in which Muhammad was taken as the type of a heroic prophet, just as Odin was made the type of a heroic divinity, the author's knowledge of the two personalities being about equal. Another apologist who acquired some popularity was Bosworth Smith,[2] who, too, was satisfied with superficial and second-hand information, and committed the error of basing his estimate of Muhammad's character and aims on the ill-recorded Meccan period instead of on the far more accurately chronicled period of Medīna. No European apologist for Muhammad seems to have possessed any proper acquaintance with the Arabic sources. Only after the definite assertion of European superiority over the world of Islām, which may be dated from the Napoleonic invasion of Egypt, and the acquisition of European nationality or its equivalent by large numbers of Muslims, has the necessity for apologies made itself felt in Muslim communities. The most prominent writer on this side is Syed Ameer Ali,[3] but there are many others. These apologists endeavour to discredit the biography of Ibn Isḥāq where it shocks the European reader; and, where this cannot easily be done, they suggest honourable motives or suppose the course followed by the Prophet to have been the least objectionable of those that were open to him at the time. Thus his toleration of polygamy is declared to have been a limitation with the view of ultimate suppression, and his attitude towards slavery is regarded as similarly intended to lead to its abolition. He has even been made to set an example of monogamy, but the ingenuity required for this is so great that the result is unconvincing.

But, while Muslim dogma, by assuming that whatever the Prophet did must necessarily have been right, renders apology unnecessary, from the earliest times there has been much edifying fiction in which the Prophet is shown to have practised all the virtues which mankind agree in admiring. The lines on which the historical character has been distorted and a mythical character substituted have in the main been three.

(1) In the Qur'ān Muhammad on the whole disclaims the character of thaumaturge, arguing that his predecessors were ordinary men, though he accepts the most important of the miracles ascribed to Moses, Jesus, and others (*e.g.*, vii. 160, iii. 43). The miracles which he claims are victories in the field, won by the assistance of angels, and the Qur'ān itself, which is a miracle either as containing historical matter to which the Prophet had no natural access or as being of unattainable eloquence (cf. xlvi. 1 ff., liii. 1 ff.). To these it is possible that one case of foretelling the future, viz. the recovery by the Romans of the territory seized by the Persians in the Nearer East (xxx. 2 f.), should be added, though the text of the Qur'ān does not insist on this as evidence of mysterious knowledge. Since the miracles of earlier prophets are attested by the Qur'ān, this scarcity of the miraculous doubtless from the first constituted a serious difficulty to Muslim controversialists, and it is likely that in Muhammad's lifetime many miracles were attributed to him which he did not himself claim; in time he was credited with the analogue of every miracle of consequence in either OT or NT, with the exception of raising the dead, which perhaps was not ascribed to him on the ground that his own resurrection never became a dogma of Islām. In works of the 4th cent. of Islām these miracles are collected and, as is usual in Muslim works, attested by chains of witnesses, under the title 'Proofs of the Mission.' The most frequently narrated of these miracles is the 'splitting of the moon,' for which it seems possible to adduce Qur'ānic attestation (liv. 1), though perhaps the text should be taken hypothetically rather than as an assertion. Another form of miracle which was popularly attributed to him was foretelling the future; even the reverse which he sustained at Uḥud was, according to the tradition, revealed to him in a dream, though the official account of that affair in *sūrah* iii. 133 ff. makes no allusion to the warning. Of marvellous experiences that which has attracted most attention is his supposed 'ascent into heaven,' which grew up round a text of the Qur'ān (xvii. 1), which merely says that God took His servant by night from the sacred place of prostration to the furthest place of prostration, usually supposed to mean from Mecca to Jerusalem. It is probable that this is the dream to which reference is made in the same *sūrah* (xvii. 62), where it is coupled with 'the accursed tree in the Qur'ān' as a temptation to the people, *i.e.* a stumbling-block to those whose faith was weak. Nothing more is known of this 'dream,' of which we should gather that the Qur'ān had contained an account which was afterwards expunged; but in the tradition it has been so expanded as to form the analogue on the one hand of the Christian Transfiguration, on the other of the colloquy of Moses on Sinai. There is even a tendency to ascribe to this ascent into heaven such non-Qur'ānic legislation as is generally adopted by Islām, in the same way as analogous Jewish legislation is called 'rules given to Moses on Sinai.' In the story that the Prophet was transferred from Mecca to Jerusalem and from Jerusalem to heaven we probably have a combination of glosses on the expression 'the furthest place of prostration,' the meaning of which is obviously obscure.

(2) The Prophet's sayings and doings were made into a source of law, corresponding with the Oral Law of the Jews, and, like the latter, not at first written down. The great collections of these precedents or rulings date from the second half of the 3rd Islāmic cent., but their accumulation goes back to the 1st cent. of the migration, when the

1 *La Vie de Mahomed*, London, 1730.
2 *Mohammed and Mohammedanism*, London, 1873.
3 *Life and Teachings of Muhammad*, London, 1891.

system of jurisprudence began to be established by the labours of jurists of Medīna. The impartial criticism of these traditions seems to lead to a purely negative result; the practice of inventing scenes in which the Prophet delivered some judgment or of fathering sayings upon him was so common from the very beginning of the Islāmic empire that any genuine sayings of his are inextricably mixed up with such as are apocryphal. The native criticism of this tradition consisted in ascertaining if possible the credibility of the persons who had handed it down. This was by no means easy, and various motives prevented those who endeavoured to criticize it from exercising their judgment freely; hence the chains which are technically regarded as strong appear to the non-Muslim critic fatally weak. The Prophet's merits as a legislator must, therefore, be judged exclusively by the Qur'ān; for, though the rest of the 'sacred code' is ascribed to him, there is little reason for thinking it to be his.

(3) The Prophet is supposed to have expressed opinions upon all sorts of subjects—*e.g.*, medicine—and writers of essays usually start by quoting these dicta. Those which have to do with the commendation of various virtues or the condemnation of vices were collected on a considerable scale by Ghazālī († 505 A.H.) in his *Revival of the Religious Sciences* (Cairo, 1282 A.H.), the standard text-book of orthodox Islāmic theology; he was, however, criticized severely for employing so many spurious dicta, many of which could be traced to fabricators.

11. The Prophet's Companions.—No account of Muhammad, however brief, could omit all notice of his Companions, the persons by whose instrumentality he accomplished so much. Many of these became historical figures, as sovereigns, governors, or generals; it is remarkable that none of them undertook the office of biographer or even collector of memoirs. The tradition implies that certain institutions were suggested to the Prophet by one or other of these adherents; but there is no evidence that he was seriously influenced by any one of them, and we should gather that their attitude towards him was that of worshippers. Although the later parts of the Qur'ān approach the character of official documents, and we actually have a State paper inserted in *sūrah* ix., it is not clear that these associates had any share in their composition. Indeed, such participation would have been at variance with the theory that the *sūrahs* were direct communications from the deity. The tradition represents Abū Bakr and 'Omar, both of whom gave their daughters to the Prophet, as the innermost cabinet; the former is said to have been regularly in favour of mild, the latter of severe, measures. Of emissaries sent to teach we hear very little; an agent was sent to Medīna to prepare for the arrival of the Prophet, but the duties of this person were probably political, at least as much as religious; and, when the policy of winning the Arab tribes had commenced, missionaries were sent to teach neophytes those portions of the Qur'ān which were to be employed in the liturgy; these missionaries appear, however, to have had in part military character. When the time had come to extend the mission outside Arabia, envoys were sent bearing copies of the Prophet's letter to all monarchs known to him; but, as these contained a command to adopt Islām on pain of being attacked, there was no occasion for the messengers to endeavour to persuade.

The theory that Islām is primarily a political adventure is borne out by the subsequent careers of its most distinguished adherents. They accumulated fortunes, and otherwise obtained conspicuous worldly success; 'Omar is credited by some historians with consummate statesmanship, and several others displayed talents as commanders of armies; but there was much rivalry for the first place, and a quarter of a century after the Prophet's death different groups of Companions led armies against each other. The later legend transforms all of them into saints and preachers, and sometimes into ascetics. This is done in particular in the case of 'Alī, of whom a sort of cult arose, especially in Persia; history, however, presents him as an ambitious libertine, endowed with personal courage, but little else that merits admiration.

12. His domestic affairs.—The women of the Prophet's family enter into the story of his career somewhat as they enter into the subsequent history; the tradition makes the first wife, Khadījah, a woman of wealth, whose acceptance of her husband's claim to a supernatural mission was an important element in determining its success. Her death is said to have occurred shortly before the migration. Since his followers at Mecca were at least to some extent persons who required temporal support, it is likely that her wealth (whatever that term may have meant) was devoted to this purpose and, indeed, consumed therein. After her death the Prophet began that course of polygamy and concubinage which has given offence to European students of his career, but does not appear to have scandalized his Arabian contemporaries, except, indeed, in the case of his marriage with the wife of his adopted son, which is defended in a Qur'ānic revelation (xxxiii. 4). On two other occasions the pages of the sacred book are devoted to the Prophet's domestic troubles—once when his girl-wife 'Ā'ishah had incurred the suspicion of unfaithfulness, and was defended by a special oracle (xxiv. 11 ff.); and another time, when, owing to the introduction of a Coptic concubine to the *ḥarīm*, the remaining members of it were so embittered that the Prophet threatened to divorce them all, and the revelation which he produced assured him that he would be able to find adequate substitutes (lxvi. 1 ff.). Since matters no less private and delicate find a place in the prophetic books of the OT (Hosea and Isaiah), perhaps their presence in the Qur'ān ought not to shock us; nevertheless the tradition states that, according to 'Ā'ishah, the Qur'ān would have profited by the omission of the affair of the adopted son, and this criticism might be extended to the others. In several of these marriages it is easy to see that political considerations were dominant. Muhammad, like other leaders, wished to unite his chief helpers to himself by as many bonds as possible, and to get a hold on dangerous opponents. Had he had sons, he would probably have utilized them in the pursuit of this policy. Of these women 'Ā'ishah, the daughter of his most faithful follower, Abū Bakr, played a historical part of great consequence, and in the first civil war herself took the field. The descendants of the Prophet, distinguished since the year 773 A.H. by green turbans, all trace their pedigree to Fāṭimah, his daughter by Khadījah; the other daughters appear to have died without issue. Fāṭimah herself, the wife of 'Alī, seems to have been cruelly treated by the first successor, and died six months after her father, being called to play a political part for which she was unfitted in supporting her husband's claim to the succession. It is curious that the exact number of his sons is unknown, though it is certain that all died in infancy. Of one, born late in his life of a Coptic concubine, sent as a present by the Byzantine governor of Egypt, the death synchronized with an eclipse of the sun, supposed to be that of 27th Jan. 632.

LITERATURE.—This, in both the Islāmic and the Christian languages, is enormous, and even a list of important works would be lengthy. Besides the sources enumerated above, the Islāmic general histories mostly devote a great deal of space to the Prophet's biography—*e.g.*, Ismā'īl **Abu'l-Fidā** († 722 A.H.), whose account, ed. with Lat. tr. by J. Gagnier, Oxford, 1723, was for more than a century the basis of European researches. Many Arabic monographs in prose and verse are enumerated by Ḥājjī Khalīfah, ed. G. Flügel, Leipzig, 1835–58, iii. 634–636. To these should be added the work called *Insān al-'Uyūn* of Burhān al-dīn al-Ḥalabī († 1044 A.H.), published Cairo, 1292, with the biography by a modern writer of Mecca, Aḥmad Zaini Dahlan, on the margin. The modern European study of the subject was started by **G. Weil**, *Mohammed der Prophet*, Stuttgart, 1843; it was popularized in English by **Washington Irving**, *Lives of Mahomet and his Successors*, London, 1850. The work of **A. Sprenger**, *Das Leben und die Lehre des Mohammad*, Berlin, 1869, claimed to be based mainly on new materials; much the same were simultaneously employed by **W. Muir**, *Life of Mahomet and Hist. of Islam*, London, 1856–61, reprinted in an abridged form, 1877, and ed. T. H. Weir, 1912. More recent biographies are those by **H. Grimme**, *Mohammed*, Munich, 1904, and **D. S. Margoliouth**, *Mohammed and the Rise of Islam*, London, 1905.

Besides biographies, numerous works deal with either the prophetic character of Muhammad or certain aspects of his work. One of the most popular of the former sort is the *Shifā fī ḥuqūq al-Muṣṭafā* of the *qāḍī* 'Iyāḍ († 544 A.H.), on which there is a vast literature, described by Ḥājjī Khalīfah, iv. 56–61; the ed. of Constantinople, 1315, in 4 vols. with the commentary of Khafājī († 1069 A.H.), is probably the best. Somewhat similar is the *Mawāhib Laduniyyah* of Qasṭallānī († 923 A.H.) with the commentary of Zurqānī, 8 vols., Cairo, 1278. Of European works mention may be made of **O. Pautz**, *Mohammeds Lehre von der Offenbarung*, Leipzig, 1898; **O. Procksch**, *Über die Blutrache und Mohammeds Stellung zu ihr*, do. 1899; **P. Casanova**, *Mohammed et la fin du monde*, Paris, 1911; **H. Lammens**, *Mohamet, fut-il sincère?*, Paris, 1914. The ninth volume of **V. Chauvin's** *Bibliographie des ouvrages arabes*, etc., Liége, 1908, contains a list of all European works on the subject from 1810 to 1885.

D. S. MARGOLIOUTH.

MUHAMMADANISM.

MUHAMMADANISM (in Central Africa).—Muhammadanism is said to have reached Central Africa from three sources—Egypt by the Nile and its affluents, Tripoli *via* Ghadames to Timbuktu, and Algeria *via* Wargla. Certain details of the dates of its introduction into various communities were collected by the traveller, H. Barth; about A.D. 1000 it found its way into Songhi, near the end of the 11th cent. into Kanem, about 1500 into Bagirmi, and not much later into Katsena. It was introduced into Logon about the beginning of the 19th century. In 1907 it was computed that the number of indigenous Muslims in British Central Africa was 50,000 as compared with 950,000 fetishists. Its introduction in certain places is connected with the names of historical personages; the chief missionary for Central Negroland was one Muḥammad b. 'Abd al-Karīm b. Maghili, a native of Buda in Tawat, who flourished about 1500.

The Islām of Central Africa seems to be everywhere of the Mālikite school; and, if it has produced a literature, few monuments of it have as yet come to light. In *Revue du monde musulman*, xii. [1910] 197 Ismaël Hamet gives a summary of the *Kitāb al-Ṭarā'if* by Muḥammad b. al-Mukhtār of the Kounta tribe of Azawad; this personage died in 1826, twenty years after the completion of his work, which consists of an edifying biography of his parents, containing the kind of matter which is usually found in hagiographies. In *Revue du monde musulman*, xiv. [1911], Hamet gives extracts from the works of a somewhat earlier writer Sīdī Muḥammad al-Yaddālī († 1752), a poem by whom in praise of the Prophet was published by L. Massignon (*ib.* viii. [1909] 199). Some contemporary poems (satires) by one Bakai were published by Barth. There appears to be nothing in these specimens that is distinctly African. In the same magazine (viii. 409) Massignon published the catalogue of a library belonging to a Central African chieftain Shaikh Sidia; the editor notices the absence of books bearing on philosophy, alchemy, and music, but otherwise it does not differ in character from other Islāmic libraries, and the want of representation of these subjects may be due to accident.

LITERATURE.—**I. Hamet**, 'La Civilisation arabe en Afrique centrale,' in *Revue du monde musulman*, xiv. [1911] 1–35.

D. S. MARGOLIOUTH.

MUHAMMADANISM (in N. Africa). — I. **History.** — The introduction of Islām into N. Africa commenced shortly after the conquest of Egypt by 'Amr b. al-'Āṣ, who in A.D. 641 penetrated as far as Barca, and in the following year took Tripoli by storm. It was not till the autumn of 647, however, that an expedition on a great scale was organized for the subjugation of Africa, where the Patricius Gregory had declared himself independent of the Byzantine emperor, and made Sbeitla (in Tunisia) his seat of government. The Arab invader, 'Abdallāh b. Abī Sarḥ, who had advanced through the interior, defeated the forces collected by Gregory in the battle of Akuba, where Gregory himself perished, took and pillaged Sbeitla, and proceeded to devastate the country southwards as far as Gafsa and Jerid and northwards as far as Marmajanna. Permanent occupation was not yet contemplated, and the conquerors were satisfied with a heavy money payment, on the receipt of which they withdrew; certain conversions, however, were made. The civil war which followed the death of 'Uthmān delayed the activities of the Muslims in this region for a time, but in 665 the first Umayyad Khalīfah, Mu'āwiyah, dispatched an expedition thither, which overcame the troops sent by the Byzantine emperor, and in 669 established a province Ifrīqiyyah, with 'Uqbah b. Nāfi' for its first governor, who for the first time employed Berber converts as soldiers, and founded the city of Kairawan. Since the Islāmic programme was carried out by this governor, who threatened the pagans with extermination, the religion began to spread fast among the Berber tribes. In 675 'Uqbah was replaced by a less vigorous governor; but he was sent back to his province by Yazīd I. shortly after his accession, and proceeded to organize an expedition which finally reached Ceuta in the extreme west of Africa, whence he turned south and saw the Atlantic before starting homeward; but he did not again reach Kairawan, as his army was attacked by superior forces and annihilated at Tehuda, N.E. of Biscra. His defeat and death (683) were followed by a general revolt of the Africans from Arab rule, and an independent Berber state, with Kairawan for capital, was able to maintain itself for five years. In 690 this city was re-taken by the Arabs, who, however, evacuated the province, which lapsed into anarchy. An end was put to this by Mūsāh b. Nuṣair, sent in 705 to Kairawan as governor of Ifrīqiyyah, who traversed as far as Ceuta the country previously invaded by 'Uqbah, penetrated as far south as the Oasis of Sijilmasa, took Tangiers, and installed a Berber convert there as governor. He returned to Kairawan in 708, having definitely won N. Africa to Islām, and put an end to Christian domination, where it still existed. The pious Umayyad 'Omar II. is said to have manifested zeal in the propagation of Islām among the inhabitants of these territories.

The Khārijites, who were giving much trouble in the eastern dominions of the Khalīfahs, also sent missionaries to the west, where they found a ready hearing among the recently converted tribes. The Ṣufrī doctrine spread among the westerly tribes, the Ibāḍī in Ifrīqiyyah proper. In 740 a revolt broke out in the extreme west against the Umayyad ruler in favour of the Khārijite doctrine, and, as it met with some initial success, it spread over Muslim Africa; a Syrian force sent by the Khalīfah Hishām to quell the rebellion was defeated on the Sebu. Another force headed by the governor of Egypt in 742 was more fortunate; but, though Kairawan was rendered secure, the Khārijites maintained themselves at Tlemsen and in the neighbouring parts of the modern Morocco, and various independent Khārijite communities established themselves to the west of the continent.

At the beginning of the 9th cent., while the dynasty of the Aghlabites was establishing itself at Kairawan, under the nominal suzerainty of the Khalīfahs of Baghdād, but virtually independent, an 'Alid dynasty called the Idrīsid became dominant in the west, and in 808 founded the city of Fez. Other petty dynasties were also established in various places. The great event in the history of Muslim Africa during this century was the arrival of the Fāṭimid missionary Abū 'Abdallāh, who won adherents among the Ketama, and by skilful organization and strategy was able to overthrow the Aghlabites, and install at Kairawan a Shī'ah dynasty, which presently substituted for Kairawan a new city, Mahdiyah, as metropolis. The petty principalities to the west of Kairawan alternated in their allegiance between the Umayyads of Spain and the Fāṭimids of Mahdiyah, but the latter remained the dominant power in N. Africa until they, having conquered Egypt, transferred their capital to Cairo, leaving in possession of Mahdiyah a dependent dynasty called the Zirids, who in the middle of the 11th cent. threw off Fāṭimid suzerainty. As the 11th cent. neared its end, the Almoravid dynasty, founded by an adventurer named Yūsuf b. Tāshifīn, with its capital at Morocco, obtained the hegemony; and this, in the middle of the 12th cent., was displaced by that of the Almohads founded by Ibn Tūmart, which under its first actual sovereign, 'Abd al-Mu'min, obtained possession of all N. Africa as well as Spain. This dynasty lasted one century only, and was succeeded by three—the Merinids with their capital at Fez, the Ziyanids with theirs at Tlemsen, and the Ḥafṣids, with theirs at Tunis —whose constant disputes kept N. Africa in a state of turbulence for some two centuries. In the 16th cent. various points on the north and west coasts were seized by Portuguese and Spanish forces and then by Turks; the three native dynasties gradually disappeared, and, whereas that of Tunis gave way to Ottoman domination, which had Algiers for its centre, in the west a new empire, that of the Sharīfs, arose. The capital of the Sharīfs was at different times Morocco and Fez, and sometimes Meknes; their first dynasty, that of the Sa'dians, lasted from 1520 until 1654, when it was ousted by that of the Ḥassānians, which became prominent in 1633. The Sharīfs and the Turks succeeded in ousting the Christian invaders from the places which they had occupied, but in 1830 Algiers was occupied by the French, whose empire has ever since been extending in N. Africa. The connexion of the Turkish settlements in N. Africa with the government of Constantinople grew constantly looser from the time of their establishment, and the pasha of Algiers had difficulty in maintaining his authority over the territories which lay to the west of that place.

The population forming the Islāmic communities has remained Berber in the main, but, besides the influx of Arabs at the time of the original invasion, the introduction of the Arab tribes Hilal and Sulaim in the 11th cent. has been of great importance for the political development of the country These tribes, which had been located in Egypt, were, it is said, sent westwards by the Fāṭimid Khalīfah Mustanṣir, by way of avenging himself on the Zirid Mu'izz, who in 1048 had accepted the suzerainty of the 'Abbāsid Khalīfah, destroyed the Ismā'īlia college at Kairawan, where the Shī'ite doctrine was taught, and burned in public all that was indicative of Shī'ism. The Arabs advanced victoriously, and compelled the Berber sovereigns to make terms with them; under the Almohads some of the divisions of these tribes were introduced into the western provinces and employed by the government as a military force.

'Far from attaching themselves to the soil as the al-Mohads had hoped, these tribes continued to live in the nomad state and to annoy the government by their turbulence' (E. Michaux-Bellaire, 'Les Tribus arabes de la vallée du Lekkous,' in *Archives marocaines*, iv. [1905] 59).

Indeed, their risings form many a chapter in the history of N. Africa. Towards the end of the 17th cent. the Ḥassānid Sharīf Ismā'īl purchased or procured a great number of Negroes, of whom he formed agricultural colonies, chiefly in the neighbourhood of Morocco, enjoying various privileges, but bound to place all male children from the age of ten at the disposal of the sovereign, to be trained for his guard, while various employments were also found for the females. By the end of his reign as many as 150,000 of these black soldiers were registered in his lists; they were placed under the patronage of Bukhārī, the author of the chief collection of traditions, whose sanctity in certain parts of the Islāmic world approaches or even exceeds that of the Prophet. The purpose of this scheme was to provide the Sulṭān with a guard unconnected with the native population, on whose fidelity he could rely. A Turkish and a Levantine element, neither very considerable in magnitude, were introduced into the eastern provinces by the Ottoman conquests.

2. Sects and orders.—It will have been seen from this sketch that during the first four centuries of Islām both Khārijite and Shī'ite opinions held sway in different parts of N. Africa. The former are still represented by certain isolated communities (see art. KHAWĀRIJ); when the Zirids asserted their independence of the Fāṭimids, Shī'ite opinions were condemned, and a general persecution of those who held them took place (1014); some years later (1045), on the occasion of a further dispute between the Zirid and the Fāṭimid monarchs, the former asserted the legitimacy of the 'Abbāsid Khalīfate and proclaimed the orthodoxy of the Mālikite system, upon which the Almoravids also insisted. The founder of the Almohad dynasty was a follower of the Ash'arite theology, and himself propagated it in Africa, displacing that of the Zahirites (Qalqashandī, *Ṣubḥ al-A'shā*, Cairo, 1915, v. 191). The further changes of dynasty appear to have produced no alteration in the dominance of these systems. The historians of the earlier period call attention to two purely African sects, both of which obtained some hold. The first of these was that founded by Ṣāliḥ b. Ṭarīf, prophet of the Bargwata in Temessna, who about A.D. 750 promulgated a Qur'ān containing *sūrahs* named after 'the Cock,' 'the Elephant,' 'the Asses,' 'Adam,' etc., and was recognized by his tribe. After a reign of forty-seven years he departed to the East, promising to return under the seventh sovereign of his dynasty and leaving his son Elias to continue his work. This successor reigned, we are told, fifty years, professing Islām, but secretly harbouring his father's heresy, which was openly professed by the third of the line, Yūnus. Yūnus endeavoured to enforce its acceptance under penalty of death, and is said to have razed numerous cities and massacred crowds of his subjects in his endeavour to propagate the doctrine. The doctrine seems to have differed from orthodox Islām in matters of ceremony chiefly. It substituted Rajab as fasting month for Ramaḍān; it prescribed ten daily and nightly prayers instead of five; its sacrificial day was 11th Muḥarram; its alms-tax was a tithe of all fruits; its ceremonial cleansing was much more elaborate than the orthodox; some of the prayers consisted of gestures without bending of the body; and the formulæ were in the vernacular of the tribe. The cock served instead of *mu'adhdhin*; its flesh was a forbidden food, whereas that of the hen was only disapproved. Eggs also were forbidden. The sect survived till the middle of the 11th cent., when it was exterminated by the Almoravids.

Another Berber author of a Qur'ān was Ḥāmīm, prophet of the Ghumarah near Tetuan, who came forward in A.D. 925; in his system prayer was only twice a day, and the only attitude adopted in it was an inclination in which the ground was touched with the back of the hands. He prescribed fasting all Thursday, and on Wednesday till noon. He reduced the fast of Ramaḍān by a number of days, abolished pilgrimage, purification, and the total ablution, and permitted sow's flesh to be eaten, on the ground that the Qur'ān of Muhammad forbade that of the boar only. Specimens of his Qur'ān, which was in the Berber language, are given in the *Kitāb al-istibṣār* (tr. E. Fagnan, Constantine, 1900, p. 143), and relics of the sect which he founded existed in the time of the historian Ibn Khaldūn (*c.* A.D. 1400), who asserts that the greater number of sorcerers came from the Jabal Ḥāmīm, which took its name from this personage, whose actual career appears to have been very short. He was defeated in the neighbourhood of Tangiers by a force sent by the Spanish Umayyad al-Nāṣir in the year 927, and his head was sent to Cordova.

In the year 1228 another prophet arose among the Ghumarah, called Muḥammad b. Abī'l-Ṭawājin, who performed miracles and instituted a code; he was, however, cursed by the saint and ascetic 'Abd al-Salām b. Mashīsh, in consequence of which most of his Berber followers withdrew from him. The prophet in retaliation caused the saint to be assassinated, but was himself shortly afterwards defeated by the garrison of Ceuta, and killed by a Berber; his descendants are still to be found in the neighbourhood of the Wad Ras, where, however, they are under a sort of ban, and forbidden access to the Jabal Alam, where the saint Ibn Mashīsh dwelt, of whose cult hatred for the Bani Ṭawājin forms a part (*Archives marocaines*, ii. [1905] 24). Ibn Khaldūn gives no details of the system which this prophet tried to establish (*History*, ed. Cairo, 1284, vi. 222). The title 'Mahdī' is said to have been taken by the first of these prophets, and, being less likely to offend popular prejudice than the title 'Prophet,' it has been assumed by many pretenders in Africa—*e.g.*, the founders of the Fāṭimid and Almohad dynasties, a contemporary of the former, 'a young man' at the commencement of the reign of the Fāṭimid Manṣūr (A.D. 946). It is noticeable that the Almohad Ma'mūn, at his triumphal entry into Morocco in 1230, definitely rejected the claim of the founder of his dynasty to this title, asserting that the only Mahdī was Jesus the Son of Mary, and that the ascription of it to Ibn Tūmart was a fable. Numerous claimants to it have risen since that time (see art. MAHDĪ).

Of an obscure sect called the Baḍaḍwa, located on the right bank of the Sebu, an account is given by G. Salmon in *Archives marocaines*, ii. [1905] 358–363. A branch of these called 'the sect of Yūsuf' is mentioned as having arisen in the 10th century (*ib.* xix. [1913] 214). Apparently they base their system on the Qur'ān, but differ from other Muslims in points of ritual.

The general dominance of the Mālikite code, of which the most familiar compendium is that of Sīdī Khalīl (Abū Ḍiyā), was not affected by the dynastic changes, except that in the provinces governed by Turks the official system of the Ottomans, that of Abū Ḥanīfah, was introduced without displacing the other; in these regions there were two *qāḍīs*. In the cities of N. Africa there were theological schools which produced orthodox writers and teachers of eminence, and such were to be found as far south as Timbuktu, which was made subject to Morocco in 1590; one of the prisoners then taken, Aḥmad Bābā, who belonged to a family of theologians, complained that the conquerors had pillaged his library, which, though containing 1600 volumes, was smaller than others which belonged to his relatives. The Islām of N. Africa was greatly influenced by the introduction of the form of Ṣūfiism connected with the name of 'Abd al-Qādir al-Jīlānī ([*q.v.*] † 561 A.H.), to whom the establishment of orders is traced. In one of the earliest European accounts of the orders (E. de Neveu, *Les Khouan: Ordres religieux chez les Musulmans de l'Algérie*, Paris, 1846) various popular beliefs about this personage are collected.

'He it is whose name is ceaselessly repeated by beggars demanding alms, and whose name is invoked by all whom any accident befalls. When a man falls, the bystanders and he himself cry out, "Ah, my lord 'Abd al-Qādir!" The miserable in their sufferings, and women in travail, pray him to intercede for them. In the month Ṣafar 380,000 evils of all sorts descend from the sky; of these he bears three-quarters himself' (p. 23 f.).

Lists of the orders established in N. Africa were made by this writer, and more complete registers were later drawn up by L. Rinn, O. Depont, and X. Coppolani. Some of these either originated in Africa or are only known to exist there.

In the 15th cent. Shādhilīism was propagated in Morocco by Muḥammad b. Sulaimān al-Jazūlī, who counts as the starting-point of all the orders and *zāwiyahs* of this region. An account of this personage, who died in 1464, and is famous throughout Islām as the author of the *Dalā'il al-Khairāt*, is given in *Archives marocaines*, xix. 277 ff., as an appendix to the treatise *Da'wat al-Nāshir* of Ibn 'Askar, which contains the lives of ascetics of Morocco; A. Graulle, who is the translator of this work, added to it as a continuation in vol. xxi. [1913] the *Nashr al-Mathānī* of Muḥammad b. al-Ṭayyib al-Qādirī, and proposes to add as another supplement the *Ghurb al-Muhtaḍar* of Ja'far al-Kittanī. The *Salwat al-anfās*, published at Fez in 1316, is of similar import. The amount of historical matter contained in these lives is small; their purpose is chiefly to edify. The growth of the orders throughout N. Africa, ultimately (according to French authorities) rendering possible a territorial division by *zāwiyahs* like parishes, does not appear to have at any time had a beneficial effect either on the religion or on the morals of the inhabitants. In an essay, 'Sur la Mentalité religieuse dans la region de Rabat et de Sale' (*Archives marocaines*, vi. [1906] 423–435), E. Mercier describes the effects which he witnessed in two towns which count as sacred.

'The people are fanatics rather than believers, haters of the non-Muslim rather than religious'; the member of an order shares the superstitions of the ignorant, but is more bigoted and, having secured his own salvation, looks down on others who are less fortunate. 'Convinced of his immense superiority, he shuts himself up in a strict formalism, scrupulous and punctual observation of the rites which take up his time and save him the trouble of reflecting' (p. 4).

It is asserted that religion occupies a much larger share of Berber than of Arab life, and the names of the dynasties, Almoravids, Almohads, bear this out. In the 16th cent. the devotees (called *murābiṭ*, or *marabout*) begin to play a political rôle of great importance; their *zāwiyahs*, or hermitages, which at times were like towns in magnitude, are regularly employed as refuges; they themselves in times of peace (so far as there were any) enjoyed divers privileges—*e.g.*, under Turkish rule the marabouts of the Amokran family in the neighhourhood of Jijeli had the right to direct the provision of timber for shipbuilding, and others had a share in the proceeds of the piracy; they were employed as envoys, as mediators, and, at times, as regents. Most frequently we hear of them as heading insurrections. The dynasty of the Sa'dian Sharīfs is said to have commenced by the inhabitants of Sus at the time of the Portuguese settlements betaking themselves to a marabout named Ibn Mubārak, whom they implored to place himself at their head and march against the Christian invaders; he referred them to the Sharīf Abu 'Abdallāh al-Qaim, then residing at Tagmadaret, whose sons undertook the duty. In 1612 the Sa'dian Sharīf al-Ma'mūn, who, in order to regain his throne, had handed over Al-Araish to the Spaniards, was assassinated by the *muqaddam* (abbot) Muḥammad b. Abī' l-Lif, at the instance, it is said, of the marabout Abū'l-Mahalli, who belonged to the Raḥmānī order, and even proclaimed himself Mahdī. This personage was able to take Morocco, where he established himself as sovereign until defeated by another marabout Yaḥyā, who espoused the cause of the Sa'dian Zaidan, and was then, not without difficulty, persuaded to return to his monastery. In 1619 an insurrection in the province Habt was headed by a marabout al-Ḥasan b. Raisun, also in favour of a Sa'dian, who undertook to restore orthodox practice; and early in the 17th cent. the marabouts of Dela, Sale, and Sijilmasa headed political parties in different parts of the Sa'dian empire. In 1639 a Turkish force dispatched from Algiers which was entrapped in the Kabiliyah was saved by the intervention of a marabout, who obtained reasonable terms from the natives for it. In 1641 the Algerian pasha Yūsuf, starting an expedition for the suppression of anarchy in the province of Constantine, obtained the good offices of the marabout Ibn Sasi of Bone. In 1664 one named Sīdī Hamud obtained a passage for the Algerian troops marching to the relief of Jijeli, which had been occupied by the French. In 1668 the marabouts of Dela were at war with the Ḥassānian Sharīf Rashīd, who defeated them and stormed their *zāwiyah*, which had grown into a populous and sumptuous town. His brother and successor, Ismā'īl, had to face an insurrection headed by one of the survivors from this monastery, named Aḥmad b. 'Abdallāh, who was defeated in the neighbourhood of Tedla. Their activity was no less marked in the 18th century. In 1757 a marabout raised the standard of revolt against the Ḥassānian Sharīf Muḥammad b. 'Abdallāh in the country of the Ghumarah. In 1777 an insurrection was started at Tlemsen by a fanatic of the Derkawī order, named Muḥammad b. 'Abdallāh, whose followers were ultimately bought off. In 1787 Salah Bey of Constantine conducted a series of campaigns, not all of them successful, against the heads of *zāwiyahs* in this province. In 1803 another Derkawī, Ibn al-Ahrash, said to be favoured by the British Government, established himself at Jijeli, and organized the natives against the bey of Constantine, whom he defeated and killed; and in 1805 the Derkawīs revolted in the province of Oran and besieged Oran itself. In 1818 the marabouts of this province gave further trouble, and many more recent instances of their activity are recorded.

In general the ostensible aim of these devotees has been to free the soil of Africa from Christian occupation; but this has not invariably been the case, as there are instances of the marabouts compromising with the Christians or even invoking their assistance against rivals (*Archives marocaines*, ii. 46).

3. Cult of saints.—Closely connected with the orders is the cult of saints, which is wide-spread in N. Africa. The tomb of Idrīs, founder of the Idrīsī dynasty, is a common place of pilgrimage, and both it and other tombs figure in the history as places of refuge. The tomb of Ibn Mashīsh (see above, p. 882[a]) is visited in the month Sha'bān, and comprehends a series of visits to those of his ancestors and descendants (*Archives marocaines*, ii. 24). A list of the tombs visited in the Gharb is given in *Archives marocaines*, xx. [1913] 246–278; of the saints thus venerated the most popular is Sīdi Qāsim b. Lallūsha († A.D. 1666). 'What is certain is that he has two sanctuaries, one on the left and one on the right bank of the Sebu' (p. 261), and that he has several festivals in the year, one of which lasts three days. A list for the province Habt is given in *Archives marocaines*, xvii. [1911] 481 ff. These saints have functions corresponding closely with those of the patron saints of Christianity.

'The *zāwiyah* Sharqāwiyah of Bū'l-Ja'd is not only a religious centre, but likewise a centre of preparation for the sacred war, and the greater number of the horsemen and shooters of the Gharb are placed under the patronage of Sīdī Bū Abid al-Sharqāwī. In this region one frequently finds the name Bū Abīd, which is considered to be of good omen for horsemen. Parents often give their children the name of a marabout under whose patronage some military exercise is placed' (*ib.* xx. 39).

An account is given (*ib.* p. 276 ff.) of various Maraboutic 'tribes,' *i.e.* groups of villages attached to some saintly cult, and not, like the *zāwiyahs*, isolated villages.

LITERATURE.—E. Mercier, *Hist. de l'Afrique septentrionale*, Paris, 1888–91, based on both native and European authorities. Much material is to be found in *Revue africaine*, nos. 1–293 [1856–1915], *Mémoires de la société archéologique de Constantine*, vols. i.–xlv. [1853–1912], *Archives marocaines*, vols. i.–xxi. [1904–13]. See also I. Hamet, *Les Musulmans français au nord de l'Afrique*, Paris, 1906; T. H. Weir, *The Shaikhs of Morocco*, London, 1904.

D. S. MARGOLIOUTH.

MUHAMMADANISM (in Arabia).—One of the results of the taking of Mecca by Muhammad was a determination on his part no longer to tolerate paganism in Arabia, and the destruction of the ancient cults took place throughout the peninsula with extraordinary rapidity; the ease with which the fetishes were discarded by their worshippers has elicited expressions of wonder from some who have chronicled the period. It is indeed suggested at times that there are still unexplored regions in Arabia whither Islām has not penetrated, but of these rumours there appears to be no confirmation. So far as the authorities before us warrant, every tradition of the older religions appears to have perished; statements about them which meet us in Arabic literature are ordinarily fictions based on Qur'ānic texts, and the so-called 'pre-Islāmic poetry' must, if genuine, have undergone wholesale expurgation. Even the revolts in Arabia which followed the Prophet's death do not appear to exhibit any recrudescence of paganism, but merely a desire for liberation from some of the more onerous exactions of Islām; and permanent relief in one matter (the number of daily prayers) is said to have been obtained by one of the rebellious tribes, though the revolt was otherwise a failure. It is worthy of notice that these rebellions were led by prophets who aimed at re-enacting Muhammad's part, not by priests or other representatives of the fallen idols. The liberation of Arabia from paganism was speedily followed by the penalizing therein of all non-Islāmic cults, even the Jews and Christians, whose rights had been respected by the Prophet, being either banished or forcibly converted in the time of the second Khalīfah.

The murder of the third of these rulers in the year 35 A.H. was an event of the greatest importance for both Arabia and Islām. On the one hand, as some of the far-sighted are said to have urged at the time, it split the community into sects; complete unity has never been restored. On the other hand, the political centre of Islām was thereby shifted to a point outside Arabia; the Assassins came from Egypt, and the battles for the succession were fought from Baṣra, Kūfa, and Damascus. These cities became the capitals of the rival claimants, and Medīna was never restored to the position which it had once held. Arabia has, therefore, ever since been a province, at a distance from the seat of government; and such principalities as have asserted their independence within the peninsula have been mediocre both in magnitude and in importance. Such talent as Arabia produced has been attracted to the political centre, whereas the persons attracted to it from outside have been mainly devotees.

There are, however, certain ways in which the influence of Arabia upon Islām has been constant or permanent. On the one hand, Mecca has maintained its position throughout history as the greatest Islāmic sanctuary; some sovereigns are said to have contemplated substituting either Jerusalem or Baghdād, but to have abandoned the idea as impracticable. This place has not only served to perpetuate the traditions which Islām took on from older times, but has also served as a rallying ground for the sects; and only occasionally has its sanctity been violated. Mecca is the place where the Islāmic world as a whole can be most easily addressed, and to this day revivalist movements, which are usually reactionary, have a tendency to materialize there.

On the other hand, Medīna remained the chief seat of Islāmic learning some generations after it had ceased to be the political capital. At this place, the residence of the Prophet's widows, several of whom survived him for many decades, and the theatre of his most eventful years, the science of tradition came into existence, and this speedily became the most important source of law, though not first in the list. In the 1st cent. of Islām Medīna produced a school of jurists who, though they left nothing in writing, by their labours prepared the way for the codes whose publication followed shortly after the foundation of Baghdād. In the middle of the 2nd cent. it was the home of the jurist Mālik, where he received as pupil Shāfi'ī; Shāfi'ī in later life went to Baghdād, where alone conspicuous ability could find its reward. With the names of these personages two of the three great Islāmic codes are connected. It is, therefore, Arabian (and indeed Medīnese) law that theoretically is observed throughout Islām, though in the more civilized States the civil and criminal portions have given way to the Code Napoléon.

The development of the other Islāmic sciences has little to do with Arabia, which in these matters has lagged behind the other provinces. The chief battles of the sects, too, have been fought outside Arabia; they could not, however, cut quite adrift from the sacred territory, where they did not, as a rule, win many enthusiastic adherents. There has, however, been always a smouldering desire to recover that hegemony which was lost after the murder of Othmān; hence there has generally been disaffection towards the ruling power. Perhaps the most serious attempt made at recovering the lost hegemony was when in the early 'Abbāsid period 'Abdallāh, son of Zubair, was able to maintain the two sacred cities for a time against the Umayyad generals. His cause perished with him; and rebellions which have since taken place in Arabia have had for their object recovery of independence within the peninsula rather than re-establishment of the political headquarters of the empire.

An account of the religious condition of Arabia in the 4th cent. of Islām is given by the geographer Muqaddasī (ed. M. J. de Goeje, Leyden, 1877, p. 96). The three great political sects, the Sunnīs, Shī'ahs, and Khārijīs (called by him Shurāt), were represented in different parts of the peninsula. One sect which has since disappeared, the Qarmaṭīs, was dominant in Hajr. The Sunnī schools were not then restricted to four, and, besides the systems of Abū Ḥanīfah and Mālik, those of Dāwūd the Ẓāhirī, Sufyān al-Thaurī, and Ibn al-Mundhir had adherents. The Shī'ites in parts of the country were also distinguished as Mu'tazilites.

Of the rise of the Khārijī power in Oman an account has been given in the art. IBĀḌĪS. Of a Khārijite who maintained himself in Yemen from 538 to 569 A.H. a notice is given by Ibn Khaldūn (tr. H. C. Kay, *Omarah's History of Yemen*, London, 1892, pp. 161–165). The branch of the Shī'ah which has maintained itself permanently in S. Arabia is the Zaidī (*q.v.*). It is called after a descendant of 'Alī, Zaid, who perished in an abortive rising of the year 122 A.H. For its history, references may be given to the work of H. C. Kay (pp. 184–190), and Khazrajī's *History of the Rasúlí Dynasty of Yaman* (tr. J. W. Redhouse, 5 vols., London, 1907–13). An account of the Qarmaṭīs in Yemen by Janadī is also translated in the work of Kay (pp. 190–212). Other sects were either at one time represented in Arabia or are still to be found there; of a Shī'ite sect called Sab'iyyah representatives are to be found in a Yemenite community called Yām (Aḥmad Rāshid, *History of Yeman and San'ā* [Turkish], Constantinople, 1291 A.H., ii. 87); their views appear to be similar to those of 'Azāqirī (Yāqūt, *Dictionary of Learned Men*, ed. D. S. Margoliouth, London, 1907–13, i. 301).

Probably the most important religious movement which has taken place in Arabia since the rise of Islām is that called Wahhābī (*q.v.*), the origin and course of which have been described by the English travellers W. G. Palgrave, Lady Anne Blunt, C. M. Doughty, and the Austrian traveller E. Nolde.

So far as the literature of these sects has hitherto been made accessible, it would appear that they have had to adopt and modify the results of the labours carried on at the great Islāmic centres, and have themselves been incapable of producing original works of any consequence. One of the few specimens as yet accessible of purely Arabian theology, *Al-'Ilm al-Shāmikh*, by Ṣāliḥ b. Mahdī of Yemen († 1108 A.H.), in which an endeavour is made to find a common ground for the sects by going behind the supposed innovations of the founders, appears to rest entirely on the older theological works, already known in Europe, the authors of which were natives of extra-Arabian provinces. We learn from this work that the Ṣūfī orders and practices, which originated in Baghdād and Baṣra, were in the author's time well represented in S. Arabia. Against these the Wahhābī movement in the centre and north of the peninsula was to some extent a revolt.

From the statements of the few travellers who have spent much time in the peninsula and have been able to familiarize themselves with its conditions, it would appear that the great bulk of the population are, in theory at any rate, fiercely Muhammadan, but that the observation of the practices which the system enjoins is much more regular in the towns than in the desert. There is, however, considerable difference between the statements of different travellers, and much variety has doubtless been occasioned by local, temporal, and personal factors. When K. Niebuhr (in the latter half of the 18th cent.) visited S. Arabia, he found that a Christian was there treated somewhat as a Jew was treated in Europe—as an inferior being, but not necessarily to be molested.[1] Perhaps the greater number of visitors in the 19th cent. either adopted or simulated Islām; and this, indeed, has been a necessity in the sacred territory, where the presence of unbelievers is not tolerated by the government. In the Wahhābī States the tendency seems to have been in the direction of intolerance; yet on this matter almost contemporary accounts are inconsistent, and it would appear that the demeanour of the traveller has largely determined the conduct of his entertainers; even a missionary who went to Ḥaiel with the avowed object of circulating the NT was only sent under escort out of the Wahhābī territory. The explorers of S. Arabia appear to have undergone little molestation on religious grounds; intertribal wars and international politics have interfered with them much more. It is worth noticing that the Cairene journal which is conducted ostensibly in the interest of the Muslim chieftains of S. Arabia has for its proprietor and editor a Christian with the unmistakable name 'Abd al-Masīḥ, 'Slave of Christ.'

LITERATURE.—This is sufficiently quoted throughout the article.

D. S. MARGOLIOUTH.

MUHAMMADANISM (in Central Asia).—In sketching the peculiarities of Islām in Central Asia, it is necessary to begin with the impression which the difference between the religious life in western and middle Asia must make upon any one who has occasion to study these wide-spread portions of the Muhammadan world. From Constantinople east a gradually increasing fanaticism and ignorance will be observed, and the deeper the penetration into Asia, the more outspoken and intense become the hatred and aversion of the believer to the adherents of a foreign creed, and the less is it possible to ignore the points of divergence separating men of various religions. In Turkey, where Christians and Muslims have lived for centuries in close proximity, a long existing and continuous intercourse with the European world has undoubtedly smoothed away many asperities, and has, to a certain extent, prepared for a mutual understanding. In spite of the temporary outbreaks of enmity between Kurds and Armenians, caused by the predatory habits of the Kurds and not by their religion—for they are very lax Muslims—the relations between Christians and Muhammadans are fair, and would be much better if the misrule of the central government on the Bosphorus and the political instigations from without did not steadily envenom the situation. In Persia Islām presents itself in quite a different form. There first appears the deep-rooted enmity between Shī'ites and Sunnites, and the fire which this schism kindled more than 1200 years ago is still raging. As for the life of the Shī'ite sect, what the present writer saw and heard during his wanderings as a dervish in Īrān gave him a very poor opinion of their piety and the moral effect of their teachings. Outward appearance and formalities, hypocrisy and fanaticism, hatred and implacability, are the main characteristics of the national religion of Persia; and, whereas in Turkey a good deal of the hierarchical power is invested in the hands of the Sultān, in Persia we find the clergy the supreme arbiters of the spiritual life, unchecked by the secular government, and very frequently its rival. During the more than 100 years' rule of the present Persian dynasty the Shāhs have striven in vain to curtail the influence of the priests; the Imām Jum'a of Iṣfahān and Karbalā were and are their equals if not superiors in power, and the Shāh's ordinances are nil without their consent.

If we turn now to Central Asia, the difference will at once appear which separates Islām there not only from Īrān—which is very natural—but also from the western portion of the Muhammadan world, in spite of their common Sunnite character and common Ḥanīfite rite. For it is only in E. Turkestan that adherents of the Shāfi'ite rite are to be met with. There we find a distinctly different religious life, the manners and customs of which do not resemble those of W. Asia. There everything bears the special stamp of extravagant fanaticism, of an exalted conception of the value of ritual trivialities, and of a deep hatred against innovations. In observing the Central Asian Muslim in his daily life, his social intercourse, his trade, and his attitude towards his government, one is tempted to believe oneself not in the 14th, but in the 2nd cent. of the Hijrah, and probably even then the prescriptions of the Qur'ān and the Sunnah were hardly so rigorously observed as they are to-day in Central Asia. Nearly one-third of the day is devoted to religious practices. Every good Muhammadan has in his room a quadrangular depression for the ritual ablutions, a niche in the wall in which to keep the Qur'ān, and a special place reserved for the *sajjādah*, or prayer carpet. Like most Orientals, he is careful to have his dress in harmony with the prescripts of his religion, and not the slightest alteration has taken place in the cut and shape of his inner and outer garments. Any deviation from the old custom, be it only in button or braid, is looked upon as an infringement of the spirit of the law. Even the material of his dress is under rigorous rule; and, as the use of pure silk is prohibited by orthodox Islām, the silk stuffs manufactured in Bukhārā and Khoqand are intermixed with a few threads of cotton. The turban, also, the *jubbah*, or overcoat, and many other garments have undergone no change for centuries, there being a predominant desire to imitate and reproduce the usage of the Muslim world of bygone ages, and particularly of Baghdād, Damascus, and the holy cities of Arabia. The case is similar as to the relations between the sexes. The separation is much more strict, and women are looked upon as mere chattels and slaves in the hand of a tyrannical master, in spite of the milder views of the Qur'ān and its expounders. They not only cover their faces with a thick impenetrable veil, but they are literally shrouded in a cloak of greater length and width than their body; and, in order not to attract the covetous glance of men, young girls even have to feign the appearance of old decrepit matrons, and very often walk leaning on a stick, as if bowed down by age or infirmities. The prohibition, also, of alcoholic drinks is very naturally more rigorously enforced than elsewhere in Islām, although in former times the ruling classes were noted for indulging freely in spirits; during the epoch of the Tīmūrids princes are mentioned who died

[1] *Description de l'Arabie*, Amsterdam, 1774, p. ix.

of *delirium tremens*; and Bābar and his followers transported this vice to the court of the Mughals. This, however, could not be said of the masses. In the present writer's time (1862–64) they were rigorously abstemious, and it is only since the annexation by Russia that the use of brandy and beer has begun to spread among the inhabitants of the towns.

In the observance, then, of the ruling prescripts of the Qur'ān and Sunnah the Muhammadan in Turkestan surpasses all his co-religionists elsewhere; his creed is the moving power in his spiritual and material life; by it he is guided in all his undertakings, thoughts, deeds, and wishes. His Muslim brother in Turkey and Persia is satisfied when he is able to perform his five daily prayers, consisting of a certain number of *rak'ahs* (bowings), and has spent three to six minutes at *murāqabah* (contemplation). The religious man in Central Asia must go far beyond this, for he has to add a few *nāfilah* (additional) *rak'ahs*; he remains from ten to fifteen minutes in contemplation, and, after having performed this extra prayer, he has to read in the forenoon either the *sūrah Yā Sīn* (xxxvi.) or *Innā Fataḥnā* (xlviii.), and in the afternoon he has to recite a portion of the *Mathnavī* of Jalāl al-Dīn Rūmī (*q.v.*), or to chant a few *ilāhīs* (hymns). This form of devotion is obligatory on every educated and respectable man, whereas the performance of the five prayers is indispensable for every Muslim irrespective of sex, age, or calling; and whoever neglects this duty, or remains ignorant of the elementary teachings of Islām, cannot escape every kind of vexation and reprobation on the part of the authorities. For this purpose a special functionary called *ra'īs* (chief) is appointed, who, accompanied by one or two servants, has to traverse the bazaars and the public places with the *dirrah*, a whip made of twisted thongs, in his hand, and, whenever he notices any one who does not go to the mosque on the first sounds of the *mu'adhdhin* (the public crier who assembles the people to prayer), he is entitled to beat the lingerer with the whip, or to put him in prison. The *ra'īs* plays, besides, the part of a public examiner: he stops at random any one in the street, puts to him a question concerning the main prescriptions of Islām, and the individual unable to answer is sent at once to school without consideration of age or profession. Full-grown and even grey-bearded men are sent to school by the religious police to learn their lesson by heart before being allowed to go. The *ra'īs*, whose office is a survival from the early Khalīfate, non-existent elsewhere in Islām, also superintends the laws of public morality. Women indecently dressed are publicly rebuked and sent home, and even children are subjected to his control. What he is still for Central Asia that the *muḥtasib* (police inspector) was for all Islām in former times; but at present, when modern European institutions are gaining ground, the office is but a nominal one in Persia as well as in Turkey. Further, not only are the prescripts of the Qur'ān more rigorously kept; they are also differently expounded. In Turkey, *e.g.*, the cutting or shaving of the beard has been practised at all times, whereas in Central Asia it is looked upon as a deadly sin, or even as apostasy. In Turkey, again, and everywhere in Islām, it suffices for the believer to wash certain parts of his body after relieving nature; in Central Asia this is much more circumstantial, for he must apply *istinjā* (cleaning with a flint or with a clod), *istinqā* (washing with water), and *istibrā* (drying). For this purpose he conceals a few clods in the fold of his turban.

But these and many other peculiarities of Islām in Central Asia are of secondary importance in comparison with one salient phase of the religious life, namely, the wide-spread and highly influential religious orders which dominate the situation, and have ever been the main moving power of the spiritual life. During many years' intimate acquaintance with the Muhammadans of Turkey and Persia, the present writer never observed such strict adherence to the rites of the different orders and such veneration for their members, generally called dervishes, as in Turkestan. In the Ottoman empire—and this is particularly the case with the genuine Turks—the Maulavī, the Baqṭāshī, the Rifā'ī, and the Qādirī orders have many votaries among the lower classes, and the respective dervishes are looked upon as saints. But the better classes, *i.e.* the Efendis and the higher dignitaries, very rarely manifest the same degree of attachment. They visit the convents on Friday afternoons, they attend the sacred ceremonies, they take advice sometimes on both worldly and spiritual matters; but they have long ago ceased to be weak instruments in the hand of the Shaikhs, and particularly of the Baqṭāshīs, who, having acted as revolutionary factors against the innovations in the time of Sulṭān Maḥmūd II., are officially interdicted and only secretly followed. Somewhat similar is the case in Persia, where the conflicts between Shī'ites and Sunnites engage too much attention to leave room for the orders, although the Shaikhīs and 'Alī Illāhīs find followers among the lower classes. The host of dervishes to be met with in towns and villages are either vagabonds, living upon the credulity and superstition of the people, or harmless idlers who conceal their laziness under the *khirqah* (mantle) of religious exaltation.

In the settled parts of Central Asia, and even among the nomads, the orders play a very different and a far more important part. There they have taken hold of the entire population; they have pushed aside the secular clergy, *i.e.* the *'ulamā*, or priests educated in the *madrasahs*, and appointed as such by the government. These, of course, are continually at war with the members of the orders, among whom the Naqshbandīs, founded by Bahā al-Dīn, best known as the author of the *Rashahat 'ain al-hayāt* ('Drops from the Fountain of Life'), occupy the foremost place. Having associated with the Naqshbandī dervishes during his stay in Central Asia, the present writer found among them various subdivisions, the character of which is expressed partly in outer appearance, partly in the way in which they fulfil their obligations. They begin as *murīds* (disciples), and as such they must forsake all worldly purposes and, clad in the *khirqah* and *kulāh* (conical hat), holding in one hand the *'aṣā* (staff) and in the other the *kashkūl* (a bowl made of a half coco-nut), have to wander about singing hymns or taking part in the *dhikr* (mentioning the name of God) and *tawḥīd* (acknowledgment of the unity of God). As the majority of the dervishes are illiterate, they learn a certain number of hymns by heart and recite them in chorus, accompanying the monotonous melody with frantic gesticulations and wild exclamations. Public places are usually selected for such performances, in order to attract attention and to collect contributions; for the dervishes, although forbidden to accept money, often betray the greatest greed, and their obtrusiveness has become proverbial. Once or twice the present writer tried to join such a howling company, but he could hardly stand the fatigue for more than an hour, whereas these adepts wander about for days without becoming exhausted. What struck him most was the endurance manifested during the *dhikrs*, and he remembers having seen one dervish crying for two nights without interruption the *Yā Hū, Yā Ḥaqq* ('He is the true and the right') without exhaustion. This, of course, refers to the lower degree of dervishes, who very rarely attain the rank of *khalīfah*, a kind of graduate, entitled to preside over a *takyah* or *khānqāh* (convent), and to lead the ritual proceedings. The title of *khalīfah* is mostly given to learned dervishes, who afterwards are addressed as *īshān* ('they,' as a polite expression instead of 'thou'), and have always a group of followers, who either stay continually with them or call on them once or twice a week. The *takyah* or *khānqāh* is really a kind of lodging-house in which there are always a few stationary dervishes, while the majority of the inmates are wandering members of the respective orders, who get a temporary shelter in an empty cell without any furniture or bedding and no regular food, except from time to time a *pilau* (rice dish), and, if deprived of all means, a piece of bread. The guests and inmates of the *takyah* regard it as a duty to assemble round the chief at the time of the five daily prayers and also at the particular exercises of the dervishes, such as the *talqīn* (recitation or instruction) and the *ḥalqah* (ring). The latter is a circle of dervishes, presided over by the *īshān*, who sing and cry so long and so vehemently that they pass into a state of excitement and hallucination; their eyes turn wildly, their mouths foam, they tremble in all their limbs, and whoever touches a dervish in this state of ecstasy is believed to have a share in his devotion, and to be cured of all kinds of infirmities. Strange to say, the spiritual leader, who presides over the exercise, always remains quiet and motionless, unaffected by the eccentricities of his disciples, and expressing his satisfaction only by a complacent nodding. Old and young women, children, greybeards, and particularly ailing people, press around; they spasmodically seize the dervishes by their arms, head, or shoulders, they cling round their necks and embrace them, crying and sobbing; and some of them actually surpass the dervishes in their ecstasies. In Turkey this excitement, bordering on madness, is seldom or never seen, nor is there a similar participation on the part of the public.

In this and in many other respects the Islām of Central Asia stands alone. Everything in it bears the stamp of extravagance, unbridled passion, and weirdness of aspect. The believer is expected to follow blindly the tenets of the Qur'ān; no discussion or explanation is permitted, nor any effort to attract. Hence we see that, whereas in Western Islām the *adhān* (call to prayer) is given from the top of a minaret in a sweet melodious song, the *mu'adhdhin* in Turkestan summons the faithful in rough and half-articulated words from the flat roof of the mosque. The performance of religious duty, they say, does not require any allurement. Austerity and draconic rigour, too, prevail with regard to neglect or trespass of the laws of Islām. In the present writer's time a Muslim convicted of the use of alcoholic drinks was sentenced to death by being hurled from a tower, and a woman caught in adultery had to undergo the penalty of *rajm* (being stoned to death). Strange to say, the Central Asians are themselves fully alive to the exceptional position which they occupy in Islām; they are even proud of it, asserting that they are the most rigorous executors of the ordinances of the Prophet, and the only Muslims whose religious belief has not been contaminated by foreign influence, but has remained as pure as in the time of the Prophet, which they call *waqt-i-sa'ādat* (the period of happiness). Accordingly, the spiritual leaders and teachers in Central Asia form a distinct class, and enjoy greater fame and reputation in Turkestan and the neighbouring countries than in the West. This refers particularly to the saints (*auliyā*), religious teachers (*khwājahs*), and chiefs of orders (*pīrs*), and not to the learned in general. They are peculiarly esteemed and venerated in Central Asia proper, and, though not unknown in the rest of Islām, may be styled the eminently national or Central Asian Muslim worthies. As such they have taken hold of the religious spirit of the people of Turkestan, Afghānistān, and India. A few of these may be mentioned here, and, first, the previously named **Bahā al-Dīn Naqshbandī**. He was Muḥammad ibn Muḥammad al-Bukhārī, and, as a pupil of Sayyid Amīr Kulāl, he was early known for his great learning and piety in Bukhārā, then the centre of Muslim letters. There he founded the order named after him. During his lifetime he became the object of great veneration, and after his death the Amīr 'Abd al-'Azīz Khān erected over his tomb in the year 1544 the famous mausoleum and convent near Bukhārā, which has since become the greatest place of pilgrimage in Central Asia, and of such sanctity that three visits to it are deemed equal to a pilgrimage to Mecca. Next to Bahā al-Dīn ranks **Khwājah Kāshānī**, known as Makhdūm A'ẓam ('the greatest lord'), born in the village of Kāshān near Andijān (Farghāna), who died A.H. 949 (A.D. 1542), and was buried in Dehbid, a village near Samarqand. In the early part of his life he acted as governor of various places, but later he devoted himself exclusively to religious contemplation and theological studies, and aroused so high a veneration that his children reached princely rank. Of these the most noted was the great saint of E. Turkestan, **Khwājah Axath** (his proper name was Hidāyat Allāh), the founder of a ruling dynasty, members of which still exist in Kashgar. Frequently mentioned and highly venerated also is **Khwājah 'Ubaid Allāh Ahrār**, one of the greatest theologians of his time († A.D. 1489 at Kumaghiran, a village near Samarqand), whose grave is still a place of pilgrimage. Similarly with the tomb at Ghijduvān of **Khwājah 'Abd al-Khāliq**, a pupil of Khwājah Kāshānī († A.H. 1010). Others are **Khwājah Abūfer Parsah**, a pupil of Bahā al-Dīn († A.H. 845), whose grave in Balkh is a place of pilgrimage, particularly for Afghans; **Khwājah 'Abd Allāh Hātifī**, a famous poet and mystic, who spent much time in India with Bābar, the founder of the Mughal dynasty, and died there in A.H. 927 (A.D. 1520); and **Juibarī** († A.H. 997 [A.D. 1588]), whose grave is in Bukhārā.

Apart from these great theological scholars, saints, and mystics, there are a number of popular spiritual worthies who are venerated by the lower classes, sedentary and nomadic, and whose plain, unadorned, and more intelligible works are the favourite reading of the masses. To these belongs **Khwājah Aḥmad Yesevī**, the Kirghiz patron-saint of the 12th cent. A.D.; his grave in Ḥaḍrat-i-Turkestan, surrounded by a huge dome now in decay, is a place of pilgrimage famous through all Central Asia. His religious poems, known as *Ḥikmat* ('Wisdom,' 'Philosophy'), are still much esteemed, although their language, mixed with Arabic and Persian expressions, is not easily understood by the uninstructed nomads. What Yesevī is to the northern part of Turkestan, **Mashrab** (personal name, Raḥīm Bābā) is for the east and south. He was a native of Namangan in Khoqand, and known as a *dīvānah*, a religious madman. A *dīvānah* wanders from place to place, behaves like a man insane, but, possessed of divine powers, works miracles, and has consequently an extraordinary influence over the ignorant masses. The present writer's own observation of these *dīvānahs* or *faqīrs* (poor) has led him to the conviction that most of them are cunning men with a lust for adventure, ready to exploit the plain people, and unwilling to submit to the sometimes rigorous monastic regulations of the orders to which they belong, or disliking the individuality of their *īshān*, or spiritual chief. It was chiefly in the villages and in the tents of the nomads that he met with these religious vagabonds; there they are highly reverenced. The *mullās*, on the other hand, accuse them of ignorance, and of breaking the precept of Islām—*Lā ruhbān fī'l-Islām*, 'There are no monks in Islām.' The majority of them are illiterate, but the present writer has met with *dīvānahs* who were versed in religious lore, had studied in *madrasahs*, and had been moved simply by wandering propensities to renounce the regular and sedentary life of a priest. Among these dervishes there is also a certain **Turk-dīvānah**, a Turk by origin, as the name indicates (date unknown), who is very often spoken of by the nomads as a saint, and who interceded with Allāh for sinful humanity. He asked Him to deliver mankind from hell, to which Allāh replied that He would when peace, justice, charity, etc., reigned supreme in the world. Further, among the latter dervishes there are many of local celebrity, though others coming from distant countries have their own influence; in fact, the farther a dervish has wandered, the greater is deemed his supernatural power, and the stronger is his grip on the masses. The reason for this extraordinary influence of the beggar-dervishes does not lie merely in the utter ignorance of the people, but rather in the tyrannic rule of the governing classes, who, lay and ecclesiastic, are everywhere hated. These unofficial servants of God, then, discredited and despised by the *mullās*, are regarded by the lower class as of themselves; they thus very naturally become popular favourites, and frequently play the part of publicly avowed protectors against oppression.

In Western Islām there is hardly a trace to be found of these roaming saints, and those whom the traveller accidentally meets in the Balkan countries, in Asia Minor, and in Syria are mostly foreigners, and principally adventurers from Central Asia, India, or Persia. The Turk himself is too lazy, too easy-tempered, and too much given to a quiet life to find pleasure in the eccentricities of the wandering dervish. The Ottoman Turk, like the Kurd and the Arab, clings with great attachment to his faith; but he is very far from giving way to the religious ecstasy and wild fanaticism which are imputed to him by his detractors. In this respect the Western Muhammadan is many hundred years ahead of his fellow-believer in Central Asia; for the latter has remained absolutely in the position of the first centuries of Islām, and, indeed, at the beginning of the past century was even more fanatical and orthodox than in the time of Hārūn al-Rashīd and al-Ma'mūn. Such, however, was not always the case. As long as the Iranian element was predominant beyond the Oxus, worldly science found many votaries, and during the reign of the Sāmānids and later Central Asia was the birthplace of literary celebrities of high standing. But with the increase of the Turkish population and under the rule of warlike Turkish chieftains, mostly of nomadic origin, a great change has set in. The place of scientific culture has been taken by exclusively theological studies and mystic speculation. There has been no want of richly endowed colleges and schools; but the students, flocking from all parts of Central Asia and India, have turned their attention to purely religious questions, neglecting even such subjects as philosophy, law, and philology, which are still cultivated in the colleges of Western Islām. Naturally, then, scientific inquiry having been gradually banished, religious eccentricity has taken its place, and Central Asia has long been the seat of fanaticism. Jalāl al-Dīn Rūmī, the author of the *Mathnavī*, was right in saying:

> 'Thou wilt to Bukhārā? O fool for thy pains!
> Thither thou goest, to be put into chains.'

Similar things were said to the present writer by his learned friends in Turkey and Persia when they heard of his intended visit to Central Asia; and when, on returning, he related to them his experiences, many of them disdainfully criticized and laughed at the overheated religious zeal of their fellow-believers. Another reason for this great difference is to be sought in the belt of dreary sand steppes, infested by nomadic robbers, which surrounds Central Asia, and has always been a great hindrance to its communication with the rest of the Muhammadan world. Whilst Western Islām has undergone essential changes in the course of time, Islām in Central Asia has remained stationary, unaffected by the temporary intellectual movements in the West, and checked by the strong conservatism of a fanatical clergy and a despotic form of government. If Shī'ite Persia had not produced its great cleft in the general Muslim body, extending from W. China to the shores of the Adriatic, Islām in Central Asia could hardly have retained its fanaticism or degenerated into these aberrations, often censured by pious Muslims of other countries, but extolled by the Central Asians themselves, who accuse their co-religionists in Turkey and Arabia of levity of mind, and proclaim with pride: 'Bukhārā is the real strength of Islām and of the faith.' This difference becomes still more important when we observe that the spirit of zealotism has extended into N. India, and has particularly infected the barbarous mountaineers of Afghānistān. When we hear of a murderous attack by some Paṭhān or Khaibarī on an unoffending British officer, we have always to think of one of those fanatics, who, anxious to become a *ghāzī*, a warrior for the faith, is ready to sacrifice his life for the title of martyr, and for the prospect of a place in Paradise. The existence of such *ghāzīs* was formerly reported among the adherents of Shaikh Shamil in the fierce struggle between the Russians and Lesghians in the N.W. Caucasus, but nowhere else in Islām. It is, therefore, to the wild influence of the Islām of Central Asia that their appearance in the north of India must be ascribed. A. VAMBÉRY.

MUHAMMADANISM (in China).—I. Historical.—China, regarded as a portion of the Muhammadan world, may be divided into (1) China proper (the 'Eighteen Provinces'), and (2) the external provinces (Turkestan, Tibet, and Mongolia). Of the external provinces only Turkestan need concern us here, for the Muhammadans resident in Tibet and Mongolia have never been more than an insignificant fraction. According to H. d'Ollone, *Revue du monde musulman*,[1] v. [1908] 94, they are to be found all along the highway to India through Tibet; thus, *e.g.*, there is a mosque at Tatsienlu for the hundred or so Muslim families living in the vicinity, while mosques are found also in Batang and Lhāsa, those in the latter city being attended, it is said, by Hindu Muhammadans. The Lāmas of Tibet are in no way hostile to Islām—a fact that need excite no surprise, since the adherents of the two religions have a common political interest in making all possible resistance to the domination of China. Nevertheless, there is no prospect of any considerable expansion of Islām in Tibet (cf. *RMM* v. 458). Hitherto, at all events, the commercial relations between Muhammadans and Tibetans

[1] Hereafter cited as *RMM*.

have brought about no conversions to Islām, though the commercial bond is far from being insignificant. In particular, the Muslims of Sung-p'an-t'ing in Sze-chuan carry on with Tibet an important traffic in tea, but in this locality the d'Ollone expedition of 1907 found only a single Tibetan convert to Islām, who, moreover, was rather lukewarm in his adherence (*RMM* v. 458 f.); on the other hand, several cases of conversion to Christianity were met with in Sung-p'an-t'ing.

Muhammadanism was introduced into Turkestan at the time when the powerful kingdom of the Sāmānids was pressing towards the east. According to the tradition—interwoven with many legendary features—which is given in the *Tezkiret al-Boghra* (extracts in R. B. Shaw, *Sketch of the Turki Language*, Calcutta, 1878–80), the Turki prince Satak Boghra was converted to Islām at the age of twelve (A.D. 966; he reigned till 1047) by a certain Abū Naṣr Sāmānī, who came from the west. It is a fact of history that the descendants of Satak Boghra, known as the Boghraids or Ilekids, maintained their power till the year 1103, and in 1070, during the reign of Tapghach (one of that dynasty), Yūsuf Khass Hajib finished his great didactic poem *Qudatku Bilik* ('Joy-giving Science'), a work imbued with the spirit of Islām. Probably the diffusion of the Persian language and civilization among the Turki population had contributed to the spread of Islām in that region. But, if Islām was here the recognized religion of the rulers, it certainly was no more than tolerated in the adjacent Turki kingdom to the east—the land of the Uigurs. Nor can the position of the Muslims have undergone any essential change by the time when the Kara-Khitai overthrew the Ilekid kingdom, since the conquered people were left in full exercise of their religious freedom as long as they paid tribute to the victors. Similar methods were practised by the Mongol conqueror Jenghiz Khān and his immediate successors. At the division of his empire Turkestan fell to his grandson, Jagatai, whose successors soon embraced Islām. Even at a later time, however, as the records conclusively show, the adherence of princes and people alike to the new faith was half-hearted, and the ideas and usages of Lāmaism (*q.v.*) were quite common among the professed Muslims. The blind superstition of the people facilitated the usurping tactics of the philosophically gifted descendants of Makhdūm 'Aẓam, who at first ruled as the spiritual advisers of the dispossessed house of Jagatai, and eventually in their own name. The dissensions that arose within the family of Makhdūm, their struggle with the Kalmuks of Zungaria, and the internal wars of the Kalmuk kingdom led (*c.* 1750) to the conquest of Zungaria by the Chinese, who shortly thereafter won Kashgaria as well, and joined the two territories together as the 'New Province' (Hsin-chian). Ever since that time the Chinese have been the ruling power there, and various attempts at revolt have proved abortive. Only for a short period, from 1864 to 1877, did the country—as Altyshahr ('Six Cities'), and subsequently Yettishahr ('Seven Cities')—figure as an independent Muhammadan State under the savage but politically capable Ya'qūb Beg, who recognized the suzerainty of the Sulṭān of Constantinople as Khalīfah; *e.g.*, the coinage was stamped with his name. The Muhammadans of these districts are nearly all Turki, though an insignificant number are Dungans (see below, pp. 891[a], 892[a]) or Chinese, and the total population is estimated at from 1,000,000 to 1,500,000.

In China proper there existed no considerable groups of Muhammadans before the Mongolian period, and the reports of an earlier immigration are altogether legendary. Chinese tradition says that Islām found its way into the country by land and sea. It tells of a maternal uncle of the Prophet, Wahb Abū Kabshah, who landed at Canton in A.D. 628 or 629, bearing presents from Muhammad to the emperor of China, together with an invitation to embrace Islām, and who then proceeded to Hsi-an-fu. Other reports say that the earliest message was brought by Sa'd Ibn Abī Waqqāṣ, whose tomb may be seen in Canton. The tradition attaches special importance to an expedition of 4000 Muslim troops which the Khalīfah Manṣūr is said to have sent to assist the emperor in a struggle with rebels (A.D. 755). The emperor permitted them to settle in the chief cities of the country; they took Chinese wives and became the progenitors of the numerous and important Muslim communities in China.

These traditions find no corroboration in the writings of Arabian historians. China and Islām, as a matter of fact, were brought into contact with each other as a result of the conditions prevailing in either sphere. About 620 a new power in Nearer Asia emerged, and another in China, each characterized by a remarkable ambition for conquest, and, advancing respectively eastwards and westwards, at length came into contact. Just as Islām (*c.* 720) conquered Transoxania, which it had been attacking incessantly after the conquest of Khurāsān, so T'ai Tsung (627–649), the second emperor of the T'ang dynasty, made himself master of Kashgaria. Of the more general incentives to mutual intercourse the strongest was commerce,[1] which was strenuously fostered by the later emperors of the Sui dynasty; another connecting link was the work of Christian missionaries, of whose bold advance into China the Nestorian stele of Hsi-an-fu (dating from 781) affords telling evidence. Against these influences, however, must be placed the impediment to intercourse arising from the tendency of both empires to rest content with their gains, and so to limit their frontiers. The emperor T'ai Tsung showed caution in rejecting the appeal of Yazdagird III. for assistance (as may be inferred from Ṭabarī, i. 2669 f., though the report of the ambassador is a fabrication; cf. i. 2876). The Muslims became more aggressive after their able general Qutaiba Ibn Muslim had subjugated Farghāna, but his expedition against Kashgar in 713 was unsuccessful. A comparison of the sources (Ṭabarī, i. 1275–1279) shows that Kashgar remained unconquered. The sending of ambassadors to the emperor of China (Hsüan Tsung, 712–756), however, is probably historical, though, as narrated by Ṭabarī (ii. 1277 ff.) in the traditional form, it is garnished with all the conventional features.[2] Under the Umayyads the Muslims had, indirectly, a good deal to do with China, since the *khāqān* of the Turki, and also the *jabghu*,[3] were vassals of the emperor. A time-honoured tale is that of the scene between Naizak and the *jabghu* on the one side, and the *shadd* (the *shad* of the Orchonian records) and the *sebel* (probably to be identified with the *ziebel* of Theophanes; cf. E. Chavannes, *Documents sur les Tou-kiue* (*Turcs*) *orientaux*, Petrograd, 1903, p. 228) on the other, in which the *shadd* makes the kow-tow before the *jabghu* (Ṭabarī, ii. 1224, year 91 [= A.D. 710]). The *jabghu*

1 Notwithstanding the surreptitious introduction of silk-culture into the Byzantine empire under Justinian, the silk merchandise of China was largely imported into Nearer Asia. It was conveyed on land by the ancient 'iter ad Seres,' or by sea through the Persian Gulf, on the north shore of which Al'ubulla (Ṭabarī, ed. Leyden, 1879–1901, i. 2384), and afterwards Sīrāf (references in G. Le Strange, *The Lands of the Eastern Caliphate*, Calcutta, 1905, p. 258 f.), was the port for such products.

2 Nothing is said, however, of an embassy from the Chinese side. At an earlier date, in the reign of Chosroës Anūshirvān there were Chinese at the Sasanian court (Ṭabarī, i. 899; cf. T. Nöldeke, *Gesch. der Perser und Araber zur Zeit der Sasaniden*, Leyden, 1879, p. 167).

3 In Ṭabarī this term is always mutilated to *jīghūyah*.

was sent to Damascus, and was probably the first Chinese, or Chinese Turki, that the Syrians had ever seen. It may be regarded as certain that it was Chinese statecraft that abetted the opposition of the Turki *khāqān* and that of the smaller nationalities in Transoxania dependent upon him or upon China itself, so that the Muslims had to maintain a ceaseless struggle. The Khottal, who are probably to be located in the Pamirs, were not dislodged till A.D. 750 (Ṭabarī, iii. 74), while Al'ikhrid, king of Kashsh, was slain in 751, his treasures—costly Chinese ware—being conveyed to Abū Muslim at Samarqand (Ṭabarī, iii. 79f.). When with the downfall of the Arabian empire the vigour of Muslim expansion had somewhat relaxed, and the central authority was busy with the maintenance and organization of what had been won, and when contemporaneously the central power of China under the T'ang emperors showed symptoms of decline, the interjacent territory was soon occupied by strong buffer States—first of all by the Uigurs, and then by the Ilekids (see above). Islām was thus placed in a very unfavourable position for making an advance into China. Weak as were the dynasties that followed the T'ang emperors, the people held firmly to the maxim, 'No foreign religion in China.' Buddhism, it is true, had made a successful entry in the face of vigorous opposition, but this is explained by the facts that (1) Buddhism was to some extent in harmony with the cult of reason (*li*), which, if hardly to be called a religion, was more widely diffused than any other, and (2) it assimilated certain elements of the national spirit and so adapted itself to the prevailing sentiment (see art. CHINA [Buddhism in]). Islām, which with its rigid doctrine of uniformity does not on principle express itself in creeds, and tends to repel by the defiant and arrogant tone of its adherents, and which, above all, contrasts with Buddhism in its being essentially a political religion, could not strike root in China save under the protection of the strong hand. The required protection was first provided by the rulers of the Mongol empire founded by Jenghiz Khān. These potentates had no religion—nothing at all events beyond the worship of their lucky star, conjoined with the egregious ambition to bring this star down from heaven. Jenghiz Khān himself saw only the advantages of a huge centralization of human beings, and, wherever it suited his purposes, he intermingled detached fragments of races without regard for nationality or religion. As a Mongol, his leading aim was the disintegration of the Chinese element and the fusion of the population, so that he might have nothing to fear from the formation of any powerful alliance against him. He found his auxiliaries—apart from his own countrymen—in the various Muslim tribes of the West, a race renowned for their courage. Among these the Turki took precedence, alike in numbers, in importance, in capacity for bearing arms, and in discipline. We shall hardly err in adding Afghan mercenaries; for the Afghans—the Paṭhāns of India—were always willing to serve for pay; and bands of warriors may also have flocked to him from the mountains of Persia—the fastnesses of the Kurds—though not the Persians in the narrower sense, the inhabitants of the plains, who had small reputation for bravery. Yet we can hardly look for definite information regarding the composition of his armies, or those of his successors, for the great Mongol rulers were not the people to lend themselves to the statistician, their great concern being with men, not with the keeping of trim muster-rolls. We may venture to assume, however, that the largest hordes of their followers were supplied by the countries lying nearest the scene of their conquests, viz. besides the land of the Turki between the Great Wall and the mountain barrier of the Thian Shan (Chinese Turkestan), Transoxania and Khurāsān. This explains also the curious phenomenon that from that day till the present Persian has been regarded by the Muslims of China as the language of polite education, and that the vernacular Chinese written by these Muslims is mixed with scraps of Persian.[1] In elucidation of this it has been supposed that at some time or other Persian immigrants had settled in the country, losing their mother tongue, but retaining vestiges of it in these numerous fragments. This, however, is certainly erroneous,[2] for the intermixture of Persian in the Muslim idiom of Chinese is due rather to the superstitious regard for the Persian language entertained by the barbarian and semi-barbarian hordes of Nearer Asia who swarmed to the camps of the Mongolian Khāns. Moreover, as soon as Kublai Khān had established his sway in China, he brought Persians in great numbers to fill the offices connected with the government and the court. Both Marco Polo and the Arabian traveller Ibn Baṭūṭah supply full information regarding these foreigners in the Chinese services.[3] To a great extent they would be full-blooded Persians, and they no doubt helped to enhance the respect accorded to their language, and to keep it alive in the very heart of the country.

As to the numbers of Muslims brought into China by the Mongol emperors, we can hardly even hazard a conjecture, although an incident now to hand may throw light upon such importations. In A.D. 1226 a young Muslim warrior, a native of Bukhārā, who claimed to be a descendant of the Prophet—a Sayyid—placed himself at the disposal of Jenghiz Khān. The latter perceived at once the outstanding ability of the youth, and, attaching him to his bodyguard, soon began to employ him on commissions of a special kind. His successor, Kublai Khān, entrusted this Sayyid (who appears as Sayyid-i Ajall in the work of Rashīd-al-Dīn, and as Sai-tien-ch'e in the Chinese sources) with the task of subjugating the province of Yün-nan, and for six years the affairs of that province were administered by this talented Muslim. He died in office, and his two tombs—the first in Yün-nan-fu, the other near Hsi-an-fu—were discovered almost simultaneously by French explorers.[4] The official employment of this Muslim from Bukhārā, who, of course, did not come single-handed, but was attended by a company of armed men, is of special interest, because his soldiers were sent on service to Yün-nan, while he himself was installed as viceroy of that province. We may accordingly infer that the influx of Islām into Yün-nan began at that time, for that it reached

1 An excellent specimen of this idiom is found in the short Chinese MS (MS Sin. Hartmann 1 of the Royal Library, Berlin) ed. A. Forke, which contains a Chinese text in Arab. script (*T'oung-pao*, II. viii. [1907] no. 8). From the nature of the language Forke inferred—wrongly, as the present writer thinks—the Persian origin of the Dungans.

2 It is no argument against the theory, however, to say that it would involve a wider diffusion of Shī'ism than we actually find, for the introduction of Shī'ism as the national religion of Persia and the dissemination of the Shī'ite principle among the people did not take place till a later period. There is also a tendency to regard all Persian writings as of Shī'ite origin—an utterly mistaken idea, as even the widely-read work, *Ma'ārij al-Nubuwwat*, 'Life of the Prophet,' by Mu'īn al-Dīn al-Miskīn († A.D. 1501), is Sunnite in character.

3 One of these officials made himself very obnoxious—Achmath [Aḥmad] 'the Bailo,' whose story is given not only in the Chinese sources (cf. J. A. M. de M. de Mailla, *Hist. générale de la Chine*, Paris, 1777–85, ix. 412 f. [tr. of *Tong-Kien-Kang-Mou*]), which might naturally be expected to take a prejudiced view, but also in a straightforward account by Marco Polo (cf. H. Yule, *The Book of Ser Marco Polo*[3], London, 1903, i. 415 ff.).

4 For reports of these discoveries see P. Berthelot, 'Note sur des inscriptions arabes, persanes et chinoises du Chen-si, du Ho-nan, et du Chan-toung,' *CAIBL*, Paris, 1905. A. Vissière has wrought the facts into a graphic and ingenious sketch (*RMM* iv. [1907] 330 ff.).

that province by sea is in the highest degree unlikely.

Now, when we take into consideration the number of Muslims in China at the present day and the isolated movement just mentioned—the only known instance of the systematic migration of Muslims into China, and there was certainly no other—we are prompted to ask how the Muslim element has attained to such vast proportions. The total number of Muslims who settled in China from the date of the earliest campaigns of Jenghiz Khān (*c.* A.D. 1200) to the fall of the Mongol dominion (*c.* A.D. 1367) cannot certainly be reckoned at more than 1,000,000. At the present day, however, the Muslims resident in China amount on the lowest estimate to 4,000,000. That this vast expansion is due entirely to natural increase is inconceivable; we must therefore look for other possible factors. (1) From time to time fresh companies of Muslims came to China, as, *e.g.*, in the retinue of Turki princesses of Muslim faith who entered the *ḥarīm* of the Chinese emperors.[1] (2) Chinese-born children were, and still are, sometimes made Muslims. (3) When great devastations occurred among the Chinese, the vacant places were filled by Muslims, as the latter, being endowed with superior vigour, were better qualified to grapple with the manifold misfortunes which throughout the centuries have fallen upon this ill-governed country. It has already been noted that the Muslims are represented as stately, strong, and brave. The high appreciation accorded to their eminent qualities by the Chinese government is shown by a recently-issued decree to the effect that Muslims are to be employed in the cultivation of sections of land adjoining the projected Ordos Road. Against these favourable conditions, however, must be set certain drawbacks. For one thing, the Chinese government has frequently been stricken with fear of the Muslims, the power of whose politico-religious organization it has good reason to know. Then there is the antagonism that arose between the Muslims of China and their co-religionists in the West; and, finally, their internal conflicts must be taken into account (see p. 894).

A word may be added regarding the names applied to the Muslims of China. It is a common notion that they are all called Dungans, and in point of fact the present writer has noted the use of this designation in Kashgar and Yarkand; by the Turki all Chinese-speaking Muslims are called 'Dungan(lar).'[2] They themselves do not use that name, but term themselves 'Hui-hui' or 'Hui-tzŭ,' and this appellation is applied by the Chinese to all Muslims, whether resident in China proper or in Turkestan. The Turki offer strong resistance to this usage, and desire to be called 'Chan-tu,' 'the turbaned,' lit. 'head-bound.'

A few details will now be given regarding the several provinces:

(1) *Kan-su.*—In this province the Muslims, according to P. Dabry (*Le Mahométisme en Chine et dans le Turkestan oriental*, Paris, 1878), number 8,350,000, *i.e.* about 85·6 per cent. The capital, Lan-chou (G. M. H. Playfair, *The Cities and Towns of China*, Hongkong, 1879, 2Shanghai, 1910, p. 3992), took no part in the insurrections of 1863–74 and 1895, and the Muslim residents received no damage. They possess a relatively high degree of culture. Lan-chou, as the terminus of the great trade-route from the West, is frequently visited by Muslims from India, Persia, and both divisions of Turkestan. Ho-chou and Kin-ki-pu (of which, however, the Chinese name is Ning-ling-t'ing; in Fu, Ning-hsia [Playfair, p. 5226]) are celebrated as centres of religious activity.[1] Kin-ki-pu was the nucleus of the sect of Ma-hua-lung (see p. 894). Hsi-ning-fu, not far from Kokonor, is a place of special interest on account of its mixed population; it affords a most fertile field for the student of ethnology and philology, since, being situated on the frontier between China and Tibet, it gives an opportunity for observing the most heterogeneous elements such as seldom occurs elsewhere. With reference to the Salars, who live compactly in twelve townships around Hsün-hua-t'ing, see below, p. 892b. In Kan-su there are also Mongolian Muslims (cf. F. Grenard, 'Note sur l'ethnographie du Kansu,' in *Mission scientifique dans la Haute Asie*, Paris, 1897–98, ii. 'Mission Dutreuil de Rhins,' p. 456).

(2) *Shen-si.*—According to Dabry, the Muslim population of Shen-si—probably largely overestimated—is 6,500,000, *i.e.* 76·7 per cent. Hsi-an-fu, the capital (Playfair, p. 2620), according to a report of the Futai (1782) to the emperor Ch'ien-lung, then contained 50,000 Muslim families (Dabry, p. 41 f.), with 7 large mosques. According to Gabriel Maurice (in H. Havret, *La Stèle chrétienne de Si-Ngan-Fou*, ii. [*Variétés sinologiques*, Shanghai, 1892–1902, no. 12] 115 ff.), the total population, including that of the four suburbs, is estimated—by mere guess-work—at some 400,000; of these one-tenth are Tatars, two-tenths Muslims, and seven-tenths Chinese. According to the tradition regarding General Kuo-tzŭ-i (697–781), who is said to have been a Christian, the Muslims had settled on the banks of the Yü-ho. When the great insurrection broke out in 1863, the Muslims of Shen-si wrought considerable damage, and, after they were overpowered, were expelled from the province. The people of Hsi-an-fu, the only city in which Muslims are now found, were kept under too strict a watch to take any part in the movement, and the Muslims were allowed to remain.

(3) *Shan-si.*—In this province the Muslims (including those of S. Mongolia) number, according to Dabry, 50,000, *i.e.* 0·41 per cent; exact data are lacking.

(4) *Chi-li.*—The available data for the Muhammadan population refer only to the Muslims in Peking, who are said to number 20,000 families, say 100,000 persons, with 11 mosques.

(5) *Shan-tung.*—Muslims are found in many towns on the Great Canal, one of their centres being the important commercial city of Lin-ch'ing-chou (Playfair, p. 4276), where there is an academy (*madrasah*), in which most of the *mullās* of Peking are trained. There are said to be 325 mosques in Shan-tung.

(6) *Sze-chuan.*—In this province the Muslims, according to *RMM* v. 91 ff., number about 70,000 families (300,000 persons), with about 400 mosques, 11 of these being in Ch'eng-tu alone (Playfair, p. 572). During the insurrections in Kan-su and Yün-nan, Sze-chuan remained passive. Visitors from Turkestan are numerous. The town of Sung-p'an-t'ing, already mentioned, is in this province; its 10,000 inhabitants, according to *RMM* v. 458, include 4000 Muslims, with 3 mosques, and about 100 *ahongs*.

(7) *Ho-nan.*—The Muslim population, according to Dabry, is 200,000.

(8) *Yün-nan.* — The Muslims here, according to Dabry, number from 350,000 to 400,000. With reference to the history of this province, the Muslim settlement of which we can trace from its starting-point, see above, p. 890b; for its more recent history we have the monograph of E. Rocher, *La Province chinoise du Yün-Nan*, Paris, 1880; cf. also d'Ollone, 'L'Islam au Yunnan,' in *RMM* iv. 285–290.

(9) In the remaining provinces Muslims are found in relatively small numbers. Dabry furnishes the following figures: Hu-nan (with Hu-pei), 50,000; Kiang-hsi, 4000; Kiang-hsu (with An-hui), 150,000; Kuang-tung, 21,000; Kuang-hsi, 15,000; Kuei-chou, 40,000; Che-kiang (with Fo-kien), 30,000. These numbers, however, are not reliable; cf. Dabry's estimate (40,000) with d'Ollone's (300,000) for the province of Sze-chuan.

2. Descriptive.—If we may regard the Muslims of China as forming a single social complex, we may indicate the main features of that complex as follows.

(*a*) *Race and language.*—Whatever be the origin of the various Muslim groups, they must all be described at the present day as Chinese. The extent to which they share the distinctive qualities of the Chinese peoples cannot be precisely determined, the requisite data not being available. In any case they all speak the language of their adopted country; they share the variation of idiom, and resemble the real Chinese in their ways of thinking, while in writing also they use almost exclusively the national language. At the same time they are differentiated from the Chinese by important characteristics, and the division of the people as a whole—exclusive, however, of the Tatars

[1] The leading instance of this is furnished by the still existing colony of Turkish Muslims which can be traced back to the reception of a Turkish princess into the *ḥarīm* of the emperor Ch'ien-lung; cf. C. Arendt, 'Peking und die westlichen Berge,' *Mitteil. der geograph. Gesellschaft Hamburg*, 1889–90, p. 64.

[2] This term may signify 'those who have come home,' *i.e.* those who have returned to the true faith, the implication being that all human beings come into the world as adherents of Islām, though some are alienated from it by their parents, and so become Jews or Christians. The word corresponds, therefore, to the Osmanic *dönmeh*, the name applied to the Jews of Saloniki who have been converted to Islām. The designation Dungan would thus seem to imply that the majority of Chinese Muslims have been converts.

[1] With reference to the history of Ho-chou see *RMM* ix. [1909] 530 ff.; cf. Kin-ki-pu, *ib.* p. 564.

(Mongols) and the aborigines of the south (Lotos, Miaotze)—into Chinese and Muslims holds good throughout. The name Dungans is applied to a large section of the Chinese Muslims, who, however, as was said above, term themselves simply Hui-hui or Hui-tzŭ, and repudiate the appellation Dungans; but they would never think of calling themselves Han ('Chinese'), nor are they ever designated so. They form, in fact, a distinct racial aggregate, co-ordinate with the Chinese and the Manchus. The name Dungans is sometimes erroneously extended also to the Turki of Turkestan, but in reality there exists a marked contrast between Dungans and Turki. The Dungans who speak Turkish—they are by no means few—use a peculiar dialect of that language; and, as regards the Chinese spoken by the Dungans, it should further be noted that the document of Dungan origin in the Berlin Royal Library (see above, p. 890b) is composed in a very corrupt Chinese. In Forke's opinion, however, its solecisms are not such as might be perpetrated by an uneducated Chinese, but are in many cases not Chinese at all, suggesting that the Dungans are of alien origin. As a special illustration of the intercourse between the Chinese Muslims and the Turki, cf. the story of Hidāyat-Allāh (Apaq Khojam) of Kāshghar, who came to Hsi-ning-fu, in MS Hartmann 1 (Forke, p. 65 f.).

The process which dominates everything found within the Great Wall is one of adaptation to Chinese standards, of assimilation to the character of the yellow race—or 'black-heads,' as they like to call themselves. This process overcame the Manchus and many other peoples who invaded the country, and it was impossible that the Muslims should altogether elude its operation. The Chinese have a capacity for dissolving racial characteristics. This holds good even of physical qualities, for Chinese sentiment does not discountenance the affiancing of native women with foreigners, while Muslim women cannot legally be given in marriage to non-Muslims. The resultant diffusion of Chinese blood among the Muslims is of vast importance, and we cannot but admire the tenacity with which the latter have kept themselves from complete absorption by the Chinese. In spite of a considerable degree of assimilation in external matters, the two peoples look at things from a fundamentally different standpoint. For the Chinese reason (*li*) is supreme; for the Muslims tradition is all. Notable, too, is the contrast in certain traits of character. The Chinese is patient to a degree, and will put up with a great deal; the Dungan has an intense self-esteem, and is a dangerous man to offend. The difference reveals itself also in the outward bearing. The Chinese not seldom gives one the impression of being a dejected and downtrodden man; the Muslim carries himself proudly, and faces the world with a frank and open countenance. The relative physical debility of the Chinese may be due in part to the opium habit. Among the Muslims this is but rarely found; tobacco smoking is prohibited, and the drinking of wine and other intoxicants, which the stringent interdict of the law does not prevent in Western Islām, is quite inconsiderable among the Muslims of China. All this testifies to a very real cleavage between the Chinese and the Muslims, and is a constant reminder that the latter are not Han-yen, but something else.

What, then, are the Muslims of China, ethnologically considered? To this question there is no answer, whether or not we postulate a connexion between the name Hui-hui (Hui-tzŭ) and the name Uigur, with all its various transcriptions in the Chinese language (Chavannes, pp. 87–94). From the time of the earliest considerable incursions of Muslims, this region of many races has been overwhelmed with so many devastations that it is now impossible to speak of any single racial type. In addition to this we must also take into account the Muslim policy of incorporating people of other faiths, notably purchased children (cf. the present writer's note in his *Der islamische Orient*, i. [Leipzig, 1905]; more recently d'Ollone, in *RMM* ix.). Such absorption of foreign elements must be regarded as a very important factor. In this connexion we should note the suggestive remark of d'Ollone to the effect that the purchased Chinese children do not exhibit a uniform Chinese type, and that the homogeneity of the Chinese 'race' is simply one of those *fables convenues* that cannot be too vehemently opposed, since in point of fact many who are not Muslims at all are no more Chinese than the Muslims themselves.

A distinct ethnological group is formed by the Salars, who live in Hsün-hua-t'ing (Playfair, p. 3110) on the right bank of the Hoang-ho, and in the surrounding villages, and who are also found on a section of the road between Hsi-ning-fu and Ho-chou. They show a racial character markedly divergent from the ordinary Chinese Muslims. In figure they are tall and spare, with nose large but not broad, eyes black and set horizontally, cheekbones not very prominent, face longish, eyebrows bushy, beard black and abundant, forehead receding, skull flattened behind, skin brown but not in any sense yellow. The Salars thus bear a striking resemblance to the Turki of Chinese Turkestan. Their chief peculiarity is their language, which may be described as a degenerate Turkish. Their style of dress is Chinese, but they shave the head completely and wear a polygonal cap (*tübe*) of white colour. In religion they are strict Ḥanīfites, and show the utmost respect to their spiritual guides (*akhons*), many of whom speak and write the Persian language; but they are given to the use of strong drink. Even the lower classes are acquainted with the Arabic script. They do not burn incense in worship, nor do they tolerate the emperor's portrait in their mosques. This form of the Muslim faith is said to have emanated from a reformer named Ma-ming-hsin (Muhammad Emin), who preached to the Salars *c.* 1750, laying great stress on the practice of praying aloud (see below, p. 894b), which led to serious disturbances. The Salars are daring brigands, and fraternize with the rabble of the upper Hoang-ho, with whom they also share a fierce hatred of the Chinese.[1]

(*b*) *Marriage, family, kinship.*—The external aspects of the sexual relation among the Muslims of China are regulated by the *sharī'ah*—in the scholastic form developed in the Ḥanīfite school—which applies to all Islām, though here the separate ordinances are not very well known to the people at large, nor, even where they are known, are they very strictly observed. As to the degree in which the Chinese environment has brought about modifications in practice, we do not possess the necessary details of information; nor would such details yield a complete and uniform picture, since the influence varies greatly in different localities.[2]

[1] Our authority for these particulars is Grenard, *Mission*, ii. 457 f. A somewhat different account is given by d'Ollone (*RMM* ix. 538 ff.), who says that the Salars are confined to twelve villages in the district of Hsün-hua-t'ing on the right bank of the Hoang-ho, but that the bulk of their traffic is with the left bank, especially the town of Hsi-ning, in which, however, there reside only five Salar families; they do not shave the head completely, but retain the pigtail; they wear, not the polygonal cap, but the turban-like head-dress of the Chinese; they have taken part in various risings; and they assert that their original home was Samarqand.

[2] With reference to the well-known canon allowing the Muslim to marry as many as four wives, and to have slaves as concubines, Dabry (ii. 266, n. 1) writes: 'In China the Muslims are forced to submit to the laws of the land regarding marriage.' This is undoubtedly a mistake in so far as it implies that

The like is true of the position of women in general. According to d'Ollone, the so-called law of veiling is not observed by Muslim women in China, who walk abroad without reserve (*RMM* ix. 540); Grenard had indicated the fact, but noted an exception in the case of the wealthier classes. In Ho-chou, however, d'Ollone found a different practice, the women there wearing a veil of black silk below the eyes (a custom which seems to the present writer to be connected with the sect of Ma-hua-lung); further, they go on the street on horseback instead of in carriages. As regards foot-binding, d'Ollone notices no difference between Muslim women and Chinese women; in Kan-su especially the practice is very common. That a Muslim should take in marriage one of alien faith is not objected to; it is rather deemed a meritorious act thus to bring an unbeliever to the true religion. The Muslim woman, on the other hand, must not be given in marriage to a non-Muslim; such a union is regarded as the most heinous of sins. In this matter, however, compromises are sometimes made with heaven: the marriage of a Turki princess with the emperor Ch'ien-lung has already been referred to; and, when the present writer passed through Minjol (a day's journey west of Kashgar) in 1902, a Chinese with a Turki wife (? concubine) was presented to him. Illicit intercourse is not punished here, any more than in other Muslim countries, with the strict legal penalty (forty whip-lashes, or stoning), but it must not be supposed that any unusual laxity of morals prevails, and the unnatural vices common among the Chinese (see an instructive chapter in J. J. Mantignon, *Superstition, crime et misère en Chine*[4], Lyons, 1902, p. 185 ff.) are less prevalent among the Muslims. No special attention is devoted to the education of children (for the schools see below (*d*)). Two very prominent features of family life are filial piety and ancestor-worship. The former is extolled in the narrative given in the Chinese-Arabic MS edited by Forke; the latter finds expression in the liturgical prayers for parents and ancestors, while use is also made of pictures of ancestors after the Chinese manner. Social distinctions are not inevitably fixed by descent, except in the case of the Prophet's descendants. The mischief wrought in other Muslim countries by surreptitious enrolment in the sacred lineage does not seem to be extensive among the Muslims of China. Nor does the veneration of Sayyids appear to have assumed any unusual forms on Chinese soil, apart at least from the case of the schismatic Ma-hua-lung, who claimed to be a Sayyid, but who failed to win such prestige as the notorious sons and grandsons of Makhdūm 'Aẓam (see above, p. 889[a]). The relative indifference to Sayyids (Sharīfs) in China is explained by the popular belief that they are for the most part converts to Islām or the descendants of converts (Dungans).

(*c*) *Industries.* — The industries in which the Chinese Muslims are engaged are (1) agriculture, (2) commerce (including handicraft and traffic in goods), and (3) transit-trade. The Muslims do not take naturally to agriculture, but here the environment has asserted itself, inasmuch as the Chinese are pre-eminently an agricultural people, and have in great measure the faculty of infecting the alien population with their own habits. Accordingly, the Chinese Muslim is everywhere one of the most industrious tillers of the soil, so that it was recently reported that those employed in colonizing the part of S. Mongolia which is to be opened by the railway-line between Kalgan and Kuei-hua-ch'eng are predominantly Muslims (*Bull. Com. Asie Franç.*, Oct. 1909, p. 456). While commerce as such is almost wholly in the hands of Chinese, who combine the qualities of the hard-working peasant with those of the astute merchant, yet the Muslims very largely monopolize the related branches of mercantile industry—the conveyance of goods from place to place and the retailing of products of their own or others' labour. Thus the Mafus, *i.e.* horse-hirers and horse-dealers, as also carriers throughout the whole of China, are principally adherents of Islām, while certain trades—especially that of slaughtering animals (not including the pig, of course)—are largely in the hands of Muslims. Their special preference, however, is for official life, though in this department they are faced by a great obstacle, viz. the number and difficulty of the examinations to be passed by aspirants to the Chinese civil service. The Muslims who could successfully undergo these tests must always have been very few. This in itself, however, does not carry any discredit, for it simply means that the Muslims have not the required degree of plodding dullness for such ordeals. On the other hand, the most capable and energetic of them were doubtless able to fulfil the conditions of entrance into the Chinese army, and to work their way to the higher ranks. From the Mongolian period onwards Muslims have often filled the more distinguished military positions. As recent instances of this, mention may be made of General Tung-fu-hsiang (see below (*d*)), as well as of Ma-ti-kai, of Yün-nan, nephew of Ma-hua-lung, and commander-general of the forces in Sze-chuan.

(*d*) *Cultus, education, etc.*—The religious attitude of the Chinese Muslims is—outwardly, at least—characterized by moderation. They make concessions to the ruling power, hoping thus to gain security for person and property, and the most capable and resolute of those who enter the government service take part in the ceremonial of the national cult. The hatred of foreigners sometimes shown by Muslim officers of high rank, like that displayed by the Chinese themselves, is to be referred, not to religious motives, but to the exasperation provoked by the high-handed way in which foreigners interfere with the internal affairs of the country. In not a few cases, indeed, the conduct of the Muslim generals is to be traced simply to a vulgar hankering after rank and wealth, as has now been made clear by the observations of d'Ollone (*RMM* vi. [1908] 7 ff., controverting the misleading note in *RMM* iv. 441 f.). Tung-fu-hsiang, *e.g.*, was in no sense a 'fanatical Muslim,' but a mere adventurer, who gained a following amid the chaos caused by the rising of 1861–74, and who, in return for the gift of a mandarinate, made himself the tool of the viceroy, Tso-tsung-t'ang, and of General Lu-song-shan. He caused Ma-hua-lung, the prime mover of the revolt, and the prophet of the 'new doctrine,' who fell into his hands in a sortie from the rebel city of Kin-ki-pu, to be beheaded. At that time Tung acquired landed estates of enormous extent. It was he also who crushed the rebellion of 1895 in Hsi-ning-fu and Ho-chou, enriching himself, as usual, with the spoils filched from his co-religionists. He received the title of 'generalissimo' (*ta jue*), and was in effect king of the country. When the Boxer rising broke out at Peking in 1900, Tung hurried thither with his henchmen—the foremost of whom was the infamous Ma-an-liang, Tongling of Ho-chou—and made himself conspicuous by his violent and malicious proceedings against the foreigners, who saw in him only a Muslim at the head of a horde of Muslims,

Chinese law would intrude upon this domain of personal rights, though it may perhaps be necessary to assert the universal validity of the imperial ordinances. These ordinances are lucidly set forth in Pierre Hoang, *Le Mariage chinois au point de vue légale* (*Var. Sinol.*, no. 14), Shanghai, 1898. The present writer has not succeeded in discovering among them anything that formally concedes an exceptional position to the Muslims.

and were quite unaware of his real relation to Islām. Having been ostensibly punished by 'banishment' to Kan-su, he lived there like a *sulṭān.* He held two fortified castles near Kin-ki-pu, and had a bodyguard of 500 veterans—as tenants of the surrounding estates which he had taken from Muslims. The local councils of Kin-ki-pu and Lin-chou could not lift a finger without his approval. After his death in February 1908, all his titles, of which he had been deprived at the instance of the European Powers, were restored, and his remains were buried with the highest honours at Kon-yuen, his birth-place (*RMM* vi. 700 ff.). Apart from adventurers of this stamp, whom probably the majority of Muslims would regard as apostates, there is a far-reaching antagonism between the indigenous and the immigrant peoples. The Chinese realize the danger involved in the Muslim aspiration of an *imperium in imperio,* while the Muslims, enjoined as they are by the Qur'ān to fight against the unbeliever, feel the ascendancy of the latter as a heavy infliction, and from time to time the strain has found expression in open revolt. The most notable and most serious of such outbreaks have been those of the north (Kan-su and Shen-si) in 1861–74, and of the south (Yün-nan) in 1856–72. It would be a mistake, however, to attribute these ruinous insurrections to religious motives alone, for racial antagonisms and the conflicting interests of different social classes were certainly no less potent factors.

The mosques resemble pagodas, the *miḥrāb* and *minbar* alone proclaiming their Muslim origin. We sometimes meet with Indo-Arabic styles, as, *e.g.*, the two cupolas above the porch of each of the mosques in Sui-fu. For occasions of prayer the *akhons* (Pers. *ākhūnd,* 'learned one'; in China, 'mosque-minister') don the white tunic; the rest of the faithful wear for the time a cap never otherwise used, which is encircled by the turban, and may be of various colours—white, blue, green, or red. This cap has two shapes: the Meccan—a round, low cowl, wholly covered by the turban—not worn by many; and the Bukharian—polygonal, being formed of four or six pieces—which hangs out from beneath the turban. It is identical with the *tübe,* or *topa,* worn by all Muslims in Russian and Chinese Turkestan.

The disruptive tendencies so common in Islām generally have made themselves felt in China. Ma-hua-lung, who was put to death during the rebellion in Kan-su, was the founder of a new sect, and his followers in Kan-su, where they are numerous, and in Sze-chuan, where as yet they are but few, regard him as the true successor of Muhammad. His descendants and disciples claim to possess superhuman powers. His teaching is called *hsin chiao,* 'new doctrine,' in contradistinction to *lao chiao,* 'ancient doctrine' (*RMM* v. 93). The nature of this new doctrine is something of a mystery. There is a tendency to regard it as an endorsement to Shī'ism, or perhaps an unusually bold representation of Ṣūfīism, but the notices of d'Ollone (*RMM* ix. 571 ff.) show that in reality it is of genuinely Sunnite character, and not a degenerate variety of the mystical philosophy so widely diffused throughout Central Asia. Ma-hua-lung was undoubtedly one of that class of visionary impostors represented in Chinese Turkestan by the Khodyas, *i.e.* the descendants of Makhdūm 'Aẓam, of whose ecclesiastico-political organization the present writer has given a detailed account in 'Ein Kirchenstaat im Islam' (in *Der islamische Orient,* i. 195 ff.). It remains an open question whether the Mahdistic idea played any part in the project of Ma-hua-lung; the reports of d'Ollone make no distinct reference to it. In any case, the pretender was regarded as an incarnation of the Spirit—a *sheng jen* ('holy man,' 'prophet') equal to, or even higher than, Muhammad himself. It speaks well for the Muslims of Kan-su that only the lower classes were duped by this charlatan, who, wholly destitute of learning, presumed to know everything, and had his answer ready for every question. As the founder of a new sect, he had to enjoin certain external forms by which his adherents might be distinguished from others. For this purpose he chose the practice of praying aloud and of holding the hands straight open and horizontal in the *qiyām* (at prayer), in contrast to the general custom of silent prayer with the hands rounded and hollow. From this practice of audible prayer is derived the usual name of the sect, viz. Ẓāhirīyah (corrupted to Chaiherinye), 'those who pray openly,' as contrasted with the Khāfīyah (vernacularly 'Hufeye'), 'those who pray secretly.' In these externals Ma-hua-lung shows a certain affinity with a movement in the West which had found its way into China at an earlier date. About 150 years previously a reformer had appeared among the Salars (see above, p. 892[b]) in the person of Muhammad Emin, known in China as Ma-ming-hsin, who introduced the custom of praying aloud, and thereby gave occasion for serious disturbances (Grenard, *loc. cit.*). Mu-hua-lung did not actually forbid his followers to attend the mosque, but he allowed prayer to be performed at home—in the 'common hall'—without special ceremonial garments. Usually three or four houses have a place of prayer in common, *i.e.* a single room set apart for worship, this arrangement being designed, it is said, to familiarize the adherents with the practice of prayer (*RMM* ix. 571). In Sung-p'an-t'ing, according to *RMM* v. 462, the followers of the new faith attend the same mosques as those of the old, while in Shen-tu, on the other hand, the breach is complete (*RMM* v. 462, ix. 561). The d'Ollone expedition had a very uncivil reception in the mosque at Ch'êng-tu; the people of the 'new doctrine' have the name of being hostile to Europeans, while the Muslims in general are friendly. After Ma-hua-lung's death in 1871, a rupture took place within the sect. His son-in-law, Ma-ta-hsi, and his grandson, Ma-mih-hsi, fought with each other for the sacred inheritance. Ma-ta-hsi, who is now (1915) sixty-two years old, has the advantage in numbers, and his place of residence, Cha-kou, near Ku-yuen, is an important religious centre, and has a *madrasah.* Ma-hua-lung's teaching was introduced into Yün-nan by his younger brother (or nephew) Talasan or Talamasan, who fell in a struggle with Ma-ju-lung. In Yün-nan, however, the sect has apparently a smaller following than in Sze-chuan, where d'Ollone met with adherents of the Hsin chiao from the boundaries of Yün-nan to Sung-p'an-t'ing on the border of Kan-su.

Alongside of the two groups of Hufeye and Chaiherinye are found two others, viz. Kuberinye and Katerinye. The meaning of 'Kuberinye' cannot be precisely determined—the word may possibly stand for Kubārī ('great'); 'Katerinye' is undoubtedly equivalent to 'Qādirīyah,' signifying the adherents of 'Abd al-Qādir al-Jīlānī (*q.v.*). It is maintained by a certain *akhon* that these four sects are respectively connected with the first four *khalīfahs*, each of whom is said to have inaugurated a particular ritual, viz. Abū Bakr that of the Hufeye, Othmān that of the Chaiherinye, 'Omar that of the Kuberinye, and 'Alī that of the Katerinye. The last-mentioned name is said to be applied also to those who venerate graves. In China, as elsewhere on Muslim soil, peculiar honour is accorded to the tombs of the eminently pious—those who have given credentials of saintship.

Thus, *e.g.*, within a mile to the north of Sung-p'an-t'ing is to be seen the tomb of an *akhon* from Medīna, who came to Sung-p'an-t'ing in 1668, lived for a time in Shen-si, and by his prayers saved the land from a drought in 1673. He died in 1680, and his tomb is guarded by an *akhon*. Another tomb, somewhat smaller, is found within the mausoleum. The orthodox *mullās* inveigh strongly against this practice (*RMM* v. 459). D'Ollone thinks that the veneration of graves is also a characteristic of the Hsin chiao sect (*RMM* ix. 533 ff.); but this cannot be admitted, and, indeed, it conflicts with other statements of the same writer. As a matter of fact, the veneration of graves is a world-wide custom, and naturally prevails here too; and that Ho-chou, the rallying-point of the new doctrine, should also contain an unusual number of sacrosanct tombs is a mere coincidence. Moreover, with reference to the name Kumbe chiao, which d'Ollone mentions as being applied to the 'new doctrine,' and upon which he bases his conclusions (*RMM* ix. 533), it remains to be shown whether the term (= 'grave-doctrine') is meant to indicate the distinctive characteristic of the sect. As regards the religious position of the ethnologically distinct Salars see above, p. 892[b].

The idea of a *khalīfah* as a single individual invested with authority over Islām as a whole is unknown to the vast majority of Chinese Muslims (*RMM* ix. 561 f.). Yet the efforts directed from Stamboul in the latter half of last century were not altogether without result. Ya'qūb Beg recognized 'Abd-al-'Azīz as commander of the faithful, while Sulaimān, the Muslim king of Yün-nan, appealed to him, as *khalīfah*—in vain, it is true—for assistance.

As the intellectual life of the Muslims bears the closest possible relation to their religion, the aim of elementary education is to inculcate the rudiments of religious doctrine, the children being taught by readings from the Qur'ān and by short catechisms. In these exercises two languages are employed—both the national language and that of the Qur'ān (or a mixed Perso-Arabic dialect). There is a considerable circulation of anthologies from the Qur'ān, either with or without a Chinese translation, and booklets containing the leading elements of doctrine in both languages are also found.[1] The life of the Chinese Muslims has no place for art. To anything in the nature of artistic activity only a single field is open—the Arabic script, which is often elaborated in pedantic forms suggestive of the Chinese method of writing, angles and loops being formed as in the native calligraphy (especially in epitaphs). The Muslims also erect ornately written Arabic tablets, which, however, often show such a divergence from the common script that they are very difficult to read. Even the experienced E. Blochet mistook an *r* for a *y* (*RMM* v. 291).

(*e*) *Political relations*.—In China proper the Muslims have never secured an independent political existence, while in Turkestan, since its annexation (*c.* 1750), they succeeded in establishing only the short-lived Muslim government of Ya'qūb Beg (see above, p. 889[a]). The object of the Muslim rising in Kan-su and Shen-si (1863–74), which was among the contributing causes of Ya'qūb Beg's success, was likewise independence; but the movement proved abortive, and, in fact, no other issue was to be expected. The necessary condition of a permanent political organization is that it shall have a basis of nationality, and no such thing exists among the Chinese Muslims. The latter, as interspersed among the Han (Chinese), form, not a national, but merely a religious, aggregate, and all history teaches that political establishments based upon religion are ephemeral. It has certainly been hinted that the Muslims of China may possibly force their religion upon the rest of the population, and thus evolve a powerful Islāmo-Chinese kingdom. It is indubitable that such an ambition is not wanting among the Muslims, and that it will continue to act in certain localities as a source of insurgent movements against the imperial government. It is regrettable that the idea has been exploited for the double purpose of acquiring religious influence among the Chinese Muslims and of furthering political ends. Considerable efforts in this direction were made—though without the least success—by Sulṭān 'Abd-al-Ḥamīd in the latter part of 1900; and minor attempts at a later date proved equally fruitless, though hopes were not abandoned even after the deposition of the Sulṭān.

[1] The present writer possesses a copy of such a bilingual catechism.

LITERATURE.—In addition to works cited in the art., reference may be made to V. P. Vasiliev, *O dviženii Magometanstva v Kitaě*, Petrograd, 1867; M. Broomhall, *Islam in China*, London, 1910; T. W. Arnold, *Preaching of Islam*², do. 1913, pp. 213 ff., 294–311; G. Devéria, 'Origine d'Islamisme en Chine, *Centenaire de l'école des langues orient. vivantes: Recueil de mémoires*, Paris, 1895, pp. 305–355; C. Schefer, 'Notice sur les relations des peuples musulmans avec les Chinois,' *ib.* pp. 1–43; E. H. Parker, 'Islam in China,' *Imp. and Asiat. Quart. Rev.* III. xxiv. [1907] 64–83; J. Anderson, 'Chinese Mohammedans,' *JAI* i. [1872] 147–162; G. Soulié, 'Les Musulmans de Yun-nan,' *RMM* ix. [1909] 209–223; Lepage, 'Biographie du Seyid Edjell Omar Chams ed-Din, introducteur de l'Islam au Yunnan,' *ib.* xi. [1910] 1–31; C. E. Bonin, 'Les Mahométans du Kansou et leur dernière révolte,' *ib.* x. [1910] 210–233; M. Hartmann, 'Vom chin. Islam,' *Welt des Islams*, i. [1913] 178–210.

M. HARTMANN.

MUHAMMADANISM (in India).—Islām was introduced into India by the Arab invaders who entered Sind under Muḥammad ibn Qāsim in A.D. 712 and founded a Muhammadan State which was eventually absorbed in the Mughal empire; but this early Arab occupation was confined to Sind, and the Muhammadan conquest of the rest of India did not begin until nearly three centuries later, with the raids of Sabuktagīn and Maḥmūd of Ghazna; when, however, Maḥmūd died in 1030, the province of Lahore was the only part of Indian territory that he bequeathed to his successor. The permanent extension of Muslim rule in India dates from the latter part of the 12th cent., when the conquests of Muḥammad Ghorī resulted in the establishment of a Muhammadan dynasty in Dihli, which continued to be a Muhammadan capital up to the extinction of the Mughal empire in 1858. The scope of this article being limited to religion and ethics, no account of the political history can be given, though the intimate connexion between Islām as a religious system and the Muhammadan governments in India makes it difficult to consider them apart. A brief reference must be made, however, to the relations between the Muslim rulers and their non-Muslim subjects. The Muhammadan invaders at times during the early stages of the conquest exhibited a brutal intolerance towards the Hindus who opposed their armies, and ruthlessly massacred Brāhmans and razed temples to the ground; but, after the savageries of conquest were over, a certain amount of toleration was allowed to their Hindu subjects. The Arabs in Sind left the Hindus in undisturbed exercise of their religion and in the enjoyment of their old rights and privileges, and the later conquerors who founded kingdoms in N. India and the Deccan were generally too much occupied with the military consolidation of their own power, or felt too little interest in spiritual matters, to turn their attention to the propagation of their own faith. Even under the settled rule of the Mughals, dynastic and financial considerations dictated their policy rather than consideration of the interests of Islām. On the other hand, the reigns of several monarchs were signalized by outbursts of fanaticism and the cruel oppression of unbelievers, their temples being destroyed and many of them converted by force. In Gujarāt Sulṭān Maḥmūd III. (1537–53) was hated by the Hindus for the stringency of his enactments against them. In Kashmīr Sulṭān Sikandar (1393–1417) acquired the designation Butshikan ('idol-smasher') by his ruthless destruction of Hindu idols and temples, and in Bengal Jalāl al-Dīn Muḥammad Shāh (1414–31) made himself notorious by his persecution of unbelievers. Aurangzīb's (1659–1707) attempt to carry out a policy of unification led to several acts of repression, and tradition attributes to him the destruction of temples and the forcible conversion of Hindus in various districts throughout the whole extent of the Mughal empire. The latest example of such fanaticism on the part of a Muhammadan ruler was that of Tīpū Sulṭān (1782–99), whose barbarities outdid anything recorded of previous monarchs after the first conquerors. Apart from such outbursts of fanaticism, the rule of the Muhammadans has generally been characterized by an attitude of toleration towards their Hindu subjects, and the adherents of the rival religions have often been closely drawn together by a spirit of amity and mutual respect.

The fact that the Muhammadan dynasties in India were almost entirely founded by foreign invaders was of great importance in the history of Islām; they brought with them a large number of foreign troops, and attracted to their courts military adventurers, poets, scholars, and others, who ultimately settled in the country. The foreign immigrants and their descendants—Arabs, Persians, Turks, Mughals, and Paṭhāns—formed an important element in the total Muhammadan population, and exercised a preponderating influence in the administration, the social organization, and the religious life. They received grants of land from the Muhammadan governments, or in times of political unrest arrogated to themselves rights of ownership, and thus formed the nucleus of an aristocracy that looked down with contempt on the native converts. The missionaries, to whose proselytizing efforts the conversion of whole tribes is attributed, and the saints, whose tombs are still venerated throughout all parts of Muslim India, were for the most part of foreign extraction. The shrines of these saints are still centres of religious influence and attract thousands of pilgrims every year; among the most famous are those of Khwājah Mu'īn al-Dīn Chishtī († 1236) at Ajmīr, Farīd al-Dīn Shakarganj († 1269) at Pākpattan, Niẓām al-Dīn Awliyā († 1325) at Dihli, and Shāh 'Ālam († 1475) near Aḥmadābād. The great family of Bukhārī Sayyids, who settled in Uch in the 13th cent., may be taken as a typical example of the wide-spread influence exercised by some of these foreign immigrants. The effect of this constant stream of foreign immigration has been to keep India in close contact with the main currents of theological thought and speculation in Islām, and the religious beliefs and practices of the educated section at least of the Muslim population, whether Sunnī or Shī'ah, have tended to conform to those in other parts of the Muslim world. A large part of the religious literature has been written in Arabic, and still more in Persian—both languages foreign to India—and the study of these languages has kept the theologians acquainted with the writings of Muslim thinkers outside India. These foreign influences have thus prevented Islām in India from taking on a provincial character, so far at least as the literate are concerned. But among the uneducated converts and the descendants of converts, of Hindu origin, especially in the country districts emote from the centres of Muslim culture, many survivals of older cults are to be found, and there the Muhammadan differs little but in name from his Hindu neighbour. He continues to worship the gods of his ancestors—particularly the village godlings, whose rites are associated with the cultivation of the soil, and the deities of disease, especially Sītalā, the dreaded goddess of smallpox —and to take part in the Hindu festivals connected with the changes of the season, such as Holi, the festival of the spring equinox, and Dasahrā, the festival of the autumn equinox. Against such Hindu beliefs and practices the orthodox have at all times protested, but the first active campaign against them appears to have been started by Sayyid Aḥmad and Ḥājī Sharī'at Allāh, who in the second decade of the 19th cent. began to disseminate in India the doctrines of the Wahhābī reforming movement. The writings of a later religious reformer, Maulavī Karāmat 'Alī († 1874), were especially influential in combating the observance of Hindu rites and ceremonies by Muhammadans. In more recent years, the greater facilities of communication between one part of the country and another, the spread of education, and the consequent growing influence of theological text-books have increased the tendency towards an orthodox uniformity, but the low level of education among the mass of the Indian Muhammadans still keeps a large proportion of them ignorant of the tenets of the faith which they profess.

The abiding influence of Hindu institutions on the converts to Islām is still further shown by their rejection of the *sharī'ah* in favour of their old tribal ordinances in regard to marriage and inheritance. As is well known, Islām is not merely a body of religious dogma but also a system of legislation, but the Muhammadanized Rājputs and Jāṭs in the Panjāb and the Mappillas on the west coast of S. India have always continued to follow the customs of their Hindu ancestors in preference to the Muslim law of succession.

The influence of Islām in India has not been confined to the Musalmāns themselves, but may be observed in sections of the population that stand outside the Muslim community. There can be little doubt that the Hindu reform movements of the 15th and 16th centuries, especially those connected with the names of Kabīr and Nānak, owed much to Muslim influences. Many low-caste Hindus, especially in N. India, worship Muhammadan saints; these saints are sometimes legendary, like Sakhī Sarwar and Shāh Mādār, or historical personages such as Pīr Shams Tabrīz of Multān, or sometimes a mixture of both as in certain enumerations of the Pañch Pīr ('five holy men'), who are represented by some thousands of Hindus to be the only divinities that they worship. An influence of a different character was that of the Mughal court upon the higher ranks of Hindu society, resulting in the adoption of many Muhammadan habits and observances such as are generally significant of adherence to the faith of Islām.

As an ethical system Islām in India presents in many ways a strong contrast to Hinduism. Both, it is true, cherish an ascetic ideal, pursued by the few, and Hindu and Muslim ascetics have often found that they have much in common, and both have often received the veneration of pious adherents of the rival creed. But the stern Puritanism of Islām has set its face rigidly against those characteristics of Hindu conduct which are set forth in the *Kāmaśāstras* and illustrated on such Hindu temples as have escaped the iconoclastic wrath of outraged Muslim sentiment. This austerity of Muslim morals runs through the whole of their social life, and lends to their outward bearing an aspect of dignity and self-respect such as springs from a constant recognition of moral obligation; at the same time it relegates women to the seclusion of the zenana, depriving social intercourse of the charm of their society, and deprecates amusements that other countries find harmless, such as dancing and card-playing. This moral fervour is capable of producing such types as that of the judge who cut himself off from all human associations lest his judgment might be influenced by consideration for a friend, the hard-worked administrative officer who gave away the whole of his official salary in charity, and the scholar who repented in bitter tears because he had made a profit out of the sale of a work on religion. The moral sanction is sought in religion, and moral precepts are based on the Qur'ān, the traditions, and the works of authoritative theologians; maxims of conduct are also frequently quoted from the poets and Ṣūfī writers. Treatises on ethics, such as *Akhlāq-i-Nāṣirī*, *Akhlāq-i-Muḥsinī*, etc., are read by the learned, and similar works—*e.g.*, *Akhlāq-i-Jahāngīrī*—were compiled in India, but acquaintance with them has been too restricted for them to have exercised much influence on the general moral consciousness of the Indian Musalmāns. This legal and didactic view of ethics may at times degenerate into formalism, and a low level of moral achievement may subsist side by side with fervid professions of piety; but the tendency of modern Muslim society in India is towards a more distinctively ethical basis for conduct and less dependence upon religious authority.

Within the narrow limits of this article it has not been possible to do more than briefly indicate some of the main characteristics of Islām in India. See, further, MISSIONS (Muhammadan), SECTS (Muhammadan).

LITERATURE.—No comprehensive work has yet been written on the religion and ethics of the Indian Muhammadans. The reader will find articles bearing on these subjects in such periodicals as *JASB* (Calcutta, 1832 ff.); *Calcutta Review* (Calcutta, 1844 ff.); *Journal of the Moslem Institute* (Calcutta, 1905 ff.); *Revue du monde musulman* (Paris, 1906 ff.); *EI* (Leyden, 1908 ff.). For the bibliography of historical works see *The History of India as told by its own Historians: The Muhammedan Period*, ed. from the papers of H. M. Elliot by John Dowson, London, 1867–77. A vast amount of material is to be found scattered throughout the official publications of the Government of India; for bibliography see F. Campbell, *Index-Catalogue of Indian Official Publications in the Library, British Museum*, do. 1900. Among separate works may be mentioned: J. H. Garcin de Tassy, *Mémoire sur les particularités de la religion musulmane dans l'Inde*[2], Paris, 1869; Mrs. Meer Hassan Ali, *Observations on the Mussulmauns of India*, London, 1832; W. W. Hunter, *The Indian Musalmans*, do. 1871; Jaffur Shurreef, *Qanoon-e-Islam, or the Customs of the Mussulmans of India*, tr. G. A. Herklots[2], Madras, 1863; Syed Ameer Ali, *The Spirit of Islam, or the Life and Teachings of Mohammed*[2], London, 1896; S. Khuda Bukhsh, *Essays Indian and Islamic*, do. 1912. A more detailed bibliography will be found in the present writer's art. 'India' in *EI*.

T. W. ARNOLD.

MUHAMMADANISM (in Persia). — Islām began in Persia very early. Within a year of Muhammad's death the Muslim armies came into collision with the Persian power, and the conflict lasted for thirty years, extending from the Tigris to the Oxus. The last Zoroastrian dynasty was overthrown in A.D. 750 in the region south of the Caspian. The conversion to Islām was a slower process, and the disappearance of Zoroastrianism was gradual. The intellectual life of Islām was very soon enriched by Persian scholars. It is significant that after the Arab conquest Nestorian missions were successfully prosecuted among Iranians described as pagans.[1] Still, Islām was identified with a foreign invasion—a fact that influenced subsequent history.

The cause of 'Alī gained adherents in Persia from the first, perhaps because Ḥusain married a Sasanian princess. In the Umayyad period revolts were frequent, many of them Khārijite in origin. The 'Abbāsid conspiracy was begun in Persia; Abū Muslim, the chief conspirator, was a Persian; and the battle of the Zāb, which decided the contest, was fought on the border of Īrān. Although revolts were common, the authority of the 'Abbāsids was generally recognized by the ruling dynasties in Persia, few of which were Shī'ite. The most determined and powerful attempt to establish Shī'ite Islām was that of the Ismā'īlians, or Assassins (*q.v.*). Persia was the greatest sufferer of all in the ruin wrought by the heathen Mongols, and Islām seemed about to perish; Tīmūr was a Sunnite Muslim, but he had mercy on none. With the rise of Ṣafawī kings (A.D. 1500) Shī'ite Islām of the Twelve was established as the State religion—a position challenged since only by the audacious Nādir († 1747), who proposed to make Shī'ite Islām a fifth sect co-ordinate with the four recognized divisions of Sunnite Islām. The paper constitution of modern Persia recognizes Shī'ite Islām as the religion of the realm.

The inner development of Shī'ite Islām has never been adequately described. From the first many Persians refused to believe that the cycle of revelation had closed with Muhammad, and the deification of 'Alī seems to have begun even before his death.[1] This mystical belief in a continuous revelation and a divine presence, different in kind from anything found in the Qur'ān, developed into the doctrine of the *imāmat* (cf. art. INCARNATION [Muslim]). In the process of the elaboration of this doctrine sects were formed, the most remarkable being that of the Ismā'īlians, which, strangely, has left scarcely a trace in modern Persia. The cult of 'Alī, and especially of Ḥusain in the celebration of 'Āshūrā (the 10th of Muḥarram), is still in process of growth. Another line of theological development has been Ṣūfiism, the great names in which are Persian (though not all Shī'ite), and which has greater influence to-day in Persia than in any other land. Important events in recent Shī'ite Islām have been the growth of Shaikhīism, the birth of Bahāism, and the attempt to join Western constitutional government to Islām.

The influence of Persia in Islām is a larger subject than Islām in Persia. Traces of Zoroastrian influence are to be found in the Qur'ān, and still more in the developed Muslim theology.

'The victory of the Abbasids was, in a sense, a conquest of the Arabs by the Persians . . . the battles of al-Qadisiya and Nahawand were avenged; Persian ideas and Persian religion began slowly to work on the faith of Muhammad.'[2]

What Islām owes to Persian Sunnites in formal theology, as well as to the dervish orders and Ṣūfiism, may be indicated by mentioning the names of al-Ghazālī, 'Abd al-Qādir al-Jīlānī, and Jalāl al-Dīn Rūmī (*qq.v.*).

Modern Persia is the resultant of the interaction of complex forces through a long period, and religiously it is far from homogeneous in character. Sunnites number a million or more. The majority of these are Kurds, some are Arabs, some Turks in Ādharbaijān, and some are Persians in the Gulf region. Among them the most numerous sect is the Shāfi'ite. Shī'ites are believers in the Twelve Imāms. Sects that are numerous and wide-spread enough to merit attention are the Mutasharī's, the Shaikhīs, and the Zahābīs. Other sects that should be mentioned are the 'Alī Illāhīs and the Bahāīs. Ṣūfiism, influential as it is, cannot be regarded as a separate sect. The dervishes are an institution that cannot be neglected (cf. art. DERVISH). The following figures are given as an approximation: Sunnites, 1,000,000; Shī'ites, Persians, Lūrs, etc., 5,000,000; Tatars, 2,000,000; 'Alī Illāhīs, 300,000; Bahāīs, 100,000.

[1] W. A. Shedd, *Islam and Oriental Churches*, Philadelphia, 1904, p. 163 f.

[1] Browne, *Literary History of Persia*, i. 220.

[2] D. B. Macdonald, *Development of Muslim Theology, Jurisprudence, and Constitutional Theory*, London, 1903, p. 133.

Even among the Sunnites (especially the Kurds) religion centres much in the cult of the Shaikhs, who are credited with miraculous powers. Many of these are connected with the dervish orders, especially the Naqshbandīs.

The great religious principle of the Shī'ites is the veneration of the family of 'Alī and the doctrine of the *imāmat.* While every community numbers its *ḥajjīs*, the great shrine for pilgrimage of the living and burial of the dead is Karbalā, which, moreover, is the place of religious authority, the seat of the chief *mujtahids*, and the centre of theological education and learning. In every city there is a *madrasah* (college), but an ambitious student completes his training at Karbalā, or at one of the neighbouring shrines that share in its importance. The unifying power of such a centre is very important. The other shrine of importance is Mashad. For the mass of the people the great religious observance is the commemoration of the battle of Karbalā on the 10th of Muḥarram and preceding days. On the spectacular side it is the carnival of the populace, and the timid disapproval of the educated is unavailing to check continual increase of the excesses of grief in cutting the head and beating the breast. Regular passion-plays are uncommon (cf. art. DRAMA [Persian]). Preaching has an important place in the mosque life, and the great topic for sermons is the life of the Imāms. Ghadīr Bairām (when Muhammad is supposed to have designated 'Alī as his successor) is at least equal to Qurbān Bairām in popular estimation. The *ḥadīth* (traditions) deal with the sayings and doings of the Imāms as well as of the Prophet, the most popular collections being those of Mullā Baqir Majlisī of Iṣfahān, made three hundred years ago. The expectation of the reappearance of the Twelfth Imām as al-Mahdī is general. The Sayyids rival the *mullās* in authority and claim the fifth of field and herd. So far the description applies to all Shī'ite sects.

The Mutasharī's, who are by far the most numerous sect, regard the *mujtahids* as the only representative of the Qā'im, or hidden Imām, and only inasmuch as they interpret the *sharī'ah* (canon law). They are conservatives and traditionalists. The Shaikhīs, Zahābīs, and minor sects hold that there is always a representative of the Imām, who possesses in some degree his divine authority. They differ as to who that representative is, and in other matters. The Shaikhīs are the intellectual mystics, interpreting, *e.g.*, the *mi'rāj* (Muhammad's ascent to heaven, deduced from Qur'ān, xvii. 1) in a spiritual way. Zahābīs resemble the dervishes in ascetic practices and in the use of the *dhikr*, both *lafẓī* and *qalbī* (spoken and silent).

'Alī Ilāhīs and Bahāīs, widely different in other respects, may be classed together as being Muslim in only a modified sense. The former recognize none of the Imāms except 'Alī, care nothing for the *sharī'ah*, pay no attention to Ramaḍān or the prayers, and have their own yearly feast, in connexion with which a common religious meal is eaten. Among Shī'ites they conform more or less, but in private they claim that they are not Shī'ite. They believe in an incarnation, but it is not very clear whether the connexion with 'Alī is not a blind. They call themselves Ahl-i Ḥaqīqah ('people of the Truth'). In practical life the reverence paid to the Sayyids, or *pīrs*, is great. Their religious centre, where the head of the sect lives, is near Kirmānshāh. They are numerous both north and south, among Kurds, Turks, and Persians, and especially in the villages and among the nomads, and are found in smaller numbers in the cities. The Bahāīs are too well known to require description. For them Muhammad and the *sharī'ah* are superseded. They are found in the cities and among the more educated classes, less often in the villages, and not at all among the nomads. They are increasing. Though only a fraction of the less numerous classes of society, their influence is not to be measured by their numbers. The Azalīs are practically extinct, and the Bahāīs, with insignificant exceptions, follow 'Abbās Efendi. Both these sects practise *taqiyyah*, or religious deception.

The Ṣūfīs (or 'Ārifs, 'γνωστικοί') are the philosophical and intellectual devotees of religion, belonging, it may be, to some sect, but not often to the Mutasharī's. Among them are many dervishes. They usually recognize some one as their guide (*murshid*). The most popular poets among them are Jalāl al-Dīn, Shams-i-Tabrīz, Farīd al-Din 'Aṭṭār, and Ḥāfiẓ. Dervishes in Persia are loosely organized, and monasteries are almost unknown. Many dervishes will claim to be *khāksārī* ('abject,' 'humble'), others to be followers of Shāh Na'mat-Allāh or of Ṣafī 'Alī Shāh, a saint of recent date.

The organization of religion is democratic, and in the last analysis it is popularity that determines rank and authority. The government exercises a control by granting titles and recognition, and the *mullās* and *mujtahids*, both as authorized expounders of the *sharī'ah* and as popular leaders, influence government. They are from the people and are susceptible to the influences that affect the people. Low birth is no bar to ecclesiastical advancement. The dervishes are to some extent controlled by the appointment from them of a *naqīb*, or civil head, in each city. Curiously, he has charge also of jugglers, mountebanks, snake-charmers, etc.

The influence of religion in moral and social matters is not easily estimated. Of course it is pervasive. The only education open to most of the people is that in the mosque schools. The pilgrimages promote intelligence and national unity. On the other hand, the shrines are centres of vice, the *mullās* are notorious for venality, the *sharī'ah* is an obstacle to progress, and religious teaching often makes wrongdoing easy rather than difficult. It may be doubted whether those who desire moral or social reform look to religion for inspiration and aid. The least religious classes are the educated and the nomads.

An influence at work that must affect the future of Islām is the rationalization of religion. It takes the form of reducing religion to the minimum of doctrine, equalizing all forms of revelation by admitting truth in each, but granting finality to none. Another tendency is what the Persians call *ṭabī'ī* ('naturalistic'), denying all revelation and taking an agnostic position on the question of God's existence. Another growing influence is the renascence of Turkish literature in the Ādharbaijān dialect in Tiflis and Baku. The reaction due to foreign dominance is also to be reckoned with. The influence of Western civilization is in many ways disintegrating. The influence of Christianity mediated by commerce, politics and literature, and missionary effort must not be forgotten. This had its part in Bābism and still more in Bahāism.

See, further, artt. BĀB, BĀBĪS, SHĪ'AHS, ṢŪFĪISM.

LITERATURE.—Besides the works cited in the article, see T. W. Arnold, *The Preaching of Islam*[2], London, 1913; E. G. Browne, *Literary History of Persia*, 2 vols., do. 1902–06, *A Year among the Persians*, do. 1893.

W. A. SHEDD.

MUHAMMADANISM (in Syria, Egypt, and Mesopotamia).—*A. SYRIA.*—Syria and Palestine have always formed one of the outlets for the superfluous population of Arabia. The invasion of the country by the Arabs in the first half of the 7th cent. A.D. was only one of a series of incursions which had been going on from time immemorial. The conquest, which took place in the Caliphate of 'Omar, only a year or two after the death of Muhammad, occupied a few years (13–15 A.H.), and was facilitated by the fact that the people of Syria came, to a large extent, both in origin and in language, of Semitic stock. The kingdom of Ghassān, which, with that of Hīra on the other side of the Syrian desert, formed a buffer State between the empires of Rome and Persia, was of pure Arab blood. When, therefore, the Arabs made their inroads into the country, they were not invading a foreign people, but rather attacking the governing classes only, the representatives of the Eastern Roman empire. Moreover, it was only a score of years since the Persians had wrested the country from the Greeks and held it for ten years. The Persian Wars had depleted the exchequer of Constantinople, and Heraclius had been compelled to withdraw the wonted subsidies from the frontier tribes—a fact which made them all the less unwilling to throw in their lot with the Arabs. When, therefore, 'Omar's forces entered the country, they did not come altogether as invaders, and to the indigenous population the issue was not subjection so much as a change of masters; and it was not impossible that the new masters might be more gentle than the old.

To the Arabs the conquest of Chaldæa was motived by the lust of plunder, the conquest of Egypt was to a large extent a necessity—had it been acquired a year or two earlier Medīna would have been saved from famine—but the conquest of Syria was largely a matter of sentiment. Within its borders were contained nearly all the holy places of Islām. Hūd and Ṣāliḥ had ministered to tribes within the boundaries of Arabia, but nearly all the remaining prophets—Abraham, Solomon, but above all Jesus—had lived and died in Palestine. Muhammad, too, had visited Syria, once as a mere boy, with his uncle Abu Ṭālib, and again as the agent of Khadījah. Jerusalem had been the goal of his mysterious night-journey, from which he had ascended to the Divine Presence, and it was from Damascus that he had turned away, saying that one could not enter Paradise twice. The reverence of the Arabs for Jerusalem is shown by the fact that it was towards it that the Muslims turned in prayer during the first two years after the arrival of Muhammad at Medīna, and that the capitulation of the city in 637 was accepted by the Caliph in person. On this occasion 'Omar visited most of the sacred places, under the guidance of the patriarch Sophronius. He is said to have identified the site of Solomon's temple, and he erected a small mosque, probably of wood and clay, for the worship of the Muslims. Jerusalem did not become the political capital of the province of Palestine. For that Ramleh was founded somewhat later. But the sacred character attributed to the ancient city by the Arabs appears in the name Bait al-Maqdis ('holy house') by which their historians always call it, or in the shortened form Al-Quds, by which it is known at the present day.

The sanctity in the eyes of the Muslims even of Jerusalem is, however, surpassed by that of Hebron, the home and place of burial of Abraham, Isaac, and Jacob, with their wives, as well as of Joseph. Hence it used to be named Masjid Ibrāhīm ('Abraham's mosque'), but now it is always called Al-Khalīl ('the friend'), abbreviated from 'the city of the friend of God.' Hebron fell into the hands of the Crusaders in A.D. 1099 and remained so until it was retaken by Saladin in 1187. The Crusaders do not seem to have had much scruple about entering the sepulchral chambers, but the curiosity of the Muslim does not exceed his sense of reverence, and one of them mentions with a feeling of the deepest awe that he had conversed with one who had with his own eyes seen Abraham. At the present day Europeans are not permitted to enter the mosque (originally a Crusaders' church), with very rare exceptions, and then only by a special *firmān*.

Under the Umayyads (A.D. 661–750) Syria attained to the hegemony of all the Arab States, and Damascus became the capital of an empire stretching from India to Spain. Mu'āwiya, the first of the line, had been governor of the country under the Caliph 'Othmān: it was to the Arabs of Syria that his dynasty owed its birth and stability, and the Caliphs of the line naturally wished to do all in their power to strengthen the position and precedency of their adopted country. Hence it was that, after the assassination of 'Alī, Mu'āwiya proclaimed himself Caliph, not at Medīna, which had been the political as well as the religious capital under the first three Caliphs, but at Jerusalem. When, on the death of his son Yazīd, the rest of the Muslim world did homage to the rival Caliph Ibn Zubair in Mecca, it was no doubt in some measure owing to the possession of the sacred city of Jerusalem and the tombs of the patriarchs at Hebron that the Umayyads were still able to maintain their position in Syria. And, whilst their rival was engaged in rebuilding the holy house at Mecca, which their armies had besieged, the Umayyad 'Abd al-Malik was building the famous Dome of the Rock upon the site of the Temple of Solomon, as the inscription, in spite of its mutilation under the 'Abbāsids, still bears witness; and it was only after the building was finished, and a substitute for the Ka'bah had been provided to which the pious Muslim might make his pilgrimage, that the rival Caliph was crushed and the Muslim world once again united under one head. Mu'āwiya had already wished to remove the pulpit of the Prophet at Medīna to his new mosque, but in deference to the religious feelings of the people he refrained from doing so. There is no reason to suppose that the Umayyad Caliph acted in this matter from merely pecuniary motives, because he wished to divert the commerce arising out of the pilgrimage to the Hijāz into his own coffers; because, as soon as he was undisputed Caliph, it would not have mattered which town became the object of pilgrimage (J. Wellhausen, *Das arabische Reich*, Berlin, 1902, p. 132 f.).

The truth is that the Umayyad Caliphs, with the exception of the pious 'Omar II., were not Muslims at heart. They sprang from the old aristocracy of Mecca, the bitterest opponents of the Prophet, who submitted to him only at the last possible moment. They did not scruple to attack and plunder the city of Medīna where he had lived and died, and even to destroy the Ka'bah itself, and they had well-nigh exterminated the family of the Prophet. They were a purely civil dynasty ruling in the name of religion, and they did not care what means they used to attain their ends. The great bulk of the population of Syria were Christians. They were, many of them, well educated, and in every way, except in fighting, more useful to the dynasty than the Arabs themselves. All the clerks in the government offices were Christians, and the State archives were written at first in Greek. A similar state of things existed in Persia and in Egypt. It was only under 'Abd al-Malik that the Arabic language began to be used exclusively, and even then the clerks continued to be non-Arabs. Some of the most influential persons about the Caliphs were also Christians. John of Damascus, as well as his father, held high office under these Arab rulers of his native city, and the panegyrist of the Umayyads was the Christian poet al-Akhṭal. Moreover, it was not that these Caliphs merely made use of their Christian subjects, whilst ignoring their religious creed. Questions of theology seem to have been discussed by the two parties in the presence of the more liberal Caliphs upon equal terms. Al-Akhtal made no attempt to conceal either his religious belief or the external emblems of his faith, when he stood before 'Abd al-Malik; and John of Damascus was an ardent defender of the use of images in divine worship, wherein he stood in opposition not only to the Caliph but to the Greek emperor as well. Such a state of things could not but react upon Muhammadanism itself, and there is little doubt that some of the less strict ways of thinking which began to prevail were due to this cause. It was to condone the delinquencies of the Umayyads that the Murjites professed to believe that there was no deadly sin for any one who made the profession of Islām, or that at any rate the sinner would not be punished until the Day of Judgment. Belief in divine predestination also began to be modified in the direction of an admission of free will. This tendency towards freedom of thought culminated in the Mu'tazilite movement under the 'Abbāsids (see SECTS [Muhammadan]). Nor was it only on the religious side that Christianity moulded Muslim life. Hishām, one of the last and best of the Umayyad Caliphs, was a notable agriculturist. His governor over 'Irāq was Khālid al-Qasrī, who was also a farmer on a grand scale. Khālid's mother was a Christian, and he built her a chapel beside the mosque at Kūfa. He employed Christians and other non-Muslim peoples in preference to Muslims, as he no doubt found them more intelligent and capable. In Hishām's days the doctrine that the Qur'ān is not eternal, which became the accepted creed for a short time under the 'Abbāsids, began to be professed. The century and more during which the Umayyads ruled the Muslim world from Damascus was the most glorious in Arabian annals, and it is not without significance that it was after the last Caliph of the line had removed the capital to his native town of Ḥarrān that the dynasty fell and was replaced by that of the 'Abbāsids.

With the fall of the Umayyads the Arabs ceased to be the ruling race and Syria became one of the provinces of the empire, not specially distinguished in the religious aspect from the rest. On the break-up of the Caliphate, with its resulting chaos, Syria became, with its many holy places, the battle-ground of Christianity and Islām. When it was prosperous and well-governed, it was generally as a dependency of Egypt, under Fāṭimid, Ayyūbid, or Mamlūk rulers. For the last four hundred years it has formed a province of Turkey.

LITERATURE.—There are no reliable reports published officially by the government. Much information is obtainable from daily and other periodicals appearing in Beirūt, mostly edited by Christians. See also A. I. S. de Sacy, *Exposé de la religion des Druzes*, Paris, 1838; G. Le Strange, *Palestine under the Moslems*, London, 1890; G. W. Chasseaud, *The Druses of the Lebanon*, do. 1855; C. H. Churchill, *Mount Lebanon*, do. 1853; J. Finn, *Stirring Times; Records from Jerusalem Consular Chronicles, 1853-56*, do. 1878; J. E. Hanauer, *Folklore of the Holy Land*, do. 1910; P. G. Baldensperger, 'The Immovable East,' in *PEFSt*, 1903 (p. 65 ff.) and foll. years; R. A. S. Macalister and E. W. G. Masterman, 'The Modern Inhabitants of Palestine,' in *PEFSt*, 1904 (p. 150 ff.) and foll. years.

B. EGYPT.—Since its conquest by the Arabs about the year A.D. 640, Egypt has, owing partly to its natural wealth and partly to its possession of the Azhar University and its frequent sovereignty over the holy places, played a leading part in the material and spiritual progress of Islām, and especially during the last hundred years it has outstripped all other countries in the direction of the Europeanizing of the faith. The people of Egypt have always been subservient to those of another race. At the beginning of the 7th cent. they had to endure twelve years of Persian domination. After the conquest was over, however, the Persians ruled, as they generally did, with moderation and tolerance, and, when the country was recovered for the Eastern empire by the conquests of Heraclius, the change of masters was a change for the worse. The natural craving of the Egyptian for a strong arm on which to lean had shown itself in the sphere of theology in their deification of Jesus Christ, which was the basis of their whole-hearted attachment to the Monophysite doctrine; when, therefore, Heraclius sought, through his instrument Cyrus, to force upon them the orthodox formula, and at the same time to increase the revenues obtained from the taxation of the country, the attempt was met by the Copts with dogged resistance, culminating in the flight of their patriarch Benjamin. It was owing to this prevailing discontent that the conquest of the country by the Arabs was a comparatively easy matter, accomplished within a couple of years, and with not more than a handful of troops. 'Amr, who had planned and carried out the expedition, became the first governor of the country. He at once granted religious toleration to the people, whose disputes he did not understand; he restored the Coptic patriarch to his office; and he, at any rate, did not increase the burden of taxation. The seat of government was removed from Alexandria to the fortress of Babylon, close to the modern Cairo, around which a town, called Fusṭāt, soon sprang up. The southern boundary of the province was at Philæ, the limit of the Christian kingdom of Nubia, with which the Arabs concluded a treaty.

The Copts did not at once go over to the faith of the conquerors. Probably they believed that the occupation would be temporary, as that of the Persians had been. Their only motives in becoming converts to Islām would have been those of self-interest, for Muslims were not subject to taxation. But it was not by any means the interest of the Arab that the subject populations should become converts to the faith, as that would endanger the source from which they drew their stipends, and lead to the bankruptcy of the government. The policy of the Arab rulers, in Egypt as elsewhere, was one of non-interference and continuity. The administration of the conquered territories was carried on, as nearly as possible, as it had been under their previous rulers. The Arabs formed a ruling class, corresponding as closely as may be to the British in India. Their business was, not to make converts to their religion, but to maintain public order, to see that justice was executed, and to collect the revenues. This was pre-eminently the case in Egypt, to such an extent that the newcomers, professed unitarians as they were, to whom images and pictures were abhorrent, did not scruple to take over even the seals of their predecessors in office, on which was frequently engraved the figure of a wolf or other animal—a rather hard nut for modern writers of Hebrew history to crack. The wise tolerance of the Arabs is shown by the fact that not only were their official documents written in Greek and Coptic as well as in Arabic, but many important positions in the government were filled by Christian natives of the country. No doubt, complaints of oppression were not wanting, but what oppression there was seems to have been due to the system which the Byzantines had bequeathed to the Arabs rather than to the manner in which the system was carried out by the latter, and sometimes the fault lay with the native intermediary.

Once more it fell to 'Amr to become the conqueror of Egypt, this time on behalf of the Umayyads, in whose hands it remained for nearly a century (A.D. 658–750). The tragic fall of the Umayyad dynasty and the massacre of their house made a deep impression upon the Christian population of Egypt, and it is not without significance that it was in Egypt that the last of the Umayyad Caliphs sought shelter from his enemies. For a century the 'Abbāsids continued to send Arab governors to Egypt, and it was not until the year 586 that non-Arab, practically independent dynasties began to be set up in the country.

Under the two centuries of Arab sway Egypt appears to have enjoyed a period of comparative prosperity and good government. The governors are no doubt often abused, but generally without justice. This is especially the case with Qurrah ibn Sharīk, who is usually described as an oppressor and persecutor, but whom numerous papyri show to have been a just, if strict, ruler. Moreover, not only was there no religious persecution of the Christians by the Arabs, but these had rescued the native Jacobite church from the hands of their co-religionists, the Greek Malkites, the free-lance nature of the Bedawī always leading him to support the more heretical side—a course which subserved his own interests also. The Arabs even discriminated in the taxation in favour of the Jacobites as against the Malkites to such an extent that not a few of the latter went over to the native church. The Arabs found Egypt in a state of feudalism. The people were serfs attached to the land, and many of the papyri are taken up with the capture of some fugitive who has escaped from his own domain. Not the least benefit which the Arabs conferred upon the Egyptians was to deliver them from their feudal lords, by converting these into mere tax-gatherers for the government.

The purely Arab government under the direct sovereignty of the Caliph was followed by a succession of dynasties of Turkish origin, the Ṭūlūnids (A.D. 868–905), whose capital Qaṭā'ī', between Fusṭāṭ (*i.e.* Latin *fossatum*) and modern Cairo, was famous for its splendour, and who for a quarter of a century ruled Syria as well as Egypt; and, after a brief interval, the Ikhshīdids (A.D. 935–969), who also ruled both Syria and the holy cities of the Hijāz, Mecca and Medīna.

The Arabs did not leave behind them much in the way of architecture to tell the visitor of their occupation of the country. The so-called 'mosque of 'Amr' may at least indicate the site on which that of the first conqueror of the country was built, but the latter was a building of very much more modest dimensions than the present spacious place of worship, and not a trace of it remains.[1] Indeed, the original Arab town of Fusṭāṭ, although it maintained an independent importance for many centuries, is now regarded as merely a part, and not the most flourishing part, of its younger sister, Cairo.

The dynasty of Ibn Ṭūlūn, on the other hand, left many memorials of their supremacy. The mosque of Ibn Ṭūlūn, said to be an imitation of the Ka'bah designed by a Christian architect, but with a dome superimposed and a minaret round which winds an external staircase resembling that of the Church of the Redeemer in Copenhagen, is still one of the sights of Cairo. Ibn Ṭūlūn's brilliant but unfortunate son also resembled the late Khedive Ismā'īl in his devotion to building and public works.

It was, however, under the Fāṭimids that Egypt rose to the height of its greatness. Claiming descent from Fāṭimah, the daughter of the Prophet, these sectaries, as they were held to be by the orthodox 'Abbāsid Caliphs, took their origin, like so many other movements, both political and religious, in N. Africa, from which they conquered Egypt (A.D. 969–1171). Mu'izz, the fourth of the dynasty, proclaimed himself Caliph, in opposition to the 'Abbāsid Caliph in Baghdād, and founded a new city close to the old capital, which he called Al-Qāhira ('the victorious'), the modern Cairo. The name bears a curious resemblance in sound to that of the ancient Egyptian town of Khere-ohe in the same neighbourhood. Like most heterodox peoples, the Fāṭimids were enlightened rulers. In spite of famine at home and the inroads of the Carmaṭians (*q.v.*) from Syria, they quickly consolidated their empire over all the countries bordering upon the shores of the Mediterranean, from Algeria to Syria, the holy cities of Arabia also acknowledging their sway. Security of life and property led to a great increase of population. Commerce was flourishing, and the trade of India, which had up till now passed through Baghdād, began to flow into Egypt, and from this period begins the decadence of the 'Abbāsid capital and the resulting aggrandizement of Cairo. 'Azīz, the son of Mu'izz, was especially distinguished for his enlightenment and religious tolerance. His reign is the culminating point of the dynasty, although it was considerably later that the prayers were said in the name of the Fāṭimid Caliphs in the 'Abbāsid capital itself, but only for one year (A.D. 1059). Under Ḥākim, the son and successor of 'Azīz, the free thinking of the Fāṭimid régime ran riot: under the malign influence of the Persian Darazi the Caliph proclaimed himself an incarnation of 'Alī, and claimed divine honours. He disappeared, but his doctrines were propagated in the sect of the Druses (see SECTS [Christian]). A persecution was also instituted against both Jews and Christians, in spirit not unlike those which the early Christians suffered for refusing to acknowledge the deification of Domitian and other Roman emperors.

The most enduring benefit which the Fāṭimids conferred upon Egypt and upon the whole Muslim world was the founding of the Azhar College. It was begun immediately after the conquest of the country, and opened in the year A.D. 972. The text of the inscription commemorating the opening has been preserved (M. van Berchem, *Corp. Inscr. Arab.*, i. [Paris, 1904] 43, no. 20). It received its name ('the fair') from an epithet of the alleged ancestress of the dynasty. Originally built as a mosque, it was transformed into a college and hospital for the poor by 'Azīz. Under the Fāṭimids the instruction imparted was naturally Shī'ite, but of this period little is known, and by a curious irony the college did not attain to full usefulness until it came under the rule of Sunnī, or orthodox, masters.

The annexation of Egypt by Saladin in the year 1169 and the consequent supersession of the Fāṭimid by the Ayyūbid dynasty, naturally led to the immediate abolition of the Shī'ite faith of the descendants of 'Alī and the establishment of the orthodox Sunnī profession, not only in the Azhar College but throughout Egypt (1171–1250). This was the more easy of accomplishment as the Egyptian Muslims were always Sunnites at heart, and had submitted to the faith of their Fāṭimid rulers only through compulsion or for the sake of peace. But, if the Fāṭimid form of faith vanished with their dynasty, they have left behind them monuments which show till the present day the greatness of their race. In addition to the Azhar mosque, the ancient city gates which are shown to the tourist date from the Fāṭimid period, as also does the mosque of Ḥākim, modelled on that of Ibn Ṭūlūn, situated between the Bāb Nasr and the Bāb Futūḥ. But their best memorial is the city of Cairo itself.

Of the four schools of doctrine which are recognized as orthodox by the Sunnite Muslims, the one

[1] See E. K. Corbett, 'The Hist. of the Mosque of Amr at Old Cairo,' in *JRAS* xxii. [1891] 759–800.

which first prevailed in Egypt was that of Mālik ibn Anas († A.D. 804). It is still the accepted rite of the rest of N. Africa, but in Egypt itself it has been replaced by that of his friend and disciple Shāfi'ī, who died in Fustāt in the year A.D. 819, and whose tomb is visited still by the pious near the foot of the Mokattam Hills. With a view to rooting out the Shī'ah doctrines and planting in their stead the orthodox faith, Saladin despoiled the Azhar of many of its privileges and endowments, and founded in its place a mosque and college round the tomb of the Imām Shāfi'ī (A.D. 1191), at the same time instituting missions to the outlying districts for the propagation of the true faith. The Azhar, however, quickly rose again into favour with the great and benevolent, and it is from the Ayyūbid rather than from the Fāṭimid period that its career of brilliance and usefulness takes its beginning. With the coming of the Mamlūks (1250–1517), who succeeded the Ayyūbids, the Ḥanīfite school (called after Abu Ḥanīfah, † in Baghdād, A.D. 767) came into prominence, and still more under the Ottoman Turks (from 1517 on). Being the least strict of the four schools and also the most inclined to monarchy, it was naturally favoured by the government, whilst the Shāfi'ite remained the popular school. As for the Ḥanbalī, the last of the four orthodox schools (founded by the fanatical Ibn Ḥanbal, † 855), it has never taken hold in Egypt, and its students in the Azhar have never been more than a handful at the most.

Meantime the Azhar University, which may be considered the intellectual barometer of Egypt, grew in importance and splendour by leaps and bounds. In the West the conquests of the Christians ending in the expulsion of the Moors from Spain by Ferdinand and Isabella in 1498, and the incursions of Jenghiz Khān at the beginning of the 13th cent. and of Tīmūr Lenk (Tamerlane) at the end of the 14th in the East, left Egypt untouched. Thus, when its rivals in Cordova and in Baghdād had been swept away, Cairo remained the undisputed mistress of Muslim learning and culture. Both its professors and students were drawn from all parts of the Muslim world, a preference even being given in some cases to those whose homes were most remote. The Muslim man of learning is cosmopolitan in his habits; he visits all countries where he may hope to pick up some crumbs of knowledge or obtain a diploma from some world-famous doctor; and the fame of the Azhar and its instructors naturally led many of these travelling students to settle in Cairo, and sometimes to lecture in its college. The best known of these is probably the philosopher-historian Ibn Khaldūn, who was a native of Tunis and was given posts in the government not only of that country, but also of Fez and Granada. He then came to Cairo, where he was given the office of *qāḍī* of the Malikīs. From there he paid a visit to Tīmūr Lenk at his camp in Syria, and finally died in Cairo in A.D. 1406.

But, while the Azhar may be considered as holding aloft the torch of learning to the whole world, both Muslim and Christian, up to the period of the Renaissance in Europe, it must be confessed that after that epoch it became a stronghold of obscurantism. This is evident from the books which continued to be studied there. The ancient poetry, which is the whole literature of pre-Islāmic Arabia, was unheard of, and even the *Assemblies* of the inimitable Ḥarīrī[1] were neglected. All study was theological (including jurisprudence) or grammatical. Even the original texts of the Qur'ān and the *Traditions* of Bukhārī were not studied so much as commentaries and super-commentaries upon these. Mathematics, natural philosophy, history, and geography were ignored. In other words, the Azhar, like the 'University' of Fez, continued to be a mediæval school after the Middle Ages had passed away.

[1] Tr. T. Chenery and F. Steingass, London, 1898.

Egypt was one of the first homes of Christian monasticism, and this religious tendency of its people showed itself also after they had largely gone over to Islām. One of the earliest and most typical mystics of Egypt is called Dhū'l-Nūn (a name of the prophet Jonah, meaning 'he of the fish'), who flourished in the first half of the 9th cent. A.D.; but perhaps the most famous is Ibn al-Fāriḍ, who is considered the greatest of all the poets of the mystics. He was born in Cairo in 1181, and died there in A.D. 1235. He was buried on the Mokattam Hills near the tomb-mosque of Shāfi'ī. His principal poem, in 671 lines, has been translated by J. von Hammer-Purgstall (Vienna, 1854). Already under Saladin not only cells and monasteries, but even convents (for divorced wives and other women), began to multiply rapidly. Būṣīrī († A.D. 1279), the author of the famous 'Ode of the Mantle,' which is known all over the Muhammadan world and has been often printed and translated into many languages, was, as his name implies, of Egyptian origin.

Although Islām is theoretically a strictly monotheistic religion, there is perhaps no faith in which the worship of saints plays a larger part. The prayer-book of Jazūlī, a native of Morocco who died in A.D. 1465, consisting of litanies in which the Arabian Prophet is a being certainly more than human, is used wherever his followers are found, and not least in Egypt. The whole of N. Africa, and indeed the Muslim world generally, is honey-combed with secret societies or brotherhoods (*ikhwān*), mostly religious in character. They form each an *ecclesia in ecclesia*. In Egypt there are four such orders named after four mystic or Ṣūfī (see ṢŪFIISM) saints of the highest rank called 'poles' (*quṭb*). The most famous of these is the Shaikh 'Abd al-Qādir al-Jīlānī († 1165), whose shrine is to this day a place of visitation in Baghdād; but the best known locally is Aḥmad al-Badawī, a native of Tunis of the 12th cent., whose tomb-mosque is at Tanta, a town of some 60,000 inhabitants, on the railway line about halfway between Alexandria and Cairo. A fair is held there annually on his saint's-day, during which the population swells to half a million, drawn from all the neighbouring countries. It resembles a fair elsewhere, shows of all kinds predominating over whatever religious motive ever existed. In Morocco the four recognized 'poles' differ from those acknowledged in Egypt, and one of them, Shādhilī, a native of the country († A.D. 1258), is also the eponym of one of the more important brotherhoods. In these shrines the room containing the catafalque of the saint is lined with banners, rosaries, ostrich eggs, and votive offerings of every description. Where the shrine has fallen into ruin and consists of four bare walls, rags and pieces of cloth are often tied to a neighbouring tree. These pious emblems represent the prayers of the faithful to the saint to intercede for them in order to obtain some much-desired object, recovery from sickness or, often, the birth of a son. The saints' tombs, which are such a marked feature of the landscape in all Muhammadan countries, are the emblems of an ineradicable superstition, and, it is said, in many cases the haunts of crime.

With the French expedition of 1798 a new era began in the history of Egypt, owing to the attempts of the Khedives to transform it into a European State. Muḥammad 'Alī sent the youth of the ruling classes to be educated in Paris, from which they too often returned imbued with the vices rather than the virtues of Europe. Ismā'īl laid down railway and telegraph lines all over the country. Under Taufīq slavery largely disappeared, and polygamy is fast becoming a thing of the past. From Taufīq also dates the liberty of the Egyptian newspaper press, a liberty which has been mostly abused. Indeed, the number of newspapers printed in Cairo is out of all proportion to the number of readers. They are, as might be expected, for the most part published in the interest of some political propaganda, nationalist (which generally means Turkish), conservative, or progressive. The best Christian newspapers are edited by Syrian immigrants. There are three or four journals published by and for women.

The progressive movement initiated by the Khedives naturally reacted on that stronghold of conservatism, the Azhar University. Incredible as it may appear, the instruction given there continued on the same lines as in the 13th century. To meet present-day needs the Gordon College was founded at Khartūm, and also a modern university in Cairo, but the latter has practically no students. Meanwhile the students of the Azhar, who have always been more or less inclined to take the law into their own hands, in 1909 went out on strike, with the result that some concessions were made to modern ideas. The last century in Egypt, however, can hardly be fairly considered as an example of Muhammadan rule, as all the ideas were European, although the instruments putting them in force were Muslim.

On the whole, it may be affirmed that Muhammadanism in Egypt has, considering the times and country, been enlightened and a source of enlightenment. Even at the period of conquest they did not put in force the iconoclastic theory of their faith, and under the Mamlūks, and even under the Fāṭimids, stone and metal work are, as may be seen by the specimens of the latter in the museum at South Kensington, of a very high order. Neither was there any scruple about making representations of living creatures. Ibn Ṭūlūn caused two plaster lions to be set over one of his gateways. Saladin introduced the eagle as an ornament in design. On one ewer, of the year A.D. 1232, in the British Museum there are over one hundred animal figures. It was from the Mamlūk artists of Egypt and Syria that this art passed into Europe. In architecture also the Mamlūks excelled. Nearly all the mosques of Cairo originated in their period, and certainly all the finest, not the least remarkable buildings being those of one of the last of the Mamlūks, Kait Bey (1468–96); yet it is on two of the oldest mosques, those of Ibn Ṭūlūn and of Ḥākīm, that are found the supposed beginnings of Gothic architecture. With the coming of the Turks a period of decadence supervened, which was only intensified under the Khedives.

With regard to their moral qualities it can be said that the Muslim rulers of Egypt, with the exception of the Caliph Ḥākīm, were not worse than Muslim rulers elsewhere; Saladin and a few other masters of the country were admirable rulers. The ancient monuments of Egypt still witness to the fact that the Arab conquerors of the country were not ruthless fanatics. The Coptic Church was not exterminated, as Zoroastrianism practically was in Persia, or Protestantism in Christian Spain. The native churches in Cairo are more magnificent than the mosques. One can only hope that the accounts of the persecution, especially under Ḥākīm, have been exaggerated; but, even if they are literally true, they would not prove that the Muslims treated Jews and Christians much worse than they treated one another. It is certainly remarkable and significant that, at the time of the British occupation, the Copts took the side of their former masters, thus bringing about an inrush of educated Syrian Christians. British writers do not give the Copts a very high character, and much prefer the Muhammadan in many ways; but this may be the result of ages of subordination. For the present, it is more than doubtful whether a Coptic government would not be more corrupt than the Muhammadan has been. The amusements of the people consist in smoking *hashīsh* (*Cannabis Indica*), which, being intoxicating, is forbidden, watching public dancers, and listening to songs and stories. All these are degrading to both spectators and performers, and it would be well if they could be put down by the government. The great want of Egypt, as of all Muslim countries, is books of fiction which are at once amusing and decent, but it would take a generation or two before a taste for such literature could be cultivated in the mind of the youthful Egyptian.

Literature.—The most reliable information in regard to present-day Egypt is to be obtained from Lord Cromer's *Modern Egypt*, London, 1908, and from his and his successors' annual Reports to the British Government (1888 ff.), as well as those of the Education and other Departments of the Government of Egypt; see also A. Milner, *England in Egypt*, London, 1892. Much information is also obtainable from E. W. Lane's notes to his tr. of *The Thousand and One Nights*, London, 1839, and his *Manners and Customs of the Modern Egyptians*, do. 1836; also Ibrahim Hilmi, *Literature of Egypt and the Sudan*, do. 1886–88; H. Jolowicz, *Bibliotheca Aegyptiaca*, Leipzig, 1858–61; M. Beiram, *Treatise on the History of the Azhar*, Cairo, 1321 A.H.; K. Vollers, in *Minerva* for 1894 (under 'Cairo'); M. Hartmann, *The Arabic Press of Egypt*, London, 1899; Artin Pasha, *L'Instruction publique en Egypte*, Paris, 1890; W. E. Jennings-Bramley, 'The Bedouins of the Sinaitic Peninsula,' *PEFSt*, 1905 (p. 126 ff.) and foll. years; T. W. Arnold, *The Preaching of Islam*[2], London, 1913; J. Ohrwalder, *Ten Years' Captivity in the Mahdi's Camp*, ed. F. R. Wingate, do. 1892; R. C. Slatin, *Fire and Sword in the Sudan*, tr. F. R. Wingate, do. 1898.

C. MESOPOTAMIA.—In the first quarter of the 7th cent. A.D. the Persians had conquered Egypt and Syria, and the Eastern Roman empire was, for the moment, almost limited by the walls of Constantinople. By a mighty effort, however, Heraclius drove the enemy from his provinces and the Persian empire was in its turn completely broken. This was the opportunity of the Arabs. Chaldæa became an easy prey, and in half a dozen years the empire, which under one dynasty and another had withstood the might of Greece and Rome for a millennium, had ceased to be.

The sudden collapse of Persia is explained by Arab writers by the decadent condition of the country, the effeminacy of the people, the tyranny of the great landowners, and the chaotic state of the government when brought face to face with the hardy nature and simple habits of the Arabs. But equally important is the fact that the population of Chaldæa was itself Arab. The Lakhmid kings, whose capital was at Hīra, near the ancient Kūfa and the present Najaf, were, like the Ghassānids on the other side of the Syrian desert, immigrants from Southern Arabia. Mesopotamia itself was peopled by the tribes of Taghlib, Iyād, and, further to the west, Nimar; and at Dūma, in the Jauf, on the route leading from Medīna to the Euphrates, was settled a branch of Kelb, the tribe which so influenced the Umayyads in Syria. All these tribes made a profession of Christianity; but how lightly their religion sat on them is clear from the nonchalance with which the tribe of Taghlib fell in with 'Omar's stipulation that they should not bring up their children in the Christian faith. Accordingly, when the Muslims set out to invade Mesopotamia, they met with little opposition and with some assistance from these tribes. The ties of blood proved stronger than those of religion.

Thus Mesopotamia quickly became a Muhammadan country, and, being peopled largely by

Arabs of the tribe of Quraish, it rapidly assumed a leading place in the Muslim world, and remained for three centuries, even when the political capital was Damascus, the intellectual and religious centre of Islām. It was generally divided into two provinces—'Irāq, the southern half, its most northerly town being Takrīt, and the northern portion, Jazīra (the Peninsula). Much the more important of the two provinces, from the point of view of the history of the faith, is 'Irāq. It has always been the storm centre of S.W. Asia, from which the majority of the great schisms and disruptions arose, and it remains to-day the seat of the Shī'ah, or party of 'Alī. Even in the days of 'Alī himself it produced the Khawārij (or Seceders), whose main principle was to oppose the established order of belief and of society, and to clamour for a theocracy, by which they really meant anarchy and nihilism. Often apparently exterminated, they continued to be a thorn in the side of the recognized Caliphate for many a day. Baghdād itself was originally built and fortified to protect the person of the Caliph against the fanatical Rawandīs, a sect of Khurāsān (A.D. 762). In the first half of the 9th cent. three of the 'Abbāsid Caliphs threw in their lot with the Mu'tazilah, or party of freedom of thought, and instituted a vigorous persecution of the orthodox believers; and in the second half of the same century a servile war broke out in the country to the north of the Persian Gulf and continued for fifteen years before it was quelled. With the 10th cent. the incursions of the terrible Carmaṭians began, who, though originating in Bahrain, quickly overspread and devastated Mesopotamia, Syria, and Egypt (see CARMAṬIANS). Meanwhile the Turkish slave-soldiers of the Caliphs had become so out of hand that the court was compelled to quit Baghdād and establish itself at Sāmarrā, some seventy-five miles further up the Tigris, and remain there for fifty-five years. By the time they returned the glory had departed from the Caliphate, and the supreme pontiff of Islām had become a puppet in the hands of the military power which happened to be supreme at the moment, until the last semblance of authority was swept away by the Mongol invasion.

But, whilst 'Irāq was the principal seat of heresy and sedition, it became for that very reason a stronghold of orthodoxy and firm government. Its turbulent population required the best brains and the strongest arm to keep them in check, and their very opinionativeness led to the necessary evolution of the particular view which eventually became accepted by the civil power. Just as some of the Caliphs liked to send their worst governors to the holy city of Medīna, so some of the best, from the point of view of the Caliph, were sent to 'Irāq. Such governors were, under the Umayyads, Ziyād, half-brother of the Caliph Mu'āwiya; the famous, if bloodthirsty, Hajjāj ibn Yūsuf, and Khālid al-Qasrī. 'Irāq, too, produced Ḥasan al-Basrī († 728), a commentator on the Qur'ān and collector of traditions about Muhammad, to whom the mystics trace their origin; and Abu'l-Ḥasan al-Ash'arī, who at first a Mu'tazilite, ended by reducing the faith to a system which was quickly acknowledged as orthodox and remains so at the present day.

The twin cities of Baṣra and Kūfa were founded immediately after the conquest of Mesopotamia by the Arabs (about A.D. 638). They were at first cantonments for the Arab garrison stationed in the territory conquered by them. These two cities, however, quickly lost their military character, and became what may be called the university towns of Islām. They have been well compared to Oxford and Cambridge, not only in their mutual rivalry, but also in the wide-spread authority which attached to their dicta. Their scholars laid down the principles of Arabic grammar, and decided, or at least pronounced upon, the proper reading of the text of the Qur'ān, those of one city often taking the view opposed to that advocated by the other. Baṣra especially was the home of free-thinking. It was there that the Arab encyclopædists published their tracts, and nowhere could the *Assemblies* of Ḥarīrī († 1122), with their airy use of expressions from the sacred volume, have been so fitly written. The Zanj and the Carmaṭian insurrections, which devastated 'Irāq, brought ruin to both towns; but, whilst Baṣra, under the enlightened 'open door' policy of native rulers, rose again, and is likely to continue an important commercial city, Kūfa never recovered.

One of the most curious facts in connexion with the history of Islām in Mesopotamia is the continuance of idolatrous rites in the midst of the true Faith at the city of Ḥarrān. Originally the seat of the worship of the moon-god, and best known from its mention in the Biblical story of Abraham, this city, from the time of Alexander, became a centre of Greek civilization. Long after Mesopotamia had become a Muslim province, Babylonian magic and Greek wisdom, Syrian paganism and Christian rites, all combined into one system of religion, continued to flourish there. Muslim governors were either kept in ignorance of these practices or bribed to remain silent regarding them. It was only in the year 830 that the Caliph Ma'mūn, when on an expedition against the Byzantines he passed by Ḥarrān, was struck by their strange garb and long hair. Then for the first time their existence became known to the central government. They were offered the alternatives of Islām—one of the tolerated sects or the sword. After some delay they declared that they were the Christians ect of the Ṣābians to whom toleration is granted in the Qur'ān. No doubt the Caliph was only too glad to let them be, as they were one of the chief means of introducing Greek learning into Islām. They produced many writers and translators, of whom perhaps the best known is Ṭābit ibn Qurrah († 901).

The 'Abbāsid was essentially a Persian dynasty. The cause had its beginnings in Khurāsān. One Caliph even wished to make the capital there. But the claims of the West were still too great for that, and so 'Irāq, the meeting-point of Semite and Persian, became and remained the seat of government. Baghdād was founded by Manṣūr in the year 762, and quickly eclipsed in grandeur all the other cities of the empire. Originally built on the west bank of the Tigris, the government offices and residence of the Caliph were later removed to the east. The insubordination of the Turkish guards at one time necessitated the withdrawal of the court to the small town of Sāmarrā further up the river. There it remained for over half a century (836–892). During this and the subsequent period nearly all the 'Abbāsid Caliphs came to a violent end at the hands of their own prætorians. Order was somewhat restored when the temporal power of the Caliphs was taken over by the Buwaihids (A.D. 945). These princes were, however, Shī'ites, whereas the population of Baghdād were Sunnites. Thus religious strife was added to civil, and was arrested only on the coming of the Seljūqs (A.D. 1055). Mesopotamia had been split up under innumerable petty chieftains, but now all Asia from Egypt to Afghanistan was under one strong ruler. The proclamation of the Fāṭimid Caliph in Baghdād in A.D. 1058 was merely a passing incident, and did not stay the march of events. The Buwaihids had already restored the old royal palace of the Khuld and turned it into a hospital, and now under the Seljūqs many colleges sprang up in Baghdād. Their famous Wazīr Niẓām al-Mulk, among his other benefactions, founded the college named after him the Niẓāmīya, which continued to be the principal college in Baghdād, until it was replaced by that of the second last of the Caliphs, Mustanṣir (A.D. 1226–42). Meantime the commercial importance of Baghdād had passed away at the same time as the temporal power of the Caliphs, and it was not the spiritual head of Islām, but the Seljūq Sulṭāns, and later Saladin, that proved the chief obstacle to the crusader.

After the fall of Baghdād and the extinction of the Caliphate by the Mongols, Mesopotamia came under the sway of Persia until these were driven back by the Ottoman Turks, who have held it for the last four hundred years. Thus the old rivalry of Constantinople and Īrān has been revived, with the added bitterness of the hatred of Shī'ah and Sunnah. To the Persian Muslim Mesopotamia is the most sacred country upon earth, holding as it does the dust of 'Alī and his son Ḥusain. 'Alī was assassinated in Kūfa in A.D. 661, but it was not until 791 that the place of his burial was discovered by Hārūn al-Rashīd, and even the authority for this statement is much later. To Alī were quickly attributed superhuman qualities, until he came not merely to be regarded as not inferior to the Prophet himself, but even to occupy the place of the second person in the Christian Trinity. Najaf or Mashhad 'Alī ("'Alī's shrine'), some four miles to the west of Kūfa, and Karbalā, the scene of the battle in which Ḥusain and most of his family perished in A.D. 680, some fifteen miles to the north of Najaf, are held, by the Persian protagonists of the divine right of Caliphs, to surpass in sacredness Medīna itself, whilst to the Turk, who now rules the land, as to some of the 'Abbāsid Caliphs, this devotion is nothing less than idolatry.

Mesopotamia, like N. Africa, has always been and still remains a forcing-house for religious fanaticism. In the strife of sects this fair province, one of the richest in the world, has almost gone out of cultivation. There is some prospect, however, that with the construction of the Euphrates valley railway and the annexation of Baṣra, the efforts to repair the system of canals, which were recently begun under W. Willcocks, will have the effect of restoring the country to what it was under its Sāsānid and Arabian rulers.

LITERATURE.—There are no reliable official reports. J. B. Fraser, *Mesopotamia and Assyria*, Edinburgh, 1842; Justin Perkins, *Eight Years in Persia*, Andover, 1843; F. R. Chesney, *Survey of Euphrates and Tigris*, London, 1850; V. Cuinet, *La Turquie d'Asie*, Paris, 1890; E. Sachau, *Am Euphrat und Tigris*, Leipzig, 1900; M. von Oppenheim, *Vom Mittelmeer zum persischen Golf*, Berlin, 1900; G. Le Strange, *Lands of the Eastern Caliphate*, Cambridge, 1905, pp. 1–126; R. P. A. Dozy and M. J. de Goeje, 'Nouveaux Documents pour l'étude de la religion des Harraniens,' in *Actes du vi^e Congrès internat. des orientalistes*, Leyden, 1888, ii. 281 f.

T. H. WEIR.

MUHAMMADANISM (in Turkey).—**1. Statistics.**—Statistics relating to Turkish conditions have hitherto been of very limited value, and in the circumstances of to-day it is virtually impossible to obtain them. The most recent computations will be found in *Die Welt des Islams*, I. i. [Berlin, 1913] 32, with which should be compared 'L'Islam en Bulgarie et dans la Roumelie orientale,' in *Revue du monde musulman*,[1] v. [1908] 482. It is unquestionable, however, that the decline of Islām in the Balkan Peninsula proceeds swiftly, and the rapidity with which the numerical decrease of a Muslim population may take place under Christian rule can be estimated from the data relating to Thessaly given by Franchet d'Espérey in *RMM* xiii. [1911] 87; thus, while in 1881 the 330,000 inhabitants of that district included 50,000 Muslims, in the present population of 381,000 there are only 3000. This shrinkage in numbers can be traced, though not in the same degree, also in Cyprus, Crete, Bulgaria, and Bosnia. It would seem to be doubtful, indeed, if the number of Muslims in the entire peninsula, even including such as are no longer Turkish subjects, would now amount to 3,000,000. As an offset, it is likely enough that there has been an increase in Anatolia. In the Muslim population of Asia Minor those of Turkish blood number about 11,000,000.

[1] Hereafter cited as *RMM*.

2. Development.—It is a manifest fact that the Turks as a people have not played so important a part in the formation of doctrine as in the popular religion. The share which they have had in the later development of Islām cannot as yet be determined, since the necessary scientific investigations have not so far been made. Nor has the protracted struggle which Sunnite orthodoxy has had to wage in Turkey with the Shī'ite faction and various sectarian movements been as yet examined in detail. On the other hand, the innovations introduced during the last century as a result of European influence have been in a measure exhaustively studied. While it is true that many of the proposed improvements were but imperfectly carried out, or were not carried out at all, they nevertheless form the most significant effort made in recent times to modernize Islām. At the outset they were ostensibly to be put in practice in the spirit of Islām, but in many cases, as a matter of fact, they ran counter to it. We are here concerned only with the reforms which come into conflict with the provisions of the *sharī'ah*, or Muhammadan law, and thus bear upon Islām as a religion. Besides a number of laws and regulations of the most diverse types there were in particular two decrees issued by the Sulṭān which, promulgated in a peculiarly impressive form, may be regarded as the pivots of modern Turkish life. These were respectively the *Ḥaṭṭ-i-sharīf* of Gulḫānah, issued on 5th Nov. 1839, and the *Ḥaṭṭ-i-humāyūn*, 18th Feb. 1856—both belonging, therefore, to the administration of 'Abd al-Majīd. While the former made promise, in a merely general way, of sundry reforms which should be in harmony with the spirit of the *sharī'ah*, the latter pledged the government to various changes in certain ordinances laid down by that legal system. These changes related to the legal oath and the military service of Christians, and to the abolition of the capital penalty for apostasy from Islām. In connexion with these points a new penal code was issued, and the suppression of slavery resolved upon, in 1858.[1]

None of these reforms sprang from the will of the Turkish people themselves; on the contrary, they were effected at the instigation of the European Powers, especially of Great Britain, and were introduced only after long temporizing on the part of the higher governing classes in Turkey. When the Western Powers had succeeded in saving Turkey in the Crimean War, they demanded, as an act of gratitude, the abrogation of the ordinances which could not but be humiliating to the Christian mind. They likewise expected that the changes would serve to intensify the nationalistic consciousness of the non-Muhammadan elements in Turkey, and thus provide a barrier to the grow-

[1] These laws were published in the *Dustūr* (Constantinople, A.H. 1289 [=A.D. 1872], 4 vols. and a supplementary vol., consisting of four books [Turkish]; Fr. version in Aristarchi Bey, *Législation ottomane*, 7 vols., do. 1873–88). The laws passed since 1908 have appeared in the *Taqwīm-i-waqāy'*; Fr. version in *Législation ottomane depuis le rétablissement de la constitution*, ed. A. Biliotti and Ahmed Sedad, Paris, 1912, i. Other useful works are: G. Young, *Corps de droit ottoman*, Oxford, 1905–06; E. Engelhardt, *La Turquie et le Tanzimat*, Paris, 1882–84; F. Eichmann, *Die Reformen des osman. Reiches*, Berlin, 1858.

ing influence of Russia. The Turkish administration was not blind to the difficulty of the undertaking, and to some extent evaded it in a very adroit fashion.

The various points were settled as follows:

In order to permit Christians to take oaths as witnesses—a privilege denied to them by the *sharīʻah*—an entirely new judicature, upon which experts had been at work for a number of years, was established. In addition to the jurisdiction of the *sharīʻah*, which thenceforward retained its competence only in certain cases arising out of the personal status of Muhammadans—such as, *e.g.*, affairs relating to marriage, alimony, divorce, inheritance, etc.—the *maḥākim-i-niẓāmīyah* were introduced, organized on European models. At these courts, instead of the sworn evidence permitted by the *sharīʻah*, documentary evidence alone was received as valid, so that it was now possible for a Christian to give his testimony even against a Muhammadan.

The abolition of capital punishment for defection from the Muslim faith was conceded in the following terms: 'As every religion and sect in my empire may practise its form of worship with complete freedom, no one shall be obstructed or molested in practising the worship of the religion to which he belongs, and no one shall be compelled to change his religion or sect' (Fr. text, § 8).

The abolition of *ḥarāj* (poll-tax) and the introduction of military service for non-Muhammadans were effected in name, but commutation (*badal-i-ʻaskarī*) was still to be allowed (cf. the present writer's art. 'Bedel-i-ʻaskeri,' in *EI*). In reality, therefore, the state of affairs remained as it was, the only modification being that the term *ḥarāj* was replaced by the expression *badal-i-ʻaskarī*. It was not till the Revolution of 1908 that military service was actually imposed upon all Turkish subjects quite independently of their religious profession—a measure certainly not conducive to the national welfare.

Similarly, the new penal code was altogether at variance with the criminal law of the *sharīʻah*. It was framed by the simple process of taking over the French *code pénal* in 1858, although as early as 1839 the *Ḥaṭṭ-i-sharīf* had promised that such a code would be drawn up, and this had in some measure been attempted. The new penal law was at length modernized by the supplementary decrees of 4th April 1911. The later code, however, did not supersede the penal ordinances of the ancient *sharīʻah*; on the contrary, the two sets of laws remain in operation side by side, and offences can be tried by either (cf. E. Nord, *Das türkische Strafgesetzbuch*, Berlin, 1912, and A. Heidborn, *Droit public et administratif de l'empire ottoman*, i., Vienna, 1909, p. 354). Of the other reforms, reference need here be made only to the enactments relating to the slave-trade. An irade of 1st Oct. 1854 forbade the buying and selling of Georgian slaves; various ministerial ordinances, dating from the years 1868, 1870, 1871, 1879, and 1889, prohibited all commerce in slaves whatsoever; since 1892 the trade has been regarded as smuggling. From 1890 Turkey has taken part in the International Conferences for the suppression of the slave-trade in Africa at Brussels.

While it is true that many of these reforms were very imperfectly carried out, or not carried out at all, yet their importance should not be underrated. In not a few cases they made a breach in the fabric of the *sharīʻah* alike in theory and in practice. A consistent application of the new laws would serve to bring Islām into line with modern ideas; but to what extent this may be effected without great religious wars, and how far Muslim theology is able and willing to deal with the fresh problems involved, the future alone can show. Hitherto Muslim theology has tacitly submitted to the reforms, and has not expressed itself openly regarding them. It is only within recent years that the aspirations of the young Turks have won support among the theologians, but no attempt has been made as yet to produce works of importance in the field of scientific theology. The views of this liberal tendency—if we may so call it—in theology find expression in the *Ṣirāṭ-i-Mustaqīm*, a periodical founded immediately after the Revolution, and from no. 183 (8th March 1912) continued under the name of *Sabīl al-Rashād* (cf. L. Bouvat, in *RMM* xx. [1912] 282–304; M. Hartmann, *Unpolitische Briefe aus der Türkei*, Leipzig, 1910, p. 137).

3. Religious organization. — Apart from the theological group just referred to, the religious ranks of Islām in Turkey have no liking for innovation. The name by which the entire class, as well as the individual member of it, is known is *ʻulamā* (the plural of *ʻalīm*, 'learned'). This long-established organization, as still existing with but little change in its main features, was founded in the reign of Sulṭān Muhammad II., the Conqueror (1451–81) (cf. J. von Hammer-Purgstall, *Des osmanischen Reichs Staatsverfassung und Staatsverwaltung*, pt. ii., Vienna, 1815, p. 373 ff.; W. Gibb, *A Hist. of Ottoman Poetry*, London, 1900–09, ii. 394; C. d'Ohsson, *Tableau général de l'empire othoman*, iv. 2, Paris, 1791, p. 482 ff.). At its head stands the Shaikh al-Islām, whose office, as now constituted, was created for him by Sulṭān Sūlaimān I. the Magnificent (1520–66), though the title had been conferred by Muhammad I., the Conqueror, upon the mufti of Constantinople. In consequence of the reforms, and especially the creation of the *maḥākim-i-niẓāmīyah* (see above), his authority has suffered a considerable decline; he now controls only the religious schools and the *sharīʻah*. The board over which he presides is called *Bāb-i-mashaiḥat-i-islāmīyah*, *Bāb-i-fatwā-panāhī*, or, popularly, *Shē-islāmqapusu*, and consists of the following departments:

(*a*) *Administrative boards*: (1) *Majlis-i-intiḥāb-i-hukkyām-i-sharʻ*, the commission for the selection of spiritual judges; (2) *Majlis-i-imtiḥān*, commission for the entrance examination for the *maktab-i-nuwāb* and the *mudarrislik*, presided over by the *dars vakīlī*; (3) *Majlis-i-maṣāliḥ-i-ṭalabah*, commission for the affairs of students; (4) *Majlis-i-mashāiḥ*, commission for the affairs of the dervish orders; (5) *Majlis-imtiḥān-i-qurrā*, commission for examining *madrasah* students with a view to their exemption from military service; (6) *Maʻmūrin-i-ʻilmīyah tāqa ʻud ṣandīghī*, superannuation fund for spiritual officials; (7) board for the administration of the property of wards. (*b*) *Judicial boards*: (1) *Rūmīlī qāḍī askarī*, the kadiasker of Rumelia; (2) *Anātūlī qāḍī ʻaskarī*, the kadiasker of Anatolia; (3) *Istāmbūl qāḍī ʻaskarī*, the *qāḍī* of Constantinople; (4) *Iʻlāmāt ōtasi*, the office for verdicts; (5) *Majlis tadqīqāt sharīʻah*, commission for revisal of the decisions of the *sharīʻah*. (*c*) *Fatvāḥānah*, office for the legal decisions of the *sharīʻah* (cf. Heidborn, i. 252 ff.).

While the standing of the Shaikh al-Islām, as of the *ʻulamā* generally, is now greatly inferior to what it once was, their influence among large masses of the people is still very considerable, and to this day they form a power which cannot safely be ignored by the politicians.

4. The dervish orders. — Perhaps an even greater influence among the people is enjoyed by the dervish orders. From the foundation of the Ottoman empire they have played a great rôle in Asia Minor, as they did to some extent even before. As a matter of fact, the gradual Muslimization of the Christian elements in Turkey has been their work; in their indifference towards the existing forms of religion, views of the most diverse character could find a refuge in their midst. Their ideas have come, in course of time, to be assimilated to those of the official and national religious organization. The order of the highest repute at the present day is the Maulavī, so called from the name of its founder, Maulānā Jalāl al-Dīn Rūmī (*q.v.*), and known in the west as the 'dancing dervishes.' The next in general regard are the Rufāʻī—the so-called 'howling dervishes.' Certain orders which at one time occupied a powerful position—*e.g.*, the Naqshbandī, the Halvatī, the Qādirī, etc.—have now sunk to a lower level; others, again, have been of late gradually growing in prestige—*e.g.*, the Malāmi (cf. Hartmann, Index).

The Baqṭāshī, an order which at one time, owing to its close connexion with the Janizaries, held a position of special prominence, sank into the background after the suppression of that force by Sulṭān Maḥmūd in 1826, but have quite recently begun to display a more active spirit. In Asia Minor, and even more decidedly in Albania, this order is constantly adding to its strength. By reason of its heterodox views it should hardly be regarded as belonging to Islām at all, but it certainly makes this claim.

It has been methodically dealt with in several recent works of great reliability, such as G. Jacob, *Beiträge zur Kenntnis des*

Derwischordens der Bektaschis, Berlin, 1908, and *Die Bektaschijje in ihrem Verhältnis zu verwandten Erscheinungen*, Munich, 1909; C. Huart, 'Les Derviches bektachis,' in *RMM* ix. [1909] 235, *Textes persans relatifs à la secte des Houroûfis*, Leyden, 1909; Ryfqy, *Bektāšī sirri*, Constantinople, A.H. 1325.

Of literature relating to the orders there is not much of a serviceable kind. J. P. Brown, *The Dervishes*, London, 1868, contains many valuable items of information, but must be read with extreme caution; and the same may be said of A. de Chatelier, *Les Confréries musulmanes du Hedjaz*, Paris, 1887.

We need not deal here with such sects as the Yezīdīs (*q.v.*), the Nuṣairīs, the Taḥtaji, the Kizil Bash (*q.v.*), etc., which, though professing certain Muslim doctrines, cannot now be included under Islām. In contrast to the Baqṭāshī, who, as has been said, still claim to rank as Muslims, these sects in general renounce the name. As the Shī'ites proper have no real standing in Turkey, they, too, lie outside the scope of this article.

5. Superstition and popular religion.—Superstition is extremely prevalent among the masses, and popular thought exhibits residua of the most diverse forms of religion. We find survivals of the ancient shamanism of the Turki peoples, as well as of Christian and Jewish superstition. This interesting side of Turkish Islām has not yet been exhaustively dealt with, but there are several compilations from which we may glean an adequate impression of it.

Besides a number of shorter papers, as, *e.g.*, F. Schrader, 'Zum vorderasiatischen Volksglauben,' in the Supplement to *AZ*, 25th Sept. 1903, the following deserve special mention: F. Mészáros, 'Osmanisch-türkischer Volksglaube,' in *Keleti Szemle*, vii. [1906] 48, 140; Wladimir Gordlewski, 'Osmanskiya skazaniya i legendy,' in *Ethnographic Review*, Moscow, 1912 (Russ., reviewed by T. Menzel in *Der Islam*, iv. [1913] 123, and F. Schrader in *Osmanischer Lloyd*, 31 Jan. 1913).

There is evidence to show, moreover, that the worship of saints (*avlīyā*) and their places of pilgrimage (*ziyāratgāh*) has a predominant place in Turkish popular belief. A large number of these saints can be traced to personages held sacred in ancient Byzantium, the names being in some cases greatly corrupted—*e.g.*, 'Toglu Dede' from St. Thekla—and the places of pilgrimage are still found on the Byzantine sites.

The religious needs of the common people, and more especially of the women, are served by a large mass of devotional literature. The principal works of this class are among the oldest literary monuments of the Osmanli Turks, and their idiom is thus frequently unintelligible to the readers of to-day—a fact which, of course, in no way detracts from their popularity. Pre-eminent among these are the *Muhammadiyah* and the *Aḥmadiyah*, as also the *History of Junus Imre* (cf. Gibb, i. 164, 389; Hartmann, Index, *s.v.* 'Junus Imre'). For the study of Turkish literary history these works are all of importance, but their theological value is of the slightest, and their contents need not further concern us here. Similarly, the '*Ilm-i-ḥal* literature requires but the briefest mention; it consists of booklets which, like our modern catechisms, set forth the leading religious doctrines in the form of question and answer.

LITERATURE.—There is as yet no systematic account of Islām in Turkey. Studies dealing with special aspects of the subject have been cited throughout the article in connexion with the particular points, and the older literature will be found in them. The numerous works designed for the general public do not fall to be mentioned here, but we may name as the best of them C. N. E. Eliot, *Turkey in Europe*, new ed., London, 1908.

F. GIESE.

MUḤYĪ AL-DĪN IBN AL-'ARABĪ.—Muḥyī al-dīn ibn al-'Arabī, the celebrated Muhammadan mystic, who is generally known by the name of Ibn al-'Arabī or Ibn 'Arabī, was born at Murcia in S. Spain in A.D. 1165. Much of his youth was spent in Seville, where he devoted himself to literary, theological, and mystical studies. After visiting Granada and other Spanish towns, as well as Tunis, Fez, and Morocco, he set out in 1201 for the East by way of Egypt, whence he made the pilgrimage to Mecca. He did not return to Spain. Many of the remaining years of his life were passed in the neighbourhood of Mecca, but he also travelled extensively in Babylonia, Asia Minor, and Syria, everywhere gaining disciples and spreading his doctrines in conversation with high and low, while, as behoved a good Muslim in the period of the Crusades, he called for repressive measures against the Christian population and encouraged his fellow-Muhammadans to persevere in their faith. He died at Damascus in A.D. 1240.

Whether we regard the extent of his theosophical writings or their influence on the subsequent development of Islāmic mysticism, Ibn al-'Arabī can justly claim the supreme position among Ṣūfī authors which posterity has accorded to him, and which is attested by the title, 'al-Shaikh al-Akbar,' conferred on him by the almost unanimous voice of those who are best qualified to judge. The list of his works drawn up by himself contains 289 titles (Brockelmann, *Gesch. der arab. Litteratur*, i. 442), and some of them are of enormous length. The most famous and important is the *Futūḥāt al-Makkīya* (4 vols., Būlāq, 1876, comprising about 3300 pages). In this, as in many of his works, Ibn al-'Arabī professes to communicate mysteries revealed to him in ecstatic vision by prophets, angels, and even God Himself (a brief résumé of part of the contents of the *Futūḥāt* will be found in H. O. Fleischer and F. Delitzsch, *Catalogus librorum manuscr. bibliothecæ senator. Lipsiensis*, Grimma, 1838, pp. 490–495). Another book, of smaller compass but equally celebrated, is the *Fuṣūṣ al-Ḥikam*, in which the author discourses upon the nature and significance of the divine revelations imparted to twenty-seven prophets, beginning with Adam and ending with Muhammad. Besides the *Futūḥāt* and the *Fuṣūṣ*, both of which contain a considerable quantity of verse, his prose writings include a mystical commentary on the Qur'ān, a collection of definitions of Ṣūfiistic technical terms, which has been edited by G. Fluegel, (Leipzig, 1845), and a short treatise on mystical psychology (Arab. text with Span. tr. by Asín Palacios, in *Actes du xive Congrès internat. des orientalistes*, iii. 151 f.). He also produced several volumes of mystical poems, one of which, the *Tarjumān al-ashwāq* (ed. with Eng. tr. by the present writer, London, 1911), has a curious history. The erotic style in which it is written gave rise to scandal, and in order to refute his accusers Ibn al-'Arabī published a second edition accompanied by a commentary in which the mystical sense of each verse is explained. Although his interpretations are often far-fetched, the poems themselves supply evidence that there was no ground for the charge brought against him, plausible as it might appear to the uninitiated. The question of his orthodoxy was keenly disputed, and, if many Muslims saw in him a dangerous heretic, others had no doubt that he was a great saint; but even his admirers recognized that the outward sense of his writings was frequently ambiguous, and that the study of them should be permitted only to mystics of ripe experience. At first sight, it seems hard to reconcile Ibn al-'Arabī's extreme conservatism in the sphere of religious law with his remarkably bold and fantastic speculations in the domain of theosophy. He belonged to the Ẓāhirite school, which rejects opinion, analogy, and authority, and takes its stand on the external (*ẓāhir*), literal meaning of the Qur'ān and the traditions. But, while his attitude in regard to legal and ritual practice was that of the literalist (*ẓāhirī*), who looks only at the outward form, in all matters of doctrine and belief he was pre-eminently the mystic (*bāṭinī*), who fixes his gaze on the inward spirit and seeks to discover the reality of which the words and letters are a symbol. As I. Goldziher has shown (*Die Ẓâhiriten*, Leipzig, 1884, p. 179 ff.), the two points of view are not mutually exclusive. The Ẓāhirite practice appealed to many Ṣūfīs, who found in it an expression of their own dislike for the hair-splitting pedantry of the rival schools of law, for the acceptance of external authority as the standard of truth, and for the method of logical demonstration as opposed to intuitive knowledge.

Ibn al-'Arabī, like other Ṣūfīs before and after him, endeavours to combine the Ash'arite theology with philosophical ideas which, in his case, are mainly derived from Plotinus and the Neo-Platonic circle. Thus he has to deal with two different conceptions of God: (1) the Allāh of the Qur'ān, endowed with attributes that are superadded to His essence, and (2) the One Being which is devoid of every attribute, quality, and relation, and which is all that exists. His God retains the attributes of Allāh, but these are reduced to mere relations, having no real existence; hence, although they are the archetypes of the sensible world, they do not affect the essential unity of God, in whom all contraries are identified. In his attempt to explain how plurality can proceed from the Simple One, Ibn al-'Arabī employs the same metaphors as Plotinus, his favourite illustration being the diffusion of light. The intelligible world is constituted by a series of seven realities: (1) God, the One Essence; (2) the First Intelligence or Universal Reason, which comprises every species of divine knowledge and, in Qur'ānic language, is the Pen that inscribes on the Tablet of Universal Soul the divine ideas whereof created things are a copy; (3) Universal Soul; (4) Universal Nature; (5) Universal Matter; (6) Universal Body; (7) Universal Figure. The entire phenomenal universe is the manifestation of those realities, which, before their manifestation, exist potentially—or, as Ibn al-'Arabī says, are non-existent—in the luminous darkness that hides eternally the essence of the Godhead. Manifestation involves relativity, and the relation of the universe to God is that of the determined to the Absolute, of the shadow to the sun. All existence is constituted by form (*ṣūrah*) and spirit (*rūḥ*). Form answers to the Aristotelian definition of matter; *i.e.*, it is essentially potential and imperfect. Spirit, on the other hand, is what Aristotle calls 'form,' the principle that gives reality and perfection to the forms produced by Universal Nature, which take their place in the order of existence according to their capacity for receiving and manifesting the life of the Universal Spirit that animates the whole. Of these forms the highest is man, who, in virtue of the microcosmic function assigned to him by his Creator, unites and displays all the divine names and attributes, so that he is the mirror in which God beholds and reveals Himself as He really is. This description refers only to the supreme type of humanity, 'the perfect man' (*al-insān al-kāmil*), whom Ibn al-'Arabī identifies with Adam as representing the class of men—prophets, saints, and theosophists—that possess a unique knowledge of God (*Fuṣūṣ al-Ḥikam*, ch. i.; cf. *EI*, art. 'al-Insān al-Kāmil'). Knowledge is a process of reminiscence. In proportion as each particular soul is purified, it receives illumination from Universal Reason by means of revelation (*waḥy*), and from Universal Soul by means of inspiration (*ilhām*). The organ of this knowledge is the reasonable soul (*al-nafs al-nāṭiqah*), which must be distinguished from the vital or animal soul (*al-rūḥ al-ḥayawānī*). While the former has only an accidental connexion with the body and is incapable of sin, the animal soul, though not consciously evil, is naturally corrupt, and suffers punishment for sins committed in the flesh.

The system of Ibn al-'Arabī may be described as a pantheistic monism. God and the world are two correlative and complementary aspects of one Absolute Reality: the world could not exist apart from God, and, if the world did not exist, God could not be manifested and known. The terms 'creator' (*al-Ḥaqq*) and 'creature' (*khalq*) are logically involved in one another as moments of the Absolute Being, not indeed of equal worth—since *al-Ḥaqq* is eternal, while *khalq* is contingent (*i.e.* eternal in the knowledge of God, and originated in respect of its manifestation)—but interchangeable subjects of predication (cf. L. Massignon, *Kitāb al-Ṭawāsīn*, Paris, 1912, p. 139 ff.). Ibn al-'Arabī delights in the daring paradoxes which this line of thought suggests to him—*e.g.*,

'He praises me and I praise Him,
And He worships me and I worship Him.
In one state I acknowledge Him,
But in the objects of sense I deny Him.
He knows me and I know Him not,
And I know Him and behold Him.
How can He be independent,
When I help and aid Him?
For that cause God brought me into existence,
Therefore I know Him and bring Him into existence'
(*Fuṣūṣ*, Cairo, 1321 A.H., ch. v. p. 78).

Although the contrary might be inferred from some passages of his writings, he makes a distinction between the divine and human natures, and his pantheism does not lead to the doctrine of incarnation (*ḥulūl*) or identification (*ittiḥād*). Man can never say with Ḥallāj, 'I am God' (*Ana 'l-Ḥaqq*), because, owing to the constitution of his mind, he is unable to think all objects of knowledge simultaneously, as God thinks them; therefore he is only 'a truth' (*ḥaqq*), not 'the Truth' (*al-Ḥaqq*), who is the counterpart of the whole universe of created things (cf. Massignon, p. 182 f.).

In view of the scanty attention that Ibn al-'Arabī has hitherto received from European scholars, it would be impossible to give a detailed account of his doctrines, and premature to make a more definite statement concerning the character of his theosophy as a whole. Much of it, of course, belongs to the common stock of Ṣūfiistic speculation, but there is also a great deal that appears to be original and based upon the immense store of his own mystical experiences, which he has so copiously recorded and analyzed (for his theory of ecstasy and the seven degrees of 'passing-away' [*fanā*] which he enumerates, see Asín Palacios, 'La Psicología segun Mohidín Abenarabi,' in *Actes du xive Congrès internat. des orientalistes*, iii. 125 ff.). Among the twenty-four heretical doctrines attributed to him by 'Alī al-Qārī' (*Risālah fī waḥdat al-wujūd*, Constantinople, 1294 A.H.) the following are noteworthy:

(*a*) That man stands to God in the same relation as the pupil of the eye, which is the instrument of vision, to the eye; *i.e.*, man is the means whereby God beholds His creation and knows Himself; and that we (mankind) are ourselves the attributes with which we endow God—excepting only the attribute of necessary and essential being—so that, 'when we contemplate Him, we contemplate ourselves, and when He contemplates us, He contemplates Himself' (*Fuṣūṣ*, ch. i.). Elsewhere Ibn al-'Arabī says: 'We are the food that sustains the being of God, and He is our food'—a further instance of the way in which he turns the principle of logical correlation to pantheistic uses.

(*b*) That God is the 'self' (*'ain*) of the things that He brought into existence, for He is the 'self' of things in manifestation, though He is not the 'self' of things in their essences. Therefore Ibn al-'Arabī holds that the true mystic, combining the doctrines of *tanzīh* and *tashbīh*, worships God both as absolutely transcendent and as externalized in nature (*Fuṣūṣ*, ch. iii.).

(*c*) That all forms of religious belief are relatively true. This follows from the proposition that God is the 'self' of all created things, whether they be sensible or intelligible. Every sectary forms some notion of God, and in praising the god which he has made he praises himself, while at the same time he blames the gods of other sects and individuals. It would be more wise and just if he perceived God in every form and in every belief, according to the verse (Qur'ān, ii. 109), 'Wheresoever ye turn, there is the face, *i.e.* the reality, of Allah' (*Fuṣūṣ*, chs. x. and xxvii.; cf. *Tarjumān al-ashwāq*, Preface, p. vi).

(*d*) That, even if the infidels shall remain in hell for ever, their torments will ultimately be transmuted into such pleasure as is enjoyed by the blessed in paradise. 'Abd al-Karīm al-Jīlī develops this theory in his *Insān al-Kāmil* (see the present writer's article, 'A Moslem Philosophy of Religion,' in *Muséon*, 3rd ser. I. i. [1915] 83 ff.). Evidently there is no room in Ibn al-'Arabī's system for the Muhammadan scheme of rewards and punishments. The fullness of the divine wisdom as manifested in creation requires that the spiritual capacities of human souls shall be infinitely various, and salvation and perdition are the effects that correspond with the capacity eternally implicit in God's knowledge of every human soul before its individualization in the material world. Ibn al-'Arabī proceeds to argue that, inasmuch as knowledge is a relation dependent on the object known, viz. the soul and its potential capacity, each individual is responsible for the good and evil which are produced by that capacity (*Fuṣūṣ*, ch. v.); but in another passage of the same work (ch. viii.) he declares that it is a more profoundly mystical thought to regard the soul as a mode of God, and its recompense as a divine illumination (*tajallī*) in the form of pleasure or pain which are felt by God Himself.

(*e*) That the saints are superior to the prophets. Ibn al-'Arabī does not state the doctrine in this absolute way. The prophets, he says, may be viewed in three aspects: as apostles, they bring a religious code to their people; as prophets, they inform them about God in proportion to their own knowledge; and, as saints, they pass away in God and abide in Him. Saintship is the inward, mystical, everlasting element in prophecy. Hence the prophet *qua* saint ranks above the prophet *qua* religious legislator or preacher of divine truth (*Fuṣūṣ*, ch. xiv.). According to 'Alī al-Qārī', Ibn al-'Arabī claimed to be the Seal of the Saints (*Khātam al-auliyā*), as Muhammad is the Seal of the Prophets.

LITERATURE.—The best general survey of Ibn al-'Arabī's theosophy is contained in two papers by Asín Palacios—'La Psicología segun Mohidín Abenarabi,' in *Actes du xive Congrès internat. des orientalistes*, Algiers, 1905, iii. 79–150, and 'Mohidín,' in *Homenaje á Menéndez y Pelayo*, Madrid, 1899, ii. 217–256. The latter volume (pp. 191–216) includes an essay by Julián Ribera, 'Origenes de la filosofía de Raimundo Lulio,' which gives much information concerning the life of Ibn al-'Arabī and the influence of his ideas upon those of Lull. See also A. von Kremer, *Gesch. der herrschenden Ideen des Islams*, Leipzig, 1868, p. 102 ff.; C. Brockelmann, *Gesch. der arab. Litteratur*, Weimar, 1898–1902, i. 441 ff.; R. A. Nicholson, *Literary History of the Arabs*, London, 1907, p. 399 ff.; D. B. Macdonald, *Development of Muslim Theology*, do. 1903, p. 261 ff.

REYNOLD A. NICHOLSON.

MUKTI.—See MOKṢA.

MULLĀ.—*Mullā* is a title of varied usage, given to officials of different ranks, but invariably to men who have received some degree of education in a *madrasah*, or higher mosque school, and hold certificates testifying thereto; it is also a generic term applied to such officials as a class.

Mullā is a proper pronunciation of the Turkish *mevla*, the Arab. *maulā* (lit. 'lord,' 'master,' 'patron'; also 'slave,' 'client'; any one standing in any sort of fixed relationship to another); it is used commonly among the Muhammadans of Turkey, Persia, Russia, India, and their spiritual dependencies. In India, however, the form *maulavī* or *mūlvī* is also used in reference to the *mullās* of the lower grades, below the rank of *'ālim* (plural = *'ulamā*). The form *mevlānā* ('our lord') is applied to the most eminent *'ulamā*, and also to eminent Ṣūfī leaders. In Turkish a distinction is further made by affixing instead of prefixing *mullā* to the name of a judge of a higher court. In Arabic-speaking countries *mullā* as a generic term is not so frequently used; in the term 'Mullā of Jerusalem,' 'of Cairo,' 'of Medīna,' etc., the reference is to the chief justice of the Muhammadan religious court of each city; while *shaikh*, a title of older usage in Muhammadanism, has persisted especially in application to a religious teacher of authority. The term 'Mad Mulla' has sometimes been applied to certain fanatical religious leaders in India and the Sūdān who, having proclaimed themselves the *Mahdī* (*q.v.*), have led revolts against the established government.

The characteristics of the *mullās* as a class are determined largely by the education which they receive. The ranks are recruited normally from the lower, less often from the middle, classes. Between the ages of eleven and fifteen, having passed through the *maktab* ('elementary school'), students are admitted as *softas* ('undergraduates') to the *madrasah* (higher mosque school). The curriculum offers training mainly in dialectics, theology, and the canon law based on the Qur'ān and traditions (*ḥadīth*); it is that of a theological seminary of the orthodox type. The Oriental languages are also taught, and in previous centuries there were *mullās* who became famous in the field of *belles-lettres*; but in more recent times the graduates have been only lawyer-theologians. The complete curriculum requires at least fifteen, in practice generally eighteen, years for fulfilment; but very few students succeed in completing the course and passing the various examinations which entitle them to a place in the higher ranks of the *'ulamā* and to appointment to the higher judicial and university positions. Owing to the Oriental veneration for scholars, as well as to certain privileges which they enjoy (such as exemption from military service, and free, though very simple, food and lodgings), many students enter the *madrasah* who are physically unable to bear the hardships of the student life and mentally unfitted for the full curriculum. Accordingly, the majority leave the *madrasah* after from one to five years of study, during which any tendency to independent thought and investigation has been discouraged and a blind devotion to traditional Muhammadanism has been made the fixed principle of life. At the end of each year's work or the completion of each professor's course, the student receives a certificate testifying to his fitness to hold some position demanding that amount of learning. Leaving the *madrasah*, he is now in the *mullā* class, and receives the support of that class in the appointment to some minor office, generally in some village or small town in the provinces. He may become an *imām*, 'leader in prayer' (though this office is not reserved exclusively for the *mullā* class), or a teacher in a primary school (and the incapacity of such teachers in the Orient is proverbial), or a lecturer in some small *madrasah*, or even a judge of one of the minor courts. It is the *mullā* as provincial mosque preacher who is regarded as typical of the class. Once in office, the *mullā* is sure of a position for life, though he may be transferred from one school or mosque to another.

Without any fixed organization, the *mullās* nevertheless form almost a caste; they are distinguished by the large turban and the flowing robe, though neither is prescribed. In influence over the masses and in devotion to formal religion, the *mullā* class has often been likened to a priesthood—a comparison which fails in accuracy only in so far as the *mullā* receives no special consecration to office, does not in any way replace the individual in offering prayer or sacrifice, cannot grant absolution, and performs no necessary part in the rites connected with birth, circumcision, marriage, or death. But, in being the teacher of these rights and duties and the accepted adviser in questions of faith as well as of daily life, the *mullā* considers himself in a position above that of the other Oriental clergy—whose equal at least he generally is in learning and whose superior he is in the persuasive powers of his dialectics.

In their conservative and reactionary tendencies the *mullās* have generally given their support to the absolutism of temporal authorities—in Turkey especially to the Sulṭān as head of both the Church and the State—and they have opposed the introduction of Western culture as encouraging religious indifferentism and ceremonial laxity, and as substituting rationalism for their own fatalism. In Persia, however, where the Shī'itic form of Muhammadanism prevails, and where, consequently, the temporal ruler is not regarded as the head of the Church, the *mullās* often exercise their popular power against the State authority, matching the despotism of the latter with their own extreme fanaticism. There the house of the *mullā*, like mosques and shrines in all Muhammadan lands, is an inviolable place of refuge; and Persian *mullās* have often been charged with harbouring outlaws, whose services they have then used in furthering their own designs. The power of the *mullās* is sometimes checked to a certain extent by that of the dervish orders, and in Turkey, India, and Egypt by the secular courts instituted in more recent times to administer the so-called *'urf* ('customary law').

The *mullās* in general, being sincere in their devotion to their calling, are seldom guilty of infractions of the moral law; indeed, they have generally been held to contrast favourably with the lower priesthood of other faiths. Moral probity is less marked among the Persian *mullās*, however, who, at heart more devoted to Persian poetry than to Muhammadan theology, hold their own functions in light esteem. In one respect, too, the *mullās* everywhere, especially those who fill the office of minor judge, are not above reproach; inasmuch as the stipend furnished by the mosque endowments, and official salaries in general, are very small, the practice of usury and acceptance of bribes is frequent—an abuse which early Muhammadanism attempted to avoid by the principle that religious teachers should always have some other means of gaining a livelihood.

Despite the reactionary tendencies and the corruptibility generally ascribed to the *mullā*, the history of Muhammadanism contains the names of many *mullās* conspicuous for nobility of character and devotion to absolute justice, who have risked their lives to rebuke the corruption and tyranny of rulers. To-day, too, the number of clear-headed, honest leaders among the Turkish, Arabic, and Indian *'ulamā* is steadily increasing; not a few *softas* have been sent from Turkey to receive part of their education in Europe; in India the *mūlvīs* have sometimes warmly advocated the innovations of the English; and everywhere in the larger cities subjected to European influence the traditional type of *mullā* is being combated by advanced Muhammadans who, even when they are rationalists, at the same time deny that they are guilty of any defection from the fundamental principles of Muhammadanism; and fatalism is often taught, practically if not logically, as a doctrine which induces fortitude in bearing the accidents and misfortunes of life, without permitting the cessation of righteous endeavour in any cause as long as Allāh has not shown, by making its failure a *fait accompli*, that His will and decree are opposed thereto.

LITERATURE.—A. Vambéry, *Western Culture in Eastern Lands*, New York, 1906; W. G. Palgrave, *Essays on Eastern Questions*, London, 1872; T. P. Hughes, *Notes on Muhammedanism*[2], do. 1875–78.

W. POPPER.

THE END OF VOL. VIII.